LECTURES & DISCOURSES BY
SWAMI VIVEKANANDA

Discovery Publisher

2019, Discovery Publisher

DISCOVERY PUBLISHER

616 Corporate Way, Suite 2-4933
Valley Cottage, New York, 10989
www.discoverypublisher.com
books@discoverypublisher.com
facebook.com/DiscoveryPublisher
twitter.com/DiscoveryPB

New York • Tokyo • Paris • Hong Kong

TABLE OF CONTENTS

Notes from Lectures & Discourses 474

Conversations & Dialogues   552

Interviews 670

Writings & Prose 694

LECTURES & DISCOURSES

SOUL, GOD AND RELIGION

Through the vistas of the past the voice of the centuries is coming down to us; the voice of the sages of the Himalayas and the recluses of the forest; the voice that came to the Semitic races; the voice that spoke through Buddha and other spiritual giants; the voice that comes from those who live in the light that accompanied man in the beginning of the earth — the light that shines wherever man goes and lives with him for ever — is coming to us even now. This voice is like the little rivulets; that come from the mountains. Now they disappear, and now they appear again in stronger flow till finally they unite in one mighty majestic flood. The messages that are coming down to us from the prophets and holy men and women of all sects and nations are joining their forces and speaking to us with the trumpet voice of the past. And the first message it brings us is: Peace be unto you and to all religions. It is not a message of antagonism, but of one united religion.

Let us study this message first. At the beginning of this century it was almost feared that religion was at an end. Under the tremendous sledge-hammer blows of scientific research, old superstitions were crumbling away like masses of porcelain. Those to whom religion meant only a bundle of creeds and meaningless ceremonials were in despair; they were at their wit's end. Everything was slipping between their fingers. For a time it seemed inevitable that the surging tide of agnosticism and materialism would sweep all before it. There were those who did not dare utter what they thought. Many thought the case hopeless and the cause of religion lost once and for ever. But the tide has turned and to the rescue has come — what? The study of comparative religions. By the study of different religions we find that in essence they are one. When I was a boy, this scepticism reached me, and it seemed for a time as if I must give up all hope of religion. But fortunately for me I studied the Christian religion, the Mohammedan, the Buddhistic, and others, and what was my surprise to find that the same foundation principles taught by my religion were also taught by all religions. It appealed to me this way. What is the truth? I asked. Is this world true? Yes. Why? Because I see it. Are the beautiful sounds we just heard (the vocal and instrumental music) true? Yes. Because we heard them. We know that man has a body, eyes, and ears, and he has a spiritual nature which we cannot see. And with his spiritual faculties he can study these different religions and find that whether a religion is taught in the forests and jungles of India or in a Christian land, in essentials all religions are one. This only shows us that religion is a constitutional necessity of the human mind. The proof of one religion depends on the proof of all the rest. For instance, if I have six fingers, and no one else has, you may well say that is abnormal. The same reasoning may be applied to the argument that only one religion is true and all others false. One religion only, like one set of six fingers in the world, would be unnatural. We see, therefore, that if one religion is true, all others must be true. There are differences in non-essentials, but in essentials they are all one. If my five fingers are true, they prove that your five fingers are true too. Wherever man is, he must develop a belief, he must develop his religious nature.

And another fact I find in the study of the various religions of the world is that there are three different stages of ideas with regard to the soul and God. In the first place, all religions admit that, apart from the body which perishes, there is a certain part or something which does not change like the body, a part that is immutable, eternal, that never dies; but some of the later religions teach that although there is a part of us that never dies, it had a beginning. But anything that has a beginning must necessarily have an end. We — the essential part of us — never had a beginning, and will never have an end. And above us all, above this eternal nature, there is another eternal Being, without end — God. People talk about the beginning of the world, the beginning of man. The word beginning simply means the beginning of the cycle. It nowhere means the beginning of the whole Cosmos. It is impossible that creation could have a beginning. No one of you can imagine a time of beginning. That which has a beginning must have an end. "Never did I not exist, nor you, nor will any of us ever hereafter cease to be," says the Bhagavad-Gita. Wherever the beginning of creation is mentioned, it means the beginning of a cycle. Your body will meet with death, but your soul, never.

Along with this idea of the soul we find another group of ideas in regard to its perfection. The soul in itself is perfect. The Old Testament of the Hebrews admits man perfect at the beginning. Man made himself impure by his own actions. But he is to regain his old nature, his pure nature. Some speak of these things in allegories, fables, and symbols. But when we begin to analyse these statements, we find that they all teach that the human soul is in its very nature perfect, and that man is to regain that original purity. How? By knowing God. Just as the Bible says, "No man can see God but through the Son." What is meant by it? That seeing God is the aim and goal of all human life. The sonship must come before we become one with the Father. Remember that man lost his purity through his own actions. When we suffer, it is because of our own acts; God is not to be blamed for it.

Closely connected with these ideas is the doctrine — which was universal before the Europeans mutilated it — the doctrine of reincarnation. Some of you may have heard of and ignored it. This idea of reincarnation runs parallel with the other doctrine of the eternity of the human soul. Nothing which ends at one point can be without a beginning and nothing that begins at one point can be without an end. We cannot believe in such a monstrous impossibility as the beginning of the human soul. The doctrine of reincarnation asserts the freedom of the soul. Suppose there was an absolute beginning. Then the whole burden of this impurity in man falls upon God. The all-merciful Father responsible for the sins of the world! If sin comes in this way, why should one suffer more than another? Why such partiality, if it comes from an all-merciful God? Why are millions trampled underfoot? Why do people starve who never did anything to cause it? Who is responsible? If they had no hand in it, surely, God would be responsible. Therefore the better explanation is that one is responsible for the miseries one suffers. If I set the wheel in motion, I am responsible for the result. And if I can bring misery, I can also stop it. It necessarily follows that we are free. There is no such thing as fate. There is nothing to compel us. What we have done, that we can undo.

To one argument in connection with this doctrine I will ask your patient attention, as it is a little intricate. We gain all our knowledge through experience; that is the only way. What we call experiences are on the plane of consciousness. For illustration: A man plays a tune on a piano, he places each finger on each key consciously. He repeats this process till the movement of the fingers becomes a habit. He then plays a tune without having to pay special attention to each particular key. Similarly, we find in regard to ourselves that our tendencies are the result of past conscious actions. A child is born with certain tendencies. Whence do they come? No child is born with a tabula rasa—with a clean, blank page—of a mind. The page has been written on previously. The old Greek and Egyptian philosophers taught that no child came with a vacant mind. Each child comes with a hundred tendencies generated by past conscious actions. It did not acquire these in this life, and we are bound to admit that it must have had them in past lives. The rankest materialist has to admit that these tendencies are the result of past actions, only they add that these tendencies come through heredity. Our parents, grandparents, and great-grandparents come down to us through this law of heredity. Now if heredity alone explains this, there is no necessity of believing in the soul at all, because body explains everything. We need not go into the different arguments and discussions on materialism and spiritualism. So far the way is clear for those who believe in an individual soul. We see that to come to a reasonable conclusion we must admit that we have had past lives. This is the belief of the great philosophers and sages of the past and of modern times. Such a doctrine was believed in among the Jews. Jesus Christ believed in it. He says in the Bible, "Before Abraham was, I am." And in another place it is said, "This is Elias who is said to have come."

All the different religions which grew among different nations under varying circumstances and conditions had their origin in Asia, and the Asiatics understand them well. When they came out from the motherland, they got mixed up with errors. The most profound and noble ideas of Christianity were never understood in Europe, because the ideas and images used by the writers of the Bible were foreign to it. Take for illustration the pictures of the Madonna. Every artist paints his Madonna according to his own pre-conceived ide-

as. I have been seeing hundreds of pictures of the Last Supper of Jesus Christ, and he is made to sit at a table. Now, Christ never sat at a table; he squatted with others, and they had a bowl in which they dipped bread—not the kind of bread you eat today. It is hard for any nation to understand the unfamiliar customs of other people. How much more difficult was it for Europeans to understand the Jewish customs after centuries of changes and accretions from Greek, Roman, and other sources! Through all the myths and mythologies by which it is surrounded it is no wonder that the people get very little of the beautiful religion of Jesus, and no wonder that they have made of it a modern shop-keeping religion.

To come to our point. We find that all religions teach the eternity of the soul, as well as that its lustre has been dimmed, and that its primitive purity is to be regained by the knowledge of God. What is the idea of God in these different religions? The primary idea of God was very vague. The most ancient nations had different Deities—sun, earth, fire, water. Among the ancient Jews we find numbers of these gods ferociously fighting with each other. Then we find Elohim whom the Jews and the Babylonians worshipped. We next find one God standing supreme. But the idea differed according to different tribes. They each asserted that their God was the greatest. And they tried to prove it by fighting. The one that could do the best fighting proved thereby that its God was the greatest. Those races were more or less savage. But gradually better and better ideas took the place of the old ones. All those old ideas are gone or going into the lumber-room. All those religions were the outgrowth of centuries; not one fell from the skies. Each had to be worked out bit by bit. Next come the monotheistic ideas: belief in one God, who is omnipotent and omniscient, the one God of the universe. This one God is extra-cosmic; he lies in the heavens. He is invested with the gross conceptions of His originators. He has a right side and a left side, and a bird in His hand, and so on and so forth. But one thing we find, that the tribal gods have disappeared for ever, and the one God of the universe has taken their place: the God of gods. Still He is only an extra-cosmic God. He is unapproachable; nothing can come near Him. But slowly this idea has changed also, and at the next stage we find a God immanent in nature.

In the New Testament it is taught, "Our Father who art in heaven"—God living in the heavens separated from men. We are living on earth and He is living in heaven. Further on we find the teaching that He is a God immanent in nature; He is not only God in heaven, but on earth too. He is the God in us. In the Hindu philosophy we find a stage of the same proximity of God to us. But we do not stop there. There is the non-dualistic stage, in which man realises that the God he has been worshipping is not only the Father in heaven, and on earth, but that "I and my Father are one." He realises in his soul that he is God Himself, only a lower expression of Him. All that is real in me is He; all that is real in Him is I. The gulf between God and man is thus bridged. Thus we find how, by knowing God, we find the kingdom of heaven within us.

In the first or dualistic stage, man knows he is a little personal soul, John, James, or Tom; and he says, "I will be John, James, or Tom to all eternity, and never anything else." As well might the murderer come along and say, "I will remain a murderer for ever." But as time goes on, Tom vanishes and goes back to the original pure Adam.

"Blessed are the pure in heart, for they shall see God." Can we see God? Of course not. Can we know God? Of course not. If God can be known, He will be God no longer. Knowledge is limitation. But I and my Father are one: I find the reality in my soul. These ideas are expressed in some religions, and in others only hinted. In some they were expatriated. Christ's teachings are now very little understood in this country. If you will excuse me, I will say that they have never been very well understood.

The different stages of growth are absolutely necessary to the attainment of purity and perfection. The varying systems of religion are at bottom founded on the same ideas. Jesus says the kingdom of heaven is within you. Again he says, "Our father who art in Heaven." How do you reconcile the two sayings? In this way: He was talking to the uneducated masses when he said the latter, the masses who were uneducated in religion. It was necessary to speak to them in their own language. The masses want concrete ideas, something the senses can grasp. A man may be the greatest philosopher in the world, but a child in religion. When a man has developed a high state of spirituality he can understand that the kingdom of heaven is within him. That is the real kingdom of the mind. Thus we see that the apparent contradictions and perplexities in every religion mark but different stages of growth. And as such we have no right to blame anyone for his religion. There are stages of growth in which forms and symbols are necessary; they are the language that the souls in that stage can understand.

The next idea that I want to bring to you is that religion does not consist in doctrines or dogmas. It is not what you read, nor what dogmas you believe that is of importance, but what you realise. "Blessed are the pure in heart, for they shall see God," yea, in this life. And that is salvation. There are those who teach that this can be gained by the mumbling of words. But no great Master ever taught that external forms were necessary for salvation. The power of attaining it is within ourselves. We live and move in God. Creeds and sects have their parts to play, but they are for children, they last but temporarily. Books never make religions, but religions make books. We must not forget that. No book ever created God, but God inspired all the great books. And no book ever created a soul. We must never forget that. The end of all religions is the realising of God in the soul. That is the one universal religion. If there is one universal truth in all religions, I place it here—in realising God. Ideals and methods may differ, but that is the central point. There may be a thousand different radii, but they all converge to the one centre, and that is the realisation of God: something behind this world of sense, this world of eternal eating and drinking and talking nonsense, this world of false shadows and selfishness. There is that beyond all books, beyond all creeds, beyond the vanities of this world and it is the realisation of God within yourself. A man may believe in all the churches in the world, he may carry in his head all the sacred books ever written, he may baptise himself in all the rivers of the earth, still, if he has no perception of God, I would class him with the rankest atheist. And a man may have never entered a church or a mosque, nor performed any ceremony, but if he feels God within himself and is thereby lifted above the vanities of the world, that man is a holy man, a saint, call him what you will. As soon as a man stands up and says he is right or his church is right, and all others are wrong, he is himself all wrong. He does not know that upon the proof of all the others depends the proof of his own. Love and charity for the whole human race, that is the test of true religiousness. I do not mean the sentimental statement that all men are brothers, but that one must feel the oneness of human life. So far as they are not exclusive, I see that the sects and creeds are all mine; they are all grand. They are all helping men towards the real religion. I will add, it is good to be born in a church, but it is bad to die there. It is good to be born a child, but bad to remain a child. Churches, ceremonies, and symbols are good for children, but when the child is grown, he must burst the church or himself. We must not remain children for ever. It is like trying to fit one coat to all sizes and growths. I do not deprecate the existence of sects in the world. Would to God there were twenty millions more, for the more there are, there will be a greater field for selection. What I do object to is trying to fit one religion to every case. Though all religions are essentially the same, they must have the varieties of form produced by dissimilar circumstances among different nations. We must each have our own individual religion, individual so far as the externals of it go.

Many years ago, I visited a great sage of our own country, a very holy man. We talked of our revealed book, the Vedas, of your Bible, of the Koran, and of revealed books in general. At the close of our talk, this good man asked me to go to the table and take up a book; it was a book which, among other things, contained a forecast of the rainfall during the year. The sage said, "Read that." And I read out the quantity of rain that was to fall. He said, "Now take the book and squeeze it." I did so and he said, "Why, my boy, not a drop of water comes out. Until the water comes out, it is all book, book. So until your religion makes you realise God, it is useless. He who only studies books for religion reminds one of the fable of the ass which carried a heavy load of sugar on its back, but did not know the sweetness of it."

Shall we advise men to kneel down and cry, "O miserable sinners that we are!" No, rather let us remind them of their divine nature. I will tell you a story. A lioness in search of prey came upon a flock of sheep, and as she jumped at one of them, she gave birth to a cub and died on the spot. The young lion was brought up in the flock, ate grass, and bleated like a sheep, and it never knew that it was a lion. One day a lion came across the flock and was astonished to see in it a huge lion eating grass and bleating like a sheep. At his sight the flock fled and the lion-sheep with them. But the lion watched his opportunity and one day found the lion-sheep asleep. He woke him up and said, "You are a lion." The other said, "No," and began to bleat like a sheep. But the stranger lion took him to a lake and asked him to look in the water at his own image and see if it did not resemble him, the stranger lion. He looked and acknowledged that it did. Then the stranger lion began to roar and asked him to do the same. The lion-sheep tried his voice and was soon roaring as grandly as the other. And he was a sheep no longer.

My friends, I would like to tell you all that you are mighty as lions.

If the room is dark, do you go about beating your chest and crying, "It is dark, dark, dark!" No, the only way to get the light is to strike a light, and then the darkness goes. The only way to realise the light above you is to strike the spiritual light within you, and the darkness of sin and impurity will flee away. Think of your higher self, not of your lower.

* * *

Some questions and answers here followed.

Q. A man in the audience said, "If ministers stop preaching hell-fire, they will have no control over their people."

A. They had better lose it then. The man who is frightened into religion has no religion at all. Better teach him of his divine nature than of his animal.

Q. What did the Lord mean when he said, "The kingdom of heaven is not of this world?"

A. That the kingdom of heaven is within us. The Jewish idea was a kingdom of heaven upon this earth. That was not the idea of Jesus.

Q. Do you believe we come up from the animals?

A. I believe that, by the law of evolution, the higher beings have come up from the lower kingdoms.

Q. Do you know of anyone who remembers his previous life?

A. I have met some who told me they did remember their previous life. They had reached a point where they could remember their former incarnations.

Q. Do you believe in Christ's crucifixion?

A. Christ was God incarnate; they could not kill him. That which was crucified was only a semblance, a mirage.

Q. If he could have produced such a semblance as that, would not that have been the greatest miracle of all?

A. I look upon miracles as the greatest stumbling-blocks in the way of truth. When the disciples of Buddha told him of a man who had performed a so-called miracle — had taken a

bowl from a great height without touching it — and showed him the bowl, he took it and crushed it under his feet and told them never to build their faith on miracles, but to look for truth in everlasting principles. He taught them the true inner light — the light of the spirit, which is the only safe light to go by. Miracles are only stumbling-blocks. Let us brush them aside.

Q. Do you believe Jesus preached the Sermon on the Mount?

A. I do believe he did. But in this matter I have to go by the books as others do, and I am aware that mere book testimony is rather shaky ground. But we are all safe in taking the teachings of the Sermon on the Mount as a guide. We have to take what appeals to our inner spirit. Buddha taught five hundred years before Christ, and his words were full of blessings: never a curse came from his lips, nor from his life; never one from Zoroaster, nor from Confucius.

THE HINDU RELIGION

My religion is to learn. I read my Bible better in the light of your Bible and the dark prophecies of my religion become brighter when compared with those of your prophets. Truth has always been universal. If I alone were to have six fingers on my hand while all of you had only five, you would not think that my hand was the true intent of nature, but rather that it was abnormal and diseased. Just so with religion. If one creed alone were to be true and all the others untrue, you would have a right to say that that religion was diseased; if one religion is true, all the others must be true. Thus the Hindu religion is your property as well as mine. Of the two hundred and ninety millions of people inhabiting India, only two millions are Christians, sixty millions Mohammedans and all the rest are Hindus.

The Hindus found their creed upon the ancient Vedas, a word derived from Vid, "to know". These are a series of books which, to our minds, contain the essence of all religion; but we do not think they alone contain the truths. They teach us the immortality of the soul. In every country and every human breast there is a natural desire to find a stable equilibrium — something that does not change. We cannot find it in nature, for all the universe is nothing but an infinite mass of changes. But to infer from that that nothing unchanging exists is to fall into the error of the Southern school of Buddhists and the Chârvâkas, which latter believe that all is matter and nothing mind, that all religion is a cheat, and morality and goodness, useless superstitions. The Vedanta philosophy teaches that man is not bound by his five senses. They only know the present, and neither the future nor the past; but as the present signifies both past and future, and all three are only demarcations of time, the present also would be unknown if it were not for something above the senses, something independent of time, which unifies the past and the future in the present.

But what is independent? Not our body, for it depends upon

outward conditions; nor our mind, because the thoughts of which it is composed are caused. It is our soul. The Vedas say the whole world is a mixture of independence and dependence, of freedom and slavery, but through it all shines the soul independent, immortal, pure, perfect, holy. For if it is independent, it cannot perish, as death is but a change, and depends upon conditions; if independent, it must be perfect, for imperfection is again but a condition, and therefore dependent. And this immortal and perfect soul must be the same in the highest God as well as in the humblest man, the difference between them being only in the degree in which this soul manifests itself.

But why should the soul take to itself a body? For the same reason that I take a looking-glass—to see myself. Thus, in the body, the soul is reflected. The soul is God, and every human being has a perfect divinity within himself, and each one must show his divinity sooner or later. If I am in a dark room, no amount of protestation will make it any brighter—I must light a match. Just so, no amount of grumbling and wailing will make our imperfect body more perfect. But the Vedanta teaches—call forth your soul, show your divinity. Teach your children that they are divine, that religion is a positive something and not a negative nonsense; that it is not subjection to groans when under oppression, but expansion and manifestation.

Every religion has it that man's present and future are modified by the past, and that the present is but the effect of the past. How is it, then, that every child is born with an experience that cannot be accounted for by hereditary transmission? How is it that one is born of good parents, receives a good education and becomes a good man, while another comes from besotted parents and ends on the gallows? How do you explain this inequality without implicating God? Why should a merciful Father set His child in such conditions which must bring forth misery? It is no explanation to say God will make amends; later on—God has no blood-money. Then, too, what becomes of my liberty, if this be my first birth? Coming into this world without the experience of a former life, my independence would be gone, for my path would be marked out by the experience of others. If I cannot be the maker of my own fortune, then I am not free. I take upon myself the blame for the misery of this existence, and say I will unmake the evil I have done in another existence. This, then, is our philosophy of the migration of the soul. We come into this life with the experience of another, and the fortune or misfortune of this existence is the result of our acts in a former existence, always becoming better, till at last perfection is reached.

We believe in a God, the Father of the universe, infinite and omnipotent. But if our soul at last becomes perfect, it also must become infinite. But there is no room for two infinite unconditional beings, and hence we believe in a Personal God, and we ourselves are He. These are the three stages which every religion has taken. First we see God in the far beyond, then we come nearer to Him and give Him omni-presence so that we live in Him; and at last we recognise that we are He. The idea of an Objective God is not untrue—in fact, every idea of God, and hence every religion, is true, as each is but a different stage in the journey, the aim of which is the perfect conception of the Vedas. Hence, too, we not only tolerate, but we Hindus accept every religion, praying in the mosque of the Mohammedans, worshipping before the fire of the Zoroastrians, and kneeling before the cross of the Christians, knowing that all the religions, from the lowest fetishism to the highest absolutism, mean so many attempts of the human soul to grasp and realise the infinite, each determined by the conditions of its birth and association, and each of them marking a stage of progress. We gather all these flowers and bind them with the twine of love, making a wonderful bouquet of worship.

If I am God, then my soul is a temple of the Highest, and my every motion should be a worship—love for love's sake, duty for duty's sake, without hope of reward or fear of punishment. Thus my religion means expansion, and expansion means realisation and perception in the highest sense—no mumbling words or genuflections. Man is to become divine, realising the divine more and more from day to day in an endless progress[1].

WHAT IS RELIGION?

A huge locomotive has rushed on over the line and a small worm that was creeping upon one of the rails saved its life by crawling out of the path of the locomotive. Yet this little worm, so insignificant that it can be crushed in a moment, is a living something, while this locomotive, so huge, so immense, is only an engine, a machine. You say the one has life and the other is only dead matter and all its powers and strength and speed are only those of a dead machine, a mechanical contrivance. Yet the poor little worm which moved upon the rail and which the least touch of the engine would have deprived of its life is a majestic being compared to that huge locomotive. It is a small part of the Infinite and, therefore, it is greater than this powerful engine. Why should that be so? How do we know the living from the dead? The machine mechanically performs all the movements its maker made it to perform, its movements are not those of life. How can we make the distinction between the living and the dead, then? In the living there is freedom, there is intelligence; in the dead all is bound and no freedom is possible, because there is no intelligence. This freedom that distinguishes us from mere machines is what we are all striving for. To be more free is the goal of all our efforts, for only in perfect freedom can there be perfection. This effort to attain freedom underlies all forms of worship, whether we know it or not.

If we were to examine the various sorts of worship all over the world, we would see that the rudest of mankind are worship-

---

1. Summary of a lecture delivered before the Ethical Society, Brooklyn, at the Pouch Gallery in Clinton Avenue, on the 30th December, 1894. Reproduced from the Brooklyn Standard Union.

ping ghosts, demons, and the spirits of their forefathers—serpent worship, worship of tribal gods, and worship of the departed ones. Why do they do this? Because they feel that in some unknown way these beings are greater, more powerful than themselves, and limit their freedom. They, therefore, seek to propitiate these beings in order to prevent them from molesting them, in other words, to get more freedom. They also seek to win favour from these superior beings, to get by gift of the gods what ought to be earned by personal effort.

On the whole, this shows that the world is expecting a miracle. This expectation never leaves us, and however we may try, we are all running after the miraculous and extraordinary. What is mind but that ceaseless inquiry into the meaning and mystery of life? We may say that only uncultivated people are going after all these things, but the question still is there: Why should it be so? The Jews were asking for a miracle. The whole world has been asking for the same these thousands of years. There is, again, the universal dissatisfaction. We make an ideal but we have rushed only half the way after it when we make a newer one. We struggle hard to attain to some goal and then discover we do not want it. This dissatisfaction we are having time after time, and what is there in the mind if there is to be only dissatisfaction? What is the meaning of this universal dissatisfaction? It is because freedom is every man's goal. He seeks it ever, his whole life is a struggle after it. The child rebels against law as soon as it is born. Its first utterance is a cry, a protest against the bondage in which it finds itself. This longing for freedom produces the idea of a Being who is absolutely free. The concept of God is a fundamental element in the human constitution. In the Vedanta, Sat-chit-ânanda (Existence-Knowledge-Bliss) is the highest concept of God possible to the mind. It is the essence of knowledge and is by its nature the essence of bliss. We have been stifling that inner voice long enough, seeking to follow law and quiet the human nature, but there is that human instinct to rebel against nature's laws. We may not understand what the meaning is, but there is that unconscious struggle of the human with the spiritual, of the lower with the higher mind, and the struggle attempts to preserve one's separate life, what we call our "individuality".

Even hells stand out with this miraculous fact that we are born rebels; and the first fact of life—the inrushing of life itself—against this we rebel and cry out, "No law for us." As long as we obey the laws we are like machines, and on goes the universe, and we cannot break it. Laws as laws become man's nature. The first inkling of life on its higher level is in seeing this struggle within us to break the bond of nature and to be free. "Freedom, O Freedom! Freedom, O Freedom!" is the song of the soul. Bondage, alas, to be bound in nature, seems its fate.

Why should there be serpent, or ghost, or demon worship and all these various creeds and forms for having miracles? Why do we say that there is life, there is being in anything? There must be a meaning in all this search, this endeavour to understand life, to explain being. It is not meaningless and vain. It is man's ceaseless endeavour to become free. The knowledge which we now call science has been struggling for thousands of years in its attempt to gain freedom, and people ask for freedom. Yet there is no freedom in nature. It is all law. Still the struggle goes on. Nay, the whole of nature from the very sun to the atoms is under law, and even for man there is no freedom. But we cannot believe it. We have been studying laws from the beginning and yet cannot—nay, will not—believe that man is under law. The soul cries ever, "Freedom, O Freedom!" With the conception of God as a perfectly free Being, man cannot rest eternally in this bondage. Higher he must go, and unless the struggle were for himself, he would think it too severe. Man says to himself, "I am a born slave, I am bound; nevertheless, there is a Being who is not bound by nature. He is free and Master of nature."

The conception of God, therefore, is as essential and as fundamental a part of mind as is the idea of bondage. Both are the outcome of the idea of freedom. There cannot be life, even in the plant, without the idea of freedom. In the plant or in the worm, life has to rise to the individual concept. It is there, unconsciously working, the plant living its life to preserve the variety, principle, or form, not nature. The idea of nature controlling every step onward overrules the idea of freedom. Onward goes the idea of the material world, onward moves the idea of freedom. Still the fight goes on. We are hearing about all the quarrels of creeds and sects, yet creeds and sects are just and proper, they must be there. The chain is lengthening and naturally the struggle increases, but there need be no quarrels if we only knew that we are all striving to reach the same goal.

The embodiment of freedom, the Master of nature, is what we call God. You cannot deny Him. No, because you cannot move or live without the idea of freedom. Would you come here if you did not believe you were free? It is quite possible that the biologist can and will give some explanation of this perpetual effort to be free. Take all that for granted, still the idea of freedom is there. It is a fact, as much so as the other fact that you cannot apparently get over, the fact of being under nature.

Bondage and liberty, light and shadow, good and evil must be there, but the very fact of the bondage shows also this freedom hidden there. If one is a fact, the other is equally a fact. There must be this idea of freedom. While now we cannot see that this idea of bondage, in uncultivated man, is his struggle for freedom, yet the idea of freedom is there. The bondage of sin and impurity in the uncultivated savage is to his consciousness very small, for his nature is only a little higher than the animal's. What he struggles against is the bondage of physical nature, the lack of physical gratification, but out of this lower consciousness grows and broadens the higher conception of a mental or moral bondage and a longing for spiritual freedom. Here we see the divine dimly shining through the veil of ignorance. The veil is very dense at first and the light may be almost obscured, but it is there, ever pure and undimmed—the radiant fire of freedom and perfection. Man personifies this as the Ruler of the Universe, the One Free Being. He does not yet know that the universe is all one, that the difference is only in degree, in the concept.

The whole of nature is worship of God. Wherever there is life, there is this search for freedom and that freedom is the same as God. Necessarily this freedom gives us mastery over all nature and is impossible without knowledge. The more we are knowing, the more we are becoming masters of nature. Mastery alone is making us strong and if there be some being entirely free and master of nature, that being must have a perfect knowledge of nature, must be omnipresent and omniscient. Freedom must go hand in hand with these, and that being alone who has acquired these will be beyond nature.

Blessedness, eternal peace, arising from perfect freedom, is the highest concept of religion underlying all the ideas of God in Vedanta—absolutely free Existence, not bound by anything, no change, no nature, nothing that can produce a change in Him. This same freedom is in you and in me and is the only real freedom.

God is still, established upon His own majestic changeless Self. You and I try to be one with Him, but plant ourselves upon nature, upon the trifles of daily life, on money, on fame, on human love, and all these changing forms in nature which make for bondage. When nature shines, upon what depends the shining? Upon God and not upon the sun, nor the moon, nor the stars. Wherever anything shines, whether it is the light in the sun or in our own consciousness, it is He. He shining, all shines after Him.

Now we have seen that this God is self-evident, impersonal, omniscient, the Knower and Master of nature, the Lord of all. He is behind all worship and it is being done according to Him, whether we know it or not. I go one step further. That at which all marvel, that which we call evil, is His worship too. This too is a part of freedom. Nay, I will be terrible even and tell you that, when you are doing evil, the impulse behind is also that freedom. It may have been misguided and misled, but it was there; and there cannot be any life or any impulse unless that freedom be behind it. Freedom breathes in the throb of the universe. Unless there is unity at the universal heart, we cannot understand variety. Such is the conception of the Lord in the Upanishads. Sometimes it rises even higher, presenting to us an ideal before which at first we stand aghast—that we are in essence one with God. He who is the colouring in the wings of the butterfly, and the blossoming of the rose-bud, is the power that is in the plant and in the butterfly. He who gives us life is the power within us. Out of His fire comes life, and the direst death is also His power. He whose shadow is death, His shadow is immortality also. Take a still higher conception. See how we are flying like hunted hares from all that is terrible, and like them, hiding our heads and thinking we are safe. See how the whole world is flying from everything terrible. Once when I was in Varanasi,

I was passing through a place where there was a large tank of water on one side and a high wall on the other. It was in the grounds where there were many monkeys. The monkeys of Varanasi are huge brutes and are sometimes surly. They now took it into their heads not to allow me to pass through their street, so they howled and shrieked and clutched at my feet as I passed. As they pressed closer, I began to run, but the faster I ran, the faster came the monkeys and they began to bite at me. It seemed impossible to escape, but just then I met a stranger who called out to me, "Face the brutes." I turned and faced the monkeys, and they fell back and finally fled. That is a lesson for all life—face the terrible, face it boldly. Like the monkeys, the hardships of life fall back when we cease to flee before them. If we are ever to gain freedom, it must be by conquering nature, never by running away. Cowards never win victories. We have to fight fear and troubles and ignorance if we expect them to flee before us.

What is death? What are terrors? Do you not see the Lord's face in them? Fly from evil and terror and misery, and they will follow you. Face them, and they will flee. The whole world worships ease and pleasure, and very few dare to worship that which is painful. To rise above both is the idea of freedom. Unless man passes through this gate he cannot be free. We all have to face these. We strive to worship the Lord, but the body rises between, nature rises between Him and us and blinds our vision. We must learn how to worship and love Him in the thunderbolt, in shame, in sorrow, in sin. All the world has ever been preaching the God of virtue. I preach a God of virtue and a God of sin in one. Take Him if you dare—that is the one way to salvation; then alone will come to us the Truth Ultimate which comes from the idea of oneness. Then will be lost the idea that one is greater than another. The nearer we approach the law of freedom, the more we shall come under the Lord, and troubles will vanish. Then we shall not differentiate the door of hell from the gate of heaven, nor differentiate between men and say, "I am greater than any being in the universe." Until we see nothing in the world but the Lord Himself, all these evils will beset us and we shall make all these distinctions; because it is only in the Lord, in the Spirit, that we are all one; and until we see God everywhere, this unity will not exist for us.

Two birds of beautiful plumage, inseparable companions, sat upon the same tree, one on the top and one below. The beautiful bird below was eating the fruits of the tree, sweet and bitter, one moment a sweet one and another a bitter. The moment he ate a bitter fruit, he was sorry, but after a while he ate another and when it too was bitter, he looked up and saw the other bird who ate neither the sweet nor the bitter, but was calm and majestic, immersed in his own glory. And then the poor lower bird forgot and went on eating the sweet and bitter fruits again, until at last he ate one that was extremely bitter; and then he stopped again and once more looked up at the glorious bird above. Then he came nearer and nearer to the other bird; and when he had come near enough, rays of light shone upon him and enveloped him, and he saw he was transformed into the higher bird. He became calm, majestic, free, and found that there had been but one bird all the time on the tree. The lower bird was but the reflection of the one above. So we are in reality one with the Lord, but the reflection makes us seem many, as when the one sun reflects in a million dew-drops and seems a million tiny suns. The reflection must vanish if we are to identify ourselves with our real nature which is divine. The universe itself can never be the limit of our satisfaction. That is why the miser gathers more and more money, that is why the robber robs, the sinner sins, that is why you are learning philosophy. All have one purpose. There is no other purpose in life, save to reach this freedom. Consciously or unconsciously, we are all striving for perfection. Every being must attain to it.

The man who is groping through sin, through misery, the man who is choosing the path through hells, will reach it, but it will take time. We cannot save him. Some hard knocks on his head will help him to turn to the Lord. The path of virtue, purity, unselfishness, spirituality, becomes known at last and what all are doing unconsciously, we are trying to do consciously. The idea is expressed by St. Paul, "The God that ye ignorantly worship, Him declare I unto you." This is the lesson for the whole world to learn. What have these philosophies and theories of nature to do, if not to help us to attain to this one goal in life? Let us come to that consciousness of the identity of everything and let man see himself in everything. Let us be no more the worshippers of creeds or sects with small limited notions of God, but see Him in everything in the universe. If you are knowers of God, you will everywhere find the same worship as in your own heart.

Get rid, in the first place, of all these limited ideas and see God in every person—working through all hands, walking through all feet, and eating through every mouth. In every being He lives, through all minds He thinks. He is self-evident, nearer unto us than ourselves. To know this is religion, is faith, and may it please the Lord to give us this faith! When we shall feel that oneness, we shall be immortal. We are physically immortal even, one with the universe. So long as there is one that breathes throughout the universe, I live in that one. I am not this limited little being, I am the universal. I am the life of all the sons of the past. I am the soul of Buddha, of Jesus, of Mohammed. I am the soul of the teachers, and I am all the robbers that robbed, and all the murderers that were hanged, I am the universal. Stand up then; this is the highest worship. You are one with the universe. That only is humility—not crawling upon all fours and calling yourself a sinner. That is the highest evolution when this veil of differentiation is torn off. The highest creed is Oneness. I am so-and-so is a limited idea, not true of the real "I". I am the universal; stand upon that and ever worship the Highest through the highest form, for God is Spirit and should be worshipped in spirit and in truth. Through lower forms of worship, man's material thoughts rise to spiritual worship and the Universal Infinite

One is at last worshipped in and through the spirit. That which is limited is material. The Spirit alone is infinite. God is Spirit, is infinite; man is Spirit and, therefore, infinite, and the Infinite alone can worship the Infinite. We will worship the Infinite; that is the highest spiritual worship. The grandeur of realising these ideas, how difficult it is! I theorise, talk, philosophize; and the next moment something comes against me, and I unconsciously become angry, I forget there is anything in the universe but this little limited self, I forget to say, "I am the Spirit, what is this trifle to me? I am the Spirit." I forget it is all myself playing, I forget God, I forget freedom.

Sharp as the blade of a razor, long and difficult and hard to cross, is the way to freedom. The sages have declared this again and again. Yet do not let these weaknesses and failures bind you. The Upanishads have declared, "Arise ! Awake ! and stop not until the goal is reached." We will then certainly cross the path, sharp as it is like the razor, and long and distant and difficult though it be. Man becomes the master of gods and demons. No one is to blame for our miseries but ourselves. Do you think there is only a dark cup of poison if man goes to look for nectar? The nectar is there and is for every man who strives to reach it. The Lord Himself tells us, "Give up all these paths and struggles. Do thou take refuge in Me. I will take thee to the other shore, be not afraid." We hear that from all the scriptures of the world that come to us. The same voice teaches us to say, "Thy will be done upon earth, as it is in heaven," for "Thine is the kingdom and the power and the glory." It is difficult, all very difficult. I say to myself, "This moment I will take refuge in Thee, O Lord. Unto Thy love I will sacrifice all, and on Thine altar I will place all that is good and virtuous. My sins, my sorrows, my actions, good and evil, I will offer unto Thee; do Thou take them and I will never forget." One moment I say, "Thy will be done," and the next moment something comes to try me and I spring up in a rage. The goal of all religions is the same, but the language of the teachers differs. The attempt is to kill the false "I", so that the real "I", the Lord, will reign. "I the Lord thy God am a jealous God. Thou shalt have no other gods before me," say the Hebrew scriptures. God must be there all alone. We must say, "Not I, but Thou," and then we should give up everything but the Lord. He, and He alone, should reign. Perhaps we struggle hard, and yet the next moment our feet slip, and then we try to stretch out our hands to Mother. We find we cannot stand alone. Life is infinite, one chapter of which is, "Thy will be done," and unless we realise all the chapters we cannot realise the whole. "Thy will be done"—every moment the traitor mind rebels against it, yet it must be said, again and again, if we are to conquer the lower self. We cannot serve a traitor and yet be saved. There is salvation for all except the traitor and we stand condemned as traitors, traitors against our own selves, against the majesty of Mother, when we refuse to obey the voice of our higher Self. Come what will, we must give our bodies and minds up to the Supreme Will. Well has it been said by the Hindu philosopher, "If man says twice,

'Thy will be done,' he commits sin." "Thy will be done," what more is needed, why say it twice? What is good is good. No more shall we take it back. "Thy will be done on earth as it is in heaven, for Thine is the kingdom and the power and the glory for evermore."

VEDIC RELIGIOUS IDEALS

What concerns us most is the religious thought—on soul and God and all that appertains to religion. We will take the Samhitâs. These are collections of hymns forming, as it were, the oldest Aryan literature, properly speaking, the oldest literature in the world. There may have been some scraps of literature of older date here and there, older than that even, but not books, or literature properly so called. As a collected book, this is the oldest the world has, and herein is portrayed the earliest feeling of the Aryans, their aspirations, the questions that arose about their manners and methods, and so on. At the very outset we find a very curious idea. These hymns are sung in praise of different gods, Devas as they are called, the bright ones. There is quite a number of them. One is called Indra, another Varuna, another Mitra, Parjanya, and so on. Various mythological and allegorical figures come before us one after the other—for instance, Indra the thunderer, striking the serpent who has withheld the rains from mankind. Then he lets fly his thunderbolt, the serpent is killed, and rain comes down in showers. The people are pleased, and they worship Indra with oblations. They make a sacrificial pyre, kill some animals, roast their flesh upon spits, and offer that meat to Indra. And they had a popular plant called Soma. What plant it was nobody knows now; it has entirely disappeared, but from the books we gather that, when crushed, it produced a sort of milky juice, and that was fermented; and it can also be gathered that this fermented Soma juice was intoxicating. This also they offered to Indra and the other gods, and they also drank it themselves. Sometimes they drank a little too much, and so did the gods. Indra on occasions got drunk. There are passages to show that Indra at one time drank so much of this Soma juice that he talked irrelevant words. So with Varuna. He is another god, very powerful, and is in the same way protecting his votaries, and they are praising him with their libations of Soma. So is the god of war, and so on. But the popular idea that strikes one as making the mythologies of the Samhitas entirely different from the other mythologies is, that along with every one of these gods is the idea of an infinity. This infinite is abstracted, and sometimes described as Âditya. At other times it is affixed, as it were, to all the other gods. Take, for example, Indra. In some of the books you will find that Indra has a body, is very strong, sometimes is wearing golden armour, and comes down, lives and eats with his votaries, fights the demons, fights the snakes, and so on. Again, in one hymn we find that Indra has been given a very high position; he is omnipresent and omnipotent, and Indra sees the heart of every being. So with Varuna. This Varuna is god of the air and is in charge of the water, just as Indra was previously; and then, all of a sudden, we find him raised up and said to be omnipresent, omnipotent, and so on. I will read one passage about this Varuna in his highest form, and you will understand what I mean. It has been translated into English poetry, so it is better that I read it in that form.

The mighty Lord on high our deeds,
as if at hand, espies;
The gods know all men do, though
men would fain their acts disguise;
Whoever stands, whoever moves,
or steals from place to place,
Or hides him in his secret cell—the
gods his movements trace.
Wherever two together plot,
and deem they are alone,
King Varuna is there, a third,
and all their schemes are known.
This earth is his, to him belong
those vast and boundless skies;
Both seas within him rest, and
yet in that small pool he lies,
Whoever far beyond the sky should
think his way to wing,
He could not there elude the grasp
of Varuna the King.
His spies, descending from the skies,
glide all this world around;
Their thousand eyes all-scanning
sweep to earth's remotest bound.

So we can multiply examples about the other gods; they all come, one after the other, to share the same fate—they first begin as gods, and then they are raised to this conception as the Being in whom the whole universe exists, who sees every heart, who is the ruler of the universe. And in the case of Varuna, there is another idea, just the germ of one idea which came, but was immediately suppressed by the Aryan mind, and that was the idea of fear. In another place we read they are afraid they have sinned and ask Varuna for pardon. These ideas were never allowed, for reasons you will come to understand later on, to grow on Indian soil, but the germs were there sprouting, the idea of fear, and the idea of sin. This is the idea, as you all know, of what is called monotheism. This monotheism, we see, came to India at a very early period. Throughout the Samhitas, in the first and oldest part, this monotheistic idea prevails, but we shall find that it did not prove sufficient for the Aryans; they threw it aside, as it were, as a very primitive sort of idea and went further on, as we Hindus think. Of course in reading books and criticisms on the Vedas written by Europeans, the Hindu cannot help smiling when he reads, that the writings of our authors are saturated with this previous education alone. Persons who have sucked in as their mother's milk the idea that the highest ideal of God is the idea of a Personal God, naturally dare not think on the lines of these ancient thinkers of India, when they find that just after the Samhitas, the monotheistic idea with which the Samhita portion is replete was thought by the Aryans to be useless and not worthy of philosophers and thinkers, and that they struggled hard for a more philosophical and transcendental idea. The monotheistic idea was much too human for them, although they gave it such descriptions as "The whole universe rests in Him," and "Thou art the keeper of all hearts." The Hindus were bold, to their great credit be it said, bold thinkers in all their ideas, so bold that one spark of their thought frightens the so-called bold thinkers of the West. Well has it been said by Prof. Max Müller about these thinkers that they climbed up to heights where their lungs only could breathe, and where those of other beings would have burst. These brave people followed reason wherever it led them, no matter at what cost, never caring if all their best superstitions were smashed to pieces, never caring what society would think about them, or talk about them; but what they thought was right and true, they preached and they talked.

Before going into all these speculations of the ancient Vedic sages, we will first refer to one or two very curious instances in the Vedas. The peculiar fact—that these gods are taken up, as it were, one after the other, raised and sublimated, till each has assumed the proportions of the infinite Personal God of the Universe—calls for an explanation. Prof. Max Müller creates for it a new name, as he thinks it peculiar to the Hindus: he calls it "Henotheism". We need not go far for the explanation. It is within the book. A few steps from the very place where we find those gods being raised and sublimated, we find the explanation also. The question arises how the Hindu mythologies should be so unique, so different from all others. In Babylonian or Greek mythologies we find one god struggling upwards, and he assumes a position and remains there, while the other gods die out. Of all the Molochs, Jehovah becomes supreme, and the other Molochs are forgotten, lost for ever; he is the God of gods. So, too, of all the Greek gods, Zeus comes to the front and assumes big proportions, becomes the God of the Universe, and all the other gods become degraded into minor angels. This fact was repeated in later times. The Buddhists and the Jains raised one of their prophets to the Godhead, and all the other gods they made subservient to Buddha, or to Jina. This is the world-wide process, but there we find an exception, as it were. One god is praised, and for the time being it is said that all the other gods obey his commands, and the very one who is said to be raised up by Varuna, is himself raised up, in the next book, to the highest position. They occupy the position of the Personal God in turns. But the explanation is there in the book, and it is a grand explanation, one that has given the theme to all subsequent thought in India, and one that will be the theme of the whole world of religions: "Ekam Sat Viprâ Bahudhâ Vadanti—That which exists is One; sages call It by various

names." In all these cases where hymns were written about all these gods, the Being perceived was one and the same; it was the perceiver who made the difference. It was the hymnist, the sage, the poet, who sang in different languages and different words, the praise of one and the same Being. "That which exists is One; sages call It by various names." Tremendous results have followed from that one verse. Some of you, perhaps, are surprised to think that India is the only country where there never has been a religious persecution, where never was any man disturbed for his religious faith. Theists or atheists, monists, dualists, monotheists are there and always live unmolested. Materialists were allowed to preach from the steps of Brahminical temples, against the gods, and against God Himself; they went preaching all over the land that the idea of God was a mere superstition, and that gods, and Vedas, and religion were simply superstitions invented by the priests for their own benefit, and they were allowed to do this unmolested. And so, wherever he went, Buddha tried to pull down every old thing sacred to the Hindus to the dust, and Buddha died of ripe old age. So did the Jains, who laughed at the idea of God. "How can it be that there is a God?" they asked; "it must be a mere superstition." So on, endless examples there are. Before the Mohammedan wave came into India, it was never known what religious persecution was; the Hindus had only experienced it as made by foreigners on themselves. And even now it is a patent fact how much Hindus have helped to build Christian churches, and how much readiness there is to help them. There never has been bloodshed. Even heterodox religions that have come out of India have been likewise affected; for instance, Buddhism. Buddhism is a great religion in some respects, but to confuse Buddhism with Vedanta is without meaning; anyone may mark just the difference that exists between Christianity and the Salvation Army. There are great and good points in Buddhism, but these great points fell into hands which were not able to keep them safe. The jewels which came from philosophers fell into the hands of mobs, and the mobs took up their ideas. They had a great deal of enthusiasm, some marvellous ideas, great and humanitarian ideas, but, after all, there is something else that is necessary—thought and intellect—to keep everything safe. Wherever you see the most humanitarian ideas fall into the hands of the multitude, the first result, you may notice, is degradation. It is learning and intellect that keep things sure. Now this Buddhism went as the first missionary religion to the world, penetrated the whole of the civilised world as it existed at that time, and never was a drop of blood shed for that religion. We read how in China the Buddhist missionaries were persecuted, and thousands were massacred by two or three successive emperors, but after that, fortune favoured the Buddhists, and one of the emperors offered to take vengeance on the persecutors, but the missionaries refused. All that we owe to this one verse. That is why I want you to remember it: "Whom they call Indra, Mitra, Varuna—That which exists is One; sages call It by various names."

It was written, nobody knows at what date, it may be 8,000 years ago, in spite of all modern scholars may say, it may be 9,000 years ago. Not one of these religious speculations is of modern date, but they are as fresh today as they were when they were written, or rather, fresher, for at that distant date man was not so civilised as we know him now. He had not learnt to cut his brother's throat because he differed a little in thought from himself; he had not deluged the world in blood, he did not become demon to his own brother. In the name of humanity he did not massacre whole lots of mankind then. Therefore these words come to us today very fresh, as great stimulating, life-giving words, much fresher than they were when they were written: "That which exists is One; sages call It by various names." We have to learn yet that all religions, under whatever name they may be called, either Hindu, Buddhist, Mohammedan, or Christian, have the same God, and he who derides any one of these derides his own God.

That was the solution they arrived at. But, as I have said, this ancient monotheistic idea did not satisfy the Hindu mind. It did not go far enough, it did not explain the visible world: a ruler of the world does not explain the world—certainly not. A ruler of the universe does not explain the universe, and much less an external ruler, one outside of it. He may be a moral guide, the greatest power in the universe, but that is no explanation of the universe; and the first question that we find now arising, assuming proportions, is the question about the universe: "Whence did it come?" "How did it come?" "How does it exist?" Various hymns are to be found on this question struggling forward to assume form, and nowhere do we find it so poetically, so wonderfully expressed as in the following hymn:

"Then there was neither aught nor naught, nor air, nor sky, nor anything. What covered all? Where rested all? Then death was not, nor deathlessness, nor change to night and day." The translation loses a good deal of the poetical beauty. "Then death was not, nor deathlessness, nor change to night and day;" the very sound of the Sanskrit is musical. "That existed, that breath, covering as it were, that God's existence; but it did not begin to move." It is good to remember this one idea that it existed motionless, because we shall find how this idea sprouts up afterwards in the cosmology, how according to the Hindu metaphysics and philosophy, this whole universe is a mass of vibrations, as it were, motions; and there are periods when this whole mass of motions subsides and becomes finer and finer, remaining in that state for some time. That is the state described in this hymn. It existed unmoved, without vibration, and when this creation began, this began to vibrate and all this creation came out of it, that one breath, calm, self-sustained, naught else beyond it.

"Gloom existed first." Those of you who have ever been in India or any tropical country, and have seen the bursting of the monsoon, will understand the majesty of these words. I remember three poets' attempts to picture this. Milton says, "No light, but rather darkness visible." Kalidasa says, "Dark-

ness which can be penetrated with a needle," but none comes near this Vedic description, "Gloom hidden in gloom." Everything is parching and sizzling, the whole creation seems to be burning away, and for days it has been so, when one afternoon there is in one corner of the horizon a speck of cloud, and in less than half an hour it has extended unto the whole earth, until, as it were, it is covered with cloud, cloud over cloud, and then it bursts into a tremendous deluge of rain. The cause of creation was described as will. That which existed at first became changed into will, and this will began to manifest itself as desire. This also we ought to remember, because we find that this idea of desire is said to be the cause of all we have. This idea of will has been the corner-stone of both the Buddhist and the Vedantic system, and later on, has penetrated into German philosophy and forms the basis of Schopenhauer's system of philosophy. It is here we first hear of it.

"Now first arose desire, the primal seed of mind.
Sages, searching in their hearts by wisdom,
found the bond,
Between existence and non-existence."

It is a very peculiar expression; the poet ends by saying that "perhaps He even does not know." We find in this hymn, apart from its poetical merits, that this questioning about the universe has assumed quite definite proportions, and that the minds of these sages must have advanced to such a state, when all sorts of common answers would not satisfy them. We find that they were not even satisfied with this Governor above. There are various other hymns where the same idea, comes in, about how this all came, and just as we have seen, when they were trying to find a Governor of the universe, a Personal God, they were taking up one Deva after another, raising him up to that position, so now we shall find that in various hymns one or other idea is taken up, and expanded infinitely and made responsible for everything in the universe. One particular idea is taken as the support, in which everything rests and exists, and that support has become all this. So on with various ideas. They tried this method with Prâna, the life principle. They expanded the idea of the life principle until it became universal and infinite. It is the life principle that is supporting everything; not only the human body, but it is the light of the sun and the moon, it is the power moving everything, the universal motive energy. Some of these attempts are very beautiful, very poetical. Some of them as, "He ushers the beautiful morning," are marvellously lyrical in the way they picture things. Then this very desire, which, as we have just read, arose as the first primal germ of creation, began to be stretched out, until it became the universal God. But none of these ideas satisfied.

Here the idea is sublimated and finally abstracted into a personality. "He alone existed in the beginning; He is the one Lord of all that exists; He supports this universe; He who is the author of souls, He who is the author of strength, whom all the gods worship, whose shadow is life, whose shadow is death; whom else shall we worship? Whose glory the snow-tops of the Himalayas declare, whose glory the oceans with all their waters proclaim." So on it goes, but, as I told you just now, this idea did not satisfy them.

At last we find a very peculiar position. The Aryan mind had so long been seeking an answer to the question from outside. They questioned everything they could find, the sun, the moon, and stars, and they found all they could in this way. The whole of nature at best could teach them only of a personal Being who is the Ruler of the universe; it could teach nothing further. In short, out of the external world we can only get the idea of an architect, that which is called the Design Theory. It is not a very logical argument, as we all know; there is something childish about it, yet it is the only little bit of anything we can know about God from the external world, that this world required a builder. But this is no explanation of the universe. The materials of this world were before Him, and this God wanted all these materials, and the worst objection is that He must be limited by the materials. The builder could not have made a house without the materials of which it is composed. Therefore he was limited by the materials; he could only do what the materials enabled him to. Therefore the God that the Design Theory gives is at best only an architect, and a limited architect of the universe; He is bound and restricted by the materials; He is not independent at all. That much they had found out already, and many other minds would have rested at that. In other countries the same thing happened; the human mind could not rest there; the thinking, grasping minds wanted to go further, but those that were backward got hold of them and did not allow them to grow. But fortunately these Hindu sages were not the people to be knocked on the head; they wanted to get a solution, and now we find that they were leaving the external for the internal. The first thing that struck them was, that it is not with the eyes and the senses that we perceive that external world, and know anything about religion; the first idea, therefore, was to find the deficiency, and that deficiency was both physical and moral, as we shall see. You do not know, says one of these sages, the cause of this universe; there has arisen a tremendous difference between you and me—why? Because you have been talking sense things and are satisfied with sense-objects and with the mere ceremonials of religion, while I have known the Purusha beyond.

Along with this progress of spiritual ideas that I am trying to trace for you, I can only hint to you a little about the other factor in the growth, for that has nothing to do with our subject, therefore I need not enlarge upon it—the growth of rituals. As those spiritual ideas progressed in arithmetical progression, so the ritualistic ideas progressed in geometrical progression. The old superstitions had by this time developed into a tremendous mass of rituals, which grew and grew till it almost killed the Hindu life And it is still there, it has got hold of and permeated every portion of our life and made

us born slaves. Yet, at the same time, we find a fight against this advance of ritual from the very earliest days. The one objection raised there is this, that love for ceremonials, dressing at certain times, eating in a certain way, and shows and mummeries of religion like these are only external religion, because you are satisfied with the senses and do not want to go beyond them. This is a tremendous difficulty with us, with every human being. At best when we want to hear of spiritual things our standard is the senses; or a man hears things about philosophy, and God, and transcendental things, and after hearing about them for days, he asks: After all, how much money will they bring, how much sense-enjoyment will they bring? For his enjoyment is only in the senses, quite naturally. But that satisfaction in the senses, says our sage, is one of the causes which have spread the veil between truth and ourselves. Devotion to ceremonials, satisfaction in the senses, and forming various theories, have drawn a veil between ourselves and truth. This is another great landmark, and we shall have to trace this ideal to the end, and see how it developed later on into that wonderful theory of Mâyâ of the Vedanta, how this veil will be the real explanation of the Vedanta, how the truth was there all the time, it was only this veil that had covered it.

Thus we find that the minds of these ancient Aryan thinkers had begun a new theme. They found out that in the external world no search would give an answer to their question. They might seek in the external world for ages, but there would be no answer to their questions. So they fell back upon this other method; and according to this, they were taught that these desires of the senses, desires for ceremonials and externalities have caused a veil to come between themselves and the truth, and that this cannot be removed by any ceremonial. They had to fall back on their own minds, and analyse the mind to find the truth in themselves. The outside world failed and they turned back upon the inside world, and then it became the real philosophy of the Vedanta; from here the Vedanta philosophy begins. It is the foundation-stone of Vedanta philosophy. As we go on, we find that all its inquiries are inside. From the very outset they seemed to declare—look not for the truth in any religion; it is here in the human soul, the miracle of all miracles in the human soul, the emporium of all knowledge, the mine of all existence—seek here. What is not here cannot be there. And they found out step by step that that which is external is but a dull reflection at best of that which is inside. We shall see how they took, as it were, this old idea of God, the Governor of the universe, who is external to the universe, and first put Him inside the universe. He is not a God outside, but He is inside; and they took Him from there into their own hearts. Here He is in the heart of man, the Soul of our souls, the Reality in us.

Several great ideas have to be understood, in order to grasp properly the workings of the Vedanta philosophy. In the first place it is not philosophy in the sense we speak of the philosophy of Kant and Hegel. It is not one book, or the work of one man. Vedanta is the name of a series of books written at different times. Sometimes in one of these productions there will be fifty different things. Neither are they properly arranged; the thoughts, as it were, have been jotted down. Sometimes in the midst of other extraneous things, we find some wonderful idea. But one fact is remarkable, that these ideas in the Upanishads would be always progressing. In that crude old language, the working of the mind of every one of the sages has been, as it were, painted just as it went; how the ideas are at first very crude, and they become finer and finer till they reach the goal of the Vedanta, and this goal assumes a philosophical name. Just at first it was a search after the Devas, the bright ones, and then it was the origin of the universe, and the very same search is getting another name, more philosophical, clearer—the unity of all things—"Knowing which everything else becomes known."

THE VEDANTA PHILOSOPHY

The Vedanta philosophy, as it is generally called at the present day, really comprises all the various sects that now exist in India. Thus there have been various interpretations, and to my mind they have been progressive, beginning with the dualistic or Dvaita and ending with the non-dualistic or Advaita. The word Vedanta literally means the end of the Vedas—the Vedas being the scriptures of the Hindus[1]. Sometimes in the West by the Vedas are meant only the hymns and rituals of the Vedas. But at the present time these parts have almost gone out of use, and usually by the word Vedas in India, the Vedanta is meant. All our commentators, when they want to quote a passage from the scriptures, as a rule, quote from the Vedanta, which has another technical name with the commentators—the Shrutis[2]. Now, all the books known by the name of the Vedanta were not entirely written after the ritualistic portions of the Vedas. For instance, one of them—the Ishâ Upanishad—forms the fortieth chapter of the Yajur-Veda, that being one of the oldest parts of the Vedas. There are other Upanishads[3] which form portions of the Brahmanas or

ritualistic writings; and the rest of the Upanishads are independent, not comprised in any of the Brahmanas or other parts of the Vedas; but there is no reason to suppose that they were entirely independent of other parts, for, as we well know, many of these have been lost entirely and many of the Brahmanas have become extinct. So it is quite possible that the independent Upanishads belonged to some Brahmanas, which in course of time fell into disuse, while the Upanishads remained. These Upanishads are also called Forest Books or Aranyakas.

The Vedanta, then, practically forms the scriptures of the Hindus, and all systems of philosophy that are orthodox have to take it as their foundation. Even the Buddhists and Jains, when it suits their purpose, will quote a passage from the Vedanta as authority. All schools of philosophy in India, although they claim to have been based upon the Vedas, took different names for their systems. The last one, the system of Vyâsa, took its stand upon the doctrines of the Vedas more than the previous systems did, and made an attempt to harmonise the preceding philosophies, such as the Sânkhya and the Nyâya, with the doctrines of the Vedanta. So it is especially called the Vedanta philosophy; and the Sutras or aphorisms of Vyasa are, in modern India, the basis of the Vedanta philosophy. Again, these Sutras of Vyasa have been variously explained by different commentators. In general there are three sorts of commentators[4] in India now; from their interpretations have arisen three systems of philosophy and sects. One is the dualistic, or Dvaita; a second is the qualified non-dualistic, or Vishishtâdvaita; and a third is the non-dualistic, or Advaita. Of these the dualistic and the qualified non-dualistic

1. The Vedas are divided mainly into two portions: the Karma-kânda and the Jnâna-kânda—the work-portion and the knowledge-portion. To the Karma-kanda belong the famous hymns and the rituals of Brâhmanas. Those books which treat of spiritual matters apart from ceremonials are called Upanishads. The Upanishads belong to the Jnana-kanda, or knowledge-portion. It is not that all the Upanishads were composed as a separate portion of the Vedas. Some are interspersed among the rituals, and at least one is in the Samhita, or hymn-portion. Sometimes the term Upanishad is applied to books which are not included in the Vedas—e.g the Gita, but as a rule it is applied to the philosophical treatises scattered through the Vedas. These treatises have been collected, and are called the Vedanta.

2. The term Shruti—meaning "that which is heard"—though including the whole of the Vedic literature, is chiefly applied by the commentators to the Upanishads.

3. The Upanishads are said to be one hundred and eight in number. Their dates cannot be fixed with certainty—only it is certain that they are older than the Buddhistic movement. Though some of the minor Upanishads contain allusions indicating a later date, yet that does not

prove the later date of the treatise, as in very many cases in Sanskrit literature, the substance of a book, though of very ancient date, receives a coating, as it were, of later events in the hands of the sectarians, to exalt their particular sect.

4. The commentaries are of various sorts such as the Bhâshya, Tikâ, Tippani, Churni, etc., of which all except the Bhashya are explanations of the text or difficult words in the text. The Bhashya is not properly a commentary, but the elucidation of a system of philosophy out of texts, the object being not to explain the words, but to bring out a philosophy. So the writer of a Bhashya expands his own system, taking texts as authorities for his system. There have been various commentaries on the Vedanta. Its doctrines found their final expression in the philosophical aphorisms of Vyasa. This treatise, called the Uttara Mimâmsâ, is the standard authority of Vedantism—nay, is the most authoritative exposition of the Hindu scriptures. The most antagonistic sects have been compelled, as it were, to take up the texts of Vyasa, and harmonise them with their own philosophy. Even in very ancient times the commentators on the Vedanta philosophy formed themselves into the three celebrated Hindu sects of dualists, qualified non-dualists, and non dualists. The ancient commentaries are perhaps lost; but they have been revived in modern times by the post-Buddhistic commentators, Shankara, Râmânuja, and Madhva. Shankara revived the nondualistic form, Ramanuja, the qualified non-dualistic form of the ancient commentator Bodhayana; and Madhva, the dualistic form. In India the sects differ mainly in their philosophy; the difference in rituals is slight, the basis of their philosophy and religion being the same.

include the largest number of the Indian people. The non-dualists are comparatively few in number. Now I will try to lay before you the ideas that are contained in all these three sects; but before going on, I will make one remark—that these different Vedanta systems have one common psychology, and that is, the psychology of the Sankhya system. The Sankhya psychology is very much like the psychologies of the Nyaya and Vaisheshika systems, differing only in minor particulars.

All the Vedantists agree on three points. They believe in God, in the Vedas as revealed, and in cycles. We have already considered the Vedas. The belief about cycles is as follows: All matter throughout the universe is the outcome of one primal matter called Âkâsha; and all force, whether gravitation, attraction or repulsion, or life, is the outcome of one primal force called Prâna. Prana acting on Akasha is creating or projecting[1] the universe. At the beginning of a cycle, Akasha is motionless, unmanifested. Then Prana begins to act, more and more, creating grosser and grosser forms out of Akasha—plants, animals, men, stars, and so on. After an incalculable time this evolution ceases and involution begins, everything being resolved back through finer and finer forms into the original Akasha and Prana, when a new cycle follows. Now there is something beyond Akasha and Prana. Both can be resolved into a third thing called Mahat—the Cosmic Mind. This Cosmic Mind does not create Akasha and Prana, but changes itself into them.

We will now take up the beliefs about mind, soul, and God. According to the universally accepted Sankhya psychology, in perception—in the case of vision, for instance—there are, first of all, the instruments of vision, the eyes. Behind the instruments—the eyes—is the organ of vision or Indriya—the optic nerve and its centres—which is not the external instrument, but without which the eyes will not see. More still is needed for perception. The mind or Manas must come and attach itself to the organ. And besides this, the sensation must be carried to the intellect or Buddhi—the determinative, reactive state of the mind. When the reaction comes from Buddhi, along with it flashes the external world and egoism. Here then is the will; but everything is not complete. Just as every picture, being composed of successive impulses of light, must be united on something stationary to form a whole, so all the ideas in the mind must be gathered and projected on something that is stationary—relatively to the body and mind—that is, on what is called the Soul or Purusha or Âtman.

According to the Sankhya philosophy, the reactive state of the mind called Buddhi or intellect is the outcome, the change, or a certain manifestation of the Mahat or Cosmic Mind. The Mahat becomes changed into vibrating thought;

and that becomes in one part changed into the organs, and in the other part into the fine particles of matter. Out of the combination of all these, the whole of this universe is produced. Behind even Mahat, the Sankhya conceives of a certain state which is called Avyakta or unmanifested, where even the manifestation of mind is not present, but only the causes exist. It is also called Prakriti. Beyond this Prakriti, and eternally separate from it, is the Purusha, the soul of the Sankhya which is without attributes and omnipresent. The Purusha is not the doer but the witness. The illustration of the crystal is used to explain the Purusha. The latter is said to be like a crystal without any colour, before which different colours are placed, and then it seems to be coloured by the colours before it, but in reality it is not. The Vedantists reject the Sankhya ideas of the soul and nature. They claim that between them there is a huge gulf to be bridged over. On the one hand the Sankhya system comes to nature, and then at once it has to jump over to the other side and come to the soul, which is entirely separate from nature. How can these different colours, as the Sankhya calls them, be able to act on that soul which by its nature is colourless? So the Vedantists, from the very first affirm that this soul and this nature are one[2]. Even the dualistic Vedantists admit that the Atman or God is not only the efficient cause of this universe, but also the material cause. But they only say so in so many words. They do not really mean it, for they try to escape from their conclusions, in this way: They say there are three existences in this universe—God, soul, and nature. Nature and soul are, as it were, the body of God. Nature and soul are, as it were, the body of God, and in this sense it may be said that God and the whole universe are one. But this nature and all these various souls remain different from each other through all eternity. Only at the beginning of a cycle do they become manifest; and when the cycle ends, they become fine, and remain in a fine state. The Advaita Vedantists—the non-dualists—reject this theory of the soul, and, having nearly the whole range of the Upanishads in their favour, build their philosophy entirely upon them. All the books contained in me Upanishads have one subject, one task before them—to prove the following theme: "Just as by the knowledge of one lump of clay we have the knowledge of all the clay in the universe, so what is that, knowing which we know everything in the universe?" The idea of the Advaitists is to generalise the whole universe into one—that something which is really the whole of this universe. And they claim that this whole universe is one, that it is one Being manifesting itself in all these various forms. They admit that what the Sankhya calls nature exists, but say that nature is God. It is this Being, the Sat, which has become con-

1. The word which is "creation", in the English language is in Sanskrit exactly "projection," because there is no sect in India which believes in creation as it is regarded in the West—a something coming out of nothing. What we mean by creation is projection of that which already existed.

2. The Vedanta and the Sankhya philosophy are very little opposed to each other. The Vedanta God developed out of the Sankhya's Purusha. All the systems take up the psychology of the Sankhya. Both the Vedanta and the Sankhya believe in the infinite soul, only the Sankhya believes there are many souls. According to the Sankhya, this universe does not require any explanation from outside. The Vedanta believes that there is the one Soul, which appears as many; and we build on the Sankhya's analysis.

verted into all this—the universe, man, soul, and everything that exists. Mind and Mahat are but the manifestations of that one Sat. But then the difficulty arises that this would be pantheism. How came that Sat which is unchangeable, as they admit (for that which is absolute is unchangeable), to be changed into that which is changeable, and perishable? The Advaitists here have a theory which they call Vivarta Vâda or apparent manifestation. According to the dualists and the Sankhyas, the whole of this universe is the evolution of primal nature. According to some of the Advaitists and some of the dualists, the whole of this universe is evolved from God. And according to the Advaitists proper, the followers of Shankaracharya, the whole universe is the apparent evolution of God. God is the material cause of this universe, but not really, only apparently. The celebrated illustration used is that of the rope and the snake, where the rope appeared to be the snake, but was not really so. The rope did not really change into the snake. Even so this whole universe as it exists is that Being. It is unchanged, and all the changes we see in it are only apparent. These changes are caused by Desha, Kâla and Nimitta (space, time, and causation), or, according to a higher psychological generalization, by Nâma and Rupa (name and form). It is by name and form that one thing is differentiated from another. The name and form alone cause the difference. In reality they are one and the same. Again, it is not, the Vedantists say, that there is something as phenomenon and something as noumenon. The rope is changed into the snake apparently only; and when the delusion ceases, the snake vanishes. When one is in ignorance, he sees the phenomenon and does not see God. When he sees God, this universe vanishes entirely for him. Ignorance or Mâyâ, as it is called, is the cause of all this phenomenon—the Absolute, the Unchangeable, being taken as this manifested universe. This Maya is not absolute zero, nor non-existence. It is defined as neither existence nor non-existence. It is not existence, because that can be said only of the Absolute, the Unchangeable, and in this sense, Maya is non-existence. Again, it cannot be said it is non-existence; for if it were, it could never produce phenomenon. So it is something which is neither; and in the Vedanta philosophy it is called Anirvachaniya or inexpressible. Maya, then, is the real cause of this universe. Maya gives the name and form to what Brahman or God gives the material; and the latter seems to have been transformed into all this. The Advaitists, then, have no place for the individual soul. They say individual souls are created by Maya. In reality they cannot exist. If there were only one existence throughout, how could it be that I am one, and you are one, and so forth? We are all one, and the cause of evil is the perception of duality. As soon as I begin to feel that I am separate from this universe, then first comes fear, and then comes misery. "Where one hears another, one sees another, that is small. Where one does not see another, where one does not hear another, that is the greatest, that is God. In that greatest is perfect happiness. In small things there is no happiness."

According to the Advaita philosophy, then, this differentiation of matter, these phenomena, are, as it were, for a time, hiding the real nature of man; but the latter really has not been changed at all. In the lowest worm, as well as in the highest human being, the same divine nature is present. The worm form is the lower form in which the divinity has been more overshadowed by Maya; that is the highest form in which it has been least overshadowed. Behind everything the same divinity is existing, and out of this comes the basis of morality. Do not injure another. Love everyone as your own self, because the whole universe is one. In injuring another, I am injuring myself; in loving another, I am loving myself. From this also springs that principle of Advaita morality which has been summed up in one word—self-abnegation. The Advaitist says, this little personalised self is the cause of all my misery. This individualised self, which makes me different from all other beings, brings hatred and jealousy and misery, struggle and all other evils. And when this idea has been got rid of, all struggle will cease, all misery vanish. So this is to be given up. We must always hold ourselves ready, even to give up our lives for the lowest beings. When a man has become ready even to give up his life for a little insect, he has reached the perfection which the Advaitist wants to attain; and at that moment when he has become thus ready, the veil of ignorance falls away from him, and he will feel his own nature. Even in this life, he will feel that he is one with the universe. For a time, as it were, the whole of this phenomenal world will disappear for him, and he will realise what he is. But so long as the Karma of this body remains, he will have to live. This state, when the veil has vanished and yet the body remains for some time, is what the Vedantists call the Jivanmukti, the living freedom. If a man is deluded by a mirage for some time, and one day the mirage disappears—if it comes back again the next day, or at some future time, he will not be deluded. Before the mirage first broke, the man could not distinguish between the reality and the deception. But when it has once broken, as long as he has organs and eyes to work with, he will see the image, but will no more be deluded. That fine distinction between the actual world and the mirage he has caught, and the latter cannot delude him any more. So when the Vedantist has realised his own nature, the whole world has vanished for him. It will come back again, but no more the same world of misery. The prison of misery has become changed into Sat, Chit, Ânanda—Existence Absolute, Knowledge Absolute, Bliss Absolute—and the attainment of this is the goal of the Advaita Philosophy.[3]

REASON AND RELIGION

Delivered in England

A sage called Nârada went to another sage named Sanatkumâra to learn about truth, and Sanatkumara inquired what

3. The above address was delivered before the Graduate Philosophical Society of Harvard University, on March 25, 1896.

he had studied already. Narada answered that he had studied the Vedas, Astronomy, and various other things, yet he had got no satisfaction. Then there was a conversation between the two, in the course of which Sanatkumara remarked that all this knowledge of the Vedas, of Astronomy, and of Philosophy, was but secondary; sciences were but secondary. That which made us realise the Brahman was the supreme, the highest knowledge. This idea we find in every religion, and that is why religion always claimed to be supreme knowledge. Knowledge of the sciences covers, as it were, only part of our lives, but the knowledge which religion brings to us is eternal, as infinite as the truth it preaches. Claiming this superiority, religions have many times looked down, unfortunately, on all secular knowledge, and not only so, but many times have refused to be justified by the aid of secular knowledge. In consequence, all the world over there have been fights between secular knowledge and religious knowledge, the one claiming infallible authority as its guide, refusing to listen to anything that secular knowledge has to say on the point, the other, with its shining instrument of reason, wanting to cut to pieces everything religion could bring forward. This fight has been and is still waged in every country. Religions have been again and again defeated, and almost exterminated. The worship of the goddess of Reason during the French Revolution was not the first manifestation of that phenomenon in the history of humanity, it was a re-enactment of what had happened in ancient times, but in modern times it has assumed greater proportions. The physical sciences are better equipped now than formerly, and religions have become less and less equipped. The foundations have been all undermined, and the modern man, whatever he may say in public, knows in the privacy of his heart that he can no more "believe". Believing certain things because an organised body of priests tells him to believe, believing because it is written in certain books, believing because his people like him to believe, the modern man knows to be impossible for him. There are, of course, a number of people who seem to acquiesce in the so-called popular faith, but we also know for certain that they do not think. Their idea of belief may be better translated as "not-thinking-carelessness". This fight cannot last much longer without breaking to pieces all the buildings of religion.

The question is: Is there a way out? To put it in a more concrete form: Is religion to justify itself by the discoveries of reason, through which every other science justifies itself? Are the same methods of investigation, which we apply to sciences and knowledge outside, to be applied to the science of Religion? In my opinion this must be so, and I am also of opinion that the sooner it is done the better. If a religion is destroyed by such investigations, it was then all the time useless, unworthy superstition; and the sooner it goes the better. I am thoroughly convinced that its destruction would be the best thing that could happen. All that is dross will be taken off, no doubt, but the essential parts of religion will emerge triumphant out of this investigation. Not only will it be made

scientific — as scientific, at least, as any of the conclusions of physics or chemistry — but will have greater strength, because physics or chemistry has no internal mandate to vouch for its truth, which religion has.

People who deny the efficacy of any rationalistic investigation into religion seem to me somewhat to be contradicting themselves. For instance, the Christian claims that his religion is the only true one, because it was revealed to so-and-so. The Mohammedan makes the same claim for his religion; his is the only true one, because it was revealed to so-and-so. But the Christian says to the Mohammedan, "Certain parts of your ethics do not seem to be right. For instance, your books say, my Mohammedan friend, that an infidel may be converted to the religion of Mohammed by force, and if he will not accept the Mohammedan religion he may be killed; and any Mohammedan who kills such an infidel will get a sure entry into heaven, whatever may have been his sins or misdeeds." The Mohammedan will retort by saying, "It is right for me to do so, because my book enjoins it. It will be wrong on my part not to do so." The Christian says, "But my book does not say so." The Mohammedan replies, "I do not know; I am not bound by the authority of your book; my book says, 'Kill all the infidels'. How do you know which is right and which is wrong? Surely what is written in my book is right and what your book says, 'Do not kill,' is wrong. You also say the same thing, my Christian friend; you say that what Jehovah declared to the Jews is right to do, and what he forbade them to do is wrong. So say I, Allah declared in my book that certain things should be done, and that certain things should not be done, and that is all the test of right and wrong." In spite of that the Christian is not satisfied; he insists on a comparison of the morality of the Sermon on the Mount with the morality of the Koran. How is this to be decided? Certainly not by the books, because the books, fighting between themselves, cannot be the judges. Decidedly then we have to admit that there is something more universal than these books, something higher than all the ethical codes that are in the world, something which can judge between the strength of inspirations of different nations. Whether we declare it boldly, clearly, or not — it is evident that here we appeal to reason.

Now, the question arises if this light of reason is able to judge between inspiration and inspiration, and if this light can uphold its standard when the quarrel is between prophet and prophet, if it has the power of understanding anything whatsoever of religion. If it has not, nothing can determine the hopeless fight of books and prophets which has been going on through ages; for it means that all religions are mere lies, hopelessly contradictory, without any constant idea of ethics. The proof of religion depends on the truth of the constitution of man, and not on any books. These books are the outgoings, the effects of man's constitution; man made these books. We are yet to see the books that made man. Reason is equally an effect of that common cause, the constitution of man, where our appeal must be. And yet, as reason alone is directly connected with this constitution, it should be resorted to, as long as it follows faithfully the same. What do I mean by reason? I mean what every educated man or woman is wanting to do at the present time, to apply the discoveries of secular knowledge to religion. The first principle of reasoning is that the particular is explained by the general, the general by the more general, until we come to the universal. For instance, we have the idea of law. If something happens and we believe that it is the effect of such and such a law, we are satisfied; that is an explanation for us. What we mean by that explanation is that it is proved that this one effect, which had dissatisfied us, is only one particular of a general mass of occurrences which we designate by the word "law". When one apple fell, Newton was disturbed; but when he found that all apples fell, it was gravitation, and he was satisfied. This is one principle of human knowledge. I see a particular being, a human being, in the street. I refer him to the bigger conception of man, and I am satisfied; I know he is a man by referring him to the more general. So the particulars are to be referred to the general, the general to the more general, and everything at last to the universal, the last concept that we have, the most universal — that of existence. Existence is the most universal concept.

We are all human beings; that is to say, each one of us, as it were, a particular part of the general concept, humanity. A man, and a cat, and a dog, are all animals. These particular examples, as man, or dog, or cat, are parts of a bigger and more general concept, animal. The man, and the cat, and the dog, and the plant, and the tree, all come under the still more general concept, life. Again, all these, all beings and all materials, come under the one concept of existence, for we all are in it. This explanation merely means referring the particular to a higher concept, finding more of its kind. The mind, as it were, has stored up numerous classes of such generalisations. It is, as it were, full of pigeon-holes where all these ideas are grouped together, and whenever we find a new thing the mind immediately tries to find out its type in one of these pigeon-holes. If we find it, we put the new thing in there and are satisfied, and we are said to have known the thing. This is what is meant by knowledge, and no more. And if we do not find that there is something like it, we are dissatisfied, and have to wait until we find a further classification for it, already existing in the mind. Therefore, as I have already pointed out, knowledge is more or less classification. There is something more. A second explanation of knowledge is that the explanation of a thing must come from inside and not from outside. There had been the belief that, when a man threw up a stone and it fell, some demon dragged it down. Many occurrences which are really natural phenomena are attributed by people to unnatural beings. That a ghost dragged down the stone was an explanation that was not in the thing itself, it was an explanation from outside; but the second explanation of gravitation is something in the nature of the stone; the explanation is coming from inside. This tendency you will find throughout modern thought; in one word, what is meant by science is that the explanations of things are in their own nature, and that no external beings or existences are required to explain what is going on in the universe. The chemist never requires demons, or ghosts, or anything of that sort, to explain his phenomena. The physicist never requires any one of these to explain the things he knows, nor does any other scientist. And this is one of the features of science which I mean to apply to religion. In this religions are found wanting and that is why they are crumbling into pieces. Every science wants its explanations from inside, from the very nature of things; and the religions are not able to supply this. There is an ancient theory of a personal deity entirely separate from the universe, which has been held from the very earliest time. The arguments in favour of this have been repeated again and again, how it is necessary to have a God entirely separate from the universe, an extra-cosmic deity, who has created the universe out of his will, and is conceived by religion to be its ruler. We find, apart from all these arguments, the Almighty God painted as the All-merciful, and at the same time, inequalities remain in the world. These things do not concern the philosopher at all, but he says the heart of the thing was wrong; it was an explanation from outside, and not inside. What is the cause of the universe? Something outside of it, some being who is moving this universe! And just as it was found insufficient to explain the phenomenon of the falling stone, so this was found insufficient to explain religion. And religions are falling to pieces, because they cannot give a better explanation than that.

Another idea connected with this, the manifestation of the same principle, that the explanation of everything comes from inside it, is the modern law of evolution. The whole meaning of evolution is simply that the nature of a thing is reproduced, that the effect is nothing but the cause in another form, that all the potentialities of the effect were present in the cause, that the whole of creation is but an evolution and not a creation. That is to say, every effect is a reproduction of a preceding cause, changed only by the circumstances, and thus it is going on throughout the universe, and we need not go outside the universe to seek the causes of these changes; they are within. It is unnecessary to seek for any cause outside. This also is breaking down religion. What I mean by breaking down religion is that religions that have held on to the idea of an extra-cosmic deity, that he is a very big man and nothing else, can no more stand on their feet; they have been pulled down, as it were.

Can there be a religion satisfying these two principles? I think there can be. In the first place we have seen that we have to satisfy the principle of generalisation. The generalisation principle ought to be satisfied along with the principle of evolution. We have to come to an ultimate generalisation, which not only will be the most universal of all generalisations, but out of which everything else must come. It will be of the same nature as the lowest effect; the cause, the highest, the ultimate, the primal cause, must be the same as the lowest and most distant of its effects, a series of evolutions. The Brahman of the Vedanta fulfils that condition, because Brahman is the last generalisation to which we can come. It has no attributes but is Existence, Knowledge, and Bliss—Absolute. Existence, we have seen, is the very ultimate generalisation which the human mind can come to. Knowledge does not mean the knowledge we have, but the essence of that, that which is expressing itself in the course of evolution in human beings or in other animals as knowledge. The essence of that knowledge is meant, the ultimate fact beyond, if I may be allowed to say so, even consciousness. That is what is meant by knowledge and what we see in the universe as the essential unity of things. To my mind, if modern science is proving anything again and again, it is this, that we are one—mentally, spiritually, and physically. It is wrong to say we are even physically different. Supposing we are materialists, for argument's sake, we shall have to come to this, that the whole universe is simply an ocean of matter, of which you and I are like little whirlpools. Masses of matter are coming into each whirlpool, taking the whirlpool form, and coming out as matter again. The matter that is in my body may have been in yours a few years ago, or in the sun, or may have been the matter in a plant, and so on, in a continuous state of flux. What is meant by your body and my body? It is the oneness of the body. So with thought. It is an ocean of thought, one infinite mass, in which your mind and my mind are like whirlpools. Are you not seeing the effect now, how my thoughts are entering into yours, and yours into mine? The whole of our lives is one; we are one, even in thought. Coming to a still further generalisation, the essence of matter and thought is their potentiality of spirit; this is the unity from which all have come, and that must essentially be one. We are absolutely one; we are physically one, we are mentally one, and as spirit, it goes without saying, that we are one, if we believe in spirit at all. This oneness is the one fact that is being proved every day by modern science. To proud man it is told: You are the same as that little worm there; think not that you are something enormously different from it; you are the same. You have been that in a previous incarnation, and the worm has crawled up to this man state, of which you are so proud. This grand preaching, the oneness of things, making us one with everything that exists, is the great lesson to learn, for most of us are very glad to be made one with higher beings, but nobody wants to be made one with lower beings. Such is human ignorance, that if anyone's ancestors were men whom society honoured, even if they were brutish, if they were robbers, even robber barons, everyone of us would try to trace our ancestry to them; but if among our ancestors we had poor, honest gentlemen, none of us wants to trace our ancestry to them. But the scales are falling from our eyes, truth is beginning to manifest itself more and more, and that is a great gain to religion. That is exactly the teaching of the Advaita, about which I am lecturing to you. The Self is the essence of this universe, the essence of all souls; He is the essence of your own life, nay, "Thou art That". You are one with this universe. He who says he is different from others, even by a hair's breadth, immediately becomes miserable. Happiness belongs to him who knows this oneness, who knows he is one with this universe.

Thus we see that the religion of the Vedanta can satisfy the demands of the scientific world, by referring it to the highest generalisation and to the law of evolution. That the explanation of a thing comes from within itself is still more completely satisfied by Vedanta. The Brahman, the God of the Vedanta, has nothing outside of Himself; nothing at all. All this indeed is He: He is in the universe: He is the universe Himself. "Thou art the man, Thou art the woman, Thou art the young man walking in the pride of youth, Thou art the old man tottering in his step." He is here. Him we see and feel: in Him we live, and move, and have our being. You have that conception in the New Testament. It is that idea, God immanent in the universe, the very essence, the heart, the soul of things. He manifests Himself, as it were, in this universe. You and I are little bits, little points, little channels, little expressions, all living inside of that infinite ocean of Existence, Knowledge, and Bliss. The difference between man and man, between angels and man, between man and animals, between animals and plants, between plants and stones is not in kind, because everyone from the highest angel to the lowest particle of matter is but an expression of that one infinite ocean, and the difference is only in degree. I am a low manifestation, you may be a higher, but in both the materials are the same. You and I are both outlets of the same channel, and that is God; as such, your nature is God, and so is mine. You are of the nature of God by your birthright; so am I. You may be an angel of purity, and I may be the blackest of demons. Nevertheless, my birthright is that infinite ocean of Existence, Knowledge, and Bliss. So is yours. You have manifested yourself more today. Wait; I will manifest myself more yet, for I have it all within me. No extraneous explanation is sought; none is asked for. The sum total of this whole universe is God Himself. Is God then matter? No, certainly not, for matter is that God perceived by the five senses; that God as perceived through the intellect is mind; and when the spirit sees, He is seen as spirit. He is not matter, but whatever is real in matter is He. Whatever is real in this chair is He, for the chair requires two things to make it. Something was outside which my senses brought to me, and to which my mind contributed something else, and the combination of these two is the chair. That which existed eternally, independent of the senses and of the intellect, was the Lord Himself. Upon Him the senses are painting chairs, and tables, and rooms, houses, and worlds, and moons, and suns, and stars, and everything else. How is it, then, that we all see this same chair, that we are all alike painting these various things on the Lord, on this Existence, Knowledge, and Bliss? It need not be that all paint the same way, but those who paint the same way are on the same plane of existence and therefore they see one another's paintings as well as one another. There may be millions of beings between you and me who do not paint the Lord in the same way, and them and their paintings we do not see.

On the other hand, as you all know, the modern physical researches are tending more and more to demonstrate that what is real is but the finer; the gross is simply appearance. However that may be, we have seen that if any theory of religion can stand the test of modern reasoning, it is the Advaita, because it fulfils its two requirements. It is the highest generalisation, beyond even personality, generalisation which is common to every being. A generalisation ending in the Personal God can never be universal, for, first of all, to conceive of a Personal God we must say, He is all-merciful, all-good. But this world is a mixed thing, some good and some bad. We cut off what we like, and generalise that into a Personal God! Just as you say a Personal God is this and that, so you have also to say that He is not this and not that. And you will always find that the idea of a Personal God has to carry with it a personal devil. That is how we clearly see that the idea of a Personal God is not a true generalisation, we have to go beyond, to the Impersonal. In that the universe exists, with all its joys and miseries, for whatever exists in it has all come from the Impersonal. What sort of a God can He be to whom we attribute evil and other things? The idea is that both good and evil are different aspects, or manifestations of the same thing. The idea that they were two was a very wrong idea from the first, and it has been the cause of a good deal of the misery in this world of ours — the idea that right and wrong are two separate things, cut and dried, independent of each other, that good and evil are two eternally separable and separate things. I should be very glad to see a man who could show me something which is good all the time, and something which is bad all the time. As if one could stand and gravely define some occurrences in this life of ours as good and good alone, and some which are bad and bad alone. That which is good today may be evil tomorrow. That which is bad today may be good tomorrow. What is good for me may be bad for you. The conclusion is, that like every other thing, there is an evolution in good and evil too. There is something which in its evolution, we call, in one degree, good, and in another, evil. The storm that kills my friend I call evil, but that may have saved the lives of hundreds of thousands of people by killing the bacilli in the air. They call it good, but I call it evil. So both good and evil belong to the relative world, to phenomena. The Impersonal God we propose is not a relative God; therefore it cannot be said that It is either good or bad, but that It is something beyond, because It is neither good nor evil. Good, however, is a nearer manifestation of It than evil.

What is the effect of accepting such an Impersonal Being, an Impersonal Deity? What shall we gain? Will religion stand as a factor in human life, our consoler, our helper? What becomes of the desire of the human heart to pray for help to some being? That will all remain. The Personal God will remain, but on a better basis. He has been strengthened by the Impersonal. We have seen that without the Impersonal, the

Personal cannot remain. If you mean to say there is a Being entirely separate from this universe, who has created this universe just by His will, out of nothing, that cannot be proved. Such a state of things cannot be. But if we understand the idea of the Impersonal, then the idea of the Personal can remain there also. This universe, in its various forms, is but the various readings of the same Impersonal. When we read it with the five senses, we call it the material world. If there be a being with more senses than five, he will read it as something else. If one of us gets the electrical sense, he will see the universe as something else again. There are various forms of that same Oneness, of which all these various ideas of worlds are but various readings, and the Personal God is the highest reading that can be attained to, of that Impersonal, by the human intellect. So that the Personal God is true as much as this chair is true, as much as this world is true, but no more. It is not absolute truth. That is to say, the Personal God is that very Impersonal God and, therefore, it is true, just as I, as a human being, am true and not true at the same time. It is not true that I am what you see I am; you can satisfy yourself on that point. I am not the being that you take me to be. You can satisfy your reason as to that, because light, and various vibrations, or conditions of the atmosphere, and all sorts of motions inside me have contributed to my being looked upon as what I am, by you. If any one of these conditions change, I am different again. You may satisfy yourself by taking a photograph of the same man under different conditions of light. So I am what I appear in relation to your senses, and yet, in spite of all these facts, there is an unchangeable something of which all these are different states of existence, the impersonal me, of which thousands of me's are different persons. I was a child, I was young, I am getting older. Every day of my life, my body and thoughts are changing, but in spite of all these changes, the sum-total of them constitutes a mass which is a constant quantity. That is the impersonal me, of which all these manifestations form, as it were, parts.

Similarly, the sum-total of this universe is immovable, we know, but everything pertaining to this universe consists of motion, everything is in a constant state of flux, everything changing and moving. At the same time, we see that the universe as a whole is immovable, because motion is a relative term. I move with regard to the chair, which does not move. There must be at least two to make motion. If this whole universe is taken as a unit there is no motion; with regard to what should it move? Thus the Absolute is unchangeable and immovable, and all the movements and changes are only in the phenomenal world, the limited. That whole is Impersonal, and within this Impersonal are all these various persons beginning with the lowest atom, up to God, the Personal God, the Creator, the Ruler of the Universe, to whom we pray, before whom we kneel, and so on. Such a Personal God can be established with a great deal of reason. Such a Personal God is explicable as the highest manifestation of the Impersonal. You and I are very low manifestations, and the Personal God is the highest of which we can conceive. Nor can you or I become that Personal God. When the Vedanta says you and I are God, it does not mean the Personal God. To take an example. Out of a mass of clay a huge elephant of clay is manufactured, and out of the same clay, a little clay mouse is made. Would the clay mouse ever be able to become the clay elephant? But put them both in water and they are both clay; as clay they are both one, but as mouse and elephant there will be an eternal difference between them. The Infinite, the Impersonal, is like the clay in the example. We and the Ruler of the Universe are one, but as manifested beings, men, we are His eternal slaves, His worshippers. Thus we see that the Personal God remains. Everything else in this relative world remains, and religion is made to stand on a better foundation. Therefore it is necessary, that we first know the Impersonal in order to know the Personal.

As we have seen, the law of reason says, the particular is only known through the general. So all these particulars, from man to God, are only known through the Impersonal, the highest generalisation. Prayers will remain, only they will get a better meaning. All those senseless ideas of prayer, the low stages of prayer, which are simply giving words to all sorts of silly desire in our minds, perhaps, will have to go. In all sensible religions, they never allow prayers to God; they allow prayers to gods. That is quite natural. The Roman Catholics pray to the saints; that is quite good. But to pray to God is senseless. To ask God to give you a breath of air, to send down a shower of rain, to make fruits grow in your garden, and so on, is quite unnatural. The saints, however, who were little beings like ourselves, may help us. But to pray to the Ruler of the Universe, prating every little need of ours, and from our childhood saying, "O Lord, I have a headache; let it go," is ridiculous. There have been millions of souls that have died in this world, and they are all here; they have become gods and angels; let them come to your help. But God! It cannot be. Unto Him we must go for higher things. A fool indeed is he who, resting on the banks of the Gangâ, digs a little well for water; a fool indeed is he who, living near a mine of diamonds, digs for bits of crystal.

And indeed we shall be fools if we go to the Father of all mercy, Father of all love, for trivial earthly things. Unto Him, therefore, we shall go for light, for strength, for love. But so long as there is weakness and a craving for servile dependence in us, there will be these little prayers and ideas of the worship of the Personal God. But those who are highly advanced do not care for such little helps, they have wellnigh forgotten all about this seeking things for themselves, wanting things for themselves. The predominant idea in them is—not I, but thou, my brother. Those are the fit persons to worship the Impersonal God. And what is the worship of the Impersonal God? No slavery there—"O Lord, I am nothing, have mercy on me." You know the old Persian poem, translated into English: "I came to see my beloved. The doors were closed. I knocked and a voice came from inside. 'Who art thou?' 'I am

so-and-so' The door was not opened. A second time I came and knocked; I was asked the same question, and gave the same answer. The door opened not. I came a third time, and the same question came. I answered, 'I am thee, my love,' and the door opened." Worship of the Impersonal God is through truth. And what is truth? That I am He. When I say that I am not Thou, it is untrue. When I say I am separate from you it is a lie, a terrible lie. I am one with this universe, born one. It is self evident to my senses that I am one with the universe. I am one with the air that surrounds me, one with heat, one with light, eternally one with the whole Universal Being, who is called this universe, who is mistaken for the universe, for it is He and nothing else, the eternal subject in the heart who says, "I am," in every heart—the deathless one, the sleepless one, ever awake, the immortal, whose glory never dies, whose powers never fail. I am one with That.

This is all the worship of the Impersonal, and what is the result? The whole life of man will be changed. Strength, strength it is that we want so much in this life, for what we call sin and sorrow have all one cause, and that is our weakness. With weakness comes ignorance, and with ignorance comes misery. It will make us strong. Then miseries will be laughed at, then the violence of the vile will be smiled at, and the ferocious tiger will reveal, behind its tiger's nature, my own Self. That will be the result. That soul is strong that has become one with the Lord; none else is strong. In your own Bible, what do you think was the cause of that strength of Jesus of Nazareth, that immense, infinite strength which laughed at traitors, and blessed those that were willing to murder him? It was that, "I and my Father are one"; it was that prayer, "Father, just as I am one with you, so make them all one with me." That is the worship of the Impersonal God. Be one with the universe, be one with Him. And this Impersonal God requires no demonstrations, no proofs. He is nearer to us than even our senses, nearer to us than our own thoughts; it is in and through Him that we see and think. To see anything, I must first see Him. To see this wall I first see Him, and then the wall, for He is the eternal subject. Who is seeing whom? He is here in the heart of our hearts. Bodies and minds change; misery, happiness, good and evil come and go; days and years roll on; life comes and goes; but He dies not. The same voice, "I am, I am," is eternal, unchangeable. In Him and through Him we know everything. In Him and through Him we see everything. In Him and through Him we sense, we think, we live, and we are. And that "I," which we mistake to be a little "I," limited, is not only my "I," but yours, the "I" of everyone, of the animals, of the angels, of the lowest of the low. That "I am" is the same in the murderer as in the saint, the same in the rich as in the poor, the same in man as in woman, the same in man as in animals. From the lowest amoeba to the highest angel, He resides in every soul, and eternally declares, "I am He, I am He." When we have understood that voice eternally present there, when we have learnt this lesson, the whole universe will have expressed its secret. Nature will have given up her secret to us.

Nothing more remains to be known. Thus we find the truth for which all religions search, that all this knowledge of material sciences is but secondary. That is the only true knowledge which makes us one with this Universal God of the Universe.

VEDANTA AS A FACTOR IN CIVILISATION

Extract from an address delivered at Airlie Lodge, Ridgeway Gardens, England

People who are capable of seeing only the gross external aspect of things can perceive in the Indian nation only a conquered and suffering people, a race of dreamers and philosophers. They seem to be incapable of perceiving that in the spiritual realm India conquers the world. No doubt it is true that just as the too active Western mind would profit by an admixture of Eastern introspect ion and the meditative habit, so the Eastern would benefit by a somewhat greater activity and energy. Still we must ask: What may be that force which causes this afflicted and suffering people, the Hindu, and the Jewish too (the two races from which have originated all the great religions of the world) to survive, when other nations perish? The cause can only be their spiritual force. The Hindus are still living though silent, the Jews are more numerous today than when they lived in Palestine. The philosophy of India percolates throughout the whole civilised world, modifying and permeating as it goes. So also in ancient times, her trade reached the shores of Africa before Europe was known, and opened communication with the rest of the world, thus disproving the belief that Indians never went outside of their own country.

It is remarkable also that the possession of India by a foreign power has always been a turning-point in the history of that power, bringing to it wealth, prosperity, dominion, and spiritual ideas. While the Western man tries to measure how much it is possible for him to possess and to enjoy, the Eastern seems to take the opposite course, and to measure how little of material possessions he can do with. In the Vedas we trace the endeavour of that ancient people to find God. In their search for Him they came upon different strata; beginning with ancestor worship, they passed on to the worship of Agni, the fire-god, of Indra, the god of thunder, and of Varuna, the God of gods. We find the growth of this idea of God, from many gods to one God, in all religions; its real meaning is that He is the chief of the tribal gods, who creates the world, rules it, and sees into every heart; the stages of growth lead up from a multiplicity of gods to monotheism. This anthropomorphic conception, however, did not satisfy the Hindus, it was too human for them who were seeking the Divine. Therefore they finally gave up searching for God in the outer world of sense and matter, and turned their attention to the inner world. Is there an inner world? And what is it? It is Âtman. It is the Self, it is the only thing an individual can be sure of. If he knows himself, he can know the universe, and not otherwise. The same question was asked in the beginning of time, even in the Rig-Veda, in another form: "Who or what existed from the beginning?" That question was gradually solved by the Vedanta philosophy. The Atman existed. That is to say, what we call the Absolute, the Universal Soul, the Self, is the force by which from the beginning all things have been and are and will be manifested.

While the Vedanta philosophers solved that question, they at the same time discovered the basis of ethics. Though all religions have taught ethical precepts, such as, "Do not kill, do not injure; love your neighbour as yourself," etc., yet none of these has given the reason. Why should I not injure my neighbour? To this question there was no satisfactory or conclusive answer forthcoming, until it was evolved by the metaphysical speculations of the Hindus who could not rest satisfied with mere dogmas. So the Hindus say that this Atman is absolute and all-pervading, therefore infinite. There cannot be two infinites, for they would limit each other and would become finite. Also each individual soul is a part and parcel of that Universal Soul, which is infinite. Therefore in injuring his neighbour, the individual actually injures himself. This is the basic metaphysical truth underlying all ethical codes. It is too often believed that a person in his progress towards perfection passes from error to truth; that when he passes on from one thought to another, he must necessarily reject the first. But no error can lead to truth. The soul passing through its different stages goes from truth to truth, and each stage is true; it goes from lower truth to higher truth. This point may be illustrated in the following way. A man is journeying towards the sun and takes a photograph at each step. How different would be the first photograph from the second and still more from the third or the last, when he reaches the real sun! But all these, though differing so widely from each other, are true, only they are made to appear different by the changing conditions of time and space. It is the recognition of this truth, which has enabled the Hindus to perceive the universal truth of all religions, from the lowest to the highest; it has made of them the only people who never had religious persecutions. The shrine of a Mohammedan saint which is at the present day neglected and forgotten by Mohammedans, is worshipped by Hindus! Many instances may be quoted, illustrating the same spirit of tolerance.

The Eastern mind could not rest satisfied till it had found that goal, which is the end sought by all humanity, namely, Unity. The Western scientist seeks for unity in the atom or the molecule. When he finds it, there is nothing further for him to discover, and so when we find that Unity of Soul or Self, which is called Atman, we can go no further. It becomes clear that everything in the sense world is a manifestation of that One Substance. Further, the scientist is brought to the necessity of recognising metaphysics, when he supposes that atoms having neither breadth nor length yet become, when combined, the cause of extension, length, and breadth. When one atom acts upon another, some medium is necessary. What is that medium? It will be a third atom. If so, then the question still remains unanswered, for how do these two act on the third? A manifest reductio ad absurdum. This contradiction in terms is also found in the hypothesis necessary to all physical science that a point is that which has neither parts nor magnitude, and a line has length without breadth. These cannot be either seen or conceived. Why? Because they do not come within the range of the senses. They are metaphysical conceptions. So we see, it is finally the mind which gives the form to all perception. When I see a chair, it is not the real chair external to my eye which I perceive, but an external something plus the mental image formed. Thus even the materialist is driven to metaphysics in the last extremity.

THE SPIRIT AND INFLUENCE OF VEDANTA

Delivered at the Twentieth Century Club, Boston

Before going into the subject of this afternoon, will you allow me to say a few words of thanks, now that I have the opportunity? I have lived three years amongst you. I have travelled over nearly the whole of America, and as I am going back from here to my own country, it is meet that I should take this opportunity of expressing my gratitude in this Athens of America. When I first came to this country, after a few days I thought I would be able to write a book on the nation. But after three years' stay here, I find I am not able to write even a page. On the other hand, I find in travelling in various countries that beneath the surface differences that we find in dress and food and little details of manners, man is man all the world over; the same wonderful human nature is everywhere represented. Yet there are certain characteristics, and in a few words I would like to sum up all my experiences here. In this land of America, no question is asked about a man's peculiarities. If a man is a man, that is enough, and they take him into their hearts, and that is one thing I have never seen in any other country in the world.

I came here to represent a philosophy of India, which is called the Vedanta philosophy. This philosophy is very, very ancient; it is the outcome of that mass of ancient Aryan literature known by the name of the Vedas. It is, as it were, the very flower of all the speculations and experiences and analyses, embodied in that mass of literature—collected and culled through centuries. This Vedanta philosophy has certain peculiarities. In the first place, it is perfectly impersonal; it does not owe its origin to any person or prophet: it does not build itself around one man as a centre. Yet it has nothing to say against philosophies which do build themselves around certain persons. In later days in India, other philosophies and systems arose, built around certain persons—such as Buddhism, or many of our present sects. They each have a certain leader to whom they owe allegiance, just as the Christians and Mohammedans have. But the Vedanta philosophy stands at the background of all these various sects, and there is no fight and no antagonism between the Vedanta and any other

system in the world.

One principle it lays down—and that, the Vedanta claims, is to be found in every religion in the world—that man is divine, that all this which we see around us is the outcome of that consciousness of the divine. Everything that is strong, and good, and powerful in human nature is the outcome of that divinity, and though potential in many, there is no difference between man and man essentially, all being alike divine. There is, as it were, an infinite ocean behind, and you and I are so many waves, coming out of that infinite ocean; and each one of us is trying his best to manifest that infinite outside. So, potentially, each one of us has that infinite ocean of Existence, Knowledge, and Bliss as our birthright, our real nature; and the difference between us is caused by the greater or lesser power to manifest that divine. Therefore the Vedanta lays down that each man should be treated not as what he manifests, but as what he stands for. Each human being stands for the divine, and, therefore, every teacher should be helpful, not by condemning man, but by helping him to call forth the divinity that is within him.

It also teaches that all the vast mass of energy that we see displayed in society and in every plane of action is really from inside out; and, therefore, what is called inspiration by other sects, the Vedantist begs the liberty to call the expiration of man. At the same time it does not quarrel with other sects; the Vedanta has no quarrel with those who do not understand this divinity of man. Consciously or unconsciously, every man is trying to unfold that divinity.

Man is like an infinite spring, coiled up in a small box, and that spring is trying to unfold itself; and all the social phenomena that we see the result of this trying to unfold. All the competitions and struggles and evils that we see around us are neither the causes of these unfoldments, nor the effects. As one of our great philosophers says—in the case of the irrigation of a field, the tank is somewhere upon a higher level, and the water is trying to rush into the field, and is barred by a gate. But as soon as the gate is opened, the water rushes in by its own nature; and if there is dust and dirt in the way, the water rolls over them. But dust and dirt are neither the result nor the cause of this unfolding of the divine nature of man. They are coexistent circumstances, and, therefore, can be remedied.

Now, this idea, claims the Vedanta, is to be found in all religions, whether in India or outside of it; only, in some of them, the idea is expressed through mythology, and in others, through symbology. The Vedanta claims that there has not been one religious inspiration, one manifestation of the divine man, however great, but it has been the expression of that infinite oneness in human nature; and all that we call ethics and morality and doing good to others is also but the manifestation of this oneness. There are moments when every man feels that he is one with the universe, and he rushes forth to express it, whether he knows it or not. This expression of oneness is what we call love and sympathy, and it is the basis of all our ethics and morality. This is summed up in the Vedanta philosophy by the celebrated aphorism, Tat Tvam Asi, "Thou art That".

To every man, this is taught: Thou art one with this Universal Being, and, as such, every soul that exists is your soul; and every body that exists is your body; and in hurting anyone, you hurt yourself, in loving anyone, you love yourself. As soon as a current of hatred is thrown outside, whomsoever else it hurts, it also hurts yourself; and if love comes out from you, it is bound to come back to you. For I am the universe; this universe is my body. I am the Infinite, only I am not conscious of it now; but I am struggling to get this consciousness of the Infinite, and perfection will be reached when full consciousness of this Infinite comes.

Another peculiar idea of the Vedanta is that we must allow this infinite variation in religious thought, and not try to bring everybody to the same opinion, because the goal is the same. As the Vedantist says in his poetical language, "As so many rivers, having their source in different mountains, roll down, crooked or straight, and at last come into the ocean—so, all these various creeds and religions, taking their start from different standpoints and running through crooked or straight courses, at last come unto THEE."

As a manifestation of that, we find that this most ancient philosophy has, through its influence, directly inspired Buddhism, the first missionary religion of the world, and indirectly, it has also influenced Christianity, through the Alexandrians, the Gnostics, and the European philosophers of the middle ages. And later, influencing German thought, it has produced almost a revolution in the regions of philosophy and psychology. Yet all this mass of influence has been given to the world almost unperceived. As the gentle falling of the dew at night brings support to all vegetable life, so, slowly and imperceptibly, this divine philosophy has been spread through the world for the good of mankind. No march of armies has been used to preach this religion. In Buddhism, one of the most missionary religions of the world, we find inscriptions remaining of the great Emperor Asoka—recording how missionaries were sent to Alexandria, to Antioch, to Persia, to China, and to various other countries of the then civilised world. Three hundred years before Christ, instructions were given them not to revile other religions: "The basis of all religions is the same, wherever they are; try to help them all you can, teach them all you can, but do not try to injure them."

Thus in India there never was any religious persecution by the Hindus, but only that wonderful reverence, which they have for all the religions of the world. They sheltered a portion of the Hebrews, when they were driven out of their own country; and the Malabar Jews remain as a result. They received at another time the remnant of the Persians, when they were almost annihilated; and they remain to this day, as a part of us and loved by us, as the modern Parsees of Bombay. There were Christians who claimed to have come with St. Thomas, the disciple of Jesus Christ; and they were allowed to settle in India and hold their own opinions; and a colony of them is even now in existence in India. And this spirit of toleration has not died out. It will not and cannot die there.

This is one of the great lessons that the Vedanta has to teach. Knowing that, consciously or unconsciously, we are struggling to reach the same goal, why should we be impatient? If one man is slower than another, we need not be impatient, we need not curse him, or revile him. When our eyes are opened and the heart is purified, the work of the same divine influence, the unfolding of the same divinity in every human heart, will become manifest; and then alone we shall be in a position to claim the brotherhood of man.

When a man has reached the highest, when he sees neither man nor woman, neither sect nor creed, nor colour, nor birth, nor any of these differentiations, but goes beyond and finds that divinity which is the real man behind every human being—then alone he has reached the universal brotherhood, and that man alone is a Vedantist.

Such are some of the practical historical results of the Vedanta.

STEPS OF HINDU PHILOSOPHIC THOUGHT

The first group of religious ideas that we see coming up—I mean recognised religious ideas, and not the very low ideas, which do not deserve the name of religion—all include the idea of inspiration and revealed books and so forth. The first group of religious ideas starts with the idea of God. Here is the universe, and this universe is created by a certain Being. Everything that is in this universe has been created by Him. Along with that, at a later stage, comes the idea of soul—that there is this body, and something inside this body which is not the body. This is the most primitive idea of religion that we know. We can find a few followers of that in India, but it was given up very early. The Indian religions take a peculiar start. It is only by strict analysis, and much calculation and conjecture, that we can ever think that that stage existed in Indian religions. The tangible state in which we find them is the next step, not the first one. At the earliest step the idea of creation is very peculiar, and it is that the whole universe is created out of zero, at the will of God; that all this universe did not exist, and out of this nothingness all this has come. In the next stage we find this conclusion is questioned. How can existence be produced out of nonexistence? At the first step in the Vedanta this question is asked. If this universe is existent it must have come out of something, because it was very easy to see that nothing comes out of nothing, anywhere. All work that is done by human hands requires materials. If a house is built, the material was existing before; if a boat is made the material existed before; if any implements are made, the materials were existing before. So the effect is produced. Naturally, therefore, the first idea that this world was created out of nothing was rejected, and some material out of which this world was created was wanted. The whole history of religion, in fact, is this search after that material.

Out of what has all this been produced? Apart from the question of the efficient cause, or God, apart from the question that God created the universe, the great question of all questions is: Out of what did He create it? All the philosophies are turning, as it were, on this question. One solution is that nature, God, and soul are eternal existences, as if three lines are running parallel eternally, of which nature and soul comprise what they call the dependent, and God the independent Reality. Every soul, like every particle of matter, is perfectly dependent on the will of God. Before going to the other steps we will take up the idea of soul, and then find that with all the Vedantic philosophers, there is one tremendous departure from all Western philosophy. All of them have a common psychology. Whatever their philosophy may have been, their psychology is the same in India, the old Sânkhya psychology. According to this, perception occurs by the transmission of the vibrations which first come to the external sense-organs, from the external to the internal organs, from the internal organs to the mind, from the mind to the Buddhi, from the Buddhi or intellect, to something which is a unit, which they call the Âtman. Coming to modern physiology, we know that it has found centres for all the different sensations. First it finds the lower centres, and then a higher grade of centres, and these two centres exactly correspond with the internal organs and the mind, but not one centre has been found which controls all the other centres. So physiology cannot tell what unifies all these centres. Where do the centres get united? The centres in the brain are all different. and there is not one centre which controls all the other centres; therefore, so far as it goes, the Indian psychology stands unchallenged upon this point. We must have this unification, some thing upon which the sensations will be reflected, to form a complete whole. Until there is that something, I cannot have any idea of you, or a picture, or anything else. If we had not that unifying something, we would only see, then after a while breathe, then hear, and so on, and while I heard a man talking I would not see him at all, because all the centres are different.

This body is made of particles which we call matter, and it is dull and insentient. So is what the Vedantists call the fine body. The fine body, according to them, is a material but transparent body, made of very fine particles, so fine that no microscope can see them. What is the use of that? It is the receptacle of the fine forces. Just as this gross body is the receptacle of the gross forces, so the fine body is the receptacle of the fine forces, which we call thought, in its various modifications. First is the body, which is gross matter, with gross force. Force cannot exist without matter. It must require some matter to exist, so the grosser forces work in the body; and those very forces become finer; the very force which is working in a gross form, works in a fine form, and becomes thought. There is no distinction between them, simply one is the gross and the other the fine

manifestation of the same thing. Neither is there any distinction between this fine body and the gross body. The fine body is also material, only very fine matter; and just as this gross body is the instrument that works the gross forces, so the fine body is the instrument that works the fine forces. From where do all these forces come? According to Vedanta philosophy, there are two things in nature, one of which they call Âkâsha, which is the substance, infinitely fine, and the other they call Prâna, which is the force. Whatever you see, or feel, or hear, as air, earth, or anything, is material—the product of Akasha. It goes on and becomes finer and finer, or grosser and grosser, changing under the action of Prana. Like Akasha, Prana is omnipresent, and interpenetrating everything. Akasha is like the water, and everything else in the universe is like blocks of ice, made out of that water, and floating in the water, and Prana is the power that changes this Akasha into all these various forms. The gross body is the instrument made out of Akasha, for the manifestation of Prana in gross forms, as muscular motion, or walking, sitting, talking, and so forth. That fine body is also made of Akasha, a very fine form of Akasha, for the manifestation of the same Prana in the finer form of thought. So, first there is this gross body. Beyond that is this fine body, and beyond that is the Jiva, the real man. Just as the nails can be pared off many times and yet are still part of our bodies, not different, so is our gross body related to the fine. It is not that a man has a fine and also a gross body; it is the one body only, the part which endures longer is the fine body, and that which dissolves sooner is the gross. Just as I can cut this nail any number of times, so, millions of times I can shed this gross body, but the fine body will remain. According to the dualists, this Jiva or the real man is very fine, minute.

So far we see that man is a being, who has first a gross body which dissolves very quickly, then a fine body which remains through aeons, and then a Jiva. This Jiva, according to the Vedanta philosophy, is eternal, just as God is eternal. Nature is also eternal, but changefully eternal. The material of nature—Prana and Akasha—is eternal, but it is changing into different forms eternally. But the Jiva is not manufactured either of Akasha or Prana; it is immaterial and, therefore, will remain for ever. It is not the result of any combination of Prana and Akasha, and whatever is not the result of combination, will never be destroyed, because destruction is going back to causes. The gross body is a compound of Akasha and Prana and, therefore, will be decomposed. The fine body will also be decomposed, after a long time, but the Jiva is simple, and will never be destroyed. It was never born for the same reason. Nothing simple can be born. The same argument applies. That which is a compound only can be born. The whole of nature comprising millions and millions of souls is under the will of God. God is all-pervading, omniscient, formless, and He is working through nature day and night. The whole of it is under His control. He is the eternal Ruler. So say the dualists. Then the question comes: If God is the ruler of this universe, why did He create such a wicked universe, why must we suffer so much? They say, it is not God's fault. It is our fault that we suffer. Whatever we sow we reap. He did not do anything to punish us. Man is born poor, or blind, or some other way. What is the reason? He had done something before, he was born that way. The Jiva has been existing for all time, was never created. It has been doing all sorts of things all the time. Whatever we do reacts upon us. If we do good, we shall have happiness, and if evil, unhappiness. So the Jiva goes on enjoying and suffering, and doing all sorts of things.

What comes after death? All these Vedanta philosophers admit that this Jiva is by its own nature pure. But ignorance covers its real nature, they say. As by evil deeds it has covered itself with ignorance, so by good deeds it becomes conscious of its own nature again. Just as it is eternal, so its nature is pure. The nature of every being is pure.

When through good deeds all its sins and misdeeds have been washed away, then the Jiva becomes pure again, and when it becomes pure, it goes to what is called Devayâna. Its organ of speech enters the mind. You cannot think without words. Wherever there is thought, there must be words. As words enter the mind, so the mind is resolved into the Prana, and the Prana into the Jiva. Then the Jiva gets quickly out of the body, and goes to the solar regions. This universe has sphere after sphere. This earth is the world sphere, in which are moons, suns, and stars. Beyond that here is the solar sphere, and beyond that another which they call the lunar sphere. Beyond that there is the sphere which they call the sphere of lightning, the electric sphere, and when the Jiva goes there, there comes another Jiva, already perfect, to receive it, and takes it to another world, the highest heaven, called the Brahmaloka, where the Jiva lives eternally, no more to be born or to die. It enjoys through eternity, and gets all sorts of powers, except the power of creation. There is only one ruler of the universe, and that is God. No one can become God; the dualists maintain that if you say you are God, it is a blasphemy. All powers except the creative come to the Jiva, and if it likes to have bodies, and work in different parts of the world, it can do so. If it orders all the gods to come before it, if it wants its forefathers to come, they all appear at its command. Such are its powers that it never feels any more pain, and if it wants, it can live in the Brahmaloka through all eternity. This is the highest man, who has attained the love of God, who has become perfectly unselfish, perfectly purified, who has given up all desires, and who does not want to do anything except worship and love God.

There are others that are not so high, who do good works, but want some reward. They say they will give so much to the poor, but want to go to heaven in return. When they die, what becomes of them? The speech enters the mind, the mind enters the Prana, the Prana enters the Jiva, and the Jiva gets out, and goes to the lunar sphere, where it has a very good time for a long period. There it enjoys happiness, so long as the effect of its good deeds endures. When the same is exhausted, it descends, and once again enters life on earth according to its desires. In the lunar sphere the Jiva becomes what we call a god, or what the Christians or Mohammedans call an angel. These gods are the names of certain positions; for instance, Indra, the king of the gods, is the name of a position; thousands of men get to that position. When a virtuous man who has performed the highest of Vedic rites dies, he becomes a king of the gods; by that time the old king has gone down again, and become man. Just as kings change here, so the gods, the Devas, also have to die. In heaven they will all die. The only deathless place is Brahmaloka, where alone there is no birth and death.

So the Jivas go to heaven, and have a very good time, except now and then when the demons give them chase. In our mythology it is said there are demons, who sometimes trouble the gods. In all mythologies, you read how these demons and the gods fought, and the demons sometimes conquered the gods, although many times, it seems, the demons did not do so many wicked things as the gods. In all mythologies, for instance, you find the Devas fond of women. So after their reward is finished, they fall down again, come through the clouds, through the rains, and thus get into some grain or plant and find their way into the human body, when the grain or plant is eaten by men. The father gives them the material out of which to get a fitting body. When the material suits them no longer, they have to manufacture other bodies. Now there are the very wicked fellows, who do, all sorts of diabolical things; they are born again as animals, and if they are very bad, they are born as very low animals, or become plants, or stones.

In the Deva form they make no Karma at all; only man makes Karma. Karma means work which will produce effect. When a man dies and becomes a Deva, he has only a period of pleasure, and during that time makes no fresh Karma; it is simply a reward for his past good Karma. When the good Karma is worked out, then the remaining Karma begins to take effect, and he comes down to earth. He becomes man again, and if he does very good works, and purifies himself, he goes to Brahmaloka and comes back no more.

The animal is a state of sojourn for the Jiva evolving from lower forms. In course of time the animal becomes man. It is a significant fact that as the human population is increasing, the animal population is decreasing. The animal souls are all becoming men. So many species of animals have become men already. Where else have they gone?

In the Vedas, there is no mention of hell. But our Purânas, the later books of our scriptures, thought that no religion could be complete, unless hells were attached to it, and so they invented all sorts of hells. In some of these, men are sawed in half, and continually tortured, but do not die. They are continually feeling intense pain, but the books are merciful enough to say it is only for a period. Bad Karma is worked out in that state and then they come back on earth, and get another chance. So this human form is the great chance. It is called the Karma-body, in which we decide our fate. We are running in a huge circle, and this is the point in the circle which determines the future. So this is considered the most important form that there is. Man is greater than the gods.

So far with dualism, pure and simple. Next comes the higher Vedantic philosophy which says, that this cannot be. God is both the material and the efficient cause of this universe. If you say there is a God who is an infinite Being, and a soul which is also infinite, and a nature which is also infinite, you can go on multiplying infinites without limit which is simply absurd; you smash all logic. So God is both the material and the efficient cause of the universe; He projects this universe out of Himself. Then how is it that God has become these walls and this table, that God has become the pig, and the murderer, and all the evil things in the world? We say that God is pure. How can He become all these degenerate things? Our answer is: just as I am a soul and have a body, and in a sense, this body is not different from me, yet I, the real I, in fact, am not the body. For instance, I say, I am a child, a young man, or an old man, but my soul has not changed. It remains the same soul. Similarly, the whole universe, comprising all nature and an infinite number of souls, is, as it were, the infinite body of God. He is inter penetrating the whole of it. He alone is unchangeable, but nature changes, and soul changes. He is unaffected by changes in nature and soul. In what way does nature change? In its forms; it takes fresh forms. But the soul cannot change that way. The soul contracts and expands in knowledge. It contracts by evil deeds. Those deeds which contract the real natural knowledge and purity of the soul are called evil deeds. Those deeds, again, which bring out the natural glory of the soul, are called good deeds. All these souls were pure, but they have become contracted; through the mercy of God, and by doing good deeds, they will expand and recover their natural purity. Everyone has the same chance, and in the long run, must get out. But this universe will not cease, because it is eternal. This is the second theory. The first is called dualism. The second holds that there are God, soul, and nature, and soul and nature form the body of God, and, therefore, these three form one unit. It represents a higher stage of religious development and goes by the name of qualified monism. In dualism, the universe is conceived as a large machine set going by God while in qualified monism, it is conceived as an organism, inter penetrated by the Divine Self.

The last are the non-dualists. They raise the question also, that God must be both the material and the efficient cause of this universe. As such, God has become the whole of this universe and there is no going against it. And when these other people say that God is the soul, and the universe is the body, and the body is changing, but God is changeless, the non-dualists say, all this is nonsense. In that case what is the use of calling God the material cause of this universe? The material cause is the cause become effect; the effect is nothing but the cause in another form. Wherever you see an effect, it is the cause reproduced. If the universe is the effect, and God the cause, it must be the reproduction of God. If you say that the universe is the body of God, and that the body becomes contracted and fine and becomes the cause, and out of that the universe is evolved, the non-dualists say that it is God Himself who has become this universe. Now comes a very fine question. If this God has become this universe, you and all these things are God. Certainly. This book is God, everything is God. My body is God, and my mind is God, and my soul is God. Then why are there so many Jivas? Has God become divided into millions of Jivas? Does that one God turn into millions of Jivas? Then how did it become so? How can that infinite power and substance, the one Being of the universe, become divided? It is impossible to divide infinity. How can that pure Being become this universe? If He has become the universe, He is changeful, and if He is changeful, He is part of nature, and whatever is nature and changeful is born and dies. If our God is changeful, He must die some day. Take note of that. Again, how much of God has become this universe ? If you say X (the unknown algebraical quantity), then God is God minus X now, and, therefore, not the same God as before this creation, because so much has become this universe.

So the non-dualists say, "This universe does not exist at all; it is all illusion. The whole of this universe, these Devas, gods, angels, and all the other beings born and dying, all this infinite number of souls coming up and going down, are all dreams." There is no Jiva at all. How can there be many? It is the one Infinity. As the one sun, reflected on various pieces of water, appears to be many, and millions of globules of water reflect so many millions of suns, and in each globule will be a perfect image of the sun, yet there is only one sun, so are all these Jivas but reflections in different minds. These different minds are like so many different globules, reflecting this one Being. God is being reflected in all these different Jivas. But a dream cannot be without a reality, and that reality is that one Infinite Existence. You, as body, mind, or soul, are a dream, but what you really are, is Existence, Knowledge, Bliss. You are the God of this universe. You are creating the whole universe and drawing it in. Thus says the Advaitist. So all these births and rebirths, coming and going are the figments of Mâyâ. You are infinite. Where can you go? The sun, the moon, and the whole universe are but drops in your transcendent nature. How can you be born or die? I never was born, never will be born. I never had father or mother, friends or foes, for I am Existence, Knowledge, Bliss Absolute. I am He, I am He. So, what is the goal, according to this philosophy? That those who receive this knowledge are one with the universe. For them, all heavens and even Brahmaloka are destroyed, the whole dream vanishes, and they find themselves the eternal God of the universe. They attain their real individuality, with its infinite knowledge and bliss, and become free. Pleasures in little things cease. We are finding pleasure in this little body, in this little individuality. How much greater the pleasure when this whole universe is my body! If there is pleasure in one body, how much more when all bodies are mine! Then is freedom attained. And this is called Advaita, the non-dualistic Vedanta philosophy.

These are the three steps which Vedanta philosophy has taken, and we cannot go any further, because we cannot go beyond unity. When a science reaches a unity, it cannot by any manner of means go any further. You cannot go beyond this idea of the Absolute.

All people cannot take up this Advaita philosophy; it is hard. First of all, it is very hard to understand it intellectually. It requires the sharpest of intellects, a bold understanding. Secondly, it does not suit the vast majority of people. So there are these three steps. Begin with the first one. Then by thinking of that and understanding it, the second will open itself. Just as a race advances, so individuals have to advance. The steps which the human race has taken to reach to the highest pinnacles of religious thought, every individual will have to take. Only, while the human race took millions of years to reach from one step to another, individuals may live the whole life of the human race in a much shorter duration. But each one of us will have to go through these steps. Those of you who are non-dualists look back to the period of your lives when you were strong dualists. As soon as you think you are a body and a mind, you will have to take the whole of this dream. If you take one portion, you must take the whole. The man who says, here is this world, and there is no (Personal) God, is a fool; because if there is a world, there will have to be a cause, and that is what is called God. You cannot have an effect without knowing that there is a cause. God will only vanish when this world vanishes; then you will become God (Absolute), and this world will be no longer for you. So long as the dream that you are a body exists, you are bound to see yourself as being born and dying; but as soon as that dream vanishes, so will the dream vanish that you are being born and dying, and so will the other dream that there is a universe vanish. That very thing which we now see as the universe will appear to us as God (Absolute), and that very God who has so long been external will appear to be internal, as our own Self.

STEPS TO REALISATION

A class-lecture delivered in America

First among the qualifications required of the aspirant for Jnâna, or wisdom, come Shama and Dama, which may be taken together. They mean the keeping of the organs in their own centres without allowing them to stray out. I shall explain to you first what the word "organ" means. Here are the eyes; the eyes are not the organs of vision but only the instruments. Unless the organs also are present, I cannot see, even if I have eyes. But, given both the organs and the instruments, unless the mind attaches itself to these two, no vision takes place. So, in each act of perception, three things are necessary—first, the external instruments, then, the internal organs, and lastly, the mind. If any one of them be absent, then there will be no

perception. Thus the mind acts through two agencies—one external, and the other internal. When I see things, my mind goes out, becomes externalised; but suppose I close my eyes and begin to think, the mind does not go out, it is internally active. But, in either case, there is activity of the organs. When I look at you and speak to you, both the organs and the instruments are active. When I close my eyes and begin to think, the organs are active, but not the instruments. Without the activity of these organs, there will be no thought. You will find that none of you can think without some symbol. In the case of the blind man, he has also to think through some figure. The organs of sight and hearing are generally very active. You must bear in mind that by the word "organ" is meant the nerve centre in the brain. The eyes and ears are only the instruments of seeing and hearing, and the organs are inside. If the organs are destroyed by any means, even if the eyes or the ears be there, we shall not see or hear. So in order to control the mind, we must first be able to control these organs. To restrain the mind from wandering outward or inward, and keep the organs in their respective centres, is what is meant by the words Shama and Dama. Shama consists in not allowing the mind to externalise, and Dama, in checking the external instruments.

Now comes Uparati which consists in not thinking of things of the senses. Most of our time is spent in thinking about sense-objects, things which we have seen, or we have heard, which we shall see or shall hear, things which we have eaten, or are eating, or shall eat, places where we have lived, and so on. We think of them or talk of them most of our time. One who wishes to be a Vedantin must give up this habit.

Then comes the next preparation (it is a hard task to be a philosopher!), Titikshâ, the most difficult of all. It is nothing less than the ideal forbearance—"Resist not evil." This requires a little explanation. We may not resist an evil, but at the same time we may feel very miserable. A man may say very harsh things to me, and I may not outwardly hate him for it, may not answer him back, and may restrain myself from apparently getting angry, but anger and hatred may be in my mind, and I may feel very badly towards that man. That is not non-resistance; I should be without any feeling of hatred or anger, without any thought of resistance; my mind must then be as calm as if nothing had happened. And only when I have got to that state, have I attained to non-resistance, and not before. Forbearance of all misery, without even a thought of resisting or driving it out, without even any painful feeling in the mind, or any remorse—this is Titiksha. Suppose I do not resist, and some great evil comes thereby; if I have Titiksha, I should no feel any remorse for not having resisted. When the mind has attained to that state, it has become established in Titiksha. People in India do extraordinary things in order to practice this Titiksha. They bear tremendous heat and cold without caring, they do not even care for snow, because they take no thought for the body; it is left to itself, as if it were a foreign thing.

The next qualification required is Shraddhâ, faith. One must have tremendous faith in religion and God. Until one has it, one cannot aspire to be a Jnâni. A great sage once told me that not one in twenty millions in this world believed in God. I asked him why, and he told me, "Suppose there is a thief in this room, and he gets to know that there is a mass of gold in the next room, and only a very thin partition between the two rooms; what will be the condition of that thief?" I answered, "He will not be able to sleep at all; his brain will be actively thinking of some means of getting at the gold, and he will think of nothing else." Then he replied, "Do you believe that a man could believe in God and not go mad to get him? If a man sincerely believes that there is that immense, infinite mine of Bliss, and that It can be reached, would not that man go mad in his struggle to reach it ?" Strong faith in God and the consequent eagerness to reach Him constitute Shraddha.

Then comes Samâdhâna, or constant practice, to hold the mind in God. Nothing is done in a day. Religion cannot be swallowed in the form of a pill. It requires hard and constant practice. The mind can be conquered only by slow and steady practice.

Next is Mumukshutva, the intense desire to be free. Those of you who have read Edwin Arnold's Light of Asia remember his translation of the first sermon of Buddha, where Buddha says,

> Ye suffer from yourselves. None else compels.
> None other holds you that ye live and die,
> And whirl upon the wheel, and hug and kiss
> Its spokes of agony,
> Its tire of tears, its nave of nothingness.

All the misery we have is of our own choosing; such is our nature. The old Chinaman, who having been kept in prison for sixty years was released on the coronation of a new emperor, exclaimed, when he came out, that he could not live; he must go back to his horrible dungeon among the rats and mice; he could not bear the light. So he asked them to kill him or send him back to the prison, and he was sent back. Exactly similar is the condition of all men. We run headlong after all sorts of misery, and are unwilling to be freed from them. Every day we run after pleasure, and before we reach it, we find it is gone, it has slipped through our fingers. Still we do not cease from our mad pursuit, but on and on we go, blinded fools that we are.

In some oil mills in India, bullocks are used that go round and round to grind the oil-seed. There is a yoke on the bullock's neck. They have a piece of wood protruding from the yoke, and on that is fastened a wisp of straw. The bullock is blindfolded in such a way that it can only look forward, and so it stretches its neck to get at the straw; and in doing so, it pushes the piece of wood out a little further; and it makes another attempt with the same result, and yet another, and so on. It never catches the straw, but goes round and round in the hope of getting it, and in so doing, grinds out the oil. In

the same way you and I who are born slaves to nature, money and wealth, wives and children, are always chasing a wisp of straw, a mere chimera, and are going through an innumerable round of lives without obtaining what we seek. The great dream is love; we are all going to love and be loved, we are all going to be happy and never meet with misery, but the more we go towards happiness, the more it goes away from us. Thus the world is going on, society goes on, and we, blinded slaves, have to pay for it without knowing. Study your own lives, and find how little of happiness there is in them, and how little in truth you have gained in the course of this wild-goose chase of the world.

Do you remember the story of Solon and Croesus? The king said to the great sage that Asia Minor was a very happy place. And the sage asked him, "Who is the happiest man? I have not seen anyone very happy." "Nonsense," said Croesus, "I am the happiest man in the world." "Wait, sir, till the end of your life; don't be in a hurry," replied the sage and went away. In course of time that king was conquered by the Persians, and they ordered him to be burnt alive. The funeral pyre was prepared and when poor Croesus saw it, he cried aloud "Solon! Solon!" On being asked to whom he referred, he told his story, and the Persian emperor was touched, and saved his life.

Such is the life-story of each one of us; such is the tremendous power of nature over us. It repeatedly kicks us away, but still we pursue it with feverish excitement. We are always hoping against hope; this hope, this chimera maddens us; we are always hoping for happiness.

There was a great king in ancient India who was once asked four questions, of which one was: "What is the most wonderful thing in the world?" "Hope," was the answer. This is the most wonderful thing. Day and nights we see people dying around us, and yet we think we shall not die; we never think that we shall die, or that we shall suffer. Each man thinks that success will be his, hoping against hope, against all odds, against all mathematical reasoning. Nobody is ever really happy here. If a man be wealthy and have plenty to eat, his digestion is: out of order, and he cannot eat. If a man's digestion be good, and he have the digestive power of a cormorant, he has nothing to put into his mouth. If he be rich, he has no children. If he be hungry and poor, he has a whole regiment of children, and does not know what to do with them. Why is it so? Because happiness and misery are the obverse and reverse of the same coin; he who takes happiness, must take misery also. We all have this foolish idea that we can have happiness without misery, and it has taken such possession of us that we have no control over the senses.

When I was in Boston, a young man came up to me, and gave me a scrap of paper on which he had written a name and address, followed by these words: "All the wealth and all the happiness of the world are yours, if you only know how to get them. If you come to me, I will teach you how to get them. Charge, $5." He gave me this and said, "What do you think of this?" I said, "Young man, why don't you get the money to print this? You have not even enough money to get this printed !" He did not understand this. He was infatuated with the idea that he could get immense wealth and happiness without any trouble. There are two extremes into which men are running; one is extreme optimism, when everything is rosy and nice and good; the other, extreme pessimism, when everything seems to be against them. The majority of men have more or less undeveloped brains. One in a million we see with a well-developed brain; the rest either have peculiar idiosyncrasies, or are monomaniacs.

Naturally we run into extremes. When we are healthy and young, we think that all the wealth of the world will be ours, and when later we get kicked about by society like footballs and get older, we sit in a corner and croak and throw cold water on the enthusiasm of others. Few men know that with pleasure there is pain, and with pain, pleasure; and as pain is disgusting, so is pleasure, as it is the twin brother of pain. It is derogatory to the glory of man that he should be going after pain, and equally derogatory, that he should be going after pleasure. Both should be turned aside by men whose reason is balanced. Why will not men seek freedom from being played upon? This moment we are whipped, and when we begin to weep, nature gives us a dollar; again we are whipped, and when we weep, nature gives us a piece of ginger-bread, and we begin to laugh again.

The sage wants liberty; he finds that sense-objects are all vain and that there is no end to pleasures and pains. How many rich people in the world want to find fresh pleasures! All pleasures are old, and they want new ones. Do you not see how many foolish things they are inventing every day, just to titillate the nerves for a moment, and that done, how there comes a reaction? The majority of people are just like a flock of sheep. If the leading sheep falls into a ditch, all the rest follow and break their necks. In the same way, what one leading member of a society does, all the others do, without thinking what they are doing. When a man begins to see the vanity of worldly things, he will feel he ought not to be thus played upon or borne along by nature. That is slavery. If a man has a few kind words said to him, he begins to smile, and when he hears a few harsh words, he begins to weep. He is a slave to a bit of bread, to a breath of air; a slave to dress, a slave to patriotism, to country, to name, and to fame. He is thus in the midst of slavery and the real man has become buried within, through his bondage. What you call man is a slave. When one realises all this slavery, then comes the desire to be free; an intense desire comes. If a piece of burning charcoal be placed on a man's head, see how he struggles to throw it off. Similar will be the struggles for freedom of a man who really understands that he is a slave of nature.

We have now seen what Mumukshutva, or the desire to be free, is. The next training is also a very difficult one. Nityân-itya-Viveka—discriminating between that which is true and that which is untrue, between the eternal and the transitory. God alone is eternal, everything else is transitory. Everything

dies; the angels die, men die, animals die, earths die, sun, moon, and stars, all die; everything undergoes constant change. The mountains of today were the oceans of yesterday and will be oceans tomorrow. Everything is in a state of flux. The whole universe is a mass of change. But there is One who never changes, and that is God; and the nearer we get to Him, the less will be the change for us, the less will nature be able to work on us; and when we reach Him, and stand with Him, we shall conquer nature, we shall be masters of phenomena of nature, and they will have no effect on us.

You see, if we really have undergone the above discipline, we really do not require anything else in this world. All knowledge is within us. All perfection is there already in the soul. But this perfection has been covered up by nature; layer after layer of nature is covering this purity of the soul. What have we to do? Really we do not develop our souls at all. What can develop the perfect? We simply take the evil off; and the soul manifests itself in its pristine purity, its natural, innate freedom.

Now begins the inquiry: Why is this discipline so necessary? Because religion is not attained through the ears, nor through the eyes, nor yet through the brain. No scriptures can make us religious. We may study all the books that are in the world, yet we may not understand a word of religion or of God. We may talk all our lives and yet may not be the better for it; we may be the most intellectual people the world ever saw, and yet we may not come to God at all. On the other hand, have you not seen what irreligious men have been produced from the most intellectual training? It is one of the evils of your Western civilisation that you are after intellectual education alone, and take no care of the heart. It only makes men ten times more selfish, and that will be your destruction. When there is conflict between the heart and the brain, let the heart be followed, because intellect has only one state, reason, and within that, intellect works, and cannot get beyond. It is the heart which takes one to the highest plane, which intellect can never reach; it goes beyond intellect, and reaches to what is called inspiration. Intellect can never become inspired; only the heart when it is enlightened, becomes inspired. An intellectual, heartless man never becomes an inspired man. It is always the heart that speaks in the man of love; it discovers a greater instrument than intellect can give you, the instrument of inspiration. Just as the intellect is the instrument of knowledge, so is the heart the instrument of inspiration. In a lower state it is a much weaker instrument than intellect. An ignorant man knows nothing, but he is a little emotional by nature. Compare him with a great professor—what wonderful power the latter possesses! But the professor is bound by his intellect, and he can be a devil and an intellectual man at the same time; but the man of heart can never be a devil; no man with emotion was ever a devil. Properly cultivated, the heart can be changed, and will go beyond intellect; it will be changed into inspiration. Man will have to go beyond intellect in the end. The knowledge of man, his powers of perception, of reasoning and intellect and heart, all are busy churning this milk of the world. Out of long churning comes butter, and this butter is God. Men of heart get the "butter", and the "buttermilk" is left for the intellectual.

These are all preparations for the heart, for that love, for that intense sympathy appertaining to the heart. It is not at all necessary to be educated or learned to get to God. A sage once told me, "To kill others one must be equipped with swords and shields, but to commit suicide a needle is sufficient; so to teach others, much intellect and learning are necessary, but not so for your own self-illumination." Are on pure? If you are pure, you will reach God. "Blessed are the pure in heart, for they shall see God." If you are not pure, and you know all the sciences in the world, that will not help you at all; you may be buried in all the books you read, but that will not be of much use. It is the heart that reaches the goal. Follow the heart. A pure heart sees beyond the intellect; it gets inspired; it knows things that reason can never know, and whenever there is conflict between the pure heart and the intellect, always side with the pure heart, even if you think what your heart is doing is unreasonable. When it is desirous of doing good to others, your brain may tell you that it is not politic to do so, but follow your heart, and you will find that you make less mistakes than by following your intellect. The pure heart is the best mirror for the reflection of truth, so all these disciplines are for the purification of the heart. And as soon as it is pure, all truths flash upon it in a minute; all truth in the universe will manifest in your heart, if you are sufficiently pure.

The great truths about atoms, and the finer elements, and the fine perceptions of men, were discovered ages ago by men who never saw a telescope, or a microscope, or a laboratory. How did they know all these things? It was through the heart; they purified the heart. It is open to us to do the same today; it is the culture of the heart, really, and not that of the intellect that will lessen the misery of the world.

Intellect has been cultured with the result that hundreds of sciences have been discovered, and their effect has been that the few have made slaves of the many—that is all the good that has been done. Artificial wants have been created; and every poor man, whether he has money or not, desires to have those wants satisfied, and when he cannot, he struggles, and dies in the struggle. This is the result. Through the intellect is not the way to solve the problem of misery, but through the heart. If all this vast amount of effort had been spent in making men purer, gentler, more forbearing, this world would have a thousandfold more happiness than it has today. Always cultivate the heart; through the heart the Lord speaks, and through the intellect you yourself speak.

You remember in the Old Testament where Moses was told, "Take off thy shoes from off thy feet, for the place whereon thou standest is holy ground." We must always approach the study of religion with that reverent attitude. He who comes with a pure heart and a reverent attitude, his heart will be opened; the doors will open for him, and he will see the truth.

If you come with intellect only, you can have a little intellectual gymnastics, intellectual theories, but not truth. Truth has such a face that any one who sees that face becomes convinced. The sun does not require any torch to show it; the sun is self-effulgent. If truth requires evidence, what will evidence that evidence? If something is necessary as witness for truth, where is the witness for that witness? We must approach religion with reverence and with love, and our heart will stand up and say, this is truth, and this is untruth.

The field of religion is beyond our senses, beyond even our consciousness. We cannot sense God. Nobody has seen God with his eyes or ever will see; nobody has God in his consciousness. I am not conscious of God, nor you, nor anybody. Where is God? Where is the field of religion? It is beyond the senses, beyond consciousness. Consciousness is only one of the many planes in which we work; you will have to transcend the field of consciousness, to go beyond the senses, approach nearer and nearer to your own centre, and as you do that, you will approach nearer and nearer to God. What is the proof of God? Direct perception, Pratyaksha. The proof of this wall is that I perceive it. God has been perceived that way by thousands before, and will be perceived by all who want to perceive Him. But this perception is no sense-perception at all; it is supersensuous, superconscious, and all this training is needed to take us beyond the senses. By means of all sorts of past work and bondages we are being dragged downwards; these preparations will make us pure and light. Bondages will fall off by themselves, and we shall be buoyed up beyond this plane of sense-perception to which we are tied down, and then we shall see, and hear, and feel things which men in the three ordinary states (viz waking, dream, and sleep) neither feel, nor see, nor hear. Then we shall speak a strange language, as it were, and the world will not understand us, because it does not know anything but the senses. True religion is entirely transcendental. Every being that is in the universe has the potentiality of transcending the senses; even the little worm will one day transcend the senses and reach God. No life will be a failure; there is no such thing as failure in the universe. A hundred times man will hurt himself, a thousand times he will tumble, but in the end he will realise that he is God. We know there is no progress in a straight line. Every soul moves, as it were, in a circle, and will have to complete it, and no soul can go so low but there will come a time when it will have to go upwards. No one will be lost. We are all projected from one common centre, which is God. The highest as well as the lowest life God ever projected, will come back to the Father of all lives. "From whom all beings are projected, in whom all live, and unto whom they all return; that is God."

VEDANTA AND PRIVILEGE

Delivered in London

We have nearly finished the metaphysical portion of the

Advaita. One point, and perhaps the most difficult to understand, remains. We have seen so far that, according to the Advaita theory, all we see around us, and the whole universe in fact, is the evolution of that one Absolute. This is called, in Sanskrit, Brahman. The Absolute has become changed into the whole of nature. But here comes a difficulty. How is it possible for the Absolute to change? What made the Absolute to change? By its very definition, the Absolute is unchangeable. Change of the unchangeable would be a contradiction. The same difficulty applies to those who believe in a Personal God. For instance, how did this creation arise? It could not have arisen out of nothing; that would be a contradiction—something coming out of nothing can never be. The effect is the cause in another form. Out of the seed, the big tree grows; the tree is the seed, plus air and water taken in. And if there were any method of testing the amount of the air, and water taken to make the body of the tree, we should find that it is exactly the same as the effect, the tree. Modern science has proved beyond doubt that it is so, that the cause is the effect in another form. The adjustment of the parts of the cause changes and becomes the effect. So, we have to avoid this difficulty of having a universe without a cause, and we are bound to admit that God has become the universe.

But we have avoided one difficulty, and landed in another. In every theory, the idea of God comes through the idea of unchangeability. We have traced historically how the one idea which we have always in mind in the search for God, even in its crudest form, is the idea of freedom; and the idea of freedom and of unchangeability is one and the same. It is the free alone which never changes, and the unchangeable alone which is free; for change is produced by something exterior to a thing, or within itself, which is more powerful than the surroundings. Everything which can be changed is necessarily bound by certain cause or causes, which cannot be unchangeable. Supposing God has become this universe, then God is here and has changed. And suppose the Infinite has become this finite universe, so much of the Infinite has gone, and, therefore, God is Infinite minus the universe. A changeable God would be no God. To avoid this doctrine of pantheism, there is a very bold theory of the Vedanta. It is that this universe, as we know and think it, does not exist, that the unchangeable has not changed, that the whole of this universe is mere appearance and not reality, that this idea of parts, and little beings, and differentiations is only apparent, not the nature of the thing itself. God has not changed at all, and has not become the universe at all. We see God as the universe, because we have to look through time, space, and causation. It is time, space, and causation that make this differentiation apparently, but not really. This is a very bold theory indeed. Now this theory ought to be explained a little more clearly. It does not mean idealism in the sense in which it is generally understood. It does not say that this universe does not exist; it exists, but at the same time it is not what we take it for. To illustrate this, the example given by the Advaita philosophy is well known. In the darkness of night, a stump of a tree is looked upon as a ghost by some superstitious person, as a policeman by a robber, as a friend by some one waiting for his companion. In all these cases, the stump of the tree did not change, but there are apparent changes, and these changes were in the minds of those who saw it. From the subjective side we can understand it better through psychology. There is something outside of ourselves, the true nature of which is unknown and unknowable to us; let us call it x. And there is something inside, which is also unknown and unknowable to us; let us call it y. The knowable is a combination of x plus y, and everything that we know, therefore, must have two parts, the x outside, and the y inside; and the x plus y is the thing we know. So, every form in the universe is partly our creation and partly something outside. Now what the Vedanta holds is that this x and this y are one and the same.

A very similar conclusion has been arrived at by some western philosophers, especially by Herbert Spencer, and some other modern philosophers. When it is said that the same power which is manifesting itself in the flower is welling up in my own consciousness, it is the very same idea which the Vedantist wants to preach, that the reality of the external world and the reality of the internal world are one and the same. Even the ideas of the internal and external exist by differentiation and do not exist in the things themselves. For instance, if we develop another sense, the whole world will change for us, showing that it is the subject which will change the object. If I change, the external world changes. The theory of the Vedanta, therefore, comes to this, that you and I and everything in the universe are that Absolute, not parts, but the whole. You are the whole of that Absolute, and so are all others, because the idea of part cannot come into it. These divisions, these limitations, are only apparent, not in the thing itself. I am complete and perfect, and I was never bound, boldly preaches the Vedanta. If you think you are bound, bound you will remain; if you know that you are free, free you are. Thus the end and aim of this philosophy is to let us know that we have been free always, and shall remain free for ever. We never change, we never die, and we are never born. What are all these changes then? What becomes of this phenomenal world? This world is admitted as an apparent world, bound by time, space, and causation, and it comes to what is called the Vivarta-vâda in Sanskrit, evolution of nature, and manifestation of the Absolute. The Absolute does not change, or re-evolve. In the little amoeba is that infinite perfection latent. It is called amoeba from its amoeba covering, and from the amoeba to the perfect man the change is not in what is inside—that remains the same, unchangeable—but the change occurs in the covering.

There is a screen here, and some beautiful scenery outside. There is a small hole in the screen through which we can only catch a glimpse of it. Suppose this hole begins to increase; as it grows larger and larger, more and more of the scenery comes into view, and when the screen has vanished, we come face to face with the whole of the scenery. This scene outside is the soul, and the screen between us and the scenery is Mâyâ—time, space, and causation. There is a little hole somewhere, through which I can catch only a glimpse of the soul. When the hole is bigger, I see more and more, and when the screen has vanished, I know that I am the soul. So changes in the universe are not in the Absolute; they are in nature. Nature evolves more and more, until the Absolute manifests Itself. In everyone It exists; in some It is manifested more than in others. The whole universe is really one. In speaking of the soul, to say that one is superior to another has no meaning. In speaking of the soul, to say that man is superior to the animal or the plant, has no meaning; the whole universe is one. In plants the obstacle to soul-manifestation is very great; in animals a little less; and in man still less; in cultured, spiritual men still less; and in perfect men, it has vanished altogether. All our struggles, exercises, pains, pleasures, tears, and smiles, all that we do and think tend towards that goal, the tearing up of the screen, making the hole bigger, thinning the layers that remain between the manifestation and the reality behind. Our work, therefore, is not to make the soul free, but to get rid of the bondages. The sun is covered by layers of clouds, but remains unaffected by them. The work of the wind is to drive the clouds away, and the more the clouds disappear, the more the light of the sun appears. There is no change whatsoever in the soul—Infinite, Absolute, Eternal, Knowledge, Bliss, and Existence. Neither can there be birth or death for the soul. Dying, and being born, reincarnation, and going to heaven, cannot be for the soul. These are different appearances, different mirages, different dreams. If a man who is dreaming of this world now dreams of wicked thoughts and wicked deeds, after a certain time the thought of that very dream will produce the next dream. He will dream that he is in a horrible place, being tortured. The man who is dreaming good thoughts and good deeds, after that period of dream is over, will dream he is in a better place; and so on from dream to dream. But the time will come when the whole of this dream will vanish. To everyone of us there must come a time when the whole universe will be found to have been a mere dream, when we shall find that the soul is infinitely better than its surroundings. In this struggle through what we call our environments, there will come a time when we shall find that these environments were almost zero in comparison with the power of the soul. It is only a question of time, and time is nothing in the Infinite. It is a drop in the ocean. We can afford to wait and be calm.

Consciously or unconsciously, therefore, the whole universe is going towards that goal. The moon is struggling to get out of the sphere of attraction of other bodies, and will come out of it, in the long run. But those who consciously strive to get free hasten the time. One benefit from this theory we practically see is that the idea of a real universal love is only possible from this point of view. All are our fellow passengers, our fellow travellers—all life, plants, animals; not only my brother man, but my brother brute, my brother plant; not only my brother the good, but my brother the evil, my brother the spiritual and my brother the wicked. They are all going to the same goal. All are in the same stream, each is hurrying towards that infinite freedom. We cannot stay the course, none can stay it, none can go back, however he may try; he will be driven forward, and in the end he will attain to freedom. Creation means the struggle to get back to freedom, the centre of our being, whence we have been thrown off, as it were. The very fact that we are here, shows that we are going towards the centre, and the manifestation of this attraction towards the centre is what we call love.

The question is asked: From what does this universe come, in what does it remain, to what does it go back? And the answer is: From love it comes, in love it remains, back it goes unto love. Thus we are in a position to understand that, whether one likes it or not, there is no going back for anyone. Everyone has to get to the centre, however he may struggle to go back. Yet if we struggle consciously, knowingly, it will smooth the passage, it will lessen the jar, and quicken the time. Another conclusion we naturally arrive at from this is that all knowledge and all power are within and not without. What we call nature is a reflecting glass—that is all the use of nature—and all knowledge is this reflection of the within on this glass of nature. What we call powers, secrets of nature, and force, are all within. In the external world are only a series of changes. There is no knowledge in nature; all knowledge comes from the human soul. Man manifests knowledge, discovers it within himself, which is pre-existing through eternity. Everyone is the embodiment of Knowledge, everyone is the embodiment of eternal Bliss, and eternal Existence. The ethical effect is just the same, as we have seen elsewhere, with regard to equality.

But the idea of privilege is the bane of human life. Two forces, as it were, are constantly at work, one making caste, and the other breaking caste; in other words, the one making for privilege, the other breaking down privilege. And whenever privilege is broken down, more and more light and progress come to a race. This struggle we see all around us. Of course there is first the brutal idea of privilege, that of the strong over the weak. There is the privilege of wealth. If a man has more money than another, he wants a little privilege over those who have less. There is the still subtler and more powerful privilege of intellect; because one man knows more than others, he claims more privilege. And the last of all, and the worst, because the most tyrannical, is the privilege of spirituality. If some persons think they know more of spirituality, of God, they claim a superior privilege over everyone else. They say, "Come down and worships us, ye common herds; we are the messengers of God, and you have to worship us." None can be Vedantists, and at the same time admit of privilege to anyone, either mental, physical, or spiritual; absolutely no privilege for anyone. The same power is in every man, the one manifesting more, the other less; the same potentiality is in everyone. Where is the claim to privilege? All knowledge is in every soul, even in the most ignorant; he has not manifested it, but, perhaps, he has not had the opportunity, the environments were not, perhaps, suitable to him. When he gets the opportunity, he will manifest it. The idea that one man is born superior to another has no meaning in the Vedanta; that between two nations one is superior and the other inferior has no meaning whatsoever. Put them in the same circumstances, and see whether the same intelligence comes out or not. Before that you have no right to say that one nation is superior to another. And as to spirituality, no privilege should be claimed there. It is a privilege to serve mankind, for this is the worship of God. God is here, in all these human souls. He is the soul of man. What privilege can men ask? There are no special messengers of God, never were, and never can be. All beings, great or small, are equally manifestations of God; the difference is only in the manifestation. The same eternal message, which has been eternally given, comes to them little by little. The eternal message has been written in the heart of every being; it is there already, and all are struggling to express it. Some, in suitable circumstances, express it a little better than others, but as bearers of the message they are all one. What claim to superiority is there? The most ignorant man, the most ignorant child, is as great a messenger of God as any that ever existed, and as great as any that are yet to come. For the infinite message is there imprinted once for all in the heart of every being. Wherever there is a being, that being contains the infinite message of the Most High. It is there. The work of the Advaita, therefore, is to break down all these privileges. It is the hardest work of all, and curious to say, it has been less active than anywhere else in the land of its birth. If there is any land of privilege, it is the land which gave birth to this philosophy—privilege for the spiritual man as well as for the man of birth. There they have not so much privilege for money (that is one of the benefits, I think), but privilege for birth and spirituality is everywhere.

Once a gigantic attempt was made to preach Vedantic ethics, which succeeded to a certain extent for several hundred years, and we know historically that those years were the best times of that nation. I mean the Buddhistic attempt to break down privilege. Some of the most beautiful epithets addressed to Buddha that I remember are, "Thou the breaker of castes, destroyer of privileges, preacher of equality to all beings." So, he preached this one idea of equality. Its power has been misunderstood to a certain extent in the brotherhood of Shramanas, where we find that hundreds of attempts have been made to make them into a church, with superiors and inferiors. Your cannot make much of a church when you tell people they are all gods. One of the good effects of Vedanta has been freedom of religious thought, which India enjoyed throughout all times of its history. It is something to glory in, that it is the land where there was never a religious persecution, where people are allowed perfect freedom in religion.

This practical side of Vedanta morality is necessary as much today as it ever was, more necessary, perhaps, than it ever was, for all this privilege-claiming has become tremendously in-

tensified with the extension of knowledge. The idea of God and the devil, or Ahura Mazda and Ahriman, has a good deal of poetry in it. The difference between God and the devil is in nothing except in unselfishness and selfishness. The devil knows as much as God, is as powerful as God; only he has no holiness—that makes him a devil. Apply the same idea to the modern world: excess of knowledge and power, without holiness, makes human beings devils. Tremendous power is being acquired by the manufacture of machines and other appliances, and privilege is claimed today as it never has been claimed in the history of the world. That is why the Vedanta wants to preach against it, to break down this tyrannising over the souls of men.

Those of you who have studied the Gita will remember the memorable passages: "He who looks upon the learned Brahmin, upon the cow, the elephant, the dog, or the outcast with the same eye, he indeed is the sage, and the wise man"; "Even in this life he has conquered relative existence whose mind is firmly fixed on this sameness, for the Lord is one and the same to all, and the Lord is pure; therefore those who have this sameness for all, and are pure, are said to be living in God." This is the gist of Vedantic morality—this sameness for all. We have seen that it is the subjective world that rules the objective. Change the subject, and the object is bound to change; purify yourself, and the world is bound to be purified. This one thing requires to be taught now more than ever before. We are becoming more and more busy about our neighbours, and less and less about ourselves. The world will change if we change; if we are pure, the world will become pure. The question is why I should see evil in others. I cannot see evil unless I be evil. I cannot be miserable unless I am weak. Things that used to make me miserable when I was a child, do not do so now. The subject changed, so the object was bound to change; so says the Vedanta. All these things which we call causes of misery and evil, we shall laugh at when we arrive at that wonderful state of equality, that sameness. This is what is called in Vedanta attaining to freedom. The sign of approaching that freedom is more and more of this sameness and equality. In misery and happiness the same, in success and defeat the same—such a mind is nearing that state of freedom.

The mind cannot be easily conquered. Minds that rise into waves at the approach of every little thing at the slightest provocation or danger, in what a state they must be! What to talk of greatness or spirituality, when these changes come over the mind? This unstable condition of the mind must be changed. We must ask ourselves how far we can be acted upon by the external world, and how far we can stand on our own feet, in spite of all the forces outside us. When we have succeeded in preventing all the forces in the world from throwing us off our balance, then alone we have attained to freedom, and not before. That is salvation. It is here and nowhere else; it is this moment. Out of this idea, out of this fountain-head, all beautiful streams of thought have flowed upon the world, generally misunderstood in their expression, apparently contradicting each other. We find hosts of brave and wonderfully spiritual souls, in every nation, taking to caves or forests for meditation, severing their connection with the external world. This is the one idea. And, on the other hand, we find bright, illustrious beings coming into society, trying to raise their fellow men, the poor, the miserable. Apparently these two methods are contradictory. The man who lives in a cave, apart from his fellow-beings, smiles contemptuously upon those who are working for the regeneration of their fellow men. "How foolish!" he says; "what work is there? The world of Maya will always remain the world of Maya; it cannot be changed." If I ask one of our priests in India, "Do you believe in Vedanta?"—he says, "That is my religion; I certainly do; that is my life." "Very well, do you admit the equality of all life, the sameness of everything?" "Certainly, I do." The next moment, when a low-caste man approaches this priest, he jumps to one side of the street to avoid that man. "Why do you jump?" "Because his very touch would have polluted me." "But you were just saying we are all the same, and you admit there is no difference in souls." He says, "Oh, that is in theory only for householders; when I go into a forest, then I will look upon everyone as the same." You ask one of your great men in England, of great birth and wealth, if he believes as a Christian in the brotherhood of mankind, since all came from God. He answers in the affirmative, but in five minutes he shouts something uncomplimentary about the common herd. Thus, it has been a theory only for several thousand years and never came into practice. All understand it, declare it as the truth, but when you ask them to practice it, they say, it will take millions of years.

There was a certain king who had a huge number of courtiers, and each one of these courtiers declared he was ready to sacrifice his life for his master, and that he was the most sincere being ever born. In course of time, a Sannyâsin came to the king. The king said to him that there never was a king who had so many sincere courtiers as he had. The Sannyasin smiled and said he did not believe that. The king said the Sannyasin could test it if he liked. So the Sannyasin declared that he would make a great sacrifice by which the king's reign would be extended very long, with the condition that there should be made a small tank into which each one of his courtiers should pour a pitcher of milk, in the dark of night. The king smiled and said, "Is this the test?" And he asked his courtiers to come to him, and told them what was to be done. They all expressed their joyful assent to the proposal and returned. In the dead of night, they came and emptied their pitchers into the tank. But in the morning, it was found full of water only. The courtiers were assembled and questioned about the matter. Each one of them had thought there would be so many pitchers of milk that his water would not be detected. Unfortunately most of us have the same idea and we do our share of work as did the courtiers in the story.

There is so much idea of equality, says the priest, that my little privilege will not be detected. So say our rich men, so say the tyrants of every country. There is more hope for the tyrannised over, than for the tyrants. It will take a very long time for tyrants to arrive at freedom, but less time for the others. The cruelty of the fox is much more terrible than the cruelty of the lion. The lion strikes a blow and is quiet for some time afterwards, but the fox trying persistently to follow his prey never misses an opportunity. Priestcraft is in its nature cruel and heartless. That is why religion goes down where priestcraft arises. Says the Vedanta, we must give up the idea of privilege, then will religion come. Before that there is no religion at all.

Do you believe what Christ says, "Sell all that thou hast, and give to the poor?" Practical equality there; no trying to torture the texts, but taking the truth as it is. Do not try to torture texts. I have heard it said that that was preached only to the handful of Jews who listened to Jesus. The same argument will apply to other things also. Do not torture texts; dare to face truth as it is. Even if we cannot reach to it, let us confess our weakness, but let us not destroy the ideal. Let us hope that we shall attain to it sometime, and strive for it. There it is—"Sell all that thou hast, and give to the poor, and follow me." Thus, trampling on every privilege and everything in us that works for privilege, let us work for that knowledge which will bring the feeling of sameness towards all mankind. You think that because you talk a little more polished language you are superior to the man in the street. Remember that when you are thinking this, you are not going towards freedom, but are forging a fresh chain for your feet. And, above all, if the pride of spirituality enters into you, woe unto you. It is the most awful bondage that ever existed. Neither can wealth nor any other bondage of the human heart bind the soul so much as this. "I am purer than others", is the most awful idea that can enter into the human heart. In what sense are you pure? The God in you is the God in all. If you have not known this, you have known nothing. How can there be difference? It is all one. Every being is the temple of the Most High; if you can see that, good, if not, spirituality has yet to come to you.

PRIVILEGE

Delivered at the Sesame Club, London

Two forces seem to be working throughout nature. One of these is constantly differentiating, and the other is as constantly unifying; the one making more and more for separate individuals, the other, as it were, bringing the individuals into a mass, bringing out sameness in the midst of all this differentiation. It seems that the action of these two forces enters into every department of nature and of human life. On the physical plane, we always find the two forces most distinctly at work, separating the individuals, making them more and more distinct from other individuals, and again making them into species and classes, and bringing out similarities of expressions, and form. The same holds good as regards the social life of man. Since the time when society began, these two forces have been at work, differentiating and unifying. Their action appears in various forms, and is called by various names, in different places, and at different times. But the essence is present in all, one making for differentiation, and the other for sameness; the one making for caste, and the other breaking it down; one making for classes and privileges, and the other destroying them. The whole universe seems to be the battle-ground of these two forces. On the one hand, it is urged, that though this unifying process exists, we ought to resist it with all our might, because it leads towards death, that perfect unity is perfect annihilation, and that when the differentiating process that is at work in this universe ceases, the universe comes to an end. It is differentiation that causes the phenomena that are before us; unification would reduce them all to a homogeneous and lifeless matter. Such a thing, of course, mankind wants to avoid. The same argument is applied to all the things and facts that we see around us. It is urged that even in physical body and social classification, absolute sameness would produce natural death and social death. Absolute sameness of thought and feeling would produce mental decay and degeneration. Sameness, therefore, is to be avoided. This has been the argument on the one side, and it has been urged in every country and in various times, with only a change of language. Practically it is the same argument which is urged by the Brahmins of India, when they want to uphold the divisions and castes, when they want to uphold the privileges of a certain portion of the community, against everybody else. The destruction of caste, they declare, would lead to destruction of society, and boldly they produce the historical fact that theirs has been the longest-lived society. So they, with some show of force, appeal to this argument. With some show of authority they declare that that alone which makes the individual live the longest life must certainly be better than that which produces shorter lives.

On the other hand, the idea of oneness has had its advocates throughout all times. From the days of the Upanishads, the Buddhas, and Christs, and all other great preachers of religion, down to our present day, in the new political aspirations, and in the claims of the oppressed and the downtrodden, and of all those who find themselves bereft of privileges—comes out the one assertion of this unity and sameness. But human nature asserts itself. Those who have an advantage want to keep it, and if they find an argument, however one-sided and crude, they must cling to it. This applies to both sides.

Applied to metaphysics, this question also assumes another form. The Buddhist declares that we need not look for anything which brings unity in the midst of these phenomena, we ought to be satisfied with this phenomenal world. This variety is the essence of life, however miserable and weak it may seem to be; we can have nothing more. The Vedantist declares that unity is the only thing that exists; variety is but phenomenal, ephemeral and apparent. "Look not to variety," says the Vedantist, "go back to unity." "Avoid unity; it is a delusion," says the Buddhist, "go to variety." The same differences of opinion in religion and metaphysics have come down to our own day, for, in fact, the sum-total of the principles of knowledge is very small. Metaphysics and metaphysical knowledge, religion and religious knowledge, reached their culmination five thousand years ago, and we are merely reiterating the same truths in different languages, only enriching them sometimes by the accession of fresh illustrations. So this is the fight, even today. One side wants us to keep to the phenomenal, to all this variation, and points out, with great show of argument, that variation has to remain, for when that stops, everything is gone. What we mean by life has been caused by variation. The other side, at the same time, valiantly points to unity.

Coming to ethics, we find a tremendous departure. It is, perhaps, the only science which makes a bold departure from this fight. For ethics is unity; its basis is love. It will not look at this variation. The one aim of ethics is this unity, this sameness. The highest ethical codes that mankind has discovered up to the present time know no variation; they have no time to stop to look into it; their one end is to make for that sameness. The Indian mind, being more analytical—I mean the Vedantic mind—found this unity as the result of all its analyses, and wanted to base everything upon this one idea of unity. But as we have seen, in the same country, there were other minds (the Buddhistic) who could not find that unity anywhere. To them all truth was a mass of variation, there was no connection between one thing and another.

I remember a story told by Prof. Max Müller in one of his books, an old Greek story, of how a Brahmin visited Socrates in Athens. The Brahmin asked, "What is the highest knowledge?" And Socrates answered, "To know man is the end and aim of all knowledge." "But how can you know man without knowing God?" replied the Brahmin. The one side, the Greek side, which is represented by modern Europe, insisted upon the knowledge of man; the Indian side, mostly represented by the old religions of the world, insisted upon the knowledge of God. The one sees God in nature, and the other sees nature in God. To us, at the present time, perhaps, has been given the privilege of standing aside from both these aspects, and taking an impartial view of the whole. This is a fact that variation exists, and so it must, if life is to be. This is also a fact that in and through these variations unity must be perceived. This is a fact that God is perceived in nature. But it is also a fact that nature is perceived in God. The knowledge of man is the highest knowledge, and only by knowing man, can we know God. This is also a fact that the knowledge of God is the highest knowledge, and knowing God alone we can know man. Apparently contradictory though these statements may appear, they are the necessity of human nature. The whole universe is a play of unity in variety, and of variety in unity. The whole universe is a play of differentiation and oneness; the whole universe is a play of the finite in the Infinite. We cannot take one without granting the other. But we cannot take them both as facts of the same perception, as facts of the same experience; yet in this way it will always go on.

Therefore, coming to our more particular purpose, which is religion rather than ethics, a state of things, where all variation has died down, giving place to a uniform, dead homogeneity, is impossible so long as life lasts. Nor is it desirable. At the same time, there is the other side of the fact, viz that this unity already exists. That is the peculiar claim—not that this unity has to be made, but that it already exists, and that you could not perceive the variety at all, without it. God is not to be made, but He already exists. This has been the claim of all religions. Whenever one has perceived the finite, he has also perceived the Infinite. Some laid stress on the finite side, and declared that they perceived the finite without; others laid stress on the Infinite side, and declared they perceived the Infinite only. But we know that it is a logical necessity that we cannot perceive the one without the other. So the claim is that this sameness, this unity, this perfection—as we may call it—is not to be made, it already exists, and is here. We have only to recognise it, to understand it. Whether we know it or not, whether we can express it in clear language or not, whether this perception assumes the force and clearness of a sense-perception or not, it is there. For we are bound by the logical necessity of our minds to confess that it is there, else, the perception of the finite would not be. I am not speaking of the old theory of substance and qualities, but of oneness; that in the midst of all this mass of phenomena, the very fact of the consciousness that you and I are different brings to us, at the same moment, the consciousness that you and I are not different. Knowledge would be impossible without that unity. Without the idea of sameness there would be neither perception nor knowledge. So both run side by side.

Therefore the absolute sameness of conditions, if that be the aim of ethics, appears to be impossible. That all men should be the same, could never be, however we might try. Men will be born differentiated; some will have more power than others; some will have natural capacities, others not; some will have perfect bodies, others not. We can never stop that. At the same time ring in our ears the wonderful words of morality proclaimed by various teachers: "Thus, seeing the same God equally present in all, the sage does not injure Self by the Self, and thus reaches the highest goal. Even in this life they have conquered relative existence whose minds are firmly fixed on this sameness; for God is pure, and God is the same to all. Therefore such are said to be living in God." We cannot deny that this is the real idea; yet at the same time comes the difficulty that the sameness as regards external forms and position can never be attained.

But what can be attained is elimination of privilege. That is really the work before the whole world. In all social lives, there has been that one fight in every race and in every country. The difficulty is not that one body of men are naturally more intelligent than another, but whether this body of men, because they have the advantage of intelligence, should take away even physical enjoyment from those who do not pos-

sess that advantage. The fight is to destroy that privilege. That some will be stronger physically than others, and will thus naturally be able to subdue or defeat the weak, is a self-evident fact, but that because of this strength they should gather unto themselves all the attainable happiness of this life, is not according to law, and the fight has been against it. That some people, through natural aptitude, should be able to accumulate more wealth than others, is natural: but that on account of this power to acquire wealth they should tyrannize and ride roughshod over those who cannot acquire so much wealth, is not a part of the law, and the fight has been against that. The enjoyment of advantage over another is privilege, and throughout ages, the aim of morality has been its destruction. This is the work which tends towards sameness, towards unity, without destroying variety.

Let all these variations remain eternally; it is the very essence of life. We shall all play in this way, eternally. You will be wealthy, and I shall be poor; you will be strong, and I shall be weak; you will be learned and I ignorant; you will be spiritual, and I, less so. But what of that? Let us remain so, but because you are physically or intellectually stronger, you must not have more privilege than I, and that you have more wealth is no reason why you should be considered greater than I, for that sameness is here, in spite of the different conditions.

The work of ethics has been, and will be in the future, not the destruction of variation and the establishment of sameness in the external world—which is impossible for it would bring death and annihilation—but to recognise the unity in spite of all these variations, to recognise the God within, in spite of everything that frightens us, to recognise that infinite strength as the property of everyone in spite of all apparent weakness, and to recognise the eternal, infinite, essential purity of the soul in spite of everything to the contrary that appears on the surface. This we have to recognise. Taking one side alone, one half only of the position, is dangerous and liable to lead to quarrels. We must take the whole thing as it is, stand on it as our basis and work it out in every part of our lives, as individuals and as unit members of society.

KRISHNA

Delivered in California, on April 1, 1900

Almost the same circumstances which gave birth to Buddhism in India surrounded the rise of Krishna. Not only this, the events of that day we find happening in our own times.

There is a certain ideal. At the same time there must always be a large majority of the human race who cannot come up to the ideal, not even intellectually...The strong ones carry it out and many times have no sympathy for the weak. The weak to the strong are only beggars. The strong ones march ahead...Of course, we see at once that the highest position to take is to be sympathetic and helpful to those who are weak. But then, in many cases the philosopher bars the way to our being sympathetic. If we go by the theory that the whole of this infinite life has to be determined by the few years' existence here and now,...then it is very hopeless for us,...and we have no time to look back upon those who are weak. But if these are not the conditions—if the world is only one of the many schools through which we have to pass, if the eternal life is to be moulded and fashioned and guided by the eternal law, and eternal law, eternal chances await everyone—then we need not be in a hurry. We have time to sympathise, to look around, stretch out a helping hand to the weak and bring them up.

With Buddhism we have two words in Sanskrit: one is translated religion, the other, a sect. It is the most curious fact that the disciples and descendants of Krishna have no name for their religion [although] foreigners call it Hinduism or Brâhmanism. There is one religion, and there are many sects. The moment you give it a name, individualise it and separate it from the rest, it is a sect, no more a religion. A sect [proclaims] its own truth and declares that there is no truth anywhere else. Religion believes that there has been, and still is, one religion in the world. There never were two religions. It is the same religion [presenting] different aspects in different places. The task is to conceive the proper understanding of the goal and scope of humanity.

This was the great work of Krishna: to clear our eyes and make us look with broader vision upon humanity in its march upward and onward. His was the first heart that was large enough to see truth in all, his the first lips that uttered beautiful words for each and all.

This Krishna preceded Buddha by some thousand years...A great many people do not believe that he ever existed. Some believe that [the worship of Krishna grew out of] the old sun worship. There seem to be several Krishnas: one was mentioned in the Upanishads, another was king, another a general. All have been lumped into one Krishna. It does not matter much. The fact is, some individual comes who is unique in spirituality. Then all sorts of legends are invented around him. But, all the Bibles and stories which come to be cast upon this one person have to be recast in [the mould of] his character. All the stories of the New Testament have to be modelled upon the accepted life [and] character of Christ. In all of the Indian stories about Buddha the one central note of that whole life is kept up—sacrifice for others...

In Krishna we find...two ideas [stand] supreme in his message: The first is the harmony of different ideas; the second is non-attachment. A man can attain to perfection, the highest goal, sitting on a throne, commanding armies, working out big plans for nations. In fact, Krishna's great sermon was preached on the battlefield.

Krishna saw plainly through the vanity of all the mummeries, mockeries, and ceremonials of the old priests; and yet he saw some good in them.

If you are a strong man, very good! But do not curse others who are not strong enough for you...Everyone says, "Woe unto you people!!" Who says, "Woe unto me that I cannot help you?" The people are doing all right to the best of their ability and means and knowledge. Woe unto me that I cannot lift them to where I am!

So the ceremonials, worship of gods, and myths, are all right, Krishna says...Why? Because they all lead to the same goal. Ceremonies, books, and forms— all these are links in the chain. Get hold! That is the one thing. If you are sincere and have really got hold of one link, do not let go; the rest is bound to come. [But people] do not get hold. They spend the time quarrelling and determining what they should get hold of, and do not get hold of anything...We are always after truth, but never want to get it. We simply want the pleasure to go about and ask. We have a lot of energy and spend it that way. That is why Krishna says: Get hold of any one of these chains that are stretched out from the common centre. No one step is greater than another...Blame no view of religion so far as it is sincere. Hold on to one of these links, and it will pull you to the centre. Your heart itself will teach all the rest. The teacher within will teach all the creeds, all the philosophies...

Krishna talks of himself as God, as Christ does. He sees the Deity in himself. And he says, "None can go a day out of my path. All have to come to me. Whosoever wants to worship in whatsoever form, I give him faith in that form, and through that I meet him..."[1] His heart is all for the masses.

Independent, Krishna stands out. The very boldness of it frightens us. We depend upon everything —...upon a few good words, upon circumstances. When the soul wants to depend upon nothing, not even upon life, that is the height of philosophy, the height of manhood. Worship leads to the same goal. Krishna lays great stress upon worship. Worship God!

Various sorts of worship we see in this world. The sick man is very worshipful to God...There is the man who loses his fortune; he also prays very much, to get money. The highest worship is that of the man who loves God for God's sake. [The question may be asked :] "Why should there be so much sorrow if there is a God?" The worshipper replies! "...There is misery in the world; [but] because of that I do not cease to love God. I do not worship Him to take away my [misery]. I love Him because He is love itself." The other [types of worship] are lower-grade; but Krishna has no condemnation for anything. It is better to do something than to stand still. The man who begins to worship God will grow by degrees and begin to love God for love's sake...

How to attain purity living this life? Shall we all go to the forest caves? What good would it do? If the mind is not under control, it is no use living in a cave because the same mind will bring all disturbances there. We will find twenty devils in the cave because all the devils are in the mind. If the mind is under control, we can have the cave anywhere, wherever we are. It is our own mental attitude which makes the world what it

1. Gita, IV. 12.

is for us. Our thoughts make things beautiful, our thoughts make things ugly. The whole world is in our own minds. Learn to see things in the proper light. First, believe in this world—that there is meaning behind everything. Everything in the world is good, is holy and beautiful. If you see something evil, think that you are not understanding it in the right light. Throw the burden on yourselves!...Whenever we are tempted to say that the world is going to the dogs, we ought to analyse ourselves, and we shall find that we have lost the faculty of seeing things as they are.

Work day and night! "Behold, I am the Lord of the Universe. I have no duty. Every duty is bondage. But I work for work's sake. If I ceased to work for a minute, [there would be chaos]."[1] So do thou work, without any idea of duty...

This world is a play. You are His playmates. Go on and work, without any sorrow, without any misery. See His play in the slums, in the saloons! Work to lift people! Not that they are vile or degraded; Krishna does not say that.

Do you know why so little good work is done? My lady goes to the slum...She gives a few ducats and says, "My poor men, take that and be happy!"...Or my fine woman, walking through the street, sees a poor fellow and throws him five cents. Think of the blasphemy of it! Blessed are we that the Lord has given us his teaching in your own Testament. Jesus says, "Inasmuch as ye have done it unto the least of these my brethren, ye have done it unto me." It is blasphemy to think that you can help anyone. First root out this idea of helping, and then go to worship. God's children are your Master's children. [And children are but different forms of the father.] You are His servant...Serve the living God! God comes to you in the blind, in the halt, in the poor, in the weak, in the diabolical. What a glorious chance for you to worship! The moment you think you are "helping", you undo the whole thing and degrade yourself. Knowing this, work. "What follows?" you say. You do not get that heartbreak, that awful misery...Then work is no more slavery. It becomes a play, and joy itself...Work! Be unattached! That is the whole secret. If you get attached, you become miserable...

With everything we do in life we identify ourselves. Here is a man who says harsh words to me. I feel anger coming on me. In a few seconds anger and I are one, and then comes misery. Attach yourselves to the Lord and to nothing else, because everything else is unreal. Attachment to the unreal will bring misery. There is only one Existence that is real, only one Life in which there is neither object nor [subject]...

But unattached love will not hurt you. Do anything—marry, have children...Do anything you like—nothing will hurt you. Do nothing with the idea of "mine". Duty for duty's sake; work for work's sake. What is that to you? You stand aside.

When we come to that non-attachment, then we can understand the marvellous mystery of the universe; how it is intense

activity and vibration, and at the same time intensest peace and calm; how it is work every moment and rest every moment. That is the mystery of the universe—the impersonal and personal in one, the infinite and finite in one. Then we shall find the secret. "He who finds in the midst of intense activity the greatest rest, and in the midst of the greatest rest intense activity, he has become a Yogi."[2] He alone is a real worker, none else. We do a little work and break ourselves. Why? We become attached to that work. If we do not become attached, side by side with it we have infinite rest...

How hard it is to arrive at this sort of non-attachment! Therefore Krishna shows us the lower ways and methods. The easiest way for everyone is to do [his or her] work and not take the results. It is our desire that binds us. If we take the results of actions, whether good or evil, we will have to bear them. But if we work not for ourselves, but all for the glory of the Lord, the results will take care of themselves. "To work you have the right, but not to the fruits thereof."[3] The soldier works for no results. He does his duty. If defeat comes, it belongs to the general, not to the soldier. We do our duty for love's sake—love for the general, love for the Lord...

If you are strong, take up the Vedanta philosophy and be independent. If you cannot do that, worship God; if not, worship some image. If you lack strength even to do that, do some good works without the idea of gain. Offer everything you have unto the service of the Lord. Fight on! "Leaves and water and one flower—whosoever lays anything on my altar, I receive it with equal delights."[4] If you cannot do anything, not a single good work, then take refuge [in the Lord]. "The Lord resides within the heart of the being, making them turn upon His wheel. Do thou with all thy soul and heart take refuge in Him...[5]

These are some of the general ideas that Krishna preached on this idea of love [in the Gita]. There are [in] other great books, sermons on love—as with Buddha, as with Jesus...

A few words about the life of Krishna. There is a great deal of similarity between the lives of Jesus and Krishna. A discussion is going on as to which borrowed of the other. There was the tyrannical king in both places. Both were born in a manger. The parents were bound in both cases. Both were saved by angels. In both cases all the boys born in that year were killed. The childhood is the same...Again, in the end, both were killed. Krishna was killed by accident; he took the man who killed him to heaven. Christ was killed, and blessed the robber and took him to heaven.

There are a great many similarities in of the New Testament and the Gita. The human thought goes the same way...I will find you the answer in the words of Krishna himself: "Whenever virtue subsides and irreligion prevails, I come down.

1. Ibid. III. 22-23.

2. Ibid. IV. 18.

3. Ibid. II. 47.

4. Ibid IX. 26.

5. Ibid XVIII. 61-62.

Again and again I come. Therefore, whenever thou seest a great soul struggling to uplift mankind, know that I am come, and worship..."[6]

At the same time, if he comes as Jesus or as Buddha, why is there so much schism? The preachings must be followed! A Hindu devotee would say: It is God himself who became Christ and Krishna and Buddha and all these [great teachers]. A Hindu philosopher would say: These are the great souls; they are already free. And though free, they refuse to accept their liberation while the whole world is suffering. They come again and again, take a human embodiment and help mankind. They know from their childhood what they are and what they come for... They do not come through bondage like we do... They come out of their own free will, and cannot help having tremendous spiritual power. We cannot resist it. The vast mass of mankind is dragged into the whirlpool of spirituality, and the vibration goes on and on because one of these [great souls] gives a push. So it continues until all mankind is liberated and the play of this planet is finished.

Glory unto the great souls whose lives we have been studying! They are the living gods of the world. They are the persons whom we ought to worship. If He comes to me, I can only recognise Him if He takes a human form. He is everywhere, but do we see Him? We can only see Him if He takes the limitation of man... If men and... animals are manifestations of God, these teachers of mankind are leaders, are Gurus. Therefore, salutations unto you, whose footstool is worshipped by angels! Salutations unto you leaders of the human race! Salutations unto you great teachers! You leaders have our salutations for ever and ever!

THE GITA—I

Delivered in San Francisco, on May 26, 1900

To understand the Gita requires its historical background. The Gita is a commentary on the Upanishads. The Upanishads are the Bible of India. They occupy the same place as the New Testament does. There are [more than] a hundred books comprising the Upanishads, some very small and some big, each a separate treatise. The Upanishads do not reveal the life of any teacher, but simply teach principles. They are [as it were] shorthand notes taken down of discussion in [learned assemblies], generally in the courts of kings. The word Upanishad may mean "sittings" [or "sitting near a teacher"]. Those of you who may have studied some of the Upanishads can understand how they are condensed shorthand sketches. After long discussions had been held, they were taken down, possibly from memory. The difficulty is that you get very little of the background. Only the luminous points are mentioned there. The origin of ancient Sanskrit is 5000 B.C.; the Upanishads [are at least] two thousand years before that. Nobody knows [exactly] how old they are. The Gita takes the ideas of the Upanishads and in [some] cases the very words. They are

6. Ibid. IV. 8; X. 41.

strung together with the idea of bringing out, in a compact, condensed, and systematic form, the whole subject the Upanishads deal with.

The [original] scriptures of the Hindus are called the Vedas. They were so vast—the mass of writings—that if the texts alone were brought here, this room would not contain them. Many of them are lost. They were divided into branches, each branch put into the head of certain priests and kept alive by memory. Such men still exist. They will repeat book after book of the Vedas without missing a single intonation. The larger portion of the Vedas has disappeared. The small portion left makes a whole library by itself. The oldest of these contains the hymns of the Rig-Veda. It is the aim of the modern scholar to restore [the sequence of the Vedic compositions]. The old, orthodox idea is quite different, as your orthodox idea of the Bible is quite different from the modern scholar's. The Vedas are divided into two portions: one the Upanishads, the philosophical portion, the other the work portion.

We will try to give a little idea of the work portion. It consists of rituals and hymns, various hymns addressed to various gods. The ritual portion is composed of ceremonies, some of them very elaborate. A great many priests are required. The priestly function became a science by itself, owing to the elaboration of the ceremonials. Gradually the popular idea of veneration grew round these hymns and rituals. The gods disappeared and in their place were left the rituals. That was the curious development in India. The orthodox Hindu [the Mimâmsaka] does not believe in gods, the unorthodox believe in them. If you ask the orthodox Hindu what the meaning is of these gods in the Vedas, [he will not be able to give any satisfactory answer]. The priests sing these hymns and pour libations and offering into the fire. When you ask the orthodox Hindu the meaning of this, he says that words have the power to produce certain effects. That is all. There is all the natural and supernatural power that ever existed. The Vedas are simply words that have the mystical power to produce effects if the sound intonation is right. If one sound is wrong it will not do. Each one must be perfect. [Thus] what in other religions is called prayer disappeared and the Vedas became the gods. So you see the tremendous importance that was attached to the words of the Vedas. These are the eternal words out of which the whole universe has been produced. There cannot be any thought without the word. Thus whatever there is in this world is the manifestation of thought, and thought can only manifest itself through words. This mass of words by which the unmanifested thought becomes manifest, that is what is meant by the Vedas. It follows that the external existence of everything [depends on the Vedas, for thought] does not exist without the word. If the word "horse" did not exist, none could think of a horse. [So] there must be [an intimate relation between] thought, word, and the external object. What are these words [in reality]? The Vedas. They do not call it Sanskrit language at all. It is Vedic language, a divine language. Sanskrit is a degenerate form. So are all other languages. There is no language older than Vedic. You may ask, "Who wrote the Vedas?" They were not written. The words are the Vedas. A word is Veda, if I can pronounce it rightly. Then it will immediately produce the [desired] effect.

This mass of Vedas eternally exists and all the world is the manifestation of this mass of words. Then when the cycle ends, all this manifestation of energy becomes finer and finer, becomes only words, then thought. In the next cycle, first the thought changes into words and then out of those words [the whole universe] is produced. If there is something here that is not in the Vedas, that is your delusion. It does not exist.

[Numerous] books upon that subject alone defend the Vedas. If you tell [their authors] that the Vedas must have been pronounced by men first, [they will simply laugh]. You never heard of any [man uttering them for the first time]. Take Buddha's words. There is a tradition that he lived and spoke these words [many times before]. If the Christian stands up and says, "My religion is a historical religion and therefore yours is wrong and ours is true," [the Mimamsaka replies], "Yours being historical, you confess that a man invented it nineteen hundred years ago. That which is true must be infinite and eternal. That is the one test of truth. It never decays, it is always the same. You confess your religion was created by such-and-such a man. The Vedas were not. By no prophets or anything... Only infinite words, infinite by their very nature, from which the whole universe comes and goes." In the abstract it is perfectly correct... The sound must be the beginning of creation. There must be germ sounds like germ plasm. There cannot be any ideas without the words... Wherever there are sensations, ideas, emotions, there must be words. The difficulty is when they say that these four books are the Vedas and nothing else. [Then] the Buddhist will stand up and say, "Ours are Vedas. They were revealed to us later on." That cannot be. Nature does not go on in that way. Nature does not manifest her laws bit by bit, an inch of gravitation today and [another inch] tomorrow. No, every law is complete. There is no evolution in law at all. It is [given] once and for ever. It is all nonsense, this "new religion and better inspiration," and all that. It means nothing. There may be a hundred thousand laws and man may know only a few today. We discover them—that is all. Those old priests with their tremendous [claims about eternal words], having dethroned the gods, took the place of the gods. [They said], "You do not understand the power of words. We know how to use them. We are the living gods of the world. Pay us; we will manipulate the words, and you will get what you want. Can you pronounce the words yourself? You cannot, for, mind you, one mistake will produce the opposite effect. You want to be rich, handsome, have a long life, a fine husband?" Only pay the priest and keep quiet!

Yet there is another side. The ideal of the first part of the Vedas is entirely different from the ideal of the other part, the Upanishads. The ideal of the first part coincides with [that of] all other religions of the world except the Vedanta. The

ideal is enjoyment here and hereafter—man and wife, husband and children. Pay your dollar, and the priest will give you a certificate, and you will have a happy time afterwards in heaven. You will find all your people there and have this merry-go-round without end. No tears, no weeping—only laughing. No stomach-ache, but yet eating. No headache, but yet [parties]. That, considered the priests, was the highest goal of man.

There is another idea in this philosophy which is according to your modern ideas. Man is a slave of nature, and slave eternally he has got to remain. We call it Karma. Karma means law, and it applies everywhere. Everything is bound by Karma. "Is there no way out?" "No! Remain slaves all through the years—fine slaves. We will manipulate the words so that you will only have the good and not the bad side of all—if you will pay [us] enough." That was the ideal of [the Mimamsakas]. These are the ideals which are popular throughout the ages. The vast mass of mankind are never thinkers. Even if they try to think, the [effect of the] vast mass of superstitions on them is terrible. The moment they weaken, one blow comes, and the backbone breaks into twenty pieces. They can only be moved by lures and threats. They can never move of their own accord. They must be frightened, horrified, or terrorised, and they are your slaves for ever. They have nothing else to do but to pay and obey. Everything else is done by the priest... How much easier religion becomes! You see, you have nothing to do. Go home and sit quietly. Somebody is doing the whole thing for you. Poor, poor animals!

Side by side, there was the other system. The Upanishads are diametrically opposite in all their conclusions. First of all, the Upanishads believe in God, the creator of the universe, its ruler. You find later on [the idea of a benign Providence]. It is an entirely opposite [conception]. Now, although we hear the priest, the ideal is much more subtle. Instead of many gods they made one God.

The second idea, that you are all bound by the law of Karma, the Upanishads admit, but they declare the way out. The goal of man is to go beyond law. And enjoyment can never be the goal, because enjoyment can only be in nature.

In the third place, the Upanishads condemn all the sacrifices and say that is mummery. That may give you all you want, but it is not desirable, for the more you get, the more you [want], and you run round and round in a circle eternally, never getting to the end—enjoying and weeping. Such a thing as eternal happiness is impossible anywhere. It is only a child's dream. The same energy becomes joy and sorrow.

I have changed my psychology a bit today. I have found the most curious fact. You have a certain idea and you do not want to have it, and you think of something else, and the idea you want to suppress is entirely suppressed. What is that idea? I saw it come out in fifteen minutes. It came out and staggered me. It was strong, and it came in such a violent and terrible fashion [that] I thought here was a madman. And when it was over, all that had happened [was a suppression of the previous emotion]. What came out? It was my own bad impression which had to be worked out. "Nature will have her way. What can suppression do?"[1] That is a terrible [statement] in the Gita. It seems it may be a vain struggle after all. You may have a hundred thousand [urges competing] at the same time. You may repress [them], but the moment the spring rebounds, the whole thing is there again.

[But there is hope]. If you are powerful enough, you can divide your consciousness into twenty parts all at the same time. I am changing my psychology. Mind grows. That is what the Yogis say. There is one passion and it rouses another, and the first one dies. If you are angry, and then happy, the next moment the anger passes away. Out of that anger you manufactured the next state. These states are always interchangeable. Eternal happiness and misery are a child's dream. The Upanishads point out that the goal of man is neither misery nor happiness, but we have to be master of that out of which these are manufactured. We must be masters of the situation at its very root, as it were.

The other point of divergence is: the Upanishads condemn all rituals, especially those that involve the killing of animals. They declare those all nonsense. One school of old philosophers says that you must kill such an animal at a certain time if the effect is to be produced. [You may reply], "But [there is] also the sin of taking the life of the animal; you will have to suffer for that." They say that is all nonsense. How do you know what is right and what is wrong? Your mind says so? Who cares what your mind says? What nonsense are you talking? You are setting your mind against the scriptures. If your mind says something and the Vedas say something else, stop your mind and believe in the Vedas. If they say, killing a man is right, that is right. If you say, "No, my conscience says [otherwise," it won't do]. The moment you believe in any book as the eternal word, as sacred, no more can you question. I do not see how you people here believe in the Bible whenever you say about [it], "How wonderful those words are, how right and how good!" Because, if you believe in the Bible as the word of God, you have no right to judge at all. The moment you judge, you think you are higher than the Bible. [Then] what is the use of the Bible to you? The priests say, "We refuse to make the comparison with your Bible or anybody's. It is no use comparing, because—what is the authority? There it ends. If you think something is not right, go and get it right according to the Vedas."

The Upanishads believe in that, [but they have a higher standard too]. On the one hand, they do not want to overthrow the Vedas, and on the other they see these animal sacrifices and the priests stealing everybody's money. But in the psychology they are all alike. All the differences have been in the philosophy, [regarding] the nature of the soul. Has it a body and a mind? And is the mind only a bundle of nerves,

the motor nerves and the sensory nerves? Psychology, they all take for granted, is a perfect science. There cannot be any difference there. All the fight has been regarding philosophy—the nature of the soul, and God, and all that.

Then another great difference between the priests and the Upanishads. The Upanishads say, renounce. That is the test of everything. Renounce everything. It is the creative faculty that brings us into all this entanglement. The mind is in its own nature when it is calm. The moment you can calm it, that [very] moment you will know the truth. What is it that is whirling the mind? Imagination, creative activity. Stop creation and you know the truth. All power of creation must stop, and then you know the truth at once.

On the other hand, the priests are all for [creation]. Imagine a species of life [in which there is no creative activity. It is unthinkable]. The people had to have a plan [of evolving a stable society. A system of rigid selection was adopted. For instance,] no people who are blind and halt can be married. [As a result] you will find so much less deformity [in India] than in any other country in the world. Epileptics and insane [people] are very rare [there]. That is owing to direct selection. The priests say, "Let them become Sannyâsins." On the other hand, the Upanishads say, "Oh no, [the] earth's best and finest [and] freshest flowers should be laid upon the altar. The strong, the young, with sound intellect and sound body—they must struggle for the truth."

So with all these divergences of opinion, I have told you that the priests already differentiated themselves into a separate caste. The second is the caste of the kings...All the Upanishadic philosophy is from the brains of kings, not priests. There [runs] an economic struggle through every religious struggle. This animal called man has some religious influence, but he is guided by economy. Individuals are guided by something else, but the mass of mankind never made a move unless economy was [involved]. You may [preach a religion that may not be perfect in every detail], but if there is an economic background [to it], and you have the most [ardent champions] to preach it, you can convince a whole country...

Whenever any religion succeeds, it must have economic value. Thousands of similar sects will be struggling for power, but only those who meet the real economic problem will have it. Man is guided by the stomach. He walks and the stomach goes first and the head afterwards. Have you not seen that? It will take ages for the head to go first. By the time a man is sixty years of age, he is called out of [the world]. The whole of life is one delusion, and just when you begin to see things the way they are, you are snatched off. So long as the stomach went first you were all right. When children's dreams begin to vanish and you begin to look at things the way they are, the head goes. Just when the head goes first, [you go out].

[For] the religion of the Upanishads to be popularised was a hard task. Very little economy is there, but tremendous altruism...

---

1. Gita, III. 33.

The Upanishads had very little kingdom, although they were discovered by kings that held all the royal power in their hands. So the struggle... began to be fiercer. Its culminating point came two thousand years after, in Buddhism. The seed of Buddhism is here, [in] the ordinary struggle between the king and the priest; and [in the struggle] all religion declined. One wanted to sacrifice religion, the other wanted to cling to the sacrifices, to Vedic gods, etc. Buddhism... broke the chains of the masses. All castes and creeds alike became equal in a minute. So the great religious ideas in India exist, but have yet to be preached: otherwise they do no good...

In every country it is the priest who is conservative, for two reasons—because it is his bread and because he can only move with the people. All priests are not strong. If the people say, "Preach two thousand gods," the priests will do it. They are the servants of the congregation who pay them. God does not pay them. So blame yourselves before blaming the priests. You can only get the government and the religion and the priesthood you deserve, and no better.

So the great struggle began in India and it comes to one of its culminating points in the Gita. When it was causing fear that all India was going to be broken up between [the] two... [groups], there rose this man Krishna, and in the Gita he tries to reconcile the ceremony and the philosophy of the priests and the people. Krishna is loved and worshipped in the same way as you do Christ. The difference is only in the age. The Hindus keep the birthday of Krishna as you do Christ's. Krishna lived five thousand years ago and his life is full of miracles, some of them very similar to those in the life of Christ. The child was born in prison. The father took him away and put him with the shepherds. All children born in that year were ordered to be killed... He was killed; that was his fate.

Krishna was a married man. There are thousands of books about him. They do not interest me much. The Hindus are great in telling stories, you see. [If] the Christian missionaries tell one story from their Bible, the Hindus will produce twenty stories. You say the whale swallowed Jonah; the Hindus say someone swallowed an elephant... Since I was a child I have heard about Krishna's life. I take it for granted there must have been a man called Krishna, and his Gita shows he has [left] a wonderful book. I told you, you can understand the character of a man by analysing the fables about him. The fables have the nature [of decorations]. You must find they are all polished and manipulated to fit into the character. For instance, take Buddha. The central idea [is] sacrifice. There are thousands of folklore, but in every case the sacrifice must have been kept up. There are thousands of stories about Lincoln, about some characteristic of that great man. You take all the fables and find the general idea and [know] that that was the central character of the man. You find in Krishna that non-attachment is the central idea. He does not need anything. He does not want anything. He works for work's sake. "Work for work's sake. Worship for worship's sake. Do good because it is good to do good. Ask no more." That must have been

the character of the man. Otherwise these fables could not be brought down to the one idea of non-attachment. The Gita is not his only sermon...

He is the most rounded man I know of, wonderfully developed equally in brain and heart and hand. Every moment [of his] is alive with activity, either as a gentleman, warrior, minister, or something else. Great as a gentleman, as a scholar, as a poet. This all-rounded and wonderful activity and combination of brain and heart you see in the Gita and other books. Most wonderful heart, exquisite language, and nothing can approach it anywhere. This tremendous activity of the man—the impression is still there. Five thousand years have passed and he has influenced millions and millions. Just think what an influence this man has over the whole world, whether you know it or not. My regard for him is for his perfect sanity. No cobwebs in that brain, no superstition. He knows the use of everything, and when it is necessary to [assign a place to each], he is there. Those that talk, go everywhere, question about the mystery of the Vedas, etc., they do not know the truth. They are no better than frauds. There is a place in the Vedas [even] for superstition, for ignorance. The whole secret is to find out the proper place for everything.

Then that heart! He is the first man, way before Buddha, to open the door of religion to every caste. That wonderful mind! That tremendously active life! Buddha's activity was on one plane, the plane of teaching. He could not keep his wife and child and become a teacher at the same time. Krishna preached in the midst of the battlefield. "He who in the midst of intense activity finds himself in the greatest calmness, and in the greatest peace finds intense activity, that is the greatest [Yogi as well as the wisest man]."[1] It means nothing to this man—the flying of missiles about him. Calm and sedate he goes on discussing the problems of life and death. Each one of the prophets is the best commentary on his own teaching. If you want to know what is meant by the doctrine of the New Testament, you go to Mr. So-and-so. [But] read again and again [the four Gospels and try to understand their import in the light of the wonderful life of the Master as depicted there]. The great men think, and you and I [also] think. But there is a difference. We think and our bodies do not follow. Our actions do not harmonise with our thoughts. Our words have not the power of the words that become Vedas... Whatever they think must be accomplished. If they say, "I do this," the body does it. Perfect obedience. This is the end. You can think yourself God in one minute, but you cannot be [God]. That is the difficulty. They become what they think. We will become [only] by [degrees].

You see, that was about Krishna and his time. In the next lecture we will know more of his book.

1. Ibid. IV. 18.

THE GITA — II

Delivered In San Francisco, on May 28, 1900

The Gîtâ requires a little preliminary introduction. The scene is laid on the battlefield of Kurukshetra. There were two branches of the same race fighting for the empire of India about five thousand years ago. The Pândavas had the right, but the Kauravas had the might. The Pandavas were five brothers, and they were living in a forest. Krishna was the friend of the Pandavas. The Kauravas would not grant them as much land as would cover the point of a needle.

The opening scene is the battlefield, and both sides see their relatives and friends—one brother on one side and another on the other side; a grandfather on one side, grandson on the other side...When Arjuna sees his own friends and relatives on the other side and knows that he may have to kill them, his heart gives way and he says that he will not fight. Thus begins the Gita.

For all of us in this world life is a continuous fight...Many a time comes when we want to interpret our weakness and cowardice as forgiveness and renunciation. There is no merit in the renunciation of a beggar. If a person who can [give a blow] forbears, there is merit in that. If a person who has, gives up, there is merit in that. We know how often in our lives through laziness and cowardice we give up the battle and try to hypnotise our minds into the belief that we are brave.

The Gita opens with this very significant verse: "Arise, O Prince! Give up this faint-heartedness, this weakness! Stand up and fight!"[2] Then Arjuna, trying to argue the matter [with Krishna], brings higher moral ideas, how non-resistance is better than resistance, and so on. He is trying to justify himself, but he cannot fool Krishna. Krishna is the higher Self, or God. He sees through the argument at once. In this case [the motive] is weakness. Arjuna sees his own relatives and he cannot strike them...

There is a conflict in Arjuna's heart between his emotionalism and his duty. The nearer we are to [beasts and] birds, the more we are in the hells of emotion. We call it love. It is self-hypnotisation. We are under the control of our [emotions] like animals. A cow can sacrifice its life for its young. Every animal can. What of that? It is not the blind, birdlike emotion that leads to perfection...[To reach] the eternal consciousness, that is the goal of man! There emotion has no place, nor sentimentalism, nor anything that belongs to the senses—only the light of pure reason. [There] man stands as spirit.

Now, Arjuna is under the control of this emotionalism. He is not what he should be—a great self-controlled, enlightened sage working through the eternal light of reason. He has become like an animal, like a baby, just letting his heart carry away his brain, making a fool of himself and trying to cover his weakness with the flowery names of "love" and so

on. Krishna sees through that. Arjuna talks like a man of little learning and brings out many reasons, but at the same time he talks the language of a fool.

"The sage is not sorry for those that are living nor for those that die."[3] [Krishna says :] "You cannot die nor can I. There was never a time when we did not exist. There will never be a time when we shall not exist. As in this life a man begins with childhood, and [passes through youth and old age, so at death he merely passes into another kind of body]. Why should a wise man be sorry?"[4] And where is the beginning of this emotionalism that has got hold of you? It is in the senses. "It is the touch of the senses that brings all this quality of existence: heat and cold, pleasure and pain. They come and go."[5] Man is miserable this moment, happy the next. As such he cannot experience the nature of the soul...

"Existence can never be non-existence, neither can non-existence ever become existence...Know, therefore, that that which pervades all this universe is without beginning or end. It is unchangeable. There is nothing in the universe that can change [the Changeless]. Though this body has its beginning and end, the dweller in the body is infinite and without end."[6]

Knowing this, stand up and fight! Not one step back, that is the idea...Fight it out, whatever comes. Let the stars move from the sphere! Let the whole world stand against us! Death means only a change of garment. What of it? Thus fight! You gain nothing by becoming cowards...Taking a step backward, you do not avoid any misfortune. You have cried to all the gods in the world. Has misery ceased? The masses in India cry to sixty million gods, and still die like dogs. Where are these gods?...The gods come to help you when you have succeeded. So what is the use? Die game...This bending the knee to superstitions, this selling yourself to your own mind does not befit you, my soul. You are infinite, deathless, birthless. Because you are infinite spirit, it does not befit you to be a slave...Arise! Awake! Stand up and fight! Die if you must. There is none to help you. You are all the world. Who can help you?

"Beings are unknown to our human senses before birth and after death. It is only in the interim that they are manifest. What is there to grieve about?[7]

"Some look at It [the Self] with wonder. Some talk of It as wonderful. Others hear of It as wonderful. Others, hearing of It, do not understand."[8]

But if you say that killing all these people is sinful, then consider this from the standpoint of your own caste-duty..."Making pleasure and misery the same, making success

---

2. Gita, II. 3.

3. Ibid. 11.

4. Ibid. 12-13.

5. Ibid. 14.

6. Ibid. 16-18.

7. Ibid. 28.

8. Ibid. 29.

and defeat the same, do thou stand up and fight.[1]

This is the beginning of another peculiar doctrine of the Gita—the doctrine of non-attachment. That is to say, we have to bear the result of our own actions because we attach ourselves to them... "Only what is done as duty for duty's sake... can scatter the bondage of Karma."[2] There is no danger that you can overdo it... "If you do even a little of it, [this Yoga will save you from the terrible round of birth and death].[3]

"Know, Arjuna, the mind that succeeds is the mind that is concentrated. The minds that are taken up with two thousand subjects (have) their energies dispersed. Some can talk flowery language and think there is nothing beyond the Vedas. They want to go to heaven. They want good things through the power of the Vedas, and so they make sacrifices."[4] Such will never attain any success [in spiritual life] unless they give up all these materialistic ideas.[5]

That is another great lesson. Spirituality can never be attained unless all material ideas are given up... What is in the senses? The senses are all delusion. People wish to retain them [in heaven] even after they are dead—a pair of eyes, a nose. Some imagine they will have more organs than they have now. They want to see God sitting on a throne through all eternity—the material body of God... Such men's desires are for the body, for food and drink and enjoyment. It is the materialistic life prolonged. Man cannot think of anything beyond this life. This life is all for the body. "Such a man never comes to that concentration which leads to freedom."[6]

"The Vedas only teach things belonging to the three Gunas, to Sattva, Rajas, and Tamas."[7] The Vedas only teach about things in nature. People cannot think anything they do not see on earth. If they talk about heaven, they think of a king sitting on a throne, of people burning incense. It is all nature, nothing beyond nature. The Vedas, therefore, teach nothing but nature. "Go beyond nature, beyond the dualities of existence, beyond your own consciousness, caring for nothing, neither for good nor for evil."[8]

We have identified ourselves with our bodies. We are only body, or rather, possessed of a body. If I am pinched, I cry. All this is nonsense, since I am the soul. All this chain of misery, imagination, animals, gods, and demons, everything, the whole world all this comes from the identification of ourselves with the body. I am spirit. Why do I jump if you pinch me?... Look at the slavery of it. Are you not ashamed? We are religious! We are philosophers! We are sages! Lord bless us! What are we? Living hells, that is what we are. Lunatics, that

is what we are!

We cannot give up the idea [of body]. We are earthbound... Our ideas are burial grounds. When we leave the body we are bound by thousands of elements to those [ideas].

Who can work without any attachment? That is the real question. Such a man is the same whether his work succeeds or fails. His heart does not give one false beat even if his whole life-work is burnt to ashes in a moment. "This is the sage who always works for work's sake without caring for the results. Thus he goes beyond the pain of birth and death. Thus he becomes free."[9] Then he sees that this attachment is all delusion. The Self can never be attached... Then he goes beyond all the scriptures and philosophies.[10] If the mind is deluded and pulled into a whirlpool by books and scriptures, what is the good of all these scriptures? One says this, another says that. What book shall you take? Stand alone! See the glory of your own soul, and see that you will have to work. Then you will become a man of firm will.[11]

Arjuna asks: "Who is a person of established will?"[12]

[Krishna answers:] "The man who has given up all desires, who desires nothing, not even this life, nor freedom, nor gods, nor work, nor anything. When he has become perfectly satisfied, he has no more cravings."[13] He has seen the glory of the Self and has found that the world, and the gods, and heaven are... within his own Self. Then the gods become no gods; death becomes no death; life becomes no life. Everything has changed. "A man is said to be [illumined] if his will has become firm, if his mind is not disturbed by misery, if he does not desire any happiness, if he is free of all [attachment], of all fear, of all anger.[14] ...

"As the tortoise can draw in his legs, and if you strike him, not one foot comes out, even so the sage can draw all his sense-organs inside,"[15] and nothing can force them out. Nothing can shake him, no temptation or anything. Let the universe tumble about him, it does not make one single ripple in his mind.

Then comes a very important question. Sometimes people fast for days... When the worst man has fasted for twenty days, he becomes quite gentle. Fasting and torturing themselves have been practiced by people all over the world. Krishna's idea is that this is all nonsense. He says that the senses will for the moment recede from the man who tortures himself, but will emerge again with twenty times more [power]... What should you do? The idea is to be natural—no asceticism. Go on, work, only mind that you are not attached. The will can never be fixed strongly in the man who has not learnt and

1. Ibid. 38.
2. Ibid. 39.
3. Ibid. 40.
4. Ibid. 41-43.
5. Ibid. 44.
6. Ibid. 44.
7. Ibid. 45.
8. Ibid. 45.

9. Ibid. 51.
10. Ibid. 52.
11. Ibid. 53.
12. Ibid. 54.
13. Ibid. 55.
14. Ibid. 56.
15. Ibid. 58.

practiced the secret of non-attachment.

I go out and open my eyes. If something is there, I must see it. I cannot help it. The mind runs after the senses. Now the senses must give up any reaction to nature.

"Where it is dark night for the [sense-bound] world, the self controlled [man] is awake. It is daylight for him…And where the world is awake, the sage sleeps."[16] Where is the world awake? In the senses. People want to eat and drink and have children, and then they die a dog's death…They are always awake for the senses. Even their religion is just for that. They invent a God to help them, to give them more women, more money, more children — never a God to help them become more godlike! "Where the whole world is awake, the sage sleeps. But where the ignorant are asleep, there the sage keeps awake"[17] — in the world of light where man looks upon himself not as a bird, not as an animal, not as a body, but as infinite spirit, deathless, immortal. There, where the ignorant are asleep, and do not have time, nor intellect, nor power to understand, there the sage is awake. That is daylight for him.

"As all the rivers of the world constantly pour their waters into the ocean, but the ocean's grand, majestic nature remains undisturbed and unchanged, so even though all the senses bring in sensations from nature, the ocean-like heart of the sage knows no disturbance, knows no fear."[18] Let miseries come in millions of rivers and happiness in hundreds! I am no slave to misery! I am no slave to happiness!

THE GITA — III

Delivered in San Francisco, on May 29, 1900

Arjuna asks: "You just advised action, and yet you uphold knowledge of Brahman as the highest form of life. Krishna, if you think that knowledge is better than action, why do you tell me to act?"[19]

[Shri Krishna]: "From ancient times these two systems have come down to us. The Sânkhya philosophers advance the theory of knowledge. The Yogis advance the theory of work. But none can attain to peace by renouncing actions. None in this life can stop activity even for a moment. Nature's qualities [Gunas] will make him act. He who stops his activities and at the same time is still thinking about them attains to nothing; he only becomes a hypocrite. But he who by the power of his mind gradually brings his sense-organs under control, employing them in work, that man is better. Therefore do thou work."[20] …

"Even if you have known the secret that you have no duty, that you are free, still you have to work for the good of others. Because whatever a great man does, ordinary people will do also.[21] If a great man who has attained peace of mind and freedom ceases to work, then all the rest without that knowledge and peace will try to imitate him, and thus confusion would arise.[22]

"Behold, Arjuna, there is nothing that I do not possess and nothing that I want to acquire. And yet I continue to work. If I stopped work for a moment, the whole universe would [be destroyed].[23] That which the ignorant do with desire for results and gain, let the wise do without any attachment and without any desire for results and gain."[24]

Even if you have knowledge, do not disturb the childlike faith of the ignorant. On the other hand, go down to their level and gradually bring them up.[25] That is a very powerful idea, and it has become the ideal in India. That is why you can see a great philosopher going into a temple and worshipping images. It is not hypocrisy.

Later on we read what Krishna says, "Even those who worship other deities are really worshipping me."[26] It is God incarnate whom man is worshipping. Would God be angry if you called Him by the wrong name? He would be no God at all! Can't you understand that whatever a man has in his own heart is God — even if he worships a stone? What of that!

We will understand more clearly if we once get rid of the idea that religion consists in doctrines. One idea of religion has been that the whole world was born because Adam ate the apple, and there is no way of escape. Believe in Jesus Christ — in a certain man's death! But in India there is quite a different idea. [There] religion means realisation, nothing else. It does not matter whether one approaches the destination in a carriage with four horses, in an electric car, or rolling on the ground. The goal is the same. For the [Christians] the problem is how to escape the wrath of the terrible God. For the Indians it is how to become what they really are, to regain their lost Selfhood…

Have you realised that you are spirit? When you say, "I do," what is meant by that — this lump of flesh called the body or the spirit, the infinite, ever blessed, effulgent, immortal? You may be the greatest philosopher, but as long as you have the idea that you are the body, you are no better than the little worm crawling under your foot! No excuse for you! So much the worse for you that you know all the philosophies and at the same time think you are the body! Body-gods, that is what you are! Is that religion?

Religion is the realisation of spirit as spirit. What are we doing now? Just the opposite, realising spirit as matter. Out of the immortal God we manufacture death and matter, and out of dead dull matter we manufacture spirit…

---

16. Ibid. 69.
17. Ibid. 69.
18. Ibid. 70.
19. Gita III. 1.
20. Ibid. 2-8.

21. Ibid. 20-21.
22. Ibid. 22-24.
23. Ibid. 22-24.
24. Ibid. 25.
25. Ibid. 26, 29.
26. Ibid. IX. 23.

If you [can realise Brahman] by standing on your head, or on one foot, or by worshipping five thousand gods with three heads each—welcome to it!...Do it any way you can! Nobody has any right to say anything. Therefore, Krishna says, if your method is better and higher, you have no business to say that another man's method is bad, however wicked you may think it.

Again, we must consider, religion is a [matter of] growth, not a mass of foolish words. Two thousand years ago a man saw God. Moses saw God in a burning bush. Does what Moses did when he saw God save you? No man's seeing God can help you the least bit except that it may excite you and urge you to do the same thing. That is the whole value of the ancients' examples. Nothing more. [Just] signposts on the way. No man's eating can satisfy another man. No man's seeing God can save another man. You have to see God yourself. All these people fighting about what God's nature is—whether He has three heads in one body or five heads in six bodies. Have you seen God? No...And they do not believe they can ever see Him. What fools we mortals be! Sure, lunatics!

[In India] it has come down as a tradition that if there is a God, He must be your God and my God. To whom does the sun belong! You say Uncle Sam is everybody's uncle. If there is a God, you ought to be able to see Him. If not, let Him go.

Each one thinks his method is best. Very good! But remember, it may be good for you. One food which is very indigestible to one is very digestible to another. Because it is good for you, do not jump to the conclusion that your method is everybody's method, that Jack's coat fits John and Mary. All the uneducated, uncultured, unthinking men and women have been put into that sort of strait jacket! Think for yourselves. Become atheists! Become materialists! That would be better. Exercises the mind!...What right have you to say that this man's method is wrong? It may be wrong for you. That is to say, if you undertake the method, you will be degraded; but that does not mean that he will be degraded. Therefore, says Krishna, if you have knowledge and see a man weak, do not condemn him. Go to his level and help him if you can. He must grow. I can put five bucketfuls of knowledge into his head in five hours. But what good will it do? He will be a little worse than before.

Whence comes all this bondage of action? Because we chain the soul with action. According to our Indian system, there are two existences: nature on the one side and the Self, the Atman, on the other. By the word nature is meant not only all this external world, but also our bodies, the mind, the will, even down to what says "I". Beyond all that is the infinite life and light of the soul—the Self, the Atman...According to this philosophy the Self is entirely separate from nature, always was and always will be...There never was a time, when the spirit could be identified even with the mind...

It is self-evident that the food you eat is manufacturing the mind all the time. It is matter. The Self is above any con-

nection with food. Whether you eat or not does not matter. Whether you think or not...does not matter. It is infinite light. Its light is the same always. If you put a blue or a green glass [before a light], what has that to do with the light? Its colour is unchangeable. It is the mind which changes and gives the different colours. The moment the spirit leaves the body, the whole thing goes to pieces.

The reality in nature is spirit. Reality itself—the light of the spirit—moves and speaks and does everything [through our bodies, minds, etc.]. It is the energy and soul and life of the spirit that is being worked upon in different ways by matter...The spirit is the cause of all our thoughts and body-action and everything, but it is untouched by good or evil, pleasure or pain, heat or cold, and all the dualism of nature, although it lends its light to everything.

"Therefore, Arjuna, all these actions are in nature. Nature...is working out her own laws in our bodies and minds. We identify ourselves with nature and say, 'I am doing this.' This way delusion seizes us."[1]

We always act under some compulsion. When hunger compels me, I eat. And suffering is still worse—slavery. That real "I" is eternally free. What can compel it to do anything? The sufferer is in nature. It is only when we identify ourselves with the body that we say, "I am suffering; I am Mr. So and-so"—all such nonsense. But he who has known the truth, holds himself aloof. Whatever his body does, whatever his mind does, he does not care. But mind you, the vast majority of mankind are under this delusion; and whenever they do any good, they feel that they are [the doers]. They are not yet able to understand higher philosophy. Do not disturb their faith! They are shunning evil and doing good. Great idea! Let them have it!...They are workers for good. By degrees they will think that there is greater glory than that of doing good. They will only witness, and things are done...Gradually they will understand. When they have shunned all evil and done all good, then they will begin to realise that they are beyond all nature. They are not the doers. They stand [apart]. They are the...witness. They simply stand and look. Nature is begetting all the universe...They turn their backs. "In the beginning, O beloved, there only existed that Existence. Nothing else existed. And That [brooding], everything else was created."[2]

"Even those who know the path act impelled by their own nature. Everyone acts according to his nature. He cannot transcend it."[3] The atom cannot disobey the law. Whether it is the mental or the physical atom, it must obey the law. "What is the use of [external restraint]?"[4]

What makes the value of anything in life? Not enjoyment, not possessions. Analyse everything. You will find there is no value except in experience, to teach us something. And in

1. Ibid. III. 27.

2. Chhândogya, VI. ii. 2-3.

3. Gita, III. 33.

4. Gita, III. 33.

many cases it is our hardships that give us better experience than enjoyment. Many times blows give us better experience than the caresses of nature... Even famine has its place and value...

According to Krishna, we are not new beings just come into existence. Our minds are not new minds... In modern times we all know that every child brings [with him] all the past, not only of humanity, but of the plant life. There are all the past chapters, and this present chapter, and there are a whole lot of future chapters before him. Everyone has his path mapped and sketched and planned out for him. And in spite of all this darkness, there cannot be anything uncaused—no event, no circumstance... It is simply our ignorance. The whole infinite chain of causation... is bound one link to another back to nature. The whole universe is bound by that sort of chain. It is the universal [chain of] cause and effect, you receiving one link, one part, I another... And that [part] is our own nature.

Now Shri Krishna says: "Better die in your own path than attempt the path of another."[5] This is my path, and I am down here. And you are way up there, and I am always tempted to give up my path thinking I will go there and be with you. And if I go up, I am neither there nor here. We must not lose sight of this doctrine. It is all [a matter of] growth. Wait and grow, and you attain everything; otherwise there will be [great spiritual danger]. Here is the fundamental secret of teaching religion.

What do you mean by "saving people" and all believing in the same doctrine? It cannot be. There are the general ideas that can be taught to mankind. The true teacher will be able to find out for you what your own nature is. Maybe you do not know it. It is possible that what you think is your own nature is all wrong. It has not developed to consciousness. The teacher is the person who ought to know... He ought to know by a glance at your face and put you on [your path]. We grope about and struggle here and there and do all sorts of things and make no progress until the time comes when we fall into that life-current and are carried on. The sign is that the moment we are in that stream we will float. Then there is no more struggle. This is to be found out. Then die in that [path] rather than giving it up and taking hold of another.

Instead, we start a religion and make a set of dogmas and betray the goal of mankind and treat everyone [as having] the same nature. No two persons have the same mind or the same body... No two persons have the same religion...

If you want to be religious, enter not the gate of any organised religions. They do a hundred times more evil than good, because they stop the growth of each one's individual development. Study everything, but keep your own seat firm. If you take my advice, do not put your neck into the trap. The moment they try to put their noose on you, get your neck out and go somewhere else. [As] the bee culling honey from many flowers remains free, not bound by any flower, be not bound... Enter not the door of any organised religion. [Religion] is only between you and your God, and no third person must come between you. Think what these organised religions have done! What Napoleon was more terrible than those religious persecutions?... If you and I organise, we begin to hate every person. It is better not to love, if loving only means hating others. That is no love. That is hell! If loving your own people means hating everybody else, it is the quintessence of selfishness and brutality, and the effect is that it will make you brutes. Therefore, better die working out your own natural religion than following another's natural religion, however great it may appear to you.[6]

"Beware, Arjuna, lust and anger are the great enemies. These are to be controlled. These cover the knowledge even of those [who are wise]. This fire of lust is unquenchable. Its location is in the sense-organs and in the mind. The Self desires nothing.[7]

"This Yoga I taught in ancient times [to Vivaswân; Vivaswan taught it to Manu]... Thus it was that the knowledge descended from one thing to another. But in time this great Yoga was destroyed. That is why I am telling it to you again today."[8]

Then Arjuna asks, "Why do you speak thus? You are a man born only the other day, and [Vivaswan was born long before you]. What do you mean that you taught him?"[9]

Then Krishna says, "O Arjuna, you and I have run the cycle of births and deaths many times, but you are not conscious of them all. I am without beginning, birthless, the absolute Lord of all creation. I through my own nature take form. Whenever virtue subsides and wickedness prevails, I come to help mankind. For the salvation of the good, for the destruction of wickedness, for the establishment of spirituality I come from time to time. Whosoever wants to reach me through whatsoever ways, I reach him through that. But know, Arjuna, none can ever swerve from my path."[10] None ever did. How can we? None swerves from His path.

... All societies are based upon bad generalisation. The law can only be formed upon perfect generalisation. What is the old saying: Every law has its exception?... If it is a law, it cannot be broken. None can break it. Does the apple break the law of gravitation? The moment a law is broken, no more universe exists. There will come a time when you will break the law, and that moment your consciousness, mind, and body will melt away.

There is a man stealing there. Why does he steal? You punish him. Why can you not make room for him and put his energy to work?... You say, "You are a sinner," and many will say he has broken the law. All this herd of mankind is forced [into uniformity] and hence all trouble, sin, and weakness... The

5. Ibid. 35.

6. Ibid. 35.

7. Ibid. 37, 40.

8. Ibid. 37, 40.

9. Ibid. 4.

10. Ibid. 5-8, 11.

world is not as bad as you think. It is we fools who have made it evil. We manufacture our own ghosts and demons, and then…we cannot get rid of them. We put our hands before our eyes and cry: "Somebody give us light." Fools! Take your hands from your eyes! That is all there is to it…We call upon the gods to save us and nobody blames himself. That is the pity of it. Why is there so much evil in society? What is it they say? Flesh and the devil and the woman. Why make these things [up]? Nobody asks you to make them [up]. "None, O Arjuna, can swerve from my path."[1] We are fools, and our paths are foolish. We have to go through all this Mâyâ. God made the heaven, and man made the hell for himself.

"No action can touch me. I have no desire for the results of action. Whosoever knows me thus knows the secret and is not bound by action. The ancient sages, knowing this secret [could safely engage in action]. Do thou work in the same fashion.[2]

"He who sees in the midst of intense activity, intense calm, and in the midst of intensest peace is intensely active [is wise indeed].[3]…This is the question: With every sense and every organ active, have you that tremendous peace [so that] nothing can disturb you? Standing on Market Street, waiting for the car with all the rush…going on around you, are you in meditation—calm and peaceful? In the cave, are you intensely active there with all quiet about you? If you are, you are a Yogi, otherwise not.

"[The seers call him wise] whose every attempt is free, without any desire for gain, without any selfishness."[4] Truth can never come to us as long as we are selfish. We colour everything with our own selves. Things come to us as they are. Not that they are hidden, not at all! We hide them. We have the brush. A thing comes, and we do not like it, and we brush a little and then look at it…We do not want to know. We paint everything with ourselves. In all action the motive power is selfishness. Everything is hidden by ourselves. We are like the caterpillar which takes the thread out of his own body and of that makes the cocoon, and behold, he is caught. By his own work he imprisons himself. That is what we are doing. The moment I say "me" the thread makes a turn. "I and mine," another turn. So it goes…

We cannot remain without action for a moment. Act! But just as when your neighbour asks you, "Come and help me!" have you exactly the same idea when you are helping yourself. No more. Your body is of no more value than that of John. Don't do anything more for your body than you do for John. That is religion.

"He whose efforts are bereft of all desire and selfishness has burnt all this bondage of action with the fire of knowledge.

He is wise."[5] Reading books cannot do that. The ass can be burdened with the whole library; that does not make him learned at all. What is the use of reading many books? "Giving up all attachment to work, always satisfied, not hoping for gain, the wise man acts and is beyond action."[6]…

Naked I came out of my mother's womb and naked I return. Helpless I came and helpless I go. Helpless I am now. And we do not know [the goal]. It is terrible for us to think about it. We get such odd ideas! We go to a medium and see if the ghost can help us. Think of the weakness! Ghosts, devils, gods, anybody—come on! And all the priests, all the charlatans! That is just the time they get hold of us, the moment we are weak. Then they bring in all the gods.

I see in my country a man becomes strong, educated, becomes a philosopher, and says, "All this praying and bathing is nonsense."…The man's father dies, and his mother dies. That is the most terrible shock a Hindu can have. You will find him bathing in every dirty pool, going into the temple, licking the dust…Help anyone! But we are helpless. There is no help from anyone. That is the truth. There have been more gods than human beings; and yet no help. We die like dogs—no help. Everywhere beastliness, famine, disease, misery, evil! And all are crying for help. But no help. And yet, hoping against hope, we are still screaming for help. Oh, the miserable condition! Oh, the terror of it! Look into your own heart! One half of [the trouble] is not our fault, but the fault of our parents. Born with this weakness, more and more of it was put into our heads. Step by step we go beyond it.

It is a tremendous error to feel helpless. Do not seek help from anyone. We are our own help. If we cannot help ourselves, there is none to help us…"Thou thyself art thy only friend, thou thyself thy only enemy. There is no other enemy but this self of mine, no other friend but myself."[7] This is the last and greatest lesson, and Oh, what a time it takes to learn it! We seem to get hold of it, and the next moment the old wave comes. The backbone breaks. We weaken and again grasp for that superstition and help. Just think of that huge mass of misery, and all caused by this false idea of going to seek for help!

Possibly the priest says his routine words and expects something. Sixty thousand people look to the skies and pray and pay the priest. Month after month they still look, still pay and pray…Think of that! Is it not lunacy? What else is it? Who is responsible? You may preach religion, but to excite the minds of undeveloped children…! You will have to suffer for that. In your heart of hearts, what are you? For every weakening thought you have put into anybody's head you will have to pay with compound interest. The law of Karma must have its pound of flesh…

There is only one sin. That is weakness. When I was a boy

1. Ibid. 11.

2. Ibid. 14-15.

3. Ibid 18.

4. Ibid. 19

5. Ibid. 19

6. Ibid. 20.

7. Ibid. VI. 5.

I read Milton's *Paradise Lost*. The only good man I had any respect for was Satan. The only saint is that soul that never weakens, faces everything, and determines to die game.

Stand up and die game!... Do not add one lunacy to another. Do not add your weakness to the evil that is going to come. That is all I have to say to the world. Be strong!... You talk of ghosts and devils. We are the living devils. The sign of life is strength and growth. The sign of death is weakness. Whatever is weak, avoid! It is death. If it is strength, go down into hell and get hold of it! There is salvation only for the brave. "None but the brave deserves the fair." None but the bravest deserves salvation. Whose hell? Whose torture? Whose sin? Whose weakness? Whose death? Whose disease?

You believe in God. If you do, believe in the real God. "Thou art the man, thou the woman, thou the young man walking in the strength of youth,... thou the old man tottering with his stick."[8] Thou art weakness. Thou art fear. Thou art heaven, and Thou art hell. Thou art the serpent that would sting. Come thou as fear! Come thou as death! Come thou as misery!...

All weakness, all bondage is imagination. Speak one word to it, it must vanish. Do not weaken! There is no other way out... Stand up and be strong! No fear. No superstition. Face the truth as it is! If death comes—that is the worst of our miseries—let it come! We are determined to die game. That is all the religion I know. I have not attained to it, but I am struggling to do it. I may not, but you may. Go on!

Where one sees another, one hears another so long as there are two, there must be fear, and fear is the mother of all [misery]. Where none sees another, where it is all One, there is none to be miserable, none to be unhappy.[9] [There is only] the One without a second. Therefore be not afraid. Awake, arise, and stop not till the goal is reached!

MOHAMMED

Delivered on March 25, 1900, in the
San Francisco Bay Area

The ancient message of Krishna is one harmonising three—Buddha's, Christ's and Mohammed's. Each of the three started an idea and carried it to its extreme. Krishna antedates all the other prophets. [Yet, we might say,] Krishna takes the old ideas and synthesises them, [although] his is the most ancient message. His message was for the time being submerged by the advance wave of Buddhism. Today it is the message peculiar to India. If you will have it so, this afternoon I will take Mohammed and bring out the particular work of the great Arabian prophet...

Mohammed [as] a young man... did not [seem to] care much for religion. He was inclined to make money. He was considered a nice young man and very handsome. There was

a rich widow. She fell in love with this young man, and they married. When Mohammed had become emperor over the larger part of the world, the Roman and Persian empires were all under his feet, and he had a number of wives. When one day he was asked which wife he liked best, he pointed to his first wife: "Because she believed [in] me first." Women have faith... Gain independence, gain everything, but do not lose that characteristic of women!...

Mohammed's heart was sick at the sin, idolatry and mock worship, superstitions and human sacrifices, and so on. The Jews were degraded by the Christians. On the other hand, the Christians were worse degraded than his own countrymen.

We are always in a hurry. [But] if any great work is to be done, there must be great preparation... After much praying, day and night, Mohammed began to have dreams and visions. Gabriel appeared to him in a dream and told him that he was the messenger of truth. He told him that the message of Jesus, of Moses, and all the prophets would be lost and asked him to go and preach. Seeing the Christians preaching politics in the name of Jesus, seeing the Persians preaching dualism, Mohammed said: "Our God is one God. He is the Lord of all that exists. There is no comparison between Him and any other."

God is God. There is no philosophy, no complicated code of ethics. "Our God is one without a second, and Mohammed is the Prophet."... Mohammed began to preach it in the streets of Mecca... They began to persecute him, and he fled into the city of [Medina]. He began to fight, and the whole race became united. [Mohammedanism] deluged the world in the name of the Lord. The tremendous conquering power!...

You... people have very hard ideas and are so superstitious and prejudiced! These messengers must have come from God, else how could they have been so great? You look at every defect. Each one of us has his defects. Who hasn't? I can point out many defects in the Jews. The wicked are always looking for defects... Flies come and seek for the [ulcer], and bees come only for the honey in the flower. Do not follow the way of the fly but that of the bee...

Mohammed married quite a number of wives afterwards. Great men may marry two hundred wives each. "Giants" like you, I would not allow to marry one wife. The characters of the great souls are mysterious, their methods past our finding out. We must not judge them. Christ may judge Mohammed. Who are you and I? Little babies. What do we understand of these great souls?...

[Mohammedanism] came as a message for the masses... The first message was equality... There is one religion—love. No more question of race, colour, [or] anything else. Join it! That practical quality carried the day... The great message was perfectly simple. Believe in one God, the creator of heaven and earth. All was created out of nothing by Him. Ask no questions...

Their temples are like Protestant churches... no music, no

---

8. Shvetâshvatara, IV. 3.

9. Chhândogya, VII. xxiii-xxiv, (adapted)

paintings, no pictures. A pulpit in the corner; on that lies the Koran. The people all stand in line. No priest, no person, no bishop...The man who prays must stand at the side of the audience. Some parts are beautiful...

These old people were all messengers of God. I fall down and worship them; I take the dust of their feet. But they are dead!...And we are alive. We must go ahead!...Religion is not an imitation of Jesus or Mohammed. Even if an imitation is good, it is never genuine. Be not an imitation of Jesus, but be Jesus, You are quite as great as Jesus, Buddha, or anybody else. If we are not...we must struggle and be. I would not be exactly like Jesus. It is unnecessary that I should be born a Jew...

The greatest religion is to be true to your own nature. Have faith in yourselves! If you do not exist, how can God exist, or anybody else? Wherever you are, it is this mind that perceives even the Infinite. I see God, therefore He exists. If I cannot think of God, He does not exist [for me]. This is the grand march of our human progress.

These [great souls] are signposts on the way. That is all they are. They say, "Onward, brothers!" We cling to them; we never want to move. We do not want to think; we want others to think for us. The messengers fulfil their mission. They ask to be up and doing. A hundred years later we cling to the message and go to sleep.

Talking about faith and belief and doctrine is easy, but it is so difficult to build character and to stem the tide of the senses. We succumb. We become hypocrites...

[Religion] is not a doctrine, [not] a rule. It is a process. That is all. [Doctrines and rules] are all for exercise. By that exercise we get strong and at last break the bonds and become free. Doctrine is of no use except for gymnastics...Through exercise the soul becomes perfect. That exercise is stopped when you say, "I believe."...

"Whenever virtue subsides and immorality abounds, I take human form. In every age I come for the salvation of the good, for the destruction of the wicked, for the establishment of spirituality."[1]

[Such] are the great messengers of light. They are our great teachers, our elder brothers. But we must go our own way!

VILVAMANGALA[2]

This is a story from one of the books of India, called "Lives of Saints". There was a young man, a Brahmin by birth, in a certain village. The man fell in love with a bad woman in another village. There was a big river between the two villages, and this man, every day, used to go to that girl, crossing this river in a ferry boat. Now, one day he had to perform the obsequies of his father, and so, although he was longing, almost dying to go to the girl, he could not. The ceremonies had to be per-

formed, and all those things had to be undergone; it is absolutely necessary in Hindu society. He was fretting and fuming and all that, but could not help it. At last the ceremony ended, and night came, and with the night, a tremendous howling storm arose. The rain was pouring down, and the river was lashed into gigantic waves. It was very dangerous to cross. Yet he went to the bank of the river. There was no ferry boat. The ferrymen were afraid to cross, but he would go; his heart was becoming mad with love for the girl, so he would go. There was a log floating down, and he got that, and with the help of it, crossed the river, and getting to the other side dragged the log up, threw it on the bank, and went to the house. The doors were closed. He knocked at the door, but the wind was howling, and nobody heard him. So he went round the walls and at last found what he thought to be a rope, hanging from the wall. He clutched at it, saying to himself, "Oh, my love has left a rope for me to climb." By the help of that rope he climbed over the wall, got to the other side, missed his footing, and fell, and noise aroused the inmates of the house, and the came out and found the man there in a faint. She revived him, and noticing that he was smelling very unpleasantly, she said, "What is the matter with you? Why this stench on your body? How did you come into the house?" He said, "Why, did not my love put that rope there?" She smiled, and said, "What love? We are for money, and do you think that I let down a rope for you, fool that you are? How did you cross the river?" "Why, I got hold of a log of wood." "Let us go and see," said the girl. The rope was a cobra, a tremendously poisonous serpent, whose least touch is death. It had its head in a hole, and was getting in when the man caught hold of its tail, and he thought it was a rope. The madness of love made him do it. When the serpent has its head in its hole, and its body out, and you catch hold of it, it will not let its head come out; so the man climbed up by it, but the force of the pull killed the serpent. "Where did you get the log?" "It was floating down the river." It was a festering dead body; the stream had washed it down and that he took for a log, which explained why he had such an unpleasant odour. The woman looked at him and said, "I never believed in love; we never do; but, if this is not love, the Lord have mercy on me. We do not know what love is. But, my friend, why do you give that heart to a woman like me? Why do you not give it to God? You will be perfect." It was a thunderbolt to the man's brain. He got a glimpse of the beyond for a moment. "Is there a God?" "Yes, yes, my friend, there is," said the woman. And the man walked on, went into a forest, began to weep and pray. "I want Thee, Oh Lord! This tide of my love cannot find a receptacle in little human beings. I want to love where this mighty river of my love can go, the ocean of love; this rushing tremendous river of my love cannot enter into little pools, it wants the infinite ocean. Thou art there; come Thou to me." So he remained there for years. After years he thought he had succeeded, he became a Sannyasin and he came into the cities. One day he was sitting on the bank of a river, at one of the bathing places,

1. Gita, IV. 7-8.

2. Found in the papers of Miss S.E. Waldo b Swami Raghavananda when he was in the U.S.A

and a beautiful young girl, the wife of a merchant of the city, with her servant, came and passed the place. The old man was again up in him, the beautiful face again attracted him. The Yogi looked and looked, stood up and followed the girl to her home. Presently the husband came by, and seeing the Sannyasin in the yellow garb he said to him, "Come in, sir, what can I do for you?" The Yogi said, "I will ask you a terrible thing." "Ask anything, sir, I am a Grihastha (householder), and anything that one asks I am ready to give." "I want to see your wife." The man said, "Lord, what is this! Well, I am pure, and my wife is pure, and the Lord is a protection to all. Welcome; come in sir." He came in, and the husband introduced him to his wife. "What can I do for you?" asked the lady. He looked and looked, and then said, "Mother, will you give me two pins from your hair?" "Here they are." He thrust them into his two eyes saying "Get away, you rascals! Henceforth no fleshy things for you. If you are to see, see the Shepherd of the groves of Vrindaban with the eyes of the soul. Those are all the eyes you have." So he went back into the forest. There again he wept and wept and wept. It was all that great flow of love in the man that was struggling to get at the truth, and at last he succeeded; he gave his soul, the river of his love, the right direction, and it came to the Shepherd. The story goes that he saw God in the form of Krishna. Then, for once, he was sorry that he had lost his eyes, and that he could only have the internal vision. He wrote some beautiful poems of love. In all Sanskrit books, the writers first of all salute their Gurus. So he saluted that girl as his first Guru.

THE SOUL AND GOD

Delivered in San Francisco, March 23, 1900

Whether it was fear or mere inquisitiveness which first led man to think of powers superior to himself, we need not discuss... These raised in the mind peculiar worship tendencies, and so on. There never have been [times in the history of mankind] without [some ideal] of worship. Why? What makes us all struggle for something beyond what we see—whether it be a beautiful morning or a fear of dead spirits?... We need not go back into prehistoric times, for it is a fact present today as it was two thousand years ago. We do not find satisfaction here. Whatever our station in life—[even if we are] powerful and wealthy—we cannot find satisfaction.

Desire is infinite. Its fulfilment is very limited.. There is no end to our desires; but when we go to fulfil them, the difficulty comes. It has been so with the most primitive minds, when their desires were [few]. Even [these] could not be accomplished. Now, with our arts and sciences improved and multiplied, our desires cannot be fulfilled [either]. On the other hand, we are struggling to perfect means for the fulfilment of desires, and the desires are increasing...

The most primitive man naturally wanted help from outside for things which he could not accomplish... He desired something, and it could not be obtained. He wanted help from other powers. The most ignorant primitive man and the most cultivated man today, each appealing to God and asking for the fulfilment of some desire, are exactly the same. What difference? [Some people] find a great deal of difference. We are always finding much difference in things when there is no difference at all. Both [the primitive man and the cultivated man] plead to the same [power]. You may call it God or Allah or Jehovah. Human beings want something and cannot get it by their own powers, and are after someone who will help them. This is primitive, and it is still present with us... We are all born savages and gradually civilise ourselves... All of us here, if we search, will find the same fact. Even now this fear does not leave us. We may talk big, become philosophers and all that; but when the blow comes, we find that we must beg for help. We believe in all the superstitions that ever existed. [But] there is no superstition in the world [that does not have some basis of truth]. If I cover my face and only the tip of my [nose] is showing, still it is a bit of my face. So [with] the superstitions—the little bits are true.

You see, the lowest sort of manifestation of religion came with the burial of the departed... First they wrapped them up and put them in mounds, and the spirits of the departed came and lived in the [mounds, at night]... Then they began to bury them... At the gate stands a terrible goddess with a thousand teeth... Then [came] the burning of the body and the flames bore the spirit up... The Egyptians brought food and water for the departed.

The next great idea was that of the tribal gods. This tribe had one god and that tribe another. The Jews had their God Jehovah, who was their own tribal god and fought against all the other gods and tribes. That god would do anything to please his own people. If he killed a whole tribe not protected by him, that was all right, quite good. A little love was given, but that love was confined to a small section.

Gradually, higher ideals came. The chief of the conquering tribe was the Chief of chiefs, God of gods... So with the Persians when they conquered Egypt. The Persian emperor was the Lord of [lords], and before the emperor nobody could stand. Death was the penalty for anyone who looked at the Persian emperor.

Then came the ideal of God Almighty and All-powerful, the omnipotent, omniscient Ruler of the universe: He lives in heaven, and man pays special tribute to his Most Beloved, who creates everything for man. The whole world is for man. The sun and moon and stars are [for him]. All who have those ideas are primitive men, not civilised and not cultivated at all. All the superior religions had their growth between the Ganga and the Euphrates... Outside of India we will find no further development [of religion beyond this idea of God in heaven]. That was the highest knowledge ever obtained outside of India. There is the local heaven where he is and [where] the faithful shall go when they die... As far as I have seen, we should call it a very primitive idea... Mumbo jumbo in Africa

[and] God in heaven — the same. He moves the world, and of course his will is being done everywhere...

The old Hebrew people did not care for any heaven. That is one of the reasons they [opposed] Jesus of Nazareth — because he taught life after death. Paradise in Sanskrit means land beyond this life. So the paradise was to make up for all this evil. The primitive man does not care [about] evil... He never questions why there should be any...

...The word devil is a Persian word... The Persians and Hindus [share the Aryan ancestry] upon religious grounds, and...they spoke the same language, only the words one sect uses for good the other uses for bad. The word Deva is an old Sanskrit word for God, the same word in the Aryan languages. Here the word means the devil...

Later on, when man developed [his inner life], he began to question, and to say that God is good. The Persians said that there were two gods — one was bad and one was good. [Their idea was that] everything in this life was good: beautiful country, where there was spring almost the whole year round and nobody died; there was no disease, everything was fine. Then came this Wicked One, and he touched the land, and then came death and disease and mosquitoes and tigers and lions. Then the Aryans left their fatherland and migrated southward. The old Aryans must have lived way to the north. The Jews learnt it [the idea of the devil] from the Persians. The Persians also taught that there will come a day when this wicked god will be killed, and it is our duty to stay with the good god and add our force to him in this eternal struggle between him and the wicked one... The whole world will be burnt out and everyone will get a new body.

The Persian idea was that even the wicked will be purified and not be bad any more. The nature of the Aryan was love and poetry. They cannot think of their being burnt [for eternity]. They will all receive new bodies. Then no more death. So that is the best about [religious] ideas outside of India...

Along with that is the ethical strain. All that man has to do is to take care of three things: good thought, good word, good deed. That is all. It is a practical, wise religion. Already there has come a little poetry in it. But there is higher poetry and higher thought.

In India we see this Satan in the most ancient part of the Vedas. He just (appears) and immediately disappears... In the Vedas the bad god got a blow and disappeared. He is gone, and the Persians took him. We are trying to make him leave the world [al]together. Taking the Persian idea, we are going to make a decent gentleman of him; give him a new body. There was the end of the Satan idea in India.

But the idea of God went on; but mind you, here comes another fact. The idea of God grew side by side with the idea of [materialism] until you have traced it up to the emperor of Persia. But on the other hand comes in metaphysics, philosophy. There is another line of thought, the idea of [the non-dual Âtman, man's] own soul. That also grows. So, out-

side of India ideas about God had to remain in that concrete form until India came to help them out a bit... The other nations stopped with that old concrete idea. In this country [America], there are millions who believe that God is [has?] a body... Whole sects say it. [They believe that] He rules the world, but there is a place where He has a body. He sits upon a throne. They light candles and sing songs just as they do in our temples.

But in India they are sensible enough never to make [their God a physical being]. You never see in India a temple of Brahmâ. Why? Because the idea of the soul always existed. The Hebrew race never questioned about the soul. There is no soul idea in the Old Testament at all. The first is in the New Testament. The Persians, they became so practical — wonderfully practical people — a fighting, conquering race. They were the English people of the old time, always fighting and destroying their neighbours — too much engaged in that sort of thing to think about the soul...

The oldest idea of [the] soul [was that of] a fine body inside this gross one. The gross one disappears and the fine one appears. In Egypt that fine one also dies, and as soon as the gross body disintegrates, the fine one also disintegrates. That is why they built those pyramids [and embalmed the dead bodies of their ancestors, thus hoping to secure immortality for the departed]...

The Indian people have no regard for the dead body at all. [Their attitude is:] "Let us take it and burn it." The son has to set fire to his father's body...

There are two sorts of races, the divine and the demonic. The divine think that they are soul and spirit. The demonic think that they are bodies. The old Indian philosophers tried to insist that the body is nothing. "As a man emits his old garment and takes a new one, even so the old body is [shed] and he takes a new one" (Gita, II. 22). In my case, all my surrounding and education were trying to [make me] the other way. I was always associated with Mohammedans and Christians, who take more care of the body...

It is only one step from [the body] to the spirit... [In India] they became insistent on this ideal of the soul. It became [synonymous with] the idea of God... If the idea of the soul begins to expand, [man must arrive at the conclusion that it is beyond name and form]... The Indian idea is that the soul is formless. Whatever is form must break some time or other. There cannot be any form unless it is the result of force and matter; and all combinations must dissolve. If such is the case, [if] your soul is [made of name and form, it disintegrates], and you die, and you are no more immortal. If it is double, it has form and it belongs to nature and it obeys nature's laws of birth and death... They find that this [soul] is not the mind... neither a double...

Thoughts can be guided and controlled... [The Yogis of India] practiced to see how far the thoughts can be guided and controlled. By dint of hard work, thoughts may be silenced altogether. If thoughts were [the real man], as soon as thought ceases, he ought to die. Thought ceases in meditation; even the mind's elements are quite quiet. Blood circulation stops. His breath stops, but he is not dead. If thought were he, the whole thing ought to go, but they find it does not go. That is practical [proof]. They came to the conclusion that even mind and thought were not the real man. Then speculation showed that it could not be.

I come, I think and talk. In the midst of all [this activity is] this unity [of the Self]. My thought and action are varied, many [fold]...but in and through them runs...that one unchangeable One. It cannot be the body. That is changing every minute. It cannot be the mind; new and fresh thoughts [come] all the time. It is neither the body nor the mind. Both body and mind belong to nature and must obey nature's laws. A free mind never will...

Now, therefore, this real man does not belong to nature. It is the person whose mind and body belong to nature. So much of nature we are using. Just as you come to use the pen and ink and chair, so he uses so much of nature in fine and in gross form; gross form, the body, and fine form, the mind. If it is simple, it must be formless. In nature alone are forms. That which is not of nature cannot have any forms, fine or gross. It must be formless. It must be omnipresent. Understand this. [Take] this glass on the table. The glass is form and the table is form. So much of the glass-ness goes off, so much of ta-ble-ness [when they break]...

The soul...is nameless because it is formless. It will neither go to heaven nor [to hell] any more than it will enter this glass. It takes the form of the vessel it fills. If it is not in space, either of two things is possible. Either the [soul permeates] space or space is in [it]. You are in space and must have a form. Space limits us, binds us, and makes a form of us. If you are not in space, space is in you. All the heavens and the world are in the person...

So it must be with God. God is omnipresent. "Without hands [he grasps] everything; without feet he can move..."[1] He [is] the formless, the deathless, the eternal. The idea of God came...He is the Lord of souls, just as my soul is the [lord] of my body. If my soul left the body, the body would not be for a moment. If He left my soul, the soul would not exist. He is the creator of the universe; of everything that dies He is the destroyer. His shadow is death; His shadow is life.

[The ancient Indian philosophers] thought:...This filthy world is not fit for man's attention. There is nothing in the universe that is [permanent—neither good nor evil]...

I told you...Satan...did not have much chance [in India]. Why? Because they were very bold in religion. They were not babies. Have you seen that characteristic of children? They are always trying to throw the blame on someone else. Baby minds [are] trying, when they make a mistake, to throw the blame upon someone [else]. On the one hand, we say, "Give me this; give me that." On the other hand, we say, "I did not do this; the devil tempted me. The devil did it." That is the history of mankind, weak mankind...

Why is evil? Why is [the world] the filthy, dirty hole? We have made it. Nobody is to blame. We put our hand in the fire. The Lord bless us, [man gets] just what he deserves. Only He is merciful. If we pray to Him, He helps us. He gives Himself to us.

That is their idea. They are [of a] poetic nature. They go crazy over poetry. Their philosophy is poetry. This philosophy is a poem...All [high thought] in the Sanskrit is written in poetry. Metaphysics, astronomy—all in poetry.

We are responsible, and how do we come to mischief? [You may say], "I was born poor and miserable. I remember the hard struggle all my life." Philosophers say that you are to blame. You do not mean to say that all this sprang up without any cause whatever? You are a rational being. Your life is not without cause, and you are the cause. You manufacture your own life all the time...You make and mould your own life. You are responsible for yourself. Do not lay the blame upon anybody, any Satan. You will only get punished a little more...

[A man] is brought up before God, and He says, "Thirty-one stripes for you,"...when comes another man. He says, "Thirty stripes: fifteen for that fellow, and fifteen for the teacher—that awful man who taught him." That is the awful thing in teaching. I do not know what I am going to get. I go all over the world. If I have to get fifteen for each one I have taught!...

We have to come to this idea: "This My Mâyâ is divine." It is My activity [My] divinity. "[My Maya] is hard to cross, but those that take refuge in me [go beyond maya]."[2] But you find out that it is very difficult to cross this ocean [of Maya by] yourself. You cannot. It is the old question - hen and egg. If you do any work, that work becomes the cause and produces the effect. That effect [again] becomes the cause and produces the effect. And so on. If you push this down, it never stops. Once you set a thing in motion, there is no more stopping. I do some work, good or bad, [and it sets up a chain reaction]...I cannot stop now.

It is impossible for us to get out from this bondage [by ourselves]. It is only possible if there is someone more powerful than this law of causation, and if he takes mercy on us and drags us out.

And we declare that there is such a one - God. There is such a being, all merciful...If there is a God, then it is possible for me to be saved. How can you be saved by your own will? Do you see the philosophy of the doctrine of salvation by grace? You Western people are wonderfully clever, but when you undertake to explain philosophy, you are so wonderfully complicated. How can you save yourself by work, if by salvation you mean that you will be taken out of all this nature? Salvation means just standing upon God, but if you understand what is meant by salvation, then you are the Self...You are not nature.

---

1. Shvetâshvatara Upanishad, III. 19.

2. Gita, VII. 14.

You are the only thing outside of souls and gods and nature. These are the external existences, and God [is] interpenetrating both nature and soul.

Therefore, just as my soul is [to] my body, we, as it were, are the bodies of God. God-souls-nature—it is one. The One, because, as I say, I mean the body, soul, and mind. But, we have seen, the law of causation pervades every bit of nature, and once you have got caught you cannot get out. When once you get into the meshes of law, a possible way of escape is not [through work done] by you. You can build hospitals for every fly and flea that ever lived...All this you may do, but it would never lead to salvation...[Hospitals] go up and they come down again. [Salvation] is only possible if there is some being whom nature never caught, who is the Ruler of nature. He rules nature instead of being ruled by nature. He wills law instead of being downed by law...He exists and he is all merciful. The moment you seek Him [He will save you].

Why has He not taken us out? You do not want Him. You want everything but Him. The moment you want Him, that moment you get Him. We never want Him. We say, "Lord, give me a fine house." We want the house, not Him. "Give me health! Save me from this difficulty!" When a man wants nothing but Him, [he gets Him]. "The same love which wealthy men have for gold and silver and possessions, Lord, may I have the same love for Thee. I want neither earth nor heaven, nor beauty nor learning. I do not want salvation. Let me go to hell again and again. But one thing I want: to love Thee, and for love's sake—not even for heaven."

Whatever man desires, he gets. If you always dream of having a body, [you will get another body]. When this body goes away he wants another, and goes on begetting body after body. Love matter and you become matter. You first become animals. When I see a dog gnawing a bone, I say, "Lord help us!" Love body until you become dogs and cats! Still degenerate, until you become minerals—all body and nothing else...

There are other people, who would have no compromise. The road to salvation is through truth. That was another watchword...

[Man began to progress spiritually] when he kicked the devil out. He stood up and took the responsibility of the misery of the world upon his own shoulders. But whenever he looked [at the] past and future and [at the] law of causation, he knelt down and said, "Lord, save me, [thou] who [art] our creator, our father, and dearest friend." That is poetry, but not very good poetry, I think. Why not? It is the painting of the Infinite [no doubt]. You have it in every language how they paint the Infinite. [But] it is the infinite of the senses, of the muscles...

"[Him] the sun [does not illumine], nor the moon, nor the stars, [nor] the flash of lightning."[1] That is another painting of the Infinite, by negative language...And the last Infinite is painted in [the] spirituality of the Upanishads. Not only

is Vedanta the highest philosophy in the world, but it is the greatest poem...

Mark today, this is the...difference between the first part of the Vedas and the second. In the first, it is all in [the domain of] sense. But all religions are only [concerned with the] infinite of the external world—nature and nature's God...[Not so Vedanta]. This is the first light that the human mind throws back [of] all that. No satisfaction [comes] of the infinite [in] space. "[The] Self-existent [One] has [created] the [senses as turned]...to the outer world. Those therefore who [seek] outside will never find that [which is within]. There are the few who, wanting to know the truth, turn their eyes inward and in their own souls behold the glory [of the Self]."[2]

It is not the infinite of space, but the real Infinite, beyond space, beyond time...Such is the world missed by the Occident...Their minds have been turned to external nature and nature's God. Look within yourself and find the truth that you had [forgotten]. Is it possible for mind to come out of this dream without the help of the gods? Once you start the action, there is no help unless the merciful Father takes us out.

That would not be freedom, [even] at the hands of the merciful God. Slavery is slavery. The chain of gold is quite as bad as the chain of iron. Is there a way out?

You are not bound. No one was ever bound. [The Self] is beyond. It is the all. You are the One; there are no two. God was your own reflection cast upon the screen of Maya. The real God [is the Self]. He [whom man] ignorantly worships is that reflection. [They say that] the Father in heaven is God. Why God? [It is because He is] your own reflection that [He] is God. Do you see how you are seeing God all the time? As you unfold yourself, the reflection grows [clearer].

"Two beautiful birds are there sitting upon the same tree. The one [is] calm, silent, majestic; the one below [the individual self], is eating the fruits, sweet and bitter, and becoming happy and sad. [But when the individual self beholds the worshipful Lord as his own true Self, he grieves no more.]"[3]

...Do not say "God". Do not say "Thou". Say "I". The language of [dualism] says, "God, Thou, my Father." The language of [non-dualism] says, "Dearer unto me than I am myself. I would have no name for Thee. The nearest I can use is I...

"God is true. The universe is a dream. Blessed am I that I know this moment that I [have been and] shall be free all eternity;...that I know that I am worshipping only myself; that no nature, no delusion, had any hold on me. Vanish nature from me, vanish [these] gods; vanish worship;...vanish superstitions, for I know myself. I am the Infinite. All these—Mrs. So-and-so, Mr. So-and-so, responsibility, happiness, misery—have vanished. I am the Infinite. How can there be death for me, or birth? Whom shall I fear? I am the One. Shall I be afraid of myself? Who is to be afraid of [whom]? I

1. Katha Upanishad, II. ii. 15.

2. Katha Upanishad, II. i. 1.

3. Mundaka Upanishad, III. i. 1-2.

Lectures & Discourses by **Swami Vivekananda**

am the one Existence. Nothing else exists. I am everything."

It is only the question of memory [of your true nature], not salvation by work. Do you get salvation? You are [already] free.

Go on saying, "I am free". Never mind if the next moment delusion comes and says, "I am bound." Dehypnotise the whole thing.

[This truth] is first to be heard. Hear it first. Think on it day and night. Fill the mind [with it] day and night: "I am It. I am the Lord of the universe. Never was there any delusion ... " Meditate upon it with all the strength of the mind till you actually see these walls, houses, everything, melt away — [until] body, everything, vanishes. "I will stand alone. I am the One." Struggle on! "Who cares! We want to be free; [we] do not want any powers. Worlds we renounce; heavens we renounce; hells we renounce. What do I care about all these powers, and this and that! What do I care if the mind is controlled or uncontrolled! Let it run on. What of that! I am not the mind, Let it go on!"

The sun [shines on the just and on the unjust]. Is he touched by the defective [character] of anyone? "I am He. Whatever [my] mind does, I am not touched. The sun is not touched by shining on filthy places, I am Existence."

This is the religion of [non-dual] philosophy. [It is] difficult. Struggle on! Down with all superstitions! Neither teachers nor scriptures nor gods [exist]. Down with temples, with priests, with gods, with incarnations, with God himself! I am all the God that ever existed! There, stand up philosophers! No fear! Speak no more of God and [the] superstition of the world. Truth alone triumphs, and this is true. I am the Infinite.

All religious superstitions are vain imaginations ... This society, that I see you before me, and [that] I am talking to you — this is all superstition; all must be given up. Just see what it takes to become a philosopher! This is the [path] of [Jnâna-] Yoga, the way through knowledge. The other [paths] are easy, slow, ... but this is pure strength of mind. No weakling [can follow this path of knowledge. You must be able to say:] "I am the Soul, the ever free; [I] never was bound. Time is in me, not I in time. God was born in my mind. God the Father, Father of the universe — he is created by me in my own mind ... "

Do you call yourselves philosophers? Show it! Think of this, talk [of] this, and [help] each other in this path, and give up all superstition!

BREATHING[4]

Delivered in San Francisco, March 28, 1900

Breathing exercises have been very popular in India from the most ancient times, so much so [that] they form a part of their religion, just as going to church and repeating certain

4. [According to SWAMI VIVEKANANDA HIS SECOND VISIT TO THE WEST (P. 461), this address was delivered on 29 March 1900 under the title "The Science of Breathing". — Ed.]

prayers ... I will try to bring those ideas before you.

I have told you how the Indian philosopher reduces the whole universe into two parts — Prâna and Âkâsha.

Prana means force — all that is manifesting itself as movement or possible movement, force, or attraction ... Electricity, magnetism, all the movements in the body, all [the movements] in the mind — all these are various manifestations of one thing called Prana. The best form of Prana, however, is in [the brain], manifesting itself as light [of understanding]. This light is under the guidance of thought.

The mind ought to control every bit of Prana that has been worked up in the body ... [The] mind should have entire control of the body. That is not [the case] with all. With most of us it is the other way. The mind should be able to control every part of [the body] just at will. That is reason, philosophy; but [when] we come to matters of fact, it is not so. For you, on the other hand, the cart is before the horse. It is the body mastering the mind. If my finger gets pinched, I become sorry. The body works upon the mind. If anything happens which I do not like to happen, I am worried; my mind [is] thrown off its balance. The body is master of the mind. We have become bodies. We are nothing else but bodies just now.

Here [comes] the philosopher to show us the way out, to teach us what we really are. You may reason it out and understand it intellectually, but there is a long way between intellectual understanding and the practical realisation of it. Between the plan of the building and the building itself there is quite a long distance. Therefore there must be various methods [to reach the goal of religion]. In the last course, we have been studying the method of philosophy, trying to bring everything under control, once more asserting the freedom of the soul ... "It is very difficult. This way is not for [every]body. The embodied mind tries it with great trouble" (Gita, XII. 5).

A little physical help will make the mind comfortable. What would be more rational than to have the mind itself accomplish the thing? But it cannot. The physical help is necessary for most of us. The system of Râja-Yoga is to utilise these physical helps, to make use of the powers and forces in the body to produce certain mental states, to make the mind stronger and stronger until it regains its lost empire. By sheer force of will if anyone can attain to that, so much the better. But most of us cannot, so we will use physical means, and help the will on its way.

... The whole universe is a tremendous case of unity in variety. There is only one mass of mind. Different [states] of that mind have different names. [They are] different little whirlpools in this ocean of mind. We are universal and individual at the same time. Thus is the play going on ... In reality this unity is never broken. [Matter, mind, spirit are all one.]

All these are but various names. There is but one fact in the universe, and we look at it from various standpoints. The same [fact] looked at from one standpoint becomes matter. The same one from another standpoint becomes mind. There are not two things. Mistaking the rope for the snake, fear came [to a man] and made him call somebody else to kill the snake. [His] nervous system began to shake; his heart began to beat...All these manifestations [came] from fear, and he discovered it was a rope, and they all vanished. This is what we see in reality. What even the senses see—what we call matter—that [too] is the Real; only not as we have seen it. The mind [which] saw the rope [and] took it for a snake was not under a delusion. If it had been, it would not have seen anything. One thing is taken for another, not as something that does not exist. What we see here is body, and we take the Infinite as matter...We are but seeking that Reality. We are never deluded. We always know truth, only our reading of truth is mistaken at times. You can perceive only one thing at a time. When I see the snake, the rope has vanished entirely. And when I see the rope, the snake has vanished. It must be one thing...

When we see the world, how can we see God? Think in your own mind. What is meant by the world is God as seen as all things [by] our senses. Here you see the snake; the rope is not. When you know the Spirit, everything else will vanish. When you see the Spirit itself, you see no matter, because that which you called matter is the very thing that is Spirit. All these variations are [superimposed] by our senses. The same sun, reflected by a thousand little wavelets, will represent to us thousands of little suns. If I am looking at the universe with my senses, I interpret it as matter and force. It is one and many at the same time. The manifold does not destroy the unity. The millions of waves do not destroy the unity of the ocean. It remains the same ocean. When you look at the universe, remember that we can reduce it to matter or to force. If we increase the velocity, the mass decreases...On the other hand, we can increase the mass and decrease the velocity...We may almost come to a point where all the mass will entirely disappear...

Matter cannot be said to cause force nor [can] force [be] the cause of matter. Both are so [related] that one may disappear in the other. There must be a third [factor], and that third something is the mind. You cannot produce the universe from matter, neither from force. Mind is something [which is] neither force nor matter, yet begetting force and matter all the time. In the long run, mind is begetting all force, and that is what is meant by the universal mind, the sum total of all minds. Everyone is creating, and [in] the sum total of all these creations you have the universe—unity in diversity. It is one and it is many at the same time.

The Personal God is only the sum total of all, and yet it is an individual by itself, just as you are the individual body of which each cell is an individual part itself.

Everything that has motion is included in Prana or force. [It is] this Prana which is moving the stars, sun, moon; Prana is gravitation...

All forces of nature, therefore, must be created by the univer-

sal mind. And we, as little bits of mind, [are] taking out that Prana from nature, working it out again in our own nature, moving our bodies and manufacturing our thought. If [you think] thought cannot be manufactured, stop eating for twenty days and see how you feel. Begin today and count...Even thought is manufactured by food. There is no doubt about it.

Control of this Prana that is working everything, control of this Prana in the body, is called Prânâyâma. We see with our common sense that it is the breath [that] is setting everything in motion. If I stop breathing, I stop. If the breath begins, [the body] begins to move. What we want to get at is not the breath itself; it is something finer behind the breath.

[There was once a minister to a great king. The] king, displeased with the minister, ordered him to be confined in the top of [a very high tower. This was done, and the minister was left there to perish. His wife came to the tower at night and called to her husband.] The minister said to her, "No use weeping." He told her to take a little honey, [a beetle], a pack of fine thread, a ball of twine, and a rope. She tied the fine thread to one of the legs of the beetle and put honey on the top of its head and let it go [with its head up]. [The beetle slowly crept onwards, in the hope of reaching the honey, until at last it reached the top of the tower, when the minister grasped the beetle, and got possession of the silken thread, then the pack thread, then the stout twine, and lastly of the rope. The minister descended from the tower by means of the rope, and made his escape. In this body of ours the breath motion is the "silken thread"; by laying hold of it we grasp the pack thread of the nerve currents, and from these the stout twine of our thoughts, and lastly the rope of Prana, controlling which we reach freedom. (Vide ante.)

By the help of things on the material plane, we have to come to finer and finer [perceptions]. The universe is one, whatever point you touch. All the points are but variations of that one point. Throughout the universe is a unity (at bottom)...Even through such a gross thing as breath I can get hold of the Spirit itself.

By the exercise of breathing we begin to feel all the movements of the body that we [now] do not feel. As soon as we begin to feel them, we begin to master them. Thoughts in the germ will open to us, and we will be able to get hold of them. Of course, not all of us have the opportunity nor the will nor the patience nor the faith to pursue such a thing; but there is the common sense idea that is of some benefit to everyone.

The first benefit is health. Ninety-nine per cent of us do not at all breathe properly. We do not inflate the lungs enough...Regularity [of breath] will purify the body. It quiets the mind...When you are peaceful, your breath is going on peacefully, [it is] rhythmic. If the breath is rhythmic, you must be peaceful. When the mind is disturbed, the breath is broken. If you can bring the breath into rhythm forcibly by practice, why can you not become peaceful? When you are disturbed, go into the room and close the door. Do not try to control the mind, but go on with rhythmic breathing for ten minutes. The heart will become peaceful. These are common sense benefits that come to everyone. The others belong to the Yogi...

Deep-breathing exercises [are only the first step]. There are about eighty-four [postures for] various exercises. Some [people] have taken up this breathing as the whole [pursuit] of life. They do not do anything without consulting the breath. They are all the time [observing] in which nostril there is more breath. When it is the right, [they] will do certain things, and when [it is] the left, they do other things. When [the breath is] flowing equally through both nostrils, they will worship.

When the breath is coming rhythmically through both nostrils, that is the time to control your mind. By means of the breath you can make the currents of the body move through any part of the body, just [at] will. Whenever [any] part of the body is ill, send the Prana to that part, all by the breath.

Various other things are done. There are sects who are trying not to breathe at all. They would not do anything that would make them breathe hard. They go into a sort of trance... Scarcely any part of the body [functions]. The heart almost ceases [to beat]... Most of these exercises are very dangerous; the higher methods [are] for acquiring higher powers. There are whole sects trying to [lighten] the whole body by withdrawal of breath and then they will rise up in the air. I have never seen anyone rise... I have never seen anyone fly through the air, but the books say so. I do not pretend to know everything. All the time I am seeing most wonderful things... [Once I observed a] man bringing out fruits and flowers, etc. [out of nowhere].

... The Yogi, when he becomes perfect, can make his body so small it will pass through this wall—this very body. He can become so heavy, two hundred persons cannot lift him. He will be able to fly through the air if he likes. [But] nobody can be as powerful as God Himself. If they could, and one created, another would destroy...

This is in the books. I can [hardly] believe them, nor do I disbelieve them. What I have seen I take...

If the study [improvement?] of things in this world is possible, it is not by competition, it is by regulating the mind. Western people say, "That is our nature; we cannot help it." Studying your social problems, [I conclude] you cannot solve them either. In some things you are worse off than we are,... and all these things do not bring the world anywhere at all...

The strong take everything; the weak go to the wall. The poor are waiting... The man who can take, will take everything. The poor hate that man. Why? Because they are waiting their turn. All the systems they invent, they all teach the same thing. The problem can only be solved in the mind of man... No law will ever make him do what he does not want to do... It is only if [man] wills to be good that he will be good. All the law and juries... cannot make him good. The almighty man says, "I

do not care."... The only solution is if we all want to be good. How can that be done?

All knowledge is within [the] mind. Who saw knowledge in the stone, or astronomy in the star? It is all in the human being.

Let us realise [that] we are the infinite power. Who put a limit to the power of mind? Let us realise we are all mind. Every drop has the whole of the ocean in it. That is the mind of man. The Indian mind reflects upon these [powers and potentialities] and wants to bring [them] all out. For himself he doesn't care what happens. It will take a great length of time [to reach perfection]. If it takes fifty thousand years, what of that!...

The very foundation of society, the formation of it, makes the defect. [Perfection] is only possible if the mind of man is changed, if he, of his own sweet will, changes his mind; and the great difficulty is, neither can he force his own mind.

You may not believe in all the claims of this Raja-Yoga. It is absolutely necessary that every individual can become divine. That is only [possible] when every individual has absolute mastery over his own thoughts... [The thoughts, the senses] should be all my servants, not my masters. Then only is it possible that evils will vanish...

Education is not filling the mind with a lot of facts. Perfecting the instrument and getting complete mastery of my own mind [is the ideal of education]. If I want to concentrate my mind upon a point, it goes there, and the moment I call, it is free [again]...

That is the great difficulty. By great struggle we get a certain power of concentration, the power of attachment of the mind to certain things. But then there is not the power of detachment. I would give half my life to take my mind off that object! I cannot. It is the power of concentration and attachment as well as the power of detachment [that we must develop]. [If] the man [is] equally powerful in both—that man has attained manhood. You cannot make him miserable even if the whole universe tumbles about his ears. What books can teach you that? You may read any amount of books... Crowd into the child fifty thousand words a moment, teach him all the theories and philosophies... There is only one science that will teach him facts, and that is psychology... And the work begins with control of the breath.

Slowly and gradually you get into the chambers of the mind and gradually get control of the mind. It is a long, [hard struggle]. It must not be taken up as something curious. When one wants to do something, he has a plan. [Raja-Yoga] proposes no faith, no belief, no God. If you believe in two thousand gods, you can try that. Why not?... [But in Raja-Yoga] it is impersonal principles.

The greatest difficulty is what? We talk and theorise The vast majority of mankind must deal with things that are concrete. For the dull people cannot see all the highest philosophy. Thus it ends. You may be graduates [in] all sciences in the world, ... but if you have not realised, you must become a baby and learn.

... If you give them things in the abstract and infinite, they get lost. Give them things [to do,] a little at a time [Tell them,] "You take [in] so many breaths, you do this." They go on, [they] understand it, and find pleasure in it. These are the kindergartens of religion. That is why breathing exercises will be so beneficial. I beg you all not to be merely curious. Practise a few days, and if you do not find any benefit, then come and curse me ...

The whole universe is a mass of energy, and it is present at every point. One grain is enough for all of us, if we know how to get what there is ...

This having to do is the poison that is killing us ... [Duty is] what pleases slaves ... [But] I am free! What I do is my play. [I am not a slave. I am] having a little fun — that is all ...

The departed spirits — they are weak, are trying to get vitality from us ...

Spiritual vitality can be given from one mind to another. The man who gives is the Guru. The man who receives is the disciple. That is the only way spiritual truth is brought into the world.

[At death] all the senses go into the [mind] and the mind goes into Prana, vitality. The soul goes out and carries part of the mind out with him. He carries a certain part of the vitality, and he carries a certain amount of very fine material also, as the germ of the spiritual body. The Prana cannot exist without some sort of [vehicle] ... It gets lodgement in the thoughts, and it will come out again. So you manufacture this new body and new brain. Through that it will manifest ...

[Departed spirits] cannot manufacture a body; and those that are very weak do not remember that they are dead ... They try to get more enjoyment from this [spirit] life by getting into the bodies of others, and any person who opens his body to them runs a terrible risk. They seek his vitality ...

In this world nothing is permanent except God ... Salvation means knowing the truth. We do not become anything; we are what we are. Salvation [comes] by faith and not by work. It is a question of knowledge! You must know what you are, and it is done. The dream vanishes. This you [and others] are dreaming here. When they die, they go to [the] heaven [of their dream]. They live in that dream, and [when it ends], they take a nice body [here], and they are good people ...

[The wise man says,] "All these [desires] have vanished from me. This time I will not go through all this paraphernalia." He tries to get knowledge and struggles hard, and he sees what a dream, what a nightmare this is - [this dreaming], and working up heavens and worlds and worse. He laughs at it.

PRACTICAL RELIGION: BREATHING AND MEDITATION

Delivered in San Francisco, April 5, 1900

Everyone's idea of practical religion is according to his theory of practicality and the standpoint he starts from. There is work. There is the system of worship. There is knowledge.

The philosopher thinks ... the difference between bondage and freedom is only caused by knowledge and ignorance. To him, knowledge is the goal, and his practicality is gaining that knowledge ... The worshipper's practical religion is the power of love and devotion. The worker's practical religion consists in doing good works. And so, as in every other thing, we are always trying to ignore the standard of another, trying to bind the whole world to our standard.

Doing good to his fellow-beings is the practical religion of the man full of love. If men do not help to build hospitals, he thinks that they have no religion at all. But there is no reason why everyone should do that. The philosopher, in the same way, may denounce every man who does not have knowledge. People may build twenty thousand hospitals, and the philosopher declares they are but ... the beasts of burden of the gods. The worshipper has his own idea and standard: Men who cannot love God are no good, whatever work they do. The [Yogi believes in] psychic [control and] the conquest of [internal] nature. "How much have you gained towards that? How much control over your senses, over your body?"— that is all the Yogi asks. And, as we said, each one judges the others by his own standard. Men may have given millions of dollars and fed rats and cats, as some do in India. They say that men can take care of themselves, but the poor animals cannot. That is their idea. But to the Yogi the goal is conquest of [internal] nature, and he judges man by that standard ...

We are always talking [about] practical religion. But it must be practical in our sense. Especially [so] in the Western countries. The Protestants' ideal is good works. They do not care much for devotion and philosophy. They think there is not much in it. "What is your knowledge!" [they say]. "Man has to do something!" ... A little humanitarianism! The churches rail day and night against callous agnosticism. Yet they seem to be veering rapidly towards just that. Callous slaves! Religion of utility! That is the spirit just now. And that is why some Buddhists have become so popular in the West. People do not know whether there is a God or not, whether there is a soul or not. [They think :] This world is full of misery. Try to help this world.

The Yoga doctrine, which we are having our lecture on, is not from that standpoint. [It teaches that] there is the soul, and inside this soul is all power. It is already there, and if we can master this body, all the power will be unfolded. All knowledge is in the soul. Why are people struggling? To lessen the misery ... All unhappiness is caused by our not having mastery over the body ... We are all putting the cart before the horse ... Take the system of work, for instance. We are trying to do good by... comforting the poor. We do not get to the cause which created the misery. It is like taking a bucket to empty out the ocean, and more [water] comes all the time. The Yogi sees that this is nonsense. [He says that] the way out of misery is to know the cause of misery first... We try to do the good we can. What for? If there is an incurable disease, why should we struggle and take care of ourselves? If the utilitarians say: "Do not bother about soul and God!" what is that to the Yogi and what is it to the world? The world does not derive any good [from such an attitude]. More and more misery is going on all the time...

The Yogi says you are to go to the root of all this. Why is there misery in the world? He answers: "It is all our own foolishness, not having proper mastery of our own bodies. That is all." He advises the means by which this misery can be [overcome]. If you can thus get mastery of your body, all the misery of the world will vanish. Every hospital is praying that more and more sick people will come there. Every time you think of doing some charity, you think there is some beggar to take your charity. If you say, "O Lord, let the world be full of charitable people!"—you mean, let the world be full of beggars also. Let the world be full of good works - let the world be full of misery. This is out-and-out slavishness!

...The Yogi says, religion is practical if you know first why misery exists. All the misery in the world is in the senses. Is there any ailment in the sun, moon, and stars? The same fire that cooks your meal burns the child. Is it the fault of the fire? Blessed be the fire! Blessed be this electricity! It gives light... Where can you lay the blame? Not on the elements. The world is neither good nor bad; the world is the world. The fire is the fire. If you burn your finger in it, you are a fool. If you [cook your meal and with it satisfy your hunger,] you are a wise man. That is all the difference. Circumstances can never be good or bad. Only the individual man can be good or bad. What is meant by the world being good or bad? Misery and happiness can only belong to the sensuous individual man.

The Yogis say that nature is the enjoyed; the soul is the enjoyer. All misery and happiness—where is it? In the senses. It is the touch of the senses that causes pleasure and pain, heat and cold. If we can control the senses and order what they shall feel—not let them order us about as they are doing now—if they can obey our commands, become our servants, the problem is solved at once. We are bound by the senses; they play upon us, make fools of us all the time.

Here is a bad odour. It will bring me unhappiness as soon as it touches my nose. I am the slave of my nose. If I am not its slave, I do not care. A man curses me. His curses enter my ears and are retained in my mind and body. If I am the master, I shall say: "Let these things go; they are nothing to me. I am not miserable. I do not bother." This is the outright, pure, simple, clear-cut truth.

The other problem to be solved is—is it practical? Can man attain to the power of mastery of the body?... Yoga says it is practical... Supposing it is not—suppose there are doubts in your mind. You have got to try it. There is no other way out...

You may do good works all the time. All the same, you will be the slave of your senses, you will be miserable and unhappy. You may study the philosophy of every religion. Men in this country carry loads and loads of books on their backs. They are mere scholars, slaves of the senses, and therefore happy and unhappy. They read two thousand books, and that is all right; but as soon as a little misery comes, they are worried, anxious... You call yourselves men! You stand up... and build hospitals. You are fools!

What is the difference between men and animals?... "Food and [sleep], procreation of the species, and fear exist in common with the animals. There is one difference: Man can control all these and become God, the master." Animals cannot do it. Animals can do charitable work. Ants do it. Dogs do it. What is the difference then? Men can be masters of themselves. They can resist the reaction to anything... The animal cannot resist anything. He is held... by the string of nature everywhere. That is all the distinction. One is the master of nature, the other the slave of nature. What is nature? The five senses...

[The conquest of internal nature] is the only way out, according to Yoga... The thirst for God is religion... Good works and all that [merely] make the mind a little quiet. To practice this—to be perfect—all depends upon our past. I have been studying [Yoga] all my life and have made very little progress yet. But I have got enough [result] to believe that this is the only true way. The day will come when I will be master of myself. If not in this life, [in another life]. I will struggle and never let go. Nothing is lost. If I die this moment, all my past struggles [will come to my help]. Have you not seen what makes the difference between one man and another? It is their past. The past habits make one man a genius and another man a fool. You may have the power of the past and can succeed in five minutes. None can predict the moment of time. We all have to attain [perfection] some time or other.

The greater part of the practical lessons which the Yogi gives us is in the mind, the power of concentration and meditation... We have become so materialistic. When we think of ourselves, we find only the body. The body has become the ideal, nothing else. Therefore a little physical help is necessary...

First, to sit in the posture In which you can sit still for a long time. All the nerve currents which are working pass along the spine. The spine is not intended to support the weight of the body. Therefore the posture must be such that the weight of the body is not on the spine. Let it be free from all pressure.

There are some other preliminary things. There is the great question of food and exercise...

The food must be simple and taken several times [a day] instead of once or twice. Never get very hungry. "He who eats too much cannot be a Yogi. He who fasts too much cannot be a Yogi. He who sleeps too much cannot be a Yogi, nor he who keeps awake too much."[1] He who does not do any work and he who works too hard cannot succeed. Proper food, proper exercise, proper sleep, proper wakefulness—these are necessary for any success.

What the proper food is, what kind, we have to determine ourselves. Nobody can determine that [for us]. As a general practice, we have to shun exciting food…We do not know how to vary our diet with our occupation. We always forget that it is the food out of which we manufacture everything we have. So the amount and kind of energy that we want, the food must determine…

Violent exercises are not all necessary…If you want to be muscular, Yoga is not for you. You have to manufacture a finer organism than you have now. Violent exercises are positively hurtful…Live amongst those who do not take too much exercise. If you do not take violent exercise, you will live longer. You do not want to burn out your lamp in muscles! People who work with their brains are the longest-lived people…Do not burn the lamp quickly. Let it burn slowly and gently…Every anxiety, every violent exercise—physical and mental—[means] you are burning the lamp.

The proper diet means, generally, simply do not eat highly spiced foods. There are three sorts of mind, says the Yogi, according to the elements of nature. One is the dull mind, which covers the luminosity of the soul. Then there is that which makes people active, and lastly, that which makes them calm and peaceful.

Now there are persons born with the tendency to sleep all the time. Their taste will be towards that type of food which is rotting—crawling cheese. They will eat cheese that fairly jumps off the table. It is a natural tendency with them.

Then active people. Their taste is for everything hot and pungent, strong alcohol…

Sâttvika people are very thoughtful, quiet, and patient. They take food in small quantities, and never anything bad.

I am always asked the question: "Shall I give up meat?" My Master said, "Why should you give up anything? It will give you up." Do not give up anything in nature. Make it so hot for nature that she will give you up. There will come a time when you cannot possibly eat meat. The very sight of it will disgust you. There will come a time when many things you are struggling to give up will be distasteful, positively loathsome.

Then there are various sorts of breathing exercises. One consists of three parts: the drawing in of the breath, the holding of the breath—stopping still without breathing—and throwing the breath out. [Some breathing exercises] are rather difficult, and some of the complicated ones are attended with great danger if done without proper diet. I would not advise you to go through any one of these except the very simple ones.

1. Gita, VI. 16.

Take a deep breath and fill the lungs. Slowly throw the breath out. Take it through one nostril and fill the lungs, and throw it out slowly through the other nostril. Some of us do not breathe deeply enough. Others cannot fill the lungs enough. These breathings will correct that very much. Half an hour in the morning and half an hour in the evening will make you another person. This sort of breathing is never dangerous. The other exercises should be practiced very slowly. And measure your strength. If ten minutes are a drain, only take five.

The Yogi is expected to keep his own body well. These various breathing exercises are a great help in regulating the different parts of the body. All the different parts are inundated with breath. It is through breath that we gain control of them all. Disharmony in parts of the body is controlled by more flow of the nerve currents towards them. The Yogi ought to be able to tell when in any part pain is caused by less vitality or more. He has to equalise that…

Another condition [for success in Yoga] is chastity. It is the corner-stone of all practice. Married or unmarried—perfect chastity. It is a long subject, of course, but I want to tell you: Public discussions of this subject are not to the taste of this country. These Western countries are full of the most degraded beings in the shape of teachers who teach men and women that if they are chaste they will be hurt. How do they gather all this?…People come to me—thousands come every year—with this one question. Someone has told them that if they are chaste and pure they will be hurt physically…How do these teachers know it? Have they been chaste? Those unchaste, impure fools, lustful creatures, want to drag the whole world down to their [level]!…

Nothing is gained except by sacrifice…The holiest function of our human consciousness, the noblest, do not make it unclean! Do not degrade it to the level of the brutes…Make yourselves decent men!…Be chaste and pure!…There is no other way. Did Christ find any other way?…If you can conserve and use the energy properly, it leads you to God. Inverted, it is hell itself…

It is much easier to do anything upon the external plane, but the greatest conqueror in the world finds himself a mere child when he tries to control his own mind. This is the world he has to conquer—the greater and more difficult world to conquer. Do not despair! Awake, arise, and stop not until the goal is reached!…

WORK AND ITS SECRET

Delivered at Los Angeles, California, January 4, 1900

One of the greatest lessons I have learnt in my life is to pay as much attention to the means of work as to its end. He was a great man from whom I learnt it, and his own life was a practical demonstration of this great principle I have been always learning great lessons from that one principle, and it appears to me that all the secret of success is there; to pay as much attention to the means as to the end.

Our great defect in life is that we are so much drawn to the ideal, the goal is so much more enchanting, so much more alluring, so much bigger in our mental horizon, that we lose sight of the details altogether.

But whenever failure comes, if we analyse it critically, in ninety-nine per cent of cases we shall find that it was because we did not pay attention to the means. Proper attention to the finishing, strengthening, of the means is what we need. With the means all right, the end must come. We forget that it is the cause that produces the effect; the effect cannot come by itself; and unless the causes are exact, proper, and powerful, the effect will not be produced. Once the ideal is chosen and the means determined, we may almost let go the ideal, because we are sure it will be there, when the means are perfected. When the cause is there, there is no more difficulty about the effect, the effect is bound to come. If we take care of the cause, the effect will take care of itself. The realization of the ideal is the effect. The means are the cause: attention to the means, therefore, is the great secret of life. We also read this in the Gita and learn that we have to work, constantly work with all our power; to put our whole mind in the work, whatever it be, that we are doing. At the same time, we must not be attached. That is to say, we must not be drawn away from the work by anything else; still, we must be able to quit the work whenever we like.

If we examine our own lives, we find that the greatest cause of sorrow is this: we take up something, and put our whole energy on it—perhaps it is a failure and yet we cannot give it up. We know that it is hurting us, that any further clinging to it is simply bringing misery on us; still, we cannot tear ourselves away from it. The bee came to sip the honey, but its feet stuck to the honey-pot and it could not get away. Again and again, we are finding ourselves in that state. That is the whole secret of existence. Why are we here? We came here to sip the honey, and we find our hands and feet sticking to it. We are caught, though we came to catch. We came to enjoy; we are being enjoyed. We came to rule; we are being ruled. We came to work; we are being worked. All the time, we find that. And this comes into every detail of our life. We are being worked upon by other minds, and we are always struggling to work on other minds. We want to enjoy the pleasures of life; and they eat into our vitals. We want to get everything from nature, but we find in the long run that nature takes everything from us—depletes us, and casts us aside.

Had it not been for this, life would have been all sunshine. Never mind! With all its failures and successes, with all its joys and sorrows, it can be one succession of sunshine, if only we are not caught.

That is the one cause of misery: we are attached, we are being caught. Therefore says the Gita: Work constantly; work, but be not attached; be not caught. Reserve unto yourself the power of detaching yourself from everything, however beloved, however much the soul might yearn for it, however great the pangs of misery you feel if you were going to leave it; still, reserve the power of leaving it whenever you want. The weak have no place here, in this life or in any other life. Weakness leads to slavery. Weakness leads to all kinds of misery, physical and mental. Weakness is death. There are hundreds of thousands of microbes surrounding us, but they cannot harm us unless we become weak, until the body is ready and predisposed to receive them. There may be a million microbes of misery, floating about us. Never mind! They dare not approach us, they have no power to get a hold on us, until the mind is weakened. This is the great fact: strength is life, weakness is death. Strength is felicity, life eternal, immortal; weakness is constant strain and misery: weakness is death.

Attachment is the source of all our pleasures now. We are attached to our friends, to our relatives; we are attached to our intellectual and spiritual works; we are attached to external objects, so that we get pleasure from them. What, again, brings misery but this very attachment? We have to detach ourselves to earn joy. If only we had power to detach ourselves at will, there would not be any misery. That man alone will be able to get the best of nature, who, having the power of attaching himself to a thing with all his energy, has also the power to detach himself when he should do so. The difficulty is that there must be as much power of attachment as that of detachment. There are men who are never attracted by anything. They can never love, they are hard-hearted and apathetic; they escape most of the miseries of life. But the wall never feels misery, the wall never loves, is never hurt; but it is the wall, after all. Surely it is better to be attached and caught, than to be a wall. Therefore the man who never loves, who is hard and stony, escaping most of the miseries of life, escapes also its joys. We do not want that. That is weakness, that is death. That soul has not been awakened that never feels weakness, never feels misery. That is a callous state. We do not want that.

At the same time, we not only want this mighty power of love, this mighty power of attachment, the power of throwing our whole soul upon a single object, losing ourselves and letting ourselves be annihilated, as it were, for other souls—which is the power of the gods—but we want to be higher even than the gods. The perfect man can put his whole soul upon that one point of love, yet he is unattached. How comes this? There is another secret to learn.

The beggar is never happy. The beggar only gets a dole with pity and scorn behind it, at least with the thought behind that the beggar is a low object. He never really enjoys what he gets.

We are all beggars. Whatever we do, we want a return. We are all traders. We are traders in life, we are traders in virtue, we are traders in religion. And alas! we are also traders in love.

If you come to trade, if it is a question of give-and-take, if it is a question of buy-and-sell, abide by the laws of buying and selling. There is a bad time and there is a good time; there is a rise and a fall in prices: always you expect the blow to come. It is like looking at the mirrors Your face is reflected: you make a grimace—there is one in the mirror; if you laugh, the mirror laughs. This is buying and selling, giving and taking.

We get caught. How? Not by what we give, but by what we expect. We get misery in return for our love; not from the fact that we love, but from the fact that we want love in return. There is no misery where there is no want. Desire, want, is the father of all misery. Desires are bound by the laws of success and failure. Desires must bring misery.

The great secret of true success, of true happiness, then, is this: the man who asks for no return, the perfectly unselfish man, is the most successful. It seems to be a paradox. Do we not know that every man who is unselfish in life gets cheated, gets hurt? Apparently, yes. "Christ was unselfish, and yet he was crucified." True, but we know that his unselfishness is the reason, the cause of a great victory—the crowning of millions upon millions of lives with the blessings of true success.

Ask nothing; want nothing in return. Give what you have to give; it will come back to you—but do not think of that now, it will come back multiplied a thousandfold—but the attention must not be on that. Yet have the power to give: give, and there it ends. Learn that the whole of life is giving, that nature will force you to give. So, give willingly. Sooner or later you will have to give up. You come into life to accumulate. With clenched hands, you want to take. But nature puts a hand on your throat and makes your hands open. Whether you will it or not, you have to give. The moment you say, "I will not", the blow comes; you are hurt. None is there but will be compelled, in the long run, to give up everything. And the more one struggles against this law, the more miserable one feels. It is because we dare not give, because we are not resigned enough to accede to this grand demand of nature, that we are miserable. The forest is gone, but we get heat in return. The sun is taking up water from the ocean, to return it in showers. You are a machine for taking and giving: you take, in order to give. Ask, therefore, nothing in return; but the more you give, the more will come to you. The quicker you can empty the air out of this room, the quicker it will be filled up by the external air; and if you close all the doors and every aperture, that which is within will remain, but that which is outside will never come in, and that which is within will stagnate, degenerate, and become poisoned. A river is continually emptying itself into the ocean and is continually filling up again. Bar not the exit into the ocean. The moment you do that, death seizes you.

Be, therefore, not a beggar; be unattached This is the most terrible task of life! You do not calculate the dangers on the path. Even by intellectually recognising the difficulties, we really do not know them until we feel them. From a distance we may get a general view of a park: well, what of that? We feel and really know it when we are in it. Even if our every attempt is a failure, and we bleed and are torn asunder, yet, through all this, we have to preserve our heart—we must assert our Godhead in the midst of all these difficulties. Nature wants us to react, to return blow for blow, cheating for cheating, lie for lie, to hit back with all our might. Then it requires a superdivine power not to hit back, to keep control, to be unattached.

Every day we renew our determination to be unattached. We cast our eyes back and look at the past objects of our love and attachment, and feel how every one of them made us miserable. We went down into the depths of despondency because of our "love"! We found ourselves mere slaves in the hands of others, we were dragged down and down! And we make a fresh determination: "Henceforth, I will be master of myself; henceforth, I will have control over myself." But the time comes, and the same story once more! Again the soul is caught and cannot get out. The bird is in a net, struggling and fluttering. This is our life.

I know the difficulties. Tremendous they are, and ninety per cent of us become discouraged and lose heart, and in our turn, often become pessimists and cease to believe in sincerity, love, and all that is grand and noble. So, we find men who in the freshness of their lives have been forgiving, kind, simple, and guileless, become in old age lying masks of men. Their minds are a mass of intricacy. There may be a good deal of external policy, possibly. They are not hot-headed, they do not speak, but it would be better for them to do so; their hearts are dead and, therefore, they do not speak. They do not curse, not become angry; but it would be better for them to be able to be angry, a thousand times better, to be able to curse. They cannot. There is death in the heart, for cold hands have seized upon it, and it can no more act, even to utter a curse, even to use a harsh word.

All this we have to avoid: therefore I say, we require super-divine power. Superhuman power is not strong enough. Superdivine strength is the only way, the one way out. By it alone we can pass through all these intricacies, through these showers of miseries, unscathed. We may be cut to pieces, torn asunder, yet our hearts must grow nobler and nobler all the time.

It is very difficult, but we can overcome the difficulty by constant practice. We must learn that nothing can happen to us, unless we make ourselves susceptible to it. I have just said, no disease can come to me until the body is ready; it does not depend alone on the germs, but upon a certain predisposition which is already in the body. We get only that for which we are fitted. Let us give up our pride and understand this, that never is misery undeserved. There never has been a blow undeserved: there never has been an evil for which I did not pave the way with my own hands. We ought to know that. Analyse yourselves and you will find that every blow you have received, came to you because you prepared yourselves for it. You did half, and the external world did the other half: that is how the blow came. That will sober us down. At the same time, from this very analysis will come a note of hope, and the note of hope is: "I have no control of the external world, but that which is in me and nearer unto me, my own world, is in my control. If the two together are required to make a failure, if the two together are necessary to give me a blow, I will not contribute the one which is in my keeping; and how then can the blow come? If I get real control of myself, the blow will never come."

We are all the time, from our childhood, trying to lay the blame upon something outside ourselves. We are always standing up to set right other people, and not ourselves. If we are miserable, we say, "Oh, the world is a devil's world." We curse others and say, "What infatuated fools!" But why should we be in such a world, if we really are so good? If this is a devil's world, we must be devils also; why else should we be here? "Oh, the people of the world are so selfish!" True enough; but why should we be found in that company, if we be better? Just think of that.

We only get what we deserve. It is a lie when we say, the world is bad and we are good. It can never be so. It is a terrible lie we tell ourselves.

This is the first lesson to learn: be determined not to curse anything outside, not to lay the blame upon any one outside, but be a man, stand up, lay the blame on yourself. You will find, that is always true. Get hold of yourself.

Is it not a shame that at one moment we talk so much of our manhood, of our being gods—that we know everything, we can do everything, we are blameless, spotless, the most unselfish people in the world; and at the next moment a little stone hurts us, a little anger from a little Jack wounds us—any fool in the street makes "these gods" miserable! Should this be so if we are such gods? Is it true that the world is to blame? Could God, who is the purest and the noblest of souls, be made miserable by any of our tricks? If you are so unselfish, you are like God. What world can hurt you? You would go through the seventh hell unscathed, untouched. But the very fact that you complain and want to lay the blame upon the external world shows that you feel the external world—the very fact that you feel shows that you are not what you claim to be. You only make your offence greater by heaping misery upon misery, by imagining that the external world is hurting you, and crying out, "Oh, this devil's world! This man hurts me; that man hurts me! " and so forth. It is adding lies to misery.

We are to take care of ourselves—that much we can do—and give up attending to others for a time. Let us perfect the means; the end will take care of itself. For the world can be good and pure, only if our lives are good and pure. It is an effect, and we are the means. Therefore, let us purify ourselves. Let us make ourselves perfect.

THE POWERS OF THE MIND

Delivered at Los Angeles, California, January 8, 1900

All over the world there has been the belief in the supernatural throughout the ages. All of us have heard of extraordinary happenings, and many of us have had some personal experience of them. I would rather introduce the subject by telling you certain facts which have come within my own experience. I once heard of a man who, if any one went to him with questions in his mind, would answer them immediately; and I was also informed that he foretold events. I was curious and went to see him with a few friends. We each had something in our minds to ask, and, to avoid mistakes, we wrote down our questions and put them in our pockets. As soon as the man saw one of us, he repeated our questions and gave the answers to them. Then he wrote something on paper, which he folded up, asked me to sign on the back, and said, "Don't look at it; put it in your pocket and keep it there till I ask for it again." And so on to each one of us. He next told us about some events that would happen to us in the future. Then he said, "Now, think of a word or a sentence, from any language you like." I thought of a long sentence from Sanskrit, a language of which he was entirely ignorant. "Now, take out the paper from your pocket," he said. The Sanskrit sentence was written there! He had written it an hour before with the remark, "In confirmation of what I have written, this man will think of this sentence." It was correct. Another of us who had been given a similar paper which he had signed and placed in his pocket, was also asked to think of a sentence. He thought of a sentence in Arabic, which it was still less possible for the man to know; it was some passage from the Koran. And my friend found this written down on the paper.

Another of us was a physician. He thought of a sentence from a German medical book. It was written on his paper.

Several days later I went to this man again, thinking possibly I had been deluded somehow before. I took other friends, and on this occasion also he came out wonderfully triumphant.

Another time I was in the city of Hyderabad in India, and I was told of a Brâhmin there who could produce numbers of things from where, nobody knew. This man was in business there; he was a respectable gentleman. And I asked him to show me his tricks. It so happened that this man had a fever, and in India there is a general belief that if a holy man puts his hand on a sick man he would be well. This Brahmin came to me and said, "Sir, put your hand on my head, so that my fever may be cured." I said, "Very good; but you show me your tricks." He promised. I put my hand on his head as desired, and later he came to fulfil his promise. He had only a strip of cloth about his loins, we took off everything else from him. I had a blanket which I gave him to wrap round himself, because it was cold, and made him sit in a corner. Twenty-five pairs of eyes were looking at him. And he said, "Now, look, write down anything you want." We all wrote down names of fruits that never grew in that country, bunches of grapes, oranges, and so on. And we gave him those bits of paper. And there came from under his blanket, bushels of grapes, oranges, and so forth, so much that if all that fruit was weighed, it would have been twice as heavy as the man. He asked us to eat the fruit. Some of us objected, thinking it was hypnotism; but the man began eating himself—so we all ate. It was all right.

He ended by producing a mass of roses. Each flower was perfect, with dew-drops on the petals, not one crushed, not one injured. And masses of them! When I asked the man for an explanation, he said, "It is all sleight of hand."

Whatever it was, it seemed to be impossible that it could be sleight of hand merely. From whence could he have got such large quantities of things?

Well, I saw many things like that. Going about India you find hundreds of similar things in different places. These are in every country. Even in this country you will find some such wonderful things. Of course there is a great deal of fraud, no doubt; but then, whenever you see fraud, you have also to say that fraud is an imitation. There must be some truth somewhere, that is being imitated; you cannot imitate nothing. Imitation must be of something substantially true.

In very remote times in India, thousands of years ago, these facts used to happen even more than they do today. It seems to me that when a country becomes very thickly populated, psychical power deteriorates. Given a vast country thinly inhabited, there will, perhaps, be more of psychical power there. These facts, the Hindus, being analytically minded. Took up and investigated. And they came to certain remarkable conclusions; that is, they made a science of it. They found out that all these, though extraordinary, are also natural; there is nothing supernatural. They are under laws just the same as any other physical phenomenon. It is not a freak of nature that a man is born with such powers. They can be systematically studied, practiced, and acquired. This science they call the science of Râja-Yoga. There are thousands of people who cultivate the study of this science, and for the whole nation it has become a part of daily worship.

The conclusion they have reached is that all these extraordinary powers are in the mind of man. This mind is a part of the universal mind. Each mind is connected with every other mind. And each mind, wherever it is located, is in actual communication with the whole world.

Have you ever noticed the phenomenon that is called thought-transference? A man here is thinking something, and that thought is manifested in somebody else, in some other place. With preparations—not by chance—a man wants to send a thought to another mind at a distance, and this other mind knows that a thought is coming, and he receives it exactly as it is sent out. Distance makes no difference. The thought goes and reaches the other man, and he understands it. If your mind were an isolated something here, and my mind were an isolated something there, and there were no connection between the two, how would it be possible for my thought to reach you? In the ordinary cases, it is not my thought that is reaching you direct; but my thought has got to be dissolved into ethereal vibrations and those ethereal vibrations go into your brain, and they have to be resolved again into your own thoughts. Here is a dissolution of thought, and there is a resolution of thought. It is a roundabout process. But in telepathy, there is no such thing; it is direct.

This shows that there is a continuity of mind, as the Yogis call it. The mind is universal. Your mind, my mind, all these little minds, are fragments of that universal mind, little waves in the ocean; and on account of this continuity, we can convey our thoughts directly to one another.

You see what is happening all around us. The world is one of influence. Part of our energy is used up in the preservation of our own bodies. Beyond that, every particle of our energy is day and night being used in influencing others. Our bodies, our virtues, our intellect, and our spirituality, all these are continuously influencing others; and so, conversely, we are being influenced by them. This is going on all around us. Now, to take a concrete example. A man comes; you know he is very learned, his language is beautiful, and he speaks to you by the hour; but he does not make any impression. Another man comes, and he speaks a few words, not well arranged, ungrammatical perhaps; all the same, he makes an immense impression. Many of you have seen that. So it is evident that words alone cannot always produce an impression. Words, even thoughts contribute only one-third of the influence in making an impression, the man, two-thirds. What you call the personal magnetism of the man—that is what goes out and impresses you.

In our families there are the heads; some of them are successful, others are not. Why? We complain of others in our failures. The moment I am unsuccessful, I say, so-and-so is the cause of the failure. In failure, one does not like to confess one's own faults and weaknesses. Each person tries to hold himself faultless and lay the blame upon somebody or something else, or even on bad luck. When heads of families fail, they should ask themselves, why it is that some persons manage a family so well and others do not. Then you will find that the difference is owing to the man—his presence, his personality.

Coming to great leaders of mankind, we always find that it was the personality of the man that counted. Now, take all the great authors of the past, the great thinkers. Really speaking, how many thoughts have they thought? Take all the writings that have been left to us by the past leaders of mankind; take each one of their books and appraise them. The real thoughts, new and genuine, that have been thought in this world up to this time, amount to only a handful. Read in their books the thoughts they have left to us. The authors do not appear to be giants to us, and yet we know that they were great giants in their days. What made them so? Not simply the thoughts they thought, neither the books they wrote, nor the speeches they made, it was something else that is now gone, that is their personality. As I have already remarked, the personality of the man is two-thirds, and his intellect, his words, are but one-third. It is the real man, the personality of the man, that runs through us. Our actions are but effects. Actions must come when the man is there; the effect is bound to follow the cause.

The ideal of all education, all training, should be this man-making. But, instead of that, we are always trying to polish up the outside. What use in polishing up the outside when there is no inside? The end and aim of all training is to make the man grow. The man who influences, who throws his magic, as it were, upon his fellow-beings, is a dynamo of power, and when that man is ready, he can do anything and everything he likes; that personality put upon anything will make it work.

Now, we see that though this is a fact, no physical laws that we know of will explain this. How can we explain it by chemical and physical knowledge? How much of oxygen, hydrogen, carbon, how many molecules in different positions, and how many cells, etc., etc. can explain this mysterious personality? And we still see, it is a fact, and not only that, it is the real man; and it is that man that lives and moves and works, it is that man that influences, moves his fellow-beings, and passes out, and his intellect and books and works are but traces left behind. Think of this. Compare the great teachers of religion with the great philosophers. The philosophers scarcely influenced anybody's inner man, and yet they wrote most marvellous books. The religious teachers, on the other hand, moved countries in their lifetime. The difference was made by personality. In the philosopher it is a faint personality that influences; in the great prophets it is tremendous. In the former we touch the intellect, in the latter we touch life. In the one case, it is simply a chemical process, putting certain chemical ingredients together which may gradually combine and under proper circumstances bring out a flash of light or may fail. In the other, it is like a torch that goes round quickly, lighting others.

The science of Yoga claims that it has discovered the laws which develop this personality, and by proper attention to those laws and methods, each one can grow and strengthen his personality. This is one of the great practical things, and this is the secret of all education. This has a universal application. In the life of the householder, in the life of the poor, the rich, the man of business, the spiritual man, in every one's life, it is a great thing, the strengthening of this personality. There are laws, very fine, which are behind the physical laws, as we know. That is to say, there are no such realities as a physical world, a mental world, a spiritual world. Whatever is, is one. Let us say, it is a sort of tapering existence; the thickest part is here, it tapers and becomes finer and finer. The finest is what we call spirit; the grossest, the body. And just as it is here in microcosm, it is exactly the same in the macrocosm. The universe of ours is exactly like that; it is the gross external thickness, and it tapers into something finer and finer until it becomes God.

We also know that the greatest power is lodged in the fine, not in the coarse. We see a man take up a huge weight, we see his muscles swell, and all over his body we see signs of exertion, and we think the muscles are powerful things. But it is the thin thread-like things, the nerves, which bring power to the muscles; the moment one of these threads is cut off from reaching the muscles, they are not able to work at all. These tiny nerves bring the power from something still finer, and that again in its turn brings it from something finer still—thought, and so on. So, it is the fine that is really the seat of power. Of course we can see the movements in the gross; but when fine movements take place, we cannot see them. When a gross thing moves, we catch it, and thus we naturally identify movement with things which are gross. But all the power is really in the fine. We do not see any movement in the fine, perhaps, because the movement is so intense that we cannot perceive it. But if by any science, any investigation, we are helped to get hold of these finer forces which are the cause of the expression, the expression itself will be under control. There is a little bubble coming from the bottom of a lake; we do not see it coming all the time, we see it only when it bursts on the surface; so, we can perceive thoughts only after they develop a great deal, or after they become actions. We constantly complain that we have no control over our actions, over our thoughts. But how can we have it? If we can get control over the fine movements, if we can get hold of thought at the root, before it has become thought, before it has become action, then it would be possible for us to control the whole. Now, if there is a method by which we can analyse, investigate, understand, and finally grapple with those finer powers, the finer causes, then alone is it possible to have control over ourselves, and the man who has control over his own mind assuredly will have control over every other mind. That is why purity and morality have been always the object of religion; a pure, moral man has control of himself. And all minds are the same, different parts of one Mind. He who knows one lump of clay has known all the clay in the universe. He who knows and controls his own mind knows the secret of every mind and has power over every mind

Now, a good deal of our physical evil we can get rid of, if we have control over the fine parts; a good many worries we can throw off, if we have control over the fine movements; a good many failures can be averted, if we have control over these fine powers. So far, is utility. Yet beyond, there is something higher.

Now, I shall tell you a theory, which I will not argue now, but simply place before you the conclusion. Each man in his childhood runs through the stages through which his race has come up; only the race took thousands of years to do it, while the child takes a few years. The child is first the old savage man—and he crushes a butterfly under his feet. The child is at first like the primitive ancestors of his race. As he grows, he passes through different stages until he reaches the development of his race. Only he does it swiftly and quickly. Now, take the whole of humanity as a race, or take the whole of the animal creation, man and the lower animals, as one whole. There is an end towards which the whole is moving. Let us call it perfection. Some men and women are born who anticipate the whole progress of mankind. Instead of waiting and being reborn over and over again for ages until the whole human race has attained to that perfection, they, as it were, rush through them in a few short years of their life. And we know that we can hasten these processes, if we be true to ourselves. If a number of men, without any culture, be left to live upon an island, and are given barely enough food, clothing, and shelter, they will gradually go on and on, evolving higher and higher stages of civilization. We know also, that this growth can be hastened by additional means. We help the growth of trees, do we not? Left to nature they would have grown, only they would have taken a longer time; we help them to grow in a shorter time than they would otherwise have taken. We are doing all the time the same thing, hastening the growth of things by artificial means. Why cannot we hasten the growth of man? We can do that as a race Why are teachers sent to other countries? Because by these means we can hasten the growth of races. Now, can we not hasten the growth of individuals? We can. Can we put a limit to the hastening? We cannot say how much a man can grow in one life. You have no reason to say that this much a man can do and no more. Circumstances can hasten him wonderfully. Can there be any limit then, till you come to perfection? So, what comes of it? — That a perfect man, that is to say, the type that is to come of this race, perhaps millions of years hence, that man can come today. And this is what the Yogis say, that all great incarnations and prophets are such men; that they reached perfection in this one life. We have had such men at all periods of the world's history and at all times. Quite recently, there was such a man who lived the life of the whole human race and reached the end — even in this life. Even this hastening of the growth must be under laws. Suppose we can investigate these laws and understand their secrets and apply them to our own needs; it follows that we grow. We hasten our growth, we hasten our development, and we become perfect, even in this life. This is the higher part of our life, and the science of the study of mind and its powers has this perfection as its real end. Helping others with money and other material things and teaching them how to go on smoothly in their daily life are mere details.

The utility of this science is to bring out the perfect man, and not let him wait and wait for ages, just a plaything in the hands of the physical world, like a log of drift-wood carried from wave to wave and tossing about in the ocean. This science wants you to be strong, to take the work in your own hand, instead of leaving it in the hands of nature, and get beyond this little life. That is the great idea.

Man is growing in knowledge, in power, in happiness. Continuously, we are growing as a race. We see that is true, perfectly true. Is it true of individuals? To a certain extent, yes. But yet, again comes the question: Where do you fix the limit? I can see only at a distance of so many feet. But I have seen a man close his eyes and see what is happening in another room. If you say you do not believe it, perhaps in three weeks that man can make you do the same. It can be taught to anybody. Some persons, in five minutes even, can be made to read what is happening in another man's mind. These facts can be demonstrated.

Now, if these things are true, where can we put a limit? If a man can read what is happening in another's mind in the corner of this room, why not in the next room? Why not anywhere? We cannot say, why not. We dare not say that it is not possible. We can only say, we do not know how it happens. Material scientists have no right to say that things like this are not possible; they can only say, "We do not know." Science has to collect facts, generalise upon them, deduce principles, and state the truth — that is all. But if we begin by denying the facts, how can a science be?

There is no end to the power a man can obtain. This is the peculiarity of the Indian mind, that when anything interests it, it gets absorbed in it and other things are neglected. You know how many sciences had their origin in India. Mathematics began there. You are even today counting 1, 2, 3, etc. to zero, after Sanskrit figures, and you all know that algebra also originated in India, and that gravitation was known to the Indians thousands of years before Newton was born.

You see the peculiarity. At a certain period of Indian history, this one subject of man and his mind absorbed all their interest. And it was so enticing, because it seemed the easiest way to achieve their ends. Now, the Indian mind became so thoroughly persuaded that the mind could do anything and everything according to law, that its powers became the great object of study. Charms, magic, and other powers, and all that were nothing extraordinary, but a regularly taught science, just as the physical sciences they had taught before that. Such a conviction in these things came upon the race that physical sciences nearly died out. It was the one thing that came before them. Different sects of Yogis began to make all sorts of experiments. Some made experiments with light, trying to find out how lights of different colours produced changes in the body. They wore a certain coloured cloth, lived under a certain colour, and ate certain coloured foods. All sorts of experiments were made in this way. Others made experiments in sound by stopping and unstopping their ears. And still others experimented in the sense of smell, and so on.

The whole idea was to get at the basis, to reach the fine parts of the thing. And some of them really showed most marvellous powers. Many of them were trying to float in the air or pass through it. I shall tell you a story which I heard from a great scholar in the West. It was told him by a Governor of Ceylon who saw the performance. A girl was brought forward and seated cross-legged upon a stool made of sticks crossed. After she had been seated for a time, the show-man began to take out, one after another, these cross-bars; and when all were taken out, the girl was left floating in the air. The Governor thought there was some trick, so he drew his sword and violently passed it under the girl; nothing was there. Now, what was this? It was not magic or something extraordinary. That is the peculiarity. No one in India would tell you that things like this do not exist. To the Hindu it is a matter of course. You know what the Hindus would often say when they have to fight their enemies— "Oh, one of our Yogis will come and drive the whole lot out!" It is the extreme belief of the race. What power is there in the hand or the sword? The power is all in the spirit.

If this is true, it is temptation enough for the mind to exert its highest. But as with every other science it is very difficult to make any great achievement, so also with this, nay much more. Yet most people think that these powers can be easily gained. How many are the years you take to make a fortune? Think of that! First, how many years do you take to learn electrical science or engineering? And then you have to work all the rest of your life.

Again, most of the other sciences deal with things that do not move, that are fixed. You can analyse the chair, the chair does not fly from you. But this science deals with the mind, which moves all the time; the moment you want to study it, it slips. Now the mind is in one mood, the next moment, perhaps, it is different, changing, changing all the time. In the midst of all this change it has to be studied, understood, grasped, and controlled. How much more difficult, then, is this science! It requires rigorous training. People ask me why I do not give them practical lessons. Why, it is no joke. I stand upon this platform talking to you and you go home and find no benefit; nor do I. Then you say, "It is all bosh." It is because you wanted to make a bosh of it. I know very little of this science, but the little that I gained I worked for thirty years of my life, and for six years I have been telling people the little that I know. It took me thirty years to learn it; thirty years of hard struggle. Sometimes I worked at it twenty hours during the twenty-four; sometimes I slept only one hour in the night; sometimes I worked whole nights; sometimes I lived in places where there was hardly a sound, hardly a breath; sometimes I had to live in caves. Think of that. And yet I know little or nothing; I have barely touched the hem of the garment of this science. But I can understand that it is true and vast and wonderful.

Now, if there is any one amongst you who really wants to study this science, he will have to start with that sort of determination, the same as, nay even more than, that which he puts into any business of life.

And what an amount of attention does business require, and what a rigorous taskmaster it is! Even if the father, the mother, the wife, or the child dies, business cannot stop! Even if the heart is breaking, we still have to go to our place of business, when every hour of work is a pang. That is business, and we think that it is just, that it is right.

This science calls for more application than any business can ever require. Many men can succeed in business; very few in this. Because so much depends upon the particular constitution of the person studying it. As in business all may not make a fortune, but everyone can make something, so in the study of this science each one can get a glimpse which will convince him of its truth and of the fact that there have been men who realised it fully.

This is the outline of the science. It stands upon its own feet and in its own light, and challenges comparison with any other science. There have been charlatans, there have been magicians, there have been cheats, and more here than in any other field. Why? For the same reason, that the more profitable the business, the greater the number of charlatans and cheats. But that is no reason why the business should not be good. And one thing more; it may be good intellectual gymnastics to listen to all the arguments and an intellectual satisfaction to hear of wonderful things. But, if any one of you really wants to learn something beyond that, merely attending lectures will not do. That cannot be taught in lectures, for it is life; and life can only convey life. If there are any amongst you who are really determined to learn it, I shall be very glad to help them.

HINTS ON PRACTICAL SPIRITUALITY

Delivered at the Home of Truth, Los Angeles, California

This morning I shall try to present to you some ideas about breathing and other exercises. We have been discussing theories so long that now it will be well to have a little of the practical. A great many books have been written in India upon this subject. Just as your people are practical in many things, so it seems our people are practical in this line. Five persons in this country will join their heads together and say, "We will have a joint-stock company", and in five hours it is done; in India they could not do it in fifty years; they are so unpractical in matters like this. But, mark you, if a man starts a system of philosophy, however wild its theory may be, it will have followers. For instance, a sect is started to teach that if a man stands on one leg for twelve years, day and night, he will get salvation—there will be hundreds ready to stand on one leg. All the suffering will be quietly borne. There are people who keep their arms upraised for years to gain religious merit. I have seen hundreds of them. And, mind you, they are not always ignorant fools, but are men who will astonish you with the depth and breadth of their intellect. So, you see, the word practical is also relative.

We are always making this mistake in judging others; we are always inclined to think that our little mental universe is all that is; our ethics, our morality, our sense of duty, our sense of utility, are the only things that are worth having. The other day when I was going to Europe, I was passing through Marseilles, where a bull-fight was being held. All the Englishmen in the steamer were mad with excitement, abusing and criticising the whole thing as cruel. When I reached England,

I heard of a party of prize-fighters who had been to Paris, and were kicked out unceremoniously by the French, who thought prize-fighting very brutal. When I hear these things in various countries, I begin to understand the marvellous saying of Christ: "Judge not that ye be not judged." The more we learn, the more he find out how ignorant we are, how multiform and multi-sided is this mind of man. When I was a boy, I used to criticise the ascetic practices of my countrymen; great preachers in our own land have criticised them; the greatest man that was ever born, Buddha himself, criticised them. But all the same, as I am growing older, I feel that I have no right to judge. Sometimes I wish that, in spite of all their incongruities, I had one fragment of their power to do and suffer. Often I think that my judgment and my criticism do not proceed from any dislike of torture, but from sheer cowardice—because I cannot do it—I dare not do it.

Then, you see that strength, power, and courage are things which are very peculiar. We generally say, "A courageous man, a brave man, a daring man", but we must bear in mind that that courage or bravery or any other trait does not always characterise the man. The same man who would rush to the mouth of a cannon shrinks from the knife of the surgeon; and another man who never dares to face a gun will calmly bear a severe surgical operation, if need be. Now, in judging others you must always define your terms of courage or greatness. The man whom I am criticising as not good may be wonderfully so in some points in which I am not.

Take another example. You often note, when people are discussing as to what man and woman can do, always the same mistake is made. They think they show man at his best because he can fight, for instance, and undergo tremendous physical exertion; and this is pitted against the physical weakness and the non-combating quality of woman. This is unjust. Woman is as courageous as man. Each is equally good in his or her way. What man can bring up a child with such patience, endurance, and love as the woman can? The one has developed the power of doing; the other, the power of suffering. If woman cannot act, neither can man suffer. The whole universe is one of perfect balance. I do not know, but some day we may wake up and find that the mere worm has something which balances our manhood. The most wicked person may have some good qualities that I entirely lack. I see that every day of my life. Look at the savage! I wish I had such a splendid physique. He eats, he drinks, to his heart's content, without knowing perhaps what sickness is, while I am suffering every minute. How many times would I have been glad to have changed my brain for his body! The whole universe is only a wave and a hollow; there can be no wave without a hollow. Balance everywhere. You have one thing great, your neighbour has another thing great. When you are judging man and woman, judge them by the standard of their respective greatness. One cannot be in other's shoes. The one has no right to say that the other is wicked. It is the same old superstition that says, "If this is done, the world will go

to ruin." But in spite of this the world has not yet come to ruin. It was said in this country that if the Negroes were freed, the country would go to ruin—but did it? It was also said that if the masses were educated, the world would come to ruin—but it was only made better. Several years ago a book came out depicting the worst thing that could happen to England. The writer showed that as workmen's wages were rising, English commerce was declining. A cry was raised that the workmen in England were exorbitant in their demands, and that the Germans worked for less wages. A commission was sent over to Germany to investigate this and it reported that the German labourers received higher wages. Why was it so? Because of the education of the masses. Then how about the world going to ruin if the masses are educated? In India, especially, we meet with old fogies all over the land. They want to keep everything secret from the masses. These people come to the very satisfying conclusion that they are the crème de la crème of this universe. They believed they cannot be hurt by these dangerous experiments. It is only the masses that can be hurt by them!

Now, coming back to the practical. The subject of the practical application of psychology has been taken up in India from very early times. About fourteen hundred years before Christ, there flourished in India a great philosopher, Patanjali by name. He collected all the facts, evidences, and researches in psychology and took advantage of all the experiences accumulated in the past. Remember, this world is very old; it was not created only two or three thousand years ago. It is taught here in the West that society began eighteen hundred years ago, with the New Testament. Before that there was no society. That may be true with regard to the West, but it is not true as regards the whole world. Often, while I was lecturing in London, a very intellectual and intelligent friend of mine would argue with me, and one day after using all his weapons against me, he suddenly exclaimed, "But why did not your Rishis come to England to teach us?" I replied, "Because there was no England to come to. Would they preach to the forests?"

"Fifty years ago," said Ingersoll to me, "you would have been hanged in this country if you had come to preach. You would have been burnt alive or you would have been stoned out of the villages."

So there is nothing unreasonable in the supposition that civilisation existed fourteen hundred years before Christ. It is not yet settled whether civilisation has always come from the lower to the higher. The same arguments and proofs that have been brought forward to prove this proposition can also be used to demonstrate that the savage is only a degraded civilised man. The people of China, for instance, can never believe that civilisation sprang from a savage state, because the contrary is within their experience. But when you talk of the civilisation of America, what you mean is the perpetuity and the growth of your own race.

It is very easy to believe that the Hindus, who have been declining for seven hundred years, were highly civilised in the past. We cannot prove that it is not so.

There is not one single instance of any civilisation being spontaneous. There was not a race in the world which became civilised unless another civilised race came and mingled with that race. The origin of civilisation must have belonged, so to say, to one or two races who went abroad, spread their ideas, and intermingled with other races and thus civilisation spread.

For practical purposes, let us talk in the language of modern science. But I must ask you to bear in mind that, as there is religious superstition, so also there is a superstition in the matter of science. There are priests who take up religious work as their speciality; so also there are priests of physical law, scientists. As soon as a great scientist's name, like Darwin or Huxley, is cited, we follow blindly. It is the fashion of the day. Ninety-nine per cent of what we call scientific knowledge is mere theories. And many of them are no better than the old superstitions of ghosts with many heads and hands, but with this difference that the latter differentiated man a little from stocks and stones. True science asks us to be cautious. Just as we should be careful with the priests, so we should be with the scientists. Begin with disbelief. Analyse, test, prove everything, and then take it. Some of the most current beliefs of modern science have not been proved. Even in such a science as mathematics, the vast majority of its theories are only working hypotheses. With the advent of greater knowledge they will be thrown away.

In 1400 B.C. a great sage made an attempt to arrange, analyse, and generalise upon certain psychological facts. He was followed by many others who took up parts of what he had discovered and made a special study of them The Hindus alone of all ancient races took up the study of this branch of knowledge in right earnest. I am teaching you now about it, but how many of you will practice it? How many days, how many months will it be before you give it up? You are impractical on this subject. In India, they will persevere for ages and ages. You will be astonished to hear that they have no churches, no Common Prayers, or anything of the kind; but they, every day, still practice the breathings and try to concentrate the mind; and that is the chief part of their devotion. These are the main points. Every Hindu must do these. It is the religion of the country. Only, each one may have a special method—a special form of breathing, a special form of concentration, and what is one's special method, even one's wife need not know; the father need not know the son's. But they all have to do these. And there is nothing occult about these things. The word "occult" has no bearing on them. Near the Gangâ thousands and thousands of people may be seen daily sitting on its banks breathing and concentrating with closed eyes. There may be two reasons that make certain practices impracticable for the generality of mankind. One is, the teachers hold that the ordinary people are not fit for them.

There may be some truth in this, but it is due more to pride. The second is the fear of persecution. A man, for instance, would not like to practice breathing publicly in this country, because he would be thought so queer; it is not the fashion here. On the other hand, in India. If a man prayed, "Give us this day our daily bread", people would laugh at him. Nothing could be more foolish to the Hindu mind than to say, "Our Father which art in Heaven." The Hindu, when he worships, thinks that God is within himself.

According to the Yogis, there are three principal nerve currents: one they call the Idâ, the other the Pingalâ, and the middle one the Sushumnâ, and all these are inside the spinal column. The Ida and the Pingala, the left and the right, are clusters of nerves, while the middle one, the Sushumna, is hollow and is not a cluster of nerves. This Sushumna is closed, and for the ordinary man is of no use, for he works through the Ida and the Pingala only. Currents are continually going down and coming up through these nerves, carrying orders all over the body through other nerves running to the different organs of the body.

It is the regulation and the bringing into rhythm of the Ida and Pingala that is the great object of breathing. But that itself is nothing—it is only so much air taken into the lungs; except for purifying the blood, it is of no more use. There is nothing occult in the air that we take in with our breath and assimilate to purify the blood; the action is merely a motion. This motion can be reduced to the unit movement we call Prâna; and everywhere, all movements are the various manifestations of this Prana. This Prana is electricity, it is magnetism; it is thrown out by the brain as thought. Everything is Prana; it is moving the sun, the moon, and the stars.

We say, whatever is in this universe has been projected by the vibration of the Prana. The highest result of vibration is thought. If there be any higher, we cannot conceive of it. The nerves, Ida and Pingala, work through the Prana. It is the Prana that is moving every part of the body, becoming the different forces. Give up that old idea that God is something that produces the effect and sits on a throne dispensing justice. In working we become exhausted because we use up so much Prana.

The breathing exercises, called Prânâyâma, bring about regulation of the breathing, rhythmic action of the Prana. When the Prana is working rhythmically, everything works properly. When the Yogis get control over their own bodies, if there is any disease in any part, they know that the Prana is not rhythmic there and they direct the Prana to the affected part until the rhythm is re-established.

Just as you can control the Prana in your own body, so, if you are powerful enough, you can control, even from here another man's Prana in India. It is all one. There is no break; unity is the law. Physically, psychically, mentally, morally, metaphysically, it is all one. Life is only a vibration. That which vibrates this ocean of ether, vibrates you. Just as in a lake, various strata of ice of various degrees of solidity are formed, or as in an ocean of vapour there are various degrees of density, so is this universe an ocean of matter. This is an ocean of ether in which we find the sun, moon, stars, and ourselves — in different states of solidity; but the continuity is not broken; it is the same throughout.

Now, when we study metaphysics, we come to know the world is one, not that the spiritual, the material, the mental, and the world of energies are separate. It is all one, but seen from different planes of vision. When you think of yourself as a body, you forget that you are a mind, and when you think of yourself as a mind, you will forget the body. There is only one thing, that you are; you can see it either as matter or body — or you can see it as mind or spirit. Birth, life, and death are but old superstitions. None was ever born, none will ever die; one changes one's position — that is all. I am sorry to see in the West how much they make of death; always trying to catch a little life. "Give us life after death! Give us life!" They are so happy if anybody tells them that they are going to live afterwards! How can I ever doubt such a thing! How can I imagine that I am dead! Try to think of yourself as dead, and you will see that you are present to see your own dead body. Life is such a wonderful reality that you cannot for a moment forget it. You may as well doubt that you exist. This is the first fact of consciousness — I am. Who can imagine a state of things which never existed? It is the most self-evident of all truths. So, the idea of immortality is inherent in man. How can one discuss a subject that is unimaginable? Why should we want to discuss the pros and cons of a subject that is self-evident?

The whole universe, therefore, is a unit, from whatever standpoint you view it. Just now, to us, this universe is a unit of Prana and Âkâsha, force and matter. And mind you, like all other basic principles, this is also self-contradictory. For what is force? — that which moves matter. And what is matter? — that which is moved by force. It is a seesaw! Some of the fundamentals of our reasoning are most curious, in spite of our boast of science and knowledge. "It is a headache without a head", as the Sanskrit proverb says. This state of things has been called Maya. It has neither existence nor non-existence. You cannot call it existence, because that only exists which is beyond time and space, which is self-existence. Yet this world satisfies to a certain degree our idea of existence. Therefore it has an apparent existence.

But there is the real existence in and through everything; and that reality, as it were, is caught in the meshes of time, space, and causation. There is the real man, the infinite, the beginningless, the endless, the ever-blessed, the ever-free. He has been caught in the meshes of time, space, and causation. So has everything in this world. The reality of everything is the same infinite. This is not idealism; it is not that the world does not exist. It has a relative existence, and fulfils all its requirements But it has no independent existence. It exists because of the Absolute Reality beyond time, space, and causation.

I have made long digressions. Now, let us return to our main subject.

All the automatic movements and all the conscious movements are the working of Prana through the nerves. Now, you see, it will be a very good thing to have control over the unconscious actions.

On some other occasions, I told you the definition of God and man. Man is an infinite circle whose circumference is nowhere, but the centre is located in one spot; and God is an infinite circle whose circumference is nowhere, but whose centre is everywhere. He works through all hands, sees through all eyes, walks on all feet, breathes through all bodies, lives in all life, speaks through every mouth, and thinks through every brain. Man can become like God and acquire control over the whole universe if he multiplies infinitely his centre of self-consciousness. Consciousness, therefore, is the chief thing to understand. Let us say that here is an infinite line amid darkness. We do not see the line, but on it there is one luminous point which moves on. As it moves along the line, it lights up its different parts in succession, and all that is left behind becomes dark again. Our consciousness; may well be likened to this luminous point. Its past experiences have been replaced by the present, or have become subconscious. We are not aware of their presence in us; but there they are, unconsciously influencing our body and mind. Every movement that is now being made without the help of consciousness was previously conscious. Sufficient impetus has been given to it to work of itself.

The great error in all ethical systems, without exception, has been the failure of teaching the means by which man could refrain from doing evil. All the systems of ethics teach, "Do not steal!" Very good; but why does a man steal? Because all stealing, robbing, and other evil actions, as a rule, have become automatic. The systematic robber, thief, liar, unjust man and woman, are all these in spite of themselves! It is really a tremendous psychological problem. We should look upon man in the most charitable light. It is not so easy to be good. What are you but mere machines until you are free? Should you be proud because you are good? Certainly not. You are good because you cannot help it. Another is bad because he cannot help it. If you were in his position, who knows what you would have been? The woman in the street, or the thief in the jail, is the Christ that is being sacrificed that you may be a good man. Such is the law of balance. All the thieves and the murderers, all the unjust, the weakest, the wickedest, the devils, they all are my Christ! I owe a worship to the God Christ and to the demon Christ! That is my doctrine, I cannot help it. My salutation goes to the feet of the good, the saintly, and to the feet of the wicked and the devilish! They are all my teachers, all are my spiritual fathers, all are my Saviours. I may curse one and yet benefit by his failings; I may bless another and benefit by his good deeds. This is as true as that I stand here. I have to sneer at the woman walking in the street, because society wants it! She, my Saviour, she, whose street-walking is the cause of the chastity of other women! Think of that. Think, men and women, of this question in your mind. It is a truth—a bare, bold truth! As I see more of the world, see more of men and women, this conviction grows stronger. Whom shall I blame? Whom shall I praise? Both sides of the shield must be seen.

The task before us is vast; and first and foremost, we must seek to control the vast mass of sunken thoughts which have become automatic with us. The evil deed is, no doubt, on the conscious plane; but the cause which produced the evil deed was far beyond in the realms of the unconscious, unseen, and therefore more potent.

Practical psychology directs first of all its energies in controlling the unconscious, and we know that we can do it. Why? Because we know the cause of the unconscious is the conscious; the unconscious thoughts are the submerged millions of our old conscious thoughts, old conscious actions become petrified—we do not look at them, do not know them, have forgotten them. But mind you, if the power of evil is in the unconscious, so also is the power of good. We have many things stored in us as in a pocket. We have forgotten them, do not even think of them, and there are many of them, rotting, becoming positively dangerous; they come forth, the unconscious causes which kill humanity. True psychology would, therefore, try to bring them under the control of the conscious. The great task is to revive the whole man, as it were, in order to make him the complete master of himself. Even what we call the automatic action of the organs within our bodies, such as the liver etc., can be made to obey our commands.

This is the first part of the study, the control of the unconscious. The next is to go beyond the conscious. Just as unconscious work is beneath consciousness, so there is another work which is above consciousness. When this superconscious state is reached, man becomes free and divine; death becomes immortality, weakness becomes infinite power, and iron bondage becomes liberty. That is the goal, the infinite realm of the superconscious.

So, therefore, we see now that there must be a twofold work. First, by the proper working of the Ida and the Pingala, which are the two existing ordinary currents, to control the subconscious action; and secondly, to go beyond even consciousness.

The books say that he alone is the Yogi who, after long practice in self-concentration, has attained to this truth. The Sushumna now opens and a current which never before entered into this new passage will find its way into it, and gradually ascend to (what we call in figurative language) the different lotus centres, till at last it reaches the brain. Then the Yogi becomes conscious of what he really is, God Himself.

Everyone without exception, everyone of us, can attain to this culmination of Yoga. But it is a terrible task. If a person wants to attain to this truth, he will have to do something more than to listen to lectures and take a few breathing exercises. Everything lies in the preparation. How long does it take to strike a light? Only a second; but how long it takes to make the candle! How long does it take to eat a dinner? Perhaps half an hour. But hours to prepare the food! We want to strike the light in a second, but we forget that the making of the candle is the chief thing.

But though it is so hard to reach the goal, yet even our smallest attempts are not in vain. We know that nothing is lost. In the Gita, Arjuna asks Krishna, "Those who fail in attaining perfection in Yoga in this life, are they destroyed like the clouds of summer?" Krishna replies, "Nothing, my friend, is lost in this world. Whatever one does, that remains as one's own, and if the fruition of Yoga does not come in this life, one takes it up again in the next birth." Otherwise, how do you explain the marvellous childhood of Jesus, Buddha, Shankara?

Breathing, posturing, etc. are no doubt helps in Yoga; but they are merely physical. The great preparations are mental. The first thing necessary is a quiet and peaceable life.

If you want to be a Yogi, you must be free, and place yourself in circumstances where you are alone and free from all anxiety. He who desires a comfortable and nice life and at the same time wants to realise the Self is like the fool who, wanting to cross the river, caught hold of a crocodile, mistaking it for a log of wood (Vivekachudâmani, 84.). "Seek ye first the kingdom of God, and everything shall be added unto you." This is the one great duty, this is renunciation. Live for an ideal, and leave no place in the mind for anything else. Let us put forth all our energies to acquire that, which never fails—our spiritual perfection. If we have true yearning for realisation, we must struggle, and through struggle growth will come. We shall make mistakes, but they may be angels unawares.

The greatest help to spiritual life is meditation (Dhyâna). In meditation we divest ourselves of all material conditions and feel our divine nature. We do not depend upon any external help in meditation. The touch of the soul can paint the brightest colour even in the dingiest places; it can cast a fragrance over the vilest thing; it can make the wicked divine—and all enmity, all selfishness is effaced. The less the thought of the body, the better. For it is the body that drags us down. It is attachment, identification, which makes us miserable. That is the secret: To think that I am the spirit and not the body, and that the whole of this universe with all its relations, with all its good and all its evil, is but as a series of paintings—scenes on a canvas—of which I am the witness.

BUDDHISTIC INDIA[1]

Delivered at the Shakespeare Club, Pasadena, California, on February 2, 1900

Buddhistic India is our subject tonight. Almost all of you, perhaps, have read Edwin Arnold's poem on the life of Bud-

1. Reproduced from the *Swami Vivekananda Centenary Memorial Volume*, published by the Swami Vivekananda Centenary, Calcutta, in 1963. The additions in square brackets have been made for purposes of clarification. Periods indicate probable omissions. —*Publisher.*

dha, and some of you, perhaps, have gone into the subject with more scholarly interest, as in English, French and German, there is quite a lot of Buddhistic literature. Buddhism itself is the most interesting of subjects, for it is the first historical outburst of a world religion. There have been great religions before Buddhism arose, in India and elsewhere, but, more or less, they are confined within their own races. The ancient Hindus or ancient Jews or ancient Persians, every one of them had a great religion, but these religions were more or less racial. With Buddhism first begins that peculiar phenomenon of religion boldly starting out to conquer the world. Apart from its doctrines and the truths it taught and the message it had to give, we stand face to face with one of the tremendous cataclysms of the world. Within a few centuries of its birth, the barefooted, shaven-headed missionaries of Buddha had spread over all the then known civilised world, and they penetrated even further—from Lapland on the one side to the Philippine Islands on the other. They had spread widely within a few centuries of Buddha's birth; and in India itself, the religion of Buddha had at one time nearly swallowed up two-thirds of the population.

The whole of India was never Buddhistic. It stood outside. Buddhism had the same fate as Christianity had with the Jews; the majority of the Jews stood aloof. So the old Indian religion lived on. But the comparison stops here. Christianity, though it could not get within its fold all the Jewish race, itself took the country. Where the old religion existed—the religion of the Jews—that was conquered by Christianity in a very short time and the old religion was dispersed, and so the religion of the Jews lives a sporadic life in different parts of the world. But in India this gigantic child was absorbed, in the long run, by the mother that gave it birth, and today the very name of Buddha is almost unknown all over India. You know more about Buddhism than ninety-nine per cent of the Indians. At best, they of India only know the name—"Oh, he was a great prophet, a great Incarnation of God"—and there it ends. The island of Ceylon remains to Buddha, and in some parts of the Himalayan country, there are some Buddhists yet. Beyond that there are none. But [Buddhism] has spread over all the rest of Asia.

Still, it has the largest number of followers of any religion, and it has indirectly modified the teachings of all the other religions. A good deal of Buddhism entered into Asia Minor. It was a constant fight at one time whether the Buddhists would prevail or the later sects of Christians. The [Gnostics] and the other sects of early Christians were more or less Buddhistic in their tendencies, and all these got fused up in that wonderful city of Alexandria, and out of the fusion under Roman law came Christianity. Buddhism in its political and social aspect is even more interesting than its [doctrines] and dogmas; and as the first outburst of the tremendous world-conquering power of religion, it is very interesting also.

I am mostly interested in this lecture in India as it has been affected by Buddhism; and to understand Buddhism and its rise a bit, we have to get a few ideas about India as it existed when this great prophet was born.

There was already in India a vast religion with an organised scripture—the Vedas; and these Vedas existed as a mass of literature and not a book—just as you find the Old Testament, the Bible. Now, the Bible is a mass of literature of different ages; different persons are the writers, and so on. It is a collection. Now, the Vedas are a vast collection. I do not know whether, if the texts were all found—nobody has found all the texts, nobody even in India has seen all the books—if all the books were known, this room would contain them. It is a huge mass of literature, carried down from generation to generation from God, who gave the scriptures. And the idea about the scriptures in India became tremendously orthodox. You complain of your orthodoxies in book-worship. If you get the Hindus' idea, where will you be? The Hindus think the Vedas are the direct knowledge of God, that God has created the whole universe in and through the Vedas, and that the whole universe exists because it is in the Vedas. The cow exists outside because the word "cow" is in the Vedas; man exists outside because of the word in the Vedas. Here you see the beginning of that theory which later on Christians developed and expressed in the text: "In the beginning was the Word and the Word was with God " It is the old, ancient theory of India. Upon that is based the whole idea of the scriptures. And mind, every word is the power of God. The word is only the external manifestation on the material plane. So, all this manifestation is just the manifestation on the material plane; and the Word is the Vedas, and Sanskrit is the language of God. God spoke once. He spoke in Sanskrit, and that is the divine language. Every other language, they consider, is no more than the braying of animals; and to denote that they call every other nation that does not speak Sanskrit [Mlechchhas], the same word as the barbarians of the Greeks. They are braying, not talking, and Sanskrit is the divine language.

Now, the Vedas were not written by anybody; they were eternally coexistent with God. God is infinite. So is knowledge, and through this knowledge is created the world. Their idea of ethics is [that a thing is good] because the law says so. Everything is bounded by that book—nothing [can go] beyond that, because the knowledge of God—you cannot get beyond that. That is Indian orthodoxy.

In the latter part of the Vedas, you see the highest, the spiritual. In the early portions, there is the crude part. You quote a passage from the Vedas—"That is not good", you say. "Why?" "There is a positive evil injunction"—the same as you see in the Old Testament. There are numbers of things in all old books, curious ideas, which we would not like in our present day. You say: "This doctrine is not at all good; why, it shocks my ethics!" How did you get your idea? [Merely] by your own thought? Get out! If it is ordained by God, what right have you to question? When the Vedas say, "Do not do this; this is immoral", and so on, no more have you the right to question at all. And that is the difficulty. If you tell a Hindu, "But our Bible does not say so", [he will reply] "Oh, your Bible! it is a babe of history. What other Bible could there be except the Vedas? What other book could there be? All knowledge is in God. Do you mean to say that He teaches by two or more Bibles? His knowledge came out in the Vedas. Do you mean to say that He committed a mistake, then? Afterwards, He wanted to do something better and taught another Bible to another nation? You cannot bring another book that is as old as Vedas. Everything else—it was all copied after that." They would not listen to you. And the Christian brings the Bible. They say: "That is fraud. God only speaks once, because He never makes mistakes."

Now, just think of that. That orthodoxy is terrible. And if you ask a Hindu that he is to reform his society and do this and that, he says: "Is it in the books? If it is not, I do not care to change. You wait. In five [hundred] years more you will find this is good." If you say to him, "This social institution that you have is not right", he says, "How do you know that?" Then he says: "Our social institutions in this matter are the better. Wait five [hundred] years and your institutions will die. The test is the survival of the fittest. You live, but there is not one community in the world which lives five hundred years together. Look here! We have been standing all the time." That is what they would say. Terrible orthodoxy! And thank God I have crossed that ocean.

This was the orthodoxy of India. What else was there? Everything was divided, the whole society, as it is today, though in a much more rigorous form then—divided into castes. There is another thing to learn. There is a tendency to make castes just [now] going on here in the West. And I myself—I am a renegade. I have broken everything. I do not believe in caste, individually. It has very good things in it. For myself, Lord help me! I would not have any caste, if He helps me. You understand what I mean by caste, and you are all trying to make it very fast. It is a hereditary trade [for] the Hindu. The Hindu said in olden times that life must be made easier and smoother. And what makes everything alive? Competition. Hereditary trade kills. You are a carpenter? Very good, your son can be only a carpenter. What are you? A blacksmith? Blacksmithing becomes a caste; your children will become blacksmiths. We do not allow anybody else to come into that trade, so you will be quiet and remain there. You are a military man, a fighter? Make a caste. You are a priest? Make a caste. The priesthood is hereditary. And so on. Rigid, high power! That has a great side, and that side is [that] it really rejects competition. It is that which has made the nation live while other nations have died—that caste. But there is a great evil: it checks individuality. I will have to be a carpenter because I am born a carpenter; but I do not like it. That is in the books, and that was before Buddha was born. I am talking to you of India as it was before Buddha. And you are trying today what you call socialism! Good things will come; but in the long run you will be a [blight] upon the race. Freedom is the watchword. Be free! A free body, a free mind,

and a free soul! That is what I have felt all my life; I would rather be doing evil freely than be doing good under bondage.

Well, these things that they are crying for now in the West, they have done ages before there. Land has been nationalised...by thousands all these things. There is blame upon this hide-bound caste. The Indian people are intensely socialistic. But, beyond that, there is a wealth of individualism. They are as tremendously individualistic—that is to say, after laying down all these minute regulations. They have regulated how you should eat, drink, sleep, die! Everything is regulated there; from early morning to when you go to bed and sleep, you are following regulations and law. Law, law. Do you wonder that a nation should [live] under that? Law is death. The more of the law in a country, the worse for the country. [But to be an individual] we go to the mountains, where there is no law, no government. The more of law you make, the more of police and socialism, the more of blackguards there are. Now this tremendous regulation of law [is] there. As soon as a child is born, he knows that he is born a slave: slave to his caste, first; slave to his nation, next. Slave, slave, slave. Every action - his drinking and his eating. He must eat under a regular method; this prayer with the first morsel, this prayer with the second, that prayer with the third, and that prayer when he drinks water. Just think of that! Thus, from day to day, it goes on and on.

But they were thinkers. They knew that this would not lead to real greatness. So they left a way out for them all. After all, they found out that all these regulations are only for the world and the life of the world. As soon as you do not want money [and] you do not want children—no business for this world—you can go out entirely free. Those that go out thus were called Sannyasins—people who have given up. They never organised themselves, nor do they now; they are a free order of men and women who refuse to marry, who refuse to possess property, and they have no law—not even the Vedas bind them. They stand on [the] top of the Vedas. They are [at] the other pole [from] our social institutions. They are beyond caste. They have grown beyond. They are too big to be bound by these little regulations and things. Only two things [are] necessary for them: they must not possess property and must not marry. If you marry, settle down, or possess property, immediately the regulations will be upon you; but if you do not do either of these two, you are free. They were the living gods of the race, and ninety-nine per cent of our great men and women were to be found among them.

In every country, real greatness of the soul means extraordinary individuality, and that individuality you cannot get in society. It frets and fumes and wants to burst society. If society wants to keep it down, that soul wants to burst society into pieces. And they made an easy channel. They say: "Well, once you get out of society, then you may preach and teach everything that you like. We only worship you from a distance. So there were the tremendous, individualistic men and women, and they are the highest persons in all society. If one of those yellow-clad shaven-heads comes, the prince even dare not remain seated in his presence; he must stand. The next half hour, one of these Sannyasins might be at the door of one of the cottages of the poorest subjects, glad to get only a piece of bread. And he has to mix with all grades; now he sleeps with a poor man in his cottage; tomorrow [he] sleeps on the beautiful bed of a king. One day he dines on gold plates in kings' palaces; the next day, he has not any food and sleeps under a tree. Society looks upon these men with great respect; and some of them, just to show their individuality, will try to shock the public ideas. But the people are never shocked so long as they keep to these principles: perfect purity and no property.

These men, being very individualistic, they are always trying new theories and plans—visiting in every country. They must think something new; they cannot run in the old groove. Others are all trying to make us run in the old groove, forcing us all to think alike. But human nature is greater than any human foolishness. Our greatness is greater than our weakness; the good things are stronger than the evil things. Supposing they succeeded in making us all think in the same groove, there we would be—no more thought to think; we would die.

Here was a society which had almost no vitality, its members pressed down by iron chains of law. They were forced to help each other. There, one was under regulations [that were] tremendous: regulations even how to breathe: how to wash face and hands; how to bathe; how to brush the teeth; and so on, to the moment of death. And beyond these regulations was the wonderful individualism of the Sannyasin. There he was. And every days new sect was rising amongst these strong, individualistic men and women. The ancient Sanskrit books tell about their standing out—of one woman who was very quaint, queer old woman of the ancient times; she always had some new thing; sometimes [she was] criticised, but always people were afraid of her, obeying her quietly. So, there were those great men and women of olden times.

And within this society, so oppressed by regulations, the power was in the hands of the priests. In the social scale, the highest caste is [that of] the priest, and that being a business—I do not know any other word, that is why I use the word "priest". It is not in the same sense as in this country, because our priest is not a man that teaches religion or philosophy. The business of a priest is to perform all these minute details of regulations which have been laid down The priest is the man who helps in these regulations. He marries you; to your funeral he comes to pray. So at all the ceremonies performed upon a man or a woman, the priest must be there. In society the ideal is marriage. [Everyone] must marry. It is the rule. Without marriage, man is not able to perform any religious ceremony; he is only half a man; [he] is not competent to officiate—even the priest himself cannot officiate as a priest, except he marries. Half a man is unfit within society.

Now, the power of the priests increased tremendously ... The general policy of our national law-givers was to give the priests this honour. They also had the same socialistic plan [you are] just ready to [try] that checked them from getting money. What [was] the motive? Social honour. Mind you, the priest in all countries is the highest in the social scale, so much so in India that the poorest Brahmin is greater than the greatest king in the country, by birth. He is the nobleman in India. But the law does not allow him ever to become rich. The law grinds him down to poverty—only, it gives him this honour. He cannot do a thousand things; and the higher is the caste in the social scale, the more restricted are its enjoyments. The higher the caste, the less the number of kinds of food that man can eat, the less the amount of food that man may eat, the less the number of occupations [he may] engage in. To you, his life would be only a perpetual train of hardships—nothing more than that. It is a perpetual discipline in eating, drinking, and everything; and all [penalties] which are required from the lower caste are required from the higher ten times more. The lowest man tells a lie; his fine is one dollar. A Brahmin, he must pay, say, a hundred dollars—[for] he knows better.

But this was a grand organisation to start with. Later on, the time came when they, these priests, began to get all the power in their hands; and at last they forgot the secret of their power: poverty. They were men whom society fed and clad so that they might simply learn and teach and think. Instead of that, they began to spread out their hands to clutch at the riches of society. They became "money-grabbers"—to use your word—and forgot all these things.

Then there was the second caste, the kingly caste, the military. Actual power was in their hands. Not only so—they have produced all of our great thinkers, and not the Brahmins. It is curious. All our great prophets, almost without one exception, belong to the kingly caste. The great man Krishna was also of that caste; Rama, he also, and all our great philosophers, almost all [sat] on the throne; thence came all the great philosophers of renunciation. From the throne came the voice that always cried, "Renounce". These military people were their kings; and they [also] were the philosophers; they were the speakers in the Upanishads. In their brains and their thought, they were greater than the priests they were more powerful, they were the kings - and yet the priests got all the power and: tried to tyrannise over them. And so that was going on: political competition between the two castes, the priests and the kings.

Another phenomenon is there. Those of you that have been to hear the first lecture already know that in India there are two great races: one is called the Aryan; the other, the non-Aryan. It is the Aryan race that has the three castes; but the whole of the rest are dubbed with one name, Shudras—no caste. They are not Aryans at all. (Many people came from outside of India, and they found the Shudras [there], the aborigines of the country). However it may be, these vast masses of non-Aryan people and the mixed people among them, they gradually became civilised and they began to scheme for the same rights as the Aryans. They wanted to enter their schools and their colleges; they wanted to take the sacred thread of the Aryans; they wanted to perform the same ceremonies as the Aryans, and wanted to have equal rights in religion and politics like the Aryans. And the Brahmin priest, he was the great antagonist of such claims. You see, it is the nature of priests in every country—they are the most conservative people, naturally. So long as it is a trade, it must be; it is to their interest to be conservative. So this tide of murmur outside the Aryan pale, the priests were trying to check with all their might. Within the Aryan pale, there was also a tremendous religious ferment, and [it was] mostly led by this military caste.

There was already the sect of Jains [who are a] conservative [force] in India [even] today. It is a very ancient sect. They declared against the validity of the scriptures of the Hindus, the Vedas. They wrote some books themselves, and they said: "Our books are the only original books, the only original Vedas, and the Vedas that now are going on under that name have been written by the Brahmins to dupe the people." And they also laid the same plan. You see, it is difficult for you to meet the arguments of the Hindus about the scriptures. They also claimed [that] the world has been created through those books. And they were written in the popular language. The Sanskrit, even then, had ceased to be a spoken language—[it had] just the same relation [to the spoken language] as Latin has to modern Italian. Now, they wrote all their books in Pali; and when a Brahmin said, "Why, your books are in Pali! ", they said, "Sanskrit is a language of the dead."

In their methods and manners they were different. For, you see, these Hindu scriptures, the Vedas, are a vast mass of accumulation—some of them crude—until you come to where religion is taught, only the spiritual. Now, that was the portion of the Vedas which these sects all claimed to preach. Then, there are three steps in the ancient Vedas: first, work; second, worship; third, knowledge. When a man purifies himself by work and worship, then God is within that man. He has realised He is already there. He only can have seen Him because the mind has become pure. Now, the mind can become purified by work and worship. That is all. Salvation is already there. We don't know it. Therefore, work, worship, and knowledge are the three steps. By work, they mean doing good to others. That has, of course, something in it, but mostly, as to the Brahmins, work means to perform these elaborate ceremonials: killing of cows and killing of bulls, killing of goats and all sorts of animals, that are taken fresh and thrown into the fire, and so on. "Now" declared the Jains, "that is no work at all, because injuring others can never be any good work"; and they said; "This is the proof that your Vedas are false Vedas, manufactured by the priests, because you do not mean to say that any good book will order us [to be] killing animals and doing these things. You do not believe it. So all this killing of animals and other things that you see in the Vedas, they have been written by the Brahmins, because they

alone are benefited. It is the priest only [who] pockets the money and goes home. So, therefore, it is all priest-craft."

It was one of their doctrines that there cannot be any God: "The priests have invented God, that the people may believe in God and pay them money. All nonsense! there is no God. There is nature and there are souls, and that is all. Souls have got entangled into this life and got round them the clothing of man you call a body. Now, do good work." But from that naturally came the doctrine that everything that is matter is vile. They are the first teachers of asceticism. If the body is the result of impurity, why, therefore the body is vile. If a man stands on one leg for some time—"All right, it is a punishment". If the head comes up bump against a wall—"Rejoice, it is a very good punishment". Some of the great founders of the [Franciscan Order]—one of them St. Francis—were going to a certain place to meet somebody; and St. Francis had one of his companions with him, and he began to talk as to whether [the person] would receive them or not, and this man suggested that possibly he would reject them. Said St. Francis: "That is not enough, brother, but if, when we go and knock at the door, the man comes and drives us away, that is not enough. But if he orders us to be bound and gives us a thorough whipping, even that is not enough. And then, if he binds us hand and foot and whips us until we bleed at every pore and throws us outside in the snow, that would be enough."

These [same] ascetic ideas prevailed at that time. These Jains were the first great ascetics; but they did some great work. "Don't injure any and do good to all that you can, and that is all the morality and ethics, and that is all the work there is, and the rest is all nonsense—the Brahmins created that. Throw it all away." And then they went to work and elaborated this one principle all through, and it is a most wonderful ideal: how all that we call ethics they simply bring out from that one great principle of non-injury and doing good.

This sect was at least five hundred years before Buddha, and he was five hundred and fifty years before Christ[1]. Now the whole of the animal creation they divide into five sections: the lowest have only one organ, that of touch; the next one, touch and taste; the next, touch, taste, and hearing; the next, touch, taste, hearing, and sight. And the next, the five organs. The first two, the one-organ and the two-organ, are invisible to the naked eye, and they art everywhere in water. A terrible thing, killing these [low forms of life]. This bacteriology has come into existence in the modern world only in the last twenty years and therefore nobody knew anything about it. They said, the lowest animals are only one-organ, touch; nothing else. The next greater [were] also invisible. And they all knew that if you boiled water these animals were ail killed. So these monks, if they died of thirst, they would never kill these animals by drinking water. But if [a monk] stands at your door and you give him a little boiled water, the sin is on

1. The dates of the Jaina and Buddha were not known accurately in those days.

you of killing the animals—and he will get the benefit. They carry these ideas to ludicrous extremes. For instance, in rubbing the body—if he bathes—he will have to kill numbers of animalcules; so he never bathes. He gets killed himself; he says that is all right. Life has no care for him; he will get killed and save life.

These Jains were there. There were various other sects of ascetics; and while this was going on, on the one hand, there was the political jealousy between the priests and the kings. And then these different dissatisfied sects [were] springing up everywhere. And there was the greater problem: the vast multitudes of people wanting the same rights as the Aryans, dying of thirst while the perennial stream of nature went flowing by them, and no right to drink a drop of water.

And that man was born—the great man Buddha. Most of you know about him, his life. And in spite of all the miracles and stories that generally get fastened upon any great man, in the first place, he is one of the most historical prophets of the world. Two are very historical: one, the most ancient, Buddha, and the other, Mohammed, because both friends and foes are agreed about them. So we are perfectly sure that there were such persons. As for the other persons, we have only to take for granted what the disciples say—nothing more. Our Krishna—you know, the Hindu prophet—he is very mythological. A good deal of his life, and everything about him, is written only by his disciples; and then there seem to be, sometimes, three or four men, who all loom into one. We do not know so clearly about many of the prophets; but as to this man, because both friends and foes write of him, we are sure that there was such a historical personage. And if we analyse through all the fables and reports of miracles and stories that generally are heaped upon a great man in this world, we will find an inside core; and all through the account of that man, he never did a thing for himself—never! How do you know that? Because, you see, when fables are fastened upon a man, the fables must be tinged with that man's general character. Not one fable tried to impute any vice or any immorality to the man. Even his enemies have favourable accounts.

When Buddha was born, he was so pure that whosoever looked at his face from a distance immediately gave up the ceremonial religion and became a monk and became saved. So the gods held a meeting. They said, "We are undone". Because most of the gods live upon the ceremonials. These sacrifices go to the gods and these sacrifices were all gone. The gods were dying of hunger and [the reason for] it was that their power was gone. So the gods said: "We must, anyhow, put this man down. He is too pure for our life." And then the gods came and said: "Sir, we come to ask you something. We want to make a great sacrifice and we mean to make a huge fire, and we have been seeking all over the world for a pure spot to light the fire on and could not find it, and now we have found it. If you will lie down, on your breast we will make the huge fire." "Granted," he says, "go on." And the gods built the fire high upon the breast of Buddha, and they

thought he was dead, and he was not. And then they went about and said, "We are undone." And all the gods began to strike him. No good. They could not kill him. From underneath, the voice comes: "Why [are you] making all these vain attempts?" "Whoever looks upon you becomes purified and is saved, and nobody is going to worship us." "Then, your attempt is vain, because purity can never be killed." This fable was written by his enemies, and yet throughout the fable the only blame that attaches to Buddha is that he was so great a teacher of purity.

About his doctrines, some of you know a little. It is his doctrines that appeal to many modern thinkers whom you call agnostics He was a great preacher of the brotherhood of mankind: "Aryan or non-Aryan, caste or no caste, and sects or no sects, every one has the same right to God and to religion and to freedom. Come in all of you." But as to other things, he was very agnostic. "Be practical." There came to him one day five young men, Brahmin born, quarrelling upon a question. They came to him to ask him the way to truth. And one said: "My people teach this, and this is the way to truth." The other said: "I have been taught this, and this is the only way to truth." "Which is the right way, sir?" "Well, you say your people taught this is truth and is the way to God?" "Yes." "But did you see God?" "No, sir." "Your father?" "No, sir." "Your grandfather?" "No, sir." "None of them saw God?" "No" "Well, and your teachers—neither [any] of them saw God?" "No." And he asked the same to the others. They all declared that none had seen God. "Well," said Buddha, "in a certain village came a young man weeping and howling and crying: 'Oh, I love her so! oh my, I love her so!' And then the villagers came; and the only thing he said was he loved her so. 'Who is she that you love?' 'I do not know.' 'Where does she live?' 'I do not know'—but he loved her so. 'How does she look?' 'That I do not know; but oh, I love her so.'" Then asked Buddha: "Young man, what would you call this young man?" "Why, sir, he was a fool!" And they all declared: "Why, sir, that young man was certainly a fool, to be crying and all that about a woman, to say he loved her so much and he never saw her or knew that she existed or anything?" "Are you not the same? You say that this God your father or your grandfather never saw, and now you are quarrelling upon a thing which neither you nor your ancestors ever knew, and you are trying to cut each other's throats about it." Then the young men asked: "What are we to do?" "Now, tell me: did your father ever teach that God is ever angry?" "No, sir." "Did your father ever teach that God is evil?" "No, sir, He is always pure." "Well, now, if you are pure and good and all that, do you not think that you will have more chance to come near to that God than by discussing all this and trying to cut each other's throats? Therefore, say I: be pure and be good; be pure and love everyone." And that was [all].

You see that non-killing of animals and charity towards animals was an already existing doctrine when he was born; but it was new with him—the breaking down of caste, that tremendous movement. And the other thing that was new: he took forty of his disciples and sent them all over the world, saying, "Go ye; mix with all races and nations and preach the excellent gospel for the good of all, for the benefit of all." And, of course, he was not molested by the Hindus. He died at a ripe old age. All his life he was a most stern man: he never yielded to weakness. I do not believe many of his doctrines; of course, I do not. I believe that the Vedantism of the old Hindus is much more thoughtful, is a grander philosophy of life. I like his method of work, but what I like [most] in that man is that, among all the prophets of mankind, here was a man who never had any cobwebs in his brain, and [who was] sane and strong. When kingdoms were at his feet, he was still the same man, maintaining "I am a man amongst men."

Why, the Hindus, they are dying to worship somebody. You will find, if you live long enough, I will be worshipped by our people. If you go there to teach them something, before you die you will be worshipped. Always trying to worship somebody. And living in that race, the world-honoured Buddha, he died always declaring that he was but man. None of his adulators could draw from him one remark that he was anything different from any other man.

Those last dying words of his always thrilled through my heart. He was old, he was suffering, he was near his death, and then came the despised outcaste—he lives on carrion, dead animals; the Hindus would not allow them to come into cities—one of these invited him to a dinner and he came with his disciples, and the poor Chanda, he wanted to treat this great teacher according to what he thought would be best; so he had a lot of pig's flesh and a lot of rice for him, and Buddha looked at that. The disciples were all [hesitating], and the Master said: "Well, do not eat, you will be hurt." But he quietly sat down and ate. The teacher of equality must eat the [outcaste] Chanda's dinner, even the pig's flesh. He sat down and ate it.

He was already dying. He found death coming on, and he asked, "Spread for me something under this tree, for I think the end is near." And he was there under the tree, and he laid himself down; he could not sit up any more. And the first thing he did, he said: "Go to that Chanda and tell him that he has been one of my greatest benefactors; for his meal, I am going to Nirvâna." And then several men came to be instructed, and a disciple said, "Do not go near now, the Master is passing away". And as soon as he heard it, the Lord said, "Let them come in". And somebody else came and the disciples would not [let them enter]. Again they came, and then the dying Lord said: "And O, thou Ananda, I am passing away. Weep not for me. Think not for me. I am gone. Work out diligently your own salvation. Each one of you is just what I am. I am nothing but one of you. What I am today is what I made myself. Do you struggle and make yourselves what I am..."

These are the memorable words of Buddha: "Believe not because an old book is produced as an authority. Believe not because your father said [you should] believe the same. Believe not because other people like you believe it. Test everything, try everything, and then believe it, and if you find it for the good of many, give it to all." And with these words, the Master passed away.

See the sanity of the man. No gods, no angels, no demons—nobody. Nothing of the kind. Stern, sane, every brain-cell perfect and complete, even at the moment of death. No delusion. I do not agree with many of his doctrines. You may not. But in my opinion—oh, if I had only one drop of that strength! The sanest philosopher the world ever saw. Its best and its sanest teacher. And never that man bent before even the power of the tyrannical Brahmins. Never that man bent. Direct and everywhere the same: weeping with the miserable, helping the miserable, singing with the singing, strong with the strong, and everywhere the same sane and able man.

And, of course, with all this I can [not] understand his doctrine. You know he denied that there was any soul in man—that is, in the Hindu sense of the word. Now, we Hindus all believe that there is something permanent in man, which is unchangeable and which is living through all eternity. And that in man we call Atman, which is without beginning and without end. And [we believe] that there is something permanent in nature [and that we call Brahman, which is also without beginning and without end]. He denied both of these. He said there is no proof of anything permanent. It is all a mere mass of change; a mass of thought in a continuous change is what you call a mind... The torch is leading the procession. The circle is a delusion. [Or take the example of a river.] It is a continuous river passing on; every moment a fresh mass of water passing on. So is this life; so is all body, so is all mind.

Well, I do not understand his doctrine—we Hindus never understood it. But I can understand the motive behind that. Oh, the gigantic motive! The Master says that selfishness is the great curse of the world; that we are selfish and that therein is the curse. There should be no motive for selfishness. You are [like a river] passing [on]—a continuous phenomenon. Have no God; have no soul; stand on your feet and do good for good's sake—neither for fear of punishment nor for [the sake of] going anywhere. Stand sane and motiveless. The motive is: I want to do good, it is good to do good. Tremendous! Tremendous! I do not sympathise with his metaphysics at all; but my mind is jealous when I think of the moral force. Just ask your minds which one of you can stand for one hour, able and daring like that man. I cannot for five minutes. I would become a coward and want a support. I am weak—a coward. And I warm to think of this tremendous giant. We cannot approach that strength. The world never saw [anything] compared to that strength. And I have not yet seen any other strength like that. We are all born cowards. If we can save ourselves [we care about nothing else]. Inside is the tremendous fear, the tremendous motive, all the time. Our own selfishness makes us the most arrant cowards; our own selfishness is the great cause of fear and cowardice. And there he stood: "Do good because it is good; ask no more questions; that is enough. A man made to do good by a fable, a story, a superstition—he will be doing evil as soon as the opportunity comes. That man alone is good who does good for good's sake, and that is the character of the man."

"And what remains of man?" was asked of the Master. "Everything—everything. But what is in the man? Not the body not the soul, but character. And that is left for all ages. All that have passed and died, they have left for us their characters, eternal possessions for the rest of humanity; and these characters are working—working all through." What of Buddha? What of Jesus of Nazareth? The world is full of their characters. Tremendous doctrine!

Let us come down a little—we have not come to the subject at all. (Laughter.) I must add not a few words more this evening…

And then, what he did. His method of work: organisation. The idea that you have today of church is his character. He left the church. He organised these monks and made them into a body. Even the voting by ballot is there five hundred and sixty years before Christ. Minute organization. The church was left and became a tremendous power, and did great missionary work in India and outside India. Then came, three hundred years after, two hundred years before Christ, the great emperor Asoka, as he has been called by your Western historians, the divinest of monarchs, and that man became entirely converted to the ideas of Buddha, and he was the greatest emperor of the world at that time. His grandfather was a contemporary of Alexander, and since Alexander's time, India had become more intimately connected with Greece… Every day in Central Asia some inscription or other is being found. India had forgotten all about Buddha and Asoka and everyone. But there were pillars, obelisks, columns, with ancient letters which nobody could read. Some of the old Mogul emperors declared they would give millions for anybody to read those; but nobody could. Within the last thirty years those have been read; they are all written in Pali.

The first inscription is: "…"

And then he writes this inscription, describing the terror and the misery of war; and then he became converted to religion. Then said he: "Henceforth let none of my descendants think of acquiring glory by conquering other races. If they want glory, let them help other races; let them send teachers of sciences and teachers of religion. A glory won by the sword is no glory at all." And next you find how he is sending missionaries even to Alexandria… You wonder that you find all over that part of the country sects rising immediately, called Theraputae, Essenes, and all those—extreme vegetarians, and so on. Now this great Emperor Asoka built hospitals for men and for animals. The inscriptions show they are ordering hospitals, building hospitals for men and for animals. That is to say, when an animal gets old, if I am poor and cannot keep it

any longer, I do not shoot it down for mercy. These hospitals are maintained by public charity. The coasting traders pay so much upon every hundredweight they sell, and all that goes to the hospital; so nobody is touched. If you have a cow that is old—anything—and do not want to keep it, send it to the hospital; they keep it, even down to rats and mice and anything you send. Only, our ladies try to kill these animals sometimes, you know. They go in large numbers to see them and they bring all sorts of cakes; the animals are killed many times by this food. He claimed that the animals should be as much under the protection of the government as man. Why should animals be allowed to be killed? [There] is no reason. But he says, before prohibiting the killing of animals for food even, [people] must be provided with all sorts of vegetables. So he sent and collected all kinds of vegetables and planted them in India; and then, as soon as these were introduced, the order was: henceforth, whosoever kills an animal will be punished. A government is to be a government; the animals must be protected also. What business has a man to kill a cow, a goat, or any other animal for food?

Thus Buddhism was and did become a great political power in India. Gradually it also fell to pieces—after all, this tremendous missionary enterprise. But to their credit it must be said, they never took up the sword to preach religion. Excepting the Buddhistic religion, there is not one religion in the world which could make one step without bloodshed—not one which could get a hundred thousand converts just by brain power alone. No, no. All through. And this is just what you are going to do in the Philippines. That is your method. Make them religious by the sword. That is what your priests are preaching. Conquer and kill them that they may get religion. A wonderful way of preaching religion!

You know how this great emperor Asoka was converted. This great emperor in his youth was not so good. [He had a brother.] And the two brothers quarrelled and the other brother defeated this one, and the emperor in vengeance wanted to kill him. The emperor got the news that he had taken shelter with a Buddhistic monk. Now, I have told you how our monks are very holy; no one would come near them. The emperor himself came. He said, "Deliver the man to me" Then the monk preached to him: "Vengeance is bad. Disarm anger with love. Anger is not cured by anger, nor hatred by hatred. Dissolve anger by love. Cure hatred by love. Friend, if for one evil thou returnest another, thou curest not the first evil, but only add one evil more to the world." The emperor said: "That is all right, fool that you are. Are you ready to give your life—to give your life for that man?" "Ready, sir." And he came out. And the emperor drew his sword, and he said: "Get ready." And just [as he] was going to strike, he looked at the face of the man. There was not a wink in those eyes. The emperor stopped, and he said: "Tell me, monk, where did you learn this strength, poor beggar, not to wink?" And then he preached again. "Go on, monk", he said, "That is nice", he said. Accordingly, he [fell under] the charm of the

Master—Buddha's charm.

There have been three things in Buddhism: the Buddha himself, his law, his church. At first it was so simple. When the Master died, before his death, they said: "What shall we do with you?" "Nothing." "What monuments shall we make over you?" He said: "Just make a little heap if you want, or just do not do anything." By and by, there arose huge temples and all the paraphernalia. The use of images was unknown before then. I say they were the first to use images. There are images of Buddha and all the saints, sitting about and praying. All this paraphernalia went on multiplying with this organisation. Then these monasteries became rich. The real cause of the downfall is here. Monasticism is all very good for a few; but when you preach it in such a fashion that every man or woman who has a mind immediately gives up social life, when you find over the whole of India monasteries, some containing a hundred thousand monks, sometimes twenty thousand monks in one building—huge, gigantic buildings, these monasteries, scattered all over India and, of course, centres of learning, and all that—who were left to procreate progeny, to continue the race? Only the weaklings. All the strong and vigorous minds went out. And then came national decay by the sheer loss of vigour.

I will tell you of this marvellous brotherhood. It is great. But theory and idea is one thing and actual working is another thing. The idea is very great: practicing nonresistance and all that, but if all of us go out in the street and practice non-resistance, there would be very little left in this city. That is to say, the idea is all right, but nobody has yet found a practical solution [as to] how to attain it.

There is something in caste, so far as it means blood; such a thing as heredity there is, certainly. Now try to [understand]—why do you not mix your blood with the Negroes, the American Indians? Nature will not allow you. Nature does not allow you to mix your blood with them. There is the unconscious working that saves the race. That was the Aryan's caste. Mind you, I do not say that they are not equal to us. They must have the same privileges and advantages, and everything; but we know that if certain races mix up, they become degraded. With all the strict caste of the Aryan and non-Aryan, that wall was thrown down to a certain extent, and hordes of these outlandish races came in with all their queer superstitions and manners and customs. Think of this: not decency enough to wear clothes, eating carrion, etc. But behind him came his fetish, his human sacrifice, his superstition, his diabolism. He kept it behind, [he remained] decent for a few years. After that he brought all [these] things out in front. And that was degrading to the whole race. And then the blood mixed; [intermarriages] took place with all sorts of unmixable races. The race fell down. But, in the long run it proved good. If you mix up with Negroes and American Indians, surely this civilisation will fall down. But hundreds and hundreds years after, out of this mixture will come a gigantic race once more, stronger than ever; but, for the time being,

you have to suffer. The Hindus believe—that is a peculiar belief, I think; and I do not know, I have nothing to say to the contrary, I have not found anything to the contrary—they believe there was only one civilised race: the Aryan. Until he gives his blood, no other race can be civilised. No teaching will do. The Aryan gives his blood to a race, and then it becomes civilised. Teaching alone will not do. He would be an example in your country: would you give your blood to the Negro race? Then he would get higher culture.

The Hindu loves caste. I may have little taint of that superstition—I do not know. I love the Master's ideal. Great! But, for me, I do not think that the working was very practical; and that was one of the great causes that led to the downfall of the Indian nation, in the long run. But then it brought about this tremendous fusion. Where so many different races are all fusing, mingling—one man white like you, or yellow, while another man as black as I am, and all grades between these two extremes, and each race keeping their customs, manners, and everything—in the long run a fusion is taking place, and out of this fusion surely will come a tremendous upheaval; but, for the time being, the giant must sleep. That is the effect of all such fusion.

When Buddhism went down that way, there came they inevitable reaction. There is but one entity in the wholes world. It is a unit world. The diversity is only eye-service. It is all one. The idea of unity and what we call monism—without duality—is the idea in India. This doctrine has: been always in India; [it was] brought forward whenever materialism and scepticism broke down everything. When Buddhism broke down everything by introducing all sorts of foreign barbarians into India—their manners and customs and things—there was a reaction, and that reaction was led by a young monk [Shankarâchârya]. And [instead] of preaching new doctrines and always thinking new thoughts and making sects, he brought back the Vedas to life: and modern Hinduism has thus an admixture of ancient Hinduism, over which the Vedantists predominate. But, you see, what once dies never comes back to life, and those ceremonials of [Hinduism] never came back to life. You will be astonished if I tell you that, according to the old ceremonials, he is not a good Hindu who does not eat beef. On certain occasions he must sacrifice a bull and eat it. That is disgusting now. However they may differ from each other in India, in that they are all one—they never eat beef. The ancient sacrifices and the ancient gods, they are all gone; modern India belongs to the spiritual part of the Vedas.

Buddhism was the first sect in India. They were the first to say: "Ours is the only path. Until you join our church, you cannot be saved." That was what they said: "It is the correct path." But, being of Hindu blood, they could not be such stony-hearted sectarians as in other countries. There will be salvation for you: nobody will go wrong for ever. No, no. [There was] too much of Hindu blood in them for that. The heart was not so stony as that. But you have to join them.

But the Hindu idea, you know, is not to join anybody. Wherever you are, that is a point from which you can start to the centre. All right. It—Hinduism—has this advantage: its secret is that doctrines and dogmas do not mean anything; what you are is what matters. If you talk all the best philosophies the world ever produced, [but] if you are a fool in your behaviour, they do not count; and if in your behaviour you are good, you have more chances. This being so, the Vedantist can wait for everybody. Vedantism teaches that there is but one existence and one thing real, and that is God. It is beyond all time and space and causation and everything. We can never define Him. We can never say what He is except [that] He is Absolute Existence, Absolute Knowledge, Absolute Blissfulness. He is the only reality. Of everything He is the reality; of you and me, of the wall and of [everything] everywhere. It is His knowledge upon which all our knowledge depends: it is His blissfulness upon which depends our pleasure; and He is the only reality. And when man realises this, he knows that "I am the only reality, because I am He—what is real in me is He also". So that when a man is perfectly pure and good and beyond all grossness, he finds, as Jesus found: "I and my Father are one." The Vedantist has patience to wait for everybody. Wherever you are, this is the highest: "I and my Father are one." Realise it. If an image helps, images are welcome. If worshipping a great man helps you, worship him. If worshipping Mohammed helps you, go on. Only be sincere; and if you are sincere, says Vedantism, you are sure to be brought to the goal. None will be left. your heart, which contains all truth, will unfold itself chapter after chapter, till you know the last truth, that "I and my Father are one". And what is salvation? To live with God. Where? Anywhere. Here this moment. One moment in infinite time is quite as good as any other moment. This is the old doctrine of the Vedas, you see. This was revived. Buddhism died out of India. It left its mark on their charity, its animals, etc. in India; and Vedantism is reconquering India from one end to the other.

THE RAMAYANA

Delivered at the Shakespeare Club, Pasadena, California, January 31, 1900

There are two great epics in the Sanskrit language, which are very ancient. Of course, there are hundreds of other epic poems. The Sanskrit language and literature have been continued down to the present day, although, for more than two thousand years, it has ceased to be a spoken language. I am now going to speak to you of the two most ancient epics, called the Râmâyana and the Mahâbhârata. They embody the manners and customs, the state of society, civilisation, etc., of the ancient Indians. The oldest of these epics is called Ramayana, "The Life of Râma". There was some poetical literature before this—most of the Vedas, the sacred books of the Hindus, are written in a sort of metre—but this book is held by common consent in India as the very beginning of poetry.

The name of the poet or sage was Vâlmiki. Later on, a great many poetical stories were fastened upon that ancient poet; and subsequently, it became a very general practice to attribute to his authorship very many verses that were not his. Notwithstanding all these interpolations, it comes down to us as a very beautiful arrangement, without equal in the literatures of the world.

There was a young man that could not in any way support his family. He was strong and vigorous and, finally, became a highway robber; he attacked persons in the street and robbed them, and with that money he supported his father, mother, wife, and children. This went on continually, until one day a great saint called Nârada was passing by, and the robber attacked him. The sage asked the robber, "Why are you going to rob me? It is a great sin to rob human beings and kill them. What do you incur all this sin for?" The robber said, "Why, I want to support my family with this money." "Now", said the sage, "do you think that they take a share of your sin also?" "Certainly they do," replied the robber. "Very good," said the sage, "make me safe by tying me up here, while you go home and ask your people whether they will share your sin in the same way as they share the money you make." The man accordingly went to his father, and asked, "Father, do you know how I support you?" He answered, "No, I do not." "I am a robber, and I kill persons and rob them." "What! you do that, my son? Get away! You outcast! "He then went to his mother and asked her, "Mother, do you know how I support you?" "No," she replied. "Through robbery and murder." "How horrible it is!" cried the mother. "But, do you partake in my sin?" said the son. "Why should I? I never committed a robbery," answered the mother. Then, he went to his wife and questioned her, "Do you know how I maintain you all?" "No," she responded. "Why, I am a highwayman," he rejoined, "and for years have been robbing people; that is how I support and maintain you all. And what I now want to know is, whether you are ready to share in my sin." "By no means. You are my husband, and it is your duty to support me."

The eyes of the robber were opened. "That is the way of the world—even my nearest relatives, for whom I have been robbing, will not share in my destiny." He came back to the place where he had bound the sage, unfastened his bonds, fell at his feet, recounted everything and said, "Save me! What can I do?" The sage said, "Give up your present course of life. You see that none of your family really loves you, so give up all these delusions. They will share your prosperity; but the moment you have nothing, they will desert you. There is none who will share in your evil, but they will all share in your good. Therefore worship Him who alone stands by us whether we are doing good or evil. He never leaves us, for love never drags down, knows no barter, no selfishness."

Then the sage taught him how to worship. And this man left everything and went into a forest. There he went on praying and meditating until he forgot himself so entirely that the ants came and built ant-hills around him and he was quite unconscious of it. After many years had passed, a voice came saying, "Arise, O sage! " Thus aroused he exclaimed, "Sage? I am a robber!" "No more 'robber'," answered the voice, "a purified sage art thou. Thine old name is gone. But now, since thy meditation was so deep and great that thou didst not re-mark even the ant-hills which surrounded thee, henceforth, thy name shall be Valmiki—'he that was born in the ant-hill'." So, he became a sage.

And this is how he became a poet. One day as this sage, Valmiki, was going to bathe in the holy river Ganga, he saw a pair of doves wheeling round and round, and kissing each other. The sage looked up and was pleased at the sight, but in a second an arrow whisked past him and killed the male dove. As the dove fell down on the ground, the female dove went on whirling round and round the dead body of its companion in grief. In a moment the poet became miserable, and look-ing round, he saw the hunter. "Thou art a wretch," he cried, "without the smallest mercy! Thy slaying hand would not even stop for love!" "What is this? What am I saying?" the poet thought to himself, "I have never spoken in this sort of way before." And then a voice came: "Be not afraid. This is poetry that is coming out of your mouth. Write the life of Rama in poetic language for the benefit of the world." And that is how the poem first began. The first verse sprang out of pits from the mouth of Valmiki, the first poet. And it was after that, that he wrote the beautiful Ramayana, "The Life of Rama".

There was an ancient Indian town called Ayodhyâ—and it exists even in modern times. The province in which it is still located is called Oudh, and most of you may have noticed it in the map of India. That was the ancient Ayodhya. There, in ancient times, reigned a king called Dasharatha. He had three queens, but the king had not any children by them. And like good Hindus, the king and the queens, all went on pilgrimag-es fasting and praying, that they might have children and, in good time, four sons were born. The eldest of them was Rama.

Now, as it should be, these four brothers were thoroughly educated in all branches of learning. To avoid future quarrels there was in ancient India a custom for the king in his own lifetime to nominate his eldest son as his successor, the Yu-varâja, young king, as he is called.

Now, there was another king, called Janaka, and this king had a beautiful daughter named Sitâ. Sita was found in a field; she was a daughter of the Earth, and was born without par-ents. The word "Sita" in ancient Sanskrit means the furrow made by a plough. In the ancient mythology of India you will find persons born of one parent only, or persons born without parents, born of sacrificial fire, born in the field, and so on—dropped from the clouds as it were. All those sorts of miraculous birth were common in the mythological lore of India.

Sita, being the daughter of the Earth, was pure and immac-ulate. She was brought up by King Janaka. When she was of a marriageable age, the king wanted to find a suitable husband for her.

There was an ancient Indian custom called Svayamvara, by which the princesses used to choose husbands. A number of princes from different parts of the country were invited, and the princess in splendid array, with a garland in her hand, and accompanied by a crier who enumerated the distinctive claims of each of the royal suitors, would pass in the midst of those assembled before her, and select the prince she liked for her husband by throwing the garland of flowers round his neck. They would then be married with much pomp and grandeur.

There were numbers of princes who aspired for the hand of Sita; the test demanded on this occasion was the breaking of a huge bow, called Haradhanu. All the princes put forth all their strength to accomplish this feat, but failed. Finally, Rama took the mighty bow in his hands and with easy grace broke it in twain. Thus Sita selected Rama, the son of King Dasharatha for her husband, and they were wedded with great rejoicings. Then, Rama took his bride to his home, and his old father thought that the time was now come for him to retire and appoint Rama as Yuvaraja. Everything was accordingly made ready for the ceremony, and the whole country was jubilant over the affair, when the younger queen Kaikeyi was remind-ed by one of her maidservants of two promises made to her by the king long ago. At one time she had pleased the king very much, and he offered to grant her two boons: "Ask any two things in my power and I will grant them to you," said he, but she made no request then. She had forgotten all about it; but the evil-minded maidservant in her employ began to work upon her jealousy with regard to Rama being installed on the throne, and insinuated to her how nice it would be for her if her own son had succeeded the king, until the queen was almost mad with jealousy. Then the servant suggested to her to ask from the king the two promised boons: one would be that her own son Bharata should be placed on the throne, and the other, that Rama should be sent to the forest and be exiled for fourteen years.

Now, Rama was the life and soul of the old king and when this wicked request was made to him, he as a king felt he could not go back on his word. So he did not know what to do. But Rama came to the rescue and willingly offered to give up the throne and go into exile, so that his father might not be guilty of falsehood. So Rama went into exile for fourteen years, accompanied by his loving wife Sita and his devoted brother Lakshmana, who would on no account be parted from him.

The Aryans did not know who were the inhabitants of these wild forests. In those days the forest tribes they called "mon-keys", and some of the so-called "monkeys", if unusually strong and powerful, were called "demons".

So, into the forest, inhabited by demons and monkeys, Rama, Lakshmana, and Sita went. When Sita had offered to accompany Rama, he exclaimed, "How can you, a princess, face hardships and accompany me into a forest full of unknown dangers!" But Sita replied, "Wherever Rama goes, there goes Sita. How can you talk of 'princess' and 'royal birth' to me? I go before you!" So, Sita went. And the younger brother, he also went with them. They penetrated far into the forest, until they reached the river Godâvari. On the banks of the river they built little cottages, and Rama and Lakshmana used to hunt deer and collect fruits. After they had lived thus for some time, one day there came a demon giantess. She was the sister of the giant king of Lanka (Ceylon). Roaming through the forest at will, she came across Rama, and seeing that he was a very handsome man, she fell in love with him at once. But Rama was the purest of men, and also he was a married man; so of course he could not return her love. In revenge, she went to her brother, the giant king, and told him all about the beautiful Sita, the wife of Rama.

Rama was the most powerful of mortals; there were no giants or demons or anybody else strong enough to conquer him. So, the giant king had to resort to subterfuge. He got hold of another giant who was a magician and changed him into a beautiful golden deer; and the deer went prancing round about the place where Rama lived, until Sita was fascinated by its beauty and asked Rama to go and capture the deer for her. Rama went into the forest to catch the deer, leaving his brother in charge of Sita. Then Lakshmana laid a circle of fire round the cottage, and he said to Sita, "Today I see something may befall you; and, therefore, I tell you not to go outside of this magic circle. Some danger may befall you if you do." In the meanwhile, Rama had pierced the magic deer with his arrow, and immediately the deer, changed into the form of a man, died.

Immediately, at the cottage was heard the voice of Rama, crying, "Oh, Lakshmana, come to my help!" and Sita said, "Lakshmana, go at once into the forest to help Rama!" "That is not Rama's voice," protested Lakshmana. But at the entreaties of Sita, Lakshmana had to go in search of Rama. As soon as he went away, the giant king, who had taken the form of a mendicant monk, stood at the gate and asked for alms. "Wait awhile," said Sita, "until my husband comes back and I will give you plentiful alms." "I cannot wait, good lady," said he, "I am very hungry, give me anything you have." At this, Sita, who had a few fruits in the cottage, brought them out. But the mendicant monk after many persuasions prevailed upon her to bring the alms to him, assuring her that she need have no fear as he was a holy person. So Sita came out of the magic circle, and immediately the seeming monk assumed his giant body, and grasping Sita in his arms he called his magic chariot, and putting her therein, he fled with the weeping Sita. Poor Sita! She was utterly helpless, nobody, was there to come to her aid. As the giant was carrying her away, she took off a few of the ornaments from her arms and at intervals dropped them to the grounds

She was taken by Râvana to his kingdom, Lanka, the island of Ceylon. He made peals to her to become his queen, and

tempted her in many ways to accede to his request. But Sita who was chastity itself, would not even speak to the giant; and he to punish her, made her live under a tree, day and night, until she should consent to be his wife.

When Rama and Lakshmana returned to the cottage and found that Sita was not there, their grief knew no bounds. They could not imagine what had become of her. The two brothers went on, seeking, seeking everywhere for Sita, but could find no trace of her. After long searching, they came across a group of "monkeys", and in the midst of them was Hanumân, the "divine monkey". Hanuman, the best of the monkeys, became the most faithful servant of Rama and helped him in rescuing Sita, as we shall see later on. His devotion to Rama was so great that he is still worshipped by the Hindus as the ideal of a true servant of the Lord. You see, by the "monkeys" and "demons" are meant the aborigines of South India.

So, Rama, at last, fell in with these monkeys. They told him that they had seen flying through the sky a chariot, in which was seated a demon who was carrying away a most beautiful lady, and that she was weeping bitterly, and as the chariot passed over their heads she dropped one of her ornaments to attract their attention. Then they showed Rama the ornament. Lakshmana took up the ornament, and said, "I do not know whose ornament this is." Rama took it from him and recognised it at once, saying, "Yes, it is Sita's." Lakshmana could not recognise the ornament, because in India the wife of the elder brother was held in so much reverence that he had never looked upon the arms and the neck of Sita. So you see, as it was a necklace, he did not know whose it was. There is in this episode a touch of the old Indian custom. Then, the monkeys told Rama who this demon king was and where he lived, and then they all went to seek for him.

Now, the monkey-king Vâli and his younger brother Sugriva were then fighting amongst themselves for the kingdom. The younger brother was helped by Rama, and he regained the kingdom from Vali, who had driven him away; and he, in return, promised to help Rama. They searched the country all round, but could not find Sita. At last Hanuman leaped by one bound from the coast of India to the island of Ceylon, and there went looking all over Lanka for Sita, but nowhere could he find her.

You see, this giant king had conquered the gods, the men, in fact the whole world; and he had collected all the beautiful women and made them his concubines. So, Hanuman thought to himself, "Sita cannot be with them in the palace. She would rather die than be in such a place." So Hanuman went to seek for her elsewhere. At last, he found Sita under a tree, pale and thin, like the new moon that lies low in the horizon. Now Hanuman took the form of a little monkey and settled on the tree, and there he witnessed how giantesses sent by Ravana came and tried to frighten Sita into submission, but she would not even listen to the name of the giant king.

Then, Hanuman came nearer to Sita and told her how he became the messenger of Rama, who had sent him to find out where Sita was; and Hanuman showed to Sita the signet ring which Rama had given as a token for establishing his identity. He also informed her that as soon as Rama would know her whereabouts, he would come with an army and conquer the giant and recover her. However, he suggested to Sita that if she wished it, he would take her on his shoulders and could with one leap clear the ocean and get back to Rama. But Sita could not bear the idea, as she was chastity itself, and could not touch the body of any man except her husband. So, Sita remained where she was. But she gave him a jewel from her hair to carry to Rama; and with that Hanuman returned.

Learning everything about Sita from Hanuman, Rama collected an army, and with it marched towards the southernmost point of India. There Rama's monkeys built a huge bridge, called Setu-Bandha, connecting India with Ceylon. In very low water even now it is possible to cross from India to Ceylon over the sand-banks there.

Now Rama was God incarnate, otherwise, how could he have done all these things? He was an Incarnation of God, according to the Hindus. They in India believe him to be the seventh Incarnation of God.

The monkeys removed whole hills, placed them in the sea and covered them with stones and trees, thus making a huge embankment. A little squirrel, so it is said, was there rolling himself in the sand and running backwards and forwards on to the bridge and shaking himself. Thus in his small way he was working for the bridge of Rama by putting in sand. The monkeys laughed, for they were bringing whole mountains, whole forests, huge loads of sand for the bridge—so they laughed at the little squirrel rolling in the sand and then shaking himself. But Rama saw it and remarked: "Blessed be the little squirrel; he is doing his work to the best of his ability, and he is therefore quite as great as the greatest of you." Then he gently stroked the squirrel on the back, and the marks of Rama's fingers, running lengthways, are seen on the squirrel's back to this day.

Now, when the bridge was finished, the whole army of monkeys, led by Rama and his brother entered Ceylon. For several months afterwards tremendous war and bloodshed followed. At last, this demon king, Ravana, was conquered and killed; and his capital, with all the palaces and everything, which were entirely of solid gold, was taken. In far-away villages in the interior of India, when I tell them that I have been in Ceylon, the simple folk say, "There, as our books tell, the houses are built of gold." So, all these golden cities fell into the hands of Rama, who gave them over to Vibhishana, the younger brother of Ravana, and seated him on the throne in the place of his brother, as a return for the valuable services rendered by him to Rama during the war.

Then Rama with Sita and his followers left Lanka. But there ran a murmur among the followers. "The test! The test!" they cried, "Sita has not given the test that she was perfectly pure in Ravana's household. "Pure! she is chastity itself" exclaimed Rama. "Never mind! We want the test," persisted the people. Subsequently, a huge sacrificial fire was made ready, into which Sita had to plunge herself. Rama was in agony, thinking that Sita was lost; but in a moment, the God of fire himself appeared with a throne upon his head, and upon the throne was Sita. Then, there was universal rejoicing, and everybody was satisfied.

Early during the period of exile, Bharata, the younger brother had come and informed Rama, of the death of the old king and vehemently insisted on his occupying the throne. During Rama's exile Bharata would on no account ascend the throne and out of respect placed a pair of Rama's wooden shoes on it as a substitute for his brother. Then Rama returned to his capital, and by the common consent of his people he became the king of Ayodhya.

After Rama regained his kingdom, he took the necessary vows which in olden times the king had to take for the benefit of his people. The king was the slave of his people, and had to bow to public opinion, as we shall see later on. Rama passed a few years in happiness with Sita, when the people again began to murmur that Sita had been stolen by a demon and carried across the ocean. They were not satisfied with the former test and clamoured for another test, otherwise she must be banished.

In order to satisfy the demands of the people, Sita was banished, and left to live in the forest, where was the hermitage of the sage and poet Valmiki. The sage found poor Sita weeping and forlorn, and hearing her sad story, sheltered her in his Âshrama. Sita was expecting soon to become a mother, and she gave birth to twin boys. The poet never told the children who they were. He brought them up together in the Brahmachârin life. He then composed the poem known as Ramayana, set it to music, and dramatised it.

The drama, in India, was a very holy thing. Drama and music are themselves held to be religion. Any song—whether it be a love-song or otherwise—if one's whole soul is in that song, one attains salvation, one has nothing else to do. They say it leads to the same goal as meditation.

So, Valmiki dramatised "The Life of Rama", and taught Rama's two children how to recite and sing it.

There came a time when Rama was going to perform a huge sacrifice, or Yajna, such as the old kings used to celebrate. But no ceremony in India can be performed by a married man without his wife: he must have the wife with him, the Sahadharmini, the "co-religionist"—that is the expression for a wife. The Hindu householder has to perform hundreds of ceremonies, but not one can be duly performed according to the Shâstras, if he has not a wife to complement it with her part in it.

Now Rama's wife was not with him then, as she had been banished. So, the people asked him to marry again. But at this request Rama for the first time in his life stood against the people. He said, "This cannot be. My life is Sita's." So, as a substitute, a golden statue of Sita was made, in order that the; ceremony could be accomplished. They arranged even a dramatic entertainment, to enhance the religious feeling in this great festival. Valmiki, the great sage-poet, came with his pupils, Lava and Kusha, the unknown sons of Rama. A stage had been erected and everything was ready for the performance. Rama and his brothers attended with all his nobles and his people—a vast audience. Under the direction of Valmiki, the life of Rama was sung by Lava and Kusha, who fascinated the whole assembly by their charming voice and appearance. Poor Rama was nearly maddened, and when in the drama, the scene of Sita's exile came about, he did not know what to do. Then the sage said to him, "Do not be grieved, for I will show you Sita." Then Sita was brought upon the stage and Rama delighted to see his wife. All of a sudden, the old murmur arose: "The test! The test!" Poor Sita was so terribly overcome by the repeated cruel slight on her reputation that it was more than she could bear. She appealed to the gods to testify to her innocence, when the Earth opened and Sita exclaimed, "Here is the test", and vanished into the bosom of the Earth. The people were taken aback at this tragic end. And Rama was overwhelmed with grief.

A few days after Sita's disappearance, a messenger came to Rama from the gods, who intimated to him that his mission on earth was finished and he was to return to heaven. These tidings brought to him the recognition of his own real Self. He plunged into the waters of Sarayu, the mighty river that laved his capital, and joined Sita in the other world.

This is the great, ancient epic of India. Rama and Sita are the ideals of the Indian nation. All children, especially girls, worship Sita. The height of a woman's ambition is to be like Sita, the pure, the devoted, the all-suffering! When you study these characters, you can at once find out how different is the ideal in India from that of the West. For the race, Sita stands as the ideal of suffering. The West says, "Do! Show your power by doing." India says, "Show your power by suffering." The West has solved the problem of how much a man can have: India has solved the problem of how little a man can have. The two extremes, you see. Sita is typical of India—the idealised India. The question is not whether she ever lived, whether the story is history or not, we know that the ideal is there. There is no other Paurânika story that has so permeated the whole nation, so entered into its very life, and has so tingled in every drop of blood of the race, as this ideal of Sita. Sita is the name in India for everything that is good, pure and holy—everything that in woman we call womanly. If a priest has to bless a woman he says, "Be Sita!" If he blesses a child, he says "Be Sita!" They are all children of Sita, and are struggling to be Sita, the patient, the all-suffering, the ever-faithful, the ever-pure wife. Through all this suffering she experiences, there is not one harsh word against Rama. She takes it as her own duty, and performs her own part in it. Think of the ter-

rible injustice of her being exiled to the forest! But Sita knows no bitterness. That is, again, the Indian ideal. Says the ancient Buddha, "When a man hurts you, and you turn back to hurt him, that would not cure the first injury; it would only create in the world one more wickedness." Sita was a true Indian by nature; she never returned injury.

Who knows which is the truer ideal? The apparent power and strength, as held in the West, or the fortitude in suffering, of the East?

The West says, "We minimise evil by conquering it." India says, "We destroy evil by suffering, until evil is nothing to us, it becomes positive enjoyment." Well, both are great ideals. Who knows which will survive in the long run? Who knows which attitude will really most benefit humanity? Who knows which will disarm and conquer animality? Will it be suffering, or doing?

In the meantime, let us not try to destroy each other's ideals. We are both intent upon the same work, which is the annihilation of evil. You take up your method; let us take up our method. Let us not destroy the ideal. I do not say to the West, "Take up our method." Certainly not. The goal is the same, but the methods can never be the same. And so, after hearing about the ideals of India, I hope that you will say in the same breath to India, "We know, the goal, the ideal, is all right for us both. You follow your own ideal. You follow your method in your own way, and Godspeed to you!" My message in life is to ask the East and West not to quarrel over different ideals, but to show them that the goal is the same in both cases, however opposite it may appear. As we wend our way through this mazy vale of life, let us bid each other Godspeed.

THE MAHABHARATA

Delivered at the Shakespeare Club, Pasadena, California, February 1, 1900

The other epic about which I am going to speak to you this evening, is called the Mahâbhârata. It contains the story of a race descended from King Bharata, who was the son of Dushyanta and Shakuntalâ. Mahâ means great, and Bhârata means the descendants of Bharata, from whom India has derived its name, Bhârata. Mahabharata means Great India, or the story of the great descendants of Bharata. The scene of this epic is the ancient kingdom of the Kurus, and the story is based on the great war which took place between the Kurus and the Panchâlas. So the region of the quarrel is not very big. This epic is the most popular one in India; and it exercises the same authority in India as Homer's poems did over the Greeks. As ages went on, more and more matter was added to it, until it has become a huge book of about a hundred thousand couplets. All sorts of tales, legends and myths, philosophical treatises, scraps of history, and various discussions have been added to it from time to time, until it is a vast, gigantic mass of literature; and through it all runs the old, original story. The central story of the Mahabharata is of a war between two families of cousins, one family, called the Kauravas, the other the Pândavas—for the empire of India.

The Aryans came into India in small companies. Gradually, these tribes began to extend, until, at last, they became the undisputed rulers of India and then arose this fight to gain the mastery, between two branches of the same family. Those of you who have studied the Gîtâ know how the book opens with a description of the battlefield, with two armies arrayed one against the other. That is the war of the Mahabharata.

There were two brothers, sons of the emperor. The elder one was called Dhritarâshtra, and the other was called Pându. Dhritarashtra, the elder one, was born blind. According to Indian law, no blind, halt, maimed, consumptive, or any other constitutionally diseased person, can inherit. He can only get a maintenance. So, Dhritarashtra could not ascend the throne, though he was the elder son, and Pandu became the emperor.

Dhritarashtra had a hundred sons, and Pandu had only five. After the death of Pandu at an early age, Dhritarashtra became king of the Kurus and brought up the sons of Pandu along with his own children. When they grew up they were placed under the tutorship of the great priestwarrior, Drona, and were well trained in the various material arts and sciences befitting princes. The education of the princes being finished, Dhritarashtra put Yudhishthira, the eldest of the sons of Pandu, on the throne of his father. The sterling virtues of Yudhishthira and the valour and devotion of his other brothers aroused jealousies in the hearts of the sons of the blind king, and at the instigation of Duryodhana, the eldest of them, the five Pandava brothers were prevailed upon to visit Vâranâvata, on the plea of a religious festival that was being held there. There they were accommodated in a palace made under Duryodhana's instructions, of hemp, resin, and lac, and other inflammable materials, which were subsequently set fire to secretly. But the good Vidura, the step-brother of Dhritarashtra, having become cognisant of the evil intentions of Duryodhana and his party, had warned the Pandavas of the plot, and they managed to escape without anyone's knowledge. When the Kurus saw the house was reduced to ashes, they heaved a sigh of relief and thought all obstacles were now removed out of their path. Then the children of Dhritarashtra got hold of the kingdom. The five Pandava brothers had fled to the forest with their mother, Kunti. They lived there by begging, and went about in disguise giving themselves out as Brâhmana students. Many were the hardships and adventures they encountered in the wild forests, but their fortitude of mind, and strength, and valour made them conquer all dangers. So things went on until they came to hear of the approaching marriage of the princess of a neighbouring country.

I told you last night of the peculiar form of the ancient Indian marriage. It was called Svayamvara, that is, the choosing of the husband by the princess. A great gathering of princes and nobles assembled, amongst whom the princess would choose her husband. Preceded by her trumpeters and heralds she would approach, carrying a garland of flowers in her hand. At the throne of each candidate for her hand, the praises of that prince and all his great deeds in battle would be declared by the heralds. And when the princess decided which prince she desired to have for a husband, she would signify the fact by throwing the marriage-garland round his neck. Then the ceremony would turn into a wedding. King Drupada was a great king, king of the Panchalas, and his daughter, Draupadi, famed far and wide for her beauty and accomplishments, was going to choose a hero.

At a Svayamvara there was always a great feat of arms or something of the kind. On this occasion, a mark in the form of a fish was set up high in the sky; under that fish was a wheel with a hole in the centre, continually turning round, and beneath was a tub of water. A man looking at the reflection of the fish in the tub of water was asked to send an arrow and hit the eye of the fish through the Chakra or wheel, and he who succeeded would be married to the princess. Now, there came kings and princes from different parts of India, all anxious to win the hand of the princess, and one after another they tried their skill, and every one of them failed to hit the mark.

You know, there are four castes in India: the highest caste is that of the hereditary priest, the Brâhmana; next is the caste of the Kshatriya, composed of kings and fighters; next, the Vaishyas, the traders or businessmen, and then Shudras, the servants. Now, this princess was, of course, a Kshatriya, one of the second caste.

When all those princes failed in hitting the mark, then the son of King Drupada rose up in the midst of the court and said: "The Kshatriya, the king caste has failed; now the contest is open to the other castes. Let a Brahmana, even a Shudra, take part in it; whosoever hits the mark, marries Draupadi."

Among the Brahmanas were seated the five Pandava brothers. Arjuna, the third brother, was the hero of the bow. He arose and stepped forward. Now, Brahmanas as a caste are very quiet and rather timid people. According to the law, they must not touch a warlike weapon, they must not wield a sword, they must not go into any enterprise that is dangerous. Their life is one of contemplation, study, and control of the inner nature. Judge, therefore, how quiet and peaceable a people they are. When the Brahmanas saw this man get up, they thought this man was going to bring the wrath of the Kshatriyas upon them, and that they would all be killed. So they tried to dissuade him, but Arjuna did not listen to them, because he was a soldier. He lifted the bow in his hand, strung it without any effort, and drawing it, sent the arrow right through the wheel and hit the eye of the fish.

Then there was great jubilation. Draupadi, the princess, approached Arjuna and threw the beautiful garland of flowers over his head. But there arose a great cry among the princes, who could not bear the idea that this beautiful princess who was a Kshatriya should be won by a poor Brahmana, from among this huge assembly of kings and princes. So, they wanted to fight Arjuna and snatch her from him by force. The brothers had a tremendous fight with the warriors, but held their own, and carried off the bride in triumph.

The five brothers now returned home to Kunti with the princess. Brahmanas have to live by begging. So they, who lived as Brahmanas, used to go out, and what they got by begging they brought home and the mother divided it among them. Thus the five brothers, with the princess, came to the cottage where the mother lived. They shouted out to her jocosely, "Mother, we have brought home a most wonderful alms today." The mother replied, "Enjoy it in common, all of you, my children." Then the mother seeing the princess, exclaimed, "Oh! what have I said! It is a girl!" But what could be done! The mother's word was spoken once for all. It must not be disregarded. The mother's words must be fulfilled. She could not be made to utter an untruth, as she never had done so. So Draupadi became the common wife of all the five brothers.

Now, you know, in every society there are stages of development. Behind this epic there is a wonderful glimpse of the ancient historic times. The author of the poem mentions the fact of the five brothers marrying the same woman, but he tries to gloss it over, to find an excuse and a cause for such an act: it was the mother's command, the mother sanctioned this strange betrothal, and so on. You know, in every nation there has been a certain stage in society that allowed polyandry—all the brothers of a family would marry one wife in common. Now, this was evidently a glimpse of the past polyandrous stage.

In the meantime, the brother of the princess was perplexed in his mind and thought: "Who are these people? Who is this man whom my sister is going to marry? They have not any chariots, horses, or anything. Why, they go on foot!" So he had followed them at a distance, and at night overheard their conversation and became fully convinced that they were really Kshatriyas. Then King Drupada came to know who they were and was greatly delighted.

Though at first much objection was raised, it was declared by Vyâsa that such a marriage was allowable for these princes, and it was permitted. So the king Drupada had to yield to this polyandrous marriage, and the princess was married to the five sons of Pandu.

Then the Pandavas lived in peace and prosperity and became more powerful every day. Though Duryodhana and his party conceived of fresh plots to destroy them, King Dhritarashtra was prevailed upon by the wise counsels of the elders to make peace with the Pandavas; and so he invited them home amidst the rejoicings of the people and gave them half of the kingdom. Then, the five brothers built for themselves a beautiful city, called Indraprastha, and extended their dominions, laying all the people under tribute to them. Then the eldest, Yudhishthira, in order to declare himself emperor over all the kings of ancient India, decided to perform a Râjasuya Yajna or Imperial Sacrifice, in which the conquered kings would have

to come with tribute and swear allegiance, and help the performance of the sacrifice by personal services. Shri Krishna, who had become their friend and a relative, came to them and approved of the idea. But there alas one obstacle to its performance. A king, Jarâsandha by name, who intended to offer a sacrifice of a hundred kings, had eighty-six of them kept as captives with him. Shri Krishna counselled an attack on Jarasandha. So he, Bhima, and Arjuna challenged the king, who accepted the challenge and was finally conquered by Bhima after fourteen days, continuous wrestling. The captive kings were then set free.

Then the four younger brothers went out with armies on a conquering expedition, each in a different direction, and brought all the kings under subjection to Yudhishthira. Returning, they laid all the vast wealth they secured at the feet of the eldest brother to meet the expenses of the great sacrifice.

So, to this Rajasuya sacrifice all the liberated kings came, along with those conquered by the brothers, and rendered homage to Yudhishthira. King Dhritarashtra and his sons were also invited to come and take a share in the performance of the sacrifice. At the conclusion of the sacrifice, Yudhishthira was crowned emperor, and declared as lord paramount. This was the sowing of the future feud. Duryodhana came back from the sacrifice filled with jealousy against Yudhishthira, as their sovereignty and vast splendour and wealth were more than he could bear; and so he devised plans to effect their fall by guile, as he knew that to overcome them by force was beyond his power. This king, Yudhishthira, had the love of gambling, and he was challenged at an evil hour to play dice with Shakuni, the crafty gambler and the evil genius of Duryodhana. In ancient India, if a man of the military caste was challenged to fight, he must at any price accept the challenge to uphold his honour. And if he was challenged to play dice, it was a point of honour to play, and dishonourable to decline the challenge. King Yudhishthira, says the Epic, was the incarnation of all virtues. Even he, the great sage-king, had to accept the challenge. Shakuni and his party had made false dice. So Yudhishthira lost game after game, and stung with his losses, he went on with the fatal game, staking everything he had, and losing all, until all his possessions, his kingdom and everything, were lost. The last stage came when, under further challenge, he had no other resources left but to stake his brothers, and then himself, and last of all, the fair Draupadi, and lost all. Now they were completely at the mercy of the Kauravas, who cast all sorts of insults upon them, and subjected Draupadi to most inhuman treatment. At last through the intervention of the blind king, they got their liberty, and were asked to return home and rule their kingdom. But Duryodhana saw the danger and forced his father to allow one more throw of the dice in which the party which would lose, should retire to the forests for twelve years, and then live unrecognised in a city for one year; but if they were found out, the same term of exile should have to be undergone once again and then only the kingdom was to be restored to the exiled.

This last game also Yudhishthira lost, and the five Pandava brothers retired to the forests with Draupadi, as homeless exiles. They lived in the forests and mountains for twelve years. There they performed many deeds of virtue and valour, and would go out now and then on a long round of pilgrimages, visiting many holy places. That part of the poem is very interesting and instructive, and various are the incidents, tales, and legends with which this part of the book is replete. There are in it beautiful and sublime stories of ancient India, religious and philosophical. Great sages came to see the brothers in their exile and narrated to them many telling stories of ancient India, so as to make them bear lightly the burden of their exile. One only I will relate to you here.

There was a king called Ashvapati. The king had a daughter, who was so good and beautiful that she was called Sâvitri, which is the name of a sacred prayer of the Hindus. When Savitri grew old enough, her father asked her to choose a husband for herself. These ancient Indian princesses were very independent, you see, and chose their own princely suitors.

Savitri consented and travelled in distant regions, mounted in a golden chariot, with her guards and aged courtiers to whom her father entrusted her, stopping at different courts, and seeing different princes, but not one of them could win the heart of Savitri. They came at last to a holy hermitage in one of those forests that in ancient India were reserved for animals, and where no animals were allowed to be killed. The animals lost the fear of man — even the fish in the lakes came and took food out of the hand. For thousands of years no one had killed anything therein. The sages and the aged went there to live among the deer and the birds. Even criminals were safe there. When a man got tired of life, he would go to the forest; and in the company of sages, talking of religion and meditating thereon, he passed the remainder of his life.

Now it happened that there was a king, Dyumatsena, who was defeated by his enemies and was deprived of his kingdom when he was struck with age and had lost his sight. This poor, old, blind king, with his queen and his son, took refuge in the forest and passed his life in rigid penance. His boy's name was Satyavân.

It came to pass that after having visited all the different royal courts, Savitri at last came to this hermitage, or holy place. Not even the greatest king could pass by the hermitages, or Âshramas as they were called, without going to pay homage to the sages, for such honour and respect was felt for these holy men. The greatest emperor of India would be only too glad to trace his descent to some sage who lived in a forest, subsisting on roots and fruits, and clad in rags. We are all children of sages. That is the respect that is paid to religion. So, even kings, when they pass by the hermitages, feel honoured to go in and pay their respects to the sages. If they approach on horseback, they descend and walk as they advance towards them. If they arrive in a chariot, chariot and armour must be left outside when they enter. No fighting man can enter unless he comes

in the manner of a religious man, quiet and gentle.

So Savitri came to this hermitage and saw there Satyavan, the hermit's son, and her heart was conquered. She had escaped all the princes of the palaces and the courts, but here in the forest-refuge of King Dyumatsena, his son, Satyavan, stole her heart.

When Savitri returned to her father's house, he asked her, "Savitri, dear daughter, speak. Did you see anybody whom you would like to marry " Then softly with blushes, said Savitri, "Yes, father." "What is the name of the prince?" "He is no prince, but the son of King Dyumatsena who has lost his kingdom — a prince without a patrimony, who lives a monastic life, the life of a Sannyasin in a forest, collecting roots and herbs, helping and feeding his old father and mother, who live in a cottage."

On hearing this the father consulted the Sage Nârada, who happened to be then present there, and he declared it was the most ill-omened choice that was ever made. The king then asked him to explain why it was so. And Narada said, "Within twelve months from this time the young man will die." Then the king started with terror, and spoke, "Savitri, this young man is going to die in twelve months, and you will become a widow: think of that! Desist from your choice, my child, you shall never be married to a short-lived and fated bridegroom." "Never mind, father; do not ask me to marry another person and sacrifice the chastity of mind, for I love and have accepted in my mind that good and brave Satyavan only as my husband. A maiden chooses only once, and she never departs from her troth." When the king found that Savitri was resolute in mind and heart, he complied. Then Savitri married prince Satyavan, and she quietly went from the palace of her father into the forest, to live with her chosen husband and help her husband's parents. Now, though Savitri knew the exact date when Satyavan was to die, she kept it hidden from him. Daily he went into the depths of the forest, collected fruits and flowers, gathered faggots, and then came back to the cottage, and she cooked the meals and helped the old people. Thus their lives went on until the fatal day came near, and three short days remained only. She took a severe vow of three nights' penance and holy fasts, and kept her hard vigils. Savitri spent sorrowful and sleepless nights with fervent prayers and unseen tears, till the dreaded morning dawned. That day Savitri could not bear him out of her sight, even for a moment. She begged permission from his parents to accompany her husband, when he went to gather the usual herbs and fuel, and gaining their consent she went. Suddenly, in faltering accents, he complained to his wife of feeling faint, "My head is dizzy, and my senses reel, dear Savitri, I feel sleep stealing over me; let me rest beside thee for a while." In fear and trembling she replied, "Come, lay your head upon my lap, my dearest lord." And he laid his burning head in the lap of his wife, and ere long sighed and expired. Clasping him to her, her eyes flowing with tears, there she sat in the lonesome forest, until the emissaries of Death approached to take away the soul of Satyavan. But they could not come near to the place where Savitri sat with the dead body of her husband, his head resting in her lap. There was a zone of fire surrounding her, and not one of the emissaries of Death could come within it. They all fled back from it, returned to King Yama, the God of Death, and told him why they could not obtain the soul of this man.

Then came Yama, the God of Death, the Judge of the dead. He was the first man that died—the first man that died on earth—and he had become the presiding deity over all those that die. He judges whether, after a man has died, he is to be punished or rewarded. So he came himself. Of course, he could go inside that charmed circle as he was a god. When he came to Savitri, he said, "Daughter, give up this dead body, for know, death is the fate of mortals, and I am the first of mortals who died. Since then, everyone has had to die. Death is the fate of man." Thus told, Savitri walked off, and Yama drew the soul out. Yama having possessed himself of the soul of the young man proceeded on his way. Before he had gone far, he heard footfalls upon the dry leaves. He turned back. "Savitri, daughter, why are you following me? This is the fate of all mortals." "I am not following thee, Father," replied Savitri, "but this is, also, the fate of woman, she follows where her love takes her, and the Eternal Law separates not loving man and faithful wife." Then said the God of Death, "Ask for any boon, except the life of your husband." "If thou art pleased to grant a boon, O Lord of Death, I ask that my father-in-law may be cured of his blindness and made happy." "Let thy pious wish be granted, duteous daughter." And then the King of Death travelled on with the soul of Satyavan. Again the same footfall was heard from behind. He looked round. "Savitri, my daughter, you are still following me?" "Yes my Father; I cannot help doing so; I am trying all the time to go back, but the mind goes after my husband and the body follows. The soul has already gone, for in that soul is also mine; and when you take the soul, the body follows, does it not?" "Pleased am I with your words, fair Savitri. Ask yet another boon of me, but it must not be the life of your husband." "Let my father-in-law regain his lost wealth and kingdom, Father, if thou art pleased to grant another supplication." "Loving daughter," Yama answered, "this boon I now bestow; but return home, for living mortal cannot go with King Yama." And then Yama pursued his way. But Savitri, meek and faithful still followed her departed husband. Yama again turned back. "Noble Savitri, follow not in hopeless woe." "I cannot choose but follow where thou takest my beloved one." "Then suppose, Savitri, that your husband was a sinner and has to go to hell. In that case goes Savitri with the one she loves?" "Glad am I to follow where he goes be it life or death, heaven or hell," said the loving wife. "Blessed are your words, my child, pleased am I with you, ask yet another boon, but the dead come not to life again." "Since you so permit me, then, let the imperial line of my father-in-law be not destroyed; let his kingdom descend to Satyavan's sons." And then the God of Death smiled. "My

daughter, thou shalt have thy desire now: here is the soul of thy husband, he shall live again. He shall live to be a father and thy children also shall reign in due course. Return home. Love has conquered Death! Woman never loved like thee, and thou art the proof that even I, the God of Death, am powerless against the power of the true love that abideth!"

This is the story of Savitri, and every girl in India must aspire to be like Savitri, whose love could not be conquered by death, and who through this tremendous love snatched back from even Yama, the soul of her husband.

The book is full of hundreds of beautiful episodes like this. I began by telling you that the Mahabharata is one of the greatest books in the world and consists of about a hundred thousand verses in eighteen Parvans, or volumes.

To return to our main story. We left the Pandava brothers in exile. Even there they were not allowed to remain unmolested from the evil plots of Duryodhana; but all of them were futile.

A story of their forest life, I shall tell you here. One day the brothers became thirsty in the forest. Yudhishthira bade his brother, Nakula, go and fetch water. He quickly proceeded towards the place where there was water and soon came to a crystal lake, and was about to drink of it, when he heard a voice utter these words: "Stop, O child. First answer my questions and then drink of this water." But Nakula, who was exceedingly thirsty, disregarded these words, drank of the water, and having drunk of it, dropped down dead. As Nakula did not return, King Yudhishthira told Sahadeva to seek his brother and bring back water with him. So Sahadeva proceeded to the lake and beheld his brother lying dead. Afflicted at the death of his brother and suffering severely from thirst, he went towards the water, when the same words were heard by him: "O child, first answer my questions and then drink of the water." He also disregarded these words, and having satisfied his thirst, dropped down dead. Subsequently, Arjuna and Bhima were sent, one after the other, on a similar quest; but neither returned, having drunk of the lake and dropped down dead. Then Yudhishthira rose up to go in search of his brothers. At length, he came to the beautiful lake and saw his brothers lying dead. His heart was full of grief at the sight, and he began to lament. Suddenly he heard the same voice saying, "Do not, O child, act rashly. I am a Yaksha living as a crane on tiny fish. It is by me that thy younger brothers have been brought under the sway of the Lord of departed spirits. If thou, O Prince, answer not the questions put by me even thou shalt number the fifth corpse. Having answered my questions first, do thou, O Kunti's son, drink and carry away as much as thou requires'." Yudhishthira replied, "I shall answer thy questions according to my intelligence. Do thou ask me" The Yaksha then asked him several questions, all of which Yudhishthira answered satisfactorily. One of the questions asked was: "What is the most wonderful fact in this world?" "We see our fellow-beings every moment falling off around us; but those that are left behind think that they will never die. This is the most curious fact: in face of death, none believes that he will die! " Another question asked was: "What is the path of knowing the secret of religion?" And Yudhishthira answered, "By argument nothing can be settled; doctrines there are many; various are the scriptures, one part contradicting the other. There are not two sages who do not differ in their opinions. The secret of religion is buried deep, as it were, in dark caves. So the path to be followed is that which the great ones have trodden." Then the Yaksha said, "I am pleased. I am Dharma, he God of Justice in the form of the crane. I came to test you. Now, your brothers, see, not one of them is dead. It is all my magic. Since abstention from injury is regarded by thee as higher than both profit and pleasure, therefore, let all thy brothers live, O Bull of the Bharata race." And at these words of the Yaksha, the Pandavas rose up.

Here is a glimpse of the nature of King Yudhishthira. We find by his answers that he was more of a philosopher, more of a Yogi, than a king.

Now, as the thirteenth year of the exile was drawing nigh, the Yaksha bade them go to Viráta's kingdom and live there in such disguises as they would think best.

So, after the term of the twelve years' exile had expired, they went to the kingdom of Virata in different disguises to spend the remaining one year in concealment, and entered into menial service in the king's household. Thus Yudhishthira became a Brâhmana courtier of the king, as one skilled in dice; Bhima was appointed a cook; Arjuna, dressed as a eunuch, was made a teacher of dancing and music to Uttarâ, the princess, and remained in the inner apartments of the king; Nakula became the keeper of the king's horses; and Sahadeva got the charge of the cows; and Draupadi, disguised as a waiting-woman, was also admitted into the queen's household. Thus concealing their identity the Pandava brothers safely spent a year, and the search of Duryodhana to find them out was of no avail. They were only discovered just when the year was out.

Then Yudhishthira sent an ambassador to Dhritarashtra and demanded that half of the kingdom should, as their share, be restored to them. But Duryodhana hated his cousins and would not consent to their legitimate demands. They were even willing to accept a single province, nay, even five villages. But the headstrong Duryodhana declared that he would not yield without fight even as much land as a needle's point would hold. Dhritarashtra pleaded again and again for peace, but all in vain. Krishna also went and tried to avert the impending war and death of kinsmen, so did the wise elders of the royal court; but all negotiations for a peaceful partition of the kingdom were futile. So, at last, preparations were made on both sides for war, and all the warlike nations took part in it.

The old Indian customs of the Kshatriyas were observed in it. Duryodhana took one side, Yudhishthira the other. From Yudhishthira messengers were at once sent to all the surrounding kings, entreating their alliance, since honourable men would

grant the request that first reached them. So, warriors from all parts assembled to espouse the cause of either the Pandavas or the Kurus according to the precedence of their requests; and thus one brother joined this side, and the other that side, the father on one side, and the son on the other. The most curious thing was the code of war of those days; as soon as the battle for the day ceased and evening came, the opposing parties were good friends, even going to each other's tents; however, when the morning came, again they proceeded to fight each other. That was the strange trait that the Hindus carried down to the time of the Mohammedan invasion. Then again, a man on horseback must not strike one on foot; must not poison the weapon; must not vanquish the enemy in any unequal fight, or by dishonesty; and must never take undue advantage of another, and so on. If any deviated from these rules he would be covered with dishonour and shunned. The Kshatriyas were trained in that way. And when the foreign invasion came from Central Asia, the Hindus treated the invaders in the selfsame way. They defeated them several times, and on as many occasions sent them back to their homes with presents etc. The code laid down was that they must not usurp anybody's country; and when a man was beaten, he must be sent back to his country with due regard to his position. The Mohammedan conquerors treated the Hindu kings differently, and when they got them once, they destroyed them without remorse.

Mind you, in those days—in the times of our story, the poem says—the science of arms was not the mere use of bows and arrows at all; it was magic archery in which the use of Mantras, concentration, etc., played a prominent part. One man could fight millions of men and burn them at will. He could send one arrow, and it would rain thousands of arrows and thunder; he could make anything burn, and so on—it was all divine magic. One fact is most curious in both these poems—the Ramayana and the Mahabharata—along with these magic arrows and all these things going on, you see the cannon already in use. The cannon is an old, old thing, used by the Chinese and the Hindus. Upon the walls of the cities were hundreds of curious weapons made of hollow iron tubes, which filled with powder and ball would kill hundreds of men. The people believed that the Chinese, by magic, put the devil inside a hollow iron tube, and when they applied a little fire to a hole, the devil came out with a terrific noise and killed many people.

So in those old days, they used to fight with magic arrows. One man would be able to fight millions of others. They had their military arrangements and tactics: there were the foot soldiers, termed the Pâda; then the cavalry, Turaga; and two other divisions which the moderns have lost and given up—there was the elephant corps—hundreds and hundreds of elephants, with men on their backs, formed into regiments and protected with huge sheets of iron mail; and these elephants would bear down upon a mass of the enemy—then, there were the chariots, of course (you have all seen pictures of those old chariots, they were used in every country). These were the four divisions of the army in those old days.

Now, both parties alike wished to secure the alliance of Krishna. But he declined to take an active part and fight in this war, but offered himself as charioteer to Arjuna, and as the friend and counsellor of the Pandavas while to Duryodhana he gave his army of mighty soldiers.

Then was fought on the vast plain of Kurukshetra the great battle in which Bhisma, Drona, Karna, and the brothers of Duryodhana with the kinsmen on both sides and thousands of other heroes fell. The war lasted eighteen days. Indeed, out of the eighteen Akshauhinis of soldiers very few men were left. The death of Duryodhana ended the war in favour of the Pandavas. It was followed by the lament of Gândhâri, the queen and the widowed women, and the funerals of the deceased warriors.

The greatest incident of the war was the marvellous and immortal poem of the Gitâ, the Song Celestial. It is the popular scripture of India and the loftiest of all teachings. It consists of a dialogue held by Arjuna with Krishna, just before the commencement of the fight on the battle-field of Kurukshetra. I would advise those of you who have not read that book to read it. If you only knew how much it has influenced your own country even! If you want to know the source of Emerson's inspiration, it is this book, the Gita. He went to see Carlyle, and Carlyle made him a present of the Gita; and that little book is responsible for the Concord Movement. All the broad movements in America, in one way or other, are indebted to the Concord party.

The central figure of the Gita is Krishna. As you worship Jesus of Nazareth as God come down as man so the Hindus worship many Incarnations of God. They believe in not one or two only, but in many, who have come down from time to time, according to the needs of the world, for the preservation of Dharma and destruction of wickedness. Each sect has one, and Krishna is one of them. Krishna, perhaps, has a larger number of followers in India than any other Incarnation of God. His followers hold that he was the most perfect of those Incarnations. Why? "Because," they say, "look at Buddha and other Incarnations: they were only monks, and they had no sympathy for married people. How could they have? But look at Krishna: he was great as a son, as a king, as a father, and all through his life he practiced the marvellous teachings which he preached." "He who in the midst of the greatest activity finds the sweetest peace, and in the midst of the greatest calmness is most active, he has known the secret of life." Krishna shows the way how to do this—by being non-attached: do everything but do not get identified with anything. You are the soul, the pure, the free, all the time; you are the Witness. Our misery comes, not from work, but by our getting attached to something. Take for instance, money: money is a great thing to have, earn it, says Krishna; struggle hard to get money, but don't get attached to it. So with children, with

wife, husband, relatives, fame, everything; you have no need to shun them, only don't get attached. There is only one attachment and that belongs to the Lord, and to none other. Work for them, love them, do good to them, sacrifice a hundred lives, if need be, for them, but never be attached. His own life was the exact exemplification of that.

Remember that the book which delineates the life of Krishna is several thousand years old, and some parts of his life are very similar to those of Jesus of Nazareth. Krishna was of royal birth; there was a tyrant king, called Kamsa, and there was a prophecy that one would be born of such and such a family, who would be king. So Kamsa ordered all the male children to be massacred. The father and mother of Krishna were cast by King Kamsa into prison, where the child was born. A light suddenly shone in the prison and the child spoke saying, "I am the Light of the world, born for the good of the world." You find Krishna again symbolically represented with cows—"The Great Cowherd," as he is called. Sages affirmed that God Himself was born, and they went to pay him homage. In other parts of the story, the similarity between the two does not continue.

Shri Krishna conquered this tyrant Kamsa, but he never thought of accepting or occupying the throne himself. He had nothing to do with that. He had done his duty and there it ended.

After the conclusion of the Kurukshetra War, the great warrior and venerable grandsire, Bhishma, who fought ten days out of the eighteen days' battle, still lay on his deathbed and gave instructions to Yudhishthira on various subjects, such as the duties of the king, the duties of the four castes, the four stages of life, the laws of marriage, the bestowing of gifts, etc., basing them on the teachings of the ancient sages. He explained Sânkhya philosophy and Yoga philosophy and narrated numerous tales and traditions about saints and gods and kings. These teachings occupy nearly one-fourth of the entire work and form an invaluable storehouse of Hindu laws and moral codes. Yudhishthira had in the meantime been crowned king. But the awful bloodshed and extinction of superiors and relatives weighed heavily on his mind; and then, under the advice of Vyasa, he performed the Ashvamedha sacrifice.

After the war, for fifteen years Dhritarashtra dwelt in peace and honour, obeyed by Yudhishthira and his brothers. Then the aged monarch leaving Yudhishthira on the throne, retired to the forest with his devoted wife and Kunti, the mother of the Pandava brothers, to pass his last days in asceticism.

Thirty-six years had now passed since Yudhishthira regained his empire. Then came to him the news that Krishna had left his mortal body. Krishna, the sage, his friend, his prophet, his counsellor, had departed. Arjuna hastened to Dwârâka and came back only to confirm the sad news that Krishna and the Yâdavas were all dead. Then the king and the other brothers, overcome with sorrow, declared that the time for them to go, too, had arrived. So they cast off the burden of royalty, placed

Parikshit, the grandson of Arjuna, on the throne, and retired to the Himalayas, on the Great Journey, the Mahâprasthâna. This was a peculiar form of Sannyâsa. It was a custom for old kings to become Sannyasins. In ancient India, when men became very old, they would give up everything. So did the kings. When a man did not want to live any more, then he went towards the Himalayas, without eating or drinking and walked on and on till the body failed. All the time thinking of God, be just marched on till the body gave way.

Then came the gods, the sages, and they told King Yudhishthira that he should go and reach heaven. To go to heaven one has to cross the highest peaks of the Himalayas. Beyond the Himalayas is Mount Meru. On the top of Mount Meru is heaven. None ever went there in this body. There the gods reside. And Yudhishthira was called upon by the gods to go there.

So the five brothers and their wife clad themselves in robes of bark, and set out on their journey. On the way, they were followed by a dog. On and on they went, and they turned their weary feet northward to where the Himalayas lifts his lofty peaks, and they saw the mighty Mount Meru in front of them. Silently they walked on in the snow, until suddenly the queen fell, to rise no more. To Yudhishthira who was leading the way, Bhima, one of the brothers, said, "Behold, O King, the queen has fallen." The king shed tears, but he did not look back. "We are going to meet Krishna," he says. "No time to look back. March on." After a while, again Bhima said, "Behold, our brother, Sahadeva has fallen." The king shed tears; but paused not. "March on," he cried.

One after the other, in the cold and snow, all the four brothers dropped down, but unshaken, though alone, the king advanced onward. Looking behind, he saw the faithful dog was still following him. And so the king and the dog went on, through snow and ice, over hill and dale, climbing higher and higher, till they reached Mount Meru; and there they began to hear the chimes of heaven, and celestial flowers were showered upon the virtuous king by the gods. Then descended the chariot of the gods, and Indra prayed him, "Ascend in this chariot, greatest of mortals: thou that alone art given to enter heaven without changing the mortal body." But no, that Yudhishthira would not do without his devoted brothers and his queen; then Indra explained to him that the brothers had already gone thither before him.

And Yudhishthira looked around and said to his dog, "Get into the chariot, child." The god stood aghast. "What! the dog?" he cried. "Do thou cast off this dog! The dog goeth not to heaven I Great King, what dost thou mean? Art thou mad? Thou, the most virtuous of the human race, thou only canst go to heaven in thy body." "But he has been my devoted companion through snow and ice. When all my brothers were dead, my queen dead, he alone never left me. How can I leave him now?" "There is no place in heaven for men with dogs. He has to be left behind. There is nothing unrighteous

in this." "I do not go to heaven," replied the king, "without the dog. I shall never give up such a one who has taken refuge with me, until my own life is at an end. I shall never swerve from righteousness, nay, not even for the joys of heaven or the urging of a god." "Then," said Indra, "on one condition the dog goes to heaven. You have been the most virtuous of mortals and he has been a dog, killing and eating animals; he is sinful, hunting, and taking other lives. You can exchange heaven with him. "Agreed," says the king. "Let the dog go to heaven."

At once, the scene changed. Hearing these noble words of Yudhishthira, the dog revealed himself as Dharma; the dog was no other than Yama, the Lord of Death and Justice. And Dharma exclaimed, "Behold, O King, no man was ever so unselfish as thou, willing to exchange heaven with a little dog, and for his sake disclaiming all his virtues and ready to go to hell even for him. Thou art well born, O King of kings. Thou hast compassion for all creatures, O Bhârata, of which this is a bright example. Hence, regions of undying felicity are thine! Thou hast won them, O King, and shine is a celestial and high goal."

Then Yudhishthira, with Indra, Dharma, and other gods, proceeds to heaven in a celestial car. He undergoes some trials, bathes in the celestial Ganga, and assumes a celestial body. He meets his brothers who are now immortals, and all at last is bliss.

Thus ends the story of the Mahabharata, setting forth in a sublime poem the triumph of virtue and defeat of vice.

In speaking of the Mahabharata to you, it is simply impossible for me to present the unending array of the grand and majestic characters of the mighty heroes depicted by the genius and master-mind of Vyasa. The internal conflicts between righteousness and filial affection in the mind of the god-fearing, yet feeble, old, blind King Dhritarashtra; the majestic character of the grandsire Bhishma; the noble and virtuous nature of the royal Yudhishthira, and of the other four brothers, as mighty in valour as in devotion and loyalty; the peerless character of Krishna, unsurpassed in human wisdom; and not less brilliant, the characters of the women — the stately queen Gandhari, the loving mother Kunti, the ever-devoted and all-suffering Draupadi — these and hundreds of other characters of this Epic and those of the Ramayana have been the cherished heritage of the whole Hindu world for the last several thousands of years and form the basis of their thoughts and of their moral and ethical ideas. In fact, the Ramayana and the Mahabharata are the two encyclopaedias of the ancient Aryan life and wisdom, portraying an ideal civilisation which humanity has yet to aspire after.

THOUGHTS ON THE GITA

During his sojourn in Calcutta in 1897, Swami Vivekananda used to stay for the most part at the Math, the headquarters of the Ramakrisnna Mission, located then at Alambazar.

During this time several young men, who had been preparing themselves for some time previously, gathered round him and took the vows of Brahmacharya and Sannyâsa, and Swamiji began to train them for future work, by holding classes on the Gîtâ and Vedanta, and initiating them into the practices of meditation. In one of these classes he talked eloquently in Bengali on the Gita. The following is the translation of the summary of the discourse as it was entered in the Math diary:

The book known as the Gita forms a part of the Mahâbhârata. To understand the Gita properly, several things are very important to know. First, whether it formed a part of the Mahabharata, i.e. whether the authorship attributed to Veda-Vyâsa was true, or if it was merely interpolated within the great epic; secondly, whether there was any historical personality of the name of Krishna; thirdly, whether the great war of Kurukshetra as mentioned in the Gita actually took place; and fourthly, whether Arjuna and others were real historical persons.

Now in the first place, let us see what grounds there are for such inquiry. We know that there were many who went by the name of Veda-Vyasa; and among them who was the real author of the Gita—the Bâdarâyana Vyasa or Dvaipâyana Vyasa? "Vyasa" was only a title. Anyone who composed a new Purâna was known by the name of Vyasa, like the word Vikramâditya, which was also a general name. Another point is, the book, Gita, had not been much known to the generality of people before Shankarâchârya made it famous by writing his great commentary on it. Long before that, there was current, according to many, the commentary on it by Bodhâyana. If this could be proved, it would go a long way, no doubt, to establish the antiquity of the Gita and the authorship of Vyasa. But the Bodhayana Bhâshya on the Vedânta Sutras—from which Râmânuja compiled his Shri-Bhâshya, which Shankaracharya mentions and even quotes in part here and there in his own commentary, and which was so greatly discussed by the Swami Dayânanda—not a copy even of that Bodhayana Bhashya could I find while travelling throughout India. It is said that even Ramanuja compiled his Bhashya from a worm-eaten manuscript which he happened to find. When even this great Bodhayana Bhashya on the Vedanta-Sutras is so much enshrouded in the darkness of uncertainty, it is simply useless to try to establish the existence of the Bodhayana Bhashya on the Gita. Some infer that Shankaracharya was the author of the Gita, and that it was he who foisted it into the body of the Mahabharata.

Then as to the second point in question, much doubt exists about the personality of Krishna. In one place in the Chhândogya Upanishad we find mention of Krishna, the son of Devaki, who received spiritual instructions from one Ghora, a Yogi. In the Mahabharata, Krishna is the king of Dwârakâ; and in the Vishnu Purâna we find a description of Krishna playing with the Gopis. Again, in the Bhâgavata, the account of his Râsalilâ is detailed at length. In very ancient times in our country there was in vogue an Utsava called Madanotsava

(celebration in honour of Cupid). That very thing was transformed into Dola and thrust upon the shoulders of Krishna. Who can be so bold as to assert that the Rasalila and other things connected with him were not similarly fastened upon him? In ancient times there was very little tendency in our country to find out truths by historical research. So any one could say what he thought best without substantiating it with proper facts and evidence. Another thing: in those ancient times there was very little hankering after name and fame in men. So it often happened that one man composed a book and made it pass current in the name of his Guru or of someone else. In such cases it is very hazardous for the investigator of historical facts to get at the truth. In ancient times they had no knowledge whatever of geography; imagination ran riot. And so we meet with such fantastic creations of the brain as sweet-ocean, milk-ocean, clarified-butter-ocean, curd-ocean, etc! In the Puranas, we find one living ten thousand years, another a hundred thousand years! But the Vedas say, शतायुर्वे पुरुषः — "Man lives a hundred years." Whom shall we follow here? So, to reach a correct conclusion in the case of Krishna is well-nigh impossible.

It is human nature to build round the real character of a great man all sorts of imaginary superhuman attributes. As regards Krishna the same must have happened, but it seems quite probable that he was a king. Quite probable I say, because in ancient times in our country it was chiefly the kings who exerted themselves most in the preaching of Brahma-Jnâna. Another point to be especially noted here is that whoever might have been the author of the Gita, we find its teachings the same as those in the whole of the Mahabharata. From this we can safely infer that in the age of the Mahabharata some great man arose and preached the Brahma-Jnâna in this new garb to the then existing society. Another fact comes to the fore that in the olden days, as one sect after another arose, there also came into existence and use among them one new scripture or another. It happened, too, that in the lapse of time both the sect and its scripture died out, or the sect ceased to exist but its scripture remained. Similarly, it was quite probable that the Gita was the scripture of such a sect which had embodied its high and noble ideas in this sacred book.

Now to the third point, bearing on the subject of the Kurukshetra War, no special evidence in support of it can be adduced. But there is no doubt that there was a war fought between the Kurus and the Panchâlas. Another thing: how could there be so much discussion about Jnâna, Bhakti, and Yoga on the battle-field, where the huge army stood in battle array ready to fight, just waiting for the last signal? And was any shorthand writer present there to note down every word spoken between Krishna and Arjuna, in the din and turmoil of the battle-field? According to some, this Kurukshetra War is only an allegory. When we sum up its esoteric significance, it means the war which is constantly going on within man between the tendencies of good and evil. This meaning, too, may not be irrational.

About the fourth point, there is enough ground of doubt as regards the historicity of Arjuna and others, and it is this: Shatapatha Brâhmana is a very ancient book. In it are mentioned somewhere all the names of those who were the performers of the Ashvamedha Yajna: but in those places there is not only no mention, but no hint even of the names of Arjuna and others, though it speaks of Janamejaya, the son of Parikshit who was a grandson of Arjuna. Yet in the Mahabharata and other books it is stated that Yudhishthira, Arjuna, and others celebrated the Ashvamedha sacrifice.

One thing should be especially remembered here, that there is no connection between these historical researches and our real aim, which is the knowledge that leads to the acquirement of Dharma. Even if the historicity of the whole thing is proved to be absolutely false today, it will not in the least be any loss to us. Then what is the use of so much historical research, you may ask. It has its use, because we have to get at the truth; it will not do for us to remain bound by wrong ideas born of ignorance. In this country people think very little of the importance of such inquiries. Many of the sects believe that in order to preach a good thing which may be beneficial to many, there is no harm in telling an untruth, if that helps such preaching, or in other words, the end justifies the means. Hence we find many of our Tantras beginning with, "Mahâdeva said to Pârvati". But our duty should be to convince ourselves of the truth, to believe in truth only. Such is the power of superstition, or faith in old traditions without inquiry into its truth, that it keeps men bound hand and foot, so much so, that even Jesus the Christ, Mohammed, and other great men believed in many such superstitions and could not shake them off. You have to keep your eye always fixed on truth only and shun all superstitions completely.

Now it is for us to see what there is in the Gita. If we study the Upanishads we notice, in wandering through the mazes of many irrelevant subjects, the sudden introduction of the discussion of a great truth, just as in the midst of a huge wilderness a traveller unexpectedly comes across here and there an exquisitely beautiful rose, with its leaves, thorns, roots, all entangled. Compared with that, the Gita is like these truths beautifully arranged together in their proper places—like a fine garland or a bouquet of the choicest flowers. The Upanishads deal elaborately with Shraddhâ in many places, but hardly mention Bhakti. In the Gita, on the other hand, the subject of Bhakti is not only again and again dealt with, but in it, the innate spirit of Bhakti has attained its culmination.

Now let us see some of the main points discussed in the Gita. Wherein lies the originality of the Gita which distinguishes it from all preceding scriptures? It is this: Though before its advent, Yoga, Jnana, Bhakti, etc. had each its strong adherents, they all quarrelled among themselves, each claiming superiority for his own chosen path; no one ever tried to seek for reconciliation among these different paths. It was the author of the Gita who for the first time tried to harmonise these. He took the best from what all the sects then existing had to offer and threaded them in the Gita. But even where Krishna failed to show a complete reconciliation (Samanvaya) among these warring sects, it was fully accomplished by Ramakrishna Paramahamsa in this nineteenth century.

The next is, Nishkâma Karma, or work without desire or attachment. People nowadays understand what is meant by this in various ways. Some say what is implied by being unattached is to become purposeless. If that were its real meaning, then heartless brutes and the walls would be the best exponents of the performance of Nishkama Karma. Many others, again, give the example of Janaka, and wish themselves to be equally recognised as past masters in the practice of Nishkama Karma! Janaka (lit. father) did not acquire that distinction by bringing forth children, but these people all want to be Janakas, with the sole qualification of being the fathers of a brood of children! No! The true Nishkama Karmi (performer of work without desire) is neither to be like a brute, nor to be inert, nor heartless. He is not Tâmasika but of pure Sattva. His heart is so full of love and sympathy that he can embrace the whole world with his love. The world at large cannot generally comprehend his all-embracing love and sympathy.

The reconciliation of the different paths of Dharma, and work without desire or attachment—these are the two special characteristics of the Gita.

Let us now read a little from the second chapter.

सञ्जय उवाच॥
तं तथा कृपयाविष्टमश्रुपूर्णाकुलेक्षणम् ।
विषीदन्तमिदं वाक्यमुवाच मधुसूदनः ॥१॥
श्रीभगवानुवाच ॥
कुतस्त्वा कश्मलमिदं विषमे समुपस्थितम् ।
अनार्यजुष्टमस्वर्ग्यमकीर्तिकरमर्जुन ॥२॥
क्लैब्यं मा स्म गमः पार्थ नैतत्त्वय्युपपद्यते ।
क्षुद्रं हृदयदौर्बल्यं त्यक्त्वोत्तिष्ठ परन्तप ॥३॥

"Sanjaya said:

To him who was thus overwhelmed with pity and sorrowing, and whose eyes were dimmed with tears, Madhusudana spoke these words.

The Blessed Lord said:

In such a strait, whence comes upon thee, O Arjuna, this dejection, un-Aryan-like, disgraceful, and contrary to the attainment of heaven?

Yield not to unmanliness, O son of Prithâ! Ill doth it become thee. Cast off this mean faint-heartedness and arise, O scorcher of thine enemies!"

In the Shlokas beginning with तं तथा कृपयाविष्टं, how poetically, how beautifully, has Arjuna's real position been painted! Then Shri Krishna advises Arjuna; and in the words क्लैब्यं मा स्म गमः पार्थ etc., why is he goading Arjuna to fight? Because it was not that the disinclination of Arjuna to fight arose out of the overwhelming predominance of pure Sattva Guna; it was all Tamas that brought on this unwillingness. The nature of a man of Sattva Guna is, that he is equally calm in all situations in life—whether it be prosperity or adversity. But Arjuna was afraid, he was overwhelmed with pity. That he had the instinct and the inclination to fight is proved by the simple fact that he came to the battle-field with no other purpose than that. Frequently in our lives also such things are seen to happen. Many people think they are Sâttvika by nature, but they are really nothing but Tâmasika. Many living in an uncleanly way regard themselves as Paramahamsas! Why? Because the Shâstras say that Paramahamsas live like one inert, or mad, or like an unclean spirit. Paramahamsas are compared to children, but here it should be understood that the comparison is one-sided. The Paramahamsa and the child are not one and non-different. They only appear similar, being the two extreme poles, as it were. One has reached to a state beyond Jnana, and the other has not got even an inkling of Jnana. The quickest and the gentlest vibrations of light are both beyond the reach of our ordinary vision; but in the one it is intense heat, and in the other it may be said to be almost without any heat. So it is with the opposite qualities of Sattva and Tamas. They seem in some respects to be the same, no doubt, but there is a world of difference between them. The Tamoguna loves very much to array itself in the garb of the Sattva. Here, in Arjuna, the mighty warrior, it has come under the guise of Dayâ (pity).

In order to remove this delusion which had overtaken Arjuna, what did the Bhagavân say? As I always preach that you should not decry a man by calling him a sinner, but that you should draw his attention to the omnipotent power that is in him, in the same way does the Bhagavan speak to Arjuna. नेतत्त्वय्युपपद्यते— "It doth not befit thee!" "Thou art Atman imperishable, beyond all evil. Having forgotten thy real nature, thou hast, by thinking thyself a sinner, as one afflicted with bodily evils and mental grief, thou hast made thyself so—this doth not befit thee!"—so says the Bhagavan: क्लैब्यं मा स्म गमः पार्थ—Yield not to unmanliness, O son of Pritha. There is in the world neither sin nor misery, neither disease nor grief; if there is anything in the world which can be called sin, it is this—'fear'; know that any work which brings out the latent power in thee is Punya (virtue); and that which makes thy body and mind weak is, verily, sin. Shake off this weakness, this faintheartedness! क्लैब्यं मा स्म गमः पार्था—Thou art a hero, a Vira; this is unbecoming of thee."

If you, my sons, can proclaim this message to the world—क्लैब्यं मा स्म गमः पार्थ नेतत्त्वय्युपपद्यते—then all this disease, grief, sin, and sorrow will vanish from off the face of the earth in three days. All these ideas of weakness will be nowhere. Now it is everywhere—this current of the vibration of fear. Reverse the current: bring in the opposite vibration, and behold the magic transformation! Thou art omnipotent—go, go to the mouth of the cannon, fear not.

Hate not the most abject sinner, fool; not to his exterior. Turn thy gaze inward, where resides the Paramâtman. Proclaim to the whole world with trumpet voice, "There is no

sin in thee, there is no misery in thee; thou art the reservoir of omnipotent power. Arise, awake, and manifest the Divinity within!"

If one reads this one Shloka —क्लैब्यं मा स्म गमः पार्थ नेतत्त्वय्युपपद्यते । क्षुद्रं हृदयदौर्बल्यं त्यक्त्वोत्तिष्ठ परंतप॥ —one gets all the merits of reading the entire Gita; for in this one Shloka lies imbedded the whole Message of the Gita.

THE STORY OF JADA BHARATA

Delivered in California

There was a great monarch named Bharata. The land which is called India by foreigners is known to her children as Bhârata Varsha. Now, it is enjoined on every Hindu when he becomes old, to give up all worldly pursuits—to leave the cares of the world, its wealth, happiness, and enjoyments to his son—and retire into the forest, there to meditate upon the Self which is the only reality in him, and thus break the bonds which bind him to life. King or priest, peasant or servant, man or woman, none is exempt from this duty: for all the duties of the householder—of the son, the brother, the husband, the father, the wife, the daughter, the mother, the sister—are but preparations towards that one stage, when all the bonds which bind the soul to matter are severed asunder for ever.

The great king Bharata in his old age gave over his throne to his son, and retired into the forest. He who had been ruler over millions and millions of subjects, who had lived in marble palaces, inlaid with gold and silver, who had drunk out of jewelled cups—this king built a little cottage with his own hands, made of reeds and grass, on the banks of a river in the Himalayan forests. There he lived on roots and wild herbs, collected by his own hands, and constantly meditated upon Him who is always present in the soul of man. Days, months, and years passed. One day, a deer came to drink water near by where the royal sage was meditating. At the same moment, a lion roared at a little distance off. The deer was so terrified that she, without satisfying her thirst, made a big jump to cross the river. The deer was with young, and this extreme exertion and sudden fright made her give birth to a little fawn, and immediately after she fell dead. The fawn fell into the water and was being carried rapidly away by the foaming stream, when it caught the eyes of the king. The king rose from his position of meditation and rescuing the fawn from the water, took it to his cottage, made a fire, and with care and attention fondled the little thing back to life. Then the kindly sage took the fawn under his protection, bringing it up on soft grass and fruits. The fawn thrived under the paternal care of the retired monarch, and grew into a beautiful deer. Then, he whose mind had been strong enough to break away from lifelong attachment to power, position, and family, became attached to the deer which he had saved from the stream. And as he became fonder and fonder of the deer, the less and less he could concentrate his mind upon the Lord. When the deer went out to graze in the forest, if it were late in returning, the mind of the royal sage would become anxious and worried. He would think, "Perhaps my little one has been attacked by some tiger—or perhaps some other danger has befallen it; otherwise, why is it late?"

Some years passed in this way, but one day death came, and the royal sage laid himself down to die. But his mind, instead of being intent upon the Self, was thinking about the deer; and with his eyes fixed upon the sad looks of his beloved deer, his soul left the body. As the result of this, in the next birth he was born as a deer. But no Karma is lost, and all the great and good deeds done by him as a king and sage bore their fruit. This deer was a born Jâtismara, and remembered his past birth, though he was bereft of speech and was living in an animal body. He always left his companions and was instinctively drawn to graze near hermitages where oblations were offered and the Upanishads were preached.

After the usual years of a deer's life had been spent, it died and was next born as the youngest son of a rich Brahmin. And in that life also, he remembered all his past, and even in his childhood was determined no more to get entangled in the good and evil of life. The child, as it grew up, was strong and healthy, but would not speak a word, and lived as one inert and insane, for fear of getting mixed up with worldly affairs. His thoughts were always on the Infinite, and he lived only to wear out his past Prârabdha Karma. In course of time the father died, and the sons divided the property among themselves; and thinking that the youngest was a dumb, good-for-nothing man, they seized his share. Their charity, however, extended only so far as to give him enough food to live upon. The wives of the brothers were often very harsh to him, putting him to do all the hard work; and if he was unable to do everything they wanted, they would treat him very unkindly. But he showed neither vexation nor fear, and neither did he speak a word. When they persecuted him very much, he would stroll out of the house and sit under a tree, by the hour, until their wrath was appeased, and then he would quietly go home again.

One day; when the wives of the brothers had treated him with more than usual unkindness, Bharata went out of the house, seated himself under the shadow of a tree and rested. Now it happened that the king of the country was passing by, carried in a palanquin on the shoulders of bearers. One of the bearers had unexpectedly fallen ill, and so his attendants were looking about for a man to replace him. They came upon Bharata seated under a tree; and seeing he was a strong young man, they asked him if he would take the place of the sick man in bearing the king's palanquin. But Bharata did not reply. Seeing that he was so able-bodied, the king's servants caught hold of him and placed the pole on his shoulders. Without speaking a word, Bharata went on. Very soon after this, the king remarked that the palanquin was not being evenly carried, and looking out of the palanquin addressed the new bearer, saying "Fool, rest a while; if thy shoulders

pain thee, rest a while." Then Bharata laying the pole of the palanquin down, opened his lips for the first time in his life, and spoke, "Whom dost thou, O King, call a fool? Whom dost thou ask to lay down the palanquin? Who dost thou say is weary? Whom dost thou address as 'thou'? If thou meanest, O King, by the word 'thee' this mass of flesh, it is composed of the same matter as thine; it is unconscious, and it knoweth no weariness, it knoweth no pain. If it is the mind, the mind is the same as thine; it is universal. But if the word 'thee' is applied to something beyond that, then it is the Self, the Reality in me, which is the same as in thee, and it is the One in the universe. Dost thou mean, O King, that the Self can ever be weary, that It can ever be tired, that It can ever be hurt? I did not want, O King—this body did not want—to trample upon the poor worms crawling on the road, and therefore, in trying to avoid them, the palanquin moved unevenly. But the Self was never tired; It was never weak; It never bore the pole of the palanquin: for It is omnipotent and omnipresent." And so he dwelt eloquently on the nature of the soul, and on the highest knowledge, etc. The king, who was proud of his learning, knowledge, and philosophy, alighted from the palanquin, and fell at the feet of Bharata, saying, "I ask thy pardon, O mighty one, I did not know that thou wast a sage, when I asked thee to carry me." Bharata blessed him and departed. He then resumed the even tenor of his previous life. When Bharata left the body, he was freed for ever from the bondage of birth.

THE STORY OF PRAHLADA

Delivered in California

Hiranyakashipu was the king of the Daityas. The Daityas, though born of the same parentage as the Devas or gods, were always, at war with the latter. The Daityas had no part in the oblations and offerings of mankind, or in the government of the world and its guidance. But sometimes they waxed strong and drove all the Devas from the heaven, and seized the throne of the gods and ruled for a time. Then the Devas prayed to Vishnu, the Omnipresent Lord of the universe, and He helped them out of their difficulty. The Daityas were driven out, and once more the gods reigned. Hiranyakashipu, king of the Daityas, in his turn, succeeded in conquering his cousins, the Devas, and seated himself on the throne of the heavens and ruled the three worlds—the middle world, inhabited by men and animals; the heavens, inhabited by gods and godlike beings; and the nether world, inhabited by the Daityas. Now, Hiranyakashipu declared himself to be the God of the whole universe and proclaimed that there was no other God but himself, and strictly enjoined that the Omnipotent Vishnu should have no worship offered to Him anywhere; and that all the worship should henceforth be given to himself only.

Hiranyakashipu had a son called Prahlâda. Now, it so happened, that this Prahlada from his infancy was devoted to

God. He showed indications of this as a child; and the king of the Daityas, fearing that the evil he wanted to drive away from the world would crop up in his own family, made over his son to two teachers called Shanda and Amarka, who were very stern disciplinarians, with strict injunctions that Prahlada was never to hear even the name of Vishnu mentioned. The teachers took the prince to their home, and there he was put to study with the other children of his age. But the little Prahlada, instead of learning from his books, devoted all the time in teaching the other boys how to worship Vishnu. When the teachers found it out, they were frightened, for the fear of the mighty king Hiranyakashipu was upon them, and they tried their best to dissuade the child from such teachings. But Prahlada could no more stop his teaching and worshipping Vishnu than he could stop breathing. To clear themselves, the teachers told the terrible fact to the king, that his son was not only worshipping Vishnu himself, but also spoiling all the other children by teaching them to worship Vishnu.

The monarch became very much enraged when he heard this and called the boy to his presence. He tried by gentle persuasions to dissuade Prahlada from the worship of Vishnu and taught him that he, the king, was the only God to worship. But it was to no purpose. The child declared, again and again, that the Omnipresent Vishnu, Lord of the universe, was the only Being to be worshipped — for even he, the king, held his throne only so long as it pleased Vishnu. The rage of the king knew no bounds, and he ordered the boy to be immediately killed. So the Daityas struck him with pointed weapons; but Prahlad's mind was so intent upon Vishnu that he felt no pain from them.

When his father, the king, saw that it was so, he became frightened but, roused to the worst passions of a Daitya, contrived various diabolical means to kill the boy. He ordered him to be trampled under foot by an elephant. The enraged elephant could not crush the body any more than he could have crushed a block of iron. So this measure also was to no purpose. Then the king ordered the boy to be thrown over a precipice, and this order too was duly carried out; but, as Vishnu resided in the heart of Prahlada, he came down upon the earth as gently as a flower drops upon the grass. Poison, fire, starvation, throwing into a well, enchantments, and other measures were then tried on the child one after another, but to no purpose. Nothing could hurt him in whose heart dwelt Vishnu.

At last, the king ordered the boy to be tied with mighty serpents called up from the nether worlds, and then cast to the bottom of the ocean, where huge mountains were to be piled high upon him, so that in course of time, if not immediately, he might die; and he ordered him to be left in this plight. Even though treated in this manner, the boy continued to pray to his beloved Vishnu: "Salutation to Thee, Lord of the universe. Thou beautiful Vishnu!" Thus thinking and meditating on Vishnu, he began to feel that Vishnu was near him, nay, that He was in his own soul, until he began to feel that he was Vishnu, and that he was everything and everywhere.

As soon as he realised this, all the snake bonds snapped asunder; the mountains were pulverised, the ocean upheaved, and he was gently lifted up above the waves, and safely carried to the shore. As Prahlada stood there, he forgot that he was a Daitya and had a mortal body: he felt he was the universe and all the powers of the universe emanated from him; there was nothing in nature that could injure him; he himself was the ruler of nature. Time passed thus, in one unbroken ecstasy of bliss, until gradually Prahlada began to remember that he had a body and that he was Prahlada. As soon as he became once more conscious of the body, he saw that God was within and without; and everything appeared to him as Vishnu.

When the king Hiranyakashipu found to his horror that all mortal means of getting rid of the boy who was perfectly devoted to his enemy, the God Vishnu, were powerless, he was at a loss to know what to do. The king had the boy again brought before him, and tried to persuade him once more to listen to his advice, through gentle means. But Prahlada made the same reply. Thinking, however, that these childish whims of the boy would be rectified with age and further training, he put him again under the charge of the teachers, Shanda and Amarka, asking them to teach him the duties of the king. But those teachings did not appeal to Prahlada, and he spent his time in instructing his schoolmates in the path of devotion to the Lord Vishnu.

When his father came to hear about it, he again became furious with rage, and calling the boy to him, threatened to kill him, and abused Vishnu in the worst language. But Prahlada still insisted that Vishnu was the Lord of the universe, the Beginningless, the Endless, the Omnipotent and the Omnipresent, and as such, he alone was to be worshipped. The king roared with anger and said: "Thou evil one, if thy Vishnu is God omnipresent, why doth he not reside in that pillar yonder?" Prahlada humbly submitted that He did do so. "If so," cried the king, "let him defend thee; I will kill thee with this sword." Thus saying the king rushed at him with sword in hand, and dealt a terrible blow at the pillar. Instantly thundering voice was heard, and lo and behold, there issued forth from the pillar Vishnu in His awful Nrisimha form — half-lion, half-man! Panic-stricken, the Daityas ran away in all directions; but Hiranyakashipu fought with him long and desperately, till he was finally overpowered and killed.

Then the gods descended from heaven and offered hymns to Vishnu, and Prahlada also fell at His feet and broke forth into exquisite hymns of praise and devotion. And he heard the Voice of God saying, "Ask, Prahlada ask for anything thou desires"; thou art My favourite child; therefore ask for anything thou mayest wish." And Prahlada choked with feelings replied, "Lord, I have seen Thee. What else can I want? Do thou not tempt me with earthly or heavenly boons." Again the Voice said: "Yet ask something, my son." And then Prahlada replied, "That intense love, O Lord, which the ignorant bear to worldly things, may I have the same love for Thee; may I have the same intensity of love for Thee, but only for love's sake!"

Then the Lord said, "Prahlada, though My intense devotees never desire for anything, here or hereafter, yet by My command, do thou enjoy the blessings of this world to the end of the present cycle, and perform works of religious merit, with thy heart fixed on Me. And thus in time, after the dissolution of thy body, thou shalt attain Me." Thus blessing Prahlada, the Lord Vishnu disappeared. Then the gods headed by Brahma installed Prahlada on the throne of the Daityas and returned to their respective spheres.

THE GREAT TEACHERS OF THE WORLD

Delivered at the Shakespeare Club, Pasadena, California, February 3, 1900

The universe, according to the theory of the Hindus, is moving in cycles of wave forms. It rises, reaches its zenith, then falls and remains in the hollow, as it were, for some time, once more to rise, and so on, in wave after wave and fall after fall. What is true of the universe is true of every part of it. The march of human affairs is like that. The history of nations is like that: they rise and they fall; after the rise comes a fall, again out of the fall comes a rise, with greater power. This motion is always going on. In the religious world the same movement exists. In every nation's spiritual life, there is a fall as well as a rise. The nation goes down, and everything seems to go to pieces. Then, again, it gains strength, rises; a huge wave comes, sometimes a tidal wave—and always on the topmost crest of the wave is a shining soul, the Messenger. Creator and created by turns, he is the impetus that makes the wave rise, the nation rise: at the same time, he is created by the same forces which make the wave, acting and interacting by turns. He puts forth his tremendous power upon society; and society makes him what he is. These are the great world-thinkers. These are the Prophets of the world, the Messengers of life, the Incarnations of God.

Man has an idea that there can be only one religion, that there can be only one Prophet, and that there can be only one Incarnation; but that idea is not true. By studying the lives of all these great Messengers, we find that each, as it were, was destined to play a part, and a part only; that the harmony consists in the sum total and not in one note. As in the life of races—no race is born to alone enjoy the world. None dare say no. Each race has a part to play in this divine harmony of nations. Each race has its mission to perform, its duty to fulfil. The sum total is the great harmony.

So, not any one of these Prophets is born to rule the world for ever. None has yet succeeded and none is going to be the ruler for ever. Each only contributes a part; and, as to that part, it is true that in the long run every Prophet will govern the world and its destinies.

Most of us are born believers in a personal religion. We talk of principles, we think of theories, and that is all right; but every thought and every movement, every one of our actions, shows that we can only understand the principle when it comes to us through a person. We can grasp an idea only when it comes to us through a materialised ideal person. We can understand the precept only through the example. Would to God that all of us were so developed that we would not require any example, would not require any person. But that we are not; and, naturally, the vast majority of mankind have put their souls at the feet of these extraordinary personalities, the Prophets, the Incarnations of God—Incarnations worshipped by the Christians, by the Buddhists, and by the Hindus. The Mohammedans from the beginning stood against any such worship. They would have nothing to do with worshipping the Prophets or the Messengers, or paying any homage to them; but, practically, instead of one Prophet, thousands upon thousands of saints are being worshipped. We cannot go against facts! We are bound to worship personalities, and it is good. Remember that word from your great Prophet to the query: "Lord, show us the Father", "He that hath seen me hath seen the Father." Which of us can imagine anything except that He is a man? We can only see Him in and through humanity. The vibration of light is everywhere in this room: why cannot lie see it everywhere? You have to see it only in that lamp. God is an Omnipresent Principle—everywhere: but we are so constituted at present that we can see Him, feel Him, only in and through a human God. And when these great Lights come, then man realises God. And they come in a different way from what we come. We come as beggars; they come as Emperors. We come here like orphans, as people who have lost their way and do not know it. What are we to do? We do not know what is the meaning of our lives. We cannot realise it. Today we are doing one thing, tomorrow another. We are like little bits of straw rocking to and fro in water, like feathers blown about in a hurricane.

But, in the history of mankind, you will find that there come these Messengers, and that from their very birth their mission is found and formed. The whole plan is there, laid down; and you see them swerving not one inch from that. Because they come with a mission, they come with a message, they do not want to reason. Did you ever hear or read of these great Teachers, or Prophets, reasoning out what they taught? No, not one of them did so. They speak direct. Why should they reason? They see the Truth. And not only do they see it but they show it! If you ask me, "Is there any God?" and I say "Yes", you immediately ask my grounds for saying so, and poor me has to exercise all his powers to provide you with some reason. If you had come to Christ and said, "Is there any God? " he would have said, "Yes"; and if you had asked, "Is there any proof?" he would have replied, "Behold the Lord! " And thus, you see, it is a direct perception, and not at all the ratiocination of reason. There is no groping in the dark, but there is the strength of direct vision. I see this table; no amount of reason can take that faith from me. It is a direct perception. Such is their faith—faith in their ideals, faith in their mission, faith in themselves, above all else. The great shining Ones believe in themselves as nobody else ever does. The people say, "Do you believe in God? Do you believe in a future life? Do you believe in this doctrine or that dogma?" But here the base is wanting: this belief in oneself. Ay, the man who cannot believe in himself, how can they expect him to believe in anything else? I am not sure of my own existence. One moment I think that I am existing and nothing can destroy me; the next moment I am quaking in fear of death. One minute I think I am immortal; the next minute, a spook appears, and then I don't know what I am, nor where I am. I don't know whether I am living or dead. One moment I think that I am spiritual, that I am moral; and the next moment, a blow comes, and I am thrown flat on my back. And why?—I have lost faith in myself, my moral backbone is broken.

But in these great Teachers you will always find this sign: that they have intense faith in themselves. Such intense faith is unique, and we cannot understand it. That is why we try to explain away in various ways what these Teachers speak of themselves; and people invent twenty thousand theories to explain what they say about their realisation. We do not think of ourselves in the same way, and, naturally, we cannot understand them.

Then again, when they speak, the world is bound to listen. When they speak, each word is direct; it bursts like a bombshell. What is in the word, unless it has the Power behind? What matters it what language you speak, and how you arrange your language? What matters it whether you speak correct grammar or with fine rhetoric? What matters it whether your language is ornamental or not? The question is whether or not you have anything to give. It is a question of giving and taking, and not listening. Have you anything to give?—that is the first question. If you have, then give. Words but convey the gift: it is but one of the many modes. Sometimes we do not speak at all. There is an old Sanskrit verse which says, "I saw the Teacher sitting under a tree. He was a young man of sixteen, and the disciple was an old man of eighty. The preaching of the Teacher was silence, and the doubts of the disciple departed."

Sometimes they do not speak at all, but yet they convey the Truth from mind to mind. They come to give. They command, they are the Messengers; you have to receive the Command. Do you not remember in your own scriptures the authority with which Jesus speaks? "Go ye, therefore, and teach all nations...teaching them to observe all things whatsoever I have commanded you." It runs through all his utterances, that tremendous faith in his own message. That you find in the life of all these great giants whom the world worships as its Prophets.

These great Teachers are the living Gods on this earth. Whom else should we worship? I try to get an idea of God in my mind, and I find what a false little thing I conceive; it would be a sin to worship that God. I open my eyes and look at the actual life of these great ones of the earth. They are higher than any conception of God that I could ever form. For, what conception of mercy could a man like me form who would go after a man if he steals anything from me and send him to jail? And what can be my highest idea of forgiveness? Nothing beyond myself. Which of you can jump out of your own bodies? Which of you can jump out of your own minds? Not one of you. What idea of divine love can you form except what you actually live? What we have never experienced we can form no idea of. So, all my best attempts at forming an idea of God would fail in every case. And here are plain facts, and not idealism—actual facts of love, of mercy, of purity, of which I can have no conception even. What wonder that I should fall at the feet of these men and worship them as God? And what else can anyone do? I should like to see the man who can do anything else, however much he may talk. Talking is not actuality. Talking about God and the Impersonal, and this and that is all very good; but these man-Gods are the real Gods of all nations and all races. These divine men have been worshipped and will be worshipped so long as man is man. Therein is our faith, therein is our hope, of a reality. Of what avail is a mere mystical principle!

The purpose and intent of what I have to say to you is this, that I have found it possible in my life to worship all of them, and to be ready for all that are yet to come. A mother recognises her son in any dress in which he may appear before her; and if one does not do so, I am sure she is not the mother of that man. Now, as regards those of you that think that you understand Truth and Divinity and God in only one Prophet in the world, and not in any other, naturally, the conclusion which I draw is that you do not understand Divinity in anybody; you have simply swallowed words and identified yourself with one sect, just as you would in party politics, as a matter of opinion; but that is no religion at all. There are some fools in this world who use brackish water although there is excellent sweet water near by, because, they say, the brackish-water well was dug by their father. Now, in my little experience I have collected this knowledge—that for all the devilry that religion is, blamed with, religion is not at all in fault: no religion ever persecuted men, no religion ever burnt witches, no religion ever did any of these things. What then incited people to do these things? Politics, but never religion; and if such politics takes the name of religion whose fault is that?

So, when each man stands and says "My Prophet is the only true Prophet," he is not correct—he knows not the alpha of religion. Religion is neither talk, nor theory, nor intellectual consent. It is realisation in the heart of our hearts; it is touching God; it is feeling, realising that I am a spirit in relation with the Universal Spirit and all Its great manifestations. If you have really entered the house of the Father, how can you have seen His children and not known them? And if you do not recognise them, you have not entered the house of the Father. The mother recognises her child in any dress and knows him however disguised. Recognise all the great, spiritual men and women in every age and country, and see that they are not really at variance with one another. Wherever there has been actual religion — this touch of the Divine, the soul coming in direct sense-contact with the Divine — there has always been a broadening of the mind which enables it to see the light everywhere. Now, some Mohammedans are the crudest in this respect, and the most sectarian. Their watchword is: "There is one God, and Mohammed is His Prophet." Everything beyond that not only is bad, but must be destroyed forthwith; at a moment's notice, every man or woman who does not exactly believe in that must be killed; everything that does not belong to this worship must be immediately broken; every book that teaches any thing else must be burnt. From the Pacific to the Atlantic, for five hundred years blood ran all over the world. That is Mohammedanism! Nevertheless, among these Mohammedans, wherever there has a philosophic man, he was sure to protest against these cruelties. In that he showed the touch of the Divine and realised a fragment of the truth; he was not playing with his religion; for it was not his father's religion he was talking, but spoke the truth direct like a man.

Side by side with tie modern theory of evolution, there is another thing: atavism. There is a tendency in us to revert to old ideas in religion. Let us think something new, even if it be wrong. It is better to do that. Why should you not try to hit the mark? We become wiser through failures. Time is infinite. Look at the wall. Did the wall ever tell a lie? It is always the wall. Man tells a lie — and becomes a god too. It is better to do something; never mind even if it proves to be wrong it is better than doing nothing. The cow never tells a lie, but she remains a cow, all the time. Do something! Think some thought; it doesn't matter whether you are right or wrong. But think something! Because my forefathers did not think this way, shall I sit down quietly and gradually lose my sense of feeling and my own thinking faculties? I may as well be dead! And what is life worth if we have no living ideas, no convictions of our own about religion? There is some hope for the atheists, because though they differ from others, they think for themselves. The people who never think anything for themselves are not yet born into the world of religion; they have a mere jelly-fish existence. They will not think; they do not care for religion. But the disbeliever, the atheist, cares, and he is struggling. So think something! Struggle Godward! Never mind if you fail, never mind if you get hold of a queer theory. If you are afraid to be called queer, keep it in your own mind — you need not go and preach it to others. But do something! Struggle Godward! Light must come. If a man feeds me every day of my life, in the long run I shall lose the use of my hands. Spiritual death is the result of following each other like a flock of sheep. Death is the result of inaction. Be active; and wherever there is activity, there must be difference. Difference is the sauce of life; it is the beauty, it is the art of everything. Difference makes all beautiful here. It is variety that is the source of life, the sign of life. Why should we be afraid of it?

Now, we are coming into a position to understand about the Prophets. Now, we see that the historical evidence is — apart from the jelly-fish existence in religion — that where there has been any real thinking, any real love for God, the soul has grown Godwards and has got as it were, a glimpse now and then, has come into direct perception, even for a second, even once in its life. Immediately, "All doubts vanish for ever, and all the crookedness of the heart is made straight, and all bondages vanish, and the results of action and Karma fly when He is seen who is the nearest of the near and the farthest of the far." That is religion, that is all of religion; the rest is mere theory, dogma, so many ways of going to that state of direct perception. Now we are fighting over the basket and the fruits have fallen into the ditch.

If two men quarrel about religion, just ask them the question: "Have you seen God? Have you seen these things?" One man says that Christ is the only Prophet: well, has he seen Christ? "Has your father seen Him?" "No, Sir." "Has your grandfather seen Him?" "No, Sir." "Have you seen Him?" "No, Sir." "Then what are you quarrelling for? The fruits have fallen into the ditch, and you are quarrelling over the basket!" Sensible men and women should be ashamed to go on quarrelling in that way!

These great Messengers and Prophets are great and true. Why? Because, each one has come to preach a great idea. Take the Prophets of India, for instance. They are the oldest of the founders of religion. We takes first, Krishna. You who have read the Gîtâ see all through the book that the one idea is non-attachment. Remain unattached. The heart's love is due to only One. To whom? To Him who never changeth. Who is that One? It is God. Do not make the mistake of giving the heart to anything that is changing, because that is misery. You may give it to a man; but if he dies, misery is the result. You may give it to a friend, but he may tomorrow become your enemy. If you give it to your husband, he may one day quarrel with you. You may give it to your wife, and she may die the day after tomorrow. Now, this is the way the world is going on. So says Krishna in the Gita: The Lord is the only One who never changes. His love never fails. Wherever we are and whatever we do, He is ever and ever the same merciful, the same loving heart. He never changes, He is never angry, whatever we do. How can God be angry with us? Your babe does many mischievous things: are you angry with that babe? Does not God know what we are going to be? He knows we are all going to be perfect, sooner or later. He has patience, infinite patience. We must love Him, and everyone that lives — only in and through Him. This is the keynote. You must love the wife, but not for the wife's sake. "Never, O Beloved, is the husband loved on account of the husband, but because the Lord is in the husband." The Vedanta philosophy says that even in the love of the husband and wife, although the wife is thinking that she is loving the husband, the real attraction is the Lord, who is present there. He is the only attraction, there is no other; but the wife in most cases does not know that it is so, but ignorantly she is doing the right thing, which is, loving the Lord. Only, when one does it ignorantly, it may bring pain. If one does it knowingly, that is salvation. This is what our scriptures say. Wherever there is love, wherever there is a spark of joy, know that to be a spark of His presence because He is joy, blessedness, and love itself. Without that there cannot be any love.

This is the trend of Krishna's instruction all the time. He has implanted that upon his race, so that when a Hindu does anything, even if he drinks water, he says "If there is virtue in it, let it go to the Lord." The Buddhist says, if he does any good deed, "Let the merit of the good deed belong to the world; if there is any virtue in what I do, let it go to the world, and let the evils of the world come to me." The Hindu says he is a great believer in God; the Hindu says that God is omnipotent and that He is the Soul of every soul everywhere; the Hindu says, If I give all my virtues unto Him, that is the greatest sacrifice, and they will go to the whole universe."

Now, this is one phase; and what is the other message of Krishna? "Whosoever lives in the midst of the world, and works, and gives up all the fruit of his action unto the Lord, he is never touched with the evils of the world. Just as the lotus, born under the water, rises up and blossoms above the water, even so is the man who is engaged in the activities of the world, giving up all the fruit of his activities unto the Lord" (Gita, V. 10).

Krishna strikes another note as a teacher of intense activity. Work, work, work day and night, says the Gita. You may ask, "Then, where is peace? If all through life I am to work like a cart-horse and die in harness, what am I here for?" Krishna says, "Yes, you will find peace. Flying from work is never the way to find peace." Throw off your duties if you can, and go to the top of a mountain; even there the mind is going—whirling, whirling, whirling. Someone asked a Sannyasin, "Sir, have you found a nice place? How many years have you been travelling in the Himalayas?" "For forty years," replied the Sannyasin. "There are many beautiful spots to select from, and to settle down in: why did you not do so?" "Because for these forty years my mind would not allow me to do so." We all say, "Let us find peace"; but the mind will not allow us to do so.

You know the story of the man who caught a Tartar. A soldier was outside the town, and he cried out when be came near the barracks, "I have caught a Tartar." A voice called out, "Bring him in." "He won't come in, sir." "Then you come in." "He won't let me come in, sir." So, in this mind of ours, we have "caught a Tartar": neither can we tone it down, nor will it let us be toned down. We have all "caught Tartars". We all say, be quiet, and peaceful, and so forth. But every baby can say that and thinks he can do it. However, that is very difficult. I have tried. I threw overboard all my duties and fled to the tops

of mountains; I lived in caves and deep forests—but all the same, I "caught a Tartar" because I had my world with me all the time. The "Tartar" is what I have in my own mind, so we must not blame poor people outside. "These circumstances are good, and these are bad," so we say, while the "Tartar" is here, within; if we can quiet him down, we shall be all right.

Therefore Krishna teaches us not to shirk our duties, but to take them up manfully, and not think of the result. The servant has no right to question. The soldier has no right to reason. Go forward, and do not pay too much attention to the nature of the work you have to do. Ask your mind if you are unselfish. If you are, never mind anything, nothing can resist you! Plunge in! Do the duty at hand. And when you have done this, by degrees you will realise the Truth: "Whosoever in the midst of intense activity finds intense peace, whosoever in the midst of the greatest peace finds the greatest activity, he is a Yogi, he is a great soul, he has arrived at perfection."

Now, you see that the result of this teaching is that all the duties of the world are sanctified. There is no duty in this world which we have any right to call menial: and each man's work is quite as good as that of the emperor on his throne.

Listen to Buddha's message—a tremendous message. It has a place in our heart. Says Buddha, "Root out selfishness, and everything that makes you selfish. Have neither wife, child, nor family. Be not of the world; become perfectly unselfish." A worldly man thinks he will be unselfish, but when he looks at the face of his wife it makes him selfish. The mother thinks she will be perfectly unselfish, but she looks at her baby, and immediately selfishness comes. So with everything in this world. As soon as selfish desires arise, as soon as some selfish pursuit is followed, immediately the whole man, the real man, is gone: he is like a brute, he is a slave' he forgets his fellow men. No more does he say, "You first and I afterwards," but it is "I first and let everyone else look out for himself."

We find that Krishna's message has also a place for us. Without that message, we cannot move at all. We cannot conscientiously and with peace, joy, and happiness, take up any duty of our lives without listening to the message of Krishna: "Be not afraid even if there is evil in your work, for there is no work which has no evil." "Leave it unto the Lord, and do not look for the results."

On the other hand, there is a corner in the heart for the other message: Time flies; this world is finite and all misery. With your good food, nice clothes, and your comfortable home, O sleeping man and woman, do you ever think of the millions that are starving and dying? Think of the great fact that it is all misery, misery, misery! Note the first utterance of the child: when it enters into the world, it weeps. That is the fact—the child-weeps. This is a place for weeping! If we listen to the Messenger, we should not be selfish.

Behold another Messenger, He of Nazareth. He teaches, "Be ready, for the Kingdom of Heaven is at hand." I have pondered over the message of Krishna, and am trying to work without attachment, but sometimes I forget. Then, suddenly, comes to me the message of Buddha: "Take care, for everything in the world as evanescent, and there is always misery in this life." I listen to that, and I am uncertain which to accept. Then again comes, like a thunderbolt, the message: "Be ready, for the Kingdom of Heaven is at hand." Do not delay a moment. Leave nothing for tomorrow. Get ready for the final event, which may overtake you immediately, even now. That message, also, has a place, and we acknowledge it. We salute the Messenger, we salute the Lord.

And then comes Mohammed, the Messenger of equality. You ask, "What good can there be in his religion?" If there were no good, how could it live? The good alone lives, that alone survives; because the good alone is strong, therefore it survives. How long is the life of an impure man, even in this life? Is not the life of the pure man much longer? Without doubt, for purity is strength, goodness is strength. How could Mohammedanism have lived, had there been nothing good in its teaching? There is much good. Mohammed was the Prophet of equality, of the brotherhood of man, the brotherhood of all Mussulmans

So we see that each Prophet, each Messenger, has a particular message. When you first listen to that message, and then look at his life, you see his whole life stands explained, radiant.

Now, ignorant fools start twenty thousand theories, and put forward, according to their own mental development, explanations to suit their own ideas, and ascribe them to these great Teachers. They take their teachings and put their misconstruction upon them. With every great Prophet his life is the only commentary. Look at his life: what he did will bear out the texts. Read the Gita, and you will find that it is exactly borne out by the life of the Teacher.

Mohammed by his life showed that amongst Mohammedans there should be perfect equality and brotherhood. There was no question of race, caste, creed, colour, or sex. The Sultan of Turkey may buy a Negro from the mart of Africa, and bring him in chains to Turkey; but should he become a Mohammedan and have sufficient merit and abilities, he might even marry the daughter of the Sultan. Compare this with the way in which the Negroes and the American Indians are treated in this country! And what do Hindus do? If one of your missionaries chance to touch the food of an orthodox person, he would throw it away. Notwithstanding our grand philosophy, you note our weakness in practice; but there You see the greatness of the Mohammedan beyond other races, showing itself in equality, perfect equality regardless of race or colour.

Will other and greater Prophets come? Certainly they will come in this world. But do not look forward to that. I should better like that each one of you became a Prophet of this real New Testament, which is made up of all the Old Testaments. Take all the old messages, supplement them with your own realisations, and become a Prophet unto others. Each one of these Teachers has been great; each has left something for us;

they have been our Gods. We salute them, we are their servants; and, all the same, we salute ourselves; for if they have been Prophets and children of God, we also are the same. They reached their perfection, and we are going to attain ours now. Remember the words of Jesus: "The Kingdom of Heaven is at hand!" This very moment let everyone of us make a staunch resolution: "I will become a Prophet, I will become a messenger of Light, I will become a child of God, nay, I will become a God!"

ON LORD BUDDHA

Delivered in Detroit

In every religion we find one type of self-devotion particularly developed. The type of working without a motive is most highly developed in Buddhism. Do not mistake Buddhism and Brâhminism. In this country you are very apt to do so. Buddhism is one of our sects. It was founded by a great man called Gautama, who became disgusted at the eternal metaphysical discussions of his day, and the cumbrous rituals, and more especially with the caste system. Some people say that we are born to a certain state, and therefore we are superior to others who are not thus born. He was also against the tremendous priestcraft. He preached a religion in which there was no motive power, and was perfectly agnostic about metaphysics or theories about God. He was often asked if there was a God, and he answered, he did not know. When asked about right conduct, he would reply, "Do good and be good." There came five Brâhmins, who asked him to settle their discussion. One said, "Sir, my book says that God is such and such, and that this is the way to come to God." Another said, "That is wrong, for my book says such and such, and this is the way to come to God"; and so the others. He listened calmly to all of them, and then asked them one by one, "Does any one of your books say that God becomes angry, that He ever injures anyone, that He is impure?" "No, Sir, they all teach that God is pure and good." "Then, my friends, why do you not become pure and good first, that you may know what God is?"

Of course I do not endorse all his philosophy. I want a good deal of metaphysics, for myself. I entirely differ in many respects, but, because I differ, is that any reason why I should not see the beauty of the man? He was the only man who was bereft of all motive power. There were other great men who all said they were the Incarnations of God Himself, and that those who would believe in them would go to heaven. But what did Buddha say with his dying breath? "None can help you; help yourself; work out your own salvation." He said about himself, "Buddha is the name of infinite knowledge, infinite as the sky; I, Gautama, have reached that state; you will all reach that too if you struggle for it." Bereft of all motive power, he did not want to go to heaven, did not want money; he gave up his throne and everything else and went about begging his bread through the streets of India, preaching for the good of men and animals with a heart as wide as the ocean.

He was the only man who was ever ready to give up his life for animals to stop a sacrifice. He once said to a king, "If the sacrifice of a lamb helps you to go to heaven, sacrificing a man will help you better; so sacrifice me." The king was astonished. And yet this man was without any motive power. He stands as the perfection of the active type, and the very height to which he attained shows that through the power of work we can also attain to the highest spirituality.

To many the path becomes easier if they believe in God. But the life of Buddha shows that even a man who does not believe in God, has no metaphysics, belongs to no sect, and does not go to any church, or temple, and is a confessed materialist, even he can attain to the highest. We have no right to judge him. I wish I had one infinitesimal part of Buddha's heart. Buddha may or may not have believed in God; that does not matter to me. He reached the same state of perfection to which others come by Bhakti—love of God—Yoga, or Jnâna. Perfection does not come from belief or faith. Talk does not count for anything. Parrots can do that. Perfection comes through the disinterested performance of action.

CHRIST, THE MESSENGER

Delivered at Los Angeles, California, 1900

The wave rises on the ocean, and there is a hollow. Again another wave rises, perhaps bigger than the former, to fall down again, similarly, again to rise—driving onward. In the march of events, we notice the rise and fall, and we generally look towards the rise, forgetting the fall. But both are necessary, and both are great. This is the nature of the universe. Whether in the world of our thoughts, the world of our relations in society, or in our spiritual affairs, the same movement of succession, of rises and falls, is going on. Hence great predominances in the march of events, the liberal ideals, are marshalled ahead, to sink down, to digest, as it were, to ruminate over the past—to adjust, to conserve, to gather strength once more for a rise and a bigger rise.

The history of nations also has ever been like that. The great soul, the Messenger we are to study this afternoon, came at a period of the history of his race which we may well designate as a great fall. We catch only little glimpses here and there of the stray records that have been kept of his sayings and doings; for verily it has been well said, that the doings and sayings of that great soul would fill the world if they had all been written down. And the three years of his ministry were like one compressed, concentrated age, which it has taken nineteen hundred years to unfold, and who knows how much longer it will yet take! Little men like you and me are simply the recipients of just a little energy. A few minutes, a few hours, a few years at best, are enough to spend it all, to stretch it out, as it were, to its fullest strength, and then we are gone for ever. But mark this giant that came; centuries and ages pass, yet the energy that he left upon the world is not yet stretched, nor yet expended to its full. It goes on adding new vigour as the ages roll on.

Now what you see in the life of Christ is the life of all the past. The life of every man is, in a manner, the life of the past. It comes to him through heredity, through surroundings, through education, through his own reincarnation—the past of the race. In a manner, the past of the earth, the past of the whole world is there, upon every soul. What are we, in the present, but a result, an effect, in the hands of that infinite past? What are we but floating waveless in the eternal current of events, irresistibly moved forward and onward and incapable of rest? But you and I are only little things, bubbles. There are always some giant waves in the ocean of affairs, and in you and me the life of the past race has been embodied only a little; but there are giants who embody, as it were, almost the whole of the past and who stretch out their hands for the future. These are the sign-posts here and there which point to the march of humanity; these are verily gigantic, their shadows covering the earth—they stand undying, eternal! As it has been said by the same Messenger, "No man hath seen God at any time, but through the Son." And that is true. And where shall we see God but in the Son? It is true that you and I, and the poorest of us, the meanest even, embody that God, even reflect that God. The vibration of light is everywhere, omnipresent; but we have to strike the light of the lamp before we can see the light. The Omnipresent God of the universe cannot be seen until He is reflected by these giant lamps of the earth—The Prophets, the man-Gods, the Incarnations, the embodiments of God.

We all know that God exists, and yet we do not see Him, we do not understand Him. Take one of these great Messengers of light, compare his character with the highest ideal of God that you ever formed, and you will find that your God falls short of the ideal, and that the character of the Prophet exceeds your conceptions. You cannot even form a higher ideal of God than what the actually embodied have practically realised and set before us as an example. Is it wrong, therefore, to worship these as God? Is it a sin to fall at the feet of these man-Gods and worship them as the only divine beings in the world? If they are really, actually, higher than all our conceptions of God, what harm is there in worshipping them? Not only is there no harm, but it is the only possible and positive way of worship. However much you may try by struggle, by abstraction, by whatsoever method you like, still so long as you are a man in the world of men, your world is human, your religion is human, and your God is human. And that must be so. Who is not practical enough to take up an actually existing thing and give up an idea which is only an abstraction, which he cannot grasp, and is difficult of approach except through a concrete medium? Therefore, these Incarnations of God have been worshipped in all ages and in all countries.

We are now going to study a little of the life of Christ, the Incarnation of the Jews. When Christ was born, the Jews were in that state which I call a state of fall between two waves; a state of conservatism; a state where the human mind is, as it were, tired for the time being of moving forward and is taking care only of what it has already; a state when the attention is more bent upon particulars, upon details, than upon the great, general, and bigger problems of life; a state of stagnation, rather than a towing ahead; a state of suffering more than of doing. Mark you, I do not blame this state of things. We have no right to criticise it—because had it not been for this fall, the next rise, which was embodied in Jesus of Nazareth would have been impossible. The Pharisees and Sadducees might have been insincere, they might have been doing things which they ought not to have done; they might have been even hypocrites; but whatever they were, these factors were the very cause, of which the Messenger was the effect. The Pharisees and Sadducees at one end were the very impetus which came out at the other end as the gigantic brain of Jesus of Nazareth.

The attention to forms, to formulas, to the everyday details of religion, and to rituals, may sometimes be laughed at; but nevertheless, within them is strength. Many times in the rushing forward we lose much strength. As a fact, the fanatic is stronger than the liberal man. Even the fanatic, therefore, has one great virtue, he conserves energy, a tremendous amount of it. As with the individual so with the race, energy is gathered to be conserved. Hemmed in all around by external enemies, driven to focus in a centre by the Romans, by the Hellenic tendencies in the world of intellect, by waves from Persia, India, and Alexandria—hemmed in physically, mentally, and morally—there stood the race with an inherent, conservative, tremendous strength, which their descendants have not lost even today. And the race was forced to concentrate and focus all its energies upon Jerusalem and Judaism. But all power when once gathered cannot remain collected; it must expend and expand itself. There is no power on earth which can be kept long confined within a narrow limit. It cannot be kept compressed too long to allow of expansion at a subsequent period.

This concentrated energy amongst the Jewish race found its expression at the next period in the rise of Christianity. The gathered streams collected into a body. Gradually, all the little streams joined together, and became a surging wave on the top of which we find standing out the character of Jesus of Nazareth. Thus, every Prophet is a creation of his own times, the creation of the past of his race; he himself is the creator of the future. The cause of today is the effect of the past and the cause for the future. In this position stands the Messenger. In him is embodied all that is the best and greatest in his own race, the meaning, the life, for which that race has struggled for ages; and he himself is the impetus for the future, not only to his own race but to unnumbered other races of the world.

We must bear another fact in mind: that my view of the great Prophet of Nazareth would be from the standpoint of the Orient. Many times you forget, also, that the Nazarene himself was an Oriental of Orientals. With all your attempts to paint him with blue eyes and yellow hair, the Nazarene was still an Oriental. All the similes, the imageries, in which the Bible is written—the scenes, the locations, the attitudes, the groups, the poetry, and symbol,—speak to you of the Orient: of the bright sky, of the heat, of the sun, of the desert, of the thirsty men and animals; of men and women coming with pitchers on their heads to fill them at the wells; of the flocks, of the ploughmen, of the cultivation that is going on around; of the water-mill and wheel, of the mill-pond, of the millstones. All these are to be seen today in Asia.

The voice of Asia has been the voice of religion. The voice of Europe is the voice of politics. Each is great in its own sphere. The voice of Europe is the voice of ancient Greece. To the Greek mind, his immediate society was all in all: beyond that, it is Barbarian. None but the Greek has the right to live. Whatever the Greeks do is right and correct; whatever else there exists in the world is neither right nor correct, nor should be allowed to live. It is intensely human in its sympathies, intensely natural, intensely artistic, therefore. The Greek lives entirely in this world. He does not care to dream. Even his poetry is practical. His gods and goddesses are not only human beings, but intensely human, with all human passions and feelings almost the same as with any of us. He loves what is beautiful, but mind you, it is always external nature: the beauty of the hills, of the snows, of the flowers, the beauty of forms and of figures, the beauty in the human face, and, more often, in the human form—that is what the Greeks liked. And the Greeks being the teachers of all subsequent Europeanism, the voice of Europe is Greek.

There is another type in Asia. Think of that vast, huge continent, whose mountain-tops go beyond the clouds, almost touching the canopy of heaven's blue; a rolling desert of miles upon miles where a drop of water cannot be found, neither will a blade of grass grow; interminable forests and gigantic rivers rushing down into the sea. In the midst of all these surroundings, the oriental love of the beautiful and of the sublime developed itself in another direction. It looked inside, and not outside. There is also the thirst for nature, and there is also the same thirst for power; there is also the same thirst for excellence, the same idea of the Greek and Barbarian, but it has extended over a larger circle. In Asia, even today, birth or colour or language never makes a race. That which makes a race is its religion. We are all Christians; we are all Mohammedans; we are all Hindus, or all Buddhists. No matter if a Buddhist is a Chinaman, or is a man from Persia, they think that they are brothers, because of their professing the same religion. Religion is the tie, unity of humanity. And then again, the Oriental, for the same reason, is a visionary, is a born dreamer. The ripples of the waterfalls, the songs of the birds, the beauties of the sun and moon and the stars and the whole earth are pleasant enough; but they are not sufficient for the oriental mind; He wants to dream a dream beyond. He wants to go beyond the present. The present, as it were, is nothing to him. The Orient has been the cradle of the human race for ages, and all the vicissitudes of fortune are there—kingdoms succeeding kingdoms, empires succeeding empires, human power, glory, and wealth, all rolling down there: a Golgotha of power and learning. That is the Orient: a Golgotha of power, of kingdoms, of learning. No wonder, the oriental mind looks with contempt upon the things of this world and naturally wants to see something that changeth not, something which dieth not, something which in the midst of this world of misery and death is eternal, blissful, undying. An oriental Prophet never tires of insisting upon these ideals; and, as for Prophets, you may also remember that without one exception, all the Messengers were Orientals.

We see, therefore, in the life of this area: Messenger of life, the first watchword: "Not this life, but something higher"; and, like the true son of the Orient, he is practical in that. You people of the West are practical in your own department, in military affairs, and in managing political circles and other things. Perhaps the Oriental is not practical in those ways, but he is practical in his own field; he is practical in religion. If one preaches a philosophy, tomorrow there are hundreds who will struggle their best to make it practical in their lives. If a man preaches that standing on one foot would lead one to salvation, he will immediately get five hundred to stand on one foot. You may call it ludicrous; but, mark you, beneath that is their philosophy—that intense practicality. In the West, plans of salvation mean intellectual gymnastics—plans which are never worked out, never brought into practical life. In the West, the preacher who talks the best is the greatest preacher.

So, we find Jesus of Nazareth, in the first place, the true son of the Orient, intensely practical. He has no faith in this evanescent world and all its belongings. No need of text-torturing, as is the fashion in the West in modern times, no need of stretching out texts until the, will not stretch any more. Texts are not India rubber, and even that has its limits. Now, no making of religion to pander to the sense vanity of the present day! Mark you, let us all be honest. If we cannot follow the ideal, let us confess our weakness, but not degrade it; let not any try to pull it down. One gets sick at heart at the different accounts of the life of the Christ that Western people give. I do not know what he was or what he was not! One would make him a great politician; another, perhaps, would make of him a great military general; another, a great patriotic Jew; and so on. Is there any warrant in the books for all such assumptions? The best commentary on the life of a great teacher is his own life. "The foxes have holes, the birds of the air have nests, but the Son of man hath not where to lay his head." That is what Christ says as they only way to salvation; he lays down no other way. Let us confess in sackcloth and ashes that we cannot do that. We still have fondness for "me and mine". We want property, money, wealth. Woe unto us! Let us confess and not put to shame that great Teacher of Humanity! He had no family ties. But do you think that, that Man had any physical ideas in him? Do you think that, this mass of light, this God and not-man, came down to earth, to be the brother of animals? And yet, people make him preach all sorts of things. He had no sex ideas! He was a soul! Nothing but a soul—just working a body for the good of humanity; and that was all his relation to the body. In the soul there is no sex. The disembodied soul has no relationship to the animal, no relationship to the body. The ideal may be far away beyond us. But never mind, keep to the ideal. Let us confess that it is our ideal, but we cannot approach it yet.

He had no other occupation in life, no other thought except that one, that he was a spirit. He was a disembodied, unfettered, unbound spirit. And not only so, but he, with his marvellous vision, had found that every man and woman, whether Jew or Gentile, whether rich or poor, whether saint or sinner, was the embodiment of the same undying spirit as himself. Therefore, the one work his whole life showed was to call upon them to realise their own spiritual nature. Give up, he says, these superstitious dreams that you are low and that you are poor. Think not that you are trampled upon and tyrannised over as if you were slaves, for within you is something that can never be tyrannised over, never be trampled upon, never be troubled, never be killed. You are all Sons of God, immortal spirit. "Know", he declared, "the Kingdom of Heaven is within you." "I and my Father are one." Dare you stand up and say, not only that "I am the Son of God", but I shall also find in my heart of hearts that "I and my Father are one"? That was what Jesus of Nazareth said. He never talks of this world and of this life. He has nothing to do with it, except that he wants to get hold of the world as it is, give it a push and drive it forward and onward until the whole world has reached to the effulgent Light of God, until everyone has realised his spiritual nature, until death is vanished and misery banished.

We have read the different stories that have been written about him; we know the scholars and their writings, and the higher criticism; and we know all that has been done by study. We are not here to discuss how much of the New Testament is true, we are not here to discuss how much of that life is historical. It does not matter at all whether the New Testament was written within five hundred years of his birth, nor does it matter even, how much of that life is true. But there is something behind it, something we want to imitate. To tell a lie, you have to imitate a truth, and that truth is a fact. You cannot imitate that which never existed. You cannot imitate that which you never perceived. But there must have been a nucleus, a tremendous power that came down, a marvellous manifestation of spiritual power—and of that we are speaking. It stands there. Therefore, we are not afraid of all the criticisms of the scholars. If I, as an Oriental, have to worship Jesus of Nazareth, there is only one way left to me, that is, to worship him as God and nothing else. Have we no right to worship him in that way, do you mean to say? If we bring him down to our own level and simply pay him a little respect as a great man, why should we worship at all? Our scriptures say, "These great children of Light, who manifest the Light themselves, who are Light themselves, they, being worshipped, become, as it were, one with us and we become one with them."

For, you see, in three ways man perceives God. At first the undeveloped intellect of the uneducated man sees God as far away, up in the heavens somewhere, sitting on a throne as a great Judge. He looks upon Him as a fire, as a terror. Now, that is good, for there is nothing bad in it. You must remember that humanity travels not from error to truth, but from truth to truth; it may be, if you like it better, from lower truth to higher truth, but never from error to truth. Suppose you start from here and travel towards the sun in a straight line. From here the sun looks only small in size. Suppose you go forward a million miles, the sun will be much bigger. At every stage the sun will become bigger and bigger. Suppose twenty thousand photographs had been taken of the same sun, from different standpoints; these twenty thousand photographs will all certainly differ from one another. But can you deny that each is a photograph of the same sun? So all forms of religion, high or low, are just different stages toward that eternal state of Light, which is God Himself. Some embody a lower view, some a higher, and that is all the difference. Therefore, the religions of the unthinking masses all over the world must be, and have always been, of a God who is outside of the universe, who lives in heaven, who governs from that place, who is a punisher of the bad and a rewarder of the good, and so on. As man advanced spiritually, he began to feel that God was omnipresent, that He must be in him, that He must be everywhere, that He was not a distant God, but dearly the Soul of all souls. As my soul moves my body, even so is God the mover of my soul. Soul within soul. And a few individuals who had developed enough and were pure enough, went still further, and at last found God. As the New Testament says, "Blessed are the pure in heart, for they shall see God." And they found at last that they and the Father were one.

You find that all these three stages are taught by the Great Teacher in the New Testament. Note the Common Prayer he taught: "Our Father which art in Heaven, hallowed be Thy name," and so on—a simple prayer, a child's prayer. Mark you, it is the "Common Prayer" because it is intended for the uneducated masses. To a higher circle, to those who had advanced a little more, he gave a more elevated teaching: "I am in my Father, and ye in me, and I in you." Do you remember that? And then, when the Jews asked him who he was, he declared that he and his Father were one, and the Jews thought that that was blasphemy. What did he mean by that? This has been also told by your old Prophets, "Ye are gods and all of you are children of the Most High." Mark the same three stages. You will find that it is easier for you to begin with the first and end with the last.

The Messenger came to show the path: that the spirit is not in forms, that it is not through all sorts of vexations and knotty problems of philosophy that you know the spirit. Better that you had no learning, better that you never read a book in your life. These are not at all necessary for salvation—nei-

ther wealth, nor position nor power, not even learning; but what is necessary is that one thing, purity. "Blessed are the pure in heart," for the spirit in its own nature is pure. How can it be otherwise? It is of God, it has come from God. In the language of the Bible, "It is the breath of God." In the language of the Koran, "It is the soul of God." Do you mean to say that the Spirit of God can ever be impure? But, alas, it has been, as it were, covered over with the dust and dirt of ages, through our own actions, good and evil. Various works which were not correct, which were not true, have covered the same spirit with the dust and dirt of the ignorance of ages. It is only necessary to clear away the dust and dirt, and then the spirit shines immediately. "Blessed are the pure in heart, for they shall see God." "The Kingdom of Heaven is within you." Where goest thou to seek for the Kingdom of God, asks Jesus of Nazareth, when it is there, within you? Cleanse the spirit, and it is there. It is already yours. How can you get what is not yours? It is yours by right. You are the heirs of immortality, sons of the Eternal Father.

This is the great lesson of the Messenger, and another which is the basis of all religions, is renunciation. How can you make the spirit pure? By renunciation. A rich young man asked Jesus, "Good Master, what shall I do that I may inherit eternal life?" And Jesus said unto him, "One thing thou lackest; go thy way, sell whatsoever thou hast, and give to the poor, and thou shalt have treasures in heaven: and come, take up thy cross, and follow Me." And he was sad at that saying and went away grieved; for he had great possessions. We are all more or less like that. The voice is ringing in our ears day and night. In the midst of our pleasures and joys, in the midst of worldly things, we think that we have forgotten everything else. Then comes a moment's pause and the voice rings in our ears "Give up all that thou hast and follow Me." "Whosoever will save his life shall lose it; and whosoever shall lose his life for My sake shall find it." For whoever gives up this life for His sake, finds the life immortal. In the midst of all our weakness there is a moment of pause and the voice rings: "Give up all that thou hast; give it to the poor and follow me." This is the one ideal he preaches, and this has been the ideal preached by all the great Prophets of the world: renunciation. What is meant by renunciation? That there is only one ideal in morality: unselfishness. Be selfless. The ideal is perfect unselfishness. When a man is struck on the right cheek, he turns the left also. When a man's coat is carried off, he gives away his cloak also.

We should work in the best way we can, without dragging the ideal down. Here is the ideal. When a man has no more self in him, no possession, nothing to call "me" or "mine", has given himself up entirely, destroyed himself as it were—in that man is God Himself; for in him self-will is gone, crushed out, annihilated. That is the ideal man. We cannot reach that state yet; yet, let us worship the ideal, and slowly struggle to reach the ideal, though, maybe, with faltering steps. It may be tomorrow, or it may be a thousand years hence; but that ideal has to be reached. For it is not only the end, but also the means. To be unselfish, perfectly selfless, is salvation itself; for the man within dies, and God alone remains.

One more point. All the teachers of humanity are unselfish. Suppose Jesus of Nazareth was teaching; and a man came and told him, "What you teach is beautiful. I believe that it is the way to perfection, and I am ready to follow it; but I do not care to worship you as the only begotten Son of God." What would be the answer of Jesus of Nazareth? "Very well, brother, follow the ideal and advance in your own way. I do not care whether you give me the credit for the teaching or not. I am not a shopkeeper. I do not trade in religion. I only teach truth, and truth is nobody's property. Nobody can patent truth. Truth is God Himself. Go forward." But what the disciples say nowadays is: "No matter whether you practise the teachings or not, do you give credit to the Man? If you credit the Master, you will be saved; if not, there is no salvation for you." And thus the whole teaching of the Master is degenerated, and all the struggle and fight is for the personality of the Man. They do not know that in imposing that difference, they are, in a manner, bringing shame to the very Man they want to honour—the very Man that would have shrunk with shame from such an idea. What did he care if there was one man in the world that remembered him or not? He had to deliver his message, and he gave it. And if he had twenty thousand lives, he would give them all up for the poorest man in the world. If he had to be tortured millions of times for a million despised Samaritans, and if for each one of them the sacrifice of his own life would be the only condition of salvation, he would have given his life. And all this without wishing to have his name known even to a single person. Quiet, unknown, silent, would he world, just as the Lord works. Now, what would the disciple say? He will tell you that you may be a perfect man, perfectly unselfish; but unless you give the credit to our teacher, to our saint, it is of no avail. Why? What is the origin of this superstition, this ignorance? The disciple thinks that the Lord can manifest Himself only once. There lies the whole mistake. God manifests Himself to you in man. But throughout nature, what happens once must have happened before, and must happen in future. There is nothing in nature which is not bound by law; and that means that whatever happens once must go on and must have been going on.

In India they have the same idea of the Incarnations of God. One of their great Incarnations, Krishna, whose grand sermon, the Bhagavad-Gîtâ, some of you might have read, says, "Though I am unborn, of changeless nature, and Lord of beings, yet subjugating My Prakriti, I come into being by My own Mâyâ. Whenever virtue subsides and immorality prevails, then I body Myself forth. For the protection of the good, for the destruction of the wicked, and for the establishment of Dharma, I come into being, in every age." Whenever the world goes down, the Lord comes to help it forward; and so He does from time to time and place to place. In another passage He speaks to this effect: Wherever thou findest a great soul of immense power and purity struggling to raise human-

ity, know that he is born of My splendour, that I am there working through him.

Let us, therefore, find God not only in Jesus of Nazareth, but in all the great Ones that have preceded him, in all that came after him, and all that are yet to come. Our worship is unbounded and free. They are all manifestations of the same Infinite God. They are all pure and unselfish; they struggled and gave up their lives for us, poor human beings. They each and all suffer vicarious atonement for every one of us, and also for all that are to come hereafter.

In a sense you are all Prophets; every one of you is a Prophet, bearing the burden of the world on your own shoulders. Have you ever seen a man, have you ever seen a woman, who is not quietly, patiently, bearing his or her little burden of life? The great Prophets were giants—they bore a gigantic world on their shoulders. Compared with them we are pigmies, no doubt, yet we are doing the same task; in our little circles, in our little homes, we are bearing our little crosses. There is no one so evil, no one so worthless, but he has to bear his own cross. But with all our mistakes, with all our evil thoughts and evil deeds, there is a bright spot somewhere, there is still somewhere the golden thread through which we are always in touch with the divine. For, know for certain, that the moment the touch of the divine is lost there would be annihilation. And because none can be annihilated, there is always somewhere in our heart of hearts, however low and degraded we may be, a little circle of light which is in constant touch with the divine.

Our salutations go to all the past Prophets whose teachings and lives we have inherited, whatever might have been their race, clime, or creed! Our salutations go to all those Godlike men and women who are working to help humanity, whatever be their birth, colour, or race! Our salutations to those who are coming in the future—living Gods—to work unselfishly for our descendants.

MY MASTER[1]

"Whenever virtue subsides and vice prevails, I come down to help mankind," declares Krishna, in the Bhagavad-Gîtâ. Whenever this world of ours, on account of growth, on account of added circumstances, requires a new adjustment, a wave of power comes; and as a man is acting on two planes, the spiritual and the material, waves of adjustment come on both planes. On the one side, of the adjustment on the material plane, Europe has mainly been the basis during modern times; and of the adjustment on the other, the spiritual plane, Asia has been the basis throughout the history of the world. Today, man requires one more adjustment on the spiritual plane; today when material ideas are at the height of their glory and power, today when man is likely to forget his divine nature, through his growing dependence on matter, and is

1. Two lectures delivered in New York and England in 1896 were combined subsequently under the present heading.

likely to be reduced to a mere money-making machine, an adjustment is necessary; the voice has spoken, and the power is coming to drive away the clouds of gathering materialism. The power has been set in motion which, at no distant date, will bring unto mankind once more the memory of its real nature; and again the place from which this power will start will be Asia.

This world of ours is on the plan of the division of labour. It is vain to say that one man shall possess everything. Yet how childish we are! The baby in its ignorance thinks that its doll is the only possession that is to be coveted in this whole universe. So a nation which is great in the possession of material power thinks that that is all that is to be coveted, that that is all that is meant by progress, that that is all that is meant by civilisation, and if there are other nations which do not care for possession and do not possess that power, they are not fit to live, their whole existence is useless! On the other hand, another nation may think that mere material civilisation is utterly useless. From the Orient came the voice which once told the world that if a man possesses everything that is under the sun and does not possess spirituality, what avails it? This is the oriental type; the other is the occidental type.

Each of these types has its grandeur, each has its glory. The present adjustment will be the harmonising, the mingling of these two ideals. To the Oriental, the world of spirit is as real as to the Occidental is the world of senses. In the spiritual, the Oriental finds everything he wants or hopes for; in it he finds all that makes life real to him. To the Occidental he is a dreamer; to the Oriental the Occidental is a dreamer playing with ephemeral toys, and he laughs to think that grown-up men and women should make so much of a handful of matter which they will have to leave sooner or later. Each calls the other a dreamer. But the oriental ideal is as necessary for the progress of the human race as is the occidental, and I think it is more necessary. Machines never made mankind happy and never will make. He who is trying to make us believe this will claim that happiness is in the machine; but it is always in the mind. That man alone who is the lord of his mind can become happy, and none else. And what, after all, is this power of machinery? Why should a man who can send a current of electricity through a wire be called a very great man and a very intelligent man? Does not nature do a million times more than that every moment? Why not then fall down and worship nature? What avails it if you have power over the whole of the world, if you have mastered every atom in the universe? That will not make you happy unless you have the power of happiness in yourself, until you have conquered yourself. Man is born to conquer nature, it is true, but the Occidental means by "nature" only physical or external nature. It is true that external nature is majestic, with its mountains, and oceans, and rivers, and with its infinite powers and varieties. Yet there is a more majestic internal nature of man, higher than the sun, moon, and stars, higher than this earth of ours, higher than the physical universe, transcending these little lives of

ours; and it affords another field of study. There the Orientals excel, just as the Occidentals excel in the other. Therefore it is fitting that, whenever there is a spiritual adjustment, it should come from the Orient. It is also fitting that when the Oriental wants to learn about machine-making, he should sit at the feet of the Occidental and learn from him. When the Occident wants to learn about the spirit, about God, about the soul, about the meaning and the mystery of this universe, he must sit at the feet of the Orient to learn.

I am going to present before you the life of one man who has put in motion such a wave in India. But before going into the life of this man, I will try to present before you the secret of India, what India means. If those whose eyes have been blinded by the glamour of material things, whose whole dedication of life is to eating and drinking and enjoying, whose ideal of possession is lands and gold, whose ideal of pleasure is that of the senses, whose God is money, and whose goal is a life of ease and comfort in this world and death after that, whose minds never look forward, and who rarely think of anything higher than the sense-objects in the midst of which they live — if such as these go to India, what do they see? Poverty, squalor, superstition, darkness, hideousness everywhere. Why? Because in their minds enlightenment means dress, education, social politeness. Whereas occidental nations have used every effort to improve their material position, India has done differently. There live the only men in the world who, in the whole history of humanity, never went beyond their frontiers to conquer anyone, who never coveted that which belonged to anyone else, whose only fault was that their lands were so fertile, and they accumulated wealth by the hard labour of their hands, and so tempted other nations to come and despoil them. They are contented to be despoiled, and to be called barbarians; and in return they want to send to this world visions of the Supreme, to lay bare for the world the secrets of human nature, to rend the veil that conceals the real man, because they know the dream, because they know that behind this materialism lives the real, divine nature of man which no sin can tarnish, no crime can spoil, no lust can taint, which fire cannot burn, nor water wet, which heat cannot dry nor death kill. And to them this true nature of man is as real as is any material object to the senses of an Occidental.

Just as you are brave to jump at the mouth of a cannon with a hurrah, just as you are brave in the name of patriotism to stand up and give up your lives for your country, so are they brave in the name of God. There it is that when a man declares that this is a world of ideas, that it is all a dream, he casts off clothes and property to demonstrate that what he believes and thinks is true. There it is that a man sits on the bank of a river, when he has known that life is eternal, and wants to give up his body just as nothing, just as you can give up a bit of straw. Therein lies their heroism, that they are ready to face death as a brother, because they are convinced that there is no death for them. Therein lies the strength that has made them invincible through hundreds of years of oppression and foreign invasion and tyranny. The nation lives today, and in that nation even in the days of the direst disaster, spiritual giants have, never failed to arise. Asia produces giants in spirituality, just as the Occident produces giants in politics, giants in science. In the beginning of the present century, when Western influence began to pour into India, when Western conquerors, sword in hand, came to demonstrate to the children of the sages that they were mere barbarians, a race of dreamers, that their religion was but mythology, and god and soul and everything they had been struggling for were mere words without meaning, that the thousands of years of struggle, the thousands of years of endless renunciation, had all been in vain, the question began to be agitated among young men at the universities whether the whole national existence up to then had been a failure, whether they must begin anew on the occidental plan, tear up their old books, burn their philosophies, drive away their preachers, and break down their temples. Did not the occidental conqueror, the man who demonstrated his religion with sword and gun, say that all the old ways were mere superstition and idolatry? Children brought up and educated in the new schools started on the occidental plan, drank in these ideas, from their childhood; and it is not to be wondered at that doubts arose. But instead of throwing away superstition and making a real search after truth, the test of truth became, "What does the West say?" The priests must go, the Vedas must be burned, because the West has said so. Out of the feeling of unrest thus produced, there arose a wave of so-called reform in India.

If you wish to be a true reformer, three things are necessary. The first is to feel. Do you really feel for your brothers? Do you really feel that there is so much misery in the world, so much ignorance and superstition? Do you really feel that men are your brothers? Does this idea come into your whole being? Does it run with your blood? Does it tingle in your veins? Does it course through every nerve and filament of your body? Are you full of that idea of sympathy? If you are, that is only the first step. You must think next if you have found any remedy. The old ideas may be all superstition, but in and round these masses of superstition are nuggets of gold and truth. Have you discovered means by which to keep that gold alone, without any of the dross? If you have done that, that is only the second step; one more thing is necessary. What is your motive? Are you sure that you are not actuated by greed of gold, by thirst for fame or power? Are you really sure that you can stand to your ideals and work on, even if the whole world wants to crush you down? Are you sure you know what you want and will perform your duty, and that alone, even if your life is at stake? Are you sure that you will persevere so long as life endures, so long as there is one pulsation left in the heart? Then you are a real reformer, you are a teacher, a Master, a blessing to mankind. But man is so impatient, so short-sighted! He has not the patience to wait, he has not the power to see. He wants to rule, he wants results immediately. Why? He wants to reap the fruits himself, and does not really care for others. Duty for duty's sake is not what he wants. "To work you have the right, but not to the fruits thereof," says Krishna. Why cling to results? Ours are the duties. Let the fruits take care of themselves. But man has no patience. He takes up any scheme. The larger number of would-be reformers all over the world can be classed under this heading.

As I have said, the idea of reform came to India when it seemed as if the wave of materialism that had invaded her shores would sweep away the teachings of the sages. But the nation had borne the shocks of a thousand such waves of change. This one was mild in comparison. Wave after wave had flooded the land, breaking and crushing everything for hundreds of years. The sword had flashed, and "Victory unto Allah" had rent the skies of India; but these floods subsided, leaving the national ideals unchanged.

The Indian nation cannot be killed. Deathless it stands, and it will stand so long as that spirit shall remain as the background, so long as her people do not give up their spirituality. Beggars they may remain, poor and poverty-stricken, dirt and squalor may surround them perhaps throughout all time, but let them not give up their God, let them not forget that they are the children of the sages. Just as in the West, even the man in the street wants to trace his descent from some robber-baron of the Middle Ages, so in India, even an Emperor on the throne wants to trace his descent from some beggar-sage in the forest, from a man who wore the bark of a tree, lived upon the fruits of the forest and communed with God. That is the type of descent we want; and so long as holiness is thus supremely venerated, India cannot die.

Many of you perhaps have read the article by Prof. Max Müller in a recent issue of the Nineteenth Century, headed "A Real Mahâtman". The life of Shri Ramakrishna is interesting, as it was a living illustration of the ideas that he preached. Perhaps it will be a little romantic for you who live in the West in an atmosphere entirely different from that of India. For the methods and manners in the busy rush of life in the West vary entirely from those of India. Yet perhaps it will be of all the more interest for that, because it will bring into a newer light, things about which many have already heard.

It was while reforms of various kinds were being inaugurated in India that a child was born of poor Brâhmin parents on the eighteenth of February, 1836, in one of the remote villages of Bengal. The father and mother were very orthodox people. The life of a really orthodox Brahmin is one of continuous renunciation. Very few things can he do; and over and beyond them the orthodox Brahmin must not occupy himself with any secular business. At the same time he must not receive gifts from everybody. You may imagine how rigorous that life becomes. You have heard of the Brahmins and their priestcraft many times, but very few of you have ever stopped to ask what makes this wonderful band of men the rulers of their fellows. They are the poorest of all the classes in the country; and the secret of their power lies in their renunciation. They never covet wealth. Theirs is the poorest priesthood in the world, and therefore the most powerful. Even in this poverty, a Brahmin's wife will never allow a poor man to pass through the village without giving him something to eat. That is considered the highest duty of the mother in India; and because she is the mother it is her duty to be served last; she must see that everyone is served before her turn comes. That is why the mother is regarded as God in India. This particular woman, the mother of our subject, was the very type of a Hindu mother. The higher the caste, the greater the restrictions. The lowest caste people can eat and drink anything they like. But as men rise in the social scale, more and more restrictions come; and when they reach the highest caste, the Brahmin, the hereditary priesthood of India, their lives, as I have said, are very much circumscribed. Compared to Western manners, their lives are of continuous asceticism. The Hindus are perhaps the most exclusive nation in the world. They have the same great steadiness as the English, but much more amplified. When they get hold of an idea they carry it out to its very conclusion, and they, keep hold of it generation after generation until they make something out of it. Once give them an idea, and it is not easy to take it back; but it is hard to make them grasp a new idea.

The orthodox Hindus, therefore, are very exclusive, living entirely within their own horizon of thought and feeling. Their lives are laid down in our old books in every little detail, and the least detail is grasped with almost adamantine firmness by them. They would starve rather than eat a meal cooked by the hands of a man not belonging to their own small section of caste. But withal, they have intensity and tremendous earnestness. That force of intense faith and religious life occurs often among the orthodox Hindus, because their very orthodoxy comes from a tremendous conviction that it is right. We may not all think that what they hold on to with such perseverance is right; but to them it is. Now, it is written in our books that a man should always be charitable even to the extreme. If a man starves himself to death to help another man, to save that man's life, it is all right; it is even held that a man ought to do that. And it is expected of a Brahmin to carry this idea out to the very extreme. Those who are acquainted with the literature of India will remember a beautiful old story about this extreme charity, how a whole family, as related in the Mahâbhârata, starved themselves to death and gave their last meal to a beggar. This is not an exaggeration, for such things still happen. The character of the father and the mother of my Master was very much like that. Very poor they were, and yet many a time the mother would starve herself a whole day to help a poor man. Of them this child was born; and he was a peculiar child from very boyhood. He remembered his past from his birth and was conscious for what purpose he came into the world, and every power was devoted to the fulfilment of that purpose.

While he was quite young, his father died; and the boy was sent to school. A Brahmin's boy must go to school; the caste restricts him to a learned profession only. The old system of education in India, still prevalent in many parts of the country, especially in connection with Sannyasins, is very different from the modern system. The students had not to pay. It was thought that knowledge is so sacred that no man ought to sell it. Knowledge must be given freely and without any price. The teachers used to take students without charge, and not only so, most of them gave their students food and clothes. To support these teachers the wealthy families on certain occasions, such as a marriage festival, or at the ceremonies for the dead, made gifts to them. They were considered the first and foremost claimants to certain gifts; and they in their turn had to maintain their students. So whenever there is a marriage, especially in a rich family, these professors are invited, and they attend and discuss various subjects. This boy went to one of these gatherings of professors, and the professors were discussing various topics, such as logic or astronomy, subjects much beyond his age. The boy was peculiar, as I have said, and he gathered this moral out of it: "This is the outcome of all their knowledge. Why are they fighting so hard? It is simply for money; the man who can show the highest learning here will get the best pair of cloth, and that is all these people are struggling for. I will not go to school any more." And he did not; that was the end of his going to school. But this boy had an elder brother, a learned professor, who took him to Calcutta, however, to study with him. After a short time the boy became fully convinced that the aim of all secular learning was mere material advancement, and nothing more, and he resolved to give up study and devote himself solely to the pursuit of spiritual knowledge. The father being dead, the family was very poor; and this boy had to make his own living. He went to a place near Calcutta and became a temple priest. To become a temple priest is thought very degrading to a Brahmin. Our temples are not churches in your sense of the word, they are not places for public worship; for, properly speaking, there is no such thing as public worship in India. Temples are erected mostly by rich persons as a meritorious religious act.

If a man has much property, he wants to build a temple. In that he puts a symbol or an image of an Incarnation of God, and dedicates it to worship in the name of God. The worship is akin to that which is conducted in Roman Catholic churches, very much like the mass, reading certain sentences from the sacred books, waving a light before the image, and treating the image in every respect as we treat a great man. This is all that is done in the temple. The man who goes to a temple is not considered thereby a better man than he who never goes. More properly, the latter is considered the more religious man, for religion in India is to each man his own private affair. In the house of every man there is either a little chapel, or a room set apart, and there he goes morning and evening, sits down in a corner, and there does his worship. And this worship is entirely mental, for another man does not hear or know what he is doing. He sees him only sitting there, and perhaps moving his fingers in a peculiar fashion, or closing his nostrils and breathing in a peculiar manner. Beyond that, he does not know what his brother is doing; even his wife, perhaps, will not know. Thus, all worship is conducted in the privacy of his own home. Those who cannot afford to have a chapel go to the banks of a river, or a lake, or the sea if they live at the seaside, but people sometimes go to worship in a temple by making salutation to the image. There their duty to the temple ends. Therefore, you see, it has been held from the most ancient times in our country, legislated upon by Manu, that it is a degenerating occupation to become a temple priest. Some of the books say it is so degrading as to make a Brahmin worthy of reproach. Just as with education, but in a far more intense sense with religion, there is the other idea behind it that the temple priests who take fees for their work are making merchandise of sacred things. So you may imagine the feelings of that boy when he was forced through poverty to take up the only occupation open to him, that of a temple priest.

There have been various poets in Bengal whose songs have passed down to the people; they are sung in the streets of Calcutta and in every village. Most of these are religious songs, and their one central idea, which is perhaps peculiar to the religions of India, is the idea of realisation. There is not a book in India on religion which does not breathe this idea. Man must realise God, feel God, see God, talk to God. That is religion. The Indian atmosphere is full of stories of saintly persons having visions of God. Such doctrines form the basis of their religion; and all these ancient books and scriptures are the writings of persons who came into direct contact with spiritual facts. These books were not written for the intellect, nor can any reasoning understand them, because they were written by men who saw the things of which they wrote, and they can be understood only by men who have raised themselves to the same height. They say there is such a thing as realisation even in this life, and it is open to everyone, and religion begins with the opening of this faculty, if I may call it so. This is the central idea in all religions, and this is why we may find one man with the most finished oratorical powers, or the most convincing logic, preaching the highest doctrines and yet unable to get people to listen to him, while we may find another, a poor man, who scarcely can speak the language of his own motherland, yet half the nation worships him in his own lifetime as God. When in India the idea somehow or other gets abroad that a man has raised himself to that state of realisation, that religion is no more a matter of conjecture to him, that he is no more groping in the dark in such momentous questions as religion, the immortality of the soul, and God, people come from all quarters to see him and gradually they begin to worship him.

In the temple was an image of the "Blissful Mother". This boy had to conduct the worship morning and evening, and by degrees this one idea filled his mind: "Is there anything behind this images? Is it true that there is a Mother of Bliss in the universe? Is it true that She lives and guides the universe, or is it all a dream? Is there any reality in religion?"

This scepticism comes to the Hindu child. It is the scepticism of our country: Is this that we are doing real? And theories will not satisfy us, although there are ready at hand almost all the theories that have ever been made with regard to God and soul. Neither books nor theories can satisfy us, the one idea that gets hold of thousands of our people is this idea of realisation. Is it true that there is a God? If it be true, can I see Him? Can I realise the truth? The Western mind may think all this very impracticable, but to us it is intensely practical. For this their lives. You have just heard how from the earliest times there have been persons who have given up all comforts and luxuries to live in caves, and hundreds have given up their homes to weep bitter tears of misery, on the banks of sacred rivers, in order to realise this idea—not to know in the ordinary sense of the word, not intellectual understanding, not a mere rationalistic comprehension of the real thing, not mere groping in the dark, but intense realisation, much more real than this world is to our senses. That is the idea. I do not advance any proposition as to that just now, but that is the one fact that is impressed upon them. Thousands will be killed, other thousands will be ready. So upon this one idea the whole nation for thousands of years have been denying and sacrificing themselves. For this idea thousands of Hindus every year give up their homes, and many of them die through the hardships they have to undergo. To the Western mind this must seem most visionary, and I can see the reason for this point of view. But though I have resided in the West, I still think this idea the most practical thing in life.

Every moment I think of anything else is so much loss to me—even the marvels of earthly sciences; everything is vain if it takes me away from that thought. Life is but momentary, whether you have the knowledge of an angel or the ignorance of an animal. Life is but momentary, whether you have the poverty of the poorest man in rags or the wealth of the richest living person. Life is but momentary, whether you are a downtrodden man living in one of the big streets of the big cities of the West or a crowned Emperor ruling over millions. Life is but momentary, whether you have the best of health or the worst. Life is but momentary, whether you have the most poetical temperament or the most cruel. There is but one solution of life, says the Hindu, and that solution is what they call God and religion. If these be true, life becomes explained, life becomes bearable, becomes enjoyable. Otherwise, life is but a useless burden. That is our idea, but no amount of reasoning can demonstrate it; it can only make it probable, and there it rests. The highest demonstration of reasoning that we have in any branch of knowledge can only make a fact probable, and nothing further. The most demonstrable facts of physical science are only probabilities, not facts yet. Facts are only in the senses. Facts have to be perceived, and we have to perceive religion to demonstrate it to ourselves. We have to sense God to be convinced that there is a God. We must sense the facts of religion to know that they are facts. Nothing else, and no amount of reasoning, but our own perception can make these things real to us, can make my belief firm as a rock. That is my idea, and that is the Indian idea.

This idea took possession of the boy and his whole life became concentrated upon that. Day after day he would weep and say, "Mother, is it true that Thou existest, or is it all poetry? Is the Blissful Mother an imagination of poets and misguided people, or is there such a Reality?" We have seen that of books, of education in our sense of the word, he had none, and so much the more natural, so much the more healthy, was his mind, so much the purer his thoughts, undiluted by drinking in the thoughts of others. Because he did not go to the university, therefore he thought for himself. Because we have spent half our lives in the university we are filled with a collection of other people's thoughts. Well has Prof. Max Müller said in the article I have just referred to that this was a clean, original man; and the secret of that originality was that he was not brought up within the precincts of a university. However, this thought — whether God can be seen — which was uppermost in his mind gained in strength every day until he could think of nothing else. He could no more conduct the worship properly, could no more attend to the various details in all their minuteness. Often he would forget to place the food-offering before the image, sometimes he would forget to wave the light; at other times he would wave it for hours, and forget everything else.

And that one idea was in his mind every day: "Is it true that Thou existest, O Mother? Why cost Thou not speak? Art Thou dead?" Perhaps some of us here will remember that there are moments in our lives when, tired of all these ratiocinations of dull and dead logic, tired of plodding through books — which after all teach us nothing, become nothing but a sort of intellectual opium-eating — we must have it at stated times or we die — tired with all this, the heart of our hearts sends out a wail: "Is there no one in this universe who can show me the light? If Thou art, show the light unto me. Why dost Thou not speak? Why dost Thou make Thyself so scarce, why send so many Messengers and not Thyself come to me? In this world of fights and factions whom am I to follow and believe? If Thou art the God of every man and woman alike, why comest Thou not to speak to Thy child and see if he is not ready?" Well, to us all come such thoughts in moments of great depression; but such are the temptations surrounding us, that the next moment we forget. For the moment it seemed that the doors of the heavens were going to be opened, for the moment it seemed as if we were going to plunge into the light effulgent; but the animal man again shakes off all these angelic visions. Down we go, animal man once more eating and drinking and dying, and dying and drinking and eating again and again. But there are exceptional minds which are not turned away so easily, which once attracted can never be turned back, whatever may be the temptation in the way, which want to see the Truth knowing that life must go. They

say, let it go in a noble conquest, and what conquest is nobler than the conquest of the lower man, than this solution of the problem of life and death, of good and evil?

At last it became impossible for him to serve in the temple. He left it and entered into a little wood that was near and lived there. About this part of his life, he told me many times that he could not tell when the sun rose or set, or how he lived. He lost all thought of himself and forgot to eat. During this period he was lovingly watched over by a relative who put into his mouth food which he mechanically swallowed.

Days and nights thus passed with the boy. When a whole day would pass, towards the evening when the peal of bells in the temples, and the voices singing, would reach the wood, it would make the boy very sad, and he would cry, "Another day is gone in vain, Mother, and Thou hast not come. Another day of this short life has gone, and I have not known the Truth." In the agony of his soul, sometimes he would rub his face against the ground and weep, and this one prayer burst forth: "Do Thou manifest Thyself in me, Thou Mother of the universe! See that I need Thee and nothing else!" Verily, he wanted to be true to his own ideal. He had heard that the Mother never came until everything had been given up for Her. He had heard that the Mother wanted to come to everyone, but they Could not have Her, that people wanted all sorts of foolish little idols to pray to, that they wanted their own enjoyments, and not the Mother, and that the moment they really wanted Her with their whole soul, and nothing else, that moment She would come. So he began to break himself into that idea; he wanted to be exact, even on the plane of matter. He threw away all the little property he had, and took a vow that he would never touch money, and this one idea, "I will not touch money", became a part of him. It may appear to be something occult, but even in after-life when he was sleeping, if I touched him with a piece of money his hand would become bent, and his whole body would become, as it were, paralysed. The other idea that came into his mind was that lust was the other enemy. Man is a soul, and soul is sexless, neither man nor woman. The idea of sex and the idea of money were the two things, he thought, that prevented him from seeing the Mother. This whole universe is the manifestation of the Mother, and She lives in every woman's body. "Every woman represents the Mother; how can I think of woman in mere sex relation?" That was the idea: Every woman was his Mother, he must bring himself to the state when he would see nothing but Mother in every woman. And he carried it out in his life.

This is the tremendous thirst that seizes the human heart. Later on, this very man said to me, "My child, suppose there is a bag of gold in one room, and a robber in the next room; do you think that the robber can sleep? He cannot. His mind will be always thinking how to get into that room and obtain possession of that gold. Do you think then that a man, firmly persuaded that there is a Reality behind all these appearances, that there is a God, that there is One who never dies, One who is infinite bliss, a bliss compared with which these pleasures of the senses are simply playthings, can rest contented without struggling to attain It? Can he cease his efforts for a moment? No. He will become mad with longing." This divine madness seized the boy. At that time he had no teacher, nobody to tell him anything, and everyone thought that he was out of his mind. This is the ordinary condition of things. If a man throws aside the vanities of the world, we hear him called mad. But such men are the salt of the earth. Out of such madness have come the powers that have moved this world of ours, and out of such madness alone will come the powers of the future that are going to move the world.

So days, weeks, months passed in continuous struggle of the soul to arrive at truth. The boy began to see visions, to see wonderful things; the secrets of his nature were beginning to open to him. Veil after veil was, as it were, being taken off. Mother Herself became the teacher and initiated the boy into the truths he sought. At this time there came to this place a woman of beautiful appearance, learned beyond compare. Later on, this saint used to say about her that she was not learned, but was the embodiment of learning; she was learning itself, in human form. There, too, you find the peculiarity of the Indian nation. In the midst of the ignorance in which the average Hindu woman lives, in the midst of what is called in Western countries her lack of freedom, there could arise a woman of supreme spirituality. She was a Sannyâsini; for women also give up the world, throw away their property, do not marry, and devote themselves to the worship of the Lord. She came; and when she heard of this boy in the grove, she offered to go and see him; and hers was the first help he received. At once she recognised what his trouble was, and she said to him. "My son blessed is the man upon whom such madness comes. The whole of this universe is mad—some for wealth, some for pleasure, some for fame, some for a hundred other things. They are mad for gold, or husbands, or wives, for little trifles, mad to tyrannise over somebody, mad to become rich, mad for every foolish thing except God. And they can understand only their own madness. When another man is mad after gold, they have fellow-feeling and sympathy for him, and they say he is the right man, as lunatics think that lunatics alone are sane. But if a man is mad after the Beloved, after the Lord, how can they understand? They think he has gone crazy; and they say, 'Have nothing to do with him.' That is why they call you mad; but yours is the right kind of madness. Blessed is the man who is mad after God. Such men are very few." This woman remained near the boy for years, taught him the forms of the religions of India, initiated him into the different practices of Yoga, and, as it were, guided and brought into harmony this tremendous river of spirituality.

Later, there came to the same grove a Sannyasin, one of the begging friars of India, a learned man, a philosopher. He was a peculiar man, he was an idealist. He did not believe that this world existed in reality; and to demonstrate that, he would never go under a roof, he would always live out of doors, in storm and sunshine alike. This man began to teach the boy the philosophy of the Vedas; and he found very soon, to his astonishment, that the pupil was in some respects wiser than the master. He spent several months with the boy, after which he initiated him into the order of Sannyasins, and took his departure.

When as a temple priest his extraordinary worship made people think him deranged in his head, his relatives took him home and married him to a little girl, thinking that that would turn his thoughts and restore the balance of his mind. But he came back and, as we have seen, merged deeper in his madness. Sometimes, in our country, boys are married as children and have no voice in the matter; their parents marry them. Of course such a marriage is little more than a betrothal. When they are married they still continue to live with their parents, and the real marriage takes place when the wife grows older, Then it is customary for the husband to go and bring his bride to his own home. In this case, however, the husband had entirely forgotten that he had a wife. In her far off home the girl had heard that her husband had become a religious enthusiast, and that he was even considered insane by many. She resolved to learn the truth for herself, so she set out and walked to the place where her husband was. When at last she stood in her husband's presence, he at once admitted her right to his life, although in India any person, man or woman, who embraces a religious life, is thereby freed from all other obligations. The young man fell at the feet of his wife and said, "As for me, the Mother has shown me that She resides in every woman, and so I have learnt to look upon every woman as Mother. That is the one idea I can have about you; but if you wish to drag me into the world, as I have been married to you, I am at your service."

The maiden was a pure and noble soul and was able to understand her husband's aspirations and sympathise with them. She quickly told him that she had no wish to drag him down to a life of worldliness; but that all she desired was to remain near him, to serve him, and to learn of him. She became one of his most devoted disciples, always revering him as a divine being. Thus through his wife's consent the last barrier was removed, and he was free to lead the life he had chosen.

The next desire that seized upon the soul of this man as to know the truth about the various religions. Up to that time he had not known any religion but his own. He wanted to understand what other religions were like. So he sought teachers of other religions. By teachers you must always remember what we mean in India, not a bookworm, but a man of realisation, one who knows truth a; first hand and not through an intermediary. He found a Mohammedan saint and placed himself under him; he underwent the disciplines prescribed by him, and to his astonishment found that when faithfully carried out, these devotional methods led him to the same goal he had already attained. He gathered similar experience from following the true religion of Jesus the Christ. He went to all the sects he could find, and whatever he took up he went into with his whole heart. He did exactly as he was told, and in every instance he arrived at the same result. Thus from actual experience, he came to know that the goal of every religion is the same, that each is trying to teach the same thing, the difference being largely in method and still more in language. At the core, all sects and all religions have the same aim; and they were only quarrelling for their own selfish purposes — they were not anxious about the truth, but about "my name" and "your name". Two of them preached the same truth, but one of them said, "That cannot be true, because I have not put upon it the seal of my name. Therefore do not listen to him." And the other man said, "Do not hear him, although he is preaching very much the same thing, yet it is not true because he does not preach it in my name."

That is what my Master found, and he then set about to learn humility, because he had found that the one idea in all religions is, "not me, but Thou", and he who says, "not me", the Lord fills his heart. The less of this little "I" the more of God there is in him. That he found to be the truth in every religion in the world, and he set himself to accomplish this. As I have told you, whenever he wanted to do anything he never confined himself to fine theories, but would enter into the practice immediately; We see many persons talking the most wonderfully fine things about charity and about equality and the rights of other people and all that, but it is only in theory. I was so fortunate as to find one who was able to carry theory into practice. He had the most wonderful faculty of carrying everything into practice which he thought was right.

Now, there was a family of Pariahs living near the place. The Pariahs number several millions in the whole of India and are a sect of people so low that some of our books say that if a Brahmin coming out from his house sees the face of a Pariah, he has to fast that day and recite certain prayers before he becomes holy again. In some Hindu cities when a Pariah enters, he has to put a crow's feather on his head as a sign that he is a Pariah, and he has to cry aloud, "Save yourselves, the Pariah is passing through the street", and you will find people flying off from him as if by magic, because if they touch him by chance, they will have to change their clothes, bathe, and do other things. And the Pariah for thousands of years has believed that it is perfectly right; that his touch will make everybody unholy. Now my Master would go to a Pariah and ask to be allowed to clean his house. The business of the Pariah is to clean the streets of the cities and to keep houses clean. He cannot enter the house by the front door; by the back door he enters; and as soon as he has gone, the whole place over which he has passed is sprinkled with and made holy by a little Gangâ water. By birth the Brahmin stands for holiness, and the Pariah for the very reverse. And this Brahmin asked to be allowed to do the menial services in the house of the Pariah. The Pariah of course could not allow that, for they all think that if they allow a Brahmin to do such menial work it will be an awful sin, and they will become extinct. The Pariah would not permit it; so in the dead of night, when all were

sleeping, Ramakrishna would enter the house. He had long hair, and with his hair he would wipe the place, saying, "Oh, my Mother, make me the servant of the Pariah, make me feel that I am even lower than the Pariah." "They worship Me best who worship My worshippers. These are all My children and your privilege is to serve them" — is the teaching of Hindu scriptures.

There were various other preparations which would take a long time to relate, and I want to give you just a sketch of his life. For years he thus educated himself. One of the Sâdhanâs was to root out the sex idea. Soul has no sex, it is neither male nor female. It is only in the body that sex exists, and the man who desires to reach the spirit cannot at the same time hold to sex distinctions. Having been born in a masculine body, this man wanted to bring the feminine idea into everything. He began to think that he was a woman, he dressed like a woman, spoke like a woman, gave up the occupations of men, and lived in the household among the women of a good family, until, after years of this discipline, his mind became changed, and he entirely forgot the idea of sex; thus the whole view of life became changed to him.

We hear in the West about worshipping woman, but this is usually for her youth and beauty. This man meant by worshipping woman, that to him every woman's face was that of the Blissful Mother, and nothing but that. I myself have seen this man standing before those women whom society would not touch, and falling at their feet bathed in tears, saying, "Mother, in one form Thou art in the street, and in another form Thou art the universe. I salute Thee, Mother, I salute Thee." Think of the blessedness of that life from which all carnality has vanished, which can look upon every woman with that love and reverence when every woman's face becomes transfigured, and only the face of the Divine Mother, the Blissful One, the Protectress of the human race, shines upon it! That is what we want. Do you mean to say that the divinity back of a woman can ever be cheated? It never was and never will be, It always asserts itself. Unfailingly it detects fraud, it detects hypocrisy, unerringly it feels the warmth of truth, the light of spirituality, the holiness of purity. Such purity is absolutely necessary if real spirituality is to be attained.

This rigorous, unsullied purity came into the life of that man. All the struggles which we have in our lives were past for him. His hard-earned jewels of spirituality, for which he had given three-quarters of his life, were now ready to be given to humanity, and then began his mission. His teaching and preaching were peculiar. In our country a teacher is a most highly venerated person, he is regarded as God Himself. We have not even the same respect for our father and mother. Father and mother give us our body, but the teacher shows us the way to salvation. We are his children, we are born in the spiritual line of the teacher. All Hindus come to pay respect to an extraordinary teacher, they crowd around him. And here was such a teacher, but the teacher had no thought whether he was to be respected or not, he had not the least idea that he was a great teacher, he thought that it was Mother who was doing everything and not he. He always said, "If any good comes from my lips, it is the Mother who speaks; what have I to do with it?" That was his one idea about his work, and to the day of his death he never gave it up. This man sought no one. His principle was, first form character, first earn spirituality and results will come of themselves. His favourite illustration was, "When the lotus opens, the bees come of their own accord to seek the honey; so let the lotus of your character be full-blown, and the results will follow." This is a great lesson to learn.

My Master taught me this lesson hundreds of times, yet I often forget it. Few understand the power of thought. If a man goes into a cave, shuts himself in, and thinks one really great thought and dies, that thought will penetrate the walls of that cave, vibrate through space, and at last permeate the whole human race. Such is the power of thought; be in no hurry therefore to give your thoughts to others. First have something to give. He alone teaches who has something to give, for teaching is not talking, teaching is not imparting doctrines, it is communicating. Spirituality can be communicated just as really as I can give you a flower. This is true in the most literal sense. This idea is very old in India and finds illustration in the West in the "theory, in the belief, of apostolic succession. Therefore first make character—that is the highest duty you can perform. Know Truth for yourself, and there will be many to whom you can teach it after wards; they will all come. This was the attitude of nay Master. He criticised no one. For years I lived with that man, but never did I hear those lips utter one word of condemnation for any sect. He had the same sympathy for all sects; he had found the harmony between them. A man may be intellectual, or devotional, or mystic, or active; the various religions represent one or the other of these types. Yet it is possible to combine all the four in one man, and this is what future humanity is going to do. That was his idea. He condemned no one, but saw the good in all.

People came by thousands to see and hear this wonderful man who spoke in a patois every word of which was forceful and instinct with light. For it is not what is spoken, much less the language in which it is spoken, but it is the personality of the speaker which dwells in everything he says that carries weight. Every one of us feels this at times. We hear most splendid orations, most wonderfully reasoned-out discourses, and we go home and forget them all. At other times we hear a few words in the simplest language, and they enter into our lives, become part and parcel of ourselves and produce lasting results. The words of a man who can put his personality into them take effect, but he must have tremendous personality. All teaching implies giving and taking, the teacher gives and the taught receives, but the one must have something to give, and the other must be open to receive.

This man came to live near Calcutta, the capital of India, the most important university town in our country which was sending out sceptics and materialists by the hundreds every year. Yet many of these university men—sceptics and agnostics—used to come and listen to him. I heard of this man, and I went to hear him. He looked just like an ordinary man, with nothing remarkable about him. He used the most simple language, and I thought "Can this man be a great teacher?"—crept near to him and asked him the question which I had been asking others all my life: "Do you believe in God, Sir?" "Yes," he replied. "Can you prove it, Sir?" "Yes." "How?" "Because I see Him just as I see you here, only in a much intenser sense." That impressed me at once. For the first time I found a man who dared to say that he saw God that religion was a reality to be felt, to be sensed in an infinitely more intense way than we can sense the world. I began to go to that man, day after day, and I actually saw that religion could be given. One touch, one glance, can change a whole life. I have read about Buddha and Christ and Mohammed, about all those different luminaries of ancient times, how they would stand up and say, "Be thou whole", and the man became whole. I now found it to be true, and when I myself saw this man, all scepticism was brushed aside. It could be done; and my Master used to say, "Religion can be given and taken more tangibly, more really than anything else in the world." Be therefore spiritual first; have something to give and then stand before the world and give it. Religion is not talk, or doctrines, or theories; nor is it sectarianism. Religion cannot live in sects and societies. It is the relation between the soul and God; how can it be made into a society? It would then degenerate into business, and wherever there are business and business principles in religion, spirituality dies. Religion does not consist in erecting temples, or building churches, or attending public worship. It is not to be found in books, or in words, or in lectures, or in organisations. Religion consists in realisation. As a fact, we all know that nothing will satisfy us until we know the truth for ourselves. However we may argue, however much we may hear, but one thing will satisfy us, and that is our own realisation; and such an experience is possible for every one of us if we will only try. The first ideal of this attempt to realise religion is that of renunciation. As far as we can, we must give up. Darkness and light, enjoyment of the world and enjoyment of God will never go together. "Ye cannot serve God and Mammon." Let people try it if they will, and I have seen millions in every country who have tried; but after all, it comes to nothing. If one word remains true in the saying, it is, give up every thing for the sake of the Lord. This is a hard and long task, but you can begin it here and now. Bit by bit we must go towards it.

The second idea that I learnt from my Master, and which is perhaps the most vital, is the wonderful truth that the religions of the world are not contradictory or antagonistic. They are but various phases of one eternal religion. That one eternal religion is applied to different planes of existence, is applied to the opinions of various minds and various races. There never was my religion or yours, my national religion or your national religion; there never existed many religions, there is only the one. One infinite religion existed all through eternity and will ever exist, and this religion is expressing itself in various countries in various ways. Therefore we must respect all religions and we must try to accept them all as far as we can. Religions manifest themselves not only according to race and geographical position, but according to individual powers. In one man religion is manifesting itself as intense activity, as work. In another it is manifesting itself as intense devotion, in yet another, as mysticism, in others as philosophy, and so forth. It is wrong when we say to others, "Your methods are not right." Perhaps a man, whose nature is that of love, thinks that the man who does good to others is not on the right road to religion, because it is not his own way, and is therefore wrong. If the philosopher thinks, "Oh, the poor ignorant people, what do they know about a God of Love, and loving Him? They do not know what they mean," he is wrong, because they may be right and he also.

To learn this central secret that the truth may be one and yet many at the same time, that we may have different visions of the same truth from different standpoints, is exactly what must be done. Then, instead of antagonism to anyone, we shall have infinite sympathy with all. Knowing that as long as there are different natures born in this world, the same religious truth will require different adaptations, we shall understand that we are bound to have forbearance with each other. Just as nature is unity in variety—an infinite variation in the phenomenal—as in and through all these variations of the phenomenal runs the Infinite, the Unchangeable, the Absolute Unity, so it is with every man; the microcosm is but a miniature repetition of the macrocosm; in spite of all these variations, in and through them all runs this eternal harmony, and we have to recognise this. This idea, above all other ideas, I find to be the crying necessity of the day. Coming from a country which is a hotbed of religious sects—and to which, through its good fortune or ill fortune, everyone who has a religious idea wants to send an advance-guard—I have been acquainted from my childhood with the various sects of the world. Even the Mormons come to preach in India. Welcome them all! That is the soil on which to preach religion. There it takes root more than in any other country. If you come and teach politics to the Hindus, they do not understand; but if you come to preach religion, however curious it may be, you will have hundreds and thousands of followers in no time, and you have every chance of becoming a living God in your lifetime. I am glad it is so, it is the one thing we want in India.

The sects among the Hindus are various, a great many in number, and some of them apparently hopelessly contradictory. Yet they all tell you they are but different manifestations of religion. "As different rivers, taking their start from different mountains, running crooked or straight, all come and mingle their waters in the ocean, so the different sects, with their different points of vied, at last all come unto Thee." This is not a theory, it has to be recognised, but not in that patronising way which we see with some people: "Oh yes, there are some very good things in it. These are what we call the ethnical religions. These ethnical religions have some good in them." Some even have the most wonderfully liberal idea that other religions are all little bits of a prehistoric evolution, but "ours is the fulfilment of things". One man says, because his is the oldest religion, it is the best: another makes the same claim, because his is the latest.

We have to recognise that each one of them has the same saving power as the other. What you have heard about their difference, whether in the temple or in the church, is a mass of superstition. The same God answers all; and it is not you, or I, or any body of men that is responsible for the safety and salvation of the least little bit of the soul; the same Almighty God is responsible for all. I do not understand how people declare themselves to be believers in God, and at the same time think that God has handed over to a little body of men all truth, and that they are the guardians of the rest of humanity. How can you call that religion? Religion is realisation; but mere talk—mere trying to believe, mere groping in darkness, mere parroting the words of ancestors and thinking it is religion, mere making a political something out of the truths of religion—is not religion at all. In every sect—even among the Mohammedans whom we always regard as the most exclusive—even among them we find that wherever there was a man trying to realise religion, from his lips have come the fiery words: "Thou art the Lord of all, Thou art in the heart of all, Thou art the guide of all, Thou art the Teacher of all, and Thou caress infinitely more for the land of Thy children than we can ever do." Do not try to disturb the faith of any man. If you can, give him something better; if you can, get hold of a man where he stands and give him a push upwards; do so, but do not destroy what he has. The only true teacher is he who can convert himself, as it were, into a thousand persons at a moment's notice. The only true teacher is he who can immediately come down to the level of the student, and transfer his soul to the student's soul and see through the student's eyes and hear through his ears and understand through his mind. Such a teacher can really teach and none else. All these negative, breaking-down, destructive teachers that are in the world can never do any good.

In the presence of my Master I found out that man could be perfect, even in this body. Those lips never cursed anyone, never even criticised anyone. Those eyes were beyond the possibility of seeing evil, that mind had lost the power of thinking evil. He saw nothing but good. That tremendous purity, that tremendous renunciation is the one secret of spirituality. "Neither through wealth, nor through progeny, but through renunciation alone, is immortality to be reached", say the Vedas. "Sell all that thou hast and give to the poor, and follow me", says the Christ. So all great saints and Prophets have expressed it, and have carried it out in their lives. How can great spirituality come without that renunciation? Renunciation is the background of all religious thought wherever it be, and you will always find that as this idea of renunciation lessens, the more will the senses creep into the field of religion, and spirituality will decrease in the same ratio.

That man was the embodiment of renunciation. In our country it is necessary for a man who becomes a Sannyasin to give up all worldly wealth and position, and this my Master carried out literally. There were many who would have felt themselves blest if he would only have accepted a present from their hands, who would gladly have given him thousands of rupees if he would have taken them, but these were the only men from whom he would turn away. He was a triumphant example, a living realisation of the complete conquest of lust and of desire for money. He was beyond all ideas of either, and such men are necessary for this century. Such renunciation is necessary in these days when men have begun to think that they cannot live a month without what they call their "necessities", and which they are increasing out of all proportion. It is necessary in a time like this that a man should arise to demonstrate to the sceptics of the world that there yet breathes a man who does not care a straw for all the gold or all the fame that is in the universe. Yet there are such men.

The other idea of his life was intense love for others. The first part of my Master's life was spent in acquiring spirituality, and the remaining years in distributing it. People in our country have not the same customs as you have in visiting a religious teacher or a Sannyasin. Somebody would come to ask him about something, some perhaps would come hundreds of miles, walking all the way, just to ask one question, to hear one word from him, "Tell me one word for my salvation." That is the way they come. They come in numbers, unceremoniously, to the place where he is mostly to be found; they may find him under a tree and question him; and before one set of people has gone, others have arrived. So if a man is greatly revered, he will sometimes have no rest day or night. He will have to talk constantly. For hours people will come pouring in, and this man will be teaching them.

So men came in crowds to hear him, and he would talk twenty hours in the twenty-four, and that not for one day, but for months and months until at last the body broke down under the pressure of this tremendous strain. His intense love for mankind would not let him refuse to help even the humblest of the thousands who sought his aid. Gradually, there developed a vital throat disorder and yet he could not be persuaded to refrain from these exertions. As soon as he heard that people were asking to see him, he would insist upon having them admitted and would answer all their questions. When expostulated with, he replied, "I do not care. I will give up twenty thousand such bodies to help one man. It is glorious to help even one man." There was no rest for him. Once a man asked him, "Sir, you are a great Yogi. Why do you not put your mind a little on your body and cure your disease? "At first he did not answer, but when the question had been repeated, he gently said, "My friend, I thought you were a sage, but you talk like other men of the world. This mind has been given to the Lord. Do you mean to say that I should take it back and put it upon the body which is but a mere cage of the soul?"

So he went on preaching to the people, and the news spread that his body was about to pass away, and the people began to flock to him in greater crowds than ever. You cannot imagine the way they come to these great religious teachers in India, how they crowd round them and make gods of them while they are yet living. Thousands wait simply to touch the hem of their garments. It is through this appreciation of spirituality in others that spirituality is produced. Whatever man wants and appreciates, he will get; and it is the same with nations. If you go to India and deliver a political lecture, however grand it may be, you will scarcely find people to listen to you but just go and teach religion, live it, not merely talk it, and hundreds will crowd just to look at you, to touch your feet. When the people heard that this holy man was likely to go from them soon, they began to come round him more than ever, and my Master went on teaching them without the least regard for his health. We could not prevent this. Many of the people came from long distances, and he would not rest until he had answered their questions. "While I can speak, I must teach them," he would say, and he was as good as his word. One day, he told us that he would lay down the body that day, and repeating the most sacred word of the Vedas he entered into Samâdhi and passed away.

His thoughts and his message were known to very few capable of giving them out. Among others, he left a few young boys who had renounced the world, and were ready to carry on his work. Attempts were made to crush them. But they stood firm, having the inspiration of that great life before them. Having had the contact of that blessed life for years, they stood their ground. These young men, living as Sannyasins, begged through the streets of the city where they were born, although some of them came from high families. At first they met with great antagonism, but they persevered and went on from day to day spreading all over India the message of that great man, until the whole country was filled with the ideas he had preached. This man, from a remote village of Bengal, without education, by the sheer force of his own determination, realised the truth and gave it to others, leaving only a few young boys to keep it alive.

Today the name of Shri Ramakrishna Paramahamsa is known all over India to its millions of people. Nay, the power of that man has spread beyond India; and if there has ever been a word of truth, a word of spirituality, that I have spoken anywhere in the world, I owe it to my Master; only the mistakes are mine.

This is the message of Shri Ramakrishna to the modern world: "Do not care for doctrines, do not care for dogmas, or sects, or churches, or temples; they count for little compared with the essence of existence in each man which is spirituality; and the more this is developed in a man, the more powerful is he for good. Earn that first, acquire that, and criticise no one, for all doctrines and creeds have some good in them. Show by your lives that religion does not mean words, or names, or sects, but that it means spiritual realisation. Only those can understand who have felt. Only those who have attained to spirituality can communicate it to others, can be great teachers of mankind. They alone are the powers of light."

The more such men are produced in a country, the more that country will be raised; and that country where such men absolutely do not exist is simply doomed nothing can save it. Therefore my Master's message to mankind is: "Be spiritual and realise truth for Yourself." He would have you give up for the sake of your fellow-beings. He would have you cease talking about love for your brother, and set to work to prove your words. The time has come for renunciation, for realisation, and then you will see the harmony in all the religions of the world. You will know that there is no need of any quarrel. And then only will you be ready to help humanity. To proclaim and make clear the fundamental unity underlying all religions was the mission of my Master. Other teachers have taught special religions which bear their names, but this great teacher of the nineteenth century made no claim for himself. He left every religion undisturbed because he had realised that in reality they are all part and parcel of the one eternal religion.

INDIAN RELIGIOUS THOUGHT

Delivered under the auspices of tile Brooklyn Ethical Society, in the Art Gallery of tile Pouch Mansion, Clinton Avenue, Brooklyn, U.S.A.

India, although only half the size of the United States, contains a population of over two hundred and ninety millions, and there are three religions which hold sway over them — the Mohammedan, the Buddhist [1], and the Hindu. The adherents of the first mentioned number about sixty millions, of the second about nine millions, while the last embrace nearly two hundred and six millions. The cardinal features of the Hindu religion are founded on the meditative and speculative philosophy and on the ethical teachings contained in the various books of the Vedas, which assert that the universe is infinite in space and eternal in duration. It never had a beginning, and it never will have an end. Innumerable have been the manifestations of the power of the spirit in the realm of matter, of the force of the Infinite in the domain of the finite; but the Infinite Spirit Itself is self-existent, eternal, and unchangeable. The passage of time makes no mark whatever on the dial of eternity. In its supersensuous region which cannot be comprehended at all by the human understanding, there is no past, and there is no future. The Vedas teach that the soul of man is immortal. The body is subject to the law of growth and decay, what grows must of necessity decay. But the in dwelling spirit is related to the infinite and eternal life; it never had a beginning and it never will have an end, One of the chief distinctions between the Hindu and the (Christian religions is that the Christian religion teaches that each human soul had its beginning at its birth into this world, whereas the Hindu religion asserts that the spirit of man is an emanation of the Eternal Being, and had no more a beginning than God Himself. Innumerable have been and will be its manifestations in its passage from one personality to another, subject to the great law of spiritual evolution, until it reaches perfection, when there is no more change.

It has been often asked: If this be so, why is it we do not remember anything of our past lives? This is our explanation: Consciousness is the name of the surface only of the mental ocean, but within its depths are stored up all our experiences, both pleasant and painful. The desire of the human soul is to find out something that is stable. The mind and the body, in fact all the various phenomena of nature, are in a condition of incessant change. But the highest aspiration of our spirit is to find out something that does not change, that has reached a state of permanent perfection. And this is the aspiration of the human soul after the Infinite! The finer our moral and intellectual development, the stronger will become this aspiration after the Eternal that changes not.

The modern Buddhists teach that everything that cannot be known by the five senses is non-existent, and that it is a delusion to suppose that man is an independent entity. The idealists, on the contrary, claim that each individual is an independent entity, and the external world does not exist outside of his mental conception. But the sure solution of this problem is that nature is a mixture of independence and dependence, of reality and idealism. Our mind and bodies are dependent on the external world, and this dependence varies according to the nature of their relation to it; but the indwelling spirit is free, as God is free, and is able to direct in a greater or lesser degree, according to the state of their development, the movements of our minds and bodies.

Death is but a change of condition. We remain in the same universe, and are subject to the same laws as before. Those who have passed beyond and have attained high planes of development in beauty and wisdom are but the advance-guard of a universal army who are following after them. The spirit of the highest is related to the spirit of the lowest, and the germ of infinite perfection exists in all. We should cultivate the optimistic temperament, and endeavour to see the good that dwells in everything. If we sit down and lament over the imperfection of our bodies and minds, we profit nothing; it is the heroic endeavour to subdue adverse circumstances that carries our spirit upwards. The object of life is to learn the laws of spiritual progress. Christians can learn from Hindus, and Hindus can learn from Christians. Each has made a contribution of value to the wisdom of the world.

Impress upon your children that true religion is positive and not negative, that it does not consist in merely refraining from evil, but in a persistent performance of noble decals. True religion comes not front the teaching of men or the reading of books; it is the awakening of the spirit within us, consequent upon pure and heroic action. Every child born into the world brings with it a certain accumulated experience from previous incarnations; and the impress of this experience is seen in the structure of its mind and body. But the feeling of independence which possesses us all shows there is something in us besides mind and body. The soul that reigns within is independent stud creates the desire for freedom. If we are not free, how can we hope to make the world better? We hold that human progress is the result of the action of the human spirit. What the world is, and what we ourselves are, are the fruits of the freedom of the spirit.

We believe in one God, the Father of us all, who is omnipresent and omnipotent, and who guides and preserves His children with infinite love. We believe in a Personal God as the Christians do, but we go further: we below that we are He! That His personality is manifested in us, that God is in us, and that we are in God We believe there is a germ of truth in all religions, and the Hindu bows down to them all; for in this world, truth is to be found not in subtraction but in addition. We would offer God a bouquet of the most beautiful flowers of all the diverse faiths. We must love God for love's sake, not for the hope of reward. We must do our duty for duty's sake not for the hope of reward. We must worship the beautiful for beauty's sake, not for the hope of reward. Thus in the purity of our hearts shall we see God. Sacrifices genuflexions, mumblings, and mutterings are not religion. They are only good if they stimulate us to the brave performance of beautiful and heroic deeds and lift our thoughts to the apprehension of the divine perfection

What good is it, if we acknowledge in our prayers that God is the Father of us all, and in our daily lives do not treat every man as our brother? Books are only made so that they may point the way to a higher life; but no good results unless the path is trodden with unflinching steps! Every human personality may be compared to a glass globe. There is the same pure white light—an emission of the divine Being—in the centre of each, but the glass being of different colours and thickness, the rays assume diverse aspects in the transmission. The equality and beauty of each central flame is the same, and the apparent inequality is only in the imperfection of the temporal instrument of its expression. As we rise higher and higher in the scale of being, the medium becomes more and more translucent.

THE BASIS FOR PSYCHIC OR SPIRITUAL RESEARCH

It was not often that Swami Vivekananda, while in the West, took part in debates. One such occasion in London when he did so was during the discussion of a lecture on, "Can Psychic Phenomena be proved from a Scientific Basis?" Referring first to a remark which he had heard in the course of this debate, not for the first time in the West, he said:

One point I want to remark upon. It is a mistaken statement that has been made to us that the Mohammedans do not believe that women have souls. I am very sorry to say it is an old mistake among Christian people, and they seem to like the mistake. That is a peculiarity in human nature, that people want to say something very bad about others whom they do not like. By the by, you know I am not a Mohammedan, but yet I have had opportunity for studying this religion, and there is not one word in the Koran which says that women have no souls, but in fact it says they have.

About the psychical things that have been the subject of discussion, I have very little to say here, for in the first place, the question is whether psychical subjects are capable of scientific demonstration. What do you mean by this demonstration? First of all, there will be the subjective and the objective side necessary. Taking chemistry and physics, with which we are so familiar, and of which we have read so much, is it true that everyone in this world is able to understand the demonstration even of the commonest subjects? Take any boor and show him one of your experiments. What will he understand of it? Nothing. It requires a good deal of previous training to be brought up to the point of understanding an experiment. Before that he cannot understand it at all. That is a area difficulty in the way. If scientific demonstration mean bringing down certain facts to a plane which is universe for all human beings, where all beings can understand it I deny that there can be any such scientific demonstration for any subject in the world. If it were so, all our universities and education would be in vain. Why are we educated if by birth we can understand everything scientific? Why so much study? It is of no use whatsoever. So, on the face of it, it is absurd if this be the meaning of scientific demonstration, the bringing down of intricate facts to the plane on which we are now. The next meaning should be the correct one, perhaps, that certain facts should be adduced as proving certain more intricate facts. There are certain more complicated intricate phenomena, which we explain by less intricate ones, and thus get, perhaps, nearer to them; in this way they are gradually brought down to the plane of our present ordinary consciousness. But even this is very complicated and very difficult, and means a training also, a tremendous amount of education. So an I have to say is that in order to have scientific explanation of psychical phenomena, we require not only perfect evidence on the side of the phenomena themselves, but a good deal of training on the part of those who want to see. All this being granted, we shall be in a position to say yea or nay, about the proof or disproof of any phenomena which are presented before us. But, before that, the most remarkable phenomena or the most oft-recorded phenomena that have happened in human society, in my opinion, would be very hard indeed to prove even in an offhand manner.

Next, as to those hasty explanations that religions are the outcome of dreams, those who have made a particular study of them would think of them but as mere guesses. We no reason to suppose that religions were the outcome of dreams as has been so easily explained. Then it would be very easy indeed to take even the agnostic's position, but unfortunately the matter cannot be explained so easily. There are many other wonderful phenomena happening, even at the present time, and these have all to be investigated, and not only have to be, but have been investigated all along. The blind man says there is no sun. That does not prove that there is no sun. These phenomena have been investigated years before. Whole races of mankind have trained themselves for centuries to become fit instruments for discovering the fine workings of the nerves; their records have been published ages ago, colleges have been created to study these subjects, and men and women there are still who are living demonstrations of these phenomena. Of course I admit that there is a good deal of hoax in the whole thing, a good deal of what is wrong and untrue in these things; but with what is this not the case? Take any common scientific phenomenon; there are two or three facts which either scientists or ordinary men may regard as absolute truths, and the rest as mere frothy suppositions. Now let the agnostic apply the same test to his own science which he would apply to what he does not want to believe. Half of it would be shaken to its foundation at once. We are bound to live on suppositions. We cannot live satisfied where we are; that is the natural growth of the human soul. We cannot become agnostics on this side and at the same time go about seeking for anything here; we have to pick. And, for this reason, we have to get beyond our limits, struggle to know what seems to be unknowable; and this struggle must continue.

In my opinion, therefore, I go really one step further than the lecturer, and advance the opinion that most of the psychical phenomena — not only little things like spirit-rappings or table-rappings which are mere child's play, not merely little things like telepathy which I have seen boys do even — most of the psychical phenomenal which the last speaker calls the higher clairvoyance, but which I would rather beg to call the experiences of the superconscious state of the mind, are the very stepping-stones to real psychological investigation. The first thing to be; seen is whether the mind can attain to that state or not. My explanation would, of course, be a little different from his, but we should probably agree when we explain terms. Not much depends on the question whether this present consciousness continues after death or not, seeing that this universe, as it is now, is not bound to this state of consciousness. Consciousness is not co-existent with existence. In my own body, and in all of our bodies, we must all admit that we are conscious of very little of the body, and of the greater part of it we are unconscious. Yet it exists. Nobody is ever conscious of his brain, for example. I never saw my brain, and I am never conscious of it. Yet I know that it exists. Therefore we may say that it is not consciousness that we want, but the existence of something which is not this gross matter; and that that knowledge can be gained even in this life, and that that knowledge has been gained and demonstrated, as far as

any science has been demonstrated, is a fact. We have to look into these things, and I would insist on reminding those who are here present on one other point. It is well to remember that very many times we are deluded on this. Certain people place before us the demonstration of a fact which is not ordinary to the spiritual nature, and we reject that fact because we say we cannot find it to be true. In many cases the fact may not be correct. But in many cases also we forget to consider whether we are fit to receive the demonstration or not, whether we have permitted our bodies and our minds to become fit subjects for their discovery.

ON ART IN INDIA

"Arts and Sciences in India" was the topic under which the Swami Vivekananda was introduced to the audience at Wendte Hall, San Francisco. The Swami held the attention of his hearers throughout as was demonstrated by the many questions which were put to him after his address.

The Swami said in part:

In the history of nations, the government at the beginning has always been in the hands of the priests. All the learning also has proceeded from the priests. Then, after the priests, the government changes hands, and the Kshatriya or the kingly power prevails, and the military rule is triumphant. This has always been true. And last comes the grasp of luxury, and the people sink down under it to be dominated by stronger and more barbarous races.

Amongst all races of the world, from the earliest time in history, India has been called the land of wisdom. For ages India itself has never gone out to conquer other nations. Its people have never been fighters. Unlike your Western people, they do not eat meat, for meat makes fighters; the blood of animals makes you restless, and you desire to do something.

Compare India and England in the Elizabethan period. What a dark age it was for your people, and how enlightened we were even then. The Anglo-Saxon people have always been badly fitted for art. They have good poetry — for instance, how wonderful is the blank verse of Shakespeare! Merely the rhyming of words is not good. It is not the most civilised thing in the world.

In India, music was developed to the full seven notes, even to half and quarter notes, ages ago. India led in music, also in drama and sculpture. Whatever is done now is merely an attempt at imitation. Everything now in India hinges on the question of how little a man requires to live upon.

IS INDIA A BENIGHTED COUNTRY?

The following is a report of a lecture at Detroit, United States, America, with the editorial comments of the Boston Evening Transcript, 5th April, 1894:

Swami Vivekananda has been in Detroit recently and made a proofed impression there. All classes flocked to hear him, and professional men in particular were greatly interested in his logic and his soundness of thought. The opera-house alone was large enough for his audience. He speaks English extremely well, and he is as handsome as he is good. The Detroit newspapers have devoted much space to the reports of his lectures. An editorial in the Detroit Evening News says: Most people will be inclined to think that Swami Vivekananda did better last night in his opera-house lecture than he did in any of his former lectures in this city. The merit of the Hindu's utterances last night lay in their clearness. He drew a very sharp line of distinction between Christianity and Christianity, and told his audience plainly wherein he himself is a Christian in one sense and not a Christian in another sense. He also drew a sharp line between Hinduism and Hinduism, carrying the implication that he desired to be classed as a Hindu only in its better sense. Swami Vivekananda stands superior to all criticism when he says, "We want missionaries of Christ. Let such come to India by the hundreds and thousands. Bring Christ's life to us and let it permeate the very core of society. Let him be preached in every village and corner of India."

When a man is as sound as that on the main question, all else that he may say must refer to the subordinate details. There is infinite humiliation in this spectacle of a pagan priest reading lessons of conduct and of life to the men who have assumed the spiritual supervision of Greenland's icy mountains and India's coral strand; but the sense of humiliation is the sine qua non of most reforms in this world. Having said what he did of the glorious life of the author of the Christian faith, Vivekananda has the right to lecture the way he has the men who profess to represent that life among the nations abroad. And after all, how like the Nazarene that sounds: "Provide neither gold nor silver, nor brass in your purses, nor scrip for your journey, neither two coats, neither shoes, nor yet staves; for the workman is worthy of his meat." Those who have become at all familiar with the religious, literature of India before the advent of Vivekananda are best prepared to understand the utter abhorrence of the Orientals of our Western commercial spirit—or what Vivekananda calls, "the shopkeeper's spirit"—in all that we do even in our very religion.

Here is a point for the missionaries which they cannot afford to ignore. They who would convert the Eastern world of paganism must live up to what they preach, in contempt for the kingdoms of this world and all the glory of them.

Brother Vivekananda considers India the most moral nation in the world. Though in bondage, its spirituality still endures. Here are extracts from the notices of some of his recent Detroit addresses: At this point the lecturer struck the great moral keynote of his discourse stating that with his people it was the belief that all non-self is good and all self is bad. This point was emphasised throughout the evening and might be termed the text of the address. "To build a home is selfish, argues the Hindu, so he builds it for the worship of God and for the entertainment of guests. To cook food is selfish, so he cooks it for the poor; he will serve himself last if any hungry stranger

applies; and this feeling extends throughout the length and breadth of the land. Any man can ask for food and shelter and any house will be opened to him.

"The caste system has nothing to do with religion. A man's occupation is hereditary—a carpenter is born a carpenter: a goldsmith, a goldsmith; a workman, a workman: and a priest, a priest.

"Two gifts are especially appreciated, the gift of learning and the gift of life. But the gift of learning takes precedence. One may save a man's life, and that is excellent; one may impart to another knowledge, and that is better. To instruct for money is an evil, and to do this would bring opprobrium upon the head of the man who barters learning for gold as though it were an article of trade. The Government makes gifts from time to time to the instructors, and the moral effect is better than it would be if the conditions were the same as exist in certain alleged civilised countries." The speaker had asked throughout the length and breadth of the land what was the definition of "civilization", and he had asked the question in many countries. Sometimes the reply has been, "What we are, that is civilization." He begged to differ in the definition of the word. A nation may conquer the waves, control the elements, develop the utilitarian problems of life seemingly to the utmost limits, and yet not realise that in the individual, the highest type of civilization is found in him who has learned to conquer self. This condition is found more in India than in any other country on earth, for there the material conditions are subservient to the spiritual, and the individual looks to the soul manifestations in everything that has life, studying nature to this end. Hence that gentle disposition to endure with indomitable patience the flings of what appears unkind fortune, the while there is a full consciousness of a spiritual strength and knowledge greater than that possessed by any other people. Therefore the existence of a country and people from which flows an unending stream that attracts the attention of thinkers far and near to approach and throw from their shoulders an oppressive earthly burden.

This lecture was prefaced with the statement that the speaker had been asked many questions. A number of these he preferred to answer privately, but three he had selected for reasons, which would appear, to answer from the pulpit. They were: "Do the people of India throw their children into the jaws of the crocodiles?" "Do they kill themselves beneath the wheels of Jagannâtha?" "Do they burn widows with their husbands?" The first question the lecturer treated in the same vein as an American abroad would in answering inquiries about Indians running round in the streets of New York and similar myths which are even today entertained by many persons on the Continent. The statement was too ludicrous to give a serious response to it. When asked by certain well-meaning but ignorant people why they gave only female children to the crocodiles, he could only ironically reply that probably it was because they were softer and more tender and could be more easily masticated by the inhabitants of the river in that benighted country. Regarding the Jagannatha legend, the lecturer explained the old practice of the Car-festival in the sacred city, and remarked that possibly a few pilgrims in their zeal to grasp the rope and participate in the drawing of the Car slipped and fell and were so destroyed. Some such mishaps had been exaggerated into the distorted versions from which the good people of other countries shrank with horror. Vivekananda denied that people burned widows. It was true, however, that widows had burned themselves. In the few cases where this had happened, they had been urged not to do so by holy men, Who were always opposed to suicide. Where the devoted widows insisted, stating that they desired to accompany their husbands in the transformation that had taken place, they were obliged to submit themselves to the fiery tests. That is, they thrust Her hands within the flames, and if they permitted them to be consumed, no further opposition was placed in the way of the fulfilment of their desires. But India is not the only country where women, who have loved, have followed immediately the beloved one to the realms of immortality; suicides in such cases have occurred in every land. It is an uncommon bit of fanaticism in any country—as unusual in India as elsewhere. "No," the speaker repeated, "the people do not burn women in India; nor have they ever burned witches."

This latter touch is decidedly acute by way of reflection. No analysis of the philosophy of the Hindu monk need be attempted here, except to say that it is based in general on the struggle of the soul to individually attain Infinity. One learned Hindu opened the Lowell Institute Course this year. What Mr. Mozoomdar began, might worthily be ended by Brother Vivekananda. This new visitor has by far the most interesting personality, although in the Hindu philosophy, of course, personality is not to be taken into consideration. At the Parliament of Religions they used to keep Vivekananda until the end of the programme to make people stay until the end of the session. On a warm day, when a prosy speaker talked too long and people began going home by hundreds, the Chairman would get up and announce that Swami Vivekananda would make a short address just before the benediction. Then he would have the peaceable hundreds perfectly in tether. The four thousand fanning people in the Hall of Columbus would sit smiling and expectant, waiting for an hour or two of other men's speeches, to listen to Vivekananda for fifteen minutes. The Chairman knew the old rule of keeping the best until the last.

THE CLAIMS OF RELIGION[1]

Sunday, 5th January

Many of you remember the thrill of joy with which in your childhood you saw the glorious rising sun; all of you, some-

1. Portions of this lecture were published in Vol. III, The published portions are reproduced here in small type. The year of the lecture is not known.

times in your life, stand and gaze upon the glorious setting sun, and at least in imagination, try to pierce through the beyond. This, in fact, is at the bottom of the whole universe—this rising from and this setting into the beyond, this whole universe coming up out of the unknown, and going back again into the unknown, crawling in as a child out of darkness, and crawling out again as an old man into darkness.

This universe of ours, the universe of the senses, the rational, the intellectual, is bounded on both sides by the illimitable, the unknowable, the ever unknown. Herein is the search, herein art the inquiries, here are the facts; from this comes the light which is known to the world as religion. Essentially, however, religion belongs to the supersensuous and not to the sense plane. It is beyond all reasoning, and not on the plane of intellect. It is a vision, an inspiration, a plunge into the unknown and unknowable making the unknowable more than known, for it can never be "known". This search has been in the human mind, as I believe from the very beginning of humanity. There cannot have been human reasoning and intellect in any period of the world's history without this struggle, this search beyond. In our little universe this human mind, we see a thought arise. Whence it rises we do not know, and when it disappears, where it goes, we know not either. The macrocosm and the microcosm are, as it were in the same groove, passing through the same stages, vibrating in the same key.

I shall try to bring before you the Hindu theory that religions do not come from without, but from within. It is my belief that religious thought is in man's very constitution, so much so that it is impossible for him to give up religion until he can give up his mind and body, until he can stop thought and life. As long as a man thinks, this struggle must go on, and so long man must have some form of religion. Thus we see various forms of religion in the world. It is a bewildering study; but it is not, as many of us think, a vain speculation. Amidst this chaos there is harmony, throughout these discordant sounds there is a note of concord; and he who is prepared to listen to it, will catch the tone.

The great question of all questions at the present time is this: Taking for granted that the knowable and the known are bounded on both sides by the unknowable and the infinitely unknown, why struggle for that unknown? Why shall we not be content with the known? Why shall we not rest satisfied with eating, drinking, and doing a little good to society? This idea is in the air. From the most learned professor to the prattling baby, we are told, "Do good to the world, that is all of religion, and don't bother your head about questions of the beyond." So much so is this the case that it has become a truism.

But fortunately we must inquire into the beyond. This present, this expressed, is only one part of that unexpressed. The sense universe is, as it were, only one portion, one bit of that infinite spiritual universe projected into the plane of sense consciousness. How can this little bit of projection be explained, be understood, without knowing that which is beyond? It is said of Socrates that one day while lecturing at Athens, he met a Brâhmana who had travelled into Greece, and Socrates told the Brahmana that the greatest study for mankind is man. And the Brahmana sharply retorted, "How can you know man until you know God?" This God, this eternally Unknowable, or Absolute, or Infinite, or without name—you may call Him by what name you like—is the rationale, the only explanation, the raison d'etre of that which is known and knowable, this present life. Take anything before you, the most material thing—take any one of these most materialistic sciences, such as chemistry or physics, astronomy or biology—study it, push the study forward and forward, and the gross forms will begin to melt and become finer and finer, until they come to a point where you are bound to make a tremendous leap from these material things into the immaterial. The gross melts into the fine, physics into metaphysics in every department of knowledge.

So with everything we have—our society, our relations With each other, our religion, and what you call ethics. There are attempts at producing a system of ethics from mere grounds of utility. I challenge any man to produce such a rational system of ethics. Do good to others. Why? Because it is the highest utility. Suppose a man says, "I do not care for utility; I want to cut the throats of others and make myself rich." What will you answer? It is out-Heroding Herod! But where is the utility of my doing good to the world? Am I a fool to work my life out that others may be happy? Why shall I myself not be happy, if there is no other sentiency beyond society, no other power in the universe beyond the five senses? What prevents me from cutting the throats of my brothers so long as I can make myself safe from the police, and make myself happy. What will you answer? You are bound to show some utility. When you are pushed from your ground you answer, "My friend, it is good to be good." What is the power in the human mind which says, "It is good to do good", which unfolds before us in glorious view the grandeur of the soul, the beauty of goodness, the all attractive power of goodness, the infinite power of goodness? That is what we call God. Is it not?

Secondly, I want to tread on a little more delicate ground. I want your attention, and ask you not to make any hasty conclusions from what I say. We cannot do much good to this world. Doing good to the world is very good. But can we do much good to the world? Have we done much good these hundreds of years that we have been struggling—have we increased the sum total of the happiness in the world? Thousands of means have been created every day to conduce to the happiness of the world, and this has been going on for hundreds and thousands of years. I ask you: Is the sum total of the happiness in the world today more than what it divas a century ago? It cannot be. Each wave that rises in the ocean must be at the expense of a hollow somewhere. If one nation becomes rich and powerful, it must be at the expense of another nation somewhere. Each piece of machinery that is invented will make twenty people rich and a twenty thousand people poor. It is the law of competition throughout. The sum total of the energy displayed remains the same throughout. It is, too, a foolhardy task. It is unreasonable to state that we can have happiness without misery. With the increase of all these means, you are increasing the want of the world, and increased wants mean insatiable thirst which will never be quenched. What can fill this want, this thirst? And so long as there is this thirst, misery is inevitable. It is the very nature of life to be happy and miserable by turns. Then again is this world left to you to do good to it? Is there no other power working in this universe? Is God dead and gone, leaving His universe to you and me—the Eternal, the Omnipotent the All-merciful, the Ever-awakened, the One who never sleeps when the universe is sleeping, whose eyes never blink? This infinite sky is, as it were, His ever-open eye. Is He dead and gone? Is He not acting in this universe? It is going on; you need not be in a hurry; you need not make yourself miserable.

[The Swami here told the story of the man who wanted a ghost to work for him, but who, when he had the ghost, could not keep him employed, until he gave him a curly dog's tail to straighten.]

Such is the case with us, with this doing good to the universe. So, my brothers, we are trying to straighten out the tail of the dog these hundreds and thousands of years. It is like rheumatism. You drive it out from the feet, and it goes to the head; you drive it from the head, and it goes somewhere else.

This will seem to many of you to be a terrible, pessimistic view of the world, but it is not. Both pessimism and optimism are wrong. Both are taking up the extremes. So long as a man has plenty to eat and drink, and good clothes to wear, he becomes a great optimist; but that very man, when he loses everything, becomes a great pessimist. When a man loses all his money and is very poor, then and then alone, with the greatest force come to him the ideas of brotherhood of humanity. This is the world, and the more I go to different countries and see of this world, and the older I get, the more I am trying to avoid both these extremes of optimism and pessimism. This world is neither good nor evil. It is the Lord's world. It is beyond both good and evil, perfect in itself. His will is going on, showing all these different pictures; and it will go on without beginning and without end. It is a great gymnasium in which you and I, and millions of souls must come and get exercises, and make ourselves strong and perfect. This is what it is for. Not that God could not make a perfect universe; not that He could not help the misery of the world. You remember the story of the young lady and the clergyman, who were both looking at the moon through the telescope, and found the moon spots. And the clergyman said, "I am sure they are the spires of some churches." "Nonsense," said the young lady, "I am sure they are the young lovers kissing each other." So we are doing with this world. When we are inside, we think we are seeing the inside. According to the plane of existence in which we are, we see the universe. Fire in the kitchen is neither good nor bad. When it cooks a meal for you, you bless the fire, and say, "How good it is!" And when it burns your finger, you say, "What a nuisance it is!" It would be equally correct and logical to say: This universe is neither good nor evil. The world is the world, and will be always so. If we open ourselves to it in such a manner that the action of the world is beneficial to us, we call it good. If we put ourselves in the position in which it is painful, we call it evil. So you will always find children, who are innocent and joyful and do not want to injure anyone, are very optimistic. They are dreaming golden dreams. Old men who have all the desires in their hearts and not the means to fulfil them, and especially those who have been thumped and bumped by the world a good deal, are very pessimistic. Religion wants to know the truth. And the first thing it has discovered is that without a knowledge of this truth there will be no life worth living.

Life will be a desert, human life will be vain, it we cannot know the beyond. It is very good to say: Be contented with the things of the present moment. The cows and the dogs are, and so are all animals, and that is what makes them animals. So if man rests content with the present and gives up all search into the beyond, mankind will all have to go back to the animal plane again. It is religion, this inquiry into the beyond, that makes the difference between man and an animal. Well has it been said that man is the only animal that naturally looks upwards; every other animal naturally looks down. That looking upward and going upward and seeking perfection are what is called salvation, and the sooner a man begins to go higher, the sooner he raises himself towards this idea of truth as salvation. It does not consist in the amount of money in your pocket, or the dress you wear, or the house You live in, but in the wealth of spiritual thought in your brain. That is what makes for human progress; that is the source of all material and intellectual progress, the motive power behind, the enthusiasm that pushes mankind forward.

What again is the goal of mankind? Is it happiness, sensuous pleasure? They used to say in the olden time that in heaven they will play on trumpets and live round a throne; in modern time I find that they think this ideal is very weak, and they have improved upon it and say that they will have marriages and all these things there. If there is any improvement in these two things, the second is an improvement for the worse. All these various theories of heaven that are being put forward show weakness in the mind. And that weakness is here: First, they think that sense happiness is the goal of life. Secondly they cannot conceive of anything that is beyond the five senses. They are as irrational as the Utilitarians. Still they are much better than the modern Atheistic Utilitarians, at any rate. Lastly, this Utilitarian position is simply childish. What right have you to say, "Here is my standard, and the whole universe must be governed by my standard?" What right have you to say that every truth shall be judged by this standard of yours—the standard that preaches mere bread, and money,

and clothes as God?

Religion does not live in bread, does not dwell in a house. Again and again you hear this objection advanced: "What good can religion do? Can it take away the poverty of the poor and give them more clothes?" Supposing it cannot, would that prove the untruth of religion? Suppose a baby stands up among you, when you are trying to demonstrate an astronomical theory, and says, "Does it bring gingerbread?" "No, it does not," you answer. "Then," says the baby, "it is useless." Babies judge the whole universe from their own standpoint, that of producing gingerbread, and so do the babies of the world.

Sad to say at the later end of this nineteenth century that these are passing for the learned, the most rational, the most logical, the most intelligent crowd ever seen on this earth.

We must not judge of higher things from this low standpoint of ours. Everything must be judged by its own standard, and the infinite must be judged by the standard of infinity. Religion permeates the whole of man's life, not only the present, but the past, present, and future. It is therefore the eternal relation between the eternal Soul, and the eternal God. Is it logical to measure its value by its action upon five minutes of human life? Certainly not. But these are all negative arguments.

Now comes the question: Can religion really do anything? It can.

Can religion really bring bread and clothes? It does. It is always doing so, and it does infinitely more than that; it brings to man eternal life. It has made man what he is, and will make of this human animal a God. That is what religion can do. Take off religion from human society, what will remain? Nothing but a forest of brutes. As I have just tried to show you that it is absurd to suppose that sense happiness is the goal of humanity, we find as a conclusion that knowledge is the goal of all life. I have tried to show to you that in these thousands of years of struggle for the search of truth and the benefit of mankind, we have scarcely made the least appreciable advance. But mankind has made gigantic advance in knowledge. The highest utility of this progress lies not in the creature comforts that it brings, but in manufacturing a god out of this animal man. Then, with knowledge, naturally comes bliss. Babies think that the happiness of the senses is the highest thing they can have. Most of you know that there is a keener enjoyment in man in the intellect than in the senses. No one of you can feel the same pleasure in eating as a dog does. You can mark that. Where does the pleasure come from in man? Not that whole-souled enjoyment of eating that the pig or the dog has. See how the pig eats. It is unconscious of the universe while it is eating; its whole soul is bound up in the food. It may be killed but it does not care when it has food. Think of the intense enjoyment that the pig has! No man has that. Where is it gone? Man has changed it into intellectual enjoyment. The pig cannot enjoy religious lectures.

That is one step higher and keener yet than intellectual pleasures, and that is the spiritual plane, spiritual enjoyment of things divine, soaring beyond reason and intellect. To procure that we shall have to lose all these sense-enjoyments. This is the highest utility. Utility is what I enjoy, and what everyone enjoys, and we run for that.

We find that man enjoys his intellect much more than an animal enjoys his senses, and we see that man enjoys his spiritual nature even more than his rational nature. So the highest wisdom must be this spiritual knowledge. With this knowledge will come bliss. All these things of this world are but the shadows, the manifestations in the third or fourth degree of the real Knowledge and Bliss.

It is this Bliss that comes to you through the love of humanity; the shadow of this spiritual Bliss is this human love, but do not confound it with that human bliss. There is that great error: We are always mistaking the: love that we have—this carnal, human love, this attachment for particles, this electrical attraction for human beings in society—for this spiritual Bliss. We are apt to mistake this for that eternal state, which it is not. For want of any other name in English, I would call it Bliss, which is the same as eternal knowledge—and that is our goal. Throughout the world, wherever there has been a religion, and wherever there will be a religion, they have all sprung and will all spring out of one source, called by various names in various countries; and that is what in the Western countries you call "inspiration". What is this inspiration? Inspiration is the only source of religious knowledge. We have seen that religion essentially belongs to the plane beyond the senses. It is "where the eyes cannot go, or the ears, where the mind cannot reach, or what words cannot express". That is the field and goal of religion, and from this comes that which we call inspiration. It naturally follows, therefore, that there must be some way to go beyond the senses. It is perfectly true that our reason cannot go beyond the senses; all reasoning is within the senses, and reason is based upon the facts which the senses reach. But can a man go beyond the senses? Can a man know the unknowable? Upon this the whole question of religion is to be and has been decided. From time immemorial there was that adamantine wall, the barrier to the senses; from time immemorial hundreds and thousands of men and women haven't dashed themselves against this wall to penetrate beyond. Millions have failed, and millions have succeeded. This is the history of the world. Millions more do not believe that anyone ever succeeded; and these are the sceptics of the present day. Man succeeds in going beyond this wall if he only tries. Man has not only reason, he has not only senses, but there is much in him which is beyond the senses. We shall try to explain it a little. I hope you will feel that it is within you also.

I move my hand, and I feel and I know that I am moving my hand. I call it consciousness. I am conscious that I am moving my hand. But my heart is moving. I am not conscious of that; and yet who is moving the heart? It must be the same being. So we see that this being who moves the hands and speaks, that is to say, acts consciously, also acts unconsciously. We find, therefore, that this being can act upon two planes—one, the plane of consciousness, and the other, the plane below that. The impulsions from the plane of unconsciousness are what we call instinct, and when the same impulsions come from the plane of consciousness, we call it reason. But there is a still higher plane, superconsciousness in man. This is apparently the same as unconsciousness, because it is beyond the plane of consciousness, but it is above consciousness and not below it. It is not instinct, it is inspiration. There is proof of it. Think of all these great prophets and sages that the world has produced, and it is well known how there will be times in their lives, moments in their existence, when they will be apparently unconscious of the external world; and all the knowledge that subsequently comes out of them, they claim, was gained during this state of existence. It is said of Socrates that while marching with the army, there was a beautiful sunrise, and that set in motion in his mind a train of thought; he stood there for two days in the sun quite unconscious. It was such moments that gave the Socratic knowledge to the world. So with all the great preachers and prophets, there are moments in their lives when they, as it were, rise from the conscious and go above it. And when they come back to the plane of consciousness, they come radiant with light; they have brought news from the beyond, and they are the inspired seers of the world.

But there is a great danger. Any man may say he is inspired; many times they say that. Where is the test? During sleep we are unconscious; a fool goes to sleep; he sleeps soundly for three hours; and when he comes back from that state, he is the same fool if not worse. Jesus of Nazareth goes into his transfiguration, and when he comes out, he has become Jesus the Christ. That is all the difference. One is inspiration, and the other is instinct. The one is a child, and the other is the old experienced man. This inspiration is possible for everyone of us. It is the source of all religions, and will ever be the source of all higher knowledge. Yet there are great dangers in the way. Sometimes fraudulent people try to impose themselves upon mankind. In these days it is becoming all too prevalent. A friend of mine had a very fine picture. Another gentleman who was rather religiously inclined, and a rich man, had his eyes upon this picture; but my friend would not sell it. This other gentleman one day comes and says to my friend, I have an inspiration and I have a message from God. "What is your message?" my friend asked. "The message is that you must deliver that picture to me." My friend was up to his mark; he immediately added, "Exactly so; how beautiful! I had exactly the same inspiration, that I should have to deliver to you the picture. Have you brought your cheque?" "Cheque? What cheque?' "Then", said my friend, "I don't think your inspiration was right. My inspiration was that I must give the picture to the man who brought a cheque for $100,000. You must bring the cheque first." The other man found he was caught, and gave up the inspiration theory. These are the dangers. A man came to me in Boston and said he had visions in which he had been talked to in the Hindu language. I said, "If I can see what he says I will believe it." But he wrote down a lot of nonsense. I tried my best to understand it, but I could not. I told him that so far as my knowledge went, such language never was and never will be in India. They had not become civilised enough to have such a language as that. He thought of course that I was a rogue and sceptic, and went away; and I would not be surprised next to hear that he was in a lunatic asylum. These are the two dangers always in this world—the danger from frauds, and the danger from fools. But that need not deter us, for all great things in this world are fraught with danger. At the same time we must take a little precaution. Sometimes I find persons perfectly wanting in logical analysis of anything. A man comes and says, "I have a message from such and such a god", and asks, "Can you deny it? Is it not possible that there will be such and such a god, and that he will give such a message? And 90 per cent of fools will swallow it. They think that that is reason enough. But one thing you ought to know, that it is possible for anything to happen - quite possible that the earth may come into contact with the Dog star in the next year and go to pieces. But if I advance this proposition, you have the right to stand up and ask me to prove it to you. What the lawyers call the onus probandi is on the man who made the proposition. It is not your duty to prove that I got my inspiration from a certain god, but mine, because I produced the proposition to you. If I cannot prove it, I should better hold my tongue. Avoid both these dangers, and you can get anywhere you please. Many of us get many messages in our lives, or think we get them, and as long as the message is regarding our own selves, go on doing what you please; but when it is in regard to our contact with and behaviour to others, think a hundred times before you act upon it; and then you will be safe.

We find that this inspiration is the only source of religion; yet it has always been fraught with many dangers; and the last and worst of all dangers is excessive claims. Certain men stand up and say they have a communication from God, and they are the mouthpiece of God Almighty, and no one else has the right to have that communication. This, on the face of it, is unreasonable. If there is anything in the universe, it must be universal; there is not one movement here that is not universal, because the whole universe is governed by laws. It is systematic and harmonious all through. Therefore what is anywhere must be everywhere. Each atom in the universe is built on the same plan as the biggest sun and the stars. If one man was ever inspired, it is possible for each and every one of us to be inspired, and that is religion. Avoid all these dangers, illusions and delusions, and fraud and making excessive claims, but come face to face with religious facts, and come into direct contact with the science of religion. Religion does not consist in believing any number of doctrines or dogmas, in going to churches or temples, in reading certain books.

Have you seen God? Have you seen the soul? If not, are you struggling for it? It is here and now, and you have not to wait for the future. What is the future but the present illimitable? What is the whole amount of time but one second repeated again and again? Religion is here and now, in this present life.

One question more: What is the goal? Nowadays it is asserted that man is progressing infinitely, forward and forward, and there is no goal of perfection to attain to. Ever approaching, never attaining, whatever that may mean, and however wonderful it may be, it is absurd on the face of it. Is there any motion in a straight line? A straight line infinitely projected becomes a circle, it returns back to the starting point. You must end where you begin; and as you began in God, you must go back to God. What remains? Detail work. Through eternity you have to do the detail work.

Yet another question: Are we to discover new truths of religion as we go on? Yea and nay. In the first place, we cannot know anything more of religion; it has been all known. In all the religions of the world you will find it claimed that there is a unity within us. Being one with the Divinity, there cannot be any further progress in that sense. Knowledge means Ending this unity in variety. I see you as men and women, and this is variety. It becomes scientific knowledge when I group you together and call you hyenas beings. Take the science of chemistry, for instance. Chemists are seeking to resolve all known substances into their original elements, and if possible, to find the one element from which all these are derived. The time may come when they will find the one element. That is the source of all other elements. Reaching that, they can go no further; the science of chemistry will have become perfect. So it is with the science of religion. If we can discover this perfect unity, then there cannot be any further progress.

When it was discovered that "I and my Father are one", the last word was said of religion. Then there only remained detail work. In true religion there is no faith or belief in the sense of blind faith. No great preacher ever preached that. That only comes with degeneracy. Fools pretend to be followers of this or that spiritual giant, and although they may be without power, endeavour to teach humanity to believe blindly. Believe what? To believe blindly is to degenerate the human soul. Be an atheist if you want, but do not believe in anything unquestioningly. Why degrade the soul to the level of animals? You not only hurt yourselves thereby, but you injure society, and make danger for those that come after you. Stand up and reason out, having no blind faith. Religion is a question of being and becoming, not of believing. This is religion, and when you have attained to that you have religion. Before that you are no better than the animals. "Do not believe in what you have heard," says the great Buddha, "do not believe in doctrines because they have been handed down to you through generations; do not believe in anything because it is followed blindly by many; do not believe because some old sage makes a statement; do not believe in truths to which you have become attached by habit; do not believe merely on the authority of your teachers and elders. Have deliberation and analyse, and when the result agrees with reason and conduces to the good of one and all, accept it and live up to it."

CONCENTRATION

Delivered at the Washington Hall, San Francisco, March 16, 1900

[This and the following two lectures (Meditation and The Practice of Religion) are reproduced here from the Vedanta and the West with the kind permission of the Vedanta Society of Southern California, by whom is reserved the copyright for America. The lectures were recorded by Ida Ansell under circumstances which she herself relates thus:

"Swami Vivekananda's second trip to the West occurred in 1899-1900. During the first half of 1900 he worked in and around San Francisco, California. I was a resident of that city, twenty-two years old at the time...I heard him lecture perhaps a score of times from March to May of 1900, and recorded seventeen of his talks. ...

"The lectures were given in San Francisco, Oakland, and Alameda, in churches, in the Alameda and San Francisco Homes of Truth, and in rented halls...Altogether Swamiji gave, besides nearly daily interviews and informal classes, at least thirty or forty major addresses in March, April, and May...

"I was long hesitant about transcribing and releasing these lectures because of the imperfectness of my notes. I was just an amateur stenographer, at the time I took them...One would have needed a speed of at least three hundred words per minute to capture all of Swamiji's torrents of eloquence. I possessed less than half the required speed, and at the time I had no idea that the material would have value to anyone but myself. In addition to his fast speaking pace, Swamiji was a superb actor. His stories and imitations absolutely forced one to stop writing, to enjoy watching him...Even though my notes were somewhat fragmentary, I have yielded to the opinion that their contents are precious and must be given for publication.

Swamiji's speaking style was colloquial, fresh, and forceful. No alterations have been made in it; no adjusting or smoothing out of his spontaneous flow for purposes of publication has been done. Where omissions were made because of some obscurity in the meaning, they have been indicated by three dots. Anything inserted for purposes of clarification has been placed in square brackets. With these qualifications, the words are exactly as Swamiji spoke them.

Everything Swamiji said had tremendous power. These lectures have slept in my old stenographer's notebook for more than fifty years. Now as they emerge, one feels that the power is still there."]

All knowledge that we have, either of the external or internal world, is obtained through only one method—by the concentration of the mind. No knowledge can be had of any science unless we can concentrate our minds upon the subject. The astronomer concentrates his mind through the telescope...and so on. If you want to study your own mind, it will be the same process. You will have to concentrate your mind and turn it back upon itself. The difference in this world between mind and mind is simply the fact of concentration. One, more concentrated than the other, gets more knowledge.

In the lives of all great men, past and present, we find this tremendous power of concentration. Those are men of genius, you say. The science of Yoga tells us that we are all geniuses if we try hard to be. Some will come into this life better fitted and will do it quicker perhaps. We can all do the same. The same power is in everyone. The subject of the present lecture is how to concentrate the mind in order to study the mind itself. Yogis have laid down certain rules and this night I am going to give you a sketch of some of these rules.

Concentration, of course, comes from various sources. Through the senses you can get concentration. Some get it when they hear beautiful music, others when they see beautiful scenery...Some get concentrated by lying upon beds of spikes, sharp iron spikes, others by sitting upon sharp pebbles. These are extraordinary cases [using] most unscientific procedure. Scientific procedure is gradually training the mind.

One gets concentrated by holding his arm up. Torture gives him the concentration he wants. But all these are extraordinary.

Universal methods have been organised according to different philosophers. Some say the state we want to attain is superconsciousness of the mind—going beyond the limitations the body has made for us. The value of ethics to the Yogi lies in that it makes the mind pure. The purer the mind, the easier it is to control it. The mind takes every thought that rises and works it out. The grosser the mind, the more difficult [it is] to control [it]. The immoral man will never be able to concentrate his mind to study psychology. He may get a little control as he begins, get a little power of hearing...and even those powers will go from him. The difficulty is that if you study closely, you see how [the] extraordinary power arrived at was not attained by regular scientific training. The men who, by the power of magic, control serpents will be killed by serpents...The man who attains any extraordinary powers will in the long run succumb to those powers. There are millions [who] receive power through all sorts of ways in India. The vast majority of them die raving lunatics. Quite a number commit suicide, the mind [being] unbalanced.

The study must be put on the safe side: scientific, slow, peaceful. The first requisite is to be moral. Such a man wants the gods to come down, and they will come down and manifest themselves to him. That is our psychology and philosophy in essence, [to be] perfectly moral. Just think what that means! No injury, perfect purity, perfect austerity! These are absolutely necessary. Just think, if a man can attain all these in perfection! What more do you want? If he is free from all enmity towards any being, ... all animals will give up their enmity [in his presence]. The Yogis lay down very strict laws ... so that one cannot pass off for a charitable man without; being charitable ...

If you believe me, I have seen a man who used to live[1] in a hole and there were cobras and frogs living with him ... Sometimes he would fast for [days and months] and then come out. He was always silent. One day there came a robber ...

My old master used to say, "When the lotus of the heart has bloomed, the bees will come by themselves." Men like that are there yet. They need not talk ... When the man is perfect from his heart, without a thought of hatred, all animals will give up their hatred [before him]. So with purity. These are necessary for our dealings with our fellow beings. We must love all ... We have no business to look at the faults of others: it does no good We must not even think of them. Our business is with the good. We are not here to deal with faults. Our business is to be good.

Here comes Miss So-and-so. She says, "I am going to be a Yogi." She tells the news twenty times, meditates fifty days, then she says, "There is nothing in this religion. I have tried it. There is nothing in it."

The very basis [of spiritual life] is not there. The foundation [must be] this perfect morality. That is the great difficulty ...

In our country there are vegetarian sects. They will take in the early morning pounds of sugar and place it on the ground for ants, and the story is, when one of them was putting sugar on the ground for ants, a man placed his foot upon the ants. The former said, "Wretch, you have killed the animals!" And he gave him such a blow, that it killed the man.

External purity is very easy and all the world rushes towards [it]. If a certain kind of dress is the kind of morality [to be observed], any fool can do that. When it is grappling with the mind itself, it is hard work.

The people who do external, superficial things are so self-righteous! I remember, when I was a boy I had great regard for the character of Jesus Christ. [Then I read about the wedding feast in the Bible.] I closed the book and said, "He ate meat and drank wine! He cannot be a good man."

We are always losing sight of the real meaning of things. The little eating and dress! Every fool can see that. Who sees that which is beyond? It is culture of the heart that we want ... One mass of people in India we see bathing twenty times a day sometimes, making themselves very pure. And they do not touch anyone ... The coarse facts, the external things! [If by bathing one could be pure,] fish are the purest beings.

Bathing, and dress, and food regulation—all these have their proper value when they are complementary to the spiritual ... That first, and these all help. But without it, no amount of eating grass ... is any good at all. They are helps

if properly understood. But improperly understood, they are derogatory ...

This is the reason why I am explaining these things: First, because in all religions everything degenerates upon being practiced by [the ignorant]. The camphor in the bottle evaporated, and they are fighting over the bottle.

Another thing: ... [Spirituality] evaporates when they say, "This is right, and that is wrong." All quarrels are [with forms and creeds] never in the spirit. The Buddhist offered for years glorious preaching; gradually, this spirituality evaporated ... [Similarly with Christianity.] And then began the quarrel whether it is three gods in one or one in three, when nobody wants to go to God Himself and know what He is. We have to go to God Himself to know whether He is three in one or one in three.

Now, with this explanation, the posture. Trying to control the mind, a certain posture is necessary. Any posture in which the person can sit easily—that is the posture for that person. As a rule, you will find that the spinal column must be left free. It is not intended to bear the weight of the body ... The only thing to remember in the sitting posture: [use] any posture in which the spine is perfectly free of the weight of the body.

Next [Prânâyâma] ... the breathing exercises. A great deal of stress is laid upon breathing ... What I am telling you is not something gleaned from some sect in India. It is universally true. Just as in this country you teach your children certain prayers, [in India] they get the children and give them certain facts etc.

Children are not taught any religion in India except one or two prayers. Then they begin to seek for somebody with whom they can get en rapport. They go to different persons and find that "This man is the man for me", and get initiation. If I am married, my wife may possibly get another man teacher and my son will get somebody else, and that is always my secret between me and my teacher. The wife's religion the husband need not know, and he would not dare ask her what her religion is. It is well known that they would never say. It is only known to that person and the teacher ... Sometimes you will find that what would be quite ludicrous to one will be just teaching for another ... Each is carrying his own burden and is to be helped according to his particular mind. It is the business of every individual, between him, his teacher, and God. But there are certain general methods which all these teachers preach. Breathing [and] meditating are universal. That is the worship in India.

On the banks of the Gangâ, we will see men, women, and children all [practicing] breathing and then meditating. Of course, they have other things to do. They cannot devote much time to this. But those who have taken this as the study of life, they practice various methods. There are eighty-four different Âsanas (postures). Those that take it up under some person, they always feel the breath and the movements in all

1. The reference is evidently to Pavhari Baba (see *Sketch of the Life of Pavhari Baba* in this volume)

the different parts of the body...

Next comes Dhâranâ [concentration]...Dharana is holding the mind in certain spots.

The Hindu boy or girl...gets initiation. He gets from his Guru a word. This is called the root word. This word is given to the Guru [by his Guru], and he gives it to his disciple. One such word is OM. All these symbols have a great deal of meaning, and they hold it secret, never write it. They must receive it through the ear — not through writing — from the teacher, and then hold it as God himself. Then they meditate on the word...

I used to pray like that at one time, all through the rainy season, four months. I used to get up and take a plunge in the river, and with all my wet clothes on repeat [the Mantra] till the sun set. Then I ate something — a little rice or something. Four months in the rainy season!

The Indian mind believes that there is nothing in the world that cannot be obtained. If a man wants money in this country, he goes to work and earns money. There, he gets a formula and sits under a tree and believes that money must come. Everything must come by the power of his [thought]. You make money here. It is the same thing. You put forth your whole energy upon money making.

There are some sects called Hatha-Yogis...They say the greatest good is to keep the body from dying...Their whole process is clinging to the body. Twelve years training! And they begin with little children, others wise it is impossible...One thing [is] very curious about the Hatha-Yogi: When he first becomes a disciple, he goes into the wilderness and lives alone forty days exactly. All they have they learn within those forty days...

A man in Calcutta claims to have lived five hundred years. The people all tell me that their grandfathers saw him...He takes a constitutional twenty miles, never walks, he runs. Goes into the water, covers himself [from] top to toe with mud. After that he plunges again into the water, again sticks himself with mud...I do not see any good in that. (Snakes, they say, live two hundred years.) He must be very old, because I have travelled fourteen years in India and wherever I went everybody knew him. He has been travelling all his life...[The Hatha-Yogi] will swallow a piece of rubber eighty inches long and take it out again. Four times a day he has to wash every part of his body, internal and external parts...

The walls can keep their bodies thousands of years...What of that? I would not want to live so long. "Sufficient unto the day is the evil thereof." One little body, with all its delusions and limitations, is enough.

There are other sects...They give you a drop of the elixir of life and you remain young...It will take me months to enumerate [all the sects]. All their activity is on this side [in the material world]. Every day a new sect...

The power of all those sects is in the mind. Their idea is to hold the mind. First concentrate it and hold it at a certain place. They generally say, at certain parts of the body along the spinal column or upon the nerve centres. By holding the mind at the nerve centres, [the Yogi] gets power over the body. The body is the great cause of disturbance to his peace, is opposite of his highest ideal, so he wants control: [to] keep the body as servant.

Then comes meditation. That is the highest state...When [the mind] is doubtful that is not its great state. Its great state is meditation. It looks upon things and sees things, not identifying itself with anything else. As long as I feel pain, I have identified myself with the body. When I feel joy or pleasure, I have identified myself with the body. But the high state will look with the same pleasure or blissfulness upon pleasure or upon pain...Every meditation is direct superconsciousness. In perfect concentration the soul becomes actually free from the bonds of the gross body and knows itself as it is. Whatever one wants, that comes to him. Power and knowledge are already there. The soul identifies itself with that which is powerless matter and thus weeps. It identifies itself with mortal shapes...But if that free soul wants to exercise any power, it will have it. If it does not, it does not come. He who has known God has become God. There is nothing impossible to such a free soul. No more birth and death for him. He is free for ever.

MEDITATION

Delivered at the Washington Hall, San Francisco,
April 3, 1900

Meditation has been laid stress upon by all religions. The meditative state of mind is declared by the Yogis to be the highest state in which the mind exists. When the mind is studying the external object, it gets identified with it, loses itself. To use the simile of the old Indian philosopher: the soul of man is like a piece of crystal, but it takes the colour of whatever is near it. Whatever the soul touches...it has to take its colour. That is the difficulty. That constitutes the bondage. The colour is so strong, the crystal forgets itself and identifies itself with the colour. Suppose a red flower is near the crystal and the crystal takes the colour and forgets itself, thinks it is red. We have taken the colour of the body and have forgotten what we are. All the difficulties that follow come from that one dead body. All our fears, all worries, anxieties, troubles, mistakes, weakness, evil, are front that one great blunder — that we are bodies. This is the ordinary person. It is the person taking the colour of the flower near to it. We are no more bodies than the crystal is the red flower.

The practice of meditation is pursued. The crystal knows what it is, takes its own colour. It is meditation that brings us nearer to truth than anything else...

In India two persons meet. In English they say, "How do you do?" The Indian greeting is, "Are you upon yourself?" The moment you stand upon something else, you run the risk of being miserable. This is what I mean by meditation — the soul trying to stand upon itself. That state must surely be the healthiest state of the soul, when it is thinking of itself, residing in its own glory. No, all the other methods that we have—by exciting emotions, prayers, and all that—really have that one end in view. In deep emotional excitement the soul tries to stand upon itself. Although the emotion may arise from anything external, there is concentration of mind.

There are three stages in meditation. The first is what is called [Dhâranâ], concentrating the mind upon an object. I try to concentrate my mind upon this glass, excluding every other object from my mind except this glass. But the mind is wavering... When it has become strong and does not waver so much, it is called [Dhyâna], meditation. And then there is a still higher state when the differentiation between the glass and myself is lost—[Samâdhi or absorption]. The mind and the glass are identical. I do not see any difference. All the senses stop and all powers that have been working through other channels of other senses [are focused in the mind]. Then this glass is under the power of the mind entirely. This is to be realised. It is a tremendous play played by the Yogis... Take for granted, the external object exists. Then that which is really outside of us is not what we see. The glass that I see is not the external object certainly. That external something which is the glass I do not know and will never know.

Something produces an impression upon me. Immediately I send the reaction towards that, and the glass is the result of the combination of these two. Action from outside—X. Action from inside—Y. The glass is XY. When you look at X, call it external world—at Y, internal world... If you try to distinguish which is your mind and which is the world—there is no such distinction. The world is the combination of you and something else...

let us take another example. You are dropping stones upon the smooth surface of a lake. Every stone you drop is followed by a reaction. The stone is covered by the little waves in the lake. Similarly, external things are like the stones dropping into the lake of the mind. So we do not really see the external... ; we see the wave only...

These waves that rise in the mind have caused many things outside. We are not discussing the [merits of] idealism and realism. We take for granted that things exist outside, but what we see is different from things that exist outside, as we see what exists outside plus ourselves.

Suppose I take my contribution out of the glass. What remains? Almost nothing. The glass will disappear. If I take my contribution from the table, what would remain of the table? Certainly not this table, because it was a mixture of the outside plus my contribution. The poor lake has got to throw the wave towards the stone whenever [the stone] is thrown in it. The mind must create the wave towards any sensation. Suppose... we can withhold the mind. At once we are masters. We refuse to contribute our share to all these phenomena... If I do not contribute my share, it has got to stop.

You are creating this bondage all the time. How? By putting in your share. We are all making our own beds, forging our own chains... When the identifying ceases between this external object and myself, then I will be able to take my contribution off, and this thing will disappear. Then I will say, "Here is the glass", and then take my mind off, and it disappears... If you can take away your share, you can walk upon water. Why should it drown you any more? What of poison? No more difficulties. In every phenomenon in nature you contribute at least half, and nature brings half. If your half is taken off, the thing must stop.

...To every action there is equal reaction...If a man strikes me and wounds me it is that man's actions and my body's reaction...Suppose I have so much power over the body that I can resist even that automatic action. Can such power be attained? The books say it can...If you stumble on [it], it is a miracle. If you learn it scientifically, it is Yoga.

I have seen people healed by the power of mind. There is the miracle worker. We say he prays and the man is healed. Another man says, "Not at all. It is just the power of the mind. The man is scientific. He knows what he is about."

The power of meditation gets us everything. If you want to get power over nature, [you can have it through meditation]. It is through the power of meditation all scientific facts are discovered today. They study the subject and forget everything, their own identity and everything, and then the great fact comes like a flash. Some people think that is inspiration. There is no more inspiration than there is expiration; and never was anything got for nothing.

The highest so-called inspiration was the work of Jesus. He worked hard for ages in previous births. That was the result of his previous work—hard work...It is all nonsense to talk about inspiration. Had it been, it would have fallen like rain. Inspired people in any line of thought only come among nations who have general education and [culture]. There is no inspiration...Whatever passes for inspiration is the result that comes from causes already in the mind. One day, flash comes the result! Their past work was the [cause].

Therein also you see the power of meditation—intensity of thought. These men churn up their own souls. Great truths come to the surface and become manifest. Therefore the practice of meditation is the great scientific method of knowledge. There is no knowledge without the power of meditation. From ignorance, superstition, etc. we can get cured by meditation for the time being and no more. [Suppose] a man has told me that if you drink such a poison you will be killed, and another man comes in the night and says, "Go drink the poison!" and I am not killed, [what happens is this:] my mind cut out from the meditation the identity between the poison and myself just for the time being. In another case of [drinking] the poison, I will be killed.

If I know the reason and scientifically raise myself up to that [state of meditation], I can save anyone. That is what the books say; but how far it is correct you must appraise.

I am asked, "Why do you Indian people not conquer these things? You claim all the time to be superior to all other people. You practice Yoga and do it quicker than anybody else. You are fitter. Carry it out! If you are a great people, you ought to have a great system. You will have to say good-bye to all the gods. Let them go to sleep as you take up the great philosophers. You are mere babies, as superstitious as the rest of the world. And all your claims are failures. If you have the claims, stand up and be bold, and all the heaven that ever existed is yours. There is the musk deer with fragrance inside, and he does not know where the fragrance [comes from]. Then after days and days he finds it in himself. All these gods and demons are within them. Find out, by the powers of reason, education, and culture that it is all in yourself. No more gods and superstitions. You want to be rational, to be Yogis, really spiritual."

[My reply is: With you too] everything is material What is more material than God sitting on a throne? You look down upon the poor man who is worshipping the image. You are no better. And you, gold worshippers, what are you? The image worshipper worships his god, something that he can see. But you do not even do that. You do not worship the spirit nor something that you can understand...Word worshippers! "God is spirit!" God is spirit and should be worshipped in spirit and faith. Where does the spirit reside? On a tree? On a cloud? What do you mean by God being ours? You are the spirit. That is the first fundamental belief you must never give up. I am the spiritual being. It is there. All this skill of Yoga and this system of meditation and everything is just to find Him there.

Why am I saying all this just now? Until you fix the location, you cannot talk. You fix it up in heaven and all the world ever except in the right place. I am spirit, and therefore the spirit of all spirits must be in my soul. Those who think it anywhere else are ignorant. Therefore it is to be sought here in this heaven; all the heaven that ever existed [is within myself]. There are some sages who, knowing this, turn their eyes inward and find the spirit of all spirits in their own spirit. That is the scope of meditation. Find out the truth about God and about your own soul and thus attain to liberation...

You are all running after life, and we find that is foolishness. There is something much higher than life even. This life is inferior, material. Why should I live at all? I am something higher than life. Living is always slavery. We always get mixed up...Everything is a continuous chain of slavery.

You get something, and no man can teach another. It is through experience [we learn]...That young man cannot be persuaded that there are any difficulties in life. You cannot persuade the old man that life is all smooth. He has had many experiences. That is the difference.

By the power of meditation we have got to control, step by step, all these things. We have seen philosophically that

all these differentiations—spirit, mind, matter, etc.—[have no real existences...Whatever exists is one. There cannot be many. That is what is meant by science and knowledge. Ignorance sees manifold. Knowledge realises one...Reducing the many into one is science...The whole of the universe has been demonstrated into one. That science is called the science of Vedanta. The whole universe is one. The one runs through all this seeming variety...

We have all these variations now and we see them—what we call the five elements: solid, liquid, gaseous, luminous, ethereal. After that the state of existence is mental and beyond that spiritual. Not that spirit is one and mind is another, ether another, and so on. It is the one existence appearing in all these variations. To go back, the solid must become liquid. The way [the elements evolved] they must go back. The solids will become liquid, etherised. This is the idea of the macrocosm—and universal. There is the external universe and universal spirit, mind, ether, gas, luminosity, liquid, solid.

The same with the mind. I am just exactly the same in the microcosm. I am the spirit; I am mind; I am the ether, solid, liquid, gas. What I want to do is to go back to my spiritual state. It is for the individual to live the life of the universe in one short life. Thus man can be free in this life. He in his own short lifetime shall have the power to live the whole extent of life...

We all struggle...If we cannot reach the Absolute, we will get somewhere, and it will be better than we are now.

Meditation consists in this practice [of dissolving every thing into the ultimate Reality—spirit]. The solid melts into liquid, that into gas, gas into ether, then mind, and mind will melt away. All is spirit.

Some of the Yogis claim that this body will become liquid etc. You will be able to do any thing with it—make it little, or gas pass through this wall—they claim. I do not know. I have never seen anybody do it. But it is in the books. We have no reason to disbelieve the books.

Possibly, some of us will be able to do it in this life. Like a flash it comes, as the result of our past work. Who knows but some here are old Yogis with just a little to do to finish the whole work. Practice!

Meditation, you know, comes by a process imagination. You go through all these processes purification of the elements—making the one melt the other, that into the next higher, that into mind, that into spirit, and then you are spirit[1].

1. This purification of the elements, known as Bhuta-shuddhi, is part of the ritualistic worship. The worshipper tries to feel that he is dissolving earth, water, fire, air, and ether with their subtle essences, and the sense-organs into mind. Mind, intellect, and sense of individual ego are merged into Mahat, the cosmic ego; Mahat is dissolved into Prakriti, the power of Brahman, and Prakriti merges into Brahman, the ultimate Reality. The Kundalini, the coiled-up power at the base of the spine, in his thoughts is led to the highest centre of consciousness in the brain, where he meditates on his oneness with the supreme Spirit.

Spirit is always free, omnipotent, omniscient. Of course, under God. There cannot be many Gods. These liberated souls are wonderfully powerful, almost omnipotent. [But] none can be as powerful as God. If one [liberated soul] said, "I will make this planet go this way", and another said, "I will make it go that way", [there would be confusion].

Don't you make this mistake! When I say in English, "I am God!" it is because I have no better word. In Sanskrit, God means absolute existence, knowledge, and wisdom, infinite self-luminous consciousness. No person. It is impersonal...

I am never Râma [never one with Ishvara, the personal aspect of God], but I am [one with Brahman, the impersonal, all-pervading existence]. Here is a huge mass of clay. Out of that clay I made a little [mouse] and you made a little [elephant]. Both are clay. Melt both down They are essentially one. "I and my Father are one." [But the clay mouse can never be one with the clay elephant.]

I stop somewhere; I have a little knowledge. You a little more; you stop somewhere. There is one soul which is the greatest of all. This is Ishvara, Lord of Yoga [God as Creator, with attributes]. He is the individual. He is omnipotent. He resides in every heart. There is no body. He does not need a body. All you get by the practice of meditation etc., you can get by meditation upon Ishvara, Lord of Yogis...

The same can be attained by meditating upon a great soul; or upon the harmony of life. These are called objective meditations. So you begin to meditate upon certain external things, objective things, either outside or inside. If you take a long sentence, that is no meditation at all. That is simply trying to get the mind collected by repetition. Meditation means the mind is turned back upon itself. The mind stops all the [thought-waves] and the world stops. Your consciousness expands. Every time you meditate you will keep your growth... Work a little harder, more and more, and meditation comes. You do not feel the body or anything else. When you come out of it after the hour, you have had the most beautiful rest you ever had in your life. That is the only way you ever give rest to your system. Not even the deepest sleep will give you such rest as that. The mind goes on jumping even in deepest sleep. Just those few minutes [in meditation] your brain has almost stopped. Just a little vitality is kept up. You forget the body. You may be cut to pieces and not feel it at all. You feel such pleasure in it. You become so light. This perfect rest we will get in meditation.

Then, meditation upon different objects. There are meditations upon different centres of the spine. [According to the Yogis, there are two nerves in the spinal column, called Idâ and Pingalâ. They are the main channels through which the afferent and efferent currents travel.] The hollow [canal called Sushumnâ] runs through the middle of the spinal column. The Yogis claim this cord is closed, but by the power of meditation it has to be opened. The energy has to be sent down to [the base of the spine], and the Kundalini rises. The world will be changed[2]...

Thousands of divine beings are standing about you. You do not see them because our world is determined by our senses. We can only see this outside. Let us call it X. We see that X according to our mental state. Let us take the tree standing outside. A thief came and what did he see in the stump? A policeman. The child saw a huge ghost. The young man was waiting for his sweetheart, and what did he see? His sweetheart. But the stump of the tree had not changed. It remained the same. This is God Himself, and with our foolishness we see Him to be man, to be dust, to be dumb, miserable.

Those who are similarly constituted will group together naturally and live in the same world. Otherwise stated, you live in the same place. All the heavens and all the hells are right here. For example: [take planes in the form of] big circles cutting each other at certain points... On this plane in one circle we can be in touch with a certain point in another [circle]. If the mind gets to the centre, you begin to be conscious on all planes. In meditation sometimes you touch another plane, and you see other beings, disembodied spirits, and so on. You get there by the power of meditation. This power is changing our senses, you see, refining our senses. If you begin to practise meditation five days, you will feel the pain from within these centres [of conciousness] and hearing [becomes finer][3]... That is why all the Indian gods have three eyes. That is the psychic eye that opens out and shows you spiritual things.

As this power of Kundalini rises from one centre to the other in the spine, it changes the senses and you begin to see this world another. It is heaven. You cannot talk. Then the Kundalini goes down to the lower centres. You are again man until the Kundalini reaches the brain, all the centres have been passed, and the whole vision vanishes and you [perceive]... nothing but the one existence. You are God. All heavens you make out of Him, all worlds out of Him. He is the one existence. Nothing else exists.

THE PRACTICE OF RELIGION

Delivered at Alameda, California, on April 18, 1900

We read many books, many scriptures. We get various ideas from our childhood, and change them every now and then. We understand what is meant by theoretical religion. We think we understand what is meant by practical religion. Now I am going to present to you my idea of practical religion.

We hear all around us about practical religion, and analysing all that, we find that it can be brought down to one conception — charity to our fellow beings. Is that all of religion? Every day we hear in this country about practical Christianity — that a man has done some good to his fellow beings. Is that all?

What is the goal of life? Is this world the goal of life? Nothing

2. See Complete Works, Vol. I.

3. See Complete Works, Vol. I.

more? Are we to be just what we are, nothing more? Is man to be a machine which runs smoothly without a hitch anywhere? Are all the sufferings he experiences today all he can have, and doesn't he want anything more?

The highest dream of many religions is the world... The vast majority of people are dreaming of the time when there will be no more disease, sickness, poverty, or misery of any kind. They will have a good time all around. Practical religion, therefore, simply means. "Clean the streets! Make it nice!" We see how all enjoy it.

Is enjoyment the goal of life? Were it so, it would be a tremendous mistake to become a man at all. What man can enjoy a meal with more gusto than the dog or the cat? Go to a menagerie and see the [wild animals] tearing the flesh from the bone. Go back and become a bird!... What a mistake then to become a man! Vain have been my years—hundreds of years—of struggle only to become the man of sense-enjoyments.

Mark, therefore, the ordinary theory of practical religion, what it leads to. Charity is great, but the moment you say it is all, you run the risk of running into materialism. It is not religion. It is no better than atheism - a little less... You Christians, have you found nothing else in the Bible than working for fellow creatures, building... hospitals?... Here stands a shopkeeper and says how Jesus would have kept the shop! Jesus would neither have kept a saloon, nor a shop, nor have edited a newspaper. That sort of practical religion is good, not bad; but it is just kindergarten religion. It leads nowhere... If you believe in God, if you are Christians and repeat everyday, "Thy will be done", just think what it means! You say every moment, "Thy will be done", really meaning, "My will be done by Thee, O God." The Infinite is working His own plans out. Even He has made mistakes, and you and I are going to remedy that! The Architect of the universe is going to be taught by the carpenters! He has left the world a dirty hole, and you are going to make it a beautiful place!

What is the goal of it all? Can senses ever be the goal? Can enjoyment of pleasure ever be the goal? Can this life ever be the goal of the soul? If it is, better die this moment; do not want this life! If that is the fate of man, that he is going to be only the perfected machine, it would just mean that we go back to being trees and stones and things like that. Did you ever hear a cow tell a lie or see a tree steal? They are perfect machines. They do not make mistakes. They live in a world where everything is finished...

What is the ideal of religion, then, if this cannot be practical [religion]? And it certainly cannot be. What are we here for? We are here for freedom, for knowledge. We want to know in order to make ourselves free. That is our life: one universal cry for freedom. What is the reason the... plant grows from the seed, overturning the ground and raising itself up to the skies? What is the offering for the earth from the sun? What is your life? The same struggle for freedom. Nature is trying all around to suppress us, and the soul wants to express itself. The struggle with nature is going on. Many things will be crushed and broken in this struggle for freedom. That is your real misery. Large masses of dust and dirt must be raised on the battlefield. Nature says, "I will conquer." The soul says, "I must be the conqueror." Nature says, "Wait! I will give you a little enjoyment to keep you quiet." The soul enjoys a little, becomes deluded a moment, but the next moment it [cries for freedom again]. Have you marked the eternal cry going on through the ages in every breast? We are deceived by poverty. We become wealthy and are deceived with wealth. We are ignorant. We read and learn and are deceived with knowledge. No man is ever satisfied. That is the cause of misery, but it is also the cause of all blessing. That is the sure sign. How can you be satisfied with this world?... If tomorrow this world becomes heaven, we will say, "Take this away. Give us something else."

The infinite human soul can never be satisfied but by the Infinite itself... Infinite desire can only be satisfied by infinite knowledge—nothing short of that. Worlds will come and go. What of that? The soul lives and for ever expands. Worlds must come into the soul. Worlds must disappear in the soul like drops in the ocean. And this world to become the goal of the soul! If we have common sense, we cannot he satisfied, though this has been the theme of the poets in all the ages, always telling us to be satisfied. And nobody has been satisfied yet! Millions of prophets have told us, "Be satisfied with your lot"; poets sing. We have told ourselves to be quiet and satisfied, yet we are not. It is the design of the Eternal that there is nothing in this world to satisfy my soul, nothing in the heavens above, and nothing beneath. Before the desire of my soul, the stars and the worlds, upper and lower, the whole universe, is but a hateful disease, nothing but that. That is the meaning. Everything is an evil unless that is the meaning. Every desire is evil unless that is the meaning, unless you understand its true importance, its goal. All nature is crying through all the atoms for one thing—its perfect freedom.

What is practical religion, then? To get to that state—freedom, the attainment of freedom. And this world, if it helps us on to that goal, [is] all right; if not—if it begins to bind one more layer on the thousands already there, it becomes an evil. Possessions, learning, beauty, everything else—as long as they help us to that goal, they are of practical value. When they have ceased helping us on to that goal of freedom, they are a positive danger. What is practical religion, then? Utilise the things of this world and the next just for one goal—the attainment of freedom. Every enjoyment, every ounce of pleasure is to be bought by the expenditure of the infinite heart and mind combined.

Look at the sum total of good and evil in this world. Has it changed? Ages have passed, and practical religion has worked for ages. The world thought that each time the problem would be solved. It is always the same problem. At best it changes its form... It trades consumption and nerve disease for twenty thousand shops… It is like old rheumatism: Drive it from one place, it goes to another. A hundred years ago man walked on foot or bought horses. Now he is happy because he rides the railroad; but he is unhappy because he has to work more and earn more. Every machine that saves labour puts more stress upon labour.

This universe, nature, or whatever you call it, must be limited; it can never be unlimited. The Absolute, to become nature, must be limited by time, space, and causation. The energy [at our disposal] is limited. You can spend it in one place, losing it in another. The sum total is always the same. Wherever there is a wave in one place, there is a hollow in another. If one nation becomes rich, others become poor. Good balances evil. The person for the moment on top of the wave thinks all is good; the person at the bottom says the world is [all evil]. But the man who stands aside sees the divine play going on. Some weep and others laugh. The latter will weep in their turn and the others laugh. What can we do? We know we cannot do anything…

Which of us do anything because we want to do good? How few! They can be counted on the fingers. The rest of us also do good, but because we are forced to do so… We cannot stop. Onward we go, knocked about from place to place. What can we do? The world will be the same world, the earth the same. It will be changed from blue to brown and from brown to blue. One language translated into another, one set of evils changed into another set of evils — that is what is going on… Six of one, half a dozen of the other. The American Indian in the forest cannot attend a lecture on metaphysics as you can, but he can digest his meal. You cut him to pieces, and the next moment he is all right. You and I, if we get scratched, we have to go to the hospital for six months…

The lower the organism, the greater is its pleasure in the senses. Think of the lowest animals and the power of touch. Everything is touch… When you come to man, you will see that the lower the civilization of the man, the greater is the power of the senses… The higher the organism, the lesser is the pleasure of the senses. A dog can eat a meal, but cannot understand the exquisite pleasure of thinking about metaphysics. He is deprived of the wonderful pleasure which you get through the intellect. The pleasures of the senses are great. Greater than those is the pleasure of the intellect. When you attend the fine fifty-course dinner in Paris, that is pleasure indeed. But in the observatory, looking at the stars, seeing… worlds coming and developing — think of that! It must be greater, for I know you forget all about eating. That pleasure must be greater than what you get from worldly things. You forget all about wives, children, husbands, and everything; you forget all about the sense-plane. That is intellectual pleasure. It is common sense that it must be greater than sense pleasure. It is always for greater joy that you give up the lesser. This is practical religion — the attainment of freedom, renunciation. Renounce!

Renounce the lower so that you may get the higher. What is the foundation of society? Morality, ethics, laws. Renounce. Renounce all temptation to take your neighbour's property, to put hands upon your neighbour, all the pleasure of tyrannising over the weak, all the pleasure of cheating others by telling lies. Is not morality the foundation of society? What is marriage but the renunciation of unchastity? The savage does not marry. Man marries because he renounces. So on and on. Renounce! Renounce! Sacrifice! Give up! Not for zero. Not for nothing. But to get the higher. But who can do this? You cannot, until you have got the higher. You may talk. You may struggle. You may try to do many things. But renunciation comes by itself when you have got the higher. Then the lesser falls away by itself.

This is practical religion. What else? Cleaning streets and building hospitals? Their value consists only in this renunciation. And there is no end to renunciation. The difficulty is they try to put a limit to it — thus far and no farther. But there is no limit to this renunciation.

Where God is, there is no other. Where the world is, there is no God. These two will never unite. [Like] light and darkness. That is what I have understood from Christianity and the life of the Teacher. Is not that Buddhism? Is not that Hinduism? Is not that Mohammedanism? Is not that the teaching of all the great sages and teachers? What is the world that is to be given up? It is here. I am carrying it all with me. My own body. It is all for this body that I put my hand voluntarily upon my fellow man, just to keep it nice and give it a little pleasure; [all for this body] that I injure others and make mistakes…

Great men have died. Weak men have died. Gods have died. Death — death everywhere. This world is a graveyard of the infinite past, yet we cling to this [body]: "I am never going to die". Knowing for sure [that the body must die] and yet clinging to it. There is meaning in that too [because in a sense we do not die]. The mistake is that we cling to the body when it is the spirit that is really immortal.

You are all materialists, because you believe that you are the body. If a man gives me a hard punch, I would say I am punched. If he strikes me, I would say I am struck. If I am not the body, why should I say so? It makes no difference if I say I am the spirit. I am the body just now. I have converted myself into matter. That is why I am to renounce the body, to go back to what I really am. I am the spirit — the soul no instrument can pierce, no sword can cut asunder, no fire can burn, no air can dry. Unborn and uncreated, without beginning and without end, deathless, birthless and omnipresent — that is what I am; and all misery comes just because I think this little lump of clay is myself. I am identifying myself with matter and taking all the consequences.

Practical religion is identifying myself with my Self. Stop this wrong identification! How far are you advanced in that? You may have built two thousand hospitals, built fifty thousand roads, and yet what of that, if you, have not realised that you are the spirit? You die a dog's; death, with the same feelings that the dog does. The dog howls and weeps because he knows that he is only matter and he is going to be dissolved.

There is death, you know, inevitable death, in water, in air, in the palace, in the prison - death everywhere. What makes you fearless? When you have realised what you are—that infinite spirit, deathless, birthless. Him no fire can burn, no instrument kill, no poison hurt. Not theory, mind you. Not reading books…[Not parroting.] My old Master used to say, "It is all very good to teach the parrot to say, 'Lord, Lord, Lord' all the time; but let the cat come and take hold of its neck, it forgets all about it" [You may] pray all the time, read all the scriptures in the world, and worship all the gods there are, [but] unless you realise the soul there is no freedom. Not talking, theorising, argumentation, but realisation. That I call practical religion.

This truth about the soul is first to be heard. If you have heard it, think about it. Once you have done that, meditate upon it. No more vain arguments! Satisfy yourself once that you are the infinite spirit. If that is true, it must be nonsense that you are the body. You are the Self, and that must be realised. Spirit must see itself as spirit. Now the spirit is seeing itself as body. That must stop. The moment you begin to realise that, you are released.

You see this glass, and you know it is simply an illusion. Some scientists tell you it is light and vibration…Seeing the spirit must be infinitely more real: than that, must be the only true state, the only true sensation, the only true vision. All these [objects you see], are but dreams. You know that now. Not the old idealists alone, but modern physicists also tell you that light is there. A little more vibration makes all the difference…

You must see God. The spirit must be realised, and that is practical religion. It is not what Christ preached that you call practical religion: "Blessed are the poor in spirit for theirs is the Kingdom of Heaven." Was it a joke? What is the practical religion you are thinking, of? Lord help us! "Blessed are the pure in heart, for they shall see God." That means street-cleaning, hospital-building, and all that? Good works, when you do them with a pure mind. Don't give the man twenty dollars and buy all the papers in San Francisco to see your name! Don't you read in your own books how no man will help you? Serve as worship of the Lord Himself in the poor, the miserable, the weak. That done, the result is secondary. That sort of work, done without any thought of gain, benefits the soul. And even of such is the Kingdom of Heaven.

The Kingdom of Heaven is within us. He is there. He is the soul of all souls. See Him in your own soul. That is practical religion. That is freedom. Let us ask each other how much we are advanced in that: how much we are worshippers of the body, or real believers in God, the spirit; how much we believe ourselves to be spirit. That is selfless. That is freedom. That is real worship. Realise yourself. That is all there is to do. Know

yourself as you are—infinite spirit. That is practical religion. Everything else is impractical, for everything else will vanish. That alone will never vanish. It Is eternal. Hospitals will tumble down. Railroad givers will all die. This earth will be blown to pieces, suns wiped out. The soul endureth for ever.

Which is higher, running after these things which perish or…worshipping that which never changes? Which is more practical, spending all the energies of life in getting things, and before you have got them death comes and you have to leave them all?—like the great [ruler] who conquered all, [who when] death came, said, "Spread out all the jars of things before me." He said "Bring me that big diamond." And he placed it on his breast and wept. Thus weeping, he died the same as the dog dies.

Man says, "I live." He knows not that it is [the fear of] death that makes him cling slavishly to life. He says "I enjoy." He never dreams that nature has enslaved him.

Nature grinds all of us. Keep count of the ounce of pleasure you get. In the long run, nature did her work through you, and when you die your body will make other plants grow. Yet we think all the time that we are getting pleasure ourselves. Thus the wheel goes round.

Therefore to realise the spirit as spirit is practical religion. Everything else is good so far as it leads to this one grand idea. That [realization] is to be attained by renunciation, by meditation—renunciation of all the senses, cutting the knots, the chains that bind us down to matter. "I do not want to get material life, do not want the sense-life, but something higher." That is renunciation. Then, by the power of meditation, undo the mischief that has been done.

We are at the beck and call of nature. If there is sound outside, I have to hear it. If something is going on, I have to see it. Like monkeys. We are two thousand monkeys concentrated, each one of us. Monkeys are very curious. So we cannot help ourselves, and call this "enjoying". Wonderful this language! We are enjoying the world! We cannot help enjoying it. Nature wants us to do it. A beautiful sound: I am hearing it. As if I could choose to hear it or not! Nature says, "Go down to the depths of misery." I become miserable in a moment…We talk about pleasures [of the senses] and possessions. One man thinks me very learned. Another thinks, "He is a fool." This degradation, this slavery, without knowing anything! In the dark room we are knocking our heads against each other.

What is meditation? Meditation is the power which enables us to resist all this. Nature may call us, "Look there is a beautiful thing!" I do not look. Now she says, "There is a beautiful smell; smell it! " I say to my nose, "Do not smell it", and the nose doesn't. "Eyes, do not see!" Nature does such an awful thing - kills one of my children, and says, "Now, rascal, sit down and weep! Go to the depths!" I say, "I don't have to." I jump up. I must be free. Try it sometimes…[In meditation], for a moment, you can change this nature. Now, if you had that power in yourself, would not that be heaven, freedom?

That is the power of meditation.

How is it to be attained? In a dozen different ways. Each temperament has its own way. But this is the general principle: get hold of the mind. The mind is like a lake, and every stone that drops into it raises waves. These waves do not let us see what we are. The full moon is reflected in the water of the lake, but the surface is so disturbed that we do not see the reflection clearly. Let it be calm. Do not let nature raise the wave. Keep quiet, and then after a little while she will give you up. Then we know what we are. God is there already, but the mind is so agitated, always running after the senses. You close the senses and [yet] you whirl and whirl about. Just this moment I think I am all right and I will meditate upon God, and then my mind goes to London in one minute. And if I pull it away from there, it goes to New York to think about the things I have done there in the past. These [waves] are to be stopped by the power of meditation.

Slowly and gradually we are to train ourselves. It is no joke—not a question of a day, or years, or maybe of births. Never mind! The pull must go on. Knowingly, voluntarily, the pull must go on. Inch by inch we will gain ground. We will begin to feel and get real possessions, which no one can take away from us—the wealth that no man can take, the wealth that nobody can destroy, the joy that no misery can hurt any more...

All these years we have depended upon others. If I have a little pleasure and that person goes away, my pleasure is gone... See the folly of man: he depends for happiness upon men! All separations are misery. Naturally. Depending upon wealth for happiness? There is fluctuation of wealth. Depending upon health or upon anything except the unchangeable spirit must bring misery today or tomorrow.

Excepting the infinite spirit, everything else is changing. There is the whirl of change. Permanence is nowhere except in yourself. There is the infinite joy, unchanging. Meditation is the gate that opens that to us. Prayers, ceremonials, and all the other forms of worship are simply kindergartens of meditation. You pray, you offer something. A certain theory existed that everything raised one's spiritual power. The use of certain words, flowers, images, temples, ceremonials like the waving of lights brings the mind to that attitude, but that attitude is always in the human soul, nowhere else. [People] are all doing it; but what they do without knowing it, do knowingly. That is the power of meditation. All knowledge you have—how did it come? From the power of meditation. The soul churned the knowledge out of its own depths. What knowledge was there ever outside of it? In the long run this power of meditation separates ourselves from the body, and then the soul knows itself as it is—the unborn, the deathless, and birthless being. No more is there any misery, no more births upon this earth, no more evolution. [The soul knows itself as having] ever been perfect and free.

THE METHODS AND PURPOSE OF RELIGION

In studying the religions of the world we generally find two methods of procedure. The one is from God to man. That is to say, we have the Semitic group of religions in which the idea of God comes almost from the very first, and, strangely enough, without any idea of soul. It was very remarkable amongst the ancient Hebrews that, until very recent periods in their history, they never evolved any idea of a human soul. Man was composed of certain mind and material particles, and that was all. With death everything ended. But, on the other hand, there was a most wonderful idea of God evolved by the same race. This is one of the methods of procedure. The other is through man to God. The second is peculiarly Aryan, and the first is peculiarly Semitic.

The Aryan first began with the soul. His ideas of God were hazy, indistinguishable, not very clear; but, as his idea of the human soul began to be clearer, his idea of God began to be clearer in the same proportion. So the inquiry in the Vedas was always through the soul. All the knowledge the Aryans got of God was through the human soul; and, as such, the peculiar stamp that has been left upon their whole cycle of philosophy is that introspective search after divinity. The Aryan man was always seeking divinity inside his own self. It became, in course of time, natural, characteristic. It is remarkable in their art and in their commonest dealings. Even at the present time, if we take a European picture of a man in a religious attitude, the painter always makes his subject point his eyes upwards, looking outside of nature for God, looking up into the skies. In India, on the other hand, the religious attitude is always presented by making the subject close his eyes. He is, as it were, looking inward.

These are the two subjects of study for man, external and internal nature; and though at first these seem to be contradictory, yet external nature must, to the ordinary man, be entirely composed of internal nature, the world of thought. The majority of philosophies in every country, especially in the West, have started with the assumption that these two, matter and mind, are contradictory existences; but in the long run we shall find that they converge towards each other and in the end unite and form an infinite whole. So it is not that by this analysis I mean a higher or lower standpoint with regard to the subject. I do not mean that those who want to search after truth through external nature are wrong, nor that those who want to search after truth through internal nature are higher. These are the two modes of procedure. Both of them must live; both of them must be studied; and in the end we shall find that they meet. We shall see that neither is the body antagonistic to the mind, nor the mind to the body, although we find, many persons who think that this body is nothing. In old times, every country was full of people who thought this body was only a disease, a sin, or something of that kind. Later on, however, we see how, as it was taught in the Vedas, this body melts into the mind, and the mind into the body.

You must remember the one theme that runs through all the Vedas: "Just as by the knowledge of one lump of clay we know all the clay that is in the universe, so what is that, knowing which we know everything else?" This, expressed more or less clearly, is the theme of all human knowledge. It is the finding of a unity towards which we are all going. Every action of our lives—the most material, the grossest as well as the finest, the highest, the most spiritual—is alike tending towards this one ideal, the finding of unity. A man is single. He marries. Apparently it may be a selfish act, but at the same time, the impulsion, the motive power, is to find that unity. He has children, he has friends, he loves his country, he loves the world, and ends by loving the whole universe. Irresistibly we are impelled towards that perfection which consists in finding the unity, killing this little self and making ourselves broader and broader. This is the goal, the end towards which the universe is rushing. Every atom is trying to go and join itself to the next atom. Atoms after atoms combine, making huge balls, the earths, the suns, the moons, the stars, the planets. They in their turn, are trying to rush towards each other, and at last, we know that the whole universe, mental and material, will be fused into one.

The process that is going on in the cosmos on a large scale, is the same as that going on in the microcosm on a smaller scale. Just as this universe has its existence in separation, in distinction, and all the while is rushing towards unity, non-separation, so in our little worlds each soul is born, as it were, cut off from the rest of the world. The more ignorant, the more unenlightened the soul, the more it thinks that it is separate from the rest of the universe. The more ignorant the person, the more he thinks, he will die or will be born, and so forth—ideas that are an expression of this separateness. But we find that, as knowledge comes, man grows, morality is evolved and the idea of non-separateness begins. Whether men understand it or not, they are impelled by that power behind to become unselfish. That is the foundation of all morality. It is the quintessence of all ethics, preached in any language, or in any religion, or by any prophet in the world. "Be thou unselfish", "Not 'I', but 'thou'"—that is the background of all ethical codes. And what is meant by this is the recognition of non-individuality—that you are a part of me, and I of you; the recognition that in hurting you I hurt myself, and in helping you I help myself; the recognition that there cannot possibly be death for me when you live. When one worm lives in this universe, how can I die? For my life is in the life of that worm. At the same time it will teach us that we cannot leave one of our fellow-beings without helping him, that in his good consists my good.

This is the theme that runs through the whole of Vedanta, and which runs through every other religion. For, you must remember, religions divide themselves generally into three parts. There is the first part, consisting of the philosophy, the essence, the principles of every religion. These principles find expression in mythology—lives of saints or heroes, demigods, or gods, or divine beings; and the whole idea of this mythology is that of power. And in the lower class of mythologies—the primitive— the expression of this power is in the muscles; their heroes are strong, gigantic. One hero conquers the whole world. As man advances, he must find expression for his energy higher than in the muscles; so his heroes also find expression in something higher. The higher mythologies have heroes who are gigantic moral men. Their strength is manifested in becoming moral and pure. They can stand alone, they can beat back the surging tide of selfishness and immorality. The third portion of all religions is symbolism, which you call ceremonials and forms. Even the expression through mythology, the lives of heroes, is not sufficient for all. There are minds still lower. Like children they must have their kindergarten of religion, and these symbologies are evolved—concrete examples which they can handle and grasp and understand, which they can see and feel as material things.

So in every religion you find there are the three stages: philosophy, mythology, and ceremonial. There is one advantage which can be pleaded for the Vedanta, that in India, fortunately, these three stages have been sharply defined. In other religions the principles are so interwoven with the mythology that it is very hard to distinguish one from the other. The mythology stands supreme, swallowing up the principles; and in course of centuries the principles are lost sight of. The explanation, the illustration of the principle, swallows up the principle, and the people see only the explanation, the prophet, the preacher, while the principles have gone out of existence almost—so much so that even today, if a man dares to preach the principles of Christianity apart from Christ, they will try to attack him and think he is wrong and dealing blows at Christianity. In the same way, if a man wants to preach the principles of Mohammedanism, Mohammedans will think the same; because concrete ideas, the lives of great men and prophets, have entirely overshadowed the principles.

In Vedanta the chief advantage is that it was not the work of one single man; and therefore, naturally, unlike Buddhism, or Christianity, or Mohammedanism, the prophet or teacher did not entirely swallow up or overshadow the principles. The principles live, and the prophets, as it were, form a secondary group, unknown to Vedanta. The Upanishads speak of no particular prophet, but they speak of various prophets and prophetesses. The old Hebrews had something of that idea; yet we find Moses occupying most of the space of the Hebrew literature. Of course I do not mean that it is bad that these prophets should take religious hold of a nation; but it certainly is very injurious if the whole field of principles is lost sight of. We can very much agree as to principles, but not very much as to persons. The persons appeal to our emotions; and the principles, to something higher, to our calm judgement. Principles must conquer in the long run, for that is the manhood of man. Emotions many times drag us down to the level of animals. Emotions have more connection with the senses than with the faculty of reason; and, therefore, when principles are entirely lost sight of and emotions prevail, religions degenerate into fanaticism and sectarianism. They are no better than party politics and such things. The most horribly ignorant notions will be taken up, and for these ideas thousands will be ready to cut the throats of their brethren. This is the reason that, though these great personalities and prophets are tremendous motive powers for good, at the same time their lives are altogether dangerous when they lead to the disregard of the principles they represent. That has always led to fanaticism, and has deluged the world in blood. Vedanta can avoid this difficulty, because it has not one special prophet. It has many Seers, who are called Rishis or sages. Seers—that is the literal translation—those who see these truths, the Mantras.

The word Mantra means "thought out", cogitated by the mind; and the Rishi is the seer of these thoughts. They are neither the property of particular persons, nor the exclusive property of any man or woman, however great he or she may be; nor even the exclusive property of the greatest spirits—the Buddhas or Christs—whom the world has produced. They are as much the property of the lowest of the low, as they are the property of a Buddha, and as much the property of the smallest worm that crawls as of the Christ, because they are universal principles. They were never created. These principles have existed throughout time; and they will exist. They are non-create—uncreated by any laws which science teaches us today. They remain covered and become discovered, but are existing through all eternity in nature. If Newton had not been born, the law of gravitation would have remained all the same and would have worked all the same. It was Newton's genius which formulated it, discovered it, brought it into consciousness, made it a conscious thing to the human race. So are these religious laws, the grand truths of spirituality. They are working all the time. If all the Vedas and the Bibles and the Korans did not exist at all, if seers and prophets had never been born, yet these laws would exist. They are only held in abeyance, and slowly but surely would work to raise the human race, to raise human nature. But they are the prophets who see them, discover them, and such prophets are discoverers in the field of spirituality. As Newton and Galileo were prophets of physical science, so are they prophets of spirituality. They can claim no exclusive right to any one of these laws; they are the common property of all nature.

The Vedas, as the Hindus say, are eternal. We now understand what they mean by their being eternal, i.e. that the laws have neither beginning nor end, just as nature has neither beginning nor end. Earth after earth, system after system, will evolve, run for a certain time, and then dissolve back again into chaos; but the universe remains the same. Millions and millions of systems are being born, while millions are being destroyed. The universe remains the same. The beginning and the end of time can be told as regards a certain planet; but as regards the universe, time has no meaning at all. So are the laws of nature, the physical laws, the mental laws, the spiritual laws. Without beginning and without end are they; and it is within a few years, comparatively speaking, a few thousand years at best, that man has tried to reveal them. The infinite mass remains before us. Therefore the one great lesson that we learn from the Vedas, at the start, is that religion has just begun. The infinite ocean of spiritual truth lies before us to be worked on, to be discovered, to be brought into our lives. The world has seen thousands of prophets, and the world has yet to see millions.

There were times in olden days when prophets were many in every society. The time is to come when prophets will walk through every street in every city in the world. In olden times, particular, peculiar persons were, so to speak, selected by the operations of the laws of society to become prophets. The time is coming when we shall understand that to become religious means to become a prophet, that none can become religious until he or she becomes a prophet. We shall come to understand that the secret of religion is not being able to think and say all these thoughts; but, as the Vedas teach, to realise them, to realise newer and higher one than have ever been realised, to discover them, bring them to society; and the study of religion should be the training to make prophets. The schools and colleges should be training grounds for prophets. The whole universe must become prophets; and until a man becomes a prophet, religion is a mockery and a byword unto him. We must see religion, feel it, realise it in a thousand times more intense a sense than that in which we see the wall.

But there is one principle which underlies all these various manifestations of religion and which has been already mapped out for us. Every science must end where it finds a unity, because we cannot go any further. When a perfect unity is reached, that science has nothing more of principles to tell us. All the work that religions have to do is to work out the details. Take any science, chemistry, for example. Suppose we can find one element out of which we can manufacture all the other elements. Then chemistry, as a science, will have become perfect. What will remain for us is to discover every day new combinations of that one material and the application of those combinations for all the purposes of life. So with religion. The gigantic principles, the scope, the plan of religion were already discovered ages ago when man found the last words, as they are called, of the Vedas—"I am He"—that there is that One in whom this whole universe of matter and mind finds its unity, whom they call God, or Brahman, or Allah, or Jehovah, or any other name. We cannot go beyond that. The grand principle has been already mapped out for us. Our work lies in filling it in, working it out, applying it to every part of our lives. We have to work now so that every one will become a prophet. There is a great work before us.

In old times, many did not understand what a prophet meant. They thought it was something by chance, that just by a fiat of will or some superior intelligence, a man gained superior knowledge. In modern times, we are prepared to demonstrate that this knowledge is the birthright of every living being, whosoever and wheresoever he be, and that there is no chance in this universe. Every man who, we think, gets something by chance, has been working for it slowly and surely through ages. And the whole question devolves upon us: "Do we want to be prophets?" If we want, we shall be.

This, the training of prophets, is the great work that lies before us; and, consciously or unconsciously, all the great systems of religion are working toward this one great goal, only with this difference, that in many religions you will find they declare that this direct perception of spirituality is not to be had in this life, that man must die, and after his death there will come a time in another world, when he will have visions of spirituality, when he will realise things which now he must believe. But Vedanta will ask all people who make such assertions, "Then how do you know that spirituality exists?" And they will have to answer that there must have been always certain particular people who, even in this life, have got a glimpse of things which are unknown and unknowable.

Even this makes a difficulty. If they were peculiar people, having this power simply by chance, we have no right to believe in them. It would be a sin to believe in anything that is by chance, because we cannot know it. What is meant by knowledge? Destruction of peculiarity. Suppose a boy goes into a street or a menagerie, and sees a peculiarly shaped animal. He does not know what it is. Then he goes to a country where there are hundreds like that one, and he is satisfied, he knows what the species is. Our knowledge is knowing the principle. Our non-knowledge is finding the particular without reference to principle. When we find one case or a few cases separate from the principle, without any reference to the principle, we are in darkness and do not know. Now, if these prophets, as they say, were peculiar persons who alone had the right to catch a glimpse of that which is beyond and no one else has the right, we should not believe in these prophets, because they are peculiar cases without any reference to a principle. We can only believe in them if we ourselves become prophets.

You, all of you, hear about the various jokes that get into the newspapers about the sea-serpent; and why should it be so? Because a few persons, at long intervals, came and told their stories about the sea-serpent, and others never see it. They have no particular principle to which to refer, and therefore the world does not believe. If a man comes to me and says a prophet disappeared into the air and went through it, I have the right to see that. I ask him, "Did your father or grandfather see it?" "Oh, no," he replies, "but five thousand years ago such a thing happened." And if I do not believe it, I have to be barbecued through eternity!

What a mass of superstition this is! And its effect is to degrade man from his divine nature to that of brutes. Why was reason given us if we have to believe? Is it not tremendously blasphemous to believe against reason? What right have we not to use the greatest gift that God has given to us? I am sure

God will pardon a man who will use his reason and cannot believe, rather than a man who believes blindly instead of using the faculties He has given him. He simply degrades his nature and goes down to the level of the beasts—degrades his senses and dies. We must reason; and when reason proves to us the truth of these prophets and great men about whom the ancient books speak in every country, we shall believe in them. We shall believe in them when we see such prophets among ourselves. We shall then find that they were not peculiar men, but only illustrations of certain principles. They worked, and that principle expressed itself naturally, and we shall have to work to express that principle in us. They were prophets, we shall believe, when we become prophets. They were seers of things divine. They could go beyond the bounds of senses and catch a glimpse of that which is beyond. We shall believe that when we are able to do it ourselves and not before.

That is the one principle of Vedanta. Vedanta declares that religion is here and now, because the question of this life and that life, of life and death, this world and that world, is merely one of superstition and prejudice. There is no break in time beyond what we make. What difference is there between ten and twelve o'clock, except what we make by certain changes in nature? Time flows on the same. So what is meant by this life or that life? It is only a question of time, and what is lost in time may be made up by speed in work. So, says Vedanta, religion is to be realised now. And for you to become religious means that you will start without any religion work your way up and realise things, see things for yourself; and when you have done that, then, and then alone, you have religion. Before that you are no better than atheists, or worse, because the atheist is sincere—he stands up and says, "I do not know about these things—while those others do not know but go about the world, saying, "We are very religious people." What religion they have no one knows, because they have swallowed some grandmother's story, and priests have asked them to believe these things; if they do not, then let them take care. That is how it is going.

Realisation of religion is the only way. Each one of us will have to discover. Of what use are these books, then, these Bibles of the world? They are of great use, just as maps are of a country. I have seen maps of England all my life before I came here, and they were great helps to me informing some sort of conception of England. Yet, when I arrived in this country, what a difference between the maps and the country itself! So is the difference between realisation and the scriptures. These books are only the maps, the experiences of past men, as a motive power to us to dare to make the same experiences and discover in the same way, if not better.

This is the first principle of Vedanta, that realisation is religion, and he who realises is the religious man; and he who does not is no better than he who says, "I do not know", if not worse, because the other says, "I do not know", and is sincere. In this realisation, again, we shall be helped very much by these books, not only as guides, but as giving instructions and exercises; for every science has its own particular method of investigation. You will find many persons in this world who will say. "I wanted to become religious, I wanted to realise these things, but I have not been able, so I do not believe anything." Even among the educated you will find these. Large numbers of people will tell you, "I have tried to be religious all my life, but there is nothing in it." At the same time you will find this phenomenon: Suppose a man is a chemist, a great scientific man. He comes and tells you this. If you say to him, "I do not believe anything about chemistry, because I have all my life tried to become a chemist and do not find anything in it", he will ask, "When did you try?" "When I went to bed, I repeated, 'O chemistry, come to me', and it never came." That is the very same thing. The chemist laughs at you and says, "Oh, that is not the way. Why did you not go to the laboratory and get all the acids and alkalis and burn your hands from time to time? That alone would have taught you." Do you take the same trouble with religion? Every science has its own method of learning, and religion is to be learnt the same way. It has its own methods, and here is something we can learn, and must learn, from all the ancient prophets of the world, every one who has found something, who has realised religion. They will give us the methods, the particular methods, through which alone we shall be able to realise the truths of religion. They struggled all their lives, discovered particular methods of mental culture, bringing the mind to a certain state, the finest perception, and through that they perceived the truths of religion. To become religious, to perceive religion, feel it, to become a prophet, we have to take these methods and practice them; and then if we find nothing, we shall have the right to say, "There is nothing in religion, for I have tried and failed."

This is the practical side of all religions. You will find it in every Bible in the world. Not only do they teach principles and doctrines, but in the lives of the saints you find practices; and when it is not expressly laid down as a rule of conduct, you will always find in the lives of these prophets that even they regulated their eating and drinking sometimes. Their whole living, their practice, their method, everything was different from the masses who surrounded them; and these were the causes that gave them the higher light, the vision of the Divine. And we, if we want to have this vision, must be ready to take up these methods. It is practice, work, that will bring us up to that. The plan of Vedanta, therefore, is: first, to lay down the principles, map out for us the goal, and then to teach us the method by which to arrive at the goal, to understand and realise religion.

Again, these methods must be various. Seeing that we are so various in our natures, the same method can scarcely be applied to any two of us in the same manner. We have idiosyncrasies in our minds, each one of us; so the method ought to be varied. Some, you will find, are very emotional in their nature; some very philosophical, rational; others cling to all sorts of ritualistic forms—want things which are concrete.

You will find that one man does not care for any ceremony or form or anything of the sort; they are like death to him. And another man carries a load of amulets all over his body; he is so fond of these symbols! Another man who is emotional in his nature wants to show acts of charity to everyone; he weeps, he laughs, and so on. And all of these certainly cannot have the same method. If there were only one method to arrive at truth, it would be death for everyone else who is not similarly constituted. Therefore the methods should be various. Vedanta understands that and wants to lay before the world different methods through which we can work. Take up any one you like; and if one does not suit you, another may. From this standpoint we see how glorious it is that there are so many religions in the world, how good it is that there are so many teachers and prophets, instead of there being only one, as many persons would like to have it. The Mohammedans want to have the whole world Mohammedan; the Christians, Christian; and the Buddhists, Buddhist; but Vedanta says, "Let each person in the world be separate, if you will; the one principle, the units will be behind. The more prophets there are, the more books, the more seers, the more methods, so much the better for the world." Just as in social life the greater the number of occupations in every society, the better for that society, the more chance is there for everyone of that society to make a living; so in the world of thought and of religion. How much better it is today when we have so many divisions of science—how much more is it possible for everyone to have great mental culture, with this great variety before us! How much better it is, even on the physical plane, to have the opportunity of so many various things spread before us, so that we may choose any one we like, the one which suits us best! So it is with the world of religions. It is a most glorious dispensation of the Lord that there are so many religions in the world; and would to God that these would increase every day, until every man had a religion unto himself!

Vedanta understands that and therefore preaches the one principle and admits various methods. It has nothing to say against anyone—whether you are a Christian, or a Buddhist, or a Jew, or a Hindu, whatever mythology you believe, whether you owe allegiance to the prophet of Nazareth, or of Mecca, or of India, or of anywhere else, whether you yourself are a prophet—it has nothing to say. It only preaches the principle which is the background of every religion and of which all the prophets and saints and seers are but illustrations and manifestations. Multiply your prophets if you like; it has no objection. It only preaches the principle, and the method it leaves to you. Take any path you like; follow any prophet you like; but have only that method which suits your own nature, so that you will be sure to progress.

THE NATURE OF THE SOUL AND ITS GOAL

The earliest idea is that a man, when he dies, is not annihilated. Something lives and goes on living even after the man is dead. Perhaps it would be better to compare the three most ancient nations—the Egyptians, the Babylonians, and the ancient Hindus—and take this idea from all of them. With the Egyptians and the Babylonians, we find a sort of soul idea—that of a double. Inside this body, according to them, there is another body which is moving and working here; and when the outer body dies, the double gets out and lives on for a certain length of time; but the life of the double is limited by the preservation of the outer body. If the body which the double has left is injured in any part, the double is sure to be injured in that part. That is why we find among the ancient Egyptians such solicitude to preserve the dead body of a person by embalming, building pyramids, etc. We find both with the Babylonians and the ancient Egyptians that this double cannot live on through eternity; it can, at best, live on for a certain time only, that is, just so long as the body it has left can be preserved.

The next peculiarity is that there is an element of fear connected with this double. It is always unhappy and miserable; its state of existence is one of extreme pain. It is again and again coming back to those that are living, asking for food and drink and enjoyments that it can no more have. It is wanting to drink of the waters of the Nile, the fresh waters which it can no more drink. It wants to get back those foods it used to enjoy while in this life; and when it finds it cannot get them, the double becomes fierce, sometimes threatening the living with death and disaster if it is not supplied with such food.

Coming to Aryan thought, we at once find a very wide departure. There is still the double idea there, but it has become a sort of spiritual body; and one great difference is that the life of this spiritual body, the soul, or whatever you may call it, is not limited by the body it has left. On the contrary, it has obtained freedom from this body, and hence the peculiar Aryan custom of burning the dead. They want to get rid of the body which the person has left, while the Egyptian wants to preserve it by burying, embalming, and building pyramids. Apart from the most primitive system of doing away with the dead, amongst nations advanced to a certain extent, the method of doing away with the bodies of the dead is a great indication of their idea of the soul. Wherever we find the idea of a departed soul closely connected with the idea of the dead body, we always find the tendency to preserve the body, and we also find burying in some form or other. On the other hand, with those in whom the idea has developed that the soul is a separate entity from the body and will not be hurt if the dead body is even destroyed, burning is always the process resorted to. Thus we find among all ancient Aryan races burning of the dead, although the Parsees changed it to exposing the body on a tower. But the very name of the tower (Dakhma) means a burning-place, showing that in ancient times they also used to burn their bodies. The other peculiarity is that among the Aryans there was no element of fear with these doubles. They are not coming down to ask for food or help; and when denied that help, they do not become ferocious or try to destroy those that are living. They rather are joyful, are glad at getting free. The fire of the funeral pyre is the symbol of disintegration. The symbol is asked to take the departed soul gently up and to carry it to the place where the fathers live, where there is no sorrow, where there is joy for ever, and so on.

Of these two ideas we see at once that they are of a similar nature, the one optimistic, and the other pessimistic—being the elementary. The one is the evolution of the other. It is quite possible that the Aryans themselves had, or may have had, in very ancient times exactly the same idea as the Egyptians. In studying their most ancient records, we find the possibility of this very idea. But it is quite a bright thing, something bright. When a man dies, this soul goes to live with the fathers and lives there enjoying their happiness. These fathers receive it with great kindness; this is the most ancient idea in India of a soul. Later on, this idea becomes higher and higher. Then it was found out that what they called the soul before was not really the soul. This bright body, fine body, however fine it might be, was a body after all; and all bodies must be made up of materials, either gross or fine. Whatever had form or shape must be limited, and could not be eternal. Change is inherent in every form. How could that which is changeful be eternal? So, behind this bright body, as it were, they found something which was the soul of man. It was called the Âtman, the Self. This Self idea then began. It had also to undergo various changes. By some it was thought that this Self was eternal; that it was very minute, almost as minute as an atom; that it lived in a certain part of the body, and when a man died, his Self went away, taking along with it the bright body. There were other people who denied the atomic nature of the soul on the same ground on which they had denied that this bright body was the soul.

Out of all these various opinions rose Sânkhya philosophy, where at once we find immense differences. The idea there is that man has first this gross body; behind the gross body is the fine body, which is the vehicle of the mind, as it were; and behind even that is the Self, the Perceiver, as the Sânkhyas call it, of the mind; and this is omnipresent. That is, your soul, my soul, everyone's soul is everywhere at the same time. If it is formless, how can it be said to occupy space? Everything that occupies space has form. The formless can only be infinite. So each soul is everywhere. The second theory put forward is still more startling. They all saw in ancient times that human beings are progressive, at least many of them. They grew in purity and power and knowledge; and the question was asked: Whence was this knowledge, this purity, this strength which men manifested? Here is a baby without any knowledge. This baby grows and becomes a strong, powerful, and wise man. Whence did that baby get its wealth of knowledge and power? The answer was that it was in the soul; the soul of the baby had this knowledge and power from the very beginning. This power, this purity, this strength were in that soul, but they were unmanifested; they have become manifested. What is meant by this manifestation or unmanifestation? That each soul is pure and perfect, omnipotent and omniscient, as they say in the Sankhya; but it can manifest itself externally only according to the mind it has got. The mind is, as it were, the reflecting mirror of the soul. My mind reflects to a certain extent the powers of my soul; so your soul, and so everyone's. That mirror which is clearer reflects the soul better. So the manifestation varies according to the mind one possesses; but the souls in themselves are pure and perfect.

There was another school who thought that this could not be. Though souls are pure and perfect by their nature, this purity and perfection become, as they say, contracted at times, and expanded at other times. There are certain actions and certain thoughts which, as it were, contract the nature of the soul; and then also other thoughts and acts, which bring its nature out, manifest it. This again is explained. All thoughts and actions that make the power and purity of the soul get contracted are evil actions, evil thoughts; and all those thoughts and actions which make the soul manifest itself—make the powers come out, as it were—are good and moral actions. The difference between the two theories is very slight; it is more of less a play on the words expansion and contraction. The one that holds that the variation only depends on the mind the soul has got is the better explanation, no doubt, but the contracting and expanding theory wants to take refuge behind the two words; and they should be asked what is meant by contraction of soul, or expansion. Soul is a spirit. You can question what is meant by contraction or expansion with regard to material, whether gross which we call matter, or fine, the mind; but beyond that, if it is not matter, that which is not bound by space or by time, how to explain the words contraction and expansion with regard to that? So it seems that this theory which holds that the soul is pure and perfect all the time, only its nature is more reflected in some minds than in others, is the better. As the mind changes, its character grows, as it were, more and more clear and gives a better reflection of the soul. Thus it goes on, until the mind has become so purified that it reflects fully the quality of the soul; then the soul becomes liberated.

This is the nature of the soul. What is the goal? The goal of the soul among all the different sects in India seems to be the same. There is one idea with all, and that is liberation. Man is infinite; and this limitation in which he exists now is not his nature. But through these limitations he is struggling upward and forward until he reaches the infinite, the unlimited, his birthright, his nature. All these combinations and recombinations and manifestations that we see round us are not the aim or the goal, but merely by the way and in passing. These combinations as earths and suns, and moons and stars, right and wrong, good and bad, our laughter and our tears, our joys and sorrows, are to enable us to gain experience through which the soul manifests its perfect nature and throws off limitation. No more, then, is it bound by laws either of internal or external nature. It has gone beyond all law, beyond all limitation, beyond all nature. Nature has come under the control of the soul, not the soul under the control of nature, as it thinks it is now. That is the one goal that the soul has; and all the succeeding steps through which it is manifesting, all the successive experiences through which it is passing in order to attain to that goal—freedom—are represented as its births. The soul is, as it were, taking up a lower body and trying to express itself through that. It finds that to be insufficient, throws it aside, and a higher one is taken up. Through that it struggles to express itself. That also is found to be insufficient, is rejected, and a higher one comes; so on and on until a body is found through which the soul manifests its highest aspirations. Then the soul becomes free.

Now the question is: If the soul is infinite and exists everywhere, as it must do, if it is a spirit, what is meant by its taking up bodies and passing through body after body? The idea is that the soul neither comes nor goes, neither is born nor dies. How can the omnipresent be born? It is meaningless nonsense to say that the soul lives in a body. How can the unlimited live in a limited space? But as a man having a book in his hands reads one page and turns it over, goes to the next page, reads that, turns it over, and so on, yet it is the book that is being turned over, the pages that are revolving, and not he—he is where he is always—even so with regard to the soul. The whole of nature is that book which the soul is reading. Each life, as it were, is one page of that book; and that read, it is turned over, and so on and on, until the whole of the book is finished, and that soul becomes perfect, having got all the experiences of nature. Yet at the same time it never moved, nor came, nor went; it was only gathering experiences. But it appears to us that we are moving. The earth is moving, yet we think that the sun is moving instead of the earth, which we know to be a mistake, a delusion of the senses. So is also this, delusion that we are born and that we die, that we come or that we go. We neither come nor go, nor have we been born. For where is the soul to go? There is no place for it to go. Where is it not already?

Thus the theory comes of the evolution of nature and the manifestation of the soul. The processes of evolution, higher and higher combinations, are not in the soul; it is already what it is. They are in nature. But as nature is evolving forward into higher and higher combinations, more and more of the majesty of the soul is manifesting itself. Suppose here is a screen, and behind the screen is wonderful scenery. There is one small hole in the screen through which we can catch only a little bit of that scenery behind. Suppose that hole becomes increased in size. As the hole increases in size, more and more of the scenery behind comes within the range of vision; and when the whole screen has disappeared, there is nothing between the scenery and you; you see the whole of it. This screen is the mind of man. Behind it is the majesty, the purity, the infinite power of the soul, and as the mind becomes clearer and clearer, purer and purer, more of the majesty of the soul manifests itself. Not that the soul is changing, but the change is in the screen. The soul is the unchangeable One, the immortal, the pure, the ever-blessed One.

So, at last, the theory comes to this. From the highest to the lowest and most wicked man, in the greatest of; human beings and the lowest of crawling worms under our feet, is the soul, pure and perfect, infinite and ever-blessed. In the worm that soul is manifesting only an infinitesimal part of its power and purity, and in the greatest man it is manifesting most of it. The difference consists in the degree of manifestation, but not in the essence. Through all beings exists the same pure and perfect soul.

There are also the ideas of heavens and other places, but these are thought to be second-rate. The idea of heaven is thought to be a low idea. It arises from the desire for a place of enjoyment. We foolishly want to limit the whole universe with our present experience. Children think that the whole universe is full of children. Madmen think the whole universe a lunatic asylum, and so on. So those to whom this world is but sense-enjoyment, whose whole life is in eating and feasting, with very little difference between them and brute beasts—such are naturally found to conceive of places where they will have more enjoyments, because this life is short. Their desire for enjoyment is infinite, so they are bound to think of places where they will have unobstructed enjoyment of the senses; and we see, as we go on, that those who want to go to such places will have to go; they will dream, and when this dream is over, they will be in another dream where there is plenty of sense-enjoyment; and when that dream breaks, they will have to think of something else. Thus they will be driving about from dream to dream.

Then comes the last theory, one more idea about the soul. If the soul is pure and perfect in its essence and nature, and if every soul is infinite and omnipresent, how is it that there can be many souls? There cannot be many infinites. There cannot be two even, not to speak of many. If there were two infinites, one would limit the other, and both become finite. The infinite can only be one, and boldly the last conclusion is approached— that it is but one and not two.

Two birds are sitting on the same tree, one on the top, the other below, both of most beautiful plumage. The one eats the fruits, while the other remains, calm and majestic, concentrated in its own glory. The lower bird is eating fruits, good and evil, going after sense-enjoyments; and when it eats occasionally a bitter fruit, it gets higher and looks up and sees the other bird sitting there calm and majestic, neither caring for good fruit nor for bad, sufficient unto itself, seeking no enjoyment beyond itself. It itself is enjoyment; what to seek beyond itself? The lower bird looks at the upper bird and wants to get near. It goes a little higher; but its old impressions are upon it, and still it goes about eating the same fruit. Again an exceptionally bitter fruit comes; it gets a shock, looks up. There the same calm and majestic one! It comes near but again is dragged

down by past actions, and continues to eat the sweet and bitter fruits. Again the exceptionally bitter fruit comes, the bird looks up, gets nearer; and as it begins to get nearer and nearer, the light from the plumage of the other bird is reflected upon it. Its own plumage is melting away, and when it has come sufficiently near, the whole vision changes. The lower bird never existed, it was always the upper bird, and what it took for the lower bird was only a little bit of a reflection.

Such is the nature of the soul. This human soul goes after sense-enjoyments, vanities of the world; like animals it lives only in the senses, lives only in momentary titillations of the nerves. When there comes a blow, for a moment the head reels, and everything begins to vanish, and it finds that the world was not what it thought it to be, that life was not so smooth. It looks upward and sees the infinite Lord a moment, catches a glimpse of the majestic One, comes a little nearer, but is dragged away by its past actions. Another blow comes, and sends it back again. It catches another glimpse of the infinite Presence, comes nearer, and as it approaches nearer and nearer, it begins to find out that its individuality—its low, vulgar, intensely selfish individuality—is melting away; the desire to sacrifice the whole world to make that little thing happy is melting away; and as it gets gradually nearer and nearer, nature begins to melt away. When it has come sufficiently near, the whole vision changes, and it finds that it was the other bird, that this infinity which it had viewed as from a distance was its own Self, this wonderful glimpse that it had got of the glory and majesty was its own Self, and it indeed was that reality. The soul then finds That which is true in everything. That which is in every atom, everywhere present, the essence of all things, the God of this universe— know that thou art He, know that thou art free.

THE IMPORTANCE OF PSYCHOLOGY

The idea of psychology in the West is very much degraded. Psychology is the science of sciences; but in the West it is placed upon the same plane as all other sciences; that is, it is judged by the same criterion—utility.

How much practical benefit will it do to humanity? How much will it add to our rapidly growing happiness? How much will it detract from our rapidly increasing pain? Such is the criterion by which everything is judged in the West.

People seem to forget that about ninety per cent of all our knowledge cannot, in the very nature of things, be applied in a practical way to add to our material happiness or to lessen our misery. Only the smallest fraction of our scientific knowledge can have any such practical application to our daily lives. This is so because only an infinitely small percentage of our conscious mind is on the sensuous plane. We have just a little bit of sensuous consciousness and imagine that to be our entire mind and life; but, as a matter of fact, it is but a drop in the mighty ocean of subconscious mind. If all there is of us were a bundle of sense-perceptions, all the knowledge we could gain could be utilised in the gratification of our sense-pleasures. But fortunately such is not the case. As we get further and further away from the animal state, our sense-pleasures become less and less; and our enjoyment, in a rapidly increasing consciousness of scientific and psychological knowledge, becomes more and more intense; and "knowledge for the sake of knowledge", regardless of the amount of sense-pleasures it may conduce to, becomes the supreme pleasure of the mind.

But even taking the Western idea of utility as a criterion by which to judge, psychology, by such a standard even, is the science of sciences. Why? We are all slaves to our senses, slaves to our own minds, conscious and subconscious. The reason why a criminal is a criminal is not because he desires to be one, but because he has not his mind under control and is therefore a slave to his own conscious and subconscious mind, and to the mind of everybody else. He must follow the dominant trend of his own mind; he cannot help it; he is forced onward in spite of himself, in spite of his own better promptings, his own better nature; he is forced to obey the dominant mandate of his own mind. Poor man, he cannot help himself. We see this in our own lives constantly. We are constantly doing things against the better side of our nature, and afterwards we upbraid ourselves for so doing and wonder what we could have been thinking of, how we could do such a thing! Yet again and again we do it, and again and again we suffer for it and upbraid ourselves. At the time, perhaps, we think we desire to do it, but we only desire it because we are forced to desire it. We are forced onward, we are helpless! We are all slaves to our own and to everybody else's mind; whether we are good or bad, that makes no difference. We are led here and there because we cannot help ourselves. We say we think, we do, etc. It is not so. We think because we have to think. We act because we have to. We are slaves to ourselves and to others. Deep down in our subconscious mind are stored up all the thoughts and acts of the past, not only of this life, but of all other lives we have lived. This great boundless ocean of subjective mind is full of all the thoughts and actions of the past. Each one of these is striving to be recognised, pushing outward for expression, surging, wave after wave, out upon the objective mind, the conscious mind. These thoughts, the stored-up energy, we take for natural desires, talents, etc. It is because we do not realise their true origin. We obey them blindly, unquestioningly; and slavery, the most helpless kind of slavery, is the result; and we call ourselves free. Free! We who cannot for a moment govern our own minds, nay, cannot hold our minds on a subject, focus it on a point to the exclusion of everything else for a moment! Yet we call ourselves free. Think of it! We cannot do as we know we ought to do even for a very short space of time. Some sense-desire will crop up, and immediately we obey it. Our conscience smites us for such weakness, but again and again we do it, we are always doing it. We cannot live up to a high standard of life, try as we will. The ghosts of past thoughts, past lives hold us down. All the misery of the world is caused by this slavery

to the senses. Our inability to rise above the sense-life—the striving for physical pleasures, is the cause of all the horrors and miseries in the world.

It is the science of psychology that teaches us to hold in check the wild gyrations of the mind, place it under the control of the will, and thus free ourselves from its tyrannous mandates. Psychology is therefore the science of sciences, without which all sciences and all other knowledge are worthless.

The mind uncontrolled and unguided will drag us down, down, for ever—rend us, kill us; and the mind controlled and guided will save us, free us. So it must be controlled, and psychology teaches us how to do it.

To study and analyse any material science, sufficient data are obtained. These facts are studied and analysed and a knowledge of the science is the result. But in the study and analysis of the mind, there are no data, no facts acquired from without, such as are equally at the command of all. The mind is analysed by itself. The greatest science, therefore, is the science of the mind, the science of psychology.

In the West, the powers of the mind, especially unusual powers, are looked upon as bordering on witchcraft and mysticism. The study of higher psychology has been retarded by its being identified with mere alleged psychic phenomena, as is done by some mystery-mongering order of Hindu fakirs.

Physicists obtain pretty much the same results the world over. They do not differ in their general facts, nor in the results which naturally follow from such facts. This is because the data of physical science are obtainable by all and are universally recognised, and the results are logical conclusions based upon these universally recognised facts. In the realm of the mind, it is different. Here there are no data, no facts observable by the physical senses, and no universally recognised materials therefore, from which to build a system of psychology after their being equally experimented upon by all who study the mind.

Deep, deep within, is the soul, the essential man, the Âtman. Turn the mind inward and become united to that; and from that standpoint of stability, the gyrations of the mind can be watched and facts observed, which are to be found in all persons. Such facts, such data, are to be found by those who go deep enough, and only by such. Among that large class of self-styled mystics the world over, there is a great difference of opinion as to the mind, its nature, powers, etc. This is because such people do not go deep enough. They have noticed some little activity of their own and others' minds and, without knowing anything about the real character of such superficial manifestations, have published them as facts universal in their application; and every religious and mystical crank has facts, data, etc., which, he claims, are reliable criteria for investigation, but which are in fact nothing more or less than his own imaginings

If you intend to study the mind, you must have systematic training; you must practice to bring the mind under your control, to attain to that consciousness from which you will be able to study the mind and remain unmoved by any of its wild gyrations. Otherwise the facts observed will not be reliable; they will not apply to all people and therefore will not be truly facts or data at all.

Among that class who have gone deeply into the study of the mind, the facts observed have been the same, no matter in what part of the world such persons may be or what religious belief they may have. The results obtained by all who go deep enough into the mind are the same.

The mind operates by perception and impulsion. For instance, the rays of the light enter by eyes, are carried by the nerves to the brain, and still I do not see the light. The brain then conveys the impulse to the mind, but yet I do not see the light; the mind then reacts, and the light flashes across the mind. The mind's reaction is impulsion, and as a result the eye perceives the object.

To control the mind you must go deep down into the subconscious mind, classify and arrange in order all the different impressions, thoughts, etc., stored up there, and control them. This is the first step. By the control of the subconscious mind you get control over the conscious.

NATURE AND MAN

The modern idea of nature includes only that part of the universe that is manifested on the physical plane. That which is generally understood to be mind is not considered to be nature.

Philosophers endeavouring to prove the freedom of the will have excluded the mind from nature; for as nature is bound and governed by law, strict unbending law, mind, if considered to be in nature, would be bound by law also. Such a claim would destroy the doctrine of free will; for how can that be free which is bound by law?

The philosophers of India have taken the reverse stand. They hold all physical life, manifest and unmanifest, to be bound by law. The mind as well as external nature, they claim, is bound by law, and by one and the same law. If mind is not bound by law, if the thoughts we think are not the necessary results of preceding thoughts, if one mental state is not followed by another which it produces, then mind is irrational; and who can claim free will and at the same time deny the operation of reason? And on the other hand, who can admit that the mind is governed by the law of causation and claim that the will is free?

Law itself is the operation of cause and effect. Certain things happen according to certain other things which have gone before. Every precedent has its consequent. Thus it is in nature. If this operation of law obtains in the mind, the mind is bound and is therefore not free. No, the will is not free. How can it be? But we all know, we all feel, that one are free. Life would have no meaning, it would not be worth living, if we were not free.

The Eastern philosophers accepted this doctrine, or rather propounded it, that the mind and the will are within time, space, and causation, the same as so-called matter; and that they are therefore bound by the law of causation. We think in time; our thoughts are bound by time; all that exists, exists in time and space. All is bound by the law of causation.

Now that which we call matter and mind are one and the same substance. The only difference is in the degree of vibration. Mind at a very low rate of vibration is what is known as matter. Matter at a high rate of vibration is what is known as mind. Both are the same substance; and therefore, as matter is bound by time and space and causation, mind which is matter at a high rate of vibration is bound by the same law.

Nature is homogeneous. Differentiation is in manifestation. The Sanskrit word for nature is Prakriti, and means literally differentiation. All is one substance, but it is manifested variously.

Mind becomes matter, and matter in its turn becomes mind, it is simply a question of vibration.

Take a bar of steel and charge it with a force sufficient to cause it to vibrate, and what would happen? If this were done in a dark room, the first thing you would be aware of would be a sound, a humming sound. Increase the force, and the bar of steel would become luminous; increase it still more, and the steel would disappear altogether. It would become mind.

Take another illustration: If I do not eat for ten days, I cannot think. Only a few stray thoughts are in my mind. I am very weak and perhaps do not know my own name. Then I eat some bread, and in a little while I begin to think; my power of mind has returned. The bread has become mind. Similarly, the mind lessens its rate of vibration and manifests itself in the body, becomes matter.

As to which is first—matter or mind, let me illustrate: A hen lays an egg; the egg brings out another hen; that hen lays another egg; that egg brings out another hen, and so on in an endless chain. Now which is first—the egg or the hen? You cannot think of an egg that was not laid by a hen, or a hen that was not hatched out of an egg. It makes no difference which is first. Nearly all our ideas run themselves into the hen and egg business.

The greatest truths have been forgotten because of their very simplicity. Great truths are simple because they are of universal application. Truth itself is always simple. Complexity is due to man's ignorance.

Man's free agency is not of the mind, for that is bound. There is no freedom there. Man is not mind, he is soul. The soul is ever free, boundless, and eternal. Herein is man's freedom, in the soul. The soul is always free, but the mind identifying itself with its own ephemeral waves, loses sight of the soul and becomes lost in the maze of time, space, and causation—Maya.

This is the cause of our bondage. We are always identifying ourselves with the mind, and the mind's phenomenal changes.

Man's free agency is established in the soul, and the soul, realising itself to be free, is always asserting the fact in spite of the mind's bondage: "I am free! I am what I am! I am what I am!" This is our freedom. The soul— ever free, boundless, eternal—through aeons and aeons is manifesting itself more and more through its instrument, the mind.

What relation then does man bear to nature? From the lowest form of life to man, the soul is manifesting itself through nature. The highest manifestation of the soul is involved in the lowest form of manifest life and is working itself outward through the process called evolution.

The whole process of evolution is the soul's struggle to manifest itself. It is a constant struggle against nature. It is a struggle against nature, and not conformity to nature that makes man what he is. We hear a great deal about living in harmony with nature, of being in tune with nature. This is a mistake. This table, this pitcher, the minerals, a tree, are all in harmony with nature. Perfect harmony there, no discord. To be in harmony with nature means stagnation, death. How did man build this house? By being in harmony with nature? No. By fighting against nature. It is the constant struggle against nature that constitutes human progress, not conformity with it.

CONCENTRATION AND BREATHING

The main difference between men and the animals is the difference in their power of concentration. All success in any line of work is the result of this. Everybody knows something about concentration. We see its results every day. High achievements in art, music, etc., are the results of concentration. An animal has very little power of concentration. Those who have trained animals find much difficulty in the fact that the animal is constantly forgetting what is told him. He cannot concentrate his mind long upon anything at a time. Herein is the difference between man and the animals—man has the greater power of concentration. The difference in heir power of concentration also constitutes the difference between man and man. Compare the lowest with the highest man. The difference is in the degree of concentration. This is the only difference.

Everybody's mind becomes concentrated at times. We all concentrate upon those things we love, and we love those things upon which we concentrate our minds. What mother is there that does not love the face of her homeliest child? That face is to her the most beautiful in the world. She loves it because she concentrates her mind on it; and if every one could concentrate his mind on that same face, every one would love it. It would be to all the most beautiful face. We all concentrate our minds upon those things we love. When we hear beautiful music, our minds become fastened upon it, and we cannot take them away. Those who concentrate their minds upon what you call classical music do not like common music, and vice versa. Music in which the notes follow each other in rapid succession holds the mind readily. A child loves lively music, because the rapidity of the notes gives the mind no chance to wander. A man who likes common music dislikes classical music, because it is more complicated and requires a greater degree of concentration to follow it.

The great trouble with such concentrations is that we do not control the mind; it controls us. Something outside of ourselves, as it were, draws the mind into it and holds it as long as it chooses. We hear melodious tones or see a beautiful painting, and the mind is held fast! We cannot take it away.

If I speak to you well upon a subject you like, your mind becomes concentrated upon what I am saying. I draw your mind away from yourself and hold it upon the subject in spite of yourself. Thus our attention is held, our minds are concentrated upon various things, in spite of ourselves. We cannot help it.

Now the question is: Can this concentration be developed, and can we become masters of it? The Yogis say, yes. The Yogis say that we can get perfect control of the mind. On the ethical side there is danger in the development of the power of concentration—the danger of concentrating the mind upon an object and then being unable to detach it at will. This state causes great suffering. Almost all our suffering is caused by our not having the power of detachment. So along with the development of concentration we must develop the power of detachment. We must learn not only to attach the mind to one thing exclusively, but also to detach it at a moment's notice and place it upon something else. These two should be developed together to make it safe.

This is the systematic development of the mind. To me the very essence of education is concentration of mind, not the collecting of facts. If I had to do my education over again, and had any voice in the matter, I would not study facts at all. I would develop the power of concentration and detachment, and then with a perfect instrument I could collect facts at will. Side by side, in the child, should be developed the power of concentration and detachment.

My development has been one-sided all along I developed concentration without the power of detaching my mind at will; and the most intense suffering of my life has been due to this. Now I have the power of detachment, but I had to learn it in later life.

We should put our minds on things; they should not draw our minds to them. We are usually forced to concentrate. Our minds are forced to become fixed upon different things by an attraction in them which we cannot resist. To control the mind, to place it just where we want it, requires special training. It cannot be done in any other way. In the study of religion the control of the mind is absolutely necessary. We have to turn the mind back upon itself in this study.

In training the mind the first step is to begin with the breathing. Regular breathing puts the body in a harmonious condition; and it is then easier to reach the mind. In practicing breathing, the first thing to consider is Âsana or posture. Any posture in which a person can sit easily is his proper position. The spine should be kept free, and the weight of the body should be supported by the ribs. Do not try by contrivances to control the mind; simple breathing is all that is necessary in that line. All austerities to gain concentration of the mind are a mistake. Do not practice them.

The mind acts on the body, and the body in its turn acts upon the mind. They act and react upon each other. Every mental state creates a corresponding state in the body, and every action in the body has its corresponding effect on the mind. It makes no difference whether you think the body and mind are two different entities, or whether you think they are both but one body— the physical body being the gross part and the mind the fine part. They act and react upon each other. The mind is constantly becoming the body. In the training of the mind, it is easier to reach it through the body. The body is easier to grapple with than the mind.

The finer the instrument, the greater the power. The mind is much finer and more powerful than the body. For this reason it is easier to begin with the body.

The science of breathing is the working through the body to reach the mind. In this way we get control of the body, and then we begin to feel the finer working of the body, the finer and more interior, and so on till we reach the mind. As we feel the finer workings of the body, they come under our control. After a while you will be able to feel the operation of the mind on the body. You will also feel the working of one half of the mind upon the other half, and also feel the mind recruiting the nerve centres; for the mind controls and governs the nervous system. You will feel the mind operating along the different nerve currents.

Thus the mind is brought under control—by regular systematic breathing, by governing the gross body first and then the fine body.

The first breathing exercise is perfectly safe and very healthful. It will give you good health, and better your condition generally at least. The other practices should be taken up slowly and carefully.

INTRODUCTION TO JNANA-YOGA

This is the rational and philosophic side of Yoga and very difficult, but I will take you slowly through it.

Yoga means the method of joining man and God. When you understand this, you can go on with your own definitions of man and God, and you will find the term Yoga fits in with every definition. Remember always, there are different Yogas for different minds, and that if one does not suit you, another may. All religions are divided into theory and practice. The Western mind has given itself up to the theory and only sees the practical part of religion as good works. Yoga is the practical part of religion and shows that religion is a practical power apart from good works.

At the beginning of the nineteenth century man tried to find God through reason, and Deism was the result. What little was left of God by this process was destroyed by Darwinism and Millism. Men were then thrown back upon historical and comparative religion. They thought, religion was derived from element worship (see Max Müller on the sun myths etc.); others thought that religion was derived from ancestor worship (see Herbert Spencer). But taken as a whole, these methods have proved a failure. Man cannot get at Truth by external methods.

"If I know one lump of clay, I know the whole mass of clay." The universe is all built on the same plan. The individual is only a part, like the lump of clay. If we know the human soul—which is one atom—its beginning and general history, we know the whole of nature. Birth, growth, development, decay, death—this is the sequence in all nature and is the same in the plant and the man. The difference is only in time. The whole cycle may be completed in one case in a day, in the other in three score years and ten; the methods are the same. The only way to reach a sure analysis of the universe is by the analysis of our own minds. A proper psychology is essential to the understanding of religion. To reach Truth by reason alone is impossible, because imperfect reason cannot study its own fundamental basis. Therefore the only way to study the mind is to get at facts, and then intellect will arrange them and deduce the principles. The intellect has to build the house; but it cannot do so without bricks and it cannot make bricks. Jnana-Yoga is the surest way of arriving at facts.

First we have the physiology of mind. We have organs of the senses, which are divided into organs of action and organs of perception. By organs I do not mean the external sense-instruments. The ophthalmic centre in the brain is the organ of sight, not the eye alone. So with every organ, the function is internal. Only when the mind reacts, is the object truly perceived. The sensory and motor nerves are necessary to perception.

Then there is the mind itself. It is like a smooth lake which when struck, say by a stone, vibrates. The vibrations gather together and react on the stone, and all through the lake they will spread and be felt. The mind is like the lake; it is constantly being set in vibrations, which leave an impression on the mind; and the idea of the Ego, or personal self, the "I", is the result of these impressions. This "I" therefore is only the very rapid transmission of force and is in itself no reality.

The mind-stuff is a very fine material instrument used for taking up the Prâna. When a man dies, the body dies; but a little bit of the mind, the seed, is left when all else is shattered; and this is the seed of the new body called by St. Paul "the spiritual body". This theory of the materiality of the mind accords with all modern theories. The idiot is lacking in intelligence because his mind-stuff is injured. Intelligence cannot be in matter nor can it be produced by any combinations of matter. Where then is intelligence? It is behind matter; it is the Jiva, the real Self, working through the instrument of matter. Transmission of force is not possible without matter, and as the Jiva cannot travel alone, some part of mind is left as a transmitting medium when all else is shattered by death.

How are perceptions made? The wall opposite sends an impression to me, but I do not see the wall until my mind reacts, that is to say, the mind cannot know the wall by mere sight. The reaction that enables the mind to get a perception of the wall is an intellectual process. In this way the whole universe is seen through our eyes plus mind (or perceptive faculty); it is necessarily coloured by our own individual tendencies. The real wall, or the real universe, is outside the mind, and is unknown and unknowable. Call this universe X, and our statement is that the seen universe is X plus mind.

What is true of the external must also apply to the internal world. Mind also wants to know itself, but this Self can only be known through the medium of the mind and is, like the wall, unknown. This self we may call Y. and the statement would then be, Y plus mind is the inner self. Kant was the first to arrive at this analysis of mind, but it was long ago stated in the Vedas. We have thus, as it were, mind standing between X and Y and reacting on both.

If X is unknown, then any qualities we give to it are only derived from our own mind. Time, space, and causation are the three conditions through which mind perceives. Time is the condition for the transmission of thought, and space for the vibration of grosser matter. Causation is the sequence in which vibrations come. Mind can only cognise through these. Anything therefore, beyond mind must be beyond time, space, and causation.

To the blind man the world is perceived by touch and sound. To us with five senses it is another world. If any of us developed an electric sense and the faculty seeing electric waves, the world would appear different. Yet the world, as the X to all of these, is still the same. As each one brings his own mind, he sees his own world. There is X plus one sense; X plus two senses, up to five, as we know humanity. The result is constantly varied, yet X remains always unchanged. Y is also beyond our minds and beyond time, space, and causation.

But, you may ask, "How do we know there are two things (X and Y) beyond time, space, and causation?" Quite true, time makes differentiation, so that, as both are really beyond time, they must be really one. When mind sees this one, it calls it variously—X, when it is the outside world, and Y, when it is the inside world. This unit exists and is looked at through the lens of minds.

The Being of perfect nature, universally appearing to us, is God, is Absolute. The undifferentiated is the perfect condition; all others must be lower and not permanent.

What makes the undifferentiated appear differentiated to mind? This is the same kind of question as what is the origin of evil and free will? The question itself is contradictory and impossible, because the question takes for granted cause and effect. There is no cause and effect in the undifferentiated; the question assumes that the undifferentiated is in the same condition as the differentiated. "Whys" and "wherefores" are in mind only. The Self is beyond causation, and It alone is free. Its light it is which percolates through every form of mind. With every action I assert I am free, and yet every action proves that I am bound. The real Self is free, yet when mixed with mind and body, It is not free. The will is the first manifestation of the real Self; the first limitation therefore of this real Self is the will. Will is a compound of Self and mind. Now, no compound can be permanent, so that when we will to live, we must die. Immortal life is a contradiction in terms, for life, being a compound, cannot be immortal. True Being is undifferentiated and eternal. How does this Perfect Being become mixed up with will, mind, thought—all defective things? It never has become mixed. You are the real you (the Y of our former statement); you never were will; you never have changed; you as a person never existed; It is illusion. Then on what, you will say, do the phenomena of illusion rest? This is a bad question. Illusion never rests on Truth, but only on illusion. Everything struggles to go back to what was before these illusions, to be free in fact. What then is the value of life? It is to give us experience. Does this view do away with evolution? On the contrary, it explains it. It is really the process of refinement of matter allowing the real Self to manifest Itself. It is as if a screen or a veil were between us and some other object. The object becomes clear as the screen is gradually withdrawn. The question is simply one of manifestation of the higher Self.

THE VEDANTA PHILOSOPHY AND CHRISTIANITY

Notes of a lecture delivered at the Unitarian Church, in Oakland, California, on February 28, 1900

Between all great religions of the world there are many points of similarity; and so startling is this likeness, at times, as to suggest the idea that in many particulars the different religions have copied from one another.

This act of imitation has been laid at the door of different religions; but that it is a superficial charge is evident from the following facts:

Religion is fundamental in the very soul of humanity; and as all life is the evolution of that which is within, it, of necessity, expresses itself through various peoples and nations.

The language of the soul is one, the languages of nations are many; their customs and methods of life are widely different. Religion is of the soul and finds expression through various nations, languages, and customs. Hence it follows that the difference between the religions of the world is one of expression and not of substance; and their points of similarity and unity are of the soul, are intrinsic, as the language of the soul is one, in whatever peoples and under whatever circumstances it manifests itself. The same sweet harmony is vibrant there also, as it is on many and diverse instruments.

The first thing in common in all great religions of the world is the possession of an authentic book. When religious systems have failed to have such a book, they have become extinct. Such was the fact of the religions of Egypt. The authentic book is the hearthstone, so to speak, of each great religious system, around which its adherents gather, and from which radiates the energy and life of the system.

Each religion, again, lays the claim that its particular book is the only authentic word of God; that all other sacred books are false and are impositions upon poor human credulity; and that to follow another religion is to be ignorant and spiritually blind.

Such bigotry is characteristic of the orthodox element of all religions. For instance, the orthodox followers of the Vedas claim that the Vedas are the only authentic word of God in the world; that God has spoken to the world only through the Vedas; not only that, but that the world itself exists by virtue of the Vedas. Before the world was, the Vedas were. Everything in the world exists because it is in the Vedas. A cow exists because the name cow is in the Vedas; that is, because the animal we know as a cow is mentioned in the Vedas. The language of the Vedas is the original language of God, all other languages are mere dialects and not of God. Every word and syllable in the Vedas must be pronounced correctly, each sound must be given its true vibration, and every departure from this rigid exactness is a terrible sin and unpardonable.

Thus, this kind of bigotry is predominant in the orthodox element of all religions. But this fighting over the letter is indulged in only by the ignorant, the spiritually blind. All who have actually attained any real religious nature never wrangle over the form in which the different religions are expressed. They know that the life of all religions is the same, and, consequently, they have no quarrel with anybody because he does not speak the same tongue.

The Vedas are, in fact, the oldest sacred books in the world. Nobody knows anything about the time when they were written or by whom. They are contained in many volumes, and I doubt that any one man ever read them all.

The religion of the Vedas is the religion of the Hindus, and the foundation of all Oriental religions; that is, all other Oriental religions are offshoots of the Vedas; all Eastern systems of religion have the Vedas as authority.

It is an irrational claim to believe in the teachings of Jesus Christ and at the same time to hold that the greater part of his teachings have no application at the present time. If you say that the reason why the powers do not follow them that believe (as Christ said they would) is because you have not faith enough and are not pure enough—that will be all right. But to say that they have no application at the present time is to be ridiculous.

I have never seen the man who was not at least my equal. I have travelled all over the world; I have been among the very worst kind of people—among cannibals—and I have never seen the man who is not at least my equal. I have done as they do—when I was a fool. Then I did not know any better; now I do. Now they do not know any better; after a while they will. Every one acts according to his own nature. We are all in process of growth. From this standpoint one man is not better than another.

WORSHIPPER AND WORSHIPPED

This lecture is reproduced from the Vedanta and the West.
Delivered in San Francisco area, April 9, 1900

We have been taking up the more analytical side of human nature. In this course we [shall] study the emotional side…The former deals with man as unlimited being, [as] principle, the latter with man as limited being…The one has no time to stop for a few tear-drops or pangs; the other cannot proceed without wiping the tear-drop, without healing that misery. One is great, so great and grand that sometimes we are staggered by the magnitude; the other [is] commonplace, and yet most beautiful and dear to us. One gets hold of us, takes us up to the heights where our lungs almost burst. We cannot breathe [in] that atmosphere. The other leaves us where we are and tries to see the objects of life, [takes the limited] view. One will accept nothing until it has the shining seal of reason; the other has faith, and what it cannot see it believes. Both are necessary. A bird cannot fly with only one wing…

What we want is to see the man who is harmoniously developed…great in heart, great in mind, [great in deed]…We want the man whose heart feels intensely the miseries and sorrows of the world…And [we want] the man who not only can feel but can find the meaning of things, who delves deeply into the heart of nature and understanding. [We want] the man who will not even stop there, [but] who wants to work out [the feeling and meaning by actual deeds]. Such a combination of head, heart, and hand is what we want. There are many teachers in this world, but you will find [that most of them] are one-sided. [One] sees the glorious midday sun of intellect [and] sees nothing else. Another hears the beautiful music of love and can hear nothing else. Another is [immersed] in activity, and has neither time to feel nor time to think. Why not [have] the giant who is equally active, equally knowing, and equally loving? Is it impossible? Certainly not. This is the man of the future, of whom there are [only a] few at present. [The number of such will increase] until the whole world is humanised.

I have been talking to you so long about intellect [and] reason. We have heard the whole of Vedanta. The veil of Maya breaks: wintry clouds vanish, and the sunlight shines on us. I have been trying to climb the heights of the Himalayas, where the peaks disappear beyond the clouds. I propose lip study with you the other side: the most beautiful valleys, the most marvellous exquisiteness in nature. [We shall study the] love that holds us here in spite of all the miseries of the world,

[the] love that has made us forge the chain of misery, this eternal martyrdom which man is suffering willingly, of his own accord. We want to study that for which man has forged the chain with his own hands, that for which he suffers, that eternal love. We do not mean to forget the other. The glacier of the Himalayas must join hands with the rice fields of Kashmir. The thunderbolt must blend its base note with the warbling of the birds.

This course will have to do with everything exquisite and beautiful. Worship is everywhere, in every soul. Everyone worships God. Whatever be the name, they are all worshipping God. The beginnings of worship—like the beautiful lotus, like life itself—are in the dirt of the earth … There is the element of fear. There is the hungering for this world's gain. There is the worship of the beggar. These are the beginnings of [the] world worshipping, [culminating in] loving God and worshipping God through man.

Is there any God? Is there anyone to be loved, any such one capable of being loved? Loving the stone would not be much good. We only love that which understands love, that which draws our love. So with worship. Never say [that] there is a man in this world of ours who worshipped a piece of stone [as stone]. He always worshipped [the omnipresent being in the stone].

We find out that the omnipresent being is in us. [But] how can we worship, unless that being is separate from us? I can only worship Thee, and not me. I can only pray to Thee, and not me. Is there any "Thou"?

The One becomes many. When we see the One, any limitations reflected through Maya disappear; but it is quite true that the manifold is not valueless. It is through the many that we reach the one …

Is there any Personal God—a God who thinks, who understands, a God who guides us? There is. The Impersonal God cannot have any one of these attributes. Each one of you is an individual: you think, you love, [you] hate, [you] are angry, sorry, etc.; yet you are impersonal, unlimited. [You are] personal and impersonal in one. You have the personal and the impersonal aspects. That [impersonal reality] cannot be angry, [nor] sorry, [nor] miserable—cannot even think misery. It cannot think, cannot know. It is knowledge itself. But the personal [aspect] knows, thinks, and dies, etc. Naturally the universal Absolute must have two aspects; the one representing the infinite reality of all things; the other, a personal aspect, the Soul of our souls, Lord of all lords. [It is] He who creates this universe. Under [His] guidance this universe exists …

He, the Infinite, the Ever-Pure, the Ever-[Free,] … He is no judge, God cannot be [a] judge. He does not sit upon a throne and judge between the good and the wicked … He is no magistrate, [no] general, [nor] master. Infinitely merciful, infinitely loving is the Personal [God].

Take it from another side. Every cell in your body has a soul conscious of the cell. It is a separate entity. It has a little will of its own, a little sphere of action of its own. All [cells] combined make up an individual. [In the same way,] the Personal God of the universe is made up of all these [many individuals].

Take it from another side. You, as I see you, are as much of your absolute nature as has been limited and perceived by one. I have limited you in order to see you through the power of my eyes, my senses. As much of you as my eyes can see, I see. As much of you as my mind can grasp is what I know to be you, and nothing more. In the same way, I am reading the Absolute, the Impersonal [and see Him as Personal]. As long as we have body and mind, we always see this triune being: God, nature, and soul. There must always be the three in one, inseparable … There is nature. There are human souls. There is again That in which nature and the human souls [are contained]

The universal soul has become embodied. My soul itself is a part of God. He is the eye of our eyes, the life of our life, the mind of our mind, the soul of our soul. This is the highest ideal of the Personal God we can have.

If you are not a dualist, [but are] a monist, you can still have the Personal God … There is the One without a second. That One wanted to love Himself. Therefore, out of that One, He made [many] … It is the big Me, the real Me, that that little me is worshipping. Thus in all systems you can have the Personal [God].

Some people are born under circumstances that make them happier than others: why should this be in the reign of a just being? There is mortality in this world. These are the difficulties in the way [These problems] have never been answered. They cannot be answered from any dualistic plane. We have to go back to philosophy to treat things as they are. We are suffering from our own Karma. It is not the fault of God. What we do is our own fault, nothing else. Why should God be blamed? …

Why is there evil? The only way you can solve [the problem] is [by saying that God is] the cause of both good and evil. The great difficulty in the theory of the Personal God is that if you say He is only good and not evil, you will be caught in the trap of your own argument. How do you know there is [a] God? You say [that He is] the Father of this universe, and you say He is good; and because there is [also] evil in the world, God must be evil … The same difficulty!

There is no good, and there is no evil. God is all there is … How do you know what is good? You feel [it]. [How do you know what is evil ? If evil comes, you feel it … We know good and evil by our feelings. There is not one man who feels only good, happy feelings. There is not one who feels only unhappy feelings …

Want and anxiety are the causes of all unhappiness and happiness too. Is want increasing or decreasing? Is life becoming simple or complex? Certainly complex. Wants are being multiplied. Your great-grandfathers did not want the same dress or the same amount of money [you do]. They had no electric cars, [nor] railroads, etc. That is why they had to work less. As soon as these things come, the want arises, and you have to work harder. More and more anxiety, and more and more competition.

It is very hard work to get money. It is harder work to keep it. You fight the whole world to get a little money together [and] fight all your life to protect it. [Therefore] there is more anxiety for the rich than for the poor... This is the way it is...

There are good and evil every where in this world. Sometimes evil becomes good, true; but other times good becomes evil also. All our senses produce evil some time or other. Let a man drink wine. It is not bad [at first], but let him go on drinking, [and] it will produce evil... A man is born of rich parents; good enough. He becomes a fool, never exercises his body or brain. That is good producing evil. Think of this love of life: We go away and jump about and live a few moments; we work hard. We are born babies, entirely incapable. It takes us years to understand things again. At sixty or seventy we open our eyes, and then comes the word, "Get out!" And there you are.

We have seen that good and evil are relative terms. The thing [that is] good for me is bad for you. If you eat the dinner that I eat, you will begin to weep, and I shall laugh... We [may] both dance, but I with joy and you with pain... The same thing is good at one part of our life and bad at another part. How can you say [that] good and evil are all cut and dried— [that] this is all good and that is all evil?

Now, who is responsible for all this good and evil, if God is ever the good? The Christians and the Mohammedans say there is a gentleman called Satan. How can you say there are two gentlemen working? There must be one... The fire that burns the child also cooks the meal. How can you call the fire good or bad, and how can you say it was created by two different persons? Who creates all [so-called] evil? God. There is no other way out. He sends death and life, plague and epidemics, and everything. If such is God, He is the good; He is the evil; He is the beautiful; He is the terrible; He is life; and He is death.

How can such a God be worshipped? We shall come to [understand] how the soul can really learn to worship the terrible; then that soul will have peace... Have you peace? Do you get rid of anxieties? Turn around, first of all, and face the terrible. Tear aside the mask and find the same [God]. He is the personal—all that is [apparently] good and all that is [apparently] bad. There is none else. If there were two Gods, nature could not stand a moment. There is not another one in nature. It is all harmony. If God played one side and the devil the other, the whole [of] nature would be [in chaos]. Who can break the law? If I break this glass, it will fall down. If anyone succeeds in throwing one atom out of place, every other atom will go out of balance... The law can never be broken. Each atom is kept in its place. Each is weighed and measured

and fulfils its [purpose] and place. Through His command the winds blow, the sun shines. Through His rule the worlds are kept in place. Through His orders death is sporting upon the earth. Just think of two or three Gods having a wrestling match in this world! It cannot be.

We now come to see that we can have the Personal God, the creator of this universe, who is merciful and also cruel... He is the good, He is the evil. He smiles, and He frowns. And none can go beyond His law. He is the creator of this universe.

What is meant by creation, something coming out of nothing? Six thousand years ago God woke up from His dream and created the world [and] before that there was nothing? What was God doing then, taking a good nap? God is the cause of the universe, and we can know the cause through the effect. If the effect is not present, the cause is not [the] cause. The cause is always known in and through the effect... Creation is infinite... You cannot think of the beginning in time or in space.

Why does He create it? Because He likes to; because He is free... You and I are bound by law, because we can work [only] in certain ways and not in others. "Without hands, He can grasp everything. Without feet, [He moves fast]." Without body, He is omnipotent. "Whom no eyes can see, but who is the cause of sight in every eye, know Him to be the Lord." You cannot worship anything else. God is the omnipotent supporter of this universe. What is called "law" is the manifestation of His will. He rules the universe by His laws.

So far [we have discussed] God and nature, eternal God and eternal nature. What about souls? They also are eternal. No soul was [ever] created; neither can [the] soul die. Nobody can even imagine his own death. The soul is infinite, eternal. How can it die? It changes bodies. As a man takes off his old, worn-out garments and puts on new and fresh ones, even so the worn-out body is thrown away and [a] fresh body is taken.

What is the nature of the soul? The soul is also [omnipotent] and omnipresent. Spirit has neither length, nor breadth, nor thickness... How can it be said to be here and there? This body falls; [the soul] works [through] another body. The soul is a circle of which the circumference is nowhere, but the centre is in the body. God is a circle whose circumference is nowhere, but whose centre is everywhere. The soul by its [very] nature is blessed, pure, and perfect; it could never be pure if its nature was impure... The soul's nature is purity; that is why souls [can] become pure. It is blessed [by nature]; that is why it [can] become blessed. It is peace; [that is why it can become peaceful]...

All of us who find ourselves in this plane, attracted to the body, work hard for a living, with jealousies and quarrels and hardships, and then death. That shows we are not what we should be. We are not free, perfectly pure, and so on. The soul, as it were, has become degraded. Then what the soul requires is expansion...

How can you do it? Can you work it out yourself? No. If a

man's face is dusty, can you wash it out with dust? If I put a seed in the ground, the seed produces a tree, the tree produces a seed, the seed another tree, etc. Hen and egg, egg and hen. If you do something good, you will have to reap the result of that, be born again and be sorry. Once started in this infinite chain, you cannot stop. You go on, ... up and down, [to] heavens and earths, and all these [bodies] ... There is no way out.

Then how can you get out of all this, and what are you here for? One idea is to get rid of misery. We are all struggling day and night to get rid of misery ... We cannot do it by work. Work will produce more work. It is only possible if there is someone who is free himself and lends us a hand. "Hear, ye children of immortality, all those that reside in this plane and all those that reside in the heavens above, I have found the secret", says the great sage. "I have found Him who is beyond all darkness. Through His mercy alone we cross this ocean of life."

In India, the idea of the goal is this: There are heavens, there are hells, there are earths, but they are not permanent. If I am sent to hell, it is not permanent. The same struggle goes on and on wherever I am. How to get beyond all this struggle is the problem. If I go to heaven, perhaps there will be a little bit of rest. If I get punished for my misdeeds, that cannot last [for ever either] ... The Indian ideal is not to go to heaven. Get out of this earth, get out of hell, and get out of heaven! What is the goal? It is freedom. You must all be free. The glory of the soul is covered up. It has to be uncovered again. The soul exists. It is everywhere. Where shall it go? ... Where can it go? It can only go where it is not. If you understand [that] it is ever present, ... [there will be] perfect happiness for ever afterwards. No more births and deaths ... No more disease, no body. [The] body itself is the biggest disease ...

The soul shall stand [as] soul. Spirit shall live as spirit. How is this to be done? By worshipping [the Lord in] the soul, who, by his [very] nature is ever present, pure, and perfect. There cannot be two almighty beings in this world. [Imagine having] two or three Gods; one will create the world, another says, "I will destroy the world." It [can] never happen. There must be one God. The soul attains to perfection; [it becomes] almost omnipotent [and] omniscient. This is the worshipper. Who is the worshipped? He, the Lord God Himself, the Omnipresent, the Omniscient, and so on. And above all, He is Love. How is [the soul] to attain this perfection? By worship.

Vedanta and the West, July-Aug. 1955.

FORMAL WORSHIP

This lecture is reproduced from the Vedanta and the West. *Delivered in San Francisco area, April 10, 1900*

All of you who are students of the Bible ... understand that the whole [of] Jewish history and Jewish' thought have been produced by two [types of] teachers—priests and prophets, the priests representing the power of conservatism, the proph-

ets the power of progress. The whole thing is that a conservative ritualism creeps in; formality gets hold of everything. This is true of every country and every religion. Then come some new seers with new visions; they preach new ideals and ideas and give a new push to society. In a few generations the followers become so faithful to their masters' ideas that they cannot see anything else. The most advanced, liberal preachers of this age within a few years will be the most conservative priests. The advanced thinkers, in their turn, will begin to hinder the man who goes a little farther. They will not let anyone go farther than what they themselves have attained. They are content to leave things as they are.

The power which works through the formative principles of every religion in every country is manifested in the forms of religion ... Principles and books, certain rules and movements—standing up, sitting down—all these belong to the same category of worship Spiritual worship becomes materialised in order that the majority of mankind can get hold of it. The vast majority of mankind in every country are never [seen] to worship spirit as spirit. It is not yet possible. I do not know if there ever will be a time when they can. How many thousands in this city are ready to worship God as spirit? Very few. They cannot; they live in the senses. You have to give them cut and dried ideas. Tell them to do something physical: Stand up twenty times; sit down twenty times. They will understand that. Tell them to breathe in through one nostril and breathe out through the other. They will understand that. All this idealism about spirit they cannot accept at all. It is not their fault ... If you have the power to worship God as spirit, good! But there was a time when you could not ... If the people are crude, the religious conceptions are crude, and the forms are uncouth and gross. If the people are refined and cultured, the forms are more beautiful. There must be forms, only the forms change according to the times.

It is a curious phenomenon that there never was a religion started in this world with more antagonism ... [to the worship of forms] than Mohammedanism ... The Mohammedans can have neither painting, nor sculpture, nor music ... That would lead to formalism. The priest never faces his audience. If he did, that would make a distinction. This way there is none. And yet it was not two centuries after the Prophet's death before saint worship [developed]. Here is the toe of the saint! There is the skin of the saint! So it goes. Formal worship is one of the stages we have to pass through.

Therefore, instead of crusading against it, let us take the best in worship and study its underlying principles.

Of course, the lowest form of worship is what is known as [tree and stone worship]. Every crude, uncultured man will take up anything and add to it some idea [of his own]; and that will help him. He may worship a bit of bone, or stone—anything. In all these crude states of worship man has never worshipped a stone as stone, a tree as tree. You know that from common sense. Scholars sometimes say that men worshipped stones and trees. That is all nonsense. Tree worship is one of the stages through which the human race passed. Never, really, was there ever worship of anything but the spirit by man.

He is spirit [and] can feel nothing but spirit. Divine mind could never make such a gross mistake as [to worship spirit as matter]. In this case, man conceived the stone as spirit or the tree as spirit. He [imagined] that some part of that Being resides in [the stone] or the tree, that [the stone or] the tree has a soul.

Tree worship and serpent worship always go together. There is the tree of knowledge. There must always be the tree, and the tree is somehow connected with the serpent. These are the oldest [forms of worship]. Even there you find that some particular tree or some particular stone is worshipped, not all the [trees or] stones in the world.

A higher state in [formal worship is that of] images [of ancestors and God]. People make images of men who have died and imaginary images of God. Then they worship those images.

Still higher is the worship of saints, of good men and women who have passed on. Men worship their relics. [They feel that] the presence of the saints is somehow in the relics, and that they will help them. [They believe that] if they touch the saint's bone, they will be healed—not that the bone itself heals, but that the saint who resides there does…

These are all low states of worship and yet worship. We all have to pass through them. It is only from an intellectual standpoint that they are not good enough. In our hearts we cannot get rid of them. [If] you take from a man all the saints and images and do not allow him to go into a temple, [he will still] imagine all the gods. He has to. A man of eighty told me he could not conceive God except as an old man with a long beard sitting on a cloud. What does that show? His education is not complete. There has not been any spiritual education, and he is unable to conceive anything except in human terms.

There is still a higher order of formal worship—the world of symbolism. The forms are still there, but they are neither trees, nor [stones], nor images, nor relics of saints. They are symbols. There are all sorts [of symbols] all over the world. The circle is a great symbol of eternity… There is the square; the well-known symbol of the cross; and two figures like S and Z crossing each other.

Some people take it into their heads to see nothing in symbols… [Others want] all sorts of abracadabra. If you tell them plain, simple truths, they will not accept them… Human nature being [what it is], the less they understand the better—the greater man [they think] you are. In all ages in every country such worshippers are deluded by certain diagrams and forms. Geometry was the greatest science of all. The vast majority of the people knew nothing [of it. They believed that if] the geometrist just drew a square and said abracadabra at the four corners, the whole world would begin to turn, the heavens would open, and God would come down and jump about and be a slave. There is a whole mass of lunatics today poring over these things day and night. All this is a sort of disease. It is not for the metaphysician at all; it is for the physician.

I am making fun, but I am so sorry. I see this problem so [grave] in India These are signs of the decay of the race, of degradation and duress. The sign of vigour, the sign of life, the sign of hope, the sign of health, the sign of everything that is good, is strength. As long as the body lives, there must be strength in the body, strength in the mind, [and strength] in the hand. In wanting to get spiritual power through [all this abracadabra] there is fear, fear of life. I do not mean that sort of symbolism.

But there is some truth in symbolistic. There cannot be any falsehood without some truth behind it. There cannot be any imitation without something real.

There is the symbolic form, of worship in the different religions. There are fresh, vigorous, poetic, healthy symbols Think of the marvellous power the symbol of the cross has had upon millions of people! Think of the symbol of the crescent! Think of the magnetism of this one symbol! Everywhere there are good and great symbols in the world. They interpret the spirit and bring [about] certain conditions of the mind; as a rule we find [they create] a tremendous power of faith and love.

Compare the Protestant with the Catholic [Church]. Who has produced more saints, more martyrs within the last four hundred years [during which] both have been in existence? The tremendous appeal of Catholic ceremonialism— all those lights, incense, candles, and the robes of the priests— has a great effect in itself. Protestantism is quite austere and unpoetic. The Protestants have gained many things, have granted a great deal more freedom in certain lines than the Catholics have, and so have a clear, more individualized conception. That is all right, but they have lost a good deal… Take the paintings in the churches. That is an attempt at poetry. If we are hungry for poetry, why not have it? Why not give the soul what it wants? We have to have music. The Presbyterians were even against music. They are the "Mohammedans" of the Christians. Down with all poetry! Down with all ceremonials! Then they produce music. It appeals to the senses. I have seen how collectively they strive for the ray of light there over the pulpit.

Let the soul have its fill of poetry and religion represented on the external plane. Why not…? You cannot fight [formal worship]. It will conquer again and again… If you do not like what the Catholics do, do better. But we will neither do anything better nor have the poetry that already exists. That is a terrible state of things! Poetry is absolutely necessary. You may be the greatest philosopher in the world. But philosophy is the highest poetry. It is not dry bones It is essence of things. The Reality itself is more poetic than any dualism…

Learning has no place in religion; for the majority learning is a block in the way...A man my have read all the libraries in the world and many not be religious at all, and another, who cannot perhaps write his own name, senses religion and realises it. The whole of religion is our own inner perception. When I use the words "man-making religion", I do not mean books, nor dogmas, nor theories. I mean the man who has realised, has fully perceived, something of that infinite presence in his own heart.

The man at whose feet I sat all my life—and it is only a few ideas of his that try to teach—could [hardly] write his name at all. All my life I have not seen another man like that, and I have travelled all over the world. When I think of that man, I feel like a fool, because I want to read books and he never did. He never wanted to lick the plates after other people had eaten. That is why he was his own book. All my life I am repeating what Jack said and John said, and never say anything myself. What glory is it that you know what John said twenty-five years ago and what Jack said five years ago? Tell me what you have to say.

Mind you, there is no value in learning. You are all mistaken in learning. The only value of knowledge is in the strengthening, the disciplining, of the mind. By all this eternal swallowing it is a wonder that we are not all dyspeptics. Let us stop, and burn all the books, and get hold of ourselves and think. You all talk [about] and get distracted over losing your "individuality". You are losing it every moment of your lives by this eternal swallowing. If any one of you believes what I teach, I will be sorry. I will only be too glad if I can excite in you the power of thinking for yourselves...My ambition is to talk to men and women, not to sheep. By men and women, I mean individuals. You are not little babies to drag all the filthy rags from the street and bind them up into a doll!

"This is a place for learning! That man is placed in the university! He knows all about what Mr. Blank said!" But Mr. Blank said nothing! If I had the choice I would...say to the professor, "Get out! You are nobody!" Remember this individualism at any cost! Think wrong if you will, no matter whether you get truth or not. The whole point is to discipline the mind. That truth which you swallow from others will not be yours. You cannot teach truth from my mouth; neither can you learn truth from my mouth. None can teach another. You have to realise truth and work it out for yourself according to your own nature...All must struggle to be individuals— strong, standing on your own feet, thinking your own thoughts, realising your own Self. No use swallowing doctrines others pass on—standing up together like soldiers in jail, sitting down together, all eating the same food, all nodding their heads at the same time. Variation is the sign of life. Sameness is the sign of death.

Once I was in an Indian city, and an old man came to me. He said, "Swami, teach me the way." I saw that that man was as dead as this table before me. Mentally and spiritually he was really dead. I said, "will you do what I ask you to do? Can you steal? Can you drink wine? Can you eat meat?"

The man [exclaimed], "What are you teaching!"

I said to him, "Did this wall ever steal? Did the wall ever drink wine?"

"No, sir."

Man steals, and he drinks wine, and becomes God. "I know you are not the wall, my friend. Do something! Do something!" I saw that if that man stole, his soul would be on the way to salvation.

How do I know that you are individuals—all saying the same thing, all standing up and sitting down together? That is the road to death! Do something for your souls! Do wrong if you please, but do something! You will understand me by and by, if you do not just now. Old age has come upon the soul, as it were. It has become rusty. The rust must be [rubbed off], and then we go on. Now you understand why there is evil in the world. Go home and think of that, just to take off that rustiness!

We pray for material things. To attain some end we worship God with shopkeeping worship. Go on and pray for food and clothes! Worship is good. Something is always better than nothing. "A blind uncle is better than no uncle at all." A very rich young man becomes ill, and then to get rid of his disease he begins to give to the poor. That is good, but it is not religion yet, not spiritual religion. It is all on the material plane. What is material, and what is not? When the world is the end and God the means to attain that end, that is material. When God is the end and the world is only the means to attain that end, spirituality has begun.

Thus, to the man who wants this [material] life enough, all his heavens are a continuance of this life. He wants to see all the people who are dead, and have a good time once more.

There was one of those ladies who bring the departed spirits down to us—a medium. She was very large, yet she was called medium. Very good! This lady liked me very much and invited me to come. The spirits were all very polite to me. I had a very peculiar experience. You understand, it was a [seance], midnight. The medium said, "...I see a ghost standing here. The ghost tells me that there is a Hindu gentleman on that bench." I stood up and said, "It required no ghost to tell you that."

There was a young man present who was married, intelligent, and well educated. He was there to see his mother. The medium said, "So-and-so's mother is here." This young man had been telling me about his mother. She was very thin when she died, but the mother that came out of the screen! You ought to have seen her! I wanted to see what this young man would do. To my surprise he jumped up and embraced this spirit and said. "Oh mother, how beautiful you have grown in the spirit land!" I said, "I am blessed that I am here. It gives me an insight into human nature!"

Going back to our formal worship...it is a low state of worship when you worship God as a means to the end, which is this life and this world... The vast majority of [people] have never had any conception of anything higher than this lump of flesh and the joys of the senses. Even in this life, all the pleasures these poor souls have are the same as the beasts... They eat animals. They love their children. Is that all the glory of man? And we worship God Almighty! What for? Just to give us these material things and defend them all the time... It means we have not gone beyond the [animals and] birds. We are no better. We do not know any better. And woe unto us, we should know better! The only difference is that they do not have a God like ours... We have the same five senses [as the animals], only theirs are better. We cannot eat a morsel of food with the relish that a dog chews a bone. They have more pleasure in life than we; so we are a little less than animals.

Why should you want to be something that any power in nature can operate better? This is the most important question for you to think about. What do you want—this life, these senses, this body, or something infinitely higher and better, something from which there is no more fall, no more change?

So what does it mean...? You say, "Lord, give me my bread, my money! Heal my diseases! Do this and that!" Every time you say that, you are hypnotising yourselves with the idea, "I am matter, and this matter is the goal." Every time you try to fulfil a material desire, you tell yourselves that you are [the] body, that you are not spirit...

Thank God, this is a dream! Thank God, for it will vanish! Thank God, there is death, glorious death, because it ends all this delusion, this dream, this fleshiness, this anguish. No dream can be eternal; it must end sooner or later. There is none who can keep his dream for ever. I thank God that it is so! Yet this form of worship is all right. Go on! To pray for something is better than nothing. These are the stages through which we pass. These are the first lessons. Gradually, the mind begins to think of something higher than the senses, the body, the enjoyments of this world.

How does [man] do it? First he becomes a thinker. When you think upon a problem, there is no sense enjoyment there, but [the] exquisite delight of thought... It is that that makes the man... Take one great idea! It deepens. Concentration comes. You no longer feel your body. Your senses have stopped. You are above all physical senses. All that was manifesting itself through the senses is concentrated upon that one idea. That moment you are higher than the animal. You get the revelation none can take from you—a direct perception of something higher than the body... Therein is the gold of mind, not upon the plane of the senses.

Thus, working through the plane of the senses, you get more and more entry into the other regions, and then this world falls away from you. You get one glimpse of that spirit, and then your senses and your sense-enjoyments, your clinging to the flesh, will all melt away from you. Glimpse after glimpse will come from the realm of spirit. You will have finished

Yoga, and spirit will stand revealed as spirit. Then you will begin the worship of God as spirit. Then you will begin to understand that worship is not to gain something. At heart, our worship was that infinite-finite element, love, which [is] an eternal sacrifice at the feet of the Lord by the soul. "Thou and not I. I am dead. Thou art, and I am not. I do not want wealth nor beauty, no, nor even learning. I do not want salvation. If it be Thy will, let me go into twenty million hells. I only want one thing: Be Thou my love!"

Vedanta and the West, Nov.-Dec. 1955.

DIVINE LOVE

This lecture is reproduced from the Vedanta and the West. *See. Delivered in San Francisco area, April 12, 1900*

[Love may be symbolised by a triangle. The first angle is,] love questions not. It is not a beggar... Beggar's love is no love at all. The first sign of love is when love asks nothing, [when it] gives everything. This is the real spiritual worship, the worship through love. Whether God is merciful is no longer questioned. He is God; He is my love. Whether God is omnipotent and almighty, limited or unlimited, is no longer questioned. If He distributes good, all right; if He brings evil, what does it matter? All other attributes vanish except that one—infinite love.

There was an old Indian emperor who on a hunting expedition came across a great sage in the forest. He was so pleased with this sage that he insisted that the latter come to the capital to receive some presents. [At first] the sage refused. [But] the emperor insisted, and at last the sage consented. When he arrived [at the palace], he was announced to the emperor who said, "Wait a minute until I finish my prayer." The emperor prayed, "Lord, give me more wealth, more [land, more health], more children." The sage stood up and began to walk out of the room. The emperor said, "You have not received my presents." The sage replied, "I do not beg from beggars. All this time you have been praying for more land, [for] more money, for this and that. What can you give me? First satisfy your own wants!"

Love never asks; it always gives... When a young man goes to see his sweetheart, ... there is no business relationship between them; theirs is a relationship of love, and love is no beggar. [In the same way], we understand that the beginning of real spiritual worship means no begging. We have finished all begging: "Lord, give me this and that." Then will religion begin.

The second [angle of the triangle of love] is that love knows no fear. You may cut me to pieces, and I [will] still love you. Suppose one of you mothers, a weak woman, sees a tiger in the street snatching your child. I know where you will be: you will face the tiger. Another time a dog appears in the street, and you will fly. But you jump at the mouth of the tiger and snatch your child away. Love knows no fear. It conquers all evil. The fear of God is the beginning of religion, but the love of God is the end of religion. All fear has died out.

The third [angle of the love-triangle is that] love is its own end. It can never be the means. The man who says, "I love you for such and such a thing", does not love. Love can never be the means; it must be the perfect end. What is the end and aim of love? To love God, that is all. Why should one love God? [There is] no why, because it is not the means. When one can love, that is salvation, that is perfection, that is heaven. What more? What else can be the end? What can you have higher than love?

I am not talking about what every one of us means by love. Little namby-pamby love is lovely. Man rails in love with woman, and woman goes to die for man. The chances are that in five minutes John kicks Jane, and Jane kicks John. This is a materialism and no love at all. If John could really love Jane, he would be perfect that moment. [His true] nature is love; he is perfect in himself. John will get all the powers of Yoga simply by loving Jane, [although] he may not know a word about religion, psychology, or theology. I believe that if a man and woman can really love, [they can acquire] all the powers the Yogis claim to have, for love itself is God. That God is omnipresent, and [therefore] you have that love, whether you know it or not.

I saw a boy waiting for a girl the other evening... I thought it a good experiment to study this boy. He developed clairvoyance and clairaudience through the intensity of his love. Sixty or seventy times he never made a mistake, and the girl was two hundred miles away. [He would say], "She is dressed this way." [Or], "There she goes." I have seen that with my own eyes.

This is the question: Is not your husband God, your child God? If you can love your wife, you have all the religion in the world. You have the whole secret of religion and Yoga in you. But can you love? That is the question. You say, "I love... Oh Mary, I die for you!" [But if you] see Mary kissing another man, you want to cut his throat. If Mary sees John talking to another girl, she cannot sleep at night, and she makes life hell for John. This is not love. This is barter and sale in sex. It is blasphemy to talk of it as love. The world talks day and night of God and religion—so of love. Making a sham of everything, that is what you are doing! Everybody talks of love, [yet in the] columns in the newspapers [we read] of divorces every day. When you love John, do you love John for his sake or for your sake? [If you love him for your sake], you expect something from John. [If you love him for his sake], you do not want anything from John. He can do anything he likes, [and] you [will] love him just the same.

These are the three points, the three angles that constitute the triangle [of love]. Unless there is love, philosophy becomes dry bones, psychology becomes a sort of [theory], and work becomes mere labour. [If there is love], philosophy becomes poetry, psychology becomes [mysticism], and work the most delicious thing in creation. [By merely] reading books [one]

becomes barren. Who becomes learned? He who can feel even one drop of love. God is love, and love is God. And God is everywhere. After seeing that God is love and God is everywhere, one does not know whether one stands on one's head or [on one's] feet—like a man who gets a bottle of wine and does not know where he stands... If we weep ten minutes for God, we will not know where we are for the next two months... We will not remember the times for meals. We will not know what we are eating. [How can] you love God and always be so nice and businesslike? ... The ... all-conquering, omnipotent power of love—how can it come? ...

Judge people not. They are all mad. Children are [mad] after their games, the young after the young, the old [are] chewing the cud of their past years; some are mad after gold. Why not some after God? Go crazy over the love of God as you go crazy over Johns and Janes. Who are they? [people] say, "Shall I give up this? Shall I give up that?" One asked, "Shall I give up marriage?" Do not give up anything! Things will give you up. Wait, and you will forget them.

[To be completely] turned into love of God—there is the real worship! You have a glimpse of that now and then in the Roman Catholic Church—some of those wonderful monks and nuns going mad with marvellous love. Such love you ought to have! Such should be the love of God—without asking anything, without seeking anything...

The question was asked: How to worship? Worship Him as dearer than all your possessions, dearer than all your relatives, [dearer than] your children. [Worship Him as] the one you love as Love itself. There is one whose name is infinite Love. That is the only definition of God. Do not care if this... universe is destroyed. What do we care as long as He is infinite love? [Do you see what worship means? All other thoughts must go. Everything must vanish except God. The love the father or mother has for the child, [the love] the wife [has] for the husband, the husband, for the wife, the friend for the friend—all these loves concentrated into one must be given to God. Now, if the woman loves the man, she cannot love another man. If the man loves the woman, he cannot love another [woman]. Such is the nature of love.

My old Master used to say, "Suppose there is a bag of gold in this room, and in the next room there is a robber. The robber is well aware that there is a bag of gold. Would the robber be able to sleep? Certainly not. All the time he would be crazy thinking how to reach the gold." ... [Similarly], if a man loves God, how can he love anything else? How can anything else stand before that mighty love of God? Everything else vanishes [before it]. How can the mind stop without going crazy to find [that love], to realise, to feel, to live in that?

This is how we are to love God: "I do not want wealth, nor [friends, nor beauty], nor possessions, nor learning, nor even salvation. If it be Thy will, send me a thousand deaths. Grant me, this—that I may love Thee and that for love's sake. That love which materialistic persons have for their worldly possessions, may that strong love come into my heart, but only for the Beautiful. Praise to God! Praise to God the Lover!" God is nothing else than that. He does not care for the wonderful things many Yogis can do. Little magicians do little tricks. God is the big magician; He does all the tricks. Who cares how many worlds [there are]? ...

There is another [way. It is to] conquer everything, [to] subdue everything —to conquer the body [and] the mind ... "What is the use of conquering everything? My business is with God!" [says the devotee.]

There was one Yogi, a great lover. He was dying of cancer of the throat. He [was] visited [by] another Yogi, who was a philosopher. [The latter] said, "Look here, my friend, why don't you concentrate your mind on that sore of yours and get it cured?" The third time this question was asked [this great Yogi] said, "Do you think it possible that the [mind] which I have given entirely to the Lord [can be fixed upon this cage of flesh and blood]?" Christ refused to bring legions of angels to his aid. Is this little body so great that I should bring twenty thousand angels to keep it two or three days more?

[From the worldly standpoint,] my all is this body. My world is this body. My God is this body. I am the body. If you pinch me, I am pinched. I forget God the moment I have a head-ache. I am the body! God and everything must come down for this highest goal—the body. From this standpoint, when Christ died on the cross and did not bring angels [to his aid], he was a fool. He ought to have brought down angels and gotten himself off the cross! But from the standpoint of the lover, to whom this body is nothing, who cares for this non-sense? Why bother thinking about this body that comes and goes? There is no more to it than the piece of cloth the Roman soldiers cast lots for.

There is a whole gamut of difference between [the worldly standpoint] and the lover's standpoint. Go on loving. If a man is angry, there is no reason why you should be angry; if he degrades himself, that is no reason why you should degrade yourself ... "Why should I become angry just because another man has made a fool of himself. Do thou resist not evil!" That is what the lovers of God say. Whatever the world does, wher-ever it goes, has no influence [on them].

One Yogi had attained supernatural powers. He said, "See my power! See the sky; I will cover it with clouds." It began to rain. [Someone] said, "My lord, you are wonderful. But teach me that, knowing which, I shall not ask for anything else." ... To get rid even of power, to have nothing, not to want power! [What this means] cannot be understood simply by intellect ... You cannot understand by reading thousands of books ... When we begin to understand, the whole world opens before us ... The girl is playing with her dolls, getting new husbands all the time; but when her real husband comes, all the dolls will be put away [for ever] ... So [with] all these goings-on here. [When] the sun of love rises, all these play-suns of power and these [cravings] all pass [away]. What shall

we do with power? Thank God if you can get rid of the power that you have. Begin to love. Power must go. Nothing must stand between me and God except love. God is only love and nothing else—love first, love in the middle, and love at the end.

[There is the] story of a queen preaching [the love of God] in the streets. Her enraged husband persecuted her, and she was hunted up and down the country. She used to sing songs describing her [love]. Her songs have been sung everywhere. "With tears in my eyes I [nourished the everlasting creeper] of love ..." This is the last, the great [goal]. What else is there? [People] want this and that. They all want to have and possess. That is why so few understand [love], so few come to it. Wake them and tell them! They will get a few more hints.

Love itself is the eternal, endless sacrifice. You will have to give up everything. You cannot take possession of anything. Finding love, you will never [want] anything [else] ... "Only be Thou my love for ever!" That is what love wants. "My love, one kiss of those lips! [For him] who has been kissed by Thee, all sorrows vanish. Once kissed by Thee, man becomes happy and forgets love of everything else. He praises Thee alone and he sees Thee alone." In the nature of human love even, [there lurk divine elements. In] the first moment of intense love the whole world seems in tune with your own heart. Every bird in the universe sings your love; the flowers bloom for you. It is infinite, eternal love itself that [human] love comes from.

Why should the lover of God fear anything—fear robbers, fear distress, fear even for his life? ... The lover [may]go to the utmost hell, but would it be hell? We all have to give up these ideas of heaven [and hell] and get greater [love] ... Hundreds there are seeking this madness of love before which everything [but God vanishes].

At last, love, lover, and beloved become one. That is the goal ... Why is there any separation between soul and man, between soul and God? ... Just to have this enjoyment of love. He wanted to love Himself, so He split Himself into many ... "This is the whole reason for creation", says the lover. "We are all one. 'I and my Father are one.' Just now I am separate in order to love God ... Which is better—to become sugar or to eat sugar? To become sugar, what fun is that:? To eat sugar—that is infinite enjoyment of love."

All the ideals of love—[God] as [our] father, mother, friend, child—[are conceived in order to strengthen devotion in us and make us feel nearer and dearer to God]. The intensest love is that between the sexes. God must be loved with that sort of love The woman loves her father; she loves her mothers she loves her child; she loves her friend. But she cannot express herself all to the father, nor to the mother, nor to the child, nor to the friend. There is only one person from whom she does not hide anything. So with the man ... The [husband-] wife relationship is the all-rounded relationship. The relation-ship of the sexes [has] all the other loves concentrated into one. In the husband, the woman has the father, the friend, the child. In the wife, the husband has mother, daughter, and something else. That tremendous complete love of the sexes must come [for God]—that same love with which a woman opens herself to a man without any bond of blood—perfectly, fearlessly, and shamelessly. No darkness! She would no more hide anything from her lover than she would from her own self. That very love must come [for God]. These things are hard and difficult to understand. You will begin to understand by and by, and all idea of sex will fall away. "Like the water drop on the sand of the river bank on a summer day, even so is this life and all its relations."

All these ideas [like] "He is the creator", are ideas fit for children. He is my love, my life itself—that must be the cry of my heart! ...

"I have one hope. They call Thee the Lord of the world, and—good or evil, great or small—I am part of the world, and Thou art also my love. My body, my mind, and my soul are all at Thy altar. Love, refuse these gifts not!"

Vedanta and the West, Sept.-Oct. 1955.

WOMEN OF INDIA

Delivered at the Shakespeare Club House, in Pasadena, California, on January 18, 1900.

Swami Vivekananda: "Some persons desire to ask questions about Hindu Philosophy before the lecture and to question in general about India after the lecture; but the chief difficulty is I do not know what I am to lecture on. I would be very glad to lecture on any subject, either on Hindu Philosophy or on anything concerning the race, its history, or its literature. If you, ladies and gentlemen, will suggest anything, I would be very glad."

Questioner: "I would like to ask, Swami, what special principle in Hindu Philosophy you would have us Americans, who are a very practical people, adopt, and what that would do for us beyond what Christianity can do."

Swami Vivekananda: "That is very difficult for me to decide; it rests upon you. If you find anything which you think you ought to adopt, and which will be helpful, you should take that. You see I am not a missionary, and I am not going about converting people to my idea. My principle is that all such ideas are good and great, so that some of your ideas may suit some people in India, and some of our ideas may suit some people here; so ideas must be cast abroad, all over the world."

Questioner: "We would like to know the result of your philosophy; has your philosophy and religion lifted your women above our women?"

Swami Vivekananda: "You see, that is a very invidious question: I like our women and your women too."

Questioner: "Well, will you tell us about your women, their customs and education, and the position they hold in the family?"

Swami Vivekananda: "Oh, yes, those things I would be very glad to tell you. So you want to know about Indian women tonight, and not philosophy and other things?"

The Lecture

I must begin by saying that you may have to bear with me a good deal, because I belong to an Order of people who never marry; so my knowledge of women in all their relations, as mother, as wife, as daughter and sister, must necessarily not be so complete as it may be with other men. And then, India, I must remember, is a vast continent, not merely a country, and is inhabited by many different races. The nations of Europe are nearer to each other, more similar to each other, than the races in India. You may get just a rough idea of it if I tell you that there are eight different languages in all India. Different languages—not dialects—each having a literature of its own. The Hindi language, alone, is spoken by 100,000,000 people; the Bengali by about 60,000,000, and so on. Then, again, the four northern Indian languages differ more from the southern Indian languages than any two European languages from each other. They are entirely different, as much different as your language differs from the Japanese, so that you will be astonished to know, when I go to southern India, unless I meet some people who can talk Sanskrit, I have to speak to them in English. Furthermore, these various races differ from each other in manners, customs, food, dress, and in their methods of thought.

Then, again, there is caste. Each caste has become, as it were, a separate racial element. If a man lives long enough in India, he will be able to tell from the features what caste a man belongs to. Then, between castes, the manners and customs are different. And all these castes are exclusive; that is to say, they would meet socially, but they would not eat or drink together, nor intermarry. In those things they remain separate. They would meet and be friends to each other, but there it would end.

Although I have more opportunity than many other men to know women in general, from my position and my occupation as a preacher, continuously travelling from one place to another and coming in contact with all grades of society —(and women, even in northern India, where they do not appear before men, in many places would break this law for religion and would come to hear us preach and talk to us)— still it would be hazardous on my part to assert that I know everything about the women of India.

So I will try to place before you the ideal. In each nation, man or woman represents an ideal consciously or unconsciously being worked out. The individual is the external expression of an ideal to be embodied. The collection of such individuals is the nation, which also represents a great ideal; towards that it is moving. And, therefore, it is rightly assumed that to understand a nation you must first understand its ideal, for each nation refuses to be judged by any other standard than its own.

All growth, progress, well-being, or degradation is but relative. It refers to a certain standard, and each man to be understood has to be referred to that standard of his perfection. You see this more markedly in nations: what one nation thinks good might not be so regarded by another nation. Cousin-marriage is quite permissible in this country. Now, in India, it is illegal; not only so, it would be classed with the most horrible incest. Widow-marriage is perfectly legitimate in this country. Among the higher castes in India it would be the greatest degradation for a woman to marry twice. So, you see, we work through such different ideas that to judge one people by the other's standard would be neither just nor practicable. Therefore we must know what the ideal is that a nation has raised before itself. When speaking of different nations, we start with a general idea that there is one code of ethics and the same kind of ideals for all races; practically, however, when we come to judge of others, we think what is good for us must be good for everybody; what we do is the right thing, what we do not do, of course in others would be outrageous. I do not mean to say this as a criticism, but just to bring the truth home. When I hear Western women denounce the confining of the feet of Chinese ladies, they never seem to think of the corsets which are doing far more injury to the race. This is just one example; for you must know that cramping the feet does not do one-millionth part of the injury to the human form that the corset has done and is doing—when every organ is displaced and the spine is curved like a serpent. When measurements are taken, you can note the curvatures. I do not mean that as a criticism but just to point out to you the situation, that as you stand aghast at women of other races, thinking that you are supreme, the very reason that they do not adopt your manners and customs shows that they also stand aghast at you.

Therefore there is some misunderstanding on both sides. There is a common platform, a common ground of understanding, a common humanity, which must be the basis of our work. We ought to find out that complete and perfect human nature which is working only in parts, here and there. It has not been given to one man to have everything in perfection. You have a part to play; I, in my humble way, another; here is one who plays a little part; there, another. The perfection is the combination of all these parts. Just as with individuals, so with races. Each race has a part to play; each race has one side of human nature to develop. And we have to take all these together; and, possibly in the distant future, some race will arise in which all these marvellous individual race perfections, attained by the different races, will come together and form a new race, the like of which the world has not yet dreamed. Beyond saying that, I have no criticism to offer about anybody. I have travelled not a little in my life; I have kept my eyes open; and the more I go about the more my mouth is closed. I have no criticism to offer.

Now, the ideal woman in India is the mother, the mother first, and the mother last. The word woman calls up to the mind of the Hindu, motherhood; and God is called Mother.

As children, every day, when we are boys, we have to go early in the morning with a little cup of water and place it before the mother, and mother dips her toe into it and we drink it.

In the West, the woman is wife. The idea of womanhood is concentrated there—as the wife. To the ordinary man in India, the whole force of womanhood is concentrated in motherhood. In the Western home, the wife rules. In an Indian home, the mother rules. If a mother comes into a Western home, she has to be subordinate to the wife; to the wife belongs the home. A mother always lives in our homes: the wife must be subordinate to her. See all the difference of ideas.

Now, I only suggest comparisons; I would state facts so that we may compare the two sides. Make this comparison. If you ask, "What is an Indian woman as wife?", the Indian asks, "Where is the American woman as mother? What is she, the all-glorious, who gave me this body? What is she who kept me in her body for nine months? Where is she who would give me twenty times her life, if I had need? Where is she whose love never dies, however wicked, however vile I am? Where is she, in comparison with her, who goes to the divorce court the moment I treat her a little badly? O American woman! where is she?" I will not find her in your country. I have not found the son who thinks mother is first. When we die, even then, we do not want our wives and our children to take her place. Our mother!— we want to die with our head on her lap once more, if we die before her. Where is she? Is woman a name to be coupled with the physical body only? Ay! the Hindu mind fears all those ideals which say that the flesh must cling unto the flesh. No, no! Woman! thou shalt not be coupled with anything connected with the flesh. The name has been called holy once and for ever, for what name is there which no lust can ever approach, no carnality ever come near, than the one word mother? That is the ideal in India.

I belong to an Order very much like what you have in the Mendicant Friars of the Catholic Church; that is to say, we have to go about without very much in the way of dress and beg from door to door, live thereby, preach to people when they want it, sleep where we can get a place—that way we have to follow. And the rule is that the members of this Order have to call every woman "mother"; to every woman and little girl we have to say "mother"; that is the custom. Coming to the West, that old habit remained and I would say to ladies, "Yes, mother", and they are horrified. I could not understand why they should be horrified. Later on, I discovered the reason: because that would mean that they are old. The ideal of womanhood in India is motherhood—that marvellous, unselfish, all-suffering, ever-forgiving mother. The wife walks behind—the shadow. She must imitate the life of the mother; that is her duty. But the mother is the ideal of love; she rules the family, she possesses the family. It is the father in India who thrashes the child and spanks when there is something done by the child, and always the mother puts herself between the father and the child. You see it is just the opposite here. It has become the mother's business to spank the children in this country, and poor father comes in between. You see, ideals are different. I do not mean this as any criticism. It is all good—this what you do; but our way is what we have been taught for ages. You never hear of a mother cursing the child; she is forgiving, always forgiving. Instead of "Our Father in Heaven", we say "Mother" all the time; that idea and that word are ever associated in the Hindu mind with Infinite Love, the mother's love being the nearest approach to God's love in this mortal world of ours. "Mother, O Mother, be merciful; I am wicked! Many children have been wicked, but there never was a wicked mother"—so says the great saint Ramprasad.

There she is—the Hindu mother. The son's wife comes in as her daughter; just as the mother's own daughter married and went out, so her son married and brought in another daughter, and she has to fall in line under the government of the queen of queens, of his mother. Even I, who never married, belonging to an Order that never marries, would be disgusted if my wife, supposing I had married, dared to displease my mother. I would be disgusted. Why? Do I not worship my mother? Why should not her daughter-in-law? Whom I worship, why not she? Who is she, then, that would try to ride over my head and govern my mother? She has to wait till her womanhood is fulfilled; and the one thing that fulfils womanhood, that is womanliness in woman, is motherhood. Wait till she becomes a mother; then she will have the same right. That, according to the Hindu mind, is the great mission of woman—to become a mother. But oh, how different! Oh, how different! My father and mother fasted and prayed, for years and years, so that I would be born. They pray for every child before it is born. Says our great law-giver, Manu, giving the definition of an Aryan, "He is the Aryan, who is born through prayer". Every child not born through prayer is illegitimate, according to the great law-giver. The child must be prayed for. Those children that come with curses, that slip into the world, just in a moment of inadvertence, because that could not be prevented—what can we expect of such progeny? Mothers of America, think of that! Think in the heart of your hearts, are you ready to be women? Not any question of race or country, or that false sentiment of national pride. Who dares to be proud in this mortal life of ours, in this world of woes and miseries? What are we before this infinite force of God? But I ask you the question tonight: Do you all pray for the children to come? Are you thankful to be mothers, or not? Do you think that you are sanctified by motherhood, or not? Ask that of your minds. If you do not, your marriage is a lie, your womanhood is false, your education is superstition, and your children, if they come without prayer, will prove a curse to humanity.

See the different ideals now coming before us. From motherhood comes tremendous responsibility. There is the basis, start from that. Well, why is mother to be worshipped so much? Because our books teach that it is the pre-natal influence that gives the impetus to the child for good or evil. Go to a hun-dred thousand colleges, read a million books, associate with all the learned men of the world—better off you are when born with the right stamp. You are born for good or evil. The child is a born god or a born demon; that is what the books say. Education and all these things come afterwards—are a mere bagatelle. You are what you are born. Born unhealth-ful, how many drug stores, swallowed wholesale, will keep you well all through your life? How many people of good, healthy lives were born of weak parents, were born of sick-ly, blood-poisoned parents? How many? None—none. We come with a tremendous impetus for good or evil: born de-mons or born gods. Education or other things are a bagatelle.

Thus say our books: direct the pre-natal influence. Why should mother be worshipped? Because she made herself pure. She underwent harsh penances sometimes to keep herself as pure as purity can be. For, mind you, no woman in India thinks of giving up her body to any man; it is her own. The English, as a reform, have introduced at present what they call "Restitution of conjugal rights", but no Indian would take advantage of it. When a man comes in physical contact with his wife, the circumstances she controls through what prayers and through what vows! For that which brings forth the child is the holiest symbol of God himself. It is the greatest prayer between man and wife, the prayer that is going to bring into the world another soul fraught with a tremendous power for good or for evil. Is it a joke? Is it a simple nervous satisfaction? Is it a brute enjoyment of the body? Says the Hindu: no, a thousand times, no!

But then, following that, there comes in another idea. The idea we started with was that the ideal is the love for the mother—herself all-suffering, all-forbearing. The worship that is accorded to the mother has its fountain-head there. She was a saint to bring me into the world; she kept her body pure, her mind pure, her food pure, her clothes pure, her im-agination pure, for years, because I would be born. Because she did that, she deserves worship. And what follows? Linked with motherhood is wifehood.

You Western people are individualistic. I want to do this thing because I like it; I will elbow every one. Why? Because I like to. I want my own satisfaction, so I marry this woman. Why? Because I like her. This woman marries me. Why? Be-cause she likes me. There it ends. She and I are the only two persons in the whole, infinite world; and I marry her and she marries me—nobody else is injured, nobody else responsible.

Your Johns and your Janes may go into the forest and there they may live their lives; but when they have to live in society, their marriage means a tremendous amount of good or evil to us. Their children may be veritable demons—burning, mur-dering, robbing, stealing, drinking, hideous, vile.

So what is the basis of the Indian's social order? It is the caste law. I am born for the caste, I live for the caste. I do not mean myself, because, having joined an Order, we are outside. I mean those that live in civil society. Born in the caste, the whole life must be lived according to caste regulation. In other words, in the present-day language of your country, the Western man is born individualistic, while the Hindu is socialistic—entirely socialistic. Now, then, the books say: if I allow you freedom to go about and marry any woman you like, and the woman to marry any man she likes, what happens? You fall in love; the father of the woman was, perchance, a lunatic or a consumptive. The girl falls in love with the face of a man whose father was a roaring drunkard. What says the law then? The law lays down that all these marriages would be illegal. The children of drunkards, consumptives, lunatics, etc., shall not be married. The deformed, humpbacked, crazy, idiotic—no marriage for them, absolutely none, says the law.

But the Mohammedan comes from Arabia, and he has his own Arabian law; so the Arabian desert law has been forced upon us. The Englishman comes with his law; he forces it upon us, so far as he can. We are conquered. He says, "Tomorrow I will marry your sister". What can we do? Our law says, those that are born of the same family, though a hundred degrees distant, must not marry, that is illegitimate, it would deteriorate or make the race sterile. That must not be, and there it stops. So I have no voice in my marriage, nor my sister. It is the caste that determines all that.

We are married sometimes when children. Why? Because the caste says: if they have to be married anyway without their consent, it is better that they are married very early, before they have developed this love: if they are allowed to grow up apart, the boy may like some other girl, and the girl some other boy, and then something evil will happen; and so, says the caste, stop it there. I do not care whether my sister is deformed, or good-looking, or bad-looking: she is my sister, and that is enough; he is my brother, and that is all I need to know. So they will love each other. You may say, "Oh! they lose a great deal of enjoyment—those exquisite emotions of a man falling in love with a woman and a woman falling in love with a man. This is a sort of tame thing, loving each other like brothers and sisters, as though they have to." So be it; but the Hindu says, "We are socialistic. For the sake of one man's or woman's exquisite pleasure we do not want to load misery on hundreds of others."

There they are—married. The wife comes home with her husband; that is called the second marriage. Marriage at an early age is considered the first marriage, and they grow up separately with women and with their parents. When they are grown, there is a second ceremony performed, called a second marriage. And then they live together, but under the same roof with his mother and father. When she becomes a mother, she takes her place in turn as queen of the family group.

Now comes another peculiar Indian institution. I have just told you that in the first two or three castes the widows are not allowed to marry. They cannot, even if they would. Of course, it is a hardship on many. There is no denying that not all the widows like it very much, because non-marrying entails upon them the life of a student. That is to say, a student must not eat meat or fish, nor drink wine, nor dress except in white clothes, and so on; there are many regulations. We are a nation of monks—always making penance, and we like it. Now, you see, a woman never drinks wine or eats meat. It was a hardship on us when we were students, but not on the girls. Our women would feel degraded at the idea of eating meat. Men eat meat sometimes in some castes; women never. Still, not being allowed to marry must be a hardship to many; I am sure of that.

But we must go back to the idea; they are intensely socialistic. In the higher castes of every country you will find the statistics show that the number of women is always much larger than the number of men. Why? Because in the higher castes, for generation after generation, the women lead an easy life. They "neither toil nor spin, yet Solomon in all his glory was not arrayed like one of them". And the poor boys, they die like flies. The girl has a cat's nine lives, they say in India. You will read in the statistics that they outnumber the boys in a very short time, except now when they are taking to work quite as hard as the boys. The number of girls in the higher castes is much larger than in the lower. Conditions are quite opposite in the lower castes. There they all work hard; women a little harder, sometimes, because they have to do the domestic work. But, mind you, I never would have thought of that, but one of your American travellers, Mark Twain, writes this about India: "In spite of all that Western critics have said of Hindu customs, I never saw a woman harnessed to a plough with a cow or to a cart with a dog, as is done in some European countries. I saw no woman or girl at work in the fields in India. On both sides and ahead (of the railway train) brown-bodied naked men and boys are ploughing in the fields. But not a woman. In these two hours I have not seen a woman or a girl working in the fields. In India, even the lowest caste never does any hard work. They generally have an easy lot compared to the same class in other nations; and as to ploughing, they never do it."

Now, there you are. Among the lower classes the number of men is larger than the number of women; and what would you naturally expect? A woman gets more chances of marriage, the number of men being larger.

Relative to such questions as to widows not marrying: among the first two castes, the number of women is disproportionately large, and here is a dilemma. Either you have a non-marriageable widow problem and misery, or the non-husband-getting young lady problem. To face the widow problem, or the old maid problem? There you are; either of the two. Now, go back again to the idea that the Indian mind is socialistic. It says, "Now look here! we take the widow problem as the lesser one." Why? "Because they have had their chance; they have been married. If they have lost their chance, at any rate they have had one. Sit down, be quiet, and consider these poor girls—they have not had one chance of marriage." Lord bless you! I remember once in Oxford Street, it was after ten o'clock, and all those ladies coming there, hundreds and thousands of them shopping; and some man, an American, looks around, and he says, "My Lord! how many of them will ever get husbands, I wonder!" So the Indian mind said to the widows, "Well, you have had your chance, and now we are very, very sorry that such mishaps have come to you, but we cannot help it; others are waiting."

Then religion comes into the question; the Hindu religion comes in as a comfort. For, mind you, our religion teaches that marriage is something bad, it is only for the weak. The very spiritual man or woman would not marry at all. So the religious woman says, "Well, the Lord has given me a better chance. What is the use of marrying? Thank God, worship God, what is the use of my loving man?" Of course, all of them cannot put their mind on God. Some find it simply impossible. They have to suffer; but the other poor people, they should not suffer for them. Now I leave this to your judgment; but that is their idea in India.

Next we come to woman as daughter. The great difficulty in the Indian household is the daughter. The daughter and caste combined ruin the poor Hindu, because, you see, she must marry in the same caste, and even inside the caste exactly in the same order; and so the poor man sometimes has to make himself a beggar to get his daughter married. The father of the boy demands a very high price for his son, and this poor man sometimes has to sell everything just to get a husband for his daughter. The great difficulty of the Hindu's life is the daughter. And, curiously enough, the word daughter in Sanskrit is "duhita". The real derivation is that, in ancient times, the daughter of the family was accustomed to milk the cows, and so the word "duhita" comes from "duh", to milk; and the word "daughter" really means a milkmaid. Later on, they found a new meaning to that word "duhita", the milkmaid—she who milks away all the milk of the family. That is the second meaning.

These are the different relations held by our Indian women. As I have told you, the mother is the greatest in position, the wife is next, and the daughter comes after them. It is a most intricate and complicated series of gradation. No foreigner can understand it, even if he lives there for years. For instance, we have three forms of the personal pronoun; they are a sort of verbs in our language. One is very respectful, one is middling, and the lowest is just like thou and thee . To children and servants the last is addressed. The middling one is used with equals. You see, these are to be applied in all the intricate relations of life. For example, to my elder sister I always throughout my life use the pronoun apani, but she never does in speaking to me; she says tumi to me. She should not, even by mistake, say apani to me, because that would mean a curse. Love, the love toward those that are superior, should always be expressed in that form of language. That is the custom. Similarly I would never dare address my elder sister or elder brother, much less my mother or father, as tu or tum or tumi. As to calling our mother and father by name, why, we would never do that. Before I knew the customs of this country, I received such a shock when the son, in a very refined family, got up and called the mother by name! However, I got used to that. That is the custom of the country. But with us, we never pronounce the name of our parents when they are present. It is always in the third person plural, even before them.

Thus we see the most complicated mesh-work in the social life of our men and our women and in our degree of relationship. We do not speak to our wives before our elders; it is only when we are alone or when inferiors are present. If I were married, I would speak to my wife before my younger sister, my nephews or nieces; but not before my elder sister or parents. I cannot talk to my sisters about their husbands at all. The idea is, we are a monastic race. The whole social organisation has that one idea before it. Marriage is thought of as something impure, something lower. Therefore the subject of love would never be talked of. I cannot read a novel before my sister, or my brothers, or my mother, or even before others. I close the book.

Then again, eating and drinking is all in the same category. We do not eat before superiors. Our women never eat before men, except they be the children or inferiors. The wife would die rather than, as she says, "munch" before her husband. Sometimes, for instance, brothers and sisters may eat together; and if I and my sister are eating, and the husband comes to the door, my sister stops, and the poor husband flies out.

These are the customs peculiar to the country. A few of these I note in different countries also. As I never married myself, I am not perfect in all my knowledge about the wife. Mother, sisters—i know what they are; and other people's wives I saw; from that I gather what I have told you.

As to education and culture, it all depends upon the man. That is to say, where the men are highly cultured, there the women are; where the men are not, women are not. Now, from the oldest times, you know, the primary education, according to the old Hindu customs, belongs to the village system. All the land from time immemorial was nationalised, as you say—belonged to the Government. There never is any private right in land. The revenue in India comes from the land, because every man holds so much land from the Government. This land is held in common by a community, it may be five, ten, twenty, or a hundred families. They govern the whole of the land, pay a certain amount of revenue to the Government, maintain a physician, a village schoolmaster, and so on.

Those of you who have read Herbert Spencer remember what he calls the "monastery system" of education that was tried in Europe and which in some parts proved a success; that is, there is one schoolmaster, whom the village keeps. These primary schools are very rudimentary, because our methods are so simple. Each boy brings a little mat; and his paper, to begin with, is palm leaves. Palm leaves first, paper is too costly. Each boy spreads his little mat and sits upon it, brings out his inkstand and his books and begins to write. A little arithmetic, some Sanskrit grammar, a little of language and accounts—these are taught in the primary school.

A little book on ethics, taught by an old man, we learnt by heart, and I remember one of the lessons: "For the good of a village, a man ought to give up his family;

For the good of a country, he ought to give up his village;

For the good of humanity, he may give up his country;

For the good of the world, everything."

Such verses are there in the books. We get them by heart, and they are explained by teacher and pupil. These things we learn, both boys and girls together. Later on, the education differs. The old Sanskrit universities are mainly composed of boys. The girls very rarely go up to those universities; but there are a few exceptions.

In these modern days there is a greater impetus towards higher education on the European lines, and the trend of opinion is strong towards women getting this higher education. Of course, there are some people in India who do not want it, but those who do want it carried the day. It is a strange fact that Oxford and Cambridge are closed to women today, so are Harvard and Yale; but Calcutta University opened its doors to women more than twenty years ago. I remember that the year I graduated, several girls came out and graduated—the same standard, the same course, the same in everything as the boys; and they did very well indeed. And our religion does not prevent a woman being educated at all. In this way the girl should be educated; even thus she should be trained; and in the old books we find that the universities were equally resorted to by both girls and boys, but later the education of the whole nation was neglected. What can you expect under foreign rule? The foreign conqueror is not there to do good to us; he wants his money. I studied hard for twelve years and became a graduate of Calcutta University; now I can scarcely make $5.00 a month in my country. Would you believe it? It is actually a fact. So these educational institutions of foreigners are simply to get a lot of useful, practical slaves for a little money—to turn out a host of clerks, postmasters, telegraph operators, and so on. There it is.

As a result, education for both boys and girls is neglected, entirely neglected. There are a great many things that should be done in that land; but you must always remember, if you will kindly excuse me and permit me to use one of your own proverbs, "What is sauce for the goose is sauce for the gander." Your foreign born ladies are always crying over the hardships of the Hindu woman, and never care for the hardships of the Hindu man. They are all weeping salt tears. But who are the little girls married to? Some one, when told that they are all married to old men, asked, "And what do the young men do? What! are all the girls married to old men, only to old men?" We are born old—perhaps all the men there.

The ideal of the Indian race is freedom of the soul. This world is nothing. It is a vision, a dream. This life is one of

many millions like it. The whole of this nature is Maya, is phantasm, a pest house of phantasms. That is the philosophy. Babies smile at life and think it so beautiful and good, but in a few years they will have to revert to where they began. They began life crying, and they will leave it crying. Nations in the vigour of their youth think that they can do anything and everything: "We are the gods of the earth. We are the chosen people." They think that God Almighty has given them a charter to rule over all the world, to advance His plans, to do anything they like, to turn the world upside down. They have a charter to rob, murder, kill; God has given them this, and they do that because they are only babes. So empire after empire has arisen—glorious, resplendent—now vanished away—gone, nobody knows where; it may have been stupendous in its ruin.

As a drop of water upon a lotus leaf tumbles about and falls in a moment, even so is this mortal life. Everywhere we turn are ruins. Where the forest stands today was once the mighty empire with huge cities. That is the dominant idea, the tone, the colour of the Indian mind. We know, you Western people have the youthful blood coursing through your veins. We know that nations, like men, have their day. Where is Greece? Where is Rome? Where that mighty Spaniard of the other day? Who knows through it all what becomes of India? Thus they are born, and thus they die; they rise and fall. The Hindu as a child knows of the Mogul invader whose cohorts no power on earth could stop, who has left in your language the terrible word "Tartar". The Hindu has learnt his lesson. He does not want to prattle, like the babes of today. Western people, say what you have to say. This is your day. Onward, go on, babes; have your prattle out. This is the day of the babies, to prattle. We have learnt our lesson and are quiet. You have a little wealth today, and you look down upon us. Well, this is your day. Prattle, babes, prattle—this is the Hindu's attitude.

The Lord of Lords is not to be attained by much frothy speech. The Lord of Lords is not to be attained even by the powers of the intellect. He is not gained by much power of conquest. That man who knows the secret source of things and that everything else is evanescent, unto him He, the Lord, comes; unto none else. India has learnt her lesson through ages and ages of experience. She has turned her face towards Him. She has made many mistakes; loads and loads of rubbish are heaped upon the race. Never mind; what of that? What is the clearing of rubbish, the cleaning of cities, and all that? Does that give life? Those that have fine institutions, they die. And what of institutions, those tinplate Western institutions, made in five days and broken on the sixth? One of these little handful nations cannot keep alive for two centuries together. And our institutions have stood the test of ages. Says the Hindu, "Yes, we have buried all the old nations of the earth and stand here to bury all the new races also, because our ideal is not this world, but the other. Just as your ideal is, so shall you be. If your ideal is mortal, if your ideal is of this earth, so shalt thou be. If your ideal is matter, matter shalt thou be. Behold!

Our ideal is the Spirit. That alone exists, nothing else exists; and like Him, we live for ever."

MY LIFE AND MISSION

Delivered at the Shakespeare Club of Pasadena, California, on January 27, 1900.

Now, ladies and gentlemen, the subject for this morning was to have been the Vedanta Philosophy. That subject itself is interesting, but rather dry and very vast.

Meanwhile, I have been asked by your president and some of the ladies and gentlemen here to tell them something about my work and what I have been doing. It may be interesting to some here, but not so much so to me. In fact, I do not quite know how to tell it to you, for this will have been the first time in my life that I have spoken on that subject.

Now, to understand what I have been trying to do, in my small way, I will take you, in imagination, to India. We have not time to go into all the details and all the ramifications of the subject; nor is it possible for you to understand all the complexities in a foreign race in this short time. Suffice it to say, I will at least try to give you a little picture of what India is like.

It is like a gigantic building all tumbled down in ruins. At first sight, then, there is little hope. It is a nation gone and ruined. But you wait and study, then you see something beyond that. The truth is that so long as the principle, the ideal, of which the outer man is the expression, is not hurt or destroyed, the man lives, and there is hope for that man. If your coat is stolen twenty times, that is no reason why you should be destroyed. You can get a new coat. The coat is unessential. The fact that a rich man is robbed does not hurt the vitality of the man, does not mean death. The man will survive.

Standing on this principle, we look in and we see — what? India is no longer a political power; it is an enslaved race. Indians have no say, no voice in their own government; they are three hundred millions of slaves — nothing more! The average income of a man in India is two shillings a month. The common state of the vast mass of the people is starvation, so that, with the least decrease in income, millions die. A little famine means death. So there, too, when I look on that side of India, I see ruin — hopeless ruin.

But we find that the Indian race never stood for wealth. Although they acquired immense wealth, perhaps more than any other nation ever acquired, yet the nation did not stand for wealth. It was a powerful race for ages, yet we find that that nation never stood for power, never went out of the country to conquer. Quite content within their own boundaries, they never fought anybody. The Indian nation never stood for imperial glory. Wealth and power, then, were not the ideals of the race.

What then? Whether they were wrong or right — that is not the question we discuss — that nation, among all the children of men, has believed, and believed intensely, that this life is not real. The real is God; and they must cling unto that God through thick and thin. In the midst of their degradation, religion came first. The Hindu man drinks religiously, sleeps religiously, walks religiously, marries religiously, robs religiously.

Did you ever see such a country? If you want to get up a gang of robbers, the leader will have to preach some sort of religion, then formulate some bogus metaphysics, and say that this method is the clearest and quickest way to get God. Then he finds a following, otherwise not. That shows that the vitality of the race, the mission of the race is religion; and because that has not been touched, therefore that race lives.

See Rome. Rome's mission was imperial power, expansion. And so soon as that was touched, Rome fell to pieces, passed out. The mission of Greece was intellect, as soon as that was touched, why, Greece passed out. So in modern times, Spain and all these modern countries. Each nation has a mission for the world. So long as that mission is not hurt, that nation lives, despite every difficulty. But as soon as its mission is destroyed, the nation collapses.

Now, that vitality of India has not been touched yet. They have not given up that, and it is still strong — in spite of all their superstitions. Hideous superstitions are there, most revolting some of them. Never mind. The national life-current is still there — the mission of the race.

The Indian nation never will be a powerful conquering people — never. They will never be a great political power; that is not their business, that is not the note India has to play in the great harmony of nations. But what has she to play? God, and God alone. She clings unto that like grim death. Still there is hope there.

So, then, after your analysis, you come to the conclusion that all these things, all this poverty and misery, are of no consequence — the man is living still, and therefore there is hope.

Well! You see religious activities going on all through the country. I do not recall a year that has not given birth to several new sects in India. The stronger the current, the more the whirlpools and eddies. Sects are not signs of decay, they are a sign of life. Let sects multiply, till the time comes when every one of us is a sect, each individual. We need not quarrel about that.

Now, take your country. (I do not mean any criticism). Here the social laws, the political formation — everything is made to facilitate man's journey in this life. He may live very happily so long as he is on this earth. Look at your streets — how clean! Your beautiful cities! And in how many ways a man can make money! How many channels to get enjoyment in this life! But, if a man here should say, "Now look here, I shall sit down under this tree and meditate; I do not want to work", why, he would have to go to jail. See! There would be no chance for him at all. None. A man can live in this society only if he falls in line. He has to join in this rush for the enjoyment of good in this life, or he dies.

Now let us go back to India. There, if a man says, "I shall go and sit on the top of that mountain and look at the tip of my nose all the rest of my days", everybody says, "Go, and Godspeed to you!" He need not speak a word. Somebody brings him a little cloth, and he is all right. But if a man says, "Behold, I am going to enjoy a little of this life", every door is closed to him.

I say that the ideas of both countries are unjust. I see no reason why a man here should not sit down and look at the tip of his nose if he likes. Why should everybody here do just what the majority does? I see no reason.

Nor why, in India, a man should not have the goods of this life and make money. But you see how those vast millions are forced to accept the opposite point of view by tyranny. This is the tyranny of the sages. This is the tyranny of the great, tyranny of the spiritual, tyranny of the intellectual, tyranny of the wise. And the tyranny of the wise, mind you, is much more powerful than the tyranny of the ignorant. The wise, the intellectual, when they take to forcing their opinions upon others, know a hundred thousand ways to make bonds and barriers which it is not in the power of the ignorant to break.

Now, I say that this thing has got to stop. There is no use in sacrificing millions and millions of people to produce one spiritual giant. If it is possible to make a society where the spiritual giant will be produced and all the rest of the people will be happy as well, that is good; but if the millions have to be ground down, that is unjust. Better that the one great man should suffer for the salvation of the world.

In every nation you will have to work through their methods. To every man you will have to speak in his own language. Now, in England or in America, if you want to preach religion to them, you will have to work through political methods — make organisations, societies, with voting, balloting, a president, and so on, because that is the language, the method of the Western race. On the other hand, if you want to speak of politics in India, you must speak through the language of religion. You will have to tell them something like this: "The man who cleans his house every morning will acquire such and such an amount of merit, he will go to heaven, or he comes to God." Unless you put it that way, they will not listen to you. It is a question of language. The thing done is the same. But with every race, you will have to speak their language in order to reach their hearts. And that is quite just. We need not fret about that.

In the Order to which I belong we are called Sannyasins. The word means "a man who has renounced". This is a very, very, very ancient Order. Even Buddha, who was 560 years before Christ, belonged to that Order. He was one of the reformers of his Order. That was all. So ancient! You find it mentioned away back in the Vedas, the oldest book in the world. In old India there was the regulation that every man and woman, towards the end of their lives, must get out of social life altogether and think of nothing except God and their own salva-

tion. This was to get ready for the great event — death. So old people used to become Sannyasins in those early days. Later on, young people began to give up the world. And young people are active. They could not sit down under a tree and think all the time of their own death, so they went about preaching and starting sects, and so on. Thus, Buddha, being young, started that great reform. Had he been an old man, he would have looked at the tip of his nose and died quietly.

The Order is not a church, and the people who join the Order are not priests. There is an absolute difference between the priests and the Sannyasins. In India, priesthood, like every other business in a social life, is a hereditary profession. A priest's son will become a priest, just as a carpenter's son will be a carpenter, or a blacksmith's son a blacksmith. The priest must always be married. The Hindu does not think a man is complete unless he has a wife. An unmarried man has no right to perform religious ceremonies.

The Sannyasins do not possess property, and they do not marry. Beyond that there is no organisation. The only bond that is there is the bond between the teacher and the taught — and that is peculiar to India. The teacher is not a man who comes just to teach me, and I pay him so much, and there it ends. In India it is really like an adoption. The teacher is more than my own father, and I am truly his child, his son in every respect. I owe him obedience and reverence first, before my own father even; because, they say, the father gave me this body, but he showed me the way to salvation, he is greater than father. And we carry this love, this respect for our teacher all our lives. And that is the only organisation that exists. I adopt my disciples. Sometimes the teacher will be a young man and the disciple a very old man. But never mind, he is the son, and he calls me "Father", and I have to address him as my son, my daughter, and so on.

Now, I happened to get an old man to teach me, and he was very peculiar. He did not go much for intellectual scholarship, scarcely studied books; but when he was a boy he was seized with the tremendous idea of getting truth direct. First he tried by studying his own religion. Then he got the idea that he must get the truth of other religions; and with that idea he joined all the sects, one after another. For the time being he did exactly what they told him to do — lived with the devotees of these different sects in turn, until interpenetrated with the particular ideal of that sect. After a few years he would go to another sect. When he had gone through with all that, he came to the conclusion that they were all good. He had no criticism to offer to any one; they are all so many paths leading to the same goal. And then he said, "That is a glorious thing, that there should be so many paths, because if there were only one path, perhaps it would suit only an individual man. The more the number of paths, the more the chance for every one of us to know the truth. If I cannot be taught in one language, I will try another, and so on". Thus his benediction was for every religion.

Now, all the ideas that I preach are only an attempt to echo his ideas. Nothing is mine originally except the wicked ones, everything I say which is false and wicked. But every word that I have ever uttered which is true and good is simply an attempt to echo his voice. Read his life by Prof. Max Muller[1].

Well, there at his feet I conceived these ideas—there with some other young men. I was just a boy. I went there when I was about sixteen. Some of the other boys were still younger, some a little older—about a dozen or more. And together we conceived that this ideal had to be spread. And not only spread, but made practical. That is to say, we must show the spirituality of the Hindus, the mercifulness of the Buddhists, the activity of the Christians, the brotherhood of the Mohammedans, by our practical lives. "We shall start a universal religion now and here," we said, "we will not wait".

Our teacher was an old man who would never touch a coin with his hands. He took just the little food offered, just so many yards of cotton cloth, no more. He could never be induced to take any other gift. With all these marvellous ideas, he was strict, because that made him free. The monk in India is the friend of the prince today, dines with him; and tomorrow he is with the beggar, sleeps under a tree. He must come into contact with everyone, must always move about. As the saying is, "The rolling stone gathers no moss". The last fourteen years of my life, I have never been for three months at a time in any one place—continually rolling. So do we all.

Now, this handful of boys got hold of these ideas, and all the practical results that sprang out of these ideas. Universal religion, great sympathy for the poor, and all that are very good in theory, but one must practise.

Then came the sad day when our old teacher died. We nursed him the best we could. We had no friends. Who would listen to a few boys, with their crank notions? Nobody. At least, in India, boys are nobodies. Just think of it—a dozen boys, telling people vast, big ideas, saying they are determined to work these ideas out in life. Why, everybody laughed. From laughter it became serious; it became persecution. Why, the parents of the boys came to feel like spanking every one of us. And the more we were derided, the more determined we became.

Then came a terrible time—for me personally and for all the other boys as well. But to me came such misfortune! On the one side was my mother, my brothers. My father died at that time, and we were left poor. Oh, very poor, almost starving all the time! I was the only hope of the family, the only one who could do anything to help them. I had to stand between my two worlds. On the one hand, I would have to see my mother and brothers starve unto death; on the other, I had believed that this man's ideas were for the good of India and the world, and had to be preached and worked out. And so the fight went on in my mind for days and months. Sometimes I would pray for five or six days and nights together without stopping.

Oh, the agony of those days! I was living in hell! The natural affections of my boy's heart drawing me to my family—i could not bear to see those who were the nearest and dearest to me suffering. On the other hand, nobody to sympathise with me. Who would sympathise with the imaginations of a boy—imaginations that caused so much suffering to others? Who would sympathise with me? None—except one.

That one's sympathy brought blessing and hope. She was a woman. Our teacher, this great monk, was married when he was a boy and she a mere child. When he became a young man, and all this religious zeal was upon him, she came to see him. Although they had been married for long, they had not seen very much of each other until they were grown up. Then he said to his wife, "Behold, I am your husband; you have a right to this body. But I cannot live the sex life, although I have married you. I leave it to your judgment". And she wept and said, "God speed you! The Lord bless you! Am I the woman to degrade you? If I can, I will help you. Go on in your work".

That was the woman. The husband went on and became a monk in his own way; and from a distance the wife went on helping as much as she could. And later, when the man had become a great spiritual giant, she came—really, she was the first disciple—and she spent the rest of her life taking care of the body of this man. He never knew whether he was living or dying, or anything. Sometimes, when talking, he would get so excited that if he sat on live charcoals, he did not know it. Live charcoals! Forgetting all about his body, all the time.

Well, that lady, his wife, was the only one who sympathised with the idea of those boys. But she was powerless. She was poorer than we were. Never mind! We plunged into the breach. I believed, as I was living, that these ideas were going to rationalise India and bring better days to many lands and foreign races. With that belief, came the realisation that it is better that a few persons suffer than that such ideas should die out of the world. What if a mother or two brothers die? It is a sacrifice. Let it be done. No great thing can be done without sacrifice. The heart must be plucked out and the bleeding heart placed upon the altar. Then great things are done. Is there any other way? None have found it. I appeal to each one of you, to those who have accomplished any great thing. Oh, how much it has cost! What agony! What torture! What terrible suffering is behind every deed of success in every life! You know that, all of you.

And thus we went on, that band of boys. The only thing we got from those around us was a kick and a curse—that was all. Of course, we had to beg from door to door for our food: got hips and haws—the refuse of everything—a piece of bread here and there. We got hold of a broken-down old house, with hissing cobras living underneath; and because that was the cheapest, we went into that house and lived there.

Thus we went on for some years, in the meanwhile making excursions all over India, trying to bring about the idea

1. *Ramakrishna: His Life and Sayings*, first published in London in 1896. Reprinted in 1951 by Advaita Ashrama.

gradually. Ten years were spent without a ray of light! Ten more years! A thousand times despondency came; but there was one thing always to keep us hopeful—the tremendous faithfulness to each other, the tremendous love between us. I have got a hundred men and women around me; if I become the devil himself tomorrow, they will say, "Here we are still! We will never give you up!" That is a great blessing. In happiness, in misery, in famine, in pain, in the grave, in heaven, or in hell who never gives me up is my friend. Is such friendship a joke? A man may have salvation through such friendship. That brings salvation if we can love like that. If we have that faithfulness, why, there is the essence of all concentration. You need not worship any gods in the world if you have that faith, that strength, that love. And that was there with us all throughout that hard time. That was there. That made us go from the Himalayas to Cape Comorin, from the Indus to the Brahmaputra.

This band of boys began to travel about. Gradually we began to draw attention: ninety per cent was antagonism, very little of it was helpful. For we had one fault: we were boys—in poverty and with all the roughness of boys. He who has to make his own way in life is a bit rough, he has not much time to be smooth and suave and polite —"my lady and my gentleman", and all that. You have seen that in life, always. He is a rough diamond, he has not much polish, he is a jewel in an indifferent casket.

And there we were. "No compromise!" was the watchword. "This is the ideal, and this has got to be carried out. If we meet the king, though we die, we must give him a bit of our minds; if the peasant, the same". Naturally, we met with antagonism.

But, mind you, this is life's experience; if you really want the good of others, the whole universe may stand against you and cannot hurt you. It must crumble before your power of the Lord Himself in you if you are sincere and really unselfish. And those boys were that.

They came as children, pure and fresh from the hands of nature. Said our Master: I want to offer at the altar of the Lord only those flowers that have not even been smelled, fruits that have not been touched with the fingers. The words of the great man sustained us all. For he saw through the future life of those boys that he collected from the streets of Calcutta, so to say. People used to laugh at him when he said, "You will see—this boy, that boy, what he becomes". His faith was unalterable: "Mother showed it to me. I may be weak, but when She says this is so—she can never make mistakes—it must be so."

So things went on and on for ten years without any light, but with my health breaking all the time. It tells on the body in the long run: sometimes one meal at nine in the evening, another time a meal at eight in the morning, another after two days, another after three days—and always the poorest and roughest thing. Who is going to give to the beggar the good things he has? And then, they have not much in India.

And most of the time walking, climbing snow peaks, sometimes ten miles of hard mountain climbing, just to get a meal. They eat unleavened bread in India, and sometimes they have it stored away for twenty or thirty days, until it is harder than bricks; and then they will give a square of that. I would have to go from house to house to collect sufficient for one meal. And then the bread was so hard, it made my mouth bleed to eat it. Literally, you can break your teeth on that bread. Then I would put it in a pot and pour over it water from the river. For months and months I existed that way—of course it was telling on the health.

Then I thought, I have tried India: it is time for me to try another country. At that time your Parliament of Religions was to be held, and someone was to be sent from India. I was just a vagabond, but I said, "If you send me, I am going. I have not much to lose, and I do not care if I lose that." It was very difficult to find the money, but after a long struggle they got together just enough to pay for my passage—and I came. Came one or two months earlier, so that I found myself drifting about in the streets here, without knowing anybody.

But finally the Parliament of Religions opened, and I met kind friends, who helped me right along. I worked a little, collected funds, started two papers, and so on. After that I went over to England and worked there. At the same time I carried on the work for India in America too.

My plan for India, as it has been developed and centralised, is this: I have told you of our lives as monks there, how we go from door to door, so that religion is brought to everybody without charge, except, perhaps, a broken piece of bread. That is why you see the lowest of the low in India holding the most exalted religious ideas. It is all through the work of these monks. But ask a man, "Who are the English?"— he does not know. He says perhaps, "They are the children of those giants they speak of in those books, are they not?" "Who governs you?" "We do not know." "What is the government?" They do not know. But they know philosophy. It is a practical want of intellectual education about life on this earth they suffer from. These millions and millions of people are ready for life beyond this world—is not that enough for them? Certainly not. They must have a better piece of bread and a better piece of rag on their bodies. The great question is: How to get that better bread and better rag for these sunken millions.

First, I must tell you, there is great hope for them, because, you see, they are the gentlest people on earth. Not that they are timid. When they want to fight, they fight like demons. The best soldiers the English have are recruited from the peasantry of India. Death is a thing of no importance to them. Their attitude is "Twenty times I have died before, and I shall die many times after this. What of that?" They never turn back. They are not given to much emotion, but they make very good fighters.

Their instinct, however, is to plough. If you rob them, murder them, tax them, do anything to them, they will be quiet and gentle, so long as you leave them free to practise their religion. They never interfere with the religion of others. "Leave us liberty to worship our gods, and take everything else!" That is their attitude. When the English touch them there, trouble starts. That was the real cause of the 1857 Mutiny — they would not bear religious repression. The great Mohammedan governments were simply blown up because they touched the Indians' religion.

But aside from that, they are very peaceful, very quiet, very gentle, and, above all, not given to vice. The absence of any strong drink, oh, it makes them infinitely superior to the mobs of any other country. You cannot compare the decency of life among the poor in India with life in the slums here. A slum means poverty, but poverty does not mean sin, indecency, and vice in India. In other countries, the opportunities are such that only the indecent and the lazy need be poor. There is no reason for poverty unless one is a fool or a blackguard — the sort who want city life and all its luxuries. They will not go into the country. They say, "We are here with all the fun, and you must give us bread". But that is not the case in India, where the poor fellows work hard from morning to sunset, and somebody else takes the bread out of their hands, and their children go hungry. Notwithstanding the millions of tons of wheat raised in India, scarcely a grain passes the mouth of a peasant. He lives upon the poorest corn, which you would not feed to your canary-birds.

Now there is no reason why they should suffer such distress — these people; oh, so pure and good! We hear so much talk about the sunken millions and the degraded women of India — but none come to our help. What do they say? They say, "You can only be helped, you can only be good by ceasing to be what you are. It is useless to help Hindus." These people do not know the history of races. There will be no more India if they change their religion and their institutions, because that is the vitality of that race. It will disappear; so, really, you will have nobody to help.

Then there is the other great point to learn: that you can never help really. What can we do for each other? You are growing in your own life, I am growing in my own. It is possible that I can give you a push in your life, knowing that, in the long run, all roads lead to Rome. It is a steady growth. No national civilisation is perfect yet. Give that civilisation a push, and it will arrive at its own goal: do not strive to change it. Take away a nation's institutions, customs, and manners, and what will be left? They hold the nation together.

But here comes the very learned foreign man, and he says, "Look here; you give up all those institutions and customs of thousands of years, and take my tomfool tinpot and be happy". This is all nonsense.

We will have to help each other, but we have to go one step farther: the first thing is to become unselfish in help. "If you do just what I tell you to do, I will help you; otherwise not." Is that help?

And so, if the Hindus want to help you spiritually, there will be no question of limitations: perfect unselfishness. I give, and there it ends. It is gone from me. My mind, my powers, my everything that I have to give, is given: given with the idea to give, and no more. I have seen many times people who have robbed half the world, and they gave $20,000 "to convert the heathen".

What for? For the benefit of the heathen, or for their own souls? Just think of that.

And the Nemesis of crime is working. We men try to hoodwink our own eyes. But inside the heart, He has remained, the real Self. He never forgets. We can never delude Him. His eyes will never be hoodwinked. Whenever there is any impulse of real charity, it tells, though it be at the end of a thousand years. Obstructed, it yet wakens once more to burst like a thunderbolt. And every impulse where the motive is selfish, self-seeking — though it may be launched forth with all the newspapers blazoning, all the mobs standing and cheering — it fails to reach the mark.

I am not taking pride in this. But, mark you, I have told the story of that group of boys. Today there is not a village, not a man, not a woman in India that does not know their work and bless them. There is not a famine in the land where these boys do not plunge in and try to work and rescue as many as they can. And that strikes to the heart. The people come to know it. So help whenever you can, but mind what your motive is. If it is selfish, it will neither benefit those you help, nor yourself. If it is unselfish, it will bring blessings upon them to whom it is given, and infinite blessings upon you, sure as you are living. The Lord can never be hoodwinked. The law of Karma can never be hoodwinked.

Well then, my plans are, therefore, to reach these masses of India. Suppose you start schools all over India for the poor, still you cannot educate them. How can you? The boy of four years would better go to the plough or to work, than to your school. He cannot go to your school. It is impossible. Self-preservation is the first instinct. But if the mountain does not go to Mohammed, then Mohammed can come to the mountain. Why should not education go from door to door, say I. If a ploughman's boy cannot come to education, why not meet him at the plough, at the factory, just wherever he is? Go along with him, like his shadow. But there are these hundreds and thousands of monks, educating the people on the spiritual plane; why not let these men do the same work on the intellectual plane? Why should they not talk to the masses a little about history — about many things? The ears are the best educators. The best principles in our lives were those which we heard from our mothers through our ears. Books came much later. Book-learning is nothing. Through the ears we get the best formative principles. Then, as they get more and more interested, they may come to your books too. First, let it roll on and on — that is my idea.

Well, I must tell you that I am not a very great believer in monastic systems. They have great merits, and also great defects. There should be a perfect balance between the monastics and the householders. But monasticism has absorbed all the power in India. We represent the greatest power. The monk is greater than the prince. There is no reigning sovereign in India who dares to sit down when the "yellow cloth" is there. He gives up his seat and stands. Now, that is bad, so much power, even in the hands of good men—although these monastics have been the bulwark of the people. They stand between the priestcraft and knowledge. They are the centres of knowledge and reform. They are just what the prophets were among the Jews. The prophets were always preaching against the priests, trying to throw out superstitions. So are they in India. But all the same so much power is not good there; better methods should be worked out. But you can only work in the line of least resistance. The whole national soul there is upon monasticism. You go to India and preach any religion as a householder: the Hindu people will turn back and go out. If you have given up the world, however, they say, "He is good, he has given up the world. He is a sincere man, he wants to do what he preaches." What I mean to say is this, that it represents a tremendous power. What we can do is just to transform it, give it another form. This tremendous power in the hands of the roving Sannyasins of India has got to be transformed, and it will raise the masses up.

Now, you see, we have brought the plan down nicely on paper; but I have taken it, at the same time, from the regions of idealism. So far the plan was loose and idealistic. As years went on, it became more and more condensed and accurate; I began to see by actual working its defects, and all that.

What did I discover in its working on the material plane? First, there must be centres to educate these monks in the method of education. For instance, I send one of my men, and he goes about with a camera: he has to be taught in those things himself. In India, you will find every man is quite illiterate, and that teaching requires tremendous centres. And what does all that mean? Money. From the idealistic plane you come to everyday work. Well, I have worked hard, four years in your country, and two in England. And I am very thankful that some friends came to the rescue. One who is here today with you is amongst them. There are American friends and English friends who went over with me to India, and there has been a very rude beginning. Some English people came and joined the orders. One poor man worked hard and died in India. There are an Englishman and an Englishwoman who have retired; they have some means of their own, and they have started a centre in the Himalayas, educating the children. I have given them one of the papers I have started—a copy you will find there on the table—the Awakened India. And there they are instructing and working among the people. I have another centre in Calcutta. Of course, all great movements must proceed from the capital. For what is a capital? It is the heart of a nation. All the blood comes into the heart and thence it is distributed; so all the wealth, all the ideas, all the education, all spirituality will converge towards the capital and spread from it.

I am glad to tell you I have made a rude beginning. But the same work I want to do, on parallel lines, for women. And my principle is: each one helps himself. My help is from a distance. There are Indian women, English women, and I hope American women will come to take up the task. As soon as they have begun, I wash my hands of it. No man shall dictate to a woman; nor a woman to a man. Each one is independent. What bondage there may be is only that of love. Women will work out their own destinies—much better, too, than men can ever do for them. All the mischief to women has come because men undertook to shape the destiny of women. And I do not want to start with any initial mistake. One little mistake made then will go on multiplying; and if you succeed, in the long run that mistake will have assumed gigantic proportions and become hard to correct. So, if I made this mistake of employing men to work out this women's part of the work, why, women will never get rid of that—it will have become a custom. But I have got an opportunity. I told you of the lady who was my Master's wife. We have all great respect for her. She never dictates to us. So it is quite safe.

That part has to be accomplished.

DISCIPLESHIP

Delivered in San Francisco, on March 29, 1900.

My subject is "Discipleship". I do not know how you will take what I have to say. It will be rather difficult for you to accept it—the ideals of teachers and disciples in this country vary so much from those in ours. An old proverb of India comes to my mind: "There are hundreds of thousands of teachers, but it is hard to find one disciple." It seems to be true. The one important thing in the attainment of spirituality is the attitude of the pupil. When the right attitude is there, illumination comes easily.

What does the disciple need in order to receive the truth? The great sages say that to attain truth takes but the twinkling of an eye—it is just a question of knowing—the dream breaks. How long does it take? In a second the dream is gone. When the illusion vanishes, how long does it take? Just the twinkling of an eye. When I know the truth, nothing happens except that the falsehood vanishes away: I took the rope for the snake, and now I see it is the rope. It is only a question of half a second and the whole thing is done. Thou art That. Thou art the Reality. How long does it take to know this? If we are God and always have been so, not to know this is most astonishing. To know this is the only natural thing. It should not take ages to find out what we have always been and what we now are.

Yet it seems difficult to realise this self-evident truth. Ages and ages pass before we begin to catch a faint glimpse of it. God is life; God is truth. We write about this; we feel in our inmost heart that this is so, that everything else than God is nothing—here today, gone tomorrow. And yet most of us remain the same all through life. We cling to untruth, and we turn our back upon truth. We do not want to attain truth. We do not want anyone to break our dream. You see, the teachers are not wanted. Who wants to learn? But if anyone wants to realise the truth and overcome illusion, if he wants to receive the truth from a teacher, he must be a true disciple.

It is not easy to be a disciple; great preparations are necessary; many conditions have to be fulfilled. Four principal conditions are laid down by the Vedantists.

The first condition is that the student who wants to know the truth must give up all desires for gain in this world or in the life to come.

The truth is not what we see. What we see is not truth as long as any desire creeps into the mind. God is true, and the world is not true. So long as there is in the heart the least desire for the world, truth will not come. Let the world fall to ruin around my ears: I do not care. So with the next life; I do not care to go to heaven. What is heaven? Only the continuation of this earth. We would be better and the little foolish dreams we are dreaming would break sooner if there were no heaven, no continuation of this silly life on earth. By going to heaven we only prolong the miserable illusions.

What do you gain in heaven? You become gods, drink nectar, and get rheumatism. There is less misery there than on earth, but also less truth. The very rich can understand truth much less than the poorer people. "It is easier for a camel to go through the eye of a needle, than for a rich man to enter into the kingdom of God." The rich man has no time to think of anything beyond his wealth and power, his comforts and indulgences. The rich rarely become religious. Why? Because they think, if they become religious, they will have no more fun in life. In the same way, there is very little chance to become spiritual in heaven; there is too much comfort and enjoyment there—the dwellers in heaven are disinclined to give up their fun.

They say there will be no more weeping in heaven. I do not trust the man who never weeps; he has a big block of granite where the heart should be. It is evident that the heavenly people have not much sympathy. There are vast masses of them over there, and we are miserable creatures suffering in this horrible place. They could pull us all out of it; but they do not. They do not weep. There is no sorrow or misery there; therefore they do not care for anyone's misery. They drink their nectar, dances go on; beautiful wives and all that.

Going beyond these things, the disciple should say, "I do not care for anything in this life nor for all the heavens that have ever existed—i do not care to go to any of them. I do not want the sense-life in any form—this identification of myself with the body—as I feel now, 'I am this body—this huge mass of flesh.' This is what I feel I am. I refuse to believe that."

The world and the heavens, all these are bound up with the senses. You do not care for the earth if you do not have any senses. Heaven also is the world. Earth, heaven, and all that is between have but one name—earth.

Therefore the disciple, knowing the past and the present and thinking of the future, knowing what prosperity means, what happiness means, gives up all these and seeks to know the truth and truth alone. This is the first condition.

The second condition is that the disciple must be able to control the internal and the external senses and must be established in several other spiritual virtues.

The external senses are the visible organs situated in different parts of the body; the internal senses are intangible. We have the external eyes, ears, nose, and so on; and we have the corresponding internal senses. We are continually at the beck and call of both these groups of senses. Corresponding to the senses are sense-objects. If any sense-objects are near by, the senses compel us to perceive them; we have no choice or independence. There is the big nose. A little fragrance is there; I have to smell it. If there were a bad odour, I would say to myself, "Do not smell it"; but nature says, "Smell", and I smell it. Just think what we have become! We have bound ourselves. I have eyes. Anything going on, good or bad, I must see. It is the same with hearing. If anyone speaks unpleasantly to me, I must hear it. My sense of hearing compels me to do so, and how miserable I feel! Curse or praise—man has got to hear. I have seen many deaf people who do not usually hear, but anything about themselves they always hear!

All these senses, external and internal, must be under the disciple's control. By hard practice he has to arrive at the stage where he can assert his mind against the senses, against the commands of nature. He should be able to say to his mind, "You are mine; I order you, do not see or hear anything", and the mind will not see or hear anything—no form or sound will react on the mind. In that state the mind has become free of the domination of the senses, has become separated from them. No longer is it attached to the senses and the body. The external things cannot order the mind now; the mind refuses to attach itself to them. Beautiful fragrance is there. The disciple says to the mind, "Do not smell", and the mind does not perceive the fragrance. When you have arrived at that point, you are just beginning to be a disciple. That is why when everybody says, "I know the truth", I say, "If you know the truth, you must have self-control; and if you have control of yourself, show it by controlling these organs."

Next, the mind must be made to quiet down. It is rushing about. Just as I sit down to meditate, all the vilest subjects in the world come up. The whole thing is nauseating. Why should the mind think thoughts I do not want it to think? I am as it were a slave to the mind. No spiritual knowledge is possible so long as the mind is restless and out of control. The disciple has to learn to control the mind. Yes, it is the function of the mind to think. But it must not think if the disciple does not want it to; it must stop thinking when he commands it to.

To qualify as a disciple, this state of the mind is very necessary.

Also, the disciple must have great power of endurance. Life seems comfortable; and you find the mind behaves well when everything is going well with you. But if something goes wrong, your mind loses its balance. That is not good. Bear all evil and misery without one murmur of hurt, without one thought of unhappiness, resistance, remedy, or retaliation. That is true endurance; and that you must acquire.

Good and evil there always are in the world. Many forget there is any evil—at least they try to forget; and when evil comes upon them, they are overwhelmed by it and feel bitter. There are others who deny that there is any evil at all and consider everything good. That also is a weakness; that also proceeds from a fear of evil. If something is evil-smelling, why sprinkle it with rose water and call it fragrant? Yes, there are good and evil in the world—god has put evil in the world. But you do not have to whitewash Him. Why there is evil is none of your business. Please have faith and keep quiet.

When my Master, Shri Ramakrishna fell ill, a Brahmin suggested to him that he apply his tremendous mental power to cure himself. He said that if my Master would only concentrate his mind on the diseased part of the body, it would heal. Shri Ramakrishna answered, "What! Bring down the mind that I've given to God to this little body!" He refused to think of body and illness. His mind was continually conscious of God; it was dedicated to Him utterly. He would not use it for any other purpose.

This craving for health, wealth, long life, and the like—the so-called good—is nothing but an illusion. To devote the mind to them in order to secure them only strengthens the delusion. We have these dreams and illusions in life, and we want to have more of them in the life to come, in heaven. More and more illusion. Resist not evil. Face it! You are higher than evil.

There is this misery in the world—it has to be suffered by someone. You cannot act without making evil for somebody. And when you seek worldly good, you only avoid an evil which must be suffered by somebody else. Everyone is trying to put it on someone else's shoulders. The disciple says, "Let the miseries of the world come to me; I shall endure them all. Let others go free."

Remember the man on the cross. He could have brought legions of angels to victory; but he did not resist. He pitied those who crucified him. He endured every humiliation and suffering. He took the burden of all upon himself: "Come unto me, all ye that labour and are heavy laden, and I will give you rest." Such is true endurance. How very high he was above this life, so high that we cannot understand it, we slaves! No sooner does a man slap me in the face than my hand hits back: bang, it goes! How can I understand the greatness and blessedness of the Glorified One? How can I see the glory of it?

But I will not drag the ideal down. I feel I am the body, resisting evil. If I get a headache, I go all over the world to have it cured; I drink two thousand bottles of medicine. How can I understand these marvellous minds? I can see the ideal, but how much of that ideal? None of this consciousness of the body, of the little self, of its pleasures and pains, its hurts and comforts, none of these can reach that atmosphere. By thinking only of the spirit and keeping the mind out of matter all the time, I can catch a glimpse of that ideal. Material thought and forms of the sense-world have no place in that ideal. Take them off and put the mind upon the spirit. Forget your life and death, your pains and pleasures, your name and fame, and realise that you are neither body nor mind but the pure spirit.

When I say "I", I mean this spirit. Close your eyes and see what picture appears when you think of your "I". Is it the picture of your body that comes, or of your mental nature? If so, you have not realised your true "I" yet. The time will come, however, when as soon as you say "I" you will see the universe, the Infinite Being. Then you will have realised your true Self and found that you are infinite. That is the truth: you are the spirit, you are not matter. There is such a thing as illusion—in it one thing is taken for another: matter is taken for spirit, this body for soul. That is the tremendous illusion. It has to go.

The next qualification is that the disciple must have faith in the Guru (teacher). In the West the teacher simply gives intellectual knowledge; that is all. The relationship with the teacher is the greatest in life. My dearest and nearest relative in life is my Guru; next, my mother; then my father. My first reverence is to the Guru. If my father says, "Do this", and my Guru says, "Do not do this", I do not do it. The Guru frees my soul. The father and mother give me this body; but the Guru gives me rebirth in the soul.

We have certain peculiar beliefs. One of these is that there are some souls, a few exceptional ones, who are already free and who will be born here for the good of the world, to help the world. They are free already; they do not care for their own salvation—they want to help others. They do not require to be taught anything. From their childhood they know everything; they may speak the highest truth even when they are babies six months old.

Upon these free souls depends the spiritual growth of mankind. They are like the first lamps from which other lamps are lighted. True, the light is in everyone, but in most men it is hidden. The great souls are shining lights from the beginning. Those who come in contact with them have as it were their own lamps lighted. By this the first lamp does not lose anything; yet it communicates its light to other lamps. A million lamps are lighted; but the first lamp goes on shining with undiminished light. The first lamp is the Guru, and the lamp that is lighted from it is the disciple. The second in turn becomes the Guru, and so on. These great ones whom you call Incarnations of God are mighty spiritual giants. They come and set in motion a tremendous spiritual current by transmitting their power to their immediate disciples and through them to generation after generation of disciples.

A bishop in the Christian Church, by the laying on of hands, claims to transmit the power which he is supposed to have received from the preceding bishops. The bishop says that Jesus Christ transmitted his power to his immediate disciples and they to others, and that that is how the Christ's power has come to him. We hold that every one of us, not bishops only, ought to have such power. There is no reason why each of you cannot be a vehicle of the mighty current of spirituality.

But first you must find a teacher, a true teacher, and you must remember that he is not just a man. You may get a teacher in the body; but the real teacher is not in the body; he is not the physical man—he is not as he appears to your eyes. It may be the teacher will come to you as a human being, and you will receive the power from him. Sometimes he will come in a dream and transmit things to the world. The power of the teacher may come to us in many ways. But for us ordinary mortals the teacher must come, and our preparation must go on till he comes.

We attend lectures and read books, argue and reason about God and soul, religion and salvation. These are not spirituality, because spirituality does not exist in books or theories or in philosophies. It is not in learning or reasoning, but in actual inner growth. Even parrots can learn things by heart and repeat them. If you become learned, what of it? Asses can carry whole libraries. So when real light will come, there will be no more of this learning from books—no book-learning. The man who cannot write even his own name can be perfectly religious, and the man with all the libraries of the world in his head may fail to be. Learning is not a condition of spiritual growth; scholarship is not a condition. The touch of the Guru, the transmittal of spiritual energy, will quicken your heart. Then will begin the growth. That is the real baptism by fire. No more stopping. You go on and go on.

Some years ago one of your Christian teachers, a friend of mine, said, "You believe in Christ?" "Yes," I answered, "but perhaps with a little more reverence." "Then why don't you be baptised?" How could I be baptised? By whom? Where is the man who can give true baptism? What is baptism? Is it sprinkling some water over you, or dipping you in water, while muttering formulas?

Baptism is the direct introduction into the life of the spirit. If you receive the real baptism, you know you are not the body but the spirit. Give me that baptism if you can. If not, you are not Christians. Even after the so-called baptism which you received, you have remained the same. What is the sense of merely saying you have been baptised in the name of the Christ? Mere talk, talk—ever disturbing the world with your foolishness! "Ever steeped in the darkness of ignorance, yet considering themselves wise and learned, the fools go round and round, staggering to and fro like the blind led by the blind."[1] Therefore do not say you are Christians, do not brag about baptism and things of that sort.

Of course there is true baptism—there was baptism in the beginning when the Christ came to the earth and taught. The illumined souls, the great ones that come to the earth from time to time, have the power to reveal the Supernal Vision to us. This is true baptism. You see, before the formulas and ceremonies of every religion, there exists the germ of universal truth. In course of time this truth becomes forgotten; it becomes as it were strangled by forms and ceremonies. The forms remain—we find there the casket with the spirit all gone. You have the form of baptism, but few can evoke the living spirit of baptism. The form will not suffice. If we want to gain the living knowledge of the living truth, we have to be truly initiated into it. That is the ideal.

The Guru must teach me and lead me into light, make me a link in that chain of which he himself is a link. The man in the street cannot claim to be a Guru. The Guru must be a man who has known, has actually realised the Divine truth, has perceived himself as the spirit. A mere talker cannot be the Guru. A talkative fool like me can talk much, but cannot be the Guru. A true Guru will tell the disciple, "Go and sin no more"; and no more can he sin, no more has the person the power to sin.

I have seen such men in this life. I have read the

Bible and all such books; they are wonderful. But the living power you cannot find in the books. The power that can transform life in a moment can be found only in the living illumined souls, those shining lights who appear among us from time to time. They alone are fit to be Gurus. You and I are only hollow talk-talk, not teachers. We are disturbing the world more by talking, making bad vibrations. We hope and pray and struggle on, and the day will come when we shall arrive at the truth, and we shall not have to speak. "The teacher was a boy of sixteen; he taught a man of eighty. Silence was the method of the teacher; and the doubts of the disciple vanished for ever."[2] That is the Guru. Just think, if you find such a man, what faith and love you ought to have for that person! Why, he is God Himself, nothing less than that! That is why Christ's disciples worshipped him as God. The disciple must worship the Guru as God Himself. All a man can know is the living God, God as embodied in man, until he himself has realised God. How else would he know God?

Here is a man in America, born nineteen hundred years after Christ, who does not even belong to the same race as Christ, the Jewish race. He has not seen Jesus or his family. He says, "Jesus was God. If you do not believe it, you will go to hell". We can understand how the disciples believed it—that Christ was God; he was their Guru, and they must have believed he was God. But what has this American got to do with the man born nineteen hundred years ago? This young man tells me

1. Katha Upanishad, I.ii.5.
2. Dakshinamurti-stotram, 12 (adapted).

that I do not believe in Jesus and therefore I shall have to go to hell. What does he know of Jesus? He is fit for a lunatic asylum. This kind of belief will not do. He will have to find his Guru.

Jesus may be born again, may come to you. Then, if you worship him as God, you are all right. We must all wait till the Guru comes, and the Guru must be worshipped as God. He is God, he is nothing less than that. As you look at him, the Guru gradually melts away and what is left? The Guru picture gives place to God Himself. The Guru is the bright mask which God wears in order to come to us. As we look steadily on, gradually the mask falls off and God is revealed. "I bow to the Guru who is the embodiment of the Bliss Divine, the personification of the highest knowledge and the giver of the greatest beatitude, who is pure, perfect, one without a second, eternal, beyond pleasure and pain, beyond all thought and all qualification, transcendental". Such is in reality the Guru. No wonder the disciple looks upon him as God Himself and trusts him, reveres him, obeys him, follows him unquestioningly. This is the relation between the Guru and the disciple.

The next condition the disciple must fulfil is to conceive an extreme desire to be free.

We are like moths plunging into the flaming fire, knowing that it will burn us, knowing that the senses only burn us, that they only enhance desire. "Desire is never satiated by enjoyment; enjoyment only increases desire as butter fed into fire increases the fire."[1] Desire is increased by desire. Knowing all this, people still plunge into it all the time. Life after life they have been going after the objects of desire, suffering extremely in consequence, yet they cannot give up desire. Even religion, which should rescue them from this terrible bondage of desire, they have made a means of satisfying desire. Rarely do they ask God to free them from bondage to the body and senses, from slavery to desires. Instead, they pray to Him for health and prosperity, for long life: "O God, cure my headache, give me some money or something!"

The circle of vision has become so narrow, so degraded, so beastly, so animal! None is desiring anything beyond this body. Oh, the terrible degradation, the terrible misery of it! What little flesh, the five senses, the stomach! What is the world but a combination of stomach and sex? Look at millions of men and women — that is what they are living for. Take these away from them and they will find their life empty, meaningless, and intolerable. Such are we. And such is our mind; it is continually hankering for ways and means to satisfy the hunger of the stomach and sex. All the time this is going on. There is also endless suffering; these desires of the body bring only momentary satisfaction and endless suffering. It is like drinking a cup of which the surface layer is nectar, while underneath all is poison. But we still hanker for all these things.

What can be done? Renunciation of the senses and desires is the only way out of this misery. If you want to be spiritual, you

must renounce. This is the real test. Give up the world — this nonsense of the senses. There is only one real desire: to know what is true, to be spiritual. No more materialism, no more this egoism, I must become spiritual. Strong, intense must be the desire. If a man's hands and feet were so tied that he could not move and then if a burning piece of charcoal were placed on his body, he would struggle with all his power to throw it off. When I shall have that sort of extreme desire, that restless struggle, to throw off this burning world, then the time will have come for me to glimpse the Divine Truth.

Look at me. If I lose my little pocketbook with two or three dollars in it, I go twenty times into the house to find that pocketbook. The anxiety, the worry, and the struggle! If one of you crosses me, I remember it twenty years, I cannot forgive and forget it. For the little things of the senses I can struggle like that. Who is there that struggles for God that way? "Children forget everything in their play. The young are mad after the enjoyment of the senses; they do not care for anything else. The old are brooding over their past misdeeds" (Shankara). They are thinking of their past enjoyments — old men that cannot have any enjoyment. Chewing the cud — that is the best they can do. None crave for the Lord in the same intense spirit with which they crave for the things of the senses.

They all say that God is the Truth, the only thing that really exists; that spirit alone is, not matter. Yet the things they seek of God are rarely spirit. They ask always for material things. In their prayers spirit is not separated from matter. Degradation — that is what religion has turned out to be. The whole thing is becoming sham. And the years are rolling on and nothing spiritual is being attained. But man should hunger for one thing alone, the spirit, because spirit alone exists. That is the ideal. If you cannot attain it now, say, "I cannot do it; that is the ideal, I know, but I cannot follow it yet." But that is not what you do. You degrade religion to your low level and seek matter in the name of spirit. You are all atheists. You do not believe in anything except the senses. "So-and-so said such-and-such — there may be something in it. Let us try and have the fun. Possibly some benefit will come; possibly my broken leg will get straight."

Miserable are the diseased people; they are great worshippers of the Lord, for they hope that if they pray to Him He will heal them. Not that that is altogether bad — if such prayers are honest and if they remember that that is not religion. Shri Krishna says in the Gita (VII.16), "Four classes of people worship Me: the distressed, the seeker of material things, the inquirer, and the knower of truth." People who are in distress approach God for relief. If they are ill, they worship Him to be healed; if they lose their wealth, they pray to Him to get it back. There are other people who ask Him for all kinds of things, because they are full of desires — name, fame, wealth, position and so on. They will say, "O Virgin Mary, I will make an offering to you if I get what I want. If you are successful in granting my prayer, I will worship God and give you a part of everything." Men not so material as that, but still with no

1. Bhagavata, IX.xix.14.

faith in God, feel inclined to know about Him. They study philosophies, read scriptures, listen to lectures, and so on. They are the inquirers. The last class are those who worship God and know Him. All these four classes of people are good, not bad. All of them worship Him.

But we are trying to be disciples. Our sole concern is to know the highest truth. Our goal is the loftiest. We have said big words to ourselves—absolute realisation and all that. Let us measure up to the words. Let us worship the spirit in spirit, standing on spirit. Let the foundation be spirit, the middle spirit, the culmination spirit. There will be no world anywhere. Let it go and whirl into space—who cares? Stand thou in the spirit! That is the goal. We know we cannot reach it yet. Never mind. Do not despair, and do not drag the ideal down. The important thing is: how much less you think of the body, of yourself as matter—as dead, dull, insentient matter; how much more you think of yourself as shining immortal being. The more you think of yourself as shining immortal spirit, the more eager you will be to be absolutely free of matter, body, and senses. This is the intense desire to be free.

The fourth and last condition of discipleship is the discrimination of the real from the unreal. There is only one thing that is real—god. All the time the mind must be drawn to Him, dedicated to Him. God exists, nothing else exists, everything else comes and goes. Any desire for the world is illusion, because the world is unreal. More and more the mind must become conscious of God alone, until everything else appears as it really is—unreal.

These are the four conditions which one who wants to be a disciple must fulfil; without fulfilling them he will not be able to come in contact with the true Guru. And even if he is fortunate enough to find him, he will not be quickened by the power that the Guru may transmit. There cannot be any compromising of these conditions. With the fulfilment of these conditions—with all these preparations—the lotus of the disciple's heart will open, and the bee shall come. Then the disciple knows that the Guru was within the body, within himself. He opens out. He realises. He crosses the ocean of life, goes beyond. He crosses this terrible ocean: and in mercy, without a thought of gain or praise, he in his turn helps others to cross.

IS VEDANTA THE FUTURE RELIGION?

Delivered in San Francisco on April 8, 1900.

Those of you who have been attending my lectures for the last month or so must, by this time, be familiar with the ideas contained in the Vedanta philosophy. Vedanta is the most ancient religion of the world; but it can never be said to have become popular. Therefore the question "Is it going to be the religion of the future?" is very difficult to answer.

At the start, I may tell you that I do not know whether it will ever be the religion of the vast majority of men. Will it ever be able to take hold of one whole nation such as the United States of America? Possibly it may. However, that is the question we want to discuss this afternoon.

I shall begin by telling you what Vedanta is not, and then I shall tell you what it is. But you must remember that, with all its emphasis on impersonal principles, Vedanta is not antagonistic to anything, though it does not compromise or give up the truths which it considers fundamental.

You all know that certain things are necessary to make a religion. First of all, there is the book. The power of the book is simply marvellous! Whatever it be, the book is the centre round which human allegiance gathers. Not one religion is living today but has a book. With all its rationalism and tall talk, humanity still clings to the books. In your country every attempt to start a religion without a book has failed. In India sects rise with great success, but within a few years they die down, because there is no book behind them. So in every other country.

Study the rise and fall of the Unitarian movement. It represents the best thought of your nation. Why should it not have spread like the Methodist, Baptist, and other Christian denominations? Because there was no book. On the other hand, think of the Jews. A handful of men, driven from one country to another, still hold together, because they have a book. Think of the Parsees—only a hundred thousand in the world. About a million are all that remain of the Jains in India. And do you know that these handfuls of Parsees and Jains still keep on just because of their books? The religions that are living at the present day—every one of them has a book.

The second requisite, to make a religion, is veneration for some person. He is worshipped either as the Lord of the world or as the great Teacher. Men must worship some embodied man! They must have the Incarnation or the prophet or the great leader. You find it in every religion today. Hindus and Christians—they have Incarnations: Buddhists, Mohammedans, and Jews have prophets. But it is all about the same—all their veneration twines round some person or persons.

The third requisite seems to be that a religion, to be strong and sure of itself, must believe that it alone is the truth; otherwise it cannot influence people.

Liberalism dies because it is dry, because it cannot rouse fanaticism in the human mind, because it cannot bring out hatred for everything except itself. That is why liberalism is bound to go down again and again. It can influence only small numbers of people. The reason is not hard to see. Liberalism tries to make us unselfish. But we do not want to be unselfish—we see no immediate gain in unselfishness; we gain more by being selfish. We accept liberalism as long as we are poor, have nothing. The moment we acquire money and power, we turn very conservative. The poor man is a democrat. When he becomes rich, he becomes an aristocrat. In religion, too, human nature acts in the same way.

A prophet arises, promises all kinds of rewards to those who will follow him and eternal doom to those who will not. Thus he makes his ideas spread. All existent religions that are spreading are tremendously fanatic. The more a sect hates other sects, the greater is its success and the more people it draws into its fold. My conclusion, after travelling over a good part of the world and living with many races, and in view of the conditions prevailing in the world, is that the present state of things is going to continue, in spite of much talk of universal brotherhood.

Vedanta does not believe in any of these teachings. First, it does not believe in a book — that is the difficulty to start with. It denies the authority of any book over any other book. It denies emphatically that any one book can contain all the truths about God, soul, the ultimate reality. Those of you who have read the Upanishads remember that they say again and again, "Not by the reading of books can we realise the Self."

Second, it finds veneration for some particular person still more difficult to uphold. Those of you who are students of Vedanta — by Vedanta is always meant the Upanishads — know that this is the only religion that does not cling to any person. Not one man or woman has ever become the object of worship among the Vedantins. It cannot be. A man is no more worthy of worship than any bird, any worm. We are all brothers. The difference is only in degree. I am exactly the same as the lowest worm. You see how very little room there is in Vedanta for any man to stand ahead of us and for us to go and worship him — he dragging us on and we being saved by him. Vedanta does not give you that. No book, no man to worship, nothing.

A still greater difficulty is about God. You want to be democratic in this country. It is the democratic God that Vedanta teaches.

You have a government, but the government is impersonal. Yours is not an autocratic government, and yet it is more powerful than any monarchy in the world. Nobody seems to understand that the real power, the real life, the real strength is in the unseen, the impersonal, the nobody. As a mere person separated from others, you are nothing, but as an impersonal unit of the nation that rules itself, you are tremendous. You are all one in the government — you are a tremendous power. But where exactly is the power? Each man is the power. There is no king. I see everybody equally the same. I have not to take off my hat and bow low to anyone. Yet there is a tremendous power in each man.

Vedanta is just that. Its God is not the monarch sitting on a throne, entirely apart. There are those who like their God that way — a God to be feared and propitiated. They burn candles and crawl in the dust before Him. They want a king to rule them — they believe in a king in heaven to rule them all. The king is gone from this country at least. Where is the king of heaven now? Just where the earthly king is. In this country the king has entered every one of you. You are all kings in this country. So with the religion of Vedanta. You are all Gods. One God is not sufficient. You are all Gods, says the Vedanta.

This makes Vedanta very difficult. It does not teach the old idea of God at all. In place of that God who sat above the clouds and managed the affairs of the world without asking our permission, who created us out of nothing just because He liked it and made us undergo all this misery just because He liked it, Vedanta teaches the God that is in everyone, has become everyone and everything. His majesty the king has gone from this country; the Kingdom of Heaven went from Vedanta hundreds of years ago.

India cannot give up his majesty the king of the earth — that is why Vedanta cannot become the religion of India. There is a chance of Vedanta becoming the religion of your country because of democracy. But it can become so only if you can and do clearly understand it, if you become real men and women, not people with vague ideas and superstitions in your brains, and if you want to be truly spiritual, since Vedanta is concerned only with spirituality.

What is the idea of God in heaven? Materialism. The Vedantic idea is the infinite principle of God embodied in every one of us. God sitting up on a cloud! Think of the utter blasphemy of it! It is materialism — downright materialism. When babies think this way, it may be all right, but when grown-up men try to teach such things, it is downright disgusting — that is what it is. It is all matter, all body idea, the gross idea, the sense idea. Every bit of it is clay and nothing but clay. Is that religion? It is no more religion than is the Mumbo Jumbo "religion" of Africa. God is spirit and He should be worshipped in spirit and in truth. Does spirit live only in heaven? What is spirit? We are all spirit. Why is it we do not realise it? What makes you different from me? Body and nothing else. Forget the body, and all is spirit.

These are what Vedanta has not to give. No book. No man to be singled out from the rest of mankind — "You are worms, and we are the Lord God!" — none of that. If you are the Lord God, I also am the Lord God. So Vedanta knows no sin. There are mistakes but no sin; and in the long run everything is going to be all right. No Satan — none of this nonsense. Vedanta believes in only one sin, only one in the world, and it is this: the moment you think you are a sinner or anybody is a sinner, that is sin. From that follows every other mistake or what is usually called sin. There have been many mistakes in our lives. But we are going on. Glory be unto us that we have made mistakes! Take a long look at your past life. If your present condition is good, it has been caused by all the past mistakes as well as successes. Glory be unto success! Glory be unto mistakes! Do not look back upon what has been done. Go ahead!

You see, Vedanta proposes no sin nor sinner. No God to be afraid of. He is the one being of whom we shall never be afraid, because He is our own Self. There is only one being of whom you cannot possibly be afraid; He is that. Then is not he really the most superstitious person who has fear of God? There may be someone who is afraid of his shadow; but even he is not afraid of himself. God is man's very Self. He is that one being whom you can never possibly fear. What is all this nonsense, the fear of the Lord entering into a man, making him tremble and so on? Lord bless us that we are not all in the lunatic asylum! But if most of us are not lunatics, why should we invent such ideas as fear of God? Lord Buddha said that the whole human race is lunatic, more or less. It is perfectly true, it seems.

No book, no person, no Personal God. All these must go. Again, the senses must go. We cannot be bound to the senses. At present we are tied down—like persons dying of cold in the glaciers. They feel such a strong desire to sleep, and when their friends try to wake them, warning them of death, they say, "Let me die, I want to sleep." We all cling to the little things of the senses, even if we are ruined thereby: we forget there are much greater things.

There is a Hindu legend that the Lord was once incarnated on earth as a pig. He had a pig mate and in course of time several little pigs were born to Him. He was very happy with His family, living in the mire, squealing with joy, forgetting His divine glory and lordship. The gods became exceedingly concerned and came to the earth to beg Him to give up the pig body and return to heaven. But the Lord would have none of that; He drove them away. He said He was very happy and did not want to be disturbed. Seeing no other course, the gods destroyed the pig body of the Lord. At once He regained His divine majesty and was astonished that He could have found any joy in being a pig.

People behave in the same way. Whenever they hear of the Impersonal God, they say, "What will become of my individuality?— my individuality will go!" Next time that thought comes, remember the pig, and then think what an infinite mine of happiness you have, each one of you. How pleased you are with your present condition! But when you realise what you truly are, you will be astonished that you were unwilling to give up your sense-life. What is there in your personality? It is any better than that pig life? And this you do not want to give up! Lord bless us all!

What does Vedanta teach us? In the first place, it teaches that you need not even go out of yourself to know the truth. All the past and all the future are here in the present. No man ever saw the past. Did any one of you see the past? When you think you are knowing the past, you only imagine the past in the present moment. To see the future, you would have to bring it down to the present, which is the only reality—the rest is imagination. This present is all that is. There is only the One. All is here right now. One moment in infinite time is quite as complete and all-inclusive as every other moment. All that is and was and will be is here in the present. Let anybody try to imagine anything outside of it—he will not succeed.

What religion can paint a heaven which is not like this earth?

And it is all art, only this art is being made known to us gradually. We, with five senses, look upon this world and find it gross, having colour, form, sound, and the like. Suppose I develop an electric sense—all will change. Suppose my senses grow finer—you will all appear changed. If I change, you change. If I go beyond the power of the senses, you will appear as spirit and God. Things are not what they seem.

We shall understand this by and by, and then see it: all the heavens—everything—are here, now, and they really are nothing but appearances on the Divine Presence. This Presence is much greater than all the earths and heavens. People think that this world is bad and imagine that heaven is somewhere else. This world is not bad. It is God Himself if you know it. It is a hard thing even to understand, harder than to believe. The murderer who is going to be hanged tomorrow is all God, perfect God. It is very hard to understand, surely; but it can be understood.

Therefore Vedanta formulates, not universal brotherhood, but universal oneness. I am the same as any other man, as any animal—good, bad, anything. It is one body, one mind, one soul throughout. Spirit never dies. There is no death anywhere, not even for the body. Not even the mind dies. How can even the body die? One leaf may fall—does the tree die? The universe is my body. See how it continues. All minds are mine. With all feet I walk. Through all mouths I speak. In everybody I reside.

Why can I not feel it? Because of that individuality, that piggishness. You have become bound up with this mind and can only be here, not there. What is immortality? How few reply, "It is this very existence of ours!" Most people think this is all mortal and dead—that God is not here, that they will become immortal by going to heaven. They imagine that they will see God after death. But if they do not see Him here and now, they will not see Him after death. Though they all believe in immortality, they do not know that immortality is not gained by dying and going to heaven, but by giving up this piggish individuality, by not tying ourselves down to one little body. Immortality is knowing ourselves as one with all, living in all bodies, perceiving through all minds. We are bound to feel in other bodies than this one. We are bound to feel in other bodies. What is sympathy? Is there any limit to this sympathy, this feeling in our bodies? It is quite possible that the time will come when I shall feel through the whole universe.

What is the gain? The pig body is hard to give up; we are sorry to lose the enjoyment of our one little pig body! Vedanta does not say, "Give it up": it says, "Transcend it". No need of asceticism—better would be the enjoyment of two bodies, better three, living in more bodies than one! When I can enjoy through the whole universe, the whole universe is my body.

There are many who feel horrified when they hear these teachings. They do not like to be told that they are not just little pig bodies, created by a tyrant God. I tell them, "Come up!" They say they are born in sin—they cannot come up except through someone's grace. I say, "You are Divine! They answer, "You blasphemer, how dare you speak so? How can a miserable creature be God? We are sinners!" I get very much discouraged at times, you know. Hundreds of men and women tell me, "If there is no hell, how can there be any religion?" If these people go to hell of their own will, who can prevent them?

Whatever you dream and think of, you create. If it is hell, you die and see hell. If it is evil and Satan, you get a Satan. If ghosts, you get ghosts. Whatever you think, that you become. If you have to think, think good thoughts, great thoughts. This taking for granted that you are weak little worms! By declaring we are weak, we become weak, we do not become better. Suppose we put out the light, close the windows, and call the room dark. Think of the nonsense! What good does it do me to say I am a sinner? If I am in the dark, let me light a lamp. The whole thing is gone. Yet how curious is the nature of men! Though always conscious that the universal mind is behind their life, they think more of Satan, of darkness and lies. You tell them the truth—they do not see it; they like darkness better.

This forms the one great question asked by Vedanta: Why are people so afraid? The answer is that they have made themselves helpless and dependent on others. We are so lazy, we do not want to do anything for ourselves. We want a Personal God, a saviour or a prophet to do everything for us. The very rich man never walks, always goes in the carriage; but in the course of years, he wakes up one day paralysed all over. Then he begins to feel that the way he had lived was not good after all. No man can walk for me. Every time one did, it was to my injury. If everything is done for a man by another, he will lose the use of his own limbs. Anything we do ourselves, that is the only thing we do. Anything that is done for us by another never can be ours. You cannot learn spiritual truths from my lectures. If you have learnt anything, I was only the spark that brought it out, made it flash. That is all the prophets and teachers can do. All this running after help is foolishness.

You know, there are bullock carts in India. Usually two bulls are harnessed to a cart, and sometimes a sheaf of straw is dangled at the tip of the pole, a little in front of the animals but beyond their reach. The bulls try continually to feed upon the straw, but never succeed. This is exactly how we are helped! We think we are going to get security, strength, wisdom, happiness from the outside. We always hope but never realise our hope. Never does any help come from the outside.

There is no help for man. None ever was, none is, and none will be. Why should there be? Are you not men and women? Are the lords of the earth to be helped by others? Are you not ashamed? You will be helped when you are reduced to dust. But you are spirit. Pull yourself out of difficulties by yourself! Save yourself by yourself! There is none to help you—never

was. To think that there is, is sweet delusion. It comes to no good.

There came a Christian to me once and said, "You are a terrible sinner." I answered, "Yes, I am. Go on." He was a Christian missionary. That man would not give me any rest. When I see him, I fly. He said, "I have very good things for you. You are a sinner and you are going to hell." I replied, "Very good, what else?" I asked him, "Where are you going?" "I am going to heaven", he answered. I said, "I will go to hell." That day he gave me up.

Here comes a Christian man and he says, "You are all doomed; but if you believe in this doctrine, Christ will help you out." If this were true—but of course it is nothing but superstition—there would be no wickedness in the Christian countries. Let us believe in it—believing costs nothing—but why is there no result? If I ask, "Why is it that there are so many wicked people?" they say, "We have to work more." Trust in God, but keep your powder dry! Pray to God, and let God come and help you out! But it is I who struggle, pray, and worship; it is I who work out my problems—and God takes the credit. This is not good. I never do it.

Once I was invited to a dinner. The hostess asked

me to say grace. I said, "I will say grace to you, madam. My grace and thanks are to you." When I work, I say grace to myself. Praise be unto me that I worked hard and acquired what I have!

All the time you work hard and bless somebody else, because you are superstitious, you are afraid. No more of these superstitions bred through thousands of years! It takes a little hard work to become spiritual. Superstitions are all materialism, because they are all based on the consciousness of body, body, body. No spirit there. Spirit has no superstitions—it is beyond the vain desires of the body.

But here and there these vain desires are being projected even into the realm of the spirit. I have attended several spiritualistic meetings. In one, the leader was a woman. She said to me, "Your mother and grandfather came to me" She said that they greeted her and talked to her. But my mother is living yet! People like to think that even after death their relatives continue to exist in the same bodies, and the spiritualists play on their superstitions. I would be very sorry to know that my dead father is still wearing his filthy body. People get consolation from this, that their fathers are all encased in matter. In another place they brought me Jesus Christ. I said, "Lord, how do you do?" It makes me feel hopeless. If that great saintly man is still wearing the body, what is to become of us poor creatures? The spiritualists did not allow me to touch any of those gentlemen. Even if these were real, I would not want them. I think, "Mother, Mother! atheists—that is what people really are! Just the desire for these five senses! Not satisfied with what they have here, they want more of the same when they die!"

What is the God of Vedanta? He is principle, not person.

You and I are all Personal Gods. The Absolute God of the universe, the creator, preserver, and destroyer of the universe, is impersonal principle. You and I, the cat, rat, devil, and ghost, all these are Its persons—all are Personal Gods. You want to worship Personal Gods. It is the worship of your own self. If you take my advice, you will never enter any church. Come out and go and wash off. Wash yourself again and again until you are cleansed of all the superstitions that have clung to you through the ages. Or, perhaps, you do not like to do so, since you do not wash yourself so often in this country—frequent washing is an Indian custom, not a custom of your society.

I have been asked many times, "Why do you laugh so much and make so many jokes?" I become serious sometimes—when I have stomach-ache! The Lord is all blissfulness. He is the reality behind all that exists, He is the goodness, the truth in everything. You are His incarnations. That is what is glorious. The nearer you are to Him, the less you will have occasions to cry or weep. The further we are from Him, the more will long faces come. The more we know of Him, the more misery vanishes. If one who lives in the Lord becomes miserable, what is the use of living in Him? What is the use of such a God? Throw Him overboard into the Pacific Ocean! We do not want Him!

But God is the infinite, impersonal being—ever existent, unchanging, immortal, fearless; and you are all His incarnations, His embodiments. This is the God of Vedanta, and His heaven is everywhere. In this heaven dwell all the Personal Gods there are—you yourselves. Exit praying and laying flowers in the temples! What do you pray for? To go to heaven, to get something, and let somebody else not have it. "Lord, I want more food! Let somebody else starve!" What an idea of God who is the reality, the infinite, ever blessed existence in which there is neither part nor flaw, who is ever free, ever pure, ever perfect! We attribute to Him all our human characteristics, functions, and limitations. He must bring us food and give us clothes. As a matter of fact we have to do all these things ourselves and nobody else ever did them for us. That is the plain truth.

But you rarely think of this. You imagine there is God of whom you are special favourites, who does things for you when you ask Him; and you do not ask of Him favours for all men, all beings, but only for yourself, your own family, your own people. When the Hindu is starving, you do not care; at that time you do not think that the God of the Christians is also the God of the Hindus. Our whole idea of God, our praying, our worshipping, all are vitiated by our ignorance, our foolish idea of ourselves as body. You may not like what I am saying. You may curse me today, but tomorrow you will bless me.

We must become thinkers. Every birth is painful. We must get out of materialism. My Mother would not let us get out of Her clutches; nevertheless we must try. This struggle is all the worship there is; all the rest is mere shadow. You are the Personal God. Just now I am worshipping you. This is the greatest prayer. Worship the whole world in that sense—by serving it. This standing on a high platform, I know, does not appear like worship. But if it is service, it is worship.

The infinite truth is never to be acquired. It is here all the time, undying and unborn. He, the Lord of the universe, is in every one. There is but one temple—the body. It is the only temple that ever existed. In this body, He resides, the Lord of souls and the King of kings. We do not see that, so we make stone images of Him and build temples over them. Vedanta has been in India always, but India is full of these temples—and not only temples, but also caves containing carved images. "The fool, dwelling on the bank of the Ganga, digs a well for water!" Such are we! Living in the midst of God—we must go and make images. We project Him in the form of the image, while all the time He exists in the temple of our body. We are lunatics, and this is the great delusion.

Worship everything as God—every form is His temple. All else is delusion. Always look within, never without. Such is the God that Vedanta preaches, and such is His worship. Naturally there is no sect, no creed, no caste in Vedanta. How can this religion be the national religion of India?

Hundreds of castes! If one man touches another man's food, he cries out, "Lord help me, I am polluted!" When I returned to India after my visit to the West, several orthodox Hindus raised a howl against my association with the Western people and my breaking the rules of orthodoxy. They did not like me to teach the truths of the Vedas to the people of the West.

But how can there be these distinctions and differences? How can the rich man turn up his nose at the poor man, and the learned at the ignorant, if we are all spirit and all the same? Unless society changes, how can such a religion as Vedanta prevail? It will take thousands of years to have large numbers of truly rational human beings. It is very hard to show men new things, to give them great ideas. It is harder still to knock off old superstitions, very hard; they do not die easily. With all his education, even the learned man becomes frightened in the dark—the nursery tales come into his mind, and he see ghosts.

The meaning of the word "Veda", from which the word "Vedanta" comes, is knowledge. All knowledge is Veda, infinite as God is infinite. Nobody ever creates knowledge. Did you ever see knowledge created? It is only discovered—what was covered is uncovered. It is always here, because it is God Himself. Past, present, and future knowledge, all exist in all of us. We discover it, that is all. All this knowledge is God Himself. The Vedas are a great Sanskrit book. In our country we go down on our knees before the man who reads the Vedas, and we do not care for the man who is studying physics. That is superstition; it is not Vedanta at all. It is utter materialism. With God every knowledge is sacred. Knowledge is God. Infinite knowledge abides within every one in the fullest measure. You are not really ignorant, though you may appear to be so. You are incarnations of God, all of you. You are incarnations of the Almighty, Omnipresent, Divine Principle. You may laugh at me now, but the time will come when you will understand. You must. Nobody will be left behind.

What is the goal? This that I have spoken of—vedanta—is not a new religion. So old—as old as God Himself. It is not confined to any time and place, it is everywhere. Everybody knows this truth. We are all working it out. The goal of the whole universe is that. This applies even to external nature—every atom is rushing towards that goal. And do you think that any of the infinite pure souls are left without knowledge of the supreme truth? All have it, all are going to the same goal—the discovery of the innate Divinity. The maniac, the murderer, the superstitious man, the man who is lynched in this country—all are travelling to the same goal. Only that which we do ignorantly we ought to do knowingly, and better.

The unity of all existence—you all have it already within yourselves. None was ever born without it. However you may deny it, it continually asserts itself. What is human love? It is more or less an affirmation of that unity: "I am one with thee, my wife, my child, my friend!" Only you are affirming the unity ignorantly. "None ever loved the husband for the husband's sake, but for the sake of the Self that is in the husband." The wife finds unity there. The husband sees himself in the wife—instinctively he does it, but he cannot do it knowingly, consciously.

The whole universe is one existence. There cannot be anything else. Out of diversities we are all going towards this universal existence. Families into tribes, tribes into races, races into nations, nations into humanity—how many wills going to the One! It is all knowledge, all science—the realisation of this unity. Unity is knowledge, diversity is ignorance. This knowledge is your birthright. I have not to teach it to you. There never were different religions in the world. We are all destined to have salvation, whether we will it or not. You have to attain it in the long run and become free, because it is your nature to be free. We are already free, only we do not know it, and we do not know what we have been doing. Throughout all religious systems and ideals is the same morality; one thing only is preached: "Be unselfish, love others." One says, "Because Jehovah commanded." "Allah," shouted Mohammed. Another cries, "Jesus". If it was only the command of Jehovah, how could it come to those who never knew Jehovah? If it was Jesus alone who gave this command, how could any one who never knew Jesus get it? If only Vishnu, how could the Jews get it, who never were acquainted with that gentleman? There is another source, greater than all of them. Where is it? In the eternal temple of God, in the souls of all beings from the lowest to the highest. It is there—that infinite unselfishness, infinite sacrifice, infinite compulsion to go back to unity.

We have seemingly been divided, limited, because of our ignorance; and we have become as it were the little Mrs. so-and-so and Mr. so-and-so. But all nature is giving this delusion the lie every moment. I am not that little man or little woman cut off from all else; I am the one universal existence. The soul in its own majesty is rising up every moment and declaring its own intrinsic Divinity.

This Vedanta is everywhere, only you must become conscious of it. These masses of foolish beliefs and superstitions hinder us in our progress. If we can, let us throw them off and understand that God is spirit to be worshipped in spirit and in truth. Try to be materialists no more! Throw away all matter! The conception of God must be truly spiritual. All the different ideas of God, which are more or less materialistic, must go. As man becomes more and more spiritual, he has to throw off all these ideas and leave them behind. As a matter of fact, in every country there have always been a few who have been strong enough to throw away all matter and stand out in the shining light, worshipping the spirit by the spirit.

If Vedanta—this conscious knowledge that all is one spirit—spreads, the whole of humanity will become spiritual. But is it possible? I do not know. Not within thousands of years. The old superstitions must run out. You are all interested in how to perpetuate all your superstitions. Then there are the ideas of the family brother, the caste brother, the national brother. All these are barriers to the realisation of Vedanta. Religion has been religion to very few.

Most of those who have worked in the field of religion all over the world have really been political workers. That has been the history of human beings. They have rarely tried to live up uncompromisingly to the truth. They have always worshipped the god called society; they have been mostly concerned with upholding what the masses believe—their superstitions, their weakness. They do not try to conquer nature but to fit into nature, nothing else. God to India and preach a new creed—they will not listen to it. But if you tell them it is from the Vedas—"That is good!" they will say. Here I can preach this doctrine, and you—how many of you take me seriously? But the truth is all here, and I must tell you the truth.

There is another side to the question. Everyone says that the highest, the pure, truth cannot be realised all at once by all, that men have to be led to it gradually through worship, prayer, and other kinds of prevalent religious practices. I am not sure whether that is the right method or not. In India I work both ways.

In Calcutta, I have all these images and temples—in the name of God and the Vedas, of the Bible and Christ and Buddha. Let it be tried. But on the heights of the Himalayas I have a place where I am determined nothing shall enter except pure truth. There I want to work out this idea about which I have spoken to you today. There are an Englishman and an Englishwoman in charge of the place. The purpose is to train seekers of truth and to bring up children without fear and without superstition. They shall not hear about Christs and Buddhas and Shivas and Vishnus—none of these. They shall learn, from the start, to stand upon their own feet. They shall learn from their childhood that God is the spirit and should be worshipped in spirit and in truth. Everyone must be looked upon as spirit. That is the ideal. I do not know what success will come of it. Today I am preaching the thing I like. I wish I had been brought up entirely on that, without all the dualistic superstitions.

Sometimes I agree that there is some good in the dualistic method: it helps many who are weak. If a man wants you to show him the polar star, you first point out to him a bright star near it, then a less bright star, then a dim star, and then the polar star. This process makes it easy for him to see it. All the various practices and trainings, Bibles and Gods, are but the rudiments of religion, the kindergartens of religion.

But then I think of the other side. How long will the world have to wait to reach the truth if it follows this slow, gradual process? How long? And where is the surety that it will ever succeed to any appreciable degree? It has not so far. After all, gradual or not gradual, easy or not easy to the weak, is not the dualistic method based on falsehood? Are not all the prevalent religious practices often weakening and therefore wrong? They are based on a wrong idea, a wrong view of man. Would two wrong make one right? Would the lie become truth? Would darkness become light?

I am the servant of a man who has passed away. I am only the messenger. I want to make the experiment. The teachings of Vedanta I have told you about were never really experimented with before. Although Vedanta is the oldest philosophy in the world, it has always become mixed up with superstitions and everything else.

Christ said, "I and my father are one", and you repeat it. Yet it has not helped mankind. For nineteen hundred years men have not understood that saying. They make Christ the saviour of men. He is God and we are worms! Similarly in India. In every country, this sort of belief is the backbone of every sect. For thousands of years millions and millions all over the world have been taught to worship the Lord of the world, the Incarnations, the saviours, the prophets. They have been taught to consider themselves helpless, miserable creatures and to depend upon the mercy of some person or persons for salvation. There are no doubt many marvellous things in such beliefs. But even at their best, they are but kindergartens of religion, and they have helped but little. Men are still hypnotised into abject degradation. However, there are some strong souls who get over that illusion. The hour comes when great men shall arise and cast off these kindergartens of religion and shall make vivid and powerful the true religion, the worship of the spirit by the spirit.

THE WOMEN OF INDIA

New Discoveries, Vol. 2, pp. 411-26.

The following lecture was delivered at Cambridge, December 17, 1894, and recorded by Miss Frances Willard's stenographer.

Swami Vivekananda faced bigotry in America on several issues of Indian culture—one was the Indian woman. Naturally he sought to correct Western misconceptions. When he lectured in his own country, however, there was no greater advocate for improving the life of Indian women than the Swami.

In speaking about the women of India, ladies and gentlemen, I feel that I am going to talk about my mothers and sisters in India to the women of another race, many of whom have been like mothers and sisters to me. But though, unfortunately, within very recent times there have been mouths only to curse the women of our country, I have found that there are some who bless them too. I have found such noble souls in this nation as Mrs. [Ole] Bull and Miss [Sarah] Farmer and Miss [Frances] Willard, and that wonderful representative of the highest aristocracy of the world, whose life reminds me of that man of India, six hundred years before the birth of Christ, who gave up his throne to mix with the people. Lady Henry Somerset has been a revelation to me. I become bold when I find such noble souls who will not curse, whose mouths are full of blessing for me, my country, our men and women, and whose hands and hearts are ever ready to do service to humanity.

I first intend to take a glimpse into times past of Indian history, and we will find something unique. All of you are aware, perhaps, that you Americans and we Hindus and this lady from Iceland [Mrs. Sigrid Magnusson] are the descendants of one common ancestry known as Aryans. Above all, we find three ideas wherever the Aryans go: the village community, the rights of women and a joyful religion[1].

The first [idea] is the system of village communities—as we have just heard from Mrs. Bull concerning the North. Each man was his own [lord?] and owned the land. All these political institutions of the world we now see, are the developments of those village systems. As the Aryans went over to different countries and settled, certain circumstances developed this institution, others that.

The next idea of the Aryans is the freedom of women. It is in the Aryan literature that we find women in ancient times taking the same share as men, and in no other literature of the world.

Going back to our Vedas—they are the oldest literature the world possesses and are composed by your and my common ancestors (they were not written in India—perhaps on the coast of the Baltic, perhaps in Central Asia—we do not know).

Their oldest portion is composed of hymns, and these

1. Since Swami Vivekananda's time there has been more research on the spread of the Aryan culture.

hymns are to the gods whom the Aryans worshipped. I may be pardoned for using the word gods; the literal translation is "the bright ones". These hymns are dedicated to Fire, to the Sun, to Varuna and other deities. The titles run: "such-and-such a sage composed this verse, dedicated to such-and-such a deity".

In the tenth chapter comes a peculiar hymn — for the sage is a woman — and it is dedicated to the one God who is at the background of all these gods. All the previous hymns are spoken in the third person, as if someone were addressing the deities. But this hymn takes a departure: God [as the Devi] is speaking for herself. The pronoun used is "I". "I am the Empress of the Universe, the Fulfiller of all prayers." (Vide "Devi Sukta", Rig-Veda 10.125)

This is the first glimpse of women's work in the Vedas. As we go on, we find them taking a greater share — even officiating as priests. There is not one passage throughout the whole mass of literature of the Vedas which can be construed even indirectly as signifying that woman could never be a priest. In fact, there are many examples of women officiating as priests.

Then we come to the last portion of these Vedas — which is really the religion of India — the concentrated wisdom of which has not been surpassed even in this century. There, too, we find women preeminent. A large portion of these books are words which have proceeded from the mouths of women. It is there — recorded with their names and teachings.

There is that beautiful story of the great sage Yâjnavalkya, the one who visited the kingdom of the great king Janaka. And there in that assembly of the learned, people came to ask him questions. One man asked him, "How am I to perform this sacrifice?" Another asked him, "How am I to perform the other sacrifice?" And after he had answered them, there arose a woman who said, "These are childish questions. Now, have a care: I take these two arrows, my two questions. Answer them if you can, and we will then call you a sage. The first is: What is the soul? The second is: What is God?" (Brihadâranyaka Upanishad 3.8.1.-12.)

Thus arose in India the great questions about the soul and God, and these came from the mouth of a woman. The sage had to pass an examination before her, and he passed well.

Coming to the next stratum of literature, our epics, we find that education has not degenerated. Especially in the caste of princes this ideal was most wonderfully held.

In the Vedas we find this idea of marrying — the girls chose for themselves; so the boys. In the next stratum they are married by their parents, except in one caste.

Even here I would ask you to look at another side. Whatever may be said of the Hindus, they are one of the most learned races the world has ever produced. The Hindu is the metaphysician; he applies everything to his intellect. Everything has to be settled by astrological calculation.

The idea was that the stars govern the fate of every man and woman. Even today when a child is born, a horoscope is cast.

That determines the character of the child. One child is born of a divine nature, another of a human, others of lower character.

The difficulty was: If a child who was of a monster-character was united with a child of a god-character, would they not have a tendency to degenerate each other?

The next difficulty was: Our laws did not allow marriage within the same clans. Not only may one not marry within his own family — or even one of his cousins — but one must not marry into the clan of his father or even of his mother.

A third difficulty was: If there had been leprosy or phthisis or any such incurable disease within six generations of either bride or bridegroom, then there must not be a marriage.

Now taking [into account] these three difficulties, the Brahmin says: "If I leave it to the choice of the boy or girl to marry, the boy or girl will be fascinated with a beautiful face. And then very likely all these circumstances will bring ruin to the family". This is the primary idea that governs our marriage laws, as you will find. Whether right or wrong, there is this philosophy at the background. Prevention is better than cure.

That misery exists in this world is because we give birth to misery. So the whole question is how to prevent the birth of miserable children. How far the rights of a society should extend over the individual is an open question. But the Hindus say that the choice of marriage should not be left in the hands of the boy or girl.

I do not mean to say that this is the best thing to do. Nor do I see that leaving it in their hands is at all a perfect solution. I have not found a solution yet in my own mind; nor do I see that any country has one.

We come next to another picture. I told you that there was another peculiar form of marriage (generally among the royalty) where the father of the girl invited different princes and noblemen and they had an assembly. The young lady, the daughter of the king, was borne on a sort of chair before each one of the princes in turn. And the herald would repeat: "This is Prince So-and-so, and these are his qualifications". The young girl would either wait or say, "Move on". And before the next prince, the crier would also give a description, and the girl would say, "Move on". (All this would be arranged beforehand; she already had the liking for somebody before this.) Then at last she would ask one of the servants to throw the garland over the head of the man, and it would be thrown to show he was accepted. (The last of these marriages was the cause of the Mohammedan invasion of India.) (Vide prince, who became the Queen of Delhi.) These marriages were specially reserved for the prince caste.

The oldest Sanskrit poem in existence, the Râmâyana, has embodied the loftiest Hindu ideal of a woman in the character of Sitâ. We have not time to go through her life of infinite patience and goodness. We worship her as God incarnate, and she is named before her husband, Râma. We say not "Mr. and Mrs.", but "Mrs. and Mr." and so on, with all the gods and goddesses, naming the woman first.

There is another peculiar conception of the Hindu. Those who have been studying with me are aware that the central conception of Hindu philosophy is of the Absolute; that is the background of the universe. This Absolute Being, of whom we can predicate nothing, has Its powers spoken of as She—that is, the real personal God in India is She. This Shakti of the Brahman is always in the feminine gender.

Rama is considered the type of the Absolute, and Sita that of Power. We have no time to go over all the life of Sita, but I will quote a passage from her life that is very much suited to the ladies of this country.

The picture opens when she was in the forest with her husband, whither they were banished. There was a female sage whom they both went to see. Her fasts and devotions had emaciated her body.

Sita approached this sage and bowed down before her. The sage placed her hand on the head of Sita and said: "It is a great blessing to possess a beautiful body; you have that. It is a greater blessing to have a noble husband; you have that. It is the greatest blessing to be perfectly obedient to such a husband; you are that. You must be happy".

Sita replied, "Mother, I am glad that God has given me a beautiful body and that I have so devoted a husband. But as to the third blessing, I do not know whether I obey him or he obeys me. One thing alone I remember, that when he took me by the hand before the sacrificial fire—whether it was a reflection of the fire or whether God himself made it appear to me—I found that I was his and he was mine. And since then, I have found that I am the complement of his life, and he of mine".

Portions of this poem have been translated into the English language. Sita is the ideal of a woman in India and worshipped as God incarnate.

We come now to Manu the great lawgiver. Now, in this book there is an elaborate description of how a child should be educated. We must remember that it was compulsory with the Aryans that a child be educated, whatever his caste. After describing how a child should be educated, Manu adds: "Along the same lines, the daughters are to be educated—exactly as the boys"[1].

I have often heard that there are other passages where women are condemned. I admit that in our sacred books there are many passages which condemn women as offering temptation; you can see that for yourselves. But there are also passages that glorify women as the power of God. And there are other passages which state that in that house where one drop of a woman's tear falls, the gods are never pleased and the house goes to ruin. Drinking wine, killing a woman and killing a Brahmin are the highest crimes in the Hindu religion. I admit there are condemnatory sentences [in some of our books]; but

here I claim the superiority of these Hindu books, for in the books of other races there is only condemnation and no good word for a woman.

Next, I will come to our old dramas. Whatever the books say, the dramas are the perfect representation of society as it then existed. In these, which were written from four hundred years before Christ onward, we find even universities full of both boys and girls. We would not [now] find Hindu women, as they have since become cut off from higher education[2]. But [at that time], they were everywhere pretty much the same as they are in this country—going out to the gardens and parks to take promenades.

There is another point which I bring before you and where the Hindu woman is still superior to all other women in the world —her rights. The right to possess property is as absolute for women in India as for men—and has been for thousands and thousands of years.

If you have any lawyer friend and can take up commentaries on the Hindu law, you will find it all for yourselves. A girl may bring a million dollars to her husband, but every dollar of that is hers. Nobody has any right to touch one dollar of that. If the husband dies without issue, the whole property of the husband goes to her, even if his father or mother is living. And that has been the law from the past to the present time. That is something which the Hindu woman has had beyond that of the women of other countries.

The older books—or even newer books—do not prohibit the Hindu widows from being married; it is a mistake to think so. They give them their choice, and that is given to both men and women. The idea in our religion is that marriage is for the weak, and I don't see any reason to give up that idea today. They who find themselves complete—what is the use of their marrying? And those that marry—they are given one chance. When that chance is over, both men and women are looked down upon if they marry again; but it is not that they are prohibited. It is nowhere said that a widow is not to marry. The widow and widower who do not marry are considered more spiritual.

Men, of course, break through this law and go and marry; whereas women—they being of a higher spiritual nature—keep to the law. For instance, our books say that eating meat is bad and sinful, but you may still eat such-and-such a meat —mutton, for instance. I have seen thousands of men who eat mutton, and never in my life have I seen a woman of higher caste who eats meat of any kind. This shows that their nature is to keep the law—keeping more towards religion. But do not judge too harshly of Hindu men. You must try to look at the Hindu law from my position too, for I am a Hindu man.

This non-marriage of widows gradually grew into a custom. And whenever in India a custom becomes rigid, it is almost

---

1. The text of this sentence is not found in the extant Manu Samhitâ. Vide Mahânirvâna Tantra 8.47.

2. Since Swami Vivekananda's time, higher education among women in India has spread rapidly.

impossible to break through it—just as in your country, you will find how hard it is to break through a five-day custom of fashion. In the lower castes, except two, the widows remarry.

There is a passage in our later law books [which states] that a woman shall not read the Vedas. But they are prohibited to even a weak Brahmin. If a Brahmin boy is not strong-minded, the law is applied to him also. But that does not show that education is prohibited to them, for the Vedas are not all that the Hindus have. Every other book women can read. All the mass of Sanskrit literature, that whole ocean of literature—science, drama, poetry—is all for them. They can go there and read everything, except the [Vedic] scriptures[1].

In later days the idea was that woman was not intended to be a priest; so what is the use of her studying the Vedas? In that, the Hindus are not so far behind other nations. When women give up the world and join our Order, they are no longer considered either men or women. They have no sex. The whole question of high or low caste, man or woman, dies out entirely.

Whatever I know of religion I learned from my master, and he learned it of a woman.

Coming back to the Rajput woman, I will try to bring to you a story from some of our old books—how during the Mohammedan conquest, one of these women was the cause of what led to the conquest of India.

A Rajput prince of Kanauj—a very ancient city—had a daughter [Samjukta]. She had heard of the military fame of Prithvi Raj [King of Ajmere and Delhi] and all his glory, and she was in love with him.

Now her father wanted to hold a Râjasuya sacrifice, so he invited all the kings in the country. And in that sacrifice, they all had to render menial service to him because he was superior over all; and with that sacrifice he declared there would be a choice by his daughter.

But the daughter was already in love with Prithvi Raj. He was very mighty and was not going to acknowledge loyalty to the king, her father, so he refused the invitation. Then the king made a golden statue of Prithvi Raj and put it near the door. He said that that was the duty he had given him to perform—that of a porter.

The upshot of the whole affair was that Prithvi Raj, like a true knight, came and took the lady behind him on his horse, and they both fled.

When the news came to her father, he gave chase with his army, and there was a great battle in which the majority of both armies was killed. And [thus the Rajputs were so weakened that] the Mohammedan empire in India began.

When the Mohammedan empire was being established in northern India, the Queen of Chitore [Râni Padmini] was famed for her beauty. And the report of her beauty reached the sultan, and he wrote a letter for the queen to be sent to

his harem. The result was a terrible war between the King of Chitore and the sultan. The Mohammedans invaded Chitore. And when the Rajputs found they could not defend themselves any more, the men all took sword in hand and killed and were killed, and the women perished in the flames.

After the men had all perished, the conqueror entered the city. There in the street was rising a horrible flame. He saw circles of women going around it, led by the queen herself. When he approached near and asked the queen to refrain from jumping into the flames, she said, "This is how the Rajput woman treats you", and threw herself into the fire.

It is said that 74,500 women perished in the flames that day to save their honour from the hands of the Mohammedans. Even today when we write a letter, after sealing it we write "74½" upon it, meaning that if one dares to open this letter, that sin of killing 74,500 women will be upon his head.

I will tell you the story of another beautiful Rajput girl[2]. There is a peculiar custom in our country called "protection". Women can send small bracelets of silken thread to men. And if a girl sends one of these to a man, that man becomes her brother.

During the reign of the last of the Mogul emperors—the cruel man who destroyed that most brilliant empire of India—he similarly heard of the beauty of a Rajput chieftain's daughter. Orders were sent that she should be brought to the Mogul harem.

Then a messenger came from the emperor to her with his picture, and he showed it to her. In derision she stamped upon it with her feet and said, "Thus the Rajput girl treats your Mogul emperor". As a result, the imperial army was marched into Rajputana.

In despair the chieftain's daughter thought of a device. She took a number of these bracelets and sent them to the Rajput princes with a message: "Come and help us". All the Rajputs assembled, and so the imperial forces had to go back again.

I will tell you a peculiar proverb in Rajputana. There is a caste in India called the shop class, the traders. They are very intelligent—some of them—but the Hindus think they are rather sharp. But it is a peculiar fact that the women of that caste are not as intelligent as the men. On the other hand, the Rajput man is not half as intelligent as the Rajput woman.

The common proverb in Rajputana is: "The intelligent woman begets the dull son, and the dull woman begets the sharp son". The fact is, whenever any state or kingdom in Rajputana has been managed by a woman, it has been managed wonderfully well.

We come to another class of women. This mild Hindu race produces fighting women from time to time. Some of you may have heard of the woman [Lakshmi Bai, Queen of Jhansi] who, during the Mutiny of 1857, fought against the Eng-

1. Today Indian women are no longer barred from reading any scriptures—Vedic or non-Vedic.

2. Chârumati, or Rupamati, daughter of Vikram Singh, King of Kishangarh, in Rajasthan. Charumati is the heroine of Râjasimha, a Bengali historical novel written by Bankim Chandra Chatterjee.

lish soldiers and held her own ground for two years—leading modern armies, managing batteries and always charging at the head of her army. This queen was a Brahmin girl.

A man whom I know lost three of his sons in that war. When he talks of them he is calm, but when he talks of this woman his voice becomes animated. He used to say that she was a goddess—she was not a human being. This old veteran thinks he never saw better generalship.

The story of Chand Bibi, or Chand Sultana [1546 - 1599], is well known in India. She was the Queen of Golconda, where the diamond mines were. For months she defended herself. At last, a breach was made in the walls. When the imperial army tried to rush in there, she was in full armour, and she forced the troops to go back[3].

In still later times, perhaps you will be astonished to know that a great English general had once to face a Hindu girl of sixteen.

Women in statesmanship, managing territories, governing countries, even making war, have proved themselves equal to men—if not superior. In India I have no doubt of that. Whenever they have had the opportunity, they have proved that they have as much ability as men, with this advantage—that they seldom degenerate. They keep to the moral standard, which is innate in their nature. And thus as governors and rulers of their state, they prove—at least in India—far superior to men. John Stuart Mill mentions this fact.

Even at the present day, we see women in India managing vast estates with great ability. There were two ladies where I was born who were the proprietors of large estates and patronesses of learning and art and who managed these estates with their own brains and looked to every detail of the business.

Each nation,beyond a general humanity, develops a certain peculiarity of character—so in religion, so in politics, so in the physical body, so in mental habitude, so in men and women, so in character. One nation develops one peculiarity of character, another takes another peculiarity. Within the last few years the world has begun to recognize this.

The very peculiarity of Hindu women, which they have developed and which is the idea of their life, is that of the mother. If you enter a Hindu's home, you will not find the wife to be the same equal companion of the husband as you find her here. But when you find the mother, she is the very pillar of the Hindu home. The wife must wait to become the mother, and then she will be everything.

If one becomes a monk, his father will have to salute him first because he has become a monk and is therefore superior to him. But to his mother he—monk or no monk—will have to go down on his knees and prostrate himself before her. He will then put a little cup of water before her feet, she will dip her toe in it, and he will have to drink of it. A Hindu

son gladly does this a thousand times over again![4]

Where the Vedas teach morality, the first words are, "Let the mother be your God" (Taittiriya Upanishad 1.11.)—and that she is. When we talk of woman in India, our idea of woman is mother. The value of women consists in their being mothers of the human race. That is the idea of the Hindu.

I have seen my old master taking little girls by the hands, placing them in a chair and actually worshipping them—placing flowers at their feet and prostrating himself before these little children—because they represented the mother God.

The mother is the God in our family. The idea is that the only real love that we see in the world, the most unselfish love, is in the mother—always suffering, always loving. And what love can represent the love of God more than the love which we see in the mother? Thus the mother is the incarnation of God on earth to the Hindu.

"That boy alone can understand God who has been first taught by his mother." I have heard wild stories about the illiteracy of our women. Till I was a boy of ten, I was taught by my mother. I saw my grandmother living and my great-grandmother living, and I assure you that there never was in my line a female ancestor who could not read or write, or who had to put "her mark" on a paper. If there was a woman who could not read or write, my birth would have been impossible. Caste laws make it imperative.

So these are wild stories which I sometimes hear—such as the statement that in the Middle Ages reading and writing were taken away from Hindu women. I refer you to Sir William Hunter's History of the English People, where he cited Indian women who could calculate a solar eclipse.

I have been told that either too much worship of the mother makes the mother selfish or too much love of the children for the mother makes them selfish. But I do not believe that. The love which my mother gave to me has made me what I am, and I owe a debt to her that I can never repay.

Why should the Hindu mother be worshipped? Our philosophers try to find a reason and they come to this definition: We call ourselves the Aryan race. What is an Aryan? He is a man whose birth is through religion. This is a peculiar subject, perhaps, in this country; but the idea is that a man must be born through religion, through prayers. If you take up our law books you will find chapters devoted to this—the prenatal influence of a mother on the child.

I know that before I was born, my mother would fast and pray and do hundreds of things which I could not even do for five minutes. She did that for two years. I believe that whatever religious culture I have, I owe to that. It was consciously that my mother brought me into the world to be what I am. Whatever good impulse I have was given to me by my mother—and consciously, not unconsciously.

3. The soldiers were so impressed with Chand Bibi's military prowess and courage that they referred to her as Chand Sultana, which means "Chand—the Empress".

4. This custom is a gesture meant to acknowledge the mother not only as the first teacher and preceptor in one's life, but also as an embodiment of the all-loving God.

"A child materially born is not an Aryan; the child born in spirituality is an Aryan." For all this trouble—because she has to make herself so pure and holy in order to have pure children—she has a peculiar claim on the Hindu child. And the rest [of her traits] is the same with all other nations: she is so unselfish. But the mother has to suffer most in our families.

The mother has to eat last. I have been asked many times in your country why the [Hindu] husband does not sit with his wife to eat—if the idea is, perhaps, that the husband thinks she is too low a being. This explanation is not at all right. You know, a hog's hair is thought to be very unclean. A Hindu cannot brush his teeth with the brushes made of it, so he uses the fibre of plants. Some traveller saw one Hindu brushing his teeth with that and then wrote that "a Hindu gets up early in the morning and gets a plant and chews it and swallows it!" Similarly, some have seen the husband and wife not eating together and have made their own explanation. There are so many explainers in this world, and so few observers—as if the world is dying for their explanations! That is why I sometimes think the invention of printing was not an unmixed blessing. The real fact is: just as in your country many things must not be done by ladies before men, so in our country the fact is that it is very indecorous to munch and munch before men. If a lady is eating, she may eat before her brothers. But if the husband comes in, she stops immediately and the husband walks out quickly. We have no tables to sit at, and whenever a man is hungry he comes in and takes his meal and goes out. Do not believe that a Hindu husband does not allow his wife to sit at the table with him. He has no table at all.

The first part of the food—when it is ready—belongs to the guests and the poor, the second to the lower animals, the third to the children, the fourth to the husband, and last comes the mother. How many times I have seen my mother going to take her first meal when it was two o'clock. We took ours at ten and she at two because she had so many things to attend to. [For example], someone knocks at the door and says, "Guest", and there is no food except what was for my mother. She would give that to him willingly and then wait for her own. That was her life and she liked it. And that is why we worship mothers as gods.

I wish you would like less to be merely petted and patronized and more to be worshipped! [You], a member of the human race!—the poor Hindu does not understand that [inclination of yours]. But when you say, "We are mothers and we command", he bows down. This is the side then that the Hindus have developed.

Going back to our theories—people in the West came about one hundred years ago to the point that they must tolerate other religions. But we know now that toleration is not sufficient toward another religion; we must accept it. Thus it is not a question of subtraction, it is a question of addition. The truth is the result of all these different sides added together. Each of all these religions represents one side, the fullness being the addition of all these. And so in every science, it is addition that is the law.

Now the Hindu has developed this side. But will this side be enough? Let the Hindu woman who is the mother become the worthy wife also, but do not try to destroy the mother. That is the best thing you can do. Thus you get a better view of the universe instead of going about all over the world, rushing into different nations and criticizing them and saying, "The horrid wretches—all fit to be barbecued for eternity!"

If we take our stand on this position—that each nation under the Lord's will is developing one part of human nature—no nation is a failure. So far they have done well, now they must do better! [Applause]

Instead of calling the Hindus "heathens", "wretches", "slaves", go to India and say, "So far your work is wonderful, but that is not all. You have much more to do. God bless you that you have developed this side of woman as a mother. Now help the other side—the wife of men".

And similarly, I think (I tell it with the best spirit) that you had better add to your national character a little more of the mother side of the Hindu nature! This was the first verse that I was taught in my life, the first day I went to school: "He indeed is a learned man who looks upon all women as his mother, who looks upon every man's property as so much dust, and looks upon every being as his own soul".

There is the other idea of the woman working with the man. It is not that the Hindus had not those ideals, but they could not develop them.

It is alone in the Sanskrit language that we find four words meaning husband and wife together. It is only in our marriage that they [both] promise, "What has been my heart now may be thine". It is there that we see that the husband is made to look at the Pole-star, touching the hand of his wife and saying, "As the Pole-star is fixed in the heavens, so may I be fixed in my affection to thee". And the wife does the same.

Even a woman who is vile enough to go into the streets can sue her husband and have a maintenance. We find the germs of these ideas in all our books throughout our nation, but we were not able to develop that side of the character.

We must go far beyond sentiment when we want to judge. We know it is not emotion alone that governs the world, but there is something behind emotion. Economic causes, surrounding circumstances and other considerations enter into the development of nations. (It is not in my present plan to go into the causes that develop woman as wife.)

So in this world, as each nation is placed under peculiar circumstances and is developing its own type, the day is coming when all these different types will be mixed up—when that vile sort of patriotism which means "rob everybody and give to me" will vanish. Then there will be no more one-sided development in the whole world, and each one of these [nations] will see that they had done right.

Let us now go to work and mix the nations up together and

let the new nation come.

Will you let me tell you my conviction? Much of the civilization that comprises the world today has come from that one peculiar race of mankind—the Aryans[1].

[Aryan] civilization has been of three types: the Roman, the Greek, the Hindu. The Roman type is the type of organization, conquest, steadiness—but lacking in emotional nature, appreciation of beauty and the higher emotions. Its defect is cruelty. The Greek is essentially enthusiastic for the beautiful, but frivolous and has a tendency to become immoral. The Hindu type is essentially metaphysical and religious, but lacking in all the elements of organization and work.

The Roman type is now represented by the Anglo-Saxon; the Greek type more by the French than by any other nation; and the old Hindus do not die! Each type has its advantage in this new land of promise. They have the Roman's organization, the power of the Greek's wonderful love for the beautiful, and the Hindu's backbone of religion and love of God. Mix these up together and bring in the new civilization.

And let me tell you, this should be done by women. There are some of our books which say that the next incarnation, and the last (we believe in ten), is to come in the form of a woman.

We see resources in the world yet remaining because all the forces that are in the world have not come into use. The hand was acting all this time while other parts of the body were remaining silent. Let the other parts of the body be awakened and perhaps in harmonious action all the misery will be cured. Perhaps, in this new land, with this new blood in your veins, you may bring in that new civilization—and, perhaps, through American women.

As to that ever blessed land which gave me this body, I look back with great veneration and bless the merciful being who permitted me to take birth in that holiest spot on earth. When the whole world is trying to trace its ancestry from men distinguished in arms or wealth, the Hindus alone are proud to trace their descent from saints.

That wonderful vessel which has been carrying for ages men and women across this ocean of life may have sprung small leaks here and there. And of that, too, the Lord alone knows how much is owing to themselves and how much to those who look down with contempt upon the Hindus.

But if such leaks there are, I, the meanest of her children, think it my duty to stop her from sinking even if I have to do it with my life. And if I find that all my struggles are in vain, still, as the Lord is my witness, I will tell them with my heartfelt benediction: "My brethren, you have done well—nay, better than any other race could have done under the same circumstances. You have given me all that I have. Grant me the privilege of being at your side to the last and let us all sink together".

1. It may be noted here that today many historians and anthropologists would describe the Aryans as a linguistic group rather than a race.——Publisher.

THE FIRST STEP TOWARDS JNANA

A Jnâna-Yoga class delivered in New York, Wednesday, December 11, 1895, and recorded by Swami Kripananda.

The word Jnâna means knowledge. It is derived from the root Jnâ—to know—the same word from which your English word to know is derived. Jnana-Yoga is Yoga by means of knowledge. What is the object of the Jnana-Yoga? Freedom. Freedom from what? Freedom from our imperfections, freedom from the misery of life. Why are we miserable? We are miserable because we are bound. What is the bondage? The bondage is of nature. Who is it that binds us? We, ourselves.

The whole universe is bound by the law of causation. There cannot be anything, any fact—either in the internal or in the external world—that is uncaused; and every cause must produce an effect.

Now this bondage in which we are is a fact. It need not be proved that we are in bondage. For instance: I would be very glad to get out of this room through this wall, but I cannot; I would be very glad if I never became sick, but I cannot prevent it; I would be very glad not to die, but I have to; I would be very glad to do millions of things that I cannot do. The will is there, but we do not succeed in accomplishing the desire. When we have any desire and not the means of fulfilling it, we get that peculiar reaction called misery. Who is the cause of desire? I, myself. Therefore, I myself am the cause of all the miseries I am in.

Misery begins with the birth of the child. Weak and helpless, he enters the world. The first sign of life is weeping. Now, how could we be the cause of misery when we find it at the very beginning? We have caused it in the past. [Here Swami Vivekananda entered into a fairly long discussion of "the very interesting theory called Reincarnation". He continued:]

To understand reincarnation, we have first to know that in this universe something can never be produced out of nothing. If there is such a thing as a human soul, it cannot be produced out of nothing. If something can be produced out of nothing, then something would disappear into nothing also. If we are produced out of nothing, then we will also go back into nothing. That which has a beginning must have an end. Therefore, as souls we could not have had any beginning. We have been existing all the time.

Then again, if we did not exist previously, there is no explanation of our present existence. The child is born with a bundle of causes. How many things we see in a child which can never be explained until we grant that the child has had past experience—for instance, fear of death and a great number of innate tendencies. Who taught the baby to drink milk and to do so in a peculiar fashion? Where did it acquire this knowledge? We know that there cannot be any knowledge without experience, for to say that knowledge is intuitive in the child, or instinctive, is what the logicians would call a "petitio principii".

It would be the same [logic] as when a man asks me why light comes through a glass, and I answer him, "Because it is transparent". That would be really no answer at all because I am simply translating his word into a bigger one. The word "transparent" means "that through which light comes"—and that was the question. The question was why light comes through the glass, and I answered him, "Because it comes through the glass".

In the same way, the question was why these tendencies are in the child. Why should it have fear of death if it never saw death? If this is the first time it was ever born, how did it know to suck the mother's milk? If the answer is "Oh, it was instinct", that is simply returning the question. If a man stands up and says, "I do not know", he is in a better position than the man who says, "It is instinct" and all such nonsense.

There is no such thing as instinct; there is no such thing as nature separate from habit. Habit is one's second nature, and habit is one's first nature too. All that is in your nature is the result of habit, and habit is the result of experience. There cannot be any knowledge but from experience.

So this baby must have had some experience too. This fact is granted even by modern materialistic science. It proves beyond doubt that the baby brings with it a fund of experience. It does not enter into this world with a "tabula rasa"—a blank mind upon which nothing is written—as some of the old philosophers believed, but ready equipped with a bundle of knowledge. So far so good.

But while modern science grants that this bundle of knowledge which the child brings with it was acquired through experience, it asserts, at the same time, that it is not its own—but its father's and its grandfather's and its great-grandfather's. Knowledge comes, they say, through hereditary transmission.

Now this is one step in advance of that old theory of "instinct", that is fit only for babies and idiots. This "instinct" theory is a mere pun upon words and has no meaning whatsoever. A man with the least thinking power and the least insight into the logical precision of words would never dare to explain innate tendencies by "instinct", a term which is equivalent to saying that something came out of nothing. But the modern theory of transmission through experience—though, no doubt, a step in advance of the old one—is not sufficient at all. Why not? We can understand a physical transmission, but a mental transmission is impossible to understand.

What causes me—who am a soul—to be born with a father who has transmitted certain qualities? What makes me come back? The father, having certain qualities, may be one binding cause. Taking for granted that I am a distinct soul that was existing before and wants to reincarnate—what makes my soul go into the body of a particular man? For the explanation to be sufficient, we have to assume a hereditary transmission of energies and such a thing as my own previous experience. This is what is called Karma, or, in English, the Law of Causation, the law of fitness.

For instance, if my previous actions have all been towards drunkenness, I will naturally gravitate towards persons who are transmitting a drunkard's character. I can only take advantage of the organism produced by those parents who have been transmitting a certain peculiar influence for which I am fit by my previous actions. Thus we see that it is true that a certain hereditary experience is transmitted from father to son, and so on. At the same time, it is my past experience that joins me to the particular cause of hereditary transmission.

A simply hereditary transmission theory will only touch the physical man and would be perfectly insufficient for the internal soul of man. Even when looking upon the matter from the purest materialistic standpoint—viz. that there is no such thing as a soul in man, and man is nothing but a bundle of atoms acted upon by certain physical forces and works like an automaton—even taking that for granted, the mere transmission theory would be quite insufficient.

The greatest difficulties regarding the simple hypothesis of mere physical transmission will be here: If there be no such thing as a soul in man, if he be nothing more than a bundle of atoms acted upon by certain forces, then, in the case of transmission, the soul of the father would decrease in ratio to the number of his children; and the man who has five, six or eight children must, in the end, become an idiot. India and China—where men breed like rats—would then be full of idiots. But, on the contrary, we find that the least amount of lunacy is in India and China.

The question is, What do we mean by the word transmission? It is a big word, but, like so many other impossible and nonsensical terms of the same kind, it has come into use without people understanding it. If I were to ask you what transmission is, you would find that you have no real conception of its meaning because there is no idea attached to it.

Let us look a little closer into the matter. Say, for instance, here is a father. A child is born to him. We see that the same qualities [which the father possesses] have entered into his child. Very good. Now how did the qualities of the father come to be in the child? Nobody knows. So this gap the modern physicists want to fill with the big word transmission. And what does this transmission mean? Nobody knows.

How can mental qualities of experience be condensed and made to live in one single cell of protoplasm? There is no difference between the protoplasm of a bird and that of a human brain. All we can say with regard to physical transmission is that it consists of the two or three protoplasmic cells cut from the father's body. That is all. But what nonsense to assume that ages and ages of past human experience got compressed into a few protoplasmic cells! It is too tremendous a pill they ask you to swallow with this little word transmission.

In olden times the churches had prestige, but today science has got it. And just as in olden times people never inquired for themselves—never studied the Bible, and so the priests had a very good opportunity to teach whatever they liked—so even now the majority of people do not study for themselves and, at the same time, have a tremendous awe and fear before anything called scientific. You ought to remember that there is a worse popery coming than ever existed in the church—the so-called scientific popery, which has become so successful that it dictates to us with more authority than religious popery.

These popes of modern science are great popes indeed, but sometimes they ask us to believe more wonderful things than any priest or any religion ever did. And one of those wonderful things is that transmission theory, which I could never understand. If I ask, "What do you mean by transmission?" they only make it a little easier by saying, "It is hereditary transmission". And if I tell them, "That is rather Greek to me", they make it still easier by saying, "It is the adherence of paternal qualities in the protoplasmic cells". In that way it becomes easier and easier, until my mind becomes muddled and disgusted with the whole thing.

Now one thing we see: we produce thought. I am talking to you this evening and it is producing thought in your brain. By this act of transmission we understand that my thoughts are being transmitted into your brain and your mind, and producing other thoughts. This is an everyday fact.

It is always rational to take the side of things which you can understand—to take the side of fact. Transmission of thought is

perfectly understandable. Therefore we are able to take up the [concept of] transmission of thought, and not of hereditary impressions of protoplasmic cells alone. We need not brush aside the theory, but the main stress must be laid upon the transmission of thought.

Now a father does not transmit thought. It is thought alone that transmits thought. The child that is born existed previously as thought. We all existed eternally as thought and will go on existing as thought.

What we think, that our body becomes. Everything is manufactured by thought, and thus we are the manufacturers of our own lives. We alone are responsible for whatever we do. It is foolish to cry out: "Why am I unhappy?" I made my own unhappiness. It is not the fault of the Lord at all.

Someone takes advantage of the light of the sun to break into your house and rob you. And then when he is caught by the policeman, he may cry: "Oh sun, why did you make me steal?" It was not the sun's fault at all, because there are thousands of other people who did much good to their fellow beings under the light of the same sun. The sun did not tell this man to go about stealing and robbing.

Each one of us reaps what we ourselves have sown. These miseries under which we suffer, these bondages under which we struggle, have been caused by ourselves, and none else in the universe is to blame. God is the least to blame for it.

"Why did God create this evil world?" He did not create this evil world at all. We have made it evil, and we have to make

it good. "Why did God create me so miserable?" He did not. He gave me the same powers as [He did] to every being. I brought myself to this pass.

Is God to blame for what I myself have done? His mercy is always the same. His sun shines on the wicked and the good alike. His air, His water, His earth give the same chances to the wicked and the good. God is always the same eternal, merciful Father. The only thing for us to do is to bear the results of our own acts.

We learn that, in the first place, we have been existing eternally; in the second place that we are the makers of our own lives. There is no such thing as fate. Our lives are the result of our previous actions, our Karma. And it naturally follows that having been ourselves the makers of our Karma, we must also be able to unmake it.

The whole gist of Jnana-Yoga is to show humanity the method of undoing this Karma. A caterpillar spins a little cocoon around itself out of the substance of its own body and at last finds itself imprisoned. It may cry and weep and howl there; nobody will come to its rescue until it becomes wise and then comes out, a beautiful butterfly. So with these our bondages. We are going around and around ourselves through countless ages. And now we feel miserable and cry and lament over our bondage. But crying and weeping will be of no avail. We must set ourselves to cutting these bondages.

The main cause of all bondage is ignorance. Man is not wicked by his own nature—not at all. His nature is pure, perfectly holy. Each man is divine. Each man that you see is a God by his very nature. This nature is covered by ignorance, and it is ignorance that binds us down. Ignorance is the cause of all misery. Ignorance is the cause of all wickedness; and knowledge will make the world good. Knowledge will remove all misery. Knowledge will make us free. This is the idea of Jnana-Yoga: knowledge will make us free! What knowledge? Chemistry? Physics? Astronomy? Geology? They help us a little, just a little. But the chief knowledge is that of your own nature. "Know thyself." You must know what you are, what your real nature is. You must become conscious of that infinite nature within. Then your bondages will burst.

Studying the external alone, man begins to feel himself to be nothing. These vast powers of nature, these tremendous changes occurring—whole communities wiped off the face of the earth in a twinkling of time, one volcanic eruption shattering to pieces whole continents—perceiving and studying these things, man begins to feel himself weak. Therefore, it is not the study of external nature that makes [one] strong. But there is the internal nature of man—a million times more powerful than any volcanic eruption or any law of nature—which conquers nature, triumphs over all its laws. And that alone teaches man what he is.

"Knowledge is power", says the proverb, does it not? It is through knowledge that power comes. Man has got to know. Here is a man of infinite power and strength. He himself is by his own nature potent and omniscient. And this he must know. And the more he becomes conscious of his own Self, the more he manifests this power, and his bonds break and at last he becomes free.

How to know ourselves? the question remains now. There are various ways to know this Self, but in Jnana-Yoga it takes the help of nothing but sheer intellectual reasoning. Reason alone, intellect alone, rising to spiritual perception, shows what we are.

There is no question of believing. Disbelieve everything — that is the idea of the Jnani. Believe nothing and disbelieve everything — that is the first step. Dare to be a rationalist. Dare to follow reason wherever it leads you.

We hear everyday people saying all around us: "I dare to reason". It is, however, a very difficult thing to do. I would go two hundred miles to look at the face of the man who dares to reason and to follow reason. Nothing is easier to say, and nothing is more difficult to do. We are bound to follow superstitions all the time — old, hoary superstitions, either national or belonging to humanity in general — superstitions belonging to family, to friends, to country, to fashion, to books, to sex and to what-not.

Talk of reason! Very few people reason, indeed. You hear a man say, "Oh, I don't like to believe in anything; I don't like to grope through darkness. I must reason". And so he reasons. But when reason smashes to pieces things that he hugs unto his breast, he says, "No more! This reasoning is all right until it breaks my ideals. Stop there!" That man would never be a Jnani. That man will carry his bondage all his life and his lives to come. Again and again he will come under the power of death. Such men are not made for Jnana. There are other methods for them — such as bhakti-yoga, Karma-Yoga, or Râja-Yoga — but not Jnana-Yoga.

I want to prepare you by saying that this method can be followed only by the boldest. Do not think that the man who believes in no church or belongs to no sect, or the man who boasts of his unbelief, is a rationalist. Not at all. In modern times it is rather bravado to do anything like that.

To be a rationalist requires more than unbelief. You must be able not only to reason, but also to follow the dictates of your reason. If reason tells you that this body is an illusion, are you ready to give it up? Reason tells you that heat and cold are mere illusions of your senses; are you ready to brave these things? If reason tells you that nothing that the senses convey to your mind is true, are you ready to deny your sense perception? If you dare, you are a rationalist.

It is very hard to believe in reason and follow truth. This whole world is full either of the superstitious or of half-hearted hypocrites. I would rather side with superstition and ignorance than stand with these half-hearted hypocrites. They are no good. They stand on both sides of the river.

Take anything up, fix your ideal and follow it out boldly unto death. That is the way to salvation. Half-heartedness never led

to anything. Be superstitious, be a fanatic if you please, but be something. Be something, show that you have something; but be not like these shilly-shallyers with truth — these jacks-of-all-trades who just want to get a sort of nervous titillation, a dose of opium, until this desire after the sensational becomes a habit.

The world is getting too full of such people. Contrary to the apostles who, according to Christ, were the salt of the earth, these fellows are the ashes, the dirt of the earth. So let us first clear the ground and understand what is meant by following reason, and then we will try to understand what the obstructions are to our following reason.

The first obstruction to our following reason is our unwillingness to go to truth. We want truth to come to us. In all my travels, most people told me: "Oh, that is not a comfortable religion you talk about. Give us a comfortable religion!"

I do not understand what they mean by this "comfortable religion". I was never taught any comfortable religion in my life. I want truth for my religion. Whether it be comfortable or not, I do not care. Why should truth be comfortable always? Truth many times hits hard — as we all know by our experience. Gradually, after a long intercourse with such persons, I came to find out what they meant by their stereotypical phrase. These people have got into a rut, and they do not dare to get out of it. Truth must apologize to them.

I once met a lady who was very fond of her children and her money and her everything. When I began to preach to her that the only way to God is by giving up everything, she stopped coming the next day. One day she came and told me that the reason for her staying away was because the religion I preached was very uncomfortable. "What sort of religion would be comfortable to you?" I asked in order to test her. She said: "I want to see God in my children, in my money, in my diamonds".

"Very good, madam", I replied. "You have now got all these things. And you will have to see these things millions of years yet. Then you will be bumped somewhere and come to reason. Until that time comes, you will never come to God. In the meantime, go on seeing God in your children and in your money and your diamonds and your dances."

It is difficult, almost impossible, for such people to give up sense enjoyment. It has grown upon them from birth to birth. If you ask a pig to give up his sty and to go into your most beautiful parlour, why it will be death to the pig. "Let go, I must live there", says the pig.

[Here Swami Vivekananda explained the story of the fishwife: "Once a fishwife was a guest in the house of a gardener who raised flowers. She came there with her empty basket, after selling fish in the market, and was asked to sleep in a room where flowers were kept. But, because of the fragrance of the flowers, she couldn't get to sleep for a long time. Her hostess saw her condition and said, 'Hello! Why are you tossing from side to side so restlessly?' The fishwife said: 'I don't know, friend. Perhaps the smell of the flowers has been disturbing my sleep. Can you give me my fish-basket? Perhaps that will put me to sleep'."]

So with us. The majority of mankind delights in this fish smell—this world, this enjoyment of the senses, this money and wealth and chattel and wife and children. All this nonsense of the world—this fishy smell—has grown upon us. We can hear nothing beyond it, can see nothing beyond it; nothing goes beyond it. This is the whole universe.

All this talk about heaven and God and soul means nothing to an ordinary man. He has heaven already here. He has no other idea beyond this world. When you tell him of something higher, he says, "That is not a comfortable religion. Give us something comfortable". That is to say that religion is nothing but what he is doing.

If he is a thief and you tell him that stealing is the highest thing we can do, he will say, "That is a comfortable religion". If he is cheating, you have to tell him that what he is doing is all right; then he will accept your teaching as a "comfortable religion". The whole trouble is that people never want to get out of their ruts—never want to get rid of the old fish-basket and smell, in order to live. If they say, "I want the truth", that simply means that they want the fish-basket.

When have you reached knowledge? When you are equipped with those four disciplines [i.e. the four qualifications for attainment discussed in Vedantic literature: discrimination between the real and the unreal, renunciation, the six treasures of virtue beginning with tranquillity, and longing for liberation]. You must give up all desire of enjoyment, either in this life or the next. All enjoyments of this life are vain. Let them come and go as they will.

What you have earned by your past actions none can take away from you. If you have deserved wealth, you can bury yourself in the forest and it will come to you. If you have deserved good food and clothing, you may go to the north pole and they will be brought to you. The polar bear will bring them. If you have not deserved them, you may conquer the world and will die of starvation. So, why do you bother about these things? And, after all, what is the use of them?

As children we all think that the world is made so very nice, and that masses of pleasures are simply waiting for our going out to them. That is every schoolboy's dream. And when he goes out into the world, the everyday world, very soon his dreams vanish. So with nations. When they see how every city is built upon ruins—every forest stands upon a city—then they become convinced of the vanity of this world.

All the power of knowledge and wealth once made has passed away—all the sciences of the ancients, lost, lost forever. Nobody knows how. That teaches us a grand lesson. Vanity of vanities; all is vanity and vexation of the spirit. If we have seen all this, then we become disgusted with this world and all it offers us. This is called Vairâgya, non-attachment, and is the first step towards knowledge.

The natural desire of man is to go towards the senses. Turning away from the senses takes him back to God. So the first lesson we have to learn is to turn away from the vanities of the world.

How long will you go on sinking and diving down and going up for five minutes, to again sink down, again come up and sink, and so on—tossed up and down? How long will you be whirled on this wheel of Karma—up and down, up and down? How many thousands of times have you been kings and rulers? How many times have you been surrounded by wealth and plunged into poverty? How many thousands of times have you been possessed of the greatest powers? But again you had to become men, rolling down on this mad rush of Karma's waters. This tremendous wheel of Karma stops neither for the widow's tears nor the orphan's cry.

How long will you go on? How long? Will you be like that old man who had spent all his life in prison and, when let out, begged to be brought back into his dark and filthy dungeon cell? This is the case with us all! We cling with all our might to this low, dark, filthy cell called this world—to this hideous, chimerical existence where we are kicked about like a football by every wind that blows.

We are slaves in the hands of nature—slaves to a bit of bread, slaves to praise, slaves to blame, slaves to wife, to husband, to child, slaves to everything. Why, I go about all over the world—beg, steal, rob, do anything—to make happy a boy who is, perhaps, hump-backed or ugly-looking. I will do every wicked thing to make him happy. Why? Because I am his father. And, at the same time, there are millions and millions of boys in this world dying of starvation—boys beautiful in body and in mind. But they are nothing to me. Let them all die. I am apt to kill them all to save this one rascal to whom I have given birth. This is what you call love. Not I. Not I. This is brutality.

There are millions of women—beautiful in body and mind, good, gentle, virtuous—dying of starvation this minute. I do not care for them at all. But that Jennie who is mine—who beats me three times a day, and scolds me the whole day—for that Jennie I am going to beg, borrow, cheat and steal so that she will have a nice gown.

Do you call that love? Not I. This is mere desire, animal desire—nothing more. Turn away from these things. Is there no end to these hideous dreams? Put a stop to them.

When the mind comes to that state of disgust with all the vanities of life, it is called turning away from nature. This is the first step. All desires must be given up—even the desire of getting heaven.

What are these heavens anyhow? Places where to sing psalms all the time. What for? To live there and have a nice healthy body with phosphorescent light or something of this kind coming out of every part, with a halo around the head, and with wings and the power to penetrate the wall?

If there be powers, they must pass away sooner or later. If

there is a heaven—as there may be many heavens with various grades of enjoyment—there cannot be a body that lives forever. Death will overtake us, even there.

Every conjunction must have a disjunction. No body, finer or coarser, can be manufactured without particles of matter coming together. Whenever two particles come together, they are held by a certain attraction; and there will come a time when those particles will separate. This is the eternal law. So, wherever there is a body—either grosser or finer, either in heaven or on earth—death will overcome it.

Therefore, all desires of enjoyment in this life, or in a life to come, should be given up. People have a natural desire to enjoy; and when they do not find their selfish enjoyments in this life, they think that after death they will have a lot of enjoyment somewhere else. If these enjoyments do not take us towards knowledge in this life, in this world, how can they bring us knowledge in another life?

Which is the goal of man? Enjoyment or knowledge? Certainly not enjoyment. Man is not born to have pleasure or to suffer pain. Knowledge is the goal. Knowledge is the only pleasure we can have.

All the sense pleasures belong to the brute. And the more the pleasure in knowledge comes, these sense pleasures fall down. The more animal a man is, the more he enjoys the pleasures of the senses. No man can eat with the same gusto as a famished dog. No man was ever born who could feel the same pleasure in eating as an ordinary bull. See how their whole soul is in that eating. Why, your millionaires would give millions for that enjoyment in eating—but they cannot have it.

This universe is like a perfectly balanced ocean. You cannot raise a wave in one place without making a hollow in another one. The sum total of energy in the universe is the same throughout. You spend it in some place, you lose it in another. The brute has got it, but he spent it on his senses; and each of his senses is a hundred times stronger than that of man.

How the dog smells at a distance! How he traces a footstep! We cannot do that. So, in the savage man. His senses are less keen than the animal's, but keener than the civilized man's.

The lower classes in every country intensely enjoy everything physical. Their senses are stronger than those of the cultured. But as you go higher and higher in the scale, you see the power of thought increasing and the powers of the senses decreasing, in the same ratio.

Take a [brute], cut him [as it were] to pieces, and in five days he is all right. But if I scratch you, it is ten to one you will suffer for weeks or months. That energy of life which he displays—you have it too. But with you, it is used in making up your brain, in the manufacture of thought. So with all enjoyments and all pleasures. Either enjoy the pleasure of the senses—live like the brute and become a brute—or renounce these things and become free.

The great civilizations—what have they died of? They went for pleasure. And they went further down and down until,

under the mercy of God, savages came to exterminate them, lest we would see human brutes growling about. Savages killed off those nations that became brutalized through sense enjoyment, lest Darwin's missing link would be found.

True civilization does not mean congregating in cities and living a foolish life, but going Godward, controlling the senses, and thus becoming the ruler in this house of the Self.

Think of the slavery in which we are [bound]. Every beautiful form I see, every sound of praise I hear, immediately attracts me; every word of blame I hear immediately repels me. Every fool has an influence over my mind. Every little movement in the world makes an impression upon me. Is this a life worth living?

So when you have realized the misery of this physical existence—when you have become convinced that such a life is not worth living—you have made the first step towards Jnana.

BHAKTI-YOGA

New Discoveries, Vol. 3, pp. 543-54. A bhakti-yoga class delivered in New York, Monday morning, January 20, 1896, and recorded by Mr. Josiah J. Goodwin.

We finished in our last [class the subject] about Pratikas. One idea more of the preparatory Bhakti, and then we will go on to the Parâ, the Supreme. This idea is what is called Nishthâ, devotion to one idea.

We know that all these ideas of worship are right and all good, and we have seen that the worship of God, and God alone, is Bhakti. The worship of any other being will not be Bhakti, but God can be worshipped in various forms and through various ideas. And we have seen that all these ideas are right and good, but the difficulty is here: If we just stop with this last conclusion, we find that in the end we have frittered away our energies and done nothing.

It is a great tendency among liberal people to become a jack-of-all-trades and master of none—to nibble a little here and there and, in the long run, find they have nothing. In this country it many times grows into a sort of disease—to hear various things and do nothing.

Here is the advice of one of our old Bhaktas: "Take the honey from all flowers, mix with all with respect, say yea, yea to all, but give not up your seat". This giving not up your own seat is what is called Nishtha. It is not that one should hate, or even criticize, the ideals of other people; he knows they are all right. But, at the same time, he must stick to his own ideal very strictly.

There is a story of Hanumân, who was a great worshipper of Râma. Just as the Christians worship Christ as the incarnation of God, so the Hindus worship many incarnations of God. According to them, God came nine times in India and will come once more. When he came as Rama, this Hanuman was his great worshipper. Hanuman lived very long and was a great Yogi.

During his lifetime, Rama came again as Krishna; and Hanuman, being a great Yogi, knew that the same God had come back again as Krishna. He came and served Krishna, but he said to him, "I want to see that Rama form of yours". Krishna said, "Is not this form enough? I am this Krishna; I am this Rama. All these forms are mine". Hanuman said, "I know that, but the Rama form is for me. The Lord of Jânaki (Janaki is a name of Sitâ.) and the Lord of Shri (Shri is a name of Laksmi.) are the same. They are both the incarnations of the Supreme Self. Yet the lotus-eyed Rama is my all in all". This is Nishtha—knowing that all these different forms of worship are right, yet sticking to one and rejecting the others. We must not worship the others at all; we must not hate or criticize them, but respect them.

The elephant has two teeth coming out from his mouth. These are only for show; he cannot eat with them. But the teeth that are inside are those with which he chews his food. So mix with all, say yea, yea to all, but join none. Stick to your own ideal of worship. When you worship, worship that ideal of God which is your own Ishta, your own Chosen Ideal. If you do not, you will have nothing. Nothing will grow.

When a plant is growing, it is necessary that it should be hedged round lest any animal should eat it up. But when it has become strong and a huge gigantic tree, do not care for any hedges—it is perfect in itself. So when just the seed of spirituality is growing, to fritter away the energies on all sorts of religious ideas—a little of this and a little of that: a little of Christianity, a little of Buddhism, and, in reality, of nothing—destroys the soul.

This [acceptance] has its good side; and in the end we will come to it. Only do not put the cart before the horse.

In the first place, we are bound to become sectarians. But this should be the ideal of sectarianism—not to avoid anyone. Each of us must have a sect, and that sect is our own Ishta—our own chosen way. However, that should not make us want to kill other people—only to hold onto our own way. It is sacred and it should not be told to our own brothers, because my choice is sacred, and his [also] is sacred. So keep that choice as your own. That should be the [attitude of] worship of everyone. When you pray to your own Ideal, your own Ishta, that is the only God you shall have. God exists in various phases, no doubt, but for the time being, your own Ishta is the only phase for you.

Then, after a long course of training in this Ishta—when this plant of spirituality has grown and the soul has become strong and you begin to realize that your Ishta is everywhere—[then] naturally all these bondages will fall down. When the fruit becomes ripe, it falls of its own weight. If you pluck an unripe fruit it is bitter, sour. So we will have to grow in this thought.

Simply hearing lectures and all this nonsense—making the Battle of Waterloo in the brain, simply unadjusted [undigested?] ideas—is no good. Devotion to one idea—those that have this will become spiritual, will see the light. You see everyone complaining: "I try this" and "I try that", and if you cross-question them as to what they try, they will say that they have heard a few lectures in one place and another, a handful of talks in one corner and another. And for three hours, or a few days, they worshipped and thought they had done enough. That is the way of fools, not the way to perfection—not the way to attain spirituality.

Take up one idea, your Ishta, and let the whole soul be devoted to it. Practise this from day to day until you see the result, until the soul grows. And if it is sincere and good, that very idea will spread till it covers the whole universe. Let it spread by itself; it will all come from the inside out. Then you will say that your Ishta is everywhere and that He is in everything.

Of course, at the same time, we must always remember that we must recognize the Ishtas of others and respect them—the other ideas of God—or else worship will degenerate into fanaticism. There is an old story of a man who was a worshipper of Shiva. There are sects in our country who worship God as Shiva, and others who worship Him as Vishnu. This man was a great worshipper of Shiva, and to that he added a tremendous hatred for all worshippers of Vishnu and would not hear the name of Vishnu pronounced. There are a great number of worshippers of Vishnu in India, and he could not avoid hearing the name. So he bored two holes in his ears and tied two little bells onto them. Whenever a man mentioned the name of Vishnu, he moved his head and rang the bells, and that prevented his hearing the name.

But Shiva told him in a dream, "What a fool you are! I am Vishnu, and I am Shiva; they are not different—only in name. There are not two Gods". But this man said, "I don't care. I will have nothing to do with this Vishnu business".

He had a little statue of Shiva and made it very nice, built an altar for it. One day he bought some beautiful incense and went home to light some of the incense for his God. While the fumes [smoke] of his incense were rising in the air, he found that the image was divided into two: one half remained Shiva, and the other half was Vishnu. Then the man jumped up and put his finger under the nostril of Vishnu so that not a particle of the smell could get there.

Then Shiva became disgusted, and the man became [was turned into] a demon. He is [known as] the father of all fanatics, the "bell-eared" demon. He is respected by the boys of India, and they worship him. It is a very peculiar kind of worship. They make a clay image and worship him with all sorts of horrible smelling flowers. There are some flowers in the forests of India which have a most pestilential smell. They worship him with these and then take big sticks and beat the image. He [the "bell-eared" demon] is the father of all fanatics who hate all other gods except their own.

This is the only danger in this Nishthâ Bhakti—becoming

this fanatical demon. The world gets full of them. It is very easy to hate. The generality of mankind gets so weak that in order to love one, they must hate another; they must take the energy out of one point in order to put it into another. A man loves one woman and then loves another; and to love the other, he has to hate the first. So with women. This characteristic is in every part of our nature, and so in our religion. The ordinary, undeveloped weak brain of mankind cannot love one without hating another. This very [characteristic] becomes fanaticism in religion. Loving their own ideal is synonymous with hating every other idea.

This should be avoided and, at the same time, the other danger should be avoided. We must not fritter away all our energies, [otherwise] religion becomes a nothing with us—just hearing lectures. These are the two dangers. The danger with the liberals is that they are too expansive and have no intensity. You see that in these days religion has become very expansive, very broad. But the ideas are so broad that there is no depth in them. Religion has become to many merely a means of doing a little charity work, just to amuse them after a hard day's labour—they get five minutes religion to amuse them. This is the danger with the liberal thought. On the other hand, the sectarians have the depth, the intensity, but that intensity is so narrow. They are very deep, but with no breadth to it. Not only that, but it draws out hatred to everyone else.

Now, if we can avoid both these dangers and become as broad as the uttermost liberals and as deep as the bluest fanatic, then we will solve the problem. Our idea is how that can be done. It is by this theory of Nishtha—knowing that all these ideals that we see are [good] and true, that all these are so many parts of the same God and, at the same time, thinking that we are not strong enough to worship Him in all these forms, and therefore must stick to one ideal and make that ideal our life. When you have succeeded in doing that, all the rest will come. Here ends the first part of Bhakti: the formal, the ceremonial and the preparatory.

You must remember that the first lesson in this Bhakti was on the disciple. Who is the disciple? What are the necessary qualifications for a disciple? You read in the scriptures: "Where the speaker is wonderful, so is the listener. When the teacher is wonderful, so is the taught. Then alone will this spirituality come".

Mankind generally thinks that everything is to be expected from the teacher. Very few people understand that they are not fit to be taught. In the disciple first this is necessary: that he must want—he must really want spirituality.

We want everything but spirituality. What is meant by want? Just as we want food. Luxuries are not wants, but necessaries are wants. Religion is a necessary thing to very few; and to the vast mass of mankind it is a luxury. There are a hundred things in life without which they can live, until they come to the shop and see a new and artistic something and they want to buy it. Ninety-nine and nine-tenths per cent of mankind

comes to religion in this way. It is one of the many luxuries they have in life. There is no harm in this. Let them have all they want; but they are entirely mistaken if they think they can fool God. He cannot be fooled. They will only fool themselves and sink down lower and lower until they become like brutes. Those therefore will become spiritual who want [spirituality]—who feel the necessity of religion, just as they feel the necessity of clothes, the necessity of work, the necessity of air to breathe.

A necessary thing is that without which we cannot live; and a luxury is that which is simply the gratification of a momentary desire.

The second qualification in the disciple is that he must be pure; and the other is that he must be persevering—he must work. Hearing is only one part; and the other part is doing.

The second necessity in Bhakti was the teacher. The teacher must be properly qualified. The main idea in that lecture was that the teacher must have the seed of spirituality. The teacher is not a talker, but the transmitter of spiritual force which he has received from his teacher, and he from others, and so on, in an unbroken current. He must be able to transmit that spiritual current.

When the teacher and the taught are both ready, then the first step in bhakti-yoga comes. The first part of bhakti-yoga is what is called the preparatory [stage], wherein you work through forms.

The next lecture was on the Name—how in all scriptures and in all religions Name has been exalted and how that Name does us good. The Bhakti-Yogi must always think that the Name itself is God—nothing different from God. The Name and God are one.

Next, it was taught how, for the Bhakti-Yogi, humility and reverence are necessary. The Bhakti-Yogi must hold himself as a dead man. A dead man never takes an insult, never retaliates; he is dead to everyone. The Bhakti-Yogi must reverence all good people, all saintly people, for the glory of the Lord shines always through His children.

The next lesson was on the Pratikas. In that it was taught that Bhakti is only when you worship God. Worshipping anyone else is not Bhakti. But we can worship anything we like if we think it is God. If we do not think it is God, that worship is not Bhakti. If you think it is God, it is all right.

There was a certain Yogi who used to practise meditation in a lonely part of the forest, on the banks of a river. There was a poor cowherd, a very ignorant man, who used to tend his herd in that forest. Every day he used to see this same Yogi meditating by the hour, practising austerities, living alone and studying. Somehow the cowherd got curious as to what he did. So he came to the Yogi and said, "Sir, can you teach me the way to God?" This Yogi was a very learned, great man, and he replied, "How will you understand God—you common cowherd? Blockhead, go home and tend your cows and don't bother your head with such things".

The poor fellow went away, but somehow a real want had come to him. So he could not rest, and he came again to the Yogi and said, "Sir, won't you teach me something about God?"

Again he was repulsed: "Oh, you blockhead, what can you understand of God? Go home". But the cowherd could not sleep; he could not eat. He must know something about God.

So he came again; and the Yogi, in order to quiet the man, as he was so insisting, said, "I'll teach you about God".

The man asked, "Sir, what sort of being is God? What is His form? How does He look?"

The Yogi said, "God is just like the big bull in your herd. That is just God. God has become that big bull".

The man believed him and went back to his herd. Day and night he took that bull for God and began to worship it. He brought the greenest grass for that bull, rested close to it and gave it light, sat near it and followed it. Thus days and months and years passed. His whole soul was there [in the bull].

One day he heard a voice, as it were, coming out of the bull. "The bull speaks!" [the cowherd thought.]"

"My son, my son."

"Why, the bull is speaking! No, the bull cannot speak."

Again he went away, and sat near meditating in great misery of his heart. He did not know anything. Again he heard the voice coming out of the bull: "My child, my child".

He went near. "No, the bull cannot speak." Then he went back again and sat despondent.

Again the voice came, and that time he found it out. It was from his own heart. He found that God was in him. Then he learned the wonderful truth of the Teacher of all teachers: "I am with thee always". And the poor cowherd learned the whole mystery.

Then he goes back to the Yogi, and when he is at some distance the Yogi sees him. The Yogi has been the most learned man in the country, practising austerity for years—meditating, studying. And this cowherd, an ignorant blockhead, never studied a book nor learned his letters. But he comes—his whole body, as it were, transfigured, his face changed, the light of heaven shining round his face. The Yogi got up. "What is this change? Where did you get this?""

Sir, you gave me that."

"How? I told you that in joke."

"But I took it seriously. And I got everything I wanted out of that bull, for is He not everywhere?"

So that bull was the Pratika. And that man worshipped the bull as his Pratika—as God—and he got everything out of it. So that intense love—that desire—brings out everything. Everything is in ourselves, and the external world and the external worship are the forms, the suggestions that call it out. When they become strong, the Lord within awakens.

The external teacher is but the suggestion. When faith in the external teacher is strong, then the Teacher of all teachers within speaks; eternal wisdom speaks in the heart of that man. He need not go any more to any books or any men or any higher beings; he need not run after supernatural or preternatural beings for instruction. The Lord Himself becomes his instructor. He gets all he wants from himself. [There is] no more need to go to any temple or church. His own body has become the greatest temple in the world, and in that temple lives the Lord of Creation. In every country great saints have been born, wonderful lives have been [lived]—coming out of the sheer power of love.

So all these external forms of Bhakti—this repetition of the Name, worship of Pratika, this Nishtha, this Ishta—are but the preparations until that eternal power wakes up. Then alone comes spirituality—when one goes beyond these laws and bounds. Then all laws fall down, all forms vanish, temples and churches crumble into dust and die away. It is good to be born in a church, but it is the worst possible fate to die in a church. It is good to be born in a sect, and the worst possible thing to die in a sect with sectarian ideas.

What sect can hold a child of the Lord? What laws bind him? What forms shall he follow? What man shall he worship? He worships the Lord Himself. He Himself teaches him. He lives in the temple of all temples, the Soul of man.

So this is the goal towards which we are going—the supreme Bhakti—and all that leads up to this is but preparation. But it is necessary. It prepares the infinite Soul to come out of this bondage of books and sects and forms; these [ultimately] fly away and leave but the Soul of man. These are superstitions of an infinite amount of time. This "my father's religion", "my country's religion", or "my book", or my this and that, are but the superstition of ages; they vanish. Just as when one is pricked with a thorn he takes another thorn to get the first out and then throws both of them away, so this superstition is in us.

In many countries—even into the soft brains of little babies—are put the most horrible and diabolical nonsense, as sect ideas. Parents think they are doing good to the child, but they are merely murdering it to satisfy Mrs. Grundy. What selfishness! There is nothing that men out of fear of themselves or out of fear of society will not do. Men will kill their own children, mothers will starve their own families, brothers will hate brothers to satisfy forms—because Mrs. So-and-so will be pleased and satisfied.

We see that the vast mass of mankind is born in some church or temple of [some religious] form and never comes out of it. Why? Have these forms helped the growth of spirituality? If through these forms we step onto the highest platform of love, where forms vanish and all these sectarian ideas go away, how is it that the vast majority of men are always grovelling in some form or another? They are all atheists; they do not want any religion.

If a man comes to this country without any friend or without knowing anyone—supposing he is a blackguard in his own country—the first thing he will do in this country will be to join a church. Will that fellow ever have religion?

Do you mean to say that those women who go to churches to show their dresses will ever have religion or will come out of forms? They will go back and back. And when they die, they will become like animals.

Do you mean to say that those men who go to church to look at the beautiful faces of women will ever have religion? Those who have certain social religions—because society requires that they shall belong to Mr. So-and-so's church or because that was their father's church—will they ever have religion? They understand certain broad views, but they must keep a certain social position—and will keep it through eternity.

What you want, you get. The Lord fulfils all desires. If you want to keep a certain position in society you will do so; if you want the church, you will get that and not Him. If you want to play the fool all your life with all these churches and foolish organizations, you will have them and have to live in them all your lives. "Those that want the departed, go to the departed and get ghosts; but those that love Him, all come to Him." So those that love Him alone will come to Him, and those that love others will go to wherever they love.

That drill business in the temples and churches—kneeling down at a certain time, standing at ease, and all that drill nonsense, all mechanical, with the mind thinking of something else—all this has nothing to do with real religion.

There was a great prophet in India, Guru Nânak, born [some] four hundred years ago. Some of you have heard of the Sikhs—the fighting people. Guru Nanak was [the founder and also] a follower of the Sikh religion.

One day he went to the Mohammedans' mosque. These Mohammedans are feared in their own country, just as in a Christian country no one dare say anything against their religion...So Guru Nanak went in and there was a big mosque, and the Mohammedans were standing in prayer. They stand in lines: they kneel down, stand up, and repeat certain words at the same times, and one fellow leads. So Guru Nanak went there. And when the mullah was saying "In the name of the most merciful and kind God, Teacher of all teachers", Guru Nanak began to smile. He says, "Look at that hypocrite". The mullah got into a passion. "Why do you smile?"

"Because you are not praying, my friend. That is why I am smiling."

"Not praying?"

"Certainly not. There is no prayer in you."

The mullah was very angry, and he went and laid a complaint before a magistrate and said, "This heathen rascal dares to come to our mosque and smiles at us when we are praying. The only punishment is instant death. Kill him".

Guru Nanak was brought before the magistrate and asked why he smiled.

"Because he was not praying."

"What was he doing?" the magistrate asked.

"I will tell you what he was doing if you will bring him before me."

The magistrate ordered the mullah to be brought. And when he came, the magistrate said, "Here is the mullah. [Now] explain why you laughed when he was praying".

Guru Nanak said, "Give the mullah a piece of the Koran [to swear on]. [In the mosque] when he was saying 'Allah, Allah', he was thinking of some chicken he had left at home".

The poor mullah was confounded. He was a little more sincere than the others, and he confessed he was thinking of the chicken, and so they let the Sikh go. "And", said the magistrate [to the mullah], "don't go to the mosque again. It is better not to go at all than to commit blasphemy there and hypocrisy. Do not go when you do not feel like praying. Do not be like a hypocrite, and do not think of the chicken and say the name of the Most Merciful and Blissful God".

A certain Mohammedan was praying in a garden. They are very regular in their prayers. When the time comes, wherever they are, they just begin, fall down on the ground and get up and fall down, and so on. One of them was in a garden when the call for prayer came, so he knelt there prostrate on the ground to pray. A girl was waiting in the garden for her lover, and she saw him on the other side. And in her hurry to reach him, she did not see the man prostrate and walked over him. He was a fanatical Mohammedan—just what you call here a Presbyterian, the same breed. Both believe in barbecuing eternally. So you can just imagine the anger of this Mohammedan when his body was walked over—he wanted to kill the girl. The girl was a smart one, and she said, "Stop that nonsense. You are a fool and a hypocrite".

"What! I am a hypocrite?"

"Yes, I am going to meet my earthly lover, and I did not see you there. But you are going to meet your heavenly lover and should not know that a girl was passing over your body."

THE MUNDAKA UPANISHAD

New Discoveries, Vol. 3, pp. 557-68. A Jnâna-Yoga class delivered in New York, January 29, 1896, and recorded by Mr. Josiah J. Goodwin.

In the last Jnana-Yoga (Vide Complete Works, II.) lecture, we read one of the Upanishads; we will read another [the Mundaka Upanishad]. Brahmâ was the first of the Devas, the Lord of this cycle and its protector. He gave this knowledge of Brahman, which is the essence of all knowledge, to his son Atharvan. The latter handed it over to his son Angiras, he to his son, Bharadvâja, and so on.

There was a man called Shaunaka, a very rich man, who went to this Angiras as a learner. He approached the teacher and asked him a question. "Tell me, sir, what is that which, being known, everything else is known?"

One [knowledge] is supreme and the other is inferior. The Rig-Veda is the name of one of the different parts of the Vedas. Shikshâ is the name of another part. All different sciences are inferior. What is the supreme science? That is the only science, the supreme science, by which we reach the Unchangeable One. But that cannot be seen, cannot be sensed, cannot be specified. Without colour, without eyes, without ears, without nose, without feet—the Eternal, the Omnipresent, the "Omnipenetrating", the Absolute—He from whom everything comes. The sages see Him, and that is the supreme knowledge.

Just as the Urnanâbhi, a species of spider, creates a thread out of his own body and takes it back, just as the plants grow by their own nature, and all these things are yet separate and apparently different (the heart is, as it were, different from the other parts of a man's body; the plants are different from the earth; the thread is different from the spider—yet they [the earth, the spider and so on] were the causes, and in them these things act), so from this Unchangeable One has come this universe.

First, out of Brahman comes the knowledge of desire and from that comes the manifestation of Creator, or the Golden Womb. From that comes intelligence, from that, matter and all these different worlds.

This is the truth—that for those who want to come to salvation or attain to other enjoyments, various ways are toldin the Vedas.

Then it [the Mundaka Upanishad] goes on to say how they will reach these blessings. When they die they will go through the sun's rays to places which are very beautiful, where after death they will go to heaven and live for some time, but from there they will again fall.

Here are two words—Ishtam and Purtam. Sacrificial and other rituals are called Ishtam, and Purtam is making roads, building hospitals and so on. "Fools are they who think that rituals and doing good work are high and that there is nothing higher." They get what they desire and go to heaven, but every enjoyment and every sorrow must have an end. And so that ends, and they fall back and back and become men again, or still lower. Those that give up the world and learn to control the senses live in a forest. Through the rays of the sun they reach that immortality where lives He who is the Absolute.

Thus the sage, examining all desires of good or evil works, throws away all duties and wants to know that, getting which there is no more return, no more change. And to know that, he goes to the Guru, the teacher, with fuel in his hand.

There is a myth in our country about going to the Guru with fuel in one's hands as a sign of helping him in making sacrifices, as he will not take presents.

Who is a teacher? He who knows the secrets of the scriptures, he whose soul has gone unto Brahman, who does not care for works or going to heaven or all these things.

Unto such a disciple, who has controlled his mind, has become peaceful and calm, has given up all this tremendous wave that rises in the mind by desire ("I will do this and that" and all those desires which are at best only disturbing, such as name and fame, which impel mankind to do all sorts of things)—to that disciple in whom all these vexatious desires have been calmed down, the teacher teaches the way which is the science of Brahman, by which he can know that One who never changes and who is the Truth.

Then comes what he [Angiras] taught:

This is the truth, O gentle one, as from a mass of burning flame myriads of sparks come out of the same nature as the fire, even so from this Unchangeable One all these forms, all these ideas, all this creation, come out; and unto Him it [the creation] goes back.

But the Eternal One is everlasting, formless, without beginning, inside and outside of every being—beyond all life, beyond all mind, the Pure One, beyond even the unchangeable, beyond everything. From Him is born the vital principle. From Him comes the mind. From Him come all organs of the senses. From Him are air, light, water and this earth which holds all beings. These heavens are, as it were, His head; His eyes, the sun and moon. The cardinal points are, as it were, His ears. The eternal knowledge of the Vedas is, as it were, His manifested speech. His life is the air. His heart is this universe; His feet, this world. He is the Eternal Self of every being.

From Him have come the different Vedas. From Him have come the gods of the Sâdhyas. The latter are superior men, much higher than ordinary men and very much like the gods.

From Him are all men. From Him are all animals. From Him is all life; from Him, all the forces in the mind; from Him all truth, all chastity. The seven organs are all from Him. The seven objects of perception are from him; the seven actions of perception are from Him. From Him are the seven worlds in which the life currents flow. From Him are all these seas and oceans. From Him are all rivers that roll into the sea; from Him are all plants and all liquids.

He is the inside. He is the inner Soul of every being. This great Purusha, this great One—He is this universe, He is the work, He is the sacrifice. He is Brahman, and He is the trinity. He who knows Him frees his own soul from the bond of ignorance and becomes free.

He is the bright one. He is inside every human soul. From Him are all name and form; all the animals and men are from Him. He is the one Supreme. He who knows Him becomes free.

How to know Him? Take this bow, which is the Upanishad, the knowledge of the Vedanta; place upon that bow the sharpened rod [arrow] of worship; stretch that bow by what?—by making the mind of the same form as He, by knowing that you are He. Thus strike at it; strike at that Brahman with this rod. This One is the bow. This human mind is the rod [arrow]. Brahman is the object which we want to hit. This object is to be hit by concentrating the mind. And just when the rod has hit [its mark], the rod penetrates into the object and becomes one with it—a unity. Even so, this soul, the rod, is to be thrown upon the object so that it will become one with It—in Whom are the heavens, this earth and the skies, in Whom are the mind and all that lives.

In the Upanishads there are certain passages which are called the great words, which are always quoted and referred to.

In Him, that One—in Him alone, the Atman—exist all other worlds. What is the use of all other talk? Know Him alone. This is the bridge over this life to reach universality.

He [Angiras] goes on to show a practical way. So far it is very figurative.

Just as all the spokes of a wheel meet at the axle, even so in this body is that place from which all the arteries flow and at which they all meet. There, meditate upon the Om that is in the heart. May thou succeed. May the gentle one with success attain the goal. May you go beyond all darkness to Him who is omniscient, the All-Knowing. His glory is in heaven, on earth and everywhere.

He who has become the mind, the Prânâ, He who is the leader in the body, He who is established in the food, the energy of life. By supreme knowledge the sages see Him whose nature is bliss, who shines as immortality.(Mundaka Upanishad 2.2.8.) (This is another of the sentences very much quoted.)

There are two words: one is Jnâna, the other Vijnâna. Jnana may be translated as science—this means intellectual [knowledge] only—and Vijnana as realization. God cannot be perceived by intellectual knowledge. He who has realized [the Self] by that supreme knowledge—what will become of that man?

All the knots of the heart will be cut asunder. All darkness will vanish forever when you have seen the Truth.

How can you doubt? How foolish and childish you will think these fights and quarrels of different sciences and different philosophies and all this. You will smile at them. All doubts will vanish, and all work will go away. All work will vanish.

Beyond, the golden sheath is there—without any impurity, without parts [indivisible]—He, the Brahman. His is the brightness, the Light of all light—the knowers of the Atman realize Him as such. And when you have done that, the sun cannot illumine, nor the moon, nor the stars. A flash of lightning cannot illumine the place; it is mental—away, deep in the mind. He shining, everything else shines; when He shines within, the whole man shines. This universe shines through His light.

Take such passages [for memorizing] later on, when studying the Upanishads.

The difference between the Hindu mind and the European mind is that whereas in the West truths are arrived at by examining the particular, the Hindu takes the opposite course. There is no [such] metaphysical sublimity as in the Upanishads.

It [the Mundaka Upanishad] leads you on, beyond the senses—infinitely more sublime than the suns and stars. First Angiras tried to describe God by sense sublimities—that His feet are the earth, His head the heavens. But that did not express what he wanted to say. It was in a sense sublime. He first gave that idea to the student and then slowly took him beyond, until he gave him the highest idea—the negative—too high to describe.

He is immortal, He is before us, He is behind us, He is on the right side, He is on the left, He is above, He is beneath.

Upon the same tree there are two birds with most beautiful wings, and the two birds always go together—always live together. Of these, one is eating the fruits of the tree; the other, without eating, is looking on. So in this body are the two birds always going together. Both have the same form and beautiful wings. One is the human soul, eating the fruits; the other is God Himself, of the same nature. He is also in this body, the Soul of our soul. He eats neither good nor evil fruits, but stands and looks on.

But the lower bird knows that he is weak and small and humble, and tells all sorts of lies. He says he is a woman, or he is a man or a boy. He says he will do good or do bad; he will go to heaven and will do a hundred sorts of things. In delirium he talks and works, and the central idea of his delirium is that he is weak.

Thus he gets all the misery because he thinks he is nobody. He is a created little being. He is a slave to somebody; he is governed by some god or gods, and so is unhappy.

But when he becomes joined with God, when he becomes a Yogi, he sees that the other bird, the Lord, is his own glory. "Why, it was my own glory whom I called God, and this little "I", this misery, was all hallucination; it never existed. I was never a woman, never a man, never any one of these things." Then he gives up all his sorrow.

When this Golden One, who is to be seen, is seen—the Creator, the Lord, the Purusha, the God of this universe—then the sage has washed off all stains of good and bad deeds. (Good deeds are as much stains as bad deeds.) Then he attains to total sameness with the Pure One. The sage knows that He who is the Soul of all souls—this Atman—shines through all.

He is the man, the woman, the cow, the dog—in all animals, in the sin and in the sinner. He is the Sannyâsin, He is in the ruler, He is everywhere.

Knowing this the sage speaks not. (He gives up criticizing anyone, scolding anyone, thinking evil of anyone.) His desires have gone into the Atman. This is the sign of the greatest knowers of Brahman—that they see nothing else but Him.

He is playing through all these things. Various forms—from the highest gods to the lowest worms—are all He. The ideas want to be illustrated.

First of all the writer showed us the idea that if we want to get to heaven and all these places, we will get there. That is to say, in the language of the Vedas, whatever one desires that he sees.

As I have told you in previous lectures, the Atman neither comes nor goes. It has neither birth nor death. You are all omnipresent, you are the Atman. You are at this moment in heaven and in the darkest places too. You are everywhere. Where are you not? Therefore how can you go anywhere? These comings and goings are all fictions—the Atman can never come nor go.

These visions change. When the mind is in a particular condition it sees a certain vision, dreams a certain dream. So in this condition, we are all seeing this world and man and animals and all these things. But in this very place, this condition will change. And the very thing we are seeing as earth, we shall see as heaven, or we may see it as the opposite place or as any place we like.

All this depends on our desires. But this dream cannot be permanent, just as we know that any dream in the night must break. Not one of these dreams will be permanent. We dream that which we think we will do. So these people who are always thinking in this life of going to heaven and meeting their friends, will have that as soon as their dream of this life is ended. And they will be compelled by their desires of this life to see these other dreams. And those who are superstitious and are frightened into all such ideas as hell will dream that they are in the hot place. Those whose ideas in this life are brutal—when they die, will become pigs and hogs and all these things. With each one, what he desires he finds.

This book starts by telling us that those who know nothing better than a little road-making or hospital-building and such good works will have a good dream when they die. They will dream that they are in a place where they will have god-bodies and can eat anything they like, jump about, go through walls and so on, and sometimes come down and startle someone.

In our mythology there are the Devas, who live in heaven, and the Devakas, who are very much the same but a little more wicked. The Devas are like your angels, only some of them from time to time become wicked and find that the daughters of men are good. Our deities are celebrated for this sort of thing. What can you expect of them? They are here—simply hospital-makers—and have no more knowledge than other men. They do some good work with the result that they become Devas. They do their good work for fame or name or some reward and get this reward, dreaming that they are in heaven and doing all these things.

Then there are demons who have done evil in this life. But our books say that these dreams will not last very long, and then they will either come back and take the old dream again as human beings, or still worse. Therefore, according to these books, it behooves every sensible, right-thinking man, once and for all, to brush aside all such foolish ideas as heavens and hells.

Two things exist in the world—dream and reality. What we call life is a succession of dreams—dream within dream. One dream is called heaven, another earth, another hell, and so on. One dream is called the human body, another the animal body, and so on—all are dreams. The reality is what is called Brahman, that Being who is Existence, Knowledge, Bliss.

He is the Guru—the sage who wants to get rid of all these dreams, to stand aside and know his own nature—who wants to go beyond this self-hypnotism.

When we desire, we are hypnotizing ourselves. Just as I desire "I will go to heaven", that hypnotizes me, and I begin to find I am in heaven directly I die, and will see angels and all sorts of things. I have seen about fifty people who have come from death's door, and they all have told me stories about being in heaven. These are the mythologies of our country, and it shows that it is all hypnotism.

Where Western people make a great mistake is here. So far as you have these ideas of heaven and hell, we agree with you. But you say this earth is real. That cannot be. If this is real, heavens and hells are real, because the proof of each of these is the same. If one is a hypnotic condition, the whole of it must be so.

Vedantists say that not only are heavens hypnotic, but so is this life and everything here. Some people want to go from one hypnotic condition to another, and these are what we call the fools of the world—the Samsârins, the travellers who go from dream to dream, from one hypnotic trance to another. For fifty years they are under the idea that they are men and women.

What nonsense is [this—] a man or a woman in the soul? It is terrible hypnotism. How can the soul have any sex? It is self-hypnotism. You have hypnotized yourself and think you are men and women. If we are fools, we will again hypnotize ourselves and want to go to heaven, and hear all this trash of gods and goddesses and all sorts of humbug, and will kneel down and pray, and have god-bodies by the millions to worship on thrones. At the end, we have to hypnotize ourselves again.

We are all in the same boat here, and all who are in the same boat see each other. Stand aside—free, beyond dream and hypnotism. Some fools have hypnotized themselves that they have bodies and wives and all these things. I also am a fool and have hypnotized myself that I have senses and all these things. So we are all in the same boat and see each other. Millions of people may be here whom we do not see, touch or feel. Just as in hypnotism there may be three books before you, but you are hypnotized and are told that one of them does not exist. And you may live for a year in that condition and never see it. Suppose thirty men are under the same hypnotic influence and are told that this book does not exist. Those who are in this condition will all fail to see the book. Men, women, animals are all hypnotized, and all see this dream because they are all in the same boat.

The Vedanta philosophy says that this whole universe—mental, physical, moral—is hypnotic. Who is the cause of this hypnotism? You yourself are to blame. This weeping and wailing and knocking your heads into corners [against brick walls, as it were] will not do you the least good.

However, knocking everything [that is hypnotic] on the head [leads to] what is called non-attachment; and clinging to more and more hypnotism is attachment. That is why in all religions you will find they wanted to give up the world, although many of them do not understand it. These fellows used to starve themselves in a forest and see the devil coming to them.

You have heard those wonderful stories of India—of how those magicians can make a man see a rope rise from the ground to the skies. I have not seen any of them. One of the Mogul emperors, Jahangir, mentions it. He says, "Allah, what do these devils do? They take a rope or a chain, and the chain is thrown up and up until it becomes firm—as if it were stuck to something. Then they let a cat go up the chain—then a dog, then a wolf, then a tiger, then a lion. All walk up the chain and vanish. Sometimes they will send men up the chain. Two men will go up and begin to fight, and then both of them vanish. And after a while you hear a noise of fighting—and [then] a head, a hand, and a foot fall. And, mind you, there are two or three thousand people present. The fellow showing it has only a loincloth on". They say this is hypnotism—throwing a net over the audience.

That is what they call their science. It exists within a certain limit. But if you go beyond this limit or come within it, you do not see it. The man who is playing does not see anything. So if you stand near him, you do not see anything. Such is the hypnotism here.

So we have first to get beyond the circle (Jnana) or stand within the circle of the hypnotism (Bhakti) with God, the great Player who is playing all these things—the whole universe He projects.

Chapter after chapter comes and goes. This is called Mâyâ, the power which creates all these tremendous things. He who is the ruler of this Maya, is God; and he who is ruled by Maya [is the soul]. Just as in the case of that chain—so the man who was standing in the centre had the power and was not deluded, but all that audience was governed by Maya. So that portion of Atman which rules Maya is called God, and the little bits of the Atman deluded by it are called souls—you and I.

The Bhakta says, Crawl nearer and nearer to the hypnotist, and when you get to the centre you do not see anything. You get clear of it.

The Jnâni does not care to undergo all this trouble—it is a dangerous way. Unless a man becomes a lunatic, when he finds himself covered with mud, will he take more mud to wash himself? So why increase the hypnotism? Get out of the circle; cut it off and be free. When you are free you will be able to play, even without being caught yourself. Now you are caught, then you will catch—that will be all the difference.

Therefore in the first part of this book, we are told that we must give up all this idea of heaven and of birth and death and so on. It is all nonsense; no man was ever born or ever died. They are all in hypnotism. So is eternal life and all this nonsense. Heaven is hypnotism and so is earth.

It is not as materialists say: that heaven is a superstition and God is a superstition, but he himself is not a superstition. If one is superstition—if one link is nonexistent—the whole chain is nonexistent. The existence of the whole chain depends on the existence of one link—and that of one link, on the whole.

If there is no heaven, there is no earth; and if there is no God, there is no man. You are under this hypnotism; and as long as you are under it, you will have to see God and nature and the soul. And when you are beyond this hypnotism, God will vanish[8]*—so will nature, and so will the soul.

Therefore, first of all, we will have to give up all these ideas of God and heaven and enjoying the fruits of these; and all that going to heaven will be one more dream.

Next, after showing these things, the book goes on to tell us how to get out of this hypnotism. And the one idea that is brought out through all these ideas is to be one with that Universal Being. The thing manifested—the Universal Being—is not anything of these; these are all nonsense—Maya. (The Swami has been discussing the two aspects of Maya. On the previous page, ([9]a few paragraphs earlier) he described Maya as the power of Brahman; here he is referring to Maya as the world-appearance.) But that upon which all these things are being played—the background upon which all this picture is written—[is we ourselves]; we are one with Him [that Universal Being]. You know you are one with Him, only you must realize it.

He gave us two words: one is intellectual knowledge, and the other is realization. That is to say, intellectual assent is within this realization, and realization is beyond it. Therefore intellectual assent is not sufficient.

Every man can say this theory is right, but that is not realization; he must realize it. We can all say we understand that this is hypnotism, but that is not realization. That will be when the hypnotism will break—even for a moment. It will come in a flash; it must come. If you struggle it will come.

When it does vanish, all idea of body will go along with it—that you have sex or body—just as a lamp blows out. Then what will become of you? If some part of your Karma remains, this world will come back again—but not with the same force. You have known that it is what it is; you will know no more bondage. So long as you have eyes you will have to see; or ears [you will have to] hear—but not with the same force.

I had read all sorts of things about the mirage, but had never seen it before until about four years ago when I was travelling in western India. Of course, as a Sannyasin I was travelling on foot, making my slow marches. So it took me about a month to travel through that country. Every day I saw such beautiful lakes and the shadows of trees on the shores of those lakes, and the whole thing was quivering in the breeze—and birds flying, and animals. Every day I saw this and thought what a beautiful country it was. But when I reached some village, I found it was all sand. I said, How is it?

One day I was very thirsty and thought I would drink a little water at the lake. But when I approached, it disappeared, and with a flash [the thought] came into my mind: "This is the mirage about which I read all my life". But the strange thing is that I was travelling for a month and could never recognize that it was a mirage—and in one moment it vanished. I was very glad to know this was the mirage about which I had read all my life.

Next morning I saw the lake again, and along with it came the idea: "That is the mirage". All that month I had been seeing the mirage and could not distinguish between reality and mirage. But in that one moment I caught the idea.

From that time, when I see a mirage, I will say, "That is a mirage", and never feel it. Such will it be with this world when the whole thing will vanish once; and after that, if you have to live out your past work, you will not be deceived.

Take a carriage with two wheels. Suppose I cut one of the wheels from the axle. The other wheel will run for some time by its past momentum and will then fall. The body is one wheel, and the soul another; and they are joined by the axle of delusion. Knowledge is the axe which will cut the axle, and the soul will stop immediately—will give up all these vain dreams.

But upon the body is that past momentum, and it will run a little, doing this and that, and then it will fall down. But only good momentum will be left, and that body can only do good. This is to warn you not to mistake a rascal for a free man. It will be impossible for that [free] man to do evil. So you must not be cheated.

When you become free the whole hypnotism has vanished and you know the distinction between the reality and the mirage. [The mirage] will no more be a bondage. The most terrible things will not be able to daunt you. A mountain [could] fall upon you, but you will not care. You will know it for a mirage.

HISTORY OF THE ARYAN RACE

A Jnâna-Yoga class delivered in London, England, on Thursday morning, May 7, 1896, and recorded by Mr. Josiah J. Goodwin.

I have told you how I would divide the subject into four Yogas, but, as the bearing of all these various Yogas is the same—the goal they want to arrive at is the same—I had better begin with the philosophical portion: the Jnana-Yoga. Jnâna means knowledge, and, before going into the principles of the Vedanta philosophy, I think it is necessary to sketch in a few words the origin and the beginning and the development—the historical portion of that system. Most of you are now familiar with the words Arya and Aryan, and many things have been written on these words.

About a century ago there was an English judge in Bengal, Sir William Jones. In India, you know, there are Mohammedans and Hindus. The Hindus were the original people, and the Mohammedans came and conquered them and ruled over them for seven hundred years. There have been many other conquests in India; and whenever there is a new conquest, the criminal laws of the country are changed. The criminal law is always the law of the conquering nation, but the civil law remains the same. So when the English conquered India, they changed the criminal law; but the civil law remained. The judges, however, were Englishmen and did not know the language of the country in which the civil laws were written, and so they had to take the help of interpreters, lawyers of India, and so on. And when any question about Indian law arose, these scholars would be referred to.

One of these judges, Sir William Jones, was a very ripe scholar, and he wanted to go to the fountain-head himself, to take up the language himself and study it, instead of relying upon these interpreters who, for instance, might be bribed to give any verdict. So he began to study the law of the Gentoos, as the Hindus were called. Gentoo is probably a form of the word gentile, used by the Portuguese and Spaniards—or "heathen", as you call it now. When the judge began to translate some of the books into English, he found that it was very hard to translate them correctly into English at first hand. What was his surprise when he found that if he translated them first into Latin, and next into English, it was much easier. Then he found in translating that a large number of Sanskrit words were almost the same as in Latin. It was he who introduced the study of Sanskrit to the Europeans. Then as the Germans were rising in scholarship—as well as the French—they took up the language and began to study it.

With their tremendous power of analysis, the Germans found that there was a similarity between Sanskrit and all the European languages. Among the ancient languages, Greek was the nearest to it in resemblance. Later, it was found that there was a language called Lithuanian, spoken somewhere on the shores of the Baltic—an independent kingdom at that time and unconnected with Russia. The language of the Lithuanians is strikingly similar to Sanskrit. Some of the Lithuanian sentences are less changed from Sanskrit forms than the northern Indian languages. Thus it was found that there is an intimate connection between all the various languages spoken in Europe and the two Asiatic languages—Persian and Sanskrit. Many theories are built upon it as to how this connection came. Theories were built up every day, and every day smashed. There is no knowing where it is going to stop.

Then came the theory that there was one race in ancient times who called themselves Aryans. They found in Sanskrit literature that there was a people who spoke Sanskrit and called themselves Aryans, and this is mentioned also in Persian literature. Thus they founded the theory that there was in ancient times a nation [of people] who called themselves Aryans and who spoke Sanskrit and lived in Central Asia. This nation, they said, broke into several branches and migrated to Europe and Persia; and wherever they went, they took their own languages. German, Greek and French are but remnants of an old tongue, and Sanskrit is the most highly developed of these languages.

These are theories and have not been proved yet; they are mere conjectures and guesses. Many difficulties come in the way—for instance, how the Indians are dark and the Europeans are fair. Even within the same nations speaking these languages—in England itself—there are many with yellow hair and many with black. Thus there are many questions which have not yet been settled.

But this is certain, that all the nations of Europe except the Basques, the Hungarians, the Tartars and the [Finns?] (Vide Complete Works, VIII.)—excepting these, all the Europeans, all the northern Indians and the Persians speak branches of the same language. Vast masses of literature are existing in all these Aryan tongues: in Greek, in Latin, in modern European languages—German, English, French—in ancient Persian, in modern Persian and in Sanskrit.

But in the first place, Sanskrit literature alone is a very big mass. Although, perhaps, three-fourths of it has been destroyed and lost through successive invasions, yet, I think, the sum total of the amount of literature in Sanskrit would outbalance any three or four European languages taken together, in number of books. No one knows how many books are there yet and where they are, because it is the most ancient of all these Aryan languages. And that branch of the Aryan race which spoke the Sanskrit language was the first to become civilized and the first to begin to write books and literature. So they went on for thousands of years. How many thousands of years they wrote no one knows. There are various guesses—from 3000 B.C. to 8000 B.C.—but all of these dates are more or less uncertain.

Each man in writing about these ancient books and dates is first of all prejudiced by his earlier education, then by his religion, then by his nationality. If a Mohammedan writes about the Hindus, anything that does not glorify his own religion he very scrupulously pushes to one side. So with the Christians—you can see that with your own writers. In the last ten years your literature has become more respectable. So long as they [the Christians] had full play, they wrote in English and were safe from Hindu criticism. But, within the last twenty years, the Hindus have begun writing in English, so they are more careful. And you will find that the tone has quite changed within the last ten or twenty years.

Another curiosity about the Sanskrit literature is that it, like any other language, has undergone many changes. Taking all the literature in these various Aryan languages—the Greek or the Latin or all these others—we find that all the European branches were of very recent date. The Greek came much later—a mere child in comparison with the Egyptian or the Babylonian.

The Egyptians and the Babylonians, of course, are not Aryans. They are separate races, and their civilizations antedate all the European civilization. But with the exception of the ancient Egyptians, they were almost coeval [with the Aryans]; in some accounts, they were even earlier. Yet in Egyptian literature, there are certain things to be accounted for—the introduction of the Indian lotus on old temples, the lotus Gangetic. It is well known that this only grows in India. Then there are the references to the land of Punt. Although very great attempts have been made to fix that land of Punt on the Arabs, it is very uncertain. And then there are the references to the monkeys and sandalwood of southern India—only to be found there.

The Jews were of a much later date than the Greek Aryans. Only one branch of the Semitic race of Babylon and this nondescript, unknowable race—the Egyptians—were much older than the Aryans, except the Hindus.

So this Sanskrit has undergone very much change as a matter of course, having been spoken and written through thousands of years. It necessarily follows that in other Aryan languages, as in Greek and Roman, the literature must be of much later date than Sanskrit. Not only so, but there is this peculiarity, that of all regular books that we have in the world, the oldest are in Sanskrit—and that is the mass of literature called the Vedas. There are very ancient pieces in the Babylonian or Egyptian literature, but they cannot be called literature or books, but just a few notes, a short letter, a few words, and so on. But as finished, cultured literature, the Vedas are the oldest.

These Vedas were written in the peculiar archaic Sanskrit, and for a long time—even today—it is thought by many European antiquarians that these Vedas were not written, but were handed down by father to son, learned by rote, and thus preserved. Within the last few years, opinion is veering round, and they are beginning to think that they must have been written in most ancient times.

Of course they have to make theories in this way. Theory after theory will have to be built up and destroyed until we reach truth. This is quite natural. But when the subject is Indian or Egyptian, the Christian philosophers rush in to make theories; while if the subject is nearer home, they think twice first. That is why they fail so much and have to keep on making fresh theories every five years. But this much is true, that this mass of literature, whether written or not, was conveyed and, not only that, but is at the present day conveyed by word of mouth. This is thought to be holy.

You find in every nation when a new idea, a new form, a new discovery or invention comes in, the old things are not brushed aside all at once, but are relegated to the religion of holiness. The ancient Hindus used to write on palm leaves and birch bark; and when paper was invented they did not throw aside all the palm leaves, but used to consider writing on palm leaves and birch bark holy. So with the Jews—they used to write only on parchment, and parchment is now used for writing in their temples. So you find when new customs come in, the old ones become holy. So this form of transmitting the literature of the Vedas from teacher to disciple by word of mouth, although antiquated and almost useless now, has become holy. The student may refresh his memory by books, but has to learn by word of mouth of a teacher. A great many modifications will always gather round such a fact to make its holiness more rational, but this is the law.

These Vedas are a vast mass of literature by themselves. That is to say, in those ancient times, in every country, religion was the first ideal to spring out of the heart of man, and all the secular knowledge that men got was made over to religion.

Secondly, people who deal with religion and in later times came to be called priests—being the first thinkers of every nation—not only thought about religious subjects, but secular matters also; and, as such, all knowledge was confined to them. These masses of knowledge—both secular and religious—will always be gathered together and made into a vast mass of literature.

In much later times, this is the case. For instance, in studying the Bible of the Jews, we find the same thing. The Talmud contained a vast mass of information on all subjects and so did the Pentateuch. In the same way, the Vedas give information on various subjects. They have come together and form one book. And in later times, when other subjects were separated from religion—when astronomy and astrology were taken out of religion—these subjects, being connected with the Vedas and being ancient, were considered very holy.

Almost the largest portion of the Vedas has been lost. The priests who carried it down to posterity were divided into so many families; and, accordingly, the Vedas were divided into so many parts. Each part was allotted to a family. The rituals, the ceremonies, the customs, the worship of that family were to be obtained from that [respective] portion of the Vedas. They preserved it and performed all the ceremonies according to that. In course of time, [some of] these families became extinct; and with them, their portion of the Vedas was lost, if these old accounts be true.

Some of you know that the Vedas are divided into four parts. One is called the Rig-Veda, another Yajur-Veda, another Sâma-Veda, and the fourth Atharva-Veda. Each one of these, again, was divided into many branches. For instance, the Sama-Veda had one thousand branches, of which only about five or six remain; the rest are all lost. So with the others. The Rig-Veda had 108, of which only one remains; and the rest are all lost.

Then [there were] these various invasions. India has been the one country to which every nation that has become strong wants to go and conquer—it being reputed to be very rich. The wealth of the people had become a fable, even in the most ancient history. [Many foreign invaders] rushed to become wealthy in India and conquered the country. Every one of these invasions destroyed one or more of these families, burned many libraries and houses. And when that was so, much literature was lost. It is only within the last few years that ideas have begun to spring up about the retention of these various religions and books. Before that, mankind had to suffer all this pillaging and breaking down. Most stupendous creations of art were lost forever. Wonderful buildings—where, from a few bits of remnants now in India, it can be imagined how wonderful they were—are completely gone...

[The fanatical belief of many of these invaders into India is] that those who do not belong to their sect have no right to live. They will go to a place where the fire will never be quenched when they die; in this life they are only fit to be made into slaves or murdered; and that they have only the right to live as slaves to "the true believers", but never as free men. So in this way, when these waves burst upon India, everything was submerged. Books and literature and civilization went down.

But there is a vitality in that race which is unique in the history of humanity, and perhaps that vitality comes from non-resistance. Non-resistance is the greatest strength. In meekness and mildness lies the greatest strength. In suffering is greater strength than in doing. In resisting one's own passions is far higher strength than in hurting others. And that has been the watchword of the race through all its difficulties, its misfortunes and its prosperity. It is the only nation that never went beyond its frontiers to cut the throats of its neighbours. It is a glorious thing. It makes me rather patriotic to think I am born a Hindu, a descendant of the only race that never went out to hurt anyone, and whose only action upon humanity has been giving and enlightening and purifying and teaching, but never robbing.

Three-quarters of the wealth of the world has come out of India, and does even now. The commerce of India has been the turning point, the pivot, of the history of the world. Whatever nation got it became powerful and civilized. The Greeks got it and became the mighty Greeks; the Romans got it and became the mighty Romans. Even in the days of the Phoenicians it was so. After the fall of Rome, the Genoese and the Venetians got it. And then the Arabs rose and created a wall between Venice and India; and in the struggle to find a new way there, America was discovered. That is how America was discovered; and the original people of America were called Indians, or "Injuns", for that reason. Even the Dutch got it—and the barbarians—and the English and they became the most powerful nation on earth. And the next nation that gets it will immediately be the most powerful.

Think of all this mass of energy that our nation displays—where does it get it? In India, they are the producers and you are the enjoyers, no doubt. They produced this—the patient, toiling millions of Hindus under the whip and slavery of everyone. Even the missionaries, who stand up to curse the millions of India, have been fattened upon the work of these millions, and they do not know how it has been done. Upon their blood the history of the world has been turning since we know history, and will have to turn for thousands of years more. What is the benefit? It gives that nation strength. They are, as it were, an example. They must suffer and stand up through all, fighting for the truths of religion—as a signpost, a beacon—to tell unto mankind that it is much higher not to resist, much higher to suffer, that if life be the goal, as even their conquerors will admit, we are the only race that can be called immortal, that can never be killed. (Vide Complete Works, IV)

Where are the Greeks today—they whose armies marched over the whole world? Gone, thousands of years—nobody knows where. Vanished, as soon as the barbarians of the north came and attacked them. Where are the mighty Romans, whose cohorts came and trampled the face of the earth? Where are they today? Gone—vanished like the morning dew, and left behind in the march.

But here are the Hindus—three hundred million strong. And think of the fertility of the race! They can increase more than the whole world can kill them. This is the vitality of the race. Although not belonging very much to our subject, I wanted to bring these things before you.

Generally the uneducated minds, the vulgar minds of every nation, like the vulgar mobs in every big city, cannot grasp, cannot see, cannot understand, any fine movement. The causes, the real movements in this world of ours, are very fine; it is only the effects that are gross and muscular. The mind is the real cause of this body, the fine movements behind. The body is the gross, the external. But everyone sees the body; very few see the mind. So with everything; the masses, the brutal, ignorant masses of every race, see a triumphant procession, stampeding horses, arms and cannonades, and these they understand. But those fine, gentle workings that are going on behind—it is only the philosopher, the highly cultivated man or woman, that can understand.

To return to our Vedanta, I have said that the Sanskrit in which the Vedas were written is not the same Sanskrit in which books were written about a thousand years later than the Vedas—the books that you read in your translations of poets and other classical writers of India. The Sanskrit of the Vedas was very simple, archaic in its composition, and possibly it was a spoken language. But the Sanskrit that we have now was never a spoken language, at least for the last three thousand years. Curiously enough, the vast mass of literature was written in a language which was dead, covering a period of three thousand years. Dramas and novels were written in this dead language. And all the time it was not spoken in the homes; it was only the language of the learned.

Even in the time of Buddha, which was about 560 years before the Christian era, we find that Sanskrit had ceased to be a spoken language. Some of his disciples wanted to teach in Sanskrit, but the master studiously refused. He wanted to teach in the language [of the people], because he said he was the prophet of the people. And that is how it has come about that the Buddhistic literature is in Pali, which was the vernacular of that time.

This vast mass of literature—the Vedas—we find in three groups. The first group is the Samhitâs, a collection of hymns. The second group is called the Brâhmanas, or the [group dealing with different kinds of] sacrifice. The word Brahmana [by usage] means [what is achieved by means of] the sacrifice. And the other group is called the Upanishads (sittings, lectures, philosophic books). Again, the first two parts together—the hymns and the rituals—are called the Karmakânda, the work portion; and the second, or philosophic portion (the Upanishads), is called the Jnânakânda, the knowledge portion. This is the same word as your English word knowledge and the Greek word gnos—just as you have the word in agnostic, and so on.

The first portion is a collection of hymns in praise of certain gods, as Agni, fire; Mitra, the sun; and so forth. They are praised and oblations are offered to them. I have said these hymns are to the gods. I have used the word gods until I make you familiar with the Sanskrit word Deva, because the word gods is very misleading. These Devas mean the "bright ones", and gods in India are less persons than positions. For instance, Indra and Agni are not names of particular persons, but particular posts in this universe. There is the post of President, the presiding post over certain elements, the presiding post over certain worlds, and so forth. According to these theologians, you and I—most of us—probably have been some of these gods several times. It is only temporarily that a soul can fill one of these positions. And after his time is over, he gives way; another soul is raised from this world by good works and takes that position—he becomes [for example] Agni. In reading Sanskrit philosophy or theology, people always get bothered by the changing of these gods. But this is the theory—that they are names of positions, that all souls will have to fill them again and again; and these gods, when the soul has attained to that position, can help mankind. So gifts and praise are offered to them. How this idea came to the Aryans we do not know, but in the earliest portion of the Rig-Veda we find this idea perfected and completed.

Behind and beyond all these Devas and men and animals and worlds is the Ruler of this universe, Ishvara—somewhat similar to what in the New Testament is called God the Creator, Preserver, the Ruler of this universe. These Devas are not to be confused with Ishvara at all, but in the English language you have the same word for both. You use the word God in the singular and the plural. But the gods are the bright ones—the Devas—and God is Ishvara. This we find even in the oldest portions of the Vedas.

Another peculiarity is that this Ishvara, this God, is manifesting Himself in all these various forms of bright ones. This idea—that the same God manifests Himself in various forms—is a very rudimentary idea of the Vedas, even in the oldest portions. There was a time when a sort of monotheistic idea entered the Vedas, but it was very quickly rejected. As we go on, perhaps you will agree with me that it was very good that it was rejected.

So we find in these oldest portions of the Samhitas that there were these various Devas—[being praised as] the manifestations of someone very much higher than they [had left] behind, so that sometimes each one of them was taken up and adjectives piled on it and at last it was said, "You are the God of the universe". Then such passages as this occurred: "I am God, worshipped as the fire", and so forth. "It is the One; sages call Him variously." "He is that one existence; the sages call Him by various names." This I ask you to remember, because this is the turning point, the key-note of all thought that India has produced—"He is that One Being; sages call Him variously." All Hindu philosophy—either theistic or atheistic or monotheistic, dualistic or nondualistic—has that as the core, the centre. And by thousands of years of culture in the race, it is impossible for the Hindu race to go [away from] that idea.

That germ became a big tree; and that is why there was never a religious persecution in India, at least by the Hindus. That explains their liberality and welcome to any religion from any part of the world which came to settle there. That is how, even at the present day, Indian Rajas go and perform Mohammedan ceremonies and enter Mohammedan mosques, although [some] Mohammedans took the first opportunity to kill a number of "the heathens".

"He is the One Being; sages call Him variously."

There have been two theories advanced in modern times with regard to the growth of religions. The one is the tribal theory; the other is the spirit theory. The tribal theory is that humanity in its savage state remains divided into many small tribes. Each tribe has a god of its own—or sometimes the same god divided into many forms, as the god of this city came to that city, and so on; Jehovah of this city and of such-and-such mountain [came to such-and-such city or mountain]. When the tribes came together, one of them became strong.

Take the case of the Jews. They were divided into so many tribes, and each tribe had a god called either Baal or Moloch which in your Old Testament is translated as "the Lord". There was the Moloch of this state and that state, of this mountain and that mountain, and there was the Moloch of the chest, who used to live in a chest. This latter tribe became strong and conquered the surrounding tribes and became triumphant. So that Moloch was proclaimed the greatest of all Molochs.

"Thou art the Java [?] of the Molochs. Thou art the ruler of all the Baals and Molochs." Yet the chest remained. So this idea was obtained from tribal gods.

There is the other theory of Spiritualism—that religion begins with the worship of ancestors. Ancestor worship was among the Egyptians, among the Babylonians, among many other races—the Hindus, the Christians. There is not one form of religion among which there has not been this ancestor worship in some form or other.

Before that they thought that this body had a double inside it and that when this body dies the double gets out and lives so long as this body exists. The double becomes very hungry or thirsty, wants food or drink, and wants to enjoy the good things of this world. So he [the double] comes to get food; and if he does not get it, he will injure even his own children. So long as the body is preserved the double will live. Naturally the first attempt, as we see, was to preserve the body, mummify the body, so that the body will live forever.

So with the Babylonians was this sort of spirit worship. Later on as the nations advanced, the cruel forms died out and better forms remained. Some place was given to that which is called heaven, and they placed food here so that it might reach the double there. Even now the pious Hindus must, one day a year at least, place food for their ancestors. And the day they leave off [this habit] will be a sorry day for the ancestors. So you also find this ancestor worship to be one cause of religion. There are in modern times philosophers who advance the theory that this has been the root of all religions. There are others who advance the theory that the root of all religions was the tribal assimilation of gods into one.

Among the Jews of the Old Testament you do not find any mention of soul. It is only in the Talmud that it is found. They got it from the Alexandrians, and the Alexandrians from the Hindus—just as the Talmud had [developed] later on the idea of transmigration of the soul. But the old Jews had grand ideas of God. The God of the Jews developed into the Great God—the Omnipotent, Omniscient, All-Merciful—and all this came to them from the Hindus, but not through the idea of the soul. So Spiritualism could not have played any part in that, because how could the man who did not believe in any soul after death have anything to do with Spiritualism?

On the other hand, in the oldest portion of the Vedas, there is very little of Spiritualism, if anything at all. These Devas [of the Vedas] were not [related to Spiritualism]—although later on they became so; and this idea of Someone behind them, of whom they were manifestations, is in the oldest parts.

Another idea is that when the body dies, the soul [which] is immortal remains beatified. The very oldest Aryan literature—whether German or Greek—has this idea of soul. The idea of soul has come from the Hindus.

Two people have given all the religion to the world—the Hindus and the Jews. But it is only with the Hindus that the idea of soul comes at first, and that was shared by the Aryan races.

The peculiarity you find is that the Semitic races and the Egyptians try to preserve the dead bodies, while the Aryans try to destroy them. The Greeks, the Germans, the Romans—your ancestors before they became Christians—used to burn the dead. It was only when Charlemagne made you Christians with the sword—and when you refused, [he] cut off a few hundred heads, and the rest jumped into the water—that burying came here. You see at once the metaphysical significance of burning the dead. The burying of the dead (Preserving the dead by the burying of the body.) can only remain when there is no idea of the soul, and the body is all. At best there came the idea later on that this very body will have another lease of life, after so many years—mummies will come out and begin to walk the streets again.

But with the Aryans the idea was from the first that the soul is not the body, but would live on. There are some old hymns in the Rig-Veda: when the bodies are burnt they say, "Take him gently, purify him, give him a bright body, take him to the land where the fathers live—wherethere is no more sorrow and where thereis joy forever". (Rig-Veda 10.16.4.)

It is curious that though in modern times many hideous and cruel forms of religion crept into India, there is one peculiar idea that divides the Aryan from all other races of the world: that their religion, in the Hindu form, accepted this Indra as one [with the Ultimate Reality]. Three-quarters of the mythology of the Vedas is the same as that of the Greeks; only the old gods became saints in the new religion. But they were originally the gods of the Samhitas.

One other peculiarity we remark—that it is a cheerful, joyful, at times almost hilarious religion; there is not a bit of pessimism in it. The earth is beautiful, the heavens are beautiful, life is immortal. Even after death they get a still more beautiful body, which has none of the imperfections of this body, and they go to live with the gods and enjoy heaven forever.

On the other hand, with the Semitic races, the very first inception of religion was one of horror. A man crouched in his little house for fear. All round his house were those doubles. The family ancestors of the Jews were there, ready to pounce upon anybody and tear him to pieces if bloody sacrifices were not given to them. Even when you find that this [double] idea coagulated into one—"Thou art the Elohim of the Jews, Thou art the Elo[him] of the [Babylonians?]"—even then the idea of sacrifice remained.

The idea of sacrifice in India was not with this first portion. But in the next portion we find the same idea in India too, in the Brahmanas. The idea of sacrifice was originally simply giving food [to the gods], but gradually it was raised and raised until it became a sacrifice to God. Philosophy came in to mystify it still more and to spin webs of logic round it. Bloody sacrifices came into vogue. Somewhere we read that three hundred bullocks have been roasted, or the gods are smelling the sacrifices and becoming very glad. Then all sorts of mystical notions got about—how the sacrifice was to be made in the form of a tri-angle or a square, a triangle within a square, a pentagon, and all sorts of figures. But the great benefit was the evolution of geometry. When they had to make all these figures—and it was laid down strictly how many bricks should be used, and how they should be laid, and how big they should be—naturally geometry came [into being]. The Egyptians evolved geometry [by] their [irrigation]—[they] made canals to take the Nile water inside their fields—and the Hindus, by their altars.

Now there is another particular difference between the idea of sacrifice in India and [that] of the Jews. The real meaning of sacrifice is worship, a form of worship by oblations. At first it was simply giving food to the bright ones, or the higher beings. They had gross food just as we have. Later on philosophy stepped in and the idea came that they, being higher beings, could not eat the same food as we do. Their bodies are made of finer particles. Our bodies cannot pass through a wall; theirs find no resistance in gross material. As such, they cannot be expected to eat in the same gross way as we do.

[Some parts of the transcription of the remaining portion of this lecture, recorded by Mr. J. J. Goodwin, were found in a severely damaged condition. Hence we have reproduced below only the legible fragments as they appeared in the original.]

…"O Indra, I offer you this oblation. O Agni, I offer you this oblation." The answer is that these words have a mystical power in Sanskrit. And when a man, in a certain state of mind, pronounces these words, he sets in motion a set of psychological causes, and these causes produce a certain effect. That is the evolution of thought.

To make it clearer, suppose a man was childless and wanted a son. He worshipped Indra, and if he got a son he said Indra gave him the son. Later on they said Indra did not exist. Who, then, gave him the son? The whole thing is a matter of cause and effect… …

They said it was not giving the gods food, but simply laying my sins upon the head of another victim. "My sins go upon the goat's head, and, if the goat be killed, my sins are forgiven." That idea of sacrifice of the Jews never entered India, and perhaps that has saved us many a pang, many a trouble.

Human nature is selfish, and the vast majority of men and women weak; and to teach vicarious sacrifice makes us more and more weak. Every child is taught that he is nothing until the poor fellow becomes hypnotized into nothing. He goes in search of somebody to cling onto, and never thinks of clinging to himself… (Vide Complete Works, VIII for similar ideas.)

THE WAY TO THE REALISATION OF A UNIVERSAL RELIGION

Delivered in the Universalist Church, Pasadena, California, 28th January 1900

No search has been dearer to the human heart than that

which brings to us light from God. No study has taken so much of human energy, whether in times past or present, as the study of the soul, of God, and of human destiny. However immersed we are in our daily occupations, in our ambitions, in our work, in the midst of the greatest of our struggles, sometimes there will come a pause; the mind stops and wants to know something beyond this world. Sometimes it catches glimpses of a realm beyond the senses, and a struggle to get at it is the result. Thus it has been throughout the ages, in all countries. Man has wanted to look beyond, wanted to expand himself; and all that we call progress, evolution, has been always measured by that one search, the search for human destiny, the search for God.

As our social struggles are represented amongst different nations by different social organizations, so is man's spiritual struggle represented by various religions; and as different social organizations are constantly quarrelling, are constantly at war with one another, so these spiritual organisations have been constantly at war with one another, constantly quarrelling. Men belonging to a particular social organisation claim that the right to live only belongs to them; and so long as they can, they want to exercise that right at the cost of the weak. We know that just now there is a fierce struggle of that sort going on in South Africa. Similarly, each religious sect has; claimed the exclusive right to live. And thus we find that though there is nothing that has brought to man more blessings than religion, yet at the same time, there is nothing that has brought more horror than religion. Nothing has made more for peace and love than religion; nothing has engendered fiercer hatred than religion. Nothing has made the brotherhood of man more tangible than religion; nothing has bred more bitter enmity between man and man than religion. Nothing has built more charitable institutions, more hospitals for men, and even for animals, than religion; nothing has deluged the world with more blood than religion. We know, at the same time, that there has always been an undercurrent of thought; there have been always parties of men, philosophers, students of comparative religion who have tried and are still trying to bring about harmony in the midst of all these jarring and discordant sects. As regards certain countries, these attempts have succeeded, but as regards the whole world, they have failed.

There are some religions which have come down to us from the remotest antiquity, which are imbued with the idea that all sects should be allowed to live, that every sect has a meaning, a great idea, imbedded within itself, and, therefore it is necessary for the good of the world and ought to be helped. In modern times the same idea is prevailing and attempts are made from time to time to reduce it to practice. These attempts do not always come up to our expectations, up to the required efficiency. Nay, to our great disappointment, we sometimes find that we are quarrelling all the more.

Now, leaving aside dogmatic study, and taking a common-sense view of the thing, we find at the start that there is

a tremendous life-power in all the great religions of the world. Some may say that they are ignorant of this, but ignorance is no excuse. If a man says "I do not know what is going on in the external world, therefore things that are going on in the external world do not exist", that man is inexcusable. Now, those of you that watch the movement of religious thought all over the world are perfectly aware that not one of the great religions of the world has died; not only so, each one of them is progressive. Christians are multiplying, Mohammedans are multiplying, the Hindus are gaining ground, and the Jews also are increasing, and by their spreading all over the world and increasing rapidly, the fold of Judaism is constantly expanding.

Only one religion of the world—an ancient, great religion—has dwindled away, and that is the religion of Zoroastrianism, the religion of the ancient Persians. Under the Mohammedan conquest of Persia about a hundred thousand of these people came and took shelter in India and some remained in ancient Persia. Those that were in Persia, under the constant persecution of the Mohammedans, dwindled down till there are at most only ten thousand; in India there are about eighty thousand of them, but they do not increase. Of course, there is an initial difficulty; they do not convert others to their religion. And then, this handful of persons living in India, with the pernicious custom of cousin marriage, do not multiply. With this single exception, all the great religions are living, spreading, and increasing. We must remember that all the great religions of the world are very ancient, not one has been formed at the present time, and that every religion of the world owes its origin to the country between the Ganga and the Euphrates; not one great religion has arisen in Europe, not one in America, not one; every religion is of Asiatic origin and belongs to that part of the world. If what the modern scientists say is true, that the survival of the fittest is the test, these religions prove by their still living that they are yet fit for some people. There is a reason why they should live, they bring good to many. Look at the Mohammedans, how they are spreading in some places in Southern Asia, and spreading like fire in Africa. The Buddhists are spreading all over Central Asia, all the time. The Hindus, like the Jews, do not convert others; still gradually, other races are coming within Hinduism and adopting the manners and customs of the Hindus and falling into line with them. Christianity, you all know, is spreading—though I am not sure that the results are equal to the energy put forth. The Christians' attempt at propaganda has one tremendous defect—and that is the defect of all Western institutions: the machine consumes ninety per cent of the energy, there is too much machinery. Preaching has always been the business of the Asiatics. The Western people are grand in organisation, social institutions, armies, governments, etc.; but when it comes to preaching religion, they cannot come near the Asiatic, whose business it has been all the time, and he knows it, and he does not use too much machinery.

This then is a fact in the present history of the human race, that all these great religions exist and are spreading and multiplying. Now, there is a meaning, certainly, to this; and had it been the will of an All-wise and All-merciful Creator that one of these religions should exist and the rest should die, it would have become a fact long, long ago. If it were a fact that only one of these religions is true and all the rest are false, by this time it would have covered the whole ground. But this is not so; not one has gained all the ground. All religions sometimes advance—sometimes decline. Now, just think of this: in your own country there are more than sixty millions of people, and only twenty-one millions professing religions of all sorts. So it is not always progress. In every country, probably, if the statistics are taken, you would find that religions are sometimes progressing and sometimes going back. Sects are multiplying all the time. If the claims of a religion that it has all the truth and God has given it all this truth in a certain book were true, why are there so many sects? Fifty years do not pass before there are twenty sects founded upon the same book. If God has put all the truth in certain books, He does not give us those books in order that we may quarrel over texts. That seems to be the fact. Why is it? Even if a book were given by God which contained all the truth about religion, it would not serve the purpose because nobody could understand the book. Take the Bible, for instance, and all the sects that exist amongst Christians; each one puts its own interpretation upon the same text, and each says that it alone understands that text and all the rest are wrong. So with every religion. There are many sects among the Mohammedans and among the Buddhists, and hundreds among the Hindus. Now, I bring these facts before you in order to show you that any attempt to bring all humanity to one method of thinking in spiritual things has been a failure and always will be a failure. Every man that starts a theory, even at the present day, finds that if he goes twenty miles away from his followers, they will make twenty sects. You see that happening all the time. You cannot make all conform to the same ideas: that is a fact, and I thank God that it is so. I am not against any sect. I am glad that sects exist, and I only wish they may go on multiplying more and more. Why? Simply because of this: If you and I and all who are present here were to think exactly the same thoughts, there would be no thoughts for us to think. We know that two or more forces must come into collision in order to produce motion. It is the clash of thought, the differentiation of thought, that awakes thought. Now, if we all thought alike, we would be like Egyptian mummies in a museum looking vacantly at one another's faces—no more than that! Whirls and eddies occur only in a rushing, living stream. There are no whirlpools in stagnant, dead water. When religions are dead, there will be no more sects; it will be the perfect peace and harmony of the grave. But so long as mankind thinks, there will be sects. Variation is the sign of life, and it must be there. I pray that they may multiply so that at last there will be as many sects as human beings, and each one will have his own method, his individual method of thought in religion.

But this thing exists already. Each one of us is thinking in his own way, but his natural course has been obstructed all the time and is still being obstructed. If the sword is not used directly, other means will be used. Just hear what one of the best preachers in New York says: he preaches that the Filipinos should be conquered because that is the only way to teach Christianity to them! They are already Catholics; but he wants to make them Presbyterians, and for this, he is ready to lay all this terrible sin of bloodshed upon his race. How terrible! And this man is one of the greatest preachers of this country, one of the best informed men. Think of the state of the world when a man like that is not ashamed to stand up and utter such arrant nonsense; and think of the state of the world when an audience cheers him! Is this civilisation? It is the old blood-thirstiness of the tiger, the cannibal, the savage, coming out once more under new names, new circumstances. What else can it be? If the state of things is such now, think of the horrors through which the world passed in olden times, when every sect was trying by every means in its power to tear to pieces the other sects. History shows that. The tiger in us is only asleep; it is not dead. When opportunities come, it jumps up and, as of old, uses its claws and fangs. Apart from the sword, apart from material weapons, there are weapons still more terrible—contempt, social hatred, and social ostracism. Now, these are the most terrible of all inflictions that are hurled against persons who do not think exactly in the same way as we do. And why should everybody think just as we do? I do not see any reason. If I am a rational man, I should be glad they do not think just as I do. I do not want to live in a grave-like land; I want to be a man in a world of men. Thinking beings must differ; difference is the first sign of thought. If I am a thoughtful man, certainly I ought to like to live amongst thoughtful persons where there are differences of opinion.

Then arises the question: How can all these varieties be true? If one thing is true, its negation is false. How can contradictory opinions be true at the same time? This is the question which I intend to answer. But I will first ask you: Are all the religions of the world really contradictory? I do not mean the external forms in which great thoughts are clad. I do not mean the different buildings, languages, rituals, books, etc. employed in various religions, but I mean the internal soul of every religion. Every religion has a soul behind it, and that soul may differ from the soul of another religion; but are they contradictory? Do they contradict or supplement each other?—that is the question. I took up the question when I was quite a boy, and have been studying it all my life. Thinking that my conclusion may be of some help to you, I place it before you. I believe that they are not contradictory; they are supplementary. Each religion, as it were, takes up one part of the great universal truth, and spends its whole force in embodying and typifying that part of the great truth. It is, therefore, addition; not exclusion. That is the idea. System after system arises, each one embodying a great idea, and ideals must be added to ideals. And this is the march of humanity. Man never progresses from error to truth, but from truth to truth, from lesser truth to higher truth—but it is never from error to truth. The child may develop more than the father, but was the father inane? The child is the father plus something else. If your present state of knowledge is much greater than it was when you were a child, would you look down upon that stage now? Will you look back and call it inanity? Why, your present stage is the knowledge of the child plus something more.

Then, again, we also know that there may be almost contradictory points of view of the same thing, but they will all indicate the same thing. Suppose a man is journeying towards the sun, and as he advances he takes a photograph of the sun at every stage. When he comes back, he has many photographs of the sun, which he places before us. We see that not two are alike, and yet, who will deny that all these are photographs of the same sun, from different standpoints? Take four photographs of this church from different corners: how different they would look, and yet they would all represent this church. In the same way, we are all looking at truth from different standpoints, which vary according to our birth, education, surroundings, and so on. We are viewing truth, getting as much of it as these circumstances will permit, colouring the truth with our own heart, understanding it with our own intellect, and grasping it with our own mind. We can only know as much of truth as is related to us, as much of it as we are able to receive. This makes the difference between man and man, and occasions sometimes even contradictory ideas; yet we all belong to the same great universal truth.

My idea, therefore, is that all these religions are different forces in the economy of God, working for the good of mankind; and that not one can become dead, not one can be killed. Just as you cannot kill any force in nature, so you cannot kill any one of these spiritual forces. You have seen that each religion is living. From time to time it may retrograde or go forward. At one time, it may be shorn of a good many of its trappings; at another time it may be covered with all sorts of trappings; but all the same, the soul is ever there, it can never be lost. The ideal which every religion represents is never lost, and so every religion is intelligently on the march.

And that universal religion about which philosophers and others have dreamed in every country already exists. It is here. As the universal brotherhood of man is already existing, so also is universal religion. Which of you, that have travelled far and wide, have not found brothers and sisters in every nation? I have found them all over the world. Brotherhood already exists; only there are numbers of persons who fail to see this and only upset it by crying for new brotherhoods. Universal religion, too, is already existing. If the priests and other people that have taken upon themselves the task of preaching different religions simply cease preaching for a few moments, we shall see it is there. They are disturbing it all the time, because

it is to their interest. You see that priests in every country are very conservative. Why is it so? There are very few priests who lead the people; most of them are led by the people and are their slaves and servants. If you say it is dry, they say it is so; if you say it is black, they say it is black. If the people advance, the priests must advance. They cannot lag behind. So, before blaming the priests—it is the fashion to blame the priest—you ought to blame yourselves. You only get what you deserve. What would be the fate of a priest who wants to give you new and advanced ideas and lead you forward? His children would probably starve, and he would be clad in rags. He is governed by the same worldly laws as you are. "If you go on," he says, "let us march." Of course, there are exceptional souls, not cowed down by public opinion. They see the truth and truth alone they value. Truth has got hold of them, has got possession of them, as it were, and they cannot but march ahead. They never look backward, and for them there are no people. God alone exists for them, He is the Light before them, and they are following that Light.

I met a Mormon gentleman in this country, who tried to persuade me to his faith. I said, "I have great respect for your opinions, but in certain points we do not agree—I belong to a monastic order, and you believe in marrying many wives. But why don't you go to India to preach?" Then he was astonished. He said, "Why, you don't believe in any marriage at all, and we believe in polygamy, and yet you ask me to go to your country!" I said, "Yes; my countrymen will hear every religious thought wherever it may come from. I wish you would go to India, first, because I am a great believer in sects. Secondly, there are many men in India who are not at all satisfied with any of the existing sects, and on account of this dissatisfaction, they will not have anything to do with religion, and, possibly, you might get some of them." The greater the number of sects, the more chance of people getting religion. In the hotel, where there are all sorts of food, everyone has a chance to get his appetite satisfied. So I want sects to multiply in every country, that more people may have a chance to be spiritual. Do not think that people do not like religion. I do not believe that. The preachers cannot give them what they need. The same man that may have been branded as an atheist, as a materialist, or what not, may meet a man who gives him the truth needed by him, and he may turn out the most spiritual man in the community. We can eat only in our own way. For instance, we Hindus eat with our fingers. Our fingers are suppler than yours, you cannot use your fingers the same way. Not only the food should be supplied, but it should be taken in your own particular way. Not only must you have the spiritual ideas, but they must come to you according to your own method. They must speak your own language, the language of your soul, and then alone they will satisfy you. When the man comes who speaks my language and gives truth in my language, I at once understand it and receive it for ever. This is a great fact.

Now from this we see that there are various grades and types of human minds and what a task religions take upon them! A man brings forth two or three doctrines and claims that his religion ought to satisfy all humanity. He goes out into the world, God's menagerie, with a little cage in hand, and says, "God and the elephant and everybody has to go into this. Even if we have to cut the elephant into pieces, he must go in." Again, there may be a sect with a few good ideas. Its followers say, "All men must come in! " "But there is no room for them." "Never mind! Cut them to pieces; get them in anyhow; if they don't get in, why, they will be damned." No preacher, no sect, have I ever met that pauses and asks, "Why is it that people do not listen to us?" Instead, they curse the people and say, "The people are wicked." They never ask, "How is it that people do not listen to my words? Why cannot I make them see the truth? Why cannot I speak in their language? Why cannot I open their eyes?" Surely, they ought to know better, and when they find people do not listen to them, if they curse anybody, it should be themselves. But it is always the people's fault! They never try to make their sect large enough to embrace every one.

Therefore we at once see why there has been so much narrow-mindedness, the part always claiming to be the whole; the little, finite unit always laying claim to the infinite. Think of little sects, born within a few hundred years out of fallible human brains, making this arrogant claim of knowledge of the whole of God's infinite truth! Think of the arrogance of it! If it shows anything, it is this, how vain human beings are. And it is no wonder that such claims have always failed, and, by the mercy of the Lord, are always destined to fail. In this line the Mohammedans were the best off; every step forward was made with the sword—the Koran in the one hand and the sword in the other: "Take the Koran, or you must die; there is no alternative! " You know from history how phenomenal was their success; for six hundred years nothing could resist them, and then there came a time when they had to cry halt. So will it be with other religions if they follow the same methods. We are such babes! We always forget human nature. When we begin life, we think that our fate will be something extraordinary, and nothing can make us disbelieve that. But when we grow old, we think differently. So with religions. In their early stages, when they spread a. little, they get the idea that they can change the minds of the whole human race in a few years, and go on killing and massacring to make converts by force; then they fail, and begin to understand better. We see that these sects did not succeed in what they started out to do, which was a great blessing. Just think if one of those fanatical sects had succeeded all over the world, where would man be today? Now, the Lord be blessed that they did not succeed! Yet, each one represents a great truth; each religion represents a particular excellence—something which is its soul. There is an old story which comes to my mind: There were some ogresses who used to kill people and do all sorts of mischief; but they themselves could not be killed, until someone found out that their souls were in certain birds, and so long as the

birds were safe nothing could destroy the ogresses. So, each one of us has, as it were, such a bird, where our soul is; has an ideal, a mission to perform in life. Every human being is an embodiment of such an ideal, such a mission. Whatever else you may lose, so long as that ideal is not lost, and that mission is not hurt, nothing can kill you. Wealth may come and go, misfortunes may pile mountains high, but if you have kept the ideal entire, nothing can kill you. You may have grown old, even a hundred years old, but if that mission is fresh and young in your heart, what can kill you? But when that ideal is lost and that mission is hurt, nothing can save you. All the wealth, all the power of the world will not save you. And what are nations but multiplied individuals? So, each nation has a mission of its own to perform in this harmony of races; and so long as that nation keeps to that ideal, that nation nothing can kill; but if that nation gives up its mission in life and goes after something else, its life becomes short, and it vanishes.

And so with religions. The fact that all these old religions are living today proves that they must have kept that mission intact; in spite of all their mistakes, in spite of all difficulties, in spite of all quarrels, in spite of all the incrustation of forms and figures, the heart of every one of them is sound—it is a throbbing, beating, living heart. They have not lost, any one of them, the great mission they came for. And it is splendid to study that mission. Take Mohammedanism, for instance. Christian people hate no religion in the world so much as Mohammedanism. They think it is the very worst form of religion that ever existed. As soon as a man becomes a Mohammedan, the whole of Islam receives him as a brother with open arms, without making any distinction, which no other religion does. If one of your American Indians becomes a Mohammedan, the Sultan of Turkey would have no objection to dine with him. If he has brains, no position is barred to him. In this country, I have never yet seen a church where the white man and the negro can kneel side by side to pray. Just think of that: Islam makes its followers all equal—so, that, you see, is the peculiar excellence of Mohammedanism. In many places in the Koran you find very sensual ideas of life. Never mind. What Mohammedanism comes to preach to the world is this practical brotherhood of all belonging to their faith. That is the essential part of the Mohammedan religion; and all the other ideas about heaven and of life etc.. are not Mohammedanism. They are accretions.

With the Hindus you will find one national idea—spirituality. In no other religion, in no other sacred books of the world, will you find so much energy spent in defining the idea of God. They tried to define the ideal of soul so that no earthly touch might mar it. The spirit must be divine; and spirit understood as spirit must not be made into a man. The same idea of unity, of the realisation of God, the omnipresent, is preached throughout. They think it is all nonsense to say that He lives in heaven, and all that. It is a mere human, anthropomorphic idea. All the heaven that ever existed is now and here. One moment in infinite time is quite as good as any other moment. If you believe in a God, you can see Him even now. We think religion begins when you have realised something. It is not believing in doctrines, nor giving intellectual assent, nor making declarations. If there is a God, have you seen Him? If you say "no", then what right have you to believe in Him? If you are in doubt whether there is a God, why do you not struggle to see Him? Why do you not renounce the world and spend the whole of your life for this one object? Renunciation and spirituality are the two great ideas of India, and it is because India clings to these ideas that all her mistakes count for so little.

With the Christians, the central idea that has been preached by them is the same: "Watch and pray, for the kingdom of Heaven is at hand"—which means, purify your minds and be ready! And that spirit never dies. You recollect that the Christians are, even in the darkest days, even in the most superstitious Christian countries, always trying to prepare themselves for the coming of the Lord, by trying to help others, building hospitals, and so on. So long as the Christians keep to that ideal, their religion lives.

Now an ideal presents itself to my mind. It may be only a dream. I do not know whether it will ever be realised in this world, but sometimes it is better to dream a dream, than die on hard facts. Great truths, even in a dream are good, better than bad facts. So, let us dream a dream.

You know that there are various grades of mind. You may be a matter-of-fact, common-sense rationalist: you do not care for forms and ceremonies; you want intellectual, hard, ringing facts, and they alone will satisfy you. Then there are the Puritans, the Mohammedans, who will not allow a picture or a statue in their place of worship. Very well! But there is another man who is more artistic. He wants a great deal of art—beauty of lines and curves, the colours, flowers, forms; he wants candles, lights, and all the insignia and paraphernalia of ritual, that he may see God. His mind takes God in those forms, as yours takes Him through the intellect. Then, there is the devotional man, whose soul is crying for God: he has no other idea but to worship God, and to praise Him. Then again, there is the philosopher, standing outside all these, mocking at them. He thinks, "What nonsense they are! What ideas about God!"

They may laugh at one another, but each one has a place in this world. All these various minds, all these various types are necessary. If there ever is going to be an ideal religion, it must be broad and large enough to supply food for all these minds. It must supply the strength of philosophy to the philosopher, the devotee's heart to the worshipper; to the ritualist, it will give all that the most marvellous symbolism can convey; to the poet, it will give as much of heart as he can take in, and other things besides. To make such a broad religion, we shall have to go back to the time when religions began and take them all in.

Our watchword, then, will be acceptance, and not exclusion.

Not only toleration, for so-called toleration is often blasphemy, and I do not believe in it. I believe in acceptance. Why should I tolerate? Toleration means that I think that you are wrong and I am just allowing you to live. Is it not a blasphemy to think that you and I are allowing others to live? I accept all religions that were in the past, and worship with them all; I worship God with every one of them, in whatever form they worship Him. I shall go to the mosque of the Mohammedan; I shall enter the Christian's church and kneel before the crucifix; I shall enter the Buddhistic temple, where I shall take refuge in Buddha and in his Law. I shall go into the forest and sit down in meditation with the Hindu, who is trying to see the Light which enlightens the heart of every one.

Not only shall I do all these, but I shall keep my heart open for all that may come in the future. Is God's book finished? Or is it still a continuous revelation going on? It is a marvellous book—these spiritual revelations of the world. The Bible, the Vedas, the Koran, and all other sacred books are but so many pages, and an infinite number of pages remain yet to be unfolded. I would leave it open for all of them. We stand in the present, but open ourselves to the infinite future. We take in all that has been in the past, enjoy the light of the present, and open every window of the heart for all that will come in the future. Salutation to all the prophets of the past, to all the great ones of the present, and to all that are to come in the future!

THE IDEAL OF A UNIVERSAL RELIGION
How It Must Embrace Different Types Of Minds And Methods

Wheresoever our senses reach, or whatsoever our minds imagine, we find therein the action and reaction of two forces, the one counteracting the other and causing the constant play of the mixed phenomena that we see around us, and of those which we feel in our minds. In the external world, the action of these opposite forces is expressing itself as attraction and repulsion, or as centripetal and centrifugal forces; and in the internal, as love and hatred, good and evil. We repel some things, we attract others. We are attracted by one, we are repelled by another. Many times in our lives we find that without any reason whatsoever we are, as it were, attracted towards certain persons; at other times, similarly, we are repelled by others. This is patent to all, and the higher the field of action, the more potent, the more remarkable, are the influences of these opposite forces. Religion is the highest plane of human thought and life, and herein we find that the workings of these two forces have been most marked. The intensest love that humanity has ever known has come from religion, and the most diabolical hatred that humanity has known has also come from religion. The noblest words of peace that the world has ever heard have come from men on the religious plane, and the bitterest denunciation that the world has ever known has been uttered by religious men. The higher the object of any religion and the finer its organisation, he more remarkable are its activities. No other human motive has deluged the world with blood so much as religion; at the same time, nothing has brought into existence so many hospitals and asylums for the poor; no other human influence has taken such care, not only of humanity, but also of the lowest of animals, as religion has done. Nothing makes us so cruel as religion, and nothing makes us so tender as religion. This has been so in the past, and will also, in all probability, be so in the future. Yet out of the midst of this din and turmoil, this strife and struggle, this hatred and jealousy of religions and sects, there have arisen, from time to time, potent voices, drowning all this noise — making themselves heard from pole to pole, as it were — proclaiming peace and harmony. Will it ever come?

Is it possible that there should ever reign unbroken harmony in this plane of mighty religious struggle. The world is exercised in the latter part of this century by the question of harmony; in society, various plans are being proposed, and attempts are made to carry them into practice; but we know how difficult it is to do so. People find that it is almost impossible to mitigate the fury of the struggle of life, to tone down the tremendous nervous tension that is in man. Now, if it is so difficult to bring harmony and peace to the physical plane of life — the external, gross, and outward side of it — then a thousand times more difficult is it to bring peace and harmony to rule over the internal nature of man. I would ask you for the time being to come out of the network of words. We have all been hearing from childhood of such things as love, peace, charity, equality, and universal brotherhood; but they have become to us mere words without meaning, words which we repeat like parrots, and it has become quite natural for us to do so. We cannot help it. Great souls, who first felt these great ideas in their hearts, manufactured these words; and at that time many understood their meaning. Later on, ignorant people have taken up those words to play with them and made religion a mere play upon words, and not a thing to be carried into practice. It becomes "my father's religion", "our nation's religion", "our country's religion", and so forth. It becomes only a phase of patriotism to profess any religion, and patriotism is always partial. To bring harmony into religion must always be difficult. Yet we will consider this problem of the harmony of religions.

We see that in every religion there are three parts — I mean in every great and recognised religion. First, there is the philosophy which presents the whole scope of that religion, setting forth its basic principles, the goal and the means of reaching it. The second part is mythology, which is philosophy made concrete. It consists of legends relating to the lives of men, or of supernatural beings, and so forth. It is the abstractions of philosophy concretised in the more or less imaginary lives of men and supernatural beings. The third part is the ritual. This is still more concrete and is made up of forms and ceremonies, various physical attitudes, flowers and incense, and many other things, that appeal to the senses. In these consists the ritual. You will find that all recognised religions have these three

elements. Some lay more stress on one, some on another. Let us now take into consideration the first part, philosophy. Is there one universal philosophy? Not yet. Each religion brings out its own doctrines and insists upon them as being the only true ones. And not only does it do that, but it thinks that he who does not believe in them must go to some horrible place. Some will even draw the sword to compel others to believe as they do. This is not through wickedness, but through a particular disease of the human brain called fanaticism. They are very sincere, these fanatics, the most sincere of human beings; but they are quite as irresponsible as other lunatics in the world. This disease of fanaticism is one of the most dangerous of all diseases. All the wickedness of human nature is roused by it. Anger is stirred up, nerves are strung high, and human beings become like tigers.

Is there any mythological similarity, is there any mythological harmony, any universal mythology accepted by all religions? Certainly not. All religions have their own mythology, only each of them says, "My stories are not mere myths." Let us try to understand the question by illustration. I simply mean to illustrate, I do not mean criticism of any religion. The Christian believes that God took the shape of a dove and came down to earth; to him this is history, and not mythology. The Hindu believes that God is manifested in the cow. Christians say that to believe so is mere mythology, and not history, that it is superstition. The Jews think that if an image be made in the form of a box, or a chest, with an angel on either side, then it may be placed in the Holy of Holies; it is sacred to Jehovah; but if the image be made in the form of a beautiful man or woman, they say, "This is a horrible idol; break it down! " This is our unity in mythology! If a man stands up and says, "My prophet did such and such a wonderful thing", others will say, "That is only superstition", but at the same time they say that their own prophet did still more wonderful things, which they hold to be historical. Nobody in the world, as far as I have seen, is able to make out the fine distinction between history and mythology, as it exists in the brains of these persons. All such stories, to whatever religion they may belong, are really mythological, mixed up occasionally, it may be with, a little history.

Next come the rituals. One sect has one particular form of ritual and thinks that that is holy, while the rituals of another sect are simply arrant superstition. If one sect worships a peculiar sort of symbol, another sect says, "Oh, it is horrible!" Take, for instance, a general form of symbol. The phallus symbol is certainly a sexual symbol, but gradually that aspect of it has been forgotten, and it stands now as a symbol of the Creator. Those nations which have this as their symbol never think of it as the phallus; it is just a symbol, and there it ends. But a man from another race or creed sees in it nothing but the phallus, and begins to condemn it; yet at the same time he may be doing something which to the so-called phallic worshippers appears most horrible. Let me take two points for illustration, the phallus symbol and the sacrament of the

Christians. To the Christians the phallus is horrible, and to the Hindus the Christian sacrament is horrible. They say that the Christian sacrament, the killing of a man and the eating of his flesh and the drinking of his blood to get the good qualities of that man, is cannibalism. This is what some of the savage tribes do; if a man is brave, they kill him and eat his heart, because they think that it will give them the qualities of courage and bravery possessed by that man. Even such a devout Christian as Sir John Lubbock admits this and says that the origin of this Christian symbol is in this savage idea. The Christians, of course, do not admit this view of its origin; and what it may imply never comes to their mind. It stands for holy things, and that is all they want to know. So even in rituals there is no universal symbol, which can command general recognition and acceptance. Where then is any universality? How is it possible then to have a universal form of religion? That, however, already exists. And let us see what it is.

We all hear about universal brotherhood, and how societies stand up especially to preach this. I remember an old story. In India, taking wine is considered very bad. There were two brothers who wished, one night, to drink wine secretly; and their uncle, who was a very orthodox man was sleeping in a room quite close to theirs. So, before they began to drink, they said to each other, "We must be very silent, or uncle will wake up." When they were drinking, they continued repeating to each other "Silence! Uncle will wake up", each trying to shout the other down. And, as the shouting increased, the uncle woke up, came into the room, and discovered the whole thing. Now, we all shout like these drunken men," Universal brotherhood! We are all equal, therefore let us make a sect." As soon as you make a sect you protest against equality, and equality is no more. Mohammedans talk of universal brotherhood, but what comes out of that in reality? Why, anybody who is not a Mohammedan will not be admitted into the brotherhood; he will more likely have his throat cut. Christians talk of universal brotherhood; but anyone who is not a Christian must go to that place where he will be eternally barbecued.

And so we go on in this world in our search after universal brotherhood and equality. When you hear such talk in the world, I would ask you to be a little reticent, to take care of yourselves, for, behind all this talk is often the intensest selfishness. "In the winter sometimes a thunder-cloud comes up; it roars and roars, but it does not rain; but in the rainy season the clouds speak not, but deluge the world with water." So those who are really workers, and really feel at heart the universal brotherhood of man, do not talk much, do not make little sects for universal brotherhood; but their acts, their movements, their whole life, show out clearly that they in truth possess the feeling of brotherhood for mankind, that they have love and sympathy for all. They do not speak, they do and they live. This world is too full of blustering talk. We want a little more earnest work, and less talk.

So far we see that it is hard to find any universal features in regard to religion, and yet we know that they exist. We are all human beings, but are we all equal? Certainly not. Who says we are equal? Only the lunatic. Are we all equal in our brains, in our powers, in our bodies? One man is stronger than another, one man has more brain power than another. If we are all equal, why is there this inequality? Who made it? We. Because we have more or less powers, more or less brain, more or less physical strength, it must make a difference between us. Yet we know that the doctrine of equality appeals to our heart. We are all human beings; but some are men, and some are women. Here is a black man, there is a white man; but all are men, all belong to one humanity. Various are our faces; I see no two alike, yet we are all human beings. Where is this one humanity? I find a man or a woman, either dark or fair; and among all these faces I know that there is an abstract humanity which is common to all. I may not find it when I try to grasp it, to sense it, and to actualise it, yet I know for certain that it is there. If I am sure of anything, it is of this humanity which is common to us all. It is through this generalised entity that I see you as a man or a woman. So it is with this universal religion, which runs through all the various religions of the world in the form of God; it must and does exist through eternity. "I am the thread that runs through all these pearls," and each pearl is a religion or even a sect thereof. Such are the different pearls, and the Lord is the thread that runs through all of them; only the majority of mankind are entirely unconscious of it.

Unity in variety is the plan of the universe. We are all men, and yet we are all distinct from one another. As a part of humanity I am one with you, and as Mr. So-and-so I am different from you. As a man you are separate from the woman; as a human being you are one with the woman. As a man you are separate from the animal, but as living beings, man, woman, animal, and plant are all one; and as existence, you are one with the whole universe. That universal existence is God, the ultimate Unity in the universe. In Him we are all one. At the same time, in manifestation, these differences must always remain. In our work, in our energies, as they are being manifested outside, these differences must always remain. We find then that if by the idea of a universal religion it is meant that one set of doctrines should be believed in by all mankind it is wholly impossible. It can never be, there can never be a time when all faces will be the same. Again, if we expect that there will be one universal mythology, that is also impossible; it cannot be. Neither can there be one universal ritual. Such a state of things can never come into existence; if it ever did, the world would be destroyed, because variety is the first principle of life. What makes us formed beings? Differentiation. Perfect balance would be our destruction. Suppose the amount of heat in this room, the tendency of which is towards equal and perfect diffusion, gets that kind of diffusion, then for all practical purposes that heat will cease to be. What makes motion possible in this universe? Lost balance. The unity of sameness can come only when this universe is destroyed, otherwise such a thing is impossible. Not only so, it would be dangerous to have it. We must not wish that all of us should think alike. There would then be no thought to think. We should be all alike, as the Egyptian mummies in a museum, looking at each other without a thought to think. It is this difference, this differentiation, this losing of the balance between us, which is the very soul of our progress, the soul of all our thought. This must always be.

What then do I mean by the ideal of a universal religion? I do not mean any one universal philosophy, or any one universal mythology, or any one universal ritual held alike by all; for I know that this world must go on working, wheel within wheel, this intricate mass of machinery, most complex, most wonderful. What can we do then? We can make it run smoothly, we can lessen the friction, we can grease the wheels, as it were. How? By recognising the natural necessity of variation. Just as we have recognised unity by our very nature, so we must also recognise variation. We must learn that truth may be expressed in a hundred thousand ways, and that each of these ways is true as far as it goes. We must learn that the same thing can be viewed from a hundred different standpoints, and yet be the same thing. Take for instance the sun. Suppose a man standing on the earth looks at the sun when it rises in the morning; he sees a big ball. Suppose he starts on a journey towards the sun and takes a camera with him, taking photographs at every stage of his journey, until he reaches the sun. The photographs of each stage will be seen to be different from those of the other stages; in fact, when he gets back, he brings with him so many photographs of so many different suns, as it would appear; and yet we know that the same sun was photographed by the man at the different stages of his progress. Even so is it with the Lord. Through high philosophy or low, through the most exalted mythology or the grossest, through the most refined ritualism or arrant fetishism, every sect, every soul, every nation, every religion, consciously or unconsciously, is struggling upward, towards God; every vision of truth that man has, is a vision of Him and of none else. Suppose we all go with vessels in our hands to fetch water from a lake. One has a cup, another a jar, another a bucket, and so forth, and we all fill our vessels. The water in each case naturally takes the form of the vessel carried by each of us. He who brought the cup has the water in the form of a cup; he who brought the jar—his water is in the shape of a jar, and so forth; but, in every case, water, and nothing but water, is in the vessel. So it is in the case of religion; our minds are like these vessels, and each one of us is trying to arrive at the realisation of God. God is like that water filling these different vessels, and in each vessel the vision of God comes in the form of the vessel. Yet He is One. He is God in every case. This is the only recognition of universality that we can get.

So far it is all right theoretically. But is there any way of practically working out this harmony in religions? We find that this recognition that all the various views of religion are true has been very very old. Hundreds of attempts have been made in India, in Alexandria, in Europe, in China, in Japan, in Tibet, and lastly in America, to formulate a harmonious religious creed, to make all religions come together in love. They have all failed, because they did not adopt any practical plan. Many have admitted that all the religions of the world are right, but they show no practical way of bringing them together, so as to enable each of them to maintain its own individuality in the conflux. That plan alone is practical, which does not destroy the individuality of any man in religion and at the same time shows him a point of union with all others. But so far, all the plans of religious harmony that have been tried, while proposing to take in all the various views of religion, have, in practice, tried to bind them all down to a few doctrines, and so have produced more new sects, fighting, struggling, and pushing against each other.

I have also my little plan. I do not know whether it will work or not, and I want to present it to you for discussion. What is my plan? In the first place I would ask mankind to recognise this maxim, "Do not destroy". Iconoclastic reformers do no good to the world. Break not, pull not anything down, but build. Help, if you can; if you cannot, fold your hands and stand by and see things go on. Do not injure, if you cannot render help. Say not a word against any man's convictions so far as they are sincere. Secondly, take man where he stands, and from there give him a lift. If it be true that God is the centre of all religions, and that each of us is moving towards Him along one of these radii, then it is certain that all of us must reach that centre. And at the centre, where all the radii meet, all our differences will cease; but until we reach there, differences there must be. All these radii converge to the same centre. One, according to his nature, travels along one of these lines, and another, along another; and if we all push onward along our own lines, we shall surely come to the centre, because, "All roads lead to Rome". Each of us is naturally growing and developing according to his own nature; each will in time come to know the highest truth for after all, men must teach themselves. What can you and I do? Do you think you can teach even a child? You cannot. The child teaches himself. Your duty is to afford opportunities and to remove obstacles. A plant grows. Do you make the plant grow? Your duty is to put a hedge round it and see that no animal eats up the plant, and there your duty ends. The plant grows of itself. So it is in regard to the spiritual growth of every man. None can teach you; none can make a spiritual man of you. You have to teach yourself; your growth must come from inside.

What can an external teacher do? He can remove the obstructions a little, and there his duty ends. Therefore help, if you can; but do not destroy. Give up all ideas that you can make men spiritual. It is impossible. There is no other teacher to you than your own soul. Recognise this. What comes of it? In society we see so many different natures. There are thousands and thousands of varieties of minds and inclinations. A thorough generalisation of them is impossible, but for our practical purpose it is sufficient to have them characterised

Lectures & Discourses by **Swami Vivekananda**

into four classes. First, there is the active man, the worker; he wants to work, and there is tremendous energy in his muscles and his nerves. His aim is to work—to build hospitals, do charitable deeds, make streets, to plan and to organise. Then there is the emotional man who loves the sublime and the beautiful to an excessive degree. He loves to think of the beautiful, to enjoy the aesthetic side of nature, and adore Love and the God of Love. He loves with his whole heart the great souls of all times, the prophets of religions, and the Incarnations of God on earth; he does not care whether reason can or cannot prove that Christ or Buddha existed; he does not care for the exact date when the Sermon on the Mount was preached, or for the exact moment of Krishna's birth; what he cares for is their personalities, their lovable figures. Such is his ideal. This is the nature of the lover, the emotional man. Then, there is the mystic whose mind wants to analyse its own self, to understand the workings of the human mind, what the forces are that are working inside, and how to know, manipulate, and obtain control over them. This is the mystical mind. Then, there is the philosopher who wants to weigh everything and use his intellect even beyond the possibilities of all human philosophy.

Now a religion, to satisfy the largest proportion of mankind, must be able to supply food for all these various types of minds; and where this capability is wanting, the existing sects all become one-sided. Suppose you go to a sect which preaches love and emotion. They sing and weep, and preach love. But as soon as you say, "My friend, that is all right, but I want something stronger than this—a little reason and philosophy; I want to understand things step by step and more rationally", they say, "Get out"; and they not only ask you to get out but would send you to the other place, if they could. The result is that that sect can only help people of an emotional turn of mind. They not only do not help others, but try to destroy them; and the most wicked part of the whole thing is that they will not only not help others, but do not believe in their sincerity. Again, there are philosophers who talk of the wisdom of India and the East and use big psychological terms, fifty syllables long, but if an ordinary man like me goes to them and says, "Can you tell me anything to make me spiritual?", the first thing they would do would be to smile and say, "Oh, you are too far below us in your reason. What can you understand about spirituality?" These are high-up philosophers. They simply show you the door. Then there are the mystical sects who speak all sorts of things about different planes of existence, different states of mind, and what the power of the mind can do, and so on; and if you are an ordinary man and say, "Show me anything good that I can do; I am not much given to speculation; can you give me anything that will suit me?", they will smile and say, "Listen to that fool; he knows nothing, his existence is for nothing." And this is going on everywhere in the world. I would like to get extreme exponents of all these different sects, and shut them up in a room, and photograph their beautiful derisive smiles!

This is the existing condition of religion, the existing condition of things. What I want to propagate is a religion that will be equally acceptable to all minds; it must be equally philosophic, equally emotional, equally mystic, and equally conducive to action. If professors from the colleges come, scientific men and physicists, they will court reason. Let them have it as much as they want. There will be a point beyond which they will think they cannot go, without breaking with reason. They will say, "These ideas of God and salvation are superstitious, guise them up! " I say, "Mr. Philosopher, this body of yours is a bigger superstition. Give it up, don't go home to dinner or to your philosophic chair. Give up the body, and if you cannot, cry quarter and sit down." For religion must be able to show how to realise the philosophy that teaches us that this world is one, that there is but one Existence in the universe. Similarly, if the mystic comes, we must welcome him, be ready to give him the science of mental analysis, and practically demonstrate it before him. And if emotional people come, we must sit, laugh, and weep with them in the name of the Lord; we must "drink the cup of love and become mad". If the energetic worker comes, we must work with him, with all the energy that we have. And this combination will be the ideal of the nearest approach to a universal religion. Would to God that all men were so constituted that in their minds all these elements of philosophy, mysticism, emotion, and of work were equally present in full! That is the ideal, my ideal of a perfect man. Everyone who has only one or two of these elements of character, I consider "one-sided; and this world is almost full of such "one-sided" men, with knowledge of that one road only in which they move; and anything else is dangerous and horrible to them. To become harmoniously balanced in all these four directions is my ideal of religion. And this religion is attained by what we, in India, call Yoga—union. To the worker, it is union between men and the whole of humanity; to the mystic, between his lower and Higher Self; to the lover, union between himself and the God of Love; and to the philosopher; it is the union of all existence. This is what is meant by Yoga. This is a Sanskrit term, and these four divisions of Yoga have in Sanskrit different names. The man who seeks after this kind of union is called a Yogi. The worker is called the Karma-Yogi. He who seeks the union through love is called the Bhakti-Yogi. He who seeks it through mysticism is called the Râja-Yogi. And he who seeks it through philosophy is called the Jnâna-Yogi So this word Yogi comprises them all.

Now first of all let me take up Râja-Yoga. What is this Raja-Yoga, this controlling of the mind? In this country you are associating all sorts of hobgoblins with the word Yoga, I am afraid. Therefore, I must start by telling you that it has nothing to do with such things. No one of these Yogas gives up reason, no one of them asks you to be hoodwinked, or to deliver your reason into the hands of priests of any type whatsoever. No one of them asks that you should give your allegiance to any superhuman messenger. Each one of them tells you to cling to your reason to hold fast to it. We find in all beings three sorts of instruments of knowledge. The first is instinct, which you find most highly developed in animals; this is the lowest instrument of knowledge. What is the second instrument of knowledge? Reasoning. You find that most highly developed in man. Now in the first place, instinct is an inadequate instrument; to animals, the sphere of action is very limited, and within that limit instinct acts. When you come to man, you see it is largely developed into reason. The sphere of action also has here become enlarged. Yet even reason is still very insufficient. Reason can go only a little way and then it stops, it cannot go any further; and if you try to push it, the result is helpless confusion, reason itself becomes unreasonable. Logic becomes argument in a circle. Take, for instance, the very basis of our perception, matter and force. What is matter? That which is acted upon by force. And force? That which acts upon matter. You see the complication, what the logicians call see-saw, one idea depending on the other, and this again depending on that. You find a mighty barrier before reason, beyond which reasoning cannot go; yet it always feels impatient to get into the region of the Infinite beyond. This world, this universe which our senses feel, or our mind thinks, is but one atom, so to say, of the Infinite, projected on to the plane of consciousness; and within that narrow limit, defined by the network of consciousness, works our reason, and not beyond. Therefore, there must be some other instrument to take us beyond, and that instrument is called inspiration. So instinct, reason, and inspiration are the three instruments of knowledge. Instinct belongs to animals, reason to man, and inspiration to God-men. But in all human beings are to be found, in a more or less developed condition, the germs of all these three instruments of knowledge. To have these mental instruments evolved, the germs must be there. And this must also be remembered that one instrument is a development of the other, and therefore does not contradict it. It is reason that develops into inspiration, and therefore inspiration does not contradict reason, but fulfils it. Things which reason cannot get at are brought to light by inspiration; and they do not contradict reason. The old man does not contradict the child, but fulfils the child. Therefore you must always bear in mind that the great danger lies in mistaking the lower form of instrument to be the higher. Many times instinct is presented before the world as inspiration, and then come all the spurious claims for the gift of prophecy. A fool or a semi-lunatic thinks that the confusion going on in his brain is inspiration, and he wants men to follow him. The most contradictory irrational nonsense that has been preached in the world is simply the instinctive jargon of confused lunatic brains trying to pass for the language of inspiration.

The first test of true teaching must be, that the teaching should not contradict reason. And you may see that such is the basis of all these Yogas. We take the Raja-Yoga, the psychological Yoga, the psychological way to union. It is a vast subject, and I can only point out to you now the central idea of this Yoga. We have but one method of acquiring knowledge. From the lowest man to the highest Yogi, all have to use the same method; and that method is what is called concentration. The chemist who works in his laboratory concentrates all the powers of his mind, brings them into one focus, and throws them on the elements; and the elements stand analysed, and thus his knowledge comes. The astronomer has also concentrated the powers of his mind and brought them into one focus; and he throws them on to objects through his telescope; and stars and systems roll forward and give up their secrets to him. So it is in every case—with the professor in his chair, the student with his book—with every man who is working to know. You are hearing me, and if my words interest you, your mind will become concentrated on them; and then suppose a clock strikes, you will not hear it, on account of this concentration; and the more you are able to concentrate your mind, the better you will understand me; and the more I concentrate my love and powers, the better I shall be able to give expression to what I want to convey to you. The more this power of concentration, the more knowledge is acquired, because this is the one and only method of acquiring knowledge. Even the lowest shoeblack, if he gives more concentration, will black shoes better; the cook with concentration will cook a meal all the better. In making money, or in worshipping God, or in doing anything, the stronger the power of concentration, the better will that thing be done. This is the one call, the one knock, which opens the gates of nature, and lets out floods of light. This, the power of concentration, is the only key to the treasure-house of knowledge. The system of Raja-Yoga deals almost exclusively with this. In the present state of our body we are so much distracted, and the mind is frittering away its energies upon a hundred sorts of things. As soon as I try to calm my thoughts and concentrate my mind upon any one object of knowledge, thousands of undesired impulses rush into the brain, thousands of thoughts rush into the mind and disturb it. How to check it and bring the mind under control is the whole subject of study in Raja-Yoga.

Now take Karma-Yoga, the attainment of God through work. It is evident that in society there are many persons who seem to be born for some sort of activity or other, whose minds cannot be concentrated on the plane of thought alone, and who have but one idea, concretised in work, visible and tangible. There must be a science for this kind of life too. Each one of us is engaged in some work, but the majority of us fritter away the greater portion of our energies, because we do not know the secret of work. Karma-Yoga explains this secret and teaches where and how to work, how to employ to the greatest advantage the largest part of our energies in the work that is before us. But with this secret we must take into consideration the great objection against work, namely that it causes pain. All misery and pain come from attachment. I want to do work, I want to do good to a human being; and it is ninety to one that that human being whom I have helped will prove ungrateful and go against me; and the result to me is pain. Such things deter mankind from working; and it spoils a good portion of the work and energy of mankind, this fear of pain and misery. Karma-Yoga teaches us how to work for work's sake, unattached, without caring who is helped, and what for. The Karma-Yogi works because it is his nature, because he feels that it is good for him to do so, and he has no object beyond that. His position in this world is that of a giver, and he never cares to receive anything. He knows that he is giving, and does not ask for anything in return and, therefore, he eludes the grasp of misery. The grasp of pain, whenever it comes, is the result of the reaction of "attachment".

There is then the Bhakti-Yoga for the man of emotional nature, the lover. He wants to love God, he relies upon and uses all sorts of rituals, flowers, incense, beautiful buildings, forms and all such things. Do you mean to say they are wrong? One fact I must tell you. It is good for you to remember, in this country especially, that the world's great spiritual giants have all been produced only by those religious sects which have been in possession of very rich mythology and ritual. All sects that have attempted to worship God without any form or ceremony have crushed without mercy everything that is beautiful and sublime in religion. Their religion is a fanaticism at best, a dry thing. The history of the world is a standing witness to this fact. Therefore do not decry these rituals and mythologies. Let people have them; let those who so desire have them. Do not exhibit that unworthy derisive smile, and say, "They are fools; let them have it." Not so; the greatest men I have seen in my life, the most wonderfully developed in spirituality, have all come through the discipline of these rituals. I do not hold myself worthy to sit at their feet, and for me to criticise them! How do I know how these ideas act upon the human minds which of them I am to accept and which to reject? We are apt to criticise everything in the world: without sufficient warrant. Let people have all the mythology they want, with its beautiful inspirations; for you must always bear in mind that emotional natures do not care for abstract definitions of the truth. God to them is something tangible, the only thing that is real; they feel, hear, and see Him, and love Him. Let them have their God. Your rationalist seems to them to be like the fool who, when he saw a beautiful statue, wanted to break it to find out of what material it was made. Bhakti-Yoga: teaches them how to love, without any ulterior motives, loving God and loving the good because it is good to do so, not for going to heaven, nor to get children, wealth, or anything else. It teaches them that love itself is the highest recompense of love — that God Himself is love. It teaches them to pay all kinds of tribute to God as the Creator, the Omnipresent, Omniscient, Almighty Ruler, the Father and the Mother. The highest phrase that can express Him, the highest idea that the human mind can conceive of Him, is that He is the God of Love. Wherever there is love, it is He. "Wherever there is any love, it is He, the Lord is present there." Where the husband kisses the wife, He is there in the kiss; where the mother kisses the child, He is there in the kiss; where friends clasp hands, He, the Lord, is present as the God of Love. When a great man loves and wishes to help mankind, He is there giving freely His bounty out of His love to mankind. Wherever the heart expands, He is there manifested. This is what the Bhakti-Yoga teaches.

We lastly come to the Jnana-Yogi, the philosopher, the thinker, he who wants to go beyond the visible. He is the man who is not satisfied with the little things of this world. His idea is to go beyond the daily routine of eating, drinking, and so on; not even the teaching of thousands of books will satisfy him. Not even all the sciences will satisfy him; at the best, they only bring this little world before him. What else will give him satisfaction? Not even myriads of systems of worlds will satisfy him; they are to him but a drop in the ocean of existence. His soul wants to go beyond all that into the very heart of being, by seeing Reality as It is; by realising It, by being It, by becoming one with that Universal Being. That is the philosopher. To say that God is the Father or the Mother, the Creator of this universe, its Protector and Guide, is to him quite inadequate to express Him. To him, God is the life of his life, the soul of his soul. God is his own Self. Nothing else remains which is other than God. All the mortal parts of him become pounded by the weighty strokes of philosophy and are brushed away. What at last truly remains is God Himself.

Upon the same tree there are two birds, one on the top, the other below. The one on the top is calm, silent, and majestic, immersed in his own glory; the one on the lower branches, eating sweet and bitter fruits by turns, hopping from branch to branch, is becoming happy and miserable by turns. After a time the lower bird eats an exceptionally bitter fruit and gets disgustful and looks up and sees the other bird, that wondrous one of golden plumage, who eats neither sweet nor bitter fruit, who is neither happy nor miserable, but calm, Self-centred, and sees nothing beyond his Self. The lower bird longs for this condition but soon forgets it, and again begins to eat the fruits. In a little while, he eats another exceptionally bitter fruit, which makes him feel miserable, and he again looks up, and tries to get nearer to the upper bird. Once more he forgets and after a time he looks up, and so on he goes again and again, until he comes very near to the beautiful bird and sees the reflection of light from his plumage playing around his own body, and he feels a change and seems to melt away; still nearer he comes, and everything about him melts away, and at last he understands this wonderful change. The lower bird was, as it were, only the substantial-looking shadow, the reflection of the higher; he himself was in essence the upper bird all the time. This eating of fruits, sweet and bitter, this lower, little bird, weeping and happy by turns, was a vain chimera, a dream: all along, the real bird was there above, calm and silent, glorious and majestic, beyond grief, beyond sorrow. The upper bird is God, the Lord of this universe; and the lower bird is the human soul, eating the sweet and bitter fruits of this world. Now and then comes a heavy blow to the soul. For a time, he stops the eating and goes towards the unknown God, and a flood of light comes. He thinks that this world is a vain show. Yet again the senses drag hint down, and he begins as before to eat the sweet and bitter fruits of the world. Again an exceptionally hard blow comes. His heart becomes open again to divine light; thus gradually he approaches God, and as he gets nearer and nearer, he finds his old self melting away. When he has come near enough, he sees that he is no other than God, and he exclaims, "He whom I have described to you as the Life of this universe, as present in the atom, and in suns and moons—He is the basis of our own life, the Soul of our soul. Nay, thou art That." This is what this Jnana-Yoga teaches. It tells man that he is essentially divine. It shows to mankind the real unity of being, and that each one of us is the Lord God Himself, manifested on earth. All of us, from the lowest worm that crawls under our feet to the highest beings to whom we look up with wonder and awe—all are manifestations of the same Lord.

Lastly, it is imperative that all these various Yogas should be carried out in, practice; mere theories about them will not do any good. First we have to hear about them, then we have to think about them. We have to reason the thoughts out, impress them on our minds, and we have to meditate on them, realise them, until at last they become our whole life. No longer will religion remain a bundle of ideas or theories, nor an intellectual assent; it will enter into our very self. By means of intellectual assent we may today subscribe to many foolish things, and change our minds altogether tomorrow. But true religion never changes. Religion is realisation; not talk, nor doctrine, nor theories, however beautiful they may be. It is being and becoming, not hearing or acknowledging; it is the whole soul becoming changed into what it believes. That is religion.

THE OPEN SECRET

Delivered at Los Angeles, Calif., 5th January 1900

Whichever way we turn in trying to understand things in their reality, if we analyse far enough, we find that at last we come to a peculiar state of things, seemingly a contradiction: something which our reason cannot grasp and yet is a fact. We take up something—we know it is finite; but as soon as we begin to analyse it, it leads us beyond our reason, and we never find an end to all its qualities, its possibilities, its powers, its relations. It has become infinite. Take even a common flower, that is finite enough; but who is there that can say he knows all about the flower? There is no possibility of anyone's getting to the end of the knowledge about that one flower. The flower has become infinite—the flower which was finite to begin with. Take a grain of sand. Analyse it. We start with the assumption that it is finite, and at last we find that it is not, it is infinite; all the same, we have looked upon it as finite. The flower is similarly treated as a finite something.

So with all our thoughts and experiences, physical and mental. We begin, we may think, on a small scale, and grasp them as little things; but very soon they elude our knowledge and plunge into the abyss of the infinite. And the greatest and the first thing perceived is ourselves. We are also in the same dilemma about existence. We exist. We see we are finite beings. We live and die. Our horizon is narrow. We are here, limited, confronted by the universe all around. Nature can crush us out of existence in a moment. Our little bodies are just held together, ready to go to pieces at a moment's notice. We know that. In the region of action how powerless we are! Our will is being thwarted at every turn. So many things we want to do, and how few we can do! There is no limit to our willing. We can will everything, want everything, we can desire to go to the dogstar. But how few of our desires can be accomplished! The body will not allow it. Well, nature is against the accomplishment of our will. We are weak. What is true of the flower, of the grain of sand, of the physical world, and of every thought, is a hundredfold more true of ourselves. We are also in the same dilemma of existence, being finite and infinite at the same time. We are like waves in the ocean; the wave is the ocean and yet not the ocean. There is not any part of the wave of which you cannot say, "It is the ocean." The name "ocean" applies to the wave and equally to every other part of the ocean, and yet it is separate from the ocean. So in this infinite ocean of existence we are like wavelets. At the same time, when we want really to grasp ourselves, we cannot—we have become the infinite.

We seem to be walking in dreams. Dreams are all right in a dream-mind; but as soon as you want to grasp one of them, it is gone. Why? Not that it was false, but because it is beyond the power of reason, the power of the intellect to comprehend it. Everything in this life is so vast that the intellect is nothing in comparison with it. It refuses to be bound by the laws of the intellect! It laughs at the bondage the intellect wants to spread around it. And a thousandfold more so is this the case with the human soul. "We ourselves"—this is the greatest mystery of the universe.

How wonderful it all is! Look at the human eye. How easily it can be destroyed, and yet the biggest suns exist only because your eyes see them. The world exists because your eyes certify that it exists. Think of that mystery! These poor little eyes! A strong light, or a pin, can destroy them. Yet the most powerful engines of destruction, the most powerful cataclysms, the most wonderful of existences, millions of suns and stars and moons and earth—all depend for their existence upon, and have to be certified by, these two little things! They say, "Nature, you exist", and we believe nature exists. So with all our senses.

What is this? Where is weakness? Who is strong? What is great and what is small? What is high and what is low in this marvellous interdependence of existence where the smallest atom is necessary for the existence of the whole? Who is great and who is small? It is past finding out! And why? Because none is great and none is small. All things are interpenetrated by that infinite ocean; their reality is that infinite; and whatever there is on the surface is but that infinite. The tree is infinite; so is everything that you see or feel—every grain of sand, every thought, every soul, everything that exists, is infinite. Infinite is finite and finite infinite. This is our existence.

Now, that may be all true, but all this feeling after the Infinite is at present mostly unconscious. It is not that we have forgotten that infinite nature of ours: none can ever do that. Who can ever think that he can be annihilated? Who can think that he will die? None can. All our relation to the Infinite works in us unconsciously. In a manner, therefore, we forget our real being, and hence all this misery comes.

In practical daily life we are hurt by small things; we are enslaved by little beings. Misery comes because we think we are finite—we are little beings. And yet, how difficult it is to believe that we are infinite beings! In the midst of all this misery and trouble, when a little thing may throw me off my balance, it must be my care to believe that I am infinite. And the fact is that we are, and that consciously or unconsciously we are all searching after that something which is infinite; we are always seeking for something that is free.

There was never a human race which did not have a religion and worship some sort of God or gods. Whether the God or gods existed or not is no question; but what is the analysis of this psychological phenomenon? Why is all the world trying to find, or seeking for, a God? Why? Because in spite of all this bondage, in spite of nature and this tremendous energy of law grinding us down, never allowing us to turn to any side—wherever we go, whatever we want to do, we are thwarted by this law, which is everywhere—in spite of all this, the human soul never forgets its freedom and is ever seeking it. The search for freedom is the search of all religions; whether they know it or not, whether they can formulate it well or ill, the idea is there. Even the lowest man, the most ignorant, seeks for something which has power over nature's laws. He wants to see a demon, a ghost, a god—somebody who can subdue nature, for whom nature is not almighty, for whom there is no law. "Oh, for somebody who can break the law!" That is the cry coming from the human heart. We are always seeking for someone who breaks the law. The rushing engine speeds along the railway track; the little worm crawls out of its way. We at once say, "The engine is dead matter, a machine; and the worm is alive," because the worm attempted to break the law. The engine, with all its power and might, can never break the law. It is made to go in any direction man wants, and it cannot do otherwise; but the worm, small and little though it was, attempted to break the law and avoid the danger. It tried to assert itself against law, assert its freedom; and there was the sign of the future God in it.

Everywhere we see this assertion of freedom, this freedom of the soul. It is reflected in every religion in the shape of God or gods; but it is all external yet—for those who only see the gods outside. Man decided that he was nothing. He was afraid that he could never be free; so he went to seek for someone outside of nature who was free. Then he thought that there were many and many such free beings, and gradually he merged them all into one God of gods and Lord of lords. Even that did not satisfy him. He came a little closer to truth, a little nearer; and then gradually found that whatever he was, he was in some way connected with the God of gods and Lord of lords; that he, though he thought himself bound and low and weak, was somehow connected with that God of gods. Then visions came to him; thought arose and knowledge advanced. And he began to come nearer and nearer to that God, and at last found out that God and all the gods, this whole psychological phenomenon connected with the search for an all-powerful free soul, was but a reflection of his own idea of himself. And then at last he discovered that it was not only true that "God made man after His own image", but that it was also true that man made God after his own image. That brought out the idea of divine freedom. The Divine Being was always within, the nearest of the near. Him we had ever been seeking outside, and at last found that He is in the heart of our hearts. You may know the story of the man who mistook his own heartbeat for somebody knocking at the door, and went to the door and opened it, but found nobody there, so he went back. Again he seemed to hear a knocking at the door, but nobody was there. Then he understood that it was his own heartbeat, and he had misinterpreted it as a knocking at the door. Similarly, man after his search finds out that this infinite freedom that he was placing in imagination all the time in the nature outside is the internal subject, the eternal Soul of souls; this Reality, he himself.

Thus at last he comes to recognise this marvellous duality of existence: the subject, infinite and finite in one—the Infinite Being is also the same finite soul. The Infinite is caught, as it were, in the meshes of the intellect and apparently manifests as finite beings, but the reality remains unchanged.

This is, therefore, true knowledge: that the Soul of our souls, the Reality that is within us, is That which is unchangeable, eternal, ever-blessed, ever-free. This is the only solid ground for us to stand upon.

This, then, is the end of all death, the advent of all immortality, the end of all misery. And he who sees that One among the many, that One unchangeable in the universe of change, he who sees Him as the Soul of his soul, unto him belongs eternal peace—unto none else.

And in the midst of the depths of misery and degradation, the Soul sends a ray of light, and man wakes up and finds that what is really his, he can never lose. No, we can never lose what is really ours. Who can lose his being? Who can lose his very existence? If I am good, it is the existence first, and then that becomes coloured with the quality of goodness. If I am evil, it is the existence first, and that becomes coloured with the quality of badness. That existence is first, last, and always; it is never lost, but ever present.

Therefore, there is hope for all. None can die; none can be

degraded for ever. Life is but a playground, however gross the play may be. However we may receive blows, and however knocked about we may be, the Soul is there and is never injured. We are that Infinite.

Thus sang a Vedantin, "I never had fear nor doubt. Death never came to me. I never had father or mother: for I was never born. Where are my foes?—for I am All. I am the Existence and Knowledge and Bliss Absolute. I am It. I am It. Anger and lust and jealousy, evil thoughts and all these things, never came to me; for I am the Existence, the Knowledge, the Bliss Absolute. I am It. I am It."

That is the remedy for all disease, the nectar that cures death. Here we are in this world, and our nature rebels against it. But let us repeat, "I am It; I am It. I have no fear, nor doubt, nor death. I have no sex, nor creed, nor colour. What creed can I have? What sect is there to which I should belong? What sect can hold me? I am in every sect!"

However much the body rebels, however much the mind rebels, in the midst of the uttermost darkness, in the midst of agonising tortures, in the uttermost despair, repeat this, once, twice, thrice, ever more. Light comes gently, slowly, but surely it comes.

Many times I have been in the jaws of death, starving, foot-sore, and weary; for days and days I had had no food, and often could walk no farther; I would sink down under a tree, and life would seem ebbing away. I could not speak, I could scarcely think, but at last the mind reverted to the idea: "I have no fear nor death; I never hunger nor thirst. I am It! I am It! The whole of nature cannot crush me; it is my servant. Assert thy strength, thou Lord of lords and God of gods! Regain thy lost empire! Arise and walk and stop not!" And I would rise up, reinvigorated, and here am I, living, today. Thus, whenever darkness comes, assert the reality and everything adverse must vanish. For, after all, it is but a dream. Mountain-high though the difficulties appear, terrible and gloomy though all things seem, they are but Mâyâ. Fear not—it is banished. Crush it, and it vanishes. Stamp upon it, and it dies. Be not afraid. Think not how many times you fail. Never mind. Time is infinite. Go forward: assert yourself again and again, and light must come. You may pray to everyone that was ever born, but who will come to help you? And what of the way of death from which none knows escape? Help thyself out by thyself. None else can help thee, friend. For thou alone art thy greatest enemy, thou alone art thy greatest friend. Get hold of the Self, then. Stand up. Don't be afraid. In the midst of all miseries and all weakness, let the Self come out, faint and imperceptible though it be at first. You will gain courage, and at last like a lion you will roar out, "I am It! I am It!" "I am neither a man, nor a woman, nor a god, nor a demon; no, nor any of the animals, plants, or trees. I am neither poor nor rich, neither learned nor ignorant. All these things are very little compared with what I am: for I am It! I am It! Behold the sun and the moon and the stars: I am the light that is shining in them! I am the beauty of the fire! I am the power in the universe! For, I am It! I am It!

"Whoever thinks that I am little makes a mistake, for the Self is all that exists. The sun exists because I declare it does, the world exists because I declare it does. Without me they cannot remain, for I am Existence, Knowledge, and Bliss Absolute—ever happy, ever pure, ever beautiful. Behold, the sun is the cause of our vision, but is not itself ever affected by any defect in the eyes of any one; even so I am. I am working through all organs, working through everything, but never does the good and evil of work attach to me. For me there is no law, nor Karma. I own the laws of Karma. I ever was and ever am.

"My real pleasure was never in earthly things—in husband, wife, children, and other things. For I am like the infinite blue sky: clouds of many colours pass over it and play for a second; they move off, and there is the same unchangeable blue. Happiness and misery, good and evil, may envelop me for a moment, veiling the Self; but I am still there. They pass away because they are changeable. I shine, because I am unchangeable. If misery comes, I know it is finite, therefore it must die. If evil comes, I know it is finite, it must go. I alone am infinite and untouched by anything. For I am the Infinite, that Eternal, Changeless Self."—So sings one of our poets.

Let us drink of this cup, this cup that leads to everything that is immortal, everything that is unchangeable. Fear not. Believe not that we are evil, that we are finite,. that we can ever die. It is not true.

"This is to be heard of, then to be thought upon, and then to be meditated upon." When the hands work,. the mind should repeat, "I am It. I am It." Think of it, dream of it, until it becomes bone of your bones and; flesh of your flesh, until all the hideous dreams of littleness, of weakness, of misery, and of evil, have entirely vanished, and no more then can the Truth be hidden from you even for a moment.

THE WAY TO BLESSEDNESS

I shall tell you a story from the Vedas tonight. The Vedas are the sacred scriptures of the Hindus and are a vast collection of literature, of which the last part is called the Vedanta, meaning the end of the Vedas. It deals with the theories contained in them, and more especially the philosophy with which we are concerned. It is written in archaic Sanskrit, and you must remember it was written thousands of years ago. There was a certain man who wanted to make a big sacrifice. In the religion of the Hindus, sacrifice plays a great part. There are various sorts of sacrifices. They make altars and pour oblations into the fire, and repeat various hymns and so forth; and at the end of the sacrifice they make a gift to the Brahmins and the poor. Each sacrifice has its peculiar gift. There was one sacrifice, where everything a man possessed had to be given up. Now this man, though rich, was miserly, and at the same time wanted to get a great name for having done this most difficult sacrifice. And when he did this sacrifice, instead of giving up everything he had, he gave away only his blind, lame, and old cows that would never more give milk. But he had a son called Nachiketas, a bright young boy, who, observing the poor gifts made by his father, and pondering on the demerit that was sure to accrue to him thereby, resolved to make amends for them by making a gift of himself. So he went to his father and said, "And to whom will you give me?" The father did not answer the boy, and the boy asked a second and a third time, when the father got vexed and said, "Thee I give unto Yama, thee I give unto Death." And the boy went straight to the kingdom of Yama. Yama was not at home, so he waited there. After three days Yama came and said to him, "O Brahmin, thou art my guest, and thou hast been here for three days without any food. I salute thee, and in order to repay thee for this trouble, I will grant thee three boons." Then the boy asked the first boon, "May my father's anger against me get calmed down," and the second boon was that he wanted to know about a certain sacrifice. And then came the third boon. "When a man dies, the question arises: What becomes of him: Some people say he ceases to exist. Others say that he exists. Please tell me what the answer is. This is the third boon that I want." Then Death answered, "The gods in ancient times tried to unravel the mystery; this mystery is so fine that it is hard to know. Ask for some other boon: do not ask this one. Ask for a long life of a hundred years. Ask for cattle and horses, ask for great kingdoms. Do not press me to answer this. Whatever man desires for his enjoyment, ask all that and I will fulfil it, but do not want to know this secret." "No sir," said the boy, man is not to be satisfied with wealth; if wealth were wanted, we should "get it, if we have only seen you. We shall also live so long as you rule. What decaying mortal, living in the world below and possessed of knowledge, having gained the company of the undecaying and the immortal, will delight in long life, knowing the nature of the pleasure produced by song and sport? Therefore, tell me this secret about the great hereafter, I do not want anything else; that is what Nachiketas wants, the mystery of death." Then the God of death was pleased. We have been saying in the last two or three lectures that this Jnâna prepares the mind. So you see here that the first preparation is that a man must desire nothing else but the truth, and truth for truth's sake. See how this boy rejected all these gifts which Death offered him; possessions, property, wealth, long life, and everything he was ready to sacrifice for this one idea, knowledge only, the truth. Thus alone can truth come. The God of death became pleased. "Here are two ways," he said, "one of enjoyment, the other of blessedness. These two in various ways draw mankind. He becomes a sage who, of these two, takes up that which leads to blessedness, and he degenerates who takes up the road to enjoyment. I praise you, Nachiketas; you have not asked for desire. In various ways I tempted you towards the path of enjoyment; you resisted them all, you have known that knowledge is much higher than a life of enjoyment.

"You have understood that the man who lives in ignorance and enjoys, is not different from the brute beast. Yet there are many who, though steeped in ignorance, in the pride of their hearts, think that they are great sages and go round and round in many crooked ways, like the blind led by the blind. This truth, Nachiketas, never shines in the heart of those who are like ignorant children, deluded by a few lumps of earth. They do not understand this world, nor the other world. They deny this and the other one, and thus again and again come under my control. Many have not even the opportunity to hear about it; and many, though hearing, cannot know it, because the teacher must be wonderful; so must he be wonderful too unto whom the knowledge is carried. If the speaker is a man who is not highly advanced, then even a hundred times heard, and a hundred times taught, the truth never illumines the soul. Do not disturb your mind by vain arguments, Nachiketas; this truth only becomes effulgent in the heart which has been made pure. He who cannot be seen without the greatest difficulty, He who is hidden, He who has entered the cave of the heart of hearts—the Ancient One—cannot be seen with the external eyes; seeing Him with the eyes of the soul, one gives up both pleasure and pain. He who knows this secret gives up all his vain desires, and attains this superfine perception, and thus becomes ever blessed. Nachiketas, that is the way to blessedness. He is beyond all virtue, beyond all vice, beyond all duties, beyond all non-duties, beyond all existence, beyond all that is to be; he who knows this, alone knows. He whom all the Vedas seek, to see whom men undergo all sorts of asceticism, I will tell you His name: It is Om. This eternal Om is the Brahman, this is the immortal One; he who knows the secret of this—whatever he desires is his. This Self of man, Nachiketas, about which you seek to know, is never born, and never dies. Without beginning, ever existing, this Ancient One is not destroyed, when the body is destroyed. If the slayer thinks that he can slay, and if the slain man thinks he is slain, both are mistaken, for neither can the Self kill, nor can It be killed. Infinitely smaller than the smallest particle, infinitely greater than the greatest existence, the Lord of all lives in the cave of the heart of every being. He who has become sinless sees Him in all His glory, through the mercy of the same Lord. (We find that the mercy of God is one of the causes of God-realisation.) Sitting He goes far, lying He goes everywhere; who else but men of purified and subtle understanding are qualified to know the God in whom all conflicting attributes meet? Without body, yet living in the body, untouched, yet seemingly in contact, omnipresent—knowing the Âtman to be such, the sage gives up all misery. This Atman is not to be attained by the study of the Vedas, nor by the highest intellect, nor by much learning. Whom the Atman seeks, he gets the Atman; unto him He discloses His glory. He who is continuously doing evil deeds, he whose mind is not calm, he who cannot meditates he who is always disturbed and fickle—he cannot understand and realise this Atman who has entered the cave of the heart. This body, O Nachiketas, is the chariot, the organs of the senses are the horses, the mind is the reins, the intellect is the charioteer, and the soul is the rider in the chariot. When the soul joins himself with the charioteer, Buddhi or intellect, and then through it with the mind, the reins, and through it again with the organs, the horses, he is said to be the enjoyer; he perceives, he works, he acts. He whose mind is not under control, and who has no discrimination, his senses are not controllable like vicious horses in the hands of a driver. But he who has discrimination, whose mind is controlled, his organs are always controllable like good horses in the hands of a driver. He who has discrimination, whose mind is always in the way to understand truth, who is always pure—he receives that truth, attaining which there is no rebirth. This, O Nachiketas, is very difficult, the way is long, and it is hard to attain. It is only those who have attained the finest perception that can see it, that can understand it. Yet do not be frightened. Awake, be up and doing. Do not stop till you have reached the goal. For the sages say that the task is very difficult, like walking on the edge of a razor. He who is beyond the senses, beyond all touch, beyond all form, beyond all taste, the Unchangeable, the Infinite, beyond even intelligence, the Indestructible—knowing Him alone, we are safe from the jaws of death."

So far, we see that Yama describes the goal that is to be attained. The first idea that we get is that birth, death, misery, and the various tossings about to which we are subject in the world can only be overcome by knowing that which is real. What is real? That which never changes, the Self of man, the Self behind the universe. Then, again, it is said that it is very difficult to know Him. Knowing does not mean simply intellectual assent, it means realisation. Again and again we have read that this Self is to be seen, to be perceived. We cannot see it with the eyes; the perception for it has to become superfine. It is gross perception by which the walls and books are perceived, but the perception to discern the truth has to be made very fine, and that is the whole secret of this knowledge. Then Yama says that one must be very pure. That is the way to making the perception superfine; and then he goes on to tell us other ways. That self-existent One is far removed from the organs. The organs or instruments see outwards, but the self-existing One, the Self, is seen inwards. You must remember the qualification that is required: the desire to know this Self by turning the eyes inwards. All these beautiful things that we see in nature are very good, but that is not the way to see God. We must learn how to turn the eyes inwards. The eagerness of the eyes to see outwards should be restricted. When you walk in a busy street, it is difficult to hear the man speak with whom you are walking, because of the noise of the passing carriages. He cannot hear you because there is so much noise. The mind is going outwards, and you cannot hear the man who is next to you. In the same way, this world around us is making such a noise that it draws the mind outwards. How can we see the Self? This going outwards must be stopped. That is what is meant by turning the eyes inwards, and then

alone the glory of the Lord within will be seen.

What is this Self? We have seen that It is even beyond the intellect. We learn from the same Upanishad that this Self is eternal and omnipresent, that you and I and all of us are omnipresent beings, and that the Self is changeless. Now this omnipresent Being can be only one. There cannot be two beings who are equally omnipresent—how could that be? There cannot be two beings who are infinite, and the result is, there is really only one Self, and you, I, and the whole universe are but one, appearing as many. "As the one fire entering into the world manifests itself in various ways, even so that one Self, the Self of all, manifests Itself in every form." But the question is: If this Self is perfect and pure, and the One Being of the universe, what becomes of It when It goes into the impure body, the wicked body, the good body, and so on? How can It remain perfect? "The one sun is the cause of vision in every eye, yet it is not touched by the defects in the eyes of any." If a man has jaundice he sees everything as yellow; the cause of his vision is the sun, but his seeing everything as yellow does not touch the sun. Even so this One Being, though the Self of every one, is not touched by the purities or impurities outside. "In this world where everything is evanescent, he who knows Him who never changes, in this world of insentience, he who knows the one sentient Being, in this world of many, he who knows this One and sees Him in his own soul, unto him belongs eternal bliss, to none else, to none else. There the sun shines not, nor the stars, nor the lightning flashes, what to speak of fire? He shining, everything shines; through His light everything becomes effulgent. When all the desires that trouble the heart cease, then the mortal becomes immortal, and here one attains Brahman. When all the crookedness of the heart disappears, when all its knots are cut asunder, then alone the mortal becomes immortal. This is the way. May this study bless us; may it maintain us; may it give us strength, may it become energy in us; may we not hate each other; peace unto all!"

This is the line of thought that you will find in the Vedanta philosophy. We see first that here is a thought entirely different from what you see anywhere else in the world. In the oldest parts of the Vedas the search was the same as in other books, the search was outside. In some of the old, old books, the question was raised, "What was in the beginning? When there was neither aught nor naught, when darkness was covering darkness, who created all this?" So the search began. And they began to talk about the angels, the Devas, and all sorts of things, and later on we find that they gave it up as hopeless. In their day the search was outside and they could find nothing; but in later days, as we read in the Vedas, they had to look inside for the self-existent One. This Is the one fundamental idea in the Vedas, that our search in the stars, the nebulae, the Milky Way, in the whole of this external universe leads to nothing, never solves the problem of life and death. The wonderful mechanism inside had to be analysed, and it revealed to them the secret of the universe; nor star or sun could do it.

Man had to be anatomised; not the body, but the soul of man. In that soul they found the answer. What was the answer they found? That behind the body, behind even the mind, there is the self-existent One. He dies not, nor is He born. The self-existent One it omnipresent, because He has no form. That which has no form or shape, that which is not limited by space or time, cannot live in a certain place. How can it? It is everywhere, omnipresent, equally present through all of us.

What is the soul of man? There was one party who held that there is a Being, God, and an infinite number of souls besides, who are eternally separate from God in essence, and form, and everything. This is dualism. This is the old, old crude idea. The answer given by another party was that the soul was a part of the infinite Divine Existence. Just as this body is a little world by itself, and behind it is the mind or thought, and behind that is the individual soul, similarly, the whole world is a body, and behind that is the universal mind, and behind that is the universal Soul. Just as this body is a portion of the universal body, so this mind is a portion of the universal mind, and the soul of man a portion of the universal Soul. This is what is called the Vishishtâdvaita, qualified monism. Now, we know that the universal Soul is infinite. How can infinity have parts? How can it be broken up, divided? It may be very poetic to say that I am a spark of the Infinite, but it is absurd to the thinking mind. What is meant by dividing Infinity? Is it something material that you can part or separate it into pieces? Infinite can never be divided. If that were possible, it would be no more Infinite. What is the conclusion then? The answer is, that Soul which is the universal is you; you are not a part but the whole of It. You are the whole of God. Then what are all these varieties? We find so many millions of individual souls. What are they? If the sun reflects upon millions of globules of water, in each globule is the form, the perfect image of the sun; but they are only images, and the real sun is only one. So this apparent soul that is in every one of us is only the image of God, nothing beyond that. The real Being who is behind, is that one God. We are all one there. As Self, there is only one in the universe. It is in me and you, and is only one; and that one Self has been reflected in all these various bodies as various different selves. But we do not know this; we think we are separate from each other and separate from Him. And so long as we think this, misery will be in the world. This is hallucination.

Then the other great source of misery is fear. Why does one man injure another? Because he fears he will not have enough enjoyment. One man fears that, perhaps, he will not have enough money, and that fear causes him to injure others and rob them. How can there be fear if there is only one existence? If a thunderbolt falls on my head, it was I who was the thunderbolt, because I am the only existence. If a plague comes, it is I; if a tiger comes, it is I. If death comes, it is I. I am both death and life. We see that fear comes with the idea that there are two in the universe. We have always heard it preached, "Love one another". What for? That doctrine was preached, but the explanation is here. Why should I love every one? Because they and I are one. Why should I love my brother? Because he and I are one. There is this oneness; this solidarity of the whole universe. From the lowest worm that crawls under our feet to the highest beings that ever lived—all have various bodies, but are the one Soul. Through all mouths, you eat; through all hands, you work; through all eyes, you see. You enjoy health in millions of bodies, you are suffering from disease in millions of bodies. When this idea comes, and we realise it, see it, feel it, then will misery cease, and fear with it. How can I die? There is nothing beyond me. Fear ceases, and then alone comes perfect happiness and perfect love. That universal sympathy, universal love, universal bliss, that never changes, raises man above everything. It has no reactions and no misery can touch it; but this little eating and drinking of the world always brings a reaction. The whole cause of it is this dualism, the idea that I am separate from the universe, separate from God. But as soon as we have realised that "I am He, I am the Self of the universe, I am eternally blessed, eternally free"—then will come real love, fear will vanish, and all misery cease.

YAJNAVALKYA AND MAITREYI

We say, "That day is indeed a bad day on which you do not hear the name of the Lord, but a cloudy day is not a bad day at all." Yâjnavalkya was a great sage. You know, the Shastras in India enjoin that every man should give up the world when he becomes old. So Yajnavalkya said to his wife, "My beloved, here is all my money, and my possessions, and I am going away." She replied, "Sir, if I had this whole earth full of wealth, would that give me immortality?" Yajnavalkya said, "No, it will not. You will be rich, and that will be all, but wealth cannot give us immortality." She replied, "what shall I do to gain that through which I shall become immortal? If you know, tell me." Yajnavalkya replied, "You have been always my beloved; you are more beloved now by this question. Come, take your seat, and I will tell you; and when you have heard, meditate upon it." He said, "It is not for the sake of the husband that the wife loves the husband, but for the sake of the Âtman that she loves the husband, because she loves the Self. None loves the wife for the sake of the wife; but it is because one loves the Self that one loves the wife. None loves the children for the children; but because one loves the Self, therefore one loves the children. None loves wealth on account of the wealth; but because one loves the Self, therefore one loves wealth. None loves the Brâhmin for the sake of the Brahmin; but because one loves the Self, one loves the Brahmin. So, none loves the Kshatriya for the sake of the Kshatriya, but because one loves the Self. Neither does any one love the world on account of the world, but because one loves the Self. None, similarly, loves the gods on account of the gods, but because one loves the Self. None loves a thing for that thing's sake; but it is for the Self that one loves it. This

Self, therefore, is to be heard, reasoned about, and meditated upon. O my Maitreyi, when that Self has been heard, when that Self has been seen, when that Self has been realised, then, all this becomes known." What do we get then? Before us we find a curious philosophy. The statement has been made that every love is selfishness in the lowest sense of the word: because I love myself, therefore I love another; it cannot be. There have been philosophers in modern times who have said that self is the only motive power in the world. That is true, and yet it is wrong. But this self is but the shadow of that real Self which is behind. It appears wrong and evil because it is small. That infinite love for the Self, which is the universe, appears to be evil, appears to be small, because it appears through a small part. Even when the wife loves the husband, whether she knows it or not, she loves the husband for that Self. It is selfishness as it is manifested in the world, but that selfishness is really but a small part of that Self-ness. Whenever one loves, one has to love in and through the Self. This Self has to be known. What is the difference? Those that love the Self without knowing what It is, their love is selfishness. Those that love, knowing what that Self is, their love is free; they are sages. "Him the Brahmin gives up who sees the Brahmin anywhere else but in the Self. Him the Kshatriya gives up who sees the Kshatriya anywhere else but in the Self. The world gives him up who sees this world anywhere but in that Atman. The gods give him up who loves the gods knowing them to be anywhere else but in the Atman. Everything goes away from him who knows everything as something else except the Atman. These Brahmins, these Kshatriyas, this world, these gods, whatever exists, everything is that Atman". Thus he explains what he means by love.

Every time we particularise an object, we differentiate it from the Self. I am trying to love a woman; as soon as that woman is particularised, she is separated from the Atman, and my love for her will not be eternal, but will end in grief. But as soon as I see that woman as the Atman, that love becomes perfect, and will never suffer. So with everything; as soon as you are attached to anything in the universe, detaching it from the universe as a whole, from the Atman, there comes a reaction. With everything that we love outside the Self, grief and misery will be the result. If we enjoy everything in the Self, and as the Self, no misery or reaction will come. This is perfect bliss. How to come to this ideal? Yajnavalkya goes on to tell us the process by which to reach that state. The universe is infinite: how can we take every particular thing and look at it as the Atman, without knowing the Atman? "As with a drum when we are at a distance we cannot catch the sound, we cannot conquer the sound; but as soon as we come to the drum and put our hand on it, the sound is conquered. When the conch-shell is being blown, we cannot catch or conquer the sound, until we come near and get hold of the shell, and then it is conquered. When the Vina is being played, when we have come to the Vina, we get to the centre whence the sound is proceeding. As when some one is burning damp fuel,

smoke and sparks of various kinds come, even so, from this great One has been breathed out knowledge; everything has come out of Him. He breathed out, as it were, all knowledge. As to all water, the one goal is the ocean; as to all touch, the skin is the one centre; as of all smell, the nose is the one centre; as of all taste, the tongue is the one goal; as of all form, the eyes are the one goal; as of all sounds, the ears are the one goal; as of all thought, the mind is the one goal; as of all knowledge, the heart is the one goal; as of all work, the hands are the one goal; as a morsel of salt put into the sea-water melts away, and we cannot take it back, even so, Maitreyi, is this Universal Being eternally infinite; all knowledge is in Him. The whole universe rises from Him, and again goes down into Him. No more is there any knowledge, dying, or death." We get the idea that we have all come just like sparks from Him, and when you know Him, then you go back and become one with Him again. We are the Universal.

Maitreyi became frightened, just as everywhere people become frightened. Said she, "Sir, here is exactly where you have thrown a delusion over me. You have frightened me by saying there will be no more gods; all individuality will be lost. There will be no one to recognise, no one to love, no one to hate. What will become of us?" "Maitreyi, I do not mean to puzzle you, or rather let it rest here. You may be frightened. Where there are two, one sees another, one hears another, one welcomes another, one thinks of another, one knows another. But when the whole has become that Atman, who is seen by whom, who is to be heard by whom, who is to be welcomed by whom, who is to be known by whom?" That one idea was taken up by Schopenhauer and echoed in his philosophy. Through whom we know this universe, through what to know Him? How to know the knower? By what means can we know the knower? How can that be? Because in and through that we know everything. By what means can we know Him? By no means, for He is that means.

So far the idea is that it is all One Infinite Being. That is the real individuality, when there is no more division, and no more parts; these little ideas are very low, illusive. But yet in and through every spark of the individuality is shining that Infinite. Everything is a manifestation of the Atman. How to reach that? First you make the statement, just as Yajnavalkya himself tells us: "This Atman is first to be heard of." So he stated the case; then he argued it out, and the last demonstration was how to know That, through which all knowledge is possible. Then, last, it is to be meditated upon. He takes the contrast, the microcosm and the macrocosm, and shows how they are rolling on in particular lines, and how it is all beautiful. "This earth is so blissful, so helpful to every being; and all beings are so helpful to this earth: all these are manifestations of that Self-effulgent One, the Atman." All that is bliss, even in the lowest sense, is but the reflection of Him. All that is good is His reflection, and when that reflection is a shadow it is called evil. There are no two Gods. When He is less manifested, it is called darkness, evil; and when He is more manifested, it is called light. That is all. Good and evil are only a question of degree: more manifested or less manifested. Just take the example of our own lives. How many things we see in our childhood which we think to be good, but which really are evil, and how many things seem to be evil which are good! How the ideas change! How an idea goes up and up! What we thought very good at one time we do not think so good now. So good and evil are but superstitions, and do not exist. The difference is only in degree. It is all a manifestation of that Atman; He is being manifested in everything; only, when the manifestation is very thick we call it evil; and when it is very thin, we call it good. It is the best, when all covering goes away. So everything that is in the universe is to be meditated upon in that sense alone, that we can see it as all good, because it is the best. There is evil and there is good; and the apex, the centre, is the Reality. He is neither evil nor good; He is the best. The best can be only one, the good can be many and the evil many. There will be degrees of variation between the good and the evil, but the best is only one, and that best, when seen through thin coverings, we call different sorts of good, and when through thick covers, we call evil. Good and evil are different forms of superstition. They have gone through all sorts of dualistic delusion and all sorts of ideas, and the words have sunk into the hearts of human beings, terrorising men and women and living there as terrible tyrants. They make us become tigers. All the hatred with which we hate others is caused by these foolish ideas which we have imbibed since our childhood—good and evil. Our judgment of humanity becomes entirely false; we make this beautiful earth a hell; but as soon as we can give up good and evil, it becomes a heaven.

"This earth is blissful ('sweet' is the literal translation) to all beings and all beings are sweet to this earth; they all help each other. And all the sweetness is the Atman, that effulgent, immortal One who is inside this earth." Whose is this sweetness? How can there be any sweetness but He? That one sweetness is manifesting itself in various ways. Wherever there is any love, any sweetness in any human being, either in a saint or a sinner, either in an angel or a murderer, either in the body, mind, or the senses, it is He. Physical enjoyments are but He, mental enjoyments are but He, spiritual enjoyments are but He. How can there be anything but He? How can there be twenty thousand gods and devils fighting with each other? Childish dreams! Whatever is the lowest physical enjoyment is He, and the highest spiritual enjoyment is He. There is no sweetness but He. Thus says Yajnavalkya. When you come to that state and look upon all things with the same eye, when you see even in the drunkard's pleasure in drink only that sweetness, then you have got the truth, and then alone you will know what happiness means, what peace means, what love means; and so long as toll make these vain distinctions, silly, childish, foolish superstitions, all sorts of misery will come. But that immortal One, the effulgent One, He is inside the earth, it is all His sweetness, and the same sweetness is in the body. This body is the earth, as it were, and inside all the powers of the body, all the enjoyments of the body, is He; the eyes see, the skin touches; what are all these enjoyments? That Self-effulgent One who is in the body, He is the Atman. This world, so sweet to all beings, and every being so sweet to it, is but the Self-effulgent; the Immortal is the bliss in that world. In us also, He is that bliss. He is the Brahman. "This air is so sweet to all beings, and all beings are so sweet to it. But He who is that Self-effulgent Immortal Being in the air—is also in this body. He is expressing Himself as the life of all beings. This sun is so sweet to all beings. All beings are so sweet to this sun. He who is the Self-effulgent Being in the sun, we reflect Him as the smaller light. What can be there but His reflection? He is in the body, and it is His reflection which makes us see the light. This moon is so sweet to all, and every one is so sweet to the moon, but that Self-effulgent and Immortal One who is the soul of that moon, He is in us expressing Himself as mind. This lightning is so beautiful, every one is so sweet to the lightning, but the Self-effulgent and Immortal One is the soul of this lightning, and is also in us, because all is that Brahman. The Atman, the Self, is the king of all beings." These ideas are very helpful to men; they are for meditation. For instance, meditate on the earth; think of the earth and at the same time know that we have That which is in the earth, that both are the same. Identify the body with the earth, and identify the soul with the Soul behind. Identify the air with the soul that is in the air and that is in me. They are all one, manifested in different forms. To realise this unity is the end and aim of all meditation, and this is what Yajnavalkya was trying to explain to Maitreyi.

SOUL, NATURE, AND GOD

According to the Vedanta philosophy, man consists of three substances, so to say. The outermost is the body, the gross form of man, in which are the instruments of sensation, such as the eyes, nose, ears, and so forth. This eye is not the organ of vision; it is only the instrument. Behind that is the organ. So, the ears are not the organs of hearing; they are the instruments, and behind them is the organ, or what, in modern physiology, is called the centre. The organs are called Indriyas in Sanskrit. If the centre which governs the eyes be destroyed, the eyes will not see; so with all our senses. The organs, again, cannot sense anything by themselves, until there be something else attached to them. That something is the mind. Many times you have observed that you were deeply engaged in a certain thought, and the clock struck and you did not hear it. Why? The ear was there; vibrations entered it and were carried into the brain, yet you did not hear, because the mind was not joined to the organ. The impressions of external objects are carried to the organs, and when the mind is attached to them, it takes the impressions and gives them, as it were, a colouring, which is called egoism, "I". Take the case of a mosquito biting me on the finger when I am engaged in some work. I do not feel it, because my mind is joined to something else. Later, when my mind is joined to the impression conveyed to the Indriyas, a reaction comes. With this reaction I become conscious of the mosquito. So even the mind joining itself to the organs is not sufficient; there must come the reaction in the form of will. This faculty from which the reaction comes, the faculty of knowledge or intellect, is called "Buddhi" First, there must be the external instrument, next the organ, next the mind must join itself to the organ, then must come the reaction of intellect, and when all these things are complete, there immediately flashes the idea, "I and the external object", and there is a perception, a concept, knowledge. The external organ, which is only the instrument, is in the body, and behind that is the internal organ which is finer; then there is the mind, then the intellectual faculty, then egoism, which says, "I"—I see, I hear, and so forth. The whole process is carried on by certain forces; you may call them vital forces; in Sanskrit they are called Prâna. This gross part of man, this body, in which are the external instruments, is called in Sanskrit, Sthula Sharira, the gross body; behind it comes the series, beginning with the organs, the mind, the intellect, the egoism. These and the vital forces form a compound which is called the fine body, the Sukshma Sharira. These forces are composed of very fine elements, so fine that no amount of injury to this body can destroy them; they survive all the shocks given to this body. The gross body we see is composed of gross material, and as such it is always being renewed and changing continuously. But the internal organs, the mind, the intellect, and the egoism are composed of the finest material, so fine that they will endure for aeons and aeons. They are so fine that they cannot be resisted by anything; they can get through any obstruction. The gross body is non-intelligent, so is the fine, being composed of fine matter. Although one part is called mind, another the intellect, and the third egoism, yet we see at a glance that no one of them can be the "Knower". None of them can be the perceiver, the witness, the one for whom action is made, and who is the seer of the action. All these movements in the mind, or the faculty of intellection, or egoism, must be for some one else. These being composed of fine matter cannot be self-effulgent. Their luminosity cannot be in themselves. This manifestation of the table, for instance, cannot be due to any material thing. Therefore there must be some one behind them all, who is the real manifester, the real seer, the real enjoyer and He in Sanskrit is called the Atman, the Soul of man, the real Self of man. He it is who really sees things. The external instruments and the organs catch the impressions and convey them to the mind, and the mind to the intellect, and the intellect reflects them as on a mirror, and back of it is the Soul that looks on them and gives His orders and His directions. He is the ruler of all these instruments, the master in the house, the enthroned king in the body. The faculty of egoism, the faculty of intellection, the faculty of cogitation, the organs, the instruments, the body, all of them obey His commands. It is He who is manifesting all of these. This is the Atman of man.

Similarly, we can see that what is in a small part of the universe must also be in the whole universe. If conformity is the law of the universe, every part of the universe must have been built on the same plan as the whole. So we naturally think that behind the gross material form which we call this universe of ours, there must be a universe of finer matter, which we call thought, and behind that there must be a Soul, which makes all this thought possible, which commands, which is the enthroned king of this universe. That soul which is behind each mind and each body is called Pratyagâtman, the individual Atman, and that Soul which is behind the universe as its guide, ruler, and governor, is God.

The next thing to consider is whence all these things come. The answer is: What is meant by coming? If it means that something can be produced out of nothing, it is impossible. All this creation, manifestation, cannot be produced out of zero. Nothing can be produced without a cause, and the effect is but the cause reproduced. Here is a glass. Suppose we break it to pieces, and pulverise it, and by means of chemicals almost annihilate it. Will it go back to zero? Certainly not. The form will break, but the particles of which it is made will be there; they will go beyond our senses, but they remain, and it is quite possible that out of these materials another glass may be made. If this is true in one case, it will be so in every case. Something cannot be made out of nothing. Nor can something be made to go back to nothing. It may become finer and finer, and then again grosser and grosser. The raindrop is drawn from the ocean in the form of vapour, and drifts away through the air to the mountains; there it changes again into water and flows back through hundreds of miles down to the mother ocean. The seed produces the tree. The tree dies, leaving only the seed. Again it comes up as another tree, which again ends in the seed, and so on. Look at a bird, how from; the egg it springs, becomes a beautiful bird, lives its life and then dies, leaving only other eggs, containing germs of future birds. So with the animals; so with men. Everything begins, as it were, from certain seeds, certain rudiments, certain fine forms, and becomes grosser and grosser as it develops; and then again it goes back to that fine form and subsides. The whole universe is going on in this way. There comes a time when this whole universe melts down and becomes finer and at last disappears entirely, as it were, but remains as superfine matter. We know through modern science and astronomy that this earth is cooling down, and in course of time it will become very cold, and then it will break to pieces and become finer and finer until it becomes ether once more. Yet the particles will all remain to form the material out of which another earth will be projected. Again that will disappear, and another will come out. So this universe will go back to its causes, and again its materials will come together and take form, like the wave that goes down, rises again, and takes shape. The acts of going back to causes and coming out again, taking form, are called in Sanskrit Sankocha and Vikâsha, which mean shrinking and expanding. The whole universe, as it were, shrinks, and then it expands again. To use the more accepted words of modern science, they are involved and evolved. You hear about evolution, how all forms grow from lower ones, slowly growing up and up. This is very true, but each evolution presupposes an involution. We know that the sum total of energy that is displayed in the universe is the same at all times, and that matter is indestructible. By no means can you take away one particle of matter. You cannot take away a foot-pound of energy or add one. The sum total is the same always. Only the manifestation varies, being involved and evolved. So this cycle is the evolution out of the involution of the previous cycle, and this cycle will again be involved, getting finer and finer, and out of that will come the next cycle. The whole universe is going on in this fashion. Thus we find that there is no creation in the sense that something is created out of nothing. To use a better word, there is manifestation, and God is the manifester of the universe. The universe, as it were, is being breathed out of Him, and again it shrinks into Him, and again He throws it out. A most beautiful simile is given in the Vedas—"That eternal One breathes out this universe and breathes it in." Just as we can breathe out a little particle of dust and breathe it in again. That is all very good, but the question may be asked: How we, it at the first cycle? The answer is: What is the meaning of a first cycle? There was none. If you can give a beginning to time, the whole concept of time will be destroyed. Try to think of a limit where time began, you have to think of time beyond that limit. Try to think where space begins, you will have to think of space beyond that. Time and space are infinite, and therefore have neither beginning nor end. This is a better idea than that God created the universe in five minutes and then went to sleep, and since then has been sleeping. On the other hand, this idea will give us God as the Eternal Creator. Here is a series of waves rising and falling, and God is directing this eternal process. As the universe is without beginning and without end, so is God. We see that it must necessarily be so, because if we say there was a time when there was no creation, either in a gross or a fine form, then there was no God, because God is known to us as Sâkshi, the Witness of the universe. When the universe did not exist, neither did He. One concept follows the other. The idea of the cause we get from the idea of the effect, and if there is no effect, there will be no cause. It naturally follows that as the universe is eternal, God is eternal.

The soul must also be eternal. Why? In the first place we see that the soul is not matter. It is neither a gross body, nor a fine body, which we call mind or thought. It is neither a physical body, nor what in Christianity is called a spiritual body. It is the gross body and the spiritual body that are liable to change. The gross body is liable to change almost every minute and dies, but the spiritual body endures through long periods, until one becomes free, when it also falls away. When a man becomes free, the spiritual body disperses. The gross body disintegrates every time a man dies. The soul not being made of any particles must be indestructible. What do we mean by destruction? Destruction is disintegration of the materials out of which anything is composed. If this glass is broken into pieces, the materials will disintegrate, and that will be the destruction of the glass. Disintegration of particles is what we mean by destruction. It naturally follows that nothing that is not composed of particles can be destroyed, can ever be disintegrated. The soul is not composed of any materials. It is unity indivisible. Therefore it must be indestructible. For the same reasons it must also be without any beginning. So the soul is without any beginning and end.

We have three entities. Here is nature which is infinite, but changeful. The whole of nature is without beginning and end, but within it are multifarious changes. It is like a river that runs down to the sea for thousands of years. It is the same river always, but it is changing every minute, the particles of water are changing their position constantly. Then there is God, unchangeable, the ruler; and there is the soul unchangeable as God, eternal but under the ruler. One is the master, the other the servant, and the third one is nature.

God being the cause of the projection, the continuance, and the dissolution of the universe, the cause must be present to produce the effect. Not only so, the cause becomes the effect. Glass is produced out of certain materials and certain forces used by the manufacturer. In the glass there are those forces plus the materials. The forces used have become the force of adhesion, and if that force goes the glass will fall to pieces; the materials also are undoubtedly in the glass. Only their form is changed. The cause has become the effect. Wherever you see an effect you can always analyze it into a cause, the cause manifests itself as the effect. It follows, if God is the cause of the universe, and the universe is the effect, that God has become the universe. If souls are the effect, and God the cause, God has become the souls. Each soul, therefore, is a part of God. "As from a mass of fire an infinite number of sparks fly, even so from the Eternal One all this universe of souls has come out."

We have seen that there is the eternal God, and there is eternal nature. And there is also an infinite number of eternal souls. This is the first stage in religion, it is called dualism, the stage when man sees himself and God eternally separate, when God is a separate entity by Him, self and man is a separate entity by himself and nature is a separate entity by itself. This is dualism, which holds that the subject and the object are opposed to each other in everything. When man looks at nature, he is the subject and nature the object. He sees the dualism between subject and object. When he looks at God, he sees God as object and himself as the subject. They are entirely separate. This is the dualism between man and God. This is generally the first view of religion.

Then comes another view which I have just shown to you. Man begins to find out that if God is the cause of the universe and the universe the effect, God Himself must have become the universe and the souls, and he is but a particle of which God is the whole. We are but little beings, sparks of that mass of fire, and the whole universe is a manifestation of God Himself. This is the next step. In Sanskrit, it is called Vishishtâdvaita. Just as I have this body and this body covers the soul, and the soul is in and through this body, so this whole universe of infinite souls and nature forms, as it were, the body of God. When the period of involution comes, the universe becomes finer and finer, yet remains the body of God. When the gross manifestation comes, then also the universe remains the body of God. Just as the human soul is the soul of the human body and minds so God is the Soul of our souls. All of you have heard this expression in every religion, "Soul of our souls". That is what is meant by it. He, as it were, resides in them, guides them, is the ruler of them all. In the first view, that of dualism, each one of us is an individual, eternally separate from God and nature. In the second view, we are individuals, but not separate from God. We are like little particles floating in one mass, and that mass is God. We are individuals but one in God. We are all in Him. We are all parts of Him, and therefore we are One. And yet between man and man, man and God there is a strict individuality, separate and yet not separate.

Then comes a still finer question. The question is: Can infinity have parts? What is meant by parts of infinity? If you reason it out, you will find that it is impossible. Infinity cannot be divided, it always remains infinite. If it could be divided, each part would be infinite. And there cannot be two infinites. Suppose there were, one would limit the other, and both would be finite. Infinity can only be one, undivided. Thus the conclusion will be reached that the infinite is one and not many, and that one Infinite Soul is reflecting itself through thousands and thousands of mirrors, appearing as so many different souls. It is the same Infinite Soul, which is the background of the universe, that we call God. The same Infinite Soul also is the background of the human mind which we call the human soul.

COSMOLOGY

There are two worlds, the microcosm, and the macrocosm, the internal and the external. We get truth from both of these by means of experience. The truth gathered from internal experience is psychology, metaphysics, and religion; from external experience, the physical sciences. Now a perfect truth should be in harmony with experiences in both these worlds. The microcosm must bear testimony to the macrocosm, and the macrocosm to the microcosm; physical truth must have its counterpart in the internal world, and the internal world must have its verification outside. Yet, as a rule, we find that many of these truths are in conflict. At one period of the world's history, the internals become supreme, and they begin to fight the externals. At the present time the externals, the physicists, have become supreme, and they have put down many claims of psychologists and metaphysicians. So far as my knowledge goes, I find that the real, essential parts of psychology are in perfect accord with the essential parts of modern physical knowledge. It is not given to one individual to be great in every respect; it is not given to one race or nation to be equally strong in the research of all fields of knowledge. The modern European nations are very strong in their research of external physical knowledge, but they are not so strong in their study of the inner nature of man. On the other hand, the Orientals have not been very strong in their researches of the external physical world, but very strong in their researches of the internal. Therefore we find that Oriental physics and other sciences are not in accordance with Occidental Sciences; nor is Occidental psychology in harmony with Oriental psychology. The Oriental physicists have been routed by Occidental scientists. At the same time, each claims to rest on truth; and as we stated before, real truth in any field of knowledge will not contradict itself; the truths internal are in harmony with the truths external.

We all know the theories of the cosmos according to the modern astronomers and physicists; and at the same time we all know how woefully they undermine the theology of Europe, how these scientific discoveries that are made act as a bomb thrown at its stronghold; and we know how theologians have in all times attempted to put down these researches.

I want here to go over the psychological ideas of the Orientals about cosmology and all that pertains to it, and you will find how wonderfully they are in accordance with the latest discoveries of modern science; and where there is disharmony, you will find that it is modern science which lacks and not they. We all use the word nature. The old Sânkhya philosophers called it by two different names, Prakriti, which is very much the same as the word nature, and the more scientific name, Avyakta, undifferentiated, from which everything proceeds, such as atoms, molecules, and forces, mind, thought, and intelligence. It is startling to find that the philosophers and metaphysicians of India stated ages ago that mind is material. What are our present materialists trying to do, but to show that mind is as much a product of nature as the body? And so is thought, and, we shall find by and by, intelligence also: all issue from that nature which is called Avyakta, the undifferentiated. The Sankhyas define it as the equilibrium of three forces, one of which is called Sattva, another Rajas, and the third Tamas. Tamas, the lowest force, is that of attraction; a little higher is Rajas, that of repulsion; and the highest is the balance of these two, Sattva; so that when these two forces, attraction and repulsion, are held in perfect control by the Sattva there is no creation, no movement in the world. As soon as this equilibrium is lost, the balance is disturbed, and one of these forces gets stronger than the other, motion sets in, and creation begins. This state of things goes on cyclically, periodically. That is to say, there is a period of disturbance of the balance, when forces begin to combine and recombine, and things project outwards. At the same time, everything has a tendency to go back to the primal state of equilibrium, and the time comes when that total annihilation of all manifestation is reached. Again, after a period, the whole thing is disturbed, projected outwards, and again it slowly goes down—like waves. All motion, everything in this universe, can be likened to waves undergoing successive rise and fall. Some of these philosophers hold that the whole universe quiets down for a period. Others hold that this quieting down applies only to systems; that is to say, that while our system here, this solar system, will quiet down and go back into the undifferentiated state, millions of other systems will go the other way, and will project outwards. I should rather favour the second opinion, that this quieting down is not simultaneous over the whole of the universe, and that in different parts different things go on. But the principle remains the same, that all we see—that is, nature herself—is progressing in successive rises and falls. The one stage, falling down, going back to balance, the perfect equilibrium, is called Pralaya, the end of a cycle. The projection and the Pralaya of the universe have been compared by theistical writers in India to the outbreathing and inbreathing of God; God, as it were, breathes out the universe, and it comes into Him again. When it quiets down, what becomes of the universe? It exists, only in finer forms, in the form of cause, as it is called in the Sankhya philosophy. It does not get rid of causation, time, and space; they are there, only it comes to very fine and minute forms. Supposing that this whole universe begins to shrink, till every one of us becomes just a little molecule, we should not feel the change at all, because everything relating to us would be shrinking at the same time. The whole thing goes down, and again projects out, the cause brings out the effect, and so it goes on.

What we call matter in modern times was called by; the ancient psychologists Bhutas, the external elements. There is one element which, according to them, is eternal ; every other element is produced out of this one. It is called Âkâsha. It is somewhat similar to the idea of ether of the moderns, though not exactly similar. Along with this element, there is the primal energy called Prâna. Prana and Akasha combine and recombine and form the elements out of them. Then at the end of the Kalpa; everything subsides, and goes back to Akasha and Prana. There is in the Rig-Veda, the oldest human writing in existence, a beautiful passage describing creation, and it is most poetical—"When there was neither aught nor naught, when darkness was rolling over darkness, what existed?" and the answer is given, "It then existed without vibration". This Prana existed then, but there was no motion in it; Ânidavâtam means "existed without vibration". Vibration had stopped. Then when the Kalpa begins, after an immense interval, the Anidavatam (unvibrating atom) commences to vibrate, and blow after blow is given by Prana to Akasha. The atoms become condensed, and as they are condensed different elements are formed. We generally find these things very curiously translated; people do not go to the philosophers or the commentators for their translation, and have not the brains to understand them themselves. A silly man reads three letters

of Sanskrit and translates a whole book. They translate the, elements as air, fire, and so on; if they would go to the commentators, they would find they do not mean air or anything of the sort.

The Akasha, acted upon by the repeated blows of Prana, produces Vâyu or vibrations. This Vayu vibrates, and the vibrations growing more and more rapid result in friction giving rise to heat, Tejas. Then this heat ends in liquefaction, Âpah. Then that liquid becomes solid. We had ether, and motion, then came heat, then it became liquefied, and then it condensed into gross matter; and it goes back in exactly the reverse way. The solid will be liquefied and will then be converted into a mass of heat, and that will slowly get back into motion; that motion will stop, and this Kalpa will be destroyed. Then, again it will come back and again dissolve into ether. Prana cannot work alone without the help of Akasha. All that we know in the form of motion, vibration, or thought is a modification of the Prana, and everything that we know in the shape of matter, either as form or as resistance, is a modification of the Akasha. The Prana cannot live alone, or act without a medium; when it is pure Prana, it has the Akasha itself to live in, and when it changes into forces of nature, say gravitation, or centrifugal force, it must have matter. You have never seen force without matter or matter without force; what we call force and matter are simply the gross manifestations of these same things, which, when superfine, are called Prana and Akasha. Prana you can call in English life, the vital force; but you must not restrict it to the life of man; at the same time you must not identify it with Spirit, Atman. So this goes on. Creation cannot have either a beginning or an end; it is an eternal on-going.

We shall state another position of these old psychologists, which is that all gross things are the results of fine ones. Everything that is gross is composed of fine things, which they call the Tanmâtras, the fine particles. I smell a flower. To smell, something must come in contact with my nose; the flower is there, but I do not see it move towards me. That which comes from the flower and in contact with my nose is called the Tanmatra, fine molecules of that flower. So with heat, light and everything. These Tanmatras can again be subdivided into atoms. Different philosophers have different theories, and we know these are only theories. It is sufficient for our purpose to know that everything gross is composed of things that are very, very fine. We first get the gross elements which we feel externally, and then come the fine elements with which the nose, eyes, and ears come in contact. Ether waves touch my eyes; I cannot see them, yet I know they must come in contact with my eyes before I can see light.

Here are the eyes, but the eyes do not see. Take away the brain centre; the eyes will still be there, as also the picture of the outside world complete on the retinae; yet the eyes will not see. So the eyes are only a secondary instrument, not the organ of vision. The organ of vision is the nerve-centre in the brain. Likewise the nose is an instrument, and there is an organ behind it. The senses are simply the external instruments. It may be said that these different organs, Indriyas, as they are called in Sanskrit, are the real seats of perception.

It is necessary for the mind to be joined to an organ to perceive. It is a common experience that we do not hear the clock strike when we happen to be buried in study. Why? The ear was there, the sound was carried through it to the brain; yet it was not heard, because the mind did not attach itself to the organ of hearing.

There is a different organ for each different instrument. For, if one served for all, we should find that when the mind joined itself to it, all the senses would be equally active. But it is not so, as we have seen from the instance of the clock. If there was only one organ for all the instruments, the mind would see and hear at the same time, would see and hear and smell at the same time, and it would be impossible for it not to do all these at one and the same time. Therefore it is necessary that there should be a separate organ for each sense. This has been borne out by modern physiology. It is certainly possible for us to hear and see at the same time, but that is because the mind attaches itself partially to the two centres.

What are the organs made of? We see that the instruments—eyes, nose, and ears—are made of gross materials. The organs are also made of matter. Just as the body is composed of gross materials, and manufactures Prana into different gross forces, so the organs are composed of the fine elements, Akasha, Vayu, Tejas, etc., and manufacture Prana into the finer forces of perception. The organs, the Prana functions, the mind and the Buddhi combined, are called the finer body of man—the Linga or Sukshma Sharira. The Linga Sharira has a real form because everything material must have a form.

The mind is called the Manas, the Chitta in Vritti or vibrating, the unsettled state. If you throw a stone in a lake, first there will be vibration, and then resistance. For a moment the water will vibrate and then it will react on the stone. So when any impression comes on the Chitta, it first vibrates a little. That is called the Manas. The mind carries the impression farther in, and presents it to the determinative faculty, Buddhi, which reacts. Behind Buddhi is Ahamkâra, egoism, the self-consciousness which says, "I am". Behind Ahamkara is Mahat, intelligence, the highest form of nature's existence. Each one is the effect of the succeeding one. In the case of the lake, every blow that comes to it is from the external world, while in the case of the mind, the blow may come either from the external or the internal world. Behind the intelligence is the Self of man, the Purusha, the Atman, the pure, the perfect, who alone is the seer, and for whom is all this change.

Man looks on all these changes; he himself is never impure; but through what the Vedantists call Adhyâsa, by reflection, by implication, he seems to be impure. It is like the appearance of a crystal when a red or a blue flower is brought before it: the colour is reflected on it, but the crystal itself is pure. We shall take it for granted that there are many selves, and each self is pure and perfect; various kinds of gross and fine matter superimpose themselves on the self and make it multicoloured. Why does nature do all this? Nature is undergoing all these changes for the development of the soul; all this creation is for the benefit of the soul, so that it may be free. This immense book which we call the universe is stretched out before man so that he may read; and he discovers eventually that he is an omniscient and omnipotent being. I must here tell you that some of our best psychologists do not believe in God in the sense in which you believe in Him. The father of our psychology, Kapila, denies the existence of God. His idea is that a Personal God is quite unnecessary; nature itself is sufficient to work out the whole of creation. What is called the Design Theory, he knocked on the head, and said that a more childish theory was never advanced. But he admits a peculiar kind of God. He says we are all struggling to get free; and when we become free, we can, as it were, melt away into nature, only to come out at the beginning of the next cycle and be its ruler. We come out omniscient and omnipotent beings. In that sense we can be called Gods; you and I and the humblest beings can be Gods in different cycles. He says such a God will be temporal; but an eternal God, eternally omnipotent and ruler of the universe cannot be. If there was such a God, there would be this difficulty: He must be either a bound spirit or a free one. A God who is perfectly free would not create: there is no necessity for it. If He were bound, He would not create, because He could not: He would be powerless. In either case, there cannot be any omniscient or omnipotent eternal ruler. In our scriptures, wherever the word God is mentioned, he says, it means those human beings who have become free.

Kapila does not believe in the unity of all souls. His analysis, so far as it goes, is simply marvellous. He is the father of Indian thinkers; Buddhism and other systems are the outcome of his thought.

According to his psychology, all souls can regain their freedom and their natural rights, which are omnipotence and omniscience. But the question arises: Where is this bondage? Kapila says it is without beginning. But if it is without beginning, it must be without end, and we shall never be free. He says that though bondage is without beginning, it is not of that constant uniform character as the soul is. In other words, nature (the cause of bondage) is without beginning and end, but not in the same sense as soul, because nature has no individuality; it is like a river which gets a fresh body of water every moment; the sum total of these bodies of water is the river, but the river is not a constant quantity. Everything in nature is constantly changing, but the soul never changes; so, as nature is always changing, it is possible for the soul to come out of its bondage.

The whole of the universe is built upon the same plan as a part of it. So, just as I have a mind, there is a cosmic mind. As in the individual, so in the universal. There is the universal gross body; behind that, a universal fine body; behind that, a universal mind; behind that, a universal egoism, or consciousness; and behind that, a universal intelligence. And all this is in nature, the manifestation of nature, not outside of it.

We have the gross bodies from our parents, as also our consciousness. Strict heredity says my body is a part of my parents' bodies, the material of my consciousness and egoism is a part of my parents'. We can add to the little portion inherited from our parents by drawing upon the universal consciousness. There is an infinite storehouse of intelligence out of which we draw what we require; there is an infinite storehouse of mental force in the universe out of which we are drawing eternally; but the seed must come from the parents. Our theory is heredity coupled with reincarnation. By the law of heredity, the reincarnating soul receives from parents the material out of which to manufacture a man.

Some of the European philosophers have asserted that this world exists because I exist; and if I do not exist, the world will not exist. Sometimes it is stated thus: If all the people in the world were to die, and there were no more human beings, and no animals with powers of perception and intelligence, all these manifestations would disappear. But these European philosophers do not know the psychology of it, although they know the principle; modern philosophy has got only a glimpse of it. This becomes easy of understanding when looked at from the Sankhya point of view. According to Sankhya, it is impossible for anything to be, which has not as its material, some portion of my mind. I do not know this table as it is. An impression from it comes to the eyes, then to, the Indriya, and then to the mind; and the mind reacts, and that reaction is what I call the table. It is just the same as throwing a stone in a lake; the lake throws a wave towards the stone; this wave is what we know. What is external nobody knows; when I try to know it, it has to become that material which I furnish. I, with my own mind, have furnished the material for my eyes. There is something which is outside, which is only, the occasion, the suggestion, and upon that suggestion I project my mind; and it takes the form that I see. How do we all see the same things? Because we all have; similar parts of the cosmic mind. Those who have like minds will see like things, and those who have not will not see alike.

A STUDY OF THE SANKHYA PHILOSOPHY

Prakriti is called by the Sânkhya philosophers indiscrete, and defined as the perfect balance of the materials in it; and it naturally follows that in perfect balance there cannot be any motion. In the primal state before any manifestation, when there was no motion but perfect balance, this Prakriti was indestructible, because decomposition or death comes from instability or change. Again, according to the Sankhya, atoms are not the primal state. This universe does not come out of atoms: they may be the secondary or the tertiary state. The primordial material may form into atoms and become grosser

and bigger things; and as far as modern investigations go, they rather point towards the same conclusion. For instance, in the modern theory of ether, if you say ether is atomic, it will not solve anything. To make it clearer, say that air is composed of atoms, and we know that ether is everywhere, interpenetrating, omnipresent, and that these air atoms are floating, as it were, in ether. If ether again be composed of atoms, there will still be spaces between every two atoms of ether. What fills up these? If you suppose that there is another ether still finer which does this, there will again be other spaces between the atoms of that finer ether which require filling up, and so it will be regressus ad infinitum, what the Sankhya philosophers call the "cause leading to nothing" So the atomic theory cannot be final. According to Sankhya, nature is omnipresent, one omnipresent mass of nature, in which are the causes of everything that exists. What is meant by cause? Cause is the fine state of the manifested state; the unmanifested state of that which becomes manifested. What do you mean by destruction? It is reverting to the cause If you have a piece of pottery and give it a blow, it is destroyed. What is meant by this is that the effects go back to their own nature, they materials out of which the pottery was created go back into their original state. Beyond this idea of destruction, any idea such as annihilation is on the face of it absurd. According to modern physical science, it can be demonstrated that all destruction means that which Kapila said ages ago — simply reverting to the cause. Going back to the finer form is all that is meant by destruction. You know how it can be demonstrated in a laboratory that matter is indestructible. At this present stage of our knowledge, if any man stands up and says that matter or this soul becomes annihilated, he is only making himself, ridiculous; it is only uneducated, silly people who would advance such a proposition; and it is curious that modern knowledge coincides with what those old philosophers taught. It must be so, and that is the proof of truth. They proceeded in their inquiry, taking up mind as the basis; they analysed the mental part of this universe and came to certain conclusions, which we, analysing the physical part, must come to, for they both must lead to the same centre.

You must remember that the first manifestation of this Prakriti in the cosmos is what the Sankhya calls "Mahat". We may call it intelligence — the great principle, its literal meaning. The first change in Prakriti is this intelligence; I would not translate it by self-consciousness, because that would be wrong. Consciousness is only a part of this intelligence. Mahat is universal. It covers all the grounds of sub-consciousness, consciousness, and super-consciousness; so any one state of consciousness, as applied to this Mahat, would not be sufficient. In nature, for instance, you note certain changes going on before your eyes which you see and understand, but there are other changes, so much finer, that no human perception can catch them. The are from the same cause, the same Mahat is making these changes. Out of Mahat comes universal egoism. These are all substance. There is no difference between matter and mind, except in degree. The substance is the same in finer or grosser form; one changes into the other, and this exactly coincides with the conclusions of modern physiological research. By believing in the teaching that the mind is not separate from the brain, you will be saved from much fighting and struggling. Egoism again changes into two varieties. In one variety it changes into the organs. Organs are of two kinds, organs of sensation and organs of reaction. They are not the eyes or the ears, but back of those are what you call brain-centres, and nerve-centres, and so on. This egoism, this matter or substance, becomes changed, and out of this material are manufactured these centres. Of the same substance is manufactured the other variety, the Tanmatras, fine particles of matter, which strike our organs of perception and bring about sensations. You cannot perceive them but only know they are there. Out of the Tanmatras is manufactured the gross matter—earth, water, and all the things that we see and feel. I want to impress this on your mind. It is very, hard to grasp it, because in Western countries the ideas are so queer about mind and matter. It is hard to get those impressions out of our brains. I myself had a tremendous difficulty, being educated in Western philosophy in my boyhood. These are all cosmic things. Think of this universal extension of matter, unbroken, one substance, undifferentiated, which is the first state of everything, and which begins to change in the same way as milk becomes curd. This first change is called Mahat. The substance Mahat changes into the grosser matter called egoism. The third change is manifested as universal sense-organs, and universal fine particles, and these last again combine and become this gross universe which with eyes, nose, and ears, we see, smell, and hear. This is the cosmic plan according to the Sankhya, and what is in the cosmos must also be microcosmic. Take an individual man. He has first a part of undifferentiated nature in him, and that material nature in him becomes changed into this Mahat, a small particle of this universal intelligence, and this particle of universal intelligence in him becomes changed into egoism, and then into the sense-organs and the fine particles of matter which combine and manufacture his body. I want this to be clear, because it is the stepping-stone to Sankhya, and it is absolutely necessary for you to understand it, because this is the basis of the philosophy of the whole world. There is no philosophy in the world that is not indebted to Kapila. Pythagoras came to India and studied this philosophy, and that was the beginning of the philosophy of the Greeks. Later, it formed the Alexandrian school, and still later, the Gnostic. It became divided into two; one part went to Europe and Alexandria, and the other remained in India; and out of this, the system of Vyasa was developed. The Sankhya philosophy of Kapila was the first rational system that the world ever saw. Every metaphysician in the world must pay homage to him. I want to impress on your mind that we are bound to listen to him as the great father of philosophy. This wonderful man, the most ancient of philosophers, is mentioned even in the Shruti: "O Lord, Thou who

produced the sage Kapila in the Beginning." How wonderful his perceptions were, and if there is ant proof required of the extraordinary power of the perception of Yogis, such men are the proof. They had no microscopes or telescopes. Yet how fine their perception was, how perfect and wonderful their analysis of things!

I will here point out the difference between Schopenhauer and the Indian philosophy. Schopenhauer says that desire, or will, is the cause of everything. It is the will to exist that make us manifest, but we deny this. The will is identical with the motor nerves. When I see an object there is no will; when its sensations are carried to the brain, there comes the reaction, which says "Do this", or "Do not do this", and this state of the ego-substance is what is called will. There cannot be a single particle of will which is not a reaction. So many things precede will. It is only a manufactured something out of the ego, and the ego is a manufacture of something still higher—the intelligence—and that again is a modification of the indiscrete nature. That was the Buddhistic idea, that whatever we see is the will. It is psychologically entirely wrong, because will can only be identified with the motor nerves. If you take out the motor nerves, a man has no will whatever. This fact, as is perhaps well known to you, has been found out after a long series of experiments made with the lower animals.

We will take up this question. It is very important to understand this question of Mahat in man, the great principle, the intelligence. This intelligence itself is modified into what we call egoism, and this intelligence is the cause of all the powers in the body. It covers the whole ground, sub-consciousness, consciousness, and super-consciousness. What are these three states? The sub-conscious state we find in animals, which we call instinct. This is almost infallible, but very limited. Instinct rarely fails. An animal almost instinctively knows a poisonous herb from an edible one, but its instinct is very limited. As soon as something new comes, it is blind. It works like a machine. Then comes a higher state of knowledge which is fallible and makes mistakes often, but has a larger scope, although it is slow, and this you call reason. It is much larger than instinct, but instinct is surer than reason. There are more chances of mistakes in reasoning than in instinct. There is a still higher state of the mind, the super-conscious, which belongs only to Yogis, to men who have cultivated it. This is infallible and much more unlimited in its scope than reason. This is the highest state. So we must remember, this Mahat is the real cause of all that is here, that which manifests itself in various ways, covers the whole ground of sub-conscious, conscious, and super-conscious, the three states in which knowledge exists.

Now comes a delicate question which is being always asked. If a perfect God created the universe, why is there imperfection in it? What we call the universe is what we see, and that is only this little plane of consciousness and reason; beyond that we do not see at all. Now the very question is an impossible one. If I take only a small portion out of a mass of some-

Lectures & Discourses by **Swami Vivekananda**

thing and look at it, it seems to be inharmonious. Naturally. The universe is inharmonious because we make it so. How? What is reason? What is knowledge? Knowledge is finding the association about things. You go into the street and see a man and say, I know this is a man; because you remember the impressions on your mind, the marks on the Chitta. You have seen many men, and each one has made an impression on your mind; and as you see this man, you refer this to your store and see many similar pictures there; and when you see them, you are satisfied, and you put this new one with the rest. When a new impression comes and it has associations in your mind, you are satisfied; and this state of association is called knowledge. Knowledge is, therefore, pigeon-holing one experience with the already existing fund of experience, and this is one of the great proofs of the fact that you cannot have any knowledge until you have already a fund in existence. If you are without experience, as some European philosophers think, and that your mind is a tabula rasa to begin with, you cannot get any knowledge, because the very fact of knowledge is the recognition of the new by means of associations already existing in the mind. There must be a store at hand to which to refer a new impression. Suppose a child is born into this world without such a fund, it would be impossible for him ever to get any knowledge. Therefore, the child must have been previously in a state in which he had a fund, and so knowledge is eternally increasing. Show me a way of getting round this argument. It is a mathematical fact. Some Western schools of philosophy also hold that there cannot be any knowledge without a fund of past knowledge. They have framed the idea that the child is born with knowledge. These Western philosophers say that the impressions with which the child comes into the world are not due to the child's past, but to the experiences of his forefathers: it is only hereditary transmission. Soon they will find out that this idea is all wrong; some German philosophers are now giving hard blows to these heredity ideas. Heredity is very good, but incomplete, it only explains the physical side. How do you explain the environments influencing us? Many causes produce one effect. Environment is one of the modifying effects. We make our own environment: as our past is, so we find the present environment. A drunken man naturally gravitates to the lowest slums of the city.

You understand what is meant by knowledge. Knowledge is pigeon-holing a new impression with old ones, recognising a new impression. What is meant by recognition? Finding associations with similar impressions that one already has. Nothing further is meant by knowledge. If that is the case, if knowledge means finding the associations, then it must be that to know anything we have to set the whole series of its similars. Is it not so? Suppose you take a pebble; to find the association, you have to see the whole series of pebbles similes to it. But with our perception of the universe as a whole we cannot do that, because in the pigeon-hole of our mind there is only one single record of the perception, we have no other

perception of the same nature or class, we cannot compare it with any other. We cannot refer it to its associations. This bit of the universe, cut off by our consciousness, is a startling new thing, because we have not been able to find its associations. Therefore, we are struggling with it, and thinking it horrible, wicked, and bad; we may sometimes think it is good, but we always think it is imperfect. It is only when we find its associations that the universe can be known. We shall recognise it when we go beyond the universe and consciousness, and then the universe will stand explained. Until we can do that, all the knocking of our heads against a wall will never explain the universe, because knowledge is the finding of similars, and this conscious plane only gives us one single perception of it. So with our idea of God. All that we see of God is only a part just as we see only one portion of the universe, and all the rest is beyond human cognition. "I, the universal; so great am I that even this universe is but a part of Me." That is why we see God as imperfect, and do not understand Him. The only way to understand Him and the universe is to go beyond reason, beyond consciousness. "When thou goest beyond the heard and the hearing, the thought and the thinking, then alone wilt thou come to Truth." "Go thou beyond the scriptures, because they teach only up to nature, up to the three qualities." When we go beyond them, we find the harmony, and not before.

The microcosm and the macrocosm are built on exactly the same plan, and in the microcosm we know only one part, the middle part. We know neither the sub-conscious, nor the super-conscious. We know the conscious only. If a man stands up and says, "I am a sinner", he makes an untrue statement because he does not know himself. He is the most ignorant of men; of himself he knows only one part, because his knowledge covers only a part of the ground he is on. So with this universe, it is possible to know only a part of it with the reason, not the whole of it; for the sub-conscious, the conscious and the super-conscious, the individual Mahat and the universal Mahat, and all the subsequent modifications, constitute the universe.

What makes nature (Prakriti) change? We see so far that everything, all Prakriti, is Jada, insentient. It is all compound and insentient. Wherever there is law, it is proof that the region of its play is insentient. Mind, intelligence, will, and everything else is insentient. But they are all reflecting the sentiency, the "Chit" of some being who is beyond all this, whom the Sankhya philosophers call "Purusha". The Purusha is the unwitting cause of all the changes in the universe. That is to say, this Purusha, taking Him in the universal sense, is the God of the universe. It is said that the will of the Lord created the universe. It is very good as a common expression, but we see it cannot be true. How could it be will? Will is the third or fourth manifestation in nature. Many things exist before it, and what created them? Will is a compound, and everything that is a compound is a product of nature. Will, therefore, could not create nature. So, to say that the will of the Lord created the universe is meaningless. Our will only covers a little portion of self-consciousness and moves our brain. It is not will that is working your body or that is working the universe. This body is being moved by a power of which will is only a manifestation in one part. Likewise in the universe there is will, but that is only one part of the universe. The whole of the universe is not guided by will; that is why we cannot explain it by the will theory. Suppose I take it for granted that it is will moving the body, then, when I find I cannot work it at will, I begin to fret and fume. It is my fault, because I had no right to take the will theory for granted. In the same way, if I take the universe and think it is will that moves it and find things which do not coincide, it is my fault. So the Purusha is not will; neither can it be intelligence, because intelligence itself is a compound. There cannot be any intelligence without some sort of matter corresponding to the brain. Wherever there is intelligence, there must be something akin to that matter which we call brain which becomes lumped together into a particular form and serves the purpose of the brain. Wherever there is intelligence, there must be that matter in some form or other. But intelligence itself is a compound. What then is this Purusha? It is neither intelligence nor will, but it is the cause of all these. It is its presence that sets them all going and combining. It does not mix with nature; it is not intelligence, or Mahat; but the Self, the pure, is Purusha. "I am the witness, and through my witnessing, nature is producing; all that is sentient and all that is insentient."

What is this sentiency in nature? We find intelligence is this sentiency which is called Chit. The basis of sentiency is in the Purusha, it is the nature of Purusha. It is that which cannot be explained but which is the cause of all that we call knowledge. Purusha is not consciousness, because consciousness is a compound; buts whatever is light and good in consciousness belongs to Purusha. Purusha is not conscious, but whatever is light in intelligence belongs to Purusha. Sentiency is in the Purusha, but the Purusha is not intelligent, not knowing. The Chit in the Purusha plus Prakriti is what we see around us. Whatever is pleasure and happiness and light in the universe belongs to Purusha; but it is a compound, because it is Purusha plus Prakriti. "Wherever there is any happiness, wherever there is any bliss, there is a spark of that immortality which is God." "Purusha is the; great attraction of the universe; though untouched by and unconnected with the universe, yet it attracts the whole; universe." You see a man going after gold, because behind it is a spark of the Purusha though mixed up with a good deal of dirt. When a man loves his children or a woman her husband, what is the attracting power? A spark of Purusha behind them. It is there, only mixed up with "dirt". Nothing else can attract. "In this world of insentiency the Purusha alone is sentient." This is the Purusha of the Sankhya. As such, it necessarily follows that the Purusha must be omnipresent. That which is not omnipresent must be limited. All limitations are caused; that which is caused must have a beginning and end. If the Purusha is limited, it will die, will not

be free, will not be final, but must have some cause. Therefore it is omnipresent. According to Kapila, there are many Purushas; not one, but an infinite number of them. You and I have each of us one, and so has everyone else; an infinite number of circles, each one infinite, running through this universe. The Purusha is neither mind nor matter, the reflex from it is all that we know. We are sure if it is omnipresent it has neither death nor birth. Nature is casting her shadow upon it, the shadow of birth and death, but it is by its nature pure. So far we have found the philosophy of the Sankhya wonderful.

Next we shall take up the proofs against it. So far the analysis is perfect, the psychology incontrovertible. We find by the division of the senses into organs and instruments that they are not simple, but compound; by dividing egoism into sense and matter, we find that this is also material and that Mahat is also a state of matter, and finally we find the Purusha. So far there is no objection. But if we ask the Sankhya the question, "Who created nature?"—the Sankhya says that the Purusha and the Prakriti are uncreate and omnipresent, and that of this Purusha there is an infinite number. We shall have to controvert these propositions, and find a better solution, and by so doing we shall come to Advaitism. Our first objection is, how can there be these two infinites? Then our argument will be that the Sankhya is not a perfect generalization, and that we have not found in it a perfect solution. And then we shall see how the Vedantists grope out of all these difficulties and reach a perfect solution, and yet all the glory really belongs to the Sankhya. It is very easy to give a finishing touch to a building when it is constructed.

SANKHYA AND VEDANTA

I shall give you a résumé of the Sânkhya philosophy, through which we have been going. We, in this lecture, want to find where its defects are, and where Vedanta comes in and supplements it. You must remember that according to Sankhya philosophy, nature is the cause of all these manifestations which we call thought, intellect, reason, love, hatred, touch, taste, and matter. Everything is from nature. This nature consists of three sorts of elements, called Sattva, Rajas, and Tamas. These are not qualities, but elements, the materials out of which the whole universe is evolved. In the beginning of a cycle these remain in equilibrium; and when creation comes, they begin to combine and recombine and manifest as the universe. The first manifestation is what the Sankhya calls the Mahat or Intelligence, and out of that comes consciousness. According to Sankhya, this is an element (Tattva). And out of consciousness are evolved Manas or mind, the organs of the senses, and the Tanmâtras (particles of sound, touch, etc.). All the fine particles are evolved from consciousness, and out of these fine particles come the gross elements which we call matter. The Tanmatras cannot be perceived; but when they become gross particles, we can feel and sense them.

The Chitta, in its threefold function of intelligence, consciousness, and mind, works and manufactures the forces called Prâna. You must at once get rid of the idea that Prana is breath. Breath is one effect of Prana. By Prana are meant the nervous forces governing and moving the whole body, which also manifest themselves as thought. The foremost and most obvious manifestation of Prana is the breathing motion. Prana acts upon air, and not air upon it. Controlling the breathing motion is prânâyâma. Pranayama is practised to get mastery over this motion; the end is not merely to control the breath or to make the lungs strong. That is Delsarte, not Pranayama. These Pranas are the vital forces which manipulate the whole body, while they in their turn are manipulated by other organs in the body, which are called mind or internal organs. So far so good. The psychology is very clear and most precise; and yet it is the oldest rational thought in the world! Wherever there is any philosophy or rational thought, it owes something or other to Kapila. Pythagoras learnt it in India, and taught it in Greece. Later on Plato got an inkling of it; and still later the Gnostics carried the thought to Alexandria, and from there it came to Europe. So wherever there is any attempt at psychology or philosophy, the great father of it is this man, Kapila. So far we see that his psychology is wonderful; but we shall have to differ with him on some points, as we go on. We find that the basic principle on which Kapila works, is evolution. He makes one thing evolve out of another, because his very definition of causation is "the cause reproduced in another form," and because the whole universe, so far as we see it, is progressive and evolving. We see clay; in another form, we call it a pitcher. Clay was the cause and the pitcher the effect. Beyond this we cannot have any idea of causation. Thus this whole universe is evolved out of a material, out of Prakriti or nature. Therefore, the universe cannot be essentially different from its cause. According to Kapila, from undifferentiated nature to thought or intellect, not one of them is what he calls the "Enjoyer" or "Enlightener". Just as is a lump of clay, so is a lump of mind. By itself the mind has no light; but ate see it reasons. Therefore there must be some one behind it, whose light is percolating through Mahat and consciousness, and subsequent modifications, and this is what Kapila calls the Purusha, the Self of the Vedantin. According to Kapila, the Purusha is a simple entity, not a compound; he is immaterial, the only one who is immaterial, and all these various manifestations are material. I see a black-board. First, the external instruments will bring that sensation to the nerve-centre, to the Indriya according to Kapila; from the centre it will go to the mind and make an impression; the mind will present it to the Buddhi, but Buddhi cannot act; the action comes, as it were, from the Purusha behind. These, so to speak, are all his servants, bringing the sensations to him, and he, as it were, gives the orders, reacts, is the enjoyer, the perceiver, the real One, the King on his throne, the Self of man, who is immaterial. Because he is immaterial, it necessarily follows that he must be infinite, he cannot have any limitation whatever. Each one of the Purushas is omnipresent; each one of us is omnipresent,

but we can act only through the Linga Sharira, the fine body. The mind, the self-consciousness, the organs, and the vital forces compose the fine body or sheath, what in Christian philosophy is called the spiritual body of man. It is this body that gets salvation, or punishment, or heaven, that incarnates and reincarnates, because we see from the very beginning that the going and the coming of the Purusha or soul are impossible. Motion means going or coming, and what goes or comes from one place to another cannot be omnipresent. Thus far we see from Kapila's psychology that the soul is infinite, and that the soul is the only thing which is not composed of nature. He is the only one that is outside of nature, but he has got bound by nature, apparently. Nature is around him, and he has identified himself with it. He thinks, "I am the Linga Sharira", "I am the gross matter, the gross body", and as such he enjoys pleasure and pain, but they do not really belong to him, they belong to this Linga Sharira or the fine body.

The meditative state is called always the highest state by the Yogi, when it is neither a passive nor an active state; in it you approach nearest to the Purusha. The soul has neither pleasure nor pain; it is the witness of everything, the eternal witness of all work, but it takes no fruits from any work. As the sun is the cause of sight of every eye, but is not itself affected by any defects in the eye or as when a crystal has red or blue flowers placed before it, the crystal looks red or blue, and yet it is neither; so, the soul is neither passive nor active, it is beyond both. The nearest way of expressing this state of the soul is that it is meditation. This is Sankhya philosophy.

Next, Sankhya says, that the manifestation of nature is for the soul; all combinations are for some third person. The combinations which you call nature, these constant changes are going on for the enjoyment of the soul, for its liberation, that it may gain all this experience from the lowest to the highest. When it has gained it, the soul finds it was never in nature, that it was entirely separate, that it is indestructible, that it cannot go and come; that going to heaven and being born again were in nature, and not in the soul. Thus the soul becomes free. All nature is working for the enjoyment and experience of the soul. It is getting this experience in order to reach the goal, and that goal is freedom. But the souls are many according to the Sankhya philosophy. There is an infinite number of souls. The other conclusion of Kapila is that there is no God as the Creator of the universe. Nature is quite sufficient by itself to account for everything. God is not necessary, says the Sankhya.

The Vedanta says that the Soul is in its nature Existence absolute, Knowledge absolute, Bliss absolute. But these are not qualities of the Soul: they are one, not three, the essence of the Soul; and it agrees with the Sankhya in thinking that intelligence belongs to nature, inasmuch as it comes through nature. The Vedanta also shows that what is called intelligence is a compound. For instance, let us examine our perceptions. I see a black-board. How does the knowledge come? What the German philosophers call "the thing-in-itself" of the black-board is unknown, I can never know it. Let us call it x. The black-board x acts on my mind, and the mind reacts. The mind is like a lake. Throw a stone in a lake and a reactionary wave comes towards the stone; this wave is not like the stone at all, it is a wave. The black-board x is like a stone which strikes the mind and the mind throws up a wave towards it, and this wave is what we call the black-board. I see you. You as reality are unknown and unknowable. You are x and you act upon my mind, and the mind throws a wave in the direction from which the impact comes, and that wave is what I call Mr. or Mrs. So-and-so. There are two elements in the perception, one coming from outside and the other from inside, and the combination of these two, x+ mind, is our external universe. All knowledge is by reaction. In the case of a whale it has been determined by calculation how long after its tail is struck, its mind reacts and the whale feels the pain. Similar is the case with internal perception. The real self within me is also unknown and unknowable. Let us call it y. When I know myself as so-and-so, it is y+ the mind. That y strikes a blow on the mind. So our whole world is x+ mind (external), and y + mind (internal), x and y standing for the thing-in-itself behind the external and the internal worlds respectively.

According to Vedanta, the three fundamental factors of consciousness are, I exist, I know, and I am blessed The idea that I have no want, that I am restful, peaceful, that nothing can disturb me, which comes from time to time, is the central fact of our being, the basic principle of our life; and when it becomes limited, and becomes a compound, it manifests itself as existence phenomenal, knowledge phenomenal, and love. Every man exists, and every man must know, and every man is mad for love. He cannot help loving. Through all existence, from the lowest to the highest, all must love. The y, the internal thing-in-itself, which, combining with mind, manufactures existence, knowledge, and love, is called by the Vedantists. Existence absolute, Knowledge absolute, Bliss absolute. That real existence is limitless, unmixed, uncombined, knows no change, is the free soul; when it gets mixed up, muddled up, as it were, with the mind, it becomes what we call individual existence. It is plant life, animal life, human life, just as universal space is cut off in a room, in a jar, and so on. And that real knowledge is not what we know, not intuition, nor reason, nor instinct. When that degenerates and is confused, we call it intuition; when it degenerates more, we call it reason; and when it degenerates still more, we call it instinct. That knowledge itself is Vijnâna, neither intuition, nor reason nor instinct. The nearest expression for it is all-knowingness. There is no limit to it, no combination in it. That bliss, when it gets clouded over, we call love, attraction for gross bodies or fine bodies, or for ideas. This is only a distorted manifestation of that blessedness. Absolute Existence, absolute Knowledge, and absolute Blessedness are not qualities of the soul, but the essence; there is no difference between them and the soul. And the three are one; we see the one thing in three different aspects. They are beyond all relative knowledge. That eternal

knowledge of the Self percolating through the brain of man becomes his intuition, reason, and so on. Its manifestation varies according to the medium through which it shines. As soul, there is no difference between man and the lowest animal, only the latter's brain is less developed and the manifestation through it which we call instinct is very dull. In a man the brain is much finer, so the manifestation is much clearer, and in the highest man it becomes entirely clear. So with existence; the existence which we know, the limited sphere of existence, is simply a reflection of that real existence which is the nature of the soul. So with bliss; that which we call love or attraction is but the rejection of the eternal blessedness of the Self. With manifestation comes limitation, but the unmanifested, the essential nature of the soul, is unlimited; to that blessedness there is no limit. But in love there is limitation. I love you one day, I hate you the next. My love increases one day and decreases the next, because it is only a manifestation.

The first point we will contend with Kapila is his idea of God. Just as the series of modifications of Prakriti, beginning with the individual intellect and ending with the individual body, require a Purusha behind, as the ruler and governor, so, in the Cosmos, the universal intellect, the universal egoism, the universal mind, all universal fine and gross materials, must have a ruler and governor. How will the cosmic series become complete without the universal Purusha behind them all as the ruler and governor? If you deny a universal Purusha behind the cosmic series, we deny your Purusha behind the individual series. If it be true that behind the series of graded, evolved individual manifestations, there stands One that is beyond them all, the Purusha who is not composed of matter, the very same logic will apply to the case of universal manifestations. This Universal Self which is beyond the universal modifications of Prakriti is what is called Ishwara, the Supreme Ruler, God.

Now comes the more important point of difference. Can there be more than one Purusha? The Purusha, we have seen, is omnipresent and infinite. The omnipresent, the infinite, cannot be two. If there are two infinites A and B, the infinite A would limit the infinite B, because the infinite B is not the infinite A, and the infinite A is not the infinite B. Difference in identity means exclusion, and exclusion means limitation. Therefore, A and B, limiting each other, cease to be infinites. Hence, there can be but one infinite, that is, one Purusha.

Now we will take up our x and y and show they are one. We have shown how what we call the external world is x + mind, and the internal world y + mind; x and y are both quantities unknown and unknowable. All difference is due to time, space, and causation. These are the constituent elements of the mind. No mentality is possible without them. You can never think without time, you can never imagine anything without space, and you can never have anything without causation. These are the forms of the mind. Take them away, and the mind itself does not exist. All difference is, therefore, due to the mind. According to Vedanta, it is the mind, its forms, that have limited x and y apparently and made them appear as external and internal worlds. But x and y, being both beyond the mind, are without difference and hence one. We cannot attribute any quality to them, because qualities are born of the mind. That which is qualityless must be one; x is without qualities, it only takes qualities of the mind; so does y; therefore these x and y are one. The whole universe is one. There is only one Self in the universe, only One Existence, and that One Existence, when it passes through the forms of time, space, and causation, is called by different names, Buddhi, fine matter, gross matter, all mental and physical forms. Everything in the universe is that One, appearing in various forms. When a little part of it comes, as it were, into this network of time, space, and causation, it takes forms; take off the network, and it is all one. Therefore in the Advaita philosophy, the whole universe is all one in the Self which is called Brahman. That Self when it appears behind the universe is called God. The same Self when it appears behind this little universe, the body, is the soul. This very soul, therefore, is the Self in man. There is only one Purusha, the Brahman of the Vedanta; God and man, analysed, are one in It. The universe is you yourself, the unbroken you; you are throughout the universe. "In all hands you work, through all mouths you eat, through all nostrils you breathe through all minds you think." The whole universe is you; the universe is your body; you are the universe both formed and unformed. You are the soul of the universe and its body also. You are God, you are the angels, you are man, you are animals, you are the plants, you are the minerals, you are everything; the manifestation of everything is you. Whatever exists is you. You are the Infinite. The Infinite cannot be divided. It can have no parts, for each part would be infinite, and then the part would be identical with the whole, which is absurd. Therefore the idea that you are Mr. So-and-so can never be true; it is a day-dream. Know this and be free. This is the Advaita conclusion. "I am neither the body, nor the organs, nor am I the mind; I am Existence, Knowledge, and Bliss absolute; I am He." This is true knowledge; all reason and intellect, and everything else is ignorance. Where is knowledge for me, for I am knowledge itself! Where is life for me, for I am life itself! I am sure I live, for I am life, the One Being, and nothing exists except through me, and in me, and as me. I am manifested through the elements, but I am the free One. Who seeks freedom? Nobody. If you think that you are bound, you remain bound; you make your own bondage. If you know that you are free, you are free this moment. This is knowledge, knowledge of freedom. Freedom is the goal of all nature.

THE GOAL

Delivered in San Francisco, March 27, 1900

We find that man, as it were, is always surrounded by something greater than himself, and he is trying to grasp the meaning of this. Man will ever [seek] the highest ideal. He knows that it exists and that religion is the search after the highest ideal. At first all his searches were in the external plane — placed in heaven, in different places — just according to [his grasp] of the total nature of man.

[Later,] man began to look at himself a little closer and began to find out that the real "me" was not the "me" that he stands for ordinarily. As he appears to the senses is not the same as he really is. He began to [search] inside of himself, and found out that … the same ideal he [had placed] outside of himself is all the time within; what he was worshipping outside was his own real inner nature. The difference between dualism and monism is that when the ideal is put outside [of oneself], it is dualism. When God is [sought] within, it is monism.

First, the old question of why and wherefore … How is it that man became limited? How did the Infinite become finite, the pure become impure? In the first place, you must never forget that this question can never be answered [by] any dualistic hypothesis.

Why did God create the impure universe? Why is man so miserable, made by a perfect, infinite, merciful Father? Why this heaven and earth, looking at which we get our conception of law? Nobody can imagine anything that he has not seen.

All the tortures we feel in this life, we put in another place and that is our hell …

Why did the infinite God make this world? [The dualist says:] Just as the potter makes pots. God the potter; we the pots … In more philosophical language the question is: How is it taken for granted that the real nature of man is pure, perfect, and infinite? This is the one difficulty found in any system of monism. Everything else is clean and clear. This question cannot be answered. The monists say the question itself is a contradiction.

Take the system of dualism — the question is asked why God created the world. This is contradictory. Why? Because — what is the idea of God? He is a being who cannot be acted upon by anything outside.

You and I are not free. I am thirsty. There is something called thirst, over which I have no control, [which] forces me to drink water. Every action of my body and even every thought of my mind is forced out of me. I have got to do it. That is why I am bound … I am forced to do this, to have this, and so on … And what is meant by why and wherefore? [Being subject to external forces.] Why do you drink water? Because thirst forces you. You are a slave. You never do anything of your own will because you are forced to do everything. Your only motive for action is some force …

The earth, by itself, would never move unless something forced it. Why does the light burn? It does not burn unless somebody comes and strikes a match. Throughout nature, everything is bound. Slavery, slavery! To be in harmony with nature is [slavery]. What is there in being the slave of nature and living in a golden cage? The greatest law and order is in the [knowledge that man is essentially free and divine] Now we see that the question why and wherefore can only be asked [in ignorance]. I can only be forced to do something through something else.

[You say] God is free. Again you ask the question why God creates the world. You contradict yourself. The meaning of God is entirely free will. The question put in logical language is this: What forced Him, who can never be forced by anybody, to create the world? You say in the same question, What forced Him? The question is nonsense. He is infinite by His very nature; He is free. We shall answer questions when you can ask them in logical language. Reason will tell you that there is only one Reality, nothing else. Wherever dualism has risen, monism came to a head and drove it out.

There is only one difficulty in understanding this. Religion is a common-sense, everyday thing. The man in the street knows it if you put it in his language and not [if it is put] in a philosopher's language. It is a common thing in human nature to [project itself]. Think of your feeling with the child. [You identify yourself with it. Then] you have two bodies. [Similarly] you can feel through your husband's mind Where can you stop? You can feel in infinite bodies.

Nature is conquered by man every day. As a race, man is manifesting his power. Try in imagination to put a limit to this power in man. You admit that man as a race has infinite power, has [an] infinite body. The only question is what you are. Are you the race or one [individual]? The moment you isolate yourself, everything hurts you. The moment you expand and feel for others, you gain help. The selfish man is the most miserable in the world. The happiest is the man who is not at all selfish. He has become the whole creation, the whole race and God [is] within him...So in dualism—Christian, Hindu, and all religions—the code of ethics...is: Do not be selfish...things for others! Expand!...

The ignorant can be made to understand [this] very easily, and the learned can be made to understand still more easily. But the man who has just got a speck of learning, him God himself cannot make understand. [The truth is,] you are not separate [from this universe]; Just as your Spirit] is [not] separate from the rest of you. If [not] so, you could not see anything, could not feel anything. Our bodies are simply little whirlpools in the ocean of matter. Life is taking a turn and passing on, in another form...The sun, the moon, the stars, you and I are mere whirlpools. Why did I select [a particular mind as mine? It is] simply a mental whirlpool in the ocean of mind.

How else is it possible that my vibration reaches you just now? If you throw a stone in the lake, it raises a vibration and [that stirs] the water into vibration. I throw my mind into the state of bliss and the tendency is to raise the same bliss in your mind. How often in your mind or heart [you have thought something] and without [verbal] communication, [others have got your thought]? Everywhere we are one...That is what we never understand. The whole [universe] is composed of time, space, and causation. And God [appears as this universe]...When did nature begin? When you [forgot your true nature and] became [bound by time, space, and causation].

This is the [rotating] circle of your bodies and yet that is your infinite nature...That is certainly nature—time, space, and causation. That is all that is meant by nature. Time began when you began to think. Space began when you got the body; otherwise there cannot be any space. Causation began when you became limited. We have to have some sort of answer. There is the answer. [Our limitation] is play. Just for the fun of it. Nothing binds you; nothing forces [you. You were] never bound. We are all acting our parts in this [play] of our own invention.

But let us bring another question about individuality. Some people are so afraid of losing their individuality. Wouldn't it be better for the pig to lose his pig-individuality if he can become God? Yes. But the poor pig does not think so at the time. Which state is my individuality? When I was a baby sprawling on the floor trying to swallow my thumb? Was that the individuality I should be sorry to lose? Fifty years hence I shall look upon this present state and laugh, just as I [now] look upon the baby state. Which of these individualities shall I keep ?...

We are to understand what is meant by this individuality...[There are two opposite tendencies:] one is the protection of the individuality, the other is the intense desire to sacrifice the individuality...The mother sacrifices all her own will for the needy baby...When she carries the baby in her arms, the call of individuality, of self-preservation is no more heard. She will eat the worst food, but her children will have the best. So for all the people we love we are ready to die.

[On the one hand] we are struggling hard to keep up this individuality; on the other hand, trying to kill it. With what result? Tom Brown may struggle hard. He is [fighting] for his individuality. Tom dies and there is not a ripple anywhere upon the surface of the earth. There was a Jew born nineteen hundred years ago, and he never moved a finger to keep his individuality...Think of that! That Jew never struggled to protect his individuality. That is why he became the greatest in the world. This is what the world does not know.

In time we are to be individuals. But in what sense? What is the individuality of man? Not Tom Brown, but God in man. That is the [true] individuality. The more man has approached that, the more he has given up his false individuality. The more he tries to collect and gain everything [for himself], the less he is an individual. The less he has thought of [himself], the more he has sacrificed all individuality during his lifetime,...the more he is an individual. This is one secret the world does not understand.

We must first understand what is meant by individuality. It is attaining the ideal. You are man now, [or] you are woman. You will change all the time. Can you stop? Do you want to keep your minds as they are now—the angels, hatreds, jealousies, quarrels, all the thousand and one things in the mind? Do you mean to say that you will keep them?...You cannot stop anywhere...until perfect conquest has been achieved, until you are pure and you are perfect.

You have no more anger when you are all love, bliss, infinite existence...Which of your bodies will you keep? You cannot stop anywhere until you come to life that never ends. Infinite life! You stop there. You have a little knowledge now and are always trying to get more. Where will you stop? Nowhere, until you become one with life itself...

Many want pleasure [as] the goal. For that pleasure they seek only the senses. On the higher planes much pleasure is to be sought. Then on spiritual planes. Then in himself—God within him. The man whose pleasure is outside of [himself] becomes unhappy when that outside thing goes. You cannot depend for this pleasure upon anything in this universe. If all my pleasures are in myself, I must have pleasure there all the time because I can never lose my Self...Mother, father, child, wife, body, wealth—everything I can lose except my self...bliss in the Self All desire is contained in the Self...This is individuality which never changes, and this is perfect.

...And how to get it? They find what the great souls of this world—all great men and women—found [through sustained discrimination]...What of these dualistic theories of twenty gods, thirty gods? It does not matter. They all had the one truth, that this false individuality must go...So this ego—the less there is of it, the nearer I am to that which I really am: the universal body. The less I think of my own individual mind, the nearer I am to that universal mind. The less I think of my own soul, the nearer I am to the universal soul.

We live in one body. We have some pain, some pleasure. Just for this little pleasure we have by living in this body, we are ready to kill everything in the universe to preserve ourselves. If we had two bodies, would not that be much better? So on and on to bliss. I am in everybody. Through all hands I work; through all feet I walk. I speak through every mouth; I live in every body. Infinite my bodies, infinite my minds. I lived in Jesus of Nazareth, in Buddha, in Mohammed—in all the great and good of the past, of the present. I am going to live in all that [may] come afterwards. Is that theory [No, it is the truth.]

If you can realise this, how infinitely more pleasurable that will be. What an ecstasy of joy! Which one body is so great that we need here anything [of] the body...After living in all the bodies of others, all the bodies there are in this world, what becomes of us? [We become one with the Infinite. And] that is the goal. That is the only way. One [man] says, "If I know the truth, I shall be melted away like butter." I wish people would be, but they are too tough to be melted so quickly!

What are we to do to be free? Free you are already...How could the free ever be bound? It is a lie. [You were] never bound. How could the unlimited ever be limited by anything? Infinite divided by infinite, added to infinite, multi-

plied by infinite [remains] infinite. You are infinite; God is infinite. You are all infinite. There cannot be two existences, only one. The Infinite can never be made finite. You are never bound. That is all...You are free already. You have reached the goal—all there is to reach. Never allow the mind to think that you have not reached the goal...

Whatever we [think] that we become. If you think you are poor sinners you hypnotise yourselves: "I am a miserable, crawling worm." Those who believe in hell are in hell when they die; those who say that they will go to heaven [go to heaven].

It is all play...[You may say,] "We have to do something; let us do good." [But] who cares for good and evil? Play! God Almighty plays. That is all...You are the almighty God playing. If you want to play on the side and take the part of a beggar, you are not [to blame someone else for making that choice]. You enjoy being the beggar. You know your real nature [to be divine]. You are the king and play you are a beggar...It is all fun. Know it and play. That is all there is to it. Then practice it. The whole universe is a vast play. All is good because all is fun. This star comes and crashes with our earth, and we are all dead. [That too is fun.] You only think fun the little things that delight your senses!...

[We are told that there is] one good god here, and one bad god there always on the watch to grab me the moment I make a mistake...When I was a child I was told by someone that God watches everything. I went to bed and looked up and expected the ceiling of the room to open. [Nothing happened.] Nobody is watching us except ourselves. No Lord except our [own Self]; no nature but what we feel. Habit is second nature; it is first nature also. It is all there is of nature. I repeat [something] two or three times; it becomes my nature. Do not be miserable! Do not repent! What is done is done. If you burn yourself, [take the consequences].

...Be sensible. We make mistakes; what of that? That is all in fun. They go so crazy over their past sins, moaning and weeping and all that. Do not repent! After having done work, do not think of it. Go on! Stop not! Don't look back! What will you gain by looking back? You lose nothing, gain nothing. You are not going to be melted like butter. Heavens and hells and incarnations—all nonsense!

Who is born and who dies? You are having fun, playing with worlds and all that. You keep this body as long as you like. If you do not like it, do not have it. The Infinite is the real; the finite is the play. You are the infinite body and the finite body in one. Know it! But knowledge will not make any difference; the play will go on...Two words—soul and body—have been joined. [Partial] knowledge is the cause. Know that you are always free. The fire of knowledge burns down all the [impurities and limitations]. I am that Infinite...

You are as free as you were in the beginning, are now, and always will be. He who knows that he is free is free; he who knows that he is bound is bound.

What becomes of God and worship and all that? They have their place. I have divided myself into God and me; I become the worshipped and I worship myself. Why not? God is I. Why not worship my Self? The universal God—He is also my Self. It is all fun. There is no other purpose.

What is the end and aim of life? None, because I [know that I am the Infinite]. If you are beggars, you can have aims. I have no aims, no want, no purpose. I come to your country, and lecture—just for fun. No other meaning. What meaning can be there? Only slaves do actions for somebody else. You do actions for nobody else. When it suits you, you worship. You can join the Christians, the Mohammedans, the Chinese, the Japanese. You can worship all the gods that ever were and are ever going to be…

I am in the sun, the moon, and the stars. I am with God and I am in all the gods. I worship my Self.

There is another side to it. I have kept it in reserve. I am the man that is going to be hanged. I am all the wicked. I am getting punished in hells. That [also] is fun. This is the goal of philosophy [to know that I am the Infinite]. Aims, motives, purposes, and duties live in the background…

This truth is first to be listened to then to be thought about. Reason, argue it out by all manner of means. The enlightened know no more than that. Know it for certain that you are in everything. That is why you should not hurt anybody, because in hurting them you hurt yourself…[Lastly,] this is to be meditated upon. Think upon it. Can you realise there will come a time when everything will crumble in the dust and you will stand alone? That moment of ecstatic joy will never leave you. You will actually find that you are without bodies. You never had bodies.

I am One, alone, through all eternity. Whom shall I fear? It is all my Self. This is continuously to be meditated upon. Through that comes realisation. It is through realisation that you become a [blessing] to others…

"Thy face shines like [that of] one who has known God."[1] That is the goal. This is not to be preached as I am doing. "Under a tree I saw a teacher, a boy of sixteen; the disciple was an old man of eighty. The teacher was teaching in silence, and the doubts of the disciple vanished."[2] And who speaks? Who lights a candle to see the sun? When the truth [dawns], no witness is necessary. You know it… That is what you are going to do: … realise it. [first think of it. Reason it out. Satisfy your curiosity. Then [think] of nothing else. I wish we never read anything. Lord help us all! Just see what [a learned] man becomes.

"This is said, and that is said…"

"What do *you* say, my friend?"

"I say nothing." [He quotes] everybody else's thought; but he thinks nothing. If this is education, what is lunacy? Look at all the men who wrote!…These modern writers, not two sentences their own! All quotations…

There is not much value in books, and in [secondhand] religion there is no value whatsoever. It is like eating. Your religion would not satisfy me Jesus saw God and Buddha saw God. If you have not seen God, you are no better than the atheist. Only he is quiet, and you talk much and disturb the world with your talk. Books and bibles and scriptures are of no use. I met an old man when I was a boy; [he did not study any scripture, but he transmitted the truth of God by a touch].

Silence ye teachers of the world. Silence ye books. Lord, Thou alone speak and Thy servant listeneth…If truth is not there, what is the use of this life? We all think we will catch it, but we do not. Most of us catch only dust. God is not there. If no God, what is the use of life? Is there any resting-place in the universe? [It is up to us to find it]; only we do not [search for it intensely. We are] like a little piece of maw carried on in the current.

If there is this truth, if there is God, it must be within us…[I must be able to say,] "I have seen Him with my eyes," Otherwise I have no religion. Beliefs, doctrines, sermons do not make religion. It is realisation, perception of God [which alone is religion]. What is the glory of all these men whom the world worships? God was no more a doctrine [for them. Did they believe] because their grandfather believed it? No. It was the realisation of the Infinite, higher than their own bodies, minds, and everything. This world is real inasmuch as it contains a little bit [of] the reflection of that God. We love the good man because in his face shines the reflection a little more. We must catch it ourselves. There is no other way.

That is the goal. Struggle for it! Have your own Bible. Have your own Christ. Otherwise you are not religious. Do not talk religion. Men talk and talk. "Some of them, steeped in darkness, in the pride of their hearts think that they have the light. And not only [that], they offer to take others upon their shoulders and both fall into the pit."[3]…

No church ever saved by itself. It is good to be born in a temple, but woe unto the person who dies in a temple or church. Out of it!…It was a good beginning, but leave it! It was the childhood place…but let it be!…Go to God directly. No theories, no doctrines. Then alone will all doubts vanish. Then alone will all crookedness be made straight…

In the midst of the manifold, he who sees that One; in the midst of this infinite death, he who sees that one life; in the midst of the manifold, he who sees that which never changes in his own soul—unto him belongs eternal peace.

UNITY, THE GOAL OF RELIGION

Delivered in New York, 1896

This universe of ours, the universe of the senses, the rational,

---

1. Chhândogya. IV. ix. 2.

2. Dakshinâmurtistotram, 12.

3. Katha, I. ii. 5.

the intellectual, is bounded on both sides by the illimitable, the unknowable, the ever unknown. Herein is the search, herein are the inquiries, here are the facts; from this comes the light which is known to the world as religion. Essentially, however, religion belongs to the supersensuous and not to the sense plane. It is beyond all reasoning and is not on the plane of intellect. It is a vision, an inspiration, a plunge into the unknown and unknowable, making the unknowable more than known for it can never be "known". This search has been in the human mind, as I believe, from the very beginning of humanity. There cannot have been human reasoning and intellect in any period of the world's history without this struggle, this search beyond. In our little universe, this human mind, we see a thought arise. Whence it arises we do not know; and when it disappears, where it goes, we know not either. The macrocosm and the microcosm are, as it were, in the same groove, passing through the same stages, vibrating in the same key.

I shall try to bring before you the Hindu theory that religions do not come from without, but from within. It is my belief that religious thought is in man's very constitution, so much so that it is impossible for him to give up religion until he can give up his mind and body, until he can give up thought and life. As long as a man thinks, this struggle must go on, and so long man must have some form of religion. Thus we see various forms of religion in the world. It is a bewildering study; but it is not, as many of us think, a vain speculation. Amidst this chaos there is harmony, throughout these discordant sounds there is a note of concord; and he who is prepared to listen to it will catch the tone.

The great question of all questions at the present time is this: Taking for granted that the known and the knowable are bounded on both sides by the unknowable and the infinitely unknown, why struggle for that infinite unknown? Why shall we not be content with the known? Why shall we not rest satisfied with eating, drinking, and doing a little good to society? This idea is in the air. From the most learned professor to the prattling baby, we are told that to do good to the world is all of religion, and that it is useless to trouble ourselves about questions of the beyond. So much is this the case that it has become a truism.

But fortunately we must inquire into the beyond. This present, this expressed, is only one part of that unexpressed. The sense universe is, as it were, only one portion, one bit of that infinite spiritual universe projected into the plane of sense consciousness. How can this little bit of projection be explained, be understood, without. Knowing that which is beyond? It is said of Socrates that one day while lecturing at Athens, he met a Brahmin who had travelled into Greece, and Socrates told the Brahmin that the greatest study for mankind is man. The Brahmin sharply retorted: "How can you know man until you know Gods" This God, this eternally Unknowable, or Absolute, or Infinite, or without name—you may call Him by what name you like—is the rationale, the only explanation, the raison d'être of that which is known and knowable, this present life. Take anything before you, the most material thing—take one of the most material sciences, as chemistry or physics, astronomy or biology—study it, push the study forward and forward, and the gross forms will begin to melt and become finer and finer, until they come to a point where you are bound to make a tremendous leap from these material things into the immaterial. The gross melts into the fine, physics into metaphysics, in every department of knowledge.

Thus man finds himself driven to a study of the beyond. Life will be a desert, human life will be vain, if we cannot know the beyond. It is very well to say: Be contented with the things of the present. The cows and the dogs are, and so are all animals; and that is what makes them animals. So if man rests content with the present and gives up all search into the beyond, mankind will have to go back to the animal plane again. It is religion, the inquiry into the beyond, that makes the difference between man and an animal. Well has it been said that man is the only animal that naturally looks upwards; every other animal naturally looks down. That looking upward and going upward and seeking perfection are what is called salvation; and the sooner a man begins to go higher, the sooner he raises himself towards this idea of truth as salvation. It does not consist in the amount of money in your pocket, or the dress you wear, or the house you live in, but in the wealth of spiritual thought in your brain. That is what makes for human progress, that is the source of all material and intellectual progress, the motive power behind, the enthusiasm that pushes mankind forward.

Religion does not live on bread, does not dwell in a house. Again and again you hear this objection advanced: "What good can religion do? Can it take away the poverty of the poor?" Supposing it cannot, would that prove the untruth of religion? Suppose a baby stands up among you when you are trying to demonstrate an astronomical theorem, and says, "Does it bring gingerbread?" "No, it does not", you answer. "Then," says the baby, "it is useless." Babies judge the whole universe from their own standpoint, that of producing gingerbread, and so do the babies of the world. We must not judge of higher things from a low standpoint. Everything must be judged by its own standard and the infinite must be judged by the standard of infinity. Religion permeates the whole of man's life, not only the present, but the past, present, and future. It is, therefore, the eternal relation between the eternal soul and the eternal God. Is it logical to measure its value by its action upon five minutes of human life? Certainly not. These are all negative arguments.

Now comes the question: Can religion really accomplish anything? It can. It brings to man eternal life. It has made man what he is, and will make of this human animal a god. That is what religion can do. Take religion from human society and what will remain? Nothing but a forest of brutes. Sense-happiness is not the goal of humanity. Wisdom (Jnâna) is the goal of all life. We find that man enjoys his intellect more than an animal enjoys its senses; and we see that man enjoys his spiritual nature even more than his rational nature. So the highest wisdom must be this spiritual knowledge. With this knowledge will come bliss. All these things of this world are but the shadows, the manifestations in the third or fourth degree of the real Knowledge and Bliss.

One question more: What is the goal? Nowadays it is asserted that man is infinitely progressing, forward and forward, and there is no goal of perfection to attain to. Ever approaching, never attaining, whatever that may mean and however wonderful it may be, it is absurd on the face of it. Is there any motion in a straight line? A straight line infinitely projected becomes a circle, it returns to the starting point. You must end where you begin; and as you began in God, you must go back to God. What remains? Detail work. Through eternity you have to do the detail work.

Yet another question: Are we to discover new truths of religion as we go on? Yea and nay. In the first place, we cannot know anything more of religion, it has all been known. In all religions of the world you will find it claimed that there is a unity within us. Being one with divinity, there cannot be any further progress in that sense. Knowledge means finding this unity. I see you as men and women, and this is variety. It becomes scientific knowledge when I group you together and call you human beings. Take the science of chemistry, for instance. Chemists are seeking to resolve all known substances into their original elements, and if possible, to find the one element from which all these are derived. The time may come when they will find one element that is the source of all other elements. Reaching that, they can go no further; the science of chemistry will have become perfect. So it is with the science of religion. If we can discover this perfect unity, there cannot be any further progress.

The next question is: Can such a unity be found? In India the attempt has been made from the earliest times to reach a science of religion and philosophy, for the Hindus do not separate these as is customary in Western countries. We regard religion and philosophy as but two aspects of one thing which must equally be grounded in reason and scientific truth.

The system of the Sânkhya philosophy is one of the most ancient in India, or in fact in the world. Its great exponent Kapila is the father of all Hindu psychology; and the ancient system that he taught is still the foundation of all accepted systems of philosophy in India today which are known as the Darshanas. They all adopt his psychology, however widely they differ in other respects.

The Vedanta, as the logical outcome of the Sankhya, pushes its conclusions yet further. While its cosmology agrees with that taught by Kapila, the Vedanta is not satisfied to end in dualism, but continues its search for the final unity which is alike the goal of science and religion.

THE FREE SOUL

Delivered in New York, 1896

The analysis of the Sânkhyas stops with the duality of existence—Nature and souls. There are an infinite number of souls, which, being simple, cannot die, and must therefore be separate from Nature. Nature in itself changes and manifests all these phenomena; and the soul, according to the Sankhyas, is inactive. It is a simple by itself, and Nature works out all these phenomena for the liberation of the soul; and liberation consists in the soul discriminating that it is not Nature. At the same time we have seen that the Sankhyas were bound to admit that every soul was omnipresent. Being a simple, the soul cannot be limited, because all limitation comes either through time, space, or causation. The soul being entirely beyond these cannot have any limitation. To have limitation one must be in space, which means the body; and that which is body must be in Nature. If the soul had form, it would be identified with Nature; therefore the soul is formless, and that which is formless cannot be said to exist here, there, or anywhere. It must be omnipresent. Beyond this the Sankhya philosophy does not go.

The first argument of the Vedantists against this is that this analysis is not a perfect one. If their Nature be absolute and the soul be also absolute, there will be two absolutes, and all the arguments that apply in the case of the soul to show that it is omnipresent will apply in the case of Nature, and Nature too will be beyond all time, space, and causation, and as the result there will be no change or manifestation. Then will come the difficulty of having two absolutes, which is impossible. What is the solution of the Vedantist? His solution is that, just as the Sankhyas say, it requires some sentient Being as the motive power behind, which makes the mind think and Nature work, because Nature in all its modifications, from gross matter up to Mahat (Intelligence), is simply insentient. Now, says the Vedantist, this sentient Being which is behind the whole universe is what we call God, and consequently this universe is not different from Him. It is He Himself who has become this universe. He not only is the instrumental cause of this universe, but also the material cause. Cause is never different from effect, the effect is but the cause reproduced in another form. We see that every day. So this Being is the cause of Nature. All the forms and phases of Vedanta, either dualistic, or qualified-monistic, or monistic, first take this position that God is not only the instrumental, but also the material cause of this universe, that everything which exists is He. The second step in Vedanta is that these souls are also a part of God, one spark of that Infinite Fire. "As from a mass of fire millions of small particles fly, even so from this Ancient One have come all these souls." So far so good, but it does not yet satisfy. What is meant by a part of the Infinite? The Infinite is indivisible; there cannot be parts of the Infinite. The Absolute cannot be divided. What is meant, therefore, by saying that all these sparks are from Him? The Advaitist, the non-dualistic Vedantist, solves the problem by maintaining that there is really no part; that each soul is really not a part of the Infinite, but actually is the Infinite Brahman. Then how can there be so many? The sun reflected from millions of globules of water appears to be millions of suns, and in each globule is a miniature picture of the sun-form; so all these souls are but reflections and not real. They are not the real "I" which is the God of this universe, the one undivided Being of the universe. And all these little different beings, men and animals etc. are but reflections, and not real. They are simply illusory reflections upon Nature. There is but one Infinite Being in the universe, and that Being appears as you and as I; but this appearance of divisions is after all a delusion. He has not been divided, but only appears to be divided. This apparent division is caused by looking at Him through the network of time, space, and causation. When I look at God through the network of time, space, and causation, I see Him as the material world. When I look at Him from a little higher plane, yet through the same network, I see Him as an animal, a little higher as a man, a little higher as a god, but yet He is the One Infinite Being of the universe, and that Being we are. I am That, and you are That. Not parts of It, but the whole of It. "It is the Eternal Knower standing behind the whole phenomena; He Himself is the phenomena." He is both the subject and the object, He is the "I" and the "You". How is this? "How to know the Knower? The Knower cannot know Himself; I see everything but cannot see myself. The Self, the Knower, the Lord of all, the Real Being, is the cause of all the vision that is in the universe, but it is impossible for Him to see Himself or know Himself, excepting through reflection. You cannot see your own face except in a mirror, and so the Self cannot see Its own nature until It is reflected, and this whole universe therefore is the Self trying to realise Itself. This reflection is thrown back first from the protoplasm, then from plants and animals, and so on and on from better and better reflectors, until the best reflector, the perfect man, is reached—just as a man who, wanting to see his face, looks first in a little pool of muddy water, and sees just an outline; then he comes to clear water, and sees a better image; then to a piece of shining metal, and sees a still better image; and at last to a looking-glass, and sees himself reflected as he is. Therefore the perfect man is the highest reflection of that Being who is both subject and object. You now find why man instinctively worships everything, and how perfect men are instinctively worshipped as God in every country. You may talk as you like, but it is they who are bound to be worshipped. That is why men worship Incarnations, such as Christ or Buddha. They are the most perfect manifestations of the eternal Self. They are much higher than all the conceptions of God that you or I can make. A perfect man is much higher than such conceptions. In him the circle becomes complete; the subject and the object become one. In him all delusions go away and in their place comes the realisation that he has always been that perfect Being. How came this bondage then? How was it possible for this perfect Being to degenerate into the imperfect? How was it possible that the free became bound? The Advaitist says, he was never bound, but was always free. Various clouds of various colours come before the sky. They remain there a minute and then pass away. It is the same eternal blue sky stretching there for ever. The sky never changes: it is the cloud that is changing. So you are always perfect, eternally perfect. Nothing ever changes your nature, or ever will. All these ideas that I am imperfect, I am a man, or a woman, or a sinner, or I am the mind, I have thought, I will think—all are hallucinations; you never think, you never had a body; you never were imperfect. You are the blessed Lord of this universe, the one Almighty ruler of everything that is and ever will be, the one mighty ruler of these suns and stars and moons and earths and planets and all the little bits of our universe. It is through you that the sun shines and the stars shed their lustre, and the earth becomes beautiful. It is through your blessedness that they all love and are attracted to each other. You are in all, and you are all. Whom to avoid, and whom to take? You are the all in all. When this knowledge comes delusion immediately vanishes.

I was once travelling in the desert in India. I travelled for over a month and always found the most beautiful landscapes before me, beautiful lakes and all that. One day I was very thirsty and I wanted to have a drink at one of these lakes; but when I approached that lake it vanished. Immediately with a blow came into my brain the idea that this was a mirage about which I had read all my life; and then I remembered and smiled at my folly, that for the last month all the beautiful landscapes and lakes I had been seeing were this mirage, but I could not distinguish them then. The next morning I again began my march; there was the lake and the landscape, but with it immediately came the idea, "This is a mirage." Once known it had lost its power of illusion. So this illusion of the universe will break one day. The whole of this will vanish, melt away. This is realization. Philosophy is no joke or talk. It has to be realised; this body will vanish, this earth and everything will vanish, this idea that I am the body or the mind will for some time vanish, or if the Karma is ended it will disappear, never to come back; but if one part of the Karma remains, then as a potter's wheel, after the potter has finished the pot, will sometimes go on from the past momentum, so this body, when the delusion has vanished altogether, will go on for some time. Again this world will come, men and women and animals will come, just as the mirage came the next day, but not with the same force; along with it will come the idea that I know its nature now, and it will cause no bondage, no more pain, nor grief, nor misery. Whenever anything miserable will come, the mind will be able to say, "I know you as hallucination." When a man has reached that state, he is called Jivanmukta, living-free", free even while living. The aim and end in this life for the Jnâna-Yogi is to become this Jivanmukta, "living-free". He is Jivanmukta who can live in this world without being attached. He is like the lotus leaves in water, which are never wetted by the water. He is the highest of human beings, nay, the highest of all beings, for he has realised his identity with the Absolute, he has realised that he is one with God. So long as you think you have the least difference from God, fear will seize you, but when you have known that you are He, that there is no difference, entirely no difference, that you are He, all of Him, and the whole of Him, all fear ceases. "There, who sees whom? Who worships whom? Who talks to whom? Who hears whom? Where one sees another, where one talks to another, where one hears another, that is little. Where none sees none, where none speaks to none, that is the highest, that is the great, that is the Brahman." Being That, you are always That. What will become of the world then? What good shall we do to the world? Such questions do not arise "What becomes of my gingerbread if I become old?" says the baby! "What becomes of my marbles if I grow? So I will not grow," says the boy! "What will become of my dolls if I grow old?" says the little child! It is the same question in connection with this world, it has no existence in the past, present, or future. If we have known the Âtman as It is, if we have known that there is nothing else but this Atman, that everything else is but a dream, with no existence in reality, then this world with its poverties, its miseries, its wickedness, and its goodness will cease to disturb us. If they do not exist, for whom and for what shall we take trouble? This is what the Jnana-Yogis teach. Therefore, dare to be free, dare to go as far as your thought leads, and dare to carry that out in your life. It is very hard to come to Jnâna. It is for the bravest and most daring, who dare to smash all idols, not only intellectual, but in the senses. This body is not I; it must go. All sorts of curious things may come out of this. A man stands up and says, "I am not the body, therefore my headache must be cured"; but where is the headache if not in his body? Let a thousand headaches and a thousand bodies come and go. What is that to me? I have neither birth nor death; father or mother I never had; friends and foes I have none, because they are all I. I am my own friend, and I am my own enemy. I am Existence-Knowledge-Bliss Absolute. I am He, I am He. If in a thousand bodies I am suffering from fever and other ills, in millions of bodies I am healthy. If in a thousand bodies I am starving, in other thousand bodies I am feasting. If in thousands of bodies I am suffering misery, in thousands of bodies I am happy. Who shall blame whom, who praise whom? Whom to seek, whom to avoid? I seek none, nor avoid any, for I am all the universe. I praise myself, I blame myself, I suffer for myself, I am happy at my own will, I am free. This is the Jnâni, the brave and daring. Let the whole universe tumble down; he smiles and says it never existed, it was all a hallucination. He sees the universe tumble down. Where was it! Where has it gone!

Before going into the practical part, we will take up one more intellectual question. So far the logic is tremendously rigorous. If man reasons, there is no place for him to stand until he comes to this, that there is but One Existence, that everything else is nothing. There is no other way left for rational mankind but to take this view. But how is it that what is infinite, ever perfect, ever blessed, Existence-Knowledge-Bliss Absolute, has come under these delusions? It is the same question that has been asked all the world over. In the vulgar form the question becomes, "How did sin come into this world?" This is the most vulgar and sensuous form of the question, and the other is the most philosophic form, but the answer is the same. The same question has been asked in various grades and fashions, but in its lower forms it finds no solution, because the stories of apples and serpents and women do not give the explanation. In that state, the question is childish, and so is the answer. But the question has assumed very high proportions now: "How did this illusion come?" And the answer is as fine. The answer is that we cannot expect any answer to an impossible question. The very question is impossible in terms. You have no right to ask that question. Why? What is perfection? That which is beyond time, space, and causation—that is perfect. Then you ask how the perfect became imperfect. In logical language the question may be put in this form: "How did that which is beyond causation become caused?" You contradict yourself. You first admit it is beyond causation, and then ask what causes it. This question can only be asked within the limits of causation. As far as time and space and causation extend, so far can this question be asked. But beyond that it will be nonsense to ask it, because the question is illogical. Within time, space, and causation it can never be answered, and what answer may lie beyond these limits can only be known when we have transcended them; therefore the wise will let this question rest. When a man is ill, he devotes himself to curing his disease without insisting that he must first learn how he came to have it.

There is another form of this question, a little lower, but more practical and illustrative: What produced this delusion? Can any reality produce delusion? Certainly not. We see that one delusion produces another, and so on. It is delusion always that produces delusion. It is disease that produces disease, and not health that produces disease. The wave is the same thing as the water, the effect is the cause in another form. The effect is delusion, and therefore the cause must be delusion. What produced this delusion? Another delusion. And so on without beginning. The only question that remains for you to ask is: Does not this break your monism, because you get two existences in the universe, one yourself and the other the delusion? The answer is: Delusion cannot be called an existence. Thousands of dreams come into your life, but do not form any part of your life. Dreams come and go; they have no existence. To call delusion existence will be sophistry. Therefore there is only one individual existence in the universe, ever free, and ever blessed; and that is what you are. This is the last conclusion reached by the Advaitists.

It may then be asked: What becomes of all these various forms of worship? They will remain; they are simply groping in the dark for light, and through this groping light will come. We have just seen that the Self cannot see Itself. Our knowledge is within the network of Mâyâ (unreality), and beyond that is freedom. Within the network there is slavery, it is all under law; beyond that there is no law. So far as the universe is concerned, existence is ruled by law, and beyond that is freedom. As long as you are in the network of time, space, and causation, to say you are free is nonsense, because in that network all is under rigorous law, sequence, and consequence. Every thought that you think is caused, every feeling has been caused; to say that the will is free is sheer nonsense. It is only when the infinite existence comes, as it were, into this network of Maya that it takes the form of will. Will is a portion of that being, caught in the network of Maya, and therefore "free will" is a misnomer. It means nothing—sheer nonsense. So is all this talk about freedom. There is no freedom in Maya.

Every one is as much bound in thought, word, deed, and mind, as a piece of stone or this table. That I talk to you now is as rigorous in causation as that you listen to me. There is no freedom until you go beyond Maya. That is the real freedom of the soul. Men, however sharp and intellectual, however clearly they see the force of the logic that nothing here can be free, are all compelled to think they are free; they cannot help it. No work can go on until we begin to say we are free. It means that the freedom we talk about is the glimpse of the blue sky through the clouds and that the real freedom—the blue sky itself— is behind. True freedom cannot exist in the midst of this delusion, this hallucination, this nonsense of the world, this universe of the senses, body, and mind. All these dreams, without beginning or end, uncontrolled and uncontrollable, ill-adjusted, broken, inharmonious, form our idea of this universe. In a dream, when you see a giant with twenty heads chasing you, and you are flying from him, you do not think it is inharmonious; you think it is proper and right. So is this law. All that you call law is simply chance without meaning. In this dream state you call it law. Within Maya, so far as this law of time, space and causation exists, there is no freedom; and all these various forms of worship are within this Maya. The idea of God and the ideas of brute and of man are within this Maya, and as such are equally hallucinations; all of them are dreams. But you must take care not to argue like some extraordinary men of whom we hear at the present time. They say the idea of God is a delusion, but the idea of this world is true. Both ideas stand or fall by the same logic. He alone has the right to be an atheist who denies this world, as well as the other. The same argument is for both. The same mass of delusion extends from God to the lowest animal, from a blade of grass to the Creator. They stand or fall by the same logic. The same person who sees falsity in the idea of God ought also to see it in the idea of his own body or his own mind. When God vanishes, then also vanish the body and mind; and when both vanish, that which is the Real Existence remains for ever. "There the eyes cannot go, nor the speech, nor the mind. We cannot see it, neither know it." And we now understand that so far as speech and thought and knowledge and intellect go, it is all within this Maya within

bondage. Beyond that is Reality. There neither thought, nor mind, nor speech, can reach.

So far it is intellectually all right, but then comes the practice. The real work is in the practice. Are any practices necessary to realise this Oneness? Most decidedly. It is not that you become this Brahman. You are already that. It is not that you are going to become God or perfect; you are already perfect; and whenever you think you are not, it is a delusion. This delusion which says that you are Mr. So-and-so or Mrs. So-and-so can be got rid of by another delusion, and that is practice. Fire will eat fire, and you can use one delusion to conquer another delusion. One cloud will come and brush away another cloud, and then both will go away. What are these practices then? We must always bear in mind that we are not going to be free, but are free already. Every idea that we are bound is a delusion. Every idea that we are happy or unhappy is a tremendous delusion; and another delusion will come—that we have got to work and worship and struggle to be free—and this will chase out the first delusion, and then both will stop.

The fox is considered very unholy by the Mohammedans and by the Hindus. Also, if a dog touches any bit of food, it has to be thrown out, it cannot be eaten by any man. In a certain Mohammedan house a fox entered and took a little bit of food from the table, ate it up, and fled. The man was a poor man, and had prepared a very nice feast for himself, and that feast was made unholy, and he could not eat it. So he went to a Mulla, a priest, and said, "This has happened to me; a fox came and took a mouthful out of my meal. What can be done? I had prepared a feast and wanted so much to eat it, and now comes this fox and destroys the whole affair." The Mulla thought for a minute and then found only one solution and said, "The only way for you is to get a dog and make him eat a bit out of the same plate, because dogs and foxes are eternally quarrelling. The food that was left by the fox will go into your stomach, and that left by the dog will go there too, and both will be purified." We are very much in the same predicament. This is a hallucination that we are imperfect; and we take up another, that we have to practice to become perfect. Then one will chase the other, as we can use one thorn to extract another and then throw both away. There are people for whom it is sufficient knowledge to hear, "Thou art That". With a flash this universe goes away and the real nature shines, but others have to struggle hard to get rid of this idea of bondage.

The first question is: Who are fit to become Jnana-Yogis? Those who are equipped with these requisites: First, renunciation of all fruits of work and of all enjoyments in this life or another life. If you are the creator of this universe, whatever you desire you will have, because you will create it for yourself. It is only a question of time. Some get it immediately; with others the past Samskâras (impressions) stand in the way of getting their desires. We give the first place to desires for enjoyment, either in this or another life. Deny that there is any life at all; because life is only another name for death. Deny that you are a living being. Who cares for life? Life is one of these hallucinations, and death is its counterpart. Joy is one part of these hallucinations, and misery the other part, and so on. What have you to do with life or death ? These are all creations of the mind. This is called giving up desires of enjoyment either in this life or another.

Then comes controlling the mind, calming it so that it will not break into waves and have all sorts of desires, holding the mind steady, not allowing it to get into waves from external or internal causes, controlling the mind perfectly, just by the power of will. The Jnana-Yogi does not take any one of these physical helps or mental helps: simply philosophic reasoning, knowledge, and his own will, these are the instrumentalities he believes in. Next comes Titikshâ, forbearance, bearing all miseries without murmuring, without complaining. When an injury comes, do not mind it. If a tiger comes, stand there. Who flies? There are men who practice Titiksha, and succeed in it. There are men who sleep on the banks of the Ganga in the midsummer sun of India, and in winter float in the waters of the Ganga for a whole day; they do not care. Men sit in the snow of the Himalayas, and do not care to wear any garment. What is heat? What is cold? Let things come and go, what is that to me, I am not the body. It is hard to believe this in these Western countries, but it is better to know that it is done. Just as your people are brave to jump at the mouth of a cannon, or into the midst of the battlefield, so our people are brave to think and act out their philosophy. They give up their lives for it. "I am Existence-Knowledge-Bliss Absolute; I am He, I am He." Just as the Western ideal is to keep up luxury in practical life, so ours is to keep up the highest form of spirituality, to demonstrate that religion is riot merely frothy words, but can be carried out, every bit of it, in this life. This is Titiksha, to bear everything, not to complain of anything. I myself have seen men who say, "I am the soul; what is the universe to me? Neither pleasure nor pain, nor virtue nor vice, nor heat nor cold is anything to me." That is Titiksha; not running after the enjoyments of the body. What is religion? To pray, "Give me this and that"? Foolish ideas of religion! Those who believe them have no true idea of God and soul. My Master used to say, "The vulture rise higher and higher until he becomes a speck, but his eye is always on the piece of rotten carrion on the earth." After all, what is the result of your ideas of religion? To cleanse the streets and have more bread and clothes? Who cares for bread and clothes? Millions come and go every minute. Who cares? Why care for the joys and vicissitudes of this little world? Go beyond that if you dare; go beyond law, let the whole universe vanish, and stand alone. "I am Existence-Absolute, Knowledge-Absolute, Bliss-Absolute; I am He, I am He."

ONE EXISTENCE APPEARING AS MANY

Delivered in New York, 1896

Vairâgya or renunciation is the turning point in all the various Yogas. The Karmi (worker) renounces the fruits of his work. The Bhakta (devotee) renounces all little loves for the almighty and omnipresent love. The Yogi renounces his experiences, because his philosophy is that the whole Nature, although it is for the experience of the soul, at last brings him to know that he is not in Nature, but eternally separate from Nature. The Jnâni (philosopher) renounces everything, because his philosophy is that Nature never existed, neither in the past, nor present, nor will It in the future. The question of utility cannot be asked in these higher themes. It is very absurd to ask it; and even if it be asked, after a proper analysis, what do we find in this question of utility? The ideal of happiness, that which brings man more happiness, is of greater utility to him than these higher things which do not improve his material conditions or bring him such great happiness. All the sciences are for this one end, to bring happiness to humanity; and that which brings the larger amount of happiness, man takes and gives up that which brings a lesser amount of happiness. We have seen how happiness is either in the body, or in the mind, or in the Âtman. With animals, and in the lowest human beings who are very much like animals, happiness is all in the body. No man can eat with the same pleasure as a famished dog or a wolf; so in the dog and the wolf the happiness is entirely in the body. In men we find a higher plane of happiness, that of thought; and in the Jnani there is the highest plane of happiness in the Self, the Atman. So to the philosopher this knowledge of the Self is of the highest utility, because it gives him the highest happiness possible. Sense-gratifications or physical things cannot be of the highest utility to him, because he does not find in them the same pleasure that he finds in knowledge itself; and after all, knowledge is the one goal and is really the highest happiness that we know. All who work in ignorance are, as it were, the draught animals of the Devas. The word Deva is here used in the sense of a wise man. All the people that work and toil and labour like machines do not really enjoy life, but it is the wise man who enjoys. A rich man buys a picture at a cost of a hundred thousand dollars perhaps, but it is the man who understands art that enjoys it; and if the rich man is without knowledge of art, it is useless to him, he is only the owner. All over the world, it is the wise man who enjoys the happiness of the world. The ignorant man never enjoys; he has to work for others unconsciously.

Thus far we have seen the theories of these Advaitist philosophers, how there is but one Atman; there cannot be two. We have seen how in the whole of this universe there is but One Existence; and that One Existence when seen through the senses is called the world, the world of matter. When It is seen through the mind, It is called the world of thoughts and ideas; and when it is seen as it is, then It is the One Infinite Being. You must bear this in mind; it is not that there is a soul in man, although I had to take that for granted in order to explain it at first, but that there is only One Existence, and that one the Atman, the Self; and when this is perceived through the senses, through sense-imageries, It is called the body. When It is perceived through thought, It is called the mind. When It is perceived in Its own nature, It is the Atman, the One Only Existence. So it is not that there are three things in one, the body and the mind and the Self, although that was a convenient way of putting it in the course of explanation; but all is that Atman, and that one Being is sometimes called the body, sometimes the mind, and sometimes the Self, according to different vision. There is but one Being which the ignorant call the world. When a man goes higher in knowledge, he calls the very same Being the world of thought. Again, when knowledge itself comes, all illusions vanish, and man finds it is all nothing but Atman. I am that One Existence. This is the last conclusion. There are neither three nor two in the universe; it is all One. That One, under the illusion of Maya, is seen as many, just as a rope is seen as a snake. It is the very rope that is seen as a snake. There are not two things there, a rope separate and a snake separate. No man sees these two things there at the same time. Dualism and non-dualism are very good philosophic terms, but in perfect perception we never perceive the real and the false at the same time. We are all born monists, we cannot help it. We always perceive the one. When we perceive the rope, we do not perceive the snake at all; and when we see the snake, we do not see the rope at all—it has vanished. When you see illusion, you do not see reality. Suppose you see one of your friends coming at a distance in the street; you know him very well, but through the haze and mist that is before you, you think it is another man. When you see your friend as another man, you do not see your friend at all, he has vanished. You are perceiving only one. Suppose your friend is Mr. A; but when you perceive Mr. A as Mr. B. you do not see Mr. A at all. In each case you perceive only one. When you see yourself as a body, you are body and nothing else; and that is the perception of the vast majority of mankind. They may talk of soul and mind, and all these things, but what they perceive is the physical form, the touch, taste, vision, and so on. Again, with certain men in certain states of consciousness, they perceive themselves as thought. You know, of course, the story told of Sir Humphrey Davy, who was making experiments before his class with laughing-gas, and suddenly one of the tubes broke, and the gas escaping, he breathed it in. For some moments he remained like a statue. Afterwards he told his class that when he was in that state, he actually perceived that the whole world is made up of ideas. The gas, for a time, made him forget the consciousness of the body, and that very thing which he was seeing as the body, he began to perceive as ideas. When the consciousness rises still higher, when this little puny consciousness is gone for ever, that which is the Reality behind shines, and we see it as the One Existence-Knowledge-Bliss, the one Atman, the Universal. "One that is only Knowledge itself, One that is Bliss itself, beyond all compare, beyond all limit, ever free, never bound, infinite as the sky, unchangeable as the sky. Such a One will manifest Himself in your heart in meditation."

How does the Advaitist theory explain these various phases of heaven and hells and these various ideas we find in all religions? When a man dies, it is said that he goes to heaven or hell, goes here or there, or that when a man dies he is born again in another body either in heaven or in another world or somewhere. These are all hallucinations. Really speaking nobody is ever born or dies. There is neither heaven nor hell nor this world; all three never really existed. Tell a child a lot of ghost stories, add let him go out into the street in the evening. There is a little stump of a tree. What does the child see? A ghost, with hands stretched out, ready to grab him. Suppose a man comes from the corner of the street, wanting to meet his sweetheart; he sees that stump of the tree as the girl. A policeman coming from the street corner sees the stump as a thief. The thief sees it as a policeman. It is the same stump of a tree that was seen in various ways. The stump is the reality, and the visions of the stump are the projections of the various minds. There is one Being, this Self; It neither comes nor goes. When a man is ignorant, he wants to go to heaven or some place, and all his life he has been thinking and thinking of this; and when this earth dream vanishes, he sees this world as a heaven with Devas and angels flying about, and all such things. If a man all his life desires to meet his forefathers, he gets them all from Adam downwards, because he creates them. If a man is still more ignorant and has always been frightened by fanatics with ideas of hell, with all sorts of punishments, when he dies, he will see this very world as hell. All that is meant by dying or being born is simply changes in the plane of vision. Neither do you move, nor does that move upon which you project your vision. You are the permanent, the unchangeable. How can you come and go? It is impossible; you are omnipresent. The sky never moves, but the clouds move over the surface of the sky, and we may think that the sky itself moves, just as when you are in a railway train, you think the land is moving. It is not so, but it is the train which is moving. You are where you are; these dreams, these various clouds move. One dream follows another without connection. There is no such thing as law or connection in this world, but we are thinking that there is a great deal of connection. All of you have probably read Alice in Wonderland. It is the most wonderful book for children that has been written in this century When I read it, I was delighted; it was always in my head to write that sort of a book for children. What pleased me most in it was what you think most incongruous, that there is no connection there. One idea comes and jumps into another, without any connection. When you were children, you thought that the most wonderful connection. So this man brought back his thoughts of childhood, which were perfectly connected to him as a child, and composed this book for children. And all these books which men write, trying to make children swallow their own ideas as men, are nonsense. We too are grown-up children, that is all. The world is the same unconnected thing—Alice in Wonderland—with no connection whatever. When we see things happen a number of times in a certain sequence, we call it cause and effect, and say that the thing will happen again. When this dream changes, another dream will seem quite as connected as this. When we dream, the things we see all seem to be connected; during the dream we never think they are incongruous; it is only when we wake that we see the want of connection. When we wake from this dream of the world and compare it with the Reality, it will be found all incongruous nonsense, a mass of incongruity passing before us, we do not know whence or whither, but we know it will end; and this is called Maya, and is like masses of fleeting fleecy clouds. They represent all this changing existence, and the sun itself, the unchanging, is you. When you look at that unchanging Existence from the outside, you call it God; and when you look at it from the inside, you call it yourself. It is but one. There is no God separate from you, no God higher than you, the real "you". All the gods are little beings to you, all the ideas of God and Father in heaven are but your own reflection. God Himself is your image. "God created man after His own image." That is wrong. Man creates God after his own image. That is right. Throughout the universe we are creating gods after our own image. We create the god and fall down at his feet and worship him; and when this dream comes, we love it!

This is a good point to understand—that the sum and substance of this lecture is that there is but One Existence, and that One-Existence seen through different constitutions appears either as the earth, or heaven, or hell, or gods, or ghosts, or men, or demons, or world, or all these things. But among these many, "He who sees that One in this ocean of death, he who sees that One Life in this floating universe, who realises that One who never changes, unto him belongs eternal peace; unto none else, unto none else." This One existence has to be realised. How, is the next question. How is it to be realised? How is this dream to be broken, how shall we wake up from this dream that we are little men and women, and all such things? We are the Infinite Being of the universe and have become materialised into these little beings, men and women, depending upon the sweet word of one man, or the angry word of another, and so forth. What a terrible dependence, what a terrible slavery! I who am beyond all pleasure and pain, whose reflection is the whole universe, little bits of whose life are the suns and moons and stars—I am held down as a terrible slave! If you pinch my body, I feel pain. If one says a kind word, I begin to rejoice. See my condition—slave of the body, slave of the mind, slave of the world, slave of a good word, slave of a bad word, slave of passion, slave of happiness, slave of life, slave of death, slave of everything! This slavery has to be broken. How? "This Atman has first to be heard, then reasoned upon, and then meditated upon." This is the method of the Advaita Jnâni. The truth has to be heard, then reflected upon, and then to be constantly asserted. Think always, "I am Brahman". Every other thought must be cast aside as weakening. Cast aside every thought that says that you are men or women. Let body go, and mind go,

and gods go, and ghosts go. Let everything go but that One Existence. "Where one hears another, where one sees another, that is small; where one does not hear another, where one does not see another, that is Infinite." That is the highest when the subject and the object become one. When I am the listener and I am the speaker, when I am the teacher and I am the taught, when I am the creator and I am the created—then alone fear ceases; there is not another to make us afraid. There is nothing but myself, what can frighten me? This is to be heard day after day. Get rid of all other thoughts. Everything else must be thrown aside, and this is to be repeated continually, poured through the ears until it reaches the heart, until every nerve and muscle, every drop of blood tingles with the idea that I am He, I am He. Even at the gate of death say, "I am He". There was a man in India, a Sannyâsin, who used to repeat "Shivoham"—"I am Bliss Eternal"; and a tiger jumped on him one day and dragged him away and killed him; but so long as he was living, the sound came, "Shivoham, Shivoham". Even at the gate of death, in the greatest danger, in the thick of the battlefield, at the bottom of the ocean, on the tops of the highest mountains, in the thickest of the forest, tell yourself, "I am He, I am He". Day and night say, "I am He". It is the greatest strength; it is religion. "The weak will never reach the Atman." Never say, "O Lord, I am a miserable sinner." Who will help you? You are the help of the universe. What in this universe can help you? Where is the man, or the god, or the demon to help you? What can prevail over you? You are the God of the universe; where can you seek for help? Never help came from anywhere but from yourself. In your ignorance, every prayer that you made and that was answered, you thought was answered by some Being, but you answered the prayer yourself unknowingly. The help came from yourself, and you fondly imagined that some one was sending help to you. There is no help for you outside of yourself; you are the creator of the universe. Like the silkworm you have built a cocoon around yourself. Who will save you? Burst your own cocoon and come out as the beautiful butterfly, as the free soul. Then alone you will see Truth. Ever tell yourself, "I am He." These are words that will burn up the dross that is in the mind, words that will bring out the tremendous energy which is within you already, the infinite power which is sleeping in your heart. This is to be brought out by constantly hearing the truth and nothing else. Wherever there is thought of weakness, approach not the place. Avoid all weakness if you want to be a Jnani.

Before you begin to practice, clear your mind of all doubts. Fight and reason and argue; and when you have established it in your mind that this and this alone can be the truth and nothing else, do not argue any more; close your mouth. Hear not argumentation, neither argue yourself. What is the use of any more arguments? You have satisfied yourself, you have decided the question. What remains? The truth has now to be realised, therefore why waste valuable time in vain arguments? The truth has now to be meditated upon, and every idea that

Lectures & Discourses by **Swami Vivekananda**

strengthens you must be taken up and every thought that weakens you must be rejected. The Bhakta meditates upon forms and images and all such things and upon God. This is the natural process, but a slower one. The Yogi meditates upon various centres in his body and manipulates powers in his mind. The Jnani says, the mind does not exist, neither the body. This idea of the body and of the mind must go, must be driven off; therefore it is foolish to think of them. It would be like trying to cure one ailment by bringing in another. His meditation therefore is the most difficult one, the negative; he denies everything, and what is left is the Self. This is the most analytical way. The Jnani wants to tear away the universe from the Self by the sheer force of analysis. It is very easy to say, "I am a Jnani", but very hard to be really one. "The way is long", it is, as it were, walking on the sharp edge of a razor; yet despair not. "Awake, arise, and stop not until the goal is reached", say the Vedas.

So what is the meditation of the Jnani? He wants to rise above every idea of body or mind, to drive away the idea that he is the body. For instance, when I say, "I Swami", immediately the idea of the body comes. What must I do then? I must give the mind a hard blow and say, "No, I am not the body, I am the Self." Who cares if disease comes or death in the most horrible form? I am not the body. Why make the body nice? To enjoy the illusion once more? To continue the slavery? Let it go, I am not the body. That is the way of the Jnani. The Bhakta says, "The Lord has given me this body that I may safely cross the ocean of life, and I must cherish it until the journey is accomplished." The Yogi says, "I must be careful of the body, so that I may go on steadily and finally attain liberation." The Jnani feels that he cannot wait, he must reach the goal this very moment. He says, "I am free through eternity, I am never bound; I am the God of the universe through all eternity. Who shall make me perfect? I am perfect already." When a man is perfect, he sees perfection in others. When he sees imperfection, it is his own mind projecting itself. How can he see imperfection if he has not got it in himself? So the Jnani does not care for perfection or imperfection. None exists for him. As soon as he is free, he does not see good and evil. Who sees evil and good? He who has it in himself. Who sees the body? He who thinks he is the body. The moment you get rid of the idea that you are the body, you do not see the world at all; it vanishes for ever. The Jnani seeks to tear himself away from this bondage of matter by the force of intellectual conviction. This is the negative way—the "Neti, Neti"—"Not this, not this."

LECTURES FROM COLOMBO TO ALMORA

FIRST PUBLIC LECTURE IN THE EAST

Delivered in Colombo

After his memorable work in the West, Swami Vivekananda landed at Colombo on the afternoon of January 15, 1897, and was given a right royal reception by the Hindu community there. The following address of welcome was then presented to him:

SRIMAT VIVEKANANDA SWAMI

Revered Sir,

In pursuance of a resolution passed at a public meeting of the Hindus of the city of Colombo, we beg to offer you a hearty welcome to this Island. We deem it a privilege to be the first to welcome you on your return home from your great mission in the West.

We have watched with joy and thankfulness the success with which the mission has, under God's blessing, been crowned. You have proclaimed to the nations of Europe and America the Hindu ideal of a universal religion, harmonising all creeds, providing spiritual food for each soul according to its needs, and lovingly drawing it unto God. You have preached the Truth and the Way, taught from remote ages by a succession of Masters whose blessed feet have walked and sanctified the soil of India, and whose gracious presence and inspiration have made her, through all her vicissitudes, the Light of the World.

To the inspiration of such a Master, Shri Ramakrishna Paramahamsa Deva, and to your self-sacrificing zeal, Western nations owe the priceless boon of being placed in living contact with the spiritual genius of India, while to many of our own countrymen, delivered from the glamour of Western civilisation, the value of Our glorious heritage has been brought home.

By your noble work and example you have laid humanity under an obligation difficult to repay, and you have shed fresh lustre upon our Motherland. We pray that the grace of God may continue to prosper you and your work, and

We remain, Revered Sir,
Yours faithfully,
for and on behalf of the Hindus of Colombo,
P. Coomara Swamy,
Member of the Legislative Council of Ceylon,
Chairman of the Meeting.
A. Kulaveerasingham, Secretary.
Colombo, January, 1897.

The Swami gave a brief reply, expressing his appreciation of the kind welcome he had received. He took advantage of the opportunity to point out that the demonstration had not been made in honour of a great politician, or a great soldier, or a millionaire, but of a begging Sannyâsin, showing the tendency of the Hindu mind towards religion. He urged the necessity of keeping religion as the backbone of the national life if the nation were to live, and disclaimed any personal character for the welcome he had received, but insisted upon its being the recognition of a principle.

On the evening of the 16th the Swami gave the following public lecture in the Floral Hall:

What little work has been done by me has not been from any inherent power that resides in me, but from the cheers, the goodwill, the blessings that have followed my path in the West from this our very beloved, most sacred, dear Motherland. Some good has been done, no doubt, in the West, but specially to myself; for what before was the result of an emotional nature, perhaps, has gained the certainty of conviction and attained the power and strength of demonstration. Formerly I thought as every Hindu thinks, and as the Hon. President has just pointed out to you, that this is the Punya Bhumi, the land of Karma. Today I stand here and say, with the conviction of truth, that it is so. If there is any land on this earth that can lay claim to be the blessed Punya Bhumi, to be the land to which all souls on this earth must come to account for Karma, the land to which every soul that is wending its way Godward must come to attain its last home, the land where humanity has attained its highest towards gentleness, towards generosity, towards purity, towards calmness, above all, the land of introspection and of spirituality—it is India. Hence have started the founders of religions from the most ancient times, deluging the earth again and again with the pure and perennial waters of spiritual truth. Hence have proceeded the tidal waves of philosophy that have covered the earth, East or West, North or South, and hence again must start the wave which is going to spiritualise the material civilisation of the world. Here is the life-giving water with which must be quenched the burning fire of materialism which is burning the core of the hearts of millions in other lands. Believe me, my friends, this is going to be.

So much I have seen, and so far those of you who are students of the history of races are already aware of this fact. The debt which the world owes to our Motherland is immense. Taking country with country, there is not one race on this earth to which the world owes so much as to the patient Hindu, the mild Hindu. "The mild Hindu" sometimes is used as an expression of reproach; but if ever a reproach concealed a wonderful truth, it is in the term, "the mild Hindu", who has always been the blessed child of God. Civilisations have arisen in other parts of the world. In ancient times and in modern times, great ideas have emanated from strong and great races. In ancient and in modern times, wonderful ideas have been carried forward from one race to another. In ancient and in modern times, seeds of great truth and power have been cast abroad by the advancing tides of national life; but mark you, my friends, it has been always with the blast of war trumpets and with the march of embattled cohorts. Each idea had to be soaked in a deluge of blood. Each idea had to wade through the blood of millions of our fellow-beings. Each word of power had to be followed by the groans of millions, by the wails of orphans, by the tears of widows. This, in the main, other nations have taught; but India has for thousands of years peacefully existed. Here activity prevailed when even Greece did not exist, when Rome was not thought of, when the very fathers of the modern Europeans lived in the forests and painted themselves blue. Even earlier, when history has no record, and tradition dares not peer into the gloom of that intense past, even from then until now, ideas after ideas have marched out from her, but every word has been spoken with a blessing behind it and peace before it. We, of all nations of the world, have never been a conquering race, and that blessing is on our head, and therefore we live.

There was a time when at the sound of the march of big Greek battalions the earth trembled. Vanished from off the face of the earth, with not every a tale left behind to tell, gone is that ancient land of the Greeks. There was a time when the Roman Eagle floated over everything worth having in this world; everywhere Rome's power was felt and pressed on the head of humanity; the earth trembled at the name of Rome. But the Capitoline Hill is a mass of ruins, the spider weaves its web where the Caesars ruled. There have been other nations equally glorious that have come and gone, living a few hours of exultant and exuberant dominance and of a wicked national life, and then vanishing like ripples on the face of the waters. Thus have these nations made their mark on the face of humanity. But we live, and if Manu came back today he would not be bewildered, and would not find himself in a foreign land. The same laws are here, laws adjusted and thought out through thousands and thousands of years; customs, the outcome of the acumen of ages and the experience of centuries, that seem to be eternal; and as the days go by, as blow after blow of misfortune has been delivered upon them, such blows seem to have served one purpose only, that of making them stronger and more constant. And to find the centre of all this, the heart from which the blood flows, the mainspring of the national life, believe me when I say after my experience of the world, that it is here.

To the other nations of the world, religion is one among the many occupations of life. There is politics, there are the enjoyments of social life, there is all that wealth can buy or power can bring, there is all that the senses can enjoy; and among all these various occupations of life and all this searching after something which can give yet a little more whetting to the cloyed senses—among all these, there is perhaps a little bit of religion. But here, in India, religion is the one and the only occupation of life. How many of you know that there has been a Sino-Japanese War? Very few of you, if any. That there are tremendous political movements and socialistic movements trying to transform Western society, how many of you know? Very few indeed, if any. But that there was a Parliament of Religions in America, and that there was a Hindu Sannyâsin sent over there, I am astonished to find that even the cooly knows of it. That shows the way the wind blows, where the national life is. I used to read books written by globe-trotting travellers, especially foreigners, who deplored the ignorance of the Eastern masses, but I found out that it was partly true and at the same time partly untrue. If you ask a ploughman in England, or America, or France, or Germany to what party he belongs, he can tell you whether he belongs to the Radicals or the Conservatives, and for whom he is going to vote. In America he will say whether he is Republican or Democrat, and he even knows something about the silver question. But if you ask him about his religion, he will tell you that he goes to church and belongs to a certain denomination. That is all he knows, and he thinks it is sufficient.

Now, when we come to India, if you ask one of our ploughmen, "Do you know anything about politics?" He will reply, "What is that?" He does not understand the socialistic movements, the relation between capital and labour, and all that; he has never heard of such things in his life, he works hard and earns his bread. But you ask, "What is your religion?" he replies, "Look here, my friend, I have marked it on my forehead." He can give you a good hint or two on questions of religion. That has been my experience. That is our nation's life.

Individuals have each their own peculiarities, and each man has his own method of growth, his own life marked out for him by the infinite past life, by all his past Karma as we Hindus say. Into this world he comes with all the past on him, the infinite past ushers the present, and the way in which we use the present is going to make the future. Thus everyone born into this world has a bent, a direction towards which he must go, through which he must live, and what is true of the individual is equally true of the race. Each race, similarly, has a peculiar bent, each race has a peculiar raison d'être, each race has a peculiar mission to fulfil in the life of the world. Each race has to make its own result, to fulfil its own mission. Political greatness or military power is never the mission of our race; it never was, and, mark my words, it never will be. But there has been the other mission given to us, which is to conserve, to preserve, to accumulate, as it were, into a dynamo, all the spiritual energy of the race, and that concentrated energy is to pour forth in a deluge on the world whenever circumstances are propitious. Let the Persian or the Greek, the Roman, the Arab, or the Englishman march his battalions, conquer the world, and link the different nations together, and the philosophy and spirituality of India is ever ready to flow along the new-made channels into the veins of the nations of the world. The Hindu's calm brain must pour out its own quota to give to the sum total of human progress. India's gift to the world is the light spiritual.

Thus, in the past, we read in history that whenever there arose a greet conquering nation uniting the different races of the world, binding India with the other races, taking her out, as it were, from her loneliness and from her aloofness from the rest of the world into which she again and again cast herself, that whenever such a state has been brought about, the result has been the flooding of the world with Indian spiritual ideas. At the beginning of this century, Schopenhauer, the great German philosopher, studying from a not very clear translation of the Vedas made from an old translation into Persian and thence by a young Frenchman into Latin, says, "In the whole world there is no study so beneficial and so elevating as that of the Upanishads. It has been the solace of my life, it will be the solace of my death." This great German sage foretold that "The world is about to see a revolution in thought more extensive and more powerful than that which was witnessed by the Renaissance of Greek Literature", and today his predictions are coming to pass. Those who keep their eyes open, those who understand the workings in the minds of different nations of the West, those who are thinkers and study the different nations, will find the immense change that has been produced in the tone, the procedure, in the methods, and in the literature of the world by this slow, never-ceasing permeation of Indian thought.

But there is another peculiarity, as I have already hinted to you. We never preached our thoughts with fire and sword. If there is one word in the English language to represent the gift of India to the world, if there is one word in the English language to express the effect which the literature of India produces upon mankind, it is this one word, "fascination". It is the opposite of anything that takes you suddenly; it throws on you, as it were, a charm imperceptibly. To many, Indian thought, Indian manners; Indian customs, Indian philosophy, Indian literature are repulsive at the first sight; but let them persevere, let them read, let them become familiar with the great principles underlying these ideas, and it is ninety-nine to one that the charm will come over them, and fascination will be the result. Slow and silent, as the gentle dew that falls in the morning, unseen and unheard yet producing a most tremendous result, has been the work of the calm, patient, all-suffering spiritual race upon the world of thought.

Once more history is going to repeat itself. For today, under the blasting light of modern science, when old and apparently strong and invulnerable beliefs have been shattered to their very foundations, when special claims laid to the allegiance of mankind by different sects have been all blown into atoms and have vanished into air, when the sledge-hammer blows of modern antiquarian researches are pulverising like masses of porcelain all sorts of antiquated orthodoxies, when religion in the West is only in the hands of the ignorant and the knowing ones look down with scorn upon anything belonging to religion, here comes to the fore the philosophy of India, which displays the highest religious aspirations of the Indian mind, where the grandest philosophical facts have been the practical spirituality of the people. This naturally is coming to the rescue, the idea of the oneness of all, the Infinite, the idea of the Impersonal, the wonderful idea of the eternal soul of man, of the unbroken continuity in the march of beings, and the infinity of the universe. The old sects looked upon the world as a little mud-puddle and thought that time began but the other day. It was there in our old books, and only there that the grand idea of the infinite range of time, space, and causation, and above all, the infinite glory of the spirit of man governed all the search for religion. When the modern tremendous theories of evolution and conservation of energy and so forth are dealing death blows to all sorts of crude theologies, what can hold any more the allegiance of cultured humanity but the most wonderful, convincing, broadening, and ennobling ideas that can be found only in that most marvellous product of the soul of man, the wonderful voice of God, the Vedanta?

At the same time, I must remark that what I mean by our religion working upon the nations outside of India comprises only the principles, the background, the foundation upon which that religion is built. The detailed workings, the minute points which have been worked out through centuries of social necessity, little ratiocinations about manners and customs and social well-being, do not rightly find a place in the category of religion. We know that in our books a clear distinction is made between two sets of truths. The one set is that which abides for ever, being built upon the nature of man, the nature of the soul, the soul's relation to God, the nature of God, perfection, and so on; there are also the principles of cosmology, of the infinitude of creation, or more correctly speaking—projection, the wonderful law of cyclical procession, and so on—these are the eternal principles founded upon the universal laws in nature. The other set comprises the minor laws which guided the working of our everyday life They belong more properly to the Purânas, to the Smritis, and not to the Shrutis. These have nothing to do with the other principles. Even in our own nation these minor laws have been changing all the time. Customs of one age, of one Yuga, have not been the customs of another, and as Yuga comes after Yuga, they will still have to change. Great Rishis will appear and lead us to customs and manners that are suited to new environments.

The great principles underlying all this wonderful, infinite, ennobling, expansive view of man and God and the world have been produced in India. In India alone man has not stood up to fight for a little tribal God, saying "My God is true and yours is not true; let us have a good fight over it." It was only here that such ideas did not occur as fighting for little gods. These great underlying principles, being based upon the eternal nature of man, are as potent today for working for the good of the human race as they were thousands of years ago, and they will remain so, so tong as this earth remains, so long as the law of Karma remains, so long as we are born as individuals and have to work out our own destiny by our individual power.

And above all, what India has to give to the world is this. If we watch the growth and development of religions in dif-

ferent races, we shall always find this that each tribe at the beginning has a god of its own. If the tribes are allied to each other, these gods will have a generic name, as for example, all the Babylonian gods had. When the Babylonians were divided into many races, they had the generic name of Baal, just as the Jewish races had different gods with the common name of Moloch; and at the same time you will find that one of these tribes becomes superior to the rest, and lays claim to its own king as the king over all. Therefrom it naturally follows that it also wants to preserve its own god as the god of all the races. Baal-Merodach, said the Babylonians, was the greatest god; all the others were inferior. Moloch-Yahveh was the superior over all other Molochs. And these questions had to be decided by the fortunes of battle. The same struggle was here also. In India the same competing gods had been struggling with each other for supremacy, but the great good fortune of this country and of the world was that there came out in the midst of the din and confusion a voice which declared एकं सद्विप्रा बहुधा वदन्ति—"That which exists is One; sages call It by various names." It is not that Shiva is superior to Vishnu, not that Vishnu is everything and Shiva is nothing, but it is the same one whom you call either Shiva, or Vishnu, or by a hundred other names. The names are different, but it is the same one. The whole history of India you may read in these few words. The whole history has been a repetition in massive language, with tremendous power, of that one central doctrine. It was repeated in the land till it had entered into the blood of the nation, till it began to tingle with every drop of blood that flowed in its veins, till it became one with the life, part and parcel of the material of which it was composed; and thus the land was transmuted into the most wonderful land of toleration, giving the right to welcome the various religions as well as all sects into the old mother-country.

And herein is the explanation of the most remarkable phenomenon that is only witnessed here—all the various sects, apparently hopelessly contradictory, yet living in such harmony. You may be a dualist, and I may be a monist. You may believe that you are the eternal servant of God, and I may declare that I am one with God Himself; yet both of us are good Hindus. How is that possible? Read then एकं सद्विप्रा बहुधा वदन्ति—"That which exists is One; sages call It by various names." Above all others, my countrymen, this is the one grand truth that we have to teach to the world. Even the most educated people of other countries turn up their noses at an angle of forty-five degrees and call our religion idolatry. I have seen that; and they never stopped to think what a mass of superstition there was in their own heads. It is still so everywhere, this tremendous sectarianism, the low narrowness of the mind. The thing which a man has is the only thing worth having; the only life worth living is his own little life of dollar-worship and mammon-worship; the only little possession worth having is his own property, and nothing else. If he can manufacture a little clay nonsense or invent a machine, that is to be admired beyond the greatest possessions. That is the case over the whole world in spite of education and learning. But education has yet to be in the world, and civilisation—civilisation has begun nowhere yet. Ninety-nine decimal nine per cent of the human race are more or less savages even now. We may read of these things in books, and we hear of toleration in religion and all that, but very little of it is there yet in the world; take my experience for that. Ninety-nine per cent do not even think of it. There is tremendous religious persecution yet in every country in which I have been, and the same old objections are raised against learning anything new. The little toleration that is in the world, the little sympathy that is yet in the world for religious thought, is practically here in the land of the Aryan, and nowhere else. It is here that Indians build temples for Mohammedans and Christians; nowhere else. If you go to other countries and ask Mohammedans or people of other religions to build a temple for you, see how they will help. They will instead try to break down your temple and you too if they can. The one great lesson, therefore, that the world wants most, that the world has yet to learn from India, is the idea not only of toleration, but of sympathy. Well has it been said in the Mahimnah-stotra: "As the different rivers, taking their start from different mountains, running straight or crooked, at last come unto the ocean, so, O Shiva, the different paths which men take through different tendencies, various though they appear, crooked or straight, all lead unto These." Though they may take various roads, all are on the ways. Some may run a little crooked, others may run straight, but at last they will all come unto the Lord, the One. Then and then alone, is your Bhakti of Shiva complete when you not only see Him in the Linga, but you see Him everywhere. He is the sage, he is the lover of Hari who sees Hari in everything and in everyone. If you are a real lover of Shiva, you must see Him in everything and in everyone. You must see that every worship is given unto Him whatever may be the name or the form; that all knees bending towards the Caaba, or kneeling in a Christian church, or in a Buddhist temple are kneeling to Him whether they know it or not, whether they are conscious of it or not; that in whatever name or form they are offered, all these flowers are laid at His feet; for He is the one Lord of all, the one Soul of all souls. He knows infinitely better what this world wants than you or I. It is impossible that all difference can cease; it must exist; without variation life must cease. It is this clash, the differentiation of thought that makes for light, for motion, for everything. Differentiation, infinitely contradictory, must remain, but it is not necessary that we should hate each other therefore; it is not necessary therefore that we should fight each other.

Therefore we have again to learn the one central truth that was preached only here in our Motherland, and that has to be preached once more from India. Why? Because not only is it in our books, but it runs through every phase of our national literature and is in the national life. Here and here alone is it practiced every day, and any man whose eyes are open can see that it is practiced here and here alone. Thus we have to teach religion. There are other and higher lessons that India can teach, but they are only for the learned. The lessons of mildness, gentleness, forbearance, toleration, sympathy, and brotherhood, everyone may learn, whether man, woman, or child, learned or unlearned, without respect of race, caste, or creed. "They call Thee by various names; Thou art One."

VEDANTISM

The following address of welcome from the Hindus of Jaffna was presented to Swami Vivekananda:

SRIMAT VIVEKANANDA SWAMI

Revered Sir,

We, the inhabitants of Jaffna professing the Hindu religion, desire to offer you a most hearty welcome to our land, the chief centre of Hinduism in Ceylon, and to express our thankfulness for your kind acceptance of our invitation to visit this part of Lanka.

Our ancestors settled here from Southern India, more than two thousand years ago, and brought with them their religion, which was patronised by the Tamil kings of Jaffna; but when their government was displaced by that of the Portuguese and the Dutch, the observance of religious rites was interfered with, public religious worship was prohibited, and the Sacred Temples, including two of the most far-famed Shrines, were razed to the ground by the cruel hand of persecution. In spite of the persistent attempts of these nations to force upon our forefathers the Christian religion, they clung to their old faith firmly, and have transmitted it to us as the noblest of our heritages Now under the rule of Great Britain, not only has there been a great and intelligent revival, but the sacred edifices have been, and are being, restored.

We take this opportunity to express our deep-felt gratitude for your noble and disinterested labours in the cause of our religion in carrying the light of truth, as revealed in the Vedas, to the Parliament of Religions, in disseminating the truths of the Divine Philosophy of India in America and England, and in making the Western world acquainted with the truths of Hinduism and thereby bringing the West in closer touch with the East. We also express our thankfulness to you for initiating a movement for the revival of our ancient religion in this materialistic age when there is a decadence of faith and a disregard for search after spiritual truth.

We cannot adequately express our indebtedness to you for making the people of the West know the catholicity of our religion and for impressing upon the minds of the savants of the West the truth that there are more things in the Philosophy of the Hin-

dus than are dreamt of in the Philosophy of the West.

We need hardly assure you that we have been carefully watching the progress of your Mission in the West and always heartily rejoicing at your devotedness and successful labours in the field of religion. The appreciative references made by the press in the great centres of intellectual activity, moral growth, and religious inquiry in the West, to you and to your valuable contributions to our religious literature, bear eloquent testimony to your noble and magnificent efforts.

We beg to express our heartfelt gratification at your visit to our land and to hope that we, who, in common with you, look to the Vedas as the foundation of all true spiritual knowledge, may have many more occasions of seeing you in our midst.

May God, who has hitherto crowned your noble work with conspicuous success, spare you long, giving you vigour and strength to continue your noble Mission.

> *We remain, Revered Sir,*
> *Yours faithfully,*
> *...*
> *for and on behalf of the Hindus Of Jaffna.*

An eloquent reply was given, and on the following evening the Swami lectured on Vedantism, a report of which is here appended:

The subject is very large and the time is short; a full analysis of the religion of the Hindus is impossible in one lecture. I will, therefore, present before you the salient points of our religion in as simple language as I can. The word Hindu, by which it is the fashion nowadays to style ourselves, has lost all its meaning, for this word merely meant those who lived on the other side of the river Indus (in Sanskrit, Sindhu). This name was murdered into Hindu by the ancient Persians, and all people living on the other side of the river Sindhu were called by them Hindus. Thus this word has come down to us; and during the Mohammedan rule we took up the word ourselves. There may not be any harm in using the word of course; but, as I have said, it has lost its significance, for you may mark that all the people who live on this side of the Indus in modern times do not follow the same religion as they did in ancient times. The word, therefore, covers not only Hindus proper, but Mohammedans, Christians, Jains, and other people who live in India. I therefore, would not use the word Hindu. What word should we use then? The other words which alone we can use are either the Vaidikas, followers of the Vedas, or better still, the Vedantists, followers of the Vedanta. Most of the great religions of the world owe allegiance to certain books which they believe are the words of God or some other supernatural beings, and which are the basis of their religion. Now of all these books, according to

the modern savants of the West, the oldest are the Vedas of the Hindus. A little understanding, therefore, is necessary about the Vedas.

This mass of writing called the Vedas is not the utterance of persons. Its date has never been fixed, can never be fixed, and, according to us, the Vedas are eternal. There is one salient point which I want you to remember, that all the other religions of the world claim their authority as being delivered by a Personal God or a number of personal beings, angels, or special messengers of God, unto certain persons; while the claim of the Hindus is that the Vedas do not owe their authority to anybody, they are themselves the authority, being eternal—the knowledge of God. They were never written, never created, they have existed throughout time; just as creation is infinite and eternal, without beginning and without end, so is the knowledge of God without beginning and without end. And this knowledge is what is meant by the Vedas (Vid to know). The mass of knowledge called the Vedanta was discovered by personages called Rishis, and the Rishi is defined as a Mantra-drashtâ, a seer of thought; not that the thought was his own. Whenever you hear that a certain passage of the Vedas came from a certain Rishi never think that he wrote it or created it out of his mind; he was the seer of the thought which already existed; it existed in the universe eternally. This sage was the discoverer; the Rishis were spiritual discoverers.

This mass of writing, the Vedas, is divided principally into two parts, the Karma Kânda and the Jnâna Kânda—the work portion and the knowledge portion, the ceremonial and the spiritual. The work portion consists of various sacrifices; most of them of late have been given up as not practicable under present circumstances, but others remain to the present day in some shape or other. The main ideas of the Karma Kanda, which consists of the duties of man, the duties of the student, of the householder, of the recluse, and the various duties of the different stations of life, are followed more or less down to the present day. But the spiritual portion of our religion is in the second part, the Jnana Kanda, the Vedanta, the end of the Vedas, the gist, the goal of the Vedas. The essence of the knowledge of the Vedas was called by the name of Vedanta, which comprises the Upanishads; and all the sects of India—Dualists, Qualified-Monists, Monists, or the Shaivites, Vaishnavites, Shâktas, Sauras, Gânapatyas, each one that dares to come within the fold of Hinduism—must acknowledge the Upanishads of the Vedas. They can have their own interpretations and can interpret them in their own way, but they must obey the authority. That is why we want to use the word Vedantist instead of Hindu. All the philosophers of India who are orthodox have to acknowledge the authority of the Vedanta; and all our present-day religions, however crude some of them may appear to be, however inexplicable some of their purposes may seem, one who understands them and studies them can trace them back to the ideas of the Upanishads. So deeply have these Upanishads sunk into our race that those of you who study the symbology of the crudest religion of the Hindus will be astonished to find sometimes figurative expressions of the Upanishads—the Upanishads become symbolised after a time into figures and so forth. Great spiritual and philosophical ideas in the Upanishads are today with us, converted into household worship in the form of symbols. Thus the various symbols now used by us, all come from the Vedanta, because in the Vedanta they are used as figures, and these ideas spread among the nation and permeated it throughout until they became part of their everyday life as symbols.

Next to the Vedanta come the Smritis. These also are books written by sages, but the authority of the Smritis is subordinate to that of the Vedanta, because they stand in the same relation with us as the scriptures of the other religions stand with regard to them. We admit that the Smritis have been written by particular sages; in that sense they are the same as the scriptures of other religions, but these Smritis are not final authority. If there is any thing in a Smriti which contradicts the Vedanta, the Smriti is to be rejected—its authority is gone. These Smritis, we see again, have varied from time to time. We read that such and such Smriti should have authority in the Satya Yuga, such and such in the Tretâ Yuga, some in the Dwâpara Yuga, and some in the Kali Yuga, and so on. As essential conditions changed, as various circumstances came to have their influence on the race, manners and customs had to be changed, and these Smritis, as mainly regulating the manners and customs of the nation, had also to be changed from time to time. This is a point I specially ask you to remember. The principles of religion that are in the Vedanta are unchangeable. Why? Because they are all built upon the eternal principles that are in man and nature; they can never change. Ideas about the soul, going to heaven, and so on can never change; they were the same thousands of years ago, they are the same today, they will be the same millions of years hence. But those religious practices which are based entirely upon our social position and correlation must change with the changes in society. Such an order, therefore, would be good and true at a certain period and not at another. We find accordingly that a certain food is allowed at one time and not another, because the food was suitable for that time; but climate and other things changed various other circumstances required to be met, so the Smriti changed the food and other things. Thus it naturally follows that if in modern times our society requires changes to be made, they must be met, and sages will come and show us the way how to meet them; but not one jot of the principles of our religion will be changed; they will remain intact.

Then there are the Purânas. पुराणं पञ्चलक्षणम्—which means, the Puranas are of five characteristics—that which treats of history, of cosmology, with various symbological illustration of philosophical principles, and so forth. These were written to popularise the religion of the Vedas. The language in which the Vedas are written is very ancient, and even among scholars very few can trace the date of these books.

The Puranas were written in the language of the people of that time, what we call modern Sanskrit. They were then meant not for scholars, but for the ordinary people; and ordinary people cannot understand philosophy. Such things were given unto them in concrete form, by means of the lives of saints and kinds and great men and historical events that happened to the race etc. The sages made use of these things to illustrate the eternal principles of religion.

There are still other books, the Tantras. These are very much like Puranas in some respects, and in some of them there is an attempt to revive the old sacrificial ideas of the Karma Kanda.

All these books constitute the scriptures of the Hindus. When there is such a mass of sacred books in a nation and a race which has devoted the greatest part of its energies to the thought of philosophy and spirituality (nobody knows for how many thousands of years), it is quite natural that there should be so many sects; indeed it is a wonder that there are not thousands more. These sects differ very much from each other in certain points. We shall not have time to understand the differences between these sects and all the spiritual details about them; therefore I shall take up the common grounds, the essential principles of all these sects which every Hindu must believe.

The first is the question of creation, that this nature, Prakriti, Mâyâ is infinite, without beginning. It is not that this world was created the other day, not that a God came and created the world and since that time has been sleeping; for that cannot be. The creative energy is still going on. God is eternally creating—is never at rest. Remember the passage in the Gita where Krishna says, "If I remain at rest for one moment, this universe will be destroyed." If that creative energy which is working all around us, day and night, stops for a second, the whole thing falls to the ground. There never was a time when that energy did not work throughout the universe, but there is the law of cycles, Pralaya. Our Sanskrit word for creation, properly translated, should be projection and not creation. For the word creation in the English language has unhappily got that fearful, that most crude idea of something coming out of nothing, creation out of nonentity, non-existence becoming existence, which, of course, I would not insult you by asking you to believe. Our word, therefore, is projection. The whole of this nature exists, it becomes finer, subsides; and then after a period of rest, as it were, the whole thing is again projected forward, and the same combination, the same evolution, the same manifestations appear and remain playing, as it were, for a certain time, only again to break into pieces, to become finer and finer, until the whole thing subsides, and again comes out. Thus it goes on backwards and forwards with a wave-like motion throughout eternity. Time, space, and causation are all within this nature. To say, therefore, that it had a beginning is utter nonsense. No question can occur as to its beginning or its end. Therefore wherever in our scriptures the words beginning and end are used, you must remember that it means the beginning and the end of one particular cycle; no more than that.

What makes this creation? God. What do I mean by the use of the English word God? Certainly not the word as ordinarily used in English—a good deal of difference. There is no other suitable word in English. I would rather confine myself to the Sanskrit word Brahman. He is the general cause of all these manifestations. What is this Brahman? He is eternal, eternally pure, eternally awake, the almighty, the all-knowing, the all-merciful, the omnipresent, the formless, the partless. He creates this universe. If he is always creating and holding up this universe, two difficulties arise. We see that there is partiality in the universe. One person is born happy, and another unhappy; one is rich, and another poor; this shows partiality. Then there is cruelty also, for here the very condition of life is death. One animal tears another to pieces, and every man tries to get the better of his own brother. This competition, cruelty, horror, and sighs rending hearts day and night is the state of things in this world of ours. If this be the creation of a God, that God is worse than cruel, worse than any devil that man ever imagined. Ay! says the Vedanta, it is not the fault of God that this partiality exists, that this competition exists. Who makes it? We ourselves. There is a cloud shedding its rain on all fields alike. But it is only the field that is well cultivated, which gets the advantage of the shower; another field, which has not been tilled or taken care of cannot get that advantage. It is not the fault of the cloud. The mercy of God is eternal and unchangeable; it is we that make the differentiation. But how can this difference of some being born happy and some unhappy be explained? They do nothing to make out that differences! Not in this life, but they did in their last birth and the difference is explained by this action in the previous life.

We now come to the second principle on which we all agree, not only all Hindus, but all Buddhists and all Jains. We all agree that life is eternal. It is not that it has sprung out of nothing, for that cannot be. Such a life would not be worth having. Everything that has a beginning in time must end in time. Of life began but yesterday, it must end tomorrow, and annihilation is the result. Life must have been existing. It does not now require much acumen to see that, for all the sciences of modern times have been coming round to our help, illustrating from the material world the principles embodied in our scriptures. You know it already that each one of us is the effect of the infinite past; the child is ushered into the world not as something flashing from the hands of nature, as poets delight so much to depict, but he has the burden of an infinite past; for good or evil he comes to work out his own past deeds. That makes the differentiation. This is the law of Karma. Each one of us is the maker of his own fate. This law knocks on the head at once all doctrines of predestination and fate and gives us the only means of reconciliation between God and man. We, we, and none else, are responsible for what we suffer. We are the effects, and we are the causes. We are free therefore. If I am unhappy, it has been of my own making, and that very thing shows that I can be happy if I will. If I am impure, that

is also of my own making, and that very thing shows that I can be pure if I will. The human will stands beyond all circumstance. Before it—the strong, gigantic, infinite will and freedom in man—all the powers, even of nature, must bow down, succumb, and become its servants. This is the result of the law of Karma.

The next question, of course, naturally would be: What is the soul? We cannot understand God in our scriptures without knowing the soul. There have been attempts in India, and outside of India too, to catch a glimpse of the beyond by studying external nature, and we all know what an awful failure has been the result. Instead of giving us a glimpse of the beyond, the more we study the material world, the more we tend to become materialised. The more we handle the material world, even the little spirituality which we possessed before vanishes. Therefore that is not the way to spirituality, to knowledge of the Highest; but it must come through the heart, the human soul. The external workings do not teach us anything about the beyond, about the Infinite, it is only the internal that can do so. Through soul, therefore, the analysis of the human soul alone, can we understand God. There are differences of opinion as to the nature of the human soul among the various sects in India, but there are certain points of agreement. We all agree that souls are without beginning and without end, and immortal by their very nature; also that all powers, blessing, purity, omnipresence, omniscience are buried in each soul. That is a grand idea we ought to remember. In every man and in every animal, however weak or wicked, great or small, resides the same omnipresent, omniscient soul. The difference is not in the soul, but in the manifestation. Between me and the smallest animal, the difference is only in manifestation, but as a principle he is the same as I am, he is my brother, he has the same soul as I have. This is the greatest principle that India has preached. The talk of the brotherhood of man becomes in India the brotherhood of universal life, of animals, and of all life down to the little ants—all these are our bodies. Even as our scripture says, "Thus the sage, knowing that the same Lord inhabits all bodies, will worship every body as such." That is why in India there have been such merciful ideas about the poor, about animals, about everybody, and everything else. This is one of the common grounds about our ideas of the soul.

Naturally, we come to the idea of God. One thing more about the soul. Those who study the English language are often deluded by the words, soul and mind. Our Âtman and soul are entirely different things. What we call Manas, the mind, the Western people call soul. The West never had the idea of soul until they got it through Sanskrit philosophy, some twenty years ago. The body is here, beyond that is the mind, yet the mind is not the Atman; it is the fine body, the Sukshma Sharira, made of fine particles, which goes from birth to death, and so on; but behind the mind is the Atman, the soul, the Self of man. It cannot be translated by the word soul or mind, so we have to use the word Atman, or, as Western philosophers have designated it, by the word Self. Whatever word you use, you must keep it clear in your mind that the Atman is separate from the mind, as well as from the body, and that this Atman goes through birth and death, accompanied by the mind, the Sukshma Sharira. And when the time comes that it has attained to all knowledge and manifested itself to perfection, then this going from birth to death ceases for it. Then it is at liberty either to keep that mind, the Sukshma Sharira, or to let it go for ever, and remain independent and free throughout all eternity. The goal of the soul is freedom. That is one peculiarity of our religion. We also have heavens and hells too; but these are not infinite, for in the very nature of things they cannot be. If there were any heavens, they would be only repetitions of this world of ours on a bigger scale, with a little more happiness and a little more enjoyment, but that is all the worse for the soul. There are many of these heavens. Persons who do good works here with the thought of reward, when they die, are born again as gods in one of these heavens, as Indra and others. These gods are the names of certain states. They also had been men, and by good work they have become gods; and those different names that you read of, such as Indra and so on, are not the names of the same person. There will be thousands of Indras. Nahusha was a great king, and when he died, he became Indra. It is a position; one soul becomes high and takes the Indra position and remains in it only a certain time; he then dies and is born again as man. But the human body is the highest of all. Some of the gods may try to go higher and give up all ideas of enjoyment in heavens; but, as in this world, wealth and position and enjoyment delude the vast majority, so do most of the gods become deluded also, and after working out their good Karma, they fall down and become human beings again. This earth, therefore, is the Karma Bhumi; it is this earth from which we attain to liberation. So even these heavens are not worth attaining to.

What is then worth having? Mukti, freedom. Even in the highest of heavens, says our scripture, you are a slave; what matters it if you are a king for twenty thousand years? So long as you have a body, so long as you are a slave to happiness, so long as time works on you, space works on you, you are a slave. The idea, therefore, is to be free of external and internal nature. Nature must fall at your feet, and you must trample on it and be free and glorious by going beyond. No more is there life; therefore more is there death. No more enjoyment; therefore no more misery. It is bliss unspeakable, in destructible, beyond everything. What we call happiness and good here are but particles of that eternal Bliss. And this eternal Bliss is our goal.

The soul is also sexless; we cannot say of the Atman that it is a man or a woman. Sex belongs to the body alone. All such ideas, therefore, as man or woman, are a delusion when spoken with regard to the Self, and are only proper when spoken of the body. So are the ideas of age. It never ages; the ancient One is always the same. How did It come down to earth?

There is but one answer to that in our scriptures. Ignorance is the cause of all this bondage. It is through ignorance that we have become bound; knowledge will cure it by taking us to the other side. How will that knowledge come? Through love, Bhakti; by the worship of God, by loving all beings as the temples of God. He resides within them. Thus, with that intense love will come knowledge, and ignorance will disappear, the bonds will break, and the soul will be free.

There are two ideas of God in our scriptures—the one, the personal; and the other, the impersonal. The idea of the Personal God is that He is the omnipresent creator, preserver, and destroyer of everything, the eternal Father and Mother of the universe, but One who is eternally separate from us and from all souls; and liberation consists in coming near to Him and living in Him. Then there is the other idea of the Impersonal, where all those adjectives are taken away as superfluous, as illogical and there remains an impersonal, omnipresent Being who cannot be called a knowing being, because knowledge only belongs to the human mind. He cannot be called a thinking being, because that is a process of the weak only. He cannot be called a reasoning being, because reasoning is a sign of weakness. He cannot be called a creating being, because none creates except in bondage. What bondage has He? None works except for the fulfilment of desires; what desires has He? None works except it be to supply some wants; what wants has He? In the Vedas it is not the word "He" that is used, but "It", for "He" would make an invidious distinction, as if God were a man. "It", the impersonal, is used, and this impersonal "It" is preached. This system is called the Advaita.

And what are our relations with this Impersonal Being?— that we are He. We and He are one. Every one is but a manifestation of that Impersonal, the basis of all being, and misery consists in thinking of ourselves as different from this Infinite, Impersonal Being; and liberation consists in knowing our unity with this wonderful Impersonality. These, in short, are the two ideas of God that we find in our scriptures.

Some remarks ought to be made here. It is only through the idea of the Impersonal God that you can have any system of ethics. In every nation the truth has been preached from the most ancient times—love your fellow-beings as yourselves—I mean, love human beings as yourselves. In India it has been preached, "love all beings as yourselves"; we make no distinction between men and animals. But no reason was forthcoming, no one knew why it would be good to love other beings as ourselves. And the reason, why, is there in the idea of the Impersonal God; you understand it when you learn that the whole world is one—the oneness of the universe—the solidarity of all life—that in hurting any one I am hurting myself, in loving any one I am loving myself. Hence we understand why it is that we ought not to hurt others. The reason for ethics, therefore, can only be had from this ideal of the Impersonal God. Then there is the question of the position of the Personal God in it. I understand the wonderful flow of love that comes from the idea of a Personal God, I thoroughly appreciate the power and potency of Bhakti on men to suit the needs of different times. What we now want in our country, however, is not so much of weeping, but a little strength. What a mine of strength is in this Impersonal God, when all superstitions have been thrown overboard, and man stands on his feet with the knowledge—I am the Impersonal Being of the world! What can make me afraid? I care not even for nature's laws. Death is a joke to me. Man stands on the glory of his own soul, the infinite, the eternal, the deathless—that soul which no instruments can pierce, which no air can dry, nor fire burn, no water melt, the infinite, the birthless, the deathless, without beginning and without end, before whose magnitude the suns and moons and all their systems appear like drops in the ocean, before whose glory space melts away into nothingness and time vanishes into non-existence. This glorious soul we must believe in. Out of that will come power. Whatever you think, that you will be. If you think yourselves weak, weak you will be; if you think yourselves strong, strong you will be; if you think yourselves impure, impure you will be; if you think yourselves pure, pure you will be. This teaches us not to think ourselves as weak, but as strong, omnipotent, omniscient. No matter that I have not expressed it yet, it is in me. All knowledge is in me, all power, all purity, and all freedom. Why cannot I express this knowledge? Because I do not believe in it. Let me believe in it, and it must and will come out. This is what the idea of the Impersonal teaches. Make your children strong from their very childhood; teach them not weakness, nor forms, but make them strong; let them stand on their feet—bold, all-conquering, all-suffering; and first of all, let them learn of the glory of the soul. That you get alone in the Vedanta—and there alone. It has ideas of love and worship and other things which we have in other religions, and more besides; but this idea of the soul is the life-giving thought, the most wonderful. There and there alone is the great thought that is going to revolutionist the world and reconcile the knowledge of the material world with religion.

Thus I have tried to bring before you the salient points of our religion—the principles. I have only to say a few words about the practice and the application As we have seen, under the circumstances existing in India, naturally many sects must appear. As a fact, we find that there are so many sects in India, and at the same time we know this mysterious fact that these sects do not quarrel with each other. The Shaivite does not say that every Vaishnavite is going to be damned, nor the Vaishnavite that every Shaivite will be damned. The Shaivite says, this is my path, and you have yours; at the end we must come together. They all know that in India. This is the theory of Ishta. It has been recognised in the most ancient times that there are various forms of worshipping God. It is also recognised that different natures require different methods. Your method of coming to God may not be my method, possibly it might hurt me. Such an idea as that there is but one way for everybody is injurious, meaningless, and entirely to be avoided. Woe unto the world when everyone is of the same religious opinion and takes to the same path. Then all religions and all thought will be destroyed. Variety is the very soul of life. When it dies out entirely, creation will die. When this variation in thought is kept up, we must exist; and we need not quarrel because of that variety. Your way is very good for you, but not for me. My way is good for me, but not for you My way is called in Sanskrit, my "Ishta". Mind you, we have no quarrel with any religion in the world. We have each our Ishta. But when we see men coming and saying, "This is the only way", and trying to force it on us in India, we have a word to say; we laugh at them. For such people who want to destroy their brothers because they seem to follow a different path towards God—for them to talk of love is absurd. Their love does not count for much. How can they preach of love who cannot bean another man to follow a different path from their own? If that is love, what is hatred? We have no quarrel with any religion in the world, whether it teaches men to worship Christ, Buddha, or Mohammed, or any other prophet. "Welcome, my brother," the Hindu says, "I am going to help you; but you must allow me to follow my way too. That is my Ishta. Your way is very good, no doubt; but it may be dangerous for me. My own experience tells me what food is good for me, and no army of doctors can tell me that. So I know from my own experience what path is the best for me." That is the goal, the Ishta, and, therefore, we say that if a temple, or a symbol, or an image helps you to realise the Divinity within, you are welcome to it. Have two hundred images if you like. If certain forms and formularies help you to realise the Divine, God speed you; have, by all means, whatever forms, and whatever temples, and whatever ceremonies you want to bring you nearer to God. But do not quarrel about them; the moment you quarrel, you are not going Godward, you are going backward, towards the brutes.

These are a few ideas in our religion. It is one of inclusion of every one, exclusion of none. Though our castes and our institutions are apparently linked with our religion, they are not so. These institutions have been necessary to protect us as a nation, and when this necessity for self-preservation will no more exist, they will die a natural death. But the older I grow, the better I seem to think of these time-honoured institutions of India. There was a time when I used to think that many of them were useless and worthless; but the older I grew, the more I seem to feel a diffidence in cursing any one of them, for each one of them is the embodiment of the experience of centuries. A child of but yesterday, destined to die the day after tomorrow, comes to me and asks me to change all my plans; and if I hear the advice of that baby and change all my surroundings according to his ideas, I myself should be a fool, and no one else. Much of the advice that is coming to us from different countries is similar to this. Tell these wiseacres: "I will hear you when you have made a stable society yourselves. You cannot hold on to one idea for two days, you quarrel and fail; you are born like moths in the spring and die like them in five minutes. You come up like bubbles and burst like bubbles too. First form a stable society like ours. First make laws and institutions that remain undiminished in their power through scores of centuries. Then will be the time to talk on the subject with you, but till then, my friend, you are only a giddy child."

I have finished what I had to say about our religion. I will end by reminding you of the one pressing necessity of the day. Praise be to Vyâsa, the great author of the Mahâbhârata, that in this Kali Yuga there is one great work. The Tapas and the other hard Yogas that were practiced in other Yugas do not work now. What is needed in this Yuga is giving, helping others. What is meant by Dana? The highest of gifts is the giving of spiritual knowledge, the next is the giving of secular knowledge, and the next is the saving of life, the last is giving food and drink. He who gives spiritual knowledge, saves the soul from many end many a birth. He who gives secular knowledge opens the eyes of human beings to wards spiritual knowledge, and far below these rank all other gifts, even the saving of life. Therefore it is necessary that you learn this and note that all other kinds of work are of much less value than that of imparting spiritual knowledge. The highest and greatest help is that given in the dissemination of spiritual knowledge. There is an eternal fountain of spirituality in our scriptures, and nowhere on earth, except in this land of renunciation, do we find such noble examples of practical spirituality. I have had a little experience of the world. Believe me, there is much talking in other lands; but the practical man of religion, who has carried it into his life, is here and here alone. Talking is not religion; parrots may talk, machines may talk nowadays. But show me the life of renunciation, of spirituality, of all-suffering, of love infinite. This kind of life indicates a spiritual man. With such ideas and such noble practical examples in our country, it would be a great pity if the treasures in the brains and hearts of all these great Yogis were not brought out to become the common property of every one, rich and poor, high and low; not only in India, but they must be thrown broadcast all over the world. This is one of our greatest duties, and you will find that the more you work to help others, the more you help yourselves. The one vital duty incumbent on you, if you really love your religion, if you really love your country, is that you must struggle hard to be up and doing, with this one great idea of bringing out the treasures from your closed books and delivering them over to their rightful heirs.

And above all, one thing is necessary. Ay, for ages we have been saturated with awful jealousy; we are always getting jealous of each other. Why has this man a little precedence, and not I? Even in the worship of God we want precedence, to such a state of slavery have we come. This is to be avoided. If there is any crying sin in India at this time it is this slavery. Every one wants to command, and no one wants to obey; and this is owing to the absence of that wonderful Brahmacharya system of yore. First, learn to obey. The command will come by itself. Always first learn to be a servant, and then you will be fit to be a master. Avoid this jealousy and you will do great works that have yet to be done. Our ancestors did most wonderful works, and we look back upon their work with veneration and pride. But we also are going to do great deeds, and let others look back with blessings and pride upon us as their ancestors. With the blessing of the Lord every one here will yet do such deeds that will eclipse those of our ancestors, great and glorious as they may have been.

REPLY TO THE ADDRESS OF WELCOME AT PAMBAN

On the arrival of Swami Vivekananda at Pamban, he was met by His Highness the Raja of Ramnad, who accorded him a hearty welcome. Preparations had been made at the landing wharf for a formal reception; and here, under a pandal which had been decorated with great taste, the following address on behalf of the Pamban people was read:

May It Please Your Holiness,

We greatly rejoice to welcome Your Holiness with hearts full of deepest gratitude and highest veneration—gratitude for having so readily and graciously consented to pay us a flying visit in spite of the numerous calls on you, and veneration for the many noble and excellent qualities that you possess and for the great work you have so nobly undertaken to do, and which you have been discharging with conspicuous ability, utmost zeal, and earnestness.

We truly rejoice to see that the efforts of Your Holiness in sowing the seeds of Hindu philosophy in the cultured minds of the great Western nations are being crowned with so much success that we already see all around the bright and cheerful aspect of the bearing of excellent fruits in great abundance, and most humbly pray that Your Holiness will, during your sojourn in Âryâvarta, be graciously pleased to exert yourself even a little more than you did in the West to awaken the minds of your brethren in this our motherland from their dreary lifelong slumber and make them recall to their minds the long-forgotten gospel of truth.

Our hearts are so full of the sincerest affection, greatest reverence, and highest admiration for Your Holiness—our great spiritual leader, that we verily find it impossible to adequately express our feelings, and, therefore, beg to conclude with an earnest and united prayer to the merciful Providence to bless Your Holiness with a long life of usefulness and to grant you everything that may tend to bring about the long-lost feelings of universal brotherhood.

The Raja added to this a brief personal welcome, which was remarkable for its depth of feeling, and then the Swami replied to the following effect:

Our sacred motherland is a land of religion and philosophy—the birthplace of spiritual giants—the land of renunciation, where and where alone, from the most ancient to the most modern times, there has been the highest ideal of life open to man.

I have been in the countries of the West—have travelled through many lands of many races; and each race and each nation appears to me to have a particular ideal—a prominent ideal running through its whole life; and this ideal is the backbone of the national life. Not politics nor military power, not commercial supremacy nor mechanical genius furnishes India with that backbone, but religion; and religion alone is all that we have and mean to have. Spirituality has been always in India.

Great indeed are the manifestations of muscular power, and marvellous the manifestations of intellect expressing themselves through machines by the appliances of science; yet none of these is more potent than the influence which spirit exerts upon the world.

The history of our race shows that India has always been most active. Today we are taught by men who ought to know better that the Hindu is mild and passive; and this has become a sort of proverb with the people of other lands. I discard the idea that India was ever passive. Nowhere has activity been more pronounced than in this blessed land of ours, and the great proof of this activity is that our most ancient and magnanimous race still lives, and at every decade in its glorious career seems to take on fresh youth—undying and imperishable. This activity manifests here in religion. But it is a peculiar fact in human nature that it judges others according to its own standard of activity. Take, for instance, a shoemaker. He understands only shoemaking and thinks there is nothing in this life except the manufacturing of shoes. A bricklayer understands nothing but bricklaying and proves this alone in his life from day to day. And there is another reason which explains this. When the vibrations of light are very intense, we do not see them, because we are so constituted that we cannot go beyond our own plane of vision. But the Yogi with his spiritual introspection is able to see through the materialistic veil of the vulgar crowds.

The eyes of the whole world are now turned towards this land of India for spiritual food; and India has to provide it for all the races. Here alone is the best ideal for mankind; and Western scholars are now striving to understand this ideal which is enshrined in our Sanskrit literature and philosophy, and which has been the characteristic of India all through the ages.

Since the dawn of history, no missionary went out of India to propagate the Hindu doctrines and dogmas; but now a wonderful change is coming over us. Shri Bhagavân Krishna says, "Whenever virtue subsides and immorality prevails, then I come again and again to help the world." Religious researches disclose to us the fact that there is not a country possessing a good ethical code but has borrowed something of it from us, and there is not one religion possessing good ideas of the immortality of the soul but has derived it directly or indirectly from us.

There never was a time in the world's history when there was so much robbery, and high-handedness, and tyranny of the strong over the weak, as at this latter end of the nineteenth century. Everybody should know that there is no salvation except through the conquering of desires, and that no man is free who is subject to the bondage of matter. This great truth all nations are slowly coming to understand and appreciate. As soon as the disciple is in a position to grasp this truth, the words of the Guru come to his help. The Lord sends help to His own children in His infinite mercy which never ceaseth and is ever flowing in all creeds. Our Lord is the Lord of all religions. This idea belongs to India alone; and I challenge any one of you to find it in any other scripture of the world.

We Hindus have now been placed, under God's providence, in a very critical and responsible position. The nations of the West are coming to us for spiritual help. A great moral obligation rests on the sons of India to fully equip themselves for the work of enlightening the world on the problems of human existence. One thing we may note, that whereas you will find that good and great men of other countries take pride in tracing back their descent to some robber-baron who lived in a mountain fortress and emerged from time to time to plunder passing wayfarers, we Hindus, on the other hand, take pride in being the descendants of Rishis and sages who lived on roots and fruits in mountains and caves, meditating on the Supreme. We may be degraded and degenerated now; but however degraded and degenerated we may be, we can become great if only we begin to work in right earnest on behalf of our religion.

Accept my hearty thanks for the kind and cordial reception you have given me. It is impossible for me to express my gratitude to H. H. the Raja of Ramnad for his love towards me. If any good work has been done by me and through me, India owes much to this good man, for it was he who conceived the idea of my going to Chicago, and it was he who put that idea into my head and persistently urged me on to accomplish it. Standing beside me, he with all his old enthusiasm is still expecting me to do more and more work. I wish there were half a dozen more such Rajas to take interest in our dear motherland and work for her amelioration in the spiritual line.

ADDRESS AT THE RAMESWARAM TEMPLE ON REAL WORSHIP

A visit was subsequently paid to the Rameswaram Temple, where the Swami was asked to address a few words to the people who had assembled there. This he did in the following terms:

It is in love that religion exists and not in ceremony, in the pure and sincere love in the heart. Unless a man is pure in body and mind, his coming into a temple and worshipping Shiva is useless. The prayers of those that are pure in mind and body will be answered by Shiva, and those that are impure and yet try to teach religion to others will fail in the end. External worship is only a symbol of internal worship; but internal worship and purity are the real things. Without them, external worship would be of no avail. Therefore you must all try to remember this.

People have become so degraded in this Kali Yuga that they think they can do anything, and then they can go to a holy place, and their sins will be forgiven. If a man goes with an impure mind into a temple, he adds to the sins that he had already, and goes home a worse man than when he left it. Tirtha (place of pilgrimage) is a place which is full of holy things and holy men. But if holy people live in a certain place, and if there is no temple there, even that is a Tirtha. If unholy people live in a place where there may be a hundred temples, the Tirtha has vanished from that place. And it is most difficult to live in a Tirtha; for if sin is committed in any ordinary place it can easily be removed, but sin committed in a Tirtha cannot be removed. This is the gist of all worship—to be pure and to do good to others. He who sees Shiva in the poor, in the weak, and in the diseased, really worships Shiva; and if he sees Shiva only in the image, his worship is but preliminary. He who has served and helped one poor man seeing Shiva in him, without thinking of his caste, or creed, or race, or anything, with him Shiva is more pleased than with the man who sees Him only in temples.

A rich man had a garden and two gardeners. One of these gardeners was very lazy and did not work; but when the owner came to the garden, the lazy man would get up and fold his arms and say, "How beautiful is the face of my master", and dance before him. The other gardener would not talk much, but would work hard, and produce all sorts of fruits and vegetables which he would carry on his head to his master who lived a long way off. Of these two gardeners, which would be the more beloved of his master? Shiva is that master, and this world is His garden, and there are two sorts of gardeners here; the one who is lazy, hypocritical, and does nothing, only talking about Shiva's beautiful eyes and nose and other features; and the other, who is taking care of Shiva's children, all those that are poor and weak, all animals, and all His creation. Which of these would be the more beloved of Shiva? Certainly he that serves His children. He who wants to serve the father must serve the children first. He who wants to serve Shiva must serve His children—must serve all creatures in this world first. It is said in the Shâstra that those who serve the servants of God are His greatest servants. So you will bear this in mind.

Let me tell you again that you must be pure and help any one who comes to you, as much as lies in your power. And this is good Karma. By the power of this, the heart becomes pure (Chitta-shuddhi), and then Shiva who is residing in every one will become manifest. He is always in the heart of every one. If there is dirt and dust on a mirror, we cannot see our image. So ignorance and wickedness are the dirt and dust that are on the mirror of our hearts. Selfishness is the chief sin, thinking of ourselves first. He who thinks, "I will eat first, I will have more money than others, and I will possess everything", he who thinks, "I will get to heaven before others I will get Mukti before others" is the selfish man. The unselfish man says, "I will be last, I do not care to go to heaven, I will even go to hell if by doing so I can help my brothers." This unselfishness is the test of religion. He who has more of this unselfishness is more spiritual and nearer to Shiva. Whether he is learned or ignorant, he is nearer to Shiva than anybody else, whether he knows it or not. And if a man is selfish, even though he has visited all the temples, seen all the places of pilgrimage, and painted himself like a leopard, he is still further off from Shiva.

REPLY TO THE ADDRESS OF WELCOME AT RAMNAD

At Ramnad the following address was presented to Swami Vivekananda by the Raja:

His Most Holiness,

Sri Paramahamsa, Yati-Râja, Digvijaya-Kolâhala, Sarvamata-Sampratipanna, Parama-Yogeeswara, Srimat Bhagavân Sree Ramakrishna Paramahamsa Karakamala Sanjâta, Râjâdhirâja-Sevita, Sree Vivekananda Swami, May It Please Your Holiness,

We, the inhabitants of this ancient and historic Samsthânam of Sethu Bandha Rameswaram, otherwise known as Râmanâthapuram or Ramnad, beg, most cordially, to welcome you to this, our motherland. We deem it a very rare privilege to be the first to pay your Holiness our heartfelt homage on your landing in India, and that, on the shores sanctified by the footsteps of that great Hero and our revered Lord—Sree Bhagavân Râmachandra.

We have watched with feelings of genuine pride and pleasure the unprecedented success which has crowned your laudable efforts in bringing home to the master-minds of the West the intrinsic merits and excellence of our time-honoured and noble religion. You have with an eloquence that is unsurpassed and in language plain and unmistakable, proclaimed to and convinced the cultured audiences in Europe and America that Hinduism fulfils all the requirements of the ideal of a universal religion and adapts itself to the temperament and needs of men and women of all races and creeds. Animated purely by a disinterested impulse, influenced by the best of motives and at considerable self-sacrifice, Your Holiness has crossed boundless seas and oceans to convey the message of truth and peace, and to plant the flag of India's spiritual triumph and glory in the rich soil of Europe and America. Your Holiness has, both by precept and practice, shown the feasibility and importance of universal brotherhood. Above all, your labours in the West have indirectly and to a great extent tended to awaken the apathetic sons and daughters of India to a sense of the greatness and glory of their ancestral faith, and to create in them a genuine interest in the study and observance of their dear and priceless religion

We feel we cannot adequately convey in words our feelings of gratitude and thankfulness to your Holiness for your philanthropic labours towards the spiritual regeneration of the East and the West. We cannot close this address without referring to the great kindness which your Holiness has always extended to our Raja, who is one of your devoted disciples, and the honour and pride he feels by this gracious act of your Holiness in landing first on his territory is indescribable.

In conclusion, we pray to the Almighty to bless your Holiness with long life, and health, and strength to enable you to carry on the good work that has been so ably inaugurated by you.

With respects and love,
We beg to subscribe ourselves,
Your Holiness' most devoted and obedient
Disciples and Servants.
Ramnad,
25th January, 1897.

The Swami's reply follows in extenso:

The longest night seems to be passing away, the sorest trouble seems to be coming to an end at last, the seeming corpse appears to be awaking and a voice is coming to us—away back where history and even tradition fails to peep into the gloom of the past, coming down from there, reflected as it were from peak to peak of the infinite Himalaya of knowledge, and of love, and of work, India, this motherland of ours—a voice is coming unto us, gentle, firm, and yet unmistakable in its utterances, and is gaining volume as days pass by, and behold, the sleeper is awakening! Like a breeze from the Himalayas, it is bringing life into the almost dead bones and muscles, the lethargy is passing away, and only the blind cannot see, or the perverted will not see, that she is awakening, this motherland of ours, from her deep long sleep. None can desist her any more; never is she going to sleep any more; no outward powers can hold her back any more; for the infinite giant is rising to her feet.

Your Highness and gentlemen of Ramnad, accept my heartfelt thanks for the cordiality and kindness with which you have received me. I feel that you are cordial and kind, for heart speaks unto heart better than any language of the mouth; spirit speaks unto spirit in silence, and yet in most unmistakable language, and I feel it in my heart of hearts. Your Highness of Ramnad, if there has been any work done by my humble self in the cause of our religion and our motherland in the Western countries, if any little work has been done in rousing the sympathies of our own people by drawing their attention to the inestimable jewels that, they know not, are lying deep buried about their own home—if, instead of dying of thirst and drinking dirty ditch water elsewhere out of the blindness of ignorance, they are being called to go and drink from the eternal fountain which is flowing perennially by their own home—if anything has been done to rouse our people towards action, to make them understand that in everything, religion and religion alone is the life of India, and when that goes India will die, in spite of politics, in spite of social reforms, in spite of Kubera's wealth poured upon the head of every one of her children—if anything has been done towards this end, India and every country where any work has been done owe much of it to you, Raja of Ramnad. For it was you who gave me the idea first, and it was you who persistently urged me on towards the work. You, as it were, intuitively understood what was going to be, and took me by the hand, helped me all along, and have never ceased to encourage me. Well is it, therefore, that you should be the first to rejoice at my success, and meet it is that I should first land in your territory on my return to India.

Great works are to be done, wonderful powers have to be worked out, we have to teach other nations many things, as has been said already by your Highness. This is the motherland of philosophy, of spirituality, and of ethics, of sweetness, gentleness, and love. These still exist, and my experience of the world leads me to stand on firm ground and make the bold statement that India is still the first and foremost of all the nations of the world in these respects. Look at this little phenomenon. There have been immense political changes within the last four or five years. Gigantic organizations undertaking to subvert the whole of existing institutions in different countries and meeting with a certain amount of success have been working all over the Western world. Ask our people if they have heard anything about them. They have heard not a word about them. But that there was a Parliament of Religions in Chicago, and that there was a Sannyasin sent over from India to that Parliament, and that he was very well received and since that time has been working in the West, the poorest beggar has known. I have heard it said that our masses are dense, that they do not want any education, and that they do not care for any information. I had at one time a foolish leaning towards that opinion myself, but I find experience is a far more glorious teacher than any amount of speculation, or any amount of books written by globe-trotters and hasty observers. This experience teaches me that they are not dense, that they are not slow, that they are as eager and thirsty for information as any race under the sun; but then each nation has its own part to play, and naturally, each nation has its own peculiarity and individuality with which it is born. Each represents, as it were, one peculiar note in this harmony of nations, and this is its very life, its vitality. In it is the backbone, the foundation, and the bed-rock of the national life, and here in this blessed land, the foundation, the backbone, the life-centre is religion and religion alone. Let others talk of politics, of the glory of acquisition of immense wealth poured in by trade, of the power and spread of commercialism, of the glorious fountain of physical liberty; but these the Hindu mind does not understand and does not want to understand. Touch him on spirituality, on religion, on God, on the soul, on the Infinite, on spiritual freedom, and I assure you, the lowest peasant in India is better informed on these subjects than many a so-called philosopher in other lands. I have said, gentlemen, that we have yet something to teach to the world. This is the very reason, the raison d'être, that this nation has lived on, in spite of hundreds of years of persecution, in spite of nearly a thousand year of foreign rule and foreign oppression. This nation still lives; the raison d'être is it still holds to God, to the treasure-house of religion and spirituality.

In this land are, still, religion and spirituality, the fountains which will have to overflow and flood the world to bring in new life and new vitality to the Western and other nations, which are now almost borne down, half-killed, and degraded by political ambitions and social scheming. From out of many voices, consonant and dissentient, from out of the medley of sounds filling the Indian atmosphere, rises up supreme, striking, and full, one note, and that is renunciation. Give up! That is the watchword of the Indian religions. This world is a delusion of two days. The present life is of five minutes. Beyond is the Infinite, beyond this world of delusion; let us seek that. This continent is illumined with brave and gigantic minds and intelligences which even think of this so called infinite universe as only a mud-puddle; beyond and still beyond they go. Time, even infinite time, is to them but non-existence. Beyond and beyond time they go. Space is nothing to them; beyond that they want to go, and this going beyond the phenomenal is the very soul of religion. The characteristic of my nation is this transcendentalism, this struggle to go beyond, this daring to tear the veil off the face of nature and have at any risk, at any price, a glimpse of the beyond. That is our ideal, but of course all the people in a country cannot give up entirely. Do you want to enthuse them, then here is the way to do so. Your talks of politics, of social regeneration, your talks of money-making and commercialism—all these will roll off like water from a duck's back. This spirituality, then, is what you have to teach the world. Have we to learn anything else, have we to learn anything from the world? We have, perhaps, to gain a little in material knowledge, in the power of organisation, in the ability to handle powers, organising powers, in bringing the best results out of the smallest of causes. This perhaps to a certain extent we may learn from the West. But if any one preaches in India the ideal of eating and drinking and making merry, if any one wants to apotheosise the material world into a God, that man is a liar; he has no place in this holy land, the Indian mind does not want to listen to him. Ay, in spite of the sparkle and glitter of Western civilisation, in spite of all its polish and its marvellous manifestation of power, standing upon this platform, I tell them to their face that it is all vain. It is vanity of vanities. God alone lives.

The soul alone lives. Spirituality alone lives. Hold on to that.

Yet, perhaps, some sort of materialism, toned down to our own requirements, would be a blessing to many of our brothers who are not yet ripe for the highest truths. This is the mistake made in every country and in every society, and it is a greatly regrettable thing that in India, where it was always understood, the same mistake of forcing the highest truths on people who are not ready for them has been made of late. My method need not be yours. The Sannyasin, as you all know, is the ideal of the Hindu's life, and every one by our Shâstras is compelled to give up. Every Hindu who has tasted the fruits of this world must give up in the latter part of his life, and he who does not is not a Hindu and has no more right to call himself a Hindu. We know that this is the ideal—to give up after seeing and experiencing the vanity of things. Having found out that the heart of the material world is a mere hollow, containing only ashes, give it up and go back. The mind is circling forward, as it were, towards the senses, and that mind has to circle backwards; the Pravritti has to stop and the Nivritti has to begin. That is the ideal. But that ideal can only be realised after a certain amount of experience. We cannot teach the child the truth of renunciation; the child is a born optimist; his whole life is in his senses; his whole life is one mass of sense-enjoyment. So there are childlike men in every society who require a certain amount of experience, of enjoyment, to see through the vanity of it, and then renunciation will come to them. There has been ample provision made for them in our Books; but unfortunately, in later times, there has been a tendency to bind every one down by the same laws as those by which the Sannyasin is bound, and that is a great mistake. But for that a good deal of the poverty and the misery that you see in India need not have been. A poor man's life is hemmed in and bound down by tremendous spiritual and ethical laws for which he has no use. Hands off! Let the poor fellow enjoy himself a little, and then he will raise himself up, and renunciation will come to him of itself. Perhaps in this line, we can be taught something by the Western people; but we must be very cautious in learning these things. I am sorry to say that most of the examples one meets nowadays of men who have imbibed the Western ideas are more or less failures.

There are two great obstacles on our path in India, the Scylla of old orthodoxy and the Charybdis of modern European civilisation. Of these two, I vote for the old orthodoxy, and not for the Europeanised system; for the old orthodox man may be ignorant, he may be crude, but he is a man, he has a faith, he has strength, he stands on his own feet; while the Europeanised man has no backbone, he is a mass of heterogeneous ideas picked up at random from every source—and these ideas are unassimilated, undigested, unharmonised. He does not stand on his own feet, and his head is turning round and round. Where is the motive power of his work?—in a few patronizing pats from the English people. His schemes of reforms, his vehement vituperations against the evils of certain social customs, have, as the mainspring, some European patronage. Why are some of our customs called evils? Because the Europeans say so. That is about the reason he gives. I would not submit to that. Stand and die in your own strength, if there is any sin in the world, it is weakness; avoid all weakness, for weakness is sin, weakness is death. These unbalanced creatures are not yet formed into distinct personalities; what are we to call them - men, women, or animals? While those old orthodox people were staunch and were men. There are still some excellent examples, and the one I want to present before you now is your Raja of Ramnad. Here you have a man than whom there is no more zealous a Hindu throughout the length and breadth of this land; here you have a prince than whom there is no prince in this land better informed in all affairs, both oriental and occidental, who takes from every nation whatever he can that is good. "Learn good knowledge with all devotion from the lowest caste. Learn the way to freedom, even if it comes from a Pariah, by serving him. If a woman is a jewel, take her in marriage even if she comes from a low family of the lowest caste." Such is the law laid down by our great and peerless legislator, the divine Manu. This is true. Stand on your own feet, and assimilate what you can; learn from every nation, take what is of use to you. But remember that as Hindus everything else must be subordinated to our own national ideals. Each man has a mission in life, which is the result of all his infinite past Karma. Each of you was born with a splendid heritage, which is the whole of the infinite past life of your glorious nation. Millions of your ancestors are watching, as it were, every action of yours, so be alert. And what is the mission with which every Hindu child is born? Have you not read the proud declaration of Manu regarding the Brahmin where he says that the birth of the Brahmin is "for the protection of the treasury of religion"? I should say that that is the mission not only of the Brahmin, but of every child, whether boy or girl, who is born in this blessed land "for the protection of the treasury of religion". And every other problem in life must be subordinated to that one principal theme. That is also the law of harmony in music. There may be a nation whose theme of life is political supremacy; religion and everything else must become subordinate to that one great theme of its life. But here is another nation whose great theme of life is spirituality and renunciation, whose one watchword is that this world is all vanity and a delusion of three days, and everything else, whether science or knowledge, enjoyment or powers, wealth, name, or fame, must be subordinated to that one theme. The secret of a true Hindu's character lies in the subordination of his knowledge of European sciences and learning, of his wealth, position, and name, to that one principal theme which is inborn in every Hindu child—the spirituality and purity of the race. Therefore between these two, the case of the orthodox man who has the whole of that life-spring of the race, spirituality, and the other man whose hands are full of Western imitation jewels but has no hold on the life-giving principle, spirituality—of these, I do not doubt that every one here will agree that we should

choose the first, the orthodox, because there is some hope in him—he has the national theme, something to hold to; so he will live, but the other will die. Just as in the case of individuals, if the principle of life is undisturbed, if the principal function of that individual life is present, any injuries received as regards other functions are not serious, do not kill the individual, so, as long as this principal function of our life is not disturbed, nothing can destroy our nation. But mark you, if you give up that spirituality, leaving it aside to go after the materialising civilisation of the West, the result will be that in three generations you will be an extinct race; because the backbone of the nation will be broken, the foundation upon which the national edifice has been built will be undermined, and the result will be annihilation all round.

Therefore, my friends, the way out is that first and foremost we must keep a firm hold on spirituality—that inestimable gift handed down to us by our ancient forefathers. Did you ever hear of a country where the greatest kings tried to trace their descent not to kings, not to robber-barons living in old castles who plundered poor travellers, but to semi-naked sages who lived in the forest? Did you ever hear of such a land? This is the land. In other countries great priests try to trace their descent to some king, but here the greatest kings would trace their descent to some ancient priest. Therefore, whether you believe in spirituality or not, for the sake of the national life, you have to get a hold on spirituality and keep to it. Then stretch the other hand out and gain all you can from other races, but everything must be subordinated to that one ideal of life; and out of that a wonderful, glorious, future India will come—I am sure it is coming—a greater India than ever was. Sages will spring up greater than all the ancient sages; and your ancestors will not only be satisfied, but I am sure, they will be proud from their positions in other worlds to look down upon their descendants, so glorious, and so great.

Let us all work hard, my brethren; this is no time for sleep. On our work depends the coming of the India of the future. She is there ready waiting. She is only sleeping. Arise and awake and see her seated here on her eternal throne, rejuvenated, more glorious than she ever was—this motherland of ours. The idea of God was nowhere else ever so fully developed as in this motherland of ours, for the same idea of God never existed anywhere else. Perhaps you are astonished at my assertion; but show me any idea of God from any other scripture equal to ours; they have only clan-Gods, the God of the Jews, the God of the Arabs, and of such and such a race, and their God is fighting the Gods of the other races. But the idea of that beneficent, most merciful God, our father, our mother, our friend, the friend of our friends, the soul of our souls, is here and here alone. And may He who is the Shiva of the Shaivites, the Vishnu of the Vaishnavites, the Karma of the Karmis, the Buddha of the Buddhists, the Jina of the Jains, the Jehovah of the Christians and the Jews, the Allah of the Mohammedans, the Lord of every sect, the Brahman of the Vedantists, He the all-pervading, whose glory has been known only in this land—may He bless us, may He help us, may He give strength unto us, energy unto us, to carry this idea into practice. May that which we have listened to and studied become food to us, may it become strength in us, may it become energy in us to help each other; may we, the teacher and the taught, not be jealous of each other! Peace, peace, peace, in the name of Hari!

REPLY TO THE ADDRESS OF WELCOME AT PARAMAKUDI

Paramakudi was the first stopping-place after leaving Ramnad, and there was a demonstration on a large scale, including the presentation of the following address:

SREEMAT VIVEKANANDA SWAMI,

We, the citizens of Paramakudi, respectfully beg to accord your Holiness a most hearty welcome to this place after your successful spiritual campaign of nearly four years in the Western world.

We share with our countrymen the feelings of joy and pride at the philanthropy which prompted you to attend the Parliament of Religions held at Chicago, and lay before the representatives of the religious world the sacred but hidden treasures of our ancient land. You have by your wide exposition of the sacred truths contained in the Vedic literature disabused the enlightened minds of the West of the prejudices entertained by them against our ancient faith, and convinced them of its universality and adaptability for intellects of all shades and in all ages.

The presence amongst us of your Western disciples is proof positive that your religious teachings have not only been understood in theory, but have also borne practical fruits. The magnetic influence of your august person reminds us of our ancient holy Rishis whose realisation of the Self by asceticism and self-control made them the true guides and preceptors of the human race.

In conclusion, we most earnestly pray to the All-Merciful that your Holiness may long be spared to continue to bless and spiritualist the whole of mankind.

With best regards.
We beg to subscribe ourselves,
Your Holiness' most obedient
and devoted Disciples and Servants.

In the course of his reply the Swami said:

It is almost impossible to express my thanks for the kindness and cordiality with which you have received me. But if I may be permitted to say so, I will add that my love for my country, and especially for my countrymen, will be the same whether they receive me with the utmost cordiality or spurn me from the country. For in the Gîtâ Shri Krishna says—men should work for work's sake only, and love for love's sake. The work that has been done by me in the Western world has been very little; there is no one present here who could not have done a hundred times more work in the West than has been done by me. And I am anxiously waiting for the day when mighty minds will arise, gigantic spiritual minds, who will be ready to go forth from India to the ends of the world to teach spirituality and renunciation—those ideas which have come from the forests of India and belong to Indian soil alone.

There come periods in the history of the human race when, as it were, whole nations are seized with a sort of world-weariness, when they find that all their plans are slipping between their fingers, that old institutions and systems are crumbling into dust, that their hopes are all blighted and everything seems to be out of joint. Two attempts have been made in the world to found social life: the one was upon religion, and the other was upon social necessity. The one was founded upon spirituality, the other upon materialism; the one upon transcendentalism, the other upon realism. The one looks beyond the horizon of this little material world and is bold enough to begin life there, even apart from the other. The other, the second, is content to take its stand on the things of the world and expects to find a firm footing there. Curiously enough, it seems that at times the spiritual side prevails, and then the materialistic side—in wave-like motions following each other. In the same country there will be different tides. At one time the full flood of materialistic ideas prevails, and everything in this life—prosperity, the education which procures more pleasures, more food—will become glorious at first and then that will degrade and degenerate. Along with the prosperity will rise to white heat all the inborn jealousies and hatreds of the human race. Competition and merciless cruelty will be the watchword of the day. To quote a very commonplace and not very elegant English proverb, "Everyone for himself, and the devil take the hindmost", becomes the motto of the day. Then people think that the whole scheme of life is a failure. And the world would be destroyed had not spirituality come to the rescue and lent a helping hand to the sinking world. Then the world gets new hope and finds a new basis for a new building, and another wave of spirituality comes, which in time again declines. As a rule, spirituality brings a class of men who lay exclusive claim to the special powers of the world. The immediate effect of this is a reaction towards materialism, which opens the door to scores of exclusive claims, until the time comes when not only all the spiritual powers of the race, but all its material powers and privileges are centred in the hands of a very few; and these few, standing on the necks of the masses of the people, want to rule them. Then society has to help itself, and materialism comes to the rescue.

If you look at India, our motherland, you will see that the same thing is going on now. That you are here today to welcome one who went to Europe to preach Vedanta would have been impossible had not the materialism of Europe opened the way for it. Materialism has come to the rescue of India in a certain sense by throwing open the doors of life to everyone, by destroying the exclusive privileges of caste, by opening up to discussion the inestimable treasures which were hidden away in the hands of a very few who have even lost the use of them. Half has been stolen and lost; and the other half which remains is in the hands of men who, like dogs in the manger, do not eat themselves and will not allow others to do so. On the other hand, the political systems that we are struggling for in India have been in Europe for ages, have been tried for centuries, and have been found wanting. One after another, the institutions, systems, and everything connected with political government have been condemned as useless; and Europe is restless, does not know where to turn. The material tyranny is tremendous. The wealth and power of a country are in the hands of a few men who do not work but manipulate the work of millions of human beings. By this power they can deluge the whole earth with blood. Religion and all things are under their feet; they rule and stand supreme. The Western world is governed by a handful of Shylocks. All those things that you hear about—constitutional government, freedom, liberty, and parliaments—are but jokes.

The West is groaning under the tyranny of the Shylocks, and the East is groaning under the tyranny of the priests; each must keep the other in check. Do not think that one alone is to help the world. In this creation of the impartial Lord, He has made equal every particle in the universe. The worst, most demoniacal man has some virtues which the greatest saint has not; and the lowest worm may have certain things which the highest man has not. The poor labourer, who you think has so little enjoyment in life, has not your intellect, cannot understand the Vedanta Philosophy and so forth; but compare your body with his, and you will see, his body is not so sensitive to pain as yours. If he gets severe cuts on his body, they heal up more quickly than yours would. His life is in the senses, and he enjoys there. His life also is one of equilibrium and balance. Whether on the ground of materialism, or of intellect, or of spirituality, the compensation that is given by the Lord to every one impartially is exactly the same. Therefore we must not think that we are the saviours of the world. We can teach the world, a good many things, and we can learn a good many things from it too. We can teach the world only what it is waiting for. The whole of Western civilisation will crumble to pieces in the next fifty years if there is no spiritual foundation. It is hopeless and perfectly useless to attempt to govern mankind with the sword. You will find that the very centres from which such ideas as government by force sprang up are the very first centres to degrade and degenerate and crumble to pieces. Europe, the centre of the manifestation of material energy, will crumble into dust within fifty years if she is not mindful to change her position, to shift her ground and make spirituality the basis of her life. And what will save Europe is the religion of the Upanishads.

Apart from the different sects, philosophies, and scriptures, there is one underlying doctrine—the belief in the soul of man, the Âtman—common to all our sects: and that can change the whole tendency of the world. With Hindus, Jains, and Buddhists, in fact everywhere in India, there is the idea of a spiritual soul which is the receptacle of all power. And you know full well that there is not one system of philosophy in India which teaches you that you can get power or purity or perfection from outside; but they all tell you that these are your birthright, your nature. Impurity is a mere superimposition under which your real nature has become hidden. But the real you is already perfect, already strong. You do not require any assistance to govern yourself; you are already self-restrained. The only difference is in knowing it or not knowing it. Therefore the one difficulty has been summed up in the word, Avidyâ. What makes the difference between God and man, between the saint and the sinner? Only ignorance. What is the difference between the highest man and the lowest worm that crawls under your feet? Ignorance. That makes all the difference. For inside that little crawling worm is lodged infinite power, and knowledge, and purity—the infinite divinity of God Himself. It is unmanifested; it will have to be manifested.

This is the one great truth India has to teach to the world, because it is nowhere else. This is spirituality, the science of the soul. What makes a man stand up and work? Strength. Strength is goodness, weakness is sin. If there is one word that you find coming out like a bomb from the Upanishads, bursting like a bomb-shell upon masses of ignorance, it is the word fearlessness. And the only religion that ought to be taught is the religion of fearlessness. Either in this world or in the world of religion, it is true that fear is the sure cause of degradation and sin. It is fear that brings misery, fear that brings death, fear that breeds evil. And what causes fear? Ignorance of our own nature. Each of us is heir-apparent to the Emperor of emperors; are of the substance of God Himself. Nay, according to the Advaita, we are God Himself though we have forgotten our own nature in thinking of ourselves as little men. We have fallen from that nature and thus made differences—I am a little better than you, or you than I, and so on. This idea of oneness is the great lesson India has to give, and mark you, when this is understood, it changes the whole aspect of things, because you look at the world through other eyes than you have been doing before. And this world is no more a battlefield where each soul is born to struggle with every other soul and the strongest gets the victory and the weakest goes to death. It becomes a playground where the Lord is playing like a child, and we are His playmates, His fellow-workers. This is only a play, however terrible, hideous, and dangerous it may appear. We have mistaken its aspect. When we have known the nature of the soul, hope comes to the weakest, to the most degraded, to the most miserable sinner. Only, declares your Shâstra, despair not. For you are the same whatever you do, and you cannot change your nature. Nature itself cannot destroy nature. Your nature is pure. It may be hidden for millions of aeons, but at last it will conquer and come out. Therefore the Advaita brings hope to every one and not despair. Its teaching is not through fear; it teaches, not of devils who are always on the watch to snatch you if you miss your footing—it has nothing to do with devils—but says that you have taken your fate in your own hands. Your own Karma has manufactured for you this body, and nobody did it for you. The Omnipresent Lord has been hidden through ignorance, and the responsibility is on yourself. You have not to think that you were brought into the world without your choice and left in this most horrible place, but to know that you have yourself manufactured your body bit by bit just as you are doing it this very moment. You yourself eat; nobody eats for you. You assimilate what you eat; no one does it for you. You make blood, and muscles, and body out of the food; nobody does it for you. So you have done all the time. One link in a chain explains the infinite chain. If it is true for one moment that you manufacture your body, it is true for every moment that has been or will come. And all the responsibility of good and evil is on you. This is the great hope. What I have done, that I can undo. And at the same time our religion does not take away from mankind the mercy of the Lord. That is always there. On the other hand, He stands beside this tremendous current of good and evil. He the bondless, the ever-merciful, is always ready to help us to the other shore, for His mercy is great, and it always comes to the pure in heart.

Your spirituality, in a certain sense, will have to form the basis of the new order of society. If I had more time, I could show you how the West has yet more to learn from some of the conclusions of the Advaita, for in these days of materialistic science the ideal of the Personal God does not count for much. But yet, even if a man has a very crude form of religion and wants temples and forms, he can have as many as he likes; if he wants a Personal God to love, he can find here the noblest ideas of a Personal God such as were never attained anywhere else in the world. If a man wants to be a rationalist and satisfy his reason, it is also here that he can find the most rational ideas of the Impersonal.

REPLY TO THE ADDRESS OF WELCOME AT SHIVAGANGA AND MANAMADURA

At Manamadura, the following address of welcome from the Zemindars and citizens of Shivaganga and Manamadura was presented to the Swami:

TO SRI SWAMI VIVEKANANDA:

Most Revered Sir,

We, the Zemindars and citizens of Shivaganga and Manamadura, beg to offer you a most hearty welcome. In the most sanguine moments of our life, in our widest dreams, we never contemplated that you, who were so near our hearts, would be in such close proximity to our homes. The first wire intimating your inability to come to Shivaganga cast a deep gloom on our hearts, and but for the subsequent silver lining to the cloud our disappointment would have been extreme. When we first heard that you had consented to honour our town with your presence, we thought we had realised our highest ambition. The mountain promised to come to Mohammed, and our joy knew no bounds. But when the mountain was obliged to withdraw its consent, and our worst fears were roused that we might not be able even to go to the mountain, you were graciously pleased to give way to our importunities.

Despite the almost insurmountable difficulties of the voyage, the noble self-sacrificing spirit with which you have conveyed the grandest message of the East to the West, the masterly way in which the mission has been executed, and the marvellous and unparalleled success which has crowned your philanthropic efforts have earned for you an undying glory. At a time when Western bread-winning materialism was making the strongest inroads on Indian religious convictions, when the sayings and writings of our sages were beginning to be numbered, the advent of a new master like you has already marked an era in the annals of religious advancement, and we hope that in the fullness of time you will succeed in disintergrating the dross that is temporarily covering the genuine gold of Indian philosophy, and, casting it in the powerful mint of intellect, will make it current coin throughout the whole globe. The catholicity with which you were able triumphantly to bear the flag of Indian philosophic thought among the heterogeneous religionists assembled in the Parliament of Religions enables us to hope that at no distant date you, just like your contemporary in the political sphere, will rule an empire over which the sun never sets, only with this difference that hers is an empire over matter, and yours will be over mind. As she has beaten all records in political history by the length and beneficience of her reign, so we earnestly pray to the Almighty that you will be spared long enough to consummate the labour of love that you have so disinterestedly undertaken and thus to outshine all your predecessors in spiritual history.

We are,
Most Revered Sir,
Your most dutiful and devoted
Servants.

The Swami's reply was to the following effect:

I cannot express the deep debt of gratitude which you have laid upon me by the kind and warm welcome which has just been accorded to me by you. Unfortunately I am not just now in a condition to make a very big speech, however much

I may wish it. In spite of the beautiful adjectives which our Sanskrit friend has been so kind to apply to me, I have a body after all, foolish though it may be; and the body always follows the promptings, conditions, and laws of matter. As such, there is such a thing as fatigue and weariness as regards the material body.

It is a great thing to see the wonderful amount of joy and appreciation expressed in every part of the country for the little work that has been done by me in the West. I look at it only in this way: I want to apply it to those great souls who are coming in the future. If the little bit of work that has been done by me receives such approbation from the nation, what must be the approbation that the spiritual giants, the world-movers coming after us, will get from this nation? India is the land of religion; the Hindu understands religion and religion alone. Centuries of education have always been in that line; and the result is that it is the one concern in life; and you all know well that it is so. It is not necessary that every one should be a shopkeeper; it is not necessary even that every one should be a schoolmaster; it is not necessary that every one should be a fighter; but in this world there will be different nations producing the harmony of result.

Well, perhaps we are fated by Divine Providence to play the spiritual note in this harmony of nations, and it rejoices me to see that we have not yet lost the grand traditions which have been handed down to us by the most glorious forefathers of whom any nation can be proud. It gives me hope, it gives me adamantine faith in the destiny of the race. It cheers me, not for the personal attention paid to me, but to know that the heart of the nation is there, and is still sound. India is still living; who says she is dead? But the West wants to see us active. If they want to see us active on the field of battle, they will be disappointed — that is not our field — just as we would be disappointed if we hoped to see a military nation active on the field of spirituality. But let them come here and see that we are equally active, and how the nation is living and is as alive as ever. We should dispel the idea that we have degenerated at all. So far so good.

But now I have to say a few harsh words, which I hope you will not take unkindly. For the complaint has just been made that European materialism has wellnigh swamped us. It is not all the fault of the Europeans, but a good deal our own. We, as Vedantists, must always look at things from an introspective viewpoint, from its subjective relations. We, as Vedantists, know for certain that there is no power in the universe to injure us unless we first injure ourselves. One-fifth of the population of India have become Mohammedans. Just as before that, going further back, two-thirds of the population in ancient times had become Buddhists, one-fifth are now Mohammedans, Christians are already more than a million.

Whose fault is it? One of our historians says in ever-memorable language: Why should these poor wretches starve and die of thirst when the perennial fountain of life is flowing by?

The question is: What did we do for these people who forsook their own religion? Why should they have become Mohammedans? I heard of an honest girl in England who was going to become a streetwalker. When a lady asked her not to do so, her reply was, "That is the only way I can get sympathy. I can find none to help me now; but let me be a fallen, downtrodden woman, and then perhaps merciful ladies will come and take me to a home and do everything they can for me." We are weeping for these renegades now, but what did we do for them before? Let every one of us ask ourselves, what have we learnt; have we taken hold of the torch of truth, and if so, how far did we carry it? We did not help them then. This is the question we should ask ourselves. That we did not do so was our own fault, our own Karma. Let us blame none, let us blame our own Karma.

Materialism, or Mohammedanism, or Christianity, or any other ism in the world could never have succeeded but that you allowed them. No bacilli can attack the human frame until it is degraded and degenerated by vice, bad food, privation, and exposure; the healthy man passes scatheless through masses of poisonous bacilli. But yet there is time to change our ways. Give up all those old discussions, old fights about things which are meaningless, which are nonsensical in their very nature. Think of the last six hundred or seven hundred years of degradation when grown-up men by hundreds have been discussing for years whether we should drink a glass of water with the right hand or the left, whether the hand should be washed three times or four times, whether we should gargle five or six times. What can you expect from men who pass their lives in discussing such momentous questions as these and writing most learned philosophies on them! There is a danger of our religion getting into the kitchen. We are neither Vedantists, most of us now, nor Paurânics, nor Tântrics. We are just "Don't-touchists". Our religion is in the kitchen. Our God is the cooking-pot, and our religion is, "Don't touch me, I am holy". If this goes on for another century, every one of us will be in a lunatic asylum. It is a sure sign of softening of the brain when the mind cannot grasp the higher problems of life; all originality is lost, the mind has lost all its strength, its activity, and its power of thought, and just tries to go round and round the smallest curve it can find. This state of things has first to be thrown overboard, and then we must stand up, be active and strong; and then we shall recognise our heritage to that infinite treasure, the treasure our forefathers have left for us, a treasure that the whole world requires today. The world will die if this treasure is not distributed. Bring it out, distribute it broadcast. Says Vyasa: Giving alone is the one work in this Kali Yuga; and of all the gifts, giving spiritual life is the highest gift possible; the next gift is secular knowledge; the next, saving the life of man; and the last, giving food to the needy. Of food we have given enough; no nation is more charitable than we. So long as there is a piece of bread in the home of the beggar, he will give half of it. Such a phenomenon can be observed only in India. We have enough of that, let us go for the other two, the gifts of spiritual and secular knowledge. And if we were all brave and had stout hearts, and with absolute sincerity put our shoulders to the wheel, in twenty-five years the whole problem would be solved, and there would be nothing left here to fight about; the whole Indian world would be once more Aryan.

This is all I have to tell you now. I am not given much to talking about plans; I rather prefer to do and show, and then talk about my plans. I have my plans, and mean to work them out if the Lord wills it, if life is given to me. I do not know whether I shall succeed or not, but it is a great thing to take up a grand ideal in life and then give up one's whole life to it. For what otherwise is the value of life, this vegetating, little, low life of man? Subordinating it to one high ideal is the only value that life has. This is the great work to be done in India. I welcome the present religious revival; and I should be foolish if I lost the opportunity of striking the iron while it is hot.

REPLY TO THE ADDRESS
OF WELCOME AT MADURA[1]

The Swami was presented with an address of welcome by the Hindus of Madura, which read as follows:

Most Revered Swami,

We, the Hindu Public of Madura, beg to offer you our most heartfelt and respectful welcome to our ancient and holy city. We realise in you a living example of the Hindu Sannyasin, who, renouncing all worldly ties and attachments calculated to lead to the gratification of the self, is worthily engaged in the noble duty of living for others and endeavouring to raise the spiritual condition of mankind. You have demonstrated in your own person that the true essence of the Hindu religion is not necessarily bound up with rules and rituals, but that it is a sublime philosophy capable of giving peace and solace to the distressed and afflicted.

You have taught America and England to admire that philosophy and that religion which seeks to elevate every man in the best manner suited to his capacities and environments. Although your teachings have for the last three years been delivered in foreign lands, they have not been the less eagerly devoured in this country, and they have not a little tended to counteract the growing materialism imported from a foreign soil.

India lives to this day, for it has a mission to fulfil in the spiritual ordering of the universe. The appearance of a soul like you at the close of this cycle of the Kali Yuga is to us a sure sign of the incarnation in the near future of great souls through whom that mission will be fulfilled.

Madura, the seat of ancient learning, Madura the favoured city of the God Sundareshwara, the holy Dwadashântakshetram of Yogis, lags behind no other Indian city in its warm admiration of your exposition of Indian Philosophy and in its grateful acknowledgments of your priceless services for humanity.

We pray that you may be blessed with a long life of vigour and strength and usefulness.

The Swami replied in the following terms:

I wish I could live in your midst for several days and fulfil the conditions that have just been pointed out by your most worthy Chairman of relating to you my experiences in the West and the result of all my labours there for the last four years. But, unfortunately, even Swamis have bodies; and the continuous travelling and speaking that I have had to undergo for the last three weeks make it impossible for me to deliver a very long speech this evening. I will, therefore, satisfy myself with thanking you very cordially for the kindness that has been shown to me, and reserve other things for some day in the future when under better conditions of health we shall have time to talk over more various subjects than we can do in so short a time this evening. Being in Madura, as the guest of one of your well-known citizens and noblemen, the Raja of Ramnad, one fact comes prominently to my mind. Perhaps most of you are aware that it was the Raja who first put the idea into my mind of going to Chicago, and it was he who all the time supported it with all his heart and influence. A good deal, therefore, of the praise that has been bestowed upon me in this address, ought to go to this noble man of Southern India. I only wish that instead of becoming a Raja he had become a Sannyasin, for that is what he is really fit for.

Wherever there is a thing really needed in one part of the world, the complement will find its way there and supply it with new life. This is true in the physical world as well as in the spiritual. If there is a want of spirituality in one part of the world, and at the same time that spirituality exists elsewhere, whether we consciously struggle for it or not, that spirituality will find its way to the part where it is needed and balance the inequality. In the history of the human race, not once or twice, but again and again, it has been the destiny of India in the past to supply spirituality to the world. We find that whenever either by mighty conquest or by commercial supremacy different parts of the world have been kneaded into one whole race and bequests have been made from one corner to the other, each nation, as it were, poured forth its own quota, either political, social, or spiritual. India's contribution to the sum total of human knowledge has been spirituality, philosophy. These she contributed even long before the rising of the Persian Empire; the second time was during the Persian Empire; for the third time during the ascendancy of the Greeks; and now for the fourth time during the ascendancy of the English, she is going to fulfil the same destiny once

1. Spelt now as Madurai.

more. As Western ideas of organization and external civilisation are penetrating and pouring into our country, whether we will have them or not, so Indian spirituality and philosophy are deluging the lands of the West. None can resist it, and no more can we resist some sort of material civilization from the West. A little of it, perhaps, is good for us, and a little spiritualisation is good for the West; thus the balance will be preserved. It is not that we ought to learn everything from the West, or that they have to learn everything from us, but each will have to supply and hand down to future generations what it has for the future accomplishment of that dream of ages — the harmony of nations, an ideal world. Whether that ideal world will ever come I do not know, whether that social perfection will ever be reached I have my own doubts; whether it comes or not, each one of us will have to work for the idea as if it will come tomorrow, and as if it only depends on his work, and his alone. Each one of us will have to believe that every one else in the world has done his work, and the only work remaining to be done to make the world perfect has to be done by himself. This is the responsibility we have to take upon ourselves.

In the meanwhile, in India there is a tremendous revival of religion. There is danger ahead as well as glory; for revival sometimes breeds fanaticism, sometimes goes to the extreme, so that often it is not even in the power of those who start the revival to control it when it has gone beyond a certain length. It is better, therefore, to be forewarned. We have to find our way between the Scylla of old superstitious orthodoxy and the Charybdis of materialism — of Europeanism, of soullessness, of the so-called reform — which has penetrated to the foundation of Western progress. These two have to be taken care of. In the first place, we cannot become Western; therefore imitating the Westerns is useless. Suppose you can imitate the Westerns, that moment you will die, you will have no more life in you. In the second place, it is impossible. A stream is taking its rise, away beyond where time began, flowing through millions of ages of human history; do you mean to get hold of that stream and push it back to its source, to a Himalayan glacier? Even if that were practicable, it would not be possible for you to be Europeanised. If you find it is impossible for the European to throw off the few centuries of culture which there is in the West, do you think it is possible for you to throw off the culture of shining scores of centuries? It cannot be. We must also remember that in every little village-god and every little superstition custom is that which we are accustomed to call our religious faith. But local customs are infinite and contradictory. Which are we to obey, and which not to obey? The Brâhmin of Southern India, for instance, would shrink in horror at the sight of another Brahmin eating meat; a Brahmin in the North thinks it a most glorious and holy thing to do — he kills goats by the hundred in sacrifice. If you put forward your custom, they are equally ready with theirs. Various are the customs all over India, but they are local. The greatest mistake made is that ignorant peo-

ple always think that this local custom is the essence of our religion.

But beyond this there is a still greater difficulty. There are two sorts of truth we find in our Shâstras, one that is based upon the eternal nature of man — the one that deals with the eternal relation of God, soul, and nature; the other, with local circumstances, environments of the time, social institutions of the period, and so forth. The first class of truths is chiefly embodied in our Vedas, our scriptures; the second in the Smritis, the Puranas. etc. We must remember that for all periods the Vedas are the final goal and authority, and if the Purânas differ in any respect from the Vedas, that part of the Puranas is to be rejected without mercy. We find, then, that in all these Smritis the teachings are different. One Smriti says, this is the custom, and this should be the practice of this age. Another one says, this is the practice of this age, and so forth. This is the Âchâra which should be the custom of the Satya Yuga, and this is the Achara which should be the custom of the Kali Yuga, and so forth. Now this is one of the most glorious doctrines that you have, that eternal truths, being based upon the nature of man, will never change so long as man lives; they are for all times, omnipresent, universal virtues. But the Smritis speak generally of local circumstances, of duties arising from different environments, and they change in the course of time. This you have always to remember that because a little social custom is going to be changed you are not going to lose your religion, not at all. Remember these customs have already been changed. There was a time in this very India when, without eating beef, no Brahmin could remain a Brahmin; you read in the Vedas how, when a Sannyasin, a king, or a great man came into a house, the best bullock was killed; how in time it was found that as we were an agricultural race, killing the best bulls meant annihilation of the race. Therefore the practice was stopped, and a voice was raised against the killing of cows. Sometimes we find existing then what we now consider the most horrible customs. In course of time other laws had to be made. These in turn will have to go, and other Smritis will come. This is one fact we have to learn that the Vedas being eternal will be one and the same throughout all ages, but the Smritis will have an end. As time rolls on, more and more of the Smritis will go, sages will come, and they will change and direct society into better channels, into duties and into paths which accord with the necessity of the age, and without which it is impossible that society can live. Thus we have to guide our course, avoiding these two dangers; and I hope that every one of us here will have breadth enough, and at the same time faith enough, to understand what that means, which I suppose is the inclusion of everything, and not the exclusion. I want the intensity of the fanatic plus the extensity of the materialist. Deep as the ocean, broad as the infinite skies, that is the sort of heart we want. Let us be as progressive as any nation that ever existed, and at the same time as faithful and conservative towards our traditions as Hindus alone know how to be.

In plain words, we have first to learn the distinction between the essentials and the non-essentials in everything. The essentials are eternal, the non-essentials have value only for a certain time; and if after a time they are not replaced by something essential, they are positively dangerous. I do not mean that you should stand up and revile all your old customs and institutions. Certainly not; you must not revile even the most evil one of them. Revile none. Even those customs that are now appearing to be positive evils, have been positively life-giving in times past; and if we have to remove these, we must not do so with curses, but with blessings and gratitude for the glorious work these customs have done for the preservation of our race. And we must also remember that the leaders of our societies have never been either generals or kings, but Rishis. And who are the Rishis? The Rishi as he is called in the Upanishads is not an ordinary man, but a Mantra-drashtâ. He is a man who sees religion, to whom religion is not merely book-learning, not argumentation, nor speculation, nor much talking, but actual realization, a coming face to face with truths which transcend the senses. This is Rishihood, and that Rishihood does not belong to any age, or time, or even to sects or caste. Vâtsyâyana says, truth must be realised; and we have to remember that you, and I, and every one of us will be called upon to become Rishis; and we must have faith in ourselves; we must become world-movers, for everything is in us. We must see Religion face to face, experience it, and thus solve our doubts about it; and then standing up in the glorious light of Rishihood each one of us will be a giant; and every word falling from our lips will carry behind it that infinite sanction of security; and before us evil will vanish by itself without the necessity of cursing any one, without the necessity of abusing any one, without the necessity of fighting any one in the world. May the Lord help us, each one of us here, to realise the Rishihood for our own salvation and for that of others!

THE MISSION OF THE VEDANTA

On the occasion of his visit to Kumbakonam, the Swamiji was presented with the following address by the local Hindu community:

Revered Swamin,

On behalf of the Hindu inhabitants of this ancient and religiously important town of Kumbakonam, we request permission to offer you a most hearty welcome on your return from the Western World to our own holy land of great temples and famous saints and sages. We are highly thankful to God for the remarkable success of your religious mission in America and in Europe, and for His having enabled you to impress upon the choicest representatives of the world's great religions assembled at Chicago that both the Hindu philosophy and religion are so broad and so rationally catholic as to have in them the power to exalt and to harmonise all ideas of God and of human spirituality.

The conviction that the cause of Truth is always safe in the hands of Him who is the life and soul of the universe has been for thousands of years part of our living faith; and if today we rejoice at the results of your holy work in Christian lands, it is because the eyes of men in and outside of India are thereby being opened to the inestimable value of the spiritual heritage of the preeminently religious Hindu nation. The success of your work has naturally added great lustre to the already renowned name of your great Guru; it has also raised us in the estimation of the civilised world; more than all, it has made us feel that we too, as a people, have reason to be proud of the achievements of our past, and that the absence of telling aggressiveness in our civilisation is in no way a sign of its exhausted or decaying condition. With clear-sighted, devoted, and altogether unselfish workers like you in our midst, the future of the Hindu nation cannot but be bright and hopeful. May the God of the universe who is also the great God of all nations bestow on you health and long life, and make you increasingly strong and wise in the discharge of your high and noble function as a worthy teacher of Hindu religion and philosophy.

A second address was also presented by the Hindu students of the town.

The Swami then delivered the following address on the Mission of the Vedanta:

A very small amount of religious work performed brings a large amount of result. If this statement of the Gita wanted an illustration, I am finding every day the truth of that great saying in my humble life. My work has been very insignificant indeed, but the kindness and the cordiality of welcome that have met me at every step of my journey from Colombo to this city are simply beyond all expectation. Yet, at the same time, it is worthy of our traditions as Hindus, it is worthy of our race; for here we are, the Hindu race, whose vitality, whose life-principle, whose very soul, as it were, is in religion. I have seen a little of the world, travelling among the races of the East and the West; and everywhere I find among nations one great ideal which forms the backbone, so to speak, of that race. With some it is politics, with others it is social culture; others again may have intellectual culture and so on for their national background. But this, our motherland, has religion and religion alone for its basis, for its backbone, for the bedrock upon which the whole building of its life has been based. Some of you may remember that in my reply to the kind address which the people of Madras sent over to me in America, I pointed out the fact that a peasant in India has, in many respects, a better religious education than many a gentleman in the West, and today, beyond all doubt, I myself am verifying my own words. There was a time when I did feel rather discontented at the want of information among the masses of India and the lack of thirst among them for information, but now I understand it. Where their interest lies, there they are more eager for information than the masses of any other race that I have seen or have travelled among. Ask our peasants about the momentous political changes in Europe, the upheavals that are going on in European society—they do not know anything of them, nor do they care to know; but the peasants, even in Ceylon, detached from India in many ways, cut off from a living interest in India—I found the very peasants working in the fields there were already acquainted with the fact that there had been a Parliament of Religions in America, that an Indian Sannyasin had gone over there, and that he had had some success.

Where, therefore, their interest is, there they are as eager for information as any other race; and religion is the one and sole interest of the people of India. I am not just now discussing whether it is good to have the vitality of the race in religious ideals or in political ideals, but so far it is clear to us that, for good or for evil, our vitality is concentrated in our religion. You cannot change it. You cannot destroy it and put in its place another. You cannot transplant a large growing tree from one soil to another and make it immediately take root there. For good or for evil, the religious ideal has been flowing into India for thousands of years; for good or for evil, the Indian atmosphere has been filled with ideals of religion for shining scores of centuries; for good or for evil, we have been born and brought up in the very midst of these ideas of religion, till it has entered into our very blood and tingled with every drop in our veins, and has become one with our constitution, become the very vitality of our lives. Can you give such religion up without the rousing of the same energy in reaction, without filling the channel which that mighty river has cut out for itself in the course of thousands of years? Do you want that the Gangâ should go back to its icy bed and begin a new course? Even if that were possible, it would be impossible for this country to give up her characteristic course of religious life and take up for herself a new career of politics or something else. You can work only under the law of least resistance, and this religious line is the line of least resistance in India. This is the line of life, this is the line of growth, and this is the line of well-being in India—to follow the track of religion.

Ay, in other countries religion is only one of the many necessities in life. To use a common illustration which I am in the habit of using, my lady has many things in her parlour, and it is the fashion nowadays to have a Japanese vase, and she must procure it; it does not look well to be without it. So my lady, or my gentleman, has many other occupations in life, and also a little bit of religion must come in to complete it. Consequently he or she has a little religion. Politics, social improvement, in one word, this world, is the goal of mankind in the West, and God and religion come in quietly as helpers to attain that goal. Their God is, so to speak, the Being who helps to cleanse and to furnish this world for them; that is apparently all the value of God for them. Do you not know how for the last hundred or two hundred years you have been hearing again and again out of the lips of men who ought to have known better, from the mouths of those who pretend

at least to know better, that all the arguments they produce against the Indian religion is this—that our religion does not conduce to well-being in this world, that it does not bring gold to us, that it does not make us robbers of nations, that it does not make the strong stand upon the bodies of the weak and feed themselves with the life-blood of the weak. Certainly our religion does not do that. It cannot send cohorts, under whose feet the earth trembles, for the purpose of destruction and pillage and the ruination of races. Therefore they say—what is there in this religion? It does not bring any grist to the grinding mill, any strength to the muscles; what is there in such a religion?

They little dream that that is the very argument with which we prove out religion, because it does not make for this world. Ours is the only true religion because, according to it, this little sense-world of three days' duration is not to be made the end and aim of all, is not to be our great goal. This little earthly horizon of a few feet is not that which bounds the view of our religion. Ours is away beyond, and still beyond; beyond the senses, beyond space, and beyond time, away, away beyond, till nothing of this world is left and the universe itself becomes like a drop in the transcendent ocean of the glory of the soul. Ours is the true religion because it teaches that God alone is true, that this world is false and fleeting, that all your gold is but as dust, that all your power is finite, and that life itself is oftentimes an evil; therefore it is, that ours is the true religion. Ours is the true religion because, above all, it teaches renunciation and stands up with the wisdom of ages to tell and to declare to the nations who are mere children of yesterday in comparison with us Hindus—who own the hoary antiquity of the wisdom, discovered by our ancestors here in India—to tell them in plain words: "Children, you are slaves of the senses; there is only finiteness in the senses, there is only ruination in the senses; the three short days of luxury here bring only ruin at last. Give it all up, renounce the love of the senses and of the world; that is the way of religion." Through renunciation is the way to the goal and not through enjoyment. Therefore ours is the only true religion.

Ay, it is a curious fact that while nations after nations have come upon the stage of the world, played their parts vigorously for a few moments, and died almost without leaving a mark or a ripple on the ocean of time, here we are living, as it were, an eternal life. They talk a great deal of the new theories about the survival of the fittest, and they think that it is the strength of the muscles which is the fittest to survive. If that were true, any one of the aggressively known old world nations would have lived in glory today, and we, the weak Hindus, who never conquered even one other race or nation, ought to have died out; yet we live here three hundred million strong! (A young English lady once told me: What have the Hindus done? They never even conquered a single race!) And it is not at all true that all its energies are spent, that atrophy has overtaken its body: that is not true. There is vitality enough, and it comes out in torrents and deluges the world when the time is ripe and requires it.

We have, as it were, thrown a challenge to the whole world from the most ancient times. In the West, they are trying to solve the problem how much a man can possess, and we are trying here to solve the problem on how little a man can live. This struggle and this difference will still go on for some centuries. But if history has any truth in it and if prognostications ever prove true, it must be that those who train themselves to live on the least and control themselves well will in the end gain the battle, and that those who run after enjoyment and luxury, however vigorous they may seem for the moment, will have to die and become annihilated. There are times in the history of a man's life, nay, in the history of the lives of nations, when a sort of world-weariness becomes painfully predominant. It seems that such a tide of world-weariness has come upon the Western world. There, too, they have their thinkers, great men; and they are already finding out that this race after gold and power is all vanity of vanities; many, nay, most of the cultured men and women there, are already weary of this competition, this struggle, this brutality of their commercial civilisation, and they are looking forward towards something better. There is a class which still clings on to political and social changes as the only panacea for the evils in Europe, but among the great thinkers there, other ideals are growing. They have found out that no amount of political or social manipulation of human conditions can cure the evils of life. It is a change of the soul itself for the better that alone will cure the evils of life. No amount of force, or government, or legislative cruelty will change the conditions of a race, but it is spiritual culture and ethical culture alone that can change wrong racial tendencies for the better. Thus these races of the West are eager for some new thought, for some new philosophy; the religion they have had, Christianity, although good and glorious in many respects, has been imperfectly understood, and is, as understood hitherto, found to be insufficient. The thoughtful men of the West find in our ancient philosophy, especially in the Vedanta, the new impulse of thought they are seeking, the very spiritual food and drink for which they are hungering and thirsting. And it is no wonder that this is so.

I have become used to hear all sorts of wonderful claims put forward in favour of every religion under the sun. You have also heard, quite within recent times, the claims put forward by Dr. Barrows, a great friend of mine, that Christianity is the only universal religion. Let me consider this question awhile and lay before you my reasons why I think that it is Vedanta, and Vedanta alone that can become the universal religion of man, and that no other is fitted for the role. Excepting our own almost all the other great religions in the world are inevitably connected with the life or lives of one or more of their founders. All their theories, their teachings, their doctrines, and their ethics are built round the life of a personal founder, from whom they get their sanction, their authority, and their power; and strangely enough, upon the historicity of the founder's life is built, as it were, all the fabric of such religions.

If there is one blow dealt to the historicity of that life, as has been the case in modern times with the lives of almost all the so-called founders of religion—we know that half of the details of such lives is not now seriously believed in, and that the other half is seriously doubted—if this becomes the case, if that rock of historicity, as they pretend to call it, is shaken and shattered, the whole building tumbles down, broken absolutely, never to regain its lost status.

Every one of the great religions in the world excepting our own, is built upon such historical characters; but ours rests upon principles. There is no man or woman who can claim to have created the Vedas. They are the embodiment of eternal principles; sages discovered them; and now and then the names of these sages are mentioned—just their names; we do not even know who or what they were. In many cases we do not know who their fathers were, and almost in every case we do not know when and where they were born. But what cared they, these sages, for their names? They were the preachers of principles, and they themselves, so far as they went, tried to become illustrations of the principles they preached. At the same time, just as our God is an Impersonal and yet a Personal God, so is our religion a most intensely impersonal one—a religion based upon principles—and yet with an infinite scope for the play of persons; for what religion gives you more Incarnations, more prophets and seers, and still waits for infinitely more? The Bhâgavata says that Incarnations are infinite, leaving ample scope for as many as you like to come. Therefore if any one or more of these persons in India's religious history, any one or more of these Incarnations, and any one or more of our prophets proved not to have been historical, it does not injure our religion at all; even then it remains firm as ever, because it is based upon principles, and not upon persons. It is in vain we try to gather all the peoples of the world around a single personality. It is difficult to make them gather together even round eternal and universal principles. If it ever becomes possible to bring the largest portion of humanity to one way of thinking in regard to religion, mark you, it must be always through principles and not through persons. Yet as I have said, our religion has ample scope for the authority and influence of persons. There is that most wonderful theory of Ishta which gives you the fullest and the freest choice possible among these great religious personalities. You may take up any one of the prophets or teachers as your guide and the object of your special adoration; you are even allowed to think that he whom you have chosen is the greatest of the prophets, greatest of all the Avatâras; there is no harm in that, but you must keep to a firm background of eternally true principles. The strange fact here is that the power of our Incarnations has been holding good with us only so far as they are illustrations of the principles in the Vedas. The glory of Shri Krishna is that he has been the best preacher of our eternal religion of principles and the best commentator on the Vedanta that ever lived in India.

The second claim of the Vedanta upon the attention of the

world is that, of all the scriptures in the world, it is the one scripture the teaching of which is in entire harmony with the results that have been attained by the modern scientific investigations of external nature. Two minds in the dim past of history, cognate to each other in form and kinship and sympathy, started, being placed in different routes. The one was the ancient Hindu mind, and the other the ancient Greek mind. The former started by analysing the internal world. The latter started in search of that goal beyond by analysing the external world. And even through the various vicissitudes of their history, it is easy to make out these two vibrations of thought as tending to produce similar echoes of the goal beyond. It seems clear that the conclusions of modern materialistic science can be acceptable, harmoniously with their religion, only to the Vedantins or Hindus as they are called. It seems clear that modern materialism can hold its own and at the same time approach spirituality by taking up the conclusions of the Vedanta. It seems to us, and to all who care to know, that the conclusions of modern science are the very conclusions the Vedanta reached ages ago; only, in modern science they are written in the language of matter. This then is another claim of the Vedanta upon modern Western minds, its rationality, the wonderful rationalism of the Vedanta. I have myself been told by some of the best Western scientific minds of the day, how wonderfully rational the conclusions of the Vedanta are. I know one of them personally who scarcely has time to eat his meal or go out of his laboratory, but who yet would stand by the hour to attend my lectures on the Vedanta; for, as he expresses it, they are so scientific, they so exactly harmonise with the aspirations of the age and with the conclusions to which modern science is coming at the present time.

Two such scientific conclusions drawn from comparative religion, I would specially like to draw your attention to: the one bears upon the idea of the universality of religions, and the other on the idea of the oneness of things. We observe in the histories of Babylon and among the Jews an interesting religious phenomenon happening. We find that each of these Babylonian and Jewish peoples was divided into so many tribes, each tribe having a god of its own, and that these little tribal gods had often a generic name. The gods among the Babylonians were all called Baals, and among them Baal Merodach was the chief. In course of time one of these many tribes would conquer and assimilate the other racially allied tribes, and the natural result would be that the god of the conquering tribe would be placed at the head of all the gods of the other tribes. Thus the so-called boasted monotheism of the Semites was created. Among the Jews the gods went by the name of Molochs. Of these there was one Moloch who belonged to the tribe called Israel, and he was called the Moloch-Yahveh or Moloch-Yava. In time, this tribe of Israel slowly conquered some of the other tribes of the same race, destroyed their Molochs, and declared its own Moloch to be the Supreme Moloch of all the Molochs. And I am sure, most of you know the amount of bloodshed, of tyranny,

and of brutal savagery that this religious conquest entailed. Later on, the Babylonians tried to destroy this supremacy of Moloch-Yahveh, but could not succeed in doing so.

It seems to me, that such an attempt at tribal self-assertion in religious matters might have taken place on the frontiers and India also. Here, too, all the various tribes of the Aryans might have come into conflict with one another for declaring the supremacy of their several tribal gods; but India's history was to be otherwise, was to be different from that of the Jews. India alone was to be, of all lands, the land of toleration and of spirituality; and therefore the fight between tribes and their gods did not long take place here. For one of the greatest sages that was ever born found out here in India even at that distant time, which history cannot reach, and into whose gloom even tradition itself dares not peep — in that distant time the sage arose and declared, एकं सद् विप्रा बहुधा वदन्ति — "He who exists is one; the sages call Him variously." This is one of the most memorable sentences that was ever uttered, one of the grandest truths that was ever discovered. And for us Hindus this truth has been the very backbone of our national existence. For throughout the vistas of the centuries of our national life, this one idea — एकं सद् विप्रा बहुधा वदन्ति — comes down, gaining in volume and in fullness till it has permeated the whole of our national existence, till it has mingled in our blood, and has become one with us. We live that grand truth in every vein, and our country has become the glorious land of religious toleration. It is here and here alone that they build temples and churches for the religions which have come with the object of condemning our own religion. This is one very great principle that the world is waiting to learn from us. Ay, you little know how much of intolerance is yet abroad. It struck me more than once that I should have to leave my bones on foreign shores owing to the prevalence of religious intolerance. Killing a man is nothing for religion's sake; tomorrow they may do it in the very heart of the boasted civilisation of the West, if today they are not really doing so. Outcasting in its most horrible forms would often come down upon the head of a man in the West if he dared to say a word against his country's accepted religion. They talk glibly and smoothly here in criticism of our caste laws. If you go, to the West and live there as I have done, you will know that even some of the biggest professors you hear of are arrant cowards and dare not say, for fear of public opinion, a hundredth part of what they hold to be really true in religious matter.

Therefore the world is waiting for this grand idea of universal toleration. It will be a great acquisition to civilisation. Nay, no civilisation can long exist unless this idea enters into it. No civilisation can grow unless fanatics, bloodshed, and brutality stop. No civilisation can begin to lift up its head until we look charitably upon one another; and the first step towards that much-needed charity is to look charitably and kindly upon the religious convictions of others. Nay more, to understand that not only should we be charitable, but positively helpful to each other, however different our religious ideas and convictions may be. And that is exactly what we do in India as I have just related to you. It is here in India that Hindus have built and are still building churches for Christians and mosques for Mohammedans. That is the thing to do. In spite of their hatred, in spite of their brutality, in spite of their cruelly, in spite of their tyranny, and in spite of the vile language they are given to uttering, we will and must go on building churches for the Christians and mosques for the Mohammedans until we conquer through love, until we have demonstrated to the world that love alone is the fittest thing to survive and not hatred, that it is gentleness that has the strength to live on and to fructify, and not mere brutality and physical force.

The other great idea that the world wants from us today, the thinking part of Europe, nay, the whole world—more, perhaps, the lower classes than the higher, more the masses than the cultured, more the ignorant than the educated, more the weak than the strong—is that eternal grand idea of the spiritual oneness of the whole universe. I need not tell you to-day, men from Madras University, how the modern researches of the West have demonstrated through physical means the oneness and the solidarity of the whole universe; how, physically speaking, you and I, the sun, moon, and stars are but little waves or waveless in the midst of an infinite ocean of matter; how Indian psychology demonstrated ages ago that, similarly, both body and mind are but mere names or little waveless in the ocean of matter, the Samashti; and how, going one step further, it is also shown in the Vedanta that behind that idea of the unity of the whole show, the real Soul is one. There is but one Soul throughout the universe, all is but One Existence This great idea of the real and basic solidarity of the whole universe has frightened many, even in this country. It even now finds sometimes more opponents than adherents. I tell you, nevertheless, that it is the one great life-giving idea which the world wants from us today, and which the mute masses of India want for their uplifting, for none can regenerate this land of ours without the practical application and effective operation of this ideal of the oneness of things.

The rational West is earnestly bent upon seeking out the rationality, the raison d' être of all its philosophy and its ethics; and you all know well that ethics cannot be derived from the mere sanction of any personage, however great and divine he may have been. Such an explanation of the authority of ethics appeals no more to the highest of the world's thinkers; they want something more than human sanction for ethical and moral codes to be binding, they want some eternal principle of truth as the sanction of ethics. And where is that eternal sanction to be found except in the only Infinite Reality that exists in you and in me and in all, in the Self, in the Soul? The infinite oneness of the Soul is the eternal sanction of all morality, that you and I are not only brothers—every literature voicing man's struggle towards freedom has preached that for you—but that you and I are really one. This is the dictate of Indian philosophy. This oneness is the rationale of all ethics and all spirituality. Europe wants it today just as much as our

downtrodden masses do, and this great principle is even now unconsciously forming the basis of all the latest political and social aspirations that are coming up in England, in Germany, in France, and in America. And mark it, my friends, that in and through all the literature voicing man's struggle towards freedom, towards universal freedom, again and again you find the Indian Vedantic ideals coming out prominently. In some cases the writers do not know the source of their inspiration, in some cases they try to appear very original, and a few there are, bold and grateful enough to mention the source and acknowledge their indebtedness to it.

When I was in America, I heard once the complaint made that I was preaching too much of Advaita, and too little of dualism. Ay, I know what grandeur, what oceans of love, what infinite, ecstatic blessings and joy there are in the dualistic love-theories of worship and religion. I know it all. But this is not the time with us to weep even in joy; we have had weeping enough; no more is this the time for us to become soft. This softness has been with us till we have become like masses of cotton and are dead. What our country now wants are muscles of iron and nerves of steel, gigantic wills which nothing can resist, which can penetrate into the mysteries and the secrets of the universe, and will accomplish their purpose in any fashion even if it meant going down to the bottom of the ocean and meeting death face to face. That is what we want, and that can only be created, established, and strengthened by understanding and realising the ideal of the Advaita, that ideal of the oneness of all. Faith, faith, faith in ourselves, faith, faith in God—this is the secret of greatness. If you have faith in all the three hundred and thirty millions of your mythological gods, and in all the gods which foreigners have now and again introduced into your midst, and still have no faith in yourselves, there is no salvation for you. Have faith in yourselves, and stand up on that faith and be strong; that is what we need. Why is it that we three hundred and thirty millions of people have been ruled for the last one thousand years by any and every handful of foreigners who chose to walk over our prostrate bodies? Because they had faith in themselves and we had not. What did I learn in the West, and what did I see behind those frothy sayings of the Christian sects repeating that man was a fallen and hopelessly fallen sinner? There I saw that inside the national hearts of both Europe and America reside the tremendous power of the men's faith in themselves. An English boy will tell you, "I am an Englishman, and I can do anything." The American boy will tell you the same thing, and so will any European boy. Can our boys say the same thing here? No, nor even the boy's fathers. We have lost faith in ourselves. Therefore to preach the Advaita aspect of the Vedanta is necessary to rouse up the hearts of men, to show them the glory of their souls. It is, therefore, that I preach this Advaita; and I do so not as a sectarian, but upon universal and widely acceptable grounds.

It is easy to find out the way of reconciliation that will not hurt the dualist or the qualified monist. There is not one system in India which does not hold the doctrine that God is within, that Divinity resides within all things. Every one of our Vedantic systems admits that all purity and perfection and strength are in the soul already. According to some, this perfection sometimes becomes, as it were, contracted, and at other times it becomes expanded again. Yet it is there. According to the Advaita, it neither contracts nor expands, but becomes hidden and uncovered now and again. Pretty much the same thing in effect. The one may be a more logical statement than the other, but as to the result, the practical conclusions, both are about the same; and this is the one central idea which the world stands in need of, and nowhere is the want more felt than in this, our own motherland.

Ay, my friends, I must tell you a few harsh truths. I read in the newspaper how, when one of our fellows is murdered or ill-treated by an Englishman, howls go up all over the country; I read and I weep, and the next moment comes to my mind the question: Who is responsible for it all? As a Vedantist I cannot but put that question to myself. The Hindu is a man of introspection; he wants to see things in and through himself, through the subjective vision. I, therefore, ask myself: Who is responsible? And the answer comes every time: Not the English; no, they are not responsible; it is we who are responsible for all our misery and all our degradation, and we alone are responsible. Our aristocratic ancestors went on treading the common masses of our country underfoot, till they became helpless, till under this torment the poor, poor people nearly forgot that they were human beings. They have been compelled to be merely hewers of wood and drawers of water for centuries, so much so, that they are made to believe that they are born as slaves, born as hewers of wood and drawers of water. With all our boasted education of modern times, if anybody says a kind word for them, I often find our men shrink at once from the duty of lifting them up, these poor downtrodden people. Not only so, but I also find that all sorts of most demoniacal and brutal arguments, culled from the crude ideas of hereditary transmission and other such gibberish from the Western world, are brought forward in order to brutalise and tyrannise over the poor all the more. At the Parliament of Religions in America, there came among others a young man, a born Negro, a real African Negro, and he made a beautiful speech. I became interested in the young man and now and then talked to him, but could learn nothing about him. But one day in England, I met some Americans; and this is what they told me. This boy was the son of a Negro chief who lived in the heart of Africa, and that one day another chief became angry with the father of this boy and murdered him and murdered the mother also, and they were cooked and eaten; he ordered the child to be killed also and cooked and eaten; but the boy fled, and after passing through great hardships and having travelled a distance of several hundreds of miles, he reached the seashore, and there he was taken into an American vessel and brought over to America. And this boy made that speech! After that, what was I to think of your doctrine of heredity!

Ay, Brâhmins, if the Brahmin has more aptitude for learning on the ground of heredity than the Pariah, spend no more money on the Brahmin's education, but spend all on the Pariah. Give to the weak, for there all the gift is needed. If the Brahmin is born clever, he can educate himself without help. If the others are not born clever, let them have all the teaching and the teachers they want. This is justice and reason as I understand it. Our poor people, these downtrodden masses of India, therefore, require to hear and to know what they really are. Ay, let every man and woman and child, without respect of caste or birth, weakness or strength, hear and learn that behind the strong and the weak, behind the high and the low, behind every one, there is that Infinite Soul, assuring the infinite possibility and the infinite capacity of all to become great and good. Let us proclaim to every soul: उत्तिष्ठत जाग्रत प्राप्य वरान्निबोधत—Arise, awake, and stop not till the goal is reached. Arise, awake! Awake from this hypnotism of weakness. None is really weak; the soul is infinite, omnipotent, and omniscient. Stand up, assert yourself, proclaim the God within you, do not deny Him! Too much of inactivity, too much of weakness, too much of hypnotism has been and is upon our race. O ye modern Hindus, de-hypnotise yourselves. The way to do that is found in your own sacred books. Teach yourselves, teach every one his real nature, call upon the sleeping soul and see how it awakes. Power will come, glory will come, goodness will come, purity will come, and everything that is excellent will come when this sleeping soul is roused to self-conscious activity. Ay, if there is anything in the Gita that I like, it is these two verses, coming out strong as the very gist, the very essence, of Krishna's teaching— "He who sees the Supreme Lord dwelling alike in all beings, the Imperishable in things that perish, he sees indeed. For seeing the Lord as the same, everywhere present, he does not destroy the Self by the Self, and thus he goes to the highest goal."

Thus there is a great opening for the Vedanta to do beneficent work both here and elsewhere. This wonderful idea of the sameness and omnipresence of the Supreme Soul has to be preached for the amelioration and elevation of the human race here as elsewhere. Wherever there is evil and wherever there is ignorance and want of knowledge, I have found out by experience that all evil comes, as our scriptures say, relying upon differences, and that all good comes from faith in equality, in the underlying sameness and oneness of things. This is the great Vedantic ideal. To have the ideal is one thing, and to apply it practically to the details of daily life is quite another thing. It is very good to point out an ideal, but where is the practical way to reach it?

Here naturally comes the difficult and the vexed question of caste and of social reformation, which has been uppermost for centuries in the minds of our people. I must frankly tell you that I am neither a caste-breaker nor a mere social reformer. I have nothing to do directly with your castes or with your social reformation. Live in any caste you like, but that is no reason why you should hate another man or another caste. It is love and love alone that I preach, and I base my teaching on the great Vedantic truth of the sameness and omnipresence of the Soul of the Universe. For nearly the past one hundred years, our country has been flooded with social reformers and various social reform proposals. Personally, I have no fault to find with these reformers. Most of them are good, well-meaning men, and their aims too are very laudable on certain points; but it is quite a patent fact that this one hundred years of social reform has produced no permanent and valuable result appreciable throughout the country. Platform speeches have been made by the thousand, denunciations in volumes after volumes have been hurled upon the devoted head of the Hindu race and its civilisation, and yet no good practical result has been achieved; and where is the reason for that? The reason is not hard to find. It is in the denunciation itself. As I told you before, in the first place, we must try to keep our historically acquired character as a people. I grant that we have to take a great many things from other nations, that we have to learn many lessons from outside; but I am sorry to say that most of our modern reform movements have been inconsiderate imitations of Western means and methods of work; and that surely will not do for India; therefore, it is that all our recent reform movements have had no result.

In the second place, denunciation is not at all the way to do good. That there are evils in our society even a child can see; and in what society are there no evils? And let me take this opportunity, my countrymen, of telling you that in comparing the different races and nations of the world I have been among, I have come to the conclusion that our people are on the whole the most moral and the most godly, and our institutions are, in their plan and purpose, best suited to make mankind happy. I do not, therefore, want any reformation. My ideal is growth, expansion, development on national lines. As I look back upon the history of my country, I do not find in the whole world another country which has done quite so much for the improvement of the human mind. Therefore I have no words of condemnation for my nation. I tell them, "You have done well; only try to do better." Great things have been done in the past in this land, and there is both time and room for greater things to be done yet. I am sure you know that we cannot stand still. If we stand still, we die. We have either to go forward or to go backward. We have either to progress or to degenerate. Our ancestors did great things in the past, but we have to grow into a fuller life and march beyond even their great achievements. How can we now go back and degenerate ourselves? That cannot be; that must not be; going back will lead to national decay and death. Therefore let us go forward and do yet greater things; that is what I have to tell you.

I am no preacher of any momentary social reform. I am not trying to remedy evils, I only ask you to go forward and to complete the practical realisation of the scheme of human progress that has been laid out in the most perfect order by our ancestors. I only ask you to work to realise more and more the Vedantic ideal of the solidarity of man and his inborn divine nature. Had I the time, I would gladly show you how everything we have now to do was laid out years ago by our ancient law-givers, and how they actually anticipated all the different changes that have taken place and are still to take place in our national institutions. They also were breakers of caste, but they were not like our modern men. They did not mean by the breaking of caste that all the people in a city should sit down together to a dinner of beef-steak and champagne, nor that all fools and lunatics in the country should marry when, where, and whom they chose and reduce the country to a lunatic asylum, nor did they believe that the prosperity of a nation is to be gauged by the number of husbands its widows get. I have yet to see such a prosperous nation.

The ideal man of our ancestors was the Brahmin. In all our books stands out prominently this ideal of the Brahmin. In Europe there is my Lord the Cardinal, who is struggling hard and spending thousands of pounds to prove the nobility of his ancestors, and he will not be satisfied until he has traced his ancestry to some dreadful tyrant who lived on a hill and watched the people passing by, and whenever he had the opportunity, sprang out on them and robbed them. That was the business of these nobility-bestowing ancestors, and my Lord Cardinal is not satisfied until he can trace his ancestry to one of these. In India, on the other hand, the greatest princes seek to trace their descent to some ancient sage who dressed in a bit of loin cloth, lived in a forest, eating roots and studying the Vedas. It is there that the Indian prince goes to trace his ancestry. You are of the high caste when you can trace your ancestry to a Rishi, and not otherwise.

Our ideal of high birth, therefore, is different from, that of others. Our ideal is the Brahmin of spiritual culture and renunciation. By the Brahmin ideal what do I mean? I mean the ideal Brahmin-ness in which worldliness is altogether absent and true wisdom is abundantly present. That is the ideal of the Hindu race. Have you not heard how it is declared that he, the Brahmin, is not amenable to law, that he has no law, that he is not governed by kings, and that his body cannot be hurt? That is perfectly true. Do not understand it in the light thrown upon it by interested and ignorant fools, but understand it in the light of the true and original Vedantic conception. If the Brahmin is he who has killed all selfishness and who lives and works to acquire and propagate wisdom and the power of love—if a country is altogether inhabited by such Brahmins, by men and women who are spiritual and moral and good, is it strange to think of that country as being above and beyond all law? What police, what military are necessary to govern them? Why should any one govern them at all? Why should they live under a government? They are good and noble, and they are the men of God; these are our ideal Brahmins, and we read that in the Satya Yuga there was only one caste, and that was the Brahmin. We read in the Mahâbhârata that the whole world was in the beginning peopled with Brahmins, and that as they began to degenerate, they became divided into different castes, and that when the cycle turns round, they will all go back to that Brahminical origin. This cycle is turning round now, and I draw your attention to this fact. Therefore our solution of the caste question is not degrading those who are already high up, is not running amuck through food and drink, is not jumping out of our own limits in order to have more enjoyment, but it comes by every one of us, fulfilling the dictates of our Vedantic religion, by our attaining spirituality, and by our becoming the ideal Brahmin. There is a law laid on each one of you in this land by your ancestors, whether you are Aryans or non-Aryans, Rishis or Brahmins, or the very lowest outcasts. The command is the same to you all, that you must make progress without stopping, and that from the highest man to the lowest Pariah, every one in this country has to try and become the ideal Brahmin. This Vedantic idea is applicable not only here but over the whole world. Such is our ideal of caste as meant for raising all humanity slowly and gently towards the realisation of that great ideal of the spiritual man who is non-resisting, calm, steady, worshipful, pure, and meditative. In that ideal there is God.

How are these things to be brought about? I must again draw your attention to the fact that cursing and vilifying and abusing do not and cannot produce anything good. They have been tried for years and years, and no valuable result has been obtained. Good results can be produced only through love, through sympathy. It is a great subject, and it requires several lectures to elucidate all the plans that I have in view, and all the ideas that are, in this connection, coming to my mind day after day I must, therefore, conclude, only reminding you of this fact that this ship of our nation, O Hindus, has been usefully plying here for ages. Today, perhaps, it has sprung a leak; today, perhaps, it has become a little worn out. And if such is the case, it behaves you and me to try our best to stop the leak and holes. Let us tell our countrymen of the danger, let them awake and help us. I will cry at the top of my voice from one part of this country to the other, to awaken the people to the situation and their duty. Suppose they do not hear me, still I shall not have one word of abuse for them, not one word of cursing. Great has been our nation's work in the past; and if we cannot do greater things in the future, let us have this consolation that we can sink and die together in peace. Be patriots, love the race which has done such great things for us in the past. Ay, the more I compare notes, the more I love you, my fellow-countrymen; you are good and pure and gentle. You have been always tyrannised over, and such is the irony of this material world of Mâyâ. Never mind that; the Spirit will triumph in the long run. In the meanwhile let us work and let us not abuse our country, let us not curse and abuse the weather-beaten and work-worn institutions of our thrice-holy motherland. Have no word of condemnation even for the most superstitious and the most irrational of its institutions, for they also must have served some good in the past.

Remember always that there is not in the world any other country whose institutions are really better in their aims and objects than the institutions of this land. I have seen castes in almost every country in the world, but nowhere is their plan and purpose so glorious as here. If caste is thus unavoidable, I would rather have a caste of purity and culture and self-sacrifice, than a caste of dollars. Therefore utter no words of condemnation. Close your lips and let your hearts open. Work out the salvation of this land and of the whole world, each of you thinking that the entire burden is on your shoulders. Carry the light and the life of the Vedanta to every door, and rouse up the divinity that is hidden within every soul. Then, whatever may be the measure of your success, you will have this satisfaction that you have lived, worked, and died for a great cause. In the success of this cause, howsoever brought about, is centred the salvation of humanity here and hereafter.

MY PLAN OF CAMPAIGN

Delivered at the Victoria Hall, Madras

As the other day we could not proceed, owing to the crowd, I shall take this opportunity of thanking the people of Madras for the uniform kindness that I have received at their hands. I do not know how better to express my gratitude for the beautiful words that have been expressed in the addresses than by praying to the Lord to make me worthy of the kind and generous expressions and by working all my life for the cause of our religion and to serve our motherland; and may the Lord make me worthy of them.

With all my faults, I think I have a little bit of boldness. I had a message from India to the West, and boldly I gave it to the American and the English peoples. I want, before going into the subject of the day, to speak a few bold words to you all. There have been certain circumstances growing around me, tending to thwart me, oppose my progress, and crush me out of existence if they could. Thank God they have failed, as such attempts will always fail. But there has been, for the last three years, a certain amount of misunderstanding, and so long as I was in foreign lands, I held my peace and did not even speak one word; but now, standing upon the soil of my motherland, I want to give a few words of explanation. Not that I care what the result will be of these words — not that I care what feeling I shall evoke from you by these words. I care very little, for I am the same Sannyâsin that entered your city about four years ago with this staff and Kamandalu; the same broad world is before me. Without further preface let me begin.

First of all, I have to say a few words about the Theosophical Society. It goes without saying that a certain amount of good work has been done to India by the Society; as such every Hindu is grateful to it, and especially to Mrs. Besant; for though I know very little of her, yet what little I know has impressed me with the idea that she is a sincere well-wisher of this motherland of ours, and that she is doing the best in her power to raise our country. For that, the eternal gratitude of every trueborn Indian is hers, and all blessings be on her and hers for ever. But that is one thing—and joining the Society of the Theosophists is another. Regard and estimation and love are one thing, and swallowing everything any one has to say, without reasoning, without criticising, without analysing, is quite another. There is a report going round that the Theosophists helped the little achievements of mine in America and England. I have to tell you plainly that every word of it is wrong, every word of it is untrue. We hear so much tall talk in this world, of liberal ideas and sympathy with differences of opinion. That is very good, but as a fact, we find that one sympathises with another only so long as the other believes in everything he has to say, but as soon as he dares to differ, that sympathy is gone, that love vanishes. There are others, again, who have their own axes to grind, and if anything arises in a country which prevents the grinding of them, their hearts burn, any amount of hatred comes out, and they do not know what to do. What harm does it do to the Christian missionary that the Hindus are trying to cleanse their own houses? What injury will it do to the Brâhmo Samâj and other reform bodies that the Hindus are trying their best to reform themselves? Why should they stand in opposition? Why should they be the greatest enemies of these movements? Why?—I ask. It seems to me that their hatred and jealousy are so bitter that no why or how can be asked there.

Four years ago, when I, a poor, unknown, friendless Sannyasin was going to America, going beyond the waters to America without any introductions or friends there, I called on the leader of the Theosophical Society. Naturally I thought he, being an American and a lover of India, perhaps would give me a letter of introduction to somebody there. He asked me, "Will you join my Society?" "No," I replied, "how can I? For I do not believe in most of your doctrines." "Then, I am sorry, I cannot do anything for you," he answered. That was not paving the way for me. I reached America, as you know, through the help of a few friends of Madras. Most of them are present here. Only one is absent, Mr. Justice Subramania Iyer, to whom my deepest gratitude is due. He has the insight of a genius and is one of the staunchest friends I have in this life, a true friend indeed, a true child of India. I arrived in America several months before the Parliament of Religions began. The money I had with me was little, and it was soon spent. Winter approached, and I had only thin summer clothes. I did not know what to do in that cold, dreary climate, for if I went to beg in the streets, the result would have been that I would have been sent to jail. There I was with the last few dollars in my pocket. I sent a wire to my friends in Madras. This came to be known to the Theosophists, and one of them wrote, "Now the devil is going to die; God bless us all." Was that paving the way for me? I would not have mentioned this now; but, as my countrymen wanted to know, it must come out. For three years I have not opened my lips about these things; silence has been my motto; but today the thing has come out. That was not all. I saw some Theosophists in the Parliament of

Religions, and I wanted to talk and mix with them. I remember the looks of scorn which were on their faces, as much as to say, "What business has the worm to be here in the midst of the gods?" After I had got name and fame at the Parliament of Religions, then came tremendous work for me; but at every turn the Theosophists tried to cry me down. Theosophists were advised not to come and hear my lectures, for thereby they would lose all sympathy of the Society, because the laws of the esoteric section declare that any man who joins that esoteric section should receive instruction from Kuthumi and Moria, of course through their visible representatives—Mr. Judge and Mrs. Besant—so that, to join the esoteric section means to surrender one's independence. Certainly I could not do any such thing, nor could I call any man a Hindu who did any such thing. I had a great respect for Mr. Judge. He was a worthy man, open, fair, simple, and he was the best representative the Theosophists ever had. I have no right to criticise the dispute between him and Mrs. Besant when each claims that his or her Mahâtmâ is right. And the strange part of it is that the same Mahatma is claimed by both. Lord knows the truth: He is the Judge, and no one has the right to pass judgement when the balance is equal. Thus they prepared the way for me all over America!

They joined the other opposition—the Christian missionaries. There is not one black lie imaginable that these latter did not invent against me. They blackened my character from city to city, poor and friendless though I was in a foreign country. They tried to oust me from every house and to make every man who became my friend my enemy. They tried to starve me out; and I am sorry to say that one of my own countrymen took part against me in this. He is the leader of a reform party in India. This gentleman is declaring every day, "Christ has come to India." Is this the way Christ is to come to India? Is this the way to reform India? And this gentleman I knew from my childhood; he was one of my best friends; when I saw him—I had not met for a long time one of my countrymen—I was so glad, and this was the treatment I received from him. The day the Parliament cheered me, the day I became popular in Chicago, from that day his tone changed; and in an underhand way, he tried to do everything he could to injure me. Is that the way that Christ will come to India? Is that the lesson that he had learnt after sitting twenty years at the feet of Christ? Our great reformers declare that Christianity and Christian power are going to uplift the Indian people. Is that the way to do it? Surely, if that gentleman is an illustration, it does not look very hopeful.

One word more: I read in the organ of the social reformers that I am called a Shudra and am challenged as to what right a Shudra has to become a Sannyasin. To which I reply: I trace my descent to one at whose feet every Brahmin lays flowers when he utters the words—यमाय धर्मराजाय चित्रगुप्ताय वै नमः—and whose descendants are the purest of Kshatriyas. If you believe in your mythology or your Paurânika scriptures, let these so-called reformers know that my caste, apart from other services in the past, ruled half of India for centuries. If my caste is left out of consideration, what will there be left of the present-day civilisation of India? In Bengal alone, my blood has furnished them with their greatest philosopher, the greatest poet, the greatest historian, the greatest archaeologist, the greatest religious preacher; my blood has furnished India with the greatest of her modern scientists. These detractors ought to have known a little of our own history, and to have studied our three castes, and learnt that the Brahmin, the Kshatriya, and the Vaishya have equal right to be Sannyasins: the Traivarnikas have equal right to the Vedas. This is only by the way. I just refer to this, but I am not at all hurt if they call me a Shudra. It will be a little reparation for the tyranny of my ancestors over the poor. If I am a Pariah, I will be all the more glad, for I am the disciple of a man, who—the Brahmin of Brahmins—wanted to cleanse the house of a Pariah. Of course the Pariah would not allow him; how could he let this Brahmin Sannyasin come and cleanse his house! And this man woke up in the dead of night, entered surreptitiously the house of this Pariah, cleansed his latrine, and with his long hair wiped the place, and that he did day after day in order that he might make himself the servant of all. I bear the feet of that man on my head; he is my hero; that hero's life I will try to imitate. By being the servant of all, a Hindu seeks to uplift himself. That is how the Hindus should uplift the masses, and not by looking for any foreign influence. Twenty years of occidental civilisation brings to my mind the illustration of the man who wants to starve his own friend in a foreign land, simply because this friend is popular, simply because he thinks that this man stands in the way of his making money. And the other is the illustration of what genuine, orthodox Hinduism itself will do at home. Let any one of our reformers bring out that life, ready to serve even a Pariah, and then I will sit at his feet and learn, and not before that. One ounce of practice is worth twenty thousand tons of big talk.

Now I come to the reform societies in Madras. They have been very kind to me. They have given me very kind words, and they have pointed out, and I heartily agree with them, that there is a difference between the reformers of Bengal and those of Madras. Many of you will remember what I have very often told you, that Madras is in a very beautiful state just now. It has not got into the play of action and reaction as Bengal has done. Here there is steady and slow progress all through; here is growth, and not reaction. In many cases, end to a certain extent, there is a revival in Bengal; but in Madras it is not a revival, it is a growth, a natural growth. As such, I entirely agree with what the reformers point out as the difference between the two peoples; but there is one difference which they do not understand. Some of these societies, I am afraid, try to intimidate me to join them. That is a strange thing for them to attempt. A man who has met starvation face to face for fourteen years of his life, who has not known where he will get a meal the next day and where to sleep, cannot be intimidated so easily. A man, almost without clothes, who dared to live where the thermometer registered thirty degrees below zero, without knowing where the next meal was to come from, cannot be so easily intimidated in India. This is the first thing I will tell them—I have a little will of my own. I have my little experience too; and I have a message for the world which I will deliver without fear and without care for the future. To the reformers I will point out that I am a greater reformer than any one of them. They want to reform only little bits. I want root-and-branch reform. Where we differ is in the method. Theirs is the method of destruction, mine is that of construction. I do not believe in reform; I believe in growth. I do not dare to put myself in the position of God and dictate to our society, "This way thou shouldst move and not that." I simply want to be like the squirrel in the building of Râma's bridge, who was quite content to put on the bridge his little quota of sand-dust. That is my position. This wonderful national machine has worked through ages, this wonderful river of national life is flowing before us. Who knows, and who dares to say whether it is good and how it shall move? Thousands of circumstances are crowding round it, giving it a special impulse, making it dull at one time and quicker at another. Who dares command its motion? Ours is only to work, as the Gita says, without looking for results. Feed the national life with the fuel it wants, but the growth is its own; none can dictate its growth to it. Evils are plentiful in our society, but so are there evils in every other society. Here the earth is soaked sometimes with widows' tears; there in the West, the air is rent with the sighs of the unmarried. Here poverty is the great bane of life; there the life-weariness of luxury is the great bane that is upon the race. Here men want to commit suicide because they have nothing to eat; there they commit suicide because they have so much to eat. Evil is everywhere; it is like chronic rheumatism. Drive it from the foot, it goes to the head; drive it from there, it goes somewhere else. It is a question of chasing it from place to place; that is all. Ay, children, to try to remedy evil is not the true way. Our philosophy teaches that evil and good are eternally conjoined, the obverse and the reverse of the same coin. If you have one, you must have the other; a wave in the ocean must be at the cost of a hollow elsewhere. Nay, all life is evil. No breath can be breathed without killing some one else; not a morsel of food can be eaten without depriving some one of it. This is the law; this is philosophy. Therefore the only thing we can do is to understand that all this work against evil is more subjective than objective. The work against evil is more educational than actual, however big we may talk. This, first of all, is the idea of work against evil; and it ought to make us calmer, it ought to take fanaticism out of our blood. The history of the world teaches us that wherever there have been fanatical reforms, the only result has been that they have defeated their own ends. No greater upheaval for the establishment of right and liberty can be imagined than the war for the abolition of slavery in America. You all know about it. And what has been its results? The slaves are a hundred times worse off today than they were before the abolition. Before the abolition, these poor negroes were the property of somebody, and, as properties, they had to be looked after, so that they might not deteriorate. Today they are the property of nobody. Their lives are of no value; they are burnt alive on mere presences. They are shot down without any law for their murderers; for they are niggers, they are not human beings, they are not even animals; and that is the effect of such violent taking away of evil by law or by fanaticism. Such is the testimony of history against every fanatical movement, even for doing good. I have seen that. My own experience has taught me that. Therefore I cannot join any one of these condemning societies. Why condemn? There are evils in every society; everybody knows it. Every child of today knows it; he can stand upon a platform and give us a harangue on the awful evils in Hindu Society. Every uneducated foreigner who comes here globe-trotting takes a vanishing railway view of India and lectures most learnedly on the awful evils in India. We admit that there are evils. Everybody can show what evil is, but he is the friend of mankind who finds a way out of the difficulty. Like the drowning boy and the philosopher—when the philosopher was lecturing him, the boy cried, "Take me out of the water first"—so our people cry: "We have had lectures enough, societies enough, papers enough; where is the man who will lend us a hand to drag us out? Where is the man who really loves us? Where is the man who has sympathy for us?" Ay, that man is wanted. That is where I differ entirely from these reform movements. For a hundred years they have been here. What good has been done except the creation of a most vituperative, a most condemnatory literature? Would to God it was not here! They have criticised, condemned, abused the orthodox, until the orthodox have caught their tone and paid them back in their own coin; and the result is the creation of a literature in every vernacular which is the shame of the race, the shame of the country. Is this reform? Is this leading the nation to glory? Whose fault is this?

There is, then, another great consideration. Here in India, we have always been governed by kings; kings have made all our laws. Now the kings are gone, and there is no one left to make a move. The government dare not; it has to fashion its ways according to the growth of public opinion. It takes time, quite a long time, to make a healthy, strong, public opinion which will solve its own problems; and in the interim we shall have to wait. The whole problem of social reform, therefore, resolves itself into this: where are those who want reform? Make them first. Where are the people? The tyranny of a minority is the worst tyranny that the world ever sees. A few men who think that certain things are evil will not make a nation move. Why does not the nation move? First educate the nation, create your legislative body, and then the law will be forthcoming. First create the power, the sanction from which the law will spring. The kings are gone; where is the new sanction, the new power of the people? Bring it up. Therefore, even for social reform, the first duty is to educate the people,

and you will have to wait till that time comes. Most of the reforms that have been agitated for during the past century have been ornamental. Every one of these reforms only touches the first two castes, and no other. The question of widow marriage would not touch seventy per cent of the Indian women, and all such questions only reach the higher castes of Indian people who are educated, mark you, at the expense of the masses. Every effort has been spent in cleaning their own houses. But that is no reformation. You must go down to the basis of the thing, to the very root of the matter. That is what I call radical reform. Put the fire there and let it burn upwards and make an Indian nation. And the solution of the problem is not so easy, as it is a big and a vast one. Be not in a hurry, this problem has been known several hundred years.

Today it is the fashion to talk of Buddhism and Buddhistic agnosticism, especially in the South. Little do they dream that this degradation which is with us today has been left by Buddhism. This is the legacy which Buddhism has left to us. You read in books written by men who had never studied the rise and fall of Buddhism that the spread of Buddhism was owing to the wonderful ethics and the wonderful personality of Gautama Buddha. I have every respect and veneration for Lord Buddha, but mark my words, the spread of Buddhism was less owing to the doctrines and the personality of the great preacher, than to the temples that were built, the idols that were erected, and the gorgeous ceremonials that were put before the nation. Thus Buddhism progressed. The little fire-places in the houses in which the people poured their libations were not strong enough to hold their own against these gorgeous temples and ceremonies; but later on the whole thing degenerated. It became a mass of corruption of which I cannot speak before this audience; but those who want to know about it may see a little of it in those big temples, full of sculptures, in Southern India; and this is all the inheritance we have from the Buddhists.

Then arose the great reformer Shankarâchârya and his followers, and during these hundreds of years, since his time to the present day, there has been the slow bringing back of the Indian masses to the pristine purity of the Vedantic religion. These reformers knew full well the evils which existed, yet they did not condemn. They did not say, "All that you have is wrong, and you must throw it away." It can never be so. Today I read that my friend Dr. Barrows says that in three hundred years Christianity overthrew the Roman and Greek religious influences. That is not the word of a man who has seen Europe, and Greece, and Rome. The influence of Roman and Greek religion is all there, even in Protestant countries, only with changed names—old gods rechristened in a new fashion. They change their names; the goddesses become Marys and the gods become saints, and the ceremonials become new; even the old title of Pontifex Maximus is there. So, sudden changes cannot be and Shankaracharya knew it. So did Râmânuja. The only way left to them was slowly to bring up to the highest ideal the existing religion. If they had sought to apply the other method, they would have been hypocrites, for the very fundamental doctrine of their religion is evolution, the soul going towards the highest goal, through all these various stages and phases, which are, therefore necessary and helpful. And who dares condemn them?

It has become a trite saying that idolatry is wrong, and every man swallows it at the present time without questioning. I once thought so, and to pay the penalty of that I had to learn my lesson sitting at the feet of a man who realised everything through idols; I allude to Ramakrishna Paramahamsa. If such Ramakrishna Paramahamsas are produced by idol-worship, what will you have—the reformer's creed or any number of idols? I want an answer. Take a thousand idols more if you can produce Ramakrishna Paramahamsas through idol worship, and may God speed you! Produce such noble natures by any means you can. Yet idolatry is condemned! Why? Nobody knows. Because some hundreds of years ago some man of Jewish blood happened to condemn it? That is, he happened to condemn everybody else's idols except his own. If God is represented in any beautiful form or any symbolic form, said the Jew, it is awfully bad; it is sin. But if He is represented in the form of a chest, with two angels sitting on each side, and a cloud hanging over it, it is the holy of holies. If God comes in the form of a dove, it is holy. But if He comes in the form of a cow, it is heathen superstition; condemn it! That is how the world goes. That is why the poet says, "What fools we mortals be!" How difficult it is to look through each other's eyes, and that is the bane of humanity. That is the basis of hatred and jealousy, of quarrel and of fight. Boys, moustached babies, who never went out of Madras, standing up and wanting to dictate laws to three hundred millions of people with thousands of traditions at their back! Are you not ashamed? Stand back from such blasphemy and learn first your lessons! Irreverent boys, simply because you can scrawl a few lines upon paper and get some fool to publish them for you, you think you are the educators of the world, you think you are the public opinion of India! Is it so? This I have to tell to the social reformers of Madras that I have the greatest respect and love for them. I love them for their great hearts and their love for their country, for the poor, for the oppressed. But what I would tell them with a brother's love is that their method is not right; It has been tried a hundred years and failed. Let us try some new method.

Did India ever stand in want of reformers? Do you read the history of India? Who was Ramanuja? Who was Shankara? Who was Nânak? Who was Chaitanya? Who was Kabir? Who was Dâdu? Who were all these great preachers, one following the other, a galaxy of stars of the first magnitude? Did not Ramanuja feel for the lower classes? Did he not try all his life to admit even the Pariah to his community? Did he not try to admit even Mohammedans to his own fold? Did not Nanak confer with Hindus and Mohammedans, and try to bring about a new state of things? They all tried, and their work is still going on. The difference is this. They had not the fanfaronade of the reformers of today; they had no curses on their lips as modern reformers have; their lips pronounced only blessings. They never condemned. They said to the people that the race must always grow. They looked back and they said, "O Hindus, what you have done is good, but, my brothers, let us do better." They did not say, "You have been wicked, now let us be good." They said, "You have been good, but let us now be better." That makes a whole world of difference. We must grow according to our nature. Vain is it to attempt the lines of action that foreign societies have engrafted upon us; it is impossible. Glory unto God, that it is impossible, that we cannot be twisted and tortured into the shape oil other nations. I do not condemn the institutions of other races; they are good for them, but not for us. What is meat for them may be poison for us. This is the first lesson to learn. With other sciences, other institutions, and other traditions behind them, they have got their present system. We, with our traditions, with thousands of years of Karma behind us, naturally can only follow our own bent, run in our own grooves; and that we shall have to do.

What is my plan then? My plan is to follow the ideas of the great ancient Masters. I have studied their work, and it has been given unto me to discover the line of action they took. They were the great originators of society. They were the great givers of strength, and of purity, and of life. They did most marvellous work. We have to do most marvellous work also. Circumstances have become a little different, and in consequence the lines of action have to be changed a little, and that is all. I see that each nation, like each individual, has one theme in this life, which is its centre, the principal note round which every other note comes to form the harmony. In one nation political power is its vitality, as in England, artistic life in another, and so on. In India, religious life forms the centre, the keynote of the whole music of national life; and if any nation attempts to throw off its national vitality—the direction which has become its own through the transmission of centuries—that nation dies if it succeeds in the attempt. And, therefore, if you succeed in the attempt to throw off your religion and take up either politics, or society, or any other things as your centre, as the vitality of your national life, the result will be that you will become extinct. To prevent this you must make all and everything work through that vitality of your religion. Let all your nerves vibrate through the backbone of your religion. I have seen that I cannot preach even religion to Americans without showing them its practical effect on social life. I could not preach religion in England without showing the wonderful political changes the Vedanta would bring. So, in India, social reform has to be preached by showing how much more spiritual a life the new system will bring; and politics has to be preached by showing how much it will improve the one thing that the nation wants—its spirituality. Every man has to make his own choice; so has every nation. We made our choice ages ago, and we must abide by it. And, after all, it is not such a bad choice. Is it such a bad choice in this world to think not of matter but of spirit, not of man but of God? That intense faith in another world, that intense hatred for this world, that intense power of renunciation, that intense faith in God, that intense faith in the immortal soul, is in you. I challenge anyone to give it up. You cannot. You may try to impose upon me by becoming materialists, by talking materialism for a few months, but I know what you are; if I take you by the hand, back you come as good theists as ever were born. How can you change your nature?

So every improvement in India requires first of all an up-heaval in religion. Before flooding India with socialistic or po-litical ideas, first deluge the land with spiritual ideas. The first work that demands our attention is that the most wonderful truths confined in our Upanishads, in our scriptures, in our Purânas must be brought out from the books, brought out from the monasteries, brought out from the forests, brought out from the possession of selected bodies of people, and scattered broadcast all over the land, so that these truths may run like fire all over the country from north to south and east to west, from the Himalayas to Comorin, from Sindh to the Brahmaputra. Everyone must know of them, because it is said, "This has first to be heard, then thought upon, and then meditated upon." Let the people hear first, and whoever helps in making the people hear about the great truths in their own scriptures cannot make for himself a better Karma today. Says our Vyasa, "In the Kali Yuga there is one Karma left. Sacrifices and tremendous Tapasyâs are of no avail now. Of Karma one remains, and that is the Karma of giving." And of these gifts, the gift of spirituality and spiritual knowledge is the highest; the next gift is the gift of secular knowledge; the next is the gift of life; and the fourth is the gift of food. Look at this wonderfully charitable race; look at the amount of gifts that are made in this poor, poor country; look at the hospitality where a man can travel from the north to the south, having the best in the land, being treated always by everyone as if he were a friend, and where no beggar starves so long as there is a piece of bread anywhere!

In this land of charity, let us take up the energy of the first charity, the diffusion of spiritual knowledge. And that diffu-sion should not be confined within the bounds of India; it must go out all over the world. This has been the custom. Those that tell you that Indian thought never went outside of India, those that tell you that I am the first Sannyasin who went to foreign lands to preach, do not know the history of their own race. Again and again this phenomenon has hap-pened. Whenever the world has required it, this perennial flood of spirituality has overflowed and deluged the world. Gifts of political knowledge can be made with the blast of trumpets and the march of cohorts. Gifts of secular knowl-edge and social knowledge can be made with fire and sword. But spiritual knowledge can only be given in silence like the dew that falls unseen and unheard, yet bringing into bloom masses of roses. This has been the gift of India to the world again and again. Whenever there has been a great conquer-

ing race, bringing the nations of the world together, making roads and transit possible, immediately India arose and gave her quota of spiritual power to the sum total of the progress of the world. This happened ages before Buddha was born, and remnants of it are still left in China, in Asia Minor, and in the heart of the Malayan Archipelago. This was the case when the great Greek conqueror united the four corners of the then known world; then rushed out Indian spirituality, and the boasted civilisation of the West is but the remnant of that deluge. Now the same opportunity has again come; the power of England has linked the nations of the world togeth-er as was never done before. English roads and channels of communication rush from one end of the world to the other. Owing to English genius, the world today has been linked in such a fashion as has never before been done. Today trade centres have been formed such as have never been before in the history of mankind. And immediately, consciously or un-consciously, India rises up and pours forth her gifts of spirit-uality; and they will rush through these roads till they have reached the very ends of the world. That I went to America was not my doing or your doing; but the God of India who is guiding her destiny sent me, and will send hundreds of such to all the nations of the world. No power on earth can resist it. This also has to be done. You must go out to preach your religion, preach it to every nation under the sun, preach it to every people. This is the first thing to do. And after preach-ing spiritual knowledge, along with it will come that secular knowledge and every other knowledge that you want; but if you attempt to get the secular knowledge without religion, I tell you plainly, vain is your attempt in India, it will never have a hold on the people. Even the great Buddhistic move-ment was a failure, partially on account of that.

Therefore, my friends, my plan is to start institutions in In-dia, to train our young men as preachers of the truths of our scriptures in India and outside India. Men, men, these are wanted: everything else will be ready, but strong, vigorous, believing young men, sincere to the backbone, are wanted. A hundred such and the world becomes revolutionized. The will is stronger than anything else. Everything must go down before the will, for that comes from God and God Himself; a pure and a strong will is omnipotent. Do you not believe in it? Preach, preach unto the world the great truths of your religion; the world waits for them. For centuries people have been taught theories of degradation. They have been told that they are nothing. The masses have been told all over the world that they are not human beings. They have been so frightened for centuries, till they have nearly become animals. Never were they allowed to hear of the Atman. Let them hear of the Atman—that even the lowest of the low have the Atman within, which never dies and never is born—of Him whom the sword cannot pierce, nor the fire burn, nor the air dry—immortal, without beginning or end, the all-pure, omnipotent, and omnipresent Atman! Let them have faith in themselves, for what makes the difference between the Englishman and you? Let them talk their religion and duty and so forth. I have found the difference. The difference is here, that the Englishman believes in himself and you do not. He believes in his being an Englishman, and he can do anything. That brings out the God within him, and he can do anything he likes. You have been told and taught that you can do nothing, and nonentities you are becoming every day. What we want is strength, so believe in yourselves. We have become weak, and that is why occultism and mysticism come to us—these creepy things; there may be great truths in them, but they have nearly destroyed us. Make your nerves strong. What we want is muscles of iron and nerves of steel. We have wept long enough. No more weeping, but stand on your feet and be men. It is a man-making religion that we want. It is man-making theories that we want. It is man-making education all round that we want. And here is the test of truth—anything that makes you weak physically, intellectually, and spiritually, reject as poison; there is no life in it, it cannot be true. Truth is strengthening. Truth is purity, truth is all-knowledge; truth must be strengthening, must be enlightening, must be invigorating. These mysticisms, in spite of some grains of truth in them, are generally weakening. Believe me, I have a lifelong experience of it, and the one conclusion that I draw is that it is weakening. I have travelled all over India, searched almost every cave here, and lived in the Himalayas. I know people who lived there all their lives. I love my nation, I cannot see you degraded, weakened any more than you are now. Therefore I am bound for your sake and for truth's sake to cry, "Hold!" and to raise my voice against this degradation of my race. Give up these weakening mysticisms and be strong. Go back to your Upanishads—the shining, the strengthening, the bright philosophy—and part from all these mysterious things, all these weakening things. Take up this philosophy; the greatest truths are the simplest things in the world, simple as your own existence. The truths of the Upanishads are before you. Take them up, live up to them, and the salvation of India will be at hand.

One word more and I have finished. They talk of patriotism. I believe in patriotism, and I also have my own ideal of patriotism. Three things are necessary for great achievements. First, feel from the heart. What is in the intellect or reason? It goes a few steps and there it stops. But through the heart comes inspiration. Love opens the most impossible gates; love is the gate to all the secrets of the universe. Feel, therefore, my would-be reformers, my would-be patriots! Do you feel? Do you feel that millions and millions of the descendants of gods and of sages have become next-door neighbours to brutes? Do you feel that millions are starving today, and millions have been starving for ages? Do you feel that ignorance has come over the land as a dark cloud? Does it make you restless? Does it make you sleepless? Has it gone into your blood, coursing through your veins, becoming consonant with your heartbeats? Has it made you almost mad? Are you seized with that one idea of the misery of ruin, and have you forgotten all about your name, your fame, your wives, your children, your property, even your own bodies? Have you done that? That is the first step to become a patriot, the very first step. I did not go to America, as most of you know, for the Parliament of Religions, but this demon of a feeling was in me and within my soul. I travelled twelve years all over India, finding no way to work for my countrymen, and that is why I went to America. Most of you know that, who knew me then. Who cared about this Parliament of Religions? Here was my own flesh and blood sinking every day, and who cared for them? This was my first step.

You may feel, then; but instead of spending your energies in frothy talk, have you found any way out, any practical solution, some help instead of condemnation, some sweet words to soothe their miseries, to bring them out of this living death?

Yet that is not all. Have you got the will to surmount mountain-high obstructions? If the whole world stands against you sword in hand, would you still dare to do what you think is right? If your wives and children are against you, if all your money goes, your name dies, your wealth vanishes, would you still stick to it? Would you still pursue it and go on steadily towards your own goal? As the great King Bhartrihari says, "Let the sages blame or let them praise; let the goddess of fortune come or let her go wherever she likes; let death come today, or let it come in hundreds of years; he indeed is the steady man who does not move one inch from the way of truth." Have you got that steadfastness? If you have these three things, each one of you will work miracles. You need not write in the newspapers, you need not go about lecturing; your very face will shine. If you live in a cave, your thoughts will permeate even through the rock walls, will go vibrating all over the world for hundreds of years, maybe, until they will fasten on to some brain and work out there. Such is the power of thought, of sincerity, and of purity of purpose.

I am afraid I am delaying you, but one word more. This national ship, my countrymen, my friends, my children—this national ship has been ferrying millions and millions of souls across the waters of life. For scores of shining centuries it has been plying across this water, and through its agency, millions of souls have been taken to the other shore, to blessedness. But today, perhaps through your own fault, this boat has become a little damaged, has sprung a leak; and would you therefore curse it? Is it fit that you stand up and pronounce malediction upon it, one that has done more work than any other thing in the world? If there are holes in this national ship, this society of ours, we are its children. Let us go and stop the holes. Let us gladly do it with our hearts' blood; and if we cannot, then let us die. We will make a plug of our brains and put them into the ship, but condemn it never. Say not one harsh word against this society. I love it for its past greatness. I love you all because you are the children of gods, and because you are the children of the glorious forefathers. How then can I curse you! Never. All blessings be upon you! I have come to you, my children, to tell you all my plans. If you hear them I am ready to work with you. But if you will not listen to them, and even kick me out of India, I will come back and tell you that we are all sinking! I am come now to sit in your midst, and if we are to sink, let us all sink together, but never let curses rise to our lips.

VEDANTA IN ITS APPLICATION TO INDIAN LIFE

There is a word which has become very common as an appellation of our race and our religion. The word "Hindu" requires a little explanation in connection with what I mean by Vedantism. This word "Hindu" was the name that the ancient Persians used to apply to the river Sindhu. Whenever in Sanskrit there is an "s", in ancient Persian it changes into "h", so that "Sindhu" became "Hindu"; and you are all aware how the Greeks found it hard to pronounce "h" and dropped it altogether, so that we became known as Indians. Now this word "Hindu" as applied to the inhabitants of the other side of the Indus, whatever might have been its meaning in ancient times has lost all its force in modern times; for all the people that live on this side of the Indus no longer belong to one religion. There are the Hindus proper, the Mohammedans, the Parsees, the Christians, the Buddhists, and Jains. The word "Hindu" in its literal sense ought to include all these; but as signifying the religion, it would not be proper to call all these Hindus. It is very hard, therefore, to find any common name for our religion, seeing that this religion is a collection, so to speak, of various religions, of various ideas, of various ceremonials and forms, all gathered together almost without a name, and without a church, and without an organisation. The only point where, perhaps, all our sects agree is that we all believe in the scriptures—the Vedas. This perhaps is certain that no man can have a right to be called a Hindu who does not admit the supreme authority of the Vedas. All these Vedas, as you are aware, are divided into two portions—the Karma Kânda and the Jnâna Kânda. The Karma Kanda includes various sacrifices and ceremonials, of which the larger part has fallen into disuse in the present age. The Jnana Kanda, as embodying the spiritual teachings of the Vedas known as the Upanishads and the Vedanta, has always been cited as the highest authority by all our teachers, philosophers, and writers, whether dualist, or qualified monist, or monist. Whatever be his philosophy or sect, every one in India has to find his authority in the Upanishads. If he cannot, his sect would be heterodox. Therefore, perhaps the one name in modern times which would designate every Hindu throughout the land would be "Vedantist" or "Vaidika", as you may put it; and in that sense I always use the words "Vedantism" and "Vedanta". I want to make it a little clearer, for of late it has become the custom of most people to identify the word Vedanta with the Advaitic system of the Vedanta philosophy. We all know that Advaitism is only one branch of the various philosophic systems that have been founded on the Upanishads. The followers of the Vishishtâd-

vaitic system have as much reverence for the Upanishads as the followers of the Advaita, and the Vishishtadvaitists claim as much authority for the Vedanta as the Advaitist. So do the dualists; so does every other sect in India. But the word Vedantist has become somewhat identified in the popular mind with the word Advaitist, and perhaps with some reason, because, although we have the Vedas for our scriptures, we have Smritis and Purânas—subsequent writings—to illustrate the doctrines of the Vedas; these of course have not the same weight as the Vedas. And the law is that wherever these Puranas and Smritis differ from any part of the Shruti, the Shruti must be followed and the Smriti rejected. Now in the expositions of the great Advaitic philosopher Shankara, and the school founded by him, we find most of the authorities cited are from the Upanishads, very rarely is an authority cited from the Smritis, except, perhaps, to elucidate a point which could hardly be found in the Shrutis. On the other hand, other schools take refuge more and more in the Smritis and less and less in the Shrutis; and as we go to the more and more dualistic sects, we find a proportionate quantity of the Smritis quoted, which is out of all proportion to what we should expect from a Vedantist. It is, perhaps, because these gave such predominance to the Paurânika authorities that the Advaitist came to be considered as the Vedantist par excellence, if I may say so.

However it might have been, the word Vedanta must cover the whole ground of Indian religious life, and being part of the Vedas, by all acceptance it is the most ancient literature that we have; for whatever might be the idea of modern scholars, the Hindus are not ready to admit that parts of the Vedas were written at one time and parts were written at another time. They of course still hold on to their belief that the Vedas as a whole were produced at the same time, rather if I may say so, that they were never produced, but that they always existed in the mind of the Lord. This is what I mean by the word Vedanta, that it covers the ground of dualism, of qualified monism, and Advaitism in India. Perhaps we may even take in parts of Buddhism, and of Jainism too, if they would come in—for our hearts are sufficiently large. But it is they that will not come in, we are ready for upon severe analysis you will always find that the essence of Buddhism was all borrowed from the same Upanishads; even the ethics, the so-called great and wonderful ethics of Buddhism, were there word for word, in some one or other of the Upanishads; and so all the good doctrines of the Jains were there, minus their vagaries. In the Upanishads, also, we find the germs of all the subsequent development of Indian religious thought. Sometimes it has been urged without any ground whatsoever that there is no ideal of Bhakti in the Upanishads. Those that have been students of the Upanishads know that that is not true at all. There is enough of Bhakti in every Upanishad if you will only seek for it; but many of these ideas which are found so fully developed in later times in the Puranas and other Smritis are only in the germ in the Upanishads. The sketch, the skeleton, was there as it were. It was filled in in some of the Puranas. But there is not one full-grown Indian ideal that cannot be traced back to the same source — the Upanishads. Certain ludicrous attempts have been made by persons without much Upanishadic scholarship to trace Bhakti to some foreign source; but as you know, these have all been proved to be failures, and all that you want of Bhakti is there, even in the Samhitas, not to speak of the Upanishads — it is there, worship and love and all the rest of it; only the ideals of Bhakti are becoming higher and higher. In the Samhita portions, now and then, you find traces of a religion of fear and tribulation; in the Samhitas now and then you find a worshipper quaking before a Varuna, or some other god. Now and then you will find they are very much tortured by the idea of sin, but the Upanishads have no place for the delineation of these things. There is no religion of fear in the Upanishads; it is one of Love and one of Knowledge.

These Upanishads are our scriptures. They have been differently explained, and, as I have told you already, whenever there is a difference between subsequent Pauranika literature and the Vedas, the Puranas must give way. But it is at the same time true that, as a practical result, we find ourselves ninety per cent Pauranika and ten per cent Vaidika — even if so much as that. And we all find the most contradictory usages prevailing in our midst and also religious opinions prevailing in our society which scarcely have any authority in the scriptures of the Hindus; and in many cases we read in books, and see with astonishment, customs of the country that neither have their authority in the Vedas nor in the Smritis or Puranas, but are simply local. And yet each ignorant villager thinks that if that little local custom dies out, he will no more remain a Hindu. In his mind Vedantism and these little local customs have been indissolubly identified. In reading the scriptures it is hard for him to understand that what he is doing has not the sanction of the scriptures, and that the giving up of them will not hurt him at all, but on the other hand will make him a better man. Secondly, there is the other difficulty. These scriptures of ours have been very vast. We read in the Mahâbhâshya of Patanjali, that great philological work, that the Sâma-Veda had one thousand branches. Where are they all? Nobody knows. So with each of the Vedas; the major portion of these books have disappeared, and it is only the minor portion that remains to us. They were all taken charge of by particular families; and either these families died out, or were killed under foreign persecution, or somehow became extinct; and with them, that branch of the learning of the Vedas they took charge of became extinct also. This fact we ought to remember, as it always forms the sheet-anchor in the hands of those who want to preach anything new or to defend anything even against the Vedas. Wherever in India there is a discussion between local custom and the Shrutis, and whenever it is pointed out that the local custom is against the scriptures, the argument that is forwarded is that it is not, that the customs existed in the branch of the Shrutis which has become extinct and so has been a recognised one. In the midst of all these varying methods of reading and commenting on our scriptures, it is very difficult indeed to find the thread that runs through all of them; for we become convinced at once that there must be some common ground underlying all these varying divisions and subdivisions. There must be harmony, a common plan, upon which all these little bits of buildings have been constructed, some basis common to this apparently hopeless mass of confusion which we call our religion. Otherwise it could not have stood so long, it could not have endured so long.

Coming to our commentators again, we find another difficulty. The Advaitic commentator, whenever an Advaitic text comes, preserves it just as it is; but the same commentator, as soon as a dualistic text presents itself, tortures it if he can, and brings the most queer meaning out of it. Sometimes the "Unborn" becomes a "goat", such are the wonderful changes effected. To suit the commentator, "Ajâ" the Unborn is explained as "Aja" a she-goat. In the same way, if not in a still worse fashion, the texts are handled by the dualistic commentator. Every dualistic text is preserved, and every text that speaks of non-dualistic philosophy is tortured in any fashion he likes. This Sanskrit language is so intricate, the Sanskrit of the Vedas is so ancient, and the Sanskrit philology so perfect, that any amount of discussion can be carried on for ages in regard to the meaning of one word. If a Pandit takes it into his head, he can render anybody's prattle into correct Sanskrit by force of argument and quotation of texts and rules. These are the difficulties in our way of understanding the Upanishads. It was given to me to live with a man who was as ardent a dualist, as ardent an Advaitist, as ardent a Bhakta, as a Jnani. And living with this man first put it into my head to understand the Upanishads and the texts of the scriptures from an independent and better basis than by blindly following the commentators; and in my opinion and in my researches, I came to the conclusion that these texts are not at all contradictory. So we need have no fear of text-torturing at all! The texts are beautiful, ay, they are most wonderful; and they are not contradictory, but wonderfully harmonious, one idea leading up to the other. But the one fact I found is that in all the Upanishads, they begin with dualistic ideas, with worship and all that, and end with a grand flourish of Advaitic ideas.

Therefore I now find in the light of this man's life that the dualist and the Advaitist need not fight each other. Each has a place, and a great place in the national life. The dualist must remain, for he is as much part and parcel of the national religious life as the Advaitist. One cannot exist without the other; one is the fulfilment of the other; one is the building, the other is the top; the one the root, the other the fruit, and so on. Therefore any attempt to torture the texts of the Upanishads appears to me very ridiculous. I begin to find out that the language is wonderful. Apart from all its merits as the greatest philosophy, apart from its wonderful merit as theology, as showing the path of salvation to mankind, the Upanishadic literature is the most wonderful painting of sublimity that the world has. Here comes out in full force that individuality of the human mind, that introspective, intuitive Hindu mind. We have paintings of sublimity elsewhere in all nations, but almost without exception you will find that their ideal is to grasp the sublime in the muscles. Take for instance, Milton, Dante, Homer, or any of the Western poets. There are wonderfully sublime passages in them; but there it is always a grasping at infinity through the senses, the muscles, getting the ideal of infinite expansion, the infinite of space. We find the same attempts made in the Samhita portion. You know some of those wonderful Riks where creation is described; the very heights of expression of the sublime in expansion and the infinite in space are attained. But they found out very soon that the Infinite cannot be reached in that way, that even infinite space, and expansion, and infinite external nature could not express the ideas that were struggling to find expression in their minds, and so they fell back upon other explanations. The language became new in the Upanishads; it is almost negative, it is sometimes, chaotic, sometimes taking you beyond the senses, pointing out to you something which you cannot grasp, which you cannot sense, and at the same time you feel certain that it is there. What passage in the world can compare with this?—न तत्र सूर्यो भाति न चंद्रतारकं नेमा विद्युतो भान्ति कुतोऽयमग्निः ।—There the sun cannot illumine, nor the moon nor the stars, the flash of lightning cannot illumine the place, what to speak of this mortal fire." Again, where can you find a more perfect expression of the whole philosophy of the world, the gist of what the Hindus ever thought, the whole dream of human salvation, painted in language more wonderful, in figure more marvellous than this?

वदा सुपर्णा सयुजा सखाया समानं वृक्षं परिषस्वजाते ।
तयोरन्यः पिप्पलं स्वाद्वत्त्यनश्नन्नन्यो अभिचाकशीति ॥
समाने वृक्षे पुरुषो निमिग्नोऽनीशया शोचति मुह्यमानः ।
जुष्टं यदा पश्यत्यन्यमीशमस्य महिमानमिति वीतशोकः ॥

Upon the same tree there are two birds of beautiful plumage, most friendly to each other, one eating the fruits, the other sitting there calm and silent without eating—the one on the lower branch eating sweet and bitter fruits in turn and becoming happy and unhappy, but the other one on the top, calm and majestic; he eats neither sweet nor bitter fruits, cares neither for happiness nor misery, immersed in his own glory. This is the picture of the human soul. Man is eating the sweet and bitter fruits of this life, pursuing gold, pursuing his senses, pursuing the vanities of life—hopelessly, madly careering he goes. In other places the Upanishads have compared the human soul to the charioteer, and the senses to the mad horses unrestrained. Such is the career of men pursuing the vanities of life, children dreaming golden dreams only to find that they are but vain, and old men chewing the cud of their past deeds, and yet not knowing how to get out of this network. This is the world. Yet in the life of every one there come golden moments; in the midst of the deepest sorrows, nay, of the deepest joys, there come moments when a part of the cloud that hides the sunlight moves away as it were, and we catch a glimpse, in spite of ourselves of something beyond—away, away beyond the life of the senses; away, away beyond its vanities, its joys, and its sorrows; away, away beyond nature, or our imaginations of happiness here or hereafter; away beyond all thirst for gold, or for fame, or for name, or for posterity. Man stops for a moment at this glimpse and sees the other bird calm and majestic, eating neither sweet nor bitter fruits, but immersed in his own glory, Self-content, Self-satisfied. As the Gita says, यस्त्वात्मरतिरेव स्यादात्मतृप्तश्च मानवः आत्मन्येव च संतुष्टस्तस्य कार्यं न विद्यते ॥—"He whose devotion is to the Atman, he who does not want anything beyond Atman, he who has become satisfied in the Atman, what work is there for him to do?" Why should he drudge? Man catches a glimpse, then again he forgets and goes on eating the sweet and bitter fruits of life; perhaps after a time he catches another glimpse, and the lower bird goes nearer and nearer to the higher bird as blows after blows are received. If he be fortunate to receive hard knocks, then he comes nearer and nearer to his companion, the other bird, his life, his friend; and as he approaches him, he finds that the light from the higher bird is playing round his own plumage; and as he comes nearer and nearer, lo! the transformation is going on. The nearer and nearer he comes, he finds himself melting away, as it were, until he has entirely disappeared. He did not really exist; it was but the reflection of the other bird who was there calm and majestic amidst the moving leaves. It was all his glory, that upper bird's. He then becomes fearless, perfectly satisfied, calmly serene. In this figure, the Upanishads take you from the dualistic to the utmost Advaitic conception.

Endless examples can be cited, but we have no time in this lecture to do that or to show the marvellous poetry of the Upanishads, the painting of the sublime, the grand conceptions. But one other idea I must note, that the language and the thought and everything come direct, they fall upon you like a sword-blade, strong as the blows of a hammer they come. There is no mistaking their meanings. Every tone of that music is firm and produces its full effect; no gyrations, no mad words, no intricacies in which the brain is lost. No signs of degradation are there—no attempts at too much allegorising, too much piling of adjectives after adjectives, making it more and more intricate, till the whole of the sense is lost, and the brain becomes giddy, and man does not know his way out from the maze of that literature. There was none of that yet. If it be human literature, it must be the production of a race which had not yet lost any of its national vigour.

Strength, strength is what the Upanishads speak to me from every page. This is the one great thing to remember, it has been the one great lesson I have been taught in my life; strength, it says, strength, O man, be not weak. Are there no human weaknesses?—says man. There are, say the Upanishads, but will more weakness heal them, would you try to wash dirt with dirt? Will sin cure sin, weakness cure weakness? Strength, O man, strength, say the Upanishads, stand up and be strong. Ay, it is the only literature in the world where you find the word "Abhih", "fearless", used again and again; in no other scripture in the world is this adjective applied either to God or to man. Abhih, fearless! And in my mind rises from the past the vision of the great Emperor of the West, Alexander the Great, and I see, as it were in a picture, the great monarch standing on the bank of the Indus, talking to one of our Sannyâsins in the forest; the old man he was talking to, perhaps naked, stark naked, sitting upon a block of stone, and the Emperor, astonished at his wisdom, tempting him with gold and honour to come over to Greece. And this man smiles at his gold, and smiles at his temptations, and refuses; and then the Emperor standing on his authority as an Emperor, says, "I will kill you if you do not come", and the man bursts into a laugh and says, "You never told such a falsehood in your life, as you tell just now. Who can kill me? Me you kill, Emperor of the material world! Never! For I am Spirit unborn and undecaying: never was I born and never do I die; I am the Infinite, the Omnipresent, the Omniscient; and you kill me, child that you are!" That is strength, that is strength! And the more I read the Upanishads, my friends, my countrymen, the more I weep for you, for therein is the great practical application. Strength, strength for us. What we need is strength, who will give us strength? There are thousands to weaken us, and of stories we have had enough. Every one of our Puranas, if you press it, gives out stories enough to fill three-fourths of the libraries of the world. Everything that can weaken us as a race we have had for the last thousand years. It seems as if during that period the national life had this one end in view, viz how to make us weaker and weaker till we have become real earthworms, crawling at the feet of every one who dares to put his foot on us. Therefore, my friends, as one of your blood, as one that lives and dies with you, let me tell you that we want strength, strength, and every time strength. And the Upanishads are the great mine of strength. Therein lies strength enough to invigorate the whole world; the whole world can be vivified, made strong, energised through them. They will call with trumpet voice upon the weak, the miserable, and the downtrodden of all races, all creeds, and all sects to stand on their feet and be free. Freedom, physical freedom, mental freedom, and spiritual freedom are the watchwords of the Upanishads.

Ay, this is the one scripture in the world, of all others, that does not talk of salvation, but of freedom. Be free from the bonds of nature, be free from weakness! And it shows to you that you have this freedom already in you. That is another peculiarity of its teachings. You are a Dvaitist; never mind, you have got to admit that by its very nature the soul is perfect; only by certain actions of the soul has it become contracted. Indeed, Râmânuja's theory of contraction and expansion is exactly what the modern evolutionists call evolution and atavism. The soul goes back, becomes contracted as it were, its powers become potential; and by good deeds and good thoughts it expands again and reveals its natural perfection.

With the Advaitist the one difference is that he admits evolution in nature and not in the soul. Suppose there is a screen, and there is a small hole in the screen. I am a man standing behind the screen and looking at this grand assembly. I can see only very few faces here. Suppose the hole increases; as it increases, more and more of this assembly is revealed to me, and in full when the hole has become identified with the screen—there is nothing between you and me in this case. Neither you changed nor I changed; all the change was in the screen. You were the same from first to last; only the screen changed. This is the Advaitist's position with regard to evolution—evolution of nature and manifestation of the Self within. Not that the Self can by any means be made to contract. It is unchangeable, the Infinite One. It was covered, as it were, with a veil, the veil of Maya, and as this Maya veil becomes thinner and thinner, the inborn, natural glory of the soul comes out and becomes more manifest. This is the one great doctrine which the world is waiting to learn from India. Whatever they may talk, however they may try to boast, they will find out day after day that no society can stand without admitting this. Do you not find how everything is being revolutionized? Do you not see how it was the custom to take for granted that everything was wicked until it proved itself good? In education, in punishing criminals, in treating lunatics, in the treatment of common diseases even, that was the old law. What is the modern law? The modern law says, the body itself is healthy; it cures diseases of its own nature. Medicine can at the best but help the storing up of the best in the body. What says it of criminals? It takes for granted that however low a criminal may be, there is still the divinity within, which does not change, and we must treat criminals accordingly. All these things are now changing, and reformatories and penitentiaries are established. So with everything. Consciously or unconsciously that Indian idea of the divinity within every one is expressing itself even in other countries. And in your books is the explanation which other nations have to accept. The treatment of one man to another will be entirely revolutionized, and these old, old ideas of pointing to the weakness of mankind will have to go. They will have received their death-blow within this century. Now people may stand up and criticise us. I have been criticised, from one end of the world to the other, as one who preaches the diabolical idea that there is no sin! Very good. The descendants of these very men will bless me as the preacher of virtue, and not of sin. I am the teacher of virtue, not of sin. I glory in being the preacher of light, and not of darkness.

The second great idea which the world is waiting to receive from our Upanishads is the solidarity of this universe. The old lines of demarcation and differentiation are vanishing rapidly. Electricity and steam-power are placing the different parts of the world in intercommunication with each other, and, as a result, we Hindus no longer say that every country beyond our own land is peopled with demons and hobgoblins, nor do the people of Christian countries say that India is only peopled by cannibals and savages. When we go out of our country, we find the same brother-man, with the same strong hand to help, with the same lips to say godspeed; and sometimes they are better than in the country in which we are born. When they come here, they find the same brotherhood, the same cheer, the same godspeed. Our Upanishads say that the cause of all misery is ignorance; and that is perfectly true when applied to every state of life, either social or spiritual. It is ignorance that makes us hate each other, it is through ignorance that we do not know and do not love each other. As soon as we come to know each other, love comes, must come, for are we not ones. Thus we find solidarity coming in spite of itself. Even in politics and sociology, problems that were only national twenty years ago can no more be solved on national grounds only. They are assuming huge proportions, gigantic shapes. They can only be solved when looked at in the broader light of international grounds. International organizations, international combinations, international laws are the cry of the day. That shows the solidarity. In science, every day they are coming to a similar broad view of matter. You speak of matter, the whole universe as one mass, one ocean of matter, in which you and I, the sun and the moon, and everything else are but the names of different little whirlpools and nothing more. Mentally speaking, it is one universal ocean of thought in which you and I are similar little whirlpools; and as spirit it moveth not, it changeth not. It is the One Unchangeable, Unbroken, Homogeneous Atman. The cry for morality is coming also, and that is to be found in our books. The explanation of morality, the fountain of ethics, that also the world wants; and that it will get here.

What do we want in India? If foreigners want these things, we want them twenty times more. Because, in spite of the greatness of the Upanishads, in spite of our boasted ancestry of sages, compared to many other races, I must tell you that we are weak, very weak. First of all is our physical weakness. That physical weakness is the cause of at least one-third of our miseries. We are lazy, we cannot work; we cannot combine, we do not love each other; we are intensely selfish, not three of us can come together without hating each other, without being jealous of each other. That is the state in which we are—hopelessly disorganised mobs, immensely selfish, fighting each other for centuries as to whether a certain mark is to be put on our forehead this way or that way, writing volumes and volumes upon such momentous questions as to whether the look of a man spoils my food or not! This we have been doing for the past few centuries. We cannot expect anything high from a race whose whole brain energy has been occupied in such wonderfully beautiful problems and researches! And are we not ashamed of ourselves? Ay, sometimes we are; but though we think these things frivolous, we cannot give them up. We speak of many things parrot-like, but never do them; speaking and not doing has become a habit with us. What is the cause of that? Physical weakness. This sort of weak brain is not able to do anything; we must strengthen it. First of

all, our young men must be strong. Religion will come afterwards. Be strong, my young friends; that is my advice to you. You will be nearer to Heaven through football than through the study of the Gita. These are bold words; but I have to say them, for I love you. I know where the shoe pinches. I have gained a little experience. You will understand the Gita better with your biceps, your muscles, a little stronger. You will understand the mighty genius and the mighty strength of Krishna better with a little of strong blood in you. You will understand the Upanishads better and the glory of the Atman when your body stands firm upon your feet, and you feel yourselves as men. Thus we have to apply these to our needs.

People get disgusted many times at my preaching Advaitism. I do not mean to preach Advaitism, or Dvaitism, or any ism in the world. The only ism that we require now is this wonderful idea of the soul—its eternal might, its eternal strength, its eternal purity, and its eternal perfection. If I had a child I would from its very birth begin to tell it, "Thou art the Pure One". You have read in one of the Puranas that beautiful story of queen Madâlasâ, how as soon as she has a child she puts her baby with her own hands in the cradle, and how as the cradle rocks to and fro, she begins to sing, "Thou art the Pure One the Stainless, the Sinless, the Mighty One, the Great One." Ay, there is much in that. Feel that you are great and you become great. What did I get as my experience all over the world, is the question. They may talk about sinners—and if all Englishmen really believed that they were sinners, Englishmen would be no better than the negroes in Central Africa. God bless them that they do not believe it! On the other hand, the Englishman believes he is born the lord of the world. He believes he is great and can do anything in the world; if he wants to go to the sun or the moon, he believes he can; and that makes him great. If he had believed his priests that he was a poor miserable sinner, going to be barbecued through all eternity, he would not be the same Englishman that he is today. So I find in every nation that, in spite of priests and superstition, the divine within lives and asserts itself. We have lost faith. Would you believe me, we have less faith than the Englishman and woman—a thousand times less faith! These are plain words; but I say these, I cannot help it. Don't you see how Englishmen and women, when they catch our ideals, become mad as it were; and although they are the ruling class, they come to India to preach our own religion notwithstanding the jeers and ridicule of their own countrymen? How many of you could do that? And why cannot you do that? Do you not know it? You know more than they do; you are more wise than is good for you, that is your difficulty! Simply because your blood is only like water, your brain is sloughing, your body is weak! You must change the body. Physical weakness is the cause and nothing else. You have talked of reforms, of ideals, and all these things for the past hundred years; but when it comes to practice, you are not to be found anywhere—till you have disgusted the whole world, and the very name of reform is a thing of ridicule! And what is the cause? Do you not know? You know too well. The only cause is that you are weak, weak, weak; your body is weak, your mind is weak, you have no faith in yourselves! Centuries and centuries, a thousand years of crushing tyranny of castes and kings and foreigners and your own people have taken out all your strength, my brethren. Your backbone is broken, you are like downtrodden worms. Who will give you strength? Let me tell you, strength, strength is what we want. And the first step in getting strength is to uphold the Upanishads, and believe—"I am the Soul", "Me the sword cannot cut; nor weapons pierce; me the fire cannot burn; me the air cannot dry; I am the Omnipotent, I am the Omniscient." So repeat these blessed, saving words. Do not say we are weak; we can do anything and everything. What can we not do? Everything can be done by us; we all have the same glorious soul, let us believe in it. Have faith, as Nachiketâ. At the time of his father's sacrifice, faith came unto Nachiketa; ay, I wish that faith would come to each of you; and every one of you would stand up a giant, a world-mover with a gigantic intellect—an infinite God in every respect. That is what I want you to become. This is the strength that you get from the Upanishads, this is the faith that you get from there.

Ay, but it was only for the Sannyâsin! Rahasya (esoteric)! The Upanishads were in the hands of the Sannyasin; he went into the forest! Shankara was a little kind and said even Grihasthas (householders) may study the Upanishads, it will do them good; it will not hurt them. But still the idea is that the Upanishads talked only of the forest life of the recluse. As I told you the other day, the only commentary, the authoritative commentary on the Vedas, has been made once and for all by Him who inspired the Vedas—by Krishna in the Gita. It is there for every one in every occupation of life. These conceptions of the Vedanta must come out, must remain not only in the forest, not only in the cave, but they must come out to work at the bar and the bench, in the pulpit, and in the cottage of the poor man, with the fishermen that are catching fish, and with the students that are studying. They call to every man, woman, and child whatever be their occupation, wherever they may be. And what is there to fear! How can the fishermen and all these carry out the ideals of the Upanishads? The way has been shown. It is infinite; religion is infinite, none can go beyond it; and whatever you do sincerely is good for you. Even the least thing well done brings marvellous results; therefore let every one do what little he can. If the fisherman thinks that he is the Spirit, he will be a better fisherman; if the student thinks he is the Spirit, he will be a better student. If the lawyer thinks that he is the Spirit, he will be a better lawyer, and so on, and the result will be that the castes will remain for ever. It is in the nature of society to form itself into groups; and what will go will be these privileges. Caste is a natural order; I can perform one duty in social life, and you another; you can govern a country, and I can mend a pair of old shoes, but that is no reason why you are greater than I, for can you mend my shoes? Can I govern the country? I am clev-

er in mending shoes, you are clever in reading Vedas, but that is no reason why you should trample on my head. Why if one commits murder should he be praised, and if another steals an apple why should he be hanged? This will have to go. Caste is good. That is the only natural way of solving life. Men must form themselves into groups, and you cannot get rid of that. Wherever you go, there will be caste. But that does not mean that there should be these privileges. They should be knocked on the head. If you teach Vedanta to the fisherman, he will say, I am as good a man as you; I am a fisherman, you are a philosopher, but I have the same God in me as you have in you. And that is what we want, no privilege for any one, equal chances for all; let every one be taught that the divine is within, and every one will work out his own salvation.

Liberty is the first condition of growth. It is wrong, a thousand times wrong, if any of you dares to say, "I will work out the salvation of this woman or child." I am asked again and again, what I think of the widow problem and what I think of the woman question. Let me answer once for all—am I a widow that you ask me that nonsense? Am I a woman that you ask me that question again and again? Who are you to solve women's problems? Are you the Lord God that you should rule over every widow and every woman? Hands off! They will solve their own problems. O tyrants, attempting to think that you can do anything for any one! Hands off! The Divine will look after all. Who are you to assume that you know everything? How dare you think, O blasphemers, that you have the right over God? For don't you know that every soul is the Soul of God? Mind your own Karma; a load of Karma is there in you to work out. Your nation may put you upon a pedestal, your society may cheer you up to the skies, and fools may praise you: but He sleeps not, and retribution will be sure to follow, here or hereafter.

Look upon every man, woman, and every one as God. You cannot help anyone, you can only serve: serve the children of the Lord, serve the Lord Himself, if you have the privilege. If the Lord grants that you can help any one of His children, blessed you are; do not think too much of yourselves. Blessed you are that that privilege was given to you when others had it not. Do it only as a worship. I should see God in the poor, and it is for my salvation that I go and worship them. The poor and the miserable are for our salvation, so that we may serve the Lord, coming in the shape of the diseased, coming in the shape of the lunatic, the leper, and the sinner! Bold are my words; and let me repeat that it is the greatest privilege in our life that we are allowed to serve the Lord in all these shapes. Give up the idea that by ruling over others you can do any good to them. But you can do just as much as you can in the case of the plant; you can supply the growing seed with the materials for the making up of its body, bringing to it the earth, the water, the air, that it wants. It will take all that it wants by its own nature. It will assimilate and grow by its own nature.

Bring all light into the world. Light, bring light! Let light come unto every one; the task will not be finished till every one has reached the Lord. Bring light to the poor and bring more light to the rich, for they require it more than the poor. Bring light to the ignorant, and more light to the educated, for the vanities of the education of our time are tremendous! Thus bring light to all and leave the rest unto the Lord, for in the words of the same Lord "To work you have the right and not to the fruits thereof." "Let not your work produce results for you, and at the same time may you never be without work."

May He who taught such grand ideas to our forefathers ages ago help us to get strength to carry into practice His commands!

THE SAGES OF INDIA

In speaking of the sages of India, my mind goes back to those periods of which history has no record, and tradition tries in vain to bring the secrets out of the gloom of the past. The sages of India have been almost innumerable, for what has the Hindu nation been doing for thousands of years except producing sages? I will take, therefore, the lives of a few of the most brilliant ones, the epoch-makers, and present them before you, that is to say, my study of them.

In the first place, we have to understand a little about our scriptures. Two ideals of truth are in our scriptures; the one is, what we call the eternal, and the other is not so authoritative, yet binding under particular circumstances, times, and places. The eternal relations which deal with the nature of the soul, and of God, and the relations between souls and God are embodied in what we call the Shrutis, the Vedas. The next set of truths is what we call the Smritis, as embodied in the words of Manu. Yâjnavalkya, and other writers and also in the Purânas, down to the Tantras. The second class of books and teachings is subordinate to the Shrutis, inasmuch as whenever any one of these contradicts anything in the Shrutis, the Shrutis must prevail. This is the law. The idea is that the framework of the destiny and goal of man has been all delineated in the Vedas, the details have been left to be worked out in the Smritis and Puranas. As for general directions, the Shrutis are enough; for spiritual life, nothing more can be said, nothing more can be known. All that is necessary has been known, all the advice that is necessary to lead the soul to perfection has been completed in the Shrutis; the details alone were left out, and these the Smritis have supplied from time to time.

Another peculiarity is that these Shrutis have many sages as the recorders of the truths in them, mostly men, even some women. Very little is known of their personalities, the dates of their birth, and so forth, but their best thoughts, their best discoveries, I should say, are preserved there, embodied in the sacred literature of our country, the Vedas. In the Smritis, on the other hand, personalities are more in evidence. Startling, gigantic, impressive, world-moving persons stand before us, as it were, for the first time, sometimes of more magnitude even than their teachings.

This is a peculiarity which we have to understand—that our religion preaches an Impersonal Personal God. It preaches any amount of impersonal laws plus any amount of personality, but the very fountain-head of our religion is in the Shrutis, the Vedas, which are perfectly impersonal; the persons all come in the Smritis and Puranas—the great Avatâras, Incarnations of God, Prophets, and so forth. And this ought also to be observed that except our religion every other religion in the world depends upon the life or lives of some personal founder or founders. Christianity is built upon the life of Jesus Christ, Mohammedanism upon Mohammed, Buddhism upon Buddha, Jainism upon the Jinas, and so on. It naturally follows that there must be in all these religions a good deal of fight about what they call the historical evidences of these great personalities. If at any time the historical evidences about the existence of these personages in ancient times become weak, the whole building of the religion tumbles down and is broken to pieces. We escaped this fate because our religion is not based upon persons but on principles. That you obey your religion is not because it came through the authority of a sage, no, not even of an Incarnation. Krishna is not the authority of the Vedas, but the Vedas are the authority of Krishna himself. His glory is that he is the greatest preacher of the Vedas that ever existed. So with the other Incarnations; so with all our sages. Our first principle is that all that is necessary for the perfection of man and for attaining unto freedom is there in the Vedas. You cannot find anything new. You cannot go beyond a perfect unity, which is the goal of all knowledge; this has been already reached there, and it is impossible to go beyond the unity. Religious knowledge became complete when Tat Twam Asi (Thou art That) was discovered, and that was in the Vedas. What remained was the guidance of people from time to time according to different times and places, according to different circumstances and environments; people had to be guided along the old, old path, and for this these great teachers came, these great sages. Nothing can bear out more clearly this position than the celebrated saying of Shri Krishna in the Gitâ: "Whenever virtue subsides and irreligion prevails, I create Myself for the protection of the good; for the destruction of all immorality I am coming from time to time." This is the idea in India.

What follows? That on the one hand, there are these eternal principles which stand upon their own foundations without depending on any reasoning even, much less on the authority of sages however great, of Incarnations however brilliant they may have been. We may remark that as this is the unique position in India, our claim is that the Vedanta only can be the universal religion, that it is already the existing universal religion in the world, because it teaches principles and not persons. No religion built upon a person can be taken up as a type by all the races of mankind. In our own country we find that there have been so many grand characters; in even a small city many persons are taken up as types by the different minds in that one city. How is it possible that one person as Mohammed or Buddha or Christ, can be taken up as the one type for the whole world, nay, that the whole of morality, ethics, spirituality, and religion can be true only from the sanction of that one person, and one person alone? Now, the Vedantic religion does not require any such personal authority. Its sanction is the eternal nature of man, its ethics are based upon the eternal spiritual solidarity of man, already existing, already attained and not to be attained. On the other hand, from the very earliest times, our sages have been feeling conscious of this fact that the vast majority of mankind require a personality. They must have a Personal God in some form or other. The very Buddha who declared against the existence of a Personal God had not died fifty years before his disciples manufactured a Personal God out of him. The Personal God is necessary, and at the same time we know that instead of and better than vain imaginations of a Personal God, which in ninety-nine cases out of a hundred are unworthy of human worship we have in this world, living and walking in our midst, living Gods, now and then. These are more worthy of worship than any imaginary God, any creation of our imagination, that is to say, any idea of God which we can form. Shri Krishna is much greater than any idea of God you or I can have. Buddha is a much higher idea, a more living and idolised idea, than the ideal you or I can conceive of in our minds; and therefore it is that they always command the worship of mankind even to the exclusion of all imaginary deities.

This our sages knew, and, therefore, left it open to all Indian people to worship such great Personages, such Incarnations. Nay, the greatest of these Incarnations goes further: "Wherever an extraordinary spiritual power is manifested by external man, know that I am there, it is from Me that that manifestation comes." That leaves the door open for the Hindu to worship the Incarnations of all the countries in the world. The Hindu can worship any sage and any saint from any country whatsoever, and as a fact we know that we go and worship many times in the churches of the Christians, and many, many times in the Mohammedan mosques, and that is good. Why not? Ours, as I have said, is the universal religion. It is inclusive enough, it is broad enough to include all the ideals. All the ideals of religion that already exist in the world can be immediately included, and we can patiently wait for all the ideals that are to come in the future to be taken in the same fashion, embraced in the infinite arms of the religion of the Vedanta.

This, more or less, is our position with regard to the great sages, the Incarnations of God. There are also secondary characters. We find the word Rishi again and again mentioned in the Vedas, and it has become a common word at the present time. The Rishi is the great authority. We have to understand that idea. The definition is that the Rishi is the Mantra-drashtâ, the seer of thought. What is the proof of religion?—this was asked in very ancient times. There is no proof in the senses was the declaration. यतो वाचो निवर्तन्ते

अप्राप्य मनसा सह—"From whence words reflect back with thought without reaching the goal." न तत्र चक्षुर्गच्छति न वागगच्छति नो मनः ।—"There the eyes cannot reach, neither can speech, nor the mind"—that has been the declaration for ages and ages. Nature outside cannot give us any answer as to the existence of the soul, the existence of God, the eternal life, the goal of man, and all that. This mind is continually changing, always in a state of flux; it is finite, it is broken into pieces. How can nature tell of the Infinite, the Unchangeable, the Unbroken, the Indivisible, the Eternal? It never can. And whenever mankind has striven to get an answer from dull dead matter, history shows how disastrous the results have been. How comes, then, the knowledge which the Vedas declare? It comes through being a Rishi. This knowledge is not in the senses; but are the senses the be-all and the end-all of the human being? Who dare say that the senses are the all-in-all of man? Even in our lives, in the life of every one of us here, there come moments of calmness, perhaps, when we see before us the death of one we loved, when some shock comes to us, or when extreme blessedness comes to us. Many other occasions there are when the mind, as it were, becomes calm, feels for the moment its real nature; and a glimpse of the Infinite beyond, where words cannot reach nor the mind go, is revealed to us. This happens in ordinary life, but it has to be heightened, practiced, perfected. Men found out ages ago that the soul is not bound or limited by the senses, no, not even by consciousness. We have to understand that this consciousness is only the name of one link in the infinite chain. Being is not identical with consciousness, but consciousness is only one part of Being. Beyond consciousness is where the bold search lies. Consciousness is bound by the senses. Beyond that, beyond the senses, men must go in order to arrive at truths of the spiritual world, and there are even now persons who succeed in going beyond the bounds of the senses. These are called Rishis, because they come face to face with spiritual truths.

The proof, therefore, of the Vedas is just the same as the proof of this table before me, Pratyaksha, direct perception. This I see with the senses, and the truths of spirituality we also see in a superconscious state of the human soul. This Rishi-state is not limited by time or place, by sex or race. Vâtsyâyana boldly declares that this Rishihood is the common property of the descendants of the sage, of the Aryan, of the non-Aryan, of even the Mlechchha. This is the sageship of the Vedas, and constantly we ought to remember this ideal of religion in India, which I wish other nations of the world would also remember and learn, so that there may be less fight and less quarrel. Religion is not in books, nor in theories, nor in dogmas, nor in talking, not even in reasoning. It is being and becoming. Ay, my friends, until each one of you has become a Rishi and come face to face with spiritual facts, religious life has not begun for you. Until the superconscious opens for you, religion is mere talk, it is nothing but preparation. You are talking second-hand, third-hand, and here applies that beautiful saying of Buddha when he had a discussion with some Brahmins. They came discussing about the nature of Brahman, and the great sage asked, "Have you seen Brahman?" "No, said the Brahmin; "Or your father?" "No, neither has he"; "Or your grandfather?" "I don't think even he saw Him." "My friend, how can you discuss about a person whom your father and grandfather never saw, and try to put each other down?" That is what the whole world is doing. Let us say in the language of the Vedanta, "This Atman is not to be reached by too much talk, no, not even by the highest intellect, no, not even by the study of the Vedas themselves."

Let us speak to all the nations of the world in the language of the Vedas: Vain are your fights and your quarrels; have you seen God whom you want to preach? If you have not seen, vain is your preaching; you do not know what you say; and if you have seen God, you will not quarrel, your very face will shine. An ancient sage of the Upanishads sent his son out to learn about Brahman, and the child came back, and the father asked, "what have you learnt?" The child replied he had learnt so many sciences. But the father said, "That is nothing, go back." And the son went back, and when he returned again the father asked the same question, and the same answer came from the child. Once more he had to go back. And the next time he came, his whole face was shining; and his father stood up and declared, "Ay, today, my child, your face shines like a knower of Brahman." When you have known God, your very face will be changed, your voice will be changed, your whole appearance will he changed. You will be a blessing to mankind; none will be able to resist the Rishi. This is the Rishihood, the ideal in our religion. The rest, all these talks and reasonings and philosophies and dualisms and monisms, and even the Vedas themselves are but preparations, secondary things. The other is primary. The Vedas, grammar, astronomy, etc., all these are secondary; that is supreme knowledge which makes us realise the Unchangeable One. Those who realised are the sages whom we find in the Vedas; and we understand how this Rishi is the name of a type, of a class, which every one of us, as true Hindus, is expected to become at some period of our life, and becoming which, to the Hindu, means salvation. Not belief in doctrines, not going to thousands of temples, nor bathing in all the rivers in the world, but becoming the Rishi, the Mantra-drashta—that is freedom, that is salvation.

Coming down to later times, there have been great world-moving sages, great Incarnations of whom there have been many; and according to the Bhâgavata, they also are infinite in number, and those that are worshipped most in India are Râma and Krishna. Rama, the ancient idol of the heroic ages, the embodiment of truth, of morality, the ideal son, the ideal husband, the ideal father, and above all, the ideal king, this Rama has been presented before us by the great sage Vâlmiki. No language can be purer, none chaster, none more beautiful and at the same time simpler than the language in which the great poet has depicted the life of Rama. And what to speak of Sitâ? You may exhaust the literature of the world that is past, and I may assure you that you will have to exhaust the literature of the world of the future, before finding another Sita. Sita is unique; that character was depicted once and for all. There may have been several Ramas, perhaps, but never more than one Sita! She is the very type of the true Indian woman, for all the Indian ideals of a perfected woman have grown out of that one life of Sita; and here she stands these thousands of years, commanding the worship of every man, woman, and child throughout the length and breadth of the land of Âryâvarta. There she will always be, this glorious Sita, purer than purity itself, all patience, and all suffering. She who suffered that life of suffering without a murmur, she the ever-chaste and ever-pure wife, she the ideal of the people, the ideal of the gods, the great Sita, our national God she must always remain. And every one of us knows her too well to require much delineation. All our mythology may vanish, even our Vedas may depart, and our Sanskrit language may vanish for ever, but so long as there will be five Hindus living here, even if only speaking the most vulgar patois, there will be the story of Sita present. Mark my words: Sita has gone into the very vitals of our race. She is there in the blood of every Hindu man and woman; we are all children of Sita. Any attempt to modernise our women, if it tries to take our women away from that ideal of Sita, is immediately a failure, as we see every day. The women of India must grow and develop in the footprints of Sita, and that is the only way.

The next is He who is worshipped in various forms, the favourite ideal of men as well as of women, the ideal of children, as well as of grown-up men. I mean He whom the writer of the Bhagavata was not content to call an Incarnation but says, "The other Incarnations were but parts of the Lord. He, Krishna, was the Lord Himself." And it is not strange that such adjectives are applied to him when we marvel at the many-sidedness of his character. He was the most wonderful Sannyasin, and the most wonderful householder in one; he had the most wonderful amount of Rajas, power, and was at the same time living in the midst of the most wonderful renunciation. Krishna can never he understood until you have studied the Gita, for he was the embodiment of his own teaching. Every one of these Incarnations came as a living illustration of what they came to preach. Krishna, the preacher of the Gita, was all his life the embodiment of that Song Celestial; he was the great illustration of non-attachment. He gives up his throne and never cares for it. He, the leader of India, at whose word kings come down from their thrones, never wants to be a king. He is the simple Krishna, ever the same Krishna who played with the Gopis. Ah, that most marvellous passage of his life, the most difficult to understand, and which none ought to attempt to understand until he has become perfectly chaste and pure, that most marvellous expansion of love, allegorised and expressed in that beautiful play at Vrindâban, which none can understand but he who has become mad with love, drunk deep of the cup of love! Who can understand the throes of the lore of the Gopis—the very ideal of love, love that wants nothing, love that even does not care for heaven, love that does not care for anything in this world or the world to come? And here, my friends, through this love of the Gopis has been found the only solution of the conflict between the Personal and the Impersonal God. We know how the Personal God is the highest point of human life; we know that it is philosophical to believe in an Impersonal God immanent in the universe, of whom everything is but a manifestation. At the same time our souls hanker after something concrete, something which we want to grasp, at whose feet we can pour out our soul, and so on. The Personal God is therefore the highest conception of human nature. Yet reason stands aghast at such an idea. It is the same old, old question which you find discussed in the Brahma-Sutras, which you find Draupadi discussing with Yudhishthira in the forest: If there is a Personal God, all-merciful, all-powerful, why is the hell of an earth here, why did He create this?—He must be a partial God. There was no solution, and the only solution that can be found is what you read about the love of the Gopis. They hated every adjective that was applied to Krishna; they did not care to know that he was the Lord of creation, they did not care to know that he was almighty, they did not care to know that he was omnipotent, and so forth. The only thing they understood was that he was infinite Love, that was all. The Gopis understood Krishna only as the Krishna of Vrindaban. He, the leader of the hosts, the King of kings, to them was the shepherd, and the shepherd for ever. "I do not want wealth, nor many people, nor do I want learning; no, not even do I want to go to heaven. Let one be born again and again, but Lord, grant me this, that I may have love for Thee, and that for love's sake." A great landmark in the history of religion is here, the ideal of love for love's sake, work for work's sake, duty for duty's sake, and it for the first time fell from the lips of the greatest of Incarnations, Krishna, and for the first time in the history of humanity, upon the soil of India. The religions of fear and of temptations were gone for ever, and in spite of the fear of hell and temptation of enjoyment in heaven, came the grandest of ideals, love for love's sake, duty for duty's sake, work for work's sake.

And what a love! I have told you just now that it is very difficult to understand the love of the Gopis. There are not wanting fools, even in the midst of us, who cannot understand the marvellous significance of that most marvellous of all episodes. There are, let me repeat, impure fools, even born of our blood, who try to shrink from that as if from something impure. To them I have only to say, first make yourselves pure; and you must remember that he who tells the history of the love of the Gopis is none else but Shuka Deva. The historian who records this marvellous love of the Gopis is one who was born pure, the eternally pure Shuka, the son of Vyâsa. So long as there its selfishness in the heart, so long is love of God impossible; it is nothing but shopkeeping: "I give

you something; O Lord, you give me something in return"; and says the Lord, "If you do not do this, I will take good care of you when you die. I will roast you all the rest of your lives. perhaps", and so on. So long as such ideas are in the brain, how can one understand the mad throes of the Gopis' love? "O for one, one kiss of those lips! One who has been kissed by Thee, his thirst for Thee increases for ever, all sorrows vanish, and he forgets love for everything else but for Thee and Thee alone." Ay, forget first the love for gold, and name and fame, and for this little trumpery world of ours. Then, only then, you will understand the love of the Gopis, too holy to be attempted without giving up everything, too sacred co be understood until the soul has become perfectly pure. People with ideas of sex, and of money, and of fame, bubbling up every minute in the heart, daring to criticise and understand the love of the Gopis! That is the very essence of the Krishna Incarnation. Even the Gita, the great philosophy itself, does not compare with that madness, for in the Gita the disciple is taught slowly how to walk towards the goal, but here is the madness of enjoyment, the drunkenness of love, where disciples and teachers and teachings and books and all these things have become one; even the ideas of fear, and God, and heaven—everything has been thrown away. What remains is the madness of love. It is forgetfulness of everything, and the lover sees nothing in the world except that Krishna and Krishna alone, when the face of every being becomes a Krishna, when his own face looks like Krishna, when his own soul has become tinged with the Krishna colour. That was the great Krishna!

Do not waste your time upon little details. Take up the framework, the essence of the life. There may be many historical discrepancies, there may be interpolations in the life of Krishna. All these things may be true; but, at the same time, there must have been a basis, a foundation for this new and tremendous departure. Taking the life of any other sage or prophet, we find that that prophet is only the evolution of what had gone before him, we find that that prophet is only preaching the ideas that had been scattered about his own country even in his own times. Great doubts may exist even as to whether that prophet existed or not. But here, I challenge any one to show whether these things, these ideals—work for work's sake, love for love's sake, duty for duty's sake, were not original ideas with Krishna, and as such, there must have been someone with whom these ideas originated. They could not have been borrowed from anybody else. They were not floating about in the atmosphere when Krishna was born. But the Lord Krishna was the first preacher of this; his disciple Vyasa took it up and preached it unto mankind. This is the highest idea to picture. The highest thing we can get out of him is Gopijanavallabha, the Beloved of the Gopis of Vrindaban. When that madness comes in your brain, when you understand the blessed Gopis, then you will understand what love is. When the whole world will vanish, when all other considerations will have died out, when you will become pure-hearted with no other aim, not even the search after truth, then and then alone will come to you the madness of that love, the strength and the power of that infinite love which the Gopis had, that love for love's sake. That is the goal. When you have got that, you have got everything.

To come down to the lower stratum — Krishna, the preacher of the Gita. Ay, there is an attempt in India now which is like putting the cart before the horse. Many of our people think that Krishna as the lover of the Gopis is something rather uncanny, and the Europeans do not like it much. Dr. So-and-so does not like it. Certainly then, the Gopis have to go! Without the sanction of Europeans how can Krishna live? He cannot! In the Mahabharata there is no mention of the Gopis except in one or two places, and those not very remarkable places. In the prayer of Draupadi there is mention of a Vrindaban life, and in the speech of Shishupâla there is again mention of this Vrindaban. All these are interpolations! What the Europeans do not want: must be thrown off. They are interpolations, the mention of the Gopis and of Krishna too! Well, with these men, steeped in commercialism, where even the ideal of religion has become commercial, they are all trying to go to heaven by doing something here; the bania wants compound interest, wants to lay by something here and enjoy it there. Certainly the Gopis have no place in such a system of thought. From that ideal lover we come down to the lower stratum of Krishna, the preacher of the Gita. Than the Gita no better commentary on the Vedas has been written or can be written. The essence of the Shrutis, or of the Upanishads, is hard to be understood, seeing that there are so many commentators, each one trying to interpret in his own way. Then the Lord Himself comes, He who is the inspirer of the Shrutis, to show us the meaning of them, as the preacher of the Gita, and today India wants nothing better, the world wants nothing better than that method of interpretation. It is a wonder that subsequent interpreters of the scriptures, even commenting upon the Gita, many times could not catch the meaning, many times could not catch the drift. For what do you find in the Gita, and what in modern commentators? One non-dualistic commentator takes up an Upanishad; there are so many dualistic passages, and he twists and tortures them into some meaning, and wants to bring them all into a meaning of his own. If a dualistic commentator comes, there are so many nondualistic texts which he begins to torture, to bring them all round to dualistic meaning. But you find in the Gita there is no attempt at torturing any one of them. They are all right, says the Lord; for slowly and gradually the human soul rises up and up, step after step, from the gross to the fine, from the fine to the finer, until it reaches the Absolute, the goal. That is what is in the Gita. Even the Karma Kanda is taken up, and it is shown that although it cannot give salvation direct; but only indirectly, yet that is also valid; images are valid indirectly; ceremonies, forms, everything is valid only with one condition, purity of the heart. For worship is valid and leads to the goal if the heart is pure and the heart is sincere; and all these various modes of worship are necessary, else why should they be there? Religions and sects are not the work of hypocrites and wicked people who invented all these to get a little money, as some of our modern men want to think. However reasonable that explanation may seem, it is not true, and they were not invented that way at all. They are the outcome of the necessity of the human soul. They are all here to satisfy the hankering and thirst of different classes of human minds, and you need not preach against them. The day when that necessity will cease, they will vanish along with the cessation of that necessity; and so long as that necessity remains, they must be there in spite of your preaching, in spite of your criticism. You may bring the sword or the gun into play, you may deluge the world with human blood, but so long as there is a necessity for idols, they must remain. These forms, and all the various steps in religion will remain, and we understand from the Lord Shri Krishna why they should.

A rather sadder chapter of India's history comes now. In the Gita we already hear the distant sound of the conflicts of sects, and the Lord comes in the middle to harmonise them all; He, the great preacher of harmony, the greatest teacher of harmony, Lord Shri Krishna. He says, "In Me they are all strung like pearls upon a thread." We already hear the distant sounds, the murmurs of the conflict, and possibly there was a period of harmony and calmness, when it broke out anew, not only on religious grounds, but roost possibly on caste grounds — the fight between the two powerful factors in our community, the kings and the priests. And from the topmost crest of the wave that deluged India for nearly a thousand years, we see another glorious figure, and that was our Gautama Shâkyamuni. You all know about his teachings and preachings. We worship him as God incarnate, the greatest, the boldest preacher of morality that the world ever saw, the greatest Karma-Yogi; as disciple of himself, as it were, the same Krishna came to show how to make his theories practical. There came once again the same voice that in the Gita preached, "Even the least bit done of this religion saves from great fear". "Women, or Vaishyas, or even Shudras, all reach the highest goal." Breaking the bondages of all, the chains of all, declaring liberty to all to reach the highest goal, come the words of the Gita, rolls like thunder the mighty voice of Krishna: "Even in this life they have conquered relativity, whose minds are firmly fixed upon the sameness, for God is pure and the same to all, therefore such are said to be living in God." "Thus seeing the same Lord equally present everywhere, the sage does not injure the Self by the self, and thus reaches the highest goal." As it were to give a living example of this preaching, as it were to make at least one part of it practical, the preacher himself came in another form, and this was Shakyamuni, the preacher to the poor and the miserable, he who rejected even the language of the gods to speak in the language of the people, so that he might reach the hearts of the people, he who gave up a throne to live with beggars, and the poor, and the downcast, he who pressed the Pariah to his breast like a second Rama.

You all know about his great work, his grand character. But the work had one great defect, and for that we are suffering even today. No blame attaches to the Lord. He is pure and glorious, but unfortunately such high ideals could not be well assimilated by the different uncivilised and uncultured races of mankind who flocked within the fold of the Aryans. These races, with varieties of superstition and hideous worship, rushed within the fold of the Aryans and for a time appeared as if they had become civilised, but before a century had passed they brought out their snakes, their ghosts, and all the other things their ancestors used to worship, and thus the whole of India became one degraded mass of superstition. The earlier Buddhists in their rage against the killing of animals had denounced the sacrifices of the Vedas; and these sacrifices used to be held in every house. There was a fire burning, and that was all the paraphernalia of worship. These sacrifices were obliterated, and in their place came gorgeous temples, gorgeous ceremonies, and gorgeous priests, and all that you see in India in modern times. I smile when I read books written by some modern people who ought to have known better, that the Buddha was the destroyer of Brahminical idolatry. Little do they know that Buddhism created Brahminism and idolatry in India.

There was a book written a year or two ago by a Russian gentleman, who claimed to have found out a very curious life of Jesus Christ, and in one part of the book he says that Christ went to the temple of Jagannath to study with the Brahmins, but became disgusted with their exclusiveness and their idols, and so he went to the Lamas of Tibet instead, became perfect, and went home. To any man who knows anything about Indian history, that very statement proves that the whole thing was a fraud, because the temple of Jagannath is an old Buddhistic temple. We took this and others over and re-Hinduised them. We shall have to do many things like that yet. That is Jagannath, and there was not one Brahmin there then, and yet we are told that Jesus Christ came to study with the Brahmins there. So says our great Russian archaeologist.

Thus, in spite of the preaching of mercy to animals, in spite of the sublime ethical religion, in spite of the hairsplitting discussions about the existence or non-existence of a permanent soul, the whole building of Buddhism tumbled down piecemeal; and the ruin was simply hideous. I have neither the time nor the inclination to describe to you the hideousness that came in the wake of Buddhism. The most hideous ceremonies, the most horrible, the most obscene books that human hands ever wrote or the human brain ever conceived, the most bestial forms that ever passed under the name of religion, have all been the creation of degraded Buddhism.

But India has to live, and the spirit of the Lords descended again. He who declared, "I will come whenever virtue subsides", came again, and this time the manifestation was in the South, and up rose that young Brahmin of whom it has been declared that at the age of sixteen he had completed all his writings; the marvellous boy Shankaracharya arose. The writings of this boy of sixteen are the wonders of the modern world, and so was the boy. He wanted to bring back the Indian world to its pristine purity, but think of the amount of the task before him. I have told you a few points about the state of things that existed in India. All these horrors that you are trying to reform are the outcome of that reign of degradation. The Tartars and the Baluchis and all the hideous races of mankind came to India and became Buddhists, and assimilated with us, and brought their national customs, and the whole of our national life became a huge page of the most horrible and the most bestial customs. That was the inheritance which that boy got from the Buddhists, and from that time to this, the whole work in India is a reconquest of this Buddhistic degradation by the Vedanta. It is still going on, it is not yet finished. Shankara came, a great philosopher, and showed that the real essence of Buddhism and that of the Vedanta are not very different, but that the disciples did not understand the Master and have degraded themselves, denied the existence of the soul and of God, and have become atheists. That was what Shankara showed, and all the Buddhists began to come back to the old religion. But then they had become accustomed to all these forms; what could be done?

Then came the brilliant Râmânuja. Shankara, with his great intellect, I am afraid, had not as great a heart. Ramanuja's heart was greater. He felt for the downtrodden, he sympathised with them. He took up the ceremonies, the accretions that had gathered, made them pure so far as they could be, and instituted new ceremonies, new methods of worship, for the people who absolutely required them. At the same time he opened the door to the highest; spiritual worship from the Brahmin to the Pariah. That was Ramanuja's work. That work rolled on, invaded the North, was taken up by some great leaders there; but that was much later, during the Mohammedan rule; and the brightest of these prophets of comparatively modern times in the North was Chaitanya.

You may mark one characteristic since the time of Ramanuja—the opening of the door of spirituality to every one. That has been the watchword of all prophets succeeding Ramanuja, as it had been the watchword of all the prophets before Shankara. I do not know why Shankara should be represented as rather exclusive; I do not find anything in his writings which is exclusive. As in the case of the declarations of the Lord Buddha, this exclusiveness that has been attributed to Shankara's teachings is most possibly not due to his teachings, but to the incapacity of his disciples. This one great Northern sage, Chaitanya, represented the mad love of the Gopis. Himself a Brahmin, born of one of the most rationalistic families of the day, himself a professor of logic fighting and gaining a word-victory—for, this he had learnt from his childhood as the highest ideal of life and yet through the mercy of some sage the whole life of that man became changed; he gave up his fight, his quarrels, his professorship of logic and became one of the greatest teachers of Bhakti the world has ever known—mad Chaitanya. His Bhakti rolled over the whole land of Bengal, bringing solace to every one. His love knew no bounds. The saint or the sinner, the Hindu or the Mohammedan, the pure or the impure, the prostitute, the streetwalker—all had a share in his love, all had a share in his mercy: and even to the present day, although greatly degenerated, as everything does become in time, his sect is the refuge of the poor, of the downtrodden, of the outcast, of the weak, of those who have been rejected by all society. But at the same time I must remark for truth's sake that we find this: In the philosophic sects we find wonderful liberalisms. There is not a man who follows Shankara who will say that all the different sects of India are really different. At the same time he was a tremendous upholder of exclusiveness as regards caste. But with every Vaishnavite preacher we find a wonderful liberalism as to the teaching of caste questions, but exclusiveness as regards religious questions.

The one had a great head, the other a large heart, and the time was ripe for one to be born, the embodiment of both this head and heart; the time was ripe for one to be born who in one body would have the brilliant intellect of Shankara and the wonderfully expansive, infinite heart of Chaitanya; one who would see in every sect the same spirit working, the same God; one who would see God in every being, one whose heart would weep for the poor, for the weak, for the outcast, for the downtrodden, for every one in this world, inside India or outside India; and at the same time whose grand brilliant intellect would conceive of such noble thoughts as would harmonise all conflicting sects, not only in India but outside of India, and bring a marvellous harmony, the universal religion of head and heart into existence. Such a man was born, and I had the good fortune to sit at his feet for years. The time was ripe, it was necessary that such a man should be born, and he came; and the most wonderful part of it was that his life's work was just near a city which was full of Western thought, a city which had run mad after these occidental ideas, a city which had become more Europeanised than any other city in India. There he lived, without any book-learning whatsoever; this great intellect never learnt even to write his own name[1], but the most graduates of our university found in him an intellectual giant. He was a strange man, this Shri Ramakrishna Paramahamsa. It is a long, long story, and I have no time to tell anything about him tonight. Let me now only mention the great Shri Ramakrishna, the fulfilment of the Indian sages, the sage for the time, one whose teaching is just now, in the present time, most beneficial. And mark the divine power working behind the man. The son of a poor priest, born in an out-of-the-way village, unknown and unthought of, today is worshipped literally by thousands in Europe and America, and tomorrow will be worshipped by thousands more. Who knows the plans of the Lord!

Now, my brothers, if you do not see the hand, the finger of Providence, it is because you are blind, born blind indeed.

1. Later research has shown that although Shri Ramakrishna was almost illiterate in the Western sense, he could read and write Bengali.

If time comes, and another opportunity, I will speak to you more fully about him. Only let me say now that if I have told you one word of truth, it was his and his alone, and if I have told you many things which were not true, which were not correct, which were not beneficial to the human race, they were all mine, and on me is the responsibility.

THE WORK BEFORE US

Delivered at the Triplicane Literary Society, Madras

The problem of life is becoming deeper and broader every day as the world moves on. The watchword and the essence have been preached in the days of yore when the Vedantic truth was first discovered, the solidarity of all life. One atom in this universe cannot move without dragging the whole world along with it. There cannot be any progress without the whole world following in the wake, and it is becoming every day clearer that the solution of any problem can never be attained on racial, or national, or narrow grounds. Every idea has to become broad till it covers the whole of this world, every aspiration must go on increasing till it has engulfed the whole of humanity, nay, the whole of life, within its scope. This will explain why our country for the last few centuries has not been what she was in the past. We find that one of the causes which led to this degeneration was the narrowing of our views narrowing the scope of our actions.

Two curious nations there have been—sprung of the same race, but placed in different circumstances and environments, working put the problems of life each in its own particular way. I mean the ancient Hindu and the ancient Greek. The Indian Aryan—bounded on the north by the snow-caps of the Himalayas, with fresh-water rivers like rolling oceans surrounding him in the plains, with eternal forests which, to him, seemed to be the end of the world—turned his vision inward; and given the natural instinct, the superfine brain of the Aryan, with this sublime scenery surrounding him, the natural result was that he became introspective. The analysis of his own mind was the great theme of the Indo-Aryan. With the Greek, on the other hand, who arrived at a part of the earth which was more beautiful than sublime, the beautiful islands of the Grecian Archipelago, nature all around him generous yet simple—his mind naturally went outside. It wanted to analyse the external world. And as a result we find that from India have sprung all the analytical sciences, and from Greece all the sciences of generalization. The Hindu mind went on in its own direction and produced the most marvellous results. Even at the present day, the logical capacity of the Hindus, and the tremendous power which the Indian brain still possesses, is beyond compare. We all know that our boys pitched against the boys of any other country triumph always. At the same time when the national vigour went, perhaps one or two centuries before the Mohammedan conquest of India, this national faculty became so much exaggerated that it degraded itself, and we find some of this degradation in everything in

India, in art, in music, in sciences, in everything. In art, no more was there a broad conception, no more the symmetry of form and sublimity of conception, but the tremendous attempt at the ornate and florid style had arisen. The originality of the race seemed to have been lost. In music no more were there the soul-stirring ideas of the ancient Sanskrit music, no more did each note stand, as it were, on its own feet, and produce the marvellous harmony, but each note had lost its individuality. The whole of modern music is a jumble of notes, a confused mass of curves. That is a sign of degradation in music. So, if you analyse your idealistic conceptions, you will find the same attempt at ornate figures, and loss of originality. And even in religion, your special field, there came the most horrible degradations. What can you expect of a race which for hundreds of years has been busy in discussing such momentous problems as whether we should drink a glass of water with the right hand or the left? What more degradation can there be than that the greatest minds of a country have been discussing about the kitchen for several hundreds of years, discussing whether I may touch you or you touch me, and what is the penance for this touching! The themes of the Vedanta, the sublimest and the most glorious conceptions of God and soul ever preached on earth, were half-lost, buried in the forests, preserved by a few Sannyâsins, while the rest of the nation discussed the momentous questions of touching each other, and dress, and food. The Mohammedan conquest gave us many good things, no doubt; even the lowest man in the world can teach something to the highest; at the same time it could not bring vigour into the race. Then for good or evil, the English conquest of India took place. Of course every conquest is bad, for conquest is an evil, foreign government is an evil, no doubt; but even through evil comes good sometimes, and the great good of the English conquest is this: England, nay the whole of Europe, has to thank Greece for its civilization. It is Greece that speaks through everything in Europe. Every building, every piece of furniture has the impress of Greece upon it; European science and art are nothing but Grecian. Today the ancient Greek is meeting the ancient Hindu on the soil of India. Thus slowly and silently the leaven has come; the broadening, the life-giving and the revivalist movement that we see all around us has been worked out by these forces together. A broader and more generous conception of life is before us; and although at first we have been deluded a little and wanted to narrow things down, we are finding out today that these generous impulses which are at work, these broader conceptions of life, are the logical interpretation of what is in our ancient books. They are the carrying out, to the rigorously logical effect, of the primary conceptions of our own ancestors. To become broad, to go out, to amalgamate, to universalist, is the end of our aims. And all the time we have been making ourselves smaller and smaller, and dissociating ourselves, contrary to the plans laid down our scriptures.

Several dangers are in the way, and one is that of the extreme conception that we are the people in the world. With all my love for India, and with all my patriotism and veneration for the ancients, I cannot but think that we have to learn many things from other nations. We must be always ready to sit at the feet of all, for, mark you, every one can teach us great lessons. Says our great law-giver, Manu: "Receive some good knowledge even from the low-born, and even from the man of lowest birth learn by service the road to heaven." We, therefore, as true children of Manu, must obey his commands and be ready to learn the lessons of this life or the life hereafter from any one who can teach us. At the same time we must not forget that we have also to teach a great lesson to the world. We cannot do without the world outside India; it was our foolishness that we thought we could, and we have paid the penalty by about a thousand years of slavery. That we did not go out to compare things with other nations, did not mark the workings that have been all around us, has been the one great cause of this degradation of the Indian mind. We have paid the penalty; let us do it no more. All such foolish ideas that Indians must not go out of India are childish. They must be knocked on the head; the more you go out and travel among the nations of the world, the better for you and for your country. If you had done that for hundreds of years past, you would not be here today at the feet of every nation that wants to rule India. The first manifest effect of life is expansion. You must expand if you want to live. The moment you have ceased to expand, death is upon you, danger is ahead. I went to America and Europe, to which you so kindly allude; I have to, because that is the first sign of the revival of national life, expansion. This reviving national life, expanding inside, threw me off, and thousands will be thrown off in that way. Mark my words, it has got to come if this nation lives at all. This question, therefore, is the greatest of the signs of the revival of national life, and through this expansion our quota of offering to the general mass of human knowledge, our contribution to the general upheaval of the world, is going out to the external world.

Again, this is not a new thing. Those of you who think that the Hindus have been always confined within the four walls of their country through all ages, are entirely mistaken; you have not studied the old books, you have not studied the history of the race aright if you think so. Each nation must give in order to live. When you give life, you will have life; when you receive, you must pay for it by giving to all others; and that we have been living for so many thousands of years is a fact that stares us in the face, and the solution that remains is that we have been always giving to the outside world, whatever the ignorant may think. But the gift of India is the gift of religion and philosophy, and wisdom and spirituality. And religion does not want cohorts to march before its path and clear its way. Wisdom and philosophy do not want to be carried on floods of blood. Wisdom and philosophy do not march upon bleeding human bodies, do not march with violence but come on the wings of peace and love, and that has always been so. Therefore we had to give. I was asked by

Lectures & Discourses by **Swami Vivekananda**

a young lady in London, "What have you Hindus done? You have never even conquered a single nation." That is true from the point of view of the Englishman, the brave, the heroic, the Kshatriya—conquest is the greatest glory that one man can have over another. That is true from his point of view, but from ours it is quite the opposite. If I ask myself what has been the cause of India's greatness, I answer, because we have never conquered. That is our glory. You are hearing every day, and sometimes, I am sorry to say, from men who ought to know better, denunciations of our religion, because it is not at all a conquering religion. To my mind that is the argument why our religion is truer than any other religion, because it never conquered, because it never shed blood, because its mouth always shed on all, words of blessing, of peace, words of love and sympathy. It is here and here alone that the ideals of toleration were first preached. And it is here and here alone that toleration and sympathy have become practical it is theoretical in every other country, it is here and here alone, that the Hindu builds mosques for the Mohammedans and churches for the Christians.

So, you see, our message has gone out to the world many a time, but slowly, silently, unperceived. It is on a par with everything in India. The one characteristic of Indian thought is its silence, its calmness. At the same time the tremendous power that is behind it is never expressed by violence. It is always the silent mesmerism of Indian thought. If a foreigner takes up our literature to study, at first it is disgusting to him; there is not the same stir, perhaps, the same amount of go that rouses him instantly. Compare the tragedies of Europe with our tragedies. The one is full of action, that rouses you for the moment, but when it is over there comes the reaction, and everything is gone, washed off as it were from your brains. Indian tragedies are like the mesmerist's power, quiet, silent, but as you go on studying them they fascinate you; you cannot move; you are bound; and whoever has dared to touch our literature has felt the bondage, and is there bound for ever. Like the gentle dew that falls unseen and unheard, and yet brings into blossom the fairest of roses, has been the contribution of India to the thought of the world. Silent, unperceived, yet omnipotent in its effect, it has revolutionised the thought of the world, yet nobody knows when it did so. It was once remarked to me, "How difficult it is to ascertain the name of any writer in India", to which I replied, "That is the Indian idea." Indian writers are not like modern writers who steal ninety percent of their ideas from other authors, while only ten per cent is their own, and they take care to write a preface in which they say, "For these ideas I am responsible". Those great master minds producing momentous results in the hearts of mankind were content to write their books without even putting their names, and to die quietly, leaving the books to posterity. Who knows the writers of our philosophy, who knows the writers of our Purânas? They all pass under the generic name of Vyâsa, and Kapila, and so on. They have been true children of Shri Krishna. They have been true followers of the Gita; they practically carried out the great mandate, "To work you have the right, but not to the fruits thereof."

Thus India is working upon the world, but one condition is necessary. Thoughts like merchandise can only run through channels made by somebody. Roads have to be made before even thought can travel from one place to another, and whenever in the history of the world a great conquering nation has arisen, linking the different parts of the world together, then has poured through these channels the thought of India and thus entered into the veins of every race. Before even the Buddhists were born, there are evidences accumulating every day that Indian thought penetrated the world. Before Buddhism, Vedanta had penetrated into China, into Persia, and the Islands of the Eastern Archipelago. Again when the mighty mind of the Greek had linked the different parts of the Eastern world together there came Indian thought; and Christianity with all its boasted civilisation is but a collection of little bits of Indian thought. Ours is the religion of which Buddhism with all its greatness is a rebel child, and of which Christianity is a very patchy imitation. One of these cycles has again arrived. There is the tremendous power of England which has linked the different parts of the world together. English roads no more are content like Roman roads to run over lands, but they have also ploughed the deep in all directions. From ocean to ocean run the roads of England. Every part of the world has been linked to every other part, and electricity plays a most marvellous part as the new messenger. Under all these circumstances we find again India reviving and ready to give her own quota to the progress and civilisation of the world. And that I have been forced, as it were, by nature, to go over and preach to America and England is the result. Every one of us ought to have seen that the time had arrived. Everything looks propitious, and Indian thought, philosophical and spiritual, roast once more go over and conquer the world. The problem before us, therefore, is assuming larger proportions every day. It is not only that we must revive our own country—that is a small matter; I am an imaginative man—and my idea is the conquest of the whole world by the Hindu race.

There have been great conquering races in the world. We also have been great conquerors. The story of our conquest has been described by that noble Emperor of India, Asoka, as the conquest of religion and of spirituality. Once more the world must be conquered by India. This is the dream of my life, and I wish that each one of you who hear me today will have the same dream in your minds, and stop not till you have realised the dream. They will tell you every day that we had better look to our own homes first and then go to work outside. But I will tell you in plain language that you work best when you work for others. The best work that you ever did for yourselves was when you worked for others, trying to disseminate your ideas in foreign languages beyond the seas, and this very meeting is proof how the attempt to enlighten other countries with your thoughts is helping your own country. One-fourth of the effect that has been produced in this country by my going to England and America would not have been brought about, had I confined my ideas only to India. This is the great ideal before us, and every one must be ready for it—the Conquest of the whole world by India—nothing less than that, and we must all get ready for it, strain every nerve for it. Let foreigners come and flood the land with their armies, never mind. Up, India, and conquer the world with your spirituality! Ay, as has been declared on this soil first, love must conquer hatred, hatred cannot conquer itself. Materialism and all its miseries can never be conquered by materialism. Armies when they attempt to conquer armies only multiply and make brutes of humanity. Spirituality must conquer the West. Slowly they are finding out that what they want is spirituality to preserve them as nations. They are waiting for it, they are eager for it. Where is the supply to come from? Where are the men ready to go out to every country in the world with the messages of the great sages of India? Where are the men who are ready to sacrifice everything, so that this message shall reach every corner of the world? Such heroic spurs are wanted to help the spread of truth. Such heroic workers are wanted to go abroad and help to disseminate the great truths of the Vedanta. The world wants it; without it the world will be destroyed. The whole of the Western world is on a volcano which may burst tomorrow, go to pieces tomorrow. They have searched every corner of the world and have found no respite. They have drunk deep of the cup of pleasure and found it vanity. Now is the time to work so that India's spiritual ideas may penetrate deep into the West. Therefore young men of Madras, I specially ask you to remember this. We must go out, we must conquer the world through our spirituality and philosophy. There is no other alternative, we must do it or die. The only condition of national life, of awakened and vigorous national life, is the conquest of the world by Indian thought.

At the same time we must not forget that what I mean by the conquest of the world by spiritual thought is the sending out of the life-giving principles, not the hundreds of superstitions that we have been hugging to our breasts for centuries. These have to be weeded out even on this soil, and thrown aside, so that they may die for ever. These are the causes of the degradation of the race and will lead to softening of the brain. That brain which cannot think high and noble thoughts, which has lost all power of originality, which has lost all vigour, that brain which is always poisoning itself with all sorts of little superstitions passing under the name of religion, we must beware of. In our sight, here in India, there are several dangers. Of these, the two, Scylla and Charybdis, rank materialism and its opposite arrant superstition, must be avoided. There is the man today who after drinking the cup of Western wisdom, thinks that he knows everything. He laughs at the ancient sages. All Hindu thought to him is arrant trash—philosophy mere child's prattle, and religion the superstition of fools. On the other hand, there is the man educated, but a sort of monomaniac, who runs to the other extreme and wants to explain the omen of this and that. He has philosophical and metaphysical, and Lord knows what other puerile explanations for every superstition that belongs to his peculiar race, or his peculiar gods, or his peculiar village. Every little village superstition is to him a mandate of the Vedas, and upon the carrying out of it, according to him, depends the national life. You must beware of this. I would rather see every one of you rank atheists than superstitious fools, for the atheist is alive and you can make something out of him. But if superstition enters, the brain is gone, the brain is softening, degradation has seized upon the life. Avoid these two. Brave, bold men, these are what we want. What we want is vigour in the blood, strength in the nerves, iron muscles and nerves of steel, not softening namby-pamby ideas. Avoid all these. Avoid all mystery. There is no mystery in religion. Is there any mystery in the Vedanta, or in the Vedas, or in the Samhitâs, or in the Puranas? What secret societies did the sages of yore establish to preach their religion? What sleight-of-hand tricks are there recorded as used by them to bring their grand truths to humanity? Mystery mongering and superstition are always signs of weakness. These are always signs of degradation and of death. Therefore beware of them; be strong, and stand on your own feet. Great things are there, most marvellous things. We may call them supernatural things so far as our ideas of nature go, but not one of these things is a mystery. It was never preached on this soil that the truths of religion were mysteries or that they were the property of secret societies sitting on the snow-caps of the Himalayas. I have been in the Himalayas. You have not been there; it is several hundreds of miles from your homes. I am a Sannyâsin, and I have been for the last fourteen years on my feet. These mysterious societies do not exist anywhere. Do not run after these superstitions. Better for you and for the race that you become rank atheists, because you would have strength, but these are degradation and death. Shame on humanity that strong men should spend their time on these superstitions, spend all their time in inventing allegories to explain the most rotten superstitions of the world. Be bold; do not try to explain everything that way. The fact is that we have many superstitions, many bad spots and sores on our body—these have to be excised, cut off, and destroyed—but these do not destroy our religion, our national life, our spirituality. Every principle of religion is safe, and the sooner these black spots are purged away, the better the principles will shine, the more gloriously. Stick to them.

You hear claims made by every religion as being the universal religion of the world. Let me tell you in the first place that perhaps there never will be such a thing, but if there is a religion which can lay claim to be that, it is only our religion and no other, because every other religion depends on some person or persons. All the other religions have been built round the life of what they think a historical man; and what they think the strength of religion is really the weakness, for disprove the historicity of the man and the whole fabric tumbles to ground. Half the lives of these great founders of religions have been broken into pieces, and the other half doubted very seriously. As such, every truth that had its sanction only in their words vanishes into air. But the truths of our religion, although we have persons by the score, do not depend upon them. The glory of Krishna is not that he was Krishna, but that he was the great teacher of Vedanta. If he had not been so, his name would have died out of India in the same way as the name of Buddha has done. Thus our allegiance is to the principles always, and not to the persons. Persons are but the embodiments, the illustrations of the principles. If the principles are there, the persons will come by the thousands and millions. If the principle is safe, persons like Buddha will be born by the hundreds and thousands. But if the principle is lost and forgotten and the whole of national life tries to cling round a so-called historical person, woe unto that religion, danger unto that religion! Ours is the only religion that does not depend on a person or persons; it is based upon principles. At the same time there is room for millions of persons. There is ample ground for introducing persons, but each one of them must be an illustration of the principles. We must not forget that. These principles of our religion are all safe, and it should be the life-work of everyone of us to keep then safe, and to keep them free from the accumulating dirt and dust of ages. It is strange that in spite of the degradation that seized upon the race again and again, these principles of the Vedanta were never tarnished. No one, however wicked, ever dared to throw dirt upon them. Our scriptures are the best preserved scriptures in the world. Compared to other books there have been no interpolations, no text-torturing, no destroying of the essence of the thought in them. It is there just as it was first, directing the human mind towards the ideal, the goal.

You find that these texts have been commented upon by different commentators, preached by great teachers, and sects founded upon them; and you find that in these books of the Vedas there are various apparently contradictory ideas. There are certain texts which are entirely dualistic, others are entirely monistic. The dualistic commentator, knowing no better, wishes to knock the monistic texts on the head. Preachers and priests want to explain them in the dualistic meaning. The monistic commentator serves the dualistic texts in a similar fashion. Now this is not the fault of the Vedas. It is foolish to attempt to prove that the whole of the Vedas is dualistic. It is equally foolish to attempt to prove that the whole of the Vedas is nondualistic. They are dualistic and non-dualistic both. We understand them better today in the light of newer ideas. These are but different conceptions leading to the final conclusion that both dualistic and monistic conceptions are necessary for the evolution of the mind, and therefore the Vedas preach them. In mercy to the human race the Vedas show the various steps to the higher goal. Not that they are contradictory, vain words used by the Vedas to delude children; they are necessary not only for children, but for many a grown-up man. So long as we have a body and so long as we are deluded by the idea of our identity with the body, so long as we have five senses and see the external world, we must have a Personal God. For if we have all these ideas, we must take as the great Râmânuja has proved, all the ideas about God and nature and the individualized soul; when you take the one you have to take the whole triangle—we cannot avoid it. Therefore as long as you see the external world to avoid a Personal God and a personal soul is arrant lunacy. But there may be times in the lives of sages when the human mind transcends as it were its own limitations, man goes even beyond nature, to the realm of which the Shruti declares, "whence words fall back with the mind without reaching it"; "There the eyes cannot reach nor speech nor mind"; "We cannot say that we know it, we cannot say that we do not know it". There the human soul transcends all limitations, and then and then alone flashes into the human soul the conception of monism: I and the whole universe are one; I and Brahman are one. And this conclusion you will find has not only been reached through knowledge and philosophy, but parts of it through the power of love. You read in the Bhâgavata, when Krishna disappeared and the Gopis bewailed his disappearance, that at last the thought of Krishna became so prominent in their minds that each one forgot her own body and thought she was Krishna, and began to decorate herself and to play as he did. We understand, therefore, that this identity comes even through love. There was an ancient Persian Sufi poet, and one of his poems says, "I came to the Beloved and beheld the door was closed; I knocked at the door and from inside a voice came, 'Who is there?' I replied, 'I am'. The door did not open. A second time I came and knocked at the door and the same voice asked, 'Who is there?' 'I am so-and-so.' The door did not open. A third time I came and the same voice asked, 'Who is there?' 'I am Thyself, my Love', and the door opened."

There are, therefore, many stages, and we need not quarrel about them even if there have been quarrels among the ancient commentators, whom all of us ought to revere; for there is no limitation to knowledge, there is no omniscience exclusively the property of any one in ancient or modern times. If there have been sages and Rishis in the past, be sure that there will be many now. If there have been Vyâsas and Vâlmikis and Shankarâchâryas in ancient times, why may not each one of you become a Shankaracharya? This is another point of our religion that you must always remember, that in all other scriptures inspiration is quoted as their authority, but this inspiration is limited to a very few persons, and through them the truth came to the masses, and we have all to obey them. Truth came to Jesus of Nazareth, and we must all obey him. But the truth came to the Rishis of India—the Mantra-drashtâs, the seers of thought—and will come to all Rishis in the future, not to talkers, not to book-swallowers, not to scholars, not to philologists, but to seers of thought. The Self is not to be reached by too much talking, not even by the highest intellects, not even by the study of the scriptures. The scriptures themselves say so. Do you find in any other scripture such a bold assertion as that—not even by the study of the Vedas will you reach the Atman? You must open your heart. Religion is not going to church, or putting marks on the forehead, or dressing in a peculiar fashion; you may paint yourselves in all the colours of the rainbow, but if the heart has not been opened, if you have not realised God, it is all vain. If one has the colour of the heart, he does not want any external colour. That is the true religious realisation. We must not forget that colours and all these things are good so far as they help; so far they are all welcome. But they are apt to degenerate and instead of helping they retard, and a man identifies religion with externalities. Going to the temple becomes tantamount to spiritual life. Giving something to a priest becomes tantamount to religious life. These are dangerous and pernicious, and should be at once checked. Our scriptures declare again and again that even the knowledge of the external senses is not religion. That is religion which makes us realise the Unchangeable One, and that is the religion for every one. He who realises transcendental truth, he who realises the Atman in his own nature, he who comes face to face with God, sees God alone in everything, has become a Rishi. And there is no religious life for you until you have become a Rishi. Then alone religion begins for you, now is only the preparation. Then religion dawns upon you, now you are only undergoing intellectual gymnastics and physical tortures.

We must, therefore, remember that our religion lays down distinctly and clearly that every one who wants salvation must pass through the stage of Rishihood—must become a Mantra-drashta, must see God. That is salvation; that is the law laid down by our scriptures. Then it becomes easy to look into the scripture with our own eyes, understand the meaning for ourselves, to analyse just what we want, and to understand the truth for ourselves. This is what has to be done. At the same time we must pay all reverence to the ancient sages for their work. They were great, these ancients, but we want to be greater. They did great work in the past, but we must do greater work than they. They had hundreds of Rishis in ancient India. We will have millions—we are going to have, and the sooner every one of you believes in this, the better for India and the better for the world. Whatever you believe, that you will be. If you believe yourselves to be sages, sages you will be tomorrow. There is nothing to obstruct you. For if there is one common doctrine that runs through all our apparently fighting and contradictory sects, it is that all glory, power, and purity are within the soul already; only according to Ramanuja, the soul contracts and expands at times, and according to Shankara, it comes under a delusion. Never mind these differences. All admit the truth that the power is there -potential or manifest it is there—and the sooner you believe that, the better for you. All power is within you; you can do anything and everything. Believe in that, do not believe that you are weak; do not believe that you are half-crazy lunatics, as most of us do nowadays. You can do anything and everything without even the guidance of any one. All power is there. Stand up and express the divinity within you.

THE FUTURE OF INDIA

This is the ancient land where wisdom made its home before it went into any other country, the same India whose influx of spirituality is represented, as it were, on the material plane, by rolling rivers like oceans, where the eternal Himalayas, rising tier above tier with their snowcaps, look as it were into the very mysteries of heaven. Here is the same India whose soil has been trodden by the feet of the greatest sages that ever lived. Here first sprang up inquiries into the nature of man and into the internal world. Here first arose the doctrines of the immortality of the soul, the existence of a supervising God, an immanent God in nature and in man, and here the highest ideals of religion and philosophy have attained their culminating points. This is the land from whence, like the tidal waves, spirituality and philosophy have again and again rushed out and deluged the world, and this is the land from whence once more such tides must proceed in order to bring life and vigour into the decaying races of mankind. It is the same India which has withstood the shocks of centuries, of hundreds of foreign invasions of hundreds of upheavals of manners and customs. It is the same land which stands firmer than any rock in the world, with its undying vigour, indestructible life. Its life is of the same nature as the soul, without beginning and without end, immortal; and we are the children of such a country.

Children of India, I am here to speak to you today about some practical things, and my object in reminding you about the glories of the past is simply this. Many times have I been told that looking into the past only degenerates and leads to nothing, and that we should look to the future. That is true. But out of the past is built the future. Look back, therefore, as far as you can, drink deep of the eternal fountains that are behind, and after that, look forward, march forward and make India brighter, greater, much higher than she ever was. Our ancestors were great. We must first recall that. We must learn the elements of our being, the blood that courses in our veins; we must have faith in that blood and what it did in the past; and out of that faith and consciousness of past greatness, we must build an India yet greater than what she has been. There have been periods of decay and degradation. I do not attach much importance to them; we all know that. Such periods have been necessary. A mighty tree produces a beautiful ripe fruit. That fruit falls on the ground, it decays and rots, and out of that decay springs the root and the future tree, perhaps mightier than the first one. This period of decay through which we have passed was all the more necessary. Out of this decay is coming the India of the future; it is sprouting, its first leaves are already out; and a mighty, gigantic tree, the Urdhvamula, is here, already beginning to appear; and it is about that that I am going to speak to you.

The problems in India are more complicated, more momentous, than the problems in any other country. Race, religion, language, government—all these together make a nation

The elements which compose the nations of the world are indeed very few, taking race after race, compared to this country. Here have been the Aryan, the Dravidian, the Tartar, the Turk, the Mogul, the European—all the nations of the world, as it were, pouring their blood into this land. Of languages the most wonderful conglomeration is here; of manners and customs there is more difference between two Indian races than between the European and the Eastern races.

The one common ground that we have is our sacred tradition, our religion. That is the only common ground, and upon that we shall have to build. In Europe, political ideas form the national unity. In Asia, religious ideals form the national unity. The unity in religion, therefore, is absolutely necessary as the first condition of the future of India. There must be the recognition of one religion throughout the length and breadth of this land. What do I mean by one religion? Not in the sense of one religion as held among the Christians, or the Mohammedans, of the Buddhists. We know that our religion has certain common grounds, common to all our sects, however varying their conclusions may be, however different their claims may be. So there are certain common grounds; and within their limitation this religion of ours admits of a marvellous variation, an infinite amount of liberty to think and live our own lives. We all know that, at least those of us who have thought; and what we want is to bring out these lifegiving common principles of our religion, and let every man, woman, and child, throughout the length and breadth of this country, understand them, know them, and try to bring them out in their lives. This is the first step; and, therefore, it has to be taken.

We see how in Asia, and especially in India, race difficulties, linguistic difficulties, social difficulties, national difficulties, all melt away before this unifying power of religion. We know that to the Indian mind there is nothing higher than religious ideals, that this is the keynote of Indian life, and we can only work in the line of least resistance. It is not only true that the ideal of religion is the highest ideal; in the case of India it is the only possible means of work; work in any other line, without first strengthening this, would be disastrous. Therefore the first plank in the making of a future India, the first step that is to be hewn out of that rock of ages, is this unification of religion. All of us have to be taught that we Hindus—dualists, qualified monists, or monists, Shaivas, Vaishnavas, or Pâshupatas—to whatever denomination we may belong, have certain common ideas behind us, and that the time has come when for the well-being of ourselves, for the well-being of our race, we must give up all our little quarrels and differences. Be sure, these quarrels are entirely wrong; they are condemned by our scriptures, forbidden by our forefathers; and those great men from whom we claim our descent, whose blood is in our veins, look down with contempt on their children quarrelling about minute differences.

With the giving up of quarrels all other improvements will come. When the life-blood is strong and pure, no disease germ can live in that body. Our life-blood is spirituality. If it flows clear, if it flows strong and pure and vigorous, everything is right; political, social, any other material defects, even the poverty of the land, will all be cured if that blood is pure. For if the disease germ be thrown out, nothing will be able to enter into the blood. To take a simile from modern medicine, we know that there must be two causes to produce a disease, some poison germ outside, and the state of the body. Until the body is in a state to admit the germs, until the body is degraded to a lower vitality so that the germs may enter and thrive and multiply, there is no power in any germ in the world to produce a disease in the body. In fact, millions of germs are continually passing through everyone's body; but so long as it is vigorous, it never is conscious of them. It is only when the body is weak that these germs take possession of it and produce disease. Just so with the national life. It is when the national body is weak that all sorts of disease germs, in the political state of the race or in its social state, in its educational or intellectual state, crowd into the system and produce disease. To remedy it, therefore, we must go to the root of this disease and cleanse the blood of all impurities. The one tendency will be to strengthen the man, to make the blood pure, the body vigorous, so that it will be able to resist and throw off all external poisons.

We have seen that our vigour, our strength, nay, our national life is in our religion. I am not going to discuss now whether it is right or not, whether it is correct or not, whether it is beneficial or not in the long run, to have this vitality in religion, but for good or evil it is there; you cannot get out of it, you have it now and for ever, and you have to stand by it, even if you have not the same faith that I have in our religion. You are bound by it, and if you give it up, you are smashed to pieces. That is the life of our race and that must be strengthened. You have withstood the shocks of centuries simply because you took great care of it, you sacrificed everything else for it. Your forefathers underwent everything boldly, even death itself, but preserved their religion. Temple alter temple was broken down by the foreign conqueror, but no sooner had the wave passed than the spire of the temple rose up again. Some of these old temples of Southern India and those like Somnâth of Gujarat will teach you volumes of wisdom, will give you a keener insight into the history of the race than any amount of books. Mark how these temples bear the marks of a hundred attacks and a hundred regenerations, continually destroyed and continually springing up out of the ruins, rejuvenated and strong as ever! That is the national mind, that is the national life-current. Follow it and it leads to glory. Give it up and you die; death will be the only result, annihilation the only effect, the moment you step beyond that life-current. I do not mean to say that other things are not necessary. I do not mean to say that political or social improvements are not necessary, but what I mean is this, and I want you to bear it in mind, that they are secondary here and that religion is primary. The Indian mind is first religious, then anything else. So this is to be strengthened, and how to do it? I will lay before you my ideas. They have been in my mind for a long time, even years before I left the shores of Madras for America, and that I went to America and England was simply for propagating those ideas. I did not care at all for the Parliament of Religions or anything else; it was simply an opportunity; for it was really those ideas of mine that took me all over the world.

My idea is first of all to bring out the gems of spirituality that are stored up in our books and in the possession of a few only, hidden, as it were, in monasteries and in forests — to bring them out; to bring the knowledge out of them, not only from the hands where it is hidden, but from the still more inaccessible chest, the language in which it is preserved, the incrustation of centuries of Sanskrit words. In one word, I want to make them popular. I want to bring out these ideas and let them be the common property of all, of every man in India, whether he knows the Sanskrit language or not. The great difficulty in the way is the Sanskrit language — the glorious language of ours; and this difficulty cannot be removed until — if it is possible — the whole of our nation are good Sanskrit scholars. You will understand the difficulty when I tell you that I have been studying this language all my life, and yet every new book is new to me. How much more difficult would it then be for people who never had time to study the language thoroughly! Therefore the ideas must be taught in the language of the people; at the same time, Sanskrit education must go on along with it, because the very sound of Sanskrit words gives a prestige and a power and a strength to the race. The attempts of the great Ramanuja and of Chaitanya and of Kabir to raise the lower classes of India show that marvellous results were attained during the lifetime of those great prophets; yet the later failures have to be explained, and cause shown why the effect of their teachings stopped almost within a century of the passing away of these great Masters. The secret is here. They raised the lower classes; they had all the wish that these should come up, but they did not apply their energies to the spreading of the Sanskrit language among the masses. Even the great Buddha made one false step when he stopped the Sanskrit language from being studied by the masses. He wanted rapid and immediate results, and translated and preached in the language of the day, Pâli. That was grand; he spoke in the language of the people, and the people understood him. That was great; it spread the ideas quickly and made them reach far and wide. But along with that, Sanskrit ought to have spread. Knowledge came, but the prestige was not there, culture was not there. It is culture that withstands shocks, not a simple mass of knowledge. You can put a mass of knowledge into the world, but that will not do it much good. There must come culture into the blood. We all know in modern times of nations which have masses of knowledge, but what of them? They are like tigers, they are like savages, because culture is not there. Knowledge is only skin-deep, as civilisation is, and a little scratch brings out the old savage. Such things happen; this is the danger. Teach the masses in the vernaculars, give them ideas; they will get information, but something more is necessary; give them culture. Until you give them that, there can be no permanence in the raised condition of the masses. There will be another caste created, having the advantage of the Sanskrit language, which will quickly get above the rest and rule them all the same. The only safety, I tell you men who belong to the lower castes, the only way to raise your condition is to study Sanskrit, and this fighting and writing and frothing against the higher castes is in vain, it does no good, and it creates fight and quarrel, and this race, unfortunately already divided, is going to be divided more and more. The only way to bring about the levelling of caste is to appropriate the culture, the education which is the strength of the higher castes. That done, you have what you want

In connection with this I want to discuss one question which it has a particular bearing with regard to Madras. There is a theory that there was a race of mankind in Southern India called Dravidians, entirely differing from another race in Northern India called the Aryans, and that the Southern India Brâhmins are the only Aryans that came from the North, the other men of Southern India belong to an entirely different caste and race to those of Southern India Brahmins. Now I beg your pardon, Mr. Philologist, this is entirely unfounded. The only proof of it is that there is a difference of language between the North and the South. I do not see any other difference. We are so many Northern men here, and I ask my European friends to pick out the Northern and Southern men from this assembly. Where is the difference? A little difference of language. But the Brahmins are a race that came here speaking the Sanskrit language! Well then, they took up the Dravidian language and forgot their Sanskrit. Why should not the other castes have done the same? Why should not all the other castes have come one after the other from Northern India, taken up the Dravidian language, and so forgotten their own? That is an argument working both ways. Do not believe in such silly things. There may have been a Dravidian people who vanished from here, and the few who remained lived in forests and other places. It is quite possible that the language may have been taken up, but all these are Aryans who came from the North. The whole of India is Aryan, nothing else.

Then there is the other idea that the Shudra caste are surely the aborigines. What are they? They are slaves. They say history repeats itself. The Americans, English, Dutch, and the Portuguese got hold of the poor Africans and made them work hard while they lived, and their children of mixed birth were born in slavery and kept in that condition for a long period. From that wonderful example, the mind jumps back several thousand years and fancies that the same thing happened here, and our archaeologist dreams of India being full of dark-eyed aborigines, and the bright Aryan came from — the Lord knows where. According to some, they came from Central Tibet, others will have it that they came from Central Asia. There are patriotic Englishmen who think that the Aryans were all red-haired. Others, according to their idea, think that they were all black-haired. If the writer happens to be a black-haired man, the Aryans were all black-haired. Of late, there was an attempt made to prove that the Aryans lived on the Swiss lakes. I should not be sorry if they had been all drowned there, theory and all. Some say now that they lived at the North Pole. Lord bless the Aryans and their habitations! As for the truth of these theories, there is not one word in our scriptures, not one, to prove that the Aryan ever came from anywhere outside of India, and in ancient India was included Afghanistan. There it ends. And the theory that the Shudra caste were all non-Aryans and they were a multitude, is equally illogical and equally irrational. It could not have been possible in those days that a few Aryans settled and lived there with a hundred thousand slaves at their command. These slaves would have eaten them up, made "chutney" of them in five minutes. The only explanation is to be found in the Mahâbhârata, which says that in the beginning of the Satya Yuga there was one caste, the Brahmins, and then by difference of occupations they went on dividing themselves into different castes, and that is the only true and rational explanation that has been given. And in the coming Satya Yuga all the other castes will have to go back to the same condition.

The solution of the caste problem in India, therefore, assumes this form, not to degrade the higher castes, not to crush out the Brahmin. The Brahminhood is the ideal of humanity in India, as wonderfully put forward by Shankaracharya at the beginning of his commentary on the Gitâ, where he speaks about the reason for Krishna's coming as a preacher for the preservation of Brahminhood, of Brahminness. That was the great end. This Brahmin, the man of God, he who has known Brahman, the ideal man, the perfect man, must remain; he must not go. And with all the defects of the caste now, we know that we must all be ready to give to the Brahmins this credit, that from them have come more men with real Brahminness in them than from all the other castes. That is true. That is the credit due to them from all the other castes. We must be bold enough, must be brave enough to speak of their defects, but at the same time we must give the credit that is due to them. Remember the old English proverb, "Give every man his due". Therefore, my friends, it is no use fighting among the castes. What good will it do? It will divide us all the more, weaken us all the more, degrade us all the more. The days of exclusive privileges and exclusive claims are gone, gone for ever from the soil of India, and it is one of the great blessings of the British Rule in India. Even to the Mohammedan Rule we owe that great blessing, the destruction of exclusive privilege. That Rule was, after all, not all bad nothing is all bad, and nothing is all good. The Mohammedan conquest of India came as a salvation to the downtrodden, to the poor. That is why one-fifth of our people have become Mohammedans. It was not the sword that did it all. It would be the height of madness to think it was all the work of sword and fire. And one-fifth—one-half—of your Madras people

will become Christians if you do not take care. Was there ever a sillier thing before in the world than what I saw in Malabar country? The poor Pariah is not allowed to pass through the same street as the high-caste man, but if he changes his name to a hodge-podge English name, it is all right; or to a Mohammedan name, it is all right. What inference would you draw except that these Malabaris are all lunatics, their homes so many lunatic asylums, and that they are to be treated with derision by every race in India until they mend their manners and know better. Shame upon them that such wicked and diabolical customs are allowed; their own children are allowed to die of starvation, but as soon as they take up some other religion they are well fed. There ought to be no more fight between the castes.

The solution is not by bringing down the higher, but by raising the lower up to the level of the higher. And that is the line of work that is found in all our books, in spite of what you may hear from some people whose knowledge of their own scriptures and whose capacity to understand the mighty plans of the ancients are only zero. They do not understand, but those do that have brains, that have the intellect to grasp the whole scope of the work. They stand aside and follow the wonderful procession of national life through the ages. They can trace it step by step through all the books, ancient and modern. What is the plan? The ideal at one end is the Brahmin and the ideal at the other end is the Chandâla, and the whole work is to raise the Chandala up to the Brahmin. Slowly and slowly you find more and more privileges granted to them. There are books where you read such fierce words as these: "If the Shudra hears the Vedas, fill his ears with molten lead, and if he remembers a line, cut his tongue out. If he says to the Brahmin, 'You Brahmin', cut his tongue out". This is diabolical old barbarism no doubt; that goes without saying; but do not blame the law-givers, who simply record the customs of some section of the community. Such devils sometimes arose among the ancients. There have been devils everywhere more or less in all ages. Accordingly, you will find that later on, this tone is modified a little, as for instance, "Do not disturb the Shudras, but do not teach them higher things". Then gradually we find in other Smritis, especially in those that have full power now, that if the Shudras imitate the manners and customs of the Brahmins they do well, they ought to be encouraged. Thus it is going on. I have no time to place before you all these workings, nor how they can be traced in detail; but coming to plain facts, we find that all the castes are to rise slowly and slowly. There are thousands of castes, and some are even getting admission into Brahminhood, for what prevents any caste from declaring they are Brahmins? Thus caste, with all its rigour, has been created in that manner. Let us suppose that there are castes here with ten thousand people in each. If these put their heads together and say, we will call ourselves Brahmins, nothing can stop them; I have seen it in my own life. Some castes become strong, and as soon as they all agree, who is to say nay? Because whatever it was, each caste was exclusive of the other. It did not meddle with others' affairs; even the several divisions of one caste did not meddle with the other divisions, and those powerful epoch-makers, Shankaracharya and others, were the great caste-makers. I cannot tell you all the wonderful things they fabricated, and some of you may resent what I have to say. But in my travels and experiences I have traced them out, and have arrived at most wonderful results. They would sometimes get hordes of Baluchis and at once make them Kshatriyas, also get hold of hordes of fishermen and make them Brahmins forthwith. They were all Rishis and sages, and we have to bow down to their memory. So, be you all Rishis and sages; that is the secret. More or less we shall all be Rishis. What is meant by a Rishi? The pure one. Be pure first, and you will have power. Simply saying, "I am a Rishi", will not do; but when you are a Rishi you will find that others obey you instinctively. Something mysterious emanates from you, which makes them follow you, makes them hear you, makes them unconsciously, even against their will, carry out your plans. That is Rishihood.

Now as to the details, they of course have to be worked out through generations. But this is merely a suggestion in order to show you that these quarrels should cease. Especially do I regret that in Moslem times there should be so much dissension between the castes. This must stop. It is useless on both sides, especially on the side of the higher caste, the Brahmin, because the day for these privileges and exclusive claims is gone. The duty of every aristocracy is to dig its own grave, and the sooner it does so, the better. The more it delays, the more it will fester and the worse death it will die. It is the duty of the Brahmin, therefore, to work for the salvation of the rest of mankind in India. If he does that, and so long as he does that, he is a Brahmin, but he is no Brahmin when he goes about making money. You on the other hand should give help only to the real Brahmin who deserves it; that leads to heaven. But sometimes a gift to another person who does not deserve it leads to the other place, says our scripture. You must be on your guard about that. He only is the Brahmin who has no secular employment. Secular employment is not for the Brahmin but for the other castes. To the Brahmins I appeal, that they must work hard to raise the Indian people by teaching them what they know, by giving out the culture that they have accumulated for centuries. It is clearly the duty of the Brahmins of India to remember what real Brahminhood is. As Manu says, all these privileges and honours are given to the Brahmin, because "with him is the treasury of virtue". He must open that treasury and distribute its valuables to the world. It is true that he was the earliest preacher to the Indian races, he was the first to renounce everything in order to attain to the higher realisation of life before others could reach to the idea. It was not his fault that he marched ahead of the other caste. Why did not the other castes so understand and do as he did? Why did they sit down and be lazy, and let the Brahmins win the race?

But it is one thing to gain an advantage, and another thing to preserve it for evil use. Whenever power is used for evil, it becomes diabolical; it must be used for good only. So this accumulated culture of ages of which the Brahmin has been the trustee, he must now give to the people at large, and it was because he did not give it to the people that the Mohammedan invasion was possible. It was because he did not open this treasury to the people from the beginning, that for a thousand years we have been trodden under the heels of every one who chose to come to India. It was through that we have become degraded, and the first task must be to break open the cells that hide the wonderful treasures which our common ancestors accumulated; bring them out and give them to everybody and the Brahmin must be the first to do it. There is an old superstition in Bengal that if the cobra that bites, sucks out his own poison from the patient, the man must survive. Well then, the Brahmin must suck out his own poison. To the non-Brahmin castes I say, wait, be not in a hurry. Do not seize every opportunity of fighting the Brahmin, because, as I have shown, you are suffering from your own fault. Who told you to neglect spirituality and Sanskrit learning? What have you been doing all this time? Why have you been indifferent? Why do you now fret and fume because somebody else had more brains, more energy, more pluck and go, than you? Instead of wasting your energies in vain discussions and quarrels in the newspapers, instead of fighting and quarrelling in your own homes—which is sinful—use all your energies in acquiring the culture which the Brahmin has, and the thing is done. Why do you not become Sanskrit scholars? Why do you not spend millions to bring Sanskrit education to all the castes of India? That is the question. The moment you do these things, you are equal to the Brahmin. That is the secret of power in India.

Sanskrit and prestige go together in India. As soon as you have that, none dares say anything against you. That is the one secret; take that up. The whole universe, to use the ancient Advaitist's simile, is in a state of self-hypnotism. It is will that is the power. It is the man of strong will that throws, as it were, a halo round him and brings all other people to the same state of vibration as he has in his own mind. Such gigantic men do appear. And what is the idea? When a powerful individual appears, his personality infuses his thoughts into us, and many of us come to have the same thoughts, and thus we become powerful. Why is it that organizations are so powerful? Do not say organization is material. Why is it, to take a case in point, that forty millions of Englishmen rule three hundred millions of people here? What is the psychological explanation? These forty millions put their wills together and that means infinite power, and you three hundred millions have a will each separate from the other. Therefore to make a great future India, the whole secret lies in organization, accumulation of power, co-ordination of wills.

Already before my mind rises one of the marvellous verses of the Rig-Veda Samhitâ which says, "Be thou all of one mind, be thou all of one thought, for in the days of yore, the gods being of one mind were enabled to receive oblations." That the gods can be worshipped by men is because they are of one mind. Being of one mind is the secret of society. And the more you go on fighting and quarrelling about all trivialities such as "Dravidian" and "Aryan", and the question of Brahmins and non-Brahmins and all that, the further you are off from that accumulation of energy and power which is going to make the future India. For mark you, the future India depends entirely upon that. That is the secret—accumulation of will-power, co-ordination, bringing them all, as it here, into one focus. Each Chinaman thinks in his own way, and a handful of Japanese all think in the same way, and you know the result. That is how it goes throughout the history of the world. You find in every case, compact little nations always governing and ruling huge unwieldy nations, and this is natural, because it is easier for the little compact nations to bring their ideas into the same focus, and thus they become developed. And the bigger the nation, the more unwieldy it is. Born, as it were, a disorganised mob, they cannot combine. All these dissensions must stop.

There is yet another defect in us. Ladies, excuse me, but through centuries of slavery, we have become like a nation of women. You scarcely can get three women together for five minutes in this country or any other country, but they quarrel. Women make big societies in European countries, and make tremendous declarations of women's power and so on; then they quarrel, and some man comes and rules them all. All over the world they still require some man to rule them. We are like them. Women we are. If a woman comes to lead women, they all begin immediately to criticise her, tear her to pieces, and make her sit down. If a man comes and gives them a little harsh treatment, scolds them now and then, it is all right, they have been used to that sort of mesmerism. The whole world is full of such mesmerists and hypnotists. In the same way, if one of our countrymen stands up and tries to become great, we all try to hold him down, but if a foreigner comes and tries to kick us, it is all right. We have been used to it, have we not? And slaves must become great masters! So give up being a slave. For the next fifty years this alone shall be our keynote—this, our great Mother India. Let all other vain gods disappear for the time from our minds. This is the only god that is awake, our own race—"everywhere his hands, everywhere his feet, everywhere his ears, he covers everything." All other gods are sleeping. What vain gods shall we go after and yet cannot worship the god that we see all round us, the Virât? When we have worshipped this, we shall be able to worship all other gods. Before we can crawl half a mile, we want to cross the ocean like Hanumân! It cannot be. Everyone going to be a Yogi, everyone going to meditate! It cannot be. The whole day mixing with the world with Karma Kânda, and in the evening sitting down and blowing through your nose! Is it so easy? Should Rishis come flying through the air, because you have blown three times through the nose? Is it a joke? It is all nonsense. What is needed is Chittashud-dhi, purification of the heart. And how does that come? The first of all worship is the worship of the Virat—of those all around us. Worship It. Worship is the exact equivalent of the Sanskrit word, and no other English word will do. These are all our gods—men and animals; and the first gods we have to worship are our countrymen. These we have to worship, instead of being jealous of each other and fighting each other. It is the most terrible Karma for which we are suffering, and yet it does not open our eyes!

Well, the subject is so great that I do not know where to stop, and I must bring my lecture to a close by placing before you in a few words the plans I want to carry out in Madras. We must have a hold on the spiritual and secular education of the nation. Do you understand that? You must dream it, you must talk it, you must think its and you must work it out. Till then there is no salvation for the race. The education that you are getting now has some good points, but it has a tremendous disadvantage which is so great that the good things are all weighed down. In the first place it is not a man-making education, it is merely and entirely a negative education. A negative education or any training that is based on negation, is worse than death. The child is taken to school, and the first thing he learns is that his father is a fool, the second thing that his grandfather is a lunatic, the third thing that all his teachers are hypocrites, the fourth that all the sacred books are lies! By the time he is sixteen he is a mass of negation, lifeless and boneless. And the result is that fifty years of such education has not produced one original man in the three Presidencies. Every man of originality that has been produced has been educated elsewhere, and not in this country, or they have gone to the old universities once more to cleanse themselves of superstitions. Education is not the amount of information that is put into your brain and runs riot there, undigested, all your life. We must have life-building, man-making, character-making assimilation of ideas. If you have assimilated five ideas and made them your life and character, you have more education than any man who has got by heart a whole library यथा खरश्चन्दनभारवाही भारस्य वेत्ता न तु चन्दनस्या—"The ass carrying its load of sandalwood knows only the weight and not the value of the sandalwood." If education is identical with information, the libraries are the greatest sages in the world, and encyclopaedias are the Rishis. The ideal, therefore, is that we must have the whole education of our country, spiritual and secular, in our own hands, and it must be on national lines, through national methods as far as practical.

Of course this is a very big scheme, a very big plan. I do not know whether it will ever work out. But we must begin the work. But how? Take Madras, for instance. We must have a temple, for with Hindus religion must come first. Then, you may say, all sects will quarrel about it. But we will make it a non-sectarian temple, having only "Om" as the symbol, the greatest symbol of any sect. If there is any sect here which believes that "Om" ought not to be the symbol, it has no right to call itself Hindu. All will have the right to interpret Hinduism, each one according to his own sect ideas, but we must have a common temple. You can have your own images and symbols in other places, but do not quarrel here with those who differ from you. Here should be taught the common grounds of our different sects, and at the same time the different sects should have perfect liberty to come and teach their doctrines, with only one restriction, that is, not to quarrel with other sects. Say what you have to say, the world wants it; but the world has no time to hear what you think about other people; you can keep that to yourselves.

Secondly, in connection with this temple there should be an institution to train teachers who must go about preaching religion and giving secular education to our people; they must carry both. As we have been already carrying religion from door to door, let us along with it carry secular education also. That can be easily done. Then the work will extend through these bands of teachers and preachers, and gradually we shall have similar temples in other places, until we have covered the whole of India. That is my plan. It may appear gigantic, but it is much needed. You may ask, where is the money. Money is not needed. Money is nothing. For the last twelve years of my life, I did not know where the next meal would come from; but money and everything else I want must come, because they are my slaves, and not I theirs; money and everything else must come. Must—that is the word. Where are the men? That is the question. Young men of Madras, my hope is in you. Will you respond to the call of your nation? Each one of you has a glorious future if you dare believe me. Have a tremendous faith in yourselves, like the faith I had when I was a child, and which I am working out now. Have that faith, each one of you, in yourself—that eternal power is lodged in every soul—and you will revive the whole of India. Ay, we will then go to every country under the sun, and our ideas will before long be a component of the many forces that are working to make up every nation in the world. We must enter into the life of every race in India and abroad; shall have to work to bring this about. Now for that, I want young men. "It is the young, the strong, and healthy, of sharp intellect that will reach the Lord", say the Vedas. This is the time to decide your future—while you possess the energy of youth, not when you are worn out and jaded, but in the freshness and vigour of youth. Work—this is the time; for the freshest, the untouched, and unsmelled flowers alone are to be laid at the feet of the Lord, and such He receives. Rouse yourselves, therefore, or life is short. There are greater works to be done than aspiring to become lawyers and picking quarrels and such things. A far greater work is this sacrifice of yourselves for the benefit of your race, for the welfare of humanity. What is in this life? You are Hindus, and there is the instinctive belief in you that life is eternal. Sometimes I have young men come and talk to me about atheism; I do not believe a Hindu can become an atheist. He may read European books, and persuade himself he is a materialist, but it is only for a time. It is not in your blood. You cannot believe what is not in your

constitution; it would be a hopeless task for you. Do not attempt that sort of thing. I once attempted it when I was a boy, but it could not be. Life is short, but the soul is immortal and eternal, and one thing being certain, death, let us therefore take up a great ideal and give up our whole life to it. Let this be our determination, and may He, the Lord, who "comes again and again for the salvation of His own people", to quote from our scriptures—may the great Krishna bless us and lead us all to the fulfilment of our aims!

ON CHARITY

During his stay in Madras the Swami presided at the annual meeting of the Chennapuri Annadâna Samâjam, an institution of a charitable nature, and in the course of a brief address referred to a remark by a previous speaker deprecating special alms-giving to the Brahmin over and above the other castes. Swamiji pointed out that this had its good as well as its bad side. All the culture, practically which the nation possessed, was among the Brahmins, and they also had been the thinkers of the nation. Take away the means of living which enabled them to be thinkers, and the nation as a whole would suffer. Speaking of the indiscriminate charity of India as compared with the legal charity of other nations, he said, the outcome of their system of relief was that the vagabond of India was contented to receive readily what he was given readily and lived a peaceful and contented life: while the vagabond in the West, unwilling to go to the poor-house—for man loves liberty more than food—turned a robber, the enemy of society, and necessitated the organisation of a system of magistracy, police, jails, and other establishments. Poverty there must be, so long as the disease known as civilisation existed: and hence the need for relief. So that they had to choose between the indiscriminate charity of India, which, in the case of Sannyâsins at any rate, even if they were not sincere men, at least forced them to learn some little of their scriptures before they were able to obtain food; and the discriminate charity of Western nations which necessitated a costly system of poor-law relief, and in the end succeeded only in changing mendicants into criminals.

ADDRESS OF WELCOME PRESENTED AT CALCUTTA AND REPLY

On his arrival in Calcutta, the Swami Vivekananda was greeted with intense enthusiasm, and the whole of his progress through the decorated streets of the city was thronged with an immense crowd waiting to have a sight of him. The official reception was held a week later, at the residence of the late Raja Radha Kanta Deb Bahadur at Sobha Bazar, when Raja Benoy Krishna Deb Bahadur took the chair. After a few brief introductory remarks from the Chairman, the following address was read and presented to him, enclosed in a silver casket:

TO SRIMAT VIVEKANANDA SWAMI:

Dear Brother,

We, the Hindu inhabitants of Calcutta and of several other places in Bengal, offer you on your return to the land of your birth a hearty welcome. We do so with a sense of pride as well as of gratitude, for by your noble work and example in various parts of the world you have done honour not only to our religion but also to our country and to our province in particular.

At the great Parliament of Religions which constituted a Section of the World's Fair held in Chicago in 1893, you presented the principles of the Aryan religion. The substance of your exposition was to most of your audience a revelation, and its manner overpowering alike by its grace and its strength. Some may have received it in a questioning spirit, a few may have criticised it, but its general effect was a revolution in the religious ideas of a large section of cultivated Americans. A new light had dawned on their mind, and with their accustomed earnestness and love of truth they determined to take full advantage of it. Your opportunities widened; your work grew. You had to meet call after call from many cities in many States, answer many queries, satisfy many doubts, solve many difficulties. You did an this work with energy, ability, and sincerity; and it has led to lasting results. Your teaching has deeply influenced many an enlightened circle in the American Commonwealth, has stimulated thought and research, and has in many instances definitely altered religious conceptions in the direction of an increased appreciation of Hindu ideals. The rapid growth of clubs and societies for the comparative study of religions and the investigation of spiritual truth is witness to your labour in the far West. You may be regarded as the founder of a College in London for the teaching of the Vedanta philosophy. Your lectures have been regularly delivered, punctually attended, and widely appreciated. Their influence has extended beyond the walls of the lecture-rooms. The love and esteem which have been evoked by your teaching are evidenced by the warm acknowledgements, in the address presented to you on the eve of your departure from London, by the students of the Vedanta philosophy in that town.

Your success as a teacher has been due not only to your deep and intimate acquaintance with the truths of the Aryan religion and your skill in exposition by speech and writing, but also, and largely, to your personality. Your lectures, your essays, and your books have high merits, spiritual and literary, and they could not but produce their effect. But it has been heightened in a manner that defies expression by the example of your simple, sincere, self-denying life, your modesty, devotion, and earnestness.

While acknowledging your services as a teacher of the sublime truths of our religion, we feel that we must render a tribute to the memory of your revered preceptor, Shri Ramakrishna Paramahamsa. To him we largely owe even you. With his rare magical insight he early discovered the heavenly spark in you and predicted for you a career which happily is now in course of realisation. He it was that unsealed the vision and the faculty divine with which God had blessed you, gave to your thoughts and aspirations the bent that was awaiting the holy touch, and aided your pursuits in the region of the unseen. His most precious legacy to posterity was yourself.

Go on, noble soul, working steadily and valiantly in the path you have chosen. You have a world to conquer. You have to interpret and vindicate the religion of the Hindus to the ignorant, the sceptical, the wilfully blind. You have begun the work in a spirit which commands our admiration, and have already achieved a success to which many lands bear witness. But a great deal yet remains to be done; and our own country, or rather we should say your own country, waits on you. The truths of the Hindu religion have to be expounded to large numbers of Hindus themselves. Brace yourself then for the grand exertion. We have confidence in you and in the righteousness of our cause. Our national religion seeks to win no material triumphs. Its purposes are spiritual; its weapon is a truth which is hidden away from material eyes and yields only to the reflective reason. Call on the world, and where necessary, on Hindus themselves, to open the inner eye, to transcend the senses, to read rightly the sacred books, to face the supreme reality, and realise their position and destiny as men. No one is better fitted than yourself to give the awakening or make the call, and we can only assure you of our hearty sympathy and loyal co-operation in that work which is apparently your mission ordained by Heaven.

We remain, dear brother,
Your loving Friends and Admirers.

The Swami's reply was as follows:

One wants to lose the individual in the universal, one renounces, flies off, and tries to cut himself off from all associations of the body of the past, one works hard to forget even that he is a man; yet, in the nears of his heart, there is a soft sound, one string vibrating, one whisper, which tells him, East or West, home is best. Citizens of the capital of this Empire, before you I stand, not as a Sannyasin, no, not even as a preacher, but I come before you the same Calcutta boy to talk to you as I used to do. Ay, I would like to sit in the dust of the streets of this city, and, with the freedom of childhood, open my mind to you, my brothers. Accept, therefore, my heartfelt thanks for this unique word that you have used, "Brother". Yes, I am your brother, and you are my brothers. I was asked by an English friend on the eve of my departure, "Swami, how do you like now your motherland after four years' experience of the luxurious, glorious, powerful West?" I could only answer, "India I loved before I came away. Now the very dust of India has become holy to me, the very air is now to me holy; it is now the holy land, the place of pilgrimage, the Tirtha." Citizens of Calcutta — my brothers — I cannot express my gratitude to you for the kindness you have shown, or rather I should not thank you at all, for you are my brothers, you have done only a brother's duty, ay, only a Hindu brother's duty; for such family ties, such relationships, such love exist nowhere beyond the bounds of this motherland of ours.

The Parliament of Religions was a great affair, no doubt. From various cities of this land, we have thanked the gentlemen who organised the meeting, and they deserved all our thanks for the kindness that has been shown to us; but yet allow me to construe for you the history of the Parliament of Religions. They wanted a horse, and they wanted to ride it. There were people there who wanted to make it a heathen show, but it was ordained otherwise; it could not help being so. Most of them were kind, but we have thanked them enough.

On the other hand, my mission in America was not to the Parliament of Religions. That was only something by the way, it was only an opening, an opportunity, and for that we are very thankful to the members of the Parliament; but really, our thanks are due to the great people of the United States, the American nation, the warm hearted, hospitable, great nation of America, where more than anywhere else the feeling of brotherhood has been developed. An American meets you for five minutes on board a train, and you are his friend, and the next moment he invites you as a guest to his home and opens the secret of his whole living there. That is the character of the American race, and we highly appreciate it. Their kindness to me is past all narration, it would take me years yet to tell you how I have been treated by them most kindly and most wonderfully. So are our thanks due to the other nation on the other side of the Atlantic. No one ever landed on English soil with more hatred in his heart for a race than I did for the English, and on this platform are present English friends who can bear witness to the fact; but the more I lived among them and saw how the machine was working — the English national life — and mixed with them, I found where the heartbeat of the nation was, and the more I loved them. There is none among you here present, my brothers, who loves the English people more than I do now. You have to see what is going on there, and you have to mix with them. As the philosophy, our national philosophy of the Vedanta, has summarised all misfortune, all misery, as coming from that one cause, ignorance,

herein also we must understand that the difficulties that arise between us and the English people are mostly due to that ignorance; we do not know them, they do not know us.

Unfortunately, to the Western mind, spirituality, nay, even morality, is eternally connected with worldly prosperity; and as soon as an Englishman or any other Western man lands on our soil and finds a land of poverty and of misery, he forthwith concludes that there cannot be any religion here, there cannot be any morality even. His own experience is true. In Europe, owing to the inclemency of the climate and many other circumstances poverty and sin go together, but not so in India. In India on the other hand, my experience is that the poorer the man the better he is in point of morality. Now this takes time to understand, and how many foreign people are there who will stop to understand this, the very secret of national existence in India? Few are there who will have the patience to study the nation and understand. Here and here alone, is the only race where poverty does not mean crime, poverty does not mean sin; and here is the only race where not only poverty does not mean crime but poverty has been deified, and the beggar's garb is the garb of the highest in the land. On the other hand, we have also similarly, patiently to study the social institutions of the West and not rush into mad judgments about them Their intermingling of the sexes, their different customs their manners, have all their meaning, have all their grand sides, if you have the patience to study them. Not that I mean that we are going to borrow their manners and customs, not that they are going to borrow ours, for the manners and customs of each race are the outcome of centuries of patient growth in that race, and each one has a deep meaning behind it; and, therefore, neither are they to ridicule our manners and customs, nor we theirs.

Again, I want to make another statement before this assembly. My work in England has been more satisfactory to me than my work in America. The bold, brave and steady Englishman, if I may use the expression, with his skull a little thicker than those of other people — if he has once an idea put into his brain, it never comes out; and the immense practicality and energy of the race makes it sprout up and immediately bear fruit. It is not so in any other country. That immense practicality, that immense vitality of the race, you do not see anywhere else. There is less of imagination, but more of work, and who knows the well-spring, the mainspring of the English heart? How much of imagination and of feeling is there! They are a nation of heroes, they are the true Kshatriyas; their education is to hide their feelings and never to show them. From their childhood they have been educated up to that. Seldom will you find an Englishman manifesting feeling, nay, even an Englishwoman. I have seen Englishwomen go to work and do deeds which would stagger the bravest of Bengalis to follow. But with all this heroic superstructure, behind this covering of the fighter, there is a deep spring of feeling in the English heart. If you once know how to reach it, if you get there, if you have personal contact and mix with him, he will open his heart, he is your friend for ever, he is your servant. Therefore in my opinion, my work in England has been more satisfactory than anywhere else. I firmly believe that if I should die tomorrow the work in England would not die, but would go on expanding all the time.

Brothers, you have touched another chord in my heart, the deepest of all, and that is the mention of my teacher, my master, my hero, my ideal, my God in life - Shri Ramakrishna Paramahamsa. If there has been anything achieved by me, by thoughts, or words, or deeds, if from my lips has ever fallen one word that has helped any one in the world, I lay no claim to it, it was his. But if there have been curses falling from my lips, if there has been hatred coming out of me, it is all mine and not his. All that has been weak has been mine, and all that has been life-giving, strengthening, pure, and holy, has been his inspiration, his words, and he himself. Yes, my friends, the world has yet to know that man. We read in the history of the world about prophets and their lives, and these come down to us through centuries of writings and workings by their disciples. Through thousands of years of chiselling and modelling, the lives of the great prophets of yore come down to us; and yet, in my opinion, not one stands so high in brilliance as that life which I saw with my own eyes, under whose shadow I have lived, at whose feet I have learnt everything —the life of Ramakrishna Paramahamsa. Ay, friends, you all know the celebrated saying of the Gitâ:

यदा यदा हि धर्मस्य ग्लानिर्भवति भारत ।
अभ्युत्थानमधर्मस्य तदात्मानं सृजाम्यहम् ॥
परित्राणाय साधूनां विनाशाय च दुष्कृताम् ।
धर्मसंस्थापनार्थाय संभवामि युगे युगे ॥

"Whenever, O descendant of Bharata, there is decline of Dharma, and rise of Adharma, then I body Myself forth. For the protection of the good, for the destruction of the wicked, and for the establishment of Dharma I come into being in every age."

Along with this you have to understand one thing more. Such a thing is before us today. Before one of these tidal waves of spirituality comes, there are whirlpools of lesser manifestation all over society. One of these comes up, at first unknown, unperceived, and unthought of, assuming proportion, swallowing, as it were, and assimilating all the other little whirlpools, becoming immense, becoming a tidal wave, and falling upon society with a power which none can resist. Such is happening before us. If you have eyes, you will see it. If your heart is open, you will receive it. If you are truth-seekers, you will find it. Blind, blind indeed is the man who does not see the signs of the day! Ay, this boy born of poor Brahmin parents in an out-of-the-way village of which very few of you have even heard, is literally being worshipped in lands which have been fulminating against heathen worship for centuries. Whose power is it? Is it mine or yours? It is none else than the power which was manifested here as Ramakrishna Paramahamsa. For, you and I, and sages and prophets, nay, even Incarna-

tions, the whole universe, are but manifestations of power more or less individualized, more or less concentrated. Here has been a manifestation of an immense power, just the very beginning of whose workings we are seeing, and before this generation passes away, you will see more wonderful workings of that power. It has come just in time for the regeneration of India, for we forget from time to time the vital power that must always work in India.

Each nation has its own peculiar method of work. Some work through politics, some through social reforms, some through other lines. With us, religion is the only ground along which we can move. The Englishman can understand even religion through politics. Perhaps the American can understand even religion through social reforms. But the Hindu can understand even politics when it is given through religion; sociology must come through religion, everything must come through religion. For that is the theme, the rest are the variations in the national life-music. And that was in danger. It seemed that we were going to change this theme in our national life, that we were going to exchange the backbone of our existence, as it were, that we were trying to replace a spiritual by a political backbone. And if we could have succeeded, the result would have been annihilation. But it was not to be. So this power became manifest. I do not care in what light you understand this great sage, it matters not how much respect you pay to him, but I challenge you face to face with the fact that here is a manifestation of the most marvellous power that has been for several centuries in India, and it is your duty, as Hindus, to study this power, to find what has been done for the regeneration, for the good of India, and for the good of the whole human race through it. Ay, long before ideas of universal religion and brotherly feeling between different sects were mooted and discussed in any country in the world, here, in sight of this city, had been living a man whose whole life was a Parliament of Religions as it should be.

The highest ideal in our scriptures is the impersonal, and would to God everyone of us here were high enough to realise that impersonal ideal; but, as that cannot be, it is absolutely necessary for the vast majority of human beings to have a personal ideal; and no nation can rise, can become great, can work at all, without enthusiastically coming under the banner of one of these great ideals in life. Political ideals, personages representing political ideals, even social ideals, commercial ideals, would have no power in India. We want spiritual ideals before us, we want enthusiastically to gather round grand spiritual names. Our heroes must be spiritual. Such a hero has been given to us in the person of Ramakrishna Paramahamsa. If this nation wants to rise, take my word for it, it will have to rally enthusiastically round this name. It does not matter who preaches Ramakrishna Paramahamsa, whether I, or you, or anybody else. But him I place before you, and it is for you to judge, and for the good of our race, for the good of our nation, to judge now, what you shall do with this great ideal of life. One thing we are to remember that it was the purest of all lives that you have ever seen, or let me tell you distinctly, that you have ever read of. And before you is the fact that it is the most marvellous manifestation of soul-power that you can read of, much less expect to see. Within ten years of his passing away, this power has encircled the globe; that fact is before you. In duty bound, therefore, for the good of our race, for the good of our religion, I place this great spiritual ideal before you. Judge him not through me. I am only a weak instrument. Let not his character be judged by seeing me. It was so great that if I or any other of his disciples spent hundreds of lives, we could not do justice to a millionth part of what he really was. Judge for yourselves; in the heart of your hearts is the Eternal Witness, and may He, the same Ramakrishna Paramahamsa, for the good of our nation, for the welfare of our country, and for the good of humanity, open your hearts, make you true and steady to work for the immense change which must come, whether we exert ourselves or not. For the work of the Lord does not wait for the like of you or me. He can raise His workers from the dust by hundreds and by thousands. It is a glory and a privilege that we are allowed to work at all under Him.

From this the idea expands. As you have pointed out to me, we have to conquer the world. That we have to! India must conquer the world, and nothing less than that is my ideal. It may be very big, it may astonish many of you, but it is so. We must conquer the world or die. There is no other alternative. The sign of life is expansion; we must go out, expand, show life, or degrade, fester, and die. There is no other alternative. Take either of these, either live or die. Now, we all know about the petty jealousies and quarrels that we have in our country. Take my word, it is the same everywhere. The other nations with their political lives have foreign policies. When they find too much quarrelling at home, they look for somebody abroad to quarrel with, and the quarrel at home stops. We have these quarrels without any foreign policy to stop them. This must be our eternal foreign policy, preaching the truths of our Shâstras to the nations of the world. I ask you who are politically minded, do you require any other proof that this will unite us as a race? This very assembly is a sufficient witness.

Secondly, apart from these selfish considerations, there are the unselfish, the noble, the living examples behind us. One of the great causes of India's misery and downfall has been that she narrowed herself, went into her shell as the oyster does, and refused to give her jewels and her treasures to the other races of mankind, refused to give the life-giving truths to thirsting nations outside the Aryan fold. That has been the one great cause; that we did not go out, that we did not compare notes with other nations—that has been the one great cause of our downfall, and every one of you knows that that little stir, the little life that you see in India, begins from the day when Raja Rammohan Roy broke through the walls of that exclusiveness. Since that day, history in India has taken another turn, and now it is growing with accelerated motion.

If we have had little rivulets in the past, deluges are coming, and none can resist them. Therefore we must go out, and the secret of life is to give and take. Are we to take always, to sit at the feet of the Westerners to learn everything, even religion? We can learn mechanism from them. We can learn many other things. But we have to teach them something, and that is our religion, that is our spirituality. For a complete civilisation the world is waiting, waiting for the treasures to come out of India, waiting for the marvellous spiritual inheritance of the race, which, through decades of degradation and misery, the nation has still clutched to her breast. The world is waiting for that treasure; little do you know how much of hunger and of thirst there is outside of India for these wonderful treasures of our forefathers. We talk here, we quarrel with each other, we laugh at and we ridicule everything sacred, till it has become almost a national vice to ridicule everything holy. Little do we understand the heart-pangs of millions waiting outside the walls, stretching forth their hands for a little sip of that nectar which our forefathers have preserved in this land of India. Therefore we must go out, exchange our spirituality for anything they have to give us; for the marvels of the region of spirit we will exchange the marvels of the region of matter. We will not be students always, but teachers also. There cannot be friendship without equality, and there cannot be equality when one party is always the teacher and the other party sits always at his feet. If you want to become equal with the Englishman or the American, you will have to teach as well as to learn, and you have plenty yet to teach to the world for centuries to come. This has to be done. Fire and enthusiasm must be in our blood. We Bengalis have been credited with imagination, and I believe we have it. We have been ridiculed as an imaginative race, as men with a good deal of feeling. Let me tell you, my friends, intellect is great indeed, but it stops within certain bounds. It is through the heart, and the heart alone, that inspiration comes. It is through the feelings that the highest secrets are reached; and therefore it is the Bengali, the man of feeling, that has to do this work.

उत्तिष्ठत जाग्रत प्राप्य वरान्निबोधत ।—Arise, awake and stop not till the desired end is reached. Young men of Calcutta, arise, awake, for the time is propitious. Already everything is opening out before us. Be bold and fear not. It is only in our scriptures that this adjective is given unto the Lord—Abhih, Abhih. We have to become Abhih, fearless, and our task will be done. Arise, awake, for your country needs this tremendous sacrifice. It is the young men that will do it. "The young, the energetic, the strong, the well-built, the intellectual"—for them is the task. And we have hundreds and thousands of such young men in Calcutta. If, as you say, I have done something, remember that I was that good-for-nothing boy playing in the streets of Calcutta. If I have done so much, how much more will you do! Arise and awake, the world is calling upon you. In other parts of India, there is intellect, there is money, but enthusiasm is only in my motherland. That must come out; therefore arise, young men of Calcutta, with enthusiasm in your blood. This not that you are poor, that you have no friends. A who ever saw money make the man? It is man that always makes money. The whole world has been made by the energy of man, by the power of enthusiasm, by the power of faith.

Those of you who have studied that most beautiful ail the Upanishads, the Katha, will remember how the king was going to make a great sacrifice, and, instead of giving away things that were of any worth, he was giving away cows and horses that were not of any use, and the book says that at that time Shraddhâ entered into the heart of his son Nachiketâ. I would not translate this word Shraddha to you, it would be a mistake; it is a wonderful word to understand, and much depends on it; we will see how it works, for immediately we find Nachiketa telling himself, "I am superior to many, I am inferior to few, but nowhere am I the last, I can also do something." And this boldness increased, and the boy wanted to solve the problem which was in his mind, the problem of death. The solution could only be got by going to the house of Death, and the boy went. There he was, brave Nachiketa waiting at the house of Death for three days, and you know how he obtained what he desired. What we want, is this Shraddha. Unfortunately, it has nearly vanished from India, and this is why we are in our present state. What makes the difference between man and man is the difference in this Shraddha and nothing else. What make one man great and another weak and low is this Shraddha. My Master used to say, he who thinks himself weak will become weak, and that is true. This Shraddha must enter into you. Whatever of material power you see manifested by the Western races is the outcome of this Shraddha, because they believe in their muscles and if you believe in your spirit, how much more will it work! Believe in that infinite soul, the infinite power, which, with consensus of opinion, your books and sages preach. That Atman which nothing can destroy, in It is infinite power only waiting to be called out. For here is the great difference between all other philosophies and the Indian philosophy. Whether dualistic, qualified monistic, or monistic, they all firmly believe that everything is in the soul itself; it has only to come out and manifest itself. Therefore, this Shraddha is what I want, and what all of us here want, this faith in ourselves, and before you is the great task to get that faith. Give up the awful disease that is creeping into our national blood, that idea of ridiculing everything, that loss of seriousness. Give that up. Be strong and have this Shraddha, and everything else is bound to follow.

I have done nothing as yet; you have to do the task. If I die tomorrow the work will not die. I sincerely believe that there will be thousands coming up from the ranks to take up the work and carry it further and further, beyond all my most hopeful imagination ever painted. I have faith in my country, and especially in the youth of my country. The youth of Bengal have the greatest of all tasks that has ever been placed on the shoulders of young men. I have travelled for the last ten years or so over the whole of India, and my conviction is that from the youth of Bengal will come the power which will raise India once more to her proper spiritual place. Ay, from the youth of Bengal, with this immense amount of feeling and enthusiasm in the blood, will come those heroes who will march from one corner of the earth to the other, preaching and teaching the eternal spiritual truths of our forefathers. And this is the great work before you. Therefore, let me conclude by reminding you once more, "Arise, awake and stop not till the desired end is reached." Be not afraid, for all great power, throughout the history of humanity, has been with he people. From out of their ranks have come all the greatest geniuses of the world, and history can only repeat itself. Be not afraid of anything. You will do marvellous work. The moment you fear, you are nobody. It is fear that is the great cause of misery in the world. It is fear that is the greatest of all superstitions. It is fear that is the cause of our woes, and it is fearlessness that brings heaven even in a moment. Therefore, "Arise, awake, and stop not till the goal is reached."

Gentlemen, allow me to thank you once more for all the kindness that I have received at your hands. It is my wish — my intense, sincere wish — to be even of the least service to the world, and above all to my own country and countrymen.

THE VEDANTA IN ALL ITS PHASES

Delivered in Calcutta

Away back, where no recorded history, nay, not even the dim light of tradition, can penetrate, has been steadily shining the light, sometimes dimmed by external circumstances, at others effulgent, but undying and steady, shedding its lustre not only over India, but permeating the whole thought-world with its power, silent, unperceived, gentle, yet omnipotent, like the dew that falls in the morning, unseen and unnoticed, yet bringing into bloom the fairest of roses: this has been the thought of the Upanishads, the philosophy of the Vedanta. Nobody knows when it first came to flourish on the soil of India. Guesswork has been vain. The guesses, especially of Western writers, have been so conflicting that no certain date can be ascribed to them. But we Hindus, from the spiritual standpoint, do not admit that they had any origin. This Vedanta, the philosophy of the Upanishads, I would make bold to state, has been the first as well as the final thought on the spiritual plane that has ever been vouchsafed to man.

From this ocean of the Vedanta, waves of light from time to time have been going Westward and Eastward. In the days of yore it travelled Westward and gave its impetus to the mind of the Greeks, either in Athens, or in Alexandria, or in Antioch. The Sânkhya system must clearly have made its mark on the minds of the ancient Greeks; and the Sankhya and all other systems in India hail that one authority, the Upanishads, the Vedanta. In India, too, in spite of all these jarring sects that we see today and all those that have been in the past, the one authority, the basis of all these systems, has yet been the Upanishads, the Vedanta. Whether you are a dualist, or a qualified monist, an Advaitist, or a Vishishtâdvaitist, a Shuddhâdvaitist, or any other Advaitist, or Dvaitist, or whatever you may call yourself, there stand behind you as authority, your Shastras, your scriptures, the Upanishads. Whatever system in India does not obey the Upanishads cannot be called orthodox, and even the systems of the Jains and the Buddhists have been rejected from the soil of India only because they did not bear allegiance to the Upanishads. Thus the Vedanta, whether we know it or not, has penetrated all the sects in India, and what we call Hinduism, this mighty banyan with its immense, almost infinite ramifications, has been throughout interpenetrated by the influence of the Vedanta. Whether we are conscious of it or not, we think the Vedanta, we live in the Vedanta, we breathe the Vedanta, and we die in the Vedanta, and every Hindu does that. To preach Vedanta in the land of India, and before an Indian audience, seems, therefore, to be an anomaly. But it is the one thing that has to be preached, and it is the necessity of the age that it must be preached. For, as I have just told you, all the Indian sects must bear allegiance to the Upanishads; but among these sects there are many apparent contradictions. Many times the great sages of yore themselves could not understand the underlying harmony of the Upanishads. Many times, even sages quarrelled, so much so that it became a proverb that there are no sages who do not differ. But the time requires that a better interpretation should be given to this underlying harmony of the Upanishadic texts, whether they are dualistic, or non-dualistic, quasi-dualistic, or so forth. That has to be shown before the world at large, and this work is required as much in India as outside of India; and I, through the grace of God, had the great good fortune to sit at the feet of one whose whole life was such an interpretation, whose life, a thousandfold more than whose teaching, was a living commentary on the texts of the Upanishads, was in fact the spirit of the Upanishads living in a human form. Perhaps I have got a little of that harmony; I do not know whether I shall be able to express it or not. But this is my attempt, my mission in life, to show that the Vedantic schools are not contradictory, that they all necessitate each other, all fulfil each other, and one, as it were, is the stepping-stone to the other, until the goal, the Advaita, the Tat Tvam Asi, is reached. There was a time in India when the Karma Kânda had its sway. There are many grand ideals, no doubt, in that portion of the Vedas. Some of our present daily worship is still according to the precepts of the Karma Kanda. But with all that, the Karma Kanda of the Vedas has almost disappeared from India. Very little of our life today is bound and regulated by the orders of the Karma Kanda of the Vedas. In our ordinary lives we are mostly Paurânikas or Tântrikas, and, even where some Vedic texts are used by the Brahmins of India, the adjustment of the texts is mostly not according to the Vedas, but according to the Tantras or the Puranas. As such, to call ourselves Vaidikas in the sense of following the Karma Kanda of the Vedas, I do not think, would be proper. But the other fact stands that we are all of us Vedantists. The people who call

themselves Hindus had better be called Vedantists, and, as I have shown you, under that one name Vaidantika come in all our various sects, whether dualists or non-dualists.

The sects that are at the present time in India come to be divided in general into the two great classes of dualists and monists. The little differences which some of these sects insist upon, and upon the authority of which want to take new names as pure Advaitists, or qualified Advaitists, and so forth, do not matter much. As a classification, either they are dualists or monists, and of the sects existing at the present time, some of them are very new, and others seem to be reproductions of very ancient sects. The one class I would present by the life and philosophy of Râmânuja, and the other by Shankarâchârya.

Ramanuja is the leading dualistic philosopher of later India, whom all the other dualistic sects have followed, directly or indirectly, both in the substance of their teaching and in the organization of their sects even down to some of the most minute points of their organization. You will be astonished if you compare Ramanuja and his work with the other dualistic Vaishnava sects in India, to see how much they resemble each other in organization, teaching, and method. There is the great Southern preacher Madhva Muni, and following him, our great Chaitanya of Bengal who took up the philosophy of the Madhvas and preached it in Bengal. There are some other sects also in Southern India, as the qualified dualistic Shaivas. The Shaivas in most parts of India are Advaitists, except in some portions of Southern India and in Ceylon. But they also only substitute Shiva for Vishnu and are Ramanujists in every sense of the term except in the doctrine of the soul. The followers of Ramanuja hold that the soul is Anu, like a particle, very small, and the followers of Shankaracharya hold that it is Vibhu, omnipresent. There have been several non-dualistic sects. It seems that there have been sects in ancient times which Shankara's movement has entirely swallowed up and assimilated. You find sometimes a fling at Shankara himself in some of the commentaries, especially in that of Vijnâna Bhikshu who, although an Advaitist, attempts to upset the Mâyâvâda of Shankara. It seems there were schools who did not believe in this Mayavada, and they went so far as to call Shankara a crypto-Buddhist, Prachchhanna Bauddha, and they thought this Mayavada was taken from the Buddhists and brought within the Vedantic fold. However that may be, in modern times the Advaitists have all ranged themselves under Shankaracharya; and Shankaracharya and his disciples have been the great preachers of Advaita both in Southern and in Northern India. The influence of Shankaracharya did not penetrate much into our country of Bengal and in Kashmir and the Punjab, but in Southern India the Smârtas are all followers of Shankaracharya, and with Varanasi as the centre, his influence is simply immense even in many parts of Northern India.

Now both Shankara and Ramanuja laid aside all claim to originality. Ramanuja expressly tells us he is only following the great commentary of Bodhâyana. भगवद् बोधायनकृतां वसितीर्णां ब्रह्मसूत्रवृत्तिं पूर्वाचार्याः संचिक्षिपुः तन्मतानुसारेण सूत्राक्षराणि व्याख्यासयन्तो—"Ancient teachers abridged that extensive commentary on the Brahma-sutras which was composed by the Bhagavân Bodhayana; in accordance with their opinion, the words of the Sutra are explained." That is what Ramanuja says at the beginning of his commentary, the Shri-Bhâshya. He takes it up and makes of it a Samkshepa, and that is what we have today. I myself never had an opportunity of seeing this commentary of Bodhayana. The late Swami Dayânanda Saraswati wanted to reject every other commentary of the Vyâsa-Sutras except that of Bodhayana; and although he never lost an opportunity of having a fling at Ramanuja, he himself could never produce the Bodhayana. I have sought for it all over India, and never yet have been able to see it. But Ramanuja is very plain on the point, and he tells us that he is taking the ideas, and sometimes the very passages out of Bodhayana, and condensing them into the present Ramanuja Bhashya. It seems that Shankaracharya was also doing the same. There are a few places in his Bhashya which mention older commentaries, and when we know that his Guru and his Guru's Guru had been Vedantists of the same school as he, sometimes corn more thorough-going, bolder even than Shankara himself on certain points, it seems pretty plain that he also was not preaching anything very original, and that even in his Bhashya he himself had been doing the same work that Ramanuja did with Bodhayana, but from what Bhashya, it cannot be discovered at the present time.

All these Darshanas that you have ever seen or heard of are based upon Upanishadic authority. Whenever they want to quote a Shruti, they mean the Upanishads. They are always quoting the Upanishads. Following the Upanishads there come other philosophies of India, but every one of them failed in getting that hold on India which the philosophy of Vyasa got, although the philosophy of Vyasa is a development out of an older one, the Sankhya, and every philosophy and every system in India—I mean throughout the world—owes much to Kapila, perhaps the greatest name in the history of India in psychological and philosophical lines. The influence of Kapila is everywhere seen throughout the world. Wherever there is a recognised system of thought, there you can trace his influence; even if it be thousands of years back, yet he stands there, the shining, glorious, wonderful Kapila. His psychology and a good deal of his philosophy have been accepted by all the sects of India with but very little differences. In our own country, our Naiyâyika philosophers could not make much impression on the philosophical world of India. They were too busy with little things like species and genus, and so forth, and that most cumbersome terminology, which it is a life's work to study. As such, they were very busy with logic and left philosophy to the Vedantists, but every one of the Indian philosophic sects in modern times has adopted the logical terminology of the Naiyayikas of Bengal. Jagadisha, Gadadhara, and Shiromani are as well known at Nadia as in some of the cities in Malabar. But the philosophy of Vyasa, the Vyasa-Sutras, is firm-seated and has attained the permanence of that which it intended to present to men, the Brahman of the Vedantic side of philosophy. Reason was entirely subordinated to the Shrutis, and as Shankaracharya declares, Vyasa did not care to reason at all. His idea in writing the Sutras was just to bring together, and with one thread to make a garland of the flowers of Vedantic texts. His Sutras are admitted so far as they are subordinate to the authority of the Upanishads, and no further.

And, as I have said, all the sects of India now hold these Vyasa-Sutras to be the great authority, and every new sect in India starts with a fresh commentary on the Vyasa-Sutras according to its light. The difference between some of these commentators is sometimes very great, sometimes the text-torturing is quite disgusting. The Vyasa-Sutras have got the place of authority, and no one can expect to found a sect in India until he can write a fresh commentary on the Vyasa-Sutras.

Next in authority is the celebrated Gita. The great glory of Shankaracharya was his preaching of the Gita. It is one of the greatest works that this great man did among the many noble works of his noble life—the preaching of the Gita and writing the most beautiful commentary upon it. And he has been followed by all founders of the orthodox sects in India, each of whom has written a commentary on the Gita.

The Upanishads are many, and said to be one hundred and eight, but some declare them to be still larger in number. Some of them are evidently of a much later date, as for instance, the Allopanishad in which Allah is praised and Mohammed is called the Rajasulla. I have been told that this was written during the reign of Akbar to bring the Hindus and Mohammedans together, and sometimes they got hold of some word, as Allah, or Illa in the Samhitâs, and made an Upanishad on it. So in this Allopanishad, Mohammed is the Rajasulla, whatever that may mean. There are other sectarian Upanishads of the same species, which you find to be entirely modern, and it has been so easy to write them, seeing that this language of the Samhitâ portion of the Vedas is so archaic that there is no grammar to it. Years ago I had an idea of studying the grammar of the Vedas, and I began with all earnestness to study Panini and the Mahâbhâshya, but to my surprise I found that the best part of the Vedic grammar consists only of exceptions to rules. A rule is made, and after that comes a statement to the effect, "This rule will be an exception". So you see what an amount of liberty there is for anybody to write anything, the only safeguard being the dictionary of Yâska. Still, in this you will find, for the must part, but a large number of synonyms. Given all that, how easy it is to write any number of Upanishads you please. Just have a little knowledge of Sanskrit, enough to make words look like the old archaic words, and you have no fear of grammar. Then you bring in Rajasulla or any other Sulla you like. In that way many Upanishads have been manufactured, and I am told that that is being done even now. In some parts of

India, I am perfectly certain, they are trying to manufacture such Upanishads among the different sects. But among the Upanishads are those, which, on the face of them, bear the evidence of genuineness, and these have been taken up by the great commentators and commented upon, especially by Shankara, followed by Ramanuja and all the rest.

There are one or two more ideas with regard to the Upanishads which I want to bring to your notice, for these are an ocean of knowledge, and to talk about the Upanishads, even for an incompetent person like myself, takes years and not one lecture only. I want, therefore, to bring to your notice one or two points in the study of the Upanishads. In the first place, they are the most wonderful poems in the world. If you read the Samhita portion of the Vedas, you now and then find passages of most marvellous beauty. For instance, the famous Shloka which describes Chaos—तम आसीत्तमसा गूढमगे etc.—"When darkness was hidden in darkness", so on it goes. One reads and feels the wonderful sublimity of the poetry. Do you mark this that outside of India, and inside also, there have been attempts at painting the sublime. But outside, it has always been the infinite in the muscles the external world, the infinite of matter, or of space. When Milton or Dante, or any other great European poet, either ancient or modern, wants to paint a picture of the infinite, he tries to soar outside, to make you feel the infinite through the muscles. That attempt has been made here also. You find it in the Samhitas, the infinite of extension most marvellously painted and placed before the readers, such as has been done nowhere else. Mark that one sentence—तम आसीत् तमसा गूढम्,—and now mark the description of darkness by three poets. Take our own Kâlidâsa—"Darkness which can be penetrated with the point of a needle"; then Milton—"No light but rather darkness visible"; but come now to the Upanishad, "Darkness was covering darkness", "Darkness was hidden in darkness". We who live in the tropics can understand it, the sudden outburst of the monsoon, when in a moment, the horizon becomes darkened and clouds become covered with more rolling black clouds. So on, the poem goes; but yet, in the Samhita portion, all these attempts are external. As everywhere else, the attempts at finding the solution of the great problems of life have been through the external world. Just as the Greek mind or the modern European mind wants to find the solution of life and of all the sacred problems of Being by searching into the external world. So also did our forefathers, and just as the Europeans failed, they failed also. But the Western people never made a move more, they remained there, they failed in the search for the solution of the great problems of life and death in the external world, and there they remained, stranded; our forefathers also found it impossible, but were bolder in declaring the utter helplessness of the senses to find the solution. Nowhere else was the answer better put than in the Upanishad: यतो वाचो निवर्तन्ते अप्राप्य मनसा सह—"From whence words come back reflected, together with the mind"; न तत्रचक्षुर्गच्छति न वाग्गच्छति—"There the eye cannot go,

nor can speech reach". There are various sentences which declare the utter helplessness of the senses, but they did not stop there; they fell back upon the internal nature of man, they went to get the answer from their own soul, they became introspective; they gave up external nature as a failure, as nothing could be done there, as no hope, no answer could be found; they discovered that dull, dead matter would not give them truth, and they fell back upon the shining soul of man, and there the answer was found.

तमेवैकं जानथ आत्मानम् अन्या वाचो वमिुञ्चथा—"Know this Atman alone," they declared, "give up all other vain words, and hear no other." In the Atman they found the solution—the greatest of all Atmans, the God, the Lord of this universe, His relation to the Atman of man, our duty to Him, and through that our relation to each other. And herein you find the most sublime poetry in the world. No more is the attempt made to paint this Atman in the language of matter. Nay, for it they have given up even all positive language. No more is there any attempt to come to the senses to give them the idea of the infinite, no more is there an external, dull, dead, material, spacious, sensuous infinite, but instead of that comes something which is as fine as even that mentioned in the saying—

न तत्र सूर्यो भाति न चन्द्रतारकं नेमा वेद्युतो भान्ति कुतोऽयमग्निं।
तमेव भान्तमनुभाति सर्वं तस्य भासा सर्वमिदं वभाती॥

What poetry in the world can be more sublime than this! "There the sun cannot illumine, nor the moon, nor the stars, there this flash of lightning cannot illumine; what to speak of this mortal fire!" Such poetry you find nowhere else. Take that most marvellous Upanishad, the Katha. What a wonderful finish, what a most marvellous art displayed in that poem! How wonderfully it opens with that little boy to whom Shraddhâ came, who wanted to see Yama, and how that most marvellous of all teachers, Death himself, teaches him the great lessons of life and death! And what was his quest? To know the secret of death.

The second point that I want you to remember is the perfectly impersonal character of the Upanishads. Although we find many names, and many speakers, and many teachers in the Upanishads, not one of them stands as an authority of the Upanishads, not one verse is based upon the life of any one of them. These are simply figures like shadows moving in the background, unfelt, unseen, unrealised, but the real force is in the marvellous, the brilliant, the effulgent texts of the Upanishads, perfectly impersonal. If twenty Yâjnavalkyas came and lived and died, it does not matter; the texts are there. And yet it is against no personality; it is broad and expansive enough to embrace all the personalities that the world has yet produced, and all that are yet to come. It has nothing to say against the worship of persons, or Avataras, or sages. On the other hand, it is always upholding it. At the same time, it is perfectly impersonal. It is a most marvellous idea, like the God it preaches, the impersonal idea of the Upanishads. For the sage, the thinker, the philosopher, for the rationalist, it is as much impersonal as any modern scientist can wish. And these are our scriptures. You must remember that what the Bible is to the Christians, what the Koran is to the Mohammedans, what the Tripitaka is to the Buddhist, what the Zend Avesta is to the Parsees, these Upanishads are to us. These and nothing but these are our scriptures. The Purânas, the Tantras, and all the other books, even the Vyasa-Sutras, are of secondary, tertiary authority, but primary are the Vedas. Manu, and the Puranas, and all the other books are to be taken so far as they agree with the authority of the Upanishads, and when they disagree they are to be rejected without mercy. This we ought to remember always, but unfortunately for India, at the present time we have forgotten it. A petty village custom seems now the real authority and not the teaching of the Upanishads. A petty idea current in a wayside village in Bengal seems to have the authority of the Vedas, and even something better. And that word "orthodox", how wonderful its influence! To the villager, the following of every little bit of the Karma Kanda is the very height of "orthodoxy", and one who does not do it is told, "Go away, you are no more a Hindu." So there are, most unfortunately in my motherland, persons who will take up one of these Tantras and say, that the practice of this Tantra is to be obeyed; he who does not do so is no more orthodox in his views. Therefore it is better for us to remember that in the Upanishads is the primary authority, even the Grihya and Shrauta Sutras are subordinate to the authority of the Vedas. They are the words of the Rishis, our forefathers, and you have to believe them if you want to become a Hindu. You may even believe the most peculiar ideas about the Godhead, but if you deny the authority of the Vedas, you are a Nâstika. Therein lies the difference between the scriptures of the Christians or the Buddhists and ours; theirs are all Puranas, and not scriptures, because they describe the history of the deluge, and the history of kings and reigning families, and record the lives of great men, and so on. This is the work of the Puranas, and so far as they agree with the Vedas, they are good. So far as the Bible and the scriptures of other nations agree with the Vedas, they are perfectly good, but when they do not agree, they are no more to be accepted. So with the Koran. There are many moral teachings in these, and so far as they agree with the Vedas they have the authority of the Puranas, but no more. The idea is that the Vedas were never written; the idea is, they never came into existence. I was told once by a Christian missionary that their scriptures have a historical character, and therefore are true, to which I replied, "Mine have no historical character and therefore they are true; yours being historical, they were evidently made by some man the other day. Yours are man-made and mine are not; their non-historicity is in their favour." Such is the relation of the Vedas with all the other scriptures at the present day.

We now come to the teachings of the Upanishads. Various texts are there. Some are perfectly dualistic, while others are monistic. But there are certain doctrines which are agreed to by all the different sects of India. First, there is the doctrine of Samsâra or reincarnation of the soul. Secondly, they all agree in their psychology; first there is the body, behind that, what they call the Sukshma Sharira, the mind, and behind that even, is the Jiva. That is the great difference between Western and Indian psychology; in the Western psychology the mind is the soul, here it is not. The Antahkarana, the internal instrument, as the mind is called, is only an instrument in the hands of that Jiva, through which the Jiva works on the body or on the external world. Here they all agree, and they all also agree that this Jiva or Atman, Jivatman as it is called by various sects, is eternal, without beginning; and that it is going from birth to birth, until it gets a final release. They all agree in this, and they also all agree in one other most vital point, which alone marks characteristically, most prominently, most vitally, the difference between the Indian and the Western mind, and it is this, that everything is in the soul. There is no inspiration, but properly speaking, expiration. All powers and all purity and all greatness—everything is in the soul. The Yogi would tell you that the Siddhis - Animâ, Laghimâ, and so on—that he wants to attain to are not to be attained, in the proper sense of the word, but are already there in the soul; the work is to make them manifest. Patanjali, for instance, would tell you that even in the lowest worm that crawls under your feet, all the eightfold Yogi's powers are already existing. The difference has been made by the body. As soon as it gets a better body, the powers will become manifest, but they are there.

नमित्तिमप्रयोजकं प्रकृतीनां वरणभेदस्तु ततः क्षेत्रकिवत्। —"Good and bad deeds are not the direct causes in the transformations of nature, but they act as breakers of obstacles to the evolutions of nature: as a farmer breaks the obstacles to the course of water, which then runs down by its own nature." Here Patanjali gives the celebrated example of the cultivator bringing water into his field from a huge tank somewhere. The tank is already filled and the water would flood his land in a moment, only there is a mud-wall between the tank and his field. As soon as the barrier is broken, in rushes the water out of its own power and force. This mass of power and purity and perfection is in the soul already. The only difference is the Âvarana—this veil—that has been cast over it. Once the veil is removed, the soul attains to purity, and its powers become manifest. This, you ought to remember, is the great difference between Eastern and Western thought. Hence you find people teaching such awful doctrines as that we are all born sinners, and because we do not believe in such awful doctrines we are all born wicked. They never stop to think that if we are by our very nature wicked, we can never be good—for how can nature change? If it changes, it contradicts itself; it is not nature. We ought to remember this. Here the dualist, and the Advaitist, and all others in India agree.

The next point, which all the sects in India believe in, is God. Of course their ideas of God will be different. The dualists believe in a Personal God, and a personal only. I want you to understand this word personal a little more. This word personal does not mean that God has a body, sits on a throne somewhere, and rules this world, but means Saguna, with qualities. There are many descriptions of the Personal God. This Personal God as the Ruler, the Creator, the Preserver, and the Destroyer of this universe is believed in by all the sects. The Advaitists believe something more. They believe in a still higher phase of this Personal God, which is personal-impersonal. No adjective can illustrate where there is no qualification, and the Advaitist would not give Him any qualities except the three —Sat-Chit-Ananda, Existence, Knowledge, and Bliss Absolute. This is what Shankara did. But in the Upanishads themselves you find they penetrate even further, and say, nothing can be predicated of it except Neti, Neti, "Not this, Not this".

Here all the different sects of India agree. But taking the dualistic side, as I have said, I will take Ramanuja as the typical dualist of India, the great modern representative of the dualistic system. It is a pity that our people in Bengal know so very little about the great religious leaders in India, who have been born in other parts of the country; and for the matter of that, during the whole of the Mohammedan period, with the exception of our Chaitanya, all the great religious leaders were born in Southern India, and it is the intellect of Southern India that is really governing India now; for even Chaitanya belonged to one of these sects, a sect of the Mâdhvas. According to Ramanuja, these three entities are eternal—God, and soul, and nature. The souls are eternal, and they will remain eternally existing, individualised through eternity, and will retain their individuality all through. Your soul will be different from my soul through all eternity, says Ramanuja, and so will this nature—which is an existing fact, as much a fact as the existence of soul or the existence of God—remain always different. And God is interpenetrating, the essence of the soul, He is the Antaryâmin. In this sense Ramanuja sometimes thinks that God is one with the soul, the essence of the soul, and these souls—at the time of Pralaya, when the whole of nature becomes what he calls Sankuchita, contracted—become contracted and minute and remain so for a time. And at the beginning of the next cycle they all come out, according to their past Karma, and undergo the effect of that Karma. Every action that makes the natural inborn purity and perfection of the soul get contracted is a bad action, and every action that makes it come out and expand itself is a good action, says Ramanuja. Whatever helps to make the Vikâsha of the soul is good, and whatever makes it Sankuchita is bad. And thus the soul is going on, expanding or contracting in its actions, till through the grace of God comes salvation. And that grace comes to all souls, says Ramanuja, that are pure and struggle for that grace.

There is a celebrated verse in the Shrutis, आहारशुद्धौ सत्त्वशुद्धिः सत्त्वशुद्धौ ध्रुवास्मृतिः "When the food is pure, then the Sattva becomes pure; when the Sattva is pure, then the Smriti" — the memory of the Lord, or the memory of our own perfection—if you are an Advaitist—"becomes truer, steadier, and absolute". Here is a great discussion. First of all, what is this

Sattva? We know that according to the Sankhya—and it has been admitted by all our sects of philosophy—the body is composed of three sorts of materials—not qualities. It is the general idea that Sattva, Rajas, and Tamas are qualities. Not at all, not qualities but the materials of this universe, and with Âhâra-shuddhi, when the food is pure, the Sattva material becomes pure. The one theme of the Vedanta is to get this Sattva. As I have told you, the soul is already pure and perfect, and it is, according to the Vedanta, covered up by Rajas and Tamas particles. The Sattva particles are the most luminous, and the effulgence of the soul penetrates through them as easily as light through glass. So if the Rajas and Tamas particles go, and leave the Sattva particles, in this state the power and purity of the soul will appear, and leave the soul more manifest.

Therefore it is necessary to have this Sattva. And the text says, "When Ahara becomes pure". Ramanuja takes this word Ahara to mean food, and he has made it one of the turning points of his philosophy. Not only so, it has affected the whole of India, and all the different sects. Therefore it is necessary for us to understand what it means, for that, according to Ramanuja, is one of the principal factors in our life, Ahara-shuddhi. What makes food impure? asks Ramanuja. Three sorts of defects make food impure—first, Jâti-dosha, the defect in the very nature of the class to which the food belongs, as the smell in onions, garlic, and suchlike. The next is Âshraya-dosha, the defect in the person from whom the food comes; food coming from a wicked person will make you impure. I myself have seen many great sages in India following strictly that advice all their lives. Of course they had the power to know who brought the food, and even who had touched the food, and I have seen it in my own life, not once, but hundreds of times. Then Nimitta-dosha, the defect of impure things or influences coming in contact with food is another. We had better attend to that a little more now. It has become too prevalent in India to take food with dirt and dust and bits of hair in it. If food is taken from which these three defects have been removed, that makes Sattva-shuddhi, purifies the Sattva. Religion seems to be a very easy task then. Then every one can have religion if it comes by eating pure food only. There is none so weak or incompetent in this world, that I know, who cannot save himself from these defects. Then comes Shankaracharya, who says this word Ahara means thought collected in the mind; when that becomes pure, the Sattva becomes pure, and not before that. You may eat what you like. If food alone would purify the Sattva, then feed the monkey with milk and rice all its life; would it become a great Yogi? Then the cows and the deer would be great Yogis. As has been said, "If it is by bathing much that heaven is reached, the fishes will get to heaven first. If by eating vegetables a man gets to heaven, the cows and the deer will get to heaven first."

But what is the solution? Both are necessary. Of course the idea that Shankaracharya gives us of Ahara is the primary idea. But pure food, no doubt, helps pure thought; it has an intimate connection; both ought to be there. But the defect is that in modern India we have forgotten the advice of Shankaracharya and taken only the "pure food" meaning. That is why people get mad with me when I say, religion has got into the kitchen; and if you had been in Madras with me, you would have agreed with me. The Bengalis are better than that. In Madras they throw away food if anybody looks at it. And with all this, I do not see that the people are any the better there. If only eating this and that sort of food and saving it from the looks of this person and that person would give them perfection, you would expect them all to be perfect men, which they are not.

Thus, although these are to be combined and linked together to make a perfect whole, do not put the cart before the horse. There is a cry nowadays about this and that food and about Varnâshrama, and the Bengalis are the most vociferous in these cries. I would ask every one of you, what do you know about this Varnashrama? Where are the four castes today in this country? Answer me; I do not see the four castes. Just as our Bengali proverb has it, "A headache without a head", so you want to make this Varnashrama here. There are not four castes here. I see only the Brâhmin and the Shudra. If there are the Kshatriyas and the Vaishyas, where are they and why do not you Brahmins order them to take the Yajnopavita and study the Vedas, as every Hindu ought to do? And if the Vaishyas and the Kshatriyas do not exist, but only the Brahmins and the Shudras, the Shastras say that the Brahmin must not live in a country where there are only Shudras; so depart bag and baggage! Do you know what the Shastras say about people who have been eating Mlechchha food and living under a government of the Mlechchhas, as you have for the past thousand years? Do you know the penance for that? The penance would be burning oneself with one's own hands. Do you want to pass as teachers and walk like hypocrisies? If you believe in your Shastras, burn yourselves first like the one great Brahmin did who went with Alexander the Great and burnt himself because he thought he had eaten the food of a Mlechchha. Do like that, and you will see that the whole nation will be at your feet. You do not believe in your own Shastras and yet want to make others believe in them. If you think you are not able to do that in this age, admit your weakness and excuse the weakness of others, take the other castes up, give them a helping hand, let them study the Vedas and become just as good Aryans as any other Aryans in the world, and be you likewise Aryans, you Brahmins of Bengal.

Give up this filthy Vâmâchâra that is killing your country. You have not seen the other parts of India. When I see how much the Vamachara has entered our society, I find it a most disgraceful place with all its boast of culture. These Vamachara sects are honeycombing our society in Bengal. Those who come out in the daytime and preach most loudly about Âchâra, it is they who carry on the horrible debauchery at night and are backed by the most dreadful books. They are ordered by the books to do these things. You who are of Bengal know it. The Bengali Shastras are the Vamachara Tan-tras. They are published by the cart-load, and you poison the minds of your children with them instead of teaching them your Shrutis. Fathers of Calcutta, do you not feel ashamed that such horrible stuff as these Vamachara Tantras, with translations too, should be put into the hands of your boys and girls, and their minds poisoned, and that they should be brought up with the idea that these are the Shastras of the Hindus? If you are ashamed, take them away from your children, and let them read the true Shastras, the Vedas, the Gita, the Upanishads.

According to the dualistic sects of India, the individual souls remain as individuals throughout, and God creates the universe out of pre-existing material only as the efficient cause. According to the Advaitists, on the other hand, God is both the material and the efficient cause of the universe. He is not only the Creator of the universe, but He creates it out of Himself. That is the Advaitist position. There are crude dualistic sects who believe that this world has been created by God out of Himself, and at the same time God is eternally separate from the universe, and everything is eternally subordinate to the Ruler of the universe. There are sects too who also believe that out of Himself God has evolved this universe, and individuals in the long run attain to Nirvâna to give up the finite and become the Infinite. But these sects have disappeared. The one sect of Advaitists that you see in modern India is composed of the followers of Shankara. According to Shankara, God is both the material and the efficient cause through Mâyâ, but not in reality. God has not become this universe; but the universe is not, and God is. This is one of the highest points to understand of Advaita Vedanta, this idea of Maya. I am afraid I have no time to discuss this one most difficult point in our philosophy. Those of you who are acquainted with Western philosophy will find something very similar in Kant. But I must warn you, those of you who have studied Professor Max Müller's writings on Kant, that there is one idea most misleading. It was Shankara who first found out the idea of the identity of time, space, and causation with Maya, and I had the good fortune to find one or two passages in Shankara's commentaries and send them to my friend the Professor. So even that idea was here in India. Now this is a peculiar theory—this Maya theory of the Advaita Vedantists. The Brahman is all that exists, but differentiation has been caused by this Maya. Unity, the one Brahman, is the ultimate, the goal, and herein is an eternal dissension again between Indian and Western thought. India has thrown this challenge to the world for thousands of years, and the challenge has been taken up by different nations, and the result is that they all succumbed and you live. This is the challenge that this world is a delusion, that it is all Maya, that whether you eat off the ground with your fingers or dine off golden plates, whether you live in palaces and are one of the mightiest monarchs or are the poorest of beggars, death is the one result; it is all the same, all Maya. That is the old Indian theme, and again and again nations are springing up trying to unsay it, to disprove it; becoming great, with enjoyment as their watchword, power in their hands, they use that power to the utmost, enjoy to the utmost, and the next moment they die. We stand for ever because we see that everything is Maya. The children of Maya live for ever, but the children of enjoyment die.

Here again is another great difference. Just as you find the attempts of Hegel and Schopenhauer in German philosophy, so you will find the very same ideas brought forward in ancient India. Fortunately for us, Hegelianism was nipped in the bud and not allowed to sprout and cast its baneful shoots over this motherland of ours. Hegel's one idea is that the one, the absolute, is only chaos, and that the individualized form is the greater. The world is greater than the non-world, Samsâra is greater than salvation. That is the one idea, and the more you plunge into this Samsara the more your soul is covered with the workings of life, the better you are. They say, do you not see how we build houses, cleanse the streets, enjoy the senses? Ay, behind that they may hide rancour, misery, horror — behind every bit of that enjoyment.

On the other hand, our philosophers have from the very first declared that every manifestation, what you call evolution, is vain, a vain attempt of the unmanifested to manifest itself. Ay, you the mighty cause of this universe, trying to reflect yourself in little mud puddles! But after making the attempt for a time you find out it was all in vain and beat a retreat to the place from whence you came. This is Vairâgya, or renunciation, and the very beginning of religion. How can religion or morality begin without renunciation itself ? The Alpha and Omega is renunciation. "Give up," says the Veda, "give up." That is the one way, "Give up". न परजया धनेन त्यागेनैके ऽमृततवमानशुः — "Neither through wealth, nor through progeny, but by giving up alone that immortality is to be reached." That is the dictate of the Indian books. Of course, there have been great givers-up of the world, even sitting on thrones. But even (King) Janaka himself had to renounce; who was a greater renouncer than he? But in modern times we all want to be called Janakas! They are all Janakas (lit. fathers) of children — unclad, ill-fed, miserable children. The word Janaka can be applied to them in that sense only; they have none of the shining, God-like thoughts as the old Janaka had. These are our modern Janakas! A little less of this Janakism now, and come straight to the mark! If you can give up, you will have religion. If you cannot, you may read all the books that are in the world, from East to West, swallow all the libraries, and become the greatest of Pandits, but if you have Karma Kanda only, you are nothing; there is no spirituality. Through renunciation alone this immortality is to be reached. It is the power, the great power, that cares not even for the universe; then it is that बरहमागाडम गोषपदायते। "The whole universe becomes like a hollow made by a cow's foot."

Renunciation, that is the flag, the banner of India, floating over the world, the one undying thought which India sends again and again as a warning to dying races, as a warning to all tyranny, as a warning to wickedness in the world. Ay, Hindus, let not your hold of that banner go. Hold it aloft. Even if you are weak and cannot renounce, do not lower the ideal. Say, "I am weak and cannot renounce the world", but do not try to be hypocrites, torturing texts, and making specious arguments, and trying to throw dust in the eyes of people who are ignorant. Do not do that, but own you are weak. For the idea is great, that of renunciation. What matters it if millions fail in the attempt, if ten soldiers or even two return victorious! Blessed be the millions dead! Their blood has bought the victory. This renunciation is the one ideal throughout the different Vedic sects except one, and that is the Vallabhâchârya sect in Bombay Presidency, and most of you are aware what comes where renunciation does not exist. We want orthodoxy — even the hideously orthodox, even those who smother themselves with ashes, even those who stand with their hands uplifted. Ay, we want them, unnatural though they be, for standing for that idea of giving up, and acting as a warning to the race against succumbing to the effeminate luxuries that are creeping into India, eating into our very vitals, and tending to make the whole race a race of hypocrites. We want to have a little of asceticism. Renunciation conquered India in days of yore, it has still to conquer India. Still it stands as the greatest and highest of Indian ideals — this renunciation. The land of Buddha, the land of Ramanuja, of Ramakrishna Paramahamsa, the land of renunciation, the land where, from the days of yore, Karma Kanda was preached against, and even today there are hundreds who have given up everything, and become Jivanmuktas — ay, will that land give up its ideals? Certainly not. There may be people whose brains have become turned by the Western luxurious ideals; there may be thousands and hundreds of thousands who have drunk deep of enjoyment, this curse of the West — the senses — the curse of the world; yet for all that, there will be other thousands in this motherland of mine to whom religion will ever be a reality, and who will be ever ready to give up without counting the cost, if need be.

Another ideal very common in all our sects, I want to place before you; it is also a vast subject. This unique idea that religion is to be realised is in India alone. नायमात्मा परवचनेन लभ्यो न मेधया न बहुना शरुतेन — "This Atman is not to be reached by too much talking, nor is it to be reached by the power of intellect, nor by much study of the scriptures." Nay, ours is the only scripture in the world that declares, not even by the study of the scriptures can the Atman be realised — not talks, not lecturing, none of that, but It is to be realised. It comes from the teacher to the disciple. When this insight comes to the disciple, everything is cleared up and realisation follows.

One more idea. There is a peculiar custom in Bengal, which they call Kula-Guru, or hereditary Guruship. "My father was your Guru, now I shall be your Guru. My father was the Guru of your father, so shall I be yours." What is a Guru? Let us go back to the Shrutis — "He who knows the secret of the Vedas", not bookworms, not grammarians, not Pandits in general, but he who knows the meaning. यथा खरशचनदनभारवाही

भारस्य वेत्ता न तु चन्दनस्य—"An ass laden with a load of sandalwood knows only the weight of the wood, but not its precious qualities"; so are these Pandits. We do not want such. What can they teach if they have no realisation? When I was a boy here, in this city of Calcutta, I used to go from place to place in search of religion, and everywhere I asked the lecturer after hearing very big lectures, "Have you seen God?" The man was taken aback at the idea of seeing God; and the only man who told me, "I have", was Ramakrishna Paramahamsa, and not only so, but he said, "I will put you in the way of seeing Him too". The Guru is not a man who twists and tortures texts. वाग्वैखरी शब्दझरी शास्त्रव्याख्यानकौशलं वैदुष्यं विदुषां तद्वद् भुक्तये न तु मुक्तये—"Different ways of throwing out words, different ways of explaining texts of the scriptures, these are for the enjoyment of the learned, not for freedom." Shrotriya, he who knows the secret of the Shrutis, Avrijina, the sinless, and Akâmahata, unpierced by desire—he who does not want to make money by teaching you—he is the Shânta, the Sâdhu, who comes as the spring which brings the leaves and blossoms to various plants but does not ask anything from the plant, for its very nature is to do good. It does good and there it is. Such is the Guru, तीर्णाः स्वयं भीमभवार्णवं जनानहेतुनान्यनपि तारयन्तः—"Who has himself crossed this terrible ocean of life, and without any idea of gain to himself, helps others also to cross the ocean." This is the Guru, and mark that none else can be a Guru, for अविद्यायामन्तरे वर्तमानाः स्वयं धीराः पण्डितिम्मन्यमानाः। दन्द्रम्यमाणाः परियन्ति मूढाः अन्धेनैव नीयमाना यथान्धाः—"Themselves steeped in darkness, but in the pride of their hearts, thinking they know everything, the fools want to help others, and they go round and round in many crooked ways, staggering to and fro, and thus like the blind leading the blind, both fall into the ditch." Thus say the Vedas. Compare that and your present custom. You are Vedantists, you are very orthodox, are you not? You are great Hindus and very orthodox. Ay, what I want to do is to make you more orthodox. The more orthodox you are, the more sensible; and the more you think of modern orthodoxy, the more foolish you are. Go back to your old orthodoxy, for in those days every sound that came from these books, every pulsation, was out of a strong, steady, and sincere heart; every note was true. After that came degradation in art, in science, in religion, in everything, national degradation. We have no time to discuss the causes, but all the books written about that period breathe of the pestilence—the national decay; instead of vigour, only wails and cries. Go back, go back to the old days when there was strength and vitality. Be strong once more, drink deep of this fountain of yore, and that is the only condition of life in India.

According to the Advaitist, this individuality which we have today is a delusion. This has been a hard nut to crack all over the world. Forthwith you tell a man he is not an individual, he is so much afraid that his individuality, whatever that may be, will be lost! But the Advaitist says there never has been an individuality, you have been changing every moment of your life. You were a child and thought in one way, now you are a man and think another way, again you will be an old man and think differently. Everybody is changing. If so, where is your individuality? Certainly not in the body, or in the mind, or in thought. And beyond that is your Atman, and, says the Advaitist, this Atman is the Brahman Itself. There cannot be two infinites. There is only one individual and it is infinite. In plain words, we are rational beings, and we want to reason. And what is reason? More or less of classification, until you cannot go on any further. And the finite can only find its ultimate rest when it is classified into the infinite. Take up a finite thing and go on analysing it, but you will find rest nowhere until you reach the ultimate or infinite, and that infinite, says the Advaitist, is what alone exists. Everything else is Maya, nothing else has real existence; whatever is of existence in any material thing is this Brahman; we are this Brahman, and the shape and everything else is Maya. Take away the form and shape, and you and I are all one. But we have to guard against the word, "I". Generally people say, "If I am the Brahman, why cannot I do this and that?" But this is using the word in a different sense. As soon as you think you are bound, no more you are Brahman, the Self, who wants nothing, whose light is inside. All His pleasures and bliss are inside; perfectly satisfied with Himself, He wants nothing, expects nothing, perfectly fearless, perfectly free. That is Brahman. In That we are all one.

Now this seems, therefore, to be the great point of difference between the dualist and the Advaitist. You find even great commentators like Shankaracharya making meanings of texts, which, to my mind, sometimes do not seem to be justified. Sometimes you find Ramanuja dealing with texts in a way that is not very clear. The idea has been even among our Pandits that only one of these sects can be true and the rest must be false, although they have the idea in the Shrutis, the most wonderful idea that India has yet to give to the world: एकं सद्विप्रा बहुधा वदन्ती—"That which exists is One; sages call It by various names." That has been the theme, and the working out of the whole of this life-problem of the nation is the working out of that theme—एकं सद्विप्रा बहुधा वदन्ती Yea, except a very few learned men, I mean, barring a very few spiritual men, in India, we always forget this. We forget this great idea, and you will find that there are persons among Pandits—I should think ninety-eight per cent—who are of opinion that either the Advaitist will be true, or the Vishishtadvaitist will be true, or the Dvaitist will be true; and if you go to Varanasi, and sit for five minutes in one of the Ghats there, you will have demonstration of what I say. You will see a regular bull-fight going on about these various sects and things.

Thus it remains. Then came one whose life was the explanation, whose life was the working out of the harmony that is the background of all the different sects of India, I mean Ramakrishna Paramahamsa. It is his life that explains that both of these are necessary, that they are like the geocentric and the heliocentric theories in astronomy. When a child is taught astronomy, he is taught the geocentric first, and works out similar ideas of astronomy to the geocentric. But when he comes to finer points of astronomy, the heliocentric will be necessary, and he will understand it better. Dualism is the natural idea of the senses; as long as we are bound by the senses we are bound to see a God who is only Personal, and nothing but Personal, we are bound to see the world as it is. Says Ramanuja, "So long as you think you are a body, and you think you are a mind, and you think you are a Jiva, every act of perception will give you the three—Soul, and nature, and something as causing both." But yet, at the same time, even the idea of the body disappears where the mind itself becomes finer and finer, till it has almost disappeared, when all the different things that make us fear, make us weak, and bind us down to this body-life have disappeared. Then and then alone one finds out the truth of that grand old teaching. What is the teaching?

इहैव तैर्जितः सर्गो येषां साम्ये स्थितं मनः।
निर्दोषं हि समं ब्रह्म तस्माद् ब्रह्मणि ते स्थिताः॥

"Even in this life they have conquered the round of birth and death whose minds are firm-fixed on the sameness of everything, for God is pure and the same to all, and therefore such are said to be living in God."

समं पश्यन् हि सर्वत्र समवस्थितमीश्वरम्।
न हिनस्त्यात्मनात्मानं ततो याति परां गतिम्॥

"Thus seeing the Lord the same everywhere, he, the sage, does not hurt the Self by the self, and so goes to the highest goal."

ADDRESS OF WELCOME AT ALMORA AND REPLY

On his arrival at Almora, Swamiji received an Address of Welcome in Hindi from the citizens of Almora, of which the following is a translation:

Great-Souled One,

Since the time we heard that, after gaining spiritual conquest in the West, you had started from England for your motherland, India, we were naturally desirous of having the pleasure of seeing you. By the grace of the Almighty, that auspicious moment has at last come. The saying of the great poet and the prince of Bhaktas, Tulasidâsa, "A person who intensely loves another is sure to find him", has been fully realised today. We have assembled here to welcome you with sincere devotion. You have highly obliged us by your kindly taking so much trouble in paying a visit to this town again. We can hardly thank you enough for your kindness. Blessed are you! Blessed, blessed is the revered Gurudeva who initiated you into Yoga. Blessed is the land of Bhârata where, even in this fearful Kali Yuga, there exist leaders of Aryan races like yourself. Even at an early period of life, you have by your simplicity, sincer-

ity, character, philanthropy, severe discipline, conduct, and the preaching of knowledge, acquired that immaculate fame throughout the world of which we feel so proud.

In truth, you have accomplished that difficult task which no one ever undertook in this country since the days of Shri Shankarâchârya. Which of us ever dreamt that a descendant of the old Indian Aryans, by dint of Tapas, would prove to the learned people of England and America the superiority of the ancient Indian religion over other creeds? Before the representatives of different religions, assembled in the world's Parliament of Religions held in Chicago, you so ably advocated the superiority of the ancient religion of India that their eyes were opened. In that great assembly, learned speakers defended their respective religions in their own way, but you surpassed them all. You completely established that no religion can compete with the religion of the Vedas. Not only this, but by preaching the ancient wisdom at various places in the continents aforesaid, you have attracted many learned men towards the ancient Aryan religion and philosophy. In England, too, you have planted the banner of the ancient religion, which it is impossible now to remove.

Up to this time, the modern civilised nations of Europe and America were entirely ignorant of the genuine nature of our religion, but you have with our spiritual teaching opened their eyes, by which they have come to know that the ancient religion, which owing to their ignorance they used to brand "as a religion of subtleties of conceited people or a mass of discourses meant for fools", is a mine of gems. Certainly, "It is better to have a virtuous and accomplished son than to have hundreds of foolish ones"; "It is the moon that singly with its light dispels all darkness and not all the stars put together." It is only the life of a good and virtuous son like yourself that is really useful to the world. Mother India is consoled in her decayed state by the presence of pious sons like you. Many have crossed the seas and aimlessly run to and fro, but it was only through the reward of your past good Karma that you have proved the greatness of our religion beyond the seas. You have made it the sole aim of your life by word, thought, and deed, to impart spiritual instruction to humanity. You are always ready to give religious instruction.

We have heard with great pleasure that you intend establishing a Math (monastery) here, and we sincerely pray that your efforts in this direction be crowned with success. The great Shankaracharya also, after his spiritual conquest, established a Math at Badarikâshrama in the Himalayas for the protection of the ancient religion. Similarly, if your desire is also fulfilled, India will be greatly benefited. By the establishment of the Math, we, Kumaonese, will derive special spiritual advantages, and we shall not see the ancient religion gradually disappearing from our midst.

From time immemorial, this part of the country has been the land of asceticism. The greatest of the Indian sages passed their time in piety and asceticism in this land; but that has become a thing of the past. We earnestly hope that by the establishment of the Math you will kindly make us realise it again. It was this sacred land which enjoyed the celebrity all over India of having true religion, Karma, discipline, and fair dealing, all of which seem to have been decaying by the efflux of time. And we hope that by your noble exertions this land will revert to its ancient religious state.

We cannot adequately express the joy we have felt at your arrival here. May you live long, enjoying perfect health and leading a philanthropic life! May your spiritual powers be ever on the increase, so that through your endeavours the unhappy state of India may soon disappear!

Two other addresses were presented, to which the Swami made the following brief reply:

This is the land of dreams of our forefathers, in which was born Pârvati, the Mother of India. This is the holy land where every ardent soul in India wants to come at the end of its life, and to close the last chapter of its mortal career. On the tops of the mountains of this blessed land, in the depths of its caves, on the banks of its rushing torrents, have been thought out the most wonderful thoughts, a little bit of which has drawn so much admiration even from foreigners, and which have been pronounced by the most competent of judges to be incomparable. This is the land which, since my very childhood, I have been dreaming of passing my life in, and as all of you are aware, I have attempted again and again to live here; and although the time was not ripe, and I had work to do and was whirled outside of this holy place, yet it is the hope of my life to end my days somewhere in this Father of Mountains where Rishis lived, where philosophy was born. Perhaps, my friends, I shall not be able to do it, in the way that I had planned before—how I wish that silence, that unknownness would be given to me—yet I sincerely pray and hope, and almost believe, that my last days will be spent here, of all places on earth.

Inhabitants of this holy land, accept my gratitude for the kind praise that has fallen from you for my little work in the West. But at the same time, my mind does not want to speak of that, either in the East or in the West. As peak after peak of this Father of Mountains began to appear before my sight, all the propensities to work, that ferment that had been going on in my brain for years, seemed to quiet down, and instead of talking about what had been done and what was going to be done, the mind reverted to that one eternal theme which the Himalayas always teach us, that one theme which is reverberating in the very atmosphere of the place, the one theme the murmur of which I hear even now in the rushing whirlpools of its rivers—renunciation! सर्वं वस्तु भयान्वितं भुवि नृणां वैराग्यमेवाभयम्— "Everything in this life is fraught with fear. It is renunciation alone that makes one fearless." Yes, this is the land of renunciation.

The time will not permit me, and the circumstances are not fitting, to speak to you fully. I shall have to conclude, there-fore, by pointing out to you that the Himalayas stand for that renunciation, and the grand lesson we shall ever teach to humanity will be renunciation. As our forefathers used to be attracted towards it in the latter days of their lives, so strong souls from all quarters of this earth, in time to come, will be attracted to this Father of Mountains, when all this fight between sects and all those differences in dogmas will not be remembered any more, and quarrels between your religion and my religion will have vanished altogether, when mankind will understand that there is but one eternal religion, and that is the perception of the divine within, and the rest is mere froth: such ardent souls will come here knowing that the world is but vanity of vanities, knowing that everything is useless except the worship of the Lord and the Lord alone.

Friends, you have been very kind to allude to an idea of mine, which is to start a centre in the Himalayas, and perhaps I have sufficiently explained why it should be so, why, above all others, this is the spot which I want to select as one of the great centres to teach this universal religion. These mountains are associated with the best memories of our race; if these Himalayas are taken away from the history of religious India, there will be very little left behind. Here, therefore, must be one of those centres, not merely of activity, but more of calmness, of meditation, and of peace; and I hope some day to realise it. I hope also to meet you at other times and have better opportunities of talking to you. For the present, let me thank you again for all the kindness that has been shown to me, and let me take it as not only kindness shown to me in person, but as to one who represents our religion. May it never leave our hearts! May we always remain as pure as we are at the present moment, and as enthusiastic for spirituality as we are just now!

VEDIC TEACHING
IN THEORY AND PRACTICE

When the Swami's visit was drawing to a close, his friends in Almora invited him to give a lecture in Hindi. He consented to make the attempt for the first time. He began slowly, and soon warmed to his theme, and found himself building his phrases and almost his words as he went along. Those best acquainted with the difficulties and limitations of the Hindi language, still undeveloped as a medium for oratory, expressed their opinion that a personal triumph had been achieved by Swamiji and that he had proved by his masterly use of Hindi that the language had in it undreamt-of possibilities of development in the direction of oratory.

Another lecture was delivered at the English Club in English, of which a brief summary follows.

The subject was "Vedic Reaching in Theory and Practice". A short historical sketch of the rise of the worship of the tribal God and its spread through conquest of other tribes was followed by am account of the Vedas. Their nature, character, and teaching were briefly touched upon. Then the Swami spoke about the soul, comparing the Western method which seeks for the solution of vital and religious mysteries in the outside world, with the Eastern method which finding no answer in nature outside turns its inquiry within. He justly claimed for his nation the glory of being the discoverers of the introspective method peculiar to themselves, and of having given to humanity the priceless treasures of spirituality which are the result of that method alone. Passing from this theme, naturally so dear to the heart of a Hindu, the Swami reached the climax of his power as a spiritual teacher when he described the relation of the soul to God, its aspiration after and real unity with God. For some time it seemed as though the teacher, his words, his audience, and the spirit pervading them all were one. No longer was there any consciousness of "I" and "Thou", of "This" or "That". The different units collected there were for the time being lost and merged in the spiritual radiance which emanated so powerfully from the great teacher and held them all more than spellbound.

Those that have frequently heard him will recall similar experiences when he ceased to be Swami Vivekananda lecturing to critical and attentive hearers, when all details and personalities were lost, names and forms disappeared, only the Spirit remaining, uniting the speaker, hearer, and the spoken word.

BHAKTI

Delivered at Sialkote, Punjab

In response to invitations from the Punjab and Kashmir, the Swami Vivekananda travelled through those parts. He stayed in Kashmir for over a month and his work there was very much appreciated by the Maharaja and his brothers. He then spent a few days in visiting Murree, Rawalpindi, and Jammu, and at each of these places he delivered lectures. Subsequently he visited Sialkote and lectured twice, once in English and once in Hindi. The subject of the Swamiji's Hindi lecture was Bhakti, a summary of which, translated into English, is given below:

The various religions that exist in the world, although they differ in the form of worship they take, are really one. In some places the people build temples and worship in them, in some they worship fire, in others they prostrate themselves before idols, while there are many who do not believe at all in God. All are true, for, if you look to the real spirit, the real religion, and the truths in each of them, they are all alike. In some religions God is not worshipped, nay, His existence is not believed in, but good and worthy men are worshipped as if they were Gods. The example worthy of citation in this case is Buddhism. Bhakti is everywhere, whether directed to God or to noble persons. Upâsana in the form of Bhakti is everywhere supreme, and Bhakti is more easily attained than Jnâna. The latter requires favourable circumstances and strenuous practice. Yoga cannot be properly practiced unless a man is physically very healthy and free from all worldly attachments. But Bhakti can be more easily practiced by persons

in every condition of life. Shândilya Rishi, who wrote about Bhakti, says that extreme love for God is Bhakti. Prahlâda speaks to the same effect. If a man does not get food one day, he is troubled; if his son dies, how agonising it is to him! The true Bhakta feels the same pangs in his heart when he yearns after God. The great quality of Bhakti is that it cleanses the mind, and the firmly established Bhakti for the Supreme Lord is alone sufficient to purify the mind. "O God, Thy names are innumerable, but in every name Thy power is manifest, and every name is pregnant with deep and mighty significance." We should think of God always and not consider time and place for doing so.

The different names under which God is worshipped are apparently different. One thinks that his method of worshipping God is the most efficacious, and another thinks that his is the more potent process of attaining salvation. But look at the true basis of all, and it is one. The Shaivas call Shiva the most powerful; the Vaishnavas hold to their all-powerful Vishnu; the worshippers of Devi will not yield to any in their idea that their Devi is the most omnipotent power in the universe. Leave inimical thoughts aside if you want to have permanent Bhakti. Hatred is a thing which greatly impedes the course of Bhakti, and the man who hates none reaches God. Even then the devotion for one's own ideal is necessary. Hanumân says, "Vishnu and Râma, I know, are one and the same, but after all, the lotus-eyed Rama is my best treasure." The peculiar tendencies with which a person is born must remain with him. That is the chief reason why the world cannot be of one religion — and God forbid that there should be one religion only — for the world would then be a chaos and not a cosmos. A man must follow the tendencies peculiar to himself; and if he gets a teacher to help him to advance along his own lines, he will progress. We should let a person go the way he intends to go, but if we try to force him into another path, he will lose what he has already attained and will become worthless. As the face of one person does not resemble that of another, so the nature of one differs from that of another, and why should he not be allowed to act accordingly? A river flows in a certain direction; and if you direct the course into a regular channel, the current becomes more rapid and the force is increased, but try to divert it from its proper course, and you will see the result; the volume as well as the force will be lessened. This life is very important, and it, therefore, ought to be guided in the way one's tendency prompts him. In India there was no enmity, and every religion was left unmolested; so religion has lived. It ought to be remembered that quarrels about religion arise from thinking that one alone has the truth and whoever does not believe as one does is a fool; while another thinks that the other is a hypocrite, for if he were not one, he would follow him.

If God wished that people should follow one religion, why have so many religions sprung up? Methods have been vainly tried to force one religion upon everyone. Even when the sword was lifted to make all people follow one religion, history tells us that ten religions sprang up in its place. One religion cannot suit all. Man is the product of two forces, action and reaction, which make him think. If such forces did not exercise a man's mind, he would be incapable of thinking. Man is a creature who thinks; Manushya (man) is a being with Manas (mind); and as soon as his thinking power goes, he becomes no better than an animal. Who would like such a man? God forbid that any such state should come upon the people of India. Variety in unity is necessary to keep man as man. Variety ought to be preserved in everything; for as long as there is variety the world will exist. Of course variety does not merely mean that one is small and the other is great; but if all play their parts equally well in their respective position in life, the variety is still preserved. In every religion there have been men good and able, thus making the religion to which they belonged worthy of respect; and as there are such people in every religion, there ought to be no hatred for any sect whatsoever.

Then the question may be asked, should we respect that religion which advocates vice? The answer will be certainly in the negative, and such a religion ought to be expelled at once, because it is productive of harm. All religion is to be based upon morality, and personal purity is to be counted superior to Dharma. In this connection it ought to be known that Âchâra means purity inside and outside. External purity can be attained by cleansing the body with water and other things which are recommended in the Shâstras. The internal man is to be purified by not speaking falsehood, by not drinking, by not doing immoral acts, and by doing good to others. If you do not commit any sin, if you do not tell lies, if you do not drink, gamble, or commit theft, it is good. But that is only your duty and you cannot be applauded for it. Some service to others is also to be done. As you do good to yourself, so you must do good to others.

Here I shall say something about food regulations. All the old customs have faded away, and nothing but a vague notion of not eating with this man and not eating; with that man has been left among our countrymen. Purity by touch is the only relic left of the good rules laid down hundreds of years ago. Three kinds of food are forbidden in the Shastras. First, the food that is by its very nature defective, as garlic or onions. If a man eats too much of them it creates passion, and he may be led to commit immoralities, hateful both to God and man. Secondly, food contaminated by external impurities. We ought to select some place quite neat and clean in which to keep our food. Thirdly, we should avoid eating food touched by a wicked man, because contact with such produces bad ideas in us. Even if one be a son of a Brahmin, but is profligate and immoral in his habits, we should not eat food from his hands.

But the spirit of these observances is gone. What is left is this, that we cannot eat from the hands of any man who is not of the highest caste, even though he be the most wise and holy person. The disregard of those old rules is ever to be found in the confectioner's shop. If you look there, you will find flies hovering all over the confectionery, and the dust from the road blowing upon the sweetmeats, and the confectioner himself in a dress that is not very clean and neat. Purchasers should declare with one voice that they will not buy sweets unless they are kept in glass-cases in the Halwai's shop. That would have the salutary effect of preventing flies from conveying cholera and other plague germs to the sweets. We ought to improve, but instead of improving we have gone back. Manu says that we should not spit in water, but we throw all sorts of filth into the rivers. Considering all these things we find that the purification of one's outer self is very necessary. The Shâstrakâras knew that very well. But now the real spirit of this observance of purity about food is lost and the letter only remains. Thieves, drunkards, and criminals can be our caste-fellows, but if a good and noble man eats food with a person of a lower caste, who is quite as respectable as himself, he will be outcasted and lost for ever. This custom has been the bane of our country. It ought, therefore, to be distinctly understood that sin is incurred by coming in contact with sinners, and nobility in the company of good persons; and keeping aloof from the wicked is the external purification.

The internal purification is a task much more severe. It consists in speaking the truth, sensing the poor, helping the needy, etc. Do we always speak the truth? What happens is often this. People go to the house of a rich person for some business of their own and flatter him by calling him benefactor of the poor and so forth, even though that man may cut the throat of a poor man coming to his house. What is this? Nothing but falsehood. And it is this that pollutes the mind. It is therefore, truly said that whatever a man says who has purified his inner self for twelve years without entertaining a single vicious idea during that period is sure to come true. This is the power of truth, and one who has cleansed both the inner and the outer self is alone capable of Bhakti. But the beauty is that Bhakti itself cleanses the mind to a great extent. Although the Jews, Mohammedans, and Christians do not set so much importance upon the excessive external purification of the body as the Hindus do, still they have it in some form or other; they find that to a certain extent it is always required. Among the Jews, idol-worship is condemned, but they had a temple in which was kept a chest which they called an ark, in which the Tables of the Law were preserved, and above the chest were two figures of angels with wings outstretched, between which the Divine Presence was supposed to manifest itself as a cloud. That temple has long since been destroyed, but the new temples are made exactly after the old fashion, and in the chest religious books are kept. The Roman Catholics and the Greek Christians have idol-worship in certain forms. The image of Jesus and that of his mother are worshipped. Among Protestants there is no idol-worship, yet they worship God in a personal form, which may be called idol-worship in another form. Among Parsees and Iranians fire-worship is carried on to a great extent. Among Mohammedans the prophets and great and noble persons are worshipped, and they turn their faces towards the Caaba when they pray. These things show that men at the first stage of religious development have to make use of something external, and when the inner self becomes purified they turn to more abstract conceptions. "When the Jiva is sought to be united with Brahman it is best, when meditation is practiced it is mediocre, repetition of names is the lowest form, and external worship is the lowest of the low." But it should be distinctly understood that even in practicing the last there is no sin. Everybody ought to do what he is able to do; and if he be dissuaded from that, he will do it in some other way in order to attain his end. So we should not speak ill of a man who worships idols. He is in that stage of growth, and, therefore, must have them; wise men should try to help forward such men and get them to do better. But there is no use in quarrelling about these various sorts of worship.

Some persons worship God for the sake of obtaining wealth, others because they want to have a son, and they think themselves Bhâgavatas (devotees). This is no Bhakti, and they are not true Bhagavatas. When a Sâdhu comes who professes that he can make gold, they run to him, and they still consider themselves Bhagavatas. It is not Bhakti if we worship God with the desire for a son; it is not Bhakti if we worship with the desire to be rich; it is not Bhakti even if we have a desire for heaven; it is not Bhakti if a man worships with the desire of being saved from the tortures of hell. Bhakti is not the outcome of fear or greediness. He is the true Bhagavata who says, "O God, I do not want a beautiful wife, I do not want knowledge or salvation. Let me be born and die hundreds of times. What I want is that I should be ever engaged in Thy service." It is at this stage—and when a man sees God in everything, and everything in God—that he attains perfect Bhakti. It is then that he sees Vishnu incarnated in everything from the microbe to Brahmâ, and it is then that he sees God manifesting Himself in everything, it is then that he feels that there is nothing without God, and it is then and then alone that thinking himself to be the most insignificant of all beings he worships God with the true spirit of a Bhakta. He then leaves Tirthas and external forms of worship far behind him, he sees every man to be the most perfect temple.

Bhakti is described in several ways in the Shastras. We say that God is our Father. In the same way we call Him Mother, and so on. These relationships are conceived in order to strengthen Bhakti in us, and they make us feel nearer and dearer to God. Hence these names are justifiable in one way, and that is that the words are simply words of endearment, the outcome of the fond love which a true Bhagavata feels for God. Take the story of Râdhâ and Krishna in Râsalilâ. The story simply exemplifies the true spirit of a Bhakta, because no love in the world exceeds that existing between a man and a woman. When there is such intense love, there is no fear, no other attachment save that one which binds that pair in an inseparable and all-absorbing bond. But with regard to parents, love is accompanied with fear due to the reverence we have for them. Why should we care whether God created anything or not, what have we to do with the fact that He is our preserver? He is only our Beloved, and we should adore Him devoid all thoughts of fear. A man loves God only when he has no other desire, when he thinks of nothing else and when he is mad after Him. That love which a man has for his beloved can illustrate the love we ought to have for God. Krishna is the God and Radha loves Him; read those books which describe that story, and then you can imagine the way you should love God. But how many understand this? How can people who are vicious to their very core and have no idea of what morality is understand all this? When people drive all sorts of worldly thoughts from their minds and live in a clear moral and spiritual atmosphere, it is then that they understand the abstrusest of thoughts even if they be uneducated. But how few are there of that nature! There is not a single religion which cannot be perverted by man. For example, he may think that the Âtman is quite separate from the body, and so, when committing sins with the body his Atman is unaffected. If religions were truly followed, there would not have been a single man, whether Hindu, Mohammedan, or Christian, who would not have been all purity. But men are guided by their own nature, whether good or bad; there is no gainsaying that. But in the world, there are always some who get intoxicated when they hear of God, and shed tears of joy when they read of God. Such men are true Bhaktas.

At the initial stage of religious development a man thinks of God as his Master and himself as His servant. He feels indebted to Him for providing for his daily wants, and so forth. Put such thoughts aside. There is but one attractive power, and that is God; and it is in obedience to that attractive power that the sun and the moon and everything else move. Everything in this world, whether good or bad, belongs to God. Whatever occurs in our life, whether good or bad, is bringing us to Him. One man kills another because of some selfish purpose. But the motive behind is love, whether for himself or for any one else. Whether we do good or evil, the propeller is love. When a tiger kills a buffalo, it is because he or his cubs are hungry.

God is love personified. He is apparent in everything. Everybody is being drawn to Him whether he knows it or not. When a woman loves her husband, she does not understand that it is the divine in her husband that is the great attractive power. The God of Love is the one thing to be worshipped. So long as we think of Him only as the Creator and Preserver, we can offer Him external worship, but when we get beyond all that and think Him to be Love Incarnate, seeing Him in all things and all things in Him, it is then that supreme Bhakti is attained.

THE COMMON BASES OF HINDUISM

On his arrival at Lahore the Swamiji was accorded a grand reception by the leaders, both of the Ârya Samâj and of the

Sanâtana Dharma Sabhâ. During his brief stay in Lahore, Swamiji delivered three lectures. The first of these was on "The Common Bases of Hinduism", the second on "Bhakti", and the third one was the famous lecture on "The Vedanta". On the first Occasion he spoke as follows:

This is the land which is held to be the holiest even in holy Âryâvarta; this is the Brahmâvarta of which our great Manu speaks. This is the land from whence arose that mighty aspiration after the Spirit, ay, which in times to come, as history shows, is to deluge the world. This is the land where, like its mighty rivers, spiritual aspirations have arisen and joined their strength, till they travelled over the length and breadth of the world and declared themselves with a voice of thunder. This is the land which had first to bear the brunt of all inroads and invasions into India; this heroic land had first to bare its bosom to every onslaught of the outer barbarians into Aryavarta. This is the land which, after all its sufferings, has not yet entirely lost its glory and its strength. Here it was that in later times the gentle Nânak preached his marvellous love for the world. Here it was that his broad heart was opened and his arms outstretched to embrace the whole world, not only of Hindus, but of Mohammedans too. Here it was that one of the last and one of the most glorious heroes of our race, Guru Govinda Singh, after shedding his blood and that of his dearest and nearest for the cause of religion, even when deserted by those for whom this blood was shed, retired into the South to die like a wounded lion struck to the heart, without a word against his country, without a single word of murmur.

Here, in this ancient land of ours, children of the land of five rivers, I stand before you, not as a teacher, for I know very little to teach, but as one who has come from the east to exchange words of greeting with the brothers of the west, to compare notes. Here am I, not to find out differences that exist among us, but to find where we agree. Here am I trying to understand on what ground we may always remain brothers, upon what foundations the voice that has spoken from eternity may become stronger and stronger as it grows. Here am I trying to propose to you something of constructive work and not destructive. For criticism the days are past, and we are waiting for constructive work. The world needs, at times, criticisms even fierce ones; but that is only for a time, and the work for eternity is progress and construction, and not criticism and destruction. For the last hundred years or so, there has been a flood of criticism all over this land of ours, where the full play of Western science has been let loose upon all the dark spots, and as a result the corners and the holes have become much more prominent than anything else. Naturally enough there arose mighty intellects all over the land, great and glorious, with the love of truth and justice in their hearts, with the love of their country, and above all, an intense love for their religion and their God; and because these mighty souls felt so deeply, because they loved so deeply, they criticised everything they thought was wrong. Glory unto these mighty spirits of the past! They have done so much

good; but the voice of the present day is coming to us, telling, "Enough!" There has been enough of criticism, there has been enough of fault-finding, the time has come for the rebuilding, the reconstructing; the time has come for us to gather all our scattered forces, to concentrate them into one focus, and through that, to lead the nation on its onward march, which for centuries almost has been stopped. The house has been cleansed; let it be inhabited anew. The road has been cleared. March children of the Aryans!

Gentlemen, this is the motive that brings me before you, and at the start I may declare to you that I belong to no party and no sect. They are all great and glorious to me, I love them all, and all my life I have been attempting to find what is good and true in them. Therefore, it is my proposal tonight to bring before you points where we are agreed, to find out, if we can, a ground of agreement; and if through the grace of the Lord such a state of things be possible, let us take it up, and from theory carry it out into practice. We are Hindus. I do not use the word Hindu in any bad sense at all, nor do I agree with those that think there is any bad meaning in it. In old times, it simply meant people who lived on the other side of the Indus; today a good many among those who hate us may have put a bad interpretation upon it, but names are nothing. Upon us depends whether the name Hindu will stand for everything that is glorious, everything that is spiritual, or whether it will remain a name of opprobrium, one designating the downtrodden, the worthless, the heathen. If at present the word Hindu means anything bad, never mind; by our action let us be ready to show that this is the highest word that any language can invent. It has been one of the principles of my life not to be ashamed of my own ancestors. I am one of the proudest men ever born, but let me tell you frankly, it is not for myself, but on account of my ancestry. The more I have studied the past, the more I have looked back, more and more has this pride come to me, and it has given me the strength and courage of conviction, raised me up from the dust of the earth, and set me working out that great plan laid out by those great ancestors of ours. Children of those ancient Aryans, through the grace of the Lord may you have the same pride, may that faith in your ancestors come into your blood, may it become a part and parcel of your lives, may it work towards the salvation of the world!

Before trying to find out the precise point where we are all agreed, the common ground of our national life, one thing we must remember. Just as there is an individuality in every man, so there is a national individuality. As one man differs from another in certain particulars, in certain characteristics of his own, so one race differs from another in certain peculiar characteristics; and just as it is the mission of every man to fulfil a certain purpose in the economy of nature, just as there is a particular line set out for him by his own past Karma, so it is with nations—each nation has a destiny to fulfil, each nation has a message to deliver, each nation has a mission to accomplish. Therefore, from the very start, we must have to understand the mission of our own race, the destiny it has to fulfil, the place it has to occupy in the march of nations, the note which it has to contribute to the harmony of races. In our country, when children, we hear stories how some serpents have jewels in their heads, and whatever one may do with the serpent, so long as the jewel is there, the serpent cannot be killed. We hear stories of giants and ogres who had souls living in certain little birds, and so long as the bird was safe, there was no power on earth to kill these giants; you might hack them to pieces, or do what you liked to them, the giants could not die. So with nations, there is a certain point where the life of a nation centres, where lies the nationality of the nation, and until that is touched, the nation cannot die. In the light of this we can understand the most marvellous phenomenon that the history of the world has ever known. Wave after wave of Barbarian conquest has rolled over this devoted land of ours. "Allah Ho Akbar!" has rent the skies for hundreds of years, and no Hindu knew what moment would be his last. This is the most suffering and the most subjugated of all the historic lands of the world. Yet we still stand practically the same race, ready to face difficulties again and again if necessary; and not only so, of late there have been signs that we are not only strong, but ready to go out, for the sign of life is expansion.

We find today that our ideas and thoughts are no more cooped up within the bounds of India, but whether we will it or not, they are marching outside, filtering into the literature of nations, taking their place among nations, and in some, even getting a commanding dictatorial position. Behind this we find the explanation that the great contribution to the sum total of the world's progress from India is the greatest, the noblest, the sublimest theme that can occupy the mind of man—it is philosophy and spirituality. Our ancestors tried many other things; they, like other nations, first went to bring out the secrets of external nature as we all know, and with their gigantic brains that marvellous race could have done miracles in that line of which the world could have been proud for ever. But they gave it up for something higher; something better rings out from the pages of the Vedas: "That science is the greatest which makes us know Him who never changes!" The science of nature, changeful, evanescent, the world of death, of woe, of misery, may be great, great indeed; but the science of Him who changes not, the Blissful One, where alone is peace, where alone is life eternal, where alone is perfection, where alone all misery ceases—that, according to our ancestors, was the sublimest science of all. After all, sciences that can give us only bread and clothes and power over our fellowmen, sciences that can teach us only how to conquer our fellow-beings, to rule over them, which teach the strong to domineer over the weak—those they could have discovered if they willed. But praise be unto the Lord, they caught at once the other side, which was grander, infinitely higher, infinitely more blissful, till it has become the national characteristic, till it has come down to us, inherited from father to

son for thousands of years, till it has become a part and parcel of us, till it tingles in every drop of blood that runs through our veins, till it has become our second nature, till the name of religion and Hindu have become one. This is the national characteristic, and this cannot be touched. Barbarians with sword and fire, barbarians bringing barbarous religions, not one of them could touch the core, not one could touch the "jewel", not one had the power to kill the "bird" which the soul of the race inhabited. This, therefore, is the vitality of I the race, and so long as that remains, there is no power under the sun that can kill the race. All the tortures and miseries of the world will pass over without hurting us, and we shall come out of the flames like Prahlâda, so long as we hold on to this grandest of all our inheritances, spirituality. If a Hindu is not spiritual I do not call him a Hindu. In other countries a man may be political first, and then he may have a little religion, but here in India the first and the foremost duty of our lives is to be spiritual first, and then, if there is time, let other things come. Bearing this in mind we shall be in a better position to understand why, for our national welfare, we must first seek out at the present day all the spiritual forces of the race, as was done in days of yore and will be done in all times to come. National union in India must be a gathering up of its scattered spiritual forces. A nation in India must be a union of those whose hearts beat to the same spiritual tune.

There have been sects enough in this country. There are sects enough, and there will be enough in the future, because this has been the peculiarity of our religion that in abstract principles so much latitude has been given that, although afterwards so much detail has been worked out, all these details are the working out of principles, broad as the skies above our heads, eternal as nature herself. Sects, therefore, as a matter of course, must exist here, but what need not exist is sectarian quarrel. Sects must be but sectarianism need not. The world would not be the better for sectarianism, but the world cannot move on without having sects. One set of men cannot do everything. The almost infinite mass of energy in the world cannot tie managed by a small number of people. Here, at once we see the necessity that forced this division of labour upon us—the division into sects. For the use of spiritual forces let there be sects; but is there any need that we should quarrel when our most ancient books declare that this differentiation is only apparent, that in spite of all these differences there is a thread of harmony, that beautified unity, running through them all? Our most ancient books have declared: एकं सद्विप्रा बहुधा वदन्ति ।—"That which exists is One; sages call Him by various names." Therefore, if there are these sectarian struggles, if there are these fights among the different sects, if there is jealousy and hatred between the different sects in India, the land where all sects have always been honoured, it is a shame on us who dare to call ourselves the descendants of those fathers.

There are certain great principles in which, I think, we—whether Vaishnavas, Shaivas, Shâktas, or Gânapatyas, whether belonging to the ancient Vedantists or the modern ones, whether belonging to the old rigid sects or the modern reformed ones—are all one, and whoever calls himself a Hindu, believes in these principles. Of course there is a difference in the interpretation, in the explanation of these principles, and that difference should be there, and it should be allowed, for our standard is not to bind every man down to our position. It would be a sin to force every man to work out our own interpretation of things, and to live by our own methods. Perhaps all who are here will agree on the first point that we believe the Vedas to be the eternal teachings of the secrets of religion. We all believe that this holy literature is without beginning and without end, coeval with nature, which is without beginning and without end; and that all our religious differences, all our religious struggles must end when we stand in the presence of that holy book; we are all agreed that this is the last court of appeal in all our spiritual differences. We may take different points of view as to what the Vedas are. There may be one sect which regards one portion as more sacred than another, but that matters little so long as we say that we are all brothers in the Vedas, that out of these venerable, eternal, marvellous books has come everything that we possess today, good, holy, and pure. Well, therefore, if we believe in all this, let this principle first of all be preached broadcast throughout the length and breadth of the land. If this be true, let the Vedas have that prominence which they always deserve, and which we all believe in. First, then, the Vedas. The second point we all believe in is God, the creating, the preserving power of the whole universe, and unto whom it periodically returns to come out at other periods and manifest this wonderful phenomenon, called the universe. We may differ as to our conception of God. One may believe in a God who is entirely personal, another may believe in a God who is personal and yet not human, and yet another may believe in a God who is entirely impersonal, and all may get their support from the Vedas. Still we are all believers in God; that is to say, that man who does not believe in a most marvellous Infinite Power from which everything has come, in which everything lives, and to which everything must in the end return, cannot be called a Hindu. If that be so, let us try to preach that idea all over the land. Preach whatever conception you have to give, there is no difference, we are not going to fight over it, but preach God; that is all we want. One idea may be better than another, but, mind you, not one of them is bad. One is good, another is better, and again another may be the best, but the word bad does not enter the category of our religion. Therefore, may the Lord bless them all who preach the name of God in whatever form they like! The more He is preached, the better for this race. Let our children be brought up in this idea, let this idea enter the homes of the poorest and the lowest, as well as of the richest and the highest—the idea of the name of God.

The third idea that I will present before you is that, unlike all other races of the world, we do not believe that this world was created only so many thousand years ago, and is going to be destroyed eternally on a certain day. Nor do we believe that the human soul has been created along with this universe just out of nothing. Here is another point I think we are all able to agree upon. We believe in nature being without beginning and without end; only at psychological periods this gross material of the outer universe goes back to its finer state, thus to remain for a certain period, again to be projected outside to manifest all this infinite panorama we call nature. This wave-like motion was going on even before time began, through eternity, and will remain for an infinite period of time.

Next, all Hindus believe that man is not only a gross material body; not only that within this there is the finer body, the mind, but there is something yet greater—for the body changes and so does the mind—something beyond, the Âtman—I cannot translate the word to you for any translation will be wrong—that there is something beyond even this fine body, which is the Atman of man, which has neither beginning nor end, which knows not what death is. And then this peculiar idea, different from that of all other races of men, that this Atman inhabits body after body until there is no more interest for it to continue to do so, and it becomes free, not to be born again, I refer to the theory of Samsâra and the theory of eternal souls taught by our Shâstras. This is another point where we all agree, whatever sect we may belong to. There may be differences as to the relation between the soul and God. According to one sect the soul may be eternally different from God, according to another it may be a spark of that infinite fire, yet again according to others it may be one with that Infinite. It does not matter what our interpretation is, so long as we hold on to the one basic belief that the soul is infinite, that this soul was never created, and therefore will never die, that it had to pass and evolve into various bodies, till it attained perfection in the human one—in that we are all agreed. And then comes the most differentiating, the grandest, and the most wonderful discovery in the realms of spirituality that has ever been made. Some of you, perhaps, who have been studying Western thought, may have observed already that there is another radical difference severing at one stroke all that is Western from all that is Eastern. It is this that we hold, whether we are Shâktas, Sauras, or Vaishnavas, even whether we are Bauddhas or Jainas, we all hold in India that the soul is by its nature pure and perfect, infinite in power and blessed. Only, according to the dualist, this natural blissfulness of the soul has become contracted by past bad work, and through the grace of God it is again going to open out and show its perfection; while according to the monist, even this idea of contraction is a partial mistake, it is the veil of Maya that causes us to think the, soul has lost its powers, but the powers are there fully manifest. Whatever the difference may be, we come to the central core, and there is at once an irreconcilable difference between all that is Western and Eastern. The Eastern is looking inward for all that is great and good. When we worship, we close our eyes and try to find

God within. The Western is looking up outside for his God. To the Western their religious books have been inspired, while with us our books have been expired; breath-like they came, the breath of God, out of the hearts of sages they sprang, the Mantra-drashtâs.

This is one great point to understand, and, my friends, my brethren, let me tell you, this is the one point we shall have to insist upon in the future. For I am firmly convinced, and I beg you to understand this one fact - no good comes out of the man who day and night thinks he is nobody. If a man, day and night, thinks he is miserable, low, and nothing, nothing he becomes. If you say yea, yea, "I am, I am", so shall you be; and if you say "I am not", think that you are not, and day and night meditate upon the fact that you are nothing, ay, nothing shall you be. That is the great fact which you ought to remember. We are the children of the Almighty, we are sparks of the infinite, divine fire. How can we be nothings? We are everything, ready to do everything, we can do everything, and man must do everything. This faith in themselves was in the hearts of our ancestors, this faith in themselves was the motive power that pushed them forward and forward in the march of civilisation; and if there has been degeneration, if there has been defect, mark my words, you will find that degradation to have started on the day our people lost this faith in themselves. Losing faith in one's self means losing faith in God. Do you believe in that infinite, good Providence working in and through you? If you believe that this Omnipresent One, the Antaryâmin, is present in every atom, is through and through, Ota-prota, as the Sanskrit word goes, penetrating your body, mind and soul, how can you lose, heart? I may be a little bubble of water, and you may be a mountain-high wave. Never mind! The infinite ocean is the background of me as well as of you. Mine also is that infinite ocean of life, of power, of spirituality, as well as yours. I am already joined—from my very birth, from the very fact of my life—I am in Yoga with that infinite life and infinite goodness and infinite power, as you are, mountain-high though you may be. Therefore, my brethren, teach this life-saving, great, ennobling, grand doctrine to your children, even from their very birth. You need not teach them Advaitism; teach them Dvaitism, or any "ism" you please, but we have seen that this is the common "ism" all through India; this marvellous doctrine of the soul, the perfection of the soul, is commonly believed in by all sects. As says our great philosopher Kapila, if purity has not been the nature of the soul, it can never attain purity afterwards, for anything that was not perfect by nature, even if it attained to perfection, that perfection would go away again. If impurity is the nature of man, then man will have to remain impure, even though he may be pure for five minutes. The time will come when this purity will wash out, pass away, and the old natural impurity will have its sway once more. Therefore, say all our philosophers, good is our nature, perfection is our nature, not imperfection, not impurity—and we should remember that. Remember the beautiful example of the great sage who, when

he was dying, asked his mind to remember all his mighty deeds and all his mighty thoughts. There you do not find that he was teaching his mind to remember all his weaknesses and all his follies. Follies there are, weakness there must be, but remember your real nature always—that is the only way to cure the weakness, that is the only way to cure the follies.

It seems that these few points are common among all the various religious sects in India, and perhaps in future upon this common platform, conservative and liberal religionists, old type and new type, may shake bands. Above all, there is another thing to remember, which I am sorry we forget from time to time, that religion, in India, means realisation and nothing short of that. "Believe in the doctrine, and you are safe", can never be taught to us, for we do not believe in that. You are what you make yourselves. You are, by the grace of God and your own exertions, what you are. Mere believing in certain theories and doctrines will not help you much. The mighty word that came out from the sky of spirituality in India was Anubhuti, realisation, and ours are the only books which declare again and again: "The Lord is to be seen". Bold, brave words indeed, but true to their very core; every sound, every vibration is true. Religion is to be realised, not only heard; it is not in learning some doctrine like a parrot. Neither is it mere intellectual assent—that is nothing; but it must come into us. Ay, and therefore the greatest proof that we have of the existence of a God is not because our reason says so, but because God has been seen by the ancients as well as by the moderns. We believe in the soul not only because there are good reasons to prove its existence, but, above all, because there have been in the past thousands in India, there are still many who have realised, and there will be thousands in the future who will realise and see their own souls. And there is no salvation for man until he sees God, realises his own soul. Therefore, above all, let us understand this, and the more we understand it the less we shall have of sectarianism in India, for it is only that man who has realised God and seen Him, who is religious. In him the knots have been cut asunder, in him alone the doubts have subsided; he alone has become free from the fruits of action who has seen Him who is nearest of the near and farthest of the far. Ay, we often mistake mere prattle for religious truth, mere intellectual perorations for great spiritual realisation, and then comes sectarianism, then comes fight. If we once understand that this realisation is the only religion, we shall look into our own hearts and find how far we are towards realising the truths of religion. Then we shall understand that we ourselves are groping in darkness, and are leading others to grope in the same darkness, then we shall cease from sectarianism, quarrel, arid fight. Ask a man who wants to start a sectarian fight, "Have you seen God? Have you seen the Atman? If you have not, what right have you to preach His name—you walking in darkness trying to lead me into the same darkness—the blind leading the blind, and both falling into the ditch?"

Therefore, take more thought before you go and find fault

with others. Let them follow their own path to realisation so long as they struggle to see truth in their own hearts; and when the broad, naked truth will be seen, then they will find that wonderful blissfulness which marvellously enough has been testified to by every seer in India, by every one who has realised the truth. Then words of love alone will come out of that heart, for it has already been touched by Him who is the essence of Love Himself. Then and then alone, all sectarian quarrels will cease, and we shall be in a position to understand, to bring to our hearts, to embrace, to intensely love the very word Hindu and every one who bears that name. Mark me, then and then alone you are a Hindu when the very name sends through you a galvanic shock of strength. Then and then alone you are a Hindu when every man who bears the name, from any country, speaking our language or any other language, becomes at once the nearest and the dearest to you. Then and then alone you are a Hindu when the distress of anyone bearing that name comes to your heart and makes you feel as if your own son were in distress. Then and then alone you are a Hindu when you will be ready to bear everything for them, like the great example I have quoted at the beginning of this lecture, of your great Guru Govind Singh. Driven out from this country, fighting against its oppressors, after having shed his own blood for the defence of the Hindu religion, after having seen his children killed on the battlefield—ay, this example of the great Guru, left even by those for whose sake he was shedding his blood and the blood of his own nearest and dearest—he, the wounded lion, retired from the field calmly to die in the South, but not a word of curse escaped his lips against those who had ungratefully forsaken him! Mark me, every one of you will have to be a Govind Singh, if you want to do good to your country. You may see thousands of defects in your countrymen, but mark their Hindu blood. They are the first Gods you will have to worship even if they do everything to hurt you, even if everyone of them send out a curse to you, you send out to them words of love. If they drive you out, retire to die in silence like that mighty lion, Govind Singh. Such a man is worthy of the name of Hindu; such an ideal ought to be before us always. All our hatchets let us bury; send out this grand current of love all round.

Let them talk of India's regeneration as they like. Let me tell you as one who has been working—at least trying to work—all his life, that there is no regeneration for India until you be spiritual. Not only so, but upon it depends the welfare of the whole world. For I must tell you frankly that the very foundations of Western civilisation have been shaken to their base. The mightiest buildings, if built upon the loose sand foundations of materialism, must come to grief one day, must totter to their destruction some day. The history of the world is our witness. Nation after nation has arisen and based its greatness upon materialism, declaring man was all matter. Ay, in Western language, a man gives up the ghost, but in our language a man gives up his body. The Western man is a body first, and then he has a soul; with us a man is a soul and

spirit, and he has a body. Therein lies a world of difference. All such civilisations, therefore, as have been based upon such sand foundations as material comfort and all that, have disappeared one after another, after short lives, from the face of the world; but the civilisation of India and the other nations that have stood at India's feet to listen and learn, namely, Japan and China, live even to the present day, and there are signs even of revival among them. Their lives are like that of the Phoenix, a thousand times destroyed, but ready to spring up again more glorious. But a materialistic civilisation once dashed down, never can come up again; that building once thrown down is broken into pieces once for all. Therefore have patience and wait, the future is in store for us.

Do not be in a hurry, do not go out to imitate anybody else. This is another great lesson we have to remember; imitation is not civilisation. I may deck myself out in a Raja's dress, but will that make me a Raja? An ass in a lion's skin never makes a lion. Imitation, cowardly imitation, never makes for progress. It is verily the sign of awful degradation in a man. Ay, when a man has begun to hate himself, then the last blow has come. When a man has begun to be ashamed of his ancestors, the end has come. Here am I, one of the least of the Hindu race, yet proud of my race, proud of my ancestors. I am proud to call myself a Hindu, I am proud that I am one of your unworthy servants. I am proud that I am a countryman of yours, you the descendants of the sages, you the descendants of the most glorious Rishis the world ever saw. Therefore have faith in yourselves, be proud of your ancestors, instead of being ashamed of them. And do not imitate, do not imitate! Whenever you are under the thumb of others, you lose your own independence. If you are working, even in spiritual things, at the dictation of others, slowly you lose all faculty, even of thought. Bring out through your own exertions what you have, but do not imitate, yet take what is good from others. We have to learn from others. You put the seed in the ground, and give it plenty of earth, and air, and water to feed upon; when the seed grows into the plant and into a gigantic tree, does it become the earth, does it become the air, or does it become the water? It becomes the mighty plant, the mighty tree, after its own nature, having absorbed everything that was given to it. Let that be your position. We have indeed many things to learn from others, yea, that man who refuses to learn is already dead. Declares our Manu: आददीत परां विद्यां प्रयत्नादवरादपि अन्त्यादपि परं धर्मं सुतरीरत्नं दुष्कुलादपि—"Take the jewel of a woman for your wife, though she be of inferior descent. Learn supreme knowledge with service even from the man of low birth; and even from the Chandâla, learn by serving him the way to salvation." Learn everything that is good from others, but bring it in, and in your own way absorb it; do not become others. Do not be dragged away out of this Indian life; do not for a moment think that it would be better for India if all the Indians dressed, ate, and behaved like another race. You know the difficulty of giving up a habit of a few years. The Lord knows how many thousands of years are in your blood; this national specialised life has been flowing in one way, the Lord knows for how many thousands of years; and do you mean to say that that mighty stream, which has nearly reached its ocean, can go back to the snows of its Himalayas again? That is impossible! The struggle to do so would only break it. Therefore, make way for the life-current of the nation. Take away the blocks that bar the way to the progress of this mighty river, cleanse its path, dear the channel, and out it will rush by its own natural impulse, and the nation will go on careering and progressing.

These are the lines which I beg to suggest to you for spiritual work in India. There are many other great problems which, for want of time, I cannot bring before you this night. For instance, there is the wonderful question of caste. I have been studying this question, its pros and cons, all my life; I have studied it in nearly every province in India. I have mixed with people of all castes in nearly every part of the country, and I am too bewildered in my own mind to grasp even the very significance of it. The more I try to study it, the more I get bewildered. Still at last I find that a little glimmer of light is before me, I begin to feel its significance just now. Then there is the other great problem about eating and drinking. That is a great problem indeed. It is not so useless a thing as we generally think. I have come to the conclusion that the insistence which we make now about eating and drinking is most curious and is just going against what the Shastras required, that is to say, we come to grief by neglecting the proper purity of the food we eat and drink; we have lost the true spirit of it.

There are several other questions which I want to bring before you and show how these problems can be solved, how to work out the ideas; but unfortunately the meeting could not come to order until very late, and I do not wish to detain you any longer now. I will, therefore, keep my ideas about caste and other things for a future occasion.

Now, one word more and I will finish about these spiritual ideas. Religion for a long time has come to be static in India. What we want is to make it dynamic. I want it to be brought into the life of everybody. Religion, as it always has been in the past, must enter the palaces of kings as well as the homes of the poorest peasants in the land. Religion, the common inheritance, the universal birthright of the race, must be brought free to the door of everybody. Religion in India must be made as free and as easy of access as is God's air. And this is the kind of work we have to bring about in India, but not by getting up little sects and fighting on points of difference. Let us preach where we all agree and leave the differences to remedy themselves. As I have said to the Indian people again and again, if there is the darkness of centuries in a room and we go into the room and begin to cry, "Oh, it is dark, it is dark!", will the darkness go? Bring in the light and the darkness will vanish at once. This is the secret of reforming men. Suggest to them higher things; believe in man first. Why start with the belief that man is degraded and degenerated? I have never failed in my faith in man in any case, even taking him

at his worst. Wherever I had faith in man, though at first the prospect was not always bright, yet it triumphed in the long run. Have faith in man, whether he appears to you to be a very learned one or a most ignorant one. Have faith in man, whether he appears to be an angel or the very devil himself. Have faith in man first, and then having faith in him, believe that if there are defects in him, if he makes mistakes, if he embraces the crudest and the vilest doctrines, believe that it is not from his real nature that they come, but from the want of higher ideals. If a man goes towards what is false, it is because he cannot get what is true. Therefore the only method of correcting what is false is by supplying him with what is true. Do this, and let him compare. You give him the truth, and there your work is done. Let him compare it in his own mind with what he has already in him; and, mark my words, if you have really given him the truth, the false must vanish, light must dispel darkness, and truth will bring the good out. This is the way if you want to reform the country spiritually; this is the way, and not fighting, not even telling people that what they are doing is bad. Put the good before them, see how eagerly they take it, see how the divine that never dies, that is always living in the human, comes up awakened and stretches out its hand for all that is good, and all that is glorious.

May He who is the Creator, the Preserver, and the Protector of our race, the God of our forefathers, whether called by the name of Vishnu, or Shiva, or Shakti, or Ganapati, whether He is worshipped as Saguna or as Nirguna, whether He is worshipped as personal or as impersonal, may He whom our forefathers knew and addressed by the words, एकं सद्विप्रा बहुधा वदन्ति । — "That which exists is One; sages call Him by various names" — may He enter into us with His mighty love; may He shower His blessings on us, may He make us understand each other, may He make us work for each other with real love, with intense love for truth, and may not the least desire for our own personal fame, our own personal prestige, our own personal advantage, enter into this great work of the spiritual regeneration of India!

BHAKTI

Delivered at Lahore on the 9th November, 1897

There is a sound which comes to us like a distant echo in the midst of the roaring torrents of the Upanishads, at times rising in proportion and volume, and yet, throughout the literature of the Vedanta, its voice, though clear, is not very strong. The main duty of the Upanishads seems to be to present before us the spirit and the aspect of the sublime, and yet behind this wonderful sublimity there come to us here and there glimpses of poetry as we read: न तत्र सूर्यो भाति न चंद्रतारकं नेमा विद्युतो भान्ति कुतोऽयमग्निः — "There the sun shines not, nor the moon, nor the stars, what to speak of this fire?" As we listen to the heart-stirring poetry of these marvellous lines, we are taken, as it were, off from the world of the senses, off even from the world of intellect, and brought to that world which can never be comprehended, and yet which is always with us. There is behind even this sublimity another ideal following as its shadow, one more acceptable to mankind, one more of daily use, one that has to enter into every part of human life, which assumes proportion and volume later on, and is stated in full and determined language in the Purâna, and that is the ideal of Bhakti. The germs of Bhakti are there already; the germs are even in the Samhitâ; the germs a little more developed are in the Upanishads; but they are worked out in their details in the Puranas.

To understand Bhakti, therefore, we have got to understand these Puranas of ours. There have been great discussions of late as to their authenticity. Many a passage of uncertain meaning has been taken up and criticised. In many places it has been pointed out that the passages cannot stand the light of modern science and so forth. But, apart from all these discussions, apart from the scientific validity of the statements of the Puranas, apart from their valid or invalid geography, apart from their valid or invalid astronomy, and so forth, what we find for a certainty, traced out bit by bit almost in every one of these volumes, is this doctrine of Bhakti, illustrated, reillustrated, stated and restated, in the lives of saints and in the lives of kings. It seems to have been the duty of the Puranas to stand as illustrations for that great ideal of the beautiful, the ideal of Bhakti, and this, as I have stated, is so much nearer to the ordinary man. Very few indeed are there who can understand end appreciate, far less live and move, in the grandeur of the full blaze of the light of Vedanta, because the first step for the pure Vedantist is to be Abhih, fearless. Weakness has got to go before a man dares to become a Vedantist, and we know how difficult that is. Even those who have given up all connection with the world, and have very few bandages to make them cowards, feel in the heart of their hearts how weak they are at moments, at times how soft they become, how cowed down; much more so is it with men who have so many bandages, and have to remain as slaves to so many hundred and thousand things, inside of themselves and outside of themselves, men every moment of whose life is dragging-down slavery. To them the Puranas come with the most beautiful message of Bhakti.

For them the softness and the poetry are spread out, for them are told these wonderful and marvellous stories of a Dhruva and a Prahlâda, and of a thousand saints, and these illustrations are to make it practical. Whether you believe in the scientific accuracy of the Puranas or not, there is not one among you whose life has not been influenced by the story of Prahlada, or that of Dhruva, or of any one of these great Paurânika saints. We have not only to acknowledge the power of the Puranas in our own day, but we ought to be grateful to them as they gave us in the past a more comprehensive and a better popular religion than what the degraded later-day Buddhism was leading us to. This easy and smooth idea of Bhakti has been written and worked upon, and we have to embrace it in our everyday practical life, for we shall see as we go on

how the idea has been worked out until Bhakti becomes the essence of love. So long as there shall be such a thing as personal and material love, one cannot go behind the teachings of the Puranas. So long as there shall be the human weakness of leaning upon somebody for support, these Puranas, in some form or other, must always exist. You can change their names; you can condemn those that are already existing, but immediately you will be compelled to write another Purana. If there arises amongst us a sage who will not want these old Puranas, we shall find that his disciples, within twenty years of his death, will make of his life another Purana. That will be all the difference.

This is a necessity of the nature of man; for them only are there no Puranas who have gone beyond all human weakness and have become what is really wanted of a Paramahamsa, brave and bold souls, who have gone beyond the bandages of Mâyâ, the necessities even of nature—the triumphant, the conquerors, the gods of the world. The ordinary man cannot do without a personal God to worship; if he does not worship a God in nature, he has to worship either a God in the shape of a wife, or a child, or a father, or a friend, or a teacher, or somebody else; and the necessity is still more upon women than men. The vibration of light may be everywhere; it may be in dark places, since cats and other animals perceive it, but for us the vibration must be in our plane to become visible. We may talk, therefore, of an Impersonal Being and so forth, but so long as we are ordinary mortals, God can be seen in man alone. Our conception of God and our worship of God are naturally, therefore, human. "This body, indeed, is the greatest temple of God." So we find that men have been worshipped throughout the ages, and although we may condemn or criticise some of the extravagances which naturally follow, we find at once that the heart is sound, that in spite of these extravagances, in spite of this going into extremes, there is an essence, there is a true, firm core, a backbone, to the doctrine that is preached. I am not asking you to swallow without consideration any old stories, or any unscientific jargon. I am not calling upon you to believe in all sorts of Vâmâchâri explanations that, unfortunately, have crept into some of the Puranas, but what I mean is this, that there is an essence which ought not to be lost, a reason for the existence of the Puranas, and that is the teaching of Bhakti to make religion practical, to bring religion from its high philosophical flights into the everyday lives of our common human beings.

Note: The lecturer defended the use of material helps in Bhakti. Would to God man did not stand where he is, but it is useless to fight against existing facts; man is a material being now, however he may talk about spirituality and all that. Therefore the material man has to be taken in hand and slowly raised, until he becomes spiritual. In these days it is hard for 99 per cent of us to understand spirituality, much more so to talk about it. The motive powers that are pushing us forward, and the efforts we are seeking to attain, are all material. We can only work, in the language of Her-bert Spencer, in the line of least resistance, and the Puranas have the good and common sense to work in the line of least resistance; and the successes that have been attained by the Puranas have been marvellous and unique. The ide-al of Bhakti is of course spiritual, but the way lies through matter and we cannot help it. Everything that is conducive to the attainment of this spirituality in the material world, therefore, is to be taken hold of and brought to the use of man to evolve the spiritual being. Having pointed out that the Shâstras start by giving the right to study the Vedas to everybody, without distinction of sex, caste, or creed, he claimed that if making a material temple helps a man more to love God, welcome; if making an image of God helps a man in attaining to this ideal of love, Lord bless him and give him twenty such images if he pleases. If anything helps him to attain to that ideal of spirituality welcome, so long as it is moral, because anything immoral will not help, but will only retard. He traced the opposition to the use of im-ages in worship in India partly at least to Kabir, but on the other hand showed that India Has had great philosophers and founders of religions who did not even believe in the existence of a Personal God and boldly preached that to the people, but yet did not condemn the use of images. At best they only said it was not a very high form of worship, and there was not one of the Puranas in which it was said that it was a very high form. Having referred historical-ly to the use of image-worship by the Jews, in their belief that Jehovah resided in a chest, he condemned the practice of abusing idol-worship merely because others said it was bad. Though an image or any other material form could be used if it helped to make a man spiritual, yet there was no one book in our religion which did not very clearly state that it was the lowest form of worship, because it was wor-ship through matter. The attempt that was made all over India to force this image-worship on everybody, he had no language to condemn; what business had anybody to direct and dictate to anyone what he should worship and through what? How could any other man know through what he would grow, whether his spiritual growth would be by wor-shipping an image, by worshipping fire, or by worshipping even a pillar? That was to be guided and directed by our own Gurus, and by the relation between the Guru and the Shishya. That explained the rule which Bhakti books laid down for what was called the Ishta, that was to say, that each man had to take up his own peculiar form of worship, his own way of going towards God, and that chosen ide-al was his Ishta Devatâ. He was to regard other forms of worship with sympathy, but at the same time to practice his own form till he reached the goal and came to the centre where no more material helps were necessary for him. In this connection a word of warning was necessary against a system prevalent in some parts of India, what was called the Kula-Guru system, a sort of hereditary Guruism. We read in the books that "He who knows the essence of the Vedas, is sinless, and does not teach another for love of gold or love of anything else, whose mercy is without any cause, who gives as the spring which does not ask anything from the plants and trees, for it is its nature to do good, and brings them out once more into life, and buds, flowers, and leaves come out, who wants nothing, but whose whole life is only to do good"—such a man could be a Guru and none else. There was another danger, for a Guru was not a teacher alone; that was a very small part of it. The Guru, as the Hindus believed, transmitted spirituality to his dis-ciples. To take a common material example, therefore, if a man were not inoculated with good virus, he ran the risk of being inoculated with what was bad and vile, so that by being taught by a bad Guru there was the risk of learning something evil. Therefore it was absolutely necessary that this idea of Kula-Guru should vanish from India. Guruism must not be a trade; that must stop, it was against the Shas-tras. No man ought to call himself a Guru and at the same time help the present state of things under the Kula-Guru system.

Speaking of the question of food, the Swami pointed out that the present-day insistence upon the strict regulations as to eating was to a great extent superficial, and missed the mark they were originally intended to cover. He par-ticularly instanced the idea that care should be exercised as to who was allowed to touch food, and pointed out that there was a deep psychological significance in this, but that in the everyday life of ordinary men it was a care difficult or impossible to exercise. Here again the mistake was made of insisting upon a general observance of an idea which was only possible to one class, those who have entirely devoted their lives to spirituality, whereas the vast majority of men were still unsatiated with material pleasures, and until they were satiated to some extent it was useless to think of forc-ing spirituality on them.

The highest form of worship that had been laid down by the Bhakta was the worship of man. Really, if there were to be any sort of worship, he would suggest getting a poor man, or six, or twelve, as their circumstances would per-mit, every day to their homes, and serving them, thinking that they were Nârâyanas. He had seen charity in many countries and the reason it did not succeed was that it was not done with a good spirit. "Here, take this, and go away"—that was not charity, but the expression of the pride of the heart, to gain the applause of the world, that the world might know they were becoming charitable. Hin-dus must know that, according to the Smritis, the giver was lower than the receiver, for the receiver was for the time be-ing God Himself. Therefore he would suggest such a form of worship as getting some of these poor Narayanas, or blind Narayanas, and hungry Narayanas into every house every day, and giving them the worship they would give to an image, feeding them and clothing them, and the next day doing the same to others. He did not condemn any form of worship, but what he went to say was that the highest form and the most necessary at present in India was this form of Narayana worship.

In conclusion, he likened Bhakti to a triangle. The first angle was that love knew no want, the second that love knew fear. Love for reward or service of any kind was the beggar's religion, the shopkeeper's religion, with very little of real religion in it. Let them not become beggars, because, in the first place, beggary was the sign of atheism. "Foolish indeed is the man who living on the banks of the Ganga digs a little well to drink water." So is the man who begs of God material objects. The Bhakta should be ready to stand up and say, "I do not want anything from you, Lord, but if you need anything from me I am ready to give." Love knew no fear. Had they not seen a weak frail, little woman passing through a street, and if a dog barked, she flew off into the next house? The next day she was in the street, perhaps, with her child at her breast. And a lion attacked her. Where was she then? In the mouth of the lion to save her child. Lastly, love was unto love itself. The Bhakta at last comes to this, that love itself is God and nothing else. Where should man go to prove the existence of God? Love was the most visible of all visible things. It was the force that was moving the sun, the moon, and the stars, manifesting itself in men, women, and in animals, everywhere and in everything. It was expressed in material forces as gravitation and so on. It was everywhere, in every atom, manifesting everywhere. It was that infinite love, the only motive power of this universe, visible everywhere, and this was God Himself[1].

THE VEDANTA

Delivered at Lahore on 12th November, 1897

Two worlds there are in which we live, one the external, the other internal. Human progress has been made, from days of yore, almost in parallel lines along both these worlds. The search began in the external, and man at first wanted to get answers for all the deep problems from outside nature. Man wanted to satisfy his thirst for the beautiful and the sublime from all that surrounded him; he wanted to express himself and all that was within him in the language of the concrete; and grand indeed were the answers he got, most marvellous ideas of God and worship, and most rapturous expressions of the beautiful. Sublime ideas came from the external world indeed. But the other, opening out for humanity later, laid out before him a universe yet sublimer, yet more beautiful, and infinitely more expansive. In the Karma Kânda portion of the Vedas, we find the most wonderful ideas of religion inculcated, we find the most wonderful ideas about an overruling Creator, Preserver, and Destroyer of the universe presented before us in language sometimes the most soul-stirring. Most

of you perhaps remember that most wonderful Shloka in the Rig-Veda Samhitâ where you get the description of chaos, perhaps the sublimest that has ever been attempted yet. In spite of all this, we find it is only a painting of the sublime outside, we find that yet it is gross, that something of matter yet clings to it. Yet we find that it is only the expression of the Infinite in; the language of matter, in the language of the finite, it is,. the infinite of the muscles and not of the mind; it is the infinite of space and not of thought. Therefore in the second portion of Jnâna Kânda, we find there is altogether a different procedure. The first was a search in external nature for the truths of the universe; it was an attempt to get the solution of the deep problems of life from the material world. यस्येते हिमवन्तो महित्वा— "Whose glory these Himalayas declare". This is a grand idea, but yet it was not grand enough for India. The Indian mind had to fall back, and the research took a different direction altogether; from the external the search came to the internal, from matter to mind. There arose the cry, "When a man dies, what becomes of him?" अस्तीत्येके नायमस्तीति चेके— "Some say that he exists, others that he is gone; say, O king of Death, what is the truth?" An entirely different procedure we find here. The Indian mind got all that could be had from the external world, but it did not feel satisfied with that; it wanted to search further, to dive into its own soul, and the final answer came.

The Upanishads, or the Vedanta, or the Âranyakas, or Rahasya is the name of this portion of the Vedas. Here we find at once that religion has got rid of all external formalities. Here we find at once that spiritual things are told not in the language of matter, but in the language of the spirit; the superfine in the language of the superfine. No more any grossness attaches to it, no more is there any compromise with things of worldly concern. Bold, brave, beyond the conception of the present day, stand the giant minds of the sages of the Upanishads, declaring the noblest truths that have ever been preached to humanity, without any compromise, without any fear. This, my countrymen, I want to lay before you. Even the Jnana Kanda of the Vedas is a vast ocean; many lives are necessary to understand even a little of it. Truly has it been said of the Upanishads by Râmânuja that they form the head, the shoulders, the crest of the Vedas, and surely enough the Upanishads have become the Bible of modern India. The Hindus have the greatest respect for the Karma Kanda of the Vedas, but, for all practical purposes, we know that for ages by Shruti has been meant the Upanishads, and the Upanishads alone. We know that all our great philosophers, whether Vyâsa, Patanjali, or Gautama, and even the father of all philosophy, the great Kapila himself, whenever they wanted an authority for what they wrote, everyone of them found it in the Upanishads, and nowhere else, for therein are the truths that remain for ever.

There are truths that are true only in a certain line, in a certain direction, under certain circumstances, and for certain times—those that are founded on the institutions of the times. There are other truths which are based on the nature

1. From the report published in *The Tribune*.

of man himself, and which must endure so long as man himself endures. These are the truths that alone can be universal, and in spite of all the changes that have come to India, as to our social surroundings, our methods of dress, our manner of eating, our modes of worship—these universal truths of the Shrutis, the marvellous Vedantic ideas, stand out in their own sublimity, immovable, unvanquishable, deathless, and immortal. Yet the germs of all the ideas that were developed in the Upanishads had been taught already in the Karma Kanda. The idea of the cosmos which all sects of Vedantists had to take for granted, the psychology which has formed the common basis of all the Indian schools of thought, had there been worked out already and presented before the world. A few words, therefore, about the Karma Kanda are necessary before we begin the spiritual portion, the Vedanta; and first of all I should like to explain the sense in which I use the word Vedanta.

Unfortunately there is the mistaken notion in modern India that the word Vedanta has reference only to the Advaita system; but you must always remember that in modern India the three Prasthânas are considered equally important in the study of all the systems of religion. First of all there are the Revelations, the Shrutis, by which I mean the Upanishads. Secondly, among our philosophies, the Sutras of Vyasa have the greatest prominence on account of their being the consummation of all the preceding systems of philosophy. These systems are not contradictory to one another, but one is based on another, and there is a gradual unfolding of the theme which culminates in the Sutras of Vyasa. Then, between the Upanishads and the Sutras, which are the systematising of the marvellous truths of the Vedanta, comes in the Gita, the divine commentary of the Vedanta.

The Upanishads, the Vyâsa-Sutras, and the Gita, therefore, have been taken up by every sect in India that wants to claim authority for orthodoxy, whether dualist, or Vishishtâdvaitist, or Advaitist; the authorities of each of these are the three Prasthanas. We find that a Shankaracharya, or a Râmânuja, or a Madhvâchârya, or a Vallabhâchârya, or a Chaitanya—any one who wanted to propound a new sect—had to take up these three systems and write only a new commentary on them. Therefore it would be wrong to confine the word Vedanta only to one system which has arisen out of the Upanishads. All these are covered by the word Vedanta. The Vishishtadvaitist has as much right to be called a Vedantist as the Advaitist; in fact I will go a little further and say that what we really mean by the word Hindu is really the same as Vedantist. I want you to note that these three systems have been current in India almost from time immemorial; for you must not believe that Shankara was the inventor of the Advaita system. It existed ages before Shankara was born; he was one of its last representatives. So with the Vishishtadvaita system: it had existed ages before Ramanuja appeared, as we already know from the commentaries he has written; so with the dualistic systems that have existed side by side with the others. And

with my little knowledge, I have come to the conclusion that they do not contradict each other.

Just as in the case of the six Darshanas, we find they are a gradual unfolding of the grand principles whose music beginning far back in the soft low notes, ends in the triumphant blast of the Advaita, so also in these three systems we find the gradual working up of the human mind towards higher and higher ideals till everything is merged in that wonderful unity which is reached in the Advaita system. Therefore these three are not contradictory. On the other hand I am bound to tell you that this has been a mistake committed by not a few. We find that an Advaitist teacher keeps intact those texts which especially teach Advaitism, and tries to interpret the dualistic or qualified non-dualistic texts into his own meaning. Similarly we find dualistic teachers trying to read their dualistic meaning into Advaitic texts. Our Gurus were great men, yet there is a saying, "Even the faults of a Guru must be told". I am of Opinion that in this only they were mistaken. We need not go into text-torturing, we need not go into any sort of religious dishonesty, we need not go into any sort of grammatical twaddle, we need not go about trying to put our own ideas into texts which were never meant for them, but the work is plain and becomes easier, once you understand the marvellous doctrine of Adhikârabheda.

It is true that the Upanishads have this one theme before them: कस्मिन्नु भगवो विज्ञाते सर्वमिदं विज्ञातं भवति—"What is that knowing which we know everything else?" In modern language, the theme of the Upanishads is to find an ultimate unity of things. Knowledge is nothing but finding unity in the midst of diversity. Every science is based upon this; all human knowledge is based upon the finding of unity in the midst of diversity; and if it is the task of small fragments of human knowledge, which we call our sciences, to find unity in the midst of a few different phenomena, the task becomes stupendous when the theme before us is to find unity in the midst of this marvellously diversified universe, where prevail unnumbered differences in name and form, in matter and spirit—each thought differing from every other thought, each form differing from every other form. Yet, to harmonise these many planes and unending Lokas, in the midst of this infinite variety to find unity, is the theme of the Upanishads. On the other hand, the old idea of Arundhati Nyâya applies. To show a man the fine star Arundhati, one takes the big and brilliant nearest to it, upon which he is asked to fix his eyes first, and then it becomes quite easy to direct his sight to Arundhati. This is the task before us, and to prove my idea I have simply to show you the Upanishads, and you will see it. Nearly every chapter begins with dualistic teaching, Upâsanâ. God is first taught as some one who is the Creator of this universe, its Preserver, and unto whom everything goes at last. He is one to be worshipped, the Ruler, the Guide of nature, external and internal, yet appearing as if He were outside of nature and external. One step further, and we find the same teacher teaching that this God is not outside of nature, but immanent in nature. And at last both ideas are discarded, and whatever is real is He; there is no difference. तत्त्वमसि श्वेतकेतो — "Shvetaketu, That thou art." That Immanent One is at last declared to be the same that is in the human soul. Here is no Compromise; here is no fear of others' opinions. Truth, bold truth, has been taught in bold language, and we need not fear to preach the truth in the same bold language today, and, by the grace of God, I hope at least to be one who dares to be that bold preacher.

To go back to our preliminaries. There are first two things to be understood — one, the psychological aspect common to all the Vedantic schools, and the other, the cosmological aspect. I will first take up the latter. Today we find wonderful discoveries of modern science coming upon us like bolts from the blue, opening our eyes to marvels we never dreamt of. But many of these are only re-discoveries of what had been found ages ago. It was only the other day that modern science found that even in the midst of the variety of forces there is unity. It has just discovered that what it calls heat, magnetism, electricity, and so forth, are all convertible into one unit force, and as such, it expresses all these by one name, whatever you may choose to call it. But this has been done even in the Samhita; old and ancient as it is, in it we meet with this very idea of force I was referring to. All the forces, whether you call them gravitation, or attraction, or repulsion, whether expressing themselves as heat, or electricity, or magnetism, are nothing but the variations of that unit energy. Whether they express themselves as thought, reflected from Antahkarana, the inner organs of man, or as action from an external organ, the unit from which they spring is what is called Prâna. Again, what is Prana? Prana is Spandana or vibration. When all this universe shall have resolved back into its primal state, what becomes of this infinite force? Do they think that it becomes extinct? Of course not. If it became extinct, what would be the cause of the next wave, because the motion is going in wave forms, rising, falling, rising again, falling again? Here is the word Srishti, which expresses the universe. Mark that the word does not mean creation. I am helpless in talking English; I have to translate the Sanskrit words as best as I can. It is Srishti, projection. At the end of a cycle, everything becomes finer and finer and is resolved back into the primal state from which it sprang, and there it remains for a time quiescent, ready to spring forth again. That is Srishti, projection. And what becomes of all these forces, the Pranas? They are resolved back into the primal Prana, and this Prana becomes almost motionless — not entirely motionless; and that is what is described in the Vedic Sukta: "It vibrated without vibrations" — Ânidavâtam. There are many technical phrases in the Upanishads difficult to understand. For instance, take this word Vâta; many times it means air and many times motion, and often people confuse one with the other. We must guard against that. And what becomes of what you call matter? The forces permeate all matter; they all dissolve into Âkâsha, from which they again come out; this Akasha is the primal matter.

Whether you translate it as ether or anything else, the idea is that this Akasha is the primal form of matter. This Akasha vibrates under the action of Prana, and when the next Srishti is coming up, as the vibration becomes quicker, the Akasha is lashed into all these wave forms which we call suns, moons, and systems.

We read again: यदिदं किंच जगत् सर्व प्राण एजति निःसृतम् — "Everything in this universe has been projected, Prana vibrating." You must mark the word Ejati, because it comes from Eja — to vibrate. Nihsritam — projected. Yadidam Kincha — whatever in this universe.

This is a part of the cosmological side. There are many details working into it. For instance, how the process takes place, how there is first ether, and how from the ether come other things, how that ether begins to vibrate, and from that Vâyu comes. But the one idea is here that it is from the finer that the grosser has come. Gross matter is the last to emerge and the most external, and this gross matter had the finer matter before it. Yet we see that the whole thing has been resolved into two, but there is not yet a final unity. There is the unity of force, Prana, there is the unity of matter, called Akasha. Is there any unity to be found among them again? Can they be melted into one? Our modern science is mute here, it has not yet found its way out; and if it is doing so, just as it has been slowly finding the same old Prana and the same ancient Akasha, it will have to move along the same lines.

The next unity is the omnipresent impersonal Being known by its old mythological name as Brahmâ, the fourheaded Brahma and psychologically called Mahat. This is where the two unite. What is called your mind is only a bit of this Mahat caught in the trap of the brain, and the sum total of all minds caught in the meshes of brains is what you call Samashti, the aggregate, the universal. Analysis had to go further; it was not yet complete. Here we were each one of us, as it were, a microcosm, and the world taken altogether is the macrocosm. But whatever is in the Vyashti, the particular, we may safely conjecture that a similar thing is happening also outside. If we had the power to analyse our own minds, we might safely conjecture that the same thing is happening in the cosmic mind. What is this mind is the question. In modern times, in Western countries, as physical science is making rapid progress, as physiology is step by step conquering stronghold after stronghold of old religions, the Western people do not know where to stand, because to their great despair, modern physiology at every step has identified the mind with the brain. But we in India have known that always. That is the first proposition the Hindu boy learns that the mind is matter, only finer. The body is gross, and behind the body is what we call the Sukshma Sharira, the fine body, or mind. This is also material, only finer; and it is not the Âtman.

I will not translate this word to you in English, because the idea does not exist in Europe; it is untranslatable. The modern attempt of German philosophers is to translate the word

Atman by the word "Self", and until that word is universally accepted, it is impossible to use it. So, call it as Self or anything, it is our Atman. This Atman is the real man behind. It is the Atman that uses the material mind as its instrument, its Antahkarana, as is the psychological term for the mind. And the mind by means of a series of internal organs works the visible organs of the body. What is this mind? It was only the other day that Western philosophers have come to know that the eyes are not the real organs of vision, but that behind these are other organs, the Indriyas, and if these are destroyed, a man may have a thousand eyes, like Indra, but there will be no sight for him. Ay, your philosophy starts with this assumption that by vision is not meant the external vision. The real vision belongs to the internal organs, the brain-centres inside. You may call them what you like, but it is not that the Indriyas are the eyes, or the nose, or the ears. And the sum total of all these Indriyas plus the Manas, Buddhi, Chitta, Ahamkâra, etc., is what is called the mind, and if the modern physiologist comes to tell you that the brain is what is called the mind, and that the brain is formed of so many organs, you need not be afraid at all; tell him that your philosophers knew it always; it is one of the very first principles of your religion.

Well then, we have to understand now what is meant by this Manas, Buddhi, Chitta, Ahamkara, etc. First of all, let us take Chitta. It is the mind-stuff—a part of the Mahat—it is the generic name for the mind itself, including all its various states. Suppose on a summer evening, there is a lake, smooth and calm, without a ripple on its surface. And suppose some one throws a stone into this lake. What happens? First there is the action, the blow given to the water; next the water rises and sends a reaction towards the stone, and that reaction takes the form of a wave. First the water vibrates a little, and immediately sends back a reaction in the form of a wave. The Chitta let us compare to this lake, and the external objects are like the stones thrown into it. As soon as it comes in contact with any external object by means of these Indriyas—the Indriyas must be there to carry these external objects inside—there is a vibration, what is called Manas, indecisive. Next there is a reaction, the determinative faculty, Buddhi, and along with this Buddhi flashes the idea of Aham and the external object. Suppose there is a mosquito sitting upon my hand. This sensation is carried to my Chitta and it vibrates a little; this is the psychological Manas. Then there is a reaction, and immediately comes the idea that I have a mosquito on my hand and that I shall have to drive it off. Thus these stones are thrown into the lake, but in the case of the lake every blow that comes to it is from the external world, while in the case of the lake of the mind, the blows may either come from the external world or the internal world. This whose series is what is called the Antahkarana.

Along with it, you ought to understand one thing more that will help us in understanding the Advaita system later on. It is this. All of you must have seen pearls and most of you know how pearls are formed. A grain of sand enters into the shell of a pearl oyster, and sets up an irritation there, and the oyster's body reacts towards the irritation and covers the little particle with its own juice. That crystallises and forms the pearl. So the whole universe is like that, it is the pearl which is being formed by us. What we get from the external world is simply the blow. Even to be conscious of that blow we have to react, and as soon as we react, we really project a portion of our own mind towards the blow, and when we come to know of it, it is really our own mind as it has been shaped by the blow. Therefore it is clear even to those who want to believe in a hard and fast realism of an external world, which they cannot but admit in these days of physiology—that supposing we represent the external world by "x", what we really know is "x" plus mind, and this mind-element is so great that it has covered the whole of that "x" which has remained unknown and unknowable throughout; and, therefore, if there is an external world, it is always unknown and unknowable. What we know of it is as it is moulded, formed, fashioned by our own mind. So with the internal world. The same applies to our own soul, the Atman. In order to know the Atman we shall have to know It through the mind; and, therefore, what little eve know of this Atman is simply the Atman plus the mind. That is to say, the Atman covered over, fashioned and moulded by the mind, and nothing more. We shall return to this a little later, but we will remember what has been told here.

The next thing to understand is this. The question arose that this body is the name of one continuous stream of matter—every moment we are adding material to it, and every moment material is being thrown oft by it—like a river continually flowing, vast masses of water always changing places; yet all the same, we take up the whole thing in imagination, and call it the same river. What do we call the river? Every moment the water is changing, the shore is changing, every moment the environment is changing, what is the river then? It is the name of this series of changes. So with the mind. That is the great Kshanika Vijnâna Vâda doctrine, most difficult to understand, but most rigorously and logically worked out in the Buddhistic philosophy; and this arose in India in opposition to some part of the Vedanta. That had to be answered and we shall see later on how it could only be answered by Advaitism and by nothing else. We will see also how, in spite of people's curious notions about Advaitism, people's fright about Advaitism, it is the salvation of the world, because therein alone is to be found the reason of things. Dualism and other isms are very good as means of worship, very satisfying to the mind, and maybe, they have helped the mind onward; but if man wants to be rational and religious at the same time, Advaita is the one system in the world for him. Well, now, we shall regard the mind as a similar river, continually filling itself at one end and emptying itself at the other end. Where is that unity which we call the Atman? The idea is this, that in spite of this continuous change in the body, and in spite of this continuous change in the mind, there is in us something that is unchangeable, which makes our ideas of things appear unchangeable. When rays of light coming from different quarters fall upon a screen, or a wall, or upon something that is not changeable, then and then alone it is possible for them to form a unity, then and then alone it is possible for them to form one complete whole. Where is this unity in the human organs, falling upon which, as it were, the various ideas will come to unity and become one complete whole? This certainly cannot be the mind itself, seeing that it also changes. Therefore there must be something which is neither the body nor the mind, something which changes not, something permanent, upon which all our ideas, our sensations fall to form a unity and a complete whole; and this is the real soul, the Atman of man. And seeing that everything material, whether you call it fine matter, or mind, must be changeful, seeing that what you call gross matter, the external world, must also be changeful in comparison to that—this unchangeable something cannot be of material substance; therefore it is spiritual, that is to say, it is not matter—it is indestructible, unchangeable.

Next will come another question: Apart from those old arguments which only rise in the external world, the arguments in support of design—who created this external world, who created matter, etc.? The idea here is to know truth only from the inner nature of man, and the question arises just in the same way as it arose about the soul. Taking for granted that there is a soul, unchangeable, in each man, which is neither the mind nor the body, there is still a unity of idea among the souls, a unity of feeling, of sympathy. How is it possible that my soul can act upon your soul, where is the medium through which it can work, where is the medium through which it can act? How is it I can feel anything about your souls? What is it that is in touch both with your soul and with my soul? Therefore there is a metaphysical necessity of admitting another soul, for it must be a soul which acts in contact all the different souls, and in and through matter—one Soul which covers and interpenetrates all the infinite number of souls in the world, in and through which they live, in and through which they sympathise, and love, and work for one another. And this universal Soul is Paramâtman, the Lord God of the universe. Again, it follows that because the soul is not made of matter, since it is spiritual, it cannot obey the laws of matter, it cannot be judged by the laws of matter. It is, therefore, unconquerable, birthless, deathless, and changeless.

नैनं छिन्दन्ति शस्त्राणि नैनं दहति पावकः।
न चैनं क्लेदयन्त्यापो न शोषयति मारुतः॥
नित्यः सर्वगतः स्थाणुरचलोऽयं सनातनः॥

— "This Self, weapons cannot pierce, nor fire can burn, water cannot wet, nor air can dry up. Changless, allpervading, unmoving, immovable, eternal is this Self of man." We learn according to the Gita and the Vedanta that this individual Self is also Vibhu, and according to Kapila, is omnipresent. Of course there are sects in India which hold that the Self is Anu, infinitely small; but what they mean is Anu in manifestation;

its real nature is Vibhu, all-pervading.

There comes another idea, startling perhaps, yet a characteristically Indian idea, and if there is any idea that is common to all our sects, it is this. Therefore I beg you to pay attention to this one idea and to remember it, for this is the very foundation of everything that we have in India. The idea is this. You have beard of the doctrine of physical evolution preached in the Western world by the German and the English savants. It tells us that the bodies of the different animals are really one; the differences that we see are but different expressions of the same series; that from the lowest worm to the highest and the most saintly man it is but one—the one changing into the other, and so on, going up and up, higher and higher, until it attains perfection. We had that idea also. Declares our Yogi Patanjali— जात्यन्तरपरिणामः प्रकृत्यापूरात्। One species—the Jâti is species—changes into another species—evolution; Parinâma means one thing changing into another, just as one species changes into another. Where do we differ from the Europeans? Patanjali says, Prakrityâpurât, "By the infilling of nature". The European says, it is competition, natural and sexual selection, etc. that forces one body to take the form of another. But here is another idea, a still better analysis, going deeper into the thing and saying, "By the infilling of nature". What is meant by this infilling of nature? We admit that the amoeba goes higher and higher until it becomes a Buddha; we admit that, but we are at the same time as much certain that you cannot get an amount of work out of a machine unless you have put it in in some shape or other. The sum total of the energy remains the same, whatever the forms it may take. If you want a mass of energy at one end, you have got to put it in at the other end; it may be in another form, but the amount of energy that should be produced out of it must be the same. Therefore, if a Buddha is the one end of the change, the very amoeba must have been the Buddha also. If the Buddha is the evolved amoeba, the amoeba was the involved Buddha also. If this universe is the manifestation of an almost infinite amount of energy, when this universe was in a state of Pralaya, it must have represented the same amount of involved energy. It cannot have been otherwise. As such, it follows that every soul is infinite. From the lowest worm that crawls under our feet to the noblest and greatest saints, all have this infinite power, infinite purity, and infinite everything. Only the difference is in the degree of manifestation. The worm is only manifesting just a little bit of that energy, you have manifested more, another god-man has manifested still more: that is all the difference. But that infinite power is there all the same. Says Patanjali: ततः क्षेत्रिकवत्—"Like the peasant irrigating his field." Through a little corner of his field he brings water from a reservoir somewhere, and perhaps he has got a little lock that prevents the water from rushing into his field. When he wants water, he has simply to open the lock, and in rushes the water of its own power. The power has not to be added, it is already there in the reservoir. So every one of us, every being, has as his own background such a reservoir of strength, infinite power, infinite purity, infinite bliss, and existence infinite—only these locks, these bodies, are hindering us from expressing what we really are to the fullest.

And as these bodies become more and more finely organised, as the Tamoguna becomes the Rajoguna, and as the Rajoguna becomes Sattvaguna, more and more of this power and purity becomes manifest, and therefore it is that our people have been so careful about eating and drinking, and the food question. It may be that the original ideas have been lost, just as with our marriage—which, though not belonging to the subject, I may take as an example. If I have another opportunity I will talk to you about these; but let me tell you now that the ideas behind our marriage system are the only ideas through which there can be a real civilisation. There cannot be anything else. If a man or a woman were allowed the freedom to take up any woman or man as wife or husband, if individual pleasure, satisfaction of animal instincts, were to be allowed to run loose in society, the result must be evil, evil children, wicked and demoniacal. Ay, man in every country is, on the one hand, producing these brutal children, and on the other hand multiplying the police force to keep these brutes down. The question is not how to destroy evil that way, but how to prevent the very birth of evil. And so long as you live in society your marriage certainly affects every member of it; and therefore society has the right to dictate whom you shall marry, and whom you shall not. And great ideas of this kind have been behind the system of marriage here, what they call the astrological Jati of the bride and bridegroom. And in passing I may remark that According to Manu a child who is born of lust is not an Aryan. The child whose very conception and whose death is according to the rules of the Vedas, such is an Aryan. Yes, and less of these Aryan children are being produced in every country, and the result is the mass of evil which we call Kali Yuga. But we have lost all these ideals—it is true we cannot carry all these ideas to the fullest length now—it is perfectly true we have made almost a caricature of some of these great ideas. It is lamentably true that the fathers and mothers are not what they were in old times, neither is society so educated as it used to be, neither has society that love for individuals that it used to have. But, however faulty the working out may be, the principle is sound; and if its application has become defective, if one method has failed, take up the principle and work it out better; why kill the principle? The same applies to the food question. The work and details are bad, very bad indeed, but that does not hurt the principle. The principle is eternal and must be there. Work it out afresh and make a re-formed application.

This is the orate great idea of the Atman which every one of our sects in India has to believe. Only, as we shall find, the dualists, preach that this Atman by evil works becomes Sankuchita, i.e. all its powers and its nature become contracted, and by good works again that nature expands. And the Advaitist says that the Atman never expands nor contracts, but seems to do so. It appears to have become contracted. That is all the

difference, but all have the one Idea that our Atman has all the powers already, not that anything will come to It from outside, not that anything will drop into It from the skies. Mark you, your Vedas are not inspired, but expired, not that they came from anywhere outside, but they are the eternal laws living in every soul. The Vedas are in the soul of the ant, in the soul of the god. The ant has only to evolve and get the body of a sage or a Rishi, and the Vedas will come out, eternal laws expressing themselves. This is the one great idea to understand that our power is already ours, our salvation is already within us. Say either that it has become contracted, or say that it has been covered with the veil of Mâyâ, it matters little; the idea is there already; you must have to believe in that, believe in the possibility of everybody—that even in the lowest man there is the same possibility as in the Buddha. This is the doctrine of the Atman.

But now comes a tremendous fight. Here are the Buddhists, who equally analyse the body into a material stream and as equally analyse the mind into another. And as for this Atman, they state that It is unnecessary; so we need not assume the Atman at all. What use of a substance, and qualities adhering to the substance? We say Gunas, qualities, and qualities alone. It is illogical to assume two causes where one will explain the whole thing. And the fight went on, and all the theories which held the doctrine of substance were thrown to the ground by the Buddhists. There was a break-up all along the line of those who held on to the doctrine of substance and qualities, that you have a soul, and I have a soul, and every one has a soul separate from the mind and body, and that each one is an individual.

So far we have seen that the idea of dualism is all right; for there is the body, there is then the fine body—the mind—there is this Atman, and in and through all the Atmans is that Paramâtman, God. The difficulty is here that this Atman and Paramatman are both called substance, to which the mind and body and so-called substances adhere like so many qualities. Nobody has ever seen a substance, none can ever conceive; what is the use of thinking of this substance? Why not become a Kshanikavâdin and say that whatever exists is this succession of mental currents and nothing more? They do not adhere to each other, they do not form a unit, one is chasing the other, like waves in the ocean, never complete, never forming one unit-whole. Man is a succession of waves, and when one goes away it generates another, and the cessation of these wave-forms is what is called Nirvana. You see that dualism is mute before this; it is impossible that it can bring up any argument, and the dualistic God also cannot be retained here. The idea of a God that is omnipresent, and yet is a person who creates without hands, and moves without feet, and so on, and who has created the universe as a Kumbhakâra (potter) creates a Ghata (pot), the Buddhist declares, is childish, and that if this is God, he is going to fight this God and not worship it. This universe is full of misery; if it is the work of a God, we are going to fight this God. And secondly, this God is illogical and impossible, as all of you are aware. We need not go into the defects of the "design theory", as all our Kshanikas have shown them full well; and so this Personal God fell to pieces.

Truth, and nothing but truth, is the watchword of the Advaitist. सत्यमेव जयते नानृतं। सत्येन पन्था वितितो देवयानः— "Truth alone triumphs, and not, untruth. Through truth alone the way to gods, Devayâna, lies." Everybody marches forward under that banner; ay, but it is only to crush the weaker man's position by his own. You come with your dualistic idea of God to pick a quarrel with a poor man who is worshipping an image, and you think you are wonderfully rational, you can confound him; but if he turns round and shatters your own Personal God and calls that an imaginary ideal, where are you? You fall back on faith and so on, or raise the cry of atheism, the old cry of a weak man—whosoever defeats him is an atheist. If you are to be rational, be rational all along the line, and if not, allow others the same privilege which you ask for yourselves. How can you prove the existence of this God? On the other hand, it can be almost disproved. There is not a shadow of a proof as to His existence, and there are very strong arguments to the contrary. How will you prove His existence, with your God, and His Gunas, and an infinite number of souls which are substance, and each soul an individual? In what are you an individual? You are not as a body, for you know today better than even the Buddhists of old knew that what may have been matter in the sun has just now become matter in you, and will go out and become matter in the plants; then where is your individuality, Mr. So-and-so? The same applies to the mind. Where is your individuality? You have one thought tonight and another tomorrow. You do not think the same way as you thought when you were a child; and old men do not think the same way as they did when they were young. Where is your individuality then? Do not say it is in consciousness, this Ahamkara, because this only covers a small part of your existence. While I am talking to you, all my organs are working and I am not conscious of it. If consciousness is the proof of existence they do not exist then, because I am not conscious of them. Where are you then with your Personal God theories? How can you prove such a God?

Again, the Buddhists will stand up and declare—not only is it illogical, but immoral, for it teaches man to be a coward and to seek assistance outside, and nobody can give him such help. Here is the universe, man made it; why then depend on an imaginary being outside whom nobody ever saw, or felt, or got help from? Why then do, you make cowards of yourselves and teach your children that the highest state of man is to be like a dog, and go crawling before this imaginary being, saying that you are weak and impure, and that you are everything vile in this universe? On the other hand, the Buddhists may urge not only that you tell a lie, but that you bring a tremendous amount of evil upon your children; for, mark you, this world is one of hypnotisation. Whatever you tell yourself, that you become. Almost the first words the great Buddha uttered were: "What you think, that you are; what you will think, that you will be." If this is true, do not teach yourself that you are nothing, ay, that you cannot do anything unless you are helped by somebody who does not live here, but sits above the clouds. The result will be that you will be more and more weakened every day. By constantly repeating, "we are very impure, Lord, make us pure", the result will be that you will hypnotise yourselves into all sorts of vices. Ay, the Buddhists say that ninety per cent of these vices that you see in every society are on account of this idea of a Personal God; this is an awful idea of the human being that the end and aim of this expression of life, this wonderful expression of life, is to become like a dog. Says the Buddhist to the Vaishnava, if your ideal, your aim and goal is to go to the place called Vaikuntha where God lives, and there stand before Him with folded hands all through eternity, it is better to commit suicide than do that. The Buddhists may even urge that, that is why he is going to create annihilation, Nirvana, to escape this. I am putting these ideas before you as a Buddhist just for the time being, because nowadays all these Advaitic ideas are said to make you immoral, and I am trying to tell you how the other side looks. Let us face both sides boldly and bravely.

We have seen first of all that this cannot be proved, this idea of a Personal God creating the world; is there any child that can believe this today? Because a Kumbhakara creates a Ghata, therefore a God created the world! If this is so, then your Kumbhakara is God also; and if any one tells you that He acts without head and hands, you may take him to a lunatic asylum. Has ever your Personal God, the Creator of the world to whom you cry all your life, helped you—is the next challenge from modern science. They will prove that any help you have had could have been got by your own exertions, and better still, you need not have spent your energy in that crying, you could have done it better without that weeping and crying. And we have seen that along with this idea of a Personal God comes tyranny and priestcraft. Tyranny and priestcraft have prevailed wherever this idea existed, and until the lie is knocked on the head, say the Buddhists, tyranny will not cease. So long as man thinks he has to cower before a supernatural being, so long there will be priests to claim rights and privileges and to make men cower before them, while these poor men will continue to ask some priest to act as interceder for them. You may do away with the Brahmin, but mark me, those who do so will put themselves in his place and will be worse, because the Brahmin has a certain amount of generosity in him, but these upstarts are always the worst of tyrannisers. If a beggar gets wealth, he thinks the whole world is a bit of straw. So these priests there must be, so long as this Personal God idea persists, and it will be impossible to think of any great morality in society. Priestcraft and tyranny go hand in hand. Why was it invented? Because some strong men in old times got people into their hands and said, you must obey us or we will destroy you. That was the long and short of it. महद्भयं वज्रमुद्यतम्—It is the idea of the thunderer who kills every one who does not obey him.

Next the Buddhist says, you have been perfectly rational up to this point, that everything is the result of the law of Karma. You believe in an infinity of souls, and that souls are without birth or death, and this infinity of souls and the belief in the law of Karma are perfectly logical no doubt. There cannot be a cause without an effect, the present must have had its cause in the past and will have its effect in the future. The Hindu says the Karma is Jada (inert) and not Chaitanya (Spirit), therefore some Chaitanya is necessary to bring this cause to fruition. Is it so, that Chaitanya is necessary to bring the plant to fruition? If I plant the seed and add water, no Chaitanya is necessary. You may say there was some original Chaitanya there, but the souls themselves were the Chaitanya, nothing else is necessary. If human souls have it too, what necessity is there for a God, as say the Jains, who, unlike the Buddhists, believe in souls and do not believe in God. Where are you logical, where are you moral? And when you criticise Advaitism and fear that it will make for immorality, just read a little of what has been done in India by dualistic sects. If there have been twenty thousand Advaitist blackguards, there have also been twenty thousand Dvaitist blackguards. Generally speaking, there will be more Dvaitist blackguards, because it takes a better type of mind to understand Advaitism, and Advaitists can scarcely be frightened into anything. What remains for you Hindus, then? There is no help for you out of the clutches of the Buddhists. You may quote the Vedas, but he does not believe in them. He will say, "My Tripitakas say otherwise, and they are without beginning or end, not even written by Buddha, for Buddha says he is only reciting them; they are eternal." And he adds, "Yours are wrong, ours are the true Vedas, yours are manufactured by the Brahmin priests, therefore out with them." How do you escape?

Here is the way to get out. Take up the first objection, the metaphysical one, that substance and qualities are different. Says the Advaitist, they are not. There is no difference between substance and qualities. You know the old illustration, how the rope is taken for the snake, and when you see the snake you do not see the rope at all, the rope has vanished. Dividing the thing into substance and quality is a metaphysical something in the brains of philosophers, for never can they be in effect outside. You see qualities if you are an ordinary man, and substance if you are a great Yogi, but you never see both at the same time. So, Buddhists, your quarrel about substance and qualities has been but a miscalculation which does not stand on fact. But if substance is unqualified, there can only be one. If you take qualities off from the soul, and show that these qualities are in the mind really, superimposed on the soul, then there can never be two souls for it is qualification that makes the difference between one soul and another. How do you know that one soul is different from the other? Owing to certain differentiating marks, certain qualities. And

where qualities do not exist, how can there be differentiation? Therefore there are not two souls, there is but One, and your Paramatman is unnecessary, it is this very soul. That One is called Paramatman, that very One is called Jivâtman, and so on; and you dualists, such as the Sânkhyas and others, who say that the soul is Vibhu, omnipresent, how can you make two infinities? There can be only one. What else? This One is the one Infinite Atman, everything else is its manifestation. There the Buddhist stops, but there it does not end.

The Advaitist position is not merely a weak one of criticism. The Advaitist criticises others when they come too near him, and just throws them away, that is all; but he propounds his own position. He is the only one that criticises, and does not stop with criticism and showing books. Here you are. You say the universe is a thing of continuous motion. In Vyashti (the finite) everything is moving; you are moving, the table is moving, motion everywhere; it is Samsâra, continuous motion; it is Jagat. Therefore there cannot be an individuality in this Jagat, because individuality means that which does not change; there cannot be any changeful individuality, it is a contradiction in terms. There is no such thing as individuality in this little world of ours, the Jagat. Thought and feeling, mind and body, men and animals and plants are in a continuous state of flux. But suppose you take the universe as a unit whole; can it change or move? Certainly not. Motion is possible in comparison with something which is a little less in motion or entirely motionless. The universe as a whole, therefore, is motionless, unchangeable. You are therefore, an individual then and then alone when you are the whole of it, when the realization of "I am the universe" comes. That is why the Vedantist says that so long as there are two, fear does not cease. It is only when one does not see another, does not feel another, when it is all one—then alone fear ceases, then alone death vanishes, then alone Samsara vanishes. Advaita teaches us, therefore, that man is individual in being universal, and not in being particular. You are immortal only when you are the whole. You are fearless and deathless only when you are the universe; and then that which you call the universe is the same as that you call God, the same that you call existence, the same that you call the whole. It is the one undivided Existence which is taken to be the manifold world which we see, as also others who are in the same state of mind as we. People who have done a little better Karma and get a better state of mind, when they die, look upon it as Svarga and see Indras and so forth. People still higher will see it, the very same thing, as Brahma-Loka, and the perfect ones will neither see the earth nor the heavens, nor any Loka at all. The universe will have vanished, and Brahman will be in its stead.

Can we know this Brahman? I have told you of the painting of the Infinite in the Samhita. Here we shall find another side shown, the infinite internal. That was the infinite of the muscles. Here we shall have the Infinite of thought. There the Infinite was attempted to be painted in language positive; here that language failed and the attempt has been to paint it in language negative. Here is this universe, and even admitting that it is Brahman, can we know it? No! No! You must understand this one thing again very clearly. Again and again this doubt will come to you: If this is Brahman, how can we know it? वज्ञिआतारमरे केन वज्ञिआनीयात्—"By what can the knower be known?" How can the knower be known? The eyes see everything; can they see themselves? They cannot: The very fact of knowledge is a degradation. Children of the Aryans, you must remember this, for herein lies a big story. All the Western temptations that come to you, have their metaphysical basis on that one thing—there is nothing higher than sense-knowledge. In the East, we say in our Vedas that this knowledge is lower than the thing itself, because it is always a limitation. When you want to know a thing, it immediately becomes limited by your mind. They say, refer back to that instance of the oyster making a pearl and see how knowledge is limitation, gathering a thing, bringing it into Consciousness, and not knowing it as a whole. This is true about all knowledge, and can it be less so about the Infinite? Can you thus limit Him who is the substance of all knowledge, Him who is the Sâkshi, the witness, without whom you cannot have any knowledge, Him who has no qualities, who is the Witness of the whole universe, the Witness in our own souls? How can you know Him? By what means can you bind Him up? Everything, the whole universe, is such a false attempt. This infinite Atman is, as it were, trying to see His own face, and all, from the lowest animals to the highest of gods, are like so many mirrors to reflect Himself in, and He is taking up still others, finding them insufficient, until in the human body He comes to know that it is the finite of the finite, all is finite, there cannot be any expression of the Infinite in the finite. Then comes the retrograde march, and this is what is called renunciation, Vairâgya. Back from the senses, back! Do not go to the senses is the watchword of Vairagya. This is the watchword of all morality, this is the watchword of all well-being; for you must remember that with us the universe begins in Tapasyâ, in renunciation, and as you go back and back, all the forms are being manifested before you, and they are left aside one after the other until you remain what you really are. This is Moksha or liberation.

This idea we have to understand: वज्ञिआतारमरे केन वज्ञिआनीयात्—"How to know the knower?" The knower cannot be known, because if it were known, it will not be the knower. If you look at your eyes in a mirror, the reflection is no more your eyes, but something else, only a reflection. Then if this soul, this Universal, Infinite Being which you are, is only a witness, what good is it? It cannot live, and move about, and enjoy the world, as we do. People cannot understand how the witness can enjoy. "Oh," they say, "you Hindus have become quiescent, and good for nothing, through this doctrine that you are witnesses! " First of all, it is only the witness that can enjoy. If there is a wrestling match, who enjoys it, those who take part in it, or those who are looking on—the outsiders? The more and more you are the witness of anything in life, the more you enjoy it. And this is Ânanda; and, therefore, infinite bliss can only be yours when you have become the witness of this universe; then alone you are a Mukta Purusha. It is the witness alone that can work without any desire, without any idea of going to heaven, without any idea of blame, without any idea of praise. The witness alone enjoys, and none else.

Coming to the moral aspect, there is one thing between the metaphysical and the moral aspect of Advaitism; it is the theory of Mâyâ. Everyone of these points in the Advaita system requires years to understand and months to explain. Therefore you will excuse me if I only just touch them en passant. This theory of Maya has been the most difficult thing to understand in all ages. Let me tell you in a few words that it is surely no theory, it is the combination of the three ideas Desha-Kâla-Nimitta—space, time, and causation—and this time and space and cause have been further reduced into Nâma-Rupa. Suppose there is a wave in the ocean. The wave is distinct from the ocean only in its form and name, and this form and this name cannot have any separate existence from the wave; they exist only with the wave. The wave may subside, but the same amount of water remains, even if the name and form that were on the wave vanish for ever. So this Maya is what makes the difference between me and you, between all animals and man, between gods and men. In fact, it is this Maya that causes the Atman to be caught, as it were, in so many millions of beings, and these are distinguishable only through name and form. If you leave it alone, let name and form go, all this variety vanishes for ever, and you are what you really are. This is Maya.

It is again no theory, but a statement of facts. When the realist states that this table exists, what he means is, that this table has an independent existence of its own, that it does not depend on the existence of anything else in the universe, and if this whole universe be destroyed and annihilated, this table will remain just as it is now. A little thought will show you that it cannot be so. Everything here in the sense-world is dependent and interdependent, relative and correlative, the existence of one depending on the other. There are three steps, therefore, in our knowledge of things; the first is that each thing is individual and separate from every other; and the next step is to find that there is a relation and correlation between all things; and the third is that there is only one thing which we see as many. The first idea of God with the ignorant is that this God is somewhere outside the universe, that is to say, the conception of God is extremely human; He does just what a man does, only on a bigger and higher scale. And we have seen how that idea of God is proved in a few words to be unreasonable and insufficient. And the next idea is the idea of a power we see manifested everywhere. This is the real Personal God we get in the Chandi, but, mark me, not a God that you make the reservoir of all good qualities only. You cannot have two Gods, God and Satan; you must have only one and dare to call Him good and bad. Have only one and take the logical consequences. We read in the Chandi: "We salute Thee, O Divine Mother, who lives in every being as peace. We salute Thee, O Divine Mother, who lives in all beings as purity." At the same time we must take the whole consequence of calling Him the All-formed. "All this is bliss, O Gârgi; wherever there is bliss there is a portion of the Divine," You may use it how you like. In this light before me, you may give a poor man a hundred rupees, and another man may forge your name, but the light will be the same for both. This is the second stage. And the third is that God is neither outside nature nor inside nature, but God and nature and soul and universe are all convertible terms. You never see two things; it is your metaphysical words that have deluded you. You assume that you are a body and have a soul, and that you are both together. How can that be? Try in your own mind. If there is a Yogi among you, he knows himself as Chaitanya, for him the body has vanished. An ordinary man thinks of himself as a body; the idea of spirit has vanished from him; but because the metaphysical ideas exist that man has a body and a soul and all these things, you think they are all simultaneously there. One thing at a time. Do not talk of God when you see matter; you see the effect and the effect alone, and the cause you cannot see, and the moment you can see the cause, the effect will have vanished. Where is the world then, and who has taken it off?

"One that is present always as consciousness, the bliss absolute, beyond all bounds, beyond all compare, beyond all qualities, ever-free, limitless as the sky, without parts, the absolute, the perfect—such a Brahman, O sage, O learned one, shines in the heart of the Jnâni in Samâdhi. (Vivekachudamani, 408).

"Where all the changes of nature cease for ever, who is thought beyond all thoughts, who is equal to all yet having no equal, immeasurable, whom Vedas declare, who is the essence in what we call our existence, the perfect—such a Brahman, O sage, O learned one, shines in the heart of the Jnani in Samadhi. (Ibid., 409)

"Beyond all birth and death, the Infinite One, incomparable, like the whole universe deluged in water in Mahâpralaya—water above, water beneath, water on all sides, and on the face of that water not a wave, not a ripple—silent and calm, all visions have died out, all fights and quarrels and the war of fools and saints have ceased for ever—such a Brahman, O sage, O learned one, shines in the heart of the Jnani in Samadhi." (Ibid., 410)

That also comes, and when that comes the world has vanished.

We have seen then that this Brahman, this Reality is unknown and unknowable, not in the sense of the agnostic, but because to know Him would be a blasphemy, because you are He already. We have also seen that this Brahman is not this table and yet is this table. Take off the name and form, and whatever is reality is He. He is the reality in everything.

"Thou art the woman, thou the man, thou art the boy, and the girl as well, thou the old man supporting thyself on a stick, thou art all in all in the universe." That is the theme of Advaitism. A few words more. Herein lies, we find, the explanation of the essence of things. We have seen how here alone we can take a firm stand against all the onrush of logic and scientific knowledge. Here at last reason has a firm foundation, and, at the same time, the Indian Vedantist does not curse the preceding steps; he looks back and he blesses them, and he knows that they were true, only wrongly perceived, and wrongly stated. They were the same truth, only seen through the glass of Maya, distorted it may be—yet truth, and nothing but truth. The same God whom the ignorant man saw outside nature, the same whom the little-knowing man saw as interpenetrating the universe, and the same whom the sage realises as his own Self, as the whole universe itself—all are One and the same Being, the same entity seen from different standpoints, seen through different glasses of Maya, perceived by different minds, and all the difference was caused by that. Not only so, but one view must lead to the other. What is the difference between science and common knowledge? Go out into the streets in the dark, and if something unusual is happening there, ask one of the passers-by what is the cause of it. If is ten to one that he will tell you it is a ghost causing the phenomenon. He is always going after ghosts and spirits outside, because it is the nature of ignorance to seek for causes outside of effects. If a stone falls, it has been thrown by a devil or a ghost, says the ignorant man, but the scientific man says it is the law of nature, the law of gravitation.

What is the fight between science and religion everywhere? Religions are encumbered with such a mass of explanations which come from outside—one angel is in charge of the sun, another of the moon, and so on ad infinitum. Every change is caused by a spirit, the one common point of agreement being that they are all outside the thing. Science means that the cause of a thing is sought out by the nature of the thing itself. As step by step science is progressing, it has taken the explanation of natural phenomena out of the hands of spirits and angels. Because Advaitism has done likewise in spiritual matters, it is the most scientific religion. This universe has not been created by any extra-cosmic God, nor is it the work of any outside genius. It is self-creating, self-dissolving, self-manifesting, One Infinite Existence, the Brahman. Tattvamasi Shvetaketo—"That thou art! O Shvetaketu!"

Thus you see that this, and this alone, and none else, can be the only scientific religion. And with all the prattle about science that is going on daily at the present time in modern half-educated India, with all the talk about rationalism and reason that I hear every day, I expect that; whole sects of you will come over and dare to be Advaitists, and dare to preach it to the world in the words of Buddha, बहुजनहिताय बहुजनसुखाय—"For the good of many, for the happiness of many." If you do not, I take you for cowards. If you cannot get over your cowardice, if your fear is your excuse, allow the same liberty to others, do not try to break up the poor idol-worshipper, do not call him a devil, do not go about preaching to every man, that does not agree entirely with you. Know first, that you are cowards yourselves, and if society frightens you, if your own superstitions of the past frighten you so much, how much more will these superstitions frighten and bind down those who are ignorant? That is the Advaita position. Have mercy on others. Would to God that the whole world were Advaitists tomorrow, not only in theory, but in realisation. But if that cannot be, let us do the next best thing; let us take the ignorant by the band, lead them always step by step just as they can go, and know that every step in all religious growth in India has been progressive. It is not from bad to good, but from good to better.

Something more has to be told about the moral relation. Our boys blithely talk nowadays; they learn from somebody—the Lord knows from whom—that Advaita makes people immoral, because if we are all one and all God, what need of morality will there be at all! In the first place, that is the argument of the brute, who can only be kept down by the whip. If you are such brutes, commit suicide rather than pass for human beings who have to be kept down by the whip. If the whip is taken away, you will all be demons! You ought all to be killed if such is the case. There is no help for you; you must always be living under this whip and rod, and there is no salvation, no escape for you.

In the second place, Advaita and Advaita alone explains morality. Every religion preaches that the essence of all morality is to do good to others. And why? Be unselfish. And why should I? Some God has said it? He is not for me. Some texts have declared it? Let them; that is nothing to me; let them all tell it. And if they do, what is it to me? Each one for himself, and somebody take the hindermost—that is all the morality in the world, at least with many. What is the reason that I should be moral? You cannot explain it except when you come to know the truth as given in the Gita: "He who sees everyone in himself, and himself in everyone, thus seeing the same God living in all, he, the sage, no more kills the Self by the self." Know through Advaita that whomsoever you hurt, you hurt yourself; they are all you. Whether you know it or not, through all hands you work, through all feet you move, you are the king enjoying in the palace, you are the beggar leading that miserable existence in the street; you are in the ignorant as well as in the learned, you are in the man who is weak, and you are in the strong; know this and be sympathetic. And that is why we must not hurt others. That is why I do not even care whether I have to starve, because there will be millions of mouths eating at the same time, and they are all mine. Therefore I should not care what becomes of me and mine, for the whole universe is mine, I am enjoying all the bliss at the same time; and who can kill me or the universe? Herein is morality. Here, in Advaita alone, is morality explained. The others teach item but cannot give you its reason. Then, so far about explanation.

What is the gain? It is strength. Take off that veil of hypnotism which you have cast upon the world, send not out thoughts and words of weakness unto humanity. Know that all sins and all evils can be summed up in that one word, weakness. It is weakness that is the motive power in all evil doing; it is weakness that is the source of all selfishness; it is weakness that makes men injure others; it is weakness that makes them manifest what they are not in reality. Let them all know what they are; let them repeat day and night what they are. Soham. Let them suck it in with their mothers' milk, this idea of strength—I am He, I am He. This is to be heard first—श्रोतव्यो मन्तव्यो निदिध्यासितव्यः etc. And then let them think of it, and out of that thought, out of that heart will proceed works such as the world has never seen. What has to be done? Ay, this Advaita is said by some to be impracticable; that is to say, it is not yet manifesting itself on the material plane. To a certain extent that is true, for remember the saying of the Vedas:

ओमित्येकाक्षरं ब्रह्म ओमित्येकाक्षरं परम्।
ओमित्येकाक्षरं ज्ञात्वा यो यदिच्छति तस्य तत् ॥

"Om, this is the Brahman; Om, this is the greatest reality; he who knows the secret of this Om, whatever he desires that he gets." Ay, therefore first know the secret of this Om, that you are the Om; know the secret of this Tattvamasi, and then and then alone whatever you want shall come to you. If you want to be great materially, believe that you are so. I may be a little bubble, and you may be a wave mountain-high, but know that for both of us the infinite ocean is the background, the infinite Brahman is our magazine of power and strength, and we can draw as much as we like, both of us, I the bubble and you the mountain-high wave. Believe, therefore, in yourselves. The secret of Advaita is: Believe in yourselves first, and then believe in anything else. In the history of the world, you will find that only those nations that have believed in themselves have become great and strong. In the history of each nation, you will always find that only those individuals who have believed in themselves have become great and strong. Here, to India, came an Englishman who was only a clerk, and for want of funds and other reasons he twice tried to blow his brains out; and when he failed, he believed in himself, he believed that he was born to do great things; and that man became Lord Clive, the founder of the Empire. If he had believed the Padres and gone crawling all his life—"O Lord, I am weak, and I am low"—where would he have been? In a lunatic asylum. You also are made lunatics by these evil teachings. I have seen, all the world over, the bad effects of these weak teachings of humility destroying the human race. Our children are brought up in this way, and is it a wonder that they become semi-lunatics?

This is teaching on the practical side. Believe, therefore, in yourselves, and if you want material wealth, work it out; it will come to you. If you want to be intellectual, work it out on the intellectual plane, and intellectual giants you shall be. And if you want to attain to freedom, work it out on the spiritual plane, and free you shall be and shall enter into Nirvana, the Eternal Bliss. But one defect which lay in the Advaita was its being worked out so long on the spiritual plane only, and nowhere else; now the time has come when you have to make it practical. It shall no more be a Rahasya, a secret, it shall no more live with monks in caves and forests, and in the Himalayas; it must come down to the daily, everyday life of the people; it shall be worked out in the palace of the king, in the cave of the recluse; it shall be worked out in the cottage of the poor, by the beggar in the street, everywhere; anywhere it can be worked out. Therefore do not fear whether you are a woman or a Shudra, for this religion is so great, says Lord Krishna, that even a little of it brings a great amount of good.

Therefore, children of the Aryans, do not sit idle; awake, arise, and stop not till the goal is reached. The time has come when this Advaita is to be worked out practically. Let us bring it down from heaven unto the earth; this is the present dispensation. Ay, the voices of our forefathers of old are telling us to bring it down from heaven to the earth. Let your teachings permeate the world, till they have entered into every pore of society, till they have become the common property of everybody, till they have become part and parcel of our lives, till they have entered into our veins and tingle with every drop of blood there.

Ay, you may be astonished to hear that as practical Vedantists the Americans are better than we are. I used to stand on the seashore at New York and look at the emigrants coming from different countries—crushed, downtrodden, hopeless, unable to look a man in the face, with a little bundle of clothes as all their possession, and these all in rags; if they saw a policeman they were afraid and tried to get to the other side of the foot-path. And, mark you, in six months those very men were walking erect, well clothed, looking everybody in the face; and what made this wonderful difference? Say, this man comes from Armenia or somewhere else where he was crushed down beyond all recognition, where everybody told him he was a born slave and born to remain in a low state all his life, and where at the least move on his part he was trodden upon. There everything told him, as it were, "Slave! you are a slave, remain so. Hopeless you were born, hopeless you must remain." Even the very air murmured round him, as it were, "There is no hope for you; hopeless and a slave you must remain", while the strong man crushed the life out of him. And when he landed in the streets of New York, he found a gentleman, well-dressed, shaking him by the hand; it made no difference that the one was in rags and the other well-clad. He went a step further and saw restaurant, that there were gentlemen dining at a table, and he was asked to take a seat at the corner of the same table. He went about and found a new life, that there was a place where he was a man among men. Perhaps he went to Washington, shook hands with the President of the United States, and perhaps there he saw men coming from distant villages, peasants, and ill clad, all shaking hands with the President. Then the veil of Maya slipped away

from him. He is Brahman, he who has been hypnotised into slavery and weakness is once more awake, and he rises up and finds himself a man in a world of men. Ay, in this country of ours, the very birth-place of the Vedanta, our masses have been hypnotised for ages into that state. To touch them is pollution, to sit with them is pollution! Hopeless they were born, hopeless they must remain! And the result is that they have been sinking, sinking, sinking, and have come to the last stage to which a human being can come. For what country is there in the world where man has to sleep with the cattle? And for this, blame nobody else, do not commit the mistake of the ignorant. The effect is here and the cause is here too. We are to blame. Stand up, be bold, and take the blame on your own shoulders. Do not go about throwing mud at others; for all the faults you suffer from, you are the sole and only cause.

Young men of Lahore, understand this, therefore, this great sin hereditary and national, is on our shoulders. There is no hope for us. You may make thousands of societies, twenty thousand political assemblages, fifty thousand institutions. These will be of no use until there is that sympathy, that love, that heart that thinks for all; until Buddha's heart comes once more into India, until the words of the Lord Krishna are brought to their practical use, there is no hope for us. You go on imitating the Europeans and their societies and their assemblages, but let me tell you a story, a fact that I saw with my own eyes. A company of Burmans was taken over to London by some persons here, who turned out to be Eurasians. They exhibited these people in London, took all the money, and then took these Burmans over to the Continent, and left them there for good or evil. These poor people did not know a word of any European language, but the English Consul in Austria sent them over to London. They were helpless in London, without knowing anyone. But an English lady got to know of them, took these foreigners from Burma into her own house, gave them her own clothes, her bed, and everything, and then sent the news to the papers. And, mark you, the next day the whole nation was, as it were, roused. Money poured in, and these people were helped out and sent back to Burma. On this sort of sympathy are based all their political and other institutions; it is the rock-foundation of love, for themselves at least. They may not love the world; and the Burmans may be their enemies, but in England, it goes without saying, there is this great love for their own people, for truth and justice and charity to the stranger at the door. I should be the most ungrateful man if I did not tell you how wonderfully and how hospitably I was received in every country in the West. Where is the heart here to build upon? No sooner do we start a little joint-stock company than we try to cheat each other, and the whole thing comes down with a crash. You talk of imitating the English and building up as big a nation as they are. But where are the foundations? Ours are only sand, and, therefore, the building comes down with a crash in no time.

Therefore, young men of Lahore, raise once more that mighty banner of Advaita, for on no other ground can you have that wonderful love until you see that the same Lord is present everywhere. Unfurl that banner of love! "Arise, awake, and stop not till the goal is reached." Arise, arise once more, for nothing can be done without renunciation. If you want to help others, your little self must go. In the words of the Christians—you cannot serve God and Mammon at the same time. Have Vairagya. Your ancestors gave up the world for doing great things. At the present time there are men who give up the world to help their own salvation. Throw away everything, even your own salvation, and go and help others. Ay you are always talking bold words, but here is practical Vedanta before you. Give up this little life of yours. What matters it if you die of starvation—you and I and thousands like us—so long as this nation lives? The nation is sinking, the curse of unnumbered millions is on our heads—those to whom we have been giving ditch-water to drink when they have been dying of thirst and while the perennial river of water was flowing past, the unnumbered millions whom we have allowed to starve in sight of plenty, the unnumbered millions to whom we have talked of Advaita and whom we have hated with all our strength, the unnumbered millions for whom we have invented the doctrine of Lokâchâra (usage), to whom we have talked theoretically that we are all the same and all are one with the same Lord, without even an ounce of practice. "Yet, my friends, it must be only in the mind and never in practice!" Wipe off this blot. "Arise and awake." What matters it if this little life goes? Everyone has to die, the saint or the sinner, the rich or the poor. The body never remains for anyone. Arise and awake and be perfectly sincere. Our insincerity in India is awful; what we want is character, that steadiness and character that make a man cling on to a thing like grim death.

"Let the sages blame or let them praise, let Lakshmi come today or let her go away, let death come just now or in a hundred years; he indeed is the sage who does not make one false step from the right path." Arise and awake, for the time is passing and all our energies will be: frittered away in vain talking. Arise and awake, let minor things, and quarrels over little details and fights over little doctrines be thrown aside, for here is the greatest of all works, here are the sinking millions. When the Mohammedans first came into India, what a great number of Hindus were here; but mark, how today they have dwindled down! Every day they will become less and less till they wholly disappear. Let them disappear, but with them will disappear the marvellous ideas, of which, with all their defects and all their misrepresentations, they still stand as representatives. And with them will disappear this marvellous Advaita, the crest-jewel of all spiritual thought. Therefore, arise, awake, with your hands stretched out to protect the spirituality of the world. And first of all, work it out for your own country. What we want is not so much spirituality as a little of the bringing down of the Advaita into the material world. First bread and then religion. We stuff them too much with religion, when the poor fellows have been starving. No dogmas will satisfy the cravings of hunger. There are two curses here: first our weakness, secondly, our hatred, our dried-up hearts. You may talk doctrines by the millions, you may have sects by the hundreds of millions; ay, but it is nothing until you have the heart to feel. Feel for them as your Veda teaches you, till you find they are parts of your own bodies, till you realise that you and they, the poor and the rich, the saint and the sinner, are all parts of One Infinite Whole, which you call Brahman.

Gentlemen, I have tried to place before you a few of the most brilliant points of the Advaita system, and now the time has come when it should be carried into practice, not only in this country but everywhere. Modern science and its sledge-hammer blows are pulverising the porcelain foundations of all dualistic religions everywhere. Not only here are the dualists torturing texts till they will extend no longer—for texts are not India-rubber—it is not only here that they are trying to get into the nooks and corners to protect themselves; it is still more so in Europe and America. And even there something of this idea will have to go from India. It has already got there. It will have to grow and increase and save their civilisations too. For in the West the old order of things is vanishing, giving way to a new order of things, which is the worship of gold, the worship of Mammon. Thus this old crude system of religion was better than the modern system, namely—competition and gold. No nation, however strong, can stand on such foundations, and the history of the world tells us that all that had such foundations are dead and gone. In the first place we have to stop the incoming of such a wave in India. Therefore preach the Advaita to every one, so that religion may withstand the shock of modern science. Not only so, you will have to help others; your thought will help out Europe and America. But above all, let me once more remind you that here is need of practical work, and the first part of that is that you should go to the sinking millions of India, and take them by the hand, remembering the words of the Lord Krishna:

इहैव तैर्जितः सर्गो येषां साम्ये स्थितं मनः।
निर्दोषं हि समं ब्रह्म तस्मात् ब्रह्मणि ते स्थिताः॥

"Even in this life they have conquered relative existence whose minds are firm-fixed on the sameness of everything, for God is pure and the same to all; therefore, such are said to be living in God."

VEDANTISM

At Khetri on 20th December 1897, Swami Vivekananda delivered a lecture on Vedantism in the hall of the Maharaja's bungalow in which he lodged with his disciples. The Swami was introduced by the Raja, who was the president of the meeting; and he spoke for more than an hour and a half. The Swami was at his best, and it was a matter of regret that no shorthand writer was present to report this interesting lecture at length. The following is a summary from notes taken down at the time:

Two nations of yore, namely the Greek and the Aryan placed in different environments and circumstances — the former, surrounded by all that was beautiful, sweet, and tempting in nature, with an invigorating climate, and the latter, surrounded on every side by all that was sublime, and born and nurtured in a climate which did not allow of much physical exercise — developed two peculiar and different ideals of civilization. The study of the Greeks was the outer infinite, while that of the Aryans was the inner infinite; one studied the macrocosm, and the other the microcosm. Each had its distinct part to play in the civilisation of the world. Not that one was required to borrow from the other, but if they compared notes both would be the gainers. The Aryans were by nature an analytical race. In the sciences of mathematics and grammar wonderful fruits were gained, and by the analysis of mind the full tree was developed. In Pythagoras, Socrates, Plato, and the Egyptian neo-Platonists, we can find traces of Indian thought.

The Swami then traced in detail the influence of Indian thought on Europe and showed how at different periods Spain, Germany, and other European countries were greatly influenced by it. The Indian prince, Dârâ-Shuko, translated the Upanishads into Persian, and a Latin translation of the same was seen by Schopenhauer, whose philosophy was moulded by these. Next to him, the philosophy of Kant also shows traces of the teachings of the Upanishads. In Europe it is the interest in comparative philology that attracts scholars to the study of Sanskrit, though there are men like Deussen who take interest in philosophy for its own sake. The Swami hoped that in future much more interest would be taken in the study of Sanskrit. He then showed that the word "Hindu" in former times was full of meaning, as referring to the people living beyond the Sindhu or the Indus; it is now meaningless, representing neither the nation nor their religion, for on this side of the Indus, various races professing different religions live at the present day.

The Swami then dwelt at length on the Vedas and stated that they were not spoken by any person, but the ideas were evolving slowly and slowly until they were embodied in book form, and then that book became the authority. He said that various religions were embodied in books: the power of books seemed to be infinite. The Hindus have their Vedas, and will have to hold on to them for thousands of years more, but their ideas about them are to be changed and built anew on a solid foundation of rock. The Vedas, he said, were a huge literature. Ninety-nine per cent of them were missing; they were in the keeping of certain families, with whose extinction the books were lost. But still, those that are left now could not be contained even in a large hall like that. They severe written in language archaic and simple; their grammar was very crude, so much so that it was said that some part of the Vedas had no meaning.

He then dilated on the two portions of the Vedas — the Karma Kânda and the Jnâna Kânda. The Karma Kanda, he said,

were the Samhitâs and the Brâhmanas. The Brahmanas dealt with sacrifices. The Samhitas were songs composed in Chhandas known as Anushtup, Trishtup, Jagati, etc. Generally they praised deities such as Varuna or Indra; and the question arose who were these deities; and if any theories were raised about them, they were smashed up by other theories, and so on it went.

The Swami then proceeded to explain different ideas of worship. With the ancient Babylonians, the soul was only a double, having no individuality of its own and not able to break its connection with the body. This double was believed to suffer hunger and thirst, feelings and emotions like those of the old body. Another idea was that if the first body was injured the double would be injured also; when the first was annihilated, the double also perished; so the tendency grew to preserve the body, and thus mummies, tombs, and graves came into existence. The Egyptians, the Babylonians, and the Jews never got any farther than this idea of the double; they did not reach to the idea of the Âtman beyond.

Prof Max Müller's opinion was that not the least trace of ancestral worship could be found in the Rig-Veda. There we do not meet with the horrid sight of mummies staring stark and blank at us. There the gods were friendly to man; communion between the worshipper and the worshipped was healthy. There was no moroseness, no want of simple joy, no lack of smiles or light in the eyes. The Swami said that dwelling on the Vedas he even seemed to hear the laughter of the gods. The Vedic Rishis might not have had finish in their expression, but they were men of culture and heart, and we are brutes in comparison to them. Swamiji then recited several Mantras in confirmation of what he had just said: "Carry him to the place where the Fathers live, where there is no grief or sorrow" etc. Thus the idea arose that the sooner the dead body was cremated the better. By degrees they came to know that there was a finer body that went to a place where there was all joy and no sorrow. In the Semitic type of religion there was tribulation and fear; it was thought that if a man saw God, he would die. But according to the Rig-Veda, when a man saw God face to face then began his real life.

Now the questions came to be asked: What were these gods? Sometimes Indra came and helped man; sometimes Indra drank too much Soma. Now and again, adjectives such as all-powerful, all-pervading, were attributed to him; the same was the case with Varuna. In this way it went on, and some of these Mantras depicting the characteristics of these gods were marvellous, and the language was exceedingly grand. The speaker here repeated the famous Nâsadiya Sukta which describes the Pralaya state and in which occurs the idea of "Darkness covering darkness", and asked if the persons that described these sublime ideas in such poetic thought were uncivilised and uncultured, then what we should call ourselves. It was not for him, Swamiji said, to criticise or pass any judgment on those Rishis and their gods — Indra or Varuna. All this was like a panorama, unfolding one scene after another, and behind them all as a background stood out एकं सव्दप्रि बहुधा वदन्ति ।—"That which exists is One; sages call It variously." The whole thing was most mystical, marvellous, and exquisitely beautiful. It seemed even yet quite unapproachable—the veil was so thin that it would rend, as it were, at the least touch and vanish like a mirage.

Continuing, he said that one thing seemed to him quite clear and possible that the Aryans too, like the Greeks, went to outside nature for their solution, that nature tempted them outside, led them step by step to the outward world, beautiful and good. But here in India anything which was not sublime counted for nothing. It never occurred to the Greeks to pry into the secrets after death. But here from the beginning was asked again and again "What am I? What will become of me after death?" There the Greek thought—the man died and went to heaven. What was meant by going to heaven? It meant going outside of everything; there was nothing inside, everything was outside; his search was all directed outside, nay, he himself was, as it were, outside himself. And when he went to a place which was very much like this world minus all its sorrows, he thought he had got everything that was desirable and was satisfied; and there all ideas of religion stopped. But this did not satisfy the Hindu mind. In its analysis, these heavens were all included within the material universe. "Whatever comes by combination", the Hindus said, "dies of annihilation". They asked external nature, "Do you know what is soul?" and nature answered, "No". "Is there any God?" Nature answered, "I do not know". Then they turned away from nature. They understood that external nature, however great and grand, was limited in space and time. Then there arose another voice; new sublime thoughts dawned in their minds. That voice said—"Neti, Neti", "Not this, not this". All the different gods were now reduced into one; the suns, moons, and stars—nay, the whole universe—were one, and upon this new ideal the spiritual basis of religion was built.

न तत्र सुर्यो भाति न चंन्द्रतारकं नेमा विद्युतो भान्ति कुतोऽयमग्नि: ।
तमेव भान्तमनुभाति सर्वं तस्य भासा सर्व मिदं विभाति ॥

— "There the sun doth not shine, neither the moon, nor stars, nor lightning, what to speak of this fire. He shining, everything doth shine. Through Him everything shineth." No more is there that limited, crude, personal idea; no more is there that little idea of God sitting in judgment; no more is that search outside, but henceforth it is directed inside. Thus the Upanishads became the Bible of India. It was a vast literature, these Upanishads, and all the schools holding different opinions in India came to be established on the foundation of the Upanishads.

The Swami passed on to the dualistic, qualified monistic, and Advaitic theories, and reconciled them by saying that each one of these was like a step by which one passed before the other was reached; the final evolution to Advaitism was the natural outcome, and the last step was "Tattvamasi". He pointed out where even the great commentators Shankarâchârya, Râmânujâchârya, and Madhvâchârya had committed mistakes. Each one believed in the Upanishads as the sole authority, but thought that they preached one thing, one path only. Thus Shankaracharya committed the mistake in supposing that the whole of the Upanishads taught one thing, which was Advaitism, and nothing else; and wherever a passage bearing distinctly the Dvaita idea occurred, he twisted and tortured the meaning to make it support his own theory. So with Ramanuja and Madhvacharya when pure Advaitic texts occurred. It was perfectly true that the Upanishads had one thing to teach, but that was taught as a going up from one step to another. Swamiji regretted that in modern India the spirit of religion is gone; only the externals remain. The people are neither Hindus nor Vedantists. They are merely don't-touchists; the kitchen is their temple and Hândi Bartans (cooking pots) are their Devatâ (object of worship). This state of things must go. The sooner it is given up the better for our religion. Let the Upanishads shine in their glory, and at the same time let not quarrels exist amongst different sects.

As Swamiji was not keeping good health, he felt exhausted at this stage of his speech; so he took a little rest for half an hour, during which time the whole audience waited patiently to hear the rest of the lecture. He came out and spoke again for half an hour, and explained that knowledge was the finding of unity in diversity, and the highest point in every science was reached when it found the one unity underlying all variety. This was as true in physical science as in the spiritual.

THE INFLUENCE OF INDIAN SPIRITUAL THOUGHT IN ENGLAND

The Swami Vivekananda presided over a meeting at which the Sister Nivedita (Miss M. E. Noble) delivered a lecture on "The Influence of Indian Spiritual Thought in England" on 11th March, 1898, at the Star Theatre, Calcutta. Swami Vivekananda on rising to introduce Miss Noble spoke as follows:

Ladies and Gentlemen,

When I was travelling through the Eastern parts of Asia, one thing especially struck me—that is the prevalence of Indian spiritual thought in Eastern Asiatic countries. You may imagine the surprise with which I noticed written on the walls of Chinese and Japanese temples some well-known Sanskrit Mantras, and possibly it will please you all the more to know that they were all in old Bengali characters, standing even in the present day as a monument of missionary energy and zeal displayed by our forefathers of Bengal.

Apart from these Asiatic countries, the work of India's spiritual thought is so widespread and unmistakable that even in Western countries, going deep below the surface, I found traces of the same influence still present. It has now become a historical fact that the spiritual ideas of the Indian people travelled towards both the East and the West in days gone by. Everybody knows now how much the world owes to India's spirituality, and what a potent factor in the present and the past of humanity have been the spiritual powers of India. These are things of the past. I find another most remarkable phenomenon, and that is that the most stupendous powers of civilisation, and progress towards humanity and social progress, have been effected by that wonderful race—I mean the Anglo-Saxon. I may go further and tell you that had it not been for the power of the Anglo-Saxons we should not have met here today to discuss, as we are doing, the influence of our Indian spiritual thought. And coming back to our own country, coming from the West to the East, I see the same Anglo-Saxon powers working here with all their defects, but retaining their peculiarly characteristic good features, and I believe that at last the grand result is achieved. The British idea of expansion and progress is forcing us up, and let us remember that the civilisation of the West has been drawn from the fountain of the Greeks, and that the great idea of Greek civilization is that of expression. In India we think—but unfortunately sometimes we think so deeply that there is no power left for expression. Gradually, therefore, it came to pass that our force of expression did not manifest itself before the world, and what is the result of that? The result is this—we worked to hide everything we had. It began first with individuals as a faculty of hiding, and it ended by becoming a national habit of hiding—there is such a lack of power of expression with us that we are now considered a dead nation. Without expression, how can we live? The backbone of Western civilization is—expansion and expression. This side of the work of the Anglo-Saxon race in India, to which I draw your attention, is calculated to rouse our nation once more to express itself, and it is inciting it to bring out its hidden treasures before the world by using the means of communication provided by the same mighty race. The Anglo-Saxons have created a future for India, and the space through which our ancestral ideas are now ranging is simply phenomenal. Ay, what great facilities had our forefathers when they delivered their message of truth and salvation? Ay, how did the great Buddha preach the noble doctrine of universal brotherhood? There were I even then great facilities here, in our beloved India, for the attainment of real happiness, and we could easily send our ideas from one end of the world to the other. Now we have reached even the Anglo-Saxon race. This is the kind of interaction now going on, and we find that our message is heard, and not only heard but is being responded to. Already England has given us some of her great intellects to help, us in our mission. Every one has heard and is perhaps familiar with my friend Miss Müller, who is now here on this platform. This lady, born of a very good family and well educated, has given her whole life to us out of love for India, and has made India her home and her family. Every one of you is familiar with the name of that noble and distinguished Englishwoman who has also given her whole life to work for the good of India and India's regeneration—I mean Mrs. Besant. Today, we meet on this platform two ladies from America who have the same mission

in their hearts; and I can assure you that they also are willing to devote their lives to do the least good to our poor country. I take this opportunity of reminding you of the name of one of our countrymen—one who has seen England and America, one in whom I have great confidence, and whom I respect and love, and who would have been present here but for an engagement elsewhere—a man working steadily and silently for the good of our country, a man of great spirituality—I mean Mr. Mohini Mohan Chatterji. And now England has sent us another gift in Miss Margaret Noble, from whom we expect much. Without any more words of mine I introduce to you Miss Noble, who will now address you.

After Sister Nivedita had finished her interesting lecture, the Swami rose and said:

I have only a few words to say. We have an idea that we Indians can do something, and amongst the Indians we Bengalis may laugh at this idea; but I do not. My mission in life is to rouse a struggle in you. Whether you are an Advaitin, whether you are a qualified monist or dualist, it does not matter much. But let me draw your attention to one thing which unfortunately we always forget: that is—"O man, have faith in yourself." That isle the way by which we can have faith in God. Whether you are an Advaitist or a dualist, whether you are a believer in the system of Yoga or a believer in Shankarâchârya, whether you are a follower of Vyâsa or Vishvâmitra, it does not matter much. But the thing is that on this point Indian thought differs from that of all the rest of the world. Let us remember for a moment that, whereas in every other religion and in every other country, the power of the soul is entirely ignored—the soul is thought of as almost powerless, weak, and inert—we in India consider the soul to be eternal and hold that it will remain perfect through all eternity. We should always bear in mind the teachings of the Upanishads.

Remember your great mission in life. We Indians, and especially those of Bengal, have been invaded by a vast amount of foreign ideas that are eating into the very vitals of our national religion. Why are we so backwards nowadays? Why are ninety-nine per cent of us made up of entirely foreign ideas and elements? This has to be thrown out if we want to rise in the scale of nations. If we want to rise, we must also remember that we have many things to learn from the West. We should learn from the West her arts and her sciences. From the West we have to learn the sciences of physical nature, while on the other hand the West has to come to us to learn and assimilate religion and spiritual knowledge. We Hindu must believe that we are the teachers of the world. We have been clamouring here for getting political rights ant many other such things. Very well. Rights and privileges and other things can only come through friendship, and friendship can only be expected between two equals When one of the parties is a beggar, what friendship can there be? It is all very well to speak so, but I say that without mutual co-operation we can never make ourselves strong men. So, I must call upon you to go out to England and America, not as beggars but as teachers of religion. The law of exchange must be applied to the best of our power. If we have to learn from them the ways and methods of making ourselves happy in this life, why, in return, should we not give them the methods and ways that would make them happy for all eternity? Above all, work for the good of humanity. Give up the so-called boast of your narrow orthodox life. Death is waiting for every one, and mark you this—the most marvellous historical fact—that all the nations of the world have to sit down patiently at the feet of India to learn the eternal truths embodied in her literature. India dies not. China dies not. Japan dies not. Therefore, we must always remember that our backbone is spirituality, and to do that we must have a guide who will show the path to us, that path about which I am talking just now. If any of you do not believe it, if there be a Hindu boy amongst us who is not ready to believe that his religion is pure spirituality, I do not call him a Hindu. I remember in one of the villages of Kashmir, while talking to an old Mohammedan lady I asked her in a mild voice, "What religion is yours?" She replied in her own language, "Praise the Lord! By the mercy of God, I am a Mussulman." And then I asked a Hindu, "What is your religion?" He plainly replied, "I am a Hindu." I remember that grand word of the Katha Upanishad—Shraddhâ or marvellous faith. An instance of Shraddha can be found in the life of Nachiketâ. To preach the doctrine of Shraddha or genuine faith is the mission of my life. Let me repeat to you that this faith is one of the potent factors of humanity and of all religions. First, have faith in yourselves. Know that though one may be a little bubble and another may be a mountain-high wave, yet behind both the bubble and the wave there is the infinite ocean. Therefore there is hope for every one. There is salvation for every one. Every one must sooner or later get rid of the bonds of Mâyâ. This is the first thing to do. Infinite hope begets infinite aspiration. If that faith comes to us, it will bring back our national life as it was in the days of Vyasa and Arjuna—the days when all our sublime doctrines of humanity were preached. Today we are far behindhand in spiritual insight and spiritual thoughts. India had plenty of spirituality, so much so that her spiritual greatness made India the greatest nation of the then existing races of the world; and if traditions and hopes are to be believed, those days will come back once more to us, and that depends upon you. You, young men of Bengal, do not look up to the rich and great men who have money. The poor did all the great and gigantic work of the world. You, poor men of Bengal, come up, you can do everything, and you must do everything. Many will follow your example, poor though you are. Be steady, and, above all, be pure and sincere to the backbone. Have faith in your destiny. You, young men of Bengal, are to work out the salvation of India. Mark that, whether you believe it or not, do not think that it will be done today or tomorrow. I believe in it as I believe in my own body and my own soul. Therefore my heart goes to you—young men of Bengal. It depends upon you who have no money; because you are poor, therefore you will work. Because you

have nothing, therefore you will be sincere. Because you are sincere, you will be ready to renounce all. That is what I am just now telling you. Once more I repeat this to you. This is your mission in life, this is my mission in life. I do not care what philosophy you take up; only I am ready to prove here that throughout the whole of India, there runs a mutual and cordial string of eternal faith in the perfection of humanity, and I believe in it myself. And let that faith spread over the whole land.

SANNYASA: ITS IDEAL AND PRACTICE

A parting Address was given to Swamiji by the junior Sannyâsins of the Math (Belur), on the eve of his leaving for the West for the second time. The following is the substance of Swamiji's reply as entered in the Math Diary on 19th June 1899:

This is not the time for a long lecture. But I shall speak to you in brief about a few things which I should like you to carry into practice. First, we have to understand the ideal, and then the methods by which we can make it practical. Those of you who are Sannyasins must try to do good to others, for Sannyasa means that. There is no time to deliver a long discourse on "Renunciation", but I shall very briefly characterise it as "the love of death". Worldly people love life. The Sannyasin is to love death. Are we to commit suicide then? Far from it. For suicides are not lovers of death, as it is often seen that when a man trying to commit suicide fails, he never attempts it for a second time. What is the love of death then? We must die, that is certain; let us die then for a good cause. Let all our actions—eating, drinking, and everything that we do—tend towards the sacrifice of our self. You nourish your body by eating. What good is there in doing that if you do not hold it as a sacrifice to the well-being of others? You nourish your minds by reading books. There is no good in doing that unless you hold it also as a sacrifice to the whole world. For the whole world is one; you are rated a very insignificant part of it, and therefore it is right for you that you should serve your millions of brothers rather than aggrandise this little self.

सर्वतः पाणिपादं तत् सर्वतोऽक्षिशिरोमुखम् ।
सर्वतः श्रुतिमल्लोके सर्वमावृत्य तिष्ठति ॥

"With hands and feet everywhere, with eyes, heads, and mouths everywhere, with ears everywhere in the universe, That exists pervading all." (Gita, XIII. 13)

Thus you must die a gradual death. In such a death is heaven, all good is stored therein—and in its opposite is all that is diabolical and evil.

Then as to the methods of carrying the ideals into practical life. First, we have to understand that we must not have any impossible ideal. An ideal which is too high makes a nation weak and degraded. This happened after the Buddhistic and the Jain reforms. On the other hand, too much practicality is also wrong. If you have not even a little imagination, if you have no ideal let guide you, you are simply a brute. So we must not lower our ideal, neither are we to lose sight of practicality. We must avoid the two extremes. In our country, the old idea is to sit in a cave and meditate and die. To go ahead of others in salvation is wrong. One must learn sooner or later that one cannot get salvation if one does not try to seek the salvation of his brothers. You must try to combine in your life immense idealism with immense practicality. You must be prepared to go into deep meditation now, and the next moment you must be ready to go and cultivate these fields (Swamiji said, pointing to the meadows of the Math). You must be prepared to explain the difficult intricacies of the Shâstras now, and the next moment to go and sell the produce of the fields in the market. You must be prepared for all menial services, not only here, but elsewhere also.

The next thing to remember is that the aim of this institution is to make men. You must not merely learn what the Rishis taught. Those Rishis are gone, and their opinions are also gone with them. You must be Rishis yourselves. You are also men as much as the greatest men that were ever born—even our Incarnations. What can mere book-learning do? What can meditation do even? What can the Mantras and Tantras do? You must stand on your own feet. You must have this new method—the method of man-making. The true man is he who is strong as strength itself and yet possesses a woman's heart. You must feel for the millions of beings around you, and yet you must be strong and inflexible and you must also possess Obedience; though it may seem a little paradoxical—you must possess these apparently conflicting virtues. If your superior order you to throw yourself into a river and catch a crocodile, you must first obey and then reason with him. Even if the order be wrong, first obey and then contradict it. The bane of sects, especially in Bengal, is that if any one happens to have a different opinion, he immediately starts a new sect, he has no patience to wait. So you must have a deep regard for your Sangha. There is no place for disobedience here. Crush it out without mercy. No disobedient members here, you must turn them out. There must not be any traitors in the camp. You must be as free as the air, and as obedient as this plant and the dog.

WHAT HAVE I LEARNT?

Delivered at Dacca, 30th March, 1901. At Dacca

Swamiji delivered two lectures in English. The first was on "What have I learnt?" and the second one was "The Religion we are born in". The following is translated from a report in Bengali by a disciple, and it contains the substance of the first lecture:

First of all, I must express my pleasure at the opportunity afforded me of coming to Eastern Bengal to acquire an intimate knowledge of this part of the country, which I hitherto lacked in spite of my wanderings through many civilised countries of the West, as well as my gratification at the sight of majestic rivers, wide fertile plains, and picturesque villages in this, my own country of Bengal, which I had not the good fortune of seeing for myself before. I did not know that there was everywhere in my country of Bengal—on land and water—so much beauty and charm. But this much has been my gain that after seeing the various countries of the world I can now much more appreciate the beauties of my own land.

In the same way also, in search of religion, I had travelled among various sects—sects which had taken up the ideals of foreign nations as their own, and I had begged at the door of others, not knowing then that in the religion of my country, in our national religion, there was so much beauty and grandeur. It is now many years since I found Hinduism to be the most perfectly satisfying religion in the world. Hence I feel sad at heart when I see existing among my own countrymen, professing a peerless faith, such a widespread indifference to our religion—though I am very well aware of the unfavourable materialistic conditions in which they pass their lives—owing to the diffusion of European modes of thought in this, our great motherland.

There are among us at the present day certain reformers who want to reform our religion or rather turn it topsyturvy with a view to the regeneration of the Hindu nation. There are, no doubt, some thoughtful people among them, but there are also many who follow others blindly and act most foolishly, not knowing what they are about. This class of reformers are very enthusiastic in introducing foreign ideas into our religion. They have taken hold of the word "idolatry", and aver that Hinduism is not true, because it is idolatrous. They never seek to find out what this so-called "idolatry" is, whether it is good or bad; only taking their cue from others, they are bold enough to shout down Hinduism as untrue. There is another class of men among us who are intent upon giving some slippery scientific explanations for any and every Hindu custom, rite, etc., and who are always talking of electricity, magnetism, air vibration, and all that sort of thing. Who knows but they will perhaps some day define God Himself as nothing but a mass of electric vibrations! However, Mother bless them all! She it is who is having Her work done in various ways through multifarious natures and tendencies.

In contradistinction to these, there is that ancient class who say, "I do not know, I do not care to know or understand all these your hair-splitting ratiocinations; I want God, I want the Atman, I want to go to that Beyond, where there is no universe, where there is no pleasure or pain, where dwells the Bliss Supreme"; who say, "I believe in salvation by bathing in the holy Gangâ with faith"; who say, "whomsoever you may worship with singleness of faith and devotion as the one God of the universe, in whatsoever form as Shiva, Râma, Vishnu, etc., you will get Moksha"; to that sturdy ancient class I am proud to belong.

Then there is a sect who advise us to follow God and the world together. They are not sincere, they do not express what they feel in their hearts. What is the teaching of the Great Ones? — "Where there is Rama, there is no Kama; where there is Kama, there Rama is not. Night and day can never exist together." The voice of the ancient sages proclaim to us, "If you desire to attain God, you will have to renounce Kâma-Kânchana (lust and possession). The Samsâra is unreal, hollow, void of substance. Unless you give it up, you can never reach God, try however you may. If you cannot do that, own that you are weak, but by no means lower the Ideal. Do not cover the corrupting corpse with leaves of gold!" So according to them, if you want to gain spirituality, to attain God, the first thing that you have to do is to give up this playing "hide-and-seek with your ideas", this dishonesty, this "theft within the chamber of thought".

What have I learnt? What have I learnt from this ancient sect? I have learnt:

दुर्लभं त्रयमेवैतत् देवानुग्रहहेतुकम्।
मनुष्यत्वं मुमुक्षुत्वं महापुरुषसंश्रयः॥

— "Verily, these three are rare to obtain and come only through the grace of God — human birth, desire to obtain Moksha, and the company of the great-souled ones." The first thing needed is Manushyatva, human birth, because it only is favourable to the attainment of Mukti. The next is Mumukshutva. Though our means of realisation vary according to the difference in sects and individuals — though different individuals can lay claim to their special rights and means to gain knowledge, which vary according to their different stations in life — yet it can be said in general without fear of contradiction that without this Mumukshutâ, realisation of God is impossible. What is Mumukshutva? It is the strong desire for Moksha — earnest yearning to get out of the sphere of pain and pleasure — utter disgust for the world. When that intense burning desire to see God comes, then you should know that you are entitled to the realisation of the Supreme.

Then another thing is necessary, and that is the coming in direct contact with the Mahâpurushas, and thus moulding our lives in accordance with those of the great-souled ones who have reached the Goal. Even disgust for the world and a burning desire for God are not sufficient. Initiation by the Guru is necessary. Why? Because it is the bringing of yourself into connection with that great source of power which has been handed down through generations from one Guru to another, in uninterrupted succession. The devotee must seek and accept the Guru or spiritual preceptor as his counsellor, philosopher, friend, and guide. In short, the Guru is the sine qua non of progress in the path of spirituality. Whom then shall I accept as my Guru? श्रोत्रियोऽवृजिनोऽकामहतो यो ब्रह्मवित्तमः — "He who is versed in the Vedas, without taint, unhurt by desire, he who is the best of the knowers of Brahman." Shrotriya — he who is not only learned in the Shâstras, but who knows their subtle secrets, who has realised their true import in his life. "Reading merely the various scriptures, they have become only parrots, and not Pandits. He indeed has become a Pandit who has gained Prema (Divine Love) by reading even one word of the Shâstras." Mere book-learned Pandits are of no avail. Nowadays, everyone wants to be a Guru; even a poor beggar wants to make a gift of a lakh of rupees! Then the Guru must be without a touch of taint, and he must be Akâmahata — unhurt by any desire — he should have no other motive except that of purely doing good to others, he should be an ocean of mercy-without-reason and not impart religious teaching with a view to gaining name or fame, or anything pertaining to selfish interest. And he must be the intense knower of Brahman, that is, one who has realised Brahman even as tangibly as an Âmalaka-fruit in the palm of the hand. Such is the Guru, says the Shruti. When spiritual union is established with such a Guru, then comes realisation of God — then god-vision becomes easy of attainment.

After initiation there should be in the aspirant after Truth, Abhyâsa or earnest and repeated attempt at practical application of the Truth by prescribed means of constant meditation upon the Chosen Ideal. Even if you have a burning thirst for God, or have gained the Guru, unless you have along with it the Abhyasa, unless you practice what you have been taught, you cannot get realisation. When all these are firmly established in you, then you will reach the Goal.

Therefore, I say unto you, as Hindus, as descendants of the glorious Âryans, do not forget the great ideal of our religion, that great ideal of the Hindus, which is, to go beyond this Samsara — not only to renounce the world, but to give up heaven too; ay, not only to give up evil, but to give up good too; and thus to go beyond all, beyond this phenomenal existence, and ultimately realise the Sat-Chit-Ânanda Brahman — the Absolute Existence-Knowledge-Bliss, which is Brahman.

THE RELIGION WE ARE BORN IN

At an open-air meeting convened at Dacca, on the 31st March, 1901, the Swamiji spoke in English for two hours on the above subject before a vast audience. The following is a translation of the lecture from a Bengali report of a disciple:

In the remote past, our country made gigantic advances in spiritual ideas. Let us, today, bring before our mind's eye that ancient history. But the one great danger in meditating over long-past greatness is that we cease to exert ourselves for new things, and content ourselves with vegetating upon that bygone ancestral glory and priding ourselves upon it. We should guard against that. In ancient times there were, no doubt, many Rishis and Maharshis who came face to face with Truth. But if this recalling of our ancient greatness is to be of real benefit, we too must become Rishis like them. Ay, not only that, but it is my firm conviction that we shall be even greater Rishis than any that our history presents to us. In the past, signal were our attainments — I glory in them, and I feel proud in thinking of them. I am not even in despair at seeing the present degradation, and I am full of hope in picturing to my mind what is to come in the future. Why? Because I know the seed undergoes a complete transformation, ay, the seed as seed is seemingly destroyed before it develops into a tree. In the same way, in the midst of our present degradation lies, only dormant for a time, the potentiality of the future greatness of our religion, ready to spring up again, perhaps more mighty and glorious than ever before.

Now let us consider what are the common grounds of agreement in the religion we are born in. At first sight we undeniably find various differences among our sects. Some are Advaitists, some are Vishishtâdvaitists, and others are Dvaitists. Some believe in Incarnations of God, some in image-worship, while others are upholders of the doctrine of the Formless. Then as to customs also, various differences are known to exist. The Jâts are not outcasted even if they marry among the Mohammedans and Christians. They can enter into any Hindu temple without hindrance. In many villages in the Punjab, one who does not eat swine will hardly be considered a Hindu. In Nepal, a Brâhmin can marry in the four Varnas; while in Bengal, a Brahmin cannot marry even among the subdivisions of his own caste. So on and so forth. But in the midst of all these differences we note one point of unity among all Hindus, and it is this, that no Hindu eats beef. In the same way, there is a great common ground of unity underlying the various forms and sects of our religion.

First, in discussing the scriptures, one fact stands out prominently—that only those religions which had one or many scriptures of their own as their basis advanced by leaps and bounds and survive to the present day notwithstanding all the persecution and repression hurled against them. The Greek religion, with all its beauty, died out in the absence of any scripture to support it; but the religion of the Jews stands undiminished in its power, being based upon the authority of the Old Testament. The same is the case with the Hindu religion, with its scripture, the Vedas, the oldest in the world. The Vedas are divided into the Karma Kânda and the Jnâna Kânda. Whether for good or for evil, the Karma Kanda has fallen into disuse in India, though there are some Brahmins in the Deccan who still perform Yajnas now and then with the sacrifice of goats; and also we find here and there, traces of the Vedic Kriyâ Kânda in the Mantras used in connection with our marriage and Shrâddha ceremonies etc. But there is no chance of its being rehabilitated on its original footing. Kumârila Bhatta once tried to do so, but he was not successful in his attempt.

The Jnana Kanda of the Vedas comprises the Upanishads and is known by the name of Vedanta, the pinnacle of the Shrutis, as it is called. Wherever you find the Âchâryas quoting a passage from the Shrutis, it is invariably from the Upanishads. The Vedanta is now the religion of the Hindus. If any sect in India wants to have its ideas established with a firm hold on the people it must base them on the authority of the Vedanta. They all have to do it, whether they are Dvaitists or Advaitists. Even the Vaishnavas have to go to Gopâlatâpini

Upanishad to prove the truth of their own theories. If a new sect does not find anything in the Shrutis in confirmation of its ideas, it will go even to the length of manufacturing a new Upanishad, and making it pass current as one of the old original productions. There have been many such in the past.

Now as to the Vedas, the Hindus believe that they are not mere books composed by men in some remote age. They hold them to be an accumulated mass of endless divine wisdom, which is sometimes manifested and at other times remains unmanifested. Commentator Sâyanâchârya says somewhere in his works यो वेदेभ्योऽखिलं जगत् निर्ममे— "Who created the whole universe out of the knowledge of the Vedas". No one has ever seen the composer of the Vedas, and it is impossible to imagine one. The Rishis were only the discoverers of the Mantras or Eternal Laws; they merely came face to face with the Vedas, the infinite mine of knowledge, which has been there from time without beginning.

Who are these Rishis? Vâtsyâyana says, "He who has attained through proper means the direct realisation of Dharma, he alone can be a Rishi even if he is a Mlechchha by birth." Thus it is that in ancient times, Vasishtha, born of an illegitimate union, Vyâsa, the son of a fisherwoman, Narada, the son of a maidservant with uncertain parentage, and many others of like nature attained to Rishihood. Truly speaking, it comes to this then, that no distinction should be made with one who has realised the Truth. If the persons just named all became Rishis, then, O ye Kulin Brahmins of the present day, how much greater Rishis you can become! Strive after that Rishihood, stop not till you have attained the goal, and the whole world will of itself bow at your feet! Be a Rishi—that is the secret of power.

This Veda is our only authority, and everyone has the right to it.

यथेमां वाचं कल्याणीमावदानि जनेभ्यः।
ब्रह्मराजन्याभ्यां शूद्राय चार्याय च स्वाय चारणाय॥

— Thus says the Shukla Yajur Veda (XXVI. 2). Can you show any authority from this Veda of ours that everyone has not the right to it? The Purânas, no doubt, say that a certain caste has the right to such and such a recension of the Vedas, or a certain caste has no right to study them, or that this portion of the Vedas is for the Satya Yuga and that portion is for the Kali Yuga. But, mark you, the Veda does not say so; it is only your Puranas that do so. But can the servant dictate to the master? The Smritis, Puranas, Tantras—all these are acceptable only so far as they agree with the Vedas; and wherever they are contradictory, they are to be rejected as unreliable. But nowadays we have put the Puranas on even a higher pedestal than the Vedas! The study of the Vedas has almost disappeared from Bengal. How I wish that day will soon come when in every home the Veda will be worshipped together with Shâlagrâma, the household Deity, when the young, the old, and the women will inaugurate the worship of the Veda!

I have no faith in the theories advanced by Western savants

with regard to the Vedas. They are today fixing the antiquity of the Vedas at a certain period, and again tomorrow upsetting it and bringing it one thousand years forward, and so on. However, about the Puranas, I have told you that they are authoritative only in so far as they agree with the Vedas, otherwise not. In the Puranas we find many things which do not agree with the Vedas. As for instance, it is written in the Puranas that some one lived ten thousand years, another twenty thousand years, but in the Vedas we find: शतायुर्वै पुरुषः — "Man lives indeed a hundred years." Which are we to accept in this case? Certainly the Vedas. Notwithstanding statements like these, I do not depreciate the Puranas. They contain many beautiful and illuminating teachings and words of wisdom on Yoga, Bhakti, Jnâna, and Karma; those, of course, we should accept. Then there are the Tantras. The real meaning of the word Tantra is Shâstra, as for example, Kâpila Tantra. But the word Tantra is generally used in a limited sense. Under the sway of kings who took up Buddhism and preached broadcast the doctrine of Ahimsâ, the performances of the Vedic Yâga-Yajnas became a thing of the past, and no one could kill any animal in sacrifice for fear of the king. But subsequently amongst the Buddhists themselves—who were converts from Hinduism—the best parts of these Yaga-Yajnas were taken up, and practiced in secret. From these sprang up the Tantras. Barring some of the abominable things in the Tantras, such as the Vâmâchâra etc., the Tantras are not so bad as people are inclined to think. There are many high and sublime Vedantic thoughts in them. In fact, the Brâhmana portions of the Vedas were modified a little and incorporated into the body of the Tantras. All the forms of our worship and the ceremonials of the present day, comprising the Karma Kanda, are observed in accordance with the Tantras.

Now let us discuss the principles of our religion a little. Notwithstanding the differences and controversies existing among our various sects, there are in them, too, several grounds of unity. First, almost all of them admit the existence of three things—three entities—Ishvara, Atman, and the Jagat. Ishvara is He who is eternally creating, preserving and destroying the whole universe. Excepting the Sânkhyas, all the others believe in this. Then the doctrine of the Atman and the reincarnation of the soul; it maintains that innumerable individual souls, having taken body after body again and again, go round and round in the wheel of birth and death according to their respective Karmas; this is Samsâravâda, or as it is commonly called the doctrine of rebirth. Then there is the Jagat or universe without beginning and without end. Though some hold these three as different phases of one only, and some others as three distinctly different entities, and others again in various other ways, yet they are all unanimous in believing in these three.

Here I should ask you to remember that Hindus, from time immemorial, knew the Atman as separate from Manas, mind. But the Occidentals could never soar beyond the mind. The West knows the universe to be full of happiness, and as such, it is to them a place where they can enjoy the most; but the East is born with the conviction that this Samsara, this ever-changing existence, is full of misery, and as such, it is nothing, nothing but unreal, not worth bartering the soul for its ephemeral joys and possessions. For this very reason, the West is ever especially adroit in organised action, and so also the East is ever bold in search of the mysteries of the internal world.

Let us, however, turn now to one or two other aspects of Hinduism. There is the doctrine of the Incarnations of God. In the Vedas we find mention of Matsya Avatâra, the Fish Incarnation only. Whether all believe in this doctrine or not is not the point; the real meaning, however, of this Avatâravâda is the worship of Man—to see God in man is the real God-vision. The Hindu does not go through nature to nature's God—he goes to the God of man through Man.

Then there is image-worship. Except the five Devatâs who are to be worshipped in every auspicious Karma as enjoined in our Shastras, all the other Devatas are merely the names of certain states held by them. But again, these five Devatas are nothing but the different names of the one God Only. This external worship of images has, however, been described in all our Shastras as the lowest of all the low forms of worship. But that does not mean that it is a wrong thing to do. Despite the many iniquities that have found entrance into the practices of image-worship as it is in vogue now, I do not condemn it. Ay, where would I have been if I had not been blessed with the dust of the holy feet of that orthodox, image-worshipping Brahmin!

Those reformers who preach against image-worship, or what they denounce as idolatry—to them I say "Brothers, if you are fit to worship God-without-form discarding all external help, do so, but why do you condemn others who cannot do the same? A beautiful, large edifice, the glorious relic of a hoary antiquity has, out of neglect or disuse, fallen into a dilapidated condition; accumulations of dirt and dust may be lying everywhere within it, maybe, some portions are tumbling down to the ground. What will you do to it? Will you take in hand the necessary cleansing and repairs and thus restore the old, or will you pull the whole edifice down to the ground and seek to build another in its place, after a sordid modern plan whose permanence has yet to be established? We have to reform it, which truly means to make ready or perfect by necessary cleansing and repairs, not by demolishing the whole thing. There the function of reform ends. When the work of renovating the old is finished, what further necessity does it serve? Do that if you can, if not, hands off!" The band of reformers in our country want, on the contrary, to build up a separate sect of their own. They have, however, done good work; may the blessings of God be showered on their heads! But why should you, Hindus, want to separate yourselves from the great common fold? Why should you feel ashamed to take the name of Hindu, which is your greatest and most glorious possession? This national ship of ours, ye children of the Immortals, my countrymen, has been plying for ages, carrying civilisation and enriching the whole world with its inestimable treasures. For scores of shining centuries this national ship of ours has been ferrying across the ocean of life, and has taken millions of souls to the other shore, beyond all misery. But today it may have sprung a leak and got damaged, through your own fault or whatever cause it matters not. What would you, who have placed yourselves in it, do now? Would you go about cursing it and quarrelling among yourselves! Would you not all unite together and put your best efforts to stop the holes? Let us all gladly give our hearts' blood to do this; and if we fail in the attempt, let us all sink and die together, with blessings and not curses on our lips.

And to the Brahmins I say, "Vain is your pride of birth and ancestry. Shake it off. Brahminhood, according to your Shastras, you have no more now, because you have for so long lived under Mlechchha kings. If you at all believe in the words of your own ancestors, then go this very moment and make expiation by entering into the slow fire kindled by Tusha (husks), like that old Kumarila Bhatta, who with the purpose of ousting the Buddhists first became a disciple of the Buddhists and then defeating them in argument became the cause of death to many, and subsequently entered the Tushânala to expiate his sins. If you are not bold enough to do that, then admit your weakness and stretch forth a helping hand, and open the gates of knowledge to one and all, and give the downtrodden masses once more their just and legitimate rights and privileges."

PRACTICAL VEDANTA

PRACTICAL VEDANTA, PART I

Delivered in London, 10th November 1896

I have been asked to say something about the practical position of the Vedanta philosophy. As I have told you, theory is very good indeed, but how are we to carry it into practice? If it be absolutely impracticable, no theory is of any value whatever, except as intellectual gymnastics. The Vedanta, therefore, as a religion must be intensely practical. We must be able to carry it out in every part of our lives. And not only this, the fictitious differentiation between religion and the life of the world must vanish, for the Vedanta teaches oneness—one life throughout. The ideals of religion must cover the whole field of life, they must enter into all our thoughts, and more and more into practice. I will enter gradually on the practical side as we proceed. But this series of lectures is intended to be a basis, and so we must first apply ourselves to theories and understand how they are worked out, proceeding from forest caves to busy streets and cities; and one peculiar feature we find is that many of these thoughts have been the outcome, not of retirement into forests, but have emanated from persons whom we expect to lead the busiest lives—from ruling monarchs.

Shvetaketu was the son of Âruni, a sage, most probably a recluse. He was brought up in the forest, but he went to the city of the Panchâlas and appeared at the court of the king, Pravâhana Jaivali. The king asked him, "Do you know how beings depart hence at death?" "No, sir." "Do you know how they return hither?" "No, sir." "Do you know the way of the fathers and the way of the gods?" "No, sir." Then the king asked other questions. Shvetaketu could not answer them. So the king told him that he knew nothing. The boy went back to his father, and the father admitted that he himself could not answer these questions. It was not that he was unwilling to answer these questions. It was not that he was unwilling to teach the boy, but he did not know these things. So he went to the king and asked to be taught these secrets. The king said that these things had been hitherto known only among kings; the priests never knew them. He, however, proceeded to teach him what he desired to know. In various Upanishads we find that this Vedanta philosophy is not the outcome of meditation in the forests only, but that the very best parts of it were thought out and expressed by brains which were busiest in the everyday affairs of life. We cannot conceive any man busier than an absolute monarch, a man who is ruling over millions of people, and yet, some of these rulers were deep thinkers.

Everything goes to show that this philosophy must be very practical; and later on, when we come to the Bhagavad-Gita—most of you, perhaps, have read it, it is the best commentary we have on the Vedanta philosophy—curiously enough the scene is laid on the battlefield, where Krishna teaches this philosophy to Arjuna; and the doctrine which stands out luminously in every page of the Gita is intense activity, but in the midst of it, eternal calmness. This is the secret of work, to attain which is the goal of the Vedanta. Inactivity, as we understand it in the sense of passivity, certainly cannot be the goal. Were it so, then the walls around us would be the most intelligent; they are inactive. Clods of earth, stumps of trees, would be the greatest sages in the world; they are inactive. Nor does inactivity become activity when it is combined with passion. Real activity, which is the goal of Vedanta, is combined with eternal calmness, the calmness which cannot be ruffled, the balance of mind which is never disturbed, whatever happens. And we all know from our experience in life that that is the best attitude for work.

I have been asked many times how we can work if we do not have the passion which we generally feel for work. I also thought in that way years ago, but as I am growing older, getting more experience, I find it is not true. The less passion there is, the better we work. The calmer we are, the better for us, and the more the amount of work we can do. When we let loose our feelings, we waste so much energy, shatter our nerves, disturb our minds, and accomplish very little work. The energy which ought to have gone out as work is spent as mere feeling, which counts for nothing. It is only when the mind is very calm and collected that the whole of its energy is spent in doing good work. And if you read the lives of the great workers which the world has produced, you will find that they were wonderfully calm men. Nothing, as it were, could throw them off their balance. That is why the man who becomes angry never does a great amount of work, and the man whom nothing can make angry accomplishes so much. The man who gives way to anger, or hatred, or any other passion, cannot work; he only breaks himself to pieces, and does nothing practical. It is the calm, forgiving, equable, well-balanced mind that does the greatest amount of work.

The Vedanta preaches the ideal; and the ideal, as we know, is always far ahead of the real, of the practical, as we may call it. There are two tendencies in human nature: one to harmonise the ideal with the life, and the other to elevate the life to the ideal. It is a great thing to understand this, for the former tendency is the temptation of our lives. I think that I can only do a certain class of work. Most of it, perhaps, is bad; most of it, perhaps, has a motive power of passion behind it, anger, or greed, or selfishness. Now if any man comes to preach to me a certain ideal, the first step towards which is to give up selfishness, to give up self-enjoyment, I think that is impractical. But when a man brings an ideal which can be reconciled with my selfishness, I am glad at once and jump at it. That is the ideal for me. As the word "orthodox" has been manipulated into various forms, so has been the word "practical". "My doxy is orthodoxy; your doxy is heterodoxy." So with practicality. What I think is practical, is to me the only practicality in the world. If I am a shopkeeper, I think shopkeeping the only practical pursuit in the world. If I am a thief, I think stealing is the best means of being practical; others are not practical. You see how we all use this word practical for things we like and can do. Therefore I will ask you to understand that Vedanta, though it is intensely practical, is always so in the sense of the ideal. It does not preach an impossible ideal, however high it be, and it is high enough for an ideal. In one word, this ideal is that you are divine, "Thou art That". This is the essence of Vedanta; after all its ramifications and intellectual gymnastics, you know the human soul to be pure and omniscient, you see that such superstitions as birth and death would be entire nonsense when spoken of in connection with the soul. The soul was never born and will never die, and all these ideas that we are going to die and are afraid to die are mere superstitions. And all such ideas as that we can do this or cannot do that are superstitions. We can do everything. The Vedanta teaches men to have faith in themselves first. As certain religions of the world say that a man who does not believe in a Personal God outside of himself is an atheist, so the Vedanta says, a man who does not believe in himself is an atheist. Not believing in the glory of our own soul is what the Vedanta calls atheism. To many this is, no doubt, a terrible idea; and most of us think that this ideal can never be reached; but the Vedanta insists that it can be realised by every one. There is neither man nor woman or child, nor difference of race or sex, nor anything that stands as a bar to the realisation of the ideal, because Vedanta shows that it is realised already, it is already there.

All the powers in the universe are already ours. It is we who have put our hands before our eyes and cry that it is dark. Know that there is no darkness around us. Take the hands away and there is the light which was from the beginning. Darkness never existed, weakness never existed. We who are fools cry that we are weak; we who are fools cry that we are impure. Thus Vedanta not only insists that the ideal is practical, but that it has been so all the time; and this Ideal, this Reality, is our own nature. Everything else that you see is false, untrue. As soon as you say, "I am a little mortal being," you are saying something which is not true, you are giving the lie to yourselves, you are hypnotising yourselves into something vile and weak and wretched.

The Vedanta recognises no sin, it only recognises error. And the greatest error, says the Vedanta, is to say that you are weak, that you are a sinner, a miserable creature, and that you have no power and you cannot do this and that. Every time you think in that way, you, as it were, rivet one more link in the chain that binds you down, you add one more layer of hypnotism on to your own soul. Therefore, whosoever thinks he is weak is wrong, whosoever thinks he is impure is wrong, and is throwing a bad thought into the world. This we must always bear in mind that in the Vedanta there is no attempt at reconciling the present life—the hypnotised life, this false life which we have assumed—with the ideal; but this false life must go, and the real life which is always existing must manifest itself, must shine out. No man becomes purer and purer, it is a matter of greater manifestation. The veil drops away, and the native purity of the soul begins to manifest itself. Everything is ours already—infinite purity, freedom, love, and power.

The Vedanta also says that not only can this be realised in the depths of forests or caves, but by men in all possible conditions of life. We have seen that the people who discovered these truths were neither living in caves nor forests, nor following the ordinary vocations of life, but men who, we have every reason to believe, led the busiest of lives, men who had to command armies, to sit on thrones, and look to the welfare of millions—and all these, in the days of absolute monarchy, and not as in these days when a king is to a great extent a mere figurehead. Yet they could find time to think out all these thoughts, to realise them, and to teach them to humanity. How much more then should it be practical for us whose lives, compared with theirs, are lives of leisure? That we cannot realise them is a shame to us, seeing that we are comparatively free all the time, having very little to do. My requirements are as nothing compared with those of an ancient absolute monarch. My wants are as nothing compared with the demands of Arjuna on the battlefield of Kurukshetra, commanding a huge army; and yet he could find time in the midst of the din and turmoil of battle to talk the highest philosophy and to carry it into his life also. Surely we ought to be able to do as much in this life of ours—comparatively free, easy, and comfortable. Most of us here have more time than we think we have, if we really want to use it for good. With the amount of freedom we have we can attain to two hundred ideals in this life, if we will, but we must not degrade the ideal to the actual. One of the most insinuating things comes to us in the shape of persons who apologise for our mistakes and teach us how to make special excuses for all our foolish wants and foolish desires; and we think that their ideal is the only ideal we need have. But it is not so. The Vedanta teaches no such thing. The actual should be reconciled to the ideal, the present life should be made to coincide with life eternal.

For you must always remember that the one central ideal of Vedanta is this oneness. There are no two in anything, no two lives, nor even two different kinds of life for the two worlds. You will find the Vedas speaking of heavens and things like that at first; but later on, when they come to the highest ideals of their philosophy, they brush away all these things. There is but one life, one world, one existence. Everything is that One, the difference is in degree and not in kind. The difference between our lives is not in kind. The Vedanta entirely denies such ideas as that animals are separate from men, and that they were made and created by God to be used for our food.

Some people have been kind enough to start an antivivisection society. I asked a member, "Why do you think, my friend, that it is quite lawful to kill animals for food, and not to kill one or two for scientific experiments?" He replied, "Vivisection is most horrible, but animals have been given to us for food." Oneness includes all animals. If man's life is immortal, so also is the animal's. The difference is only in degree and not in kind. The amoeba and I are the same, the difference is only in degree; and from the standpoint of the highest life, all these differences vanish. A man may see a great deal of difference between grass and a little tree, but if you mount very high, the grass and the biggest tree will appear much the same. So, from the standpoint of the highest ideal, the lowest animal and the highest man are the same. If you believe there is a God, the animals and the highest creatures must be the same. A God who is partial to his children called men, and cruel to his children called brute beasts, is worse than a demon. I would rather die a hundred times than worship such a God. My whole life would be a fight with such a God But there is no difference, and those who say there is, are irresponsible, heartless people who do not know. Here is a case of the word practical used in a wrong sense. I myself may not be a very strict vegetarian, but I understand the ideal. When I eat meat I know it is wrong. Even if I am bound to eat it under certain circumstances, I know it is cruel. I must not drag my ideal down to the actual and apologise for my weak conduct in this way. The ideal is not to eat flesh, not to injure any being, for all animals are my brothers. If you can think of them as your brothers, you have made a little headway towards the brotherhood of all souls, not to speak of the brotherhood of man! That is child's play. You generally find that this is not

very acceptable to many, because it teaches them to give up the actual, and go higher up to the ideal. But if you bring out a theory which is reconciled with their present conduct, they regard it as entirely practical.

There is this strongly conservative tendency in human nature: we do not like to move one step forward. I think of mankind just as I read of persons who become frozen in snow; all such, they say, want to go to sleep, and if you try to drag them up, they say, "Let me sleep; it is so beautiful to sleep in the snow", and they die there in that sleep. So is our nature. That is what we are doing all our life, getting frozen from the feet upwards, and yet wanting to sleep. Therefore you must struggle towards the ideal, and if a man comes who wants to bring that ideal down to your level, and teach a religion that does not carry that highest ideal, do not listen to him. To me that is an impracticable religion. But if a man teaches a religion which presents the highest ideal, I am ready for him. Beware when anyone is trying to apologise for sense vanities and sense weaknesses. If anyone wants to preach that way to us, poor, sense-bound clods of earth as we have made ourselves by following that teaching, we shall never progress. I have seen many of these things, have had some experience of the world, and my country is the land where religious sects grow like mushrooms. Every year new sects arise. But one thing I have marked, that it is only those that never want to reconcile the man of flesh with the man of truth that make progress. Wherever there is this false idea of reconciling fleshly vanities with the highest ideals, of dragging down God to the level of man, there comes decay. Man should not be degraded to worldly slavery, but should be raised up to God.

At the same time, there is another side to the question. We must not look down with contempt on others. All of us are going towards the same goal. The difference between weakness and strength is one of degree; the difference between virtue and vice is one of degree, the difference between heaven and hell is one of degree, the difference between life and death is one of degree, all differences in this world are of degree, and not of kind, because oneness is the secret of everything. All is One, which manifests Itself, either as thought, or life, or soul, or body, and the difference is only in degree. As such, we have no right to look down with contempt upon those who are not developed exactly in the same degree as we are. Condemn none; if you can stretch out a helping hand, do so. If you cannot, fold your hands, bless your brothers, and let them go their own way. Dragging down and condemning is not the way to work. Never is work accomplished in that way. We spend our energies in condemning others. Criticism and condemnation is a vain way of spending our energies, for in the long run we come to learn that all are seeing the same thing, are more or less approaching the same ideal, and that most of our differences are merely differences of expression.

Take the idea of sin. I was telling you just now the Vedantic idea of it, and the other idea is that man is a sinner. They are practically the same, only the one takes the positive and the other the negative side. One shows to man his strength and the other his weakness. There may be weakness, says the Vedanta, but never mind, we want to grow. Disease was found out as soon as man was born. Everyone knows his disease; it requires no one to tell us what our diseases are. But thinking all the time that we are diseased will not cure us—medicine is necessary. We may forget anything outside, we may try to become hypocrites to the external world, but in our heart of hearts we all know our weaknesses. But, says the Vedanta, being reminded of weakness does not help much; give strength, and strength does not come by thinking of weakness all the time. The remedy for weakness is not brooding over weakness, but thinking of strength. Teach men of the strength that is already within them. Instead of telling them they are sinners, the Vedanta takes the opposite position, and says, "You are pure and perfect, and what you call sin does not belong to you." Sins are very low degrees of Self-manifestation; manifest your Self in a high degree. That is the one thing to remember; all of us can do that. Never say, "No", never say, "I cannot", for you are infinite. Even time and space are as nothing compared with your nature. You can do anything and everything, you are almighty.

These are the principles of ethics, but we shall now come down lower and work out the details. We shall see how this Vedanta can be carried into our everyday life, the city life, the country life, the national life, and the home life of every nation. For, if a religion cannot help man wherever he may be, wherever he stands, it is not of much use; it will remain only a theory for the chosen few. Religion, to help mankind, must be ready and able to help him in whatever condition he is, in servitude or in freedom, in the depths of degradation or on the heights of purity; everywhere, equally, it should be able to come to his aid. The principles of Vedanta, or the ideal of religion, or whatever you may call it, will be fulfilled by its capacity for performing this great function.

The ideal of faith in ourselves is of the greatest help to us. If faith in ourselves had been more extensively taught and practiced, I am sure a very large portion of the evils and miseries that we have would have vanished. Throughout the history of mankind, if any motive power has been more potent than another in the lives of all great men and women, it is that of faith in themselves. Born with the consciousness that they were to be great, they became great. Let a man go down as low as possible; there must come a time when out of sheer desperation he will take an upward curve and will learn to have faith in himself. But it is better for us that we should know it from the very first. Why should we have all these bitter experiences in order to gain faith in ourselves? We can see that all the difference between man and man is owing to the existence or non-existence of faith in himself. Faith in ourselves will do everything. I have experienced it in my own life, and am still doing so; and as I grow older that faith is becoming stronger and stronger. He is an atheist who does not believe in himself. The old religions said that he was an atheist who did not be-

lieve in God. The new religion says that he is the atheist who does not believe in himself. But it is not selfish faith because the Vedanta, again, is the doctrine of oneness. It means faith in all, because you are all. Love for yourselves means love for all, love for animals, love for everything, for you are all one. It is the great faith which will make the world better. I am sure of that. He is the highest man who can say with truth, "I know all about myself." Do you know how much energy, how many powers, how many forces are still lurking behind that frame of yours? What scientist has known all that is in man? Millions of years have passed since man first came here, and yet but one infinitesimal part of his powers has been manifested. Therefore, you must not say that you are weak. How do you know what possibilities lie behind that degradation on the surface? You know but little of that which is within you. For behind you is the ocean of infinite power and blessedness.

"This Âtman is first to be heard of." Hear day and night that you are that Soul. Repeat it to yourselves day and night till it enters into your very veins, till it tingles in every drop of blood, till it is in your flesh and bone. Let the whole body be full of that one ideal, "I am the birthless, the deathless, the blissful, the omniscient, the omnipotent, ever-glorious Soul." Think on it day and night; think on it till it becomes part and parcel of your life. Meditate upon it, and out of that will come work. "Out of the fullness of the heart the mouth speaketh," and out of the fullness of the heart the hand worketh also. Action will come. Fill yourselves with the ideal; whatever you do, think well on it. All your actions will be magnified, transformed, deified, by the very power of the thought. If matter is powerful, thought is omnipotent. Bring this thought to bear upon your life, fill yourselves with the thought of your almightiness, your majesty, and your glory. Would to God no superstitions had been put into your head! Would to God we had not been surrounded from our birth by all these superstitious influences and paralysing ideas of our weakness and vileness! Would to God that mankind had had an easier path through which to attain to the noblest and highest truths! But man had to pass through all this; do not make the path more difficult for those who are coming after you.

These are sometimes terrible doctrines to teach. I know people who get frightened at these ideas, but for those who want to be practical, this is the first thing to learn. Never tell yourselves or others that you are weak. Do good if you can, but do not injure the world. You know in your inmost heart that many of your limited ideas, this humbling of yourself and praying and weeping to imaginary beings are superstitions. Tell me one case where these prayers have been answered. All the answers that came were from your own hearts. You know there are no ghosts, but no sooner are you in the dark than you feel a little creepy sensation. That is so because in our childhood we have had all these fearful ideas put into our heads. But do not teach these things to others through fear of society and public opinion, through fear of incurring the hatred of friends, or for fear of losing cherished superstitions.

Be masters of all these. What is there to be taught more in religion than the oneness of the universe and faith in one's self? All the works of mankind for thousands of years past have been towards this one goal, and mankind is yet working it out. It is your turn now and you already know the truth. For it has been taught on all sides. Not only philosophy and psychology, but materialistic sciences have declared it. Where is the scientific man today who fears to acknowledge the truth of this oneness of the universe? Who is there who dares talk of many worlds? All these are superstitions. There is only one life and one world, and this one life and one world is appearing to us as manifold. This manifoldness is like a dream. When you dream, one dream passes away and another comes. You do not live in your dreams. The dreams come one after another, scene after scene unfolds before you. So it is in this world of ninety per cent misery and ten per cent happiness. Perhaps after a while it will appear as ninety per cent happiness, and we shall call it heaven, but a time comes to the sage when the whole thing vanishes, and this world appears as God Himself, and his own soul as God. It is not therefore that there are many worlds, it is not that there are many lives. All this manifoldness is the manifestation of that One. That One is manifesting Himself as many, as matter, spirit, mind, thought, and everything else. It is that One, manifesting Himself as many. Therefore the first step for us to take is to teach the truth to ourselves and to others.

Let the world resound with this ideal, and let superstitions vanish. Tell it to men who are weak and persist in telling it. You are the Pure One; awake and arise, O mighty one, this sleep does not become you. Awake and arise, it does not befit you. Think not that you are weak and miserable. Almighty, arise and awake, and manifest your own nature. It is not fitting that you think yourself a sinner. It is not fitting that you think yourself weak. Say that to the world, say it to yourselves, and see what a practical result comes, see how with an electric flash everything is manifested, how everything is changed. Tell that to mankind, and show them their power. Then we shall learn how to apply it in our daily lives.

To be able to use what we call Viveka (discrimination), to learn how in every moment of our lives, in every one of our actions, to discriminate between what is right and wrong, true and false, we shall have to know the test of truth, which is purity, oneness. Everything that makes for oneness is truth. Love is truth, and hatred is false, because hatred makes for multiplicity. It is hatred that separates man from man; therefore it is wrong and false. It is a disintegrating power; it separates and destroys.

Love binds, love makes for that oneness. You become one, the mother with the child, families with the city, the whole world becomes one with the animals. For love is Existence, God Himself; and all this is the manifestation of that One Love, more or less expressed. The difference is only in degree, but it is the manifestation of that One Love throughout. Therefore in all our actions we have to judge whether it is making for diversity or for oneness. If for diversity we have to give it up, but if it makes for oneness we are sure it is good. So with our thoughts; we have to decide whether they make for disintegration, multiplicity, or for oneness, binding soul to soul and bringing one influence to bear. If they do this, we will take them up, and if not, we will throw them off as criminal.

The whole idea of ethics is that it does not depend on anything unknowable, it does not teach anything unknown, but in the language of the Upanishad, "The God whom you worship as an unknown God, the same I preach unto thee." It is through the Self that you know anything. I see the chair; but to see the chair, I have first to perceive myself and then the chair. It is in and through the Self that the chair is perceived. It is in and through the Self that you are known to me, that the whole world is known to me; and therefore to say this Self is unknown is sheer nonsense. Take off the Self and the whole universe vanishes. In and through the Self all knowledge comes. Therefore it is the best known of all. It is yourself, that which you call I. You may wonder how this I of me can be the I of you. You may wonder how this limited I can be the unlimited Infinite, but it is so. The limited is a mere fiction. The Infinite has been covered up, as it were, and a little of It is manifesting as the I. Limitation can never come upon the unlimited; it is a fiction. The Self is known, therefore, to every one of us—man, woman, or child—and even to animals. Without knowing Him we can neither live nor move, nor have our being; without knowing this Lord of all, we cannot breathe or live a second. The God of the Vedanta is the most known of all and is not the outcome of imagination.

If this is not preaching a practical God, how else could you teach a practical God? Where is there a more practical God than He whom I see before me—a God omnipresent, in every being, more real than our senses? For you are He, the Omnipresent God Almighty, the Soul of your souls, and if I say you are not, I tell an untruth. I know it, whether at all times I realise it or not. He is the Oneness, the Unity of all, the Reality of all life and all existence.

These ideas of the ethics of Vedanta have to be worked out in detail, and, therefore, you must have patience. As I have told you, we want to take the subject in detail and work it up thoroughly, to see how the ideas grow from very low ideals, and how the one great Ideal of oneness has developed and become shaped into the universal love; and we ought to study these in order to avoid dangers. The world cannot find time to work it up from the lowest steps. But what is the use of our standing on higher steps if we cannot give the truth to others coming afterwards? Therefore, it is better to study it in all its workings; and first, it is absolutely necessary to clear the intellectual portion, although we know that intellectuality is almost nothing; for it is the heart that is of most importance. It is through the heart that the Lord is seen, and not through the intellect. The intellect is only the street-cleaner, cleansing the path for us, a secondary worker, the policeman; but the policeman is not a positive necessity for the workings of society. He is only to stop disturbances, to check wrong-doing, and that is all the work required of the intellect. When you read intellectual books, you think when you have mastered them, "Bless the Lord that I am out of them", because the intellect is blind and cannot move of itself, it has neither hands nor feet. It is feeling that works, that moves with speed infinitely superior to that of electricity or anything else. Do you feel?—that is the question. If you do, you will see the Lord: It is the feeling that you have today that will be intensified, deified, raised to the highest platform, until it feels everything, the oneness in everything, till it feels God in itself and in others. The intellect can never do that. "Different methods of speaking words, different methods of explaining the texts of books, these are for the enjoyment of the learned, not for the salvation of the soul" (Vivekachudâmani, 58).

Those of you who have read Thomas a Kempis know how in every page he insists on this, and almost every holy man in the world has insisted on it. Intellect is necessary, for without it we fall into crude errors and make all sorts of mistakes. Intellect checks these; but beyond that, do not try to build anything upon it. It is an inactive, secondary help; the real help is feeling, love. Do you feel for others? If you do, you are growing in oneness. If you do not feel for others, you may be the most intellectual giant ever born, but you will be nothing; you are but dry intellect, and you will remain so. And if you feel, even if you cannot read any book and do not know any language, you are in the right way. The Lord is yours.

Do you not know from the history of the world where the power of the prophets lay? Where was it? In the intellect? Did any of them write a fine book on philosophy, on the most intricate ratiocinations of logic? Not one of them. They only spoke a few words. Feel like Christ and you will be a Christ; feel like Buddha and you will be a Buddha. It is feeling that is the life, the strength, the vitality, without which no amount of intellectual activity can reach God. Intellect is like limbs without the power of locomotion. It is only when feeling enters and gives them motion that they move and work on others. That is so all over the world, and it is a thing which you must always remember. It is one of the most practical things in Vedantic morality, for it is the teaching of the Vedanta that you are all prophets, and all must be prophets. The book is not the proof of your conduct, but you are the proof of the book. How do you know that a book teaches truth? Because you are truth and feel it. That is what the Vedanta says. What is the proof of the Christs and Buddhas of the world? That you and I feel like them. That is how you and I understand that they were true. Our prophet-soul is the proof of their prophet-soul. Your godhead is the proof of God Himself. If you are not a prophet, there never has been anything true of God. If you are not God, there never was any God, and never will be. This, says the Vedanta, is the ideal to follow. Every one of us will have to become a prophet, and you are that already. Only know it. Never think there is anything impossible for the soul. It is the greatest heresy to think so. If there is sin, this is the only sin—to say that you are weak, or others are weak.

PRACTICAL VEDANTA, PART II

Delivered in London, 12th November 1896

I will relate to you a very ancient story from the Chhândogya Upanishad, which tells how knowledge came to a boy. The form of the story is very crude, but we shall find that it contains a principle. A young boy said to his mother, "I am going to study the Vedas. Tell me the name of my father and my caste." The mother was not a married woman, and in India the child of a woman who has not been married is considered an outcast; he is not recognised by society and is not entitled to study the Vedas. So the poor mother said, "My child, I do not know your family name; I was in service, and served in different places; I do not know who your father is, but my name is Jabâlâ and your name is Satyakâma." The little child went to a sage and asked to be taken as a student. The sage asked him, "What is the name of your father, and what is your caste?" The boy repeated to him what he had heard from his mother. The sage at once said, "None but a Brâhmin could speak such a damaging truth about himself. You are a Brahmin and I will teach you. You have not swerved from truth." So he kept the boy with him and educated him.

Now come some of the peculiar methods of education in ancient India. This teacher gave Satyakama four hundred lean, weak cows to take care of, and sent him to the forest. There he went and lived for some time. The teacher had told him to come back when the herd would increase to the number of one thousand. After a few years, one day Satyakama heard a big bull in the herd saying to him, "We are a thousand now; take us back to your teacher. I will teach you a little of Brahman." "Say on, sir," said Satyakama. Then the bull said, "The East is a part of the Lord, so is the West, so is the South, so is the North. The four cardinal points are the four parts of Brahman. Fire will also teach you something of Brahman." Fire was a great symbol in those days, and every student had to procure fire and make offerings. So on the following day, Satyakama started for his Guru's house, and when in the evening he had performed his oblation, and worshipped at the fire, and was sitting near it, he heard a voice come from the fire, "O Satyakama." "Speak, Lord," said Satyakama. (Perhaps you may remember a very similar story in the Old Testament, how Samuel heard a mysterious voice.) "O Satyakama, I am come to teach you a little of Brahman. This earth is a portion of that Brahman. The sky and the heaven are portions of It. The ocean is a part of that Brahman." Then the fire said that a certain bird would also teach him something. Satyakama continued his journey and on the next day when he had performed his evening sacrifice a swan came to him and said, "I will teach you something about Brahman. This fire which you worship, O Satyakama, is a part of that Brahman. The sun is a part, the moon is a part, the lightning is a part of that Brahman. A bird called Madgu will tell you more about it." The next evening that bird came, and a similar voice was heard by Satyakama, "I will tell you something about Brahman. Breath is a part of Brahman, sight is a part, hearing is a part, the mind is a part." Then the boy arrived at his teacher's place and presented himself before him with due reverence. No sooner had the teacher seen this disciple than he remarked: "Satyakama, thy face shines like that of a knower of Brahman! Who then has taught thee?" "Beings other than men," replied Satyakama. "But I wish that you should teach me, sir. For I have heard from men like you that knowledge which is learnt from a Guru alone leads to the supreme good." Then the sage taught him the same knowledge which he had received from the gods. "And nothing was left out, yea, nothing was left out."

Now, apart from the allegories of what the bull, the fire, and the birds taught, we see the tendency of the thought and the direction in which it was going in those days. The great idea of which we here see the germ is that all these voices are inside ourselves. As we understand these truths better, we find that the voice is in our own heart, and the student understood that all the time he was hearing the truth; but his explanation was not correct. He was interpreting the voice as coming from the external world, while all the time, it was within him. The second idea that we get is that of making the knowledge of the Brahman practical. The world is always seeking the practical possibilities of religion, and we find in these stories how it was becoming more and more practical every day. The truth was shown through everything with which the students were familiar. The fire they were worshipping was Brahman, the earth was a part of Brahman, and so on.

The next story belongs to Upakosala Kâmalâyana, a disciple of this Satyakama, who went to be taught by him and dwelt with him for some time. Now Satyakama went away on a journey, and the student became very downhearted; and when the teacher's wife came and asked him why he was not eating, the boy said, "I am too unhappy to eat." Then a voice came from the fire he was worshipping, saying "This life is Brahman, Brahman is the ether, and Brahman is happiness. Know Brahman." "I know, sir," the boy replied, "that life is Brahman, but that It is ether and happiness I do not know." Then it explained that the two words ether and happiness signified one thing in reality, viz. the sentient ether (pure intelligence) that resides in the heart. So, it taught him Brahman as life and as the ether in the heart. Then the fire taught him, "This earth, food, fire, and sun whom you worship, are forms of Brahman. The person that is seen in the sun, I am He. He who knows this and meditates on Him, all his sins vanish and he has long life and becomes happy. He who lives in the cardinal points, the moon, the stars, and the water, I am He. He who lives in this life, the ether, the heavens, and the lightning, I am He." Here too we see the same idea of practical religion. The things which they were worshipping, such as the fire, the sun, the moon, and so forth, and the voice with which they were familiar, form the subject of the stories which explain them and give them a higher meaning. And this is the real, practical side of Vedanta. It does not destroy the world, but it explains it; it does not destroy the person, but explains him; it does not destroy the individuality, but explains it by showing the real individuality. It does not show that this world is vain and does not exist, but it says, "Understand what this world is, so that it may not hurt you." The voice did not say to Upakosala that the fire which he was worshipping, or the sun, or the moon, or the lightning, or anything else, was all wrong, but it showed him that the same spirit which was inside the sun, and moon, and lightning, and the fire, and the earth, was in him, so that everything became transformed, as it were, in the eyes of Upakosala. The fire which was merely a material fire before, in which to make oblations, assumed a new aspect and became the Lord. The earth became transformed, life became transformed, the sun, the moon, the stars, the lightning, everything became transformed and deified. Their real nature was known. The theme of the Vedanta is to see the Lord in everything, to see things in their real nature, not as they appear to be. Then another lesson is taught in the Upanishads: "He who shines through the eyes is Brahman; He is the Beautiful One, He is the Shining One. He shines in all these worlds." A certain peculiar light, a commentator says, which comes to the pure man, is what is meant by the light in the eyes, and it is said that when a man is pure such a light will shine in his eyes, and that light belongs really to the Soul within, which is everywhere. It is the same light which shines in the planets, in the stars, and suns.

I will now read to you some other doctrine of these ancient Upanishads, about birth and death and so on. Perhaps it will interest you. Shvetaketu went to the king of the Panchâlas, and the king asked him, "Do you know where people go when they die? Do you know how they come back? Do you know why the other world does not become full?" The boy replied that he did not know. Then he went to his father and asked him the same questions. The father said, "I do not know," and he went to the king. The king said that this knowledge was never known to the priests, it was only with the kings, and that was the reason why kings ruled the world. This man stayed with the king for some time, for the king said he would teach him. "The other world, O Gautama, is the fire. The sun is its fuel. The rays are the smoke. The day is the flame. The moon is the embers. And the stars are the sparks. In this fire the gods pour libation of faith and from this libation king Soma is born." So on he goes. "You need not make oblation to that little fire: the whole world is that fire, and this oblation, this worship, is continually going on. The gods, and the angels, and everybody is worshipping it. Man is the greatest symbol of fire, the body of man." Here also we see the ideal becoming practical and Brahman is seen in everything. The principle that underlies all these stories is that invented symbolism may be good and helpful, but already better symbols exist than any we can invent. You may invent an image through which to worship God, but a better image already exists, the living man. You may build a temple in which to worship God, and that may be good, but a better one, a much higher one, already exists, the human body.

You remember that the Vedas have two parts, the ceremonial and the knowledge portions. In time ceremonials had multiplied and become so intricate that it was almost hopeless to disentangle them, and so in the Upanishads we find that the ceremonials are almost done away with, but gently, by explaining them. We see that in old times they had these oblations and sacrifices, then the philosophers came, and instead of snatching away the symbols from the hands of the ignorant, instead of taking the negative position, which we unfortunately find so general in modern reforms, they gave them something to take their place. "Here is the symbol of fire," they said. "Very good! But here is another symbol, the earth. What a grand, great symbol! Here is this little temple, but the whole universe is a temple; a man can worship anywhere. There are the peculiar figures that men draw on the earth, and there are the altars, but here is the greatest of altars, the living, conscious human body, and to worship at this altar is far higher than the worship of any dead symbols."

We now come to a peculiar doctrine. I do not understand much of it myself. If you can make something out of it, I will read it to you. When a man dies, who has by meditation purified himself and got knowledge, he first goes to light, then from light to day, from day to the light half of the moon, from that to the six months when the sun goes to the north, from that to the year, from the year to the sun, from the sun to the moon, from the moon to the lightning, and when he comes to the sphere of lightning, he meets a person who is not human, and that person leads him to (the conditioned) Brahman. This is the way of the gods. When sages and wise persons die, they go that way and they do not return. What is meant by this month and year, and all these things, no one understands clearly. Each one gives his own meaning, and some say it is all nonsense. What is meant by going to the world of the moon and of the sun, and this person who comes to help the soul after it has reached the sphere of lightning, no one knows. There is an idea among the Hindus that the moon is a place where life exists, and we shall see how life has come from there. Those that have not attained to knowledge, but have done good work in this life, first go, when they die, through smoke, then to night, then to the dark fifteen days, then to the six months when the sun goes to the south, and from that they go to the region of their forefathers, then to ether, then to the region of the moon, and there become the food of the gods, and later, are born as gods and live there so long as their good works will permit. And when the effect of the good work has been finished, they come back to earth by the same route. They first become ether, and then air, and then smoke, and then mist, then cloud, and then fall upon the earth as raindrops; then they get into food, which is eaten up by human beings, and finally become their children. Those whose works have been very good take birth in good families,

and those whose works have been bad take bad births, even in animal bodies. Animals are continually coming to and going from this earth. That is why the earth is neither full nor empty.

Several ideas we can get also from this, and later on, perhaps, we shall be able to understand it better, and we can speculate a little upon what it means. The last part which deals with how those who have been in heaven return, is clearer, perhaps, than the first part; but the whole idea seems to be this that there is no permanent heaven without realising God. Now some people who have not realised God, but have done good work in this world, with the view of enjoying the results, go, when they die, through this and that place, until they reach heaven, and there they are born in the same way as we are here, as children of the gods, and they live there as long as their good works will permit. Out of this comes one basic idea of the Vedanta that everything which has name and form is transient. This earth is transient, because it has name and form, and so the heavens must be transient, because there also name and form remain. A heaven which is eternal will be contradictory in terms, because everything that has name and form must begin in time, exist in time, and end in time. These are settled doctrines of the Vedanta, and as such the heavens are given up.

We have seen in the Samhitâ that the idea of heaven was that it was eternal, much the same as is prevalent among Mohammedans and Christians. The Mohammedans concretise it a little more. They say it is a place where there are gardens, beneath which rivers run. In the desert of Arabia water is very desirable, so the Mohammedan always conceives of his heaven as containing much water. I was born in a country where there are six months of rain every year. I should think of heaven, I suppose, as a dry place, and so also would the English people. These heavens in the Samhita are eternal, and the departed have beautiful bodies and live with their forefathers, and are happy ever afterwards. There they meet with their parents, children, and other relatives, and lead very much the same sort of life as here, only much happier. All the difficulties and obstructions to happiness in this life have vanished, and only its good parts and enjoyments remain. But however comfortable mankind may consider this state of things, truth is one thing and comfort is another. There are cases where truth is not comfortable until we reach its climax. Human nature is very conservative It does something, and having once done that, finds it hard to get out of it. The mind will not receive new thoughts, because they bring discomfort.

In the Upanishads, we see a tremendous departure made. It is declared that these heavens in which men live with the ancestors after death cannot be permanent. Seeing that everything which has name and form must die. If there are heavens with forms, these heavens must vanish in course of time; they may last millions of years, but there must come a time when they will have to go. With this idea came another that these souls must come back to earth, and that heavens are places where they enjoy the results of their good works, and after these effects are finished they come back into this earth life again. One thing is clear from this that mankind had a perception of the philosophy of causation even at the early time. Later on we shall see how our philosophers bring that out in the language of philosophy and logic, but here it is almost in the language of children. One thing you may remark in reading these books that it is all internal perception. If you ask me if this can be practical, my answer is, it has been practical first, and philosophical next. You can see that first these things have been perceived and realised and then written. This world spoke to the early thinkers. Birds spoke to them, animals spoke to them, the sun and the moon spoke to them; and little by little they realised things, and got into the heart of nature. Not by cogitation not by the force of logic, not by picking the brains of others and making a big book, as is the fashion in modern times, not even as I do, by taking up one of their writings and making a long lecture, but by patient investigation and discovery they found out the truth. Its essential method was practice, and so it must be always. Religion is ever a practical science, and there never was nor will be any theological religion. It is practice first, and knowledge afterwards. The idea that souls come back is already there. Those persons who do good work with the idea of a result, get it, but the result is not permanent. There we get the idea of causation very beautifully put forward, that the effect is only commensurate with the cause. As the cause is, so the effect will be. The cause being finite, the effect must be finite. If the cause is eternal the effect can be eternal, but all these causes, doing good work, and all other things, are only finite causes, and as such cannot produce infinite result.

We now come to the other side of the question. As there cannot be an eternal heaven, on the same grounds, there cannot be an eternal hell. Suppose I am a very wicked man, doing evil every minute of my life. Still, my whole life here, compared with my eternal life, is nothing. If there be an eternal punishment, it will mean that there is an infinite effect produced by a finite cause, which cannot be. If I do good all my life, I cannot have an infinite heaven; it would be making the same mistake. But there is a third course which applies to those who have known the Truth, to those who have realised It. This is the only way to get beyond this veil of Mâyâ — to realise what Truth is; and the Upanishads indicate what is meant by realising the Truth.

It means recognising neither good nor bad, but knowing all as coming from the Self; Self is in everything. It means denying the universe; shutting your eyes to it; seeing the Lord in hell as well as in heaven; seeing the Lord in death as well as in life. This is the line of thought in the passage I have read to you; the earth is a symbol of the Lord, the sky is the Lord, the place we fill is the Lord, everything is Brahman. And this is to be seen, realised, not simply talked or thought about. We can see as its logical consequence that when the soul has realised that everything is full of the Lord, of Brahman, it will not care whether it goes to heaven, or hell, or anywhere else; whether it be born again on this earth or in heaven. These things have ceased to have any meaning to that soul, because every place is the same, every place is the temple of the Lord, every place has become holy and the presence of the Lord is all that it sees in heaven, or hell, or anywhere else. Neither good nor bad, neither life nor death — only the one infinite Brahman exists.

According to the Vedanta, when a man has arrived at that perception, he has become free, and he is the only man who is fit to live in this world. Others are not. The man who sees evil, how can he live in this world? His life is a mass of misery. The man who sees dangers, his life is a misery; the man who sees death, his life is a misery. That man alone can live in this world, he alone can say, "I enjoy this life, and I am happy in this life". Who has seen the Truth, and the Truth in everything. By the by, I may tell you that the idea of hell does not occur in the Vedas anywhere. It comes with the Purânas much later. The worst punishment according to the Vedas is coming back to earth, having another chance in this world. From the very first we see the idea is taking the impersonal turn. The ideas of punishment and reward are very material, and they are only consonant with the idea of a human God, who loves one and hates another, just as we do. Punishment and reward are only admissible with the existence of such a God. They had such a God in the Samhita, and there we find the idea of fear entering, but as soon as we come to the Upanishads, the idea of fear vanishes, and the impersonal idea takes its place. It is naturally the hardest thing for man to understand, this impersonal idea, for he is always clinging on to the person. Even people who are thought to be great thinkers get disgusted at the idea of the Impersonal God. But to me it seems so absurd to think of God as an embodied man. Which is the higher idea, a living God, or a dead God? A God whom nobody sees, nobody knows, or a God Known?

The Impersonal God is a living God, a principle. The difference between personal and impersonal is this, that the personal is only a man, and the impersonal idea is that He is the angel, the man, the animal, and yet something more which we cannot see, because impersonality includes all personalities, is the sum total of everything in the universe, and infinitely more besides. "As the one fire coming into the world is manifesting itself in so many forms, and yet is infinitely more besides," so is the Impersonal.

We want to worship a living God. I have seen nothing but God all my life, nor have you. To see this chair you first see God, and then the chair in and through Him He is everywhere saying, "I am". The moment you feel "I am", you are conscious of Existence. Where shall we go to find God if we cannot see Him in our own hearts and in every living being? "Thou art the man, Thou art the woman, Thou art the girl, and Thou art the boy. Thou art the old man tottering with a stick. Thou art the young man walking in the pride of his strength." Thou art all that exists, a wonderful living God who is the only fact in the universe. This seems to many to be a terrible contradiction to the traditional God who lives behind a veil somewhere and whom nobody ever sees. The priests only give us an assurance that if we follow them, listen to their admonitions, and walk in the way they mark out for us—then when we die, they will give us a passport to enable us to see the face of God! What are all these heaven ideas but simply modifications of this nonsensical priestcraft?

Of course the impersonal idea is very destructive, it takes away all trade from the priests, churches, and temples. In India there is a famine now, but there are temples in each one of which there are jewels worth a king's ransom! If the priests taught this Impersonal idea to the people, their occupation would be gone. Yet we have to teach it unselfishly, without priestcraft. You are God and so am I; who obeys whom? Who worships whom? You are the highest temple of God; I would rather worship you than any temple, image, or Bible. Why are some people so contradictory in their thought? They are like fish slipping through our fingers. They say they are hard-headed practical men. Very good. But what is more practical than worshipping here, worshipping you? I see you, feel you, and I know you are God. The Mohammedan says, there is no God but Allah. The Vedanta says, there is nothing that is not God. It may frighten many of you, but you will understand it by degrees. The living God is within you, and yet you are building churches and temples and believing all sorts of imaginary nonsense. The only God to worship is the human soul in the human body. Of course all animals are temples too, but man is the highest, the Taj Mahal of temples. If I cannot worship in that, no other temple will be of any advantage. The moment I have realised God sitting in the temple of every human body, the moment I stand in reverence before every human being and see God in him—that moment I am free from bondage, everything that binds vanishes, and I am free.

This is the most practical of all worship. It has nothing to do with theorising and speculation. Yet it frightens many. They say it is not right. They go on theorising about old ideals told them by their grandfathers, that a God somewhere in heaven had told some one that he was God. Since that time we have only theories. This is practicality according to them, and our ideas are impractical! No doubt, the Vedanta says that each one must have his own path, but the path is not the goal. The worship of a God in heaven and all these things are not bad, but they are only steps towards the Truth and not the Truth itself. They are good and beautiful, and some wonderful ideas are there, but the Vedanta says at every point, "My friend, Him whom you are worshipping as unknown, I worship as thee. He whom you are worshipping as unknown and are seeking for, throughout the universe, has been with you all the time. You are living through Him, and He is the Eternal Witness of the universe" "He whom all the Vedas worship, nay, more, He who is always present in the eternal 'I'. He existing, the whole universe exists. He is the light and life of the universe. If the 'I' were not in you, you would not see the sun, everything would be a dark mass. He shining, you see the world."

One question is generally asked, and it is this that this may lead to a tremendous amount of difficulty. Everyone of us will think, "I am God, and whatever I do or think must be good, for God can do no evil." In the first place, even taking this danger of misinterpretation for granted, can it be proved that on the other side the same danger does not exist? They have been worshipping a God in heaven separate from them, and of whom they are much afraid. They have been born shaking with fear, and all their life they will go on shaking. Has the world been made much better by this? Those who have understood and worshipped a Personal God, and those who have understood and worshipped an Impersonal God, on which side have been the great workers of the world—gigantic workers, gigantic moral powers? Certainly on the Impersonal. How can you expect morality to be developed through fear? It can never be. "Where one sees another, where one hears another, that is Maya. When one does not see another, when one does not hear another, when everything has become the Atman, who sees whom, who perceives whom?" It is all He, and all I, at the same time. The soul has become pure. Then, and then alone we understand what love is. Love cannot come through fear, its basis is freedom. When we really begin to love the world, then we understand what is meant by brotherhood or mankind, and not before.

So, it is not right to say that the Impersonal idea will lead to a tremendous amount of evil in the world, as if the other doctrine never lent itself to works of evil, as if it did not lead to sectarianism deluging the world with blood and causing men to tear each other to pieces. "My God is the greatest God, let us decide it by a free fight." That is the outcome of dualism all over the world. Come out into the broad open light of day, come out from the little narrow paths, for how can the infinite soul rest content to live and die in small ruts? Come out into the universe of Light. Everything in the universe is yours, stretch out your arms and embrace it with love. If you ever felt you wanted to do that, you have felt God.

You remember that passage in the sermon of Buddha, how he sent a thought of love towards the south, the north, the east, and the west, above and below, until the whole universe was filled with this lose, so grand, great, and infinite. When you have that feeling, you have true personality. The whole universe is one person; let go the little things. Give up the small for the Infinite, give up small enjoyments for infinite bliss. It is all yours, for the Impersonal includes the Personal. So God is Personal and Impersonal at the same time. And Man, the Infinite, Impersonal Man, is manifesting Himself as person. We the infinite have limited ourselves, as it were, into small parts. The Vedanta says that Infinity is our true nature; it will never vanish, it will abide for ever. But we are limiting ourselves by our Karma, which like a chain round our necks has dragged us into this limitation. Break that chain and be free. Trample law under your feet. There is no law in human nature, there is no destiny, no fate. How can there be law in infinity? Freedom is its watchword. Freedom is its nature, its birthright. Be free, and then have any number of personalities you like. Then we will play like the actor who comes upon the stage and plays the part of a beggar. Contrast him with the actual beggar walking in the streets. The scene is, perhaps, the same in both cases, the words are, perhaps, the same, but yet what difference! The one enjoys his beggary while the other is suffering misery from it. And what makes this difference? The one is free and the other is bound. The actor knows his beggary is not true, but that he has assumed it for play, while the real beggar thinks that it is his too familiar state and that he has to bear it whether he wills it or not. This is the law. So long as we have no knowledge of our real nature, we are beggars, jostled about by every force in nature; and made slaves of by everything in nature; we cry all over the world for help, but help never comes to us; we cry to imaginary beings, and yet it never comes. But still we hope help will come, and thus in weeping, wailing, and hoping, one life is passed, and the same play goes on and on.

Be free; hope for nothing from anyone. I am sure if you look back upon your lives you will find that you were always vainly trying to get help from others which never came. All the help that has come was from within yourselves. You only had the fruits of what you yourselves worked for, and yet you were strangely hoping all the time for help. A rich man's parlour is always full; but if you notice, you do not find the same people there. The visitors are always hoping that they will get something from those wealthy men, but they never do. So are our lives spent in hoping, hoping, hoping, which never comes to an end. Give up hope, says the Vedanta. Why should you hope? You have everything, nay, you are everything. What are you hoping for? If a king goes mad, and runs about trying to find the king of his country, he will never find him, because he is the king himself. He may go through every village and city in his own country, seeking in every house, weeping and wailing, but he will never find him, because he is the king himself. It is better that we know we are God and give up this fool's search after Him; and knowing that we are God we become happy and contented. Give up all these mad pursuits, and then play your part in the universe, as an actor on the stage.

The whole vision is changed, and instead of an eternal prison this world has become a playground; instead of a land of competition it is a land of bliss, where there is perpetual spring, flowers bloom and butterflies flit about. This very world becomes heaven, which formerly was hell. To the eyes of the bound it is a tremendous place of torment, but to the eyes of the free it is quite otherwise. This one life is the universal life, heavens and all those places are here. All the gods are here, the prototypes of man. The gods did not create man after their type, but man created gods. And here are the prototypes, here is Indra, here is Varuna, and all the gods of the universe. We have been projecting our little doubles, and we are the originals of these gods, we are the real, the only gods to be worshipped. This is the view of the Vedanta, and this its practicality. When we have become free, we need not go mad and throw up society and rush off to die in the forest or the cave; we shall remain where we were, only we shall understand the whole thing. The same phenomena will remain, but with a new meaning. We do not know the world yet; it is only through freedom that we see what it is, and understand its nature. We shall see then that this so-called law, or fate, or destiny occupied only an infinitesimal part of our nature. It was only one side, but on the other side there was freedom all the time. We did not know this, and that is why we have been trying to save ourselves from evil by hiding our faces in the ground, like the hunted hare. Through delusion we have been trying to forget our nature, and yet we could not; it was always calling upon us, and all our search after God or gods, or external freedom, was a search after our real nature. We mistook the voice. We thought it was from the fire, or from a god or the sun, or moon, or stars, but at last we have found that it was from within ourselves. Within ourselves is this eternal voice speaking of eternal freedom; its music is eternally going on. Part of this music of the Soul has become the earth, the law, this universe, but it was always ours and always will be. In one word, the ideal of Vedanta is to know man as he really is, and this is its message, that if you cannot worship your brother man, the manifested God, how can you worship a God who is unmanifested?

Do you not remember what the Bible says, "If you cannot love your brother whom you have seen, how can you love God whom you have not seen?" If you cannot see God in the human face, how can you see him in the clouds, or in images made of dull, dead matter, or in mere fictitious stories of our brain? I shall call you religious from the day you begin to see God in men and women, and then you will understand what is meant by turning the left cheek to the man who strikes you on the right. When you see man as God, everything, even the tiger, will be welcome. Whatever comes to you is but the Lord, the Eternal, the Blessed One, appearing to us in various forms, as our father, and mother, and friend, and child—they are our own soul playing with us.

As our human relationships can thus be made divine, so our relationship with God may take any of these forms and we can look upon Him as our father, or mother, or friend, or beloved. Calling God Mother is a higher ideal than calling Him Father; and to call Him Friend is still higher; but the highest is to regard Him as the Beloved. The highest point of all is to see no difference between lover and beloved. You may remember, perhaps, the old Persian story, of how a lover came and knocked at the door of the beloved and was asked, "Who are you?" He answered, "It is I", and there was no response. A second time he came, and exclaimed, "I am here", but the door was not opened. The third time he came, and the voice asked from inside, "Who is there?" He replied, "I am thyself, my beloved", and the door opened. So is the relation between God and ourselves. He is in everything, He is everything.

Every man and woman is the palpable, blissful, living God. Who says God is unknown? Who says He is to be searched after? We have found God eternally. We have been living in Him eternally; everywhere He is eternally known, eternally worshipped.

Then comes another idea, that other forms of worship are not errors. This is one of the great points to be remembered, that those who worship God through ceremonials and forms, however crude we may think them to be, are not in error. It is the journey from truth to truth, from lower truth to higher truth. Darkness is less light; evil is less good; impurity is less purity. It must always be borne in mind that we should see others with eyes of love, with sympathy, knowing that they are going along the same path that we have trodden. If you are free, you must know that all will be so sooner or later, and if you are free, how can you see the impermanent? If you are really pure, how do you see the impure? For what is within, is without. We cannot see impurity without having it inside ourselves. This is one of the practical sides of Vedanta, and I hope that we shall all try to carry it into our lives. Our whole life here is to carry this into practice, but the one great point we gain is that we shall work with satisfaction and contentment, instead of with discontent and dissatisfaction, for we know that Truth is within us, we have It as our birthright, and we have only to manifest It, and make It tangible.

PRACTICAL VEDANTA, PART III

Delivered in London, 17th November 1896

In the Chhâdogya Upanishad we read that a sage called Nârada came to another called Sanatkumâra, and asked him various questions, of which one was, if religion was the cause of things as they are. And Sanatkumara leads him, as it were, step by step, telling him that there is something higher than this earth, and something higher than that, and so on, till he comes to Âkâsha, ether. Ether is higher than light, because in the ether are the sun and the moon, lightning and the stars; in ether we live, and in ether we die. Then the question arises, if there is anything higher than that, and Sanatkumara tells him of Prâna. This Prana, according to the Vedanta, is the principle of life. It is like ether, an omnipresent principle; and all motion, either in the body or anywhere else, is the work of this Prana. It is greater than Akasha, and through it everything lives. Prana is in the mother, in the father, in the sister, in the teacher, Prana is the knower.

I will read another passage, where Shvetaketu asks his father about the Truth, and the father teaches him different things, and concludes by saying, "That which is the fine cause in all these things, of It are all these things made. That is the All, that is Truth, thou art That, O Shvetaketu." And then he gives various examples. "As a bee, O Shvetaketu, gathers honey from different flowers, and as the different honeys do not know that they are from various trees, and from various flowers, so all of us, having come to that Existence, know not

that we have done so. Now, that which is that subtle essence, in It all that exists has its self. It is the True. It is the Self and thou, O Shvetaketu, are That." He gives another example of the rivers running down to the ocean. "As the rivers, when they are in the ocean, do not know that they have been various rivers, even so when we come out of that Existence, we do not know that we are That. O Shvetaketu, thou art That." So on he goes with his teachings.

Now there are two principles of knowledge. The one principle is that we know by referring the particular to the general, and the general to the universal; and the second is that anything of which the explanation is sought is to be explained so far as possible from its own nature. Taking up the first principle, we see that all our knowledge really consists of classifications, going higher and higher. When something happens singly, we are, as it were, dissatisfied. When it can be shown that the same thing happens again and again, we are satisfied and call it law. When we find that one apple falls, we are dissatisfied; but when we find that all apples fall, we call it the law of gravitation and are satisfied. The fact is that from the particular we deduce the general.

When we want to study religion, we should apply this scientific process. The same principle also holds good here, and as a fact we find that that has been the method all through. In reading these books from which I have been translating to you, the earliest idea that I can trace is this principle of going from the particular to the general. We see how the "bright ones" became merged into one principle; and likewise in the ideas of the cosmos we find the ancient thinkers going higher and higher—from the fine elements they go to finer and more embracing elements, and from these particulars they come to one omnipresent ether, and from that even they go to an all embracing force, or Prana; and through all this runs the principle, that one is not separate from the others. It is the very ether that exists in the higher form of Prana, or the higher form of Prana concretes, so to say, and becomes ether; and that ether becomes still grosser, and so on.

The generalization of the Personal God is another case in point. We have seen how this generalization was reached, and was called the sum total of all consciousness. But a difficulty arises—it is an incomplete generalization. We take up only one side of the facts of nature, the fact of consciousness, and upon that we generalise, but the other side is left out. So, in the first place it is a defective generalization. There is another insufficiency, and that relates to the second principle. Everything should be explained from its own nature. There may have been people who thought that every apple that fell to the ground was dragged down by a ghost, but the explanation is the law of gravitation; and although we know it is not a perfect explanation, yet it is much better than the other, because it is derived from the nature of the thing itself, while the other posits an extraneous cause. So throughout the whole range of our knowledge; the explanation which is based upon the nature of the thing itself is a scientific explanation, and an explanation which brings in an outside agent is unscientific.

So the explanation of a Personal God as the creator of the universe has to stand that test. If that God is outside of nature, having nothing to do with nature, and this nature is the outcome of the command of that God and produced from nothing, it is a very unscientific theory, and this has been the weak point of every Theistic religion throughout the ages. These two defects we find in what is generally called the theory of monotheism, the theory of a Personal God, with all the qualities of a human being multiplied very much, who, by His will, created this universe out of nothing and yet is separate from it. This leads us into two difficulties.

As we have seen, it is not a sufficient generalization, and secondly, it is not an explanation of nature from nature. It holds that the effect is not the cause, that the cause is entirely separate from the effect. Yet all human knowledge shows that the effect is but the cause in another form. To this idea the discoveries of modern science are tending every day, and the latest theory that has been accepted on all sides is the theory of evolution, the principle of which is that the effect is but the cause in another form, a readjustment of the cause, and the cause takes the form of the effect. The theory of creation out of nothing would be laughed at by modern scientists.

Now, can religion stand these tests? If there be any religious theories which can stand these two tests, they will be acceptable to the modern mind, to the thinking mind. Any other theory which we ask the modern man to believe, on the authority of priests, or churches, or books, he is unable to accept, and the result is a hideous mass of unbelief. Even in those in whom there is an external display of belief, in their hearts there is a tremendous amount of unbelief. The rest shrink away from religion, as it were, give it up, regarding it as priestcraft only.

Religion has been reduced to a sort of national form. It is one of our very best social remnants; let it remain. But the real necessity which the grandfather of the modern man felt for it is gone; he no longer finds it satisfactory to his reason. The idea of such a Personal God, and such a creation, the idea which is generally known as monotheism in every religion, cannot hold its own any longer. In India it could not hold its own because of the Buddhists, and that was the very point where they gained their victory in ancient times. They showed that if we allow that nature is possessed of infinite power, and that nature can work out all its wants, it is simply unnecessary to insist that there is something besides nature. Even the soul is unnecessary.

The discussion about substance and qualities is very old, and you will sometimes find that the old superstition lives even at the present day. Most of you have read how, during the Middle Ages, and, I am sorry to say, even much later, this was one of the subjects of discussion, whether qualities adhered to substance, whether length, breadth, and thickness adhered to the substance which we call dead matter, whether, the substance remaining, the qualities are there or not. To this our Buddhist says, "You have no ground for maintaining the existence of such a substance; the qualities are all that exist; you do not see beyond them." This is just the position of most of our modern agnostics. For it is this fight of the substance and qualities that, on a higher plane, takes the form of the fight between noumenon and phenomenon. There is the phenomenal world, the universe of continuous change, and there is something behind which does not change; and this duality of existence, noumenon and phenomenon, some hold, is true, and others with better reason claim that you have no right to admit the two, for what we see, feel, and think is only the phenomenon. You have no right to assert there is anything beyond phenomenon; and there is no answer to this. The only answer we get is from the monistic theory of the Vedanta. It is true that only one exists, and that one is either phenomenon or noumenon. It is not true that there are two—something changing, and, in and through that, something which does not change; but it is the one and the same thing which appears as changing, and which is in reality unchangeable. We have come to think of the body, and mind, and soul as many, but really there is only one; and that one is appearing in all these various forms. Take the well-known illustration of the monists, the rope appearing as the snake. Some people, in the dark or through some other cause, mistake the rope for the snake, but when knowledge comes, the snake vanishes and it is found to be a rope. By this illustration we see that when the snake exists in the mind, the rope has vanished, and when the rope exists, the snake has gone. When we see phenomenon, and phenomenon only, around us, the noumenon has vanished, but when we see the noumenon, the unchangeable, it naturally follows that the phenomenon has vanished. Now, we understand better the position of both the realist and the idealist. The realist sees the phenomenon only, and the idealist looks to the noumenon. For the idealist, the really genuine idealist, who has truly arrived at the power of perception, whereby he can get away from all ideas of change, for him the changeful universe has vanished, and he has the right to say it is all delusion, there is no change. The realist at the same time looks at the changeful. For him the unchangeable has vanished, and he has a right to say this is all real.

What is the outcome of this philosophy? It is that the idea of Personal God is not sufficient. We have to get to something higher, to the Impersonal idea. It is the only logical step that we can take. Not that the personal idea would be destroyed by that, not that we supply proof that the Personal God does not exist, but we must go to the Impersonal for the explanation of the personal, for the Impersonal is a much higher generalization than the personal. The Impersonal only can be Infinite, the personal is limited. Thus we preserve the personal and do not destroy it. Often the doubt comes to us that if we arrive at the idea of the Impersonal God, the personal will be destroyed, if we arrive at the idea of the Impersonal man, the personal will be lost. But the Vedantic idea is not the destruction of the individual, but its real preservation. We cannot prove the individual by any other means but by referring to the universal, by proving that this individual is really the universal. If we think of the individual as separate from everything else in the universe, it cannot stand a minute. Such a thing never existed.

Secondly, by the application of the second principle, that the explanation of everything must come out of the nature of the thing, we are led to a still bolder idea, and one more difficult to understand. It is nothing less than this, that the Impersonal Being, our highest generalization, is in ourselves, and we are That. "O Shvetaketu, thou art That." You are that Impersonal Being; that God for whom you have been searching all over the universe is all the time yourself—yourself not in the personal sense but in the Impersonal. The man we know now, the manifested, is personalised, but the reality of this is the Impersonal. To understand the personal we have to refer it to the Impersonal, the particular must be referred to the general, and that Impersonal is the Truth, the Self of man.

There will be various questions in connection with this, and I shall try to answer them as we go on. Many difficulties will arise, but first let us clearly understand the position of monism. As manifested beings we appear to be separate, but our reality is one, and the less we think of ourselves as separate from that One, the better for us. The more we think of ourselves as separate from the Whole, the more miserable we become. From this monistic principle we get at the basis of ethics, and I venture to say that we cannot get any ethics from anywhere else. We know that the oldest idea of ethics was the will of some particular being or beings, but few are ready to accept that now, because it would be only a partial generalization. The Hindus say we must not do this or that because the Vedas say so, but the Christian is not going to obey the authority of the Vedas. The Christian says you must do this and not do that because the Bible says so. That will not be binding on those who do not believe in the Bible. But we must have a theory which is large enough to take in all these various grounds. Just as there are millions of people who are ready to believe in a Personal Creator, there have also been thousands of the brightest minds in this world who felt that such ideas were not sufficient for them, and wanted something higher, and wherever religion was not broad enough to include all these minds, the result was that the brightest minds in society were always outside of religion; and never was this so marked as at the present time, especially in Europe.

To include these minds, therefore, religion must become broad enough. Everything it claims must be judged from the standpoint of reason. Why religions should claim that they are not bound to abide by the standpoint of reason, no one knows. If one does not take the standard of reason, there cannot be any true judgment, even in the case of religions. One religion may ordain something very hideous. For instance, the Mohammedan religion allows Mohammedans to kill all who are not of their religion. It is clearly stated in the Koran, "Kill the infidels if they do not become Mohammedans." They must be put to fire and sword. Now if we tell a Mohammedan that this is wrong, he will naturally ask, "How do you know that? How do you know it is not good? My book says it is." If you say your book is older, there will come the Buddhist, and say, my book is much older still. Then will come the Hindu, and say, my books are the oldest of all. Therefore referring to books will not do. Where is the standard by which you can compare? You will say, look at the Sermon on the Mount, and the Mohammedan will reply, look at the Ethics of the Koran. The Mohammedan will say, who is the arbiter as to which is the better of the two? Neither the New Testament nor the Koran can be the arbiter in a quarrel between them. There must be some independent authority, and that cannot be any book, but something which is universal; and what is more universal than reason? It has been said that reason is not strong enough; it does not always help us to get at the Truth; many times it makes mistakes, and, therefore, the conclusion is that we must believe in the authority of a church! That was said to me by a Roman Catholic, but I could not see the logic of it. On the other hand I should say, if reason be so weak, a body of priests would be weaker, and I am not going to accept their verdict, but I will abide by my reason, because with all its weakness there is some chance of my getting at truth through it; while, by the other means, there is no such hope at all.

We should, therefore, follow reason and also sympathise with those who do not come to any sort of belief, following reason. For it is better that mankind should become atheist by following reason than blindly believe in two hundred millions of gods on the authority of anybody. What we want is progress, development, realisation. No theories ever made men higher. No amount of books can help us to become purer. The only power is in realisation, and that lies in ourselves and comes from thinking. Let men think. A clod of earth never thinks; but it remains only a lump of earth. The glory of man is that he is a thinking being. It is the nature of man to think and therein he differs from animals. I believe in reason and follow reason having seen enough of the evils of authority, for I was born in a country where they have gone to the extreme of authority.

The Hindus believe that creation has come out of the Vedas. How do you know there is a cow? Because the word cow is in the Vedas. How do you know there is a man outside? Because the word man is there. If it had not been, there would have been no man outside. That is what they say. Authority with a vengeance! And it is not studied as I have studied it, but some of the most powerful minds have taken it up and spun out wonderful logical theories round it. They have reasoned it out, and there it stands—a whole system of philosophy; and thousands of the brightest intellects have been dedicated through thousands of years to the working out of this theory. Such has been the power of authority, and great are the dangers thereof. It stunts the growth of humanity, and we must not forget that we want growth. Even in all relative truth, more than the truth itself, we want the exercise. That is our life.

The monistic theory has this merit that it is the most rational of all the religious theories that we can conceive of. Every other theory, every conception of God which is partial and little and personal is not rational. And yet monism has this grandeur that it embraces all these partial conceptions of God as being necessary for many. Some people say that this personal explanation is irrational. But it is consoling; they want a consoling religion and we understand that it is necessary for them. The clear light of truth very few in this life can bear, much less live up to. It is necessary, therefore, that this comfortable religion should exist; it helps many souls to a better one. Small minds whose circumference is very limited and which require little things to build them up, never venture to soar high in thought. Their conceptions are very good and helpful to them, even if only of little gods and symbols. But you have to understand the Impersonal, for it is in and through that alone that these others can be explained. Take, for instance, the idea of a Personal God. A man who understands and believes in the Impersonal—John Stuart Mill, for example—may say that a Personal God is impossible, and cannot be proved. I admit with him that a Personal God cannot be demonstrated. But He is the highest reading of the Impersonal that can be reached by the human intellect, and what else is the universe but various readings of the Absolute? It is like a book before us, and each one has brought his intellect to read it, and each one has to read it for himself. There is something which is common in the intellect of all men; therefore certain things appear to be the same to the intellect of mankind. That you and I see a chair proves that there is something common to both our minds. Suppose a being comes with another sense, he will not see the chair at all; but all beings similarly constituted will see the same things. Thus this universe itself is the Absolute, the unchangeable, the noumenon; and the phenomenon constitutes the reading thereof. For you will first find that all phenomena are finite. Every phenomenon that we can see, feel, or think of, is finite, limited by our knowledge, and the Personal God as we conceive of Him is in fact a phenomenon. The very idea of causation exists only in the phenomenal world, and God as the cause of this universe must naturally be thought of as limited, and yet He is the same Impersonal God. This very universe, as we have seen, is the same Impersonal Being read by our intellect. Whatever is reality in the universe is that Impersonal Being, and the forms and conceptions are given to it by our intellects. Whatever is real in this table is that Being, and the table form and all other forms are given by our intellects.

Now, motion, for instance, which is a necessary adjunct of the phenomenal, cannot be predicated of the Universal. Every little bit, every atom inside the universe, is in a constant state of change and motion, but the universe as a whole is unchangeable, because motion or change is a relative thing; we can only think of something in motion in comparison with something which is not moving. There must be two things in order to understand motion. The whole mass of the universe, taken as a unit, cannot move. In regard to what will it move? It cannot be said to change. With regard to what will it change? So the whole is the Absolute; but within it every particle is in a constant state of flux and change. It is unchangeable and changeable at the same time, Impersonal and Personal in one. This is our conception of the universe, of motion and of God, and that is what is meant by "Thou art That". Thus we see that the Impersonal instead of doing away with the personal, the Absolute instead of pulling down the relative, only explains it to the full satisfaction of our reason and heart. The Personal God and all that exists in the universe are the same Impersonal Being seen through our minds. When we shall be rid of our minds, our little personalities, we shall become one with It. This is what is meant by "Thou art That". For we must know our true nature, the Absolute.

The finite, manifested man forgets his source and thinks himself to be entirely separate. We, as personalised, differentiated beings, forget our reality, and the teaching of monism is not that we shall give up these differentiations, but we must learn to understand what they are. We are in reality that Infinite Being, and our personalities represent so many channels through which this Infinite Reality is manifesting Itself; and the whole mass of changes which we call evolution is brought about by the soul trying to manifest more and more of its infinite energy. We cannot stop anywhere on this side of the Infinite; our power, and blessedness, and wisdom, cannot but grow into the Infinite. Infinite power and existence and blessedness are ours, and we have not to acquire them; they are our own, and we have only to manifest them.

This is the central idea of monism, and one that is so hard to understand. From my childhood everyone around me taught weakness; I have been told ever since I was born that I was a weak thing. It is very difficult for me now to realise my own strength, but by analysis and reasoning I gain knowledge of my own strength, I realise it. All the knowledge that we have in this world, where did it come from? It was within us. What knowledge is outside? None. Knowledge was not in matter; it was in man all the time. Nobody ever created knowledge; man brings it from within. It is lying there. The whole of that big banyan tree which covers acres of ground, was in the little seed which was, perhaps, no bigger than one eighth of a mustard seed; all that mass of energy was there confined. The gigantic intellect, we know, lies coiled up in the protoplasmic cell, and why should not the infinite energy? We know that it is so. It may seem like a paradox, but is true. Each one of us has come out of one protoplasmic cell, and all the powers we possess were coiled up there. You cannot say they came from food; for if you heap up food mountains high, what power comes out of it? The energy was there, potentially no doubt, but still there. So is infinite power in the soul of man, whether he knows it or not. Its manifestation is only a question of being conscious of it. Slowly this infinite giant is, as it were, waking up, becoming conscious of his power, and arousing himself; and with his growing consciousness, more and more of his bonds are breaking, chains are bursting asunder, and the day is sure to come when, with the full consciousness of his infinite power and wisdom, the giant will rise to his feet and stand erect. Let us all help to hasten that glorious consummation.

PRACTICAL VEDANTA, PART IV

Delivered in London, 18th November 1896

We have been dealing more with the universal so far. This morning I shall try to place before you the Vedantic ideas of the relation of the particular to the universal. As we have seen, in the dualistic form of Vedic doctrines, the earlier forms, there was a clearly defined particular and limited soul for every being. There have been a great many theories about this particular soul in each individual, but the main discussion was between the ancient Vedantists and the ancient Buddhists, the former believing in the individual soul as complete in itself, the latter denying in toto the existence of such an individual soul. As I told you the other day, it is pretty much the same discussion you have in Europe as to substance and quality, one set holding that behind the qualities there is something as substance, in which the qualities inhere; and the other denying the existence of such a substance as being unnecessary, for the qualities may live by themselves. The most ancient theory of the soul, of course, is based upon the argument of self-identity—"I am I"—that the I of yesterday is the I of today, and the I of today will be the I of tomorrow; that in spite of all the changes that are happening to the body, I yet believe that I am the same I. This seems to have been the central argument with those who believed in a limited, and yet perfectly complete, individual soul.

On the other hand, the ancient Buddhists denied the necessity of such an assumption. They brought forward the argument that all that we know, and all that we possibly can know, are simply these changes. The positing of an unchangeable and unchanging substance is simply superfluous, and even if there were any such unchangeable thing, we could never understand it, nor should we ever be able to cognise it in any sense of the word. The same discussion you will find at the present time going on in Europe between the religionists and the idealists on the one side, and the modern positivists and agnostics on the other; one set believing there is something which does not change (of whom the latest representative is your Herbert Spencer), that we catch a glimpse of something which is unchangeable. And the other is represented by the modern Comtists and modern Agnostics. Those of you who were interested a few years ago in the discussions between Herbert Spencer and Frederick Harrison might have noticed that it was the same old difficulty, the one party standing for a substance behind the changeful, and the other party denying the necessity for such an assumption. One party says we

cannot conceive of changes without conceiving of something which does not change; the other party brings out the argument that this is superfluous; we can only conceive of something which is changing, and as to the unchanging, we can neither know, feel, nor sense it.

In India this great question did not find its solution in very ancient times, because we have seen that the assumption of a substance which is behind the qualities, and which is not the qualities, can never be substantiated; nay, even the argument from self-identity, from memory,—that I am the I of yesterday because I remember it, and therefore I have been a continuous something—cannot be substantiated. The other quibble that is generally put forward is a mere delusion of words. For instance, a man may take a long series of such sentences as "I do", "I go", "I dream", "I sleep", "I move", and here you will find it claimed that the doing, going, dreaming etc., have been changing, but what remained constant was that "I". As such they conclude that the "I" is something which is constant and an individual in itself, but all these changes belong to the body. This, though apparently very convincing and clear, is based upon the mere play on words. The "I" and the doing, going, and dreaming may be separate in black and white, but no one can separate them in his mind.

When I eat, I think of myself as eating—am identified with eating. When I run, I and the running are not two separate things. Thus the argument from personal identity does not seem to be very strong. The other argument from memory is also weak. If the identity of my being is represented by my memory, many things which I have forgotten are lost from that identity. And we know that people under certain conditions forget their whole past. In many cases of lunacy a man will think of himself as made of glass, or as being an animal. If the existence of that man depends on memory, he has become glass, which not being the case we cannot make the identity of the Self depend on such a flimsy substance as memory. Thus we see that the soul as a limited yet complete and continuing identity cannot be established as separate from the qualities. We cannot establish a narrowed-down, limited existence to which is attached a bunch of qualities.

On the other hand, the argument of the ancient Buddhists seems to be stronger—that we do not know, and cannot know, anything that is beyond the bunch of qualities. According to them, the soul consists of a bundle of qualities called sensations and feelings. A mass of such is what is called the soul, and this mass is continually changing.

The Advaitist theory of the soul reconciles both these positions. The position of the Advaitist is that it is true that we cannot think of the substance as separate from the qualities, we cannot think of change and not-change at the same time; it would be impossible. But the very thing which is the substance is the quality; substance and quality are not two things. It is the unchangeable that is appearing as the changeable. The unchangeable substance of the universe is not something separate from it. The noumenon is not something different from the phenomena, but it is the very noumenon which has become the phenomena. There is a soul which is unchanging, and what we call feelings and perceptions, nay, even the body, are the very soul, seen from another point of view. We have got into the habit of thinking that we have bodies and souls and so forth, but really speaking, there is only one.

When I think of myself as the body, I am only a body; it is meaningless to say I am something else. And when I think of myself as the soul, the body vanishes, and the perception of the body does not remain. None can get the perception of the Self without his perception of the body having vanished, none can get perception of the substance without his perception of the qualities having vanished.

The ancient illustration of Advaita, of the rope being taken for a snake, may elucidate the point a little more. When a man mistakes the rope for a snake, the rope has vanished, and when he takes it for a rope, the snake has vanished, and the rope only remains. The ideas of dual or treble existence come from reasoning on insufficient data, and we read them in books or hear about them, until we come under the delusion that we really have a dual perception of the soul and the body; but such a perception never really exists. The perception is either of the body or of the soul. It requires no arguments to prove it, you can verify it in your own minds.

Try to think of yourself as a soul, as a disembodied something. You will find it to be almost impossible, and those few who are able to do so will find that at the time when they realise themselves as a soul they have no idea of the body. You have heard of, or perhaps have seen, persons who on particular occasions had been in peculiar states of mind, brought about by deep meditation, self-hypnotism, hysteria, or drugs. From their experience you may gather that when they were perceiving the internal something, the external had vanished for them. This shows that whatever exists is one. That one is appearing in these various forms, and all these various forms give rise to the relation of cause and effect. The relation of cause and effect is one of evolution—the one becomes the other, and so on. Sometimes the cause vanishes, as it were, and in its place leaves the effect. If the soul is the cause of the body, the soul, as it were vanishes for the time being, and the body remains; and when the body vanishes, the soul remains. This theory fits the arguments of the Buddhists that were levelled against the assumption of the dualism of body and soul, by denying the duality, and showing that the substance and the qualities are one and the same thing appearing in various forms.

We have seen also that this idea of the unchangeable can be established only as regards the whole, but never as regards the part. The very idea of part comes from the idea of change or motion. Everything that is limited we can understand and know, because it is changeable; and the whole must be unchangeable, because there is no other thing besides it in rela-

tion to which change would be possible. Change is always in regard to something which does not change, or which changes relatively less.

According to Advaita, therefore, the idea of the soul as universal, unchangeable, and immortal can be demonstrated as far as possible. The difficulty would be as regards the particular. What shall we do with the old dualistic theories which have such a hold upon us, and which we have all to pass through—these beliefs in limited, little, individual souls?

We have seen that we are immortal with regard to the whole; but the difficulty is, we desire so much to be immortal as parts of the whole. We have seen that we are Infinite, and that that is our real individuality. But we want so much to make these little souls individual. What becomes of them when we find in our everyday experience that these little souls are individuals, with only this reservation that they are continuously growing individuals? They are the same, yet not the same. The I of yesterday is the I of today, and yet not so, it is changed somewhat. Now, by getting rid of the dualistic conception, that in the midst of all these changes there is something that does not change, and taking the most modern of conceptions, that of evolution, we find that the "I" is a continuously changing, expanding entity.

If it be true that man is the evolution of a mollusc, the mollusc individual is the same as the man, only it has to become expanded a great deal. From mollusc to man it has been a continuous expansion towards infinity. Therefore the limited soul can be styled an individual which is continuously expanding towards the Infinite Individual. Perfect individuality will only be reached when it has reached the Infinite, but on this side of the Infinite it is a continuously changing, growing personality. One of the remarkable features of the Advaitist system of Vedanta is to harmonise the preceding systems. In many cases it helped the philosophy very much; in some cases it hurt it. Our ancient philosophers knew what you call the theory of evolution; that growth is gradual, step by step, and the recognition of this led them to harmonise all the preceding systems. Thus not one of these preceding ideas was rejected. The fault of the Buddhistic faith was that it had neither the faculty nor the perception of this continual, expansive growth, and for this reason it never even made an attempt to harmonise itself with the preexisting steps towards the ideal. They were rejected as useless and harmful.

This tendency in religion is most harmful. A man gets a new and better idea, and then he looks back on those he has given up, and forthwith decides that they were mischievous and unnecessary. He never thinks that, however crude they may appear from his present point of view, they were very useful to him, that they were necessary for him to reach his present state, and that everyone of us has to grow in a similar fashion, living first on crude ideas, taking benefit from them, and then arriving at a higher standard. With the oldest theories, therefore, the Advaita is friendly. Dualism and all systems that had preceded it are accepted by the Advaita not in a patronising way, but with the conviction that they are true manifestations of the same truth, and that they all lead to the same conclusions as the Advaita has reached.

With blessing, and not with cursing, should be preserved all these various steps through which humanity has to pass. Therefore all these dualistic systems have never been rejected or thrown out, but have been kept intact in the Vedanta; and the dualistic conception of an individual soul, limited yet complete in itself, finds its place in the Vedanta.

According to dualism, man dies and goes to other worlds, and so forth; and these ideas are kept in the Vedanta in their entirety. For with the recognition of growth in the Advaitist system, these theories are given their proper place by admitting that they represent only a partial view of the Truth.

From the dualistic standpoint this universe can only be looked upon as a creation of matter or force, can only be looked upon as the play of a certain will, and that will again can only be looked upon as separate from the universe. Thus a man from such a standpoint has to see himself as composed of a dual nature, body and soul, and this soul, though limited, is individually complete in itself. Such a man's ideas of immortality and of the future life would necessarily accord with his idea of soul. These phases have been kept in the Vedanta, and it is, therefore, necessary for me to present to you a few of the popular ideas of dualism. According to this theory, we have a body, of course, and behind the body there is what they call a fine body. This fine body is also made of matter, only very fine. It is the receptacle of all our Karma, of all our actions and impressions, which are ready to spring up into visible forms. Every thought that we think, every deed that we do, after a certain time becomes fine, goes into seed form, so to speak, and lives in the fine body in a potential form, and after a time it emerges again and bears its results. These results condition the life of man. Thus he moulds his own life. Man is not bound by any other laws excepting those which he makes for himself. Our thoughts, our words and deeds are the threads of the net which we throw round ourselves, for good or for evil. Once we set in motion a certain power, we have to take the full consequences of it. This is the law of Karma. Behind the subtle body, lives Jiva or the individual soul of man. There are various discussions about the form and the size of this individual soul. According to some, it is very small like an atom; according to others, it is not so small as that; according to others, it is very big, and so on. This Jiva is a part of that universal substance, and it is also eternal; without beginning it is existing, and without end it will exist. It is passing through all these forms in order to manifest its real nature which is purity. Every action that retards this manifestation is called an evil action; so with thoughts. And every action and every thought that helps the Jiva to expand, to manifest its real nature, is good. One theory that is held in common in India by the crudest dualists as well as by the most advanced non-dualists is that all the possibilities and powers of the soul are within it, and do not come from any external source. They are in the soul in potential form, and the whole work of life is simply directed towards manifesting those potentialities.

They have also the theory of reincarnation which says that after the dissolution of this body, the Jiva will have another, and after that has been dissolved, it will again have another, and so on, either here or in some other worlds; but this world is given the preference, as it is considered the best of all worlds for our purpose. Other worlds are conceived of as worlds where there is very little misery, but for that very reason, they argue, there is less chance of thinking of higher things there. As this world contains some happiness and a good deal of misery, the Jiva some time or other gets awakened, as it were, and thinks of freeing itself. But just as very rich persons in this world have the least chance of thinking of higher things, so the Jiva in heaven has little chance of progress, for its condition is the same as that of a rich man, only more intensified; it has a very fine body which knows no disease, and is under no necessity of eating or drinking, and all its desires are fulfilled. The Jiva lives there, having enjoyment after enjoyment, and so forgets all about its real nature. Still there are some higher worlds, where in spite of all enjoyments, its further evolution is possible. Some dualists conceive of the goal as the highest heaven, where souls will live with God for ever. They will have beautiful bodies and will know neither disease nor death, nor any other evil, and all their desires will be fulfilled. From time to time some of them will come back to this earth and take another body to teach human beings the way to God; and the great teachers of the world have been such. They were already free, and were living with God in the highest sphere; but their love and sympathy for suffering humanity was so great that they came and incarnated again to teach mankind the way to heaven.

Of course we know that the Advaita holds that this cannot be the goal or the ideal; bodilessness must be the ideal. The ideal cannot be finite. Anything short of the Infinite cannot be the ideal, and there cannot be an infinite body. That would be impossible, as body comes from limitation. There cannot be infinite thought, because thought comes from limitation. We have to go beyond the body, and beyond thought too, says the Advaita. And we have also seen that, according to Advaita, this freedom is not to be attained, it is already ours. We only forget it and deny it. Perfection is not to be attained, it is already within us. Immortality and bliss are not to be acquired, we possess them already; they have been ours all the time.

If you dare declare that you are free, free you are this moment. If you say you are bound, bound you will remain. This is what Advaita boldly declares. I have told you the ideas of the dualists. You can take whichever you like.

The highest ideal of the Vedanta is very difficult to understand, and people are always quarrelling about it, and the greatest difficulty is that when they get hold of certain ideas, they deny and fight other ideas. Take up what suits you, and let others take up what they need. If you are desirous of clinging to this little individuality, to this limited manhood, remain in it, have all these desires, and be content and pleased with them. If your experience of manhood has been very good and nice, retain it as long as you like; and you can do so, for you are the makers of your own fortunes; none can compel you to give up your manhood. You will be men as long as you like; none can prevent you. If you want to be angels, you will be angels, that is the law. But there may be others who do not want to be angels even. What right have you to think that theirs is a horrible notion? You may be frightened to lose a hundred pounds, but there may be others who would not even wink if they lost all the money they had in the world. There have been such men and still there are. Why do you dare to judge them according to your standard? You cling on to your limitations, and these little worldly ideas may be your highest ideal. You are welcome to them. It will be to you as you wish. But there are others who have seen the truth and cannot rest in these limitations, who have done with these things and want to get beyond. The world with all its enjoyments is a mere mud-puddle for them. Why do you want to bind them down to your ideas? You must get rid of this tendency once for all. Accord a place to everyone.

I once read a story about some ships that were caught in a cyclone in the South Sea Islands, and there was a picture of it in the Illustrated London News. All of them were wrecked except one English vessel, which weathered the storm. The picture showed the men who were going to be drowned, standing on the decks and cheering the people who were sailing through the storm.[1] Be brave and generous like that. Do not drag others down to where you are. Another foolish notion is that if we lose our little individuality, there will be no morality, no hope for humanity. As if everybody had been dying for humanity all the time! God bless you! If in every country there were two hundred men and women really wanting to do good to humanity, the millennium would come in five days. We know how we are dying for humanity! These are all tall talks, and nothing else. The history of the world shows that those who never thought of their little individuality were the greatest benefactors of the human race, and that the more men and women think of themselves, the less are they able to do for others. One is unselfishness, and the other selfishness. Clinging on to little enjoyments, and to desire the continuation and repetition of this state of things is utter selfishness. It arises not from any desire for truth, its genesis is not in kindness for other beings, but in the utter selfishness of the human heart, in the idea, "I will have everything, and do not care for anyone else." This is as it appears to me. I would like to see more moral men in the world like some of those grand old prophets and sages of ancient times who would have given up a hundred lives if they could by so doing benefit one little animal! Talk of morality and doing good to others! Silly talk

of the present time!

I would like to see moral men like Gautama Buddha, who did not believe in a Personal God or a personal soul, never asked about them, but was a perfect agnostic, and yet was ready to lay down his life for anyone, and worked all his life for the good of all, and thought only of the good of all. Well has it been said by his biographer, in describing his birth, that he was born for the good of the many, as a blessing to the many. He did not go to the forest to meditate for his own salvation; he felt that the world was burning, and that he must find a way out. "Why is there so much misery in the world ?"—was the one question that dominated his whole life. Do you think we are so moral as the Buddha?

The more selfish a man, the more immoral he is. And so also with the race. That race which is bound down to itself has been the most cruel and the most wicked in the whole world. There has not been a religion that has clung to this dualism more than that founded by the Prophet of Arabia, and there has not been a religion which has shed so much blood and been so cruel to other men. In the Koran there is the doctrine that a man who does not believe these teachings should be killed; it is a mercy to kill him! And the surest way to get to heaven, where there are beautiful houris and all sorts of sense-enjoyments, is by killing these unbelievers. Think of the bloodshed there has been in consequence of such beliefs!

In the religion of Christ there was little of crudeness; there is very little difference between the pure religion of Christ and that of the Vedanta. You find there the idea of oneness; but Christ also preached dualistic ideas to the people in order to give them something tangible to take hold of, to lead them up to the highest ideal. The same Prophet who preached, "Our Father which art in heaven", also preached, "I and my Father are one", and the same Prophet knew that through the "Father in heaven" lies the way to the "I and my Father are one". There was only blessing and love in the religion of Christ; but as soon as crudeness crept in, it was degraded into something not much better than the religion of the Prophet of Arabia. It was crudeness indeed—this fight for the little self, this clinging on to the "I", not only in this life, but also in the desire for its continuance even after death. This they declare to be unselfishness; this the foundation of morality! Lord help us, if this be the foundation of morality! And strangely enough, men and women who ought to know better think all morality will be destroyed if these little selves go and stand aghast at the idea that morality can only stand upon their destruction. The watchword of all well-being, of all moral good is not "I" but "thou". Who cares whether there is a heaven or a hell, who cares if there is a soul or not, who cares if there is an unchangeable or not? Here is the world, and it is full of misery. Go out into it as Buddha did, and struggle to lessen it or die in the attempt. Forget yourselves; this is the first lesson to be learnt, whether you are a theist or an atheist, whether you are an agnostic or a Vedantist, a Christian or a Mohammedan. The one lesson obvious to all is the destruction of the little self

---

1. H.M.S. Calliope and the American men-of-war at Samoa. — Ed

and the building up of the Real Self.

Two forces have been working side by side in parallel lines. The one says "I", the other says "not I". Their manifestation is not only in man but in animals, not only in animals but in the smallest worms. The tigress that plunges her fangs into the warm blood of a human being would give up her own life to protect her young. The most depraved man who thinks nothing of taking the lives of his brother men will, perhaps, sacrifice himself without any hesitation to save his starving wife and children. Thus throughout creation these two forces are working side by side; where you find the one, you find the other too. The one is selfishness, the other is unselfishness. The one is acquisition, the other is renunciation. The one takes, the other gives. From the lowest to the highest, the whole universe is the playground of these two forces. It does not require any demonstration; it is obvious to all.

What right has any section of the community to base the whole work and evolution of the universe upon one of these two factors alone, upon competition and struggle? What right has it to base the whole working of the universe upon passion and fight, upon competition and struggle? That these exist we do not deny; but what right has anyone to deny the working of the other force? Can any man deny that love, this "not I", this renunciation is the only positive power in the universe? That other is only the misguided employment of the power of love; the power of love brings competition, the real genesis of competition is in love. The real genesis of evil is in unselfishness. The creator of evil is good, and the end is also good. It is only misdirection of the power of good. A man who murders another is, perhaps, moved to do so by the love of his own child. His love has become limited to that one little baby, to the exclusion of the millions of other human beings in the universe. Yet, limited or unlimited, it is the same love.

Thus the motive power of the whole universe, in what ever way it manifests itself, is that one wonderful thing, unselfishness, renunciation, love, the real, the only living force in existence. Therefore the Vedantist insists upon that oneness. We insist upon this explanation because we cannot admit two causes of the universe. If we simply hold that by limitation the same beautiful, wonderful love appears to be evil or vile, we find the whole universe explained by the one force of love. If not, two causes of the universe have to be taken for granted, one good and the other evil, one love and the other hatred. Which is more logical? Certainly the one-force theory.

Let us now pass on to things which do not possibly belong to dualism. I cannot stay longer with the dualists. I am afraid. My idea is to show that the highest ideal of morality and unselfishness goes hand in hand with the highest metaphysical conception, and that you need not lower your conception to get ethics and morality, but, on the other hand, to reach a real basis of morality and ethics you must have the highest philosophical and scientific conceptions. Human knowledge is not antagonistic to human well-being. On the contrary, it is knowledge alone that will save us in every department of life—in knowledge is worship. The more we know the better for us. The Vedantist says, the cause of all that is apparently evil is the limitation of the unlimited. The love which gets limited into little channels and seems to be evil eventually comes out at the other end and manifests itself as God. The Vedanta also says that the cause of all this apparent evil is in ourselves. Do not blame any supernatural being, neither be hopeless and despondent, nor think we are in a place from which we can never escape unless someone comes and lends us a helping hand. That cannot be, says the Vedanta. We are like silkworms; we make the thread out of our own substance and spin the cocoon, and in course of time are imprisoned inside. But this is not for ever. In that cocoon we shall develop spiritual realisation, and like the butterfly come out free. This network of Karma we have woven around ourselves; and in our ignorance we feel as if we are bound, and weep and wail for help. But help does not come from without; it comes from within ourselves. Cry to all the gods in the universe. I cried for years, and in the end I found that I was helped. But help came from within. And I had to undo what I had done by mistake. That is the only way. I had to cut the net which I had thrown round myself, and the power to do this is within. Of this I am certain that not one aspiration, well-guided or ill-guided in my life, has been in vain, but that I am the resultant of all my past, both good and evil. I have committed many mistakes in my life; but mark you, I am sure of this that without every one of those mistakes I should not be what I am today, and so am quite satisfied to have made them. I do not mean that you are to go home and wilfully commit mistakes; do not misunderstand me in that way. But do not mope because of the mistakes you have committed, but know that in the end all will come out straight. It cannot be otherwise, because goodness is our nature, purity is our nature, and that nature can never be destroyed. Our essential nature always remains the same.

What we are to understand is this, that what we call mistakes or evil, we commit because we are weak, and we are weak because we are ignorant. I prefer to call them mistakes. The word sin, although originally a very good word, has got a certain flavour about it that frightens me. Who makes us ignorant? We ourselves. We put our hands over our eyes and weep that it is dark. Take the hands away and there is light; the light exists always for us, the self-effulgent nature of the human soul. Do you not hear what your modern scientific men say? What is the cause of evolution? Desire. The animal wants to do something, but does not find the environment favourable, and therefore develops a new body. Who develops it? The animal itself, its will. You have developed from the lowest amoeba. Continue to exercise your will and it will take you higher still. The will is almighty. If it is almighty, you may say, why cannot I do everything? But you are thinking only of your little self. Look back on yourselves from the state of the amoeba to the human being; who made all that? Your own will. Can you deny then that it is almighty? That which has made you come up so high can make you go higher still. What you want is character, strengthening of the will.

If I teach you, therefore, that your nature is evil, that you should go home and sit in sackcloth and ashes and weep your lives out because you took certain false steps, it will not help you, but will weaken you all the more, and I shall be showing you the road to more evil than good. If this room is full of darkness for thousands of years and you come in and begin to weep and wail, "Oh the darkness", will the darkness vanish? Strike a match and light comes in a moment. What good will it do you to think all your lives, "Oh, I have done evil, I have made many mistakes"? It requires no ghost to tell us that. Bring in the light and the evil goes in a moment. Build up your character, and manifest your real nature, the Effulgent, the Resplendent, the Ever-Pure, and call It up in everyone that you see. I wish that everyone of us had come to such a state that even in the vilest of human beings we could see the Real Self within, and instead of condemning them, say, "Rise thou effulgent one, rise thou who art always pure, rise thou birthless and deathless, rise almighty, and manifest thy true nature. These little manifestations do not befit thee." This is the highest prayer that the Advaita teaches. This is the one prayer, to remember our true nature, the God who is always within us, thinking of it always as infinite, almighty, ever-good, ever-beneficent, selfless, bereft of all limitations. And because that nature is selfless, it is strong and fearless; for only to selfishness comes fear. He who has nothing to desire for himself, whom does he fear, and what can frighten him? What fear has death for him? What fear has evil for him? So if we are Advaitists, we must think from this moment that our old self is dead and gone. The old Mr., Mrs., and Miss So-and-so are gone, they were mere superstitions, and what remains is the ever-pure, the ever-strong, the almighty, the all-knowing—that alone remains for us, and then all fear vanishes from us. Who can injure us, the omnipresent? All weakness has vanished from us, and our only work is to arouse this knowledge in our fellow beings. We see that they too are the same pure self, only they do not know it; we must teach them, we must help them to rouse up their infinite nature. This is what I feel to be absolutely necessary all over the world. These doctrines are old, older than many mountains possibly. All truth is eternal. Truth is nobody's property; no race, no individual can lay any exclusive claim to it. Truth is the nature of all souls. Who can lay an, special claim to it? But it has to be made practical, to be made simple (for the highest truths are always simple), so that it may penetrate every pore of human society, and become the property of the highest intellects and the commonest minds, of the man, woman, and child at the same time. All these ratiocinations of logic, all these bundles of metaphysics, all these theologies and ceremonies may have been good in their own time, but let us try to make things simpler and bring about the golden days when every man will be a worshipper, and the Reality in every man will be the object of worship.

ON BHAKTI-YOGA

THE PREPARATION

The best definition given of Bhakti-Yoga is perhaps embodied in the verse: "May that love undying which the non-discriminating have for the fleeting objects of the senses never leave this heart of mine—of me who seek after Thee!" We see what a strong love men, who do not know any better, have for sense-objects, for money, dress, their wives, children, friends, and possessions. What a tremendous clinging they have to all these things! So in the above prayer the sage says, "I will have that attachment, that tremendous clinging, only to Thee." This love, when given to God, is called Bhakti. Bhakti is not destructive; it teaches us that no one of the faculties we have has been given in vain, that through them is the natural way to come to liberation. Bhakti does not kill out our tendencies, it does not go against nature, but only gives it a higher and more powerful direction. How naturally we love objects of the senses! We cannot but do so, because they are so real to us. We do not ordinarily see anything real about higher things, but when a man has seen something real beyond the senses, beyond the universe of senses, the idea is that he can have a strong attachment, only it should be transferred to the object beyond the senses, which is God. And when the same kind of love that has before been given to sense-objects is given to God, it is called Bhakti. According to the sage Râmânuja, the following are the preparations for getting that intense love.

The first is Viveka. It is a very curious thing, especially to people of the West. It means, according to Ramanuja, "discrimination of food". Food contains all the energies that go to make up the forces of our body and mind; it has been transferred, and conserved, and given new directions in my body, but my body and mind have nothing essentially different from the food that I ate. Just as the force and matter we find in the material world become body and mind in us, so, essentially, the difference between body and mind and the food we eat is only in manifestation. It being so, that out of the material particles of our food we construct the instrument of thought, and that from the finer forces lodged in these particles we manufacture thought itself, it naturally follows, that both this thought and the instrument will be modified by the food we take. There are certain kinds of food that produce a certain change in the mind; we see it every day. There are other sorts which produce a change in the body, and in the long run have a tremendous effect on the mind. It is a great thing to learn; a good deal of the misery we suffer is occasioned by the food we take. You find that after a heavy and indigestible meal it is very hard to control the mind; it is running, running all the time. There are certain foods which are exciting; if you eat such food, you find that you cannot control the mind. It is obvious that after drinking a large quantity of wine, or other alcoholic beverage, a man finds that his mind would not be controlled; it runs away from his control.

Lectures & Discourses by **Swami Vivekananda**

According to Ramanuja, there are three things in food we must avoid. First, there is Jâti, the nature, or species of the food, that must be considered. All exciting food should be avoided, as meat, for instance; this should not be taken because it is by its very nature impure. We can get it only by taking the life of another. We get pleasure for a moment, and another creature has to give up its life to give us that pleasure. Not only so, but we demoralise other human beings. It would be rather better if every man who eats meat killed the animal himself; but, instead of doing so, society gets a class of persons to do that business for them, for doing which, it hates them. In England no butcher can serve on a jury, the idea being that he is cruel by nature. Who makes him cruel? Society. If we did not eat beef and mutton, there would be no butchers. Eating meat is only allowable for people who do very hard work, and who are not going to be Bhaktas; but if you are going to be Bhaktas, you should avoid meat. Also, all exciting foods, such as onions, garlic, and all evil-smelling food, as "sauerkraut". Any food that has been standing for days, till its condition is changed, any food whose natural juices have been almost dried ups any food that is malodorous, should be avoided.

The next thing that is to be considered as regards food is still more intricate to Western minds—it is what is called Âshraya, i.e. the person from whom it comes This is rather a mysterious theory of the Hindus. The idea is that each man has a certain aura round him, and whatever thing he touches, a part of his character, as it were, his influence, is left on it. It is supposed that a man's character emanates from him, as it were, like a physical force, and whatever he touches is affected by it. So we must take care who touches our food when it is cooked; a wicked or immoral person must not touch it. One who wants to be a Bhakta must not dine with people whom he knows to be very wicked, because their infection will come through the food.

The other form of purity to be observed is Nimitta, or instruments. Dirt and dust must not be in food. Food should not be brought from the market and placed on the table unwashed. We must be careful also about the saliva and other secretions. The lips ought never, for instance, to be touched with the fingers. The mucous membrane is the most delicate part of the body, and all tendencies are conveyed very easily by the saliva. Its contact, therefore, is to be regarded as not only offensive, but dangerous. Again, we must not eat food, half of which has been eaten by someone else. When these things are avoided in food, it becomes pure; pure food brings a pure mind, and in a pure mind is a constant memory of God.

Let me tell you the same thing as explained by another commentator, Shankarâchârya, who takes quite another view. This word for food, in Sanskrit, is derived from the root, meaning to gather. Âhâra means "gathered in". What is his explanation? He says, the passage that when food is pure the mind will become pure really means that lest we become subject to the senses we should avoid the following: First as to attachment; we must not be extremely attached to anything excepting God. See everything, do everything, but be not attached. As soon as extreme attachment comes, a man loses himself, he is no more master of himself, he is a slave. If a woman is tremendously attached to a man, she becomes a slave to that man. There is no use in being a slave. There are higher things in this world than becoming a slave to a human being. Love and do good to everybody, but do not become a slave. In the first place, attachment degenerates us, individually, and in the second place, makes us extremely selfish. Owing to this failing, we want to injure others to do good to those we love. A good many of the wicked deeds done in this world are really done through attachment to certain persons. So all attachment excepting that for good works should be avoided; but love should be given to everybody. Then as to jealousy. There should be no jealousy in regard to objects of the senses; jealousy is the root of all evil, and a most difficult thing to conquer. Next, delusion. We always take one thing for another, and act upon that, with the result that we bring misery upon ourselves. We take the bad for the good. Anything that titillates our nerves for a moment we think; as the highest good, and plunge into it immediately, but find, when it is too late, that it has given us a tremendous blow. Every day, we run into this error, and we often continue in it all our lives. When the senses, without being extremely attached, without jealousy, or without delusion, work in the world, such work or collection of impressions is called pure food, according to Shankaracharya. When pure food is taken, the mind is able to take in objects and think about them without attachment, jealousy or delusion; then the mind becomes pure, and then there is constant memory of God in that mind.

It is quite natural for one to say that Shankara's meaning is the best, but I wish to add that one should not neglect Ramanuja's interpretation either. It is only when you take care of the real material food that the rest will come. It is very true that mind is the master, but very few of us are not bound by the senses. We are all controlled by matter; and as long as we are so controlled, we must take material aids; and then, when we have become strong, we can eat or drink anything we like. We have to follow Ramanuja in taking care about food and drink; at the same time we must also take care about our mental food. It is very easy to take care about material food, but mental work must go along with it; then gradually our spiritual self will become stronger and stronger, and the physical self less assertive. Then will food hurt you no more. The great danger is that every man wants to jump at the highest ideal, but jumping is not the way. That ends only in a fall. We are bound down here, and we have to break our chains slowly. This is called Viveka, discrimination.

The next is called Vimoka, freedom from desires. He who wants to love God must get rid of extreme desires, desire nothing except God. This world is good so far as it helps one to go to the higher world. The objects of the senses are good so far as they help us to attain higher objects. We always forget that this world is a means to an end, and not an end itself. If this were the end we should be immortal here in our physical body; we should never die. But we see people every moment dying around us, and yet, foolishly, we think we shall never die; and from that conviction we come to think that this life is the goal. That is the case with ninety-nine per cent of us. This notion should be given up at once. This world is good so far as it is a means to perfect ourselves; and as soon as it has ceased to be so, it is evil. So wife, husband, children, money and learning, are good so long as they help us forward; but as soon as they cease to do that, they are nothing but evil. If the wife help us to attain God, she is a good wife; so with a husband or a child. If money help a man to do good to others, it is of some value; but if not, it is simply a mass of evil, and the sooner it is got rid of, the better.

The next is Abhyâsa, practice. The mind should always go towards God. No other things have any right to withhold it. It should continuously think of God, though this is a very hard task; yet it can be done by persistent practice. What we are now is the result of our past practice. Again, practice makes us what we shall be. So practice the other way; one sort of turning round has brought us this way, turn the other way and get out of it as soon as you can. Thinking of the senses has brought us down here—to cry one moment, to rejoice the next, to be at the mercy of every breeze, slave to everything. This is shameful, and yet we call ourselves spirits. Go the other way, think of God; let the mind not think of any physical or mental enjoyment, but of God alone. When it tries to think of anything else, give it a good blow, so that it may turn round and think of God. As oil poured from one vessel to another falls in an unbroken line, as chimes coming from a distance fall upon the ear as one continuous sound, so should the mind flow towards God in one continuous stream. We should not only impose this practice on the mind, but the senses too should be employed. Instead of hearing foolish things, we must hear about God; instead of talking foolish words, we must talk of God. Instead of reading foolish books, we must read good ones which tell of God.

The greatest aid to this practice of keeping God in memory is, perhaps, music. The Lord says to Nârada, the great teacher of Bhakti, "I do not live in heaven, nor do I live in the heart of the Yogi, but where My devotees sing My praise, there am I". Music has such tremendous power over the human mind; it brings it to concentration in a moment. You will find the dull, ignorant, low, brute-like human beings, who never steady their mind for a moment at other times, when they hear attractive music, immediately become charmed and concentrated. Even the minds of animals, such as dogs, lions, cats, and serpents, become charmed with music.

The next is Kriyâ, work—doing good to others. The memory of God will not come to the selfish man. The more we come out and do good to others, the more our hearts will be purified, and God will be in them. According to our scriptures, there are five sorts of work, called the fivefold sacrifice. First, study. A man must study every day something holy and good. Second, worship of God, angels, or saints, as it may be. Third, our duty to our forefathers. Fourth, our duty to human beings. Man has no right to live in a house himself, until he builds for the poor also, or for anybody who needs it. The householder's house should be open to everybody that is poor and suffering; then he is a real householder. If he builds a house only for himself and his wife to enjoy, he will never be a lover of God. No man has the right to cook food only for himself; it is for others, and he should have what remains. It is a common practice in India that when the season's produce first comes into the market, such as strawberries or mangoes, a man buys some of them and gives to the poor. Then he eats of them; and it is a very good example to follow in this country. This training will make a man unselfish, and at the same time, be an excellent object-lesson to his wife and children. The Hebrews in olden times used to give the first fruits to God. The first of everything should go to the poor; we have only a right to what remains. The poor are God's representatives; anyone that suffers is His representative. Without giving, he who eats and enjoys eating, enjoys sin. Fifth, our duty to the lower animals. It is diabolical to say that all animals are created for men to be killed and used in any way man likes. It is the devil's gospel, not God's. Think how diabolical it is to cut them up to see whether a nerve quivers or not, in a certain part of the body. I am glad that in our country such things are not countenanced by the Hindus, whatever encouragement they may get from the foreign government they are under. One portion of the food cooked in a household belongs to the animals also. They should be given food every day; there ought to be hospitals in every city in this country for poor, lame, or blind horses, cows, dogs, and cats, where they should be fed and taken care of.

Then there is Kalyâna, purity, which comprises the following: Satya, truthfulness. He who is true, unto him the God of truth comes. Thought, word, and deed should be perfectly true. Next Ârjava, straightforwardness, rectitude. The word means, to be simple, no crookedness in the heart, no double-dealing. Even if it is a little harsh, go straightforward, and not crookedly. Dayâ, pity, compassion. Ahimsâ, not injuring any being by thought, word, or deed. Dâna, charity. There is no higher virtue than charity. The lowest man is he whose hand draws in, in receiving; and he is the highest man whose hand goes out in giving. The hand was made to give always. Give the last bit of bread you have even if you are starving. You will be free in a moment if you starve yourself to death by giving to another. Immediately you will be perfect, you will become God. People who have children are bound already. They cannot give away. They want to enjoy their children, and they must pay for it. Are there not enough children in the world? It is only selfishness which says, "I'll have a child for myself".

The next is Anavasâda—not desponding, cheerfulness. Despondency is not religion, whatever else it may be. By being pleasant always and smiling, it takes you nearer to God, near-

Lectures & Discourses by **Swami Vivekananda**

er than any prayer. How can those minds that are gloomy and dull love? If they talk of love, it is false; they want to hurt others. Think of the fanatics; they make the longest faces, and all their religion is to fight against others in word and act. Think of what they have done in the past, and of what they would do now if they were given a free hand. They would deluge the whole world in blood tomorrow if it would bring them power. By worshipping power and making long faces, they lose every bit of love from their hearts. So the man who always feels miserable will never come to God. It is not religion, it is diabolism to say, "I am so miserable." Every man has his own burden to bear. If you are miserable, try to be happy, try to conquer it.

God is not to be reached by the weak. Never be weak. You must be strong; you have infinite strength within you. How else will you conquer anything? How else will you come to God? At the same time you must avoid excessive merriment, Uddharsha, as it is called. A mind in that state never becomes calm; it becomes fickle. Excessive merriment will always be followed by sorrow. Tears and laughter are near kin. People so often run from one extreme to the other. Let the mind be cheerful, but calm. Never let it run into excesses, because every excess will be followed by a reaction.

These, according to Ramanuja, are the preparations for Bhakti.

THE FIRST STEPS

The philosophers who wrote on Bhakti defined it as extreme love for God. Why a man should love God is the question to be solved; and until we understand that, we shall not be able to grasp the subject at all. There are two entirely different ideals of life. A man of any country who has any religion knows that he is a body and a spirit also. But there is a great deal of difference as to the goal of human life.

In Western countries, as a rule, people lay more stress on the body aspect of man; those philosophers who wrote on Bhakti in India laid stress on the spiritual side of man; and this difference seems to be typical of the Oriental and Occidental nations. It is so even in common language. In England, when speaking of death it is said, a man gave up his ghost; in India, a man gave up his body. The one idea is that man is a body and has a soul; the other that man is a soul and has a body. More intricate problems arise out of this. It naturally follows that the ideal which holds that man is a body and has a soul lays all the stress on the body. If you ask why man lives, you will be told it is to enjoy the senses, to enjoy possessions and wealth. He cannot dream of anything beyond even if he is told of it; his idea of a future life would be a continuation of this enjoyment. He is very sorry that it cannot continue all the time here, but he has to depart; and he thinks that somehow or other he will go to some place where the same thing will be renewed. He will have the same enjoyments, the same senses, only heightened and strengthened. He wants to worship God, because God is the means to attain this end. The goal of his life is enjoyment of sense-objects, and he comes to know there is a Being who can give him a very long lease of these enjoyments, and that is why he worships God.

On the other hand the Indian idea is that God is the goal of life; there is nothing beyond God, and the sense-enjoyments are simply something through which we are passing now in the hope of getting better things. Not only so; it would be disastrous and terrible if man had nothing but sense-enjoyments. In our everyday life we find that the less the sense-enjoyments, the higher the life of the man. Look at the dog when he eats. No man ever ate with the same satisfaction. Observe the pig giving grunts of satisfaction as he eats; it is his heaven, and if the greatest archangel came and looked on, the pig would not even notice him. His whole existence is in his eating. No man was ever born who could eat that way. Think of the power of hearing in the lower animals, the power of seeing; all their senses are highly developed. Their enjoyment of the senses is extreme; they become simply mad with delight and pleasure. And the lower the man also, the more delight he finds in the senses. As he gets higher, the goal becomes reason and love. In proportion as these faculties develop, he loses the power of enjoying the senses.

For illustration's sake, if we take for granted that a certain amount of power is given to man, and that can be spent either on the body, or the mind, or the spirit, then all the powers spent on any one of these leaves just so much less to be expended on the others. The ignorant or savage races have much stronger sensual faculties than the civilised races, and this is, in fact, one of the lessons we learn from history that as a nation becomes civilised the nerve organisation becomes finer, and they become physically weaker. Civilise a savage race, and you will find the same thing; another barbarian race comes up and conquers it. It is nearly always the barbarian race that conquers. We see then that if we desire only to have sense-enjoyments all the time, we degrade ourselves to the brute state. A man does not know what he is asking for when he says, he wants to go to a place where his sense-enjoyments will be intensified; that he can only have by going down to the brutes.

So with men desiring a heaven full of sense-pleasures. They are like swine wallowing in the mire of the senses, unable to see anything beyond. This sense-enjoyment is what they want, and the loss of it is the loss of heaven to them. These can never be Bhaktas in the highest sense of the word; they can never be true lovers of God. At the same time, though this lower ideal be followed for a time, it will also in course of time change, each man will find that there is something higher, of which he did not know, and so this clinging to life and to things of the senses will gradually die away. When I was a little boy at school, I had a fight with another schoolfellow about some sweetmeats, and he being the stronger boy snatched them from my hand. I remember the feeling I had; I thought that boy was the most wicked boy ever born, and that as soon as I grew strong enough I would punish him;

there was no punishment sufficient for his wickedness. We have both grown up now, and we are fast friends. This world is full of babies to whom eating and drinking, and all these little cakes are everything. They will dream of these cakes, and their idea of future life is where these cakes will be plentiful. Think of the American Indian who believes that his future life will be in a place which is a very good hunting ground. Each one of us has an idea of a heaven just as we want it to be; but in course of time, as we grow older and see higher things, we catch higher glimpses beyond. But let us not dispense with our ideas of future life in the ordinary way of modern times, by not believing in anything—that is destruction. The agnostic who thus destroys everything is mistaken, the Bhakta sees higher. The agnostic does not want to go to heaven, because he has none; while the Bhakta does not want to go to heaven, because he thinks it is child's play. What he wants is God.

What can be a higher end than God? God Himself is the highest goal of man; see Him, enjoy Him. We can never conceive anything higher, because God is perfection. We cannot conceive of any higher enjoyment than that of love, but this word love has different meanings. It does not mean the ordinary selfish love of the world; it is blasphemy to call that love. The love for our children and our wives is mere animal love; that love which is perfectly unselfish is the only love, and that is of God. It is a very difficult thing to attain to. We are passing through all these different loves—love of children, father, mother, and so forth. We slowly exercise the faculty of love; but in the majority of cases we never learn anything from it, we become bound to one step, to one person. In some cases men come out of this bondage. Men are ever running after wives and wealth and fame in this world; sometimes they are hit very hard on the head, and they find out what this world really is. No one in this world can really love anything but God. Man finds out that human love is all hollow. Men cannot love though they talk of it. The wife says she loves her husband and kisses him; but as soon as he dies, the first thing she thinks about is the bank account, and what she shall do the next day. The husband loves the wife; but when she becomes sick and loses her beauty, or becomes haggard, or makes a mistake, he ceases to care for her. All the love of the world is hypocrisy and hollowness.

A finite subject cannot love, nor a finite object be loved. When the object of the love of a man is dying every moment, and his mind also is constantly changing as he grows, what eternal love can you expect to find in the world? There cannot be any real love but in God: why then all these loves? These are mere stages. There is a power behind impelling us forward, we do not know where to seek for the real object, but this love is sending us forward in search of it. Again and again we find out our mistake. We grasp something, and find it slips through our fingers, and then we grasp something else. Thus on and on we go, till at last comes light; we come to God, the only One who loves. His love knows no change and is ever ready to take us in. How long would any of you bear with me if I injured you? He in whose mind is no anger, hatred, or envy, who never loses his balance, dies, or is born, who is he but God? But the path to God is long and difficult, and very few people attain Him. We are all babies struggling. Millions of people make a trade of religion. A few men in a century attain to that love of God, and the whole country becomes blessed and hallowed. When a son of God appears, a whole country becomes blessed. It is true that few such are born in any one century in the whole world, but all should strive to attain that love of God. Who knows but you or I may be the next to attain? Let us struggle therefore.

We say that a wife loves her husband. She thinks that her whole soul is absorbed in him: a baby comes and half of it goes out to the baby, or more. She herself will feel that the same love of husband does not exist now. So with the father. We always find that when more intense objects of love come to us, the previous love slowly vanishes. Children at school think that some of their schoolfellows are the dearest beings that they have in life, or their fathers or mothers are so; then comes the husband or wife, and immediately the old feeling disappears, and the new love becomes uppermost. One star arises, another bigger one comes, and then a still bigger one, and at last the sun comes, and all the lesser lights vanish. That sun is God. The stars are the smaller loves. When that Sun bursts upon him, a man becomes mad what Emerson calls "a God-intoxicated man". Man becomes transfigured into God, everything is merged in that one ocean of love. Ordinary love is mere animal attraction. Otherwise why is the distinction between the sexes? If one kneels before an image, it is dreadful idolatry; but if one kneels before husband or wife, it is quite permissible!

The world presents to us manifold stages of love. We have first to clear the ground. Upon our view of life the whole theory of love will rest. To think that this world is the aim and end of life is brutal and degenerating. Any man who starts in life with that idea degenerates himself He will never rise higher, he will never catch this glimpse from behind, he will always be a slave to the senses. He will struggle for the dollar that will get him a few cakes to eat. Better die than live that life. Slaves of this world, slaves of the senses, let us rouse ourselves; there is something higher than this sense-life. Do you think that man, the Infinite Spirit was born to be a slave to his eyes, his nose, and his ears? There is an Infinite, Omniscient Spirit behind that can do everything, break every bond; and that Spirit we are, and we get that power through love. This is the ideal we must remember. We cannot, of course, get it in a day. We may fancy that we have it, but it is a fancy after all; it is a long, long way off. We must take man where he stands, and help him upwards. Man stands in materialism; you and I are materialists. Our talking about God and Spirit is good; but it is simply the vogue in our society to talk thus: we have learnt it parrot-like and repeat it. So we have to take ourselves where we are as materialists, and must take the help of matter and go on slowly until we become real spiritualists, and

Lectures & Discourses by **Swami Vivekananda**

feel ourselves spirits, understand the spirit, and find that this world which we call the infinite is but a gross external form of that world which is behind.

But something besides that is necessary. You read in the Sermon on the Mount, "Ask, and it shall be given (to) you; seek, and ye shall find; knock, and it shall be opened unto you." The difficulty is, who seeks, who wants? We all say we know God. One man writes a book to disprove God, another to prove Him. One man thinks it his duty to prove Him all his life; another, to disprove Him, and he goes about to teach man there is no God. What is the use of writing a book either to prove or disprove God? What does it matter to most people whether there is a God or not? The majority of men work just like a machine with no thought of God and feeling no need of Him. Then one day comes Death and says, "Come." The man says, "Wait a little, I want a little more time. I want to see my son grow a little bigger." But Death says, "Come at once." So it goes on. So goes poor John. What shall we say to poor John? He never found anything in which God was the highest; perhaps he was a pig in the past, and he is much better as a man. But there are some who get a little awakening. Some misery comes, someone whom we love most dies, that upon which we had bent our whole soul, that for which we had cheated the whole world and perhaps our own brother, that vanishes, and a blow comes to us. Perhaps a voice comes in our soul and asks, "What after this?" Sometimes death comes without a blow, but such cases are few. Most of us, when anything slips through our fingers, say, "What next?" How we cling to the senses! You have heard of a drowning man clutching at a straw; a man will clutch at a straw first, and when it fails, he will say someone must help him. Still people must, as the English phrase goes, "sow their wild oats", before they can rise to higher things.

Bhakti is a religion. Religion is not for the many, that is impossible. A sort of knee-drill, standing up and sitting down, may be suited for the many; but religion is for the few. There are in every country only a few hundreds who can be, and will be religious. The others cannot be religious, because they will not be awakened, and they do not want to be. The chief thing is to want God. We want everything except God, because our ordinary wants are supplied by the external world; it is only when our necessities have gone beyond the external world that we want a supply from the internal, from God. So long as our needs are confined within the narrow limits of this physical universe, we cannot have any need for God; it is only when we have become satiated with everything here that we look beyond for a supply. It is only when the need is there that the demand will come. Have done with this child's play of the world as soon as you can, and then you will feel the necessity of something beyond the world, and the first step in religion will come.

There is a form of religion which is fashionable. My friend has much furniture in her parlour; it is the fashion to have a Japanese vase, so she must have one even if it costs a thousand dollars. In the same way she will have a little religion and join a church. Bhakti is not for such. That is not want. Want is that without which we cannot live. We want breath, we want food, we want clothes; without them we cannot live. When a man loves a woman in this world, there are times when he feels that without her he cannot live, although that is a mistake. When a husband dies, the wife thinks she cannot live without him; but she lives all the same. This is the secret of necessity: it is that without which we cannot live; either it must come to us or we die. When the time comes that we feel the same about God, or in other words, we want something beyond this world, something above all material forces, then we may become Bhaktas. What are our little lives when for a moment the cloud passes away, and we get one glimpse from beyond, and for that moment all these lower desires seem like a drop in the ocean? Then the soul grows, and feels the want of God, and must have Him.

The first step is: What do we want? Let us ask ourselves this question every day, do we want God? You may read all the books in the universe, but this love is not to be had by the power of speech, not by the highest intellect, not by the study of various sciences. He who desires God will get Love, unto him God gives Himself. Love is always mutual, reflective. You may hate me, and if I want to love you, you repulse me. But if I persist, in a month or a year you are bound to love me. It is a wellknown psychological phenomenon. As the loving wife thinks of her departed husband, with the same love we must desire the Lord, and then we will find God, and all books and the various sciences would not be able to teach us anything. By reading books we become parrots; no one becomes learned by reading books. If a man reads but one word of love, he indeed becomes learned. So we want first to get that desire.

Let us ask ourselves each day, "Do we want Gods" When we begin to talk religion, and especially when we take a high position and begin to teach others, we must ask ourselves the same question. I find many times that I don't want God, I want bread more. I may go mad if I don't get a piece of bread; many ladies will go mad if they don't get a diamond pin, but they do not have the same desire for God; they do not know the only Reality that is in the universe. There is a proverb in our language—If I want to be a hunter, I'll hunt the rhinoceros; if I want to be a robber, I'll rob the king's treasury. What is the use of robbing beggars or hunting ants? So if you want to love, love God. Who cares for these things of the world? This world is utterly false; all the great teachers of the world found that out; there is no way out of it but through God. He is the goal of our life; all ideas that the world is the goal of life are pernicious. This world and this body have their own value, a secondary value, as a means to an end; but the world should not be the end. Unfortunately, too often we make the world the end and God the means. We find people going to church and saying, "God, give me such and such; God, heal my disease." They want nice healthy bodies; and because they hear that someone will do this work for them, they go and pray to Him. It is better to be an atheist than to have such an idea of religion. As I have told you, this Bhakti is the highest ideal; I don't know whether we shall reach it or not in millions of years to come, but we must make it our highest ideal, make our senses aim at the highest. If we cannot get to the end, we shall at least come nearer to it. We have slowly to work through the world and the senses to reach God.

THE TEACHER OF SPIRITUALITY

Every soul is destined to be perfect, and every being, in the end, will attain to that state. Whatever we are now is the result of whatever we have been or thought in the past; and whatever we shall be in the future will be the result of what we do or think now. But this does not preclude our receiving help from outside; the possibilities of the soul are always quickened by some help from outside, so much so that in the vast majority of cases in the world, help from outside is almost absolutely necessary. Quickening influence comes from outside, and that works upon our own potentialities; and then the growth begins, spiritual life comes, and man becomes holy and perfect in the end. This quickening impulse which comes from outside cannot be received from books; the soul can receive impulse only from another soul, and from nothing else. We may study books all our lives, we may become very intellectual, but in the end we find we have not developed at all spiritually. It does not follow that a high order of intellectual development always shows an equivalent development of the spiritual side of man; on the other hand, we find cases almost every day where the intellect has become very highly developed at the expense of the spirit.

Now in intellectual development we can get much help from books, but in spiritual development, almost nothing. In studying books, sometimes we are deluded into thinking that we are being spiritually helped; but if we analyse ourselves, we shall find that only our intellect has been helped, and not the spirit. That is the reason why almost everyone of us can speak most wonderfully on spiritual subjects, but when the time of action comes, we find ourselves so woefully deficient. It is because books cannot give us that impulse from outside. To quicken the spirit, that impulse must come from another soul.

That soul from which this impulse comes is called the Guru, the teacher; and the soul to which the impulse is conveyed is called the disciple, the student. In order to convey this impulse, in the first place, the soul from which it comes must possess the power of transmitting it, as it were, to another; and in the second place, the object to which it is transmitted must be fit to receive it. The seed must be a living seed, and the field must be ready ploughed; and when both these conditions are fulfilled, a wonderful growth of religion takes place. "The speaker of religion must be wonderful, so must the hearer be"; and when both of these are really wonderful, extraordinary, then alone will splendid spiritual growth come,

and not otherwise. These are the real teachers, and these are the real students. Besides these, the others are playing with spirituality—just having a little intellectual struggle, just satisfying a little curiosity—but are standing only on the outward fringe of the horizon of religion. There is some value in that; real thirst for religion may thus be awakened; all comes in course of time. It is a mysterious law of nature that as soon as the field is ready the seed must come, as soon as the soul wants religion, the transmitter of religious force must come. "The seeking sinner meeteth the seeking Saviour." When the power that attracts in the receiving soul is full and ripe, the power which answers to that attraction must come.

But there are great dangers in the way. There is the danger to the receiving soul of mistaking its momentary emotion for real religious yearning. We find that in ourselves. Many times in our lives, somebody dies whom we loved; we receive a blow; for a moment we think that this world is slipping between our fingers, and that we want something higher, and that we are going to be religious. In a few days that wave passes away, and we are left stranded where we were. We often times mistake such impulses for real thirst after religion, but so long as these momentary emotions are thus mistaken, that continuous, real want of the soul will not come, and we shall not find the "transmitter".

So when we complain that we have not got the truth, and that we want it so much, instead of complaining, our first duty ought to be to look into our own souls and find whether we really want it. In the vast majority of cases we shall find that we are not fit; we do not want; there was no thirst after the spiritual.

There are still more difficulties for the "transmitter". There are many who, though immersed in ignorance, yet, in the pride of their hearts, think they know everything, and not only do not stop there, but offer to take others on their shoulders, and thus "the blind leading the blind, they both fall into the ditch". The world is full of these; everyone wants to be a teacher, every beggar wants to make a gift of a million dollars. Just as the latter is ridiculous, so are these teachers.

How are we to know a teacher then? In the first place, the sun requires no torch to make it visible. We do not light a candle to see the sun. When the sun rises, we instinctively become aware of its rising; and when a teacher of men comes to help us, the soul will instinctively know that it has found the truth. Truth stands on its own evidences; it does not require any other testimony to attest it; it is self-effulgent. It penetrates into the inmost recesses of our nature, and the whole universe stands up and says, "This is Truth." These are the very great teachers, but we can get help from the lesser ones also; and as we ourselves are not always sufficiently intuitive to be certain of our judgment of the man from whom we receive, there ought to be certain tests. There are certain conditions necessary in the taught, and also in the teacher.

The conditions necessary in the taught are purity, a real thirst after knowledge, and perseverance. No impure soul can be religious; that is the one great condition; purity in every way is absolutely necessary. The other condition is a real thirst after knowledge. Who wants? That is the question. We get whatever we want—that is an old, old law. He who wants, gets. To want religion is a very difficult thing, not so easy as we generally think. Then we always forget that religion does not consist in hearing talks, or in reading books, but it is a continuous struggle, a grappling with our own nature, a continuous fight till the victory is achieved. It is not a question of one or two days, of years, or of lives, but it may be hundreds of lifetimes, and we must be ready for that. It may come immediately, or it may not come in hundreds of lifetimes; and we must be ready for that. The student who sets out with such a spirit finds success.

In the teacher we must first see that he knows the secret of the scriptures. The whole world reads scriptures—Bibles, Vedas, Korans, and others; but they are only words, external arrangement, syntax, the etymology, the philology, the dry bones of religion. The teacher may be able to find what is the age of any book, but words are only the external forms in which things come. Those who deal too much in words and let the mind run always in the force of words lose the spirit. So the teacher must be able to know the spirit of the scriptures. The network of words is like a huge forest in which the human mind loses itself and finds no way out. The various methods of joining words, the various methods of speaking a beautiful language, the various methods of explaining the dicta of the scriptures, are only for the enjoyment of the learned. They do not attain perfection; they are simply desirous to show their learning, so that the world may praise them and see that they are learned men. You will find that no one of the great teachers of the world went into these various explanations of texts; on their part there is no attempt at "text-torturing", no saying, "This word means this, and this is the philological connection between this and that word." You study all the great teachers the world has produced, and you will see that no one of them goes that way. Yet they taught, while others, who have nothing to teach, will take up a word and write a three-volume book on its origin and use. As my Master used to say, what would you think of men who went into a mango orchard and busied themselves in counting the leaves and examining the colour of the leaves, the size of the twigs, the number of branches, and so forth, while only one of them had the sense to begin to eat the mangoes? So leave this counting of leaves and twigs and this note-taking to others. That work has its own value in its proper place, but not here in the spiritual realm. Men never become spiritual through such work; you have never once seen a strong spiritual man among these "leaf-counters". Religion is the highest aim of man, the highest glory, but it does not require "leaf-counting". If you want to be a Christian, it is not necessary to know whether Christ was born in Jerusalem or Bethlehem or just the exact date on which he pronounced the Sermon on the Mount; you only require to feel the Sermon on the Mount. It is not necessary to read two thousand words on when it was delivered. All that is for the enjoyment of the learned. Let them have it; say amen to that. Let us eat the mangoes.

The second condition necessary in the teacher is that he must be sinless. The question was once asked me in England by a friend, "Why should we look to the personality of a teacher? We have only to judge of what he says, and take that up." Not so. If a man wants to teach me something of dynamics or chemistry or any other physical science, he may be of any character; he can still teach dynamics or any other science. For the knowledge that the physical sciences require is simply intellectual and depends on intellectual strength; a man can have in such a case a gigantic intellectual power without the least development of his soul. But in the spiritual sciences it is impossible from first to last that there can be any spiritual light in that soul which is impure. What can such a soul teach? It knows nothing. Spiritual truth is purity. "Blessed are the pure in heart, for they shall see God". In that one sentence is the gist of all religions. If you have learnt that, all that has been said in the past and all that it is possible to say in the future, you have known; you need not look into anything else, for you have all that is necessary in that one sentence; it could save the world, were all the other scriptures lost. A vision of God, a glimpse of the beyond never comes until the soul is pure. Therefore in the teacher of spirituality, purity is the one thing indispensable; we must see first what he is, and then what he says. Not so with intellectual teachers; there we care more for what he says than what he is. With the teacher of religion we must first and foremost see what he is, and then alone comes the value of the words, because he is the transmitter. What will he transmit, if he has not flat spiritual power in him? To give a simile: If a heater is hot, it can convey heat vibrations, but if not, it is impossible to do so. Even so is the case with the mental vibrations of the religious teacher which he conveys to the mind of the taught. It is a question of transference, and not of stimulating only our intellectual faculties. Some power, real and tangible, goes out from the teacher and begins to grow in the mind of the taught. Therefore the necessary condition is that the teacher must be true.

The third condition is motive. We should see that he does not teach with any ulterior motive, for name, or fame, or anything else, but simply for love, pure love for you. When spiritual forces are transmitted from the teacher to the taught, they can only be conveyed through the medium of love; there is no other medium that can convey them. Any other motive, such as gain or name, would immediately destroy the conveying medium; therefore all must be done through love. One who has known God can alone be a teacher. When you see that in the teacher these conditions are fulfilled, you are safe; if they are not fulfilled, it is unwise to accept him. There is a great risk, if he cannot convey goodness, of his conveying wickedness sometimes. This must be guarded against; therefore it naturally follows that we cannot be taught by anybody and everybody.

The preaching of sermons by brooks and stones may be true as a poetical figure but no one can preach a single grain of truth until he has it in himself. To whom do the brooks preach sermons? To that human soul only whose lotus of life has already opened. When the heart has been opened, it can receive teaching from the brooks or the stones—it can get some religious teaching from all these; but the unopened heart will see nothing but brooks and rolling stones. A blind man may come to a museum, but he comes and goes only; if he is to see, his eyes must first be opened. This eye-opener of religion is the teacher. With the teacher, therefore, our relationship is that of ancestor and descendant; the teacher is the spiritual ancestor, and the disciple is the spiritual descendant. It is all very well to talk of liberty and independence, but without humility, submission, veneration, and faith, there will not be any religion. It is a significant fact that where this relation still exists between the teacher and the taught, there alone gigantic spiritual souls grow; but in those who have thrown it off religion is made into a diversion. In nations and churches where this relation between teacher and taught is not maintained spirituality is almost an unknown quantity. It never comes without that feeling; there is no one to transmit and no one to be transmitted to, because they are all independent. Of whom can they learn? And if they come to learn, they come to buy learning. Give me a dollar's worth of religion; cannot I pay a dollar for it? Religion cannot be got that way!

There is nothing higher and holier than the knowledge which comes to the soul transmitted by a spiritual teacher. If a man has become a perfect Yogi it comes by itself, but it cannot be got in books. You may go and knock your head against the four corners of the world, seek in the Himalayas, the Alps, the Caucasus, the Desert of Gobi or Sahara, or the bottom of the sea, but it will not come until you find a teacher. Find the teacher, serve him as a child, open your heart to his influence, see in him God manifested. Our attention should be fixed on the teacher as the highest manifestation of God; and as the power of attention concentrates there, the picture of the teacher as man will melt away; the frame will vanish, and the real God will be left there. Those that come to truth with such a spirit of veneration and love—for them the Lord of truth speaks the most wonderful words. "Take thy shoes from off thy feet, for the place whereon thou standest is holy ground". Wherever His name is spoken, that place is holy. How much more so is a man who speaks His name, and with what veneration ought we to approach a man out of whom come spiritual truths! This is the spirit in which we are to be taught. Such teachers are few in number, no doubt, in this world, but the world is never altogether without them. The moment it is absolutely bereft of these, it will cease to be, it will become a hideous hell and will just drop. These teachers are the fair flowers of human life and keep the world going; it is the strength that is manifested from these hearts of life that keeps the bounds of society intact.

Beyond these is another set of teachers, the Christs of the world. These Teachers of all teachers represent God Himself in the form of man. They are much higher; they can transmit spirituality with a touch, with a wish, which makes even the lowest and most degraded characters saints in one second. Do you not read of how they used to do these things? They are not the teachers about whom I was speaking; they are the Teachers of all teachers, the greatest manifestations of God to man; we cannot see God except through them. We cannot help worshipping them, and they are the only beings we are bound to worship.

No man hath "seen" God but as He is manifested in the Son. We cannot see God. If we try to see Him, we make a hideous caricature of God. There is an Indian story that an ignorant man was asked to make an image of the God Shiva, and after days of struggle he made an image of a monkey. So whenever we attempt to make an image of God, we make a caricature of Him, because we cannot understand Him as anything higher than man so long as we are men. The time will come when we transcend our human nature and know Him as He is; but so long as we are men we must worship Him in man. Talk as we may, try as we may, we cannot see God except as a man. We may deliver great intellectual speeches, become very great rationalists, and prove that these tales of God as all nonsense, but let us come to practical common sense. What is behind this remarkable intellect? Zero, nothing, simply so much froth. When next you hear a man delivering great intellectual lectures against this worship of God, get hold of him and ask him what is his idea of God, what he means by "omnipotence", and "omniscience", and "omnipresent love", and so forth, beyond the spelling of the words. He means nothing, he cannot formulate an idea, he is no better than the man in the street who has not read a single book. That man in the street, however, is quiet and does not disturb the world, while the other man's arguments cause disturbance. He has no actual perception, and both are on the same plane.

Religion is realisation, and you must make the sharpest distinction between talk and realisation. What you perceive in your soul is realisation. Man has no idea of the Spirit, he has to think of it with the forms he has before him. He has to think of the blue skies, or the expansive fields, or the sea, or something huge. How else can you think of God? So what are you doing in reality? You are talking of omnipresence, and thinking of the sea. Is God the sea? A little more common sense is required. Nothing is so uncommon as common sense, the world is too full of talk. A truce to all this frothy argument of the world. We are by our present constitution limited and bound to see God as man. If the buffaloes want to worship God, they will see Him as a huge buffalo. If a fish wants to worship God, it will have to think of Him as a big fish. You and I, the buffalo, the fish, each represents so many different vessels. All these go to the sea to be filled with water according to the shape of each vessel. In each of these vessels is nothing but water. So with God. When men see Him, they see Him as man, and the animals as animal—each according to his ideal. That is the only way you can see Him; you have to worship Him as man, because there is no other way out of it. Two classes of men do not worship God as man—the human brute who has no religion, and the Paramahamsa (highest Yogi) who has gone beyond humanity, who has thrown off his mind and body and gone beyond the limits of nature. All nature has become his Self. He has neither mind nor body, and can worship God as God, as can a Jesus or a Buddha. They did not worship God as man. The other extreme is the human brute. You know how two extremes look alike. Similar is the case with the extreme of ignorance and the other extreme of knowledge; neither of these worships anybody. The extremely ignorant do not worship God, not being developed enough to feel the need for so doing. Those that have attained the highest knowledge also do not worship God—having realised and become one with God. God never worships God. Between these two poles of existence, if anyone tells you he is not going to worship God as man, take care of him. He is an irresponsible talker, he is mistaken; his religion is for frothy thinkers, it is intellectual nonsense.

Therefore it is absolutely necessary to worship God as man, and blessed are those races which have such a "God-man" to worship. Christians have such a God-man in Christ; therefore cling close to Christ; never give up Christ. That is the natural way to see God; see God in man. All our ideas of God are concentrated there. The great limitation Christians have is that they do not heed other manifestations of God besides Christ. He was a manifestation of God; so was Buddha; so were some others, and there will be hundreds of others. Do not limit God anywhere. Pay all the reverence that you think is due to God, to Christ; that is the only worship we can have. God cannot be worshipped; He is the immanent Being of the universe. It is only to His manifestation as man that we can pray. It would be a very good plan, when Christians pray, to say, "in the name of Christ". It would be wise to stop praying to God, and only pray to Christ. God understands human failings and becomes a man to do good to humanity. "Whenever virtue subsides and immorality prevails, then I come to help mankind", says Krishna. He also says, "Fools, not knowing that I, the Omnipotent and Omnipresent God of the universe, have taken this human form, deride Me and think that cannot be." Their minds have been clouded with demoniacal ignorance, so they cannot see in Him the Lord of the universe. These great Incarnations of God are to be worshipped. Not only so, they alone can be worshipped; and on the days of their birth, and on the days when they went out of this world, we ought to pay more particular reverence to them. In worshipping Christ I would rather worship Him just as He desires; on the day of His birth I would rather worship Him by fasting than by feasting—by praying. When these are thought of, these great ones, they manifest themselves in our souls, and they make us like unto them. Our whole nature changes, and we become like them.

But you must not mix up Christ or Buddha with hobgoblins flying through the air and all that sort of nonsense. Sacrilege! Christ coming into a spiritualistic seance to dance! I have seen that presence in this country. It is not in that way that these manifestations of God come. The very touch of one of them will be manifest upon a man; when Christ touches, the whole soul of man will change, that man will be transfigured just as He was. His whole life will be spiritualised; from every pore of his body spiritual power will emanate. What were the great powers of Christ in miracles and healing, in one of his character? They were low, vulgar things that He could not help doing because He was among vulgar beings. Where was this miracle-making done? Among the Jews; and the Jews did not take Him. Where was it not done? In Europe. The miracle-making went to the Jews, who rejected Christ, and the Sermon on the Mount to Europe, which accepted Him. The human spirit took on what was true and rejected what was spurious. The great strength of Christ is not in His miracles or His healing. Any fool could do those things. Fools can heal others, devils can heal others. I have seen horrible demoniacal men do wonderful miracles. They seem to manufacture fruits out of the earth. I have known fools and diabolical men tell the past, present, and future. I have seen fools heal at a glance, by the will, the most horrible diseases. These are powers, truly, but often demoniacal powers. The other is the spiritual power of Christ which will live and always has lived - an almighty, gigantic love, and the words of truth which He preached. The action of healing men at a glance is forgotten, but His saying, "Blessed are the pure in heart", that lives today. These words are a gigantic magazine of power—inexhaustible. So long as the human mind lasts, so long as the name of God is not forgotten, these words will roll on and on and never cease to be. These are the powers Jesus taught, and the powers He had. The power of purity; it is a definite power. So in worshipping Christ, in praying to Him, we must always remember what we are seeking. Not those foolish things of miraculous display, but the wonderful powers of the Spirit, which make man free, give him control over the whole of nature, take from him the badge of slavery, and show God unto him.

THE NEED OF SYMBOLS

Bhakti is divided into two portions. One is called Vaidhi, formal or ceremonial; the other portion is called Mukhyâ, supreme. The word Bhakti covers all the ground between the lowest form of worship and the highest form of life. All the worship that you have seen in any country in the world, or in any religion, is regulated by love. There is a good deal that is simple ceremony; there is also a good deal which, though not ceremony, is still not love, but a lower state. Yet these ceremonies are necessary. The external part of Bhakti is absolutely necessary to help the soul onward. Man makes a great mistake when he thinks that he can at once jump to the highest state. If a baby thinks he is going to be an old man in a day, he is mistaken; and I hope you will always bear in mind this one ideal, that religion is neither in books, nor in intellectual consent, nor in reasoning. Reason, theories, documents, doctrines, books, religious ceremonies, are all helps to religion: religion itself consists in realisation. We all say, "There is a God." Have you seen God? That is the question. You hear a man say, "There is God in heaven." You ask him if he has seen Him, and if he says he has, you would laugh at him and say he is a maniac. With most people religion is a sort of intellectual assent and goes no further than a document. I would not call it religion. It is better to be an atheist than to have that sort of religion. Religion does not depend on our intellectual assent or dissent. You say there is a soul. Have you seen the soul? How is it we all have souls and do not see them? You have to answer the question and find out the way to see the soul. If not, it is useless to talk of religion. If any religion is true, it must be able to show us the soul and show us God and the truth in ourselves. If you and I fight for all eternity about one of these doctrines or documents, we shall never come to any conclusion. People have been fighting for ages, and what is the outcome? Intellect cannot reach there at all. We have to go beyond the intellect; the proof of religion is in direct perception. The proof of the existence of this wall is that we see it; if you sat down and argued about its existence or non-existence for ages, you could never come to any conclusion; but directly you see it, it is enough. If all the men in the world told you it did not exist, you would not believe them, because you know that the evidence of your own eyes is superior to that of all the doctrines and documents in the world.

To be religious, you have first to throw books overboard. The less you read of books, the better for you; do one thing at a time. It is a tendency in Western countries, in these modern times, to make a hotchpotch of the brain; all sorts of unassimilated ideas run riot in the brain and form a chaos without ever obtaining a chance to settle down and crystallise into a definite shape. In many cases it becomes a sort of disease, but this is not religion. Then some want a sensation. Tell them about ghosts and people coming from the North Pole or any other remote place, with wings or in any other form, and that they are invisibly present and watching over them, and make them feel uncanny, then they are satisfied and go home; but within twenty-four hours they are ready for a fresh sensation. This is what some call religion. This is the way to the lunatic asylum, and not to religion. The Lord is not to be reached by the weak, and all these weird things tend to weakness. Therefore go not near them; they only make people weak, bring disorder to the brain, weaken the mind, demoralise the soul, and a hopeless muddle is the result. You must bear in mind that religion does not consist in talk, or doctrines, or books, but in realisation; it is not learning, but 'being. Everybody knows, "Do not steal", but what of it? That man has really known who has not stolen. Everybody knows, "Do not injure others", but of what value is it? Those who have not done so have realised it, they know it and have built their character

on it. Religion is realising; and I will call you a worshipper of God when you have become able to realise the Idea. Before that it is the spelling of the weird, and no more. It is this power of realisation that makes religion. No amount of doctrines or philosophies or ethical books, that you may have stuffed into your brain, will matter much, only what you are and what you have realised. So we have to realise religion, and this realisation of religion is a long process. When men hear of something very high and wonderful, they all think they will get that, and never stop for a moment to consider that they will have to work their way up to it; they all want to jump there. If it is the highest, we are for it. We never stop to consider whether we have the power, and the result is that we do not do anything. You cannot take a man with a pitchfork and push him up there; we all have to work up gradually. Therefore the first part of religion is Vaidhi Bhakti, the lower phase of worship.

What are these lower phases of worship? They are various. In order to attain to the state where we can realise, we must pass through the concrete—just as you see children learn through the concrete first—and gradually come to the abstract. If you tell a baby that five times two is ten, it will not understand; but if you bring ten things and show how five times two is ten, it will understand. Religion is a long, slow process. We are all of us babies here; we may be old, and have studied all the books in the universe, but we are all spiritual babies. We have learnt the doctrines and dogmas, but realised nothing in our lives. We shall have to begin now in the concrete, through forms and words, prayers and ceremonies; and of these concrete forms there will be thousands; one form need not be for everybody. Some may be helped by images, some may not. Some require an image outside, others one inside the brain. The man who puts it inside says, "I am a superior man. When it is inside it is all right; when it is outside, it is idolatry, I will fight it." When a man puts an image in the form of a church or a temple, he thinks it is holy; but when it is in a human form, he objects to it!

So there are various forms through which the mind will take this concrete exercise; and then, step by step, we shall come to the abstract understanding, abstract realisation. Again, the same form is not for everyone; there is one form that will suit you, and another will suit somebody else, and so on. All forms, though leading to the same goal, may not be for all of us. Here is another mistake we generally make. My ideal does not suit you; and why should I force it on you? My fashion of building churches or reading hymns does not suit you; why should I force it on you? Go into the world and every fool will tell you that his form is the only right one, that every other form is diabolical, and he is the only chosen man ever born in the universe. But in fact, all these forms are good and helpful. Just as there are certain varieties in human nature, so it is necessary that there should be an equal number of forms in religion; and the more there are, the better for the world. If there are twenty forms of religion in the world, it is very good; if there are four hundred, so much the better—there will be the more to choose from. So we should rather be glad when the number of religions and religious ideas increase and multiply, because they will then include every man and help mankind more. Would to God that religions multiplied until every man had his own religion, quite separate from that of any other! This is the idea of the Bhakti-Yogi.

The final idea is that my religion cannot be yours, or yours mine. Although the goal and the aim are the same, yet each one has to take a different road, according to the tendencies of his mind; and although these roads are various, they must all be true, because they lead to the same goal. It cannot be that one is true and the rest not. The choosing of one's own road is called in the language of Bhakti, Ishta, the chosen way.

Then there are words. All of you have heard of the power of words, how wonderful they are! Every book—the Bible, the Koran, and the Vedas—is full of the power of words. Certain words have wonderful power over mankind. Again, there are other forms, known as symbols. Symbols have great influence on the human mind. But great symbols in religion were not created indefinitely. We find that they are the natural expressions of thought. We think symbolically. All our words are but symbols of the thought behind, and different people have come to use different symbols without knowing the reason why. It was all behind, and these symbols are associated with the thoughts; and as the thought brings the symbol outside, so the symbol, on the contrary, can bring the thought inside. So one portion of Bhakti tells about these various subjects of symbols and words and prayers. Every religion has prayers, but one thing you must bear in mind—praying for health or wealth is not Bhakti, it is all Karma or meritorious action. Praying for any physical gain is simply Karma, such as a prayer for going to heaven and so forth. One that wants to love God, to be a Bhakta, must discard all such prayers. He who wants to enter the realms of light must first give up this buying and selling this "shopkeeping" religion, and then enter the gates. It is not that you do not get what you pray for; you get everything, but such praying is a beggar's religion. "Foolish indeed is he who, living on the banks of the Ganga, digs a little well for water. A fool indeed is the man who, coming to a mine of diamonds, seeks for glass beads." This body will die some time, so what is the use of praying for its health again and again? What is there in health and wealth? The wealthiest man can use and enjoy only a little portion of his wealth. We can never get all the things of this world; and if not, who cares? This body will go, who cares for these things? If good things come, welcome; if they go away, let them go. Blessed are they when they come, and blessed are they when they go. We are striving to come into the presence of the King of kings. We cannot get there in a beggar's dress. Even if we wanted to enter the presence of an emperor, should we be admitted? Certainly not. We should be driven out. This is the Emperor of emperors, and in these beggar's rags we cannot enter. Shopkeepers never have admission there; buying and selling have no place there. As you read in the Bible, Jesus drove the buyers and sellers out of the Temple. Do not pray for little things. If you seek only bodily comforts, where is the difference between men and animals? Think yourselves a little higher than that.

So it goes without saying that the first task in becoming a Bhakta is to give up all desires of heaven and other things. The question is how to get rid of these desires. What makes men miserable? Because they are slaves, bound by laws, puppets in the hand of nature, tumbled about like playthings. We are continually taking care of this body that anything can knock down; and so we are living in a constant state of fear. I have read that a deer has to run on the average sixty or seventy miles every day, because it is frightened. We ought to know that we are in a worse plight than the deer. The deer has some rest, but we have none. If the deer gets grass enough it is satisfied, but we are always multiplying our wants. It is a morbid desire with us to multiply our wants. We have become so unhinged and unnatural that nothing natural will satisfy us. We are always grasping after morbid things, must have unnatural excitement—unnatural food, drink, surroundings, and life. As to fear, what are our lives but bundles of fear? The deer has only one class of fear, such as that from tigers, wolves, etc. Man has the whole universe to fear.

How are we to free ourselves from this is the question. Utilitarians say, "Don't talk of God and hereafter; we don't know anything of these things, let us live happily in this world." I would be the first to do so if we could, but the world will not allow us. As long as you are a slave of nature, how can you? The more you struggle, the more enveloped you become. You have been devising plans to make you happy, I do not know for how many years, but each year things seem to grow worse. Two hundred years ago in the old world people had few wants; but if their knowledge increased in arithmetical progression, their wants increased in geometrical progression. We think that in salvation at least our desires will be fulfilled, so we desire to go to heaven. This eternal, unquenchable thirst! Always wanting something! When a man is a beggar, he wants money. When he has money, he wants other things, society; and after that, something else. Never at rest. How are we to quench this? If we get to heaven, it will only increase desire. If a poor man gets rich, it does not quench his desires, it is only like throwing butter on the fire, increasing its bright flames. Going to heaven means becoming intensely richer, and then desire comes more and more. We read of many human things in heaven in the different Bibles of the world; they are not always very good there; and after all, this desire to go to heaven is a desire after enjoyment. This has to be given up. It is too little, too vulgar a thing for you to think of going to heaven. It is just the same as thinking, I will become a millionaire and lord it over people. There are many of these heavens, but through them you cannot gain the right to enter the gates of religion and love.

THE CHIEF SYMBOLS

There are two Sanskrit words, Pratika and Pratimâ. Pratika means coming towards, nearing. In all countries you find various grades of worship. In this country, for instance, there are people who worship images of saints, there are people who worship certain forms and symbols. Then there are people who worship different beings who are higher than men, and their number is increasing very rapidly — worshippers of departed spirits. I read that there are something like eight millions of them here. Then there are other people who worship certain beings of higher grade — the angels, the gods, and so forth. Bhakti-Yoga does not condemn any one of these various grades, but they are all classed under one name, Pratika. These people are not worshipping God, but Pratika, something which is near, a step towards God. This Pratika worship cannot lead us to salvation and freedom; it can only give us certain particular things for which we worship them. For instance, if a man worships his departed ancestors or departed friends, he may get certain powers or certain information from them. Any particular gift that is got from these objects of worship is called Vidyâ, particular knowledge; but freedom, the highest aim, comes only by worship of God Himself. Some Orientalists think, in expounding the Vedas, that even the Personal God Himself is a Pratika. The Personal God may be a Pratika, but the Pratikas are neither the Personal nor Impersonal God. They cannot be worshipped as God. So it would be a great mistake if people thought that by worshipping these different Pratikas, either as angels, or ancestors, or Mahâtmâs (holy men, saints), etc., or departed spirits, they could ever reach to freedom. At best they can only reach to certain powers, but God alone can make us free. But because of that they are not to be condemned, their worship produces some result. The man who does not understand anything higher may get some power, some enjoyment, by the worship of these Pratikas; and after a long course of experience, when he will be ready to come to freedom, he will of his own accord give up the Pratikas.

Of these various Pratikas the most prevalent form is the worship of departed friends. Human nature — personal love, love for our friends — is so strong in us that when they die, we wish to see them once more — clinging on to their forms. We forget that these forms while living were constantly changing, and when they die, we think they become constant, and that we shall see them so. Not only so, but if I have a friend or a son who has been a scoundrel, as soon as he dies, I begin to think he is the saintliest person in existence; he becomes a god. There are people in India who, if a baby dies, do not burn it, but bury it and build a temple over it; and that little baby becomes the god of that temple. This is a very prevalent form of religion in many countries, and there are not wanting philosophers who think this has been the origin of all religions. Of course they cannot prove it. We must remember, however, that this worship of Pratikas can never bring us to salvation or to freedom.

Secondly, it is very dangerous. The danger is that these Pratikas, "nearing-stages", so far as they lead us on to a further stage, are all right; but the chances are ninety-nine to one that we shall stick to the Pratikas all our lives. It is very good to be born in a church, but it is very bad to die there. To make it clearer, it is very good to be born in a certain sect and have its training — it brings out our higher qualities; but in the vast majority of cases we die in that little sect, we never come out or grow. That is the great danger of all these worships of Pratikas. One says that these are all stages which one has to pass, but one never gets out of them; and when one becomes old, one still sticks to them. If a young man does not go to church, he ought to be condemned. But if an old man goes to church, he also ought to be condemned; he has no business with this child's play any more; the church should have been merely a preparation for something higher. What business has he any more with forms and Pratikas and all these preliminaries?

Book worship is another strong form of this Pratika, the strongest form. You find in every country that the book becomes the God. There are sects in my country who believe that God incarnates and becomes man, but even God incarnate as man must conform to the Vedas, and if His teachings do not so conform, they will not take Him. Buddha is worshipped by the Hindus, but if you say to them, "If you worship Buddha, why don't you take His teachings?" they will say, because they, the Buddhists, deny the Vedas. Such is the meaning of book worship. Any number of lies in the name of a religious book are all right. In India if I want to teach anything new, and simply state it on my own authority, as what I think, nobody will come to listen to me; but if I take some passage from the Vedas, and juggle with it, and give it the most impossible meaning, murder everything that is reasonable in it, and bring out my own ideas as the ideas that were meant by the Vedas, all the fools will follow me in a crowd. Then there are men preaching a sort of Christianity that would frighten the ordinary Christian out of his wits; but they say, "This is what Jesus Christ meant", and many come round them. People do not want anything new, if it is not in the Vedas or the Bible It is a case of nerves: when you hear a new and striking thing, you are startled; or when you see a new thing, you are startled; it is constitutional. It is much more so with thoughts. The mind has been running in ruts, and to take up a new idea is too much of a strain; so the idea has to be put near the ruts, and then we slowly take it. It is a good policy, but bad morality. Think of the mass of incongruities that reformers, and what you call the liberal preachers, pour into society today. According to Christian Scientists, Jesus was a great healer; according to the Spiritualists, He was a great psychic; according to the Theosophists, He was a Mahâtmâ. All these have to be deduced from the same text. There is a text in the Vedas which says, "Existence (Sat) alone existed, O beloved, nothing else existed in the beginning". Many different meanings are given to the word Sat in this text. The Atomists say the word meant "atoms", and out of these atoms the world has been produced. The Naturalists say it meant "nature", and out of nature everything has come. The Shunyavâdins (maintainers of the Void) say it meant "nothing", "zero", and out of nothing everything has been produced. The Theists say it meant "God", and the Advaitists say it was "Absolute Existence", and all refer to the same text as their authority.

These are the defects of book worship. But there is, on the other hand, a great advantage in it: it gives strength. All religious sects have disappeared excepting those that have a book. Nothing seems to kill them. Some of you have heard of the Parsees. They were the ancient Persians, and at one time there were about a hundred millions of them. The majority of them were conquered by the Arabs, and converted to Mohammedanism. A handful fled from their persecutors with their book, which is still preserving them. A book is the most tangible form of God. Think of the Jews; if they had not had a book, they would have simply melted into the world. But that keeps them up; the Talmud keeps them together, in spite of the most horrible persecution. One of the great advantages of a book is that it crystallises everything in tangible and convenient form, and is the handiest of all idols. Just put a book on an altar and everyone sees it; a good book everyone reads. I am afraid I may be considered partial. But, in my opinion books have produced more evil than good. They are accountable for many mischievous doctrines. Creeds all come from books, and books are alone responsible for the persecution and fanaticism in the world. Books in modern times are making liars everywhere. I am astonished at the number of liars abroad in every country.

The next thing to be considered is the Pratima, or image, the use of images. All over the world you will find images in some form or other. With some, it is in the form of a man, which is the best form. If I wanted to worship an image I would rather have it in the form of a man than of an animal, or building, or any other form. One sect thinks a certain form is the right sort of image, and another thinks it is bad. The Christian thinks that when God came in the form of a dove it was all right, but if He comes in the form of a fish, as the Hindus say, it is very wrong and superstitious. The Jews think if an idol be made in the form of a chest with two angels sitting on it, and a book on it, it is all right, but if it is in the form of a man or a woman, it is awful. The Mohammedans think that when they pray, if they try to form a mental image of the temple with the Caaba, the black stone in it, and turn towards the west, it is all right, but if you form the image in the shape of a church it is idolatry. This is the defect of image-worship. Yet all these seem to be necessary stages.

In this matter it is of supreme importance to think what we ourselves believe. What we have realised, is the question. What Jesus, or Buddha, or Moses did is nothing to us, unless we too do it for ourselves. It would not satisfy our hunger to shut ourselves up in a room and think of what Moses ate, nor would what Moses thought save us. My ideas are very radical on these points. Sometimes I think that I am right when I agree with all the ancient teachers, at other times I think they are right when they agree with me. I believe in thinking independently. I believe in becoming entirely free from the holy teachers; pay all reverence to them, but look at religion as an independent research. I have to find my light, just as they found theirs. Their finding the light will not satisfy us at all. You have to become the Bible, and not to follow it, excepting as paying reverence to it as a light on the way, as a guide-post, a mark: that is all the value it has. But these images and other things are quite necessary. You may try to concentrate your mind, or even to project any thought. You will find that you naturally form images in your mind. You cannot help it. Two sorts of persons never require any image — the human animal who never thinks of any religion, and the perfected being who has passed through these stages. Between these two points all of us require some sort of ideal, outside and inside. It may be in the form of a departed human being, or of a living man or woman. This is clinging to personality and bodies, and is quite natural. We are prone to concretise. How could we be here if we did not concretise? We are concreted spirits, and so we find ourselves here on this earth. Concretisation has brought us here, and it will take us out. Going after things of the senses has made us human beings, and we are bound to worship personal beings, whatever we may say to the contrary. It is very easy to say "Don't be personal"; but the same man who says so is generally most personal. His attachment for particular men and women is very strong; it does not leave him when they die, he wants to follow them beyond death. That is idolatry; it is the seed, the very cause of idolatry; and the cause being there it will come out in some form. Is it not better to have a personal attachment to an image of Christ or Buddha than to an ordinary man or woman? In the West, people say that it is bad to kneel before images, but they can kneel before a woman and say, "You are my life, the light of my eyes, my soul." That is worse idolatry. What ifs this talk about my soul my life? It will soon go away. It is only sense-attachment. It is selfish love covered by a mass of flowers. Poets give it a good name and throw lavender-water and all sorts of attractive things over it. Is it not better to kneel before a statue of Buddha or the Jina conqueror and say, "Thou art my life"? I would rather do that.

There is another sort of Pratika which is not recognised in Western countries, bout is taught in our books. This teaches the worship of mind as God. Anything that is worshipped as God is a stage, a nearing, as it were. An example of this is the method of showing the fine star known as Arundhati, near the group Pleiades. One is shown a big star near to it, and when he has fixed his attention on this and has come to know it, he is shown a finer and still nearer star; and when he has fixed his attention on that, he is led up to Arundhati. So all these various Pratikas and Pratimas lead to God. The worship of Buddha and of Christ constitute a Pratika. A drawing near to the worship of God. But this worship of Buddha and of

Christ will not save a man, he must go beyond them to Him who manifested Himself as Jesus Christ, for God alone can give us freedom. There are even some philosophers who say these should he regarded as God; they are not Pratikas, but God Himself. However, we can take all these different Pratikas, these different stages of approach, and not be hurt by them: but if we think while we are worshipping them that we are worshipping God, we are mistaken. If a man worships Jesus Christ, and thinks he will be saved by that, he is mistaken entirely. If a man thinks that by worshipping an idol or the ghosts or spirits of the departed he will be saved, he is entirely mistaken. We may worship anything by seeing God in it, if we can forget the idol and see God there. We must not project any image upon God. But we may fill any image with that Life which is God. Only forget the image, and you are right enough—for "Out of Him comes everything". He is everything. We may worship a picture as God, but not God as the picture. God in the picture is right, but the picture as God is wrong. God in the image is perfectly right. There is no danger there. This is the real worship of God. But the image-God is a mere Pratika.

The next great thing to consider in Bhakti is the "word", the Nâmashakti, the power of the name. The whole universe is composed of name and form. Whatever we see is either a compound of name and form, or simply name with form which is a mental image. So, after all, there is nothing that is not name and form. We all believe God to be without form or shape, but as soon as we begin to think of Him, He acquires both name and form The Chitta is like the calm lake, thoughts being like waves upon this Chitta—and name and form are the normal ways in which these waves arise; no wave can rise without name and form. The uniform cannot be thought of; it is beyond thought; as soon as it becomes thought and matter, it must have name and form. We cannot separate these. It is said in many books that God created the universe out of the Word. Shabdabrahman, in Sanskrit, is the Christian theory of the Word. An old Indian theory, it was taken to Alexandria by Indian preachers and was planted there. Thus the idea of the Word and the Incarnation became fixed there.

There is deep meaning in the thought that God created everything out of the Word. God Himself being formless, this is the best way to describe the projection of forms, or the creation. The Sanskrit word for creation is Srishti, projection. What is meant by "God created things out of nothing"? The universe is projected out of God. He becomes the universe, and it all returns to Him, and again it proceeds forth, and again returns. Through all eternity it will go on in that way. We have seen that the projection of anything in the mind cannot be without name and form. Suppose the mind to be perfectly calm, entirely without thought; nevertheless, as soon as thought begins to rise it will immediately take name and form. Every thought has a certain name and a certain form. In the same way the very fact of creation, the very fact of projection is eternally connected with name and form. Thus we find

that every idea that man has, or can have, must be connected with a certain name or word as its counterpart. This being so, it is quite natural to suppose that this universe is the outcome of mind, just as your body is the outcome of your idea—your idea, as it were, made concrete and externalised. If it be true, moreover, that the whole universe is built on the same plan, then, if you know the manner in which one atom is built, you can understand how the whole universe is built. If it is true that in you, the body forms the gross part outside and the mind forms the fine part inside, and both are eternally inseparable, then, when you cease to have the body, you will cease to have the mind also. When a man's brain is disturbed, his ideas also get disturbed, because they are but one, the finer and the grosser parts. There are not two such things as matter and mind. As in a high column of air there are dense and rarefied strata of one and the same element air, so it is with the body; it is one thing throughout, layer on layer, from grosser to finer. Again, the body is like the finger nails. As these continue growing even when they are cut, so from our subtle ideas grows body after body. The finer a thing the more persistent it is; we find that always. The grosser it is the less persistent. Thus, form is the grosser and name the finer state of a single manifesting power called thought. But these three are one; it is the Unity and the Trinity, the three degrees of existence of the same thing. Finer, more condensed, and most condensed. Wherever the one is, the others are there also. Wherever name is, there is form and thought.

It naturally follows that if the universe is built upon the same plan as the body, the universe also must have the same divisions of form, name, and thought. The "thought" is the finest part of the universe, the real motive power. The thought behind our body is called soul, and the thought behind the universe is called God. Then after that is the name, and last of all is the form which we see and feel. For instance, you are a particular person, a little universe in this universe, a body with a particular form; then behind that a name, John or Jane, and behind that again a thought; similarly there is this whole universe, and behind that is the name, what is called the "Word" in all religions, and behind that is God. The universal thought is Mahat, as the Sânkhyas call it, universal consciousness. What is that name? There must be some name. The world is homogeneous, and modern science shows beyond doubt that each atom is composed of the same material as the whole universe. If you know one lump of clay you know the whole universe. Man is the most representative being in the universe, the microcosm, a small universe in himself. So in man we find there is the form, behind that the name, and behind that the thought, the thinking being. So this universe must be on exactly the same plan. The question is: What is that name? According to the Hindus that word is Om. The old Egyptians also believed that. The Katha Upanishad says, "That, seeking which a man practices Brahmacharya, I will tell you in short what that is, that is Om... This is Brahman, the Immutable One, and is the highest; knowing this Immutable One, whatever one desires one gets."

This Om stands for the name of the whole universe, or God. Standing midway between the external world and God, it represents both. But then we can take the universe piecemeal, according to the different senses, as touch, as colour, as taste, and in various other ways. In each case we can make of this universe millions of universes from different standpoints, each of which will be a complete universe by itself, and each one will have a name, and a form, and a thought behind. These thoughts behind are Pratikas. Each of them has a name. These names of sacred symbols are used in Bhakti-Yoga. They have almost infinite power. Simply by repetition of these words we can get anything we desire, we can come to perfection. But two things are necessary. "The teacher must be wonderful, so also must be the taught", says the Katha Upanishad. Such a name must come from a person to whom it has descended through right succession. From master to disciple, the spiritual current has been coming; from ancient times, bearing its power. The person from whom such a word comes is called a Guru, and the person to whom it goes is called Shishya, the disciple. When the word has been received in the regular way, and when it has been repeated, much advance has been made in Bhakti-Yoga. Simply by the repetition of that word will come even the highest state of Bhakti. "Thou hast so many names. Thou understandest what is meant by them all these names are Thine, and in each is Thine infinite power; there is neither time nor place for repeating these names, for all times and places are holy. Thou art so easy, Thou art so merciful, how unfortunate am I, that I have no love for Thee!"

THE ISHTA

The theory of Ishta, which I briefly referred to before, is a subject requiring careful attention because with a proper understanding of this, all the various religions of the world can be understood. The word Ishta is derived from the root Ish, to desire, choose. The ideal of all religions, all sects, is the same—the attaining of liberty and cessation of misery. Wherever you find religion, you find this ideal working in one form or other. Of course in lower stages of religion it is not so well expressed; but still, well or ill-expressed, it is the one goal to which every religion approaches. All of us want to get rid of misery; we are struggling to attain to liberty—physical, mental, spiritual. This is the whole idea upon which the world is working. Through the goal is one and the same, there may be many ways to reach it, and these ways are determined by the peculiarities of our nature. One man's nature is emotional, another's intellectual, another's active, and so forth. Again, in the same nature there may be many subdivisions. Take for instance love, with which we are specially concerned in this subject of Bhakti. One man's nature has a stronger love for children; another has it for wife, another for mother, another for father, another for friends. Another by nature has love for country, and a few love humanity in the broadest sense; they are of course very few, although everyone of us talks of it as if it were the guiding motive power of our lives. Some few sages have experienced it. A few great souls among mankind feel this universal love, and let us hope that this world will never be without such men.

We find that even in one subject there are so many different ways of attaining to its goal. All Christians believe in Christ; but think, how many different explanations they have of him. Each church sees him in a different light, from different standpoints. The Presbyterian's eyes are fixed upon that scene in Christ's life when he went to the money-changers; he looks on him as a fighter. If you ask a Quaker, perhaps he will say, "He forgave his enemies." The Quaker takes that view, and so on. If you ask a Roman Catholic, what point of Christ's life is the most pleasing to him, he, perhaps, will say, "When he gave the keys to Peter". Each sect is bound to see him in its own way.

It follows that there will be many divisions and subdivisions even of the same subject. Ignorant persons take one of these subdivisions and take their stand upon it, and they not only deny the right of every other man to interpret the universe according to his own light, but dare to say that others are entirely wrong, and they alone are right. If they are opposed, they begin to fight. They say that they will kill any man who does not believe as they believe, just as the Mohammedans do. These are people who think they are sincere, and who ignore all others. But what is the position we want to take in this Bhakti-Yoga? Not only that we would not tell others that they are wrong, but that we would tell them that they are right—all of these who follow their own ways. That way, which your nature makes it absolutely necessary for you to take, is the right way. Each one of us is born with a peculiarity of nature as the result of our past existence. Either we call it our own reincarnated past experience or a hereditary past; whatever way we may put it, we are the result of the past - that is absolutely certain, through whatever channels that past may have come. It naturally follows that each one of us is an effect, of which our past has been the cause; and as such, there is a peculiar movement, a peculiar train, in each one of us; and therefore each one will have to find way for himself.

This way, this method, to which each of us is naturally adapted, is called the "chosen way". This is the theory of Ishta, and that way which is ours we call our own Ishta. For instance, one man's idea of God is that He is the omnipotent Ruler of the universe. His nature is perhaps such. He is an overbearing man who wants to rule everyone; he naturally finds God an omnipotent Ruler. Another man, who was perhaps a schoolmaster, and severe, cannot see any but a just God, a God of punishment, and so on Each one sees God according to his own nature; and this vision, conditioned by our own nature, is our Ishta. We have brought ourselves to a position where we can see that vision of God, and that alone; we cannot see any other vision. You will perhaps sometimes think of the teaching of a man that it is the best and fits you exactly, and the next day you ask one of your friends to go and hear him; but he comes away with the idea that it was the worst teaching he had ever heard. He is not wrong, and it is useless to quarrel with him. The teaching was all right, but it was not fitted to that man. To extend it a little further, we must understand that truth seen from different standpoints can be truth, and yet not the same truth.

This would seem at first to be a contradiction in terms, but we must remember that an absolute truth is only one, while relative truths are necessarily various. Take your vision of this universe, for instance. This universe, as an absolute entity, is unchangeable, and unchanged, and the same throughout. But you and I and everybody else hear and see, each one his own universe. Take the sun. The sun is one; but when you and I and a hundred other people stand at different places and look at it, each one of us sees a different sun. We cannot help it. A very little change of place will change a man's whole vision of the sun. A slight change in the atmosphere will make again a different vision. So, in relative perception, truth always appears various. But the Absolute Truth is only one. Therefore we need not fight with others when we find they; are telling something about religion which is not exactly according to our view of it. We ought to remember that both of us may be true, though apparently contradictors. There may be millions of radii converging towards the same centre in the sun. The further they are from the centre, the greater is the distance between any two. But as they all meet at the centre, all difference vanishes. There is such a centre, which is the absolute goal of mankind. It is God. We are the radii. The distances between the radii are the constitutional limitations through which alone we can catch the vision of God. While standing on this plane, we are bound each one of us to have a different view of the Absolute Reality; and as such, all views are true, and no one of us need quarrel with another. The only solution lies in approaching the centre. If we try to settle our differences by argument or quarrelling, we shall find that we can go on for hundreds of years without coming to a conclusion. History proves that. The only solution is to march ahead and go towards the centre; and the sooner we do that the sooner our differences will vanish.

This theory of Ishta, therefore, means allowing a man to choose his own religion. One man should not force another to worship what he worships. All attempts to herd together human beings by means of armies, force, or arguments, to drive them pell-mell into the same enclosure and make them worship the same God have failed and will fail always, because it is constitutionally impossible to do so. Not only so, there is the danger of arresting their growth. You scarcely meet any man or woman who is not struggling for some sort of religion; and how many are satisfied, or rather how few are satisfied! How few find anything! And why? Simply because most of them go after impossible tasks. They are forced into these by the dictation of others. For instance, when I am a child, my father puts a book into my hand which says God is such

and such. What business has he to put that into my mind? How does he know what way I would develop? And being ignorant of my constitutional development, he wants to force his ideas on my brain, with the result that my growth is stunted. You cannot make a plant grow in soil unsuited to it. A child teaches itself. But you can help it to go forward in its own way. What you can do is not of the positive nature, but of the negative. You can take away the obstacles, but knowledge comes out of its own nature. Loosen the soil a little, so that it may come out easily. Put a hedge round it; see that it is not killed by anything, and there your work stops. You cannot do anything else. The rest is a manifestation from within its own nature. So with the education of a child; a child educates itself. You come to hear me, and when you go home, compare what you have learnt, and you will find you have thought out the same thing; I have only given it expression. I can never teach you anything: you will have to teach yourself, but I can help you perhaps in giving expression to that thought.

So in religion—more so—I must teach myself religion. What right has my father to put all sorts of nonsense into my head? What right has my master or society to put things into my head? Perhaps they are good, but they may not be my way. Think of the appalling evil that is in the world today, of the millions and millions of innocent children perverted by wrong ways of teaching. How many beautiful things which would have become wonderful spiritual truths have been nipped in the bud by this horrible idea of a family religion, a social religion, a national religion, and so forth. Think of what a mass of superstition is in your head just now about your childhood's religion, or your country's religion, and what an amount of evil it does, or can do. Man does not know what a potent power lies behind each thought and action. The old saying is true that, "Fools rush in where angels fear to tread." This should be kept in view from the very first. How? By this belief in Ishta. There are so many ideals; I have no right to say what shall be your ideal, to force any ideal on you. My duty should be to lay before you all the ideals I know of and enable you to see by your own constitution what you like best, and which is most fitted to you. Take up that one which suits you best and persevere in it. This is your Ishta, your special ideal.

We see then that a congregational religion can never be. The real work of religion must be one's own concern. I have an idea of my own, I must keep it sacred and secret, because I know that it need not be your idea. Secondly, why should I create a disturbance by wanting to tell everyone what my idea is? Other people would come and fight me. They cannot do so if I do not tell them; but if I go about telling them what my ideas are, they will all oppose me. So what is the use of talking about them? This Ishta should be kept secret, it is between you and God. All theoretical portions of religion can be preached in public and made congregational, but higher religion cannot be made public. I cannot get ready my religious feelings at a moment's notice. What is the result of this mummery and mockery? It is making a joke of religion, the worst of blasphemy. The result is what you find in the churches of the present day. How can human beings stand this religious drilling? It is like soldiers in a barrack. Shoulder arms, kneel down, take a book, all regulated exactly. Five minutes of feeling, five minutes of reason, five minutes of prayer, all arranged beforehand. These mummeries have driven out religion. Let the churches preach doctrines, theories, philosophies to their hearts' content, but when it comes to worship, the real practical part of religion, it should be as Jesus says, "When thou prayest, enter into thy closet, and when thou hast shut thy door, pray to thy Father which is in secret"

This is the theory of Ishta. It is the only way to make religion meet practically the necessities of different constitutions, to avoid quarrelling with others, and to make real practical progress in spiritual life. But I must warn you that you do not misconstrue my words into the formation of secret societies. If there were a devil, I would look for him within a secret society—as the invention of secret societies. They are diabolical schemes. The Ishta is sacred, not secret. But in what sense? Why should I not speak of my Ishta to others? Because it is my own most holy thing. It may help others, but how do I know that it will not rather hurt them? There may be a man whose nature is such that he cannot worship a Personal God, but can only worship as an Impersonal God his own highest Self. Suppose I leave him among you, and he tells you that there is no Personal God, but only God as the Self in you or me. You will be shocked. His idea is sacred, but not secret. There never was a great religion or a great teacher that formed secret societies to preach God's truths. There are no such secret societies in India. Such things are purely Western in idea, and merely foisted upon India. We never knew anything about them. Why indeed should there be secret societies in India? In Europe, people were not allowed to talk a word about religion that did not agree with the views of the Church. So they were forced to go about amongst the mountains in hiding and form secret societies, that they might follow their own kind of worship. There was never a time in India when a man was persecuted for holding his own views on religion. There were never secret religious societies in India, so any idea of that sort you must give up at once. These secret societies always degenerate into the most horrible things. I have seen enough of this world to know what evil they cause, and how easily they slide into free love societies and ghost societies, how men play into the hands of other men or women, and how their future possibilities of growth in thought and act are destroyed, and so on. Some of you may be displeased with me for talking in this way, but I must tell you the truth. Perhaps only half a dozen men and women will follow me in all my life; but they will be real men and women, pure and sincere, and I do not want a crowd. What can crowds do? The history of the world was made by a few dozens, whom you can count on your fingers, and the rest were a rabble. All these secret societies and humbugs make men and women impure, weak and narrow; and the weak have no will, and can never work.

Therefore have nothing to do with them. All this false love of mystery should be knocked on the head the first time it comes into your mind. No one who is the least impure will ever become religious. Do not try to cover festering sores with masses of roses. Do you think you can cheat God? None can. Give me a straightforward man or woman; but Lord save me from ghosts, flying angels, and devils. Be common, everyday, nice people.

There is such a thing as instinct in us, which we have in common with the animals, a reflex mechanical movement of the body. There is again a higher form of guidance, which we call reason, when the intellect obtains facts and then generalises them. There is a still higher form of knowledge which we call inspiration, which does not reason, but knows things by flashes. That is the highest form of knowledge. But how shall we know it from instinct? That is the great difficulty. Everyone comes to you, nowadays, and says he is inspired, and puts forth superhuman claims. How are we to distinguish between inspiration and deception? In the first place, inspiration must not contradict reason. The old man does not contradict the child, he is the development of the child. What we call inspiration is the development of reason. The way to intuition is through reason. Instinctive movements of your body do not oppose reason. As you cross a street, how instinctively you move your body to save yourself from the cars. Does your mind tell you it was foolish to save your body that way? It does not. Similarly, no genuine inspiration ever contradicts reason. Where it does it is no inspiration. Secondly, inspiration must be for the good of one and all, and not for name or fame, or personal gain. It should always be for the good of the world, and perfectly unselfish. When these tests are fulfilled, you are quite safe to take it as inspiration. You must remember that there is not one in a million that is inspired, in the present state of the world. I hope their number will increase. We are now only playing with religion. With inspiration we shall begin to have religion. Just as St. Paul says, "For now we see through a glass darkly, but then face to face." But in the present state of the world they are few and far between who attain to that state; yet perhaps at no other period were such false claims made to inspiration, as now. It is said that women have intuitive faculties, while men drag themselves slowly upward by reason. Do not believe it. There are just as many inspired men as women, though women have perhaps more claim to peculiar forms of hysteria and nervousness. You had better die as an unbeliever than be played upon by cheats and jugglers. The power of reasoning was given you for use. Show then that you have used it properly. Doing so, you will be able to take care of higher things.

We must always remember that God is Love. "A fool indeed is he who, living on the banks of the Ganga, seeks to dig a little well for water. A fool indeed is the man who, living near a mine of diamonds, spends his life in searching for beads of glass." God is that mine of diamonds. We are fools indeed to give up God for legends of ghosts or flying hobgoblins. It is a disease, a morbid desire. It degenerates the race, weakens the nerves and the brain, living in incessant morbid fear of hob-goblins, or stimulating the hunger for wonders; all these wild stories about them keep the nerves at an unnatural tension—a slow and sure degeneration of the race. It is degeneration to think of giving up God, purity, holiness, and spirituality, to go after all this nonsense! Reading other men's thoughts! If I must read everyone else's thoughts for five minutes at a time I shall go crazy. Be strong and stand up and seek the God of Love. This is the highest strength. What power is higher than the power of purity? Love and purity govern the world. This love of God cannot be reached by the weak; therefore, be not weak, either physically, mentally, morally or spiritually. The Lord alone is true. Everything else is untrue; everything else should be rejected for the salve of the Lord. Vanity of vanities, all is vanity. Serve the Lord and Him alone.

ON JNANA-YOGA[1]

Part I

Om Tat Sat! To know the Om is to know the secret of the universe. The object of Jnana-Yoga is the same as that of Bhakti and Raja Yogas, but the method is different. This is the Yoga for the strong, for those who are neither mystical nor devotional, but rational. As the Bhakti-Yogi works his way to complete oneness with the Supreme through love and devotion, so the Jnana-yogi forces his way to the realisation of God by the power of pure reason. He must be prepared to throw away all old idols, all old beliefs and superstitions, all desire for this world or another, and be determined only to find freedom. Without Jnana (knowledge) liberation cannot be ours. It consists in knowing what we really are, that we are beyond fear, beyond birth, beyond death. The highest good is the realisation of the Self. It is beyond sense, beyond thought. The real "I" cannot be grasped. It is the eternal subject and can never become the object of knowledge, because knowledge is only of the related, not of the Absolute. All sense-knowledge is limitation, it is an endless chain of cause and effect. This world is a relative world, a shadow of the real; still, being the plane of equipoise where happiness and misery are about evenly balanced, it is the only plane where man can realise his true Self and know that he is Brahman.

This world is "the evolution of nature and the manifestation of God". It is our interpretation of Brahman or the Absolute, seen through the veil of Maya or appearance. The world is not zero, it has a certain reality; it only appears because Brahman is .

How shall we know the knower? The Vedanta says, "We are It, but can never know It, because It can never become the object of knowledge." Modern science also says that It cannot be known. We can, however, have glimpses of It from time to time. When the delusion of this world is once broken, it will come back to us, but no longer will it hold any reality for us. We shall know it as a mirage. To reach behind the mirage is the aim of all religions. That man and God are one is the constant teaching of the Vedas, but only few are able to penetrate behind the veil and reach the realisation of this truth.

The first thing to be got rid of by him who would be a Jnani is fear. Fear is one of our worst enemies. Next, believe in nothing until you know it. Constantly tell yourself, "I am not the body, I am not the mind, I am not thought, I am not even consciousness; I am the Atman." When you can throw away all, only the true Self will remain. The Jnani's meditation is of two sorts: (1) to deny and think away everything we are not; (2) to insist upon what we really are—the Atman, the One Self—existence, Knowledge, and Bliss. The true rationalist must go on and fearlessly follow his reason to its farthest limits. It will not answer to stop anywhere on the road. When we begin to deny, all must go until we reach what cannot be thrown away or denied, which is the real "I". That "I" is the witness of the universe, it is unchangeable, eternal, infinite. Now, layer after layer of ignorance covers it from our eyes, but it remains ever the same.

Two birds sat on one tree. The bird at the top was calm, majestic, beautiful, perfect. The lower bird was always hopping from twig to twig, now eating sweet fruits and being happy, now eating bitter fruits and being miserable. One day, when he had eaten a fruit more bitter than usual, he glanced up at the calm majestic upper bird and thought, "How I would like to be like him!" and he hopped up a little way towards him. Soon he forgot all about his desire to be like the upper bird, and went on as before, eating sweet and bitter fruits and being happy and miserable. Again he looked up, again he went up a little nearer to the calm and majestic upper bird. Many times was this repeated until at last he drew very near the upper bird; the brilliancy of his plumage dazzled him, seemed to absorb him, and finally, to his wonder and surprise, he found there was only one bird—he was the upper bird all the time and had but just found it out. Man is like that lower bird, but if he perseveres in his efforts to rise to the highest ideal he can conceive of, he too will find that he was the Self all the time and the other was but a dream. To separate ourselves utterly from matter and all belief in its reality is true Jnana. The Jnani must keep ever in his mind the "Om Tat Sat", that is, Om the only real existence. Abstract unity is the foundation of Jnana-yoga. This is called Advaitism ("without dualism or dvaitism"). This is the corner-stone of the Vedanta philosophy, the Alpha and the Omega. "Brahman alone is true, all else is false and I am Brahman." Only by telling ourselves this until we make it a part of our very being, can we rise beyond all duality, beyond both good and evil, pleasure and pain, joy and sorrow, and know ourselves as the One, eternal, unchanging, infinite—the "One without a second".

---

1. These were originally recorded by a prominent American disciple of the Swami, Miss S.E. Waldo. Swami Saradananda, while he was in America (1896), copied them out from her notebook—Ed.

The Jnana-yogi must be as intense as the narrowest sectarian, yet as broad as the heavens. He must absolutely control his mind, be able to be a Buddhist or a Christian, to have the power to consciously divide himself into all these different ideas and yet hold fast to the eternal harmony. Constant drill alone can enable us to get this control. All variations are in the One, but we must learn not to identify ourselves with what we do, and to hear nothing, see nothing, talk of nothing but the thing in hand. We must put in our whole soul and be intense. Day and night tell yourself, "I am He, I am He."

Part II

The greatest teacher of the Vedanta philosophy was Shankaracharya. By solid reasoning he extracted from the Vedas the truths of Vedanta, and on them built up the wonderful system of Jnana that is taught in his commentaries. He unified all the conflicting descriptions of Brahman and showed that there is only one Infinite Reality. He showed too that as man can only travel slowly on the upward road, all the varied presentations are needed to suit his varying capacity. We find something akin to this in the teachings of Jesus, which he evidently adapted to the different abilities of his hearers. First he taught them of a Father in heaven and to pray to Him. Next he rose a step higher and told them, "I am the vine, you are the branches", and lastly he gave them the highest truth: "I and my Father are one", and "The Kingdom of Heaven is within you." Shankara taught that three things were the great gifts of God: (1) human body, (2) thirst after God, and (3) a teacher who can show us the light. When these three great gifts are ours, we may know that our redemption is at hand. Only knowledge can free and save us, but with knowledge must go virtue.

The essence of Vedanta is that there is but one Being and that every soul is that Being in full, not a part of that Being. All the sun is reflected in each dew-drop. Appearing in time, space and causality, this Being is man, as we know him, but behind all appearance is the one Reality. Unselfishness is the denial of the lower or apparent self. We have to free ourselves from this miserable dream that we are these bodies. We must know the truth, "I am He". We are not drops to fall into the ocean and be lost; each one is the whole , infinite ocean, and will know it when released from the fetters of illusion. Infinity cannot be divided, the "One without a second" can have no second, all is that One. This knowledge will come to all, but we should struggle to attain it now, because until we have it, we cannot really give mankind the best help. The Jivanmukta ('the living free' or one who knows) alone is able to give real love, real charity, real truth, and it is truth alone that makes us free. Desire makes slaves of us, it is an insatiable tyrant and gives its victims no rest; but the Jivanmukta has conquered all desire by rising to the knowledge that he is the One and there is nothing left to wish for.

The mind brings before us all our delusions—body, sex, creed, caste, bondage; so we have to tell the truth to the mind incessantly, until it is made to realise it. Our real nature is all bliss, and all the pleasure we know is but a reflection, an atom, of that bliss we get from touching our real nature. That is beyond both pleasure and pain. It is the "witness" of the universe, the unchanging reader before whom turn the leaves of the book of life.

Through practice comes Yoga, through Yoga comes knowledge, through knowledge love, and through love bliss. "Me and mine" is a superstition; we have lived in it so long that it is well-nigh impossible to shake it off. Still we must get rid of it if we would rise to the highest. We must be bright and cheerful, long faces do not make religion. Religion should be the most joyful thing in the world, because it is the best. Asceticism cannot make us holy. Why should a man who loves God and who is pure be sorrowful? He should be like a happy child, be truly a child of God. The essential thing in religion is making the heart pure; the Kingdom of Heaven is within us, but only the pure in heart can see the King. While we think of the world, it is only the world for us; but let us come to it with the feeling that the world is God, and we shall have God. This should be our thought towards everyone and everything—parents, children, husbands, wives, friends, and enemies. Think how it would change the whole universe for us if we could consciously fill it with God! See nothing but God! All sorrow, all struggle, all pain would be for ever lost to us!

Jnana is "creedlessness", but that does not mean that it despises creeds. It only means that a stage above and beyond creeds has been gained. The Jnani seeks not to destroy, but to help all. As all rivers roll their waters into the sea and become one, so all creeds should lead to Jnana and become one.

The reality of everything depends upon Brahman, and only as we really grasp this truth, have we any reality. When we cease to see any differences, then we know that "I and the Father are One".

Jnana is taught very clearly by Krishna in the Bhagavad-gita. This great poem is held to be the Crown jewel of all Indian literature. It is a kind of commentary on the Vedas. It shows us that our battle for spirituality must be fought out in this life; so we must not flee from it, but rather compel it to give us all that it holds. As the Gita typifies this struggle for higher things, it is highly poetical to lay the scene in a battlefield. Krishna in the guise of a charioteer to Arjuna, leader of one of the opposing armies, urges him not to be sorrowful, not to fear death, since he knows he is immortal, that nothing which changes can be in the real nature of man. Through chapter after chapter, Krishna teaches the higher truths of philosophy and religion to Arjuna. It is these teachings which make this poem so wonderful; practically the whole of the Vedanta philosophy is included in them. The Vedas teach that the soul is infinite and in no way affected by the death of the body. The soul is a circle whose circumference is nowhere, but whose centre is in some body. Death (so-called) is but a change of centre. God is a circle whose circumference is nowhere and whose centre is everywhere, and when we can get out of the narrow centre of body, we shall realise God—our true Self.

The present is only a line of demarcation between the past and the future; so we cannot rationally say that we care only for the present, as it has no existence apart from the past and the future. It is all one complete whole, the idea of time being merely a condition imposed upon us by the form of our understanding.

Part III

Jnana teaches that the world should be given up, but not on that account to be abandoned. To be in the world, but not of it, is the true test of the Sannyasin. This idea of renunciation has been in some form common to nearly all religions. Jnana demands that we look upon all alike, that we see only "sameness". Praise and blame, good and bad, even heat and cold, must be equally acceptable to us. In India there are many holy men of whom this is literally true. They wander on the snow-clad heights of the Himalayas or over the burning desert sands, entirely unclothed and apparently entirely unconscious of any difference in temperature.

We have first of all to give up this superstition of body; we are not the body. Next must go the further superstition that we are mind. We are not mind; it is but the "silken body", not any part of the soul. The mere word "body", applied to nearly all things, includes something common among all bodies. This is existence .

Our bodies are symbols of thought behind, and the thoughts themselves are in their turn symbols of something behind them, that is, the one Real Existence, the Soul of our soul, the Self of the universe, the Life of our life, our true Self. As long as we believe ourselves to be even the least different from God, fear remains with us; but when we know ourselves to be the One, fear goes: of what can we be afraid? By sheer force of will the Jnani rises beyond body, beyond mind, making this universe zero. Thus he destroys Avidya and knows his true Self, the Atman. Happiness and misery are only in the senses, they cannot touch our real Self. The soul is beyond time, space, and causality—therefore unlimited, omnipresent.

The Jnani has to come out of all forms, to get beyond all rules and books, and be his own book. Bound by forms, we crystallise and die. Still the Jnani must never condemn those who cannot yet rise above forms. He must never even think of another, "I am holier than thou".

These are the marks of the true Jnana-yogi: (1) He desires nothing, save to know. (2) All his senses are under perfect restraint; he suffers everything without murmuring, equally content if his bed be the bare ground under the open sky, or if he is lodged in a king's palace. He shuns no suffering, he stands and bears it—he has given up all but the Self. (3) He knows that all but the One is unreal. (4) He has an intense desire for freedom. With a strong will, he fixes his mind on higher things and so attains to peace. If we know not peace, what are we more than the brutes? He does everything for others—for the Lord—giving up all fruits of work and looking for no result, either here or hereafter. What can the universe give us more than our own soul? Possessing that, we possess all. The Vedas teach that the Atman, or Self, is the One Undivided Existence. It is beyond mind, memory, thought, or even consciousness as we know it. From it are all things. It is that through which (or because of which) we see, hear, feel, and think. The goal of the universe is to realise oneness with the "Om" or One Existence. The Jnani has to be free from all forms; he is neither a Hindu, a Buddhist, nor a Christian, but he is all three. All action is renounced, given up to the Lord; then no action has power to bind. The Jnani is a tremendous rationalist; he denies everything. He tells himself day and night, "There are no beliefs, no sacred words, no heaven, no hell, no creed, no church—there is only Atman." When everything has been thrown away until what cannot be thrown away is reached, that is the Self. The Jnani takes nothing for granted; he analyses by pure reason and force of will, until he reaches Nirvana which is the extinction of all relativity. No description or even conception of this state is possible. Jnana is never to be judged by any earthly result. Be not like the vulture which soars almost beyond sight, but which is ever ready to swoop downwards at the sight of a bit of carrion. Ask not for healing, or longevity, or prosperity, ask only to be free.

We are "Existence, Knowledge, Bliss" (Sachchidananda). Existence is the last generalisation in the universe; so we exist, we know it; and bliss is the natural result of existence without alloy. Now and then we know a moment of supreme bliss, when we ask nothing, give nothing, and know nothing but bliss. Then it passes and we again see the panorama of the universe going on before us and we know it is but a "mosaic work set upon God, who is the background of all things". When we return to earth and see the Absolute as relative, we see Sachchidananda as Trinity—father, Son, Holy Ghost. Sat = the creating principle; Chit = the guiding principle; Ananda = the realising principle, which joins us again to the One. No one can know "existence" (Sat) except through "knowledge" (Chit), and hence the force of the saying of Jesus, No man can see the Father save through the Son. The Vedanta teaches that Nirvana can be attained here and now, that we do not have to wait for death to reach it. Nirvana is the realisation of the Self, and after having once, if only for an instant, known this, never again can one be deluded by the mirage of personality. Having eyes, we must see the apparent; but all the time we know it for what it is, we have found out its true nature. It is the "screen" that hides the Self which is unchanging. The screen opens and we find the Self behind it—all change is in the screen. In the saint the screen is thin and the Reality can almost shine through; but in the sinner it is thick, and we are apt to lose sight of the truth that the Atman is there, as well as behind the saint.

All reasoning ends only in finding Unity; so we first use

analysis, then synthesis. In the world of science, the forces are gradually narrowed down in the search for one underlying force. When physical science can perfectly grasp the final unity, it will have reached an end, for reaching unity we find rest. Knowledge is final.

Religion, the most precious of all sciences, long ago discovered that final unity, to reach which is the object of Jnana-yoga. There is but one Self in the universe, of which all lower selves are but manifestations. The Self, however, is infinitely more than all of its manifestations. All is the Self or Brahman. The saint, the sinner, the lamb, the tiger, even the murderer, as far as they have any reality, can be nothing else, because there is nothing else. "That which exists is One, sages call It variously." Nothing can be higher than this knowledge, and in those purified by Yoga it comes in flashes to the soul. The more one has been purified and prepared by Yoga and meditation, the clearer are these flashes of realisation. This was dis -

covered 4,000 years ago, but has not yet become the property of the race; it is still the property of some individuals only.

Part IV

All men, so-called, are not yet really human beings. Every one has to judge of this world through his own mind. The higher understanding is extremely difficult. The concrete is more to most people than the abstract. As an illustration of this, a story is told of two men in Bombay—one a Hindu and the other a Jain—who were playing chess in the house of a rich merchant of Bombay. The house was near the sea, the game long; the ebb and flow of the tide under the balcony where they sat attracted the attention of the players. One explained it by a legend that the gods in their play threw the water into a great pit and then threw it out again. The other said: No, the gods draw it up to the top of a high mountain to use it, and then when they have done with it, they throw it down again. A young student present began to laugh at them and said, "Do you not know that the attraction of the moon causes the tides?" At this, both men turned on him in a fury and inquired if he thought they were fools. Did he suppose that they believed the moon had any ropes to pull up the tides, or that it could reach so far? They utterly refused to accept any such foolish explanation. At this juncture the host entered the room and was appealed to by both parties. He was an educated man and of course knew the truth, but seeing plainly the impossibility of making the chess-players understand it, he made a sign to the student and then proceeded to give an explanation of the tides that proved eminently satisfactory to his ignorant hearers. "You must know", he told them, "that afar off in the middle of the ocean, there is a huge mountain of sponge—you have both seen sponge, and know what

I mean. This mountain of sponge absorbs a great deal of the water and then the sea falls; by and by the gods come down and dance on the mountain and their weight squeezes all the water out and the sea rises again. This, gentlemen, is the cause of the tides, and you can easily see for yourselves how rea-

sonable and simple is this explanation." The two men who ridiculed the power of the moon to cause the tides, found nothing incredible in a mountain of sponge, danced upon by the gods! The gods were real to them, and they had actually seen sponge; what was more likely than their joint effect upon the sea! "Comfort" is no test of truth; on the contrary, truth is often far from being "comfortable". If one intends to really find truth, one must not cling to comfort. It is hard to let all go, but the Jnani must do it. He must become pure, kill out all desires and cease to identify himself with the body. Then and then only, the higher truth can shine in his soul. Sacrifice is necessary, and this immolation of the lower self is the underlying truth that has made sacrifice a part of all religions. All the propitiatory offerings to the gods were but dimly understood types of the only sacrifice that is of any real value, the surrender of the apparent self, through which alone we can realise the higher Self, the Atman. The Jnani must not try to preserve the body, nor even wish to do so. He must be strong and follow truth, though the universe fall. Those who follow "fads" can never do this. It is a life-work, nay, the work of a hundred lives! Only the few dare to realise the God within, to renounce heaven and Personal God and all hope of reward. A firm will is needed to do this; to be even vacillating is a sign of tremendous weakness. Man always is perfect, or he never could become so; but he had to realise it. If man were bound by external causes, he could only be mortal. Immortality can only be true of the unconditioned. Nothing can act on the Atman—the idea is pure delusion; but man must identify himself with that, not with body or mind. Let him know that he is the witness of the universe, then he can enjoy the beauty of the wonderful panorama passing before him. Let him even tell himself, "I am the universe, I am Brahman." When man really identifies himself with the One, the Atman, everything is possible to him and all matter becomes his servant. As Shri Ramakrishna has said: After the butter is churned, it can be put in water or milk and will never mix with either; so when man has once realised the Self, he can no more be contaminated by the world. "From a balloon, no minor distinctions are visible, so when man rises high enough, he will not see good and evil people." "Once the pot is burned, no more can it be shaped; so with the mind that has once touched the Lord and has had a baptism of fire, no more can it be changed." Philosophy in Sanskrit means "clear vision", and religion is practical philosophy. Mere theoretic, speculative philosophy is not much regarded in India. There is no church, no creed, no dogma. The two great divisions are the "Dvaitists" and the "Advaitists". The former say, "The way to salvation is through the mercy of God; the law of causation, once set in motion, can never be broken; only God, who is not bound by this law, by His mercy helps us to break it". The latter say, "Behind all this nature is something that is free; and finding that which is beyond all law gets us freedom; and freedom is salvation." Dualism is only one phase, Advaitism goes to the ultimate. To become pure is the shortest path to freedom. Only that is ours which we earn. No authority can save us, no beliefs. If there is a God, all can find Him. No one needs to be told it is warm; each one can discover it for himself. So it should be with God. He should be a fact in the consciousness of all men. The Hindus do not recognise "sin", as it is understood by the Western mind. Evil deeds are not "sins", we are not offending some Ruler in committing these; we are simply injuring ourselves, and we must suffer the penalty. It is not a sin to put one's finger in the fire, but he who does so will surely suffer just as much as if it were. All deeds produce certain results, and "every deed returns to the doer". "Trinitarianism" is an advance on "Unitarianism" (which is dualism, God and man for ever separate). The first step upwards is when we recognise ourselves as the children of God; the last step is when we realise ourselves as the One, the Atman.

Part V

The question why there cannot be eternal bodies is in itself illogical, as "body" is a term applied to a certain combination of elements, changeable and in its very nature impermanent. When we are not passing through changes, we will not have bodies (so-called). "Matter" beyond the limit of time, space, and causality will not be matter at all. Time and space exist only in us, we are the one Permanent Being. All forms are transitory, that is why all religions say, "God has no form". Menander was a Greco-bactrian king. He was converted to Buddhism about 150 B.C. by one of the Buddhist missionary monks and was called by them "Milinda". He asked a young monk, his teacher, "Can a perfect man (such as Buddha) be in error or make mistakes?" The young monk's answer was : The perfect man can remain in ignorance of minor matters not in his experience, but he can never be in error as to what his insight has actually realised. He is perfect here and now. He knows the whole mystery, the Essence of the universe, but he may not know the mere external variation through which that Essence is manifested in time and space. He knows the clay itself, but has not had experience of every shape it may be wrought into. The perfect man knows the Soul itself, but not every form and combination of its manifestation. He would have to attain more relative knowledge just as we do, though on account of his immense power, he would learn it far more quickly.

The tremendous "search-light" of a perfectly controlled mind, when thrown on any subject, would rapidly reduce it to possession. It is very important to understand this, because it saves so much foolish explanation as to how a Buddha or a Jesus could be mistaken in ordinary relative Knowledge, as we well know they were. The disciples should not be blamed as having put down the sayings erroneously. It is humbug to say that one thing is true and another untrue in their statements. Accept the whole account, or reject it. How can we pick out the true from the false?

If a thing happens once, it can happen again. If any human being has ever realised perfection, we too can do so. If we cannot become perfect here and now, we never can in any state or heaven or condition we may imagine. If Jesus Christ was not perfect, then the religion bearing his name falls to the ground. If he was perfect, then we too can become perfect. The perfect man does not reason or "know", as we count "knowing", for all our knowledge is mere comparison, and there is no comparison, no classification, possible in the Absolute. Instinct is less liable to error than reason, but reason is higher and leads to intuition, which is higher still. Knowledge is the parent of intuition, which like instinct, is also unerring, but on a higher plane. There are three grades of manifestation in living beings: (1) subconscious—mechanical, unerring; (2) conscious—knowing, erring; (3) superconscious—intuitional, unerring; and these are illustrated in an animal, man, and God. For the man who has become perfect, nothing remains but to apply his understanding. He lives only to help the world, desiring nothing for himself. What distinguishes is negative—the positive is ever wider and wider. What we have in common is the widest of all, and that is "Being". "Law is a mental shorthand to explain a series of phenomena"; but law as an entity, so to speak, does not exist. We use the word to express the regular succession of certain occurrences in the phenomenal world. We must not let law become a superstition, a something inevitable, to which we must submit. Error must accompany reason, but the very struggle to conquer error makes us gods. Disease is the struggle of nature to cast out something wrong; so sin is the struggle of the divine in us to throw off the animal. We must "sin" (that is, make mistakes) in order to rise to Godhood.

Do not pity anyone. Look upon all as your equal, cleanse yourself of the primal sin of inequality. We are all equal and must not think, "I am good and you are bad, and I am trying to reclaim you". Equality is the sign of the free. Jesus came to publicans and sinners and lived with them. He never set himself on a pedestal. Only sinners see sin. See not man, see only the Lord. We manufacture our own heaven and can make a heaven even in hell. Sinners are only to be found in hell, and as long as we see them around us, we are there ourselves. Spirit is not in time, nor in space. Realise "I am Existence Absolute, Knowledge Absolute, Bliss Absolute—i am He, I am He". Be glad at birth, be glad at death, rejoice always in the love of God. Get rid of the bondage of body; we have become slaves to it and learnt to hug our chains and love our slavery; so much so that we long to perpetuate it, and go on with "body" "body" for ever. Do not cling to the idea of "body", do not look for a future existence in any way like this one; do not love or want the body, even of those dear to us. This life is our teacher, and dying only makes room to begin over again. Body is our schoolmaster, but to commit suicide is folly, it is only killing the "schoolmaster". Another will take his place. So until we have learnt to transcend the body, we must have it, and losing one, will get another. Still we must not identify ourselves with the body, but look upon it only as an instrument to be used in reaching perfection. Hanuman, the devotee of Rama, summed up his philosophy in these words: When I identify myself with the body, O Lord, I am Thy creature, eternally separate from Thee. When I identify myself with the soul, I am a spark of that Divine Fire which Thou art. But when I identify myself with the Atman, I and Thou art one.

Therefore the Jnani strives to realise the Self and nothing else.

Part VI

Thought is all important, for "what we think we become". There was once a Sannyasin, a holy man, who sat under a tree and taught the people. He drank milk, and ate only fruit, and made endless "Pranayamas", and felt himself to be very holy. In the same village lived an evil woman. Every day the Sannyasin went and warned her that her wickedness would lead her to hell. The poor woman, unable to change her method of life which was her only means of livelihood, was still much moved by the terrible future depicted by the Sannyasin. She wept and prayed to the Lord, begging Him to forgive her because she could not help herself. By and by both the holy man and the evil woman died. The angels came and bore her to heaven, while the demons claimed the soul of the Sannyasin. "Why is this!" he exclaimed, "have I not lived a most holy life, and preached holiness to everybody? Why should I be taken to hell while this wicked woman is taken to heaven?" "Because," answered the demons, "while she was forced to commit unholy acts, her mind was always fixed on the Lord and she sought deliverance, which has now come to her. But you, on the contrary, while you performed only holy acts, had your mind always fixed on the wickedness of others. You saw only sin, and thought only of sin, so now you have to go to that place where only sin is." The moral of the story is obvious: The outer life avails little. The heart must be pure and the pure heart sees only good, never evil. We should never try to be guardians of mankind, or to stand on a pedestal as saints reforming sinners. Let us rather purify ourselves, and the result must be that in so doing we shall help others.

Physics is bounded on both sides by metaphysics. So it is with reason — it starts from non-reason and ends with non-reason. If we push inquiry far enough in the world of perception, we must reach a plane beyond perception. Reason is really stored up and classified perception, preserved by memory. We can never imagine or reason beyond our sense-perceptions. Nothing beyond reason can be an object of sense-knowledge. We feel the limited character of reason, yet it does bring us to a plane where we get a glimpse of something beyond. The question then arises: Has man an instrument that transcends reason? It is very probable that in man there is a power to reach beyond reason; in fact the saints in all ages assert the existence of this power in themselves. But it is impossible in the very nature of things to translate spiritual ideas and perceptions into the language of reason; and these saints, each and all, have declared their inability to make known their spiritual experiences. Language can, of course, supply no words for them, so that it can only be asserted that these are actual experiences and can be had by all. Only in that way can they become known, but they can never be described. Religion is the science which learns the transcendental in nature through the transcendental in man. We know as yet but little of man, consequently but little of the universe. When we know more of man, we shall probably know more of the universe. Man is the epitome of all things and all knowledge is in him. Only for the infinitesimal portion of the universe, which comes into sense-perception, are we able to find a reason; never can we give the reason for any fundamental principle. Giving a reason for a thing is simply to classify it and put it in a pigeon-hole of the mind. When we meet a new fact, we at once strive to put it in some existing category and the attempt to do this is to reason. When we succeed in placing the fact, it gives a certain amount of satisfaction, but we can never go beyond the physical plane in this classification. That man can transcend the limits of the senses is the emphatic testimony of all past ages. The Upanishads told 5,000 years ago that the realisation of God could never be had through the senses. So far, modern agnosticism agrees, but the Vedas go further than the negative side and assert in the plainest terms that man can and does transcend this sense-bound, frozen universe. He can, as it were, find a hole in the ice, through which he can pass and reach the whole ocean of life. Only by so transcending the world of sense, can he reach his true Self and realise what he really is.

Jnana is never sense-knowledge. We cannot know Brahman, but we are Brahman, the whole of It, not a piece. The unextended can never be divided. The apparent variety is but the reflection seen in time and space, as we see the sun reflected in a million dewdrops, though we know that the sun itself is one and not many. In Jnana we have to lose sight of the variety and see only the Unity. Here there is no subject, no object, no knowing, no thou or he or I, only the one, absolute Unity. We are this all the time; once free,

ever free. Man is not bound by the law of causation. Pain and misery are not in man, they are but as the passing cloud throwing its shadow over the sun, but the cloud passes, the sun is unchanged; and so it is with man. He is not born, he does not die, he is not in time and space. These ideas are mere reflections of the mind, but we mistake them for the reality and so lose sight of the glorious truth they obscure. Time is but the method of our thinking, but we are the eternally present tense. Good and evil have existence only in relation to us. One cannot be had without the other, because neither has meaning or existence apart from the other. As long as we recognise duality, or separate God and man, so long we must see good and evil. Only by going to the centre, by unifying ourselves with God can we escape the delusions of the senses. When we let go the eternal fever of desire, the endless thirst that gives us no rest, when we have for ever quenched desire, we shall escape both good and evil, because we shall have transcended both. The satisfaction of desire only increases it, as oil poured on fire but makes it burn more fiercely. The further from the centre, the faster goes the wheel, the less the rest. Draw near the centre, check desire, stamp it out, let the false self go, then our vision will clear and we shall see God. Only through renunciation of this life and of all life to come (heaven etc.), can we reach the point where we stand firmly on the true Self. While we hope for anything, desire still rules us. Be for one moment really "hopeless", and the mist will clear. For what to hope when one is the all of existence? The secret of Jnana is to give up all and be sufficient unto ourselves. Say "not", and you become "not"; say "is", and you become "is". Worship the Self within, naught else exists. All that binds us is Maya — delusion.

Part VII

The Self is the condition of all in the universe, but It can never be conditioned. As soon as we know that we are It, we are free. As mortals we are not and never can be free. Free mortality is a contradiction in terms, for mortality implies change, and only the changeless can be free. The Atman alone is free, and that is our real essence. We feel this inner freedom; in spite of all theories, all beliefs, we know it, and every action proves that we know it. The will is not free, its apparent freedom is but a reflection from the Real. If the world were only an endless chain of cause and effect, where could one stand to help it? There must needs be a piece of dry land for the rescuer to stand on, else how can he drag anyone out of the rushing stream and save him from drowning? Even the fanatic who cries "I am a worm", thinks that he is on the way to become a saint. He sees the saint even in the worm.

There are two ends or aims of human life, real knowing (Vijnana) and bliss. Without freedom, these two are impossible. They are the touchstone of all life. We should feel the Eternal Unity so much, that we should weep for all sinners, knowing that it is we who are sinning. The eternal law is self-sacrifice, not self-assertion. What self to assert when all is one? There are no "rights", all is love. The great truths that Jesus taught have never been lived. Let us try his method and see if the world will not be saved. The contrary method has nearly destroyed it. Selflessness only, not selfishness, can solve the question. The idea of "right" is a limitation; there is really no "mine" and "thine", for I am thou and thou art I. We have "responsibility", not "rights". We should say, "I am the universe", not "I am John" or "I am Mary". These limitations are all delusions and are what holds us in bondage, for as soon as I think, "I am John", I want exclusive possession of certain things and begin to say "me and mine", and continually make new distinctions in so doing. So our bondage goes on increasing with every fresh distinction, and we get further and further away from the central Unity, the undivided Infinite. There is only one Individual, and each of us is That. Oneness alone is love and fearlessness; separation leads us to hatred and fear. Oneness fulfils the law. Here, on earth, we strive to enclose little spaces and exclude outsiders, but we cannot do that

in the sky, though that is what sectarian religion tries to do when it says, "Only this way leads to salvation, all others are wrong". Our aim should be to wipe out these little enclosures to widen the boundaries until they are lost sight of, and to realise that all religions lead to God. This little puny self must be sacrificed. This is the truth symbolised by baptism into a new life, the death of the old man, the birth of the new — the perishing of the false self, the realisation of the Atman, the one Self of the universe.

The two great divisions of the Vedas are Karma Kanda — the portion pertaining to doing or work, and Jnana Kanda — the portion treating of knowing, true knowledge. In the Vedas we can find the whole process of the growth of religious ideas. This is because when a higher truth was reached, the lower perception that led to it, was still preserved. This was done, because the sages realised that the world of creation being eternal, there would always be those who needed the first steps to knowledge, that the highest philosophy, while open to all, could never be grasped by all. In nearly every other religion, only the last or highest realisation of truth has been preserved, with the natural consequence that the older ideas were lost, while the newer ones were only understood by the few and gradually came to have no meaning for the many. We see this result illustrated in the growing revolt against old traditions and authorities.

Instead of accepting them, the man of today boldly challenges them to give reasons for their claims, to make clear the grounds upon which they demand acceptance. Much in Christianity is the mere application of new names and meanings to old pagan beliefs and customs. If the old sources had been preserved and the reasons for the transitions fully explained, many things would have been clearer. The Vedas preserved the old ideas and this fact necessitated huge commentaries to explain them and why they were kept. It also led to many superstitions, through clinging to old forms after all sense of their meaning had been lost. In many ceremonials, words are repeated which have survived from a now forgotten language and to which no real meaning can now be attached. The idea of evolution was to be found in the Vedas long before the Christian era; but until Darwin said it was true, it was regarded as a mere Hindu superstition.

All external forms of prayer and worship are included in the Karma Kanda. These are good when performed in a spirit of unselfishness and not allowed to degenerate into mere formality. They purify the heart. The Karma-yogi wants everyone to be saved before himself. His only salvation is to help others to salvation. "To serve Krishna's servants is the highest worship." One great saint prayed, "Let me go to hell with the sins of the whole world, but let the world be saved." This true worship leads to intense self-sacrifice. It is told of one sage that he was willing to give all his virtues to his dog, that it might go to heaven, because it had long been faithful to him, while he himself was content to go to hell.

The Jnana Kanda teaches that knowledge alone can save, in other words, that he must become "wise unto salvation". Knowledge is first objective, the Knower knowing Himself. The Self, the only subject, is in manifestation seeking only to know Itself. The better the mirror, the better reflection it can give; so man is the best mirror, and the purer the man, the more clearly he can reflect God. Man makes the mistake of separating himself from God and identifying himself with the body. This mistake arises through Maya, which is not exactly delusion but might be said to be seeing the real as something else and not as it is. This identifying of ourselves with the body leads to inequality, which inevitably leads to struggle and jealousy, and so long as we see inequality, we can never know happiness. "Ignorance and inequality are the two sources of all misery", says Jnana.

When man has been sufficiently buffeted by the world, he awakes to a desire for freedom; and searching for means of escape from the dreary round of earthly existence, he seeks knowledge, learns what he really is, and is free. After that he looks at the world as a huge machine, but takes good care to keep his fingers out of the wheels. Duty ceases for him who is free; what power can constrain the free being? He does good, because it is his nature, not because any fancied duty commands it. This does not apply to those who are still in the bondage of the senses. Only for him, who has transcended the lower self, is this freedom. He stands on his own soul, obeys no law; he is free and perfect. He has undone the old superstitions and got out of the wheel. Nature is but the mirror of our own selves. There is a limit to the working power of human beings, but no limit to desire; so we strive to get hold of the working powers of others and enjoy the fruits of their labours, escaping work ourselves. Inventing machinery to work for us can never increase well-being, for in gratifying desire, we only find it, and then we want more and more without end. Dying, still filled with ungratified desires, we have to be born again and again in the vain search for satisfaction. "Eight Millions of bodies have we had, before we reached the human", say the Hindus. Jnana says, "Kill desire and so get rid of it". That is the only way. Cast out all causation and realise the Atman. Only freedom can produce true morality. If there were only an endless chain of cause and effect, Nirvana could not be. It is extinction of the seeming self, bound by this chain. That is what constitutes freedom, to get beyond causality.

Our true nature is good, it is free, the pure being that can never be or do wrong. When we read God with our eyes and minds, we call Him this or that; but in reality there is but One, all variations are our interpretations of that One. We become nothing; we regain our true Self. Buddha's summary of misery as the outcome of "ignorance and caste" (inequality) has been adopted by the Vedantists, because it is the best ever made. It manifests the wonderful insight of this greatest among men. Let us then be brave and sincere: whatever path we follow with devotion, must take us to freedom. Once lay hold of one link of the chain and the whole must come after

it by degrees. Water the root of the tree and the whole tree is watered. It is of little advantage to waste time to water each leaf. In other words, seek the Lord and getting Him we get all. Churches, doctrines, forms—these are merely the hedges to protect the tender plant of religion; but later on they must all be broken down, that the little plant may become a tree. So the various religious sects, Bibles, Vedas, and scriptures are just "tubs" for the little plant; but it has to get out of the tub and fill the world.

We must learn to feel ourselves as much in the sun, in the stars, as here. Spirit is beyond all time and space; every eye seeing is my eye; every mouth praising the Lord is my mouth; every sinner is I. We are confined nowhere, we are not body. The universe is our body. We are just the pure crystal reflecting all, but itself

ever the same. We are magicians waving magic wands and creating scenes before us at will, but we have to go behind appearances and know the Self. This world is like water in a kettle, beginning to boil; first a bubble comes, then another, then many until all is in ebullition and passes away in steam. The great teachers are like the bubbles as they begin—here one, there one; but in the end every creature has to be a bubble and escape. Creation, ever new, will bring new water and go through the process all over again. Buddha and Christ are the two greatest "bubbles" the world has known. They were great souls who having realised freedom helped others to escape. Neither was perfect, but they are to be judged by their virtues, never by their defects. Jesus fell short, because he did not always live up to his own highest ideal; and above all, because he did not give woman an equal place with man. Woman did everything for him, yet not one was made an apostle. This was doubtless owing to his Semitic origin. The great Aryans, Buddha among the rest, have always put woman in an equal position with man. For them sex in religion did not exist. In the Vedas and Upanishads, women taught the highest truths and received the same veneration as men.

Part VIII

Both happiness and misery are chains, the one golden, the other iron; but both are equally strong to bind us and hold us back from realising our true nature. The Atman knows neither happiness nor misery. These are mere "states", and states must ever change. The nature of the soul is bliss and peace unchanging. We have not to get it; we have it; let us wash away the dross from our eyes and see it. We must stand ever on the Self and look with perfect calmness upon all the panorama of the world. It is but baby's play and ought never to disturb us. If the mind is pleased by praise, it will be pained by blame. All pleasures of the senses or even of the mind are evanescent, but within ourselves is the one true unrelated pleasure, dependent on nothing outside. "The pleasure of the Self is what the world calls religion." The more our bliss is within, the more spiritual we are. Let us not depend upon the world for pleasure.

Some poor fishwives, overtaken by a violent storm, found refuge in the garden of a rich man. He received them kindly, fed them, and left them to rest in a summer-house, surrounded by exquisite flowers which filled all the air with their rich perfume. The women lay down in this sweet-smelling paradise, but could not sleep. They missed something out of their lives and could not be happy without it. At last one of the women arose and went to the place where they had left their fish baskets, brought them to the summer-house, and then once more happy in the familiar smell, they were all soon sound asleep.

Let not the world be our "fish basket" which we have to depend upon for enjoyment. This is Tamasika, or being bound by the lowest of the three qualities (or Gunas). Next higher come the egotistical who talk always about "I", "I". Sometimes they do good work and may become spiritual. These are Rajasika or active. Highest come the introspective nature (Sattvika), those who live only in the Self. These three qualities are in every human being in varying proportions, and different ones predominate at different times. We must strive to overcome Tamas with Rajas and then to submerge both in Sattva.

Creation is not a "making" of something, it is the struggle to regain equilibrium, as when atoms of cork are thrown to the bottom of a pail of water: they rush to the top singly and in clusters, and when all have reached the top and equilibrium has been regained, all motion or "life" ceases. So with creation; if equilibrium were reached, all change would cease and life, so-called, would end. Life must be accompanied with evil, for when the balance is regained, the world must end, as sameness and destruction are one. There is no possibility of ever having pleasure without pain, or good without evil, for living itself is just the lost equilibrium. What we want is freedom, not life, nor pleasure, nor good. Creation is eternal, without beginning, without end, the ever moving ripple in an infinite lake. There are yet unreached depths and others where stillness has been regained, but the ripple is ever progressing, the struggle to regain the balance is eternal. Life and death are but different names for the same fact, they are the two sides of one coin. Both are Maya, the inexplicable state of striving at one point to live and a moment later to die. Beyond all this is the true nature, the Atman. We enter into creation, and then, for us, it becomes living. Things are dead in themselves, only we give them life, and then, like fools, we turn round and are afraid of them or enjoy them! The world is neither true nor untrue, it is the shadow of truth. "Imagination is the gilded shadow of truth", says the poet. The internal universe, the Real, is infinitely greater than the external one, which is but the shadowy projection of the true one. When we see the "rope", we do not see the "serpent", and when the "serpent" is, the "rope" is not. Both cannot exist at the same time; so while we see the world we do not realise the Self, it is only an intellectual concept. In the realisation of Brahman, the personal "I" and all sense of the world is lost. The Light does not know the darkness, because it has no existence in the light; so Brahman is all. While we recognise a God, it is really only the Self that we have separated from ourselves and worship as outside of us; but all the time it is our own true Self, the one and only God. The nature of the brute is to remain where he is, of man to seek good and avoid evil, of God to neither seek nor avoid, but just to be blissful eternally. Let us be Gods, let us make our hearts like an ocean, to go beyond all the trifles of the world and see it only as a picture. We can then enjoy it without being in any way affected by it. Why look for good in the world, what can we find there? The best it has to offer is only as if children playing in a mud puddle found a few glass beads. They lose them again and have to begin the search anew. Infinite strength is religion and God. We are only souls if we are free, there is immortality only if we are free, there is God only if He is free.

Until we give up the world manufactured by the ego, never can we enter the Kingdom of Heaven. None ever did, none ever will. To give up the world is to utterly forget the ego, to know it not at all, living in the body but not being ruled by it. This rascal ego must be obliterated. Power to help mankind is with the silent ones who only live and love and withdraw their own personality entirely. They never say "me" or "mine", they are only blessed in being the instruments to help others. They are wholly identified with God, asking nothing and not consciously doing anything. They are the true Jivanmuktas—the absolutely selfless, their little personality thoroughly blown away, ambition non-existent. They are all principle, with no personality. The more we sink the "little self", the more God comes. Let us get rid of the little "I" and let only the great "I" live in us. Our best work and our greatest influence is when we are without a thought of self. It is the "desireless" who bring great results to pass. Bless men when they revile you. Think how much good they are doing by helping to stamp out the false ego. Hold fast to the real Self, think only pure thoughts, and you will accomplish more than a regiment of mere preachers. Out of purity and silence comes the word of power.

Part IX

Expression is necessarily degeneration, because spirit can only be expressed by the "letter", and as St. Paul said, "the letter killeth". Life cannot be in the "letter" which is only a reflection. Yet, principle must be clothed in matter to be "known". We lose sight of the Real in the covering and come to consider that as the Real, instead of as the symbol. This is an almost universal mistake. Every great Teacher knows this and tries to guard against it; but humanity, in general, is prone to worship the seen rather than the unseen. This is why a succession of prophets have come to the world to point again and again to the principle behind the personality and to give it a new covering suited to the times. Truth remains ever unchanged, but it can only be presented in a "form"; so from time to time a new "form" or expression is given to Truth, as the progress of mankind makes them ready to receive it. When we free ourselves from name and form, especially when we no longer need a body of any kind, good or bad, coarse or fine, then only do we escape from bondage. "Eternal progression" would be eternal bondage. We must get beyond all differentiation and reach eternal "sameness" or homogeneity or Brahman. The Atman is the unity of all personalities and is unchangeable, the "One without a second". It is not life, but it is coined into life. It is beyond life and death and good and bad. It is the Absolute Unity. Dare to seek Truth even through hell. Freedom can never be true of name and form, of the related. No form can say, "I am free as a form." Not until all idea of form is lost, does freedom come. If our freedom hurts others, we are not free there. We must not hurt others. While real perception is only one, relative perceptions must be many. The fountain of all knowledge is in every one of us—in the ant as in the highest angel. Real religion is one; all quarrel is with the forms, the symbols, the "illustrations". The millennium exists already for those who find it. The truth is, we have lost ourselves and think the world to be lost. "Fool! Hearest not thou? In thine own heart, day and night, is singing that Eternal Music—sachchidananda, Soham, Soham, (Existence, Knowledge, and Bliss, I am He, I am He)!"

To try to think without a phantasm is to try to make the impossible possible. Each thought has two parts—the thinking and the word, and we must have both. Neither idealists nor materialists are able to explain the world; to do that, we must take both idea and expression. All knowledge is of the reflected as we can only see our own faces reflected in a mirror. So no one can know his Self or Brahman; but each is that Self and must see it reflected in order to make it an object of knowledge. This seeing the illustrations of the unseen Principle is what leads to idolatry—so-called. The range of idols is wider than is usually supposed. They range from wood and stone to great personalities as Jesus or Buddha. The introduction of idols into India was the result of Buddha's constantly inveighing against a Personal God. The Vedas knew them not, but the reaction against the loss of God as Creator and Friend led to making idols of the great teachers, and Buddha himself became an idol and is worshipped as such by millions of people. Violent attempts at reform always end in retarding true reform. To worship is inherent in every man's nature; only the highest philosophy can rise to pure abstraction. So man will ever personify his God in order to worship Him. This is very good, as long as the symbol, be it what it may, is worshipped as a symbol of the Divinity behind and not in and for itself. Above all, we need to free ourselves from the superstition of believing because "it is in the books". To try to make everything—science, religion, philosophy, and all—conform to what any book says, is a most horrible tyranny. Book-worship is the worst form of idolatry. There was once a stag, proud and free, and he talked in a lordly fashion to his child, "Look at me, see my powerful horns! With one thrust I can kill a man; it is a fine thing to be a stag!" Just then the sound of the huntsman's bugle was heard in the distance, and the stag precipitately fled, followed by his wondering child. When they had reached a place of safety, he inquired, "Why do you fly before man, O my father, when you are so strong and brave?" The stag answered, "My child, I know I am strong and powerful, but when I hear that sound, something seizes me and makes me fly whether I will or no." So with us. We hear the "bugle" of the laws laid down in the books, habits and old superstitions lay hold of us; and before we know it, we are fast bound and forget our real nature which is freedom.

Knowledge exists eternally. The man who discovers a spiritual truth is what we call "inspired", and what he brings to the world is revelation. But revelation too is eternal and is not to be crystallised as final and then blindly followed. Revelation may come to any man who has fitted himself to receive it. Perfect purity is the most essential thing, for only "the pure in heart shall see God". Man is the highest being that exists and this is the greatest world, for here can man realise freedom. The highest concept we can have of God is man. Every attribute we give Him belongs also to man, only in a lesser degree. When we rise higher and want to get out of this concept of God, we have to get out of the body, out of mind and imagination, and leave this world out of sight. When we rise to be the absolute, we are no longer in the world—all is Subject, without object.

Man is the apex of the only "world" we can ever know. Those who have attained "sameness" or perfection, are said to be "living in God". All hatred is "killing the self by the self"; therefore, love is the law of life. To rise to this is to be perfect; but the more "perfect" we are, the less work can we do. The Sattvika see and know that all this world is mere child's play and do not trouble themselves about that. We are not much disturbed when we see two puppies fighting and biting each other. We know it is not a serious matter. The perfect one knows that this world is Maya. Life is called Samsara—it is the result of the conflicting forces acting upon us. Materialism says, "The voice of freedom is a delusion." Idealism says, "The voice that tells of bondage is but a dream." Vedanta says, "We are free and not free at the same time." That means that we are never free on the earthly plane, but ever free on the spiritual side. The Self is beyond both freedom and bondage. We are Brahman, we are immortal knowledge beyond the senses, we are Bliss Absolute.

ON RAJA-YOGA[1]

Raja-Yoga is as much a science as any in the world. It is an analysis of the mind, a gathering of the facts of the supersen-

1. These lessons are composed of notes of class talks given by Swami Vivekananda to an intimate audience in the house of Mrs. Sara C. Bull, a devoted American disciple, and were preserved by her and finally printed in 1913 for private circulation——Ed.

suous world and so building up the spiritual world. All the great spiritual teachers the world has known said, "I see and I know." Jesus, Paul, and Peter all claimed actual perception of the spiritual truths they taught.

This perception is obtained by Yoga.

Neither memory nor consciousness can be the limitation of existence. There is a superconscious state. Both it and the unconscious state are sensationless, but with a vast difference between them—the difference between ignorance and knowledge. Present Yoga as an appeal to reason, as a science.

Concentration of the mind is the source of all knowledge.

Yoga teaches us to make matter our slave, as it ought to be. Yoga means "yoke", "to join", that is, to join the soul of man with the supreme Soul or God.

The mind acts in and under consciousness. What we call consciousness is only one link in the infinite chain that is our nature.

This "I" of ours covers just a little consciousness and a vast amount of unconsciousness, while over it, and mostly unknown to it, is the superconscious plane.

Through faithful practice, layer after layer of the mind opens before us, and each reveals new facts to us. We see as it were new worlds created before us, new powers are put into our hands, but we must not stop by the way or allow ourselves to be dazzled by these "beads of glass" when the mine of diamonds lies before us.

God alone is our goal. Failing to reach God, we die.

Three things are necessary to the student who wishes to succeed. First. Give up all ideas of enjoyment in this world and the next, care only for God and Truth. We are here to know truth, not for enjoyment. Leave that to brutes who enjoy as we never can. Man is a thinking being and must struggle on until he conquers death, until he sees the light. He must not spend himself in vain talking that bears no fruit. Worship of society and popular opinion is idolatry. The soul has no sex, no country, no place, no time.

Second. Intense desire to know Truth and God. Be eager for them, long for them, as a drowning man longs for breath. Want only God, take nothing else, let not "seeming" cheat you any longer. Turn from all and seek only God.

Third. The six trainings: First—restraining the mind from going outward. Second—restraining the senses. Third—turning the mind inward. Fourth—suffering everything without murmuring. Fifth—fastening the mind to one idea. Take the subject before you and think it out; never leave it. Do not count time. Sixth—think constantly of your real nature. Get rid of superstition. Do not hypnotise yourself into a belief in your own inferiority. Day and night tell yourself what you really are, until you realise (actually realise) your oneness with God.

Without these disciplines, no results can be gained.

We can be conscious of the Absolute, but we can never express It. The moment we try to express It, we limit It and It ceases to be Absolute.

We have to go beyond sense limit and transcend even reason, and we have the power to do this.

After practising the first lesson in breathing a week, the pupil reports to the teacher.

FIRST LESSON

This is a lesson seeking to bring out the individuality. Each individuality must be cultivated. All will meet at the centre. "Imagination is the door to inspiration and the basis of all thought." All prophets, poets, and discoverers have had great imaginative power. The explanation of nature is in us; the stone falls outside, but gravitation is in us, not outside. Those who stuff themselves, those who starve themselves, those who sleep too much, those who sleep too little, cannot become Yogis. Ignorance, fickleness, jealousy, laziness, and excessive attachment are the great enemies to success in Yoga practice. The three great requisites are:

First. Purity, physical and mental; all uncleanness, all that would draw the mind down, must be abandoned.

Second. Patience: At first there will be wonderful manifestations, but they will all cease. This is the hardest period, but hold fast; in the end the gain is sure if you have patience.

Third. Perseverance: Persevere through thick and thin, through health and sickness, never miss a day in practice.

The best time for practice is the junction of day and night, the calmest time in the tides of our bodies, the zero point between two states. If this cannot be done, practise upon rising and going to bed. Great personal cleanliness is necessary—a daily bath.

After bathing, sit down and hold the seat firm, that is, imagine that you sit as firm as a rock, that nothing can move you. Hold the head and shoulders and the hips in a straight line, keeping the spinal column free; all action is along it, and it must not be impaired.

Begin with your toes and think of each part of your body as perfect; picture it so in your mind, touching each part if you prefer to do so. Pass upward bit by bit until you reach the head, thinking of each as perfect, lacking nothing. Then think of the whole as perfect, an instrument given to you by God to enable you to attain Truth, the vessel in which you are to cross the ocean and reach the shores of eternal truth. When this has been done, take a long breath through both nostrils, throw it out again, and then hold it out as long as you comfortably can. Take four such breaths, then breathe naturally and pray for illumination. "I meditate on the glory of that being who created this universe; may he illuminate my mind." Sit and meditate on this ten or fifteen minutes.

Tell your experiences to no one but your Guru.

Talk as little as possible.

Keep your thoughts on virtue; what we think we tend to

become.

Holy meditation helps to burn out all mental impurities. All who are not Yogis are slaves; bond after bond must be broken to make us free.

All can find the reality beyond. If God is true, we must feel him as a fact, and if there is a soul, we ought to be able to see it and feel it.

The only way to find if there be a soul is to be something which is not the body.

The Yogis class our organs under two chief heads: organs of sense and organs of motion, or knowledge and action.

The internal organ or mind has four aspects. First—manas, the cogitating or thinking faculty, which is usually almost entirely wasted, because uncontrolled; properly governed, it is a wonderful power. Second—buddhi, the will (sometimes called the intellect). Third—ahamkara, the self-conscious egotism (from Aham). Fourth—chitta, the substance in and through which all the faculties act, the floor of the mind as it were; or the sea in which the various faculties are waves.

Yoga is the science by which we stop Chitta from assuming, or becoming transformed into, several faculties. As the reflection of the moon on the sea is broken or blurred by the waves, so is the reflection of the Atman, the true Self, broken by the mental waves. Only when the sea is stilled to mirror-like calmness, can the reflection of the moon be seen, and only when the "mind-stuff", the Chitta is controlled to absolute calmness, is the Self to be recognised.

The mind is not the body, though it is matter in a finer form. It is not eternally bound by the body. This is proved as we get occasionally loosened from it. We can learn to do this at will by controlling the senses.

When we can do that fully, we shall control the universe, because our world is only what the senses bring us. Freedom is the test of the higher being. Spiritual life begins when you have loosened yourself from the control of the senses. He whose senses rule him is worldly—is a slave.

If we could entirely stop our mind-stuff from breaking into waves, it would put an end to our bodies. For millions of years we have worked so hard to manufacture these bodies that in the struggle we have forgotten our real purpose in getting them, which was to become perfect. We have grown to think that body-making is the end of our efforts. This is Maya. We must break this delusion and return to our original aim and realise we are not the body, it is our servant.

Learn to take the mind out and to see that it is

separate from the body. We endow the body with sensation and life and then think it is alive and real. We have worn it so long that we forget that it is not identical with us. Yoga is to help us put off our body when we please and see it as our servant, our instrument, not our ruler. Controlling the mental powers is the first great aim in Yoga practices. The second is concentrating them in full force upon any subject.

You cannot be a Yogi if you talk much.

SECOND LESSON

This Yoga is known as the eightfold Yoga, because it is divided into eight principal parts. These are:

First—Yama. This is most important and has to govern the whole life; it has five divisions:

- 1st. Not injuring any being by thought, word, or deed.
- 2nd. Non-covetousness in thought, word, or deed.
- 3rd. Perfect chastity in thought, word, or deed.
- 4th. Perfect truthfulness in thought, word, or deed.
- 5th. Non-receiving of gifts.

Second—Niyama. The bodily care, bathing daily, dietary, etc.

Third—Asana, posture. Hips, shoulders, and head must be held straight, leaving the spine free.

Fourth—pranayama, restraining the breath (in order to get control of the Prana or vital force).

Fifth—Pratyahara, turning the mind inward and restraining it from going outward, revolving the matter in the mind in order to understand it.

Sixth—Dharana, concentration on one subject.

Seventh—Dhyana, meditation.

Eighth—Samadhi, illumination, the aim of all our efforts.

Yama and Niyama are for lifelong practice. As for the others, we do as the leech does, not leave one blade of grass before firmly grasping another. In other words, we have thoroughly to understand and practise one step before taking another.

The subject of this lesson is Pranayama, or controlling the Prana. In Raja-Yoga breathing enters the psychic plane and brings us to the spiritual. It is the fly-wheel of the whole bodily system. It acts first upon the lungs, the lungs act on the heart, the heart acts upon the circulation, this in turn upon the brain, and the brain upon the mind. The will can produce an outside sensation, and the outside sensation can arouse the will. Our wills are weak; we do not realise their power, we are so much bound up in matter. Most of our action is from outside in. Outside nature throws us off our balance, and we cannot (as we ought) throw nature off her balance. This is all wrong; the stronger power is really within.

The great saints and teachers were those who had conquered this world of thought within themselves and so spake with power. The story[1] of the minister confined in a high tower, who was released through the efforts of his wife who brought him a beetle, honey, a silken thread, a cord, and a rope, illustrates the way we gain control of our mind by using first the physical regulation of the breath as the silken thread. That enables us to lay hold on one power after another until the rope of concentration delivers us from the prison of the body

1. For the story see *Complete Works of Swami Vivekananda*, Vol. I, p. 143.

and we are free. Reaching freedom, we can discard the means used to bring us there.

Pranayama has three parts:

- 1st. Puraka — inhaling
- 2nd. Kumbhaka — restraining
- 3rd. Rechaka — exhaling

There are two currents passing through the brain and circulating down the sides of the spine, crossing at the base and returning to the brain. One of these currents, called the "sun" (Pingala), starts from the left hemisphere of the brain, crosses at the base of the brain to the right side of the spine, and recrosses at the base of the spine, like one-half of the figure eight.

The other current, the "moon" (Ida), reverses this action and completes this figure eight. Of course, the lower part is much longer than the upper. These currents flow day and night and make deposits of the great life forces at different points, commonly known as "plexuses"; but we are rarely conscious of them. By concentration we can learn to feel them and trace them over all parts of the body. These "sun" and "moon" currents are intimately connected with breathing, and by regulating this we get control of the body.

In the Katha Upanishad the body is described as the chariot, the mind is the reins, the intellect is the charioteer, the senses are the horses, and the objects of the senses their road. The self is the rider, seated in the chariot. Unless the rider has understanding and can make the charioteer control his horses, he can never attain the goal; but the senses, like vicious steeds, will drag him where they please and may even destroy him. These two currents are the great "check rein" in the hands of the charioteer, and he must get control of this to control the horses. We have to get the power to become moral; until we do that, we cannot control our actions. Yoga alone enables us to carry into practice the teachings of morality. To become moral is the object of Yoga. All great teachers were Yogis and controlled every current. The Yogis arrest these currents at the base of the spine and force them through the centre of the spinal column. They then become the current of knowledge, which only exists in the Yogi.

Second Lesson in Breathing: One method is not for all. This breathing must be done with rhythmic regularity, and the easiest way is by counting; as that is purely mechanical, we repeat the sacred word "Om" a certain number of times instead.

The process of Pranayama is as follows: Close the right nostril with the thumb and then slowly inhale through the left nostril, repeating the word "Om" four times.

Then firmly close both nostrils by placing the forefinger on the left one and hold the breath in, mentally repeating "Om" eight times.

Then, removing the thumb from the right nostril, exhale slowly through that, repeating "Om" four times.

As you close the exhalation, draw in the abdomen forcibly to expel all the air from the lungs. Then slowly inhale through the right nostril, keeping the left one closed, repeating "Om" four times. Next close the right nostril with the thumb and hold the breath while repeating "Om" eight times. Then unclose the left nostril and slowly exhale, repeating "Om" four times, drawing in the abdomen as before. Repeat this whole operation twice at each sitting, that is, making four Pranayamas, two for each nostril. Before taking your seat it is well to begin with prayer.

This needs to be practised a week; then gradually increase the duration of breathing, keeping the same ratio, that is, if you repeat "Om" six times at inhalation, then do the same at exhalation and twelve times during Kumbhaka. These exercises will make us more spiritual, more pure, more holy. Do not be led aside into any byways or seek after power. Love is the only power that stays by us and increases. He who seeks to come to God through Raja-yoga must be strong mentally, physically, morally, and spiritually. Take every step in that light.

Of hundreds of thousands only one soul will say, "I will go beyond, and I will penetrate to God." Few can face the truth; but to accomplish anything, we must be willing to die for Truth.

THIRD LESSON

Kundalini: Realise the soul not as matter, but as it is. We are thinking of the soul as body, but we must separate it from sense and thought. Then alone can we know we are immortal. Change implies the duality of cause and effect, and all that changes must be mortal. This proves that the body cannot be immortal, nor can the mind, because both are constantly changing. Only the unchangeable can be immortal, because there is nothing to act upon it.

We do not become it, we are it; but we have to clear away the veil of ignorance that hides the truth from us. The body is objectified thought. The "sun" and "moon" currents bring energy to all parts of the body. The surplus energy is stored at certain points (plexuses) along the spinal column commonly known as nerve centres.

These currents are not to be found in dead bodies and can only be traced in a healthy organism.

The Yogi has an advantage; for he is able not only to feel them, but actually to see them. They are luminous in his life, and so are the great nerve centres.

There is conscious as well as unconscious action. The Yogis possess a third kind, the superconscious, which in all countries and in all ages has been the source of all religious knowledge. The superconscious state makes no mistakes, but whereas the action of the instinct would be purely mechanical, the former is beyond consciousness.

It has been called inspiration, but the Yogi says, "This faculty is in every human being, and eventually all will enjoy it."

We must give a new direction to the "sun" and "moon" currents and open for them a new passage through the centre of the spinal cord. When we succeed in bringing the currents

Lectures & Discourses by **Swami Vivekananda**

through this passage called "Sushumna", up to the brain, we are for the time being separated entirely from the body.

The nerve centre at the base of the spine near the sacrum is most important. It is the seat of the generative substance of the sexual energy and is symbolised by the Yogi as a triangle containing a tiny serpent coiled up in it. This sleeping serpent is called Kundalini, and to raise this Kundalini is the whole object of Raja-yoga.

The great sexual force, raised from animal action and sent upward to the great dynamo of the human system, the brain, and there stored up, becomes Ojas or spiritual force. All good thought, all prayer, resolves a part of that animal energy into Ojas and helps to give us spiritual power. This Ojas is the real man and in human beings alone is it possible for this storage of Ojas to be accomplished. One in whom the whole animal sex force has been transformed into Ojas is a god. He speaks with power, and his words regenerate the world.

The Yogi pictures this serpent as being slowly lifted from stage to stage until the highest, the pineal gland, is reached. No man or woman can be really spiritual until the sexual energy, the highest power possessed by man, has been converted into Ojas.

No force can be created; it can only be directed. Therefore we must learn to control the grand powers that are already in our hands and by will power make them spiritual instead of merely animal. Thus it is clearly seen that chastity is the corner-stone of all morality and of all religion. In Raja-yoga especially, absolute chastity in thought, word, and deed is a sine qua non. The same laws apply to the married and the single. If one wastes the most potent forces of one's being, one cannot become spiritual.

All history teaches us that the great seers of all ages were either monks and ascetics or those who had given up married life; only the pure in life can see God.

Just before making the Pranayama, endeavour to visualise the triangle. Close your eyes and picture it vividly in your imagination. See it surrounded by flames and with the serpent coiled in the middle. When you can clearly see the Kundalini, place it in imagination at the base of the spine, and when restraining the breath in Kumbhaka, throw it forcibly down on the head of the serpent to awaken it. The more powerful the imagination, the more quickly will the real result be attained and the Kundalini be awakened. Until it does, imagine it does: try to feel the currents and try to force them through the Sushumna. This hastens their action.

FOURTH LESSON

Before we can control the mind we must study it.

We have to seize this unstable mind and drag it from its wanderings and fix it on one idea. Over and over again this must be done. By power of will we must get hold of the mind and make it stop and reflect upon the glory of God.

The easiest way to get hold of the mind is to sit quiet and let it drift where it will for a while. Hold fast to the idea, "I am the witness watching my mind drifting. The mind is not I." Then see it think as if it were a thing entirely apart from yourself. Identify yourself with God, never with matter or with the mind.

Picture the mind as a calm lake stretched before you and the thoughts that come and go as bubbles rising and breaking on its surface. Make no effort to control the thoughts, but watch them and follow them in imagination as they float away. This will gradually lessen the circles. For the mind ranges over wide circles of thought and those circles widen out into ever-increasing circles, as in a pond when we throw a stone into it. We want to reverse the process and starting with a huge circle make it narrower until at last we can fix the mind on one point and make it stay there. Hold to the idea, "I am not the mind, I see that I am thinking, I am watching my mind act", and each day the identification of yourself with thought and feeling will grow less, until at last you can entirely separate yourself from the mind and actually know it to be apart from yourself.

When this is done, the mind is your servant to control as you will. The first stage of being a Yogi is to go beyond the senses. When the mind is conquered, he has reached the highest stage.

Live alone as much as possible. The seat should be of comfortable height; put first a grass mat, then a skin (fur), next a silken cover. It is better that the seat has no back and it must stand firm.

Thoughts being pictures, we should not create them. We have to exclude all thought from the mind and make it a blank; as fast as a thought comes we have to banish it. To be able to accomplish this, we must transcend matter and go beyond our body. The whole life of man is really an effort to do this.

Each soul has its own meaning: In our nature these two things are connected.

The highest ideal we have is God. Meditate on Him. We cannot know the Knower, but we are He.

Seeing evil, we are creating it. What we are, we see outside, for the world is our mirror. This little body is a little mirror we have created, but the whole universe is our body. We must think this all the time; then we shall know that we cannot die or hurt another, because he is our own. We are birthless and deathless and we ought only to love. "This whole universe is my body; all health, all happiness is mine, because all is in the universe." Say, "I am the universe." We finally learn that all action is from us to the mirror.

Although we appear as little waves, the whole sea is at our back, and we are one with it. No wave can exist of itself.

Imagination properly employed is our greatest friend; it goes beyond reason and is the only light that takes us everywhere.

Inspiration is from within and we have to inspire ourselves by our own higher faculties.

FIFTH LESSON

Pratyahara and Dharana: Krishna says, "All who seek me by whatever means will reach me", "All must reach me." Pratyahara is a gathering toward, an attempt to get hold of the mind and focus it on the desired object. The first step is to let the mind drift; watch it; see what it thinks; be only the witness. Mind is not soul or spirit. It is only matter in a finer form, and we own it and can learn to manipulate it through the nerve energies.

The body is the objective view of what we call mind (subjective). We, the Self, are beyond both body and mind; we are "Atman", the eternal, unchangeable witness. The body is crystallised thought.

When the breath is flowing through the left nostril, it is the time for rest; when through the right, for work; and when through both, the time to meditate. When we are calm and breathing equally through both nostrils, we are in the right condition for quiet meditation. It is no use trying to concentrate at first. Control of thought will come of itself.

After sufficient practice of closing the nostrils with the thumb and forefinger, we shall be able to do it by the power of will, through thought alone.

Pranayama is now to be slightly changed. If the student has the name of his "Ishta" (Chosen Ideal), he should use that instead of "Om" during inhalation and exhalation, and use the word "Hum" (pronounced Hoom) during Kumbhaka.

Throw the restrained breath forcibly down on the head of the Kundalini at each repetition of the word Hum and imagine that this awakens her. Identify yourself only with God. After a while thoughts will announce their coming, and we shall learn the way they begin and be aware of what we are going to think, just as on this plane we can look out and see a person coming. This stage is reached when we have learnt to separate ourselves from our minds and see ourselves as one and thought as something apart. Do not let the thoughts grasp you; stand aside, and they will die away.

Follow these holy thoughts; go with them; and when they melt away, you will find the feet of the Omnipotent God. This is the superconscious state; when the idea melts, follow it and melt with it.

Haloes are symbols of inner light and can be seen by the Yogi. Sometimes we may see a face as if surrounded by flames and in them read the character and judge without erring. We may have our Ishta come to us as a vision, and this symbol will be the one upon which we can rest easily and fully concentrate our minds.

We can imagine through all the senses, but we do so mostly through the eyes. Even imagination is half material. In other words, we cannot think without a phantasm. But since animals appear to think, yet have no words, it is probable that there is no inseparable connection between thought and images.

Try to keep up the imagination in Yoga, being careful to keep it pure and holy. We all have our peculiarities in the way of imaginative power; follow the way most natural to you; it will be the easiest.

We are the results of all reincarnations through Karma: "One lamp lighted from another", says the Buddhist—different lamps, but the same light.

Be cheerful, be brave, bathe daily, have patience, purity, and perseverance, then you will become a Yogi in truth. Never try to hurry, and if the higher powers come, remember that they are but side-paths. Do not let them tempt you from the main road; put them aside and hold fast to your only true aim—god. Seek only the Eternal, finding which we are at rest for ever; having the all, nothing is left to strive for, and we are for ever in free and perfect existence—existence absolute, Knowledge absolute, Bliss absolute.

SIXTH LESSON

Sushumna: It is very useful to meditate on the Sushumna. You may have a vision of it come to you, and this is the best way. Then meditate for a long time on that. It is a very fine, very brilliant thread, this living passage through the spinal cord, this way of salvation through which we have to make the Kundalini rise.

In the language of the Yogi, the Sushumna has its ends in two lotuses, the lower lotus surrounding the triangle of the Kundalini and the top one in the brain surrounding the pineal gland; between these two are four other lotuses, stages on the way:

- 6th. Pineal Gland.
- 5th. Between the Eyes.
- 4th. Bottom of the Throat.
- 3rd. Level with the Heart.
- 2nd. Opposite the Navel.
- 1st. Base of Spine.

We must awaken the Kundalini, then slowly raise it from one lotus to another till the brain is reached. Each stage corresponds to a new layer of the mind.

ON THE EAST AND THE WEST

I—INTRODUCTION

Vast and deep rivers—swelling and impetuous—charming pleasure-gardens by the river banks, putting to shame the celestial Nandana-Kânana; amidst these pleasure-gardens rise, towering to the sky, beautiful marble palaces, decorated with the most exquisite workmanship of fine art; on the sides, in front, and behind, clusters of huts, with crumbling mud-walls and dilapidated roofs, the bamboos of which, forming their skeletons, as it were, are exposed to view; moving about here and there emaciated figures of young and old in tattered rags, whose faces bear deep-cut lines of the despair and poverty of hundreds of years; cows, bullocks, buffaloes everywhere—ay, the same melancholy look in their eyes, the same feeble physique; on the wayside refuse and dirt: This is our present-day India!

Worn-out huts by the very side of palaces, piles of refuse in the near proximity of temples, the Sannyâsin clad with only a little loin-cloth, walking by the gorgeously dressed, the pitiful gaze of lustreless eyes of the hunger-stricken at the well-fed and the amply-provided: This is our native land!

Devastation by violent plague and cholera; malaria eating into the very vitals of the nation; starvation and semi-starvation as second nature; death-like famine often dancing its tragic dance; the Kurukshetra (battlefield) of malady and misery, the huge cremation ground, strewn with the dead bones of lost hope, activity, joy, and courage; and in the midst of that, sitting in august silence, the Yogi, absorbed in deep communion with the Spirit, with no other goal in life than Moksha: This is what meets the eye of the European traveller in India.

A conglomeration of three hundred million souls, resembling men only in appearance, crushed out of life by being downtrodden by their own people and foreign nations, by people professing their own religion and by others of foreign faiths; patient in labour and suffering and devoid of initiative like the slave; without any hope, without any past, without any future; desirous only of maintaining the present life anyhow, however precarious; of malicious nature befitting a slave, to whom the prosperity of their fellow-men is unbearable; bereft of Shraddhâ, like one with whom all hope is dead, faithless; whose weapon of defence is base trickery, treachery, and slyness like that of a fox; the embodiment of selfishness; licking the dust of the feet of the strong, withal dealing a death-blow to those who are comparatively weak; full of ugly, diabolical superstitions which come naturally to those who are weak and hopeless of the future; without any standard of morality as their backbone; three hundred millions of souls such as these are swarming on the body of India like so many worms on a rotten, stinking carcass: This is the picture concerning us, which naturally presents itself to the English official!

Maddened with the wine of newly acquired powers; devoid of discrimination between right and wrong; fierce like wild beasts, henpecked, lustful; drenched in liquor, having no idea of chastity or purity, nor of cleanly ways and habits; believing in matter only, with a civilisation resting on matter and its various applications; addicted to the aggrandisement of self by exploiting others' countries, others' wealth, by force, trick, and treachery; having no faith in the life hereafter, whose Âtman (Self) is the body, whose whole life is only in the senses and creature comforts: Thus, to the Indian, the Westerner is the veriest demon (Asura).

These are the views of observers on both sides—views born of mutual indiscrimination and superficial knowledge or ig-

norance. The foreigners, the Europeans, come to India, live in palatial buildings in the perfectly clean and healthy quarters of our towns and compare our "native" quarters with their neat and beautifully laid-out cities at home; the Indians with whom they come in contact are only of one class—those who hold some sort of employment under them. And, indeed, distress and poverty are nowhere else to be met with as in India; besides that, there is no gainsaying that dirt and filth are everywhere. To the European mind, it is inconceivable that anything good can possibly be amidst such dirt, such slavery, and such degradation.

We, on the other hand, see that the Europeans eat without discrimination whatever they get, have no idea of cleanliness as we have, do not observe caste distinctions, freely mix with women, drink wine, and shamelessly dance at a ball, men and women held in each other's arms: and we ask ourselves in amazement, what good can there be in such a nation?

Both these views are derived from without, and do not look within and below the surface. We do not allow foreigners to mix in our society, and we call them Mlechchhas; they also in their turn hate us as slaves and call us "niggers". In both of these views there must be some truth, though neither of the parties has seen the real thing behind the other.

With every man, there is an idea; the external man is only the outward manifestation, the mere language of this idea within. Likewise, every nation has a corresponding national idea. This idea is working for the world and is necessary for its preservation. The day when the necessity of an idea as an element for the preservation of the world is over, that very day the receptacle of that idea, whether it be an individual or a nation, will meet destruction. The reason that we Indians are still living, in spite of so much misery, distress, poverty, and oppression from within and without is that we have a national idea, which is yet necessary for the preservation of the world. The Europeans too have a national idea of their own, without which the world will not go on; therefore they are so strong. Does a man live a moment, if he loses all his strength? A nation is the sum total of so many individual men; will a nation live if it has utterly lost all its strength and activity? Why did not this Hindu race die out, in the face of so many troubles and tumults of a thousand years? If our customs and manners are so very bad, how is it that we have not been effaced from the face of the earth by this time? Have the various foreign conquerors spared any pains to crush us out? Why, then, were not the Hindus blotted out of existence, as happened with men in other countries which are uncivilised? Why was not India depopulated and turned into a wilderness? Why, then foreigners would have lost no time to come and settle in India, and till her fertile lands in the same way as they did and are still doing in America, Australia, and Africa! Well, then, my foreigner, you are not so strong as you think yourself to be; it is a vain imagination. First understand that India has strength as well, has a substantial reality of her own yet. Furthermore, understand that India is still living, because she has her own quota yet to give to the general store of the world's civilisation. And you too understand this full well, I mean those of our countrymen who have become thoroughly Europeanised both in external habits and in ways of thought and ideas, and who are continually crying their eyes out and praying to the European to save them—"We are degraded, we have come down to the level of brutes; O ye European people, you are our saviours, have pity on us and raise us from this fallen state!" And you too understand this, who are singing Te Deums and raising a hue and cry that Jesus is come to India, and are seeing the fulfilment of the divine decree in the fullness of time. Oh, dear! No! neither Jesus is come nor Jehovah; nor will they come; they are now busy in saving their own hearths and homes and have no time to come to our country. Here is the selfsame Old Shiva seated as before, the bloody Mother Kâli worshipped with the selfsame paraphernalia, the pastoral Shepherd of Love, Shri Krishna, playing on His flute. Once this Old Shiva, riding on His bull and laboring on His Damaru travelled from India, on the one side, to Sumatra, Borneo, Celebes, Australia, as far as the shores of America, and on the other side, this Old Shiva battened His bull in Tibet, China, Japan, and as far up as Siberia, and is still doing the same. The Mother Kali is still exacting Her worship even in China and Japan: it is She whom the Christians metamorphosed into the Virgin Mary, and worship as the mother of Jesus the Christ. Behold the Himalayas! There to the north is Kailâs, the main abode of the Old Shiva. That throne the ten-headed, twenty-armed, mighty Ravana could not shake—now for the missionaries to attempt the task?—Bless my soul! Here in India will ever be the Old Shiva laboring on his Damaru, the Mother Kali worshipped with animal sacrifice, and the lovable Shri Krishna playing on His flute. Firm as the Himalayas they are; and no attempts of anyone, Christian or other missionaries, will ever be able to remove them. If you cannot bear them—avaunt! For a handful of you, shall a whole nation be wearied out of all patience and bored to death? Why don't you make your way somewhere else where you may find fields to graze upon freely—the wide world is open to you! But no, that they won't do. Where is that strength to do it? They would eat the salt of that Old Shiva and play Him false, slander Him, and sing the glory of a foreign Saviour—dear me! To such of our countrymen who go whimpering before foreigners—"We are very low, we are mean, we are degraded, everything we have is diabolical"—to them we say: "Yes, that may be the truth, forsooth, because you profess to be truthful and we have no reason to disbelieve you; but why do you include the whole nation in that We? Pray, sirs, what sort of good manner is that?"

First, we have to understand that there are not any good qualities which are the privileged monopoly of one nation only. Of course, as with individuals, so with nations, there may be a prevalence of certain good qualities, more or less in one nation than in another.

With us, the prominent idea is Mukti; with the Westerners, it is Dharma. What we desire is Mukti; what they want is Dharma. Here the word "Dharma" is used in the sense of the Mimâmsakas. What is Dharma? Dharma is that which makes man seek for happiness in this world or the next. Dharma is established on work, Dharma is impelling man day and night to run after and work for happiness.

What is Mukti? That which teaches that even the happiness of this life is slavery, and the same is the happiness of the life to come, because neither this world nor the next is beyond the laws of nature; only, the slavery of this world is to that of the next as an iron chain is to a golden one. Again, happiness, wherever it may be, being within the laws of nature, is subject to death and will not last ad infinitum. Therefore man must aspire to become Mukta, he must go beyond the bondage of the body; slavery will not do. This Mokshapath is only in India and nowhere else. Hence is true the oft-repeated saying that Mukta souls are only in India and in no other country. But it is equally true that in future they will be in other countries as well; that is well and good, and a thing of great pleasure to us. There was a time in India when Dharma was compatible with Mukti. There were worshippers of Dharma, such as Yudhishthira, Arjuna, Duryodhana, Bhishma, and Karna, side by side with the aspirants of Mukti, such as Vyâsa, Shuka, and Janaka. On the advent of Buddhism, Dharma was entirely neglected, and the path of Moksha alone became predominant. Hence, we read in the Agni Purâna, in the language of similes, that the demon Gayâsura—that is, Buddha[1]—tried to destroy the world by showing the path of Moksha to all; and therefore the Devas held a council and by stratagem set him at rest for ever. However, the central fact is that the fall of our country, of which we hear so much spoken, is due to the utter want of this Dharma. If the whole nation practices and follows the path of Moksha, that is well and good; but is that possible? Without enjoyment, renunciation can never come; first enjoy and then you can renounce. Otherwise, if the whole nation, all of a sudden, takes up Sannyâsa, it does not gain what it desires, but it loses what it had into the bargain—the bird in the hand is fled, nor is that in the bush caught. When, in the heyday of Buddhistic supremacy, thousands of Sannyâsins lived in every monastery, then it was that the country was just on the verge of its ruin! The Bauddhas, the Christians, the Mussulmans, and the Jains prescribe, in their folly, the same law and the same rule for all. That is a great mistake; education, habits, customs, laws, and rules should be different for different men and nations, in conformity with their difference of temperament. What will it avail, if one tries to make them all uniform by compulsion? The Bauddhas declared, "Nothing is more desirable in life than Moksha; whoever you are, come one and all to take it." I ask, "Is that ever possible?" "You are a householder, you must not concern yourself much with things of that sort: you do your Svadharma (natural duty)"—

---

1. Swamiji afterwards changed this view with reference to Buddha, as is evident from the letter dated Varanasi, the 9th February, 1902, in this volume.

thus say the Hindu scriptures. Exactly so! He who cannot leap one foot, is going to jump across the ocean to Lankâ in one bound! Is it reason? You cannot feed your own family or dole out food to two of your fellow-men, you cannot do even an ordinary piece of work for the common good, in harmony with others—and you are running after Mukti! The Hindu scriptures say, "No doubt, Moksha is far superior to Dharma; but Dharma should be finished first of all". The Bauddhas were confounded just there and brought about all sorts of mischief. Non-injury is right; "Resist not evil" is a great thing—these are indeed grand principles; but the scriptures say, "Thou art a householder; if anyone smites thee on thy cheek, and thou dost not return him an eye for an eye, a tooth for a tooth, thou wilt verily be a sinner." Manu says, "When one has come to kill you, there is no sin in killing him, even though he be a Brâhmin" (Manu, VIII. 350). This is very true, and this is a thing which should not be forgotten. Heroes only enjoy the world. Show your heroism; apply, according to circumstances, the fourfold political maxims of conciliation, bribery, sowing dissensions, and open war, to win over your adversary and enjoy the world—then you will be Dhârmika (righteous). Otherwise, you live a disgraceful life if you pocket your insults when you are kicked and trodden down by anyone who takes it into his head to do so; your life is a veritable hell here, and so is the life hereafter. This is what the Shastras say. Do your Svadharma—this is truth, the truth of truths. This is my advice to you, my beloved co-religionists. Of course, do not do any wrong, do not injure or tyrannise over anyone, but try to do good to others as much as you can. But passively to submit to wrong done by others is a sin—with the householder. He must try to pay them back in their own coin then and there. The householder must earn money with great effort and enthusiasm, and by that must support and bring comforts to his own family and to others, and perform good works as far as possible. If you cannot do that, how do you profess to be a man? You are not a householder even—what to talk of Moksha for you!!

We have said before that Dharma is based on work. The nature of the Dharmika is constant performance of action with efficiency. Why, even the opinion of some Mimamsakas is that those parts of the Vedas which do not enjoin work are not, properly speaking, Vedas at all. One of the aphorisms of Jaimini runs thus: "आम्नायस्य क्रियार्थत्वादानर्थक्यमतदर्थानाम्—The purpose of the Vedas being work, those parts of the Vedas that do not deal with work miss the mark."

"By constant repetition of the syllable Om and by meditating on its meaning, everything can be obtained"; "All sins are washed away by uttering the name of the Lord"; "He gets all, who resigns himself to the Will of God"—yes, these words of the Shastras and the sages are, no doubt, true. But, do you see, thousands of us are, for our whole life, meditating on Om, are getting ecstatic in devotion in the name of the Lord, and are crying, "Thy Will be done, I am fully resigned to Thee! "—and what are they actually getting in return? Absolutely

nothing! How do you account for this? The reason lies here, and it must be fully understood. Whose meditation is real and effective? Who can really resign himself to the Will of God? Who can utter with power irresistible, like that of a thunderbolt, the name of the Lord? It is he who has earned Chitta-shuddhi, that is, whose mind has been purified by work, or in other words, he who is the Dharmika.

Every individual is a centre for the manifestation of a certain force. This force has been stored up as the resultant of our previous works, and each one of us is born with this force at his back. So long as this force has not worked itself out, who can possibly remain quiet and give up work? Until then, he will have to enjoy or suffer according to the fruition of his good or bad work and will be irresistibly impelled to do work. Since enjoyment and work cannot be given up till then, is it not better to do good rather than bad works—to enjoy happiness rather than suffer misery? Shri Râmprasâd[2] used to say, "They speak of two works, 'good' and 'bad'; of them, it is better to do the good."

Now what is that good which is to be pursued? The good for him who desires Moksha is one, and the good for him who wants Dharma is another. This is the great truth which the Lord Shri Krishna, the revealer of the Gita, has tried therein to explain, and upon this great truth is established the Varnâshrama[3] system and the doctrine of Svadharma etc. of the Hindu religion.

अद्वेष्टा सर्वभूतानां मैत्रः करुण एव च ।
निर्ममो निरहंकारः समदुःखसुखः क्षमी ॥ (Gita, XII.13.)

—"He who has no enemy, and is friendly and compassionate towards all, who is free from the feelings of 'me and mine', even-minded in pain and pleasure, and forbearing"—these and other epithets of like nature are for him whose one goal in life is Moksha.

क्लैब्यं मा स्म गमः पार्थ नैतत्त्वय्युपपद्यते ।
क्षुद्रं हृदयदौर्बल्यं त्यक्त्वोत्तिष्ठ परन्तप ॥ (Gita, II. 3.)

—"Yield not to unmanliness, O son of Prithâ! Ill cloth it befit thee. Cast off this mean faint-heartedness and arise. O scorcher of thine enemies."

तस्मात्त्वमुत्तिष्ठ यशो लभस्व जित्वा शत्रून् भुङ्क्ष्व राज्यं समृद्धम् ।
मयैवैते निहताः पूर्वमेव निमित्तमात्रं भव सव्यसाचिन् ॥ (Gita, XI. 33.)

—"Therefore do thou arise and acquire fame. After conquering thy enemies, enjoy unrivalled dominion; verily, by Myself have they been already slain; be thou merely the instrument, O Savyasâchin (Arjuna)." In these and similar passages in the Gita the Lord is showing the way to Dharma. Of course, work is always mixed with good and evil, and to work, one has to incur sin, more or less. But what of that? Let it be so. Is not something better than nothing? Is not insufficient food better

2. A Bengali saint, devotee of Kâli, and an inspired poet who composed songs in praise of the Deity, expressing the highest truths of religion in the simplest words.

3. Four castes and four stages of life.

than going without any? Is not doing work, though mixed with good and evil, better than doing nothing and passing an idle and inactive life, and being like stones? The cow never tells a lie, and the stone never steals, but, nevertheless, the cow remains a cow and the stone a stone. Man steals and man tells lies, and again it is man that becomes a god. With the prevalence of the Sâttvika essence, man becomes inactive and rests always in a state of deep Dhyâna or contemplation; with the prevalence of the Rajas, he does bad as well as good works; and with the prevalence of the Tamas again, he becomes inactive and inert. Now, tell me, looking from outside, how are we to understand, whether you are in a state wherein the Sattva or the Tamas prevails? Whether we are in the state of Sattvika calmness, beyond all pleasure and pain, and past all work and activity, or whether we are in the lowest Tâmasika state, lifeless, passive, dull as dead matter, and doing no work, because there is no power in us to do it, and are, thus, silently and by degrees, getting rotten and corrupted within—I seriously ask you this question and demand an answer. Ask your own mind, and you shall know what the reality is. But, what need to wait for the answer? The tree is known by its fruit. The Sattva prevailing, the man is inactive, he is calm, to be sure; but that inactivity is the outcome of the centralization of great powers, that calmness is the mother of tremendous energy. That highly Sattivka man, that great soul, has no longer to work as we do with hands and feet—by his mere willing only, all his works are immediately accomplished to perfection. That man of predominating Sattva is the Brahmin, the worshipped of all. Has he to go about from door to door, begging others to worship him? The Almighty Mother of the universe writes with Her own hand, in golden letters on his forehead, "Worship ye all, this great one, this son of Mine", and the world reads and listens to it and humbly bows down its head before him in obedience. That man is really—

अद्वेष्टा सर्वभूतानां मैत्रः करुण एव च ।
निर्ममो निरहंकारः समदुःखसुखः क्षमी ॥ (Gita, XII.13.)

—"He who has no enemy, and is friendly and compassionate towards all, who is free from the feelings of 'me and mine', even-minded in pain and pleasure, and forbearing." And mark you, those things which you see in pusillanimous, effeminate folk who speak in a nasal tone chewing every syllable, whose voice is as thin as of one who has been starving for a week, who are like a tattered wet rag, who never protest or are moved even if kicked by anybody—those are the signs of the lowest Tamas, those are the signs of death, not of Sattva—all corruption and stench. It is because Arjuna was going to fall into the ranks of these men that the Lord is explaining matters to him so elaborately in the Gita. Is that not the fact? Listen to the very first words that came out of the mouth of the Lord, "क्लैब्यं मा स्म गमः पार्थ नेतत्त्वय्युपपद्यते—Yield not to unmanliness, O Pârtha! Ill, doth it befit thee!" and then later, "तस्मात्त्वमुत्तिष्ठ यशो लभस्व—Therefore do thou arise and acquire fame." Coming under the influence of the Jains, Buddhas, and others, we have joined the lines of those

Tamasika people. During these last thousand years, the whole country is filling the air with the name of the Lord and is sending its prayers to Him; and the Lord is never lending His ears to them. And why should He? When even man never hears the cries of the fool, do you think God will? Now the only way out is to listen to the words of the Lord in the Gita, "क्लैब्यं मा स्म गमः पार्थ—Yield not to unmanliness, O Partha!" "तस्मात्त्वमुत्तिष्ठ यशो लभस्व—Therefore do thou arise and acquire fame."

Now let us go on with our subject-matter—the East and the West. First see the irony of it. Jesus Christ, the God of the Europeans, has taught: Have no enemy, bless them that curse you; whosoever shall smite thee on thy right cheek, turn to him the other also; stop all your work and be ready for the next world; the end of the world is near at hand. And our Lord in the Gita is saying: Always work with great enthusiasm, destroy your enemies and enjoy the world. But, after all, it turned out to be exactly the reverse of what Christ or Krishna implied. The Europeans never took the words of Jesus Christ seriously. Always of active habits, being possessed of a tremendous Râjasika nature, they are gathering with great enterprise and youthful ardour the comforts and luxuries of the different countries of the world and enjoying them to their hearts' content. And we are sitting in a corner, with our bag and baggage, pondering on death day and night, and singing, "नलिनीदलगतजलमतितरलं तद्वज्जीवितमतिशयचपलम्—Very tremulous and unsteady is the water on the lotus-leaf; so is the life of man frail and transient"—with the result that it is making our blood run cold and our flesh creep with the fear of Yama, the god of death; and Yama, too, alas, has taken us at our word, as it were—plague and all sorts of maladies have entered into our country! Who are following the teachings of the Gita?—the Europeans. And who are acting according to the will of Jesus Christ?—The descendants of Shri Krishna! This must be well understood. The Vedas were the first to find and proclaim the way to Moksha, and from that one source, the Vedas, was taken whatever any great Teacher, say, Buddha or Christ, afterwards taught. Now, they were Sannyasins, and therefore they "had no enemy and were friendly and compassionate towards all". That was well and good for them. But why this attempt to compel the whole world to follow the same path to Moksha? "Can beauty be manufactured by rubbing and scrubbing? Can anybody's love be won by threats or force?" What does Buddha or Christ prescribe for the man who neither wants Moksha nor is fit to receive it?—Nothing! Either you must have Moksha or you are doomed to destruction—these are the only two ways held forth by them, and there is no middle course. You are tied hand and foot in the matter of trying for anything other than Moksha. There is no way shown how you may enjoy the world a little for a time; not only all openings to that are hermetically sealed to you, but, in addition, there are obstructions put at every step. It is only the Vedic religion which considers ways and means and lays down rules for the fourfold attainment of man, comprising Dharma, Artha, Kama, and Moksha. Buddha ruined us, and so did Christ ruin Greece and Rome! Then, in due course of time, fortunately, the Europeans became Protestants, shook off the teachings of Christ as represented by Papal authority, and heaved a sigh of relief. In India, Kumârila again brought into currency the Karma-Mârga, the way of Karma only, and Shankara and Râmânuja firmly re-established the Eternal Vedic religion, harmonising and balancing in due proportions Dharma, Artha, Kama, and Moksha. Thus the nation was brought to the way of regaining its lost life; but India has three hundred million souls to wake, and hence the delay. To revive three hundred millions—can it be done in a day?

The aims of the Buddhistic and the Vedic religions are the same, but the means adopted by the Buddhistic are not right. If the Buddhistic means were correct, then why have we been thus hopelessly lost and ruined? It will not do to say that the efflux of time has naturally wrought this. Can time work, transgressing the laws of cause and effect?

Therefore, though the aims are the same, the Bauddhas for want of right means have degraded India. Perhaps my Bauddha brothers will be offended at this remark, and fret and fume; but there's no help for it; the truth ought to be told, and I do not care for the result. The right and correct means is that of the Vedas—the Jâti Dharma, that is, the Dharma enjoined according to the different castes—the Svadharma, that is, one's own Dharma, or set of duties prescribed for man according to his capacity and position—which is the very basis of Vedic religion and Vedic society. Again, perhaps, I am offending many of my friends, who are saying, I suppose, that I am flattering my own countrymen. Here let me ask them once for all: What do I gain by such flattery? Do they support me with any money or means? On the contrary, they try their best to get possession of money which I secure by begging from outside of India for feeding the famine-stricken and the helpless; and if they do not get it, they abuse and slander! Such then, O my educated countrymen, are the people of my country. I know them too well to expect anything from them by flattery. I know they have to be treated like the insane; and anyone who administers medicine to a madman must be ready to be rewarded with kicks and bites; but he is the true friend who forces the medicine down the throats of such and bears with them in patience.

Now, this Jati Dharma, this Svadharma, is the path of welfare of all societies in every land, the ladder to ultimate freedom. With the decay of this Jati Dharma, this Svadharma, has come the downfall of our land. But the Jati Dharma or Svadharma as commonly understood at present by the higher castes is rather a new evil, which has to be guarded against. They think they know everything of Jati Dharma, but really they know nothing of it. Regarding their own village customs as the eternal customs laid down by the Vedas, and appropriating to themselves all privileges, they are going to their doom! I am not talking of caste as determined by qualitative distinction, but of the hereditary caste system. I admit that the qualitative caste system is the primary one; but the pity is qualities yield to birth in two or three generations. Thus the vital point of our national life has been touched; otherwise, why should we sink to this degraded state? Read in the Gita, "संकरस्य च कर्ता स्यामुपहन्यामिमाः प्रजाः—I should then be the cause of the admixture of races, and I should thus ruin these beings." How came this terrible Varna-Sâmkarya—this confounding mixture of all castes—and disappearance of all qualitative distinctions? Why has the white complexion of our forefathers now become black? Why did the Sattvaguna give place to the prevailing Tamas with a sprinkling, as it were, of Rajas in it? That is a long story to tell, and I reserve my answer for some future occasion. For the present, try to understand this, that if the Jati Dharma be rightly and truly preserved, the nation shall never fall. If this is true, then what was it that brought our downfall? That we have fallen is the sure sign that the basis of the Jati Dharma has been tampered with. Therefore, what you call the Jati Dharma is quite contrary to what we have in fact. First, read your own Shastras through and through, and you will easily see that what the Shastras define as caste-Dharma, has disappeared almost everywhere from the land. Now try to bring back the true Jati Dharma, and then it will be a real and sure boon to the country. What I have learnt and understood, I am telling you plainly. I have not been imported from some foreign land to come and save you, that I should countenance all your foolish customs and give scientific explanations for them; it does not cost our foreign friends anything, they can well afford to do so. You cheer them up and heap applause upon them, and that is the acme of their ambition. But if dirt and dust be flung at your faces, it falls on mine too! Don't you see that?

I have said elsewhere that every nation has a national purpose of its own. Either in obedience to the Law of nature, or by virtue of the superior genius of the great ones, the social manners and customs of every nation are being moulded into shape, so as to bring that purpose to fruition. In the life of every nation, besides that purpose and those manners and customs that are essentially necessary to effect that purpose, all others are superfluous. It does not matter much whether those superfluous customs and manners grow or disappear; but a nation is sure to die when the main purpose of its life is hurt.

When we were children, we heard the story of a certain ogress who had her soul living in a small bird, and unless the bird was killed, the ogress would never die. The life of a nation is also like that. Again another thing you will observe, that a nation will never greatly grudge if it be deprived of these rights which have not much to do with its national purpose, nay, even if all of such are wrested from it; but when the slightest blow is given to that purpose on which rests its national life, that moment it reacts with tremendous power.

Take for instance the case of the three living nations, of whose history you know more or less, viz. the French, the English, and the Hindu. Political independence is the backbone of the French character. French subjects bear calmly all oppressions. Burden them with heavy taxes, they will not raise the least voice against them; compel the whole nation to join the army, they never complain; but the instant anyone meddles with that political independence, the whole nation will rise as one man and madly react. No one man shall be allowed to usurp authority over us; whether learned or ignorant, rich or poor, of noble birth or of the lower classes, we have equal share in the Government of our country, and in the independent control of our society—this is the root-principle of the French character. He must suffer Who will try to interfere with this freedom.

In the English character, the "give and take" policy, the business principle of the trader, is principally inherent. To the English, just and equitable distribution of wealth is of essential interest. The Englishman humbly submits to the king and to the privileges of the nobility; only if he has to pay a farthing from his pocket, he must demand an account of it. There is the king; that is all right; he is ready to obey and honour him; but if the king wants money, the Englishman says: All right, but first let me understand why it is needed, what good it will bring; next, I must have my say in the matter of how it is to be spent, and then I shall part with it. The king, once trying to exact money from the English people by force, brought about a great revolution. They killed the king.

The Hindu says that political and social independence are well and good, but the real thing is spiritual independence—Mukti. This is our national purpose; whether you take the Vaidika, the Jaina, or the Bauddha, the Advaita, the Vishishtâdvaita, or the Dvaita—there, they are all of one mind. Leave that point untouched and do whatever you like, the Hindu is quite unconcerned and keeps silence; but if you run foul of him there, beware, you court your ruin. Rob him of everything he has, kick him, call him a "nigger" or any such name, he does not care much; only keep that one gate of religion free and unmolested. Look here, how in the modern period the Pathan dynasties were coming and going, but could not get a firm hold of their Indian Empire, because they were all along attacking the Hindu's religion. And see, how firmly based, how tremendously strong was the Mogul Empire. Why? Because the Moguls left that point untouched. In fact, Hindus were the real prop of the Mogul Empire; do you not know that Jahangir, Shahjahan, and Dara Shikoh were all born of Hindu mothers? Now then observe—as soon as the ill-fated Aurangzeb again touched that point, the vast Mogul Empire vanished in an instant like a dream. Why is it that the English throne is so firmly established in India? Because it never touches the religion of the land in any way. The sapient Christian missionaries tried to tamper a little with this point, and the result was the Mutiny of 1857. So long as the English understand this thoroughly and act accordingly, their throne in India will remain unsullied and unshaken. The wise and far-seeing among the English also comprehend this and admit it—read Lord Roberts's Forty-one Years in India[1].

1. Vide 30th and 31st Chapters.

Now you understand clearly where the soul of this ogress is—it is in religion. Because no one was able to destroy that, therefore the Hindu nation is still living, having survived so many troubles and tribulations. Well, One Indian scholar asks, "what is the use of keeping the soul of the nation in religion? Why not keep it in social or political independence, as is the case with other nations?" It is very easy to talk like that. If it be granted, for the sake of argument, that religion and spiritual independence, and soul, God, and Mukti are all false, even then see how the matter stands. As the same fire is manifesting itself in different forms, so the same one great Force is manifesting itself as political independence with the French, as mercantile genius and expansion of the sphere of equity with the English, and as the desire for Mukti or spiritual independence with the Hindu. Be it noted that by the impelling of this great Force, has been moulded the French and the English character, through several centuries of vicissitudes of fortune; and also by the inspiration of that great Force, with the rolling of thousands of centuries, has been the present evolution of the Hindu national character. I ask in all seriousness—which is easier, to give up our national character evolved out of thousands of centuries, or your grafted foreign character of a few hundred years? Why do not the English forget their warlike habits and give up fighting and bloodshed, and sit calm and quiet concentrating their whole energy on making religion the sole aim of their life?

The fact is, that the river has come down a thousand miles from its source in the mountains; does it, or can it go back to its source? If it ever tries to trace back its course, it will simply dry up by being dissipated in all directions. Anyhow the river is sure to fall into the ocean, sooner or later, either by passing through open and beautiful plaints or struggling through grimy soil. If our national life of these ten thousand years has been a mistake, then there is no help for it; and if we try now to form a new character, the inevitable result will be that we shall die.

But, excuse me if I say that it is sheer ignorance and want of proper understanding to think like that, namely, that our national ideal has been a mistake. First go to other countries and study carefully their manners and conditions with your own eyes—not with others'—and reflect on them with a thoughtful brain, if you have it: then read your own scriptures, your ancient literature travel throughout India, and mark the people of her different parts and their ways and habits with the wide-awake eye of an intelligent and keen observer—not with a fool's eye—and you will see as clear as noonday that the nation is still living intact and its life is surely pulsating. You will find there also that, hidden under the ashes of apparent death, the fire of our national life is yet smouldering and that the life of this nation is religion, its language religion, and its idea religion; and your politics, society, municipality, plague-prevention work, and famine-relief work—all these things will be done as they have been done all along here, viz. only through religion; otherwise all your frantic yelling and bewailing will end in nothing, my friend!

Besides, in every country, the means is the same after all, that is, whatever only a handful of powerful men dictate becomes the *fait accompli*; the rest of the men only follow like a flock of sheep, that's all. I have seen your Parliament, your Senate, your vote, majority, ballot; it is the same thing everywhere, my friend. The powerful men in every country are moving society whatever way they like, and the rest are only like a flock of sheep. Now the question is this, who are these men of power in India?—they who are giants in religion. It is they who lead our society; and it is they again who change our social laws and usages when necessity demands: and we listen to them silently anti do what they command. The only difference with ours is, that we have not that superfluous fuss and bustle of the majority, the vote, ballot, and similar concomitant tugs-of-war as in other countries. That is all.

Of course we do not get that education which the common people in the West do, by the system of vote and ballot etc., but, on the other hand, we have not also amongst us that class of people who, in the name of politics, rob others and fatten themselves by sucking the very life-blood of the masses in all European countries. If you ever saw, my friend that shocking sight behind the scene of acting of these politicians—that revelry of bribery, that robbery in broad daylight, that dance of the Devil in man, which are practiced on such occasions—you would be hopeless about man! "Milk goes abegging from door to door, while the grog-shop is crowded; the chaste woman seldom gets the wherewithal to hide her modesty, while the woman of the town flutters about in all her jewelry!" They that have money have kept the government of the land under their thumb, are robbing the people and sending them as soldiers to fight and be slain on foreign shores, so that, in case of victory; their coffers may be full of gold bought by the blood of the subject-people on the field of battle. And the subject-people? Well, theirs is only to shed their blood. This is politics! Don't be startled, my friend; don't be lost in its mazes.

First of all, try to understand this: Does man make laws, or do laws make man? Does man make money, or does money make man? Does man make name and fame, or name and fame make man?

Be a man first, my friend, and you will see how all those things and the rest will follow of themselves after you. Give up that hateful malice, that dog-like bickering and barking at one another, and take your stand on goal purpose, right means, righteous courage, and be brave When you are born a man, leave some indelible mark behind you. "When you first came to this world, O Tulsi[2], the world rejoiced and you cried; now live your life in doing such acts that when you will leave this world, the world will cry for you and you will leave it laughing." If you can do that, then you are a man; otherwise, what good are you?

---

2. A poet and a devotee—the author of the Ramcharitmanasa. Here the poet is addressing himself.

Next, you must understand this, my friend, that we have many things to learn from other nations. The man who says he has nothing more to learn is already at his last grasp. The nation that says it knows everything is on the very brink of destruction! "As long as I live, so long do I learn." But one point to note here is that when we take anything from others, we must mould it after our own way. We shall add to our stock what others have to teach, but we must always be careful to keep intact what is essentially our own. For instance, Suppose I want to have my dinner cooked in the European fashion. When taking food, the Europeans sit on chairs, and we are accustomed to squat on the floor. To imitate the Europeans, if I order my dinner to be served, on a table and have to sit on a chair more than an hour, my feet will be in a fair way of going to Yama's door, as they say, and I shall writhe in torture; what do you say to that? So I must squat on the floor in my own style, while having their dishes. Similarly, whenever we learn anything from others, we must mould it after our own fashion, always preserving in full our characteristic nationality. Let me ask, "Does man wear clothes or do clothes make the man?" The man of genius in any, dress commands respect; but nobody cares for fools like me, though carrying, like the washerman's ass, a load of clothes on my back.

II — CUSTOMS: EASTERN AND WESTERN

The foregoing, by way of an introduction, has come to be rather long; but after all this talk it will be easier for us to compare the two nations. They are good, and we are also good. "You can neither praise the one nor blame the other; both the scales are equal." Of course, there are gradations and varieties of good, this is all.

According to us, there are three things in the makeup of man. There is the body, there is the mind, and there is the soul. First let us consider the body, which is the most external thing about man.

First, see how various are the differences with respect to the body. How many varieties of nose, face, hair, height, complexion, breadth, etc., there are!

The modern ethnologists hold that variety of complexion is due to intermixture of blood. Though the hot or cold climate of the place to a certain extent affects the complexion, no doubt, yet the main cause of its change is heredity. Even in the coldest parts of the world, people with dark complexions are seen, and again in the hottest countries white men are seen to live. The complexion of the aboriginal tribes of Canada, in America, and of the Eskimos of the Northern Polar regions, is not white. While islands, such as Borneo, Celebes, etc., situated in the equatorial regions are peopled by white aborigines.

According to the Hindu Shastras, the three Hindu castes, Brahmana, Kshatriya, and Vaishya, and the several nations outside India, to wit, Cheen, Hun, Darad, Pahlava, Yavana, and Khâsh are all Aryas. This Cheen of our Shastras is not the modern Chinaman. Besides, in those days, the Chinamen did not call themselves Cheen at all. There was a distinct, powerful nation, called Cheen, living in the north-eastern parts of Kashmir, and the Darads lived where are now seen the hill-tribes between India and Afghanistan. Some remnants of the ancient Cheen are yet to be found in very small numbers, and Daradisthan is yet in existence. In the Râjatarangini, the history of Kashmir, references are often made to the supremacy of the powerful Darad-Raj. An ancient tribe of Huns reigned for a long period in the north-western parts of India. The Tibetans now call themselves Hun, but this Hun is perhaps "Hune". The fact is, that the Huns referred to in Manu are not the modern Tibetans, but it is quite probable that the modern Tibetans are the product of a mixture of the ancient Aryan Huns and some other Mogul tribes that came to Tibet from Central Asia. According to Prjevalski and the Duc d' Orleans, the Russian and French travellers, there are still found in some parts of Tibet tribes with faces and eyes of the Aryan type. "Yavana" was the name given to the Greeks. There has been much dispute about the origin of this name. Some say that the name Yavana was first used to designate a tribe of Greeks inhabiting the place called "Ionia", and hence, in the Pâli writs of the Emperor Asoka, the Greeks are named "Yonas", and afterwards from this "Yona" the Sanskrit word Yavana, was derived. Again, according to some of our Indian antiquarians, the word Yavana does not stand for the Greeks. But all these views are wrong. The original word is Yavana itself; for not only the Hindus but the ancient Egyptians and the Babylonians as well called the Greeks by that name. By the word Pahlava is meant the ancient Parsees, speaking the Pahlavi tongue. Even now, Khash denotes the semi-civilised Aryan tribes living in mountainous regions and in the Himalayas, and the word is still used in this sense. In that sense, the present Europeans are the descendants of the Khash; in other words, those Aryan tribes that were uncivilised in ancient days are all Khash.

In the opinion of modern savants, the Aryans had reddish-white complexion, black or red hair, straight noses, well-drawn eyes, etc.; and the formation of the skull varied a little according to the colour of the hair. Where the complexion is dark, there the change has come to pass owing to the mixture of the pure Aryan blood with black races. They hold that there are still some tribes to the west of the Himalayan borders who are of pure Aryan blood, and that the rest are all of mixed blood; otherwise, how could they be dark? But the European Pundits ought to know by this time that, in the southern parts of India, many children are born with red hair, which after two or three years changes into black, and that in the Himalayas many have red hair and blue or grey eyes.

Let the Pundits fight among themselves; it is the Hindus who have all along called themselves Aryas. Whether of pure or mixed blood, the Hindus are Aryas; there it rests. If the Europeans do not like us, Aryas, because we are dark, let them take another name for themselves—what is that to us?

Whether black or white, it does not matter; but of all the nations of the world, the Hindus are the handsomest and finest in feature. I am not bragging nor saying anything in exaggeration because they belong to my own nationality, but this fact is known all over the world. Where else can one find a higher percentage of fine-featured men and women than in India? Besides, it has to be taken into consideration how much more is required in our country to make us look handsome than in other countries, because our bodies are so much more exposed. In other countries, the attempt is always to make ugly persons appear beautiful under cover of elaborate dresses and clothes.

Of course, in point of health, the Westerners are far superior to us. In the West, men of forty years and women of fifty years are still young. This is, no doubt, because they take good food, dress well and live in a good climate, and above all, the secret is that they do not marry at an early age. Ask those few strong tribes among ourselves and see what their marriageable age is. Ask the hill tribes, such as, the Goorkhas, the Punjabis, the Jats, and the Afridis, what their marriageable age is. Then read your own Shastras—thirty is the age fixed for the Brahmana, twenty-five for the Kshatriya, and twenty for the Vaishya. In point of longevity and physical and mental strength, there is a great difference between the Westerners and ourselves. As soon as we attain to forty, our hope and physical and mental strength are on the decline. While, at that age, full of youthful vigour and hope, they have only made a start.

We are vegetarians—most of our diseases are of the stomach; our old men and women generally die of stomach complaints. They of the West take meat—most of their diseases are of the heart; their old men and women generally die of heart or lung diseases. A learned doctor of the West observes that the people who have chronic stomach complaints generally tend to a melancholy and renouncing nature, and the people suffering from complaints of the heart and the upper parts of the body have always hope and faith to the last; the cholera patient is from the very beginning afraid of death, while the consumptive patient hopes to the last moment that he will recover. "Is it owing to this," my doctor friend may with good reasoning ask, "that the Indians always talk and think of death and renunciation?" As yet I have not been able to find a satisfactory answer to this; but the question seems to have an air of truth about it, and demands serious consideration.

In our country, people suffer little from diseases of the teeth and hair; in the West, few people have natural, healthy teeth, and baldness is met with everywhere. Our women bore their noses and ears for wearing ornaments; in the West, among the higher classes, the women do not do those things much, nowadays; but by squeezing the waist, making the spine crooked, and thus displacing the liver and spleen and disfiguring the form, they suffer the torment of death to make themselves shapely in appearance and added to that is the burden of dress, over which they have to show their features to the best advantage. Their Western dress is, however, more suited for work. With the exception of the dress worn in society by the ladies of the wealthy classes, the dress of the women in general is ugly. The Sâri of our women, and the Chogâ, Châpkan, and turban of our men defy comparison as regards beauty in dress. The tight dresses cannot approach in beauty the loose ones that fall in natural folds. But all our dresses being flowing, and in folds, are not suited for doing work; in doing work, they are spoiled and done for. There is such a thing as fashion in the West. Their fashion is in dress, ours in ornaments, though nowadays it is entering a little into clothes also. Paris is the centre of fashion for ladies' dress and London for men's. The actresses of Paris often set the fashions. What new fashion of dress a distinguished actress of the time would wear, the fashionable world would greedily imitate. The big firms of dressmakers set the fashions nowadays. We can form no idea of the millions of pounds that are spent every year in the making of dress in the West. The dress-making business has become a regular science. What colour of dress will suit with the complexion of the girl and the colour of her hair, what special feature of her body should be disguised, and what displayed to the best advantage—these and many other like important points, the dressmakers have seriously to consider. Again, the dress that ladies of very high position wear, others have to wear also, otherwise they lose their caste! This is FASHION.

Then again, this fashion is changing every day, so to say; it is sure to change four times with the four seasons of the year, and, besides, many other times as well. The rich people have their dresses made after the latest fashion by expert firms; those who belong to the middle classes have them often done at home by women-tailors, or do them themselves. If the new fashion approaches very near to their last one, then they just change or adjust their clothes accordingly; otherwise, they buy new ones. The wealthy classes give away their dresses which have gone out of fashion to their dependents and servants. The ladies' maids and valets sell them, and those are exported to the various colonies established by the Europeans in Africa, Asia, and Australia, and there they are used again. The dresses of those who are immensely rich are all ordered from Paris; the less wealthy have them copied in their own country by their own dressmakers. But the ladies' hats must be of French make. As a matter of fact, the dress of the English and the German women is not good; they do not generally follow the Paris fashions—except, of course, a few of the rich and the higher classes. So, the women of other countries indulge in jokes at their expense. But men in England mostly dress very well. The American men and women, without distinction, wear very fashionable dress. Though the American Government imposes heavy duties on all dresses imported from London or Paris, to keep out foreign goods from the country—yet, all the same, the women order their dress from Paris, and men, from London. Thousands of men and women are employed in daily introducing into the market woollen and silk fabrics of various kinds and colours, and thousands, again, are manufacturing all sorts of dresses out of them. Unless the dress is exactly up to date, ladies and gentle-

men cannot walk in the street without being remarked upon by the fashionable. Though we have not all this botheration of the fashion in dress in our country, we have, instead, a fashion in ornaments, to a certain extent. The merchants dealing in silk, woollen, and other materials in the West have their watchful eyes always fixed on the way the fashion changes, and what sort of things people have begun to like; or they hit upon a new fashion, out of their own brain, and try to draw the attention of the people thereto. When once a merchant succeeds in gaining the eyes of the people to the fashion brought into the market by him, he is a made man for life. At the time of the Emperor Napoleon III of France, his wife, the Empress Eugenie, was the universally recognised avatar of fashion of the West. The shawl, of Kashmir were her special favourites, and therefore shawls worth millions of rupees used to be exported every year, in her time, from Kashmir to Europe. With the fall of Napoleon III, the fashion has changed, and Kashmir shawls no longer sell. And as for the merchants of our country, they always walk in the old rut. They could not opportunely hit upon any new style to catch the fancy of the West under the altered circumstances, and so the market was lost to them. Kashmir received a severe shock and her big and rich merchants all of a sudden failed.

This world, if you have the eyes to see, is yours—if not, it is mine; do you think that anyone waits for another? The Westerners are devising new means and methods to attract the luxuries and the comforts of different parts of the world. They watch the situation with ten eyes and work with two hundred hands, as it were; while we will never do what the authors of Shastras have not written in books, and thus we are moving in the same old groove, and there is no attempt to seek anything original and new; and the capacity to do that is lost to us now. The whole nation is rending the skies with the cry for food and dying of starvation. Whose fault is it? Ours! What means are we taking in hand to find a way out of the pitiable situation? Zero! Only making great noise by our big and empty talk! That is all that we are doing. Why not come put of your narrow comer and see, with your eyes open, how the world is moving onwards? Then the mind will open and the power of thinking and of timely action will come of itself. You certainly know the story of the Devas and the Asuras. The Devas have faith in their soul, in God, and in the after-life, while the Asuras give importance to this life, and devote themselves to enjoying this world and trying to have bodily comforts in every possible way. We do not mean to discuss here whether the Devas are better than the Asuras, or the Asuras than the Devas, but, reading their descriptions in the Purânas, the Asuras seem to be, truth to tell, more like MEN, and far more manly than the Devas; the Devas are inferior, without doubt, to the Asuras, in many respects. Now, to understand the East and the West, we cannot do better than interpret the Hindus as the sons of the Devas and the Westerners as the sons of the Asuras.

First, let us see about their respective ideas of cleanliness of the body. Purity means cleanliness of mind and body; the latter is effected by the use of water etc. No nation in the world is as cleanly in the body as the Hindu, who uses water very freely. Taking a plunge bath is wellnigh scarce in other nations, with a few exceptions. The English have introduced it into their country after coming in contact with India. Even now, ask those of our students who have resided in England for education, and they will tell you how insufficient the arrangements for bathing are there. When the Westerners bathe—and that is once a week—they change their inner clothing. Of course, nowadays, among those who have means, many bathe daily and among Americans the number is larger; the Germans once in a week, the French and others very rarely! Spain and Italy are warm countries, but there it is still less! Imagine their eating of garlic in abundance, profuse perspiration day and night, and yet no bath! Ghosts must surely run away from them, what to say of men! What is meant by bath in the West? Why, the washing of face, head, and hands, i.e. only those parts which are exposed. A millionaire friend of mine once invited me to come over to Paris: Paris, which is the capital of modern civilisation—Paris, the heaven of luxury, fashion, and merriment on earth—the centre of arts and sciences. My friend accommodated me in a huge palatial hotel, where arrangements for meals were in a right royal style, but, for bath—well, no name of it. Two days I suffered silently—till at last I could bear it no longer, and had to address my friend thus: "Dear brother, let this royal luxury be with you and yours! I am panting to get out of this situation. Such hot weather, and no facility of bathing; if it continues like this, I shall be in imminent danger of turning mad like a rabid dog." Hearing this, my friend became very sorry for me and annoyed with the hotel authorities, and said: "I won't let you stay here any more, let us go and find out a better place". Twelve of the chief hotels were seen, but no place for bathing was there in any of them. There are independent bathing-houses, where one can go and have a bath for four or five rupees. Good heavens! That very afternoon I read in a paper that an old lady entered into the bath-tub and died then and there! Whatever the doctors may say, I am inclined to think that perhaps that was the first occasion in her life to come into contact with so much water, and the frame collapsed by the sudden shock! This is no exaggeration. Then, the Russians and some others are awfully unclean in that line. Starting from Tibet, it is about the same all over those regions. In every boarding house in America, of course, there is a bathroom, and an arrangement of pipe-water.

See, however, the difference here. Why do we Hindus bathe? Because of the fear of incurring sin. The Westerners wash their hands and face for cleanliness' sake. Bathing with us means pouring water over the body, though the oil and the dirt may stick on and show themselves. Again, our Southern Indian brothers decorate themselves with such long and wide caste-marks that it requires, perchance the use of a pumice-stone to rub them off. Our bath, on the other hand, is an easy matter—to have a plunge in, anywhere; but not so, in the West. There they have to put off a load of clothes, and how many buttons and hooks and eyes are there! We do not feel any delicacy to show our body; to them it is awful, but among men, say, between father and son, there is no impropriety; only before women you have to cover yourself cap-a-pie.

This custom of external cleanliness, like all other customs, sometimes turns out to be, in the long run, rather a tyranny or the very reverse of Âchâra (cleanliness). The European says that all bodily matters have to be attended to in private. Well and good. "It is vulgar to spit before other people. To rinse your mouth before others is disgraceful." So, for fear of censure, they do not wash their mouth after meals, and the result is that the teeth gradually decay. Here is non-observance of cleanliness for fear of society or civilisation. With us, it is the other extreme—to rinse and wash the mouth before all men, or sitting in the street, making a noise as if you were sick—this is rather tyranny. Those things should, no doubt, be done privately and silently, but not to do them for fear of society is also equally wrong.

Again, society patiently bears and accommodates itself to those customs which are unavoidable in particular climates. In a warm country like ours, we drink glass after glass of water; now, how can we help eructating; but in the West, that habit is very ungentlemanly. But there, if you blow the nose and use your pocket handkerchief at the time of eating—that is not objectionable, but with us, it is disgusting. In a cold country like theirs, one cannot avoid doing it now and then.

We Hindus hold dirt in abomination very much, but, all the same, we are, in point of fact, frequently dirty ourselves. Dirt is so repugnant to us that if we touch it we bathe; and so to keep ourselves away from it, we leave a heap of it to rot near the house—the only thing to be careful about is not to touch it; but, on the other hand, do we ever think that we are living virtually in hell? To avoid one uncleanliness, we court another and a greater uncleanliness; to escape from one evil, we follow on the heels of another and a greater evil. He who keeps dirt heaped in his house is a sinner, no doubt about that. And for his retribution he has not to wait for the next life; it recoils on his head betimes—in this very life.

The grace of both Lakshmi (goddess of fortune) and Sarasvati (goddess of learning) now shines on the peoples of the Western countries. They do not stop at the mere acquisition of the objects of enjoyment, but in all their actions they seek for a sort of beauty and grace. In eating and drinking, in their homes and surroundings, in everything, they want to see an all-round elegance. We also had that trait once—when there was wealth and prosperity in the land. We have now too much poverty, but, to make matters worse, we are courting our ruin in two ways—namely, we are throwing away what we have as our own, and labouring in vain to make others' ideals and habits ours. Those national virtues that we had are gradually disappearing, and we are not acquiring any of the

Western ones either? In sitting, walking, talking, etc., there was in the olden days a traditional, specific trait of our own; that is now gone, and withal we have not the ability to take in the Western modes of etiquette. Those ancient religious rites, practices, studies, etc., that were left to us, you are consigning to the tide-waters to be swept away—and yet something new and suitable to the exigencies of the time, to make up for them, is not striking its roots and becoming stable with us. In oscillating between these two lines, all our present distress lies. The Bengal that is to be has not as yet got a stable footing. It is our arts that have fared the worst of all. In the days gone by, our old women used to paint the floors, doors, and walls of their houses with a paste of rice-powder, drawing various beautiful figures; they used to cut plantain leaves in an artistic manner, to serve the food on; they used to lavish their art in nicely arranging the different comestibles on the plates. Those arts, in these days, have gradually disappeared or are doing so.

Of course new things have to be learnt, have to be introduced and worked out; but is that to be done by sweeping away all that is old, just because it is old? What new things have you learnt? Not any—save and except a jumble of words! What really useful science or art have you acquired? Go, and see, even now in the distant villages, the old woodwork and brickwork. The carpenters of your towns cannot even turn out a decent pair of doors. Whether they are made for a hut or a mansion is hard to make out! They are only good at buying foreign tools, as if that is all of carpentry! Alas! That state of things has come upon all matters in our country. What we possessed as our own is all passing away, and yet, all that we have learnt from foreigners is the art of speechifying. Merely reading and talking! The Bengalis, and the Irish in Europe, are races cast in the same mould—only talking and talking, and bandying words. These two nations are adepts in making grandiloquent speeches. They are nowhere, when a jot of real practical work is required—over and above that, they are barking at each other and fighting among themselves all the days of their life!

In the West, they have a habit of keeping everything about themselves neat and clean, and even the poorest have an eye towards it. And this regard for cleanliness has to be observed; for, unless the people have clean suits of clothes, none will employ them in their service. Their servants, maids, cooks, etc., are all dressed in spotlessly clean clothes. Their houses are kept trim and tidy by being daily brushed, washed and dusted. A part of good breeding consists in not throwing things about, but keeping them in their proper places. Their kitchens look clean and bright—vegetable peelings and such other refuse are placed, for the time being in a separate receptacle, and taken, later on, by a scavenger to a distance and thrown away in a proper place set apart for the purpose. They do not throw such things about in their yards or on the roads.

The houses and other buildings of those who are wealthy are really a sight worth seeing—these are, night and day, a marvel of orderliness and cleanliness! Over and above that, they are in the habit of collecting art treasures from various countries, and adorning their rooms with them. As regards ourselves, we need not, of course, at any rate for the present, go in for collecting works of art as they do; but should we, or should we not, at least preserve those which we possess from going to ruin? It will take up a long time yet to become as good and efficient as they are in the arts of painting and sculpture. We were never very skilful in those two departments of art. By imitating the Europeans we at the utmost can only produce one or two Ravi Varmas among us! But far better than such artists are our Patuas (painter) who do the Châlchitras[1] of our goddesses, in Bengal. They display in their work at least a boldness in the brilliancy of their colours. The paintings of Ravi Varma and others make one hide one's face from shame! Far better are those gilded pictures of Jaipur and the Chalchitra of the goddess Durgâ that we have had from old times. I shall reserve my reflections on the European arts of sculpture and painting for some future occasion. That is too vast a subject to enter upon here.

III — FOOD AND COOKING

Now hear something about the Western art of cooking. There is greater purity observed in our cooking than in any other country; on the other hand, we have not that perfect regularity, method and cleanliness of the English table. Every day our cook first bathes and changes his clothes before entering the kitchen; he neatly cleanses all the utensils and the hearth with water and earth, and if he chances to touch his face, nose, or any part of his body, he washes his hands before he touches again any food. The Western cook scarcely bathes; moreover, he tastes with a spoon the cooking he is engaged in, and does not think much of redipping the spoon into the pot. Taking out his handkerchief he blows his nose vigorously, and again with the same hand he, perchance, kneads the dough. He never thinks of washing his hands when he comes from outside, and begins his cooking at once. But all the same, he has snow-white clothes and cap. Maybe, he is dancing on the dough—why, because he may knead it thoroughly well with the whole pressure of his body, no matter if the sweat of his brow gets mixed with it! (Fortunately nowadays, machines are widely used for the task.) After all this sacrilege, when the bread is finished, it is placed on a porcelain dish covered with a snow-white napkin and is carried by the servant dressed in a spotless suit of clothes with white gloves on; then it is laid upon the table spread over with a clean table-cloth. Mark here, the gloves—lest the man touches anything with his bare fingers!

Observe ours on the other hand. Our Brahmin cook has first purified himself with a bath, and then cooked the dinner in thoroughly cleansed utensils, but he serves it to you on a plate on the bare floor which has been pasted over with earth and

1. Arch shaper frames over the images of deities, with Paurânika pictures.

cow-dung; and his cloth, albeit daily washed, is so dirty that it looks as if it were never washed. And if the plantain-leaf, which sometimes serves the purpose of a plate, is torn, there is a good chance of the soup getting mixed up with the moist floor and cow-dung paste and giving rise to a wonderful taste!

After taking a nice bath we put on a dirty-looking cloth, almost sticky with oil; and in the West, they put on a perfectly clean suit on a dirty body, without having had a proper bath. Now, this is to be understood thoroughly—for here is the point of essential difference between the Orient and the Occident. That inward vision of the Hindu and the outward vision of the West, are manifest in all their respective manners and customs. The Hindu always looks inside, and the Westerner outside. The Hindu keeps diamonds wrapped in a rag, as it were; the Westerner preserves a lump of earth in a golden casket! The Hindu bathes to keep his body clean, he does not care how dirty his cloth may be; the Westerner takes care to wear clean clothes—what matters it if dirt remains on his body! The Hindu keeps neat and clean the rooms, doors, floors, and everything inside his house; what matters it if a heap of dirt and refuse lies outside his entrance door! The Westerner looks to covering his floors with bright and beautiful carpets, the dirt and dust under them is all right if concealed from view! The Hindu lets his drains run open over the road, the bad smell does not count much! The drains in the West are underground—the hotbed of typhoid fever! The Hindu cleanses the inside, the Westerner cleanses the outside.

What is wanted is a clean body with clean clothes. Rinsing the mouth, cleansing the teeth and all that must be done—but in private. The dwelling-houses must be kept clean, as well as the streets and thoroughfares and all outlying places. The cook must keep his clothes clean as well as his body. Moreover, the meals must be partaken of in spotless cups and plates, sitting in a neat and tidy place. Achara or observance of the established rules of conduct in life is the first step to religion, and of that again, cleanliness of body and mind, cleanliness in everything, is the most important factor. Will one devoid of Achara ever attain to religion? Don't you see before your very eyes the miseries of those who are devoid of Achara? Should we not, thus paying dearly for it, learn the lesson? Cholera, malaria, and plague have made their permanent home in India, and are carrying away their victims by millions. Whose fault is it? Ours, to be sure. We are sadly devoid of Achara!

All our different sects of Hinduism admit the truth of the celebrated saying of the Shruti[1], "आहारशुद्धौ सत्त्वशुद्धिः सत्त्वशुद्धौ ध्रुवा स्मृतिः—When the food is pure, then the inner-sense gets purified; on the purification of the innersense, memory (of the soul's perfection) becomes steady." Only, according to Shankarâchârya, the word Ahâra means the sense-perceptions, and Râmânuja takes the word to mean food. But what is the solution? All sects agree that both are necessary, and both ought to be taken into account. Without pure food, how can the Indriyas (organs) perform their respective functions properly? Everyone knows by experience that impure food weakens the power of receptivity of the Indriyas or makes them act in opposition to the will. It is a well-known fact that indigestion distorts the vision of things and makes one thing appeal as another, and that want of food makes the eyesight and other powers of the senses dim and weak. Similarly, it is often seen that some particular kind of food brings on some particular state of the body and the mind. This principle is at the root of those many rules which are so strictly enjoined in Hindu society—that we should take this sort and avoid that sort of food—though in many cases, forgetting their essential substance, the kernel, we are now busy only with quarelling about the shell and keeping watch and ward over it.

Râmânujâchârya asks us to avoid three sorts at defects which, according to him, make food impure. The first defect is that of the Jâti, i.e. the very nature or the species to which the food belongs, as onion, garlic, and so on. These have an exciting tendency and, when taken, produce restlessness of the mind, or in other words perturb the intellect. The next is that of Âshraya, i.e. the nature of the person from whom the food comes. The food coming from a wicked person will make one impure and think wicked thoughts, while the food coming from a good man will elevate one's thoughts. Then the other is Nimitta-dosha, i.e. impurity in food due to such agents in it as dirt and dust, worms or hair; taking such food also makes the mind impure. Of these three defects, anyone can eschew the Jati and the Nimitta, but it is not easy for all to avoid the Ashraya. It is only to avoid this Ashraya-dosha, that we have so much of "Don't-touchism" amongst us nowadays. "Don't touch me! Don't touch me!"

But in most cases, the cart is put before the horse; and the real meaning of the principle being misunderstood, it becomes in time a queer and hideous superstition. In these cases, the Acharas of the great Âchâryas, the teachers of mankind, should be followed instead of the Lokâchâras. i.e. the customs followed by the people in general. One ought to read the lives of such great Masters as Shri Chaitanya Deva and other similarly great religious teachers and see how they behaved themselves with their fellow-men in this respect. As regards the Jati-dosha in food, no other country in the world furnishes a better field for its observation than India. The Indians, of all nations, take the purest of foods and, all over the world, there is no other country where the purity as regards the Jati is so well observed as in India. We had better attend to the Nimitta-dosha a little more now in India, as it is becoming a source of serious evil with us. It has become too common with us to buy food from the sweets-vendor's shop in the bazaar, and you can judge for yourselves how impure these confections are from the point of view of the Nimitta-dosha; for, being kept exposed, the dirt and dust of the roads as well as dead insects adhere to them, and how stale and polluted they must sometimes be. All this dyspepsia that you notice in every home and the prevalence of diabetes from which the townspeople suffer so much now-

---

1. Chhândogya Upanishad, VII. xxvi. 2.

adays are due to the taking of impure food from the bazaars; and that the village-people are not as a rule so subject to these complaints is principally due to the fact that they have not these bazaars near them, where they can buy at their will such poisonous food as Loochi, Kachoori, etc. I shall dwell on this in detail later on.

This is, in short, the old general rule about food. But there were, and still are, many differences of opinion about it. Again, as in the old, so in the present day, there is a great controversy whether it is good or bad to take animal food or live only on a vegetable diet, whether we are benefited or otherwise by taking meat. Besides, the question whether it is right or wrong to kill animals has always been a matter of great dispute. One party says that to take away life is a sin, and on no account should it be done. The other party replies: "A fig for your opinion! It is simply impossible to live without killing." The Shastras also differ, and rather confuse one, on this point. In one place the Shastra dictates, "Kill animals in Yajnas", and again, in another place it says, "Never take away life". The Hindus hold that it is a sin to kill animals except in sacrifices, but one can with impunity enjoy the pleasure of eating meat after the animal is sacrificed in a Yajna. Indeed, there are certain rules prescribed for the householder in which he is required to kill animals on occasions, such as Shraddha and so on; and if he omits to kill animals at those times, he is condemned as a sinner. Manu says that if those that are invited to Shraddha and certain other ceremonies do not partake of the animal food offered there, they take birth in an animal body in their next.

On the other hand, the Jains, the Buddhists, and the Vaishnavas protest, saying, "We do not believe in the dictates of such Hindu Shastras; on no account should the taking away of life be tolerated." Asoka, the Buddhist emperor, we read, punished those who would perform Yajnas or offer meat to the invited at any ceremony. The position in which the modern Vaishnavas find themselves is rather one of difficulty. Instances are found in the Râmâyana[2] and the Mahâbhârata[3] of the drinking of wine and the taking of meat by Rama and Krishna, whom they worship as God. Sita Devi vows meat, rice, and a thousand jars of wine to the river-goddess, Gangâ[4]!

In the West, the contention is whether animal food is injurious to health or not, whether it is more strengthening than vegetable diet or not, and so on. One party says that those that take animal food suffer from all sorts of bodily complaints. The other contradicts this and says, "That is all fiction. If that were true, then the Hindus would have been the healthiest race, and the powerful nations, such as the English, the Americans, and others, whose principal food is meat, would have succumbed to all sorts of maladies and ceased to exist by this time." One says that the flesh of the goat makes the intellect like that of the goat, the flesh of the swine like that of the swine, and fish like that of the fish. The other declares that it can as well be argued then that the potato makes a potato-like brain, that vegetables make a vegetable-like brain—resembling dull and dead matter. Is it not better to have the intelligence of a living animal than to have the brain dull and inert like dead matter? One party says that those things which are in the chemical composition of animal food are also equally present in the vegetables. The other ridicules it and exclaims. "Why, they are in the air too. Go then and live on air only". One argues that the vegetarians are very painstaking and can go through hard and long-sustained labour. The other says, "If that were true, then the vegetarian nations would occupy the foremost rank, which is not the case, the strongest and foremost nations being always those that take animal food." Those who advocate animal food contend: "Look at the Hindus and the Chinamen, how poor they are. They do not take meat, but live somehow on the scanty diet of rice and all sorts of vegetables. Look at their miserable condition. And the Japanese were also in the same plight, but since they commenced taking meat, they turned over a new leaf. In the Indian regiments there are about a lac and a half of native sepoys; see how many of them are vegetarians. The best parts of them, such as the Sikhs and the Goorkhas, are never vegetarians". One party says, "Indigestion is due to animal food". The other says, "That is all stuff and nonsense. It is mostly the vegetarians who suffer from stomach complaints." Again, "It may be the vegetable food acts as an effective purgative to the system. But is that any reason that you should induce the whole world to take it?"

Whatever one or the other may say, the real fact, however, is that the nations who take the animal food are always, as a rule, notably brave, heroic and thoughtful. The nations who take animal food also assert that in those days when the smoke from Yajnas used to rise in the Indian sky and the Hindus used to take the meat of animals sacrificed, then only great religious geniuses and intellectual giants were born among them; but since the drifting of the Hindus into the Bâbâji's

---

2. सीतामादाय बाहुभ्यां मधुमैरेयकं शुचि ।
पाययामास काकुत्स्थः श्चीमनिन्द्रो यथामृतम् ॥
मांसानि च सुमृष्टानि विविधानि फलानि च ।
रामस्याभयवहारार्थं किंकिरास्तूर्णमाहरन् ॥

"Embracing Sitâ with both his arms, Kâkutstha (Râma) made her drink pure Maireya wine, even as Indra makes Shachi partake of nectar.

Servants quickly served flesh-meat variously dressed, and fruits of various kinds for the use of Rama."

3. उभौ मध्वासवकृपितावुभौ चन्दनरूषितौ ।
सरगर्विनौ वरवस्त्रौ तौ दिव्याभरणभूषितौ ॥

"(I saw) both of them (Krishna and Arjuna) drunk with Madhvâsava (sweet spirituous liquor made from honey), both adorned with sandal paste, garlanded, and wearing costly garments and beautiful ornaments." (Udyoga, LVIII. 5).

4. सुराघटसहस्रेण मांसभूतौदनेन च ।
यक्षये त्वां परीयता देवि पुरीं पुनरुपागता॥

"Be merciful to us, O goddess, and I shall, on my return home, worship thee with a thousand jars of arrack (spirituous liquor) and rice well-dressed with flesh-meat" (Ramayana).

vegetarianism, not one great, original man arose midst them. Taking this view into account, the meat-eaters in our country are afraid to give up their habitual diet. The Ârya Samâjists are divided amongst themselves on this point, and a controversy is raging within their fold—one party holding that animal food is absolutely necessary, and the opposite party denouncing it as extremely wrong and unjust.

In this way, discussions of a conflicting character, giving rise to mutual abuses, quarrels, and fights, are going on. After carefully scrutinising all sides of the question and setting aside all fanaticism that is rampant on this delicate question of food, I must say that my conviction tends to confirm this view—that the Hindus are, after all right; I mean that injunction of the Hindu Shastras which lays down the rule that food, like many other things, must be different according to the difference of birth and profession; this is the sound conclusion. But the Hindus of the present day will neither follow their Shastras nor listen to what their great Acharyas taught.

To eat meat is surely barbarous and vegetable food is certainly purer—who can deny that? For him surely is a strict vegetarian diet whose one end is to lead solely a spiritual life. But he who has to steer the boat of his life with strenuous labour through the constant life-and-death struggles and the competition of this world must of necessity take meat. So long as there will be in human society such a thing as the triumph of the strong over the weak, animal food is required; otherwise, the weak will naturally be crushed under the feet of the strong. It will not do to quote solitary instances of the good effect of vegetable food on some particular person or persons: compare one nation with another and then draw conclusions.

The vegetarians, again, are also divided amongst themselves. Some say that rice, potatoes, wheat, barley, maize, and other starchy foods are of no use; these have been produced by man, and are the source of all maladies. Starchy food which generates sugar in the system is most injurious to health. Even horses and cows become sickly and diseased if kept within doors and fed on wheat and rice; but they get well again if allowed to graze freely on the tender and growing herbage in the meadows. There is very little starchy substance in grass and nuts and other green edible herbs. The orang-outang eats grass and nuts and does not usually eat potato and wheat, but if he ever does so, he eats them before they are ripe, i.e. when there is not much starch in them. Others say that taking roast meat and plenty of fruit and milk is best suited to the attainment longevity. More especially, they who take much fruit regularly, do not so soon lose their youth, as the acid of fruit dissolves the foul crust formed on the bones which is mainly the cause of bringing on old age.

All these contentions have no end; they are going on unceasingly. Now the judicious view admitted by all in regard to this vexed question is, to take such food as is substantial and nutritious and at the same time, easily digested. The food should be such as contains the greatest nutriment in the smallest compass, and be at the same time quickly assimilable;

otherwise, it has necessarily to be taken in large quantity, and consequently the whole day is required only to digest it. If all the energy is spent only in digesting food, what will there be left to do other works?

All fried things are really poisonous. The sweets-vendor's shop is Death's door. In hot countries, the less oil and clarified butter (ghee) taken the better. Butter is more easily digested than ghee. There is very little substance in snow-white flour; whole-wheat flour is good as food. For Bengal, the style and preparation of food that are still in vogue in our distant villages are commendable. What ancient Bengali poet do you find singing the praise of Loochi and Kachoori? These Loochis and Kachooris have been introduced into Bengal from the North-Western Provinces; but even there, people take them only occasionally. I have never seen even there anyone who lives mainly on things fried in ghee, day after day. The Chaube wrestlers of Mathura are, no doubt, fond of Loochis and sweetmeats; but in a few years Chaubeji's power of digestion is ruined, and he has to drug himself with appetising preparations called Churans.

The poor die of starvation because they can get nothing to eat, and the rich die of starvation because what they take is not food. Any and every stuff eaten is not food; that is real food which, when eaten, is well assimilated. It is better to fast rather than stuff oneself with anything and everything. In the delicacies of the sweetmeat shops there is hardly anything nourishing; on the other hand, there is—poison! Of old, people used to take those injurious things only occasionally; but now, the townspeople, especially those who come from villages to live in towns, are the greatest sinners in this respect, as they take them every day. What wonder is there that they die prematurely of dyspepsia! If you are hungry, throw away all sweets and things fried in ghee into the ditch, and buy a pice worth of Moorhi (popped rice)—that will be cheaper and more nutritious food. It is sufficient food to have rice, Dâl (lentils), whole-wheat Châpâtis (unfermented bread), fish, vegetables, and milk. But Dal has to be taken as the Southern Indians take it, that is, the soup of it only; the rest of the preparation give to the cattle. He may take meat who can afford it, but not making it too rich with heating spices, as the North-Western people do. The spices are no food at all; to take them in abundance is only due to a bad habit. Dal is a very substantial food but hard to digest. Pea-soup prepared of tender peas is easily digested and pleasant to the taste. In Paris this pea-soup is a favourite dish. First, boil the peas well, then make a paste of them and mix them with water. Now strain the soup through a wire-strainer, like that in which milk is strained and all the outer skin will be separated. Then add some spices, such as turmeric, black pepper, etc., according to taste, and broil it with a little ghee in the pan—and you get a pleasant and wholesome Dal. The meat-eaters can make it delicious by cooking it with the head of a goat or fish.

That we have so many cases of diabetes in India is chiefly due to indigestion; of course there are solitary instances in which excessive brain work is the cause, but with the majority it is indigestion. Pot-belly is the foremost sign of indigestion. Does eating mean stuffing oneself? That much which on can assimilate is proper food for one. Growing thin or fat is equally due to indigestion. Do not give yourself up as lost because some symptoms of diabetes are noticeable in you; those are nothing in our country anti should not be taken seriously into account. Only, pay more attention to your diet so that you may avoid indigestion. Be in the open air as much as possible, and take good long walks and work hard. The muscles of the leg should be as hard as iron. If you are in service, take leave when possible and make a pilgrimage to the Badarikâshrama in the Himalayas. If the journey is accomplished on foot through the ascent and descent of two hundred miles in the hills, you will see that this ghost of diabetes will depart from you. Do not let the doctors come near you; most of them will harm you more than do any good; and so far as possible, never take medicines, which in most cases kill the patient sooner than the illness itself. If you can, walk all the way from town to your native village every year during the Puja vacation. To be rich in our country has come to be synonymous with being the embodiment of laziness and dependence. One who has to walk being supported by another, or one who has to be fed by another, is doomed to be miserable—is a veritable in valid. He who eats cautiously only the finer coating of the Loochi, for fear that the whole will not agree with him, is already dead in life. Is he a man or a worm who cannot walk twenty miles at a stretch. Who can save one who invites illness and premature death of his own will?

And as for fermented bread, it is also poison; do not touch it at all! Flour mixed with yeast becomes injurious. Never take any fermented thing; in this respect the prohibition in our Shastras of partaking of any such article of food is a fact of great importance. Any sweet thing which has turned sour is called in the Shastras "Shukta", and that is prohibited to be taken, excepting curd, which is good and beneficial. If you have to take bread, toast it well over the fire.

Impure water and impure food are the cause of all maladies. In America, nowadays, it has become a craze to purify the drinking water. The filter has had its day and is now discredited, because it only strains the water through, while all the finer germs of diseases such as cholera, plague, remain intact in it; moreover, the filter itself gradually becomes the hotbed of these germs. When the filter was first introduced in Calcutta, for five years, it is said there was no outbreak of cholera; since then it has become as bad as ever, for the reason that the huge filter itself has now come to be the vehicle of cholera germs. Of all kinds, the simple method that we have of placing three earthen jars one over another on a three-footed bamboo frame, is the best; but every second or third day the sand and charcoal should be changed, or used again after heating them. The method of straining water through a cloth containing a lump of alum in it, that we find in vogue in the villages along the banks of the Ganga in the vicinity of Cal-

cutta, is the best of all. The particles of alum taking with them all earth and impurities and the disease germs, gradually settle at the bottom of the deep jar as sediment; this simple system brings into disrepute pipewater and excels all your foreign filters. Moreover, if the water is boiled it becomes perfectly safe. Boil the water when the impurities are settled down by the alum, and then drink it, and throw away filters and such other things into the ditch. Now in America, the drinking water is first turned into vapour by means of huge machines; then the vapour is cooled down into water again, and through another machine pure air is pressed into it to substitute that air which goes out during the process of vaporization. This water is very pure and is used in every home.

In our country, he who has some means, feeds his children with all sorts of sweets and ghee-fried things, because, perchance, it is a shame—just think what the people will say!—to let them have only rice and Chapatis! What can you expect children fed like that to be but disproportionate in figure, lazy, worthless idiots, with no backbone of their own? The English people, who are so strong a race, who work so hard day and night, and whose native place is a cold country—even they hold in dread the very name of sweetmeats and food fried in butter! And we, who live in the zone of fire, as it were, who do not like to move from one place to another—what do we eat?—Loochis, Kachooris, sweets, and other things, all fried in ghee or oil! Formerly, our village zemindars in Bengal would think nothing of walking twenty or thirty miles, and would eat twice-twenty Koi-fish, bones and all—and they lived to a hundred years. Now their sons and grandsons come to Calcutta and put on airs, wear spectacles, eat the sweets from the bazaars, hire a carriage to go from one street to another, and then complain of diabetes—and their life is cut short; this is the result of their being "civilised, Calcutta-ised" people. And doctors and Vaidyas hasten their ruin too. They are all-knowing, they think they can cure anything with medicine. If there is a little flatulence, immediately some medicine is prescribed. Alas, it never enters into the heads of these Vaidyas to advise them to keep away from medicine, and go and have a good walk of four or five miles, or so.

I am seeing many countries, and many ways and preparations of food; but none of them approaches the admirable cooking of our various dishes of Bengal, and it is not too much to say that one should like to take rebirth for the sake of again enjoying their excellence. It is a great pity that one does not appreciate the value of teeth when one has them! Why should we imitate the West as regards food—and how many can afford to do so? The food which is suitable in our part of the country is pure Bengali food, cheap, wholesome, and nourishing, like that of the people of Eastern Bengal. Imitate their food as much as you can; the more you lean westwards to copy the modes of food, the worse you are, and the more uncivilized you become. You are Calcutta-ites, civilised, forsooth! Carried away by the charm of that destructive net which is of your own creation, the bazaar sweets, Bankura has consigned its popped-rice to the river Damodar, its Kalâi Dâl has been cast into the ditch, and Dacca and Vikrampur have thrown to the dogs their old dishes—or in other words, they have become "civilised"! You have gone to rack and ruin, and are leading others in the same path, toll townspeople, and you pride yourselves on your being "civilized"! And these provincial people are so foolish that they will eat all the refuse of Calcutta and suffer from dyspepsia and dysentery, but will not admit that it is not suiting them, and will defend themselves by saying that the air of Calcutta is damp and "saline"! They must by all means be townspeople in every respect!

So far, in brief, about the merits of food and other customs. Now I shall say something in the matter of what the Westerners generally eat, and how by degrees it has changed.

The food of the poor in all countries is some species of corn; herbs, vegetables, and fish and meat fall within the category of luxuries and are used in the shape of chutney. The crop which grows in abundance and is the chief produce of a country is the staple food of its poorer classes; as in Bengal, Orissa, Madras, and the Malabar coasts, the prime food is rice, pulse, and vegetables, and sometimes, fish and meat are used for chutney only. The food of the well-to-do class in other parts of India is Chapatis (unfermented bread) of wheat, and rice, of the people in general, mainly Chapatis of Bazrâ, Marhuâ, Janâr, Jhingorâ, and other corns.

All over India, herbs, vegetables, pulse, fish, and meat are used only to make tasteful the Roti (unfermented bread), or the rice, as the case may be, and hence they are called in Sanskrit, "Vyanjana", i.e. that which seasons food. In the Punjab, Rajputana, and the Deccan, though the rich people and the princes take many kinds of meat every day, yet with them even, the principal food is Roti or rice. He who takes daily one pound of meat, surely takes two pounds of Chapatis along with it.

Similarly in the West, the chief foods of the people in poor countries, and especially of the poor class in the rich parts, are bread and potatoes; meat is rarely taken, and, if taken, is considered as a chutney. In Spain, Portugal, Italy, and in other comparatively warm countries, grapes grow profusely, and the wine made of grapes is very cheap. These wines are not intoxicating (i.e.. unless one drinks a great quantity, one will not get intoxicated) and are very nutritious. The poor of those countries, therefore, use grape juice as a nourishment instead of fish and meat. But in the northern parts of Europe, such as Russia, Sweden, and Norway, bread made of rye, potatoes, and a little dried fish form the food of the poor classes.

The food of the wealthy classes of Europe, and of all the classes of America is quite different, that is to say, their chief food is fish and meat, and bread, rice, and other things are taken as chutney. In America, bread is taken very little. When fish is served, it is served by itself, or when meat is served, it is served by itself and is often taken without bread or rice. Therefore the plate has to be changed frequently; if there are ten sorts of food, the plate has to be changed as many times. If we were to take our food in this way, we should have to serve like this—suppose the Shukta (bitter curry) is first brought, and, changing that plate, Dal is served on another; in the same way the soup arrives; and again a little rice by itself, or a few Loochis, and so on. One benefit of this way of serving is that a little only of many varieties is taken, and it saves one from eating too much of anything. The French take coffee, and one or two slices of bread and butter in the morning, fish and meat, etc., in a moderate way about midday, and the principal meal comes at night. With the Italians and Spaniards, the custom is the same as that of the French. The Germans eat a good deal, five or six times a day, with more or less meat every time; the English, three times, the breakfast being rather small, but tea or coffee between; and the Americans also three times, but the meal is rather large every time, with plenty of meat. In all these countries, the principal meal is, however, dinner; the rich have French cooks and have food cooked after the French fashion. To begin with, a little salted fish or roe, or some sort of chutney or vegetable—this is by way of stimulating the appetite; soup follows; then, according to the present day fashion, fruit; next comes fish; then a meat-curry; after which a joint of roast meat, and with it some vegetables; afterwards game birds, or venison, etc., then sweets, and finally, delicious ice-cream. At the table of the rich, the wine is changed every time the dish changes—and hock, claret, and iced champagne are served with the different courses. The spoon and knife and fork are also changed each time with the plate. After dinner—coffee without milk and liqueurs in very tiny glasses are brought in, and smoking comes last. The greater the variety of wines served with the various dishes, the greater will the host be regarded as a rich and wealthy man of fashion. As much money is spent over there in giving a dinner as would ruin a moderately rich man of our country.

Sitting cross-legged on a wooden seat on the ground, with a similar one to lean his back against, the Arya used to take his food on a single metal plate, placed on a slightly-raised wooden stool. The same custom is still in rogue in the Punjab, Rajputana, Mahârâshtra, and Gujarat. The people of Bengal, Orissa, Telinga, and Malabar, etc., do not use wooden stools to put the plates on, but take their food on a plate or a plantain-leaf placed on the ground. Even the Maharaja of Mysore does the same. The Mussulmans sit on a large, white sheet, when taking their food. The Burmese and the Japanese place their plates on the ground and sit supporting themselves on their knees and feet only, and not flat on their haunches like the Indians. The Chinamen sit on chairs, with their dishes placed on a table, and use spoons and wooden chop-sticks in taking their food. In the olden times, the Romans and Greeks had a table before them and, reclining on a couch, used to eat their food with their fingers. The Europeans also, sitting on chairs, used to take their food with their fingers from the table; now they have spoons and forks. The Chinese mode of eating is really an exercise requiring skill. As our

Lectures & Discourses by **Swami Vivekananda**

Pân (betel)-vendors make, by dexterity of hand, two separate pieces of thin iron-sheets work like scissors in the trimming of Pan leaves, so the Chinese manipulate two sticks between two fingers and the palm of the right hand, in such a way as to make them act like tongs to carry the vegetables up to their mouths. Again, putting the two together, and holding a bowl of rice near the mouth, they push the rice in with the help of those sticks formed like a little shovel.

The primitive ancestors of every nation used to eat, it is said, whatever they could get. When they killed a big animal, they would make it last for a month and would not reject it even after it got rotten. Then gradually they became civilised and learnt cultivation. Formerly, they could not get their food every day by hunting and would, like the wild animals, gorge themselves one day and then starve four or five days in the week. Later they escaped that, for they could get their food every day by cultivation; but it remained a standing custom to take with food something like rotten meat or other things of the old days. Primarily, rotten meat was an indispensable article of food; now that or something else in its place became, like the sauce, a favourite relish. The Eskimos live in the snowy regions, where no kind of corn can be produced; their daily food is fish and flesh. Once in a way when they lose their appetite, they take just a piece of rotten flesh to recover their lost appetite. Even now, Europeans do not immediately cook wild birds, game, and venison, while fresh, but they keep them hanging till they begin to smell a little. In Calcutta the rotten meat of a deer is sold out as soon as brought to the market, and people prefer some fish when slightly rotten. In some parts of Europe, the cheese which smells a little is regarded as very tasty. Even the vegetarians like to have a little onion and garlic; the Southern Indian Brahmin must have them in his cooking. But the Hindu Shastras prohibited that too, making it a sin to take onions, garlic, domestic fowl, and pork to one caste (the Brahmin); they that would take them would lose their caste. So the orthodox Hindus gave up onions and garlic, and substituted in their place asafoetida, a thing which is more strikingly offensive in smell than either of the other two! The orthodox Brahmins of the Himalayas similarly took to a kind of dried grass smelling just like garlic! And what harm in that? The scriptures do not say anything against taking these things!

Every religion contains some rules regarding the taking of certain foods, and the avoiding of others; only Christianity is an exception. The Jains and the Bauddhas will by no means take fish or meat. The Jains, again, will not even eat potatoes, radishes, or other vegetable roots, which grow underground, lest in digging them up worms are killed. They will not eat at night lest some insect get into their mouths in the dark. The Jews do not eat fish that have no scales, do not eat pork, nor the animals that are not cloven-hoofed and do not ruminate. Again, if milk or any preparation of milk be brought into the kitchen where fish or flesh is being cooked, the Jews will throw away everything cooked there. For this reason, the

orthodox Jews do not eat the food cooked by other nations. Like the Hindus, too, they do not take flesh which is simply slaughtered and not offered to God. In Bengal and the Punjab, another name of flesh that is offered to the Goddess is Mahâprasâda, lit., the "great offering". The Jews do not eat flesh, unless it is Mahaprasada, i.e. unless it is properly offered to God. Hence, they, like the Hindus, are not permitted to buy flesh at any and every shop. The Mussulmans obey many rules similar to the Jews, but do not, like them, go to extremes; they do not take milk and fish or flesh at the same meal, but do not consider it so much harmful if they are in the same kitchen or if one touches another. There is much similarity respecting food between the Hindus and the Jews. The Jews, however, do not take wild boar, which the Hindus do. In the Punjab, on account of the deadly animosity between the Hindus and the Mussulmans, the former do what the latter will not, and the wild boar has come to be one of the very essential articles of food with the Hindus there. With the Rajputs, hunting the wild boar and partaking of its flesh is rather an act of Dharma. The taking of the flesh of even the domesticated pig prey ails to a great extent in the Deccan among all castes except the Brahmins. The Hindus eat the wild fowl (cock or hen), but not domesticated fowls.

The people of India from Bengal to Nepal and in the Himalayas as far as the borders of Kashmir, follow the same usages regarding food. In these parts, the customs of Manu are in force to a large extent even up to this day. But they obtain more especially in the parts from Kumaon to Kashmir than in Bengal, Bihar, Allahabad, or Nepal. For example, the Bengalis do not eat fowl or fowl's eggs, but they eat duck's eggs; so do the Nepalese; but from Kumaon upwards, even that is not allowed. The Kashmiris eat with pleasure eggs of the wild duck, but not of the domesticated bird. Of the people of India, beginning from Allahabad, excepting in the Himalayas, they who take the flesh of goat take fowl as well.

All these rules and prohibitions with respect to food are for the most part meant, no doubt, in the interests of good health; of course, in each and every instance, it is difficult accurately to determine which particular food is conducive to health and which is not. Again, swine and fowls eat anything and everything and are very unclean; so they are forbidden. No one sees what the wild animals eat in the forest; so they are not disallowed. Besides, the wild animals are healthier and less sickly than the domesticated ones. Milk is very difficult of digestion, especially when one is suffering from acidity, and cases have happened when even by gulping down a glass of milk in haste, life has been jeopardised. Milk should be taken as a child does from its mother's breast; if it is sucked or sipped by degrees, it is easily digestible, otherwise not. Being itself hard of digestion, it becomes the more so when taken with flesh; so the Jews are prohibited from taking flesh and milk at the same meal.

The foolish and ignorant mother who forces her baby to swallow too much milk beats her breast in despair within a few months, on seeing that there is little hope of her darling's life! The modern medical authorities prescribe only a pint of milk even for an adult, and that is to be taken as slowly as possible; and for babies a "feeding-bottle" is the best means. Our mothers are too busy with household duties, so the maid-servant puts the crying baby in her lap and not unfrequently holds it down with her knee, and by means of a spoon makes it gulp down as much milk as she can. And the result is that generally it is afflicted with liver complaint and seldom grows up—that milk proves to be its doom; only those that have sufficient vitality to survive this sort of dangerous feeding attain a strong and healthy manhood. And think of our old-fashioned confinement rooms, of the hot fomentations given to the baby, and treatments of like nature. It was indeed a wonder and must have been a matter of special divine grace that the mother and the baby survived these severe trials and could become strong and healthy!

IV—CIVILISATION IN DRESS

In every country the respectability of a person is determined, to a certain extent, by the nature of the dress he wears. As our village-folk in Bengal say in their patois, "How can a gentleman be distinguished from one of low birth unless his income is known?" And not only income, "Unless it is seen how one dresses oneself, how can it be known if one is a gentleman?" This is the same all over the world, more or less. In Bengal, no gentleman can walk in the streets with only a loincloth on; while in other parts of India, no one goes out of doors but with a turban on his head. In the West, the French have all along taken the lead in everything—their food and their dress are imitated by others. Even now, though different parts of Europe have got different modes of clothes and dress of their own, yet when one earns a good deal of money and becomes a "gentleman", he straightaway rejects his former native dress and substitutes the French mode in its place. The Dutch farmer whose native dress somewhat resembles the paijâmâs of the Kabulis, the Greek clothed in full skirts, the Russ dressed somewhat after the Tibetan fashion—as soon as they become "genteel", they wear French coats and pantaloons. Needless to speak of women—no sooner do they get rich than they must by any means have their dresses made in Paris. America, England, France, and Germany are now the rich countries in the West, and the dress of the people of these countries, one and all, is made after the French fashion, which is slowly and surely making its way into every part of Europe. The whole of Europe seems to be an imitation of France. However, men's clothes are better made nowadays in London than Paris, so men have them "London-made", and women in the Parisian style. Those who are very rich have their dresses sent from those two places. America enforces an exorbitant tax upon the importation of foreign dresses; notwithstanding that, the American women must have them from Paris and London. This, only the Americans can afford to do, for America is now

the chief home of Kubera, the god of wealth.

The ancient Aryans used to put on the Dhoti and Châdar[1]. The Kshatriyas used to wear trousers and long coats when fighting. At other times they would use only the Dhoti and Chadar; and they wore the turban. The same custom is still in vogue, except in Bengal, among the people in all parts of India; they are not so particular about the dress for the rest of the body, but they must have a turban for the head. In former times, the same was also the custom for both the man and the women. In the sculptured figures of the Buddhistic period, the men and the women are seen to wear only a piece of Kaupin. Even Lord Buddha's father, though a king, is seen in some sculptures, sitting on a throne, dressed in the same way; so also the mother, only has, in addition, ornaments on her feet and arms; but they all have turbans! The Buddhist Emperor, Dharmâshoka, is seen sitting on a drum-shaped seat with only a Dhoti on, and a Chadar round his neck, and looking at damsels performing a dance before him; the dancing girls are very little clothed, having only short pieces of loose material hanging from the waist; but the glory is—that the turban is there, and it makes the principal feature of their dress. The high officials of the State who attended the royal court, are, however, dressed in excellent trousers and Chogas, or long coats. When the King Nala, was disguised as a charioteer in to service of the King Rituparna, he drove the chariot at such a tremendous speed that the Chadar of the king Rituparna was blown away to such a distance that it could not be recovered; and as he had set out to marry, or join a Svayamvara, he had to do so, perchance, without a Chadar. The Dhoti and the Chadar are the time-honored dress of the Aryans. Hence, at the time of the performance of any religious ceremony, the rule among the Hindus even now is to put on the Dhoti and Chadar only.

The dress of the ancient Greeks and Romans was Dhoti and Chadar—one broad piece of cloth and another smaller one made in the form of the toga, from which the word Choga is derived. Sometimes they used also a shirt, and at the time of fighting, trousers and coats. The dress of the women was a long and sufficiently broad, square-shaped garment, similar to that formed by sewing two sheets lengthwise, which they slipped over the head and tied round, once under the breast and again round the waist. Then they fastened the upper parts which were open, over both the arms by means of large pins, in much the same way as the hill tribes of the northern Himalayas still wear their blankets. There was a Chadar over this long garment. This dress was very simple and elegant.

From the very old days, only the Iranians used shaped dresses. Perhaps they learnt it from the Chinese. The Chinese were the primeval teachers of civilisation in dress and other things pertaining to various comforts and luxuries. From time immemorial, the Chinese took their meals at a table, sitting

1. Dhoti is a piece of cloth about four or five yards long, worn by the Indians round the loins instead of breeches, and Chadar is a piece of cloth three yards long, used as a loose upper garment.

on chairs, with many elaborate auxiliaries, and wore shaped dresses of many varieties—coat, cap, trousers, and so on.

On conquering Iran, Alexander gave up the old Greek Dhoti and Chadar and began using trousers. At this, his Greek soldiers became so disaffected towards him that they were on the point of mutiny. But Alexander was not the man to yield, and by the sheer force of his authority he introduced trousers and coats as a fashion in dress.

In a hot climate, the necessity of clothes is not so much felt. A mere Kaupin is enough for the purpose of decency; other clothes serve more as embellishments. In cold countries, as a matter of unavoidable necessity, the people, when uncivilised, clothe themselves with the skins of animals, and when they gradually become civilised, they learn the use of blankets, and by degrees, shaped dresses, such as pantaloons, coats, and so on. Of course it is impossible in cold countries to display the beauty of ornaments, which have to be worn on the bare body, for if they did so they would suffer severely from cold. So the fondness for ornaments is transfered to, and is satisfied by, the niceties of dress. As in India the fashions in ornaments change very often, so in the West the fashions in dress change every moment.

In cold countries, therefore, it is the rule that one should not appear before others without covering oneself from head to foot. In London, a gentleman or a lady cannot go out without conforming himself or herself exactly to what society demands. In the West, it is immodest for a woman to show her feet in society, but at a dance it is not improper to expose the face, shoulders, and upper part of the body to view. In our country, on the other hand, for a woman to show her face is a great shame, (hence that rigorous drawing of the veil), but not so the feet. Again, in Rajputana and the Himalayas they cover the whole body except the waist!

In the West, actresses and dancing-girls are very thinly covered, to attract men. Their dancing often means exposing their limbs in harmonious movements accompanied by music. In our country, the women of gentle birth are not so particular in covering themselves thoroughly, but the dancing-girls are entirely covered. In the West, women are always completely clothed in the daytime; so attraction is greater in their being thinly covered. Our women remain in the house most of the time, and much dressing themselves is unusual; so with us, attraction is greater in their fully covering themselves. In Malabar, men and women have only a piece of cloth round their loins. With the Bengalis it is about the same, and before men, the women scrupulously draw their veils, and cover their bodies.

In all countries except China, I notice many queer and mysterious ideas of propriety—in some matters they are carried too far, in others again, what strikes one as being very incorrect is not felt to be so at all.

The Chinese of both sexes are always fully covered from head to foot. The Chinese are the disciples of Confucius, are the disciples of Buddha, and their morality is quite strict and refined. Obscene language, obscene books or pictures, any conduct the least obscene—and the offender is punished then and there. The Christian missionaries translated the Bible into the Chinese tongue. Now, in the Bible there are some passages so obscene as to put to shame some of the Purânas of the Hindus. Reading those indecorous passages, the Chinamen were so exasperated against Christianity that they made a point of never allowing the Bible to be circulated in their country. Over and above that, missionary women wearing evening dress and mixing freely with men invited the Chinese to their parties. The simpleminded Chinese were disgusted, and raised a cry, saying: Oh, horror! This religion is come to us to ruin our young boys, by giving them this Bible to read, and making them fall an easy prey to the charms of these half clothed wily women! This is why the Chinese are so very indignant with the Christians. Otherwise, the Chinese are very tolerant towards other religions. I hear that the missionaries have now printed an edition, leaving out the objectionable parts; but this step has made the Chinese more suspicious than before.

V—ETIQUETTE AND MANNERS

Again, in the West, ideas of decency and etiquette vary in accordance with the different countries. With the English and Americans they are of one type, is with the French of another, with the Germans again different. The Russians and the Tibetans have much in common; and the Turks have their own quite distinct customs, and so on.

In Europe and America, the people are extremely particular in observing privacy, much more than we are. We are vegetarians, and so eat a quantity of vegetables etc., and living in a hot country we frequently drink one or two glasses of water at a time. The peasant of the Upper Provinces eats two pounds of powdered barley, and then sets to drawing and drinking water from the shell every now and again, as he feels so thirsty. In summer we keep open places in our house for distributing water to the thirsty, through a hollowed bamboo stem. These ways make the people not so very particular about privacy; they cannot help it. Compare cowsheds and horses' stables with lions' and tigers' cages. Compare the dog with the goat. The food of the Westerners is chiefly meat, and in cold countries they hardly drink any water. Gentlemen take a little wine in small glasses. The French detest water; only Americans drink it in great quantities, for their country is very warm in summer. New York is even hotter than Calcutta. The Germans drink a good deal of beer, but not with their meals.

In cold countries, men are always susceptible to catching cold, so they cannot help sneezing; in warm countries people have to drink much water at meals, consequently we cannot help eructating. Now note the etiquette: if you do that in a Western society, your sin is unpardonable; but if you bring out your pocket handkerchief and blow your nose vigorously, it will see nothing objectionable in that. With us, the host will not feel satisfied, so to say, unless he sees you doing the former, as that is taken as a sign of a full meal; but what would you think of doing the latter when having a meal in the company of others?

In England and America, no mention of indigestion or any stomach complaints, you may be suffering from, should be made before women; it is a different matter, of course, if your friend is an old woman, or if she is quite well known to you. They are not so sensitive about these things in France. The Germans are even less particular.

English and American men are very guarded in their conversation before women; you cannot even speak of a "leg". The French, like us, are very free in conversation; the Germans and the Russians will use vulgar terms in the presence of anybody.

But conversations on being in love are freely carried on between mother and son, between brothers and sisters, and between them and their fathers. The father asks the daughter many questions about her lover (the future bridegroom) and cuts all sorts of jokes about her engagement. On such occasions, the French maiden modestly laughs down her head, the English maiden is bashful, and the American maiden gives him sharp replies to his face. Kissing and even embrace are not so very objectionable; these things can be talked of in society. But in our country, no talk, nor even all indirect hint of love affairs, is permissible before superior relations.

The Westerners are now rich people. Unless one's dress is very clean and in conformity with strict etiquette, one will not be considered a gentleman and cannot mix in society. A gentleman must change his collar and shirt twice or thrice every day; the poor people, of course, cannot do this. On the outer garment there must not be stains or even a crease. However much you may suffer from heat, you must go out with gloves for fear of getting your hands dirty in the streets, and to shake hands with a lady with hands that are not clean is very ungentlemanlike. In polite society, if the act of spitting or rinsing the mouth or picking the teeth be ever indulged in—the offender will be marked as a Chandâla, a man of low caste, and shunned!

The Dharma of the Westerners is worship of Shakti—the Creative Power regarded as the Female Principle. It is with them somewhat like the Vâmâchâri's worship of woman. As the Tântrika says. "On the left side the women...on the right, the cup full of wine; in short, warm meat with ingredients...the Tantrika religion is very mysterious, inscrutable even to the Yogis." It is this worship of Shakti that is openly and universally practised. The idea of motherhood, i.e. the relation of a son to his mother, is also noticed in great measure. Protestantism as a force is not very significant in Europe, where the religion is, in fact, Roman Catholic. In the religion, Jehovah, Jesus, and the Trinity are secondary; there, the worship is for the Mother—She, the Mother, with the Child

Jesus in her arms. The emperor cries "Mother", the field-marshal cries "Mother", the soldier with the flag in his hand cries "Mother", the seaman at the helm cries "Mother", the fisherman in his rags cries "Mother", the beggar in the street cries "Mother"! A million voices in a million ways, from a million places—from the palace, from the cottage, from the church, cry "Mother", "Mother", "Mother"! Everywhere is the cry "Ave Maria"; day and night, "Ave Maria", "Ave Maria"!

Next is the worship of the woman. This worship of Shakti is not lust, but is that Shakti-Pujâ, that worship of the Kumâri (virgin) and the Sadhavâ (the married woman whose husband is living), which is done in Varanasi, Kalighat, and other holy places. It is the worship of the Shakti, not in mere thought, not in imagination, but in actual, visible form. Our Shakti-worship is only in the holy places, and at certain times only is it performed; but theirs is in every place and always, for days, weeks, months, and years. Foremost is the woman's state, foremost is her dress, her seat, her food, her wants, and her comforts; the first honours in all respects are accorded to her. Not to speak of the noble-born, not to speak of the young and the fair, it is the worship of any and every woman, be she an acquaintance or a stranger. This Shakti-worship the Moors, the mixed Arab race, Mohammedan in religion, first introduced into Europe when they conquered Spain and ruled her for eight centuries. It was the Moors who first sowed in Europe the seeds of Western civilisation and Shakti-worship. In course of time, the Moors forgot this Shakti-Worship and fell from their position of strength, culture and glory, to live scattered and unrecognised in an unnoticed corner of Africa, and their power and civilisation passed over to Europe. The Mother, leaving the Moors, smiled Her loving blessings on the Christians and illumined their homes.

VI—FRANCE—PARIS

What is this Europe? Why are the black, the bronze, the yellow, the red inhabitants of Asia, Africa, and America bent low at the feet of the Europeans? Why are they the sole rulers in this Kali-Yuga? To understand this Europe one has to understand her through France, the fountain-head of everything that is highest in the West. The supreme power that rules the world is Europe, and of this Europe the great centre is Paris. Paris is the centre of Western civilization. Here, in Paris, matures and ripens every idea of Western ethics, manners and customs, light or darkness, good or evil. This Paris is like a vast ocean, in which there is many a precious gem, coral, and pearl, and in which, again, there are sharks and other rapacious sea-animals as well. Of Europe, the central field of work, the Karmakshetra, is France. A picturesque country, neither very cold nor very warm, very fertile, weather neither excessively wet nor extremely dry, sky clear, sun sweet, elms and oaks in abundance, grass-lands charming, hills and rivers small, springs delightful. Excepting some parts of China, no other country in the world have I seen that is so beautiful as France. That play of beauty in water and fascination in land, that madness in the air, that ecstasy in the sky! Nature so lovely—the men so fond of beauty! The rich and the poor, the young and the old, keep their houses, their rooms, the streets, the fields, the gardens, the walks, so artistically neat and clean—the whole country looks like a picture. Such love of nature and art have I seen nowhere else, except in Japan. The palatial structures, the gardens resembling Indra's paradise, the groves, even the farmer's fields—everywhere and in everything there is an attempt at beauty, an attempt at art, remarkable and effected with success, too.

From ancient times, France has been the scene of conflict among the Gauls, the Romans, the Franks, and other nations. After the destruction of the Roman Empire, the Franks obtained absolute dominion over Europe. Their King, Charlemagne, forced Christianity into Europe, by the power of the sword. Europe was made known in Asia by these Franks. Hence we still call the Europeans Franki, Feringi, Planki or Filinga, and so on.

Ancient Greece, the fountain-head of Western civilisation, sank into oblivion from the pinnacle of her glory, the vast empire of Rome was broken into pieces by the dashing waves of the barbarian invaders—the light of Europe went out; it was at this time that another barbarous race rose out of obscurity in Asia—the Arabs. With extraordinary rapidity, that Arab tide began to spread over the different parts of the world. Powerful Persia had to kiss the ground before the Arabs and adopt the Mohammedan religion, with the result that the Mussulman religion took quite a new shape; the religion of the Arabs and the civilisation of Persia became intermingled.

With the sword of the Arabs, the Persian civilisation began to disseminate in all directions. That Persian civilisation had been borrowed from ancient Greece and India. From the East and from the West, the waves of Mussulman invaders dashed violently on Europe and along them also, the light of wisdom and civilisation began dispersing the darkness of blind and barbarous Europe. The wisdom, learning, and arts of ancient Greece entered into Italy, overpowered the barbarians, and with their quickening impulse, life began to pulsate in the dead body of the world-capital of Rome. The pulsation of this new life took a strong and formidable shape in the city of Florence—old Italy began showing signs of new life. This is called Renaissance, the new birth. But this new birth was for Italy only a rebirth; while for the rest of Europe, it was the first birth. Europe was born in the sixteenth century A.D. i.e. about the time when Akbar, Jehangir, Shahjahan, and other Moghul Emperors firmly established their mighty empire in India.

Italy was an old nation. At the call of the Renaissance, she woke up and gave her response, but only to turn over on her side in bed, as it were, and fall fast asleep again. For various reasons, India also stirred up a little at this time. For three ruling generations from Akbar, learning, wisdom, and arts came to be much esteemed in India. But India was also a very old nation; and for some reason or other, she also did the same as Italy and slept on again.

In Europe, the tide of revival in Italy struck the powerful, young and new nation, the Franks. The torrent of civilisation, flowing from all quarters to Florence and there uniting, assumed a new form; but Italy had not the power within herself to hold that stupendous mass of fresh energy. The revival would have, as in India, ended there, had it not been for the good fortune of Europe that the new nation of the Franks gladly took up that energy, and they in vigour of their youthful blood boldly floated their national ship on the tide; and the current of that progress gradually gathered in volume and strength—from one it swelled into a thousand courses. The other nations of Europe greedily took the water of that tide into their own countries by cutting new channels, and increased its volume and speed by pouring their own lifeblood into it. That tidal wave broke, in the fullness of time, on the shores of India. It reached as far as the coast of Japan, and she became revitalised by bathing in its water. Japan is the new nation of Asia.

Paris is the fountain-head of European civilisation, as Gomukhi is of the Ganga. This huge metropolis is a vision of heaven on earth, the city of constant rejoicing. Such luxury, such enjoyments, such mirthfulness are neither in London nor in Berlin nor anywhere else. True, there is wealth in London and in New York, in Berlin there is learning and wisdom; but nowhere is that French soil, and above all, nowhere is that genius of the French man. Let there be wealth in plenty, let there be learning and wisdom, let there be beauty of nature also, elsewhere—but where is the man? This remarkable French character is the incarnation of the ancient Greek, as it were, that had died to be born again—always joyful, always full of enthusiasm, very light and silly, yet again exceedingly grave, prompt, and resolute to do every work, and again despondent at the least resistance. But that despondency is only for a moment with the Frenchman, his face soon after glowing again with fresh hope and trust.

The Paris University is the model of European universities. All the Academies of Science that are in the world are imitations of the French Academy. Paris is the first teacher of the founding of colonial empires. The terms used in military art in all languages are still mostly French. The style and diction of French writings are copied in all the European languages. Of science, philosophy, and art, this Paris is the mine. Everywhere, in every respect, there is imitation of the French. As if the French were the townspeople, and the other nations only villagers compared with them! What the French initiate, the Germans, the English, and other nations imitate, may be fifty or twenty-five years later, whether it be in learning, or in art, or in social matters. This French civilisation reached Scotland, and when the Scottish king became the king of England, it awoke and roused England; it was during the reign of the Stuart Dynasty of Scotland that the Royal Society and other institutions were established in England.

Again, France is the home of liberty. From here, the city of Paris, travelled with tremendous energy the power of the People, and shook the very foundations of Europe. From that time the face of Europe has completely changed and a new Europe has collie into existence. "Liberté, Equalité, Fraternité" is no more heard in France; she is now pursuing other ideas and other purposes, while the spirit of tile French Revolution is still working among the other nations of Europe.

One distinguished scientist of England told me the other day that Paris was the centre of the world, and that the more a nation would succeed in establishing its connection with the city of Paris, the more would that nation's progress in national life be achieved. Though such assertion is a partial exaggeration of fact, yet it is certainly true that if anyone has to give to the world any new idea, this Paris is the place for its dissemination. If one can gain the approbation of the citizens of Paris, that voice the whole of Europe is sure to echo back. The sculptor, the painter the musician the dancer, or any artist, if he can first obtain celebrate in Paris, acquires very easily the esteem and eulogy of other countries.

We hear only of the darker side of this Paris in our country—that it is a horrible place, a hell on earth. Some of the English hold this view; and the wealthy people of other countries, in whose eyes no other enjoyment is possible in life except the gratification of the senses, naturally see Paris as the home of immorality and enjoyments.

But it is the same in all big cities of the West, such as London, Berlin, Vienna, New York. The only difference is: in other countries the means of enjoyment are commonplace and vulgar, but the very dirt of civilised Paris is coated over with gold leaf. To compare tile refined enjoyments of Paris with the barbarity, in this respect, of other cities is to compare the wild boar's wallowing in the mire with the peacock's dance spreading out its feathers like a fan.

What nation in the world has not the longing to enjoy and live a life of pleasure? Otherwise, why should those who get rich hasten to Paris of all places? Why do kings and emperors, assuming other names come to Paris and live incognito and feel themselves happy by bathing in this whirlpool of sense-enjoyment? The longing is in all countries, and no pains are spared to satisfy it; the only difference is: the French have perfected it as a science, they know how to enjoy, they have risen to the highest rung of the ladder of enjoyment.

Even then, most of the vulgar dances and amusements are for the foreigner; the French people are very cautious, they never waste money for nothing. All those luxuries, those expensive hotels and cafés, at which the cost of a dinner is enough to ruin one, are for the rich foolish foreigner. The French are highly refined, profuse in etiquette, polished and suave in their manners, clever in drawing money from one's pocket; and when they do, they laugh in their sleeve.

Besides, there is another thing to note. Society, as it is among the Americans, Germans, and the English, is open to all nations; so the foreigner can quickly see the ins and outs of it. After an acquaintance of a few days, the American will invite one to live in his house for a while; the Germans also do the same; and the English do so after a longer acquaintance. But it is very different with the French; a Frenchman will never invite one to live with his family unless he is very intimately acquainted with him. But when a foreigner gets such all opportunity and has occasion and time enough to see and know the family, he forms quite a different opinion from what he generally hears. Is it not equally foolish of foreigners to venture an opinion on our national character, as they do, by seeing only the low quarters of Calcutta? So with Paris. The unmarried women in France are as well guarded as in our country, they cannot even mix flatly in society; only after marriage can they do so in company with their husbands. Like us, their negotiations for marriage are carried on by their parents. Being a jolly people, none of their big social functions will be complete without professional dancers, as with us performances of dancing-girls are given on the occasions of marriage and Puja. Living in a dark foggy country, the English are gloomy, make long faces and remark that such dances at one's home are very improper, but at a theatre they are all right. It should lie noted here that their dances may appear improper to our eyes, but not so with them, they being accustomed to them. The girl may, at a dance, appear in a dress showing the to neck and shoulders, and that is not taken as improper; and the English and Americans would not object to attending such dances, but on going hone, might not refrain from condemning tile French customs!

Again, the idea is the same everywhere regarding the chastity; of women, whose deviation from it is fraught with danger, but in the case of men it does not matter so much. The Frenchman is, no doubt, a little freer in this respect, and like the rich men of other countries cares not for criticism. Generally speaking, in Europe, the majority of men do not regard a little lax conduct as so very bad, and in the West, the same is the case with bachelors. The parents of young students consider it rather a drawback if the latter fight shy of women, lest they become effeminate. The one excellence which a man must have, in the West, is courage. Their word "virtue" and our word "Viratva" (heroism) are one and the same. Look to the derivation of the word "virtue" and see what they call goodness in man. For women, they hold chastity as the most important virtue, no doubt. One man marrying more than one wife is not so injurious to society as a woman having more than one husband at the same time, for the latter leads to the gradual decay of the race. Therefore, in all countries good care is taken to preserve the chastity of women. Behind this attempt of every society to preserve the chastity of women is seen the hand of nature. The tendency of nature is to multiply the population, and the chastity of women helps that tendency. Therefore, in being more anxious about the purity of women than of men, every society is only assisting nature in the fulfilment of her purpose.

The object of my speaking of these things is to impress upon you the fact that the life of each nation has a moral purpose of its own, and the manners and customs of a nation must be judged from the standpoint of that purpose. The Westerners should be seen through their eyes; to see them through our eyes, and for them to see us with theirs—both these are mistakes. The purpose of our life is quite the opposite of theirs. The Sanskrit name for a student, Brahmachârin, is synonymous with the Sanskrit word Kâmajit[1]. Our goal of life is Moksha; how can that be ever attained without Brahmacharya or absolute continence? Hence it is imposed upon our boys and youth as an indispensable condition during their studentship. The purpose of life in the West is Bhoga, enjoyment; hence much attention to strict Brahmacharya is not so indispensably necessary with them as it is with us.

Now, to return to Paris. There is no city in the world that can compare with modern Paris. Formerly it was quite different from what it is now—it was somewhat like the Bengali quarters of Varanasi, with zigzag lanes and streets, two houses joined together by an arch over the lane here and there, wells by the side of walls, and so on. In the last Exhibition they showed a model of old Paris, but that Paris has completely disappeared by gradual changes; the warfare and revolutions through which the city has passed have, each time, caused ravages in one part or another, razing every thing to the ground, and again, new Paris has risen in its place, cleaner and more extensive.

Modern Paris is, to a great extent, the creation of Napoleon III. He completed that material transformation of the city which had already been begun at the fall of the ancient monarchy. The student of the history of France need not be reminded how its people were oppressed by the absolute monarchs of France prior to the French Revolution. Napoleon III caused himself to be proclaimed Emperor by sheer force of arms, wading through blood. Since the first French Revolution, the French people were always fickle and thus a source of alarm to the Empire. Hence the Emperor, in order to keep his subjects contented and to please the ever-unstable masses of Paris by giving them work, went on continually making new and magnificent public roads and embankments and building gateways, theatres, and many other architectural structures, leaving the monuments of old Paris as before. Not only was the city traversed in all directions by new thoroughfares, straight and wide, with sumptuous houses raised or restored, but a line of fortification was built doubling the area of the city. Thus arose the boulevards, and the fine quarters of d'Antin and other neighbourhoods; and the avenue of the Champs Elysées, which is unique in the world was reconstructed. This avenue is so broad that down the middle and on both sides of it run gardens all along, and in one place it has taken a circular shape which comprises the city front, toward the West,

1. One who has full control over his passions.

called Place de la Concorde. Round this Place de la Concorde are statues in the form of women representing the eight chief towns of France. One of these statues represents the district of Strasburg. This district was wrested from the hands of the French by the Germans after the battle of 1870. The pain of this loss the French have not yet been able to get over, and that statue is still covered with flowers and garlands offered in memory of its dead spirit, as it were. As men place garlands over the tombs of their dead relations, so garlands are placed on that statue, at one time or another.

It seems to me that the Chandni Chauk of Delhi might have been at one time somewhat like this Place de la Concorde. Here and there columns of victory, triumphal arches and sculptural art in the form of huge statues of man and women, lions, etc., adorn the square.

A very big triumphal column in imitation of Trajan's Column, made of gun-metal (procured by melting 1,200 guns), is erected in Place Vendome in memory of the great hero, Napoleon I; on the sides are engraved the victories of his reign, and on the top is the figure of Napoleon Bonaparte. In the Place de la Bastille stands the Column of July (in memory of the Revolution of July 1789) on the side of the old fortress, "The Bastille", afterwards used as a State prison. Here were imprisoned those who incurred the king's displeasure. In those old days, without any trial or anything of the kind, the king would issue a warrant bearing the royal seal, called "Lettre de Cachet". Then, without any inquiry as to what good acts the victim had done for his country, or whether he was really guilty or not, without even any question as to what he actually did to incur the king's wrath, he would be at once thrown into tile Bastille. If the fair favourites of the kings were displeased with anyone, they could obtain by request a "Lettre de Cachet" from the king against that man, and the poor man would at once be sent to the Bastille. Of the unfortunate who were imprisoned there, very few ever came out. When, afterwards, the whole country rose as one man in revolt against such oppression and tyranny and raised the cry of "Individual liberty, All are equal, No one is high or low", the people of Paris in their mad excitement attacked the king and queen. The very first thing the mob did was to pull down the Bastille, the symbol of extreme tyranny of man over man, and passed the night in dancing, singing, and feasting on the spot. The king tried to escape, but the people managed to catch him, and hearing that the father-in-law of the king, the Emperor of Austria, was sending soldiers to aid his son-in-law, became blind with rage and killed the king and the queen. The whole French nation became mad in the name of liberty and equality—France became a republic—they killed all the nobility whom they could get hold of, and many of the nobility gave up their titles and rank and made common cause with the subject people. Not only so, they called all the nations of the world to rise—"Awake, kill the kings who are all tyrants, let all be free and have equal rights." Then all the kings of Europe began to tremble in fear lest this fire might spread into their countries, lest it might bum their thrones; and hence, determined to put it down, they attacked France from all directions. On the other side, the leaders of the French Republic proclaimed, "Our native land is in peril, come one and all", and the proclamation soon spread like the flames of a conflagration throughout the length and breadth of France. The young, the old, the men, the women, the rich, the poor, the high, the low, singing their martial song, La Marseillaise, the inspiring national song of France, came out—crowds of the poor French people, in rags, barefooted, in that severe cold, and half-starved—came out with guns on their shoulders—परतिरागाय... वनिशाय च दुष्कृताम् for the destruction of the wicked and the salvation of their homes—and boldly faced the vast united force of Europe. The whole of Europe could not stand the onrush of that French army. At the head and front of the French army, stood a hero at the movement of whose finger the whole world trembled. He was Napoleon. With the edge of the sword and at the point of the bayonet, he thrust "Liberty, Equality, and Fraternity" into the very bone and marrow of Europe—and thus the victory of the tri-coloured Cocarde was achieved. Later, Napoleon became the Emperor of France and successfully accomplished the consolidation of the French Empire.

Subsequently, not being favoured with an heir to the throne, he divorced the partner of his life in weal and woe, the guiding angel of his good fortune, the Empress Josephine, and married the daughter of the Emperor of Austria. But the wheel of his luck turned with his desertion of Josephine, his army died in the snow and ice during his expedition against Russia. Europe, getting this opportunity, forced him to abdicate his throne, sent him as an exile to an island, and put on the throne one of the old royal dynasty. The wounded lion escaped from the island and presented himself again in France; the whole of France welcomed him and rallied under his banner, and the reigning king fled. But this luck was broken once for all, and it never returned. Again the whole of Europe united against him and defeated him at the battle of Waterloo. Napoleon boarded an English man-of-war and surrendered himself; the English exiled him and kept him as a lifelong prisoner in the distant island of St. Helena. Again a member of the old royal family of France was reinstated as king. Later on, the French people became restless under the old monarchy, rose in rebellion, drove away the king and his family and re-established the Republic In the course of time a nephew of the great Napoleon became a favourite with the people, and by means of intrigues he proclaimed himself Emperor. He was Napoleon III. For some time his reign was very powerful; but being defeated in conflict with the Germans he lost his throne, and France became once more a republic; and since then down to the present day she has continued to be republican.

VII—PROGRESS OF CIVILISATION

The theory of evolution, which is the foundation of almost all the Indian schools of thought, has now made its way into the physical science of Europe. It has been held by the religions of all other countries except India that the universe in its entirety is composed of parts distinctly separate from each other. God, nature, man—each stands by itself, isolated from one another; likewise, beasts, birds, insects, trees, the earth, stones, metals, etc., are all distinct from one another; God created them separate from the beginning.

Knowledge is to find unity in the midst of diversity—to establish unity among things which appear to us to be different from one another. That particular relation by which man finds this sameness is called Law. This is what is known as Natural Law.

I have said before that our education, intelligence, and thought are all spiritual, all find expression in religion. In the West, their manifestation is in the external—in the physical and social planes. Thinkers in ancient India gradually came to understand that that idea of separateness was erroneous, that there was a connection among all those distinct objects—there was a unity which pervaded the whole universe—trees, shrubs, animals, men, Devas, even God Himself; the Advaitin reaching the climax in this line of thought declared all to be but the manifestations of the One. In reality, the metaphysical and the physical universe are one, and the name of this One is Brahman; and the perception of separateness is an error—they called it Mâyâ, Avidyâ or nescience. This is the end of knowledge.

If this matter is not comprehended at the present day by anyone outside India—for India we leave out of consideration—how is one to be regarded as a Pandit? However, most of the erudite men in the West are coming to understand this, in their own way—through physical science. But how that One has become the many—neither do we understand, nor do they. We, too, have offered the solution of this question by saying that it is beyond our understanding, which is limited. They, too, have done the same. But the variations that the One has undergone, the different sorts of species and individuality It is assuming—that can be understood, and the enquiry into this is called Science.

So almost all are now evolutionists in the West. As small animals through gradual steps change into bigger ones, and big animals sometimes deteriorate and become smaller and weaker, and in the course of time die out—so also, man is not born into a civilised state all on a sudden; in these days an assertion to the contrary is no longer believed in by anybody among the thoughtful in the West, especially because the evidence that their ancestors were in a savage state only a few centuries ago, and from that state such a great transformation has taken place in so short a time. So they say that all men must have gradually evolved, and are gradually evolving from the uncivilised state.

Primitive men used to mange their work with implements of wood and stone; they wore skins and leaves, and lived in mountain-caves or in huts thatched with leaves made somewhat after the fashion of birds' nests, and thus somehow passed their days. Evidence in proof of this is being obtained in all countries by excavating the earth, and also in some few places, men at that same primitive stage are still living. Gradually men learnt to use metal—soft metals such as tin and copper—and found out how to make tools and weapons by fusing them. The ancient Greeks, the Babylonians, and the Egyptians did not know the use of iron for a long time—even when they became comparatively civilised and wrote books and used gold and silver. At that time, the Mexicans, the Peruvians, the Mayas, and other races among the aborigines of the New World were comparatively civilised and used to build large temples; the use of gold and silver was quite common amongst them (in fact the greed for their gold and silver led the Spaniards to destroy them). But they managed to make all these things, toiling very hard with flint instruments—they did not know iron even by name.

In the primitive stage, man used to kill wild animals and fish by means of bows and arrows, or by the use of a net, and live upon them. Gradually, he learnt to till the ground and tend the cattle. Taming wild animals, he made them work for him or reared them for his own eating when necessary; the cow, horse, hog, elephant, camel, goat, sheep, fowls, birds, and other animals became domesticated; of all these, the dog is the first friend of man.

So, in course of time, the tilling of the soil came into existence. The fruits, roots, herbs, vegetables, and the various cereals eaten by man are quite different now from what they were when they grew in a wild state. Through human exertion and cultivation wild fruits gained in size and acquired toothsomeness, and wild grass was transformed into delicious rice. Constant changes are going on, no doubt, in nature, by its own processes. Few species of trees and plants, birds and beasts are being always created in nature through changes, brought about by time, environment and other causes. Thus before the creation of man, nature was changing the trees, plants, and other animals by slow and gentle degrees, but when man came on the scene, he began to effect changes with rapid strides. He continually transported the native fauna and flora of one country to another, and by crossing them various new species of plants and animals were brought into existence.

In the primitive stage there was no marriage, but gradually matrimonial relations sprang up. At first, the matrimonial relation depended, amongst all communities, on the mother. There was not much fixity about the father, the children were named after the mother: all the wealth was in the hands of the women, for they were to bring up the children. In the course of time, wealth, the women included, passed into the hands of the male members. The male said, "All this wealth and grain are mine; I have grown these in the fields or got them by plunder and other means; and if anyone dispute my claims and want to have a share of them, I will fight him." In the same way he said, "All these women are exclusively mine; if anyone encroach upon my right in them, I will fight him." Thus there originated the modern marriage system. Women became as much the property of man as his slaves and chattels. The ancient marriage custom was that the males of one tribe married the women of another; and even then the women were snatched away by force. In course of time, this business of taking away the bride by violence dropped away, and marriage was contracted with the mutual consent of both parties. But every custom leaves a faint trace of itself behind, and even now we find in every country a mock attack is made on such occasions upon the bridegroom. In Bengal and Europe, handfuls of rice are thrown at the bridegroom, and in Northern India the bride's women friends abuse the bridegroom's party calling them names, anti so on.

Society began to be formed and it varied according to different countries. Those who lived on the sea-shore mostly earned their livelihood by fishing in the sea, those on the plains by agriculture. The mountaineers kept large flocks of sheep, and the dwellers in the desert tended goats and camels. Others lived in the forests and maintained themselves by hunting. The dwellers on the plain learnt agriculture; their struggle for existence became less keen; they had time for thought and culture, and thus became more and more civilised. But with the advance of civilisation their bodies grew weaker and weaker. The difference in physique between those who always lived in the open air and whose principal article of food was animal diet, and others who dwelt in houses and lived mostly on grains and vegetables, became greater and greater. The hunter, the shepherd, the fisherman turned robbers or pirates whenever food became scarce and plundered the dwellers in the plains. These, in their turn, united themselves in bands of large numbers for the common interest of self-preservation; and thus little kingdoms began to be formed.

The Devas lived on grains and vegetables, were civilised, dwelt in villages, towns, and gardens, and wore woven clothing. The Asuras[1] dwelt in the hills and mountains, deserts or on the sea-shores, lived on wild animals, and the roots and fruits of the forests, and on what cereals they could get from the Devas in exchange for these or for their cows and sheep, and wore the hides of wild animals. The Devas were weak in body and could not endure hardships; the Asuras, on the other hand, were hardy with frequent fasting and were quite capable of suffering all sorts of hardships.

Whenever food was scarce among the Asuras, they set out from their hills and sea-shores to plunder towns and villages. At times they attacked the Devas for wealth and grains and whenever the Devas failed to unite themselves in large numbers against them, they were sure to die at the hands of the Asuras. But the Devas being stronger in intelligence,

1. The terms "Devas" and "Asuras" are used here in the sense in which they occur in the Gitâ (XVI), i.e. races in which the Daivi (divine) or the Âsuri (non-divine) traits preponderate.

commenced inventing, all sorts of machines for warfare. The Brahmâstra, Garudâstra Vaishnavâstra, Shaivâstra—all these weapons of miraculous power belonged to the Devas. The Asuras fought with ordinary weapons, but they were enormously strong. They defeated the Devas repeatedly, but they never cared to become civilised, or learn agriculture, or cultivate their intellect. If the victorious Asuras tried to reign over the vanquished Devas in Svarga, they were sure to be outwitted by the Devas' superior intellect and skill, and, before long, turned into their slaves. At other times, the Asuras returned to their own places after plundering. The Devas, whenever they were united, forced them to retire, mark you, either into the hills or forests, or to the sea-shore. Gradually each party gained in numbers and became stronger and stronger; millions of Devas were united, and so were millions of Asuras. Violent conflicts and fighting went on, and along with them, the intermingling of these two forces.

From the fusion of these different types and races our modern societies, manners, and customs began to be evolved. New ideas sprang up and new sciences began to be cultivated. One class of men went on manufacturing articles of utility and comfort, either by manual or intellectual labour. A second class took upon themselves the charge of protecting them, and all proceeded to exchange these things. And it so happened that a band of fellows who were very clever undertook to take these things from one place to another and on the plea of remuneration for this, appropriated the major portion of their profit as their due. One tilled the ground, a second guarded the produce from being robbed, a third took it to another place and a fourth bought it. The cultivator got almost nothing; he who guarded the produce took away as much of it as he could by force; the merchant who brought it to the market took the lion's share; and the buyer had to pay out of all proportion for the things, and smarted under the burden! The protector came to be known as the king; he who took the commodities from one place to another was the merchant. These two did not produce anything—but still snatched away the best part of things and made themselves fat by virtually reaping most of the fruits of the cultivator's toil and labour. Tile poor fellows who produced all these things had often to go without his meals and cry to God for help!

Now, with the march of events, all these matters' grew more and more involved, knots upon knots multiplied, and out of this tangled network has evolved our modern complex society. But the marks of a bygone: character persist and do not die out completely. Those who in their former births tended sheep or lived by fishing or the like take to habits of piracy, robbery, and similar occupations in their civilised incarnation also. With no forests to hunt in, no hills or mountains in the neighbourhood on which to tend the flocks—by the accident of birth in a civilised society, he cannot get enough opportunity for either hunting, fishing, or grazing, cattle—he is obliged therefore to rob or steal, impelled by his own nature; what else can he do? And the worthy daughters of those far-famed ladies[1] of the Paurânika age, whose names we are to repeat every morning—they can no longer marry more than one husband at a time, even if they want to, and so they turn unchaste. In these and other ways, men of different types and dispositions, civilised and savage, born with the nature of the Devas and the Asuras have become fused together and form modern society. And that is why we see, in every society, God plating in these various forms—the Sâdhu Nârâyana, the robber Narayana, and so on. Again, the character of any particular society came to be determined as Daivi (divine) or Âsuri (non-divine) quality, in proportion as one or the other of these two different types of persons preponderated within it.

The whole of tile Asian civilization was first evolved on the plains near large rivers and on fertile soils—on the banks of the Ganga, the Yangtse-Kiang, and the Euphrates. The original foundation of all these civilisations is agriculture, and in all of there the Daivi nature predominates. Most of the European civilization, on the other hand, originated either in hilly countries or on the sea coasts—piracy and robbery form the basis of this civilisation; there the Asuri nature is preponderant.

So far as can be inferred in modern times, Central Asia and the deserts of Arabia seem to have been the home of the Asuras. Issuing from their fastnesses, these shepherds and hunters, the descendants of the Asuras, being united in hordes after hordes, chased the civilized Devas and scattered them all over the world.

Of course there was a primitive race of aborigines in the continent of Europe. They lived in mountain-caves, and the more intelligent among them erected platforms by planting sticks in tile comparatively shallow parts of the water and built houses thereon. They used arrows, spearheads, knives, and axes, all made of flint, and managed every kind of work with them.

Gradually the current of the Asian races began to break forth upon Europe, and as its effects, some parts became comparatively civilised; the language of a certain people in Russia resembles the languages of Southern India.

But for the most part these barbarians remained as barbarous as ever, till a civilised race from Asia Minor conquered the adjacent parts of Europe and founded a high order of new civilization: to us they are known as Yavanas, to the Europeans as Greeks.

Afterwards, in Italy, a barbarous tribe known as the Romans conquered the civilised Etruscans, assimilated their culture and learning, and established a civilization of their own on the ruins of that of the conquered race. Gradually, the Romans carried their victorious arms in all directions; all the barbarous tribes in the southwest of Europe came under the suzerainty of Rome; only the barbarians of the forests living in the northern regions retained independence. In the efflux of time, however, the Romans became enervated by being slaves to wealth and luxury, and at that time Asia again let loose

1. Ahalyâ, Târâ, Mandodari, Kunti, and Draupadi.

Lectures & Discourses by **Swami Vivekananda**

her armies of Asuras on Europe. Driven from their homes by the onslaught of these Asuras, the barbarians of Northern Europe fell upon the Roman Empire, and Rome was destroyed. Encountered by the force of this Asian invasion, a new race sprang up through the fusion of the European barbarians with the remnants of the Romans and Greeks. At that time, the Jews being conquered and driven away from their homes by the Romans, scattered themselves throughout Europe, and with them their new religion, Christianity, also spread all over Europe. All these different races and their creeds and ideas, all these different hordes of Asuras, heated by the fire of constant struggle and warfare, began to melt and fuse in Mahâmâyâ's crucible; and from that fusion the modern European race has sprung up.

Thus a barbarous, very barbarous European race came into existence, with all shades of complexion from the swarthy colour of the Hindus to the milk-white colour of the North, with black, brown, red, or white hair, black, grey, or blue eyes, resembling the fine features of face, the nose and eyes of the Hindus, or the flat faces of the Chinese. For some time they continued to tight among themselves; those of the north leading the life of pirates harassed and killed the comparatively civilised races. In the meantime, however, the two heads of the Christian Churches, the Pope (in French and Italian, Pape[2]) of Italy and the Patriarch of Constantinople, insinuating themselves, began to exercise their authority over these brutal barbarian hordes, over their kings, queens, and peoples.

On the other side, again Mohammedanism arose in the deserts of Arabia. The wild Arabs, inspired by tile teachings of a great sage, bore down upon the earth with all irresistible force and vigour. That torrent, carrying everything before it, entered Europe from both the East and the West, and along with this tide the learning and culture of India and ancient Greece were carried into Europe.

A tribe of Asuras from Central Asia known as the Seljuk Tartars, accepted Mohammedanism and conquered Asia Minor and other countries of Asia. The various attempts of the Arabs to conquer India proved unsuccessful. The wave of Mohammedan conquest, which had swallowed the whole earth, had to fall back before India. They attacked Sindh once, but could not told it: and they did not make any other attempt after that.

But a few centuries afterwards, when the Turks and other Tartar races were converted from Buddhism to Mohammedanism—at that time they conquered the Hindus, Persians, and Arabs, and brought all of them alike under their subjection. Of all the Mohammedan conquerors of India, none was an Arab or a Persian; they were all Turks and Tartars. In Rajputana, all the Mohammedan invaders were called Turks, and that is a true and historical fact. The Chârans of Rajputana sang "turuganko bodhi jor —The Turks are very powerful"—and that was true. From Kutubuddin down to the

2. pronounced as *Pâp*.

Mogul Emperors—all of them are Tartars. They are the same race to which the Tibetans belong; only they have become Mohammedans and changed their flat round faces by intermarrying with the Hindus and Persians. They are the same ancient races of Asuras. Even today they are reigning on the thrones of Kabul, Persia, Arabia, and Constantinople, and the Gândhâris (natives of Kandahar) and Persians are still the slaves of the Turks. The vast Empire of China, too, is lying at the feet of the Manchurian Tartars; only these Manchus have not given up their religion, have not become Mohammedans, they are disciples of the Grand Lama. These Asuras never care for learning and cultivation of the intellect; the only thing they understand is fighting. Very little of the warlike spirit is possible without a mixture of that blood; and it is that Tartar blood which is seen in the vigorous, martial spirit of Northern Europe, especially in the Russians, who have three-fourths of Tartar blood in their veins. The fight between the Devas and the Asuras will continue yet for a long time to come. The Devas marry the Asura girls and the Asuras snatch away Deva brides—it is this that leads to the formation of powerful mongrel races.

The Tartars seized and occupied the throne of tile Arabian Caliph, took possession of Jerusalem, the great Christian place of pilgrimage, and other plates, would not allow pilgrims to visit the holy sepulchre, and killed many Christians. The heads of the Christian Churches grew mad with rage and roused their barbarian disciples throughout Europe, who in their turn inflamed the kings and their subjects alike. Hordes of European barbarians rushed towards Asia Minor to deliver Jerusalem from the hands of the infidels. A good portion of them cut one another's throats, others died of disease, while the rest were killed by the Mohammedans. However, the blood was up of the wild barbarians, and no sooner had the Mohammedans killed them than they arrived in fresh numbers—with that clogged obstinacy of a wild savage. They thought nothing even of plundering their own men, and making meals of Mohammedans when they found nothing better. It is well known that the English king Richard had a liking for Mohammedan flesh.

Here the result was the same, as usually happens in a war between barbarians and civilised men. Jerusalem and other places could not be conquered. But Europe began to be civilised. The English, French, German, and other savage nations who dressed themselves in hides and ate raw flesh, came in contact with Asian civilisation. An order of Christian soldiers of Italy and other countries, corresponding to our Nâgâs, began to learn philosophy; and one of their sects, the Knights Templars, became confirmed Advaita Vedantists, and ended by holding Christianity up to ridicule. Moreover, as they had amassed enormous riches, the kings of Europe, at the orders of the Pope, and under the pretext of saving religion, robbed and exterminated them.

On the other side, a tribe of Mohammedans, called the Moors, established a civilised kingdom in Spain, cultivated various branches of knowledge, and founded the first university in Europe. Students flocked from all parts, from Italy, France, and even from far-off England. The sons of royal families came to learn manners, etiquette civilisation, and the art of war. Houses, temples, edifices, and other architectural buildings began to be built after a new style.

But the whole of Europe was gradually transformed into a vast military camp—and this is even now the case. When the Mohammedans conquered any kingdom, their king kept a large part for himself, and the rest he distributed among his generals. These men did not pay any rent but had to supply the king with a certain number of soldiers in time of need. Thus the trouble of keeping a standing army always ready was avoided, and a powerful army was created which served only in time of war. This same idea still exists to a certain extent in Rajputana, and it was brought into the West by the Mohammedans. The Europeans took this system from the Mohammedans. But whereas with the Mohammedans there were the king and his groups of feudatory chiefs and their armies, and the rest—the body of the people—were ordinary subjects who were left unmolested in time of war—in Europe, on the other hand, the king and his groups of feudatory chiefs were on one side, and they turned all the subject people into their slaves. Everyone had to live under the shelter of a military feudatory chief, as his man, and then only was he allowed to live; he had to be always ready to fight at any time, at the word of command.

What is the meaning of the "Progress of Civilisation" which the Europeans boast so much about? The meaning of it is the successful accomplishment of the desired object by the justification of wrong means, i.e. by making the end justify the means. It makes acts of theft, falsehood, and hanging appear proper under certain circumstances; it vindicates Stanley's whipping of the hungry Mohammedan guards who accompanied him, for stealing a few mouthfuls of bread; it guides and justifies the well-known European ethics which says, "Get out from this place, I want to come in and possess it", the truth of which is borne out by the evidence of history, that where-ever the Europeans have gone, there has followed the extinction of the aboriginal races. In London, this "progress of civilisation" regards unfaithfulness in conjugal life, and, in Paris, the running away of a man, leaving his wife and children helpless and committing suicide as a mistake and not a crime.

Now compare the first three centuries of the quick spread of the civilisation of Islam with the corresponding period of Christianity. Christianity, during its first three centuries, was not even successful ill making itself known to the world; and since the day when the sword of Constantine made a place for it in his kingdom, what support has Christianity ever lent to the spread of civilisation, either spiritual or secular? What reward did the Christian religion offer to that European Pandit who sought to prove for the first time that the Earth is a revolving planet? What scientist has ever been hailed with approval and enthusiasm by the Christian Church? Can the

literature of the Christian flock consistently meet the requirements of legal jurisprudence, civil or criminal, or of arts and trade policies? Even now the "Church" does not sanction the diffusion of profane literature. Is it possible, still, for a man who has penetrated deep into modern learning and science to be an absolutely sincere Christian? In the New Testament there is no covert or overt praise of any arts and sciences. But there is scarcely any science or branch of art that is not sanctioned and held up for encouragement, directly or indirectly, in the Koran, or in the many passages of the Hadis, the traditional sayings of Mohammed. The greatest thinkers of Europe—Voltaire, Darwin, Büchner, Flammarion, Victor Hugo, anti a host of others like them—are in the present times denounced by Christianity and are victims of the vituperative tongues of its orthodox community. On the other hand, Islam regards such people to be believers in the existence of God, but only wanting in faith in the Prophet. Let there be a searching investigation into the respective merits of the two religions as regards their helpfulness, or the throwing of obstacles in the path of progress, and it will be seen that wherever Islam has gone, there it has preserved the aboriginal inhabitants—there those races still exist, their language and their nationality abide even to the present day.

Where can Christianity show such an achievement? Where are, today, the Arabs of Spain, and the aboriginal races of America? What treatment are the Christians according to the European Jews? With the single exception of charitable organisations no other line of work in Europe is in harmony with the teachings of the Gospel. Whatever heights of progress Europe has attained, every one of them has been gained by its revolt against Christianity—by its rising against the gospel. If Christianity had its old paramount sway in Europe today, it would have lighted the fire of the Inquisition against such modern scientists as Pasteur and Koch, and burnt Darwin and others of his school at the stake. In modern Europe Christianity and civilisation are two different things. Civilisation has now girded up her loins to destroy her old enemy, Christianity, to overthrow the clergy, and to wring educational and charitable institutions from their hands. But for the ignorance-ridden rustic masses, Christianity would never have been able for a moment to support its present despised existence, and would have been pulled out by its roots; for the urban poor are, even now, enemies of the Christian Church! Now compare this with Islam. In the Mohammedan countries, all the ordinances are firmly established upon the Islamic religion, and its own preachers are greatly venerated by all the officials of the State, and teachers of other religions also are respected.

The European civilisation may be likened to a piece of cloth, of which these are the materials: its loom is a vast temperate hilly country on the sea-shore; its cotton, a strong warlike mongrel race formed by the intermixture of various races; its warp is warfare in defence of one's self and one's religion. The one who wields the sword is great, and the one who cannot, gives up his independence and lines under the protection of some warrior's sword. Its woof is commerce. The means to this civilisation is the sword; its auxiliary—courage and strength; its aim enjoyment here and thereafter.

And how is it with us? The Aryans are lovers of peace, cultivators of the soil, and are quite happy and contented if they can only rear their families undisturbed. In such a life they have ample leisure, and therefore greater opportunity of being thoughtful and civilised. Our King Janaka tilled the soil with his own hands, and he was also the greatest of the knowers of Truth, of his time. With us, Rishis, Munis, and Yogis have been born from the very beginning; they have known from the first that the world is a chimera. Plunder and fight as you may, the enjoyment that you are seeking is only in peace; and peace, in the renunciation of physical pleasures. Enjoyment lies not in physical development, but in the culture of the mind and the intellect.

It was the knowers who reclaimed the jungles for cultivation. Then, over that cleared plot of land was built the Vedic altar; in that pure sky of Bhârata, up rose the sacred smoke of Yajnas; in that air breathing peace, the Vedic Mantras echoed and re-echoed—and cattle and other beasts grazed without any fear of danger. The place of the sword was assigned at the feet of learning and Dharma. Its only work was to protect Dharma and save the lives of men and cattle The hero was the protector of the weak in danger—the Kshatriya. Ruling over the plough and the sword was Dharma, the protector of all. He is the King of kings; he is ever-awake even while the world sleeps. Everyone was free under the protection of Dharma.

And what your European Pundits say about the Aryan's swooping down from some foreign land, snatching away the lands of the aborigines and settling in India by exterminating them, is all pure nonsense, foolish talk! Strange, that our Indian scholars, too, say amen to them; and all these monstrous lies are being taught to our boys! This is very bad indeed.

I am an ignoramus myself; I do not pretend to any scholarship; but with the little that I understand, I strongly protested against these ideas at the Paris Congress. I have been talking with the Indian and European savants on the subject, and hope to raise many objections to this theory in detail, when time permits. And this I say to you—to our Pundits—also, "You are learned men, hunt up your old books and scriptures, please, and draw your own conclusions."

Whenever the Europeans find an opportunity, they exterminate the aborigines and settle down in ease and comfort on their lands; and therefore they think the Aryans must have done the same! The Westerners would be considered wretched vagabonds if they lived in their native homes depending wholly on their own internal resources, and so they have to run wildly about the world seeking how they can feed upon the fat of the land of others by spoliation and slaughter; and therefore they conclude the Aryans must have done the same! But where is your proof? Guess-work? Then keep your fanciful guesses to yourselves!

In what Veda, in what Sukta, do you find that the Aryans came into India from a foreign country? Where do you get the idea that they slaughtered the wild aborigines? What do you gain by talking such nonsense? Vain has been your study of the Râmâyana; why manufacture a big fine story out of it?

Well, what is the Ramayana? The conquest of the savage aborigines of Southern India by the Aryans! Indeed! Râmachandra is a civilised Aryan king, and with whom is he fighting? With King Râvana of Lankâ. Just read the Ramayana, and you will find that Ravana was rather more and not less civilised than Ramachandra. The civilisation of Lanka was rather higher, and surely not lower, than that of Ayodhyâ. And then, when were these Vânaras (monkeys) and other Southern Indians conquered? They were all, on the other hand, Ramachandra's friends and allies. Say which kingdoms of Vâli and Guhaka were annexed by Ramachandra?

It was quiet possible, however, that in a few places there were occasional fights between the Aryans and the aborigines; quite possible, that one or two cunning Munis pretended to meditate with closed eyes before their sacrificial fires in the jungles of the Râkshasas, waiting, however, all the time to see when the Rakshasas would throw stones and pieces of bone at them. No sooner had this been done than they would go whining to the kings. The mail clad kings armed with swords and weapons of steel would come on fiery steeds. But how long could the aborigines fight with their sticks and stones? So they were killed or chased away, and the kings returned to their capital. Well, all this may have been, hut how does this prove that their lands were taken away by the Aryans? Where in the Ramayana do you find that?

The loom of the fabric of Aryan civilisation is a vast, warm, level country, interspersed with broad, navigable rivers. The cotton of this cloth is composed of highly civilised, semi-civilised, and barbarian tribes, mostly Aryan. Its warp is Varnâshramâchâra[1], and its woof, the conquest of strife and competition in nature.

And may I ask you, Europeans, what country you have ever raised to better conditions? Wherever you have found weaker races, you have exterminated them by the roots, as it were. You have settled on their lands, and they are gone for ever. What is the history of your America, your Australia, and New Zealand, your Pacific islands and South Africa? Where are those aboriginal races there today? They are all exterminated, you have killed them outright, as if they were wild beasts. It is only where you have not the power to do so, and there only, that other nations are still alive.

But India has never done that. The Aryans were kind and generous; and in their hearts which were large and unbound-

---

1. The old Aryan institution of the four castes and stages of life. The former comprise the Brâhmin, Kshatriya, Vaishya, and Shudra, and the latter, Brahmacharya (student life), Gârhasthya (house-holder's life), Vânaprastha (hermit life), and Sannyâsa (life of renunciation).

ed as the ocean, and in their brains, gifted with superhuman genius, all these ephemeral and apparently pleasant but virtually beastly processes never found a place. And I ask you, fools of my own country, would there have been this institution of Varnashrama if the Aryans had exterminated the aborigines in order to settle on their lands?

The object of the peoples of Europe is to exterminate all in order to live themselves. The aim of the Aryans is to raise all up to their own level, nay, even to a higher level than themselves. The means of European civilisation is the sword; of the Aryans, the division into different Varnas. This system of division into different Varnas is the stepping-stone to civilisation, making one rise higher and higher in proportion to one's learning and culture. In Europe, it is everywhere victory to the strong and death to the weak. In the land of Bhârata, every social rule is for the protection of the weak.

INSPIRED TALKS

UNTITLED TALK I

RECORDED BY MISS S. E. WALDO, A DISCIPLE

This day marks the beginning of the regular teaching given daily by Swami Vivekananda to his disciples at Thousand Island Park. We had not yet all assembled there, but the Master's heart was always in his work, so he commenced at once to teach the three or four who were with him. He came on this first morning with the Bible in his hand and opened to the Book of John, saying that since we were all Christians, it was proper that he should begin with the Christian scriptures.

WEDNESDAY, June 19, 1895.

"In the beginning was the Word, and the Word was with God, and the Word was God." The Hindu calls this Mâyâ, the manifestation of God, because it is the power of God. The Absolute reflecting through the universe is what we call nature. The Word has two manifestations—the general one of nature, and the special one of the great Incarnations of God—Krishna, Buddha, Jesus, and Ramakrishna. Christ, the special manifestation of the Absolute, is known and knowable. The absolute cannot be known: we cannot know the Father, only the Son. We can only see the Absolute through the "tint of humanity", through Christ.

In the first five verses of John is the whole essence of Christianity: each verse is full of the profoundest philosophy.

The Perfect never becomes imperfect. It is in the darkness, but is not affected by the darkness. God's mercy goes to all, but is not affected by their wickedness. The sun is not affected by any disease of our eyes which may make us see it distorted. In the twenty-ninth verse, "taketh away the sin of the world" means that Christ would show us the way to become perfect. God became Christ to show man his true nature, that we too are God. We are human coverings over the Divine; but as the

divine Man, Christ and we are one.

The Trinitarian Christ is elevated above us; the Unitarian Christ is merely a moral man; neither can help us. The Christ who is the Incarnation of God, who has not forgotten His divinity, that Christ can help us, in Him there is no imperfection. These Incarnations are always conscious of their own divinity; they know it from their birth. They are like the actors whose play is over, but who, after their work is done, return to please others. These great Ones are untouched by aught of earth; they assume our form and our limitations for a time in order to teach us; but in reality they are never limited, they are ever free…

Good is near Truth, but is not yet Truth. After learning not to be disturbed by evil, we have to learn not to be made happy by good. We must find that we are beyond both evil and good; we must study their adjustment and see that they are both necessary.

The idea of dualism is from the ancient Persians.[6]* Really good and evil are one (Because they are both chains and products of Maya.) and are in our own mind. When the mind is self-poised, neither good nor bad affects it. Be perfectly free; then neither can affect it, and we enjoy freedom and bliss. Evil is the iron chain, good is the gold one; both are chains. Be free, and know once for all that there is no chain for you. Lay hold of the golden chain to loosen the hold of the iron one, then throw both away. The thorn of evil is in our flesh; take another thorn from the same bush and extract the first thorn; then throw away both and be free…

In the world take always the position of the giver. Give everything and look for no return. Give love, give help, give service, give any little thing you can, but keep out barter. Make no conditions, and none will be imposed. Let us give out of our own bounty, just as God gives to us.

The Lord is the only Giver, all the men in the world are only shopkeepers. Get His cheque, and it must be honoured everywhere.

"God is the inexplicable, inexpressible essence of love", to be known, but never defined.

* * *

In our miseries and struggles the world seems to us a very dreadful place. But just as when we watch two puppies playing and biting we do not concern ourselves at all, realising that it is only fun and that even a sharp nip now and then will do no actual harm, so all our struggles are but play in God's eyes. This world is all for play and only amuses God; nothing in it can make God angry.

* * *

"Mother! In the sea of life my bark is sinking. The whirlwind of illusion, the storm of attachment is growing every moment.

My five oarsmen (senses) are foolish, and the helmsman (mind) is weak.

My bearings are lost, my boat is sinking. O Mother! Save me!"

"Mother, Thy light stops not for the saint or the sinner; it animates the lover and the murderer." Mother is ever manifesting through all. The light is not polluted by what it shines on, nor benefited by it. The light is ever pure, ever changeless. Behind every creature is the "Mother", pure, lovely, never changing. "Mother, manifested as light in all beings, we bow down to Thee!" She is equally in suffering, hunger, pleasure, sublimity. "When the bee sucks honey, the Lord is eating." Knowing that the Lord is everywhere, the sages give up praising and blaming. Know that nothing can hurt you. How? Are you not free? Are you not Âtman? He is the Life of our lives, the hearing of our ears, the sight of our eyes.

We go through the world like a man pursued by a policeman and see the barest glimpses of the beauty of it. All this fear that pursues us comes from believing in matter. Matter gets its whole existence from the presence of mind behind it. What we see is God percolating through nature. (Here "nature" means matter and mind.)

UNTITLED TALK II

RECORDED BY MISS S. E. WALDO, A DISCIPLE
SUNDAY, June 23, 1895.

Be brave and be sincere; then follow any path with devotion, and you must reach the Whole. Once lay hold of one link of the chain, and the whole chain must come by degrees. Water the roots of the tree (that is, reach the Lord), and the whole tree is watered; getting the Lord, we get all.

One-sidedness is the bane of the world. The more sides you can develop the more souls you have, and you can see the universe through all souls—through the Bhakta (devotee) and the Jnâni (philosopher). Determine your own nature and stick to it. Nishthâ (devotion to one ideal) is the only method for the beginner; but with devotion and sincerity it will lead to all. Churches, doctrines, forms, are the hedges to protect the tender plant, but they must later be broken down that the plant may become a tree. So the various religions, Bibles, Vedas, dogmas—all are just tubs for the little plant; but it must get out of the tub. Nishthâ is, in a manner, placing the plant in the tub, shielding the struggling soul in its path...

Look at the "ocean" and not at the "wave"; see no difference between ant and angel. Every worm is the brother of the Nazarene. How say one is greater and one less? Each is great in his own place. We are in the sun and in the stars as much as here. Spirit is beyond space and time and is everywhere. Every mouth praising the Lord is my mouth, every eye seeing is my eye. We are confined nowhere; we are not body, the universe is our body. We are magicians waving magic wands and creating scenes before us at will. We are the spider in his huge web, who can go on the varied strands wheresoever he desires. The spider is now only conscious of the spot where he is, but he will in time become conscious of the whole web. We are now conscious only where the body is, we can use only one brain; but when we reach ultraconsciousness, we know all, we can use all brains. Even now we can "give the push" in consciousness, and it goes beyond and acts in the superconscious.

We are striving "to be" and nothing more, no "I" ever—just pure crystal, reflecting all, but ever the same, When that state is reached, there is no more doing; the body becomes a mere mechanism, pure without care for it; it cannot become impure.

Know you are the Infinite, then fear must die. Say ever, "I and my Father are one."

* * *

In time to come Christs will be in numbers like bunches of grapes on a vine; then the play will be over and will pass out—as water in a kettle beginning to boil shows first one bubble, then another then more and more, until all is in ebullition and passes out as steam. Buddha and Christ are the two biggest "bubbles" the world has yet produced. Moses was a tiny bubble, greater and greater ones came. Sometime, however, all will be bubbles and escape; but creation, ever new, will bring new water to go through the process all over again.

UNTITLED TALK III

RECORDED BY MISS S. E. WALDO, A DISCIPLE
MONDAY, June 24, 1895.

The reading today was from the Bhakti-Sutras by Nârada.

"Extreme love to God is Bhakti, and this love is the real immortality, getting which a man becomes perfectly satisfied, sorrows for no loss, and is never jealous; knowing which man becomes mad."

My Master used to say, "This world is a huge lunatic asylum where all men are mad, some after money, some after women, some after name or fame, and a few after God. I prefer to be mad after God. God is the philosophers' stone that turns us to gold in an instant; the form remains, but the nature is changed—the human form remains, but no more can we hurt or sin."

"Thinking of God, some weep, some sing, some laugh, some dance, some say wonderful things, but all speak of nothing but God."

Prophets preach, but the Incarnations like Jesus, Buddha, Ramakrishna, can give religion; one glance, one touch is enough. That is the power of the Holy Ghost, the "laying on of hands"; the power was actually transmitted to the disciples by the Master—the "chain of Guru-power". That, the real baptism, has been handed down for untold ages.

"Bhakti cannot be used to fulfil any desires, itself being the check to all desires." Narada gives these as the signs of love: "When all thoughts, all words, and all deeds are given up unto the Lord, and the least forgetfulness of God makes one intensely miserable, then love has begun."

"This is the highest form of love because therein is no desire for reciprocity, which desire is in all human love."

"A man who has gone beyond social and scriptural usage, he is a Sannyâsin. When the whole soul goes to God, when we take refuge only in God, then we know that we are about to get this love."

Obey the scriptures until you are strong enough to do without them; then go beyond them. Books are not an end-all. Verification is the only proof of religious truth. Each must verify for himself; and no teacher who says, "I have seen, but you cannot", is to be trusted, only that one who says, "You can see too". All scriptures, all truths are Vedas in all times, in all countries; because these truths are to be seen, and any one may discover them.

"When the sun of Love begins to break on the horizon, we want to give up all our actions unto God; and when we forget Him for a moment, it grieves us greatly."

Let nothing stand between God and your love for Him. Love Him, love Him, love Him; and let the world say what it will. Love is of three sorts — one demands, but gives nothing; the second is exchange; and the third is love without thought of return — love like that of the moth for the light.

"Love is higher than work, than Yoga, than knowledge."

Work is merely a schooling for the doer; it can do no good to others. We must work out our own problem; the prophets only show us how to work. "What you think, you become", so if you throw your burden on Jesus, you will have to think of Him and thus become like Him — you love Him.

"Extreme love and highest knowledge are one."

But theorising about God will not do; we must love and work. Give up the world and all worldly things, especially while the "plant" is tender. Day and night think of God and think of nothing else as far as possible. The daily necessary thoughts can all be thought through God. Eat to Him, drink to Him, sleep to Him, see Him in all. Talk of God to others; this is most beneficial.

Get the mercy of God and of His greatest children: these are the two chief ways to God. The company of these children of light is very hard to get; five minutes in their company will change a whole life; and if you really want it enough, one will come to you. The presence of those who love God makes a place holy, "such is the glory of the children of the Lord". They are He; and when they speak, their words are scriptures. The place where they have been becomes filled with their vibrations, and those going there feel them and have a tendency to become holy also.

"To such lovers there is no distinction of caste, learning, beauty, birth, wealth, or occupation; because all are His."

Give up all evil company, especially at the beginning. Avoid worldly company, that will distract your mind. Give up all "me and mine". To him who has nothing in the universe the

Lord comes. Cut the bondage of all worldly affections; go beyond laziness and all care as to what becomes of you. Never turn back to see the result of what you have done. Give all to the Lord and go on and think not of it. The whole soul pours in a continuous current to God; there is no time to seek money, or name, or fame, no time to think of anything but God; then will come into our hearts that infinite, wonderful bliss of Love. All desires are but beads of glass. Love of God increases every moment and is ever new, to be known only by feeling it. Love is the easiest of all, it waits for no logic, it is natural. We need no demonstration, no proof. Reasoning is limiting something by our own minds. We throw a net and catch something, and then say that we have demonstrated it; but never, never can we catch God in a net.

Love should be unrelated. Even when we love wrongly, it is of the true love, of the true bliss; the power is the same, use it as we may. Its very nature is peace and bliss. The murderer when he kisses his baby forgets for an instant all but love. Give up all self, all egotisms get out of anger, lust, give all to God. "I am not, but Thou art; the old man is all gone, only Thou remainest." "I am Thou." Blame none; if evil comes, know the Lord is playing with you and be exceeding glad.

Love is beyond time and space, it is absolute.

UNTITLED TALK IV

RECORDED BY MISS S. E. WALDO, A DISCIPLE
TUESDAY, June 25, 1895.

After every happiness comes misery; they may be far apart or near. The more advanced the soul, the more quickly does one follow the other. What we want is neither happiness nor misery. Both make us forget our true nature; both are chains — one iron, one gold; behind both is the Atman, who knows neither happiness nor misery. These are states and states must ever change; but the nature of the Soul is bliss, peace, unchanging. We have not to get it, we have it; only wash away the dross and see it.

Stand upon the Self, then only can we truly love the world. Take a very, very high stand; knowing out universal nature, we must look with perfect calmness upon all the panorama of the world. It is but baby's play, and we know that, so cannot be disturbed by it. If the mind is pleased with praise, it will be displeased with blame. All pleasures of the senses or even of the mind are evanescent but within ourselves is the one true unrelated pleasure, dependent upon nothing. It is perfectly free, it is bliss. The more our bliss is within, the more spiritual we are. The pleasure of the Self is what the world calls religion.

The internal universe, the real, is infinitely greater than the external, which is only a shadowy projection of the true one. This world is neither true nor untrue, it is the shadow of truth. "Imagination is the gilded shadow of truth", says the poet.

We enter into creation, and then for us it becomes living. Things are dead in themselves; only we give them life, and then, like fools, we turn around and are afraid of them, or enjoy them. But be not like certain fisher-women, who, caught in a storm on their way home from market, took refuge in the house of a florist. They were lodged for the night in a room next to the garden where the air was full of the fragrance of flowers. In vain did they try to rest, until one of their number suggested that they wet their fishy baskets and place them near their heads. Then they all fell into a sound sleep.

The world is our fish basket, we must not depend upon it for enjoyment. Those who do are the Tâmasas or the bound. Then there are the Râjasas or the egotistical, who talk always about "I", "I". They do good work sometimes and may become spiritual. But the highest are the Sâttvikas, the introspective, those who live only in the Self. These three qualities, Tamas, Rajas, and Sattva (idleness, activity, and illumination), are in everyone, and different ones predominate at different times.

Creation is not a "making" of something, it is the struggle to regain the equilibrium, as when atoms of cork are thrown to the bottom of a pail of water and rush to rise to the top, singly or in clusters. Life is and must be accompanied by evil. A little evil is the source of life; the little wickedness that is in the world is very good; for when the balance is regained, the world will end, because sameness and destruction are one. When this world goes, good and evil go with it; but when we can transcend this world, we get rid of both good and evil and have bliss.

There is no possibility of ever having pleasure without pain, good without evil; for living itself is just the lost equilibrium. What we want is freedom, not life, nor pleasure, nor good. Creation is infinite, without beginning and without end—the ever-moving ripple in an infinite lake. There are yet unreached depths and others where the equilibrium has been regained; but the ripple is always progressing, the struggle to regain the balance is eternal. Life and death are only different names for the same fact, the two sides of the one coin. Both are Maya, the inexplicable state of striving at one time to live, and a moment later to die. Beyond this is the true nature, the Atman. While we recognise a God, it is really only the Self which we have separated ourselves from and worship as outside of us; but it is our true Self all the time—the one and only God.

To regain the balance we must counteract Tamas by Rajas; then conquer Rajas by Sattva, the calm beautiful state that will grow and grow until all else is gone. Give up bondage; become a son, be free, and then you can "see the Father", as did Jesus. Infinite strength is religion and God. Avoid weakness and slavery. You are only a soul, if you are free; there is immortality for you, if you are free; there is God, if He is free...

The world for me, not I for the world. Good and evil are our slaves, not we theirs. It is the nature of the brute to remain where he is (not to progress); it is the nature of man to seek good and avoid evil; it is the nature of God to seek neither, but just to be eternally blissful. Let us be God! Make the heart like an ocean, go beyond all the trifles of the world, be mad with joy even at evil; see the world as a picture and then enjoy its beauty, knowing that nothing affects you. Children finding glass beads in a mud puddle, that is the good of the world. Look at it with calm complacency; see good and evil as the same—both are merely "God's play"; enjoy all.

* * *

My Master used to say, "All is God; but tiger-God is to be shunned. All water is water; but we avoid dirty water for drinking."

The whole sky is the censer of God, and sun and moon are the lamps. What temple is needed? All eyes are Thine, yet Thou hast not an eye; all hands are Thine; yet Thou hast not a hand.

Neither seek nor avoid, take what comes. It is liberty to be affected by nothing; do not merely endure, be unattached. Remember the story of the bull. A mosquito sat long on the horn of a certain bull. Then his conscience troubled him, and he said, "Mr. Bull, I have been sitting here a long time, perhaps I annoy you. I am sorry, I will go away." But the bull replied, "Oh no, not at all! Bring your whole family and live on my horn; what can you do to me?"

UNTITLED TALK V

RECORDED BY MISS S. E. WALDO, A DISCIPLE
WEDNESDAY, June 26, 1895.

Our best work is done, our greatest influence is exerted, when we are without thought of self. All great geniuses know this. Let us open ourselves to the one Divine Actor, and let Him act, and do nothing ourselves. "O Arjuna! I have no duty in the whole world", says Krishna. Be perfectly resigned, perfectly unconcerned; then alone can you do any true work. No eyes can see the real forces, we can only see the results. Put out self, lose it, forget it; just let God work, it is His business. We have nothing to do but stand aside and let God work. The more we go away, the more God comes in. Get rid of the little "I", and let only the great "I" live.

We are what our thoughts have made us; so take care of what you think. Words are secondary. Thoughts live, they travel far. Each thought we think is tinged with our own character, so that for the pure and holy man, even his jests or abuse will have the twist of his own love and purity and do good.

Desire nothing; think of God and look for no return. It is the desireless who bring results. The begging monks carry religion to every man's door; but they think that they do nothing, they claim nothing, their work is unconsciously done. If they should eat of the tree of knowledge, they would become egoists, and all the good they do would fly away. As soon as we say "I", we are humbugged all the time; and we call it "knowable", but it is only going round and round like a bullock tied to a tree. The Lord has hidden Himself best, and His work is best; so he who hides himself best, accomplishes most. Conquer yourself, and the whole universe is yours.

In the state of Sattva we see the very nature of things, we go beyond the senses and beyond reason. The adamantine wall that shuts us in is egoism; we refer everything to ourselves, thinking. "I do this, that, and the other." Get rid of this puny "I"; kill this diabolism in us; "Not I, but Thou"—say it, feel it, live it. Until we give up the world manufactured by the ego, never can we enter the kingdom of heaven. None ever did, none ever will. To give up the world is to forget the ego, to know it not at all—living in the body, but not of it. This rascal ego must be obliterated. Bless men when they revile you. Think how much good they are doing you; they can only hurt themselves. Go where people hate you, let them thrash the ego out of you, and you will get nearer to the Lord. Like the mother-monkey, we hug our "baby", the world, as long as we can, but at last when we are driven to put it under our feet and step on it[6]* then we are ready to come to God. Blessed it is to be persecuted for the sake of righteousness. Blessed are we if we cannot read, we have less to take us away from God.

Enjoyment is the million-headed serpent that we must tread under foot. We renounce and go on, then find nothing and despair; but hold on, hold on. The world is a demon. It is a kingdom of which the puny ego is king. Put it away and stand firm. Give up lust and gold and fame and hold fast to the Lord, and at last we shall reach a state of perfect indifference. The idea that the gratification of the senses constitutes enjoyment is purely materialistic. There is not one spark of real enjoyment there; all the joy there is, is a mere reflection of the true bliss.

Those who give themselves up to the Lord do more for the world than all the so-called workers. One man who has purified himself thoroughly accomplishes more than a regiment of preachers. Out of purity and silence comes the word of power.

"Be like a lily—stay in one place and expand your petals; and the bees will come of themselves." There was a great contrast between Keshab Chandra Sen and Shri Ramakrishna. The second never recognised any sin or misery in the world, no evil to fight against. The first was a great ethical reformer, leader, and founder of the Brahmo-Samaj. After twelve years the quiet prophet of Dakshineswar had worked a revolution not only in India, but in the world. The power is with the silent ones, who only live and love and then withdraw their personality. They never say "me" and "mine"; they are only blessed in being instruments. Such men are the makers of Christs and Buddhas, ever living fully identified with God, ideal existences, asking nothing, and not consciously doing anything. They are the real movers, the Jivanmuktas, (Literally, free even while living.) absolutely selfless, the little personality entirely blown away, ambition non-existent. They are all principle, no personality.

UNTITLED TALK VI

RECORDED BY MISS S. E. WALDO, A DISCIPLE
THURSDAY, June 27, 1895.

The Swami brought the New Testament this morning and talked again on the book of John.)

Mohammed claimed to be the "Comforter" that Christ promised to send. He considered it unnecessary to claim a supernatural birth for Jesus. Such claims have been common in all ages and in all countries. All great men have claimed gods for their fathers.

Knowing is only relative; we can be God, but never know Him. Knowledge is a lower state; Adam's fall was when he came to "know". Before that he was God, he was truth, he was purity. We are our own faces, but can see only a reflection, never the real thing. We are love, but when we think of it, we have to use a phantasm, which proves that matter is only externalised thought.

Nivritti is turning aside from the world. Hindu mythology says that the four first-created (The four first-created were Sanaka, Sanandana, Sanâtana, and Sanatkumâra.) were warned by a Swan (God Himself) that manifestation was only secondary; so they remained without creating. The meaning of this is that expression is degeneration, because Spirit can only be expressed by the letter and then the "letter killeth" (Bible, 2 Cor. III. 6.); yet principle is bound to be clothed in matter, though we know that later we shall lose sight of the real in the covering. Every great teacher understands this, and that is why a continual succession of prophets has to come to show us the principle and give it a new covering suited to the times. My Master taught that religion is one; all prophets teach the same; but they can only present the principle in a form; so they take it out of the old form and put it before us in a new one. When we free ourselves from name and form, especially from a body—when we need no body, good or bad—then only do we escape from bondage. Eternal progression is eternal bondage; annihilation of form is to be preferred. We must get free from any body, even a "god-body". God is the only real existence, there cannot be two. There is but One Soul, and I am That.

Good works are only valuable as a means of escape; they do good to the doer, never to any other.

Knowledge is mere classification. When we find many things of the same kind we call the sum of them by a certain name and are satisfied; we discover "facts", never "why". We take a circuit in a wider field of darkness and think we know something! No "why" can be answered in this world; for that we must go to God. The Knower can never be expressed; it is as when a grain of salt drops into the ocean, it is at once merged in the ocean.

Differentiation creates; homogeneity or sameness is God. Get beyond differentiation; then you conquer life and death and reach eternal sameness and are in God, are God. Get freedom, even at the cost of life. All lives belong to us as leaves to a book; but we are unchanged, the Witness, the Soul, upon whom the impression is made, as when the impression of a circle is made upon the eyes when a firebrand is rapidly whirled round and round. The Soul is the unity of all personalities, and because It is at rest, eternal, unchangeable. It is God, Atman. It is not life, but It is coined into life. It is not pleasure, but It is manufactured into pleasure…

Today God is being abandoned by the world because He does not seem to be doing enough for the world. So they say, "Of what good is He?" Shall we look upon God as a mere municipal authority?

All we can do is to put down all desires, hates, differences; put down the lower self, commit mental suicide, as it were; keep the body and mind pure and healthy, but only as instruments to help us to God; that is their only true use. Seek truth for truth's sake alone, look not for bliss. It may come, but do not let that be your incentives. Have no motive except God. Dare to come to Truth even through hell.

UNTITLED TALK VII

RECORDED BY MISS S. E. WALDO, A DISCIPLE
FRIDAY, June 28, 1895.

The entire party went on a picnic for the day, and although the Swami taught constantly, as he did wherever he was, no notes were taken and no record, therefore, of what he said remains. As he began his breakfast before setting out, however, he remarked:

Be thankful for all food, it is Brahman. His universal energy is transmuted into our individual energy and helps us in all that we do.

UNTITLED TALK VIII

RECORDED BY MISS S. E. WALDO, A DISCIPLE
SATURDAY, June 29, 1895.

The Swami came this morning with a Gita in his hand.

Krishna, the "Lord of souls", talks to Arjuna or Gudâkesha, "lord of sleep" (he who has conquered sleep). The "field of virtue" (the battlefield) is this world; the five brothers (representing righteousness) fight the hundred other brothers (all that we love and have to contend against); the most heroic brother, Arjuna (the awakened soul), is the general. We have to fight all sense-delights, the things to which we are most attached, to kill them. We have to stand alone; we are Brahman, all other ideas must be merged in this one.

Krishna did everything but without any attachment; he was in the world, but not of it. "Do all work but without attachment; work for work's sake, never for yourself."

Freedom can never be true of name and form; it is the clay out of which we (the pots) are made; then it is limited and not free, so that freedom can never be true of the related. One pot can never say "I am free" as a pot; only as it loses all ideas of form does it become free. The whole universe is only the Self with variations, the one tune made bearable by variation; sometimes there are discords, but they only make the subsequent harmony more perfect. In the universal melody three ideas stand out — freedom, strength, and sameness.

If your freedom hurts others, you are not free there. You must not hurt others.

"To be weak is to be miserable", says Milton. Doing and suffering are inseparably joined. (Often, too, the man who laughs most is the one who suffers most.) "To work you have the right, not to the fruits thereof."

* * *

Evil thoughts, looked at materially, are the disease bacilli.

Each thought is a little hammer blow on the lump of iron which our bodies are, manufacturing out of it what we want it to be.

We are heirs to all the good thoughts of the universe, if we open ourselves to them.

The book is all in us. Fool, hearest not thou? In thine own heart day and night is singing that Eternal Music — Sachchidânanda, soham, soham — Existence-Knowledge-Bliss Absolute, I am He, I am He.

The fountain of all knowledge is in every one of us, in the ant as in the highest angel. Real religion is one, but we quarrel with the forms, the symbols, the illustrations. The millennium exists already for those who find it; we have lost ourselves and then think the world is lost.

Perfect strength will have no activity in this world; it only is, it does not act.

While real perfection is only one, relative perfections must be many.

UNTITLED TALK IX

RECORDED BY MISS S. E. WALDO, A DISCIPLE
SUNDAY, June 30, 1895.

To try to think without a phantasm is to try to make the impossible possible. We cannot think "mammalia" without a concrete example. So with the idea of God.

The great abstraction of ideas in the world is what we call God.

Each thought has two parts—the thinking and the word; and we must have both. Neither idealists nor materialists are right; we must take both idea and expression.

All knowledge is of the reflected, as we can only see our face in a mirror. No one will ever know his own Self or God; but we are that own Self, we are God.

In Nirvana you are when you are not. Buddha said, "You are best, you are real, when you are not" — when the little self is gone.

The Light Divine within is obscured in most people. It is like a lamp in a cask of iron, no gleam of light can shine through.

Gradually, by purity and unselfishness we can make the obscuring medium less and less dense, until at last it becomes as transparent as glass. Shri Ramakrishna was like the iron cask transformed into a glass cask through which can be seen the inner light as it is. We are all on the way to become the cask of glass and even higher and higher reflections. As long as there is a "cask" at all, we must think through material means. No impatient one can ever succeed.

* * *

Great saints are the object-lessons of the Principle. But the disciples make the saint the Principle, and then they forget the Principle in the person.

The result of Buddha's constant inveighing against a personal God was the introduction of idols into India. In the Vedas they knew them not, because they saw God everywhere, but the reaction against the loss of God as Creator and Friend was to make idols, and Buddha became an idol—so too with Jesus. The range of idols is from wood and stone to Jesus and Buddha, but we must have idols.

* * *

Violent attempts at reform always end by retarding reform. Do not say, "You are bad"; say only, "You are good, but be better."

Priests are an evil in every country, because they denounce and criticise, pulling at one string to mend it until two or three others are out of place. Love never denounces, only ambition does that. There is no such thing as "righteous" anger or justifiable killing.

If you do not allow one to become a lion, he will become a fox. Women are a power, only now it is more for evil because man oppresses woman; she is the fox, but when she is not longer oppressed, she will become the lion.

Ordinarily speaking, spiritual aspiration ought to be balanced through the intellect; otherwise it may degenerate into mere sentimentality...

All theists agree that behind the changeable there is an Unchangeable, though they vary in their conception of the Ultimate. Buddha denied this in toto. "There is no Brahman, no Atman, no soul," he said.

As a character Buddha was the greatest the world has ever seen; next to him Christ. But the teachings of Krishna as taught by the Gita are the grandest the world has ever known. He who wrote that wonderful poem was one of those rare souls whose lives sent a wave of regeneration through the world. The human race will never again see such a brain as his who wrote the Gita.

* * *

There is only one Power, whether manifesting as evil or good. God and the devil are the same river with the water flowing in opposite directions.

UNTITLED TALK X

RECORDED BY MISS S. E. WALDO, A DISCIPLE
MONDAY, July 1, 1895. (Shri Ramakrishna Deva)

Shri Ramakrishna was the son of a very orthodox Brahmin, who would refuse even a gift from any but a special caste of Brahmins; neither might he work, nor even be a priest in a temple, nor sell books, nor serve anyone. He could only have "what fell from the skies" (alms), and even then it must not come through a "fallen" Brahmin. Temples have no hold on the Hindu religion; if they were all destroyed, religion would not be affected a grain. A man must only build a house for "God and guests", to build for himself would be selfish; therefore he erects temples as dwelling places for God.

Owing to the extreme poverty of his family, Shri Ramakrishna was obliged to become in his boyhood a priest in a temple dedicated to the Divine Mother, also called Prakriti, or Kâli, represented by a female figure standing with feet on a male figure, indicating that until Maya lifts, we can know nothing. Brahman is neuter, unknown and unknowable, but to be objectified He covers Himself with a veil of Maya, becomes the Mother of the Universe, and so brings forth the creation. The prostrate figure (Shiva or God) has become Shava (dead or lifeless) by being covered by Maya. The Jnâni says, "I will uncover God by force" (Advaitism); but the dualist says, "I will uncover God by praying to Mother, begging Her to open the door to which She alone has the key."

The daily service of the Mother Kali gradually awakened such intense devotion in the heart of the young priest that he could no longer carry on the regular temple worship. So he abandoned his duties and retired to a small woodland in the temple compound, where he gave himself up entirely to meditation. These woods were on the bank of the river Ganga; and one day the swift current bore to his very feet just the necessary materials to build him a little enclosure. In this enclosure he stayed and wept and prayed, taking no thought for the care of his body or for aught except his Divine Mother. A relative fed him once a day and watched over him. Later came a Sannyasini or lady ascetic, to help him find his "Mother". Whatever teachers he needed came to him unsought; from every sect some holy saint would come and offer to teach him and to each he listened eagerly. But he worshipped only Mother; all to him was Mother.

Shri Ramakrishna never spoke a harsh word against anyone. So beautifully tolerant was he that every sect thought that he belonged to them. He loved everyone. To him all religions were true. He found a place for each one. He was free, but free in love, not in "thunder". The mild type creates, the thundering type spreads. Paul was the thundering type to spread the light. (And it has been said by many that Swami Vivekananda himself was a kind of St. Paul to Shri Ramakrishna.)

The age of St. Paul, however, is gone; we are to be the new lights for this day. A self-adjusting organisation is the great need of our time. When we can get one, that will be the last religion of the world. The wheel must turn, and we should help it, not hinder. The waves of religious thought rise and fall, and on the topmost one stands the "prophet of the period". Ramakrishna came to teach the religion of today, constructive, not destructive. He had to go afresh to Nature to ask for facts, and he got scientific religion which never says "believe", but "see"; "I see, and you too can see." Use the same means and you will reach the same vision. God will come to everyone, harmony is within the reach of all. Shri Ramakrishna's teachings are "the gist of Hinduism"; they were not peculiar to him. Nor did he claim that they were; he cared naught for name or fame.

He began to preach when he was about forty; but he never went out to do it. He waited for those who wanted his teachings to come to him. In accordance with Hindu custom, he was married by his parents in early youth to a little girl of five, who remained at home with her family in a distant village, unconscious of the great struggle through which her young husband was passing. When she reached maturity, he was already deeply absorbed in religious devotion. She travelled on foot from her home to the temple at Dakshineswar where he was then living; and as soon as she saw him, she recognised what he was, for she herself was a great soul, pure and holy, who only desired to help his work, never to drag him down to the level of the Grihastha (householder).

Shri Ramakrishna is worshipped in India as one of the great Incarnations, and his birthday is celebrated there as a religious festival...

A curious round stone is the emblem of Vishnu, the omnipresent. Each morning a priest comes in, offers sacrifice to the idol, waves incense before it, then puts it to bed and apologises to God for worshipping Him in that way, because he can only conceive of Him through an image or by means of some material object. He bathes the idol, clothes it, and puts his divine self into the idol "to make it alive".

* * *

There is a sect which says, "It is weakness to worship only the good and beautiful, we ought also to love and worship the hideous and the evil." This sect prevails all over Tibet, and they have no marriage. In India proper they cannot exist openly, but organise secret societies. No decent men will belong to them except sub rosa. Thrice communism was tried in Tibet, and thrice it failed. They use Tapas and with immense success as far as power is concerned.

Tapas means literally "to burn". It is a kind of penance to "heat" the higher nature. It is sometimes in the form of a sunrise to sunset vow, such as repeating Om all day incessantly. These actions will produce a certain power that you can convert into any form you wish, spiritual or material. This idea of Tapas penetrates the whole of Hindu religion. The Hindus even say that God made Tapas to create the world. It is a mental instrument with which to do everything. "Everything in the three worlds can be caught by Tapas."...

People who report about sects with which they are not in sympathy are both conscious and unconscious liars. A believer in one sect can rarely see truth in others.

* * *

A great Bhakta (Hanuman) once said when asked what day of the month it was, "God is my eternal date, no other date I care for."

UNTITLED TALK XI

RECORDED BY MISS S. E. WALDO, A DISCIPLE
TUESDAY, July 2, 1895. (The Divine Mother.)

Shâktas worship the Universal Energy as Mother, the sweetest name they know; for the mother is the highest ideal of womanhood in India. When God is worshipped as "Mother", as Love, the Hindus call it the "right-handed" way, and it leads to spirituality but never to material prosperity. When God is worshipped on His terrible side, that is, in the "left-handed" way, it leads usually to great material prosperity, but rarely to spirituality; and eventually it leads to degeneration and the obliteration of the race that practices it.

Mother is the first manifestation of power and is considered a higher idea than father. With the name of Mother comes the idea of Shakti, Divine Energy and Omnipotence, just as the baby believes its mother to be all-powerful, able to do anything. The Divine Mother is the Kundalini ("coiled up" power) sleeping in us; without worshipping Her we can never know ourselves. All-merciful, all-powerful, omnipresent are attributes of Divine Mother. She is the sum total of the energy in the universe. Every manifestation of power in the universe is "Mother". She is life, She is intelligence, She is Love. She is in the universe yet separate from it. She is a person and can be seen and known (as Shri Ramakrishna saw and knew Her). Established in the idea of Mother, we can do anything. She quickly answers prayer.

She can show; Herself to us in any form at any moment. Divine Mother can have form (Rupa) and name (Nâma) or name without form; and as we worship Her in these various aspects we can rise to pure Being, having neither form nor name.

The sum total of all the cells in an organism is one person; so each soul is like one cell and the sum of them is God, and beyond that is the Absolute. The sea calm is the Absolute; the same sea in waves is Divine Mother. She is time, space, and causation. God is Mother and has two natures, the conditioned and the unconditioned. As the former, She is God, nature, and soul (man). As the latter, She is unknown and unknowable. Out of the Unconditioned came the trinity—God, nature, and soul, the triangle of existence. This is the Vishishtâdvaitist idea.

A bit of Mother, a drop, was Krishna, another was Buddha, another was Christ. The worship of even one spark of Mother in our earthly mother leads to greatness. Worship Her if you want love and wisdom.

UNTITLED TALK XII

RECORDED BY MISS S. E. WALDO, A DISCIPLE
WEDNESDAY, July 3, 1895.

Generally speaking, human religion begins with fear. "The fear of the Lord is the beginning of wisdom." But later comes the higher idea. "Perfect love casteth out fear." Traces of fear will remain with us until we get knowledge, know what God is. Christ, being man, had to see impurity and denounced it; but God, infinitely higher, does not see iniquity and cannot be angry. Denunciation is never the highest. David's hands were smeared with blood; he could not build the temple. (Bible, Samuel, Chap. XVII—end.)

The more we grow in love and virtue and holiness, the more we see love and virtue and holiness outside. All condemnation of others really condemns ourselves. Adjust the microcosm (which is in your power to do) and the macrocosm will adjust itself for you. It is like the hydrostatic paradox, one drop of water can balance the universe. We cannot see outside what we are not inside. The universe is to us what the huge engine is to the miniature engine; and indication of any error in the tiny engine leads us to imagine trouble in the huge one.

Every step that has been really gained in the world has been gained by love; criticising can never do any good, it has been tried for thousand of years. Condemnation accomplishes nothing.

A real Vedantist must sympathise with all. Monism, or absolute oneness is the very soul of Vedanta. Dualists naturally tend to become intolerant, to think theirs as the only way. The Vaishnavas in India, who are dualists, are a most intolerant sect. Among the Shaivas, another dualistic sect, the story is told of a devotee by the name of Ghantâkarna or the Bell-eared, who was so devout a worshipper of Shiva that he did not wish even to hear the name of any other deity; so he wore two bells tied to his ears in order to drown the sound of any voice uttering other Divine names. On account of his intense devotion to Shiva, the latter wanted to teach him that there was no difference between Shiva and Vishnu, so He appeared before him as half Vishnu and half Shiva. At that moment the devotee was waving incense before Him, but so great was the bigotry of Ghantakarna that when he saw the fragrance of the incense entering the nostril of Vishnu, he thrust his finger into it to prevent the god from enjoying the sweet smell...

The meat-eating animal, like the lion, gives one blow and subsides, but the patient bullock goes on all day, eating and sleeping as it walks. The "live Yankee" cannot compete with the rice-eating Chinese coolie. While military power dominates, meat-eating still prevail; but with the advance of science, fighting will grow less, and then the vegetarians will come in.

* * *

We divide ourselves into two to love God, myself loving my Self. God has created me and I have created God. We create God in our image; it is we who create Him to be our master, it is not God who makes us His servants. When we know that we are one with God, that we and He are friends, then come equality and freedom. So long as you hold yourself separated by a hair's breadth from this Eternal One, fear cannot go.

Never ask that foolish question, what good will it do to the world? Let the world go. Love and ask nothing; love and look for nothing further. Love and forget all the "isms". Drink the cup of love and become mad. Say "Thine, O Thine for ever O Lord!" and plunge in, forgetting all else. The very idea of God is love. Seeing a cat loving her kittens stand and pray. God has become manifest there; literally believe this. Repeat "I am Thine, I am Thine", for we can see God everywhere. Do not seek for Him, just see Him.

"May the Lord ever keep you alive, Light of the world, Soul of the universe!" ...

The Absolute cannot be worshipped, so we must worship a manifestation, such a one as has our nature. Jesus had our nature; he became the Christ; so can we, and so must we. Christ and Buddha were the names of a state to be attained; Jesus and Gautama were the persons to manifest it. "Mother" is the first and highest manifestation, next the Christs and Buddhas. We make our own environment, and we strike the fetters off. The Atman is the fearless. When we pray to a God outside, it is good, only we do not know what we do. When we know the Self, we understand. The highest expression of love is unification.

"There was a time when I was a woman and he was a man. Still love grew until there was neither he nor I; Only I remember faintly there was a time when there were two. But love came between and made them one."—Persian Sufi Poem

Knowledge exists eternally and is co-existent with God. The man who discovers a spiritual law is inspired, and what he brings is revelation; but revelation too is eternal, not to be crystallised as final and then blindly followed. The Hindus have been criticised so many years by their conquerors that they (the Hindus) dare to criticise their religion themselves, and this makes them free. Their foreign rulers struck off their fetters without knowing it. The most religious people on earth, the Hindus have actually no sense of blasphemy; to speak of holy things in any way is to them in itself a sanctification. Nor have they any artificial respect for prophets or books, or for hypocritical piety.

The Church tries to fit Christ into it, not the Church into Christ; so only those writings were preserved that suited the purpose in hand. Thus the books are not to be depended upon and book-worship is the worst kind of idolatry to bind our feet. All has to conform to the book—science, religion, philosophy; it is the most horrible tyranny, this tyranny of the Protestant Bible. Every man in Christian countries has a huge cathedral on his head and on top of that a book, and yet man lives and grows! Does not this prove that man is God?

Man is the highest being that exists, and this is the greatest world. We can have no conception of God higher than man, so our God is man, and man is God. When we rise and go beyond and find something higher, we have to jump out of the mind, out of body and the imagination and leave this world; when we rise to be the Absolute, we are no longer in this world. Man is the apex of the only world we can ever know. All we know of animals is only by analogy, we judge them by what we do and feel ourselves.

The sum total of knowledge is ever the same, only sometimes it is more manifested and sometimes less. The only source of it is within, and there only is it found.

* * *

All poetry, painting, and music is feeling expressed through words, through colour, through sound...

Blessed are those upon whom their sins are quickly visited, their account is the sooner balanced! Woe to those whose punishment is deferred, it is the greater!

Those who have attained sameness are said to be living in God. All hatred is killing the "Self by the self", therefore love is the law of life. To rise to this is to be perfect; but the more perfect we are, less work (so-called) can we do. The Sâttvika see and know that all is mere child's play and do not trouble themselves about anything.

It is easy to strike a blow, but tremendously hard to stay the hand, stand still, and say, "In Thee, O Lord, I take refuge", and then wait for Him to act.

UNTITLED TALK XIII

RECORDED BY MISS S. E. WALDO, A DISCIPLE
FRIDAY, July 5, 1895.

Until you are ready to change any minute, you can never see the truth; but you must hold fast and be steady in the search for truth...

Chârvâkas, a very ancient sect in India, were rank materialists. They have died out now, and most of their books are lost. They claimed that the soul, being the product of the body and its forces, died with it; that there was no proof of its further existence. They denied inferential knowledge accepting only perception by the senses.

* * *

Samâdhi is when the Divine and human are in one, or it is "bringing sameness"...

Materialism says, the voice of freedom is a delusion. Idealism says, the voice that tells of bondage is delusion. Vedanta says, you are free and not free at the same time—never free on the earthly plane, but ever free on the spiritual.

Be beyond both freedom and bondage.

We are Shiva, we are immortal knowledge beyond the senses.

Infinite power is back of everyone; pray to Mother, and it will come to you.

"O Mother, giver of Vâk (eloquence), Thou self-existent, come as the Vak upon my-lips," (Hindu invocation).

"That Mother whose voice is in the thunder, come Thou in me! Kali, Thou time eternal, Thou force irresistible, Shakti, Power!"

UNTITLED TALK XIV

RECORDED BY MISS S. E. WALDO, A DISCIPLE
SATURDAY, July 6, 1895.

Today we had Shankaracharya's commentary on Vyâsa's Vedânta Sutras.

Om tat sat! According to Shankara, there are two phases of the universe, one is I and the other thou; and they are as contrary as light and darkness, so it goes without saying that neither can be derived from the other. On the subject, the object has been superimposed; the subject is the only reality, the other a mere appearance. The opposite view is untenable. Matter and the external world are but the soul in a certain state; in reality there is only one.

All our world comes from truth and untruth coupled together. Samsâra (life) is the result of the contradictory forces acting upon us, like the diagonal motion of a ball in a parallelogram of forces. The world is God and is real, but that is not the world we see; just as we see silver in the mother-of-pearl where it is not. This is what is known as Adhyâsa or superimposition, that is, a relative existence dependent upon a real one, as when we recall a scene we have seen; for the time it exists for us, but that existence is not real. Or some say, it is as when we imagine heat in water, which does not belong to it; so really it is something which has been put where it does not belong, "taking the thing for what it is not". We see reality, but distorted by the medium through which we see it.

You can never know yourself except as objectified. When we mistake one thing for another, we always take the thing before us as the real, never the unseen; thus we mistake the object for the subject. The Atman never becomes the object. Mind is the internal sense, the outer senses are its instruments. In the subject is a trifle of the objectifying power that enables him to know "I am"; but the subject is the object of its own Self, never of the mind or the senses. You can, however, superimpose one idea on another idea, as when we say, "The sky is blue", the sky itself being only an idea. Science and nescience there are, but the Self is never affected by any nescience. Relative knowledge is good, because it leads to absolute knowledge; but neither the knowledge of the senses, nor of the mind, nor even of the Vedas is true, since they are all within the realm of relative knowledge. First get rid of the delusion, "I am the body", then only can we want real knowledge. Man's knowledge is only a higher degree of brute knowledge.

* * *

One part of the Vedas deals with Karma—form and ceremonies. The other part deals with the knowledge of Brahman and discusses religion. The Vedas in this part teach of the Self; and because they do, their knowledge is approaching real knowledge. Knowledge of the Absolute depends upon no book, nor upon anything; it is absolute in itself. No amount of study will give this knowledge; is not theory, it is realization. Cleanse the dust from the mirror, purify your own mind, and in a flash you know that you are Brahman.

God exists, not birth nor death, not pain nor misery, nor murder, nor change, nor good nor evil; all is Brahman. We take the "rope for the serpent", the error is ours...We can only do good when we love God and He reflects our love. The murderer is God, and the "clothing of murderer" is only superimposed upon him. Take him by the hand and tell him the truth.

Soul has no caste, and to think it has is a delusion; so are life and death, or any motion or quality. The Atman never changes, never goes nor comes. It is the eternal Witness of all Its own manifestations, but we take It for the manifestation; an eternal illusion, without beginning or end, ever going on. The Vedas, however, have to come down to our level, for if they told us the highest truth in the highest way, we could not understand it.

Heaven is a mere superstition arising from desire, and desire is ever a yoke, a degeneration. Never approach any thing except as God; for if we do, we see evil, because we throw a veil of delusion over what we look at, and then we see evil. Get free from these illusions; be blessed. Freedom is to lose all illusions.

In one sense Brahman is known to every human being; he knows, "I am"; but man does not know himself as he is. We all know we are, but not how we are. All lower explanations are partial truths; but the flower, the essence of the Vedas, is that the Self in each of us is Brahman. Every phenomenon is included in birth, growth, and death—appearance, continuance and disappearance. Our own realisation is beyond the Vedas, because even they depend upon that. The highest Vedanta is the philosophy of the Beyond.

To say that creation has any beginning is to lay the axe at the root of all philosophy.

Maya is the energy of the universe, potential and kinetic. Until Mother releases us, we cannot get free.

The universe is ours to enjoy. But want nothing. To want is weakness. Want makes us beggars, and we are sons of the king, not beggars.

UNTITLED TALK XV

RECORDED BY MISS S. E. WALDO, A DISCIPLE
SUNDAY MORNING, July 7, 1895.

Infinite manifestation dividing itself in portion still remains infinite, and each portion is infinite.

Brahman is the same in two forms—changeable and unchangeable, expressed and unexpressed. Know that the Knower and the known are one. The Trinity—the Knower, the known, and knowing—is manifesting as this universe. That God the Yogi sees in meditation, he sees through the power of his own Self.

What we call nature, fate, is simply God's will.

So long as enjoyment is sought, bondage remains. Only imperfection can enjoy, because enjoyment is the fulfilling of desire. The human soul enjoys nature. The underlying reality of nature, soul, and God is Brahman; but It (Brahman) is unseen, until we bring It out. It may be brought out by Pramantha or friction, just as we can produce fire by friction. The body is the lower piece of wood, Om is the pointed piece and Dhyâna (meditation) is the friction. When this is used, that light which is the knowledge of Brahman will burst forth in the soul. Seek it through Tapas. Holding the body upright, sacrifice the organs of sense in the mind. The sense-centres are within, and their organs without; drive them into the mind and through Dhârâna (concentration) fix the mind in Dhyana. Brahman is omnipresent in the universe as is butter in milk, but friction makes It manifest in one place. As churning brings out the butter in the milk, so Dhyana brings the realisation of Brahman in the soul.

All Hindu philosophy declares that there is a sixth sense, the superconscious, and through it comes inspiration.

* * *

The universe is motion, and friction will eventually bring everything to an end; then comes a rest; and after that all begins again...

So long as the "skin sky" surrounds man, that is, so long as he identifies himself with his body, he cannot see God.

SUNDAY AFTERNOON

There are six schools of philosophy in India that are regarded as orthodox, because they believe in the Vedas.

Vyasa's philosophy is par excellence that of the Upanishads. He wrote in Sutra form, that is, in brief algebraical symbols without nominative or verb. This caused so much ambiguity that out of the Sutras came dualism, mono-dualism, and monism or "roaring Vedanta"; and all the great commentators in these different schools were at times "conscious liars" in order to make the texts suit their philosophy.

The Upanishads contain very little history of the doings of any man, but nearly all other scriptures are largely personal histories. The Vedas deal almost entirely with philosophy. Religion without philosophy runs into superstition; philosophy without religion becomes dry atheism.

Vishishta-advaita is qualified Advaita (monism). Its expounder was Râmânuja. He says, "Out of the ocean of milk of the Vedas, Vyasa has churned this butter of philosophy, the better to help mankind." He says again, "All virtues and all qualities belong to Brahman, Lord of the universe. He is the greatest Purusha.

Madhva is a through-going dualist or Dvaitist. He claims that even women might study the Vedas. He quotes chiefly from the Purânas. He says that Brahman means Vishnu, not Shiva at all, because there is no salvation except through Vishnu.

UNTITLED TALK XVI

RECORDED BY MISS S. E. WALDO, A DISCIPLE
MONDAY, July 8, 1895.

There is no place for reasoning in Madhva's explanation, it is all taken from the revelation in the Vedas.

Ramanuja says, the Vedas are the holiest study. Let the sons of the three upper castes get the Sutra (The holy thread.) and at eight, ten, or eleven years of age begin the study, which means going to a Guru and learning the Vedas word for word, with perfect intonation and pronunciation.

Japa is repeating the Holy Name; through this the devotee rises to the Infinite. This boat of sacrifice and ceremonies is very frail, we need more than that to know Brahman, which alone is freedom. Liberty is nothing more than destruction of ignorance, and that can only go when we know Brahman. It is not necessary to go through all these ceremonials to reach the meaning of the Vedanta. Repeating Om is enough.

Seeing difference is the cause of all misery, and ignorance is the cause of seeing difference. That is why ceremonials are not needed, because they increase the idea of inequality; you practice them to get rid of something or to obtain something.

Brahman is without action, Atman is Brahman, and we are Atman; knowledge like this takes off all error. It must be heard, apprehended intellectually, and lastly realised. Cogitating is applying reason and establishing this knowledge in ourselves by reason. Realising is making it a part of our lives by constant thinking of it. This constant thought or Dhyana is as oil that pours in one unbroken line from vessel to vessel; Dhyana rolls the mind in this thought day and night and so helps us to attain to liberation. Think always "Soham, Soham"; this is almost as good as liberation. Say it day and night; realisation will come as the result of this continuous cogitation. This absolute and continuous remembrance of the Lord is what is meant by Bhakti.

This Bhakti is indirectly helped by all good works. Good thoughts and good works create less differentiation than bad ones; so indirectly they lead to freedom. Work, but give up the results to the Lord. Knowledge alone can make us perfect. He who follows the God of Truth with devotion, to him the God of Truth reveals Himself... We are lamps, and our burning is what we call "life". When the supply of oxygen gives out, then the lamp must go out. All we can do is to keep the lamp clean. Life is a product, a compound, and as such must resolve itself into its elements.

UNTITLED TALK XVII

RECORDED BY MISS S. E. WALDO, A DISCIPLE
TUESDAY, July 9, 1895.

Man as Atman is really free; as man he is bound, changed by every physical condition. As man, he is a machine with an idea of freedom; but this human body is the best and the human mind the highest mind there is. When a man attains to the Atman state, he can take a body, making it to suit himself; he is above law. This is a statement and must be proved. Each one must prove it for himself; we may satisfy ourselves, but we cannot satisfy another. Râja-Yoga is the only science of religion that can be demonstrated; and only what I myself have proved by experience, do I teach. The full ripeness of reason is intuition, but intuition cannot antagonise reason.

Work purifies the heart and so leads to Vidyâ (wisdom). The Buddhists said, doing good to men and to animals were the only works; the Brahmins said that worship and all ceremonials were equally "work" and purified the mind. Shankara declares that "all works, good and bad, are against knowledge". Actions tending to ignorance are sins, not directly, but as causes, because they tend to increase Tamas and Rajas. With Sattva only, comes wisdom. Virtuous deeds take off the veil from knowledge, and knowledge alone can make us see God.

Knowledge can never be created, it can only be discovered; and every man who makes a great discovery is inspired. Only, when it is a spiritual truth he brings, we call him a prophet; and when it is on the physical plane, we call him a scientific man, and we attribute more importance to the former, although the source of all truth is one.

Shankara says, Brahman is the essence, the reality of all knowledge, and that all manifestations as knower, knowing, and known are mere imaginings in Brahman. Ramanuja attributes consciousness to God; the real monists attribute nothing, not even existence in any meaning that we can attach to it. Ramanuja declares that God is the essence of conscious knowledge. Undifferentiated consciousness, when differentiated, becomes the world...

Buddhism, one of the most philosophical religions in the world, spread all through the populace, the common people of India. What a wonderful culture there must have been among the Aryans twenty-five hundred years ago, to be able to grasp ideas!

Buddha was the only great Indian philosopher who would not recognise caste, and not one of his followers remains in India. All the other philosophers pandered more or less to social prejudices; no matter how high they soared, still a bit of the vulture remained in them. As my Master used to say, "The vulture soars high out of sight in the sky, but his eye is ever on a bit of carrion on the earth."

* * *

The ancient Hindus were wonderful scholars, veritable living encyclopaedias. They said, "Knowledge in books and money in other people's hands is like no knowledge and no money at all."

Shankara was regarded by many as an incarnation of Shiva.

UNTITLED TALK XVIII

RECORDED BY MISS S. E. WALDO, A DISCIPLE
WEDNESDAY, July 10, 1895.

There are sixty-five million Mohammedans in India, some of them Sufis.[6]* Sufis identify man with God, and through them this idea came into Europe. They say, "I am that Truth"; but they have an esoteric as well as an exoteric doctrine, although Mohammed himself did not hold it.

"Hashshashin" has become our word "assassin", because an old sect of Mohammedanism killed nonbelievers as a part of its creed.

A pitcher of water has to be present in the Mohammedan worship as a symbol of God filling the universe.

The Hindus believe that there will be ten Divine Incarnations. Nine have been and the tenth is still to come.

* * *

Shankara sometimes resorts to sophistry in order to prove that the ideas in the books go to uphold his philosophy. Buddha was more brave and sincere than any teacher. He said: "Believe no book; the Vedas are all humbug. If they agree with me, so much the better for the books. I am the greatest book; sacrifice and prayer are useless." Buddha was the first human being to give to the world a complete system of morality. He was good for good's sake, he loved for love's sake.

Shankara says: God is to be reasoned on, because the Vedas say so. Reason helps inspiration; books and realised reason—or individualized perception—both are proofs of God. The Vedas are, according to him, a sort of incarnation of universal knowledge. The proof of God is that He brought forth the Vedas, and the proof of the Vedas is that such wonderful books could only have been given out by Brahman. They are the mine of all knowledge, and they have come out of Him as a man breathes out air; therefore we know that He is infinite in power and knowledge. He may or may not have created the world, that is a trifle; to have produced the Vedas is more important! The world has come to know God through the Vedas; no other way there is.

And so universal is this belief, held by Shankara, in the all-inclusiveness of the Vedas that there is even a Hindu proverb that if a man loses his cow, he goes to look for her in the Vedas!

Shankara further affirms that obedience to ceremonial is not knowledge. Knowledge of God is independent of moral duties, or sacrifice or ceremonial, or what we think or do not think, just as the stump is not affected when one man takes it for a ghost and another sees it as it is.

Vedanta is necessary because neither reasoning nor books can show us God. He is only to be realised by superconscious perception, and Vedanta teaches how to attain that. You must get beyond personal God (Ishvara) and reach the Absolute Brahman. God is the perception of every being: He is all there is to he perceived. That which says "I" is Brahman, but although we, day and night, perceive Him; we do not know that we are perceiving Him. As soon as we become aware of this truth, all misery goes; so we must get knowledge of the truth. Reach unity; no more duality will come. But knowledge does not come by sacrifice, but by seeking, worshipping, knowing the Atman.

Brahmavidyâ is the highest knowledge, knowing the Brahman; lower knowledge is science. This is the teaching of the Mundakopanishad or the Upanishad for Sannyâsins. There are two sorts of knowledge—principal and secondary. The unessential is that part of the Vedas dealing with worship and ceremonial, also all secular knowledge. The essential is that by which we reach the Absolute. It (the Absolute) creates all from Its own nature; there is nothing to cause, nothing outside. It is all energy, It is all there is. He who makes all sacrifices to himself, the Atman, he alone knows Brahman. Fools think outside worship the highest; fools think works can give us God. Only those who go through the Sushumnâ (the "path" of the Yogis) reach the Atman. They must go to a Guru to learn. Each part has the same nature as the whole; all springs from the Atman. Meditation is the arrow, the whole soul going out to God is the bow, which speeds the arrow to its mark, the Atman. As finite, we can never express the Infinite, but we are the Infinite. Knowing this we argue with no one.

Divine wisdom is to be got by devotion, meditation, and chastity. "Truth alone triumphs, and not untruth. Through truth alone the way is spread to Brahman"—where alone love and truth are.

UNTITLED TALK XIX

RECORDED BY MISS S. E. WALDO, A DISCIPLE
THURSDAY, July 11, 1895.

Without mother-love no creation could continue. Nothing is entirely physical, nor yet entirely metaphysical; one presupposes the other and explains the other. All Theists agree that there is a background to this visible universe, they differ as to the nature or character of that background. Materialists say there is no background.

In all religions the superconscious state is identical. Hindus, Christians, Mohammedans, Buddhists, and even those of no creed, all have the very same experience when they transcend the body...

The purest Christians in the world were established in India by the Apostle Thomas about twenty-five years after the death of Jesus. This was while the Anglo-Saxons were still savages, painting their bodies and living in caves. The Christians in India once numbered about three millions, but now there are about one million.

Christianity is always propagated by the sword. How wonderful that the disciples of such a gentle soul should kill so much! The three missionary religions are the Buddhist, Mohammedan, and Christian. The three older ones, Hinduism, Judaism and Zoroastrianism, never sought to make converts. Buddhists never killed, but converted three-quarters of the world at one time by pure gentleness.

The Buddhists were the most logical agnostics. You can really stop nowhere between nihilism and absolutism. The Buddhists were intellectually all-destroyers, carrying their theory to its ultimate logical issue. The Advaitists also worked out their theory to its logical conclusion and reached the Absolute—one identified Unit Substance out of which all phenomena are being manifested. Both Buddhists and Advaitists have a feeling of identity and non-identity at the same time; one of these feelings must be false, and the other true. The nihilist puts the reality in non-identity, the realist puts the reality in identity; and this is the fight which occupies the whole world. This is the "tug-of-war".

The realist asks, "How does the nihilist get any idea of identity?" How does the revolving light appear a circle? A point of rest alone explains motion. The nihilist can never explain the genesis of the delusion that there is a background; neither can the idealist explain how the One becomes the many. The only explanation must come from beyond the sense-plane; we must rise to the superconscious, to a state entirely beyond sense-perception. That metaphysical power is the further instrument that the idealist alone can use. He can experience the Absolute; the man Vivekananda can resolve himself into the Absolute and then come back to the man again. For him, then the problem is solved and secondarily for others, for he can show the way to others. Thus religion begins where philosophy ends. The "good of the world" will be that what is now superconscious for us will in ages to come be the conscious for all. Religion is therefore the highest work the world has; and because man has unconsciously felt this, he has clung through all the ages to the idea of religion.

Religion, the great milch cow, has given many kicks, but never mind, it gives a great deal of milk. The milkman does not mind the kick of the cow which gives much milk. Religion is the greatest child to be born, the great "moon of realisation"; let us feed it and help it grow, and it will become a giant. King Desire and King Knowledge fought, and just as the latter was about to be defeated, he was reconciled to Queen Upanishad and a child was born to him, Realisation, who saved the victory to him.(From the Prabodha-chandrodaya, a Vedantic Sanskrit masque.)

Love concentrates all the power of the will without effort, as when a man falls in love with a woman.

The path of devotion is natural and pleasant. Philosophy is taking the mountain stream back to its force. It is a quicker method but very hard. Philosophy says, "Check everything." Devotion says, "Give the stream, have eternal self-surrender." It is a longer way, but easier and happier.

"Thine am I for ever; henceforth whatever I do, it is Thou doing it. No more is there any me or mine."

"Having no money to give, no brains to learn, no time to practice Yoga, to Thee, O sweet One, I give myself, to Thee my body and mind."

No amount of ignorance or wrong ideas can put a barrier between the soul and God. Even if there be no God, still hold fast to love. It is better to die seeking a God than as a dog seeking only carrion. Choose the highest ideal, and give your life up to that. "Death being so certain, it is the highest thing to give up life for a great purpose."

Love will painlessly attain to philosophy; then after knowledge comes Parâbhakti (supreme devotion).

Knowledge is critical and makes a great fuss over everything; but Love says, "God will show His real nature to me" and accepts all.

RABBIA

Rabbia, sick upon her bed,
By two saints was visited —
Holy Malik, Hassan wise —
Men of mark in Moslem eyes.

Hassan said, "Whose prayer is pure
Will God's chastisements endure."
Malik, from a deeper sense
Uttered his experience:
"He who loves his master's choice
Will in chastisement rejoice."

Rabbia saw some selfish will
In their maxims lingering still,
And replied "O men of grace,
He who sees his Master's face,
Will not in his prayers recall
That he is chastised at all !"

— Persian Poem

UNTITLED TALK XX

RECORDED BY MISS S. E. WALDO, A DISCIPLE
FRIDAY, July 12, 1895. (Shankara's Commentary.)

Fourth Vyasa Sutra. "Âtman (is) the aim of all."

Ishvara is to be known from the Vedanta; all Vedas point to Him (Who is the Cause; the Creator, Preserver and Destroyer). Ishvara is the unification of the Trinity, known as Brahmâ, Vishnu, and Shiva, which stand at the head of the Hindu Pantheon. "Thou art our Father who takest us to the other shore of the dark ocean" (Disciple's words to the Master).

The Vedas cannot show you Brahman, you are That already; they can only help to take away the veil that hides the truth from our eyes. The first veil to vanish is ignorance; and when that is gone, sin goes; next desire ceases, selfishness ends, and all misery disappears. This cessation of ignorance can only come when I know that God and I are one; in other words, identify yourself with Atman, not with human limitations. Dis-identify yourself with the body, and all pain will cease. This is the secret of healing. The universe is a case of hypnotisation; de-hypnotise yourself and cease to suffer.

In order to be free we have to pass through vice to virtue, and then get rid of both. Tamas is to be conquered by Rajas, both are to be submerged in Sattva; then go beyond the three qualities. Reach a state where your very breathing is a prayer.

Whenever you learn (gain anything) from another man's words, know that you had the experience in a previous existence, because experience is the only teacher.

With all powers comes further misery, so kill desire. Getting any desire is like putting a stick into a nest of hornets. Vairâgya is finding, out that desires are but gilded balls of poison.

"Mind is not God" (Shankara). "Tat tvam asi" "Aham Brahmâsmi" ("That thou art", "I am Brahman"). When a man realises this, all the knots of his heart are cut asunder, all his doubts vanish". Fearlessness is not possible as long as we have even God over us; we must be God. What is disjoined will be for ever disjoined; if you are separate from God, then you can never be one with Him, and vice versa. If by virtue you are joined to God, when that ceases, disjunction will come. The junction is eternal, and virtue only helps to remove the veil. We are âzâd (free), we must realise it. "Whom the Self chooses" means we are the Self and choose ourselves.

Does seeing depend upon our own efforts or does it depend upon something outside? It depends upon ourselves; our efforts take off the dust, the mirror does not change. There is neither knower, knowing, nor known. "He who knows that he does not know, knows It." He who has a theory knows nothing.

The idea that we are bound is only an illusion.

Religion is not of this world; it is "heart-cleansing", and its effect on this world is secondary. Freedom is inseparable from the nature of the Atman. This is ever pure, ever perfect, ever unchangeable. This Atman you can never know. We can say nothing about the Atman but "not this, not this".

"Brahman is that which we can never drive out by any power of mind or imagination." (Shankara).

* * *

The universe is thought, and the Vedas are the words of this thought. We can create and uncreate this whole universe. Repeating the words, the unseen thought is aroused, and as a result a seen effect is produced. This is the claim of a certain sect of Karmis. They think that each one of us is a creator. Pronounce the words, the thought which corresponds will arise, and the result will become visible. "Thought is the power of the word, the word is the expression of the thought," say Mimâmsakas, a Hindu philosophical sect.

UNTITLED TALK XXI

RECORDED BY MISS S. E. WALDO, A DISCIPLE
SATURDAY, July 13th, 1895.

Everything we know is a compound, and all sense-knowledge comes through analysis. To think that mind is a simple, single, or independent is dualism. Philosophy is not got by studying books; the more you read books, the more muddled becomes the mind. The idea of unthinking philosophers was that the mind was a simple, and this led them to believe in free-will. Psychology, the analysis of the mind, shows the mind to be a compound, and every compound must be held together by some outside force; so the will is bound by the combination of outside forces. Man cannot even will to eat unless he is hungry. Will is subject to desire. But we are free; everyone feels it.

The agnostic says this idea is a delusion. Then, how do you prove the world? Its only proof is that we all see it and feel it; so just as much we all feel freedom. If universal consensus affirms this world, then it must be accepted as affirming freedom; but freedom is not of the will as it is. The constitutional belief of man in freedom is the basis of all reasoning. Freedom is of the will as it was before it became bound. The very idea of free-will shows every moment man's struggle against bondage. The free can be only one, the Unconditioned, the Infinite, the Unlimited. Freedom in man is now a memory, an attempt towards freedom.

Everything in the universe is struggling to complete a circle, to return to its source, to return to its only real Source, Atman. The search for happiness is a struggle to find the balance, to restore the equilibrium. Morality is the struggle of the bound will to get free and is the proof that we have come from perfection ...

The idea of duty is the midday sun of misery scorching the very soul. "O king, drink this one drop of nectar and be happy." ("I am not the doer", this is the nectar.)

Let there be action without reaction; action is pleasant, all misery is reaction. The child puts its hand in the flame, that is pleasure; but when its system reacts, then comes the pain of burning. When we can stop that reaction, then we have nothing to fear. Control the brain and do not let it read the record; be the witness and do not react, only thus can you be happy. The happiest moments we ever know are when we entirely forget ourselves. Work of your own free will, not from duty. We have no duty. This world is just a gymnasium in which we play; our life is an eternal holiday.

The whole secret of existence is to have no fear. Never fear what will become of you, depend on no one. Only the moment you reject all help are you free. The full sponge can absorb no more.

* * *

Even fighting in self-defence is wrong, though it is higher than fighting in aggression. There is no "righteous" indignation, because indignation comes from not recognising sameness in all things.

UNTITLED TALK XXII

RECORDED BY MISS S. E. WALDO, A DISCIPLE
SUNDAY, July 14, 1895.

Philosophy in India means that through which we see God, the rationale of religion; so no Hindu could ever ask for a link between religion and philosophy.

Concrete, generalised, abstract are the three stages in the process of philosophy. The highest abstraction in which all things agree is the One. In religion we have first, symbols and forms; next, mythologies; and last, philosophy. The first two are for the time being; philosophy is the underlying basis of all, and the others are only stepping stones in the struggle to reach the Ultimate.

In Western religion the idea is that without the New Testament and Christ there could be no religion. A similar belief exists in Judaism with regard to Moses and the Prophets, because these religions are dependent upon mythology only. Real religion, the highest, rises above mythology; it can never rest upon that. Modern science has really made the foundations of religion strong. That the whole universe is one, is scientifically demonstrable. What the metaphysicians call "being", the physicist calls "matter", but there is no real fight between the two, for both are one. Though an atom is invisible, unthinkable, yet in it are the whole power and potency of the universe. That is exactly what the Vedantist says of Atman. All sects are really saying the same thing in different words.

Vedanta and modern science both posit a self-evolving Cause. In Itself are all the causes. Take for example the potter shaping a pot. The potter is the primal cause, the clay the material cause, and the wheel the instrumental cause; but the Atman is all three. Atman is cause and manifestation too. The Vedantist says the universe is not real, it is only apparent. Nature is God seen through nescience. The Pantheists say, God has become nature or this world; the Advaitists affirm that God is appearing as this world, but He is not this world.

We can only know experience as a mental process, a fact in the mind as well as a mark in the brain. We cannot push the brain back or forward, but we can the mind; it can stretch over all time—past, present, and future; and so facts in the mind are eternally preserved. All facts are already generalised in mind, which is omnipresent.[6]*

Kant's great achievement was the discovery that "time, space, and causation are modes of thought," but Vedanta taught this ages ago and called it "Maya." Schopenhauer stands on reason only and rationalises the Vedas... Shankara maintained the orthodoxy of the Vedas.

* * *

"Treeness" or the idea of "tree", found out among trees is knowledge, and the highest knowledge is One...

Personal God is the last generalization of the universe, only hazy, not clear-cut and philosophic...

Unity is self-evolving, out of which everything comes.

Physical science is to find out facts, metaphysics is the thread to bind the flowers into a bouquet. Every abstraction is metaphysical; even putting manure at the root of a tree involves a process of abstraction...

Religion includes the concrete, the more generalized and the ultimate unity. Do not stick to particularisations. Get to the principle, to the One...

Devils are machines of darkness, angels are machines of light; but both are machines. Man alone is alive. Break the machine, strike the balance[7]* and then man can become free. This is the only world where man can work out his salvation.

"Whom the Self chooses" is true. Election is true, but put it within. As an external and fatalistic doctrine, it is horrible.

UNTITLED TALK XXIII

RECORDED BY MISS S. E. WALDO, A DISCIPLE
MONDAY, July 15, 1895.

Where there is polyandry, as in Tibet, women are physically stronger than the men. When the English go there, these women carry large men up the mountains.

In Malabar, although of course polyandry does not obtain there, the women lead in everything. Exceptional cleanliness is apparent everywhere and there is the greatest impetus to learning. When I myself was in that country, I met many women who spoke good Sanskrit, while in the rest of India not one woman in a million can speak it. Mastery elevates, and servitude debases. Malabar has never been conquered either by the Portuguese or by the Mussulmans.

The Dravidians were a non-Aryan race of Central Asia who preceded the Aryans, and those of Southern India were the most civilised. Women with them stood higher than men. They subsequently divided, some going to Egypt, others to Babylonia, and the rest remaining in India.

UNTITLED TALK XXIV

RECORDED BY MISS S. E. WALDO, A DISCIPLE
TUESDAY, July 16, 1895. (Shankara)

The "unseen cause" (Or mass of subtle impressions.) leads us to sacrifice and worship, which in turn produce seen results; but to attain liberation we must first hear, then think or reason, and then meditate upon Brahman.

The result of works and the result of knowledge are two different things. "Do" and "Do not do" are the background of all morality, but they really belong only to the body and the mind. All happiness and misery are inextricably connected with the senses, and body is necessary to experience them. The higher the body, the higher the standard of virtue, even up to Brahma; but all have bodies. As long as there is a body, there must be pleasure and pain; only when one has got rid of the body can one escape them. The Atman is bodiless, says Shankara.

No law can make you free, you are free. Nothing can give you freedom, if you have it not already. The Atman is self-illumined. Cause and effect do not reach there, and this dis-embodiedness is freedom. Beyond what was, or is, or is to be, is Brahman. As an effect, freedom would have no value; it would be a compound, and as such would contain the seeds of bondage. It is the one real factor. Not to be attained, hut the real nature of the soul.

Work and worship, however, are necessary to take away the veil, to lift oh the bondage and illusion. They do not give us freedom; but all the same, without effort on our own part we do not open our eyes and see what we are. Shankara says further that Advaita-Vedanta is the crowning glory of the Vedas; hut the lower Vedas are also necessary, because they teach work and worship, and through these many come to the Lord. Others may come without any help but Advaita. Work and worship lead to the same result as Advaita.

Books cannot teach God, but they can destroy ignorance; their action is negative. To hold to the books and at the same time open the way to freedom is Shankara's great achievement. But after all, it is a kind of hair-splitting. Give man first the concrete, then raise him to the highest by slow degrees. This is the effort of the various religions and explains their existence and why each is suited to some stage of development. The very books are a part of the ignorance they help to dispel. Their duty is to drive out the ignorance that has come upon knowledge. "Truth shall drive out untruth." You are free and cannot he made so. So long as you have a creed, you have no God. "He who knows he knows, knows nothing." Who can know the Knower? There are two eternal facts in existence, God and the universe, the former unchangeable, the latter changeable. The world exists eternally. Where your mind cannot grasp the amount of change, you call it eternally … You see the stone or the bas-relief on it, but not both at once; yet both are one.

* * *

Can you make yourself at rest even for a second? All Yogis say you can …

The greatest sin is to think yourself weak. No one is greater: realise you are Brahman. Nothing has power except what you give it. We are beyond the sun, the stars, the universe. Teach the Godhood of man. Deny evil, create none. Stand up and say, I am the master, the master of all. We forge the chain, and we alone can break it.

No action can give you freedom; only knowledge can make you free, Knowledge is irresistible; the mind cannot take it or reject it. When it comes the mind has to accept it; so it is not a work of the mind; only, its expression comes in the mind.

Work or worship is to bring you back to your own nature. It is an entire illusion that the Self is the body; so even while living here in the body, we can be free. The body has nothing in common with the Self. Illusion is taking the real for the unreal—not "nothing at all".

UNTITLED TALK XXIV

RECORDED BY MISS S. E. WALDO, A DISCIPLE
WEDNESDAY, July 17, 1895.

Râmânuja divides the universe into Chit, Achit, and Ishvara—man, nature, and God; conscious, subconscious, and superconscious. Shankara, on the contrary, says that Chit, the soul, is the same as God. God is truth, is knowledge, is infinity; these are not qualities. Any thought of God is a qualification, and all that can be said of Him is "Om tat sat".

Shankara further asks, can you see existence separate from everything else? Where is the differentiation between two objects? Not in sense-perception, else all would be one in it. We have to perceive in sequence. In getting knowledge of what a thing is, we get also something which it is not. The differentiae are in the memory and are got by comparison with what is stored there. Difference is not in the nature of a thing, it is in the brain. Homogeneous one is outside, differentiae are inside (in the mind); so the idea of "many" is the creation of the mind.

Differentiae become qualities when they are separate but joined in one object. We cannot say positively what differentiation is. All that we see and feel about things is pure and simple existence, "isness". All else is in us. Being is the only positive proof we have of anything. All differentiation is really "secondary reality", as the snake in the rope, because the serpent, too, had a certain reality, in that something was seen although misapprehended. When the knowledge of the rope becomes negative, the knowledge of the snake becomes positive, and vice versa; but the fact that you see only one does not prove that the other is non-existent. The idea of the world is an obstruction covering the idea of God and is to be removed, but it does have an existence.

Shankara says again, perception is the last proof of existence. It is self-effulgent and self-conscious, because to go beyond the senses we should still need perception. Perception is independent of the senses, of all instruments, unconditioned. There can be no perception without consciousness; perception has self-luminosity, which in a lesser degree is called consciousness. Not one act of perception can be unconscious; in fact, consciousness is the nature of perception. Existence and perception are one thing, not two things joined together. That which is infinite; so, as perception is the last it is eternal. It is always subjective; is its own perceiver. Perception is not: perception brings mind. It is absolute, the only knower, so perception is really the Atman. Perception itself perceives, but the Atman cannot be a knower, because a "knower" becomes such by the action of knowledge; but, Shankara says, "This

Atman is not I", because the consciousness "I am" (Aham) is not in the Atman. We are but the reflections of that Atman; and Atman and Brahman are one.

When you talk and think of the Absolute, you have to do it in the relative; so all these logical arguments apply. In Yoga, perception and realisation are one. Vishishtâdvaita, of which Ramanuja is the exponent, is seeing partial unity and is a step toward Advaita. Vishishta means differentiation. Prakriti is the nature of the world, and change comes upon it. Change-ful thoughts expressed in changeful words can never prove the Absolute. You reach only something that is minus certain qualities, not Brahman Itself; only a verbal unification, the highest abstraction, but not the nonexistence of the relative.

UNTITLED TALK XXV

RECORDED BY MISS S. E. WALDO, A DISCIPLE
THURSDAY, July 18, 1895.

The lesson today was mainly Shankara's argument against the conclusion of the Sânkhya philosophy.

The Sankhyas say that consciousness is a compound, and beyond that, the last analysis gives us the Purusha, Witness, but that there are many Purushas—each of us is one. Advaita, on the contrary, affirms that Purushas can be only One, that Purusha cannot be conscious, unconscious, or have any qual-ification, for either these qualities would bind, or they would eventually cease; so the One must be without any qualities, even knowledge, and It cannot be the cause of the universe or of anything. "In the beginning, existence only, One without a second", says the Vedas.

* * *

The presence of Sattva with knowledge does not prove that Sattva is the cause of knowledge; on the contrary, Sattva calls out what was already existing in man, as the fire heats an iron ball placed near it by arousing the heat latent in it, not by entering into the ball.

Shankara says, knowledge is not a bondage, because it is the nature of God. The world ever is, whether manifested or un-manifested; so an eternal object exists.

Jnâna-bala-kriyâ (knowledge, power, activity) is God. Nor does He need form, because the finite only needs form to interpose as an obstruction to catch and hold infinite knowl-edge; but God really needs no such help. There is no "moving soul", there is only one Atman. Jiva (individual soul) is the conscious ruler of this body, in whom the five life principles come into unity, and yet that very Jiva is the Atman, because all is Atman. What you think about it is your delusion and not in the Jiva. You are God, and whatever else you may think is wrong. You must worship the Self in Krishna, not Krishna as Krishna. Only by worshipping the Self can freedom be won. Even personal God is but the Self objectified. "Intense search after my own reality is Bhakti", says Shankara.

All the means we take to reach God are true; it is only like trying to find the pole-star by locating it through the stars that are around it.

* * *

The Bhagavad-Gita is the best authority on Vedanta.

UNTITLED TALK XXVI

RECORDED BY MISS S. E. WALDO, A DISCIPLE
FRIDAY, July 19, 1895.

So long as I say "you", I have the right to speak of God protecting us. When I see another, I must take all the conse-quences and put in the third, the ideal, which stands between us; that is the apex of the triangle. The vapour becomes snow, then water, then Ganga; but when it is vapour, there is no Ganga, and when it is water, we think of no vapour in it. The idea of creation or change is inseparably connected with will. So long as we perceive this world in motion, we have to con-ceive will behind it. Physics proves the utter delusion of the senses; nothing really is as ever see, hear, feel, smell, taste it. Certain vibrations producing certain results affect our senses; we know only relative truth.

The Sanskrit word for truth is "isness" (Sat). From our pres-ent standpoint, this world appears to us as will and conscious-ness. Personal God is as much an entity for Himself as we are for ourselves, and no more. God can also be seen as a form, just as we are seen. As men, we must have a God; as God, we need none. This is why Shri Ramakrishna constantly saw the Divine Mother ever present with him, more real than any other thing around him; but in Samâdhi all went but the Self. Personal God comes nearer and nearer until He melts away, and there is no more Personal God and no more "I", all is merged in Self.

Consciousness is a bondage. The argument from design claims that intelligence precedes form; but if intelligence is the cause of anything, it itself is in its turn an effect. It is Maya. God creates us, and we create God, and this is Maya. The circle is unbroken; mind creates body, and body creates mind; the egg brings the chicken, the chicken the egg; the tree the seed, the seed the tree. The world is neither entire-ly differentiated nor yet entirely homogeneous. Man is free and must rise above both sides. Both are right in their place; but to reach truth, "isness", we must transcend all that we now know of existence, will, consciousness, doing, going, knowing. There is no real individuality of the Jiva (separate soul); eventually it, as a compound, will go to pieces. Only that which is beyond further analysis is "simple", and that alone is truth, freedom, immortality, bliss. All struggles for the preservation of this illusive individuality are really vices. All struggles to lose this individuality are virtues. Everything in the universe is trying to break down this individuality, ei-ther consciously or unconsciously. All morality is based upon the destruction of separateness or false individuality, because that is the cause of all sin. Morality exists first; later, religion codifies it. Customs come first, and then mythology follows to explain them. While things are happening, they come by a higher law than reasoning; that arises later in the attempt to understand them. Reasoning is not the motive power, it is "chewing the cud" afterwards. Reason is the historian of the actions of the human beings.

* * *

Buddha was a great Vedantist (for Buddhism was really only an offshoot of Vedanta), and Shankara is often called a "hidden Buddhist". Buddha made the analysis, Shankara made the synthesis out of it. Buddha never bowed down to anything—neither Veda, nor caste, nor priest, nor custom. He fearlessly reasoned so far as reason could take him. Such a fearless search for truth and such love for every living thing the world has never seen. Buddha was the Washington of the religious world; he conquered a throne only to give it to the world, as Washington did to the American people. He sought nothing for himself.

UNTITLED TALK XXVII

RECORDED BY MISS S. E. WALDO, A DISCIPLE
SATURDAY, July 20, 1895.

Perception is our only real knowledge or religion. Talking about it for ages will never make us know our soul. There is no difference between theories and atheism. In fact, the atheist is the truer man. Every step I take in the light is mine for ever. When you go to a country and see it, then it is yours. We have each to see for ourselves; teachers can only "bring the food", we must eat it to be nourished. Argument can never prove God save as a logical conclusion.

It is impossible to find God outside of ourselves. Our own souls contribute all the divinity that is outside of us. We are the greatest temple. The objectification is only a faint imitation of what we see within ourselves.

Concentration of the powers of the mind is our only instrument to help us see God. If you know one soul (your own), you know all souls, past, present, and to come. The will concentrates the mind, certain things excite and control this will, such as reason, love, devotion, breathing. The concentrated mind is a lamp that shows us every corner of the soul.

No one method can suit all. These different methods are not steps necessary to be taken one after another. Ceremonials are the lowest form; next God external, and after that God internal. In some cases gradation may be needed, but in many only one way is required. It would be the height of folly to say to everyone, "You must pass through Karma and Bhakti before you can reach Jnana."

Stick to your reason until you reach something higher; and you will know it to be higher, because it will not jar with reason. The stage beyond consciousness is inspiration (Samâ-dhi); but never mistake hysterical trances for the real thing. It is a terrible thing to claim this inspiration falsely, to mistake instinct for inspiration. There is no external test for inspiration, we know it ourselves; our guardian against mistake is negative—the voice of reason. All religion is going beyond reason, but reason is the only guide to get there. Instinct is like ice, reason is the water, and inspiration is the subtlest form or vapour; one follows the other. Everywhere is this eternal sequence—unconsciousness, consciousness, intelligence—matter, body, mind—and to us it seems as if the chain began with the particular link we first lay hold of. Arguments on both sides are of equal weight, and both are true. We must reach beyond both, to where there is neither the one nor the other. These successions are all Maya.

Religion is above reason, supernatural. Faith is not belief, it is the grasp on the Ultimate, an illumination. First hear, then reason and find out all that reason can give about the Atman; let the flood of reason flow over It, then take what remains. If nothing remains, thank God you have escaped a superstition. When you have determined that nothing can take away the Atman, that It stands every test, hold fast to this and teach it to all. Truth cannot be partial; it is for the good of all. Finally, in perfect rest and peace meditate upon It, concentrate your mind upon It, make yourself one with It. Then no speech is needed; silence will carry the truth. Do not spend your energy in talking, but meditate in silence; and do not let the rush of the outside world disturb you. When your mind is in the highest state, you are unconscious of it. Accumulate power in silence and become a dynamo of spirituality. What can a beggar give? Only a king can give, and he only when he wants nothing himself.

Hold your money merely as custodian for what is God's. Have no attachment for it. Let name and fame and money go; they are a terrible bondage. Feel the wonderful atmosphere of freedom. You are free, free, free! Oh, blessed am I! Freedom am I! I am the Infinite! In my soul I can find no beginning and no end. All is my Self. Say this unceasingly.

UNTITLED TALK XXVIII

RECORDED BY MISS S. E. WALDO, A DISCIPLE
SUNDAY, July 21, 1895. (Patanjali's Yoga Aphorisms)

Yoga is the science of restraining the Chitta (mind) from breaking into Vrittis (modifications). Mind is a mixture of sensation and feelings, or action and reaction; so it cannot be permanent. The mind has a fine body and through this it works on the gross body. Vedanta says that behind the mind is the real Self. It accepts the other two, but posits a third, the Eternal, the Ultimate, the last analysis, the unit, where there is no further compound. Birth is re-composition, death is de-composition, and the final analysis is where Atman is found; there being no further division possible, the perdurable is reached.

The whole ocean is present at the back of each wave, and all manifestations are waves, some very big, some small; yet all are the ocean in their essence, the whole ocean; but as waves each is a part. When the waves are stilled, then all is one; "a spectator without a spectacle", says Patanjali. When the mind is active, the Atman is mixed up with it. The repetition of old forms in quick succession is memory.

Be unattached. Knowledge is power, and getting one you get the other. By knowledge you can even banish the material world. When you can mentally get rid of one quality after another from any object until all are gone, you can at will make the object itself disappear from your consciousness.

Those who are ready, advance very quickly and can become Yogis in six months. The less developed may take several years; and anyone by faithful work and by giving up everything else and devoting himself solely to practice can reach the goal in twelve years. Bhakti will bring you there without any of these mental gymnastics, but it is a slower way.

Ishvara is the Atman as seen or grasped by mind. His highest name is Om; so repeat it, meditate on it, and think of all its wonderful nature and attributes. Repeating the Om continually is the only true worship. It is not a word, it is God Himself.

Religion gives you nothing new; it only takes off obstacles and lets you see your Self. Sickness is the first great obstacle; a healthy body is the best instrument. Melancholy is an almost insuperable barrier. If you have once known Brahman, never after can you be melancholy. Doubt, want of perseverance, mistaken ideas are other obstacles.

* * *

Prânas are subtle energies, sources of motion. There are ten in all, five inward and five outward. One great current flows upwards, and the other downwards. Prânâyâma is controlling the Pranas through breathing. Breath is the fuel, Prana is the steam, and the body is the engine. Pranayama has three parts, Puraka (in-breathing), Kumbhaka (holding the breath), Rechaka (out-breathing)...

The Guru is the conveyance in which the spiritual influence is brought to you. Anyone can teach, but the spirit must be passed on by the Guru to the Shishya (disciple), and that will fructify. The relation between Shishyas is that of brotherhood, and this is actually accepted by law in India. The Guru passes the thought power, the Mantra, that he has received from those before him; and nothing can be done without a Guru. In fact, great danger ensues. Usually without a Guru, these Yoga practices lead to lust; but with one, this seldom happens. Each Ishta has a Mantra. The Ishta is the ideal peculiar to the particular worshipper; the Mantra is the external word to express it. Constant repetition of the word helps to fix the ideal firmly in the mind. This method of worship prevails among religious devotees all over India.

UNTITLED TALK XXIX

RECORDED BY MISS S. E. WALDO, A DISCIPLE
TUESDAY, July 23, 1895. (Bhagavad-Gita, Karma-Yoga)

To attain liberation through work, join yourself to work but without desire, looking for no result. Such work leads to knowledge, which in turn brings emancipation. To give up work before you know, leads to misery. Work done for the Self gives no bondage. Neither desire pleasure nor fear pain from work. It is the mind and body that work, not I. Tell yourself this unceasingly and realise it. Try not to know that you work.

Do all as a sacrifice or offering to the Lord. Be in the world, but not of it, like the lotus leaf whose roots are in the mud but which remains always pure. Let your love go to all, whatever they do to you. A blind man cannot see colour, so how can we see evil unless it is in us? We compare what we see outside with what we find in ourselves and pronounce judgment accordingly. If we are pure, we cannot see impurity. It may exist, but not for us. See only God in every man, woman and child; see it by the antarjyotis, "inner light", and seeing that, we can see naught else. Do not want this world, because what you desire you get. Seek the Lord and the Lord only. The more power there is, the more bondage, the more fear. How much more afraid and miserable are we than the ant! Get out of it all and come to the Lord. Seek the science of the maker and not that of the made.

"I am the doer and the deed." "He who can stem the tide of lust and anger is a great Yogi."

"Only by practice and non-attachment can we conquer mind." ...

Our Hindu ancestors sat down and thought on God and morality, and so have we brains to use for the same ends; but in the rush of trying to get gain, we are likely to lose them again.

* * *

The body has in itself a certain power of curing itself and many things can rouse this curative power into action, such as mental conditions, or medicine, or exercise, etc. As long as we are disturbed by physical conditions, so long we need the help of physical agencies. Not until we have got rid of bondage to the nerves, can we disregard them.

There is the unconscious mind, but it is below consciousness, which is just one part of the human organism. Philosophy is guess-work about the mind. Religion is based upon sense contact, upon seeing, the only basis of knowledge. What comes in contact with the superconscious mind is fact. Âptas are those who have "sensed" religion. The proof is that if you follow their method, you too will see. Each science requires its own particular method and instruments. An astronomer cannot show you the rings of Saturn by the aid of all the pots and pans in the kitchen. He needs a telescope. So, to see the great facts of religion, the methods of those who have already seen must be followed. The greater the science the more varied the means of studying it. Before we came into the world, God provided the means to get out; so all we have to do is to find the means. But do not fight over methods. Look only for realisation and choose the best method you can find to suit you. Eat the mangoes and let the rest quarrel over the basket. See Christ, then you will be a Christian. All else is talk; the less talking the better.

The message makes the messenger. The Lord makes the temple; not vice versa.

Learn until "the glory of the Lord shines through your face", as it shone through the face of Shvetaketu.

Guess against guess makes fight; but talk of what you have been, and no human heart can resist it. Paul was converted against his will by realisation.

TUESDAY AFTERNOON

After dinner there was a short conversation in the course of which the Swami said:

Delusion creates delusion. Delusion creates itself and destroys itself, such is Maya. All knowledge (so-called), being based on Maya, is a vicious circle, and in time that very knowledge destroys itself. "Let go the rope", delusion cannot touch the Atman. When we lay hold of the rope—identify ourselves with Maya—she has power over us. Let go of it, be the Witness only, then you can admire the picture of the universe undisturbed.

UNTITLED TALK XXX

RECORDED BY MISS S. E. WALDO, A DISCIPLE
WEDNESDAY, July 24, 1895.

The powers acquired by the practice of Yoga are not obstacles for the Yogi who is perfect, but are apt to be so for the beginner, through the wonder and pleasure excited by their exercise. Siddhis are the powers which mark success in the practice; and they may be produced by various means, such as the repetition of a Mantra, by Yoga practice, meditation, fasting, or even by the use of herbs and drugs. The Yogi, who has conquered all interest in the powers acquired and who renounces all virtue arising from his actions, comes into the "cloud of virtue" (name of one of the states of Samadhi) and radiates holiness as a cloud rains water.

Meditation is on a series of objects, concentration is on one object.

Mind is cognised by the Atman, but it is not self-illuminated. The Atman cannot be the cause of anything. How can it be? How can the Purusha join itself to Prakriti (nature)? It does not; it is only illusively thought to do so...

Learn to help without pitying or feeling that there is any misery. Learn to be the same to enemy and to friend; then when you can do that and no longer have any desire, the goal is attained.

Cut down the banyan tree of desire with the axe of non-attachment, and it will vanish utterly. It is all illusion. "He from whom blight and delusion have fallen, he who has conquered the evils of association, he alone is âzâd (free)."

To love anyone personally is bondage. Love all alike, then all desires fall off.

Time, the "eater of everything", comes, and all has to go. Why try to improve the earth, to paint the butterfly? It all has to go at last. Do not be mere white mice in a treadmill, working always and never accomplishing anything. Every desire is fraught with evil, whether the desire itself be good or evil. It is like a dog jumping for a piece of meat which is ever receding from his reach, and dying a dog's death at last. Do not be like that. Cut off all desire.

* * *

Paramâtman as ruling Maya is Ishvara; Paramâtman as under Maya is Jivâtman. Maya is the sum total of manifestation and will utterly vanish.

Tree-nature is Maya, it is really God-nature which we see under the veil of Maya. The "why" of anything is in Maya. To ask why Maya came is a useless question, because the answer can never be given in Maya, and beyond Maya who will ask it? Evil creates "why", not "why" the evil, and it is evil that asks "why". Illusion destroys illusion. Reason itself, being based upon contradiction, is a circle and has to kill itself. Sense-perception is an inference, and yet all inference comes from perception.

Ignorance reflecting the light of God is seen; but by itself it is zero. The cloud would not appear except as the sunlight falls on it.

There were four travellers who came to a high wall. The first one climbed with difficulty to the top and without looking back, jumped over. The second clambered up the wall, looked over, and with a shout of delight disappeared. The third in his turn climbed to the top, looked where his companions had gone, laughed with joy, and followed them. But the fourth one came back to tell what had happened to his fellow-travellers. The sign to us that there is something beyond is the laugh that rings back from those great ones who have plunged from Maya's wall.

* * *

Separating ourselves from the Absolute and attributing certain qualities to It give us Ishvara. It is the Reality of the universe as seen through our mind. Personal devil is the misery of the world seen through the minds of the superstitious.

UNTITLED TALK XXXI

RECORDED BY MISS S. E. WALDO, A DISCIPLE
THURSDAY, July 25, 1895. (Patanjali's Yoga Aphorisms)

"Things may be done, caused to be done, or approved of", and the effect upon us is nearly equal.

Complete continence gives great intellectual and spiritual power. The Brahmachârin must be sexually pure in thought, word, and deed. Lose regard for the body; get rid of the consciousness of it so far as possible.

Âsana (posture) must be steady and pleasant; and constant practice, identifying the mind with the Infinite, will bring this about.

Continual attention to one object is contemplation.

When a stone is thrown into still water, many circles are made, each distinct but all interacting; so with our minds; only in us the action is unconscious, while with the Yogi it is conscious. We are spiders in a web, and Yoga practice will enable us like the spider to pass along any strand of the web we please. Non-Yogis are bound to the particular spot where they are.

* * *

To injure another creates bondage and hides the truth. Negative virtues are not enough; we have to conquer Maya, and then she will follow us. We only deserve things when they cease to bind us. When the bondage ceases, really and truly, all things come to us. Only those who want nothing are masters of nature.

Take refuge in some soul who has already broken his bondage, and in time he will free you through his mercy. Higher still is to take refuge in the Lord (Ishvara), but it is the most difficult; only once in a century can one be found who has really done it. Feel nothing, know nothing, do nothing, have nothing, give up all to God, and say utterly, "Thy will be done". We only dream this bondage. Wake up and let it go. Take refuge in God, only so can we cross the desert of Maya. "Let go thy hold, Sannyasin bold, say, Om tat sat, Om!"

It is our privilege to be allowed to be charitable, for only so can we grow. The poor man suffers that we may be helped; let the giver kneel down and give thanks, let the receiver stand up and permit. See the Lord back of every being and give to Him. When we cease to see evil, the world must end for us, since to rid us of that mistake is its only object. To think there is any imperfection creates it. Thoughts of strength and perfection alone can cure it. Do what good you can, some evil will inhere in it; but do all without regard to personal result, give up all results to the Lord, then neither good nor evil will affect you.

Doing work is not religion, but work done rightly leads to freedom. In reality all pity is darkness, because whom to pity? Can you pity God? And is there anything else? Thank God for giving you this world as a moral gymnasium to help your development, but never imagine you can help the world. Be grateful to him who curses you, for he gives you a mirror to show what cursing is, also a chance to practise self-restraint; so bless him and be glad. Without exercise, power cannot come out; without the mirror, we cannot see ourselves.

Unchaste imagination is as bad as unchaste action. Con-trolled desire leads to the highest result. Transform the sexual energy into spiritual energy, but do not emasculate, because that is throwing away the power. The stronger this force, the more can be done with it. Only a powerful current of water can do hydraulic mining.

What we need today is to know there is a God and that we can see and feel Him here and now. A Chicago professor says, "Take care of this world, God will take care of the next." What nonsense! If we can take care of this world, what need of a gratuitous Lord to take care of the other!

UNTITLED TALK XXXII

RECORDED BY MISS S. E. WALDO, A DISCIPLE
FRIDAY, July 26, 1895. (Brihadâranyakopanishad.)

Love all things only through and for the Self. Yâjnavalkya said to Maitreyi, his wife, "Through the Atman we know all things." The Atman can never be the object of knowledge, nor can the Knower be known. He who knows he is the Atman, he is law unto himself. He knows he is the universe and its creator...

Perpetuating old myths in the form of allegories and giving them undue importance fosters superstition and is really weakness. Truth must have no compromise. Teach truth and make no apology for any superstition; neither drag truth to the level of the listener.

UNTITLED TALK XXXIII

RECORDED BY MISS S. E. WALDO, A DISCIPLE
SATURDAY, July 27, 1895. (Kathopanishad)

Learn not the truth of the Self save from one who has realised it; in all others it is mere talk. Realisation is beyond virtue and vice, beyond future and past; beyond all the pairs of opposites. "The stainless one sees the Self, and an eternal calm comes in the Soul." Talking, arguing, and reading books, the highest flights of the intellect, the Vedas themselves, all these cannot give knowledge of the Self.

In us are two — The God-soul and the man-soul. The sages know that the latter is but the shadow, that the former is the only real Sun.

Unless we join the mind with the senses, we get no report from eyes, nose, ears, etc. The external organs are used by the power of the mind. Do not let the senses go outside, and then you can get rid of body and the external world.

This very "x" which we see here as an external world, the departed see as heaven or hell according to their own mental states. Here and hereafter are two dreams, the latter modelled on the former; get rid of both, all is omnipresent, all is now. Nature, body, and mind go to death, not we; we never go nor come. The man Swami Vivekananda is in nature, is born, and dies; but the self which we see as Swami Vivekananda is never born and never dies. It is the eternal and unchangeable Reality.

The power of the mind is the same whether we divide it into five senses or whether we see only one. A blind man says, "Everything has a distinct echo, so I clap my hands and get that echo, and then I can tell everything that is around me." So in a fog the blind man can safely lead the seeing man. Fog or darkness makes no difference to him.

Control the mind, cut off the senses, then you are a Yogi; after that, all the rest will come. Refuse to hear, to see, to smell, to taste; take away the mental power from the external organs. You continually do it unconsciously as when your mind is absorbed; so you can learn to do it consciously. The mind can put the senses where it pleases. Get rid of the fundamental superstition that we are obliged to act through the body. We are not. Go into your own room and get the Upanishads out of your own Self. You are the greatest book that ever was or ever will be, the infinite depository of all that is. Until the inner teacher opens, all outside teaching is in vain. It must lead to the opening of the book of the heart to have any value.

The will is the "still small voice", the real Ruler who says "do" and "do not". It has done all that binds us. The ignorant will leads to bondage, the knowing will can free us. The will can be made strong in thousands of ways; every way is a kind of Yoga, but the systematised Yoga accomplishes the work more quickly. Bhakti, Karma, Raja, and Jnana-Yoga get over the ground more effectively. Put on all powers, philosophy, work, prayer, meditation—crowd all sail, put on all head of steam—reach the goal. The sooner, the better...

Baptism is external purification symbolising the internal. It is of Buddhist origin.

The Eucharist is a survival of a very ancient custom of savage tribes. They sometimes killed their great chiefs and ate their flesh in order to obtain in themselves the qualities that made their leaders great. They believed that in such a way the characteristics that made the chief brave and wise would become theirs and make the whole tribe brave and wise, instead of only one man. Human sacrifice was also a Jewish idea and one that clung to them despite many chastisements from Jehovah. Jesus was gentle and loving, but to fit him into Jewish beliefs, the idea of human sacrifice, in the form of atonement or as a human scapegoat, had to come in. This cruel idea made Christianity depart from the teachings of Jesus himself and develop a spirit of persecution and bloodshed...

Say, "it is my nature", never say, "It is my duty"—to do anything whatever.

"Truth alone triumphs, not untruth." Stand upon Truth, and you have got God.

* * *

From the earliest times in India the Brahmin caste have held themselves beyond all law; they claim to be gods. They are poor, but their weakness is that they seek power. Here are about sixty millions of people who are good and moral and hold no property, and they are what they are because from their birth they are taught that they are above law, above punishment. They feel themselves to be "twice-born", to be sons of God.

UNTITLED TALK XXXIV

RECORDED BY MISS S. E. WALDO, A DISCIPLE
SUNDAY, July 28, 1895.

Avadhuta Gita or "Song of the Purified" by Dattâtreya (Dattatreya, the son of Atri and Anasuyâ, was an incarnation of Brahmâ, Vishnu and Shiva.)

"All knowledge depends upon calmness of mind."

"He who has filled the universe, He who is Self in self, how shall I salute Him!"

To know the Atman as my nature is both knowledge and realisation. "I am He, there is not the least doubt of it."

"No thought, no word, no deed, creates a bondage for me. I am beyond the senses, I am knowledge and bliss."

There is neither existence nor non-existence, all is Atman. Shake off all ideas of relativity; shake off all superstitions; let caste and birth and Devas and all else vanish. Why talk of being and becoming? Give up talking of dualism and Advaitism! When were you two, that you talk of two or one? The universe is this Holy One and He alone. Talk not of Yoga to make you pure; you are pure by your very nature. None can teach you.

Men like him who wrote this song are what keep religion alive. They have actually realised; they care for nothing, feel nothing done to the body, care not for heat and cold or danger or anything. They sit still and enjoy the bliss of Atman, while red-hot coals burn their body, and they feel them not.

"When the threefold bondage of knower, knowledge, and known ceases, there is the Atman."

"Where the delusion of bondage and freedom ceases, there the Atman is."

"What if you have controlled the mind, what if you have not? What if you have money, what if you have not? You are the Atman ever pure. Say, 'I am the Atman. No bondage ever came near me. I am the changeless sky; clouds of belief may pass over me, but they do not touch me.'"

"Burn virtue, burn vice. Freedom is baby talk. I am that immortal Knowledge. I am that purity."

"No one was ever bound, none was ever free. There is none but me. I am the Infinite, the Ever-free. Talk not to me! What can change me, the essence of knowledge! Who can teach, who can be taught?"

Throw argument, throw philosophy into the ditch.

"Only a slave sees slaves, the deluded delusion, the impure impurity."

Place, time causation are all delusions. It is your disease that you think you are bound and will be free. You are the Unchangeable. Talk not. Sit down and let all things melt away, they are but dreams. There is no differentiation, no distinction, it is all superstition; therefore be silent and know what you are.

"I am the essence of bliss." Follow no ideal, you are all there is. Fear naught, you are the essence of existence. Be at peace. Do not disturb yourself. You never were in bondage, you never were virtuous or sinful. Get rid of all these delusions and be at peace. Whom to worship? Who worships? All is the Atman. To speak, to think is superstition. Repeat over and over, "I am Atman", "I am Atman". Let everything else go.

UNTITLED TALK XXXV

RECORDED BY MISS S. E. WALDO, A DISCIPLE
MONDAY, July 29, 1895.

We sometimes indicate a thing by describing its surroundings. When we say "Sachchidananda" (Existence-Knowledge-Bliss), we are merely indicating the shores of an indescribable Beyond. Not even can we say "is" about it, for that too is relative. Any imagination, any concept is in vain. Neti, neti ("Not this, not this") is all that can be said, for even to think is to limit and so to lose.

The senses cheat you day and night. Vedanta found that out ages ago; modern science is just discovering the same fact. A picture has only length and breadth, and the painter copies nature in her cheating by artificially giving the appearance of depth. No two people see the same world. The highest knowledge will show you that there is no motion, no change in anything; that the very idea of it is all Maya. Study nature as a whole, that is, study motion. Mind and body are not our real self; both belong to nature, but eventually we can know the ding an sich. Then mind and body being transcended, all that they conceive goes. When you cease utterly to know and see the world, then you realise Atman. The superseding of relative knowledge is what we want. There is no infinite mind or infinite knowledge, because both mind and knowledge are limited. We are now seeing through a veil; then we reach the "x", which is the Reality of all our knowing.

If we look at a picture through a pin-hole in a cardboard, we get an utterly mistaken notion; yet what we see is really the picture. As we enlarge the hole, we get a clearer and clearer idea. Out of the reality we manufacture the different views in conformity with our mistaken perceptions of name and form. When we throw away the cardboard, we see the same picture, but we see it as it is. We put in all the attributes, all the errors; the picture itself is unaltered thereby. That is because Atman is the reality of all; all we see is Atman, but not as we see it, as name and form; they are all in our veil, in Maya.

They are like spots in the object-glass of a telescope, yet it is the light of the sun that shows us the spots; we could not even see the illusion save for the background of reality which is Brahman. Swami Vivekananda is just the speck on the object-glass; I am Atman, real, unchangeable, and that reality alone enables me to see Swami Vivekananda. Atman is the essence of every hallucination; but the sun is never identified with the spots on the glass, it only shows them to us. Our actions, as they are evil or good, increase or decrease the "spots"; but they never affect the God within us. Perfectly cleanse the mind of spots and instantly we see, "I and my father are one".

We first perceive, then reason later. We must have this perception as a fact, and it is called religion, realisation. No matter if one never heard of creed or prophet or book. Let him get this realisation, and he needs no more. Cleanse the mind, this is all of religion; and until we ourselves clear off the spots, we cannot see the Reality as it is. The baby sees no sun; he has not yet the measure of it in himself. Get rid of the defects within yourself, and you will not be able to see any without. A baby sees robbery done, and it means nothing to him. Once you find the hidden object in a puzzle picture, you see it ever more; so when once you are free and stainless, you see only freedom and purity in the world around. That moment all the knots of the heart are cut asunder, all crooked places are made straight, and this world vanishes as a dream. And when we awake, we wonder how we ever came to dream such trash!

"Getting whom, misery mountain high has no power to move the soul."

With the axe of knowledge cut the wheels asunder, and the Atman stands free, even though the old momentum carries on the wheel of mind and body. The wheel can now only go straight, can only do good. If that body does anything bad, know that the man is not Jivanmukta; he lies if he makes that claim. But it is only when the wheels have got a good straight motion (from cleansing the mind) that the axe can be applied. All purifying action deals conscious or unconscious blows on delusion. To call another a sinner is the worst thing you can do. Good action done ignorantly produces the same result and helps to break the bondage.

To identify the sun with the spots on the object-glass is the fundamental error. Know the sun, the "I", to be ever unaffected by anything, and devote yourself to cleansing the spots. Man is the greatest being that ever can be. The highest worship there is, is to worship man as Krishna, Buddha, Christ. What you want, you create. Get rid of desire...

The angels and the departed are all here, seeing this world as heaven. The same "x" is seen by all according to their mental attitude. The best vision to be had of the "x" is here on this earth. Never want to go to heaven, that is the worst delusion. Even here, too much wealth and grinding poverty are both bondages and hold us back from religion. Three great gifts we have: first, a human body. (The human mind is the nearest reflection of God, we are "His own image".) Second, the desire to be free. Third, the help of a noble soul, who has crossed the ocean of delusion, as a teacher. When you have these three, bless the Lord; you are sure to be free.

What you only grasp intellectually may be overthrown by a new argument; but what you realise is yours for ever.

Talking, talking religion is but little good. Put God behind everything—man, animal, food, work; make this a habit.

Ingersoll once said to me: "I believe in making the most out of this world, in squeezing the orange dry, because this world is all we are sure of." I replied: "I know a better way to squeeze the orange of this world than you do, and I get more out of it. I know I cannot die, so I am not in a hurry; I know there is no fear, so I enjoy the squeezing. I have no duty, no bondage of wife and children and property; I can love all men and women. Everyone is God to me. Think of the joy of loving man as God! Squeeze your orange this way and get ten thousandfold more out of it. Get every single drop."

That which seems to be the will is the Atman behind, it is really free.

MONDAY AFTERNOON

Jesus was imperfect because he did not live up fully to his own ideal, and above all because he did not give woman a place equal to man. Women did everything for him, and yet he was so bound by the Jewish custom that not one was made an apostle. Still he was the greatest character next to Buddha, who in his turn was not fully perfect. Buddha, however, recognised woman's right to an equal place in religion, and his first and one of his greatest disciples was his own wife, who became the head of the whole Buddhistic movement among the women of India. But we ought not to criticise these great ones, we should only look upon them as far above ourselves. Nonetheless we must not pin our faith to any man, however great; we too must become Buddhas and Christs.

No man should be judged by his defects. The great virtues a man has are his especially, his errors are the common weaknesses of humanity and should never be counted in estimating his character.

* * *

Vira, the Sanskrit word for "heroic", is the origin of our word "virtue", because in ancient times the best fighter was regarded as the most virtuous man.

UNTITLED TALK XXXVI

RECORDED BY MISS S. E. WALDO, A DISCIPLE
TUESDAY, July 30, 1895.

Christs and Buddhas are simply occasions upon which to objectify our own inner powers. We really answer our own prayers.

It is blasphemy to think that if Jesus had never been born, humanity would not have been saved. It is horrible to forget thus the divinity in human nature, a divinity that must come out. Never forget the glory of human nature. We are the greatest God that ever was or ever will be. Christs and Buddhas are but waves on the boundless ocean which I am. Bow down to nothing but your own higher Self. Until you know that you are that very God of gods, there will never be any freedom for you.

All our past actions are really good, because they lead us to what we ultimately become. Of whom to beg? I am the real existence, and all else is a dream save as it is I. I am the whole ocean; do not call the little wave you have made "I"; know it for nothing but a wave. Satyakâma (lover of truth) heard the inner voice telling him, "You are the infinite, the universal is in you. Control yourself and listen to the voice of your true Self."

The great prophets who do the fighting have to be less perfect than those who live silent lives of holiness, thinking great thoughts and so helping the world. These men, passing out one after another, produce as final outcome the man of power who preaches.

* * *

Knowledge exists, man only discovers it. The Vedas are the eternal knowledge through which God created the world. They talk high philosophy—the highest—and make this tremendous claim...

Tell the truth boldly, whether it hurts or not. Never pander to weakness. If truth is too much for intelligent people and sweeps them away, let them go; the sooner the better. Childish ideas are for babies and savages; and these are not all in the nursery and the forests, some of them have fallen into the pulpits.

It is bad to stay in the church after you are grown up spiritually. Come out and die in the open air of freedom.

All progression is in the relative world. The human form is the highest and man the greatest being, because here and now we can get rid of the relative world entirely, can actually attain freedom, and this is the goal. Not only we can, but some have reached perfection; so no matter what finer bodies come, they could only be on the relative plane and could do no more than we, for to attain freedom is all that can be done.

The angels never do wicked deeds, so they never get punished and never get saved. Blows are what awaken us and help to break the dream. They show us the insufficiency of this world and make us long to escape, to have freedom...

A thing dimly perceived we call by one name; the same thing when fully perceived we call by another. The higher the moral nature, the higher the perception and the stronger the will.

TUESDAY AFTERNOON

The reason of the harmony between thought and matter is that they are two sides of one thing, call it "x", which divides itself into the internal and the external.

The English word "paradise" comes from the Sanskrit pa-ra-desa, which was taken over into the Persian language and means literally "the land beyond", or the other world. The old Aryans always believed in a soul, never that man was the body. Their heavens and hells were all temporary, because no effect can outlast its cause and no cause is eternal; therefore all effects must come to an end.

The whole of the Vedanta Philosophy is in this story: Two birds of golden plumage sat on the same tree. The one above, serene, majestic, immersed in his own glory; the one below restless and eating the fruits of the tree, now sweet, now bitter. Once he ate an exceptionally bitter fruit, then he paused and looked up at the majestic bird above; but he soon forgot about the other bird and went on eating the fruits of the tree as before. Again he ate a bitter fruit, and this time he hopped up a few boughs nearer to the bird at the top. This happened many times until at last the lower bird came to the place of the upper bird and lost himself. He found all at once that there had never been two birds, but that he was all the time that upper bird, serene, majestic, and immersed in his own glory.

UNTITLED TALK XXXVII

RECORDED BY MISS S. E. WALDO, A DISCIPLE
WEDNESDAY, July 31, 1895.

Luther drove a nail into religion when he took away renunciation and gave us morality instead. Atheists and materialists can have ethics, but only believers in the Lord can have religion.

The wicked pay the price of the great soul's holiness. Think of that when you see a wicked man. Just as the poor man's labour pays for the rich man's luxury, so is it in the spiritual world. The terrible degradation of the masses in India is the price nature pays for the production of great souls like Mirâbâi, Buddha, etc.

* * *

"I am the holiness of the holy" (Gita). I am the root, each uses it in his own way, but all is I. "I do everything, you are but the occasion."

Do not talk much, but feel the spirit within you; then you are a Jnani. This is knowledge, all else is ignorance. All that is to be known is Brahman. It is the all...

Sattva binds through the search for happiness and knowledge, Rajas binds through desire, Tamas binds through wrong perception and laziness. Conquer the two lower by Sattva, and then give up all to the Lord and be free.

The Bhakti-Yogi realises Brahman very soon and goes beyond the three qualities. (Gita, Chapter XII.)

The will, the consciousness, the senses, desire, the passions, all these combined make what we call the "soul".

There is first, the apparent self (body); second, the mental self who mistakes the body for himself (the Absolute bound by Maya); third, the Atman, the ever pure, the ever free. Seen partially, It is nature; seen wholly, all nature goes, even the memory of it is lost. There is the changeable (mortal), the eternally changeable (nature), and the Unchangeable (Atman).

Be perfectly hopeless, that is the highest state. What is there to hope for? Burst asunder the bonds of hope, stand on your Self, be at rest, never mind what you do, give up all to God, but have no hypocrisy about it.

Svastha, the Sanskrit word for "standing on your own Self", is used colloquially in India to inquire, "Are you well, are you happy?" And when Hindus would express, "I saw a thing", they say, "I saw a word-meaning (Padârtha)." Even this universe is a "word-meaning".

* * *

A perfect man's body mechanically does right; it can do only good because it is fully purified. The past momentum that carries on the wheel of body is all good. All evil tendencies are burnt out.

* * *

"That day is indeed a bad day when we do not speak of the Lord, not a stormy day."

Only love for the Supreme Lord is true Bhakti. Love for any other being, however great, is not Bhakti. The "Supreme Lord" here means Ishvara, the concept of which transcends what you in the West mean by the personal God. "He from whom this universe proceeds, in whom it rests, and to whom it returns, He is Ishvara, the Eternal, the Pure, the All-Merciful, the Almighty, the Ever-Free, the All-Knowing, the Teacher of all teachers, the Lord who of His own nature is inexpressible Love."

Man does not manufacture God out of his own brain; but he can only see God in the light of his own capacity, and he attributes to Him the best of all he knows. Each attribute is the whole of God, and this signifying the whole by one quality is the metaphysical explanation of the personal God. Ishvara is without form yet has all forms, is without qualities yet has all qualities. As human beings, we have to see the trinity of existence — God, man, nature; and we cannot do otherwise.

But to the Bhakta all these philosophical distinctions are mere idle talk. He cares nothing for argument, he does not reason, he "senses", he perceives. He wants to love himself in pure love of God, and there have been Bhaktas who maintain that this is more to be desired than liberation, who say, "I do not want to be sugar. I want to taste sugar; I want to love and enjoy the Beloved."

In Bhakti-Yoga the first essential is to want God honestly and intensely. We want everything but God, because our ordinary desires are fulfilled by the external world. So long as our needs are confined within the limits of the physical universe, we do not feel any need for God; it is only when we have had hard blows in our lives and are disappointed with everything here that we feel the need for something higher; then we seek God.

Bhakti is not destructive; it teaches that all our faculties may become means to reach salvation. We must turn them all towards God and give to Him that love which is usually wasted on the fleeting objects of sense.

Bhakti differs from your Western idea of religion in that Bhakti admits no elements of fear, no Being to be appeased or propitiated. There are even Bhaktas who worship God as their own child, so that there may remain no feeling even of awe or reverence. There can be no fear in true love, and so long as there is the least fear, Bhakti cannot even begin. In Bhakti there is also no place for begging or bargaining with God. The idea of asking God for anything is sacrilege to a Bhakta. He will not pray for health or wealth or even to go to heaven.

One who wants to love God, to be a Bhakta, must make a bundle of all these desires and leave them outside the door and then enter. He who wants to enter the realms of light must make a bundle of all "shop-keeping" religion and cast it away before he can pass the gates. It is not that you do not get what you pray for; you get everything, but it is low, vulgar, a beggar's religion. "Fool indeed is he, who, living on the banks of the Ganga, digs a little well for water. Fool indeed is the man who, coming to a mine of diamonds, begins to search for glass beads." These prayers for health and wealth and material prosperity are not Bhakti. They are the lowest form of Karma. Bhakti is a higher thing. We are striving to come into the presence of the King of kings. We cannot get there in a beggar's dress. If we wanted to enter the presence of an emperor, would we be admitted in a beggar's rags? Certainly not. The lackey would drive us out of the gates. This is the Emperor of emperors and never can we come before Him in a beggar's garb. Shop-keepers never have admission there, buying and selling will not do there at all. You read in the Bible that Jesus drove the buyers and sellers out of the temple.

So it goes without saying that the first task in becoming a Bhakta is to give up all desires of heaven and so on. Such a heaven would be like this place, this earth, only a little better. The Christian idea of heaven is a place of intensified enjoyment. How can that be God? All this desire to go to heaven is a desire for enjoyment. This has to be given up. The love of the Bhakta must be absolutely pure and unselfish, seeking nothing for itself either here or hereafter.

"Giving up the desire of pleasure and pain, gain or loss, worship God day and night; not a moment is to be lost in vain."

"Giving up all other thoughts, the whole mind day and night worships God. Thus being worshipped day and night, He reveals Himself and makes His worshippers feel Him."

UNTITLED TALK XXXVIII

RECORDED BY MISS S. E. WALDO, A DISCIPLE
THURSDAY, August 1, 1895.

The real Guru is the one through whom we have our spiritual descent. He is the channel through which the spiritual current flows to us, the link which joins us to the whole spiritual world. Too much faith in personality has a tendency to produce weakness and idolatry, but intense love for the Guru makes rapid growth possible, he connects us with the internal Guru. Adore your Guru if there be real truth in him; that Guru-bhakti (devotion to the teacher) will quickly lead you to the highest.

Sri Ramakrishna's purity was that of a baby. He never touched money in his life, and lust was absolutely annihilated in him. Do not go to great religious teachers to learn physical science, their whole energy has gone to the spiritual. In Sri Ramakrishna Paramahamsa the man was all dead and only God remained; he actually could not see sin, he was literally "of purer eyes than to behold iniquity". The purity of these few Paramahamsa (Monks of the highest order) is all that holds the world together. If they should all die out and leave it, the world would go to pieces. They do good by simply being, and they know it not; they just are...

Books suggest the inner light and the method of bringing that out, but we can only understand them when we have earned the knowledge ourselves. When the inner light has flashed for you, let the books go, and look only within. You have in you all and a thousand times more than is in all the books. Never lose faith in yourself, you can do anything in this universe. Never weaken, all power is yours.

If religion and life depend upon books or upon the existence of any prophet whatsoever, then perish all religion and books! Religion is in us. No books or teachers can do more than help us to find it, and even without them we can get all truth within. You have gratitude for books and teachers without bondage to them; and worship your Guru as God, but do not obey him blindly; love him all you will, but think for yourself. No blind belief can save you, work out your own salvation. Have only one idea of God—that He is an eternal help.

Freedom and highest love must go together, then neither can become a bondage. We can give nothing to God; He gives all to us. He is the Guru of Gurus. Then we find that He is the "Soul of our souls", our very Self. No wonder we love Him, He is the Soul of our souls; whom or what else can we love? We want to be the "steady flame, burning without heat and without smoke". To whom can you do good, when you see only God? You cannot do good to God! All doubt goes, all is, "sameness". If you do good at all, you do it to yourself; feel that the receiver is the higher one. You serve the other because you are lower than he, not because he is low and you are high. Give as the rose gives perfume, because it is its own nature, utterly unconscious of giving.

The great Hindu reformer, Raja Ram Mohan Roy, was a wonderful example of this unselfish work. He devoted his whole life to helping India. It was he who stopped the burning of widows. It is usually believed that this reform was due entirely to the English; but it was Raja Ram Mohan Roy who started the agitation against the custom and succeeded in obtaining the support of the Government in suppressing it. Until he began the movement, the English had done nothing. He also founded the important religious Society called the Brahmo-Samaj, and subscribed a hundred thousand dollars to found a university. He then stepped out and told them to go ahead without him. He cared nothing for fame or for results to himself.

THURSDAY AFTERNOON

There are endless series of manifestations, like "merry-go-round", in which the souls ride, so to speak. The series are eternal; individual souls get out, but the events repeat themselves eternally; and that is how one's past and future can be read, because all is really present. When the soul is in a certain chain, it has to go through the experiences of that chain. From one series souls go to other series; from some series they escape for ever by realising that they are Brahman. By getting hold of one prominent event in a chain and holding on to it, the whole chain can be dragged in and read. This power is easily acquired, but it is of no real value; and to practise it takes just so much from our spiritual forces. Go not after these things, worship God.

UNTITLED TALK XXXIX

RECORDED BY MISS S. E. WALDO, A DISCIPLE
FRIDAY, August 2, 1895.

Nishthâ (devotion to one ideal) is the beginning of realisation. "Take the honey out of all flowers; sit and be friendly with all, pay reverence to all, say to all, 'Yes, brother, yes, brother', but keep firm in your own way." A higher stage is actually to take the position of the other. If I am all, why can I not really and actively sympathise with my brother and see with his eyes? While I am weak, I must stick to one course (Nishthâ), but when I am strong, I can feel with every other and perfectly sympathise with his ideas.

The old idea was: "Develop one idea at the expense of all the rest". The modern way is "harmonious development". A third way is to "develop the mind and control it", then put it where you will; the result will come quickly. This is developing yourself in the truest way. Learn concentration and use it in any direction. Thus you lose nothing. He who gets the whole must have the parts too. Dualism is included in Advaitism (monism).

"I first saw him and he saw me. There was a flash of eye from me to him and from him to me."

This went on until the two souls became so closely united that they actually became one...

There are two kinds of Samadhi—I concentrate on myself, then I concentrate and there is a unity of subject and object.

You must be able to sympathise fully with each particular, then at once to jump back to the highest monism. After having perfected yourself, you limit yourself voluntarily. Take the whole power into each action. Be able to become a dualist for the time being and forget Advaita, yet be able to take it up again at will.

* * *

Cause and effect are all Maya, and we shall grow to understand that all we see is as disconnected as the child's fairy tales now seem to us. There is really no such thing as cause and effect and we shall come to know it. Then if you can, lower your intellect to let any allegory pass through your mind without questioning about connection. Develop love of imagery and beautiful poetry and then enjoy all mythologies as poetry. Come not to mythology with ideas of history and reasoning. Let it flow as a current through your mind, let it be whirled as a candle before your eyes, without asking who holds the candle, and you will get the circle; the residuum of truth will remain in your mind.

The writers of all mythologies wrote in symbols of what they saw and heard, they painted flowing pictures. Do not try to pick out the themes and so destroy the pictures; take them as they are and let them act on you. Judge them only by the effect and get the good out of them.

* * *

Your own will is all that answers prayer, only it appears under the guise of different religious conceptions to each mind. We may call it Buddha, Jesus, Krishna, Jehovah, Allah, Agni, but it is only the Self, the "I"...

Concepts grow, but there is no historical value in the allegories which present them. Moses' visions are more likely to be wrong than ours are, because we have more knowledge and are less likely to be deceived by illusions.

Books are useless to us until our own book opens; then all other books are good so far as they confirm our book. It is the strong that understand strength, it is the elephant that understands the lion, not the rat. How can we understand Jesus until we are his equals? It is all in the dream to feed five thousand with two loaves, or to feed two with five loaves; neither is real and neither affects the other. Only grandeur appreciates grandeur, only God realises God. The dream is only the dreamer, it has no other basis. It is not one thing and the dreamer another. The keynote running through the music is—"I am He, I am He", all other notes are but variations and do not affect the real theme. We are the living books and books are but the words we have spoken. Everything is the living God, the living Christ; see it as such. Read man, he is the living poem. We are the light that illumines all the Bibles and Christs and Buddhas that ever were. Without that, these would be dead to us, not living.

Stand on your own Self.

The dead body resents nothing; let us make our bodies dead and cease to identify ourselves with them.

UNTITLED TALK XL

RECORDED BY MISS S. E. WALDO, A DISCIPLE
SATURDAY, August 3, 1895.

Individuals who are to get freedom in this life have to live thousands of years in one lifetime. They have to be ahead of their times, but the masses can only crawl. Thus we have Christs and Buddhas...

There was once a Hindu queen, who so much desired that all her children should attain freedom in this life that she herself took all the care of them; and as she rocked them to sleep, she sang always the one song to them—"Tat tvam asi, Tat tvam asi" ("That thou art, That thou art").

Three of them became Sannyasins, but the fourth was taken away to be brought up elsewhere to become a king. As he was leaving home, the mother gave him a piece of paper which he was to read when he grew to manhood. On that piece of paper was written, "God alone is true. All else is false. The soul never kills or is killed. Live alone or in the company of holy ones." When the young prince read this, he too at once renounced the world and became a Sannyasin.

Give up, renounce the world. Now we are like dogs strayed into a kitchen and eating a piece of meat, looking round in fear lest at any moment some one may come and drive them out. Instead of that, be a king and know you own the world. This never comes until you give it up and it ceases to bind. Give up mentally, if you do not physically. Give up from the heart of your hearts. Have Vairâgya (renunciation). This is the real sacrifice, and without it, it is impossible to attain spirituality. Do not desire, for what you desire you get, and with it comes terrible bondage. It is nothing but bringing "noses on us,"[6]* as in the case of the man who had three boons to ask. We never get freedom until we are self-contained. "Self is the Saviour of self, none else."

Learn to feel yourself in other bodies, to know that we are all one. Throw all other nonsense to the winds. Spit out your actions, good or bad, and never think of them again. What is done is done. Throw off superstition. Have no weakness even in the face of death. Do not repent, do not brood over past deeds, and do not remember your good deeds; be âzâd (free). The weak, the fearful, the ignorant will never reach Atman. You cannot undo, the effect must come, face it, but be careful never to do the same thing again. Give up the burden of all deeds to the Lord; give all, both good and bad. Do not keep the good and give only the bad. God helps those who do not help themselves.

"Drinking the cup of desire, the world becomes mad." Day and night never come together, so desire and the Lord can never come together. Give up desire.

* * *

There is a vast difference between saying "food, food" and eating it, between saying "water, water" and drinking it. So by merely repeating the words "God, God" we cannot hope to attain realisation. We must strive and practise.

Only by the wave falling back into the sea can it become unlimited, never as a wave can it be so. Then after it has become the sea, it can become the wave again and as big a one as it pleases. Break the identification of yourself with the current and know that you are free.

True philosophy is the systematising of certain perceptions. Intellect ends where religion begins. Inspiration is much higher than reason, but it must not contradict it. Reason is the rough tool to do the hard work; inspiration is the bright light which shows us all truth. The will to do a thing is not necessarily inspiration...

Progression in Maya is a circle that brings you back to the starting point; but you start ignorant and come to the end with all knowledge. Worship of God, worship of the holy ones, concentration and meditation, and unselfish work, these are the ways of breaking away from Maya's net; but we must first have the strong desire to get free. The flash of light that will illuminate the darkness for us is in us; it is the knowledge that is our nature—there is no "birthright", we were never born. All that we have to do is to drive away the clouds that cover it.

Give up all desire for enjoyment in earth or heaven. Control the organs of the senses and control the mind. Bear every misery without even knowing that you are miserable. Think of nothing but liberation. Have faith in Guru, in his teachings, and in the surety that you can get free. Say "Soham, Soham" whatever comes. Tell yourself this even in eating, walking, suffering; tell the mind this incessantly—that what we see never existed, that there is only "I". Flash—the dream will break! Think day and night, this universe is zero, only God is. Have intense desire to get free.

All relatives and friends are but "old dry wells"; we fall into them and get dreams of duty and bondage, and there is no end. Do not create illusion by helping anyone. It is like a banyan tree, that spreads on and on. If you are a dualist, you are a fool to try to help God. If you are a monist, you know that you are God; where find duty? You have no duty to husband, child, friend. Take things as they come, lie still, and when your body floats, go; rise with the rising tide, fall with falling tide. Let the body die; this idea of body is but a worn-out fable. "Be still and know that you are God."

The present only is existent. There is no past or future even in thought, because to think it, you have to make it the present. Give up everything, and let it float where it will. This world is all a delusion, do not let it fool you again. You have known it for what it is not, now know it for what it is. If the body is dragged anywhere, let it go; do not care where the body is. This tyrannical idea of duty is a terrible poison and is destroying the world.

Do not wait to have a harp and rest by degrees; why not take a harp and begin here? Why wait for heaven? Make it here. In heaven there is no marrying or giving in marriage; why not begin at once and have none here? The yellow robe of the Sannyasin is the sign of the free. Give up the beggar's dress of the world; wear the flag of freedom, the ochre robe.

UNTITLED TALK XLI

RECORDED BY MISS S. E. WALDO, A DISCIPLE
SUNDAY, August 4, 1895.

"Whom the ignorant worship, Him I preach unto thee."

This one and only God is the "knownest" of the known. He is the one thing we see everywhere. All know their own Self, all know, "I am", even animals. All we know is the projection of the Self. Teach this to the children, they can grasp it. Every religion has worshipped the Self, even though unconsciously, because there is nothing else.

This indecent clinging to life as we know it here, is the source of all evil. It causes all this cheating and stealing. It makes money a god and all vices and fears ensue. Value nothing material and do not cling to it. If you cling to nothing, not even life, then there is no fear. "He goes from death to death who sees many in this world." There can be no physical death for us and no mental death, when we see that all is one. All bodies are mine; so even body is eternal, because the tree, the animal, the sun, the moon, the universe itself is my body; then how can it die? Every mind, every thought is mine, then how can death come? The Self is never born and never dies. When we realise this, all doubts vanish. "I am, I know, I love"—these can never be doubted. There is no hunger, for all that is eaten is eaten by me. If a hair falls out, we do not think we die; so if one body dies, it is but a hair falling…

The superconscious is God, is beyond speech beyond thought, beyond consciousness… There are three states,—brutality (Tamas), humanity (Rajas), and divinity (Sattva). Those attaining the highest state simply are. Duty dies there; they only love and as a magnet draw others to them. This is freedom. No more you do moral acts, but whatever you do is moral. The Brahmavit (knower of God) is higher than all gods. The angels came to worship Jesus when he had conquered delusion and had said, "Get thee behind me, Satan." None can help a Brahmavit, the universe itself bows down before him. His every desire is fulfilled, his spirit purifies others; therefore worship the Brahmavit if you wish to attain the highest. When we have the three great "gifts of God"—a human body, intense desire to be free, and the help of a great soul to show us the way—then liberation is certain for us. Mukti is ours.

* * *

Death of the body for ever is Nirvana. It is the negative side and says, "I am not this, nor this, nor this." Vedanta takes the further step and asserts the positive side—Mukti or freedom. "I am Existence absolute, Knowledge absolute, Bliss absolute, I am He", this is Vedanta, the cap-stone of the perfect arch.

The great majority of the adherents of Northern Buddhism believe in Mukti and are really Vedantists. Only the Ceylonese accept Nirvana as annihilation.

No belief or disbelief can kill the "I". That which comes with belief and goes with disbelief is only delusion. Nothing teaches the Atman. "I salute my own Self." "Self-illuminated, I salute myself, I am Brahman." The body is a dark room; when we enter it, it becomes illuminated, it becomes alive. Nothing can ever affect the illumination; it cannot be destroyed. It may be covered, but never destroyed.

* * *

At the present time God should be worshipped as "Mother", the Infinite Energy. This will lead to purity, and tremendous energy will come here in America. Here no temples weigh us down, no one suffers as they do in poorer countries. Woman has suffered for aeons, and that has given her infinite patience and infinite perseverance. She holds on to an idea. It is this which makes her the support of even superstitious religions and of the priests in every land, and it is this that will free her. We have to become Vedantists and live this grand thought; the masses must get it, and only in free America can this be done. In India these ideas were brought out by individuals like Buddha, Shankara, and others, but the masses did not retain them. The new cycle must see the masses living Vedanta, and this will have to come through women.

"Keep the beloved beautiful Mother in the heart of your hearts with all care."

"Throw out everything but the tongue, keep that to say, "Mother, Mother!""

"Let no evil counsellors enter; let you and me, my heart, alone see Mother."

"Thou art beyond all that lives!"

"My Moon of life, my Soul of soul!"

SUNDAY AFTERNOON

Mind is an instrument in the hand of Atman, just as body is an instrument in the hand of mind. Matter is motion outside, mind is motion inside. All change begins and ends in time. If the Atman is unchangeable, It must be perfect; if perfect, It must be infinite; and if It be infinite, It must be only One; there cannot be two infinites. So the Atman, the Self, can be only One. Though It seems to be various, It is really only One. If a man were to go toward the sun, at every step he would see a different sun, and yet it would be the same sun after all.

Asti, "isness", is the basis of all unity; and just as soon as the basis is found, perfection ensues. If all colour could be resolved into one colour, painting would cease. The perfect oneness is rest; we refer all manifestations to one Being. Taoists, Confucianists, Buddhists, Hindus, Jews, Mohammedans, Christians, and Zoroastrians, all preached the golden rule and in almost the same words; but only the Hindus have given the rationale, because they saw the reason: Man must love others because those others are himself. There is but One.

Of all the great religious teachers the world has known, only Lao-tze, Buddha, and Jesus transcended the golden rule and said, "Do good to your enemies", "Love them that hate you."

Principles exist; we do not create them, we only discover them...Religion consists solely in realisation. Doctrines are methods, not religion. All the different religions are but applications of the one religion adapted to suit the requirements of different nations. Theories only lead to fighting; thus the name of God that ought to bring peace has been the cause of half the bloodshed of the world. Go to the direct source. Ask God what He is. Unless He answers, He is not; but every religion teaches that He does answer.

Have something to say for yourself, else how can you have any idea of what others have said? Do not cling to old superstitions; be ever ready for new truths. "Fools are they who would drink brackish water from a well that their forefathers have digged and would not drink pure water from a well that others have digged." Until we realise God for ourselves, we can know nothing about Him. Each man is perfect by his nature; prophets have manifested this perfection, but it is potential in us. How can we understand that Moses saw God unless we too see Him? If God ever came to anyone, He will come to me. I will go to God direct; let Him talk to me. I cannot take belief as a basis; that is atheism and blasphemy. If God spake to a man in the deserts of Arabia two thousand years ago, He can also speak to me today, else how can I know that He has not died? Come to God any way you can; only come. But in coming do not push anyone down.

The knowing ones must have pity on the ignorant. One who knows is willing to give up his body even for an ant, because he knows that the body is nothing.

UNTITLED TALK XLII

RECORDED BY MISS S. E. WALDO, A DISCIPLE
MONDAY, August 5, 1895.

The question is: Is it necessary to pass through all the lower stages to reach the highest, or can a plunge be taken at once? The modern American boy takes twenty-five years to attain that which his forefathers took hundreds of years to do. The present-day Hindu gets in twenty years to the height reached in eight thousand years by his ancestors. On the physical side, the embryo goes from the amoeba to man in the womb. These are the teachings of modern science. Vedanta goes further and tells us that we not only have to live the life of all past humanity, but also the future life of all humanity. The man who does the first is the educated man, the second is the Jivanmukta, for ever free (even while living).

Time is merely the measure of our thoughts, and thought being inconceivably swift, there is no limit to the speed with which we can live the life ahead. So it cannot be stated how long it would take to live all future life. It might be in a second, or it might take fifty lifetimes. It depends on the intensity of the desire. The teaching must therefore be modified according to the needs of the taught. The consuming fire is ready for all, even water and chunks of ice quickly consume. Fire a mass of bird-shot, one at least will strike; give a man a whole muse-

um of truths, he will at once take what is suited to him. Past lives have moulded our tendencies; give to the taught in accordance with his tendency. Intellectual, mystical, devotional, practical—make one the basis, but teach the others with it. Intellect must be balanced with love, the mystical nature with reason, while practice must form part of every method. Take every one where he stands and push him forward. Religious teaching must always be constructive, not destructive.

Each tendency shows the life-work of the past, the line or radius along which that man must move. All radii lead to the centre. Never even attempt to disturb anyone's tendencies; to do that puts back both teacher and taught. When you teach Jnana, you must become a Jnani and stand mentally exactly where the taught stands. Similarly in every other Yoga. Develop every faculty as if it were the only one possessed, this is the true secret of so-called harmonious development. That is, get extensity with intensity, but not at its expense. We are infinite. There is no limitation in us, we can be as intense as the most devoted Mohammedan and as broad as the most roaring atheist.

The way to do this is not to put the mind on any one subject, but to develop and control the mind itself; then you can turn it on any side you choose. Thus you keep the intensity and extensity. Feel Jnana as if it were all there was, then do the same with Bhakti, with Raja (-Yoga), with Karma. Give up the waves and go to the ocean, then you can have the waves as you please. Control the "lake" of your own mind, else you cannot understand the lake of another's mind.

The true teacher is one who can throw his whole force into the tendency of the taught. Without real sympathy we can never teach well. Give up the notion that man is a responsible being, only the perfect man is responsible. The ignorant have drunk deep of the cup of delusion and are not sane. You, who know, must have infinite patience with these. Have nothing but love for them and find out the disease that has made them see the world in a wrong light, then help them to cure it and see aright. Remember always that only the free have free will; all the rest are in bondage and are not responsible for what they do. Will as will is bound. The water when melting on the top of the Himalayas is free, but becoming the river, it is bound by the banks; yet the original impetus carries it to the sea, and it regains its freedom. The first is the "fall of man", the second is the "resurrection". Not one atom can rest until it finds its freedom.

Some imaginations help to break the bondage of the rest. The whole universe is imagination, but one set of imaginations will cure another set. Those which tell us that there is sin and sorrow and death in the world are terrible; but the other set which says ever, "I am holy, there is God, there is no pain", these are good and help to break the bondage of the others. The highest imagination that can break all the links of the chain is that of Personal God.

"Om tat sat" is the only thing beyond Maya, but God exists

eternally. As long as the Niagara Falls exist, the rainbow will exist; but the water continually flows away. The falls are the universe, and the rainbow is personal God; and both are eternal. While the universe exists, God must exist. God creates the universe, and the universe creates God; and both are eternal. Maya is neither existence nor non-existence. Both the Niagara Falls and the rainbow are eternally changeable... Brahman seen through Maya. Persians and Christians split Maya into two and call the good half "God" and the bad half the "devil". Vedanta takes Maya as a whole and recognises a unity beyond it—Brahman...

Mohammed found that Christianity was straying out from the Semitic fold and his teachings were to show what Christianity ought to be as a Semitic religion, that it should hold to one God. The Aryan idea that "I and my Father are one" disgusted and terrified him. In reality the conception of the Trinity was a great advance over the dualistic idea of Jehovah, who was for ever separate from man. The theory of incarnation is the first link in the chain of ideas leading to the recognition of the oneness of God and man. God appearing first in one human form, then re-appearing at different times in other human forms, is at last recognised as being in every human form, or in all men. Monistic is the highest stage, monotheistic is a lower stage. Imagination will lead you to the highest even more rapidly and easily than reasoning.

Let a few stand out and live for God alone and save religion for the world. Do not pretend to be like Janaka when you are only the "progenitor" of delusions. (The name Janaka means "progenitor" and belonged to a king who, although he still held his kingdom for the sake of his people, had given up everything mentally.) Be honest and say, "I see the ideal but I cannot yet approach it"; but do not pretend to give up when you do not. If you give up, stand fast. If a hundred fall in the fight, seize the flag and carry it on. God is true for all that, no matter who fails. Let him who falls hand on the flag to another to carry on; it can never fall.

When I am washed and clean, why shall impurity be added on to me? Seek first the kingdom of Heaven, and let everything else go. Do not want anything "added into you"; be only glad to get rid of it. Give up and know that success will follow, even if you never see it. Jesus left twelve fishermen, and yet those few blew up the Roman Empire.

Sacrifice on God's altar earth's purest and best. He who struggles is better than he who never attempts. Even to look on one who has given up has a purifying effect. Stand up for God; let the world go. Have no compromise. Give up the world, then alone you are loosened from the body. When it dies, you are âzâd, free. Be free. Death alone can never free us. Freedom must be attained by our own efforts during life; then, when the body falls, there will be no rebirth for the free.

Truth is to be judged by truth and by nothing else. Doing good is not the test of truth; the Sun needs no torch by which to see it. Even if truth destroys the whole universe, still it is truth; stand by it.

Practising the concrete forms of religion is easy and attracts the masses; but really there is nothing in the external.

"As the spider throws her web out of herself and draws it in, even so this universe is thrown out and drawn in by God."

UNTITLED TALK XLIII

RECORDED BY MISS S. E. WALDO, A DISCIPLE
TUESDAY, August 6, 1895.

Without the "I" there can be no "you" outside. From this some philosophers came to the conclusion that the external world did not exist save in the subject; that the "you" existed only in the "I". Others have argued that the "I" can only be known through the "you" and with equal logic. These two views are partial truths, each wrong in part and each right in part. Thought is as much material and as much in nature as body is. Both matter and mind exist in a third, a unity which divides itself into the two. This unity is the Atman, the real Self.

There is being, "x", which is manifesting itself as both mind and matter. Its movements in the seen are along certain fixed lines called law. As a unity, it is free; as many, it is bound by law. Still, with all this bondage, an idea of freedom is ever present, and this is Nivritti, or the "dragging from attachment". The materialising forces which through desire lead us to take an active part in worldly affairs are called Pravritti.

That action is moral which frees us from the bondage of matter and vice versa. This world appears infinite, because everything is in a circle; it returns to whence it came. The circle meets, so there is no rest or peace here in any place. We must get out. Mukti is the one end to be attained...

Evil changes in form but remains the same in quality. In ancient times force ruled, today it is cunning. Misery in India is not so bad as in America, because the poor man here sees the greater contrast to his own bad condition.

Good and evil are inextricably combined, and one cannot be had without the other. The sum total of energy in this universe is like a lake, every wave inevitably leads to a corresponding depression. The sum total is absolutely the same; so to make one man happy is to make another unhappy. External happiness is material and the supply is fixed; so that not one grain can be had by one person without taking from another. Only bliss beyond the material world can be had without loss to any. Material happiness is but a transformation of material sorrow.

Those who are born in the wave and kept in it do not see the depression and what is there. Never think, you can make the world better and happier. The bullock in the oil-mill never reaches the wisp of hay tied in front of him, he only grinds out the oil. So we chase the will-o'-the-wisp of happiness that always eludes us, and we only grind nature's mill, then die, merely to begin again. If we could get rid of evil, we should never catch a glimpse of anything higher; we would be satisfied and never struggle to get free. When man finds that all search for happiness in matter is nonsense, then religion begins. All human knowledge is but a part of religion.

In the human body the balance between good and evil is so even that there is a chance for man to wish to free himself from both.

The free never became bound; to ask how he did, is an illogical question. Where no bondage is, there is no cause and effect. "I became a fox in a dream and a dog chased me." Now how can I ask why the dog chased me? The fox was a part of the dream, and the dog followed as a matter of course; but both belong to the dream and have no existence outside. Science and religion are both attempts to help us out of the bondage; only religion is the more ancient, and we have the superstition that it is the more holy. In a way it is, because it makes morality a vital point, and science does not.

"Blessed are the pure in heart, for they shall see God." This sentence alone would save mankind if all books and prophets were lost. This purity of heart will bring the vision of God. It is the theme of the whole music of this universe. In purity is no bondage. Remove the veils of ignorance by purity, then we manifest ourselves as we really are and know that we were never in bondage. The seeing of many is the great sin of all the world. See all as Self and love all; let all idea of separateness go...

The diabolical man is a part of my body as a wound or a burn is. We have to nurse it and get it better; so continually nurse and help the diabolical man, until he "heals" and is once happy and healthy.

While we think on the relative plane, we have the right to believe that as bodies we can be hurt by relative things and equally that we can be helped by them. This idea of help, abstracted, is what we call God. The sum total of all ideas of help is God.

God is the abstract compound of all that is merciful and good and helpful; that should be the sole idea. As Atman, we have no body; so to say, "I am God, and poison does not hurt me", is an absurdity. While there is a body and we see it, we have not realised God. Can the little whirlpool remain after the river vanishes? Cry for help, and you will get it; and at last you will find that the one crying for help has vanished, and so has the Helper, and the play is over; only the Self remains.

This once done, come back and play as you will. This body can then do no evil, because it is not until the evil forces are all burned out that liberation comes. All dross has been burned out and there remains "flame without heat and without smoke".

The past momentum carries on the body, but it can only do good, because the bad was all gone before freedom came. The dying thief on the cross reaped the effects of his past actions. He had been a Yogi and had slipped; then he had to be born again; again he slipped and became a thief; but the past good he had done bore fruit, and he met Jesus in the moment when liberation could come, and one word made him free.

Buddha set his greatest enemy free, because he, by hating him (Buddha) so much, kept constantly thinking of him; that thought purified his mind, and he became ready for freedom. Therefore think of God all the time, and that will purify you...

(Thus ended the beautiful lessons of our beloved Guru. The following Monday he left Thousand Island Park and returned to New York.)

NOTES FROM LECTURES & DISCOURSES

Swami Vivekananda delivered scores of lectures and classes during his relatively short ministry. Unfortunately the Swami was not always accompanied by a professional stenographer who could keep pace with the exceptional speed of his extempore deliveries. However, a few students managed to take notes of some lectures and classes, which are today the only available records of works that would otherwise have been lost to the world.

The original quotation marks of the note-takers have been reproduced. — Publisher

ON KARMA-YOGA

Isolation of the soul from all objects, mental and physical, is the goal; when that is attained, the soul will find that it was alone all the time, and it required no one to make it happy. As long as we require someone else to make us happy, we are slaves. When the Purusha finds that It is free, and does not require anything to complete Itself, that this nature is quite unnecessary, then freedom (Kaivalya) is attained.

Men run after a few dollars and do not think anything of cheating a fellow-being to get those dollars; but if they would restrain themselves, in a few years they would develop such characters as would bring them millions of dollars—if they wanted them. Then their will would govern the universe. But we are all such fools!

What is the use of talking of one's mistakes to the world? They cannot thereby be undone. For what one has done one must suffer; one must try and do better. The world sympathises only with the strong and the powerful.

It is only work that is done as a free-will offering to humanity and to nature that does not bring with it any binding attachment.

Duty of any kind is not to be slighted. A man who does the lower work is not, for that reason only, a lower man than he who does the higher work; a man should not be judged by the nature of his duties, but by the manner in which he does them. His manner of doing them and his power to do them are indeed the test of a man. A shoemaker who can turn out a strong, nice pair of shoes in the shortest possible time is a better man, according to his profession and his work, than a professor who talks nonsense every day of his life.

Every duty is holy, and devotion to duty is the highest form of the worship of God; it is certainly a source of great help in enlightening and emancipating the deluded and ignorance-encumbered souls of the Baddhas—the bound ones.

By doing well the duty which is nearest to us, the duty which is in our hands now, we make ourselves stronger and improving our strength in this manner step by step, we may even reach a state in which it shall be our privilege to do the most coveted and honoured duties in life and in society.

Nature's justice is uniformly stern and unrelenting.

The most practical man would call life neither good nor evil.

Every successful man must have behind him somewhere tremendous integrity, tremendous sincerity, and that is the cause of his signal success in life. He may not have been perfectly unselfish; yet he was tending towards it. If he had been perfectly unselfish, his would have been as great a success as that of the Buddha or of the Christ. The degree of unselfishness marks the degree of success everywhere.

The great leaders of mankind belong to higher fields than the field of platform work.

However we may try, there cannot be any action which is perfectly pure or any which is perfectly impure, taking purity or impurity in the sense of injury or non-injury. We cannot breathe or live without injuring others, and every morsel of food we eat is taken from another's mouth; our very lives are crowding out some other lives. It may be those of men, or animals, or small fungi, but someone somewhere we have to crowd out. That being the case, it naturally follows that perfection can never be attained by work. We may work through all eternity, but there will be no way out of this intricate maze: we may work on and on and on, but there will be no end.

The man who works through freedom and love cares nothing for results. But the slave wants his whipping; the servant wants his pay. So with all life; take for instance the public life. The public speaker wants a little applause or a little hissing and hooting. If you keep him in a corner without it, you kill him, for he requires it. This is working through slavery. To expect something in return, under such conditions, becomes second nature. Next comes the work of the servant, who requires some pay; I give this, and you give me that. Nothing is easier to say, "I work for work's sake", but nothing is so difficult to attain. I would go twenty miles on my hands and knees to look on the face of the man who can work for work's sake. There is a motive somewhere. If it is not money, it is power. If it is not power, it is gain. Somehow, somewhere, there is a motive power. You are my friend, and I want to work for you and with you. This is all very well, and every moment I may make protestation of my sincerity. But take care, you must be sure to agree with me! If you do not, I shall no longer take care of you or live for you! This kind of work for a motive brings misery. That work alone brings unattachment and bliss, wherein we work as masters of our own minds.

The great lesson to learn is that I am not the standard by which the whole universe is to be judged; each man is to be judged by his own idea, each race by its own standard and ideal, each custom of each country by its own reasoning and conditions. American customs are the result of the environment in which the Americans live and Indian customs are the result of the environment in which the Indians are; and so of China, Japan, England, and every other country.

We all find ourselves in the position for which we are fit, each ball finds its own hole; and if one has some capacity above another, the world will find that out too, in this universal adjusting that goes on. So it is no use to grumble. There may be a rich man who is wicked, yet there must be in that man certain qualities that made him rich; and if any other man has the same qualities, he will also become rich. What is the use of fighting and complaining? That will not help us to better things. He who grumbles at the little thing that has fallen to his lot to do will grumble at everything. Always grumbling, he will lead a miserable life, and everything will be a failure. But that man who does his duty as he goes, putting, his shoulder to the wheel, will see the light, and higher and higher duties will fall to his share.

ON FANATICISM

There are fanatics of various kinds. Some people are wine fanatics and cigar fanatics. Some think that if men gave up smoking cigars, the world would arrive at the millennium. Women are generally amongst these fanatics. There was a young lady here one day, in this class. She was one of a number of ladies in Chicago who have built a house where they take in the working people and give them music and gymnastics. One day this young lady was talking about the evils of the world and said she knew the remedy. I asked, "How do you know?" and she answered, "Have you seen Hull House?" In her opinion, this Hull House is the one panacea for all the evils that flesh is heir to. This will grow upon her. I am sorry for her. There are some fanatics in India who think that if a woman could marry again when her husband died, it would cure all evil. This is fanaticism.

When I was a boy I thought that fanaticism was a great element in work, but now, as I grow older, I find out that it is not.

There may be a woman who would steal and make no objection to taking someone else's bag and going away with it. But perhaps that woman does not smoke. She becomes a smoke fanatic, and as soon as she finds a man smoking, she strongly disapproves of him, because he smokes a cigar. There may be a man who goes about cheating people; there is no trusting him; no woman is safe with him. But perhaps this scoundrel does not drink wine. If so, he sees nothing good in anyone who drinks wine. All these wicked things that he himself does are of no consideration. This is only natural human selfishness and one-sidedness.

You must also remember that the world has God to govern it, and He has not left it to our charity. The Lord God is its Governor and Maintainer, and in spite of these wine fanatics and cigar fanatics, and all sorts of marriage fanatics, it would go on. If all these persons were to die, it would go on none the worse.

Do you not remember in your own history how the "Mayflower" people came out here, and began to call themselves Puritans? They were very pure and good as far as they went, until they began to persecute other people; and throughout the history of mankind it has been the same. Even those that run away from persecution indulge in persecuting others as soon as a favourable opportunity to do so occurs.

In ninety cases out of a hundred, fanatics must have bad livers, or they are dyspeptics, or are in some way diseased. By degrees even physicians will find out that fanaticism is a kind of disease. I have seen plenty of it. The Lord save me from it!

My experience comes to this, that it is rather wise to avoid all sorts of fanatical reforms. This world is slowly going on; let it go slowly. Why are you in a hurry? Sleep well and keep your nerves in good order; eat right food, and have sympathy with the world. Fanatics only make hatred. Do you mean to say that the temperance fanatic loves these poor people who become drunkards? A fanatic is a fanatic simply because he expects to get something for himself in return. As soon as the battle is over, he goes for the spoil. When you come out of the company of fanatics you may learn how really to love and sympathise. And the more you attain of love and sympathy, the less will be your power to condemn these poor creatures; rather you will sympathise with their faults. It will become possible for you to sympathise with the drunkard and to know that he is also a man like yourself. You will then try to understand the many circumstances that are dragging him down, and feel that if you had been in his place you would perhaps have committed suicide. I remember a woman whose husband was a great drunkard, and she complained to me of his becoming so. I replied, "Madam, if there were twenty millions of wives like yourself, all husbands would become drunkards." I am convinced that a large number of drunkards are manufactured by their wives. My business is to tell the truth and not to flatter anyone. These unruly women from whose minds the words bear and forbear are gone for ever, and whose false ideas of independence lead them to think that men should be at their feet, and who begin to howl as soon as men dare to say anything to them which they do not like—such women are becoming the bane of the world, and it is a wonder that they do not drive half the men in it to commit suicide. In this way things should not go on. Life is not so easy as they believe it to be; it is a more serious business!

A man must not only have faith but intellectual faith too. To make a man take up everything and believe it, would be to make him a lunatic. I once had a book sent me, which said I must believe everything told in it. It said there was no soul, but that there were gods and goddesses in heaven, and a thread of light going from each of our heads to heaven! How did the writer know all these things? She had been inspired, and wanted me to believe it too; and because I refused, she said, "You must be a very bad man; there is no hope for you!" This is fanaticism.

WORK IS WORSHIP

The highest man cannot work, for there is no binding element, no attachment, no ignorance in him. A ship is said to have passed over a mountain of magnet ore, and all the bolts and bars were drawn out, and it went to pieces. It is in ignorance that struggle remains, because we are all really atheists.

Real theists cannot work. We are atheists more or less. We do not see God or believe in Him. He is G-O-D to us, and nothing more. There are moments when we think He is near, but then we fall down again. When you see Him, who struggles for whom? Help the Lord! There is a proverb in our language, "Shall we teach the Architect of the universe how to build?" So those are the highest of mankind who do not work. The next time you see these silly phrases about the world and how we must all help God and do this or that for Him, remember this. Do not think such thoughts; they are too selfish. All the work you do is subjective, is done for your own benefit. God has not fallen into a ditch for you and me to help Him out by building a hospital or something of that sort. He allows you to work. He allows you to exercise your muscles in this great gymnasium, not in order to help Him but that you may help yourself. Do you think even an ant will die for want of your help? Most arrant blasphemy! The world does not need you at all. The world goes on you are like a drop in the ocean. A leaf does not move, the wind does not blow without Him. Blessed are we that we are given the privilege of working for Him, not of helping Him. Cut out this word "help" from your mind. You cannot help; it is blaspheming. You are here yourself at His pleasure. Do you mean to say, you help Him? You worship. When you give a morsel of food to the dog, you worship the dog as God. God is in that dog. He is the dog. He is all and in all. We are allowed to worship Him. Stand in that reverent attitude to the whole universe, and then will come perfect non-attachment. This should be your duty. This is the proper attitude of work. This is the secret taught by Karma-Yoga.

WORK WITHOUT MOTIVE

At the forty-second meeting of the Ramakrishna Mission held at the premises No. 57 Râmkânta Bose Street, Baghbazar, Calcutta, on the 20th March, 1898, Swami Vivekananda gave an address on "Work without Motive", and spoke to the following effect:

When the Gita was first preached, there was then going on a great controversy between two sects. One party considered the Vedic Yajnas and animal sacrifices and such like Karmas to constitute the whole of religion. The other preached that the killing of numberless horses and cattle cannot be called religion. The people belonging to the latter party were mostly Sannyâsins and followers of Jnâna. They believed that the giving up of all work and the gaining of the knowledge of the Self was the only path to Moksha By the preaching of His great doctrine of work without motive, the Author of the Gita set at rest the disputes of these two antagonistic sects.

Many are of opinion that the Gita was not written at the time of the Mahâbhârata, but was subsequently added to it. This is not correct. The special teachings of the Gita are to be found in every part of the Mahabharata, and if the Gita is to be expunged, as forming no part of it, every other portion of it which embodies the same teachings should be similarly treated.

Now, what is the meaning of working without motive? Nowadays many understand it in the sense that one is to work in such a way that neither pleasure nor pain touches his mind. If this be its real meaning, then the animals might be said to work without motive. Some animals devour their own offspring, and they do not feel any pangs at all in doing so. Robbers ruin other people by robbing them of their possessions; but if they feel quite callous to pleasure or pain, then they also would be working without motive. If the meaning of it be such, then one who has a stony heart, the worst of criminals, might be considered to be working without motive. The walls have no feelings of pleasure or pain, neither has a stone, and it cannot be said that they are working without motive. In the above sense the doctrine is a potent instrument in the hands of the wicked. They would go on doing wicked deeds, and would pronounce themselves as working without a motive. If such be the significance of working without a motive, then a fearful doctrine has been put forth by the preaching of the Gita. Certainly this is not the meaning. Furthermore, if we look into the lives of those who were connected with the preaching of the Gita, we should find them living quite a different life. Arjuna killed Bhishma and Drona in battle, but withal, he sacrificed all his self-interest and desires and his lower self millions of times.

Gita teaches Karma-Yoga. We should work through Yoga (concentration). In such concentration in action (Karma-Yoga), there is no consciousness of the lower ego present. The consciousness that I am doing this and that is never present when one works through Yoga. The Western people do not understand this. They say that if there be no consciousness of ego, if this ego is gone, how then can a man work? But when one works with concentration, losing all consciousness of oneself the work that is done will be infinitely better, and this every one may have experienced in his own life. We perform many works subconsciously, such as the digestion of food etc., many others consciously, and others again by becoming immersed in Samâdhi as it were, when there is no consciousness of the smaller ego. If the painter, losing the consciousness of his ego, becomes completely immersed in his painting, he will be able to produce masterpieces. The good cook concentrates his whole self on the food-material he handles; he loses all other consciousness for the time being. But they are only able to do perfectly a single work in this way, to which they are habituated. The Gita teaches that all works should be done thus. He who is one with the Lord through Yoga performs all his works by becoming immersed in concentration, and does not seek any personal benefit. Such a performance of work brings only good to the world, no evil can come out of it. Those who work thus never do anything for themselves.

The result of every work is mixed with good and evil. There is no good work that has not a touch of evil in it. Like smoke round the fire, some evil always clings to work. We should engage in such works as bring the largest amount of good and the smallest measure of evil. Arjuna killed Bhishma and Drona; if this had not been done Duryodhana could not have been conquered, the force of evil would have triumphed over the force of good, and thus a great calamity would have fallen on the country. The government of the country would have been usurped by a body of proud unrighteous kings, to the great misfortune of the people. Similarly, Shri Krishna killed Kamsa, Jarâsandha, and others who were tyrants, but not a single one of his deeds was done for himself. Every one of them was for the good of others. We are reading the Gita by candle-light, but numbers of insects are being burnt to death. Thus it is seen that some evil clings to work. Those who work without any consciousness of their lower ego are not affected with evil, for they work for the good of the world. To work without motive, to work unattached, brings the highest bliss and freedom. This secret of Karma-Yoga is taught by the Lord Shri Krishna in the Gita.

SADHANAS OR PREPARATIONS FOR HIGHER LIFE

If atavism gains, you go down; if evolution gains, you go on. Therefore, we must not allow atavism to take place. Here, in my own body, is the first work of the study. We are too busy trying to mend the ways of our neighbours, that is the difficulty. We must begin with our own bodies. The heart, the liver, etc., are all atavistic; bring them back into consciousness, control them, so that they will obey your commands and act up to your wishes. There was a time when we had control of the liver; we could shake the whole skin, as can the cow. I have seen many people bring the control back by sheer hard practice. Once an impress is made, it is there. Bring back all the submerged activities—the vast ocean of action. This is the first part of the great study, and it is absolutely necessary for our social well-being. On the other hand, only the consciousness need not be studied all the time.

Then there is the other part of study, not so necessary in our social life, which tends to liberation. Its direct action is to free the soul, to take the torch into the gloom, to clean out what is behind, to shake it up or even defy it, and to make us march onward piercing the gloom. That is the goal—the superconscious. Then when that state is reached, this very man becomes divine, becomes free. And to the mind thus trained to transcend all, gradually this universe will begin to give up its secrets; the book of nature will be read chapter after chapter, till the goal is attained, and we pass from this valley of life and death to that One, where death and life do not exist, and we know the Real and become the Real.

The first thing necessary is a quiet and peaceable life. If I have to go about the world the whole day to make a living, it is hard for me to attain to anything very high in this life. Perhaps in another life I shall be born under more propitious circumstances. But if I am earnest enough, these very circumstances will change even in this birth. Was there anything you did not get which you really wanted? It could not be. For it is the want that creates the body. It is the light that has bored the holes, as it were, in your head, called the eyes. If the light had not existed, you would have had no eyes. It is sound that had made the ears. The object of perception existed first, before you made the organ. In a few hundred thousand years or earlier, we may have other organs to perceive electricity and other things. There is no desire for a peaceful mind. Desire will not come unless there is something outside to fulfil it. The outside something just bores a hole in the body, as it were, and tries to get into the mind. So, when the desire will arise to have a peaceful, quiet life, that shall come where everything shall be propitious for the development of the mind—you may take that as my experience. It may come after thousands of lives, but it must come. Hold on to that, the desire. You cannot have the strong desire if its object was not outside for you already. Of course you must understand, there is a difference between desire and desire. The master said, "My child, if you desire after God, God shall come to you." The disciple did not understand his master fully. One day both went to bathe in a river, and the master said, "Plunge in", and the boy did so. In a moment the master was upon him, holding him down. He would not let the boy come up. When the boy struggled and was exhausted, he let him go. "Yes, my child, how did you feel there;" "Oh, the desire for a breath of air!" "Do you have that kind of desire for God?" "No, sir." "Have that kind of desire for God and you shall have God."

That, without which we cannot live, must come to us. If it did not come to us, life could not go on.

If you want to be a Yogi, you must be free and place yourself in circumstances where you are alone and free from all anxiety. He who desires for a comfortable and nice life and at the same time wants to realise the Self is like the fool who, wanting to cross the river, caught hold of a crocodile mistaking it for a log of wood. "Seek ye first the Kingdom of God and His righteousness, and all these things shall be added unto you." Unto him everything who does not care for anything. Fortune is like a flirt; she cares not for him who wants her, but she is at the feet of him who does not care for her. Money comes and showers itself upon one who does not care for it; so does fame come in abundance until it is a trouble and a burden. They always come to the Master. The slave never gets anything. The Master is he who can live in spite of them, whose life does not depend upon the little, foolish things of the world. Live for an ideal, and that one ideal alone. Let it be so great, so strong, that there may be nothing else left in the mind; no place for anything else, no time for anything else.

How some people give all their energies, time, brain, body, and everything, to become rich! They have no time for breakfast! Early in the morning they are out and at work! They die in the attempt—ninety per cent of them—and the rest when they make money, cannot enjoy it. That is grand! I do not say it is bad to try to be rich. It is marvellous, wonderful.

Why, what does it show? It shows that one can have the same amount of energy and struggle for freedom as one has for money. We know we have to give up money and all other things when we die, and yet, see the amount of energy we can put forth for them. But we, the same human beings, should we not put forth a thousandfold more strength and energy to acquire that which never fades, but which remains to us for ever? For this is the one great friend, our own good deeds, our own spiritual excellence, that follows us beyond the grave. Everything else is left behind here with the body.

That is the one great first step—the real desire for the ideal. Everything comes easy after that. That the Indian mind found out; there, in India, men go to any length to find truth. But here, in the West, the difficulty is that everything is made so easy. It is not truth, but development, that is the great aim. The struggle is the great lesson. Mind you, the great benefit in this life is struggle. It is through that we pass. If there is any road to Heaven, it is through Hell. Through Hell to Heaven is always the way. When the soul has wrestled with circumstance and has met death, a thousand times death on the way, but nothing daunted has struggled forward again and again and yet again—then the soul comes out as a giant and laughs at the ideal he has been struggling for, because he finds how much greater is he than the ideal. I am the end, my own Self, and nothing else, for what is there to compare to me own Self? Can a bag of gold be the ideal of my Soul? Certainly not! My Soul is the highest ideal that I can have. Realising my own real nature is the one goal of my life.

There is nothing that is absolutely evil. The devil has a place here as well as God, else he would not be here. Just as I told you, it is through Hell that we pass to Heaven. Our mistakes have places here. Go on! Do not look back if you think you have done something that is not right. Now, do you believe you could be what you are today, had you not made those mistakes before? Bless your mistakes, then. They have been angels unawares. Blessed be torture! Blessed be happiness! Do not care what be your lot. Hold on to the ideal. March on! Do not look back upon little mistakes and things. In this battlefield of ours, the dust of mistakes must be raised. Those who are so thin-skinned that they cannot bear the dust, let them get out of the ranks.

So, then, this tremendous determination to struggle a hundredfold more determination than that which you put forth to gain anything which belongs to this life, is the first great preparation.

And then along with it, there must be meditation Meditation is the one thing. Meditate! The greatest thing is meditation. It is the nearest approach to spiritual life—the mind meditating. It is the one moment in our daily life that we are not at all material—the Soul thinking of Itself, free from all matter—this marvellous touch of the Soul!

The body is our enemy, and yet is our friend. Which of you can bear the sight of misery? And which of you cannot do so when you see it only as a painting? Because it is unreal, we do not identify ourselves with it, eve know it is only a painting; it cannot bless us, it cannot hurt us. The most terrible misery painted upon a price of canvas, we may even enjoy; we praise the technique of the artist, we wonder at his marvellous genius, even though the scene he paints is most horrible. That is the secret; that non-attachment. Be the Witness.

No breathing, no physical training of Yoga, nothing is of any use until you reach to the idea, "I am the Witness." Say, when the tyrant hand is on your neck, "I am the Witness! I am the Witness!" Say, "I am the Spirit! Nothing external can touch me." When evil thoughts arise, repeat that, give that sledge-hammer blow on their heads, "I am the Spirit! I am the Witness, the Ever-Blessed! I have no reason to do, no reason to suffer, I have finished with everything, I am the Witness. I am in my picture gallery—this universe is my museum, I am looking at these successive paintings. They are all beautiful. Whether good or evil. I see the marvellous skill, but it is all one. Infinite flames of the Great Painter!" Really speaking, there is naught—neither volition, nor desire. He is all. He—She—the Mother, is playing, and we are like dolls, Her helpers in this play. Here, She puts one now in the garb of a beggar, another moment in the garb of a king, the next moment in the garb of a saint, and again in the garb of a devil. We are putting on different garbs to help the Mother Spirit in Her play.

When the baby is at play, she will not come even if called by her mother. But when she finishes her play, she will rush to her mother, and will have no play. So there come moments in our life, when we feel our play is finished, and we want to rush to the Mother. Then all our toil here will be of no value; men, women, and children—wealth, name, and fame, joys and glories of life—punishments and successes—will be no more, and the whole life will seem like a show. We shall see only the infinite rhythm going on, endless and purposeless, going we do not know where. Only this much shall we say; our play is done.

THE COSMOS AND THE SELF

Everything in nature rises from some fine seed-forms, becomes grosser and grosser, exists for a certain time, and again goes back to the original fine form. Our earth, for instance, has come out of a nebulous form which, becoming colder and colder, turned into this crystallised planet upon which we live, and in the future it will again go to pieces and return to its rudimentary nebulous form. This is happening in the universe, and has been through time immemorial. This is the whole history of man, the whole history of nature, the whole history of life.

Every evolution is preceded by an involution. The whole of the tree is present in the seed, its cause. The whole of the human being is present in that one protoplasm. The whole of this universe is present in the cosmic fine universe. Everything is present in its cause, in its fine form. This evolution, or gradual unfolding of grosser and grosser forms, is true, but each case has been preceded by an involution. The whole of this universe must have been involute before it came out, and has unfolded itself in all these various forms to be involved again once more. Take, for instance, the life of a little plant. We find two things that make the plant a unity by itself—its growth and development, its decay and death. These make one unity the plant life. So, taking that plant life as only one link in the chain of life, we may take the whole series as one life, beginning in the protoplasm and ending in the most perfect man. Man is one link, and the various beasts, the lower animals, and plants are other links. Now go back to the source, the finest particles from which they started, and take the whole series as but one life, and you will find that every evolution here is the evolution of something which existed previously.

Where it begins, there it ends. What is the end of this universe? Intelligence, is it not? The last to come in the order of creation, according to the evolutionists, was intelligence. That being so, it must be the cause, the beginning of creation also. At the beginning that intelligence remains involved, and in the end it gets evolved. The sum total of the intelligence displayed in the universe must therefore be the involved universal intelligence unfolding itself, and this universal intelligence is what we call God, from whom we come and to whom we return, as the scriptures say. Call it by any other name, you cannot deny that in the beginning there is that infinite cosmic intelligence.

What makes a compound? A compound is that in which the causes have combined and become the effect. So these compound things can be only within the circle of the law of causation; so far as the rules of cause and effect go, so far can we have compounds and combinations. Beyond that it is impossible to talk of combinations, because no law holds good therein. Law holds good only in that universe which we see, feel, hear, imagine, dream, and beyond that we cannot place any idea of law. That is our universe which we sense or imagine, and we sense what is within our direct perception, and we imagine what is in our mind. What is beyond the body is beyond the senses, and what is beyond the mind is beyond the imagination, and therefore is beyond our universe, and therefore beyond the law of causation. The Self of man being beyond the law of causation is not a compound, is not the effect of any cause, and therefore is ever free and is the ruler of everything that is within law. Not being a compound, it will never die, because death means going back to the component parts, destruction means going back to the cause. Because it cannot die, it cannot live; for both life and death are modes of manifestation of the same thing. So the Soul is beyond life and death. You were never born, and you will never die. Birth and death belong to the body only.

The doctrine of monism holds that this universe is all that exists; gross or fine, it is all here; the effect and the cause are both here; the explanation is here. What is known as the particular is simply repetition in a minute form of the universal. We get our idea of the universe from the study of our own Souls, and what is true there also holds good in the outside universe. The ideas of heaven and all these various places, even if they be true, are in the universe. They altogether make this Unity. The first idea, therefore, is that of a Whole, a Unit, composed of various minute particles, and each one of us is a part, as it were, of this Unit. As manifested beings we appear separate, but as a reality we are one. The more we think ourselves separate from this Whole, the more miserable we become. So, Advaita is the basis of ethics.

WHO IS A REAL GURU?

A real Guru is one who is born from time to time as a repository of spiritual force which he transmits to future generations through successive links of Guru and Shishya (disciple). The current of this spirit-force changes its course from time to time, just as a mighty stream of water opens up a new channel and leaves the old one for good. Thus it is seen that old sects of religion grow lifeless in the course of time, and new sects arise with the fire of life in them. Men who are truly wise commit themselves to the mercy of that particular sect through which the current of life flows. Old forms of religion are like the skeletons of once mighty animals, preserved in museums. They should be regarded with the due honour. They cannot satisfy the true cravings of the soul for the Highest, just as a dead mango-tree cannot satisfy the cravings of a man for luscious mangoes.

The one thing necessary is to be stripped of our vanities—the sense that we possess any spiritual wisdom—and to surrender ourselves completely to the guidance of our Guru. The Guru only knows what will lead us towards perfection. We are quite blind to it. We do not know anything. This sort of humility will open the door of our heart for spiritual truths. Truth will never come into our minds so long as there will remain the faintest shadow of Ahamkâra (egotism). All of you should try to root out this devil from your heart. Complete self-surrender is the only way to spiritual illumination.

ON ART

The secret of Greek Art is its imitation of nature even to the minutest details; whereas the secret of Indian Art is to represent the ideal. The energy of the Greek painter is spent in perhaps painting a piece of flesh, and he is so successful that a dog is deluded into taking it to be a real bit of meat and so goes to bite it. Now, what glory is there in merely imitating nature? Why not place an actual bit of flesh before the dog?

The Indian tendency, on the other hand, to represent the ideal, the supersensual, has become degraded into painting grotesque images. Now, true Art can be compared to a lily which springs from the ground, takes its nourishment from the ground, is in touch with the ground, and yet is quite high above it. So Art must be in touch with nature—and wherever that touch is gone, Art degenerates—yet it must be above nature.

Art is—representing the beautiful. There must be Art in everything.

The difference between architecture and building is that the former expresses an idea, while the latter is merely a structure built on economical principles. The value of matter depends solely on its capacities of expressing ideas.

The artistic faculty was highly developed in our Lord Shri Ramakrishna, and he used to say that without this faculty none can be truly spiritual.

ON LANGUAGE

Simplicity is the secret. My ideal of language is my Master's language, most colloquial and yet most expressive. It must express the thought which is intended to be conveyed.

The attempt to make the Bengali language perfect in so short a time will make it cut and dried. Properly speaking, it has no verbs. Michael Madhusudan Dutt attempted to remedy this in poetry. The greatest poet in Bengal was Kavikankana. The best prose in Sanskrit is Patanjali's Mahâbhâshya. There the language is vigorous. The language of Hitopadesha is not bad, but the language of Kâdambari is an example of degradation.

The Bengali language must be modelled not after the Sanskrit, but rather after the Pâli, which has a strong resemblance to it. In coining or translating technical terms in Bengali, one must, however, use all Sanskrit words for them, and an attempt should be made to coin new words. For this purpose, if a collection is made from a Sanskrit dictionary of all those technical terms, then it ill help greatly the constitution of the Bengali language.

THE SANNYASIN

In explanation of the term Sannyâsin, the Swami in the course of one of his lectures in Boston said:

When a man has fulfilled the duties and obligations of that stage of life in which he is born, and his aspirations lead him to seek a spiritual life and to abandon altogether the worldly pursuits of possession, fame, or power, when, by the growth of insight into the nature of the world, he sees its impermanence, its strife, its misery, and the paltry nature of its prizes, and turns away from all these—then he seeks the True, the Eternal Love, the Refuge. He makes complete renunciation (Sannyâsa) of all worldly position, property, and name, and wanders forth into the world to live a life of self-sacrifice and to persistently seek spiritual knowledge, striving to excel in love and compassion and to acquire lasting insight. Gaining these pearls of wisdom by years of meditation, discipline, and inquiry, he in his turn becomes a teacher and hands on to disciples, lay or professed, who may seek them from him, all that he can of wisdom and beneficence.

A Sannyasin cannot belong to any religion, for his is a life of independent thought, which draws from all religions; his is a life of realisation, not merely of theory or belief, much less of dogma.

THE SANNYASIN AND
THE HOUSEHOLDER

The men of the world should have no voice in the affairs of the Sannyâsins. The Sannyasin should have nothing to do with the rich, his duty is with the poor. He should treat the poor with loving care and serve them joyfully with all his might. To pay respects to the rich and hang on them for support has been the bane of all the Sannyasin communities of our country. A true Sannyasin should scrupulously avoid that. Such conduct becomes a public woman rather than one who professes to have renounced the world. How should a man immersed in Kâma-Kânchana (lust and greed) become a devotee of one whose central ideal is the renunciation of Kama-Kanchana? Shri Ramakrishna wept and prayed to the Divine Mother to send him such a one to talk with as would not have in him the slightest tinge of Kama-Kanchana; for he would say, "My lips burn when I talk with the worldly-minded." He also used to say that he could not even bear the touch of the worldly-minded and the impure. That King of Sannyasins (Shri Ramakrishna) can never be preached by men of the world. The latter can never be perfectly sincere; for he cannot but have some selfish motives to serve. If Bhagavân (God) incarnates Himself as a householder, I can never believe Him to be sincere. When a householder takes the position of the leader of a religious sect, he begins to serve his own interests in the name of principle, hiding the former in the garb of the latter, and the result is the sect becomes rotten to the core. All religious movements headed by householders have shared the same fate. Without renunciation religion can never stand.

Here Swamiji was asked—What are we Sannyasins to understand by renunciation of Kanchana (wealth)? He answered as follows:With a view to certain ends we have to adopt certain means. These means vary according to the conditions of time, place, individual, etc.; but the end always remains unaltered. In the case of the Sannyasin, the end is the liberation of the Self and doing good to humanity—"आत्मनो मोक्षार्थं जगद्धिताय च"; and of the ways to attain it, the renunciation of Kama-Kanchana is the most important. Remember, renunciation consists in the total absence of all selfish motives and not in mere abstinence from external contact, such as avoiding to touch one's money kept with another at the same time enjoying all its benefits. Would that be renunciation? For accomplishing the two above-mentioned ends, the begging excursion would be a great help to a Sannyasin at a time when the householders strictly obeyed the injunctions of Manu and other law-givers, by setting apart every day a portion of their meal for ascetic guests. Nowadays things have changed considerably, especially, as in Bengal, where no Mâdhukari[1] system prevails. Here it would be mere waste of energy to try to live on Madhukari, and you would profit nothing by it. The injunction of Bhikshâ (begging) is a means to serve the above two ends, which will not be served by that way now. It does not, therefore, go against the principle of renunciation under such circumstances if a Sannyasin provides for mere necessaries of life and devotes all his energy to the accomplishment of his ends for which he took Sannyasa. Attaching too much importance ignorantly to the means brings confusion. The end should never be lost sight of.

THE EVILS OF ADHIKARIVADA

In one of his question classes the talk drifted on to the Adhikârivâda, or the doctrine of special rights and privileges, and Swamiji in pointing out vehemently the evils that have resulted from it spoke to the following effect:

With all my respects for the Rishis of yore, I cannot but denounce their method in instructing the people. They always enjoined upon them to do certain things but took care never to explain to them the reason for it. This method was pernicious to the very core; and instead of enabling men to attain the end, it laid upon their shoulders a mass of meaningless nonsense. Their excuse for keeping the end hidden from view was that the people could not have understood their real meaning even if they had presented it to them, not being worthy recipients. The Adhikarivada is the outcome of pure selfishness. They knew that by this enlightenment on their special subject they would lose their superior position of instructors to the people. Hence their endeavour to support this theory. If you consider a man too weak to receive these lessons, you should try the more to teach and educate him; you should give him the advantage of more teaching, instead of less, to train up his intellect, so as to enable him to comprehend the more subtle problems. These advocates of Adhikarivada ignored the tremendous fact of the infinite possibilities of the human soul. Every man is capable of receiving knowledge if it is imparted in his own language. A teacher who cannot convince others should weep on account of his own inability to teach the people in their own language, instead of cursing them and dooming them to live in ignorance and superstition, setting up the plea that the higher knowledge is not for them. Speak out the truth boldly, without any fear that it will puzzle the weak. Men are selfish; they do not want others to come up to the same level of their knowledge, for fear of losing their own privilege and prestige over others. Their contention is that the knowledge of the highest spiritual truths will bring about confusion in the understanding of the weak-minded men, and so the Shloka goes:

"न बुद्धिभेदं जनयेदज्ञानां कर्मसङ्गिनाम् ।

जोषयेत्सर्वकर्माणि विद्वान्युक्तः समाचरन् ॥३- २६॥"

— "One should not unsettle the understanding of the ignorant, attached to action (by teaching them Jnâna): the wise man, himself steadily acting, should engage the ignorant in all work" (Gita, III. 26).

I cannot believe in the self-contradictory statement that light brings greater darkness. It is like losing life in the ocean of Sachchidânanda, in the ocean of Absolute Existence and Immortality. How absurd! Knowledge means freedom from the errors which ignorance leads to. Knowledge paving the way to error! Enlightenment leading to confusion! Is it possible? Men are not bold enough to speak out broad truths, for fear of losing the respect of the people. They try to make a compromise between the real, eternal truths and the nonsensical prejudices of the people, and thus set up the doctrine that Lokâchâras (customs of the people) and Deshâchâras (customs of the country) must be adhered to. No compromise! No whitewashing! No covering of corpses beneath flowers! Throw away such texts as, "तथापि लोकाचारः —Yet the customs of the people have to be be followed." Nonsense! The result of this sort of compromise is that the grand truths are soon buried under heaps of rubbish, and the latter are eagerly held as real truths. Even the grand truths of the Gita, so boldly preached by Shri Krishna, received the gloss of compromise in the hands of future generations of disciples, and the result is that the grandest scripture of the world is now made to yield many things which lead men astray.

This attempt at compromise proceeds from arrant downright cowardice. Be bold! My children should be brave, above all. Not the least compromise on any account. Preach the highest truths broadcast. Do not fear losing your respect or causing unhappy friction. Rest assured that if you serve truth in spite of temptations to forsake it, you will attain a heavenly strength in the face of which men will quail to speak before you things which you do not believe to be true. People will be convinced of what you will say to them if you can strictly serve truth for fourteen years continually, without swerving from it. Thus you will confer the greatest blessing on the masses, unshackle their bandages, and uplift the whole nation.

ON BHAKTI-YOGA

The dualist thinks you cannot be moral unless you have a God with a rod in His hand, ready to punish you. How is that? Suppose a horse had to give us a lecture on morality, one of those very wretched cab-horses who move only with the whip, to which he has become accustomed. He begins to speak about human beings and says that they must be very immoral. Why? "Because I know they are not whipped regularly." The fear of the whip only makes one more immoral.

You all say there is a God and that He is an omnipresent Being. Close your eyes and think what He is. What do you find? Either you are thinking, in bringing the idea of omnipresence

---

1. Literally, 'bee-like'. The system of begging one's food piecemeal from several houses, so as not to tax the householder, as a bee gathers honey from different flowers.

in your mind, of the sea, or the blue sky, or an expanse of meadow, or such things as you have seen in your life. If that is so, you do not mean anything by omnipresent God; it has no meaning at all to you. So with every other attribute of God. What idea have we of omnipotence or omniscience? We have none. Religion is realising, and I shall call you a worshipper of God when you have become able to realise the Idea. Before that it is the spelling of words and no more. It is this power of realisation that makes religion; no amount of doctrines or philosophies, or ethical books, that you may have stuffed into your brain, will matter much—only what you are and what you have realised.

The Personal God is the same Absolute looked at through the haze of Mâyâ. When we approach Him with the five senses, we can see Him only as the Personal God. The idea is that the Self cannot be objectified. How can the Knower know Itself? But It can cast a shadow, as it were, if that can be called objectification. So the highest form of that shadow, that attempt at objectifying Itself, is the Personal God. The Self is the eternal subject, and we are struggling all the time to objectify that Self. And out of that struggle has come this phenomenal universe and what we call matter, and so on. But these are very weak attempts, and the highest objectification of the Self possible to us is the Personal God. This objectification is an attempt to reveal our own nature. According to the Sânkhya, nature is showing all these experiences to the soul, and when it has got real experience it will know its own nature. According to the Advaita Vedantist, the soul is struggling to reveal itself. After long struggle, it finds that the subject must always remain the subject; and then begins non-attachment, and it becomes free.

When a man has reached that perfect state, he is of the same nature as the Personal God. "I and my Father are one." He knows that he is one with Brahman, the Absolute, and projects himself as the Personal God does. He plays—as even the mightiest of kings may sometimes play with dolls.

Some imaginations help to break the bondage of the rest. The whole universe is imagination, but one set of imaginations will cure another set. Those that tell us that there is sin and sorrow and death in the world are terrible. But the other set—thou art holy, there is God, there is no pain—these are good, and help to break the bondage of the others. The highest imagination that can break all the links of the chain is that of the Personal God.

To go and say, "Lord, take care of this thing and give me that; Lord, I give you my little prayer and you give me this thing of daily necessity; Lord, cure my headache", and all that—these are not Bhakti. They are the lowest states of religion. They are the lowest form of Karma. If a man uses all his mental energy in seeking to satisfy his body and its wants, show me the difference between him and an animal. Bhakti is a higher thing higher than even desiring heaven. The idea of heaven is of a place of intensified enjoyment. How can that be God?

Only the fools rush after sense-enjoyments. It is easy to live in the senses. It is easier to run in the old groove, eating and drinking; but what these modern philosophers want to tell you is to take these comfortable ideas and put the stamp of religion on them. Such a doctrine is dangerous. Death lies in the senses. Life on the plane of the Spirit is the only life, life on any other plane is mere death; the whole of this life can be only described as a gymnasium. We must go beyond it to enjoy real life.

As long as touch-me-not-ism is your creed and the kitchen-pot your deity, you cannot rise spiritually. All the petty differences between religion and religion are mere word-struggles, nonsense. Everyone thinks, "This is my original idea", and wants to have things his own way. That is how struggles come.

In criticising another, we always foolishly take one especially brilliant point as the whole of our life and compare that with the dark ones in the life of another. Thus we make mistakes in judging individuals.

Through fanaticism and bigotry a religion can be propagated very quickly, no doubt, but the preaching of that religion is firm-based on solid ground, which gives everyone liberty to his opinions and thus uplifts him to a higher path, though this process is slow

First deluge the land (India) with spiritual ideas, then other ideas will follow The gift of spirituality and spiritual knowledge is the highest, for it saves from many and many a birth; the next gift is secular knowledge, as it opens the eyes of human beings towards that spiritual knowledge; the next is the saving of life; and the fourth is the gift of food.

Even if the body goes in practicing Sâdhanâs (austerities for realisation), let it go; what of that? Realisation will come in the fullness of time, by living constantly in the company of Sâdhus (holy men). A time comes when one understands that to serve a man even by preparing a Chhilam (earthen pipe) of tobacco is far greater than millions of meditations. He who can properly prepare a Chhilam of tobacco can also properly meditate.

Gods are nothing but highly developed dead men. We can get help from them.

Anyone and everyone cannot be an Âchârya (teacher of mankind); but many may become Mukta (liberated). The whole world seems like a dream to the liberated, but the Acharya has to take up his stand between the two states. He must have the knowledge that the world is true, or else why should he teach? Again, if he has not realised the world as a dream, then he is no better than an ordinary man, and what could he teach? The Guru has to bear the disciple's burden of sin; and that is the reason why diseases and other ailments appear even in the bodies of powerful Acharyas. But if he be imperfect, they attack his mind also, and he falls. So it is a difficult thing to be an Acharya.

It is easier to become a Jivanmukta (free in this very life)

than to be an Acharya. For the former knows the world as a dream and has no concern with it; but an Acharya knows it as a dream and yet has to remain in it and work. It is not possible for everyone to be an Acharya. He is an Acharya through whom the divine power acts. The body in which one becomes an Acharya is very different from that of any other man. There is a science for keeping that body in a perfect state. His is the most delicate organism, very susceptible, capable of feeling intense joy and intense suffering. He is abnormal.

In every sphere of life we find that it is the person within that triumphs, and that personality is the secret of all success.

Nowhere is seen such sublime unfoldment of feeling as in Bhagavân Shri Krishna Chaitanya, the Prophet of Nadia.

Shri Ramakrishna is a force. You should not think that his doctrine is this or that. But he is a power, living even now in his disciples and working in the world. I saw him growing in his ideas. He is still growing. Shri Ramakrishna was both a Jivanmukta and an Acharya.

ISHVARA AND BRAHMAN

In reply to a question as to the exact position of Ishvara in Vedantic Philosophy, the Swami Vivekananda, while in Europe, gave the following definition: "Ishvara is the sum total of individuals, yet He is an Individual, as the human body is a unit, of which each cell is an individual. Samashti or collected equals God; Vyashti or analysed equals the Jiva. The existence of Ishvara, therefore, depends on that of Jiva, as the body on the cell, and vice versa. Thus, Jiva and Ishvara are coexistent beings; when one exists, the other must. Also, because, except on our earth, in all the higher spheres, the amount of good being vastly in excess of the amount of evil, the sum total (Ishvara) may be said to be all-good. Omnipotence and omniscience are obvious qualities and need no argument to prove from the very fact of totality. Brahman is beyond both these and is not a conditioned state; it is the only Unit not composed of many units, the principle which runs through all from a cell to God, without which nothing can exist; and whatever is real is that principle, or Brahman. When I think I am Brahman, I alone exist; so with others. Therefore, each one is the whole of that principle."

ON JNANA-YOGA

All souls are playing, some consciously, some unconsciously. Religion is learning to play consciously.

The same law which holds good in our worldly life also holds good in our religious life and in the life of the cosmos. It is one, it is universal. It is not that religion is guided by one law and the world by another. The flesh and the devil are but degrees of difference from God Himself.

Theologians, philosophers, and scientists in the West are ransacking everything to get a proof that they live afterwards! What a storm in a tea-cup! There are much higher things to think of. What silly superstition is this, that you ever die! It requires no priests or spirits or ghosts to tell us that we shall not die. It is the most self-evident of all truths. No man can imagine his own annihilation. The idea of immortality is inherent in man.

Wherever there is life, with it there is death. Life is the shadow of death, and death, the shadow of life. The line of demarcation is too fine to determine, too difficult to grasp, and most difficult to hold on to.

I do not believe in eternal progress, that we are growing on ever and ever in a straight line. It is too nonsensical to believe. There is no motion in a straight line. A straight line infinitely projected becomes a circle. The force sent out will complete the circle and return to its starting place.

There is no progress in a straight line. Every soul moves in a circle, as it were, and will have to complete it; and no soul can go so low but that there will come a time when it will have to go upwards. It may start straight down, but it has to take the upward curve to complete the circuit. We are all projected from a common centre, which is God, and will come back after completing the circuit to the centre from which we started.

Each soul is a circle. The centre is where the body is, and the activity is manifested there. You are omnipresent, though you have the consciousness of being concentrated in only one point. That point has taken up particles of matter and formed them into a machine to express itself. That through which it expresses itself is called the body. You are everywhere. When one body or machine fails you, the centre moves on and takes up other particles of matter, finer or grosser, and works through them. Here is man. And what is God? God is a circle with circumference nowhere and centre everywhere. Every point in that circle is living, conscious, active, and equally working. With our limited souls only one point is conscious, and that point moves forward and backward.

The soul is a circle whose circumference is nowhere (limitless), but whose centre is in some body. Death is but a change of centre. God is a circle whose circumference is nowhere, and whose centre is everywhere. When we can get out of the limited centre of body, we shall realise God, our true Self.

A tremendous stream is flowing towards the ocean, carrying little bits of paper and straw hither and thither on it. They may struggle to go back, but in the long run they; must flow down to the ocean. So you and I and all nature are like these little straws carried in mad currents towards that ocean of Life, Perfection, and God. We may struggle to go back, or float against the current and play all sorts of pranks, but in the long run we must go and join this great ocean of Life and Bliss.

Jnâna (knowledge) is "creedlessness"; but that does not mean that it despises creeds. It only means that a stage above and beyond creeds has been gained. The Jnâni (true philosopher) strives to destroy nothing but to help all. All rivers roll their waters into the sea and become one. So all creeds should lead to Jnana and become one. Jnana teaches that the world should be renounced but not on that account abandoned. To live in the world and not to be of it is the true test of renunciation.

I cannot see how it can be otherwise than that all knowledge is stored up in us from the beginning. If you and I are little waves in the ocean, then that ocean is the background.

There is really no difference between matter, mind, and Spirit. They are only different phases of experiencing the One. This very world is seen by the five senses as matter, by the very wicked as hell, by the good as heaven, and by the perfect as God.

We cannot bring it to sense demonstration that Brahman is the only real thing; but we can point out that this is the only conclusion that one can come to. For instance, there must be this oneness in everything, even in common things. There is the human generalisation, for example. We say that all the variety is created by name and form; yet when we want to grasp and separate it, it is nowhere. We can never see name or form or causes standing by themselves. So this phenomenon is Mâyâ—something which depends on the noumenon and apart from it has no existence. Take a wave in the ocean. That wave exists so long as that quantity of water remains in a wave form; but as soon as it goes down and becomes the ocean, the wave ceases to exist. But the whole mass of water does not depend so much on its form. The ocean remains, while the wave form becomes absolute zero.

The real is one. It is the mind which makes it appear as many. When we perceive the diversity, the unity has gone; and as soon as we perceive the unity, the diversity has vanished. Just as in everyday life, when you perceive the unity, you do not perceive the diversity. At the beginning you start with unity. It is a curious fact that a Chinaman will not know the difference in appearance between one American and another; and you will not know the difference between different Chinamen.

It can be shown that it is the mind which makes things knowable. It is only things which have certain peculiarities that bring themselves within the range of the known and knowable. That which has no qualities is unknowable. For instance, there is some external world, X, unknown and unknowable. When I look at it, it is X plus mind. When I want to know the world, my mind contributes three quarters of it. The internal world is Y plus mind, and the external world X plus mind. All differentiation in either the external or internal world is created by the mind, and that which exists is unknown and unknowable. It is beyond the range of knowledge, and that which is beyond the range of knowledge can have no differentiation. Therefore this X outside is the same as the Y inside, and therefore the real is one.

God does not reason. Why should you reason if you know? It is a sign of weakness that we have to go on crawling like worms to get a few facts, and then the whole thing tumbles down again. The Spirit is reflected in mind and in everything.

It is the light of the Spirit that makes the mind sentient. Everything is an expression of the Spirit; the minds are so many mirrors. What you call love, fear, hatred, virtue, and vice are all reflections of the Spirit. When the reflector is base, the reflection is bad.

The real Existence is without manifestation. We cannot conceive It, because we should have to conceive through the mind, which is itself a manifestation. Its glory is that It is inconceivable. We must remember that in life the lowest and highest vibrations of light we do not see, but they are the opposite poles of existence. There are certain things which we do not know now, but which we can know. It is due to our ignorance that we do not know them. There are certain things which we can never know, because they are much higher than the highest vibrations of knowledge. But we are the Eternal all the time, although we cannot know it. Knowledge will be impossible there. The very fact of the limitations of the conception is the basis for its existence. For instance, there is nothing so certain in me as my Self; and yet I can only conceive of it as a body and mind, as happy or unhappy, as a man or a woman. At the same time, I try to conceive of it as it really is and find that there is no other way of doing it but by dragging it down; yet I am sure of that reality. "No one, O beloved, loves the husband for the husband's sake, but because the Self is there. It is in and through the Self that she loves the husband. No one, O beloved, loves the wife for the wife's sake, but in and through the Self." And that Reality is the only thing we know, because in and through It we know everything else; and yet we cannot conceive of It. How can we know the Knower? If we knew It, It would not be the knower, but the known; It would be objectified.

The man of highest realisation exclaims, "I am the King of kings; there is no king higher than I, I am the God of gods; there is no God higher than I I alone exist, One without a second." This monistic idea of the Vedanta seems to many, of course, very terrible, but that is on account of superstition.

We are the Self, eternally at rest and at peace. We must not weep; there is no weeping for the Soul. We in our imagination think that God is weeping on His throne out of sympathy. Such a God would not be worth attaining. Why should God weep at all? To weep is a sign of weakness, of bondage.

Seek the Highest, always the Highest, for in the Highest is eternal bliss. If I am to hunt, I will hunt the lion. If I am to rob, I will rob the treasury of the king. Seek the Highest.

Oh, One that cannot be confined or described! One that can be perceived in our heart of hearts! One beyond all compare, beyond limit, unchangeable like the blue sky! Oh, learn the All, holy one I Seek for nothing else!

Where changes of nature cannot reach, thought beyond all thought, Unchangeable, Immovable; whom all books declare, all sages worship; Oh, holy one, seek for nothing else!

Beyond compare, Infinite Oneness! No comparison is possible. Water above, water below, water on the right, water on the left; no wave on that water, no ripple, all silence; all eternal bliss. Such will come to thy heart. Seek for nothing else!

Why weepest thou, brother? There is neither death nor disease for thee. Why weepest thou, brother? There is neither misery nor misfortune for thee. Why weepest thou, brother? Neither change nor death was predicated of thee. Thou art Existence Absolute.

I know what God is—I cannot speak Him to you. I know not what God is—how can I speak Him to you? But seest thou not, my brother, that thou art He, thou art; He? Why go seeking God here and there? Seek not, and that is God. Be your own Self.

Thou art Our Father, our Mother, our dear Friend. Thou bearest the burden of the world. Help us to bear the burden of our lives. Thou art our Friend, our Lover, our Husband, Thou art ourselves!

THE CAUSE OF ILLUSION

The question—what is the cause of Mâyâ (illusion)?—has been asked for the last three thousand years; and the only answer is: when the world is able to formulate a logical question, we shall answer it. The question is contradictory. Our position is that the Absolute has become this relative only apparently, that the Unconditioned has become the conditioned only in Maya. By the very admission of the Unconditioned, we admit that the Absolute cannot be acted upon by anything else. It is uncaused, which means that nothing outside Itself can act upon It. First of all, if It is unconditioned, It cannot have been acted upon by anything else. In the Unconditioned there cannot be time, space, or causation. That granted your question will be: "What caused that which cannot be caused by anything to be changed into this?" Your question is only possible in the conditioned. But you take it out of the conditioned, and want to ask it in the Unconditioned. Only when the Unconditioned becomes conditioned, and space, time, and causation come in, can the question be asked. We can only say ignorance makes the illusion. The question is impossible. Nothing can have worked on the Absolute. There was no cause. Not that we do not know, or that we are ignorant; but It is above knowledge, and cannot be brought down to the plane of knowledge. We can use the words, "I do not know" in two senses. In one way, they mean that we are lower than knowledge, and in the other way, that the thing is above knowledge. The X-rays have become known now. The very causes of these are disputed, but we are sure that we shall know them. Here we can say we do not know about the X-rays. But about the Absolute we cannot know. In the case of the X-rays we do not know, although they are within the range of knowledge; only we do not know them yet. But, in the other case, It is so much beyond knowledge that It ceases to be a matter of knowing. "By what means can the Knower be known?" You are always yourself and cannot objectify yourself. This was one of the arguments used by our philosophers to prove immortality. If I try to think I am lying dead, what have I to imagine? That I am standing and looking down at myself, at some dead body. So that I cannot objectify myself.

EVOLUTION

In the matter of the projection of Akâsha and Prâna into manifested form and the return to fine state, there is a good deal of similarity between Indian thought and modern science. The moderns have their evolution, and so have the Yogis. But I think that the Yogis' explanation of evolution is the better one. "The change of one species into another is attained by the infilling of nature." The basic idea is that we are changing from one species to another, and that man is the highest species. Patanjali explains this "infilling of nature" by the simile of peasants irrigating fields. Our education and progression simply mean taking away the obstacles, and by its own nature the divinity will manifest itself. This does away with all the struggle for existence. The miserable experiences of life are simply in the way, and can be eliminated entirely. They are not necessary for evolution. Even if they did not exist, we should progress. It is in the very nature of things to manifest themselves. The momentum is not from outside, but comes from inside. Each soul is the sum total of the universal experiences already coiled up there; and of all these experiences, only those will come out which find suitable circumstances.

So the external things can only give us the environments. These competitions and struggles and evils that we see are not the effect of the involution or the cause, but they are in the way. If they did not exist, still man would go on and evolve as God, because it is the very nature of that God to come out and manifest Himself. To my mind this seems very hopeful, instead of that horrible idea of competition. The more I study history, the more I find that idea to be wrong. Some say that if man did not fight with man, he would not progress. I also used to think so; but I find now that every war has thrown back human progress by fifty years instead of hurrying it forwards. The day will come when men will study history from a different light and find that competition is neither the cause nor the effect, simply a thing on the way, not necessary to evolution at all.

The theory of Patanjali is the only theory I think a rational man can accept. How much evil the modern system causes! Every wicked man has a licence to be wicked under it. I have seen in this country (America) physicists who say that all criminals ought to be exterminated and that that is the only way in which criminality can be eliminated from society. These environments can hinder, but they are not necessary to progress. The most horrible thing about competition is that one may conquer the environments, but that where one may conquer, thousands are crowded out. So it is evil at best. That cannot be good which helps only one and hinders the majority. Patanjali says that these struggles remain only through our ignorance, and are not necessary, and are not part of the evolution of man. It is just our impatience which creates them. We have not the patience to go and work our way out. For instance, there is a fire in a theatre, and only a few escape. The rest in trying to rush out crush one another down. That crush was not necessary for the salvation of the building nor of the two or three who escaped. If all had gone out slowly, not one would have been hurt. That is the case in life. The doors are open for us, and we can all get out without the competition and struggle; and yet we struggle. The struggle we create through our own ignorance, through impatience; we are in too great a hurry. The highest manifestation of strength is to keep ourselves calm and on our own feet.

BUDDHISM AND VEDANTA

The Vedanta philosophy is the foundation of Buddhism and everything else in India; but what we call the Advaita philosophy of the modern school has a great many conclusions of the Buddhists. Of course, the Hindus will not admit that—that is the orthodox Hindu, because to them the Buddhists are heretics. But there is a conscious attempt to stretch out the whole doctrine to include the heretics also.

The Vedanta has no quarrel with Buddhism. The idea of the Vedanta is to harmonise all. With the Northern Buddhists we have no quarrel at all. But the Burmese and Siamese and all the Southern Buddhists say that there is a phenomenal world, and ask what right we have to create a noumenal world behind this. The answer of the Vedanta is that this is a false statement. The Vedanta never contended that there was a noumenal and a phenomenal world. There is one. Seen through the senses it is phenomenal, but it is really the noumenal all the time. The man who sees the rope does not see the snake. It is either the rope or the snake, but never the two. So the Buddhistic statement of our position, that we believe there are two worlds, is entirely false. They have the right to say it is the phenomenal if they like, but no right to contend that other men have not the right to say it is the noumenal.

Buddhism does not want to have anything except phenomena. In phenomena alone is desire. It is desire that is creating all this. Modern Vedantists do not hold this at all. We say there is something which has become the will. Will is a manufactured something, a compound, not a "simple". There cannot be any will without an external object. We see that the very position that will created this universe is impossible. How could it? Have you ever known will without external stimulus? Desire cannot arise without stimulus, or in modern philosophic language, of nerve stimulus. Will is a sort of reaction of the brain, what the Sânkhya philosophers call Buddhi. This reaction must be preceded by action, and action presupposes an external universe. When there is no external universe, naturally there will be no will; and yet, according to your theory, it is will that created the universe. Who creates the will? Will is co-existent with the universe. Will is one phenomenon caused by the same impulse which created the universe. But philosophy must not stop there. Will is entirely personal; therefore we cannot go with Schopenhauer at all. Will is a compound—a mixture of the internal and the external. Suppose a man were born without any senses, he would have no will at all. Will requires something from outside, and the brain will get some energy from inside; therefore will is a compound, as much a compound as the wall or anything else. We do not agree with the will-theory of these German philosophers at all. Will itself is phenomenal and cannot be the Absolute. It is one of the many projections. There is something which is not will, but is manifesting itself as will. That I can understand. But that will is manifesting itself as everything else, I do not understand, seeing that we cannot have any conception of will, as separate from the universe. When that something which is freedom becomes will, it is caused by time, space, and causation. Take Kant's analysis. Will is within time, space, and causation. Then how can it be the Absolute? One cannot will without willing in time.

If we can stop all thought, then we know that we are beyond thought. We come to this by negation. When every phenomenon has been negatived, whatever remains, that is It. That cannot be expressed, cannot be manifested, because the manifestation will be, again, will.

ON THE VEDANTA PHILOSOPHY

The Vedantist says that a man is neither born nor dies nor goes to heaven, and that reincarnation is really a myth with regard to the soul. The example is given of a book being turned over. It is the book that evolves, not the man. Every soul is omnipresent, so where can it come or go? These births and deaths are changes in nature which we are mistaking for changes in us.

Reincarnation is the evolution of nature and the manifestation of the God within.

The Vedanta says that each life is built upon the past, and that when we can look back over the whole past we are free. The desire to be free will take the form of a religious disposition from childhood. A few years will, as it were, make all truth clear to one. After leaving this life, and while waiting for the next, a man is still in the phenomenal.

We would describe the soul in these words: This soul the sword cannot cut, nor the spear pierce; the fire cannot burn nor water melt it; indestructible, omnipresent is this soul. Therefore weep not for it.

If it has been very bad, we believe that it will become good in the time to come. The fundamental principle is that there is eternal freedom for every one. Every one must come to it. We have to struggle, impelled by our desire to be free. Every other desire but that to be free is illusive. Every good action, the Vedantist says, is a manifestation of that freedom.

I do not believe that there will come a time when all the evil in the world will vanish. How could that be? This stream goes on. Masses of water go out at one end, but masses are coming in at the other end.

The Vedanta says that you are pure and perfect, and that there is a state beyond good and evil, and that is your own nature. It is higher even than good. Good is only a lesser differentiation than evil.

We have no theory of evil. We call it ignorance.

So far as it goes, all dealing with other people, all ethics, is in the phenomenal world. As a most complete statement of truth, we would not think of applying such things as ignorance to God. Of Him we say that He is Existence, Knowledge, and Bliss Absolute. Every effort of thought and speech will make the Absolute phenomenal and break Its character.

There is one thing to be remembered: that the assertion—I am God—cannot be made with regard to the sense-world. If you say in the sense-world that you are God, what is to prevent your doing wrong? So the affirmation of your divinity applies only to the noumenal. If I am God, I am beyond the tendencies of the senses and will not do evil. Morality of course is not the goal of man, but the means through which this freedom is attained. The Vedanta says that Yoga is one way that makes men realise this divinity. The Vedanta says this is done by the realisation of the freedom within and that everything will give way to that. Morality and ethics will all range themselves in their proper places.

All the criticism against the Advaita philosophy can be summed up in this, that it does not conduce to sense-enjoyments; and we are glad to admit that.

The Vedanta system begins with tremendous pessimism, and ends with real optimism. We deny the sense-optimism but assert the real optimism of the Supersensuous. That real happiness is not in the senses but above the senses; and it is in every man. The sort of optimism which we see in the world is what will lead to ruin through the senses.

Abnegation has the greatest importance in our philosophy. Negation implies affirmation of the Real Self. The Vedanta is pessimistic so far as it negatives the world of the senses, but it is optimistic in its assertion of the real world.

The Vedanta recognises the reasoning power of man a good deal, although it says there is something higher than intellect; but the road lies through intellect.

We need reason to drive out all the old superstitions; and what remains is Vedantism. There is a beautiful Sanskrit poem in which the sage says to himself: "Why weepest thou, my friend? There is no fear nor death for thee. Why weepest thou? There is no misery for thee, for thou art like the infinite blue sky, unchangeable in thy nature. Clouds of all colours come before it, play for a moment, and pass away; it is the same sky. Thou hast only to drive away the clouds."

We have to open the gates and clear the way. The water will rush in and fill in by its own nature, because it is there already.

Man is a good deal conscious, partly unconscious, and there is a possibility of getting beyond consciousness. It is only when we become men that we can go beyond all reason. The words higher or lower can be used only in the phenomenal world. To say them of the noumenal world is simply contradictory, because there is no differentiation there. Man-manifestation is the highest in the phenomenal world. The Vedantist says he is higher than the Devas. The gods will all have to die and will become men again, and in the man-body alone they will become perfect.

It is true that we create a system, but we have to admit that it is not perfect, because the reality must be beyond all systems. We are ready to compare it with other systems and are ready to show that this is the only rational system that can be; but it is not perfect, because reason is not perfect. It is, however, the only possible rational system that the human mind can conceive.

It is true to a certain extent that a system must disseminate itself to be strong. No system has disseminated itself so much as the Vedanta. It is the personal contact that teaches even now. A mass of reading does not make men; those who were real men were made so by personal contact. It is true that there are very few of these real men, but they will increase. Yet you cannot believe that there will come a day when we shall all be philosophers. We do not believe that there will come a time when there will be all happiness and no unhappiness.

Now and then we know a moment of supreme bliss, when we ask nothing, give nothing, know nothing but bliss. Then it passes, and we again see the panorama of the universe moving before us; and we know that it is but a mosaic work set upon God, who is the background of all things.

The Vedanta teaches that Nirvâna can be attained here and now, that we do not have to wait for death to reach it. Nirvana is the realisation of the Self; and after having once known that, if only for an instant, never again can one be deluded by the mirage of personality. Having eyes, we must see the apparent, but all the time we know what it is; we have found out its true nature. It is the screen that hides the Self, which is unchanging. The screen opens, and we find the Self behind it. All change is in the screen. In the saint the screen is thin, and the reality can almost shine through. In the sinner the screen is thick, and we are liable to lose sight of the truth that the Atman is there, as well as behind the saint's screen. When the screen is wholly removed, we find it really never existed—that we were the Atman and nothing else, even the screen is forgotten.

The two phases of this distinction in life are—first, that the man who knows the real Self, will not be affected by anything; secondly, that that man alone can do good to the world. That man alone will have seen the real motive of doing good to others, because there is only one, it cannot be called egoistic, because that would be differentiation. It is the only selflessness. It is the perception of the universal, not of the individual. Every case of love and sympathy is an assertion of this universal. "Not I, but thou." Help another because you are in him and he is in you, is the philosophical way of putting it. The real Vedantist alone will give up his life for a fellow-man without any compunction, because he knows he will not die. As long as there is one insect left in the world, he is living; as long as one mouth eats, he eats. So he goes on doing good to others; and is never hindered by the modern ideas of caring for the body. When a man reaches this point of abnegation, he goes beyond the moral struggle, beyond everything. He sees in the most learned priest, in the cow, in the dog, in the most miserable places, neither the learned man, nor the cow, nor the dog, nor the miserable place, but the same divinity manifesting itself in them all. He alone is the happy man; and the man who has acquired that sameness has, even in this life, conquered all existence. God is pure; therefore such a man is said to be living in God. Jesus says, "Before Abraham was, I am." That means that Jesus and others like him are free spirits; and Jesus of Nazareth took human form, not by the compulsion of his past actions, but just to do good to mankind. It is not that when a man becomes free, he will stop and become a dead lump; but he will be more active than any other being, because every other being acts only under compulsion, he alone through freedom.

If we are inseparable from God, have we no individuality? Oh, yes: that is God. Our individuality is God. This is not the individuality you have now; you are coming towards that. Individuality means what cannot be divided. How can you call this individuality? One hour you are thinking one way, and the next hour another way, and two hours after, another way. Individuality is that which changes not—is beyond all things, changeless. It would be tremendously dangerous for this state to remain in eternity, because then the thief would always remain a thief and the blackguard a blackguard. If a baby died, he would have to remain a baby. The real individuality is that which never changes and will never change; and that is the God within us.

Vedantism is an expansive ocean on the surface of which a man-of-war could be near a catamaran. So in the Vedantic ocean a real Yogi can be by the side of an idolater or even an atheist. What is more, in the Vedantic ocean, the Hindu, Mohammedan, Christian, and Parsee are all one, all children of the Almighty God.

LAW AND FREEDOM

The struggle never had meaning for the man who is free. But for us it has a meaning, because it is name-and-form that creates the world.

We have a place for struggle in the Vedanta, but not for fear. All fears will vanish when you begin to assert your own nature. If you think that you are bound, bound you will remain. If you think you are free, free you will be.

That sort of freedom which we can feel when we are yet in the phenomenal is a glimpse of the real but not yet the real.

I disagree with the idea that freedom is obedience to the laws of nature. I do not understand what it means. According to the history of human progress, it is disobedience to nature that has constituted that progress. It may be said that the conquest of lower laws was through the higher. But even there, the conquering mind was only trying to be free; and as soon as it found that the struggle was also through law, it wanted to conquer that also. So the ideal was freedom in every case. The trees never disobey law. I never saw a cow steal. An oyster never told a lie. Yet they are not greater than man. This life is a tremendous assertion of freedom; and this obedience to law, carried far enough, would make us simply matter—either in society, or in politics, or in religion. Too many laws are a sure sign of death. Wherever in any society there are too many laws, it is a sure sign that that society will soon die. If you study the characteristics of India, you will find that no nation possesses so many laws as the Hindus, and national death is the result. But the Hindus had one peculiar idea—they never made any doctrines or dogmas in religion; and the latter has had the greatest growth. Eternal law cannot be freedom, because to say that the eternal is inside law is to limit it.

There is no purpose in view with God, because if there were some purpose, He would be nothing better than a man. Why should He need any purpose? If He had any, He would be bound by it. There would be something besides Him which was greater. For instance, the carpet-weaver makes a piece of carpet. The idea was outside of him, something greater. Now where is the idea to which God would adjust Himself? Just as the greatest emperors sometimes play with dolls, so He is playing with this nature; and what we call law is this. We call it law, because we can see only little bits which run smoothly. All our ideas of law are within the little bit. It is nonsense to say that law is infinite, that throughout all time stones will fall. If all reason be based upon experience, who was there to see if stones fell five millions of years ago? So law is not constitutional in man. It is a scientific assertion as to man that where we begin, there we end. As a matter of fact, we get gradually outside of law, until we get out altogether, but with the added experience of a whole life. In God and freedom we began, and freedom and God will be the end. These laws are in the middle state through which we have to pass. Our Vedanta is the assertion of freedom always. The very idea of law will frighten the Vedantist; and eternal law is a very dreadful thing for him, because there would be no escape. If there is to be an eternal law binding him all the time, where is the difference between him and a blade of grass? We do not believe in that abstract idea of law.

We say that it is freedom that we are to seek, and that that freedom is God. It is the same happiness as in everything else; but when man seeks it in something which is finite, he gets only a spark of it. The thief when he steals gets the same happiness as the man who finds it in God; but the thief gets only a little spark with a mass of misery. The real happiness is God.

Love is God, freedom is God; and everything that is bondage is not God.

Man has freedom already, but he will have to discover it. He has it, but every moment forgets it. That discovering, consciously or unconsciously, is the whole life of every one. But the difference between the sage and the ignorant man is that one does it consciously and the other unconsciously. Every one is struggling for freedom—from the atom to the star. The ignorant man is satisfied if he can get freedom within a certain limit—if he can get rid of the bondage of hunger or of being thirsty. But that sage feels that there is a stronger bondage which has to be thrown off. He would not consider the freedom of the Red Indian as freedom at all.

According to our philosophers, freedom is the goal. Knowledge cannot be the goal, because knowledge is a compound. It is a compound of power and freedom, and it is freedom alone that is desirable. That is what men struggle after. Simply the possession of power would not be knowledge. For instance, a scientist can send an electric shock to a distance of some miles; but nature can send it to an unlimited distance. Why do we not build statues to nature then? It is not law that we want but ability to break law. We want to be outlaws. If you are bound by laws, you will be a lump of clay. Whether you are beyond law or not is not the question; but the thought that we are beyond law—upon that is based the whole history of humanity. For instance, a man lives in a forest, and never has had any education or knowledge. He sees a stone falling down—a natural phenomenon happening— and he thinks it is freedom. He thinks it has a soul, and the central idea in that is freedom. But as soon as he knows that it must fall, he calls it nature—dead, mechanical action. I may or may not go into the street. In that is my glory as a man. If I am sure that I must go there, I give myself up and become a machine. Nature with its infinite power is only a machine; freedom alone constitutes sentient life.

The Vedanta says that the idea of the man in the forest is the right one; his glimpse is right, but the explanation is wrong. He holds to this nature as freedom and not as governed by law. Only after all this human experience we will come back to think the same, but in a more philosophical sense. For instance, I want to go out into the street. I get the impulse of my will, and then I stop; and in the time that intervenes between the will and going into the street, I am working uniformly. Uniformity of action is what we call law. This uniformity of my actions, I find, is broken into very short periods, and so I do not call my actions under law. I work through freedom. I walk for five minutes; but before those five minutes of walking, which are uniform, there was the action of the will, which gave the impulse to walk. Therefore man says he is free, because all his actions can be cut up into small periods; and although there is sameness in the small periods, beyond the period there is not the same sameness. In this perception of non-uniformity is the idea of freedom. In nature we see only very large periods of uniformity; but the beginning and end must be free impulses. The impulse of freedom was given just at the beginning, and that has rolled on; but this, compared with our periods, is much longer. We find by analysis on philosophic grounds that we are not free. But there will remain this factor, this consciousness that I am free. What we have to explain is, how that comes. We will find that we have these two impulsions in us. Our reason tells us that all our actions are caused, and at the same time, with every impulse we are asserting our freedom. The solution of the Vedanta is that there is freedom inside—that the soul is really free—but that that soul's actions are percolating through body and mind, which are not free.

As soon as we react, we become slaves. A man blames me, and I immediately react in the form of anger. A little vibration which he created made me a slave. So we have to demonstrate our freedom. They alone are the sages who see in the highest, most learned man, or the lowest animal, or the worst and most wicked of mankind, neither a man nor a sage nor an animal, but the same God in all of them. Even in this life they have conquered relativity, and have taken a firm stand upon this equality. God is pure, the same to all. Therefore such a sage would be a living God. This is the goal towards which we are going; and every form of worship, every action of mankind, is a method of attaining to it. The man who wants money is striving for freedom —to get rid of the bondage of poverty. Every action of man is worship, because the idea is to attain to freedom, and all action, directly or indirectly, tends to that. Only, those actions that deter are to be avoided. The whole universe is worshipping, consciously or unconsciously; only it does not know that even while it is cursing, it is in another form worshipping the same God it is cursing, because those who are cursing are also struggling for freedom. They never think that in reacting from a thing they are making themselves slaves to it. It is hard to kick against the pricks.

If we could get rid of the belief in our limitations, it would be possible for us to do everything just now. It is only a question of time. If that is so, add power, and so diminish time. Remember the case of the professor who learnt the secret of the development of marble and who made marble in twelve years, while it took nature centuries.

THE GOAL AND METHODS OF REALISATION

The greatest misfortune to befall the world would be if all mankind were to recognise and accept but one religion, one universal form of worship, one standard of morality. This would be the death-blow to all religious and spiritual progress. Instead of trying to hasten this disastrous event by inducing persons, through good or evil methods, to conform to our own highest ideal of truth, we ought rather to endeavour to remove all obstacles which prevent men from developing in accordance with their own highest ideals, and thus make their attempt vain to establish one universal religion.

The ultimate goal of all mankind, the aim and end of all religions, is but one—re-union with God, or, what amounts to the same, with the divinity which is every man's true nature. But while the aim is one, the method of attaining may vary with the different temperaments of men.

Both the goal and the methods employed for reaching it are called Yoga, a word derived from the same Sanskrit root as the English "yoke", meaning "to join", to join us to our reality, God. There are various such Yogas, or methods of union—but the chief ones are—Karma-Yoga, Bhakti-Yoga, Râja-Yoga, and Jnâna-Yoga.

Every man must develop according to his own nature. As every science has its methods, so has every religion. The methods of attaining the end of religion are called Yoga by us, and the different forms of Yoga that we teach, are adapted to the different natures and temperaments of men. We classify them in the following way, under four heads:

1. Karma-Yoga—The manner in which a man realises his own divinity through works and duty.
2. Bhakti-Yoga—The realisation of the divinity through devotion to, and love of, a Personal God.
3. Raja-Yoga—The realisation of the divinity through the control of mind.
4. Jnana-Yoga—The realisation of a man's own divinity through knowledge.

These are all different roads leading to the same centre—God. Indeed, the varieties of religious belief are an advantage, since all faiths are good,so far as they encourage man to lead a religious life. The more sects there are, the more opportunities there are for making successful appeals to the divine instinct in all men.

WORLD-WIDE UNITY

Speaking of the world-wide unity, before the Oak Beach Christian Unity, Swami Vivekananda said:All religions are, at the bottom, alike. This is so, although the Christian Church, like the Pharisee in the parable, thanks God that it alone is right and thinks that all other religions are wrong and in need of Christian light. Christianity must become tolerant before the world will be willing to unite with the Christian Church in a common charity. God has not left Himself without a witness in any heart, and men, especially men who follow Jesus Christ, should be willing to admit this. In fact, Jesus Christ was willing to admit every good man to the family of God. It is not the man who believes a certain something, but the man who does the will of the Father in heaven, who is right. On this basis—being right and doing right—the whole world can unite.

THE AIM OF RAJA-YOGA

Yoga has essentially to do with the meditative side of religion, rather than the ethical side, though, of necessity, a little of the latter has to be considered. Men and women are growing to desire more than mere revelation, so called. They want facts in their own consciousness. Only through experience can there be any reality in religion. Spiritual facts are to be gathered mostly from the superconscious state of mind. Let us put ourselves into the same condition as did those who claim to have had special experiences; then if we have similar experiences, they become facts for us. We can see all that another has seen; a thing that happened once can happen again, nay, must, under the same circumstances. Raja-Yoga teaches us how to reach the superconscious state. All the great religions recognise this state in some form; but in India, special attention is paid to this side of religion. In the beginning, some mechanical means may help us to acquire this state; but mechanical means alone can never accomplish much. Certain positions, certain modes of breathing, help to harmonise and concentrate the mind, but with these must go purity and strong desire for God, or realisation. The attempt to sit down and fix the mind on one idea and hold it there will prove to most people that there is some need for help to enable them to do this successfully. The mind has to be gradually and systematically brought under control. The will has to be strengthened by slow, continuous, and persevering drill. This is no child's play, no fad to be tried one day and discarded the next. It is a life's work; and the end to be attained is well worth all that it can cost us to reach it; being nothing less than the realisation of our absolute oneness with the Divine. Surely, with this end in view, and with the knowledge that we can certainly succeed, no price can be too great to pay.

RELIGION AND SCIENCE

Experience is the only source of knowledge. In the world, religion is the only source where there is no surety, because it is not taught as a science of experience. This should not be. There is always, however, a small group of men who teach religion from experience. They are called mystics, and these mystics in every religion speak the same tongue and teach the same truth. This is the real science of religion. As mathematics in every part of the world does not differ, so the mystics do not differ. They are all similarly constituted and similarly situated. Their experience is the same; and this becomes law.

In the church, religionists first learn a religion, then begin to practise it; they do not take experience as the basis of their belief. But the mystic starts out in search of truth, experiences it first, and then formulates his creed. The church takes the experience of others; the mystic has his own experience. The church goes from the outside in; the mystic goes from the inside out.

Religion deals with the truths of the metaphysical world just as chemistry and the other natural sciences deal with the truths of the physical world. The book one must read to learn chemistry is the book of nature. The book from which to learn religion is your own mind and heart. The sage is often ignorant of physical science, because he reads the wrong book—the book within; and the scientist is too often ignorant of religion, because he too reads the wrong book—the book without.

All science has its particular methods; so has the science of religion. It has more methods also, because it has more material to work upon. The human mind is not homogeneous like the external world. According to the different nature, there must be different methods. As some special sense predominates in a person—one person will see most, another will hear most—so there is a predominant mental sense; and through this gate must each reach his own mind. Yet through all minds runs a unity, and there is a science which may be applied to all. This science of religion is based on the analysis of the human soul. It has no creed.

No one form of religion will do for all. Each is a pearl on a string. We must be particular above all else to find individuality in each. No man is born to any religion; he has a religion in his own soul. Any system which seeks to destroy individuality is in the long run disastrous. Each life has a current running though it, and this current will eventually take it to God. The end and aim of all religions is to realise God. The greatest of all training is to worship God alone. If each man chose his own ideal and stuck to it, all religious controversy would vanish.

RELIGION IS REALISATION

The greatest name man ever gave to God is Truth. Truth is the fruit of realisation; therefore seek it within the soul. Get away from all books and forms and let your soul see its Self. "We are deluded and maddened by books", Shri Krishna declares. Be beyond the dualities of nature. The moment you think creed and form and ceremony the "be-all" and "end-all", then you are in bondage. Take part in them to help others, but take care they do not become a bondage. Religion is one, but its application must be various. Let each one, therefore, give his message; but find not the defects in other religions. You must come out from all form if you would see the Light. Drink deep of the nectar of the knowledge of God. The man who realises, "I am He", though clad in rags, is happy. Go forth into the Eternal and come back with eternal energy. The slave goes out to search for truth; he comes back free.

RELIGION IS SELF-ABNEGATION

One cannot divide the rights of the universe. To talk of "right" implies limitation. It is not "right" but "responsibility". Each is responsible for the evil anywhere in the world. No one can separate himself from his brother. All that unites with the universal is virtue; all that separates is sin. You are a part of the Infinite. This is your nature. Hence you are your brother's keeper.

The first end of life is knowledge; the second end of life is happiness. Knowledge and happiness lead to freedom. But not one can attain liberty until every being (ant or dog) has liberty. Not one can be happy until all are happy. When you hurt anyone you hurt yourself, for you and your brother are one. He is indeed a Yogi who sees himself in the whole universe and the whole universe in himself. Self-sacrifice, not self-assertion, is the law of the highest universe. The world is so evil because Jesus' teaching, "Resist not evil", has never been tried. Selflessness alone will solve the problem. Religion comes with intense self-sacrifice. Desire nothing for yourself. Do all for others. This is to live and move and have your being in God.

UNSELFISH WORK IS TRUE RENUNCIATION

This world is not for cowards. Do not try to fly. Look not for success or failure. Join yourself to the perfectly unselfish will and work on. Know that the mind which is born to succeed joins itself to a determined will and perseveres. You have the right to work, but do not become so degenerate as to look for results. Work incessantly, but see something behind the work. Even good deeds can find a man in great bondage. Therefore be not bound by good deeds or by desire for name and fame. Those who know this secret pass beyond this round of birth and death and become immortal.

The ordinary Sannyasin gives up the world, goes out, and thinks of God. The real Sannyasin lives in the world, but is not of it. Those who deny themselves, live in the forest, and chew the cud of unsatisfied desires are not true renouncers. Live in the midst of the battle of life. Anyone can keep calm in a cave or when asleep. Stand in the whirl and madness of action and reach the Centre. If you have found the Centre, you cannot be moved.

FREEDOM OF THE SELF

As we cannot know except through effects that we have eyes, so we cannot see the Self except by Its effects. It cannot be brought down to the low plane of sense-perception. It is the condition of everything in the universe, though Itself unconditioned. When we know that we are the Self, then we are free. The Self can never change. It cannot be acted on by a cause, because It is Itself the cause. It is self-caused. If we can find in ourself something that is not acted on by any cause, then we have known the Self.

Freedom is inseparably connected with immortality. To be free one must be above the laws of nature. Law exists so long as we are ignorant. When knowledge comes, then we find that law nothing but freedom in ourselves. The will can never be free, because it is the slave of cause and effect. But the "I" behind the will is free; and this is the Self. "I am free"—that is the basis on which to build and live. And freedom means immortality.

NOTES ON VEDANTA

The cardinal features of the Hindu religion are founded on the meditative and speculative philosophy and on the ethical teachings contained in the various books of the Vedas, which assert that the universe is infinite in space and eternal in duration. It never had a beginning, and it never will have an end. Innumerable have been the manifestations of the power of the Spirit in the realm of matter, of the force of the Infinite in the domain of the finite, but the Infinite Itself is self - existent, eternal, and unchangeable. The passage of time makes no mark whatever on the dial of eternity. In its supersensuous region, which cannot be comprehended at all by the human understanding, there is no past and there is no future.

The Vedas teach that the soul of man is immortal. The body is subject to the law of growth and decay; what grows must of necessity decay. But the indwelling spirit is related to the infinite and eternal life; it never had a beginning, and it will never have an end. One of the chief distinctions between the Vedic and the Christian religion is that the Christian religion teaches that each human soul had its beginning at its birth into this world; whereas the Vedic religion asserts that the spirit of man is an emanation of the Eternal Being and had no more a beginning than God Himself. Innumerable have been and will be its manifestations in its passage from one personality to another, subject to the great law of spiritual evolution, until it reaches perfection, when there is no more change.

HINDU AND GREEK

Three mountains stand as typical of progress — the Himalayas of Indo-aryan, Sinai of Hebrew, and Olympus of Greek civilisation. When the Aryans reached India, they found the climate so hot that they could not work incessantly, so they began to think; thus they became introspective and developed religion. They discovered that there was no limit to the power of mind; they therefore sought to master that; and through it they learnt that there was something infinite coiled up in the frame we call man, which was seeking to become kinetic. To evolve this became their chief aim. Another branch of the Aryans went into the smaller and more picturesque country of Greece, where the climate and natural conditions were more favorable; so their activity turned outwards, and they developed the external arts and outward liberty. The Greek sought political liberty. The Hindu has always sought spiritual liberty. Both are one - sided. The Indian cares not enough for national protection or patriotism, he will defend only his religion; while with the Greek and in Europe (where the Greek civilisation finds its continuation) the country comes first. To care only for spiritual liberty and not for social liberty is a defect, but the opposite is a still greater defect. Liberty of both soul and body is to be striven for.

THOUGHTS ON THE VEDAS AND UPANISHADS

The Vedic sacrificial altar was the origin of Geometry.

The invocation of the Devas, or bright ones, was the basis of worship. The idea is that one invoked is helped and helps.

Hymns are not only words of praise but words of power, being pronounced with the right attitude of mind.

Heaven are only other states of existence with added senses and heightened powers.

All higher bodies also are subject to disintegration as is the physical. Death comes to all forms of bodies in this and other lives. Devas are also mortal and can only give enjoyment.

Behind all Devas there is the Unit Being—god, as behind this body there is something higher that feels and sees.

The powers of creation, preservation, and destruction of the Universe, and the attributes, such as omnipresence, omniscience, and omnipotence, make God of gods. "Hear ye children of Immortality! Hear ye Devas who live in higher spheres!" (Shvetashvatara, II.5). "I have found out a ray beyond all darkness, beyond all doubt. I have found the Ancient One" (ibid. III.8). The way to this is contained in the Upanishads.

On earth we die. In heaven we die. In the highest heaven we die. It is only when we reach God that we attain life and become immortal.

The Upanisads treat of this alone. The path of the Upanishads is the pure path. Many manners, customs, and local allusions cannot be understood today. Through them, however, truth becomes clear. Heavens and Earth are all thrown off in order to come to Light.

The Upanisads declare:

"He the Lord has interpenetrated the universe. It is all His."

"He the Omnipresent, the One without a second, the One without a body, pure, the great poet of the universe, whose metre is the suns and stars, is giving to each what he deserves" (Isha Upanishad, 8, adapted).

"They are groping in utter darkness who try to reach the Light by ceremonials. And they who think this nature is all are in darkness. They who wish to come out of nature through this thought are groping in still deeper darkness" (Isha, 9).

Are then ceremonials bad? No, they will benefit those who are coming on.

In one of the Upanishads (i.e. Katha) this question is asked by Nachiketa, a youth: "Some say of a dead man, he is gone; others, he is still living. You are Yama, Death.

You know the truth; do answer me." Yama replied, "Even the Devas, many of them, know not—much less men. Boy, do not ask of me this answer." But Nachiketa persists. Yama again replies, "The enjoyments of the gods, even these I offer you. Do not insist upon your query." But Nachiketa was firm as a rock. Then the god of death said, "My boy, you have declined, for the third time, wealth, power, long life, fame, family. You are brave enough to ask the highest truth. I will teach you. There are two ways, one of truth, one of enjoyment. You have choosen the former."

Now note here the conditions of imparting the truth. First, the purity—a boy, a pure, unclouded soul, asking the secret of the universe. Second, that he must take truth for truth's sake alone. Until the truth has come through one who has had realisation, from one who has perceived it himself, it cannot become fruitful. Books cannot give it, argument cannot establish it. Truth comes unto him who knows the secret of it.

After you have received it, be quiet. Be not ruffled by vain argument. Come to your own realisation. You alone can do it.

Neither happiness nor misery, vice nor virtue, knowledge nor non - knowledge is it. You must realise it. How can I describe it to you?

He who cries out with his whole heart, "O Lord, I want but Thee"—to him the Lord reveals Himself. Be pure, be calm; the mind when ruffled cannot reflect the Lord. "He whom the Vedas declare, He, to reach whom, we serve with prayer and sacrifice, Om is the sacred name of that indescribable One. This word is the holiest of all words. He who knows the secret of this word receives that which he desires." Take refuge in this word. Whoso takes refuge in this word, to him the way opens.

ON RAJA-YOGA

The first stage of Yoga is Yama.

To master Yama five things are necessary:

1. Non-injuring any being by thought, word, and deed.
2. Speaking the truth in thought, word, and deed.
3. Non-covetousness in thought, word, and deed.
4. Perfect chastity in thought, word, and deed.
5. Perfect sinlessness in thought, word, and deed.

Holiness is the greatest power. Everything else quails before it. Then comes Asana, or posture, of a devotee. The seat must be firm, the head, ribs, and body in a straight line, erect. Say to yourself that you are firmly seated, and that nothing can move you. Then mention the perfection of the body, bit by bit, from head to foot. Think of it as being clear as crystal, and as a perfect vessel to sail over the sea of life.

Pray to God and to all the prophets and saviors of the world and holy spirits in the universe to help you.

Then for half an hour practice Pranayama or the suspending, restraining, and controlling of the breath, mentally repeating the word Om as you inhale and exhale the breath. Words charged with spirit have wonderful power.

The other stages of Yoga are: (1) Pratyahara or the restraint of the organs of sense from all outward things, and directing them entirely to mental impressions; (2) Dharana or steadfast concentration; (3) Dhyana or meditation; (4) Samadhi or abstract meditation. It is the highest and last stage of Yoga. Samadhi is perfect absorption of thought into the Supreme Spirit, when one realises, "I and my Father are one."

Do one thing at a time and while doing it put your whole soul into it to the exclusion of all else.

ON BHAKTI-YOGA

Bhakti-Yoga is the path of systematised devotion for the attainment of union with the Absolute. It is the easiest and surest path to religion or realisation.

Love to God is the one essential to be perfect in this path.

There are five stages of love.

- First, man wants help and has a little fear.
- Second, when God is seen as Father.
- Third, when God is seen as Mother. Then all women are looked upon as reflections of the Mother-god. With the idea of Mother-god real love begins.
- Fourth, love for love's sake. Love for love's sake transcends all qualities.
- Fifth, love in Divine-union. It leads to oneness or super-consciousness.

God is both Personal and Impersonal as we are personal and impersonal.

Prayer and praise are the first means of growth. Repeating the names of God has wonderful power.

Mantra is a special word, or sacred text, or name of God choosen by the Guru for repetition and reflection by the disciple. The disciple must concentrate on a personality for prayer and praise, and that is his Ishta.

These words (Mantras) are not sounds of words but God Himself, and we have them within us. Think of Him, speak of Him. No desire for the world! Buddhas's Sermon on the Mount was, "As thou thinkest, so art thou."

After attaining superconsiousness the Bhakta descends again to love and worship.

Pure love has no motive. It has nothing to gain.

After prayer and praise comes meditation. Then comes reflection on the name and on the Ishta of the individual.

Pray that that manifestation which is our Father, our Mother, may cut our bonds.

Pray, "Take us by the hand as a father takes his son, and leave us not."

Pray, "I do not want wealth or beauty, this world or another, but Thee, O God! Lord! I have become weary. Oh, take me by the hand, Lord, I take shelter with Thee. Make me Thy servant. Be Thou my refuge."

Pray, "Thou our Father, our Mother, our dearest Friend! Thou who bearest this universe, help us to bear the little burden of this our life. Leave us not. Let us never be separated from Thee. Let us always dwell in Thee."

When love to God is revealed and is all, this world appears like a drop.

Pass from non-existence to existence, from darkness to light.

ON JNANA-YOGA

First, meditation should be of a negative nature. Think away everything. Analyse everything that comes in the mind by the sheer action of the will.

Next, assert what we really are—existence, knowledge, and bliss—being, knowing, and loving.

Meditation is the means of unification of the subject and object. Meditate:

Above, it is full of me; below, it is full of me; in the middle, it is full of me. I am in all beings, and all beings are in me. Om Tat Sat, I am It. I am existence above mind. I and the one spirit of the universe. I am neither pleasure nor pain.

The body drinks, eats, and so on. I am not the body. I am not mind. I am He.

I am the witness. I look on. When health comes I am the witness. When disease comes I am the witness.

I am Existence, Knowledge, Bliss.

I am the essence and nectar of knowledge. Through eternity I change not. I am calm, resplendent, and unchanging.

THE REALITY AND SHADOW

That which differentiates one thing from another is time, space, and causation.

The differentiation is in the form, not in the substance. You may destroy the form and it disappears for ever; but the substance remains the same. You can never destroy the substance.

Evolution is in nature, not in the soul—evolution of nature, manifestation of the soul.

Maya is not illusion as it is popularly interpreted. Maya is real, yet it is not real. It is real in that the Real is behind it and gives it its appearance of reality. That which is real in Maya is the Reality in and through Maya. Yet the Reality is never seen ; and hence that which is seen is unreal, and it has no real independent existence of itself, but is dependent upon the Real for its existence.

Maya then is a paradox—real, yet not real, an illusion, yet not an illusion.

He who knows the Real sees in Maya not illusion, but reality. He who knows not the Real sees in Maya illusion and thinks it real.

HOW TO BECOME FREE

All things in nature work according to law. Nothing is excepted. The mind as well as everything in external nature is governed and controlled by law.

Internal and external nature, mind and matter, are in time and space, and are bound by the law of causation.

The freedom of the mind is a delusion. How can the mind be free when it is controlled and bound by law?

The law of Karma is the law of causation.

We must become free. We are free; the work is to know it. We must give up all slavery, all bondage of whatever kind. We must not only give up our bondage to earth and everything and everybody on earth, but also to all ideas of heaven and happiness.

We are bound to earth by desire and also to God, heaven, and the angels. A slave is a slave whether to man, to God, or to angels.

The idea of heaven must pass away. The idea of heaven after death where the good live a life of eternal happiness is a vain dream, without a particle of meaning or sense in it. Wherever there is happiness there must follow unhappiness sometime. Wherever there is pleasure there must be pain. This is absolutely certain, every action has its reaction somehow.

The idea of freedom is the only true idea of salvation—freedom from everything, the senses, whether of pleasure or pain, from good as well as evil.

More than this even, we must be free from death; and to be free from death, we must be free from life. Life is but a dream of death. Where there is life, there will be death; so get away from life if you would be rid of death.

We are ever free if we would only believe it, only have faith enough. You are the soul, free and eternal, ever free, ever blessed. Have faith enough and you will be free in a minute.

Everything in time, space, and causation is bound. The soul is beyond all time, all space, all causation. That which is bound is nature, not the soul.

Therefore proclaim your freedom and be what you are—ever free, ever blessed.

Time, space, and causation we call Maya.

SOUL AND GOD

Anything that is in space has form. Space itself has form. Either you are in space, or space is in you. The soul is beyond all space. Space is in the soul, not the soul in space.

Form is confined to time and space and is bound by the law of causation. All time is in us, we are not in time. As the soul is not in time and space, all time and space are within the soul. The soul is therefore omnipresent.

Our idea of God is the reflection of ourselves.

Old Persian and Sanskrit have affinities.

The primitive idea of God was identifying God with different forms of nature—nature-worship. The next stage was the tribal God. The next stage, the worship of kings.

The idea of God in heaven is predominant in all nations except in India. The idea is very crude.

The idea of the continuity of life is foolish. We can never get rid of death until we get rid of life.

THE GOAL

Dualism recognises God and nature to be eternally separate:

the universe and nature eternally dependent upon God.

The extreme monists make no such distinction. In the last analysis, they claim, all is God: the universe becomes lost in God; God is the eternal life of the universe.

With them infinite and finite are mere terms. The universe, nature, etc. exist by virtue of differentiation. Nature is itself differentiation.

Such questions as, "Why did God create the universe?" "Why did the All-perfect create the imperfect?" etc., can never be answered, because such questions are logical absurdities. Reason exists in nature; beyond nature it has no existence. God is omnipotent, hence to ask why He did so and so is to limit Him; for it implies that there is a purpose in His creating the universe. If He has a purpose, it must be a means to an end, and this would mean that He could not have the end without the means. The questions, why and wherefore, can only be asked of something which depends upon something else.

ON PROOF OF RELIGION

The great question about religion is: What makes it so unscientific? If religion is a science, why is it not as certain as other sciences? All beliefs in God, heaven, etc., are mere conjectures, mere beliefs. There seems to be nothing certain about it. Our ideas concerning religion are changing all the time. The mind is in a constant state of flux.

Is man a soul, an unchanging substance, or is he a constantly changing quantity? All religions, except primitive Buddhism, believe that man is a soul, an identity, a unit that never dies but is immortal.

The primitive Buddhists believe that man is a constantly changing quantity, and that his consciousness consists in an almost infinite succession of incalculably rapid changes, each change, as it were, being unconnected with the others, standing alone, thus precluding the theory of the law of sequence or causation.

If there is a unit, there is a substance. A unit is always simple. A simple is not a compound of anything. It does not depend on anything else. It stands alone and is immortal.

Primitive Buddhists contend that everything is unconnected; nothing is a unit; and that the theory of man being a unit is a mere belief and cannot be proved.

Now the great question is : Is man a unit, or is he a constantly changing mass?

There is but one way to prove this, to answer this question. Stop the gyrations of the mind, and the theory that a man is a unit, a simple, will be demonstrated. All changes are in me, in the Chitta, the mind-substance. I am not the changes. If I were, I could not stop them.

Everyone is trying to make himself and everybody else believe that this world is all very fine, that he is perfectly happy. But when man stops to question his motives in life, he will see that the reason he is struggling after this and that is because he

cannot help himself. He must move on. He cannot stop, so he tries to make himself believe that he really wants this and that. The one who actually succeeds in making himself believe that he is having a good time is the man of splendid physical health. This man responds to his desires instantly, without question. He acts in response to that power within him, urging him on without a thought, as though he acted because he wanted to. But when he has been knocked about a good deal by nature, when he has received a good many wounds and bruises, he begins to question the meaning of all this; and as he gets hurt more and thinks more, he sees that he is urged on by a power beyond his control and that he acts simply because he must. Then he begins to rebel, and the battle begins.

Now if there is a way out of all this trouble, it is within ourselves. We are always trying to realise the Reality. Instinctively we are always trying to do that. It is creation in the human soul that covers up God; that is why there is so much difference in God-ideals. Only when creation stops can we find the Absolute. The Absolute is in the soul, not in creation. So by stopping creation, we come to know the Absolute. When we think of ourselves, we think of the body; and when we think of God, we think of Him as body. To stop the gyrations of the mind, so that the soul may become manifested, is the work. Training begins with the body. Breathing trains the body, gets it into a harmonious condition. The object of the breathing exercises is to attain meditation and concentration. If you can get absolutely still for just one moment, you have reached the goal. The mind may go on working after that; but it will never be the same mind again. You will know yourself as you are—your true Self. Still the mind but for one moment, and the truth of your real nature will flash upon you, and freedom is at hand: no more bondage after that. This follows from the theory that if you can know an instant of time, you know all time, as the whole is the rapid succession of one. Master the one, know thoroughly one instant—and freedom is reached.

All religions believe in God and the soul except the primitive Buddhist. The modern Buddhists believe in God and the soul. Among the primitive Buddhists are the Burmese, Siamese, Chinese, etc.

Arnold's book, *The Light of Asia*, represents more of Vedantism than Buddhism.

THE DESIGN THEORY

The idea that nature in all her orderly arrangements shows design on the part of the Creator of the universe is good as a kindergarten teaching to show the beauty, power, and glory of God, in order to lead children in religion up to a philosophical conception of God; but apart from that, it is not good, and perfectly illogical. As a philosophical idea, it is entirely without foundation, if God is taken to be omnipotent.

If nature shows the power of God in creating the universe, (then) to have a design in so doing also shows His weakness. If God is omnipotent, He needs no design, no scheme, to do anything. He has but to will it, and it is done. No question, no scheme, no plan, of God in nature.

The material universe is the result of the limited consciousness of man. When man becomes conscious of his divinity, all matter, all nature, as we know it, will cease to exist.

The material world, as such, has no place in the consciousness of the All-presence as a necessity of any end. If it had, God would be limited by the universe. To say that nature exists by His permission is not to say that it exists as a necessity for Him to make man perfect, or for any other reason.

It is a creation for man's necessity, not God's. There is no scheme of God in the plan of the universe. How could there be any if He is omnipotent? Why should He have need of a plan, or a scheme, or a reason to do anything? To say that He has is to limit Him and to rob Him of His character of omnipotence.

For instance, if you came to a very wide river, so wide that you could not get across it except by building a bridge, the very fact that you would have to build the bridge to get across the river would show your limitation, would show your weakness, even if the ability to build the bridge did show your strength. If you were not limited but could just fly or jump across, you would not be under the necessity of building a bridge; and to build the bridge just to exhibit your power to do so would show your weakness again by showing your vanity, more than it would show anything else.

Monism and dualism are essentially the same. The difference consists in the expression. As the dualists hold the Father and Son to be two, the monists hold them to be really one. Dualism is in nature, in manifestation, and monism is pure spirituality in the essence.

The idea of renunciation and sacrifice is in all religions as a means to reach God.

SPIRIT AND NATURE

Religion is the realisation of Spirit as Spirit; not Spirit as matter.

Religion is a growth. Each one must experience it himself. The Christians believe that Jesus Christ died to save man. With you it is belief in a doctrine, and this belief constitutes your salvation. With us doctrine has nothing whatever to do with salvation. Each one may believe in whatever doctrine he likes; or in no doctrine.

What difference does it make to you whether Jesus Christ lived at a certain time or not? What has it to do with you that Moses saw God in the burning bush? The fact that Moses saw God in the burning bush does not constitute your seeing Him, does it? If it does, then the fact that Moses ate is enough for you; you ought to stop eating. One is just as sensible as the other. Records of great spiritual men of the past do us no good whatever except that they urge us onward to do the same, to experience religion ourselves. Whatever Christ or Moses or anybody else did does not help us in the least, except to urge us on.

Each one has a special nature peculiar to himself, which he must follow and through which he will find his way to freedom. Your teacher should be able to tell you what your particular path in nature is and to put you in it. He should know by your face where you belong and should be able to indicate it to you. You should never try to follow another's path, for that is his way, not yours. When that path is found, you have nothing to do but fold your arms, and the tide will carry you to freedom. Therefore when you find it, never swerve from it. You way is the best for you, but that is no sign that it is the best for others.

The truly spiritual see Spirit as Spirit, not as matter. It is Spirit that makes nature move; It is the reality in nature. So action is in nature; not in the Spirit. Spirit is always the same, changeless, eternal. Spirit and matter are in reality the same; but Spirit, as such, never becomes matter; and matter, as such, never becomes Spirit.

The Spirit never acts. Why should it? It merely is, and that is sufficient. It is pure existence absolute and has no need of action.

You are not bound by law. That is in your nature. The mind is in nature and is bound by law. All nature is bound by law, the law of its own action; and this law can never be broken. If you could break a law of nature, all nature would come to an end in an instant. There would be no more nature. He who attains freedom breaks the law of nature, and for him nature fades away and has no more power over him. Each one will break the law but once and for ever; and that will end his trouble with nature.

Governments, societies, etc. are comparative evils. All societies are based on bad generalisation. The moment you form yourselves into an organisation, you begin to hate everybody outside of that organisation. When you join an organisation, you are putting bounds upon yourself, you are limiting your own freedom. The greatest goodness is the highest freedom. Our aim should be to allow the individual to move towards this freedom. More of goodness, less of artificial laws. Such laws are not laws at all. If it were a law, it could not be broken. The fact that these so-called laws are broken, shows clearly that they are not laws. A law is that which cannot be broken.

Whenever you suppress a thought, it is simply pressed down out of sight, in a coil like a spring, only to spring out again at a moment's notice, with all the pent-up force resulting from the suppression, and do in a few moments what it would have done in a much longer period.

Every ounce of pleasure brings its pound of pain. It is the same energy that at one time manifests itself as pleasure, at another time as pain. As soon as one set of sensations stops, another begins. But in some cases, in more advanced persons, one may have two, yea, even a hundred different thoughts entering into active operation at the same time.

Mind is action of its own nature. Mind-activity means creation. The thought is followed by the word, and the word by the form. All of this creating will have to stop, both mental and physical, before the mind can reflect the soul.

THE PRACTICE OF RELIGION

At Alameda, Calif., March 18, 1900

We read many books, but that does not bring us knowledge. We may read all the Bibles in the world, but that will not give us religion. Theoretical religion is easy enough to get, any one may get that. What we want is practical religion.

The Christian idea of a practical religion is in doing good works—worldly utility.

What good is utility? Judged from a utilitarian standpoint, religion is a failure. Every hospital is a prayer that more people may come there. What is meant by charity? Charity is not fundamental. It is really helping on the misery of the world, not eradicating it. One looks for name and fame and covers his efforts to obtain them with the enamel of charity and good works. He is working for himself under the pretext of working for others. Every so-called charity is an encouragement of the very evil it claims to operate against.

Men and women go to balls and dance all night in honor of some hospital or other charitable institution, then go home, behave like beasts, and bring devils into the world to fill jails, insane asylums, and hospitals. So it goes on, and it is called good works—building hospital, etc. The ideal of good works is to lessen, or eradicate, the misery of the world. The Yogi says, all misery comes from not being able to control the mind. The Yogi's ideal is freedom from nature. Conquest of nature is his standard of work. The Yogi says that all power is in the soul, and by the controlling of the mind and body one conquers nature by the power of the soul.

Every ounce of muscle in excess of what is beyond the needs of one's physical work is that much less of brain. Do not exercise too hard; it is injurious. The one who does not work hard will live the longest. Eat less food and work less. Store up brain food.

Household work is enough for women.

Do not make the lamp burn fast; let it burn slowly.

Proper diet means simple diet, not highly spiced.

FRAGMENTARY NOTES ON THE RAMAYANA

Worship Him who alone stands by us, whether we are doing good or are doing evil; who never leaves us even; as love never pulls down, as love knows no barter, no selfishness.

Rama was the soul of the old king; but he was a king, and he could not go back on his word. "Wherever Rama goes, there go I", says Lakshmana, the younger brother.

The wife of the elder brother to us Hindus is just like a mother. At last he found Sita, pale and thin, like a bit of the moon that lies low at the foot of the horizon.

Sita was chastity itself; she would never touch the body of another man except that of her husband. "Pure? She is chastity itself", says Rama.

Drama and music are by themselves religion; any song, love song or any song, never mind; if one's whole soul is in that song, he attains salvation, just by that; nothing else he has to do; if a man's whole soul is in that, his soul gets salvation. They say it leads to the same goal.

Wife—the co-religionist. Hundreds of ceremonies the Hindu has to perform, and not one can be performed if he has not a wife. You see the priests tie them up together, and they go round temples and make very great pilgrimages tied together.

Rama gave up his body and joined Sita in the other world.

Sita—the pure, the pure, the all-suffering!

Sita is the name in India for everything that is good, pure, and holy; everything that in woman we call woman.

Sita—the patient, all-suffering, ever-faithful, ever-pure wife! Through all the suffering she had, there was not one harsh word against Rama.

Sita never returned injury.

"Be Sita!"

NOTES TAKEN DOWN IN MADRAS

1892-93

The three essentials of Hinduism are belief in God, in the Vedas as revelation, in the doctrine of Karma and transmigration.

If one studies the Vedas between the lines, one sees a religion of harmony.

One point of difference between Hinduism and other religions is that in Hinduism we pass from truth to truth—from a lower truth to a higher truth—and never from error to truth.

The Vedas should be studied through the eye-glass of evolution. They contain the whole history of the progress of religious consciousness, until religion has reached perfection in unity.

The Vedas are Anadi, eternal. The meaning of the statement is not, as is erroneously supposed by some, that the words of the Vedas are Anadi, but that the spiritual laws inculcated by the Vedas are such. These laws which are immutable and eternal have been discovered at various times by great men or Rishis, though some of them are forgotten now, while others are preserved.

When a number of people from various angles and distances have a look at the sea, each man sees a portion of it according to his horizon. Though each man may say that what he sees is the real sea, all of them speak the truth, for all of them see portions of the same wide expanse. So the religious scriptures, though they seem to contain varying and conflicting statements, speak the truth, for they are all descriptions of that one infinite Reality.

When one sees a mirage for the first time, he mistakes it for a reality, and after vainly trying to quench his thirst in it, learns that it is a mirage. But whenever he sees such a phenomenon in future, in spite of the apparent reality, the idea that he sees a mirage always presents itself to him. So is the world of Maya to a Jivanmukta (the liberated in life).

Some of the Vedic secrets were known to certain families only, as certain powers naturally exist in some families. With the extinction of these families, those secrets have died away.

Vedic anatomy was no less perfect than the Ayurvedic.

There were many names for many parts of the organs, because they had to cut up animals for sacrifice. The sea is described as full of ships. Sea voyage was prohibited later on, partly because there came the fear that people might thereby become Buddhists.

Buddhism was the rebellion of newly-formed Kshatriyas against Vedic priestcraft.

Hinduism threw away Buddhism after taking its sap. The attempt of all the Southern Acharyas was to effect a reconciliation between the two. Shankaracharya's teaching shows the influence of Buddhism. His disciples perverted his teaching and carried it to such an extreme point that some of the later reformers were right in calling the Acharya's followers "crypto-buddhists".

***

What is Spencer's unknowable? It is our Maya. Western philosophers are afraid of the unknowable, but our philosophers have taken a big jump into the unknown, and they have conquered.

Western philosophers are like vultures soaring high in the sky, but all the while, with their eye fixed on the carrion beneath. They cannot cross the unknown, and they therefore turn back and worship the almighty dollar.

There have been two lines of progress in this world—political and religious. In the former the Greeks are everything, the modern political institutions being only the development of the Grecian; in the latter the Hindus are everything.

My religion is one of which Christianity is an offshoot and Buddhism a rebel child.

Chemistry ceases to improve when one element is found from which all others are deductible. Physics ceases to progress when one force is found of which all others are manifestations. So religion ceases to progress when unity is reached, which is the case with Hinduism.

There is no new religious idea preached anywhere which is not found in the Vedas.

In everything, there are two kinds of development—analytical and synthetical. In the former the Hindus excel other nations. In the latter they are nil[1].

The Hindus have cultivated the power of analysis and abstraction. No nation has yet produced a grammar like that of Panini.

Ramanuja's important work is the conversion of Jains and Buddhists to Hinduism. He is a great advocate of image-worship. He introduced love and faith as potent means of salvation.

Even in the Bhagavata, twenty-four Avatars are mentioned corresponding to the twenty-four Tirthankaras of the Jains, the name of Rishabhadeva being common to both.

The practice of Yoga gives the power of abstraction. The superiority of a Siddha over others consists in his being able to separate attributes from objects and think of them independently, giving them objective reality.

***

The opposite extremes always meet and resemble each other. The greatest self-forgotten devotee whose mind is absorbed in the contemplation of the infinite Brahman and the most debased, drunken maniac present the same externals. At times we are surprised with the analogical transition from one to the other.

Extremely nervous men succeed as religious men. They become fervent over whatever they take into their head. "All are mad in this world; some are mad after gold, others after women, and some are after God; if drowning is to be the fate of man, it is better to be drowned in an ocean of milk than in a pool of dung", a devotee replied who was charged with madness.

The God of Infinite Love and the object of Love sublime and infinite are painted blue. Krishna is painted blue, so also Solomon's[2] God of Love. It is a natural law that anything sublime and infinite is associated with blue colour. Take a handful of water, it is absolutely colourless. But look at the deep wide ocean; it is as blue as anything. Examine the space near you; it is colourless. But look at the infinite expanse of the sky; it is blue.

That the Hindus, absorbed in the ideal, lacked in realistic observation is evident from this. Take painting and sculpture. What do you see in the Hindu paintings? All sorts of grotesque and unnatural figures. What do you see in a Hindu temple? A Chaturbhanga[3] Narayana or some such thing. But take into consideration any Italian picture or Grecian statue—what a study of nature you find in them! A gentleman for twenty years sat burning a candle in his hand, in order to paint a lady carrying a candle in her hand.

The Hindus progressed in the subjective sciences.

1. Here by the term "synthesis" is meant a scientific generalisation, and by the term "analysis" an ontological reduction of facts and objects to their immanent principles.—Ed.

2. See Old Testament, The Song of Solomon, I. 5,7,14.

3. Lit. bent at four places or joints of the body.

There are as many different conducts taught in the Vedas as there are differences in human nature. What is taught to an adult cannot be taught to a child.

A Guru should be a doctor of men. He should understand the nature of his disciple and teach him the method which suits him best.

There are infinite ways of practicing Yoga. Certain methods have produced successful result with certain men. But two are of general importance with all: (1) Reaching the reality by negativing every known experience, (2) Thinking that you are everything, the whole universe. The second method, though it leads to the goal sooner than the first, is not the safest one. It is generally attended with great dangers which may lead a man astray and deter him from obtaining his aim.

There is this difference between the love taught by Christianity and that taught by Hinduism: Christianity teaches us to love our neighbours as we should wish them to love us; Hinduism asks us to love them as ourselves, in fact to see ourselves in them.

A mongoose is generally kept in a glass-case with a long chain attached to it, so that it may go about freely. When it scents danger as it wanders about, with one jump it goes into the glass case. So is a Yogi in this world.

***

The whole universe is one chain of existence, of which matter forms one pole and God the other; the doctrine of Vishishtadvaitism may be explained by some such ideas.

The Vedas are full of passages which prove the existence of a Personal God. The Rishis, who through long devotion saw God, had a peep into the unknown and threw their challenge to the world. It is only presumptuous men, who have not walked in the path described by the Rishis and who have not followed their teachings, that criticise them and oppose them. No man has yet come forward who would dare to say that he has properly followed their directions and has not seen anything and that these men are liars. There are men who have been under trial at various times and have felt that they have not been forsaken by God. The world is such that if faith in God does not offer us any consolation, it is better to commit suicide.

A pious missionary went out on business. All of a sudden his three sons died of cholera. His wife covered the three dead bodies of her beloved children with a sheet and was awaiting her husband at the gate. When he returned, she detained him at the gate and put him the question, "My dear husband, some one entrusts something to you and in your absence suddenly takes it back. Will you feel sorry?" He replied, "Certainly I would not". Then she took him in, removed the sheet and showed the three corpses. He bore this calmly and buried the bodies. Such is the strength of mind of those who hold firm faith in the existence of an all-merciful God who disposes of everything in the universe.

The Absolute can never be thought of. We can have no idea of a thing unless it is finite. God the infinite can only be conceived and worshipped as the finite.

John the Baptist was an Essene—a sect of Buddhists. The Christian cross is nothing but the Shivalinga converted into two across. Remnants of Buddhist worship are still to be found among the relics of ancient Rome.

In South India, some of the Ragas (tunes) are sung and remembered as independent Ragas, whereas they are derivations of the six primary ones. In their music, there is very little of Murchhana, or oscillating touches of sound.

Even the use of the perfect instrument of music is rare. The Vina of the South is not the real Vina. We have no martial music, no martial poetry either. Bhavabhuti is a little martial.

***

Christ was a Sannyasin, and his religion is essentially fit for Sannyasins only. His teachings may be summed up as: "Give up"; nothing more—being fit for the favoured few. "Turn the other cheek also!"—impossible, impracticable! The Westerners know it. It is meant for those who hunger and thirst after righteousness, who aim at perfection. "Stand on your rights", is the rule for the ordinary men. One set of moral rules cannot be preached to all—sadhus and householders.

All sectarian religions take for granted that all men are equal. This is not warranted by science. There is more difference between minds than between bodies. One fundamental doctrine of Hinduism is that all men are different, there being unity in variety. Even for a drunkard, there are some Mantras—even for a man going to a prostitute!

Morality is a relative term. Is there anything like absolute morality in this world? The idea is a superstition. We have no right to judge every man in every age by the same standard.

Every man, in every age, in every country is under peculiar circumstances. If the circumstances change, ideas also must change. Beef-eating was once moral. The climate was cold, and the cereals were not much known. Meat was the chief food available. So in that age and clime, beef was in a manner indispensable. But beef-eating is held to be immoral now.

The one thing unchangeable is God. Society is moving.

Jagat (world) means that which is moving. God is Achala (immovable).

What I say is not, "Reform", but, "Move on". Nothing is too bad to reform. Adaptability is the whole mystery of life—the principle underneath which serves to unfold it. Adjustment or adaptation is the outcome of the Self pitted against external forces tending to suppress It. He who adjusts himself best lives the longest. Even if I do not preach this, society is changing, it must change. It is not Christianity nor science, it is necessity, that is working underneath, the necessity that people must have to live or starve.

***

The best scenery in the world can be seen on the sublime heights of the Himalayas. If one lives there for a time, he is sure to have mental calmness, however restless he might have been before. God is the highest form of generalised law. When once this law is known, all others can be explained as being subordinate to it. God is to religion what Newton's law of gravity is to falling bodies.

Every worship consists of prayer in the highest form. For a man who cannot make Dhyana or mental worship, Puja or ceremonial worship is necessary. He must have the thing concrete.

The brave alone can afford to be sincere. Compare the lion and the fox.

Loving only the good in God and nature—even a child does that. You should love the terrible and the painful as well. A father loves the child, even when he is giving him trouble.

Shri Krishna was God, incarnated to save mankind. Gopi-li-la (his disport with cowherd maids) is the acme of the religion of love in which individuality vanishes and there is communion. It is in this Lila that Shri Krishna shows what he preaches in the Gita: "Give up every other tie for me." Go and take shelter under Vrindavana-Lila to understand Bhakti. On this subject a great number of books is extant. It is the religion of India. The larger number of Hindus follow Shri Krishna.

Shri Krishna is the God of the poor, the beggar, the sinner, the son, the father, the wife, and of everyone. He enters intimately into all our human relations and makes everything holy and in the end brings us to salvation. He is the God who hides himself from the philosopher and the learned and reveals himself to the ignorant and the children. He is the God of faith and love and not of learning. With the Gopis, love and God were the same thing—they knew Him to be love incarnate.

In Dwaraka, Shri Krishna teaches duty; in Vrindavana, love. He allowed his sons to kill each other, they being wicked.

God, according to the Jewish and Mohammedan idea, is a big Session Judge. Our God is rigorous on the surface, but loving and merciful at heart.

There are some who do not understand Advaitism and make a travesty of its teachings. They say, "What is Shuddha and Ashuddha (pure and impure)—what is the difference between virtue and vice? It is all human superstition", and observe no moral restraint in their actions. It is downright roguery; and any amount of harm is done by the preaching of such things.

This body is made up of two sorts of Karma consisting of virtue and vice—injurious vice and non-injurious virtue. A thorn is pricking my body, and I take another thorn to take it out and then throw both away. A man desiring to be perfect takes a thorn of virtue and with it takes off the thorn of vice. He still lives, and virtue alone being left, the momentum of action left to him must be of virtue. A bit of holiness is left to the Jivanmukta, and he lives, but everything he does must be holy.

Virtue is that which tends to our improvement, and vice to our degeneration. Man is made up of three qualities—brutal, human, and godly. That which tends to increase the divinity in you is virtue, and that which tends to increase brutality in you is vice. You must kill the brutal nature and become human, that is, loving and charitable. You must transcend that too and become pure bliss, Sachchidananda, fire without burning, wonderfully loving, but without the weakness of human love, without the feeling of misery.

Bhakti is divided into Vaidhi and Raganuga Bhakti.

Vaidhi Bhakti is implicit belief in obedience to the teachings of the Vedas.

Raganuga Bhakti is of five kinds:

1. Shanta as illustrated by the religion of Christ;
2. Dasya as illustrated by that of Hanuman to Rama;
3. Sakhya as illustrated by that of Arjuna to Shri Krishna;
4. Vatsalya as illustrated by that of Vasudeva to Shri Krishna;
5. Madhura (that of the husband and wife) in the lives of Shri Krishna and the Gopikas.

Keshab Chandra Sen compared society to an ellipse. God is the central sun. Society is sometimes in the aphelion and sometimes in the perihelion. An Avatar comes and takes it to the perihelion. Then it goes back again. Why should it be so? I cannot say. What necessity for an Avatara? What necessity was there to create? Why did He not create us all perfect? It is Lila (sport), we do not know.

Men can become Brahman but not God. If anybody becomes God, show me his creation. Vishvamitra's creation is his own imagination. It should have obeyed Vishvamitra's law. If anybody becomes a Creator, there would be an end of the world, on account of the conflict of laws. The balance is so nice that if you disturb the equilibrium of one atom, the whole world will come to an end.

There were great men—so great that no number nor human arithmetic could state the difference between them and us. But compared with God, they were geometrical points. In comparison with the Infinite, everything is nothing. Compared with God, what is Vishvamitra but a human moth?

Patanjali is the father of the theory of evolution, spiritual and physical.

Generally the organism is weaker than the environment. It is struggling to adjust itself. Sometimes it over-adjusts itself. Then the whole body changes into another species. Nandi was a man whose holiness was so great that the human body could not contain it. So those molecules changed into a god-body.

The tremendous engine of competition will destroy everything. If you are to live at all, you must adjust yourself to the times. If we are to live at all, we must be a scientific nation. Intellectual power is the force. You must learn the power of organisation of the Europeans. You must become educated and must educate your women. You must abolish child marriage.

All these ideas are floating over society. You all know it, yet dare not act. Who is to bell the cat? In the fullness of time a wonderful man will come. Then all the rats will be made bold.

Whenever a great man comes, the circumstances are ready under his feet. He is the last straw to break the camel's back. He is the spark of the cannon. There is something in the talking—we are preparing for him.

Was Krishna cunning? No, he was not cunning. He tried his best to prevent war. It was Duryodhana who forced the war. But, when once in the thing, you should not recede—that is the man of duty. Do not run away, it is cowardice. When in the thing, you must do it. You should not budge an inch—of course not for a wrong thing; this was a righteous war.

The devil comes in many guises—anger in the form of justice—passion in the form of duty. When it first comes, the man knows and then he forgets. Just as your pleaders' conscience; at first they know it is all Badmashi (roguery), then it is duty to their clients; at last they get hardened.

Yogis live on the banks of the Narmada—the best place for them, because the climate is very even. Bhaktas live in Vrindavana.

Sipahis (sepoys) die soon—nature is full of defect—the athletes die soon. The gentlemen class are the strongest, while the poor are the hardiest. Fruit diet may agree with a costive man. Civilised man needs rest for intellectual work. For food he has to take spices and condiments. The savage walks forty or fifty miles a day. He relishes the blandest foods.

Our fruits are all artificial, and the natural mango is a poor affair. Wheat also is artificial.

Save the spiritual store in your body by observing continence.

The rule for a householder about the expenditure of his income is, one-fourth of the income for his family, one-fourth for charity, one-fourth to be saved, one-fourth for self.

Unity in variety is the plan of creation, individuality in universality.

Why deny the cause only? Deny the effect also. The cause must contain everything that is in the effect.

Christ's public life extended only over eighteen months, and for this he had silently been preparing himself for thirty-two years. Mohammed was forty years old before he came out.

***

It is true that the caste system becomes essential in the ordinary course of nature. Those that have aptitudes for a particular work form a class. But who is to settle the class of a particular individual? If a Brahmin thinks that he has a special aptitude for spiritual culture, why should he be afraid to meet a Shudra in an open field? Will a horse be afraid of running a race with a jade?

Refer to the life of the author of Krishna-karnamrita, Vil-

vamangala—a devotee who plucked his eyes out because he could not see God. His life illustrates the principle that even misdirected love leads in the end to love proper.

Too early religious advancement of the Hindus and that superfineness in everything which made them cling to higher alternatives, have reduced them to what they are. The Hindus have to learn a little bit of materialism from the West and teach them a little bit of spirituality.

Educate your women first and leave them to themselves; then they will tell you what reforms are necessary for them. In matters concerning them, who are you?

Who reduced the Bhangis and the Pariahs to their present degraded condition? Heartlessness in our behavior and at the same time preaching wonderful Advaitism—is it not adding insult to injury?

Form and formless are intertwined in this world. The formless can only be expressed in form and form can only be thought with the formless. The world is a form of our thoughts. The idol is the expression of religion.

In God all natures are possible. But we can see Him only through human nature. We can love Him as we love a man—as father, son. The strongest love in the world is that between man and woman, and that also when it is clandestine. This is typified in the love between Krishna and Radha.

Nowhere is it said in the Vedas that man is born a sinner. To say so is a great libel on human nature.

It is not an easy task to reach the state of seeing the Reality face to face. The other day one could not find the hidden cat in a whole picture, though it occupied the major portion of the picture.

***

You cannot injure anybody and sit quietly. It is a wonderful machinery—you cannot escape God's vengeance.

Kama (lust) is blind and leads to hell. Prema is love, it leads to heaven.

There is no idea of lust or sympathy in the love of Krishna and Radha. Radha says to Krishna, "If you place your feet on my heart, all lust will vanish."

When abstraction is reached lust dies and there is only love.

A poet loved a washerwoman. Hot Dal fell upon the feet of the woman and the feet of the poet were scalded.

Shiva is the sublime aspect of God, Krishna the beautiful aspect of God. Love crystallises into blueness. Blue colour is expressive of intense love. Solomon saw "Krishna". Here Krishna came to be seen by all.

Even now, when you get love, you see Radha. Become Radha and be saved. There is no other way, Christians do not understand Solomon's song. They call it prophecy symbolising Christ's love for the Church. They think it nonsense and father some story upon it.

Hindus believe Buddha to be an Avatara.

Hindus believe in God positively. Buddhism does not try to know whether He is or not.

Buddha came to whip us into practice. Be good, destroy the passions. Then you will know for yourself whether Dvaita or Advaita philosophy is true—whether there is one or there are more than one.

Buddha was a reformer of Hinduism.

In the same man the mother sees a son, while the wife at the same time sees differently with different results. The wicked see in God wickedness. The virtuous see in Him virtue. He admits of all forms. He can be moulded according to the imagination of each person. Water assumes various shapes in various vessels. But water is in all of them. Hence all religions are true.

God is cruel and not cruel. He is all being and not being at the same time. Hence He is all contradictions. Nature also is nothing but a mass of contradictions.

***

Freedom of the will—it is as you feel you are free to act. But this freedom is a species of necessity. There is one infinite link before, after, and between the thought and the action, but the latter takes the name of freedom—like a bird flitting through a bright room. We feel the freedom and feel it has no other cause. We cannot go beyond consciousness, therefore we feel we are free. We can trace it no further than consciousness. God alone feels the real freedom. Mahapurushas (saints) feel themselves identified with God; hence they also feel the real freedom.

You may stop the water flowing out of the fountain by closing that part of the stream and gathering it all in the fountain; you have no liberty beyond it. But the source remains unchanged. Everything is predestination—and a part of that predestination is that you shall have such feeling—the feeling of freedom. I am shaping my own action. Responsibility is the feeling of reaction. There is no absolute power. Power here is the conscious feeling of exercising any faculty which is created by necessity. Man has the feeling "I act"; what he means by power of freedom is the feeling. The power is attended with responsibility. Whatever may be done through us by predestination, we feel the reaction. A ball thrown by one, itself feels the reaction.

But this innate necessity which comes to us as our freedom does not affect also the conscious relations we form with our surroundings. The relativity is not changed. Either everybody is free or everybody is under necessity. That would not matter. The relations would be the same. Vice and virtue would be the same. If a thief pleads that he was under the necessity of stealing, the magistrate would say that he was under the necessity to punish. We are seated in a room, and the whole room is moving—the relation between us is unchanged. To get out of this infinite chain of causation is Mukti (freedom). Muktas (free souls) are not actuated by necessity, they are like

god. They begin the chain of cause and effect. God is the only free being—the first source of their will—and is always experienced by them as such.

The feeling of want is the real prayer, not the words. But you must have patience to wait and see if your prayers are answered.

You should cultivate a noble nature by doing your duty. By doing our duty we get rid of the idea of duty; and then and then only we feel everything as done by God. We are but machines in His hand. This body is opaque, God is the lamp. Whatever is going out of the body is God's. You do not feel it. You feel "I". This is delusion. You must learn calm submission to the will of God. Duty is the best school for it. This duty is morality. Drill yourself to be thoroughly submissive. Get rid of the "I". No humbuggism. Then you can get rid of the idea of duty; for all is His. Then you go on naturally, forgiving, forgetting, etc.

Our religion always presents different gradations of duty and religion to different people.

Light is everywhere visible only in the men of holiness. A Mahapurusha is like crystal glass—full rays of God passing and repassing through. Why not worship a Jivanmukta?

Contact with holy men is good. If you go near holy men, you will find holiness overflowing unconsciously in everything there.

Resist not evil done to yourself, but you may resist evil done to others.

If you wish to become a saint, you should renounce all kinds of pleasures. Ordinarily, you may enjoy all, but pray to God for guidance, and He will lead you on.

The universe fills only a small portion of the heart which craves for something beyond and above the world.

Selfishness is the devil incarnate in every man. Every bit of self, bit by bit, is devil. Take off self by one side and God enters by the other. When the self is got rid of, only God remains. Light and darkness cannot remain together.

Forgetting the little "I" is a sign of healthy and pure mind. A healthy child forgets its body.

Sita—to say that she was pure is a blasphemy. She was purity itself embodied—the most beautiful character that ever lived on earth.

A Bhakta should be like Sita before Rama. He might be thrown into all kinds of difficulties. Sita did not mind her sufferings; she centreed herself in Rama.

***

Buddhism proves nothing about the Absolute Entity. In a stream the water is changing; we have no right to call the stream one. Buddhist deny the one, and say, it is many. We say it is one and deny the many. What they call Karma is what we call the soul. According to Buddhism, man is a series of waves. Every wave dies, but somehow the first wave causes the second. That the second wave is identical with the first is illusion. To get rid of illusion good Karma is necessary. Buddhists do not postulate anything beyond the world. We say, beyond the relative there is the Absolute. Buddhism accepts that there is misery, and sufficient it is that we can get rid of this Duhkha (misery); whether we get Sukha (happiness) or not, we do not know. Buddha preached not the soul preached by others. According to the Hindus, soul is an entity or substance, and God is absolute. Both agree in this, that they destroy the relative. But Buddhists do not give what is the effect of that destruction of the relative.

Present-day Hinduism and Buddhism were growths from the same branch. Buddhism degenerated, and Shankara lopped it off!

Buddha is said to have denied the Vedas because there is so much Himsa (killing) and other things. Every page of Buddhism is a fight with the Vedas (the ritualistic aspect). But he had no authority to do so.

Buddha is expressly agnostic about God; but God is everywhere preached in our religion. The Vedas teach God—both personal and impersonal. God is everywhere preached in the Gita. Hinduism is nothing without God. The Vedas are nothing without Him. That is the only way to salvation. Sannyasins have to repeat the following, several times: I, wishing for Mukti, take refuge in God, who created the world, who breathed out the Vedas.

Buddha, we may say now, ought to have understood the harmony of religions. He introduced sectarianism.

Modern Hinduism, modern Jainism, and Buddhism branched off at the same time. For some period, each seemed to have wanted to outdo the others in grotesqueness and humbuggism.

***

We cannot imagine anything which is not God. He is all that we can imagine with our five senses, and more. He is like a chameleon; each man, each nation, sees one face of Him and at different times, in different forms. Let each man see and take of God whatever is suitable to him. Compare each animal absorbing from nature whatever food is suitable to it.

The fault with all religions like Christianity is that they have one set of rules for all. But Hindu religion is suited to all grades of religious aspiration and progress. It contains all the ideals in their perfect form. For example, the ideal of Shanta or blessedness is to be found in Vasishtha; that of love in Krishna; that of duty in Rama and Sita; and that of intellect in Shukadeva. Study the characters of these and of other ideal men. Adopt one which suits you best.

Follow truth wherever it may lead you; carry ideas to their utmost logical conclusions. Do not be cowardly and hypocritical. You must have a great devotion to your ideal, devotion not of the moment, but calm, persevering, and steady devotion, like that of a Chataka (a kind of bird) which looks into the sky in the midst of thunder and lightening and would drink no water but from the clouds. Perish in the struggle to be holy; a thousand times welcome death. Be not disheartened. When good nectar is unattainable, it is no reason why we should eat poison. There is no escape. This world is as unknown as the other.

Charity never faileth; devotion to an ideal never fails in sympathy, never becomes weary of sympathising with others. Love to enemies is not possible for ordinary men: they drive out others in order to live themselves. Only a very few men lived in the world who practised both. King Janaka was one of them. Such a man is superior even to Sannyasins. Shukadeva, who was purity and renunciation embodied, made Janaka his Guru; and Janaka said to him, "You are a born Siddha; whatever you know and your father taught you, is true. I assure you of this."

***

Individuality in universality is the plan of creation. Each cell has its part in bringing about consciousness. Man is individual and at the same time universal. It is while realising our individual nature that we realise even our national and universal nature. Each is an infinite circle whose centre is everywhere and circumference nowhere. By practice one can feel universal Selfhood which is the essence of Hinduism. He who sees in every being his own Self is a Pandita (sage).

Rishis are discoverers of spiritual laws.

In Advaitism, there is no Jivatma; it is only a delusion. In Dvaitism, there is Jiva infinitely distinct from God. Both are true. One went to the fountain, another to the tank. Apparently we are all Dvaitists as far as our consciousness goes. But beyond? Beyond that we are Advaitists. In reality, this is the only truth. According to Advaitism, love every man as your own Self and not as your brother as in Christianity. Brotherhood should be superseded by universal Selfhood. Not universal brotherhood, but universal Selfhood is our motto. Advaitism may include also the "greatest happiness" theory.

So'ham—I am He. Repeat the idea constantly, voluntarily at first; then it becomes automatic in practice. It percolates to the nerves. So this idea, by rote, by repetition, should be driven even into the nerves.

Or, first begin with Dvaitism that is in your consciousness; second stage, Vishishtadvaitism—"I in you, you in me, and all is God." This is the teaching of Christ.

The highest Advaitism cannot be brought down to practical life. Advaitism made practical works from the plane of Vishishtadvaitism. Dvaitism—small circle different from the big circle, only connected by Bhakti; Vishishtadvaitism—small circle within big circle, motion regulated by the big circle; Advaitism—small circle expands and coincides with the big circle. In Advaitism "I" loses itself in God. God is here, God is there, God is "I".

***

One way for attaining Bhakti is by repeating the name of God a number of times. Mantras have effect—the mere repetition of words. Jalagiman Chetti's powers are due to the repetition of the Mantra—repetition of certain words with certain ceremonies. The powers of the Astras or Banas (missiles, arrows, etc.) of ancient war were due to Mantra. This is taken for granted throughout our Shastras. That we should take all these Shastras to be imagination is superstition.

To obtain Bhakti, seek the company of holy men who have Bhakti, and read books like the Gita and the Imitation of Christ; always think of the attributes of God.

The Vedas contain not only the means how to obtain Bhakti but also the means for obtaining any earthly good or evil. Take whatever you want.

Bengal is a land of Bhakti or Bhaktas. The stone on which Chaitanya used to stand in the temple of Jagannatha to see the image was worn by his tears of love and devotion. When he took Sannyasa, he showed his fitness for it to his Guru by keeping sugar on his tongue for some time without its being dissolved. He discovered Vrindavana by the power of insight he had acquired through devotion.

I will tell you something for your guidance in life. Everything that comes from India take as true, until you find congent reasons for disbelieving it. Everything that comes from Europe take as false, until you find congent reasons for believing it. Do not be carried away by European fooleries. Think for yourselves. Only one thing is lacking: you are slaves; you follow whatever Europeans do. That is simply an impotent state of mind. Society may take up materials from any quarter but should grow in its own way.

To be shocked by a new custom is the father of all superstition, the first road to hell. It leads to bigotry and fanaticism. Truth is heaven. Bigotry is hell.

CONCENTRATION

Concentration is the essence of all knowledge; nothing can be done without it. Ninety per cent of thought force is wasted by the ordinary human being, and therefore he is constantly committing blunders; the trained man or mind never makes a mistake. When the mind is concentrated and turned backward on itself, all within us will be our servants, not our masters. The Greeks applied their concentration to the external world, and the result was perfection in art, literature, etc. The Hindu concentrated on the internal world, upon the unseen realms in the Self, and developed the science of Yoga. Yoga is controlling the senses, will and mind. The benefit of its study is that we learn to control instead of being controlled. Mind seems to be layer on layer. Our real goal is to cross all these intervening strata of our being and find God. The end and aim of Yoga is to realise God. To do this we must go beyond relative knowledge, go beyond the sense-world. The world is awake to the senses, the children of the Lord are asleep on that plane. The world is asleep to the Eternal, the children of the Lord are awake in that realm. These are the sons of God. There is but one way to control the senses—to see Him who is the Reality in the universe. Then and only then can we really conquer our senses.

Concentration is restraining the mind into smaller and smaller limits. There are eight processes for thus restraining the mind. The first is Yama, controlling the mind by avoiding externals. All morality is included in this. Beget no evil. Injure no living creature. If you injure nothing for twelve years, then even lions and tigers will go down before you. Practise truthfulness. Twelve years of absolute truthfulness in thought, word, and deed gives a man what he wills. Be chaste in thought, word, and action. Chastity is the basis of all religions. Personal purity is imperative. Next in Niyama, not allowing the mind to wander in any direction. Then Asana, posture. There are eighty-four postures: but the best is most natural to each one; that is, which can be kept longest with the greatest ease.

After this comes Pranayama, restraint of breath. Then Pratyahara, drawing in of the organs from their objects. Then Dharana, concentration. Then Dhyana, contemplation or meditation. (This is the kernel of the Yoga system.) And last, Samadhi, superconsciousness. The purer the body and mind, the quicker the desired result will be obtained. You must be perfectly pure. Do not think of evil things, such thoughts will surely drag you down. If you are perfectly pure and practise faithfully, your mind can finally be made a searchlight of infinite power. There is no limit to its scope. But there must be constant practice and non-attachment to the world. When a man reaches the superconscious state, all feeling of body melts away. Then alone does he become free and immortal. To all external appearances, unconsciousness and superconsciousness are the same; but they differ as a lump of clay from a lump of gold. The one whose whole soul is given up to God has reached the superconscious plane.

THE POWER OF THE MIND

The cause becomes the effect. The cause is not one thing and the effect something else that exists as a result. The effect is always the cause worked out. Always, the cause becomes the effect. The popular idea is that the effect is the result of the operation of a cause which is something independent and aloof from the effect. This is not so. The effect is always the cause worked out into another condition.

The universe is really homogeneous. Heterogeneity is only in appearance. There seen to be different substances, different powers, etc. throughout nature. But take two different substances, say a piece of glass and a piece of wood, grind them up together fine enough, reduce them till there is nothing more to reduce, and the substance remaining appears homogeneous. All substances in the last analysis are one. Homogeneity is the substance, the reality; heterogeneity is the appearance of many things as though they were many substances. The One is homogeneity; the appearance of the One as many is heterogeneity.

Hearing, seeing, or tasting, etc. is the mind in different states of action.

The atmosphere of a room may be hypnotised so that everybody who enters it will see all sorts of things—men and objects flying through the air.

Everybody is hypnotised already. The work of attaining freedom, of realising one's real nature, consists in de-hypnotisation.

One thing to be remembered is that we are not gaining powers at all. We have them already. The whole process of growth is de-hypnotisation.

The purer the mind, the easier it is to control. Purity of the mind must be insisted upon if you would control it. Do not think covetously about mere mental powers. Let them go. One who seeks the powers of the mind succumbs to them. Almost all who desire powers become ensnared by them.

Perfect morality is the all in all of complete control over mind. The man who is perfectly moral has nothing more to do; he is free. The man who is perfectly moral cannot possibly hurt anything or anybody. Non-injuring has to be attained by him who would be free. No one is more powerful than he who has attained perfect non-injuring. No one could fight, no one could quarrel, in his presence. Yes, his very presence, and nothing else, means peace, means love wherever he may be. Nobody could be angry or fight in his presence. Even the animals, ferocious animals, would be peaceful before him.

I once knew a Yogi, a very old man, who lived in a hole in the ground all by himself[1]. All he had was a pan or two to cook his meals in. He ate very little, and wore scarcely anything, and spent most of his time meditating.

With him all people were alike. He had attained to non-injuring. What he saw in everything, in every person, in every animal, was the Soul, the Lord of the Universe. With him, every person and every animal was "my Lord". He never addressed any person or animal in any other way. Well, one day a thief came his way and stole one of his pans. He saw him and ran after him. The chase was a long one. At last the thief from exhaustion had to stop, and the Yogi, running up to him, fell on his knees before him and said, "My Lord, you do me a great honour to come my way. Do me the honour to accept the other pan. It is also yours." This old man is dead now. He was full of love for everything in the world. He would have died for an ant. Wild animals instinctively knew this old man to be their friend. Snakes and ferocious animals would go into his hold and sleep with him. They all loved him and never fought in his presence.

Never talk about the faults of others, no matter how bad they may be. Nothing is ever gained by that. You never help one by talking about his fault; you do him an injury, and injure yourself as well.

All regulations in eating, practising, etc., are all right so long as they are complementary to a spiritual aspiration, but they are not ends in themselves; they are only helps.

Never quarrel about religion. All quarrels and disputation concerning religion simply show that spirituality is not present. Religious quarrels are always over the husks. When purity, when spirituality goes, leaving the soul dry, quarrels begin, and not before.

LESSONS ON RAJA-YOGA[2]

Prana

The theory of creation is that matter is subject to five conditions: ether, luminous ether, gaseous, liquid, and solid. They are all evoked out of one primal element, which is very finest ether.

The name of the energy in the universe is Prana, which is the force residing in these elements. Mind is the great instrument for using the Prana. Mind is material. Behind the mind is Atman which takes hold of the Prana. Prana is the driving power of the world, and can be seen in every manifestation of life. The body is mortal and the mind is mortal; both, being compounds, must die. Behind all is the Atman which never dies. The Atman is pure intelligence controlling and directing Prana. But the intelligence we see around us is always imperfect. When intelligence is perfect, we get the Incarnation—the Christ. Intelligence is always trying to manifest itself, and in order to do this it is creating minds and bodies of different degrees of development. In reality, and at the back of all things, every being is equal.

Mind is very fine matter; it is the instrument for manifesting Prana. Force requires matter for manifestation.

The next point is how to use this Prana. We all use it, but how sadly we waste it! The first doctrine in the preparatory stage is that all knowledge is the outcome of experience. Whatever is beyond the five senses must also be experienced in order to become true to us.

Our mind is acting on three planes: the subconscious, conscious, and superconscious. Of men, the Yogi alone is superconscious. The whole theory of Yoga is to go beyond the mind. These three planes can be understood by considering the vibrations of light or sound. There are certain vibrations of light too slow to become visible; then as they get faster, we see them as light; and then they get too fast for us to see them at all. The same with sound.

How to transcend the senses without disturbing the health is what we want to learn. The Western mind has stumbled into acquiring some of the psychic gifts which in them are abnormal and are frequently the sign of disease. The Hindu has studied and made perfect this subject of science, which all may now study without fear or danger.

---

1. Pavhari Baba of Ghazipur. (See Vol. IV. pp. 283-95).

2. These lessons and those on Bhakti-Yoga that follow are made out of class notes preserved in England—Ed.

Mental healing is a fine proof of the superconscious state; for the thought which heals is a sort of vibration in the Prana, and it does not go as a thought but as something higher for which we have no name.

Each thought has three states. First, the rising or beginning, of which we are unconscious; second, when the thought rises to the surface; and third, when it goes from us. Thought is like a bubble rising to the surface. When thought is joined to will, we call it power. That which strikes the sick person whom you are trying to help is not thought, but power. The self-man running through it all is called in Sanskrit Sutratma, the "Thread-self".

The last and highest manifestation of Prana is love. The moment you have succeeded in manufacturing love out of Prana, you are free. It is the hardest and the greatest thing to gain. You must not criticise others; you must criticise yourself. If you see a drunkard, do not criticise him; remember he is you in another shape. He who has not darkness sees no darkness in others. What you have inside you is that you see in others. This is the surest way of reform. If the would-be reformers who criticise and see evil would themselves stop creating evil, the world would be better. Beat this idea into yourself.

The Practice of Yoga

The body must be properly taken care of. The people who torture their flesh are demoniacal. Always keep your mind joyful; if melancholy thoughts come, kick them out. A Yogi must not eat too much, but he also must not fast; he must not sleep too much, but he must not go without any sleep. In all things only the man who holds the golden mean can become a Yogi.

What is the best time for practice in Yoga? The junction time of dawn and twilight, when all nature becomes calm. Take help of nature. Take the easiest posture in sitting. Have the three parts straight—the ribs, the shoulders, and the head—leaving the spine free and straight, no leaning backwards or forwards. Then mentally hold the body as perfect, part by part. Then send a current of love to all the world; then pray for enlightenment. And lastly, join your mind to your breath and gradually attain the power of concentrating your attention on its movements. The reason for this will be apparent by degrees

The Ojas

The "Ojas" is that which makes the difference between man and man. The man who has much Ojas is the leader of men. It gives a tremendous power of attraction. Ojas is manufactured from the nerve-currents. It has this peculiarity: it is most easily made from that force which manifests itself in the sexual powers. If the powers of the sexual centres are not frittered away and their energies wasted (action is only thought in a grosser state), they can be manufactured into Ojas. The two great nerve currents of the body start from the brain, go down on each side of the spinal cord, but they cross in the shape of the figure 8 at the back of the head. Thus the left side of the body is governed by the right side of the head. At the lowest point of the circuit is the sexual centre, the Sacral Plexus. The energy conveyed by these two currents of nerves comes down, and a large amount is continually being stored in the Sacral Plexus. The last bone in the spine is over the Sacral Plexus and is described in symbolic language as a triangle; and as the energy is stored up beside it, this energy is symbolised by a serpent. Consciousness and subconsciousness work through these two nerve-currents. But superconsciousness takes off the nerve-current when it reaches the lower end of the circuit, and instead of allowing it to go up and complete the circuit, stops and forces it up the spinal cord as Ojas from the Sacral Plexus. The spinal cord is naturally closed, but it can be opened to form a passage for this Ojas. As the current travels from one centre of the spinal cord to another, you can travel from one plane of existence to another. This is why the human being is greater than others, because all planes, all experiences, are possible to the spirit in the human body. We do not need another; for man can, if he likes, finish in his body his probation and can after that become pure spirit. When the Ojas has gone from centre to centre and reaches the Pineal Gland (a part of the brain to which science can assign no function), man then becomes neither mind nor body, he is free from all bondage.

The great danger of psychic powers is that man stumbles, as it were, into them, and knows not how to use them rightly. He is without training and without knowledge of what has happened to him. The danger is that in using these psychic powers, the sexual feelings are abnormally roused as these powers are in fact manufactured out of the sexual centre. The best and safest way is to avoid psychic manifestations, for they play the most horrible pranks on their ignorant and untrained owners.

To go back to symbols. Because this movement of the Ojas up the spinal cord feels like a spiral one, it is called the "snake". The snake, therefore, or the serpent, rests on the bone or triangle. When it is roused, it travels up the spinal cord; and as it goes from centre to centre, a new natural world is opened inside us—the Kundalini is roused.

Pranayama

The practice of Pranayama is the training of the superconscious mind. The physical practice is divided into three parts and deals entirely with the breath. It consists of drawing in, holding, and throwing out the breath. The breath must be drawn in by one nostril whilst you count four, then held whilst you count sixteen, and thrown away by the other nostril whilst you count eight. Then reverse the process closing the other nostril while you breathe in. You will have to begin by holding one nostril with your thumb; but in time your breathing will obey your mind. Make four of these Pranayamas morning and evening.

Metagnosticism

"Repent, for the Kingdom of Heaven is at hand." The word "repent" is in Greek "metanoeite" ("meta" means behind, after, beyond) and means literally "go beyond knowledge"—the knowledge of the (five) senses—"and look within where you will find the kingdom of heaven".

Sir William Hamilton says at the end of a philosophical work, "Here philosophy ends, here religion begins". Religion is not, and never can be, in the field of intellect. Intellectual reasoning is based on facts evident to the senses. Now religion has nothing to do with the senses. The agnostics say they cannot know God, and rightly, for they have exhausted the limits of their senses and yet get no further in knowledge of God. Therefore in order to prove religion—that is, the existence of God, immortality, etc.—we have to go beyond the knowledge of the senses. All great prophets and seers claim to have "seen God", that is to say, they have had direct experience. There is no knowledge without experience, and man has to see God in his own soul. When man has come face to face with the one great fact in the universe, then alone will doubts vanish and crooked things become straight. This is "seeing God". Our business is to verify, not to swallow. Religion, like other sciences, requires you to gather facts, to see for yourself, and this is possible when you go beyond the knowledge which lies in the region of the five senses. Religious truths need verification by everyone. To see God is the one goal. Power is not the goal. Pure Existence-knowledge-and-love is the goal; and Love is God.

Thought, Imagination, and Meditation

The same faculty that we employ in dreams and thoughts, namely, imagination, will also be the means by which we arrive at Truth. When the imagination is very powerful, the object becomes visualised. Therefore by it we can bring our bodies to any state of health or disease. When we see a thing, the particles of the brain fall into a certain position like the mosaics of a kaleidoscope. Memory consists in getting back this combination and the same setting of the particles of the brain. The stronger the will, the greater will be the success in resetting these particles of the brain. There is only one power to cure the body, and that is in every man. Medicine only rouses this power. Disease is only the manifest struggle of that power to throw off the poison which has entered the body. Although the power to overthrow poison may be roused by medicine, it may be more permanently roused by the force of thought. Imagination must hold to the thought of health and strength in order that in case of illness the memory of the ideal of health may be roused and the particles re-arranged in the position into which they fell when healthy. The tendency of the body is then to follow the brain.

The next step is when this process can be arrived at by another's mind working on us. Instances of this may be seen every day. Words are only a mode of mind acting on mind.

Good and evil thoughts are each a potent power, and they fill the universe. As vibration continues, so thought remains in the form of thought until translated into action. For example, force is latent in the man's arm until he strikes a blow, when he translates it into activity. We are the heirs of good and evil thought. If we make ourselves pure and the instruments of good thoughts, these will enter us. The good soul will not be receptive to evil thoughts. Evil thoughts find the best field in evil people; they are like microbes which germinate and increase only when they find a suitable soil. Mere thoughts are like little wavelets; fresh impulses to vibration come to them simultaneously, until at last one great wave seems to stand up and swallow up the rest. These universal thought-waves seem to recur every five hundred years, when invariably the great wave typifies and swallows up the others. It is this which constitutes a prophet. He focuses in his own mind the thought of the age in which he is living and gives it back to mankind in concrete form. Krishna, Buddha, Christ, Mohammed, and Luther may be instanced as the great waves that stood up above their fellows (with a probable lapse of five hundred years between them). Always the wave that is backed by the greatest purity and the noblest character is what breaks upon the world as movement of social reform. Once again in our day there is a vibration of the waves of thought and the central idea is that of the Immanent God, and this is everywhere cropping up in every form and every sect. In these waves, construction alternates with destruction; yet the construction always makes an end of the work of destruction. Now, as a man dives deeper to reach his spiritual nature, he feels no longer bound by superstition. The majority of sects will be transient, and last only as bubbles because the leaders are not usually men of character. Perfect love, the heart never reacting, this is what builds character. There is no allegiance possible where there is no character in the leader, and perfect purity ensures the most lasting allegiance and confidence.

Take up an idea, devote yourself to it, struggle on in patience, and the sun will rise for you.

***

To return to imagination:

We have to visualise the Kundalini. The symbol is the serpent coiled on the triangular bone.

Then practice the breathing as described before, and, while holding the breath, imagine that breath like the current which flows down the figure 8; when it reaches the lowest point, imagine that it strikes the serpent on the triangle and causes the serpent to mount up the channel within the spinal cord. Direct the breath in thought to this triangle.

We have now finished the physical process and from this point it becomes mental.

The first exercise is called the "gathering-in". The mind has to be gathered up or withdrawn from wandering.

After the physical process, let the mind run on and do not

restrain it; but keep watch on your mind as a witness watching its action. This mind is thus divided into two—the player and the witness. Now strengthen the witnessing part and do not waste time in restraining your wanderings. The mind must think; but slowly and gradually, as the witness does its part, the player will come more and more under control, until at last you cease to play or wander. 2nd Exercise: Meditation—which may be divided into two. We are concrete in constitution and the mind must think in forms. Religion admits this necessity and gives the help of outward forms and ceremonies. You cannot meditate on God without some form. One will come to you, for thought and symbol are inseparable. Try to fix your mind on that form. 3rd Exercise: This is attained by practicing meditation and is really "one-pointedness". The mind usually works in a circle; make it remain on one point.

The last is the result. When the mind has reached this, all is gained—healing, clairvoyance, and all psychic gifts. In a moment you can direct this current of thought to anyone, as Jesus did, with instantaneous result.

People have stumbled upon these gifts without previous training, but I advise you to wait and practise all these steps slowly; then you will get everything under your control. You may practise healing a little if love is the motive, for that cannot hurt. Man is very short-sighted and impatient. All want power, but few will wait to gain it for themselves. He distributes but will not store up. It takes a long time to earn and but a short time to distribute. Therefore store up your powers as you acquire them and do not dissipate them.

Every wave of passion restrained is a balance in your favor. It is therefore good policy not to return anger for anger, as with all true morality. Christ said, "Resist not evil", and we do not understand it until we discover that it is not only moral but actually the best policy, for anger is loss of energy to the man who displays it. You should not allow your minds to come into those brain-combinations of anger and hatred.

When the primal element is discovered in chemical science, the work of the chemist will be finished. When unity is discovered, perfection in the science of religion is reached, and this was attained thousands of years ago. Perfect unity is reached when man says, "I and my Father are one".

LESSONS ON BHAKTI-YOGA

The Yoga Through Devotion

We have been considering Raja-Yoga and the physical exercises. Now we shall consider Yoga through devotion. But you must remember that no one system is necessary (for all). I want to set before you many systems, many ideals, in order that you may find one that will suit you; if one does not, perhaps another may.

We want to become harmonious beings, with the psychical, spiritual, intellectual, and working (active) sides of our nature equally developed. Nations and individuals typify one of these sides or types and cannot understand more than that one. They get so built up into one ideal that they cannot see any other. The ideal is really that we should become many-sided. Indeed the cause of the misery of the world is that we are so one-sided that we cannot sympathise with one another. Consider a man looking at the sun from beneath the earth, up the shaft of a mine; he sees one aspect of the sun. Then another man sees the sun from the earth's level, another through mist and fog, another from the mountain top. To each the sun has a different appearance. So there are many appearances, but in reality there is only one sun. There is diversity of vision, but one object; and that is the sun.

Each man, according to his nature, has a peculiar tendency and takes to certain ideals and a certain path by which to reach them. But the goal is always the same to all. The Roman Catholic is deep and spiritual, but he has lost breadth. The Unitarian is wide, but he has lost spirituality and considers religion as of divided importance. What we want is the depth of the Roman Catholic and the breadth of the Unitarian. We must be as broad as the skies, as deep as the ocean; we must have the zeal of the fanatic, the depth of the mystic, and the width of the agnostic. The word "toleration" has acquired an unpleasant association with the conceited man who, thinking himself in a high position, looks down on his fellow-creatures with pity. This is a horrible state of mind. We are all travelling the same way, towards the same goal, but by different paths made by the necessities of the case to suit diverse minds. We must become many-sided, indeed we must become protean in character, so as not only to tolerate, but to do what is much more difficult, to sympathise, to enter into another's path, and feel with him in his aspirations and seeking after God. There are two elements in every religion—a positive and a negative. In Christianity, for instance, when you speak of the Incarnation, of the Trinity, of salvation through Jesus Christ, I am with you. I say, "Very good, that I also hold true." But when you go on to say, "There is no other true religion, there is no other revelation of God", then I say, "Stop, I cannot go with you when you shut out, when you deny." Every religion has a message to deliver, something to teach man; but when it begins to protest, when it tries to disturb others, then it takes up a negative and therefore a dangerous position, and does not know where to begin or where to end.

Every force completes a circuit. The force we call man starts from the Infinite God and must return to Him. This return to God must be accomplished in one of two ways—either by slowly drifting back, going with nature, or by our own inward power, which causes us to stop on our course, which would, if left alone, carry us in a circuit back to God, and violently turn round and find God, as it were, by a short cut. This is what the Yogi does.

I have said that every man must choose his own ideal which is in accord with his nature. This ideal is called a man's Ishta. You must keep it sacred (and therefore secret) and when you worship God, worship according to your Ishta. How are we to find out the particular method? It is very difficult, but as you persevere in your worship, it will come of itself. Three things are the special gifts of God to man—the human body, the desire to be free, and the blessing of help from one who is already free. Now, we cannot have devotion without a Personal God. There must be the lover and the beloved. God is an infinitised human being. It is bound to be so, for so long as we are human, we must have a humanised God, we are forced to see a Personal God and Him only. Consider how all that we see in this world is not the object pure and simple, but the object plus our own mind. The chair plus the chair's reaction on your mind is the real chair. You must colour everything with your mind, and then alone you can see it. (Example: The white, square, shiny, hard box, seen by the man with three senses, then by the man with four senses, then by him with five senses. The last alone sees it with all the enumerated qualities, and each one before has seen an additional one to the previous man. Now suppose a man with six senses sees the same box, he would see still another quality added.)

Because I see love and knowledge, I know the universal cause is manifesting that love and knowledge. How can that be loveless which causes love in me? We cannot think of the universal cause without human qualities. To see God as separate from ourselves in the universe is necessary as a first step. There are three visions of God: the lowest vision, when God seems to have a body like ourselves (see Byzantine art); a higher vision when we invest God with human qualities; and then on and on, till we come to the highest vision, when we see God.

But remember that in *all* these steps we are seeing God and God alone; there is no illusion in it, no mistake. Just as when we saw the sun from different points, it was still the sun and not the moon or anything else.

We cannot help seeing God as we are—infinitised, but still as we are. Suppose we tried to conceive God as the

Absolute, we should have again to come back to the relative state in order to enjoy and love.

The devotion to God as seen in every religion is divided into two parts: the devotion which works through forms and ceremonies and through words, and that which works through love. In this world we are bound by laws, and we are always striving to break through these laws, we are always trying to disobey, to trample on nature. For instance, nature gives us no houses, we build them. Nature made us naked, we clothe ourselves. Man's goal is to be free, and just in so far as we are incompetent to break nature's laws shall we suffer. We only obey nature's law in order to be *outlawed*—beyond law. The whole struggle of life is *not* to obey. (That is why I sympathise with Christian Scientists, for they teach the liberty of man and the divinity of soul.) The soul is superior to all environment. "The universe is my father's kingdom; I am the heir-apparent"—that is the attitude for man to take. "My own soul can subdue all."

We must work through law before we come to liberty. External helps and methods, forms, ceremonies, creeds, doctrines, all have their right place and are meant to support and strengthen us until we become strong. Then they are no more necessary. They are our nurses, and as such indispensable in youth. Even books are nurses, medicines are nurses. But we must work to bring about the time when man shall recognise his mastery over his own body. Herbs and medicines have power over us as long as we allow them; when we become strong, these external methods are no more necessary.

Worships Through Words and Love

Body is only mind in a grosser form, mind being composed of finer layers and the body being the denser layers; and when man has perfect control over his mind, he will also have control over his body. Just as each mind has its own peculiar body, so to each word belongs a particular thought. We talk in double consonants when we are angry—"stupid", "fool", "idiot", etc.; in soft vowels when we are sad—"Ah me!" These are momentary feelings, of course; but there are eternal feelings, such as love, peace, calmness, joy, holiness; and these feelings have their word-expression in all religions, the word being only the embodiment of these, man's highest feelings. Now the thought has produced the word, and in their turn these words may produce the thoughts or feelings. This is where the help of words come in. Each of such words covers one ideal. These sacred mysterious words we all recognise and know, and yet if we merely read them in books, they have no effect on us. To be effective, they must be charged with spirit, touched and used by one who has himself been touched by the Spirit of God and who now *lives*. It is only he who can set the current in motion. The "laying on of hands" is the continuation of that current which was set in motion by Christ. The one who has the power of transmitting this current is called a Guru. With great teachers the use of words is not necessary—as with Jesus. But the "small fry" transmit this current through words.

Do not look on the faults of others. You cannot judge a man by his faults. (Example: Suppose we were to judge of an apple tree by the rotten, unripe, unformed apples we find on the ground. Even so do the faults of a man not show what the man's character is.) Remember, the wicked are always the same all over the world. The thief and the murderer are the same in Asia and Europe and America. They form a nation by themselves. It is only in the good and the pure and the strong that you find variety. Do not recognise wickedness in others. Wickedness is ignorance, weakness. What is the good of telling people they are weak?

Criticism and destruction are of no avail. We must give them something higher; tell them of their own glorious nature, their birthright. Why do not more people come to God? The reason is that so few people have any enjoyments outside their five senses. The majority *cannot* see with their eyes nor hear with their ears in the inner world.

We now come to *Worship through Love*.

It has been said, "It is good to be born in a church, but not to

Lectures & Discourses by **Swami Vivekananda**

die in it." The tree receives support and shelter from the hedge that surrounds it when young; but unless the hedge is removed, the growth and strength of that tree will be hindered. Formal worship, as we have seen, is a necessary stage, but gradually by slow growth we outgrow it and come to a higher platform. When love to God becomes perfect, we think no more of the qualities of God—that He is omnipotent, omnipresent, and all those big adjectives. We do not want anything of God, so we do not care to notice these qualities. Just all we want is love of God. But anthropomorphism still follows us. We cannot get away from our humanity, we cannot jump out of our bodies; so we must love God as we love one another.

There are five steps in human love.

1. The lowest, most commonplace, "peaceful" love, when we look up to our Father for all we want—protection, food, etc.
2. The love which makes us want to serve. Man wants to serve God as his master, the longing to serve dominating every other feeling; and we are indifferent whether the master is good or bad, kind or unkind.
3. The love of a friend, the love of equals—companions, playmates. Man feels God to be his companion.
4. Motherly love. God is looked upon as a child. In India this is considered a higher love than the foregoing, because it has absolutely no element of fear.
5. The love of husband and wife; love for love's sake—god the perfect, beloved one.

It has been beautifully expressed: "Four eyes meet, a change begins to come into two souls; love comes in the middle between these two souls and makes them *one*."

When a man has this last and most perfect form of love, then all desires vanish, forms and doctrines and churches drop away, even the desire for freedom (the end and aim of all religions is freedom from birth and death and other things) is given up. The highest love is the love that is sexless, for it is perfect unity that is expressed in the highest love, and sex differentiates bodies. It is therefore only in spirit that union is possible. The less we have of the physical idea, the more perfect will be our love; at last all physical thought will be forgotten, and the two souls will become one. We love, love always. Love comes and penetrates through the forms and sees beyond. It has been said, "The lover sees Helen's beauty in an Ethiopian's brow." The Ethiopian is the suggestion and upon that suggestion the man throws his love. As the oyster throws over the irritants, it finds in its shell, the substance that turns the irritants into beautiful pearls, so man throws out love, and it is always man's highest ideal that he loves, and the highest ideal is always selfless; so man loves love. God is love, and we love God—or love love. We only see love, love cannot be expressed. "A dumb man eating butter" cannot tell you what butter is like. Butter is butter, and its qualities cannot be expressed to those who have not tasted it. Love for love's sake cannot be expressed to those who have not felt it.

Love may be symbolised by a triangle. The first angle is, love never begs, never asks for anything; the second, love knows no fear; the third and the apex, love for love's sake.

Through the power of love the senses become finer and higher. The perfect love is very rare in human relation, for human love is almost always interdependent and mutual. But God's love is a constant stream, nothing can hurt or disturb it. When man loves God as his highest ideal, as no beggar, wanting nothing, then is love carried to the extreme of evolution, and it becomes a great power in the universe. It takes a long time to get to these things, and we have to begin by that which is nearest to our nature; some are born to service, some to be mothers in love. Anyhow, the result is with God. We must take advantage of nature.

On Doing Good to the World

We are asked: What good is your Religion to society? Society is made a test of truth. Now this is very illogical. Society is only a stage of growth through which we are passing. We might just as well judge the good or utility of a scientific discovery by its use to the baby. It is simply monstrous. If the social state were permanent, it would be the same as if the baby remained a baby. There can be no perfect man-baby; the words are a contradiction in terms, so there can be no perfect society. Man must and will grow out of such early stages. Society is good at a certain stage, but it cannot be our ideal; it is a constant flux. The present mercantile civilisation must die, with all its pretensions and humbug—all a kind of "Lord Mayor's Show". What the world wants is thought-power through individuals. My Master used to say, "Why don't you help your own lotus flower to bloom? The bees will then come of themselves." The world needs people who are mad with love of God. You must believe in yourself, and then you will believe in God. The history of the world is that of six men of faith, six men of deep pure character. We need to have three things; the heart to feel, the brain to conceive, the hand to work. First we must go out of the world and make ourselves fit instruments. Make yourself a dynamo. *Feel* first for the world. At a time when all men are ready to work, where is the man of *feeling*? Where is the feeling that produced an Ignatius Loyola? Test your love and humility. That man is not humble or loving who is jealous. Jealousy is a terrible, horrible sin; it enters a man so mysteriously. Ask yourself, does your mind react in hatred or jealousy? Good works are continually being undone by the tons of hatred and anger which are being poured out on the world. If you are pure, if you are strong, *you*, *one* man, are equal to the whole world.

The brain to conceive the next condition of doing good works is only a dry Sahara after all; it cannot do anything alone unless it has the *feeling* behind it. Take love, which has never failed; and then the brain will conceive, and the hand will work righteousness. Sages have dreamed of and have *seen* the vision of God. "The pure in heart shall see God." All the great ones claim to have seen God. Thousands of years ago has the vision been seen, and the unity which lies beyond has been recognised; and now the only thing we can do is to fill in these glorious outlines.

MOTHER-WORSHIP[1]

The two conjoint facts of perception we can never get rid of are happiness and unhappiness—things which bring us pain also bring pleasure. Our world is made up of these two. We cannot get rid of them; with every pulsation of life they are present. The world is busy trying to reconcile these opposites, sages trying to find solution of this commingling of the opposites. The burning heat of pain is intermitted by flashes of rest, the gleam of light breaking the darkness in intermittent flashes only to make the gloom deeper.

Children are born optimists, but the rest of life is a continuous disillusionment; not one ideal can be fully attained, not one thirst can be quenched. So on they go trying to solve the riddle, and religion has taken up the task.

In religions of dualism, among the Persians, there was a God and a Satan. This through the Jews has gone all over Europe and America. It was a working hypothesis thousands of years ago; but now we know, that is not tenable. There is nothing absolutely good or evil; it is good to one and evil to another, evil today, good tomorrow, and vice versa…

God was first of course a clan-god, then He became God of gods. With ancient Egyptians and Babylonians, this idea (of a dual God and Satan) was very practically carried out. Their Moloch became God of gods and the captured gods were forced to do homage in His temple.

Yet the riddle remains: Who presides over this Evil? Many are hoping against hope that all is good and that we do not understand. We are clutching at a straw, burying our heads in the sand. Yet we all follow morality and the gist of morality is sacrifice—not I but thou. Yet how it clashes with the great good God of the universe! He is so selfish, the most vengeful person that we know, with plagues, famines, war!

We all have to get experiences in this life. We may try to fly bitter experiences, but sooner or later they catch us. And I pity the man who does not face the whole.

Manu Deva of the Vedas, was transformed in Persia as Ahriman. So the mythological explanation of the question was dead; but the question remained, and there was no reply, no solution.

But there was the other idea in the old Vedic hymn to the Goddess: "I am the light. I am the light of the sun and moon; I am the air which animates all beings." This is the germ which afterwards develops into Mother-worship. By Mother-worship is not meant difference between father and mother. The first idea connoted by it is that of energy—I am the power that is in all beings.

1. Based on fragmentary notes of a class talk by Swami Vivekananda in New York.

The baby is a man of nerves. He goes on and on till he is a man of power. The idea of good and evil was not at first differentiated and developed. An advancing consciousness showed power as the primal idea. Resistance and struggle at every step is the law. We are the resultant of the two—energy and resistance, internal and external power. Every atom is working and resisting every thought in the mind. Everything we see and know is but the resultant of these two forces.

This idea of God is something new. In the Vedic hymns Varuna and Indra shower the choicest gifts and blessings on devotees, a very human idea, more human than man himself.

This is the new principle. There is one power behind all phenomena. Power is power everywhere, whether in the form of evil or as Saviour of the world. So this is the new idea; the old idea was man-god. Here is the first opening out of the idea of one universal power. "I stretch the bows of Rudra when He desires to destroy evil" (Rig-veda, X.125, *Devi-Sukta*).

Very soon in the Gita (IX.19, also X.4-5) we find, "O Arjuna, I am the Sat and I am the Asat, I am the good and I am the bad, I am the power of saints, I am the power of the wicked." But soon the speaker patches up truth, and the idea goes to sleep. I am power in good so long as it is doing good works.

In the religion of Persia, there was the idea of Satan, but in India, no conception of Satan. Later books began to realise this new idea. Evil exists, and there is no shirking the fact. The universe is a fact; and if a fact, it is a huge composition of good and evil. Whoever rules must rule over good and evil. If that power makes us live, the same makes us die. Laughter and tears are kin, and there are more tears than laughter in this world. Who made flowers, who made the Himalayas?—a very good God. Who made my sins and weaknesses?—karma, Satan, self. The result is a lame, one-legged universe, and naturally the God of the universe, a one-legged God.

The view of the absolute separation of good and evil, two cut and dried and separate existences, makes us brutes of unsympathetic hearts. The good woman jumps aside from the streetwalker. Why? She may be infinitely better than you in some respects. This view brings eternal jealousy and hatred in the world, eternal barrier between man and man, between the good man and the comparatively less good or evil man. Such brutal view is pure evil, more evil than evil itself. Good and evil are not separate existences, but there is an evolution of good, and what is less good we call evil.

Some are saints and some sinners. The sun shines on good and evil alike. Does he make any distinction?

The old idea of the fatherhood of God is connected with the sweet notion of God presiding over happiness. We want to deny facts. Evil is non-existent, is zero. The "I" is evil. And the "I" exists only too much. Am I zero? Every day I try to find myself so and fail.

All these ideas are attempts to fly evil. But we have to face it. Face the whole! Am I under contract to anyone to offer partial love to God only in happiness and good, not in misery and evil?

The lamp by the light of which one forges a name and another writes a cheque for a thousand dollars for famine, shines on both, knows no difference. Light knows no evil; you and I make it good or evil.

This idea must have a new name. It is called Mother, because in a literal sense it began long ago with a feminine writer elevated to a goddess. Then came Samkhya, and with it all energy is female. The magnet is still, the iron filings are active.

The highest of all feminine types in India is mother, higher than wife. Wife and children may desert a man, but his mother never. Mother is the same or loves her child perhaps a little more. Mother represents colourless love that knows no barter, love that never dies. Who can have such love?—only mother, not son, nor daughter, nor wife. "I am the Power that manifests everywhere", says the Mother—she who is bringing out this universe, and She who is bringing forth the following destruction. No need to say that destruction is only the beginning of creation. The top of a hill is only the beginning of a valley.

Be bold, face facts as facts. Do not be chased about the universe by evil. Evils are evils. What of that?

After all, it is only Mother's play. Nothing serious after all. What could move the Almighty? What made Mother create the universe? She could have no goal. Why? Because the goal is something that is not yet attained. What is this creation for? Just fun. We forget this and begin to quarrel and endure misery. We are the playmates of the Mother.

Look at the torture the mother bears in bringing up the baby. Does she enjoy it? Surely. Fasting and praying and watching. She loves it better than anything else. Why? Because there is no selfishness.

Pleasure will come—good: who forbids? Pain will come: welcome that too. A mosquito was sitting on a bull's horn; then his conscience troubled him and he said, "Mr. Bull, I have been sitting here a long time. Perhaps I annoy you. I am sorry, I will go away." But the bull replied, "Oh, no, not at all! Bring your whole family and live on my horn; what can you do to me?"

Why can we not say that to misery? To be brave is to have faith in the Mother! "I am Life, I am Death." She it is whose shadow is life and death. She is the pleasure in all pleasure. She is the misery in all misery. If life comes, it is the Mother; if death comes, it is the Mother. If heaven comes, She is. If hell comes, there is the Mother; plunge in. We have not faith, we have not patience to see this. We trust the man in the street; but there is one being in the universe we never trust and that is God. We trust Him when He works just our way. But the time will come when, getting blow after blow, the self-sufficient mind will die. In everything we do, the serpent ego is rising up. We are glad that there are so many thorns on the path. They strike the hood of the cobra.

Last of all will come self-surrender. Then we shall be able to give ourselves up to the Mother. If misery comes, welcome; if happiness comes, welcome. Then, when we come up to this love, all crooked things shall be straight. There will be the same sight for the Brahmin, the Pariah, and the dog. Until we love the universe with samesightedness, with impartial, undying love, we are missing again and again. But then all will have vanished, and we shall see in all the same infinite eternal Mother.

NARADA-BHAKTI-SUTRAS

A free translation dictated by Swamiji in America

Chapter I

1. Bhakti is intense love for God.

2. It is the nectar of love;

3. Getting which man becomes perfect, immortal, and satisfied for ever;

4. Getting which man desires no more, does not become jealous of anything, does not take pleasure in vanities:

5. Knowing which man becomes filled with spirituality, becomes calm, and finds pleasure only in God.

6. It cannot be used to fill any desire, itself being the check to all desires.

7. Sannyasa is giving up both the popular and the scriptural forms of worship.

8. The Bhakti-sannyasin is the one whose whole soul goes unto God, and whatever militates against love to God, he rejects.

9. Giving up all other refuge, he takes refuge in God.

10. Scriptures are to be followed as long as one's life has not become firm;

11. Or else there is danger of doing evil in the name of liberty.

12. When love becomes established, even social forms are given up, except those which are necessary for the preservation of life.

13. There have been many definitions of love, but Narada gives these as the signs of love: When all thoughts, all words, and all deeds are given up unto the Lord, and the least forgetfulness of God makes one intensely miserable, then love has begun.

14. As the Gopis had it—

15. Because, although worshipping God as their lover, they never forgot his God-nature;

16. Otherwise they would have committed the sin of unchastity.

17. This is the highest form of love, because there is no desire of reciprocity, which desire is in all human love.

Chapter II

1. Bhakti is greater than Karma, greater than Jnana, greater

than Yoga (Raja-Yoga), because Bhakti itself is its result, because Bhakti is both the means and the end (fruit).

2. As a man cannot satisfy his hunger by simple knowledge or sight of food, so a man cannot be satisfied by the knowledge or even the perception of God until love comes; therefore love is the highest.

Chapter III

1. These, however, the Masters have said about Bhakti:

2. One who wants this Bhakti must give up sense-enjoyments and even the company of people.

3. Day and night he must think about Bhakti and nothing else.

4. (He must) go where they sing or talk of God.

5. The principle cause of Bhakti is the mercy of a great (or free) soul.

6. Meeting with a great soul is hard to obtain, and never fails to save the soul.

7. Through the mercy of God we get such Gurus.

8. There is no difference between Him and His (own) ones.

9. Seek, therefore, for this.

10. Evil company is always to be shunned;

11. Because it leads to lust and anger, illusion, forgetfulness of the goal, destruction of the will (lack of perseverance), and destruction of everything.

12. These disturbances may at first be like ripples, but evil company at last makes them like the sea.

13. He gets across Maya who gives up all attachment, serves the great ones, lives alone, cuts the bondages of this world, goes beyond the qualities of nature, and depends upon the Lord for even his living.

14. He who gives up the fruits of work, he who

15. gives up all work and the dualism of joy and misery, who gives up even the scriptures, gets that unbroken love for God;

16. He crosses this river and helps others to cross it.

Chapter IV

1. The nature of love is inexpressible.

2. As the dumb man cannot express what he tastes, but his actions betray his feelings, so man cannot express this love in words, but his actions betray it.

3. In some rare persons it is expressed.

4. Beyond all qualities, all desires, ever increasing, unbroken, the finest perception is love.

5. When a man gets this love, he sees love everywhere, he hears love everywhere, he talks love everywhere, he thinks love everywhere.

6. According to the qualities or conditions, this love manifests itself differently.

7. The qualities are: Tamas (dullness, heaviness), Rajas (restlessness, activity), Sattva (serenity, purity); and the conditions are: Arta (afflicted), Artarthi (wanting something), Jijnasu (searching truth), Jnani (knower).

8. Of these the latter are higher than the preceding ones.

9. Bhakti is the easiest way of worship.

10. It is its own proof and does not require any other.

11. Its nature is peace and perfect bliss.

12. Bhakti never seeks to injure anyone or anything, not even the popular modes of worship.

13. Conversation about lust, or doubt of God or about one's enemies must not be listened to.

14. Egotism, pride, etc. must be given up.

15. If those passions cannot be controlled, place them upon God, and place all your actions on Him.

16. Merging the trinity of Love, Lover, and Beloved, worship God as His eternal servant, His eternal bride—thus love is to be made unto God.

Chapter V

1. That love is highest which is concentrated upon God.

2. When such speak of God, their voices stick in their throats, they cry and weep; and it is they who give holy places their holiness; they make good works, good books better, because they are permeated with God.

3. When a man loves God so much, his forefathers rejoice, the gods dance, and the earth gets a Master!

4. To such lovers there is no difference of caste, sex, knowledge, form, birth, or wealth;

5. Because they are all God's.

6. Arguments are to be avoided;

7. Because there is no end to them, and they lead to no satisfactory result.

8. Read books treating of this love, and do deeds which increase it.

9. Giving up all desires of pleasure and pain, gain and loss, worship God day and night. Not a moment is to be spent in vain.

10. Ahimsa (non-killing), truthfulness, purity, mercy, and godliness are always to be kept.

11. Giving up all other thoughts, the whole mind should day and night worship God. Thus being worshipped day and night, He reveals Himself and makes His worshippers feel Him.

12. In past, present, and future, Love is greatest!

Thus following the ancient sages, we have dared to preach the doctrine of Love, without fearing the jeers of the world.

ON ART

In art, interest must be centred on the principal theme. Drama is the most difficult of all arts. In it two things are to be satisfied—first, the ears, and second, the eyes. To paint a scene, if one thing be painted, it is easy enough; but to paint different things and yet to keep up the central interest is very difficult. Another difficult thing is stage-management, that is, combining different things in such a manner as to keep the central interest intact.

ON MUSIC

There is science in Dhrupad, Kheyal, etc., but it is in Kirtana, i.e. in Mathura and Viraha and other like compositions that there is real music—for there is feeling. Feeling is the soul, the secret of everything. There is more music in common people's songs, and they should be collected together. The science of Dhrupad etc., applied to the music of Kirtana will produce the perfect music.

ON MANTRA & MANTRA-CHAITANYA

The Mantra-shastris (upholders of the Mantra theory) believe that some words have been handed down through a succession of teachers and disciples, and the mere utterance of them will lead to some form of realisation. There are two different meanings of the word Mantra-chaitanya. According to some, if you practise the repetition of a certain Mantra, you will see the Ishta-devata who is the object or deity of that Mantra. But according to others, the word means that if you practise the repetition of a certain Mantra received from a Guru not competent, you will have to perform certain ceremonials by which that Mantra will become Chetana or living, and then its repetition will be successful. Different Mantras, when they are thus "living", show different signs, but the general sign is that one will be able to repeat it for a long time without feeling any strain and that his mind will very soon be concentrated. This is about the Tantrika Mantras.

From the time of the Vedas, two different opinions have been held about Mantras. Yaska and others say that the Vedas have meanings, but the ancient Mantra-shastris say that they have no meaning, and that their use consists only in uttering them in connection with certain sacrifices, when they will surely produce effect in the form of various material enjoyments or spiritual knowledge. The latter arises from the utterance of the Upanishads.

ON CONCEPTIONS OF GODHEAD

Man's inner hankering is to find some one who is free, that is, beyond the laws of nature. The Vedantins believe in such an Eternal Ishvara, while the Buddhists and the Sankhyas believe only a Janyeshvara (created God), that is, a God who was a man before, but has become God through spiritual practice. The Puranas reconcile these two positions by the doctrine of Incarna-tion. That is, they say that the Janyeshvara is nothing but the Nitya (Eternal) Ishvara, taking by Maya the form of a Janyeshvara. The argument of the Sankhyas against the doc-trine of Eternal Ishvara, viz "how a liberated soul can create the universe", is based on false grounds. For you cannot dictate anything to a liberated soul. He is free, that is, he may do whatever he likes. According to the Vedanta, the Janyeshvaras cannot create, preserve, or destroy the universe.

ON FOOD

You preach to others to be men but cannot give them good food. I have been thinking over this problem for the last four years. I wish to make an experiment whether something of the nature of flattened rice can be made out of wheat. Then we can get a different food every day. About drinking water, I searched for a filter which would suit our country. I found one pan-like porcelain vessel through which water was made to pass, and all the bacilli remained in the porcelain pan. But gradually that filter would itself become the hotbed of all germs. This is the danger of all filters. After continued searching I found one method by which water was distilled and then oxygen was passed into it. After this the water became so pure that great improvement of health was sure to result from its use.

ON SANNYASA AND FAMILY LIFE

Talking of the respective duties of a monk and a householder, Swamiji said:

A Sannyasin should avoid the food, bedding, etc., which have been touched or used by householders, in order to save himself—not from hatred towards them—so long as he has not risen to the highest grade, that is, become a Paramahamsa. A householder should salute him with "Namo Narayanaya", and a Sannyasin should bless the former.

मेरुसरषपयोर्यद्यत् सूर्यखद्योतयोरवि।
सरतिसागर्योर्यद्यत् तथा भिक्षुगृहस्थयो:॥

— Like the difference between the biggest mountain and a mustard-seed, between the sun and a glow-worm, between the ocean and a streamlet, is the wide gulf between a Sannyasin and a householder.

Swami Vivekananda made everyone utter this and, chanting some Vedanta stanzas, said, "You should always repeat to yourselves these Shlokas. 'Shravana' not only means hearing from the Guru, but also repetition to our own selves. 'आवृत्तरसिकृदुपदेशात्— scriptural truth should be often repeated for such has been repeatedly enjoined'— in this Sutra of Vedanta, Vyasa lays stress on repetition."

ON QUESTIONING THE COMPETENCY OF THE GURU

In the course of a conversation Swamiji spiritedly remarked, "Leave off your commercial calculating ideas. If you can get rid of your attachment to a single thing, you are on the way to liberation. Do not see a public woman, or sinner, or Sadhu.

That vile woman also is the Divine Mother. A Sannyasin says once, twice, that she is Mother; then he gets deluded again and says, 'Hence, O vile, unchaste woman!' At a moment all your ignorance may vanish. It is foolish talk that ignorance disperses gradually. There are disciples who have been devoted to the Guru even when he has fallen from the ideal. I have seen in Rajputana one whose spiritual teacher had turned a Christian, but who nevertheless went on giving him his regular dues. Give up your Western ideas. Once you have pledged your faith to a particular teacher, stick to him with all force. It is children who say that there is no morality in the Vedanta. Yes, they are right. Vedanta is above morality. Talk of high things, as you have become Sannyasins."

SHRI RAMAKRISHNA: THE SIGNIFICANCE OF HIS LIFE AND TEACHINGS

In a narrow society there is depth and intensity of spirituality. The narrow stream is very rapid. In a catholic society, along with the breadth of vision we find a proportionate loss in depth and intensity. But the life of Sri Ramakrishna upsets all records of history. It is a remarkable phenomenon that in Sri Ramakrishna there has been an assemblage of ideas deeper than the sea and vaster than the skies.

We must interpret the Vedas in the light of the experience of Sri Ramakrishna. Shankaracharya and all other commentators made the tremendous mistake to think that the whole of the Vedas spoke the same truth. Therefore they were guilty of torturing those of the apparently conflicting Vedic texts which go against their own doctrines, into the meaning of their particular schools. As, in the olden times, it was the Lord alone, the deliverer of the Gita , who partially harmonised these apparently conflicting statements, so with a view to completely settling this dispute, immensely magnified in the process of time, He Himself has come as Sri Ramakrishna. Therefore no one can truly understand the Vedas and Vedanta, unless one studies them in the light of the utterance of Sri Ramakrishna who first exemplified in his life and taught that these scriptural statements which appear to the cursory view as contradictory, are meant for different grades of aspirants and are arranged in the order of evolution. The whole world will undoubtedly forget its fights and disputes and be united in a fraternal tie in religious and other matters as a consequence of these teachings.

If there is anything which Sri Ramakrishna has urged us to give up as carefully as lust and wealth, it is the limiting of the infinitude of God by circumscribing it within narrow bounds. Whoever, therefore, will try to limit the infinite ideals of Sri Ramakrishna in that way, will go against him and be his enemy.

One of his own utterances is that those who have seen the chameleon only once, know only one colour of the animal, but those who have lived under the tree, know all the colours that it puts on. For this reason, no saying of Sri Ramakrishna can be accepted as authentic, unless it is verified by those who constantly lived with him and whom he brought up to fulfil his life's mission.

Such a unique personality, such a synthesis of the utmost of Jnana, Yoga, Bhakti and Karma, has never before appeared among mankind. The life of Sri Ramakrishna proves that the greatest breadth, the highest catholicity and the utmost intensity can exist side by side in the same individual, and that society also can be constructed like that, for society is nothing but an aggregate of individuals.

He is the true disciple and follower of Sri Ramakrishna, whose character is perfect and all-sided like this. The formation of such a perfect character is the ideal of this age, and everyone should strive for that alone.

ON SHRI RAMAKRISHNA & HIS VIEWS

By force, think of one thing at least as Brahman. Of course it is easier to think of Ramakrishna as God, but the danger is that we cannot form Ishvara-buddhi (vision of Divinity) in others. God is eternal, without any form, omnipresent. To think of Him as possessing any form is blasphemy. But the secret of image-worship is that you are trying to develop your vision of Divinity in one thing.

Shri Ramakrishna used to consider himself as an Incarnation in the ordinary sense of the term, though I could not understand it. I used to say that he was Brahman in the Vedantic sense; but just before his passing away, when he was suffering from the characteristic difficulty in breathing, he said to me as I was cogitating in my mind whether he could even in that pain say that he was an Incarnation, "He who was Rama and Krishna has now actually become Ramakrishna—but not in your Vedantic sense!" He used to love me intensely, which made many quite jealous of me. He knew one's character by sight, and never changed his opinion. He could perceive, as it were, supersensual things, while we try to know one's character by reason, with the result that our judgments are often fallacious. He called some persons his Antarangas or 'belonging to the inner circle', and he used to teach them the secrets of his own nature and those of Yoga. To the outsiders or Bahirangas he taught those parables now known as "Sayings". He used to prepare those young men (the former class) for his work, and though many complained to him about them, he paid no heed. I may have perhaps a better opinion of a Bahiranga than an Antaranga through his actions, but I have a superstitious regard for the latter. "Love me, love my dog", as they say. I love that Brahmin priest intensely, and therefore, love whatever he used to love, whatever he used to regard! He was afraid about me that I might create a sect, if left to myself.

He used to say to some, "You will not attain spirituality in this life." He sensed everything, and this will explain his apparent partiality to some. He, as a scientist, used to see that different people required different treatment. None except those of the "inner circle" were allowed to sleep in his room. It is not true that those who have not seen him will not attain salvation; neither is it true that a man who has seen him thrice will attain Mukti (liberation).

Devotion as taught by Narada, he used to preach to the masses, those who were incapable of any higher training.

He used generally to teach dualism. As a rule, he never taught Advaitism. But he taught it to me. I had been a dualist before.

SHRI RAMAKRISHNA: THE NATION'S IDEAL

In order that a nation may rise, it must have a high ideal. Now, that ideal is, of course, the abstract Brahman. But as you all cannot be inspired by an abstract ideal, you must have a personal ideal. You have got that, in the person of Shri Ramakrishna. The reason why other personages cannot be our ideal now is, that their days are gone; and in order that Vedanta may come to everyone, there must be a person who is in sympathy with the present generation. This is fulfilled in Shri Ramakrishna. So now you should place him before everyone. Whether one accepts him as a Sadhu or an Avatara does not matter.

He said he would come once more with us. Then, I think, he will embrace Videha-mukti (Absolute Emancipation). If you wish to work, you must have such an Ishta-devata, or Guardian Angel, as the Christian nations call it. I sometimes imagine that different nations have different Ishta-devatas, and these are each trying for supremacy. Sometimes I fancy, such an Ishta-devata becomes powerless to do service to a nation.

NOTES OF LECTURES
MERCENARIES IN RELIGION

Delivered in Minneapolis on November 26, 1893: Reported in the Minneapolis Journal.

The Unitarian church was crowded yesterday morning by an audience anxious to learn something of eastern religious thought as outlined by Swami Vivekananda, a Brahmin priest, who was prominent in the Parliament of Religions at Chicago last summer. The distinguished representative of the Brahmin faith was brought to Minneapolis by the Peripatetic Club, and he addressed that body last Friday evening. He was induced to remain until this week, in order that he might deliver the address yesterday ... Dr. H.M. Simmons, the pastor, ... read from Paul's lesson of faith, hope and charity, and "the greatest of these is charity", supplementing that reading by a selection from the Brahmin scripture which teaches the same lesson, and also a selection from the Moslem faith, and poems from the Hindu literature, all of which are in harmony with Paul's utterances.

After a second hymn Swami Vivekandi [sic] was introduced. He stepped to the edge of the platform and at once had his audience interested by the recital of a Hindu story. He said

in excellent English: "I will tell you a story of five blind men. There was a procession in a village in India, and all the people turned out to see the procession, and specially the gaily caparisoned elephant. The people were delighted, and as the five blind men could not see, they determined to touch the elephant that they might acquaint themselves with its form. They were given the privilege, and after the pro-cession had passed, they returned home together with the people, and they began to talk about the elephant. 'It was just like a wall,' said one. 'No it wasn't,' said another, 'it was like a piece of rope.' 'You are mistaken,' said a third, 'I felt him and it was just a serpent.' The discussion grew excited, and the fourth declared the elephant was like a pillow. The argument soon broke into more angry expressions, and the five blind men took to fighting. Along came a man with two eyes, and he said, 'My friends, what is the matter?' The disputation was explained, whereupon the new-comer said, 'Men, you are all right: the trouble is you touched the elephant at different points. The wall was the side, the rope was the tail, the serpent was the trunk, and the toes were the pillow. Stop your quarrelling; you are all right, only you have been viewing the elephant from different standpoints."

Religion, he said, had become involved in such a quarrel. The people of the West thought they had the only religion of God, and the people of the East held the same prejudice. Both were wrong; God was in every religion.

There were many bright criticisms on Western thought. The Christians were characterised as having a "shopkeeping religion". They were always begging of God —"O God, give me this and give me that; O God, do this and do that." The Hindu couldn't understand this. He thought it wrong to be begging of God. Instead of begging, the religious man should give. The Hindu believed in giving to God, to his fellows, instead of asking God to give to them. He had observed that the people of the West, very many of them, thought a great deal of God, so long as they got along all right, but when the reverse came, then God was forgotten: not so with the Hindu, who had come to look upon God as a being of love. The Hindu faith recognised the motherhood of God as well as the fatherhood, because the former was a better fulfilment of the idea of love. The Western Christian would work all the week for the dollar, and when he succeeded he would pray, "O God, we thank thee for giving us this benefit", and then he would put all the money into his pocket; the Hindu would make the money and then give it to God by helping the poor and the less fortunate. And so comparisons were made between the ideas of the West and the ideas of the East. In speaking of God, Vivekanandi said in substance: "You people of the West think you have God. What is it to have God? If you have Him, why is it that so much criminality exists, that nine out of ten people are hypocrites? Hypocrisy cannot exist where God is. You have your palaces for the worship of God, and you attend them in part for a time once a week, but how few go to worship God. It is the fashion in the West to attend church, and many of you attend for no other reason. Have you then, you people of the West, any right to lay exclusive claim to the possession of God?"

Here the speaker was interrupted by spontaneous applause. He proceeded: "We of the Hindu faith believe in worshipping God for love's sake, not for what He gives us, but because God is love, and no nation, no people, no religion has God until it is willing to worship Him for love's sake. You of the West are practical in business, practical in great inventions, but we of the East are practical in religion. You make commerce your business; we make religion our business. If you will come to India and talk with the workman in the field, you will find he has no opinion on politics. He knows nothing of politics. But you talk to him of religion, and the humblest knows about monotheism, deism, and all the isms of religion. You ask: "'What government do you live under?' and he will reply: 'I don't know. I pay my taxes, and that's all I know about it.' I have talked with your labourers, your farmers, and I find that in politics they are all posted. They are either Democrat or Republican, and they know whether they prefer free silver or a gold standard. But you talk to them of religion; they are like the Indian farmer, they don't know, they attend such a church, but they don't know what it believes; they just pay their pew rent, and that's all they know about it—or God."

The superstitions of India were admitted, "but what nation doesn't have them?" he asked. In summing up, he held that the nations had been looking at God as a monopoly. All nations had God, and any impulse for good was God. The Western people, as well as the Eastern people, must learn to "want God", and this "want" was compared to the man under water, struggling for air; he wanted it, he couldn't live without it. When the people of the West "wanted" God in that manner, then they would be welcome in India, because the missionaries would then come to them with God, not with the idea that India knows not God, but with love in their hearts and not dogma.

THE DESTINY OF MAN

Delivered in Memphis on January 17, 1894:
Reported in Appeal-Avalanche.

The audience was moderately large, and was made up of the best literary and musical talent of the city, including some of the most distinguished members of the legal fraternity and financial institutions.

The speaker differs in one respect in particular from some American orators. He advances his ideas with as much deliberation as a professor of mathematics demon-strates an example in algebra to his students. Kananda[1] speaks with perfect faith in his own powers and ability to hold successfully his position against all argument. He advances no ideas, nor make assertions that he does not follow up to a logical conclusion. Much

1. In those days Swamiji was generally referred to by American press as Vive Kananda.

of his lecture is something on the order of Ingersoll's philosophy. He does not believe in future punishment nor in God as Christians believe in Him. He does not believe the mind is immortal, from the fact that it is dependent, and nothing can be immortal except it is independent of all things. He says: "God is not a king sitting away in one corner of the universe to deal out punishment or rewards according to a man's deeds here on earth, and the time will come when man will know the truth, and stand up and say, 'I am God,' am life of His life. Why teach that God is far away when our real nature, our immortal principle is God? "Be not deluded by your religion teaching original sin, for the same religion teaches original purity. When Adam fell, he fell from purity. (Applause) Purity is our real nature, and to regain that is the object of all religion. All men are pure; all men are good. Some objections can be raised to them, and you ask why some men are brutes? That man you call a brute is like the diamond in the dirt and dust—brush the dust off and it is a diamond, just as pure as if the dust had never been on it, and we must admit that every soul is a big diamond. "Nothing is baser than calling our brother a sinner. A lioness once fell upon a flock of sheep and killed a lamb. A sheep found a very young lion, and it followed her, and he gave it suck, and it grew up with the sheep and learned to eat grass like a sheep. One day an old lion saw the sheep lion and tried to get it away from the sheep, but it ran away as he approached. The big lion waited till he caught the sheep lion alone, and he seized it and carried it to a clear pool of water and said, 'You are not a sheep, but a lion; look at your picture in the water.' The sheep lion, seeing its picture reflected from the water, said, 'I am a lion and not a sheep.' Let us not think we are sheep, but be lions, and don't bleat and eat grass like a sheep. "For four months I have been in America. In Massachusetts I visited a reformatory prison. The jailor at that prison never knows for what crimes the prisoners are incarcerated. The mantle of charity is thrown around them. In another city there were three newspapers, edited by very learned men, trying to prove that severe punishment was a necessity, while one other paper contended that mercy was better than punishment. The editor of one paper proved by statistics that only fifty per cent of criminals who received severe punishment returned to honest lives, while ninety per cent of those who received light punishment returned to useful pursuits in life. "Religion is not the outcome of the weakness of human nature; religion is not here because we fear a tyrant; religion is love, unfolding, expanding, growing. Take the watch—within the little case is machinery and a spring. The spring, when wound up, tries to regain its natural state. You are like the spring in the watch, and it is not necessary that all watches have the same kind of a spring, and it is not necessary that we all have the same religion. And why should we quarrel? If we all had the same ideas the world would be dead. External motion we call action; internal motion is human thought. The stone falls to the earth. You say it is caused by the law of gravitation. The horse draws the cart and God draws the horse. That is the law of motion. Whirlpools show the strength of the current; stop the current and stag-nation ensues. Motion is life. We must have unity and variety. The rose would smell as sweet by any other name, and it does not matter what your religion is called. "Six blind men lived in a village. They could not see the elephant, but they went out and felt of him. One put his hand on the elephant's tail, one of them on his side, one on his tongue[trunk], one on his ear. They began to describe the elephant. One said he was like a rope; one said he was like a great wall; one said he was like a boa constrictor, and another said he was like a fan. They finally came to blows and went to pummelling each other. A man who could see came along and inquired the trouble, and the blind men said they had seen the elephant and disagreed because one accused the other of lying. 'Well,' said the man, 'you have all lied; you are blind, and neither of you have seen it.' That is what is the matter with our religion. We let the blind see the elephant. (Applause). "A monk of India said, 'I would believe you if you were to say that I could press the sands of the desert and get oil, or that I could pluck the tooth from the mouth of the crocodile without being bitten, but I cannot believe you when you say a bigot can be changed.' You ask why is there so much variance in religions? The answer is this: The little streams that ripple down a thousand mountain sides are destined to come at last to the mighty ocean. So with the different religions. They are destined at last to bring us to the bosom of God. For 1,900 years you have been trying to crush the Jews. Why could you not crush them? Echo answers: Ignorance and bigotry can never crush truth."

The speaker continued in this strain of reasoning for nearly two hours, and concluded by saying: "Let us help, and not destroy."

REINCARNATION

Delivered in Memphis on January 19, 1894:
Reported in Appeal-Avalanche.

Swami Vive Kananda, the beturbaned and yellow-robed monk, lectured again last night to a fair-sized and appreciative audience at the La Salette Academy on Third street.

The subject was "Transmigration of the Soul, or "metempsychosis". Possibly Vive Kananda never appeared to greater advantage than in this role, so to speak. Metempsychosis is one of the most widely-accepted beliefs among the Eastern races, and one that they are ever ready to defend, at home or abroad. As Kananda said: "Many of you do not know that it is one of the oldest religious doctrines of all the old religions. It was known among the Pharisees, among the Jews, among the first fathers of the Christian Church, and was a common belief among the Arabs. And it lingers still with the Hindus and the Buddhists. "This state of things went on until the days of science which is merely a contemplation of energies. Now, you Western people believe this doctrine to be subversive of morality. In order to have a full survey of the argument, its

logical and metaphysical features, we will have to go over all the ground. All of us believe in a moral governor of this universe; yet nature reveals to us instead of justice, injustice. One man is born under the best of circumstances. Throughout his entire life circumstances come ready made to his hands—all conducive to happiness and a higher order of things. Another is born, and at every point his life is at variance with that of his neighbour. He dies in depravity, exiled from society. Why so much impartiality [partiality] in the distribution of happiness? "The theory of metempsychosis reconciles this dis-

harmonious chord in your common beliefs. Instead of making us immoral, this theory give us the idea of justice. Some of you say: 'It is God's will.' This is no answer. It is unscientific. Everything has a cause. The sole cause and whole theory of causation being left with God, makes Him a most immoral creature. But materialism is as much illogical as the other. So far as we go, perception [causation?] involves all things. Therefore, this doctrine of the transmigration of the soul is necessary on these grounds. Here we are all born. Is this the first creation? Is creation something coming out of nothing? Analysed completely, this sentence is nonsense. It is not creation, but manifestation. "A something cannot be the effect of a cause that is not. If I put my finger in the fire, the burn is a simultaneous effect, and I know that the cause of the burn was the action of my placing my finger in contact with the fire. And as in the case of nature, there never was a time when nature did not exist, because the cause has always existed. But for argument['s] sake, admit that there was a time when there was no existence. Where was all this mass of matter? To create something new would be the introduction of so much more energy into the universe. This is impossible. Old things can be re-created, but there can be no addition to the universe. "No mathematical demonstration could be made that would have this theory of metempsychosis. According to logic, hypothesis and theory must not be believed. But my contention is that no better hypothesis has been forwarded by the human intellect to explain the phenomena of life. "I met with a peculiar incident while on a train leaving the city of Minneapolis. There was a cowboy on the train. He was a rough sort of a fellow and a Presbyterian of the blue nose type. He walked up and asked me where I was from. I told him India. 'What are you?' he said. 'Hindu', I replied. 'Then you must go to hell', he remarked. I told him of this theory, and after [my] explaining it, he said he had always believed in it because he said that one day when he was chopping a log, his little sister came out in her clothes and said that she used to be a man. That is why he believed in the transmigration of souls. The whole basis of the theory is this: If a man's actions be good, he must be a higher being, and vice versa. "There is another beauty in this theory—the moral motor [motive] it supplies. What is done is done. It says, 'Ah, that it were done better.' Do not put your finger in the fire again. Every moment is a new chance."

Vive Kananda spoke in this strain for some time, and he was frequently applauded.

Swami Vive Kananda will lecture again this afternoon at 4 o'clock at La Salette Academy on "The Manners and Customs of India."

COMPARATIVE THEOLOGY

Delivered in Memphis on January 21, 1894:
Reported in Appeal-Avalanche.

"Comparative Theology" was the subject of a discourse last night by Swami Vive Kananda at the Young Men's Hebrew Association Hall. It was the blue-ribbon lecture of the series, and no doubt increased the general admiration the people of this city entertain for the learned gentleman.

Heretofore Vive Kananda has lectured for the benefit of one charity-worthy object or another, and it can be safely said that he has rendered them material aid. Last night, however, he lectured for his own benefit. The lecture was planned and sustained by Mr. Hu L. Brinkley, one of Vive Kananda's warmest friends and most ardent admirers. In the neighbourhood of two hundred gathered at the hall last night to hear the eminent Easterner for the last time in this city.

The first question the speaker asserted in connection with the subject was: "Can there be such a distinction between religions as their creeds would imply?"

He asserted that no differences existed now, and he retraced the line of progress made by all religions and brought it back to the present day. He showed that such variance of opinion must of necessity have existed with primitive man in regard to the idea of God, but that as the world advanced step by step in a moral and intellectual way, the distinctions became more and more indistinct, until finally it had faded away entirely, and now there was one all-prevalent doctrine — that of an absolute existence. "No savage", said the speaker, "can be found who does not believe in some kind of a god." "Modern science does not say whether it looks upon this as a revelation or not. Love among savage nations is not very strong. They live in terror. To their superstitious imaginations is pictured some malignant spirit, before the thought of which they quake in fear and terror. Whatever he likes he thinks will please the evil spirit. What will pacify him he thinks will appease the wrath of the spirit. To this end he labours even against his fellow-savage."

The speaker went on to show by historical facts that the savage man went from ancestral worship to the worship of elephants, and later to gods, such as the God of Thunder and Storms. Then the religion of the world was polytheism. "The beauty of the sunrise, the grandeur of the sunset, the mystifying appearance of the star-bedecked skies, and the weirdness of thunder and lightning[nature] impressed primitive man with a force that he could not explain, and suggested the idea of a higher and more powerful being controlling the infinities that flocked before his gaze," said Vive Kananda.

Then came another period — the period of monotheism. All the gods disappeared and blended into one, the God of Gods, the ruler of the universe. Then the speaker traced the Aryan race up to that period, where they said: "We live and move in God. He is motion." Then there came another period known to metaphysics as the "period of Pantheism". This race rejected Polytheism and Monotheism, and the idea that God was the universe, and said "the soul of my soul is the only true existence. My nature is my existence and will expand to me."

Vive Kananda then took up Buddhism. He said that they neither asserted nor denied the existence of a God. Buddha would simply say, when his counsel was sought: "You see misery. Then try to lessen it." To a Buddhist misery is ever present, and society measures the scope of his existence. Mohammedans, he said, believed in the Old Testament of the Hindu [Hebrew] and the New Testament of the Christian. They do not like the Christians, for they say they are heretics and teach man-worship. Mohammed ever forbade his followers having a picture of himself. "The next question that arises," said he, "are these religions true or are some of them true and some of them false? They have all reached one conclusion, that of an absolute and infinite existence. Unity is the object of religion. The multiple of phenomena that is seen at every hand is only the infinite variety of unity. an analysis of religion shows that man does not travel from fallacy to truth, but from a lower truth to a higher truth. "A man brings in a coat to a lot of people. Some say the coat does not fit them. Well, you get out; you can't have a coat. Ask one Christian minister what is the matter with all the other sects that are opposed to his doctrines and dogmas, and he will answer: 'Oh, they're not Christians.' But we have better instruction than these. Our own natures, love, and science — they teach us better. Like the eddies to a river, take them away and stagnation follows. Kill the difference in opinions, and it is the death of thought. Motion is necessity. Thought is the motion of the mind, and when that ceases death begins. "If you put a simple molecule of air in the bottom of a glass of water it at once begins a struggle to join the infinite atmosphere above. So it is with the soul. It is struggling to regain its pure nature and to free itself from this material body. It wants to regain its own infinite expansion. This is everywhere the same. Among Christians, Buddhists, Mohammedans, agnostic, or priest, the soul is struggling. A river flows a thousand miles down the circuitous mountain side to where it joins the seas, and a man is standing there to tell it to go back and start anew and assume a more direct course! That man is a fool. You are a river that flows from the heights of Zion. I flow from the lofty peaks of the Himalayas. I don't say to you, go back and come down as I did, you're wrong. That is more wrong than foolish. Stick to your beliefs. The truth is never lost. Books may perish, nations may go down in a crash, but the truth is preserved and is taken up by some man and handed back to society, which proves a grand and continuous revelation of God."

THE SCIENCE OF YOGA[1]

*Delivered at Tucker Hall, Alameda, California,
on April 13, 1900.*

The old Sanskrit word Yoga is defined as [Chittavrit-tinirodha]. It means that Yoga is the science that teaches us to bring the Chitta under control from the state of change. The Chitta is the stuff from which our minds are made and which is being constantly churned into waves by external and internal influences. Yoga teaches us how to control the mind so that it is not thrown out of balance into wave forms...

What does this mean? To the student of religion almost ninety-nine per cent of the books and thoughts of religion are mere speculations. One man thinks religion is this and another, that. If one man is more clever than the others, he overthrows their speculations and starts a new one. Men have been studying new religious systems for the last two thousand, four thousand, years—how long exactly nobody knows... When they could not reason them out, they said, "Believe!" If they were powerful, they forced their beliefs. This is going on even now.

But there are a set of people who are not entirely satisfied with this sort of thing. "Is there no way out?" they ask. You do not speculate that way in physics, chemistry, and mathematics. Why cannot the science of religion be like any other science? They proposed this way: If such a thing as the soul of man really exists, if it is immortal, if God really exists as the ruler of this universe—he must be [known] here; and all that must be [realised] in [your own] consciousness.

The mind cannot be analysed by any external machine. Supposing you could look into my brain while I am thinking, you would only see certain molecules interchanged. You could not see thought, consciousness, ideas, images. You would simply see the mass of vibrations—chemical and physical changes. From this example we see that this sort of analysis would not do.

Is there any other method by which the mind can be analysed as mind? If there is, then the real science of religion is possible. The science of Raja-yoga claims there is such a possibility. We can all attempt it and succeed to a certain degree. There is this great difficulty: In external sciences the object is [comparatively easy to observe]. The instruments of analysis are rigid; and both are external. But in the analysis of the mind the object and the instruments of analysis are the same thing... The subject and the object become one...

External analysis will go to the brain and find physical and chemical changes. It would never succeed [in answering the questions]: What is the consciousness? What is your imagination? Where does this vast mass of ideas you have come from, and where do they go? We cannot deny them. They are facts. I never saw my own brain. I have to take for granted I have one. But man can never deny his own conscious imagination...

The great problem is ourselves. Am I the long chain I do not see—one piece following the other in rapid succession but quite unconnected? Am I such a state of consciousness [for ever in a flux]? Or am I something more than that—a substance, an entity, what we call the soul? In other words, has man a soul or not? Is he a bundle of states of consciousness without any connection, or is he a unified substance? That is the great controversy. If we are merely bundles of consciousness,... such a question as immortality would be merely delusion... On the other hand, if there is something in me which is a unit, a substance, then of course I am immortal. The unit cannot be destroyed or broken into pieces. Only compounds can be broken up...

All religions except Buddhism believe and struggle in some way or other to reach such a substance. Buddhism denies the substance and is quite satisfied with that. It says, this business about God, the soul, immortality, and all that—do not vex yourselves with such questions. But all the other religions of the world cling to this substance. They all believe that the soul is the substance in man in spite of all the changes, that God is the substance which is in the universe. They all believe in the immortality of the soul. These are speculations. Who is to decide the controversy between the Buddhists and the Christians? Christianity says there is a substance that will live for ever. The Christian says, "My Bible says so." The Buddhist says, "I do not believe in your book."...

The question is: Are we the substance [the soul] or this subtle matter, the changing, billowing mind?... Our minds are constantly changing. Where is the substance within? We do not find it. I am now this and now that. I will believe in the substance if for a moment you can stop these changes...

Of course all the beliefs in God and heaven are little beliefs of organised religions. Any scientific religion never proposes such things.

Yoga is the science that teaches us to stop the Chitta [the mind-stuff] from getting into these changes. Suppose you succeed in leading the mind to a perfect state of Yoga. That moment you have solved the problem. You have known what you are. You have mastered all the changes. After that you may let the mind run about, but it is not the same mind any more. It is perfectly under your control. No more like wild horses that dash you down... You have seen God. This is no longer a matter of speculation. There is no more Mr. So-and-so,... no more books or Vedas, or controversy of preachers, or anything. You have been yourself: I am the substance beyond all these changes. I am not the changes; if I were, I could not stop them. I can stop the changes, and therefore I can never be the changes. This is the proposition of the science of Yoga...

We do not like these changes. We do not like changes at all. Every change is being forced upon us... In our country bullocks carry a yoke on their shoulders [which is connected by a pole with an oil press]. From the yoke projects a piece of wood [to which is tied a bundle of grass] just far enough

1. Fragmentary notes of a lecture recorded by Ida Ansell and reprinted from Vedanta and the West, July-August, 1957.

to tempt the bullock, but he cannot reach it. He wants to eat the grass and goes a little farther [thereby turning the oil press]...We are like these bullocks, always trying to eat the grass and stretching our necks to reach it. We go round and round this way. Nobody likes these changes. Certainly not!...All these changes are forced upon us...We cannot help it. Once we have put ourselves in the machine, we must go on and on. The moment we stop, there is greater evil than if we continued forward...

Of course misery comes to us. It is all misery because it is all unwilling. It is all forced. Nature orders us and we obey, but there is not much love lost between us and nature. All our work is an attempt to escape nature. We say we are enjoying nature. If we analyse ourselves, we find that we are trying to escape everything and invent ways to enjoy this and that...[Nature is] like the Frenchman who had invited an English friend and told him of his old wines in the cellar. He called for a bottle of old wine. It was so beautiful, and the light sparkled inside like a piece of gold. His butler poured out a glass, and the Englishman quietly drank it. The butler had brought in a bottle of castor oil! We are drinking castor oil all the time; we cannot help it...[People in general]...are so reduced to machinery they do not...even think. Just like cats, dogs and other animals, they are also driven with the whip by nature. They never disobey, never think of it. But even they have some experience of life...[Some, however,] begin to question: What is this? What are all these experiences for? What is the Self? Is there any escape? Any meaning to life?...

The good will die. The wicked will die. Kings will die, and beggars will die. The great misery is death...All the time we are trying to avoid it. And if we die in a comfortable religion, we think we will see Johns and Jacks afterwards and have a good time.

In your country they bring Johns and Jacks down to show you [in Seances]. I saw such people numbers of times and shook hands with them. Many of you may have seen them. They bang the piano and sing "Beulah Land": America is a vast land. My home is on the other side of the world. I do not know where Beulah Land is. You will not find it in any geography. See our good comfortable religion! The old, old moth-eaten belief!

Those people cannot think. What can be done for them? They have been eaten up by the world. There is nothing in them to think. Their bones have become hollow, their brains are like cheese...I sympathise with them. Let them have their comfort! Some people are evidently very much comforted by seeing their ancestors from Beulah Land.

One of these mediums offered to bring my ancestors down to me. I said, "Stop there. Do anything you like, but if you bring my ancestors, I don't know if I can restrain myself." The medium was very kind and stopped.

In our country, when we begin to get worried by things, we pay something to the priests and make a bargain with God...For the time being we feel comforted, otherwise we will not pay the priests. A little comfort comes, but [it turns] into reaction shortly...So again misery comes. The same misery is here all the time. Your people in our country says, "If you believe in our doctrine you are safe." Our people among the lower classes believe in your doctrines. The only change is that they become beggars...But is that religion? It is politics—not religion. You may call it religion, dragging the word religion down to that sense. But it is not spiritual.

Among thousands of men and women a few are inclined to something higher than this life. The others are like sheep...Some among thousands try to understand things, to find a way out. The question is: Is there a way out? If there is a way out, it is in the soul and nowhere else. The ways out from other sources have been tried enough, and all [have been found wanting]. People do not find satisfaction. The very fact that those myriads of theories and sects exist show that people do not find satisfaction.

The science of Yoga proposes this, that the one way out is through ourselves. We have to individualise ourselves. If there is any truth, we can [realise it as our very essence]...We will cease being driven about by nature from place to place...

The phenomenal world is always changing: [to reach the Changeless] that is our goal. We want to be That, to realise that Absolute, the [changeless] Reality. What is preventing us from realising that Reality? It is the fact of creation. The creative mind is creating all the time and gets mixed up with its own creation. [But we must also remember that] it is creation that discovered God. It is creation that discovered the Absolute in every individual soul...

Going back to our definition: Yoga is stopping the Chitta, the mind-stuff, from getting into these changes. When all this creation has been stopped—if it is possible to stop it—then we shall see for ourselves what we are in reality...The Uncreated, the One that creates, manifests itself.

The methods of Yoga are various. Some of them are very difficult; it takes long training to succeed. Some are easy. Those who have the perseverance and strength to follow it through attain to great results. Those who do not may take a simpler method and get some benefit out of it.

As to the proper analysis of the mind, we see at once how difficult it is to grapple with the mind itself. We have become bodies. That we are souls we have forgotten entirely. When we think of ourselves, it is the body that comes into our imagination. We behave as bodies. We talk as bodies. We are all body. From this body we have to separate the soul. Therefore the training begins with the body itself, [until ultimately] the spirit manifests itself...The central idea in all this training is to attain to that power of concentration, the power of meditation.

When Will Christ Come Again?

I never take much notice of these things. I have come to deal with principles. I have only to preach that God comes again and again, and that He came in India as Krishna, Rama, and Buddha, and that He will come again. It can almost be demonstrated that after each 500 years the world sinks, and a tremendous spiritual wave comes, and on the top of the wave is a Christ.

There is a great change now coming all over the world, and this is a cycle. Men are finding that they are losing hold of life; which way will they turn, down or up? Up, certainly. How can it be down? Plunge into the breach; fill up the breach with your body, your life. How should you allow the world to go down when you are living?

The Difference Between Man and Christ

There is much difference in manifested beings. As a manifested being you will never be Christ. Out of clay, manufacture a clay elephant, out of the same clay, manufacture a clay mouse. Soak them in water, they become one. As clay, they are eternally one; as fashioned things, they are eternally different. The Absolute is the material of both God and man. As Absolute, Omnipresent Being, we are all one; and as personal beings, God is the eternal master, and we are the eternal servants.

You have three things in you: (1) the body, (2) the mind, (3) the spirit. The spirit is intangible, the mind comes to birth and death, and so does the body. You are that spirit, but often you think you are the body.

When a man says, "I am here", he thinks of the body. Then comes another moment when you are on the highest plane; you do not say, "I am here". But if a man abuses you or curses you and you do not resent it, you are the spirit. "When I think I am the mind, I am one spark of that eternal fire which Thou art; and when I feel that I am the spirit, Thou and I are one"— so says a devotee to the Lord. Is the mind in advance of the spirit?

God does not reason; why should you reason if you knew? It is a sign of weakness that we have to go on crawling like worms to get a few facts and build generalisations, and then the whole thing tumbles down again. The spirit is reflected in the mind and everything. It is the light of the spirit that makes the mind sensate. Everything is an expression of the spirit; the minds are so many mirrors. What you call love and fear, hatred, virtue, and vice are all reflections of the spirit; only when the reflector is base the reflection is bad.

Are Christ and Buddha Identical?

It is my particular fancy that the same Buddha became Christ. Buddha prophesied, "I will come again in five hundred years", and Christ came here in five hundred years. These are the two Lights of the whole human nature. Two men have been produced, Buddha and Christ; these are the two giants, huge gigantic personalities, two Gods. Between them they divide the whole world. Wherever there is the least knowledge in the world, people bow down either to Buddha or Christ. It would be very hard to produce more like them, but I hope there will be. Mohammed came five hundred years after, five hundred years after came Luther with his Protestant wave, and this is five hundred years after that again. It is a great thing in a few thousand years to produce two such men as Jesus and Buddha. Are not two such enough? Christ and Buddha were Gods, the others were prophets. Study the life of these two and see the manifestation of power in them—calm and non-resisting, poor beggars owning nothing, without a cent in their pockets, despised all their lives, called heretic and fool—and think of the immense spiritual power they have wielded over humanity.

Salvation From Sin

We are to be saved from sin by being saved from ignorance. Ignorance is the cause of which sin is the result.

Coming Back to the Divine Mother

When a nurse takes a baby out into the garden and plays with the baby, the Mother may send a word to the baby to come indoors. The baby is absorbed in play, and says, "I won't come; I don't want to eat." After a while the baby becomes tired with his play and says, "I will go to Mother." The nurse says, "Here is a new doll", but the baby says, "I don't care for dolls any more. I will go to Mother", and he weeps until he goes. We are all babies. The Mother is God. We are absorbed in seeking for money, wealth, and all these things; but the time will come when we will awaken; and then this nature will try to give us more dolls, and we will say, "No, I have had enough; I will go to God."

No Individuality Apart From God

If we are inseparable from God, and always one, have we no individuality? Oh yes; that is God. Our individuality is God. This is not real individuality which you have now. You are coming towards that true one. Individuality means what cannot be divided. How can you call this state—we are now—individuality? One hour you are thinking one way, and the next hour another way, and two hours after another way. Individuality is that which changes not. It would be tremendously dangerous for the present state to remain in eternity, then the thief would always remain a thief, and the blackguard, a blackguard. If a baby died, it would have to remain a baby. The real individuality is that which never changes, and will never change; and that is God within us.

MAN THE MAKER OF HIS DESTINY

There was a very powerful dynasty in Southern India. They made it a rule to take the horoscope of all the prominent men living from time to time, calculated from the time of their birth. In this way they got a record of leading facts predicted, and compared them afterwards with events as they happened. This was done for a thousand years, until they found certain agreements; these were generalised and recorded and made into a huge book. The dynasty died out, but the family of astrologers lived and had the book in their possession. It seems possible that this is how astrology came into existence. Excessive attention to the minutiae of astrology is one of the superstitions which has hurt the Hindus very much.

I think the Greeks first took astrology to India and took from the Hindus the science of astronomy and carried it back with them from Europe. Because in India you will find old altars made according to a certain geometrical plan, and certain things had to be done when the stars were in certain positions, therefore I think the Greeks gave the Hindus astrology, and the Hindus gave them astronomy.

I have seen some astrologers who predicted wonderful things; but I have no reason to believe they predicted them only from the stars, or anything of the sort. In many cases it is simply mind-reading. Sometimes wonderful predictions are made, but in many cases it is arrant trash.

In London, a young man used to come to me and ask me, "What will become of me next year?" I asked him why he asked me so. "I have lost all my money and have become very, very poor." Money is the only God of many beings. Weak men, when they lose everything and feel themselves weak, try all sorts of uncanny methods of making money, and come to astrology and all these things. "It is the coward and the fool who says, 'This is fate'"—so says the Sanskrit proverb. But it is the strong man who stands up and says, "I will make my fate." It is people who are getting old who talk of fate. Young men generally do not come to astrology. We may be under planetary influence, but it should not matter much to us. Buddha says, "Those that get a living by calculation of the stars by such art and other lying tricks are to be avoided"; and he ought to know, because he was the greatest Hindu ever born. Let stars come, what harm is there? If a star disturbs my life, it would not be worth a cent. You will find that astrology and all these mystical things are generally signs of a weak mind; therefore as soon as they are becoming prominent in our minds, we should see a physician, take good food and rest.

If you can get an explanation of a phenomenon from within its nature, it is nonsense to look for an explanation from outside. If the world explains itself, it is nonsense to go outside for an explanation. Have you found any phenomena in the life of a man that you have ever seen which cannot be explained by the power of the man himself? So what is the use of going to the stars or anything else in the world? My own Karma is sufficient explanation of my present state. So in the case of Jesus himself. We know that his father was only a carpenter. We need not go to anybody else to find an explanation of his power. He was the outcome of his own past, all of which was a preparation for that Jesus. Buddha goes back and back to

animal bodies and tells us how he ultimately became Buddha. So what is the use of going to stars for explanation? They may have a little influence; but it is our duty to ignore them rather than hearken to them and make ourselves nervous. This I lay down as the first essential in all I teach: anything that brings spiritual, mental, or physical weakness, touch it not with the toes of your feet. Religion is the manifestation of the natural strength that is in man. A spring of infinite power is coiled up and is inside this little body, and that spring is spreading itself. And as it goes on spreading, body after body is found insufficient; it throws them off and takes higher bodies. This is the history of man, of religion, civilisation, or progress. That giant Prometheus, who is bound, is getting himself unbound. It is always a manifestation of strength, and all these ideas such as astrology, although there may be a grain of truth in them, should be avoided.

There is an old story of an astrologer who came to a king and said, "You are going to die in six months." The king was frightened out of his wits and was almost about to die then and there from fear. But his minister was a clever man, and this man told the king that these astrologers were fools. The king would not believe him. So the minister saw no other way to make the king see that they were fools but to invite the astrologer to the palace again. There he asked him if his calculations were correct. The astrologer said that there could not be a mistake, but to satisfy him he went through the whole of the calculations again and then said that they were perfectly correct. The king's face became livid. The minister said to the astrologer, "And when do you think that you will die?" "In twelve years", was the reply. The minister quickly drew his sword and separated the astrologer's head from the body and said to the king, "Do you see this liar? He is dead this moment."

If you want your nation to live, keep away from all these things. The only test of good things is that they make us strong. Good is life, evil is death. These superstitious ideas are springing like mushrooms in your country, and women wanting in logical analysis of things are ready to believe them. It is because women are striving for liberation, and women have not yet established themselves intellectually. One gets by heart a few lines of poetry from the top of a novel and says she knows the whole of Browning. Another attends a course of three lectures and then thinks she knows everything in the world. The difficulty is that they are unable to throw off the natural superstition of women. They have a lot of money and some intellectual learning, but when they have passed through this transition stage and get on firm ground, they will be all right. But they are played upon by charlatans. Do not be sorry; I do not mean to hurt anyone, but I have to tell the truth. Do you not see how open you are to these things? Do you not see how sincere these women are, how that divinity latent in all never dies? It is only to know how to appeal to the Divine.

The more I live, the more I become convinced every day that

every human being is divine. In no man or woman, however vile, does that divinity die. Only he or she does not know how to reach it and is waiting for the Truth. And wicked people are trying to deceive him or her with all sorts of fooleries. If one man cheats another for money, you say he is a fool and a blackguard. How much greater is the iniquity of one who wants to fool others spiritually! This is too bad. It is the one test, that truth must make you strong and put you above superstition. The duty of the philosopher is to raise you above superstition. Even this world, this body and mind are superstitions; what infinite souls you are! And to be tricked by twinkling stars! It is a shameful condition. You are divinities; the twinkling stars owe their existence to you.

I was once travelling in the Himalayas, and the long road stretched before us. We poor monks cannot get any one to carry us, so we had to make all the way on foot. There was an old man with us. The way goes up and down for hundreds of miles, and when that old monk saw what was before him, he said, "Oh sir, how to cross it; I cannot walk any more; my chest will break." I said to him, "Look down at your feet." He did so, and I said, "The road that is under your feet is the road that you have passed over and is the same road that you see before you; it will soon be under your feet." The highest things are under your feet, because you are Divine Stars; all these things are under your feet. You can swallow the stars by the handful if you want; such is your real nature. Be strong, get beyond all superstitions, and be free.

GOD: PERSONAL & IMPERSONAL

My idea is that what you call a Personal God is the same as the Impersonal Being, a Personal and Impersonal God at the same time. We are personalised impersonal beings. If you use the word in the absolute sense, we are impersonal; but if you use it in a relative meaning, we are personal. Each one of you is a universal being, each one is omnipresent. It may seem staggering at first, but I am as sure of this as that I stand before you. How can the spirit help being omnipresent? It has neither length, nor breadth, nor thickness, nor any material attribute whatsoever; and if we are all spirits we cannot be limited by space. Space only limits space, matter matter. If we were limited to this body we would be a material something. Body and soul and everything would be material, and such words as "living in the body", "embodying the soul" would be only words used for convenience; beyond that they would have no meaning. Many of you remember the definition I gave of the soul; that each soul is a circle whose centre is in one point and circumference nowhere. The centre is where the body is, and the activity is manifested there. You are omnipresent; only you have the consciousness of being concentrated in one point. That point has taken up particles of matter, and formed them into a machine to express itself. That through which it expresses itself is called the body. So you are everywhere; when one body or machine fails, you, the centre,

move on and take up other particles of matter, finer or grosser, and work through that. This is man. And what is God? God is a circle with its circumference nowhere and centre everywhere. Every point in that circle is living, conscious, active, and equally working; with us limited souls, only one point is conscious, and that point moves forward and backward. As the body has a very infinitesimal existence in comparison with that of the universe, so the whole universe, in comparison with God, is nothing. When we talk of God speaking, we say He speaks through His universe; and when we speak of Him beyond all limitations of time and space, we say He is an Impersonal Being. Yet He is the same Being.

To give an illustration: We stand here and see the sun. Suppose you want to go towards the sun. After you get a few thousand miles nearer, you will see another sun, much bigger. Supposing you proceed much closer, you will see a much bigger sun. At last you will see the real sun, millions and millions of miles big. Suppose you divide this journey into so many stages, and take photographs from each stage, and after you have taken the real sun, come back and compare them; they will all appear to be different, because the first view was a little red ball, and the real sun was millions of miles bigger; yet it was the same sun. It is the same with God: the Infinite Being we see from different standpoints, from different planes of mind. The lowest man sees Him as an ancestor; as his vision gets higher, as the Governor of the planet; still higher as the Governor of the universe, and the highest man sees Him as himself. It was the same God, and the different realisations were only degrees and differences of vision.

THE DIVINE INCARNATION
OR AVATARA

Jesus Christ was God—the Personal God become man. He has manifested Himself many times in different forms and these alone are what you can worship. God in His absolute nature is not to be worshipped. Worshipping such God would be nonsense. We have to worship Jesus Christ, the human manifestation, as God. You cannot worship anything higher than the manifestation of God. The sooner you give up the worship of God separate from Christ, the better for you. Think of the Jehovah you manufacture and of the beautiful Christ. Any time you attempt to make a God beyond Christ, you murder the whole thing. God alone can worship God. It is not given to man, and any attempt to worship Him beyond His ordinary manifestations will be dangerous to mankind. Keep close to Christ if you want salvation; He is higher than any God you can imagine. If you think that Christ was a man, do not worship Him; but as soon as you can realise that He is God, worship Him. Those who say He was a man and then worship Him commit blasphemy; there is no half-way house for you; you must take the whole strength of it. "He that hath seen the Son hath seen the Father", and without seeing the Son, you cannot see the Father. It would be only tall talk and frothy philosophy and dreams and speculations. But if you want to have a hold on spiritual life, cling close to God as manifest in Christ.

Philosophically speaking, there was no such human being living as Christ or Buddha; we saw God through them. In the Koran, Mohammed again and again repeats that Christ was never crucified, it was a semblance; no one could crucify Christ.

The lowest state of philosophical religion is dualism;

the highest form is the Triune state. Nature and the human soul are interpenetrated by God, and this we see as the Trinity of God, nature, and soul. At the same time you catch a glimpse that all these three are products of the One. Just as this body is the covering of the soul, so this is, as it were, the body of God. As I am the soul of nature, so is God the soul of my soul. You are the centre through which you see all nature in which you are. This nature, soul, and God make one individual being, the universe. Therefore they are a unity; yet at the same time they are separate. Then there is another sort of Trinity which is much like the Christian Trinity. God is absolute. We cannot see God in His absolute nature, we can only speak of that as "not this, not this". Yet we can get certain qualities as the nearest approach to God. First is existence, second is knowledge, third is bliss—very much corresponding to your Father, Son, and Holy Ghost. Father is the existence out of which everything comes; Son is that knowledge. It is in Christ that God will be manifest. God was everywhere, in all beings, before Christ; but in Christ we became conscious of Him. This is God. The third is bliss, the Holy Spirit. As soon as you get this knowledge, you get bliss. As soon as you begin to have Christ within you, you have bliss; and that unifies the three.

PRANAYAMA

First of all we will try to understand a little of the meaning of Pranayama. Prana stands in metaphysics for the sum total of the energy that is in the universe. This universe, according to the theory of the philosophers, proceeds in the form of waves; it rises, and again it subsides, melts away, as it were; then again it proceeds out in all this variety; then again it slowly returns. So it goes on like a pulsation. The whole of this universe is composed of matter and force; and according to Sanskrit philosophers, everything that we call matter, solid and liquid, is the outcome of one primal matter which they call Akasha or ether; and the primordial force, of which all the forces that we see in nature are manifestations, they call Prana. It is this Prana acting upon Akasha, which creates this universe, and after the end of a period, called a cycle, there is a period of rest. One period of activity is followed by a period of rest; this is the nature of everything. When this period of rest comes, all these forms that we see in the earth, the sun, the moon, and the stars, all these manifestations melt down until they become ether again. They become dissipated as ether. All these forces, either in the body or in the mind, as gravitation, attraction, motion, thought, become dissipated, and go off into the primal Prana. We can understand from this the importance of this Pranayama. Just as this ether encompasses us everywhere and we are interpenetrated by it, so everything we see is composed of this ether, and we are floating in the ether like pieces of ice floating in a lake. They are formed of the water of the lake and float in it at the same time. So everything that exists is composed of this Akasha and is floating in this ocean. In the same way we are surrounded by this vast ocean of Prana—force and energy. It is this Prana by which we breathe and by which the circulation of the blood goes on; it is the energy in the nerves and in the muscles, and the thought in the brain. All forces are different manifestations of this same Prana, as all matter is a different manifestation of the same Akasha. We always find the causes of the gross in the subtle. The chemist takes a solid lump of ore and analyses it; he wants to find the subtler things out of which that gross is composed. So with our thought and our knowledge; the explanation of the grosser is in the finer. The effect is the gross and the cause the subtle. This gross universe of ours, which we see, feel, and touch, has its cause and explanation behind in the thought. The cause and explanation of that is also further behind. So in this human body of ours, we first find the gross movements, the movements of the hands and lips; but where are the causes of these? The finer nerves, the movements of which we cannot perceive at all, so fine that we cannot see or touch or trace them in any way with our senses, and yet we know they are the cause of these grosser movements. These nerve movements, again, are caused by still finer movements, which we call thought; and that is caused by something finer still behind, which is the soul of man, the Self, the Atman. In order to understand ourselves we have first to make our perception fine. No microscope or instrument that was ever invented will make it possible for us to see the fine movements that are going on inside; we can never see them by any such means. So the Yogi has a science that manufactures an instrument for the study of his own mind, and that instrument is in the mind. The mind attains to powers of finer perception which no instrument will ever be able to attain.

To attain to this power of superfine perception we have to begin from the gross. And as the power becomes finer and finer, we go deeper and deeper inside our own nature; and all the gross movements will first be tangible to us, and then the finer movements of the thought; we will be able to trace the thought before its beginning, trace it where it goes and where it ends. For instance, in the ordinary mind a thought arises. The mind does not know how it began or whence it comes. The mind is like the ocean in which a wave rises, but although the man sees the wave, he does not know how the wave came there, whence its birth, or whither it melts down again; he cannot trace it any further. But when the perception becomes finer, we can trace this wave long, long before it comes to the surface; and we will be able to trace it for a long distance after it has disappeared, and then we can understand psychology as it truly is. Nowadays men think this or that and write many volumes, which are entirely misleading, because they have not the power to analyse their own minds and are talking of things they have never known, but only theorised about. All science must be based on facts, and these facts must be observed and generalised. Until you have some facts to generalise upon, what are you going to do? So all these attempts at generalising are based upon knowing the things we generalise. A man proposes a theory, and adds theory to theory, until the whole book is patchwork of theories, not one of them with the least meaning. The science of Raja-yoga says, first you must gather facts about your own mind, and that can be done by analysing your mind, developing its finer powers of perception and seeing for yourselves what is happening inside; and when you have got these facts, then generalise; and then alone you will have the real science of psychology.

As I have said, to come to any finer perception we must take the help of the grosser end of it. The current of action which is manifested on the outside is the grosser.

If we can get hold of this and go on further and further, it becomes finer and finer, and at last the finest. So this body and everything we have in this body are not different existences, but, as it were, various links in the same chain proceeding from fine to gross. You are a complete whole; this body is the outside manifestation, the crust, of the inside; the external is grosser and the inside finer; and so finer and finer until you come to the Self. And at last, when we come to the Self, we come to know that it was only the Self that was manifesting all this; that it was the Self which became the mind and became the body; that nothing else exists but the Self, and all these others are manifestations of that Self in various degrees, becoming grosser and grosser. So we will find by analogy that in this whole universe there is the gross manifestation, and behind that is the finer movement, which we can call the will of God. Behind that even, we will find that Universal Self. And then we will come to know that the Universal Self becomes God and becomes this universe; and that it is not that this universe is one and God another and the Supreme Self another, but that they are different states of the manifestation of the same Unity behind.

All this comes of our Pranayama. These finer movements that are going on inside the body are connected with the breathing; and if we can get hold of this breathing and manipulate it and control it, we will slowly get to finer and finer motions, and thus enter, as it were, by getting hold of that breathing, into the realms of the mind.

The first breathing that I taught you in our last lesson was simply an exercise for the time being. Some of these breathing exercises, again, are very difficult, and I will try to avoid all the difficult ones, because the more difficult ones require a great deal of dieting and other restrictions which it is impossible for most of you to keep to. So we will take the slower paths and the simpler ones. This breathing consists of three parts. The first is breathing in, which is called in Sanskrit Puraka, filling; and the second part is called Kumbhaka, retaining, filling the lungs and stopping the air from coming out; the third is called Rechaka, breathing out. The first exercise which I will give you today is simply breathing in and stopping the breath and throwing it out slowly. Then there is one step more in the breathing which I will not give you today, because you cannot remember them all; it would be too intricate. These three parts of breathing make one Pranayama. This breathing should be regulated, because if it is not, there is danger in the way to yourselves. So it is regulated by numbers, and I will give you first the lowest numbers. Breathe in four seconds, then hold the breath for eight seconds, then again throw it out slowly in four seconds[1]. Then begin again, and do this four times in the morning and four times in the evening. There is one thing more. Instead of counting by one, two, three, and all such meaningless things, it is better to repeat any word that is holy to you. In our country we have symbolical words, "Om" for instance, which means God. If that be pronounced instead of one, two, three, four, it will serve your purpose very well. One thing more. This breathing should begin through the left nostril and should turn out through the right nostril, and the next time is should be drawn in through the right and thrown out through the left. Then reverse again, and so on. In the first place you should be able to drive your breathing through either nostril at will, just by the power of the will. After a time you will find it easy; but now I am afraid you have not that power. So we must stop the one nostril while breathing through the other with the finger and during the retention, of course, both nostrils.

The first two lessons should not be forgotten. The

first thing is to hold yourselves straight; second to think of the body as sound and perfect, as healthy and strong. Then throw a current of love all around, think of the whole universe being happy. Then if you believe in God, pray. Then breathe.

In many of you certain physical changes will come, twitchings all over the body, nervousness; some of you will feel like weeping, sometimes a violent motion will come. Do not be afraid; these things have to come as you go on practicing. The whole body will have to be rearranged as it were. New channels for thought will be made in the brain, nerves which have not acted in your whole life will begin to work, and a whole new series of changes will come in the body itself.

---

1. This process is more difficult when the ratio is two, eight, and four; for further remarks see later.

WOMEN OF THE EAST[1]

Report of a lecture in the Chicago Daily Inter-Ocean,
September 23, 1893.

Swami Vivekananda, at a special meeting, discussed the present and future of the women of the East. He said, "The best thermometer to the progress of a nation is its treatment of its women. In ancient Greece there was absolutely no difference in the state of man and woman. The idea of perfect equality existed. No Hindu can be a priest until he is married, the idea being that a single man is only half a man, and imperfect. The idea of perfect womanhood is perfect independence. The central idea of the life of a modern Hindu lady is her chastity. The wife is the centre of a circle, the fixity of which depends upon her chastity. It was the extreme of this idea which caused Hindu widows to be burnt. The Hindu women are very spiritual and very religious, perhaps more so than any other women in the world. If we can preserve these beautiful characteristics and at the same time develop the intellects of our women, the Hindu woman of the future will be the ideal woman of the world."

CONGRESS OF RELIGIOUS UNITY

Report of a lecture in the Chicago Sunday Herald,
September 24, 1893.

Swami Vivekananda said, "All the words spoken at this parliament come to the common conclusion that the brotherhood of man is the much-to-be-desired end. Much has been said for this brotherhood as being a natural condition, since we are all children of one God. Now, there are sects that do not admit of the existence of God — that is, a Personal God.

---

1. As many women as could crowd into Hall 7 yesterday afternoon flocked thither to hear something as to the lives of their sisters of the Orient. Mrs. Potter Palmer and Mrs. Charles Henrotin sat upon the platform, surrounded by turbanned representatives of the women of the East. It may interest the reader to know that the published addresses of Swami Vivekananda at the Parliament of Religions in Chicago are not exhaustive and many addresses, specially those delivered at the Scientific Section of the Parliament were not all reported. The Scientific Sessions were conducted simultaneously with the open session at the Hall of Columbus. Swami Vivekananda spoke on the following subjects at the Scientific Section: 1. Orthodox Hinduism and the Vedanta Philosophy.——Friday, September 22, 1893, at 10:30 a.m. 2. The Modern Religions of India.——Friday, September 22, 1893 afternoon session. 3. On the subject of the foregoing addresses.——Saturday, September 23, 1893. 4. The Essence of the Hindu Religion.——Monday, September 25, 1893. The Chicago Daily Inter-ocean of September 23, 1893 published the following note on the first lecture. "In the Scientific Section yesterday morning Swami Vivekananda spoke on 'Orthodox Hinduism'. Hall III was crowded to overflowing and hundreds of questions were asked by auditors and answered by the great Sannyasin with wonderful skill and lucidity. At the close of the session he was thronged with eager questioners who begged him to give a semi-public lecture somewhere on the subject of his religion. He said that he already had the project under consideration."

Unless we wish to leave those sects out in the cold — and in that case our brotherhood will not be universal — we must have our platform broad enough to embrace all mankind. It has been said here that we should do good to our fellow men, because every bad or mean deed reacts on the doer. This appears to me to savour of the shopkeeper — ourselves first, our brothers afterwards. I think we should love our brother whether we believe in the universal fatherhood of God or not, because every religion and every creed recognises man as divine, and you should do him no harm that you might not injure that which is divine in him."

THE LOVE OF GOD — I

Report of a lecture in the Chicago Herald,
September 25, 1893.

An audience that filled the auditorium of the Third Unitarian Church at Laflin and Monroe streets heard Swami Vivekananda preach yesterday morning. The subject of his sermon was the love of God, and his treatment of the theme was eloquent and unique. He said that God was worshipped in all parts of the world, but by different names and in different ways. It is natural for men, he said, to worship the grand and the beautiful, and that religion was a portion of their nature. The need of God was felt by all, and His love prompted them to deeds of charity, mercy, and justice. All men loved God because He was love itself. The speaker had heard since coming to Chicago a great deal about the brotherhood of man. He believed that a still stronger tie connected them, in that all are the offsprings of the love of God. The brotherhood of man was the logical sequence of God as the Father of all. The speaker said he had travelled in the forests of India and slept in caves, and from his observation of nature he had drawn the belief that there was something above the natural law that kept men from wrong, and that, he concluded, was the love of God. If God had spoken to Christ, Mohammed, and the Rishis of the Vedas, why did He not speak also to him, one of his children? "Indeed, he does speak to me", the Swami continued, "and to all His children. We see Him all around us and are impressed continually by the boundlessness of His love, and from that love we draw the inspiration for our well-being and well-doing."

THE LOVE OF GOD — II

A lecture delivered in the Unitarian Church of Detroit on
February 20, 1894 and reported in the Detroit Free Press.

Vivekananda delivered a lecture on "The Love of God" at the Unitarian Church last night before the largest audience that he has yet had. The trend of the lecturer's remarks was to show that we do not accept God because we really want Him, but because we have need of Him for selfish purposes. Love, said the speaker, is something absolutely unselfish, that which has no thought beyond the glorification and adoration of the object upon which our affections are bestowed. It is a quality which bows down and worships and asks nothing in return. Merely to love is the sole request that true love has to ask.

It is said of a Hindu saint that when she was married, she said to her husband, the king, that she was already married. "To whom?" asked the king. "To God", was the reply. She went among the poor and the needy and taught the doctrine of extreme love for God. One of her prayers is significant, showing the manner in which her heart was moved: "I ask not for wealth; I ask not for position; I ask not for salvation; place me in a hundred hells if it be Thy wish, but let me continue to regard Thee as my love." The early language abounds in beautiful prayers of this woman. When her end came, she entered into Samadhi on the banks of a river. She composed a beautiful song, in which she stated that she was going to meet her Beloved.

Men are capable of philosophical analysis of religion. A woman is devotional by nature and loves God from the heart and soul and not from the mind. The songs of Solomon are one of the most beautiful parts of the Bible. The language in them is much of that affectionate kind which is found in the prayers of the Hindu woman saint. And yet I have heard that Christians are going to have these incomparable songs removed. I have heard an explanation of the songs in which it is said that Solomon loved a young girl and desired her to return his royal affection. The girl, however, loved a young man and did not want to have anything to do with Solomon. This explanation is excellent to some people, because they cannot understand such wondrous love for God as is embodied in the songs. Love for God in India is different from love for God elsewhere, because when you get into a country where the thermometer reads 40 degrees below zero, the temperament of the people changes. The aspirations of the people in the climate where the books of the Bible are said to have been written were different from the aspirations of the cold-blooded Western nations, who are more apt to worship the almighty dollar with the warmth expressed in the songs than to worship God. Love for God seems to be based upon a basis of "what can I get out of it?" In their prayers they ask for all kinds of selfish things.

Christians are always wanting God to give them something. They appear as beggars before the throne of the Almighty. A story is told of a beggar who applied to an emperor for alms. While he was waiting, it was time for the emperor to offer up prayers. The emperor prayed, "O God, give me more wealth; give me more power; give me a greater empire." The beggar started to leave. The emperor turned and asked him, "Why are you going?" "I do not beg of beggars", was the reply.

Some people find it really difficult to understand the frenzy of religious fervour which moved the heart of Mohammed.

He would grovel in the dust and writhe in agony. Holy men who have experienced these extreme emotions have been called epileptic. The absence of the thought of self is the essen-

tial characteristic of the love for God. Religion nowadays has become a mere hobby and fashion. People go to church like a flock of sheep. They do not embrace God because they need Him. Most persons are unconscious atheists who self-complacently think that they are devout believers.

INDIA

Report of a lecture delivered at Detroit on Thursday, February 15, 1894, with the editorial comments of the Detroit Free Press.

An audience that filled the Unitarian Church heard the renowned monk, Swami Vivekananda, deliver a lecture last night on the manners and customs of his country. His eloquent and graceful manner pleased his listeners, who followed him from beginning to end with the closest attention, showing approval from time to time by outbursts of applause. While his lecture was more popular in character than the celebrated Address before the religious congress in Chicago, it was highly entertaining, especially where the speaker diverted from the instructive portions and was led to an eloquent narration of certain spiritual conditions of his own people. It is upon matters religious and philosophic (and necessarily spiritual) that the Eastern brother is most impressive, and, while outlining the duties that follow the conscientious consideration of the great moral law of nature, his softly modulated tones, a peculiarity of his people, and his thrilling manner are almost prophetic. He speaks with marked deliberation, except when placing before his listeners some moral truth, and then his eloquence is of the highest kind.

It seemed somewhat singular that the Eastern monk, who is so outspoken in his disapproval of missionary labour on the part of the Christian church in India (where, he affirms, the morality is the highest in the world), should have been introduced by Bishop Ninde who in June will depart for China in the interest of foreign Christian missions. The Bishop expects to remain away until

December; but if he should stay longer he will go to India. The Bishop referred to the wonders of India and the intelligence of the educated classes there, introducing Vivekananda in a happy manner. When that dusky gentleman arose, dressed in his turban and bright gown, with handsome face and bright, intelligent eyes, he presented an impressive figure. He returned thanks to the Bishop for his words and proceeded to explain race divisions in his own country, the manners of the people, and the different languages. Principally there are four northern tongues and four southern, but there is one common religion. Four-fifths of the population of 300 million people are Hindus and the Hindu is a peculiar person. He does everything in a religious manner. He eats religiously; he sleeps religiously; he rises in the morning religiously; he does good things religiously; and he also does bad things religiously. At this point the lecturer struck the great moral keynote of his discourse, stating that with his people it was the belief that all non-self is good and all self is bad. This point was emphasised throughout the evening and might be termed the text of the address. To build a home is selfish, argues the Hindu; so he builds it for the worship of God and for the entertainment of guests. To cook food is selfish, so he cooks for the poor; he will serve himself last if any hungry stranger applies, and this feeling extends throughout the length and breadth of the land. Any man can ask for food and shelter, and any house will be opened to him.

The caste system has nothing to do with religion. A man's occupation is hereditary: a carpenter is born a carpenter; a goldsmith, a goldsmith; a workman, a workman; and a priest, a priest. But this is a comparatively modern social evil, since it has existed only about 1,000 years. This period of time does not seem so great in India as in this and other countries. Two gifts are especially appreciated—the gift of learning and the gift of life. But the gift of learning takes precedence. One may save a man's life, and that is excellent; one may impart to another knowledge, and that is better. To instruct for money is an evil, and to do this would bring opprobrium on the head of the man who barters learning for gold, as though it were an article of trade. The government makes gifts from time to time to the instructors, and the moral effect is better than it would be if the conditions were the same as exist in certain alleged civilised countries. The speaker had asked through the length and breadth of the land what was the definition of civilisation, and he had asked the question in many countries. Sometimes the reply had been given: What we are, that is civilisation. He begged to differ in the definition of the word. A nation may control the elements, develop utilitarian problems of life seemingly to the limit, and yet not realise that in the individual the highest type of civilisation is found in him who has learnt to conquer self. This condition is found in India more than in any country on earth, for there the material conditions are subservient to the spiritual, and the individual looks for the soul manifestations in everything that has life, studying nature to this end. Hence that gentle disposition to endure with indomitable patience the flings of what appears unkind fortune, the while there is a full consciousness of a spiritual strength and knowledge greater than those possessed by any other people; hence the existence of a country and a people from which flows an unending stream that attracts the attention of thinkers far and near to approach and throw from their shoulders an oppressive earthly burden. The early king, who in 260 B.C. commanded that there should be no more bloodshed, no more wars, and who sent forth instead of soldiers an army of instructors, acted wisely, although in material things the land has suffered. But though in bondage to brutal nations who conquer by force, the Indian's spirituality endures for ever, and nothing can take it away from him. There is something Christlike in the humility of the people to endure the stings and arrows of outraged fortune, the while the soul is advancing towards the brighter goal. Such a country has no need of Christian missionaries to "preach ideas", for

theirs is a religion that makes men gentle, sweet, considerate, and affectionate towards all God's creatures, whether man or beast. Morally, said the speaker, India is head and shoulders above the United States or any other country on the globe. Missionaries would do well to come there and drink of the pure waters, and see what a beautiful influence upon a great community have the lives of the multitude of holy men.

Then marriage condition was described; and the privileges extended to women in ancient times when the system of co-education flourished. In the records of the saints in India there is the unique figure of the prophetess. In the Christian creed they are all prophets, while in India the holy women occupy a conspicuous place in the holy books. The householder has five objects for worship. One of them is learning and teaching. Another is worship of dumb creatures. It is hard for Americans to understand the last worship, and it is difficult for Europeans to appreciate the sentiment. Other nations kill animals by wholesale and kill one another; they exist in a sea of blood. A European said that the reason why in India animals were not killed was because it was supposed that they contained the spirits of ancestors. This reason was worthy of a savage nation who are not many steps from the brute. The fact was that the statement was made by a set of atheists in India who thus carped at the Vedic idea of non-killing and transmigration of souls. It was never a religious doctrine, it was an idea of a materialistic creed. The worship of dumb animals was pictured in a vivid manner. The hospitable spirit—the Indian golden rule, was illustrated by a story. A Brahmin, his wife, his son, and his son's wife had not tasted food for some time on account of a famine. The head of the house went out and after a search found a small quantity of barley. He brought this home and divided it into four portions, and the small family was about to eat, when a knock was heard at the door. It was a guest. The different portions were set before him, and he departed with his hunger satisfied, while the quartette who had entertained him perished. This story is told in India to illustrate what is expected in the sacred name of hospitality.

The speaker concluded in an eloquent manner. Throughout, his speech was simple; but whenever he indulged in imagery, it was delightfully poetic, showing that the Eastern brother has been a close and attentive observer of the beauties of nature. His excessive spirituality is a quality which makes itself felt with his auditors, for it manifests itself in the love for animate and inanimate things and in the keen insight into the mysterious workings of the divine law of harmony and kindly intentions.

HINDUS AND CHRISTIANS

*A lecture delivered at Detroit on February 21, 1894,
and reported in the Detroit Free Press.*

Of the different philosophies, the tendency of the Hindu is not to destroy, but to harmonise everything. If any new idea comes into India, we do not antagonise it, but simply try to take it in, to harmonise it, because this method was taught first by our prophet, God incarnate on earth, Shri Krishna. This Incarnation of God preached himself first: "I am the God Incarnate, I am the inspirer of all books, I am the inspirer of all religions." Thus we do not reject any.

There is one thing which is very dissimilar between us and Christians, something which we never taught. That is the idea of salvation through Jesus' blood, or cleansing by any man's blood. We had our sacrifice as the Jews had. Our sacrifices mean simply this: Here is some food I am going to eat, and until some portion is offered to God, it is bad; so I offer the food. This is the pure and simple idea. But with the Jew the idea is that his sin be upon the lamb, and let the lamb be sacrificed and him go scot-free. We never developed this beautiful idea in India, and I am glad we did not. I, for one, would not come to be saved by such a doctrine. If anybody would come and say, "Be saved by my blood", I would say to him, "My brother, go away; I will go to hell; I am not a coward to take innocent blood to go to heaven; I am ready for hell." So that doctrine never cropped up amongst us, and our prophet says that whenever evil and immortality prevail on earth, He will come down and support His children; and this He is doing from time to time and from place to place. And whenever on earth you see an extraordinary holy man trying to uplift humanity, know that He is in him.

So you see that is the reason why we never fight any religion. We do not say that ours is the only way to salvation. Perfection can be had by everybody, and what is the proof? Because we see the holiest of men in all countries, good men and women everywhere, whether born in our faith or not. Therefore it cannot be held that ours is the only way to salvation. "Like so many rivers flowing from different mountains, all coming and mingling their waters in the sea, all the different religions, taking their births from different standpoints of fact, come unto Thee." This is a part of the child's everyday prayer in India. With such everyday prayers, of course, such ideas as fighting because of differences of religion are simply impossible. So much for the philosophers of India. We have great regard for all these men, especially this prophet, Shri Krishna, on account of his wonderful catholicity in harmonising all the preceding revelations.

Then the man who is bowing down before the idol. It is not in the same sense as you have heard of the Babylonian and the Roman idolatry. It is peculiar to the Hindus. The man is before the idol, and he shuts his eyes and tries to think, "I am He; I have neither life nor death; I have neither father nor mother; I am not bound by time or space; I am Existence infinite, Bliss infinite, and Knowledge infinite; I am He, I am He. I am not bound by books, or holy places, or pilgrimages, or anything whatsoever; I am the Existence Absolute, Bliss Absolute; I am He, I am He." This he repeats and then says, "O Lord, I cannot conceive Thee in myself; I am a poor man." Religion does not depend upon knowledge. It is the soul itself, it is God, not to be attained by simple book-knowledge or powers of speech. You may take the most learned man you have and ask him to think of spirit as spirit; he cannot. You may imagine spirit, he may imagine spirit. It is impossible to think of spirit without training. So no matter how much theology you may learn—you may be a great philosopher and greater theologian—but the Hindu boy would say, "Well, that has nothing to do with religion." Can you think of spirit as spirit? Then alone all doubt ceases, and all crookedness of the heart is made straight. Then only all fears vanish, and all doubtings are for ever silent when man's soul and God come face to face.

A man may be wonderfully learned in the Western sense, yet he may not know the A B C of religion. I would tell him that. I would ask him, "Can you think of spirit as such? Are you advanced in the science of the soul? Have you manifested your own soul above matter?" If he has not, then I say to him, "Religion has not come to you; it is all talk and book and vanity." But this poor Hindu sits before that idol and tries to think that he is That, and then says, "O Lord, I cannot conceive Thee as spirit, so let me conceive of Thee in this form"; and then he opens his eyes and see this form, and prostrating himself he repeats his prayers. And when his prayer is ended, he says, "O Lord, forgive me for this imperfect worship of Thee."

You are always being told that the Hindu worships blocks of stone. Now what do you think of this fervent nature of the souls of these people? I am the first monk to come over to these Western countries—it is the first time in the history of the world that a Hindu monk has crossed the ocean. But we hear such criticism and hear of these talks, and what is the general attitude of my nation towards you? They smile and say, "They are children; they may be great in physical science; they may build huge things; but in religion they are simply children." That is the attitude of my people.

One thing I would tell you, and I do not mean any unkind criticism. You train and educate and clothe and pay men to do what? To come over to my country to curse and abuse all my forefathers, my religion, and everything. They walk near a temple and say, "You idolaters, you will go to hell." But they dare not do that to the Mohammedans of India; the sword would be out. But the Hindu is too mild; he smiles and passes on, and says, "Let the fools talk." That is the attitude. And then you who train men to abuse and criticise, if I just touch you with the least bit of criticism, with the kindest of purpose, you shrink and cry, "Don't touch us; we are Americans. We criticise all the people in the world, curse them and abuse them, say anything; but do not touch us; we are sensitive plants." You may do whatever you please; but at the same time I am going to tell you that we are content to live as we are; and in one thing we are better off—we never teach our children to swallow such horrible stuff: "Where every prospect pleases and man alone is vile." And whenever your ministers criticise us, let them remember this: If all India stands up and takes all the mud that is at the bottom of the Indian Ocean and throws it up against the Western countries, it will not be doing an infinitesimal part of that which you are doing to us. And what for? Did we ever send one missionary to convert anybody in the world? We say to you, "Welcome to your religion, but allow me to have mine." You call yours an aggressive religion. You are aggressive, but how many have you taken? Every sixth man in the world is a Chinese subject, a Buddhist; then there are Japan, Tibet, and Russia, and Siberia, and Burma, and Siam; and it may not be palatable, but this Christian morality, the Catholic Church, is all derived from them. Well, and how was this done? Without the shedding of one drop of blood! With all your brags and boastings, where has your Christianity succeeded without the sword? Show me one place in the whole world. One, I say, throughout the history of the Christian religion—one; I do not want two. I know how your forefathers were converted. They had to be converted or killed; that was all. What can you do better than Mohammedanism, with all your bragging? "We are the only one!" And why? "Because we can kill others." The Arabs said that; they bragged. And where is the Arab now? He is the bedouin. The Romans used to say that, and where are they now? Blessed are the peace-makers; they shall enjoy the earth. Such things tumble down; it is built upon sands; it cannot remain long.

Everything that has selfishness for its basis, competition as its right hand, and enjoyment as its goal, must die sooner or later. Such things must die. Let me tell you, brethren, if you want to live, if you really want your nation to live, go back to Christ. You are not Christians. No, as a nation you are not. Go back to Christ. Go back to him who had nowhere to lay his head. "The birds have their nests and the beasts their lairs, but the Son of Man has nowhere to lay his head." Yours is religion preached in the name of luxury. What an irony of fate! Reverse this if you want to live, reverse this. It is all hypocrisy that I have heard in this country. If this nation is going to live, let it go back to him. You cannot serve God and Mammon at the same time. All this prosperity, all this from Christ! Christ would have denied all such heresies. All prosperity which comes with Mammon is transient, is only for a moment. Real permanence is in Him. If you can join these two, this wonderful prosperity with the ideal of Christ, it is well. But if you cannot, better go back to him and give this up. Better be ready to live in rags with Christ than to live in palaces without him.

CHRISTIANITY IN INDIA

A lecture delivered at Detroit on March 11, 1894
and reported in the Detroit Free Press.

"Vive Kananda spoke to a crowded audience at the Detroit Opera House last night. He was given an extremely cordial reception and delivered his most eloquent address here. He spoke for two hours and a half.

Hon. T. W. Palmer, in introducing the distinguished visitor, referred to the old tale of the shield that was copper on one side and silver on the other and the contest which ensued. If we look on both sides of a question there would be less dispute. It is possible for all men to agree. The matter of foreign missions has been dear to the religious heart. Vive Kananda, from the Christian standpoint, said Mr. Palmer, was a pagan. It would be pleasant to hear from a gentleman who spoke about the copper side of the shield.

Vive Kananda was received with great applause." ...

I do not know much about missionaries in Japan and China, but I am well posted about India. The people of this country look upon India as a vast waste, with many jungles and a few civilised Englishmen. India is half as large as the United States, and there are three hundred million people. Many stories are related, and I have become tired of denying these. The first invaders of India, the Aryans, did not try to exterminate the population of India as the Christians did when they went into a new land, but the endeavour was made to elevate persons of brutish habits. The Spaniards came to Ceylon with Christianity. The Spaniards thought that their God commanded them to kill and murder and to tear down heathen temples. The Buddhists had a tooth a foot long, which belonged to their Prophet, and the Spaniards threw it into the sea, killed a few thousand persons, and converted a few scores. The Portuguese came to Western India. The Hindus have a belief in the Trinity and had a temple dedicated to their sacred belief. The invaders looked at the temple and said it was a creation of the devil; and so they brought their cannon to bear upon the wonderful structure and destroyed a portion of it. But the invaders were driven out of the country by the enraged population. The early missionaries tried to get hold of the land, and in their effort to secure a foothold by force, they killed many people and converted a number. Some of them became Christians to save their lives. Ninety-nine percent of the Christians converted by the Portuguese sword were compelled to be so, and they said, "We do not believe in Christianity, but we are forced to call ourselves Christians." But Catholic Christianity soon relapsed.

The East India Company got possession of a part of India with the idea of making hay while the sun shone. They kept the missionaries away. The Hindus were the first to welcome the missionaries, not the Englishmen, who were engaged in trade. I have great admiration for some of the first missionaries of the later period, who were true servants of Jesus and did not vilify the people or spread vile falsehoods about them.

They were gentle, kindly men. When Englishmen became masters of India, the missionary enterprise began to become stagnant, a condition which characterises the missionary efforts in India today. Dr. Long, an early missionary, stood by the people. He translated a Hindu drama describing the evils perpetuated in India by indigo-planters, and what was the result? He was placed in jail by the English. Such missionaries were of benefit to the country, but they have passed away. The Suez Canal opened up a number of evils.

Now goes the missionary, a married man, who is hampered because he is married. The missionary knows nothing about the people, he cannot speak the language, so he invariably settles in the little white colony. He is forced to do this because he is married. Were he not married, he could go among the people and sleep on the ground if necessary. So he goes to India to seek company for his wife and children. He stays among the English-speaking people. The great heart of India is today absolutely untouched by missionary effort. Most of the missionaries are incompetent. I have not met a single missionary who understands Sanskrit. How can a man absolutely ignorant of the people and their traditions, get into sympathy with them? I do not mean any offense, but Christians send men as missionaries, who are not persons of ability. It is sad to see money spent to make converts when no real results of a satisfactory nature are reached.

Those who are converted, are the few who make a sort of living by hanging round the missionaries. The converts who are not kept in service in India, cease to be converts. That is about the entire matter in a nutshell. As to the way of converting, it is absolutely absurd. The money the missionaries bring is accepted. The colleges founded by missionaries are all right, so far as the education is concerned. But with religion it is different. The Hindu is acute; he takes the bait but avoids the hook! It is wonderful how tolerant the people are. A missionary once said, "That is the worst of the whole business. People who are self-complacent can never be converted."

As regards the lady missionaries, they go into certain houses, get four shillings a month, teach them something of the Bible, and show them how to knit. The girls of India will never be converted. Atheism and skepticism at home is what is pushing the missionary into other lands.

When I came into this country I was surprised to meet so many liberal men and women. But after the Parliament of Religions a great Presbyterian paper came out and gave me the benefit of a seething article. This the editor called enthusiasm. The missionaries do not and cannot throw off nationality—they are not broad enough—and so they accomplish nothing in the way of converting, although they may have a nice sociable time among themselves. India requires help from Christ, but not from the antichrist; these men are not Christlike. They do not act like Christ; they are married and come over and settle down comfortably and make a fair livelihood. Christ and his disciples would accomplish much good in India, just as many of the Hindu saints do; but these men are not of that sacred character. The Hindus would welcome the Christ of the Christians gladly, because his life was holy and beautiful; but they cannot and will not receive the narrow utterances of the ignorant, hypocritical or self-deceiving men.

Men are different. If they were not, the mentality of the world would be degraded. If there were not different religions, no religion would survive. The Christian requires his religion; the Hindu needs his own creed. All religions have struggled against one another for years. Those which were founded on a book, still stand. Why could not the Christians convert the Jews? Why could they not make the Persians Christians? Why could they not convert Mohammedans? Why cannot any impression be made upon China or Japan? Buddhism, the first missionary religion, numbers double the number of converts of any other religion, and they did not use the sword. The Mohammedans used the greatest violence. They number the least of the three great missionary religions. The Mohammedans have had their day. Every day you read of Christian nations acquiring land by bloodshed. What missionaries preach against this? Why should the most blood-thirsty nation exalt an alleged religion which is not the religion of Christ? The Jews and the Arabs were the fathers of Christianity, and how they have been persecuted by the Christians! The Christians have been weighed in the balance in India and have been found wanting. I do not mean to be unkind, but I want to show the Christians how they look in others' eyes. The missionaries who preach the burning pit are regarded with horror. The Mohammedans rolled wave after wave over India waving the sword, and today where are they?

The furthest that all religions can see is the existence of a spiritual entity. So no religion can teach beyond that point. In every religion there is the essential truth and the non-essential casket in which this jewel lies. Believing in the Jewish book or in the Hindu book is non-essential. Circumstances change; the receptacle is different; but the central truth remains. The essentials being the same, the educated people of every community retain the essentials. If you ask a Christian what his essentials are, he should reply, "The teachings of Lord Jesus." Much of the rest is nonsense. But the nonsensical part is right; it forms the receptacle. The shell of the oyster is not attractive, but the pearl is within it. The Hindu will never attack the life of Jesus; he reverences the Sermon on the Mount. But how many Christians know or have heard of the teachings of the Hindu holy men? They remain in a fool's paradise. Before a small fraction of the world was converted, Christianity was divided into many creeds. That is the law of nature. Why take a single instrument from the great religious orchestra of the earth? Let the grand symphony go on. Be pure. Give up superstition and see the wonderful harmony of nature. Superstition gets the better of religion. All the religions are good, since the essentials are the same. Each man should have the perfect exercise of his individuality, but these individualities form a perfect whole. This marvelous condition is already in existence. Each creed has something to add to the wonderful structure.

I pity the Hindu who does not see the beauty in Jesus Christ's character. I pity the Christian who does not reverence the Hindu Christ. The more a man sees of himself, the less he sees of his neighbors. Those that go about converting, who are very busy saving the souls of others, in many instances forget their own souls. I was asked by a lady why the women of India were not more elevated. It is in a great degree owing to the barbarous invaders through different ages; it is partly due to the people in India themselves. But our women are any day better than the ladies of this country who devotees of novels and balls. Where is the spirituality one would expect in a country which is so boastful of its civilisation? I have not found it. "Here" and "here-after" are words to frighten children. It is all "here". To live and move in God—even here, even in this body! All self should go out; all superstition should be banished. Such men live in India. Where are such in this country? Your preachers speak against "dreamers". The people of this country would be better off if there were more "dreamers". If a man here followed literally the instruction of his Lord, he would be called a fanatic. There is a good deal of difference between dreaming and the brag of the nineteenth century. The bees look for the flowers. Open the lotus! The whole world is full of God and not of sin. Let us help each other. Let us love each other. A beautiful prayer of the Buddhist is: I bow down to all the saints; I bow down to all the prophets; I bow down to all the holy men and women all over the world!

THE RELIGION OF LOVE

Notes of a lecture delivered in London,
November 16, 1895.

Just as it is necessary for a man to go through symbols and ceremonies first in order to arrive at the depth of realisation, so we say in India, "It is good to be born in a church, but bad to die in one". A sapling must be hedged about for protection, but when it becomes a tree, a hedge would be a hindrance. So there is no need to criticise and condemn the old forms. We forget that in religion there must be growth.

At first we think of a Personal God, and call Him Creator, Omnipotent, Omniscient, and so forth. But when loves comes, God is only love. The loving worshipper does not care what God is, because he wants nothing from Him. Says an Indian saint, "I am no beggar!" Neither does he fear. God is loved as a human being.

Here are some of the systems founded on love. (1) Shanta, a common, peaceful love, with such thoughts as those of fatherhood and help; (2) Dasya, the ideal of service; God as master or general or sovereign, giving punishments and rewards; (3) Vatsalya, God as mother or child. In India the mother never punishes. In each of these stages, the worshipper forms an ideal of God and follows it. Then (4) Sakhya, God as friend.

There is here no fear. There is also the feeling of equality and familiarity. There are some Hindus who worship God as friend and playmate. Next comes (5) Madhura, sweetest love, the love of husband and wife. Of this St. Teresa and the ecstatic saints have been examples. Amongst the Persians, God has been looked upon as the wife, amongst the Hindus as the husband. We may recall the great queen Mira Bai, who preached that the Divine Spouse was all. Some carry this to such an extreme that to call God "mighty" or "father" seems to them blasphemy. The language of this worship is erotic. Some even use that of illicit passion. To this cycle belongs the story of Krishna and the Gopi-girls. All this probably seems to you to entail great degeneration on the worshipper. And so it does. Yet many great saints have been developed by it. And no human institution is beyond abuse. Would you cook nothing because there are beggars? Would you possess nothing because there are thieves? "O Beloved, one kiss of Thy lips, once tasted, hath made me mad!"

The fruit of this idea is that one can no longer belong to any sect, or endure ceremonial. Religion in India culminates in freedom. But even this comes to be given up, and all is love for love's sake.

Last of all comes love without distinction, the Self. There is a Persian poem that tells how a lover came to the door of his beloved, and knocked. She asked, "Who art thou?" and he replied, "I am so and so, thy beloved!" and she answered only, "Go! I know none such!" But when she had asked for the fourth time, he said, "I am thyself, O my Beloved, therefore open thou to me!" And the door was opened.

A great saint said, using the language of a girl, describing love: "Four eyes met. There were changes in two souls. And now I cannot tell whether he is a man and I am a woman, or he is a woman and I a man. This only I remember, two souls were. Love came, and there was one."

In the highest love, union is only of the spirit. All love of any other kind is quickly evanescent. Only the spiritual lasts, and this grows.

Love sees the Ideal. This is the third angle of the triangle. God has been Cause, Creator, Father. Love is the culmination. The mother regrets that her child is humpbacked, but when she has nursed him for a few days, she loves him and thinks him most beautiful. The lover sees the beauty of Helen in the brow of Ethiopia. We do not commonly realise what happens. The brow of Ethiopia is merely a suggestion: the man sees Helen. His ideal is thrown upon the suggestion and covers it, as the oyster makes sand into a pearl. God is this ideal, through which man may see all.

Hence we come to love love itself. This love cannot be expressed. No words can utter it. We are dumb about it.

The senses become very much heightened in love. Human love, we must remember, is mixed up with attributes. It is dependent, too, on the other's attitude. Indian languages have words to describe this interdependence of love. The lowest love is selfish; it consists in pleasure of being loved. We say in India, "One gives the cheek, the other kisses." Above this is mutual love. But this also ceases mutually. True love is all giving. We do not even want to see the other, or to do anything to express our feeling. It is enough to give. It is almost impossible to love a human being like this, but it is possible to love God.

In India there is no idea of blasphemy if boys fighting in the street use the name of God. We say, "Put your hand into the fire, and whether you feel it or not, you will be burnt. So to utter the name of God can bring nothing but good."

The notion of blasphemy comes from the Jews, who were impressed by the spectacle of Persian loyalty. The ideas that God is judge and punisher are not in themselves bad, but they are low and vulgar. The three angles of the triangle are: Love begs not; Love knows no fear; Love is always the ideal. "Who would be able to live one second,

Who would be able to breathe one moment,

If the Loving one had not filled the universe?"

Most of us will find that we were born for service. We must leave the results to God. The work was done only for love of God. If failure comes, there need be no sorrow. The work was done only for love of God.

In women, the mother-nature is much developed. They worship God as the child. They ask nothing, and will do anything.

The Catholic Church teaches many of these deep things, and though it is narrow, it is religious in the highest sense. In modern society, Protestantism is broad but shallow. To judge truth by what good it does is as bad as to question the value of a scientific discovery to a baby.

Society must be outgrown. We must crush law and become outlaws. We allow nature, only in order to conquer her. Renunciation means that none can serve both God and Mammon.

Deepen your own power of thought and love. Bring your own lotus to blossom: the bees will come of themselves. Believe first in yourself, then in God. A handful of strong men will move the world. We need a heart to feel, a brain to conceive, and a strong arm to do the work. Buddha gave himself for the animals. Make yourself a fit agent to work. But it is God who works, not you. One man contains the whole universe. One particle of matter has all the energy of the universe at its back. In a conflict between the heart and the brain follow your heart.

Yesterday, competition was the law. Today, cooperation is the law. Tomorrow there is no law. Let sages praise thee, or let the world blame. Let fortune itself come, or let poverty and rags stare thee in the face.

Eat the herbs of the forest, one day, for food; and the next, share a banquet of fifty courses. Looking neither to right hand nor to the left, follow thou on!

The Swami began by telling, in answer to questions, the sto-ry of how Pavhari Baba snatched up his own vessels and ran after the thief, only to fall at his feet and say: "O Lord, I knew not that Thou wert there! Take them! They are Thine! Pardon me, Thy child!"

Again he told how the same saint was bitten by a cobra, and when, towards nightfall he recovered, he said, "A messenger came to me from the Beloved."

JNANA AND KARMA

Notes of a lecture delivered in London,
November 23, 1895.

The greatest force is derived from the power of thought. The finer the element, the more powerful it is . The silent power of thought influences people even at a distance, because mind is one as well as many. The universe is a cobweb; minds are spiders.

The universe equals the phenomena of one Universal Being. He, seen through our senses, is the universe. This is Maya. So the world is illusion, that is, the imperfect vision of the Real, a semi-revelation, even as the sun in the morning is a red ball. Thus all evils and wickedness are but weakness, the imperfect vision of goodness.

A straight line projected infinitely becomes a circle. The search for good comes back to Self. I am the whole mystery, God. I am a body, the lower self; and I am the Lord of the universe.

Why should a man be moral and pure? Because this strengthens his will. Everything that strengthens the will by revealing the real nature is moral. Everything that does the reverse is immoral. The standard varies from country to country, from individual to individual. Man must recover from his state of slavery to laws, to words, and so on. We have no freedom of the will now, but we shall have when we are free. Renunciation is this giving up of the world. Through the senses, anger comes, and sorrow comes. As long as renunciation is not there, self and the passion animating it are different. At last they become identified, and the man is an animal at once. Become possessed with the feeling of renunciation.

I once had a body, was born, struggled and died: What awful hallucinations! To think that one was cramped in a body, weeping for salvation!

But does renunciation demand that we all become ascetics? Who then is to help others? Renunciation is not asceticism. Are all beggars Christ? Poverty is not a synonym for holiness; often the reverse. Renunciation is of the mind. How does it come? In a desert, when I was thirsty, I saw a lake. It was in the midst of a beautiful landscape. There were trees surrounding it, and their reflections could be seen in the water, upside down. But the whole thing proved to be a mirage. Then I knew that every day for a month I had seen this; and only that day, being thirsty, I had learnt it to be unreal. Every day for a month I should see it again. But I should never take it to be real. So, when we reach God, the idea of the universe, the body and so on, will vanish. It will return afterwards. But next time we shall know it to be unreal.

The history of the world is the history of persons like Buddha and Jesus. The passionless and unattached do most for the world. Picture Jesus in the slums. He sees beyond the misery, "You, my brethren, are all divine." His work is calm. He removes causes. You will be able to work for the good of the world when you know for a fact that this work is all illusion. The more unconscious this work, the better, because it is then the more superconscious. Our search is not for good or evil; but happiness and good are nearer to truth than their opposites. A man ran a thorn into his finger, and with another thorn took it out. The first thorn is Evil. The second thorn is Good. The Self is that Peace which passeth beyond both evil and good. The universe is melting down: man draws nearer to God. For one moment he is real—god. He is re-differentiated—a prophet. Before him, now, the world trembles. A fool sleeps and wakes a fool—a man unconscious; and superconscious, he returns with infinite power, purity, and love—the God-man. This is the use of the superconscious state.

Wisdom can be practised even on a battlefield. The Gita was preached so. There are three states of mind: the active, the passive, and the serene. The passive state is characterised by slow vibrations; the active by quick vibrations, and the serene by the most intense vibrations of all. Know that the soul is sitting in the chariot. The body is the chariot; the outer senses are the horses; and the mind the reins; and the intellect the charioteer. So man crosses the ocean of Maya. He goes beyond. He reaches God. When a man is under the control of his senses, he is of this world. When he has controlled the senses, he has renounced.

Even forgiveness, if weak and passive, is not true: fight is better. Forgive when you could bring legions of angels to the victory. Krishna, the charioteer of Arjuna, hears him say, "Let us forgive our enemies", and answers, "You speak the words of wise men, but you are not a wise man, but a coward". As a lotus-leaf, living in the water yet untouched by it, so should the soul be in the world. This is a battlefield, fight your way out. Life in this world is an attempt to see God. Make your life a manifestation of will strengthened by renunciation.

We must learn to control all our brain-centres consciously. The first step is the joy of living. Asceticism is fiendish. To laugh is better than to pray. Sing. Get rid of misery. Do not for heaven's sake infect others with it. Never think God sells a little happiness and a little unhappiness. Surround yourself with flowers and pictures and incense. The saints went to the mountain tops to enjoy nature.

The second step is purity.

The third is full training of the mind. Reason out what is true from what is untrue. See that God alone is true. If for a moment you think you are not God, great terror will seize you. As soon as you think "I am He ", great peace and joy will come to you. Control the senses. If a man curses me, I should still see in him God, whom through my weakness I see as a curser. The poor man to whom you do good is extending a privilege to you. He allows you, through His mercy, to worship Him thus.

The history of the world is the history of a few men who had faith in themselves. That faith calls out the divinity within. You can do anything. You fail only when you do not strive sufficiently to manifest infinite power. As soon as a man or a nation loses faith, death comes.

There is a divine within that cannot be overcome either by church dogmas or by blackguardism. A handful of Greeks speak wherever there is civilisation. Some mistakes there must always be. Do not grieve. Have great insight. Do not think, "What is done is done. Oh, that 'twere done better!" If man had not been God, humanity would by this time have become insane, with its litanies and its penitence.

None will be left, none destroyed. All will in the end be made perfect. Say, day and night, "Come up, my brothers! You are the infinite ocean of purity! Be God! Manifest as God!"

What is civilisation? It is the feeling of the divine within. When you find time, repeat these ideas to yourself and desire freedom. That is all. Deny everything that is not God. Assert everything that is God. Mentally assert this, day and night. So the veil grows thinner: "I am neither man nor angel. I have no sex nor limit. I am knowledge itself. I am He. I have neither anger nor hatred. I have neither pain nor pleasure. Death or birth I never had. For I am Knowledge Absolute, and Bliss Absolute. I am He, my soul, I am He!"

Find yourself bodiless. You never had a body. It was all superstition. Give back the divine consciousness to all the poor, the downtrodden, the oppressed, and the sick.

Apparently, every five hundred years or so, a wave of this thought comes over the world. Little waves arise in many directions: but one swallows up all the others and sweeps over society. That wave does this which has most character at its back.

Confucius, Moses, and Pythagoras; Buddha, Christ, Mohammed; Luther, Calvin, and the Sikhs; Theosophy, Spiritualism, and the like; all these mean only the preaching of the Divine-in-man.

Never say man is weak. Wisdom-yoga is no better than the others. Love is the ideal and requires no object. Love is God. So even through devotion we reach the subjective God. I am He! How can one work, unless one loves city, country, animals, the universe? Reason leads to the finding of unity in variety. Let the atheist and the agnostic work for the social good. So God comes.

But this you must guard against: Do not disturb the faith of any. For you must know that religion is not in doctrines. Religion lies in being and becoming, in realisation. All men are born idolaters. The lowest man is an animal. The highest man is perfect. And between these two, all have to think in sound and colour, in doctrine and ritual.

The test of having ceased to be an idolater is: "When you say 'I', does the body come into your thought or not? If it does, then you are still a worshipper of idols." Religion is not intellectual jargon at all, but realisation. If you think about God, you are only a fool. The ignorant man, by prayer and devotion, can reach beyond the philosopher. To know God, no philosophy is necessary. Our duty is not to disturb the faith of others. Religion is experience. Above all and in all, be sincere; identification brings misery, because it brings desire. Thus the poor man sees gold, and identifies himself with the need of gold. Be the witness. Learn never to react.

THE CLAIMS OF VEDANTA ON THE MODERN WORLD

Report of a lecture delivered in Oakland on Sunday, February 25, 1900, with editorial comments of the Oakland Enquirer.

The announcement that Swami Vivekananda, a distinguished savant of the East, would expound the philosophy of Vedanta in the Parliament of Religions at the Unitarian Church last evening, attracted an immense throng. The main auditorium and ante-rooms were packed, the annexed auditorium of Wendte Hall was thrown open, and this was also filled to overflowing, and it is estimated that fully 500 persons, who could not obtain seats or standing room where they could hear conveniently, were turned away.

The Swami created a marked impression. Frequently he received applause during the lecture, and upon concluding, held a levee of enthusiastic admirers. He said in part, under the subject of "The Claims of Vedanta on the Modern World":

Vedanta demands the consideration of the modern world. The largest number of the human race is under its influence. Again and again, millions upon millions have swept down on its adherents in India, crushing them with their great force, and yet the religion lives.

In all the nations of the world, can such a system be found? Others have risen to come under its shadow. Born like mushrooms, today they are alive and flourishing, and tomorrow they are gone. Is this not the survival of the fittest?

It is a system not yet complete. It has been growing for thousands of years and is still growing. So I can give you but an idea of all I would say in one brief hour.

First, to tell you of the history of the rise of Vedanta. When it arose, India had already perfected a religion. Its crystallisation had been going on many years. Already there were elaborate ceremonies; already there had been perfected a system of morals for the different stages of life. But there came a rebellion against the mummeries and mockeries that enter into many religions in time, and great men came forth to proclaim through the Vedas the true religion. Hindus received their religion from the revelation of these Vedas. They were told that the Vedas were without beginning and without end. It may sound ludicrous to this audience—how a book can be without beginning or end; but by the Vedas no books are meant. They mean the accumulated treasury of spiritual laws discovered by different persons in different times.

Before these men came, the popular ideas of a God ruling the universe, and that man was immortal, were in existence. But there they stopped. It was thought that nothing more could be known. Here came the daring of the expounders of Vedanta. They knew that religion meant for children is not good for thinking men; that there is something more to man and God.

The moral agnostic knows only the external dead nature. From that he would form the law of the universe. He might as well cut off my nose and claim to form an idea of my whole body, as argue thus. He must look within. The stars that sweep through the heavens, even the universe is but a drop in the bucket. Your agnostic sees not the greatest, and he is frightened at the universe.

The world of spirit is greater than all—the God of the universe who rules—our Father, our Mother. What is this heathen mummery we call the world? There is misery everywhere. The child is born with a cry upon its lips; it is its first utterance. This child becomes a man, and so well used to misery that the pang of the heart is hidden by a smile on the lips.

Where is the solution of this world? Those who look outside will never find it; they must turn their eyes inward and find truth. Religion lives inside.

One man preaches, if you chop your head off, you get salvation. But does he get any one to follow him? Your own Jesus says, "Give all to the poor and follow me." How many of you have done this? You have not followed out this command, and yet Jesus was the great teacher of your religion. Every one of you is practical in his own life, and you find this would be impracticable.

But Vedanta offers you nothing that is impracticable. Every science must have its own matter to work upon. Everyone needs certain conditions and much of training and learning; but any Jack in the street can tell you all about religion. You may want to follow religion and follow an expert, but you may only care to converse with Jack, for he can talk it.

You must do with religion as with science, come in direct contact with facts, and on that foundation build a marvellous structure. To have a true religion you must have instruments. Belief is not in question; of faith you can make nothing, for you can believe anything.

We know that in science as we increase the velocity, the mass decreases; and as we increase the mass, the velocity decreases. Thus we have matter and force. The matter, we do not know how, disappears into force, and force into matter. Therefore there is something which is neither force nor matter, as these two may not disappear into each other. This is what we call mind—the universal mind.

Your body and my body are separate, you say. I am but a little whirlpool in the universal ocean of mankind. A whirlpool, it is true, but a part of the great ocean. You stand by moving water where every particle is changing, and yet you call it a stream. The water is changing, it is true, but the banks remain the same. The mind is not changing, but the body—how quick its growth! I was a baby, a boy, a man, and soon I will be an old man, stooped and aged. The body is changing, and you say, is the mind not changing also? When I was a child, I was thinking, I have become larger, because my mind is a sea of impressions.

There is behind nature a universal mind. The spirit is simply a unit and it is not matter. For man is a spirit. The question, "Where does the soul go after death?" should be answered like the boy when he asked, "Why does not the earth fall down?" The questions are alike, and their solutions alike; for where could the soul go to?

To you who talk of immortality I would ask when you go home to endeavour to imagine you are dead. Stand by and touch your dead body. You cannot, for you cannot get out of yourself. The question is not concerning immortality, but as to whether Jack will meet his Jenny after death.

The one great secret of religion is to know for yourself that you are a spirit. Do not cry out, "I am a worm, I am nobody!" As the poet says, "I am Existence, Knowledge, and Truth." No man can do any good in the world by crying out, "I am one of its evils." The more perfect, the less imperfections you see.

THE LAWS OF LIFE AND DEATH

Report of a lecture delivered in Oakland on March 7, 1900, with editorial comments of the Oakland Tribune.

Swami Vivekananda delivered a lecture last evening on the subject, "The Laws of Life and Death". The Swami said: "How to get rid of this birth and death—not how to go to heaven, but how one can stop going to heaven—this is the object of the search of the Hindu."

The Swami went on to say that nothing stands isolated—everything is a part of the never-ending procession of cause and effect. If there are higher beings than man, they also must obey the laws. Life can only spring from life, thought from thought, matter from matter. A universe cannot be created out of matter. It has existed for ever. If human beings came into the world fresh from the hands of nature, they would come without impressions; but we do not come in that way, which shows that we are not created afresh. If human souls are created out of nothing, what is to prevent them from going back into nothing? If we are to live all the time in the future, we must have lived all the time in the past.

It is the belief of the Hindu that the soul is neither mind nor body. What is it which remains stable—which can say, "I am I"? Not the body, for it is always changing; and not the mind, which changes more rapidly than the body, which never has

the same thoughts for even a few minutes. There must be an identity which does not change—something which is to man what the banks are to the river—the banks which do not change and without whose immobility we would not be conscious of the constantly moving stream. Behind the body, behind the mind, there must be something, viz the soul, which unifies the man. Mind is merely the fine instrument through which the soul—the master—acts on the body. In India we say a man has given up his body, while you say, a man gives up his ghost. The Hindus believe that a man is a soul and has a body, while Western people believe he is a body and possesses a soul.

Death overtakes everything which is complex. The soul is a single element, not composed of anything else, and therefore it cannot die. By its very nature the soul must be immortal. Body, mind, and soul turn upon the wheel of law—none can escape. No more can we transcend the law than can the stars, than can the sun—it is all a universe of law. The law of Karma is that every action must be followed sooner or later by an effect. The Egyptian seed which was taken from the hand of a mummy after 5000 years and sprang into life when planted is the type of the never-ending influence of human acts. Action can never die without producing action. Now, if our acts can only produce their appropriate effects on this plane of existence, it follows that we must all come back to round out the circle of causes and effects. This is the doctrine of reincarnation. We are the slaves of law, the slaves of conduct, the slaves of thirst, the slaves of desire, the slaves of a thousand things. Only by escaping from life can we escape from slavery to freedom. God is the only one who is free. God and freedom are one and the same.

THE REALITY AND THE SHADOW

Report of a lecture delivered in Oakland on March 8, 1900, with editorial comments of the Oakland Tribune.

Swami Vivekananda, the Hindu philosopher, delivered another lecture in Wendte Hall last evening. His subject was: "The Reality and The Shadow". He said: "The soul of man is ever striving after certainty, to find something that does not change. It is never satisfied. Wealth, the gratification of ambition or of appetite are all changeable. Once these are attained, man is not content. Religion is the science which teaches us whence to satisfy this longing after the unchangeable. Behind all the local colours and derivations they teach the same thing—that there is reality only in the soul of man. "The philosophy of Vedanta teaches that there are two worlds, the external or sensory, and the internal or subjective—the thought world. "It posits three fundamental concepts—time, space, and causation. From these is constituted Maya, the essential groundwork of human thought, not the product of thought. This same conclusion was arrived at a later date by the great German philosopher Kant. "My reality, that of nature and of God, is the same, the difference is in form of manifestation.

The differentiation is caused by Maya. The contour of the shore may shape the ocean into bay, strait, or inlet; but when this shaping force or Maya is removed, the separate form disappears, the differentiation ceases, all is ocean again."

The Swami then spoke of the roots of the theory of evolution to be found in the Vedanta philosophy. "All modern religions start with the idea," continued the speaker, "that man was once pure, he fell, and will become pure again. I do not see where they get this idea. The seat of knowledge is the soul; external circumstance simply stimulates the soul; knowledge is the power of the soul. Century after century it has been manufacturing bodies. The various forms of incarnation are merely successive chapters of the story of the life of the soul. We are constantly building our bodies. The whole universe is in a state of flux, of expansion and contraction, of change. Vedanta holds that the soul never changes in essence, but it is modified by Maya. Nature is God limited by mind. The evolution of nature is the modification of the soul. The soul in essence is the same in all forms of being. Its expression is modified by the body. This unity of soul, this common substance of humanity, is the basis of ethics and morality. In this sense all are one, and to hurt one's brother is to hurt one's Self. "Love is simply an expression of this infinite unity. Upon what dualistic system can you explain love? One of the European philosophers says that kissing is a survival of cannibalism, a kind of expression of 'how good you taste'. I do not believe it. "What is it we all seek? Freedom. All the effort and struggle of life is for freedom. It is the march universal of races, of worlds, and of systems. "If we are bound, who bound us? No power can bind the Infinite but Itself."

After the discourse an opportunity was afforded for asking questions of the speaker, who devoted half an hour to answering them.

WAY TO SALVATION

Report of a lecture delivered in Oakland on Monday, March 12, 1900, with editorial comments of the Oakland Enquirer.

Wendte Hall of the First Unitarian Church was crowded last evening with a large audience to hear the "Way to Salvation" from the standpoint of the Hindu priest, Swami Vivekananda. This was the last lecture of a series of three which the Swami has delivered. He said in part:

One man says God is in heaven, another that God is in nature and everywhere present. But when the great crisis comes, we find the goal is the same. We all work on different plans, but the end is not different.

The two great watchwords of every great religion are renunciation and self-sacrifice. We all want the truth, and we know that it must come, whether we want it or not. In a way we are all striving for that good. And what prevents our reaching it? It is ourselves. Your ancestors used to call it the devil; but it is our own false self.

We live in slavery, and we would die if we were out of it. We are like the man who lived in total darkness for ninety years and when taken out into the warm sunshine of nature, prayed to be taken back to his dungeon. You would not leave this old life to go into a newer and greater freedom which opens out.

The great difficulty is to go to the heart of things. These little degraded delusions of Jack So-and-so's, who thinks he has an infinite soul, however small he is with his different religions. In one country, all as a matter of religion, a man has many wives; in another one woman has many husbands. So some men have two gods, some one God, and some no God at all.

But salvation is in work and love. You learn something thoroughly; in time you may not be able to call that thing to memory. Yet it has sunk into your inner consciousness and is a part of you. So as you work, whether it be good or bad, you shape your future course of life. If you do good work with the idea of work—work for work's sake—you will go to heaven of your idea and dream of heaven.

The history of the world is not of its great men, of its demigods, but it is the little islands of the sea, which build themselves to great continents from fragments of the sea drift. Then the history of the world is in the little acts of sacrifice performed in every household. Man accepts religion because he does not wish to stand on his own judgment. He takes it as the best way of getting out of a bad place.

The salvation of man lies in the great love with which he loves his God. Your wife says, "O John, I could not live without you." Some men when they lose their money have to be sent to the asylum. Do you feel that way about your God? When you can give up money, friends, fathers and mothers, brothers and sisters, all that is in the world and only pray to God that He grant you something of His love, then you have found salvation.

THE PEOPLE OF INDIA

Report of a lecture delivered in Oakland on Monday, March 19, 1900, with editorial comments of the Oakland Enquirer.

The lecture which the Swami Vivekananda gave Monday night in his new course on "The People of India", was interesting, not only for what he had to relate of the people of that country, but for the insight into their mental attitude and prejudices which the speaker gave without really meaning it. It is apparent that the Swami, educated and intellectual man that he is, is no admirer of Western civilisation. He has evidently been a good deal embittered by the talk about child widows, the oppression of women, and other barbarisms alleged against the people of India, and is somewhat inclined to resort to the tu quoque in reply.

In commencing his talk, he gave his hearers an idea of the racial characteristics of the people. He said that the bond of unity in India, as in other countries of Asia, is not language or race, but religion. In Europe the race makes the nation, but in Asia people of diverse origin and different tongues become one nation if they have the same religion. The people of Northern India are divided into four great classes, while in Southern India the languages are so entirely different from those of Northern India that there is no kinship whatever. The people of Northern India belong to the great Aryan race, to which all of the people of Europe, except the Basques in the Pyrennees, and the Finns, are supposed to belong. The Southern India people belong to the same race as the ancient Egyptians and the Semites. To illustrate the difficulties of learning one another's languages in India, the Swami said that when he had occasion to go into Southern India, he always talked with the native people in English, unless they belonged to the select few who could speak Sanskrit.

A good deal of the lecture was taken up in a discussion of the caste system which the Swami characterised by saying that it had its bad side, but that its benefits outweighed its disadvantages. In brief, this caste system had grown by the practice of the son always following the business of the father. In course of time the community came thus to be divided into a series of classes, each held rigidly within its own boundaries. But while this divided the people, it also united them, because all the members of a caste were bound to help their fellows in case of need. And as no man could rise out of his caste, the Hindus have no such struggles for social or personal supremacy as embitter the people of other countries.

The worst feature of the caste is that is suppresses competition, and the checking of competition has really been the cause of the political downfall of India and its conquest by foreign races.

Respecting the much-discussed subject of marriage, the Hindus are socialistic and see nothing good in matches being made by a couple of young people who might be attached to one another, without regard to the welfare of the community, which is more important than that of any two persons. "Because I love Jennie and Jennie loves me", said the Swami, "is no reason why we should be married."

He denied that the condition of the child widows is as bad as has been represented, saying that in India the position of widows in general is one of a great deal of influence, because a large part of the property in the country is held by widows. In fact, so enviable is the position of widows that a woman or a man either might almost pray to be made a widow.

The child widows, or women who have been betrothed to children who died before marriage, might be pitied if a marriage were the only real object in life, but, according to the Hindu way of thinking, marriage is rather a duty than a privilege, and the denial of the right of child widows to marry is no particular hardship.

I AM THAT I AM

Notes of a lecture given in San Francisco on March 20, 1900.

The subject tonight is man, man in contrast with nature. For a long time the word "nature" was used almost exclusively to denote external phenomena. These phenomena were found to behave methodically; and they often repeated themselves: that which had happened in the past happened again — nothing happened only once. Thus it was concluded that nature was uniform. Uniformity is closely associated with the idea of nature; without it natural phenomena cannot be understood. This uniformity is the basis of what we call law.

Gradually the word "nature" and the idea of uniformity came to be applied also to internal phenomena, the phenomena of life and mind. All that is differentiated is nature. Nature is the quality of the plant, the quality of the animal, and the quality of man. Man's life behaves according to definite methods; so does his mind. Thoughts do not just happen, there is a certain method in their rise, existence and fall. In other words, just as external phenomena are bound by law, internal phenomena, that is to say, the life and mind of man, are also bound by law.

When we consider law in relation to man's mind and existence, it is at once obvious that there can be no such thing as free will and free existence. We know how animal nature is wholly regulated by law. The animal does not appear to exercise any free will. The same is true of man; human nature also is bound by law. The law governing functions of the human mind is called the law of Karma.

Nobody has ever seen anything produced out of nothing; if anything arises in the mind, that also must have been produced from something. When we speak of free will, we mean the will is not caused by anything. But that cannot be true, the will is caused; and since it is caused, it cannot be free — it is bound by law. That I am willing to talk to you and you come to listen to me, that is law. Everything that I do or think or feel, every part of my conduct or behaviour, my every movement — all is caused and therefore not free. This regulation of our life and mind — that is the law of Karma.

If such a doctrine had been introduced in olden times into a Western community, it would have produced a tremendous commotion. The Western man does not want to think his mind is governed by law. In India it was accepted as soon as it was propounded by the most ancient Indian system of philosophy. There is no such thing as freedom of the mind; it cannot be. Why did not this teaching create any disturbance in the Indian mind? India received it calmly; that is the speciality of Indian thought, wherein it differs from every other thought in the world.

The external and internal natures are not two different things; they are really one. Nature is the sum total of all phenomena. "Nature" means all that is, all that moves. We make a tremendous distinction between matter and mind; we think that the mind is entirely different from matter. Actually, they are but one nature, half of which is continually acting on the other half. Matter is pressing upon the mind in the form of various sensations. These sensations are nothing but force. The force from the outside evokes the force within. From the will to respond to or get away from the outer force, the inner force becomes what we call thought.

Both matter and mind are really nothing but forces; and if you analyse them far enough, you will find that at root they are one. The very fact that the external force can somehow evoke the internal force shows that somewhere they join each other—they must be continuous and, therefore, basically the same force. When you get to the root of things, they become simple and general. Since the same force appears in one form as matter and in another form as mind, there is no reason to think matter and mind are different. Mind is changed into matter, matter is changed into mind. Thought force becomes nerve force, muscular force; muscular and nerve force become thought force. Nature is all this force, whether expressed as matter or mind.

The difference between the subtlest mind and the grossest matter is only one of degree. Therefore the whole universe may be called either mind or matter, it does not matter which. You may call the mind refined matter, or the body concretised mind; it makes little difference by which name you call which. All the troubles arising from the conflict between materialism and spirituality are due to wrong thinking. Actually, there is no difference between the two. I and the lowest pig differ only in degree. It is less manifested, I am more. Sometimes I am worse, the pig is better.

Nor is it any use discussing which comes first—mind or matter. Is the mind first, out of which matter has come? Or is matter first, out of which the mind has come? Many of the philosophical arguments proceed from these futile questions. It is like asking whether the egg or the hen is first. Both are first, and both last—mind and matter, matter and mind. If I say matter exists first and matter, growing finer and finer, becomes mind, then I must admit that before matter there must have been mind. Otherwise, where did matter come from? Matter precedes mind, mind precedes matter. It is the hen and the egg question all through.

The whole of nature is bound by the law of causation and is in time and space. We cannot see anything outside of space, yet we do not know space. We cannot perceive anything outside of time, yet we do not know time. We cannot understand anything except in terms of causality, yet we do not know what causation is. These three things—time, space, and causality—are in and through every phenomena, but they are not phenomena. They are as it were the forms or moulds in which everything must be cast before it can be apprehended. Matter is substance plus time, space, and causation. Mind is substance plus time, space and causation.

This fact can be expressed in another way. Everything is substance plus name and form. Name and form come and go, but substance remains ever the same. Substance, form, and name make this pitcher. When it is broken, you do not call it pitcher any more, nor do you see its pitcher form. Its name and form vanish, but its substance remains. All the differentiation in substance is made by name and form. There are not real, because they vanish. What we call nature is not the substance, unchanging and indestructible. Nature is time, space and causation. Nature is name and form. Nature is Maya. Maya means name and form, into which everything is cast. Maya is not real. We could not destroy it or change it if it were real. The substance is the noumenon, Maya is phenomena. There is the real "me" which nothing can destroy, and there is the phenomenal "me" which is continually changing and disappearing.

The fact is, everything existing has two aspects. One is noumenal, unchanging and indestructible; the other is phenomenal, changing and destructible. Man in his true nature is substance, soul, spirit. This soul, this spirit, never changes, is never destroyed; but it appears to be clothed with a form and to have a name associated with it. This form and name are not immutable or indestructible; they continually change and are destroyed.

Yet men foolishly seek immortality in this changeable aspect, in the body and mind—they want to have an eternal body. I do not want that kind of immortality.

What is the relation between me and nature? In so far as nature stands for name and form or for time, space, and causality, I am not part of nature, because I am free, I am immortal, I am unchanging and infinite. The question does not arise whether I have free will or not; I am beyond any will at all. Wherever there is will, it is never free. There is no freedom of will whatever. There is freedom of that which becomes will when name and form get hold of it, making it their slave. That substance—the soul—as it were moulds itself, as it were throws itself into the cast of name and form, and immediately becomes bound, whereas it was free before. And yet its original nature is still there. That is why it says, "I am free; in spite of all this bondage, I am free." And it never forgets this.

But when the soul has become the will, it is no more really free. Nature pulls the strings, and it has to dance as nature wants it to. Thus have you and I danced throughout the years. All the things that we see, do, feel, know, all our thoughts and actions, are nothing but dancing to the dictates of nature. There has been, and there is, no freedom in any of this. From the lowest to the highest, all thoughts and actions are bound by law, and none of these pertain to our real Self.

My true Self is beyond all law. Be in tune with slavery, with nature, and you live under law, you are happy under law. But the more you obey nature and its dictates, the more bound you become; the more in harmony with ignorance you are, the more you are at the beck and call of everything in the universe. Is this harmony with nature, this obedience to law, in accord with the true nature and destiny of man? What mineral ever quarrelled with and disputed any law? What tree or plant ever defied any law? This table is in harmony with nature, with law; but a table it remains always, it does not become any better. Man begins to struggle and fight against nature. He makes many mistakes, he suffers. But eventually he conquers nature and realises his freedom. When he is free, nature becomes his slave.

The awakening of the soul to its bondage and its effort to stand up and assert itself—this is called life. Success in this struggle is called evolution. The eventual triumph, when all the slavery is blown away, is called salvation, Nirvana, freedom. Everything in the universe is struggling for liberty. When I am bound by nature, by name and form, by time, space and causality, I do not know what I truly am. But even in this bondage my real Self is not completely lost. I strain against the bonds; one by one they break, and I become conscious of my innate grandeur. Then comes complete liberation. I attain to the clearest and fullest consciousness of myself—i know that I am the infinite spirit, the master of nature, not its slave. Beyond all differentiation and combination, beyond space, time and causation, I am that I am.

UNITY

Notes of a lecture delivered at the Vedanta Society, New York, in June, 1900.

The different sectarian systems of India all radiate from one central idea of unity or dualism.

They are all under Vedanta, all interpreted by it. Their final essence is the teaching of unity. This, which we see as many, is God. We perceive matter, the world, manifold sensation. Yet there is but one existence.

These various names mark only differences of degree in the expression of that One. The worm of today is the God of tomorrow. These distinctions which we do love are all parts of one infinite fact, and only differ in the degree of expression. That one infinite fact is the attainment of freedom.

However mistaken we may be as to the method, all our struggle is really for freedom. We seek neither misery nor happiness, but freedom. This one aim is the secret of the insatiable thirst of man. Man's thirst, says the Hindu, man's thirst, says the Buddhist, is a burning, unquenchable thirst for more and more. You Americans are always looking for more pleasure, more enjoyment. You cannot be satisfied, true; but at bottom what you seek is freedom.

This vastness of his desire is really the sign of man's own infinitude. It is because he is infinite, that he can only be satisfied when his desire is infinite and its fulfilment infinite.

What then can satisfy man? Not gold. Not enjoyment. Not beauty. One Infinite alone can satisfy him, and that Infinite is Himself. When he realises this, then alone comes freedom. "This flute, with the sense-organs as its keyholes,

With all its sensations, perceptions, and song,

Is singing only one thing. It longs to go back to the wood whence it was cut!"

"Deliver thou thyself by thyself!

Ah, do not let thyself sink!

For thou art thyself thy greatest friend.

And thou thyself thy greatest enemy."

Who can help the Infinite? Even the hand that comes to you through the darkness will have to be your own.

Fear and desire are the two causes of all this, and who creates them? We ourselves. Our lives are but a passing from dream to dream. Man the infinite dreamer, dreaming finite dreams!

Oh, the blessedness of it, that nothing external can be eternal! They little know what they mean, whose hearts quake when they hear that nothing in this relative world can be eternal.

I am the infinite blue sky. Over me pass these clouds of various colours, remain a moment, and vanish. I am the same eternal blue. I am the witness, the same eternal witness of all. I see, therefore nature exists. I do not see, therefore she does not. Not one of us could see or speak if this infinite unity were broken for a moment.

THE WORSHIP OF THE DIVINE MOTHER

Fragmentary notes taken on a Sunday afternoon in New York in June, 1900.

From the tribal or clan-god, man arrives, in every religion, at the sum, the God of gods.

Confucius alone has expressed the one eternal idea of ethics. "Manu Deva" was transformed into Ahriman. In India, the mythological expression was suppressed; but the idea remained. In an old Veda is found the Mantra, "I am the empress of all that lives, the power in everything."

Mother-worship is a distinct philosophy in itself. Power is the first of our ideas. It impinges upon man at every step; power felt within is the soul; without, nature. And the battle between the two makes human life. All that we know or feel is but the resultant of these two forces. Man saw that the sun shines on the good and evil alike. Here was a new idea of God, as the Universal Power behind all—the Mother-idea was born.

Activity, according to Sankhya, belongs to Prakriti, to nature, not to Purusha or soul. Of all feminine types in India, the mother is pre-eminent. The mother stands by her child through everything. Wife and children may desert a man, but his mother never! Mother, again, is the impartial energy of the universe, because of the colourless love that asks not, desires not, cares not for the evil in her child, but loves him the more. And today Mother-worship is the worship of all the highest classes amongst the Hindus.

The goal can only be described as something not yet attained. Here, there is no goal. This world is all alike the play of Mother. But we forget this. Even misery can be enjoyed when there is no selfishness, when we have become the witness of our own lives. The thinker of this philosophy has been struck by the idea that one power is behind all phenomena. In our thought of God, there is human limitation, personality: with Shakti comes the idea of One Universal Power. "I stretch the bow of Rudra when He desires to kill", says Shakti. The Upanisads did not develop this thought; for Vedanta does not care for the God-idea. But in the Gita comes the significant saying to Arjuna, "I am the real, and I am the unreal. I bring good, and I bring evil."

Again the idea slept. Later came the new philosophy. This universe is a composite fact of good and evil; and one Power must be manifesting through both. "A lame one-legged universe makes only a lame one-legged God." And this, in the end, lands us in want of sympathy and makes us brutal. The ethics built upon such a concept is an ethics of brutality. The saint hates the sinner, and the sinner struggles against the saint. Yet even this leads onward. For finally the wicked self-sufficient mind will die, crushed under repeated blows; and then we shall awake and know the Mother.

Eternal, unquestioning self-surrender to Mother alone can give us peace. Love Her for Herself, without fear or favour. Love Her because you are Her child. See Her in all, good and bad alike. Then alone will come "Sameness" and Bliss Eternal that is Mother Herself when we realise Her thus. Until then, misery will pursue us. Only resting in Mother are we safe.

THE ESSENCE OF RELIGION

Report of a lecture delivered in America.

In France the "rights of man" was long a watchword of the race; in America the rights of women still beseech the public ear; in India we have concerned ourselves always with the rights of Gods. The Vedanta includes all sects. We have a peculiar idea in India. Suppose I had a child; I should not teach him any religion, but the practice of concentrating his mind; and just one line of prayer—not prayer in your sense, but this: "I meditate on Him who is the Creator of the universe; may He enlighten my mind." Then, when old enough, he goes about hearing the different philosophies and teachings, till he finds that which seems the truth to him. He then becomes the Shishya or disciple of the Guru (teacher) who is teaching this truth. He may choose to worship Christ or Buddha or Mohammed: we recognise the rights of each of these, and the right of all souls to their own Ishta or chosen way. It is, therefore, quite possible for my son to be a Buddhist, my wife to be a Christian, and myself a Mohammedan at one and the same time with absolute freedom from friction.

We are all glad to remember that all roads lead to God; and that the reformation of the world does not depend upon all seeing God through our eyes. Our fundamental idea is that your doctrine cannot be mine, nor mine yours. I am my own sect. It is true that we have created a system of religion in In-

dia which we believe to be the only rational religious system extant; but our belief in its rationality rests upon its all-inclusion of the searchers after God; its absolute charity towards all forms of worship, and its eternal receptivity of those ideas trending towards the evolution of God in the universe. We admit the imperfection of our system, because the reality must be beyond all system; and in this admission lies the portent and promise of an eternal growth. Sects, ceremonies, and books, so far as they are the means of a man's realising his own nature, are all right; when he has realised that, he gives up everything. "I reject the Vedas!" is the last word of the Vedanta philosophy. Ritual, hymns, and scriptures, through which he has travelled to freedom, vanish for him. "So'ham, So'ham"— i am He, I am He—bursts from his lips, and to say "Thou" to God is blasphemy, for he is "one with the Father".

Personally, I take as much of the Vedas as agree with reason. Parts of the Vedas are apparently contradictory. They are not considered as inspired in the Western sense of the word, but as the sum total of the knowledge of God, omniscience, which we possess. But to say that only those books which we call the Vedas contain this knowledge is mere sophistry. We know it is shared in varying degrees by the scriptures of all sects. Manu says, that part only of the Vedas which agrees with reason is Vedas; and many of our philosophers have taken this view. Of all the scriptures of the world, it is the Vedas alone which declare that the study of the Vedas is secondary.

The real study is that "by which we realise the Unchangeable", and that is neither by reading, nor believing, nor reasoning, but by superconscious perception and Samadhi. When a man has reached that perfect state, he is of the same nature as the Personal God: "I and my Father are one." He knows himself one with Brahman, the Absolute, and projects himself as does the Personal God. The Personal God is the Absolute looked at through the haze of Maya—ignorance.

When we approach Him with the five senses, we can only see Him as the Personal God. The idea is that the Self cannot be objectified. How can the knower know himself? But he can cast a shadow, as it were, and the highest form of that shadow, that attempt of objectifying one's Self is the Personal God. The Self is the eternal subject, and we are eternally struggling to objectify that Self, and out of that struggle has come this phenomenon of the universe: that which we call matter. But these are weak attempts, and the highest objectification of the Self, possible to us, is the Personal God. "An honest God's the noblest work of man", said one of your Western thinkers. God is as man is. No man can see God but through these human manifestations. Talk as you may, try as you may, you cannot think of God but as a man; and as you are, He is. An ignorant man was asked to make an image of the God Shiva; and after many days of hard struggle he succeeded only in manufacturing the image of a monkey! So, when we try to think of God as He is in His absolute perfection, we meet with miserable failure, because we are limited and bound by our present constitution to see God as man. If the buffaloes desire to worship

God, they, in keeping with their own nature, will see Him as a huge buffalo; if a fish wishes to worship God, its concept of Him would inevitably be a big fish; and man must think of Him as man. Suppose man, the buffalo, and the fish represent so many different vessels; that these vessels all go to the sea of God to be filled, each according to its shape and capacity. In man the water takes the shape of man; in the buffalo the shape of the buffalo; and in the fish the shape of the fish; but in each of these vessels is the same water of the sea of God.

Two kinds of mind do not worship God as man—the human brute who has no religion, and the Paramahamsa who has transcended the limits of his own human nature.

To him all nature has become his own Self; he alone can worship God as He is. The human brute does not worship because of his ignorance, and the Jivanmuktas (free souls) do not worship because they have realised God in themselves. "So'ham, So'ham"—i am He, I am He—they say; and how shall they worship themselves?

I will tell you a little story. There was once a baby lion left by its dying mother among some sheep. The sheep fed it and gave it shelter. The lion grew apace and said "Ba-a-a" when the sheep said "Ba-a-a". One day another lion came by. "What do you do here?" said the second lion in astonishment: for he heard the sheep-lion bleating with the rest. "Ba-a-a," said the other. "I am a little sheep, I am a little sheep, I am frightened." "Nonsense!" roared the first lion, "come with me; I will show you." And he took him to the side of a smooth stream and showed him that which was reflected therein. "You are a lion; look at me, look at the sheep, look at yourself." And the sheep-lion looked, and then he said, "Ba-a-a, I do not look like the sheep—it is true, I am a lion!" and with that he roared a roar that shook the hills to their depths.

That is it. We are lions in sheep's clothing of habit, we are hypnotised into weakness by our surroundings. And the province of Vedanta is the self-dehypnotisation. The goal to be reached is freedom. I disagree with the idea that freedom is obedience to the laws of nature. I do not understand what that means. According to the history of human progress, it is disobedience to nature that has constituted that progress. It may be said that the conquest of lower laws was through the higher, but even there the conquering mind was still seeking freedom; as soon as it found the struggle was through law, it wished to conquer that also. So the ideal is always freedom. The trees never disobey law. I never saw a cow steal. An oyster never told a lie. Yet these are not greater than man.

Obedience to law, in the last issue, would make of us simply matter—either in society, or in politics, or religion. This life is a tremendous assertion of freedom; excess of laws means death. No nation possesses so many laws as the Hindus, and the result is the national death. But the Hindus had one peculiar idea—they never made any doctrines or dogmas in religion; and the latter has had the greatest growth. Therein are we practical—wherein you are impractical—in our religion.

A few men come together in America and say, "We will have a stock company"; in five minutes it is done. In India twenty men may discuss a stock company for as many weeks, and it may not be formed; but if one believes that by holding up his hands in air for forty years he will attain wisdom, it will be done! So we are practical in ours, you in your way.

But the way of all ways to realisation is love. When one loves the Lord, the whole universe becomes dear to one, because it is all His. "Everything is His, and He is my Lover; I love Him", says the Bhakta. In this way everything becomes sacred to the Bhakta, because all things are His. How, then, may we hurt any one? How, then, may we not love another? With the love of God will come, as its effect, the love of every one in the long run. The nearer we approach God, the more do we begin to see that all things abide in Him, our heart will become a perennial fountain of love. Man is transformed in the presence of this Light of Love and realises at last the beautiful and inspiring truth that Love, Lover, and the Beloved are really one.

THE RELIGION OF INDIA

New Discoveries, Vol. 2, pp. 145-49, 155-56.

These notes of daily morning classes delivered at Greenacre, Maine, in the summer of 1894 and recorded by Miss Emma Thursby were discovered among Miss Emma Thursby's papers at the New-York Historical Society. They have been lightly edited in order to conform to the style of the Complete Works.

Notes taken miscellaneously from discourses given by Swami Vivekananda under the "Pine" at Greenacre in July and August 1894.

The name of Swami's master was Ramakrishna Paramahamsa. The signification of Vivekananda is conscious bliss.

Meditation is a sort of prayer and prayer is meditation. The highest meditation is to think of nothing. If you can remain one moment without thought, great power will come. The whole secret of knowledge is concentration. Soul best develops itself by loving God with all the heart. Soul is the thinking principle in man, of which mind is a function. Soul is only the conduit from Spirit to mind.

All souls are playing, some consciously, some unconsciously. Religion is learning to play consciously.

The Guru is your own higher Self.

Seek the highest, always the highest, for in the highest is eternal bliss. If I am to hunt, I will hunt the rhinoceros. If I am to rob, I will rob the treasury of the king. Seek the highest.

[Some of the following passages are the Swami's free translations from Indian scriptures, including the Avadhuta-Gitâ of Dattâtreya.]

If you know you are bound [you are bound]; if you know you are free, you are free. My mind was never bound by yearnings of this world; for like the eternal blue sky, I am the essence of Knowledge, of Existence and of Bliss. Why weepest thou, Brother? Neither death nor disease for thee. Why weepest thou, Brother? Neither misery nor misfortune for thee. Why weepest thou, Brother? Neither change nor death was predicated of thee. Thou Art Existence Absolute.

I know what God is; I cannot speak [of] Him to you. I know not [what] God is; how can I speak [of] Him to you? But seest not thou, my brother, that thou wert He, thou wert He? Why go seeking God here and there? Seek not, and that is God. Be your own Self—One that cannot be confessed or described, One that can be perceived in our heart of hearts. One beyond all compare, beyond limit, unchangeable like the blue sky. Oh! learn the All Holy One. Seek for nothing else.

Where changes of nature cannot reach, thought beyond all thought, unchangeable, immovable, whom all books declare, all sages worship, O Holy One! Seek for nothing else.

Beyond compare, Infinite Oneness—no comparison is possible. Water above, water beneath, water on the right, water on the left. No wave on that water, no ripple. All silence, all eternal bliss. Such will come to thy heart. Seek for nothing else. Thou art our father, our mother, our dear friend. Thou bearest the burden of this world. Help us to bear the burden of our lives. Thou art our friend, our lover, our husband. Thou art ourselves. Four sorts of people worship Me. Some want the delights of the physical world. Some want money, some want religion. Some worship Me because they love Me.

Real love is love for love's sake. I do not ask health or money or life or salvation. Send me to a thousand hells, but let me love Thee for love's sake. Mirâ Bâi, the great queen, taught the doctrine of love for love's sake.

Our present consciousness is only a little bit of an infinite sea of mind. Do not be limited to this consciousness.

Three great things [are] to be desired to develop the soul: First, human birth; second, thirst for the highest; third, to find one who has reached the highest—a Mahâtmâ, one whose mind, word and deed are full of the nectar of virtue, whose only pleasure is in doing good to the universe, who looks upon others' virtues, be they only as a mustard seed, even as though they were a mountain, thus expanding his own self and helping others to expand. Thus is the Mahatma.

The word Yoga is the root of which our word yoke is a derivation—meaning "to join"—and Yoga means "joining ourselves with God"—joining me with my real Self.

All actions now involuntary or automatic were once voluntary, and our first step is to gain a knowledge of the automatic actions—the real idea being to revivify and make voluntary all automatic actions, to bring them into consciousness. Many Yogis can control the actions of their hearts.

To go back into consciousness and bring out things we have forgotten is ordinary power, but this can be heightened. All knowledge—all that—can be brought out of the inner consciousness, and to do this is Yoga. The majority of actions and thoughts is automatic, or acting behind consciousness. The seat of automatic action is in the medulla oblongata and down the spinal cord.

The question is, how to find our way back to our inner consciousness. We have come out through spirit, soul, mind, and body, and now we must go back from body to spirit. First, get hold of the air [breath], then the nervous system, then the mind, then the Atman, or spirit. But in this effort we must be perfectly sincere in desiring the highest.

The law of laws is concentration. First, concentrate all the nerve energies and all power lodged in the cells of the body into one force and direct it at will. Then bring the mind, which is thinner matter, into one center. The mind has layer after layer. When the nerve force concentrated is made to pass through the spinal column, one layer of the mind is open. When it is concentrated in one bone [plexus, or "lotus"], another part of the world is open. So from world to world it goes until it touches the pineal gland in the center of the brain. This is the seat of conservation of potential energy, the source of both activity and passivity.

Start with the idea that we can finish all experience in this world, in this incarnation. We must aim to become perfect in this life, this very moment. Success only comes to that life amongst men who wants to do this, this very moment. It is acquired by him who says, "Faith, I wait upon faith come what may". Therefore, go on knowing you are to finish this very moment. Struggle hard and then if you do not succeed, you are not to blame. Let the world praise or blame you. Let all the wealth of the earth come to your feet, or let you be made the poorest on earth. Let death come this moment or hundreds of years hence. Swerve not from the path you have taken. All good thoughts are immortal and go to make Buddhas and Christs.

Law is simply a means of [your] expression [of] various phenomena brought into your mind. Law is your method of grasping material phenomena and bringing them into unity. All law is finding unity in variety. The only method of knowledge is concentration on the physical, mental, and spiritual planes; and concentrating the powers of the mind to discover one in many, is what is called knowledge.

Everything that makes for unity is moral, everything that makes for diversity is immoral. Know the One without a second, that is perfection. The One who manifests in all is the basis of the universe; and all religion, all knowledge, must come to this point.

The following are some of the disconnected notes taken by Miss Emma Thursby during the last of the Swami's Greenacre classes, delivered Sunday morning, August 12, 1894.

I am Existence Absolute Kundalini

Bliss Absolute Circle mother I am He, Shivoham

I am He, Shivoham

He is the learned man who sees that every man's property is nothing. Every woman his Mother.

Shanti—peace—

We meditate on the Glory of Hrim (A Bija Mantra, or seed word, for the Divine Mother.)

Mother

Buddhistic Prayer

I bow to all the saint[s] on Earth

I bow down to the founders of Religion

to all holy men and women

Prophets of Religion

who have been on Earth

Hindu prayer

I meditate on the Glory of the producer of this Universe may He enlighten our minds.

CHRIST'S MESSAGE TO THE WORLD

New Discoveries, Vol. 5, p. 379.

From Mr. Frank Rhodehamel's notes of a lecture delivered in San Francisco, California, on March 11, 1900.

Everything progresses in waves. The march of civilization, the progression of worlds, is in waves. All human activities likewise progress in waves—art, literature, science, religion.

Great waves succeed each other, and between these great waves is a quiet, a calm, a period of rest, a period of recuperation.

All manifest life seems to require a period of sleep, of calm, in which to gain added strength, renewed vigour, for the next manifestation, or awakening to activity. Thus is the march of all progress, of all manifest life—in waves, successive waves, [of] activity and repose. Waves succeed each other in an endless chain of progression.

Religion, like everything else, progresses in waves; and at the summit of each great wave stands an illumined soul, a mighty spiritual leader and teacher of men. Such a one was Jesus of Nazareth.

MOHAMMED'S MESSAGE TO THE WORLD

New Discoveries, Vol. 5, pp. 401-3. Cf. "Mohammed", Complete Works, I.

Excerpts of Ida Ansell's first transcript of Swami Vivekananda's San Francisco lecture delivered Sunday, March 25, 1900.

Mohammed

After stating that he would "take Mohammed and bring out the particular work of the great Arabian prophet", Swami Vivekananda continued his lecture.

Each great messenger not only creates a new order of things, but is himself the creation of a certain order of things. There is no such thing as an independent, active cause. All causes are cause and effect in turn. Father is father and son in turn. Mother is mother and daughter in turn. It is necessary to un-

derstand the surroundings and circumstances into which they [the great messengers] come…

This is the peculiarity of civilization. One wave of a race will go from its birthplace to a distant land and make a wonderful civilization. The rest will be left in barbarism. The Hindus came into India and the tribes of Central Asia were left in barbarism. Others came to Asia Minor and Europe. Then, you remember the coming out of Egypt of the Israelites. Their home was the Arabian desert. Out of that springs a new work…All civilizations grow that way. A certain race becomes civilized. Then comes a nomad race. Nomads are always ready to fight. They come and conquer a race. They bring better blood, stronger physiques. They take up the mind of the conquered race and add that to their body and push civilization still further. One race becomes cultured and civilized until the body is worn out. Then like a whirlwind comes a race strong in the physical, and they take up the arts and the sciences and the mind, and push civilization further. This must be. Otherwise the world would not be.

* * *

The moment a great man rises, they build a beautiful [mythology] around him. Science and truth is all the religion that exists. Truth is more beautiful than any mythology in the world…

The old Greeks had disappeared already, the whole nation [lay] under the feet of the Romans who were learning their science and art. The Roman was a barbarian, a conquering man. He had no eye for poetry or art. He knew how to rule and how to get everything centralized into that system of Rome and to enjoy that. That was sweet. And that Roman Empire is gone, destroyed by all sorts of difficulties, luxury, a new foreign religion, and all that. Christianity had been already six hundred years in the Roman Empire…

Whenever a new religion tries to force itself upon another race, it succeeds if the race is uncultured. If it [the race] is cultured, it will destroy the [religion]…The Roman Empire was a case in point, and the Persian people saw that. Christianity was another thing with the barbarians in the north. [But] the Christianity of the Roman Empire was a mixture of everything, something from Persia, from the Jews, from India, from Greece, everything.

* * *

The race is always killed by [war]. War takes away the best men, gets them killed, and the cowards are left at home. Thus comes the degeneration of the race…Men became small. Why? All the great men became [warriors]. That is how war kills races, takes their best into the battlefields.

Then the monasteries. They all went to the desert, to the caves for meditation. The monasteries gradually became the centres of wealth and luxury…

The Anglo-Saxon race would not be Anglo-Saxon but

for these monasteries. Every weak man was worse than a slave.…In that state of chaos these monasteries were centres of light and protection.

Where [cultures] differ very much they do not quarrel. All these warring, jarring elements [were originally] all one.

In the midst of all this chaos was born the prophet…

[This concluded the first part of the Swami's lecture. Vide "Mohammed"]

CLASS LESSONS IN MEDITATION BY SWAMI VIVEKANANDA

New Discoveries, Vol. 6, p. 10.

Mr. Frank Rhodehamel's notes of a class delivered in San Francisco, California, on Monday, March 26, 1900.

The first point is the position. Sit with the spine perfectly free, with the weight resting on the hips. The next step is breathing. Breathe in the left nostril and out the right. Fill the lungs full and eject all the breath. Clear the lungs of all impure air. Breathe full and deep. The next thing is to think of the body as luminous, filled with light. The next thing is to concentrate on the base of the spine, not from the outside, but look down the spinal column inside to the base of the spine.

THE GITA

New Discoveries, Vol. 6, pp. 175-76.

Mr. Frank Rhodehamel's notes of a Bhagavad-Gîtâ class delivered Thursday, May 24, 1900, in San Francisco, California

The Gîtâ is the gist of the Vedas. It is not our Bible; the Upanishads are our Bible. It [the Gita] is the gist of the Upanishads and harmonizes the many contradictory parts of the Upanishads.

The Vedas are divided into two portions—the work portion and the knowledge portion. The work portion contains ceremonials, rules as to eating, living, doing charitable work, etc. The knowledge came afterwards and was enunciated by kings.

The work portion was exclusively in the hands of the priests and pertained entirely to the sense life. It taught to do good works that one might go to heaven and enjoy eternal happiness. Anything, in fact, that one might want could be provided for him by the work or ceremonials. It provided for all classes of people good and bad. Nothing could be obtained through the ceremonials except by the intercession of the priests. So if one wanted anything, even if it was to have an enemy killed, all he had to do was to pay the priest; and the priest through these ceremonials would procure the desired results. It was therefore in the interests of the priests that the ceremonial portion of the Vedas should be preserved. By it they had their living. They consequently did all in their power to preserve that portion intact. Many of these ceremonials were very complicated, and it took years to perform some of them.

The knowledge portion came afterwards and was promulgated exclusively by kings. It was called the Knowledge of Kings. The great kings had no use for the work portion with all its frauds and superstitions and did all in their power to destroy it. This knowledge consisted of a knowledge of God, the soul, the universe, etc. These kings had no use for the ceremonials of the priests, their magical works, etc. They pronounced it all humbug; and when the priests came to them for gifts, they questioned the priests about God, the soul, etc., and as the priests could not answer such questions they were sent away. The priests went back to their fathers to enquire about the things the kings asked them, but could learn nothing from them, so they came back again to the kings and became their disciples. Very little of the ceremonials are followed today. They have been mostly done away with, and only a few of the more simple ones are followed today.

Then in the Upanishads there is the doctrine of Karma. Karma is the law of causation applied to conduct. According to this doctrine we must work forever, and the only way to get rid of pain is to do good works and thus to enjoy the good effects; and after living a life of good works, die and go to heaven and live forever in happiness. Even in heaven we could not be free from Karma, only it would be good Karma, not bad.

The philosophical portion denounces all work however good, and all pleasure, as loving and kissing wife, husband or children, as useless. According to this doctrine all good works and pleasures are nothing but foolishness and in their very nature impermanent. "All this must come to an end sometime, so end it now; it is vain." So says the philosophical portion of the Upanishads. It claims all the pain in the world is caused by ignorance, therefore the cure is knowledge.

This idea of one being held down fast by past Karma, or work, is all nonsense. No matter how dense one may be, or how bad, one ray of light will dissipate it all. A bale of cotton, however large, will be utterly destroyed by a spark. If a room has been dark for untold ages, a lamp will end it all. So with each soul, however benighted he may be, he is not absolutely bound down by his past Karma to work for ages to come. "One ray of Divine Light will free him, reveal to him his true nature."

Well, the Gita harmonizes all these conflicting doctrines. As to Krishna, whether or not he ever lived, I do not know. "A great many stories are told of him, but I do not believe them."

"I doubt very much that he ever lived and think it would be a good thing if he never did. There would have been one less god in the world."

THE GITA—I

New Discoveries, Vol. 6, pp. 205-7. Cf. Ida Ansell's notes of "The Gita I", Complete Works, I.

Mr. Frank Rhodehamel's notes of a Bhagavad-Gîtâ lecture delivered Saturday, May 26, 1900, in San Francisco, California.

The Gîtâ is to the Hindus what the New Testament is to the Christians. It is about five thousand years old, and the day of religious celebrations with the Hindus is the anniversary of the Battle of Kurukshetra about five thousand years ago. As I said, the Vedas are divided into two great divisions, the philosophical and the Karmakânda, or work portion.

Between the kings, who promulgated the philosophic portion, and the priests a great conflict arose. The priests had the people on their side because they had all the utility which appealed to the popular mind. The kings had all the spirituality and none of the economic element; but as they were powerful and the rulers of the nation, the struggle was a hard and bitter one. The kings gradually gained a little ground, but their ideas were too elevated for the masses, so the ceremonial, or work portion, always had the mass of the people.

Always remember this, that whenever a religious system gains ground with the people at large, it has a strong economic side to it. It is the economic side of a religion that finds lodgement with the people at large, and never its spiritual, or philosophic, side. If you should preach the grandest philosophy in the streets for a year, you would not have a handful of followers. But you could preach the most arrant nonsense, and if it had an economic element, you would have the whole people with you.

None knows by whom the Vedas were written; they are so ancient. According to the orthodox Hindus, the Vedas are not the written words at all, but they consist of the words themselves orally spoken with the exact enunciation and intonation. This vast mass of religion has been written and consists of thousands upon thousands of volumes. Anyone who knows the precise pronunciation and intonation knows the Vedas, and no one else. In ancient times certain royal families were the custodians of certain parts of the Vedas. The head of the family could repeat every word of every volume he had, without missing a word or an intonation. These men had giant intellects, wonderful memories.

The strictly orthodox believers in the Vedas, the Karmakanda, did not believe in God, the soul or anything of the sort, but that we as we are were the only beings in the universe, material or spiritual. When they were asked what the many allusions to God in the Vedas mean, they say that they mean nothing at all; that the words properly articulated have a magical power, a power to create certain results. Aside from that they have no meaning.

Whenever you suppress a thought, you simply press it down out of sight in a coil, like a spring, only to spring out again at a moment's notice with all the pent up force as the result of the suppression, and do in a few moments what it would have done in a much longer period.

Every ounce of pleasure brings its pound of pain. It is the same energy that at one time manifests itself as pleasure and at another time as pain. As soon as one set of sensations stops, another begins. But in some cases, in more advanced persons, one may have two, yes, or even a hundred different thoughts enter into active operation at the same time. When one thought is suppressed, it is merely coiled up ready to spring forth with pent up fury at any time.

"Mind is of its own nature. Mind activity means creation. The thought is followed by the word, and the word by the form. All of this creating will have to stop, both mental and physical, before the mind can reflect the soul."

"My old master (Shri Ramakrishna.) could not write his own name without making a mistake. He made three mistakes in spelling, in writing his own name."

"Yet that is the kind of man at whose feet I sat."

"You will break the law of nature but once, and it will be the last time. Nature will then be nothing to you."

THE GITA—III

New Discoveries, Vol. 6, pp. 213-16. Cf.

Ida Ansell's notes of "The Gita III", Complete Works, I. Mr. Frank Rhodehamel's notes of the Bhagavad-Gîtâ lecture delivered Tuesday, May 29, 1900, in San Francisco, California.

1. "If you know everything, disturb not the childlike faith of the innocent."
2. "Religion is the realization of Spirit as Spirit. Not spirit as matter."
3. "You are spirit. Realize yourselves as spirit. Do it any way you can."
4. "Religion is a growth": each one must experience it himself.
5. "Everyone thinks 'my method is the best'. That is so, but it is the best for you."
6. "Spirit must stand revealed as spirit."
7. "There never was a time when spirit could be identified with matter."
8. "What is real in nature is the spirit."
9. "Action is in nature."
10. "'In the beginning there was That Existence. He looked and everything was created.'"
11. "Everyone works according to his own nature."
12. "You are not bound by law. That is in your nature. The mind is in nature and is bound by law."
13. "If you want to be religious, keep out of religious arguments."
14. "Governments, societies, etc., are evils." "All societies are based on bad generalizations." "A law is that which cannot be broken."
15. "Better never love, if that love makes us hate others."
16. "The sign of death is weakness; the sign of life is strength."

4. The Christian believes that Jesus Christ died to save him. With you it is belief in a doctrine, and this belief constitutes your salvation. With us, doctrine has nothing whatever to do with salvation. Each one may believe in whatever doctrine he likes or in no doctrine. With us realization is religion, not doctrine. What difference does it make to you whether Jesus Christ lived at a certain time? What has it to do with you that Moses saw God in a burning bush? The fact that Moses saw God in the burning bush does not constitute your seeing Him, does it? If it does, then the fact that Moses ate is enough for you; you ought to stop eating. One is just as sensible as the other. Records of great spiritual men of the past do us no good whatever except that they urge us onward to do the same, to experience religion ourselves. Whatever Christ or Moses or anybody else did does not help us in the least except to urge us on.

5. Each one has a special nature peculiar to himself which he must follow and through which he will find his way to freedom. Your teacher should be able to tell you what your particular path in nature is and to put you in it. He should know by your face where you belong and should be able to indicate it to you. We should never try to follow another's path for that is his way, not yours. When that path is found, you have nothing to do but fold your arms and the tide will carry you to freedom. Therefore when you find it, never swerve from it. Your way is the best for you, but that is no sign it is the best for another.

6. The truly spiritual see spirit as spirit, not as matter. Spirit as such can never become matter, though matter is spirit at a low rate of vibration. It is spirit that makes nature move; it is the Reality in nature, so action is in nature but not in the spirit. Spirit is always the same, changeless, eternal. Spirit and matter are in reality the same, but spirit, as such, never becomes matter, and matter, as such, never becomes spirit. Matter, as such, never becomes spirit as such, for it is simply a mode of spirit, or spirit at a low rate of vibration. You take food and it becomes mind, and mind in turn becomes the body. Thus mind and body, spirit and matter are distinct though either may give place to the other; but they are not to be identified.

8. "What is real in nature is the Spirit." The spirit is the life in all action in nature. It is the spirit that gives nature its reality and power of action.

9. "Action is in nature." "The spirit never acts. Why should it?" It merely is, and that is sufficient. It is pure existence absolute and has no need of action.

12. All nature is bound by law, the law of its own action; and this law can never be broken. If you could break a law of nature, all nature would come to an end in an instant. There would be no more nature. He who attains freedom breaks the law of nature and for him nature fades away and has no more power over him. Each one will break the law but once and forever and that will end his trouble with nature. "You are not bound by law. That is in your nature. The mind is in nature and is bound by law."

14. The moment you form yourselves into an organization, you begin to hate everybody outside of that organization. When you join an organization you are putting bonds upon yourself, you are limiting your own freedom. Why should you form yourselves into an order having rules and regulations, thus limiting every one as to his independent action? If one breaks a law of an order or society he is hated by the rest. What right has anyone to lay down rules and laws governing others? Such laws are not laws at all. If it were a law it could not be broken. The fact that these so-called laws are broken shows clearly they are not laws.

GITA CLASS

New Discoveries, Vol. 6, pp. 275-76.

Sister Nivedita's notes of a New York Bhagavad-Gitâ class, recorded in a June 16, 1900 letter to Miss Josephine MacLeod.

This morning the lesson on the Gitâ was grand. It began with a long talk on the fact that the highest ideals are not for all. Non-resistance is not for the man who thinks the replacing of the maggot in the wound by the leprous saint with "Eat, Brother!" disgusting and horrible. Non-resistance is practised by a mother's love towards an angry child. It is a travesty in the mouth of a coward, or in the face of a lion.

Let us be true. Nine-tenths of our life's energy is spent in trying to make people think us that which we are not. That energy would be more rightly spent in becoming that which we would like to be. And so it went—beginning with the salutation to an incarnation:

Salutation to thee—the Guru of the universe, Whose footstool is worshipped by the gods.

Thou one unbroken Soul,

Physician of the world's diseases.

Guru of even the gods,

To thee our salutation.

Thee we salute. Thee we salute. Thee we salute. In the Indian tones—by Swami himself.

There was an implication throughout the talk that Christ and Buddha were inferior to Krishna—in the grasp of problems—inasmuch as they preached the highest ethics as a world path, whereas Krishna saw the right of the whole, in all its parts—to its own differing ideals.

CONVERSATIONS & DIALOGUES

DISCUSSION AT THE GRADUATE PHILOSOPHICAL SOCIETY OF HARVARD UNIVERSITY

Q.—I should like to know something about the present activity of philosophic thought in India. To what extent are these questions discussed?

A.—As I have said, the majority of the Indian people are practically dualists, and the minority are monists. The main subject of discussion is Mâyâ and Jiva. When I came to this country, I found that the labourers were informed of the present condition of politics; but when I asked them, "What is religion, and what are the doctrines of this and that particular sect?" they said, "We do not know; we go to church." In India if I go to a peasant and ask him, "Who governs you?" he says, "I do not know; I pay my taxes." But if I ask him what is his religion, he says, "I am a dualist", and is ready to give you the details about Maya and Jiva. He cannot read or write, but he has learned all this from the monks and is very fond of discussing it. After the day's work, the peasants sit under a tree and discuss these questions.

Q.—What does orthodoxy mean with the Hindus?

A.—In modern times it simply means obeying certain caste laws as to eating, drinking, and marriage. After that the Hindu can believe in any system he likes. There was never an organised church in India; so there was never a body of men to formulate doctrines of orthodoxy. In a general way, we say that those who believe in the Vedas are orthodox; but in reality we find that many of the dualistic sects believe more in the Purânas than in the Vedas alone.

Q.—What influence had your Hindu philosophy on the Stoic philosophy of the Greeks?

A.—It is very probable that it had some influence on it through the Alexandrians. There is some suspicion of Pythagoras' being influenced by the Sânkhya thought. Anyway, we think the Sankhya philosophy is the first attempt to harmonise the philosophy of the Vedas through reason. We find Kapila mentioned even in the Vedas: "Knowledge, the first-born sage Kapila."

Q.—What is the antagonism of this thought with Western science?

A.—No antagonism at all. We are in harmony with it. Our theory of evolution and of Âkâsha and Prâna is exactly what your modern philosophies have. Your belief in evolution is among our Yogis and in the Sankhya philosophy. For instance, Patanjali speaks of one species being changed into another by the infilling of nature—""जात्यन्तरपरिणामः प्रकृत्यापूरात्"; only he differs from you in the explanation. His explanation of this evolution is spiritual. He says that just as when a farmer wants to water his field from the canals that pass near, he has only to lift up gate— "निमित्तमप्रयोजकं प्रकृतीनां वरणभेदस्तु ततः क्षेत्रिकवत्" —so each man is the Infinite already, only these bars and bolts and different circumstances shut him in; but as soon as they are removed, he rushes out and expresses himself.

In the animal, the man was held in abeyance; but as soon as good circumstances came, he was manifested as man. And again, as soon as fitting circumstances came, the God in man manifested itself. So we have very little to quarrel with in the new theories. For instance, the theory of the Sankhya as to perception is very little different from modern physiology.

Q.—But your method is different?

A.—Yes. We claim that concentrating the powers of the mind is the only way to knowledge. In external science, concentration of mind is—putting it on something external; and in internal science, it is—drawing towards one's Self. We call this concentration of mind Yoga.

Q.—In the state of concentration does the truth of these principles become evident?

A.—The Yogis claim a good deal. They claim that by concentration of the mind every truth in the universe becomes evident to the mind, both external and internal truth.

Q.—What does the Advaitist think of cosmology?

A.—The Advaitist would say that all this cosmology and everything else are only in Maya, in the phenomenal world. In truth they do not exist. But as long as we are bound, we have to see these visions. Within these visions things come in a certain regular order. Beyond them there is no law and order, but freedom.

Q.—Is the Advaita antagonistic to dualism?

A.—The Upanishads not being in a systematised form, it was easy for philosophers to take up texts when they liked to form a system. The Upanishads had always to be taken, else there would be no basis. Yet we find all the different schools of thought in the Upanishads. Our solution is that the Advaita is not antagonistic to the Dvaita (dualism). We say the latter is only one of three steps. Religion always takes three steps. The first is dualism. Then man gets to a higher state, partial non-dualism. And at last he finds he is one with the universe. Therefore the three do not contradict but fulfil.

Q.—Why does Maya or ignorance exist?

A.—"Why" cannot be asked beyond the limit of causation. It can only be asked within Maya. We say we will answer the question when it is logically formulated. Before that we have no right to answer.

Q.—Does the Personal God belong to Maya?

A.—Yes; but the Personal God is the same Absolute seen through Maya. That Absolute under the control of nature is what is called the human soul; and that which is controlling nature is Ishvara, or the Personal God. If a man starts from here to see the sun, he will see at first a little sun; but as he proceeds he will see it bigger and bigger, until he reaches the real one. At each stage of his progress he was seeing apparently a different sun; yet we are sure it was the same sun he was seeing. So all these things are but visions of the Absolute, and as such they are true. Not one is a false vision, but we can only say they were lower stages.

Q.—What is the special process by which one will come to know the Absolute?

A.—We say there are two processes. One is the positive, and the other, the negative. The positive is that through which the whole universe is going— that of love. If this circle of love is increased indefinitely, we reach the one universal love. The other is the "Neti", "Neti"—"not this", "not this" —stopping every wave in the mind which tries to draw it out; and at last the mind dies, as it were, and the Real discloses Itself. We call that Samâdhi, or superconsciousness.

Q.—That would be, then, merging the subject in the object!

A.—Merging the object in the subject, not merging the subject in the object. Really this world dies, and I remain. I am the only one that remains.

Q.—Some of our philosophers in Germany have thought that the whole doctrine of Bhakti (Love for the Divine) in India was very likely the result of occidental influence.

A.—I do not take any stock in that—the assumption was ephemeral. The Bhakti of India is not like the Western Bhakti. The central idea of ours is that there is no thought of fear. It is always, love God. There is no worship through fear, but always through love, from beginning to end. In the second place, the assumption is quite unnecessary. Bhakti is spoken of in the oldest of the Upanishads, which is much older than the Christian Bible. The germs of Bhakti are even in the Samhitâ (the Vedic hymns). The word Bhakti is not a Western word. It was suggested by the word Shraddhâ.

Q.—What is the Indian idea of the Christian faith?

A.—That it is very good. The Vedanta will take in every one. We have a peculiar idea in India. Suppose I had a child. I should not teach him any religion; I should teach him breathings—the practice of concentrating the mind, and just one line of prayer—not prayer in your sense, but simply something like this, "I meditate on Him who is the Creator of this universe: may He enlighten my mind I" That way he would be educated, and then go about hearing different philosophers and teachers. He would select one who, he thought, would suit him best; and this man would become his Guru or teacher, and he would become a Shishya or disciple. He would say to that man, "This form of philosophy which you preach is the best; so teach me." Our fundamental idea is that your doctrine cannot be mine, or mine yours. Each one must have his own way. My daughter may have one method, and my son another, and I again another. So each one has an Ishta or chosen way, and we keep it to ourselves. It is between me and my teacher, because we do not want to create a fight. It will not help any one to tell it to others, because each one will have to find his own way. So only general philosophy and general methods can be taught universally. For instance, giving a ludicrous example, it may help me to stand on one leg. It would be ludicrous to you if I said every one must do that, but it may suit me. It is quite possible for me to be a dualist and for my wife to be a monist, and so on. One of my son

may worship Christ or Buddha or Mohammed, so long as he obeys the caste laws. That is his own Ishta.

Q.—Do all Hindus believe in caste?

A.—They are forced to. They may not believe, but they have to obey.

Q.—Are these exercises in breathing and concentration universally practiced?

A.—Yes; only some practice only a little, just to satisfy the requirements of their religion. The temples in India are not like the churches here. They may all vanish tomorrow, and will not be missed. A temple is built by a man who wants to go to heaven, or to get a son, or something of that sort. So he builds a large temple and employs a few priests to hold services there. I need not go there at all, because all my worship is in the home. In every house is a special room set apart, which is called the chapel. The first duty of the child, after his initiation, is to take a bath, and then to worship; and his worship consists of this breathing and meditating and repeating of a certain name. And another thing is to hold the body straight. We believe that the mind has every power over the body to keep it healthy. After one has done this, then another comes and takes his seat, and each one does it in silence. Sometimes there are three or four in the same room, but each one may have a different method. This worship is repeated at least twice a day.

Q.—This state of oneness that you speak of, is it an ideal or something actually attained?

A.—We say it is within actuality; we say we realise that state. If it were only in talk, it would be nothing. The Vedas teach three things: this Self is first to be heard, then to be reasoned, and then to be meditated upon. When a man first hears it, he must reason on it, so that he does not believe it ignorantly, but knowingly; and after reasoning what it is, he must meditate upon it, and then realise it. And that is religion. Belief is no part of religion. We say religion is a superconscious state.

Q.—If you ever reach that state of superconsciousness, can you ever tell about it?

A.—No; but we know it by its fruits. An idiot, when he goes to sleep, comes out of sleep an idiot or even worse. But another man goes into the state of meditation, and when he comes out he is a philosopher, a sage, a great man. That shows the difference between these two states.

Q. —I should like to ask, in continuation of Professor—'s question, whether you know of any people who have made any study of the principles of self-hypnotism, which they undoubtedly practiced to a great extent in ancient India, and what has been recently stated and practiced in that thing. Of course you do not have it so much in modern India.

A.—What you call hypnotism in the West is only a part of the real thing. The Hindus call it self-hypnotisation. They say you are hypnotised already, and that you should get out of it and de-hypnotise yourself. "There the sun cannot illume, nor the moon, nor the stars; the flash of lightning cannot il-

Lectures & Discourses by Swami Vivekananda

lume that; what to speak of this mortal fire! That shining, everything else shines" (Katha Upanishad, II ii. 15). That is not hypnotisation, but de-hypnotisation. We say that every other religion that preaches these things as real is practicing a form of hypnotism. It is the Advaitist alone that does not care to be hypnotised. His is the only system that more or less understands that hypnotism comes with every form of dualism. But the Advaitist says, throw away even the Vedas, throw away even the Personal God, throw away even the universe, throw away even your own body and mind, and let nothing remain, in order to get rid of hypnotism perfectly. "From where the mind comes back with speech, being unable to reach, knowing the Bliss of Brahman, no more is fear." That is de-hypnotisation. "I have neither vice nor virtue, nor misery nor happiness; I care neither for the Vedas nor sacrifices nor ceremonies; I am neither food nor eating nor eater, for I am Existence Absolute, Knowledge Absolute, Bliss Absolute; I am He, I am He." We know all about hypnotism. We have a psychology which the West is just beginning to know, but not yet adequately, I am sorry to say.

Q.—What do you call the astral body?

A.—The astral body is what we call the Linga Sharira. When this body dies, how can it come to take another body? Force cannot remain without matter. So a little part of the fine matter remains, through which the internal organs make another body—for each one is making his own body; it is the mind that makes the body. If I become a sage, my brain gets changed into a sage's brain; and the Yogis say that even in this life a Yogi can change his body into a god-body.

The Yogis show many wonderful things. One ounce of practice is worth a thousand pounds of theory. So I have no right to say that because I have not seen this or that thing done, it is false. Their books say that with practice you can get all sorts of results that are most wonderful. Small results can be obtained in a short time by regular practice, so that one may know that there is no humbug about it, no charlatanism. And these Yogis explain the very wonderful things mentioned in all scriptures in a scientific way. The question is, how these records of miracles entered into every nation. The man, who says that they are all false and need no explanation, is not rational. You have no right to deny them until you can prove them false. You must prove that they are without any foundation, and only then have you the right to stand up and deny them. But you have not done that. On the other hand, the Yogis say they are not miracles, and they claim that they can do them even today. Many wonderful things are done in India today. But none of them are done by miracles. There are many books on the subject. Again, if nothing else has been done in that line except a scientific approach towards psychology, that credit must be given to the Yogis.

Q.—Can you say in the concrete what the manifestations are which the Yogi can show?

A.—The Yogi wants no faith or belief in his science but that which is given to any other science, just enough gentlemanly faith to come and make the experiment. The ideal of the Yogi is tremendous. I have seen the lower things that can be done by the power of the mind, and therefore, I have no right to disbelieve that the highest things can be done. The ideal of the Yogi is eternal peace and love through omniscience and omnipotence. I know a Yogi who was bitten by a cobra, and who fell down on the ground. In the evening he revived again, and when asked what happened, he said: "A messenger came from my Beloved." All hatred and anger and jealousy have been burnt out of this man. Nothing can make him react; he is infinite love all the time, and he is omnipotent in his power of love. That is the real Yogi. And this manifesting different things is accidental on the way. That is not what he wants to attain. The Yogi says, every man is a slave except the Yogi. He is a slave of food, to air, to his wife, to his children, to a dollar, slave to a nation, slave to name and fame, and to a thousand things in this world. The man who is not controlled by any one of these bandages is alone a real man, a real Yogi. "They have conquered relative existence in this life who are firm-fixed in sameness. God is pure and the same to all. Therefore such are said to be living in God" (Gita, V. 19).

Q.—Do the Yogis attach any importance to caste?

A.—No; caste is only the training school for undeveloped minds.

Q.—Is there no connection between this idea of super. consciousness and the heat of India?

A.—I do not think so; because all this philosophy was thought out fifteen thousand feet above the level of the sea, among the Himalayas, in an almost Arctic temperature.

Q.—Is it practicable to attain success in a cold climate?

A.—It is practicable, and the only thing that is practicable in this world. We say you are a born Vedantist, each one of you. You are declaring your oneness with everything each moment you live. Every time that your heart goes out towards the world, you are a true Vedantist, only you do not know it. You are moral without knowing why; and the Vedanta is the philosophy which analysed and taught man to be moral consciously. It is the essence of all religions.

Q.—Should you say that there is an unsocial principle in our Western people, which makes us so pluralistic, and that Eastern people are more sympathetic than we are?

A.—I think the Western people are more cruel, and the Eastern people have more mercy towards all beings. But that is simply because your civilisation is very much more recent. It takes time to make a thing come under the influence of mercy. You have a great deal of power, and the power of control of the mind has especially been very little practiced. It will take time to make you gentle and good. T his feeling tingles in every drop of blood in India. If I go to the villages to teach the people politics, they will not understand; but if I go to teach them Vedanta, they will say, "Now, Swami, you are all right". That Vairâgya, non-attachment, is everywhere in India, even today. We are very much degenerated now; but kings will give up their thrones and go about the country without anything.

In some places the common village-girl with her spinning-wheel says, "Do not talk to me of dualism; my spinning-wheel says 'Soham, Soham'—'I am He, I am He.'" Go and talk to these people, and ask them why it is that they speak so and yet kneel before that stone. They will say that with you religion means dogma, but with them realisation. "I will be a Vedantist", one of them will say, "only when all this has vanished, and I have seen the reality. Until then there is no difference between me and the ignorant. So I am using these stones and am going to temples, and so on, to come to realisation. I have heard, but I want to see and realise." "Different methods of speech, different manners of explaining the meaning of the scriptures—these are only for the enjoyment of the learned, not for freedom" (Shankara). It is realisation which leads us to that freedom.

Q.—Is this spiritual freedom among the people consistent with attention to caste?

A.—Certainly not. They say there should be no caste. Even those who are in caste say it is not a very perfect institution. But they say, when you find us another and a better one, we will give it up. They say, what will you give us instead? Where is there no caste? In your nation you are struggling all the time to make a caste. As soon as a man gets a bag of dollars, he says, "I am one of the Four Hundred." We alone have succeeded in making a permanent caste. Other nations are struggling and do not succeed. We have superstitions and evils enough. Would taking the superstitions and evils from your country mend matters? It is owing to caste that three hundred millions of people can find a piece of bread to eat yet. It is an imperfect institution, no doubt. But if it had not been for caste, you would have had no Sanskrit books to study. This caste made walls, around which all sorts of invasions rolled and surged, but found it impossible to break through. That necessity has not gone yet; so caste remains. The caste we have now is not that of seven hundred years ago. Every blow has riveted it. Do you realise that India is the only country that never went outside of itself to conquer? The great emperor Asoka insisted that none of his descendants should go to conquer. If people want to send us teachers, let them help, but not injure. Why should all these people come to conquer the Hindus? Did they do any injury to any nation? What little good they could do, they did for the world. They taught it science, philosophy, religion, and civilised the savage hordes of the earth. And this is the return—only murder and tyranny, and calling them heathen rascals. Look at the books written on India by Western people and at the stories of many travellers who go there; in retaliation for what injuries are these hurled at them?

Q.—What is the Vedantic idea of civilisation?

A.—You are philosophers, and you do not think that a bag of gold makes the difference between man and man. What is the value of all these machines and sciences? They have only

one result: they spread knowledge. You have not solved the problem of want, but only made it keener. Machines do not solve the poverty question; they simply make men struggle the more. Competition gets keener. What value has nature in itself? Why do you go and build a monument to a man who sends electricity through a wire? Does not nature do that millions of times over? Is not everything already existing in nature? What is the value of your getting it? It is already there. The only value is that it makes this development. This universe is simply a gymnasium in which the soul is taking exercise; and after these exercises we become gods. So the value of everything is to be decided by how far it is a manifestation of God. Civilisation is the manifestation of that divinity in man.

Q.—Have the Buddhists any caste laws?

A.—The Buddhists never had much caste, and there are very few Buddhists in India. Buddha was a social reformer. Yet in Buddhistic countries I find that there have been strong attempts to manufacture caste, only they have failed. The Buddhists' caste is practically nothing, but they take pride in it in their own minds.

Buddha was one of the Sannyâsins of the Vedanta. He started a new sect, just as others are started even today. The ideas which now are called Buddhism were not his. They were much more ancient. He was a great man who gave the ideas power. The unique element in Buddhism was its social element. Brahmins and Kshatriyas have always been our teachers, and most of the Upanishads were written by Kshatriyas, while the ritualistic portions of the Vedas came from the Brahmins. Most of our great teachers throughout India have been Kshatriyas, and were always universal in their teachings; whilst the Brahmana prophets with two exceptions were very exclusive. Râma, Krishna, and Buddha—worshipped as Incarnations of God—were Kshatriyas.

Q.—Are sects, ceremonies, and scriptures helps to realisation?

A.—When a man realises, he gives up everything. The various sects and ceremonies and books, so far as they are the means of arriving at that point, are all right. But when they fail in that, we must change them. "The knowing one must not despise the condition of those who are ignorant, nor should the knowing one destroy the faith; of the ignorant in their own particular method, but by proper action lead them and show them the path to comes to where he stands" (Gita, III. 26).

Q.—How does the Vedanta explain individuality and ethics?

A.—The real individual is the Absolute; this personalisation is through Maya. It is only apparent; in reality it is always the Absolute. In reality there is one, but ins Maya it is appearing as many. In Maya there is this variation. Yet even in this Maya there is always the tendency to, get back to the One, as expressed in all ethics and all morality of every nation, because it is the constitutional necessity of the soul. It is finding its oneness; and this struggle to find this oneness is what we call ethics and morality. Therefore we must always practice them.

Q.—Is not the greater part of ethics taken up with the relation between individuals?

A.—That is all it is. The Absolute does not come within Maya.

Q.—You say the individual is the Absolute, and I was going to ask you whether the individual has knowledge.

A.—The state of manifestation is individuality, and the light in that state is what we call knowledge. To use, therefore, this term knowledge for the light of the Absolute is not precise, as the absolute state transcends relative knowledge.

Q.—Does it include it?

A.—Yes, in this sense. Just as a piece of gold can be changed into all sorts of coins, so with this. The state can be broken up into all sorts of knowledge. It is the state of superconsciousness, and includes both consciousness and unconsciousnes. The man who attains that state has all that we call knowledge. When he wants to realise that consciousness of knowledge, he has to go a step lower. Knowledge is a lower state; it is only in Maya that we can have knowledge.

AT THE TWENTIETH CENTURY CLUB OF BOSTON

Q.—Did Vedanta exert any influence over Mohammedanism?

A.—This Vedantic spirit of religious liberality has very much affected Mohammedanism. Mohammedanism in India is quite a different thing from that in any other country. It is only when Mohammedans come from other countries and preach to their co-religionists in India about living with men who are not of their faith that a Mohammedan mob is aroused and fights.

Q.—Does Vedanta recognise caste?

A.—The caste system is opposed to the religion of the Vedanta. Caste is a social custom, and all our great preachers have tried to break it down. From Buddhism downwards, every sect has preached against caste, and every time it has only riveted the chains. Caste is simply the outgrowth of the political institutions of India; it is a hereditary trade guild. Trade competition with Europe has broken caste more than any teaching.

Q.—What is the peculiarity of the Vedas?

A.—One peculiarity of the Vedas is that they are the only scriptures that again and again declare that you must go beyond them. The Vedas say that they were written just for the child mind; and when you have grown, you must go beyond them.

Q.—Do you hold the individual soul to be eternally real?

A.—The individual soul consists of a man's thoughts, and they are changing every moment. Therefore, it cannot be eternally real. It is real only in the phenomenal. The individual consists of memory and thought, how can that be real?

Q.—Why did Buddhism as a religion decline in India?

A.—Buddhism did not really decline in India; it was only a gigantic social movement. Before Buddha great numbers of animals were killed for sacrifice and other reasons, and people drank wine and ate meat in large quantities. Since Buddha's teaching drunkenness has almost disappeared, and the killing of animals has almost gone.

AT THE BROOKLYN ETHICAL SOCIETY, BROOKLYN

Q.—How can you reconcile your optimistic views with the existence of evil, with the universal prevalence of sorrow and pain?

A. —I can only answer the question if the existence of evil be first proved; but this the Vedantic religion does not admit. Eternal pain unmixed with pleasure would be a positive evil; but temporal pain and sorrow, if they have contributed an element of tenderness and nobility tending towards eternal bliss, are not evils: on the contrary, they may be supreme good. We cannot assert that anything is evil until we have traced its sequence into the realm of eternity.

Devil worship is not a part of the Hindu religion. The human race is in process of development; all have not reached the same altitude. Therefore some are nobler and purer in their earthly lives than others. Every one has an opportunity within the limits of the sphere of his present development of making himself better. We cannot unmake ourselves; we cannot destroy or impair the vital force within us, but we have the freedom to give it different directions.

Q.—Is not the reality of cosmic matter simply the imagining of our own minds?

A.—In my opinion the external world is certainly an entity and has an existence outside of our mental conceptions. All creation is moving onwards and upwards, obedient to the great law of spirit evolution, which is different from the evolution of matter. The latter is symbolical of, but does not explain, the process of the former. We are not individuals now, in our present earthly environment. We shall not have reached individuality until we shall have ascended to the higher state, when the divine spirit within us will have a perfect medium for the expression of its attributes.

Q.—What is your explanation of the problem presented to Christ, as to whether it was the infant itself or its parents that had sinned, that it was born blind?

A.—While the question of sin does not enter into the problem, I am convinced that the blindness was due to some act on the part of the spirit of the child in a previous incarnation. In my opinion such problems are only explicable on the hypothesis of a prior earthly existence.

Q.—Do our spirits pass at death into a state of happiness?

A.—Death is only a change of condition: time and space are

in you, you are not in time and space. It is enough to know that as we make our lives purer and nobler, either in the seen or the unseen world, the nearer we approach God, who is the centre of all spiritual beauty and eternal joy.

Q.—What is the Hindu theory of the transmigration of souls?

A.—It is on the same basis as the theory of conservation is to the scientist. This theory was first produced by a philosopher of my country. The ancient sages did not believe in a creation. A creation implies producing something out of nothing. That is impossible. There was no beginning of creation as there was no beginning of time. God and creation are as two lines without end, without beginning, and parallel. Our theory of creation is "It is, it was, and is to be". All punishment is but reaction. People of the West should learn one thing from India and that is toleration. All the religions are good, since the essentials are the same.

Q.—Why are the women of India not much elevated?

A.—It is in a great degree owing to the barbarous invaders through different ages; it is partly due to the people of India themselves.

When it was pointed out to Swamiji in America that Hinduism is not a proselytising religion, he replied:

"I have a message to the West as Buddha had a message to the East."

Q.—Do you intend to introduce the practices and rituals of the Hindu religion into this country (America)?

A.—I am preaching simply philosophy.

Q.—Do you not think if the fear of future hell-fire were taken from man there would be no controlling him?

A.—No! On the contrary, I think he is made far better through love and hope than through fear.

SELECTIONS FROM THE MATH DIARY

Q.—Whom can we call a Guru?

A.—He who can tell your past and future is your Guru.

Q.—How can one have Bhakti?

A.—There is Bhakti within you, only a veil of lust-and-wealth covers it, and as soon as that is removed Bhakti will manifest by itself.

Q.—What is the true meaning of the assertion that we should depend on ourselves?

A.—Here self means the eternal Self. But even dependence on the non-eternal self may lead gradually to the right goal, as the individual self is really the eternal Self under delusion.

Q.—If unity is the only reality, how could duality which is perceived by all every moment have arisen?

A.—Perception is never dual; it is only the representation of perception that involves duality. If perception were dual, the known could have existed independently of the knower, and vice versa.

Q.—How is harmonious development of character to be best effected?

A.—By association with persons whose character has been so developed.

Q.—What should be our attitude to the Vedas?

A.—The Vedas, i.e. only those portions of them which agree with reason, are to be accepted as authority. Other Shâstras, such as the Purânas etc., are only to be accepted so far as they do not go against the Vedas. All the religious thoughts that have come subsequent to the Vedas, in the world, in whatever part of it have been derived from the Vedas.

Q.—Is the division of time into four Yugas astronomical or arbitrary calculation?

A.—There is no mention of such divisions in the Vedas. They are arbitrary assumptions of Paurânika times.

Q.—Is the relation between concepts and words necessary and immutable, or accidental and conventional?

A.—The point is exceedingly debatable. It seems that there is a necessary relation, but not absolutely so, as appears from the diversity of language. There may be some subtle relation which we are not yet able to detect.

Q.—What should be the principle to be followed in working within India?

A.— First of all, men should be taught to be practical and physically strong. A dozen of such lions will conquer the world, and not millions of sheep can do so. Secondly, men should not be taught to imitate a personal ideal, however great.

Then Swamiji went on to speak of the corruptions of some of the Hindu symbols. He distinguished between the path of knowledge and the path of devotion. The former belonged properly to the Aryas, and therefore was so strict in the selection of Adhikâris (qualified aspirants), and the latter coming from the South, or non-Aryan sources, made no such distinction.

Q.—What part will the Ramakrishna Mission take in the regenerating work of India?

A.—From this Math will go out men of character who will deluge the world with spirituality. This will be followed by revivals in other lines. Thus Brahmins, Kshatriyas, and Vaishyas will be produced. The Shudra caste will exist no longer—their work being done by machinery. The present want of India is the Kshatriya force.

Q.—Is retrograde reincarnation from the human stage possible?

A.—Yes. Reincarnation depends on Karma. If a man accumulates Karma akin to the beastly nature, he will be drawn thereto.

In one of the question-classes (1898) Swamiji traced image-worship to Buddhistic sources. First, there was the Chaitya; second, the Stupa ; and then came the temple of Buddha. Along with it arose the temples of the Hindu deities.

Q.—Does the Kundalini really exist in the physical body?

A.—Shri Ramakrishna used to say that the so celled lotuses of the Yogi do not really exist in the human body, but that they are created within oneself by Yoga powers.

Q.—Can a man attain Mukti by image-worship?

A.—Image-worship cannot directly give Mukti; it may be an indirect cause, a help on the way. Image-worship should not be condemned, for, with many, it prepares the mind for the realisation of the Advaita which alone makes man perfect.

Q.—What should be our highest ideal of character?

A.—Renunciation.

Q.—How did Buddhism leave the legacy of corruption in India?

A.—The Bauddhas tried to make everyone in India a monk or a nun. We cannot expect that from every one. This led to gradual relaxation among monks and nuns. It was also caused by their imitating Tibetan and other barbarous customs in the name of religion. They went, to preach in those places and assimilated their corruptions, and then introduced them into India.

Q.—Is Mâyâ without beginning and end?

A.—Maya is eternal both ways, taken universally, ask genus; but it is non-eternal individually.

Q.—Brahman and Maya cannot be cognised simultaneously. How could the absolute reality of either be proved as arising out of the one or the other?

A.—It could be proved only by realisation. When one realises Brahman, for him Maya exists no longer, just as once the identity of the rope is found out, the illusion of the serpent comes no more.

Q.—What is Maya?

A.—There is only one thing, call it by any name—matter, or spirit. It is difficult or rather impossible to think the one independent of the other. This is Maya, or ignorance.

Q.—What is Mukti (liberation)?

A.—Mukti means entire freedom—freedom from the bondages of good and evil. A golden chain is as much a chain as an iron one. Shri Ramakrishna used to say that, to pick out one thorn which has stuck into the foot, another thorn is requisitioned, and when the thorn is taken out, both are thrown away. So the bad tendencies are to be counteracted by the good ones, but after that, the good tendencies have also to be conquered.

Q.—Can salvation (Mukti) be obtained without the grace of God?

A.—Salvation has nothing to do with God. Freedom already is.

Q.—What is the proof of the self in us not being the product of the body etc.?

A.—The "ego" like its correlative "non-ego", is the product of the body, mind etc. The only proof of the existence of the real Self is realisation.

Q.—Who is a true Jnâni, and who is a true Bhakta?

A.—The true Jnani is he who has the deepest love within his heart and at the same time is a practical seer of Advaita in his outward relations. And the true Bhakta (lover) is he who, realising his own soul as identified with the universal Soul, and thus possessed of the true Jnana within, feels for and loves everyone. Of Jnana and Bhakti he who advocates one and denounces the other cannot be either a Jnani or a Bhakta, but he is a thief and a cheat.

Q.—Why should a man serve Ishvara?

A.—If you once admit that there is such a thing as Ishvara (God), you have numberless occasions to serve Him. Service of the Lord means, according to all the scriptural authorities, remembrance (Smarana). If you believe in the existence of God, you will be reminded of Him at every step of your life.

Q.—Is Mâyâvâda different from Advaitâvada?

A.—No. They are identical. There is absolutely no other explanation of Advaitavada except Mayavada.

Q.—How is it possible for God who is infinite to be limited in the form of a man (as an Avatâra)?

A.—It is true that God is infinite, but not in the sense in which you comprehend it. You have confounded your idea of infinity with the materialistic idea of vastness. When you say that God cannot take the form of a man, you understand that a very, very large substance or form (as if material in nature), cannot be compressed into a very, very small compass. God's infinitude refers to the unlimitedness of a purely spiritual entity, and as such, does not suffer in the least by expressing itself in a human form.

Q.—Some say, "First of all become a Siddha (one who has realised the Truth), and then you have the right to Karma, or work for others", while others say that one should work for others even from the beginning. How can both these views be reconciled?

A.—You are confusing one thing with the other. Karma means either service to humanity or preaching. To real preaching, no doubt, none has the right except the Siddha Purusha, i.e. one who has realised the Truth. But to service every one has the right, and not only so, but every one is under obligation to serve others, so long as he is accepting service from others.

YOGA, VAIRAGYA, TAPASYA, LOVE

Q. — Does Yoga serve to keep the body in its full health and vitality?

A. — It does. It staves off disease. As objectification of one's own body is difficult, it is very effective in regard to others. Fruit and milk are the best food for Yogis.

Q. — Is the attainment of bliss synchronous with that of Vairagya?

A.—The first step in Vairagya is very painful. When perfected, it yields supreme bliss.

Q.—What is Tapasyâ?

A.—Tapasya is threefold—of the body, of speech and of mind. The first is service of others; the second truthfulness; and third, control and concentration.

Q.—Why do we not see that the same consciousness pervades the ant as well as the perfected sage?

A.—Realising the unity of this manifestation is a question of time only.

Q.—Is preaching possible without gaining perfection?

A.—No. May the Lord grant that all the Sannyasin disciples of my Master and of myself be perfected, so that they may be fit for missionary work!

Q.—Is the divine majesty expressed in the Universal Form of Shri Krishna in the Gita superior to the expression of love unattended with other attributes, embodied in the form of Shri Krishna, for instance, in His relation with the Gopis?

A.—The feeling of love, unattended with the idea of divinity, in respect to the person loved, is assuredly inferior to the expression of divine majesty. If it were not so, all lovers of the flesh would have obtained freedom.

IN ANSWER TO NIVEDITA

Q.—I cannot remember what parts Prithvi Rai and Chând disguised themselves to play, when they determined to attend the Svayamvara at Kanauj.

A.—Both went as minstrels.

Q.—Also did Prithvi Rai determine to marry Samyuktâ partly because she was the daughter of his rival and partly for the fame of her great beauty? Did he then send a woman-servant to obtain the post of her maid? And did this old nurse set herself to make the princess fall in love with Prithvi Rai?

A.—They had fallen in love with each other, hearing deeds and beauty and seeing portraits. Falling in love through portraits is an old Indian game.

Q.—How did Krishna come to be brought up amongst the shepherds?

A.—His father had to flee with the baby to save it from the tyrant Kamsa, who ordered all the babes (male) from that year to be killed, as (through prophecy) he was afraid one of them would be Krishna and dethrone him. He kept Krishna's father and mother in prison (who were his cousins) for fear of that prophecy.

Q.—How did this part of his life terminate?

A.—He came with his brother Baladeva and Nanda, his foster-father, invited by the tyrant to a festival. (The tyrant had plotted his destruction.) He killed the tyrant and instead of taking the throne placed the nearest heir on it. Himself he never took any fruit of action.

Q.—Can you give me any dramatic incident of this period?

A.—This period is full of miracles. He as a baby was once naughty and the cowherd-mother tried to tie him with her churning string and found she could not bind him with all the strings she had. Then her eyes opened and she saw that she was going to bind him who had the whole universe in his body. She began to pray and tremble. Immediately the Lord touched her with his Maya and she saw only the child.

Brahmâ, the chief of gods, disbelieving that the Lord had become a cowherd, stole one day all the cows and cowherd boys and put them to sleep in a cave. When he came back, he found the same boys and cows round Krishna. Again he stole the new lot and hid them away. He came back and saw there the same again. Then his eyes opened and began to see numerous worlds and heavens and Brahmans by the thousands, one greater than the preceding, in the body of the Lord.

He danced on the serpent Kâliya who had been poisoning the water of the Yamunâ, and he held up the mount Govardhana in defiance of Indra whose worship he had forbidden and who in revenge wanted to kill all the people of Vraja by deluge of rain. They were all sheltered by Krishna under the hill Govardhana which he upheld with a finger on their head.

He from his childhood was against snake-worship and Indra-worship. Indra-worship is a Vedic ritual. Throughout the Gita he is not favourable to Vedic ritual.

This is the period of his love to Gopis. He was eleven years of age.

GURU, AVATARA, YOGA, JAPA, SEVA

Q.—How can Vedanta be realised?

A.—By "hearing, reflection, and meditation". Hearing must take place from a Sad-guru. Even if one is not a regular disciple, but is a fit aspirant and hears the Sad-guru's words, he is liberated.

Q.—Who is a Sad-guru?

A.—A Sad-guru is one on whom the spiritual power has descended by Guru-paramparâ, or an unbroken chain of discipleship.

To play the role of a spiritual teacher is a very difficult thing. One has to take on oneself the sins of others. There is every chance of a fall in less advanced men. If merely physical pain ensues, then he should consider himself fortunate.

Q.—Cannot the spiritual teacher make the aspirant fit?

A.—An Avatâra can. Not an ordinary Guru.

Q.—Is there no easy way to liberation?

A.—"There is no royal road to Geometry"—except for those who have been fortunate enough to come in contact with an Avatara. Paramahamsa Deva used to say, "One who is having his last birth shall somehow or other see me."

Q.—Is not Yoga an easy path to that?

A.—(Jokingly) You have said well, I see!—Yoga an easy path! If your mind be not pure and you try to follow Yoga, you will perhaps attain some supernatural power, but that will be a hindrance. Therefore purity of mind is the first thing necessary.

Q.—How can this be attained?

A.—By good work. Good work is of two kinds, positive and negative. "Do not steal"—that is a negative mandate, and "Do good to others"—is a positive one.

Q.—Should not doing good to others be performed in a higher stage, for if performed in a lower stage, it may bind one to the world?

A.—It should be performed in the first stage. One who has any desire at first gets deluded and becomes bound, but not others. Gradually it will become very natural.

Q.—Sir, last night you said, "In you is everything." Now, if I want to be like Vishnu, shall I have to meditate on the form also, or only on the idea?

A.—According to capacity one may follow either way.

Q.—What is the means of realisation?

A.—The Guru is the means of realisation. "There is no knowledge without a teacher."

Q.—Some say that there is no necessity of practicing meditation in a worship-room. How far is it true?

A.—Those who have already realised the Lord's presence may not require it, but for others it is necessary. One, however, should go beyond the form and meditate on the impersonal aspect of God, for no form can grant liberation. You may get worldly prosperity from the sight of the form. One who ministers to his mother succeeds in this world; one who worships his father goes to heaven; but the worshipper of a Sâdhu (holy man) gets knowledge and devotion.

Q.—What is the meaning of "कृपामहि सज्जनसंगतरिका"—"Even a moment's association with the holy ones serves to take one beyond this relative existence"?

A.—A fit person coming in contact with a true Sadhu attains to liberation. True Sadhus are very rare, but their influence is such that a great writer has said, "Hypocrisy is the tribute which vice pays to virtue." But Avataras are Kapâlamochanas, that is, they can alter the doom of people. They can stir the whole world. The least dangerous and best form of worship is worshipping man. One who has got the idea of Brahman in a man has realised it in the whole universe. Monasticism and the householder's life are both good, according to different circumstances. Knowledge is the only thing necessary.

Q.—Where should one meditate—inside the body or outside it? Should the mind be withdrawn inside or held outside?

A.—We should try to meditate inside. As for the mind being here or there, it will take a long time before we reach the mental plane. Now our struggle is with the body. When one acquires a perfect steadiness in posture, then and then alone one begins to struggle with the mind. Âsana (posture) being conquered, one's limbs remain motionless, and one can sit as long as one pleases.

Q.—Sometimes one gets tired of Japa (repetition of the Mantra). Should one continue it or read some good book instead?

A.—One gets tired of Japa for two reasons. Sometimes one's brain is fatigued, sometimes it is the result of idleness. If the former, then one should give up Japa for the time being, for persistence in it at the time results in seeing hallucinations, or in lunacy etc. But if the latter, the mind should be forced to continue Japa.

Q.—Sometimes sitting at Japa one gets joy at first, but then one seems to be disinclined to continue the Japa owing to that joy. Should it be continued then?

A.—Yes, that joy is a hindrance to spiritual practice, its name being Rasâsvâdana (tasting of the sweetness). One must rise above that.

Q.—Is it good to practice Japa for a long time, though the mind may be wandering?

A.—Yes. As some people break a wild horse by always keeping his seat on his back.

Q.—You have written in your Bhakti-Yoga that if a weak-bodied man tries to practice Yoga, a tremendous reaction comes. Then what to do?

A.—What fear if you die in the attempt to realise the Self! Man is not afraid of dying for the sake of learning and many other things, and why should you fear to die for religion?

Q.—Can Jiva-sevâ (service to beings) alone give Mukti?

A.—Jiva-seva can give Mukti not directly but indirectly, through the purification of the mind. But if you wish to do a thing properly, you must, for the time being, think that that is all-sufficient. The danger in any sect is want of zeal. There must be constancy (Nishthâ), or there will be no growth. At present it has become necessary to lay stress on Karma.

Q.—What should be our motive in work—compassion, or any other motive?

A.—Doing good to others out of compassion is good, but the Seva (service) of all beings in the spirit of the Lord is better.

Q.—What is the efficacy of prayer?

A.—By prayer one's subtle powers are easily roused, and if consciously done, all desires may be fulfilled by it; but done unconsciously, one perhaps in ten is fulfilled. Such prayer, however, is selfish and should therefore be discarded.

Q.—How to recognise God when He has assumed a human form?

A.—One who can alter the doom of people is the Lord. No Sadhu, however advanced, can claim this unique position. I do not see anyone who realises Ramakrishna as God. We sometimes feel it hazily, that is all. To realise Him as God and yet be attached to the world is inconsistent.

The following Conversations & Dialogues are translated from the contributions of disciples to the Udbodhan, the Bengali organ of the Ramakrishna Math and Mission.

SHRI SURENDRA NATH DAS GUPTA

Think of Death Always and New Life Will Come within—Work for Others—God the Last Refuge

Shri Suredra Nath Das Gupta

One day, with some of my young friends belonging to different colleges, I went to the Belur Math to see Swamiji. We sat round him; talks on various subjects were going on. No sooner was any question put to him than he gave the most conclusive answer to it. Suddenly he exclaimed, pointing to us, "You are all studying different schools of European philosophy and metaphysics and learning new facts about nationalities and countries; can you tell me what is the grandest of all the truths in life?"

We began to think, but could not make out what he wanted us to say. As none put forth any reply, he exclaimed in his inspiring language:

"Look here—we shall all die! Bear this in mind always, and then the spirit within will wake up. Then only, meanness will vanish from you, practicality in work will come, you will get new vigour in mind and body, and those who come in contact with you will also feel that they have really got something uplifting from you."

Then the following conversation took place between him and myself:

Myself: But, Swamiji, will not the spirit break down at the thought of death and the heart be overpowered by despondency?

Swamiji: Quite so. At first, the heart will break down, and despondency and gloomy thoughts will occupy your mind. But persist; let days pass like that —and then? Then you will see that new strength has come into the heart, that the constant thought of death is giving you a new life and is making you more and more thoughtful by bringing every moment before your mind's eye the truth of the saying, "Vanity of vanities, all is vanity!" Wait! Let days, months, and years pass, and you will feel that the spirit within is waking up with the strength of a lion, that the little power within has transformed itself into a mighty power! Think of death always, and you will realise the truth of every word I say. What more shall I say in words!

One of my friends praised Swamiji in a low voice.

Swamiji: Do not praise me. Praise and censure have no value in this world of ours. They only rock a man as if in a swing. Praise I have had enough of; showers of censure I have also had to bear; but what avails thinking of them! Let everyone go on doing his own duty unconcerned. When the last moment arrives, praise and blame will be the same to you, to me, and to others. We are here to work, and will have to leave all when the call comes

Myself: How little we are, Swamiji!

Swamiji: True! You have well said! Think of this infinite universe with its millions and millions of solar systems, and think with what an infinite, incomprehensible power they are impelled, running as if to touch the Feet of the One Unknown—and how little we are! Where then is room here to allow ourselves to indulge in vileness and mean-mindedness? What should we gain here by fostering mutual enmity and party-spirit? Take my advice: Set yourselves wholly to the service of others, when you come from your colleges. Believe me, far greater happiness would then be yours than if you had had a whole treasury full of money and other valuables at your command. As you go on your way, serving others, you will advance accordingly in the path of knowledge.

Myself: But we are so very poor, Swamiji!

Swamiji: Leave aside your thoughts of poverty! In what respect are you poor? Do you feel regret because you have not a coach and pair or a retinue of servants at your beck and call? What of that? You little know how nothing would be impossible for you in life if you labour day and night for others with your heart's blood! And lo and behold! the other side of the hallowed river of life stands revealed before your eyes—the screen of Death has vanished, and you are the inheritors of the wondrous realm of immortality!

Myself: Oh, how we enjoy sitting before you, Swamiji, and hearing your life-giving words!

Swamiji: You see, in my travels throughout India all these years, I have come across many a great soul, many a heart overflowing with loving kindness, sitting at whose feet I used to feel a mighty current of strength coursing into my heart, and the few words I speak to you are only through the force of that current gained by coming in contact with them! Do not think I am myself something great!

Myself: But we look upon you, Swamiji, as one who has realised God!

No sooner did I say these words than those fascinating eyes of his were filled with tears (Oh, how vividly I, see that scene before my eyes even now), and he with a heart overflowing with love, softly and gently spoke: "At those Blessed Feet is the perfection of Knowledge, sought by the Jnanis! At those Blessed Feet also is the fulfilment of Love sought by the Lovers! Oh, say, where else will men and women go for refuge but to those Blessed Feet!"

After a while he again said, "Alas! what folly for men in this world to spend their days fighting and quarrelling with one another as they do! But how long can they go in that way? In the evening of life[1] they must all come home, to the arms of the Mother."

---

1. At the end of one's whole course of transmigratory existence.

SHRI SURENDRA NATH SEN

The Loss of Shraddha in India and Need of Its Revival—Men We Want—Real Social Reform

Shri Surendra Nath Sen —from private dairy

Saturday, the 22nd January, 1898.

Early in the morning I came to Swamiji who was then staying in the house of Balaram Babu at 57 Ramkanta Bose Street, Calcutta. The room was packed full with listeners. Swamiji was saying, "We want Shraddhâ, we want faith in our own selves. Strength is life, weakness is death. 'We are the Âtman, deathless and free; pure, pure by nature. Can we ever commit any sin? Impossible!'—such a faith is needed. Such a faith makes men of us, makes gods of us. It is by losing this idea of Shraddha that the country has gone to ruin."

Question: How did we come to lose this Shraddha?

Swamiji: We have had a negative education all along from our boyhood. We have only learnt that we are nobodies. Seldom are we given to understand that great men were ever born in our country. Nothing positive has been taught to us. We do not even know how to use our hands and feet! We master all the facts and figures concerning the ancestors of the English, but we are sadly unmindful about our own. We have learnt only weakness. Being a conquered race, we have brought ourselves to believe that we are weak and have no independence in anything. So, how can it be but that the Shraddha is lost? The idea of true Shraddha must be brought back once more to us, the faith in our own selves must be reawakened, and, then only, all the problems which face our country will gradually be solved by ourselves.

Q. How can that ever be? How will Shraddha alone remedy the innumerable evils with which our society is beset? Besides, there are so many crying evils in the country, to remove which the Indian National Congress and other patriotic associations are carrying on a strenuous agitation and petitioning the British government. How better can their wants be made known? What has Shraddha to do with the matter?

Swamiji: Tell me, whose wants are those—yours or the ruler's? If yours, will the ruler supply them for you, or will you have to do that for yourselves?

Q. But it is the ruler's duty to see to the wants of the subject people. Whom should we look up to for everything, if not to the king?

Swamiji: Never are the wants of a beggar fulfilled. Suppose the government give you all you need, where are the men who are able to keep up the things demanded? So make men first. Men we want, and how can men be made unless Shraddha is there?

Q. But such is not the view Of the majority, sir.

Swamiji: What you call majority is mainly composed of fools and men of common intellect. Men who have brains to think for themselves are few, everywhere. These few men with brains are the real leaders in everything and in every department of work; the majority are guided by them as with a string, and that is good, for everything goes all right when they follow in the footsteps of these leaders. Those are only fools who think themselves too high to bend their heads to anyone, and they bring on their own ruin by acting on their own judgment. You talk of social reform? But what do you do? All that you mean by your social reform is either widow remarriage, or female emancipation, or something of that sort. Do you not? And these again are directed within the confines of a few of the castes only. Such a scheme of reform may do good to a few no doubt, but of what avail is that to the whole nation? Is that reform or only a form of selfishness—somehow to cleanse your own room and keep it tidy and let others go from bad to worse!

Q. Then, you mean to say that there is no need of social reform at all?

Swamiji: Who says so? Of course there is need of it. Most of what you talk of as social reform does not touch the poor masses; they have already those things—the widow remarriage, female emancipation, etc.—which you cry for. For this reason they will not think of those things as reforms at all. What I mean to say is that want of Shraddha has brought in all the evils among us, and is bringing in more and more. My method of treatment is to take out by the roots the very causes of the disease and not to keep them merely suppressed. Reforms we should have in many ways; who will be so foolish as to deny it? There is, for example, a good reason for intermarriage in India, in the absence of which the race is becoming physically weaker day by day.

Since it was a day of a solar eclipse, the gentleman who was asking these questions saluted Swamiji and left saying "I must go now for a bath in the Ganga. I shall, however, come another day."

Reconciliation of Jnana-Yoga and Bhakti-Yoga—God in Good and in Evil Too—Use Makes a Thing Good or Evil—Karma—Creation—God—Maya

Shri Surendra Nath Sen —from private dairy

Sunday, The 23rd January, 1898.

It was evening and the occasion of the weekly meeting of the Ramakrishna Mission, at the house of Balaram Babu of Baghbazar. Swami Turiyananda, Swami Yogananda, Swami Premananda, and others had come from the Math. Swamiji was seated in the verandah to the east, which was now full of people, as were the northern and the southern sections of the verandah. But such used to be the case every day when Swamiji stayed in Calcutta.

Many of the people who came to the meeting had heard that Swamiji could sing well, and so were desirous of hearing him. Knowing this, Master Mahâshaya (M.) whispered to a few gentlemen near him to request Swamiji to sing; but he saw through their intention and playfully asked, "Master Mahashaya, what are you talking about among yourselves in whispers? Do speak out." At the request of Master Mahashaya, Swamiji now began in his charming voice the song—"Keep with loving care the darling Mother Shyâmâ in thy heart..." It seemed as if a Vinâ was playing. At its close, he said to Master Mahashaya, "Well, are you now satisfied? But no more singing! Otherwise, being in the swing of it, I shall be carried away by its intoxication. Moreover, my voice is now spoilt be frequent lecturing in the West. My voice trembles a great deal..."

Swamiji then asked one of his Brahmacharin disciples to speak on the real nature of Mukti. So, the Brahmacharin stood up and spoke at some length. A few others followed him. Swamiji then invited discussion on the subject of the discourse, and called upon one of his householder disciples to lead it; but as the latter tried to advocate the Advaita and Jnâna and assign a lower place to dualism and Bhakti, he met with a protest from one of the audience. As each of the two opponents tried to establish his own viewpoint, a lively word-fight ensued. Swamiji watched them for a while but, seeing that they were getting excited, silenced them with the following words:

Why do you get excited in argument and spoil everything? Listen! Shri Ramakrishna used to say that pure knowledge and pure Bhakti are one and the same. According to the doctrine of Bhakti, God is held to be "All-Love". One cannot even say, "I love Him", for the reason that He is All-Love. There is no love outside of Himself; the love that is in the heart with which you love Him is even He Himself. In a similar way, whatever attractions or inclinations one feels drawn by, are all He Himself. The thief steals, the harlot sells her body to prostitution, the mother loves her child—in each of these too is He! One world system attracts another—there also is He. Everywhere is He. According to the doctrine of Jnana also, He is realised by one everywhere. Here lies the reconciliation of Jnana and Bhakti. When one is immersed in the highest ecstasy of divine vision (Bhâva), or is in the state of Samâdhi, then alone the idea of duality ceases, and the distinction between the devotee and his God vanishes. In the scriptures on Bhakti, five different paths of relationship are mentioned, by any of which one can attain to God; but another one can very well be added to them, viz. the path of meditation on the non-separateness, or oneness with God. Thus the Bhakta can call the Advaitins Bhaktas as well, but of the non-differentiating type. As long as one is within the region of Mâya, so long the idea of duality will no doubt remain. Space-time-causation, or name-and-form, is what is called Maya. When one goes beyond this Maya, then only the Oneness is realised, and then man is neither a dualist nor an Advaitist—to him all is One. All this difference that you notice between a Bhakta and a Jnani is in the preparatory stage—one sees God outside, and the other sees Him within. But there is another point: Shri Ramakrishna used to say that there is another stage of Bhakti which is called the Supreme Devotion (Parâbhakti)

i.e. to love Him after becoming established in the consciousness of Advaita and after having attained Mukti. It may seem paradoxical, and the question may be raised here why such a one who has already attained Mukti should be desirous of retaining the spirit of Bhakti? The answer is: The Mukta or the Free is beyond all law; no law applies in his case, and hence no question can be asked regarding him. Even becoming Mukta, some, out of their own free will, retain Bhakti to taste of its sweetness.

Q. God may be in the love of the mother for her child; but, sir, this idea is really perplexing that God is even in thieves and the harlots in the form of their natural inclinations to sin! It follows then that God is as responsible for the sin as for all the virtue in this world.

Swamiji: That consciousness comes in a stage of highest realization, when one sees that whatever is of the nature of love or attraction is God. But one has to reach that state to see and realise that idea for oneself in actual life.

Q. But still one has to admit that God is also in the sin!

Swamiji: You see, there are, in reality, no such different things as good and evil. They are mere conventional terms. The same thing we call bad, and again another time we call good, according to the way we make use of it. Take for example this lamplight; because of its burning, we are able to see and do various works of utility; this is one mode of using the light. Again, if you put your fingers in it, they will be burnt; that is another mode of using the same light. So we should know that a thing becomes good or bad according to the way we use it. Similarly with virtue and vice. Broadly speaking, the proper use of any of the faculties of our mind and body is termed virtue, and its improper application or waste is called vice.

Thus questions after questions were put and answered. Someone remarked, "The theory that God is even there, where one heavenly body attracts another, may or may not be true as a fact, but there is no denying the exquisite poetry the idea conveys."

Swamiji: No, my dear sir, that is not poetry. One can see for oneself its truth when one attains knowledge.

From what Swamiji further said on this point, I understood him to mean that matter and spirit, though to all appearances they seem to be two distinct things, are really two different forms of one substance; and similarly, all the different forces that are known to us, whether in the material or in the internal world, are but varying forms of the manifestation of one Force. We call a thing matter, where that spirit force is manifested less; and living, where it shows itself more; but there is nothing which is absolutely matter at all times and in all conditions. The same Force which presents itself in the material world as attraction or gravitation is felt in its finer and subtler state as love and the like in the higher spiritual stages of realisation.

Q. Why should there be even this difference relating to individual use? Why should there be at all this tendency in man to make bad or improper use of any of his faculties?

Swamiji: That tendency comes as a result of one's own past actions (Karma); everything one has is of his own doing. Hence it follows that it is solely in the hands of every individual to control his tendencies and to guide them properly.

Q. Even if everything is the result of our Karma, still it must have had a beginning, and why should our tendencies have been good or bad at the beginning?

Swamiji: How do you know that there is a beginning? The Srishti (creation) is without beginning—this is the doctrine of the Vedas. So long as there is God, there is creation as well.

Q. Well, sir, why is this Maya here, and whence has it come?

Swamiji: It is a mistake to ask "why" with respect to God; we can only do so regarding one who has wants or imperfections. How can there be an, "why" concerning Him who has no wants and who is the One Whole? No such question as "Whence has Maya come?" can be asked. Time-space-causation is what is called Maya. You, I, and everyone else are within this Maya; and you are asking about what is beyond Maya! How can you do so while living within Maya?

Again, many questions followed. The conversation turned on the philosophies of Mill, Hamilton, Herbert Spencer, etc., and Swamiji dwelt on them to the satisfaction of all. Everyone wondered at the vastness of his Western philosophical scholarship and the promptness of his replies.

The meeting dispersed after a short conversation on miscellaneous subjects.

Intermarriage Among Subdivisions of a Varna—Against Early Marriage—The Education that Indians Need—Brahmacharya

Shri Surendra Nath Sen —from private dairy

Monday, The 24th January, 1898.

The same gentleman who was asking questions of Swamiji on Saturday last came again. He raised again the topic of intermarriage and enquired, "How should intermarriage be introduced between different nationalities?"

Swamiji: I do not advise our intermarriage with nations professing an alien religion. At least for the present, that will, of a certainty, slacken the ties of society and be a cause of manifold mischief. It is the intermarriage between people of the same religion that I advocate.

Q. Even then, it will involve much perplexity. Suppose I have a daughter who is born and brought up in Bengal, and I marry her to a Marathi or a Madrasi. Neither will the girl understand her husband's language nor the husband the girl's. Again, the difference in their individual habits and customs is so great. Such are a few of the troubles in the case of the married couple. Then as regards society, it will make confusion worse confounded.

Swamiji: The time is yet very long in coming when marriages of that kind will be widely possible. Besides, it is not judicious now to go in for that all of a sudden. One of the secrets of work is to go along the line of least resistance. So, first of all, let there be marriages within the sphere of one's own caste-people. Take for instance, the Kayasthas of Bengal. They have several subdivisions amongst them, such as, the Uttar-rârhi, Dakshin-rârhi, Bangaja, etc., and they do not intermarry with each other. Now, let there be intermarriages between the Uttar-rarhis and the Dakshin-rarhis, and if that is not possible at present, let it be between the Bangajas and the Dakshin-rarhis. Thus we are to build up that which is already existing, and which is in our hands to reduce into practice—reform does not mean wholesale breaking down.

Q. Very well, let it be as you say: but what corresponding good can come of it?

Swamiji: Don't you see how in our society, marriage, being restricted for several hundreds of years within the same subdivisions of each caste, has come to such a pass nowadays as virtually to mean marital alliance between cousins and near relations; and how for this very reason the race is getting deteriorated physically, and consequently all sorts of disease and other evils are finding a ready entrance into it? The blood having had to circulate within the narrow circle of a limited number of individuals has become vitiated; so the new-born children inherit from their very birth the constitutional diseases of their fathers. Thus, born with poor blood, their bodies have very little power to resist the microbes of any disease, which are ever ready to prey upon them. It is only by widening the circle of marriage that we can infuse a new and a different kind of blood into our progeny, so that they may be saved from the clutches of many of our present-day diseases and other consequent evils.

Q. May I ask you, sir, what is your opinion about early marriage?

Swamiji: Amongst the educated classes in Bengal, the custom of marrying their boys too early is dying out gradually. The girls are also given in marriage a year or two older than before, but that has been under compulsion —from pecuniary want. Whatever might be the reason for it, the age of marrying girls should be raised still higher. But what will the poor father do? As soon as the girl grows up a little, every one of the female sex, beginning with the mother down to the relatives and neighbours even, will begin to cry out that he must find a bridegroom for her, and will not leave him in peace until he does so! And, about your religious hypocrites, the less said the better. In these days no one hears them, but still they will take up the role of leaders themselves. The rulers passed the Age of Consent Bill prohibiting a man under the threat of penalty to live with a girl of twelve years, and at once all these so-called leaders of your religion raised a tremendous hue and cry against it, sounding the alarm, "Alas, our religion is lost! As if religion consisted in making a girl a mother at the age of twelve or thirteen! So the rulers also naturally think, "Goodness gracious! What a religion is theirs! And these people lead political agitations and demand political rights!"

Q. Then, in your opinion, both men and women should be married at an advanced age?

Swamiji: Certainly. But education should be imparted along with it, otherwise irregularity and corruption will ensue. By education I do not mean the present system, but something in the line of positive teaching. Mere book-learning won't do. We want that education by which character is formed, strength of mind is increased, the intellect is expanded, and by which one can stand on one's own feet.

Q. We have to reform our women in many ways.

Swamiji: With such an education women will solve their own problems. They have all the time been trained in help-lessness, servile dependence on others, and so they are good only to weep their eyes out at the slightest approach of a mis-hap or danger. Along with other things they should acquire the spirit of valour and heroism. In the present day it has be-come necessary for them also to learn self-defence. See how grand was the Queen of Jhansi!

Q. What you advise is quite a new departure, and it will, I am afraid, take a very long time yet to train our women in that way.

Swamiji: Anyhow, we have to try our best. We have not only to teach them but to teach ourselves also. Mere beget-ting children does not make a father; a great many respon-sibilities have to be taken upon one's shoulders as well. To make a beginning in women's education: our Hindu women easily understand what chastity means, because it is their her-itage. Now, first of all, intensify that ideal within them above everything else, so that they may develop a strong character by the force of which, in every stage of their life, whether married, or single if they prefer to remain so, they will not be in the least afraid even to give up their lives rather than flinch an inch from their chastity. Is it little heroism to be able to sacrifice one's life for the sake of one's ideal whatever that ideal may be? Studying the present needs of the age, it seems im-perative to train some women up in the ideal of renunciation, so that they will take up the vow of lifelong virginity, fired with the strength of that virtue of chastity which is innate in their life-blood from hoary antiquity. Along with that they should be taught sciences and other things which would be of benefit, not only to them but to others as well, and knowing this they would easily learn these things and feel pleasure in doing so. Our motherland requires for her well-being some of her children to become such pure-souled Brahmachârins and Brahmachârinis.

Q. In what way will that conduce to her well-being?

Swamiji: By their example and through their endeavours to hold the national ideal before the eyes of the people, a revo-lution in thoughts and aspirations will take place. How do matters stand now? Somehow, the parents must dispose of a girl in marriage, if she he nine or ten years of age! And what a rejoicing of the whole family if a child is born to her at the age of thirteen! If the trend of such ideas is reversed, then only there is some hope for the ancient Shraddhâ to return. And what to talk of those who will practice Brahmacharya as defined above—think how much faith in themselves will be theirs! And what a power for good they will be!

The questioner now saluted Swamiji and was ready to take leave. Swamiji asked him to come now and then "Certainly, sir," replied the gentleman, "I feel so much benefited. I have heard from you many new things, which I have not been told anywhere before." I also went home as it was about time for dinner.

Madhura-Bhava—Prema—Namakirtana— Its Danger—Bhakti Tempered With Jnana— A Curious Dream

Shri Surendra Nath Sen —from private dairy

Monday, The 24th January, 1898.

In the afternoon I came again to Swamiji and saw quite a good gathering round him. The topic was the Madhura-Bhâ-va or the way of worshipping God as husband, as in vogue with some followers of Shri Chaitanya. His occasional bons mots were raising laughter, when someone remarked, "What is there to make so much fun of about the Lord's doings? Do you think that he was not a great saint, and that he did not do everything for the good of humanity?"

Swamiji: Who is that! Should I poke fun at you then, my dear sir! You only see the fun of it, do you? And you, sir, do not see the lifelong struggle through which I have passed to mould this life after his burning ideal of renunciation of wealth and lust, and my endeavours to infuse that ideal into the people at large! Shri Chaitanya was a man of tremendous renunciation and had nothing to do with woman and carnal appetites. But, in later times, his disciples admitted women into their order, mixed indiscriminately with them in his name, and made an awful mess of the whole thing. And the ideal of love which the Lord exemplified in his life was perfectly selfless and bereft of any vestige of lust; that sexless love can never be the property of the masses. But the subsequent Vaishnava Gurus, instead of laying particular stress first on the aspect of renunciation in the Master's life, bestowed all their zeal on preaching and infusing his ideal of love among the masses, and the conse-quence was that the common people could not grasp and as-similate that high ideal of divine love, and naturally made of it the worst form of love between man and woman.

Q. But, sir, he preached the name of the Lord Hari to all, even to the Chandâlas; so why should not the common mass-es have a right to it?

Swamiji: I am talking not of his preaching, but of his great ideal of love —the Râdhâ-prema[1], with which he used to re-main intoxicated day and night, losing his individuality in Radha.

Q. Why may not that be made the common property of all?

1. The divine love which Radha had towards Shri Krishna.

Swamiji: Look at this nation and see what has been the outcome of such an attempt. Through the preaching of that love broadcast, the whole nation has become effeminate—a race of women! The whole of Orissa has been turned into a land of cowards; and Bengal, running after the Radha-prema, these past four hundred years, has almost lost all sense of manliness! The people are very good only at crying and weeping; that has become their national trait. Look at their literature, the sure index of a nation's thoughts and ideas. Why, the refrain of the Bengali literature for these four hundred years is strung to that same tune of moaning and crying. It has failed to give birth to any poetry which breathes a true heroic spirit!

Q. Who are then truly entitled to possess that Prema (love)?

Swamiji: There can be no love so long as there is lust—even as speck of it, as it were, in the heart. None but men of great renunciation, none but mighty giants among men, have a right to that Love Divine. If that highest ideal of love is held out to the masses, it will indirectly tend to stimulate its worldly prototype which dominates the heart of man—for, meditating on love to God by thinking of oneself as His wife or beloved, one would very likely be thinking most of the time of one's own wife—the result is too obvious to point out.

Q. Then is it impossible for householders to realise God through that path of love, worshipping God as one's husband or lover and considering oneself as His spouse?

Swamiji : With a few exceptions; for ordinary householders it is impossible no doubt. And why lay so much stress on this delicate path, above all others? Are there no other relationships by which to worship God, except this Madhura idea of love? Why not follow the four other paths, and take the name of the Lord with all your heart? Let the heart be opened first, and all else will follow of itself. But know this for certain, that Prema cannot come while there is lust. Why not try first to get rid of carnal desires? You will say, "How is that possible? I am a householder." Nonsense! Because one is a householder, does it mean that one should be a personification of incontinence, or that one has to live in marital relations all one's life? And, after all, how unbecoming of a man to make of himself a woman, so that he may practice this Madhura love!

Q. True, sir. Singing God's name in a party (Nâmakirtana) is an excellent help and gives one a joyous feeling. So say our scriptures, and so did Shri Chaitanya Deva also preach to the masses. When the Khole (drum) is played upon, it makes the heart leap with such a transport that one feels inclined to dance.

Swamiji: That is all right, but don't think that Kirtana means dancing only. It means singing the glories of God, in whatever way that suits you. That vehement stirring up of feeling and that dancing of the Vaishnavas are good and very catching no doubt; but there is also a danger in practising them, from which you must save yourself. The danger lies here—in the reaction. On the one hand, the feelings are at once roused to the highest pitch, tears flow from the eyes, the head reels as it were

under intoxication—on the other hand, as soon as the Sankirtan stops, that mass of feeling sinks down as precipitately as it rose. The higher the wave rises on the ocean, the lower it falls, with equal force. It is very difficult at that stage to contain oneself against the shock of reaction; unless one has proper discrimination, one is likely to succumb to the lower propensities of lust etc. I have noticed the same thing in America also. Many would go to church, pray with much devotion, sing with great feeling, and even burst into tears when hearing the sermons; but after coming out of church, they would have a great reaction and succumb to carnal tendencies.

Q. Then, sir, do instruct us which of the ideas preached by Shri Chaitanya we should take up as well suited to us, so that we may not fall into errors.

Swamiji: Worship God with Bhakti tempered with Jnâna. Keep the spirit of discrimination along with Bhakti. Besides this, gather from Shri Chaitanya, his heart, his loving kindness to all beings, his burning passion for God, and make his renunciation the ideal of your life.

The questioner now addressed the Swamiji with folded hands, "I beg your pardon, sir. Now I come to see you are right. Seeing you criticise in a playful mood the Madhura love of the Vaishnavas, I could not at first understand the drift of your remarks; hence I took exception to them."

Swamiji: Well, look here, if we are to criticise at all, it is better to criticise God or God-men. If you abuse me I shall very likely get angry with you, and if I abuse you, you will try to retaliate. Isn't it so? But God or God-men will never return evil for evil. The gentleman now left, after bowing down at the feet of Swamiji. I have already said that such a gathering was an everyday occurrence when Swamiji used to stay in Calcutta. From early in the morning till eight or nine at night, men would flock to him at every hour of the day. This naturally occasioned much irregularity in the time of his taking his meals; so, many desiring to put a stop to this state of things, strongly advised Swamiji not to receive visitors except at appointed hours. But the loving heart of Swamiji, ever ready to go to any length to help others, was so melted with compassion at the sight of such a thirst for religion in the people, that in spite of ill health, he did not comply with any request of the kind. His only reply was, "They take so much trouble to come walking all the way from their homes, and can I, for the consideration of risking my health a little, sit here and not speak a few words to them?"

At about 4 p.m. the general conversation came to a close, and the gathering dispersed, except for a few gentlemen with whom Swamiji continued his talk on different subjects, such as England and America, and so on. In the course of conversation he said:

"I had a curious dream on my return voyage from England. While our ship was passing through the Mediterranean Sea, in my sleep, a very old and venerable looking person, Rishi-like in appearance, stood before me and said, 'Do ye come and effect our restoration. I am one of that ancient order of Therâputtas (Theraputae) which had its origin in the teachings of the Indian Rishis. The truths and ideals preached by us have been given out by Christians as taught by Jesus; but for the matter of that, there was no such personality by the name of Jesus ever born. Various evidences testifying to this fact will be brought to light by excavating here.' 'By excavating which place can those proofs and relics you speak of be found?' I asked. The hoary-headed one, pointing to a locality in the vicinity of Turkey, said, 'See here.' Immediately after, I woke up, and at once rushed to the upper deck and asked the Captain, 'What neighbourhood is the ship in just now?' 'Look yonder', the Captain replied, 'there is Turkey and the Island of Crete.'"

Was it but a dream, or is there anything in the above vision? Who knows!

SHRI PRIYA NATH SINHA

Reminiscences—The Problem of Famines in India and Self-Sacrificing Workers—East and West—Is it Sattva or Tamas—A Nation of Mendicants—The "Give and Take" Policy—Tell a Man his Defects Directly but Praise his Virtues Before Others—Vivekananda Everyone may Become—Unbroken Brahmacharya is the Secret of Power—Samadhi and Work

Shri Priya Nath Sinha

Our house was very close to Swamiji's, and since we were boys of the same section of the town, I often used to play with him. From my boyhood I had a special attraction for him, and I had a sincere belief that he would become a great man. When he became a Sannyasin we thought that the promise of a brilliant career for such a man was all in vain.

Afterwards, when he went to America, I read in newspapers reports of his lectures at the Chicago Parliament of Religions and others delivered in various place, of America, and I thought that fire can never remain hidden under a cloth; the fire that was within Swamiji had now burst into a flame; the bud after so many years had blossomed.

After a time I came to know that he had returned to India, and had been delivering fiery lectures at Madras. I read them and wondered that such sublime truths existed in the Hindu religion and that they could be explained so lucidly. What an extraordinary power he had! Was he a man or a god?

A great enthusiasm prevailed when Swamiji came to Calcutta, and we followed him to the Sil's garden-house, on the Ganga, at Cossipore. A few days later, at the residence of Raja Radhakanta Dev, the "Calcutta boy" delivered an inspiring lecture to a huge concourse of people in reply to an address of welcome, and Calcutta heard him for the first time and was lost in admiration. But these are facts known to all.

After his coming to Calcutta, I was very anxious to see him once alone and be able to talk freely with him as in our boyhood. But there was always a gathering of eager inquirers about him, and conversations were going on without a break; so I did not get an opportunity for some time, until one day when we went out for a walk in the garden on the Ganga side. He at once began to talk, as of old, to me, the playmate of his boyhood. No sooner had a few words passed between us than repeated calls came, informing him that many gentlemen had come to see him. He became a little impatient at last and told the messenger, "Give me a little respite, my son; let me speak a few words with this companion of my boyhood; let me stay in the open air for a while. Go and give a welcome to those who have come, ask them to sit down, offer them tobacco, and request them to wait a little."

When we were alone again, I asked him, "Well, Swamiji, you are a Sâdhu (holy man). Money was raised by subscription for your reception here, and I thought, in view of the famine in this country, that you would wire, before arriving in Calcutta, saying, 'Don't spend a single pice on my reception, rather contribute the whole sum to the famine relief fund'; but I found that you did nothing of the kind. How was that?"

Swamiji: Why, I wished rather that a great enthusiasm should be stirred up. Don't you see, without some such thing how would the people be drawn towards Shri Ramakrishna and be fired in his name? Was this ovation done for me personally, or was not his name glorified by this? See how much thirst has been created in the minds of men to know about him! Now they will come to know of him gradually, and will not that be conducive to the good of the country? If the people do not know him who came for the welfare of the country, how can good befall them? When they know what he really was, then men—real men—will be made; and when will be such men, how long will it take to drive away famines etc. from the land? So I say that I rather desired that there should be some bustle and stir in Calcutta, so that the public might be inclined to believe in the mission of Shri Ramakrishna; otherwise what was the use of making so much fuss for my sake? What do I care for it? Have I become any greater now than when I used to play with you at your house? I am the same now as I was before. Tell me, do you find any change in me?

Though I said, "No, I do not find much change to speak of", yet in my mind I thought, "You have now, indeed, become a god."

Swamiji continued: "Famine has come to be a constant quantity in our country, and now it is, as it were, a sort of blight upon us. Do you find in any other country such frequent ravages of famine? No, because there are men in other countries, while in ours, men have become akin to dead matter, quite inert. Let the people first learn to renounce their selfish nature by studying Shri Ramakrishna, by knowing him as he really was, and then will proceed from them real efforts trying to stop the frequently recurring famines. By and by I shall make efforts in that direction too; you will see."

Myself: That will be good. Then you are going to deliver

many lectures here, I presume; otherwise, how will his name be preached?

Swamiji: What nonsense! Nothing of the kind!

Has anything left undone by which his name can be known? Enough has been done in that line. Lectures won't do any good in this country. Our educated countrymen would hear them and, at best, would cheer and clap their hands, saying, "Well done"; that is all. Then they would go home and digest, as we say, everything they had heard, with their meal! What good will hammering do on a piece of rusty old iron? It will only crumble into pieces. First, it should be made red-hot, and then it can be moulded into any shape by hammering. Nothing will avail in our country without setting a glowing and living example before the people. What we want are some young men who will renounce everything and sacrifice their lives for their country's sake. We should first form their lives and then some real work can be expected.

Myself: Well, Swamiji, it has always puzzled me that, while men of our country, unable to understand their own religion, were embracing alien religions, such as Christianity, Mohammedanism, etc., you, instead of doing anything for them, went over to England and America to preach Hinduism.

Swamiji: Don't you see that circumstances have changed now? Have the men of our country the power left in them to take up and practice true religion? What they have is only pride in themselves that they are very Sâttvika. Time was when they were Sattvika, no doubt, but now they have fallen very low. The fall from Sattva brings one down headlong into Tamas! That is what has happened to them. Do you think that a man who does not exert himself at all, who only takes the name of Hari, shutting himself up in a room, who remains quiet and indifferent even when seeing a huge amount of wrong and violence done to others before his very eyes, possesses the quality of Sattva? Nothing of the kind, he is only enshrouded in dark Tamas. How can the people of a country practice religion who do not get even sufficient food to appease their hunger? How can renunciation come to the people of a country in whose minds the desires for Bhoga (enjoyment) have not been in the least satisfied? For this reason, find out, first of all, the ways and means by which men may get enough to eat and have enough luxuries to enable them to enjoy life a little; and then gradually, true Vairâgya (dispassion) will come, and they will be fit and ready to realise religion in life. The people of England and America, how full of Rajas they are! They have become satiated with all sorts of worldly enjoyment. Moreover, Christianity, being a religion of faith and superstition, occupies the same rank as our religion of the Purânas. With the spread of education and culture, the people of the West can no more find peace in that. Their present condition is such that, giving them one lift will make them reach the Sattva. Then again, in these days, would you accept the words of a Sannyasin clad in rags, in the same degree as you would the words of a white-face (Westerner) who might come and speak to you on your own religion?

Myself: Just so, Swamiji! Mr. N. N. Ghosh[1] also speaks exactly to the same effect.

Swamiji: Yes, when my Western disciples after acquiring proper training and illumination will come in numbers here and ask you, "What are you all doing? Why are you of so little faith? How are your rites and religion, manners, customs, and morals in any way inferior? We even regard your religion to be the highest!"—then you will see that lots of our big and influential folk will hear them. Thus they will be able to do immense good to this country. Do not think for a moment that they will come to take up the position of teachers of religion to you. They will, no doubt, be your Guru regarding practical sciences etc., for the improvement of material conditions, and the people of our country will be their Guru in everything pertaining to religion. This relation of Guru and disciple in the domain of religion will for ever exist between India and the rest of the world. Myself: How can that be, Swamiji? Considering the feeling of hatred with which they look upon us, it does not seem probable that they will ever do good to us, purely from an unselfish motive.

Swamiji: They find many reasons to hate us, and so they may justify themselves in doing so. In the first place, we are a conquered race, and moreover there is nowhere in the world such a nation of mendicants as we are! The masses who comprise the lowest castes, through ages of constant tyranny of the higher castes and by being treated by them with blows and kicks at every step they took, have totally lost their manliness and become like professional beggars; and those who are removed one stage higher than these, having read a few pages of English, hang about the thresholds of public offices with petitions in their hands. In the case of a post of twenty or thirty rupees falling vacant, five hundred B.A.s and M.A.s will apply for it! And, dear me! how curiously worded these petitions are! "I have nothing to eat at home, sir, my wife and children are starving; I most humbly implore you, sir, to give me some means to provide for myself and my family, or we shall die of starvation!" Even when they enter into service, they cast all self-respect to the winds, and servitude in its worst form is what they practice. Such is the condition, then, of the masses. The highly-educated, prominent men among you form themselves into societies and clamour at the top of their voices: "Alas, India is going to ruin, day by day! O English rulers, admit our country men to the higher offices of the State, relieve us from famines" and so on, thus rending the air, day and night, with the eternal cry of "Give" and "Give"! The burden of all their speech is, "Give to us, give more to us, O Englishmen!" Dear me! what more will they give to you? They have given railways, telegraphs, well-ordered administration to the country—have almost entirely suppressed robbers, have given education in science—what more will they give? What does anyone give to others with perfect unselfishness?

1. A celebrated barrister, journalist, and educationalist of Calcutta.

Well, they have given you so much; let me ask, what have you given to them in return?

Myself: What have we to give, Swamiji? We pay taxes.

Swamiji: Do you, really? Do you give taxes to them of your own will, or do they exact them by compulsion because they keep peace in the country? Tell me plainly, what do you give them in return for all that they have done for you? You also have something to give them that they have not. You go to England, but that is also in the garb of a beggar—praying for education. Some go, and what they do there at the most is, perchance, to applaud the Westerner's religion in some speeches and then come back. What an achievement, indeed! Why, have you nothing to give them? An inestimable treasure you have, which you can give—give them your religion, give them your philosophy! Study the history of the whole world, and you will see that every high ideal you meet with anywhere had its origin in India. From time immemorial India has been the mine of precious ideas to human society; giving birth to high ideas herself, she has freely distributed them broadcast over the whole world. The English are in India today, to gather those higher ideals, to acquire a knowledge of the Vedanta, to penetrate into the deep mysteries of that eternal religion which is yours. Give those invaluable gems in exchange for what you receive from them. The Lord took me to their country to remove this opprobrium of the beggar that is attributed by them to us. It is not right to go to England for the purpose of begging only. Why should they always give us alms? Does anyone do so for ever? It is not the law of nature to be always taking gifts with outstretched hands like beggars. To give and take is the law of nature. Any individual or class or nation that does not obey this law never prospers in life. We also must follow that law That is why I went to America. So great is now the thirst for religion in the people there that there is room enough even if thousands of men like me go. They have been for a long time giving you of what wealth they possess, and now is the time for you to share your priceless treasure with them. And you will see how their feelings of hatred will be quickly replaced by those of faith, devotion, and reverence towards you, and how they will do good to your country even unasked. They are a nation of heroes —never do they forget any good done to them.

Myself: Well, Swamiji, in your lectures in the West you have frequently and eloquently dwelt on our characteristic talents and virtues, and many convincing proofs you have put forward to show our whole-souled love of religion; but now you say that we have become full of Tamas; and at the same time you are accrediting us as the teachers of the eternal religion of the Rishis to the world! How is that?

Swamiji: Do you mean to say that I should go about from country to country, expatiating on your failings before the public? Should I not rather hold up before them the characteristic virtues that mark you as a nation? It is always good to tell a man his defects in a direct way and in a friendly spirit to make him convinced of them, so that he may correct himself—but you should trumpet forth his virtues before others. Shri Ramakrishna used to say that if you repeatedly tell a bad man that he is good, he turns in time to be good; similarly, a good man becomes bad if he is incessantly called so. There, in the West, I have said enough to the people of their short-comings. Mind, up to my time, all who went over to the West from our country have sung paeans to them in praise of their virtues and have trumpeted out only our blemishes to their ears. Consequently, it is no wonder that they have learnt to hate us. For this reason I have laid before them your virtues, and pointed out to them their vices, just as I am now telling you of your weaknesses and their good points. However full of Tamas you may have become, something of the nature of the ancient Rishis, however little it may be, is undoubtedly in you still—at least the framework of it. But that does not show that one should be in a hurry to take up at once the role of a teacher of religion and go over to the West to preach it. First of all, one must completely mould one's religious life in solitude, must be perfect in renunciation and must preserve Brahmacharya without a break. The Tamas has entered into you—what of that? Cannot the Tamas be destroyed? It can be done in less than no time! It was for the destruction of this Tamas that Bhagavân Shri Ramakrishna came to us.

Myself: But who can aspire to be like you, Swamiji?

Swamiji: Do you think that there will be no more Vivekanandas after I die! That batch of young men who came and played music before me a little while ago, whom you all despise for being addicted to intoxicating drugs and look upon as worthless fellows, if the Lord wishes, each and everyone of them may become a Vivekananda! There will be no lack of Vivekanandas, if the world needs them—thousands and millions of Vivekanandas will appear—from where, who knows! Know for certain that the work done by me is not the work of Vivekananda, it is His work—the Lord's own work! If one governor-general retires, another is sure to be sent in his place by the Emperor. Enveloped in Tamas however much you may be, know all that will clear away if you take refuge in Him by being sincere to the core of your heart. The time is opportune now, as the physician of the world-disease has come. Taking His name, if you set yourself to work, He will accomplish everything Himself through you. Tamas itself will be transformed into the highest Sattva!

Myself: Whatever you may say, I cannot bring myself to believe in these words. Who can come by that oratorical power of expounding philosophy which you have?

Swamiji: You don't know! That power may come to all. That power comes to him who observes unbroken Brahmacharya for a period of twelve years, with the sole object of realising God I have practiced that kind of Brahmacharya myself, and so a screen has been removed, as it were, from my brain. For that reason, I need not any more think over or prepare myself for any lectures on such a subtle subject as philosophy. Suppose I have to lecture tomorrow; all that I shall speak about will pass tonight before my eyes like so many pictures; and the next day I put into words during my lecture all those things that I saw. So you will understand now that it is not any power which is exclusively my own. Whoever will practice unbroken Brahmacharya for twelve years will surely have it. If you do so, you too will get it. Our Shâstras do not say that only such and such a person will get it and not others!

Myself: Do you remember, Swamiji, one day, before you took Sannyâsa, we were sitting in the house of—, and you were trying to explain the mystery of Samâdhi to us. And when I called in question the truth of your words, saying that Samadhi was not possible in this Kali Yuga, you emphatically demanded: "Do you want to see Samadhi or to have it yourself? I get Samadhi myself, and I can make you have it!" No sooner had you finished saying so than a stranger came up and we did not pursue that subject any further.

Swamiji: Yes, I remember the occasion.

Later, on my pressing him to make me get Samadhi, he said, "You see, having continually lectured and worked hard for several years, the quality of Rajas has become too predominant in me. Hence that power is lying covered, as it were, in me now. If I leave all work and go to the Himalayas and meditate in solitude for some time, then that power will again come out in me."

Reminiscences—Pranayama—Thought-Reading— Knowledge of Previous Births

A day or two later, as I was coming out of my house intending to pay a visit to Swamiji, I met two of my friends who expressed a wish to accompany me, for they wanted to ask Swamiji something about Prânâyâma. I had heard that one should not visit a temple or a Sannyâsin without taking something as an offering; so we took some fruits and sweets with us and placed them before him. Swamiji took them in his hands, raised them to his head, and bowed to us before even we made our obeisance to him. One of the two friends with me had been a fellow-student of his. Swamiji recognised him at once and asked about his health and welfare Then he made us sit down by him. There were many others there who had come to see and hear him. After replying to a few questions put by some of the gentlemen, Swamiji, in the course of his conversation, began to speak about Pranayama. First of all, he explained through modern science the origin of matter from the mind, and then went on to show what Pranayama is. All three of us had carefully read beforehand his book called Râja-Yoga. But from what we heard from him that day about Pranayama, it seemed to me that very little of the knowledge that was in him had been recorded in that book. I understand also that what he said was not mere book-learning, for who could explain so lucidly and elaborately all the intricate problems of religion, even with the help of science, without himself realising the Truth?

His conversation on Pranayama went on from half past three o'clock till half past seven in the evening. When the meeting dissolved and we came away, my companions asked me how Swamiji could have known the questions that were in their hearts, and whether I had communicated to him their desire for asking those questions.

A few days after this occasion, I saw Swamiji in the house of the late Priya Nath Mukherjee at Baghbazar. There were present Swami Brahmananda, Swami Yogananda, Mr. G. C. Ghosh, Atul Babu, and one or two other friends. I said, "Well, Swamiji, the two gentlemen who went to see you the other day wanted to ask you some questions about Pranayama, which had been raised in their minds by reading your book on Raja-Yoga some time before you returned to this country, and they had then told me of them. But that day, before they asked you anything, you yourself raised those doubts that had occurred to them and solved them! They were very much surprised and inquired of me if I had let you know their doubts beforehand." Swamiji replied: "Similar occurrences having come to pass many times in the West, people often used to ask me, 'How could you know the questions that were agitating our minds?' This knowledge does not happen to me so often, but with Shri Ramakrishna it was almost always there."

In this connection Atul Babu asked him: "You have said in Raja-Yoga that one can come to know all about one's previous births. Do you know them yourself?"

Swamiji: Yes, I do.

Atul Babu: What do you know? Have you any objection to tell?

Swamiji: I can know them—I do know them—but I prefer not to say anything in detail.

The Art and Science of Music, Eastern and Western

It was an evening in July 1898, at the Math, in Nilambar Mukerjee's garden-house, Belur. Swamiji with all his disciples had been meditating, and at the close of the meditation came out and sat in one of the rooms. As it was raining hard and a cold wind was blowing, he shut the door and began to sing to the accompaniment of Tânpurâ. The singing being over, a long conversation on music followed. Swami Shivananda asked him, "What is Western music like?"

Swamiji: Oh, it is very good; there is in it a perfection of harmony, which we have not attained. Only, to our untrained ears, it does not sound well, hence we do not like it, and think that the singers howl like jackals. I also had the same sort of impression, but when I began to listen to the music with attention and study it minutely, I came more and more to understand it, and I was lost in admiration. Such is the case with every art. In glancing at a highly finished painting we cannot understand where its beauty lies. Moreover, unless the eye is, to a certain extent, trained, one cannot appreciate the subtle touches and blendings, the inner genius of a work of art. What real music we have lies in Kirtana and Dhrupada; the rest has been spoiled by being modulated according to the Islamic methods. Do you think that singing the short and light airs of Tappâ songs in a nasal voice and flitting like lightning from one note to another by fits and starts are the best things in the world of music? Not so. Unless each note is given full play in every scale, all the science of music is marred. In painting, by keeping in touch with nature, you can make it as artistic as you like; there is no harm in doing that, and the result will be nothing but good. Similarly, in music, you can display any amount of skill by keeping to science, and it will be pleasing to the ear. The Mohammedans took up the different Râgas and Râginis after coming into India. But they put such a stamp of their own colouring on the art of Tappa songs that all the science in music was destroyed.

Q. Why, Mahârâj (sir)? Who has not a liking for music in Tappa?

Swamiji: The chirping of crickets sounds very good to some. The Santâls think their music also to be the best of all. You do not seem to understand that when one note comes upon another in such quick succession, it not only robs music of all grace, but, on the other hand, creates discordance rather. Do not the permutation and combination of the seven keynotes form one or other of the different melodies of music, known as Ragas and Raginis? Now, in Tappa, if one slurs over a whole melody (Raga) and creates a new tune, and over and above that, if the voice is raised to the highest pitch by tremulous modulation, say, how can the Raga be kept intact? Again, the poetry of music is completely destroyed if there be in it such profuse use of light and short strains just for effect. To sing by keeping to the idea, meant to be conveyed by a song, totally disappeared from our country when Tappas came into vogue. Nowadays, it seems, the true art is reviving a little with the improvement in theatres; but, on the other hand, all regard for Ragas and Raginis is being more and more flung to the winds.

Accordingly, to those who are past masters in the art of singing Dhrupada, it is painful to hear Tappas. But in our music the cadence, or a duly regulated rise and fall of voice or sound, is very good. The French detected and appreciated this trait first, and tried to adapt and introduce it in their music. After their doing this, the whole of Europe has now thoroughly mastered it.

Q. Maharaj, their music seems to be pre-eminently martial, whereas that element appears to be altogether absent in ours.

Swamiji: Oh, no, we have it also. In martial music, harmony is greatly needed. We sadly lack harmony, hence it does not show itself so much. Our music had been improving steadily. But when the Mohammedans came, they took possession of it in such a way that the tree of music could grow no further. The music of the Westerners is much advanced. They have the sentiment of pathos as well as of heroism in their music, which is as it should be. But our antique musical instrument made from the gourd has been improved no further.

Q. Which of the Ragas and Raginis are martial in tune?

Swamiji: Every Raga may be made martial if it is set in harmony and the instruments are tuned accordingly. Some of the Raginis can also become martial.

The conversation was then closed, as it was time for supper. After supper, Swamiji enquired as to the sleeping arrangements for the guests who had come from Calcutta to the Math to pass the night, and he then retired to his bedroom.

The Old Institution of Living with the Guru—The Present University System—Lack of Shraddha—We have a National History—Western Science Coupled with Vedanta—The So-called Higher Education—The Need of Technical Education and Education on National Lines—The Story of Satyakama—Mere Book-Learning and Education under Tyagis—Shri Ramakrishna and the Pandits—Establishment of Maths with Sadhus in Charge of Colleges—Text-Books for Boys to be Compiled—Stop Early Marriage!—Plan of Sending Unmarried Graduates to Japan—The Secret of Japan's Greatness—Art, Asian and European—Art and Utility—Styles of Dress—The Food Question and Poverty

It was about two years after the new Math had been constructed and while all the Swamis were living there that I came one morning to pay a visit to my Guru. Seeing me, Swamiji smiled and after inquiring of my welfare etc., said, "You are going to stay today, are you not?"

"Certainly", I said, and after various inquiries I asked, "Well, Mahârâj, what is your idea of educating our boys?"

Swamiji: Guru-griha-vâsa—living with the Guru.

Q. How?

Swamiji: In the same way as of old. But with this education has to be combined modern Western science. Both these are necessary.

Q. Why, what is the defect in the present university system?

Swamiji: It is almost wholly one of defects. Why, it is nothing but a perfect machine for turning out clerks. I would even thank my stars if that were all. But no! See how men are becoming destitute of Shraddhâ and faith. They assert that the Gita is only an interpolation, and that the Vedas are but rustic songs! They like to master every detail concerning things and nations outside of India, but if you ask them, they do not know even the names of their own forefathers up to the seventh generation, not to speak of the fourteenth!

Q. But what does that matter? What if they do not know the names of their forefathers?

Swamiji: Don't think so. A nation that has no history of its own has nothing in this world. Do you believe that one who has such faith and pride as to feel, "I come of noble descent", can ever turn out to be bad? How could that be? That faith in himself would curb his actions and feelings, so much so that he would rather die than commit wrong. So a national history keeps a nation well-restrained and does not allow it to sink so low. Oh, I know you will say, "But we have not such a history!" No, there is not any, according to those who think like you. Neither is there any, according to your big university scholars; and so also think those who, having travelled through the West in one great rush, come back dressed in European style and assert, "We have nothing, we are barbarians." Of course, we have no history exactly like that of other countries. Suppose we take rice, and the Englishmen do not. Would you for that reason imagine that they all die of starvation, and are going to be exterminated? They live quite well on what they can easily procure or produce in their own country and what is suited to them. Similarly, we have our own history exactly as it ought to have been for us. Will that history be made extinct by shutting your eyes and crying, "Alas! we have no history!" Those who have eyes to see, find a luminous history there, and on the strength of that they know the nation is still alive. But that history has to be rewritten. It should be restated and suited to the understanding and ways of thinking which our men have acquired in the present age through Western education.

Q. How has that to be done?

Swamiji: That is too big a subject for a talk now. However, to bring that about, the old institution of "living with the Guru" and similar systems of imparting education are needed. What we want are Western science coupled with Vedanta, Brahmacharya as the guiding motto, and also Shraddhâ and faith in one's own self. Another thing that we want is the abolition of that system which aims at educating our boys in the same manner as that of the man who battered his ass, being advised that it could thereby be turned into a horse.

Q. What do you mean by that?

Swamiji: You see, no one can teach anybody. The teacher spoils everything by thinking that he is teaching. Thus Vedanta says that within man is all knowledge—even in a boy it is so—and it requires only an awakening, and that much is the work of a teacher. We have to do only so much for the boys that they may learn to apply their own intellect to the proper use of their hands, legs, ears, eyes, etc., and finally everything will become easy. But the root is religion. Religion is as the rice, and everything else, like the curries. Taking only curries causes indigestion, and so is the case with taking rice alone. Our pedagogues are making parrots of our boys and ruining their brains by cramming a lot of subjects into them. Looking from one standpoint, you should rather be grateful to the Viceroy[1] for his proposal of reforming the university system, which means practically abolishing higher education; the country will, at least, feel some relief by having breathing time. Goodness gracious! What a fuss and fury about graduating, and after a few days all cools down! And after all that, what is it they learn but that what religion and customs we have are all bad, and what the Westerners have are all good!

1. Lord Curzon, who took steps to raise the standard of university education so high as to make it very expensive and hence almost inaccessible to boys of the middle classes.

At last, they cannot keep the wolf from the door! What does it matter if this higher education remains or goes? It would be better if the people got a little technical education, so that they might find work and earn their bread, instead of dawdling about and crying for service.

Q. Yes, the Marwaris are wiser, since they do not accept service and most of them engage themselves in some trade.

Swamiji: Nonsense! They are on the way to bringing ruin on the country. They have little understanding of their own interests. You are much better, because you have more of an eye towards manufactures. If the money that they lay out in their business and with which they make only a small percentage of profit were utilised in conducting a few factories and workshops, instead of filling the pockets of Europeans by letting them reap the benefit of most of the transactions, then it would not only conduce to the well-being of the country but bring by far the greater amount of profit to them, as well. It is only the Kabulis who do not care for service—the spirit of independence is in their very bone and marrow. Propose to anyone of them to take service, and you will see what follows!

Q. Well, Maharaj, in case higher education is abolished, will not the men become as stupid as cows, as they were before?

Swamiji: What nonsense! Can ever a lion become a jackal? What do you mean? Is it ever possible for the sons of the land that has nourished the whole world with knowledge from time immemorial to turn as stupid as cows, because of the abolition of higher education by Lord Curzon?

Q. But think what our people were before the advent of the English, and what they are now.

Swamiji: Does higher education mean mere study of material sciences and turning out things of everyday use by machinery? The use of higher education is to find out how to solve the problems of life, and this is what is engaging the profound thought of the modern civilised world, but it was solved in our country thousands of years ago.

Q. But your Vedanta also was about to disappear?

Swamiji: It might be so. In the efflux of time the light of Vedanta now and then seems as if about to be extinguished, and when that happens, the Lord has to incarnate Himself in the human body; He then infuses such life and strength into religion that it goes on again for some time with irresistible vigour. That life and strength has come into it again.

Q. What proof is there, Maharaj, that India has freely contributed her knowledge to the rest of the world?

Swamiji: History itself bears testimony to the fact. All the soul-elevating ideas and the different branches of knowledge that exist in the world are found on proper investigation to have their roots in India.

Aglow with enthusiasm, Swamiji dwelt at length on this topic. His health was very bad at the time, and moreover owing to the intense heat of summer, he was feeling thirsty and drinking water too often. At last he said "Dear Singhi, get a glass of iced water for me please, I shall explain everything to you clearly." After drinking the iced water he began afresh.

Swamiji: What we need, you know, is to study, independent of foreign control, different branches of the knowledge that is our own, and with it the English language and Western science; we need technical education and all else that may develop industries So that men, instead of seeking for service, may earn enough to provide for themselves, and save something against a rainy day.

Q. What were you going to say the other day about the tol (Sanskrit boarding school) system?

Swamiji: Haven't you read the stories from the Upanishads? I will tell you one. Satyakâma went to live the life of a Brahmachârin with his Guru. The Guru gave into his charge some cows and sent him away to the forest with them. Many months passed by, and when Satyakama saw that the number of cows was doubled he thought of returning to his Guru. On his way back, one of the bulls, the fire, and some other animals gave him instructions about the Highest Brahman. When the disciple came back, the Guru at once saw by a mere glance at his face that the disciple had learnt the knowledge of the Supreme Brahman[1]. Now, the moral this story is meant to teach is that true education is gained by constant living in communion with nature.

Knowledge should be acquired in that way, otherwise by educating yourself in the tol of a Pandit you will be only a human ape all your life. One should live from his very boyhood with one whose character is like a blazing fire and should have before him a living example of the highest teaching. Mere reading that it is a sin to tell a lie will be of no use. Every boy should be trained to practice absolute Brahmacharya, and then, and then only, faith —Shraddha—will come. Otherwise, why will not one who has no Shraddha speak an untruth? In our country, the imparting of knowledge has always been through men of renunciation. Later, the Pandits, by monopolising all knowledge and restricting it to the tols, have only brought the country to the brink of ruin. India had all good prospects so long as Tyâgis (men of renunciation) used to impart knowledge.

Q. What do you mean, Maharaj? There are no Sannyâsins in other countries, but see how by dint of their knowledge India is laid prostrate at their feet!

Swamiji: Don't talk nonsense, my dear, hear what I say. India will have to carry others' shoes for ever on her head if the charge of imparting knowledge to her sons does not again fall upon the shoulders Of Tyâgis. Don't you know how an illiterate boy, possessed of renunciation, turned the heads of your great old Pandits? Once at the Dakshineswar Temple the Brâhmana who was in charge of the worship of Vishnu broke a leg of the image. Pandits were brought together at a meeting to give their opinions, and they, after consulting old books and manuscripts, declared that the worship of this bro-

ken image could not be sanctioned according to the Shâstras and a new image would have to be consecrated. There was, consequently, a great stir. Shri Ramakrishna was called at last. He heard and asked, "Does a wife forsake her husband in case he becomes lame?" What followed? The Pandits were struck dumb, all their Shâstric commentaries and erudition could not withstand the force of this simple statement. If what you say was true, why should Shri Ramakrishna come down to this earth, and why should he discourage mere book-learning so much? That new life-force which he brought with him has to be instilled into learning and education, and then the real work will be done.

Q. But that is easier said than done.

Swamiji: Had it been easy, it would not have been necessary for him to come. What you have to do now is to establish a Math in every town and in every village. Can you do that? Do something at least. Start a big Math in the heart of Calcutta. A well-educated Sâdhu should be at the head of that centre and under him there should be departments for teaching practical science and arts, with a specialist Sannyasin in charge of each of these departments.

Q. Where will you get such Sadhus?

Swamiji: We shall have to manufacture them. Therefore, I always say that some young men with burning patriotism and renunciation are needed. None can master a thing perfectly in so short a time as the Tyagis will.

After a short silence Swamiji said, "Singhi, there are so many things left to be done for our country that thousands like you and me are needed. What will mere talk do? See to what a miserable condition the country is reduced; now do something! We haven't even got a single book well suited for the little boys."

Q. Why, there are so many books of Ishwar Chandra Vidyâsâgar for the boys!

No sooner had I said this than he laughed out and said: Yes, there you read "Ishvar Nirakar Chaitanya Svarup"—(God is without form and of the essence of pure knowledge); "Subal ati subodh bâlak"—(Subal is a very good boy), and so on. That won't do. We must compose some books in Bengali as also in English with short stories from the Râmâyana, the Mahâbhârata, the Upanishads, etc., in very easy and simple language, and these are to be given to our little boys to read.

It was about eleven o'clock by this time. The sky became suddenly overcast, and a cool breeze began to blow. Swamiji was greatly delighted at the prospect of rain. He got up and said, "Let us, Singhi, have a stroll by the side of the Ganga." We did so, and he recited many stanzas from the Meghaduta of Kâlidâsa, but the one undercurrent of thought that was all the time running through his mind was the good of India. He exclaimed, "Look here, Singhi, can you do one thing? Can you put a stop to the marriage of our boys for some time?"

I said, "Well, Maharaj, how can we think of that when the Babus are trying, on the other hand, all sorts of means to

1. Chhândogya, IV. ix. 2.

make marriage cheaper?"

Swamiji : Don't trouble your head on that score; who can stem the tide of time! All such agitations will end in empty sound, that is all. The dearer the marriages become, the better for the country. What a hurry-scurry of passing examinations and marrying right off! It seems as if no one was to be left a bachelor, but it is just the same thing again, next year!

After a short silence, Swamiji again said, "if I can get some unmarried graduates, I may try to send them over to Japan and make arrangements for their technical education there, so that when they come back, they may turn their knowledge to the best account for India. What a good thing that would be!"

Q. Why, Maharaj, is it better for us to go to Japan than to England?

Swamiji: Certainly! In my opinion, if all our rich and educated men once go and see Japan, their eyes will be opened.

Q. How?

Swamiji: There, in Japan, you find a fine assimilation of knowledge, and not its indigestion, as we have here. They have taken everything from the Europeans, but they remain Japanese all the same, and have not turned European; while in our country, the terrible mania of becoming Westernised has seized upon us like a plague.

I said: "Maharaj, I have seen some Japanese paintings; one cannot but marvel at their art. Its inspiration seems to be something which is their own and beyond imitation."

Swamiji: Quite so. They are great as a nation because of their art. Don't you see they are Asians, as we are? And though we have lost almost everything, yet what we still have is wonderful. The very soul of the Asian is interwoven with art. The Asian never uses a thing unless there be art in it. Don't you knew that art is, with us, a part of religion? How greatly is a lady admired, among us, who can nicely paint the floors and walls, on auspicious occasions, with the paste of rice powder? How great an artist was Shri Ramakrishna himself!

Q. The English art is also good, is it not?

Swamiji: What a stupid fool you are! But what is the use of blaming you when that seems to be the prevailing way of thinking! Alas, to such a state is our country reduced! The people will look upon their own gold as brass, while the brass of the foreigner it gold to them! This is, indeed, the magic wrought by modern education! Know that since the time the Europeans have come into contact with Asia, they are trying to infuse art into their own life.

Myself: If others hear you talk like this, Maharaj they will think that you take a pessimistic view of things.

Swamiji: Naturally! What else can they think who move in a rut! How I wish I could show you everything through my eyes! Look at their buildings—how commonplace, how meaningless, they are! Look at those big government buildings; can you, just by seeing their outside, make out any meaning for which each of them stands? No, because they are all so unsymbolical. Take again the dress of Westerners: their stiff coats and straight pants fitting almost tightly to the body, are, in our estimation hardly decent. Is it not so? And, oh, what beauty indeed, in that! Now, go all over our motherland and see if you cannot read aright, from their very appearance, the meaning for which our buildings stand, and hew much art there is in them! The glass is their drinking vessel, and ours is the metal Ghati (pitcher-shaped); which of the two is artistic? Have you seen the farmers' homes in our villages?

Myself: Yes, I have, of course.

Swamiji: What have you seen of them?

I did not know what to say. However, I replied, "Maharaj, they are faultlessly neat and clean, the yards and floors being daily well plastered over".

Swamiji: Have you seen their granaries for keeping paddy? What an art is there in them! What a variety of paintings even on their mud walls! And then, if you go and see how the lower classes live in the West, you would at once mark the difference. Their ideal is utility, ours art. The Westerner looks for utility in everything, whereas with us art is everywhere. With the Western education, those beautiful Ghatis of ours have been discarded, and enamel glasses have usurped their place in our homes! Thus the ideal of utility has been imbibed by us to such an extent as to make it look little short of the ridiculous. Now what we need is the combination of art and utility. Japan has done that very quickly, and so she has advanced by giant strides. Now, in their turn, the Japanese are going to teach the Westerners.

Q. Maharaj, which nation in the world dresses best?

Swamiji: The Aryans do; even the Europeans admit that. How picturesquely their dresses hang in folds! The royal costumes of most nations are, to some extent, a sort of imitation of the Aryans,'—the same attempt is made there to keep them in folds, and those costumes bear a marked difference to their national style.

By the by, Singhi, leave off that wretched habit of wearing those European shirts.

Q. Why, Maharaj?

Swamiji: For the reason that they are used by the Westerners only as underwear. They never like to see them worn outside. How mistaken of the Bengalis to do so! As if one should wear anything and everything, as if there was no unwritten law about dress, as if there was no ancestral style to follow! Our people are out-casted by taking the food touched by the lower classes it would have been very well if the same law applied to their wearing any irregular style of dress. Why can't you adapt your dress in some way to our own style? What sense is there in your adopting European shirts and coats?

It began to rain now, and the dinner-bell also rang. So we went in to partake of the Prasâda (consecrated food) with others. During the meal, Swamiji said, addressing me: "Concentrated food should be taken. To fill the stomach with a large quantity of rice is the root of laziness." A little while after he said again, "Look at the Japanese, they take rice with the soup of split peas, twice or thrice a day. But even the strongly built take a little at a time, though the number of meals may be more. Those who are well-to-do among them take meat daily. While we stuff ourselves twice a day up to the throat, as it were, and the whole of our energy is exhausted in digesting such a quantity of rice!"

Q. Is it feasible for us Bengalis, poor as we are, to take meat?

Swamiji: Why not? You can afford to have it in small quantities. Half a pound a day is quite enough. The real evil is idleness, which is the principal cause of our poverty. Suppose the head of a firm gets displeased with someone and decreases his pay; or out of three or four bread-winning sons in a family one suddenly dies; what do they do? Why, they at once curtail the quantity of milk for the children, or live on one meal a day, having a little popped rice or so at night!

Q. But what else can they do under the circumstances?

Swamiji: Why can't they exert themselves and earn more to keep up their standard of food? But no! They must go to their local Âddâs (rendezvous) and idle hours away! Oh, if they only knew how they wasted their time!

The Discrimination of the Four Castes According to Jati and Guna—Brahmanas and Kshatriyas in the West—The Kula-Guru System in Bengal

Once I went to see Swamiji while he was staying in Calcutta at the house of the late Balaram Basu. After a long conversation about Japan and America, I asked him, "Well, Swamiji, how many disciples have you in the West?"

Swamiji: A good many.

Q. Two or three thousands?

Swamiji: Maybe more than that.

Q. Are they all initiated by you with Mantras?

Swamiji: Yes.

Q. Did you give them permission to utter Pranava (Om)?

Swamiji: Yes.

Q. How did you, Mahârâj? They say that the Shudras have no right to Pranava, and none has except the Brâhmins. Moreover, the Westerners are Mlechchhas, not even Shudras.

Swamiji: How do you know that those whom I have initiated are not Brahmins?

Myself: Where could you get Brahmins outside India, in the lands of the Yavanas and Mlechchhas?

Swamiji: My disciples are all Brahmins! I quite admit the truth of the words that none except the Brahmins has the right to Pranava. But the son of a Brahmin is not necessarily always a Brahmin; though there is every possibility of his being one, he may not become so. Did you not hear that the nephew of Aghore Chakravarti of Baghbazar became a sweeper and actually used to do all the menial services of his adopted caste? Was he not the son of a Brahmin?

The Brahmin caste and the Brâhmanya qualities are two distinct things. In India, one is held to be a Brahmin by one's caste, but in the West, one should be known as such by one's Brahmanya qualities. As there are three Gunas—Sattva, Rajas, and Tamas—so there are Gunas which show a man to be a Brahmin, Kshatriya, Vaishya or Shudra. The qualities of being a Brahmin or a Kshatriya are dying out from the country; but in the West they have now attained to Kshatriyahood, from which the next step is Brahminhood; and many there are who have qualified themselves for that.

Q. Then you call those Brahmins who are Sâttvika by nature.

Swamiji: Quite so. As there are Sattva, Rajas, and Tamas—one or other of these Gunas more or less—in every man, so the qualities which make a Brahmin, Kshatriya, Vaishya, or Shudra are inherent in every man, more or less. But at times one or other of these qualities predominates in him in varying degrees, and it is manifested accordingly. Take a man in his different pursuits, for example: when he is engaged in serving another for pay, he is in Shudrahood; when he is busy transacting some piece of business for profit, on his own account, he is a Vaishya; when he fights to right wrongs, then the qualities of a Kshatriya come out in him; and when he meditates on God or passes his time in conversation about Him, then he is a Brahmin. Naturally, it is quite possible for one to be changed from one caste into another. Otherwise, how did Vishvâmitra become a Brahmin and Parashurâma a Kshatriya?

Q. What you say seems to be quite right, but why then do not our Pandits and family-Gurus teach us the same thing?

Swamiji: That is one of the great evils of our country. But let the matter rest now.

Swamiji here spoke highly of the Westerners' spirit of practicality, and how, when they take up religion also, that spirit shows itself.

Myself: True, Maharaj, I have heard that their spiritual and psychic powers are very quickly developed when they practice religion. The other day Swami Saradananda showed me a letter written by one of his Western disciples, describing the spiritual powers highly developed in the writer through the Sâdhanâs practiced for only four months.

Swamiji: So you see! Now you understand whether there are Brahmins in the West or not. You have Brahmins here also, but they are bringing the country down to the verge of ruin by their awful tyranny, and consequently what they have naturally is vanishing away by degrees. The Guru initiates his disciple with a Mantra, but that has come to be a trade with him. And then, how wonderful is the relation nowadays between a Guru and his disciple! Perchance, the Guru has nothing to eat at home, and his wife brings the matter to his notice and says, "Pray, go once again to your disciples, dear. Will your playing at dice all day long save us from hunger?" The Brahmin in reply says, "Very well, remind me of it tomorrow morning. I have come to hear that my disciple so-and-so is having a run of luck, and, moreover, I have not been to him for a long time." This is what your Kula-Guru system has come to in Bengal! Priestcraft in the West is not so degenerated, as yet; it is on the whole better than your kind!

FROM THE DIARY OF A DISCIPLE, SHRI SARAT CHANDRA CHAKRAVARTY

(Translated from Bengali)

India Wants not Lecturing but Work—The Crying Problem in India is Poverty—Young Sannyasins to be Trained Both as Secular And Spiritual Teachers and Workers for the Masses—Exhortations to Young Men to WORK for Others

From the Diary of a disciple. The disciple in this and the following conversations is Sharat Chandra Chakravarty.

Disciple: How is it, Swamiji, that you do not lecture in this country? You have stirred Europe and America with your lectures, but coming back here you have kept silence.

Swamiji: In this country, the ground should be prepared first; then if the seed is sown, the plant will come out best. The ground in the West, in Europe and America is very fertile and fit for sowing seeds. There they have reached the climax of Bhoga (enjoyment). Being satiated with Bhoga to the full, their minds are not getting peace now even in those enjoyments, and they feel as if they wanted something else. In this country you have neither Bhoga nor Yoga (renunciation). When one is satiated with Bhoga, then it is that one will listen to and understand the teachings on Yoga. What good will lectures do in a country like India which has become the birthplace of disease, sorrow, and affliction, and where men are emaciated through starvation, and weak in mind?

Disciple: How is that? Do you not say that ours is the land of religion and that here the people understand religion as they do nowhere else? Why then will not this country be animated by your inspiring eloquence and reap to the full the fruits thereof?

Swamiji: Now understand what religion means. The first thing required is the worship of the Kurma (tortoise) Incarnation, and the belly-god is this Kurma, as it were. Until you pacify this, no one will welcome your words about religion. India is restless with the thought of how to face this spectre of hunger. The draining of the best resources of the country by the foreigners, the unrestricted exports of merchandise, and, above all, the abominable jealousy natural to slaves are eating into the vitals of India. First of all, you must remove this evil of hunger and starvation, this constant anxiety for bare existence, from those to whom you want to preach religion; otherwise, lectures and such things will be of no benefit.

Disciple: What should we do then to remove that evil?

Swamiji: First, some young men full of the spirit of renunciation are needed —those who will be ready to sacrifice their lives for others, instead of devoting themselves to their own happiness. With this object in view I shall establish a Math to train young Sannyâsins, who will go from door to door and make the people realise their pitiable condition by means of facts and reasoning, and instruct them in the ways and means for their welfare, and at the same time will explain to them as clearly as possible, in very simple and easy language, the higher truths of religion. The masses in our country are like the sleeping Leviathan. The education imparted by the present university system reaches one or two per cent of the masses only. And even those who get that do not succeed in their endeavours of doing any good to their country. But it is not their fault, poor fellows! As soon as they come out of their college, they find themselves fathers of several children! Somehow or other they manage to secure the position of a clerk, or at the most, a deputy magistrate. This is the finale of education! With the burden of a family on their backs, they find no time to do anything great or think anything high. They do not find means enough to fulfil their personal wants and interests; so what can be expected of them in the way of doing anything for others?

Disciple: Is there then no way out for us?

Swamiji: Certainly there is. This is the land of Religion Eternal. The country has fallen, no doubt, but will as surely rise again, and that upheaval will astound the world. The lower the hollows the billows make, the higher and with greater force will they rise again.

Disciple: How will India rise again?

Swamiji: Do you not see? The dawn has already appeared in the eastern sky, and there is little delay in the sun's rising. You all set your shoulders to the wheel! What is there in making the world all in all, and thinking of "My Samsâra (family and property), my Samsâra"? Your duty at present is to go from one part of the country to another, from village to village, and make the people understand that mere sitting idly won't do any more. Make them understand their real condition and say, "O ye brothers, arise! Awake! How much longer would you remain asleep!" Go and advise them how to improve their own condition, and make them comprehend the sublime truths of the Shâstras (scriptures), by presenting them in a lucid and popular way. So long the Brahmins have monopolised religion; but since they cannot hold their ground against the strong tide of time, go and take steps so that one and all in the land may get that religion. Impress upon their minds that they have the same right to religion as the Brahmins. Initiate all, even down to the Chandâlas (people of the lowest castes), in these fiery Mantras. Also instruct them, in simple words, about the necessities of life, and in trade, commerce, agriculture, etc. If you cannot do this then lie upon your education and culture, and lie upon your studying the Vedas and Vedanta!

Disciple: But where is that strength in us? I should have felt myself blessed if I had a hundredth part of your powers, Swamiji.

Swamiji: How foolish! Power and things like that will come by themselves. Put yourself to work, and you will final such tremendous power coming to you that you will feel it hard to bear. Even the least work done for others awakens the power within; even thinking the least good of others gradually instils into the heart the strength of a lion. I lore you all ever so much, but I wish you all to die working for others—I should rather be glad to see you do that!

Disciple: What will become of those, then, who depend on me?

Swamiji: If you are ready to sacrifice your life for others, God will certainly provide some means for them. Have you not read in the Gita (VI. 40) the words of Shri Krishna, "न हि कल्याणाकृत्कश्चिति तात गच्छति—Never does a doer of good, O my beloved, come to grief"?

Disciple: I see, sir.

Swamiji: The essential thing is renunciation. With out renunciation none can pour out his whole heart in working for others. The man of renunciation sees all with an equal eye and devotes himself to the service of all. Does not our Vedanta also teach us to see all with an equal eye? Why then do you cherish the idea that the wife and children are your own, more than others? At your very threshold, Nârâyana Himself in the form of a poor beggar is dying of starvation! Instead of giving him anything, would you only satisfy the appetites of your wife and children with delicacies? Why, that is beastly!

Disciple: To work for others requires a good deal of money at times, and where shall I get that?

Swamiji: Why not do as much as lies within your power? Even if you cannot give to others for want of money, surely you can at least breathe into their ears some good words or impart some good instruction, can't you? Or does that also require money?

Disciple: Yes, sir, that I can do.

Swamiji: But saying, "I can", won't do. Show me through action what you can do, and then only I shall know that your coming to me is turned to some good account. Get up, and put your shoulders to the wheel—how long is this life for? As you have come into this world, leave some mark behind. Otherwise, where is the difference between you and the trees and stones? They, too, come into existence, decay and die. If you like to be born and to die like them, you are at liberty to do so. Show me by your actions that your reading the Vedanta has been fruitful of the highest good. Go and tell all, "In every one of you lies that Eternal Power", and try to wake It up. What will you do with individual salvation? That is sheer selfishness. Throw aside your meditation, throw away your salvation and such things! Put your whole heart and soul in the work to which I have consecrated myself.

With bated breath the disciple heard these inspiring words, and Swamiji went on with his usual fire and eloquence.

Swamiji: First of all, make the soil ready, and thousands of Vivekanandas will in time be born into this world to deliver lectures on religion. You needn't worry yourself about that! Don't you see why I am starting orphanages, famine-relief works, etc.? Don't you see how Sister Nivedita, a British lady, has learnt to serve Indians so well, by doing even menial work for them? And can't you, being Indians, similarly serve your own fellow-countrymen? Go, all of you, wherever there is an outbreak of plague or famine, or wherever the people are in distress, and mitigate their sufferings. At the most you may die in the attempt—what of that? How many like you are being born and dying like worms every day? What difference does that make to the world at large? Die you must, but have a great ideal to die for, and it is better to die with a great ideal in life. Preach this ideal from door to door, and you will yourselves be benefited by it at the same time that you are doing good to your country. On you lie the future hopes of our country. I feel extreme pain to see you leading a life of inaction. Set yourselves to work—to work! Do not tarry—the time of death is approaching day by day! Do not sit idle, thinking that everything will be done in time, later on! Mind—nothing will be done that way!

Reconciliation of Jnana and Bhakti—Sat-Chit-Ananda—How Sectarianism Originates—Bring in Shraddha and the Worship of Shakti and avataras—The Ideal of the Hero We Want Now, not the Madhura-Bhava—Shri Ramakrishna—Avataras

Disciple: Pray, Swamiji, how can Jnâna and Bhakti be reconciled? We see the followers of the path of devotion (Bhaktas) close their ears at the name of Shankara, and again, the followers of the path of knowledge (Jnanis) call the Bhaktas fanatics, seeing them weep in torrents, or sing and dance in ecstasy, in the name of the Lord.

Swamiji: The thing is, all this conflict is in the preliminary (preparatory) stages of Jnana and Bhakti. Have you not heard Shri Ramakrishna's story about Shiva's demons and Râma's monkeys[1]?

Disciple: Yes, sir, I have.

Swamiji: But there is no difference between the supreme Bhakti and the supreme Jnana. The supreme Bhakti is to realise God as the form of Prema (love) itself. If you see the loving form of God manifest everywhere and in everything, how can you hate or injure others? That realisation of love can never come so long as there is the least desire in the heart, or what Shri Ramakrishna used to say, attachment for Kâma-Kânchana (sense-pleasure and wealth). In the perfect realisation of love, even the consciousness of one's own body does not exist. Also, the supreme Jnana is to realise the oneness everywhere, to see one's own self as the Self in everything. That too cannot come so long as there is the least consciousness of the ego (Aham).

1. There was once a fight between Shiva and Rama. Shiva was the Guru of Rama, and Rama was the Guru of Shiva. They fought but became friendly again. But there was no end to the quarrels and wranglings between the demons of Shiva and the monkeys of Rama!

Disciple: Then what you call love is the same as supreme knowledge?

Swamiji: Exactly so. Realisation of love comes to none unless one becomes a perfect Jnani. Does not the Vedanta say that Brahman is Sat-Chit-Ânanda— the absolute Existence-Knowledge-Bliss?

Disciple: Yes, sir.

Swamiji: The phrase Sat-Chit-Ananda means—Sat, i.e. existence, Chit, i.e. consciousness or knowledge, and Ananda, i.e. bliss which is the same as love. There is no controversy between the Bhakta and the Jnani regarding the Sat aspect of Brahman. Only, the Jnanis lay greater stress on His aspect of Chit or knowledge, while the Bhaktas keep the aspect of Ananda or love more in view. But no sooner is the essence of Chit realised than the essence of Ananda is also realised. Because what is Chit is verily the same as Ananda.

Disciple: Why then is so much sectarianism prevalent in India? And why is there so much controversy between the scriptures on Bhakti and Jnana?

Swamiji: The thing is, all this waging of war and controversy is concerning the preliminary ideals, i.e. those ideals which men take up to attain the real Jnana or real Bhakti. But which do you think is the higher—the end or the means? Surely, the means can never be higher than the end, because the means to realise the same end must be numerous, as they vary according to the temperament or mental capacities of individual followers. The counting of beads, meditation, worship, offering oblations in the sacred fire—all these and such other things are the limbs of religion; they are but means; and to attain to supreme devotion (Parâ-Bhakti) or to the highest realisation of Brahman is the pre-eminent end. If you look a little deeper, you will understand what they are fighting about. One says, "If you pray to God facing the East, then you will reach Him." "No," says another, "you will have to sit facing the West, and then only you will see Him." Perhaps someone realised God in meditation, ages ago, by sitting with his face to the East, and his disciples at once began to preach this attitude, asserting that none can ever see God unless he assumes this position. Another party comes forward and inquires, "How is that? Such and such a person realised God while facing the West, and we have seen this ourselves." In this way all these sects have originated. Someone might have attained supreme devotion by repeating the name of the Lord as Hari, and at once it entered into the composition of the Shâstra as:

हरेर्नाम हरेर्नाम हरेर्नामैव केवलम् । कलौ नास्त्येव नास्त्येव नास्त्येव गतिरन्यथा ॥

—"The name of the Lord Hari, the name of the Lord Hari, the name of the Lord Hari alone. Verily, there is no other, no other, no other path than this in the age of Kali."

Someone, again, let us suppose, might have attained perfection with the name of Allah, and immediately another creed originated by him began to spread, and so on. But we have to see what is the end to which all these forms of worship and other religious practices are intended to lead. The end is Shraddhâ. We have not any synonym in our Bengali language to express the Sanskrit word Shraddha. The (Katha) Upanishad says that Shraddha entered into the heart of Nachiketâ. Even with the word Ekâgratâ (one-pointedness) we cannot express the whole significance of the word Shraddha. The word Ekâgranishthâ (one-pointed devotion) conveys, to a certain extent, the meaning of the word Shraddha. If you meditate on any truth with steadfast devotion and concentration, you will see that the mind is more and more tending onwards to Oneness, i.e. taking you towards the realisation of the absolute Existence-Knowledge-Bliss. The scriptures on Bhakti or Jnana give special advice to men to take up in life the one or the other of such Nishthas (scrupulous persistence) and make it their own. With the lapse of ages, these great truths become distorted and gradually transform themselves into Deshâchâras or the prevailing customs of a country. It has happened, not only in India, but in every nation and every society in the world. And the common people, lacking in discrimination, make these the bone of contention and fight among themselves. They have lost sight of the end, and hence sectarianism, quarrels, and fights continue.

Disciple: What then is the saving means, Swamiji?

Swamiji: That true Shraddha, as of old, has to be brought back again. The weeds have to be talker up by the roots. In every faith and in every path, there are, no doubt, truths which transcend time and space, but a good deal of rubbish has accumulated over them. This has to be cleared away, and the true eternal principles have to be held before the people; and then only, our religion and our country will be really benefited.

Disciple: How will that be effected?

Swamiji: Why, first of all, we have to introduce the worship of the great saints. Those great-souled ones who have realised the eternal truths are to be presented before the people as the ideas to be followed; as in the case of India—Shri Râmachandra, Shri Krishna, Mahâvira and Shri Ramakrishna, among others. Can you bring in the worship of Shri Ramachandra and Mahavira in this country? Keep aside for the present the Vrindâvan aspect of Shri Krishna, and spread far and wide the worship of Shri Krishna roaring the Gita out, with the voice of a Lion. And bring into daily use the worship of Shakti—the divine Mother, the source of all power.

Disciple: Is the divine play of Shri Krishna with the Gopis of Vrindavan not good, then?

Swamiji: Under the present circumstances, that worship is of no good to you. Playing on the flute and so on will not regenerate the country. We now mostly need the ideal of a hero with the tremendous spirit of Rajas thrilling through his veins from head to foot—the hero who will dare and die to know the Truth—the hero whose armour is renunciation, whose sword is wisdom. We want now the spirit of the brave warrior in the battlefield of life, and not of the wooing lover who looks upon life as a pleasure-garden!

Disciple: Is then the path of love, as depicted in the ideal of the Gopis, false?

Swamiji: Who says so? Not I! That is a very superior form of worship (Sâdhanâ). In this age of tremendous attachment to sense-pleasure and wealth, very few are able even to comprehend those higher ideals.

Disciple: Then are not those who are worshipping God as husband or lover (Madhura) following the proper path?

Swamiji: I dare say not. There may be a few honourable exceptions among them, but know, that the greater part of them are possessed of dark Tâmasika nature. Most of them are full of morbidity and affected with exceptional weakness. The country must be raised. The worship of Mahavira must be introduced; the Shakti-pujâ must form a part of our daily practice; Shri Ramachandra must be worshipped in every home. Therein lies your welfare, therein lies the good of the country—there is no other way.

Disciple: But I have heard that Bhagavan Shri Ramakrishna used to sing the name of God very much?

Swamiji: Quite so, but his was a different case. What comparison can there be between him and ordinary men? He practiced in his life all the different ideals of religion to show that each of them leads but to the One Truth. Shall you or I ever be able to do all that he has done? None of us has understood him fully. So, I do not venture to speak about him anywhere and everywhere. He only knows what he himself really was; his frame was a human one only, but everything else about him was entirely different from others.

Disciple: Do you, may I ask, believe him to be an Avatara (Incarnation of God)?

Swamiji: Tell me first—what do you mean by an Avatara?

Disciple: Why, I mean one like Shri Ramachandra, Shri Krishna, Shri Gauranga, Buddha, Jesus, and others.

Swamiji: I know Bhagavan Shri Ramakrishna to be even greater than those you have just named. What to speak of believing, which is a petty thing—I know! Let us, however, drop the subject now; more of it another time.

After a pause Swamiji continued: To re-establish the Dharma, there come Mahâpurushas (great teachers of humanity), suited to the needs of the times and society. Call them what you will—either Mahapurushas or Avataras—it matters little. They reveal, each in his life, the ideal. Then, by degrees, shapes are moulded in their matrices—MEN are made! Gradually, sects arise and spread As time goes on, these sects degenerate, and similar reformers come again. This has been the law flowing in uninterrupted succession, like a current, down the ages.

Disciple: Why do you not preach Shri Ramakrishna as an Avatara? You have, indeed, power, eloquence, and everything else needed to do it.

Swamiji: Truly, I tell you, I have understood him very little. He appears to me to have been so great that, whenever I have to speak anything of him, I am afraid lest I ignore or explain away the truth, lest my little power does not suffice, lest in trying to extol him I present his picture by painting him according to my lights and belittle him thereby!

Disciple: But many are now preaching him as an Avatara.

Swamiji: Let them do so if they like. They are doing it in the light in which they have understood him. You too can go and do the same, if you have understood him.

Disciple: I cannot even grasp you, what to say of Shri Ramakrishna! I should consider myself blessed in this life if I get a little of Your grace.

Brahman and Differentiation—Personal Realisation of Oneness—Supreme Bliss is the Goal of All—Think Always, I am Brahman—Discrimination and Renunciation are the Means—Be Fearless

Disciple: Pray, Swamiji, if the one Brahman is the only Reality, why then exists all this differentiation in the world?

Swamiji: Are you not considering this question from the point of view of phenomenal existence? Looking from the phenomenal side of existence, one can, through reasoning and discrimination, gradually arrive at the very root of Unity. But if you were firmly established in that Unity, how from that standpoint, tell me, could you see this differentiation?

Disciple: True, if I had existed in the Unity, how should I be able to raise this question of "why"? As I put this question, it is already taken for granted that I do so by seeing this diversity.

Swamiji: Very well. To enquire about the root of Oneness through the diversity of phenomenal existence is named by the Shâstras as Vyatireki reasoning, or the process of arguing by the indirect method, that is, Adhyâropa and Apavâda, first taking for granted something that is nonexistent or unreal as existing or real, and then showing through the course of reasoning that that is not a substance existing or real. You are talking of the process of arriving at the truth through assuming that which is not-true as true—are you not?

Disciple: To my mind, the state of the existing or the seen seems to be self-evident, and hence true, and that which is opposite to it seems, on the other hand, to be unreal.

Swamiji: But the Vedas say, "One only without a second". And if in reality there is the One only that exists—the Brahman—then, your differentiation is false. You believe in the Vedas, I suppose?

Disciple: Oh, yes, for me self I hold the Vedas as the highest authority; but if, in argument, one does not accept them to be so, one must, in that case, have to be refuted by other means.

Swamiji: That also can be done. Look here, a time comes when what you call differentiation vanishes, and we cannot perceive it at all. I have experienced that state in my own life.

Disciple: When have you done so?

Swamiji: One day in the temple-garden at Dakshineswar Shri Ramakrishna touched me over the heart, and first of all I began to see that the houses —rooms, doors, windows, verandahs—the trees, the sun, the moon—all were flying off, shattering to pieces as it were—reduced to atoms and molecules—and ultimately became merged in the Âkâsha. Gradually again, the Akasha also vanished, and after that, my consciousness of the ego with it; what happened next I do not recollect. I was at first frightened. Coming back from that state, again I began to see the houses, doors, windows, verandahs, and other things. On another occasion, I had exactly the same realisation by the side of a lake in America.

Disciple: Might not this state as well be brought about by a derangement of the brain? And I do not understand what happiness there can be in realising such a state.

Swamiji: A derangement of the brain! How can you call it so, when it comes neither as the result of delirium from any disease, nor of intoxication from drinking, nor as an illusion produced by various sorts of queer breathing exercises—but when it comes to a normal man in full possession of his health and wits? Then again, this experience is in perfect harmony with the Vedas. It also coincides with the words of realisation of the inspired Rishis and Âchâryas of old. Do you take me, at last, to be a crack-brained man? (smiling).

Disciple: Oh, no, I did not mean that of course. When there are to be found hundreds of illustrations about such realisation of Oneness in the Shastras, and when you say that it can be as directly realised as a fruit in the palm of one's hand, and when it has been your own personal experience in life, perfectly coinciding with the words of the Vedas and other Shastras—how dare I say that it is false? Shri Shankaracharya also realising that state has said, "Where is the universe vanished?" and so on.

Swamiji: Know—this knowledge of Oneness is what the Shastras speak of as realisation of the Brahman, by knowing which, one gets rid of fear, and the shackles of birth and death break for ever. Having once realised that Supreme Bliss, one is no more overwhelmed by pleasure and pain of this world. Men being fettered by base lust-and-wealth cannot enjoy that Bliss of Brahman.

Disciple: If it is so, and if we are really of the essence of the Supreme Brahman, then why do we not exert ourselves to gain that Bliss? Why do we again and again run into the jaws of death, being decoyed by this worthless snare of lust-and-wealth?

Swamiji: You speak as if man does not desire to have that Bliss! Ponder over it, and you will see that whatever anyone is doing, he is doing in the hope of gaining that Supreme Bliss. Only, not everyone is conscious of it and so cannot understand it. That Supreme Bliss fully exists in all, from Brahmâ down to the blade of grass. You are also that undivided Brahman. This very moment you can realise if you think yourself truly and absolutely to be so. It is all mere want of direct perception. That you have taken service and work so hard for the sake of your wife also shows that the aim is ultimately to attain to that Supreme Bliss of Brahman. Being again and again entangled in the intricate maze of delusion and hard hit by sorrows and afflictions, the eye will turn of itself to one's own real nature, the Inner Self. It is owing to the presence of this desire for bliss in the heart, that man, getting hard shocks one after another, turns his eye inwards—to his own Self. A time is sure to come to everyone, without exception, when he will do so to one it may be in this life, to another, after thousands of incarnations.

Disciple: It all depends upon the blessings of the Guru and the grace of the Lord!

Swamiji: The wind of grace of the Lord is blowing on, for ever and ever. You just need to spread your sail. Whenever you do anything, do it with your whole heart concentrated on it. Think day and night, "I am of the essence of that Supreme Existence-Knowledge-Bliss—what fear and anxiety have I? This body, mind, and intellect are all transient, and That which is beyond these is myself."

Disciple: Thoughts like these come only for a while now and then, but quickly vanish, and I think all sorts of trash and nonsense.

Swamiji: It happens like that in the initial stage, but gradually it is overcome. But from the beginning, intensity of desire in the mind is needed. Think always, "I am ever-pure, ever-knowing, and ever-free; how can I do anything evil? Can I ever be befooled like ordinary men with the insignificant charms of lust and wealth?" Strengthen the mind with such thoughts. This will surely bring real good.

Disciple: Once in a while strength of mind comes. But then again I think that if I would appear at the Deputy Magistrateship Examination, wealth and name and fame would come and I should live well and happy

Swamiji: Whenever such thoughts come in the mind, discriminate within yourself between the real and the unreal. Have you not read the Vedanta? Even when you sleep, keep the sword of discrimination at the head of your bed, so that covetousness cannot approach you even in dream. Practising such strength, renunciation will gradually come, and then you will see—the portals of heaven are wide open to you.

Disciple: If it is so, Swamiji, how is it then that the texts on Bhakti say that too much of renunciation kills the feelings that make for tenderness?

Swamiji: Throw away, I say, texts which teach things like that! Without renunciation, without burning dispassion for sense-objects, without turning away from wealth and lust as from filthy abomination— न सिध्यति ब्रह्मशतान्तरेऽपि—never can one attain salvation even in hundreds of Brahma's cycles". Repeating the names of the Lord, meditation, worship, offering libations in sacred fire, penance—all these are for bringing forth renunciation. One who has not gained renunciation, know his efforts to be like unto those of the man who is pulling at the oars all the while that the boat is at anchor. "न प्रजया धनेन त्यागेनेके अमृतत्वमानशुः—neither by progeny nor by wealth, but by renunciation alone some (rare ones) attained immortality" (Kaivalya Upanishad, 3).

Disciple: Will mere renouncing of wealth and lust accomplish everything?

Swamiji: There are other hindrances on the path even after renouncing those two; then, for example, comes name and fame. Very few men, unless of exceptional strength, can keep their balance under that. People shower honours upon them, and various enjoyments creep in by degrees. It is owing to this that three-fourths of the Tyâgis are debarred from further progress! For establishing this Math and other things, who knows but that I may have to come back again!

Disciple: If you say things like that, then we are undone!

Swamiji: What fear? "अभीरभीरभी—Be fearless, be fearless, be fearless!" You have seen Nâg Mahâshaya how even while living the life of a householder, he is more than a Sannyâsin! This is very uncommon; I have rarely seen one like him. If anyone wants to be a householder, let him be like Nag Mahashaya. He shines like a brilliant luminary in the spiritual firmament of East Bengal. Ask the people of that part of the country to visit him often; that will do much good to them.

Disciple: Nag Mahashaya, it seems, is the living personification of humility in the play of Shri Ramakrishna's divine drama on earth.

Swamiji: Decidedly so, without a shadow of doubt! I have a wish to go and see him once. Will you go with, me? I love to see fields flooded over with water in the rains. Will you write to him?

Disciple: Certainly I will. He is always mad with joy when he hears about you, and says that East Bengal will be sanctified into a place of pilgrimage by the dust of your feet.

Swamiji: Do you know, Shri Ramakrishna used to speak of Nag Mahashaya as a "flaming fire"?

Disciple: Yes, so I have heard.

At the request of Swamiji, the disciple partook of some Prasâda (consecrated food), and left for Calcutta late in the evening; he was deeply thinking over the message of fearlessness that he had heard from the lips of the inspired teacher—"I am free!" "I am free!"

Renunciation of Kama-kanchana—God's Mercy Falls on Those Who Struggle for Realisation—Unconditional Mercy and Brahman Are One

Disciple: Shri Ramakrishna used to say, Swamiji, that a man cannot progress far towards religious realisation unless he first relinquishes Kâma-Kânchana (lust and greed). If so, what will become of householders? For their whole minds are set on these two things.

Swamiji: It is true that the mind can never turn to God until the desire for lust and wealth has gone from it, be the man a householder or a Sannyâsin. Know this for a fact, that as long as the mind is caught in these, so long true devotion, firmness,

and Shraddhâ (faith) can never come.

Disciple: Where will the householders be, then? What way are they to follow?

Swamiji: To satisfy our smaller desires and have done with them for ever, and to relinquish the greater ones by discrimination—that is the way. Without renunciation God can never be realised—यदि ब्रह्मा स्वयं वदेत्—even if Brahmâ himself enjoined otherwise!

Disciple: But does renunciation of everything come as soon as one becomes a monk?

Swamiji: Sannyasins are at least struggling to make themselves ready for renunciation, whereas householders are in this matter like boatmen who work at their oars while the boat lies at anchor. Is the desire for enjoyment ever appeased? "भूय एवाभिवर्धते—It increases ever and ever" (Bhâgavata, IX. xix. 14).

Disciple: Why? May not world-weariness come, after enjoying the objects of the senses over and over for a long time?

Swamiji: To how many does that come? The mind becomes tarnished by constant contact with the objects of the senses and receives a permanent moulding and impress from them. Renunciation, and renunciation alone, is the real secret, the Mulamantra, of all Realisation.

Disciple: But there are such injunctions of the seers in the scriptures as these: "गृहेषु पञ्चेन्द्रयनिग्रहस्तप:—To restrain the five senses while living with one's wife and children is Tapas." "निवृत्ततरागस्य गृहं तपोवनम्—For him whose desires are under control, living in the midst of his family is the same as retiring into a forest for Tapasya."

Swamiji: Blessed indeed are those who can renounce Kama-Kanchana, living in their homes with their family! But how many can do that?

Disciple: But then, what about the Sannyasins? Are they all able to relinquish lust and love for riches fully?

Swamiji: As I said just now, Sannyasins are on the path of renunciation, they have taken the field, at least, to fight for the goal; but householders, on the other hand, having no knowledge as yet of the danger that comes through lust and greed, do not even attempt to realise the Self; that they must struggle to get rid of these is an idea that has not yet entered their minds.

Disciple: But many of them are struggling for it.

Swamiji: Oh, yes, and those who are doing so will surely renounce by degrees; their inordinate attachment for Kama-Kanchana will diminish gradually. But for those who procrastinate, saying, "Oh, not so soon! I shall do it when the time comes", Self-realisation is very far off. "Let me realise the Truth this moment! In this very life!"—these are the words of a hero. Such heroes are ever ready to renounce the very next moment, and to such the scripture (Jâbâla Upanishad, 3.) says, "यदहरेव विरजेत् तदहरेव प्रव्रजेत्— The moment you feel disgust for the vanities of the world, leave it all and take to the life of a monk."

Disciple: But was not Shri Ramakrishna wont to say, "All these attachments vanish through the grace of God when one prays to Him?"

Swamiji: Yes, it is so, no doubt, through His mercy, but one needs to be pure first before one can receive this mercy—pure in thought, word, and deed; then it is that His grace descends on one.

Disciple: But of what necessity is grace to him who can control himself in thought, word, and deed? For then he would be able to develop himself in the path of spirituality by means of his own exertions!

Swamiji: The Lord is very merciful to him whom He sees struggling heart and soul for Realisation. But remain idle, without any struggle, and you will see that His grace will never come.

Disciple: Everyone longs to be good, yet the mind for some inscrutable reasons, turns to evil! Does not everyone wish to be good—to be perfect —to realise God?

Swamiji: Know them to be already struggling who desire this. God bestows His mercy when this struggle is maintained.

Disciple: In the history of the Incarnations, we find many persons who, we should say, had led very dissipated lives and yet were able to realise God without much trouble and without performing any Sâdhanâ or devotion. How is this accounted for?

Swamiji: Yes, but a great restlessness must already have come upon them; long enjoyment of the objects of the senses must already have created in them deep disgust. Want of peace must have been consuming their very hearts. So deeply they had already felt this void in their hearts that life even for a moment had seemed unbearable to them unless they could gain that peace which follows in the train of the Lord's mercy. So God was kind to them. This development took place in them direct from Tamas to Sattva.

Disciple: Then, whatever was the path, they may be said to have realised God truly in that way?

Swamiji: Yes, why not? But is it not better to enter into a mansion by the main entrance than by its doorway of dishonour?

Disciple: No doubt that is true. Yet, the point is established that through mercy alone one can realise God.

Swamiji: Oh, yes, that one can, but few indeed are there who do so!

Disciple: It appears to me that those who seek to realise God by restraining their senses and renouncing lust and wealth hold to the (free-will) theory of self-exertion and self-help; and that those who take the name of the Lord and depend on Him are made free by the Lord Himself of all worldly attachments, and led by Him to the supreme stage of realisation.

Swamiji: True, those are the two different standpoints, the former held by the Jnânis, and the latter by the Bhaktas. But the ideal of renunciation is the keynote of both.

Disciple: No doubt about that! But Shri Girish Chandra Ghosh[1] once said to me that there could be no condition in God's mercy; there could be no law for it! If there were, then it could no longer be termed mercy. The realm of grace or mercy must transcend all law.

Swamiji: But there must be some higher law at work in the sphere alluded to by G. C. of which we are ignorant. Those are words, indeed, for the last stage of development, which alone is beyond time, space, and causation. But, when we get there, who will be merciful, and to whom, where there is no law of causation? There the worshipper and the worshipped, the meditator and the object of meditation, the knower and the known, all become one—call that Grace or Brahman, if you will. It is all one uniform homogeneous entity!

Disciple: Hearing these words from you, Swamiji, I have come to understand the essence of all philosophy and religion (Vedas and Vedanta); it seems as if I had hitherto been living in the midst of high-sounding words without any meaning.

Doctrine of Ahimsa and Meat-Eating—Sattva, Rajas, Tamas in Man—Food And Spirituality— 'Âhâra'—Three Defects in Food—Don't-Touchism and Caste-Prejudices—Restoring the Old Chaturvarnya and the Laws of the Rishis

Disciple: Pray, Swamiji, do tell me if there is any relation between the discrimination of food taken and the development of spirituality in man.

Swamiji: Yes, there is, more or less.

Disciple: Is it proper or necessary to take fish and meat?

Swamiji: Ay, take them, my boy! And if there be any harm in doing so, I will take care of that. Look at the masses of our country! What a look of sadness on their faces and want of courage and enthusiasm in their hearts, with large stomachs and no strength in their hands and feet—a set of cowards frightened at every trifle!

Disciple: Does the taking of fish and meat give strength? Why do Buddhism and Vaishnavism preach "अहिंसा परमो धर्मः—Non-killing is the highest virtue"?

Swamiji: Buddhism and Vaishnavism are not two different things. During the decline of Buddhism in India, Hinduism took from her a few cardinal tenets of conduct and made them her own, and these have now come to be known as Vaishnavism. The Buddhist tenet, "Non-killing is supreme virtue", is very good, but in trying to enforce it upon all by legislation without paying any heed to the capacities of the people at large, Buddhism has brought ruin upon India. I have come across many a "religious heron"[2] in India, who fed

1. The great Bengali actor-dramatist, a staunch devotee of Shri Ramakrishna.

2. Meaning, religious hypocrite. The heron, so the story goes, gave it out to the fishes that he had forsaken his old habit of catching fish and turned highly religious. So he took his stand on the brink of the water

ants with sugar, and at the same time would not hesitate to bring ruin on his own brother for the sake of "filthy lucre"!

Disciple: But in the Vedas as well as in the laws of Manu, there are injunctions to take fish and meat.

Swamiji: Ay, and injunctions to abstain from killing as well. For the Vedas enjoin, "मा हिंस्यात् सर्वभूतानि—Cause no injury to any being"; Manu also says, "निवृत्तिस्तु महाफला—Cessation of desire brings great results." Killing and non-killing have both been enjoined, according to the individual capacity, or fitness and adaptability on those who will observe the one practice or the other.

Disciple: It is the fashion here nowadays to give up fish and meat as soon as one takes to religion, and to many it is more sinful not to do so than to commit such great sins as adultery. How, do you think, such notions came into existence?

Swamiji: What's the use of your knowing how they came, when you see clearly, do you not, that such notions are working ruin to our country and our society? Just see—the people of East Bengal eat much fish, meat, and turtle, and they are much healthier than those of this part of Bengal. Even the rich men of East Bengal have not yet taken to Loochis or Châpâtis at night, and they do not suffer from acidity and dyspepsia like us. I have heard that in the villages of East Bengal the people have not the slightest idea of what dyspepsia means!

Disciple: Quite so, Swamiji. We never complain of dyspepsia in our part of the country. I first heard of it after coming to these parts. We take fish with rice, mornings and evenings.

Swamiji: Yes, take as much of that as you can, without fearing criticism. The country has been flooded with dyspeptic Bâbâjis living on vegetables only. That is no sign of Sattva, but of deep Tamas—the shadow of death. Brightness in the face, undaunted enthusiasm in the heart, and tremendous activity—these result from Sattva; whereas idleness, lethargy, inordinate attachment, and sleep are the signs of Tamas.

Disciple: But do not fish and meat increase Rajas in man?

Swamiji: That is what I want you to have. Rajas is badly needed just now! More than ninety per cent of those whom you now take to be men with the Sattva, quality are only steeped in the deepest Tamas. Enough, if you find one-sixteenth of them to be really Sâttvika! What we want now is an immense awakening of Râjasika energy, for the whole country is wrapped in the Râjasika of Tamas. The people of this land must be fed and clothed—must be awakened —must be made more fully active. Otherwise they will become inert, as inert as trees and stones. So, I say, eat large quantities of fish and meat, my boy!

Disciple: Does a liking for fish and meat remain when one has fully developed the Sattva quality?

Swamiji: No, it does not. All liking for fish and meat disappears when pure Sattva is highly developed, and these are the signs of its manifestation in a soul: sacrifice of everything and feigned to be meditating, while in reality he was always hatching his opportunity to catch the unwary fish.

for others, perfect non-attachment to lust and wealth, want of pride and egotism. The desire for animal food goes when these things are seen in a man. And where such indications are absent, and yet you find men sidings with the non-killing party, know it for a certainty that herein, there is either hypocrisy or a show of religion. When you yourself come to that stage of pure Sattva, give up fish and meat, by all means.

Disciple: In the Chhândogya Upanishad (VII. xxvi. 2) there is this passage, "आहारशुद्धौ सत्त्वशुद्धिः—Through pure food the Sattva quality in a man becomes pure."

Swamiji: Yes, I know. Shankarâchârya has said that the word Âhâra there means "objects of the senses", whereas Shri Râmânuja has taken the meaning of Ahara to be "food". In my opinion we should take that meaning of the word which reconciles both these points of view. Are we to pass our lives discussing all the time about the purity and impurity of food only, or are we to practice the restraining of our senses? Surely, the restraining of the senses is the main object; and the discrimination of good and bad, pure and impure foods, only helps one, to a certain extent, in gaining that end. There are, according to our scriptures, three things which make food impure: (1) Jâti-dosha or natural defects of a certain class of food, like onions, garlic, etc.; (2) Nimitta-dosha or defects arising from the presence of external impurities in it, such as dead insects, dust, etc. that attach to sweetmeats bought from shops; (3) Âshraya-dosha or defects that arise by the food coming from evil sources, as when it has been touched and handled by wicked persons. Special care should be taken to avoid the first and second classes of defects. But in this country men pay no regard just to these two, and go on fighting for the third alone, the very one that none but a Yogi could really discriminate! The country from end to end is being bored to extinction by the cry, "Don't touch", "Don't touch", of the non-touchism party. In that exclusive circle of theirs, too, there is no discrimination of good and bad men, for their food may be taken from the hands of anyone who wears a thread round his neck and calls himself a Brâhmin! Shri Ramakrishna was quite unable to take food in this indiscriminate way from the hands of any and all. It happened many a time that he would not accept food touched by a certain person or persons, and on rigorous investigation it would turn out that these had some particular stain to hide. Your religion seems nowadays to be confined to the cooking-pot alone. You put on one side the sublime truths of religion and fight, as they say, for the skin of the fruit and not for the fruit itself!

Disciple: Do you mean, then, that we should eat the food handled by anyone and everyone?

Swamiji: Why so? Look here. You being Brahmin of a certain class, say, of the Bhattâcharya class, why should you not eat rice cooked by Brahmins of all classes? Why should you, who belong to the Rârhi section, object to taking rice cooked by a Brahmin of the Barendra section, or why should a Barendra object to taking your rice? Again, why should not the other subcastes in the west and south of India, e.g. the Marathi, Telangi, Kanouji, do the same? Do you not see that hundreds of Brahmins and Kâyasthas in Bengal now go secretly to eat dainties in public restaurants, and when they come out of those places pose as leaders of society and frame rules to support don't-touchism. Must our society really be guided by laws dictated by such hypocrites? No, I say. On the contrary we must turn them out. The laws laid down by the great Rishis of old must be brought back and be made to rule supreme once more. Then alone can national well-being be ours.

Disciple: Then, do not the laws laid down by the Rishis rule and guide our present society?

Swamiji: Vain delusion! Where indeed is that the case nowadays? Nowhere have I found the laws of the Rishis current in India, even when during my travels I searched carefully and thoroughly. The blind and not unoften meaningless customs sanctioned by the peoples local prejudices and ideas, and the usages and ceremonials prevalent amongst women, are what really govern society everywhere! How many care to read the Shâstras or to lead society according to their ordinances after careful study?

Disciple: What are we to do, then?

Swamiji: We must revive the old laws of the Rishis. We must initiate the whole people into the codes of our old Manu and Yâjnavalkya, with a few modifications here and there to adjust them to the changed circumstances of the time. Do you not see that nowhere in India now are the original four castes (Châturvarnya) to be found? We have to redivide the whole Hindu population, grouping it under the four main castes, of Brahmins, Kshatriyas, Vaishyas, and Shudras, as of old. The numberless modern subdivisions of the Brahmins that split them up into so many castes, as it were, have to be abolished and a single Brahmin caste to be made by uniting them all. Each of the three remaining castes also will have to be brought similarly into single groups, as was the case in Vedic times. Without this will the Motherland be really benefited by your simply crying as you do nowadays, "We won't touch you!; We won't take him back into our caste!"? Never, my boy!

UNTITLED CONVERSATION I

The disciple is Sharatchandra Chakravarty, who published his records in a Bengali book, Swami-Shishya-Samvâda, in two parts. The present series of "Conversations and Dialogues" is a revised translation from this book. Five dialogues of this series have already appeared in the Vol. V.

Place: Calcutta, the house of the late Babu Priyanath Mukhopadhyaya, Baghbazar.

Year: 1897.

It is three or four days since Swamiji has set his foot in Calcutta (On February 20, 1897.) after his first return from the West. The joy of the devotees of Shri Ramakrishna knows no bounds at enjoying his holy presence after a long time. And the well-to-do among them are considering themselves blessed to cordially invite Swamiji to their own houses. This afternoon Swamiji had an invitation to the house of Srijut Priyanath Mukhopadhyaya, a devotee of Shri Ramakrishna, at Rajballabhpara in Baghbazar. Receiving this news, many devotees assembled today in his house.

The disciple also, informed of it through indirect sources, reached the house of Mr. Mukherjee at about 2-30 p.m. He had not yet made his acquaintance with Swamiji. So this was to be his first meeting with the Swami.

On the disciple's reaching there, Swami Turiyananda took him to Swamiji and introduced him. After his return to the Math, the Swami had already heard about him, having read a Hymn on Shri Ramakrishna composed by the disciple.

Swamiji also had come to know that the disciple used to visit Nâg Mahâshaya, a foremost devotee of Shri Ramakrishna[1].

When the disciple prostrated himself before him and took his seat, Swamiji addressed him in Sanskrit and asked him about Nag Mahashaya and his health, and while referring to his superhuman renunciation, his unbounded love for God, and his humility, he said:

"वयं तत्त्वान्वेषात् हता मधुकर त्वं खलु कृती।"

(Words addressed by King Dushyanta to the bee which was teasing Shakuntalâ by darting at her lips—Kalidasa's Shâkuntalam.)

—"We are undone by our vain quest after reality; while, O bee, you are indeed blessed with success!" He then asked the disciple to send these words to Nag Mahashaya. Afterwards, finding it rather inconvenient to talk to the disciple in the crowd, he called him and Swami Turiyananda to a small room to the west and, addressing himself to the disciple, began to recite these words from the Vivekachudâmani (43):

मा भैष्ट वद्विद्वंस्तव नास्त्यपायः
संसारसिन्धोस्तरणेऽस्त्युपायः।
येनैव याता यतयोऽस्य पारं
तमेव मार्गं तव निर्दिशामि॥

—"O wise one, fear not; you have not to perish. Means there are for crossing the ocean of this round of birth and death. I shall show you the same way by which holy men of renunciation have crossed this ocean." He then asked him to read Âchârya Shankara's work named Vivekachudâmani.

At these words, the disciple went on musing within himself. Was the Swami in this way hinting at the desirability of his own formal initiation? The disciple was at that time a staunch orthodox man in his ways, and a Vedantin. He had not yet settled his mind as regards the adoption of a Guru and was a devoted advocate of Varnâshrama or caste ordinances.

While various topics were going on, a man came in and an-

1. Durgacharan Nag, the great saint and perfected soul, living as a householder, who wonderfully reflected in his life—in many of its phases—the greatness of the Master, Shri Ramakrishna.

nounced that Mr. Narendranath Sen, the Editor of the Mirror, had come for an interview with Swamiji. Swamiji asked the bearer of this news to show him into that small room. Narendra Babu came and taking a seat there introduced various topics about England and America. In answer to his questions Swamiji said, "Nowhere in the world is to be found another nation like the Americans, so generous, broad-minded, hospitable, and so sincerely eager to accept new ideas." "Wherever work", he went on, "has been done in America has not been done through my power. The people of America have accepted the ideas of Vedanta, because they are so good-hearted." Referring to England he said, "There is no nation in the world so conservative as the English. They do not like so easily to accept any new idea, but if through perseverance they can be once made to understand any idea, they will never give it up by any means. Such firm determination you will find in no other nation. This is why they occupy the foremost position in the world in power and civilization."

Then declaring that if qualified preachers could be had, there was greater likelihood of the Vedanta work being permanently established in England than in America, he continued, "I have only laid the foundation of the work. If future preachers follow my path, a good deal of work may be done in time."

Narendra Babu asked, "What future prospect is there for us in preaching religion in this way?"

Swamiji said: "In our country there is only this religion of Vedanta. Compared with the Western civilisation, it may be said, we have hardly got anything else. But by the preaching of this universal religion of Vedanta, a religion which gives equal rights to acquire spirituality to men of all creeds and all paths of religious practice, the civilised West would come to know what a wonderful degree of spirituality once developed in India and how that is still existing. By the study of this religion, the Western nations will have increasing regard and sympathy for us. Already these have grown to some extent. In this way, if we have their real sympathy and regard, we would learn from them the sciences bearing on our material life, thereby qualifying ourselves better for the struggle for existence. On the other hand, by learning this Vedanta from us, they will be enabled to secure their own spiritual welfare."

Narendra Babu asked, "Is there any hope of our political progress in this kind of interchange?"

Swamiji said, "They (the Westerners) are the children of the great hero Virochana![1] Their power makes the five elements play like puppets in their hands. If you people believe that we shall in case of conflict with them gain freedom by applying those material forces, you are profoundly mistaken. Just as a little piece of stone figures before the Himalayas, so we differ from them in point of skill in the use of those forces. Do you

know what my idea is? By preaching the profound secrets of the Vedanta religion in the Western world, we shall attract the sympathy and regard of these mighty nations, maintaining for ever the position of their teacher in spiritual matters, and they will remain our teachers in all material concerns. The day when, surrendering the spiritual into their hands, our countrymen would sit at the feet of the West to learn religion, that day indeed the nationality of this fallen nation will be dead and gone for good. Nothing will come of crying day and night before them, 'Give me this or give me that.' When there will grow a link of sympathy and regard between both nations by this give-and-take intercourse, there will be then no need for these noisy cries. They will do everything of their own accord. I believe that by this cultivation of religion and the wider diffusion of Vedanta, both this country and the West will gain enormously. To me the pursuit of politics is a secondary means in comparison with this. I will lay down my life to carry out this belief practically. If you believe in any other way of accomplishing the good of India, well, you may go on working your own way."

Narendra Babu shortly left, expressing his unqualified agreement with Swamiji's ideas. The disciple, hearing the above words from Swamiji, astonishingly contemplated his luminous features with steadfast gaze.

When Narendra Babu had departed, an enthusiastic preacher belonging to the society for the protection of cows came for an interview with Swamiji. He was dressed almost like a Sannyasin, if not fully so—with a Geruâ turban on the head; he was evidently an up-country Indian. At the announcement of this preacher of cow-protection Swamiji came out to the parlour room. The preacher saluted Swamiji and presented him with a picture of the mother-cow. Swamiji took that in his hand and, making it over to one standing by, commenced the following conversation with the preacher:

Swamiji: What is the object of your society ?

Preacher: We protect the mother-cows of our country from the hands of the butcher. Cow-infirmaries have been founded in some places where the diseased, decrepit mother-cows or those bought from the butchers are provided for.

Swamiji: That is very good indeed. What is the source of your income?

Preacher: The work of the society is carried on only by gifts kindly made by great men like you.

Swamiji: What amount of money have you now laid by?

Preacher: The Marwari traders' community are the special supporters of this work. They have given a big amount for this good cause.

Swamiji: A terrible famine has now broken out in Central India. The Indian Government has published a death-roll of nine lakhs of starved people. Has your society done anything to render help in this time of famine?

Preacher: We do not help during famine or other distresses. This society has been established only for the protection of

---

1. In ancient Indian tradition Virochana was the first great king of the Asuras, possessing supernatural powers. Recent investigations in Assyrian mythology prove the existence of a tradition in Assyrian history about such a king, called Berosus in certain ancient generalogies.

Lectures & Discourses by Swami Vivekananda

mother-cows.

Swamiji: During a famine when lakhs of people, your own brothers and sisters, have fallen into the jaws of death, you have not thought it your duty, though having the means, to help them in that terrible calamity with food!

Preacher: No. This famine broke out as a result of men's Karma, their sins. It is a case of "like Karma, like fruit".

Hearing the words of the preacher, sparks of fire, as it were, scintillated in Swamiji's large eyes; his face became flushed. But he suppressed his feeling and said: "Those associations which do not feel sympathy for men and, even seeing their own brothers dying from starvation, do not give them a handful of rice to save their lives, while giving away piles of food to save birds and beasts, I have not the least sympathy for, and I do not believe that society derives any good from them. If you make a plea of Karma by saying that men die through their Karma, then it becomes a settled fact that it is useless to try or struggle for anything in this world; and your work for the protection of animals is no exception. With regard to your cause also, it can be said—the mother-cows through their own Karma fall into the hands of the butchers and die, and we need not do anything in the matter."

The preacher was a little abashed and said: "Yes, what you say is true, but the Shâstras say that the cow is our mother."

Swamiji smilingly said, "Yes, that the cow is our mother, I understand: who else could give birth to such accomplished children?"

The up-country preacher did not speak further on the subject; perhaps he could not understand the point of Swamiji's poignant ridicule. He told Swamiji that he was begging something of him for the objects of the society.

Swamiji: I am a Sannyasin, a fakir. Where shall I find money enough to help you? But if ever I get money in my possession, I shall first spend that in the service of man. Man is first to be saved; he must be given food, education, and spirituality. If any money is left after doing all these, then only something would be given to your society.

At these words, the preacher went away after saluting Swamiji. Then Swamiji began to speak to us: "What words, these, forsooth! Says he that men are dying by reason of their Karma, so what avails doing any kindness to them! This is decisive proof that the country has gone to rack and ruin! Do you see how much abused the Karma theory of your Hinduism has been? Those who are men and yet have no feeling in the heart for man, well, are such to be counted as men at all?" While speaking these words, Swamiji's whole body seemed to shiver in anguish and grief.

Then, while smoking, Swamiji said to the disciple, "Well, see me again."

Disciple: Where will you be staying, sir? Perhaps you might put up in some rich man's house. Will he allow me there?

Swamiji: At present, I shall be living either at the Alambazar Math or at the garden-house of Gopal Lal Seal at Cossipore. You may come to either place.

Disciple: Sir, I very much wish to speak with you in solitude.

Swamiji: All right. Come one night. We shall speak plenty of Vedanta.

Disciple: Sir, I have heard that some Europeans and Americans have come with you. Will they not get offended at my dress or my talk?

Swamiji: Why, they are also men, and moreover they are devoted to the Vedanta religion. They will be glad to converse with you.

Disciple: Sir, Vedanta speaks of some distinctive qualifications for its aspirants; how could these come out in your Western disciples? The Shastras say—he who has studied the Vedas and the Vedanta, who has formally expiated his sins, who has performed all the daily and occasional duties enjoined by the scriptures, who is self-restrained in his food and general conduct, and specially he who is accomplished in the four special Sâdhanâs (preliminary disciplines), he alone has a right to the practice of Vedanta. Your Western disciples are in the first place non-Brahmins, and then they are lax in point of proper food and dress; how could they understand the system of Vedanta?

Swamiji: When you speak with them, you will know at once whether they have understood Vedanta or not.

Swamiji, perhaps, could now see that the disciple was rigidly devoted to the external observances of orthodox Hinduism. Swamiji then, surrounded by some devotees of Shri Ramakrishna, went over to the house of Srijut Balaram Basu of Baghbazar. The disciple bought the book Vivekachudamani at Bat-tala and went towards his own home at Darjipara.

UNTITLED CONVERSATION II

Translated from Bengali From the Diary of a Disciple

The disciple is Sharatchandra Chakravarty, who published his records in a Bengali book, Swami-Shishya-Samvâda, in two parts. The present series of "Conversations and Dialogues" is a revised translation from this book. Five dialogues of this series have already appeared in the Complete Works, Volume V.

Place: On the way from Calcutta to Cossipore and in the garden of the late Gopal Lal Seal.

Year: 1897.

Today Swamiji was taking rest at noon in the house of Srijut Girish Chandra Ghosh[2]. The disciple arriving there saluted him and found that Swamiji was just ready to go to the garden-house of Gopal Lal Seal. A carriage was waiting outside. He said to the disciple, "Well come with me." The disciple agreeing, Swamiji got up with him into the carriage and it started. When it drove up the Chitpur road, on see-

---

2. The famous actor and dramatist of Bengal and a foremost devotee of Shri Ramakrishna.

ing the Gangâ, Swamiji broke forth in a chant, self-involved: गङ्गातरङ्ग-रमणीय-जटा-कलापं etc.[1] The disciple listened in silent wonder to that wave of music, when after a short while, seeing a railway engine going towards the Chitpur hydraulic bridge, Swamiji said to the disciple, "Look how it goes majestically like a lion!" The disciple replied, "But that is inert matter. Behind it there is the intelligence of man working, and hence it moves. In moving thus, what credit is there for it?"

Swamiji: Well, say then, what is the sign of consciousness?

Disciple: Why, sir, that indeed is conscious which acts through intelligence.

Swamiji: Everything is conscious which rebels against nature: there, consciousness is manifested. Just try to kill a little ant, even it will once resist to save its life. Where there is struggle, where there is rebellion, there is the sign of life, there consciousness is manifested.

Disciple: Sir, can that test be applied also in the case of men and of nations?

Swamiji: Just read the history of the world and see whether it applies or not. You will find that excepting yours, it holds good in the case of all other nations. It is you only who are in this world lying prostrate today like inert matter. You have been hypnotised. From very old times, others have been telling you that you are weak, that you have no power, and you also, accepting that, have for about a thousand years gone on thinking, "We are wretched, we are good for nothing." (Pointing to his own body:) This body also is born of the soil of your country; but I never thought like that. And hence you see how, through His will, even those who always think us low and weak, have done and are still doing me divine honour. If you can think that infinite power, infinite knowledge and indomitable energy lie within you, and if you can bring out that power, you also can become like me.

Disciple: Where is the capacity in us for thinking that way, sir? Where is the teacher or preceptor who from our childhood will speak thus before us and make us understand? What we have heard and have learnt from all is that the object of having an education nowadays is to secure some good job.

Swamiji: For that reason is it that we have come forward with quite another precept and example. Learn that truth from us, understand it, and realise it and then spread that idea broadcast, in cities, in towns, and in villages. Go and preach to all, "Arise, awake, sleep no more; within each of you there is the power to remove all wants and all miseries. Believe this, and that power will be manifested." Teach this to all, and, with that, spread among the masses in plain language the central truths of science, philosophy, history, and geography. I have a plan to open a centre with the unmarried youths; first of all I shall teach them, and then carry on the work through them.

Disciple: But that requires a good deal of money. Where will you get this money?

Swamiji: What do you talk! Isn't it man that makes moneys Where did you ever hear of money making man? If you can make your thoughts and words perfectly at one, if you can, I say, make yourself one in speech and action, money will pour in at your feet of itself, like water.

Disciple: Well, sir, I take it for granted that money will come, and you will begin that good work. But what will that matter? Before this, also, many great men carried out many good deeds. But where are they now? To be sure, the same fate awaits the work which you are going to start. Then what is the good of such an endeavour?

Swamiji: He who always speculates as to what awaits him in future, accomplishes nothing whatsoever. What you have understood as true and good, just do that at once. What's the good of calculating what may or may not befall in future? The span of life is so, so short—and can anything be accomplished in it if you go on forecasting and computing results. God is the only dispenser of results; leave it to Him to do all that. What have you got to do with on working.

While he was thus going on, the cab reached the garden-house. Many people from Calcutta came to the garden that day to see Swamiji. Swamiji got down from the carriage, took his seat in the room, and began conversation with them all. Mr. Goodwin, a Western disciple of Swamiji, was standing near by, like the embodiment of service, as it were. The disciple had already made his acquaintance; so he came to Mr. Goodwin, and both engaged in a variety of talk about Swamiji.

In the evening Swamiji called the disciple and asked him, "Have you got the Katha Upanishad by heart?"

Disciple: No, sir, I have only read it with Shankara's commentary.

Swamiji: Among the Upanishads, one finds no other book so beautiful as this. I wish you would all get it by heart. What will it do only to read it? Rather try to bring into your life the faith, the courage, the discrimination, and the renunciation of Nachiketâ.

Disciple: Give your blessings, please, that I may realise these.

Swamiji: You have heard of Shri Ramakrishna's words, haven't you? He used to say, "The breeze of mercy is already blowing, do you only hoist the sail." Can anybody, my boy, thrust realization upon another? One's destiny is' in one's own hands—the Guru only makes this much understood. Through the power of the seed itself the tree grows, the air and water are only aids.

Disciple: There is, sir, the necessity also of extraneous help.

Swamiji: Yes, there is. But you should know that if there be no substance within, no amount of outside help will avail anything. Yet there comes a time for everyone to realise the Self. For everyone is Brahman. The distinction of higher and lower is only in the degree of manifestation of that Brahman. In time, everyone will have perfect manifestation. Hence the Shâstras say, "कालेनात्मनि विन्दति"—In time, That is realised in

1. From Vyâsa's Hymn to Vishvanâtha, meaning "whose matted locks look charming with the waves of the Ganga playing among them".

one's self."

Disciples When, alas, will that happen, sir? From the Shastras we hear how many births we have had to pass in ignorance!

Swamiji: What's the fear? When you have come here this time, the goal shall be attained in this life. Liberation or Samâdhi—all this consists in simply doing away with the obstacles to the manifestation of Brahman. Otherwise the Self is always shining forth like the sun. The cloud of ignorance has only veiled it. Remove the cloud and the sun will manifest. Then you get into the state of "भिद्यते हृदयग्रन्थिः" ("the knot of the heart is broken") etc. The various paths that you find, all advise you to remove the obstacles on the way. The way by which one realises the Self, is the way which he preached to all. But the goal of all is the knowledge of the Self, the realization of this Self. To it all men, all beings have equal right. This is the view acceptable to all.

Disciple: Sir, when I read or hear these words of the Shastras, the thought that the Self has not yet been realised makes the heart very disconsolate.

Swamiji: This is what is called longing. The more it grows the more will the cloud of obstacles be dispelled, and stronger will faith be established. Gradually the Self will be realised like a fruit on the palm of one's hand. This realisation alone is the soul of religion. Everyone can go on abiding by some observances and formalities. Everyone can fulfil certain injunctions and prohibitions but how few have this longing for realization! This intense longing—becoming mad after realising God or getting the knowledge of the Self—is real spirituality. The irresistible madness which the Gopis had for the Lord, Shri Krishna, yea, it is intense longing like that which is necessary for the realization of the Self! Even in the Gopis' mind there was a slight distinction of man and woman. But in real Self-knowledge, there is not the slightest distinction of sex.

While speaking thus, Swamiji introduced the subject of Gita-Govindam (of Jayadeva) and continued saying:

Jayadeva was the last poet in Sanskrit literature though he often cared more for the jingling of words than for depth of sentiment. But just see how the poet has shown the culmination of love and longing in the Shloka "पतति पतत्रे" etc.[2] Such love indeed is necessary for Self-realisation. There must be fretting and pining within the heart. Now from His playful life at Vrindaban come to the Krishna of Kurukshetra, and see how that also is fascinating—how, amidst all that horrible din and uproar of fighting, Krishna remains calm, balanced, and peaceful. Ay, on the very battlefield, He is speaking the Gita to Arjuna and getting him on to fight, which is the Dharma of a Kshatriya! Himself an agent to bring about this terrible warfare, Shri Krishna remains unattached to action—He did

not take up arms! To whichsoever phase of it you look, you will find the character of Shri Krishna perfect. As if He was the embodiment of knowledge, work, devotion, power of concentration, and everything! In the present age, this aspect of Shri Krishna should be specially studied. Only contemplating the Krishna of Vrindaban with His flute won't do nowadays—that will not bring salvation to humanity. Now is needed the worship of Shri Krishna uttering forth the lion-roar of the Gita, of Râma with His bow and arrows, of Mahâvira, of Mother Kâli. Then only will the people grow strong by going to work with great energy and will. I have considered the matter most carefully and come to the conclusion that of those who profess and talk of religion nowadays in this country, the majority are full of morbidity— crack-brained or fanatic. Without development of an abundance of Rajas, you have hopes neither in this world, nor in the next. The whole country is enveloped in intense Tamas; and naturally the result is—servitude in this life and hell in the next.

Disciple: Do you expect in view of the Rajas in the Westerners that they will gradually become Sâttvika?

Swamiji: Certainly. Possessed of a plenitude of Rajas, they have now reached the culmination of Bhoga, or enjoyment. Do you think that it is not they, but you, who are going to achieve Yoga—you who hang about for the sake of your bellies? At the sight of their highly refined enjoyment, the delineation in Meghaduta—"विद्युद्वनतं ललितवसनाः" etc.[3] —comes to my mind. And your Bhoga consists in lying on a ragged bed in a muggy room, multiplying progeny every year like a hog!—Begetting a band of famished beggars and slaves! Hence do I say, let people be made energetic and active in nature by the stimulation of Rajas. Work, work, work; "नान्यः पन्था विद्यतेऽयनाय"—There is no other path of liberation but this."

Disciple: Sir, did our forefathers possess this kind of Rajas?

Swamiji: Why, did they not? Does not history tell us that they established colonies in many countries, and sent preachers of religion to Tibet, China, Sumatra, and even to far-off Japan? Do you think there is any other means of achieving progress except through Rajas?

As conversation thus went on, night approached; and mean-

---

2. "पतति पतत्रे विचलति पत्रे शङ्कितभवदुपयानम् ।
रचयति शयनं सचकितनयनं पश्यति तव पन्थानम् ॥"

— "At the flying of a bird or the stirring of a leaf, she fancies you are coming; she arranges your bed with eyes all alert looking towards the way you would come."

3. विद्युद्वनतं ललितवसनाः सेन्द्रचापं सचित्राः
सङ्गीताय प्रहतमुरजाः स्निग्धगम्भीरघोषम् ।
अन्तस्तोयं मणिमयभुवस्तुङ्गमभ्रंलिहाग्रा:
प्रासादास्त्वां तुलयितुमलं यत्र तैस्तैर्विशेषैः ॥

— "The mansions of that city may well be compared with you, O cloud, there is correspondence in features: while flashes of lightning play within you, they have charmingly attired damsels moving within them; while you have the rainbow, they have their paintings; you have your deep, rolling rumble, they have their drums sounding forth music, you contain pellucid water within you, they have their interior bedecked with transparent gems; you soar so high, their roofs also kiss the sky" (Meghaduta, II. 1). Kalidasa thus introduces his description of the enjoyments of Alakâpuri. So the reference here is not only to the first verse quoted but also to the whole description which follows.

while Miss Müller came there. She was an English lady, having great reverence for Swamiji. Swamiji introduced the disciple to her, and after a short talk Miss Müller went upstairs.

Swamiji: See, to what a heroic nation they belong! How far-off is her home, and she is the daughter of a rich man—yet how long a way has she come, only with the hope of realising the spiritual ideal!

Disciple: Yes, sir, but your works are stranger still! How so many Western ladies and gentlemen are always eager to serve you! For this age, it is very strange indeed!

Swamiji: If this body lasts, you will see many more things. If I can get some young men of heart and energy, I shall revolutionize the whole country. There are a few in Madras. But I have more hope in Bengal. Such clear brains are to be found scarcely in any other country. But they have no strength in their muscles. The brain and muscles must develop simultaneously. Iron nerves with an intelligent brain—and the whole world is at your feet.

Word was brought that supper was ready for Swamiji. He said to the disciple, "Come and have a look at my food." While going on with the supper, he said, "It is not good to take much fatty or oily substance. Roti is better than Luchi. Luchi is the food of the sick. Take fish and meat and fresh vegetables, but sweets sparingly." While thus talking, he inquired, "Well, how many Rotis have I taken? Am I to take more? He did not remember how much he took and did not feel even it he yet had any appetite. The sense of body faded away so much while he was talking!

He finished after taking a little more. The disciple also took leave and went back to Calcutta. Getting no cab for hire, he had to walk; and while walking, he thought over in his mind how soon again he could come the next day to see Swamiji.

UNTITLED CONVERSATION III

Translated from Bengali From the Diary of a Disciple

The disciple is Sharatchandra Chakravarty, who published his records in a Bengali book, Swami-Shishya-Samvâda, in two parts. The present series of "Conversations and Dialogues" is a revised translation from this book. Five dialogues of this series have already appeared in the Complete Works, Volume V.

Place: Cossipore, at the garden of the late Gopal Lal Seal.

Year: 1897.

After his first return from the West, Swamiji resided for a few days at the garden of the late Gopal Lal Seal at Cossipore. Some well-known Pundits living at Barabazar, Calcutta, came to the garden one day with a view to holding a disputation with him. The disciple was present there on the occasion.

All the Pundits who came there could speak in Sanskrit fluently. They came and greeting Swamiji, who sat surrounded by a circle of visitors, began their conversation in Sanskrit. Swamiji also responded to them in melodious Sanskrit. The disciple cannot remember now the subject on which the Pundits argued with him that day. But this much he remembers that the Pundits, almost all in one strident voice, were rapping out to Swamiji in Sanskrit subtle questions of philosophy, and he, in a dignified serious mood, was giving out to them calmly his own well argued conclusions about those questions.

In the discussion with the Pundits Swamiji represented the side of the Siddhânta or conclusions to be established, while the Pundits represented that of the Purvapaksha or objections to be raised. The disciple remembers that, while arguing, Swamiji wrongly used in one place the word Asti instead of Svasti, which made the Pundits laugh out. At this, Swamiji at once submitted: पाखण्डितानां दासोऽहं कृपन्तवयमेतत् सखलनम्—I am but a servant of the Pundits, please excuse this mistake." The Pundits also were charmed at this humility of Swamiji. After a long dispute, the Pundits at last admitted that the conclusions of the Siddhanta side were adequate, and preparing to depart, they made their greetings to Swamiji.

After the Pundits had left, the disciple learnt from Swamiji that these Pundits who took the side of the Purvapaksha were well versed in the Purva-Mimâmsâ Shâstras, Swamiji advocated the philosophy of the Uttara-Mimâmsâ or Vedanta and proved to them the superiority of the path of knowledge, and they were obliged to accept his conclusions.

About the way the Pundits laughed at Swamiji, picking up one grammatical mistake, he said that this error of his was due to the fact of his not having spoken in Sanskrit for many years together. He did not blame the Pundits a bit for all that. But he pointed out in this connection that in the West it would imply a great incivility on the part of an opponent to point out any such slip in language, deviating from the real issue of dispute. A civilised society in such cases would accept the idea, taking no notice of the language. "But in your country, all the fighting is going on over the husk, nobody searches for the kernel within." So saying, Swamiji began to talk with the disciple in Sanskrit. The disciple also gave answers in broken Sanskrit. Yet Swamiji praised him for the sake of encouragement. From that day, at the request of Swamiji, the disciple used to speak with him in Sanskrit off and on.

In reply to the question, what is civilisation, Swamiji said that day: "The more advanced a society or nation is in spirituality, the more is that society or nation civilised. No nation can be said to have become civilised only because it has succeeded in increasing the comforts of material life by bringing into use lots of machinery and things of that sort. The present-day civilization of the West is multiplying day by day only the wants and distresses of men. On the other hand, the ancient Indian civilisation by showing people the way to spiritual advancement, doubtless succeeded, if not in removing once for all, at least in lessening, in a great measure, the material needs of men. In the present age, it is to bring into coalition both these civilisations that Bhagavan Shri Ramakrishna was born. In this age, as on the one hand people have to be intensely practical, so on the other hand they have to acquire deep spiritual knowledge." Swamiji made us clearly understand that day that from such interaction of the Indian civilization with that of the West would dawn on the world a new era. In the course of dilating upon this, he happened to remark in one place, "Well, another thing. People there in the West think that the more a man is religious, the more demure he must be in his outward bearing—no word about anything else from his lips! As the priests in the West would on the one hand be struck with wonder at my liberal religious discourses, they would be as much puzzled on the other hand when they found me, after such discourses, talking frivolities with my friends. Sometimes they would speak out to my face: 'Swami, you are a priest, you should not be joking and laughing in this way like ordinary men. Such levity does not look well in you.' To which I would reply, 'We are children of bliss, why should we look morose and sombre?' But I doubt if they could rightly catch the drift of my words."

That day Swamiji spoke many things about Bhâva Samâdhi and Nirvikalpa Samadhi as well. These are produced below as far as possible:

Suppose a man is cultivating that type of devotion to God which Hanumân represents. The more intense the attitude becomes, the more will the pose and demeanour of that aspirant, nay even his physical configuration, be cast in that would. It is in this way that transmutation of species takes place. Taking up any such emotional attitude, the worshipper becomes gradually shaped into the very form of his ideal. The ultimate stage of any such sentiment is called Bhava Samadhi. While the aspirant in the path of Jnana, pursuing the process of Neti, Neti, "not this, not this", such as "I am not the body, nor the mind, nor the intellect", and so on, attains to the Nirvikalpa Samadhi when he is established in absolute consciousness. It requires striving through many births to reach perfection or the ultimate stage with regard to a single one of these devotional attitudes. But Shri Ramakrishna, the king of the realm of spiritual sentiment, perfected himself in no less than eighteen different forms of devotion! He also used to say that his body would not have endured, had he not held himself on to this play of spiritual sentiment.

The disciple asked that day, "Sir, what sort of food did you use to take in the West?"

Swamiji: The same as they take there. We are Sannyasins and nothing can take away our caste!

On the subject of how he would work in future in this country, Swamiji said that day that starting two centres, one in Madras and another in Calcutta, he would rear up a new type of Sannyasins for the good of all men in all its phases. He further said that by a destructive method no progress either for the society or for the country could be achieved. In all ages and times progress has been effected by the constructive process, that is, by giving a new mould to old methods and customs. Every religious preacher in India, during the past ages, worked in that line. Only the religion of Bhagavan Buddha was destructive. Hence that religion has been extirpated from India.

The disciple remembers that while thus speaking on, he remarked, "If the Brahman is manifested in one man, thousands of men advance, finding their way out in that light. Only the knowers of Brahman are the spiritual teachers of mankind. This is corroborated by all scriptures and by reason too. It is only the selfish Brahmins who have introduced into this country the system of hereditary Gurus, which is against the Vedas and against the Shastras. Hence it is that even through their spiritual practice men do not now succeed in perfecting themselves or in realising Brahman. To remove all this corruption in religion, the Lord has incarnated Himself on earth in the present age in the person of Shri Ramakrishna. The universal teachings that he offered, if spread all over the world, will do good to humanity and the world. Not for many a century past has India produced so great, so wonderful, a teacher of religious synthesis."

A brother-disciple of Swamiji at that time asked him, "Why did you not publicly preach Shri Ramakrishna as an Avatâra in the West?"

Swamiji: They make much flourish and fuss over their science and philosophy. Hence, unless you first knock to pieces their intellectual conceit through reasoning, scientific argument, and philosophy, you cannot build anything there. Those who finding themselves off their moorings through their utmost intellectual reasoning would approach me in a real spirit of truth-seeking, to them alone, I would speak of Shri Ramakrishna. If, otherwise, I had forthwith spoken of the doctrine of incarnation, they might have said, "Oh, you do not say anything new—why, we have our Lord Jesus for all that!"

After thus spending some three or four delightful hours, the disciple came back to Calcutta that day along with the other visitors.

UNTITLED CONVERSATION IV

Translated from Bengali From the Diary of a Disciple

The disciple is Sharatchandra Chakravarty, who published his records in a Bengali book, Swami-Shishya-Samvâda, in two parts. The present series of "Conversations and Dialogues" is a revised translation from this book. Five dialogues of this series have already appeared in the Complete Works, Volume V.

Place: The Kali-temple at Dakshineswar and the Alambazar Math.

Year: 1897, March.

When Swamiji returned from England for the first time, the Ramakrishna Math was located at Alambazar. The birthday anniversary of Bhagavan Shri Ramakrishna was being celebrated this year at the Kali-temple of Rani Râsmani at Dakshineswar. Swamiji with some of his brother disciples reached there from the Alambazar Math at about 9 or 10 a.m. He was barefooted, with a yellow turban on his head. Crowds of people were waiting to see and hear him. In the temple of Mother Kali, Swamiji prostrated himself before the Mother of the Universe, and thousands of heads, following him, bent low. Then after prostrating himself before Râdhâkântaji he came into the room which Shri Ramakrishna used to occupy. There was not the least breathing space in the room.

Two European ladies who accompanied Swamiji to India attended the festival. Swamiji took them along with himself to show them the holy Panchavati and the Vilva tree.[1] Though the disciple was not yet quite familiar with Swamiji, he followed him, and presented him with the copy of a Sanskrit Ode about the Utsava (celebration) composed by himself. Swamiji read it while walking towards the Panchavati. And on the way he once looked aside towards the disciple and said, "Yes, it's done well. Attempt others like it."

The householder devotees of Shri Ramakrishna happened to be assembled on one side of the Panchavati, among whom was Babu Girish Chandra Ghosh. Swamiji, accompanied by a throng, came to Girish Babu and saluted him, saying, "Hello! here is Mr. Ghosh." Girish Babu returned his salutation with folded hands. Reminding Girish Babu of the old days, Swamiji said, "Think of it, Mr. Ghosh—from those days to these, what a transition!" Girish Babu endorsed Swamiji's sentiment and said, "Yes, that is true; but yet the mind longs to see more of it." After a short conversation, Swamiji proceeded towards the Vilva tree situated on the north-east of the Panchavati.

Now a huge crowd stood in keen expectancy to hear lecture from Swamiji. But though he tried his utmost, Swamiji could not speak louder than the noise and clamour of the people. Hence he had to give up attempting a lecture and left with the two European ladies to show them sites connected with Shri Ramakrishna's spiritual practices and introduce them to particular devotees and followers of the Master.

After 3 p.m. Swamiji said to the disciple, "Fetch me a cab, please; I must go to the Math now." The disciple brought one accordingly. Swamiji himself sat on one side and asked Swami Niranjanananda and the disciple to sit on the other and they drove towards the Alambazar Math. On the way, Swamiji said to the disciple, "It won't do to live on abstract ideas merely. These festivals and the like are also necessary; for then only, these ideas will spread gradually among the masses. You see, the Hindus have got their festivals throughout the year, and the secret of it is to infuse the great ideals of religion gradually into the minds of the people. It has also its drawback, though. For people in general miss their inner significance and become so much engrossed in externals that no sooner are these festivities over than they become their old selves again. Hence it is true that all these form the outer covering of religion, which in a way hide real spirituality and self-knowledge.

"But there are those who cannot at all understand in the abstract what 'religion' is or what the 'Self' is, and they try to realise spirituality gradually through these festivals and ceremonies. Just take this festival celebrated today; those that attended it will at least once think of Shri Ramakrishna. The thought will occur to their mind as to who he was, in whose name such a great crowd assembled and why so many people came at all in his name. And those who will not feel that much even, will come once in a year to see all the devotional dancing and singing, or at least to partake of the sacred food-offerings, and will also have a look at the devotees of Shri Ramakrishna. This will rather benefit them than do any harm."

Disciple: But, sir, suppose somebody thinks these festivals and ceremonies to be the only thing essential, can he possibly advance any further? They will gradually come down to the level of commonplace observances, like the worship in our country of (the goddesses) Shashthi, Mangala-chandi, and the like. People are found to observe these rites till death; but where do we find even one among them rising through such observances to the knowledge of Brahman?

Swamiji: Why? In India so many spiritual heroes were born, and did they not make them the means of scaling the heights of greatness? When by persevering in practice through these props they gained a vision of the Self, they ceased to be keen on them. Yet, for the preservation of social balance even great men of the type of Incarnations follow these observances.

Disciple: Yes, they may observe these for appearance only. But when to a knower of the Self even this world itself becomes unreal like magic, is it possible for him to recognise these external observances as true?

Swamiji: Why not? Is not our idea of truth also a relative one, varying in relation to time, place, and person? Hence all observances have their utility, relatively to the varying qualifications in men. It is just as Shri Ramakrishna used to say, that the mother cooks Polâo and Kâlia (rich dishes) for one son, and sago for another.

Now the disciple understood at last and kept quiet. Meanwhile the carriage arrived at the Alambazar Math. The disciple followed Swamiji into the Math where Swamiji, being thirsty, drank some water. Then putting off his coat, he rested recumbent on the blanket spread on the floor. Swami Niranjanananda, seated by his side, said, "We never had such a great crowd in any year's Utsava before! As if the whole of Calcutta flocked there!"

Swamiji: It was quite natural; stranger things will happen hereafter.

Disciple: Sir, in every religious sect are found to exist external festivals of some kind or other. But there is no amity between one sect and another in this matter. Even in the case of such a liberal religion as that of Mohammed, I have found in Dacca that the Shiâs and Sunnis go to loggerheads with each other.

Swamiji: That is incidental more or less wherever you have

---

1. Panchavati is a grove of five special trees arranged and grown to serve purposes of spiritual practice. The Vilva is also a holy tree of that sort.

sects. But do you know what the ruling sentiment amongst us is? — non-sectarianism. Our Lord was born to point that out. He would accept all forms, but would say withal that, looked at from the standpoint of the knowledge of Brahman, they were only like illusory Mâyâ.

Disciple: Sir, I can't understand your point. Sometimes it seems to me that, by thus celebrating these festivals, you are also inaugurating another sect round the name of Shri Ramakrishna. I have heard it from the lips of Nâg Mahâshaya that Shri Ramakrishna did not belong to any sect. He used to pay great respect to all creeds such as the Shâktas, the Vaishnavas, the Brahmos, the Mohammedans, and the Christians.

Swamiji: How do you know that we do not also hold in great esteem all the religious creeds?

So saying, Swamiji called out in evident amusement to Swami Niranjanananda: "Just think what this Bângâl[2] is saying!"

Disciple: Kindly make me understand, sir, what you mean.

Swamiji: Well, you have, to be sure, read my lectures. But where have I built on Shri Ramakrishna's name? It is only the pure Upanishadic religion that I have gone about preaching in the world.

Disciple: That's true, indeed. But what I find by being familiar with you is that you have surrendered yourself, body and soul, to Ramakrishna. If you have understood Shri Ramakrishna to be the Lord Himself, why not give it out to the people at large?

Swamiji: Well, I do preach what I have understood. And if you have found the Advaitic principles of Vedanta to be the truest religion, then why don't you go out and preach it to all men?

Disciple: But I must realise, before I can preach it to others. I have only studied Advaitism in books.

Swamiji: Good; realise first and then preach. Now, therefore, you have no right to say anything of the beliefs each man tries to live by. For you also proceed now by merely putting your faith on some such beliefs.

Disciple: True, I am also living now by believing in something; but I have the Shâstras for my authority. I do not accept any faith opposed to the Shastras.

Swamiji: What do you mean by the Shastras? If the Upanishads are authority, why not the Bible or the Zend-Avesta equally so?

Disciple: Granted these scriptures are also good authority, they are not, however, as old as the Vedas. And nowhere, moreover, is the theory of the Âtman better established than in the Vedas.

Swamiji: Supposing I admit that contention of yours, what right have you to maintain that truth can be found nowhere except in the Vedas?

2. This term as used of people hailing from East Bengal is too often supposed to have a ring of derision. But in the case of the disciple, it very easily and naturally grew to be a term of peculiar endearment. — Ed.

Disciple: Yes, truth may also exist in all the scriptures other than the Vedas, and I don't say anything to the contrary. But as for me, I choose to abide by the teachings of the Upanishads, for I have very great faith in them.

Swamiji: Quite welcome to do that, but if somebody else has "very great" faith in any other set of doctrines, surely you should allow him to abide by that. You will discover that in the long run both he and yourself will arrive at the same goal. For haven't you read in the Mahimnah-stotram, "त्वमसि पयसामर्णव इव — Thou art as the ocean to the rivers falling into it?"

UNTITLED CONVERSATION V

Translated from Bengali From the Diary of a Disciple

The disciple is Sharatchandra Chakravarty, who published his records in a Bengali book, Swami-Shishya-Samvâda, in two parts. The present series of "Conversations and Dialogues" is a revised translation from this book. Five dialogues of this series have already appeared in the Complete Works, Volume V.

Place: Alambazar Math.

Year: 1897, May.

It was the 19th Vaishâkha (April-May) of the year 1303 B.S. Swamiji had agreed to initiate the disciple today. So, early in the morning, he reached the Alambazar Math. Seeing the disciple Swamiji jocosely said, "Well, you are to be 'sacrificed' today, are you not?"

After this remark to the disciple, Swamiji with a smile resumed his talk with others about American subjects. And in due relevancy came along such topics also as how one-pointed in devotion one has to be in order to build up a spiritual life, how firm faith and strong devotion to the Guru have to be kept up, how deep reliance has to be placed on the words of the Guru, and how even one's life has to be laid down for his sake. Then putting some questions to the disciple, Swamiji began to test his heart: "Well, are you ready to do my bidding to your utmost, whatever it be and whenever it may come? If I ask you to plunge into the Ganga or to jump from the roof of a house, meaning it all for your good, could you do even that without any hesitations Just think of it even now; otherwise don't rush forward on the spur of the moment to accept me as your Guru." And the disciple nodded assent to all questions of the kind.

Swamiji then continued: "The real Guru is he who leads you beyond this Mâyâ of endless birth and death — who graciously destroys all the griefs and maladies of the soul. The disciple of old used to repair to the hermitage of the Guru, fuel in hand; and the Guru, after ascertaining his competence, would teach him the Vedas after initiation, fastening round his waist the threefold filament of Munja, a kind of grass, as the emblem of his vow to keep his body, mind, and speech in control. With the help of this girdle, the disciples used to tie up their Kaupinas. Later on, the custom of wearing the sacred thread superseded this girdle of Munja grass."

Disciple: Would you, then, say, sir, that the use of the holy thread we have adopted is not really a Vedic custom?

Swamiji: Nowhere is there mention of thread being so used in the Vedas. The modern author of Smritis, Raghunandana Bhattacharya, also puts it thus: "At this stage,[1] the sacrificial girdle should be put on." Neither in Gobhila's Grihya-Sutras do we find any mention of the girdle made of thread. In the Shâstras, this first Vedic Samskâra (purification ceremony) before the Guru has been called the Upanayana; but see, to what a sad pass our country has been brought! Straying away from the true path of the Shastras, the country has been overwhelmed with usages and observances originating in particular localities, or popular opinion, or with the womenfolk! That's why I ask you to proceed along the path of the Shastras as in olden times. Have faith within yourselves and thereby bring it back into the country. Plant in your heart the faith of Nachiketâ. Even go up to the world of Yama like him. Yes, if to know the secrets of the Atman, to liberate your soul, to reach the true solution of the mystery of birth and death, you have to go to the very jaws of death and realise the truth thereby, well, go there with an undaunted heart. It is fear alone that is death. You have to go beyond all fear. So from this day be fearless. Off at once, to lay down your life for your own liberation and for the good of others. What good is it carrying along a load of bones and flesh! Initiated into the Mantra of extreme self-sacrifice for the sake of God, go, lay down for others this body of flesh and bones like the Muni Dadhichi! Those alone, say the Shastras, are the real Gurus, who have studied the Vedas and the Vedanta, who are knowers of the Brahman, who are able to lead others beyond to fearlessness; when such are at hand, get yourself initiated, "no speculation in such a case". Do you know what has become of this principle now? — "like the blind leading the blind"!

* * *

The initiation ceremony was duly gone through in the chapel. After this Swamiji spoke out: "Give me the Guru-dakshinâ."[2] The disciple replied, "Oh, what shall I give?" On this Swamiji suggested, "Well, fetch any fruit from the store-room." So the disciple ran to the store-room and came back into the chapel with ten or twelve lichis. These Swamiji took from his hand and ate them one by one, saying, "Now, your Guru-dakshina is made."

A member of the Math, Brahmachâri (now Swami) Shuddhananda, also had his initiation from Swamiji on this occasion.

Swamiji then had his dinner and went to take a short rest.

After the siesta, he came and sat in the hall of the upper storey. The disciple finding this opportunity asked, "Sir, how and whence came the ideas of virtue and vice?"

Swamiji: It is from the idea of the manifold that these have evolved. The more a man advances towards oneness, the more ideas of "I" and "you" subside, ideas from which all these pairs of opposites such as virtue and vice have originated. When the idea that So-and-so is different from me comes to the mind, all other ideas of distinction begin to manifest, while with the complete realisation of oneness, no more grief or illusion remains for man, "तत्र को मोहः कः शोकः एकत्वमनुपश्यतः—For him who sees oneness, where is there any grief or any delusion?" Sin may be said to be the feeling of every kind of weakness. From this weakness spring jealousy, malice, and so forth. Hence weakness is sin. The Self within is always shining forth resplendent. Turning away from that people say "I", "I", "I", with their attention held up by this material body, this queer cage of flesh and bones. This is the root of all weakness. From that habit only, the relative outlook on life has emerged in this world. The absolute Truth lies beyond that duality.

Disciple: Well, is then all this relative experience not true?

Swamiji: As long as the idea of "I" remains, it is true. And the instant the realisation of "I" as the Atman comes, this world of relative existence becomes false. What people speak of as sin is the result of weakness — is but another form of the egoistic idea, "I am the body". When the mind gets steadfast in the truth, "I am the Self", then you go beyond merit and demerit, virtue and vice. Shri Ramakrishna used to say, "When the 'I' dies, all trouble is at an end."

Disciple: Sir, this "I" has a most tenacious life. It is very difficult to kill it.

Swamiji: Yes, in one sense, it is very difficult, but in another sense, it is quite easy. Can you tell me where this "I" exists? How can you speak of anything being killed, which never exists at all? Man only remains hypnotised with the false idea of an ego. When this ghost is off from us, all dreams vanish, and then it is found that the one Self only exists from the highest Being to a blade of grass. This will have to be known, to be realised. All practice or worship is only for taking off this veil. When that will go, you will find that the Sun of Absolute Knowledge is shining in Its own lustre. For the Atman only is self-luminous and has to be realised by Itself. How can that, which can be experienced only by itself be known with the help of any other thing? Hence the Shruti says, says, "विज्ञातारमरे केन विजानीयात्—Well, through what means is that to be known which is the Knower?" Whatever you know, you know through the instrumentality of your mind. But mind is something material. It is active only because there is the pure Self behind it. So, how can you know that Self through your mind? But this only becomes known, after all, that the mind cannot reach the pure Self, no, nor even the intellect. Our relative knowledge ends just there. Then, when the mind is free from activity or functioning, it vanishes, and the Self is revealed. This state has been described by the commentator

1. Referring, that is to say, to some steps in the Vedic ceremony of a Brahmin's initiation.

2. The special gift which a disciple has to make to his Guru as the symbol of the mutual relation being consummated.

Shankara as अपरोक्षानुभूति: or supersensuous perception.

Disciple: But, sir, the mind itself is the "I". If that mind is gone, then the "I" also cannot remain.

Swamiji: Yes, the state that comes then is the real nature of the ego. The "I" that remains then is omnipresent, all-pervading, the Self of all. Just as the Ghatâkâsha, when the jar is broken, becomes the Mahâkâsha,[3] for with the destruction of the jar the enclosed space is not destroyed. The puny "I" which you were thinking of as confined in the body, becomes spread out and is thus realised in the form of the all pervading "I" or the Self. Hence what matters it to the real "I" or the Self, whether the mind remains or is destroyed? What I say you will realise in course of time. "कालेनात्मनि विन्दति—It is realised within oneself in due time." As you go on with Shravana and Manana (proper hearing and proper thinking), you will fully understand it in due time and then you will go beyond mind. Then there will be no room for any such question.

Hearing all this, the disciple remained quiet on his seat, and Swamiji, as he gently smoked, continued: "How many Shastras have been written to explain this simple thing, and yet men fail to understand it! How they are vesting this precious human life on the fleeting pleasures of some silver coins and the frail beauty of women! Wonderful is the influence of Mahâmâyâ (Divine Illusion)! Mother! Oh Mother!"

UNTITLED CONVERSATION VI

Translated from Bengali

The disciple is Sharatchandra Chakravarty, who published his records in a Bengali book, Swami-Shishya-Samvâda, in two parts. The present series of "Conversations and Dialogues" is a revised translation from this book. Five dialogues of this series have already appeared in the Complete Works, Volume V.

Place: Baghbazar, Calcutta.

Year: 1897.

Swamiji has been staying for some days at the house of the late Balaram Babu. At his wish, a large number of devotees of Shri Ramakrishna have assembled at the house at 3 p.m. (on May 1, 1897). Swami Yogananda is amongst those present here. The object of Swamiji is to form an Association. When all present had taken their seats, Swamiji proceeded to speak as follows:

"The conviction has grown in my mind after all my travels in various lands that no great cause can succeed without an organisation. In a country like ours, however, it does not seem quite practicable to me to start an organisation at once with a democratic basis or work by general voting. People in the West are more educated in this respect, and less jealous of

one another than ourselves. They have learnt to respect merit. Take for instance my case. I was just an insignificant man there, and yet see how cordially they received and entertained me. When with the spread of education the masses in our country grow more sympathetic and liberal, when they learn to have their thoughts expanded beyond the limits of sect or party, then it will be possible to work; on the democratic basis of organization. For this reason it is necessary to have a dictator for this Society. Everybody should obey him, and then in time we may work on the principle of general voting.

"Let this Association be named after him, in whose name indeed, we have embraced the monastic life, with whom as your Ideal in life you all toil on the field of work from your station in family life, within twenty years of whose passing away a wonderful diffusion of his holy name and extraordinary life has taken place both in the East and the West. We are the servants of the Lord. Be you all helpers In this cause."

When Srijut Girish Chandra Ghosh and all other householder disciples present had approved of the above proposal, the future programme of the Society of Shri Ramakrishna was taken up for discussion. The Society was named the Ramakrishna Mission.

Swamiji himself became the general president of the Mission and other office-bearers also were elected. The rule was laid down that the Association should hold meetings at the house of Balaram Babu every Sunday at 4 p.m. Needless to say that Swamiji used to attend these meetings whenever convenient.

When the meeting had broken up and the members departed, addressing Swami Yogananda, Swamiji said, "So the work is now begun this way; let us see how far it succeeds by the will of Shri Ramakrishna."

Swami Yogananda. You are doing these things with Western methods. Should you say Shri Ramakrishna left us any such instructions?

Swamiji: Well, how do you know that all this is not on Shri Ramakrishna's lines? He had an infinite breadth of feeling, and dare you shut him up within your own limited views of life. I will break down these limits and scatter broadcast over the earth his boundless inspiration. He never instructed me to introduce any rites of his own worship. We have to realise the teachings he has left us about religious practice and devotion, concentration and meditation, and such higher ideas and truths, and then preach these to all men. The infinite number of faiths are only so many paths. I haven't been born to found one more sect in a world already teeming with sects. We have been blessed with obtaining refuge at the feet of the Master, and we are born to carry his message to the dwellers of the three worlds.

Swami Yogananda uttered no word of dissent, and so Swamiji continued: Time and again have I received in this life marks of his grace. He stands behind and gets all this work done by me. When lying helpless under a tree in an agony of hunger, when I had not even a scrap of cloth for Kaupina,

---

3. Ghatâkâsha and Mahâkâsha are technical terms in Vedanta, meaning the space enclosed by the jar and the omnipresent. The two are one and the same, only the former is limited by the Upâdhi (adjunct) of the Ghata or jar.

when I was resolved on travelling penniless round the world, even then help came in all ways by the grace of Shri Ramakrishna. And again when crowds jostled with one another in the streets of Chicago to have a sight of this Vivekananda, then also, just because I had his grace, I could digest without difficulty all that honour—a hundredth part of which would have been enough to turn mad any ordinary man; and by his will, victory followed everywhere. Now I must conclude by doing something in this country. So casting all doubt away, please help my work; and you will find everything fulfilled by his will.

Swami Yogananda: Yes, whatever you will, shall be fulfilled; and are we not all ever obedient to you? Now and then I do clearly see how Shri Ramakrishna is getting all these things done through you. And yet, to speak plainly, some misgiving rises at intervals, for as we saw it, his was of doing things different. So I question myself: "Are we sure that we are not going astray from Shri Ramakrishna's teachings?" And so I take the opposing attitude and warn you.

Swamiji: You see, the fact is that Shri Ramakrishna is not exactly what the ordinary followers have comprehended him to be. He had infinite moods and phases. Even if you might form an idea of the limits of Brahmajnâna, the knowledge of the Absolute, you could not have any idea of the unfathomable depths of his mind! Thousands of Vivekanandas may spring forth through one gracious glance of his eyes! But instead of doing that, he has chosen to get things done this time through me as his single instrument, and what can I do in this matter you see?

Saying this, Swamiji left to attend to something else waiting for him, and Swami Yogananda went on praising Swamiji's versatile gifts.

Meanwhile Swamiji returned and asked the disciple, "Do the people in your part of the country know much of Shri Ramakrishna?"

Disciple: Only one man, Nâg Mahâshaya, came to Shri Ramakrishna from our part of Bengal;[1] it is from him that many came to hear of him and had their curiosity excited to know more. But that Shri Ramakrishna was the Incarnation of God, the people there have not yet come to know and some would not believe it even if told so.

Swamiji: Do you think it is an easy matter to believe so? We who had actual dealings with him in every respect we who heard of that fact again and again from his own lips, we who lived and stayed with him for twenty-four hours of the day—even we off and on have doubts about it coming over us! So what to speak of others!

Disciple: Did Shri Ramakrishna, out of his own lips ever say that he was God, the all-perfect Brahman?

Swamiji: Yes, he did so many times. And he said this to all

of us. One day while was staying at the Cossipore garden, his body in imminent danger of falling off for ever, by the side of his bed I was saying in my mind, "Well, now if you can declare that you are God, then only will I believe you are really God Himself." It was only two days before he passed away. Immediately, he looked up towards me all on a sudden and said, "He who was Rama, He who was Krishna, verily is He now Ramakrishna in this body. And that not merely from the standpoint of your Vedanta!"[2] At this I was struck dumb. Even we haven't had yet the perfect faith, after hearing it again and again from the holy lips of our Lord himself—our minds still get disturbed now and then with doubt and despair—and so, what shall we speak of others being slow to believe? It is indeed a very difficult matter to be able to declare and believe a man with a body like ours to be God Himself. We may just go to the length of declaring him to be a "perfected one", or a "knower of Brahman". Well, it matters nothing, whatever you may call him or think of him, a saint, or a knower of Brahman, or anything. But take it from me, never did come to this earth such an all-perfect man as Shri Ramakrishna! In the utter darkness of the world, this great man is like the shining pillar of illumination in this age! And by his light alone will man now cross the ocean of Samsâra!

Disciple: To me it seems, sir, that true faith comes only after actually seeing or hearing something. Mathur[3] Babu, I have heard, actually saw so many things about Shri Ramakrishna, and thus he had that wonderful faith in him.

Swamiji: He who believes not, believes not even after seeing, and thinks that it is all hallucination, or dream and so on. The great transfiguration of Krishna—the Vishvarupa (form universal)—was seen alike by Duryodhana and by Arjuna. But only Arjuna believed, while Duryodhana took it to be magic! Unless He makes us understand, nothing can be stated or understood. Somebody comes to the fullest faith even without seeing or hearing, while somebody else remains plunged in doubt even after witnessing with his own eyes various extraordinary powers for twelve years! The secret of it all is His grace! But then one must persevere, so that the grace may be received.

Disciple: Is there, sir, any law of graces

Swamiji: Yes and no.

Disciple: How is that ?

Swamiji: Those who are pure always in body, mind, and speech, who have strong devotion, who discriminate between the real and the unreal, who persevere in meditation and contemplation—upon them alone the grace of the Lord descends. The Lord, however, is beyond all natural laws—is not under any rules and regulations, or just as Shri Ramakrishna used to say, He has the child's nature—and that's why we find

1. This is not quite correct, for at least two more disciples, viz Nityagopal Goswami and Pundit Kaliprasad Chakravarty are known to have come from Dacca. — Ed.

2. In the sense that a knower of Brahman may declare his identity with any being, such as Manu and so forth. Vide the Vedanta-Sutras I. i. 30.

3. Mathura Nath Biswas, son-in-law of Rani Rasmani, the foundress of the temple at Dakshineswar.

some failing to get any response even after calling on Him for millions of births, while some one else whom we regard as a sinful or penitent man or a disbeliever, would have Illumination in a flash!—On the latter the Lord perhaps lavishes His grace quite unsolicited! You may argue that this man had good merits stored up from previous life, but the mystery is really difficult to understand. Shri Ramakrishna used to say sometimes, "Do rely on Him; be like the dry leaf at the mercy of the wind"; and again he would say, "The wind of His grace is always blowing, what you need to do is to unfurl your sail."

Disciple: But, sir, this is a most tremendous statement. No reasoning, I see, can stand here.

Swamiji: Ah, all reasoning and arguing is within the limit of the realm of Maya; it lies within the categories of space, time, and causation. But He is beyond these categories. We speak of His law, still He is beyond all law. He creates, or becomes, all that we speak of as laws of nature, and yet He is outside of them all. He on whom His grace descends, in a moment goes beyond all law. For this reason there is no condition in grace. It is as His play or sport. And this creation of the universe is like His play—लोकवक्तु लीलाकैवल्यम्—It is the pure delight of sport, as in the case of men" (Vedanta-Sutras, II. i. 33). Is it not possible for Him who creates and destroys the universe as if in play to grant salvation by grace to the greatest sinner? But then it is just His pleasure, His play, to get somebody through the practice of spiritual discipline and somebody else without it.

Disciple: Sir, I can't understand this.

Swamiji: And you needn't. Only get your mind to cling to Him as far as you can. For then only the great magic of this world will break of itself. But then, you must persevere. You must take off your mind from lust and lucre, must discriminate always between the real and the unreal—must settle down into the mood of bodilessness with the brooding thought that you are not this body, and must always have the realisation that you are the all-pervading Atman. This persevering practice is called Purushakâra (self-exertion—as distinguished from grace). By such self-exertion will come true reliance on Him, and that is the goal of human achievement.

After a pause Swamiji resumed: Had you not been receiving His grace, why else would you come here at all? Shri Ramakrishna used to say, "Those who have had the grace of God cannot but come here. Wherever they might be, whatever they might be doing, they are sure to be affected by words or sentiments uttered from here."[4] Just take your own case—do you think it is possible without the grace of God to have the blessed company of Nag Mahashaya, a man who rose to spiritual perfection through the strength of divine grace and came to know fully what this grace really means? "अनेकजन्मसंसिद्धस्ततो

यातिं परां गतिम्—One attains the highest stage after being perfected by the practice of repeated births" (Gita, VI. 45). It is only by virtue of great religious merit acquired through many births that one comes across a great soul like him. All the characteristics of the highest type of Bhakti, spoken of in the scriptures, have manifested themselves in Nag Mahashaya. It is only in him that we actually see fulfilled the widely quoted text, "तृणादपि सुनीचेन". ("Lowlier than the lowly stalk of grass.") Blessed indeed is your East Bengal to have been hallowed by the touch of Nag Mahashaya's feet!

While speaking thus, Swamiji rose to pay a visit to the great poet, Babu Girish Chandra Ghosh. Swami Yogananda and the disciple followed him. Reaching Girish Babu's place, Swamiji seated himself and said "You see, G. C., the impulse is constantly coming nowadays to my mind to do this and to do that, to scatter broadcast on earth the message of Shri Ramakrishna and so on. But I pause again to reflect, lest all this give rise to another sect in India. So I have to work with a good deal of caution. Sometimes I think, what if a sect does grow up. But then again the thought comes! 'No. Shri Ramakrishna never disturbed anybody's own spiritual outlook; he always looked at the inner sameness.' Often do I restrain myself with this thought. Now, what do you say?"

Girish Babu: What can I say to this? You are the instrument in his hand. You have to do just what he would have you do. I don't trouble myself over the detail. But I see that the power of the Lord is getting things done by you, I see it clear as daylight.

Swamiji: But I think we do things according to our own will. Yet, that in misfortunes and adversities, in times of want and poverty, he reveals himself to us and guides us along the true path—this I have been able to realise. But alas, I still fail to comprehend in any way the greatness of his power.

Girish Babu: Yes, he said, "If you understand it to the full, everything will at once vanish. Who will work then or who will be made to work?"

After this the talk drifted on to America. And Swamiji grew warm on his subject and went on describing the wonderful wealth of the country, the virtues and defects of men and women there, their luxury and so on.

UNTITLED CONVERSATION VII

Translated from Bengali From the Diary of a Disciple

The disciple is Sharatchandra Chakravarty, who published his records in a Bengali book, Swami-Shishya-Samvâda, in two parts. The present series of "Conversations and Dialogues" is a revised translation from this book. Five dialogues of this series have already appeared in the Complete Works, Volume V.

Place: Calcutta.

Year: 1897.

For some days past, Swamiji has been staying at Balaram

---

4. With his egoism perfectly merged in the consciousness of the Mother, the use of to word "here" by Shri Ramakrishna would often stand for the ordinary reference to self. By "here" is evidently meant the centre of the Mother's self-revelation.

Bose's house, Baghbazar. There will be a total eclipse of the sun today. The disciple is to cook for Swamiji this morning, and on his presenting himself, Swamiji said, "Well, the cooking must be in the East Bengal style; and we must finish our dinner before the eclipse starts."

The inner apartments of the house were all unoccupied now. So the disciple went inside into the kitchen and started his cooking. Swamiji also was looking in now and then with a word of encouragement and sometimes with a joke, as, "Take care, the soup[1] must be after the East Bengal fashion."

The cooking had been almost completed, when Swamiji came in after his bath and sat down for dinner, putting up his own seat and plate. "Do bring in anything finished, quick," he said, "I can't wait, I'm burning with hunger!" While eating, Swamiji was pleased with the curry with bitters and remarked, "Never have I enjoyed such a nice thing! But none of the things is so hot as your soup." "It's just after the style of the Burdwan District", said Swamiji tasting the sour preparation. He then brought his dinner to a close and after washing sat on the bedstead inside the room. While having his after-dinner smoke, Swamiji remarked to the disciple, "Whoever cannot cook well cannot become a good Sâdhu; unless the mind is pure, good tasteful cooking is not possible. "

Soon after this, the sound of bells and conch-shells, etc., rose from all quarters, when Swamiji said, "Now that the eclipse has begun, let me sleep, and you please massage my feet!" Gradually the eclipse covered the whole of the sun's disc and all around fell the darkness of dusk.

While there were fifteen or twenty minutes left for the eclipse to pass off, Swamiji rose from his siesta, and after washing, jocosely said while taking a smoke, "Well, people say that whatever one does during an eclipse, one gets that millionfold in future; so I thought that the Mother, Mahâmâyâ, did not ordain that this body might have good sleep, and if I could get some sleep during the eclipse, I might have plenty of it in future. But it all failed, for I slept only for fifteen minutes a. the most."

After this, at the behest of Swamiji some short speeches were made. There was yet an hour left before dusk. When all had assembled in the parlour, Swamiji told them to put him any question they liked.

Swami Shuddhananda asked, "What is the real nature of meditation, sir?"

Swamiji: Meditation is the focusing of the mind on some object. If the mind acquires concentration on one object, it can be so concentrated on any object whatsoever.

Disciple: Mention is made in the scriptures of two kinds of meditation—one having some object and the other objectless. What is meant by all that, and which of the two is the higher one?

Swamiji: First, the practice of meditation has to proceed

with some one object before the mind. Once I used to concentrate my mind on some black point. Ultimately, during those days, I could not see the point any more, nor notice that the point was before me at all—the mind used to be no more—no wave of functioning would rise, as if it were all an ocean without any breath of air. In that state I used to experience glimpses of supersensuous truth. So I think, the practice of meditation even with some trifling external object leads to mental concentration. But it is true that the mind very easily attains calmness when one practices meditation with anything on which one's mind is most apt to settle down. This is the reason why we have in this country so much worship of the images of gods and goddesses. And what wonderful art developed from such worship! But no more of that now. The fact, however, is that the objects of meditation can never be the same in the case of all men. People have proclaimed and preached to others only those external objects to which they held on to become perfected in meditation. Oblivious of the fact, later on, that these objects are aids to the attainment of perfect mental calmness, men have extolled them beyond everything else. They have wholly concerned themselves with the means, getting comparatively unmindful of the end. The real aim is to make the mind functionless, but this cannot be got at unless one becomes absorbed in some object.

Disciple: But if the mind becomes completely engrossed and identified with some object, how can it give us the consciousness of Brahman?

Swamiji: Yes, though the mind at first assumes the form of the object, yet later on the consciousness of that object vanishes. Then only the experience of pure "isness" remains.

Disciple: Well, sir, how is it that desires rise even after mental concentration is acquired?

Swamiji: Those are the outcome of previous Samskâras (deep-rooted impressions or tendencies). When Buddha was on the point of merging in Samadhi (superconsciousness), Mâra made his appearance. There was really no Mara extraneous to the mind; it was only the external reflection of the mind's previous Samskaras.

Disciple: But one hears of various fearful experiences prior to the attainment of perfection. Are they all mental projections?

Swamiji: What else but that? The aspiring soul, of course, does not make out at that time that all these are external manifestations of his own mind. But all the same, there is nothing outside of it. Even what you see as this world does not exist outside. It is all a mental projection. When the mind becomes functionless, it reflects the Brahman-consciousness. Then the vision of all spheres of existence may supervene, "यं यं लोकं मनसा संविभाति—Whatsoever sphere one may call up in mind" (Mundaka, III. i. 10). Whatsoever is resolved on becomes realised at once. He who, even on attaining this state of unfalsified self-determination, preserves his watchfulness and is free from the bondage of desire, verily attains to the knowledge of Brahman. But he who loses his balance after reaching this

1. The Bengali expression has a peculiar pronunciation in East Bengal which gives the point of the joke.

Lectures & Discourses by **Swami Vivekananda**

state gets the manifold powers, but falls off from the Supreme goal.

So saying, Swamiji began to repeat "Shiva, Shiva", and then continued: There is no way, none whatsoever, to the solution of the profound mystery of this life except through renunciation. Renunciation, renunciation and renunciation—let this be the one motto of your lives. सर्वं वस्तु भयान्वितं भुवि नृणां वैराग्यमेवाभयम्—For men, all things on earth are infected with fear, Vairâgya (renunciation) alone constitutes fearlessness" (Vairâgya-Shatakam).

UNTITLED CONVERSATION VIII

Translated from Bengali From the Diary of a Disciple

The disciple is Sharatchandra Chakravarty, who published his records in a Bengali book, Swami-Shishya-Samvâda, in two parts. The present series of "Conversations and Dialogues" is a revised translation from this book. Five dialogues of this series have already appeared in the Complete Works, Volume V.

Place: Calcutta.

Year: 1897, March or April.

Today the disciple came to meet Swamiji at Baghbazar, but found him ready for a visiting engagement. "Well, come along with me", were the words with which Swamiji accosted him as he went downstairs, and the disciple followed. They then put themselves into a hired cab which proceeded southwards.

Disciple: Sir, where are you going to visit, please?

Swamiji: Well, come with me and you will see.

Thus keeping back the destination from the disciple, Swamiji opened the following conversation as the carriage reached the Beadon Street: One does not find any real endeavour in your country to get the women educated. You, the men are educating yourselves to develop your manhood, but what are you doing to educate and advance those who share all your happiness and misery, who lay down their lives to serve you in your homes?

Disciple: Why, sir, just see how many schools and colleges hare sprung up nowadays for our women, and how many of them are getting degrees of B.A. and M.A.

Swamiji: But all that is in the Western style. How many schools have been started on your own national lines, in the spirit of your own religious ordinances? But alas, such a system does not obtain even among the men of your country, what to speak of women! It is seen from the official statistics that only three or four per cent of the people in India are educated, and not even one per cent of the women.

Otherwise, how could the country come to such a fallen condition? How can there be any progress of the country without the spread of education, the dawning of knowledge? Even no real effort or exertion in the cause is visible among the few in your country who are the promise of the future, you who have received the blessings of education. But know

for certain that absolutely nothing can be done to improve the state of things, unless there is spread of education first among the women and the masses. And so I have it in my mind to train up some Brahmachârins and Brahmachârinis, the former of whom will eventually take the vow of Sannyâsa and try to carry the light of education among the masses, from village to village, throughout the country, while the latter will do the same among women. But the whole work must be done in the style of our own country. Just as centres have to be started for men, so also centres have to be started for teaching women. Brahmacharinis of education and character should take up the task of teaching at these different centres. History and the Purânas, housekeeping and the arts, the duties of home-life and principles that make for the development of an ideal character have to be taught with the help of modern science, and the women students must be trained up in ethical and spiritual life. We must see to their growing up as ideal matrons of home in time. The children of such mothers will make further progress in the virtues that distinguish the mothers. It is only in the homes of educated and pious mothers that great men are born. And you have reduced your women to something like manufacturing machines; alas, for heaven's sake, is this the outcome of your education? The uplift of the women, the awakening of the masses must come first, and then only can any real good come about for the country, for India.

Near Chorebagan Swamiji gave it out to the disciple that the foundress of the Mahâkali Pâthashâlâ, the Tapasvini Mâtâji (ascetic mother), had invited him to visit her institution. When our carriage stopped at its destination, three or four gentlemen greeted Swamiji and showed him up to the first door. There the Tapasvini mother received him standing. Presently she escorted him into one of the classes, where all the maidens stood up in greeting. At a word from Mataji all of them commenced reciting the Sanskrit meditation of Lord Shiva with proper intonation. Then they demonstrated at the instance of the Mother how they were taught the ceremonies of worship in their school. After watching all this with much delight and interest, Swamiji proceeded to visit the other classes. After this, Mataji sent for some particular girl and asked her to explain before Swamiji the first verse of the third canto of Kalidasa's Raghavamsham, which she did in Sanskrit. Swamiji expressed his great appreciation of the measure of success Mataji had attained by her perseverance and application in the cause of diffusing education among women. In reply, she said with much humility, "In my service to my students, I look upon them as the Divine Mother; well, in starting the school I have neither fame nor any other object in view."

Being asked by Mataji, Swamiji recorded his opinion about the institution in the Visitors' Book, the last line of which was: "The movement is in the right direction."

After saluting Mataji, Swamiji went back to his carriage, which then proceeded towards Baghbazar, while the following conversation took place between Swamiji and the disciple.

Swamiji: How far is the birthplace of this venerable lady! She has renounced everything of her worldly life, and yet how diligent in the service of humanity! Had she not been a woman, could she ever have undertaken the teaching of women in the way she is doing? What I saw here was all good, but that some male householders should be pitchforked as teachers is a thing I cannot approve of. The duty of teaching in the school ought to devolve in every respect on educated widows and Brahmacharinis. It is good to avoid in this country any association of men with women's schools.

Disciple: But, sir, how would you get now in thin country learned and virtuous women like Gârgi, Khanâ or Lilâvati?

Swamiji: Do you think women of the type don't exist now in the country? Still on this sacred soil of India, this land of Sitâ and Sâvitri, among women may be found such character, such spirit of service, such affection, compassion, contentment, and reverence, as I could not find anywhere else in the world! In the West, the women did not very often seem to me to be women at all, they appeared to be quite the replicas of men! Driving vehicles, drudging in offices, attending schools, doing professional duties! In India alone the sight of feminine modesty and reserve soothes the eye! With such materials of great promise, you could not, alas, work out their uplift! You did not try to infuse the light of knowledge into them. If they get the right sort of education, they may well turn out to be the ideal women in the world.

Disciple: Do you think, sir, the same consummation would be reached through the way Mataji is educating her students? These students would soon grow up and get married and would presently shade into the likeness of all other women of the common run. So I think, if these girls might be made to adopt Brahmacharya, then only could they devote their lives to the cause of the country's progress and attain to the high ideals preached in our sacred books.

Swamiji: Yes, everything will come about in time. Such educated men are not yet born in this country, who can keep their girls unmarried without fear of social punishment. Just see how before the girls exceed the age of twelve or thirteen, people hasten to give them away in marriage out of this fear of their social equals. Only the other day, when the Age of Consent Bill was being passed, the leaders of society massed together millions of men to send up the cry "We don't want the Bill." Had this been in any other country, far from getting up meetings to send forth a cry like that, people would have hidden their heads under their roofs in shame, that such a calumny could yet stain their society.

Disciple: But, sir, I don't think the ancient law-givers supported this custom of early marriage without any rhyme or reason. There must have been some secret meaning in this attitude of theirs.

Swamiji: Well, what might have been this secret meaning, please?

Disciple: Take it, for instance, in the first place that if the girls are married at an early age, they may come over to their husbands' home to learn the particular ways and usages of the family from the early years of their life. They may acquire adequate skill in the duties of the household under the guidance of their parents-in-law. In the homes of their own parents, on the other hand, there is the likelihood of grown-up daughters going astray. But married early, they have no chance of thus going wrong, and over and above this, such feminine virtues as modesty, reserve, fortitude, and diligence are apt to develop in them.

Swamiji: In favour of the other side of the question, again, it may be argued that early marriage leads to premature child-bearing, which accounts for most of our women dying early; their progeny also, being of low vitality, go to swell the ranks of our country's beggars! For if the physique of the parents be not strong and healthy, how can strong and healthy children be born at all? Married a little later and bred in culture, our mothers will give birth to children who would be able to achieve the real good of the country. The reason why you have so many widows in every home lies here, in this custom of early marriage. If the number of early marriages declines, that of widows is bound to follow suit.

Disciple: But, sir, it seems to me, if our women are married late in life, they are apt to be less mindful of their household duties. I have heard that the mothers-in-law in Calcutta very often do all the cooking, while the educated daughters-in-law sit idle with red paint round their feet! But in our East Bengal such a thing is never allowed to take place.

Swamiji: But everywhere under the sun you find the same blending of the good and the bad. In my opinion society in every country shapes itself out of its own initiative. So we need not trouble our heads prematurely about such reforms as the abolition of early marriage, the remarriage of widows, and so on. Our part of the duty lies in imparting true education to all men and women in society. As an outcome of that education, they will of themselves be able to know what is good for them and what is bad, and will spontaneously eschew the latter. It will not be then necessary to pull down or set up anything in society by coercion.

Disciple: What sort of education, do you think, is suited to our women?

Swamiji: Religion, arts, science, housekeeping, cooking, sewing, hygiene—the simple essential points in these subjects ought to be taught to our women. It is not good to let them touch novels and fiction. The Mahakali Pathashala is to a great extent moving in the right direction. But only teaching rites of worship won't do; their education must be an eye-opener in all matters. Ideal characters must always be presented before the view of the girls to imbue them with a devotion to lofty principles of selflessness. The noble examples of Sita, Savitri, Damavanti, Lilavati, Khana, and Mirâ should be brought home to their minds and they should be inspired to mould their own lives in the light of these.

Our cab now reached the house of the late Babu Balaram Bose at Baghbazar. Swamiji alighted from it and went upstairs. There he recounted the whole of his experience at the Mahakali Pathashala to those who had assembled there to see him.

Then while discussing what the members of the newly formed Ramakrishna Mission should do, Swamiji proceeded to establish by various arguments the supreme importance of the 'gift of learning" and the "gift of knowledge".[1] Turning to the disciple he said, "Educate, educate, 'नान्यः पन्था विद्यतेऽयनाय—Than this there is no other way'." And referring in banter to the party who do not favour educational propaganda, he said, "Well, don't go into the party of Prahlâdas!" Asked as to the meaning of the expression he replied, "Oh, haven't you heard? Tears rushed out of the eyes of Prahlada at the very sight of the first letter 'Ka' of the alphabet as it reminded him Of Krishna; so how could any studies be proceeded with? But then the tears in Prahlada's eyes were tears of love, while your fools affect tears in fright! Many of the devotees are also like that." All of those present burst out laughing on hearing this, and Swami Yogananda said to Swamiji, "Well, once you have the urge within towards anything to be done, you won't have any peace until you see the utmost done about it. Now what you have a mind to have done shall be done no doubt."

UNTITLED CONVERSATION IX

Translated from Bengali From the Diary of a Disciple

The disciple is Sharatchandra Chakravarty, who published his records in a Bengali book, Swami-Shishya-Samvâda, in two parts. The present series of "Conversations and Dialogues" is a revised translation from this book. Five dialogues of this series have already appeared in the Complete Works, Volume V.

Place: Calcutta.

Year: 1897.

For the last ten days, the disciple had been studying Sâyana's commentary on the Rig-Veda with Swamiji, who was staying then at the house of the late Babu Balaram Bose at Baghbazar. Max Müller's volumes on the Rig-Veda had been brought from a wealthy friend's private library. Swamiji was correcting the disciple every now and then and giving him the true pronunciation or construction as necessary. Sometimes while explaining the arguments of Sayana to establish the eternity of the Vedas, Swamiji was praising very highly the commentator's wonderful ingenuity; sometimes again while arguing out the deeper significance of the doctrine, he was putting forward a difference in view and indulging in an innocent squib at Sayana.

While our study had proceeded thus for a while, Swamiji raised the topic about Max Müller and continued thus: Well,

---

1. The allusion here is to the classification of various gifts, mentioned by Manu.

do you know, my impression is that it is Sayana who is born again as Max Müller to revive his own commentary on the Vedas? I have had this notion for long. It became confirmed in my mind, it seems, after I had seen Max Müller. Even here in this country, you don't find a scholar so persevering, and so firmly grounded in the Vedas and the Vedanta. Over and above this, what a deep, unfathomable respect for Sri Ramakrishna! Do you know, he believes in his Divine Incarnation! And what great hospitality towards me when I was his guest! Seeing the old man and his lady, it seemed to me that they were living their home-life like another Vasishtha and Arundhati! At the time of parting with me, tears came into the eyes of the old man.

Disciple: But, sir, if Sayana himself became Max Müller, then why was he born as a Mlechchha instead of being born in the sacred land of India?

Swamiji: The feeling and the distinction that I am an Aryan and the other is a Mlechchha come from ignorance. But what are Varnâshrama and caste divisions to one who is the commentator of the Vedas, the shining embodiment of knowledge? To him they are wholly meaningless, and he can assume human birth wherever he likes for doing good to mankind. Specially, if he did not choose to be born in a land which excelled both in learning and wealth, where would he secure the large expenses for publishing such stupendous volumes? Didn't you hear that the East India Company paid nine lakhs of rupees in cash to have the Rig-Veda published? Even this money was not enough. Hundreds of Vedic Pundits had to be employed in this country on monthly stipends. Has anybody seen in this age, here in this country, such profound yearning for knowledge, such prodigious investment of money for the sake of light and learning? Max Müller himself has written it in his preface, that for twenty-five years he prepared only the manuscripts. Then the printing took another twenty years! It is not possible for an ordinary man to drudge for fortyfive years of his life with one publication. Just think of it! Is it an idle fancy of mine to say he is Sayana himself?

After this talk about Max Müller the leading of the Vedas was resumed. Now Swamiji began variously to support the view of Sayana that creation proceeded out of the Vedas. He said: Veda means the sum total of eternal truths; the Vedic Rishis experienced those truths; they can be experienced only by seers of the supersensuous and not by common men like us. That is why in the Vedas the term Rishi means "the seer of the truth of the Mantras", and not any Brahmin with the holy thread hanging down the neck. The division of society into castes came about later on. Veda is of the nature of Shabda or of idea. It is but the sum total of ideas. Shabda, according to the old Vedic meaning of the term, is the subtle idea, which reveals itself by taking the gross form later on. So owing to the dissolution of the creation the subtle seeds of the future creation become involved in the Veda. Accordingly, in the Puranas you find that during the first Divine Incarnation, the Minâvatâra, the Veda is first made manifest. The Vedas having been first revealed in this Incarnation, the other creative manifestations followed. Or in other words, all the created objects began to take concrete shape out of the Shabdas or ideas in the Veda. For in Shabda or idea, all gross objects have their subtle forms. Creation had proceeded in the same way in all previous cycles or Kalpas. This you find in the Sandhyâ Mantra of the Vedas:

सूर्याचन्द्रमसौ धाता यथापूर्वमकल्पयत् पृथिवीं दिवं चान्तरीक्षमथो स्वः—The Creator projected the sun, the moon, the earth, the atmosphere, the heaven, and the upper spheres in the same manner and process as in previous cycles." Do you understand?

Disciple: But, sir, how in the absence of an actual concrete object can the Shabda or idea be applied and for what? And how can the names too be given at all?

Swamiji: Yes. that is what on first thought seems to be the difficulty. But just think of this. Supposing this jug breaks into pieces; does the idea of a jug become null and void? No. Because, the jug is the gross effect, while the idea, "jug", is the subtle state or the Shabda-state of the jug. In the same way, the Shabda-state of every object is its subtle state, and the things we see, hear, touch, or perceive in any manner are the gross manifestations of entities in the subtle or Shabda-state. Just as we may speak of the effect and its cause. Even when the whole creation is annihilated, the Shabda, as the consciousness of the universe or the subtle reality of all concrete things, exists in Brahman as the cause. At the point of creative manifestation, this sum total of causal entities vibrates into activity, as it were, and as being the sonant, material substance of it all, the eternal, primal sound of "Om" continues to come out of itself. And then from the causal totality comes out first the subtle image or Shabda-form of each particular thing and then its gross manifestation. Now that causal Shabda, or word-consciousness, is Brahman, and it is the Veda. This is the purport of Sayana. Do you now understand?

Disciple: No, sir, I can't clearly comprehend it.

Swamiji: Well, you understand, I suppose, that even if all the jugs in the universe were to be destroyed, the idea or Shabda, "jug", would still exist. So if the universe be destroyed—I mean if all the things making up the universe be smashed to atoms—why should not the ideas or Shabdas representing all of them in consciousness, be still existing; And why cannot a second creation be supposed to come out of them in time?

Disciple: But, sir, if one cries out "jug", "jug", that does not cause any jug to be produced!

Swamiji: No, nothing is produced if you or I cry out like that; but a jug must be revealed if the idea of it rises in Brahman which is perfect in Its creative determinations. When we see even those established in the practice of religion (Sâdhakas) bring about by will-power things otherwise impossible to happen, what to speak of Brahman with perfect creativeness of will? At the point of creation Brahman becomes manifest as Shabda (Idea), and then assumes the form of "Nâda" or

"Om". At the next stage, the particular Shabdas or ideas, that variously existed in former cycles, such as Bhuh, Bhuvah, Svah, cow, man, etc., begin to come out of the "Om". As soon as these ideas appear in Brahman endowed with perfect will, the corresponding concrete things also appear, and gradually the diversified universe becomes manifest. Do you now understand how Shabda is the source of creation?

Disciple: Yes, I just form some idea of it, but there is no clear comprehension in the mind.

Swamiji: Well, clear comprehension, inward realisation, is no small matter, my son. When the mind proceeds towards self-absorption in Brahman, it passes through all these stages one by one to reach the absolute (Nirvikalpa) state at last. In the process of entering into Samadhi, first the universe appears as one mass of ideas; then the whole thing loses itself in a profound "Om". Then even that melts away, even that seems to be between being and non-being. That is the experience of the eternal Nada. And then the mind becomes lost in the Reality of Brahman, and then it is done! All is peace!

The disciple sat mute, thinking that none could express and explain it in the way Swamiji was doing, unless the whole thing were a matter of one's own experience!

Swamiji then resumed the subject: Great men like Avatâras, in coming back from Samadhi to the realm of "I" and "mine", first experience the unmanifest Nada, which by degrees grows distinct and appears as Om, and then from Omkâra, the subtle form of the universe as a mass of ideas becomes experienced, and last, the material universe comes into perception. But ordinary Sadhakas somehow reach beyond Nada through immense practice, and when once they attain to the direct realisation of Brahman, they cannot again come back to the lower plane of material perception. They melt away in Brahman, क्षीरे नीरवत्—Like water in milk".

When all this talk on the theory of creation was going on, the great dramatist, Babu Girish Chandra Ghosh, appeared on the scene. Swamiji gave him his courteous greetings and continued his lessons to the disciple.

Shabdas are again divided into two classes, the Vedic Shabdas and those in common human use. I found this position in the Nyâya book called Shabdashaktiprakâshikâ. There the arguments no doubt indicate great power of thought; but, oh, the terminology confounds the brain!

Now turning to Girish Babu Swamiji said: What do you say, G. C.? Well, you do not care to study all this, you pass your days with your adoration of this and that god, eh?

Girish Babu: What shall I study, brother? I have neither time nor understanding enough to pry into all that. But this time, with Shri Ramakrishna's grace, I shall pass by with greetings to your Vedas and Vedanta, and take one leap to the far beyond! He gets you through all these studies, because he wants to get many a thing done by you. But we have no need of them. Saying this, Girish Babu again and again touched the big Rig-Veda volumes with his head, uttering, "All Victory to

Ramakrishna in the form of Veda!"

Swamiji was now in a sort of deep reverie, when Girish Babu suddenly called out to him and said: Well, hear me, please. A good deal of study you have made in the Vedas and Vedanta, but say, did you find anywhere in them any way for us out of all these profound miseries in the country, all these wailings of grief, all this starvation, all these crimes of adultery, and the many horrible sins?

Saying this he painted over and over again the horrid pictures of society. Swamiji remained perfectly quiet and speechless, while at the thought of the sorrows and miseries of his fellow men, tears began to flow out of his eyes, and seemingly to hide his feelings from us, he rose and left the room.

Meanwhile, addressing the disciple, Girish Babu said: Did you see, Bângâl? What a great loving heart! I don't honour your Swamiji simply for being a Pundit versed in the Vedas; but I honour him for that great heart of his which just made him retire weeping at the sorrows of his fellow beings.

The disciple and Girish Babu then went on conversing with each other, the latter proving that knowledge and love were ultimately the same.

In the meantime, Swamiji returned and asked the disciple, "Well, what was all this talk going on between you?" The disciple said, "Sir, we are talking about the Vedas, and the wonder of it is that our Girish Babu has not studied these books but has grasped the ultimate truths with clean precision!"

Swamiji: All truths reveal themselves to him who has got real devotion to the Guru; he has hardly any need of studies. But such devotion and faith are very rare in this world. He who possesses those in the measure of our friend here need not study the Shastras. But he who rushes forward to imitate him will only bring about his own ruin. Always follow his advice, but never attempt to imitate his ways.

Disciple: Yes, sir,

Swamiji: No saying ditto merely! Do grasp dearly the words I say. Don't nod assent like a fool to everything said. Don't put implicit faith, even if I declare something. First clearly grasp and then accept. Shri Ramakrishna always used to insist on my accepting every word of his only after clear comprehension of it. Walk on your path, only with what sound principle, clear reasoning, and scripture all declare as true. Thus by constant reflection, the intellect will become dear, and then only can Brahman be reflected therein. Do you understand?

Disciple: Yes, sir, I do. But the brain gets puzzled with the different views of different men. This very moment I was being told by Girish Babu, "What will you do with all this studying?" And then you come and say, "Reflect on what you hear and read about." So what exactly am I to do?

Swamiji: Both what he and I have advised you are true. The only difference is that the advice of both has been given from different standpoints. There is a stage of spiritual life where all reasonings are hushed; "मूकास्वादनवत्—Like some delicious taste enjoyed by the dumb". And there is another mode of

spiritual life in which one has to realise the Truth through the pursuit of scriptural learning, through studying and teaching. You have to proceed through studies and reflection, that is your way to realisation. Do you see?

Receiving such a mandate from Swamiji, the disciple in his folly took it to imply Girish Babu's discomfiture, and so turning towards him said: "Do you hear, sir? Swamiji's advice to me plainly is just to study and reflect on the Vedas and Vedanta."

Girish Babu: Well, you go on doing so; with Swamiji's blessings, you will, indeed, succeed in that way.

Swami Sadananda arrived there at that moment, and seeing him, Swamiji at once said, "Do you know, my heart is sorely troubled by the picture of our country's miseries G. C. was depicting just now; well, can you do anything for our country?"

Sadananda: Mahârâj, let the mandate once go forth; your slave is ready.

Swamiji: First, on a pretty small scale, start a relief centre, where the poor and the distressed may obtain relief and the diseased may be nursed. Helpless people having none to look after them will be relieved and served there, irrespective of creed or colour, do you see?

Sadananda: Just as you command, sir.

Swamiji: There is no greater Dharma than this service of living beings. If this Dharma can be practiced in the real spirit, then "मुक्तिः करफलायते—Liberation comes as a fruit on the very palm of one's hand".

Addressing Girish Babu now, Swamiji said, "Do you know, Girish Babu, it occurs to me that even if a thousand births have to be taken in order to relieve the sorrows of the world, surely I will take them. If by my doing that, even a single soul may have a little bit of his grief relieved, why, I will do it. Well, what avails it all to have only one's own liberation? All men should be taken along with oneself on that way. Can you say why a feeling like this comes up foremost in my mind?

Girish Babu: Ah, otherwise why should Shri Ramakrishna declare you to be greater than all others in spiritual competence?

Saying this, Girish Babu took leave of us all to go elsewhere on some business.

UNTITLED CONVERSATION X

Translated from Bengali From the Diary of a Disciple

The disciple is Sharatchandra Chakravarty, who published his records in a Bengali book, Swami-Shishya-Samvâda, in two parts. The present series of "Conversations and Dialogues" is a revised translation from this book. Five dialogues of this series have already appeared in the Complete Works, Volume V.

Place: The Alambazar Math.

Year: 1897.

After Swamiji's first return to Calcutta from the West, he always used to place before the zealous young men who visited him the lofty ideals of renunciation, and anyone expressing his desire of accepting Sannyasa would receive from him great encouragement and kindness. So, inspired by his enthusiasm some young men of great good fortune gave up their worldly life in those days and became initiated by him into Sannyasa. The disciple was present at the Alambazar Math the day the first four of this batch were given Sannyasa by Swamiji.

Often has the disciple heard it from the Sannyasins of the Math that Swamiji was repeatedly requested by his brother-monks not to admit one particular candidate into Sannyasa, whereupon Swamiji replied: "Ah, if even we shrink from working out the salvation of the sinful, the heavy-laden, the humiliated, and the afflicted in soul, who else are to take care of them in this world? No, don't you please stand against me in this matter." So Swamiji's strong opinion triumphed, and always the refuge of the helpless, he resolved out of his great love to give him Sannyasa.

The disciple had been staying at the Math for the last two days, when Swamiji called him and said: "Well, you belong to the priestly class; tomorrow you get them to perform their Shrâddha, and the next day I shall give them Sannyasa. So get yourself ready by consulting the books of ceremonials today." The disciple bowed this mandate of Swamiji, and the ceremony was duly gone through.

But the disciple became very much depressed at the thought of the great sternness of Sannyasa. Swamiji detecting his mental agitation asked him, "Well, I see, you feel some dread in your mind at all this experience, is it not so?" And when the disciple confessed it to be so Swamiji said: "From this day these four are dead to the world, and new bodies, new thoughts, new garments will be theirs from tomorrow—and shining in the glory of Brahman they will live like flaming fire! '— Not by work, nor by progeny, nor by wealth, but by renunciation alone some (rare ones) attained Immortality' (Kaivalya Upanishad)."

After the ceremony, the four Brahmacharins bowed at the feet of Swamiji. He blessed them and said, "You have the enthusiasm to embrace the loftiest vow of human life; blessed indeed is your birth, blessed your family, blessed the mothers who held you in their womb! '— The whole family-line becomes hallowed, the mother achieves her highest!'"

That day after supper, Swamiji talked of the ideal of Sannyasa alone. To the zealous candidates for Sannyasa, he said: The real aim of Sannyasa is "— For one's highest freedom and for the good of the world". Without having Sannyasa none can really be a knower of Brahman—this is what the Vedas and the Vedanta proclaim. Don't listen to the words of those who say, "We shall both live the worldly life and be knowers of Brahman." That is the flattering self-consolation of cryptopleasure-seekers. He who has the slightest desire for worldly pleasures, even a shred of some such craving, will feel frightened at the thought of the path you are going to tread; so, to give himself some consolation he goes about preaching that impossible creed of harmonising Bhoga and Tyâga. That is all the raving of lunatics, the frothing of the demented—idle theories contrary to the scriptures, contrary to the Vedas. No freedom without renunciation. Highest love for God can never be achieved without renunciation. Renunciation is the word— "नान्यः पन्था विद्यते अयनाय—There's no other way than this." Even the Gita says, "— The sages know Sannyasa to be the giving up of all work that has desire for its end."

Nobody attains freedom without shaking off the coils of worldly worries. The very fact that somebody lives the worldly life proves that he is tied down to it as the bond-slave of some craving or other. Why otherwise will he cling to that life at all? He is the slave either of lust or of gold, of position or of fame, of learning or of scholarship. It is only after freeing oneself from all this thraldom that one can get on along the way of freedom. Let people argue as loud as they please, I have got this conviction that unless all these bonds are given up, unless the monastic life is embraced, none is going to be saved, no attainment of Brahmajnâna is possible.

Disciple: Do you mean, sir, that merely taking up Sannyasa will lead one to the goal?

Swamiji: Whether the goal is attained or not is not the point before us now. But until you get out of this wheel of Samsâra, until the slavery of desire is shaken off, you can't attain either Bhakti or Mukti. To the knower of Brahman, supernatural powers or prosperity are mere trivialities.

Disciple: Sir, is there any special time for Sannyasa, and are there different kinds of it?

Swamiji: There is no special time prescribed for a life of Sannyasa. The Shruti says: "— Directly the spirit of renunciation comes, you should take to Sannyasa." The Yogavâsishtha also says:

— "Owing to life itself being frail and uncertain, one should be devoted to religion even in one's youth. For who knows when one's body may fall off?"

The Shâstras are found to speak of four kinds of Sannyasa: (1) Vidvat, (2) Vividishâ, (3) Markata, (4) Âtura. The awakening of real renunciation all at once and the consequent giving up of the world through Sannyasa is something that never happens unless there are strong Samskâras or tendencies, developed from previous birth. And this is called the Vidvat Sannyasa. Vividisha Sannyasa is the case of one who, out of a strong yearning for the knowledge of the Self through the pursuit of scriptural study and practice, goes to the man of realisation and from him embraces Sannyasa to give himself up to those pursuits. Markata Sannyasa is the case of a man who is driven out of the world by some of its chastisements such as the death of a relative or the like and then takes to Sannyasa, though in such a case the renouncing spirit does not endure long. Shri Ramakrishna used to say of it, "With this kind of renunciation one hastens away to the up-country and then happens to get hold of a nice job; and then eventually perhaps arranges to get his wife brought over to him or perhaps takes to a new one!" And last, there is another kind of Sannyasa which the Shastras prescribe for a man who is lying on his death-bed, the hope of whose life has been given up. For then, if he dies, he dies with the holiest of vows upon him, and in his next birth the merit of it will accrue to him. And in case he recovers, he shall not go back to his old life again but live the rest of his days in the noble endeavour after Brahmajnana. Swami Shivananda gave this kind of Sannyasa to your uncle. The poor man died; but through that initiation he will come to a new birth of higher excellence. After all there is no other way to the knowledge of the Self but through Sannyasa.

Disciple: What then, sir, will be the fate of the householders?

Swamiji: Why, through the merit of good Karma, they shall have this renunciation in some future birth of theirs. And directly this renunciation comes, there is an end of all troubles—with no further delay he gets across this mystery of life and death. But then all rules have their exceptions. A few men, one or two, may be seen to attain the highest freedom by the true fulfilment of the householder's Dharma, as we have amongst us Nâg Mahâshaya, for instance.

Disciple: Sir, even the Upanishads etc. do not clearly teach about renunciation and Sannyasa.

Swamiji: You are talking like a madman! Renunciation is the very soul of the Upanishads. Illumination born of discriminative reflection is the ultimate aim of Upanishadic knowledge. My belief, however, is that it was since the time of Buddha that the monastic vow was preached more thoroughly all over India, and renunciation, the giving up of sense-enjoyment, was recognised as the highest aim of religious life. And Hinduism has absorbed into itself this Buddhistic spirit of renunciation. Never was a great man of such renunciation born in this world as Buddha.

Disciple: Do you then mean, sir, that before Buddha's advent there was very little of the spirit of renunciation in the country, and there were hardly any Sannyasins at all?

Swamiji: Who says that? The monastic institution was there, but the generality of people did not recognise it as the goal of life; there was no such staunch spirit for it, there was no such firmness in spiritual discrimination. So even when Buddha betook himself to so many Yogis and Sâdhus, nowhere did he acquire the peace he wanted. And then to realise the Highest he fell back on his own exertions, and seated on a spot with the famous words, "— Let my body wither away on this seat" etc., rose from it only after becoming the Buddha, the Illumined One. The many monasteries that you now see in India occupied by monks were once in the possession of Buddhism. The Hindus have only made them their own now by modifying them in their own fashion. Really speaking, the institution of Sannyasa originated with Buddha; it was he who breathed life into the dead bones of this institution.

Swami Ramakrishnananda, a brother-disciple of Swami-

ji, interposed, "But the ancient law-books and Puranas are good authority that all the four Ashramas had existed in India before Buddha was born." Swamiji replied, "Most of the Puranas, the codes of Manu and others, as well as much of the Mahâbhârata form but recent literature. Bhagavân Buddha was much earlier than all that." "On that supposition," rejoined Swami Ramakrishnananda, "discussions about Buddhism would be found in the Vedas, Upanishads, the law-books, Puranas, and the like. But since such discussions are not found in these ancient books, how can you say that Buddha antedated them all? In a few old Puranas, of course, accounts of the Buddhistic doctrine are partially given; but from these, it can't be concluded that the scriptures of the Hindus such as the law-books and Puranas are of recent date."

Swamiji: Please read history, (Evidently, during the argumentation, Swamiji was taking his stand on the conclusions of modern historical studies, thereby giving his encouragement and support to such new efforts and methods. But we know from one of his letters to Swami Swarupananda (C.W. modern scholars and worked out the pre-Buddhiscic origin of much of modern Hinduism.) and you will find that Hinduism has become so great only by absorbing all the ideas of Buddha.

Swami Ramakrishnananda: It seems to me that Buddha has only left revivified the great Hindu ideas, by thoroughly practicing in his life such principles as renunciation, non-attachment, and so on.

Swamiji: But this position can't be proved. For we don't get any history before Buddha was born. If we accept history only as authority, we have to admit that in the midst of the profound darkness of the ancient times, Buddha only shines forth as a figure radiant with the light of knowledge.

Now the topic of Sannyasa was resumed and Swamiji said: Wheresoever might lie the origin of Sannyasa, the goal of human life is to become a knower of Brahman by embracing this vow of renunciation. The supreme end is to enter the life of Sannyasa. They alone are blessed indeed who have broken off from worldly life through a spirit of renunciation.

Disciple: But many people are of opinion nowadays, sir, that with the increase of wandering monks in the country, much harm has been done to its material progress. They assert it on the ground that these monks idly roam about depending on householders for their living, that these are of no help to the cause of social and national advancement.

Swamiji: But will you explain to me first what is meant by the term material or secular advancement?

Disciple: Yes, it is to do as people in the West are doing by securing the necessaries of life through education, and promoting through science such objects in life as commerce, industry, communications, and so on.

Swamiji: But can all these be ever brought about, if real Rajas is not awakened in man? Wandering all over India, nowhere I found this Rajas manifesting itself. It is all Tamas and

Tamas! The masses lie engulfed in Tamas, and only among the monks could I find this Rajas and Sattva. These people are like the backbone of the country. The real Sannyasin is a teacher of householders. It is with the light and teaching obtained from them that householders of old triumphed many a time in the battles of life. The householders give food and clothing to the Sadhus, only in return for their invaluable teachings. Had there been no such mutual exchange in India, her people would have become extinct like the American Indians by this time. It is because the householders still give a few morsels of food to the Sadhus that they are yet able to keep their foothold on the path of progress. The Sannyasins are not idle. They are really the fountain-head of all activity. The householders see lofty ideals carried into practice in the lives of the Sadhus and accept from them such noble ideas; and this it is that has up till now enabled them to fight their battle of life from the sphere of Karma. The example of holy Sadhus makes them work out holy ideas in life and imbibe real energy for work. The Sannyasins inspire the householders in all noble causes by embodying in their lives the highest principle of giving up everything for the sake of God and the good of the world, and as a return the householders give them a few doles of food. And the very disposition and capacity to grow that food develops in the people because of the blessings and good wishes of the all-renouncing monks. It is because of their failure to understand the deeper issues that people blame the monastic institution. Whatever may be the case in other countries, in this land the bark of householders' life does not sink only because the Sannyasins are at its helm.

Disciple: But, sir, how many monks are to be found who are truly devoted to the good of men?

Swamiji: Ah, quite enough if one great Sannyasin like Shri Ramakrishna comes in a thousand years! For a thousand years after his advent, people may well guide themselves by those ideas and ideals he leaves behind. It is only because this monastic institution exists in the country that men of his greatness are born here. There are defects, more or less, in all the institutions of life. But what is the reason that in spite of its faults, this noble institution stands yet supreme over all the other institutions of life? It is because the true Sannyasins forgo even their own liberation and live simply for doing good to the world. If you don't feel grateful to such a noble institution, lie on you again and again!

While speaking these words, Swamiji's countenance became aglow. And before the eyes of the disciple he shone as the very embodiment of Sannyasa.

Then, as if realising deep within his soul the greatness of this institution, self-absorbed, he broke forth in sweetest symphony:

— "Brooding blissful in mind over the texts of the Vedanta, quite contented with food obtained as alms and wandering forth with a heart untouched by any feeling of grief, thrice blessed are the Sannyasins, with only their loin-cloth for dress."

Resuming the talk, he went on: For the good of the many, for the happiness of the many is the Sannyasin born. His life is all vain, indeed, who, embracing Sannyasa, forgets this ideal. The Sannyasin, verily, is born into this world to lay down his life for others, to stop the bitter cries of men, to wipe the tears of the widow, to bring peace to the soul of the bereaved mother, to equip the ignorant masses for the struggle for existence, to accomplish the secular and spiritual well-being of all through the diffusion of spiritual teachings and to arouse the sleeping lion of Brahman in all by throwing in the light of knowledge. Addressing then his brothers of the Order, he said: Our life is "— for the sake of our self-liberation as well as for the good of the world". So what are you sitting idle for? Arise, awake; wake up yourselves, and awaken others. Achieve the consummation of human life before you pass off— "Arise, awake, and stop not till the goal is reached."

UNTITLED CONVERSATION XI

Translated from Bengali From the Diary of a Disciple

The disciple is Sharatchandra Chakravarty, who published his records in a Bengali book, Swami-Shishya-Samvâda, in two parts. The present series of "Conversations and Dialogues" is a revised translation from this book. Five dialogues of this series have already appeared in the Complete Works, Volume V.

Place: The house of the late Babu Navagopal Ghosh, Ramakrishnapur, Howrah.

Year: 6th February, 1898.

Today the festival of installing the image of Shri Ramakrishna was to come off at the residence of Babu Navagopal Ghosh of Ramakrishnapur, Howrah. The Sannyasins of the Math and the householder devotees of Shri Ramakrishna had all been invited there.

Swamiji with his party reached the bathing ghat at Ramakrishnapur. He was dressed in the simplest garb of ochre with turban on his head and was barefooted On both sides of the road were standing multitudes of people to see him. Swamiji commenced singing the famous Nativity Hymn on Shri Ramakrishna— "Who art Thou laid on the lap of a poor Brahmin mother", etc., and headed a procession, himself playing on the Khol. (A kind of Indian drum elongated and narrows at both ends.) All the devotees assembled there followed, joining in the; chorus.

Shortly after the procession reached its destination, Swamiji went upstairs to see the chapel. The chapel was floored with marble. In the centre was the throne and upon it was the porcelain image of Shri Ramakrishna. The arrangement of materials was perfect and Swamiji was much pleased to see this.

The wife of Navagopal Babu prostrated herself before Swamiji with the other female members of the house and then took to fanning him. Hearing Swamiji speaking highly of every arrangement, she addressed him and said, "What have we got to entitle us to the privilege of worshipping Thâkur (the Master,

Lord)? — A poor home and poor means! Do bless us please by installing him here out of your own kindness!

In reply to this, Swamiji jocosely said, "Your Thakur never had in his fourteen generations such a marble floored house to live in! He had his birth in that rural thatched cottage and lived his days on indifferent means. And if he does not live here so excellently served, where else should he live?" Swamiji's words made everybody laugh out.

Now, with his body rubbed with ashes and gracing the seat of the priest, Swamiji himself conducted the worship, with Swami Prakashananda to assist him. After the worship was over, Swamiji while still in the worship-room composed extempore this Mantra for prostration before Bhagavan Shri Ramakrishna:

— "I bow down to Ramakrishna, who established the religion, embodying in himself the reality of all religions and being thus the foremost of divine Incarnations."

All prostrated before Shri Ramakrishna with this Mantra. In the evening Swamiji returned to Baghbazar.

UNTITLED CONVERSATION XII

Translated from Bengali From the Diary of a Disciple

The disciple is Sharatchandra Chakravarty, who published his records in a Bengali book, Swami-Shishya-Samvâda, in two parts. The present series of "Conversations and Dialogues" is a revised translation from this book. Five dialogues of this series have already appeared in the Complete Works, Volume V.

Place: Balaram Babu's residence, Calcutta.

Year: 1898.

Swamiji had been staying during the last two days at Balaram Babu's residence at Baghbazar. He was taking a short stroll on the roof of the house, and the disciple with four or five others was in attendance. While walking to and fro, Swamiji took up the story of Guru Govind Singh and with his great eloquence touched upon the various points in his life — how the revival of the Sikh sect was brought about by his great renunciation, austerities, fortitude, and life-consecrating labours — how by his initiation he re-Hinduised Mohammedan converts and took them back into the Sikh community — and how on the banks of the Narmada he brought his wonderful life to a close. Speaking of the great power that used to be infused in those days into the initiates of Guru Govind, Swamiji recited a popular Dohâ (couplet) of the Sikhs:

The meaning is: "When Guru Govind gives the Name, i.e. the initiation, a single man becomes strong enough to triumph over a lakh and a quarter of his foes." Each disciple, deriving from his inspiration a real spiritual devotion, had his soul filled with such wonderful heroism! While holding forth thus on the glories of religion, Swamiji's eyes dilating with enthusiasm seemed to be emitting fire, and his hearers, dumb-stricken and looking at his face, kept watching the wonderful sight.

After a while the disciple said: "Sir, it was very remarkable that Guru Govind could unite both Hindus and Mussulmans within the fold of his religion and lead them both towards the same end. In Indian history, no other example of this can be found."

Swamiji: Men can never be united unless there is a bond of common interest. You can never unite people merely by getting up meetings, societies, and lectures if their interests be not one and the same. Guru Govind made it understood everywhere that the men of his age, be they Hindus or Mussulmans, were living under a regime of profound injustice and oppression. He did not create any common interest, he only pointed it out to the masses. And so both Hindus and Mussulmans followed him. He was a great worshipper of Shakti. Yet, in Indian history, such an example is indeed very rare.

Finding then that it was getting late into the night, Swamiji came down with others into the parlour on the first floor, where the following conversation on the subject of miracles took place.

Swamiji said, "It is possible to acquire miraculous powers by some little degree of mental concentration", and turning to the disciple he asked, "Well, should you like to learn thought-reading? I can teach that to you in four or five days."

Disciple: Of what avail will it be to me, sir?

Swamiji: Why, you will be able to know others' minds.

Disciple: Will that help my attainment of the knowledge of Brahman?

Swamiji: Not a bit.

Disciple: Then I have no need to learn that science. But, sir, I would very much like to hear about what you have yourself seen of the manifestation of such psychic powers.

Swamiji: Once when travelling in the Himalayas I had to take up my abode for a night in a village of the hill-people. Hearing the beating of drums in the village some time after nightfall, I came to know upon inquiring of my host that one of the villagers had been possessed by a Devatâ or good spirit. To meet his importunate wishes and to satisfy my own curiosity, we went out to see what the matter really was. Reaching the spot, I found a great concourse of people. A tall man with long, bushy hair was pointed out to me, and I was told that person had got the Devata on him. I noticed an axe being heated in fire close by the man; and after a while, I found the red-hot thing being seized and applied to parts of his body and also to his hair! But wonder of wonders, no part of his body or hair thus branded with the red-hot axe was found to be burnt, and there was no expression of any pain in his face! I stood mute with surprise. The headman of the village, meanwhile, came up to me and said, "Mahârâj, please exorcise this man out of your mercy." I felt myself in a nice fix, but moved to do something, I had to go near the possessed man. Once there, I felt a strong impulse to examine the axe rather closely, but the instant I touched it, I burnt my fingers, although the thing had been cooled down to blackness. The smarting made me restless and all my theories about the axe phenomenon were spirited away from my mind! However, smarting with the burn, I placed my hand on the head of the man and repeated for a short while the Japa. It was a matter of surprise to find that the man came round in ten or twelve minutes. Then oh, the gushing reverence the villagers showed to me! I was taken to be some wonderful man! But, all the same, I couldn't make any head or tail of the whole business. So without a word one way or the other, I returned with my host to his hut. It was about midnight, and I went to bed. But what with the smarting burn in the hand and the impenetrable puzzle of the whole affair, I couldn't have any sleep that night. Thinking of the burning axe failing to harm living human flesh, it occurred again and again to my mind, "There are more things in heaven and earth, Horatio, than are dreamt of in your philosophy."

Disciple: But, could you later on ever explain the mystery, sir?

Swamiji: No. The event came back to me in passing just now, and so I related it to you.

He then resumed: But Shri Ramakrishna used to disparage these supernatural powers; his teaching was that one cannot attain to the supreme truth if the mind is diverted to the manifestation of these powers. The layman mind, however, is so weak that, not to speak of householders, even ninety per cent of the Sâdhus happen to be votaries of these powers. In the West, men are lost in wonderment if they come across such miracles. It is only because Shri Ramakrishna has mercifully made us understand the evil of these powers as being hindrances to real spirituality that we are able to take them at their proper value. Haven't you noticed how for that reason the children of Shri Ramakrishna pay no heed to them?

Swami Yogananda said to Swamiji at this moment, "Well, why don't you narrate to our Bângâl (Lit. A man from East Bengal, i.e. the disciple.) that incident of yours in Madras when you met the famous ghost-tamer?"

At the earnest entreaty of the disciple Swamiji was persuaded to give the following account of his experience:

Once while I was putting up at Manmatha Babu's (Babu Manmatha Nath Bhattacharya, M.A., late Accountant General, Madras.) place, I dreamt one night that my mother had died. My mind became much distracted. Not to speak of corresponding with anybody at home, I used to send no letters in those days even to our Math. The dream being disclosed to Manmatha, he sent a wire to Calcutta to ascertain facts about the matter. For the dream had made my mind uneasy on the one hand, and on the other, our Madras friends, with all arrangements ready, were insisting on my departing for America immediately, and I felt rather unwilling to leave before getting any news of my mother. So Manmatha who discerned this state of my mind suggested our repairing to a man living some way off from town, who having acquired mystic pow-

ers over spirits could tell fortunes and read the past and the future of a man's life. So at Manmatha's request and to get rid of my mental suspense, I agreed to go to this man. Covering the distance partly by railway and partly on foot, we four of us—Manmatha, Alasinga, myself, and another—managed to reach the place, and what met our eyes there was a man with a ghoulish, haggard, soot-black appearance, sitting close to a cremation ground. His attendants used some jargon of South Indian dialect to explain to us that this was the man with perfect power over the ghosts. At first the man took absolutely no notice of us; and then, when we were about to retire from the place, he made a request for us to wait. Our Alasinga was acting as the interpreter, and he explained the requests to us. Next, the man commenced drawing some figures with a pencil, and presently I found him getting perfectly still in mental concentration. Then he began to give out my name, my genealogy, the history of my long line of forefathers and said that Shri Ramakrishna was keeping close to me all through my wanderings, intimating also to me good news about my mother. He also foretold that I would have to go very soon to far-off lands for preaching religion. Getting good news thus about my mother, we all travelled back to town, and after arrival received by wire from Calcutta the assurance of mother's doing well.

Turning to Swami Yogananda, Swamiji remarked, "Everything that the man had foretold came to be fulfilled to the letter, call it some fortuitous concurrence or anything you will."

Swami Yogananda said in reply, "It was because you would not believe all this before that this experience was necessary for you."

Swamiji: Well, I am not a fool to believe anything and everything without direct proof. And coming into this realm of Mahâmâya, oh, the many magic mysteries I have come across alongside this bigger magic conjuration of a universe! Maya, it is all Maya! Goodness! What rubbish we have been talking so long this day! By thinking constantly of ghosts, men become ghosts themselves, while whoever repeats day and night, knowingly or unknowingly, "I am the eternal, pure, free, self-illumined Atman", verily becomes the knower of Brahman.

Saying this, Swamiji affectionately turned to the disciple and said, "Don't allow all that worthless nonsense to occupy your mind. Always discriminate between the real and the unreal, and devote yourself heart and soul to the attempt to realise the Atman. There is nothing higher than this knowledge of the Atman; all else is Maya, mere jugglery. The Atman is the one unchangeable Truth. This I have come to understand, and that is why I try to bring it home to you all. "One Brahman there is without a second", "There is nothing manifold in existence" (Brihadâranyaka, IV. iv. 19)

All this conversation continued up to eleven o'clock at highs. After that, his meal being finished, Swamiji retired for rest.

The disciple bowed down at his feet to bid him good-bye. Swamiji asked, "Are you not coming tomorrow?"

Disciple: Yes, sir, I am coming, to be sure. The mind longs so much to meet you at least once before the day is out.

Swamiji: So good night now, it is getting very late.

The following conversations were taken from the Diary of a Disciple (Shri Sharat Chandra Chakravarty, B.A.)

UNTITLED CONVERSATION XIII

Swamiji was staying at the time at the rented garden-house of Nilambar Babu where the Math had been removed from Alambazar. Arrangements had been made for Shri Ramakrishna's Tithipuja (Nativity) on a grand scale. On the morning of the auspicious day, Swamiji personally inspected the preliminaries of the worship. The inspection over, Swamiji asked the disciple, "Well, you have brought the holy threads, I hope?"

Disciple: Yes, sir, I have. Everything is ready, as you desired. But, sir, I can't make out why so many holy threads are in requisition.

Swamiji: Every Dwijati[1] (twice-born) has a right to investiture with the holy thread. The Vedas themselves are authority in this matter. Whoever will come here on this sacred birthday of Shri Ramakrishna, I shall invest him with the holy thread. These people have fallen from their true status, and the scriptures say that after proper expiation, those fallen in the way earn the right to investiture with the holy thread. This is the great day of Shri Ramakrishna's nativity, and men will be purified by taking his name. So the assembled devotees are to be invested with the holy thread today; do you now understand?

Disciple: I have collected, Sir, quite a good number of holy threads according to your instructions, and after the worship I shall with your permission invest the Bhaktas with them.

Swamiji: To the Bhaktas who are not Brahmins, give this Mantra of Gayatri (here Swamiji communicated to the disciple the special Gayatris for them.) By degrees all the people of the land have to be lifted to the position of Brahmins, not to speak of the Bhaktas of Shri Ramakrishna. Each Hindu, I say, is a brother of every other, and it is we who have degraded them by our outcry, "Don't touch, don't touch!" And so the whole country has been plunged to the utmost depths of meanness, cowardice, and ignorance. These men have to be uplifted; words of hope and faith have to be proclaimed to them. We have to tell them, "You are men like us, and you have all the rights that we have." Do you understand?

Disciple: Yes, sir, it should be so.

Swamiji: Now, ask those who will take the holy thread to finish their bath in the Ganga. Than after prostration before Shri Ramakrishna, they will have their investiture.

About forty to fifty Bhaktas then duly received the Gayatri

1. Brahmins, Kshatriyas, and Vaishyas are the Dwijatis.

from the disciple and were invested with the holy thread. When receiving them, Swamiji's face beamed with profound delight. A little after this, Shri Girish Chandra Ghosh arrived at the Math from Calcutta.

Now arrangements for music were made at the desire of Swamiji, and Sannyasins of the Math decorated Swamiji as a Yogin.

Swamiji now chanted with the sweetest intonation to the accompaniment of the Tanpura, the Sanskrit hymn beginning with [(Sanskrit)] ("repeating in a low tone the name of Rama" etc.), and when the chanting came to a close, he went on repeating with exquisite charm the holy words "Rama, Rama, Shri Rama, Rama". His eyes were half-closed, and the natural sublimity of his countenance seemed today to have deepened a hundredfold. Everybody remained spelled for over a half an hour.

After the chanting of Shri Rama's name, Swamiji continued to sing a song of Tulsidas on Shri Ramachandra in the same intoxicated strain of mind. Then other music followed.

After this, Swamiji suddenly took to putting off all the decorations he had on his person and began to dress Girish Babu with them. Then he declared, "Paramahamsa-deva used to say our brother is the incarnation of Bhairava[2]. There's no distinction between us and him." Girish Babu sat speechless all the time. A piece of gerua cloth was also brought, and he was draped in it and uttered no word of remonstrance. For he had merged his self fully today in the wishes of his brother disciples. Swamiji now said, "Well, G. C., you are to speak to us today about Thakur (Lord). And all of you (turning all round himself) sit quiet and attentive." Even then, Girish Babu sat motionless, voiceless like marble, absolutely lost in joy. And when at last he opened his lips, he did so to say, "Ah, what can this humble self speak of our Lord of unbounded mercy! Verily in this alone I realise his mercy, that to me, this lowly creature, He has extended the privilege of sitting and mixing on the same footing with you Sannyasins, pure from your childhood, who have renounced all lust and lucre." While speaking thus, the words choked in his throat, and he could not speak anything more.

After this, some pieces of Hindu music were rendered by Swamiji. The devotees were now called to partake of refreshments. After refreshments, Swamiji came and took his seat in the parlour on the ground-floor, and all the many visitors sat round him. Accosting a house-holder friend who had his investiture with the holy thread that day, Swamiji said, "Really you all belong to the twice-born castes, only it is long since you lost your status. From this day again you become the twice-born. Repeat the Gayatri at least a hundred times daily, won't you?" The householder expressed his assent.

Meanwhile Srijut Mahendranath Gupta (Master Mahashaya [Venerable], or "M") appeared on the scene. Swamiji cordially received him and made him take his seat. "Master Mahash-

2. Divine companion of Shiva.

aya," said Swamiji, "this is the anniversary of Shri Ramakrishna's birthday. So you shall have to relate to us something about him." Master Mahashaya bent his head down smilingly in reply.

Just then it was announced that Swami Akhandananda had come from Murshidabad with two Pantuas[1] which weighed one maund and a half! All of us hurried out to see these prodigious Pantuas. When they were shown to Swamiji, he said, "Take them up to the chapel for offering."

Making Swami Akhandananda the subject of his remarks, Swamiji said to the disciple, "Mark you, what a great hero he is in work! Of fear, death and the like he has no cognisance—doggedly going on doing his own work —'work for the welfare of the many, for the happiness of the many'."

Disciple: Sir, that power must have come to him as the result of a good deal of austerities.

Swamiji: True, power comes of austerities; but again, working for the sake of others itself constitutes Tapasya (practice of austerity). The karma-yogins regard work itself as part of Tapasya. As on the one hand the practice of Tapasya intensifies altruistic feelings in the devotee and actuates him to unselfish work, so also the pursuit of work for the sake of others carries the worker to the last fruition of Tapasya, namely the purification of the heart, and leads him thus to the realisation of the supreme Atman (Self).

Disciple: But, sir, how few of us can work whole-heartedly for the sake of others from the very outset! How difficult it is for such broad-mindedness to come at all as will make men sacrifice the desire for their own happiness and devote their lives for others!

Swamiji: And how many have their minds going after Tapasya? With the attraction for lust and lucre working the other way, how many long for the realisation of God? In fact, disinterested work is quite as difficult as Tapasya. So you have no right to say anything against those who go in for work in the cause of others. If you find Tapasya to be to your liking, well, go on with it. Another may find work as congenial to himself, and you have no right to make a prohibition in his case. You seem to have the settled idea in your mind that work is no Tapasya at all!

Disciple: Yes, sir, before this I used to mean quite a different thing by Tapasya.

Swamiji: As by continuing our religious practices we gradually develop a certain determined tendency for it, so by performing disinterested work over and over again, even unwillingly, we gradually find the will merging itself in it. The inclination to work for others develops in this way, do you see? Just do some such work even though unwillingly, and then see if the actual fruit of Tapasya is realised within or not. As the outcome of work for the sake of others, the angularities of the mind get smoothed down, and men are gradually prepared for sincere self-sacrifice for the good of others.

Disciple: But, sir, what is the necessity at all for doing good to others?

Swamiji: Well, it is necessary for one's own good. We become forgetful of the ego when we think of the body as dedicated to the service of others—the body with which most complacently we identify the ego. And in the long run comes the consciousness of disembodiness. The more intently you think of the well-being of others, the more oblivious of self you become. In this way, as gradually your heart gets purified by work, you will come to feel the truth that your own Self is pervading all beings and all things. Thus it is that doing good to others constitutes a way, a means of revealing one's own Self or Atman. Know this also to be one of the spiritual practices, a discipline for God-realisation. Its aim also is Self-realisation. Exactly as that aim is attained by Jnana (knowledge), Bhakti (devotion) and so on, also by work for the sake of others.

Disciple: But, sir, if I am to keep thinking of others day and night, when shall I contemplate on the Atman? If I rest wholly occupied with something particular and relative, how can I realise the Atman which is Absolute?

Swamiji: The highest aim of all disciplines, all spiritual paths, is the attainment of the knowledge of Atman. If you, by being devoted to the service of others and by getting your heart purified by such work, attain to the vision of all beings as the Self, what else remains to be attained in the way of Self-realisation? Would you say that Self-realisation is the state of existing as inert matter, as this wall or as this piece of wood, for instance?

Disciple: Though that is not the meaning, yet what the scriptures speak of as the withdrawal of the Self into Its real nature consists in the arresting of all mind-functions and all work.

Swamiji: Yes, this Samadhi of which the scriptures speak is a state not at all easy to attain. When very rarely it appears in somebody, it does not last for long; so what will he keep himself occupied with? Thus it is that after realising that state described in the scriptures, the saint sees the Self in all beings and in that consciousness devotes himself to service, so that any Karma that was yet left to be worked out through the body may exhaust itself. It is this state which has been described by the authors of the Shastras (scriptures) as Jivanmukti, "Freedom while living".

Disciple: So after all it comes about, sir, that unless this state of Jivanmukti is attained, work for the sake of others can never be pursued in the truest sense of the term.

Swamiji: Yes, that is what the Shastras say, but they also say that work or service for the good of others leads to this state of Jivanmukti. Otherwise there would be no need on the part of the Shastras to teach a separate path of religious practice, called the Karma-yoga.

The disciple now understood the point and became silent, and Swamiji giving up the point commenced rendering in a voice of superhuman sweetness the song composed by Babu

---

1. A sweetmeat usually about two inches in length, made mostly of fresh cheese fried in ghee and put in syrup.

Girish Chandra Ghosh to commemorate Shri Ramakrishna's Nativity, and beginning:

"Who art Thou lying on the lap of the poor Brahmin matron."

UNTITLED CONVERSATION XIV

Today Swamiji is to perform a sacrifice and install Shri Ramakrishna on the site of the new Math. The disciple has been staying at the Math since the night before, with a view to witnessing the installation ceremony.

In the morning Swamiji had his bath in the Ganga and entered the worship-room. Then he made offerings to the sacred Padukas (slippers) of Shri Ramakrishna and fell to meditation.

Meditation and worship over, preparations were now made for going to the new Math premises. Swamiji himself took on his right shoulder the ashes of Shri Ramakrishna's body preserved in a copper casket, and led the van. The disciple in company with other Sannyasins brought up the rear. There was the music of bells and conchs. On his way Swamiji said to the disciple, "Shri Ramakrishna said to me, 'Wherever you will take me on your shoulders, there I will go and stay, be it under a tree or in a hut.' It is therefore that I am myself carrying him on my shoulders to the new Math grounds. Know it for certain that Shri Ramakrishna will keep his seat fixed there, for the welfare of many, for a long time to come."

Disciple: When was it that he said this to you?

Swamiji: Didn't you hear from them? It was at the Cossipur garden.

Disciple: I see. It was on this occasion, I suppose, that the split took place between Shri Ramakrishna's Sannyasin and householder disciples regarding the privilege of serving him?

Swamiji: Yes, but not exactly a "split"— it was only a misunderstanding, that's all. Rest assured that among those that are Shri Ramakrishna's devotees, and have truly obtained his grace, there is no sect or schism, there cannot be— be they householders or Sannyasins. As to that kind of slight misunderstanding, do you know what it was due to? Well, each devotee colours Shri Ramakrishna in the light of his own understanding and each forms his own idea of him from his peculiar standpoint. He was, as it were, a great Sun and each one of us is eyeing him, as it were, through a different kind of colored glass and coming to look upon that one Sun as particoloured. Of course, it is quite true that this leads to schism in course of time. But then, such schisms rarely occur in the lifetime of those who are fortunate enough to have come in direct contact with an Avatara. The effulgence of that Personality, who takes pleasure only in his Self, dazzles their eyes and sweeps away pride, egotism, and narrow-mindedness from their minds. Consequently they find no opportunity to create sects and party factions. They are content to offer him their heart's worship, each in his own fashion.

Disciple: Sir, do the devotees of the Avatara, then, view him differently notwithstanding their knowing him to be God, and does this lead to the succeeding generations of their followers to limit themselves within narrow bounds and form various little sects?

Swamiji: Quite so. Hence sects are bound to form in course of time. Look, for instance, how the followers of Chaitanya Deva have been divided into two or three hundred sects; and those of Jesus hold thousands of creeds. But all those sects without exception follow Chaitanya Deva or Jesus, and none else.

Disciple: Then, perhaps, Shri Ramakrishna's followers, too, will be divided in course of time into various sects?

Swamiji: Well, of course. But then this Math that we are building will harmonise all creeds, all standpoints. Just as Shri Ramakrishna held highly liberal views, this Math too, will be a center for propagating similar ideas. The blazing light of universal harmony that will emanate from here will flood the whole world.

While all this was going on, the party reached the Math premises. Swamiji took the casket down from his shoulder, placed in on the carpet spread on the ground, and bowed before it touching the ground with his forehead. Others too followed suit.

Then Swamiji again sat for worship. After going through the Puja (worship), he lighted the sacrificial fire, made oblations to it, and himself cooking Payasa (milk-rice with sugar) with the help of his brother-disciples, offered it to Shri Ramakrishna. Probably also he initiated certain householders on the spot that day. All this ceremony being done, Swamiji cordially addressed the assembled gentlemen and said, "Pray today all of you, heart and soul, to the holy feet of Shri Ramakrishna, that the great Avatara of this cycle that he is, he may "For the welfare of the many, and for the happiness of the many— [(Sanskrit)]", reside in this holy spot from this day for a great length of time, and ever continue to make it the unique center of harmony amongst all religions." Everyone prayed like that with folded palms. Swamiji next called the disciple and said, "None of us (Sannyasins) have any longer the right to take back this casket of Shri Ramakrishna, for we have installed him here today. It behoves you, therefore, to take it on your head back (to Nilambar Babu's garden)". Seeing that the disciple hesitated to touch the casket, Swamiji said, "No fear, touch it, you have my order." The disciple gladly obeyed the injunction, lifted the casket on his head, and moved on. He went first, next came Swamiji, and the rest followed. Swamiji said to the disciple on the way, "Shri Ramakrishna has today sat on your head and is blessing you. Take care, never let your mind think of anything transitory, from this day forth." Before crossing a small bridge, Swamiji again said to him, "Beware, now, you must move very cautiously."

Thus all safely reached the Math and rejoiced. Swamiji now entered into a conversation with the disciple, in the course of which he said, "Through the will of Shri Ramakrishna, his Dharmakshetra—sanctified spot—has been established to-day. A twelve years' anxiety is off my head. Do you know what I am thinking of at this moment?— this Math will be a center of learning and spiritual discipline. Householders of a virtuous turn like yourselves will build houses on the surrounding land and live there, and Sannyasins, men of renunciation, will live in the center, while on that plot of land on the south of the Math, buildings will be erected for English and American disciples to live in. How do you like this idea?

Disciple: Sir, it is indeed a wonderful fancy of yours.

Swamiji: A fancy do you call it? Not at all, everything will come about in time. I am but laying the foundation. There will be lots of further developments in future. Some portion of it I shall live to work out. And I shall infuse into you fellows various ideas, which you will work out in future. It will not do merely to listen to great principles. You must apply them in the practical field, turn them into constant practice. What will be the good of cramming the high-sounding dicta of the scriptures? You have first to grasp the teachings of the Shastras, and then to work them out in practical life. Do you understand? This is called practical religion.

Thus the talk went on, and gradually drifted to the topic of Shankaracharya. The disciple was a great adherent of Shankara, almost to the point of fanaticism. He used to look upon Shankara's Advaita philosophy as the crest of all philosophies and could not bear any criticism of him. Swamiji was aware of this, and, as was his wont, wanted to break this one-sidedness of the disciple.

Swamiji: Shankara's intellect was sharp like the razor. He was a good arguer and a scholar, no doubt of that, but he had no great liberality; his heart too seems to have been like that. Besides, he used to take great pride in his Brahmanism—much like a southern Brahmin of the priest class, you may say. How he has defended in his commentary on the Vedanta-sutras that the non-brahmin castes will not attain to a supreme knowledge of Brahman! And what specious arguments! Referring to Vidura[1] he has said that he became a knower of Brahman by reason of his Brahmin body in the previous incarnation. Well, if nowadays any Shudra attains to a knowledge of Brahman, shall we have to side with your Shankara and maintain that because he had been a Brahmin in his previous birth, therefore he has attained to this knowledge? Goodness! What is the use of dragging in Brahminism with so much ado? The Vedas have entitled any one belonging to the three upper castes to study the Vedas and the realisation of Brahman, haven't they? So Shankara had no need whatsoever of displaying this curious bit of pedantry on this subject, contrary to the Vedas. And such was his heart that he burnt to death lots of Buddhist monks—by defeating them in argument! And the Buddhists, too, were foolish enough to burn themselves to death, simply because they were worsted in argument! What can you call such an action on Shankara's part except fanaticism? But look at Buddha's heart! Ever ready to give his own life to save the life of even a kid—what to speak of "[(Sanskrit)]—for the welfare of the many, for the happiness of the many"! See, what a large heartedness—what a compassion!

Disciple: Can't we call that attitude of the Buddha, too, another kind of fanaticism, sir? He went to the length of sacrificing his own body for the sake of a beast!

Swamiji: But consider how much good to the world and its beings came out of that 'fanaticism' of his—how many monasteries and schools and colleges, how many public hospitals and veterinary refuges were established, how developed architecture became—think of that. What was there in this country before Buddha's advent? Only a number of religious principles recorded on bundles of palm leaves—and those too known only to a few. It was Lord Buddha who brought them down to the practical field and showed how to apply them in the everyday life of the people. In a sense, he was the living embodiment of true Vedanta.

Disciple: But, sir, it was he who by breaking down the Varnashrama Dharma (duty according to caste and order of life) brought about a revolution within the fold of Hinduism in India, and there seems to be some truth also in the remark that the religion he preached was for this reason banished in course of time from the soil of India.

Swamiji: It was not through his teachings that Buddhism came to such degradation, it was the fault of his followers. By becoming too philosophic they lost much of their breadth of heart. Then gradually the corruption known as Vamachara (unrestrained mixing with women in the name of religion) crept in and ruined Buddhism. Such diabolical rites are not to be met with in any modern Tantra! One of the principal centres of Buddhism was Jagannatha or Puri, and you have simply to go there and look at the abominable figures carved on the temple walls to be convinced of this. Puri has come under the sway of the Vaishnavas since the time of Ramanuja and Shri Chaitanya. Through the influence of great personages like these the place now wears an altogether different aspect.

Disciple: Sir, the Shastras tell us of various special influences attaching to places of pilgrimage. How far is this claim true?

Swamiji: When the whole world is the Form Universal of the Eternal Atman, the Ishvara (God), what is there to wonder at in special influences attaching to particular places? There are places where He manifests Himself specially, either spontaneously or through the earnest longing of pure souls, and the ordinary man, if he visits those places with eagerness, attains his end quite easily. Therefore it may lead to the development of the Self in time to have recourse to holy places. But know it for certain that there is no greater Tirtha (holy spot) than the body of man. Nowhere else is the Atman so manifest as here. That car of Jagannatha that you see is but a concrete symbol of this corporeal car. You have to behold the Atman in this

---

1. Uncle of the Pandava brothers, and a most saintly character, considered to be an incarnation of Dharma.

car of the body. Haven't you read "[(Sanskrit)]—know the Atman to be seated on the chariot" etc., "[(Sanskrit)]—all the gods worship the Vamana (the Supreme Being in a diminutive form) seated in the interior of the body"? The sight of the Atman is the real vision of Jagannatha. And the statement "[(Sanskrit)]—seeing the Vamana on the car, one is no more subject to rebirth", means that if you can visualise the Atman which is within you, and disregarding which you are always identifying yourself with this curious mass of matter, this body of yours—if you can see that, then there is no more rebirth for you. If the sight of the Lord's image on a wooden framework confers liberation on people, then crores of them would be liberated every year—specially with such facility of communication by rail nowadays! But I do not mean to say that the notion which devotees in general entertain towards Shri Jagannatha is either nothing or erroneous. There is a class of people who gradually rise to higher and higher truths with the help of that image. So it is an undoubted fact that in and through that image there is a special manifestation of the Lord.

Disciple: Sir, are there different religions then for the ignorant and the wise?

Swamiji: Quite so. Otherwise why do your scriptures go to such lengths over the specification of the qualifications of an aspirant? All is truth no doubt, but relative truth, different in degrees. Whatever man knows to be truth is of a like nature: some are lesser truths, others, higher ones in comparison with them, while the Absolute Truth is God alone. This Atman is altogether dormant in matter; in man, designated as a living being, It is partially conscious; while in personages like Shri Krishna, Buddha, and Shankara the same Atman has reached the superconscious stage. There is a state even beyond that, which cannot be expressed in terms of thought or language—[(Sanskrit)].

Disciple: Sir, there are certain Bhakti sects who hold that we must practise devotion by placing ourselves in a particular attitude or relation with God. They do not understand anything about the glory of the Atman and so forth, and exclusively recommend this constant devotional attitude.

Swamiji: What they say is true to their own case. By continued practice along this line, they too shall feel an awakening of Brahman within them. And what we (Sannyasins) are doing is another kind of practice. We have renounced the world. So how will it suit us to practise by putting ourselves in some worldly relation—such as that of mother, or father, or wife or son, and so forth—with God? To us all these ideals appear to be narrow. Of course it is very difficult to qualify for the worship of God in His absolute, unconditioned aspect. But must we go in for poison because we get no nectar? Always talk and hear and reason about this Atman. By continuing to practise in this way, you will find in time that the Lion (Brahman) will wake up in you too. Go beyond all those relative attitudes—mere sports of the mind. Listen to what Yama says

in the Katha Upanisad: [(Sanskrit)][2] Arise! Awake! and stop not until the goal is reached!

Here the subject was brought to a close. The bell for taking Prasada (consecrated food) rang, and Swamiji went to partake of it, followed by the disciple.

UNTITLED CONVERSATION XV

Swamiji has removed the Math from Alambazar to Nilambar Babu's garden at Belur. He is very glad to have come to these new premises. He said to the disciple when the latter came, "See how the Ganga flows by and what a nice building! I like this place. This is the ideal kind of place for a Math." It was then afternoon.

In the evening the disciple found Swamiji alone in the upper storey, and the talk went on, on various topics, in the course of which he wanted to know about Swamiji's boyhood days. Swamiji began to say, "From my very boyhood I was a dare-devil sort of fellow. Otherwise, do you think I could make a tour round the world without a single copper in my pocket?"

In boyhood Swamiji had a great predilection for hearing the chanting of the Ramayana by professional singers. Wherever such chanting would take place in the neighborhood, he would attend it, leaving sport and all. Swamiji related how, while listening to the Ramayana, on some days, he would be so deeply engrossed in it as to forget all about home, and would have no idea that it was late at night, and that he must return home, and so forth. One day during the chant he heard that the monkey-god Hanuman lived in banana orchards. Forthwith he was so much convinced that when the chant was over, he did not go home straight that night, but loitered in a banana orchard close to his house, with the hope of catching sight of Hanuman, till it was very late in the night.

In his student life he used to pass the day-time only in playing and gambolling with his mates, and study at night bolting the doors. And none could know when he prepared his lessons.

The disciple asked, "Did you see any visions, sir, during your school days?"

Swamiji: While at school, one night I was meditating within closed doors and had a fairly deep concentration of mind. How long I meditated in that way, I cannot say. It was over, and I still kept my seat, when from the southern wall of that room a luminous figure stepped out and stood in front of me. There was a wonderful radiance on its visage, yet there seemed to be no play of emotion on it. It was the figure of a Sannyasin absolutely calm, shaven-headed, and staff and Kamandalu (a Sannyasin's wooden water-bowl) in hand. He gazed at me for some time and seemed as if he would address me. I too gazed at him in speechless wonder. Then a kind of fright seized me, I opened the door, and hurried out of the room. Then it struck

---

2. Arise, awake, and learn by approaching the elite.

me that it was foolish of me to run away like that, that perhaps he might say something to me. But I have never met that figure since. Many a time and often I have thought that if again I saw him, I would no more be afraid but would speak to him. But I met him no more.

Disciple: Did you ever think on the matter afterwards?

Swamiji: Yes, but I could find no clue to its solution. I now think it was the Lord Buddha whom I saw.

After a short pause, Swamiji said, "When the mind is purified, when one is free from the attachment for lust and gold, one sees lots of visions, most wonderful ones! But one should not pay heed to them. The aspirant cannot advance further if he sets his mind constantly on them. Haven't you heard that Shri Ramakrishna used to say, 'Countless jewels lie uncared for in the outer courts of my beloved Lord's sanctum'? We must come face to face with the Atman; what is the use of setting one's mind on vagaries like those?"

After saying these words, Swamiji sat silent for a

while, lost in thought over something. He then resumed:

"Well, while I was in America I had certain wonderful powers developed in me. By looking into people's eyes I could fathom in a trice the contents of their minds. The workings of everybody's mind would be potent to me, like a fruit on the palm of one's hand. To some I used to give out these things, and of those to whom I communicated these, many would become my disciples; whereas those who came to mix with me with some ulterior motive would not, on coming across this power of mine, even venture into my presence any more. "When I began lecturing in Chicago and other cities, I had to deliver every week some twelve or fifteen or even more lectures at times. This excessive strain on the body and mind would exhaust me to a degree. I seemed to run short of subjects for lectures and was anxious where to find new topics for the morrow's lecture. New thoughts seemed altogether scarce. One day, after the lecture, I lay thinking of what means to adopt next. The thought induced a sort of slumber, and in that state I heard as if somebody standing by me was lecturing—many new ideas and new veins of thought, which I had scarcely heard or thought of in my life. On awaking I remembered them and reproduced them in my lecture. I cannot enumerate how often this phenomenon took place. Many, many days did I hear such lectures while lying in bed. Sometimes the lecture would be delivered in such a loud voice that the inmates of adjacent rooms would hear the sound and ask me the next day, "With whom, Swamiji, were you talking so loudly last night?" I used to avoid the question somehow. Ah, it was a wonderful phenomenon."

The disciple was wonder-struck at Swamiji's words and after thinking deeply on the matter said, "Sir, then you yourself must have lectured like that in your subtle body, and sometimes it would be echoed by the gross body also."

Swamiji listened and replied, "Well, may be."

The topic of his American experiences came up. Swami-ji said, "In that country the women are more learned than men. They are all well versed in science and philosophy, and that is why they would appreciate and honour me so much. The men are grinding all day at their work and have very little leisure, whereas the women, by studying and teaching in schools and colleges, have become highly learned. Whichever side you turn your eyes in America, you see the power and influence of women."

Disciple: Well, sir, did not the bigoted Christians oppose you?

Swamiji: Yes, they did. When people began to honour me, then the Padris were after me. They spread many slanders about me by publishing them in the newspapers. Many asked me to contradict these slanders. But I never took the slightest notice of them. It is my firm conviction that no great work is accomplished in this world by low cunning; so without paying any heed to these vile slanders, I used to work steadily at my mission. The upshot I used to find was that often my slanderers, feeling repentant afterwards, would surrender to me and offer apologies, by themselves contradicting the slanders in the papers. Sometimes it so happened that learning that I had been invited to a certain house, somebody would communicate those slanders to my host, who hearing them, would leave home, locking his door. When I went there to attend the invitation, I found it was deserted and nobody was there. Again a few days afterwards, they themselves, learning the truth, would feel sorry for their previous conduct and come to offer themselves as disciples. The fact is, my son, this whole world is full of mean ways of worldliness. But men of real moral courage and discrimination are never deceived by these. Let the world say what it chooses, I shall tread the path of duty—know this to be the line of action for a hero. Otherwise, if one has to attend day and night to what this man says or that man writes, no great work is achieved in this world. Do you know this Sanskrit Shloka: "Let those who are versed in the ethical codes praise or blame, let Lakshmi, the goddess of Fortune, come or go wherever she wisheth, let death overtake him today or after a century, the wise man never swerves from the path of rectitude."[1] Let people praise you or blame you, let fortune smile or frown upon you, let your body fall today or after a Yuga, see that you do not deviate from the path of Truth. How much of tempest and waves one has to weather, before one reaches the haven of Peace! The greater a man has become, the fiercer ordeal he has had to pass through. Their lives have been tested true by the touchstone of practical life, and only then have they been acknowledged great by the world. Those who are faint-hearted and cowardly sink their barks near the shore, frightened by the raging of waves on the sea. He who is a hero never casts a glance at these. Come what may, I must attain my ideal first—this is Purushakara, manly endeavour; without such manly endeavor no amount of Divine help will be of any avail to banish your inertia.

---

1. Bhartrihari's Nitishataka.

Disciple: Is, then, reliance on Divine help a sign of weakness?

Swamiji: In the Shastras real self-surrender and reliance on God has been indicated as the culmination of human achievement. But in your country nowadays the way people speak of Daiva or reliance on Divine dispensation is a sign of death, the outcome of great cowardliness; conjuring up some monstrous idea of God-head and trying to saddle that with all your faults and shortcomings. Haven't you heard Shri Ramakrishna's story about "the sin of killing a cow"?[2] In the end the owner of the garden had to suffer for the sin of killing the cow. Nowadays everybody says: "I am acting as I am being directed by the Lord", and thus throws the burden of both his sins and virtues on the Lord. As if he is himself the lotus-leaf in the water (untouched by it)! If everybody can truly live always in this mood, then he is a Free Soul. But what really happens is that for the "good" I have the credit, but the "bad" Thou, God, art responsible! Praise be to such reliance on God! Without the attainment of the fullness of Knowledge or Divine Love, such a state of absolute reliance on the Lord does not come. He who is truly and sincerely reliant on the Lord goes beyond all idea of the duality of good and bad. The brightest example of the attainment of this state among us at the present time is Nag Mahashaya.[3]

Then the conversation drifted to the subject of Nag Mahashaya. Swamiji said, "One does not find a second devoted Bhakta like him—oh, when shall I see him again!"

Disciple: He will soon come to Calcutta to meet you, so mother (Nag Mahashaya's wife) has written to me.

Swamiji: Shri Ramakrishna used to compare him to King Janaka. A man with such control over all the senses one does not hear of even, much less come across. You must associate with him as much as you can. He is one of Shri Ramakrishna's nearest disciples.

Disciple: Many in our part of the country call him a madcap. But I have known him to be a great soul since the very first day of my meeting him. He loves me much, and I have his fervent blessings.

Swamiji: Since you have attained the company of such a Mahapurusha (holy soul), what more have you to fear about? As an effect of many lives of Tapasya one is blessed with the company of such a great soul. How does he live at home?

Disciple: Sir, he has got no business or anything of the kind. He is always busy in serving the guests who come to

his house. Beyond the small sum the Pal Babus give him, he has no other means of subsistence; his expenses, however, are like those in a rich family. But he does not spend a pice for his own enjoyment, all that expense is for the service of others. Service—service of others—this seems to be the great mission of his life. It sometimes strikes me that realising the Atman in all creatures, he is engrossed in serving the whole world as a part and parcel of himself. In the service of others he works incessantly and is not conscious even of his body. I suppose, he always lives on the plane which you, sir, call the superconscious state of the mind.

Swamiji: Why should not that be? How greatly was he beloved of Shri Ramakrishna! In your East Bengal, one of Shri Ramakrishna's divine companions has been born in the person of Nag Mahashaya. By his radiance Eastern Bengal has become effulgent.

UNTITLED CONVERSATION XVI

It is two or three days since Swamiji has returned from Kashmir. His health is indifferent. When the disciple came to the Math, Swami Brahmananda said, "Since returning from Kashmir, Swamiji does not speak to anybody, he sits in one place rapt in thought; you go to him and by conversation try to draw his mind a little towards worldly objects."

The disciple coming to Swamiji's room in the upper storey found him sitting as if immersed in deep mediation. There was no smile on his face, his brilliant eyes had no outward look, as if intent on seeing something within. Seeing the disciple, he only said, "You have come, my son? Please take your seat", and lapsed into silence. The disciple seeing the inside of his left eye reddened asked, "How is it that your eye is red?" "That is nothing", said Swamiji and was again silent. When even after along time Swamiji did not speak, the disciple was a little troubled at heart and touching his feet said, "Won't you relate to me what things you have seen at Amarnath?" By the disciple's touching his feet, the tensity of his mood was broken a little, as if his attention was diverted a little outwards. He said, "Since visiting Amarnath, I feel as if Shiva is sitting on my head for twenty-four hours and would not come down." The disciple heard it with speechless wonder.

Swamiji: I underwent great religious austerities at Amarnath and then in the temple of Kshir Bhavani. Go and prepare me some tobacco, I will relate everything to you.

The disciple joyfully obeyed the order. Swamiji slowly smoking began to say, "On the way to Amarnath, I made a very steep ascent on the mountain. Pilgrims do not generally travel by that path. But the determination came upon me that I must go by that path, and so I did. The labour of the strenuous ascent has told on my body. The cold there is so biting that you feel it like pin-pricks."

Disciple: I have heard that it is the custom to visit the image of Amarnath naked; is it so?

---

2. A man had laid out a beautiful garden into which a cow strayed one day and did much injury. The man in rage gave some blows to the cow which killed her. Then to avoid the terrible sin he bethought himself of a trick; knowing that Indra was the presiding deity of the hand, he tried to lay the blame on him. Indra perceiving his sophistry appeared on the scene in the guise of a Brahmin and by a number of questions drew from him the answer that each and every item in connection with that garden was the man's own handiwork; whereupon Indra exposed his cunning with the cutting remark, "Well, everything here has been done by you, and Indra alone is responsible for the killing of the cow, eh!"

3. Durga Charan Nag, a disciple of Shri Ramakrishna.

Swamiji: Yes, I entered the cave with only my Kaupina on and my body smeared with holy ash; I did not then feel any cold or heat. But when I came out of the temple, I was benumbed by the cold.

Disciple: Did you see the holy pigeons? I have heard, in that cold no living creatures are found to live, but a flight of pigeons from some unknown place frequents the place occasionally.

Swamiji: Yes, I saw three or four white pigeons; whether they live in the cave or the neighboring hills, I could not ascertain.

Disciple: Sir, I have heard people say that the sight of pigeons on coming out of the temple indicates that one has really been blessed with the vision of Shiva.

Swamiji: I have heard that the sight of the pigeons brings to fruition whatever desires one may have.

Then Swamiji said that on the way back he returned to Srinagar by the common route by which the pilgrims return. A few days after returning to Srinagar, he went to visit Kshir Bhavani Devi and staying there for seven days worshipped the Devi and made Homa to her with offerings of Kshira (condensed milk). Every day he used to worship the Devi with a maund of Kshira as offering. One day, while worshipping, the thought arose in Swamiji's mind: "Mother Bhavani has been manifesting Her Presence here for untold years. The Mohammedans came and destroyed her temple, yet the people of the place did nothing to protect Her. Alas, if I were then living I could never have borne it silently." When, thinking in this strain, his mind was much oppressed with sorrow and anguish, he distinctly heard the voice of the Mother saying, "It was according to My desire that the Mohammedans destroyed this temple. It is My desire that I should live in a dilapidated temple, otherwise, can I not immediately erect a seven-storeyed temple of gold here if I like? What can you do? Shall I protect you or shall you protect me!" Swamiji said, "Since hearing that divine voice, I cherish no more plans. The idea of building Maths etc. I have given up; as Mother wills, so it will be." The disciple, speechless with wonder, began to think, "Did he not one day tell me that whatever I saw and heard was but the echo of the Atman within me, that there was nothing outside?"— and fearlessly spoke it out also —"Sir, you used to say that Divine Voices are the echo of our inward thoughts and feelings." Swamiji gravely said, "Whether it be internal or external, if you actually hear with your ears such a disembodied voice, as I have done, can you deny it and call it false? Divine Voices are actually heard, just as you and I are talking."

The disciple, without controverting accepted Swamiji's words, for his words always carried conviction.

He then brought up the subject of departed spirits, and said, "Sir, these ghosts and departed spirits we hear about—which the Shastras also amply corroborate—are all these true or not?

Swamiji: Certainly they are true. Whatever you don't see, are they all false for that? Beyond your sight, millions of universes are revolving at great distances. Because you do not see them, are they non-existent for that? But then, do not put your mind on these subjects of ghosts and spirits. Your mental attitude towards them should be one of indifference. You duty is to realise the Atman within this body. When you realise the Atman, ghosts and spirits will be your slaves.

Disciple: But sir, I think that, if one sees them, it strengthens one's belief in the hereafter, and dispels all doubts about it.

Swamiji: You are heroes; do you mean to say that even you shall have to strengthen your belief in the hereafter by seeing ghosts and spirits! You have read so many sciences and scriptures—have mastered so many secrets of this infinite universe—even with such knowledge, you have to acquire the knowledge of the Atman by seeing ghosts and spirits! What a shame!

Disciple: Well, sir, have you ever seen ghosts and spirits?

Swamiji narrated that a certain deceased relative of his used to come to him as a disembodied spirit. Sometimes it used to bring him information about distant events. But on verification, some of its information was not found to be correct. Afterwards at a certain place of pilgrimage Swamiji prayed for it mentally, wishing it might be released—since then he did not see it again. The disciple then questioned Swamiji if Shraddha or other obsequial ceremonies appeased the departed spirits in any way. Swamiji replied, "That is not impossible." On the disciple's asking for the grounds of that belief Swamiji said, "I will explain the subject to you at length some day. There are irrefutable arguments to prove that the Shraddha ceremony appeases the departed beings. Today I don't feel well. I shall explain it to you another day." But the disciple did not get another opportunity to ask that question to Swamiji.

UNTITLED CONVERSATION XVII

The Math is still situated in Nilambar Babu's garden house at Belur. It is the month of November. Swamiji is now much engaged in the study and discussion of Sanskrit scriptures. The couplet beginning with "Achandala-pratihatarayah", he composed about this time. Today Swamiji composed the hymn, "Om Hring Ritam "etc., and handing it over to the disciple said, "See if there is any metrical defect in these stanzas." The disciple made a copy of the poem for this purpose.

On this day it seemed as if the goddess of learning had manifested herself on his tongue. With the disciple he fluently talked about two hours at a stretch in exceedingly melodious Sanskrit. After the disciple had copied the hymn, Swamiji said, "You see, as I write immersed in thought, grammatical slips sometimes occur; therefore I ask you all to look over them."

Disciple: Sir, these are not slips, but the licence of genius.

Swamiji: You may say so; but why will other people assent to that? The other day I wrote an essay on "What is Hinduism", and some amongst you even are complaining that it was written in a very stiff Bengali. I think, language and thought also, like all other things, become lifeless and monotonous in course of time. Such a state seems to have happened now in this country. On the advent of Shri Ramakrishna, however, a new current has set in, in thought and language. Everything has now to be recast in new moulds. Everything has to be propagated with the stamp of new genius. Look, for example, how the old modes of Sannyasins are breaking, yielding place to a new mould by degrees. The Sannyasins of the present day have to go to distant countries for preaching, and if they go in an ash-besmeared, half-nude body like the Sadhus (holy men) of old, in the first place they won't be taken on board the ships, and even if they anyhow reach foreign countries in that dress, they will have to stay in jail. Everything requires to be changed a little according to place, time, and civilisation. Henceforth I am thinking of writing essays in Bengali. Litterateurs will perhaps rail at them. Never mind—I shall try to cast the Bengali language in a new mould. Nowadays, Bengali writers use too many verbs in their writings; this takes away the force of the language. If one can express the ideas of verbs with adjectives, it adds to the force of the language; henceforth try to write in that style. Try to write articles in that style in the Udbodhan. Do you know the meaning of the use of verbs in language? It gives a pause to the thought; hence the use of too many verbs in language is the sign of weakness, like quick breathing, and indicates that there is not much vitality in the language; that is why one cannot lecture well in the Bengali language. He who has control over his language, does not make frequent breaks in his thoughts. As your physique has been rendered languid by living on a dietary of boiled rice and dal, similar is the case with your language. In food, in modes of life, in thought, and in language, energy has to be infused. With the infusion of vitality all round and the circulation of blood in all arteries and veins, one should feel the throbbing of new life in everything—then only will the people of this land be able to survive the present terrible struggle for existence; otherwise the country and the race will vanish in the enveloping shadows of death at no distant date.

Disciple: Sir, the constitution of the people of this country has been moulded in a peculiar way through long ages. Is it possible to change that within a short time?

Swamiji: If you have known the old ways to be wrong, then why don't you, as I say, learn to live in a better way? By your example ten other people will follow suit, and by theirs another fifty people will learn. By this process in course of time the new idea will awaken in the hearts of the whole race. But even if after understanding, you do not act accordingly, I shall know that you are wise in words only—but practically you are fools.

Disciple: Your words, sir, infuse great courage, enthusiasm, energy and strength into the heart.

Swamiji: By degrees the heart has to be strengthened. If one man is made, it equals the result of a hundred thousand lec-

tures. Making the mind and lips at one, the ideas have to be practised in life. This is what Shri Ramakrishna meant by "allowing no theft in the chamber of thought". You have to be practical in all spheres of work. The whole country has been ruined by masses of theories. He who is the true son of Shri Ramakrishna will manifest the practical side of religious ideas and will set to work with one-pointed devotion without paying heed to the prattling of men or of society. Haven't you heard of the couplet of Tulsidas: "The elephant walks the market-place and a thousand curs bark at him; so the Sadhus have no ill-feeling if worldly people slander them." You have to walk in this way. No count should be taken of the words of people. If one has to pay heed to their praise or blame, no great work can be accomplished in this life. "नायमात्मा बलहीनेन लभ्य:— the Atman is not to be gained by the weak." If there is no strength in the body and mind, the Atman cannot be realised. First you have to build the body by good nutritious food—then only will the mind be strong. The mind is but the subtle part of the body. You must retain great strength in your mind and words. "I am low, I am low"— repeating these ideas in the mind, man belittles and degrades himself. Therefore, the Shastra (Ashtavakra Samhita, I.11) says:

मुक्ताभिमानी मुक्तो हि बद्धो बद्धाभिमान्यपि।
किंवदन्तीह सत्येयं या मति: सा गतिर्भवेत॥

— He who thinks himself free, free he becomes; he who thinks himself bound, bound he remains—this popular saying is true: 'As one thinks, so one becomes'." He alone who is always awake to the idea of freedom, becomes free; he who thinks he is bound, endures life after life in the state of bondage. It is a fact. This truth holds good both in spiritual and temporal matters. Those who are always down-hearted and dispirited in this life can do no work; from life to life they come and go wailing and moaning. "The earth is enjoyed by heroes"— this is the unfailing truth. Be a hero. Always say, "I have no fear." Tell this to everybody —"Have no fear". Fear is death, fear is sin, fear is hell, fear is unrighteousness, fear is wrong life. All the negative thoughts and ideas that are in this world have proceeded from this evil spirit of fear. This fear alone has kept the sun, air and death in their respective places and functions, allowing none to escape from their bounds. Therefore the Shruti says (Katha Upanishad, II.iii,3) says:

"भयादस्याग्निस्तपति भयात्तपति सूर्य:।
भयादिन्द्रश्च वायुश्च मृत्युर्धावति पञ्चम:॥

— Through fear of this, fire burns, the sun heats; through fear Indra and Vayu are carrying on their functions, and Death stalks upon this earth." When the gods Indra, Chandra, Vayu, Varuna will attain to fearlessness, then will they be one with Brahman, and all this phantasm of the world will vanish. Therefore I say, "Be fearless, be fearless."

Swamiji, in saying these words, appeared in the eyes of the disciple like the very embodiment of "fearlessness", and he thought, "How in his presence even the fear of death leaves one and vanishes into nothingness!"

Swamiji continued: In this embodied existence, you will be tossed again and again on the waves of happiness and misery, prosperity and adversity—but know them all to be of momentary duration. Never care for them. "I am birthless, the deathless Atman, whose nature is Intelligence"— implanting this idea firmly in your heart, you should pass the days of your life. "I have no birth, no death, I am the Atman untouched by anything"— lose yourself completely in this idea. If you can once become one with this idea, then in the hour of sorrow and tribulation, it will rise of itself in your mind, and you will not have to strive with difficulty to bring it up. The other day, I was a guest of Babu Priyanath Mukherjee at Baidyanath. There I had such a spell of asthma that I felt like dying. But from within, with every breath arose the deep-toned sound, "I am He, I am He". Resting on the pillow, I was waiting for the vital breath to depart, and observing all the time that from within was being heard the sound of "I am He, I am He!" I could hear all along एकमेवाद्वयं ब्रह्म नेह नानास्ति किञ्चन—the Brahman, the One without a second, alone exists, nothing manifold exists in the world."

The disciple, struck with amazement said, "Sir, talking with you and listening to your realisations, I feel no necessity for the study of scriptures."

Swamiji: No! Scriptures have to be studied also. For the attainment of Jnana, study of scriptures is essential. I shall soon open classes in the Math for them. The Vedas, Upanishads, the Gita, and Bhagavata should be studied in the classes, and I shall teach the Panini's Ashtadhyayai.

Disciple: Have you studied the Ashtadhayayi of Panini?

Swamiji: When I was in Jaipur, I met a great grammarian and felt a desire to study Sanskrit grammar with him. Although he was a great scholar in that branch, he had not much aptitude for teaching. He explained to me the commentary on the first aphorism for three days continuously, still I could not grasp a bit of it. On the fourth day the teacher got annoyed and said, "Swamiji, I could not make you understand the meaning of the first aphorism even in three days; I fear, you will not be much benefited by my teaching." Hearing these words, a great self-reproach came over me. Putting food and sleep aside, I set myself to study the commentary on the first aphorism independently. Within three hours the sense of the commentary stood explained before me as clearly as anything; then going to my teacher I gave him the sense of the whole commentary. My teacher, hearing me, said, "How could you gather the sense so excellently within three hours, which I failed to explain to you in three days?" After that, every day I began to read chapter after chapter, with the greatest ease. Through concentration of mind everything can be accomplished—even mountains can be crushed to atoms.

Disciple: Sir, everything is wonderful about you.

Swamiji: There is nothing wonderful in this universe. Ignorance constitutes the only darkness, which confers all things and makes them look mysterious. When everything is lighted by Knowledge, the sense of mystery vanishes from the face of things. Even such an inscrutable thing as Maya, which brings the most impossible things to pass, disappears. Know Him, think of Him, by knowing whom everything else is known. And when that Atman is realised, the purport of all scriptures will be perceived as clearly as a fruit on the palm of one's hand. The Rishis of old attained realisation, and must we fail? We are also men. What has happened once in the life of one individual must, through proper endeavour, be realised in the life of others. History repeats itself. This Atman is the same in all, there is only a difference of manifestation in different individuals. Try to manifest this Atman, and you will see your intellect penetrating into all subjects. The intellect of one who has not realised the Atman is one-sided, whereas the genius of the knower of Atman is all-embracing. With the manifestation of the Atman you will find that science, philosophy, and everything will be easily mastered. Proclaim the glory of the Atman with the roar of a lion, and impart fearlessness unto all beings by saying, "Arise, awake, and stop not till the goal is reached."

UNTITLED CONVERSATION XVIII

The disciple is staying with Swamiji at the garden-house of Nilambar Babu at Belur for the last two days.

Today, Swamiji has given permission to the disciple to stay in his room at night. When the disciple was serving Swamiji and massaging his feet, he spoke to him: "What folly! Leaving such a place as this, you want to go back to Calcutta! See what an atmosphere of holiness is here—the pure air of the Ganga—what an assemblage of Sadhus—will you find anywhere a place like this!"

Disciple: Sir, as the fruition of great austerities in past lives, I have been blessed with your company. Now bless me that I may not be overcome by ignorance and delusion any more. Now my mind sometimes is seized with a great longing for some direct spiritual realisation.

Swamiji: I also felt like that many times. One day in the Cossipore garden, I had expressed my prayer to Shri Ramakrishna with great earnestness. Then in the evening, at the hour of meditation, I lost the consciousness of the body, and felt that it was absolutely non-existent. I felt that the sun, moon, space, time, ether, and all had been reduced to a homogeneous mass and then melted far away into the unknown; the body-consciousness had almost vanished, and I had nearly merged in the Supreme. But I had just a trace of the feeling of Ego, so I could again return to the world of relativity from the Samadhi. In this state of Samadhi all the difference between "I" and the "Brahman" goes away, everything is reduced into unity, like the waters of the Infinite Ocean—water everywhere, nothing else exists—language and thought, all fail there. Then only is the state "beyond mind and speech" realised in its actuality. Otherwise, so long as the religious aspirant thinks or says, "I am the Brahman"—"I" and "the Brahman", these two entities persist—there is the involved semblance of duality. After that experience, even after trying repeatedly, I failed to bring back the state of Samadhi. On informing Shri Ramakrishna about it, he said, "If you remain day and night in that state, the work of the Divine Mother will not be accomplished; therefore you won't be able to induce that state again; when your work is finished, it will come again."

Disciple: On the attainment of the absolute and transcendent Nirvikalpa Samadhi can none return to the world of duality through the consciousness of Egoism?

Swamiji: Shri Ramakrishna used to say that the Avataras alone can descend to the ordinary plane from that state of Samadhi, for the good of the world. Ordinary Jivas do not; immersed in that state, they remain alive for a period of twenty-one days; after that, their body drops like a sere leaf from the tree of Samsara (world).

Disciple: When in Samadhi the mind is merged, and there remain no waves on the surface of consciousness, where then is the possibility of mental activity and returning to the world through the consciousness of Ego? When there is no mind, then who will descend from Samadhi to the relative plane, and by what means?

Swamiji: The conclusion of the Vedanta is that when there is absolute samadhi and cessation of all modifications, there is no return from that state; as the Vedanta Aphorism says: "अनावृत्तिः शब्दात्—there is non-return, from scriptural texts." But the Avataras cherish a few desires for the good of the world. By taking hold of that thread, they come down from the superconscious to the conscious state.

Disciple: But, sir, if one or two desires remain, how can that state be called the absolute, transcendent Samadhi? For the scriptures say that in that state all the modifications of the mind and all desires are stamped out.

Swamiji: How then can there be projection of the universe after Mahapralaya (final dissolution)? At Maha-pralaya everything is merged in the Brahman. But even after that, one hears and reads of creation in the scriptures, that projection and contraction (of the universe) go on in wave forms. Like the fresh creation and dissolution of the universe after Mahapralaya, the superconscious and conscious states of Avataras also stand to reason.

Disciple: If I argue that at the time of dissolution the seeds of further creation remain almost merged in Brahman, and that it is not absolute dissolution or Nirvikalpa Samadhi?

Swamiji: Then I shall ask you to answer how the projection of the universe is possible from Brahman in which there is no shadow of any qualification—which is unaffected and unqualified.

Disciple: Why, this is but a seeming projection. The reply to the question is given in the scriptures in this way, that the manifestation of creation from Brahman is only an appearance like the mirage in the desert, but really there has been no creation or anything of the kind. This illusion is produced by Maya, which is the negation of the eternally existing Brahman, and hence unreal.

Swamiji: If the creation is false, then you can also regard the Nirvikalpa Samadhi of Jiva and his return therefrom as seeming appearances. Jiva is Brahman by his nature. How can he have any experience of bondage? Your desire to realise the truth that you are Brahman is also a hallucination in that case—for the scripture says, "You are already that." Therefore, "अयमेव हि ते बन्ध समाधिमनुतिष्ठसि—this is verily your bondage that you are practising the attainment of Samadhi."

Disciple: This is a great dilemma. If I am Brahman, why don't I always realise it?

Swamiji: In order to attain to that realisation in the conscious plane, some instrumentality is required. The mind is that instrument in us. But it is a non-intelligent substance. It only appears to be intelligent through the light of the Atman behind. Therefore the author of the Panchadashi (III.40) says: "चिच्छायावेशतः शक्तिश्चेतनेव विभाति सा—the Shakti appears to be intelligent by the reflection of the intelligence of the Atman." Hence the mind also appears to us like an intelligent substance. Therefore it is certain that you won't be able to know the Atman, the Essence of Intelligence, through the mind. You have to go beyond the mind—for only the Atman exists there—there the object of knowledge becomes the same as the instrument of knowledge. The knower, knowledge, and the instrument of knowledge become one and the same. It is therefore that the Shruti says, "विज्ञातारमरे केन विजानीयात्—through what are you to know the Eternal Subject?" The real fact is that there is a state beyond the conscious plane, where there is no duality of the knower, knowledge, and the instrument of knowledge etc. When the mind is merged, that state is perceived. I say it is "perceived," because there is no other word to express that state. Language cannot express that state. Shankaracharya has styled it "Transcendent Perception" (Aparokshanubhuti). Even after that transcendent perception Avataras descend to the relative plane and give glimpses of that—therefore it is said that the Vedas and other scriptures have originated from the perception of Seers. The case of ordinary Jivas is like that of the salt-doll which attempting to sound the depths of the ocean melted into it. Do you see? The sum and substance of it is—you have only got to know that you are Eternal Brahman.

You are already that, only the intervention of a non-intelligent mind (which is called Maya in the scriptures) is hiding that knowledge. When the mind composed of subtle matter is quelled, the Atman is effulgent by Its own radiance. One proof of the fact that Maya or mind is an illusion is that the mind by itself is non-intelligent and of the nature of darkness; and it is the light of the Atman behind, that makes it appear as intelligent. When you will understand this, the mind will merge in the unbroken Ocean of Intelligence; then you will realise: "[(Sanskrit)]—this Atman is Brahman."

Then Swamiji, addressing the disciple, said, "You feel sleepy, then go to sleep."

In the night the disciple had a wonderful dream, as a result of which he earnestly begged Swamiji's permission to worship him. Swamiji had to acquiesce, and after the ceremony was over he said to the disciple, "Well, your worship is finished, but Premananda will be in a rage at your sacrilegious act of worshipping my feet in the flower-tray meant for Shri Ramakrishna's worship." Before his words were finished, Swami Premananda came there, and Swamiji said to him, "See what a sacrilege he has committed! With the requisites of Shri Ramakrishna's worship, he has worshipped me!" Swami Premananda, smiling, said, "Well done! Are you and Shri Ramakrishna different?"—hearing which the disciple felt at ease.

The disciple is an orthodox Hindu. Not to speak of prohibited food, he does not even take food touched by another. Therefore Swamiji sometimes used to refer to him as "priest". Swamiji, while he was eating biscuits with his breakfast, said to Swami Sadananda, "Bring the priest in here." When the disciple came to Swamiji, he gave some portion of his food to him to eat. Finding the disciple accepting it without any demur, Swamiji said, "Do you know what you have eaten now? These are made from eggs." In reply, the disciple said, "Whatever may be in it, I have no need to know; taking this sacramental food from you, I have become immortal."

Thereupon Swamiji said, "I bless you that from this day all your egoism of caste, colour, high birth, religious merit and demerit, and all, may vanish for ever!" ...

UNTITLED CONVERSATION XIX

The disciple has come to the Math this morning. As soon as he stood after touching the feet of Swamiji, Swamiji said, "What's the use of your continuing in service any more? Why not go in for some business?" The disciple was then employed as a private tutor in some family. Asked about the profession of teaching, Swamiji said, "If one does the work of teaching boys for a long time, one gets blunt in intellect; one's intelligence is not manifested. If one stays among a crowd of boys day and night, gradually one gets obtuse. So give up the working of teaching boys."

Disciple: What shall I do, then?

Swamiji; Why, if you want to live the life of a worldly man and have a desire for earning money, then go over to America. I shall give you directions for business. You will find that in five years you will get together a lot of money.

Disciple: What business shall I go in for? And where am I to get the money from?

Swamiji: What nonsense are you talking? Within you lies indomitable power. Only thinking, "I am nothing, I am nothing", you have become powerless. Why, you alone! The whole race has become so. Go round the world once, and you will find how vigorously the life-current of other nations is flowing. And what are you doing? Even after learning so much, you go about the doors of others, crying, "Give me employment". Trampled under others' feet doing slavery for others, are you men any more? You are not worth a pin's head! In this fertile country with abundant water-supply, where nature produces wealth and harvest a thousand times more than in others, you have no food for your stomach, no clothes to cover your body! In this country of abundance, the produce of which has been the cause of the spread of civilisation in other countries, you are reduced to such straits! Your condition is even worse than that of a dog. And you glory in your Vedas and Vedanta! A nation that cannot provide for its simple food and clothing, which always depends on others for its subsistence—what is there for it to vaunt about? Throw your religious observances overboard for the present and be first prepared for the struggle for existence. People of foreign countries are turning out such golden results from the raw materials produced in your country, and you, like asses of burden, are only carrying their load. The people of foreign countries import Indian raw goods, manufacture various commodities by bringing their intelligence to bear upon them, and become great; whereas you have locked up your intelligence, thrown away your inherited wealth to others, and roam about crying piteously for food.

Disciple: In what way, sir, can the means of subsistence be procured?

Swamiji: Why, the means are in your hands. You blindfold your eyes, and said, "I am blind and can see nothing." Tear off the folds from your eyes and you will see the whole world lighted by the rays of the midday sun. If you cannot procure money, go to foreign countries, working your passage as a Lascar. Take Indian cloth, towels, bamboo-work, and other indigenous products, and peddle in the streets of Europe and America; you will find how greatly Indian products are appreciated in foreign markets even now. In America I found, some Mohammedans of the Hooghly district had grown rich by peddling Indian commodities in this way. Have you even less intelligence than they? Take, for example, such excellent fabric as the Varanasi-made Saris of India, the like of which are not produced anywhere else in the world. Go to America with this cloth. Have gowns made out of this fabric and sell them, and you will see how much you earn.

Disciple: Sir, why will they wear gowns made of the Saris of Varanasi? I have heard that clothes designed diversely are not to the taste of the ladies in those countries.

Swamiji: Whether they will receive or not, I shall look to that. It is for you to exert yourself and go over there. I have many friends in that country, to whom I shall introduce you. At first I shall request them to take this cloth up among themselves. Then you will find many will follow suit, and at last you won't be able to keep the supply up to the enormous demand.

Disciple: Where shall I get the capital for the business?

Swamiji: I shall somehow give you a start; for the rest you

must depend on your own exertions. "If you die, you get to heaven; and if you win, you enjoy the earth" (Gita). Even if you die in this attempt, well and good, many will take up the work, following your example. And if you succeed, you will live a life of great opulence.

Disciple: Yes, sir, so it is. But I cannot muster sufficient courage.

Swamiji: That is what I say, my son, you have no Shraddha — no faith in yourselves. What will you achieve? You will have neither material nor spiritual advancement. Either put forth your energy in the way I have suggested and be successful in life, or give up all and take to the path we have chosen. Serve the people of all countries through spiritual instruction — then only will you get your dole of food like us. If there is no mutual exchange, do you think anybody cares for anybody else? You observe in our case, that because we give the householders some spiritual instructions, they in return give us some morsels of food. If you do nothing, why will they give you food? You observe so much misery in mere service and slavery of others, still you are not waking up; and so your misery also is never at an end. This is certainly the delusive power of Maya! In the West I have found that those who are in the employment of others have their seats fixed in the back rows in the Parliament, while the front seats are reserved for those who have made themselves famous by self-exertion, or education, or intelligence. In Western countries there is no botheration of caste. Those on whom Fortune smiles for their industry and exertion are alone regarded as leaders of the country and the controllers of its destiny. Whereas in your country, you are simply vaunting your superiority in caste, till at last you cannot even get a morsel of food! You have not the capacity to manufacture a needle, and you dare to criticise the English! Fools! Sit at their feet and learn from them the arts, industries, and the practicality necessary for the struggle for existence. You will be esteemed once more when you will become fit. Then they too will pay heed to your words. Without the necessary preparation, what will mere shouting in the Congress avail?

Disciple: But, sir, all the educated men of the country have joined it.

Swamiji: Well, you consider a man as educated if only he can pass some examinations and deliver good lectures. The education which does not help the common mass of people to equip themselves for the struggle for life, which does not bring out strength of character, a spirit of philanthropy, and the courage of a lion — is it worth the name? Real education is that which enables one to stand on one's own legs. The education that you are receiving now in schools and colleges is only making you a race of dyspeptics. You are working like machines merely, and living a jelly-fish existence.

The peasant, the shoemaker, the sweeper, and such other lower classes of India have much greater capacity for work and self-reliance than you. They have been silently working through long ages and producing the entire wealth of the land, without a word of complaint. Very soon they will get above you in position. Gradually capital is drifting into their hands, and they are not so much troubled with wants as you are. Modern education has changed your fashion, but new avenues of wealth lie yet undiscovered for want of the inventive genius. You have so long oppressed these forbearing masses; now is the time for their retribution. And you will become extinct in your vain search for employment, making it the be — all and end — all of your life.

Disciple: Sir, although our power of originality is less than that of other countries, still the lower classes of India are being guided by our intelligence. So where will they get the power and culture to overcome the higher classes in the struggle for existence?

Swamiji: Never mind if they have not read a few books like you — if they have not acquired your tailor-made civilisation. What do these matter? But they are the backbone of the nation in all countries. If these lower classes stop work, from where will you get your food and clothing? If the sweepers of Calcutta stop work for a day, it creates a panic; and if they strike for three days, the whole town will be depopulated by the outbreak of epidemics. If the labourers stop work, your supply of food and clothes also stops. And you regard them as low-class people and vaunt your own culture!

Engrossed in the struggle for existence, they had not the opportunity for the awakening of knowledge. They have worked so long uniformly like machines guided by human intelligence, and the clever educated section have taken the substantial part of the fruits of their labour. In every country this has been the case. But times have changed. The lower classes are gradually awakening to this fact and making a united front against this, determined to exact their legitimate dues. The masses of Europe and America have been the first to awaken and have already begun the fight. Signs of this awakening have shown themselves in India, too, as is evident from the number of strikes among the lower classes nowadays. The upper classes will no longer be able to repress the lower, try they ever so much. The well-being of the higher classes now lies in helping the lower to get their legitimate rights.

Therefore I say, set yourselves to the task of spreading education among the masses. Tell them and make them understand, "You are our brothers — a part and parcel of our bodies, and we love you and never hate you." If they receive this sympathy from you, their enthusiasm for work will be increased a hundredfold. Kindle their knowledge with the help of modern science. Teach them history, geography, science, literature, and along with these the profound truths of religion. In exchange for that teaching, the poverty of the teachers will also disappear. By mutual exchange both parties will become friendly to each other.

Disciple: But, sir, with the spread of learning among them, they too will in course of time have fertile brains but become idle and inactive like us and live on the fruits of the labour of the next lower classes.

Swamiji: Why shall it be so? Even with the awakening of knowledge, the potter will remain a potter, the fisherman a fisherman, the peasant a peasant. Why should they leave their hereditary calling? "(Sanskrit)—don't give up the work to which you were born, even if it be attended with defects." If they are taught in this way, why should they give up their respective callings? Rather they will apply their knowledge to the better performance of the work to which they have been born. A number of geniuses are sure to arise from among them in the course of time. You (the higher classes) will take these into your own fold. The Brahmins acknowledged the valiant king Vishvamitra as a Brahmin, and think how grateful the whole Kshatriya race became to the Brahmins for this act! By such sympathy and co-operation even birds and beasts become one's own—not to speak of men!

Disciple: Sir, what you say is true, but there yet seems to be a wide gulf between the higher and lower classes. To bring the higher classes to sympathise with the lower seems to be a difficult affair in India.

Swamiji: But without that there is no well-being for your upper classes. You will be destroyed by internecine quarrels and fights—which you have been having so long. When the masses will wake up, they will come to understand your oppression of them, and by a puff of their mouth you will be entirely blown away! It is they who have introduced civilisation amongst you; and it is they who will then pull it down. Think how at the hands of the Gauls the mighty ancient Roman civilisation crumbled into dust! Therefore I say, try to rouse these lower classes from slumber by imparting learning and culture to them. When they will awaken—and awaken one day they must—they also will not forget your good services to them and will remain grateful to you.

After such conversation Swamiji, addressing the disciple, said: Let these subjects drop now—come, tell me what you have decided. Do something, whatever it be. Either go in for some business, or like us come to the path of real Sannyasa, "[(Sanskrit)]—for one's own liberation and for the good of the world." The latter path is of course the best way there is. What good will it do to be a worthless householder? You have understood that everything in life is transitory: "[(Sanskrit)]—life is as unstable as the water on the lotus leaf." Therefore if you have the enthusiasm for acquiring this knowledge of the Atman, do not wait any more but come forward immediately. "[(Sanskrit)]—the very day that you feel dispassion for the world, that very day renounce and take to Sannyasa" (Jabalopanishad, 4). Sacrifice your life for the good of others and go round to the doors of people carrying this message of fearlessness "[(Sanskrit)]—arise, awake, and stop not till the goal is reached."

UNTITLED CONVERSATION XX

Swamiji accompanied by Sister Nivedita, Swami Yogananda, and others has come to visit the Zoological Gardens at Alipur in the afternoon. Rai Rambrahma Sanyal Bahadur, Superintendent of the Gardens, cordially received them and took them round the Gardens. Swamiji, as he went on seeing the various species of animals, casually referred to the Darwinian theory of the gradual evolution of animals. The disciple remembers how, entering the room for snakes, he pointed to a huge python with circular rings on its body, with the remark: "From this the tortoise has evolved in course of time. That very snake, by remaining stationary at one spot for a long time, has gradually turned hard-backed." He further said in fun to the disciple, "You eat tortoises, don't you? Darwin holds that it is this snake that has evolved into the tortoise in the process of time—then you eat snakes too!" The disciple protested, "Sir, when a thing is metamorphosed into another thing through evolution, it has no more its former shape and habits; then how can you say that eating tortoise means eating snakes also?"

This answer created laughter among the party. After seeing some other things, Swamiji went to Rambrahma Babu's quarters in the Gardens, where he took tea, and others also did the same. Finding that the disciples hesitated to sit at the same table and partake of the sweets and tea which Sister Nivedita had touched, Swamiji repeatedly urged him to take them, which he was induced to do, and drinking water himself, he gave the rest of it to the disciple to drink. After this there was a short conversation on Darwin's evolution theory.

Rambrahma Babu: What is your opinion of the evolution theory of Darwin and the causes he has put forward for it?

Swamiji: Taking for granted that Darwin is right, I cannot yet admit that it is the final conclusion about the causes of evolution.

Rambrahma Babu: Did the ancient scholars of our country discuss this subject?

Swamiji: The subject has been nicely discussed in the Samkhya Philosophy. I am of opinion that the conclusion of the ancient Indian philosophers is the last word on the causes of evolution. Rambrahma Babu: I shall be glad to hear of it, if it can be explained in a few words.

Swamiji: You are certainly aware of the laws of struggle for existence, survival of the fittest, natural selection, and so forth, which have been held by the Western scholars to be the causes of elevating a lower species to a higher. But none of these has been advocated as the cause of that in the system of Patanjali. Patanjali holds that the transformation of one species into another is effected by the "in-filling of nature" [(Sanskrit)]. It is not that this is done by the constant struggle against obstacles. In my opinion, struggle and competition sometimes stand in the way of a being's attaining its perfection. If the evolution of an animal is effected by the destruction of a thousand others, then one must confess that this evolution is doing very little good to the world. Taking it for granted that it conduces to physical well-being, we cannot help admitting that it is a serious obstacle to spiritual development. According to the philosophers of our country, every being is a perfect Soul, and the diversity of evolution and manifestation of nature is simply due to the difference in the degree of manifestation of this Soul. The moment the obstacles to the evolution and manifestation of nature are completely removed, the Soul manifests Itself perfectly. Whatever may happen in the lower strata of nature's evolutions, in the higher strata at any rate, it is not true that it is only by constantly struggling against obstacles that one has to go beyond them. Rather it is observed that there the obstacles give way and a greater manifestation of the Soul takes place through education and culture, through concentration and meditation, and above all through sacrifice. Therefore, to designate the obstacles not as the effects but as the causes of the Soul-manifestation, and describe them as aiding this wonderful diversity of nature, is not consonant with reason. The attempt to remove evil from the world by killing a thousand evil-doers, only adds to the evil in the world. But if the people can be made to desist from evil-doing by means of spiritual instruction, there is no more evil in the world. Now, see how horrible the Western struggle theory becomes!

Rambrahma Babu was astonished to hear Swamiji's words and said at length, "India badly needs at the present moment men well versed in the Eastern and Western philosophies like you. Such men alone are able to point out the mistakes of the educated people who see only one side of the shield. I am extremely delighted to hear your original explanation of the evolution theory."

Shortly after, Swamiji with the party left for Baghbazar and reached Balaram Bose's house at about 8 p.m. After a short rest, he came to the drawing-room, where there was a small gathering, all eager to hear of the conversation at the Zoological Gardens in detail. When Swamiji came to the room, the disciple, as the spokesman of the meeting, raised that very topic.

Disciple: Sir, I have not been able to follow all your remarks about the evolution theory at the Zoo. Will you kindly recapitulate them in simple words?

Swamiji: Why, which points did you fail to grasp?

Disciple: You have often told us that it is the power to struggle with the external forces which constitutes the sign of life and the first step towards improvement. Today you seem to have spoken just the opposite thing.

Swamiji: Why should I speak differently? It was you who could not follow me. In the animal kingdom we really see such laws as struggle for existence, survival of the fittest, etc., evidently at work. Therefore Darwin's theory seems true to a certain extent. But in the human kingdom, where there is the manifestation of rationality, we find just the reverse of those laws. For instance, in those whom we consider really great men

or ideal characters, we scarcely observe any external struggle. In the animal kingdom instinct prevails; but the more a man advances, the more he manifests rationality. For this reason, progress in the rational human kingdom cannot be achieved, like that in the animal kingdom, by the destruction of others! The highest evolution of man is effected through sacrifice alone. A man is great among his fellows in proportion as he can sacrifice for the sake of others, while in the lower strata of the animal kingdom, that animal is the strongest which can kill the greatest number of animals. Hence the struggle theory is not equally applicable to both kingdoms. Man's struggle is in the mental sphere. A man is greater in proportion as he can control his mind. When the mind's activities are perfectly at rest, the Atman manifests Itself. The struggle which we observe in the animal kingdom for the preservation of the gross body obtains in the human plane of existence for gaining mastery over the mind or for attaining the state of balance. Like a living tree and its reflection in the water of a tank, we find opposite kinds of struggle in the animal and human kingdoms.

Disciple: Why then do you advocate so much the improvement of our physique?

Swamiji: Well, do you consider yourselves as men? You have got only a bit of rationality—that's all. How will you struggle with the mind unless the physique be strong? Do you deserve to be called men any longer—the highest evolution in the world? What have you got besides eating, sleeping, and satisfying the creature-comforts? Thank your stars that you have not developed into quadrupeds yet! Shri Ramakrishna used to say, "He is the man who is conscious of his dignity". You are but standing witnesses to the lowest class of insect-like existence of which the scripture speaks, that they simply undergo the round of births and deaths without being allowed to go to any of the higher spheres! You are simply living a life of jealousy among yourselves and are objects of hatred in the eyes of the foreigner. You are animals, therefore I recommend you to struggle. Leave aside theories and all that. Just reflect calmly on your own everyday acts and dealings with others and find out whether you are not a species of beings intermediate between the animal and human planes of existence! First build up your own physique. Then only you can get control over the mind. "नायमात्मा बलहीनेन लभ्यः—this Self is not to be attained by the weak" (Katha Upanishad, I.ii.23).

Disciple: But, sir, the commentator (Shankara) has interpreted the word "weak" to mean "devoid of Brahmacharya or continence".

Swamiji: Let him. I say, "The physically weak are unfit for the realisation of the Self."

Disciple: But many dull-headed persons also have strong bodies.

Swamiji: If you can take the pains to give them good ideas once, they will be able to work them out sooner than physically unfit people. Don't you find that in a weak physique it is difficult to control the sex-appetite or anger? Lean people are quickly incensed and are quickly overcome by the sex instinct.

Disciple: But we find exceptions to the rule also.

Swamiji: Who denies it? Once a person gets control over the mind, it matters little whether the body remains strong or becomes emaciated. The gist of the thing is that unless one has a good physique one can never aspire to Self-realisation. Shri Ramakrishna used to say, "One fails to attain realisation if there be but a slight defect in the body".

Finding that Swamiji had grown excited, the disciple did not dare to push the topic further, but remained quiet accepting Swamiji's view. Shortly after, Swamiji, addressing those present, said, "By the bye, have you heard that this `priest' has today taken food which was touched by Nivedita? That he took the sweets touched by her did not matter so much, but—here he addressed the disciple—"how did you drink the water she had touched?"

Disciple: But it was you, sir, who ordered me to do so. Under the Guru's orders I can do anything. I was unwilling to drink the water though. But you drank it and I had to take it as Prasada.

Swamiji: Well, your caste is gone for ever. Now nobody will respect you as a Brahmin of the priest class.

Disciple: I don't care if they do not. I can take the rice from the house of a Pariah if you order me to.

These words set Swamiji and all those present in a roar of laughter.

The conversation lasted till it was past midnight, when the disciple came back to his lodging, only to find it bolted. So he had to pass the night out of doors.

The wheel of Time has rolled on in its unrelenting course, and Swamiji, Swami Yogananda, and Sister Nivedita are now no more on earth. Only the sacred memory of their lives remains—and the disciple considers himself blessed to be able to record, in ever so meagre a way, these reminiscences.

UNTITLED CONVERSATION XXI

The disciple has come to the Math (monastery) today. It has now been removed to Nilambar Babu's garden-house, and the site of the present Math has recently been purchased. Swamiji is out visiting the new Math-grounds at about four o'clock, taking the disciple with him. The site was then mostly jungle, but on the north side of it there was a one-storeyed brick-built house. Swamiji began to walk over the site and to discuss in the course of conversation the plan of work of the future Math and its rules and regulations.

Reaching by degrees the veranda on the east side of the one-storeyed house, Swamiji said, "Here would be the place for the Sadhus to live. It is my wish to convert this Math into a chief centre of spiritual practices and the culture of knowledge. The power that will have its rise from here will flood the whole world and turn the course of men's lives into different channels; from this place will spring forth ideals which will be the harmony of Knowledge, Devotion, Yoga, and Work; at a nod from the men of this Math a life-giving impetus will in time be given to the remotest corners of the globe; while all true seekers after spirituality will in course of time assemble here. A thousand thoughts like these are arising in my mind. "Yonder plot of land on the south side of the Math will be the centre of learning, where grammar, philosophy, science, literature, rhetoric, the Shrutis, Bhakti scriptures, and English will be taught. This Temple of Learning will be fashioned after the Tols of old days. Boys who are Brahmacharins from their childhood will live there and study the scriptures. Their food and clothing and all will be supplied from the Math. After a course of five years' training these Brahmacharins may, if they like, go back to their homes and lead householders' lives; or they may embrace the monastic life with the sanction of the venerable Superiors of the Math. The authorities of the Math will have the power to turn out at once any of these Brahmacharins who will be found refractory or of a bad character. Teaching will be imparted here irrespective of caste or creed, and those who will have objection to this will not be admitted. But those who would like to observe their particular caste-rites, should make separate arrangements for their food, etc. They will only attend the classes along with the rest. The Math authorities shall keep a vigilant watch over the character of these also. None but those that are trained here shall be eligible for Sannyasa. Won't it be nice when by degrees this Math will begin to work like this?"

Disciple: Then you want to reintroduce into the country the ancient institution of living a Brahmacharin's life in the house of the Guru?

Swamiji: Exactly. The modern system of education gives no facility for the development of the knowledge of Brahman. We must found Brahmacharya Homes as in times of old. But now we must lay their foundations on a broad basis, that is to say, we must introduce a good deal of change into it to suit the requirements of the times. Of this I shall speak to you later on. "That piece of land to the south of the Math," Swamiji resumed, "we must also purchase in time. There we shall start an Annasatra—a Feeding Home. There arrangements will be made for serving really indigent people in the spirit of God. The Feeding Home will be named after Shri Ramakrishna. Its scope will at first be determined by the amount of funds. For the matter of that, we may start it with two or three inmates. We must train energetic Brahmacharins to conduct this Home. They will have to collect the funds for its maintenance—ay, even by begging. The Math will not be allowed to give any pecuniary help in this matter. The Brahmacharins themselves shall have to raise funds for it. Only after completing their five years' training in this Home of Service, will they be allowed to join the Temple of Learning branch. After a training of ten years—five in the Feeding Home and five in the Temple of Learning—they will be allowed to enter the life of Sannyasa, having initiation from the Math authorities—provided of course they have a mind to become Sannyasins and the Math authorities consider them fit for Sannyasa and are willing to admit them into it. But the Head of the Math will be free to confer Sannyasa on any exceptionally meritorious Brahmacharin, at any time, in defiance of this rule. The ordinary Brahmacharins, however, will have to qualify themselves for Sannyasa by degrees, as I have just said. I have all these ideas in my brain."

Disciple: Sir, what will be the object of starting three such sections in the Math?

Swamiji: Didn't you understand me? First of all, comes the gift of food; next is the gift of learning, and the highest of all is the gift of knowledge. We must harmonise these three ideals in the Math. By continuously practising the gift of food, the Brahmacharins will have the idea of practical work for the sake of others and that of serving all beings in the spirit of the Lord firmly impressed on their minds. This will gradually purify their minds and lead to the manifestation of Sattvika (pure and unselfish) ideas. And having this the Brahmacharins will in time acquire the fitness for attaining the knowledge of Brahman and become eligible for Sannyasa.

Disciple: Sir, if, as you say, the gift of (spiritual) knowledge is the highest, why then start sections for the gift of food and the gift of learning?

Swamiji: Can't you understand this point even now? Listen. If in these days of food scarcity you can, for the disinterested service of others, get together a few morsels of food by begging or any other means, and give them to the poor and suffering, that will not only be doing good to yourself and the world, but you will at the same time get everybody's sympathy for this noble work. The worldly-minded people, tied down to lust and wealth, will have faith in you for this labour of love and come forward to help you. You will attract a thousand times as many men by this unasked-for gift of food, as you will by the gift of learning or of (spiritual) knowledge. In no other work will you get so much public sympathy as you will in this. In a truly noble work, not to speak of men, even God Himself befriends the doer. When people have thus been attracted, you will be able to stimulate the desire for learning and spirituality in them. Therefore the gift of food comes first.

Disciple; Sir, to start Feeding Homes we want a site first, then buildings, and then the funds to work them. Where will so much money come from?

Swamiji: The southern portion of the Math premises I am leaving at your disposal immediately, and I am getting a thatched house erected under that Bael tree. You just find out one or two blind or infirm people and apply yourself to their service. Go and beg food for them yourself; cook with your own hands and feed them. If you continue this for some days, you will find that lots of people will be coming forward to assist you with plenty of money. "[(Sanskrit)]—never, my son, does a doer of good come to grief." (Gita, VI.40)

Disciple: Yes, it is true. But may not that kind of continuous work become a source of bondage in the long run?

Swamiji: If you have no eye to the fruits of work, and if you have a passionate longing to go beyond all selfish desires, then these good works will help to break your bonds, I tell you. How thoughtless of you to say that such work will lead to bondage! Such disinterested work is the only means of rooting out the bondage due to selfish work. "[(Sanskrit)] There is no other way out" (Shvetasvatara Upanishad, III.8).

Disciple: Your words encourage me to hear in detail about your ideas of the Feeding Home and Home of Service.

Swamiji: We must build small well-ventilated rooms for the poor. Only two or three of them will live in each room. They must be given good bedding, clean clothes, and so on. There will be a doctor for them, who will inspect them once or twice a week according to his convenience. The Sevashrama (Home of Service) will be as a ward attached to the Annasatra, where the sick will be nursed. Then, gradually, as funds will accumulate, we shall build a big kitchen. The Annasatra must be astir with constant shouts of food demanded and supplied. The rice-gruel must run into the Ganga and whiten its water! When I see such a Feeding Home started, it will bring solace to my heart.

Disciple: When you have this kind of desire, most likely it will materialise into action in course of time.

Hearing the disciple's words, Swamiji remained motionless for a while, gazing on the Ganga. Then with a beaming countenance he addressed the disciple, saying: "Who knows which of you will have the lion roused up in him, and when? If in a single one amongst you Mother rouses the fire, there will be hundreds of Feeding Homes like that. Knowledge and Power and Devotion—everything exists in the fullest measure in all beings. We only notice the varying degrees of their manifestation and call one great and another little. In the minds of all creatures a screen intervenes as it were and hides the perfect manifestation from view. The moment that is removed, everything is settled; whatever you want, whatever you will desire, will come to pass."

Swamiji continued: "If the Lord wills, we shall make this Math a great centre of harmony. Our Lord is the visible embodiment of the harmony of all ideals. He will be established on earth if we keep alive that spirit of harmony here. We must see to it that people of all creeds and sects, from the Brahmana down to the Chandala, may come here and find their respective ideals manifested. The other day when I installed Shri Ramakrishna on the Math grounds, I felt as if his ideas shot forth from this place and flooded the whole universe, sentient and insentient. I, for one, am doing my best, and shall continue to do so—all of you too explain to people the liberal ideas of Shri Ramakrishna; what is the use of merely reading the Vedanta? We must prove the truth of pure Advaitism in practical life. Shankara left this Advaita philosophy in the hills and forests, while I have come to bring it out of those places and scatter it broadcast before the workaday world and society. The lion-roar of Advaita must resound in every hearth and home, in meadows and groves, over hills and plains. Come all of you to my assistance and set yourselves to work."

Disciple: Sir, it appeals to me rather to realise that state through meditation than to manifest it in action.

Swamiji: That is but a state of stupefaction, as under liquor. What will be the use of merely remaining like that? Through the urge of Advaitic realisation, you should sometimes dance wildly and sometimes remain lost to outward sense. Does one feel happy to taste of a good thing by oneself? One should share it with others. Granted that you attain personal liberation by means of the realisation of the Advaita, but what matters it to the world? You must liberate the whole universe before you leave this body. Then only you will be established in the eternal Truth. Has that bliss any match, my boy? You will be established in that bliss of the Infinite which is limitless like the skies. You will be struck dumb to find your presence everywhere in the world of soul and matter. You will feel the whole sentient and insentient world as your own self. Then you can't help treating all with the same kindness as you show towards yourself. This is indeed practical Vedanta. Do you understand me? Brahman is one, but is at the same time appearing to us as many, on the relative plane. Name and form are at the root of this relativity. For instance, what do you find when you abstract name and form from a jar? Only earth, which is its essence. Similarly, through delusion you are thinking of and seeing a jar, a cloth, a monastery, and so on. The phenomenal world depends on this nescience which obstructs knowledge and which has no real existence. One sees variety such as wife, children, body, mind—only in the world created by nescience by means of name and form. As soon as this nescience is removed, the realisation of Brahman which eternally exists is the result.

Disciple: Where has the nescience come from?

Swamiji: Where it has come from I shall tell you later on. When you began to run, mistaking the rope for the snake, did the rope actually turn into a snake? Or was it not your ignorance which put you to flight in that way?

Disciple: I did it from sheer ignorance.

Swamiji: Well, then, consider whether, when you will again come to know the rope as rope, you will not laugh at your previous ignorance. Will not name and form appear to be a delusion then?

Disciple: They will.

Swamiji: If that be so, the name and form turn out to be unreal. Thus Brahman, the Eternal Existence, proves to be the only reality. Only through this twilight of nescience you think this is your wife, that is your child, this is your own, that is not your own, and so on, and fail to realise the existence of the Atman, the illuminator of everything. When through the Guru's instructions and your own conviction you will see, not this world of name and form, but the essence which lies as its substratum then only you will realise your

identity with the whole universe from the Creator down to a clump of grass, then only you will get the state in which "[(Sanskrit)]—the knots of the heart are cut asunder and all doubts are dispelled".

Disciple: Sir, one wishes to know of the origin and cessation of this nescience.

Swamiji: You have understood, I presume, that a thing that ceases to exist afterwards is a phenomenon merely? He who has truly realised Brahman will say—where is nescience, in faith? He sees the rope as rope only, and never as the snake. And he laughs at the alarm of those who see it as the snake. For this reason, nescience has no absolute reality. You can call nescience neither real nor unreal; "[(Sanskrit)]—neither real, nor unreal, nor a mixture of both". About a thing that is thus proved to be false, neither question nor answer is of any significance. Moreover, any question on such a thing is unreasonable. I shall explain how. Are not this question and answer made from the standpoint of name and form, of time and space? And can you explain Brahman which transcends time and space, by means of questions and answers? Hence the Shastras and Mantras and such other things are only relatively, and not absolutely, true. Nescience has verily no essence to call its own; how then can you understand it? When Brahman will manifest Itself, there will be no more room for such questions. Have you not heard that story of Shri Ramakrishna about the shoemaker coolie?[1] The moment one recognises nescience, it vanishes.

Disciple: But, sir, whence has this nescience come?

Swamiji: How can that come which has no existence at all? It must exist first, to admit the possibility of coming.

Disciple: How then did this world of souls and matter originate?

Swamiji: There is only one Existence—brahman. You are but seeing That under different forms and names, through the veil of name and form which are unreal.

Disciple: But why this unreal name and form? Whence have they come?

Swamiji: The Shastras have described this ingrained notion or ignorance as almost endless in a series. But it has a termination, while Brahman ever remains as It is, without suffering

---

1. Once a Brahmin, desirous of going to a disciple's house, was in need of a coolie to carry his load. Not finding anyone belonging to a good caste, he at last asked a shoemaker to perform the function. The man at first refused on the ground that he was a man belonging to an untouchable caste. But the Brahmin insisted on engaging him, telling him that he would escape detection by keeping perfectly silent. The man was at last persuaded to go, and when the party reached their destination, someone asked the shoemaker-servant to remove a pair of shoes. The servant who thought it best to keep silent, as instructed, paid no attention to the order, which was repeated, whereupon the man getting annoyed shouted out, "Why dost thou not hear me, sirrah? Art thou a shoemaker?" "O Master," cried the bewildered shoemaker, "I am discovered. I cannot stay any longer." Saying this he immediately took to his heels.

the least change, like the rope which causes the delusion of the snake. Therefore the conclusion of the Vedanta is that the whole universe has been superimposed on Brahman—appearing like a juggler's trick. It has not caused the least aberration of Brahman from Its real nature. Do you understand me?

Disciple: One thing I cannot yet understand.

Swamiji: What is that?

Disciple: You have just said that creation, maintenance, and dissolution, etc. are superimposed on Brahman, and have no absolute existence. But how can that be? One can never have the delusion of something that one has not already experienced. Just as one who has never seen a snake cannot mistake a rope for a snake, so how can one who has not experienced this creation, come to mistake Brahman for the creation? Therefore creation must have been, or is, to have given rise to the delusion of creation. But this brings in a dualistic position.

Swamiji: The man of realisation will in the first place refute your objection by stating that to his vision creation and things of that sort do not at all appear. He sees Brahman and Brahman alone. He sees the rope and not the snake. If you argue that you, at any rate, are seeing this creation, or snake—then he will try to bring home to you the real nature of the rope, with a view to curing your defective vision. When through his instructions and your reasoning you will be able to realise the truth of the rope, or Brahman, then this delusive idea of the snake, or creation, will vanish. At that time, what else can you call this delusive idea of creation, maintenance, and dissolution, but a superimposition on the Brahman? If this appearance of creation etc. has continued as a beginningless series, let it do so; no advantage will be gained by settling this question. Until Brahman is realised as vividly as a fruit on the palm of one's hand this question cannot be adequately settled, and then neither such a question crops up, nor is there need for a solution. The tasting of the reality of Brahman is then like a dumb man tasting something nice, but without the power to express his feelings.

Disciple: What then will be the use of reasoning about it so much?

Swamiji: Reasoning is necessary to understand the point intellectually. But the Reality transcends reasoning: "[(Sanskrit)]—this conviction cannot be reached through reasoning."

In the course of such conversation Swamiji reached the Math, accompanied by the disciple. Swamiji then explained to the Sannyasins and Brahmacharins of the Math the gist of the above discussion on Brahman. While going upstairs, he remarked to the disciple, "[(Sanskrit)]—this Atman cannot be attained by the weak."

UNTITLED CONVERSATION XXII

The Bengali fortnightly magazine, Udbodhan, was just started by Swami Trigunatita under the direction of Swamiji for spreading the religious views of Shri Ramakrishna among the general public. After the first number came out the disciple came to the Math at Nilambar Babu's garden one day. Swamiji started the following conversation with him about the Udbodhan.

Swamiji: (Humorously caricaturing the name of the magazine) Have you seen the Udbandhana[2]?

Disciple: Yes, sir; it is a good number.

Swamiji: We must mould the ideas, language, and everything of this magazine in a new fashion.

Disciple: How?

Swamiji: Not only must we give out Shri Ramakrishna's ideas to all, but we must also introduce a new vigour into the Bengali language. For instance, the frequent use of verbs diminishes the force of a language. We must restrict the use of verbs by the use of adjectives. Begin to write articles in that way, and show them to me before you give them to print in the Udbodhan.

Disciple: Sir, it is impossible for any other man to labour for this magazine in the way Swami Trigunatita does.

Swamiji: Do you think these Sannyasin children of Shri Ramakrishna are born simply to sit under trees lighting Dhuni-fires? Whenever any of them will take up some work, people will be astonished to see their energy. Learn from them how to work. Here, for instance, Trigunatita has given up his spiritual practices, his meditation and everything, to carry out my orders, and has set himself to work. Is this a matter of small sacrifice? What an amount of love for me is at the back of this spirit of work, do you see? He will not stop short of success! Have you householders such determination?

Disciple: But, sir, it looks rather odd in our eyes that Sannyasins in ochre robe should go about from door to door as the Swami is doing.

Swamiji: Why? The circulation of the magazine is only for the good of the householders. By the spread of new ideas within the country the public at large will be benefited. Do you think this unselfish work is any way inferior to devotional practices? Our object is to do good to humanity. We have no idea of making money from the income of this paper. We have renounced everything and have no wives or children to provide for after our death. If the paper be a success, the whole of its income will be spent in the service of humanity. Its surplus money will be profitably spent in the opening of monasteries and homes of service in different places and all sorts of work of public utility. We are not certainly working like householders with the plan of filling our own pockets. Know for certain that all our movements are for the good of others.

Disciple: Even then, all will not be able to appreciate this spirit.

Swamiji: What if they cannot? It neither adds nor takes away

2. The word means "suicide by hanging".

anything from us. We do not take up any work with an eye to criticism.

Disciple: So this magazine will be a fortnightly. We should like it to be a weekly.

Swamiji: Yes, but where are the funds? If through the grace of Shri Ramakrishna funds are raised, it can be made into a daily even, in future. A hundred thousand copies may be struck off daily and distributed free in every street and lane of Calcutta.

Disciple: This idea of yours is a capital one.

Swamiji: I have a mind to make the paper self-supporting first, and then set you up as its editor. You have not yet got the capacity to make any enterprise stand on its legs. That is reserved only for these all-renouncing Sannyasins to do. They will work themselves to death, but never yield. Whereas a little resistance or just a trifle of criticism is bewildering to you.

Disciple: Sir, the other day I saw that Swami Trigunatita worshipped the photograph of Sri Ramakrishna in the Press before opening the work and asked for your blessings for the success of the work.

Swamiji: Well, Shri Ramakrishna is our centre. Each one of us is a ray of that light-centre. So Trigunatita worshipped Shri Ramakrishna before beginning the work, did he? It was excellently done. But he told me nothing of it.

Disciple: Sir, he fears you and yesterday he told me to come to you and ask your opinion of the first issue of the magazine, after which, he said, he would see you.

Swamiji: Tell him when you go that I am exceedingly delighted with his work. Give him my loving blessings. And all of you help him as far as you can. You will be doing Shri Ramakrishna's work by that.

Immediately after saying these words Swamiji called Swami Brahmananda to him and directed him to give Swami Trigunatita more money for the Udbodhan if it was needed.

The same evening, after supper, Swamiji again referred to the topic of Udbodhan in the following words: "In the Udbodhan we must give the public only positive ideas. Negative thoughts weaken men. Do you not find that where parents are constantly taxing their sons to read and write, telling them they will never learn anything, and calling them fools and so forth, the latter do actually turn out to be so in many cases? If you speak kind words to boys and encourage them, they are bound to improve in time. What holds good of children, also holds good of children in the region of higher thoughts. If you can give them positive ideas, people will grow up to be men and learn to stand on their own legs. In language and literature, in poetry and the arts, in everything we must point out not the mistakes that people are making in their thoughts and actions, but the way in which they will gradually be able to do these things better. Pointing out mistakes wounds a man's feelings. We have seen how Shri Ramakrishna would encourage even those whom we considered as worthless and change the very course of their lives thereby! His very method

of teaching was a unique phenomenon."

After a short pause, Swamiji continued, "Never take the preaching of religion to mean the turning up of one's nose at everything and at everybody. In matters physical, mental, and spiritual—in everything we must give men positive ideas and never hate anybody. It is your hatred of one another that has brought about your degradation. Now we shall have to raise men by scattering broadcast only positive thoughts. First we must raise the whole Hindu race in this way and then the whole world. That is why Shri Ramakrishna incarnated. He never destroyed a single man's special inclinations. He gave words of hope and encouragement even to the most degraded of persons and lifted them up. We too must follow in his footsteps and lift all up, and rouse them. Do you understand? "Your history, literature, mythology, and all other Shastras are simply frightening people. They are only telling them, 'You will go to hell, you are doomed!' Therefore has this lethargy crept into the very vitals of India. Hence we must explain to men in simple words the highest ideas of the Vedas and the Vedanta. Through the imparting of moral principles, good behaviour, and education we must make the Chandala come up to the level of the Brahmana. Come, write out all these things in the Udbodhan and awaken everyone, young and old, man and woman. Then only shall I know that your study of the Vedas and Vedanta has been a success. What do you say? Will you be able to do this?"

Disciple: Through your blessings and command I think I shall succeed in everything.

Swamiji: Another thing. You must learn to make the physique very strong and teach the same to others. Don't you find me exercising every day with dumb-bells even now? Walk in the morning and evenings and do physical labour. Body and mind must run parallel. It won't do to depend on others in everything. When the necessity of strengthening the physique is brought home to people, they will exert themselves of their own accord. It is to make them feel this need that education is necessary at the present moment.

UNTITLED CONVERSATION XXIII

Disciple: Why is it, Swamiji, that our society and country have come to such degradation?

Swamiji: It is you who are responsible for it.

Disciple: How, sir? You surprise me.

Swamiji: You have been despising the lower classes of the country for a very long time and, as a result, you have now become the objects of contempt in the eyes of the world.

Disciple: When did you find us despising them?

Swamiji: Why, you priest-class never let the non-brahmin class read the Vedas and Vedanta and all such weighty Shastras—never touch them even. You have only kept them down. It is you who have always done like that through selfishness. It was the Brahmins who made a monopoly of the religious books and kept the question of sanction and prohibition in their own hands. And repeatedly calling the other races of India low and vile, they put this belief into their heads that they were really such. If you tell a man, "You are low, you are vile", in season and out of season, then he is bound to believe in course of time that he is really such. This is called hypnotism. The non-brahmin classes are now slowly rousing themselves. Their faith in Brahminical scriptures and Mantras is getting shaken. Through the spread of Western education all the tricks of the Brahmins are giving way, like the banks of the Padma in the rainy season. Do you not see that?

Disciple: Yes, sir, the stricture of orthodoxy is gradually lessening nowadays.

Swamiji: It is as it should be. The Brahmins, in fact, gradually took a course of gross immorality and oppression. Through selfishness they introduced a large number of strange, non-vedic, immoral, and unreasonable doctrines—simply to keep intact their own prestige. And the fruits of that they are reaping forthwith.

Disciple: What may these fruits be, sir?

Swamiji: Don't you perceive them? It is simply due to your having despised the masses of India that you have now been living a life of slavery for the last thousand years; it is therefore that you are the objects of hatred in the eyes of foreigners and are looked upon with indifference by your countrymen.

Disciple: But, sir, even now it is the Brahmins who direct all ceremonials, and people are observing them according to the opinions of the Brahmins. Why then do you speak like that?

Swamiji: I don't find it. Where do the tenfold Samskaras or purifying ceremonies enjoined by the Shastras obtain still? Well, I have travelled the whole of India, and everywhere I have found society to be guided by local usages which are condemned by the Shrutis and Smritis. Popular customs, local usages, and observances prevalent among women only—have not these taken the place of the Smritis everywhere? Who obeys, and whom? If you can but spend enough money, the priest-class is ready to write out whatever sanctions or prohibitions you want! How many of them read the Vedic Kalpa (Ritual), Grihya and Shrauta Sutras? Then, look, here in Bengal the code of Raghunandana is obeyed; a little farther on you will find the code of Mitakshara in vogue; while in another part the code of Manu holds sway! You seem to think that the same laws hold good everywhere! What I want therefore is to introduce the study of the Vedas by stimulating a greater regard for them in the minds of the people, and to pass everywhere the injunctions of the Vedas.

Disciple: Sir, is it possible nowadays to set them going?

Swamiji: It is true that all the ancient Vedic laws will not have a go, but if we introduce additions and alterations in them to suit the needs of the times, codify them, and hold them up as a new model to society, why will they not pass current?

Disciple: Sir, I was under the impression that at least the injunctions of Manu were being obeyed all over India even now.

Swamiji: Nothing of the kind. Just look to your own province and see how the Vamachara (immoral practices) of the Tantras has entered into your very marrow. Even modern Vaishnavism, which is the skeleton of the defunct Buddhism, is saturated with Vamachara! We must stem the tide of this Vamachara, which is contrary to the spirit of the Vedas.

Disciple: Sir, is it possible now to cleanse this Aegean stable?

Swamiji: What nonsense do you say, you coward! You have well-nigh thrown the country into ruin by crying, 'It is impossible, it is impossible!' What cannot human effort achieve?

Disciple: But, sir, such a state of things seems impossible unless sages like Manu and Yajnavalkya are again born in the country.

Swamiji: Goodness gracious! Was it not purity and unselfish labour that made them Manu and Yajnavalkya, or was it something else? Well, we ourselves can be far greater than even Manu and Yajnavalkya if we try to; why will not our views prevail then?

Disciple: Sir, it is you who said just now that we must revive the ancient usages and observances within the country. How then can we think lightly of sages like Manu and the rest?

Swamiji: What an absurd deduction! You altogether miss my point. I have only said that the ancient Vedic customs must be remodelled according to the need of the society and the times, and passed under a new form in the land. Have I not?

Disciple: Yes, sir.

Swamiji: What, then, were you talking? You have read the Shastras, and my hope and faith rest in men like you. Understand my words in their true spirit, and apply yourselves to work in their light.

Disciple: But, sir, who will listen to us? Why should our countrymen accept them?

Swamiji: If you can truly convince them and practise what you preach, they must. If, on the contrary, like a coward you simply utter Shlokas as a parrot, be a mere talker and quote authority only, without showing them in action—then who will care to listen to you?

Disciple: Please give me some advice in brief about social reform.

Swamiji: Why, I have given you advice enough; now put at least something in practice. Let the world see that your reading of the scriptures and listening to me has been a success. The codes of Manu and lots of other books that you have read—what is their basis and underlying purpose? Keeping that basis intact, compile in the manner of the ancient Rishis the essential truths of them and supplement them with thoughts that are suited to the times; only take care that all races and all sects throughout India be really benefited by following these rules. Just write out a Smriti like that; I shall revise it.

Disciple: Sir, it is not an easy task; and even if such a Smriti be written, will it be accepted?

Swamiji: Why not? Just write it out. "[(Sanskrit)]—time is infinite, and the world is vast." If you write it in the proper way, there must come a day when it will be accepted. Have faith in yourself. You people were once the Vedic Rishis. Only, you have come in different forms, that's all. I see it clear as daylight that you all have infinite power in you. Rouse that up; arise, arise—apply yourselves heart and soul, gird up your loins. What will you do with wealth and fame that are so transitory? Do you know what I think? I don't care for Mukti and all that. My mission is to arouse within you all such ideas; I am ready to undergo a hundred thousand rebirths to train up a single man.

Disciple: But, sir, what will be the use of undertaking such works? Is not death stalking behind?

Swamiji: Fie upon you! If you die, you will die but once. Why will you die every minute of your life by constantly harping on death like a coward?

Disciple: All right, sir, I may not think of death, but what good will come of any kind of work in this evanescent world?

Swamiji: My boy, when death is inevitable, is it not better to die like heroes than as stocks and stones? And what is the use of living a day or two more in this transitory world? It is better to wear out than to rust out—specially for the sake of doing the least good to others.

Disciple: It is true, sir. I beg pardon for troubling you so much.

Swamiji: I don't feel tired even if I talk for two whole nights to an earnest inquirer; I can give up food and sleep and talk and talk. Well, if I have a mind, I can sit up in Samadhi in a Himalayan cave. And you see that nowadays through the Mother's grace I have not to think about food, it comes anyhow. Why then don't I do so? And why am I here? Only the sight of the country's misery and the thought of its future do not let me remain quiet any more!— even Samadhi and all that appear as futile—even the sphere of Brahma with its enjoyments becomes insipid! My vow of life is to think of your welfare. The day that vow will be fulfilled, I shall leave this body and make a straight run up!

Hearing Swamiji's words the disciple sat speechless for a while, gazing at him, wondering in his heart. Then, with a view to taking his leave, he saluted Swamiji reverently and asked his permission to go.

Swamiji: Why do you want to go? Why not live in the Math? Your mind will again be polluted if you go back to the worldly-minded. See here, how fresh is the air, there is the Ganga, and the Sadhus (holy men) are practising meditation, and holding lofty talks! While the moment you will go to Calcutta, you will be thinking of nasty stuff.

The disciple joyfully replied, "All right, sir, I shall stay today at the Math."

Swamiji: Why "today"? Can't you live here for good? What is the use of going back to the world?

The disciple bent down his head, hearing Swamiji's words. Various thoughts crowded into his brain and kept him speechless.

UNTITLED CONVERSATION XXIV

Today Swamiji is walking round the new Math grounds in the afternoon in company with the disciple. Standing at a little distance off the Bael tree Swamiji took to singing slowly a Bengali song[1]: "O Himalaya,

Ganesh is auspicious to me" etc., ending with the line —"And many Dandis (Sannyasins) and Yogis with matted hair will also come." While singing the song Swamiji repeated this line to the disciple and said, "Do you understand? In course of time many Sadhus and Sannyasins will come here." Saying this he sat under the tree and remarked, "The ground under the Bilva tree is very holy. Meditating here quickly brings about an awakening of the religious instinct. Shri Ramakrishna used to say so."

Disciple: Sir, those who are devoted to the discrimination between the Self and not-self—have they any need to consider the auspiciousness of place, time, and so forth?

Swamiji: Those who are established in the knowledge of the Atman have no need for such discrimination, but that state is not attained off-hand. It comes as the result of long practice. Therefore in the beginning one has to take the help of external aids and learn to stand on one's own legs. Later on, when one is established in the knowledge of the Atman, there is no more need for any external aid.

The various methods of spiritual practice that have been laid down in the scriptures are all for the attainment of the knowledge of the Atman. Of course these practices vary according to the qualifications of different aspirants. But they also are a kind of work, and so long as there is work, the Atman is not discovered. The obstacles to the manifestation of the Atman are overcome by practices as laid down in the scriptures; but work has no power of directly manifesting the Atman, it is only effective in removing some veils that cover knowledge. Then the Atman manifests by Its own effulgence. Do you see? Therefore does your commentator (Shankara) say, "In our knowledge of Brahman, there cannot be the least touch of work."

Disciple: But, sir, since the obstacles to Self-manifestation are not overcome without the performance of work in some form or other, therefore indirectly work stands as a means to knowledge.

Swamiji: From the standpoint of the causal chain, it so appears prima facie. Taking up this view it is stated in the Purva-mimamsa that work for a definite end infallibly produces a definite result. But the vision of the Atman which is

---

1. This is one of the songs sung in the homes of Bengal on the eve of Durga Puja.

Absolute is not to be compassed by means of work. For the rule with regard to a seeker of the Atman is that he should undergo spiritual practice, but have no eye to its results. It follows thence that these practices are simply the cause of the purification of the aspirant's mind. For if the Atman could be directly realised as a result of these practices, then scriptures would not have enjoined on the aspirant to give up the results of work. So it is with a view to combating the Purva-mimamsa doctrine of work with motive producing results, that the philosophy of work without motive has been set forth in the Gita. Do you see?

Disciple: But, sir, if one has to renounce the fruits of work, why should one be induced to undertake work which is always troublesome?

Swamiji: In this human life, one cannot help doing some kind of work always. When man has perforce to do some work, Karma-yoga enjoins on him to do it in such a way as will bring freedom through the realisation of the Atman. As to your objection that none will be induced to work—the answer is, that whatever work you do has some motive behind it; but when by the long performance of work, one notices that one work merely leads to another, through a round of births and rebirths, then the awakened discrimination of man naturally begins to question itself, "Where is the end to this interminable chain of work?" It is then that he appreciates the full import of the words of the Lord in the Gita: "Inscrutable is the course of work."Therefore when the aspirant finds that work with motive brings no happiness, then he renounces action. But man is so constituted that to him the performance of work is a necessity, so what work should he take up? He takes up some unselfish work, but gives up all desire for its fruits. For he has known then that in those fruits of work lie countless seeds of future births and deaths. Therefore the knower of Brahman renounces all actions. Although to outward appearances he engages himself in some work, he has no attachment to it. Such men have been described in the scriptures as Karma-yogins.

Disciple: Is then the work without motive of the unselfish knower of Brahman like the activities of a lunatic?

Swamiji: Why so? Giving up the fruits of work means not to perform work for the good of one's own body or mind. The knower of Brahman never seeks his own happiness. But what is there to prevent him from doing work for the welfare of others? Whatever work he does without attachment for its fruits brings only good to the world—it is all "for the good of the many, for the happiness of the many". Shri Ramakrishna used to say, "They never take a false step". Haven't you read in the Uttara-rama-charita "[(Sanskrit)] — the words of the ancient Rishis have always some meaning, they are never false?" When the mind is merged in the Atman by the suppression of all modifications, it produces "a dispassion for the enjoyment of fruits of work here or hereafter"; there remains no desire in the mind for any enjoyment here, or, after death,

in any heavenly sphere. There is no action and interaction of desires in the mind. But when the mind descends from the superconscious state into the world of "I and mine", then by the momentum of previous work or habit, or Samskaras (impressions), the functions of the body go on as before. The mind then is generally in the superconscious state; eating and other functions of the body are done from mere necessity, and the body-consciousness is very much attenuated. Whatever work is done after reaching this transcendental state is done rightly; it conduces to the real well-being of men and the world; for then the mind of the doer is not contaminated by selfishness or calculation of personal gain or loss. The Lord has created this wonderful universe, remaining always in the realm of superconsciousness; therefore there is nothing imperfect in this world. So I was saying that the actions which the knower of the Atman does without attachment for fruits are never imperfect, but they conduce to the real well-being of men and the world.

Disciple: Sir, you said just now that knowledge and work are contradictory, that in the supreme knowledge there is no room at all for work, or in other words, that by means of work the realisation of Brahman cannot be attained. Why then do you now and then speak words calculated to awaken great Rajas (activity)? You were telling me the other day, "Work, work, work—there is no other way."

Swamiji: Going round the whole world, I find that people of this country are immersed in great Tamas (inactivity), compared with people of other countries. On the outside, there is a simulation of the Sattvika (calm and balanced) state, but inside, downright inertness like that of stocks and stones—what work will be done in the world by such people? How long can such an inactive, lazy, and sensual people live in the world? First travel in Western countries, then contradict my words. How much of enterprise and devotion to work, how much enthusiasm and manifestation of Rajas are there in the lives of the Western people! While, in your own country, it is as if the blood has become congealed in the heart, so that it cannot circulate in the veins—as if paralysis has overtaken the body and it has become languid. So my idea is first to make the people active by developing their Rajas, and thus make them fit for the struggle for existence. With no strength in the body, no enthusiasm at heart, and no originality in the brain, what will they do—these lumps of dead matter! By stimulating them I want to bring life into them—to this I have dedicated my life. I will rouse them through the infallible power of Vedic Mantras. I am born to proclaim to them that fearless message —"Arise! Awake!" Be you my helpers in this work! Go from village to village, from one portion of the country to another, and preach this message of fearlessness to all, from the Brahmin to the Chandala. Tell each and all that infinite power resides within them, that they are sharers of immortal Bliss. Thus rouse up the Rajas within them—make them fit for the struggle for existence, and then speak to them about salvation. First make the people of the country stand on their legs by rousing their inner power, first let them learn to have good food and clothes and plenty of enjoyment—then tell them how to be free from this bondage of enjoyment.

Laziness, meanness, and hypocrisy have covered the whole length and breadth of the country. Can an intelligent man look on all this and remain quiet? Does it not bring tears to the eyes? Madras, Bombay, Punjab, Bengal—whichever way I look, I see no signs of life. You are thinking yourselves highly educated. What nonsense have you learnt? Getting by heart the thoughts of others in a foreign language, and stuffing your brain with them and taking some university degrees, you consider yourselves educated! Fie upon you! Is this education? What is the goal of your education? Either a clerkship, or being a roguish lawyer, or at the most a Deputy Magistracy, which is another form of clerkship—isn't that all? Open your eyes and see what a piteous cry for food is rising in the land of Bharata, proverbial for its wealth! Will your education fulfil this want? Never.

With the help of Western science set yourselves to dig the earth and produce food-stuffs—not by means of mean servitude of others—but by discovering new avenues to production, by your own exertions aided by Western science. Therefore I teach the people of this country to be full of activities, so as to be able to produce food and clothing for themselves. For want of food and clothing and plunged in anxiety for it, the country has come to ruin—what are you doing to remedy this? Throw aside your scriptures in the Ganga and teach the people first the means of procuring their food and clothing, and then you will find time to read to them the scriptures. If their material wants are not removed by the rousing of intense activity, none will listen to words of spirituality. Therefore I say, first rouse the inherent power of the Atman within you, then, rousing the faith of the general people in that power as much as you can, teach them first of all to make provision for food, and then teach them religion. There is no time to sit idle—who knows when death will overtake one?

While saying these words, a mingled expression of remorse, sorrow, compassion, and power shone on his face. Looking at his majestic appearance, the disciple was awed into silence. A little while afterwards Swamiji said again, "That activity and self-reliance must come in the people of the country in time—I see it clearly. There is no escape. The intelligent man can distinctly see the vision of the next three Yugas (ages) ahead. Ever since the advent of Shri Ramakrishna the eastern horizon has been aglow with the dawning rays of the sun which in course of time will illumine the country with the splendour of the midday sun."

UNTITLED CONVERSATION XXV

The present Math buildings are almost complete now.

Swamiji is not in good health; therefore doctors have advised him to go out on a boat in the mornings and evenings on the Ganga.

Today is Sunday. The disciple is sitting in Swamiji's room and conversing with him. About this time Swamiji framed certain rules for the guidance of the Sannyasins and Brahmacharins of the Math, the object of which was to keep them from indiscriminate mixing with worldly people. The conversation turned on this topic.

Swamiji: Nowadays I feel a peculiar smell of lax self-control in the dress and clothes of worldly people; therefore I have made it a rule in the Math that householders should not sit or lie on the beds of Sadhus. Formerly I used to read in the Shastras that such a smell is felt, and therefore Sannyasins cannot bear the smell of householders. Now I see it is true. By strictly observing the rules that have been framed, the Brahmacharins will in time grow into genuine Sannyasins. When they are established in the ideal of Sannyasa, they will be able to mix on an equal footing with worldly men without any harm. But now if they are not kept within the barriers of strict rules, they will all go wrong. In order to attain to ideal Brahmacharya one has in the beginning to observe strict rules regarding chastity. Not only should one keep oneself strictly aloof from the least association with the opposite sex, but also give up the company of married people even.

The disciple who was a householder was awed at these words of Swamiji, felt dejected that he would not be able to associate freely as before with the Sadhus of the Math and said, "Sir, I feel more intimacy with the Math and its inmates than with my own family. As if they are known to me from a long long time. The unbounded freedom that I enjoy in the Math, I feel nowhere else in the world."

Swamiji: All those who are pure in spirit will feel like that here. Those who do not feel so must be taken as not belonging to this Math and its ideals. That is the reason why many people come here out of mere sensation-mongering and then run away. Those who are devoid of continence and are running after money day and night will never be able to appreciate the ideals of the Math, nor regard the Math people as their own. The Sannyasins of this Math are not like those of old, ash-besmeared, with matted hair and iron tongs in their hands, and curing disease by medicinal titbits; therefore seeing the contrast, people cannot appreciate them. The ways, movements and ideas of our Master were all cast in a new mould, so we are also of a new type. Sometimes dressed like gentlemen, we are engaged in lecturing; at other times, throwing all aside, with "Hara, Hara, Vyom Vyom" on the lips, ash-clad, we are immersed in meditation and austerities in mountains and forests.

Now it won't do to merely quote the authority of our ancient books. The tidal wave of Western civilisation is now rushing over the length and breadth of the country. It won't do now simply to sit in meditation on mountain tops without realising in the least its usefulness. Now is wanted—as said in the Gita by the Lord—intense Karma-yoga, with unbounded courage and indomitable strength in the heart. Then only will the people of the country be roused, otherwise they will continue to be as much in the dark as you are.

The day is nearly ended. Swamiji came downstairs, dressed for the boating excursion on the Ganga. Swamiji, accompanied by the disciple and two others, boarded the boat, which passed the Dakshineswar temple and reached Panihati where it was anchored below the garden-house of Babu Govinda Kumar Chaudhury. It has once been proposed to rent this house for the use of the Math. Swamiji descended from the boat, went round the house and the garden and looking over the place minutely said, "The garden is nice but is at a great distance from Calcutta. The devotees of Shri Ramakrishna would have been put to trouble to walk such a long distance from Calcutta. It is fortunate that the Math has not been established here." The boat then returned to the Math amid the enveloping darkness.

UNTITLED CONVERSATION XXVI

The disciple has today come to the Math with Nag Mahashaya in company.

Swamiji to Nag Mahashaya (saluting him): You are all right, I hope?

Nag Mahashaya: I have come today to visit you. Glory to Shankara! Glory to Shankara! I am blessed today verily with the sight of Shiva!

Saying these words, Nag Mahashaya out of reverence stood with joined hands before him.

Swamiji: How is your health?

Nag Mahashaya: Why are you asking about this trifling body—this cage of flesh and bones? Verily I am blessed today to see you.

Saying these words, Nag Mahashaya prostrated before Swamiji.

Swamiji (lifting him up): Why are you doing that to me?

Nag Mahashaya: I see with my inner eye that today I am blessed with the vision of Shiva Himself. Glory to Ramakrishna!

Swamiji (addressing the disciple): Do you see? How real Bhakti transforms human nature! Nag Mahashaya has lost himself in the Divine, his body-consciousness has vanished altogether. (To Swami Premananda) Get some Prasada for Nag Mahashaya.

Nag Mahashaya: Prasada! (To Swamiji with folded hands) Seeing you, all my earthly hunger has vanished today.

The Brahmacharins and Sannyasins of the Math were studying the Upanishads. Swamiji said to them, "Today a great devotee of Shri Ramakrishna has come amongst us. Let it be a holiday in honour of Nag Mahashaya's visit to the Math." So all closed their books and sat in a circle round Nag Mahashaya; Swamiji also sat in front of him.

Swamiji (addressing all): Do you see? Look at Nag Mahash-

aya; he is a householder, yet he has no knowledge of the mundane existence; he always lives lost in Divine consciousness. (To Nag Mahashaya) Please tell us and these Brahmacharins something about Shri Ramakrishna.

Nag Mahashaya (in reverence): What do you say, sir? What shall I say? I have come to see you—the hero, the helper in the divine play of Shri Ramakrishna. Now will people appreciate his message and teachings. Glory to Ramakrishna!

Swamiji: It is you who have really appreciated and understood Shri Ramakrishna. We are only spent in useless wanderings.

Nag Mahashaya: What do you say, sir? You are the image of Shri Ramakrishna—the obverse and reverse of the same coin. Those who have eyes, let them see.

Swamiji: Is the starting of these Maths and Ashramas etc. a step in the right direction?

Nag Mahashaya: I am an insignificant being, what do I understand? Whatever you do, I know for a certainty, will conduce to the well-being of the world—ay, of the world.

Many out of reverence proceeded to take the dust of Nag Mahashaya's feet, which made him much agitated. Swamiji, addressing all, said, "Don't act so as to cause pain to Nag Mahashaya; he feels uncomfortable." Hearing this everybody desisted.

Swamiji: Do please come and stay at the Math. You will be an object-lesson to the boys here.

Nag Mahashaya: I once asked Shri Ramakrishna about that, to which he replied, "Stay as a householder as you are doing." Therefore I am continuing in that life. I see you all occasionally and feel myself blessed.

Swamiji: I will go to your place once.

Nag Mahashaya, mad with joy, said, "Shall such a day dawn? My place will be made holy by your visit, like Varanasi. Shall I be so fortunate as that!"

Swamiji: Well, I have the desire. Now it depends on "Mother" to take me there.

Nag Mahashaya: Who will understand you? Unless the inner vision opens, nobody can understand you. Only Shri Ramakrishna understood you; all else have simply put faith in his words, but none has understood you really.

Swamiji: Now my one desire is to rouse the country—the sleeping leviathan that has lost all faith in his power and makes no response. If I can wake it up to a sense of the Eternal Religion then I shall know that Shri Ramakrishna's advent and our birth are fruitful. That is the one desire in my heart: Mukti and all else appear of no consequence to me. Please give me your blessings that I may succeed.

Nag Mahashaya: Your will and his have become one. Whatever is your will is his. Glory to Shri Ramakrishna!

Swamiji: To work one requires a strong body; since coming to this country, I am not doing well; in the West I was in very good health.

Nag Mahashaya: "Whenever one is born in a body," Shri Ramakrishna used to say, "one has to pay the house tax." Disease and sorrow are the tax. But your body is a box of gold mohurs, and very great care should be taken of it. But who will do it? Who will understand? Only Shri Ramakrishna understood. Glory to Ramakrishna!

Swamiji: All at the Math take great care of me.

Nag Mahashaya: It will be to their good if they do it, whether they know it or not. If proper attention is not paid to your body, then the chances are that it will fall off.

Swamiji: Nag Mahashaya, I do not fully understand whether what I am doing is right or not. At particular times I feel a great inclination to work in a certain direction, and I work according to that. Whether it is for good or evil, I cannot understand.

Nag Mahashaya: Well, Shri Ramakrishna said, "The treasure is now locked."— therefore he does not let you know fully. The moment you know it, your play of human life will be at an end.

Swamiji was pondering something with steadfast gaze. Then Swami Premananda brought some Prasada for Nag Mahashaya who was ecstatic with joy. Shortly after Nag Mahashaya found Swamiji slowly digging the ground with a spade near the pond, and held him by the hand saying, "When we are present, why should you do that?" Swamiji leaving the spade walked about the garden talking the while, and began to narrate to a disciple, "After Shri Ramakrishna's passing away we heard one day that Nag Mahashaya lay fasting in his humbled tiled lodgings in Calcutta. Myself, Swami Turiyananda, and another went together and appeared at Nag Mahashaya's cottage. Seeing us he rose from his bed. We said, 'We shall have our Bhiksha (food) here today.' At once Nag Mahashaya brought rice, cooking pot, fuel, etc. from the bazaar and began to cook. We thought that we would eat and make Nag Mahashaya also eat. Cooking over, he gave the food to us; we set apart something for him and then sat down to eat. After this, we requested him to take food; he at once broke the pot of rice and striking his forehead began to say: 'Shall I give food to the body in which God has not been realised?' Seeing this we were struck with amazement. Later on after much persuasion we induced him to take some food and then returned."

Swamiji: Will Nag Mahashaya stay in the Math tonight?

Disciple: No, he has some work; he must return today.

Swamiji: Then look for a boat. It is getting dark. When the boat came, the disciple and Nag Mahashaya saluted

UNTITLED CONVERSATION XXVII

Swamiji is now in very good health. The disciple has come to the Math on a Sunday morning. After visiting Swamiji he has come downstairs and is discussing the Vedantic scriptures with Swami Nirmalananda. At this moment Swamiji himself came downstairs and addressing the disciple, said, "What were you discussing with Nirmalananda?"

Disciple: Sir, he was saying, "The Brahman of the Vedanta is only known to you and your Swamiji. We on the contrary know that "(Sanskrit)— shri Krishna is the Lord Himself."

Swamiji: What did you say?

Disciple: I said that the Atman is the one Truth, and that Krishna was merely a person who had realised this Atman. Swami Nirmalananda is at heart a believer in the Advaita Vedanta, but outwardly he takes up the dualistic side. His first idea seems to be to moot the personal aspect of the Ishvara and then by a gradual process of reasoning to strengthen the foundations of Vedanta.

But as soon as he calls me a "Vaishnava" I forget his real intention and begin a heated discussion with him.

Swamiji: He loves you and so enjoys the fun of teasing you. But why should you be upset by his words? You will also answer, "You, sir, are an atheist, a believer in Nihility."

Disciple: Sir, is there any such statement in the Upanishads that Ishvara is an all-powerful Person? But people generally believe in such an Ishvara.

Swamiji: The highest principle, the Lord of all, cannot be a Person. The Jiva is an individual and the sum total of all Jivas is the Ishvara. In the Jiva, Avidya, or nescience, is predominant, but Ishvara controls Maya composed of Avidya and Vidya and independently projects this world of moving and immovable things out of Himself. But Brahman transcends both the individual and collective aspects, the Jiva and Ishvara. In Brahman there is no part. It is for the sake of easy comprehension that parts have been imagined in It. That part of Brahman in which there is the superimposition of creation, maintenance and dissolution of the universe has been spoken of as Ishvara in the scriptures, while the other unchangeable portion, with reference to which there is no thought of duality, is indicated as Brahman. But do not on that account think that Brahman is a distinct and separate substance from the Jivas and the universe. The Qualified Monists hold that it is Brahman that has transformed Itself into Jivas and the universe. The Advaitins on the contrary maintain that Jivas and the universe have been merely superimposed on Brahman. But in reality there has been no modification in Brahman. The Advaitin says that the universe consists only of name and form. It endures only so long as there are name and form. When through meditation and other practices name and form are dissolved, then only the transcendent Brahman remains. Then the separate reality of Jivas and the universe is felt no longer. Then it is realised that one is the Eternal Pure Essence of Intelligence, or Brahman. The real nature of the Jiva is Brahman. When the veil of name and form vanishes through meditation etc., then that idea is simply realised. This is the substance of pure Advaita. The Vedas, the Vedanta and all other scriptures only explain this idea in different ways.

Disciple: How then is it true that Ishvara is an almighty Person?

Swamiji: Man is man in so far as he is qualified by the limiting adjunct of mind. Through the mind he has to understand and grasp everything, and therefore whatever he thinks must be limited by the mind. Hence it is the natural tendency of man to argue, from the analogy of his own personality, the personality of Ishvara (God). Man can only think of his ideal as a human being. When buffeted by sorrow in this world of disease and death he is driven to desperation and helplessness, then he seeks refuge with someone, relying on whom he may feel safe. But where is that refuge to be found? The omnipresent Atman which depends on nothing else to support It is the only Refuge. At first man does not find that. When discrimination and dispassion arise in the course of meditation and spiritual practices, he comes to know it. But in whatever way he may progress on the path of spirituality, everyone is unconsciously awakening Brahman within him. But the means may be different in different cases. Those who have faith in the Personal God have to undergo spiritual practices holding on to that idea. If there is sincerity, through that will come the awakening of the lion of Brahman within. The knowledge of Brahman is the one goal of all beings but the various ideas are the various paths to it. Although the real nature of the Jiva is Brahman, still as he has identification with the qualifying adjunct of the mind, he suffers from all sorts of doubts and difficulties, pleasure and pain. But everyone from Brahma down to a blade of grass is advancing towards the realisation of his real nature. And none can escape the round of births and deaths until he realises his identity with Brahman. Getting the human birth, when the desire for freedom becomes very strong, and along with it comes the grace of a person of realisation, then man's desire for Self-knowledge becomes intensified. Otherwise the mind of men given to lust and greed never inclines that way. How should the desire to know Brahman arise in one who has the hankering in his mind for the pleasures of family life, for wealth and for fame? He who is prepared to renounce all, who amid the strong current of the duality of good and evil, happiness and misery, is calm, steady, balanced, and awake to his Ideal, alone endeavours to attain to Self-knowledge. He alone by the might of his own power tears asunder the net of the world. "[(Sanskrit)] — breaking the barriers of Maya, he emerges like a mighty lion."

Disciple: Well then, is it true that without Sannyasa, there can be no knowledge of Brahman?

Swamiji: That is true, a thousand times. One must have both internal and external Sannyasa — renunciation in spirit as also formal renunciation. Shankaracharya, in commenting on the Upanishadic text, "Neither by Tapas (spiritual practice) devoid of the necessary insignia",[1] has said that by practising Sadhana without the external badge of Sannyasa (the Geruarobe, the staff, Kamandalu, etc.), Brahman, which is difficult to attain, is not realised. Without dispassion for the world, without renunciation, without giving up the desire for enjoyment, absolutely nothing can be accomplished in the spiritual life. "It is not like a sweetmeat in the hands of a child which you can snatch by a trick."[2]

Disciple: But, sir, in the course of spiritual practices, that renunciation may come.

Swamiji: Let those to whom it will come gradually have it that way. But why should you sit and wait for that? At once begin to dig the channel which will bring the waters of spirituality to your life. Shri Ramakrishna used to deprecate lukewarmness in spiritual attainments as, for instance, saying that religion would come gradually, and that there was no hurry for it. When one is thirsty, can one sit idle? Does he not run about for water? Because your thirst for spirituality has not come, therefore you are sitting idly. The desire for knowledge has not grown strong, therefore you are satisfied with the little pleasures of family life.

Disciple: Really I do not understand why I don't get that idea of renouncing everything. Do make some way for that, please.

Swamiji: The end and the means are all in your hands. I can only stimulate them. You have read so many scriptures and are serving and associating with such Sadhus who have known Brahman; if even this does not bring the idea of renunciation, then your life is in vain. But it will not be altogether vain; the effects of this will manifest in some way or other in time.

The disciple was much dejected and again said to Swamiji: "Sir, I have come under your refuge, do open the path of Mukti for me — that I may realise the Truth in this body."

Swamiji: What fear is there? Always discriminate — your body, your house, these Jivas and the world are all absolutely unreal like a dream. Always think that this body is only an inert instrument. And the self-contained Purusha within is your real nature. The adjunct of mind is His first and subtle covering, then, there is this body which is His gross, outer covering. The indivisible changeless, self-effulgent Purusha is lying hidden under these delusive veils, therefore your real nature is unknown to you. The direction of the mind which always runs after the senses has to be turned within. The mind has to be killed. The body is but gross — it dies and dissolves into the five elements. But the bundle of mental impressions, which is the mind, does not die soon. It remains for some time in seed-form and then sprouts and grows in the form of a tree — it takes on another physical body and goes the round of birth and death, until Self-knowledge arises. Therefore I say, by meditation and concentration and by the power of philosophical discrimination plunge this mind in the Ocean of Existence-knowledge-bliss Absolute. When the mind dies, all limiting adjuncts vanish and you are established in Brahman.

Disciple: Sir, it is so difficult to direct this uncontrolled mind towards Brahman.

---

1. Mundaka Upanishad, III. ii. 4.

2. Song of Ramprasad.

Swamiji: Is there anything difficult for the hero? Only men of faint hearts speak so. "[(Sanskrit)]—mukti is easy of attainment only to the hero—but not to cowards." Says the Gita (VI. 35), "[(Sanskrit)]—by renunciation and by practice is the mind brought under control, O Arjuna." The Chitta or mind-stuff is like a transparent lake, and the waves which rise in it by the impact of sense-impressions constitute Manas or the mind. Therefore the mind consists of a succession of thought-waves. From these mental waves arises desire. Then that desire transforms itself into will and works through its gross instrument, the body. Again, as work is endless, so its fruits also are endless. Hence the mind is always being tossed by countless myriads of waves—the fruits of work. This mind has to be divested of all modifications (Vrittis) and reconverted into the transparent lake, so that there remains not a single wave of modification in it. Then will Brahman manifest Itself. The scriptures give a glimpse of this state in such passages as: "Then all the knots of the heart are cut asunder", etc. Do you understand?

Disciple: Yes, sir, but meditation must base itself on some object?

Swamiji: You yourself will be the object of your meditation. Think and meditate that you are the omnipresent Atman. "I am neither the body, nor the mind, nor the Buddhi (determinative faculty), neither the gross nor the subtle body"—by this process of elimination, immerse your mind in the transcendent knowledge which is your real nature. Kill the mind by thus plunging it repeatedly in this. Then only you will realise the Essence of Intelligence, or be established in your real nature. Knower and known, meditator and the object meditated upon will then become one, and the cessation of all phenomenal superimpositions will follow. This is styled in the Shastras as the transcendence of the triad or relative knowledge (Triputibheda). There is no relative or conditioned knowledge in this state. When the Atman is the only knower, by what means can you possibly know It? The Atman is Knowledge, the Atman is Intelligence, the Atman is Sachchidananda. It is through the inscrutable power of Maya, which cannot be indicated as either existent or non-existent, that the relative consciousness has come upon the Jiva who is none other than Brahman. This is generally known as the conscious state. And the state in which this duality of relative existence becomes one in the pure Brahman is called in the scriptures the superconscious state and described in such words as, "[(Sanskrit)]—it is like an ocean perfectly at rest and without a name" (Vivekachudamani, 410).

Swamiji spoke these words as if from the profound depths of his realisation of Brahman.

Swamiji: All philosophy and scriptures have come from the plane of relative knowledge of subject and object. But no thought or language of the human mind can fully express the Reality which lies beyond the plane of relative Knowledge! Science, philosophy, etc. are only partial truths. So they can never be the adequate channels of expression for the transcendent Reality. Hence viewed from the transcendent standpoint, everything appears to be unreal—religious creeds, and works, I and thou, and the universe—everything is unreal! Then only it is perceived: "I am the only reality; I am the all-pervading Atman, and I am the proof of my own existence." Where is the room for a separate proof to establish the reality of my existence? I am, as the scriptures say, "[(Sanskrit)]—always known to myself as the eternal subject" (Vivekachudamani, 409). I have seen that state, realised it. You also see and realise it and preach this truth of Brahman to all. Then only will you attain to peace.

While speaking these words, Swamiji's face wore a serious expression and he was lost in thought. After some time he continued: "Realise in your own life this knowledge of Brahman which comprehends all theories and is the rationale of all truths, and preach it to the world. This will conduce to your own good and the good of others as well. I have told you today the essence of all truths; there is nothing higher than this."

Disciple: Sir, now you are speaking of Jnana; but sometimes you proclaim the superiority of Bhakti, sometimes of Karma, and sometimes of Yoga. This confuses our understanding.

Swamiji: Well, the truth is this. The knowledge of Brahman is the ultimate goal—the highest destiny of man. But man cannot remain absorbed in Brahman all the time. When he comes out of it, he must have something to engage himself. At that time he should do such work as will contribute to the real well-being of people. Therefore do I urge you in the service of Jivas in a spirit of oneness. But, my son, such are the intricacies of work, that even great saints are caught in them and become attached.

Therefore work has to be done without any desire for results. This is the teaching of the Gita. But know that in the knowledge of Brahman there is no touch of any relation to work. Good works, at the most, purify the mind. Therefore has the commentator Shankara so sharply criticised the doctrine of the combination of Jnana and Karma. Some attain to the knowledge of Brahman by the means of unselfish work. This is also a means, but the end is the realisation of Brahman. Know this thoroughly that the goal of the path of discrimination and of all other modes of practice is the realisation of Brahman.

Disciple: Now, sir, please tell me about the utility of Raja-yoga and Bhakti-yoga.

Swamiji: Striving in these paths also some attain to the realisation of Brahman. The path of Bhakti or devotion of God is a slow process, but is easy of practice. In the path of Yoga there are many obstacles; perhaps the mind runs after psychic powers and thus draws you away from attaining your real nature. Only the path of Jnana is of quick fruition and the rationale of all other creeds; hence it is equally esteemed in all countries and all ages. But even in the path of discrimination there is the chance of the mind getting stuck in the interminable net of vain argumentation. Therefore along with it, meditation should be practised. By means of discrimination and meditation, the goal or Brahman has to be reached. One is sure to reach the goal by practising in this way. This, in my opinion, is the easy path ensuring quick success.

Disciple: Now please tell me something about the doctrine of Incarnation of God.

Swamiji: You want to master everything in a day, it seems!

Disciple: Sir, if the doubts and difficulties of the mind be solved in one day, then I shall not have to trouble you time and again.

Swamiji: Those by whose grace the knowledge of Atman, which is extolled so much in the scriptures, is attained in a minute are the moving Tirthas (seats of holiness)— the Incarnations. From their very birth they are knowers of Brahman, and between Brahman and the knower of Brahman there is not the least difference. "[(Sanskrit)]—he who knows the Brahman becomes the Brahman" (Mundaka, III.ii.9). The Atman cannot be known by the mind for It is Itself the Knower—this I have already said. Therefore man's relative knowledge reached up to the Avataras—those who are always established in the Atman. The highest ideal of Ishvara which the human mind can grasp is the Avatara. Beyond this there is no relative knowledge. Such knowers of Brahman are rarely born in the world. And very few people can understand them. They alone are the proof of the truths of the scriptures—the towers of light in the ocean of the world. By the company of such Avataras and by their grace, the darkness of the mind disappears in a trice and realisation flashes immediately in the heart. Why or by what process it comes cannot be ascertained. But it does come. I have seen it happen like that. Shri Krishna spoke the Gita, establishing Himself in the Atman. Those passages of the Gita where He speaks with the word "I", invariably indicate the Atman: "Take refuge in Me alone" means, "Be established in the Atman". This knowledge of the Atman is the highest aim of the Gita. The references to Yoga etc. are but incidental to this realisation of the Atman. Those who have not this knowledge of the Atman are "suicides". "They kill themselves by the clinging to the unreal"; they lose their life in the noose of sense-pleasures. You are also men, and can't you ignore this trash of sensual enjoyment that won't last for two days? Should you also swell the ranks of those who are born and die in utter ignorance? Accept the "beneficial" and discard the "pleasant". Speak of this Atman to all, even to the lowest. By continued speaking your own intelligence also will clear up. And always repeat the great Mantras —"[(Sanskrit)]—thou art That", "[(Sanskrit)]—I am That", "[(Sanskrit)]—all this is verily Brahman"— and have the courage of a lion in the heart. What is there to fear? Fear is death—fear is the greatest sin. The human soul, represented by Arjuna, was touched with fear. Therefore Bhagavan Shri Krishna, established in the Atman, spoke to him the teachings of the Gita. Still his fear would not leave him. Later, when Arjuna saw the Universal Form of the Lord, and became established in the Atman, then with all bondages of Karma burnt by the fire of knowledge, he fought the battle.

Disciple: Sir, can a man do work even after realisation?

Swamiji: After realisation, what is ordinarily called work does not persist. It changes its character. The work which the Jnani does only conduces to the well-being of the world. Whatever a man of realisation says or does contributes to the welfare of all. We have observed Shri Ramakrishna; he was, as it were "[(Sanskrit)]—in the body, but not of it!" About the motive of the actions of such personages only this can be said: "[(Sanskrit)]—everything they do like men, simply by way of sport" (Brahma-Sutras , II.i.33).

UNTITLED CONVERSATION XXVIII

The disciple has come to the Math today accompanied by Shri Ranadaprasad Das Gupta, the founder and professor of the Jubilee Art Academy, Calcutta. Ranada Babu is an expert artist, a learned man and an admirer of Swamiji. After the exchange of courtesies Swamiji began to talk with Ranada Babu on various topics relating to art.

Swamiji: I had the opportunity of seeing the beauties

of art of nearly every civilised country in the world, but I saw nothing like the development of art which took place in our country during the Buddhistic period. During the regime of the Mogul Emperors also, there was a marked development of art—and the Taj and the Jumma Masjid etc. are standing monuments of that culture.

Art has its origin in the expression of some idea in whatever man produces. Where there is no expression of idea, however much there may be a display of colours and so on, it cannot be styled as true art. Even the articles of everyday use, such as water vessels, or cups and saucers, should be used to express an idea. In the Paris Exhibition I saw a wonderful figure carved in marble. In explanation of the figure, the following words were inscribed underneath: Art unveiling Nature. That is how art sees the inner beauty of nature by drawing away with its own hands the covering veils. The work has been so designed as to indicate that the beauty of nature has not yet become fully unveiled; but the artist is fascinated, as it were, with the beauty of the little that has become manifest. One cannot refrain from praising the sculptor who has tried to express this exquisite idea. You should also try to produce something original like this.

Ranada Babu: Yes, I also have the desire to do some original modelling at leisure. But I meet with no encouragement in this country; it is a poor country and there is want of appreciation. Swamiji: If you can with your whole heart produce one real thing, if you can rightly express a single idea in art, it must win appreciation in course of time. A real thing never suffers from want of appreciation in this world. It is also heard that some artists have gained appreciation for their works a thousand years after their death!

Ranada Babu: That is true. But we have become so worthless that we haven't got the courage to spend a lot of energy to no purpose. Through these five years' struggle I have succeeded to some extent. Bless me that my efforts be not in vain.

Swamiji: If you set to work in right earnest, then you are sure to be successful. Whoever works at a thing heart and soul not only achieves success in it, but through his absorption in that he also realises the supreme Truth—brahman. Whoever works at a thing with his whole heart receives help from God.

Ranada Babu: What difference did you find between the art of the West and that of India?

Swamiji: It is nearly the same everywhere. Originality is rarely found. In those countries pictures are painted with the help of models obtained by photographing various objects. But no sooner does one take the help of machinery than all originality vanishes—one cannot give expression to one's ideas. The ancient artists used to evolve original ideas from their brains and try to express them in their paintings. Now the picture being a likeness of photographs, the power of originality and the attempt to develop are getting scarce. But each nation has a characteristic of its own. In its manners and customs, in its mode of living, in painting and sculpture is found the expression of that characteristic idea. For instance, music and dancing in the West are all pointed in their expression. In dance, they look as if jerking the limbs; in instrumental music, the sounds prick the ear like a sword thrust, as it were; so also in vocal music. In this country, on the other hand, the dance has a rolling wave-like movement, and there is the same rounded movement in the varieties of pitch in vocal song. So also in instrumental music. Hence with regard to art also, a different expression is found among different people. People who are very materialistic take nature as their ideal, and try to express in art ideas allied thereto, while the people whose ideal is the transcendent Reality beyond nature try to express that in art through the powers of nature. With regard to the former class of people, nature is the primary basis of art, while with the second class, ideality is the principal motive of artistic development. Thus, though starting with two different ideals in art, they have advanced in it each in its own way. Seeing some paintings in the West you will mistake them for real natural objects. With respect to this country also, when in ancient times sculpture attained a high degree of perfection, if you look at a statue of the period it will make you forget the material world and transport you to a new ideal world. As in Western countries paintings like those of former times are not produced now, so in our country also, attempts to give expression to original ideas in art are no longer seen. For example, the paintings from your art school have got no expression, as it were. It would be well if you try to paint the objects of everyday meditation of the Hindus by giving in them the expression of ancient ideals.

Ranada Babu: I feel much encouraged by your words. I shall try to act up to your suggestions.

Swamiji: Take, for instance, the figure of Mother Kali. In it there is the union of the blissful and the terrible aspects. But in none of the pictures can be seen the true expression of these two aspects. Far from this, there is no attempt to express adequately even one of these two aspects! I have tried to put down some ideas of the terrible aspects of Mother Kali in my English poem, Kali the Mother. Can you express those ideas in a picture?

Ranada Babu: Please let me know them.

Swamiji had the poem brought from the library, and began to read it out most impressively to Ranada Babu. Ranada Babu silently listened to the poem, and after a while, as if visualising the figure with his mind's eye, he turned to Swamiji with a frightened look.

Swamiji: Well, will you be able to express this idea in the picture?

Ranada Babu: Yes, I shall try[1]; but it turns one's head even to imagine the idea.

Swamiji: After drawing the picture, please show it to me. Then I will tell you about the points necessary to perfect it.

Then Swamiji had the design which he had sketched for the seal[2] of the Ramakrishna Mission brought, showed it to Ranada Babu and asked his opinion on it. It depicted a lake in which a lotus blossomed, and there was a swan, and the whole was encircled by a serpent. Ranada Babu at first could not catch the significance of it and asked Swamiji to explain. Swamiji said, "The wavy waters in the picture are symbolic of Karma; the lotus, of Bhakti; and the rising-sun, of Jnana. The encircling serpent is indicative of Yoga and the awakened Kundalini Shakti, while the swan in the picture stands for the Paramatman (Supreme Self). Therefore the idea of the picture is that by the union of Karma, Jnana, Bhakti, and Yoga, the vision of the Paramatman is obtained."

Ranada Babu kept silent, gratified to hear the motif of the picture. After a while he said, "I wish I could learn about art from you!"

Then Swamiji showed to Ranada Babu a drawing, depicting his plan of the future Ramakrishna Temple and Math. Then he began to say, "In the building of this prospective Temple and Math I have the desire to bring together all that is best in Eastern and Western art. I shall try to apply in its construction all the ideas about architecture which I have gathered in my travels all over the world. A big prayer-hall will be built with roof supported on numerous clustered pillars. In its walls, hundreds of lotuses will be in full bloom. It must be big enough to accommodate a thousand persons sitting in meditation. The Ramakrishna temple and prayer-hall should be built together in such a way that from a distance it would taken for a representation of the symbol, "Om". Within the

1. Ranada Babu began to paint this picture the very next day, but it was never finished, nor shown to Swamiji.

2. Printed on the title-page of this volume.

temple there would be a figure of Shri Ramakrishna seated on a swan. On the two sides of the door will be represented the figure of a lion and a lamb licking each other's body in love-expressing the idea that great power and gentleness have become united in love. I have these ideas in my mind; and if I live long enough I shall carry them out. Otherwise future generations will try if they can do it by degrees. It is my opinion that Shri Ramakrishna was born to vivify all branches of art and culture in this country. Therefore this Math has to be built up in such a way that religion, work, learning, Jnana, and Bhakti may spread over the world from this centre. Be you my helpers in this work."

Ranada Babu and the assembled Sannyasins and Brahmacharins listened to Swamiji in mute wonder. After a while Swamiji resumed, "I am discussing the subject at length with you as you are yourself an adept in the line. Now please tell me what you have learnt about the highest ideals of art as the result of your long study of it."

Ranada Babu: What new thing can I tell you? On the contrary, it is you who have opened my eyes on this subject. I have never heard such instructive words on the subject of art in my life. Bless me, sir, that I can work out the ideas that I have got from you.

Then Swamiji got up from his seat and paced the lawn, remarking to the disciple, "He is a very spirited young man."

Disciple: Sir, he is astonished to hear your words.

Swamiji, without answering the disciple, began to hum the lines of a song which Shri Ramakrishna used to sing, "The controlled mind is a great treasure, the philosopher's stone, which yields whatever you want."

After walking a while, Swamiji, washing his face, entered his room with the disciple in company and read the article on Art in the Encyclopaedia Britannica for some time. After finishing it, he began to make fun with the disciple, caricaturing the words and accents of East Bengal.

UNTITLED CONVERSATION XXIX

Swamiji has just returned from East Bengal and Assam a few days back. He is ill, and his feet have swollen. Coming to the Math, the disciple went upstairs and prostrated himself at Swamiji's feet. In spite of his ill health, Swamiji wore his usual smiling face and affectionate look.

Disciple: How are you, Swamiji?

Swamiji: What shall I speak of my health, my son? The body is getting unfit for work day by day. It has been born on the soil of Bengal, and some disease or other is always overtaking it. The physique of this country is not at all good. If you want to do some strenuous work, it cannot bear the strain. But the few days that the body lasts, I will work for you. I shall die in harness. Disciple: If you give up work for some time and take rest, then you will be all right. Your life means good to the world.

Swamiji: Am I able to sit quiet, my son! Two or three days before Shri Ramakrishna's passing away, She whom he used to call "Kali" entered this body. It is She who takes me here and there and makes me work, without letting me remain quiet or allowing me to look to my personal comforts.

Disciple: Are you speaking metaphorically ?

Swamiji: Oh, no; two or three days before his leaving the body, he called me to his side one day, and asking me to sit before him, looked steadfastly at me and fell into Samadhi. Then I really felt that a subtle force like an electric shock was entering my body! In a little while, I also lost outward consciousness and sat motionless. How long I stayed in that condition I do not remember; when consciousness returned I found Shri Ramakrishna shedding tears. On questioning him, he answered me affectionately, "Today, giving you my all, I have become a beggar. With this power you are to do many works for the world's good before you will return." I feel that power is constantly directing me to this or that work. This body has not been made for remaining idle.

Hearing these words with speechless wonder the disciple thought—who knows how common people will take these words? Thereupon he changed the topic and said, "Sir, how did you like our East Bengal?"

Swamiji: I liked it on the whole. The fields, I saw, were rich in crops, the climate also is good, and the scenery on the hillside is charming. The Brahmaputra Valley is incomparable in its beauty. The people of East Bengal are a little stronger and more active than those of this part. It may be due to their taking plenty of fish and meat. Whatever they do, they do with great persistence. They use a great deal of oil and fat in their food, which is not good, because taking too much of oily and fatty food produces fat in the body.

Disciple: How did you find their religious consciousness?

Swamiji: About religious ideas, I noticed the people are very conservative, and many have turned into fanatics in trying to be liberal in religion. One day a young man brought to me, in the house of Mohini Babu at Dacca, a photograph and said, "Sir, please tell me who he is. Is he an Avatara?" I told him gently many times that I know nothing of it. When even on my telling him three or four times the boy did not cease from his persistent questioning, I was constrained to say at last, "My boy, henceforth take a little nutritious food and then your brain will develop. Without nourishing food, I see your brain has become dried up." At these words the young man may have been much displeased. But what could I do? Unless I spoke like this to the boys, they would turn into madcaps by degrees.

Disciple: In our East Bengal a great many Avataras have cropped up recently.

Swamiji: People may call their Guru an Avatara; they may have any idea of him they like. But Incarnations of God are not born anywhere and everywhere and at all seasons. At Dacca itself I heard there were three or four Avataras!

Disciple: How did you find the women of that side?

Swamiji: The women are very nearly the same everywhere. I found Vaishnavism strong at Dacca. The wife of H__ seemed to be very intelligent. With great care she used to prepare food and send it to me.

Disciple: I heard you have been to Nag Mahashaya's place.

Swamiji: Yes, going so far, should I not visit the birthplace of such a great soul? His wife fed me with many delicacies prepared by her own hand. The house is charming, like a peace retreat. There I took a swimming bath in a village pond. After that I had such a sound sleep that I woke at half past two in the afternoon. Of the few days I had sound sleep in my life, that in Nag Mahashaya's house was one. Rising from sleep I had a plentiful repast. Nag Mahashaya's wife presented me a cloth which I tied round my head as a turban and started for Dacca. I found that the photograph of Nag Mahashaya was being worshipped there. The place where his remains lie interred ought to be well kept. Even now it is not as it should be.

Disciple: The people of that part have not been able to appreciate Nag Mahashaya.

Swamiji: How can ordinary people appreciate a great man like him? Those who had his company are blessed indeed.

Disciple: What did you see at Kamakhya?

Swamiji: The Shillong hills are very beautiful. There I met Sir Henry Cotton, the Chief Commissioner of Assam. He asked me, "Swamiji, after travelling through Europe and America, what have you come to see here in these distant hills?" Such a good and kind-hearted man as Sir Henry Cotton is rarely found. Hearing of my illness, he sent the Civil Surgeon and inquired after my health mornings and evenings. I could not do much lecturing there, because my health was very bad. On the way Nitai served and looked after me nicely.

Disciple: What did you find the religious ideas of that part to be?

Swamiji: It is the land of the Tantras. I heard of one "Hankar Deva" who is worshipped there as an Avatara. I heard his sect is very wide-spread. I could not ascertain if "Hankar Deva" was but another form of the name Shankaracharya. They are monks — perhaps Tantrika Sannyasins, or perhaps one of the Shankara sects.

Disciple: The people of East Bengal have not been able to appreciate you as is the case with Nag Mahashaya.

Swamiji: Whether they appreciate me or not, the people there are more active and energetic than those of these parts. In time it will develop more. What are nowadays known as refined or civilised ways have not yet thoroughly entered those parts. Gradually they will. In all times, etiquette and fashion spread to the countryside from the capital. And this is happening in East Bengal also. The land that has produced a great soul like Nag Mahashaya is blessed and has a hopeful future. By the light of his personality Eastern Bengal is radiant.

Disciple: But, sir, ordinary people did not know him as a great soul. He hid himself in great obscurity.

Swamiji: There they used to make much fuss about my food and say, "Why should you eat that food or eat from the hands of such and such?"— and so on. To which I had to reply, "I am a Sannyasin and a mendicant friar and what need have I to observe so much outward formality with regard to food etc.? Do not your scriptures say, "[(Sanskrit)]—one should beg one's food from door to door, ay even from the house of an outcast"? But of course external forms are necessary in the beginning, for the inner realisation of religion, in order to make the truth of the scriptures practical in one's life. Haven't you heard of Shri Ramakrishna's story of "wringing out the almanac for water"?[1] Outward forms and observances are only for the manifestation of the great inner powers of man. The object of all scriptures is to awaken those inner powers and make him understand and realise his real nature. The means are of the nature of ordinances and prohibitions. If you lose sight of the ideal fight over the means only, what will it avail? In every country I have visited, I find this fighting over the means going on, and people have no eye on the ideal. Shri Ramakrishna came to show the truth of this.

Realisation of the truth is the essential thing. Whether you bathe in the Ganga for a thousand years or live on vegetable food for a like period, unless it helps towards the manifestation of the Self, know that it is all of no use. If on the other hand, any one can realise the Atman, without the observance of outward forms, then that very non-observance of forms is the best means. But even after the realisation of Atman, one should observe outward forms to a certain extent for setting an example to the people. The thing is you must make the mind steadfast on something. If it is steadfast on one object, it attains to concentration, that is, its other modifications die out and there is a uniform flow in one direction. Many become wholly preoccupied with the outward forms and observances merely and fail to direct their mind to thoughts of the Atman! If you remain day and night within the narrow groove of ordinances and prohibitions, how will there be any expression of the soul? The more one has advanced in the realisation of the Atman, the less is he dependent on the observances of forms. Shankaracharya also has said, "[(Sanskrit)]—where is there any ordinance or prohibition for him whose mind is always above the play of the Gunas?" Therefore the essential truth is realisation. Know that to be the goal. Each distinct creed is but a way to the Truth. The test of progress is the amount of renunciation that one has attained. Where you find the attraction for lust and wealth considerably diminished, to whatever creed he may belong, know that his inner spirit is awakening. The door of Self-realisation has surely opened for him. On the contrary if you observe a thousand outward rules and quote a thousand scriptural texts, still, if it has not

1. The Bengali almanac makes a forecast of the annual rainfall but not a drop comes out of squeezing its pages! Similarly scriptures are useless unless their truths are realised in life.

brought the spirit of renunciation in you, know that your life is in vain. Be earnest over this realisation and set your heart on it. Well, you have read enough of scriptures. But tell me, of what avail has it been? Some perhaps thinking of money have become millionaires, whereas you have become a Pundit by thinking of scriptures. But both are bondages. Attain the supreme knowledge and go beyond Vidya and Avidya, relative knowledge and ignorance.

Disciple: Sir, through your grace I understand it all, but my past Karma does not allow me to assimilate these teachings.

Swamiji: Throw aside your Karma and all such stuff. If it is a truth that by your own past action you have got this body; then, nullifying the effects of evil works by good works, why should you not be a Jivanmukta in this very body? Know that freedom or Self-knowledge is in your own hands. In real knowledge there is no touch of work. But those who work after being Jivanmuktas do so for the good of others. They do not look to the results of works. No seed of desire finds any room in their mind. And strictly speaking it is almost impossible to work like that for the good of the world from the householder's position. In the whole of Hindu scriptures there is the single instance of King Janaka in this respect. But you nowadays want to pose as Janakas (lit. fathers) in every home by begetting children year after year, while he was without the body-consciousness!

Disciple: Please bless me that I may attain Self-realisation in this very life.

Swamiji: What fear? If there is sincerity of spirit, I tell you, for a certainty, you will attain it in this very life. But manly endeavour is wanted. Do you know what it is? "I shall certainly attain Self-knowledge. Whatever obstacles may come, I shall certainly overcome them"— a firm determination like this is Purushakara. "Whether my mother, father, friends, brothers, wife, and children live or die, whether this body remains or goes, I shall never turn back till I attain to the vision of the Atman"— this resolute endeavour to advance towards one's goal, setting at naught all other considerations, is termed manly endeavour. Otherwise, endeavour for creature comforts even beasts and birds show. Man has got this body simply to realise Self-knowledge. If you follow the common run of people in the world and float with the general current, where then is your manliness? Well, the common people are going to the jaws of death! But you have come to conquer it! Advance like a hero. Don't be thwarted by anything. How many days will this body last, with its happiness and misery? When you have got the human body, then rouse the Atman within and say— I have reached the state of fearlessness! Say— I am the Atman in which my lower ego has become merged for ever. Be perfect in this idea; and then as long as the body endures, speak unto others this message of fearlessness: "Thou art That", "Arise, awake, and stop not till the goal is reached!" If you can achieve this, then shall I know that you are really a tenacious East Bengal man.

UNTITLED CONVERSATION XXX

Swamiji is in indifferent health since his return to the Math from the Shillong Hills. His feet have swollen. All this has made his brother-disciples very anxious. At the request of Swami Niranjanananda, Swamiji has agreed to take Ayurvedic medicine. He is to begin this treatment from next Tuesday and entirely give up taking water and salt. Today is Sunday. The disciple asked him, "Sir, it is terribly hot now and you drink water very frequently; it will be unbearable for you now to stop taking water altogether for this treatment."

Swamiji: What do you say? I shall make a firm resolve, on the morning of the day I shall begin this treatment, not to take any water. After that no water shall pass down the throat any more. For three weeks not a drop of water shall be able to go down the throat. The body is but an outer covering of the mind and whatever the mind will dictate to it, it will have to carry out. So there is nothing to be afraid of. At the request of Niranjan I have to undergo this treatment. Well, I cannot be indifferent to the request of my brother-disciples.

It is now about ten o'clock. Swamiji cheerfully raised the topic of his future Math for women, saying, "With the Holy Mother as the centre of inspiration, a Math is to be established on the eastern bank of the Ganga. As Brahmacharins and Sadhus will be trained in this Math here, so in the other Math also, Brahmacharinis and Sadhvis will be trained."

Disciple: Sir, history does not tell us of any Maths for women in India in ancient times. Only during the Buddhistic period one hears of Maths for women; but from it in course of time many corruptions arose. The whole country was overrun by great evil practices.

Swamiji: It is very difficult to understand why in this country so much difference is made between men and women, whereas the Vedanta declares that one and the same conscious Self is present in all beings. You always criticise the women, but say what have you done for their uplift? Writing down Smritis etc., and binding them by hard rules, the men have turned the women into mere manufacturing machines! If you do not raise the women, who are the living embodiment of the Divine Mother, don't think that you have any other way to rise.

Disciple: Women are a bondage and a snare to men. By their Maya they cover the knowledge and dispassion of men. It is for this, I suppose, that scriptural writers hint that knowledge and devotion are difficult of attainment to them.

Swamiji: In what scriptures do you find statements that women are not competent for knowledge and devotion? In the period of degradation, when the priests made other castes incompetent for the study of the Vedas, they deprived the women also of all their rights. Otherwise you will find that in the Vedic or Upanishad age Maitreyi, Gargi, and other ladies of revered memory have taken the places of Rishis through their skill in discussing about Brahman. In an assembly of a thousand Brahmanas who were all erudite in the Vedas,

Gargi boldly challenged Yajnavalkya in a discussion about Brahman. Since such ideal women were entitled to spiritual knowledge, why shall not the women have the same privilege now? What has happened once can certainly happen again. History repeats itself. All nations have attained greatness by paying proper respect to women. That country and that nation which do not respect women have never become great, nor will ever be in future. The principal reason why your race has so much degenerated is that you have no respect for these living images of Shakti. Manu says, "Where women are respected, there the gods delight; and where they are not, there all works and efforts come to naught."[1] There is no hope of rise for that family or country where there is no estimation of women, where they live in sadness. For this reason, they have to be raised first; and an ideal Math has to be started for them.

Disciple: Sir, when you first returned from the West, in your lecture at the Star Theatre you sharply criticised the Tantras. Now by your supporting the worship of women, as taught in the Tantras, you are contradicting yourself.

Swamiji: I denounced only the present corrupted form of Vamachara of the Tantras. I did not denounce the Mother-worship of the Tantras, or even the real Vamachara. The purport of the Tantras is to worship women in a spirit of Divinity. During the downfall of Buddhism, the Vamachara became very much corrupted, and that corrupted form obtains to the present day. Even now the Tantra literature of India is influenced by those ideas. I denounced only these corrupt and horrible practices—which I do even now. I never objected to the worship of women who are the living embodiment of Divine Mother, whose external manifestations, appealing to the senses have maddened men, but whose internal manifestations, such as knowledge, devotion, discrimination and dispassion make man omniscient, of unfailing purpose, and a knower of Brahman. "एषा प्रसन्ना वरदा नृणां भवति मुक्तये—she, when pleased, becomes propitious and the cause of the freedom of man" (Chandi, I. 57). Without propitiating the Mother by worship and obeisance, not even Brahma and Vishnu have the power to elude Her grasp and attain to freedom. Therefore for the worship of these family goddesses, in order to manifest the Brahman within them, I shall establish the women's Math.

Disciple: It may be a good idea but where will you get the women inmates? With the present hard restrictions of society, who will permit the ladies of their household to join your Math?

Swamiji: Why so? Even now there are women disciples of Shri Ramakrishna. With their help I shall start this Math. The Holy Mother will be their central figure and the wives and daughters of the devotees of Shri Ramakrishna will be its first inmates. For they will easily appreciate the usefulness of such a Math. After that, following their example, many householders will help in their noble work.

---

1. Manu, III. 56.

Disciple: The devotees of Shri Ramakrishna will certainly join this work. But I don't think the general public will help in this work.

Swamiji: No great work has been done in the world without sacrifice. Who on seeing the tiny sprout of the banyan can imagine that in course of time it will develop into a gigantic banyan tree? At present I shall start the Math in this way. Later on you will see that after a generation or two people of this country will appreciate the worth of this Math. My women disciples will lay down their lives for it. Casting off fear and cowardice, you also be helpers in this noble mission and hold this high ideal before all. You will see, it will shed its lustre over the whole country in time.

Disciple: Sir, please tell me all about your plan of this Math for women.

Swamiji: On the other side of the Ganga a big plot of land will be acquired, where unmarried girls or Brahmacharini widows will live; devout married women will also be allowed to stay now and then. Men will have no concern with this Math. The elderly Sadhus of the Math will manage the affairs of this Math from a distance. There shall be a girls' school attached to this women's Math, in which religious scriptures, literature, Sanskrit, grammar, and even some amount of English should be taught. Other matters such as sewing, culinary art, rules of domestic work, and upbringing of children, will also be taught while Japa, worship, meditation, etc. shall form an indispensable part of the teaching. Those who will be able to live here permanently, renouncing home and family ties, will be provided with food and clothing from the Math. Those who will not be able to do that will be allowed to study in this Math as day-scholars. With the permission of the head of the Math, the latter will be allowed even to stay in the Math occasionally, and during such stay will be maintained by the Math. The elder Brahmacharinis will take charge of the training of the girl students in Brahmacharya. After five or six years' training in this Math, the guardians of the girls may marry them. If deemed fit for Yoga and religious life, with the permission of the guardians they will be allowed to stay in this Math, taking the vow of celibacy. These celibate nuns will in time be the teachers and preachers of the Math. In villages and towns they will open centres and strive for the spread of female education. Through such devout preachers of character there will be the real spread of female education in the country. So long as the students will remain in association with this Math, they must observe Brahmacharya as the basic ideal of this Math.

Spirituality, sacrifice, and self-control will be the motto of the pupils of this Math, and service or Seva-dharma the vow of their life. In view of such ideal lives, who will not respect and have faith in them? If the life of the women of this country be moulded in such fashion, then only will there be the reappearance of such ideal characters as Sita, Savitri and Gargi. To what straits the strictures of local usages have reduced the women of this country, rendering them lifeless and inert, you could understand if only you visited the Western countries. You alone are responsible for this miserable condition of the women, and it rests with you also to raise them again. Therefore I say, set to work. What will it do to memorise a few religious books like the Vedas and so on?

Disciple: Sir, if the girl students after being trained in this Math marry, how will one find ideal characters in them? Will it not be better if the rule is made that those who will be educated in this Math shall not marry?

Swamiji: Can that be brought about all at once? They must be given education and left to themselves. After that they will act as they think best. Even after marriage and entering the world, the girls educated as above will inspire their husbands with noble ideals and be the mothers of heroic sons. But there must be this rule that the guardians of the students in the women's Math must not even think of marrying them before they attain the age of fifteen.

Disciple: Sir, then those girls will not command reputation in society. Nobody would like to marry them.

Swamiji: Why will not they be wanted in marriage? You have not yet understood the trend of society. These learned and accomplished girls will never be in want of bridegrooms. Society nowadays does not follow the texts recommending child-marriage nor will do so in future. Even now don't you see?

Disciple: But there is sure to be a violent opposition against this in the beginning.

Swamiji: Let it be. What is there to be afraid of in that? Opposition to a righteous work initiated with moral courage will only awaken the moral power of the initiators the more. That which meets with no obstruction, no opposition, only takes men to the path of moral death. Struggle is the sign of life.

Disciple: Yes, sir.

Swamiji: In the highest reality of the Parabrahman, there is no distinction of sex. We notice this only in the relative plane. And the more the mind becomes introspective, the more that idea of difference vanishes. Ultimately, when the mind is wholly merged in the homogeneous and undifferentiated Brahman, such ideas as this is a man or that a woman do not remain at all. We have actually seen this in the life of Shri Ramakrishna. Therefore do I say that though outwardly there may be difference between men and women, in their real nature there is none. Hence, if a man can be a knower of Brahman, why cannot a woman attain to the same knowledge? Therefore I was saying that if even one amongst the women became a knower of Brahman, then by the radiance of her personality thousands of women would be inspired and awakened to truth, and great well-being of the country and society would ensue. Do you understand?

Disciple: Sir, your teachings have opened my eyes today.

Swamiji: Not fully yet. When you realise that all-illumining reality of the Atman, then you will see that this idea of sex-distinction has vanished altogether, then only will you look upon women as the veritable manifestation of Brahman. We have seen in Shri Ramakrishna how he had this idea of divine motherhood in every woman, of whatever caste she might be, or whatever might be her worth. It is because I have seen this that I ask you all so earnestly to do likewise and open girls' schools in every village and try to uplift them. If the women are raised, then their children will by their noble actions glorify the name of the country—then will culture, knowledge, power, and devotion awaken in the land.

Disciple: But, sir, contrary results appear to have come out of the present female education. With just a smattering of education, they take merely to the Western modes of living, but it is not clear how far they are advancing in the spirit of renunciation, self-control, austerity, Brahmacharya and other qualities conducive to Brahmajnana.

Swamiji: In the beginning a few mistakes like that are unavoidable. When a new idea is preached in the country, some, failing to grasp it properly, go wrong in that way. But what matters it to the well-being of society at large? Well, those who are pioneers of the little bit of female education that now obtains in the country were undoubtedly very great-hearted. But the truth is that some defect or other must creep into that learning or culture which is not founded on a religious basis. But now female education is to be spread with religion as its centre. All other training should be secondary to religion. Religious training, the formation of character and observance of the vow of celibacy—these should be attended to. In the female education which has obtained up till now in India, it is religion that has been made a secondary concern, hence those defects you were speaking of have crept in. But no blame attaches therefore to the women. Reformers having proceeded to start female education without being Brahmacharins themselves have stumbled like that. Founders of all good undertakings, before they launch on their desired work, must attain to the knowledge of the Atman through rigorous self-discipline. Otherwise defects are bound to occur in their work.

Disciple: Yes, sir, it is observed that many educated women spend their time in reading novels and so on; but in East Bengal even with education women have not given up their religious observances. Is it so here in this part?

Swamiji: In every country, nations have their good and bad sides. Ours is to do good works in our lives and hold an example before others. No work succeeds by condemnation. It only repels people. Let anybody say what he likes, don't contradict him. In this world of Maya, whatever work you will take up will be attended with some defect. "[(Sanskrit)]—all works are covered with defects as fire is with smoke" (Gita, XVIII.48). Every fire has a chance of being attended with smoke. But will you, on that account, sit inactive? As far as you can, you must go on doing good work.

Disciple: What is this good work?

Swamiji: Whatever helps in the manifestation of Brahman

is good work. Any work can be done so as to help, if not directly, at least indirectly, the manifestation of the Atman. But following the path laid down by the Rishis, that knowledge of the Atman manifests quickly; on the contrary, the doing of works which have been indicated by the scriptural writers as wrong, brings only bondage of the soul and sometimes this bondage of delusion does not vanish even in many lives. But in all ages and climes, freedom is sure to be attained by Jivas ultimately. For the Atman is the real nature of the Jiva. Can anybody give up his own nature? If you fight with your shadow for a thousand years, can you drive it away from you?—it will always remain with you.

Disciple: But, sir, according to Shankara, Karma is antagonistic to Jnana. He has variously refuted the intermingling of Jnana and Karma. So how can Karma be helpful to the manifestation of Jnana?

Swamiji: Shankara after saying so has again described Karma as indirect help to the manifestation of Jnana and the means for the purification of the mind. But I do not contradict his conclusion that in transcendent knowledge there is no touch of any work whatsoever. So long as man is within the realm of the consciousness of action, agent, and the result of action, he is powerless to sit idle without doing some work. So, as work is thus ingrained in the very nature of man, why don't you go on doing such works as are helpful to the manifestation of the knowledge of the Atman? That all work is the effect of ignorance may be true from the absolute standpoint, but within the sphere of relative consciousness it has a great utility. When you will realise the Atman, the doing or non-doing of work will be within your control, and whatever you will do in that state will be good work, conducive to the well-being of Jivas and the world. With the manifestation of Brahman, even the breath you draw will be to the good of Jiva. Then you will no longer have to work by means of conscious planning. Do you understand?

Disciple: Yes, it is a beautiful conclusion reconciling Karma and Jnana from the Vedantic standpoint.

At this time, the bell for supper rang, and the disciple, before going to partake of it, prayed with folded hands, "Bless me, sir, that I may attain to the knowledge of Brahman in this very life." Swamiji placing his hand on the disciple's head said, "Have no fear, my son. You are not like ordinary worldly men—neither householders, nor exactly Sannyasins—but quite a new type."

UNTITLED CONVERSATION XXXI

Swamiji is in indifferent health. At the earnest request of Swami Niranjanananda he has been taking

Ayurvedic medicines for six or seven days. According to this treatment, the drinking of water is strictly forbidden. He has to appease his thirst with milk.

The disciple has come to the Math early in the day. Swamiji on seeing him spoke with affection, "Oh, you have come? Well done, I was thinking of you."

Disciple: I hear that you are living on milk for the last six or seven days.

Swamiji: Yes, at the earnest entreaty of Niranjan, I had to take to this medicine! I cannot disregard their request.

Disciple: You were in the habit of taking water very frequently. How could you give it up altogether?

Swamiji: When I heard that according to this treatment water had to be given up, I made a firm resolve immediately not to take water. Now the idea of drinking water does not even occur to the mind.

Disciple: The treatment is doing you good I hope?

Swamiji: That I don't know. I am simply obeying the orders of my brother-disciples.

Disciple: I think that indigenous drugs such as the Vaidyas use, are very well-suited to our constitution.

Swamiji: My idea is that it is better even to die under the treatment of a scientific doctor than expect recovery from the treatment of laymen who know nothing of modern science, but blindly go by the ancient books, without gaining a mastery of the subject—even though they may have cured a few cases.

Swamiji cooked certain dishes, one of which was prepared with vermicelli. When the disciple, who partook of it, asked Swamiji what it was, he replied, "It is a few English earthworms which I have brought dried from London." This created laughter among those present at the expense of the disciple. Despite his spare food and scanty sleep, Swamiji is very active. A few days ago, a new set of the Encyclopaedia Brittanica had been bought for the Math. Seeing the new shining volumes, the disciple said to Swamiji, "It is almost impossible to read all these books in a single lifetime." He was unaware that Swamiji had already finished ten volumes and had begun the eleventh.

Swamiji: What do you say? Ask me anything you like from these ten volumes, and I will answer you all.

The disciple asked in wonder, "Have you read all these books?" Swamiji: Why should I ask you to question me otherwise?

Being examined, Swamiji not only reproduced the sense, but at places the very language of the difficult topics selected from each volume. The disciple, astonished, put aside the books, saying, "This is not within human power!"

Swamiji: Do you see, simply by the observance of strict Brahmacharya (continence) all learning can be mastered in a very short time—one has an unfailing memory of what one hears or knows but once. It is owing to this want of continence that everything is on the brink of ruin in our country.

Disciple: Whatever you may say, sir, the manifestation of such superhuman power cannot be the result of mere Brahmacharya, something else there must be.

Swamiji did not say anything in reply.

Then Swamiji began to explain lucidly to the disciple the arguments and conclusions about the difficult points in all philosophies. In course of the conversation Swami Brahmananda entered the room and said to the disciple, "You are a nice man! Swamiji is unwell, and instead of trying to keep his mind cheerful by light talk, you are making him talk incessantly, raising the most abstruse subjects!" The disciple was abashed. But Swamiji said to Swami Brahmananda, "Keep your regulation of Ayurvedic treatment aside. These are my children; and if my body goes in teaching them, I don't care." After this, some light talk followed. Then arose the topic of the place of Bharatchandra in Bengali literature. From the beginning Swamiji began to ridicule Bharatchandra in various ways and satirised the life, manners, marriage-customs, and other usages of society at the time of Bharatchandra, who was an advocate of child-marriage. He expressed the opinion that the poems of Bharatchandra, being full of bad taste and obscenities, had not found acceptance in any cultured society except in Bengal, and he said, "Care should be taken that such books do not come into the hands of boys." Then raising the topic of Michael Madhusudan Dutt, he added, "That was a wonderful genius born in your province. There is not another epic in Bengali literature like the Meghnabadh, no mistake in that; and it is difficult to come across a poem like that in the whole of modern European literature."

Disciple: But, sir, I think Michael was very fond of a bombastic style.

Swamiji: Well, if anybody in your country does anything new, you at once hoot him. First examine well what he is saying, but instead of that, the people of the country will chase after anything which is not quite after the old modes. For example, in order to bring to ridicule this Meghnabadh Kavya, which is the gem of Bengali literature, the parody of Chhuchhundaribadh Kavya (The Death of a Mole) was written. They may caricature as much as they like, it does not matter. But the Meghnadbadh Kavya still stands unshaken in its reputation like the Himalayas while the opinions and writings of carping critics who are busy picking holes in it have been washed away into oblivion. What will the vulgar public understand of this epic Michael has written in such a vigorous diction and an original metre? And at the present time

Girish Babu is writing wonderful books in a new metre which your overwise Pundits are criticising and finding fault with. But does G.C. care for that? People will appreciate the book afterwards.

Thus speaking on the subject of Michael he said, "Go and get the Meghnadbadh Kavya from the library downstairs." On the disciple's bringing it he said, "Now read, let me see how you can read it."

The disciple read a portion, but the reading not being to the liking of Swamiji, he took the book and showed him how to read and asked him to read again. Then he asked him,

"Now, can you say which portion of the Kavya is best?" The disciple failing to answer, Swamiji said, "That portion of the book which describes how Indrajit has been killed in battle and Mandodari, beside herself with grief, is dissuading Ravana from the battle—but Ravana casting off forcibly from his mind the grief for his son is firmly resolved on battle like a great hero, and forgetting in a fury of rage and vengeance all about his wife and children, is ready to rush out for battle—that is the most finely conceived portion of the book. Come what may, I shall not forget my duty, whether the world remains or dissolves—these are the words of a great hero. Inspired by such feelings, Michael has written that portion."

Saying this, Swamiji opened the particular passage and began to read it in the most impressive manner.

UNTITLED CONVERSATION XXXII

Swamiji is much better under the Ayurvedic treatment. The disciple is at the Math. While attending on Swamiji, he asked, "The Atman is all-pervading, the very life of the life of all beings, and so very near. Still why is It not perceived?"

Swamiji: Do you see yourself that you have eyes?

When others speak of the eyes, then you are reminded that you have got eyes. Again when dust or sand enters into them and sets up an irritation, then you feel quite well that you have got eyes. Similarly the realisation of this universal Atman which is inner than the innermost is not easily attained. Reading from scriptures or hearing from the lips of the preceptor, one has some idea of It, but when the hard lashes of the bitter sorrow and pain of the world make the heart sore, when on the death of one's near and dear relatives, man thinks himself helpless, when the impenetrable and insurmountable darkness about the future life agitates his mind, then does the Jiva pant for a realisation of the Atman. Therefore is sorrow helpful to the knowledge of the Atman. But one should remember the bitter lesson of experience. Those who die, merely suffering the woes of life like cats and dogs, are they men? He is a man who even when agitated by the sharp interaction of pleasure and pain is discriminating, and knowing them to be of an evanescent nature, becomes passionately devoted to the Atman. This is all the difference between men and animals. That which is nearest is least observed. The Atman is the nearest of the near, therefore the careless and unsteady mind of man gets no clue to It. But the man who is alert, calm, self-restrained, and discriminating, ignores the external world and diving more and more into the inner world, realises the glory of the Atman and becomes great. Then only he attains to the knowledge of the Atman and realises the truth of such scriptural texts as, "I am the Atman", "Thou art That, O Shvetaketu," and so on. Do you understand?

Disciple: Yes, sir. But why this method of attaining Self-knowledge through the path of pain and suffering? Instead of all this, it would have been well if there had been no creation at all. We were all at one time identified with Brahman. Why then this desire for creation on the path of Brahman? Why again this going forth of the Jiva (who is no other than Brahman) along the path of birth and death, amidst the interaction of the dualities of life?

Swamiji: When a man is intoxicated, he sees many hallucinations; but when the intoxication goes off, he understands them as the imaginations of a heated brain. Whatever you see of this creation which is without a beginning, but has an end, is only an effect of your state of intoxication; when that passes off, such questions will not arise at all.

Disciple: Then is there no reality in the creation, and preservation, etc. of the Universe?

Swamiji: Why should not there be? So long as you identify yourself with the body and have the ego-consciousness, all these will remain. But when you are bereft of the body-consciousness and devoted to the Atman and live in the Atman, then with respect to you none of these will remain, and such questions as whether there is any creation or birth or death will have no room. Then you will have to say—[Sanskrit]—"Where is it gone, by whom is it taken, wherein is the world merged? It was just observed by me and is it non-existent now? What a wonder!" (Vivekachudamani 483).

Disciple: If there is no knowledge of the existence of the universe, how can it be said, "Wherein is the world merged?"

Swamiji: Because one has to express the idea in language, therefore that mode of expression has been used. The author has tried to express in thought and language about the state where thought or language cannot reach, and therefore he has stated the fact that the world is wholly unreal, in a relative mode like the above. The world has no absolute reality which only belongs to Brahman, which is beyond the reach of mind and speech. Say what more you have to ask. Today I will put an end to all your arguments.

The bell of the evening service in the worship-room rang at the time, and everybody made for it. But the disciple stayed in Swamiji's room, noticing which Swamiji said, "Won't you go to the worship-room?"

Disciple: I should like to stay here.

Swamiji: All right.

After some time the disciple looking outside of the room said, "It is the new-moon night and all the quarters are overspread with darkness. It is the night for the worship of Mother Kali."

Swamiji without saying anything gazed at the eastern sky for some time and said, "Do you see what a mysterious and solemn beauty there is in this darkness!" Saying this and continuing to look at the dense mass of darkness, he stood enwrapt. After some minutes had passed, Swamiji slowly began to sing a Bengali song, "O Mother, in deep darkness flashes Thy formless beauty", etc. After the song Swamiji entered his room and sat down with an occasional word like "Mother, Mother", or "Kali, Kali", on his lips.

Uneasy at Swamiji's profoundly abstracted mood, the disciple said, "Now, sir, please speak with me."

Swamiji smilingly said, "Can you fathom the beauty and profundity of the Atman whose external manifestation is so sweet and beautiful?" The disciple wished for a change of topic, noticing which, Swamiji began another song of Kali: "O Mother, Thou flowing stream of nectar, in how many forms and aspects dost Thou play in manifestation!" After the song he said, "This Kali is Brahman in manifestation. Haven't you heard Shri Ramakrishna's illustration of the `snake moving and the snake at rest' (representing the dynamic and static aspects of the same thing)?"

Disciple: Yes, sir.

Swamiji: This time, when I get well, I shall worship the Mother with my heart's blood, then only will She be pleased. Your Raghunandan also says like that. The Mother's child shall be a hero, a Mahavira. In unhappiness, sorrow, death, and desolation, the Mother's child shall always remain fearless.

UNTITLED CONVERSATION XXXIII

Swamiji is staying at the Math nowadays. His health is not very good, but he goes out for a walk in the mornings and evenings. The disciple, after bowing at the feet of Swamiji, inquired about his health.

Swamiji: Well, this body is in such a pitiable condition, but none of you are stepping forward to help in my work! What shall I do single-handed? This time the body has come out of the soil of Bengal, so can it bear the strain of much work? You who come here are pure souls; and if you do not become my helpers in this work, what shall I do alone?

Disciple: Sir, these self-sacrificing Brahmacharins and Sannyasins are standing behind you, and I think that each one of them can devote his life to your work—still why do you speak in this way?

Swamiji: Well, I want a band of young Bengal—who alone are the hope of this country. My hope of the future lies in the youths of character—intelligent, renouncing all for the service of others, and obedient—who can sacrifice their lives in working out my ideas and thereby do good to themselves and the country at large. Otherwise, boys of the common run are coming in groups and will come. Dullness is written on their faces—their hearts are devoid of energy, their bodies feeble and unfit for work, and minds devoid of courage. What work will be done by these? If I get ten or twelve boys with the faith of Nachiketa, I can turn the thoughts and pursuits of this country in a new channel.

Disciple: Sir, so many young men are coming to you, and do you find none among them of such a nature?

Swamiji: Among those who appear to me to be of good calibre, some have bound themselves by matrimony; some have sold themselves for the acquisition of worldly name, fame, or wealth; while some are of feeble bodies. The rest, who form the majority, are unable to receive any high idea. You are no doubt fit to receive my high ideas, but you are not able to work them out in the practical field. For these reasons sometimes an anguish comes into the mind, and I think that taking this human body, I could not do much work through untowardness of fortune. Of course, I have not yet wholly given up hope, for, by the will of God, from among these very boys may arise in time great heroes of action and spirituality who will in future work out my ideas.

Disciple: It is my firm belief that your broad and liberal ideas must find universal acceptance some day or other. For I see they are all-sided and infusing vigour into every department of thought and activity. And the people of the country are accepting, either overtly or covertly, your ideas, and teaching them to the people.

Swamiji: What matters it if they acknowledge my name or not? It is enough if they accept my ideas. Ninety-nine per cent of the Sadhus, even after renouncing lust and wealth, get bound at the last by the desire of name and fame. "Fame... that last infirmity of noble mind"— haven't you read? We shall have to work, giving up altogether all desire for results. People will call us both good and bad. But we shall have to work like lions, keeping the ideal before us, without caring whether "the wise ones praise or blame us".

Disciple: What ideal should we follow now?

Swamiji: You have now to make the character of Mahavira your ideal. See how at the command of Ramachandra he crossed the ocean. He had no care for life or death! He was a perfect master of his senses and wonderfully sagacious. You have now to build your life on this great ideal of personal service. Through that, all other ideals will gradually manifest in life. Obedience to the Guru without questioning, and strict observance of Brahmacharya— this is the secret of success. As on the one hand Hanuman represent the ideal of service, so on the other hand he represents leonine courage, striking the whole world with awe. He has not the least hesitation in sacrificing his life for the good of Rama. A supreme indifference to everything except the service of Rama, even to the attainment of the status of Brahma and Shiva, the great World-gods! Only the carrying out of Shri Rama's best is the one vow of this life! Such whole-hearted devotion is wanted. Playing on the Khol and Kartal and dancing in the frenzy of Kirtana has degenerated the whole people. They are, in the first place, a race of dyspeptics— and if in addition to this they dance and jump in that way, how can they bear the strain? In trying to imitate the highest Sadhana, the preliminary qualification for which is absolute purity, they have been swallowed in dire Tamas. In every district and village you may visit, you will find only the sound of the Khol and Kartal! Are not drums made in the country? Are not trumpets and kettle-drums available in India? Make the boys hear the deep-toned sound of these instruments. Hearing from boyhood the sound of these effemi-

nate forms of music and listening to the kirtana, the country is well-nigh converted into a country of women. What more degradation can you expect? Even the poet's imagination fails to draw this picture! The Damaru[1] and horn have to be sounded, drums are to be beaten so as to raise the deep and martial notes, and with "Mahavira, Mahavira" on your lips and shouting "Hara, Hara, Vyom, Vyom", the quarters are to be reverberated. The music which awakens only the softer feelings of man is to be stopped now for some time. Stopping the light tunes such as Kheal and Tappa for some time, the people are to be accustomed to hear the Dhrupad music. Through the thunder-roll of the dignified Vedic hymns, life is to be brought back into the country. In everything the austere spirit of heroic manhood is to be revived. In following such an ideal lies the good of the people and the country. If you can build your character after such an ideal, then a thousand others will follow. But take care that you do not swerve an inch from the ideal. Never lose heart. In eating, dressing, or lying, in singing or playing, in enjoyment or disease, always manifest the highest moral courage. Then only will you attain the grace of Mahashakti, the Divine Mother.

Disciple: Sir, at times I am overcome by low spirits, I don't know how.

Swamiji: Then think like this: "Whose child am I? I associate with him and shall I have such weak-mindedness and lowness of spirits?" Stamping down such weakness of mind and heart, stand up, saying, "I am possessed of heroism— I am possessed of a steady intellect— I am a knower of Brahman, a man of illumination." Be fully conscious of your dignity by remembering, "I am the disciple of such and such who is the companion-in-life of Shri Ramakrishna, the conqueror of lust and wealth." This will produce a good effect. He who has not this pride has no awakening of Brahman within him. Haven't you heard Ramprasad's song? He used to say, "Whom do I fear in the world, whose sovereign is the Divine Mother!" Keep such a pride always awake in the mind. Then weakness of mind and heart will no longer be able to approach you. Never allow weakness to overtake your mind. Remember Mahavira, remember the Divine Mother! And you will see that all weakness, all cowardice will vanish at once.

Saying these words, Swamiji came downstairs and took his accustomed seat on a cot in the courtyard. Then, addressing the assembled Sannyasins and Brahmacharins, he said, "Here is the unveiled presence of Brahman. Fie upon those who disregarding It set their mind on other things! Ah! here is Brahman as palpable as a fruit in one's palm. Don't you see? Here!"

These words were spoken in such an appealing way, that every one stood motionless like a figure painted on canvas and felt as if he were suddenly drawn into the depth of meditation... After some time that tension of feeling passed and they regained their normal consciousness.

Next, in the course of a walk, Swamiji spoke to the disciple.

---

1. An hour-glass-shaped drum, held in Shiva's hand.

"Did you see how everybody had become concentrated to-day? These are all children of Shri Ramakrishna, and on the very uttering of the words, they felt the truth."

Disciple: Sir, not to speak of them, even my heart was overflowing with an unearthly bliss! But now it appears like a vanished dream.

Swamiji: Everything will come in time. Now, go on working. Set yourself to some work for the good of men sunk in ignorance and delusion. You will see that such experiences will come of themselves.

Disciple: I feel nervous to enter into its labyrinths—neither have I the strength. The scriptures also say, "Impenetrable is the path of Karma".

Swamiji: What do you wish to do then?

Disciple: To live and hold discussion with one like

you, who has realised the truth of all scriptures and through hearing, thinking, and meditating on the Truth to realise Brahman in this very life. I have no enthusiasm, nor perhaps the strength, for anything else.

Swamiji: If you love that, well, you can go on doing it. And speak about your thoughts and conclusions about the Shastras to others, it will benefit them. So long as there is the body, one cannot live without doing some work or other; therefore one should do such work as is conducive to the good of others. Your own realisations and conclusions about scriptural truths may benefit many a seeker after Truth. Put them into writing which may help many others.

Disciple: First let me realise the Truth, then I shall write. Shri Ramakrishna used to say; "Without the badge of authority, none will listen to you."

Swamiji: There may be many in the world who have got stuck in that stage of spiritual discipline and reasoning through which you are passing, without being able to pass beyond that stage. Your experience and way of thinking, if recorded, may be of benefit to them at least. If you put down in easy language the substance of the discussions which you hold with the Sadhus of this Math, it may help many.

Disciple: Since you wish it, I shall try to do it.

Swamiji: What is the good of that spiritual practice or realisation which does not benefit others, does not conduce to the well-being of people sunk in ignorance and delusion, does not help in rescuing them from the clutches of lust and wealth? Do you think, so long as one Jiva endures in bondage, you will have any liberation? So long as he is not liberated—it may take several lifetimes—you will have to be born to help him, to make him realise Brahman. Every Jiva is part of yourself—which is the rationale of all work for others. As you desire the whole-hearted good of your wife and children, knowing them to be your own, so when a like amount of love and attraction for every Jiva will awaken in you, then I shall know that Brahman is awakening in you, not a moment before. When this feeling of the all-round good of all without

respect for caste or colour will awaken in your heart, then I shall know you are advancing towards the ideal.

Disciple: Sir, it is a most tremendous statement that without the salvation of all, there shall be no salvation for an individual! I have never heard of such a wonderful proposition.

Swamiji: There is a class of Vedantists who hold such a view. They say that individual liberation is not the real and perfect form of liberation, but universal and collective liberation is true Mukti. Of course, both merits and defects can be pointed out in that view.

Disciple: According to Vedanta, the state of individualised existence is the root of bondage, and the Infinite Intelligence, through desires and effects of works, appears bound in that limiting condition. When by means of discrimination that limiting condition vanishes and the Jiva is bereft of all adjuncts, then how can there be bondage for the Atman which is of the essence of transcendent Intelligence? He for whom the idea of the Jiva and the world is a persisting reality may think that without the liberation of all he has no liberation. But when the mind becomes bereft of all limiting adjuncts and is merged in Brahman, where is there any differentiation for him? So nothing can operate as a bar to his Mukti.

Swamiji: Yes, what you say is right, and most Vedantins hold that view, which is also flawless. In that view, individual liberation is not barred. But just consider the greatness of his heart who thinks that he will take the whole universe with him to liberation!

Disciple: Sir, it may indicate boldness of heart, but it is not supported by the scriptures.

Swamiji was in an abstracted mood and did not listen to the words. After some time he said: "Day and night think and meditate on Brahman, meditate with great one-pointedness of mind. And during the time of awakeness to outward life, either do some work for the sake of others or repeat in your mind, 'Let good happen to Jivas and the world!' 'Let the mind of all flow in the direction of Brahman!' Even by such continuous current of thought the world will be benefited. Nothing good in the world becomes fruitless, be it work or thought. Your thought-currents will perhaps rouse the religious feeling of someone in America."

Disciple: Sir, please bless me that my mind may be concentrated on the Truth.

Swamiji: So it will be. If you have earnestness of desire, it will certainly be.

UNTITLED CONVERSATION XXXIV

At the time Belur Math was established, many among the orthodox Hindus were wont to make sharp criticism of the ways of life in the Math. Hearing the report of such criticism from the disciple, Swamiji would say (in the words of the couplet of Tulasidas), "The elephant passes in the market-place, and a thousand curs begin barking after him; so the Sadhus have no ill-feeling when worldly people slander then." Or again he would say, "Without persecution no beneficent idea can enter into the heart of a society." He would exhort everybody, "Go on working without an eye to results. One day you are sure to reap the fruits of it." Again, on the lips of Swamiji were very often heard the words of the Gita, "A doer of good never comes to grief, my son."

In May or June, 1901, seeing the disciple at the Math Swamiji said, "Bring me a copy of Ashtavimshati-tattva (Twenty-eight Categories) of Raghunandan at an early date."

Disciple: Yes, sir, but what will you do with the Raghunandan Smriti, which the present educated India calls a heap of superstition?

Swamiji: Why? Raghunandan was a wonderful scholar of his time. Collecting the ancient Smritis, he codified the customs and observances of the Hindus, adapting them to the needs of the changed times and circumstances. All Bengal is following the rules laid down by him. But in the iron grip of his rules regulating the life of a Hindu from conception to death, the Hindu society was much oppressed. In matters of eating and sleeping, in even the ordinary functions of life, not to speak of the important ones, he tried to regulate every one by rules. In the altered circumstances of the times, that did not last long. At all times in all countries the Karma-kanda, comprising the social customs and observances, changes form. Only the Jnana-kanda endures. Even in the Vedic age you find that the rituals gradually changed in form. But the philosophic portion of the Upanishads has remained unchanged up till now—only there have been many interpreters, that is all.

Disciple: What will do you with the Smriti of Raghunandan?

Swamiji: This time I have a desire to celebrate the Durga Puja (worship of goddess Durga). If the expenses are forthcoming, I shall worship the Mahamaya. Therefore I have a mind to read the ceremonial forms of that worship. When you come to the Math next Sunday, you must bring a copy of the book with you.

Disciple: All right, sir.

Next Saturday the disciple brought a copy of the book, and Swamiji was much pleased to get it. Meeting the disciple a week after this he said, "I have finished the Raghunandan Smriti presented by you. If possible, I shall celebrate the Puja of the Divine Mother."

The Durga Puja took place with great eclat at the proper time.

Shortly after this Swamiji performed a Homa before the Mother Kali at Kalighat. Referring this incident he spoke to the disciple, "Well, I was glad to see that there was yet a liberality of view at Kalighat. The temple authorities did not object in the least to my entering the temple, though they knew that I was a man who had returned from the West. On the contrary, they very cordially took me into the holy precincts and helped me to worship the Mother to my heart's content."

UNTITLED CONVERSATION XXXV

Today is the anniversary celebration of Shri Ramakrishna—the last that Swamiji ever saw. The disciple presented an invocatory hymn on Shri Ramakrishna to Swamiji. He then proceeded to rub Swamiji's feet gently. Before starting to read the poem, Swamiji spoke to him: "Do it very gently as the feet have become very tender."

After reading the poem Swamiji said, "It is well done."

Swamiji's illness had increased so much that the disciple, observing it, felt sore at heart. Understanding his inner feeling, Swamiji said, "What are you thinking? This body is born and it will die. If I have been able to instil a few of my ideas into you all, then I shall know that my birth has not been in vain."

Disciple: Are we fit objects of your mercy? If you bless me, without taking my fitness into consideration, then I will consider myself fortunate.

Swamiji: Always remember that renunciation is the root idea. Unless one is initiated into this idea, not even Brahma and the World-gods have the power to attain Mukti.

Disciple: It is a matter of deep regret that even hearing this from you almost every day, I have not been able to realise it.

Swamiji: Renunciation must come, but in the fulness of time. "[(Sanskrit)]—in the fulness of time one attains to knowledge within himself." When the few Samskaras (tendencies) of the previous life are spent, then renunciation sprouts up in the heart.

After some time he said, "Why should you go outside and see the big concourse of people? Stay with me now. And ask Niranjan to sit at the door, so that nobody may disturb me today."

Then the following conversation took place between Swamiji and the disciple:

Swamiji: I think that it will be better if from now the anniversary is celebrated in a different way. The celebration should extend to four or five days instead of one. On the first day, there may be study and interpretation of scriptures; on the second, discussion on the Vedas and the Vedanta and the solution of the problems in connection with them; on the third day, there may be a question class. The fourth day may be fixed for lectures. On the last day, there will be a festival on the present lines. This will be like the Durga Puja extending over four or five days. Of course, if the celebration is on the above lines, none but the devotees of Shri Ramakrishna will be able to attend on the other days except the last. But that does not matter. A large promiscuous crowd of people does not mean a great propagation of the message of Shri Ramakrishna.

Disciple: Sir, it is a beautiful idea. Next time it will be done according to your wishes.

Swamiji: Now, my son, you all will carry them out. I have no more inclination for these things.

Disciple: Sir, this year many Kirtana parties have come.

Hearing these words Swamiji stood up holding the iron bars of the window and looked at the assembled crowd of devotees. After some time he sat down.

Swamiji: You are the actors in the Divine Lila (play) of Shri Ramakrishna. After this, not to speak of ours, people will take your names also. These hymns which you are writing will afterwards be read by people for the acquirement of love and knowledge. Know that the attainment of the knowledge of the Atman is the highest object of life. If you have devotion for the Avataras who are the world-teachers, that knowledge will manifest of itself in time.

Disciple: Sir, shall I attain to such knowledge?

Swamiji: By the blessings of Shri Ramakrishna you shall attain to divine love and knowledge. You will not find much happiness in the worldly life.

Disciple: Sir, if you condescend to destroy the weakness of my mind, then only there is hope for me.

Swamiji: What fear! When you have chanced to come here, you shall be free.

Disciple (with great entreaty): You must save me and lift me from ignorance in this very life.

Swamiji: Say, who can save anybody? The Guru can only take away some covering veils. When these veils are removed, the Atman shines in Its own glory and manifests like the sun.

Disciple: Then why do we find mention of grace in the scriptures?

Swamiji: Grace means this. He who has realised the Atman becomes a storehouse of great power. Making him the centre and with a certain radius a circle is formed, and whoever comes within the circle becomes animated with the ideas of that saint, i.e. they are overwhelmed by his ideas. Thus without much religious striving, they inherit the results of his wonderful spirituality. If you call this grace, you may do so.

Disciple: Is there no other grace than this?

Swamiji: Yes, there is. When the Avatara comes, then with him are born liberated persons as helpers in his world-play. Only Avataras have the power to dispel the darkness of a million souls and give them salvation in one life. This is known as grace. Do you understand?

Disciple: Yes, sir. But what is the way for those who have not been blessed with the sight of him?

Swamiji: The way for them is to call on him. Calling on him, many are blessed with his vision—can see him in human form just like ours and obtain his grace.

Disciple: Have you ever had a vision of Shri Ramakrishna after his passing away?

Swamiji: After leaving the body, I associated for some time with Pavhari Baba of Ghazipur. There was a garden not far distant from his Ashrama where I lived. People used to say it was a haunted garden, but as you know, I am a sort of demon myself and have not much fear of ghosts. In the garden there were many lemon trees which bore numerous fruits. At that time I was suffering from diarrhoea, and there no food could be had except bread. So, to increase the digestive powers, I used to take plenty of lemons. Mixing with Pavhari Baba, I liked him very much, and he also came to love me deeply. One day I thought that I did not learn any art for making this weak body strong, even though I lived with Shri Ramakrishna for so many years. I had heard that Pavhari Baba knew the science of Hatha-yoga. So I thought I would learn the practices of Hatha-yoga from him, and through them strengthen the body. You know, I have a dogged resolution, and whatever I set my heart on, I always carry out. On the eve of the day on which I was to take initiation, I was lying on a cot thinking; and just then I saw the form of Sri Ramakrishna standing on my right side, looking steadfastly at me, as if very much grieved. I had dedicated myself to him, and at the thought that I was taking another Guru I was much ashamed and kept looking at him. Thus perhaps two or three hours passed, but no words escaped from my mouth. Then he disappeared all on a sudden. My mind became upset seeing Shri Ramakrishna that night, so I postponed the idea of initiation from Pavhari Baba for the day. After a day or two again the idea of initiation from Pavhari Baba arose in the mind—and again in the night there was the appearance of Shri Ramakrishna as on the previous occasion. Thus when for several nights in succession I had the vision of Shri Ramakrishna, I gave up the idea of initiation altogether, thinking that as every time I resolved on it, I was getting such a vision, then no good but harm would come from it.

After some time he addressed the disciple, saying, "Those who have seen Shri Ramakrishna are really blessed. Their family and birth have become purified by it. All of you will also get his vision. The very fact that you have come here, shows that you are very near to him. Nobody has been able to understand who came on earth as Sri Ramakrishna. Even his own nearest devotees have got no real clue to it. Only some have got a little inkling of it. All will understand it afterwards."

The conversation was thus going on when Swami Niranjanananda knocked at the door. The disciple rose and inquired, "Who has come?" Swami Niranjanananda replied, "Sister Nivedita and some other English ladies." They were admitted into the room, sat on the floor and inquired about the health of Swamiji. After a few more words they went away. Then Swamiji said to the disciple, "See how cultured they are! If they were Bengalis, they would have made me talk at least for half an hour, even though they found me unwell."

It is about half past two now, and there is a great gathering of people outside. Understanding the disciple's mind, Swamiji said, "Just go and have a look round—but come back soon."

UNTITLED CONVERSATION XXXVI

After returning from Eastern Bengal Swamiji stayed in the Math and lived a simple childlike life. Every year some Santal labourers used to work in the Math. Swamiji would joke and make fun with them and loved to hear their tales of weal and woe. One day several noted gentlemen of Calcutta came to visit Swamiji in the Math. That day Swamiji had started such a warm talk with the Santals that, when he was informed of the arrival of those gentlemen, he said, "I shan't be able to go now. I am happy with these men." Really that day Swamiji did not leave the poor Santals to see those visitors.

One among the Santals was named Keshta. Swamiji loved Keshta very much. Whenever Swamiji came to talk with them, Keshta used to say to Swamiji, "O my Swamiji, do not come to us when we are working, for while talking with you our work stops and the supervising Swami rebukes us afterwards." Swamiji would be touched by these words and say, "No, no, he will not say anything; tell me a little about your part of the country"— saying which he used to introduce the topic of their worldly affairs.

One day Swamiji said to Keshta, "Well, will you take food here one day?" Keshta said, "We do not take food touched by you; if you put salt in our food and we eat it, we shall lose our caste." Swamiji said, "Why should you take salt? We will prepare curry for you without salt, will you then take it?" Keshta agreed to it. Then at orders of Swamiji, bread, curry, sweets, curd, etc. were arranged for the Santals, and he made them sit before him to eat. While eating, Keshta said, "Whence have you got such a thing? We never tasted anything like this." Feeding them sumptuously, Swamiji said, "You are Narayanas, God manifest; today I have offered food to Narayana." The service of "Daridra Narayana"— god in the poor—about which Swamiji spoke, he himself performed one day like this.

After their meal, the Santals went for rest, and Swamiji, addressing the disciple, said, "I found them the veritable embodiment of God—such simplicity, such sincere guileless love I have seen nowhere else." Then, addressing the Sannyasins of the Math, he said, "See how simple they are. Can you mitigate their misery a little? Otherwise, of what good is the wearing of the Gerua robe? Sacrifice of everything for the good of others is real Sannyasa. They have never enjoyed any good thing in life. Sometimes I feel a desire to sell the Math and everything, and distribute the money to the poor and destitute. We have made the tree our shelter. Alas! the people of the country cannot get anything to eat, and how can we have the heart to raise food to our mouths? When I was in the Western countries, I prayed to the Divine Mother, "People here are sleeping on a bed of flowers, they eat all kinds of delicacies, and what do they not enjoy, while people in our country are dying of starvation. Mother, will there be no way for them! One of the objects of my going to the West to preach religion was to see if I could find any means for feeding the people of this country. "Seeing the poor people of our country starving for food, a desire comes to me to overthrow all ceremonial worship and learning, and go round from village to village collecting money from the rich by convincing them through force of character and Sadhana, and to spend the whole life in serving the poor. "Alas! nobody thinks of the poor of this land. They are the backbone of the country, who by their labour are producing food—these poor people, the sweepers and labourers, who if they stop work for one day will create a panic in the town. But there is none to sympathise with them, none to console them in their misery. Just see, for want of sympathy from the Hindus, thousands of Pariahs in Madras are turning Christians. Don't think this is simply due to the pinch of hunger; it is because they do not get any sympathy from us. We are day and night calling out to them, 'Don't touch us! Don't touch us!' Is there any compassion or kindliness of heart in the country? Only a class of 'Don't-touchists'; kick such customs out! I sometimes feel the urge to break the barriers of 'Don't-touchism', to go at once and call out, 'Come, all who are poor, miserable, wretched, and down-trodden', and to bring them all together in the name of Shri Ramakrishna. Unless they rise, the Mother won't awaken. We could not make any provision for food and clothes for these—what have we done then? Alas! they know nothing of worldliness, and therefore even after working day and night cannot provide themselves with food and clothes. Let us open their eyes. I see clear as daylight that there is the one Brahman in all, in them and in me—one Shakti dwells in all. The only difference is of manifestation. Unless the blood circulates over the whole body, has any country risen at any time? If one limb is paralysed, then even with the other limbs whole, not much can be done with that body—know this for certain."

Disciple: Sir, there is such a diversity of religions and ideas among the people of this country that it is a difficult affair to bring harmony among them.

Swamiji (in anger): If you think any work difficult, then do not come here. Through the grace of God all paths become easy. Your work is to serve the poor and miserable, without any distinction of caste or colour, and you have no need to think about the results. Your duty is to go on working, and then everything will follow of itself. My method of work is to construct and not to pull down. Read the history of the world, and you will find that a great soul stood as the central figure in a certain period of a country. Animated by his ideas, hundreds of people did good to the world. You are all intelligent boys, and have been coming here for a long time. Say, what have you done? Couldn't you give one life for the service of others? In the next life you may read Vedanta and other philosophies. Give this life for the service of others, then I shall know that your coming here has not been in vain.

Saying these words, Swamiji sat silent, wrapt in deep thought. After some time, he added, "After so much austerity, I have understood this as the real truth—god is present in every Jiva; there is no other God besides that. 'Who serves Jiva, serves God indeed'." After some pause Swamiji, addressing the disciple, said, "What I have told you today, inscribe in your heart. See that you do not forget it."

UNTITLED CONVERSATION XXXVII

It was Saturday, and the disciple came to the Math just before evening. An austere routine was being followed now at the Math regarding spiritual practices. Swamiji had issued an order that all Brahmacharins and Sannyasins should get up very early in the morning and practise Japa and meditation in the worship-room. Swamiji was having little sleep during these days, and would rise from bed at three in the morning.

On the disciple saluting Swamiji just after his

appearance at the Math, he said, "Well, see how they are practising religious exercises here nowadays. Everyone passes a considerable time in Japa and meditation on mornings and evenings. Look there—a bell has been procured, which is used for rousing all from sleep. Everyone has to get up before dawn. Shri Ramakrishna used to say, 'In the morning and evening the mind remains highly imbued with Sattva ideas; those are the times when one should meditate with earnestness.' "After the passing away of Shri Ramakrishna we underwent a lot of religious practice at the Baranagore Math. We used to get up at 3 a.m. and after washing our face etc.— some after bath, and others without it—we would sit in the worship-room and become absorbed in Japa and meditation. What a strong spirit of dispassion we had in those days! We had no thought even as to whether the world existed or not. Ramakrishnananda busied himself day and night with the duties pertaining to Shri Ramakrishna's worship and service, and occupied the same position in the Math as the mistress of the house does in a family. It was he who would procure, mostly by begging, the requisite articles for Shri Ramakrishna's worship and our subsistence. There have been days when the Japa and meditation continued from morning till four or five in the afternoon. Ramakrishnananda waited and waited with our meals ready, till at last he would come and snatch us from our meditation by sheer force. Oh, what a wonderful constancy of devotion we have noticed in him!"

Disciple: Sir, how did you use to meet the Math expenses then?

Swamiji: What a question! Well, we were Sadhus, and what would come by begging and other means, would be utilised for defraying the Math expenses. Today both Suresh Babu (Surendra Nath Mitra) and Balaram Babu are no more; had they been alive they would have been exceedingly glad to see this Math. You have doubtless heard Suresh Babu's name. It was he who used to bear all the expenses of the Baranagore Math. It was this Suresh Mitra who used to think most for us in those days. His devotion and faith have no parallel!

Disciple; Sir, I have heard that you did not see him very often while he was dying.

Swamiji: We could only do so if we were allowed (by his relatives). Well, it is a long tale. But know this for certain that among worldly people it is of little count to your relatives and kinsmen whether you live or die. If you succeed in leaving some property, you will find even in your lifetime that there

has been set up a brawl over it in your household. You will have no one to console you in your death-bed—not even your wife and sons! Such is the way of the world!

Referring to the past condition of the Math, Swamiji went on, "Owing to want of funds I would sometimes fight for abolishing the Math altogether. But I could never induce Ramakrishnananda to accede to the proposal. Know Ramakrishnananda to be the central figure of the Math. There have been days when the Math was without a grain of food. If some rice was collected by begging, there was no salt to take it with! On some days there would be only rice and salt, but nobody cared for it in the least. We were then being carried away by a tidal wave of spiritual practice. Boiled Bimba leaves, rice, and salt—this was the menu for a month at a stretch. Oh, those wonderful days! The austerities of that period were enough to dismay supernatural beings, not to speak of men. But it is a tremendous truth that if there be real worth in you, the more are circumstances against you, the more will that inner power manifest itself. But the reason why I have provided for beds and a tolerable living in this Math is that the Sannyasins that are enrolling themselves nowadays will not be able to bear so much strain as we did. There was the life of Shri Ramakrishna before us, and that was why we did not care much for privations and hardships. Boys of this generation will not be able to undergo so much hardship. Hence it is that I have provided for some sort of habitation and a bare subsistence for them. If they get just enough food and clothing, the boys will devote themselves to religious practice and will learn to sacrifice their lives for the good of humanity."

Disciple: Sir, outside people say a good deal against this sort of bedding and furniture.

Swamiji: Let them say. Even in jest they will at least once think of this Math. And they say, it is easier to attain liberation through cherishing a hostile spirit. Shri Ramakrishna used to say, "Men should be ignored like worms." Do you mean we have to conduct ourselves according to the chance opinion of others? Pshaw!

Disciple: Sir, you sometimes say, "All are Narayanas, the poor and the needy are my Narayanas", and again you say, "Men should be ignored like worms." What do you really mean?

Swamiji: Well, there is not the least doubt that all are Narayanas. But all Narayanas do not criticise the furniture of the Math. I shall go on working for the good of men, without caring in the least for the criticisms of others—it is in this sense that the expression, "Men are to be ignored like worms", has been used. He who has a dogged determination like that shall have everything. Only some may have it sooner, and others a little later, that is all. But one is bound to reach the goal. It is because we had such a determination that we have attained the little that we have. Otherwise, what dire days of privation we have had to pass through! One day, for want of food I fainted in the outer platform of a house on the roadside and quite a shower of rain had passed over my head before I recovered my senses! Another day, I had to do odd jobs in Calcutta for the whole day without food, and had my meal on my return to the Math at ten or eleven in the night. And these were not solitary instances.

Saying these words, Swamiji sat for a while pursuing some trend of thought. Then he resumed:

Real monasticism is not easy to attain. There is no order of life so rigorous as this. If you stumble ever so little, you are hurled down a precipice—and are smashed to pieces. One day I was travelling on foot from Agra to Vrindaban. There was not a farthing with me. I was about a couple of miles from Vrindaban when I found a man smoking on the roadside, and I was seized with a desire to smoke. I said to the man, "Hallo, will you let me have a puff at your Chillum?" He seemed to be hesitating greatly and said, "Sire, I am a sweeper." Well, there was the influence of old Samskaras, and I immediately stepped back and resumed my journey without smoking. I had gone a short distance when the thought occurred to me that I was a Sannyasin, who had renounced caste, family, prestige, and everything—and still I drew back as soon as the man gave himself out as a sweeper, and could not smoke at the Chillum touched by him! The thought made me restless at heart; then I had walked on half a mile. Again I retraced my steps and came to the sweeper whom I found still sitting there. I hastened to tell him, "Do prepare a Chillum of tobacco for me, my dear friend." I paid no heed to his objections and insisted on having it. So the man was compelled to prepare a Chillum for me. Then I gladly had a puff at it and proceeded to Vrindaban. When one has embraced the monastic life, one has to test whether one has gone beyond the prestige of caste and birth, etc. It is so difficult to observe the monastic vow in right earnest! There must not be the slightest divergence between one's words and actions.

Disciple: Sir, you sometimes hold before us the householder's ideal and sometimes the ideal of the Sannyasin. Which one are we to adopt?

Swamiji: Well, go on listening to all. Then stick to that one which appeals to you—grip it hard like a bulldog.

Swamiji came downstairs accompanied by the disciple, while speaking these words, and began to pace to and fro, uttering now and then the name of Shiva or humming a song on the Divine Mother, such as, "Who knows how diversely Thou playest, O Mother, Thou flowing stream of nectar", and so on.

UNTITLED CONVERSATION XXXVIII

The disciple passed the preceding night in Swamiji's room. At 4 a.m. Swamiji roused him and said "Go and knock up the Sadhus and Brahmacharins from sleep with the bell." In pursuance of the order, the disciple rang the bell near the Sadhus who slept. The monastic inmates hastened to go to the worship-room for meditation.

According to Swamiji's instructions, the disciple rang the bell lustily near Swami Brahmananda's bed, which made the latter exclaim, "Good heavens! The Bangal[1] has made it too hot for us to stay in the Math!" On the disciple's communicating this to Swamiji, he burst out into a hearty laugh, saying, "Well done!"

Then Swamiji, too, washed his face and entered the chapel accompanied by the disciple.

The Sannyasins—swami Brahmananda and others—were already seated for meditation. A separate seat was kept for Swamiji, on which he sat facing the east, and pointing to a seat in front to the disciple, said, "Go and meditate, sitting there."

Shortly after taking his seat, Swamiji became perfectly calm and motionless, like a statue, and his breathing became very slow. Everyone else kept his seat.

After about an hour and a half, Swamiji rose from meditation with the words "Shiva, Shiva". His eyes were flushed, the expression placid, calm, and grave. Bowing before Shri Ramakrishna he came downstairs and paced the courtyard of the Math. After a while he said to the disciple. "Do you see how the Sadhus are practising meditation etc. nowadays? When the meditation is deep, one sees many wonderful things. While meditating at the Baranagore Math, one day I saw the nerves Ida and Pingala. One can see them with a little effort. Then, when one has a vision of the Shushumna, one can see anything one likes. If a man has unflinching devotion to the Guru, spiritual practices—meditation, Japa, and so forth—come quite naturally; one need not struggle for them. 'The Guru is Brahma, the Guru is Vishnu, and the Guru is Shiva Himself.'"

Then the disciple prepared tobacco for Swamiji and when he returned with it, Swamiji spoke as he puffed at it, "Within there is the lion—the eternally pure, illumined, and ever free Atman; and directly one realises Him through meditation and concentration, this world of Maya vanishes. He is equally present in all; and the more one practises, the quicker does the Kundalini (the `coiled-up' power) awaken in him. When this power reaches the head, one's vision is unobstructed—one realises the Atman."

Disciple: Sir, I have only read of these things in the scriptures, but nothing has been realised as yet.

Swamiji: कालेनात्मनि विन्दति—it is bound to come in time. But some attain this early, and others are a little late. One must stick to it—determined never to let it go. This is true manliness. You must keep the mind fixed on one object, like an unbroken stream of oil. The ordinary man's mind is scattered on different objects, and at the time of meditation, too, the mind is at first apt to wander. But let any desire whatever arise in the mind, you must sit calmly and watch what sort of ideas are coming. By continuing to watch in that way, the

---

1. Meaning an East Bengal man, used as a term of endearing reproach for the disciple.

mind becomes calm, and there are no more thought-waves in it. These waves represent the thought-activity of the mind. Those things that you have previously thought deeply, have transformed themselves into a subconscious current, and therefore these come up in the mind in meditation. The rise of these waves, or thoughts, during meditation is an evidence that your mind is tending towards concentration. Sometimes the mind is concentrated on a set of ideas—this is called meditation with Vikalpa or oscillation. But when the mind becomes almost free from all activities, it melts in the inner Self, which is the essence of infinite Knowledge, One, and Itself Its own support. This is what is called Nirvikalpa Samadhi, free from all activities. In Shri Ramakrishna we have again and again noticed both these forms of Samadhi. He had not to struggle to get these states. They came to him spontaneously, then and there. It was a wonderful phenomenon. It was by seeing him that we could rightly understand these things. Meditate every day alone. Everything will open up of itself. Now the Divine Mother—the embodiment of illumination—is sleeping within, hence you do not understand this. She is the Kundalini. When, before meditating, you proceed to "purify the nerves", you must mentally strike hard on the Kundalini in the Muladhara (sacral plexus), and repeat, "Arise, Mother, arise!" One must practise these slowly. During meditation, suppress the emotional side altogether. This is a great source of danger. Those that are very emotional no doubt have their Kundalini rushing quickly upwards, but it is as quick to come down as to go up. And when it does come down, it leaves the devotee in a state of utter ruin. It is for this reason that Kirtanas and other auxiliaries to emotional development have a great drawback. It is true that by dancing and jumping, etc. through a momentary impulse, that power is made to course upwards, but it is never enduring. On the contrary when it traces back its course, it rouses violent lust in the individual. Listening to my lectures in America, through temporary excitement many among the audience used to get into an ecstatic state, and some would even become motionless like statues. But on inquiry I afterwards found that many of them had an excess of the carnal instinct immediately after that state. But this happens simply owing to a lack of steady practice in meditation and concentration.

Disciple: Sir, in no scriptures have I ever read these secrets of spiritual practice. Today I have heard quite new things.

Swamiji: Do you think the scriptures contain all the secrets of spiritual practice? These are being handed down secretly through a succession of Gurus and disciples. Practise meditation and concentration with the utmost care. Place fragrant flowers in front and burn incense. At the outset take such external help as will make the mind pure. As you repeat the name of your Guru and Ishta, say, "Peace be to all creatures and the universe!" First send impulses of these good wishes to the north, south, east, west, above, below—in all directions, and then sit down to meditate. One has to do this during the early stages. Then sitting still (you may face in any direction),

meditate in the way I have taught you while initiating. Don't leave out a single day. If you have too much pressing work, go through the spiritual exercises for at least a quarter of an hour. Can you reach the goal without steadfast devotion, my son?

Now Swamiji went upstairs, and as he did so, he said, "You people will have your spiritual insight opened without much trouble. Now that you have chanced to come here, you have liberation and all under your thumb. Besides practising meditation, etc., set yourselves heart and soul to remove to a certain extent the miseries of the world, so full of wails. Through hard austerities I have almost ruined this body. There is hardly any energy left in this pack of bones and flesh. You set yourselves to work now, and let me rest a while. If you fail to do anything else, well, you can tell the world at large about the scriptural truths you have studied so long. There is no higher gift than this, for the gift of knowledge is the highest gift in the world."

UNTITLED CONVERSATION XXXIX

Swamiji was now staying at the Math. The disciple came to the Math and towards the evening accompanied Swamiji and Swami Premananda for a walk. Finding Swamiji absorbed in thought, the disciple entered into a conversation with Swami Premananda on what Shri Ramakrishna used to say of Swamiji's greatness. After walking some distance Swamiji turned to go back to the Math. Seeing Swami Premananda and the disciple near by, he said, "Well, what were you talking?" The disciple said, "We were talking about Shri Ramakrishna and his words." Swamiji only heard the reply, but again lapsed into thought and walking along the road returned to the Math. He sat on the camp-cot placed under the mango-tree and, resting there some time, washed his face and then, pacing the upper verandah, spoke to the disciple thus: "Why do you not set about propagating Vedanta in your part of the country? There Tantrikism prevails to a fearful extent. Rouse and agitate the country with the lion-roar of Advaitavada (monism). Then I shall know you to be a Vedantist. First open a Sanskrit school there and teach the Upanishads and the Brahma-sutras . Teach the boys the system of Brahmacharya. I have heard that in your country there is much logic-chopping of the Nyaya school. What is there in it? Only Vyapti (pervasiveness) and Anumana (inference)— on these subjects the Pandits of the Nyaya school discuss for months! What does it help towards the Knowledge of the Atman? Either in your village or Nag Mahashaya's, open a Chatushpathi (indigenous school) in which the scriptures will be studied and also the life and teachings of Shri Ramakrishna. In this way you will advance your own good as well as the good of the people, and your fame will endure.

Disciple: Sir, I cherish no desire for name or fame. Only, sometimes I feel to do as you are saying. But by marriage I have got so entangled in the world that I fear my desire will always remain in the mind only.

Swamiji: What if you have married? As you are maintaining your parents and brothers with food and clothing, so do for your wife likewise; and by giving her religious instruction draw her to your path. Think her to be a partner and helper in the living of your religious life. At other times look upon her with an even eye with others. Thinking thus all the unsteadiness of the mind will die out. What fear?

The disciple felt assured by these words. After his meal, Swamiji sat on his own bed, and the disciple had an opportunity of doing some personal service for him.

Swamiji began to speak to the disciple, enjoining him to be reverential to the Math members: "These children of Shri Ramakrishna whom you see, are wonderful Tyagis (selfless souls), and by service to them you will attain to the purification of mind and be blessed with the vision of the Atman. You remember the words of the Gita: `By interrogation and service to the great soul'. Therefore you must serve them, by which you will attain your goal; and you know how much they love you."

Disciple: But I find it very difficult to understand them. Each one seems to be of a different type.

Swamiji: Shri Ramakrishna was a wonderful gardener. Therefore he has made a bouquet of different flowers and formed his Order. All different types and ideas have come into it, and many more will come. Shri Ramakrishna used to say, "Whoever has prayed to God sincerely for one day, must come here." Know each of those who are here to be of great spiritual power. Because they remain shrivelled before me, do not think them to be ordinary souls. When they will go out, they will be the cause of the awakening of spirituality in people. Know them to be part of the spiritual body of Shri Ramakrishna, who was the embodiment of infinite religious ideas. I look upon them with that eye. See, for instance, Brahmananda, who is here—even I have not the spirituality which he has. Shri Ramakrishna looked upon him as his mind-born son; and he lived and walked, ate and slept with him. He is the ornament of our Math—our king. Similarly Premananda, Turiyananda, Trigunatitananda, Akhandananda, Saradananda, Ramakrishnananda, Subodhananda, and others; you may go round the world, but it is doubtful if you will find men of such spirituality and faith in God like them. They are each a centre of religious power, and in time that power will manifest.

The disciple listened in wonder, and Swamiji said again: "But from your part of the country, except Nag Mahashaya none came to Shri Ramakrishna. A few others who saw Shri Ramakrishna could not appreciate him." At the thought of Nag Mahashaya, Swamiji kept silent for some time. It was only four or five months since he had passed away. Swamiji had heard that on one occasion a spring of Ganga water rose in the house of Nag Mahashaya, and recollecting this he asked the disciple, "Well, how did that event take place? Tell me about it."

Disciple: I only heard about it, but did not see it with my own eyes. I heard that in a Mahavaruni Yoga Nag Mahashaya started with his father for Calcutta.

But not getting any accommodation in the railway train he stayed for three or four days in Narayangunge in vain and returned home. Then Nag Mahashaya said to his father, "If the mind is pure, then the Mother Ganga will appear here." Then at the auspicious hour of the holy bath, a jet of water rose, piercing the ground of his courtyard. Many of those who saw it are living today. But that was many years before I met him.

Swamiji: There was nothing strange in it. He was a saint of unfalsified determination. I do not consider such a phenomenon at all strange in his case.

Saying this, Swamiji, feeling sleepy, lay on his side. At this the disciple came down to take his supper.

UNTITLED CONVERSATION XL

While walking on the banks of the Ganga at Calcutta one afternoon, the disciple saw a Sannyasin in the distance approaching towards Ahiritola Ghat. While he came near, the disciple found the Sannyasin to be no other than his Guru, Swami Vivekananda. In his left hand he had a leaf receptacle containing fried gram, which he was eating like a boy, and was walking in great joy. When he stood before him, the disciple fell at his feet and asked the reason for his coming to Calcutta unexpectedly.

Swamiji: I came on business. Come, will you go to the Math? Eat a little of the fried gram. It has a nice saline and pungent taste. The disciple took the food with gladness and agreed to go to the Math with him.

Swamiji: Then look for a boat.

The disciple hurried to hire a boat. He was settling

the amount of the boat-hire with the boatman, who demanded eight annas, when Swamiji also appeared on the scene and stopped the disciple saying, "Why are you higgling with them?" and said to the boatman, "Very well, I will give you eight annas", and got into the boat. That boat proceeded slowly against the current and took nearly an hour and half to reach the Math. Being alone with Swamiji in the boat, the disciple had an opportunity of asking him freely about all subjects. Raising the topic of the glorificatory poem which the disciple had recently composed singing the greatness of the devotees of Shri Ramakrishna, Swamiji asked him, "How do you know that those whom you have named in your hymn are the near and intimate disciples of Shri Ramakrishna?"

Disciple: Sir, I have associated with the Sannyasin and householder disciples of Shri Ramakrishna for so many years; I have heard from them that they are all devotees of Shri Ramakrishna.

Swamiji: Yes, they are devotees of Shri Ramakrishna. But all devotees do not belong to the group of his most intimate and nearest disciples. Staying in the Cossipore Garden, Shri Ramakrishna said to us, "The Divine Mother showed me that all of these are not my inner devotees." Shri Ramakrishna said so that day with respect to both his men and women devotees.

Then speaking of the way Shri Ramakrishna would indicate different grades among devotees, high and low, Swamiji began to explain to the disciple at length the great difference there is between the householder's and the Sannyasin's life.

Swamiji: Is it possible that one would serve the path of lust and wealth and understand Shri Ramakrishna aright at the same time? Or will it ever be possible? Never put your faith in such words. Many among the devotees of Shri Ramakrishna are now proclaiming themselves as Ishvara-koti (of Divine class), Antaranga (of inner circle), etc. They could not imbibe his great renunciation or dispassion, yet they say they are his intimate devotees! Sweep away all such words. He was a prince of Tyagis (self-renouncers), and obtaining his grace can anybody spend his life in the enjoyment of lust and wealth?

Disciple: Is it then, sir, that those who came to him at Dakshineswar were not his devotees?

Swamiji: Who says that? Everybody who has gone to Shri Ramakrishna has advanced in spirituality, is advancing, and will advance. Shri Ramakrishna used to say that the perfected Rishis of a previous Kalpa (cycle) take human bodies and come on earth with the Avataras. They are the associates of the Lord. God works through them and propagates His religion. Know this for a truth that they alone are the associates of the Avatara who have renounced all self for the sake of others, who, giving up all sense-enjoyments with repugnance, spend their lives for the good of the world, for the welfare of the Jivas. The disciples of Jesus were all Sannyasins. The direct recipients of the grace of Shankara, Ramanuja, Shri Chaitanya and Buddha were the all-renouncing Sannyasins. It is men of this stamp who have been through succession of disciples spreading the Brahma-vidya (knowledge of Brahman) in the world. Where and when have you heard that a man being the slave of lust and wealth has been able to liberate another or to show the path of God to him? Without himself free, how can he make others free? In Veda, Vedanta, Itihasa (history), Purana (ancient tradition), you will find everywhere that the Sannyasins have been the teachers of religion in all ages and climes. History repeats itself. It will also be likewise now. The capable Sannyasin children of Shri Ramakrishna, the teacher of the great synthesis of religions, will be honoured everywhere as the teachers of men. The words of others will dissipate in the air like an empty sound. The real self-sacrificing Sannyasins of the Math will be the centre of the preservation and spread of religious ideas. Do you understand?

Disciple: Then is it not true—what the householder devotees of Shri Ramakrishna are preaching about him in diverse ways?

Swamiji: It can't be said that they are altogether false; but what they are saying about Shri Ramakrishna is only partial truth. According to one's own capacity, one has understood Shri Ramakrishna and so is discussing about him. It is not bad either to do so. But if any of his devotees has concluded that what he has understood of him is the only truth, then he is an object of pity. Some are saying that Shri Ramakrishna was a Tantrika and Kaula, some that he was Shri Chaitanya born on earth to preach "Naradiya Bhakti" (Bhakti as taught by Narada); some again that to undertake spiritual practices is opposed to faith in him as an Avatara while some are opining that it is not agreeable to his teachings to take to Sannyasa. You will hear such words from the householder devotees, but do not listen to such one-sided estimates. He was the concentrated embodiment of how many previous Avataras! Even spending the whole life in religious austerity, we could not understand it. Therefore one has to speak about him with caution and restraint. As are one's capacities, so he fills one with spiritual ideas. One spray from the full ocean of his spirituality, if realised, will make gods of men. Such a synthesis of universal ideas you will not find in the history of the world again. Understand from this who was born in the person of Shri Ramakrishna. When he used to instruct his Sannyasin disciples, he would rise from his seat and look about to see if any householder was coming that way or not. If he found none, then in glowing words he would depict the glory of renunciation and austerity. As a result of the rousing power of that fiery dispassion, we have renounced the world and become averse to worldliness.

Disciple: He used to make such distinctions between householders and Sannyasins!

Swamiji: Ask and learn from the householder devotees themselves about it. And you yourself can think and know which are greater—those of his children who for the realisation of God have renounced all enjoyments of the worldly life and are spending themselves in the practice of austerities on hills and forests, Tirthas and Ashramas (holy places and hermitages), or those who are praising and glorifying his name and practising his remembrance, but are not able to rise above the delusion and bondage of the world? Which are greater—those who are coming forward in the service of humanity, regarding them as the Atman, those who are continent since early age, who are the moving embodiments of renunciation and dispassion, or those who like flies are at one time sitting on a flower, and at the next moment on a dung heap? You can yourself think and come to a conclusion.

Disciple: But, sir, what does the world really mean to those who have obtained his grace? Whether they remain in the householder's life or take to Sannyasa, it is immaterial—so it appears to me. Swamiji: The mind of those who have truly received his grace cannot be attached to worldliness. The test of his grace is—unattachment to lust or wealth. If that has not come in anyone's life, then he has not truly received his grace.

When the above discussion ended thus, the disciple raising another topic, asked Swamiji, "Sir, what is the outcome of all your labours here and in foreign countries?"

Swamiji: You will see only a little manifestation of what has been done. In time the whole world must accept the universal and catholic ideas of Shri Ramakrishna and of this, only the beginning has been made. Before this flood everybody will be swept off.

Disciple: Please tell me more about Shri Ramakrishna. I like very much to hear of him from your lips.

Swamiji: You are hearing so much about him all the time, what more? He himself is his own parallel. Has he any exemplar?

Disciple: What is the way for us who have not seen him?

Swamiji: You have been blessed with the company of these Sadhus who are the direct recipients of his grace. How then can you say you have not seen him? He is present among his Sannyasin disciples. By service to them, he will in time be revealed in your heart. In time you will realise everything.

Disciple: But, sir, you speak about others who have received his grace, but never about what he used to say about yourself.

Swamiji: What shall I say about myself? You see, I must be one of his demons. In his presence even, I would sometimes speak ill of him, hearing which he would laugh.

Saying thus Swamiji's face assumed a grave aspect, and he looked towards the river with an absent mind and sat still for some time. Within a short time the evening fell and the boat also reached the Math. Swamiji was then humming a tune to himself, "Now in the evening of life, take the child back to his home."

When the song was finished, Swamiji said, "In your part of the country (East Bengal) sweet-voiced singers are not born. Without drinking the water of mother Ganga, a sweet, musical voice is not acquired."

After paying the hire, Swamiji descended from the boat and taking off his coat sat in the western verandah of the Math. His fair complexion and ochre robe presented a beautiful sight.

UNTITLED CONVERSATION XLI

Today is the first of Asharh (June-July). The disciple has come to the Math before dusk from Bally, with his office-dress on, as he has not found time to change it. Coming to the Math, he prostrated himself at the feet of Swamiji and inquired about his health. Swamiji replied that he was well, but looking at his dress, he said, "You put on coat and trousers, why don't you put on collars?" Saying this, he called Swami Saradananda who was near and said, "Give him tomorrow two collars from my stock." Swami Saradananda bowed assent to his order.

The disciple then changed his office-dress and came to Swamiji, who, addressing him, said, "By giving up one's national costume and ways of eating and living, one gets denationalised. One can learn from all, but that learning which leads to denationalisation does not help one's uplift but becomes the cause of degradation."

Disciple: Sir, one cannot do without putting on dress approved by superior European officers in official quarters.

Swamiji: No one prevents that. In the interests of your service, you put on official dress in official quarters. But on returning home you should be a regular Bengali Babu—with flowing cloth, a native shirt, and with the Chudder on the shoulder. Do you understand?

Disciple: Yes, sir.

Swamiji: You go about from house to house only with the European shirt on. In the West, to go about visiting people with simply the shirt on is ungentlemanly—one is considered naked. Without putting on a coat over the shirt, you will not be welcomed in a gentleman's house. What nonsense have you learnt to imitate in the matter of dress! Boys and young men nowadays adopt a peculiar manner of dress which is neither Indian nor Western, but a queer combination.

After such talk Swamiji began to pace the bank of the river, and the disciple was alone with him. He was hesitating to ask Swamiji a question about religious practices.

Swamiji: What are you thinking? Out with it.

The disciple with great delicacy said, "Sir, I have been thinking that if you can teach me some method by which the mind becomes calm within a short time, by which I may be immersed in meditation quickly, I shall feel much benefited. In the round of worldly duties, I feel it difficult to make the mind steady in meditation at the time of spiritual practice."

Swamiji seemed delighted at this humility and earnestness of the disciple. In reply he affectionately said, "After some time come to me when I am alone upstairs, I will talk to you about it."

Coming up shortly after, the disciple found that Swamiji was sitting in meditation, facing the west. His face wore a wonderful expression, and his whole body was completely motionless. The disciple stood by, looking with speechless wonder on the figure of Swamiji in meditation, and when even after standing long he found no sign of external consciousness in Swamiji, he sat noiselessly by. After half an hour, Swamiji seemed to show signs of a return to external consciousness. The disciple found that his folded hands began to quiver, and a few minutes later Swamiji opened his eyes and looking at the disciple said, "When did you come?"

Disciple: A short while ago.

Swamiji: Very well, get me a glass of water.

The disciple hurriedly brought a glass of water and Swamiji drinking a little, asked the disciple to put the glass back in its proper place. The disciple did so and again sat by Swamiji.

Swamiji: Today I had a very deep meditation.

Disciple: Sir, please teach me so that my mind also may get absorbed in meditation.

Swamiji: I have already told you all the methods. Meditate every day accordingly, and in the fulness of time you will feel like that. Now tell me what form of Sadhana appeals to you most.

Disciple: Sir, I practise every day as you have told me, still I don't get a deep meditation. Sometimes I think it is useless for me to practise meditation. So I feel that I shall not fare well in it, and therefore now desire only eternal companionship with you.

Swamiji: Those are weaknesses of the mind. Always try to get absorbed in the eternally present Atman. If you once get the vision of the Atman, you will get everything—the bonds of birth and death will be broken.

Disciple: You bless me to attain to it. You asked me, still I don't get a deep meditation. By some means, do please make my mind steady.

Swamiji: Meditate whenever you get time. If the mind once enters the path of Sushumna, everything will get right. You will not have to do much after that.

Disciple: You encourage me in many ways. But shall I be blessed with a vision of the Truth? Shall I get freedom by attaining true knowledge?

Swamiji: Yes, of course. Everybody will attain Mukti, from a worm up to Brahma, and shall you alone fail? These are weaknesses of the mind; never think of such things.

After this, he said again: "Be possessed of Shraddha (faith), of Virya (courage), attain to the knowledge of the Atman, and sacrifice your life for the good of others—this is my wish and blessing."

The bell for the meal ringing at this moment, Swamiji asked the disciple to go and partake of it. The disciple, prostrating himself at the feet of Swamiji, prayed for his blessings. Swamiji putting his hand on his head blessed him and said, "If my blessings be of any good to you, I say—may Bhagavan Shri Ramakrishna give you his grace! I know of no blessing higher than this." After meals, the disciple did not go upstairs to Swamiji, who had retired early that night. Next morning the disciple, having to return to Calcutta in the interests of his business appeared before Swamiji upstairs.

Swamiji: Will you go immediately?

Disciple: Yes, sir.

Swamiji: Come again next Sunday, won't you?

Disciple: Yes, certainly.

Swamiji: All right, there is a boat coming.

The disciple took leave of Swamiji. He did not know that this was to be his last meeting with his Ishtadeva (chosen Ideal) in the physical body. Swamiji with a glad heart bade him farewell and said, "Come on Sunday." The disciple replied, "Yes, I will," and got downstairs.

The boatmen were calling for him, so he ran for the boat. Boarding it, he saw Swamiji pacing the upper verandah, and saluting him he entered the boat.

Seven days after this, Swamiji passed away from mortal life. The disciple had no knowledge of the impending catastrophe. Getting the news on the second day of Swamiji's passing away,

he came to the Math, and therefore he had not the good fortune to see his physical form again!

CONVERSATION XLII: SHRI PRIYA NATH SINHA

of Swamiji had a talk with him one day at the Math on this subject. Swamiji remarked, "You see, we have an old adage: 'If your son is not inclined to study, put him in the Durbars (Sabha).' The word Sabha here does not mean social meetings, such as take place occasionally at people's houses—it means royal Durbars. In the days of the independent kings of Bengal, they used to hold their courts mornings and evenings. There all the affairs of the State were discussed in the morning—and as there were no newspapers at that time, the king used to converse with the leading gentry of the capital and gather from them all information regarding the people and the State. These gentlemen had to attend these meetings, for if they did not do so, the king would inquire into the reason of their non-attendance. Such Durbars were the centres of culture in every country and not merely in ours. In the present day, the western parts of India, especially Rajputana, are much better off in this respect than Bengal, as something similar to these old Durbars still obtains there."

Q.— then, Maharaj, have our people lost their own good manners because we have no kings of our own?

Swamiji: It is all a degeneration which has its root in selfishness. That in boarding a steamer one follows the vulgar maxim, "Uncle, save thy own precious skin", and in music and moments of recreation everyone tries to make a display of himself, is a typical picture of our mental state. Only a little training in self-sacrifice would take it away. It is the fault of the parents who do not teach their children good manners. Self-sacrifice, indeed, is the basis of all civilisation.

On the other hand, owing to the undue domination exercised by the parents, our boys do not get free scope for growth. The parents consider singing as improper. But the son, when he hears a fine piece of music, at once sets his whole mind on how to learn it, and naturally he must look out for an Adda. [1] Then again, "It is a sin to smoke!" So what else can the young man do than mix with the servants of the house, to indulge in this habit in secret? In everyone there are infinite tendencies, which require proper scope for satisfaction. But in our country that is not allowed; and to bring about a different order of things would require a fresh training of the parents. Such is the condition! What a pity! We have not yet developed a high grade of civilisation; and in spite of this, our educated Babus want the British to hand over the government to them to manage! It makes me laugh and cry as well. Well, where is that martial spirit which, at the very outset, requires one to know how to serve and obey and to practise self-restraint! The martial spirit is not self-assertion but self-sacrifice. One must be ready to advance and lay down one's life at the word of command, before he can command the hearts and lives of others. One must sacrifice himself first.

A devotee of Shri Ramakrishna once passed some severe remarks, in a book written by him, against those who did not believe in Shri Ramakrishna as an Incarnation of God. Swamiji summoned the writer to his presence and addressed him thus in a spirited manner:

What right had you to write like that, abusing others? What matters it if they do not believe in your Lord? Have we created a sect? Are we Ramakrishnites, that we should look upon anyone who will not worship him, as our enemy? By your bigotry you have only lowered him, and made him small. If your Lord is God Himself, then you ought to know that in whatsoever name one is calling upon him, it is his worship only—and who are you to abuse others? Do you think they will hear you if you inveigh against them? How foolish! You can only win others' hearts when you have sacrificed yourself to them, otherwise why should they hear you?

Regaining his natural composure after a short while, Swamiji spoke in a sorrowful tone:

Can anyone, my dear friend, have faith or resignation in the Lord, unless he himself is a hero? Never can hatred and malice vanish from one's heart unless one becomes a hero, and unless one is free from these, how can one become truly civilised? Where in this country is that sturdy manliness, that spirit of heroism? Alas, nowhere. Often have I looked for that, and I found only one instance of it, and only one.

Q.— in whom have you found it, Swamiji?

Swamiji: In G. C. alone I have seen that true resignation—that true spirit of a servant of the Lord. And was it not because he was ever ready to sacrifice himself that Shri Ramakrishna took upon himself all his responsibility? What a unique spirit of resignation to the Lord! I have not met his parallel. From him have I learnt the lesson of self-surrender.

So saying, Swamiji raised his folded hands to his head out of respect to him.

UNTITLED CONVERSATION XLIII

Swamiji: A very funny thing happened today. I

went to a friend's house. He has had a picture painted, the subject of which is "Shri Krishna addressing Arjuna on the battlefield of Kurukshetra". Shri Krishna stands on the chariot, holding the reins in His hand and preaching the Gita to Arjuna. He showed me the picture and asked me how I liked it. "Fairly well", I said. But as he insisted on having my criticism on it, I had to give my honest opinion by saying, "There is nothing in it to commend itself to me; first, because the chariot of the time of Shri Krishna was not like the modern pagoda-shaped car, and also, there is no expression in the figure of Shri Krishna."

Q.— Was not the pagoda-chariot in use then?

Swamiji: Don't you know that since the Buddhistic era, there has been a great confusion in everything in our country? The

kings never used to fight in pagoda-chariots. There are chariots even today in Rajputana that greatly resemble the chariots of old. Have you seen the chariots in the pictures of Grecian mythology? They have two wheels, and one mounts them from behind; we had that sort of chariot. What good is it to paint a picture if the details are wrong? An historical picture comes up to a standard of excellence when after making proper study and research, things are portrayed exactly as they were at that period. The truth must be represented, otherwise the picture is nothing. In these days, our young men who go in for painting are generally those who were unsuccessful at school, and who have been given up at home as good-for-nothing; what work of art can you expect from them? To paint a really good picture requires as much talent as to produce a perfect drama.

Q.— how then should Shri Krishna be represented in the picture in question?

Swamiji: Shri Krishna ought to be painted as He really was, the Gita personified; and the central idea of the Gita should radiate from His whole form as He was teaching the path of Dharma to Arjuna, who had been overcome by infatuation and cowardice.

So saying Swamiji posed himself in the way in which Shri Krishna should be portrayed, and continued: "Look here, thus does he hold the bridle of the horses—so tight that they are brought to their haunches, with their forelegs fighting the air, and their mouths gaping. This will show a tremendous play of action in the figure of Shri Krishna. His friend, the world-renowned hero, casting aside his bow and arrows, has sunk down like a coward on the chariot, in the midst of the two armies. And Shri Krishna, whip in one hand and tightening the reins with the other, has turned Himself towards Arjuna, with his childlike face beaming with unworldly love and sympathy, and a calm and serene look—and is delivering the message of the Gita to his beloved comrade. Now, tell me what idea this picture of the Preacher of the Gita conveys to you."

The friend: Activity combined with firmness and serenity.

Swamiji: Ay, that's it! Intense action in the whole body, and withal a face expressing the profound calmness and serenity of the blue sky. This is the central idea of the Gita—to be calm and steadfast in all circumstances, with one's body, mind, and soul centred at His hallowed Feet! [(Sanskrit)] (Gita IV.18)

He who even while doing action can keep his mind calm, and in whom, even when not doing any outward action, flows the current of activity in the form of the contemplation of Brahman, is the intelligent one among men, he indeed is the Yogi, he indeed is the perfect worker.

At this moment, the man who had been sent to arrange a boat returned and said that it was ready; so Swamiji told his friend, "Now let us go to the Math.

You must have left word at home that you were going there with me?"

They continued their talk as they walked to the boat.

Swamiji: This idea must be preached to everyone—work, work, endless work—without looking at results, and always keeping the whole mind and soul steadfast at the lotus feet of the Lord!

Q.— but is this not Karma-yoga?

Swamiji: Yes, this is Karma-yoga; but without spiritual practices you will never be able to do this Karma-yoga. You must harmonise the four different Yogas; otherwise how can you always keep your mind and heart wholly on the Lord?

Q.— it is generally said that work according to the Gita means the performance of Vedic sacrifices and religious exercises; any other kind of work is futile.

Swamiji: All right; but you must make it more comprehensive. Who is responsible for every action you do, every breath you take, and every thought you think? Isn't it you yourself?

The friend: Yes and no. I cannot solve this clearly. The truth about it is that man is the instrument and the Lord is the agent. So when I am directed by His will, I am not at all responsible for my actions.

Swamiji: Well, that can be said only in the highest state of realisation. When the mind will be purified by work and you will see that it is He who is causing all to work, then only you will have a right to speak like that. Otherwise it is all bosh, a mere cant.

Q.— why so, if one is truly convinced by reasoning that the Lord alone is causing all actions to be done?

Swamiji: It may hold good when one has been so convinced. But it only lasts for that moment, and not a whit afterwards. Well, consider this thoroughly, whether all that you do in your everyday life, you are not doing with an egoistic idea that you yourself are the agent.

How long do you remember that it is the Lord who is making you work? But then, by repeatedly analysing like that, you will come to a state when the ego will vanish and in its place the Lord will come in. Then you will be able to say with justice "Thou, Lord, art guarding all my actions from within." But, my friend, if the ego occupies all the space within your heart, where forsooth will there be room enough for the Lord to come in? The Lord is verily absent!

Q.— But it is He who is giving me the wicked impulse?

Swamiji: No, by no means. It would be blaspheming the Lord to think in that way. He is not inciting you to evil action, it is all the creation of your desire for self-gratification. If one says the Lord is causing everything to be done, and wilfully persists in wrong-doing, it only brings ruin on him. That is the origin of self-deception. Don't you feel an elation after you have done a good deed? You then give yourself the credit of doing something good—you can't help it, it is very human. But how absurd to take the credit of doing the good act on oneself and lay the blame for the evil act on the Lord! It is a most dangerous idea—the effect of ill-digested Gita and Vedanta. Never hold that view. Rather say that He is causing

the good work to be done while you are responsible for the evil action. That will bring on devotion and faith, and you will see His grace manifested at every step. The truth about it is that no one has created you—you have created yourself. This is discrimination, this is Vedanta. But one does not understand it before realisation. Therefore the aspirant should begin with the dualistic standpoint, that the Lord is causing the good actions, while he is doing the evil. This is the easiest way to the purification of the mind. Hence you find dualism so strong among the Vaishnavas. It is very difficult to entertain Advaitic (non-dualistic) ideas at the outset. But the dualistic standpoint gradually leads to the realisation of the Advaita.

Hypocrisy is always a dangerous thing. If there is no wilful self-deception, that is to say, if one sincerely believes that the most wicked impulse is also prompted by the Lord, rest assured that one will not have to do those mean acts for long. All the impurities of the mind are quickly destroyed. Our ancient scriptural writers understood this well. And I think that the Tantrika form of worship originated from the time that Buddhism began to decline and, through the oppression of the Buddhists, people began to perform their Vedic sacrifices in secret. They had no more opportunity to conduct them for two months at a stretch, so they made clay images, worshipped them, and consigned them to the water—finishing everything in one night, without leaving the least trace! Man longs for a concrete symbol, otherwise his heart is not satisfied. So in every home that one-night sacrifice began to take place. As Shri Ramakrishna used to say, "Some enter the house by the scavenger's entrance", so the spiritual teachers of that time saw that those who could not perform any religious rite owing to their evil propensities, also needed some way of coming round by degrees to the path of virtue. For them those queer Tantrika rites came to be invented.

Q.— They went on doing evil actions thinking them to be good. So how could this remove their evil tendencies?

Swamiji: Why, they gave a different direction to their propensities; they did them, but with the object of realising the Lord.

Q.— Can this really be done?

Swamiji: It comes to the same thing. The motive must be right. And what should prevent them from succeeding?

Q.— But many are caught in the temptation for wine, meat, etc. in trying to get along with such means.

Swamiji: It was therefore that Shri Ramakrishna came. The days of practising the Tantra in that fashion are gone. He, too, practised the Tantra, but not in that way. Where there is the injunction of drinking wine, he would simply touch his forehead with a drop of it. The Tantrika form of worship is a very slippery ground. Hence I say that this province has had enough of the Tantra. Now it must go beyond. The Vedas should be studied. A harmony of the four kinds of Yogas must be practised and absolute chastity must be preserved.

Q.— What do you mean by the harmony of the four Yogas?

Swamiji: Discrimination between the real and the unreal, dispassion and devotion, work and practices in concentration, and along with these there must be a reverential attitude towards women.

Q.— How can one look with reverence on women?

Swamiji: Well, they are the representatives of the Divine Mother. And real well-being of India will commence from the day that the worship of the Divine Mother will truly begin, and every man will sacrifice himself at the altar of the Mother...

Q.— Swamiji, in your boyhood, when we asked you to marry, you would reply, "I won't, but you will see what I shall become." You have actually verified your words.

Swamiji: Yes, dear brother, you saw how I was in want of food, and had to work hard besides. Oh, the tremendous labour! Today the Americans out of love have given me this nice bed, and I have something to eat also. But, also, I have not been destined to enjoy physically—and lying on the mattress only aggravates my illness. I feel suffocated, as it were. I have to come down and lie on the floor for relief!

CONVERSATION XLIV: VENGEANCE OF HISTORY (MRS. WRIGHT)

"It was the other day," he said, in his musical voice, "only just the other day—not more than four hundred years ago." And then followed tales of cruelty and oppression, of a patient race and a suffering people, and of a judgment to come! "Ah, the English!" he said. "Only just a little while ago they were savages, the vermin crawled on the ladies' bodies,... and they scented themselves to disguise the abominable odour of their persons... Most hor-r-ible! Even now they are barely emerging from barbarism." "Nonsense," said one of his scandalised hearers, "that was at least five hundred years ago." "And did I not say `a little while ago'? What are a few hundred years when you look at the antiquity of the human soul?" Then with a turn of tone, quite reasonable and gentle, "They are quite savage", he said. "The frightful cold, the want and privation of their northern climate", going on more quickly and warmly, "has made them wild . They only think to kill... Where is their religion? They take the name of that Holy One, they claim to love their fellowmen, they civilise—by Christianity!— no! It is their hunger that has civilised them, not their God. The love of man is on their lips, in their hearts there is nothing but evil and every violence. `I love you my brother, I love you!' ...and all the while they cut his throat! Their hands are red with blood."...Then, going on more slowly, his beautiful voice deepening till it sounded like a bell, "But the judgment of God will fall upon them. `Vengeance is mine; I will repay, saith the Lord', and destruction is coming. What are your Christians? Not one third of the world. Look at those Chinese, millions of them. They are the vengeance of God that will light upon you. There will be another invasion of the Huns", adding, with a little chuckle, "they will sweep over Europe, they will not leave one stone standing upon another. Men, women, children, all will go and the dark ages will come again." His voice was indescribably sad and pitiful; then suddenly and flippantly, dropping the seer, "Me—i don't care! The world will rise up better from it, but it is coming. The vengeance of God, it is coming soon." "Soon?" they all asked.

"It will not be a thousand years before it is done."

They drew a breath of relief. It did not seem imminent.

"And God will have vengeance", he went on. "You may not see it in religion, you may not see it in politics, but you must see it in history, and as it has been; it will come to pass. If you grind down the people, you will suffer. We in India are suffering the vengeance of God. Look upon these things. They ground down those poor people for their own wealth, they heard not the voice of distress, they ate from gold and silver when the people cried for bread, and the Mohammedans came upon them slaughtering and killing: slaughtering and killing they overran them. India has been conquered again and again for years, and last and worst of all came the Englishman. You look about India, what has the Hindu left? Won-derful temples, everywhere. What has the Mohammedan left? Beautiful palaces. What has the Englishman left? Nothing but mounds of broken brandy bottles! And God has had no mercy upon my people because they had no mercy. By their cruelty they degraded the populace; and when they needed them, the common people had no strength to give for their aid. If man cannot believe in the Vengeance of God, he certainly cannot deny the Vengeance of History. And it will come upon the English; they have their heels on our necks, they have sucked the last drop of our blood for their own pleasures, they have carried away with them millions of our money, while our people have starved by villages and provinces. And now the Chinaman is the vengeance that will fall upon them; if the Chinese rose today and swept the English into the sea, as they well deserve, it would be no more than justice."

And then, having said his say, the Swami was silent. A babble of thin-voiced chatter rose about him, to which he listened, apparently unheeding. Occasionally he cast his eye up to the roof and repeated softly, "Shiva! Shiva!" and the little company, shaken and disturbed by the current of powerful feelings and vindictive passion which seemed to be flowing like molten lava beneath the silent surface of this strange being, broke up, perturbed.

He stayed days [actually it was only a long weekend]...All through, his discourses abounded in picturesque illustrations and beautiful legends...

One beautiful story he told was of a man whose wife reproached him with his troubles, reviled him because of the success of others, and recounted to him all his failures. "Is this what your God has done for you", she said to him, "after you have served Him so many years?" Then the man answered, "Am I a trader in religion? Look at the mountain. What does it do for me, or what have I done for it? And yet I love it be-cause I am so made that I love the beautiful. Thus I love God." ... There was another story he told of a king who offered a gift to a Rishi. The Rishi refused, but the king insisted and begged that he would come with him. When they came to the palace, he heard the king praying, and the king begged for wealth, for power, for length of days from God. The Rishi listened, wondering, until at last he picked up his mat and started away. Then the king opened his eyes from his prayers and saw him. "Why are you going?" he said. "You have not asked for your gift." "I", said the Rishi, "ask from a beggar?"

When someone suggested to him that Christianity was a saving power, he opened his great dark eyes upon him and said, "If Christianity is a saving power in itself, why has it not saved the Ethiopians, the Abyssinians?"

Often on Swamiji's lips was the phrase, "They would not dare to do this to a monk." ... At times he even expressed a great longing that the English government would take him and shoot him. "It would be the first nail in their coffin", he would say, with a little gleam of his white teeth. "and my death would run through the land like wild fire."

His great heroine was the dreadful [?] Ranee of the Indian mutiny, who led her troops in person. Most of the old mutineers, he said, had become monks in order to hide themselves, and this accounted very well for the dangerous quality of the monks' opinions. There was one man of them who had lost four sons and could speak of them with composure, but whenever he mentioned the Ranee, he would weep, with tears streaming down his face. "That woman was a goddess", he said, "a devi. When overcome, she fell on her sword and died like a man." It was strange to hear the other side of the Indian mutiny, when you would never believe that there was another side to it, and to be assured that a Hindu could not possibly kill a woman ...

CONVERSATION XLV: RELIGION, CIVILISATION, AND MIRACLES (THE APPEAL-AVALANCHE)

"I am a monk," he said, as he sat in the parlors of La Salette Academy, (On January 21, 1894.) which is his home while in Memphis, "and not a priest. When at home I travel from place to place, teaching the people of the villages and towns through which I pass. I am dependent upon them for my sustenance, as I am not allowed to touch money."

"I was born," he continued, in answer to a question, "in Bengal and become a monk and a celibate from choice. At my birth my father had a horoscope taken of my life, but would never tell me what it was. Some years ago when I visited my home, my father having died, I came across the chart among some papers in my mother's possession and saw from it that I was destined to become a wanderer on the face of the earth."

There was a touch of pathos in the speaker's voice and a murmur of sympathy ran around the group of listeners. Kananda (American reporters generally spelt his name as Vivekananda)

in those days.) knocked the ashes from his cigar and was silent for a space.

Presently some one asked:

"If your religion is all that you claim it is, if it is the only true faith, how is it that your people are not more advanced in civilisation than we are? Why has it not elevated them among the nations of the world?"

"Because that is not the sphere of any religion," replied the Hindu gravely. "My people are the most moral in the world, or quite as much as any other race. They are more considerate of their fellow man's rights, and even those of dumb animals, but they are not materialists. No religion has ever advanced the thought or inspiration of a nation or people. In fact, no great achievement has ever been attained in the history of the world that religion has not retarded. Your boasted Christianity has not proven an exception in this respect. Your Darwins, your Mills, your Humes, have never received the endorsement of your prelates. Why, then, criticise my religion on this account?"

"I would not give a fig for a faith that does not tend to elevate mankind's lot on earth as well as his spiritual condition," said one of the group, 'and therein I am not prepared to admit the correctness of your statements. Christianity has founded colleges, hospitals and raised the degenerate. It has elevated the downcast and helped its followers to live."

"You are right there to a certain extent," replied the monk calmly, "and yet it is not shown that these things are directly the result of your Christianity. There are many causes operating in the West to produce these results.

"Religious thought should be directed to developing man's spiritual side. Science, art, learning and metaphysical research all have their proper functions in life, but if you seek to blend them, you destroy their individual characteristics until, in time, you eliminate the spiritual, for instance, from the religious altogether. You Americans worship what? The dollar. In the mad rush for gold, you forget the spiritual until you have become a nation of materialists. Even your preachers and churches are tainted with the all-pervading desire. Show me one in the history of your people, who has led the spiritual lives that those whom I can name at home have done. Where are those who, when death comes, could say, 'O Brother Death, I welcome thee.' Your religion helps you to build Ferris wheels and Eiffel towers, but does it aid you in the development of your inner lives?"

The monk spoke earnestly, and his voice, rich and well modulated, came through the dusk that pervaded the apartment, half-sadly, half-accusingly. There was something of the weird in the comments of this stranger from a land whose history dates back 6,000 years upon the civilisation of the Nineteenth Century America.

"But, in pursuing the spiritual, you lost sight of the demands of the present," said some one. "Your doctrine does not help men to live."

"It helps them to die," was the answer.

"We are sure of the present."

"You are sure of nothing."

"The aim of the ideal religion should be to help one to live and to prepare one to die at the same time."

"Exactly," said the Hindu, quickly, "and it is that which we are seeking to attain. I believe that the Hindu faith has developed the spiritual in its devotees at the expense of the material, and I think that in the Western world the contrary is true. By uniting the materialism of the West with the spiritualism of the East I believe much can be accomplished. It may be that in the attempt the Hindu faith will lose much of its individuality."

"Would not the entire social system of India have to be revolutionised to do what you hope to do?"

"Yet, probably, still the religion would remain unimpaired."

The conversation here turned upon the form of worship of the Hindus, and Kananda gave some interesting information on this subject. There are agnostics and atheists in India as well as elsewhere. "Realisation" is the one thing essential in the lives of the followers of Brahma. Faith is not necessary. Theosophy is a subject with which Kananda is not versed, nor is it a part of his creed unless he chooses to make it so. It is more of a separate study. Kananda never met Mme. Blavatsky, but has met Col. Olcott of the American Theosophical Society. He is also acquainted with Annie Besant. Speaking of the "fakirs" of India, the famous jugglers or musicians [magicians?], whose feats have made for them a world-wide reputation, Kananda told of a few episodes that had come within his observation and which almost surpass belief.

"Five months ago," he said, when questioned on this subject, "or just one month before I left India to come to this country, I happened in company in a caravan or party of 25 to sojourn for a space in a city in the interior. While there we learned of the marvellous work of one of these itinerant magicians and had him brought before us. He told us he would produce for us any article we desired. We stripped him, at his request, until he was quite naked and placed him in the corner of the room. I threw my travelling blanket about him and then we called upon him to do as he had promised. He asked what we should like, and I asked for a bunch of California [?] grapes, and straightway the fellow brought them forth from under his blanket. Oranges and other fruits were produced, and finally great dishes of steaming rice."

Continuing, the monk said he believed in the existence of a "sixth sense" and in telepathy. He offered no explanation of the feats of the fakirs, merely saying that they were very wonderful. The subject of idols came up and the monk said that idols formed a part of his religion insomuch as the symbol is concerned.

"What do you worship?" said the monk, "What is your idea of God?"

"The spirit," said a lady quietly.

"What is the spirit? Do you Protestants worship the words of the Bible or something beyond? We worship the God through the idol."

"That is, you attain the subjective through the objective," said a gentleman who had listened attentively to the words of the stranger.

"Yes, that is it," said the monk, gratefully.

Vivekananda discussed further in the same strain until the call terminated as the hour for the Hindu's lecture approached.

"I was born," he continued, in answer to a question, "in Bengal and become a monk and a celibate from choice. At my birth my father had a horoscope taken of my life, but would never tell me what it was. Some years ago when I visited my home, my father having died, I came across the chart among some papers in my mother's possession and saw from it that I was destined to become a wanderer on the face of the earth."

There was a touch of pathos in the speaker's voice and a murmur of sympathy ran around the group of listeners. Kananda[1] knocked the ashes from his cigar and was silent for a space.

Presently some one asked:

"If your religion is all that you claim it is, if it is the only true faith, how is it that your people are not more advanced in civilisation than we are? Why has it not elevated them among the nations of the world?" "Because that is not the sphere of any religion," replied the Hindu gravely. "My people are the most moral in the world, or quite as much as any other race. They are more considerate of their fellow man's rights, and even those of dumb animals, but they are not materialists. No religion has ever advanced the thought or inspiration of a nation or people. In fact, no great achievement has ever been attained in the history of the world that religion has not retarded. Your boasted Christianity has not proven an exception in this respect. Your Darwins, your Mills, your Humes, have never received the endorsement of your prelates. Why, then, criticise my religion on this account?" "I would not give a fig for a faith that does not tend to elevate mankind's lot on earth as well as his spiritual condition," said one of the group, 'and therein I am not prepared to admit the correctness of your statements. Christianity has founded colleges, hospitals and raised the degenerate. It has elevated the downcast and helped its followers to live." "You are right there to a certain extent," replied the monk calmly, "and yet it is not shown that these things are directly the result of your Christianity. There are many causes operating in the West to produce these results. "Religious thought should be directed to developing man's spiritual side. Science, art, learning and metaphysical research all have their proper functions in life, but if you seek to blend them, you destroy their individual characteristics until, in time, you eliminate the spiritual, for instance, from the religious altogether. You Americans

---

1. American reporters generally spelt his name as Vive Kananda in those days.

worship what? The dollar. In the mad rush for gold, you forget the spiritual until you have become a nation of materialists. Even your preachers and churches are tainted with the all-pervading desire. Show me one in the history of your people, who has led the spiritual lives that those whom I can name at home have done. Where are those who, when death comes, could say, 'O Brother Death, I welcome thee.' Your religion helps you to build Ferris wheels and Eiffel towers, but does it aid you in the development of your inner lives?"

The monk spoke earnestly, and his voice, rich and well modulated, came through the dusk that pervaded the apartment, half-sadly, half-accusingly. There was something of the weird in the comments of this stranger from a land whose history dates back 6,000 years upon the civilisation of the Nineteenth Century America. "But, in pursuing the spiritual, you lost sight of the demands of the present," said some one. "Your doctrine does not help men to live." "It helps them to die," was the answer.

"We are sure of the present."

"You are sure of nothing."

"The aim of the ideal religion should be to help one to live and to prepare one to die at the same time." "Exactly," said the Hindu, quickly, "and it is that which we are seeking to attain. I believe that the Hindu faith has developed the spiritual in its devotees at the expense of the material, and I think that in the Western world the contrary is true. By uniting the materialism of the West with the spiritualism of the East I believe much can be accomplished. It may be that in the attempt the Hindu faith will lose much of its individuality." "Would not the entire social system of India have to be revolutionised to do what you hope to do?" "Yet, probably, still the religion would remain unimpaired."

The conversation here turned upon the form of worship of the Hindus, and Kananda gave some interesting information on this subject. There are agnostics and atheists in India as well as elsewhere. "Realisation" is the one thing essential in the lives of the followers of Brahma. Faith is not necessary. Theosophy is a subject with which Kananda is not versed, nor is it a part of his creed unless he chooses to make it so. It is more of a separate study. Kananda never met Mme. Blavatsky, but has met Col. Olcott of the American Theosophical Society. He is also acquainted with Annie Besant. Speaking of the "fakirs" of India, the famous jugglers or musicians [magicians?], whose feats have made for them a world-wide reputation, Kananda told of a few episodes that had come within his observation and which almost surpass belief. "Five months ago," he said, when questioned on this subject, "or just one month before I left India to come to this country, I happened in company in a caravan or party of 25 to sojourn for a space in a city in the interior. While there we learned of the marvellous work of one of these itinerant magicians and had him brought before us. He told us he would produce for us any article we desired. We stripped him, at his request, until he was quite naked and

placed him in the corner of the room. I threw my travelling blanket about him and then we called upon him to do as he had promised. He asked what we should like, and I asked for a bunch of California [?] grapes, and straightway the fellow brought them forth from under his blanket. Oranges and other fruits were produced, and finally great dishes of steaming rice." Continuing, the monk said he believed in the existence of a "sixth sense" and in telepathy. He offered no explanation of the feats of the fakirs, merely saying that they were very wonderful. The subject of idols came up and the monk said that idols formed a part of his religion insomuch as the symbol is concerned.

"What do you worship?" said the monk, "What is your idea of God?" "The spirit," said a lady quietly.

"What is the spirit? Do you Protestants worship the words of the Bible or something beyond? We worship the God through the idol." "That is, you attain the subjective through the objective," said a gentleman who had listened attentively to the words of the stranger. "Yes, that is it," said the monk, gratefully.

Vivekananda discussed further in the same strain until the call terminated as the hour for the Hindu's lecture approached.

CONVERSATION XLVI: RELIGIOUS HARMONY (THE DETROIT FREE PRESS, FEBRUARY 14, 1894)

"I make the distinction between religion and creed. Religion is the acceptance of all existing creeds, seeing in them the same striving towards the same destination. Creed is something antagonistic and combative. There are different creeds, because there are different people, and the creed is adapted to the commonwealth where it furnishes what people want. As the world is made up of infinite variety of persons of different natures, intellectually, spiritually, and materially, so these people take to themselves that form of belief in the existence of a great and good moral law, which is best fitted for them. Religion recognizes and is glad of the existence of all these forms because of the beautiful underlying principle.

The same goal is reached by different routes and my way would not be suited perhaps to the temperament of my Western neighbour, the same that his route would not commend itself to my disposition and philosophical way of thinking. I belong to the Hindu religion. That is not the Buddhists' creed, one of the sects of the Hindu religion. We never indulge in missionary work. We do not seek to thrust the principles of our religion upon anyone. The fundamental principles of our religion forbid that. Nor do we say anything against any missionaries whom you send from this country anywhere. For all of us they are entirely welcome to penetrate the innermost recesses of the earth. Many come to us, but we do not struggle for them; we have no missionaries striving to bring anyone to our way of thinking. With no effort from us many forms of the Hindu religion are spreading far and wide, and these manifestations have taken the form of Christian science, theosophy, and Edwin Arnold's Light of Asia. Our religion is older than most religions and the Christian creed—i do not call it religion, because of its antagonistic features—came directly from the Hindu religion. It is one of the great offshoots. The Catholic religion also takes all its forms from us—the confessional, the belief in saints and so on—and a Catholic priest who saw this absolute similarity and recognised the truth of the origin of the Catholic religion was dethroned from his position because he dared to publish a volume explaining all that he observed and was convinced of." "You recognise agnostics in your religion?" was asked.

"Oh, yes; philosophical agnostics and what you call infidels. When Buddha, who is with us a saint, was asked by one of his followers: `Does God exist?' He replied: `God. When have I spoken to you about God? This I tell you, be good and do good.' The philosophical agnostics—there are many of us—believe in the great moral law underlying everything in nature and in the ultimate perfection. All the creeds which are accepted by all people are but the endeavours of humanity to realise that infinity of Self which lies in the great future." "Is it beneath the dignity of your religion to resort to missionary effort?"

For reply the visitor from the Orient turned to a little volume and referred to an edict among other remarkable edicts. "This," he said, "was written 200 B.C., and will be the best answer I can give you on that question."

In delightfully clear, well modulated tones, he read:

"The King Piyadasi, beloved of the gods, honours all sects, both ascetics and householders; he propitiates them by alms and other gifts, but he attaches less importance to gifts and honours than to endeavour to promote the essential moral virtues. It is true the prevalence of essential virtues differs in different sects, but there is a common basis. That is, gentleness, moderation in language and morality. Thus one should not exalt one's own sect and decry others, but tender them on every occasion the honour they deserve. Striving thus, one promotes the welfare of his own sect, while serving the others. Striving otherwise, one does not serve his own sect, while disserving others; and whosoever, from attachment to his own sect and with a view to promoting it, decries others, only deals rude blows to his own sect. Hence concord alone is meritorious, so that all bear and love to bear the beliefs of each other. It is with this purpose that this edict has been inscribed; that all people, whatever their fate may be, should be encouraged to promote the essential moral doctrines in each and mutual respects for all other sects. It is with this object that the ministers of religion, the inspectors and other bodies of officers should all work."

After reading this impressive passage Swami Vive Kananda remarked that the same wise king who had caused this edict to be inscribed had forbidden the indulgence of war, as its horrors were antagonistic to all the principles of the great and universal moral doctrine. "For this reason," remarked the visitor, "India has suffered in its material aspect. Where brute strength and bloodshed has advanced other nations, India has deprecated such brutal manifestations; and by the law of the survival of the fittest, which applies to nations as well as to individuals, it has fallen behind as a power on the earth in the material sense." "But will it not be an impossibility to find in the great combative Western countries, where such tremendous energy is needed to develop the pressing practical necessities of the nineteenth century, this spirit which prevails in placid India?"

The brilliant eyes flashed, and a smile crossed the features of the Eastern brother. "May not one combine the energy of the lion with the gentleness of the lamb?" he asked.

Continuing, he intimated that perhaps the future holds the conjunction of the East and the West, a combination which would be productive of marvellous results. A condition which speaks well for the natures of the Western nation is the reverence in which women are held and the gentle consideration with which they are treated.

He says with the dying Buddha, "Work out your own salvation. I cannot help you. No man can help you. Help yourself." Harmony and peace, and not dissension, is his watchword.

The following story is one which he related recently regarding the practice of fault-finding among creeds: "A frog lived in a well. It had lived there for a long time. It was born there and brought up there, and yet was a little, small frog. Of course the evolutionists were not there to tell us whether the frog lost its eyes or not, but, for our story's sake, we must take it for granted that it had eyes, and that it every day cleansed the waters of all the worms and bacilli that lived in it, with an energy that would give credit to our modern bacteriologists. In this way it went on and became a little sleek and fat—perhaps as much so as myself. Well, one day another frog that lived in the sea, came and fell into the well. "`Whence are you from?'

"`I am from the sea.'

"`The sea? How big is that? Is it as big as my well?' and he took a leap from one side of the well to the other. "`My friend,' says the frog of the sea, `how do you compare the sea with your little well?' "`Then the frog took another leap and asked; `Is your sea so big?' "`What nonsense you speak to compare the sea with your well.' "`Well, then,' said the frog of the well, `nothing can be bigger than my well; there can be nothing bigger than this; this fellow is a liar, so turn him out.' "That has been the difficulty all the while.

"I am a Hindu. I am sitting in my own little well, and thinking that the world is my well. The Christian sits in his little well and the whole world is his well. The Mohammedan sits in his well and thinks the whole world that. I have to thank you of America for the great attempt you are making to break down the barriers of this little world of ours, and hope that, in the future, the Lord will help you to accomplish that purpose."

CONVERSATION XLVII: FALLEN WOMEN (THE DETROIT TRIBUNE, MARCH 17, 1894)

The story of which the sentences that precede this one are a paragraph, was written in India. They were written by Rudyard Kipling, from whom most of us have learned all that we definitely know about India, with the exception of the fact that India raises wheat enough to be a great competitor of our own farmers, that men work there for two cents a day and that women throw their babies into the Ganga, which is the sacred river of the country.

But Vive Kananda, since he came to this country, has exploded the story about the women of India feeding their babies to the alligators, and now he says that he never heard of Rudyard Kipling until he came to America, and that it is not proper in India to talk of such a profession as that of Lalun, out of which Mr. Kipling has made one of his most delightful and instructive tales. "In India," said Kananda yesterday, "we do not discuss such things. No one ever speaks of those unfortunate women. When a woman is discovered to be unchaste in India, she is hurled out from her caste. No one thereafter can touch or speak to her. If she went into the house, they would take up and clean the carpets and wash the walls she breathed against. No one can have anything to do with such a person. There are no women who are not virtuous in Indian society. It is not at all as it is in this country. Here there are bad women living side by side with virtuous women in your society. One cannot know who is bad and who is good in America. But in India once a woman slips, she is an outcast for ever—she and her children, sons and daughters. It is terrible, I admit, but it keeps society pure." "How about the men?" was asked. "Does the same rule hold in regard to them? Are they outcast when they are proven to be unchaste?" "Oh, no. It is quite different with them. It would be so, perhaps, if they could be found out. But the men move about. They can go from place to place. It is not possible to discover them. The women are shut up in the house. They are certainly discovered if they do anything wrong. And when they are discovered, they are thrown out. Nothing can save them. Sometimes it is very hard when a father has to give up his daughter or a husband his wife. But if they do not give them up, they will be banished with them too. It is very different in this country. Women cannot go about there and make associations as they do here. It is very terrible, but it makes society pure. "I think that unchastity is the one great sin of your country. It must be so, there is so much luxury here. A poor girl would sell herself for a new bonnet. It must be so where there is so much luxury."

Mr. Kipling says this about Lalun and her profession:

"Lalun's real husband, for even ladies of Lalun's profession have husbands in the East, was a great, big jujube tree. Her mama, who had married a fig, spent ten thousand rupees on Lalun's wedding, which was blessed by forty-seven clergymen of mama's church, and distributed 5,000 rupees in charity to the poor. And that was a custom of the land."

In India when a woman is unfaithful to her husband she loses her caste, but none of her civil or religious rights. She can still own property and the temples are still open to her. 'Yes," said Kananda, "a bad woman is not allowed to marry. She cannot marry any one without their being an outcast like herself, so she marries a tree, or sometimes a sword. It is the custom. Sometimes these women grow very rich and become very charitable, but they can never regain their caste. In the interior towns, where they still adhere to the old customs, she cannot ride in a carriage, no matter how wealthy she may be; the best that she is allowed is a pair of bullocks. And then in India she has to wear a dress of her own, so that she can be distinguished. You can see these people going by, but no one ever speaks to them. The greatest number of these women is in the cities. A good many of them are Jews too, but they all have different quarters of the cities, you know. They all live apart. It is a singular thing that, bad as they are, wretched as some of these women are, they will not admit a Christian lover. They will not eat with them or touch them—the 'omnivorous barbarians', as they call them. They call them that because they eat everything. Do you know what that disease, the unspeakable disease, is called in India? It is called 'Bad Faringan', which means 'the Christian disease'. It was the Christian that brought it into India. "Has there been any attempt in India to solve this question? Is it a public question the way it is in America?" "No, there has been very little done in India. There is a great field for women missionaries if they would convert prostitutes in India. They do nothing in India—very little. There is one sect, the Veshnava [Vaishnava][1], who try to reclaim these women. This is a religious sect. I think about 90 per cent [?] of all prostitutes belong to this sect. This sect does not believe in caste and they go everywhere without reference to caste. There are certain temples, as the temple of Jagatnot [Jagannath], where there is no caste. Everybody who goes into that town takes off his caste while he is there, because that is holy ground and everything is supposed to be pure there. When he goes outside, he resumes it again, for caste is a mere worldly thing. You know some of the castes are so particular that they will not eat any food unless it is prepared by themselves. They will not touch any one outside their caste. But in the city they all live together. This is the only sect in India that makes proselytes. It makes everybody a member of its church. It goes into the Himalayas and converts the wild men. You perhaps did not know that there were wild men in India. Yes, there are. They dwell at the foot of the Himalayas." "Is there any ceremony by which a woman is declared unchaste, a civil process?" Kananda was asked. "No, it is not a civil process. It is just custom. Sometimes there is a formal ceremony and sometimes there is not. They simply make pariahs out of them. When any woman is suspected sometimes they get together and give her a sort of trial, and if it is decided that she is guilty, then a note is sent around to all the other members

1. Words in square brackets are ours.- ed.

of the caste, and she is banished. "Mind you," he exclaimed, "I do not mean to say that this is a solution of the question. The custom is terribly rigid. But you have no solution of the question, either. It is a terrible thing. It is a great wrong of the Western world."

INTERVIEWS

FIRST MEETING WITH MADAME EMMA CALVE

New Discoveries, Vol. 1, pp. 484-86.

The story of the first meeting of Swami Vivekananda and Madame Emma Calvé, as told in Calvé's autobiography, My Life.

…[Swami Vivekananda] was lecturing in Chicago one year when I was there; and as I was at that time greatly depressed in mind and body, I decided to go to him.

…Before going I had been told not to speak until he addressed me. When I entered the room, I stood before him in silence for a moment. He was seated in a noble attitude of meditation, his robe of saffron yellow falling in straight lines to the floor, his head swathed in a turban bent forward, his eyes on the ground. After a pause he spoke without looking up.

"My child", he said, "what a troubled atmosphere you have about you. Be calm. It is essential".

Then in a quiet voice, untroubled and aloof, this man who did not even know my name talked to me of my secret problems and anxieties. He spoke of things that I thought were unknown even to my nearest friends. It seemed miraculous, supernatural.

"How do you know all this?" I asked at last. "Who has talked of me to you?"

He looked at me with his quiet smile as though I were a child who had asked a foolish question.

"No one has talked to me", he answered gently. "Do you think that it is necessary? I read in you as in an open book."

Finally it was time for me to leave.

"You must forget", he said as I rose. "Become gay and happy again. Build up your health. Do not dwell in silence upon your sorrows. Transmute your emotions into some form of external expression. Your spiritual health requires it. Your art demands it."

I left him deeply impressed by his words and his personality. He seemed to have emptied my brain of all its feverish complexities and placed there instead his clear and calming thoughts. I became once again vivacious and cheerful, thanks to the effect of his powerful will. He did not use any of the hypnotic or mesmeric influences. It was the strength of his character, the purity and intensity of his purpose that carried conviction. It seemed to me, when I came to know him better, that he lulled one's chaotic thoughts into a state of peaceful acquiescence, so that one could give complete and undivided attention to his words.

FIRST MEETING WITH JOHN D. ROCKEFELLER

An excerpt from Madame Verdier's journal quoted in the New Discoveries, Vol. 1, pp. 487-88.

As told by Madame Emma Calvé, to Madame Drinette Verdier.

Mr. X, in whose home Swamiji was staying in Chicago, was a partner or an associate in some business with John D. Rockefeller. Many times John D. heard his friends talking about this extraordinary and wonderful Hindu monk who was staying with them, and many times he had been invited to meet Swamiji but, for one reason or another, always refused. At that time Rockefeller was not yet at the peak of his fortune, but was already powerful and strong-willed, very difficult to handle and a hard man to advise.

But one day, although he did not want to meet Swamiji, he was pushed to it by an impulse and went directly to the house of his friends, brushing aside the butler who opened the door and saying that he wanted to see the Hindu monk.

The butler ushered him into the living room, and, not waiting to be announced, Rockefeller entered into Swamiji's adjoining study and was much surprised, I presume, to see Swamiji behind his writing table not even lifting his eyes to see who had entered.

After a while, as with Calvé, Swamiji told Rockefeller much of his past that was not known to any but himself, and made him understand that the money he had already accumulated was not his, that he was only a channel and that his duty was to do good to the world—that God had given him all his wealth in order that he might have an opportunity to help and do good to people.

Rockefeller was annoyed that anyone dared to talk to him that way and tell him what to do. He left the room in irritation, not even saying goodbye. But about a week after, again without being announced, he entered Swamiji's study and, finding him the same as before, threw on his desk a paper which told of his plans to donate an enormous sum of money toward the financing of a public institution.

"Well, there you are", he said. "You must be satisfied now, and you can thank me for it."

Swamiji didn't even lift his eyes, did not move. Then taking the paper, he quietly read it, saying: "It is for you to thank me". That was all. This was Rockefeller's first large donation to the public welfare.

A DUSKY PHILOSOPHER FROM INDIA

New Discoveries, Vol. 5, pp. 389-94.

To preserve the historical authenticity of the newspaper reports in this section, their original spelling has been largely retained; however, their punctuation has been made consistent with the style of the Complete Works. — Publisher.

An interview by Blanche Partington, San Francisco Chronicle, March 18, 1900.

… Bowing very low in Eastern fashion on his entrance to the room, then holding out his hand in good American style, the dusky philosopher from the banks of the Ganges gave friendly greeting to the representative of that thoroughly Occidental institution, the daily press.

… I asked for a picture to illustrate this article, and when someone handed me a certain "cut" which has been extensively used in lecture advertisements here, he uttered a mild protest against its use.

"But that does not look like you", said I.

"No, it is as if I wished to kill someone", he said smiling, "like — like —"

"Othello", I inserted rashly. But the little audience of friends only smiled as the Swami made laughing recognition of the absurd resemblance of the picture to the jealous Moor. But I do not use that picture.

"Is it true, Swami", I asked, "that when you went home after lecturing in the Congress of Religions after the World's Fair, princes knelt at your feet, a half dozen of the ruling sovereigns of India dragged your carriage through the streets, as the papers told us? We do not treat our priests so".

"That is not good to talk of", said the Swami. "But it is true that religion rules there, not dollars."

"What about caste?"

"What of your Four Hundred?" he replied, smiling. "Caste in India is an institution hardly explicable or intelligible to the Occidental mind. It is acknowledged to be an imperfect institution, but we do not recognize a superior social result from your attempts at class distinction. India is the only country which has so far succeeded in imposing a permanent caste upon her people, and we doubt if an exchange for Western superstitions and evils would be for her advantage."

"But under such regime—where a man may not eat this nor drink that, nor marry the other—the freedom you teach would be impossible", I ventured.

"It is impossible", assented the Swami; "but until India has outgrown the necessity for caste laws, caste laws will remain". "Is it true that you may not eat food cooked by a foreigner—unbeliever?" I asked.

"In India the cook—who is not called a servant—must be of the same or higher caste than those for whom the food is cooked, as it is considered that whatever a man touches is impressed by his personality, and food, with which a man builds up the body through which he expresses himself, is regarded as being liable to such impression. As to the foods we eat, it is assumed that certain kinds of food nourish certain properties worthy of cultivation, and that others retard our spiritual growth. For instance, we do not kill to eat. Such food would be held to nourish the animal body, at the expense of the spiritual body, in which the soul is said to be clothed on its departure from this physical envelope, besides laying the sin of blood-guiltiness upon the butcher."

"Ugh!" I exclaimed involuntarily, an awful vision of reproachful little lambs, little chicken ghosts, hovering cow spirits—I was always afraid of cows anyway—rising up before me.

"You see", explained the Brahmin [Kshatriya], "the universe is all one, from the lowest insect to the highest Yogi. It is all one, we are all one, you and I are one —". Here the Occidental audience smiled, the unconscious monk chanting the oneness of things in Sanskrit and the consequent sin of taking any life.

… He was pacing up and down the room most of the time during our talk, occasionally standing over the register—it was a chill morning for this child of the sun—and doing with grace and freedom whatever occurred to him, even, at length, smoking a little.

"You, yourself, have not yet attained supreme control over all desires", I ventured. The Swami's frankness is infectious.

"No, madam", and he smiled the broad and brilliant smile of a child; "Do I look it?" But the Swami, from the land of hasheesh and dreams, doubtless did not connect my query with its smoky origin.

"Is it usual among the Hindoo priesthood to marry?" I ventured again.

"It is a matter of individual choice", replied this member of the Hindoo priesthood. "One does not marry that he may not be in slavery to a woman and children, or permit the slavery of a woman to him."

"But what is to become of the population?" urged the anti-Malthusian.

"Are you so glad to have been born?" retorted the Eastern thinker, his large eyes flashing scorn. "Can you conceive of nothing higher than this warring, hungry, ignorant world? Do not fear that the you may be lost, though the sordid, miserable consciousness of the now may go. What worth having [would be] gone?

"The child comes crying into the world. Well may he cry! Why should we weep to leave it? Have you thought"—here the sunny smile came back—"of the different modes of East and West of expressing the passing away? We say of the dead man, 'He gave up his body'; you put it, 'he gave up the ghost'. How can that be? Is it the dead body that permits the ghost to depart? What curious inversion of thought!"

"But, on the whole, Swami, you think it better to be comfortably dead than a living lion?" persisted the defender of populations.

"Swâhâ, Swaha, so be it!" shouted the monk.

"But how is it that under such philosophy men consent to live at all?"

"Because a man's own life is sacred as any other life, and one may not leave chapters unlearned", returned the philosopher. "Add power and diminish time, and the school days are shorter; as the learned professor can make the marble in twelve years which nature took centuries to form. It is all a question of time."

"India, which has had this teaching so long, has not yet learned her lesson?"

"No, though she is perhaps nearer than any other country, in that she has learned to love mercy."

"What of England in India?" I asked.

"But for English rule I could not be here now", said the monk, "though your lowest free-born American Negro holds higher position in India politically than is mine. Brahmin and coolie, we are all 'natives'. But it is all right, in spite of the misunderstanding and oppression. England is the Tharma [Karma?] of India, attracted inevitably by some inherent weakness, past mistakes, but from her blood and fibre will come the new national hope for my countrymen. I am a loyal subject of the Empress of India!" and here the Swami salaamed before an imaginary potentate, bowing very low, perhaps too low for reverence.

"But such an apostle of freedom—", I murmured.

"She is the widow for many years, and such we hold in high worth in India", said the philosopher seriously. "As to freedom, yes, I believe the goal of all development is freedom, law and order. There is more law and order in the grave than anywhere else—try it."

"I must go", I said. "I have to catch a train".

"That is like all Americans", smiled the Swami, and I had a glimpse of all eternity in his utter restfulness. "You must catch this car or that train always. Is there not another, later?"

But I did not attempt to explain the Occidental conception of the value of time to this child of the Orient, realizing its utter hopelessness and my own renegade sympathy. It must be delightful beyond measure to live in the land of "time enough". In the Orient there seems time to breathe, time to think, time to live; as the Swami says, what have we in exchange? We live in time; they in eternity.

"WE ARE HYPNOTIZED INTO WEAKNESS BY OUR SURROUNDINGS"

New Discoveries, Vol. 5, pp. 396-98.

An interview by the San Francisco Examiner, March 18, 1900.

Hindoo Philosopher Who Strikes at the Root of Some Occidental Evils and Tells How We Must Worship God Simply and Not with Many Vain Prayers.

...

One American friend he may be assured of—the Swami is a charming person to interview.

Pacing about the little room where he is staying, he kept the small audience of interviewer and friend entertained for a couple of hours.

"Tell you about the English in India? But I do not wish to talk of politics. But from the higher standpoint, it is true that but for the English rule I could not be here. We natives know that it is through the intermixture of English blood and ideas that the salvation of India will come. Fifty years ago, all the literature and religion of the race were locked up in the Sanskrit language; today the drama and the novel are written in the vernacular, and the literature of religion is being translated. That is the work of the English, and it is unnecessary, in America, to descant upon the value of the education of the masses."

"What do you think of the Boers War?" was asked.

"Oh! Have you seen the morning paper? But I do not wish to discuss politics. English and Boers are both in the wrong. It is terrible—terrible—the bloodshed! English will conquer, but at what fearful cost! She seems the nation of Fate."

And the Swami with a smile, began chanting the Sanskrit for an unwillingness to discuss politics.

Then he talked long of ancient Russian history, and of the wandering tribes of Tartary, and of the Moorish rule in Spain, and displaying an astonishing memory and research. To this childlike interest in all things that touch him is doubtless due much of the curious and universal knowledge that he seems to possess.

MARRIAGE

New Discoveries, Vol. 5, p. 138.

From Miss Josephine MacLeod's February 1908 letter to Mary Hale, in which she described Swami Vivekananda's response to Alberta Sturges's question:

ALBERTA STURGES: Is there no happiness in marriage?

SWAMI VIVEKANANDA: Yes, Alberta, if marriage is entered into as a great austerity—and everything is given up—even principle!

LINE OF DEMARCATION

New Discoveries, Vol. 5, p. 225.

From Mrs. Alice Hansbrough's reminiscences of a question-answer exchange following the class entitled "Hints on Practical Spirituality":

Q: Swami, if all things are one, what is the difference between a cabbage and a man?

A: Stick a knife into your leg, and you will see the line of demarcation.

GOD IS!

New Discoveries, Vol. 5, p. 276.

Alice Hansbrough's record of a question-answer session after a class lecture:

Q: Then, Swami, what you claim is that all is good?

A: By no means. My claim is that all is not—only God is! That makes all the difference.

RENUNCIATION

New Discoveries, Vol. 6, p. 11-12.

From Alice Hansbrough's reminiscences of a question-answer session following one of Swami Vivekananda's San Francisco classes pertaining to renunciation:

WOMAN STUDENT: Well, Swami, what would become of the world if everyone renounced?

SWAMI VIVEKANANDA: Madam, why do you come to me with that lie on your lips? You have never considered anything in this world but your own pleasure!

SHRI RAMAKRISHNA'S DISCIPLE

New Discoveries, Vol. 6, p. 12.

Mrs. Edith Allan described a teacher-student exchange in one of Swami Vivekananda's San Francisco classes:

SWAMI VIVEKANANDA: I am the disciple of a man who could not write his own name, and I am not worthy to undo his shoes. How often have I wished I could take my intellect and throw it into the Ganges!

STUDENT: But, Swami, that is the part of you I like best.

SWAMI VIVEKANANDA: That is because you are a fool, Madam—like I am.

THE MASTER'S DIVINE INCARNATION

New Discoveries, Vol. 6, p. 17.

From Mrs. Edith Allan's reminiscences:

SWAMI VIVEKANANDA: I have to come back once more. The Master said I am to come back once more with him.

MRS. ALLAN: You have to come back because Shri Ramakrishna says so?

SWAMI VIVEKANANDA: Souls like that have great power, Madam.

A PRIVATE ADMISSION

New Discoveries, Vol. 6, p. 121.

From Mrs. Edith Allan's reminiscences of Swami Vivekananda's stay in northern California, 1900:

WOMAN STUDENT: Oh, if I had only lived earlier, I could have seen Shri Ramakrishna!

SWAMI VIVEKANANDA (turning quietly to her): You say that, and you have seen me?

A GREETING

New Discoveries, Vol. 6, p. 136.

From Mr. Thomas Allan's reminiscences of Swami Vivekananda's visit to Alameda, California, 1900:

MR. ALLAN: Well, Swami, I see you are in Alameda!

SWAMI VIVEKANANDA: No, Mr. Allan, I am not in Alameda; Alameda is in me.

"THIS WORLD IS A CIRCUS RING"

New Discoveries, Vol. 6, p. 156.

From Mrs. Alice Hansbrough's reminiscences of Swami Vivekananda's conversation with Miss Bell at Camp Taylor, California, in May 1900:

MISS BELL: This world is an old schoolhouse where we come to learn our lessons.

SWAMI VIVEKANANDA: Who told you that? [Miss Bell could not remember.] Well, I don't think so. I think this world is a circus ring in which we are the clowns tumbling.

MISS BELL: Why do we tumble, Swami?

SWAMI VIVEKANANDA: Because we like to tumble. When we get tired, we will quit.

ON KALI

The Complete Works of Sister Nivedita, Vol. I, p. 118.

Sister Nivedita's reminiscence of a conversation with Swami Vivekananda at the time she was learning the Kâli worship:

SISTER NIVEDITA: Perhaps, Swamiji, Kali is the vision of Shiva! Is She?

SWAMI VIVEKANANDA: Well! Well! Express it in your own way. Express it in your own way!

TRAINING UNDER SHRI RAMAKRISHNA

The Complete Works of Sister Nivedita, Vol. I, pp. 159-60.

While on board a ship to England, Swami Vivekananda was touched by the childlike devotion of the ship's servants:

SWAMI VIVEKANANDA: You see, I love our Mohammedans!

SISTER NIVEDITA: Yes, but what I want to understand is this habit of seeing every people from their strongest aspect. Where did it come from? Do you recognize it in any historical character? Or is it in some way derived from Shri Ramakrishna?

SWAMI VIVEKANANDA: It must have been the training under Ramakrishna Paramahamsa. We all went by his path to some extent. Of course it was not so difficult for us as he made it for himself. He would eat and dress like the people he wanted to understand, take their initiation, and use their language. "One must learn", he said, "to put oneself into another man's very soul". And this method was his own! No one ever before in India became Christian and Mohammedan and Vaishnava, by turn!

MIRACLES

The Memphis Commercial, 15th January, 1894

Asked by the reporter for his impressions of America, he said:

"I have a good impression of this country especially of the American women. I have especially remarked on the absence of poverty in America."

The conversation afterward turned to the subject of religions. Swami Vive Kananda expressed the opinion that the World's Parliament of Religions had been beneficial in that it had done much toward broadening ideas.

"What", asked the reporter, "is the generally accepted view held by those of your faith as to the fate after death of one holding the Christian religion?"

"We believe that if he is a good man he will be saved. Even an atheist, if he is a good man, we believe must be saved. That is our religion. We believe all religions are good, only those who hold them must not quarrel."

Swami Vive Kananda was questioned concerning the truthfulness of the marvelous stories of the performance of wonderful feats of conjuring, levitation, suspended animation, and the like in India. Vive Kananda said:

"We do not believe in miracles at all but that apparently strange things may be accomplished under the operation of natural laws. There is a vast amount of literature in India on these subjects, and the people there have made a study of these things.

"Thought-reading and the foretelling of events are successfully practiced by the Hathayogis.

"As to levitation, I have never seen anyone overcome gravitation and rise by will into the air, but I have seen many who were trying to do so. They read books published on the subject and spend years trying to accomplish the feat. Some of them in their efforts nearly starve themselves and become so thin that if one presses his finger upon their stomachs he can actually feel the spine.

"Some of these Hathayogis live to a great age."

The subject of suspended animation was broached and the Hindu monk told the Commercial reporter that he himself had known a man who went into a sealed cave, which was then closed up with a trap door, and remained there for many years without food. There was a decided stir of interest among those who heard this assertion. Vive Kananda entertained not the slightest doubt of the genuineness of this case. He says that in the case of suspended animation, growth is for the time arrested. He says the case of the man in India who was buried with a crop of barley raised over his grave and who was finally taken out still alive is perfectly well authenticated. He thinks the studies which enabled persons to accomplish that feat were suggested by the hibernating animals.

Vive Kananda said that he had never seen the feat which some writers have claimed has been accomplished in India, of throwing a rope into the air and the thrower climbing up the rope and disappearing out of sight in the distant heights.

A lady present when the reporter was interviewing the monk said some one had asked her if he, Vive Kananda, could perform wonderful tricks, and if he had been buried alive as a part of his installation in the Brotherhood. The answer to both questions was a positive negative. "What have those things to do with religion?" he asked. "Do they make a man purer? The Satan of your Bible is powerful, but differs from God in not being pure."

Speaking of the sect of Hathayoga, Vive Kananda said there was one thing, whether a coincidence or not, connected with the initiation of their disciples, which was suggestive of the one passage in the life of Christ. They make their disciples live alone for just forty days.

AN INDIAN YOGI IN LONDON

The Westminster Gazette, 23rd October, 1895

Indian philosophy has in recent years had a deep and growing fascination for many minds, though up to the present time its exponents in this country have been entirely Western in their thought and training, with the result that very little is really known of the deeper mysteries of the Vedanta wisdom, and that little only by a select few. Not many have the courage or the intuition to seek in heavy translations, made greatly in the interests of philologists, for that sublime knowledge which they really reveal to an able exponent brought up in all the traditions of the East.

It was therefore with interest and not without some curiosity, writes a correspondent, that I proceeded to interview an exponent entirely novel to Western people in the person of the Swami Vivekananda, an actual Indian Yogi, who has boldly undertaken to visit the Western world to expound the traditional teaching which has been handed down by ascetics and Yogis through many ages and who in pursuance of this object, delivered a lecture last night in the Princes' Hall.

The Swami Vivekananda is a striking figure with his turban (or mitre-shaped black cloth cap) and his calm but kindly features.

On my inquiring as to the significance, if any, of his name, the Swami said: "Of the name by which I am now known (Swami Vivekananda), the first word is descriptive of a Sannyâsin, or one who formally renounces the world, and the second is the title I assumed — as is customary with all Sannyasins — on my renunciation of the world, it signifies, literally, 'the bliss of discrimination'."

"And what induced you to forsake the ordinary course of the world, Swami?" I asked.

"I had a deep interest in religion and philosophy from my childhood," he replied, "and our books teach renunciation as the highest ideal to which man can aspire. It only needed the meeting with a great Teacher—Ramakrishna Paramahamsa—to kindle in me the final determination to follow the path he himself had trod, as in him I found my highest ideal realised."

"Then did he found a sect, which you now represent?"

"No", replied the Swami quickly. "No, his whole life was spent in breaking down the barriers of sectarianism and dogma. He formed no sect. Quite the reverse. He advocated and strove to establish absolute freedom of thought. He was a great Yogi."

"Then you are connected with no society or sect in this country? Neither Theosophical nor Christian Scientist, nor any other?"

"None whatever!" said the Swami in clear and impressive tones. (His face lights up like that of a child, it is so simple, straightforward and honest.) "My teaching is my own interpretation of our ancient books, in the light which my Master shed upon them. I claim no supernatural authority. Whatever in my teaching may appeal to the highest intelligence and be accepted by thinking men, the adoption of that will be my reward." "All religions", he continued, "have for their object the teaching either of devotion, knowledge, or Yoga, in a concrete form. Now, the philosophy of Vedanta is the abstract science which embraces all these methods, and this it is that I teach, leaving each one to apply it to his own concrete form. I refer each individual to his own experiences, and where reference is made to books, the latter are procurable, and may be studied by each one for himself. Above all, I teach no authority proceeding from hidden beings speaking through visible agents, any more than I claim learning from hidden books or manuscripts. I am the exponent of no occult societies, nor do I believe that good can come of such bodies. Truth stands on its own authority, and truth can bear the light of day."

"Then you do not propose to form any society. Swami?" I suggested.

"None; no society whatever. I teach only the Self hidden in the heart of every individual and common to all. A handful of strong men knowing that Self and living in Its light would revolutionise the world, even today, as has been the case by single strong men before each in his day."

"Have you just arrived from India?" I inquired—for the Swami is suggestive of Eastern suns.

"No," he replied, "I represented the Hindu religion at the Parliament of Religions held at Chicago in 1893. Since then I have been travelling and lecturing in the United States. The American people have proved most interested audiences and sympathetic friends, and my work there has so taken root that I must shortly return to that country."

"And what is your attitude towards the Western religions, Swami?"

"I propound a philosophy which can serve as a basis to every possible religious system in the world, and my attitude towards all of them is one of extreme sympathy—my teaching is antagonistic to none. I direct my attention to the individual, to make him strong, to teach him that he himself is divine, and I call upon men to make themselves conscious of this divinity within. That is really the ideal—conscious or unconscious—of every religion."

"And what shape will your activities take in this country?"

"My hope is to imbue individuals with the teachings to which I have referred, and to encourage them to express these to others in their own way; let them modify them as they will; I do not teach them as dogmas; truth at length must inevitably prevail.

"The actual machinery through which I work is in the hands of one or two friends. On October 22, they have arranged for me to deliver an address to a British audience at Princes' Hall, Piccadilly, at 8-30 p.m. The event is being advertised. The subject will be on the key of my philosophy—'Self-Knowledge'. Afterwards I am prepared to follow any course that opens—to attend meetings in people's drawing-rooms or elsewhere, to answer letters, or discuss personally. In a mercenary age I may venture to remark that none of my activities are undertaken for a pecuniary reward."

I then took my leave from one of the most original of men that I have had the honour of meeting.

INDIA'S MISSION

Sunday Times, London, 1896

English people are well acquainted with the fact that they send missionaries to India's "coral strands". Indeed, so thoroughly do they obey the behest, "Go ye forth into all the world and preach the Gospel", that none of the chief British sects are behindhand in obedience to the call to spread Christ's teaching. People are not so well aware that India also sends missionaries to England.

By accident, if the term may be allowed, I fell across the Swami Vivekananda in his temporary home at 63 St. George's Road, S. W., and as he did not object to discuss the nature of his work and visit to England, I sought him there and began our talk with an expression of surprise at his assent to my request.

"I got thoroughly used to the interviewer in America. Because it is not the fashion in my country, that is no reason why I should not use means existing in any country I visit, for spreading what I desire to be known! There I was representative of the Hindu religion at the World's Parliament of Religions at Chicago in 1893. The Raja of Mysore and some other friends sent me there. I think I may lay claim to having had some success in America. I had many invitations to other great American cities besides Chicago; my visit was a very long one, for, with the exception of a visit to England last summer, repeated as you see this year, I remained about three years in America. The American civilisation is, in my opinion a very great one. I find the American mind peculiarly susceptible to new ideas; nothing is rejected because it is new. It is examined on its own merits, and stands or falls by these alone."

"Whereas in England—you mean to imply something?"

"Yes, in England, civilisation is older, it has gathered many accretions as the centuries have rolled on. In particular, you have many prejudices that need to be broken through, and whoever deals with you in ideas must lay this to his account."

"So they say. I gather that you did not found anything like a church or a new religion in America."

"That is true. It is contrary to our principles to multiply organizations, since, in all conscience, there are enough of them. And when organizations are created they need individuals to look after them. Now, those who have made Sannyâsa—that is, renunciation of all worldly position, property, and name—whose aim is to seek spiritual knowledge, cannot undertake this work, which is, besides, in other hands."

"Is your teaching a system of comparative religion?"

"It might convey a more definite idea to call it the kernel of all forms of religion, stripping from them the non-essential, and laying stress on that which is the real basis. I am a disciple of Ramakrishna Paramahamsa, a perfect Sannyâsin whose influence and ideas I fell under. This great Sannyasin never assumed the negative or critical attitude towards other religions, but showed their positive side—how they could be carried into life and practiced. To fight, to assume the antagonistic attitude, is the exact contrary of his teaching, which dwells on the truth that the world is moved by love. You know that the Hindu religion never persecutes. It is the land where all sects may live in peace and amity. The Mohammedans brought murder and slaughter in their train, but until their arrival peace prevailed. Thus the Jains, who do not believe in a God and who regard such belief as a delusion, were tolerated, and still are there today. India sets the example of real strength, that is meekness. Dash, pluck, fight, all these things are weakness."

"It sounds very like Tolstoy's doctrine; it may do for individuals, though personally I doubt it. But how will it answer for nations?"

"Admirably for them also. It was India's Karma, her fate, to be conquered, and in her turn, to conquer her conqueror. She has already done so with her Mohammedan victors: Educated Mohammedans are Sufis, scarcely to be distinguished from Hindus. Hindu thought has permeated their civilisation; they assumed the position of learners. The great Akbar, the Mogul Emperor, was practically a Hindu. And England will be conquered in her turn. Today she has the sword, but it is worse than useless in the world of ideas. You know what Schopenhauer said of Indian thought. He foretold that its influence would be as momentous in Europe, when it became well known, as the revival of Greek and Latin; culture after the Dark Ages."

"Excuse me saying that there do not seem many signs; of it just now."

"Perhaps not", said the Swami, gravely. "I dare say a good many people saw no signs of the old Renaissance and did not know it was there, even after it had come. But there is a great movement, which can be discerned by those who know the signs of the times. Oriental research has of recent years made great progress. At present it is in the hands of scholars, and it seems dry and heavy in the work they have achieved. But gradually the light of comprehension will break"

"And India is to be the great conqueror of the future? Yet she does not send out many missionaries to preach her ideas. I presume she will wait until the world comes to her feet?"

"India was once a great missionary power. Hundreds' of years before England was converted to Christianity, Buddha sent out missionaries to convert the world of Asia to his doctrine. The world of thought is being converted. We are only at the beginning as yet. The number of those who decline to adopt any special form of religion is greatly increasing, and this movement is among the educated classes. In a recent American census, a large number of persons declined to class themselves as belonging to any form of religion. All religions are different expressions of the same truth; all march on or die out. They are the radii of the same truth, the expression that variety of minds requires."

"Now we are getting near it. What is that central truth?"

"The Divine within; every being, however degraded, is the expression of the Divine. The Divinity becomes covered, hidden from view. I call to mind an incident of the Indian Mutiny. A Swami, who for years had fulfilled a vow of eternal silence, was stabbed by a Mohammedan. They dragged the murderer before his victim and cried out, 'Speak the word, Swami, and he shall die.' After many years of silence, he broke it to say with his last breath: 'My children, you are all mistaken. That man is God Himself.' The great lesson is, that unity is behind all. Call it God, Love, Spirit. Allah, Jehovah—it is the same unity that animates all life from the lowest animal to the noblest man. Picture to yourself an ocean ice-bound, pierced with many different holes. Each of these is a soul, a man, emancipated according to his degree of intelligence, essaying to break through the ice."

"I think I see one difference between the wisdom of the East and that of the West. You aim at producing very perfect individuals by Sannyasa, concentration, and so forth. Now the ideal of the West seems to be the perfecting of the social state; and so we work at political and social questions, since we think that the permanence of our civilisation depends upon the well-being of the people."

"But the basis of all systems, social or political," said the Swami with great earnestness, "rests upon the goodness of men. No nation is great or good because Parliament enacts this or that, but because its men are great and good. I have visited China which had the most admirable organisation of all nations. Yet today China is like a disorganised mob, because her men are not equal to the system contrived in the olden days. Religion goes to the root of the matter. If it is right, all is right."

"It sounds just a little vague and remote from practical life, that the Divine is within everything but covered. One can't be looking for it all the time."

"People often work for the same ends but fail to recognise the fact. One must admit that law, government, politics are phases not final in any way. There is a goal beyond them where law is not needed. And by the way, the very word Sannyasin means the divine outlaw, one might say, divine nihilist, but that miscomprehension pursues those that use such a word. All great Masters teach the same thing. Christ saw that the basis is not law, that morality and purity are the only strength. As for your statement that the East aims at higher self-development and the West at the perfecting of the social state, you do not of course forget that there is an apparent Self and a real Self."

"The inference, of course, being that we work for the apparent, you for the real?"

"The mind works through various stages to attain its fuller development. First, it lays hold of the concrete, and only gradually deals with abstractions. Look, too, how the idea of universal brotherhood is reached. First it is grasped as brotherhood within a sect—hard, narrow, and exclusive. Step by step we reach broad generalizations and the world of abstract ideas."

"So you think that those sects, of which we English are so fond, will die out. You know what the Frenchman said, 'England, the land of a thousand sects and but one sauce'."

"I am sure that they are bound to disappear. Their existence is founded on non-essentials; the essential part of them will remain and be built up into another edifice. You know the old saying that it is good to be born in a church, but not to die in it."

"Perhaps you will say how your work is progressing in England?"

"Slowly, for the reasons I have already named. When you deal with roots and foundations, all real progress must be slow. Of course, I need not say that these ideas are bound to spread by one means or another, and to many of us the right moment for their dissemination seems now to have come."

Then I listened to an explanation of how the work is carried on. Like many an old doctrine, this new one is offered without money and without price, depending entirely upon the voluntary efforts of those who embrace it.

The Swami is a picturesque figure in his Eastern dress. His simple and cordial manner, savouring of anything but the popular idea of asceticism, an unusual command of English and great conversational powers add not a little to an interesting personality ... His vow of Sannyasa implies renunciation of position, property, and name, as well as the persistent search for spiritual knowledge.

INDIA AND ENGLAND

India, London, 1896

During the London season, Swami Vivekananda has been teaching and lecturing to considerable numbers of people who have been attracted by his doctrine and philosophy. Most English people fancy that England has the practical monopoly of missionary enterprise, almost unbroken save for a small effort on the part of France. I therefore sought the Swami in his temporary home in South Belgravia to enquire what message India could possibly send to England, apart from the remonstrances she has too often had to make on the subject of home charges, judicial and executive functions combined in one person, the settlement of expenses connected with Sudanese and other expeditions.

"It is no new thing", said the Swami composedly, "that India should send forth missionaries. She used to do so under the Emperor Asoka, in the days when the Buddhist faith was young, when she had something to teach the surrounding nation."

"Well, might one ask why she ever ceased doing so, and why she has now begun again?"

"She ceased because she grew selfish, forgot the principle that nations and individuals alike subsist and prosper by a system of give and take. Her mission to the world has always been the same. It is spiritual, the realm of introspective thought has been hers through all the ages; abstract science, metaphysics, logic, are her special domain. In reality, my mission to England is an outcome of England's to India. It has been hers to conquer, to govern, to use her knowledge of physical science to her advantage and ours. In trying to sum up India's contribution to the world, I am reminded of a Sanskrit and an English idiom. When you say a man dies, your phrase is, 'He gave up the ghost', whereas we say, 'He gave up the body'. Similarly, you more than imply that the body is the chief part of man by saying it possesses a soul. Whereas we say a man is a soul and possesses a body. These are but small ripples on the surface, yet they show the current of your national thought. I should like to remind you how Schopenhauer predicted that the influence of Indian philosophy upon Europe would be as momentous when it became well known as was the revival of Greek and Latin learning at the close of the Dark Ages. Oriental research is making great progress; a new world of ideas is opening to the seeker after truth."

"And is India finally to conquer her conquerors?"

"Yes, in the world of ideas. England has the sword, the material world, as our Mohammedan conquerors had before her. Yet Akbar the Great became practically a Hindu; educated Mohammedans, the Sufis, are hardly to be distinguished from the Hindus; they do not eat beef, and in other ways conform to our usages. Their thought has become permeated by ours."

"So, that is the fate you foresee for the lordly Sahib? Just at this moment he seems to be a long way off it."

"No, it is not so remote as you imply. In the world of religious ideas, the Hindu and the Englishman have much in common, and there is proof of the same thing among other religious communities. Where the English ruler or civil servant has had any knowledge of India's literature, especially her philosophy, there exists the ground of a common sympathy, a territory constantly widening. It is not too much to say that only ignorance is the cause of that exclusive—sometimes even contemptuous—attitude assumed by some."

"Yes, it is the measure of folly. Will you say why you went to America rather than to England on your mission?"

"That was a mere accident—a result of the World's Parliament of Religions being held in Chicago at the time of the World's Fair, instead of in London, as it ought to have been. The Raja of Mysore and some other friends sent me to America as the Hindu representative. I stayed there three years, with the exception of last summer and this summer, when I came to lecture in London. The Americans are a great people, with a future before them. I admire them very much, and found many kind friends among them. They are less prejudiced than the English, more ready to weigh end examine anew idea, to value it in spite of its newness. They are most hospitable too; far less time is lost in showing one's credentials, as it were. You travel in America, as I did, from city to city, always lecturing among friends. I saw Boston, New York, Philadelphia, Baltimore, Washington, Des Moines, Memphis, and numbers of other places."

"And leaving disciples in each of them?"

"Yes, disciples, but not organizations. That is no part of my work. Of these there are enough in all conscience. Organisations need men to manage them; they must seek power, money, influence. Often they struggle for domination, and even fight."

"Could the gist of this mission of yours be summed up in a few words? Is it comparative religion you want to preach?"

"It is really the philosophy of religion, the kernel of all its outward forms. All forms of religion have an essential and a non-essential part. If we strip from them the latter, there remains the real basis of all religion, which all forms of religion possess in common. Unity is behind them all. We may call it God, Allah, Jehovah, the Spirit, Love; it is the same unity that animates all life, from its lowest form to its noblest manifestation in man. It is on this unity that we need to lay stress, whereas in the West, and indeed everywhere, it is on the non-essential that men are apt to lay stress. They will fight and kill each other for these forms, to make their fellows con-

form. Seeing that the essential is love of God and love of man, this is curious, to say the least."

"I suppose a Hindu could never persecute."

"He never yet has done so; he is the most tolerant of all the races of men. Considering how profoundly religious he is, one might have thought that he would persecute those who believe in no God. The Jains regard such belief as sheer delusion, yet no Jain has ever been persecuted. In India the Mohammedans were the first who ever took the sword."

"What progress does the doctrine of essential unity make in England? Here we have a thousand sects."

"They must gradually disappear as liberty and knowledge increase. They are founded on the nonessential, which by the nature of things cannot survive. The sects have served their purpose, which was that of an exclusive brotherhood on lines comprehended by those within it. Gradually we reach the idea of universal brotherhood by flinging down the walls of partition which separate such aggregations of individuals. In England the work proceeds slowly, possibly because the time is not yet ripe for it; but all the same, it makes progress. Let me call your attention to the similar work that England is engaged upon in India. Modern caste distinction is a barrier to India's progress. It narrows, restricts, separates. It will crumble before the advance of ideas.

"Yet some Englishmen, and they are not the least sympathetic to India nor the most ignorant of her history, regard caste as in the main beneficent. One may easily be too much Europeanised. You yourself condemn many of our ideals as materialistic."

"True. No reasonable person aims at assimilating India to England; the body is made by the thought that lies behind it. The body politic is thus the expression of national thought, and in India, of thousands of years of thought. To Europeanise India is therefore an impossible and foolish task: the elements of progress were always actively present in India. As soon as a peaceful government was there, these have always shown themselves. From the time of the Upanishads down to the present day, nearly all our great Teachers have wanted to break through the barriers of caste, i.e. caste in its degenerate state, not the original system. What little good you see in the present caste clings to it from the original caste, which was the most glorious social institution. Buddha tried to re-establish caste in its original form. At every period of India's awakening, there have always been great efforts made to break down caste. But it must always be we who build up a new India as an effect and continuation of her past, assimilating helpful foreign ideas wherever they may be found. Never can it be they; growth must proceed from within. All that England can do is to help India to work out her own salvation. All progress at the dictation of another, whose hand is at India's throat, is valueless in my opinion. The highest work can only degenerate when slave-labour produces it."

"Have you given any attention to the Indian National Congress movement?"

"I cannot claim to have given much; my work is in another part of the field. But I regard the movement as significant, and heartily wish it success. A nation is being made out of India's different races. I sometimes think they are no less various than the different peoples of Europe. In the past, Europe has struggled for Indian trade, a trade which has played a tremendous part in the civilisation of the world; its acquisition might almost be called a turning-point in the history of humanity. We see the Dutch, Portuguese, French, and English contending for it in succession. The discovery of America may be traced to the indemnification the Venetians sought in the far distant West for the loss they suffered in the East."

"Where will it end?"

"It will certainly end in the working out of India's homogeneity, in her acquiring what we may call democratic ideas. Intelligence must not remain the monopoly of the cultured few; it will be disseminated from higher to lower classes. Education is coming, and compulsory education will follow. The immense power of our people for work must be utilised. India's potentialities are great and will be called forth"

"Has any nation ever been great without being a great military power?"

"Yes," said the Swami without a moment's hesitation, "China has. Amongst other countries, I have travelled in China and Japan. Today, China is like a disorganised mob; but in the heyday of her greatness she possessed the most admirable organisation any nation has yet known Many of the devices and methods we term modern were practiced by the Chinese for hundreds and even thousands of years. Take competitive examination as an illustration."

"Why did she become disorganized?"

"Because she could not produce men equal to the system. You have the saying that men cannot be made virtuous by an Act of Parliament; the Chinese experienced it before you. And that is why religion is of deeper importance than politics, since it goes to the root, and deals with the essential of conduct."

"Is India conscious of the awakening that you allude to?"

"Perfectly conscious. The world perhaps sees it chiefly in the Congress movement and in the field of social reform; but the awakening is quite as real in religion, though it works more silently."

"The West and East have such different ideals of life. Ours seems to be the perfecting of the social state. Whilst we are busy seeing to these matters, Orientals are meditating on abstractions. Here has Parliament been discussing the payment of the Indian army in the Sudan. All the respectable section of the Conservative press has made a loud outcry against the unjust decision of the Government, whereas you probably think the whole affair not worth attention."

"But you are quite wrong", said the Swami, taking the paper and running his eyes over extracts from the Conservative Journals. "My sympathies in this matter are naturally with my country. Yet it reminds one of the old Sanskrit proverb: 'You have sold the elephant, why quarrel over the goad?' India always pays. The quarrels of politicians are very curious. It will take ages to bring religion into politics."

"One ought to make the effort very soon all the same."

"Yes, it is worth one's while to plant an idea in the heart of this great London, surely the greatest governing machine that has ever been set in motion. I often watch it working, the power and perfection with which the minutest vein is reached, its wonderful system of circulation and distribution. It helps one to realise how great is the Empire and how great its task. And with all the rest, it distributes thought. It would be worth a man's while to place some ideas in the heart of this great machine, so that they might circulate to the remotest part."

The Swami is a man of distinguished appearance. Tall, broad, with fine features enhanced by his picturesque Eastern dress, his personality is very striking. By birth, he is a Bengali, and by education, a graduate of the Calcutta University. His gifts as an orator are high. He can speak for an hour and a half without a note or the slightest pause for a word.

—C.S.B

INDIAN MISSIONARY'S MISSION TO ENGLAND

The Echo, London, 1896

...I presume that in his own country the Swami would live under a tree, or at most in the precincts of a temple, his head shaved, dressed in the costume of his country. But these things are not done in London, so that I found the Swami located much like other people, and, save that he wears a long coat of a dark orange shade, dressed like other mortals likewise. He laughingly related that his dress, especially when he wears a turban, does not commend itself to the London street arab, whose observations are scarcely worth repeating. I began by asking the Indian Yogi to spell his name very slowly...

"Do you think that nowadays people are laying much stress on the non-essential?"

"I think so among the backward nations, and among the less cultured portion of the civilised people of the West. Your question implies that among the cultured and the wealthy, matters are on a different footing. So they are; the wealthy are either immersed in the enjoyment of health or grubbing for more. They, and a large section of the busy people, say of religion that it is rot, stuff, nonsense, and they honestly think so The only religion that is fashionable is patriotism and Mrs. Grundy. People merely go to church when they are marrying or burying somebody."

"Will your message take them oftener to church?"

"I scarcely think it will. Since I have nothing whatever to do with ritual or dogma; my mission is to show that religion is everything and in everything... And what can we say of the system here in England? Everything goes to show that Socialism or some form of rule by the people, call it what you will, is coming on the boards. The people will certainly want the satisfaction of their material needs, less work, no oppression, no war, more food. What guarantee have we that this or any civilisation will last, unless it is based on religion, on the goodness of man? Depend on it, religion goes to the root of the matter. If it is right, all is right."

"It must be difficult to get the essential, the metaphysical, part of religion into the minds of the people. It is remote from their thoughts and manner of life."

"In all religions we travel from a lesser to a higher truth, never from error to truth. There is a Oneness behind all creation, but minds are very various. 'That which exists is One, sages call It variously.' What I mean is that one progresses from a smaller to a greater truth. The worst religions are only bad readings of the froth. One gets to understand bit by bit. Even devil-worship is but a perverted reading of the ever-true and immutable Brahman. Other phases have more or less of the truth in them. No form of religion possesses it entirely."

"May one ask if you originated this religion you have come to preach to England?"

"Certainly not. I am a pupil of a great Indian sage, Ramakrishna Paramahamsa. He was not what one might call a very learned man, as some of our sages are, but a very holy one, deeply imbued with the spirit of the Vedanta philosophy. When I say philosophy, I hardly know whether I ought not to say religion, for it is really both. You must read Professor Max Müller's account of my Master in a recent number of the Nineteenth Century. Ramakrishna was born in the Hooghly district in 1836 and died in 1886. He produced a deep effect on the life of Keshab Chandra Sen and others. By discipline of the body and subduing of the mind he obtained a wonderful insight into the spiritual world. His face was distinguished by a childlike tenderness, profound humility, and remarkable sweetness of expression. No one could look upon it unmoved."

"Then your teaching is derived from the Vedas?"

"Yes, Vedanta means the end of the Vedas, the third section or Upanishads, containing the ripened ideas which we find more as germs in the earlier portion. The most ancient portion of the Vedas is the Samhitâ, which is in very archaic Sanskrit, only to be understood by the aid of a very old dictionary, the Nirukta of Yâska."

"I fear that we English have rather the idea that India has much to learn from us; the average man is pretty ignorant as to what may be learnt from India."

"That is so, but the world of scholars know well how much is to be learnt and how important the lesson. You would not find Max Müller, Monier Williams, Sir William Hunter, or German Oriental scholars making light of Indian abstract science."

... The Swami gives his lecture at 39 Victoria Street. All are made welcome, and as in ancient apostolic times, the new teaching is without money and without price. The Indian missionary is a mall of exceptionally fine physique; his command of English can only be described as perfect.

—C.S.B

WITH THE SWAMI VIVEKANANDA AT MADURA

The Hindu, Madras, February, 1897

Q. — The theory that the universe is false seems to be understood in the following senses: (a) the sense in which the duration of perishing forms and names is infinitesimally small with reference to eternity; (b) the sense in which the period between any two Pralayas (involution of the universe) is infinitesimally small with reference to eternity; (c) the sense in which the universe is ultimately false though it has an apparent reality at present, depending upon one sort of consciousness, in the same way as the idea of silver superimposed on a shell or that of a serpent on a rope, is true for the time being, and, in effect, is dependent upon a particular condition of mind; (d) the sense in which the universe is a phantom just like the son of a barren woman or like the horns of a hare.

In which of these senses is the theory understood in the Advaita philosophy?

A. — There are many classes of Advaitists and each has understood the theory in one or the other sense. Shankara taught the theory in the sense (c), and it is his teaching that the universe, as it appears, is real for all purposes for every one in his present consciousness, but it vanishes when the consciousness assumes a higher form. You see the trunk of a tree standing before you, and you mistake it for a ghost. The idea of a ghost is for the time being real, for it works on your mind and produces the same result upon it as if it were a ghost. As soon as you discover it to be a stump, the idea of the ghost disappears. The idea of a stump and that of the ghost cannot co-exist, and when one is present, the other is absent.

Q. — Is not the sense (d) also adopted in some of the writings of Shankara?

A. — No. Some other men who, by mistake, carried Shankara's notion to an extreme have adopted the sense (d) in their writing. The senses (a) and (b) are peculiar to the writings of some other classes of Advaita philosophers but never received Shankara's sanction.

Q. — What is the cause of the apparent reality?

A. — What is the cause of your mistaking a stump for a ghost? The universe is the same, in fact, but it is your mind that creates various conditions for it.

Q. — What is the true meaning of the statement that the Vedas are beginningless and eternal? Does it refer to the Vedic utterances or the statements contained in the Vedas? If it refers to the truth involved in such statements, are not the sciences, such as Logic, Geometry, Chemistry, etc., equally beginningless and eternal, for they contain an everlasting truth?

A. — There was a time when the Vedas themselves were considered eternal in the sense in which the divine truths contained therein were changeless and permanent and were only revealed to man. At a subsequent time, it appears that the utterance of the Vedic hymns with the knowledge of its meaning was important, and it was held that the hymns themselves must have had a divine origin. At a still later period the meaning of the hymns showed that many of them could not be of divine origin, because they inculcated upon mankind performance of various unholy acts, such as torturing animals, and we can also find many ridiculous stories in the Vedas. The correct meaning of the statement "The Vedas are beginningless and eternal" is that the law or truth revealed by them to man is permanent and changeless. Logic, Geometry, Chemistry, etc., reveal also a law or truth which is permanent and changeless, and in that sense they are also beginningless and eternal. But no truth or law is absent from the Vedas, and I ask any one of you to point out to me any truth which is not treated of in them.

Q. — What is the notion of Mukti, according to the Advaita philosophy, or in other words, is it a conscious state? Is there any difference between the Mukti of the Advaitism and the Buddhistic Nirvâna?

A. — There is a consciousness in Mukti, which we call superconsciousness. It differs from your present consciousness. It is illogical to say that there is no consciousness in Mukti. The consciousness is of three sorts — the dull, mediocre, and intense — as is the case of light. When vibration is intense, the brilliancy is so very powerful as to dazzle the sight itself and in effect is as ineffectual as the dullest of lights. The Buddhistic Nirvana must have the same degree of consciousness whatever the Buddhists may say. Our definition of Mukti is affirmative in its nature, while the Buddhistic Nirvana has a negative definition.

Q. — Why should the unconditioned Brahman choose to assume a condition for the purpose of manifestation of the world's creation?

A. — The question itself is most illogical. Brahman is Avâng-manasogocharam, meaning that which is incapable of being grasped by word and mind. Whatever lies beyond the region of space, time and causation cannot be conceived by the human mind, and the function of logic and enquiry lies only within the region of space, time, and causation. While that is so, it is a vain attempt to question about what lies beyond the possibilities of human conception.

Q. — Here and there attempts are made to import into the Purânas hidden ideas which are said to have been allegorically represented. Sometimes it is said that the Puranas need not contain any historical truth, but are mere representations of the highest ideals illustrated with fictitious characters. Take for instance, Vishnupurâna, Râmâyana, or Bhârata. Do they contain historical veracity or are they mere allegorical representations of metaphysical truths, or are they representations of the highest ideals for the conduct of humanity, or are they mere epic poems such as those of Homer?

A. — Some historical truth is the nucleus of every Purana. The object of the Puranas is to teach mankind the sublime truth in various forms; and even if they do not contain any historical truth, they form a great authority for us in respect of the highest truth which they inculcate. Take the Râmâyana, for illustration, and for viewing it as an authority on building character, it is not even necessary that one like Rama should have ever lived. The sublimity of the law propounded by Ramayana or Bharata does not depend upon the truth of any personality like Rama or Krishna, and one can even hold that such personages never lived, and at the same time take those writings as high authorities in respect of the grand ideas which they place before mankind. Our philosophy does not depend upon any personality for its truth. Thus Krishna did not teach anything new or original to the world, nor does Ramayana profess anything which is not contained in the Scriptures. It is to be noted that Christianity cannot stand without Christ, Mohammedanism without Mohammed, and Buddhism without Buddha, but Hinduism stands independent of any man, and for the purpose of estimating the philosophical truth contained in any Purana, we need not consider the question whether the personages treated of therein were really material men or were fictitious characters. The object of the Puranas was the education of mankind, and the sages who constructed them contrived to find some historical personages and to superimpose upon them all the best or worst qualities just as they wanted to, and laid down the rules of morals for the conduct of mankind. Is it necessary that a demon with ten heads (Dashamukha) should have actually lived as stated in the Ramayana? It is the representation of some truth which deserves to be studied, apart from the question whether Dashamukha was a real or fictitious character. You can now depict Krishna in a still more attractive manner, and the description depends upon the sublimity of your ideal, but there stands the grand philosophy contained in the Puranas.

Q. — Is it possible for a man, if he were an adept, to remember the events connected with his past incarnations? The physiological brain, which he owned in his previous incarnation, and in which the impressions of his experience were stored, is no longer present. In this birth he is endowed with a new physiological brain, and while that is so, how is it possible for the present brain to get at the impressions received by another apparatus which is not existence at present?

Swami — What do you mean by an adept?

Correspondent — One that has developed the hidden powers of his nature.

Swami — I cannot understand how the hidden powers can be developed. I know what you mean, but I should always desire that the expressions used are precise and accurate. You may say that the powers hidden are uncovered. It is possible for those that have uncovered the hidden powers of their nature to remember the incidents connected with their past incarnations, for their present brain had its Bija (seed) in the Sukshma man after death.

Q.—Does the spirit of Hinduism permit the proselytism of strangers into it? And can a Brâhmin listen to the exposition of philosophy made by a Chandâla?

A.—Proselytism is tolerated by Hinduism. Any man, whether he be a Shudra or Chandala, can expound philosophy even to a Brahmin. The truth can be learnt from the lowest individual, no matter to what caste or creed he belongs.

Here the Swami quoted Sanskrit verses of high authority in support of his position.

The discourse ended, as the time appointed in the programme for his visiting the Temple had already arrived. He accordingly took leave of the gentlemen present and proceeded to visit the Temple.

THE ABROAD AND THE PROBLEMS AT HOME

The Hindu, Madras, February, 1897

Our representative met the Swami Vivekananda in the train at the Chingleput Station and travelled with him to Madras. The following is the report of the interview:

"What made you go to America, Swamiji?"

"Rather a serious question to answer in brief. I can only answer it partly now. Because I travelled all over India, I wanted to go over to other countries. I went to America by the Far East."

"What did you see in Japan, and is there any chance of India following in the progressive steps of Japan?"

"None whatever, until all the three hundred millions of India combine together as a whole nation. The world has never seen such a patriotic and artistic race as the Japanese, and one special feature about them is this that while in Europe and elsewhere Art generally goes with dirt, Japanese Art is Art plus absolute cleanliness. I would wish that every one of our young men could visit Japan once at least in his lifetime. It is very easy to go there. The Japanese think that everything Hindu is great and believe that India is a holy land. Japanese Buddhism is entirely different from what you see in Ceylon. It is the same as Vedanta. It is positive and theistic Buddhism, not the negative atheistic Buddhism of Ceylon.

"What is the key to Japan's sudden greatness?"

"The faith of the Japanese in themselves, and their love for their country. When you have men who are ready to sacrifice their everything for their country, sincere to the backbone—when such men arise, India will become great in every respect. It is the men that make the country! What is there in the country? If you catch the social morality and the political morality of the Japanese, you will be as great as they are. The Japanese are ready to sacrifice everything for their country, and they have become a great people. But you are not; you cannot be, you sacrifice everything only for your own families and possessions."

"Is it your wish that India should become like Japan?"

"Decidedly not. India should continue to be what she is. How could India ever become like Japan, or any nation for the matter of that? In each nation, as in music, there is a main note, a central theme, upon which all others turn. Each nation has a theme: everything else is secondary. India's theme is religion. Social reform and everything else are secondary. Therefore India cannot be like Japan. It is said that when 'the heart breaks', then the flow of thought comes. India's heart must break, and the flow of spirituality will come out. India is India. We are not like the Japanese, we are Hindus. India's very atmosphere is soothing. I have been working incessantly here, and amidst this work I am getting rest. It is only from spiritual work that we can get rest in India. If your work is material here, you die of—diabetes!"

"So much for Japan. What was your first experience of America, Swamiji?"

"From first to last it was very good. With the exception of the missionaries and 'Church-women' the Americans are most hospitable, kind-hearted, generous, and good-natured."

"Who are these 'Church-women' that you speak of, Swamiji?"

"When a woman tries her best to find a husband, she goes to all the fashionable seaside resorts and tries all sorts of tricks to catch a man. When she fails in her attempts, she becomes, what they call in America, an 'old maid', and joins the Church. Some of them become very 'Churchy'. These 'Church-women' are awful fanatics. They are under the thumb of the priests there. Between them and the priests they make hell of earth and make a mess of religion. With the exception of these, the Americans are a very good people. They loved me, and I love them a great deal. I felt as if I was one of them."

"What is your idea about the results of the Parliament of Religions?"

"The Parliament of Religions, as it seems to me, was intended for a 'heathen show' before the world: but it turned out that the heathens had the upper hand and made it a Christian show all around. So the Parliament of Religions was a failure from the Christian standpoint, seeing that the Roman Catholics, who were the organisers of that Parliament, are, when there is a talk of another Parliament at Paris, now steadily opposing it. But the Chicago Parliament was a tremendous success for India and Indian thought. It helped on the tide of Vedanta, which is flooding the world. The American people—of course, minus the fanatical priests and Church-women—are very glad of the results of the Parliament."

"What prospects have you, Swamiji, for the spread of your mission in England?"

"There is every prospect. Before many years elapse a vast majority of the English people will be Vedantins. There is a greater prospect of this in England than there is in America. You see, Americans make a fanfaronade of everything, which is not the case with Englishmen. Even Christians cannot understand their New Testament, without understanding the Vedanta. The Vedanta is the rationale of all religions. Without the Vedanta every religion is superstition; with it everything becomes religion."

"What is the special trait you noticed in the English character?"

"The Englishman goes to practical work as soon as he believes in something. He has tremendous energy for practical work. There is in the whole world no human being superior to the English gentleman or lady. That is really the reason of my faith in them. John Bull is rather a thick-headed gentleman to deal with. You must push and push an idea till it reaches his brain, but once there, it does not get out. In England, there was not one missionary or anybody who said anything against me; not one who tried to make a scandal about me. To my astonishment, many of my friends belong to the Church of England. I learn, these missionaries do not come from the higher classes in England. Caste is as rigorous there as it is here, and the English churchmen belong to the class of gentlemen. They may differ in opinion from you, but that is no bar to their being friends with you; therefore, I would give a word of advice to my countrymen, which is, not to take notice of the vituperative missionaries, now that I have known that they are. We have 'sized' them, as the Americans say. Non-recognition is the only attitude to assume towards them."

"Will you kindly enlighten me, Swamiji, on the Social Reform movements in America and England?"

"Yes. All the social upheavalists, at least the leaders of them, are trying to find that all their communistic or equalising theories must have a spiritual basis, and that spiritual basis is in the Vedanta only. I have been told by several leaders, who used to attend my lectures, that they required the Vedanta as the basis of the new order of things."

"What are your views with regard to the Indian masses?"

"Oh, we are awfully poor, and our masses are very ignorant about secular things. Our masses are very good because poverty here is not a crime. Our masses are not violent. Many times I was near being mobbed in America and England, only on account of my dress. But I never heard of such a thing in India as a man being mobbed because of peculiar dress. In every other respect, our masses are much more civilised than the European masses."

"What will you propose for the improvement of our masses?"

"We have to give them secular education. We have to follow the plan laid down by our ancestors, that is, to bring all the ideals slowly down among the masses. Raise them slowly up, raise them to equality. Impart even secular knowledge through religion."

"But do you think, Swamiji, it is a task that can be easily accomplished?"

"It will, of course, have gradually to be worked out. But if there are enough self-sacrificing young fellows, who, I hope, will work with me, it can be done tomorrow. It all depends upon the zeal and the self-sacrifice brought to the task."

"But if the present degraded condition is due to their past Karma, Swamiji, how do you think they could get out of it easily, and how do you propose to help them?"

The Swamiji readily answered "Karma is the eternal assertion of human freedom. If we can bring ourselves down by our Karma, surely it is in our power to raise ourselves by it. The masses, besides, have not brought themselves down altogether by their own Karma. So we should give them better environments to work in. I do not propose any levelling of castes. Caste is a very good thing. Caste is the plan we want to follow. What caste really is, not one in a million understands. There is no country in the world without caste. In India, from caste we reach to the point where there is no caste. Caste is based throughout on that principle. The plan in India is to make everybody a Brahmin, the Brahmin being the ideal of humanity. If you read the history of India you will find that attempts have always been made to raise the lower classes. Many are the classes that have been raised. Many more will follow till the whole will become Brahmin. That is the plan. We have only to raise them without bringing down anybody. And this has mostly to be done by the Brahmins themselves, because it is the duty of every aristocracy to dig its own grave; and the sooner it does so, the better for all. No time should be lost. Indian caste is better than the caste which prevails in Europe or America. I do not say it is absolutely good. Where would you be if there were no caste? Where would be your learning and other things, if there were no caste? There would be nothing left for the Europeans to study if caste had never existed! The Mohammedans would have smashed everything to pieces. Where do you find the Indian society standing still? It is always on the move. Sometimes, as in the times of foreign invasions, the movement has been slow, at other times quicker. This is what I say to my countrymen. I do not condemn them. I look into their past. I find that under the circumstances no nation could do more glorious work. I tell them that they have done well. I only ask them to do better."

"What are your views, Swamiji, in regard to the relation of caste to rituals?"

"Caste is continually changing, rituals are continually changing, so are forms. It is the substance, the principle, that does not change. It is in the Vedas that we have to study our religion. With the exception of the Vedas every book must change. The authority of the Vedas is for all time to come; the authority of every one of our other books is for the time being. For instance; one Smriti is powerful for one age, another for another age. Great prophets are always coming and pointing the way to work. Some prophets worked for the lower classes, others like Madhva gave to women the right to study the Vedas. Caste should not go; but should only be readjusted occasionally. Within the old structure is to be found life enough for the building of two hundred thousand new ones. It is sheer nonsense to desire the abolition of caste. The new method is— evolution of the old."

"Do not Hindus stand in need of social reform?"

"We do stand in need of social reform. At times great men would evolve new ideas of progress, and kings would give them the sanction of law. Thus social improvements had been in the past made in India, and in modern times to effect such progressive reforms, we will have first to build up such an authoritative power. Kings having gone, the power is the people's. We have, therefore, to wait till the people are educated, till they understand their needs and are ready and able to solve their problems. The tyranny of the minority is the worst tyranny in the world. Therefore, instead of frittering away our energies on ideal reforms, which will never become practical, we had better go to the root of the evil and make a legislative body, that is to say, educate our people, so that they may be able to solve their own problems. Until that is done all these ideal reforms will remain ideals only. The new order of things is the salvation of the people by the people, and it takes time to make it workable, especially in India, which has always in the past been governed by kings."

"Do you think Hindu society can successfully adopt European social laws?"

"No, not wholly. I would say, the combination of the Greek mind represented by the external European energy added to the Hindu spirituality would be an ideal society for India. For instance, it is absolutely necessary for you, instead of frittering away your energy and often talking of idle nonsense, to learn from the Englishman the idea of prompt obedience to leaders, the absence of jealousy, the indomitable perseverance and the undying faith in himself. As soon as he selects a leader for a work, the Englishman sticks to him through thick and thin and obeys him. Here in India, everybody wants to become a leader, and there is nobody to obey. Everyone should learn to obey before he can command. There is no end to our jealousies; and the more important the Hindu, the more jealous he is. Until this absence of jealousy and obedience to leaders are learnt by the Hindu, there will be no power of organization. We shall have to remain the hopelessly confused mob that we are now, hoping and doing nothing. India has to learn from Europe the conquest of external nature, and Europe has to learn from India the conquest of internal nature. Then there will be neither Hindus nor Europeans— there will be the ideal humanity which has conquered both the natures, the external and the internal. We have developed one phase of humanity, and they another. It is the union of the two that is wanted. The word freedom which is the watchword of our religion really means freedom physically, mentally, and spiritually."

"What relation, Swamiji, does ritual bear to religion?"

"Rituals are the kindergarten of religion. They are absolutely necessary for the world as it is now; only we shall have to give people newer and fresher rituals. A party of thinkers must undertake to do this. Old rituals must be rejected and new ones substituted."

"Then you advocate the abolition of rituals, don't you?"

"No, my watchword is construction, not destruction. Out of the existing rituals, new ones will have to be evolved. There is infinite power of development in everything; that is my belief. One atom has the power of the whole universe at its back. All along, in the history of the Hindu race, there never was any attempt at destruction, only construction. One sect wanted to destroy, and they were thrown out of India: They were the Buddhists. We have had a host of reformers— Shankara, Râmânuja, Madhva, and Chaitanya. These were great reformers, who always were constructive and built according to the circumstances of their time. This is our peculiar method of work. All the modern reformers take to European destructive reformation, which will never do good to anyone and never did. Only once was a modern reformer mostly constructive, and that one was Raja Ram Mohan Ray. The progress of the Hindu race has been towards the realisation of the Vedantic ideals. All history of Indian life is the struggle for the realisation of the ideal of the Vedanta through good or bad fortune. Whenever there was any reforming sect or religion which rejected the Vedantic ideal, it was smashed into nothing."

"What is your programme of work here?"

"I want to start two institutions, one in Madras and one in Calcutta, to carry out my plan; and that plan briefly is to bring the Vedantic ideals into the everyday practical life of the saint or the sinner, of the sage or the ignoramus, of the Brahmin or the Pariah."

Our representative here put to him a few questions relative to Indian politics; but before the Swami could attempt anything like an answer, the train steamed up to the Egmore platform, and the only hurried remark that fell from the Swami was that he was dead against all political entanglements of Indian and European problems. The interview then terminated.

THE MISSIONARY WORK OF THE FIRST HINDU SANNYASIN TO THE WEST AND HIS PLAN OF REGENERATION OF INDIA

Madras Times, February, 1897

For the past few weeks, the Hindu public of Madras have been most eagerly expecting the arrival of Swami Vivekananda, the great Hindu monk of world-wide fame. At the present moment his name is on everybody's lips. In the school, in the college, in the High Court, on the marina, and in the streets and bazars of Madras, hundreds of inquisitive spirits may be seen asking when the Swami will be coming. Large numbers of students from the mofussil, who have come up for the University examinations are staying here, awaiting the Swami, and increasing their hostelry bills, despite the urgent call of their parents to return home immediately. In a few days the Swami will be in our midst. From the nature of the receptions received elsewhere in this Presidency, from the preparations being made here, from the triumphal arches erected at Castle Kernan, where the "Prophet" is to be lodged at the cost of the Hindu public, and from the interest taken in the movement by the leading Hindu gentlemen of this city, like the Hon'ble Mr. Justice Subramaniya Iyer, there is no doubt that the Swami will have a grand reception. It was Madras that first recognised the superior merits of the Swami and equipped him for Chicago. Madras will now have again the honour of welcoming the undoubtedly great man who has done so much to raise the prestige of his motherland. Four year ago, when the Swami arrived here, he was practically an obscure individual. In an unknown bungalow at St. Thome he spent nearly two months, all along holding conversations on religious topics and teaching and instructing all comers who cared to listen to him. Even then a few educated young men with "a keener eye" predicted that there was something in the man, "a power", that would lift him above all others, that would pre-eminently enable him to be the leader of men. These young men, who were then despised as "misguided enthusiasts", "dreamy revivalists", have now the supreme satisfaction of seeing their Swami, as they love to call him, return to them with a great European and American fame. The mission of the Swami is essentially spiritual. He firmly believes that India, the motherland of spirituality, has a great future before her. He is sanguine that the West will more and more come to appreciate what he regards as the sublime truths of Vedanta. His great motto is "Help, and not Fight" "Assimilation, and not Destruction", "Harmony and Peace, and not Dissension". Whatever difference of opinion followers of other creeds may have with him, few will venture to deny that the Swami has done yeoman's service to his country in opening the eyes of the Western world to "the good in the Hindu". He will always be remembered as the first Hindu Sannyâsin who dared to cross the sea to carry to the West the message of what he believes in as a religious peace.

A representative of our paper interviewed the Swami Vivekananda, with a view to eliciting from him an account of the success of his mission in the West. The Swami very courteously received our representative and motioned him to a chair by his side. The Swami was dressed in yellow robes, was calm, serene, and dignified, and appeared inclined to answer any questions that might be put to him. We have given the Swami's words as taken down in shorthand by our representative.

"May I know a few particulars about your early life?" asked our representative.

The Swami said: "Even while I was a student at Calcutta, I was of a religious temperament. I was critical even at that time of my life, mere words would not satisfy me. Subsequently I met Ramakrishna Paramahamsa, with whom I lived for a long time and under whom I studied. After the death of my father I gave myself up to travelling in India and started a little monastery in Calcutta. During my travels, I came to Madras, where I received help from the Maharaja of Mysore and the Raja of Ramnad."

"What made Your Holiness carry the mission of Hinduism to Western countries?"

"I wanted to get experience. My idea as to the keynote of our national downfall is that we do not mix with other nations—that is the one and the sole cause. We never had opportunity to compare notes. We were Kupa-Mandukas (frogs in a well)."

"You have done a good deal of travelling in the West?"

"I have visited a good deal of Europe, including Germany and France, but England and America were the chief centres of my work. At first I found myself in a critical position, owing to the hostile attitude assumed against the people of this country by those who went there from India. I believe the Indian nation is by far the most moral and religious nation in the whole world, and it would be a blasphemy to compare the Hindus with any other nation. At first, many fell foul of me, manufactured huge lies against me by saying that I was a fraud, that I had a harem of wives and half a regiment of children. But my experience of these missionaries opened my eyes as to what they are capable of doing in the name of religion. Missionaries were nowhere in England. None came to fight me. Mr. Lund went over to America to abuse me behind my back, but people would not listen to him. I was very popular with them. When I came back to England, I thought this missionary would be at me, but the Truth silenced him. In England the social status is stricter than caste is in India. The English Church people are all gentlemen born, which many of the missionaries are not. They greatly sympathised with me. I think that about thirty English Church clergymen agree entirely with me on all points of religious discussion. I was agreeably surprised to find that the English clergymen, though they differed from me, did not abuse me behind my back and stab me in the dark. There is the benefit of caste and hereditary culture."

"What has been the measure of your success in the West?"

"A great number of people sympathised with me in America—much more than in England. Vituperation by the low-caste missionaries made my cause succeed better. I had no money, the people of India having given me my bare passage-money, which was spent in a very short time. I had to live just as here on the charity of individuals. The Americans are a very hospitable people. In America one-third of the people are Christians, but the rest have no religion, that is they do not belong to any of the sects, but amongst them are to be found the most spiritual persons. I think the work in England is sound. If I die tomorrow and cannot send any more Sannyasins, still the English work will go on. The Englishman is a very good man. He is taught from his childhood to suppress all his feelings. He is thickheaded, and is not so quick as the Frenchman or the American. He is immensely practical. The American people are too young to understand renunciation. England has enjoyed wealth and luxury for ages. Many people there are ready for renunciation. When I first lectured in England I had a little class of twenty or thirty, which was kept going when I left, and when I went back from America I could get an audience of one thousand. In America I could get a much bigger one, as I spent three years in America and only one year in England. I have two Sannyasins—one in England and one in America, and I intend sending Sannyasins to other countries.

"English people are tremendous workers. Give them an idea, and you may be sure that that idea is not going to be lost, provided they catch it. People here have given up the Vedas, and all your philosophy is in the kitchen. The religion of India at present is 'Don't-touchism'—that is a religion which the English people will never accept. The thoughts of our forefathers and the wonderful life-giving principles that they discovered, every nation will take. The biggest guns of the English Church told me that I was putting Vedantism into the Bible. The present Hinduism is a degradation. There is no book on philosophy, written today, in which something of our Vedantism is not touched upon—even the works of Herbert Spencer contain it. The philosophy of the age is Advaitism, everybody talks of it; only in Europe, they try to be original. They talk of Hindus with contempt, but at the same time swallow the truths given out by the Hindus. Professor Max Müller is a perfect Vedantist, and has done splendid work in Vedantism. He believes in re-incarnation."

"What do you intend doing for the regeneration of India?"

"I consider that the great national sin is the neglect of the masses, and that is one of the causes of our downfall. No amount of politics would be of any avail until the masses in India are once more well educated, well fed, and well cared for. They pay for our education, they build our temples, but in return they get kicks. They are practically our slaves. If we want to regenerate India, we must work for them. I want to start two central institutions at first—one at Madras and the other at Calcutta—for training young men as preachers. I have funds for starting the Calcutta one. English people will find funds for my purpose.

"My faith is in the younger generation, the modern generation, out of them will come my workers. They will work out the whole problem, like lions. I have formulated the idea and have given my life to it. If I do not achieve success, some better one will come after me to work it out, and I shall be content to struggle. The one problem you have is to give to the masses their rights. You have the greatest religion which the world ever saw, and you feed the masses with stuff and nonsense. You have the perennial fountain flowing, and you give them ditch-water. Your Madras graduate would not touch a low-caste man, but is ready to get out of him the money for his education. I want to start at first these two institutions for educating missionaries to be both spiritual and secular instructors to our masses. They will spread from centre to centre, until we have covered the whole of India. The great thing is to have faith in oneself, even before faith in God; but the difficulty seems to be that we are losing faith in ourselves day by day. That is my objection against the reformers. The orthodox have more faith and more strength in themselves, in spite of their crudeness; but the reformers simply play into the hands of Europeans and pander to their vanity. Our masses are gods as compared with those of other countries. This is the only country where poverty is not a crime. They are mentally and physically handsome; but we hated and hated them till they have lost faith in themselves. They think they are born slaves. Give them their rights, and let them stand on their rights. This is the glory of the American civilization. Compare the Irishman with knees bent, half-starved, with a little stick and bundle of clothes, just arrived from the ship, with what he is, after a few months' stay in America. He walks boldly and bravely. He has come from a country where he was a slave to a country where he is a brother.

"Believe that the soul is immortal, infinite and all-powerful. My idea of education is personal contact with the teacher - Gurugriha-Vâsa. Without the personal life of a teacher there would be no education. Take your Universities. What have they done during the fifty years of their existences. They have not produced one original man. They are merely an examining body. The idea of the sacrifice for the common weal is not yet developed in our nation."

"What do you think of Mrs. Besant and Theosophy?"

"Mrs. Besant is a very good woman. I lectured at her Lodge in London. I do not know personally much about her. Her knowledge of our religion is very limited; she picks up scraps here and there; she never had time to study it thoroughly. That she is one of the most sincere of women, her greatest enemy will concede. She is considered the best speaker in England. She is a Sannyâsini. But I do not believe in Mahâtmâs and Kuthumis. Let her give up her connection with the Theosophical Society, stand on her own footing, and preach what she thinks right."

Speaking of social reforms, the Swami expressed himself about widow-marriage thus: "I have yet to see a nation whose fate is determined by the number of husbands their widows get."

Knowing as he did that several persons were waiting downstairs to have an interview with the Swami, our representative withdrew, thanking the Swami for the kindness with which he had consented to the journalistic torture.

The Swami, it may be remarked, is accompanied by Mr. and Mrs. J. H. Sevier, Mr. T. G. Harrison, a Buddhist gentleman of Colombo, and Mr. J. J. Goodwin. It appears that Mr. and Mrs. Sevier accompany the Swami with a view to settling in the Himalayas, where they intend building a residence for the Western disciples of the Swami, who may have an inclination to reside in India. For twenty years, Mr. and Mrs. Sevier had followed no particular religion, finding satisfaction in none of those that were preached; but on listening to a course of lectures by the Swami, they professed to have found a religion that satisfied their heart and intellect. Since then they have accompanied the Swami through Switzerland, Germany, and Italy, and now to India. Mr. Goodwin, a journalist in England, became a disciple of the Swami fourteen months ago, when he first met him at New York. He gave up his journalism and devotes himself to attending the Swami and taking down his lectures in shorthand. He is in every sense a true "disciple", saying that he hopes to be with the Swami till his death.

REAWAKENING OF HINDUISM ON A NATIONAL BASIS

Prabuddha Bharata, September, 1898

In an interview which a representative of Prabuddha Bharata had recently with the Swami Vivekananda, that great Teacher was asked: "What do you consider the distinguishing feature of your movement, Swamiji?"

"Aggression," said the Swami promptly, "aggression in a religious sense only. Other sects and parties have carried spirituality all over India, but since the days of Buddha we have been the first to break bounds and try to flood the world with missionary zeal."

"And what do you consider to be the function of your movement as regards India?'

"To find the common bases of Hinduism and awaken the national consciousness to them. At present there are three parties in India included under the term 'Hindu' — the orthodox, the reforming sects of the Mohammedan period, and the reforming sects of the present time. Hindus from North to South are only agreed on one point, viz. on not eating beef."

"Not in a common love for the Vedas?"

"Certainly not. That is just what we want to reawaken. India has not yet assimilated the work of Buddha. She is hypnotised by his voice, not made alive by it."

"In what way do you see this importance of Buddhism in India today?"

"It is obvious and overwhelming. You see India never loses anything; only she takes time to turn everything into bone and muscle. Buddha dealt a blow at animal sacrifice from which India has never recovered; and Buddha asked people not to kill cows for sacrifice… not to kill beyond what they needed for consumption.', and cow-killing is an impossibility with us."[1]

"With which of the three parties you name do you identify yourself, Swamiji?"

"With all of them. We are orthodox Hindus," said the Swami, "but", he added suddenly with great earnestness and emphasis, "we refuse entirely to identify ourselves with 'Don't-touchism'. That is not Hinduism: it is in none of our books; it is an unorthodox superstition which has interfered with national efficiency all along the line."

"Then what you really desire is national efficiency?"

"Certainly. Can you adduce any reason why India should lie in the ebb-tide of the Aryan nations? Is she inferior in intellect? Is she inferior in dexterity? Can you look at her art, at her mathematics, at her philosophy, and answer 'yes'? All that is needed is that she should de-hypnotise herself and wake up from her age-long sleep to take her true rank in the hierarchy of nations."

"But India has always had her deep inner life. Are you not afraid, Swamiji, that in attempting to make her active you may take from her, her one great treasure?"

"Not at all. The history of the past has gone to develop the inner life of India and the activity (i.e. the outer life) of the West. Hitherto these have been divergent. The time has now come for them to unite. Ramakrishna Paramahamsa was alive to the depths of being, yet on the outer plane who was more active? This is the secret. Let your life be as deep as the ocean, but let it also be as wide as the sky.

"It is a curious thing", continued the Swami, "that the inner life is often most profoundly developed where the outer conditions are most cramping and limiting. But this is an accidental — not an essential — association, and if we set ourselves right here in India, the world will be 'tightened'. For are we not all one?"

"Your last remarks, Swamiji, raise another question. In what sense is Shri Ramakrishna a part of this awakened Hinduism?"

"That is not for me to determine", said the Swami. "I have never preached personalities. My own life is guided by the enthusiasm of this great soul; but others will decide for themselves how far they share in this attitude. Inspiration is not filtered out to the world through one channel, however great. Each generation should be inspired afresh. Are we not all God?"

"Thank you. I have only one question more to ask you. You have defined the attitude and function of your movement with regard to your own people. Could you in the same way characterise your methods of action as a whole?"

"Our method", said the Swami, "is very easily described. It simply consists in reasserting the national life. Buddha preached renunciation. India heard, and yet in six centuries she reached heir greatest height. The secret lies there. The national ideals of India are renunciation and service. Intensify her in those channels, and the rest will take carte of itself. The banner of the spiritual cannot be raised too high in this country. In it alone is salvation.

1. Source- http://qz.com/366659/history-says-most-hindus-never-had-any-beef-with-beef/

ON INDIAN WOMEN—THEIR PAST, PRESENT AND FUTURE

Prabuddha Bharata, December, 1898

It was early one Sunday morning, writes our representative, in a beautiful Himalayan valley, that I was at last able to carry out the order of the Editor, and call on the Swami Vivekananda, to ascertain something of his views on the position and prospects of Indian Women.

"Let us go for a walk", said the Swami, when I had announced my errand, and we set out at once amongst some of the most lovely scenery in the world.

By sunny and shady ways we went, through quiet villages, amongst playing children and across the golden cornfields. Here the tall trees seemed to pierce the blue above, and there a group of peasant girls stooped, sickle in hand, to cut and carry off the plume-tipped stalks of maize-straw for the winter stores. Now the road led into an apple orchard, where great heaps of crimson fruit lay under the trees for sorting, and again we were out in the open, facing the snows that rose in august beauty above the white clouds against the sky.

At last my companion broke the silence. "The Aryan and Semitic ideals of woman", he said, "have always been diametrically opposed. Amongst the Semites the presence of woman is considered dangerous to devotion, and she may not perform any religious function, even such as the killing of a bird for food: according to the Aryan a man cannot perform a religious action without a wife."

"But Swamiji!" said I—startled at an assertion so sweeping and so unexpected—"is Hinduism not an Aryan faith?"

"Modern Hinduism", said the Swami quietly, "is largely Paurânika, that is, post-Buddhistic in origin. Dayânanda Saraswati pointed out that though a wife is absolutely necessary in the Sacrifice of the domestic fire, which is a Vedic rite, she may not touch the Shâlagrâma Shilâ, or the household-idol, because that dates from the later period of the Purânas."

"And so you consider the inequality of woman amongst us as entirely due to the influence of Buddhism?"

"Where it exists, certainly," said the Swami, "but we should not allow the sudden influx of European criticism and our consequent sense of contrast to make us acquiesce too readily in this notion of the inequality of our women. Circumstances have forced upon us, for many centuries, the woman's need of protection. This, and not her inferiority, is the true reading of our customs."

"Are you then entirely satisfied with the position of women amongst us, Swamiji?"

"By no means," said the Swami, "but our right of interference is limited entirely to giving education. Women must be put in a position to solve their own problems in their own way. No one can or ought to do this for them. And our Indian women are as capable of doing it as any in the world."

"How do you account for the evil influence which you attribute to Buddhism?"

"It came only with the decay of the faith", said the Swami. "Every movement triumphs by dint of some unusual characteristic, and when it falls, that point of pride becomes its chief element of weakness. The Lord Buddha—greatest of men—was a marvellous organiser and carried the world by this means. But his religion was the religion of a monastic order. It had, therefore, the evil effect of making the very robe of the monk honoured. He also introduced for the first time the community life of religious houses and thereby necessarily made women inferior to men, since the great abbesses could take no important step without the advice of certain abbots. It ensured its immediate object, the solidarity of the faith, you see, only its far-reaching effects are to be deplored."

"But Sannyâsa is recognised in the Vedas!"

"Of course it is, but without making any distinction between men and women. Do you remember how Yâjnavalkya was questioned at the Court of King Janaka? His principal examiner was Vâchaknavi, the maiden orator—Brahmavâdini, as the word of the day was. 'Like two shining arrows in the hand of the skilled archer', she says, 'are my questions.' Her sex is not even commented upon. Again, could anything be more complete than the equality of boys and girls in our old forest universities? Read our Sanskrit dramas—read the story of Shakuntala, and see if Tennyson's 'Princess' has anything to teach us! "

"You have a wonderful way of revealing the glories of our past, Swamiji!"

"Perhaps, because I have seen both sides of the world," said the Swami gently, "and I know that the race that produced Sitâ—even if it only dreamt of her—has a reverence for woman that is unmatched on the earth. There is many a burden bound with legal tightness on the shoulders of Western women that is utterly unknown to ours. We have our wrongs and our exceptions certainly, but so have they. We must never forget that all over the globe the general effort is to express love and tenderness and uprightness, and that national customs are only the nearest vehicles of this expression. With regard to the domestic virtues I have no hesitation in saying that our Indian methods have in many ways the advantage over all others."

"Then have our women any problems at all, Swamiji?"

"Of course, they have many and grave problems, but none that are not to be solved by that magic word 'education'. The true education, however, is not yet conceived of amongst us."

"And how would you define that?"

"I never define anything", said the Swami, smiling. "Still, it may be described as a development of faculty, not an accumulation of words, or as a training of individuals to will rightly and efficiently. So shall we bring to the need of India great fearless women—women worthy to continue the traditions of Sanghamittâ, Lilâ, Ahalyâ Bâi, and Mirâ Bâi—women fit to be mothers of heroes, because they are pure and selfless, strong with the strength that comes of touching the feet of God."

"So you consider that there should be a religious element in education, Swamiji?"

"I look upon religion as the innermost core of education", said the Swami solemnly. "Mind, I do not mean my own, or any one else's opinion about religion. I think the teacher should take the pupil's starting-point in this, as in other respects, and enable her to develop along her own line of least resistance."

"But surely the religious exaltation of Brahmacharya, by taking the highest place from the mother and wife and giving it to those who evade those relations, is a direct blow dealt at woman?"

"You should remember", said the Swami, "that if religion exalts Brahmacharya for woman, it does exactly the same for man Moreover, your question shows a certain confusion in your own mind. Hinduism indicates one duty, only one, for the human soul. It is to seek to realise the permanent amidst the evanescent. No one presumes to point out any one way in which this may be done. Marriage or non-marriage, good or evil, learning or ignorance, any of these is justified, if it leads to the goal. In this respect lies the great contrast between it and Buddhism, for the latter's outstanding direction is to realise the impermanence of the external, which, broadly speaking, can only be done in one way. Do you recall the story of the young Yogi in the Mahâbhârata who prided himself on his psychic powers by burning the bodies of a crow and crane by his intense will, produced by anger? Do you remember that the young saint went into the town and found first a wife nursing her sick husband and then the butcher Dharma-Vyâdha, both of whom had obtained enlightenment in the path of common faithfulness and duty?"

"And so what would you say, Swamiji, to the women of this country?

"Why, to the women of this country." said the Swami, "I would say exactly what I say to the men. Believe in India and in our Indian faith. Be strong and hopeful and unashamed, and remember that with something to take, Hindus have immeasurably more to give than any other people in the world."

ON THE BOUNDS OF HINDUISM

Prabuddha Bharata, April, 1899

Having been directed by the Editor, writes our representative, to interview Swami Vivekananda on the question of converts to Hinduism, I found an opportunity one evening on the roof of a Ganga houseboat. It was after nightfall, and we had stopped at the embankments of the Ramakrishna Math, and there the Swami came down to speak with me.

Time and place were alike delightful. Overhead the stars, and around—the rolling Ganga; and on one side stood the dimly lighted building, with its background of palms and lofty shade-trees.

"I want to see you, Swami", I began, "on this matter of receiving back into Hinduism those who have been perverted from it. Is it your opinion that they should be received?"

"Certainly," said the Swami, "they can and ought to be taken."

He sat gravely for a moment, thinking, and then resumed. "Besides," he said, "we shall otherwise decrease in numbers. When the Mohammedans first came, we are said—I think on the authority of Ferishta, the oldest Mohammedan historian—to have been six hundred millions of Hindus. Now we are about two hundred millions. And then every man going out of the Hindu pale is not only a man less, but an enemy the more.

"Again, the vast majority of Hindu perverts to Islam and Christianity are perverts by the sword, or the descendants of these. It would be obviously unfair to subject these to disabilities of any kind. As to the case of born aliens, did you say? Why, born aliens have been converted in the past by crowds, and the process is still going on.

"In my own opinion, this statement not only applies to aboriginal tribes, to outlying nations, and to almost all our conquerors before the Mohammedan conquest, but also in the Purânas. I hold that they have been aliens thus adopted.

"Ceremonies of expiation are no doubt suitable in the case of willing converts, returning to their Mother-Church, as it were; but on those who were alienated by conquest—as in Kashmir and Nepal—or on strangers wishing to join us, no penance should be imposed."

"But of what caste would these people be, Swamiji?" I ventured to ask. "They must have some, or they can never be assimilated into the great body of Hindus. Where shall we look for their rightful place?"

"Returning converts", said the Swami quietly, "will gain their own castes, of course. And new people will make theirs. You will remember," he added, "that this has already been done in the case of Vaishnavism. Converts from different castes and aliens were all able to combine under that flag and form a caste by themselves—and a very respectable one too. From Râmânuja down to Chaitanya of Bengal, all great Vaishnava Teachers have done the same."

"And where should these new people expect to marry?" I asked.

"Amongst themselves, as they do now", said the Swami quietly.

"Then as to names," I enquired, "I suppose aliens and perverts who have adopted non-Hindu names should be named newly. Would you give them caste-names, or what?"

"Certainly," said the Swami, thoughtfully, "there is a great deal in a name!" and on this question he would say no more.

But my next enquiry drew blood. "Would you leave these new-comers, Swamiji, to choose their own form of religious belief out of many-visaged Hinduism, or would you chalk out a religion for them?"

"Can you ask that?" he said. "They will choose for themselves. For unless a man chooses for himself, the very spirit of Hinduism is destroyed. The essence of our Faith consists simply in this freedom of the Ishta."

I thought the utterance a weighty one, for the man before me has spent more years than any one else living I fancy, in studying the common bases of Hinduism in a scientific and sympathetic spirit—and the freedom of the Ishta is obviously a principle big enough to accommodate the world.

But the talk passed to other matters, and then with a cordial good night this great teacher of religion lifted his lantern and went back into the monastery, while I by the pathless paths of the Ganga, in and out amongst her crafts of many sizes, made the best of my way back to my Calcutta home.

WRITINGS & PROSE

IS THE SOUL IMMORTAL?[1]

"None has power to destroy the unchangeable."
— *Bhagavad-Gîtâ.*

In the great Sanskrit epic, the Mahâbhârata, the story is told how the hero, Yudhishthira, when asked by Dharma to tell what was the most wonderful thing in the world, replied, that it was the persistent belief of man kind in their own deathlessness in spite of their witnessing death everywhere around them almost every moment of their lives. And, in fact, this is the most stupendous wonder in human life. In spite of all arguments to the contrary urged in different times by different schools, in spite of the inability of reason to penetrate the veil of mystery which will ever hang between the sensuous and the supersensuous worlds, man is thoroughly persuaded that he cannot die.

We may study all our lives, and in the end fail to bring the problem of life and death to the plane of rational demonstration, affirmative or negative. We may talk or write, preach or teach, for or against the permanency or impermanency of human existence as much as we like; we may become violent partisans of this side or that; we may invent names by the hundred, each more intricate than its predecessor, and lull ourselves into a momentary rest under the delusion of our having solved the problem once for all; we may cling with all our powers to any one of the curious religious superstitions or the far more objectionable scientific superstitions — but in the end, we find ourselves playing an external game in the bowling alley of reason and raising intellectual pin after pin, only to be knocked over again and again.

But behind all this mental strain and torture, not infrequently productive of more dangerous results than mere games, stands a fact unchallenged and unchallengeable — the fact, the wonder, which the Mahabharata points out as the inability of our mind to conceive our own annihilation. Even to imagine my own annihilation I shall have to stand by and look on as a witness.

Now, before trying to understand what this curious phenomenon means, we want to note that upon this one fact the whole world stands. The permanence of the external world is inevitably joined to the permanence of the internal; and, however plausible any theory of the universe may seem which asserts the permanence of the one and denies that of the other, the theorist himself will find that in his own mechanism not one conscious action is possible, without the permanence of both the internal and the external worlds being one of the factors in the motive cause. Although it is perfectly true that when the human mind transcends its own limitations, it finds the duality reduced to an indivisible unity, on this side of the unconditioned, the whole objective world — that is to say, the world we know — is and can be alone known to us as existing for the subject, and therefore, before we would be able to conceive the annihilation of the subject we are bound to conceive the annihilation of the object.

So far it is plain enough. But now comes the difficulty. I cannot think of myself ordinarily as anything else but a body. My idea of my own permanence includes my idea of myself as a body. But the body is obviously impermanent, as is the whole of nature — a constantly vanishing quantity.

Where, then, is this permanence?

There is one more wonderful phenomenon connected with our lives, without which "who will be able to live, who will be able to enjoy life a moment?" — the idea of freedom.

This is the idea that guides each footstep of ours, makes our movements possible, determines our relations to each other — nay, is the very warp and woof in the fabric of human life. Intellectual knowledge tries to drive it inch by inch from its territory, post after post is snatched away from its domains, and each step is made fast and ironbound with the railroadings of cause and effect. But it laughs at all our attempts, and, lo, it keeps itself above all this massive pile of law and causation with which we tried to smother it to death! How can it be otherwise? The limited always requires a higher generalization of the unlimited to explain itself. The bound can only be explained by the free, the caused by the uncaused. But again, the same difficulty is also here. What is free? The body or even the mind? It is apparent to all that they are as much bound by law as anything else in the universe.

Now the problem resolves itself into this dilemma: either the whole universe is a mass of never-ceasing change and nothing more, irrevocably bound by the law of causation, not one particle having a unity of itself, yet is curiously producing an ineradicable delusion of permanence and freedom, or there is in us and in the universe something which is permanent and free, showing that the basal constitutional belief of the human mind is not a delusion. It is the duty of science to explain facts by bringing them to a higher generalization. Any explanation, therefore that first wants to destroy a part of the fact given to be explained, in order to fit itself to the remainder, is not scientific, whatever else it may be.

So any explanation that wants to overlook the fact of this persistent and all-necessary idea of freedom commits the above-mentioned mistake of denying a portion of the fact in order to explain the rest, and is, therefore, wrong. The only other alternative possible, then, is to acknowledge, in harmony with our nature, that there is something in us which is free and permanent.

But it is not the body; neither is it the mind. The body is dying every minute. The mind is constantly changing. The body is a combination, and so is the mind, and as such can never reach to a state beyond all change. But beyond this momentary sheathing of gross matter, beyond even the finer covering of the mind is the Âtman, the true Self of man, the permanent, the ever free. It is his freedom that is percolat-

1. The Swamiji's contribution to the discussion of this question, carried on in the pages of *The New York Morning Advertiser.*

ing through layers of thought and matter, and, in spite of the colourings of name and form, is ever asserting its unshackled existence. It is his deathlessness, his bliss, his peace, his divinity that shines out and makes itself felt in spite of the thickest layers of ignorance. He is the real man, the fearless one, the deathless one, the free.

Now freedom is only possible when no external power can exert any influence, produce any change. Freedom is only possible to the being who is beyond all conditions, all laws, all bondages of cause and effect. In other words, the unchangeable alone can be free and, therefore, immortal. This Being, this Atman, this real Self of man, the free, the unchangeable is beyond all conditions, and as such, it has neither birth nor death.

"Without birth or death, eternal, ever-existing is this soul of man."

REINCARNATION[1]

"Both you and I have passed through many births;
you know them not, I know them all."
— *Bhagavad-Gîtâ*

Of the many riddles that have perplexed the intellect of man in all climes and times, the most intricate is himself. Of the myriad mysteries that have called forth his energies to struggle for solution from the very dawn of history, the most mysterious is his own nature. It is at once the most insoluble enigma and the problem of all problems. As the starting-point and the repository of all we know and feel and do, there never has been, nor will be, a time when man's own nature will cease to demand his best and foremost attention.

Though through hunger after that truth, which of all others has the most intimate connection with his very existence, though through an all-absorbing desire for an inward standard by which to measure the outward universe though through the absolute and inherent necessity of finding a fixed point in a universe of change, man has sometimes clutched at handfuls of dust for gold, and even when urged on by a voice higher than reason or intellect, he has many times failed rightly to interpret the real meaning of the divinity within—still there never was a time since the search began, when some race, or some individuals, did not hold aloft the lamp of truth.

Taking a one-sided, cursory and prejudiced view of the surroundings and the unessential details, sometimes disgusted also with the vagueness of many schools and sects, and often, alas, driven to the opposite extreme by the violent superstitions of organised priestcraft—men have not been wanting, especially among advanced intellects, in either ancient or modern times, who not only gave up the search in despair, but declared it fruitless and useless. Philosophers might fret and sneer, and priests ply their trade even at the point of the sword, but truth comes to those alone who worship at her

1. Contributed to the *Metaphysical Magazine*, New York, March, 1895

shrine for her sake only, without fear and without shopkeeping.

Light comes to individuals through the conscious efforts of their intellect; it comes, slowly though, to the whole race through unconscious percolations. The philosophers show the volitional struggles of great minds; history reveals the silent process of permeation through which truth is absorbed by the masses.

Of all the theories that have been held by man about himself, that of a soul entity, separate from the body and immortal, has been the most widespread; and among those that held the belief in such a soul, the majority of the thoughtful had always believed also in its pre-existence.

At present the greater portion of the human race, having organised religion, believe in it; and many of the best thinkers in the most favoured lands, though nurtured in religions avowedly hostile to every idea of the preexistence of the soul, have endorsed it. Hinduism and Buddhism have it for their foundation; the educated classes among the ancient Egyptians believed in it; the ancient Persians arrived at it; the Greek philosophers made it the corner-stone of their philosophy; the Pharisees among the Hebrews accepted it; and the Sufis among the Mohammedans almost universally acknowledged its truth.

There must be peculiar surroundings which generate and foster certain forms of belief among nations. It required ages for the ancient races to arrive at any idea about a part, even of the body, surviving after death; it took ages more to come to any rational idea about this something which persists and lives apart from the body. It was only when the idea was reached of an entity whose connection with the body was only for a time, and only among those nations who arrived at such a conclusion, that the unavoidable question arose: Whither? Whence?

The ancient Hebrews never disturbed their equanimity by questioning themselves about the soul. With them death ended all. Karl Heckel justly says, "Though it is true that in the Old Testament, preceding the exile, the Hebrews distinguish a life-principle, different from the body, which is sometimes called 'Nephesh', or 'Ruakh', or 'Neshama', yet all these words correspond rather to the idea of breath than to that of spirit or soul. Also in the writings of the Palestinean Jews, after the exile, there is never made mention of an individual immortal soul, but always only of a life-breath emanating from God, which, after the body is dissolved, is reabsorbed into the Divine 'Ruakh'."

The ancient Egyptians and the Chaldeans had peculiar beliefs of their own about the soul; but their ideas about this living part after death must not be confused with those of the ancient Hindu, the Persian, the Greek, or any other Aryan race. There was, from the earliest times, a broad distinction between the Âryas and the non-Sanskrit speaking Mlechchhas in the conception of the soul. Externally it was typified by their disposal of the dead—the Mlechchhas mostly trying their best to preserve the dead bodies either by careful burial or by the more elaborate processes of mummifying, and the Aryas generally burning their dead.

Herein lies the key to a great secret—the fact that no Mlechchha race, whether Egyptian, Assyrian, or Babylonian, ever attained to the idea of the soul as a separate entity which can live independent of the body, without he help of the Aryas, especially of the Hindus.

Although Herodotus states that the Egyptians were the first to conceive the idea of the immortality of the soul, and states as a doctrine of the Egyptians "that the soul after the dissolution of the body enters again and again into a creature that comes to life; then, that the soul wanders through all the animals of the land and the sea and through all the birds, and finally after three thousand years returns to a human body," yet, modern researches into Egyptology have hitherto found no trace of metempsychosis in the popular Egyptian religion. On the other hand, the most recent researches of Maspero, A. Erman, and other eminent Egyptologists tend to confirm the supposition that the doctrine of palingenesis was not at home with the Egyptians.

With the ancient Egyptians the soul was only a double, having no individuality of its own, and never able to break its connection with the body. It persists only so long as the body lasts; and if by chance the corpse is destroyed, the departed soul must suffer a second death and annihilation. The soul after death was allowed to roam freely all over the world, but always returning at night to where the corpse was, always miserable, always hungry and thirsty, always extremely desirous to enjoy life once more, and never being able to fulfil the desire. If any part of its old body was injured, the soul was also invariably injured in its corresponding part. And this idea explains the solicitude of the ancient Egyptians to preserve their dead. At first the deserts were chosen as the burial-place, because the dryness of the air did not allow the body to perish soon, thus granting to the departed soul a long lease of existence. In course of time one of the gods discovered the process of making mummies, through which the devout hoped to preserve the dead bodies of their ancestors for almost an infinite length of time, thus securing immortality to the departed ghost, however miserable it might be.

The perpetual regret for the world, in which the soul can take no further interest, never ceased to torture the deceased. "O. my brother," exclaims the departed "withhold not thyself from drinking and eating, from drunkenness, from love, from all enjoyment, from following thy desire by night and by day; put not sorrow within thy heart, for, what are the years of man upon earth? The West is a land of sleep and of heavy shadows, a place wherein the inhabitants, when once installed, slumber on in their mummy forms, never more waking to see their brethren; never more to recognise their fathers and mothers, with hearts forgetful of their wives and children The living water, which earth giveth to all who dwell upon it, is for me stagnant and dead; that water floweth to all who are on earth, while for me it is but liquid putrefaction, this water that is mine. Since I came into this funeral valley I know not where nor what I am. Give me to drink of running water…let me be placed by the edge of the water with my face to the North, that the breeze may caress me and my heart be refreshed from its sorrow."[2]

Among the Chaldeans also, although they did not speculate so much as the Egyptians as to the condition of the soul after death, the soul is still a double and is bound to its sepulchre. They also could not conceive of a state without this physical body, and expected a resurrection of the corpse again to life; and though the goddess Ishtar, after great perils and adventures, procured the resurrection of her shepherd, husband, Dumuzi, the son of Ea and Damkina, "The most pious votaries pleaded in rain from temple to temple, for the resurrection of their dead friends."

Thus we find, that the ancient Egyptians or Chaldeans never could entirely dissociate the idea of the soul from the corpse of the departed or the sepulchre. The state of earthly existence was best after all; and the departed are always longing to have a chance once more to renew it; and the living are fervently hoping to help them in prolonging the existence of the miserable double and striving the best they can to help them.

This is not the soil out of which any higher knowledge of the soul could spring. In the first place it is grossly materialistic, and even then it is one of terror and agony. Frightened by the almost innumerable powers of evil, and with hopeless, agonised efforts to avoid them, the souls of the living, like their ideas of the souls of the departed—wander all over the world though they might—could never get beyond the sepulchre and the crumbling corpse.

We must turn now for the source of the higher ideas of the soul to another race, whose God was an all-merciful, all-pervading Being manifesting Himself through various bright, benign, and helpful Devas, the first of all the human race who addressed their God as Father "Oh, take me by the hands even as a father takes his dear son"; with whom life was a hope and not a despair; whose religion was not the intermittent groans escaping from the lips of an agonised man during the intervals of a life of mad excitement; but whose ideas come to us redolent with the aroma of the field and forest; whose songs of praise—spontaneous, free, joyful, like the songs which burst forth from the throats of the birds when they hail this beautiful world illuminated by the first rays of the lord of the day—come down to us even now through the vista of eighty centuries as fresh calls from heaven; we turn to the ancient Aryas.

"Place me in that deathless, undecaying world where is the

2. This text has been translated into German by Brugsch, *Die Egyptische Gräberwelt*, pp. 39, 40, and into French by Maspero, *Études Égyptiennes*, vol. I., pp. 181-90.

light of heaven, and everlasting lustre shines"; "Make me immortal in that realm where dwells the King Vivasvân's son, where is the secret shrine of heaven"; "Make me immortal in that realm where they move even as they list"; "In the third sphere of inmost heaven, where worlds are full of light, make me immortal in that realm of bliss"— These are the prayers of the Aryas in their oldest record, the Rig-Veda Samhitâ.

We find at once a whole world of difference between the Mlechchha and the Aryan ideals. To the one, this body and this world are all that are real, and all that are desirable. A little life-fluid which flies off from the body at death, to feel torture and agony at the loss of the enjoyments of the senses, can, they fondly hope, be brought back if the body is carefully preserved; and thus a corpse became more an object of care than the living man. The other found out that, that which left the body was the real man; and when separated from the body, it enjoyed a state of bliss higher than it ever enjoyed when in the body. And they hastened to annihilate the corrupted corpse by burning it.

Here we find the germ out of which a true idea of the soul could come. Here it was—where the real man was not the body, but the soul, where all ideas of an inseparable connection between the real man and the body were utterly absent—that a noble idea of the freedom of the soul could rise. And it was when the Aryas penetrated even beyond the shining cloth of the body with which the departed soul was enveloped, and found its real nature of a formless, individual, unit principle, that the question inevitably arose: Whence?

It was in India and among the Aryas that the doctrine of the pre-existence, the immortality, and the individuality of the soul first arose. Recent researches in Egypt have failed to show any trace of the doctrines of an independent and individual soul existing before and after the earthly phase of existence. Some of the mysteries were no doubt in possession of this idea, but in those it has been traced to India.

"I am convinced", says Karl Heckel, "that the deeper we enter into the study of the Egyptian religion, the clearer it is shown that the doctrine of metempsychosis was entirely foreign to the popular Egyptian religion; and that even that which single mysteries possessed of it was not inherent to the Osiris teachings, but derived from Hindu sources."

Later on, we find the Alexandrian Jews imbued with the doctrine of an individual soul, and the Pharisees of the time of Jesus, as already stated, not only had faith in an individual soul, but believed in its wandering through various bodies; and thus it is easy to find how Christ was recognised as the incarnation of an older Prophet, and Jesus himself directly asserted that John the Baptist was the Prophet Elias come back again. "If ye will receive it, this is Elias, which was for to come."—Matt. XI. 14.

The ideas of a soul and of its individuality among the Hebrews, evidently came through the higher mystical teachings of the Egyptians, who in their turn derived it from India. And

that it should come through Alexandria is significant, as the Buddhistic records clearly show Buddhistic missionary activity in Alexandria and Asia Minor.

Pythagoras is said to have been the first Greek who taught the doctrine of palingenesis among the Hellenes. As an Aryan race, already burning their dead and believing in the doctrine of an individual soul, it was easy for the Greeks to accept the doctrine of reincarnation through the Pythagorean teachings. According to Apuleius, Pythagoras had come to India, where he had been instructed by the Brâhmins.

So far we have learnt that wherever the soul was held to be an individual, the real man, and not a vivifying part of the body only, the doctrine of its pre-existence had inevitably come, and that externally those nations that believed in the independent individuality of the soul had almost always signified it by burning the bodies of the departed. Though one of the ancient Aryan races, the Persian, developed at an early period and without any; Semitic influence a peculiar method of disposing of the bodies of the dead, the very name by which they call their "Towers of silence", comes from the root Dah, to burn.

In short, the races who did not pay much attention to the analysis of their own nature, never went beyond the material body as their all in all, and even when driven by higher light to penetrate beyond, they only came to the conclusion that somehow or other, at some distant period of time, this body will become incorruptible.

On the other hand, that race which spent the best part of its energies in the inquiry into the nature of man as a thinking being—the Indo-Aryan—soon found out that beyond this body, beyond even the shining body which their forefathers longed after, is the real man, the principle, the individual who clothes himself with this body, and then throws it off when worn out. Was such a principle created? If creation means something coming out of nothing, their answer is a decisive "No". This soul is without birth and without death; it is not a compound or combination but an independent individual, and as such it cannot be created or destroyed. It is only travelling through various states.

Naturally, the question arises: Where was it all this time? The Hindu philosophers say, "It was passing through different bodies in the physical sense, or, really and metaphysically speaking, passing through different mental planes."

Are there any proofs apart from the teachings of the Vedas upon which the doctrine of reincarnation has been founded by the Hindu philosophers? There are, and we hope to show later on that there are grounds as valid for it as for any other universally accepted doctrine. But first we will see what some of the greatest of modern European thinkers have thought about reincarnation.

I. H. Fichte, speaking about the immortality of the soul, says:

"It is true there is one analogy in nature which might be

brought forth in refutation of the continuance. It is the well-known argument that everything that has a beginning in time must also perish at some period of time; hence, that the claimed past existence of the soul necessarily implies its pre-existence. This is a fair conclusion, but instead of being an objection to, it is rather an additional argument for its continuance. Indeed, one needs only to understand the full meaning of the metaphysico-physiological axiom that in reality nothing can be created or annihilated, to recognise that the soul must have existed prior to its becoming visible in a physical body."

Schopenhauer, in his book, *Die Welt als Wille und Vorstellung*, speaking about palingenesis, says:

"What sleep is for the individual, death is for the 'will'. It would not endure to continue the same actions and sufferings throughout an eternity without true gain, if memory and individuality remained to it. It flings them off, and this is Lethe, and through this sleep of death it reappears fitted out with another intellect as a new being; a new day tempts to new shores. These constant new births, then, constitute the succession of the life-dreams of a will which in itself is indestructible, until instructed and improved by so much and such various successive knowledge in a constantly new form, it abolishes and abrogates itself... It must not be neglected that even empirical grounds support a palingenesis of this kind. As a matter of fact, there does exist a connection between the birth of the newly appearing beings and the death of those that are worn out. It shows itself in the great fruitfulness of the human race which appears as a consequence of devastating diseases. When in the fourteenth century the Black Death had for the most part depopulated the Old World, a quite abnormal fruitfulness appeared among the human race, and twin-births were very frequent. The circumstance was also remarkable that none of the children born at this time obtained their full number of teeth; thus nature, exerting itself to the utmost, was niggardly in details. This is related by F. Schnurrer in his Chronik der Seuchen, 1825. Casper, also, in his Ueber die Wahrscheinliche Lebensdauer des Menschen, 1835, confirms the principle that the number of births in a given population has the most decided influence upon the length of life and mortality in it, as this always keeps pace with mortality; so that always and everywhere the deaths and the births increase and decrease in like proportion, which he places beyond doubt by an accumulation of evidence collected from many lands and their various provinces. And yet it is impossible that there can be physical, causal connection between my early death and the fruitfulness of a marriage with which I have nothing to do, or conversely. Thus here the metaphysical appears undeniable, and in a stupendous manner, as the immediate ground of explanation of the physical. Every new-born being comes fresh and blithe into the new existence, and enjoys it as a free gift; but there is and can be nothing freely given. Its fresh existence is paid for by the old age and death of a worn-out existence which has perished, but which contained the indestructible seed out of which the new existence has arisen; they are one being."

The great English philosopher Hume, nihilistic though he was, says in the sceptical essay on immortality, "The metempsychosis is therefore the only system of this kind that philosophy can listen to." The philosopher Lessing, with a deep poetical insight, asks, "Is this hypothesis so laughable merely because it is the oldest, because the human understanding, before the sophistries of the schools had dissipated and debilitated it, lighted upon it at once?...Why should not I come back as often as I am capable of acquiring fresh knowledge, fresh experience? Do I bring away so much from once that there is nothing to repay the trouble of coming back?"

The arguments for and against the doctrine of a preexisting soul reincarnating through many lives have been many, and some of the greatest thinkers of all ages have taken up the gauntlet to defend it; and so far as we can see, if there is an individual soul, that it existed before seems inevitable. If the soul is not an individual but a combination of "Skandhas" (notions), as the Mâdhyamikas among the Buddhists insist, still they find pre-existence absolutely necessary to explain their position.

The argument showing the impossibility of an infinite existence beginning in time is unanswerable, though attempts have been made to ward it off by appealing to the omnipotence of God to do anything, however contrary to reason it may be. We are sorry to find this most fallacious argument proceeding from some of the most thoughtful persons.

In the first place, God being the universal and common cause of all phenomena, the question was to find the natural causes of certain phenomena in the human soul, and the Deus ex machina theory is, therefore, quite irrelevant. It amounts to nothing less than confession of ignorance. We can give that answer to every question asked in every branch of human knowledge and stop all inquiry and, therefore, knowledge altogether.

Secondly, this constant appeal to the omnipotence of God is only a word-puzzle. The cause, as cause, is and can only be known to us as sufficient for the effect, and nothing more. As such we have no more idea of an infinite effect than of an omnipotent cause. Moreover, all our ideas of God are only limited; even the idea of cause limits our idea of God. Thirdly, even taking the position for granted, we are not bound to allow any such absurd theories as "Something coming out of nothing", or "Infinity beginning in time", so long as we can give a better explanation.

A so-called great argument is made against the idea of pre-existence by asserting that the majority of mankind are not conscious of it. To prove the validity of this argument, the party who offers it must prove that the whole of the soul of man is bound up in the faculty of memory. If memory be the test of existence, then all that part of our lives which is not now in it must be non-existent, and every, person who in a state of coma or otherwise loses his memory must be non-existent also.

The premises from which the inference is drawn of a previous existence, and that too on the plane of conscious' action, as adduced by the Hindu philosophers, are chiefly these:

First, how else to explain this world of inequalities? Here is one child born in the province of a just and merciful God, with every circumstance conducing to his becoming a good and useful member of the human race, and perhaps at the same instant and in the same city another child is born under circumstances every one of which is against his becoming good. We see children born to suffer, perhaps all their lives, and that owing to no fault of theirs. Why should it be so? What is the cause? Of whose ignorance is it the result? If not the child's, why should it suffer for its parents' actions?

It is much better to confess ignorance than to try to evade the question by the allurements of future enjoyments in proportion to the evil here, or by posing "mysteries". Not only undeserved suffering forced upon us by any agent is immoral—not to say unjust—but even the future-makingup theory has no legs to stand upon.

How many of the miserably born struggle towards a higher life, and how many more succumb to the circumstances they are placed under? Should those who grow worse and more wicked by being forced to be born under evil circumstances be rewarded in the future for the wickedness of their lives? In that case the more wicked the man is here, the better will be his deserts hereafter.

There is no other way to vindicate the glory and the liberty of the human soul and reconcile the inequalities and the horrors of this world than by placing the whole burden upon the legitimate cause—our own independent actions or Karma. Not only so, but every theory of the creation of the soul from nothing inevitably leads to fatalism and preordination, and instead of a Merciful Father, places before us a hideous, cruel, and an ever-angry God to worship. And so far as the power of religion for good or evil is concerned, this theory of a created soul, leading to its corollaries of fatalism and predestination, is responsible for the horrible idea prevailing among some Christians and Mohammedans that the heathens are the lawful victims of their swords, and all the horrors that have followed and are following it still.

But an argument which the philosophers of the Nyâya school have always advanced in favour of reincarnations and which to us seems conclusive, is this: Our experiences cannot be annihilated. Our actions (Karma) though apparently disappearing, remain still unperceived (Adrishta), and reappear again in their effect as tendencies (Pravrittis). Even little babies come with certain tendencies—fear of death, for example.

Now if a tendency is the result of repeated actions, the tendencies with which we are born must be explained on that ground too. Evidently we could not have got them in this life; therefore we must have to seek for their genesis in the past.

Now it is also evident that some of our tendencies are the effects of the self-conscious efforts peculiar to man; and if it is true that we are born with such tendencies, it rigorously follows that their causes were conscious efforts in the past—that is, we must have been on the same mental plane which we call the human plane, before this present life.

So far as explaining the tendencies of the present life by past conscious efforts goes, the reincarnationists of India and the latest school of evolutionists are at once; the only difference is that the Hindus, as spiritualists, explain it by the conscious efforts of individual souls, and the materialistic school of evolutionists, by a hereditary physical transmission. The schools which hold to the theory of creation out of nothing are entirely out of court.

The issue has to be fought out between the reincarnationists who hold that all experiences are stored up as; tendencies in the subject of those experiences, the individual soul, and are transmitted by reincarnation of that unbroken individuality—and the materialists who hold that the brain is the subject of all actions and the theory of the transmission through cells.

It is thus that the doctrine of reincarnation assumes an infinite importance to our mind, for the fight between reincarnation and mere cellular transmission is, in reality, the fight between spiritualism and materialism. If cellular transmission is the all-sufficient explanation, materialism is inevitable, and there is no necessity for the theory of a soul. If it is not a sufficient explanation, the theory of an individual soul bringing into this life the experiences of the past is as absolutely true. There is no escape from the alternative, reincarnation or materialism. Which shall we accept?

ON DR. PAUL DEUSSEN[1]

More than a decade has passed since a young German student, one of eight children of a not very well-to-do clergyman, heard on a certain day Professor Lassen lecturing on a language and literature new—very new even at that time—to European scholars, namely, Sanskrit. The lectures were of course free; for even now it is impossible for any one in any European University to make a living by teaching Sanskrit, unless indeed the University backs him.

Lassen was almost the last of that heroic band of German scholars, the pioneers of Sanskrit scholarship in Germany. Heroic certainly they were—what interest except their pure and unselfish love of knowledge could German scholars have had at that time in Indian literature? The veteran Professor was expounding a chapter of Shakuntalâ; and on that day there was no one present more eagerly and attentively listening to Lassen's exposition than our young student. The subject-matter of the exposition was of course interesting and wonderful, but more wonderful was the strange language, the strange sounds of which, although uttered with all those dif-

1. Written for the *Brahmavâdin*, 1896.

ficult peculiarities that Sanskrit consonants are subjected to in the mouths of unaccustomed Europeans, had strange fascination for him. He returned to his lodgings, but that night sleep could not make him oblivious of what he had heard. A glimpse of a hitherto unknown land had been given to him, a land far more gorgeous in its colours than any he had yet seen, and having a power of fascination never yet experienced by his young and ardent soul.

Naturally his friends were anxiously looking forward to the ripening of his brilliant parts, and expected that he would soon enter a learned profession which might bring him respect, fame, and, above all, a good salary and a high position. But then there was this Sanskrit! The vast majority of European scholars had not even heard of it then; as for making it pay — I have already said that such a thing is impossible even now. Yet his desire to learn it was strong.

It has unfortunately become hard for us modern Indians to understand how it could be like that; nevertheless, there are to be met with in Varanasi and Nadia and other places even now, some old as well as young persons among our Pandits, and mostly among the Sannyasins, who are mad with this kind of thirst for knowledge for its own sake. Students, not placed in the midst of the luxurious surroundings and materials of the modern Europeanised Hindu, and with a thousand times less facilities for study, poring over manuscripts in the flickering light of an oil lamp, night after night, which alone would have been enough to completely destroy the eye-sight of the students of any other nation; travelling on foot hundreds of miles, begging their way all along, in search of a rare manuscript or a noted teacher; and wonderfully concentrating all the energy of their body and mind upon their one object of study, year in and year out, till the hair turns grey and the infirmity of age overtakes them — such students have not, through God's mercy, as yet disappeared altogether from our country. Whatever India now holds as a proud possession, has been undeniably the result of such labour on the part of her worthy sons in days gone by; and the truth of this remark will become at once evident on comparing the depth and solidity as well as the unselfishness and the earnestness of purpose of India's ancient scholarship with the results attained by our modern Indian Universities. Unselfish and genuine zeal for real scholarship and honest earnest thought must again become dominant in the life of our countrymen if they are ever to rise to occupy among nations a rank worthy of their own historic past. It is this kind of desire for knowledge which has made Germany what she is now — one of the foremost, if not the foremost, among the nations of the world.

Yes, the desire to learn Sanskrit was strong in the heart of this German student. It was long, uphill work — this learning of Sanskrit; with him too it was the same world-old story of successful scholars and their hard work, their privations and their indomitable energy — and also the same glorious conclusion of a really heroic achievement. He thus achieved success; and now — not only Europe, but all India knows this man, Paul Deussen, who is the Professor of Philosophy in the University of Kiel. I have seen professors of Sanskrit in America and in Europe. Some of them are very sympathetic towards Vedantic thought. I admire their intellectual acumen and their lives of unselfish labour. But Paul Deussen — or as he prefers to be called in Sanskrit, Deva-Sena — and the veteran Max Müller have impressed me as being the truest friends of India and Indian thought. It will always be among the most pleasing episodes in my life — my first visit to this ardent Vedantist at Kiel, his gentle wife who travelled with him in India, and his little daughter, the darling of his heart — and our travelling together through Germany and Holland to London, and the pleasant meetings we had in and about London.

The earliest school of Sanskritists in Europe entered into the study of Sanskrit with more imagination than critical ability. They knew a little, expected much from that little, and often tried to make too much of what little they knew. Then, in those days even, such vagaries as the estimation of Shakuntala as forming the high watermark of Indian philosophy were not altogether unknown! These were naturally followed by a reactionary band of superficial critics, more than real scholars of any kind, who knew little or nothing of Sanskrit, expected nothing from Sanskrit studies, and ridiculed everything from the East. While criticising the unsound imaginativeness of the early school to whom everything in Indian literature was rose and musk, these, in their turn, went into speculations which, to say the least, were equally highly unsound and indeed very venturesome. And their boldness was very naturally helped by the fact that these over-hasty and unsympathetic scholars and critics were addressing an audience whose entire qualification for pronouncing any judgment in the matter was their absolute ignorance of Sanskrit. What a medley of results from such critical scholarship! Suddenly, on one fine morning, the poor Hindu woke up to find that everything that was his was gone; one strange race had snatched away from him his arts, another his architecture, and a third, whatever there was of his ancient sciences; why, even his religion was not his own! Yes — that too had migrated into India in the wake of a Pehlevi cross of stone! After a feverish period of such treading-on-each-other's-toes of original research, a better state of things has dawned. It has now been found out that mere adventure without some amount of the capital of real and ripe scholarship produces nothing but ridiculous failure even in the business of Oriental research, and that the traditions in India are not to be rejected with supercilious contempt, as there is really more in them than most people ever dream of.

There is now happily coming into existence in Europe a new type of Sanskrit scholars, reverential, sympathetic, and learned — reverential because they are a better stamp of men, and sympathetic because they are learned. And the link which connects the new portion of the chain with the old one is, of course, our Max Müller. We Hindus certainly owe more to him than to any other Sanskrit scholar in the West, and I am simply astonished when I think of the gigantic task which he, in his enthusiasm, undertook as a young man and brought to a successful conclusion in his old age. Think of this man without any help, poring over old manuscripts, hardly legible to the Hindus themselves, and in a language to acquire which takes a lifetime even in India — without even the help of any needy Pandit whose "brains could be picked", as the Americans say, for ten shillings a month, and a mere mention of his name in the introduction to some book of "very new researches" — think of this man, spending days and sometimes months in elucidating the correct reading and meaning of a word or a sentence in the commentary of Sâyana (as he has himself told me), and in the end succeeding in making an easy road through the forest of Vedic literature for all others to go along; think of him and his work, and then say what he really is to us! Of course we need not all agree with him in all that he says in his many writings; certainly such an agreement is impossible. But agreement or no agreement, the fact remains that this one man has done a thousand times more for the preservation, spreading, and appreciation of the literature of our forefathers than any of us can ever hope to do, and he has done it all with a heart which is full of the sweet balm of love and veneration.

If Max Müller is thus the old pioneer of the new movement, Deussen is certainly one of its younger advance-guard. Philological interest had hidden long from view the gems of thought and spirituality to be found in the mine of our ancient scriptures. Max Müller brought out a few of them and exhibited them to the public gaze, compelling attention to them by means of his authority as the foremost philologist. Deussen, unhampered by any philological leanings and possessing the training of a philosopher singularly well versed in the speculations of ancient Greece and modern Germany, took up the cue and plunged boldly into the metaphysical depths of the Upanishads, found them to be fully safe and satisfying, and then — equally boldly declared that fact before the whole world. Deussen is certainly the freest among scholars in the expression of his opinion about the Vedanta. He never stops to think about the "What they would say" of the vast majority of scholars. We indeed require bold men in this world to tell us bold words about truth; and nowhere, is this more true now than in Europe where, through the fear of social opinion and such other causes, there has been enough in all conscience of the whitewashing and apologising attitude among scholars towards creeds and customs which, in all probability, not many among them really believe in. The greater is the glory, therefore, to Max Müller and to Deussen for their bold and open advocacy of truth! May they be as bold in showing to us our defects, the later corruptions in our thought-systems in India, especially in their application to our social needs! Just now we very much require the help of such genuine friends as these to check the growing virulence of the disease, very prevalent in India, of running either to the one extreme of slavish panegyrists who cling to every village superstition as the innermost essence of the Shâstras, or to the

other extreme of demoniacal denouncers who see no good in us and in our history, and will, if they can, at once dynamite all the social and spiritual organizations of our ancient land of religion and philosophy.

ON PROFESSOR MAX MÜLLER[1]

Though the ideal of work of our Brahmavâdin should always be "कर्मण्येवाधिकारस्ते मा फलेषु कदाचन—To work thou hast the right, but never to the fruits thereof", yet no sincere worker passes out of the field of activity without making himself known and catching at least a few rays of light.

The beginning of our work has been splendid, and the steady earnestness shown by our friends is beyond all praise. Sincerity of conviction and purity of motive will surely gain the day; and even a small minority, armed with these, is surely destined to prevail against all odds.

Keep away from all insincere claimants to supernatural illumination; not that such illumination is impossible, but, my friends, in this world of ours "lust, or gold, or fame" is the hidden motive behind ninety per cent of all such claims, and of the remaining ten per cent, nine per cent are cases which require the tender care of physicians more than the attention of metaphysicians.

The first great thing to accomplish is to establish a character, to obtain, as we say, the परतिष्ठिता परज्ञा (established Wisdom). This applies equally to individuals and to organised bodies of individuals. Do not fret because the world looks with suspicion at every new attempt, even though it be in the path of spirituality. The poor world, how often has it been cheated! The more the संसार that is, the worldly aspect of life, looks at any growing movement with eyes of suspicion, or, even better still, presents to it a semi-hostile front, so much the better is it for the movement. If there is any truth this movement has to disseminate, any need it is born to supply, soon will condemnation be changed into praise, and contempt converted into love. People in these days are apt to take up religion as a means to some social or political end. Beware of this. Religion is its own end. That religion which is only a means to worldly well-being is not religion, whatever else it may be; and it is sheer blasphemy against God and man to hold that man has no other end than the free and full enjoyment of all the pleasure of his senses.

Truth, purity, and unselfishness—wherever these are present, there is no power below or above the sun to crush the possessor thereof. Equipped with these, one individual is able to face the whole universe in opposition.

Above all, beware of compromises. I do not mean that you are to get into antagonism with anybody, but you have to hold on to your own principles in weal or woe and never adjust them to others' "fads" through the greed of getting supporters. Your Âtman is the support of the universe—whose support do you stand in need of? Wait with patience and love

1. Written for the *Brahmâvadin*, from London, June 6, 1896.

and strength; if helpers are not ready now, they will come in time. Why should we be in a hurry? The real working force of all great work is in its almost unperceived beginnings.

Whoever could have thought that the life and teachings of a boy born of poor Brâhmin parents in a wayside Bengal village would, in a few years, reach such distant lands as our ancestors never even dreamed of? I refer to Bhagavan Ramâkrishna. Do you know that Prof. Max Müller has already written an article on Shri Ramakrishna for the Nineteenth Century, and will be very glad to write a larger and fuller account of his life and teachings if sufficient materials are forthcoming? What an extraordinary man is Prof. Max Müller! I paid a visit to him a few days ago. I should say, that I went to pay my respects to him, for whosoever loves Shri Ramakrishna, whatever be his or her sect, or creed, or nationality, my visit to that person I hold as a pilgrimage. "मद्भक्तानां च ये भक्तास्ते मे भक्ततमा मताः—They who are devoted to those who love Me—they are My best devotees." Is that not true?

The Professor was first induced to inquire about the power behind, which led to sudden and momentous changes in the life of the late Keshab Chandra Sen, the great Brâhmo leader; and since then, he has been an earnest student and admirer of the life and teachings of Shri Ramakrishna. "Ramakrishna is worshipped by thousands today, Professor", I said. "To whom else shall worship be accorded, if not to such", was the answer. The Professor was kindness itself, and asked Mr. Sturdy and myself to lunch with him. He showed us several colleges in Oxford and the Bodleian library. He also accompanied us to the railway station; and all this he did because, as he said, "It is not every day one meets a disciple of Ramakrishna Paramahamsa."

The visit was really a revelation to me. That nice little house in its setting of a beautiful garden, the silverheaded sage, with a face calm and benign, and forehead smooth as a child's in spite of seventy winters, and every line in that face speaking of a deep-seated mine of spirituality somewhere behind; that noble wife, the helpmate of his life through his long and arduous task of exciting interest, overriding opposition and contempt, and at last creating a respect for the thoughts of the sages of ancient India—the trees, the flowers, the calmness, and the clear sky—all these sent me back in imagination to the glorious days of Ancient India, the days of our Brahmarshis and Râjarshis, the days of the great Vânaprasthas, the days of Arundhatis and Vasishthas.

It was neither the philologist nor the scholar that I saw, but a soul that is every day realising its oneness with the Brahman, a heart that is every moment expanding to reach oneness with the Universal. Where others lose themselves in the desert of dry details, he has struck the well-spring of life. Indeed his heartbeats have caught the rhythm of the Upanishads "तमेवैकं जानथ जात्मानमन्या वाचो विमुञ्चथ—Know the Atman alone, and leave off all other talk."

Although a world-moving scholar and philosopher, his learning and philosophy have only led him higher and higher to the realisation of the Spirit, his अपरा विदिया (lower knowledge) has indeed helped him to reach the परा विदिया (higher knowledge). This is real learning. विदिया ददाति विनियम्—"Knowledge gives humility." Of what use is knowledge if it does not show us the way to the Highest?

And what love he bears towards India! I wish I had a hundredth part of that love for my own motherland! Endued with an extraordinary, and at the same time intensely active mind, he has lived and moved in the world of Indian thought for fifty years or more, and watched the sharp interchange of light and shade in the interminable forest of Sanskrit literature with deep interest and heartfelt love, till they have all sunk into his very soul and coloured his whole being.

Max Müller is a Vedantist of Vedantists. He has, indeed, caught the real soul of the melody of the Vedanta, in the midst of all its settings of harmonies and discords—the one light that lightens the sects and creeds of the world, the Vedanta, the one principle of which all religions are only applications. And what was Ramakrishna Paramahamsa? The practical demonstration of this ancient principle, the embodiment of India that is past, and a foreshadowing of the India that is to be, the bearer of spiritual light unto nations. The jeweller alone can understand the worth of jewels; this is an old proverb. Is it a wonder that this Western sage does study and appreciate every new star in the firmament of Indian thought, before even the Indians themselves realise its magnitude?

"When are you coming to India? Every heart there would welcome one who has done so much to place the thoughts of their ancestors in the true light", I said. The face of the aged sage brightened up—there was almost a tear in his eyes, a gentle nodding of the head, and slowly the words came out: "I would not return then; you would have to cremate me there." Further questions seemed an unwarrantable intrusion into realms wherein are stored the holy secrets of man's heart. Who knows but that it was what the poet has said—

$$\text{तच्चेतमा समरति नूनमबोधपूर्वं ।}$$
$$\text{भावस्थिराणि जननान्तरसौहृदानि ॥}$$

—"He remembers with his mind the friendships of former births, firmly rooted in his heart."

His life has been a blessing to the world; and may it be many, many years more, before he changes the present plane of his existence!

SKETCH OF THE LIFE OF PAVHARI BABA

To help the suffering world was the gigantic task to which the Buddha gave prominence, brushing aside for the time being almost all other phases of religion; yet he had to spend years in self-searching to realise the great truth of the utter hollowness of clinging to a selfish individuality. A more unselfish and untiring worker is beyond our most sanguine imagination: yet who had harder struggles to realise the meaning of things than he? It holds good in all times that the greater the work, the more must have been the power of realisation behind. Working out the details of an already laid out masterly plan may not require much concentrated thought to back it, but the great impulses are only transformed great concentrations. The theory alone perhaps is sufficient for small exertions, but the push that creates the ripple is very different from the impulsion that raises the wave, and yet the ripple is only the embodiment of a bit of the power that generates the wave.

Facts, naked facts, gaunt and terrible may be; truth, bare truth, though its vibrations may snap every chord of the heart; motive selfless and sincere, though to reach it, limb after limb has to be lopped off—such are to be arrived at, found, and gained, before the mind on the lower plane of activity can raise huge work-waves. The fine accumulates round itself the gross as it rolls on through time and becomes manifest, the unseen crystallises into the seen, the possible becomes the practical, the cause the effect, and thought, muscular work.

The cause, held back by a thousand circumstances, will manifest itself, sooner or later, as the effect; and potent thought, however powerless at present, will have its glorious day on the plane of material activity. Nor is the standard correct which judges of everything by its power to contribute to our sense-enjoyment.

The lower the animal, the more is its enjoyment in the senses, the more it lives in the senses. Civilisation, true civilization, should mean the power of taking the animal-man out of his sense-life—by giving him visions and tastes of planes much higher—and not external comforts.

Man knows this instinctively. He may not formulate it to himself under all circumstances. He may form very divergent opinions about the life of thought. But it is there, pressing itself to the front in spite of everything, making him pay reverence to the hoodoo-worker, the medicine-man, the magician, the priest, or the professor of science. The growth of man can only be gauged by his power of living in the higher atmosphere where the senses are left behind, the amount of the pure thought-oxygen his lungs can breathe in, and the amount of time he can spend on that height.

As it is, it is an obvious fact that, with the exception of what is taken up by the necessities of life, the man of culture is loth to spend his time on so-called comforts, and even necessary actions are performed with lessened zeal, as the process moves forward.

Even luxuries are arranged according to ideas and ideals, to make them reflect as much of thought-life as possible—and this is Art.

"As the one fire coming into the universe is manifesting itself in every form, and yet is more besides"—yes, infinitely more besides! A bit, only a small bit, of infinite thought can be made to descend to the plane of matter to minister to our comfort—the rest will not allow itself to be rudely handled. The superfine always eludes our view and laughs at our at-

tempts to bring it down. In this case, Mohammed must go to the mountain, and no "nay". Man must raise himself to that higher plane if he wants to enjoy its beauties, to bathe in its light, to feel his life pulsating in unison with the Cause-Life of the universe.

It is knowledge that opens the door to regions of wonder, knowledge that makes a god of an animal: and that knowledge which brings us to That, "knowing which everything else is known" (the heart of all knowledge—whose pulsation brings life to all sciences—the science of religion) is certainly the highest, as it alone can make man live a complete and perfect life in thought. Blessed be the land which has styled it "supreme science"!

The principle is seldom found perfectly expressed in the practical, yet the ideal is never lost. On the one hand, it is our duty never to lose sight of the ideal, whether we can approach it with sensible steps, or crawl towards it with imperceptible motion: on the other hand, the truth is, it is always loosening in front of us—though we try our best to cover its light with our hands before our eyes.

The life of the practical is in the ideal. It is the ideal that has penetrated the whole of our lives, whether we philosophise, or perform the hard, everyday duties of life. The rays of the ideal, reflected and refracted in various straight or tortuous lines, are pouring in through every aperture and windhole, and consciously or unconsciously, every function has to be performed in its light, every object has to be seen transformed, heightened, or deformed by it. It is the ideal that has made us what we are, and will make us what we are going to be. It is the power of the ideal that has enshrouded us, and is felt in our joys or sorrows, in our great acts or mean doings, in our virtues and vices.

If such is the power of the ideal over the practical, the practical is no less potent in forming the ideal. The truth of the ideal is in the practical. The fruition of the ideal has been through the sensing of the practical. That the ideal is there is a proof of the existence of the practical somehow, somewhere. The ideal may be vaster, yet it is the multiplication of little bits of the practical. The ideal mostly is the summed-up, generalized, practical units.

The power of the ideal is in the practical. Its work on us is in and through the practical. Through the practical, the ideal is brought down to our sense-perception, changed into a form fit for our assimilation. Of the practical we make the steps to rise to the ideal. On that we build our hopes; it gives us courage to work.

One man who manifests the ideal in his life is more powerful than legions whose words can paint it in the most beautiful colours and spin out the finest principles.

Systems of philosophy mean nothing to mankind, or at best only intellectual gymnastics, unless they are joined to religion and can get a body of men struggling to bring them down to practical life with more or less success. Even systems having not one positive hope, when taken up by groups and made somewhat practical, had always a multitude; and the most elaborate positive systems of thought withered away without it.

Most of us cannot keep our activities on a par with our thought-lives. Some blessed ones can. Most of us seem to lose the power of work as we think deeper, and the power of deep thought if we work more. That is why most great thinkers have to leave to time the practical realisation of their great ideals. Their thoughts must wait for more active brains to work them out and spread them. Yet, as we write, comes before us a vision of him, the charioteer of Arjuna, standing in his chariot between the contending hosts, his left hand curbing the fiery steeds—a mail-clad warrior, whose eagle-glance sweeps over the vast army, and as if by instinct weighs every detail of the battle array of both parties—at the same time that we hear, as it were, falling from his lips and thrilling the awestruck Arjuna, that most marvellous secret of work: "He who finds rest in the midst of activity, and activity in rest, he is the wise amidst men, he the Yogi, he is the doer of all work" (Gita, IV. 18).

This is the ideal complete. But few ever reach it. We must take things as they are, therefore, and be contented to piece together different aspects of human perfection, developed in different individuals.

In religion we have the man of intense thought, of great activity in bringing help to others, the man of boldness and daring self-realisation, and the man of meekness and humility.

The subject of this sketch was a man of wonderful humility and intense self-realisation.

Born of Brâhmin parents in a village near Guzi, Varanasi, Pavhâri Bâbâ, as he was called in after life, came to study and live with his uncle in Ghazipur, when a mere boy. At present, Hindu ascetics are split up into the main divisions of Sannyâsins, Yogis, Vairâgis, and Panthis. The Sannyasins are the followers of Advaitism after Shankarâchârya; the Yogis, though following the Advaita system, are specialists in practicing the different systems of Yoga; the Vairagis are the dualistic disciples of Râmânujâchârya and others; the Panthis, professing either philosophy, are orders founded during the Mohammedan rule. The uncle of Pavhari Baba belonged to the Ramanuja or Shri sect, and was a Naishthika Brahmachârin, i.e. one who takes the vow of lifelong celibacy. He had a piece of land on the banks of the Ganga, about two miles to the north of Ghazipur, and had established himself there. Having several nephews, he took Pavhari Baba into his home and adopted him, intending him to succeed to his property and position.

Not much is known of the life of Pavhari Baba at this period. Neither does there seem to have been any indication of those peculiarities which made him so well known in after years. He is remembered merely as a diligent student of Vyâkarana and Nyâya, and the theology of his sect, and as an active lively boy whose jollity at times found vent in hard practical jokes at the expense of his fellow-students.

Thus the future saint passed his young days, going through the routine duties of Indian students of the old school; and except that he showed more than ordinary application to his studies, and a remarkable aptitude for learning languages, there was scarcely anything in that open, cheerful, playful student life to foreshadow the tremendous seriousness which was to culminate in a most curious and awful sacrifice.

Then something happened which made the young scholar feel, perhaps for the first time, the serious import of life, and made him raise his eyes, so long riveted on books, to scan his mental horizon critically and crave for something in religion which was a fact, and not mere book-lore. His uncle passed away. One face on which all the love of that young heart was concentrated had gone, and the ardent boy, struck to the core with grief, determined to supply the gap with a vision that can never change.

In India, for everything, we want a Guru. Books, we Hindus are persuaded, are only outlines. The living secrets must be handed down from Guru to disciple, in every art, in every science, much more so in religion. From time immemorial earnest souls in India have always retired to secluded spots, to carry on uninterrupted their study of the mysteries of the inner life, and even today there is scarcely a forest, a hill, or a sacred spot which rumour does not consecrate as the abode of a great sage. The saying is well known:

"The water is pure that flows.

The monk is pure that goes."

As a rule, those who take to the celibate religious life in India spend a good deal of their life in journeying through various countries of the Indian continent, visiting different shrines—thus keeping themselves from rust, as it were, and at the same time bringing religion to the door of everyone. A visit to the four great sacred places, situated in the four corners of India, is considered almost necessary to all who renounce the world.

All these considerations may have had weight with our young Brahmacharin, but we are sure that the chief among them was the thirst for knowledge. Of his travels we know but little, except that, from his knowledge of Dravidian languages, in which a good deal of the literature of his sect is written, and his thorough acquaintance with the old Bengali of the Vaishnavas of Shri Chaitanya's order, we infer that his stay in Southern India and Bengal could not have been very short.

But on his visit to one place, the friends of his youth lay great stress. It was on the top of mount Girnâr in Kathiawar, they say, that he was first initiated into the mysteries of practical Yoga.

It was this mountain which was so holy to the Buddhists. At its foot is the huge rock on which is inscribed the first-deciphered edict of the "divinest of monarchs", Asoka. Beneath it, through centuries of oblivion, lay the conclave of gigantic Stupas, forest covered, and long taken for hillocks of the Girnar range. No less sacred is it still held by the sect of which

Buddhism is now thought to be a revised edition, and which strangely enough did not venture into the field of architectural triumphs till its world-conquering descendant had melted away into modern Hinduism. Girnar is celebrated amongst Hindus as having been sanctified by the stay of the great Avadhuta Guru Dattâtreya, and rumour has it that great and perfected Yogis are still to be met with by the fortunate on its top.

The next turning-point in the career of our youthful Brahmacharin we trace to the banks of the Ganga some where near Varanasi, as the disciple of a Sannyasin who practiced Yoga and lived in a hole dug in the high bank of the river. To this yogi can be traced the after-practice of our saint, of living inside a deep tunnel, dug out of the ground on the bank of the Ganga near Ghazipur. Yogis have always inculcated the advisability of living in caves or other spots where the temperature is even, and where sounds do not disturb the mind. We also learn that he was about the same time studying the Advaita system under a Sannyasin in Varanasi.

After years of travel, study, and discipline, the young Brahmacharin came back to the place where he had been brought up. Perhaps his uncle, if alive, would have found in the face of the boy the same light which of yore a greater sage saw in that of his disciple and exclaimed, "Child, thy face today shines with the glory of Brahman!" But those that welcomed him to his home were only the companions of his boyhood — most of them gone into, and claimed for ever by, the world of small thought and eternal toil.

Yet there was a change, a mysterious — to them an awe-inspiring — change, in the whole character and demeanour of that school-day friend and playmate whom they had been wont to understand. But it did not arouse in them emulation, or the same research. It was the mystery of a man who had gone beyond this world of trouble and materialism, and this was enough. They instinctively respected it and asked no questions.

Meanwhile, the peculiarities of the saint began to grow more and more pronounced. He had a cave dug in the ground, like his friend near Varanasi, and began to go into it and remain there for hours. Then began a process of the most awful dietary discipline. The whole day he worked in his little Âshrama, conducted the worship of his beloved Râmachandra, cooked good dinners — in which art he is said to have been extraordinarily proficient — distributed the whole of the offered food amongst his friends and the poor, looked after their comforts till night came, and when they were in their beds, the young man stole out, crossed the Ganga by swimming, and reached the other shore. There he would spend the whole night in the midst of his practices and prayers, come back before daybreak and wake up his friends, and then begin once more the routine business of "worshipping others", as we say in India.

His own diet, in the meanwhile, was being attenuated every day, till it came down, we are told, to a handful of bitter Nim-ba leaves, or a few pods of red pepper, daily. Then he gave up going nightly to the woods on the other bank of the river and took more and more to his cave. For days and months, we are told, he would be in the hole, absorbed in meditation, and then come out. Nobody knows what he subsisted on during these long intervals, so the people called him Pav-âhâri (or air-eater) Bâbâ (or father).

He would never during his life leave this place. Once, however, he was so long inside the cave that people gave him up as dead, but after a long time, the Baba emerged and gave a Bhândârâ (feast) to a large number of Sâdhus.

When not absorbed in his meditations, he would be living in a room above the mouth of his cave, and during this time he would receive visitors. His fame began to spread, and to Rai Gagan Chandra Bahadur of the Opium Department, Ghazipur — a gentleman whose innate nobility and spirituality have endeared him to all — we owe our introduction to the saint.

Like many others in India, there was no striking or stirring external activity in this life. It was one more example of that Indian ideal of teaching through life and not through words, and that truth bears fruit in those lives only which have become ready to receive. Persons of this type are entirely averse to preaching what they know, for they are for ever convinced that it is internal discipline alone that leads to truth, and not words. Religion to them is no motive to social conduct, but an intense search after and realisation of truth in this life. They deny the greater potentiality of one moment over another, and every moment in eternity being equal to every other, they insist on seeing the truths of religion face to face now and here, not waiting for death.

The present writer had occasion to ask the saint the reason of his not coming out of his cave to help the world. At first, with his native humility and humour, he gave the following strong reply:

"A certain wicked person was caught in some criminal act and had his nose cut off as a punishment. Ashamed to show his noseless features to the world and disgusted with himself, he fled into a forest; and there, spreading a tiger-skin on the ground, he would feign deep meditation whenever he thought anybody was about. This conduct, instead of keeping people off, drew them in crowds to pay their respects to this wonderful saint; and he found that his forest-life had brought him once again an easy living. Thus years went by. At last the people around became very eager to listen to some instruction from the lips of the silent meditative saint; and one young man was specially anxious to be initiated into the order. It came to such a pass that any more delay in that line would undermine the reputation of the saint. So one day he broke his silence and asked the enthusiastic young man to bring on the morrow a sharp razor with him. The young man, glad at the prospect of the great desire of his life being speedily fulfilled, came early the next morning with the razor. The noseless saint led him to a very retired spot in the forest, took the razor in his hand, opened it, and with one stroke cut off his nose, repeating in a solemn voice, 'Young man, this has been my initiation into the order. The same I give to you. Do you transmit it diligently to others when the opportunity comes!' The young man could not divulge the secret of this wonderful initiation for shame, and carried out to the best of his ability the injunctions of his master. Thus a whole sect of nose-cut saints spread over the country. Do you want me to be the founder of another such?"

Later on, in a more serious mood, another query brought the answer: "Do you think that physical help is the only help possible? Is it not possible that one mind can help other minds even without the activity of the body?"

When asked on another occasion why he, a great Yogi, should perform Karma, such as pouring oblations into the sacrificial fire, and worshipping the image of Shri Raghunâthji, which are practices only meant for beginners, the reply came: "Why do you take for granted that everybody makes Karma for his own good? Cannot one perform Karma for others?"

Then again, everyone has heard of the thief who had come to steal from his Ashrama, and who at the sight of the saint got frightened and ran away, leaving the goods he had stolen in a bundle behind; how the saint took the bundle up, ran after the thief, and came up to him after miles of hard running; how the saint laid the bundle at the feet of the thief, and with folded hands and tears in his eyes asked his pardon for his own intrusion, and begged hard for his acceptance of the goods, since they belonged to him, and not to himself.

We are also told, on reliable authority, how once he was bitten by a cobra; and though he was given up for hours as dead, he revived; and when his friends asked him about it, he only replied that the cobra "was a messenger from the Beloved".

And well may we believe this, knowing as we do the extreme gentleness, humility, and love of his nature. All sorts of physical illness were to him only "messengers from the Beloved", and he could not even bear to hear them called by any other name, even while he himself suffered tortures from them. This silent love and gentleness had conveyed themselves to the people around, and those who have travelled through the surrounding villages can testify to the unspoken influence of this wonderful man. Of late, he did not show himself to anyone. When out of his underground retiring-place, he would speak to people with a closed door between. His presence above, ground was always indicated by the rising smoke of oblations in the sacrificial fire, or the noise of getting things ready for worship.

One of his great peculiarities was his entire absorption at the time in the task in hand, however trivial. The same amount of care and attention was bestowed in cleaning a copper pot as in the worship of Shri Raghunathji, he himself being the best example of the secret he once told us of work: "The means should be loved and cared for as if it were the end itself."

Neither was his humility kindred to that which means pain and anguish or self-abasement. It sprang naturally from the realization of that which he once so beautifully explained to us, "O King, the Lord is the wealth of those who have nothing—yes, of those", he continued, "who have thrown away all desires of possession, even that of one's own soul." He would never directly teach, as that would be assuming the role of a teacher and placing himself in a higher position than another. But once the spring was touched, the fountain welled up with infinite wisdom; yet always the replies were indirect.

In appearance he was tall and rather fleshy, had but one eye, and looked much younger than his real age. His voice was the sweetest we have ever heard. For the last ten years or more of his life, he had withdrawn himself entirely from the gaze of mankind. A few potatoes and a little butter were placed behind the door of his room, and sometimes during the night this was taken in when he was not in Samâdhi and was living above ground. When inside his cave, he did not require even these. Thus, this silent life went on, witnessing to the science of Yoga, and a living example of purity, humility, and love.

The smoke, which, as we have said already, indicated his coming out of Samadhi, one day smelled of burning flesh. The people around could not guess what was happening; but when the smell became overpowering, and the smoke was seen to rise up in volumes, they broke open the door, and found that the great Yogi had offered himself as the last oblation to his sacrificial fire, and very soon a heap of ashes was all that remained of his body.

Let us remember the words of Kâlidâsa: "Fools blame the actions of the great, because they are extraordinary and their reasons past the finding-out of ordinary mortals."

Yet, knowing him as we do, we can only venture to suggest that the saint saw that his last moments had come, and not wishing to cause trouble to any, even after death, performed this last sacrifice of an Ârya, in full possession of body and mind.

The present writer owes a deep debt of gratitude to the departed saint and dedicates these lines, however unworthy, to the memory of one of the greatest Masters he has loved and served.

ARYANS AND TAMILIANS

A veritable ethnological museum! Possibly, the half-ape skeleton of the recently discovered Sumatra link will be found on search here, too. The Dolmens are not wanting. Flint implements can be dug out almost anywhere. The lake-dwellers—at least the river-dwellers—must have been abundant at one time. The cave-men and leaf-wearers still persist. The primitive hunters living in forests are in evidence in various parts of the country. Then there are the more historical varieties—the Negrito-Kolarian, the Dravidian, and the Aryan. To these have been added from time to time dashes of nearly all the known races, and a great many yet unknown—various breeds of Mongoloids, Mongols, Tartars, and the so-called Aryans of the philologists. Well, here are the Persian, the Greek, the Yunchi, the Hun, the Chin, the Scythian, and many more, melted and fused, the Jews, Parsees, Arabs, Mongols, down to the descendants of the Vikings and the lords of the German forests, yet undigested—an ocean of humanity, composed of these race-waves seething, boiling, struggling, constantly changing form, rising to the surface, and spreading, and swallowing little ones, again subsiding—this is the history of India.

In the midst of this madness of nature, one of the contending factions discovered a method and, through the force of its superior culture, succeeded in bringing the largest number of Indian humanity under its sway.

The superior race styled themselves the Âryas or nobles, and their method was the Varnâshramâchâra—the so-called caste.

Of course the men of the Aryan race reserved for themselves, consciously or unconsciously a good many privileges; yet the institution of caste has always been very flexible, sometimes too flexible to ensure a healthy uprise of the races very low in the scale of culture.

It put, theoretically at least, the whole of India under the guidance—not of wealth, nor of the sword—but of intellect—intellect chastened and controlled by spirituality. The leading caste in India is the highest of the Aryans—the Brahmins.

Though apparently different from the social methods of other nations, on close inspection, the Aryan method of caste will not be found so very different except on two points:

The first is, in every other country the highest honour belongs to the Kshatriya—the man of the sword. The Pope of Rome will be glad to trace his descent to some robber baron on the banks of the Rhine. In India, the highest honour belongs to the man of peace—the Sharman the Brahmin, the man of God.

The greatest Indian king would be gratified to trace his descent to some ancient sage who lived in the forest, probably a recluse, possessing nothing, dependent upon the villagers for his daily necessities, and all his life trying to solve the problems of this life and the life hereafter.

The second point is, the difference of unit. The law of caste in every other country takes the individual man or woman as the sufficient unit. Wealth, power, intellect, or beauty suffices for the individual to leave the status of birth and scramble up to anywhere he can.

Here, the unit is all the members of a caste community.

Here, too, one has every chance of rising from a low caste to a higher or the highest: only, in this birth-land of altruism, one is compelled to take his whole caste along with him.

In India, you cannot, on account of your wealth, power, or any other merit, leave your fellows behind and make common cause with your superiors; you cannot deprive those who

helped in your acquiring the excellence of any benefit therefrom and give them in return only contempt. If you want to rise to a higher caste in India, you have to elevate all your caste first, and then there is nothing in your onward path to hold you back.

This is the Indian method of fusion, and this has been going on from time immemorial. For in India, more there elsewhere. Such words as Aryans and Dravidians are only of philological import, the so-called craniological differentiation finding no solid ground to work upon.

Even so are the names Brahmin, Kshatriya, etc. They simply represent the status of a community in itself continuously fluctuating, even when it has reached the summit and all further endeavours are towards fixity of the type by non-marriage, by being forced to admit fresh groups, from lower castes or foreign lands, within its pale.

Whatever caste has the power of the sword, becomes Kshatriya; whatever learning, Brahmin; whatever wealth, Vaishya.

The groups that have already reached the coveted goal, indeed, try to keep themselves aloof from the newcomers, by making sub-divisions in the same caste, but the fact remains that they coalesce in the long run. This is going on before our own eyes, all over India.

Naturally, a group having raised itself would try to preserve the privileges to itself. Hence, whenever it was possible to get the help of a king, the higher castes, especially the Brahmins, have tried to put down similar aspirations in lower castes, by the sword if practicable. But the question is: Did they succeed? Look closely into your Purânas and Upa-puranas, look especially into the local Khandas of the big Puranas, look round and see what is happening before your eyes, and you will find the answer.

We are, in spite of our various castes, and in spite of the modern custom of marriage restricted within the sub-divisions of a caste (though this is not universal), a mixed race in every sense of the word.

Whatever may be the import of the philological terms "Aryan" and "Tamilian", even taking for granted that both these grand sub-divisions of Indian humanity came from outside the Western frontier, the dividing line had been, from the most ancient times, one of language and not of blood. Not one of the epithets expressive of contempt for the ugly physical features of the Dasyus of the Vedas would apply to the great Tamilian race; in fact if there be a toss for good looks between the Aryans and Tamilians, no sensible man would dare prognosticate the result.

The super-arrogated excellence of birth of any caste in India is only pure myth, and in no part of India has it, we are sorry to say, found such congenial soil, owing to linguistic differences, as in the South.

We purposely refrain from going into the details of this social tyranny in the South, just as we have stopped ourselves from scrutinising the genesis of the various modern Brahmins and other castes. Sufficient for us to note the extreme tension of feeling that is evident between the Brahmins and non-Brahmins of the Madras Presidency.

We believe in Indian caste as one of the greatest social institutions that the Lord gave to man. We also believe that though the unavoidable defects, foreign persecutions, and, above all, the monumental ignorance and pride of many Brahmins who do not deserve the name, have thwarted, in many ways, the legitimate fructification of this most glorious Indian institution, it has already worked wonders for the land of Bharata and is destined to lead Indian humanity to its goal.

We earnestly entreat the Brahmins of the South not to forget the ideal of India — the production of a universe of Brahmins, pure as purity, good as God Himself: this was at the beginning, says the Mahâbhârata, and so will it be in the end.

Then anyone who claims to be a Brahmin should prove his pretensions, first by manifesting that spirituality, and next by raising others to the same status. On the face of this, it seems that most of them are only nursing a false pride of birth; and any schemer, native or foreign, who can pander to this vanity and inherent laziness by fulsome sophistry, appears to satisfy most.

Beware, Brahmins, this is the sign of death! Arise and show your manhood, your Brahminhood, by raising the non-Brahmins around you — not in the spirit of a master — not with the rotten canker of egotism crawling with superstitions and the charlatanry of East and West — but in the spirit of a servant. For verily he who knows how to serve knows how to rule.

The non-Brahmins also have been spending their energy in kindling the fire of caste hatred — vain and useless to solve the problem — to which every non-Hindu is only too glad to throw on a load of fuel.

Not a step forward can be made by these inter-caste quarrels, not one difficulty removed; only the beneficent onward march of events would be thrown back, possibly for centuries, if the fire bursts out into flames

It would be a repetition of Buddhistic political blunders.

In the midst of this ignorant clamour and hatred, we are delighted to find Pandit D. Savariroyan pursuing the only legitimate and the only sensible course. Instead of wasting precious vitality in foolish and meaningless quarrels, Pandit Savariroyan has undertaken in his articles on the "Admixture of the Aryan with Tamilian" in the Siddhânta Deepikâ, to clear away not only a lot of haze, created by a too adventurous Western philology, but to pave the way to a better understanding of the caste problem in the South.

Nobody ever got anything by begging. We get only what we deserve. The first step to deserve is to desire: and we desire with success what we feel ourselves worthy to get.

A gentle yet clear brushing off of the cobwebs of the so-called Aryan theory and all its vicious corollaries is therefore absolutely necessary, especially for the South, and a proper self-respect created by a knowledge of the past grandeur of one of the great ancestors of the Aryan race — the great Tamilians.

We stick, in spite of Western theories, to that definition of the word "Arya" which we find in our sacred books, and which includes only the multitude we now call Hindus. This Aryan race, itself a mixture of two great races, Sanskrit-speaking and Tamil-speaking, applies to all Hindus alike. That the Shudras have in some Smritis been excluded from this epithet means nothing, for the Shudras were and still are only the waiting Aryas — Aryas in novitiate.

Though we know Pandit Savariroyan is walking over rather insecure ground, though we differ from many of his sweeping explanations of Vedic names and races, yet we are glad that he has undertaken the task of beginning a proper investigation into the culture of the great mother of Indian civilisation — if the Sanskrit-speaking race was the father.

We are glad also that he boldly pushes forward the Accado-Sumerian racial identity of the ancient Tamilians. And this makes us proud of the blood of the great civilisation which flowered before all others — compared to whose antiquity the Aryans and Semites are babies.

We would suggest, also, that the land of Punt of the Egyptians was not only Malabar, but that the Egyptians as a race bodily migrated from Malabar across the ocean and entered the delta along the course of the Nile from north to south, to which Punt they have been always fondly looking back as the home of the blessed.

This is a move in the right direction. Detailed and more careful work is sure to follow with a better study of the Tamilian tongues and the Tamilian elements found in the Sanskrit literature, philosophy, and religion. And who are more competent to do this work than those who learn the Tamilian idioms as their mother-tongue?

As for us Vedântins and Sannyâsins, ore are proud of our Sanskrit-speaking ancestors of the Vedas; proud of our Tamil-speaking ancestors whose civilization is the oldest yet known; we are proud of our Kolarian ancestors older than either of the above — who lived and hunted in forests; we are proud of our ancestors with flint implements — the first of the human race; and if evolution is true, we are proud of our animal ancestors, for they antedated man himself. We are proud that we are descendants of the whole universe, sentient or insentient. Proud that we are born, and work, and suffer — prouder still that we die when the task is finished and enter forever the realm where there is no more delusion.

THE SOCIAL CONFERENCE ADDRESS

"God created the native, God created the European, but somebody else created the mixed breed" — we heard a horribly blasphemous Englishman say.

Before us lies the inaugural address of Mr. Justice Ranade, voicing the reformatory zeal of tie Indian Social Conference. In it there is a huge array of instances of inter-caste marriages of yore, a good leaf about the liberal spirit of the ancient Kshatriyas, good sober advice to students, all expressed with an earnestness of goodwill and gentleness of language that is truly admirable.

The last part, however, which offers advice as to the creation of a body of teachers for the new movement strong in the Punjab, which we take for granted is the Ârya Samâj, founded by a Sannyâsin, leaves us wondering and asking ourselves the question:

It seems God created the Brâhmin, God created the Kshatriya, but who created the Sannyasin?

There have been and are Sannyasins or monks in every known religion. There are Hindu monks, Buddhist monks, Christian monks, and even Islam had to yield its rigorous denial and take in whole orders of mendicant monks.

There are the wholly shaved, the partly shaved, the long hair, short hair, matted hair, and various other hirsute types.

There are the sky-clad, the rag-clad, the ochre-clad, the yellow-clad (monks), the black-clad Christian and the blue-clad Mussulman. Then there have been those that tortured their flesh in various ways, and others who believed in keeping their bodies well and healthy. There was also, in odd days in every country, the monk militant. The same spirit and similar manifestations haste run in parallel lines with the women, too—the nuns. Mr. Ranade is not only the President of the Indian Social Conference but a chivalrous gentleman also: the nuns of the Shrutis and Smritis seem to have been to his entire satisfaction. The ancient celibate Brahmavâdinis, who travelled from court to court challenging great philosophers, do not seem to him to thwart the central plan of the Creator—the propagation of species; nor did they seem to have lacked in the variety and completeness of human experience, in Mr. Ranade's opinion, as the stronger sex following the same line of conduct seem to have done.

We therefore dismiss the ancient nuns and their modern spiritual descendants as having passed muster.

The arch-offender, man alone, has to bear the brunt of Mr. Ranade's criticism, and let us see whether he survives it or not.

It seems to be the consensus of opinion amongst savants that this world-wide monastic institution had its first inception in this curious land of ours, which appears to stand so much in need of "social reform".

The married teacher and the celibate are both as old as the Vedas. Whether the Soma-sipping married Rishi with his "all-rounded" experience was the first in order of appearance, or the lack-human-experience celibate Rishi was the primeval form, is hard to decide just now. Possibly Mr. Ranade will solve the problem for us independently of the hearsay of the so-called Western Sanskrit scholars; till then the question stands a riddle like the hen and egg problem of yore.

But whatever be the order of genesis, the celibate teachers of the Shrutis and Smritis stand on an entirely different platform from the married ones, which is perfect chastity, Brahmacharya.

If the performance of Yajnas is the corner-stone of the work-portion of the Vedas, as surely is Brahmacharya the foundation of the knowledge-portion.

Why could not the blood-shedding sacrificers be the exponents of the Upanishads—why?

On the one side was the married Rishi, with his meaningless, bizarre, nay, terrible ceremonials, his misty sense of ethics, to say the least; on the other hand, the celibate monks tapping, in spite of their want of human experience, springs of spirituality and ethics at which the monastic Jinas, the Buddhas, down to Shankara, Ramanuja, Kabir, and Chaitanya, drank deep and acquired energy to propagate their marvellous spiritual and social reforms, and which, reflected third-hand, fourth-hand from the West, is giving our social reformers the power even to criticise the Sannyasins.

At the present day, what support, what pay, do the mendicants receive in India, compared to the pay and privilege of our social reformers? And what work does the social reformer do, compared to the Sannyasin's silent selfless labour of love?

But they have not learnt the modern method of self-advertisement!!

The Hindu drank in with his mother's milk that this life is as nothing—a dream! In this he is at one with the Westerners; but the Westerner sees no further and his conclusion is that of the Chârvâka—to "make hay while the sun shines". "This world being a miserable hole, let us enjoy to the utmost what morsels of pleasure are left to us." To the Hindu, on the other hand, God and soul are the only realities, infinitely more real than this world, and he is therefore ever ready to let this go for the other.

So long as this attitude of the national mind continues, and we pray it will continue for ever, what hope is there in our anglicised compatriots to check the impulse in Indian men and women to renounce all "for the good of the universe and for one's own freedom"?

And that rotten corpse of an argument against the monk—used first by the Protestants in Europe, borrowed by the Bengali reformers, and now embraced by our Bombay brethren—the monk on account of his celibacy must lack the realisation of life "in all its fullness and in all its varied experience!" We hope this time the corpse will go for good into the Arabian Sea, especially in these days of plague, and notwithstanding the filial love one may suppose the foremost clan of Brahmins there may have for ancestors of great perfume, if the Paurânika accounts are of any value in tracing their ancestry.

By the bye, in Europe, between the monks and nuns, they have brought up and educated most of the children, whose parents, though married people, were utterly unwilling to taste of the "varied experiences of life".

Then, of course, every faculty has been given to us by God for some use. Therefore the monk is wrong in not propagating the race—a sinner! Well, so also have been given us the faculties of anger, lust, cruelty, theft, robbery, cheating, etc., every one of these being absolutely necessary for the maintenance of social life, reformed or unreformed. What about these? Ought they also to be maintained at full steam, following the varied-experience theory or not? Of course the social reformers, being in intimate acquaintance with God Almighty and His purposes, must answer the query in the positive. Are we to follow Vishvâmitra, Atri, and others in their ferocity and the Vasishtha family in particular in their "full and varied experience" with womankind? For the majority of married Rishis are as celebrated for their liberality in begetting children wherever and whenever they could, as for their hymn-singing and Soma-bibbing; or are we to follow the celibate Rishis who upheld Brahmacharya as the sine qua non of spirituality?

Then there are the usual backsliders, who ought to come in for a load of abuse—monks who could not keep up to their ideal—weak, wicked.

But if the ideal is straight and sound, a backsliding monk is head and shoulders above any householder in the land, on the principle, "It is better to have loved and lost."

Compared to the coward that never made the attempt, he is a hero.

If the searchlight of scrutiny were turned on the inner workings of our social reform conclave, angels would have to take note of the percentage of backsliders as between the monk and the householder; and the recording angel is in our own heart.

But then, what about this marvellous experience of standing alone, discarding all help, breasting the storms of life, of working without any sense of recompense, without any sense of putrid duty? Working a whole life, joyful, free—not goaded on to work like slaves by false human love or ambition?

This the monk alone can have. What about religion? Has it to remain or vanish? If it remains, it requires its experts, its soldiers. The monk is the religious expert, having made religion his one métier of life. He is the soldier of God. What religion dies so long as it has a band of devoted monks?

Why are Protestant England and America shaking before the onrush of the Catholic monk?

Vive Ranade and the Social Reformers!—but, O India! Anglicised India! Do not forget, child, that there are in this society problems that neither you nor your Western Guru can yet grasp the meaning of—much less solve!

INDIA'S MESSAGE TO THE WORLD

The following notes were discovered among Swami Vivekananda's papers. He intended to write a book and jotted down forty-two points as a syllabus for the work, but only a few points were dealt with as an introduction by him and the work was left unfinished. We give the manuscript as found.

Syllabus

1. Bold has been my message to the people of the West. Bolder to those at home.

2. Four years of residence in the marvellous West has made India only the better understood. The shades are deeper and the lights brighter.

3. The survey—it is not true that the Indians have degenerated.

4. The problem here has been as it has been everywhere else—the assimilation of various races, but nowhere has it been so vast as here.

5. Community of language, government and, above all, religion has been the power of fusion.

6. In other lands this has been attempted by "force", that is, the enforcement of the culture of one race only over the rest. The result being the production of a short-lived vigorous national life; then, dissolution.

7. In India, on the other hand, the attempts have been as gentle as the problem vast, and from the earliest times, the customs, and especially the religions, of the different elements tolerated.

8. Where it was a small problem and force was sufficient to form a unity, the effect really was the nipping in the bud of various healthy types in the germ of all the elements except the dominant one. It was only one set of brains using the vast majority for its own good, thus losing the major portion of the possible amount of development, and thus when the dominant type had spent itself, the apparently impregnable building tottered to its ruins, e.g., Greece, Rome, the Norman.

9. A common language would be a great desideratum; but the same criticism applies to it, the destruction of the vitality of the various existing ones.

10. The only solution to be reached was the finding of a great sacred language of which all the others would be considered as manifestations, and that was found in the Sanskrit.

11. The Dravidian languages may or may not have been originally Sanskritic, but for practical purposes they are so now, and every day we see them approaching the ideal more and more, yet keeping their distinctive vital peculiarities.

12. A racial background was found—the Âryas.

13. The speculation whether there was a distinct, separate race called the Aryas living in Central Asia to the Baltic.

14. The so-called types. Races were always mixed.

15. The "blonde" and the "brunette".

16. Coming to practical common sense from so-called historical imagination. The Aryas in their oldest records were in the land between Turkistan and the Punjab and N. W. Tibet.

17. This leads to the attempt at fusion between races and tribes of various degrees of culture.

18. Just as Sanskrit has been the linguistic solution, so the Arya the racial solution. So the Brâhminhood is the solution of the varying degrees of progress and culture as well as that of all social and political problems.

19. The great ideal of India — Brahminhood.

20. Property-less, selfless, subject to no laws, no king except the moral.

21. Brahminhood by descent — various races have claimed and acquired the right in the past as well as in the present.

22. No claim is made by the doer of great deeds, only by lazy worthless fools.

23. Degradation of Brahminhood and Kshatriyahood. The Puranas said there will be only non-Brahmins in the Kali Yuga, and that is true, becoming truer every day. Yet a few Brahmins remain, and in India alone.

24. Kshatriyahood — we must pass through that to become a Brahmin. Some may have passed through in the past, but the present must show that.

25. But the disclosure of the whole plan is to be found in religion.

26. The different tribes of the same race worship similar gods, under a generic name as the Baals of the Babylonians, the Molochs of the Hebrews.

27. The attempt in Babylonia of making all the Baals merge in Baal-Merodach — the attempt of the Israelites to merge all the Molochs in the Moloch Yavah or Yahu.

28. The Babylonians destroyed by the Persians; and the Hebrews who took the Babylonian mythology and adapted it to their own needs, succeeded in producing a strict monotheistic religion.

29. Monotheism like absolute monarchy is quick in executing orders, and a great centralization of force, but it grows no farther, and its worst feature is its cruelty and persecution. All nations coming within its influence perish very soon after a flaring up of a few years.

30. In India the same problem presented itself - the solution found — एकं सद्विप्रा बहुधा वदन्ति।

    This is the keynote to everything which has succeeded, and the keystone of the arch.

31. The result is that wonderful toleration of the Vedantist.

32. The great problem therefore is to harmonise and unify without destroying the individuality of these various elements.

33. No form of religion which depends Upon persons, either of this earth or even of heaven, is able to do that.

34. Here is the glory of the Advaita system preaching a principle, not a person, yet allowing persons, both human and divine, to have their full play.

35. This has been going on all the time; in this sense we have been always progressing. The Prophets during the Mohammedan rule.

36. It was fully conscious and vigorous in old days, and less so of late; in this sense alone we have degenerated.

37. This is going to be in the future. If the manifestation of the power of one tribe utilising the labours of the rest produced wonderful results at least for a certain length of time, here is going to be the accumulation and the concentration of all the races that have been slowly and inevitably getting mixed up in blood and ideas, and in my mind's eye, I see the future giant slowly maturing. The future of India, the youngest and the most glorious of the nations of earth as well as the oldest.

38. The way — we will have to work. Social customs as barriers, some as founded upon the Smritis. But none from the Shrutis. The Smritis must change with time. This is the admitted law.

39. The principles of the Vedanta not only should be preached everywhere in India, but also outside. Our thought must enter into the make-up of the minds of every nation, not through writings, but through persons.

40. Gift is the only Karma in Kali Yuga. None attaining knowledge until purified by Karma.

41. Gift of spiritual and secular knowledge.

42. Renunciation — Renouncers — the national call.

Introduction

Bold has been my message to the people of the West, bolder is my message to you, my beloved countrymen. The message of ancient India to new Western nations I have tried my best to voice — ill done or well done the future is sure to show; but the mighty voice of the same future is already sending forward soft but distinct murmurs, gaining strength as the days go by, the message of India that is to be to India as she is at present.

Many wonderful institutions and customs, and many wonderful manifestations of strength and power it has been my good fortune to study in the midst of the various races I have seen, but the most wonderful of all was to find that beneath all these apparent variations of manners and customs, of culture and power, beats the same mighty human heart under the impulsion of the same joys and sorrows, of the same weakness and strength

Good and evil are everywhere and the balance is wondrously even; but, above all, is the glorious soul of man everywhere which never fails to understand any one who knows how to speak its own language. Men and women are to be found in every race whose lives are blessings to humanity, verifying the words of the divine Emperor Asoka: "In every land dwell Brâhmins and Shramanas."

I am grateful to the lands of the West for the many warm hearts that received me with all the love that pure and disinterested souls alone could give; but my life's allegiance is to this my motherland; and if I had a thousand lives, every moment of the whole series would be consecrated to your service, my countrymen, my friends.

For to this land I owe whatever I possess, physical, mental, and spiritual; and if I have been successful in anything, the glory is yours, not mine. Mine alone are my weaknesses and failures, as they come through my inability of profiting by the mighty lessons with which this land surrounds one, even from his very birth.

And what a land! Whosoever stands on this sacred land, whether alien or a child of the soil, feels himself surrounded—unless his soul is degraded to the level of brute animals—by the living thoughts of the earth's best and purest sons, who have been working to raise the animal to the divine through centuries, whose beginning history fails to trace. The very air is full of the pulsations of spirituality. This land is sacred to philosophy, to ethics and spirituality, to all that tends to give a respite to man in his incessant struggle for the preservation of the animal to all training that makes man throw off the garment of brutality and stand revealed as the spirit immortal, the birthless, the deathless, the ever-blessed—the land where the cup of pleasure was full, and fuller has been the cup of misery, until here, first of all, man found out that it was all vanity; here, first of all in the prime of youth, in the lap of luxury, in the height of glory and plenitude of power, he broke through the fetters of delusion. Here, in this ocean of humanity, amidst the sharp interaction of strong currents of pleasure and pain, of strength and weakness, of wealth and poverty, of joy and sorrow, of smile and tear, of life and death, in the melting rhythm of eternal peace and calmness, arose the throne of renunciation! Here in this land, the great problems of life and death, of the thirst for life, and the vain mad struggles to preserve it only resulting in the accumulation of woes were first grappled with and solved—solved as they never were before and never will be hereafter; for here and here alone was discovered that even life itself is an evil, the shadow only of something which alone is real. This is the land where alone religion was practical and real, and here alone men and women plunged boldly in to realise the goal, just as in other lands they madly plunge in to realise the pleasures of life by robbing their weaker brethren. Here and here alone the human heart expanded till it included not only the human, but birds, beasts, and plants; from the highest gods to grains of sand, the highest and the lowest, all find a place in the heart of man, grown great, infinite. And here alone, the human soul studied the universe as one unbroken unity whose every pulse was his own pulse.

We all hear so much about the degradation of India. There was a time when I also believed in it. But today standing on the vantage-ground of experience, with eyes cleared of obstructive predispositions and above all, of the highly-coloured pictures of other countries toned down to their proper shade and light by actual contact, I confess in all humility that I was wrong. Thou blessed land of the Aryas, thou wast never degraded. Sceptres have been broken and thrown away, the ball of power has passed from hand to hand, but in India, courts and kings always touched only a few; the vast mass of the people, from the highest to the lowest, has been left to pursue its own inevitable course, the current of national life flowing at times slow and half-conscious, at others, strong and awakened. I stand in awe before the unbroken procession of scores of shining centuries, with here and there a dim link in the chain, only to flare up with added brilliance in the next, and there she is walking with her own majestic steps—my motherland—to fulfil her glorious destiny, which no power on earth or in heaven can check—the regeneration of man the brute into man the God.

Ay, a glorious destiny, my brethren, for as far back as the days of the Upanishads we have thrown the challenge to the world: न प्रजया धनेन त्यागेनेके अमृतत्वमानशुः— "Not by progeny, not by wealth, but by renunciation alone immortality is reached." Race after race has taken the challenge up and tried their utmost to solve the world-riddle on the plane of desires. They have all failed in the past—the old ones have become extinct under the weight of wickedness and misery, which lust for power and gold brings in its train, and the new ones are tottering to their fall. The question has yet to be decided whether peace will survive or war; whether patience will survive or non-forbearance, whether goodness will survive or wickedness; whether muscle will survive or brain; whether worldliness will survive or spirituality. We have solved our problem ages ago, and held on to it through good or evil fortune, and mean to hold on to it till the end of time. Our solution is unworldliness—renunciation.

This is the theme of Indian life-work, the burden of her eternal songs, the backbone of her existence, the foundation of her being, the raison d'être of her very existence—the spiritualisation of the human race. In this her life-course she has never deviated, whether the Tartar ruled or the Turk, whether the Mogul ruled or the English.

And I challenge anybody to show one single period of her national life when India was lacking in spiritual giants capable of moving the world. But her work is spiritual, and that cannot be done with blasts of war-trumpets or the march of cohorts. Her influence has always fallen upon the world like that of the gentle dew, unheard and scarcely marked, yet bringing into bloom the fairest flowers of the earth. This influence, being in its nature gentle, would have to wait for a fortunate combination of circumstances, to go out of the country into other lands, though it never ceased to work within the limits of its native land. As such, every educated person knows that whenever the empire-building Tartar or Persian or Greek or Arab brought this land in contact with the outside world, a mass of spiritual influence immediately flooded the world from here. The very same circumstances have presented themselves once more before us. The English high roads over land and sea and the wonderful power manifested by the inhabitants of that little island have once more brought India in contact with the rest of the world, and the same work has already begun. Mark my words, this is but the small beginning, big things are to follow; what the result of the present work outside India will be I cannot exactly state, but this I know for certain that millions, I say deliberately, millions in every civilised land are waiting for the message that will save them from the hideous abyss of materialism into which modern money-worship is driving them headlong, and many of the leaders of the new social movements have already discovered that Vedanta in its highest form can alone spiritualise their social aspirations. I shall have to return to this towards the end I take up therefore the other great subject, the work within the country.

The problem assumes a twofold aspect, not only spiritualisation but assimilation of the various elements of which the nation is composed. The assimilation of different races into one has been the common task in the life of every nation.

STRAY REMARKS ON THEOSOPHY[1]

The Theosophists are having a jubilee time of it this year, and several press-notices are before us of their goings and doings for the last twenty-five years.

Nobody has a right now to say that the Hindus are not liberal to a fault. A coterie of young Hindus has been found to welcome even this graft of American Spiritualism, with its panoply of taps and raps and hitting back and forth with Mahâtmic pellets.

The Theosophists claim to possess the original divine knowledge of the universe. We are glad to learn of it, and gladder still that they mean to keep it rigorously a secret. Woe unto us, poor mortals, and Hindus at that, if all this is at once let out on us! Modern Theosophy is Mrs. Besant. Blavatskism and Olcottism seem to have taken a back seat. Mrs. Besant means well at least—and nobody can deny her perseverance and zeal.

There are, of course, carping critics. We on our part see nothing but good in Theosophy—good in what is directly beneficial, good in what is pernicious, as they say, indirectly good as we say—the intimate geographical knowledge of various heavens, and other places, and the denizens thereof; and the dexterous finger work on the visible plane accompanying ghostly communications to live Theosophists—all told. For Theosophy is the best serum we know of, whose injection never fails to develop the queer moths finding lodgment in some brains attempting to pass muster as sound.

We have no wish to disparage the good work of the Theosophical or any other society. Yet exaggeration has been in the past the bane of our race and if the several articles on the work of the Theosophical Society that appeared in the Advocate of Lucknow be taken as the temperamental gauge of Lucknow, we are sorry for those it represents, to say the least; foolish depreciation is surely vicious, but fulsome praise is equally loathsome.

1. Found among Swami Vivekananda's papers.

This Indian grafting of American Spiritualism—with only a few Sanskrit words taking the place of spiritualistic jargon—Mahâtmâ missiles taking the place of ghostly raps and taps, and Mahatmic inspiration that of obsession by ghosts.

We cannot attribute a knowledge of all this to the writer of the articles in the Advocate, but he must not confound himself and his Theosophists with the great Hindu nation, the majority of whom have clearly seen through the Theosophical phenomena from the start and, following the great Swami Dayânanda Sarasvati who took away his patronage from Blavatskism the moment he found it out, have held themselves aloof.

Again, whatever be the predilection of the writer in question, the Hindus have enough of religious teaching and teachers amidst themselves even in this Kali Yuga, and they do not stand in need of dead ghosts of Russians and Americans.

The articles in question are libels on the Hindus and their religion. We Hindus—let the writer, like that of the articles referred to, know once for all—have no need nor desire to import religion from the West. Sufficient has been the degradation of importing almost everything else.

The importation in the case of religion should be mostly on the side of the West, we are sure, and our work has been all along in that line. The only help the religion of the Hindus got from the Theosophists in the West was not a ready field, but years of uphill work, necessitated by Theosophical sleight-of-hand methods. The writer ought to have known that the Theosophists wanted to crawl into the heart of Western Society, catching on to the skirts of scholars like Max Müller and poets like Edwin Arnold, all the same denouncing these very men and posing as the only receptacles of universal wisdom. And one heaves a sigh of relief that this wonderful wisdom is kept a secret. Indian thought, charlatanry, and mango-growing fakirism had all become identified in the minds of educated people in the West, and this was all the help rendered to Hindu religion by the Theosophists.

The great immediate visible good effect of Theosophy in every country, so far as we can see, is to separate, like Prof. Koch's injections into the lungs of consumptives, the healthy, spiritual, active, and patriotic from the charlatans, the morbids, and the degenerates posing as spiritual beings.

REPLY TO THE ADDRESS OF THE MAHARAJA OF KHETRI

INDIA—THE LAND OF RELIGION

During the residence of the Swamiji in America, the following Address from the Maharaja of Khetri (Rajputana), dated March 4th, 1895, was received by him:

My dear Swamiji,

As the head of this Durbar (a formal stately assemblage) held today for this special purpose, I have much pleasure in conveying to you, in my own name and that of my subjects, the heartfelt thanks of this State for your worthy representation of Hinduism at the Parliament of Religions, held at Chicago, in America.

I do not think the general principles of Hinduism could be expressed more accurately and clearly in English than what you have done, with all the restrictions imposed by the very natural shortcomings of language itself.

The influence of your speech and behaviour in foreign lands has not only spread admiration among men of different countries and different religions, but has also served to familiarise you with them, to help in the furtherance of your unselfish cause. This is very highly and inexpressibly appreciated by us all, and we should feel to be failing in our duty, were I not to write to you formally at least these few lines, expressing our sincere gratitude for all the trouble you have taken in going to foreign countries, and to expound in the American Parliament of Religions the truths of our ancient religion which we ever hold so dear. It is certainly applicable to the pride of India that it has been fortunate in possessing the privilege of having secured so able a representative as yourself.

Thanks are also due to those noble souls whose efforts succeeded in organising the Parliament of Religions, and who accorded to you a very enthusiastic reception. As you were quite a foreigner in that continent, their kind treatment of you is due to their love of the several qualifications you possess, and this speaks highly of their noble nature.

I herewith enclose twenty printed copies of this letter and have to request that, keeping this one with yourself you will kindly distribute the other copies among your friends.

With best regards,
I remain,
Yours very sincerely,
Raja Ajit Singh Bahadur of Khetri .

The Swamiji sent the following reply:

"Whenever virtue subsides, and wickedness raises its head, I manifest Myself to restore the glory of religion"—are the words, O noble Prince, of the Eternal One in the holy Gîtâ, striking the keynote of the pulsating ebb and flow of the spiritual energy in the universe.

These changes are manifesting themselves again and again in rhythms peculiar to themselves, and like every other tremendous change, though affecting, more or less, every particle within their sphere of action, they show their effects more intensely upon those particles which are naturally susceptible to their power.

As in a universal sense, the primal state is a state of sameness of the qualitative forces—a disturbance of this equilibrium and all succeeding struggles to regain it, composing what we call the manifestation of nature, this universe, which state of things remains as long as the primitive sameness is not reached—so, in a restricted sense on our own earth, differentiation and its inevitable counterpart, this struggle towards homogeneity, must remain as long as the human race shall remain as such, creating strongly marked peculiarities between ethnic divisions, sub-races and even down to individuals in all parts of the world.

In this world of impartial division and balance, therefore, each nation represents, as it were, a wonderful dynamo for the storage and distribution of a particular species of energy, and amidst all other possessions that particular property shines forth as the special characteristic of that race. And as any upheaval in any particular part of human nature, though affecting others more or less, stirs to its very depth that nation of which it is a special characteristic, and from which as a centre it generally starts, so any commotion in the religious world is sure to produce momentous changes in India, that land which again and again has had to furnish the centre of the wide-spread religious upheavals; for, above all, India is the land of religion.

Each man calls that alone real which helps him to realise his ideal. To the worldly-minded, everything that can be converted into money is real, that which cannot be so converted is unreal. To the man of a domineering spirit, anything that will conduce to his ambition of ruling over his fellow men is real—the rest is naught; and man finds nothing in that which does not echo back the heartbeats of his special love in life.

Those whose only aim is to barter the energies of life for gold, or name, or any other enjoyment; those to whom the tramp of embattled cohorts is the only manifestation of power; those to whom the enjoyments of the senses are the only bliss that life can give—to these, India will ever appear as an immense desert whose every blast is deadly to the development of life, as it is known by them.

But to those whose thirst for life has been quenched for ever by drinking from the stream of immortality that flows from far away beyond the world of the senses, whose souls have cast away—as a serpent its slough—the threefold bandages of lust, gold, and fame, who, from their height of calmness, look with love and compassion upon the petty quarrels and jealousies and fights for little gilded puff-balls, filled with dust, called "enjoyment" by those under a sense-bondage; to those whose accumulated force of past good deeds has caused the scales of ignorance to fall off from their eyes, making them see through the vanity of name and form—to such wheresoever they be, India, the motherland and eternal mine of spirituality, stands transfigured, a beacon of hope to everyone in search of Him who is the only real Existence in a universe of vanishing shadows.

The majority of mankind can only understand power when it is presented to them in a concrete form, fitted to their perceptions. To them, the rush and excitement of war, with its power and spell, is something very tangible, and any manifestation of life that does not come like a whirlwind, bearing down everything before it, is to them as death. And India, for centuries at the feet of foreign conquerors, without any idea or hope of resistance, without the least solidarity among its masses, without the least idea of patriotism, must needs appear to such, as a land of rotten bones, a lifeless putrescent mass.

It is said—the fittest alone survive. How is it, then, that this most unfitted of all races, according to commonly accepted ideas, could bear the most awful misfortunes that ever befall a race, and yet not show the least signs of decay? How is it that, while the multiplying powers of the so-called vigorous and active races are dwindling every day, the immoral (?) Hindu shows a power of increase beyond them all? Great laurels are due, no doubt, to those who can deluge the world with blood at a moment's notice; great indeed is the glory of those who, to keep up a population of a few millions in plenty, have to starve half the population of the earth, but is no credit due to those who can keep hundreds of millions in peace and plenty, without snatching the bread from the mouth of anyone else? Is there no power displayed in bringing up and guiding the destinies of countless millions of human beings, through hundreds of centuries, without the least violence to others?

The mythologists of all ancient races supply us with fables of heroes whose life was concentrated in a certain small portion of their bodies, and until that was touched they remained invulnerable. It seems as if each nation also has such a peculiar centre of life, and so long as that remains untouched, no amount of misery and misfortune can destroy it.

In religion lies the vitality of India, and so long as the Hindu race do not forget the great inheritance of their forefathers, there is no power on earth to destroy them.

Nowadays everybody blames those who constantly look back to their past. It is said that so much looking back to the past is the cause of all India's woes. To me, on the contrary, it seems that the opposite is true. So long as they forgot the past, the Hindu nation remained in a state of stupor; and as soon as they have begun to look into their past, there is on every side a fresh manifestation of life. It is out of this past that the future has to be moulded; this past will become the future.

The more, therefore, the Hindus study the past, the more glorious will be their future, and whoever tries to bring the past to the door of everyone, is a great benefactor to his nation. The degeneration of India came not because the laws and customs of the ancients were bad, but because they were not allowed to be carried to their legitimate conclusions.

Every critical student knows that the social laws of India have always been subject to great periodic changes. At their inception, these laws were the embodiment of a gigantic plan, which was to unfold itself slowly through time. The great seers of ancient India saw so far ahead of their time that the world has to wait centuries yet to appreciate their wisdom, and it is this very inability on the part of their own descendants to appreciate the full scope of this wonderful plan that is the one and only cause of the degeneration of India.

Ancient India had for centuries been the battlefield for the ambitious projects of two of her foremost classes—the Brâhmins and the Kshatriyas.

On the one hand, the priesthood stood between the lawless social tyranny of the princes over the masses whom the Kshatriyas declared to be their legal food. On the other hand, the Kshatriya power was the one potent force which struggled with any success against the spiritual tyranny of the priesthood and the ever-increasing chain of ceremonials which they were forging to bind down the people with.

The tug of war began in the earliest periods of the history of our race, and throughout the Shrutis it can be distinctly traced. A momentary lull came when Shri Krishna, leading the faction of Kshatriya power and of Jnâna, showed the way to reconciliation. The result was the teachings of the Gita—the essence of philosophy, of liberality, of religion. Yet the causes were there, and the effect must follow.

The ambition of these two classes to be the masters of the poor and ignorant was there, and the strife once more became fierce. The meagre literature that has come down to us from that period brings to us but faint echoes of that mighty past strife, but at last it broke out as a victory for the Kshatriyas, a victory for Jnana, for liberty—and ceremonial had to go down, much of it for ever. This upheaval was what is known as the Buddhistic reformation. On the religious side, it represented freedom from ceremonial; on the political side, overthrow of the priesthood by the Kshatriyas.

It is a significant fact that the two greatest men ancient India produced, were both Kshatriyas—Krishna and Buddha—and still more significant is the fact that both of these God-men threw open the door of knowledge to everyone, irrespective of birth or sex.

In spite of its wonderful moral strength, Buddhism was extremely iconoclastic; and much of its force being spent in merely negative attempts, it had to die out in the land of its birth, and what remained of it became full of superstitions and ceremonials, a hundred times cruder than those it was intended to suppress. Although it partially succeeded in putting down the animal sacrifices of the Vedas, it filled the land with temples, images, symbols, and bones of saints.

Above all, in the medley of Aryans, Mongols, and aborigines which it created, it unconsciously led the way to some of the hideous Vâmâchâras. This was especially the reason why this travesty of the teaching of the great Master had to be driven out of India by Shri Shankara and his band of Sannyâsins.

Thus even the current of life, set in motion by the greatest soul that ever wore a human form, the Bhagavân Buddha himself, became a miasmatic pool, and India had to wait for centuries until Shankara arose, followed in quick succession by Râmânuja and Madhva.

By this time, an entirely new chapter had opened in the history of India. The ancient Kshatriyas and the Brahmins had disappeared. The land between the Himalayas and the Vindhyas, the home of the Âryas, the land which gave birth to Krishna and Buddha, the cradle of great Râjarshis and Brahmarshis, became silent, and from the very farther end of the Indian Peninsula, from races alien in speech and form, from families claiming descent from the ancient Brahmins, came the reaction against the corrupted Buddhism.

What had become of the Brahmins and Kshatriyas of Âryâvarta? They had entirely disappeared, except here and there a few mongrel clans claiming to be Brahmins and Kshatriyas, and in spite of their inflated, self-laudatory assertions that the whole world ought to learn from एतद्देशप्रसूतस्य सकाशादग्रजन्मनः, they had to sit in sackcloth and ashes, in all humility, to learn at the feet of the Southerners. The result was the bringing back of the Vedas to India—a revival of Vedânta, such as India never before had seen; even the householders began to study the Âranyakas.

In the Buddhistic movement, the Kshatriyas were the real leaders, and whole masses of them became Buddhists. In the zeal of reform and conversion, the popular dialects had been almost exclusively cultivated to the neglect of Sanskrit, and the larger portion of Kshatriyas had become disjointed from the Vedic literature and Sanskrit learning. Thus this wave of reform, which came from the South, benefited to a certain extent the priesthood, and the priests only. For the rest of India's millions, it forged more chains than they had ever known before.

The Kshatriyas had always been the backbone of India, so also they had been the supporters of science and liberty, and their voices had rung out again and again to clear the land from superstitions; and throughout the history of India they ever formed the invulnerable barrier to aggressive priestly tyranny.

When the greater part of their number sank into ignorance, and another portion mixed their blood with savages from Central Asia and lent their swords to establish the rules of priests in India, her cup became full to the brim, and down sank the land of Bharata, not to rise again, until the Kshatriya rouses himself, and making himself free, strikes the chains from the feet of the rest. Priestcraft is the bane of India. Can man degrade his brother, and himself escape degradation?

Know, Rajaji, the greatest of all truths, discovered by your ancestors, is that the universe is one. Can one injure anyone without injuring himself? The mass of Brahmin and Kshatriya tyranny has recoiled upon their own heads with compound interest; and a thousand years of slavery and degradation is what the inexorable law of Karma is visiting upon them.

This is what one of your ancestors said: "Even in this life, they have conquered relativity whose mind is fixed in sameness"—one who is believed to be God incarnate. We all believe it. Are his words then vain and without meaning? If not, and we know they are not, any attempt against this perfect equality of all creation, irrespective of birth, sex, or even qualification, is a terrible mistake, and no one can be saved until he has attained to this idea of sameness.

Follow, therefore, noble Prince, the teachings of the Vedanta, not as explained by this or that commentator, but as the Lord within you understands them. Above all, follow this great doctrine of sameness in all things, through all beings, seeing the same God in all.

This is the way to freedom; inequality, the way to bondage. No man and no nation can attempt to gain physical freedom without physical equality, nor mental freedom without mental equality.

Ignorance, inequality, and desire are the three causes of human misery, and each follows the other in inevitable union. Why should a man think himself above any other man, or even an animal? It is the same throughout:

$$\text{त्वं स्त्री त्वं पुमानसि त्वं कुमार उत वा कुमारी।}$$

—"Thou art the man, Thou the woman, Thou art the young man, Thou the young woman."

Many will say, "That is all right for the Sannyasins, but we are householders." No doubt, a householder having many other duties to perform, cannot as fully attain to this sameness; yet this should be also their ideal, for it is the ideal of all societies, of all mankind, all animals, and all nature, to attain to this sameness. But alas! they think inequality is the way to attain equality as if they could come to right by doing wrong!

This is the bane of human nature, the curse upon mankind, the root of all misery—this inequality. This is the source of all bondage, physical, mental, and spiritual.

$$\text{समं पश्यन् हि सर्वत्र समवस्थितमीश्वरम् ।}$$
$$\text{न हिनस्त्यात्मनात्मानं ततो याति परां गतिम् ॥}$$

— "Since seeing the Lord equally existent everywhere he injures not Self by self, and so goes to the Highest Goal" (Gita, XIII. 28).

This one saying contains, in a few words, the universal way to salvation.

You, Rajputs, have been the glories of ancient India. With your degradation came national decay, and India can only be raised if the descendants of the Kshatriyas co-operate with the descendants of the Brahmins, not to share the spoils of pelf and power, but to help the weak to enlighten the ignorant, and to restore the lost glory of the holy land of their forefathers.

And who can say but that the time is propitious? Once more the wheel is turning up, once more vibrations have been set in motion from India, which are destined at no distant day to reach the farthest limits of the earth. One voice has spoken, whose echoes are rolling on and gathering strength every day, a voice even mightier than those which have preceded it, for it is the summation of them all. Once more the voice that spoke to the sages on the banks of the Sarasvati, the voice whose echoes reverberated from peak to peak of the "Father of Mountains", and descended upon the plains through Krishna Buddha, and Chaitanya in all-carrying floods, has spoken again. Once more the doors have opened. Enter ye into the realms of light, the gates have been opened wide once more.

And you, my beloved Prince—you the scion of a race who are the living pillars upon which rests the religion eternal, its sworn defenders and helpers, the descendants of Râma and Krishna, will you remain outside? I know, this cannot be. Yours, I am sure, will be the first hand that will be stretched forth to help religion once more. And when I think of you, Raja Ajit Singh, one in whom the well-known scientific attainments of your house have been joined to a purity of character of which a saint ought to be proud, to an unbounded love for humanity, I cannot help believing in the glorious renaissance of the religion eternal, when such hands are willing to rebuild it again.

May the blessings of Ramakrishna be on you and yours for ever and ever, and that you may live long for the good of many, and for the spread of truth is the constant prayer of—

Vivekananda.

REPLY TO THE MADRAS ADDRESS[1]

Friends, Fellow-Countrymen and Co-Religionists of Madras,

It is most gratifying to me to find that my insignificant service to the cause of our religion has been accept able to you, not because it is as a personal appreciation of me and my work in a foreign and distant land, but as a sure sign that, though whirlwind after whirlwind of foreign invasion has passed over the devoted head of India, though centuries of neglect on our part and contempt on the part of our conquerors have visibly dimmed the glories of ancient Âryâvarta, though many a stately column on which it rested, many a beautiful arch, and many a marvellous corner have been washed away by the inundations that deluged the land for centuries—the centre is all sound, the keystone is unimpaired. The spiritual foundation upon which the marvellous monument of glory to God and charity to all beings has been reared stands unshaken, strong as ever. Your generous appreciation of Him whose message to India and to the whole world, I, the most unworthy of His servants, had the privilege to bear shows your innate spiritual instinct which saw in Him and His message the first murmurs of that tidal wave of spirituality which is destined at no distant future to break upon India in all its irresistible powers, carrying away in its omnipotent flood all that is weak

and defective, and raising the Hindu race to the platform it is destined to occupy in the providence of God, crowned with more glory than it ever had even in the past, the reward of centuries of silent suffering, and fulfilling its mission amongst the races of the world—the evolution of spiritual humanity.

The people of Northern India are especially grateful to you of the South, as the great source to which most of the impulses that are working in India today can be traced. The great Bhâshyakâras, epoch-making Âchâryas, Shankara, Râmânuja, and Madhva were born in Southern India. Great Shankara to whom every Advâitavâdin in the world owes allegiance; great Ramanuja whose heavenly touch converted the downtrodden pariahs into Âlwârs; great Madhva whose leadership was recognised even by the followers of the only Northern Prophet whose power has been felt all over the length and breadth of India—Shri Krishna Chaitanya. Even at the present day it is the South that carries the palm in the glories of Varanasi—your renunciation controls the sacred shrines on the farthest peaks of the Himalayas, and what wonder that with the blood of Prophets running in your veins, with your lives blessed by such Acharyas, you are the first and foremost to appreciate and hold on to the message of Bhagavân Shri Ramakrishna.

The South had been the repository of Vedic learning, and you will understand me when I state that, in spite of the reiterated assertions of aggressive ignorance, it is the Shruti still that is the backbone of all the different divisions of the Hindu religion.

However great may be the merits of the Samhitâ and the Brâhmana portions of the Vedas to the ethnologists or the philologists, however desirable may be the results that the अग्नमीमीले[2] or इषेत्वोर्जेत्वा[3] or ग्ननो देवीरभीष्टये[4] in conjunction with the different Vedis (altars) and sacrifices and libations produce—it was all in the way of Bhoga; and no one ever contended that it could produce Moksha. As such, the Jnâna-Kânda, the Âranyakas, the Shrutis par excellence which teach the way to spirituality, the Moksha-Mârga, have always ruled and will always rule in India.

Lost in the mazes and divisions of the "Religion Eternal", by prepossession and prejudice unable to grasp the meaning of the only religion whose universal adaptation is the exact shadow of the अगोरगीयान् महतो महीयान्[5] God it preaches, groping in the dark with a standard of spiritual truth borrowed second-hand from nations who never knew anything but rank materialism, the modern young Hindu struggles in vain to understand the religion of his forefathers, and gives up the

---

1. When the success of the Swami in America became well known in India, several meetings were held and addresses of thanks and congratulations were forwarded to him. The first reply which he wrote was that to the Address of the Hindus of Madras.

2. ओं अग्नमीले पुरोहितं यज्ञस्य देवमृत्वजिम्। होतारं रत्नधातमम्॥ ऋग्वेद:।१।१।१।

3. ओं इषेत्वोर्जेत्वा वायवः स्थोपायवः स्थ देवो वः सविता प्रार्पयतु श्रेष्ठतमाय कर्मणो। यजुर्वेद:।१।१।१।

4. ओं ग्ननो देवीरमीष्टये आपो भवन्तु पीतये श्ंयोरभिसित्रवन्तु नः॥ अथर्ववेद:।१।१।१।

5. Smaller than the smallest, greater than the greatest (Katha, II. 20).

quest altogether, and becomes a hopeless wreck of an agnostic, or else, unable to vegetate on account of the promptings of his innate religious nature, drinks carelessly of some of those different decoctions of Western materialism with an Eastern flavour, and thus fulfils the prophecy of the Shruti:

परियन्ति मूढा अन्धेनेव नीयमाना यथान्धाः।

— "Fools go staggering to and fro, like blind men led by the blind."

They alone escape whose spiritual nature has been touched and vivified by the life-giving touch of the "Sad-Guru"[6].

Well has it been said by Bhagavan Bhashyakara:

दुर्लभं त्रयमेवैतत् देवानुग्रहहेतुकम्।
मनुष्यत्वं मुमुक्षुत्वं महापुरुषसंश्रयः॥

— "These three are difficult to obtain in this world, and depend on the mercy of the gods — the human birth, the desire for salvation, and the company of the great-souled ones."

Either in the sharp analysis of the Vaisheshikas, resulting in the wonderful theories about the Paramânus, Dvyanus, and Trasarenus[7], or the still more wonderful analysis displayed in the discussions of the Jâti, Dravya, Guna, Samavâya[8], and to the various categories of the Naiyâyikas, rising to the solemn march of the thought of the Sânkhyas, the fathers of the theories of evolution, ending with the ripe fruit, the result of all these researches, the Sutras of Vyâsa — the one background to all these different analyses and syntheses of the human mind is still the Shrutis. Even in the philosophical writings of the Buddhists or Jains, the help of Shrutis is never rejected, and at least in some of the Buddhistic schools and in the majority of the Jain writings, the authority of the Shrutis is fully admitted, excepting what they call the Himsaka Shrutis, which they hold to be interpolations of the Brahmins. In recent times, such a view has been held by the late great Swami Dayânanda Saraswati.

If one be asked to point out the system of thought towards which as a centre all the ancient and modern Indian thoughts have converged, if one wants to see the real backbone of Hinduism in all its various manifestations, the Sutras of Vyasa will unquestionably be pointed out as constituting all that.

Either one hears the Advaita-Keshari roaring in peals of thunder — the Asti, Bhâti, and Priya[9] — amidst the heart-stopping solemnities of the Himalayan forests, mixing with the solemn cadence of the river of heaven, or listens to the cooing of the Piyâ, Pitam in the beautiful bowers of the grove of Vrindâ: whether one mingles with the sedate meditations of the monasteries of Varanasi or the ecstatic dances of the followers of the Prophet of Nadia; whether one sits at the feet of the teacher of the Vishishtâdvaita system with its Vadakale, Tenkale[10], and all the other subdivisions, or listens with reverence to the Acharyas of the Mâdhva school; whether one hears the martial "Wâ Guruki Fateh"[11] of the secular Sikhs or the sermons on the Grantha Sâhib of the Udâsis and Nirmalâs; whether he salutes the Sannyâsin disciples of Kabir with "Sat Sâhib" and listens with joy to the Sâkhis (Bhajans); whether he pores upon the wonderful lore of that reformer of Rajputana, Dâdu, or the works of his royal disciple, Sundaradâsa, down to the great Nishchaladâsa, the celebrated author of Vichâra sâgara, which book has more influence in India than any that has been written in any language within the last three centuries; if even one asks the Bhangi Mehtar of Northern India to sit down and give an account of the teachings of his Lâlguru — one will find that all these various teachers and schools have as their basis that system whose authority is the Shruti, Gitâ its divine commentary, the Shâriraka-Sutras its organised system, and all the different sects in India, from the Paramahamsa Parivrâjakâchâryas to the poor despised Mehtar disciples of Lâlguru, are different manifestations.

The three Prasthânas[12], then, in their different explanations as Dvaita, Vishishtadvaita, or Advaita, with a few minor recensions, form the "authorities" of the Hindu religion. The Purânas, the modern representations of the ancient Nârâsamsi (anecdote portion of the Vedas), supply the mythology, and the Tantras, the modern representations of the Brâhmanas (ritual and explanatory portion of the Vedas), supply the ritual. Thus the three Prasthanas, as authorities, are common to all the sects; but as to the Puranas and Tantras, each sect has its own.

The Tantras, as we have said, represent the Vedic rituals in a modified form; and before any one jumps into the most absurd conclusions about them, I will advise him to read the Tantras in conjunction with the Brahmanas, especially the Adhvaryu portion. And most of the Mantras, used in the Tantras, will be found taken verbatim from their Brahmanas. As to their influence, apart from the Shrauta and Smârta rituals, all the forms of the rituals in vogue from the Himalayas to the Comorin have been taken from the Tantras, and they direct the worship of the Shâkta, or Shaiva, or Vaishnava, and all the others alike.

Of course, I do not pretend that all the Hindus are thoroughly acquainted with these sources of their religion. Many, especially in lower Bengal, have not heard of the names of these sects and these great systems; but consciously or unconsciously, it is the plan laid down in the three Prasthanas that they are all working out.

Wherever, on the other hand, the Hindi language is spoken,

6. The good teacher.

7. Atoms, Entities composed of two atoms, Entities composed of three atoms.

8. Genus, Substance, Quality, Inhesion or Inseparability.

9. Exists (Sat), Shines (Chit), Is beloved (Ânanda) — the three indicatives of Brahman.

10. The two divisions of the Ramanuja sect.

11. Victory to the Guru

12. "Courses", viz, the Upanishad (Shruti), the Gita, and the *Shariraka-Sutras*.

even the lowest classes have more knowledge of the Vedantic religion than many of the highest in lower Bengal.

And why so?

Transported from the soil of Mithilâ to Navadvipa, nurtured and developed by the fostering genius of Shiromani, Gadâdhara, Jagadisha, and a host of other great names, an analysis of the laws of reasoning, in some points superior to every other system in the whole world, expressed in a wonderful and precise mosaic of language, stands the Nyâya of Bengal, respected and studied throughout the length and breadth of Hindusthân. But, alas, the Vedic study was sadly neglected, and until within the last few years, scarcely anyone could be found in Bengal to teach the Mahâbhâshya of Patanjali. Once only a mighty genius rose above the never-ending Avachchhinnas and Avachchhedakas[1] — Bhagavân Shri Krishna Chaitanya. For once the religious lethargy of Bengal was shaken, and for a time it entered into a communion with the religious life of other parts of India.

It is curious to note that though Shri Chaitanya obtained his Sannyâsa from a Bhârati, and as such was a Bharati himself, it was through Mâdhavendra Puri that his religious genius was first awakened.

The Puris seem to have a peculiar mission in rousing the spirituality of Bengal. Bhagavan Shri Ramakrishna got his Sannyâsâshrama from Totâ Puri.

The commentary that Shri Chaitanya wrote on the Vyâsa-Sutras has either been lost or not found yet. His disciples joined themselves to the Madhvas of the South, and gradually the mantles of such giants as Rupa and Sanâtana and Jiva Goswâmi fell on the shoulders of Bâbâjis, and the great movement of Shri Chaitanya was decaying fast, till of late years there is a sign of revival. Hope that it will regain its lost splendour.

The influence of Shri Chaitanya is all over India. Wherever the Bhakti-Mârga is known, there he is appreciated, studied, and worshipped. I have every reason to believe that the whole of the Vallabhâchârya recension is only a branch of the sect founded by Shri Chaitanya. But most of his so-called disciples in Bengal do not know how his power is still working all over India; and how can they? The disciples have become Gadiâns (Heads of monasteries), while he was preaching barefooted from door to door in India, begging Âchandâlas (all down to the lowest) to love God.

The curious and unorthodox custom of hereditary Gurus that prevails in Bengal, and for the most part in Bengal alone, is another cause of its being cut off from the religious life of the rest of India.

The greatest cause of all is that the life of Bengal never received an influx from that of the great brotherhood of Sannyasins who are the representatives and repositories of the highest Indian spiritual culture even at the present day.

Tyâga (renunciation) is never liked by the higher classes of Bengal. Their tendency is for Bhoga (enjoyment). How can they get a deep insight into spiritual things? त्यागेनेके अमृतत्वमानशुः — "By renunciation alone immortality was reached." How can it be otherwise?

On the other hand, throughout the Hindi-speaking world, a succession of brilliant Tyâgi teachers of far-reaching influence has brought the doctrines of the Vedanta to every door. Especially the impetus given to Tyaga during the reign of Ranjit Singh of the Punjab has made the highest teachings of the Vedantic philosophy available for the very lowest of the low. With true pride, the Punjabi peasant girl says that even her spinning wheel repeats: "Soham", "Soham". And I have seen Mehtar Tyagis in the forest of Hrishikesh wearing the garb of the Sannyasin, studying the Vedanta. And many a proud high-class man would be glad to sit at their feet and learn. And why not? अन्त्यादपि परं धर्मं — "Supreme knowledge (can be learnt) even from the man of low birth."

Thus it is that the North-West and the Punjab have a religious education which is far ahead of that of Bengal, Bombay, or Madras. The ever-travelling Tyagis of the various orders, Dashanâmis or Vairâgis or Panthis bring religion to everybody's door, and the cost is only a bit of bread. And how noble and disinterested most of them are! There is one Sannyasin belonging to the Kachu Panthis or independents (who do not identify themselves with any sect), who has been instrumental in the establishing of hundreds of schools and charitable asylums all over Rajputana. He has opened hospitals in forests, and thrown iron bridges over the gorges in the Himalayas, and this man never touches a coin with his hands, has no earthly possession except a blanket, which has given him the nickname of the "Blanket Swami", and begs his bread from door to door. I have never known him taking a whole dinner from one house, lest it should be a tax on the householder. And he is only one amongst many. Do you think that so long as these Gods on earth live in India and protect the "Religion Eternal" with the impenetrable rampart of such godly characters, the old religion will die?

In this country[2], the clergymen sometimes receive as high salaries as rupees thirty thousand, forty thousand, fifty thousand, even ninety thousand a year, for preaching two hours on Sunday only, and that only six months in a year. Look at the millions upon millions they spend for the support of their religion, and Young Bengal has been taught that these God-like, absolutely unselfish men like Kambli-Swami are idle vagabonds. मद्भक्तानाञ्च च ये भक्तास्ते मे भक्ततमा मताः — "Those who are devoted to My worshippers are regarded as the best of devotees."

Take even an extreme case, that of an extremely ignorant Vairagi. Even he, when he goes into a village tries his best to impart to the villagers whatever he knows, from Tulasidâsa, or Chaitanya-Charitâmrita or the Âlwârs in Southern India. Is that not doing some good? And all this for only a bit of bread

1. In Nyaya, 'Determined', and 'determining attribute'.

2. United States of America

and a rag of cloth. Before unmercifully criticising them, think how much you do, my brother, for your poor fellow-country-men, at whose expense you have got your education, and by grinding whose face you maintain your position and pay your teachers for teaching you that the Babajis are only vagabonds.

A few of your fellow-countrymen in Bengal have criticised what they call a new development of Hinduism. And well they may. For Hinduism is only just now penetrating into Bengal, where so long the whole idea of religion was a bundle of Deshâchâras (local customs) as to eating and drinking and marriage.

This short paper has not space for the discussion of such a big subject as to whether the view of Hinduism, which the disciples of Ramakrishna have been preaching all over India, was according to the "Sad-Shâstras" or not. But I will give a few hints to our critics, which may help them in understanding our position better.

In the first place, I never contended that a correct idea of Hinduism can be gathered from the writings of Kâshidâsa or Krittivâsa, though their words are "Amrita Samâna" (like nectar), and those that hear them are "Punyavâns" (virtuous). But we must go to Vedic and Dârshanika authorities, and to the great Acharyas and their disciples all over India.

If, brethren, you begin with the Sutras of Gautama, and read his theories about the Âptas (inspired) in the light of the commentaries of Vâtsyâyana, and go up to the Mimâmsakas with Shabara and other commentators, and find out what they say about the अलौककिपरत्यक्षम् (supersensuous realisation), and who are Aptas, and whether every being can become an Apta or not, and that the proof of the Vedas is in their being the words of such Aptas if you have time to look into the introduction of Mahidhara to the Yajur-Veda, you will find a still more lucid discussion as to the Vedas being laws of the inner life of man, and as such they are eternal.

As to the eternity of creation—this doctrine is the corner-stone not only of the Hindu religion, but of the Buddhists and Jains also.

Now all the sects in India can be grouped roughly as following the Jnâna-Mârga or the Bhakti-Mârga. If you will kindly look into the introduction to the Shâriraka-Bhâshya of Shri Shankarâchârya, you will find there the Nirapekshatâ (transcendence) of Jnana is thoroughly discussed, and the conclusion is that realisation of Brahman or the attainment of Moksha do not depend upon ceremonial, creed, caste, colour, or doctrine. It will come to any being who has the four Sâdhanâs, which are the most perfect moral culture.

As to the Bhaktas, even Bengali critics know very well that some of their authorities even declared that caste or nationality or sex, or, as to that, even the human birth, was never necessary to Moksha. Bhakti is the one and only thing necessary.

Both Jnana and Bhakti are everywhere preached to be unconditioned, and as such there is not one authority who lays down the conditions of caste or creed or nationality in attaining Moksha. See the discussion on the Sutra of Vyâsa—अन्तरा चापि तु तद्दृष्टेः[3] by Shankara, Ramanuja, and Madhva.

Go through all the Upanishads, and even in the Samhitas, nowhere you will find the limited ideas of Moksha which every other religion has. As to toleration, it is everywhere, even in the Samhita of the Adhvaryu Veda, in the third or fourth verse of the fortieth chapter, if my memory does not fail; it begins with न बुध्दभिदं जनयेदज्ञानां कर्मसंगनिनाम्[4]. This is running through every where. Was anybody persecuted in India for choosing his Ishta Devatâ, or becoming an atheist or agnostic even, so long as he obeyed the social regulations? Society may punish anybody by its disapprobation for breaking any of its regulations, but no man, the lowest Patita (fallen), is ever shut out from Moksha. You must not mix up the two together. As to that, in Malabar a Chandâla is not allowed to pass through the same street as a high-caste man, but let him become a Mohammedan or Christian, he will be immediately allowed to go anywhere; and this rule has prevailed in the dominion of a Hindu sovereign for centuries. It may be queer, but it shows the idea of toleration for other religions even in the most untoward circumstances.

The one idea the Hindu religions differ in from every other in the world, the one idea to express which the sages almost exhaust the vocabulary of the Sanskrit language, is that man must realise God even in this life. And the Advaita texts very logically add, "To know God is to become God."

And here comes as a necessary consequence the broadest and most glorious idea of inspiration—not only as asserted and declared by the Rishis of the Vedas, not only by Vidura and Dharmavyâdha and a number of others, but even the other day Nischaladâsa, a Tyagi of the Dâdu panthi sect, boldly declared in his Vichâra-Sâgara: "He who has known Brahman has become Brahman. His words are Vedas, and they will dispel the darkness of ignorance, either expressed in Sanskrit or any popular dialect."

Thus to realise God, the Brahman, as the Dvaitins say, or to become Brahman, as the Advaitins say—is the aim and end of the whole teaching of the Vedas; and every other teaching, therein contained, represents a stage in the course of our progress thereto. And the great glory of Bhagavan Bhashyakara Shankaracharya is that it was his genius that gave the most wonderful expression to the ideas of Vyasa.

As absolute, Brahman alone is true; as relative truth, all the different sects, standing upon different manifestations of the same Brahman, either in India or elsewhere, are true. Only

3. "But also (persons standing) between (are qualified for knowledge); for that is seen (in scripture)."—— III. iv. 36. A person even if he does not belong to an Ashrama (possessing not the means to entitle him to one or other of the Ashramas, stages of life) and thus stands between, as it were, is qualified for the knowledge of Brahman; for we meet scriptural passages declaring that persons of such a class possessed the knowledge of Brahman. Vide Chhând. Upa. IV. i; Bri. Upa. III. vi. & viii.

4. "(The wise one) should not unsettle the understanding of the ignorant, attached to action." The line also occurs in the Gita (III. 26).

some are higher than others. Suppose a man starts straight towards the sun. At every step of his journey he will see newer and newer visions of the sun—the size, the view, and light will every moment be new, until he reaches the real sun. He saw the sun at first like a big ball, and then it began to increase in size. The sun was never small like the ball he saw; nor was it ever like all the succession of suns he saw in his journey. Still is it not true that our traveller always saw the sun, and nothing but the sun? Similarly, all these various sects are true—some nearer, some farther off from the real sun which is our एकमेवाद्वतीयम्—"One without a second".

And as the Vedas are the only scriptures which teach this real absolute God, of which all other ideas of God are but minimised and limited visions; as the सर्वलोकहितैषिणी[1] Shruti takes the devotee gently by the hand, and leads him from one stage to another, through all the stages that are necessary for him to travel to reach the Absolute; and as all other religions represent one or other of these stages in an unprogressive and crystallized form, all the other religions of the world are included in the nameless, limitless, eternal Vedic religion.

Work hundreds of lives out, search every corner of your mind for ages—and still you will not find one noble religious idea that is not already imbedded in that infinite mine of spirituality.

As to the so-called Hindu idolatry—first go and learn the forms they are going through, and where it is that the worshippers are really worshipping, whether in the temple, in the image, or in the temple of their own bodies. First know for certain what they are doing—which more than ninety per cent of the revilers are thoroughly ignorant of—and then it will explain itself in the light of the Vedantic philosophy.

Still these Karmas are not compulsory. On the other hand, open your Manu and see where it orders every old man to embrace the fourth Ashrama, and whether he embraces it or not, he must give up all Karma. It is reiterated everywhere that all these Karmas ज्ञाने परिसमाप्यते—"finally end in Jnana".

As to the matter of that, a Hindu peasant has more religious education than many a gentleman in other countries. A friend criticised the use of European terms of philosophy and religion in my addresses. I would have been very glad to use Sanskrit terms; it would have been much more easy, as being the only perfect vehicle of religious thought. But the friend forgot that I was addressing an audience of Western people; and although a certain Indian missionary declared that the Hindus had forgotten the meaning of their Sanskrit books, and that it was the missionaries who unearthed the meaning, I could not find one in that large concourse of missionaries who could understand a line in Sanskrit—and yet some of them read learned papers criticising the Vedas, and all the sacred sources of the Hindu religion!

It is not true that I am against any religion. It is equally untrue that I am hostile to the Christian missionaries in In-

dia. But I protest against certain of their methods of raising money in America. What is meant by those pictures in the school-books for children where the Hindu mother is painted as throwing her children to the crocodiles in the Ganga? The mother is black, but the baby is painted white, to arouse more sympathy, and get more money. What is meant by those pictures which paint a man burning his wife at a stake with his own hands, so that she may become a ghost and torment the husband's enemy? What is meant by the pictures of huge cars crushing over human beings? The other day a book was published for children in this country, where one of these gentlemen tells a narrative of his visit to Calcutta. He says he saw a car running over fanatics in the streets of Calcutta. I have heard one of these gentlemen preach in Memphis that in every village of India there is a pond full of the bones of little babies.

What have the Hindus done to these disciples of Christ that every Christian child is taught to call the Hindus "vile", and "wretches", and the most horrible devils on earth? Part of the Sunday School education for children here consists in teaching them to hate everybody who is not a Christian, and the Hindus especially, so that, from their very childhood they may subscribe their pennies to the missions. If not for truth's sake, for the sake of the morality of their own children, the Christian missionaries ought not to allow such things going on. Is it any wonder that such children grow up to be ruthless and cruel men and women? The greater a preacher can paint the tortures of eternal hell—the fire that is burning there, the brimstone - the higher is his position among the orthodox. A servant-girl in the employ of a friend of mine had to be sent to a lunatic asylum as a result of her attending what they call here the revivalist-preaching. The dose of hell-fire and brimstone was too much for her. Look again at the books published in Madras against the Hindu religion. If a Hindu writes one such line against the Christian religion, the missionaries will cry fire and vengeance.

My countrymen, I have been more than a year in this country. I have seen almost every corner of the society, and, after comparing notes, let me tell you that neither are we devils, as the missionaries tell the world we are, nor are they angels, as they claim to be. The less the missionaries talk of immorality, infanticide, and the evils of the Hindu marriage system, the better for them. There may be actual pictures of some countries before which all the imaginary missionary pictures of the Hindu society will fade away into light. But my mission in life is not to be a paid reviler. I will be the last man to claim perfection for the Hindu society. No man is more conscious of the defects that are therein, or the evils that have grown up under centuries of misfortunes. If, foreign friends, you come with genuine sympathy to help and not to destroy, Godspeed to you. But if by abuses, incessantly hurled against the head of a prostrate race in season and out of season, you mean only the triumphant assertion of the moral superiority of your own nation, let me tell you plainly, if such a comparison be insti-

---

1. The well-wisher to all the world.

Lectures & Discourses by Swami Vivekananda

tuted with any amount of justice, the Hindu will be found head and shoulders above all other nations in the world as a moral race.

In India religion was never shackled. No man was ever challenged in the selection of his Ishta Devatâ, or his sect, or his preceptor, and religion grew, as it grew nowhere else. On the other hand, a fixed point was necessary to allow this infinite variation to religion, and society was chosen as that point in India. As a result, society became rigid and almost immovable. For liberty is the only condition of growth.

On the other hand, in the West, the field of variation was society, and the constant point was religion. Conformity was the watchword, and even now is the watchword of European religion, and each new departure had to gain the least advantage only by wading through a river of blood. The result is a splendid social organisation, with a religion that never rose beyond the grossest materialistic conceptions.

Today the West is awakening to its wants; and the "true self of man and spirit" is the watchword of the advanced school of Western theologians. The student of Sanskrit philosophy knows where the wind is blowing from, but it matters not whence the power comes so longs as it brings new life.

In India, new circumstances at the same time are persistently demanding a new adjustment of social organisations. For the last three-quarters of a century, India has been bubbling over with reform societies and reformers. But, alas, every one of them has proved a failure. They did not know the secret. They had not learnt the great lesson to be learnt. In their haste, they laid all the evils in our society at the door of religion; and like the man in the story, wanting to kill the mosquito that sat on a friend's forehead, they were trying to deal such heavy blows as would have killed man and mosquito together. But in this case, fortunately, they only dashed themselves against immovable rocks and were crushed out of existence in the shock of recoil. Glory unto those noble and unselfish souls who have struggled and failed in their misdirected attempts. Those galvanic shocks of reformatory zeal were necessary to rouse the sleeping leviathan. But they were entirely destructive, and not constructive, and as such they were mortal, and therefore died.

Let us bless them and profit by their experience. They had not learnt the lesson that all is a growth from inside out, that all evolution is only a manifestation of a preceding involution. They did not know that the seed can only assimilate the surrounding elements, but grows a tree in its own nature. Until all the Hindu race becomes extinct, and a new race takes possession of the land, such a thing can never be—try East or West, India can never be Europe until she dies.

And will she die—this old Mother of all that is noble or moral or spiritual, the land which the sages trod, the land in which Godlike men still live and breathe? I will borrow the lantern of the Athenian sage and follow you, my brother, through the cities and villages, plains and forests, of this broad world—show me such men in other lands if you can. Truly have they said, the tree is known by its fruits. Go under every mango tree in India; pick up bushels of the worm-eaten, unripe, fallen ones from the ground, and write hundreds of the most learned volumes on each one of them—still you have not described a single mango. Pluck a luscious, full-grown, juicy one from the tree, and now you have known all that the mango is.

Similarly, these Man-Gods show what the Hindu religion is. They show the character, the power, and the possibilities of that racial tree which counts culture by centuries, and has borne the buffets of a thousand years of hurricane, and still stands with the unimpaired vigour of eternal youth.

Shall India die? Then from the world all spirituality will be extinct, all moral perfection will be extinct, all sweet-souled sympathy for religion will be extinct, all ideality will be extinct; and in its place will reign the duality of lust and luxury as the male and female deities, with money as its priest, fraud, force, and competition its ceremonies, and the human soul its sacrifice. Such a thing can never be. The power of suffering is infinitely greater than the power of doing; the power of love is infinitely of greater potency than the power of hatred. Those that think that the present revival of Hinduism is only a manifestation of patriotic impulse are deluded.

First, let us study the quaint phenomenon.

Is it not curious that, whilst under the terrific onset of modern scientific research, all the old forts of Western dogmatic religions are crumbling into dust; whilst the sledge-hammer blows of modern science are pulverising the porcelain mass of systems whose foundation is either in faith or in belief or in the majority of votes of church synods; whilst Western theology is at its wit's end to accommodate itself to the ever-rising tide of aggressive modern thought; whilst in all other sacred books the texts have been stretched to their utmost tension under the ever-increasing pressure of modern thought, and the majority of them are broken and have been stored away in lumber rooms; whilst the vast majority of thoughtful Western humanity have broken asunder all their ties with the church and are drifting about in a sea of unrest, the religions which have drunk the water of life at that fountain of light, the Vedas—Hinduism and Buddhism—alone are reviving?

The restless Western atheist or agnostic finds in the Gîtâ or in the Dhammapada the only place where his soul can anchor.

The tables have been turned, and the Hindu, who saw through tears of despair his ancient homestead covered with incendiary fire, ignited by unfriendly hands, now sees, when the searchlight of modern thought has dispersed the smoke, that his home is the one that is standing in all its strength, and all the rest have either vanished or are building their houses anew after the Hindu plan. He has wiped away his tears, and has found that the axe that tried to cut down to the roots the ऊर्ध्वमूलमधःशाखमश्वत्थं प्राहुरव्ययम् (Gita, XV. 1) has proved the merciful knife of the surgeon.

He has found that he has neither to torture texts nor commit any other form of intellectual dishonesty to save his religion. Nay, he may call all that is weak in his scriptures, weak, because they were meant to be so by the ancient sages, to help the weak, under the theory of अरुन्धतीदर्शनन्याय[1]. Thanks to the ancient sages who have discovered such an all-pervading, ever-expanding system of religion that can accommodate all that has been discovered in the realm of matter, and all that is to be known; he has begun to appreciate them anew, and discover anew, that those discoveries which have proved so disastrous to every limited little scheme of religion are but re-discoveries, in the plane of intellect and sense-consciousness, of truths which his ancestors discovered ages ago in the higher plane of intuition and superconsciousness.

He has not, therefore, to give up anything, nor go about seeking for anything anywhere, but it will be enough for him if he can utilise only a little from the infinite store he has inherited and apply it to his needs. And that he has begun to do and will do more and more. Is this not the real cause of this revival?

Young men of Bengal, to you I especially appeal. Brethren, we know to our shame that most of the real evils for which the foreign races abuse the Hindu nation are only owing to us. We have been the cause of bringing many undeserved calumnies on the head of the other races in India. But glory unto God, we have been fully awakened to it, and with His blessings, we will not only cleanse ourselves, but help the whole of India to attain the ideals preached in the religion eternal.

Let us wipe off first that mark which nature always puts on the forehead of a slave — the stain of jealousy. Be jealous of none. Be ready to lend a hand to every worker of good. Send a good thought for every being in the three worlds.

Let us take our stand on the one central truth in our religion — the common heritage of the Hindus, the Buddhists, and Jains alike — the spirit of man, the Atman of man, the immortal, birthless, all-pervading, eternal soul of man whose glories the Vedas cannot themselves express, before whose majesty the universe with its galaxy upon galaxy of suns and stars and nebulae is as a drop. Every man or woman, nay, from the highest Devas to the worm that crawls under our feet, is such a spirit evoluted or involuted. The difference is not in kind, but in degree.

This infinite power of the spirit, brought to bear upon matter evolves material development, made to act upon thought evolves intellectuality, and made to act upon itself makes of man a God.

1. When a bride is brought to the house of her husband for the first time he shows her a very tiny star, called Arundhati. To do this, he has to direct her gaze the right way, which he does by asking her to look at something near and something big in the direction of the star, e.g., a branch of a tree. Next he draws her attention to a large bright star observed beyond this branch and so on, till by several steps he succeeds in leading her eyes to the right thing. This method of leading to a subtle object through easy and gradual steps is called Arundhati Nyaya

First, let us be Gods, and then help others to be Gods. "Be and make." Let this be our motto. Say not man is a sinner. Tell him that he is a God. Even if there were a devil, it would be our duty to remember God always, and not the devil.

If the room is dark, the constant feeling and repeating of darkness will not take it away, but bring in the light. Let us know that all that is negative, all that is destructive, all that is mere criticism, is bound to pass away; it is the positive, the affirmative, the constructive that is immortal, that will remain for ever. Let us say, "We are" and "God is" and "We are God", "Shivoham, Shivoham", and march on. Not matter but spirit. All that has name and form is subject to all that has none. This is the eternal truth the Shrutis preach. Bring in the light; the darkness will vanish of itself. Let the lion of Vedanta roar; the foxes will fly to their holes. Throw the ideas broadcast, and let the result take care of itself. Let us put the chemicals together; the crystallization will take its own course. Bring forth the power of the spirit, and pour it over the length and breadth of India; and all that is necessary will come by itself.

Manifest the divinity within you, and everything will be harmoniously arranged around it. Remember the illustration of Indra and Virochana in the Vedas; both were taught their divinity. But the Asura, Virochana, took his body for his God. Indra, being a Deva, understood that the Atman was meant. You are the children of India. You are the descendants of the Devas. Matter can never be your God; body can never be your God.

India will be raised, not with the power of the flesh, but with the power of the spirit; not with the flag of destruction, but with the flag of peace and love, the garb of the Sannyâsin; not by the power of wealth, but by the power of the begging bowl. Say not that you are weak. The spirit is omnipotent. Look at that handful of young men called into existence by the divine touch of Ramakrishna's feet. They have preached the message from Assam to Sindh, from the Himalayas to Cape Comorin. They have crossed the Himalayas at a height of twenty thousand feet, over snow and ice on foot, and penetrated into the mysteries of Tibet. They have begged their bread, covered themselves with rags; they have been persecuted, followed by the police, kept in prison, and at last set free when the Government was convinced of their innocence.

They are now twenty. Make them two thousand tomorrow. Young men of Bengal, your country requires it. The world requires it. Call up the divinity within you, which will enable you to bear hunger and thirst, heat and cold. Sitting in luxurious homes, surrounded with all the comforts of life, and doling out a little amateur religion may be good for other lands, but India has a truer instinct. It intuitively detects the mask. You must give up. Be great. No great work can be done without sacrifice. The Purusha Himself sacrificed Himself to create this world. Lay down your comforts, your pleasures, your names, fame or position, nay even your lives, and make a bridge of human chains over which millions will cross this ocean of life. Bring all the forces of good together. Do not care under what banner you march. Do not care what be your colour—green, blue, or red—but mix up all the colours and produce that intense glow of white, the colour of love. Ours is to work. The results will take care of themselves. If any social institution stands in your way of becoming God, it will give way before the power of Spirit. I do not see into the future; nor do I care to see. But one vision I see dear as life before me: that the ancient Mother has awakened once more, sitting on Her throne rejuvenated, more glorious than ever. Proclaim Her to all the world with the voice of peace and benediction.

Yours ever in love and labour,
Vivekananda.

A MESSAGE OF SYMPATHY TO A FRIEND[2]

"Naked came I out of my mother's womb, and naked shall I return thither; the Lord gave and the Lord hath taken away; blessed be the name of the Lord." Thus said the old Jewish saint when suffering the greatest calamities that could befall man, and he erred not. Herein lies the whole secret of Existence. Waves may roll over the surface and tempest rage, but deep down there is the stratum of infinite calmness, infinite peace, and infinite bliss. "Blessed are they that mourn, for they shall be comforted." And why? Because it is during these moments of visitations when the heart is wrung by hands which never stop for the father's cries or the mother's wail, when under the load of sorrow, dejection, and despair, the world seems to be cut off from under our feet, and when the whole horizon seems to be nothing but an impenetrable sheet of misery and utter despair—that the internal eyes open, light flashes all of a sudden, the dream vanishes, and intuitively we come face to face with the grandest mystery in nature—Existence. Yes, then it is—when the load would be sufficient to sink a lot of frail vessels—that the man of genius, of strength, the hero, sees that infinite, absolute, ever-blissful Existence per se, that infinite being who is called and worshipped under different names in different climes. Then it is, the shackles that bind the soul down to this hole of misery break, as it were, for a time, and unfettered it rises and rises until it reaches the throne of the Lord, "Where the wicked cease from troubling and the weary are at rest". Cease not, brother, to send up petitions day and night, cease not to say day and night—THY WILL BE DONE.

"Ours not to question why,
Ours but to do and die."

Blessed be Thy name, O Lord! And Thy will be done. Lord, we know that we are to submit; Lord, we know that it is the Mother's hand that is striking, and "The spirit is willing but the flesh is weak." There is. Father of Love, an agony at the heart which is fighting against that calm resignation which

Thou teaches". Give us strength, O Thou who sawest Thy whole family destroyed before Thine eyes, with Thine hands crossed on Thy breast. Come, Lord, Thou Great Teacher, who has taught us that the soldier is only to obey and speak not. Come, Lord, come Arjuna's Charioteer, and teach me as Thou once taughtest him, that resignation in Thyself is the highest end and aim of this life, so that with those great ones of old, I may also firmly and resignedly cry, Om Shri Krishnârpan-amastu.

May the Lord send you peace is the prayer day and night of —

Vivekananda.

WHAT WE BELIEVE IN[3]

I agree with you so far that faith is a wonderful insight and that it alone can save; but there is the danger in it of breeding fanaticism and barring further progress.

Jnâna is all right; but there is the danger of its becoming dry intellectualism. Love is great and noble; but it may die away in meaningless sentimentalism.

A harmony of all these is the thing required. Ramakrishna was such a harmony. Such beings are few and far between; but keeping him and his teachings as the ideal, we can move on. And if amongst us, each one may not individually attain to that perfection, still we may get it collectively by counter-acting, equipoising, adjusting, and fulfilling one another. This would be harmony by a number of persons and a decided advance on all other forms and creeds.

For a religion to be effective, enthusiasm is necessary. At the same time we must try to avoid the danger of multiplying creeds. We avoid that by being a nonsectarian sect, having all the advantages of a sect and the broadness of a universal religion.

God, though everywhere, can be known to us in and through human character. No character was ever so perfect as Ramakr-ishna's, and that should be the centre round which we ought to rally, at the same time allowing everybody to regard him in his own light, either as God, saviour, teacher, model, or great man, just as he pleases. We preach neither social equality nor inequality, but that every being has the same rights, and insist upon freedom of thought and action in every way.

We reject none, neither theist, nor pantheist, monist, poly-theist, agnostic, nor atheist; the only condition of being a disciple is modelling a character at once the broadest and the most intense. Nor do we insist upon particular codes of mo-rality as to conduct, or character, or eating and drinking, ex-cept so far as it injures others.

Whatever retards the onward progress or helps the down-ward fall is vice; whatever helps in coming up and becoming harmonised is virtue.

We leave everybody free to know, select, and follow whatever

---

2. Written from Bombay on 23rd May,1893 to D. R. Balaji Rao who just had a severe domestic affliction.

3. Written to "Kidi" on March 3, 1894, from Chicago.

suits and helps him. Thus, for example, eating meat may help one, eating fruit another. Each is welcome to his own peculiarity, but he has no right to criticise the conduct of others, because that would, if followed by him, injure him, much less to insist that others should follow his way. A wife may help some people in this progress, to others she may be a positive injury. But the unmarried man has no right to say that the married disciple is wrong, much less to force his own ideal of morality upon his brother.

We believe that every being is divine, is God. Every soul is a sun covered over with clouds of ignorance, the difference between soul and soul is owing to the difference in density of these layers of clouds. We believe that this is the conscious or unconscious basis of all religions, and that this is the explanation of the whole history of human progress either in the material, intellectual, or spiritual plane—the same Spirit is manifesting through different planes.

We believe that this is the very essence of the Vedas.

We believe that it is the duty of every soul to treat, think of, and behave to other souls as such, i.e. as Gods, and not hate or despise, or vilify, or try to injure them by any manner or means. This is the duty not only of the Sannyasin, but of all men and women.

The soul has neither sex, nor caste, nor imperfection

We believe that nowhere throughout the Vedas, Darshanas, or Purânas, or Tantras, is it ever said that the soul has any sex, creed, or caste. Therefore we agree with those who say, "What has religion to do with social reforms?" But they must also agree with us when we tell them that religion has no business to formulate social laws and insist on the difference between beings, because its aim and end is to obliterate all such fictions and monstrosities.

If it be pleaded that through this difference we would reach the final equality and unity, we answer that the same religion has said over and over again that mud cannot be washed with mud. As if a man can be moral by being immoral!

Social laws were created by economic conditions under the sanction of religion. The terrible mistake of religion was to interfere in social matters. But how hypocritically it says and thereby contradicts itself, "Social reform is not the business of religion"! True, what we want is that religion should not be a social reformer, but we insist at the same time that society has no right to become a religious law-giver. Hands off! Keep yourself to your own bounds and everything would come right.

Education is the manifestation of the perfection already in man.

Religion is the manifestation of the Divinity already in man.

Therefore the only duty of the teacher in both cases is to remove all obstructions from the way. Hands off! as I always say, and everything will be right. That is, our duty is to clear the way. The Lord does the rest.

Especially, therefore, you must bear in mind that religion has to do only with the soul and has no business to interfere in social matters; you must also bear in mind that this applies completely to the mischief which has already been done. It is as if a man after forcibly taking possession of another's property cries through the nose when that man tries to regain it—and preaches the doctrine of the sanctity of human right!

What business had the priests to interfere (to the misery of millions of human beings) in every social matter?

You speak of the meat-eating Kshatriya. Meat or no meat, it is they who are the fathers of all that is noble and beautiful in Hinduism. Who wrote the Upanishads? Who was Râma? Who was Krishna? Who was Buddha? Who were the Tirthankaras of the Jains? Whenever the Kshatriyas have preached religion, they have given it to everybody; and whenever the Brahmins wrote anything, they would deny all right to others. Read the Gitâ and the Sutras of Vyâsa, or get someone to read them to you. In the Gita the way is laid open to all men and women, to all caste and colour, but Vyasa tries to put meanings upon the Vedas to cheat the poor Shudras. Is God a nervous fool like you that the flow of His river of mercy would be dammed up by a piece of meat? If such be He, His value is not a pie!

Hope nothing from me, but I am convinced as I have written to you, and spoken to you, that India is to be saved by the Indians themselves. So you, young men of the motherland, can dozens of you become almost fanatics over this new ideal? Take thought, collect materials, write a sketch of the life of Ramakrishna, studiously avoiding all miracles. The life should be written as an illustration of the doctrines he preached. Only his—do not bring me or any living persons into that. The main aim should be to give to the world what he taught, and the life as illustrating that. I, unworthy though I am, had one commission—to bring out the casket of jewels that was placed in my charge and make it over to you. Why to you? Because the hypocrites, the jealous, the slavish, and the cowardly, those who believe in matter only, can never do anything. Jealousy is the bane of our national character, natural to slaves. Even the Lord with all His power could do nothing on account of this jealousy. Think of me as one who has done all his duty and is now dead and gone. Think that the whole work is upon your shoulders. Think that you, young men of our motherland, are destined to do this. Put yourselves to the task. Lord bless you. Leave me, throw me quite out of sight. Preach the new ideal, the new doctrine, the new life. Preach against nobody, against no custom. Preach neither for nor against caste or any other social evil. Preach to let "hands off", and everything will come right.

My blessings on you all, my brave, steadfast, and loving souls.

OUR DUTY TO THE MASSES[1]

Shri Nârâyana bless you and yours. Through your Highness' kind help it has been possible for me to come to this country. Since then I have become well known here, and the hospitable people of this country have supplied all my wants. It is a wonderful country, and this is a wonderful nation in many respects. No other nation applies so much machinery in their everyday work as do the people of this country. Everything is machine. Then again, they are only one-twentieth of the whole population of the world. Yet they have fully one-sixth of all the wealth of the world. There is no limit to their wealth and luxuries. Yet everything here is so dear. The wages of labour are the highest in the world; yet the fight between labour and capital is constant.

Nowhere on earth have women so many privileges as in America. They are slowly taking everything into their hands; and, strange to say, the number of cultured women is much greater than that of cultured men. Of course, the higher geniuses are mostly from the rank of males. With all the criticism of the Westerners against our caste, they have a worse one—that of money. The almighty dollar, as the Americans say, can do anything here.

No country on earth has so many laws, and in no country are they so little regarded. On the whole our poor Hindu people are infinitely more moral than any of the Westerners. In religion they practice here either hypocrisy or fanaticism. Sober-minded men have become disgusted with their superstitious religions and are looking forward to India for new light. Your Highness cannot realise without seeing how eagerly they take in any little bit of the grand thoughts of the holy Vedas, which resist and are unharmed by the terrible onslaughts of modern science. The theories of creation out of nothing, of a created soul, and of the big tyrant of a God sitting on a throne in a place called heaven, and of the eternal hell-fires have disgusted all the educated; and the noble thoughts of the Vedas about the eternity of creation and of the soul, and about the God in our own soul, they are imbibing fast in one shape or other. Within fifty years the educated of the world will come to believe in the eternity of both soul and creation, and in God as our highest and perfect nature, as taught in our holy Vedas. Even now their learned priests are interpreting the Bible in that way. My conclusion is that they require more spiritual civilisation, and we, more material.

The one thing that is at the root of all evils in India is the condition of the poor. The poor in the West are devils; compared to them ours are angels, and it is therefore so much the easier to raise our poor. The only service to be done for our lower classes is to give them education, to develop their lost individuality. That is the great task between our people and princes. Up to now nothing has been done in that direction. Priest-power and foreign conquest have trodden them down for centuries, and at last the poor of India have forgotten that they are human beings. They are to be given ideas; their eyes are to be opened to what is going on in the world around them; and then they will work out their own salvation. Every nation, every man and every woman must work out their own salvation. Give them ideas—that is the only help they require, and then the rest must follow as the effect. Ours is to put the chemicals together, the crystallization comes in the law of nature. Our duty is to put ideas into their heads, they will do the rest. This is what is to be done in India. It is this idea that has been in my mind for a long time. I could not accomplish it in India, and that was the reason of my coming to this country. The great difficulty in the way of educating the poor is this. Supposing even your Highness opens a free school in every village, still it would do no good, for the poverty in India is such, that the poor boys would rather go to help their fathers in the fields, or otherwise try to make a living, than come to the school. Now if the mountain does not come to Mohammed, Mohammed must go to the mountain. If the poor boy cannot come to education, education must go to him. There are thousands of single-minded, self-sacrificing Sannyâsins in our own country, going from village to village, teaching religion. If some of them can be organised as teachers of secular things also, they will go from place to place, from door to door, not only preaching, but teaching also. Suppose two of these men go to a village in the evening with a camera, a globe, some maps, etc. They can teach a great deal of astronomy and geography to the ignorant. By telling stories about different nations, they can give the poor a hundred times more information through the ear than they can get in a lifetime through books. This requires an organization, which again means money. Men enough there are in India to work out this plan, but alas! they have no money. It is very difficult to set a wheel in motion; but when once set, it goes on with increasing velocity. After seeking help in my own country and failing to get any sympathy from the rich, I came over to this country through your Highness' aid. The Americans do not care a bit whether the poor of India die or live. And why should they, when our own people never think of anything but their own selfish ends?

My noble Prince, this life is short, the vanities of the world are transient, but they alone live who live for others, the rest are more dead than alive. One such high, noble-minded, and royal son of India as your Highness can do much towards raising India on her feet again and thus leave a name to posterity which shall be worshipped.

That the Lord may make your noble heart feel intensely for the suffering millions of India, sunk in ignorance, is the prayer of —

Vivekananda.

---

1. Written from Chicago to H. H. the Maharaja of Mysore on June 23, 1894.

REPLY TO THE CALCUTTA ADDRESS[1]

I am in receipt of the resolutions that were passed at the recent Town Hall meeting in Calcutta and the kind words my fellow-citizens sent over to me.

Accept, sir, my most heartfelt gratitude for your appreciation of my insignificant services.

I am thoroughly convinced that no individual or nation can live by holding itself apart from the community of others, and whenever such an attempt has been made under false ideas of greatness, policy, or holiness — the result has always been disastrous to the secluding one.

To my mind, the one great cause of the downfall and the degeneration of India was the building of a wall of custom — whose foundation was hatred of others — round the nation, and the real aim of which in ancient times was to prevent the Hindus from coming in contact with the surrounding Buddhistic nations.

Whatever cloak ancient or modern sophistry may try to throw over it, the inevitable result — the vindication of the moral law, that none can hate others without degenerating himself — is that the race that was foremost amongst the ancient races is now a byword, and a scorn among nations. We are object-lessons of the violation of that law which our ancestors were the first to discover and disseminate.

Give and take is the law; and if India wants to raise herself once more, it is absolutely necessary that she brings out her treasures and throws them broadcast among the nations of the earth, and in return be ready to receive what others have to give her. Expansion is life, contraction is death. Love is life, and hatred is death. We commenced to die the day we began to hate other races; and nothing can prevent our death unless we come back to expansion, which is life.

We must mix, therefore, with all the races of the earth. And every Hindu that goes out to travel in foreign parts renders more benefit to his country than hundreds of men who are bundles of superstitions and selfishness, and whose one aim in life seems to be like that of the dog in the manger. The wonderful structures of national life which the Western nations have raised, are supported by the strong pillars of character, and until we can produce members of such, it is useless to fret and fume against this or that power.

Do any deserve liberty who are not ready to give it to others? Let us calmly and in a manly fashion go to work, instead of dissipating our energy in unnecessary frettings and fumings. I, for one, thoroughly believe that no power in the universe can withhold from anyone anything he really deserves. The past was great no doubt, but I sincerely believe that the future will be more glorious still.

May Shankara keep us steady in purity, patience, and perseverance!

1. Written from New York on Nov. 18, 1894, to Raja Pyari Mohan Mukherji, President of the public meeting held on Sept. 5, 1894 at the Calcutta Town Hall in appreciation of Swami Vivekananda's work in the West.

TO MY BRAVE BOYS[2]

Push on with the organization. Nothing else is necessary but these — love, sincerity, and patience. What is life but growth, i.e. expansion, i.e. love? Therefore all love is life, it is the only law of life; all selfishness is death, and this is true here or hereafter. It is life to do good, it is death not to do good to others. Ninety per cent of human brutes you see are dead, are ghosts — for none lives, my boys, but he who loves. Feel, my children, feel; feel for the poor, the ignorant, the downtrodden; feel till the heart stops and the brain reels and you think you will go mad — then pour the soul out at the feet of the Lord, and then will come power, help, and indomitable energy. Struggle, struggle, was my motto for the last ten years. Struggle, still say I. When it was all dark, I used to say, struggle; when light is breaking in, I still say, struggle. Be not afraid, my children. Look not up in that attitude of fear towards that infinite starry vault as if it would crush you. Wait! In a few hours more, the whole of it will be under your feet. Wait, money does not pay, nor name; fame does not pay, nor learning. It is love that pays; it is character that cleaves its way through adamantine walls of difficulties.

Now the question before us is this. There cannot be any growth without liberty. Our ancestors freed religious thought, and we have a wonderful religion. But they put a heavy chain on the feet of society, and our society is, in a word, horrid, diabolical. In the West, society always had freedom, and look at them. On the other hand, look at their religion.

Liberty is the first condition of growth. Just as man must have liberty to think and speak, so he must have liberty in food, dress, and marriage, and in every other thing, so long as he does not injure others.

We talk foolishly against material civilisation. The grapes are sour. Even taking all that foolishness for granted, in all India there are, say, a hundred thousand really spiritual men and women. Now, for the spiritualisation of these, must three hundred millions be sunk in savagery and starvation? Why should any starve? How was it possible for the Hindus to have been conquered by the Mohammedans? It was due to the Hindus' ignorance of material civilization. Even the Mohammedans taught them to wear tailor-made clothes. Would the Hindus had learnt from the Mohammedans how to eat in a cleanly way without mixing their food with the dust of the streets! Material civilization, nay, even luxury, is necessary to create work for the poor. Bread! Bread! I do not believe in a God, who cannot give me bread here, giving me eternal bliss in heaven! Pooh! India is to be raised, the poor are to be fed, education is to be spread, and the evil of priestcraft is to be removed. No priestcraft, no social tyranny! More bread, more opportunity for everybody! Our young fools organise meetings to get more power from the English. They only laugh. None deserves liberty who is not ready to give liberty.

2. Written to Alasinga Perumal from New York on 19th November, 1894.

Suppose the English give over to you all the power. Why, the powers that be then, will hold the people down, and let them not have it. Slaves want power to make slaves.

Now, this is to be brought about slowly, and by only insisting on our religion and giving liberty to society. Root up priest-craft from the old religion, and you get the best religion in the world. Do you understand me? Can you make a European society with India's religion? I believe it is possible, and must be.

The grand plan is to start a colony in Central India, where you can follow your own ideas independently, and then a little leaven will leaven all. In the meanwhile form a Central Association and go on branching off all over India. Start only on religious grounds now, and do not preach any violent social reform at present; only do not countenance foolish superstitions. Try to revive society on the old grounds of universal salvation and equality as laid down by the old Masters, such as Shankarâchârya, Râmânuja, and Chaitanya.

Have fire and spread all over. Work, work. Be the servant while leading. Be unselfish, and never listen to one friend in private accusing another. Have infinite patience, and success is yours.

Now take care of this: Do not try to "boss" others, as the Yankees say. Because I always direct my letters to you, you need not try to show your consequence over my other friends. I know you never can be such a fool, but still I think it my duty to warn you. This is what kills all organizations. Work, work, for, to work only for the good of others is life.

I want that there should be no hypocrisy, no Jesuitism, no roguery. I have depended always on the Lord, always on Truth broad as the light of day. Let me not die with stains on my conscience for having played Jesuitism to get up name or fame, or even to do good. There should not be a breath of immorality, nor a stain of policy which is bad.

No shilly-shally, no esoteric blackguardism, no secret humbug, nothing should be done in a corner. No special favouritism of the Master, no Master at that, even. Onward, my brave boys—money or no money—men or no men! Have you love? Have you God? Onward and forward to the breach, you are irresistible.

How absurd! The Theosophical magazines saying that they, the Theosophists, prepared the way to my success! Indeed! Pure nonsense! Theosophists prepared the way!

Take care! Beware of everything that is untrue; stick to truth and we shall succeed, maybe slowly, but surely. Work on as if I never existed. Work as if on each of you depended the whole work. Fifty centuries are looking on you, the future of India depends on you. Work on. I do not know when I shall be able to come. This is a great field for work. They can at best praise in India, but they will not give a cent for anything; and where shall they get it, beggars themselves? Then, they have lost the faculty of doing public good for the last two thousand years or more. They are just learning the ideas of nation, public, etc. So I need not blame them.

Blessings to you all!

A PLAN OF WORK FOR INDIA[3]

It is with a heart full of love, gratitude, and trust that I take up my pen to write to you. Let me tell you first, that you are one of the few men that I have met in my life who are thorough in their convictions. You have a whole-souled possession of a wonderful combination of feeling and knowledge, and withal a practical ability to bring ideas into realised forms. Above all, you are sincere, and as such I confide to you some of my ideas.

The work has begun well in India, and it should not only be kept up, but pushed on with the greatest vigour. Now or never is the time. After taking a far and wide view of things, my mind has now been concentrated on the following plan. First, it would be well to open a Theological College in Madras, and then gradually extend its scope, to give a thorough education to young men in the Vedas and the different Bhâshyas and philosophies, including a knowledge of the other religions of the world. At the same time a paper in English and the vernacular should be started as an organ of the College.

This is the first step to be taken, and huge things grow out of small undertakings. Madras just now is following the golden mean by appreciating both the ancient and modern phases of life.

I fully agree with the educated classes in India that a thorough overhauling of society is necessary. But how to do it? The destructive plans of reformers have failed. My plan is this. We have not done badly in the past, certainly not. Our society is not bad but good, only I want it to be better still. Not from error to truth, nor from bad to good, but from truth to higher truth, from good to better, best. I tell my countrymen that so far they have done well—now is the time to do better.

Now, take the case of caste—in Sanskrit, Jâti, i.e. species. Now, this is the first idea of creation. Variation (Vichitratâ), that is to say Jati, means creation. "I am One, I become many" (various Vedas). Unity is before creation, diversity is creation. Now if this diversity stops, creation will be destroyed. So long as any species is vigorous and active, it must throw out varieties. When it ceases or is stopped from breeding varieties, it dies. Now the original idea of Jati was this freedom of the individual to express his nature, his Prakriti, his Jati, his caste; and so it remained for thousands of years. Not even in the latest books is inter-dining prohibited; nor in any of the older books is inter-marriage forbidden. Then what was the cause of India's downfall?—the giving up of this idea of caste. As Gitâ says, with the extinction of caste the world will be destroyed. Now does it seem true that with the stoppage of these variations the world will be destroyed? The present caste is not the real Jati, but a hindrance to its progress. It really has prevented the free action of Jati, i.e. caste or variation. Any crystallized custom or privilege or hereditary class in any shape really prevents caste (Jati) from having its full sway; and whenever any

3. Written to Justice Sir Subrahmanya Iyer from Chicago, 3rd Jan., 1895.

nation ceases to produce this immense variety, it must die. Therefore what I have to tell you, my countrymen, is this, that India fell because you prevented and abolished caste. Every frozen aristocracy or privileged class is a blow to caste and is not-caste. Let Jati have its sway; break down every barrier in the way of caste, and we shall rise. Now look at Europe. When it succeeded in giving free scope to caste and took away most of the barriers that stood in the way of individuals, each developing his caste—Europe rose. In America, there is the best scope for caste (real Jati) to develop, and so the people are great. Every Hindu knows that astrologers try to fix the caste of every boy or girl as soon as he or she is born. That is the real caste—the individuality, and Jyotisha (astrology) recognises that. And we can only rise by giving it full sway again. This variety does not mean inequality, nor any special privilege.

This is my method—to show the Hindus that they have to give up nothing, but only to move on in the line laid down by the sages and shake off their inertia, the result of centuries of servitude. Of course, we had to stop advancing during the Mohammedan tyranny, for then it was not a question of progress but of life and death. Now that that pressure has gone, we must move forward, not on the lines of destruction directed by renegades and missionaries, but along our own line, our own road. Everything is hideous because the building is unfinished. We had to stop building during centuries of oppression. Now finish the building and everything will look beautiful in its own place. This is all my plan. I am thoroughly convinced of this. Each nation has a main current in life; in India it is religion. Make it strong and the waters on either side must move along with it. This is one phase of my line of thought. In time, I hope to bring them all out, but at present I find I have a mission in this country also. Moreover, I expect help in this country and from here alone. But up to date I could not do anything except spreading my ideas. Now I want that a similar attempt be made in India.

I do not know when I shall go over to India. I obey the leading of the Lord. I am in His hands.

"In this world in search of wealth, Thou art, O Lord, the greatest jewel I have found. I sacrifice myself unto Thee."

"In search of some one to love, Thou art the One Beloved I have found. I sacrifice myself unto Thee." (Yajurveda Samhitâ).

May the Lord bless you for ever and ever!

FUNDAMENTALS OF RELIGION[1]

My mind can best grasp the religions of the world, ancient or modern, dead or living, through this fourfold division:

1. Symbology—The employment of various external aids to preserve and develop the religious faculty of man.

2. History—The philosophy of each religion as illustrated in the lives of divine or human teachers acknowledged by each religion. This includes mythology; for what is mythology to one race, or period, is or was history to other races or periods. Even in cases of human teachers, much of their history is taken as mythology by successive generations.

3. Philosophy—The rationale of the whole scope of each religion.

4. Mysticism—The assertion of something superior to sense-knowledge and reason which particular persons, or all persons under certain circumstances, possess; runs through the other divisions also.

All the religions of the world, past or present, embrace one or more of these principles, the highly developed ones having all the four.

Of these highly developed religions again, some had no sacred book or books and they have disappeared; but those which were based on sacred books are living to the present day. As such, all the great religions of the world today are founded on sacred books.

- The Vedic on the Vedas (misnamed the Hindu or Brahminic).
- The Avestic on the Avesta.
- The Mosaic on the Old Testament.
- The Buddhistic on the Tripitaka.
- The Christian on the New Testament.
- The Mohammedan on the Koran.

The Taoists and the Confucianists in China, having also books, are so inextricably mixed up with the Buddhistic form of religion as to be catalogued with Buddhism.

Again, although strictly speaking there are no absolutely racial religions, yet it may be said that, of this group, the Vedic, the Mosaic, and the Avestic religions are confined to the races to which they originally belonged; while the Buddhistic, the Christian, and the Mohammedan religions have been from their very beginning spreading religions.

The struggle will be between the Buddhists and Christians and Mohammedans to conquer the world, and the racial religions also will have unavoidably to join in the struggle. Each one of these religions, racial or spreading, has been already split into various branches and has undergone vast changes consciously or unconsciously to adapt itself to varying circumstances. This very fact shows that not one of them is fitted alone to be the religion of the entire human race. Each religion being the effect of certain peculiarities of the race it sprang from, and being in turn the cause of the intensification and preservation of those very peculiarities, not one of them can fit the universal human nature. Not only so, but there is a negative element in each. Each one helps the growth of a certain part of human nature, but represses everything else which the race from which it sprang had not. Thus one religion to become universal

1. This incomplete article was found in the papers of Miss S. E. Waldo. The heading is inserted by us—*Publisher*.

would be dangerous and degenerating to man.

Now the history of the world shows that these two dreams—that of a universal political Empire and that of a universal religious Empire—have been long before mankind, but that again and again the plans of the greatest conquerors had been frustrated by the splitting up of his territories before he could conquer only a little part of the earth; and similarly every religion has been split into sects before it was fairly out of its cradle.

Yet it seems to be true, that the solidarity of the human race, social as well as religious, with a scope for infinite variation, is the plan of nature; and if the line of least resistance is the true line of action, it seems to me that this splitting up of each religion into sects is the preservation of religion by frustrating the tendency to rigid sameness, as well as the dear indication to us of the line of procedure.

The end seems, therefore, to be not destruction but a multiplication of sects until each individual is a sect unto himself. Again a background of unity will come by the fusion of all the existing religions into one grand philosophy. In the mythologies or the ceremonials there never will be unity, because we differ more in the concrete than in the abstract. Even while admitting the same principle, men will differ as to the greatness of each of his ideal teacher.

So, by this fusion will be found out a union of philosophy as the basis of union, leaving each at liberty to choose his teacher or his form as illustrations of that unity. This fusion is what is naturally going on for thousands of years; only, by mutual antagonism, it has been woefully held back.

Instead of antagonising, therefore, we must help all such interchange of ideas between different races, by sending teachers to each other, so as to educate humanity in all the various religions of the world; but we must insist as the great Buddhist Emperor of India, Asoka, did, in the second century before Christ, not to abuse others, or to try to make a living out of others' faults; but to help, to sympathise, and to enlighten.

There is a great outcry going over the world against metaphysical knowledge as opposed to what is styled physical knowledge. This crusade against the metaphysical and the beyond-this-life, to establish the present life and the present world on a firmer basis, is fast becoming a fashion to which even the preachers of religion one after the other are fast succumbing. Of course, the unthinking multitude are always following things which present to them a pleasing surface; but when those who ought to know better, follow unmeaning fashions, pseudo-philosophical though they profess to be, it becomes a mournful fact.

Now, no one denies that our senses, as long as they are normal, are the most trustworthy guides we have, and the facts they gather in for us form the very foundation of the structure of human knowledge. But if they mean that all human knowledge is only sense-perception and nothing but that, we deny it. If by physical sciences are meant systems of knowledge which are entirely based and built upon sense-perception, and nothing but that, we contend that such a science never existed nor will ever exist. Nor will any system of knowledge, built upon sense-perception alone, ever be a science.

Senses no doubt cull the materials of knowledge and find similarities and dissimilarities; but there they have to stop. In the first place the physical gatherings of facts are conditioned by certain metaphysical conceptions, such as space and time. Secondly, grouping facts, or generalisation, is impossible without some abstract notion as the background. The higher the generalization, the more metaphysical is the abstract background upon which the detached facts are arranged. Now, such ideas as matter, force, mind, law, causation, time, and space are the results of very high abstractions, and nobody has ever sensed any one of them; in other words, they are entirely metaphysical. Yet without these metaphysical conceptions, no physical fact is possible to be understood. Thus a certain motion becomes understood when it is referred to a force; certain sensations, to matter; certain changes outside, to law; certain changes in thought, to mind; certain order singly, to causation—and joined to time, to law. Yet nobody has seen or even imagined matter or force, law or causation, time or space.

It may be urged that these, as abstracted concepts do not exist, and that these abstractions are nothing separate or separable from the groups of which they are, so to say, only qualities.

Apart from the question whether abstractions are possible or not, or whether there is something besides the generalized groups or not, it is plain that these notions of matter or force, time or space, causation, law, or mind, are held to be units abstracted and independent (by themselves) of the groups, and that it is only when they are thought of as such, they furnish themselves as explanations of the facts in sense-perception. That is to say, apart from the validity of these notions, we see two facts about them—first, they are metaphysical; second, that only as metaphysical do they explain the physical and not otherwise.

Whether the external conforms to the internal, or the internal to the external, whether matter conforms to mind, or mind to matter, whether the surroundings mould the mind, or the mind moulds the circumstances, is old, old question, and is still today as new and vigorous as it ever was. Apart from the question of precedence or causation—without trying to solve the problem as to whether the mind is the cause of matter or matter the cause of mind—it is evident that whether the external was formed by the internal or not, it must conform itself to the internal for us to be able to know it. Supposing that the external world is the cause of the internal, yet we shall of have to admit that the external world, as cause of ours mind, is unknown and unknowable, because the mind can only know that much or that view of the external or that view which conforms to or is a reflection of its own nature. That which is its own reflection could not have been its cause. Now that view of the whole mass of existence, which is cut off by mind and known, certainly cannot be the cause of mind, as its very existence is known in and through the mind.

Thus it is impossible to deduce a mind from matter. Nay, it is absurd. Because on the very face of it that portion of existence which is bereft of the qualities of thought and life and endowed with the quality of externality is called matter, and that portion which is bereft of externality and endowed with the qualities of thought and life is called mind. Now to prove matter from mind, or mind from matter, is to deduce from each the very qualities we have taken away from each; and, therefore, all the fight about the causality of mind or matter is merely a word puzzle and nothing more. Again, throughout all these controversies runs, as a rule, the fallacy of imparting different meanings to the words mind and matter. If sometimes the word mind is used as something opposed and external to matter, at others as something which embraces both the mind and matter, i.e. of which both the external and internal are parts on the materialistic side; the word matter is sometimes used in is the restricted sense of something external which we sense, and again it means something which is the cause of all the phenomena both external and internal. The materialist frightens the idealist by claiming to derive his mind from the elements of the laboratory, while all the time he is struggling to express something higher than all elements and atoms, something of which both the external and the internal phenomena are results, and which he terms matter. The idealist, on the other hand, wants to derive all the elements and atoms of the materialist from his own thought, even while catching glimpses of something which is the cause of both mind and matter, and which he ofttimes calls God. That is to say, one party wants to explain the whole universe by a portion of it which is external, the other by another portion which is internal. Both of these attempts are impossible. Mind and matter cannot explain each other. The only explanation is to be sought for in something which will embrace both matter and mind.

It may be argued that thought cannot exist without mind, for supposing there was a time when there was no thought, matter, as we know it, certainly could not have existed. On the other hand, it may be said that knowledge being impossible without experience, and experience presupposing the external world, the existence of mind, as we know it, is impossible without the existence of matter.

Nor is it possible that either of them had a beginning. Generalisation is the essence of knowledge. Generalisation is impossible without a storage of similarities. Even the fact of comparison is impossible without previous experience.

Knowledge thus is impossible without previous knowledge—and knowledge necessitating the existence of both thought and matter, both of them are without beginning.

Again generalization, the essence of sense-knowledge, is impossible without something upon which the detached facts of perception unite. The whole world of external perceptions requires something upon which to unite in order to form a concept of the world, as painting must have its canvas. If thought or mind be this canvas to the external world, it, in its turn requires another. Mind being a series of different feelings and willing—and not a unit, requires something besides itself as its background of unity. Here all analysis is bound to stop, for a real unity has been found. The analysis of a compound cannot stop until an indivisible unit has been reached. The fact that presents us with such a unity for both thought and matter must necessarily be the last indivisible basis of every phenomenon, for we cannot conceive any further analysis; nor is any further analysis necessary, as this includes an analysis of all our external and internal perceptions.

So far then, we see that a totality of mental and material phenomena, and something beyond, upon which they are both playing, are the results of our investigation.

Now this something beyond is not in sense-perception; it is a logical necessity, and a feeling of its indefinable presence runs through all our sense-perceptions. We see also that to this something we are driven by the sheer necessity of being true to our reason and generalising faculty.

It may be urged that there is no necessity whatsoever of postulating any such substance or being beyond the mass of mental and material phenomena. The totality of phenomena is all that we know or can know, and it requires nothing beyond itself to explain itself. An analysis beyond the senses is impossible, and the feeling of a substance in which everything inheres is simply an illusion.

We see, that from the most ancient times, there has been these two schools among thinkers. One party claims that the unavoidable necessity of the human mind to form concepts and abstractions is the natural guide to knowledge, and that it can stop nowhere until we have transcended all phenomena and formed a concept which is absolute in all directions, transcending time and space and causality. Now if this ultimate concept is arrived at by analysing the whole phenomena of thought and matter, step by step, taking the cruder first and resolving it into a finer, and still finer, until we arrive at something which stands as the solution of everything else, it is obvious that everything else beyond this final result is a momentary modification of itself, and as such, this final result alone is real and everything else is but its shadow. The reality, therefore, is not in the senses but beyond them.

On the other hand, the other party holds that the only reality in the universe is what our senses bring to us, and although a sense of something beyond hangs on to all our sense-perceptions, that is only a trick of the mind, and therefore unreal.

Now a changing something can never be understood, without the idea of something unchanging; and if it be said that that unchanging something, to which the changing is referred, is also a changing phenomenon only relatively unchanging, and is therefore to be referred to something else, and so on, we say that however infinitely long this series be, the very fact of our inability to understand a changeable without an unchangeable forces us to postulate one as the background of all the changeable. And no one has the right to take one part of a whole as right and reject the other at will. If one takes the obverse he must take the reverse of the same coin also, however he may dislike it.

Again, with every movement, man asserts his freedom. From the highest thinker to the most ignorant man everyone knows that he is free. Now every man at the same time finds out with a little thinking that every action of his had motives and conditions, and given those motives and conditions his particular action can be as rigorously deduced as any other fact in causation.

Here, again, the same difficulty occurs. Man's will is as rigorously bound by the law of causation as the growth of any little plant or the falling of a stone, and yet, through all this bondage runs the indestructible idea of freedom. Here also the totality side will declare that the idea of freedom is an illusion and man is wholly a creature of necessity.

Now, on one hand, this denial of freedom as an illusion is no explanation; on the other hand, why not say that the idea of necessity or bondage or causation is an illusion of the ignorant? Any theory which can fit itself to facts which it wants to explain, by first cutting as many of them as prevents its fitting itself into them, is on the face of it wrong. Therefore the only way left to us is to admit first that the body is not free, neither is the will but that there must be something beyond both the mind and body which is free and *(incomplete)*.

THE PROBLEM OF MODERN INDIA AND ITS SOLUTION[1]

The ancient history of India is full of descriptions of the gigantic energies and their multifarious workings, the boundless spirit, the combination of indomitable action and reaction of the various forces, and, above all, the profound thoughtfulness of a godly race. If the word history is understood to mean merely narratives of kings and emperors, and pictures of society — tyrannised over from time to time by the evil passions, haughtiness, avarice, etc., of the rulers of the time, portraying

1. The above is a translation of the first Bengali article written by Swami Vivekananda as an introduction to the *Udbodhana*, when it was started on the 14th of January, 1899, as the Bengali fortnightly (afterwards monthly) journal of the Ramakrishna Order.

the acts resulting from their good or evil propensities, and how these reacted upon the society of that time — such a history India perhaps does not possess. But every line of that mass of the religious literature of India, her ocean of poetry, her philosophies and various scientific works reveal to us — a thousand times more clearly than the narratives of the life-incidents and genealogies of particular kings and emperors can ever do — the exact position and every step made in advance by that vast body of men who, even before the dawn of civilisation, impelled by hunger and thirst, lust and greed, etc., attracted by the charm of beauty, endowed with a great and indomitable mental power, and moved by various sentiments, arrived through various ways and means at that stage of eminence. Although the heaps of those triumphal flags which they gathered in their innumerable victories over nature with which they had been waging war for ages, have, of late, been torn and tattered by the violent winds of adverse circumstances and become worn out through age, yet they still proclaim the glory of Ancient India.

Whether this race slowly proceeded from Central Asia, Northern Europe, or the Arctic regions, and gradually came down and sanctified India by settling there at last, or whether the holy land of India was their original native place, we have no proper means of knowing now. Or whether a vast race living in or outside India, being displaced from its original abode, in conformity with natural laws, came in the course of time to colonise and settle over Europe and other places — and whether these people were white or black, blue-eyed or dark-eyed, golden-haired or black-haired — all these matters — there is no sufficient ground to prove now, with the one exception of the fact of the kinship of Sanskrit with a few European languages. Similarly, it is not easy to arrive at a final conclusion as to the modern Indians, whether they all are the pure descendants of that race, or how much of the blood of that race is flowing in their veins, or again, what races amongst them have any of that even in them.

However, we do not, in fact, lose much by this uncertainty.

But there is one fact to remember. Of that ancient Indian race, upon which the rays of civilisation first dawned, where deep thoughtfulness first revealed itself in full glory, there are still found hundreds of thousands of its children, born of its mind — the inheritors of its thoughts and sentiments — ready to claim them.

Crossing over mountains, rivers, arid oceans, setting at naught, as it were, the obstacles of the distance of space and time, the blood of Indian thought has flowed, and is still flowing into the veins of other nations of the globe, whether in a distinct or in some subtle unknown way. Perhaps to us belongs the major portion of the universal ancient inheritance.

In a small country lying in the eastern corner of the Mediterranean Sea, beautiful and adorned by nature, and garlanded by well-formed and beautiful-looking islands, lived a race of men who were few in number, but of a very charming aspect, perfectly formed, and strong in muscles and sinews, light of body, yet possessing steadiness and perseverance, and who were unrivalled for the creation of all earthly beauties, as well as endowed with extraordinary practicality and intellect. The other ancient nations used to call them Yavanas, but they called themselves Greeks. This handful of a vigorous and wonderful race is a unique example in the annals of man. Wherever and in whatever nation there has been, or is, any advance made in earthly science up to the present day — such as social, martial, political, sculptural, etc. — there the shadow of ancient Greece has fallen. Let us leave apart the consideration of ancient times, for even in this modern age, we, the Bengalis, think ourselves proud and enlightened simply by following the footmarks of these Yavana Gurus for these last fifty years, illumining our homes with what light of theirs is reaching us through the European literature.

The whole of Europe nowadays is, in every respect, the disciple of ancient Greece, and her proper inheritor; so much so that a wise man of England had said, "Whatever nature has not created, that is the creation of the Greek mind."

These two gigantic rivers (Aryans and Yavanas), issuing from far-away and different mountains (India and Greece), occasionally come in contact with each other, and whenever such confluence takes place, a tremendous intellectual or spiritual tide, rising in human societies, greatly expands the range of civilisation and confirms the bond of universal brotherhood among men.

Once in far remote antiquity, the Indian philosophy, coming in contact with Greek energy, led to the rise of the Persian, the Roman, and other great nations. After the invasion of Alexander the Great, these two great waterfalls colliding with each other, deluged nearly half of the globe with spiritual tides, such as Christianity. Again, a similar commingling, resulting in the improvement and prosperity of Arabia, laid the foundation of modern European civilisation. And perhaps, in our own day, such a time for the conjunction of these two gigantic forces has presented itself again. This time their centre is India.

The air of India pre-eminently conduces to quietness, the nature of the Yavana is the constant expression of power; profound meditation characterises the one, the indomitable spirit of dexterous activity, the other; one's motto is "renunciation", the other's "enjoyment". One's whole energy is directed inwards, the other's, outwards; one's whole learning consists in the knowledge of the Self or the Subject, the other's, in the knowledge of the not-Self or the object (perishable creation); one loves Moksha (spiritual freedom), the other loves political independence; one is unmindful of gaining prosperity in this world, the other sets his whole heart on making a heaven of this world; one, aspiring after eternal bliss, is indifferent to all the ephemeral pleasures of this life, and the other, doubting the existence of eternal bliss, or knowing it to be far away, directs his whole energy to the attainment of earthly pleasures

as much as possible.

In this age, both these types of mankind are extinct, only their physical and mental children, their works and thoughts are existing.

Europe and America are the advanced children of the Yavanas, a glory to their forefathers; but the modern inhabitants of the land of Bharata are not the glory of the ancient Aryas. But, as fire remains intact under cover of ashes, so the ancestral fire still remains latent in these modern Indians. Through the grace of the Almighty Power, it is sure to manifest itself in time.

What will accrue when that ancestral fire manifests itself?

Would the sky of India again appear clouded over by waving masses of smoke springing from the Vedic sacrificial fire? Or is the glory of Rantideva again going to be revived in the blood of the sacrificed animals? Are the old customs of Gomedha, Ashvamedha, or perpetuating the lineage from a husband's brother, and other usages of a like nature to come back again? Or is the deluge of a Buddhistic propaganda again going to turn the whole of India into a big monastery? Are the laws of Manu going to be rehabilitated as of yore? Or is the discrimination of food, prescribed and forbidden, varying in accordance with geographical dimensions, as it is at the present day, alone going to have its all-powerful domination over the length and breadth of the country? Is the caste system to remain, and is it going to depend eternally upon the birthright of a man, or is it going to be determined by his qualification? And again in that caste system, is the discrimination of food, its touchableness or untouchableness, dependent upon the purity or the impurity of the man who touches it, to be observed as it is in Bengal, or will it assume a form more strict as it does in Madras? Or, as in the Punjab, will all such restrictions be obliterated? Are the marriages of the different Varnas to take place from the upper to the lower Varna in the successive order, as in Manu's days, and as it is still in vogue in Nepal? Or, as in Bengal and other places, are they to be kept restricted to a very limited number of individuals constituting one of the several communities of a certain class of the Varna? To give a conclusive answer to all these questions is extremely difficult. They become the more difficult of solution, considering the difference in the customs prevailing in different parts of the country — nay, as we find even in the same part of the country such a wide divergence of customs among different castes and families.

Then what is to be?

What we should have is what we have not, perhaps what our forefathers even had not — that which the Yavanas had; that, impelled by the life-vibration of which, is issuing forth in rapid succession from the great dynamo of Europe, the electric flow of that tremendous power vivifying the whole world. We want that. We want that energy, that love of independence, that spirit of self-reliance, that immovable fortitude, that dexterity in action, that bond of unity of purpose, that thirst for improvement. Checking a little the constant looking back to the past, we want that expansive vision infinitely projected forward; and we want—that intense spirit of activity (Rajas) which will flow through our every vein, from head to foot.

What can be a greater giver of peace than renunciation? A little ephemeral worldly good is nothing in comparison with eternal good; no doubt of that. What can bring greater strength than Sattva Guna (absolute purity of mind)? It is indeed true that all other kinds of knowledge are but non-knowledge in comparison with Self-knowledge. But I ask: How many are there in the world fortunate enough to gain that Sattva Guna? How many in this land of Bharata? How many have that noble heroism which can renounce all, shaking off the idea of "I and mine"? How many are blessed enough to possess that far-sight of wisdom which makes the earthly pleasures appear to be but vanity of vanities? Where is that broad-hearted man who is apt to forget even his own body in meditating over the beauty and glory of the Divine? Those who are such are but a handful in comparison to the population of the whole of India; and in order that these men may attain to their salvation, will the millions and millions of men and women of India have to be crushed under the wheel of the present-day society and religion?

And what good can come out of such a crushing?

Do you not see—talking up this plea of Sattva, the country has been slowly and slowly drowned in the ocean of Tamas or dark ignorance? Where the most dull want to hide their stupidity by covering it with a false desire for the highest knowledge which is beyond all activities, either physical or mental; where one, born and bred in lifelong laziness, wants to throw the veil of renunciation over his own unfitness for work; where the most diabolical try to make their cruelty appear, under the cloak of austerity, as a part of religion; where no one has an eye upon his own incapacity, but everyone is ready to lay the whole blame on others; where knowledge consists only in getting some books by heart, genius consists in chewing the cud of others' thoughts, and the highest glory consists in taking the name of ancestors: do we require any other proof to show that that country is being day by day drowned in utter Tamas?

Therefore Sattva or absolute purity is now far away from us. Those amongst us who are not yet fit, but who hope to be fit, to reach to that absolutely pure Paramahamsa state—for them the acquirement of Rajas or intense activity is what is most beneficial now. Unless a man passes through Rajas, can he ever attain to that perfect Sâttvika state? How can one expect Yoga or union with God, unless one has previously finished with his thirst for Bhoga or enjoyment? How can renunciation come where there is no Vairâgya or dispassion for all the charms of enjoyment?

On the other hand, the quality of Rajas is apt to die down as soon as it comes up, like a fire of palm leaves. The presence of Sattva and the Nitya or Eternal Reality is almost in a state of juxtaposition—Sattva is nearly Nitya. Whereas the nation in which the quality of Rajas predominates is not so long-lived, but a nation with a preponderance of Sattva is, as it were, immortal. History is a witness to this fact.

In India, the quality of Rajas is almost absent: the same is the case with Sattva in the West. It is certain, therefore, that the real life of the Western world depends upon the influx, from India, of the current of Sattva or transcendentalism; and it is also certain that unless we overpower and submerge our Tamas by the opposite tide of Rajas, we shall never gain any worldly good or welfare in this life; and it is also equally certain that we shall meet many formidable obstacles in the path of realisation of those noble aspirations and ideals connected with our after-life.

The one end and aim of the Udbodhana is to help the union and intermingling of these two forces, as far as it lies in its power.

True, in so doing there is a great danger—lest by this huge wave of Western spirit are washed away all our most precious jewels, earned through ages of hard labour; true, there is fear lest falling into its strong whirlpool, even the land of Bharata forgets itself so far as to be turned into a battlefield in the struggle after earthly enjoyments; ay, there is fear, too, lest going to imitate the impossible and impracticable foreign ways, rooting out as they do our national customs and ideals, we lose all that we hold dear in this life and be undone in the next!

To avoid these calamities we must always keep the wealth of our own home before our eyes, so that every one down to the masses may always know and see what his own ancestral property is. We must exert ourselves to do that; and side by side, we should be brave to open our doors to receive all available light from outside. Let rays of light come in, in sharp-driving showers from the four quarters of the earth; let the intense flood of light flow in from the West—what of that? Whatever is weak and corrupt is liable to die—what are we to do with it? If it goes, let it go, what harm does it do to us? What is strong and invigorating is immortal. Who can destroy that?

How many gushing springs and roaring cataracts, how many icy rivulets and ever-flowing streamlets, issuing from the eternal snow-capped peaks of the Himalayas, combine and flow together to form the gigantic river of the gods, the Gangâ, and rush impetuously towards the ocean! So what a variety of thoughts and ideas, how many currents of forces, issuing from innumerable saintly hearts, and from brains of geniuses of various lands have already enveloped India, the land of Karma, the arena for the display of higher human activities! Look! how under the dominion of the English, in these days of electricity, railroad, and steamboat, various sentiments, manners, customs, and morals are spreading all over the land with lightning speed. Nectar is coming, and along with it, also poison; good is coming, as well as evil. There has been enough of angry opposition and bloodshed; the power of stemming this tide is not in Hindu society. Everything, from water filtered by machinery and drawn from hydrants, down to sugar purified with bone-ash, is being quietly and freely taken by almost every one, in spite of much show of verbal protest. Slowly and slowly, by the strong dint of law, many of our most cherished customs are falling off day by day—we have no power to withstand that. And why is there no power? Is truth really powerless? "Truth alone conquers and not falsehood."—Is this Divine Vedic saying false? Or who knows but that those very customs which are being swept away by the deluge of the power of Western sovereignty or of Western education were not real Âchâras, but were Anâchâras after all. This also is a matter for serious consideration.

बहुजनहिताय बहुजनसुखाय— "For the good of the many, as well as for the happiness of the many"—in an unselfish manner, with a heart filled with love and reverence, the Udbodhana invites all wise and large-hearted men who love their motherland to discuss these points and solve these problems; and, being devoid of the feeling of hatred or antagonism, as well as turning itself away from the infliction of abusive language directed towards any individual, or society, or any sect, it offers its whole self for the service of all classes.

To work we have the right, the result is in the hands of the Lord. We only pray: "O Thou Eternal Spirit, make us spiritual; O Thou Eternal Strength, make us strong; O Thou Mighty One, make us mighty."

RAMAKRISHNA: HIS LIFE AND SAYINGS[1]

Among the Sanskrit scholars of the West, Professor Max Müller takes the lead. The Rig-Veda Samhitâ, the whole of which no one could even get at before, is now very neatly printed and made accessible to the public, thanks to the munificent generosity of the East India Company and to the Professor's prodigious labours extending over years. The alphabetical characters of most of the manuscripts, collected from different parts of India, are of various forms, and many words in them are inaccurate. We cannot easily comprehend how difficult it is for a foreigner, however learned he may be, to find out the accuracy or inaccuracy of these Sanskrit characters, and more especially to make out clearly the meaning of an extremely condensed and complicated commentary. In the life of Professor Max Müller, the publication of the Rig-Veda is a great event. Besides this, he has been dwelling, as it were, and spending his whole lifetime amidst ancient Sanskrit literature; but notwithstanding this, it does not imply that in the Professor's imagination India is still echoing as of old with Vedic hymns, with her sky clouded with sacrificial smoke, with many a Vasishtha, Vishvâmitra, Janaka, and Yâjnavalkya, with her every home blooming with a Gârgi or a Maitreyi and herself guided by the Vedic rules or canons of Grihya-Sutra.

The Professor, with ever-watchful eyes, keeps himself well-informed of what new events are occurring even in the out-of-

the-way corners of modern India, half-dead as she is, trodden down by the feet of the foreigner professing an alien religion, and all but bereft of her ancient manners, rites, and customs. As the Professor's feet never touched these shores, many Anglo-Indians here show an unmixed contempt for his opinions on the customs, manners, and codes of morality of the Indian people. But they ought to know that, even after their lifelong stay, or even if they were born and brought up in this country, except any particular information they may obtain about that stratum of society with which they come in direct contact, the Anglo-Indian authorities have to remain quite ignorant in respect of other classes of people; and the more so, when, of this vast society divided into so many castes, it is very hard even among themselves for one caste to properly know the manners and peculiarities of another.

Some time ago, in a book, named, Residence in India, written by a well-known Anglo-Indian officer, I came across such a chapter as "Native Zenana Secrets". Perhaps because of that strong desire in every human heart for knowledge of secrets, I read the chapter, but only to find that this big Anglo-Indian author is fully bent upon satisfying the intense curiosity of his own countrymen regarding the mystery of a native's life by describing an affaire d'amour, said to have transpired between his sweeper, the sweeper's wife, and her paramour! And from the cordial reception given to the book by the Anglo-Indian community, it seems the writer's object has been gained, and he feels himself quite satisfied with his work "God-speed to you, dear friends!"—What else shall we say? Well has the Lord said in the Gita:

$$\text{ध्यायतो विषयान्पुंसः सङ्गस्तेषूपजायते ।}$$
$$\text{सङ्गात्संजायते कामः कामात्क्रोधोऽभिजायते ॥}$$

—"Thinking of objects, attachment to them is formed in a man. From attachment longing, and from longing anger grows."

Let such irrelevant things alone. To return to our subject: After all, one wonders at Professor Max Müller's knowledge of the social customs and codes of law, as well as the contemporaneous occurrences in the various provinces of present-day India; this is borne out by our own personal experiences.

In particular, the Professor observes with a keen eye what new waves of religion are rising in different parts of India, and spares no pains in letting the Western world not remain in the dark about them. The Brâhmo Samaj guided by Debendranâth Tagore and Keshab Chandra Sen, the Ârya Samaj established by Swami Dayânanda Sarasvati, and the Theosophical movement—have all come under the praise or censure of his pen. Struck by the sayings and teachings of Shri Ramakrishna published in the two well-established journals, the Brahmavâdin and the Prabuddha Bhârata, and reading what the Brahmo preacher, Mr. Pratâp Chandra Mazumdâr, wrote about Shri Ramakrishna,[2] he was attracted by the sage's life.

---

1. Translation of a review of *Ramakrishna: His Life and Sayings* by Prof. Max Müller, contributed to the *Udbodhana*, 14th March, 1899.

2. "Paramahamsa Sreemat Ramakrishna"—Theistic Quarterly Review, October, 1879.

Some time ago, a short sketch of Shri Ramakrishna's life[3] also appeared in the well-known monthly journal of England, The Imperial and Asiatic Quarterly Review, contributed by Mr. C. H. Tawney, M.A., the distinguished librarian of the India House. Gathering a good deal of information from Madras and Calcutta, the Professor discussed Shri Ramakrishna's life and his teachings in a short article[4] in the foremost monthly English journal, The Nineteenth Century. There he expressed himself to the effect that this new sage easily won his heart by the originality of his thoughts, couched in novel language and impregnate with fresh spiritual power which he infused into India when she was merely echoing the thoughts of her ancient sages for several centuries past, or, as in recent times, those of Western scholars. He, the Professor, had read often India's religious literature and thereby well acquainted himself with the life-stories of many of her ancient sages and saints; but is it possible to expect such lives again in this age in this India of modern times? Ramakrishna's life was a reply in the affirmative to such a question. And it brought new life by sprinkling water, as it were, at the root of the creeper of hope regarding India's future greatness and progress, in the heart of this great-souled scholar whose whole life has been dedicated to her.

There are certain great souls in the West who sincerely desire the good of India, but we are not aware whether Europe can point out another well-wisher of India who feels more for India's well-being than Professor Max Müller. Not only is Max Müller a well-wisher of India, but he has also a strong faith in Indian philosophy and Indian religion. That Advaitism is the highest discovery in the domain of religion, the Professor has many times publicly admitted. That doctrine of reincarnation, which is a dread to the Christian who has identified the soul with the body, he firmly believes in because of his having found conclusive proof in his own personal experience. And what more, perhaps, his previous birth was in India; and lest by coming to India, the old frame may break down under the violent rush of a suddenly aroused mass of past recollections - is the fear in his mind that now stands foremost in the way of his visit to this country. Still as a worldly man, whoever he may be, he has to look to all sides and conduct himself accordingly. When, after a complete surrender of all worldly interests, even the Sannyasin, when performing any practices which he knows to be purest in themselves, is seen to shiver in fear of public opinion, simply because they are held with disapproval by the people among whom he lives; when the consideration of gaining name and fame and high position, and the fear of losing them regulate the actions of even the greatest ascetic, though he may verbally denounce such consideration as most filthy and detestable—what wonder then that the man of the world who is universally honoured, and is ever anxious not to incur the displeasure of society, will have to be very cautious in ventilating the views which he personally cherishes. It is not a fact that the Professor is an utter disbeliever in such subtle subjects as the mysterious psychic powers of the Yogis.

It is not many years since Professor Max Müller "felt called upon to say a few words on certain religious movements, now going on in India"—"which has often and not unjustly, been called a country of philosophers"— which seemed to him "to have been very much misrepresented and misunderstood at home". In order to remove such misconceptions and to protest against "the wild and overcharged accounts of saints and sages living and teaching at present in India, which had been published and scattered broadcast in Indian, American, and English papers"; and "to show at the same time that behind such strange names as Indian Theosophy, and Esoteric Buddhism, and all the rest, there was something real something worth knowing"—or in other words, to point out to the thoughtful section of Europe that India was not a land inhabited only by "quite a new race of human beings who had gone through a number of the most fearful ascetic exercises", to carry on a lucrative profession by thus acquiring the powers of working such "very silly miracles" as flying through the air like the feathered race, walking on or living fishlike under the water, healing all sorts of maladies by means of incantations, and, by the aid of occult arts fabricating gold, silver, or diamond from baser materials, or by the power of Siddhis bestowing sturdy sons to rich families—but that men, who had actually realised in their life great transcendental truths, who were real knowers of Brahman, true Yogis, real devotees of God, were never found wanting in India: and, above all, to show that the whole Aryan population of India had not as yet come down so low as to be on the same plane as the brute creation, that, rejecting the latter, the living Gods in human shape, they "the high and the low" were, day and night, busy licking the feet of the first-mentioned performers of silly juggleries,—Professor Max Müller presented Shri Ramakrishna's life to the learned European public, in an article entitled "A Real Mahâtman", which appeared in The Nineteenth Century in its August number, 1896.

The learned people of Europe and America read the article with great interest and many have been attracted towards its subject, Shri Ramakrishna Deva, with the result that the wrong ideas of the civilised West about India as a country full of naked, infanticidal, ignorant, cowardly race of men who were cannibals and little removed from beasts, who forcibly burnt their widows and were steeped in all sorts of sin and darkness—towards the formation of which ideas, the Christian missionaries and, I am as much ashamed as pained to confess, some of my own countrymen also have been chiefly instrumental—began to be corrected. The veil of the gloom of ignorance, which was spread across the eyes of the Western people by the strenuous efforts of these two bodies of men, has been slowly and slowly rending asunder. "Can the country that has produced a great world-teacher like Shri Bhagavân Ramakrishna Deva be really full of such abominations as we

---

3. "A Modern Hindu Saint"—January, 1896.

4. "A Real Mahâtman."

have been asked to believe in, or have we been all along duped by interested organised bodies of mischief-makers, and kept in utter obscurity and error about the real India?"— Such a question naturally arises in the Western mind.

When Professor Max Müller, who occupies in the West the first rank in the field of Indian religion, philosophy, and literature, published with a devoted heart a short sketch of Shri Ramakrishna's life in The Nineteenth Century for the benefit of Europeans and Americans, it is needless to say that a bitter feeling of burning rancour made its appearance amongst those two classes of people referred to above.

By improper representation of the Hindu gods and goddesses, the Christian missionaries were trying with all their heart and soul to prove that really religious men could never be produced from among their worshippers; but like a straw before a tidal wave, that attempt was swept away; while that class of our countrymen alluded to above, which set itself to devise means for quenching the great fire of the rapidly spreading power of Shri Ramakrishna, seeing all its efforts futile, has yielded to despair. What is human will in opposition to the divine?

Of course from both sides, unintermittent volleys of fierce attack were opened on the aged Professor's devoted head; the old veteran, however, was not the one to turn his back. He had triumphed many times in similar contests. This time also he has passed the trial with equal ease. And to stop the empty shouts of his inferior opponents, he has published, by way of a warning to them, the book, Ramakrishna: His Life and Sayings, in which he has collected more complete information and given a fuller account of his life and utterances, so that the reading public may get a better knowledge of this great sage and his religious ideas—the sage "who has lately obtained considerable celebrity both in India and America where his disciples have been actively engaged in preaching his gospel and winning converts to his doctrines even among Christian audiences". The Professor adds, "This may seem very strange, nay, almost incredible to us...Yet every human heart has its religious yearnings; it has a hunger for religion, which sooner or later wants to be satisfied. Now the religion taught by the disciples of Ramakrishna comes to these hungry souls without any untoward authority", and is therefore, welcomed as the "free elixir of life" ... "Hence, though there may be some exaggeration in the number of those who are stated to have become converted to the religion of Ramakrishna, ... there can be no doubt that a religion which can achieve such successes in our time, while it calls itself with perfect truth the oldest religion and philosophy of the world, viz the Vedanta, the end or highest object of the Vedas, deserves our careful attention."

After discussing, in the first part of the book, what is meant by the Mahatman, the Four Stages of Life, Ascetic Exercises or Yoga, and after making some mention about Dayananda Sarasvati, Pavhâri Bâbâ, Debendranath Tagore, and Rai Shâligrâm Sâheb Bahadur, the leader of the Râdhâswami sect, the Professor enters on Shri Ramakrishna's life.

The Professor greatly fears lest the Dialogic Process—the transformation produced in the description of the facts as they really happened by too much favourableness or unfavourableness of the narrator towards them—which is invariably at work in all history as a matter of inevitable course, also influences this present sketch of life. Hence his unusual carefulness about the collection of facts. The present writer is an insignificant servant of Shri Ramakrishna. Though the materials gathered by him for Ramakrishna's life have been well-pounded in the mortar of the Professor's logic and impartial judgment, still he (Max Müller) has not omitted to add that there may be possible "traces of what I call the Dialogic Process and the irrepressible miraculising tendencies of devoted disciples" even in "his unvarnished description of his Master". And, no doubt, those few harsh-sweet words which the Professor has said in the course of his reply to what some people, with the Brâhmo-Dharma preacher, the Rev. Pratap Chandra Mazumdar, at their head, wrote to him in their anxiety to make out a "not edifying side" of Ramakrishna's character—demand thoughtful consideration from those amongst us of Bengal who, being full of jealousy, can with difficulty bear the sight of others' weal.

Shri Ramakrishna's life is presented in the book in very brief and simple language. In this life, every word of the wary historian is weighed, as it were, before being put on paper; those sparks of fire, which are seen here and there to shoot forth in the article, "A Real Mahatman", are this time held in with the greatest care. The Professor's boat is here plying between the Scylla of the Christian missionaries on the one hand, and the Charybdis of the tumultuous Brahmos on the other. The article, "A Real Mahatman" brought forth from both the parties many hard words and many carping remarks on the Professor. It is a pleasure to observe that there is neither the attempt made here to retort on them, nor is there any display of meanness—as the refined writers of England are not in the habit of indulging in that kind of thing—but with a sober, dignified, not the least malignant, yet firm and thundering voice, worthy of the aged scholar, he has removed the charges that were levelled against some of the uncommon ideas of the great-soured sage—swelling forth from a heart too deep for ordinary grasp.

And the charges are, indeed, surprising to us. We have heard the great Minister of the Brahmo Samaj, the late revered Âchârya Shri Keshab Chandra Sen, speaking in his charming way that Shri Ramakrishna's simple, sweet, colloquial language breathed a superhuman purity; though in his speech could be noticed some such words as we term obscene, the use of those words, on account of his uncommon childlike innocence and of their being perfectly devoid of the least breath of sensualism, instead of being something reproachable, served rather the purpose of embellishment—yet, this is one of the mighty charges!

Another charge brought against him is that his treatment of his wife was barbarous because of his taking the vow of leading a Sannyasin's life! To this the Professor has replied that he took the vow of Sannyasa with his wife's assent, and that during the years of his life on this earth, his wife, bearing a character worthy of her husband, heartily received him as her Guru (spiritual guide) and, according to his instructions, passed her days in infinite bliss and peace, being engaged in the service of God as a lifelong Brahmachârini. Besides, he asks, "Is love between husband and wife really impossible without the procreation of children?" "We must learn to believe in Hindu honesty" — in the matter that, without having any physical relationship, a Brahmachari husband can live a life of crystal purity, thus making his Brahmacharini wife a partner in the immortal bliss of the highest spiritual realisation, Brahmânanda — "however incredulous we might justly be on such matters in our own country". May blessings shower on the Professor for such worthy remarks! Even he, born of a foreign nationality and living in a foreign land, can understand the meaning of our Brahmacharya as the only way to the attainment of spirituality, and belies that it is not even in these days rare in India, whilst the hypocritical heroes of our own household are unable to see anything else than carnal relationship in the matrimonial union! "As a man thinketh in his mind, so he seeth outside."

Again another charge put forward is that "he did not show sufficient moral abhorrence of prostitutes". To this the Professor's rejoinder is very very sweet indeed: he says that in this charge Ramakrishna "does not stand quite alone among the founders of religion! " Ah! How sweet are these words — they remind one of the prostitute Ambâpâli, the object of Lord Buddha's divine grace, and of the Samaritan woman who won the grace of the Lord Jesus Christ.

Yet again, another charge is that he did not hate those who were intemperate in their habits. Heaven save the mark! One must not tread even on the shadow of a man, because he took a sip or two of drink — is not that the meaning? A formidable accusation indeed! Why did not the Mahâpurusha kick away and drive off in disgust the drunkards, the prostitutes, the thieves, and all the sinners of the world! And why did he not, with eyes closed, talk in a set drawl after the never-to-be-varied tone of the Indian flute-player, or talk in conventional language concealing his thoughts! And above all, the crowning charge is why did he not "live maritalement" all his life!

Unless life can be framed after the ideal of such strange purity and good manners as set forth by the accusers, India is doomed to go to ruin. Let her, if she has to rise by the help of such ethical rules!

The greater portion of the book has been devoted to the collection of the sayings, rather than to the life itself. That those sayings have attracted the attention of many of the English-speaking readers throughout the world can be easily inferred from the rapid sale of the book. The sayings, falling direct from his holy lips, are impregnate with the strongest spiritual force and power, and therefore they will surely exert their divine influence in every part of the world. "For the good of the many, for the happiness of the many" great-souled men take their birth; their lives and works are past the ordinary human run, and the method of their preaching is equally marvellous.

And what are we doing? The son of a poor Brahmin, who has sanctified us by his birth, raised us by his work, and has turned the sympathy of the conquering race towards us by his immortal sayings — what are we doing for him? Truth is not always palatable, still there are times when it has to be told: some of us do understand that his life and teachings are to our gain, but there the matter ends. It is beyond our power even to make an attempt to put those precepts into practice in our own lives, far less to consign our whole body and soul to the huge waves of harmony of Jnâna and Bhakti that Shri Ramakrishna has raised. This play of the Lord, those who have understood or are trying to understand, to them we say, "What will mere understanding do? The proof of understanding is in work. Will others believe you if it ends only in verbal expressions of assurance or is put forward as a matter of personal faith? Work argues what one feels; work out what you feel and let the world see." All ideas and feelings coming out of the fullness of the heart are known by their fruits — practical works.

Those who, knowing themselves very learned, think lightly of this unlettered, poor, ordinary temple-priest, to them our submission is: "The country of which one illiterate temple-priest, by virtue of his own strength, has in so short a time caused the victory of the ancient Sanâtana Dharma of your forefathers to resound even in lands far beyond the seas — of that country, you are the heroes of heroes, the honoured of all, mighty, well-bred, the learned of the learned — how much therefore must you be able to perform far more uncommon, heroic deeds for the welfare of your own land and nation, if you but will its Arise, therefore, come forward, display the play of your superior power within, manifest it, and we are standing with offerings of deepest veneration in hand ready to worship you. We are ignorant, poor, unknown, and insignificant beggars with only the beggar's garb as a means of livelihood; whereas you are supreme in riches and influence, of mighty power, born of noble descent, centres of all knowledge and learning! Why not rouse yourselves? Why not take the lead? Show the way, show us that example of perfect renunciation for the good of the world, and we will follow you like bond-slaves!"

On the other hand, those who are showing unjustified signs of causeless, rancorous hostilities out of absolute malice and envy — natural to a slavish race — at the success and the celebrity of Shri Ramakrishna and his name — to them we say, "Dear friends, vain are these efforts of yours! If this infinite, unbounded, religious wave that has engulfed in its depths the very ends of space — on whose snow-white crest shineth this divine form in the august glow of a heavenly presence—if this be the effect brought about by our eager endeavours in pursuit of personal name, fame, or wealth, then, without your or any others' efforts, this wave shall in obedience to the insuperable law of the universe, soon die in the infinite womb of time, never to rise again! But if, again, this tide, in accordance with the will and under the divine inspiration of the One Universal Mother, has begun to deluge the world with the flood of the unselfish love of a great man's heart, then, O feeble man, what power cost thou possess that thou shouldst thwart the onward progress of the Almighty Mother's will?"

THE PARIS CONGRESS OF THE HISTORY OF RELIGIONS[1]

In the Paris Exhibition, the Congress of the History of Religions recently sat for several days together. At the Congress, there was no room allowed for the discussions on the doctrines and spiritual views of any religion; its purpose was only to inquire into the historic evolution of the different forms of established faiths, and along with it other accompanying facts that are incidental to it. Accordingly, the representation of the various missionary sects of different religions and their beliefs was entirely left out of account in this Congress. The Chicago Parliament of Religions was a grand affair, and the representatives of many religious sects from all parts of the world were present at it. This Congress, on the other hand, was attended only by such scholars as devote themselves to the study of the origin and the history of different religions. At the Chicago Parliament the influence of the Roman Catholics was great, and they organised it with great hopes for their sect. The Roman Catholics expected to establish their superiority over the Protestants without much opposition; by proclaiming their glory and strength and laying the bright side of their faith before the assembled Christians, Hindus, Buddhists, Mussulmans, and other representatives of the world-religions and publicly exposing their weakness, they hoped to make firm their own position. But the result proving otherwise, the Christian world has been deplorably hopeless of the reconciliation of the different religious systems; so the Roman Catholics are now particularly opposed to the repetition of any such gathering. France is a Roman Catholic country; hence in spite of the earnest wish of the authorities, no religious congress was convened on account of the vehement opposition on the part of the Roman Catholic world.

The Congress of the History of Religions at Paris was like the Congress of Orientalists which is convened from time to time and at which European scholars, versed in Sanskrit, Pali, Arabic, and other Oriental languages, meet; only the antiquarianism of Christianity was added to this Paris Congress.

From Asia only three Japanese Pandits were present at the Congress. From India there was the Swami Vivekananda.

The conviction of many of the Sanskrit scholars of the West

is that the Vedic religion is the outcome of the worship of the fire, the sun, and other awe-inspiring objects of natural phenomena.

Swami Vivekananda was invited by the Paris Congress to contradict this conviction, and he promised to read a paper on the subject. But he could not keep his promise on account of ill health, and with difficulty was only able to be personally present at the Congress, where he was most warmly received by all the Western Sanskrit scholars, whose admiration for the Swami was all the greater as they had already gone through many of his lectures on the Vedanta.

At the Congress, Mr. Gustav Oppert, a German Pandit, read a paper on the origin of the Shâlagrâma-Shilâ. He traced the origin of the Shalagrama worship to that of the emblem of the female generative principle. According to him, the Shiva-Linga is the phallic emblem of the male and the Shalagrama of the female generative principle. And thus he wanted to establish that the worship of the Shiva-Linga and that of the Shalagrama—both are but the component parts of the worship of Linga and Yoni! The Swami repudiated the above two views and said that though he had heard of such ridiculous explanations about the Shiva-Linga, the other theory of the Shalagrama-Shila was quite new and strange, and seemed groundless to him.

The Swami said that the worship of the Shiva-Linga originated from the famous hymn in the Atharva-Veda Samhitâ sung in praise of the Yupa-Stambha, the sacrificial post. In that hymn a description is found of the beginningless and endless Stambha or Skambha, and it is shown that the said Skambha is put in place of the eternal Brahman. As afterwards the Yajna (sacrificial) fire, its smoke, ashes, and flames, the Soma plant, and the ox that used to carry on its back the wood for the Vedic sacrifice gave place to the conceptions of the brightness of Shiva's body, his tawny matted-hair, his blue throat, and the riding on the bull of the Shiva, and so on—just so, the Yupa-Skambha gave place in time to the Shiva-Linga, and was deified to the high Devahood of Shri Shankara. In the Atharva-Veda Samhita, the sacrificial cakes are also extolled along with the attributes of the Brahman.

In the Linga Purâna, the same hymn is expanded in the shape of stories, meant to establish the glory of the great Stambha and the superiority of Mahâdeva.

Again, there is another fact to be considered. The Buddhists used to erect memorial topes consecrated to the memory of Buddha; and the very poor, who were unable to build big monuments, used to express their devotion to him by dedicating miniature substitutes for them. Similar instances are still seen in the case of Hindu temples in Varanasi and other sacred places of India where those, who cannot afford to build temples, dedicate very small temple-like constructions instead. So it might be quite probable that during the period of Buddhistic ascendancy, the rich Hindus, in imitation of the Buddhists, used to erect something as a memorial resembling

---

1. Translated from a Paris letter written to the *Udbodhana*.

their Skambha, and the poor in a similar manner copied them on a reduced scale, and afterwards the miniature memorials of the poor Hindus became a new addition to the Skambha.

One of the names of the Buddhist Stupas (memorial topes) is Dhâtu-garbha, that is, "metal-wombed". Within the Dhâtu-garbha, in small cases made of stone, shaped like the present Shalagrama, used to be preserved the ashes, bones, and other remains of the distinguished Buddhist Bhikshus, along with gold, silver, and other metals. The Shalagrama-Shilas are natural stones resembling in form these artificially-cut stone-cases of the Buddhist Dhatu-garbha, and thus being first worshipped by the Buddhists, gradually got into Vaishnavism, like many other forms of Buddhistic worship that found their way into Hinduism. On the banks of the Narmadâ and in Nepal, the Buddhistic influence lasted longer than in other parts of India; and the remarkable coincidence that the Narmadeshvara Shiva-Linga, found on the banks of the Narmadâ and hence so called, and the Shalagrama-Shilas of Nepal are given preference to by the Hindus to those found elsewhere in India is a fact that ought to be considered with respect to this point of contention.

The explanation of the Shalagrama-Shila as a phallic emblem was an imaginary invention and, from the very beginning, beside the mark. The explanation of the Shiva-Linga as a phallic emblem was brought forward by the most thoughtless, and was forthcoming in India in her most degraded times, those of the downfall of Buddhism. The filthiest Tântrika literature of Buddhism of those times is yet largely found and practiced in Nepal and Tibet.

The Swami gave another lecture in which he dwelt on the historic evolution of the religious ideas in India, and said that the Vedas are the common source of Hinduism in all its varied stages, as also of Buddhism and every other religious belief in India. The seeds of the multifarious growth of Indian thought on religion lie buried in the Vedas. Buddhism and the rest of India's religious thought are the outcome of the unfolding and expansion of those seeds, and modern Hinduism also is only their developed and matured form. With the expansion or the contraction of society, those seeds lie more or less expanded at one place or more or less contracted at another.

He said a few words about the priority of Shri Krishna to Buddha. He also told the Western scholars that as the histories of the royal dynasties described in the Vishnu Purâna were by degrees being admitted as proofs throwing light on the ways of research of the antiquarian, so, he said, the traditions of India were all true, and desired that Western Sanskrit scholars, instead of writing fanciful articles, should try to discover their hidden truths.

Professor Max Müller says in one of his books that, whatever similarities there may be, unless it be demonstrated that some one Greek knew Sanskrit, it cannot be concluded that ancient India helped ancient Greece in any way. But it is curious to observe that some Western savants, finding several terms of Indian astronomy similar to those of Greek astronomy, and coming to know that the Greeks founded a small kingdom on the borders of India, can clearly read the help of Greece on everything Indian, on Indian literature, Indian astronomy, Indian arithmetic. Not only so; one has been bold enough to go so far as to declare that all Indian sciences as a rule are but echoes of the Greek!

On a single Sanskrit Shloka —

म्लेच्छा वे यवनाः तेषु एषा विद्या प्रतिष्ठिता। ऋषिवत् तेऽपि पूज्यन्ते...

— "The Yavanas are Mlechchhas, in them this science is established, (therefore) even they deserve worship like Rishis, ..."—how much the Westerners have indulged their unrestrained imagination! But it remains to be shown how the above Shloka goes to prove that the Aryas were taught by the Mlechchhas. The meaning may be that the learning of the Mlechchha disciples of the Aryan teachers is praised here, only to encourage the Mlechchhas in their pursuit of the Aryan science.

Secondly, when the germ of every Aryan science is found in the Vedas and every step of any of those sciences can be traced with exactness from the Vedic to the present day, what is the necessity for forcing the far-fetched suggestion of the Greek influence on them? "What is the use of going to the hills in search of honey if it is available at home?" as a Sanskrit proverb says.

Again, every Greek-like word of Aryan astronomy can be easily derived from Sanskrit roots. The Swami could not understand what right the Western scholars had to trace those words to a Greek source, thus ignoring their direct etymology.

In the same manner, if on finding mention of the word Yavanikâ (curtain) in the dramas of Kâlidâsa and other Indian poets, the Yâvanika (Ionian or Greek) influence on the whole of the dramatic literature of the time is ascertained, then one should first stop to compare whether the Aryan dramas are at all like the Greek. Those who have studied the mode of action and style of the dramas of both the languages must have to admit that any such likeness, if found, is only a fancy of the obstinate dreamer, and has never any real existence as a matter of fact. Where is that Greek chorus? The Greek Yavanika is on one side of the stage, the Aryan diametrically on the other. The characteristic manner of expression of the Greek drama is one thing, that of the Aryan quite another. There is not the least likeness between the Aryan and the Greek dramas: rather the dramas of Shakespeare resemble to a great extent the dramas of India. So the conclusion may also be drawn that Shakespeare is indebted to Kalidasa and other ancient Indian dramatists for all his writings, and that the whole Western literature is only an imitation of the Indian.

Lastly, turning Professor Max Müller's own premises against him, it may be said as well that until it is demonstrated that some one Hindu knew Greek some time one ought not to talk even of Greek influence.

Likewise, to see Greek influence in Indian sculpture is also entirely unfounded.

The Swami also said that the worship of Shri Krishna is much older than that of Buddha, and if the Gitâ be not of the same date as the Mahâbhârata, it is surely much earlier and by no means later. The style of language of the Gita is the same as that of the Mahabharata. Most of the adjectives used in the Gita to explain matters spiritual are used in the Vana and other Parvans of the Mahabharata, respecting matters temporal. Such coincidence is impossible without the most general and free use of those words at one and the same time. Again, the line of thought in the Gita is the same as in the Mahabharata; and when the Gita notices the doctrines of all the religious sects of the time, why does it not ever mention the name of Buddhism?

In spite of the most cautious efforts of the writers subsequent to Buddha, reference to Buddhism is not withheld and appears somewhere or other, in some shape or other, in histories, stories, essays, and every book of the post-Buddhistic literature. In covert or overt ways, some allusion is sure to be met with in reference to Buddha and Buddhism. Can anyone show any such reference in the Gita? Again, the Gita is an attempt at the reconciliation of all religious creeds, none of which is slighted in it. Why, it remains to be answered, is Buddhism alone denied the tender touch of the Gita-writer?

The Gita wilfully scorns none. Fear?—Of that there is a conspicuous absence in it. The Lord Himself, being the interpreter and the establisher of the Vedas, never hesitates to even censure Vedic rash presumptuousness if required. Why then should He fear Buddhism?

As Western scholars devote their whole life to one Greek work, let them likewise devote their whole life to one Sanskrit work, and much light will flow to the world thereby. The Mahabharata especially is the most invaluable work in Indian history; and it is not too much to say that this book has not as yet been even properly read by the Westerners.

After the lecture, many present expressed their opinions for or against the subject, and declared that they agreed with most of what the Swami had said, and assured the Swami that the old days of Sanskrit Antiquarianism were past and gone. The views of modern Sanskrit scholars were largely the same as those of the Swami's, they said. They believed also that there was much true history in the Puranas and the traditions of India

Lastly, the learned President, admitting all other points of the Swami's lecture, disagreed on one point only, namely, on the contemporaneousness of the Gita with the Mahabharata. But the only reason he adduced was that the Western scholars were mostly of the opinion that the Gita was not a part of the Mahabharata.

The substance of the lecture will be printed in French in the General Report of the Congress.

KNOWLEDGE: ITS SOURCE AND ACQUIREMENT[1]

Various have been the theories propounded as regards the primitive source of knowledge. We read in the Upanishads that Brahmâ, who was the first and the foremost among the Devas, held the key to all knowledge, which he revealed to his disciples and which, being handed down in succession, has been bequeathed as a legacy to the subsequent age. According to the Jains, during an indefinite period of cycle of Time, which comprises between one thousand and two thousand billions of "oceans" of years, are born some extraordinary, great, perfected beings whom they call Jinas, and through them the door to knowledge is now and shell opened to human society. Likewise Buddhism believes in, and expects at regular intervals, the appearance of the Buddhas, that is, persons possessed of infinite universal wisdom. The same is the reason also of the introduction of Incarnations of God by the Paurânika Hindus, who ascribe to them, along with other missions, the special function of restoring the lost spiritual knowledge by its proper adjustment to the needs of the time. Outside India, we find the great-souled Zoroaster bringing down the light of knowledge from above to the mortal world. So also did Moses, Jesus, and Mohammed, who, possessed of heavenly authority, proclaim to fallen humanity the tidings of divine wisdom in their own unique ways.

Brahma is the name of a high position among the Devas, to which every man can aspire by virtue of meritorious deeds. Only a selected few can become Jinas, while others can never attain to Jinahood; but they can only go so far as to gain the state of Mukti. The state of being a Buddha is open to one and all without distinction. Zoroaster, Moses, Jesus, and Mohammed are great personalities who incarnated themselves for the fulfilment of some special mission; so also did the Incarnations of God mentioned by the Pauranika sages. For others to look up to that seat of these divine personages with a longing eye is madness.

Adam got his knowledge through the tasting of the forbidden fruit. Noah was taught social science by the grace of Jehovah. In India, the theory is that every science has its presiding deity; their founders are either Devas or perfected beings; from the most menial arts as that of a cobbler to the most dignified office of the spiritual guide, everything depends on the kind intervention of the gods or supreme beings. "No knowledge is possible without a teacher." There is no way to the attainment of knowledge unless it is transmitted through an apostolic succession from disciple to disciple, unless it comes through the mercy of the Guru and direct from his mouth.

Then again, the Vedantic and other philosophers of the Indian schools hold that knowledge is not to be acquired from without. It is the innate nature of the human soul and the essential birthright of every man. The human soul is the repos-

1. Translated from a Bengali contribution by Swami Vivekananda to the *Udbodhana*, 12th February, 1899.

itory of infinite wisdom; what external agency can illuminate it? According to some schools, this infinite wisdom remains always the same and is never lost; and man is not ordinarily; conscious of this, because a veil, so to speak, has fallen over it on account of his evil deeds, but as soon as the veil is removed it reveals itself. Others say that this infinite wisdom, though potentially present in a human soul, has become contracted through evil deeds and it becomes expanded again by the mercy of God gained by good deeds. We also read in our scriptures various other methods of unfolding this inborn infinite power and knowledge, such as devotion to God, performance of work without attachment, practicing the eightfold accessories of the Yoga system, or constant dwelling on this knowledge, and so on. The final conclusion, however, is this, that through the practice of one or more or all of these methods together man gradually becomes conscious of his inborn real nature, and the infinite power and wisdom within, latent or veiled, becomes at last fully manifest.

On the other side, the modern philosophers have analysed the human mind as the source of infinitely possible manifestations and have come to the conclusion that when the individual mind on the one hand, and favourable time, place, and causation on the other can act and react upon one another, then highly developed consciousness of knowledge is sure to follow. Nay, even the unfavourableness of time and place can be successfully surmounted by the vigour and firmness of the individual. The strong individual, even if he is thrown amidst the worst conditions of place or time, overcomes them and affirms his own strength. Not only so, all the heavy burdens heaped upon the individual, the acting agent, are being made lighter and lighter in the course of time, so that any individual, however weak he may be in the beginning, is sure to reach the goal at the end if he assiduously applies himself to gain it. Look at the uncivilised and ignorant barbarians of the other day! How through close and studious application they are making long strides into the domains of civilisation, how even those of the lower strata are making their way and are occupying with an irresistible force the most exalted positions in it! The sons of cannibal parents are turning out elegant and educated citizens; the descendants of the uncivilised Santals, thanks to the English Government, have been nowadays meeting in successful competition our Bengali students in the Indian Universities. As such, the partiality of the scientific investigators of the present day to the doctrine of hereditary transmission of qualities is being gradually diminished.

There is a certain class of men whose conviction is that from time eternal there is a treasure of knowledge which contains the wisdom of everything past, present, and future. These men hold that it was their own forefathers who had the sole privilege of having the custody of this treasure. The ancient sages, the first possessors of it, bequeathed in succession this treasure and its true import to their descendants only. They are, therefore, the only inheritors to it; as such, let the rest of the world worship them.

May we ask these men what they think should be the condition of the other peoples who have not got such forefathers? "Their condition is doomed", is the general answer. The more kind-hearted among them is perchance pleased to rejoin, "Well, let them come and serve us. As a reward for such service, they will be born in our caste in the next birth. That is the only hope we can hold out to them." "Well, the moderns are making many new and original discoveries in the field of science and arts, which neither you dreamt of, nor is there any proof that your forefathers ever had knowledge of. What do you say to that?" "Why certainly our forefathers knew all these things, the knowledge of which is now unfortunately lost to us. Do you want a proof? I can show you one. Look! Here is the Sanskrit verse ... " Needless to add that the modern party, who believes in direct evidence only, never attaches any seriousness to such replies and proofs.

Generally, all knowledge is divided into two classes, the Aparâ, secular, and the Parâ, spiritual. One pertains to perishable things, and the other to the realm of the spirit. There is, no doubt, a great difference these two classes of knowledge, and the way to the attainment of the one may be entirely different from the way to the attainment of the other. Nor can it be denied that no one method can be pointed out as the sole and universal one which will serve as the key to all and every door in the domain of knowledge. But in reality all this difference is only one of degree and not of kind. It is not that secular and spiritual knowledge are two opposite and contradictory things; but they are the same thing—the same infinite knowledge which is everywhere fully present from the lowest atom to the highest Brahman—they are the same knowledge in its different stages of gradual development. This one infinite knowledge we call secular when it is in its lower process of manifestation, and spiritual when it reaches the corresponding higher phase.

"All knowledge is possessed exclusively by some extraordinary great men, and those special personages take birth by the command of God, or in conformity to a higher law of nature, or in some preordained order of Karma; except through the agency of these great ones, there is no other way of attaining knowledge." If such a view be correct and certain, there seems to be no necessity for any individual to strive hard to find any new and original truth—all originality is lost to society for want of exercise and encouragement; and the worst of all is that, society tries to oppose and stop any attempt in the original direction, and thus the faculty of the initiative dies out. If it is finally settled that the path of human welfare is for ever chalked out by these omniscient men, society naturally fears its own destruction if the least deviation be made from the boundary line of the path, and so it tries to compel all men through rigid laws and threats of punishment to follow that path with unconditional obedience. If society succeeds in imposing such obedience to itself by confining all men within the narrow groove of these paths, then the destiny of mankind becomes no better than that of a machine. If every act in a man's life has been all previously determined, then what need is there for the culture of the faculty of thought—where is the field for the free play of independent thought and action? In course of time, for want of proper use, all activity is given up, all originality is lost, a sort of Tâmasika dreamy lifelessness hovers over the whole nation, and headlong it goes down and down. The death of such a nation is not far to seek.

On the other hand, if the other extreme were true that that society prospers the most which is not guided by the injunctions of such divinely-inspired souls, then civilisation, wisdom, and prosperity—deserting the Chinese, Hindus, Egyptians, Babylonians, Iranians, Greeks, Romans, and other great nations of ancient and modern times, who have always followed the path laid down by their sages—would have embraced the Zulus, the Kafirs, the Hottentots, and the aboriginal tribes of the Andamans and the Australian islands who have led a life of guideless independence.

Considering all these points, it must be admitted that though the presence of knowledge everywhere in every individual is an eternal truism, yet the path pointed out by the great ones of the earth has the glory peculiar to it, and that there is a peculiar interest attached to the transmission of knowledge through the succession of teachers and their disciples. Each of them has its place in the development of the sum total of knowledge; and we must learn to estimate them according to their respective merits. But, perhaps, being carried away by their over-zealous and blind devotion to their Masters, the successors and followers of these great ones sacrifice truth before the altar of devotion and worship to them, and misrepresent the true meaning of the purpose of those great lives by insisting on personal worship, that is, they kill the principle for the person.

This is also a fact of common experience that when man himself has lost all his own strength, he naturally likes to pass his days in idle remembrance of his forefathers' greatness. The devoted heart gradually becomes the weakest in its constant attempt to resign itself in every respect to the feet of its ancestors, and at last a time comes when this weakness teaches the disabled yet proud heart to make the vainglory of its ancestors' greatness as the only support of its life. Even if it be true that your ancestors possessed all knowledge, which has in the efflux of time been lost to you, it follows that you, their descendants, must have been instrumental in this disappearance of knowledge, and now it is all the same to you whether you have it or not. To talk of having or losing this already lost knowledge serves no useful purpose at present. You will have to make new efforts, to undergo troubles over again, if you want to recover it.

True, that spiritual illumination shines of itself in a pure heart, and, as such, it is not something acquired from without; but to attain this purity of heart means long struggle and constant practice. It has also been found, on careful inquiry in the sphere of material knowledge, that those higher truths which have now and then been discovered by great scientific men have flashed like sudden floods of light in their mental atmosphere, which they had only to catch and formulate. But such truths never appear in the mind of an uncultured and wild savage. All these go to prove that hard Tapasyâ, or practice of austerities in the shape of devout contemplation and constant study of a subject is at the root of all illumination in its respective spheres.

What we call extraordinary, superconscious inspiration is only the result of a higher development of ordinary consciousness, gained by long and continued effort. The difference between the ordinary and the extraordinary is merely one of degree in manifestation. Conscious efforts lead the way to superconscious illumination.

Infinite perfection is in every man, though unmanifested. Every man has in him the potentiality of attaining to perfect saintliness, Rishihood, or to the most exalted position of an Avatâra, or to the greatness of a hero in material discoveries. It is only a question of time and adequate well-guided investigation, etc., to have this perfection manifested. In a society where once such great men were born, there the possibility of their reappearance is greater. There can be no doubt that a society with the help of such wise guides advances faster than the one without it. But it is equally certain that such guides will rise up in the societies that are now without them and will lead them to equally rapid progress in the future.

MODERN INDIA

Translated from a Bengali contribution to the Udbodhana, March 1899

The Vedic priests base their superior strength on the knowledge of the sacrificial Mantras[1]. By the power of these Mantras, the Devas are made to come down from their heavenly abodes, accept the drink and food offerings, and grant the prayers of the Yajamânas[2]. The kings as well as their subjects are, therefore, looking up to these priests for their welfare during their earthly life. Raja Soma[3] is worshipped by the priest and is made to thrive by the power of his Mantras. As such, the Devas, whose favourite food is the juice of the Soma plant offered in oblation by the priest, are always kind to him and bestow his desired boons. Thus strengthened by divine grace, he defies all human opposition; for what can the power of mortals do against that of the gods? Even the king, the centre of all earthly power, is a supplicant at his door. A kind look from him is the greatest help; his mere blessing a tribute to the State, pre-eminent above everything else.

Now commanding the king to be engaged in affairs fraught

---

1. Vedic hymns uttered by the priests to invoke the Devas at the time of sacrifice.

2. The men who perform sacrifices.

3. The name of the Soma plant as commonly found in the Vedas. The priests offered to the Devas the juice of this plant at the time of sacrifice.

with death and ruin, now standing by him as his fastest friend with kind and wise counsels, now spreading the net of subtle, diplomatic statesmanship in which the king is easily caught—the priest is seen, oftentimes, to make the royal power totally subservient to him. Above all, the worst fear is in the knowledge that the name and fame of the royal forefathers and of himself and his family lie at the mercy of the priest's pen. He is the historian. The king might have paramount power; attaining a great glory in his reign, he might prove himself as the father and mother in one to his subjects; but if the priest is not appeased, his sun of glory goes down with his last breath for ever; all his worth and usefulness deserving of universal approbation are lost in the great womb of time, like unto the fall of gentle dew on the ocean. Others who inaugurated the huge sacrifices lasting over many years, the performers of the Ashvamedha and so on—those who showered, like incessant rain in the rainy season, countless wealth on the priests—their names, thanks to the grace of priests, are emblazoned in the pages of history. The name of Priyadarshi Dharmâshoka[4], the beloved of the gods, is nothing but a name in the priestly world, while Janamejaya[5], son of Parikshit, is a household word in every Hindu family.

To protect the State, to meet the expenses of the personal comforts and luxuries of himself and his long retinue, and, above all, to fill to overflowing the coffers of the all-powerful priesthood for its propitiation, the king is continually draining the resources of his subjects, even as the sun sucks up moisture from the earth. His especial prey—his milch cows—are the Vaishyas.

Neither under the Hindu kings, nor under the Buddhist rule, do we find the common subject-people taking any part in expressing their voice in the affairs of the State. True, Yudhishthira visits the houses of Vaishyas and even Shudras when he is in Vâranâvata; true, the subjects are praying for the installation of Râmachandra to the regency of Ayodhyâ; nay, they are even criticising the conduct of Sitâ and secretly making plans for the bringing about of her exile: but as a recognised rule of the State they have no direct voice in the supreme government. The power of the populace is struggling to express itself in indirect and disorderly ways without any method. The people have not as yet the conscious knowledge of the existence of this power. There is neither the attempt on their part to organise it into a united action, nor have they got the will to do so; there is also a complete absence of that capacity, that skill, by means of which small and incoherent centres of force are united together, creating insuperable strength as their resultant.

Is this due to want of proper laws?—no, that is not it. There are laws, there are methods, separately and distinctly assigned for the guidance of different departments of government,

there are laws laid down in the minutest detail for everything, such as the collection of revenue, the management of the army, the administration of justice, punishments and rewards. But at the root of all, is the injunction of the Rishi—the word of divine authority, the revelation of God coming through the inspired Rishi. The laws have, it can almost be said, no elasticity in them. Under the circumstances, it is never possible for the people to acquire any sort of education by which they can learn to combine among themselves and be united for the accomplishment of any object for the common good of the people, or by which they can have the concerted intellect to conceive the idea of popular right in the treasures collected by the king from his subjects, or even such education by which they can be fired with the aspiration to gain the right of representation in the control of State revenues and expenditure. Why should they do such things? Is not the inspiration of the Rishi responsible for their prosperity and progress?

Again, all those laws are in books. Between laws as codified in books and their operation in practical life, there is a world of difference. One Ramachandra is born after thousands of Agnivarnas[6] pass away! Many kings show us the life of Chandâshoka[7]; Dharmâshokas are rare! The number of kings like Akbar, in whom the subjects find their life, is far less than that of kings like Aurangzeb who live on the blood of their people!

Even if the kings be of as godlike nature as that of Yudhishthira, Ramachandra, Dharmashoka, or Akbar under whose benign rule the people enjoyed safety and prosperity, and were looked after with paternal care by their rulers, the hand of him who is always fed by another gradually loses the power of taking the food to his mouth. His power of self-preservation can never become fully manifest who is always protected in every respect by another. Even the strongest youth remains but a child if he is always looked after as a child by his parents. Being always governed by kings of godlike nature, to whom is left the whole duty of protecting and providing for the people, they can never get any occasion for understanding the principles of self-government. Such a nation, being entirely dependent on the king for everything and never caring to exert itself for the common good or for self-defence, becomes gradually destitute of inherent energy and strength. If this state of dependence and protection continues long, it becomes the cause of the destruction of the nation, and its ruin is not far to seek.

Of course, it can be reasonably concluded that, when the government a country, is guided by codes of laws enjoined by Shâstras which are the outcome of knowledge inspired by the

4. The name given to the great king, Asoka, after he embraced Buddhism.

5. The performer of the great snake-sacrifice of Mahâbhârata.

6. Agnivarna was a prince of the Solar race, who never used to come out of the seraglio, and died of consumption due to excessive indulgence.

7. The great king Asoka was at first called Chandashoka, i.e. Fierce Asoka, because of his ascending the throne by killing his brother and his other cruel deeds. After nine years of reign he became a convert to Buddhism and his character underwent a complete transformation; he was thenceforth known for his good deeds by the name of Dharmashoka, Virtuous Asoka.

divine genius of great sages, such a government must lead to the unbroken welfare of the rich and the poor, the wise and the ignorant, the king and the subjects alike. But we have seen already how far the operation of those laws was, or may be, possible in practical life. The voice of the ruled in the government of their land—which is the watchword of the modern Western world, and of which the last expression has been echoed with a thundering voice in the Declaration of the American Government, in the words, "That the government of the people of this country must be by the people and for the good of the people"—cannot however be said to have been totally unrecognised in ancient India. The Greek travellers and others saw many independent small States scattered all over this country, and references are also found to this effect in many places of the Buddhistic literature. And there cannot be the least doubt about it that the germ of self-government was at least present in the shape of the village Panchâyat[1], which is still to be found in existence in many places of India. But the germ remained for ever the germ; the seed though put in the ground never grew into a tree. This idea of self-government never passed beyond the embryo state of the village Panchayat system and never spread into society at large.

In the religious communities, among Sannyasins in the Buddhist monasteries, we have ample evidence to show that self-government was fully developed. Even now, one wonders to see how the power of the Panchayat system of the principles of self-government, is working amongst the Nâgâ Sannyasins—what deep respect the "Government by the Five" commands from them, what effective individual rights each Naga can exercise within his own sect, what excellent working of the power of organisation and concerted action they have among themselves!

With the deluge which swept the land at the advent of Buddhism, the priestly power fell into decay and the royal power was in the ascendant. Buddhist priests are renouncers of the world, living in monasteries as homeless ascetics, unconcerned with secular affairs. They have neither the will nor the endeavour to bring and keep the royal power under their control through the threat of curses or magic arrows. Even if there were any remnant of such a will, its fulfilment has now become an impossibility. For Buddhism has shaken the thrones of all the oblation-eating gods and brought them down from their heavenly positions. The state of being a Buddha is superior to the heavenly positions of many a Brahmâ or an Indra, who vie with each other in offering their worship at the feet of the Buddha, the God-man! And to this Buddhahood, every man has the privilege to attain; it is open to all even in this life. From the descent of the gods, as a natural consequence, the superiority of the priests who were supported by them is gone.

Accordingly, the reins of that mighty sacrificial horse—the royal power—are no longer held in the firm grasp of the Ve-

1. Literally, "government by five", in which the village-men sit together and decide among themselves, all disputes.

dic priest; and being now free, it can roam anywhere by its unbridled will. The centre of power in this period is neither with the priests chanting the Sâma hymns and performing the Yajnas according to the Yajur-Veda; nor is the power vested in the hands of Kshatriya kings separated from each other and ruling over small independent States. But the centre of power in this age is in emperors whose unobstructed sway extend over vast areas bounded by the ocean, covering the whole of India from one end to the other. The leaders of this age are no longer Vishvâmitra or Vasishtha, but emperors like Chandragupta, Dharmashoka, and others. There never were emperors who ascended the throne of India and led her to the pinnacle of her glory such as those lords of the earth who ruled over her in paramount sway during the Buddhistic period. The end of this period is characterised by the appearance of Râjput power on the scene and the rise of modern Hinduism. With the rise of Rajput power, on the decline of Buddhism, the sceptre of the Indian empire, dislodged from its paramount power, was again broken into a thousand pieces and wielded by small powerless hands. At this time, the Brâhminical (priestly) power again succeeded in raising its head, not as an adversary as before, but this time as an auxiliary to the royal supremacy.

During this revolution, that perpetual struggle for supremacy between the priestly and the royal classes, which began from the Vedic times and continued through ages till it reached its climax at the time of the Jain and Buddhist revolutions, has ceased for ever. Now these two mighty powers are friendly to each other; but neither is there any more that glorious Kshatra (warlike) velour of the kings, nor that spiritual brilliance which characterised the Brahmins; each has lost his former intrinsic strength. As might be expected, this new union of the two forces was soon engaged in the satisfaction of mutual self-interests, and became dissipated by spending its vitality on extirpating their common opponents, especially the Buddhists of the time, and on similar other deeds. Being steeped in all the vices consequent on such a union, e.g., the sucking of the blood of the masses, taking revenge on the enemy, spoliation of others' property, etc., they in vain tried to imitate the Râjasuya and other Vedic sacrifices of the ancient kings, and only made a ridiculous farce of them. The result was that they were bound hand and foot by a formidable train of sycophantic attendance and its obsequious flatteries, and being entangled in an interminable net of rites and ceremonies with flourishes of Mantras and the like, they soon became a cheap and ready prey to the Mohammeden invaders from the West.

That priestly power which began its strife for superiority with the royal power from the Vedic times and continued it down the ages, that hostility against the Kshatra power, Bhagavân Shri Krishna succeeded by his super-human genius in putting a stop to, at least for the tired being, during his earthly existence. That Brâhmanya power was almost effaced from its field of work in India during the Jain and Buddhist revolutions, or, perhaps, was holding its feeble stand by being subservient to the strong antagonistic religions. That Brahmanya power, since this appearance of Rajput power, which held sway over India under the Mihira dynasty and others, made its last effort to recover its lost greatness; and in its effort to establish that supremacy, it sold itself at the feet of the fierce hordes of barbarians newly come from Central Asia, and to win their pleasure introduced in the land their hateful manners and customs. Moreover, it, the Brahmanya; power, solely devoting itself to the easy means to dupe ignorant barbarians, brought into vogue mysterious rites and ceremonies backed by its new Mantras and the like; and in doing so, itself lost its former wisdom, its former vigour and vitality, and its own chaste habits of long acquirement. Thus it turned the whole Âryâvarta into a deep and vast whirlpool of the most vicious, the most horrible, the most abominable, barbarous customs; and as the inevitable consequence of countenancing these detestable customs and superstitions, it soon lost all its own internal strength and stamina and became the weakest of the weak. What wonder that it should be broken into a thousand pieces and fall at the mere touch of the storm of Mussulman invasions from the West! That great Brahmanya power fell—who knows, if ever to rise again?

The resuscitation of the priestly power under the Mussulman rule was, on the other hand, an utter impossibility. The Prophet Mohammed himself was dead against the priestly class in any shape and tried his best for the total destruction of this power by formulating rules and injunctions to that effect. Under the Mussulman rule, the king himself was the supreme priest; he was the chief guide in religious matters; and when he became the emperor, he cherished the hope of being the paramount leader in all matters over the whole Mussulman world. To the Mussulman, the Jews or the Christians are not objects of extreme detestation; they are, at the worst, men of little faith. But not so the Hindu. According to him, the Hindu is idolatrous, the hateful Kafir; hence in this life he deserves to be butchered; and in the next, eternal hell is in store for him. The utmost the Mussulman kings could do as a favour to the priestly class—the spiritual guides of these Kafirs—was to allow them somehow to pass their life silently and wait for the last moment. This was again sometimes considered too, much kindness! If the religious ardour of any king was a little more uncommon, there would immediately follow arrangements for a great Yajna by way of Kafir-slaughter!

On one side, the royal power is now centred in kings professing a different religion and given to different customs. On the other, the priestly power has been entirely displaced from its influential position as the controller and lawgiver of the society. The Koran and its code of laws have taken the place of the Dharma Shâstras of Manu and others. The Sanskrit language has made room for the Persian and the Arabic. The Sanskrit language has to remain confined only to the purely religious writings and religious matters of the conquered and detested Hindu and, as such, has since been living a precarious life at the hands of the neglected priest. The priest himself, the relic

of the Brahmanya power, fell back upon the last resource of conducting only the comparatively unimportant family ceremonies, such as the matrimonial etc., and that also only so long and as much as the mercy of the Mohammedan rulers permitted.

In the Vedic and the adjoining periods, the royal power could not manifest itself on account of the grinding pressure of the priestly power. We have seen how, during the Buddhistic revolution, resulting in the fall of the Brahminical supremacy, the royal power in India reached its culminating point. In the interval between the fall of the Buddhistic and the establishment of the Mohammedan empire, we have seen how the royal power was trying to raise its head through the Rajputs in India, and how it failed in its attempt. At the root of this failure, too, could be traced the same old endeavours of the Vedic priestly class to bring back and revive with a new life their original (ritualistic) days.

Crushing the Brahminical supremacy under his feet the Mussulman king was able to restore to a considerable extent the lost glories of such dynasties of emperors as the Maurya, the Gupta, the Andhra, and the Kshâtrapa[2].

Thus the priestly power—which sages like Kumârila, Shankara, and Râmânuja tried to re-establish, which for some time was supported by the sword of the Rajput power, and which tried to rebuild its structure on the fall of its Jain and Buddhist adversaries—was under Mohammedan rule laid to sleep for ever, knowing no awakening. In this period, the antagonism or warfare is not between kings and priests, but between kings and kings. At the end of this period, when Hindu power again raised its head, and, to some extent, was successful in regenerating Hinduism through the Mahrattas and the Sikhs, we do not find much play of the priestly power with these regenerations. On the contrary, when the Sikhs admitted any Brahmin into their sect, they, at first, compelled him publicly to give up his previous Brahminical signs and adopt the recognised signs of their own religion.

In this manner, after an age-long play of action and reaction between these two forces, the final victory of the royal power was echoed on the soil of India for several centuries, in the name of foreign monarchs professing an entirely different religion from the faith of the land. But at the end of this Mohammedan period, another entirely new power made its appearance on the arena and slowly began to assert its prowess in the affairs of the Indian world.

This power is so new, its nature and workings are so foreign to the Indian mind, its rise so inconceivable, and its vigour so insuperable that though it wields the suzerain power up till now, only a handful of Indians understand what this power is.

We are talking of the occupation of India by England.

From very ancient times, the fame of India's vast wealth and her rich granaries has enkindled in many powerful foreign nations the desire for conquering her. She has been, in

2. The Persian governors of Âryâvarta and Gujarat.

fact, again and again conquered by foreign nations. Then why should we say that the occupation of India by England was something new and foreign to the Indian mind?

From time immemorial Indians have seen the mightiest royal power tremble before the frown of the ascetic priest, devoid of worldly desire, armed with spiritual strength — the power of Mantras (sacred formulas) and religious lore — and the weapon of curses. They have also seen the subject people silently obey the commands of their heroic all-powerful suzerains, backed by their arms and armies, like a flock of sheep before a lion. But that a handful of Vaishyas (traders) who, despite their great wealth, have ever crouched awe stricken not only before the king but also before any member of the royal family, would unite, cross for purposes of business rivers and seas, would, solely by virtue of their intelligence and wealth, by degrees make puppets of the long-established Hindu and Mohammedan dynasties; not only so, but that they would buy as well the services of the ruling powers of their own country and use their valour and learning as powerful instruments for the influx of their own riches — this is a spectacle entirely novel to the Indians, as also the spectacle that the descendants of the mighty nobility of a country, of which a proud lord, sketched by the extraordinary pen of its great poet, says to a common man, "Out, dunghill! darest thou brave a nobleman?" would, in no distant future, consider it the zenith of human ambition to be sent to India as obedient servants of a body of merchants, called The East India Company — such a sight was, indeed, a novelty unseen by India before!

According to the prevalence, in greater or lesser degree, of the three qualities of Sattva, Rajas, and Tamas in man, the four castes, the Brahmin, Kashatriya, Vaishya, and Shudra, are everywhere present at all times, in all civilised societies. By the mighty hand of time, their number and power also vary at different times in regard to different countries. In some countries the numerical strength or influence of one of these castes may preponderate over another; at some period, one of the classes may be more powerful than the rest. But from a careful study of the history of the world, it appears that in conformity to the law of nature the four castes, the Brahmin, Kshatriya, Vaishya, and Shudra do, in every society, one after another in succession, govern the world.

Among the Chinese, the Sumerians, the Babylonians, the Egyptians, the Chaldeans, the Areas, the Iranians, the Jews, the Arabs — among all these ancient nations, the supreme power of guiding society is, in the first period of their history, in the hands of the Brahmin or the priest. In the second period, the ruling power is the Kshatriya, that is, either absolute monarchy or oligarchical government by a chosen body of men. Among the modern Western nations, with England at their head, this power of controlling society has been, for the first time, in the hands of the Vaishyas or mercantile communities, made rich through the carrying on of commerce.

Though Troy and Carthage of ancient times and Venice and similar other small commercial States of comparatively modern times became highly powerful, yet, amongst them, there was not the real rising of the Vaishya power in the proper sense of the term.

Correctly speaking, the descendants of the royal family had the sole monopoly of the commerce of those old days by employing the common people and their servants under them to carry on the trade; and they appropriated to themselves the profits accruing from it. Excepting these few men, no one was allowed to take any part or voice an opinion even in the government of the country and kindred affairs. In the oldest countries like Egypt, the priestly power enjoyed unmolested supremacy only for a short period, after which it became subjugated to the royal power and lived as an auxiliary to it. In China, the royal power, centralised by the genius of Confucius, has been controlling and guiding the priestly power, in accordance with its absolute will, for more than twenty-five centuries; and during the last two centuries, the all-absorbing Lamas of Tibet, though they are the spiritual guides of the royal family, have been compelled to pass their days, being subject in every way to the Chinese Emperor.

In India, the royal power succeeded in conquering the priestly power and declaring its untrammelled authority long after the other ancient civilised nations had done so; and therefore the inauguration of the Indian Empire came about long after the Chinese, Egyptian, Babylonian, and other Empires had risen. It was only with the Jewish people that the royal power, though it tried hard to establish its supremacy over the priestly, had to meet a complete defeat in the attempt. Not even the Vaishyas attained the ruling power with the Jews. On the other hand, the common subject people, trying to free themselves from the shackles of priestcraft, were crushed to death under the internal commotion of adverse religious movements like Christianity and the external pressure of the mighty Roman Empire.

As in the ancient days the priestly power, in spite of its long-continued struggle, was subdued by the more powerful royal power, so, in modern times, before the violent blow of the newly-risen Vaishya power, many a kingly crown has to kiss the ground, many a sceptre is for ever broken to pieces. Only those few thrones which are allowed still to exercise some power in some of the civilised countries and make a display of their royal pomp and grandeur are all maintained solely by the vast hordes of wealth of these Vaishya communities — the dealers in salt, oil, sugar, and wine — and kept up as a magnificent and an imposing front, and as a means of glorification to the really governing body behind, the Vaishyas.

That mighty newly-risen Vaishya power — at whose command, electricity carries messages in an instant from one pole to another, whose highway is the vast ocean, with its mountain-high waves, at whose instance, commodities are being carried with the greatest ease from one part of the globe to another, and at whose mandate, even the greatest monarchs tremble—on the white foamy crest of that huge wave the all-conquering Vaishya power, is installed the majestic throne of England in all its grandeur.

Therefore the conquest of India by England is not a conquest by Jesus or the Bible as we are often asked to believe. Neither is it like the conquest of India by the Moguls and the Pathans. But behind the name of the Lord Jesus, the Bible, the magnificent palaces, the heavy tramp of the feet of armies consisting of elephants, chariots, cavalry, and infantry, shaking the earth, the sounds of war trumpets, bugles, and drums, and the splendid display of the royal throne, behind all these, there is always the virtual presence of England—that England whose war flag is the factory chimney, whose troops are the merchantmen, whose battlefields are the market-places of the world, and whose Empress is the shining Goddess of Fortune herself! It is on this account I have said before that it is indeed an unseen novelty, this conquest of India by England. What new revolution will be effected in India by her clash with the new giant power, and as the result of that revolution what new transformation is in store for future India, cannot be inferred from her past history.

I have stated previously that the four castes, Brahmin, Kshatriya, Vaishya, and Shudra do, in succession, rule the world. During the period of supreme authority exercised by each of these castes, some acts are accomplished which conduce to the welfare of the people, while others are injurious to them.

The foundation of the priestly power rests on intellectual strength, and not on the physical strength of arms. Therefore, with the supremacy of the priestly power, there is a great prevalence of intellectual and literary culture. Every human heart is always anxious for communication with, and help from, the supersensuous spiritual world. The entrance to that world is not possible for the generality of mankind; only a few great souls who can acquire a perfect control over their sense-organs and who are possessed with a nature preponderating with the essence of Sattva Guna are able to pierce the formidable wall of matter and come face to face, as it were, with the supersensuous—it is only they who know the workings of the kingdom that bring the messages from it and show the way to others. These great souls are the priests, the primitive guides, leaders, and movers of human societies.

The priest knows the gods and communicates with them; he is therefore worshipped as a god. Leaving behind the thoughts of the world, he has no longer to devote himself to the earning of his bread by the sweat of his brow. The best and foremost parts of all food and drink are due as offerings to the gods; and of these gods, the visible proxies on earth are the priests. It is through their mouths that they partake of the offerings. Knowingly or unknowingly, society gives the priest abundant leisure, and he can therefore get the opportunity of being meditative and of thinking higher thoughts. Hence the development of wisdom and learning originates first with the supremacy of the priestly power. There stands the priest

between the dreadful lion—the king—on the one hand, and the terrified flock of sheep—the subject people—on the other. The destructive leap of the lion is checked by the controlling rod of spiritual power in the hands of the priest. The flame of the despotic will of the king, maddened in the pride of his wealth and men, is able to burn into ashes everything that comes in his way; but it is only a word from the priest, who has neither wealth nor men behind him but whose sole strength is his spiritual power, that can quench the despotic royal will, as water the fire.

With the ascendancy of the priestly supremacy are seen the first advent of civilisation, the first victory of the divine nature over the animal, the first mastery of spirit over matter, and the first manifestation of the divine power which is potentially present in this very slave of nature, this lump of flesh, to wit, the human body. The priest is the first discriminator of spirit from matter, the first to help to bring this world in communion with the next, the first messenger from the gods to man, and the intervening bridge that connects the king with his subjects. The first offshoot of universal welfare and good is nursed by his spiritual power, by his devotion to learning and wisdom, by his renunciation, the watchword of his life and, watered even by the flow of his own life-blood. It is therefore that in every land it was he to whom the first and foremost worship was offered. It is therefore that even his memory is sacred to us!

There are evils as well. With the growth of life is sown simultaneously the seed of death. Darkness and light always go together. Indeed, there are great evils which, if not checked in proper time, lead to the ruin of society. The play of power through gross matter is universally experienced; everyone sees, everyone understands, the mighty manifestation of gross material force as displayed in the play of battle-axes and swords, or in the burning properties of fire and lightning. Nobody doubts these things, nor can there ever be any question about their genuineness. But where the repository of power and the centre of its play are wholly mental, where the power is confined to certain special words, to certain special modes of uttering them, to the mental repetition of certain mysterious syllables, or to other similar processes and applications of the mind, there light is mixed with shade, there the ebb and flow naturally disturb the otherwise unshaken faith, and there even when things are actually seen or directly perceived, still sometimes doubts arise as to their real occurrence. Where distress, fear, anger, malice, spirit of retaliation, and the like passions of man, leaving the palpable force of arms, leaving the gross material methods to gain the end in view which every one can understand, substitute in their stead the mysterious mental processes like Stambhana, Uchchâtana, Vashikarana, and Mârana[1] for their fructification—there a cloud of smoky indistinctness, as it were, naturally envelops

1. Suppression of any bodily faculty, thereby causing a person's ruin, removing him from a position, subduing and getting mastery over him, and killing him by means of magical incantations.

the mental atmosphere of these men who often live and move in such hazy worlds of obscure mysticism. No straight line of action presents itself before such a mind; even if it does, the mind distorts it into crookedness. The final result of all this is insincerity—that very limited narrowness of the heart—and above all, the most fatal is the extreme intolerance born of malicious envy at the superior excellence of another.

The priest naturally says to himself: "Why should I part with the power that has made the Devas subservient to me, has given me mastery over physical and mental illnesses, and has gained for me the service of ghosts, demons, and other unseen spirits? I have dearly bought this power by the price of extreme renunciation. Why should I give to others that to get which I had to give up my wealth, name, fame, in short, all my earthly comforts and happiness?" Again, that power is entirely mental. And how many opportunities are there of keeping it a perfect secret! Entangled in this wheel of circumstances, human nature becomes what it inevitably would: being used to practice constant self-concealment, it becomes a victim of extreme selfishness and hypocrisy, and at last succumbs to the poisonous consequences which they bring in their train. In time, the reaction of this very desire to concealment rebounds upon oneself. All knowledge, all wisdom is almost lost for want of proper exercise and diffusion, and what little remains is thought to have been obtained from some supernatural source; and, therefore, far from making fresh efforts to go in for originality and gain knowledge of new sciences, it is considered useless and futile to attempt even to improve the remnants of the old by cleansing them of their corruptions. Thus lost to former wisdom, the former indomitable spirit of self-reliance, the priest, now glorifying himself merely in the name of his forefathers, vainly struggles to preserve untarnished for himself the same glory, the same privilege, the same veneration, and the same supremacy as was enjoyed by his great forefathers. Consequently, his violent collision with the other castes.

According to the law of nature, wherever there is an awakening of a new and stronger life, there it tries to conquer and take the place of the old and the decaying. Nature favours the dying out of the unfit and the survival of the fittest. The final result of such conflict between the priestly and the other classes has been mentioned already.

That renunciation, self-control, and asceticism of the priest which during the period of his ascendancy were devoted to the pursuance of earnest researches of truth are on the eve of his decline employed anew and spent solely in the accumulation of objects of self-gratification and in the extension of privileged superiority over others. That power, the centralization of which in himself gave him all honour and worship, has now been dragged down from its high heavenly position to the lowest abyss of hell. Having lost sight of the goal, drifting aimless, the priestly power is entangled, like the spider, in the web spun by itself. The chain that has been forged from generation to generation with the greatest care to be put on others' feet is now tightened round its own in a thousand coils, and is thwarting its own movement in hundreds of ways. Caught in the endless thread of the net of infinite rites, ceremonies, and customs, which it spread on all sides as external means for purification of the body and the mind with a view to keeping society in the iron grasp of these innumerable bonds—the priestly power, thus hopelessly entangled from head to foot, is now asleep in despair! There is no escaping out of it now. Tear the net, and the priesthood of the priest is shaken to its foundation! There is implanted in every man, naturally, a strong desire for progress; and those who, finding that the fulfilment of this desire is an impossibility so long as one is trammelled in the shackles of priesthood, rend this net and take to the profession of other castes in order to earn money thereby—them, the society immediately dispossesses of their priestly rights. Society has no faith in the Brahminhood of the so-called Brahmins who, instead of keeping the Shikhâ[1], part their hair, who, giving up their ancient habits and ancestral customs, clothe themselves in semi European dress and adopt the newly introduced usages from the West in a hybrid fashion. Again, in those parts of India, wherever this new-comer, the English Government, is introducing new modes of education and opening up new channels for the coming in of wealth, there hosts of Brahmin youths are giving up their hereditary priestly profession and trying to earn their livelihood and become rich by adopting the callings of other castes, with the result that the habits and customs of the priestly class, handed down from their distant forefathers, are scattered to the winds and are fast disappearing from the land.

In Gujarat, each secondary sect of the Brahmins is divided into two subdivisions, one being those who still stick to the priestly profession, while the other lives by other professions. There only the first subdivisions, carrying on the priestly profession, are called "Brâhmanas", and though the other subdivisions are by lineage descendants from Brahmin fathers, yet the former do not link themselves in matrimonial relation with the latter. For example, by the name of "Nâgara Brâhmana" are meant only those Brahmins who are priests living on alms; and by the name "Nâgara" only are meant those Brahmins who have accepted service under the Government, or those who have been carrying on the Vaishya's profession. But it appears that such distinctions will not long continue in these days in Gujarat. Even the sons of the "Nagara Brahmanas" are nowadays getting English education, and entering into Government service, or adopting some mercantile business. Even orthodox Pandits of the old school, undergoing pecuniary difficulties, are sending their sons to the colleges of the English universities or making them choose the callings of Vaidyas, Kâyasthas, and other non-Brahmin castes. If the current of affairs goes on running in this course, then it is a question of most serious reflection, no doubt, how long more will the priestly class continue on India's soil. Those who lay

1. The sacred tuft or lock of hair left on the crown of the head at tonsure.

Lectures & Discourses by **Swami Vivekananda**

the fault of attempting to bring down the supremacy of the priestly class at the door of any particular person or body of persons other than themselves ought to know that, in obedience to the inevitable law of nature, the Brahmin caste is erecting with its own hands its own sepulchre; and this is what ought to be. It is good and appropriate that every caste of high birth and privileged nobility should make it its principal duty to raise its own funeral pyre with its own hands. Accumulation of power is as necessary as its diffusion, or rather more so. The accumulation of blood in the heart is an indispensable condition for life; its non-circulation throughout the body means death. For the welfare of society, it is absolutely necessary at certain times to have all knowledge and power concentrated in certain families or castes to the exclusion of others, but that concentrated power is focussed for the time being, only to be scattered broadcast over the whole of society in future. If this diffusion be withheld, the destruction of that society is, without doubt, near at hand.

On the other side, the king is like the lion; in him are present both the good and evil propensities of the lord of beasts. Never for a moment his fierce nails are held back from tearing to pieces the heart of innocent animals, living on herbs and grass, to allay his thirst for blood when occasion arises; again, the poet says, though himself stricken with old age and dying with hunger, the lion never kills the weakest fox that throws itself in his arms for protection. If the subject classes, for a moment, stand as impediments in the way of the gratification of the senses of the royal lion, their death knell is inevitably tolled; if they humbly bow down to his commands, they are perfectly safe. Not only so. Not to speak of ancient days, even in modern times, no society can be found in any country where the effectiveness of individual self-sacrifice for the good of the many and of the oneness of purpose and endeavour actuating every member of the society for the common good of the whole have been fully realised. Hence the necessity of the kings who are the creations of the society itself. They are the centres where all the forces of society, otherwise loosely scattered about, are made to converge, and from which they start and course through the body politic and animate society.

As during the Brâhminical supremacy, at the first stage is the awakening of the first impulse for search after knowledge, and later the continual and careful fostering of the growth of that impulse still in its infancy—so, during the Kshatriya supremacy, a strong desire for pleasure pursuits has made its appearance at the first stage, and later have sprung up inventions and developments of arts and sciences as the means for its gratification. Can the king, in the height of his glory, hide his proud head within the lowly cottages of the poor? Or can the common good of his subjects ever minister to his royal appetite with satisfaction?

He whose dignity bears no comparison with anyone else on earth, he who is divinity residing in the temple of the human body—for the common man, to cast even a mere glance at his, the king's, objects of pleasure is a great sin; to think of ever possessing them is quite out of the question. The body of the king is not like the bodies of other people, it is too sacred to be polluted by any contamination; in certain countries it is even believed never to come under the sway of death. A halo of equal sacredness shines around the queen, so she is scrupulously guarded from the gaze of the common folk, not even the sun may cast a glance on her beauty! Hence the rising of magnificent palaces to take the place of thatched cottages. The sweet harmonious strain of artistic music, flowing as it were from heaven, silenced the disorderly jargon of the rabble. Delightful gardens, pleasant groves, beautiful galleries, charming paintings, exquisite sculptures, fine and costly apparel began to displace by gradual steps the natural beauties of rugged woods and the rough and coarse dress of the simple rustic. Thousands of intelligent men left the toilsome task of the ploughman and turned their attention to the new field of fine arts, where they could display the finer play of their intellect in less laborious and easier ways. Villages lost their importance; cities rose in their stead.

It was in India, again, that the kings, after having enjoyed for some time earthly pleasures to their full satisfaction, were stricken at the latter part of their lives with heavy world-weariness, as is sure to follow on extreme sense-gratification; and thus being satiated with worldly pleasures, they retired at their old age into secluded forests, and there began to contemplate the deep problems of life. The results of such renunciation and deep meditation were marked by a strong dislike for cumbrous rites and ceremonials and an extreme devotion to the highest spiritual truths which we find embodied in the Upanishads, the Gita, and the Jain and the Buddhist scriptures. Here also was a great conflict between the priestly and the royal powers. Disappearance of the elaborate rites and ceremonials meant a death-blow to the priest's profession. Therefore, naturally, at all times and in every country, the priests gird up their loins and try their best to preserve the ancient customs and usages, while on the other side stand in opposition kings like Janaka, backed by Kshatriya prowess as well as spiritual power. We have dealt at length already on this bitter antagonism between the two parties.

As the priest is busy about centralising all knowledge and learning at a common centre, to wit, himself, so the king is ever up and doing in collecting all the earthly powers and focusing them in a central point, i.e. his own self. Of course, both are beneficial to society. At one time they are both needed for the common good of society, but that is only at its infant stage. But if attempts be made, when society has passed its infant stage and reached its vigorous youthful condition, to clothe it by force with the dress which suited it in its infancy and keep it bound within narrow limits, then either it bursts the bonds by virtue of its own strength and tries to advance, or where it fails to do so, it retraces its footsteps and by slow degrees returns to its primitive uncivilised condition.

Kings are like parents to their subjects, and the subjects are the kings' children. The subjects should, in every respect, look up to the king and stick to their king with unreserved obedience, and the king should rule them with impartial justice and look to their welfare and bear the same affection towards them as he would towards his own children. But what rule applies to individual homes applies to the whole society as well, for society is only the aggregate of individual homes. "When the son attains the age of sixteen, the father ought to deal with him as his friend and equal"[1]—if that is the rule, does not the infant society ever attain that age of sixteen? It is the evidence of history that at a certain time every society attains its manhood, when a strong conflict ensues between the ruling power and the common people. The life of the society, its expansion and civilisation, depend on its victory or defeat in this conflict.

Such changes, revolutionizing society, have been happening in India again and again, only in this country they have been effected in the name of religion, for religion is the life of India, religion is the language of this country, the symbol of all its movements. The Chârvâka, the Jain, the Buddhist, Shankara, Ramanuja, Kabir, Nânak, Chaitanya, the Brâhmo Samâj, the Arya Samaj—of all these and similar other sects, the wave of religion, foaming, thundering, surging, breaks in the front, while in the rear follows the filling-up of social wants. If all desires can be accomplished by the mere utterance of some meaningless syllables, then who will exert himself and go through difficulties to work out the fulfilment of his desires? If this malady enters into the entire body of any social system, then that society becomes slothful and indisposed to any exertion, and soon hastens to it, ruin. Hence the slashing sarcasm of the Charvakas, who believed only in the reality of sense-perceptions and nothing beyond. What could have saved Indian society from the ponderous burden of omnifarious ritualistic ceremonialism, with its animal and other sacrifices, which all but crushed the very life out of it, except the Jain revolution which took its strong stand exclusively on chaste morals and philosophical truth? Or without the Buddhist revolution what would have delivered the suffering millions of the lower classes from the violent tyrannies of the influential higher castes? When, in course of time, Buddhism declined and its extremely pure and moral character gave place to equally bad, unclean, and immoral practices, when Indian society trembled under the infernal dance of the various races of barbarians who were allowed into the Buddhistic fold by virtue of its universal all-embracing spirit of equality—then Shankara, and later Ramanuja, appeared on the scene and tried their best to bring society back to its former days of glory and re-establish its lost status. Again, it is an undoubted fact that if there had not been the advent of Kabir, Nanak, and Chaitanya in the Mohammedan period, and the

establishment of the Brahmo Samaj and the Arya Samaj in our own day, then, by this time, the Mohammedans and the Christians would have far outnumbered the Hindus of the present day in India.

What better material is there than nourishing food to build up the body composed of various elements, and the mind which sends out infinite waves of thought? But if that food which goes to sustain the body and strengthen the mind is not properly assimilated, and the natural functions of the body do not work properly, then that very thing becomes the root of all evil.

The individual's life is in the life of the whole, the individual's happiness is in the happiness of the whole; apart from the whole, the individual's existence is inconceivable—this is an eternal truth and is the bed-rock on which the universe is built. To move slowly towards the infinite whole, bearing a constant feeling of intense sympathy and sameness with it, being happy with its happiness and being distressed in its affliction, is the individual's sole duty. Not only is it his duty, but in its transgression is his death, while compliance with this great truth leads to life immortal. This is the law of nature, and who can throw dust into her ever-watchful eyes? None can hoodwink society and deceive it for any length of time. However much there may have accumulated heaps of refuse and mud on the surface of society—still, at the bottom of those heaps the life-breath of society is ever to be found pulsating with the vibrations of universal love and self-denying compassion for all. Society is like the earth that patiently bears incessant molestations; but she wakes up one day, however long that may be in coming, and the force of the shaking tremors of that awakening hurls off to a distance the accumulated dirt of self-seeking meanness piled up during millions of patient and silent years!

We ignore this sublime truth; and though we suffer a thousand times for our folly, yet, in our absurd foolishness, impelled by the brute in us, we do not believe in it. We try to deceive, but a thousand times we find we are deceived ourselves, and yet we do not desist! Mad that we are, we imagine we can impose on nature' With our shortsighted vision we think ministering to the self at any cost is the be-all and end-all of life.

Wisdom, knowledge, wealth, men, strength, prowess and whatever else nature gathers and provides us with, are all only for diffusion, when the moment of need is at hand. We often forget this fact, put the stamp of "mine only" upon the entrusted deposits, and pari passu, we sow the seed of our own ruin!

The king, the centre of the forces of the aggregate of his subjects, soon forgets that those forces are only stored with him so that he may increase and give them back a thousandfold in their potency, so that they may spread over the whole community for its good. Attributing all Godship to himself, in

---

1. Taken from one of the well-known didactic verses of the statesman-Pandit, Chânakya, which runs thus: "Let the father treat with tenderness the child till he is five, let him (the father) reprove him (the child) for the next ten years; when the son attains the age of sixteen, the father ought to deal with him as his friend."

Lectures & Discourses by **Swami Vivekananda**

his pride, like the king Vena[2] he looks upon other people as wretched specimens of humanity who should grovel before him; any opposition to his will, whether good or bad, is a great sin on the part of his subjects. Hence oppression steps into the place of protection—sucking their blood in place of preservation. If the society is weak and debilitated, it silently suffers all ill-treatment at the hands of the king, and as the natural consequence, both the king and his people go down and down and fall into the most degraded state, and thus become an easy prey to any nation stronger than themselves. Where the society is healthy and strong, there soon follows a fierce contest between the king and his subjects, and, by its reaction and convulsion, are flung away the sceptre and the crown; and the throne and the royal paraphernalia become like past curiosities preserved in the museum galleries.

As the result of this contest—as its reaction—is the appearance of the mighty power of the Vaishya, before whose angry glance the crowned heads, the lords of heroes, tremble like an aspen leaf on their thrones—whom the poor as well as the prince humbly follow in vain expectation of the golden jar in his hands, that like Tantalus's fruit always recedes from the grasp.

The Brahmin said, "Learning is the power of all powers; that learning is dependent upon me, I possess that learning, so the society must follow my bidding." For some days such was the case. The Kshatriya said, "But for the power of my sword, where would you be, O Brahmin, with all your power of lore? You would in no time be wiped off the face of the earth. It is I alone that am the superior." Out flew the flaming sword from the jingling scabbard—society humbly recognised it with bended head. Even the worshipper of learning was the first to turn into the worshipper of the king. The Vaishya is saying, "You, madmen I what you call the effulgent all-pervading deity is here, in my hand, the ever-shining gold, the almighty sovereign. Behold, through its grace, I am also equally all-powerful. O Brahmin! even now, I shall buy through its grace all your wisdom, learning, prayers, and meditation. And, O great king! your sword, arms, valour, and prowess will soon be employed, through the grace of this, my gold, in carrying out my desired objects. Do you see those lofty and extensive mills? Those are my hives. See, how, swarms of millions of bees, the Shudras, are incessantly gathering honey for those hives. Do you know for whom? For me, this me, who in due course of time will squeeze out every drop of it for my own use and profit."

As during the supremacy of the Brahmin and the Kshatriya, there is a centralization of learning and advancement of civilization, so the result of the supremacy of the Vaishya is accumulation of wealth. The power of the Vaishya lies in the possession of that coin, the charm of whose clinking sound works with an irresistible fascination on the minds of the four castes. The Vaishya is always in fear lest the Brahmin swindles him out of this, his only possession, and lest the Kshatriya usurps it by virtue of his superior strength of arms. For self-preservation, the Vaishyas as a body are, therefore, of one mind. The Vaishya commands the money; the exorbitant interest that he can exact for its use by others, as with a lash in his hand, is his powerful weapon which strikes terror in the heart of all. By the power of his money, he is always busy curbing the royal power. That the royal power may not anyhow stand in the way of the inflow of his riches, the merchant is ever watchful. But, for all that, he has never the least wish that the power should pass on from the kingly to the Shudra class.

To what country does not the merchant go? Though himself ignorant, he carries on his trade and transplants the learning, wisdom, art, and science of one country to another. The wisdom, civilization, and arts that accumulated in the heart of the social body during the Brahmin and the Kshatriya supremacies are being diffused in all directions by the arteries of commerce to the different market-places of the Vaishya. But for the rising of this Vaishya power, who would have carried today the culture, learning, acquirements, and articles of food and luxury of one end of the world to the other?

And where are they through whose physical labour only are possible the influence of the Brahmin, the prowess of the Kshatriya, and the fortune of the Vaishya? What is their history, who, being the real body of society, are designated at all times in all countries as "baseborn"?—for whom kind India prescribed the mild punishments, "Cut out his tongue, chop off his flesh", and others of like nature, for such a grave offence as any attempt on their part to gain a share of the knowledge and wisdom monopolised by her higher classes—those "moving corpses" of India and the "beasts of burden" of other countries—the Shudras, what is their lot in life? What shall I say of India? Let alone her Shudra class, her Brahmins to whom belonged the acquisition of scriptural knowledge are now the foreign professors, her Kshatriyas the ruling Englishmen, and Vaishyas, too, the English in whose bone and marrow is the instinct of trade, so that, only the Shudra-ness—the-beast-of-burdenness—is now left with the Indians themselves.

A cloud of impenetrable darkness has at present equally enveloped us all. Now there is neither firmness of purpose nor boldness of enterprise, neither courage of heart nor strength of mind, neither aversion to maltreatments by others nor dislike for slavery, neither love in the heart nor hope nor manliness; but what we have in India are only deep-rooted envy and strong antipathy against one another, morbid desire to ruin by hook or by crook the weak, and to lick dog-like the feet of the strong. Now the highest satisfaction consists in the display of wealth and power, devotion in self-gratification, wisdom in the accumulation of transitory objects, Yoga in hideous di-

2. His story occurs in the Bhâgavata. The King Vena thought himself higher than Brahmâ, Vishnu, and Maheshvara, and declared accordingly that all worship should be offered to him. The Rishis once sought him and tried by good advice to make him give up such egoism, but he in return insulted them and ordered them to worship him, whereupon, it is said, he was destroyed by the fire of the anger of the Rishis.

abolical practices, work in the slavery of others, civilisation in base imitation of foreign nations, eloquence in the use of abusive language, the merit of literature in extravagant flatteries of the rich or in the diffusion of ghastly obscenities! What to speak separately of the distinct Shudra class of such a land, where the whole population has virtually come down to the level of the Shudra? The Shudras of countries other than India have become, it seems, a little awake; but they are wanting in proper education and have only the mutual hatred of men of their own class—a trait common to Shudras. What avails it if they greatly outnumber the other classes? That unity, by which ten men collect the strength of a million, is yet far away from the Shudra; hence, according to the law of nature, the Shudras invariably form the subject race.

But there is hope. In the mighty course of time, the Brahmin and the other higher castes, too, are being brought down to the lower status of the Shudras, and the Shudras are being raised to higher ranks. Europe, once the land of Shudras enslaved by Rome, is now filled with Kshatriya valour. Even before our eyes, powerful China, with fast strides, is going down to Shudra-hood, while insignificant Japan, rising with the sudden start of a rocket, is throwing off her Shudra nature and is invading by degrees the rights of the higher castes. The attaining of modern Greece and Italy to Kshatriya-hood and the decline of Turkey, Spain, and other countries, also, deserve consideration here.

Yet, a time will come when there will be the rising of the Shudra class, with their Shudra-hood; that is to say, not like that as at present when the Shudras are becoming great by acquiring the characteristic qualities of the Vaishya or the Kshatriya, but a time will come when the Shudras of every country, with their inborn Shudra nature and habits—not becoming in essence Vaishya or Kshatriya, but remaining as Shudras—will gain absolute supremacy in every society. The first glow of the dawn of this new power has already begun to break slowly upon the Western world, and the thoughtful are at their wits' end to reflect upon the final issue of this fresh phenomenon. Socialism, Anarchism, Nihilism[1], and other like sects are the vanguard of the social revolution that is to follow. As the result of grinding pressure and tyranny, from time out of mind, the Shudras, as a rule, are either meanly senile, licking dog-like the feet of the higher class, or otherwise are as inhuman as brute beasts. Again, at all times their hopes and aspirations are baffled; hence a firmness of purpose and perseverance in action they have none.

In spite of the spread of education in the West, there is a great hindrance in the way of the rising of the Shudra class, and that is the recognition of caste as determined by the inherence of more or less good or bad qualities. By this very qualitative caste system which obtained in India in ancient days, the Shudra class was kept down, bound hand and foot.

1. Socialism took its birth in 1835 A.D. The initiator of Anarchism was Bakunin, who was born in 1814 A.D. Nihilism was first inaugurated in Russia in 1862.

In the first place, scarcely any opportunity was given to the Shudra for the accumulation of wealth or the earning of proper knowledge and education; to add to this disadvantage, if ever a man of extraordinary parts and genius were born of the Shudra class, the influential higher sections of the society forthwith showered titular honours on him and lifted him up to their own circle. His wealth and the power of his wisdom were employed for the benefit of an alien caste—and his own caste-people reaped no benefits of his attainments; and not only so, the good-for-nothing people, the scum and refuse of the higher castes, were cast off and thrown into the Shudra class to swell their number. Vasishtha, Nârada, Satyakâma Jâbâla, Vyâsa, Kripa, Drona, Karna, and others of questionable parentage[2] were raised to the position of a Brahmin or a Kshatriya, in virtue of their superior learning or valour; but it remains to be seen how the prostitute, maidservant, fisherman, or the charioteer[3] class was benefited by these upliftings. Again, on the other hand, the fallen from the Brahmin, the Kshatriya, or the Vaishya class were always brought down to fill the ranks of the Shudras.

In modern India, no one born of Shudra parents, be he a millionaire or a great Pandit, has ever the right to leave his own society, with the result that the power of his wealth, intellect, or wisdom, remaining confined within his own caste limits, is being employed for the betterment of his own community. This hereditary caste system of India, being thus unable to overstep its own bounds, is slowly but surely conducing to the advancement of the people moving within the same circle. The improvement of the lower classes of India will go on, in this way, so long as India will be under a government dealing with its subjects irrespective of their caste and position.

Whether the leadership of society be in the hands of those who monopolise learning or wield the power of riches or arms, the source of its power is always the subject masses. By so much as the class in power severs itself from this source, by so much is it sure to become weak. But such is the strange irony of fate, such is the queer working of Mâyâ, that they from whom this power is directly or indirectly drawn, by fair

2. (1) Vasishtha's father was Brahmâ and mother unknown. (2) Narada's mother was a maidservant and father unknown. (3) Satyakama Jabala's mother was a maidservant, by name Jabâlâ, and father unknown. (4) Vyasa's father was a Brahmin sage Parâshara, and mother Matsyagandhâ, the virgin daughter of a fisherman. (5) Kripa s father was a Brahmin sage, Sharadvân Gautama, and mother the goddess Jânapadi. (6) Drona's father was the Brahmin sage, Bharadvâja, and mother the goddess Ghritâchi. (7) Karna's mother was Kunti, who conceived during her maidenhood, and father the god sun. For detailed information vide the accounts of their births: for (1), see chapter 174, Âdiparva, Mahabharata, or in Rigveda, 7, 33, 11-13; for (2), chapter 6, Skandha I, Srimad Bhagavata, for (3) section 4 Prapâthaka iv, Chhândogya Upanishad; for (4), (5), (6) and (7) chapters 105, 130, 130 and 111, respectively of the Âdiparva of the Mahabharata.

3. In her anxiety to save her reputation, Kunti threw the newborn child Karna, into water. A charioteer found the child in his pitiable condition and adopted him as his son.

means or foul—by deceit, stratagem, force, or by voluntary gift—they soon cease to be taken into account by the leading class. When in course of time, the priestly power totally estranged itself from the subject masses, the real dynamo of its power, it was overthrown by the then kingly power taking its stand on the strength of the subject people; again, the kingly power, judging itself to be perfectly independent, created a gaping chasm between itself and the subject people, only to be itself destroyed or become a mere puppet in the hands of the Vaishyas, who now succeeded in securing a relatively greater co-operation of the mass of the people. The Vaishyas have now gained their end; so they no longer deign to count on help from the subject people and are trying their best to dissociate themselves from them; consequently, here is being sown the seed of the destruction of this power as well.

Though themselves the reservoir of all powers, the subject masses, creating an eternal distance between one another, have been deprived of all their legitimate rights; and they will remain so as long as this sort of relation continues.

A common danger, or sometimes a common cause of hatred or love, is the bond that binds people together. By the same law that herds beasts of prey together, men also unite into a body and form a caste or a nation of their own. Zealous love for one's own people and country, showing itself in bitter hatred against another—as of Greece against Persia, or Rome against Carthage, of the Arab against the Kafir, of Spain against the Moor, of France against Spain, of England and Germany against France, and of America against England—is undoubtedly one of the main causes which lead to the advancement of one nation over another, by way of uniting itself in hostilities against another.

Self-love is the first teacher of self-renunciation. For the preservation of the individual's interest only one looks first to the well-being of the whole. In the interest of one's own nation is one's own interest; in the well-being of one's own nation is one's own well-being. Without the co-operation of the many, most words can by no means go on—even self-defence becomes an impossibility. The joining of friendly hands in mutual help for the protection of this self-interest is seen in every nation, and in every land. Of course, the circumference of this self-interest varies with different people. To multiply and to have the opportunity of somehow dragging on a precarious existence, and over and above this, the condition that the religious pursuits of the higher castes may not suffer in any way, is of the highest gain and interest for Indians! For modern India, there is no better hope conceivable; this is the last rung of the ladder of India's life!

The present government of India has certain evils attendant on it, and there are some very great and good parts in it as well. Of highest good is this, that after the fall of the Pâtaliputra Empire till now, India was never under the guidance of such a powerful machinery of government as the British, wielding the sceptre throughout the length and breadth of the land.

And under this Vaishya supremacy, thanks to the strenuous enterprise natural to the Vaishya, as the objects of commerce are being brought from one end of the world to another, so at the same time, as its natural sequence, the ideas and thoughts of different countries are forcing their way into the very bone and marrow of India. Of these ideas and thoughts, some are really most beneficial to her, some are harmful, while others disclose the ignorance and inability of the foreigners to determine what is truly good for the inhabitants of this country.

But piercing through the mass of whatever good or evil there may be is seen rising the sure emblem of India's future prosperity—that as the result of the action and reaction between her own old national ideals on the one hand, and the newly-introduced strange ideals of foreign nations on the other, she is slowly and gently awakening from her long deep sleep. Mistakes she will make, let her: there is no harm in that; in all our actions, errors and mistakes are our only teachers. Who commits mistaken the path of truth is attainable by him only. Trees never make mistakes, nor do stones fall into error; animals are hardly seen to transgress the fixed laws of nature; but man is prone to err, and it is man who becomes God-on-earth. If our every movement from the nursery to the death-bed, if our every thought from rising at day-break till retirement at midnight, be prescribed and laid down for us in minutest detail by others—and if the threat of the king's sword be brought into requisition to keep us within the iron grasp of those prescribed rules—then, what remains for us to think independently for ourselves? What makes a man a genius, a sage? Isn't it because he thinks, reasons, wills? Without exercise, the power of deep thinking is lost. Tamas prevails, the mind gets dull and inert, the spirit is brought down to the level of matter. Yet, even now, every religious preacher, every social leader is anxious to frame new laws and regulations for the guidance of society! Does the country stand in want of rules? Has it not enough of them? Under the oppression of rules, the whole nation is verging on its ruin—who stops to understand this?

In the case of an absolute and arbitrary monarchy, the conquered race is not treated with so much contempt by the ruling power. Under such an absolute government, the rights of all subjects are equal, in other words, no one has any right to question or control the governing authority. So there remains very little room for special privileges of caste and the like. But where the monarchy is controlled by the voice of the ruling race, or a republican form of government rules the conquered race, there a wide distance is created between the ruling and the ruled; and the most part of that power, which, if employed solely for the well-being of the ruled classes, might have done immense good to them within a short time, is wasted by the government in its attempts and applications to keep the subject race under its entire control. Under the Roman Emperorship, foreign subjects were, for this very reason, happier than under the Republic of Rome. For this very reason, St. Paul, the Christian Apostle, though born of the conquered Jewish race, obtained permission to appeal to the Roman Emperor, Caesar, to judge of the charges laid against him[1] Because some individual Englishman may call us "natives" or "niggers" and hate us as uncivilized savages, we do not gain or lose by that. We, on account of caste distinctions, have among ourselves far stronger feelings of hatred and scorn against one another; and who can say that the Brahmins, if they get some foolish unenlightened Kshatriya king on their side, will not graciously try again to "cut out the Shudras' tongues and chop off their limbs"? That recently in Eastern Aryavarta, the different caste-people seem to develop a feeling of united sympathy amidst themselves with a view to ameliorating their present social condition — that in the Mahratta country, the Brahmins have begun to sing paeans in praise of the "Marâthâ" race — these, the lower castes cannot yet believe to be the outcome of pure disinterestedness.

But gradually the idea is being formed in the minds of the English public that the passing away of the Indian Empire from their sway will end in imminent peril to the English nation, and be their ruin. So, by any means whatsoever, the supremacy of England must be maintained in India. The way to effect this, they think, is by keeping uppermost in the heart of every Indian the mighty prestige and glory of the British nation. It gives rise to both laughter and tears simultaneously to observe how this ludicrous and pitiful sentiment is gaining ground among the English, and how they are steadily extending their modus operandi for the carrying out of this sentiment into practice. It seems as if the Englishmen resident in India are forgetting that so long as that fortitude, that perseverance, and that intense national unity of purpose, by which Englishmen have earned this Indian Empire — and that ever wide-awake commercial genius aided by science' which has turned even India, the mother of all riches, into the principal mart of England — so long as these characteristics are not eliminated from their national life, their throne in India is unshakable. So long as these qualities are inherent in the British character, let thousands of such Indian Empires be lost, thousands will be earned again. But if the flow of the stream of those qualifier be retarded, shall an Empire be governed by the mere emblazoning of British prestige and glory? Therefore when such remarkable traits of character are still predominant in the English as a nation, it is utterly useless to spend so much energy and power for the mere preservation of meaningless "prestige". If that power were employed for the welfare of the subject-people, that, would certainly have been a great gain for both the ruling and the ruled races.

It has been said before that India is slowly awakening through her friction with the outside nations; and as the result of this little awakening, is the appearance, to a certain extent, of free and independent thought in modern India. On one side is modern Western science, dazzling the eyes with the brilliancy of myriad suns and driving in the chariot of hard and fast facts collected by the application of tangible pow-

1. The Acts, xxv. 11.

ers direct in their incision, on the other are the hopeful and strengthening traditions of her ancient forefathers, in the days when she was at the zenith of her glory — traditions that have been brought out of the pages of her history by the great sages of her own land and outside, that run for numberless years and centuries through her every vein with the quickening of life drawn from universal love — traditions that reveal unsurpassed valour, superhuman genius, and supreme spirituality, which are the envy of the gods — these inspire her with future hopes. On one side, rank materialism, plenitude of fortune, accumulation of gigantic power, and intense sense-pursuits have, through foreign literature, caused a tremendous stir; on the other, through the confounding din of all these discordant sounds, she hears, in low yet unmistakable accents, the heart-rending cries of her ancient gods, cutting her to the quick. There lie before her various strange luxuries introduced from the West — celestial drinks, costly well-served food, splendid apparel, magnificent palaces, new modes of conveyance, new manners, new fashions dressed in which moves about the well-educated girl in shameless freedom — all these are arousing unfelt desires. Again, the scene changes, and in its place appear, with stern presence, Sitâ, Sâvitri, austere religious vows, fastings, the forest retreat, the matted locks and orange garb of the semi-naked Sannyasin, Samâdhi and the search after the Self. On one side is the independence of Western societies based on self-interest; on the other is the extreme self-sacrifice of the Aryan society. In this violent conflict, is it strange that Indian society should be tossed up and down? Of the West, the goal is individual independence, the language money-making education, the means politics; of India, the goal is Mukti, the language the Veda, the means renunciation. For a time, Modern India thinks, as it were, I am ruining this worldly life of mine in vain expectation of uncertain spiritual welfare hereafter which has spread its fascination over one; and again, lo! spellbound she listens —

इति संसारे स्फुटतरदोषः कथमिह मानव तव सन्तोषः —"Here, in this world of death and change, O man, where is thy happiness?"

On one side, new India is saying, "We should have full freedom in the selection of husband and wife; because the marriage, in which are involved the happiness and misery of all our future life, we must have the right to determine according to our own free will." On the other, old India is dictating, "Marriage is not for sense-enjoyment, but to perpetuate the race. This is the Indian conception of marriage. By the producing of children, you are contributing to, and are responsible for, the future good or evil of the society. Hence society has the right to dictate whom you shall marry and whom you shall not. That form of marriage obtains in society which is conducive most to its well-being; do you give up your desire of individual pleasure for the good of the many."

On one side, new India is saying, "If we only adopt Western ideas, Western language, Western food, Western dress, and Western manners, we shall be as strong and powerful as the

Western nations"; on the other, old India is saying, "Fools! By imitation, other's ideas never become one's own; nothing, unless earned, is your own. Does the ass in the lion's skin become the lion?"

On one side, new India is saving, "What the Western nations do is surely good, otherwise how did they become so great?" On the other side, old India is saying, "The flash of lightning is intensely bright, but only for a moment; look out, boys, it is dazzling your eyes. Beware!"

Have we not then to learn anything from the West? Must we not needs try and exert ourselves for better things? Are we perfect? Is our society entirely spotless, without any flaw. There are many things to learn, he must struggle for new and higher things till we die—struggle is the end of human life. Shri Ramakrishna used to say, "As long as I live, so long do I learn." That man or that society which has nothing to learn is already in the jaws of death. Yes, learn we must many things from the West: but there are fears as well.

A certain young man of little understanding used always to blame the Hindu Shâstras before Shri Ramakrishna. One day he praised the Bhagavad-Gita, on which Shri Ramakrishna said, "Methinks, some European Pandit has praised the Gita, and so he has also followed suit."

O India, this is your terrible danger. The spell of imitating the West is getting such a strong hold upon you that what is good or what is bad is no longer decided by reason, judgment, discrimination, or reference to the Shastras. Whatever ideas, whatever manners the white men praise or like are good; whatever things they dislike or censure are bad. Alas! what can be a more tangible proof of foolishness than this?

The Western ladies move freely everywhere, therefore that is good; they choose for themselves their husbands, therefore that is the highest step of advancement; the Westerners disapprove of our dress, decorations, food, and ways of living, therefore they must be very bad; the Westerners condemn image-worship as sinful, surely then, image-worship is the greatest sin, there is no doubt of it!

The Westerners say that worshipping a single Deity is fruitful of the highest spiritual good, therefore let us throw our gods and goddesses into the river Ganga! The Westerners hold caste distinctions to be obnoxious, therefore let all the different castes be jumbled into one! The Westerners say that child-marriage is the root of all evils, therefore that is also very bad, of a certainty it is!

We are not discussing here whether these customs deserve continuance or rejection; but if the mere disapproval of the Westerners be the measure of the abominableness of our manners and customs, then it is our duty to raise our emphatic protest against it.

The present writer has, to some extent, personal experience of Western society. His conviction resulting from such experience has been that there is such a wide divergence between the Western society and the Indian as regards the primal course and goal of each, that any sect in India, framed after the Western model, will miss the aim. We have not the least sympathy with those who, never leaving lived in Western society and, therefore, utterly ignorant of the rules and prohibitions regarding the association of men and women that obtain there, and which act as safeguards to preserve the purity of the Western women, allow a free rein to the unrestricted intermingling of men and women in our society.

I have observed in the West also that the children of weaker nations, if born in England, give themselves out as Englishmen, instead of Greek, Portuguese, Spaniard, etc., as the case may be. All drift towards the strong. That the light of glory which shines in the glorious may anyhow fall and reflect on one's own body, i.e. to shine in the borrowed light of the great, is the one desire of the weak. When I see Indians dressed in European apparel and costumes, the thought comes to my mind, perhaps they feel ashamed to own their nationality and kinship with the ignorant, poor, illiterate, downtrodden people of India! Nourished by the blood of the Hindu for the last fourteen centuries, the Parsee is no longer a "native"! Before the arrogance of the casteless, who pretend to be and glorify themselves in being Brahmins, the true nobility of the old, heroic, high-class Brahmin melts into nothingness! Again, the Westerners have now taught us that those stupid, ignorant, low-caste millions of India, clad only in loin-cloths, are non-Aryans. They are therefore no more our kith and kin!

O India! With this mere echoing of others, with this base imitation of others, with this dependence on others this slavish weakness, this vile detestable cruelty—wouldst thou, with these provisions only, scale the highest pinnacle of civilisation and greatness? Wouldst thou attain, by means of thy disgraceful cowardice, that freedom deserved only by the brave and the heroic? O India! Forget not that the ideal of thy womanhood is Sita, Savitri, Damayanti; forget not that the God thou worshippest is the great Ascetic of ascetics, the all-renouncing Shankara, the Lord of Umâ; forget not that thy marriage, thy wealth, thy life are not for sense-pleasure, are not for thy individual personal happiness; forget not that thou art born as a sacrifice to the Mother's altar; forget not that thy social order is but the reflex of the Infinite Universal Motherhood; forget not that the lower classes, the ignorant, the poor, the illiterate, the cobbler, the sweeper, are thy flesh and blood, thy brothers. Thou brave one, be bold, take courage, be proud that thou art an Indian, and proudly proclaim, "I am an Indian, every Indian is my brother." Say, "The ignorant Indian, the poor and destitute Indian, the Brahmin Indian, the Pariah Indian, is my brother." Thou, too, clad with but a rag round thy loins proudly proclaim at the top of thy voice: "The Indian is my brother, the Indian is my life, India's gods and goddesses are my God. India's society is the cradle of my infancy, the pleasure-garden of my youth, the sacred heaven, the Varanasi of my old age." Say, brother: "The soil of India is my highest heaven, the good of India is my good," and repeat and pray day and night, "O Thou Lord of Gauri, O Thou Mother of the Universe, vouchsafe manliness unto me! O Thou Mother of Strength, take away my weakness, take away my unmanliness, and make me a Man!"

THE EDUCATION THAT INDIA NEEDS[1]

In reply to your questions about the methods of work, the most important thing I have to say is that the work should be started on a scale which would be commensurate with the results desired. I have heard much of your liberal mind, patriotism, and steady perseverance from my friend Miss Müller; and the proof of your erudition is evident. I look upon it as a great good fortune that you are desirous to know what little this insignificant life has been able to attempt; I shall state it to you here, as far as I can. But first I shall lay before you my mature convictions for your deliberation.

We have been slaves for ever, i.e. it has never been given to the masses of India to express the inner light which is their inheritance. The Occident has been rapidly advancing towards freedom for the last few centuries. In India, it was the king who used to prescribe everything from Kulinism down to what one should eat and what one should not. In Western countries, the people do everything themselves.

The king now has nothing to say in any social matter; on the other hand, the Indian people have not yet even the least faith in themselves, what to say of self-reliance. The faith in one's own Self, which is the basis of Vedânta, has not yet been even slightly carried into practice. It is for this reason that the Western method—i.e. first of all, discussion about the wished-for end, then the carrying it out by the combination of all the forces—is of no avail even now in this country: it is for this reason that we appear so greatly conservative under foreign rule. If this be true, then it is a vain attempt to do any great work by means of public discussion. "There is no chance of a headache where there is no head"—where is the public? Besides, we are so devoid of strength that our whole energy is exhausted if we undertake to discuss anything, none is left for work. It is for this reason, I suppose, we observe in Bengal almost always—"Much cry but little wool." Secondly, as I have written before, I do not expect anything from the rich people of India. It is best to work among the youth in whom lies our hope—patiently, steadily, and without noise.

Now about work. From the day when education and culture etc. began to spread gradually from patricians to plebeians, grew the distinction between the modern civilisation as of Western countries, and the ancient civilisation as of India, Egypt, Rome, etc. I see it before my eyes, a nation is advanced in proportion as education and intelligence spread among the masses. The chief cause of India's ruin has been the monopolising of the whole education and intelligence of the land, by dint of pride and royal authority, among a handful of men. If we are to rise again, we shall have to do it in the same way,

i.e. by spreading education among the masses. A great fuss has been made for half a century about social reform. Travelling through various places of India these last ten years, I observed the country full of social reform associations. But I did not find one association for them by sucking whose blood the people known as "gentlemen" have become and continue to be gentlemen! How many sepoys were brought by the Mussulmans? How many Englishmen are there? Where, except in India, can be had millions of men who will cut the throats of their own fathers and brothers for six rupees? Sixty millions of Mussulmans in seven hundred years of Mohammedan rule, and two millions of Christians in one hundred years of Christian rule—what makes it so? Why has originality entirely forsaken the country? Why are our deft-fingered artisans daily becoming extinct, unable to compete with the Europeans? By what power again has the German labourer succeeded in shaking the many-century-grounded firm footing of the English labourer?

Education, education, education alone! Travelling through many cities of Europe and observing in them the comforts and education of even the poor people, there was brought to my mind the state of our own poor people, and I used to shed tears. What made the difference? Education was the answer I got. Through education comes faith in one's own Self, and through faith in one's own Self the inherent Brahman is waking up in them, while the Brahman in us is gradually becoming dormant. In New York I used to observe the Irish colonists come—downtrodden, haggard-looking, destitute of all possessions at home, penniless, and wooden-headed—with their only belongings, a stick and a bundle of rags hanging at the end of it, fright in their steps, alarm in their eyes. A different spectacle in six months—the man walks upright, his attire is changed! In his eyes and steps there is no more sign of fright. What is the cause? Our Vedanta says that that Irishman was kept surrounded by contempt in his own country—the whole of nature was telling him with one voice, "Pat, you have no more hope, you are born a slave and will remain so." Having been thus told from his birth, Pat believed in it and hypnotised himself that he was very low, and the Brahman in him shrank away. While no sooner had he landed in America than he heard the shout going up on all sides, "Pat, you are a man as we are. It is man who has done all, a man like you and me can do everything: have courage!" Pat raised his head and saw that it was so, the Brahman within woke up. Nature herself spoke, as it were, "Arise, awake, and stop not till the goal is reached" (Katha Upanishad, I. ii. 4.)

Likewise the education that our boys receive is very negative. The schoolboy learns nothing, but has everything of his own broken down—want of Shraddhâ is the result. The Shraddha which is the keynote of the Veda and the Vedanta—the Shraddha which emboldened Nachiketâ to face Yama and question him, through which Shraddha this world moves the annihilation of that Shraddha!

1. Written to Shrimati Saralâ Ghosal, B.A., Editor, *Bhârati*, from Darjeeling, 24th April, 1897. Translated from Bengali.

अज्ञश्चाश्रद्दधानश्च संशयात्मा वनिश्यति

— "The ignorant, the man devoid of Shraddha, the doubting self runs to ruin." Therefore are we so near destruction. The remedy now is the spread of education. First of all, Self-knowledge. I do not mean thereby, matted hair, staff, Kamandalu, and mountain caves which the word suggests. What do I mean then? Cannot the knowledge, by which is attained even freedom from the bondage of worldly existence, bring ordinary material prosperity? Certainly it can. Freedom, dispassion, renunciation all these are the very highest ideals, but

स्वल्पमप्यस्य धर्मस्य त्रायते महतो भयात्

— "Even a little of this Dharma saves one from the great fear (of birth and death)." Dualist, qualified-monist, monist, Shaiva, Vaishnava, Shâkta, even the Buddhist and the Jain and others—whatever sects have arisen in India—are all at one in this respect that infinite power is latent in this Jivatman (individualised soul); from the ant to the perfect man there is the same Âtman in all, the difference being only in manifestation. "As a farmer breaks the obstacles (to the course of water)" (Patanjali's Yoga-Sutra, Kaivalsapâda, 3). That power manifests as soon as it gets the opportunity and the right place and time. From the highest god to the meanest grass, the same power is present in all—whether manifested or not. We shall have to call forth that power by going from door to door.

Secondly, along with this, education has to be imparted. That is easy to say, but how to reduce it into practice? There are thousands of unselfish, kind-hearted men in our country who has renounced every thing. In the same way as they travel about and give religious instructions without any remuneration, so at least half of them can be trained as teachers or bearers of such education as we need most. For that, we want first of all a centre in the capital of each Presidency, from whence to spread slowly throughout the whole of India. Two centres have recently been started in Madras and Calcutta; there is hope of more soon. Then, the greater part of the education to the poor should be given orally, time is not yet ripe for schools. Gradually in these main centres will be taught agriculture, industry, etc., and workshops will be established for the furtherance of arts. To sell the manufactures of those workshops in Europe and America, associations will be started like those already in existence. It will be necessary to start centres for women, exactly like those for men. But you are aware how difficult that is in this country. Again, "The snake which bites must take out its own poison"—and that this is going to be is my firm conviction; the money required for these works would have to come from the West. And for that reason our religion should be preached in Europe and America. Modern science has undermined the basis of religions like Christianity. Over and above that, luxury is about to kill the religious instinct itself. Europe and America are now looking towards India with expectant ewes: this is the time for philanthropy, this is the time to occupy the hostile strongholds.

In the West, women rule; all influence and power are theirs. If bold and talented women like yourself versed in Vedanta, go to England to preach, I am sure that every year hundreds of men and women will become blessed by adopting the religion of the land of Bharata. The only woman who went over from our country was Ramâbâi; her knowledge of English, Western science and art was limited; still she surprised all. If anyone like you goes, England will be stirred, what to speak of America! If an Indian woman in Indian dress preach there the religion which fell from the lips of the Rishis of India—I see a prophetic vision—there will rise a great wave which will inundate the whole Western world. Will there be no women in the land of Maitreyi, Khanâ, Lilâvati, Sâvitri, and Ubhayabhârati, who will venture to do this? The Lord knows. England we shall conquer, England we shall possess, through the power of spirituality.

नान्यः पन्था विद्यतेऽयनाय

— "There is no other way of salvation." Can salvation ever come by getting up meetings and societies? Our conquerors must be made Devas by the power of our spirituality. I am a humble mendicant, an itinerant monk; I am helpless and alone. What can I do? You have the power of wealth, intellect, and education; will you forgo this opportunity? Conquest of England, Europe, and America—this should be our one supreme Mantra at present, in it lies the well-being of the country. Expansion is the sign of life, and we must spread over the world with our spiritual ideals. Alas! this frame is poor, moreover, the physique of a Bengali; even under this labour a fatal disease has attacked it, but there is the hope:

उत्पत्स्यतेऽस्ति मम कोऽपि समानधर्मा।
कालो ह्ययं निरवधिर्विपुला च पृथ्वी॥

—"A kindred spirit is or will be born out of the limitless time and populous earth to accomplish the work" (Bhavabhuti).

About vegetarian diet I have to say this—first, my Master was a vegetarian; but if he was given meat offered to the Goddess, he used to hold it up to his head. The taking of life is undoubtedly sinful; but so long as vegetable food is not made suitable to the human system through progress in chemistry, there is no other alternative but meat-eating. So long as man shall have to live a Râjasika (active) life under circumstances like the present, there is no other way except through meat-eating. It is true that the Emperor Asoka saved the lives of millions of animals by the threat of the sword; but is not the slavery of a thousand years more dreadful than that? Taking the life of a few goats as against the inability to protect the honour of one's own wife and daughter, and to save the morsels for one's children from robbing hands—which of these is more sinful? Rather let those belonging to the upper ten, who do not earn their livelihood by manual labour, not take meat; but the forcing of vegetarianism upon those who have to earn their bread by labouring day and night is one of the causes of the loss of our national freedom. Japan is an example of what good and nourishing food can do.

May the All-powerful Vishveshvari inspire your heart!

OUR PRESENT SOCIAL PROBLEMS[1]

स ईशोऽनिर्वचनीयप्रेमस्वरूपः

— "The Lord whose nature is unspeakable love."

That this characteristic of God mentioned by Nârada is manifest and admitted on all hands is the firm conviction of my life. The aggregate of many individuals is called Samashti (the whole), and each individual is called Vyashti (a part). You and I—each is Vyashti, society is Samashti. You, I, an animal, a bird, a worm, an insect, a tree, a creeper, the earth, a planet, a star—each is Vyashti, while this universe is Samashti, which is called Virât, Hiranyagarbha, or Ishvara in Vedânta, and Brahmâ, Vishnu, Devi, etc., in the Purânas. Whether or not Vyashti has individual freedom, and if it has, what should be its measure, whether or not Vyashti should completely sacrifice its own will, its own happiness for Samashti—are the perennial problems before every society. Society everywhere is busy finding the solution of these problems. These, like big waves, are agitating modern Western society. The doctrine which demands the sacrifice of individual freedom to social supremacy is called socialism, while that which advocates the cause of the individual is called individualism.

Our motherland is a glowing example of the results and consequence of the eternal subjection of the individual to society and forced self-sacrifice by dint of institution and discipline. In this country men are born according to Shâstric injunctions, they eat and drink by prescribed rules throughout life, they go through marriage and kindred functions in the same way; in short, they even die according to Shastric injunctions. The hard discipline, with the exception of one great good point, is fraught with evil. The good point is that men can do one or two things well with very little effort, having practiced them every day through generations. The delicious rice and curry which a cook of this country prepares with the aid of three lumps of earth and a few sticks can be had nowhere else. With the simple mechanism of an antediluvian loom, worth one rupee, and the feet put in a pit, it is possible to make kincobs worth twenty rupees a yard, in this country alone. A torn mat, an earthen lamp, and that fed by castor oil—with the aid of materials such as these, wonderful savants are produced in this country alone. An all-forbearing attachment to an ugly and deformed wife, and a lifelong devotion to a worthless and villainous husband are possible in this country alone. Thus far the bright side.

But all these things are done by people guided like lifeless machines. There is no mental activity, no unfoldment of the heart, no vibration of life, no flux of hope; there is no strong stimulation of the will, no experience of keen pleasure, nor the contact of intense sorrow; there is no stir of inventive genius, no desire for novelty, no appreciation of new things. Clouds never pass away from this mind, the radiant picture of the morning sun never charms this heart. It never even occurs to this mind if there is any better state than this; where it does, it cannot convince; in the event of conviction, effort is lacking; and even where there is effort, lack of enthusiasm kills it out.

If living by rule alone ensures excellence, if it be virtue to follow strictly the rules and customs handed down through generations, say then, who is more virtuous than a tree, who is a greater devotee, a holier saint, than a railway train? Who has ever seen a piece of stone transgress a natural law? Who has ever known cattle to commit sin?

The huge steamer, the mighty railway engine—they are non-intelligent; they move, turn, and run, but they are without intelligence. And yonder tiny worm which moved away from the railway line to save its life, why is it intelligent? There is no manifestation of will in the machine, the machine never wishes to transgress law; the worm wants to oppose law—rises against law whether it succeeds or not; therefore it is intelligent. Greater is the happiness, higher is the Jiva, in proportion as this will is more successfully manifest. The will of God is perfectly fruitful; therefore He is the highest.

What is education? Is it book-learning? No. Is it diverse knowledge? Not even that. The training by which the current and expression of will are brought under control and become fruitful is called education. Now consider, is that education as a result of which the will, being continuously choked by force through generations, is well-nigh killed out; is that education under whose sway even the old ideas, let alone the new ones, are disappearing one by one; is that education which is slowly making man a machine? It is more blessed, in my opinion, even to go wrong, impelled by one's free will and intelligence than to be good as an automaton. Again, can that be called society which is formed by an aggregate of men who are like lumps of clay, like lifeless machines, like heaped up pebbles? How can such society fare well? Were good possible, then instead of being slaves for hundreds of years, we would have been the greatest nation on earth, and this soil of India, instead of being a mine of stupidity, would have been the eternal fountain-head of learning.

Is not self-sacrifice, then, a virtue? Is it not the most virtuous deed to sacrifice the happiness of one, the welfare of one, for the sake of the many? Exactly, but as the Bengali adage goes, "Can beauty be manufactured by rubbing and scrubbing? Can love be generated by effort and compulsion?" What glory is there in the renunciation of an eternal beggar? What virtue is there in the sense control of one devoid of sense-power? What again is the self-sacrifice of one devoid of idea, devoid of heart, devoid of high ambition, and devoid of the conception of what constitutes society? What expression of devotedness to a husband is there by forcing a widow to commit Sati? Why make people do virtuous deeds by teach-

---

1. Translated from a Bengali letter written to Shrimati Mrinalini Bose from Deoghar (Vaidyanâth), on 23rd December, 1898.

ing superstitions? I say, liberate, undo the shackles of people as much as you can. Can dirt be washed by dirt? Can bondage be removed by bondage? Where is the instance? When you would be able to sacrifice all desire for happiness for the sake of society, then you would be the Buddha, then you would be free: that is far off. Again, do you think the way to do it lies through oppression? "Oh, what examples or self-denial are our widows! Oh, how sweet is child-marriage! Is another such custom possible! Can there be anything but love between husband and wife in such a marriage!" such is the whine going round nowadays. But as to the men, the masters of the situation, there is no need of self-denial for them! Is there a virtue higher than serving others? But the same does not apply to Brâhmins — you others do it! The truth is that in this country parents and relatives can ruthlessly sacrifice the best interests of their children and others for their own selfish ends to save themselves by compromise to society; and the teaching of generations rendering the mind callous has made it perfectly easy. He, the brave alone, can deny self. The coward, afraid of the lash, with one hand wipes his eyes and gives with the other. Of what avail are such gifts? It is a far cry to love universal. The young plant should be hedged in and taken care of. One can hope gradually to attain to universal love if one can learn to love one object unselfishly. If devotion to one particular Ishta-Deva is attained, devotion to the universal Virat is gradually possible.

Therefore, when one has been able to deny self for an individual, one should talk of self-sacrifice for the sake of society, not before. It is action with desire that leads to action without desire. Is the renunciation of desire possible if desire did not exist in the beginning? And what could it mean? Can light have any meaning if there is no darkness?

Worship with desire, with attachment, comes first. Commence with the worship of the little, then the greater will come of itself.

Mother, be not anxious. It is against the big tree that the great wind strikes. "Poking a fire makes it burn better"; "A snake struck on the head raises its hood" — and so on. When there comes affliction in the heart, when the storm of sorrow blows all around, and it seems light will be seen no more, when hope and courage are almost gone, it is then, in the midst of this great spiritual tempest, that the light of Brahman within gleams. Brought up in the lap of luxury, lying on a bed of roses and never shedding a tear, who has ever become great, who has ever unfolded the Brahman within? Why do you fear to weep? Weep! Weeping clears the eyes and brings about intuition. Then the vision of diversity — man, animal, tree — slowly melting away, makes room for the infinite realisation of Brahman everywhere and in everything. Then —

समं पश्यन् हि सर्वत्र समवस्थितमीश्वरम् ।

न हिनस्त्यात्मनात्मानं ततो याति परां गतिम् ॥

— "Verily, seeing the same God equally existent every where,

he does not injure the Self by the self, and so goes to the Supreme Goal" (Gitâ, XIII. 28).

HISTORICAL EVOLUTION OF INDIA

OM TAT SAT

Om Namo Bhagavate Râmakrishnâya

नासतः सत् जायते — Existence cannot be produced by non-existence.

Non-existence can never be the cause of what exists. Something cannot come out of nothing. That the law of causation is omnipotent and knows no time or place when it did not exist is a doctrine as old as the Aryan race, sung by its ancient poet-seers, formulated by its philosophers, and made the corner-stone upon which the Hindu man even of today builds his whole scheme of life.

There was an inquisitiveness in the race to start with, which very soon developed into bold analysis, and though, in the first attempt, the work turned out might be like the attempts with shaky hands of the future master-sculptor, it very soon gave way to strict science, bold attempts, and startling results.

Its boldness made these men search every brick of their sacrificial altars; scan, cement, and pulverise every word of their scriptures; arrange, re-arrange, doubt, deny, or explain the ceremonies. It turned their gods inside out, and assigned only a secondary place to their omnipotent, omniscient, omnipresent Creator of the universe, their ancestral Father-in-heaven; or threw Him altogether overboard as useless, and started a world-religion without Him with even now the largest following of any religion. It evolved the science of geometry from the arrangements of bricks to build various altars, and startled the world with astronomical knowledge that arose from the attempts accurately to time their worship and oblations. It made their contribution to the science of mathematics the largest of any race, ancient or modern, and to their knowledge of chemistry, of metallic compounds in medicine, their scale of musical notes, their invention of the bow-instruments — (all) of great service in the building of modern European civilisation. It led them to invent the science of building up the child-mind through shining fables, of which every child in every civilised country learns in a nursery or a school and carries an impress through life.

Behind and before this analytical keenness, covering it as in a velvet sheath, was the other great mental peculiarity of the race — poetic insight. Its religion, its philosophy, its history, its ethics, its politics were all inlaid in a flower-bed of poetic imagery — the miracle of language which was called Sanskrit or "perfected", lending itself to expressing and manipulating them better than any other tongue. The aid of melodious numbers was invoked even to express the hard facts of mathematics.

This analytical power and the boldness of poetical visions which urged it onward are the two great internal causes in the make-up of the Hindu race. They together formed, as it were, the keynote to the national character. This combination is what is always making the race press onwards beyond the senses — the secret of those speculations which are like the steel blades the artisans used to manufacture — cutting through bars of iron, yet pliable enough to be easily bent into a circle.

They wrought poetry in silver and gold; the symphony of jewels, the maze of marble wonders, the music of colours, the fine fabrics which belong more to the fairyland of dreams than to the real — have back of them thousands of years of working of this national trait.

Arts and sciences, even the realities of domestic life, are covered with a mass of poetical conceptions, which are pressed forward till the sensuous touches the supersensuous and the real gets the rose-hue of the unreal.

The earliest glimpses we have of this race show it already in the possession of this characteristic, as an instrument of some use in its hands. Many forms of religion and society must have been left behind in the onward march, before we find the race as depicted in the scriptures, the Vedas.

An organised pantheon, elaborate ceremonials, divisions of society into hereditary classes necessitated by a variety of occupations, a great many necessaries and a good many luxuries of life are already there.

Most modern scholars are agreed that surroundings as to climate and conditions, purely Indian, were not yet working on the race.

Onwards through several centuries, we come to a multitude surrounded by the snows of Himalayas on the north and the heat of the south — vast plains, interminable forests, through which mighty rivers roll their tides. We catch a glimpse of different races — Dravidians, Tartars, and Aboriginals pouring in their quota of blood, of speech, of manners and religions. And at last a great nation emerges to our view — still keeping the type of the Aryan — stronger, broader, and more organised by the assimilation. We find the central assimilative core giving its type and character to the whole mass, clinging on with great pride to its name of "Aryan", and, though willing to give other races the benefits of its civilisation, it was by no means willing to admit them within the "Aryan" pale.

The Indian climate again gave a higher direction to the genius of the race. In a land where nature was propitious and yielded easy victories, the national mind started to grapple with and conquer the higher problems of life in the field of thought. Naturally the thinker, the priest, became the highest class in the Indian society, and not the man of the sword. The priests again, even at that dawn of history, put most of their energy in elaborating rituals; and when the nation began to find the load of ceremonies and lifeless rituals too heavy — came the first philosophical speculations, and the royal race was the first to break through the maze of killing rituals.

On the one hand, the majority of the priests impelled by economical considerations were bound to defend that form of religion which made their existence a necessity of society and assigned them the highest place in the scale of caste; on the other hand, the king-caste, whose strong right hand guarded and guided the nation and who now found itself as leading in the higher thoughts also, were loath to give up the first place to men who only knew how to conduct a ceremonial. There were then others, recruited from both the priests and king-castes, who ridiculed equally the ritualists and philosophers, declared spiritualism as fraud and priestcraft, and upheld the attainment of material comforts as the highest goal of life. The people, tired of ceremonials and wondering at the philosophers, joined in masses the materialists. This was the beginning of that caste question and that triangular fight in India between ceremonials, philosophy, and materialism which has come down unsolved to our own days.

The first solution of the difficulty attempted was by applying the eclecticism which from the earliest days had taught the people to see in differences the same truth in various garbs. The great leader of this school, Krishna — himself of royal race — and his sermon, the Gîtâ, have after various vicissitudes, brought about by the upheavals of the Jains, the Buddhists, and other sects, fairly established themselves as the "Prophet" of India and the truest philosophy of life. Though the tension was toned down for the time, it did not satisfy the social wants which were among the causes — the claim of the king-race to stand first in the scale of caste and the popular intolerance of priestly privilege. Krishna had opened the gates of spiritual knowledge and attainment to all irrespective of sex or caste, but he left undisturbed the same problem on the social side. This again has come down to our own days, in spite of the gigantic struggle of the Buddhists, Vaishnavas, etc. to attain social equality for all.

Modern India admits spiritual equality of all souls — but strictly keeps the social difference.

Thus we find the struggle renewed all along the line in the seventh century before the Christian era and finally in the sixth, overwhelming the ancient order of things under Shâkya Muni, the Buddha. In their reaction against the privileged priesthood, Buddhists swept off almost every bit of the old ritual of the Vedas, subordinated the gods of the Vedas to the position of servants to their own human saints, and declared the "Creator and Supreme Ruler" as an invention of priestcraft and superstition.

But the aim of Buddhism was reform of the Vedic religion by standing against ceremonials requiring offerings of animals, against hereditary caste and exclusive priesthood, and against belief in permanent souls. It never attempted to destroy that religion, or overturn the social order. It introduced a vigorous method by organising a class of Sannyâsins into a strong monastic brotherhood, and the Brahmavâdinis into a body of nuns — by introducing images of saints in the place of altar-fires.

It is probable that the reformers had for centuries the majority of the Indian people with them. The older forces were never entirely pacified, but they underwent a good deal of modification during the centuries of Buddhistic supremacy.

In ancient India the centres of national life were always the intellectual and spiritual and not political. Of old, as now, political and social power has been always subordinated to spiritual and intellectual. The outburst of national life was round colleges of sages and spiritual teachers. We thus find the Samitis of the Panchâlas, of the Kâshyas (of Varanasi), the Maithilas standing out as great centres of spiritual culture and philosophy, even in tile Upanishads. Again these centres in turn became the focus of political ambition of the various divisions of the Aryans.

The great epic Mahâbhârata tells us of the war of the Kurus and Panchalas for supremacy over the nation, in which they destroyed each other. The spiritual supremacy veered round and centred in the East among the Magadhas and Maithilas, and after the Kuru-Panchala war a sort of supremacy was obtained by the kings of Magadha.

The Buddhist reformation and its chief field of activity were also in the same eastern region; and when the Maurya kings, forced possibly by the bar sinister on their escutcheon, patronised and led the new movement, the new priest power joined hands with the political power of the empire of Pataliputra. The popularity of Buddhism and its fresh vigour made the Maurya kings the greatest emperors that India ever had. The power of the Maurya sovereigns made Buddhism that world-wide religion that we see even today.

The exclusiveness of the old form of Vedic religions debarred it from taking ready help from outside. At the same time it kept it pure and free from many debasing elements which Buddhism in its propagandist zeal was forced to assimilate.

This extreme adaptability in the long run made Indian Buddhism lose almost all its individuality, and extreme desire to be of the people made it unfit to cope with the intellectual forces of the mother religion in a few centuries. The Vedic party in the meanwhile got rid of a good deal of its most objectionable features, as animal sacrifice, and took lessons from the rival daughter in the judicious use of images, temple processions, and other impressive performances, and stood ready to take within her fold the whole empire of Indian Buddhism, already tottering to its fall.

And the crash came with the Scythian invasions and the total destruction of the empire of Pataliputra.

The invaders, already incensed at the invasion of their central Asiatic home by the preachers of Buddhism, found in the sun-worship of the Brahmins a great sympathy with their own solar religion—and when the Brahminist party were ready to adapt and spiritualise many of the customs of the new-comers, the invaders threw themselves heart and soul into the Brahminic cause.

Then there is a veil of darkness and shifting shadows; there are tumults of war, rumours of massacres; and the next scene rises upon a new phase of things.

The empire of Magadha was gone. Most of northern India was under the rule of petty chiefs always at war with one another. Buddhism was almost extinct except in some eastern and Himalayan provinces and in the extreme south and the nation after centuries of struggle against the power of a hereditary priesthood awoke to find itself in the clutches of a double priesthood of hereditary Brahmins and exclusive monks of the new regime, with all the powers of the Buddhistic organisation and without their sympathy for the people.

A renascent India, bought by the velour and blood of the heroic Rajputs, defined by the merciless intellect of a Brahmin from the same historical thought-centre of Mithila, led by a new philosophical impulse organised by Shankara and his bands of Sannyasins, and beautified by the arts and literature of the courts of Mâlavâ—arose on the ruins of the old.

The task before it was profound, problems vaster than any their ancestors had ever faced. A comparatively small and compact race of the same blood and speech and the same social and religious aspiration, trying to save its unity by unscalable walls around itself, grew huge by multiplication and addition during the Buddhistic supremacy; and (it) was divided by race, colour, speech, spiritual instinct, and social ambitions into hopelessly jarring factions. And this had to be unified and welded into one gigantic nation. This task Buddhism had also come to solve, and had taken it up when the proportions were not so vast.

So long it was a question of Aryanising the other types that were pressing for admission and thus, out of different elements, making a huge Aryan body. In spite of concessions and compromises, Buddhism was eminently successful and remained the national religion of India. But the time came when the allurements of sensual forms of worship, indiscriminately taken in along with various low races, were too dangerous for the central Aryan core, and a longer contact would certainly have destroyed the civilisation of the Aryans. Then came a natural reaction for self-preservation, and Buddhism and separate sect ceased to live in most parts of its land of birth.

The reaction-movement, led in close succession by Kumârila in the north, and Shankara and Râmânuja in the south, has become the last embodiment of that vast accumulation of sects and doctrines and rituals called Hinduism. For the last thousand years or more, its great task has been assimilation, with now and then an outburst of reformation. This reaction first wanted to revive the rituals of the Vedas—failing which, it made the Upanishads or the philosophic portions of the Vedas its basis. It brought Vyasa's system of Mimâmsâ philosophy and Krishna's sermon, the Gita, to the forefront; and all succeeding movements have followed the same. The movement of Shankara forced its way through its high intellectuality; but it could be of little service to the masses, because of its adherence to strict caste-laws, very small scope for ordinary emotion, and making Sanskrit the only vehicle of communication. Ramanuja on the other hand, with a most practical philosophy, a great appeal to the emotions, an entire denial of birthrights before spiritual attainments, and appeals through the popular tongue completely succeeded in bringing the masses back to the Vedic religion.

The northern reaction of ritualism was followed by the fitful glory of the Malava empire. With the destruction of that in a short time, northern India went to sleep as it were, for a long period, to be rudely awakened by the thundering onrush of Mohammedan cavalry across the passes of Afghanistan. In the south, however, the spiritual upheaval of Shankara and Ramanuja was followed by the usual Indian sequence of united races and powerful empires. It was the home of refuge of Indian religion and civilisation, when northern India from sea to sea lay bound at the feet of Central Asiatic conquerors. The Mohammedan tried for centuries to subjugate the south, but can scarcely be said to have got even a strong foothold; and when the strong and united empire of the Moguls was very near completing its conquest, the hills and plateaus of the south poured in their bands of fighting peasant horsemen, determined to die for the religion which Râmdâs preached and Tukâ sang; and in a short time the gigantic empire of the Moguls was only a name.

The movements in northern India during the Mohammedan period are characterised by their uniform attempt to hold the masses back from joining the religion of the conquerors—which brought in its train social and spiritual equality for all.

The friars of the orders founded by Râmânanda, Kabir, Dâdu, Chaitanya, or Nânak were all agreed in preaching the equality of man, however differing from each other in philosophy. Their energy was for the most part spent in checking the rapid conquest of Islam among the masses, and they had very little left to give birth to new thoughts and aspirations. Though evidently successful in their purpose of keeping the masses within the fold of the old religion, and tempering the fanaticism of the Mohammedans, they were mere apologists, struggling to obtain permission to live.

One great prophet, however, arose in the north, Govind Singh, the last Guru of the Sikhs, with creative genius; and the result of his spiritual work was followed by the well-known political organisation of the Sikhs. We have seen throughout the history of India, a spirtitual upheaval is almost always succeeded by a political unity extending over more or less area of the continent, which in its turn helps to strengthen the spiritual aspiration that brings it to being. But the spiritual aspiration that preceded the rise of the Mahratta or the Sikh empire was entirely reactionary. We seek in vain to find in the court of Poona or Lahore even a ray of reflection of that intellectual glory which surrounded the courts of the Muguls, much less the brilliance of Malava or Vidyânagara. It was

intellectually the darkest period of Indian history; and both these meteoric empires, representing the upheaval of mass-fanaticism and hating culture with all their hearts, lost all their motive power as soon as they had succeeded in destroying the rule of the hated Mohammedans.

Then there came again a period of confusion. Friends and foes, the Mogul empire and its destroyers, and the till then peaceful foreign traders, French and English, all joined in a mêlée of fight. For more than half a century there was nothing but war and pillage and destruction. And when the smoke and dust cleared, England was stalking victorious over the rest. There has been half a century of peace and law and order under the sway of Britain. Time alone will prove if it is the order of progress or not.

There have been a few religious movements amongst the Indian people during the British rule, following the same line that was taken up by northern Indian sects during the sway of the empire of Delhi. They are the voices of the dead or the dying—the feeble tones of a terrorised people, pleading for permission to live. They are ever eager to adjust their spiritual or social surroundings according to the tastes of the conquerors—if they are only left the right to live, especially the sects under the English domination, in which social differences with the conquering race are more glaring than the spiritual. The Hindu sects of the century seem to have set one ideal of truth before them—the approval of their English masters. No wonder that these sects have mushroom lives to live. The vast body of the Indian people religiously hold aloof from them, and the only popular recognition they get is the jubilation of the people when they die.

But possibly, for some time yet, it cannot be otherwise.

THE STORY OF THE BOY GOPALA

"O mother! I am so afraid to go to school through the woods alone; other boys have servants or somebody to bring them to school or take them home-why cannot I have someone to bring me home?"-thus said Gopâla, a little Brahmin boy, to his mother one winter afternoon when he was getting ready for school. The school hours were in the morning and afternoon. It was dark when the school closed in the afternoon, and the path lay through the woods.

Gopala's mother was a widow. His father who had lived as a Brahmin should-never caring for the goods of the world, studying and teaching, worshipping and helping others to worship—died when Gopala was a baby. And the poor widow retired entirely from the concerns of the world-even from that little she ever had-her soul given entirely to God, and waiting patiently with prayers, fasting, and discipline, for the great deliverer death, to meet in another life, him who was the eternal companion of her joys and sorrows, her partner in the good and evil of the beginningless chain of lives. She lived in her little cottage. A small rice-field her husband received as sacred gift to learning brought her sufficient rice; and the piece of land that surrounded her cottage, with its clumps of bamboos, a few cocoanut palms, a few mangoes, and lichis, with the help of the kindly village folk, brought forth sufficient vegetables all the year round. For the rest, she worked hard every day for hours at the spinning-wheel.

She was up long before the rosy dawn touched the tufted heads of the palms, long before the birds had begun to warble in their nests, and sitting on her bed-a mat on the ground covered with a blanket-repeated the sacred names of the holy women of the past, saluted the ancient sages, recited the sacred names of Nârâyana the Refuge of mankind, of Shiva the merciful, of Târâ the Saviour Mother; and above all, (she) prayed to Him whom her heart most loved, Krishna, who had taken the form of Gopala, a cowherd, to teach and save mankind, and rejoiced that by one day she was nearer to him who had gone ahead, and with him nearer by a day to Him, the Cowherd.

Before the light of the day, she had her bath in the neighbouring stream, praying that her mind might be made as clean by the mercy of Krishna, as her body by the water. Then she put on her fresh-washed whiter cotton garment, collected some flowers, rubbed a piece of sandalwood on a circular stone with a little water to make a fragrant paste, gathered a few sweet-scented Tulasi leaves, and retired into a little room in the cottage, kept apart for worship. In this room she kept her Baby Cowherd; on a small wooden throne under a small silk canopy; on a small velvet cushion, almost covered with flowers, was placed a bronze image of Krishna as a baby. Her mother's heart could only be satisfied by conceiving God as her baby. Many and many a time her learned husband had talked to her of Him who is preached in the Vedas, the formless, the infinite, the impersonal. She listened with all attention, and the conclusion was always the same-what is written in the Vedas must be true; but, oh! it was so immense, so far off, and she, only a weak, ignorant woman; and then, it was also written: "In whatsoever form one seeks Me, I reach him in that form, for all mankind are but following the paths I laid down for them"-and that was enough. She wanted to know no more. And there she was-all of the devotion, of faith, of love her heart was capable of, was there in Krishna, the Baby Cowherd, and all that heart entwined round the visible Cowherd, this little bronze image. Then again she had heard: "Serve Me as you would a being of flesh and blood, with love and purity, and I accept that all." So she served as she would a master, a beloved teacher, above all, as she would serve the apple of her eye, her only child, her son.

So she bathed and dressed the image, burned incense before it, and for offering?-oh, she was so poor!-but with tears in her eyes she remembered her husband reading from the books: "I accept with gladness even leaves and flowers, fruits and water, whatever is offered with love", and she offered: "Thou for whom the world of flowers bloom, accept my few common flowers. Thou who feedest the universe, accept my poor offerings of fruits. I am weak, I am ignorant. I do not know how to

approach Thee, how to worship Thee, my God, my Cowherd, my child; let my worship be pure, my love for Thee selfless; and if there is any virtue in worship, let it be Thine, grant me only love, love that never asks for anything-'never seeks for anything but love'." Perchance the mendicant in his morning call was singing in the little yard:

Thy knowledge, man! I value not,
It is thy love I fear;
It is thy love that shakes My throne,
Brings God to human tear.
For love behold the Lord of all,
The formless, ever free,
Is made to take the human form
To play and live with thee.
What learning, they of Vrindâ's groves,
The herdsmen, ever got?
What science, girls that milked the kine?
They loved, and Me they bought.

Then, in the Divine, the mother-heart found her earthly son Gopala (lit. cowherd), named after the Divine Cowherd. And the soul which would almost mechanically move among its earthly surroundings-which, as it were, was constantly floating in a heavenly ether ready to drift away from contact of things material found its earthly moorings in her child. It was the only thing left to her to pile all her earthly joys and love on. Were not her movements, her thoughts, her pleasures, her very life for that little one that bound her to life?

For years she watched over the day-to-day unfolding of that baby life with all a mother's care; and now that he was old enough to go to school, how hard she worked for months to get the necessaries for the young scholar!

The necessaries however were few. In a land where men contentedly pass their lives poring over books in the the light of a mud lamp, with an ounce of oil in which is a thin cotton wick-a rush mat being the only furniture about them-the necessaries of a student are not many. Yet there were some, and even those cost many a day of hard work to the poor mother.

How for days she toiled over her wheel to buy Gopala a new cotton Dhoti and a piece of cotton Châdar, the under and upper coverings, the small mat in which Gopala was to put his bundle of palm leaves for writing and his reed pens, and which he was to carry rolled up under his arm to be used as his seat at school-and the inkstand. And what joy to her it was, when on a day of good omen Gopal attempted to write his first letters, only a mother's heart, a poor mother's, can know!

But today there is a dark shadow in her mind. Gopala is frightened to go alone through the wood. Never before had she felt her widowhood, her loneliness, her poverty so bitter. For a moment it was all dark, but she recalled to her mind what she had heard of the eternal promise: "Those that depend on Me giving up all other thoughts, to them I Myself carry whatever is necessary." And she was one of the souls who could believe.

So the mother wiped her tears and told her child that he need not fear. For in those woods lived another son of hers tending cattle, and also called Gopala; and if he was ever afraid passing through them, he had only to call on brother Gopala!

The child was that mother's son, and he believed.

That day, coming home from school through the wood, Gopala was frightened and called upon his brother Gopala, the cowherd: "Brother cowherd, are you here? Mother said you are, and I am to call on you: I am frightened being alone." And a voice came from behind the trees: "Don't be afraid, little brother, I am here; go home without fear."

Thus every day the boy called, and the voice answered. The mother heard of it with wonder and love; and she instructed her child to ask the brother of the wood to show himself the next time.

The next day the boy, when passing through the woods, called upon his brother. The voice came as usual, but the boy asked the brother in the woods to show himself to him. The voice replied, "I am busy today, brother, and cannot come." But the boy insisted, and out of the shade of the trees came the Cowherd of the woods, a boy dressed in the garb of cowherds, with a little crown on his head in which were peacock's feathers, and the cowherd's flute in his hands.

And they were so happy: they played together for hours in the woods, climbing trees, gathering fruits and flowers-the widow's Gopala and the Gopala of the woods, till it was almost late for school. Then the widow's Gopala went to school with a reluctant heart, and nearly forgot all his lesson, his mind eager to return to the woods and play with his brother.

Months passed this wise. The poor mother heard of it day by day and, in the joy of this Divine mercy, forgot her widowhood, her poverty, and blessed her miseries a thousand times.

Then there came some religious ceremonies which the teacher had to perform in honour of his ancestors. These village teachers, managing alone a number of boys and receiving no fixed fees from them, have to depend a great deal upon presents when the occasion requires them.

Each pupil brought in his share, in goods or money. And Gopala, the orphan, the widow's son!-the other boys smiled a smile of contempt on him when they talked of the presents they were bringing.

That night Gopala's heart was heavy, and he asked his mother for some present for the teacher, and the poor mother had nothing.

But she determined to do what she had been doing all her life, to depend on the Cowherd, and told her son to ask from his brother Gopala in the forests for some present for the teacher.

The next day, after Gopala had met the Cowherd boy in the woods as usual and after they had some games together, Gopala told his brother of the forest the grief that was in his mind and begged him to give him something to present his teacher with.

"Brother Gopala," said the cowherd, "I am only a cowherd you see, and have no money, but take this pot of cream as from a poor cowherd and present it to your teacher."

Gopala, quite glad that he now had something to give his teacher, more so because it was a present from his brother in the forest, hastened to the home of the teacher and stood with an eager heart behind a crowd of boys handing over their presents to the teacher. Many and varied were the presents they had brought, and no one thought of looking even at the present of the orphan.

The neglect was quite disheartening; tears stood in the eyes of Gopala, when by a sudden stroke of fortune the teacher happened to take notice of him. He took the small pot of cream from Gopala's hand, and poured the cream into a big vessel, when to his wonder the pot filled up again! Again he emptied the contents into a bigger vessel, again it was full; and thus it went on, the small pot filling up quicker than he could empty it.

Then amazement took hold of everyone; and the teacher took the poor orphan in his arms and inquired about the pot of cream.

Gopala told his teacher all about his brother Cowherd in the forest, how he answered his call, how he played with him, and how at last he gave him the pot of cream.

The teacher asked Gopala to take him to the woods and show him his brother of the woods, and Gopala was only too glad to take his teacher there.

The boy called upon his brother to appear, but there was no voice even that day. He called again and again. No answer. And then the boy entreated his brother in the forest to speak, else the teacher would think he was not speaking the truth. Then came the voice as from a great distance:

"Gopala, thy mother's and thy love and faith brought Me to thee; but tell thy teacher, he will have to wait a long while yet."

HINDUISM AND SHRI RAMAKRISHNA

Translated from Bengali

By the word "Shastras" the Vedas without beginning or end are meant. In matters of religious duty the Vedas are the only capable authority.

The Puranas and other religious scriptures are all denoted by the word "Smriti". And their authority goes so far as they follow the Vedas and do not contradict them.

Truth is of two kinds: (1) that which is cognisable by the five ordinary senses of man, and by reasonings based thereon; (2) that which is cognisable by the subtle, supersensuous power of Yoga.

Knowledge acquired by the first means is called science; and knowledge acquired by the second is called the Vedas.

The whole body of supersensuous truths, having no beginning or end, and called by the name of the Vedas, is ever-existent. The Creator Himself is creating, preserving, and destroying the universe with the help of these truths.

The person in whom this supersensuous power is manifested is called a Rishi, and the supersensuous truths which he realises by this power are called the Vedas.

This Rishihood, this power of supersensuous perception of the Vedas, is real religion. And so long as this does not develop in the life of an initiate, so long is religion a mere empty word to him, and it is to be understood that he has not taken yet the first step in religion.

The authority of the Vedas extends to all ages, climes and persons; that is to say, their application is not confined to any particular place, time, and persons.

The Vedas are the only exponent of the universal religion.

Although the supersensuous vision of truths is to be met with in some measure in our Puranas and Itihasas and in the religious scriptures of other races, still the fourfold scripture known among the Aryan race as the Vedas being the first, the most complete, and the most undistorted collection of spiritual truths, deserve to occupy the highest place among all scriptures, command the respect of all nations of the earth, and furnish the rationale of all their respective scriptures.

With regard to the whole Vedic collection of truths discovered by the Aryan race, this also has to be understood that those portions alone which do not refer to purely secular matters and which do not merely record tradition or history, or merely provide incentives to duty, form the Vedas in the real sense.

The Vedas are divided into two portions, the Jnâna-kânda (knowledge-portion) and the Karma-kânda (ritual-portion). The ceremonies and the fruits of the Karma-kanda are confined within the limits of the world of Mâyâ, and therefore they have been undergoing and will undergo transformation according to the law of change which operates through time, space, and personality.

Social laws and customs likewise, being based on this Karma-kanda, have been changing and will continue to change hereafter. Minor social usages also will be recognised and accepted when they are compatible with the spirit of the true scriptures and the conduct and example of holy sages. But blind allegiance only to usages such as are repugnant to the spirit of the Shastras and the conduct of holy sages has been one of the main causes of the downfall of the Aryan race.

It is the Jnana-kanda or the Vedanta only that has for all time commanded recognition for leading men across Maya and bestowing salvation on them through the practice of Yoga, Bhakti, Jnana, or selfless work; and as its validity and authority remain unaffected by any limitations of time, place or persons, it is the only exponent of the universal and eternal religion for all mankind.

The Samhitas of Manu and other sages, following the lines laid down in the Karma-kanda, have mainly ordained rules of conduct conducive to social welfare, according to the exigencies of time, place, and persons. The Puranas etc. have taken up the truths imbedded in the Vedanta and have explained them in detail in the course of describing the exalted life and deeds of Avataras and others. They have each emphasised, besides, some out of the infinite aspects of the Divine Lord to teach men about them.

But when by the process of time, fallen from the true ideals and rules of conduct and devoid of the spirit of renunciation, addicted only to blind usages, and degraded in intellect, the descendants of the Aryans failed to appreciate even the spirit of these Puranas etc. which taught men of ordinary intelligence the abstruse truths of the Vedanta in concrete form and diffuse language and appeared antagonistic to one another on the surface, because of each inculcating with special emphasis only particular aspects of the spiritual ideal —

And when, as a consequence, they reduced India, the fair land of religion, to a scene of almost infernal confusion by breaking up piecemeal the one Eternal Religion of the Vedas (Sanâtana Dharma), the grand synthesis of all the aspects of the spiritual ideal, into conflicting sects and by seeking to sacrifice one another in the flames of sectarian hatred and intolerance —

Then it was that Shri Bhagavan Ramakrishna incarnated himself in India, to demonstrate what the true religion of the Aryan race is; to show where amidst all its many divisions and offshoots, scattered over the land in the course of its immemorial history, lies the true unity of the Hindu religion, which by its overwhelming number of sects discordant to superficial view, quarrelling constantly with each other and abounding in customs divergent in every way, has constituted itself a misleading enigma for our countrymen and the butt of contempt for foreigners; and above all, to hold up before men, for their lasting welfare, as a living embodiment of the Sanatana Dharma, his own wonderful life into which he infused the universal spirit and character of this Dharma, so long cast into oblivion by the process of time.

In order to show how the Vedic truths — eternally existent as the instrument with the Creator in His work of creation, preservation, and dissolution — reveal themselves spontaneously in the minds of the Rishis purified from all impressions of worldly attachment, and because such verification and confirmation of the scriptural truths will help the revival, reinstatement, and spread of religion — the Lord, though the very embodiment of the Vedas, in this His new incarnation has thoroughly discarded all external forms of learning.

That the Lord incarnates again and again in human form for the protection of the Vedas or the true religion, and of Brahminhood or the ministry of that religion—is a doctrine well established in the Puranas etc.

The waters of a river falling in a cataract acquire greater velocity, the rising wave after a hollow swells higher; so after every spell of decline, the Aryan society recovering from all the evils by the merciful dispensation of Providence has risen the more glorious and powerful—such is the testimony of history.

After rising from every fall, our revived society is expressing more and more its innate eternal perfection, and so also the omnipresent Lord in each successive incarnation is manifesting Himself more and more.

Again and again has our country fallen into a swoon, as it were, and again and again has India's Lord, by the manifestation of Himself, revivified her.

But greater than the present deep dismal night, now almost over, no pall of darkness had ever before enveloped this holy land of ours. And compared with the depth of this fall, all previous falls appear like little hoof-marks.

Therefore, before the effulgence of this new awakening' the glory of all past revivals in her history will pale like stars before the rising sun; and compared with this mighty manifestation of renewed strength, all the many past epochs of such restoration will be as child's play.

The various constituent ideals of the Religion Eternal, during its present state of decline, have been lying scattered here and there for want of competent men to realise them—some being preserved partially among small sects and some completely lost.

But strong in the strength of this new spiritual renaissance, men, after reorganising these scattered and disconnected spiritual ideals, will be able to comprehend and practice them in their own lives and also to recover from oblivion those that are lost. And as the sure pledge of this glorious future, the all-merciful Lord has manifested in the present age, as stated above, an incarnation which in point of completeness in revelation, its synthetic harmonising of all ideals, and its promoting of every sphere of spiritual culture, surpasses the manifestations of all past ages.

So at the very dawn of this momentous epoch, the reconciliation of all aspects and ideals of religious thought and worship is being proclaimed; this boundless, all embracing idea had been lying inherent, but so long concealed, in the Religion Eternal and its scriptures, and now rediscovered, it is being declared to humanity in a trumpet voice.

This epochal new dispensation is the harbinger of great good to the whole world, specially to India; and the inspirer of this dispensation, Shri Bhagavan Ramakrishna, is the reformed and remodelled manifestation of all the past great epoch-makers in religion. O man, have faith in this, and lay to heart.

The dead never return; the past night does not reappear; a spent-up tidal wave does not rise anew; neither does man inhabit the same body over again. So from the worship of the dead past, O man, we invite you to the worship of the living present; from the regretful brooding over bygones, we invite you to the activities of the present; from the waste of energy in retracing lost and demolished pathways, we call you back to broad new-laid highways lying very near. He that is wise, let him understand.

Of that power, which at the very first impulse has roused distant echoes from all the four quarters of the globe, conceive in your mind the manifestation in its fullness; and discarding all idle misgivings, weaknesses, and the jealousies characteristic of enslaved peoples, come and help in the turning of this mighty wheel of new dispensation!

With the conviction firmly rooted in your heart that you are the servants of the Lord, His children, helpers in the fulfilment of His purpose, enter the arena of work.

THE BENGALI LANGUAGE

Written for the "Udbodhan"

In our country, owing to all learning being in Sanskrit from the ancient times, there has arisen an immeasurable gulf between the learned and the common folk. All the great personages, from Buddha down to Chaitanya and Ramakrishna, who came for the well-being of the world, taught the common people in the language of the people themselves. Of course, scholarship is an excellent thing; but cannot scholarship be displayed through any other medium than a language that is stiff and unintelligible, that is unnatural and merely artificial? Is there no room for art in the spoken language? What is the use of creating an unnatural language to the exclusion of the natural one? Do you not think out your scholastic researches in the language which you are accustomed to speak at home? Why then do you introduce such a queer and unwieldy thing when you proceed to put them in black and white? The language in which you think out philosophy and science in your mind, and argue with others in public—is not that the language for writing philosophy and science? If it is not, how then do you reason out those truths within yourselves and in company of others in that very language? The language in which we naturally express ourselves, in which we communicate our anger, grief, or love, etc.— there cannot be a fitter language than that. We must stick to that idea, that manner of expression, that diction and all. No artificial language can ever have that force, and that brevity and expressiveness, or admit of being given any turn you please, as that spoken language. Language must be made like pure steel—turn and twist it any way you like, it is again the same—it cleaves a rock in twain at one stroke, without its edge being turned. Our language is becoming artificial by imitating the slow and pompous movement—and only that—of Sanskrit. And language is the chief means and index of a nation's progress.

If you say, "It is all right, but there are various kinds of dialects in different parts of Bengal—which of them to accept?"—the answer is: We must accept that which is gaining strength and spreading through natural laws, that is to say, the language of Calcutta. East or west, from wheresoever people may come, once they breathe in the air of Calcutta, they are found to speak the language in vogue there; so nature herself points out which language to write in. The more railroads and facilities of communication there are, the more will the difference of east and west disappear, and from Chittagong to Baidyanath there will be that one language, viz that of Calcutta. It is not the question which district possesses a language most approaching Sanskrit—you must see which language is triumphing. When it is evident that the language of Calcutta will soon become the language of the whole of Bengal, then, if one has to make the written and spoken language the same, one would, if one is intelligent enough certainly make the language of Calcutta one's foundation. Here local jealousies also should be thrown overboard. Where the welfare of the whole province is concerned, you must overlook the claims to superiority of your own district or village.

Language is the vehicle of ideas. It is the ideas that are of prime importance, language comes after. Does it look well to place a monkey on a horse that has trappings of diamonds and pearls? Just look at Sanskrit. Look at the Sanskrit of the Brâhmanas, at Shabara Swâmi's commentary on the Mimâmsâ philosophy, the Mahâbhâshya of Patanjali, and, finally, at the great Commentary of Achârya Shankara: and look also at the Sanskrit of comparatively recent times. You will at once understand that so long as a man is alive, he talks a living language, but when he is dead, he speaks a dead language. The nearer death approaches, the more does the power of original thinking wane, the more is there the attempt to bury one or two rotten ideas under a heap of flowers and scents. Great God! What a parade they make! After ten pages of big adjectives, all on a sudden you have—"There lived the King!" Oh, what an array of spun-out adjectives, and giant compounds, and skilful puns! They are symptoms of death. When the country began to decay, then all these signs became manifest. It was not merely in language—all the arts began to manifest them. A building now neither expressed any idea nor followed any style; the columns were turned and turned till they had all their strength taken out of them. The ornaments pierced the nose and the neck and converted the wearer into a veritable ogress; but oh, the profusion of leaves and foliage carved fantastically in them! Again, in music, nobody, not even the sage Bharata, the originator of dramatic performances, could understand whether it was singing, or weeping, or wrangling, and what meaning or purpose it sought to convey! And what an abundance of intricacies in that music! What labyrinths of flourishes—enough to strain all one's nerves! Over and above that, that music had its birth in the nasal tone uttered through the teeth compressed, in imitation of the Mohammedan musical experts! Nowadays there is an indication of correcting these; now will people gradually understand that a language, or art, or music that expresses no meaning and is lifeless is of no good. Now they will understand that the more strength is

infused into the national life, the more will language art, and music, etc. become spontaneously instinct with ideas and life. The volume of meaning that a couple of words of everyday use will convey, you may search in vain in two thousand set epithets. Then every image of the Deity will inspire devotion, every girl decked in ornaments will appear to be a goddess, and every house and room and furniture will be animated with the vibration of life.

MATTER FOR SERIOUS THOUGHT

Translated from Bengali

A man presented himself to be blessed by a sight of the Deity. He had an access of joy and devotion at the sight; and perhaps to pay back the good he received, he burst out into a song. In one corner of the hall, reclining against a pillar, was Chobeji dozing. He was the priest in the temple, an athlete, a player on the guitar, was a good hand in swallowing two jugfuls of Bhâng (an intoxicating drink.), and had various other qualifications besides. All on a sudden, a dreadful noise assailing his tympanum, the fantastic universe conjured up under the influence of the inebriating liquor vanished for a moment from Chobeji's enormous chest of two and forty inches! And casting his crimson-tinged, languid eyes around in search of the cause of disturbance to his tranquil mind, Chobeji discovered that in front of the God was a man singing, overwhelmed with his own feelings, in a tune as touching as the scouring of cauldrons in a festive house, and, in so doing, he was subjecting the shades of the whole host of musical masters like Nârada, Bharata, Hanumân, Nâyaka, and the rest to ineffable anguish. The mortified Chobeji in a sharp reprimanding tone addressed the man who had been the direct obstacle to his enjoyment of that peculiar bliss of inebriation, "Hello, my friend, what are you shouting like that for, without caring for time or tune?" Quick came the response, "What need I care for time or tune? I am trying to win the Lord's heart." "Humph!" retorted Chobeji, "do you think the Lord is such a fool? You must be mad! You could not win my heart even—and has the Lord less brains than I?"

***

The Lord has declared unto Arjuna: "Take thou refuge in Me, thou hast nothing else to do. And I shall deliver thee." Bholâchand is mighty glad to hear this from some people; he now and then yells out in a trenchant note: "I have taken refuge in the Lord. I shall not have to do anything further." Bholachand is under the: impression that it is the height of devotion to bawl out those words repeatedly in the harshest tone possible. Moreover, he does not fail to make it known now and then in the aforesaid pitch that he is ever ready to lay down his life even, for the Lord's sake, and that if the Lord does not voluntarily surrender Himself to this tie of devotion, everything would be hollow and false. And a few foolish satellites of his also share the same opinion. But Bholachand is not prepared to give up a single piece of wickedness for the sake of the Lord. Well, is the Lord really such a fool? Why, this is not enough to hoodwink us even!

**

Bholâ Puri an out and out Vedantin—in everything he is careful to trumpet his Brahminhood. If all people are about to starve for food around Bhola Puri, it does not touch him even in the least; he expounds the unsubstantiality of pleasure and pain. If through disease, or affliction, or starvation people die by the thousand, what matters even that to him? He at once reflects on the immortality of the soul! If the strong overpower the weak and even kill them before his very eyes, Bhola Puri is lost in the profound depths of the meaning of the spiritual dictum, "The soul neither kills nor is killed." He is exceedingly averse to action of any kind. If hard pressed, he replies that he finished all actions in his previous births. But Bhola Puri's realisation of unity of the Self suffers a terrible check when he is hurt in one point. When there is some anomaly in the completeness of his Bhikshâ, or when the householder is unwilling to offer him worship according to his expectations, then, in the opinion of Puriji, there are no more despicable creatures on earth than householders, and he is at a loss to make out why the village that failed to offer adequate worship to him should, even for a moment add to the world's burden.

He, too, has evidently thought the Lord more foolish than ourselves.

**

"I say, Râm Charan, you have neither education nor the means to set up a trade, nor are you fit for physical labour. Besides, you cannot give up indulging in intoxications, nor do away with your wickednesses. Tell me, how do you manage to make your living?"

RAM CHARAN—"That is an easy job, sir; I preach unto all."

What has Ram Charan taken the Lord for?

**

The city of Lucknow is astir with the festivities of the Mohurrum. The gorgeous decorations and illumination in the principal mosque, the Imambara, know no bounds. Countless people have congregated. Hindus, Mohammedans, Christians, Jews—all sorts of people—men, women, and children of all races and creeds have crowded today to witness the Mohurrum. Lucknow is the capital of the Shias, and wailings in the name of the illustrious Hassan and Hossain rend the skies today. Who was there whose heart was not touched by the lamentation and beating of breasts that took place on this mournful occasion? The tale of the Kârbâlâ, now a thousand years old, has been renovated today.

Among this crowd of spectators were two Rajput gentlemen, who had come from a far-off village to see the festival. The Thakur Sahibs were—as is generally the case with village zemindârs (landlords)—innocent of learning. That Mohammedan culture, the shower of euphuistic phraseology with its nice and correct pronunciation, the varieties of fashionable dress—the loose-fitting cloaks and tight trousers and turbans, of a hundred different colours, to suit the taste of the townsfolk—all these had not yet found their way to such a remote village to convert the Thakur Sahibs. The Thakurs were, therefore, simple and straightforward, always fond of hunting, stalwart and hardy, and of exceedingly tough hearts.

The Thakurs had crossed the gate and were about to enter the mosque, when the guard interrupted them. Upon inquiring into the reasons, he answered, "Look here, this giant figure that you see standing by the doorway, you must give it five kicks first, and then you can go in." "Whose is the statue, pray?" "It is the statue of the nefarious Yejid who killed the illustrious Hassan and Hossain a thousand years ago. Therefore is this crying and this mourning." The guard thought that after this elaborate explanation the statue of Yejid was sure to merit ten kicks instead of five. But mysterious are the workings of Karma, and everything was sadly misunderstood. The Thakurs reverentially put their scarfs round their neck and prostrated and rolled themselves at the feet of the statue of Yeiid, praying with faltering accents: "What is the use of going in any more? What other gods need be seen? Bravo Yejid! Thou alone art the true God. Thou hast thrashed the rascals so well that they are weeping till now!"

**

There is the towering temple of the Eternal Hindu Religion, and how many ways of approaching it! And what can you not find there? From the Absolute Brahman of the Vedantin down to Brahma, Vishnu, Shiva, Shakti, Uncle Sun, (The Sun is popularly given this familiar appellation.) the rat-riding Ganesha, and the minor deities such as Shashthi and Mâkâl, and so forth—which is lacking there? And in the Vedas, in the Vedanta, and the Philosophies, in the Puranas and the Tantras, there are lots of materials, a single sentence of which is enough to break one's chain of transmigration for ever. And oh, the crowd! Millions and millions of people are rushing towards the temple. I, too, had a curiosity to see and join in the rush. But what was this that met my eyes when I reached the spot! Nobody was going inside the temple! By the side of the door, there was a standing figure, with fifty heads, a hundred arms, two hundred bellies, and five hundred legs, and everyone was rolling at the feet of that. I asked one for the reason and got the reply: "Those deities that you see in the interior, it is worship enough for them to make a short prostration, or throw in a few flowers from a distance. But the real worship must be offered to him who is at the gate; and those Vedas, the Vedanta, and the Philosophies, the Puranas and other scriptures that you see—there is no harm if you hear them read now and then; but you must obey the mandate of this one." Then I asked again, "Well, what is the name of this God of gods?" "He is named Popular Custom"—came the reply. I was reminded of the Thakur Sahibs, and exclaimed, "Bravo, Popular Custom! Thou hast thrashed them so well", etc.

***

Gurguré Krishnavyâl Bhattâchârya is a vastly learned man, who has the knowledge of the whole world at his finger-ends. His frame is a skeleton; his friends say it is through the rigours of his austerities, but his enemies ascribe it to want of food. The wicked, again, are of opinion that such a physique is but natural to one who has a dozen issues every year. However that may be, there is nothing on earth that Krishnavyal does not know; specially, he is omniscient about the flow of electric magnetic currents all over the human body, from the hair-tuft to its furthest nook and corner. And being possessed of this esoteric knowledge, he is incomparably the best authority for giving a scientific explanation all things—from a certain earth used in the worship of the goddess Durga down to the reasonable age of puberty of a girl being ten, and sundry inexplicable and mysterious rites pertaining to allied matters. And as for adducing precedents, well, he has made the thing so clear that even boys could understand it. There is forsooth no other land for religion than India, and within India itself none but the Brahmins have the qualification for understanding religion and among Brahmins, too, all others excepting the Krishnavyal family are as nothing and, of these latter again, Gurguré has the pre-eminent claim! Therefore whatever Gurguré Krishnavyal says is self-evident truth.

Learning is being cultivated to a considerable extent, and people are becoming a bit conscious and active, so that they want to understand anal taste everything; so Krishnavyal is assuring everybody: "Discard all fear! Whatever doubts are arising in your minds, I am giving scientific explanations for them. You remain just as you were. Sleep to your heart's content and never mind anything else. Only, don't forget my honorarium." The people exclaimed: "Oh, what a relief! What a great danger did really confront us! We should have had to sit up, and walk, and move—what a pest!" So they said, "Long live Krishnavyal", and turned on one side on the bed once more. The habit of a thousand years was not to go so soon. The body itself would resent it. The inveterate obtuseness of the mind of a thousand years was not to pass away at a moment's notice. And is it not for this that the Krishnavyal class are held in repute? "Bravo, Habit! Thou hast thrashed them so well", etc.

SHIVA'S DEMON

This incomplete story was found among Swamiji's papers after he had passed away. It is printed as the last article in the Bengali book Bhâbbâr Kathâ.

Baron K— lived in a district of Germany. Born in all aristocratic family, he inherited high rank, honour and wealth even in early youth; besides, he was highly cultured and endowed with many accomplishments. A good many charming, afflu-

ent, and young women of rank craved for his love. And which father or mother does not wish for a son-in-law of such parts, culture, handsomeness, social position, lineage, and youthful age? An aristocratic beauty had attracted Baron K— also, but the marriage was still far off. In spite of all rank and wealth, Baron K— had none to call his own, except a sister who was exquisitely beautiful and educated. The Baron had taken a vow that he would marry only after his sister had chosen her fiancé and the marriage celebrated with due éclat and rich dowries from him. She had been the apple of her parents' eyes. Baron K— did not want to enjoy a married life, before her wedding. Besides, the custom in this Western country is that the son does not live in his father's or in any relative's family after marriage; the couple live separately. It may be possible for the husband to live with his wife in his father-in-law's house but a wife will never live in her father-in-law's. So K— postponed his marriage till his sister's.

***

For some months K— had no news of his sister. Foregoing the life of ease, comfort, and happiness in a palace served by a big retinue, and snatching herself from the affection of her only brother, she had absconded. All search had been in vain. That brought K— untold sorrow. He had no more any relish for the pleasures of life; he was ever unhappy and dejected. His relatives now gave up all hope of the sister's return, and tried to make the Baron cheerful. They were very anxious about him, and his fiancée was ever full of apprehension.

***

It was the time of the Paris Exhibition. The elite of all countries assembled there. The art-treasures, and artistic products were brought to Paris from all quarters. Baron K—'s relatives advised him to go to Paris where his despondent heart would regain its normal health and buoyancy, once it was in contact with that active, invigorating current of joy. The Baron bowed down to their wishes and started for Paris with his friends.

MEMOIRS OF EUROPEAN TRAVEL

Swami Vivekananda left Calcutta for the West, for the second time, on the 20th June, 1899, by the BISN steamship Golconda. In reading these pages the reader should remember that Swamiji wrote them in alight, humorous tone in Bengali, which it is impossible to render in English.

The second section of these memoirs, relates to his return journey from the West at the end of 1900.

These were originally published in the Udbodhan.

—Editor.

Part I

Om Namo Nârâyanâya, ("Salutations to the Lord"; the usual form of addressing a Sannyasin. These memoirs of his second journey to the West were addressed to Swami Trigunatitananda, Editor, Udbodhan and hence this form of address.) Swâmi.—Pronounce the last syllable of the second word in a high pitch, brother, in the Hrishikesh fashion. For seven days we have been on board the ship and every day I think of writing to you something about our mode of life, and of writing materials also you have given me enough, but the characteristic lethargy of a Bengali stands in the way and foils everything. In the first place, there is idleness; every day I think of writing—what do you call it—a diary, but then, on account of various preoccupations, it is postponed to the endless "tomorrow", and does not progress an inch. In the second place, I do not remember the dates etc., at all; you must do me the favour to fill these up yourselves. And, besides, if you be very generous, you may think that like the great devotee, Hanuman, it is impossible for me to remember dates and such other trivialities—owing to the presence of the Lord in the heart. But the real truth is that it is due to my foolishness and idleness. What nonsense! What comparison can there be between "the Solar Dynasty" (Swamiji here refers to Kâlidâsa's famous line of the Raghuvamsham: "O the difference between the majestic Solar Dynasty and my poor intellect!")—I beg your pardon—between Hanuman with his whole heart given to Shri Râma, the crown of the Solar Dynasty, and me, the lowest of the low! But then he crossed at one bound the ocean extending a hundred Yojanas, while we are crossing it confined within a wooden house, so to say, being pitched this side and that and somehow keeping ourselves on our feet with the help of posts and pillars. But there is one point of superiority on our side in that he had the blessed sight of Râkshasas and Râkshasis after reaching Lankâ, whereas we are going in company with them. At dinner time that glittering of a hundred knives and the clattering of a hundred forks frightened brother T __ (Turiyananda) out of his wits. He now and then started lest his neighbour with auburn hair and grey, cat-like eyes, through inadvertence might plunge her knife into his flesh, and the more so, as he is rather sleek and fat. I say, did Hanuman have sea-sickness while crossing the sea? Do the ancient books say anything on that? You are all well-read men, proficient in the Ramayana and other scriptures, so you may settle that question. But our modern authorities are silent on that point. Perhaps he had not; but then the fact of his having entered into the jaws of somebody raises a doubt. Brother T__ is also of opinion that when the prow of the ship suddenly heaves up towards heaven as if to consult with the king of gods, and immediately after plunges to the bottom of the ocean as if to pierce king Vali, residing in the nether worlds—he at that time feels that he is being swallowed by the terrible and wide-gaping jaws of somebody.

I beg your pardon, you have entrusted your work to a nice man! I owe you a description of the sea-voyage for seven days which will be full of poetry and interest, and be written in a polished, rhetorical style, but instead of that I am talking at random. But the fact is, having striven all my life to eat the kernel of Brahman, after throwing away the shell of Maya, how shall I now get the power of appreciating nature's beauties all

of a sudden? All my life I have been on the move all over India, "from Varanasi to Kashmir, and thence to Khorasan, and Gujarat (Tulsidâs.)". How many hills and rivers, mountains and springs, and valleys and dales, how many cloud-belted peaks covered in perpetual snow, and oceans tempestuous, roaring and foamy, have I not seen, and heard of, and crossed! But sitting on a shabby wooden bedstead in a dark room of the ground floor, requiring a lamp to be lighted in the daytime, with the walls variegated by the stain of chewed betel leaves and made noisy by the squeaking and tickling of rats and moles and lizards, by the side of the main street resounding with the rattle of hackneys and tram-cars and darkened by clouds of dust—in such poetic environment, the pictures of the Himalayas, oceans, meadows, deserts, etc., that poet Shyamacharan, puffing at the all too familiar hookah, has drawn with such lifelike precision, to the glory of the Bengalis—it is vain for us to try to imitate them! Shyamacharan in his boyhood went for a change to the up-country, where the water is so stimulating to the digestive functions that if you drink a tumblerful of it even after a very heavy meal, every bit of it will be digested and you will feel hungry again. Here it was that Shyamacharan's intuitive genius caught a glimpse of the sublime and beautiful aspects of nature. But there is one fly in the pot—they say that Shyamacharan's peregrinations extended as far as Burdwan (in Bengal) and no further!

But at your earnest request and also to prove that I am not wholly devoid of the poetic instinct either, I set myself to the task with God's name, and you, too, be all attention.

No ship generally leaves the port in the night—specially from a commercial port like Calcutta and in a river like the Hooghly or Ganga. Until the ship reaches the sea, it is in the charge of the pilot, who acts as the Captain, and he gives the command. His duty ends in either piloting the ship down to the sea or, if it be an incoming ship, from the mouth of the sea to the port. We have got two great dangers towards the mouth of the Hooghly—first, the James and Mary Banks near Budge-Budge, and second, the sandbank near the entrance to Diamond Harbour. Only in the high tide and during the day, the pilot can very carefully steer his ship, and in no other condition; consequently it took us two days to get out of the Hooghly.

Do you remember the Ganga at Hrishikesh? That clear bluish water—in which one can count the fins of fishes five yards below the surface—that wonderfully sweet, ice-cold "charming water of the Ganga (From Valmiki's hymn.)", and that wonderful sound of "Hara, Hara" of the running water, and the echo of "Hara, Hara" from the neighbouring mountain-falls? Do you remember that life in the forest, the begging of Mâdhukari (Meaning, collected from door to door, in small bits.) alms, eating on small islands of rock in the bed of the Ganga, hearty drinking of that water with the palms, and the fearless wandering of fishes all round for crumbs of bread? You remember that love for Ganga water, that glory of the Ganga, the touch of its water that makes the mind dispassionate, that Ganga flowing over the Himalayas, through Srinagar, Tehri, Uttarkasi, and Gangotri—some of you have seen even the source of the Ganga! But there is a certain unforgettable fascination in our Ganga of Calcutta, muddy, and whitish—as if from contact with Shiva's body—and bearing a large number of ships on her bosom. Is it merely patriotism or the impressions of childhood?—Who knows? What wonderful relation is this between mother Ganga and the Hindus? Is it merely superstition? May be. They spend their lives with the name of Ganga on their lips, they die immersed in the waters of the Ganga, men from far off places take away Ganga water with them, keep it carefully in copper vessels, and sip drops of it on holy festive occasions. Kings and princes keep it in jars, and at considerable expense take the water from Gangotri to pour it on the head of Shiva at Rameshwaram! The Hindus visit foreign countries—Rangoon, Java, Hongkong, Madagascar, Suez, Aden, Malta—and they take with them Ganga water and the Gîtâ.

The Gita and the sacred waters of the Ganga constitute the Hinduism of the Hindus. Last time I went to the West, I also took a little of it with me, fearing it might be needed, and whenever opportunities occurred I used to drink a few drops of it. And every time I drank, in the midst of the stream of humanity, amid that bustle of civilisation, that hurry of frenzied footsteps of millions of men and women in the West, the mind at once became calm and still, as it were. That stream of men, that intense activity of the West, that clash and competition at every step, those seats of luxury and celestial opulence—Paris, London, New York, Berlin, Rome—all would disappear and I used to hear that wonderful sound of "Hara, Hara", to see that lonely forest on the sides of the Himalayas, and feel the murmuring heavenly river coursing through the heart and brain and every artery of the body and thundering forth, "Hara, Hara, Hara!"

This time you, too, I see, have sent Mother Ganga, for Madras. But, dear brother, what a strange vessel have you put Mother in! Brother T__ is a Brahmachârin from his boyhood, and looks "like burning fire through the force of his spirituality (Kâlidâsa's Kumârasambhavam.)". Formerly as a Brâhmana he used to be saluted as "Namo Brahmané", and now it is—oh, the sublimity of it!—"Namo Nârâyanâya", as he is a Sannyâsin. And it is perhaps due to that, that Mother, in his custody, has left her seat in the Kamandalu of Brahmâ, and been forced to enter a jar! Anyhow, getting up from bed late at night I found that Mother evidently could not bear staying in that awkward vessel and was trying to force her passage out of it. I thought it most dangerous, for if Mother chose to re-enact here those previous scenes of her life, such as piercing the Himalayas, washing away the great elephant Airâvata, and pulling down the hut of the sage Jahnu, then it would be a terrible affair. I offered many prayers to Mother and said to her in various supplicatory phrases, "Mother, do wait a little, let us reach Madras tomorrow, and there you can do whatever you like. There are many there more thick-skulled than elephants—most of them with huts like that of Jahnu—while those half-shaven, shining heads with ample hair-tufts are almost made of stone, compared to which even the Himalayas would be soft as butter! You may break them as much as you like; now pray wait a little." But all my supplications were in vain. Mother would not listen to them. Then I hit upon a plan, and said to her, "Mother, look at those turbaned servants with jackets on, moving to and fro on the ship, they are Mohammedans, real, beef-eating Mohammedans, and those whom you find moving about sweeping and cleaning the rooms etc., are real scavengers, disciples of Lâl Beg; and if you do not hear me, I will call them and ask them to touch you! Even if that is not sufficient to quiet you, I will just send you to your father's home; you see that room there, if you are shut in there, you will get back to your primitive condition in the Himalayas, when all your restlessness will be silenced, and you shall remain frozen into a block of ice." That silenced her. So it is everywhere, not only in the case of gods, but among men also—whenever they get a devotee, they take an undue advantage over him.

See, how I have again strayed from my subject and am talking at random. I have already told you at the outset that those things are not in my line, but if you bear with me, I shall try again.

There is a certain beauty in one's own people which is not to be found anywhere else. Even the denizens of Paradise cannot compare in point of beauty with our brothers and sisters, or sons and daughters, however uncouth they may be. But, if, even roaming over Paradise and seeing the people there, you find your own people coming out really beautiful, then there is no bound to your delight. There is also a special beauty in our Bengal, covered with endless verdant stretches of grass, and bearing as garlands a thousand rivers and streams. A little of this beauty one finds in Malabar, and also in Kashmir. Is there not beauty in water? When there is water everywhere, and heavy showers of rain are running down arum leaves, while clumps of cocoanut and date palms slightly bend their heads under that downpour, and there is the continuous croaking of frogs all round—is there no beauty in such a scene as this? And one cannot appreciate the beauty of the banks of our Ganga, unless one is returning from foreign countries and entering the river by its mouth at Diamond Harbour. That blue, blue sky, containing in its bosom black clouds, with golden-fringed whitish clouds below them, underneath which clumps of cocoanut and date palms toss their tufted heads like a thousand chowries, and below them again is an assemblage of light, deep, yellowish, slightly dark, and other varieties of green massed together—these being the mango, lichi, blackberry, and jack-fruit trees, with an exuberance of leaves and foliage that entirely hide the trunk, branches, and twigs—while, close by, clusters of bamboos toss in the wind, and at the foot of all lies that grass, before whose soft and glossy surface the carpets of Yarkand, Persia, and Turkistan are almost as nothing—as far as the eye can reach that green, green grass looking as even as if some one had trimmed and pruned it, and stretching right down to the edge of the river—as far down the banks as where the gentle waves of the Ganga have submerged and are pushing playfully against, the land is framed with green grass, and just below this is the sacred water of the Ganga. And if you sweep your eye from the horizon right up to the zenith, you will notice within a single line such a play of diverse colours, such manifold shades of the same colour, as you have witnessed nowhere else. I say, have you ever come under the fascination of colours—the sort of fascination which impels the moths to die in the flame, and the bees to starve themselves to death in the prison of flowers? I tell you one thing—if you want to enjoy the beauty of Gangetic scenery, enjoy it to your heart's content now, for very soon the whole aspect will be altered. In the hands of money-grabbing merchants, everything will disappear. In place of that green grass, brick kilns will be reared and burrow-pits for the brickfields will be sunk. Where, now, the tiny wavelets of the Ganga are playing with the grass, there will be moored the jute-laden flats and those cargo-boats; and those variegated colours of cocoanuts and palms, of mangoes and lichis, that blue sky, the beauty of the clouds—these you will altogether miss hereafter; and you will find instead the enveloping smoke of coal, and standing ghostlike in the midst of that smoke, the half-distinct chimneys of the factories!

Now our ship has reached the sea. The description, which you read in Kalidasa's Raghuvamsham of the shores "of the sea appearing blue with forests of palm and other trees" and "looking like a slender rim of rust on the tyre of an iron wheel" etc.—is not at all accurate and faithful. With all my respects for the great poet, it is my belief that he never in his life saw either the ocean or the Himalayas. (Swamiji afterwards changed his opinion with regard to the last part, i.e. Kalidasa's acquaintance with the Himalayas.)

Here there is a blending of white and black waters, somewhat resembling the confluence of the Ganga and Jamuna at Allahabad. Though Mukti (liberation) may be rare in most places, it is sure at "Hardwar, Allahabad, and the mouth of the Ganga". But they say that this is not the real mouth of the river. However, let me salute the Lord here, for "He has His eyes, and head and face everywhere (Gita, XIII. 13.)".

How beautiful! As far as the eye reaches, the deep blue waters of the sea are rising into foamy waves and dancing rhythmically to the winds. Behind us lie the sacred waters of the Ganga, whitened with the ashes of Shiva's body, as we read in the description, "Shiva's matted locks whitened by the foam of the Ganga (Shankaracharya's hymn.)". The water of the Ganga is comparatively still. In front of us lies the parting line between the waters. There ends the white water. Now begin the blue waters of the ocean—before, behind and all round there is only blue, blue water everywhere, breaking incessantly into waves. The sea has blue hair, his body is of a blue complexion, and his garment is also blue. We read in the Puranas that millions of Asuras hid themselves under the ocean through fear

of the gods. Today their opportunity has come, today Neptune is their ally, and Aeolus is at their back. With hideous roars and thundering shouts they are today dancing a terrible war-dance on the surface of the ocean, and the foamy waves are their grim laughter! In the midst of this tumult is our ship, and on board the ship, pacing the deck with lordly steps, are men and women of that nation which rules the sea-girt world, dressed in charming attire, with a complexion like the moonbeams—looking like self-reliance and self-confidence personified, and appearing to the black races as pictures of pride and haughtiness. Overhead, the thunder of the cloudy monsoon sky, on all sides the dance and roar of foam-crested waves, and the din of the powerful engines of our ship setting at naught the might of the sea—it was a grand conglomeration of sounds, to which I was listening, lost in wonder, as if in a half-waking state, when, all of a sudden, drowning all these sounds, there fell upon my ears the deep and sonorous music of commingled male and female voices singing in chorus the national anthem, "Rule Britannia, Britannia rules the waves!" Startled, I looked around and found that the ship was rolling heavily, and brother T__, holding his head with his hands was struggling against an attack of sea-sickness.

In the second class are two Bengali youths going to the West for study, whose condition is worse. One of them looks so frightened that he would be only too glad to scuttle straight home if he were allowed to land. These two lads and we two are the only Indians on the ship—the representatives of modern India. During the two days the ship was in the Ganga, brother T__, under the secret instructions of the Editor, Udbodhan, used to urge me very much to finish my article on "Modern India" quickly. I too found an opportunity today and asked him, "Brother, what do you think is the condition of modern India?" And he, casting a look towards the second class and another at himself, said, with a sigh, "Very sad, getting very much muddled up!"

The reason why so much importance is attached to the Hooghly branch of the Ganga, instead of the bigger one, Padmâ, is, according to many, that the Hooghly was the primary and principal course of the river, and latterly the river shifted its course, and created an outlet by the Padma. Similarly the present "Tolley's Nullah" represents the ancient course of the Ganga, and is known as the Âdi-Gangâ. The sailing merchant, the hero of Kavikankan's work, makes his voyage to Ceylon along that channel. Formerly the Ganga was navigable for big ships up to Triveni. The ancient port of Saptagrâm was situated a little distance off Triveni ghat, on the river Saraswati. From very ancient times Saptagram was the principal port for Bengal's foreign trade. Gradually the mouth of the Saraswati got silted up. In the year 1539 it silted up so much that the Portuguese settlers had to take up a site further down the Ganga, for their ships to come up. The site afterwards developed into the famous town of Hooghly. From the commencement of the sixteenth century both Indian and foreign merchants were feeling much anxiety about the silting up of the Ganga. But what of that? Human engineering skill has hitherto proved ineffectual against the gradual silting up of the river-bed which continues to the present day. In 1666 a French Missionary writes that the Ganga near Suti got completely silted up at the time. Holwell, of Black-Hole fame, on his way to Murshidabad was compelled to resort to small country-boats on account of the shallowness of the river at Santipur. In 1797 Captain Colebrook writes that country-boats could not ply in the Hooghly and the Jalangi during summer. During the years 1822-1884, the Hooghly was closed to all boat-traffic. For twenty-four years within this period the water was only two or three feet deep. In the seventeenth century, the Dutch planted a trade settlement at Chinsura, one mile below Hooghly. The French, who came still later, established their settlement at Chandernagore, still further down the river. In 1723 the German Ostend Company opened a factory at Bankipore, five miles below Chandernagore on the other side of the river. In 1616 the Danes had started a factory at Serampore, eight miles below Chandernagore, and then the English established the city of Calcutta still further down the river. None of the above places are now accessible to ships, only Calcutta being open now. But everybody is afraid of its future.

There is one curious reason why there remains so much water in the Ganga up to about Santipur even during summer. When the flow of the surface water has ceased, large quantities of water percolating through the subsoil find their way into the river. The bed of the Ganga is even now considerably below the level of the land on either side. If the level of the river-bed should gradually rise owing to the subsidence of fresh soil, then the trouble will begin. And there is talk about another danger. Even near Calcutta, through earthquakes or other causes, the river at times dried up so much that one could wade across. It is said that in 1770 such a state of things happened. There is another report that on Thursday, the 9th October, 1734, during ebb-tide in the noon, the river dried up completely. Had it happened a little later, during the inauspicious last portion of the day, I leave it to you to infer the result. Perhaps then the river would not have returned to its bed again.

So far, then, as regards the upper portion of the Hooghly; now as regards the portion below Calcutta. The great dangers to be faced in this portion are the James and Mary Banks. Formerly the river Damodar had its confluence with the Ganga thirty miles above Calcutta, but now, through the curious transformations of time, the confluence is over thirty-one miles to the south of it. Some six miles below this point the Rupnarayan pours its waters into the Ganga. The fact is there, that these two feeders rush themselves into the Ganga in happy combination—but how shall this huge quantity of mud be disposed of? Consequently big sandbanks are formed in the bed of the river, which constantly shift their position and are sometimes rather loose and sometimes a compact mass, causing no end of fear. Day and night soundings of the river's depth are being taken, the omission of which for a few days, through carelessness, would mean the destruction of ships. No sooner will a ship strike against them than it will either capsize or be straightway swallowed up in them! Cases are even recorded that within half an hour of a big three-masted ship striking one of these sandbanks, the whole of it disappeared in the sand, leaving only the top of the masts visible. These sandbanks may rightly be considered as the mouth of the Damodar-Rupnarayan. (There is a pun on the words Damodar-Rupnarayan which not only imply the two rivers, but also mean "Narayana as Damodara, or swallowing everything (Damodara-rupa-Narayana).") The Damodar is not now satisfied with Santhal villages, and is swallowing ships and steamers etc. as a sauce by way of variety. In 1877 a ship named "County of Sterling", with a cargo of 1,444 tons of wheat from Calcutta, had no sooner struck one of these terrible sandbanks than within eight minutes there was no trace left of it. In 1874 a steamer carrying a load of 2,400 tons suffered the same fate in two minutes. Blessed be thy mouth, O Mother Ganga! I salute thee for allowing us to get off scot-free. Brother T__ says, "Sir, a goat ought to be offered to the Mother for her benignity." I replied, "Exactly so, brother, but why offer only one day, instead of everyday!" Next day brother T__ readverted to the topic, but I kept silent. The next day after that I pointed out to him at dinner-time to what an extent the offering of goats was progressing. Brother seemed rather puzzled and said, "What do you mean? It is only you who are eating." Then at considerable pains I had to explain to him how it was said that a youth of Calcutta once visited his father-in-law's place in a remote village far from the Ganga. There at dinner-time he found people waiting about with drums etc., and his mother-in-law insisted on his taking a little milk before sitting to dinner. The son-in-law considered it might perhaps be a local custom which he had better obey; but no sooner had he taken a sip of the milk than the drums began to play all around and his mother-in-law, with tears of joy, placed her hand on his head and blessed him, saying, "My son, you have really discharged the duties of a son today; look here, you have in your stomach the water of the Ganga, as you live on its banks, and in the milk there was the powdered bone of your deceased father-in-law; so by this act of yours his bones have reached the Ganga and his spirit has obtained all the merits thereof." So here was a man from Calcutta, and on board the ship there was plenty of meat preparations and every time one ate them, meat was being offered to mother Ganga. So he need not be at all anxious on the subject. Brother T__ is of such a grave disposition that it was difficult to discover what impression the lecture made on him.

What a wonderful thing a ship is! The sea, which from the shore looks so fearful, in the heart of which the sky seems to bend down and meet, from whose bosom the sun slowly rises and in which it sinks again, and the least frown of which makes the heart quail—that sea has been turned into a highway, the cheapest of all routes, by ships. Who invented the ship? No one in particular. That is to say, like all machinery indispensable to men—without which they cannot do for a single moment, and by the combination and adjustment of which all kinds of factory plants have been constructed—the ship also is the outcome of joint labour. Take for instance the wheels; how absolutely indispensable they are! From the creaking bullock-cart to the car of Jagannath, from the spinning wheel to the stupendous machinery of factories, everywhere there is use for the wheel. Who invented the wheel? No one in particular, that is to say, all jointly. The primitive man used to fell trees with axes, roll big trunks along inclined planes; by degrees they were cut into the shape of solid wheels, and gradually the naves and spokes of the modern wheel came into vogue. Who knows how many millions of years it took to do this? But in India all the successive stages of improvement are preserved. However much they may be improved or transformed, there are always found men to occupy the lower stages of evolution, and consequently the whole series is preserved. First of all a musical instrument was formed with a string fixed to a piece of bamboo. Gradually it came to be played by a horsehair bow, and the first violin was made; then it passed through various transformations, with different sorts of strings and guts, and the bow also assumed different forms and names, till at last the highly finished guitar and sarang etc., came into existence. But in spite of this, do not the Mohammedan cabmen even now with a shabby horsehair bow play on the crude instrument made of a bamboo pipe fixed to an earthen pot, and sing the story of Majwar Kahar weaving his fishing net? Go to the Central Provinces, and you will find even now solid wheels rolling on the roads—though it bespeaks a dense intellect on the part of the people, specially in these days of rubber tyres.

In very ancient times, that is, in the golden age, when the common run of people were so sincere and truthful that they would not even cover their bodies for fear of hypocrisy—making the exterior look different from the interior—would not marry lest they might contract selfishness, and banishing all ideas of distinction between meum and tuum always used to look upon the property of others "as mere clods of earth", on the strength of bludgeons, stones, etc. (Swamiji is ironically describing the naked primitive man, to whom marriage was unknown, and who had no respect for person or property.);—in those blessed times, for voyaging over water, they constructed canoes and rafts and so forth, burning out the interior of a tree, or by fastening together a few logs of trees. Haven't you seen catamarans along the sea-coast from Orissa to Colombo? And you must have observed how far into the sea the rafts can go. There you have rudiments of ship-building.

And that boat of the East Bengal boatmen boarding which you have to call on the five patron-saints of the river for your safety; your house-boat manned by Chittagong boatmen, which even in a light storm makes its helmsmen declare his inability to control the helm, and all the passengers are asked to take the names of their respective gods as a last resort; that big up-country boat with a pair of fantastic brass eyes at the prow, rowed by the oarsmen in a standing posture; that boat of merchant Shrimanta's voyage (according to Kavikankan, Shrimanta crossed the Bay of Bengal simply by rowing, and was about to be drowned owing to his boat getting caught in the antennae of a shoal of lobsters, and almost capsizing! Also he mistook a shell for a tiny fish, and so on), in other words the Gangasagar boat—nicely roofed above and having a floor of split bamboos, and containing in its hold rows of jars filled with Ganga water (which is deliciously cool, I beg your pardon, you visit Gangasagar during hard winter, and the chill north wind drives away all your relish for cooling drinks); and that small-sized boat which daily takes the Bengali Babus to their office and brings them back home, and is superintended over by the boatman of Bally, very expert and very clever—no sooner does he sight a cloud so far away as Konnagar than he puts the boat in safety!—they are now passing into the hands of the strong-bodied men from Jaunpur who speak a peculiar dialect, and whom your Mahant Maharaj, out of fun ordered to catch a heron—which he facetiously styled as "Bakâsur (A demon of the shape of a big heron, mentioned in the Bhagavâta.)", and this puzzled them hopelessly and they stammered out, "Please, sire, where are we to get this demon? It is an enigma to us"; then that bulky, slow-moving (cargo) boat nicknamed "Gâdhâ (donkey)" in Bengali, which never goes straight, but always goes sideways; and that big species of boats, like the schooner, having from one to three masts, which imports cargoes of cocoanuts, dates and dried fish from Ceylon, the Maldives, or Arabia;—these and many others too numerous to mention, represent the subsequent development in naval construction.

To steer a ship by means of sails is a wonderful discovery. To whichever direction the wind may be blowing, by a clever manipulation of the sails, the ship is sure to reach her destination. But she takes more time when the wind is contrary. A sailing ship is a most beautiful sight, and from a distance looks like a many-winged great bird descending from the skies. Sails, however, do not allow a ship to steer straight ahead, and if the wind is a little contrary, she has to take a zigzag course. But when there is a perfect lull, the ship is helpless and has to lower her sails and stand still. In the equatorial regions it frequently happens even now. Nowadays sailing ships also have very little of wood in them and are mostly made of iron. It is much more difficult to be the captain or sailor of a sailing ship than in a steamer, and no one can be a good captain in sailing ship without experience. To know the direction of the wind at every step and to be on one's guard against danger-spots long ahead—these two qualifications are indispensably necessary in a sailing ship, more than in a steamer. A steamer is to a great extent under human control—the engines can be stopped in a moment. It can be steered ahead, or astern, sideways or in any desired direction, within a very short time, but the sailing ship is at the mercy of the wind. By the time the sails can be lowered or the helm turned, the ship may strike a bank or run up on a submarine rock or collide with another ship. Nowadays sailing ships very seldom carry passengers, except coolies. They generally carry cargo, and that also inferior stuff, such as salt etc. Small sailing ships such as the schooner, do coasting trade. Sailing ships cannot afford to hire steamers to tow them along the Suez Canal and spend thousands of rupees as toll, so they can go to England in six months by rounding Africa.

Due to all these disadvantages of sailing ships, naval warfare in the past was a risky affair. A slight change in the course of the wind or in the ocean-current would decide the fate of a battle. Again, those ships, being made of wood, would frequently catch fire, which had to be put out. Their construction also was of a different type; one end was flat and very high, with five or six decks. On the uppermost deck at this end there used to be a wooden verandah, in front of which were the commander's room and office and on either side were the officers' cabins. Then there was a large open space, at the other end of which were a few cabins. The lower decks also had similar roofed halls, one underneath the other. In the lowermost deck or hold were the sailor's sleeping and dining rooms, etc. On either side of each deck were ranged cannon, their muzzles projecting through the rows of apertures in the ships' walls; and on both sides were heaps of cannon balls (and powder bags in times of war). All the decks of these ancient men-of-war had very low roofs and one had to carry his head down when moving about. Then it was a troublesome business to secure marines for naval warfare. There was a standing order of the Government to enlist men by force or guile wherever they could be found. Sons were violently snatched away from their mothers, and husbands from their wives. Once they were made to board the ship, (which perhaps the poor fellows had never done in their lives), they were ordered straightway to climb the masts! And if through fear they failed to carry out the order, they were flogged. Some would also die under the ordeal. It was the rich and influential men of the country who made these laws, it was they who would appropriate the benefits of commerce, or ravage, or conquest of different countries, and the poor people were simply to shed their blood and sacrifice their lives — as has been the rule throughout the world's history! Now those laws exist no longer, and the name of the Pressgang does not now send a shiver through the hearts of the peasantry and poor folk. Now it is voluntary service, but many juvenile criminals are trained as sailors in men-of-war, instead of being thrown into prison.

Steam-power has revolutionised all this, and sails are almost superfluous ornaments in ships nowadays. They depend very little on winds now, and there is much less danger from gales and the like. Ships have now only to take care that they do not strike against submarine rocks. And men-of-war of the present day are totally different from those of the past. In the first place, they do not at all look like ships, but rather like floating iron fortresses of varying dimensions. The number of cannon also has been much reduced, but compared with the modern turret-guns, those of the past were mere child's play. And how fast these men-of-war are! The smallest of these are the torpedo-boats; those that are a little bigger are for capturing hostile merchant-ships, and the big ones are the ponderous instruments for the actual naval fight.

During the Civil War of the United States of America, the Unionist party fixed rows of iron rails against the outer walls of a wooden ship so as to cover them. The enemy's cannon-balls striking against them were repulsed without doing any harm to the ship. After this, as a rule, the ship's sides began to be clad in iron, so that hostile balls might not penetrate the wood. The ship's cannon also began to improve — bigger and bigger cannon were constructed and the work of moving, loading, and firing them came to be executed by machinery, instead of with the hand. A cannon which even five hundred men cannot move an inch, can now be turned vertically or horizontally, loaded and fired by a little boy pressing a button, and all this in a second! As the iron wall of ships began to increase in thickness, so cannon with the power of thunder also began to be manufactured. At the present day, a battle-ship is a fortress with walls of steel, and the guns are almost as Death itself. A single shot is enough to smash the biggest ship into fragments. But this "iron bridal-chamber" — which Nakindar's father (in the popular Bengali tale) never even dreamt of, and which, instead of standing on the top of "Sâtâli Hill" moves dancing on seventy thousand mountain-like billows, even this is mortally afraid of torpedoes! The torpedo is a tube somewhat shaped like a cigar, and if fired at an object travels under water like a fish. Then, the moment it hits its object, the highly explosive materials it contains explode with a terrific noise, and the ship under which this takes place is reduced to its original condition, that is, partly into iron and wooden fragments, and partly into smoke and fire! And no trace is found of the men who are caught in this explosion of the torpedo — the little that is found, is almost in a state of mincemeat! Since the invention of these torpedoes, naval wars cannot last long. One or two fights, and a big victory is scored or a total defeat. But the wholesale loss of men of both parties in naval fight which men apprehended before the introduction of these men-of-war has been greatly falsified by facts.

If a fraction of the volley of balls discharged during a field-fight from the guns and rifles of each hostile army on the opponents hit their aim, then both rival armies would be killed to a man in two minutes. Similarly if only one of five hundred shots fired from a battle-ship in action hit its mark, then no trace would be left of the ships on both sides. But the wonder is that, as guns and rifles are improving in quality, as the latter are being made lighter, and the rifling in their barrels finer, as the range is increasing, as machinery for loading is being multiplied, and rate of firing quickened — the more they seem to miss their aim! Armed with the old fashioned unusually long-barrelled musket — which has to be supported on a two-legged wooden stand while firing, and ignited by actually setting fire and blowing into it — the Barakhjais and the Afridis can fire with unerring precision, while the modern trained soldier with the highly complex machine-guns of the present day fires 150 rounds in a minute and serves merely to heat the atmosphere! Machinery in a small proportion is good, but too much of it kills man's initiative and makes a lifeless machine of him. The men in factories are doing the same monotonous work, day after day, night after night, year after year, each batch of men doing one special bit of work—such as fashioning the heads of pins, or uniting the ends of threads, or moving backwards or forwards with the loom—for a whole life. And the result is that the loss of that special job means death to them—they find no other means of living and starve. Doing routine work like a machine, one becomes a lifeless machine. For that reason, one serving as a schoolmaster or a clerk for a whole lifetime ends by turning a stupendous fool.

The form of merchantmen and passenger-ships is of a different type. Although some merchant-ships are so constructed that in times of war they can easily be equipped with a few guns and give chase to unarmed hostile merchant-ships, for which they get remuneration from their respective Governments, still they generally differ widely from warships. These are now mostly steamships and generally so big and expensive that they are seldom owned by individuals, but by companies. Among the carrying companies for Indian and European trade, the P. & O. Company is the oldest and richest, then comes the B. I. S. N. Company, and there are many others. Among those of foreign nationalities, the Messageries Maritimes (French) the Austrian Lloyd, the German Lloyd, and the Rubattino Company (Italian), are the most famous. Of these the passenger-ships of the P. & O. Company are generally believed to be the safest and fastest. And the arrangements of food in the Messageries Maritimes are excellent.

When we left for Europe this time, the last two companies had stopped booking "native" passengers for fear of the plague-infection. And there is a law of the Indian Government that no "native" of India can go abroad without a certificate from the Emigration Office, in order to make sure that nobody is enticing him away to foreign countries to sell him as a slave or to impress him as a coolie, but that he is going of his own free will. This written document must be produced before they will take him into the ship. This law was so long silent against the Indian gentry going to foreign countries. Now on account of the plague epidemic it has been revived, so that the Government may be informed about every "native" going out. Well, in our country we hear much about some people belonging to the gentry and some to the lower classes. But in the eyes of the Government all are "natives" without exception. Maharajas, Rajas, Brahmins, Kshatriyas, Vaishyas, Shudras—all belong to one and the same class—that of "natives". The law, and the test which applies to coolies, is applicable to all "natives" without distinction. Thanks to you, O English Government, through your grace, for a moment at least I feel myself one with the whole body of "natives". It is all the more welcome, because this body of mine having come of a Kâyastha family, I have become the target of attack of many sections. Nowadays we hear it from the lips of people of all castes in India that they are all full-blooded Aryans—only there is some difference of opinion amongst them about the exact percentage of Aryan blood in their veins, some claiming to have the full measure of it, while others may have one ounce more or less than another—that is all. But in this they are all unanimous that their castes are all superior to the Kayastha! And it is also reported that they and the English race belong to the same stock—that they are cousins-german to each other, and that they are not "natives". And they have come to this country out of humanitarian principles, like the English. And such evil customs as child-marriage, polygamy, image-worship, the sutti, the zenana-system, and so forth have no place in their religion—but these have been introduced by the ancestors of the Kayasthas, and people of that ilk. Their religion also is of the same pattern as that of the English! And their forefathers looked just like the English, only living under the tropical sun of India has turned them black! Now come forward with your pretensions, if you dare! "You are all natives", the Government says. Amongst that mass of black, a shade deeper or lighter cannot be distinguished. The Government says, "They are all natives". Now it is useless for you to dress yourselves after the English fashion. Your European hats etc., will avail you little henceforth. If you throw all the blame on the Hindus, and try to fraternise with the English, you would thereby come in for a greater share of cuffs and blows and not less. Blessings to you, O English Government! You have already become the favoured child of Fortune; may your prosperity increase ever more! We shall be happy once more to wear our loin-cloth and Dhoti—the native dress. Through your grace we shall continue to travel from one end of the country to the other, bare-headed, and barefooted, and heartily eat our habitual food of rice and Dâl with our fingers, right in the Indian fashion. Bless the Lord! We had well-nigh been tempted by Anglo-Indian fashions and been duped by its glamour. We heard it said that no sooner did we give up our native dress, native religion, and native manners and customs, than the English people would take us on their shoulders and lionise us. And we were about to do so, when smack came the whip of the Englishman and the thud of British boots—and immediately men were seized by a panic and turned away, bidding good-bye to English ways, eager to confess their "native" birth.

"The English ways we'd copy with such pains, The British boots did stamp out from our brains!"

Blessed be the English Government! May their throne be firm and their rule permanent. And the little tendency that remained in me for taking to European ways vanished, thanks to the Americans. I was sorely troubled by an overgrown beard, but no sooner did I peep into a hair-cutting saloon than somebody called out, "This is no place for such shabby-looking people as you." I thought that perhaps seeing me so quaintly dressed in turban and Gerua cloak, the man was prejudiced against me. So I should go and buy an English coat and hat. I was about to do this when fortunately I met an American gentleman who explained to me that it was much better that I was dressed in my Gerua cloak, for now the gentlemen would not take me amiss, but if I dressed in European fashion, everybody would chase me away. I met the same kind of treatment in one or two other saloons. After which I began the practice of shaving with my own hands. Once I was burning with hunger, and went into a restaurant, and asked for a particular thing, whereupon the man said, "We do not stock it." "Why, it is there." "Well, my good man, in plain language it means there is no place here for you to sit and take your meal." "And why?" "Because nobody will eat at the same table with you, for he will be outcasted." Then America began to look agreeable to me, somewhat like my own caste-ridden country. Out with these differences of white and black, and this nicety about the proportion of Aryan blood among the "natives"! How awkward it looks for slaves to be over-fastidious about pedigree! There was a Dom (a man of the sweeper-caste) who used to say, "You won't find anywhere on earth a caste superior to ours. You must know we are Dom-m-m-s!" But do you see the fun of it? The excesses about caste distinctions obtain most among peoples who are least honoured among mankind.

Steamships are generally much bigger than sailing ships. The steamships that ply across the Atlantic are just half as much bigger than the "Golconda". (The B. I. S. N. steamer in which Swami Vivekananda went to the West for the second time.) The ship on which I crossed the Pacific from Japan was also very big. In the centre of the biggest ships are the first class compartments with some open space on either side; then comes the second class, flanked by the "steerage" on either side. At one end are the sailors' and servants' quarters. The steerage corresponds to the third class, in which very poor people go as passengers, as, for instance, those who are emigrating to America, Australia, etc. The accommodation for them is very small and the food is served not on tables but from hand to hand. There is no steerage in ships which ply between England and India, but they take deck-passengers. The open space between the first and second classes is used by them for sitting or sleeping purposes. But I did not notice a single deck-passenger bound for a long journey. Only in 1893, on my way to China, I found a number of Chinamen going as deck-passengers from Bombay to Hongkong.

During stormy weather, the deck-passengers suffer great inconvenience, and also to a certain extent at ports when the cargo is unloaded. Excepting in the hurricane-deck which is on top of all, there is a square opening in all other decks, through which cargo is loaded and unloaded, at which times the deck-passengers are put to some trouble. Otherwise, it is very pleasant on the deck at night from Calcutta to Suez, and in summer, through Europe also. When the first and second class passengers are about to melt in their furnished compartments on account of the excessive heat, then the deck is almost a heaven in comparison. The second class in ships of this type is very uncomfortable. Only, in the ships of the newly started German Lloyd Company plying between Bergen, in Germany and Australia, the second class arrangements are excellent; there are cabins even in the hurricane-deck, and food arrangements are almost on a par with those of the first class in the "Golconda". That line touches Colombo on the way.

In the "Golconda" there are only two cabins on the hurricane-deck, one on each side; one is for the doctor, and the other was allotted to us. But owing to the excessive heat, we had to take shelter in the lower deck, for our cabin was just above the engine-room of the ship. Although the ship is made of iron, yet the passengers' cabins are made of wood. And there are many holes along the top and bottom of the wooden walls of these, for the free passage of air. The walls are painted over with ivory-paint which has cost nearly £25 per room. There is a small carpet spread on the floor and against one of the walls are fixed two frameworks somewhat resembling iron bedsteads without legs, one on top of the other. Similarly on the opposite wall. Just opposite the entrance there is a wash-basin, over which there is a looking-glass, two bottles, and two tumblers for drinking water. Against the sides of each bed is attached a netting in brass frames which can be fixed up to the wall and again lowered down. In it the passengers put their watch and other important personal necessaries before retiring. Below the lower bedstead, there is room for storing the trunks and bags. The second class arrangements are on a similar plan, only the space is narrower and the furniture of an inferior quality. The shipping business is almost a monopoly of the English. Therefore in the ships constructed by other nations also, the food arrangements, as well as the regulation of the time, have to be made in the English fashion, to suit the large number of English passengers in them. There are great differences between England, France, Germany, and Russia, as regards food and time. Just as in our country, there are great differences between Bengal, Northern India, the Mahratta country, and Gujarat. But these differences are very little observed in the ships, because there, owing to a majority of English-speaking passengers, everything is being moulded after the English fashion.

The Captain is the highest authority in a ship. Formerly the Captain used to rule in the ship in the high seas, punishing offenders, hanging pirates, and so forth. Now he does not go so far, but his word is law on board a ship. Under him are four officers (or malims, in Indian vernacular). Then come four or five engineers, the chief engineer ranking equally with an officer and getting first class food. And there are four or five steersmen (sukanis, in Indian vernacular) who hold the helm by turns—they are also Europeans. The rest, comprising the servants, the sailors, and the coalmen are all Indian, and all of them Mohammedans; Hindu sailors I saw only on the Bombay side, in P. & O. ships. The servants and the sailors are from Calcutta, while the coalmen belong to East Bengal;

the cooks also are Catholic Christians of East Bengal. There are four sweepers besides, whose duty it is to clear out dirty water from the compartments, make arrangements for bath and keep the latrines etc. clean and tidy. The Mohammedan servants and lascars do not take food cooked by Christians; besides, every day there are preparations of ham or bacon on board the ship. But they manage to set up some sort of privacy for themselves. They have no objection to taking bread prepared in the ship's kitchen, and those servants from Calcutta who have received the "new light" of civilisation, do not observe any restrictions in matters of food. There are three messes for the men, one for the servants, one for the sailors, and one for the coalmen. The company provides each mess with a cook and a servant; every mess has got a separate place for cooking. A few Hindu passengers, were going from Calcutta to Colombo, and they used to do their cooking in one of these kitchens after the servants had finished theirs. The servants draw their own drinking water. On every deck two pumps are fixed against the wall, one on each side; the one is for sweet and the other for salt water, and the Mohammedans draw sweet water from this for their own use. Those Hindus who have no objection to taking pipe-water can very easily go on these ships to England and elsewhere, observing all their orthodoxy in matters of food and drink. They can get a kitchen, and drinking water free from the touch of any, and even the bathing water need not be touched by anybody else; all kinds of food such as rice, pulse, vegetables, fish, meat, milk, and ghee are available on the ship, especially on these ships where mostly Indians are employed, to whom rice, pulse, radish, cabbage, and potato, etc. have to be supplied every day. The one thing necessary is money. With money you can proceed anywhere alone, observing full orthodoxy.

These Bengali servants are employed nowadays in almost all ships that ply between Calcutta and Europe. They are gradually forming into a class by themselves. Several nautical terms also are being coined by them; for instance, the captain is termed bariwallah (landlord); the officer malim; the mast 'dôl'; a sail sarh; bring down aria; raise habish (heave), etc.

The body of lascars and coalmen have each a head who is called serang, under whom are two or three tindals, and under these come the lascars and coalmen.

The head of the khansamas, or "boys", is the butler, over whom there is a European steward. The lascars wash and cleanse the ship, throw or wind up the cables, set down or lift the boats and hoist or strike sail (though this last is a rare occurrence in steamships) and do similar kind of work. The Serang and the Tindal are always moving about watching them and assisting in their work. The coalmen keep the fire steady in the engine-room; their duty is to fight day and night with fire and to keep the engines neat and clean. And it is no easy task to keep that stupendous engine and all its parts neat and tidy. The Serang and his assistant (or "Brother", in the lascar's parlance) are from Calcutta and speak Bengali; they look gentlemanly and can read and write, having studied in school; they speak tolerable English also. The Serang has a son, thirteen years of age, who is a servant of the Captain and waits at his door as an orderly. Seeing these Bengali lascars, coalmen, servants, and boys at work, the feeling of despair with regard to my countrymen which I had, was much abated. How they are slowly developing their manhood, with a strong physique—how fearless, yet docile! That cringing, sycophant attitude common to "natives" even the sweepers do not possess—what a transformation!

The Indian lascars do excellent work without murmur, and go on a quarter of a European sailor's pay. This has dissatisfied many in England, especially as many Europeans are losing their living thereby. They sometimes set up an agitation. Having nothing else to say against them—for the lascars are smarter in work than Europeans—they only complain that in rough weather, when the ship is in danger, they lose all courage. Good God! In actual circumstances, that infamy is found to be baseless. In times of danger, the European sailors freely drink through fear and make themselves stupid and out of use. Indian sailors never take a drop of liquor in their life, and up to now, not one of them has ever shown cowardice in times of great danger. Does the Indian soldier display any cowardice on the field of battle? No, but they must have leaders. An English friend of mine, named General Strong, was in India during the Sepoy Mutiny. He used to tell many stories about it. One day, in the course of conversation, I asked him how it was that the sepoys who had enough of guns, ammunition, and provisions at their disposal, and were also trained veterans, came to suffer such a defeat. He replied that the leaders among them, instead of advancing forward, only kept shouting from a safe position in the rear, "Fight on, brave lads", and so forth; but unless the commanding officer goes ahead and faces death, the rank and file will never fight with heart. It is the same in every branch. "A captain must sacrifice his head," they say. If you can lay down your life for a cause, then only you can be a leader. But we all want to be leaders without making the necessary sacrifice. And the result is zero—nobody listens to us!

However much you may parade your descent from Aryan ancestors and sing the glories of ancient India day and night, and however much you may be strutting in the pride of your birth, you, the upper classes of India, do you think you are alive? You are but mummies ten thousand years old! It is among those whom your ancestors despised as "walking carrion" that the little of vitality there is still in India is to be found; and it is you who are the real "walking corpses". Your houses, your furniture, look like museum specimens, so lifeless and antiquated they are; and even an eye-witness of your manners and customs, your movements and modes of life, is inclined to think that he is listening to a grandmother's tale! When, even after making a personal acquaintance with you, one returns home, one seems to think one had been to visit the paintings in an art gallery! In this world of Maya, you are the real illusions, the mystery, the real mirage in the desert, you, the upper classes of India! You represent the past tense, with all its varieties of form jumbled into one. That one still seems to see you at the present time, is nothing but a nightmare brought on by indigestion. You are the void, the unsubstantial nonentities of the future. Denizens of the dreamland, why are you loitering any longer? Fleshless and bloodless skeletons of the dead body of Past India you are, why do you not quickly reduce yourselves into dust and disappear in the air? Ay, on your bony fingers are some priceless rings of jewel, treasured up by your ancestors, and within the embrace of your stinking corpses are preserved a good many ancient treasure-chests. Up to now you have not had the opportunity to hand them over. Now under the British rule, in these days of free education and enlightenment, pass them on to your heirs, ay, do it as quickly as you can. You merge yourselves in the void and disappear, and let New India arise in your place. Let her arise—out of the peasants' cottage, grasping the plough; out of the huts of the fisherman, the cobbler, and the sweeper. Let her spring from the grocer's shop, from beside the oven of the fritter-seller. Let her emanate from the factory, from marts, and from markets. Let her emerge from groves and forests, from hills and mountains. These common people have suffered oppression for thousands of years—suffered it without murmur, and as a result have got wonderful fortitude. They have suffered eternal misery, which has given them unflinching vitality. Living on a handful of grain, they can convulse the world; give them only half a piece of bread, and the whole world will not be big enough to contain their energy; they are endowed with the inexhaustible vitality of a Raktabija. (A demon, in the Durgâ-Saptashati, every drop of whose blood falling on the ground produced another demon like him.) And, besides, they have got the wonderful strength that comes of a pure and moral life, which is not to be found anywhere else in the world. Such peacefulness, such contentment, such love, such power of silent and incessant work, and such manifestation of lion's strength in times of action—where else will you find these! Skeletons of the Past, there, before you, are your successors, the India that is to be. Throw those treasure-chests of yours and those jewelled rings among them, as soon as you can; and you vanish into the air, and be seen no more—only keep your ears open. No sooner will you disappear than you will hear the inaugural shout of Renaissant India, ringing with the voice of a million thunders and reverberating throughout the universe, "Wah Guru Ki Fateh"—victory to the Guru!

Our ship is now in the Bay of Bengal, which is reported to be very deep. The little of it that was shallow has been silted up by the Ganga crumbling the Himalayas and washing down the North-Western Provinces (U.P.). That alluvial region is our Bengal. There is no indication of Bengal extending further beyond the Sunderbans. Some say that the Sunderbans were formerly the site of many villages and towns and were an elevated region. But many do not admit this now. However, the Sunderbans and the northern part of the Bay of Bengal have been the scene of many historic events. These were the rendezvous of the Portuguese pirates; the king of Arakan made repeated attempts to occupy this region, and here also the representative of the Mogul Emperor tried his best to punish the Portuguese pirates headed by Gonzalez; and this has frequently been the scene of many fights between the Christians, Moguls, Mugs, and Bengalis.

The Bay of Bengal is naturally rough, and to add to this, it is the monsoon season, so our ship is rolling heavily. But then, this is only the beginning and there is no knowing what is to follow, as we are going to Madras. The greater part of Southern India belongs now to the Madras Presidency. What is there in mere extent of land? Even a desert turns into heaven when it falls to the care of a fortunate owner. The unknown petty village of Madras, formerly called Chinnapattanam or Madraspattanam, was sold by the Raja of Chandragiri to a company of merchants. Then the English had their principal trade in Java, and Bantam was the centre of England's Asiatic trade. Madras and other English trade settlements in India were under the control of Bantam. Where is that Bantam now? And what development that Madras has made! It is not whole truth to say that fortune favours the enterprising man; behind there must be the strength that comes of the Divine Mother. But I also admit that it is the enterprising men unto whom Mother gives strength.

Madras reminds one of a typical South Indian province; though even at the Jagannath Ghat of Calcutta, one can get a glimpse of the South by seeing the Orissa Brahmin with his border-shaven head and tufted hair, his variously painted forehead, the involuted slippers, in which only the toes may enter; that nose irritated with snuff and with that habit of covering the bodies of their children with sandalpaste prints. The Gujarati Brahmin, the jet-black Maharashtra Brahmin, and the exceptionally fair, cat-eyed square-headed Brahmin of Konkan—though all of them dress in the same way, and are all known as Deccanis, yet the typical southern Brahmin is to be found in Madras. That forehead covered over with the ample caste-mark of the Ramanuja sect—which to the uninitiated looks anything but sublime, (and whose imitation—the caste-mark of the Ramananda sect of Northern India—is hailed with many a facetious rhyme—and which completely throws into the shade the custom prevailing in Bengal among leaders of the Vaishnavite sect, of frightfully imprinting their whole body); that Telugu, Tamil, and Malayalam speech of which you won't understand a single syllable even if you hear it spoken for six years and in which there is a play of all possible varieties of 'l' and 'd' sounds; that eating of rice with 'black-peppered dal soup'—each morsel of which sends a shiver through the heart (so pungent and so acid!); that addition of margosa leaves, oats, etc., by way of flavour, that taking of "rice-and-curd" etc., that bath with gingili oil rubbed over the body, and the frying of fish in the same oil—without these how can one conceive the southern country?

Again, the South has Hinduism alive during the Mohammedan rule and even for some time previous to it. It was in the South that Shankaracharya was born, among that caste who wear a tuft on the front of the head and eat food prepared with cocoanut oil: this was the country that produced Ramanuja: it was also the birthplace of Madhva Muni. Modern Hinduism owes its allegiance to these alone. The Vaishnavas of the Chaitanya sect form merely a recension of the Madhva sect; the religious reformers of the North such as Kabir, Dadu, Nanak, and Ramsanehi are all an echo of Shankaracharya; there you find the disciples of Ramanuja occupying Ayodhya and other places. These Brahmins of the South do not recognise those of the North as true Brahmins, nor accept them as disciples, and even to the other day would not admit them to Sannyasa. The people of Madras even now occupy the principal seats of religion. It was in the South that when people of North India were hiding themselves in woods and forests, giving up their treasures, their household deities, and wives and children, before the triumphant war-cry of Mohammedan invaders—the suzerainty of the King of Vidyânagar was established firm as ever. In the South, again, was born the wonderful Sâyanâchârya—the strength of whose arms, vanquishing the Mohammedans, kept King Bukka on his throne, whose wise counsels gave stability to the Vidyanagar Kingdom, whose state-policy established lasting peace and prosperity in the Deccan, whose superhuman genius and extraordinary industry produced the commentaries on the whole Vedas—and the product of whose wonderful sacrifice, renunciation, and researches was the Vedanta treatise named Panchadashi—that Sannyasin Vidyâranya Muni or Sayana (According to some, Sayana, the commentator of the Vedas, was the brother of Vidyaranya Muni.) was born in this land. The Madras Presidency is the habitat of that Tamil race whose civilisation was the most ancient, and a branch of whom, called the Sumerians, spread a vast civilisation on the banks of the Euphrates in very ancient times; whose astrology, religious lore, morals, rites, etc., furnished the foundation for the Assyrian and Babylonian civilisations; and whose mythology was the source of the Christian Bible. Another branch of these Tamils spread from the Malabar coast and gave rise to the wonderful Egyptian civilisation, and the Aryans also are indebted to this race in many respects. Their colossal temples in the South proclaim the triumph of the Veera Shaiva and Veera Vaishnava sects. The great Vaishnava religion of India has also sprung from a Tamil Pariah—Shathakopa—"who was a dealer in winnowing-fans but was a Yogin all the while". And the Tamil Alwars or devotees still command the respect of the whole Vaishnava sect. Even now the study of the Dvaita, Vishishtâdvaita and Advaita systems of Vedanta is cultivated more in South India than anywhere else. Even now the thirst for religion is stronger here than in any other place.

In the night of the 24th June, our ship reached Madras. Getting up from bed in the morning, I found that we were within the enclosed space of the Madras harbour. Within the harbour the water was still, but without, towering waves were roaring, which occasionally dashing against the harbour-wall were shooting up fifteen or twenty feet high into the air and breaking in a mass of foam. In front lay the well-known Strand Road of Madras. Two European Police Inspectors, a Jamadar of Madras and a dozen Constables boarded our ship and told me with great courtesy that "natives" were not allowed to land on the shore, but the Europeans were. A "native", whoever he might be, was of such dirty habits that there was every chance of his carrying plague germs about; but the Madrasis had asked for a special permit for me, which they might obtain. By degrees the friends of Madras began to come near our vessel on boats in small groups. As all contact was strictly forbidden, we could only speak from the ship, keeping some space between. I found all my friends—Alasinga, Biligiri, Narasimhachary, Dr. Nanjunda Rao, Kidi, and others on the boats. Basketfuls of mangoes, plantains, cocoanuts, cooked rice-and-curd, and heaps of sweet and salt delicacies, etc. began to come in. Gradually the crowd thickened—men, women, and children in boats everywhere. I found also Mr. Chamier, my English friend who had come out to Madras as a barrister-at-law. Ramakrishnananda and Nirbhayananda made some trips near to the ship. They insisted on staying on the boat the whole day in the hot sun, and I had to remonstrate with them, when they gave up the idea. And as the news of my not being permitted to land got abroad, the crowd of boats began to increase still more. I, too, began to feel exhaustion from leaning against the railings too long. Then I bade farewell to my Madrasi friends and entered my cabin. Alasinga got no opportunity to consult me about the Brahmavadin and the Madras work; so he was going to accompany me to Colombo. The ship left the harbour in the evening, when I heard a great shout, and peeping through the cabin-window, I found that about a thousand men, women, and children of Madras who had been sitting on the harbour-walls, gave this farewell shout when the ship started. On a joyous occasion the people of Madras also, like the Bengalis, make the peculiar sound with the tongue known as the Hulu.

It took us four days to go from Madras to Ceylon. That rising and heaving of waves which had commenced from the mouth of the Ganga began to increase as we advanced, and after we had left Madras it increased still more. The ship began to roll heavily, and the passengers felt terribly sea-sick, and so did the two Bengali boys. One of them was certain he was going to die, and we had to console him with great difficulty, assuring him that there was nothing to be afraid of, as it was quite a common experience and nobody ever died of it. The second class, again, was right over the screw of the ship. The two Bengali lads, being natives, were put into a cabin almost like a black-hole, where neither air nor light had any access. So the boys could not remain in the room, and on the deck the rolling was terrible. Again, when the prow of the ship settled into the hollow of a wave and the stern was pitched up, the screw rose clear out of the water and continued to wheel in the air, giving a tremendous jolting to the whole vessel. And the second class then shook as when a rat is seized by a cat and shaken.

However, this was the monsoon season. The more the ship would proceed westwards, the more gale and wind she would have to encounter. The people of Madras had given plenty of fruits, the greater part of which, and the sweets, and rice-and-curd, etc., I gave to the boys. Alasinga had hurriedly bought a ticket and boarded the ship barefooted. He says he wears shoes now and then. Ways and manners differ in different countries. In Europe it is a great shame on the part of ladies to show their feet, but they feel no delicacy in exposing half their bust. In our country, the head must be covered by all means, no matter if the rest of the body is well covered or not. Alasinga, the editor of the Brahmavadin, who is a Mysore Brahmin of the Ramanuja sect, having a fondness for Rasam (Pungent and sour dal soup.) with shaven head and forehead overspread with the caste-mark of the Tengale sect, has brought with him with great care, as his provision for the voyage, two small bundles, in one of which there is fried flattened rice, and in another popped rice and fried peas! His idea is to live upon these during the voyage to Ceylon, so that his caste may remain intact. Alasinga had been to Ceylon once before, at which his caste-people tried to put him into some trouble, without success. That is a saving feature in the caste-system of India — if one's caste-people do not object, no one else has any right to say anything against him. And as for the South India castes — some consist of five hundred souls in all, some even hundred, or at most a thousand, and so circumscribed is their limit that for want of any other likely bride, one marries one's sister's daughter! When railways were first introduced in Mysore, the Brahmins who went from a distance to see the trains were outcasted! However, one rarely finds men like our Alasinga in this world — one so unselfish, so hard-working and devoted to his Guru, and such an obedient disciple is indeed very rare on earth. A South Indian by birth, with his head shaven so as to leave a tuft in the centre, bare-footed, and wearing the Dhoti, he got into the first class; he was strolling now and then on the deck and when hungry, was chewing some of the popped rice and peas! The ship's servants generally take all South Indians to be Chettis (merchants) and say that they have lots of money, but will not spend a bit of it on either dress or food! But the servants are of opinion that in our company Alasinga's purity as a Brahmin is getting contaminated. And it is true — for the South Indians lose much of their caste-rigours through contact with us.

Alasinga did not feel sea-sick. Brother T__ felt a little trouble at the beginning but is now all right. So the four days passed in various pleasant talks and gossip. In front of us is Colombo. Here we have Sinhal — Lanka. Shri Ramachandra crossed over to Lanka by building a bridge across and conquered Ravana, her King. Well, I have seen the bridge, and also, in the palace of the Setupati Maharaja of Ramnad, the stone slab on which Bhagavan Ramachandra installed his ancestor as Setupati for

the first time. But the Buddhist Ceylonese of these sophisticated times will not admit this. They say that in their country there is not even a tradition to indicate it. But what matters their denial? Are not our "old books" authorities enough? Then again, they call their country Sinhal and will not term it Lanka (Means also "Chillies" in Bengal.) — and how should they? There is no piquancy either in their words, or in their work, or in their nature, or in their appearance! Wearing gowns, with plaited hair, and in that a big comb — quite a feminine appearance! Again, they have slim, short, and tender womanlike bodies. These — the descendants of Ravana and Kumbhakarna! Not a bit of it! Tradition says they have migrated from Bengal — and it was well done. That new type of people who are springing in Bengal — dressed like women, speaking in soft and delicate accents, walking with a timid, faltering gait, unable to look any one in the face and from their very birth given to writing love poems and suffering the pangs of separation from their beloved — well, why do they not go to Ceylon, where they will find their fellows! Are the Government asleep? The other day they created a great row trying to capture some people in Puri. Why, in the metropolis itself are many worth seizing and packing off!

There was a very naughty Bengali Prince, named Vijaya Sinha, who quarrelled with his father, and getting together a few more fellows like him set sail in a ship, and finally came upon the Island of Ceylon. That country was then inhabited by an aboriginal tribe whose descendants are now known as the Bedouins. The aboriginal king received him very cordially and gave him his daughter in marriage. There he remained quietly for some time, when one night, conspiring with his wife, with a number of fellows, he took the king and his nobles by surprise and massacred them. Then Vijaya Sinha ascended the throne of Ceylon. But his wickedness did not end here. After a time he got tired of his aboriginal queen, and got more men and more girls from India and himself married a girl named Anurâdhâ, discarding his first aboriginal wife. Then he began to extirpate the whole race of the aborigines, almost all of whom were killed, leaving only a small remnant who are still to be met with in the forests and jungles. In this way Lanka came to be called Sinhal and became, to start with, colony of Bengali ruffians!

In course of time, under the regime of Emperor Asoka, his son Mahinda and his daughter Sanghamittâ, who had taken the vow of Sannyasa, came to the Island of Ceylon as religious missionaries. Reaching there, they found the people had grown quite barbarous, and, devoting their whole lives, they brought them back to civilisation as far as possible; they framed good moral laws for them and converted them to Buddhism. Soon the Ceylonese grew very staunch Buddhists, and built a great city in the centre of the island and called it Anuradhapuram. The sight of the remains of this city strikes one dumb even today — huge stupas, and dilapidated stone building extending for miles and miles are standing to this day; and a great part of it is overgrown with jungles which have not yet been cleared.

Shaven-headed monks and nuns, with the begging bowl in hand and clothed in yellow robes, spread all over Ceylon. In places colossal temples were reared containing huge figure of Buddha in meditation, of Buddha preaching the Law, and of Buddha in a reclining posture—entering into Nirvana. And the Ceylonese, out of mischief, painted on the walls of the temples the supposed state of things in Purgatory—some are being thrashed by ghosts, some are being sawed, some burnt, some fried in hot oil, and some being flayed—altogether a hideous spectacle! Who could know that in this religion, which preached "noninjury as the highest virtue", there would be room for such things! Such is the case in China, too, so also in Japan. While preaching non-killing so much in theory, they provide for such an array of punishments as curdles up one's blood to see. Once a thief broke into the house of a man of this non-killing type. The boys of the house caught hold of the thief and were giving him a sound beating. The master hearing a great row came out on the upper balcony and after making inquiries shouted out, "Cease from beating, my boys. Don't beat him. Non-injury is the highest virtue." The fraternity of junior non-killers stopped beating and asked the master what they were to do with the thief. The master ordered, "Put him in a bag, and throw him into water." The thief, much obliged at this humane dispensation, with folded hands said, "Oh! How great is the master's compassion!" I had heard that the Buddhists were very quiet people and equally tolerant of all religions. Buddhist preachers come to Calcutta and abuse us with choice epithets, although we offer them enough respect. Once I was preaching at Anuradhapuram among the Hindus—not Buddhists—and that in an open maidan, not on anybody's property—when a whole host of Buddhist monks and laymen, men and women, came out beating drums and cymbals and set up an awful uproar. The lecture had to stop, of course, and there was the imminent risk of bloodshed. With great difficulty I had to persuade the Hindus that we at any rate might practise a bit of non-injury, if they did not. Then the matter ended peacefully.

Gradually Tamilian Hindus from the north began slowly to migrate into Ceylon. The Buddhists, finding themselves in untoward circumstances, left their capital to establish a hill-station called Kandy, which, too, the Tamilians wrested from them in a short time and placed a Hindu king on the throne. Then came hordes of Europeans—the Spaniards, the Portuguese, and the Dutch. Lastly the English have made themselves kings. The royal family of Kandy have been sent to Tanjore, where they are living on pension and Mulagutanni Rasam.

In northern Ceylon there is a great majority of Hindus, while in the southern part, Buddhists and hybrid Eurasians of different types preponderate. The principal seat of the Buddhists is Colombo, the present capital, and that of the Hindus is Jaffna. The restrictions of caste are here much less than in India; the Buddhists have a few in marriage affairs, but none in matters of food, in which respect the Hindus observe some restrictions. All the butchers of Ceylon were formerly Buddhists; now the number is decreasing owing to the revival of Buddhism. Most of the Buddhists are now changing their anglicised titles for native ones. All the Hindu castes have mixed together and formed a single Hindu caste, in which, like the Punjabi Jats, one can marry a girl of any caste—even a European girl at that. The son goes into a temple, puts the sacred trilinear mark on the forehead, utters "Shiva, Shiva", and becomes a Hindu. The husband may be a Hindu, while the wife is a Christian. The Christian rubs some sacred ash on the forehead, utters "Namah Pârvatipatayé" (salutation to Shiva), and she straightway becomes a Hindu. This is what has made the Christian missionaries so cross with you. Since your coming into Ceylon, many Christians, putting sacred ash on their head and repeating "Salutation to Shiva", have become Hindus and gone back to their caste. Advaitavâda and Vira-Shaivavâda are the prevailing religions here. In place of the word "Hindu" one has to say "Shiva". The religious dance and Sankirtana which Shri Chaitanya introduced into Bengal had their origin in the South, among the Tamil race. The Tamil of Ceylon is pure Tamil and the religion of Ceylon is equally pure Tamil religion. That ecstatic chant of a hundred thousand men, and their singing of devotional hymns to Shiva, the noise of a thousand Mridangas (A kind of Indian drum.) with the metallic sound of big cymbals, and the frenzied dance of these ash-covered, red-eyed athletic Tamilians with stout rosaries of Rudrâksha beads on their neck, looking just like the great devotee, Hanuman—you can form no idea of these, unless you personally see the phenomenon.

Our Colombo friends had procured a permit for our landing, so we landed and met our friends there. Sir Coomara Swami is the foremost man among the Hindus: his wife is an English lady, and his son is barefooted and wears the sacred ashes on his forehead. Mr. Arunachalam and other friends came to meet me. After a long time I partook of Mulagutanni and the king-cocoanut. They put some green cocoanuts into my cabin. I met Mrs. Higgins and visited her boarding school for Buddhist girls. I also visited the monastery and school of our old acquaintance, the Countess of Canovara. The Countess' house is more spacious and furnished than Mrs. Higgins's. The Countess has invested her own money, whereas Mrs. Higgins has collected the money by begging. The Countess herself wears a Gerua cloth after the mode of the Bengali Sari. The Ceylonese Buddhists have taken a great fancy to this fashion, I found. I noticed carriage after carriage of women, all wearing the same Bengali Sari.

The principal place of pilgrimage for the Buddhists is the Dalada Maligawa or Tooth-temple at Kandy, which contains a tooth of Lord Buddha. The Ceylonese say it was at first in the Jagannath Temple at Puri and after many vicissitudes reached Ceylon, where also there was no little trouble over it. Now it is lying safe. The Ceylonese have kept good historical records of themselves, not like those of ours—merely cock and bull stories. And the Buddhist scriptures also are well preserved here in the ancient Magadhi dialect. From here the Buddhist religion spread to Burma, Siam, and other countries. The Ceylonese Buddhists recognise only Shâkyamuni mentioned in their scriptures and try to follow his precepts. They do not, like the people of Nepal, Sikkim, Bhutan, Ladak, China, and Japan, worship Shiva and do not know the worship with mystical Mantras of such goddesses as Târâ Devi and so forth. But they believe in possession by spirits and things of that sort. The Buddhists have now split into two schools, the Northern and the Southern; the Northern school calls itself the Mahâyâna, and the Southern school, comprising the Ceylonese, Burmese, Siamese, etc., Hinâyâna. The Mahâyâna branch worships Buddha in name only; their real worship is of Tara Devi and of Avalokiteshwara (whom the Japanese, Chinese and Koreans call Wanyin); and there is much use of various cryptic rites and Mantras. The Tibetans are the real demons of Shiva. They all worship Hindu gods, play the Damaru, (A tabor shaped like an hour-glass.) keep human skulls, blow horns made of the bones of dead monks, are much given to wine and meat, and are always exorcising evil spirits and curing diseases by means of mystical incantations. In China and Japan, on the walls of all the temples I have observed various monosyllabic Mantras written in big gilt letters, which approach the Bengali characters so much that you can easily make out the resemblance.

Alasinga returned to Madras from Colombo, and we also got on board our ship, with presents of some lemons from the orchard of Coomara Swami, some king-cocoanuts, and two bottles of syrup, etc. (The god Kârtikeya has various names, such as Subrahmanya, Kamâra Swâmi etc. In the South the worship of this god is much in vogue; they call Kartikeya an incarnation of the sacred formula "Om".)

The ship left Colombo on the morning of 25th June. Now we have to encounter full monsoon conditions. The more our ship is advancing, the more is the storm increasing and the louder is the wind howling—there is incessant rain, and enveloping darkness; huge waves are dashing on the ship's deck with a terrible noise, so that it is impossible to stay on the deck. The dining table has been divided into small squares by means of wood partitions, placed lengthwise and breadthwise, called fiddle, out of which the food articles are jumping up. The ship is creaking, as if it were going to break to pieces. The Captain says, "Well, this year's monsoon seems to be unusually rough". The Captain is a very interesting person who spent many years in the Chinese Sea and Indian Ocean; a very entertaining fellow, very clever in telling cock and bull stories. Numerous stories of pirates—how Chinese coolies used to kill ship's officers, loot the whole ship and escape—and other stories of that ilk he is narrating. And there is nothing else to do, for reading or writing is out of the question in such heavy rolling. It is extremely difficult to sit inside the cabin; the window has been shut for fear of the waves getting in. One day Brother T__ kept it slightly ajar and a fragment of a wave entered and flooded the whole cabin! And who can describe the heaving and tossing on the deck! Amid such conditions, you must remember, the work for your Udbodhan is going on to a certain extent.

There are two Christian missionary passengers on our ship, one of whom is an American, with a family—a very good man, named Bogesh. He has been married seven years, and his children number half-a-dozen. The servants call it God's special grace—though the children perhaps, feel differently. Spreading a shabby bed on the deck, Mrs. Bogesh makes all the children lie on it and goes away. They make themselves dirty and roll on the deck, crying aloud. The passengers on the deck are always nervous and cannot walk about on the deck, lest they might tread on any of Bogesh's children. Making the youngest baby lie in a square basket with high sides, Mr. and Mrs. Bogesh sit in a corner for four hours, huddled together. One finds it hard to appreciate your European civilisation. If we rinse our mouth or wash our teeth in public—they say it is barbarous, these things ought to be done in private. All right, but I put it to you, if it is not also decent to avoid such acts as the one above referred to, in public. And you run after this civilisation! However you cannot understand what good Protestantism has done to North Europe, unless you see the Protestant clergy. If then ten crores of English people die, and only the priests survive, in twenty years another ten crores will be raised!

Owing to the rolling of the ship most of the passengers are suffering from headache. A little girl named Tootle is accompanying her father; she has lost her mother. Our Nivedita has become a mother to Tootle and Bogesh's children. Tootle has been brought up in Mysore with her father who is a planter. I asked her, "Tootle, how are you?" She replied, "This Bungalow is not good and rolls very much, which makes me sick." To her every house is a bungalow. One sickly child of Bogesh suffers specially from want of care; the poor thing is rolling on the wooden deck the whole day. The old Captain now and then comes out of his cabin and feeds him with some soup with a spoon, and pointing to his slender legs says, "What a sickly child—how sadly neglected!"

Many desire eternal happiness. But if happiness were eternal, misery also would be eternal, just think of that. Could we in that case have ever reached Aden! Fortunately neither happiness nor misery is eternal; therefore in spite of our six days' journey being prolonged into fourteen days, and our buffeting terrible wind and rain night and day, we at last did reach Aden. The more we were ahead of Colombo, the more the storm and rain increased, the sky became a lake, and the wind and the waves grew fierce; and it was almost impossible for the ship to proceed, breasting such wind and wave, and her speed was halved. Near the island of Socotra, the monsoon was at its worst. The Captain remarked that this was the centre of the monsoon, and that if we could pass this, we should gradually reach calmer waters. And so we did. And this nightmare also ended.

On the evening of the 8th, we reached Aden. No one, white or black, is allowed to land, neither is any cargo allowed into the ship. And there are not many things worth seeing here. You have only barren stretches of sand, bearing some resemblance to Rajputana, and treeless, verdureless hills. In between the hills there are forts and on the top are the soldiers' barracks. In front are the hotels and shops arranged in the form of a crescent, which are discernible from the ship. Many ships are lying in anchor. One English, and one German man-of-war came in; the rest are either cargo or passenger ships. I had visited the town last time. Behind the hills are the native barracks and the bazar. A few miles from there, there are big pits dug into the sides of the hills, where the rain-water accumulates. Formerly that was the only source of water. Now by means of an apparatus they distil the sea water and get good fresh water, which, however, is very dear. Aden is just like an Indian town—with its large percentage of Indian civil and military population. There are a good many Parsee shopkeepers and Sindhi merchants. Aden is a very ancient place—the Roman Emperor Constantius sent a batch of missionaries here to preach Christianity. Then the Arabs rose and killed these Christians, whereupon the Roman Emperor asked the King of Abyssinia—long a Christian country—to punish them. The Abyssinian King sent an army and severely punished the Arabs of Aden. Afterwards Aden passed into the hands of the Samanidi Kings of Persia. It is they who are reputed to have first excavated those caves for the accumulation of water. Then, after the rise of Mohammedanism, Aden passed into the hands of the Arabs. After a certain time, a Portuguese general made ineffectual attempts to capture the place. Then the Sultan of Turkey made the place a naval base with the object of expelling the Portuguese from the Indian Ocean.

Again it passed into the possession of the neighbouring Arabian ruler. Afterwards, the English purchased it and they built the present town. Now the warships of all the powerful nations are cruising all over the world, and everyone wants to have a voice in every trouble that arises in any part of it. Every nation wants to safeguard its supremacy, political interest, and commerce. Hence they are in need of coal every now and then. As it would not be possible to get a supply of coal from an enemy country in times of war, every Power wants to have a coaling station of its own. The best sites have been already occupied by the English; the French have come in for the next best; and after them the other Powers of Europe have secured, and are securing, sites for themselves either by force or by purchase, or by friendly overture. The Suez Canal is now the link between Europe and Asia, and it is under the control of the French. Consequently the English have made their position very strong at Aden, and the other Powers also have each made a base for themselves along the Red Sea. Sometimes this rage for land brings disastrous consequences. Italy, trodden under foreign feet for seven centuries, stood on her legs after enormous difficulties. But immediately after doing this, she began to think a lot of herself and became ambitious of foreign conquest. In Europe no nation can seize a bit of land belonging to another; for all the Powers would unite to crush the usurper. In Asia also, the big Powers—the English, Russians, French, and Dutch—have left little space unoccupied. Now there remained only a few bits of Africa, and thither Italy directed her attention. First she tried in North Africa, where she met with opposition from the French and desisted. Then the English gave her a piece of land on the Red Sea, with the ulterior object that from that centre Italy might absorb the Abyssinian territory. Italy, too, came on with an army. But the Abyssinian King, Manalik, gave her such a beating that Italy found it difficult to save herself by fleeing from Africa. Besides, Russian and Abyssinian Christianity being, as is alleged, very much alike, the Russian Czar is an ally of the Abyssinians at bottom.

Well, our ship is now passing through the Red Sea. The missionary said, "This is the Red Sea, which the Jewish leader Moses crossed on foot with his followers. And the army which the Egyptian King Pharaoh sent for their capture was drowned in the sea, the wheels of their war-chariots having stuck in the mud"—like Karna's in the Mahâbhârata story. He further said that this could now be proved by modern scientific reasons. Nowadays in every country it has become a fashion to support the miracles of religion by scientific argument. My friend, if these phenomena were the outcome of natural forces, where then is there room for their intervention of your god "Yave"? A great dilemma!—If they are opposed to science, those miracles are mere myths, and your religion is false. And even if they are borne out by science, the glory of your god is superfluous, and they are just like any other natural phenomena. To this, Priest Bogesh replied, "I do not know all the issues involved in it, I simply believe." This is all right—one can tolerate that. But then there is a party of men, who are very clear in criticising others' views and bringing forward arguments against them, but where they themselves are concerned, they simply say, "I only believe, my mind testifies to their veracity." These are simply unbearable. Pooh! What weight has their intellect? Absolutely nothing! They are very quick to label the religious beliefs of others as superstitious, especially those which have been condemned by the Europeans, while in their own case they concoct some fantastic notions of Godhead and are beside themselves with emotions over them.

The ship is steadily sailing north. The borders of this Red Sea were a great centre of ancient civilisation. There, on the other side, are the deserts of Arabia, and on this—Egypt. This is that ancient Egypt. Thousands of years ago, these Egyptians starting from Punt (probably Malabar) crossed the Red Sea, and steadily extended their kingdom till they reached Egypt. Wonderful was the expansion of their power, their territory, and their civilisation. The Greeks were the disciples of these. The wonderful mausoleums of their kings, the Pyramids, with figures of the Sphinx, and even their dead bodies are preserved to this day. Here lived the ancient Egyptian peoples, with curling hair and ear-rings, and wearing snow-white dhotis without one end being tucked up behind. This is Egypt—the memorable stage where the Hyksos, the Pharaohs, the Persian Emperors, Alexander the Great, and the Ptolemies, and the Roman and Arab conquerors played their part. So many centuries ago, they left their history inscribed in great detail in hieroglyphic characters on papyrus paper, on stone slabs, and on the sides of earthen vessels.

This is the land where Isis was worshipped and Horus flourished. According to these ancient Egyptians, when a man dies, his subtle body moves about; but any injury done to the dead body affects the subtle body, and the destruction of the former means the total annihilation of the latter. Hence they took so much pains to preserve the corpse. Hence the pyramids of the kings and emperors. What devices, how much labour—alas, all in vain! Lured by the treasures, robbers have dug into the pyramids, and penetrating the mysteries of the labyrinths, have stolen the royal bodies. Not now—it was the work of the ancient Egyptians themselves. Some five or six centuries ago, these desiccated mummies the Jewish and Arab physicians looked upon as possessing great medicinal virtues and prescribed them for patients all over Europe. To this day, perhaps, it is the genuine "Mumia" of Unani and Hakimi methods of treatment!

Emperor Asoka sent preachers to this Egypt during the reign of the Ptolemy dynasty. They used to preach religion, cure diseases, live on vegetable food, lead celibate lives, and make Sannyasin disciples. They came to found many sects—the Therapeutae, Essenes, Manichaeans, and the like; from which modern Christianity has sprung. It was Egypt that became, during the Ptolemaic rule, the nursery of all learning. Here was that city of Alexandria, famous all over the world for its university, its library, and its literati—that Alexandria which, falling into the hands of illiterate, bigoted, and vulgar Christians suffered destruction, with its library burnt to ashes and learning stamped out! Finally, the Christians killed the lady servant, Hypatia, subjected her dead body to all sorts of abominable insult, and dragged it through the streets, till every bit of flesh was removed from the bones!

And to the south lie the deserts of Arabia—the mother of heroes. Have you ever seen a Bedouin Arab, with a cloak on, and a big kerchief tied on his head with a bunch of woollen strings?—That gait, that pose of standing, and that look, you will find in no other country. From head to foot emanates the freedom of open unconfined desert air—there you have the Arab. When the bigotry of the Christians and the barbarity of the Goths extinguished the ancient Greek and Roman civilisation, when Persia was trying to hide her internal putrefaction by adding layer after layer of gold-leaf upon it, when, in India, the sun of splendour of Pataliputra and Ujjain had set, leaving some illiterate, tyrant kings to rule over her, and the corruptions of dreadful obscenities and the worship of lust festering within—when such was the state of the world, this insignificant, semi-brutal Arab race spread like lightning over

its surface.

There you see a steamer coming from Mecca, with a cargo of pilgrims; behold—the Turk in European dress, the Egyptian in half-European costume, the Syrian Mussalman in Iranian attire, and the real Arab wearing a cloth reaching down the knee. Before the time of Mohammed, it was the custom to circumambulate round the Cabba temple in a state of nudity; since his time they have to wrap round a cloth. It is for this reason, that our Mohammedans unloose the strings of their trousers, and let their cloth hang down to the feet. Gone are those days for the Arabs. A continual influx of Kaffir, Sidi, and Abyssinian blood has changed their physique, energy, and all—the Arab of the desert is completely shorn of his former glory. Those that live in the north are peaceful citizens of the Turkish State. But the Christian subjects of the Sultan hate the Turks and love the Arabs. They say that the Arabs are amenable to education, become gentlemen, and are not so troublesome, while the real Turks oppress the Christians very much.

Though the desert is very hot, that heat is not enervating. There is no further trouble if you cover your body and head against it. Dry heat is not only not enervating, on the contrary it has a marked toning effect. The people of Rajputana, Arabia, and Africa are illustrations of this. In certain districts of Marwar, men, cattle, horses, and all are strong and of great stature. It is a joy to look at the Arabs and Sidis. Where the heat is moist, as in Bengal, the body is very much enervated, and every animal is weak.

The very name of the Red Sea strikes terror into the hearts of the passengers—it is so dreadfully hot, specially in summer, as it is now. Everyone is seated on the deck and recounts a story of some terrible accident, according to his knowledge. The Captain has outbidden them all. He says that a few days ago a Chinese man-of-war was passing through the Red Sea, and her Captain and eight sailors who worked in the coal-room died of heat.

Indeed, those who work in the coal-room have in the first place to stand in a pit of fire, and then there is the terrible heat of the Red Sea. Sometimes they run mad, rush up to the deck, plunge into the sea, and are drowned; or sometimes they die of heat in the engine-room itself.

These stories were enough to throw us out of our wits, nearly. But fortunately we did not experience so much heat. The breeze, instead of being a south-wind, continued to blow from the north, and it was the cool breeze of the Mediterranean.

On the 14th of July the steamer cleared the Red Sea and reached Suez. In front is the Suez Canal. The steamer has cargo for Suez. Well, Egypt is now under a visitation of plague, and possibly we are also carrying its germs. So there is the risk of contagion on both sides. Compared with the precautions taken here against mutual contact, well, those of our country are as nothing. The goods have to be unloaded, but the coolie of Suez must not touch the ship. It meant a good deal of extra trouble for the ship's sailors. They have to serve as coolies, lift up the cargo by means of cranes and drop it, without touching, on the Suez boats which carry it ashore. The agent of the Company has come near the ship in a small launch, but he is not allowed to board her. From the launch he is talking with the Captain who is in his ship. You must know this is not India, where the white man is beyond the plague regulations and all—here is the beginning of Europe. And all this precaution is taken lest the rat-borne plague finds an entrance into this heaven. The incubation period of plague-germs is ten days; hence the quarantine for ten days. We have however passed that period, so the disaster has been averted for us. But we shall be quarantined for ten days more if we but touch any Egyptian. In that case no passengers will be landed either at Naples or at Marseilles. Therefore every kind of work is being done from a distance, free from contact. Consequently it will take them the whole day to unload the cargo in this slow process. The ship can easily cross the Canal in the night, if she be provided with a searchlight; but if that is to be fitted, the Suez people will have to touch the ship—there, you have ten days' quarantine. She is therefore not to start in the night, and we must remain as we are in this Suez harbour for twenty-four hours! This is a very beautiful natural harbour, surrounded almost on three sides by sandy mounds and hillocks, and the water also is very deep. There are innumerable fish and sharks swimming in it. Nowhere else on earth are sharks in such plenty as in this port and in the port of Sydney, in Australia—they are ready to swallow men at the slightest opportunity! Nobody dares to descend into the water. Men, too, on their part are dead against the snakes and sharks and never let slip an opportunity to kill them.

In the morning, even before breakfast, we came to learn that big sharks were moving about behind the ship. I had never before an opportunity to see live sharks—the last time I came, the ship called at Suez for only a very short time, and that too, close to the town. As soon as we heard of the sharks, we hastened to the spot. The second class was at the stern of the ship, and from its deck, crowds of men, women and children were leaning over the railings to see the sharks. But our friends, the sharks, had moved off a little when we appeared on the spot, which damped our spirit very much. But we noticed that shoals of a kind of fish with bill-like heads were swimming in the water, and there was a species of very tiny fish in great abundance. Now and then a big fish, greatly resembling the hilsa, was flitting like an arrow hither and thither. I thought, he might be a young shark, but on inquiry I found it was not. Bonito was his name. Of course I had formerly read of him, and this also I had read that he was imported into Bengal from the Maldives as dried fish, on big-sized boats. It was also a matter of report that his meat was red and very tasteful. And we were now glad to see his energy and speed. Such a large fish was flitting through the water like an arrow, and in that glassy sea-water every movement of his body was noticeable. We were thus watching the bonito's

circuits and the restless movements of the tiny fish for twenty minutes of half an hour. Half an hour—three quarters—we were almost tired of it, when somebody announced—there he was. About a dozen people shouted, "There he is coming!" Casting my eyes I found that at some distance a huge black thing was moving towards us, six or seven inches below the surface of the water. Gradually the thing approached nearer and nearer. The huge flat head was visible; now massive his movement, there was nothing of the bonito's flitting in it. But once he turned his head, a big circuit was made. A gigantic fish; on he comes in a solemn gait, while in front of him are one or two small fish, and a number of tiny ones are playing on his back and all about his body. Some of them are holding fast on to his neck. He is your shark with retinue and followers. The fish which are preceding him are called the pilot fish. Their duty is to show the shark his prey, and perhaps be favoured with crumbs of his meal. But as one looks at the terrible gaping jaws of the shark, one doubts whether they succeed much in this latter respect. The fish which are moving about the shark and climbing on his back, are the "suckers". About their chest there is a flat, round portion, nearly four by two inches, which is furrowed and grooved, like the rubber soles of many English shoes. That portion the fish applies to the shark's body and sticks to it; that makes them appear as if riding on the shark's body and back. They are supposed to live on the worms etc. that grow on the shark's body. The shark must always have his retinue of these two classes of fish. And he never injures them, considering them perhaps as his followers and companions. One of these fish was caught with a small hook and line. Someone slightly pressed the sole of his shoe against its chest and when he raised his foot, it too was found to adhere to it. In the same way it sticks to the body of the shark.

The second class passengers have got their mettle highly roused. One of them is a military man and his enthusiasm knows no bounds. Rummaging the ship they found out a terrible hook—it outvied the hooks that are used in Bengal for recovering water-pots that have accidentally dropped into wells. To this they tightly fastened about two pounds of meat with a strong cord, and a stout cable was tied to it. About six feet from it, a big piece of wood was attached to act as a float. Then the hook with the float was dropped in the water. Below the ship a police boat was keeping guard ever since we came, lest there might be any contact between us and the people ashore. On this boat there were two men comfortably asleep, which made them much despised in the eyes of the passengers. At this moment they turned out to be great friends. Roused by the tremendous shouts, our friend, the Arab, rubbed his eyes and stood up. He was preparing to tuck up his dress, imagining some trouble was at hand, when he came to understand that so much shouting was nothing more than a request to him to remove the beam that was meant as a float to catch the shark, along with the hook, to a short distance. Then he breathed a sigh of relief, and grinning from ear to ear he managed to push the float to some distance by means of a pole. While we in eagerness stood on tiptoe, leaning over the railing, and anxiously waited for the shark—"watching his advent with restless eyes"; (From Jayadeva, the famous Sanskrit Poet of Bengal.) and as is always the case with those for whom somebody may be waiting with suspense, we suffered a similar fate—in other words, "the Beloved did not turn up". But all miseries have an end, and suddenly about a hundred yards from the ship, something of the shape of a water-carrier's leather bag, but much larger, appeared above the surface of the water, and immediately there was the hue and cry, "There is the shark!" "Silence, you boys and girls!—the shark may run off".—"Hallo, you people there, why don't you doff your white hats for a while?—the shark may shy".—While shouts like these were reaching the ear, the shark, denizen of the salt sea, rushed close by, like a boat under canvas, with a view to doing justice to the lump of pork attached to the hook. Seven or eight feet more and the shark's jaws would touch the bait. But that massive tail moved a little, and the straight course was transformed into a curve. Alas, the shark has made off! Again the tail slightly moved, and the gigantic body turned and faced the hook. Again he is rushing on—gaping, there, he is about to snap at the bait! Again the cursed tail moved, and the shark wheeled his body off to a distance. Again he is taking a circuit and coming on, he is gaping again; look now, he has put the bait into his jaws, there, he is tilting on his side; yes, he has swallowed the bait—pull, pull, forty or fifty pull together, pull on with all your might! What tremendous strength the fish has, what struggles he makes, how widely he gapes! Pull, pull! He is about to come above the surface, there he is turning in the water, and again turning on his side, pull, pull! Alas, he has extricated himself from the bait! The shark has fled. Indeed, what fussy people you all are! You could not wait to give him some time to swallow the bait! And you were impatient enough to pull so soon as he turned on his side! However, it is no use crying over spilt milk. The shark was rid of the hook and made a clean run ahead. Whether he taught the pilot fish a good lesson, we have got no information, but the fact was that the shark was clean off. And he was tiger-like, having black stripes over his body like a tiger. However, the "Tiger", with a view to avoiding the dangerous vicinity of the hook, disappeared, with his retinue of pilots and suckers.

But there is no need of giving up hopes altogether, for there, just by the side of the retreating "Tiger" is coming on another, a huge flat-headed creature! Alas, sharks have no language! Otherwise "Tiger" would surely have made an open breast of his secret to the newcomer and thus warned him. He would certainly have said, "Hallo, my friend, beware there is a new creature come over there, whose flesh is very tasteful and savoury, but what hard bones! Well, I have been born and brought up as a shark these many years and have devoured lots of animals—living, dead, and half-dead, and filled my stomach with lots of bones, bricks, and stones, and wooden stuff; but compared with these bones they are as butter, I tell you. Look, what has become of my teeth and jaws". And along with this he would certainly have shown to the new-comer those gaping jaws reaching almost to half his body. And the other too, with characteristic experience of maturer years, would have prescribed for him one or other of such infallible marine remedies as the bile of one fish, the spleen of another, the cooling broth of oysters, and so forth. But since nothing of the kind took place, we must conclude that either the sharks are sadly in want of a language, or that they may have one, but it is impossible to talk under water; therefore until some characters fit for the sharks are discovered, it is impossible to use that language. Or it may be that "Tiger", mixing too much in human company, has imbibed a bit of human disposition too, and therefore, instead of giving out the real truth, asked "Flat-head", with a smile, if he was doing well, and bade him good-bye: "Shall I alone be befooled?"

Then Bengali poem has it, "First goes Bhagiratha blowing his conch, then comes Ganga bringing up the rear" etc. Well, of course, no blowing of the conch is heard, but first are going the pilot fish, and behind them comes "Flat-head", moving his massive body, while round about him dance the suckers. Ah, who can resist such a tempting bait? For a space of five yards on all sides, the surface of the sea is glossy with a film of fat, and it is for "Flat-head" himself to say how far the fragrance thereof has spread. Besides, what a spectacle it is! White, and red, and yellow—all in one place! It was real English pork, tied round a huge black hook, heaving under water most temptingly!

Silence now, every one—don't move about, and see that you don't be too hasty. But take care to keep close to the cable. There, he is moving near the hook, and examining the bait, putting it in his jaws! Let him do so. Hush—now he has turned on his side—look, he is swallowing it whole, silence—give him time to do it. Then, as "Flat-head", turning on his side, had leisurely swallowed the bait, and was about to depart, immediately there was the pull behind! " Flat-head", astonished, jerked his head and wanted to throw the bait off, but it made matters worse! The hook pierced him, and from above, men, young and old, began to pull violently at the cable. Look, the head of the shark is above water—pull, brothers, pull! There, about half the shark's body is above water! Oh, what jaws! It is all jaws and throat, it seems! Pull on! Ah, the whole of it is clear of water. There, the hook has pierced his jaws through and through—pull on! Wait, wait!—Hallo, you Arab Police boatman, will you tie a string round his tail?—He is such a huge monster that it is difficult to haul him up otherwise. Take care, brother, a blow from that tail is enough to fracture a horse's leg! Pull on—Oh, how very heavy! Good God, what have we here! Indeed, what is it that hangs down from under the shark's belly? Are they not the entrails! His own weight has forced them out! All right, cut them off, and let them drop into the sea, that will make the weight lighter. Pull on, brothers! Oh, it is a fountain of blood! No, there is no use trying to save the clothes. Pull, he is almost within reach. Now, set him on the deck; take care, brother, be very careful, if he but charges on anybody, he will bite off a whole arm! And beware of that tail! Now, slacken the rope—thud! Lord! What a big shark! And with what a thud he fell on board the ship! Well, one cannot be too careful—strike his head with that beam—hallo, military man, you are a soldier, you are the man to do it.—"Quite so". The military passenger, with body and clothes splashed with blood, raised the beam and began to land heavy blows on the shark's head. And the women went on shrieking, "Oh dear! How cruel! Don't kill him!" and so forth, but never stopped seeing the spectacle. Let that gruesome scene end here. How the shark's belly was ripped open, how a torrent of blood flowed, how the monster continued to shake and move for a long time even after his entrails and heart had been taken off and his body dismembered, how from his stomach a heap of bones, skin, flesh, and wood, etc. came out—let all these topics go. Suffice it to say, that I had my meal almost spoilt that day—everything smelt of that shark.

This Suez Canal is a triumph of canal engineering. It was dug by a French engineer, Ferdinand de Lesseps. By connecting the Mediterranean with the Red Sea, it has greatly facilitated the commerce between Europe and India.

Of all the causes which have worked for the present state of human civilisation from the ancient times, the commerce of India is perhaps the most important. From time immemorial India has beaten all other countries in point of fertility and commercial industries. Up till a century ago, the whole of the world's demand for cotton cloth, cotton, jute, indigo, lac, rice, diamonds, and pearls, etc. used to be supplied from India. Moreover, no other country could produce such excellent silk and woollen fabrics, like the kincob etc. as India. Again, India has been the land of various spices such as cloves, cardamom, pepper, nutmeg, and mace. Naturally, therefore, from very ancient times, whatever country became civilised at any particular epoch, depended upon India for those commodities. This trade used to follow two main routes—one was through land, via Afghanistan and Persia, and the other was by sea—through the Red Sea. After his conquest of Persia, Alexander the Great despatched a general named Niarchus to explore a sea-route, passing by the mouth of the Indus, across the ocean, and through the Red Sea. Most people are ignorant of the extent to which the opulence of ancient countries like Babylon, Persia, Greece, and Rome depended on Indian commerce. After the downfall of Rome, Baghdad in Mohammedan territory, and Venice and Genoa in Italy, became the chief Western marts of Indian commerce. And when the Turks made themselves masters of the Roman Empire and closed the trade-route to India for the Italians, then Christopher Columbus (Christobal Colon), a Spaniard or Genoese, tried to explore a new route to India across the Atlantic, which resulted in the discovery of the American continent. Even after reaching America, Columbus could not get rid of the delusion that it was India. It is therefore that the aborigines of America are to this day designated as Indians. In the Vedas we find both names, "Sindhu" and "Indu", for the Indus; the Persians transformed them into "Hindu", and the Greeks into "Indus", whence we derived the words "India" and "Indian". With the rise of Mohammedanism the word "Hindu" became degraded and meant "a dark-skinned fellow", as is the case with the word "native" now.

The Portuguese, in the meantime, discovered a new route to India, doubling Africa. The fortune of India smiled on Portugal—then came the turn of the French, the Dutch, the Danes, and the English. Indian commerce, Indian revenue and all are now in the possession of the English; it is therefore that they are the foremost of all nations now. But now, Indian products are being grown in countries like America and elsewhere, even better than in India, and she has therefore lost something of her prestige. This the Europeans are unwilling to admit. That India, the India of "natives", is the chief means and resources of their wealth and civilisation, is a fact which they refuse to admit, or even understand. We too, on our part, must not cease to bring it home to them.

Just weigh the matter in your mind. Those uncared-for lower classes of India—the peasants and weavers and the rest, who have been conquered by foreigners and are looked down upon by their own people—it is they who from time immemorial have been working silently, without even getting the remuneration of their labours! But what great changes are taking place slowly, all over the world, in pursuance of nature's law! Countries, civilisations, and supremacy are undergoing revolutions. Ye labouring classes of India, as a result of your silent, constant labours Babylon, Persia, Alexandria, Greece, Rome, Venice, Genoa, Baghdad, Samarqand, Spain, Portugal, France, Denmark, Holland, and England have successively attained supremacy and eminence! And you?—Well, who cares to think of you! My dear Swami, your ancestors wrote a few philosophical works, penned a dozen or so epics, or built a number of temples—that is all, and you rend the skies with triumphal shouts; while those whose heart's blood has contributed to all the progress that has been made in the world—well, who cares to praise them? The world-conquering heroes of spirituality, war, and poetry are in the eyes of all, and they have received the homage of mankind. But where nobody looks, no one gives a word of encouragement, where everybody hates—that living amid such circumstances and displaying boundless patience, infinite love, and dauntless practicality, our proletariat are doing their duty in their homes day and night, without the slightest murmur—well, is there no heroism in this? Many turn out to be heroes when they have got some great task to perform. Even a coward easily gives up his life, and the most selfish man behaves disinterestedly, when there is a multitude to cheer them on; but blessed indeed is he who manifests the same unselfishness and devotion to duty in the smallest of acts, unnoticed by all—and it is you who are actually doing this ye ever-trampled labouring classes of India! I bow to you.

Lectures & Discourses by **Swami Vivekananda**

This Suez Canal is also a thing of remote antiquity. During the reign of the Pharaohs in Egypt, a number of lagoons were connected with one another by a channel and formed a canal touching both seas. During the rule of the Roman Empire in Egypt also, attempts were made now and then to keep that channel open. Then the Mohammedan General Amru, after his conquest of Egypt, dug out the sand and changed certain features of it, so that it became almost transformed.

After that nobody paid much attention to it. The present canal was excavated by Khedive Ismail of Egypt, the Viceroy of the Sultan of Turkey, according to the advice of the French, and mostly through French capital. The difficulty with this canal is that owing to its running through a desert, it again and again becomes filled with sand. Only one good-sized merchant-ship can pass through it at a time, and it is said that very big men-of-war or merchantmen can never pass through it. Now, with a view to preventing incoming and outgoing ships from colliding against each other, the whole canal has been divided into a number of sections, and at both ends of each section there are open spaces broad enough for two or three ships to lie at anchor together. The Head Office is at the entrance to the Mediterranean, and there are stations in every section like railway stations. As soon as a ship enters the canal, messages are continually wired to this Head Office, where reports of how many ships are coming in and how many are going out, with their position at particular moments are telegraphed, and are marked on a big map. To prevent one ship confronting another, no ship is allowed to leave any station without a line-clear.

The Suez Canal is in the hands of the French. Though the majority of shares of the Canal Company are now owned by the English, yet, by a political agreement, the entire management rests with the French.

Now comes the Mediterranean. There is no more memorable region than this, outside India. It marks the end of Asia, Africa, and of ancient civilisation. One type of manners and customs and modes of living ends here and another type of features and temperament, food and dress, customs and habits begins — we enter Europe. Not only this, but here also is the great centre of that historical admixture of colours, races, civilisations, culture, and customs, which extending over many centuries has led to the birth of modern civilisation. That religion, and culture, and civilisation, and extraordinary prowess which today have encircled the globe were born here in the regions surrounding the Mediterranean. There, on the south, is the very, very ancient Egypt, the birthplace of sculpture — overflowing in wealth and food-stuffs; on the east is Asia Minor, the ancient arena of the Phoenician, Philistine, Jewish, valiant Babylonian, Assyrian, and Persian civilisations; and on the north, the land where the Greeks — wonders of the world — flourished in ancient times.

Well, Swami, you have had enough of countries, and rivers, and mountains, and seas — now listen to a little of ancient history. Most wonderful are these annals of ancient days; not fiction, but truth — the true history of the human race. These ancient countries were almost buried in oblivion for eternity — the little that people knew of them consisted almost exclusively of the curiously fictitious compositions of the ancient Greek historians, or the miraculous descriptions of the Jewish mythology called the Bible. Now the inscriptions on ancient stones, buildings, rooms, and tiles, and linguistic analysis are voluble in their narration of the history of those countries. This recounting has but just commenced, but even now it has unearthed most wonderful tales, and who knows what more it will do in future? Great scholars of all countries are puzzling their heads day and night over a bit of rock inscription or a broken utensil, a building or a tile, and discovering the tales of ancient days sunk in oblivion.

When the Mohammedan leader Osman occupied Constantinople, and the banner of Islam began to flutter triumphantly over the whole of eastern Europe, then those books and that learning and culture of the ancient Greeks which were kept hidden with their powerless descendants spread over western Europe in the wake of the retreating Greeks. Though subjected for a long time to the Roman rule, the Greeks were the teachers of the Romans in point of learning and culture. So much so that owing to the Greeks embracing Christianity and the Christian Bible being written in the Greek tongue, Christianity got a hold over the whole Roman Empire. But the ancient Greeks, whom we call the Yavanas, and who were the first teachers of European civilisation, attained the zenith of their culture long before the Christians. Ever since they became Christians, all their learning and culture was extinguished. But as some part of the culture of their ancestors is still preserved in the Hindu homes, so it was with the Christian Greeks; these books found their way all over Europe. This it was that gave the first impetus to civilisation among the English, German, French, and other nations. There was a craze for learning the Greek language and Greek arts. First of all, they swallowed everything that was in those books. Then, as their own intelligence began to brighten up, and sciences began to develop, they commenced researches as to the date, author, subject, and authenticity, etc. of those books. There was no restriction whatever in passing free opinions on all books of the non-Christian Greeks, barring only the scriptures of the Christians, and consequently there cropped up a new science — that of external and internal criticism.

Suppose, for instance, that it is written in a book that such and such an incident took place on such and such a date. But must a thing be accepted as authentic, simply because some one has been pleased to write something about it in a book? It was customary with people, specially of those times, to write many things from imagination; moreover, they had very scanty knowledge about nature, and even of this earth we live in. All these raised grave doubts as to the authenticity of the subject-matter of a book. Suppose, for instance, that a Greek historian has written that on such and such a date there was a king in India called Chandragupta. If now, the books of India, too, mention that king under that particular date, the matter is certainly proved to a great extent. If a few coins of Chandragupta's reign be found, or a building of his time which contains references to him, the veracity of the matter is then assured.

Suppose another book records a particular incident as taking place in the reign of Alexander the Great, but there is mention of one or two Roman Emperors in such a way that they cannot be taken as interpolations—then that book is proved not to belong to Alexander's time.

Or again, language. Every language undergoes some change through the lapse of time, and authors have also their own peculiar style. If in any book there is suddenly introduced a description which has no bearing on the subject, and is in a style quite different from the author's, it will readily be suspected as an interpolation. Thus a new science of ascertaining the truth about a book, by means of doubting and testing and proving in various ways, was discovered.

To add to this, modern science began, with rapid strides, to throw new light on things from all sides, with the results that any book that contained a reference to supernatural incidents came to be wholly disbelieved.

To crown all, there were the entrance of the tidal wave of Sanskrit into Europe and the deciphering of ancient lapidary inscriptions found in India, on the banks of the Euphrates, and in Egypt, as well as the discovery of temples etc., hidden for ages under the earth or on hill-sides, and the correct reading of their history.

I have already said that this new science of research set the Bible or the New Testament books quite apart. Now there are no longer the tortures of the Inquisition, there is only the fear of social obloquy; disregarding that, many scholars have subjected those books also to a stringent analysis. Let us hope that as they mercilessly hack the Hindu and other scriptures to pieces, they will in time show the same moral courage towards the Jewish and Christian scriptures also. Let me give an illustration to explain why I say this. Maspero, a great savant and a highly reputed author on Egyptology, has written a voluminous history of the Egyptians and Babylonians entitled Histoire Ancienne Orientale. A few years ago I read an English translation of the book by an English archaeologist. This time, on my asking a Librarian of the British Museum about certain books on Egypt and Babylon, Maspero's book was mentioned. And when he learnt that I had with me an English translation of the book, he said that it would not do, for the translator was a rather bigoted Christian, and wherever Maspero's researches hit Christianity in any way, he (the translator) had managed to twist and torture those passages! He recommended me to read the book in original French. And on reading I found it was just as he had said—a terrible problem indeed! You know very well what a queer thing religious bigotry is; it makes a mess of truth and untruth. Thenceforth

my faith in the translations of those research works has been greatly shaken.

Another new science has developed—ethnology, that is, the classification of men from an examination of their colour, hair, physique, shape of the head, language, and so forth.

The Germans, though masters in all sciences, are specially expert in Sanskrit and ancient Assyrian culture; Benfey and other German scholars are illustrations of this. The French are skilled in Egyptology—scholars like Maspero are French. The Dutch are famous for their analysis of Jewish and ancient Christian religions—writers like Kuenen have attained a world-celebrity. The English inaugurate many sciences and then leave off.

Let me now tell you some of the opinions of these scholars. If you do not like their views, you may fight them; but pray, do not lay the blame on me. According to the Hindus, Jews, ancient Babylonians, Egyptians, and other ancient races, all mankind have descended from the same primaeval parents. People do not much believe in this now.

Have you ever seen jet-black, flat-nosed, thick-lipped, curly-haired Kaffirs with receding foreheads? And have you seen the Santals, and Andamanese, and Bhils with about the same features, but of shorter stature, and with hair less curly? The first class are called Negroes; these live in Africa. The second class are called Negritos (little Negroes); in ancient times these used to inhabit certain parts of Arabia, portions of the banks of the Euphrates, the southern part of Persia, the whole of India, the Andamans, and other islands, even as far as Australia. In modern times they are to be met with in certain forests and jungles of India, in the Andamans, and in Australia.

Have you seen the Lepchas, Bhutias, and Chinese—white or yellow in colour, and with straight black hair? They have dark eyes—but these are set so as to form an angle—scanty beard and moustache, a flat face, and very prominent malar bones. Have you seen the Nepalese, Burmese, Siamese, Malays, and Japanese? They have the same shape, but have shorter stature.

The two species of this type are called Mongols and Mongoloids (little Mongols). The Mongolians have now occupied the greater part of Asia. It is they who, divided into many branches such as the Mongols, Kalmucks, Huns, Chinese, Tartars, Turks, Manchus, Kirghiz, etc. lead a nomadic life, carrying tents, and tending sheep, goats, cattle, and horses, and whenever an opportunity occurs, sweep like a swarm of locusts and unhinge the world. These Chinese and Tibetans alone are an exception to this. They are also known by the name of Turanians. It is the Turan which you find in the popular phrase, "Iran and Turan."

A race of a dark colour but with straight hair, straight nose and straight dark eyes, used to inhabit ancient Egypt and ancient Babylonia and now live all over India, specially in the southern portion; in Europe also one finds traces of them in rare places. They form one race, and have the technical name of Dravidians.

Another race has white colour, straight eyes, but ears and noses curved and thick towards the tip, receding foreheads, and thick lips—as, for instance, the people of north Arabia, the modern Jews and the ancient Babylonians, Assyrians, Phoenicians, etc.; their languages also have a common stock; these are called the Semitic race.

And those who speak a language allied to Sanskrit, who have straight noses, mouths, and eyes, a white complexion, black or brown hair, dark or blue eyes, are called Aryans.

All the modern races have sprung from an admixture of these races. A country which has a preponderance of one or other of these races, has also its language and physiognomy mostly like those of that particular race.

It is not a generally accepted theory in the West that a warm country produces dark complexion and a cold country white complexion. Many are of opinion that the existing shades between black and white have been the outcome of a fusion of races.

According to scholars, the civilisations of Egypt and ancient Babylonia are the oldest. Houses and remains of buildings are to be met with in these countries dating 6,000 B.C. or even earlier. In India the oldest building that may have been discovered date back to Chandragupta's time at the most; that is, only 300 B.C. Houses of greater antiquity have not yet been discovered. (The ancient remains at Harappa, Mohenjo-daro etc., in the Indus Valley in North-west India, which prove the existence of an advanced city civilisation in India dating back to more than 3000 B.C., were not dug out before 1922.—Ed.) But there are books, etc., of a far earlier date, which one cannot find in any other country. Pandit Bal Gangadhar Tilak has brought evidence to show that the Vedas of the Hindus existed in the present form at least five thousand years before the Christian era.

The borders of this Mediterranean were the birthplace of that European civilisation which has now conquered the world. On these shores the Semitic races such as the Egyptians, Babylonians, Phoenicians, and Jews, and the Aryan races such as the Persians, Greeks, and Romans, fused together—to form the modern European civilisation.

A big stone slab with inscriptions on it, called the Rosetta Stone, was discovered in Egypt. On this there are inscriptions in hieroglyphics, below which there is another kind of writing, and below them all there are inscriptions resembling Greek characters. A scholar conjectured that those three sets of inscriptions presented the same thing, and he deciphered these ancient Egyptian inscriptions with the help of Coptic characters—the Copts being the Christian race who yet inhabit Egypt and who are known as the descendants of the ancient Egyptians. Similarly the cuneiform characters inscribed on the bricks and tiles of the Babylonians were also gradually deciphered. Meanwhile certain Indian inscriptions in plough-shaped characters were discovered as belonging to the time of

Emperor Asoka. No earlier inscriptions than these have been discovered in India. (The Indus script is now known to be contemporary with Sumerian and Egyptian.—Ed.) The hieroglyphics inscribed on various kinds of temples, columns, and sarcophagi all over Egypt are being gradually deciphered and making Egyptian antiquity more lucid.

The Egyptians entered into Egypt from a southern country called Punt, across the seas. Some say that that Punt is the modern Malabar, and that the Egyptians and Dravidians belong to the same race. Their first king was named Menes, and their ancient religion too resembles in some parts our mythological tales. The god Shibu was enveloped by the goddess Nui; later on another god Shu came and forcibly removed Nui. Nui's body became the sky, and her two hands and two legs became the four pillars of that sky. And Shibu became the earth. Osiris and Isis, the son and daughter of Nui, are the chief god and goddess in Egypt, and their son Horus is the object of universal worship. These three used to be worshipped in a group. Isis, again, is worshipped in the form of the cow.

Like the Nile on earth there is another Nile in the sky, of which the terrestrial Nile is only a part. According to the Egyptians, the Sun travels round the earth in a boat; now and then a serpent called Ahi devours him, then an eclipse takes place. The Moon is periodically attacked by a boar and torn to pieces, from which he takes fifteen days to recover. The deities of Egypt are some of them jackal-faced, some hawk-faced, others cow-faced, and so on.

Simultaneously with this, another civilisation had its rise on the banks of the Euphrates. Baal, Moloch, Istarte, and Damuzi were the chief of deities here. Istarte fell in love with a shepherd named Damuzi. A boar killed the latter and Istarte went to Hades, below the earth, in search of him. There she was subjected to various tortures by the terrible goddess Alat. At last Istarte declared that she would no more return to earth unless she got Damuzi back. This was a great difficulty; she was the goddess of sex-impulse, and unless she went back, neither men, nor animals, nor vegetables would multiply. Then the gods made a compromise that every year Damuzi was to reside in Hades for four months and live on earth during the remaining eight months. Then Istarte returned, there was the advent of spring and a good harvest followed.

Thus Damuzi again is known under the name of Adunoi or Adonis! The religion of all the Semitic races, with slight minor variations, was almost the same. The Babylonians, Jews, Phoenicians, and Arabs of a later date used the same form of worship. Almost every god was called Moloch—the word which persists to this day in the Bengali language as Mâlik (ruler), Mulluk (kingdom) and so forth—or Baal; but of course there were minor differences. According to some, the god called Alat afterwards turned into Allah of the Arab.

The worship of these gods also included certain terrible and abominable rites. Before Moloch or Baal children used to be burnt alive. In the temple of Istarte the natural and unnatural satisfaction of lust was the principal feature.

The history of the Jewish race is much more recent than that of Babylon. According to scholars the scripture known as the Bible was composed from 500 B.C. to several years after the Christian era. Many portions of the Bible which are generally supposed to be of earlier origin belong to a much later date. The main topics of the Bible concern the Babylonians. The Babylonian cosmology and description of the Deluge have in many parts been incorporated wholesale into the Bible. Over and above this, during the rule of the Persian Emperors in Asia Minor, many Persian doctrines found acceptance among the Jews. According to the Old Testament, this world is all; there is neither soul nor an after-life. In the New Testament there is mention of the Parsee doctrines of an after-life and resurrection of the dead, while the theory of Satan exclusively belongs to the Parsis.

The principal feature of the Jewish religion is the worship of Yave-Moloch. But this name does not belong to the Jewish language; according to some it is an Egyptian word. But nobody knows whence it came. There are descriptions in the Bible that the Israelites lived confined in Egypt for a long time, but all this is seldom accepted now, and the patriarchs such as Abraham, and Isaac, and Joseph are proved to be mere allegories.

The Jews would not utter the name "Yave", in place of which they used to say "Adunoi". When the Jews became divided into two branches, Israel and Ephraim, two principal temples were constructed in the two countries. In the temple that was built by the Israelites in Jerusalem, an image of Yave, consisting of a male and female figure united, was preserved in a coffer (ark), and there was a big phallic column at the door. In Ephraim, Yave used to be worshipped in the form of a gold-covered Bull.

In both places it was the practice to consign the eldest son alive to the flames before the god, and a band of women used to live in both the temples, within the very precincts of which they used to lead most immoral lives and their earnings were utilised for temple expenditure.

In course of time there appeared among the Jews a class of men who used to invoke the presence of deities in their person by means of music or dance. They were called Prophets. Many of these, through association with the Persians, set themselves against image-worship, sacrifice of sons, immorality, prostitution, and such other practices. By degrees, circumcision took the place of human sacrifice; and prostitution and image-worship etc. gradually disappeared. In course of time from among these Prophets Christianity had its rise.

There is a great dispute as to whether there ever was born a man with the name of Jesus. Of the four books comprising the New Testament, the Book of St. John has been rejected by some as spurious. As to the remaining three, the verdict is that they have been copied from some ancient book; and that, too,

long after the date ascribed to Jesus Christ.

Moreover, about the time that Jesus is believed to have been born among the Jews themselves, there were born two historians, Josephus and Philo. They have mentioned even petty sects among the Jews, but not made the least reference to Jesus or the Christians, or that the Roman Judge sentenced him to death on the cross. Josephus' book had a single line about it, which has now been proved to be an interpolation. The Romans used to rule over the Jews at that time, and the Greeks taught all sciences and arts. They have all written a good many things about the Jews, but made no mention of either Jesus or the Christians.

Another difficulty is that the sayings, precepts, or doctrines which the New Testament preaches were already in existence among the Jews before the Christian era, having come from different quarters, and were being preached by Rabbis like Hillel and others. These are what scholars say; but they cannot, with safety to their reputation, give oracular verdicts off-hand on their own religion, as they are wont to do with regard to alien religions. So they proceed slowly. This is what is called Higher Criticism.

The Western scholars are thus studying the religions, customs, races, etc., of different and far-off countries. But we have nothing of the kind in Bengali! And how is it possible? If a man after ten years of hard labour translates a book of this kind, well, what will he himself live upon, and where will he get the funds to publish his book?

In the first place, our country is very poor, and in the second place, there is practically no cultivation of learning. Shall such a day dawn for our country when we shall be cultivating various kinds of arts and sciences? — "She whose grace makes the dumb eloquent and the lame to scale mountains" — She, the Divine Mother, only knows!

The ship touched Naples — we reached Italy. The capital of Italy is Rome — Rome, the capital of that ancient, most powerful Roman Empire, whose politics, military science, art of colonisation, and foreign conquest are to this day the model for the whole world!

After leaving Naples the ship called at Marseilles, and thence straight at London.

You have already heard a good deal about Europe — what they eat, how they dress, what are their manners and customs, and so forth — so I need not write on this. But about European civilisation, its origin, its relation to us, and the extent to which we should adopt it — about such things I shall have much to say in future. The body is no respecter of persons, dear brother, so I shall try to speak about them some other time. Or what is the use? Well, who on earth can vie with us (specially the Bengalis) as regards talking and discussing? Show it in action if you can. Let your work proclaim, and let the tongue rest. But let me mention one thing in passing, viz. that Europe began to advance from the date that learning and power began to flow in among the poor lower classes. Lots of suffering poor people of other countries, cast off like refuse as it were, find a house and shelter in America, and these are the very backbone of America! It matters little whether rich men and scholars listen to you, understand you, and praise or blame you—they are merely the ornaments, the decorations of the country!—It is the millions of poor lower class people who are its life. Numbers do not count, nor does wealth or poverty; a handful of men can throw the world off its hinges, provided they are united in thought, word, and deed—never forget this conviction. The more opposition there is, the better. Does a river acquire velocity unless there is resistence? The newer and better a thing is, the more opposition it will meet with at the outset. It is opposition which foretells success. Where there is no opposition there is no success either. Good-bye!

Part II

We have an adage among us that one that has a disc-like pattern on the soles of his feet becomes a vagabond. I fear, I have my soles inscribed all over with them. And there is not much room for probability, either. I have tried my best to discover them by scrutinising the soles, but all to no purpose—the feet have been dreadfully cracked through the severity of cold, and no discs or anything of the kind could be traced. However, when there is the tradition, I take it for granted that my soles are full of those signs. But the results are quite patent—it was my cherished desire to remain in Paris for some time and study the French language and civilisation; I left my old friends and acquaintances and put up with a new friend, a Frenchman of ordinary means, who knew no English, and my French—well, it was something quite extraordinary! I had this in mind that the inability to live like a dumb man would naturally force me to talk French, and I would attain fluency in that language in no time—but on the contrary I am now on a tour through Vienna, Turkey, Greece, Egypt, and Jerusalem! Well, who can stem the course of the inevitable!—And this letter I am writing to you from the last remaining capital of Mohammedan supremacy—from Constantinople!

I have three travelling companions—two of them French and the third an American. The American is Miss MacLeod whom you know very well; the French male companion is Monsieur Jules Bois, a famous philosopher and litterateur of France; and the French lady friend is the world-renowned singer, Mademoiselle Calvé. "Mister" is "Monsieur" in the French language, and "Miss" is "Mademoiselle"—with a Z-sound. Mademoiselle Calvé is the foremost singer—opera singer—of the present day. Her musical performances are so highly appreciated that she has an annual income of three to four lakhs of rupees, solely from singing. I had previously been acquainted with her. The foremost actress in the West, Madame Sarah Bernhardt, and the foremost singer, Calvé, are both of them of French extraction, and both totally ignorant of English, but they visit England and America occasionally and earn millions of dollars by acting and singing. French is the language of the civilised world, the mark of gentility in the West, and everybody knows it; consequently these two ladies have neither the leisure nor the inclination to learn English. Madame Bernhardt is an aged lady; but when she steps on the stage after dressing, her imitation of the age and sex of the role she plays is perfect! A girl or a boy—whatever part you want her to play, she is an exact representation of that. And that wonderful voice! People here say her voice has the ring of silver strings! Madame Bernhardt has a special regard for India; she tells me again and again that our country is "trés ancien, tres civilisé"—very ancient and very civilised. One year she performed a drama touching on India, in which she set up a whole Indian street-scene on the stage—men, women, and children, Sadhus and Nagas, and everything—an exact picture of India! After the performance she told me that for about a month she had visited every museum and made herself acquainted with the men and women and their dress, the streets and bathing ghats and everything relating to India. Madame Bernhardt has a very strong desire to visit India.—"C'est mon rave!—It is the dream of my life", she says. Again, the Prince of Wales (His late Majesty King Edward VII, the then Prince of Wales.) has promised to take her over to a tiger and elephant hunting excursion. But then she said she must spend some two lakhs of rupees if she went to India! She is of course in no want of money. "La divine Sarah"—the divine Sarah—is her name; how can she want money, she who never travels but by a special train! That pomp and luxury many a prince of Europe cannot afford to indulge in! One can only secure a seat for her performance by paying double the fees, and that a month in advance! Well, she is not going to suffer want of money! But Sarah Bernhardt is given to spending lavishly. Her travel to India is therefore put off for the present.

Mademoiselle Calvé will not sing this winter, she will take a rest and is going to temperate climates like Egypt etc. I am going as her guest. Calvé has not devoted herself to music alone, she is sufficiently learned and has a great love for philosophical and religious literature. She was born amidst very poor circumstances; gradually, through her own genius and undergoing great labour and much hardship, she has now amassed a large fortune and has become the object of adoration of kings and potentates!

There are famous lady singers, such as Madame Melba, Madame Emma Ames, and others; and very distinguished singers, such as Jean de Reszke, Plancon, and the rest—all of whom earn two or three lakhs of rupees a year! But with Calvé's art is coupled a unique genius. Extraordinary beauty, youth, genius, and a celestial voice—all these have conspired to raise Calvé to the forefront of all singers. But there is no better teacher than pain and poverty! That extreme penury and pain and hardship of childhood, a constant struggle against which has won for Calvé this victory, have engendered a remarkable sympathy and a profound seriousness in her life. Again, in the West, there are ample opportunities along with the enterprising spirit. But in our country, there is a sad dearth of opportunities, even if the spirit of enterprise be not absent. The Bengali woman may be keen after acquiring education, but it comes to nought for want of opportunities. And what is there to learn from in the Bengali language? At best some poor novels and dramas! Then again, learning is confined at present to a foreign tongue or to Sanskrit and is only for the chosen few. In these Western countries there are innumerable books in the mother-tongue; over and above that, whenever something new comes out in a foreign tongue, it is at once translated and placed before the public.

Monsieur Jules Bois is a famous writer; he is particularly an adept in the discovery of historical truths in the different religions and superstitions. He has written a famous book putting into historical form the devil-worship, sorcery, necromancy, incantation, and such other rites that were in vogue in Mediaeval Europe, and the traces of those that obtain to this day. He is a good poet, and is an advocate of the Indian Vedantic ideas that have crept into the great French poets, such as Victor Hugo and Lamartine and others, and the great German poets, such as Goethe, Schiller, and the rest. The influence of Vedanta on European poetry and philosophy is very great. Every good poet is a Vedantin, I find; and whoever writes some philosophical treatise has to draw upon Vedanta in some shape or other. Only some of them do not care to admit this indebtedness, and want to establish their complete originality, as Herbert Spencer and others, for instance. But the majority do openly acknowledge. And how can they help it—in these days of telegraphs and railways and newspapers? M. Jules Bois is very modest and gentle, and though a man of ordinary means, he very cordially received me as a guest into his house in Paris. Now he is accompanying us for travel.

We have two other companions on the journey as far as Constantinople—Père Hyacinthe and his wife. Père, i.e. Father Hyacinthe was a monk of a strict ascetic section of the Roman Catholic Church. His scholarship, extraordinary eloquence, and great austerities won for him a high reputation in France and in the whole Catholic Order. The great poet, Victor Hugo, used to praise the French style of two men—one of these was Père Hyacinthe. At forty years of age Père Hyacinthe fell in love with an American woman and eventually married her. This created a great sensation, and of course the Catholic Order immediately gave him up. Discarding his ascetic garb of bare feet and loose-fitting cloak, Père Hyacinthe took up the hat, coat, and boots of the householder and became—Monsieur Loyson. I, however, call him by his former name. It is an old, old tale, and the matter was the talk of the whole continent. The Protestants received him with honour, but the Catholics began to hate him. The Pope, in consideration of his attainments, was unwilling to part with him and asked him to remain a Greek Catholic priest, and not abandon the Roman Church. (The priests of the Greek Catholic section are allowed to marry but once, but do not get any high position). Mrs. Loyson, however, forcibly dragged him

out of the Pope's fold. In course of time they had children and grandchildren; now the very aged Loyson is going to Jerusalem to try to establish cordial relations among the Christians and Mussulmans. His wife had perhaps seen many visions that Loyson might possibly turn out to be a second Martin Luther and overthrow the Pope's throne—into the Mediterranean. But nothing of the kind took place; and the only result was, as the French say, that he was placed between two stools. But Madame Loyson still cherishes her curious daydreams! Old Loyson is very affable in speech, modest, and of a distinctly devotional turn of mind. Whenever he meets me, he holds pretty long talks about various religions and creeds. But being of a devotional temperament, he is a little afraid of the Advaita. Madame Loyson's attitude towards me is, I fear, rather unfavourable. When I discuss with the old man such topics as renunciation and monasticism etc., all those long-cherished sentiments wake up in his aged breast, and his wife most probably smarts all the while. Besides, all French people, of both sexes, lay the whole blame on the wife; they say, "That woman has spoilt one of our great ascetic monks!" Madame Loyson is really in a sorry predicament—specially as they live in Paris, in a Catholic country. They hate the very sight of a married priest; no Catholic would ever tolerate the preaching of religion by a man with family. And Madame Loyson has a bit of animus also. Once she expressed her dislike of an actress, saying, "It is very bad of you to live with Mr. So-and-so without marrying him". The actress immediately retorted, "I am a thousand times better than you. I live with a common man; it may be, I have not legally married him; whereas you are a great sinner—you have made such a great monk break his religious vows! If you were so desperately in love with the monk, why, you might as well live as his attending maid; but why did you bring ruin on him by marrying him and thus converting him into a householder?"

However I hear all and keep silent. But old Père Hyacinthe is a really sweet-natured and peaceful man, he is happy with his wife and family—and what can the whole French people have to say against this? I think, everything would be settled if but his wife climbed down a bit. But one thing I notice, viz. that men and women, in every country, have different ways of understanding and judging things. Men have one angle of vision, women another; men argue from one standpoint, women from another. Men extenuate women and lay the blame on men; while women exonerate men and heap all the blame on women.

One special benefit I get from the company of these ladies and gentlemen is that, except the one American lady, no one knows English; talking in English is wholly eschewed, (It is not etiquette in the West to talk in company any language but one known to all party.) and consequently somehow or other I have to talk as well as hear French.

From Paris our friend Maxim has supplied me with letters of introduction to various places, so that the countries may be properly seen. Maxim is the inventor of the famous Maxim gun—the gun that sends off a continuous round of balls and is loaded and discharged automatically without intermission. Maxim is by birth an American; now he has settled in England, where he has his gun-factories etc. Maxim is vexed if anybody alludes too frequently to his guns in his presence and says, "My friend, have I done nothing else except invent that engine of destruction?" Maxim is an admirer of China and India and is a good writer on religion and philosophy etc. Having read my works long since, he holds me in great—I should say, excessive—admiration. He supplies guns to all kings and rulers and is well known in every country, though his particular friend is Li Hung Chang, his special regard is for China and his devotion, for Confucianism. He is in the habit of writing occasionally in the newspapers, under Chinese pseudonyms, against the Christians—about what takes them to China, their real motive, and so forth. He cannot at all bear the Christian missionaries preaching their religion in China! His wife also is just like her husband in her regard for China and hatred of Christianity! Maxim has no issue; he is an old man, and immensely rich.

The tour programme was as follows—from Paris to Vienna, and thence to Constantinople, by rail; then by steamer to Athens and Greece, then across the Mediterranean to Egypt, then Asia Minor, Jerusalem, and so on. The "Oriental Express" runs daily from Paris to Constantinople, and is provided with sleeping, sitting, and dining accommodations after the American model. Though not perfect like the American cars, they are fairly well furnished. I am to leave Paris by that train on October 24 (1900).

Today is the 23rd October; tomorrow evening I am to take leave of Paris. This year Paris is a centre of the civilised world, for it is the year of the Paris Exhibition, and there has been an assemblage of eminent men and women from all quarters of the globe. The master-minds of all countries have met today in Paris to spread the glory of their respective countries by means of their genius. The fortunate man whose name the bells of this great centre will ring today will at the same time crown his country also with glory, before the world. And where art thou, my Motherland, Bengal, in the great capital city swarming with German, French, English, Italian, and other scholars? Who is there to utter thy name? Who is there to proclaim thy existence? From among that white galaxy of geniuses there stepped forth one distinguished youthful hero to proclaim the name of our Motherland, Bengal—it was the world-renowned scientist, Dr. (Later, Sir.) J. C. Bose! Alone, the youthful Bengali physicist, with galvanic quickness, charmed the Western audience today with his splendid genius; that electric charge infused pulsations of new life into the half-dead body of the Motherland! At the top of all physicists today is—Jagadish Chandra Bose, an Indian, a Bengali! Well done, hero! Whichever countries, Dr. Bose and his accomplished, ideal wife may visit, everywhere they glorify India—add fresh laurels to the crown of Bengal. Blessed pair!

And the daily reunion of numbers of distinguished men and women which Mr. Leggett brought about at an enormous expense in his Parisian mansion, by inviting them to at-homes—that too ends today.

All types of distinguished personages—poets, philosophers, scientists, moralists, politicians, singers, professors, painters, artists, sculptors, musicians, and so on, of both sexes—used to be assembled in Mr. Leggett's residence, attracted by his hospitality and kindness. That incessant outflow of words, clear and limpid like a mountainfall, that expression of sentiments emanating from all sides like sparks of fire, bewitching music, the magic current of thoughts from master minds coming into conflict with one another—which used to hold all spellbound, making them forgetful of time and place—these too shall end.

Everything on earth has an end. Once again I took a round over the Paris Exhibition today—this accumulated mass of dazzling ideas, like lightning held steady as it were, this unique assemblage of celestial panorama on earth!

It has been raining in Paris for the last two or three days. During all this time the sun who is ever kind to France has held back his accustomed grace. Perhaps his face has been darkened over with clouds in disgust to witness the secretly flowing current of sensuality behind this assemblage of arts and artists, learning and learned folk, or perhaps he has hid his face under a pall of cloud in grief over the impending destruction of this illusive heaven of particoloured wood and canvas.

We too shall be happy to escape. The breaking up of the Exhibition is a big affair; the streets of this heaven on earth, the Eden-like Paris, will be filled with knee-deep mud and mortar. With the exception of one or two main buildings, all the houses and their parts are but a display of wood and rags and whitewashing—just as the whole world is! And when they are demolished, the lime-dust flies about and is suffocating; rags and sand etc. make the streets exceedingly dirty; and, if it rains in addition, it is an awful mess.

In the evening of October 24 the train left Paris. The night was dark and nothing could be seen. Monsieur Bois and myself occupied one compartment—and early went to bed. On awakening from sleep we found we had crossed the French frontier and entered German territory. I had already seen Germany thoroughly; but Germany, after France, produces quite a jarring effect. "On the one hand the moon is setting" (यात्येकतोऽस्तशिखरं पतिरोषधीनां—From Kalidasa's Shakuntalā.)—the world-encompassing France is slowly consuming herself in the fire of contemplated retribution—while on the other hand, centralised, young, and mighty Germany has begun her upward march above the horizon with rapid strides. On one side is the artistic workmanship of the dark-haired, comparatively short-statured, luxurious, highly civilised French people, to whom art means life; and on the other, the clumsy daubing, the unskilful manipulation, of tawny-haired, tall, gigantic German. After Paris there is no other city in the

Western world; everywhere it is an imitation of Paris—or at least an attempt at it. But in France that art is full of grace and ethereal beauty, while in Germany, England, and America the imitation is coarse and clumsy. Even the application of force on the part of the French is beautiful, as it were, whereas the attempt of the Germans to display beauty even is terrible. The countenance of French genius, even when frowning in anger, is beautiful; that of German genius, even when beaming with smiles, appears frightful, as it were. French civilisation is full of nerve, like camphor or musk—it volatilises and pervades the room in a moment; while German civilisation is full of muscle, heavy like lead or mercury—it remains motionless and inert wherever it lies. The German muscle can go on striking small blows untiringly, till death; the French have tender, feminine bodies, but when they do concentrate and strike, it is a sledge-hammer blow and is irresistible.

The Germans are constructing after the French fashion big houses and mansions, and placing big statues, equestrian figures, etc. on top of them, but on seeing a double-storeyed German building one is tempted to ask—is it a dwelling-house for men, or a stable for elephants and camels, while one mistakes a five-storeyed French stable for elephants and horses as a habitation for fairies.

America is inspired by German ideals; hundreds of thousand Germans are in every town. The language is of course English, but nevertheless America is being slowly Germanised. Germany is fast multiplying her population and is exceptionally hardy. Today Germany is the dictator to all Europe, her place is above all! Long before all other nations, Germany has given man and woman compulsory education, making illiteracy punishable by law, and today she is enjoying the fruits of that tree. The German army is the foremost in reputation, and Germany has vowed to become foremost in her navy also. German manufacture of commodities has beaten even England! German merchandise and the Germans themselves are slowly obtaining a monopoly even in the English colonies. At the behest of the German Emperor all the nations have ungrudgingly submitted to the lead of the German Generalissimo in the battle-fields of China!

The whole day the train rushed through Germany, till in the afternoon it reached the frontiers of Austria, the ancient sphere of German supremacy, but now an alien territory. There are certain troubles in travelling through Europe. In every country enormous duties are levied upon certain things, or some articles of merchandise are the monopoly of the Government, as for instance, tobacco. Again, in Russia and Turkey, you are totally forbidden to enter without a royal passport; a passport you must always have. Besides, in Russia and Turkey, all your books and papers will be seized; and when on perusal the authorities are satisfied that there is nothing in them against the Russian or Turkish Government and religion, then only they will be returned, otherwise they will all be confiscated. In other countries your tobacco is a source of great trouble. You must open your chest, and trunk and

packages for inspection whether they contain tobacco etc. or not. And to come to Constantinople one has to pass through two big States—Germany and Austria, and many petty ones; the latter had formerly been districts of Turkey, but later on the independent Christian kings made a common cause and wrested as many of these Christian districts from Mohammedan hands as they could. The bite of these tiny ants is much worse than even that of the bigger ones.

In the evening of October 25 the train reached Vienna, the capital of Austria. The members of the royal family in Austria and Russia are styled Archdukes and Archduchesses. Two Archdukes are to get down at Vienna by this train; and until they have done so the other passengers are not allowed to get down. So we had to wait. A few officers in laced uniform and some soldiers with feathered caps were waiting for the Archdukes, who got down surrounded by them. We too felt relieved and made haste to get down and have our luggage passed. There were few passengers, and it did not take us much time to show our luggage and have it passed. A hotel had already been arranged for, and a man from the hotel was waiting for us with a carriage. We reached the hotel duly. It was out of the question to go out for sight-seeing during the night; so the next morning we started to see the town. In all hotels, and almost in all the countries of Europe except England and Germany, the French fashion prevails. They eat twice a day like the Hindus; in the morning by twelve o'clock, and in the evening by eight. Early in the morning, that is, about eight or nine, they take a little coffee. Tea is very little in vogue except in England and Russia. The morning meal is called in French déjeuner—that is, breakfast, and the evening meal dîner—that is, dinner. Tea is very much in use in Russia—it is too cold, and China is near enough. Chinese tea is excellent, and most of it goes to Russia. The Russian mode of drinking tea is also analogous to the Chinese, that is, without mixing milk. Tea or coffee becomes injurious like poison if you mix milk with it. The real tea-drinking races, the Chinese, Japanese, Russians, and the inhabitants of Central Asia, take tea without milk. Similarly, the original coffee-drinking races, such as the Turks, drink coffee without milk. Only in Russia they put a slice of lemon and a lump of sugar into the tea. The poor people place a lump of sugar in the mouth and drink tea over it, and when one has finished drinking, one passes that lump on to another, who repeats the process.

Vienna is a small city after the model of Paris. But the Austrians are German by race. The Austrian Emperor was hitherto the Emperor of almost the whole of Germany. In the present times, owing to the far-sightedness of King Wilhelm of Prussia, the wonderful diplomacy of his able minister, Bismark, and the military genius of General Von Moltke, the King of Prussia is the Emperor of the whole of Germany barring Austria. Austria, shorn of her glory and robbed of her power, is somehow maintaining her ancient name and prestige. The Austrian royal line—the Hapsburg Dynasty—is the oldest and most aristocratic dynasty in Europe. It was this Austrian dynasty which hitherto rules Germany as Emperors—Germany whose princes are seated on the thrones of almost all the countries of Europe, and whose petty feudatory chiefs even occupy the thrones of such powerful empires as England and Russia. The desire for that honour and prestige Austria still cherishes in full, only she lacks the power. Turkey is called "the sick man" of Europe; then Austria should be called "the sick dame". Austria belongs to the Catholic sect, and until recently the Austrian Empire used to be called "the Holy Roman Empire". Modern Germany has a preponderance of Protestants. The Austrian Emperor has always been the right-hand man of the Pope, his faithful follower, and the leader of the Roman Catholic sect. Now the Austrian Emperor is the only Catholic Ruler in Europe; France, the eldest daughter of the Catholic Church, is now a Republic, while Spain and Portugal are downfallen! Italy has given only room enough for the Papal throne to be established, robbing the Pope's entire splendour and dominion; between the King of Italy and the Pope of Rome there is no love lost, they cannot bear each other's sight. Rome, the capital of the Pope, is now the capital of Italy. The King lives in the Pope's ancient palace which he has seized, and the ancient Italian kingdom of the Pope is now confined within the precincts of the Vatican. But the Pope has still great influence in religious matters—and the chief supporter of this is Austria. As a result of the struggle against Austria—against the age-long thraldom of Austria, the ally of the Pope—up rose modern Italy. Consequently Austria is against Italy—against, because she lost her. Unfortunately, however, young Italy, under England's misdirection, set herself to create a powerful army and navy. But where was the money? So, involved in debt, Italy is on the way to ruin; and to her misfortune, she brought on herself a fresh trouble by proceeding to extend her empire in Africa. Defeated by the Abyssinian monarch, she has sunk down, bereft of glory and prestige. Prussia in the meantime defeated Austria in a great war and thrust her off to a great distance. Austria is slowly dying, while Italy has similarly fettered herself by the misuse of her new life.

The Austrian royal line is still the proudest of all European royal families. It boasts of being a very ancient and very aristocratic dynasty. The marriages and other connections of this line are contracted with the greatest circumspection, and no such relationship can be established with families that are not Roman Catholic. It was the glamour of a connection with this line that led to the fall of Napoleon the Great. Quaintly enough, he took it into his head to marry a daughter of some noble royal family and found a great dynasty through a succession of descendents. The hero who, questioned as to his pedigree, had replied, "I owe the title to my nobility to none—I am to be the founder of a great dynasty"—that is to say, that he would originate a powerful dynasty, and that he was not born to glorify himself with the borrowed plumes of some ancestor—that hero fell into this abyss of family prestige.

The divorce of the Empress Josephine, the defeat of the Austrian Emperor in battle and taking his daughter to wife, the marriage of Bonaparte in great pomp with Marie Louise, the Princess of Austria, the birth of a son, the installation of the new-born babe as the King of Rome, the fall of Napoleon, the enmity of his father-in-law, Leipsic, Waterloo, St. Helena, Empress Marie Louise living in her father's house with her child, the marriage of Napoleon's royal consort with an ordinary soldier, the death of his only son, the King of Rome, in the house of his maternal grandfather—all these are well-known incidents of history.

Fallen in a comparatively weakened condition, France is now ruminating on her past glory—nowadays there are very many books on Napoleon. Dramatists like Sardou are writing many dramas on Napoleon dead and gone; and actresses like Madame Bernhardt and Réjane are performing those plays every night before bumper houses. Recently Madame Bernhardt has created a great attraction in Paris by playing a drama entitled L'aiglon (the Young Eagle).

The young Eagle is the only son of Napoleon, practically interned in his maternal grandfather's residence, the Palace of Vienna. The Austrian Emperor's minister, the Machiavellian Metternich, is always careful not to allow the tales of heroism of his father to enter into the boy's mind. But a few of Bonaparte's veterans contrived to get themselves admitted into the boy's service in the Schönbrunn Palace, incognito; their idea was to somehow take the boy over to France and found the Bonaparte line by driving out the Bourbons reinstated by the combined European potentates. The child was the son of a great hero, and very soon that latent heroism woke up in him to hear the glorious tales of battle of his father. One day the boy fled from the Schönbrunn Palace accompanied by the conspirators. But Metternich's keen intellect had already scented the matter, and he cut off the journey. The son of Bonaparte was carried back to the Schönbrunn Palace and the Young Eagle, with his wings tied, as it were, very soon died of a broken heart!

This Schönbrunn Palace is an ordinary palace. Of course, the rooms etc. are lavishly decorated; in one of them perhaps one meets with only Chinese workmanship, in another only works of Hindu art, in a third the productions of some other country, and so on; and the garden attached to the Palace is very charming indeed. But all the people that now go to visit this Palace go there with the object of seeing the room where Bonaparte's son used to lie, or his study, or the room in which he died, and so forth. Many thoughtless French men and women are interrogating the guard, which room belonged to "L'aiglon", which bed did "L'aiglon" use to occupy, and so on. What silly questions, these! The Austrians only know that he was the son of Bonaparte, and the relation was established by forcibly taking their girl in marriage; that hatred they have not yet forgotten. The Prince was a grandchild of the Emperor, and homeless, so they could not help giving him a shelter, but they could give him no such title as "King of Rome";

only, being the grandson of the Austrian Emperor, he was an Archduke, that was all. It may be that you French people have now written a book on him, making him the Young Eagle, and the addition of imaginary settings and the genius of Madame Bernhardt have created a great interest in the story, but how should an Austrian guard know that name? Besides, it has been written in that book that the Austrian Emperor, following the advice of his minister Metternich, in a way killed Napoleon's son!

Hearing the name "L'aiglon", the guard put on a long face and went on showing the rooms and other things thoroughly disgusted at heart; what else could he do? — it was too much for him to give up the tips. Moreover, in countries like Austria etc., the military department is too poorly paid, they have to live almost on a bare pittance; of course they are allowed to go back home after a few years' service. The guard's countenance darkened as an expression of his patriotism, but the hand instinctively moved towards the tip. The French visitors put some silver pieces into the guard's hand and returned home talking of "L'aiglon" and abusing Metternich, while the guard shut the doors with a long salute. In his heart he must have given sweet names to the ancestors of the whole French people.

The thing most worth seeing in Vienna is the Museum, specially the Scientific Museum, an institution of great benefit to the student. There is a fine collection of the skeletons of various species of ancient extinct animals. In the Art Gallery, paintings by Dutch artists form the major portion. In the Dutch school, there is very little attempt at suggestiveness; this school is famous for its exact copy of natural objects and creatures. One artist has spent years over the drawing of a basketful of fish, or a lump of flesh, or a tumbler of water — and that fish, or flesh, or water in the tumbler is wonderful. But the female figures of the Dutch school look just like athletes.

There is of course German scholarship and German intellectuality in Vienna, but the causes which helped the gradual decay of Turkey are at work here also — that is to say, the mixture of various races and languages. The population of Austria proper speaks German; the people of Hungary belong to the Tartar stock, and have a different language; while there are some who are Greek-speaking and are Christians belonging to the Greek Church. Austria has not the power to fuse together so many different sects. Hence she has fallen.

In the present times a huge wave of nationalism is sweeping over Europe, where people speaking the same tongue, professing the same religion, and belonging to the same race want to unite together. Wherever such union is being effectively accomplished, there is great power being manifested; and where this is impossible, death is inevitable. After the death of the present Austrian Emperor, (Francis Joseph II died in 1916) Germany will surely try to absorb the German-speaking portion of the Austrian Empire — and Russia and others are sure to oppose her; so there is the possibility of a dreadful war. The present Emperor being very old, that catastrophe may take place very early. The German Emperor is nowadays an ally of the Sultan of Turkey; and when Germany will attempt to seize Austrian territory, Turkey, which is Russia's enemy, will certainly offer some resistance to Russia; so the German Emperor is very friendly towards Turkey.

Three days in Vienna were sufficient to tire me. To visit Europe after Paris is like tasting an inferior preparation after a sumptuous feast — that dress, and style of eating, that same fashion everywhere; throughout the land you meet with that same black suit, and the same queer hat — disgusting! Besides, you have clouds above, and this swarm of people with black hats and black coats below — one feels suffocated, as it were. All Europe is gradually taking up that same style of dress, and that same mode of living! It is a law of nature that such are the symptoms of death! By hundreds of years of drill, our ancestors have so fashioned us that we all clean our teeth, wash our face, eat our meals, and do everything in the same way, and the result is that we have gradually become mere automata; the life has gone out, and we are moving about, simply like so many machines! Machines never say "yea" or "nay", never trouble their heads about anything, they move on "in the way their forefathers have gone", and then rot and die. The Europeans too will share the same fate! "The course of time is ever changing! If all people take to the same dress, same food, same manner of talking, and same everything, gradually they will become like so many machines, will gradually tread the path their forefathers have trod", and as an inevitable consequence of that — they will rot and die!

On the 28th October, at 9 p.m., we again took that Orient Express train, which reached Constantinople on the 30th. These two nights and one day the train ran through Hungary, Serbia, and Bulgaria. The people of Hungary are subjects of the Austrian Emperor, whose title, however, is "Emperor of Austria and King of Hungary". The Hungarians and Turks are of the same race, akin to the Tibetans. The Hungarians entered Europe along the north of the Caspian Sea, while the Turks slowly occupied Europe through the western borders of Persia and through Asia Minor. The people of Hungary are Christians, and the Turks are Mohammedans, but the martial spirit characteristic of Tartar blood is noticeable in both. The Hungarians have fought again and again for separation from Austria and are now but nominally united. The Austrian Emperor is King of Hungary in name only. Their capital, Budapest, is a very neat and beautiful city. The Hungarians are a pleasure-loving race and fond of music, and you will find Hungarian bands all over Paris.

Serbia, Bulgaria, and the rest were districts of Turkey and have become practically independent after the Russo-Turkish War; but the Sultan of Turkey is yet their Emperor; and Serbia and Bulgaria have no right regarding foreign affairs. There are three civilised nations in Europe — the French, the Germans, and the English. The rest are almost as badly off as we are, and the majority of them are so uncivilised that you can find

Lectures & Discourses by Swami Vivekananda

no race in Asia so degraded. Throughout Serbia and Bulgaria you find the same mud houses, and people dressed in tattered rags, and heaps of filth—and I was almost inclined to think I was back to India! Again, as they are Christians, they must have a number of hogs; and a single hog will make a place more dirty than two hundred barbarous men will be able to do. Living in a mud house with mud roof, with tattered rags on his person, and surrounded by hogs—there you have your Serb or Bulgarian! After much bloodshed and many wars, they have thrown off the yoke of Turkey; but along with this they have got a serious disadvantage—they must construct their army after the European model, otherwise the existence of not one of them is safe for a day. Of course, sooner or later they will all one day be absorbed by Russia; but even this two days' existence is impossible without an army. So they must have conscription.

In an evil hour, did France suffer defeat from Germany. Through anger and fear she made every citizen a soldier. Every man must serve for some time in the army and learn the military science; there is no exemption for anybody. He must have to live in the barracks for three years and learn to fight, shouldering his gun, be he a millionaire by birth. The government will provide for his food and clothing, and the salary will be a centime (one pice) a day. After this he must be always ready for active service for two years at his home; and another fifteen years he must be ready to present himself for service at the first call. Germany set a lion to fury, so she too had to be ready. In other countries also conscription has been introduced in mutual dread of one another—so throughout Europe, excepting only England. England, being an island, is continually strengthening her navy, but who knows if the lessons of the Boer War will not force her to introduce conscription. Russia has the largest population of all, so she can amass the biggest army in Europe. Now, the titular states, like Serbia and Bulgaria, which the European Powers are creating by dismembering Turkey—they, too, as soon as they are born, must have up-to-date trained and well-equipped armies and guns etc. But ultimately who is to supply the funds? Consequently the peasants have had to put on tattered rags—while in the towns you will find soldiers dressed in gorgeous uniforms. Throughout Europe there is a craze for soldiers—soldiers everywhere. Still, liberty is one thing and slavery another; even best work loses its charm if one is forced to do it by another. Without the idea of personal responsibility, no one can achieve anything great. Freedom with but one meal a day and tattered rags on is a million times better than slavery in gold chains. A slave suffers the miseries of hell both here and hereafter. The people of Europe joke about the Serbs and Bulgarians etc., and taunt them with their mistakes and shortcomings. But can they attain proficiency all in a day, after so many years of servitude? Mistakes they are bound to commit—ay, by the hundreds—but they will learn through these mistakes and set them right when they have learnt. Give him responsibility and the weakest man will become strong, and the ignorant man sagacious.

The train is traversing Hungary, Rumania, and other countries. Among the races that inhabit the moribund Austrian Empire, the Hungarians yet possess vitality. All the races of Europe, except one or two small ones, belong to the great stock which European scholars term the Indo-European or Aryan race. The Hungarians are among the few races which do not speak a Sanskritic language. The Hungarians and Turks, as already stated, belong to the same race. In comparatively modern times this very powerful race established their sovereignty in Asia and Europe. The country now called Turkistan, lying to the north of the Western Himalayas and the Hindukush range, was the original home of the Turks. The Turkish name for that country is Chagwoi. The Mogul dynasty of Delhi, the present Persian royal line, the dynasty of the Turkish Sultan of Constantinople, and the Hungarians have all gradually extended their dominion from that country, beginning with India, and pushing right up to Europe, and even today these dynasties style themselves as Chagwois and speak a common language. Of course these Turks were uncivilised ages ago, and used to roam with herds of sheep, horses, and cattle, taking their wives and children and every earthly possession with them, and encamp for some time wherever they could find enough pasture for their beasts. And when grass and water ran short there, they used to remove somewhere else. Even now many families of this race lead nomadic lives in this way in Central Asia. They have got a perfect similarity with the races of Central Asia as regards language, but some difference in point of physiognomy. The Turk's face resembles that of the Mongolian in the shape of the head and in the prominence of the cheek-bone, but the Turk's nose is not flat, but rather long, and the eyes are straight and large, though the space between the eyes of comparatively wide, as with the Mongolians. It appears that from a long time past Aryan and Semitic blood has found its way into this Turkish race. From time immemorial the Turks have been exceedingly fond of war. And the mixture with them of Sanskrit-speaking races and the people of Kandahar and Persia has produced the war-loving races such as the Afghans, Khiljis, Hazaras, Barakhais, Usufjais, etc., to whom war is a passion and who have frequently oppressed India.

In very ancient times this Turkish race repeatedly conquered the western provinces of India and founded extensive kingdoms. They were Buddhists, or would turn Buddhists after occupying Indian territory. In the ancient history of Kashmir there is mention of these famous Turkish Emperors, Hushka, Yushka, and Kanishka. It was this Kanishka who founded the Northern school of Buddhism called the Mahâyâna. Long after, the majority of them took to Mohammedanism and completely devastated the chief Buddhistic seats of Central Asia such as Kandahar and Kabul. Before their conversion to Mohammedanism they used to imbibe the learning and culture of the countries they conquered, and by assimilating the culture of other countries would try to propagate civilisation.

But ever since they became Mohammedans, they have only the instinct for war left in them; they have not got the least vestige of learning and culture; on the contrary, the countries that come under their sway gradually have their civilisation extinguished. In many places of modern Afghanistan and Kandahar etc., there yet exist wonderful Stupas, monasteries, temples and gigantic statues built by their Buddhistic ancestors. As a result of Turkish admixture and their conversion to Mohammedanism, those temples etc. are almost in ruins, and the present Afghans and allied races have grown so uncivilised and illiterate that far from imitating those ancient works of architecture, they believe them to be the creation of supernatural spirits like the Jinn etc., and are firmly convinced that such great undertakings are beyond the power of man to accomplish. The principal cause of the present degradation of Persia is that the royal line belongs to the powerful, uncivilised Turkish stock, whereas the subjects are the descendants of the highly civilised ancient Persians, who were Aryans. In this way the Empire of Constantinople—the last political arena of the Greeks and Romans, the descendants of civilised Aryans—has been ruined under the blasting feet of powerful, barbarous Turkey. The Mogul Emperors of India were the only exceptions to this rule; perhaps that was due to an admixture of Hindu ideas and Hindu blood. In the chronicles of Rajput bards and minstrels all the Mohammedan dynasties who conquered India are styled as Turks. This is a very correct appellation, for, or whatever races the conquering Mohammedan armies might be made up, the leadership was always vested in the Turks alone.

What is called the Mohammedan invasion, conquest, or colonisation of India means only this that, under the leadership of Mohammedan Turks who were renegades from Buddhism, those sections of the Hindu race who continued in the faith of their ancestors were repeatedly conquered by the other section of that very race who also were renegades from Buddhism or the Vedic religion and served under the Turks, having been forcibly converted to Mohammedanism by their superior strength. Of course, the language of the Turks has, like their physiognomy, been considerably mixed up; specially those sections that have gone farthest from their native place. Chagwoi have got the most hybrid form of language. This year the Shah of Persia visited the Paris Exhibition and returned to his country by rail via Constantinople. Despite the immense difference in time and place, the Sultan and the Shah talked with each other in their ancient Turkish mother tongue. But the Sultan's Turkish was mixed up with Persian, Arabic, and a few Greek words, while that of the Shah was comparatively pure.

In ancient times these Chagwoi Turks were divided into two sections; one was called the "white sheep", and the other, "black sheep". But these sections started from their birthplace on the north of Kashmir, tending their flocks of sheep and ravaging countries, till they reached the shore of the Caspian Sea. The "white sheep" penetrated into Europe along the north of the Caspian Sea and founded the Kingdom of Hungary, seizing a fragment of the Roman Empire then almost in ruins, while the "black sheep", advancing along the south of the Caspian Sea, gradually occupied the western portion of Persia and, crossing the Caucasus, by degrees made themselves masters of Arabian territory such as Asia Minor and so forth; gradually they seized the throne of the Caliph, and bit by bit annexed the small remnant of the western Roman Empire. In very remote ages these Turks were great snake-worshippers. Most probably it was these dynasties whom the ancient Hindus used to designate as Nagas and Takshakas. Later on they became Buddhists; and afterwards they very often used to embrace the religion of any particular country they might conquer at any particular time. In comparatively recent times, of the two sections we are speaking about, the "white sheep" conquered the Christians and became converts to Christianity, while the "black sheep" conquered the Mohammedans and adopted their religion. But in their Christianity or Mohammedanism one may even now trace on research the strata of serpent-worship and of Buddhism.

The Hungarians, though Turks by race and language, are Christians—Roman Catholics—in religion. In the past, religious fanaticism had no respect for any tie—neither the tie of language, nor that of blood, nor that of country. The Hungarians are ever the deadly enemies of Turkey; and but for the Hungarians' aid Christian states, such as Austria etc., would not have been able to maintain their existence on many an occasion. In modern times, owing to the spread of education and the discovery of Linguistics and Ethnology, people are being more attracted to the kinship of language and blood, while religious solidarity is gradually slackening. So, among the educated Hungarians and Turks, there is growing up a feeling of racial unity. Though a part of the Austrian Empire, Hungary has repeatedly tried to cut off from her. The result of many revolutions and rebellions has been that Hungary is now only nominally a province of the Austrian Empire, but practically independent in all respects. The Austrian Emperor is styled "the Emperor of Austria and King of Hungary". Hungary manages all her internal affairs independently of Austria and in these the subjects have full power. The Austrian Emperor continues to be a titular leader here, but even this bit of relation, it appears, will not last long. Skill in war, magnanimity and other characteristic virtues of the Turkish race are sufficiently present in the Hungarian also. Besides, not being converted to Mohammedanism they do not consider such heavenly arts as music etc. as the devil's snare, and consequently the Hungarians are great adepts in music and are renowned for this all over Europe.

Formerly I had the notion that people of cold climates did not take hot chillies, which was merely a bad habit of warm climate people. But the habit of taking chillies, which we observed to begin with Hungary and which reached its climax in Rumania and Bulgaria etc., appeared to me to beat even your South Indians.

ADDENDA

These interesting jottings were found among Swamiji's papers —Editor.

The first view of Constantinople we had from the train. It is an ancient city, with big drains running across the walls, narrow and crooked lanes full of dirt, and wooden houses, etc., but in them there is a certain beauty owing to their novelty. At the station we had great trouble over our books. Mademoiselle Calvé and Jules Bois tried much, in French, to reason with the octroi officers, which gradually led to a quarrel between the parties. The head of the officers was a Turk, and his dinner was ready; so the quarrel ended without further complications. They returned all the books with the exception of two which they held back. They promised to send them to the hotel immediately, which they never did. We went round the town and bazar of Stamboul or Constantinople. Beyond the Pont or creek is the Pera or foreigners' quarters, hotels, etc., whence we got into a carriage, saw the town, and then took some rest. In the evening we went to visit Woods Pasha, and the next day started on an excursion along the Bosphorus in a boat. It was extremely cold and there was a strong wind. So I and Miss MacLeod got down at the first station. It was decided that we would cross over to Scutari and see Père Hyacinthe. Not knowing the language we engaged a boat by signs merely, crossed over, and hired a carriage. On the way we saw the seat of a Sufi Fakir. These Fakirs cure people's diseases, which they do in the following manner. First they read a portion of their scriptures, moving their body backward and forward; then they begin to dance and gradually get a sort of inspiration, after which they heal the disease by treading on the patient's body.

We had a long talk with Père Hyacinthe about the American Colleges, after which we went to an Arab shop where we met a Turkish student. Then we returned from Scutari.—We had found out a boat, but it failed to reach its exact destination. However, we took a tram from the place where we were landed and returned to our quarters at the hotel at Stamboul. The Museum at Stamboul is situated where the ancient harem of the Greek Emperors once stood. We saw some remarkable sarcophagi and other things, and had a charming view of the city from above Topkhana. I enjoyed taking fried chick peas here after such a long time, and had spiced rice and some other dishes, prepared in the Turkish fashion. After visiting the cemetery of Scutari we went to see the ancient walls. Within the walls was the prison—a dreadful place. Next we met Woods Pasha and started for the Bosphorus. We had our dinner with the French chargé d'affaires and met a Greek Pasha and an Albanian gentleman. The Police have prohibited Père Hyacinthe's lectures; so I too cannot lecture. We saw Mr. Devanmall and Chobeji—a Gujarâti Brahmin. There are a good many Indians here—Hindustanis, Mussalmans, etc. We had a talk on Turkish Philosophy and heard of Noor Bey, whose gradfather was a Frenchman. They say he is as handsome as a

Kashmari. The women here have got no purdah system and are very free. Prostitution is chiefly a Mohammedan practice. We heard of Kurd Pasha and the massacre of Armenians. The Armenians have really no country of their own, and those countries which they inhabit have generally a preponderating Mohammedan population. A particular tract called Armenia is unknown. The present Sultan is constructing a Hamidian cavalry out of the Kurds who will be trained in the manner of the Cossacks and they will be exempted from conscription.

The Sultan called the Armenian and Greek Patriarchs and proposed to them conscription as an alternative for payment of taxes. They might thus serve to protect their motherland. They replied that if they went as soldiers to fight and died by the side of the Mohammedans, there would be some confusion about the interment of Christian soldiers. The Sultan's rejoinder to this was that it might be remedied by providing for both Mohammedan and Christian priests in each regiment, who would conduct the funeral service together when in the exigencies of battle the dead bodies of Christian and Mohammedan soldiers would have to be buried in a heap all together, and there could possibly be no harm if the souls of men of one religion heard in addition the funeral services meant for those of the other religion. But the Christians did not agree—so they continue to pay taxes. The surest reason of their not acquiescing in the proposal was their fear lest by living with the Mohammedans they might turn Mohammedan wholesale. The present Sultan of Stamboul is a very hard-working man and he personally supervises everything, including even the arrangement of amusements, such as theatrical performances etc., in the palace. His predecessor, Murad, was really a most unfit man, but the present Sultan is very intelligent. The amount of improvement he has made in the condition of the State in which he found it at his accession is simply wonderful. The Parliamentary system will not be successful in this country.

At 10 in the morning we left Constantinople, passing a night and a day on the sea, which was perfectly placid. By degrees we reached the Golden Horn and the Sea of Marmora. In one of the islands of the Marmora we saw a monastery of the Greek religion. Formerly there was ample opportunity for religious education here, for it was situated between Asia on one side and Europe on the other. While out in the morning on a visit of the Mediterranean Archipelago we came across Professor Liper, whose acquaintance I had already made in the Pachiappa College at Madras. In one of the islands we came upon the ruins of a temple, which had probably been dedicated to Neptune, judging from its position on the seashore. In the evening we reached Athens, and after passing a whole night under quarantine we obtained permission for landing in the morning. Port Peiraeus is a small town, but very beautiful, having a European air about it in all respects, except that one meets now and then with one or two Greeks dressed in gowns. From there we drove five miles to have a look at the ancient walls of Athens which used to connect the city with the port. Then we went through the town; the Acropolis, the hotels, houses, and streets, and all were very neat and clean. The palace is a small one. The same day, again, we climbed the hillock and had a view of the Acropolis, the temple of the Wingless Victory, and the Parthenon, etc. The temple is made of white marble. Some standing remains of columns also we saw. The next day we again went to see these with Mademoiselle Melcarvi, who explained to us various historical facts relating thereto. On the second day we visited the temple of Olympian Zeus, Theatre Dionysius etc., as far as the sea-shore. The third day we set out for Eleusis, which was the chief religious seat of the Greeks. Here it was that the famous Eleusinian Mysteries used to be played. The ancient theatre of this place has been built anew by a rich Greek. The Olympian games too have been revived in the present times. They are held at a place near Sparta, the Americans carrying off the palm in them in many respects. But the Greeks won in the race from that place to this theatre of Athens. This year they gave undisputed proof of this trait of theirs in a competition with the Turks also. At 10 a.m. on the fourth day we got on board the Russian steamer, Czar, bound for Egypt. After reaching the dock we came to learn that the steamer was to start at 4 a.m. — perhaps we were too early or there would be some extra delay in loading the cargo. So, having no other alternative, we went round and made a cursory acquaintance with the sculpture of Ageladas and his three pupils, Phidias, Myron, and Polycletus, who had flourished between 576 B.C. and 486 B.C. Even here we began to feel the great heat. In a Russian ship the first class is over the screw, and the rest is only deck — full of passengers, and cattle, and sheep. Besides, no ice was available in this steamer.

From a visit to the Louvre Museum in Paris I came to understand the three stages of Greek art. First, there was the Mycenoean art, then Greek art proper. The Achaean kingdom had spread its sway over the neighbouring islands and also mastered all the arts that flourished there, being imported from Asia. Thus did art first make its appearance in Greece. From the prehistoric times up to 776 B.C. was the age of the Mycenoean art. This art principally engaged itself in merely copying Asiatic art. Then from 776 B.C. to 146 B.C. was the age of Hellenic or true Greek art. After the destruction of the Achaean Empire by the Dorian race, the Greeks living on the continent and in the Archipelago founded many colonies in Asia. This led to a close conflict between them and Babylon and Egypt, which first gave rise to Greek art. This art in course of time gave up its Asiatic tinge and applied itself to an exact imitation of nature. The difference between Greek art and the art of other countries consists in this, that the former faithfully delineates the living phenomena of natural life.

From 776 B.C. to 475 B.C. is the age of Archaic Greek art. The figures are yet stiff — not lifelike. The lips are slightly parted, as if always in smiles. In this respect they resemble the works of Egyptian artists. All the statues stand erect on their legs — quite stiff. The hair and beard etc. and all carved in regular lines and the clothes in the statues are all wrapped close round the body, in a jumble — not like flowing dress.

Next to Archaic Greek art comes the age of Classic Greek art — from 475 B.C. to 323 B.C., that is to say, from the hegemony of Athens up to the death of Alexander the Great. Peloponnesus and Attica were the states where the art of this period flourished most. Athens was the chief city of Attica. A learned French art critic has written, "(Classic) Greek art at its highest development freed itself completely from the fetters of all established canons and became independent. It then recognised the art regulations of no country, nor guided itself according to them. The more we study the fifth century B.C., so brilliant in its art development — during which period all the perfect specimens of sculpture were turned out — the more is the idea brought home to our mind that Greek art owed its life and vigour to its cutting loose from the pale of stereotyped rules". This Classic Greek art had two schools — first, the Attic, and second, the Peloponnesian. In the Attic school, again, there were two different types — the first was the outcome of the genius of the gifted sculptor, Phidias, which a French scholar has described in the following terms: "A marvel of perfection in beauty and a glorious specimen of pure and sublime ideas, which will never lose their hold upon the human mind". The masters in the second type of the Attic school were Scopas and Praxiteles. The work of this school was to completely divorce art from religion and keep it restricted to the delineation of merely human life.

The chief exponents of the second or Peloponnesian school of Classic Greek art were Polycletus and Lysippus. One of these was born in the fifth century B.C., and the other in the fourth century B.C. They chiefly aimed at laying down the rule that the proportion of the human body must be faithfully reproduced in art.

From 323 B.C. to 146 B.C., that is, from the death of Alexander to the conquest of Attica by the Romans, is the period of decadence in Greek art. One notices in the Greek art of this period an undue attention to gorgeous embellishments, and an attempt to make the statues unusually large in bulk. Then at the time of the Roman occupation of Greece, Greek art contented itself merely by copying the works of previous artists of that country; and the only novelty there was, consisted in reproducing exactly the face of some particular individual.

THE STRUGGLE FOR EXPANSION[1]

The old dilemma, whether the tree precedes the seed or the seed the tree, runs through all our forms of knowledge. Whether intelligence is first in the order of being or matter; whether the ideal is first or the external manifestation; whether freedom is our true nature or bondage of law; whether thought creates matter or matter thought; whether the incessant change in nature precedes the idea of rest or the idea of

1. Written by the Swami during his first visit to America in answer to questions put by a Western disciple.

rest precedes the idea of change—all these are questions of the same insoluble nature. Like the rise and fall of a series of waves, they follow one another in an invariable succession and men take this side or that according to their tastes or education or peculiarity of temperaments.

For instance, if it be said on the one hand that, seeing the adjustment in nature of different parts, it is clear that it is the effect of intelligent work; on the other hand it may be argued that intelligence itself being created by matter and force in the course of evolution could not have been before this world. If it be said that the production of every form must be preceded by an ideal in the mind, it can be argued, with equal force, that the ideal was itself created by various external experiences. On the one hand, the appeal is to our ever-present idea of freedom; on the other, to the fact that nothing in the universe being causeless, everything, both mental and physical, is rigidly bound by the law of causation. If it be affirmed that, seeing the changes of the body induced by volition, it is evident that thought is the creator of this body, it is equally clear that as change in the body induces a change in the thought, the body must have produced the mind. If it be argued that the universal change must be the outcome of a preceding rest, equally logical argument can be adduced to show that the idea of unchangeability is only an illusory relative notion, brought about by the comparative differences in motion.

Thus in the ultimate analysis all knowledge resolves itself into this vicious circle: the indeterminate interdependence of cause and effect. Judging by the laws of reasoning, such knowledge is incorrect; and the most curious fact is that this knowledge is proved to be incorrect, not by comparison with knowledge which is true, but by the very laws which depend for their basis upon the selfsame vicious circle. It is clear, therefore, that the peculiarity of all our knowledge is that it proves its own insufficiency. Again, we cannot say that it is unreal, for all the reality we know and can think of is within this knowledge. Nor can we deny that it is sufficient for all practical purposes. This state of human knowledge which embraces within its scope both the external and the internal worlds is called Maya. It is unreal because it proves its own incorrectness. It is real in the sense of being sufficient for all the needs of the animal man.

Acting in the external world Maya manifests itself as the two powers of attraction and repulsion. In the internal its manifestations are desire and non-desire (Pravritti and Nivritti). The whole universe is trying to rush outwards. Each atom is trying to fly off from its centre. In the internal world, each thought is trying to go beyond control. Again each particle in the external world is checked by another force, the centripetal, and drawn towards the centre. Similarly in the thought-world the controlling power is checking all these outgoing desires.`

Desires of materialisation, that is, being dragged down more and more to the plane of mechanical action, belong to the animal man. It is only when the desire to prevent all such bondage to the senses arises that religion dawns in the heart of man. Thus we see that the whole scope of religion is to prevent man from falling into the bondage of the senses and to help him to assert his freedom. The first effort of this power of Nivritti towards that end is called morality. The scope of all morality is to prevent this degradation and break this bondage. All morality can be divided into the positive and the negative elements; it says either, "Do this" or "Do not do this". When it says, "Do not", it is evident that it is a check to a certain desire which would make a man a slave. When it says, "Do", its scope is to show the way to freedom and to the breaking down of a certain degradation which has already seized the human heart.

Now this morality is only possible if there be a liberty to be attained by man. Apart from the question of the chances of attaining perfect liberty, it is clear that the whole universe is a case of struggle to expand, or in other words, to attain liberty. This infinite space is not sufficient for even one atom. The struggle for expansion must go on eternally until perfect liberty is attained. It cannot be said that this struggle to gain freedom is to avoid pain or to attain pleasure. The lowest grade of beings, who can have no such feeling, are also struggling for expansion; and according to many, man himself is the expansion of these very beings.

THE BIRTH OF RELIGION[2]

The beautiful flowers of the forest with their many-coloured petals, nodding their heads, jumping, leaping, playing with every breeze; the beautiful birds with their gorgeous plumage, their sweet songs echoing through every forest glade—they were there yesterday, my solace, my companions, and today they are gone—where? My playmates, the companions of my joys and sorrows, my pleasures and pastime—they also are gone—where? Those that nursed me when I was a child, who all through their lives had but one thought for me—that of doing everything for me—they also are gone. Everyone, everything is gone, is going, and will go. Where do they go? This was the question that pressed for an answer in the mind of the primitive man. "Why so?" you may ask, "Did he not see everything decomposed, reduced to dust before him? Why should he have troubled his head at all about where they went?"

To the primitive man everything is living in the first place, and to him death in the sense of annihilation has no meaning at all. People come to him, go away, and come again. Sometimes they go away and do not come. Therefore in the most ancient language of the world death is always expressed by some sort of going. This is the beginning of religion. Thus the primitive man was searching everywhere for a solution of his difficulty—where do they all go?

There is the morning sun radiant in his glory, bringing light

2. Written by the Swami during his first visit to America in answer to questions put by a Western disciple.

and warmth and joy to a sleeping world. Slowly he travels and, alas, he also disappears, down, down below!

But the next day he appears again—glorious, beautiful! And there is the lotus—that wonderful flower in the Nile, the Indus, and the Tigris, the birth-places of civilisation—opening in the morning as the solar rays strike its closed petals and with the waning sun shutting up again. Some were there then who came and went and got up from their graves revivified. This was the first solution. The sun and the lotus are, therefore, the chief symbols in the most ancient religions. Why these symbols? because abstract thought, whatever that be, when expressed, is bound to come clad in visible, tangible, gross garments. This is the law. The idea of the passing out as not out of existence but in it, had to be expressed only as a change, a momentary transformation; and reflexively, that object which strikes the senses and goes vibrating to the mind and calls up a new idea is bound to be taken up as the support, the nucleus round which the new idea spreads itself for an expression. And so the sun and the lotus were the first symbols.

There are deep holes everywhere—so dark and so dismal; down is all dark and frightful; under water we cannot see, open our eyes though we may; up is light, all light, even at night the beautiful starry hosts shedding their light. Where do they go then, those I love? Not certainly down in the dark, dark place, but up, above in the realm of Everlasting Light. That required a new symbol. Here is fire with its glowing wonderful tongues of flame—eating up a forest in a short time, cooking the food, giving warmth, and driving wild animals away—this life-giving, life-saving fire; and then the flames—they all go upwards, never downwards. Here then was another—this fire that carries them upwards to the places of light—the connecting link between us and those that have passed over to the regions of light. "Thou Ignis", begins the oldest human record, "our messenger to the bright ones." So they put food and drink and whatever they thought would be pleasing to these "bright ones" into the fire. This was the beginning of sacrifice.

So far the first question was solved, at least as far as to satisfy the needs of these primitive men. Then came the other question: Whence has all this come? Why did it not come first? Because we remember a sudden change more. Happiness, joy, addition, enjoyment make not such a deep impression on our mind as unhappiness, sorrow, and subtraction. Our nature is joy, enjoyment, pleasure, and happiness. Anything that violently breaks it makes a deeper impression than the natural course. So the problem of death was the first to be solved as the great disturber. Then with more advancement came the other question: Whence they came? Everything that lives moves: we move; our will moves our limbs; our limbs manufacture forms under the control of our will. Everything then that moved had a will in it as the motor, to the man-child of ancient times as it is to the child-man of the present day. The wind has a will; the cloud, the whole of nature, is full

of separate wills, minds, and souls. They are creating all this just as we manufacture many things; they—the "Devas", the "Elohims" are the creators of all this.

Now in the meanwhile society was growing up. In society there was the king—why not among the bright ones, the Elohims? Therefore there was a supreme "Deva", an Elohim-jahveh, God of gods—the one God who by His single will has created all this—even the "bright ones". But as He has appointed different stars and planets, so He has appointed different "Devas" or angels to preside over different functions of nature—some over death, some over birth, etc. One supreme being, supreme by being infinitely more powerful than the rest, is the common conception in the two great sources of all religions, the Aryan and Semitic races. But here the Aryans take a new start, a grand deviation.

Their God was not only a supreme being, but He was the Dyaus Pitar, the Father in heaven. This is the beginning of Love. The Semitic God is only a thunderer, only the terrible one, the mighty Lord of hosts. To all these the Aryan added a new idea, that of a Father . And the divergence becomes more and more obvious all through further progress, which in fact stopped at this place in the Semitic branch of the human race. The God of the Semitic is not to be seen—nay, it is death to see Him; the God of the Aryan cannot only be seen, but He is the goal of being; the one aim of life is to see Him. The Semitic obeys his King of kings for fear of punishment and keeps His commandments. The Aryan loves his father; and further on he adds mother, his friend. And "Love me, love my dog", they say. So each one of His creatures should be loved, because they are His. To the Semitic, this life is an outpost where we are posted to test our fidelity; to the Aryan this life is on the way to our goal. To the Semitic, if we do our duty well, we shall have an ever-joyful home in heaven. To the Aryan, that home is God Himself. To the Semitic, serving God is a means to an end, namely, the pay, which is joy and enjoyment. To the Aryan, enjoyment, misery—everything—is a means, and the end is God. The Semitic worships God to go to heaven. The Aryan rejects heaven to go to God. In short, this is the main difference. The aim and end of the Aryan life is to see God, to see the face of the Beloved, because without Him he cannot live. "Without Thy presence, the sun, the moon, and the stars lose their light."

FOUR PATHS OF YOGA[1]

Our main problem is to be free. It is evident then that until we realise ourselves as the Absolute, we cannot attain to deliverance. Yet there are various ways of attaining to this realisation. These methods have the generic name of Yoga (to join, to join ourselves to our reality). These Yogas, though divided into various groups, can principally be classed into four; and as each is only a method leading indirectly to the realisation

1. Written by the Swami during his first visit to America in answer to questions put by a Western disciple.

of the Absolute, they are suited to different temperaments. Now it must be remembered that it is not that the assumed man becomes the real man or Absolute. There is no becoming with the Absolute. It is ever free, ever perfect; but the ignorance that has covered Its nature for a time is to be removed. Therefore the whole scope of all systems of Yoga (and each religion represents one) is to clear up this ignorance and allow the Atman to restore its own nature. The chief helps in this liberation are Abhyasa and Vairagya. Vairagya is non-attachment to life, because it is the will to enjoy that brings all this bondage in its train; and Abhyasa is constant practice of any one of the Yogas.

Karma-yoga . Karma-yoga is purifying the mind by means of work. Now if any work is done, good or bad, it must produce as a result a good or bad effect; no power can stay it, once the cause is present. Therefore good action producing good Karma, and bad action, bad Karma, the soul will go on in eternal bondage without ever hoping for deliverance. Now Karma belongs only to the body or the mind, never to the Atman (Self); only it can cast a veil before the Atman.

The veil cast by bad Karma is ignorance. Good Karma has the power to strengthen the moral powers. And thus it creates non-attachment; it destroys the tendency towards bad Karma and thereby purifies the mind. But if the work is done with the intention of enjoyment, it then produces only that very enjoyment and does not purify the mind or Chitta. Therefore all work should be done without any desire to enjoy the fruits thereof. All fear and all desire to enjoy here or hereafter must be banished for ever by the Karma-yogi. Moreover, this Karma without desire of return will destroy the selfishness, which is the root of all bondage. The watchword of the Karma-yogi is "not I, but Thou", and no amount of self-sacrifice is too much for him. But he does this without any desire to go to heaven, or gain name or fame or any other benefit in this world. Although the explanation and rationale of this unselfish work is only in Jnana-yoga, yet the natural divinity of man makes him love all sacrifice simply for the good of others, without any ulterior motive, whatever his creed or opinion. Again, with many the bondage of wealth is very great; and Karma-yoga is absolutely necessary for them as breaking the crystallisation that has gathered round their love of money.

Next is Bhakti-Yoga . Bhakti or worship or love in some form or other is the easiest, pleasantest, and most natural way of man. The natural state of this universe is attraction; and that is surely followed by an ultimate disunion. Even so, love is the natural impetus of union in the human heart; and though itself a great cause of misery, properly directed towards the proper object, it brings deliverance. The object of Bhakti is God. Love cannot be without a subject and an object. The object of love again must be at first a being who can reciprocate our love. Therefore the God of love must be in some sense a human God. He must be a God of love. Aside from the question whether such a God exists or not, it is a fact that to those who have love in their heart this Absolute appears as a God of love, as personal.

The lower forms of worship, which embody the idea of God as a judge or punisher or someone to be obeyed through fear, do not deserve to be called love, although they are forms of worship gradually expanding into higher forms. We pass on to the consideration of love itself. We will illustrate love by a triangle, of which the first angle at the base is fearlessness. So long as there is fear, it is not love. Love banishes all fear. A mother with her baby will face a tiger to save her child. The second angle is that love never asks, never begs. The third or the apex is that love loves for the sake of love itself. Even the idea of object vanishes. Love is the only form in which love is loved. This is the highest abstraction and the same as the Absolute.

Next is Raja-Yoga . This Yoga fits in with every one of these Yogas. It fits inquirers of all classes with or without any belief, and it is the real instrument of religious inquiry. As each science has its particular method of investigation, so is this Raja-yoga the method of religion. This science also is variously applied according to various constitutions. The chief parts are the Pranayama, concentration, and meditation. For those who believe in God, a symbolical name, such as Om or other sacred words received from a Guru, will be very helpful. Om is the greatest, meaning the Absolute. Meditating on the meaning of these holy names while repeating them is the chief practice.

Next is Jnana-Yoga. This is divided into three parts. First: hearing the truth—that the Atman is the only reality and that everything else is Maya (relativity). Second: reasoning upon this philosophy from all points of view. Third: giving up all further argumentation and realising the truth. This realisation comes from (1) being certain that Brahman is real and everything else is unreal; (2) giving up all desire for enjoyment; (3) controlling the senses and the mind; (4) intense desire to be free. Meditating on this reality always and reminding the soul of its real nature are the only ways in this Yoga. It is the highest, but most difficult. Many persons get an intellectual grasp of it, but very few attain realisation.

CYCLIC REST AND CHANGE[2]

This whole universe is a case of lost balance. All motion is the struggle of the disturbed universe to regain its equilibrium, which, as such, cannot be motion. Thus in regard to the internal world it would be a state which is beyond thought, for thought itself is a motion. Now when all indication is towards perfect equilibrium by expansion and the whole universe is rushing towards it, we have no right to say that that state can never be attained. Again it is impossible that there should be any variety whatsoever in that state of equilibrium. It must be homogeneous; for as long as there are even two atoms, they will attract and repel each other and disturb the balance.

2. Written by the Swami during his first visit to America in answer to questions put by a Western disciple.

Therefore this state of equilibrium is one of unity, of rest, and of homogeneity. In the language of the internal, this state of equilibrium is not thought, nor body, nor anything which we call an attribute. The only thing which we can say it will retain is what is its own nature as existence, self-consciousness, and blissfulness.

This state in the same way cannot be two. It must only be a unit, and all fictitious distinctions of I, thou, etc., all the different variations must vanish, as they belong to the state of change or Maya. It may be said that this state of change has come now upon the Self, showing that, before this, it had the state of rest and liberty; that at present the state of differentiation is the only real state, and the state of homogeneity is the primitive crudeness out of which this changeful state is manufactured; and that it will be only degeneration to go back to the state of undifferentiation. This argument would have had some weight if it could be proved that these two states, viz homogeneity and heterogeneity, are the only two states happening but once through all time. What happens once must happen again and again. Rest is followed by change—the universe. But that rest must have been preceded by other changes, and this change will be succeeded by other rests. It would be ridiculous to think that there was a period of rest and then came this change which will go on for ever. Every particle in nature shows that it is coming again and again to periodic rest and change.

This interval between one period of rest and another is called a Kalpa. But this Kalpic rest cannot be one of perfect homogeneity, for in that case there would be an end to any future manifestation. Now to say that the present state of change is one of great advance in comparison to the preceding state of rest is simply absurd, because in that case the coming period of rest being much more advanced in time must be much more perfect! There is no progression or digression in nature. It is showing again and again the same forms. In fact, the word law means this. But there is a progression with regard to souls. That is to say, the souls get nearer to their own natures, and in each Kalpa large numbers of them get deliverance from being thus whirled around. It may be said, the individual soul being a part of the universe and nature, returning again and again, there cannot be any liberty for the soul, for in that case the universe has to be destroyed. The answer is that the individual soul is an assumption through Maya, and it is no more a reality than nature itself. In reality, this individual soul is the unconditioned absolute Brahman (the Supreme).

All that is real in nature is Brahman, only it appears to be this variety, or nature, through the superimposition of Maya. Maya being illusion cannot be said to be real, yet it is producing the phenomena. If it be asked, how can Maya, herself being illusion, produce all this, our answer is that what is produced being also ignorance, the producer must also be that. How can ignorance be produced by knowledge? So this Maya is acting in two ways as nescience and science (relative knowledge); and this science after destroying nescience or ignorance is itself also destroyed. This Maya destroys herself and what remains is the Absolute, the Essence of existence, knowledge, and bliss. Now whatever is reality in nature is this Absolute, and nature comes to us in three forms, God, conscious, and unconscious, i.e. God, personal souls, and unconscious beings. The reality of all these is the Absolute; through Maya it is seen to be diverse. But the vision of God is the nearest to the reality and the highest. The idea of a Personal God is the highest idea which man can have. All the attributes attributed to God are true in the same sense as are the attributes of nature. Yet we must never forget that the Personal God is the very Absolute seen through Maya.

A PREFACE TO *THE IMITATION OF CHRIST*[1]

The Imitation of Christ is a cherished treasure of the Christian world. This great book was written by a Roman Catholic monk. "Written", perhaps, is not the proper word. It would be more appropriate to say that each letter of the book is marked deep with the heart's blood of the great soul who had renounced all for his love of Christ. That great soul whose words, living and burning, have cast such a spell for the last four hundred years over the hearts of myriads of men and women; whose influence today remains as strong as ever and is destined to endure for all time to come; before whose genius and Sâdhâna (spiritual effort) hundred of crowned have bent down in reverence; and before whose matchless purity the jarring sects of Christendom, whose name is legion, have sunk their differences of centuries in common veneration to a common principle—that great soul, strange to say, has not thought fit to put his name to a book such as this. Yet there is nothing strange here after all, for why should he? Is it possible for one who totally renounced all earthly joys and despised the desire for the bauble fame as so much dirt and filth—is it possible for such a soul to care for that paltry thing, a mere author's name? Posterity, however, has guessed that the author was Thomas à Kempis, a Roman Catholic monk. How far the guess is true is known only to God. But be he who he may, that he deserves the world's adoration is a truth that can be gainsaid by none.

We happen to be the subjects of a Christian government now. Through its favour it has been our lot to meet Christians of so many sects, native as well as foreign. How startling the divergence between their profession and practice! Here stands the Christian missionary preaching: "Sufficient unto the day is the evil thereof. Take no thought for the morrow"—and then busy soon after, making his pile and framing his budget for ten years in advance! There he says that he follows him who "hath not where to lay his head", glibly talking of the

1. Translated from an original Bengali writing of the Swami in 1889. The passage is the preface to his Bengali translation of *The Imitation* of *Christ* which he contributed to a Bengali monthly. He translated only six chapters with quotations of parallel passages from the Hindu scriptures.

glorious sacrifice and burning renunciation of the Master, but in practice going about like a gay bridegroom fully enjoying all the comforts the world can bestow! Look where we may, a true Christian nowhere do we see. The ugly impression left on our mind by the ultra-luxurious, insolent, despotic, barouche-and-brougham-driving Christians of the Protestant sects will be completely removed if we but once read this great book with the attention it deserves.

All wise men think alike. The reader, while reading this book, will hear the echo of the Bhagavad-Gitâ over and over again. Like the Bhagavad-Gita it says, "Give up all Dharmas and follow Me". The spirit of humility, the panting of the distressed soul, the best expression of Dâsya Bhakti (devotion as a servant) will be found imprinted on every line of this great book and the reader's heart will be profoundly stirred by the author's thoughts of burning renunciation, marvellous surrender, and deep sense of dependence on the will of God. To those of my countrymen, who under the influence of blind bigotry may seek to belittle this book because it is the work of a Christian, I shall quote only one aphorism of Vaisheshika Darshana and say nothing more. The aphorism is this: आप्तोपदेशवाक्यं शब्द—which means that the teachings of Siddha Purushas (perfected souls) have a probative force and this is technically known as Shabda Pramâna (verbal evidence). Rishi Jaimini, the commentator, says that such Âpta Purushas (authorities) may be born both among the Aryans and the Mlechchhas.

If in ancient times Greek astronomers like Yavanâchârya could have been so highly esteemed by our Aryan ancestors, then it is incredible that this work of the lion of devotees will fail to be appreciated by my countrymen.

Be that as it may, we shall place the Bengali translation of this book before our readers seriatim. We trust that the readers of Bengal will spend over it at least one hundredth part of the time they waste over cart-loads of trashy novels and dramas.

I have tried to make the translation as literal as possible, but I cannot say how far I have succeeded. The allusions to the Bible in several passages are given in the footnotes.

AN INTERESTING CORRESPONDENCE[2]

Now Sister Mary,

2. In order to truly appreciate this correspondence, the reader has to be informed of the occasion which gave rise to it and also to remember the relation that existed between the correspondents. At the outset of the first letter the Swami speaks of "the hard raps" that he gave to his correspondent. These were nothing but a very strong letter which he wrote to her in vindication of his position, on the 1st of February, 1895, which will be found reproduced in the fifth volume of the Complete Works of the Swami. It was a very beautiful letter full of the fire of a Sannyasin's spirit, and we request our readers to go through it before they peruse the following text. Mary Hale, to whom the Swami wrote, was one of the two daughters of Mr. and Mrs. Hale whom the Swami used to address as Father Pope and Mother Church. The Misses Hales and their two cousins were like sisters to him, and they also in their turn

You need not be sorry
For the hard raps I gave you,
You know full well,
Though you like me tell,
With my whole heart I love you.
The babies I bet,
The best friends I met,
Will stand by me in weal and woe.
And so will I do,
You know it too.
Life, name, or fame, even heaven forgo
For the sweet sisters four
Sans reproche et sans peur,
The truest, noblest, steadfast, best.
The wounded snake its hood unfurls,
The flame stirred up doth blaze,
The desert air resounds the calls
Of heart-struck lion's rage.
The cloud puts forth its deluge strength
When lightning cleaves its breast,
When the soul is stirred to its inmost depth
Great ones unfold their best.
Let eyes grow dim and heart grow faint,
And friendship fail and love betray,
Let Fate its hundred horrors send,
And clotted darkness block the way.
All nature wear one angry frown,
To crush you out—still know, my soul,
You are Divine. March on and on,
Nor right nor left but to the goal.
Nor angel I, nor man, nor brute,
Nor body, mind, nor he or she,
The books do stop in wonder mute
To tell my nature; I am He.
Before the sun, the moon, the earth,
Before the stars or comets free,
Before e'en time has had its birth,
I was, I am, and I will be.
The beauteous earth, the glorious sun,
The calm sweet moon, the spangled sky,
Causation's laws do make them run;
They live in bonds, in bonds they die.
And mind its mantle dreamy net

held the Swami in great love and reverence. Some of the finest letters of the Swami were written to them. In the present correspondence the Swami is seen in a new light, playful and intensely human, yet keyed to the central theme of his life, Brahmajnana. The first letter was written from New York, 15th February 1895—— Ed.

Cast o'er them all and holds them fast.
In warp and woof of thought are set,
Earth, hells, and heavens, or worst or best.
Know these are but the outer crust —
All space and time, all effect, cause.
I am beyond all sense, all thoughts,
The witness of the universe.
Not two or many, 'tis but one,
And thus in me all me's I have;
I cannot hate, I cannot shun
Myself from me, I can but love.
From dreams awake, from bonds be free,
Be not afraid. This mystery,
My shadow, cannot frighten me,
Know once for all that I am He.

Well, so far my poetry. Hope you are all right. Give my love
to mother and Father Pope. I am busy to death and have almost no time to write even a line. So excuse me if later on I
am rather late in writing.

Yours eternally,
Vivekananda.

Miss M.B.H. sent Swami the following doggerel in reply:

The monk he would a poet be
And wooed the muse right earnestly;
In thought and word he could well beat her,
What bothered him though was the metre.
His feet were all too short too long,
The form not suited to his song;
He tried the sonnet, lyric, epic,
And worked so hard, he waxed dyspeptic.
While the poetic mania lasted
He e'en from vegetables fasted,
Which Leon[1] had with tender care
Prepared for Swami's dainty fare.
One day he sat and mused alone —
Sudden a light around him shone,
The "still small voice" his thoughts inspire
And his words glow like coals of fire.
And coals of fire they proved to be
Heaped on the head of contrite me —
My scolding letter I deplore
And beg forgiveness o'er and o'er.
The lines you sent to your sisters four
Be sure they'll cherish evermore

---

1. Leon Landsberg, a disciple of the Swami who lived with him for
some time.

For you have made them clearly see
The one main truth that "all is He".
Then Swami:
In days of yore,
On Ganga's shore preaching,
A hoary priest was teaching
How Gods they come
As Sita Ram,
And gentle Sita pining, weeping.
The sermons end,
They homeward wend their way —
The hearers musing, thinking.
When from the crowd
A voice aloud
This question asked beseeching, seeking —
"Sir, tell me, pray,
Who were but they
These Sita Ram you were teaching, speaking!"
So Mary Hale,
Allow me tell,
You mar my doctrines wronging, baulking.
I never taught
Such queer thought
That all was God — unmeaning talking!
But this I say,
Remember pray,
That God is true, all else is nothing,
This world's a dream
Though true it seem,
And only truth is He the living!
The real me is none but He,
The real me is none but He,
And never, never matter changing!
With undying love and gratitude to you all …
Vivekananda.
And then Miss M.B.H.:
The difference I clearly see
'Twixt tweedledum and tweedledee —
That is a proposition sane,
But truly 'tis beyond my vein
To make your Eastern logic plain.
If "God is truth, all else is naught,"
This "world a dream", delusion up wrought,
What can exist which God is not?
All those who "many" see have much to fear,
He only lives to whom the "One" is clear.
So again I say

In my poor way,
I cannot see but that all's He,
If I'm in Him and He in me.
Then the Swami replied:
Of temper quick, a girl unique,
A freak of nature she,
A lady fair, no question there,
Rare soul is Miss Mary.

Her feelings deep she cannot keep,
But creep they out at last,
A spirit free, I can foresee,
Must be of fiery cast.

Tho' many a lay her muse can bray,
And play piano too,
Her heart so cool, chills as a rule
The fool who comes to woo.

Though, Sister Mary, I hear they say
The sway your beauty gains,
Be cautious now and do not bow,
However sweet, to chains.

For 'twill be soon, another tune
The moon-struck mate will hear
If his will but clash, your words will hash
And smash his life I fear.

These lines to thee, Sister Mary,
Free will I offer, take
"Tit for tat"— a monkey chat,
For monk alone can make.

A HYMN TO SHRI RAMAKRISHNA

In Sanskrit

1. He who was Shri Rama, whose stream of love flowed with resistless might even to the Chandala (the outcaste); Oh, who ever was engaged in doing good to the world though superhuman by nature, whose renown there is none to equal in the three worlds, Sita's beloved, whose body of Knowledge Supreme was covered by devotion sweet in the form of Sita.

2. He who quelled the noise, terrible like that at the time of destruction, arising from the battle (of Kurukshetra), who destroyed the terrible yet natural night of ignorance (of Arjuna) and who roared out the Gita sweet and appeasing; That renowned soul is born now as Shri Ramakrishna.

3. Hail, O Lord of Men! Victory unto You! I surrender myself to my Guru, the physician for the malady of Samsara (relative existence) who is, as it were, a wave rising in the ocean of Shakti (Power), who has shown various sports of Love Divine, and who is the weapon to destroy the demon of doubt.

Hail, O Lord of Men! Victory unto You!

4. Hail, O Lord of Men! Victory unto you! I surrender myself to my Guru the Man-god, the physician for the malady of this Samsara (relative existence), whose mind ever dwelt on the non-dualistic Truth, whose personality was covered by the cloth of Supreme Devotion, who was ever active (for the good of humanity) and whose actions were all superhuman.

Hail, O Lord of Men! Victory unto You!

THE ETHER[2]

This article first appeared anonymously in the February 1895 issue of the New York Medical Times, a prestigious monthly medical journal founded and edited by Dr. Egbert Guernsey.

Classification or grouping of phenomena by their similarities is the first step in scientific knowledge—perhaps it is all. An organized grouping, revealing to us a similarity running through the whole group, and a conviction that under similar circumstances the group will arrange itself in the same form—stretched over all time, past, present and future—is what we call law.

This finding of unity in variety is really what we call knowledge. These different groups of similars are stowed away in the pigeon-holes of the mind, and when a new fact comes before us we begin to search for a similar group already existing in one of the pigeon-holes of the mind. If we succeed in finding one ready-made, we take the newcomer in immediately. If not, we either reject the new fact, or wait till we find more of his kind, and form a new place for the group.

Facts which are extraordinary thus disturb us; but and when we find many like them, they cease to disturb, even when our knowledge about their cause remains the same as before.

The ordinary experiences of our lives are no less wonderful than any miracles recorded in any sacred book of the world; nor are we any more enlightened as to the cause of these ordinary experiences than of the so-called miracles. But the miraculous is "extraordinary", and the everyday experience is "ordinary". The "extraordinary" startles the mind, the "ordinary" satisfies.

The field of knowledge is so varied, and the more the difference is from the centre, the more widely the radii diverge.

At the start the different sciences were thought to have no connection whatever with each other; but as more and more knowledge comes in—that is, the more and more we come nearer the centre—the radii are converging more and more, and it seems that they are on the eve of finding a common centre. Will they ever find it?

The study of the mind was, above all, the science to which the sages of India and Greece had directed their attention. All religions are the outcome of the study of the inner man. Here

2. Reprinted in New Discoveries, Vol. 3, pp. 55-59. Because the Swami's original handwritten article is unavailable, we have made the spelling, punctuation and grammar of his published version conform to the style of the Complete Works. — Publisher.

we find the attempt at finding the unity, and in the science of religion, as taking its stand upon general and massive propositions, we find the boldest and the most vigorous manifestation of this tendency at finding the unity.

Some religions could not solve the problem beyond the finding of a duality of causes, one good, the other evil. Others went as far as finding an intelligent personal cause, a few went still further beyond intellect, beyond personality, and found an infinite being.

In those, and only those systems which dared to transcend beyond the personality of a limited human consciousness, we find also an attempt to resolve all physical phenomena into unity.

The result was the "Akâsha" of the Hindus and the "Ether" of the Greeks.

This "Akasha" was, after the mind, the first material manifestation, said the Hindu sages, and out of this "Akasha" all this has been evolved.

History repeats itself; and again during the latter part of the nineteenth century, the same theory is coming with more vigour and fuller light.

It is being proved more clearly than ever that as there is a co-relation of physical forces there is also a co-relation of different [branches of] knowledge, and that behind all these general groups there is a unity of knowledge.

It was shown by Newton[1] that if light consisted of material particles projected from luminous bodies, they must move faster in solids and liquids than in air, in order that the laws of refraction might be satisfied.

Huyghens[2], on the other hand, showed that to account for the same laws on the supposition that light consisted in the undulating motion of an elastic medium, it must move more slowly in solids and fluids than in gases. Fizeau[3] and Foucault[4] found Huyghens's predictions correct.

Light, then, consists in the vibrating motion of a medium, which must, of course, fill all space. This is called the ether.

In the fact that the theory of a cosmic ether explains fully all the phenomena of radiation, refraction, diffraction and polarization of light is the strongest argument in favour of the theory.

Of late, gravitation, molecular action, magnetic, electric, and electro-dynamic attractions and repulsions have thus been explained.

Sensible and latent heat, electricity and magnetism themselves have been of late almost satisfactorily explained by the theory of the all-pervading ether.

Zöllner[5], however, basing his calculations upon the data supplied by the researches of Wilhelm Weber[6], thinks that the transmission of life force between the heavenly bodies is effected both ways, by the undulation of a medium and by the actual evidence of particles.

Weber found that the molecules, the smallest particles of bodies, were composed of yet smaller particles, which he called the electric particles, and which in the molecules are in a constant circular motion. These electric particles are partly positive, partly negative.

Those of the same electricity repulse those of different electricity; attracting each other, each molecule contains the same amount of electric particles, with a small surplus of either positive or negative quickly changing the balance.

Upon this Zöllner builds these propositions:

(1) The molecules are composed of a very great number of particles—the so-called electric particles, which are in constant circular motion around each other within the molecule.

(2) If the inner motion of a molecule increases over a certain limit, then electric particles are emitted. They then travel from one heavenly body through space until they reach another heavenly body, where they are either reflected or absorbed by other molecules.

(3) The electric particles thus traversing space are the ether of the physicist.

(4) These ether particles have a twofold motion: first, their proper motion; second, an undulatory motion, for which they receive the impulse from the ether particles rotating in the molecules.

(5) The motion of the smallest particles corresponds to that of the heavenly bodies.

The corollary is:

The law of attraction which holds good for the heavenly bodies also holds good for the smallest particles.

Under these suppositions, that which we call space is really filled with electric particles, or ether.

Zöllner also found the following interesting calculation for the electric atoms:

Velocity: 50,143 geographical miles per second.

Amount of ether particles in a water molecule: 42,000 million.

Distance from each other: 0.0032 millimeter.

So far as it goes, then, the theory of a universal cosmic ether is the best at hand to explain the various phenomena of nature.

As far as it goes, the theory that this ether consists of particles, electric or otherwise, is also very valuable. But on all suppositions, there must be space between two particles of ether, however small; and what fills this inter-ethereal space? If particles still finer, we require still more fine ethereal particles to fill up the vacuum between every two of them, and so on.

1. Isaac Newton, 1642 – 1727.

2. Christian Huyghens, 1629 – 1695.

3. Armand Hippolyte Louis Fizeau, 1819 – 1896.

4. Jean Bernard Léon Foucault, 1819 – 1868.

5. Johann K. F. Zöllner, 1834 – 1882.

6. Wilhelm Eduard Weber, 1804 – 1891.

Thus the theory of ether, or material particles in space, though accounting for the phenomena in space, cannot account for space itself.

And thus we are forced to find that the ether which comprehends the molecules explains the molecular phenomena, but itself cannot explain space because we cannot but think of ether as in space. And, therefore, if there is anything which will explain this space, it must be something that comprehends in its infinite being the infinite space itself. And what is there that can comprehend even the infinite space but the Infinite Mind?

NOTES[7]

An undated and untitled, one-page manuscript in Swami Vivekananda's own handwriting.

My nerves act on my brain—the brain sends back a reaction which, on the mental side, is this world.

Something—x—acts on the brain through the nerves, the reaction is this world.

Why not the x be also in the body—why outside?

Because we find the already created outside world (as the result of a previous reaction of the brain) acts on us calling on a further reaction.

Thus inside becomes outside and creates another action, which interior action created another reaction, which again becomes outside and again acts inside.

The only way of reconciling idealism and realism is to hold that one brain can be affected by the world created as reaction by another brain from inside, i.e., the mixture x + mind which one brain throws out can affect another, to which it's similarly external.

Therefore as soon as we come within the influence of this hypnotic circle, or influence, created by hundreds of preceding brains we begin to feel this world as they see it.

Mind is only a phase of matter, i.e., of the ever-changing phenomena of which matter and mind are different states or views. There must be something in whose presence this eternal, phenomenal net is spread—that is the Substance, the Brahman.

LECTURE NOTES

New Discoveries, Vol. 4, pp. 213-14.

Probably at the turn of the century, Miss Ellen Waldo gave these undated notes in Swami Vivekananda's handwriting to her friend Sister Devamata, a member of the Boston Vedanta Centre, where they were later made available for publication.

Man will need a religion so long as he is constituted as at present. The forms will change from time to time.

The dissatisfaction with the senses.

The yearning beyond.

There were encroachments of religion on the domains of physical science—these [encroachments] religion is giving up every day. Yet there is a vast field covered by religion where physical science[s] are mute.

The [vain?] attempt to keep man strictly within the limits of the senses—Because—there are men who catch a glimpse now and then of the infinite beyond.

The types of men.

The worker—the mystic the emotional the intellectual. Each type is necessary for the well—being of society. The dangers of each —

A mixture minimizes the danger.

The East is too full of mystics and meditative the West of workers—An exchange will be for the good of both.

The necessity of religion —

The four types of men

that come to religion —

the basis of Unity—the Divinity

in man. Why use this term?

the western Society has work

and intellectual philosophy —

But work must not be destructive

of others.

Philosophy—must not be only dry intellectuality.

MACROCOSM AND MICROCOSM

The Life of Swami Vivekananda, Vol. I. p. 250.

After his experience of the macrocosm within the microcosm while absorbed in meditation under the peepul tree at Kakrighat, in 1890, Swami Vivekananda jotted down in Bengali fragments of his realization in his notebook.

In the beginning was the Word etc.

The microcosm and the macrocosm are built on the same plan. Just as the individual soul is encased in the living body, so is the universal Soul in the Living Prakriti [Nature]—the objective universe. Shivâ [i.e. Kâli] is embracing Shiva: this is not a fancy. This covering of the one [Soul] by the other [Nature] is analogous to the relation between an idea and the word expressing it: they are one and the same; and it is only by a mental abstraction that one can distinguish them. Thought is impossible without words. Therefore, in the beginning was the Word etc.

This dual aspect of the Universal Soul is eternal. So what we perceive or feel is this combination of the Eternally Formed and the Eternally Formless.

7. *New Discoveries*, Vol. 3, pp. 440-41.

SWAMI VIVEKANANDA'S FOOTNOTES TO *THE IMITATION OF CHRIST*[1]

In 1889, Swami Vivekananda translated into Bengali selections from Book I, chapters 1-6 of Thomas à Kempis's *The Imitation of Christ*. They were published along with a preface in a now-defunct Bengali monthly magazine, *Sâhitya Kalpadruma*. The Swami's preface and Bengali translation, entitled "Ishânusharana"[2], were later published in the Bengali Complete Works (first edition), VI, pp. 16-28. However, only the preface to The Imitation of Christ was published in the English edition of the Complete Works, VIII.

Swami Vivekananda's partial Bengali translation of The Imitation of Christ includes as footnotes quotations from Hindu scriptures that parallel à Kempis's ideas, comments or commentary. For the sake of clarity, these footnotes (numbered 1 through 17) have been appended to their respective verses in The Imitation of Christ (indicated in parentheses), arranged under their appropriate chapter headings in the book, and reproduced here in bold.

Many of the Sanskrit footnotes to the Bengali translation were later rendered into English during the course of Swami Vivekananda's lecturing or writing. For the sake of interest, these English translations have also been added to the Swami's restored footnote text. Otherwise, Sanskrit verses have been translated by the Publisher for the convenience of the reader.
—Publisher

BOOK I[3]

Chapter 1

Of the Imitation of Christ and Contempt of all the Vanities of the World

1. "He that followeth Me, walketh not in darkness", saith the Lord [John 8.12]. (The Imitation of Christ V.1.)

Swami Vivekananda's Footnote: Bhagavad-Gita 7.14

देवी ह्येषा गुणमयी मम माया दुरत्यया ।
मामेव ये प्रपद्यन्ते मायामेतां तरन्ति ते ॥

Swami Vivekananda's Translation: This My Mâyâ is divine, made up of qualities and very difficult to cross. Yet those who come unto Me, cross the river of life[4].

2. Let therefore our chief endeavour be to meditate upon the life of Jesus Christ. (The Imitation of Christ V.1.)

---

1. *Prabuddha Bharata*, September 1982, pp. 390-93.

2. In Bengali, the word Ishâ means Christ and Anusharana, "to follow"; hence Ishânusharana means "to follow Christ".

3. Verses are cited from Thomas à Kempis's *Of the Imitation of Christ* (London: Oxford University Press, 1961.) This translation—based on that of F. B. (the Jesuit Anthony Hoskins), which first appeared c. 1613—has been lightly edited in order to conform to the grammar, punctuation and style of the *Complete Works*—Publisher.

4. Vide "Maya and Freedom", *Complete Works*, II:123.

Swami Vivekananda's Footnote: Adhyâtma Râmâyana, Uttara-Kanda 5.54 (RamaGita)

ध्यायेत्रेवमात्मानमहर्निशं मुनिः ।
तष्ठित्तेत्सदा मुक्तसमस्तबन्धनः ॥

Publisher's Translation: Thus meditating upon the Self day and night, let the sage abide free from all bondage.

3. The doctrine of Christ exceedeth all the doctrines of holy men; and he that hath the Spirit will find therein the hidden manna. (The Imitation of Christ V.2.)

Swami Vivekananda's Footnote:

When the Israelites were afflicted by want of food in a desert, God showered on them a kind of "manna".

4. But it falleth out, that many who often hear the Gospel of Christ, are yet but little affected, because they are void of the Spirit of Christ. But whosoever would fully and feelingly understand the words of Christ, must endeavour to conform his life wholly to the life of Christ. (The Imitation of Christ V.2.)

Swami Vivekananda's Footnote (a): Bhagavad-Gita 2.29

श्रुत्वाप्येनं वेद न चैव कश्चित् ।

Swami Vivekananda'S Translation: Others, hearing of It, do not understand[5].

Swami Vivekananda's Footnote (b): Vivekachudâmani 62.

न गच्छति विना पानं व्याधिरौषधशब्दतः ।
विनाऽपरोक्षानुभवं ब्रह्मशब्देर्न मुच्यते ॥

Publisher's Translation: A disease does not leave the body by simply repeating the name of the medicine; one must take the medicine. Similarly, liberation does not come by merely saying the word Brahman. Brahman must be experienced.

Swami Vivekananda's Footnote (c): Mahabharata(critical edition) 12.309.91.

श्रुतेन किं येन न धर्ममाचरेत् ।

Publisher's Translation: Of what avail is reading the Vedas without practising religion?

5. What will it avail thee to dispute profoundly of the Trinity if thou be void of humility and art thereby displeasing to the Trinity? (The Imitation of Christ V.3.)

Swami Vivekananda's Footnote:

According to the Christians, God the Father, Holy Ghost, and God the Son are One in three and Three in One.

6. Surely great words do not make a man holy and just; but a virtuous life maketh him dear to God. (The Imitation of Christ V.3.)

Swami Vivekananda's Footnote: Vivekachudamani 58.

वाग्वेखरी शब्दझरी शास्तरव्याख्यानकौशलम्।
वेदुष्यं विदुषां तद्वद् भुक्तये न तु मुक्तये॥

Swami Vivekananda's Translation: Wonderful methods of

---

5. Vide "The Gita II", *Complete Works*, I.

joining words, rhetorical powers, and explaining texts of the books in various ways—these are only for the enjoyment of the learned, and not religion[6].

7. If thou didst know the whole Bible by heart and the sayings of all the philosophers, what would it profit thee without the love of God and without grace? (The Imitation of Christ V.3.)

Swami Vivekananda's Footnote: [reference only]

—I Corinthians 13.2.

8. "Vanity of vanities, all is vanity" (Eccles.) except to love God and to serve Him only. (The Imitation of Christ V.3.)

Swami Vivekananda's Footnote: Maniratnamâlâ

के सन्ति सन्तोऽखिलवीतरागाः ।
अपास्तमोहाः श्रवितत्त्वनिष्ठाः ॥

Publisher's Translation: They alone are holy men (Sâdhus) who are devoid of any longing for worldly objects, free from delusion and are devoted to the truth of Shiva.

9. Call often to mind that proverb "The eye is not satisfied with seeing, nor the ear filled with hearing". (The Imitation of Christ V.5.)

Swami Vivekananda's Footnote: [reference only]

—Eccles. 1.8.

10. Endeavour, therefore, to withdraw thy heart from the love of visible things and to turn thyself to the invisible. For they that follow their lusts stain their own consciences and lose the grace of God. (The Imitation of Christ V.5.)

Swami Vivekananda's Footnote: Mahabharata, 2.63.

(Yayatigatha)

न जातु कामः कामानुपभोगेन शाम्यति ।
हविषा कृष्णवर्त्मेव भूय एवाभिवर्धते ॥

Swami Vivekananda's Translation: Desire is never satisfied by the enjoyment of desires; it only increases the more, as fire when butter is poured upon it[7].

Chapter 3
Of the Doctrine of Truth

11. What availeth it to cavil and dispute much about dark and hidden things; for ignorance of which we shall not be reproved at the day of judgement?(The Imitation of Christ V.1.)

Swami Vivekananda's Footnote:

According to the Christian view, God will judge all beings on the last day (the day of the dissolution of the world), and will award heaven or hell according to the virtues or vices of different individuals.

12. He to whom the Eternal Word speaketh is delivered from many an opinion.(The Imitation of Christ V.2.)

Swami Vivekananda's Footnote:

6. Vide "Realization", *Complete Works*, II:164

7. Vide "Maya and Illusion", *Complete Works*, II.

This Word is somewhat similar to the Maya of the Vedantists. This Itself was manifested in the form of Christ.

Chapter 5
Of the Reading of Holy Scriptures

13. Truth, not eloquence, is to be sought for in Holy Scripture. Each part of the Scripture is to be read with the same Spirit wherewith it was written. (The Imitation of Christ V.1.)

Swami Vivekananda's Footnote: Katha Upanishad 1.2.9.

नैषा तर्केण मतिरापनेया ।

Swami Vivekananda's Translation: Neither is the mind to be disturbed by vain arguments, for it is no more a question of argument; it is a question of fact[8].

14. Let not the authority of the writer offend thee, whether he be of great or small learning; but let the love of pure truth draw thee to read. (The Imitation of Christ V.1.)

Swami Vivekananda's Footnote: Laws of Manu 2.238.

आददीत शुभां विद्यां प्रयत्नादवरादपि।

Swami Vivekananda's Translation: Learn supreme knowledge with service even from the man of low birth[9].

Chapter 6
Of Inordinate Affections

15. Whensoever a man desireth anything inordinately, he becometh presently disquieted in himself. (The Imitation of Christ V.1.)

Swami Vivekananda's Footnote: Bhagavad-Gita 2.67.

इन्द्रियाणां हि चरतां यन्मनोऽनु विधीयते ।
तदस्य हरति प्रज्ञां वायुर्नावमिवाम्भसि ॥

Swami Vivekananda's Translation: For the mind which follows in the wake of the wandering senses carries away his discrimination as a wind (carries away from its course) a boat on the waters.

16. The proud and covetous can never rest. The poor and humble in spirit live together in all peace.

The man that is not yet perfectly dead to himself, is quickly tempted and overcome in small and trifling things. (The Imitation of Christ V.1.)

Swami Vivekananda's Footnote: Bhagavad-Gita 2.62-63.

ध्यायतो विषयान्पुंसः संगस्तेषूपजायते ।
संगात्संजायते कामः कामात्क्रोधोऽभिजायते ॥
क्रोधाद्भवति संमोहः संमोहात्स्मृतिविभ्रमः ।
स्मृतिभ्रंशाद् बुद्धिनाशो बुद्धिनाशात्प्रणश्यति ॥

Publisher's Translation: By thinking about sense objects, at-

8. Vide "Realization", Complete Works, II:162

9. Vide "The Common Bases of Hinduism", *Complete Works*, III. 381-382

tachment to them is formed. From attachment comes longing, and longing breeds anger. From anger comes delusion, and from delusion, confused memory. From confused memory comes the ruin of discrimination; and from the ruin of discrimination, a man perishes.

17. There is then no peace in the heart of a carnal man, nor in him that is addicted to outward things, but in the spiritual and devout man. (The Imitation of Christ V.2.)

Swami Vivekananda's Footnote: Bhagavad-Gita 2.60.

यततो ह्यपि कौन्तेय पुरुषस्य विपश्चितः ।
इन्द्रियाणि प्रमाथीनि हरन्ति प्रसभं मनः ॥

Publisher's Translation: The turbulent senses, O son of Kunti, violently carry away the mind of even a wise man striving after perfection.

THE PLAGUE MANIFESTO

Om Salutations to Bhagavan Shri Ramakrishna!

Brothers of Calcutta!

1. We feel happy when you are happy, and we suffer when you suffer. Therefore, during these days of extreme adversity, we are striving and ceaselessly praying for your welfare and an easy way to save you from disease and the fear of an epidemic.

2. If that grave disease — fearing which both the high and the low, the rich and the poor are all fleeing the city — ever really comes in our midst, then even if we perish while serving and nursing you, we will consider ourselves fortunate because you are all embodiments of God. He who thinks otherwise — out of vanity, superstition or ignorance — offends God and incurs great sin. There is not the slightest doubt about it.

3. We humbly pray to you — please do not panic due to unfounded fear. Depend upon God and calmly try to find the best means to solve the problem. Otherwise, join hands with those who are doing that very thing.

4. What is there to fear? The terror that has entered people's hearts due to the occurrence of the plague has no real ground. Through God's will, nothing of the terrible form that plague takes, as seen in other places, has occurred in Calcutta. The government authorities have also been particularly helpful to us. So what is there to fear?

5. Come, let us give up this false fear and, having faith in the infinite compassion of God, gird our loins and enter the field of action. Let us live pure and clean lives. Disease, fear of an epidemic, etc., will vanish into thin air by His grace.

6. (a) Always keep the house and its premises, the rooms, clothes, bed, drain, etc., clean.

(b) Do not eat stale, spoiled food; take fresh and nutritious food instead. A weak body is more susceptible to disease.

(c) Always keep the mind cheerful. Everyone will die once. Cowards suffer the pangs of death again and again, solely due to the fear in their own minds.

(d) Fear never leaves those who earn their livelihoods by unethical means or who cause harm to others. Therefore, at this time when we face the great fear of death, desist from all such behaviour.

(e) During the period of epidemic, abstain from anger and from lust — even if you are householders.

(f) Do not pay any heed to rumours.

(g) The British government will not vaccinate anyone by force. Only those who are willing will be vaccinated.

(h) There will be no lack of effort in treating the afflicted patients in our hospital under our special care and supervision, paying full respect to religion, caste and the modesty (Purdah) of women. Let the wealthy run away! But we are poor; we understand the heartache of the poor. The Mother of the Universe is Herself the support of the helpless. The Mother is assuring us: "Fear not! Fear not!"

7. Brother, if there is no one to help you, then send information immediately to the servants of Shri Bhagavan Ramakrishna at Belur Math. There will be no dearth of help that is physically possible. By the grace of the Mother, monetary help will also be possible.

— N. B. In order to remove the fear of the epidemic, you should sing Nâma Sankirtanam [the name of the Lord] every evening and in every locality.

Discovery Publisher is a multimedia publisher whose mission is to inspire and support personal transformation, spiritual growth and awakening. We strive with every title to preserve the essential wisdom of the author, spiritual teacher, thinker, healer, and visionary artist.

71106622R10452

Made in the USA
Columbia, SC
24 August 2019